THE

GOSPEL

ACCORDING TO

JOHN.

BY

JOHN PETER LANGE, D.D.,

PROFESSOR OF THEOLOGY AT THE UNIVERSITY OF BONN.

TRANSLATED FROM THE GERMAN,

REVISED, ENLARGED, AND EDITED

BY

PHILIP SCHAFF, D.D.,

PROFESSOR OF THEOLOGY IN THE UNION THEOLOGICAL SEMINARY, NEW YORK

Wipf & Stock

PUBLISHERS

Eugene, Oregon

Wipf and Stock Publishers
199 W 8th Ave, Suite 3
Eugene, OR 97401

The Gospel according to John
an Exegetical and Doctrinal Commentary
By Lange, John Peter
ISBN 13: 978-1-55635-413-7
ISBN 10: 1-55635-413-4
Publication date 4/6/2007
Previously published by Charles Scribner, 1871

SPECIAL INTRODUCTION TO THE AMERICAN EDITION.

THE GOSPEL OF JOHN.

THE four canonical Gospels are representations of one and the same Gospel, in its fourfold aspect and relation to the human race, and may be called, with Irenæus, "the fourfold Gospel" (τετράμορφον εὐαγγέλιον). Taken together, they give us a complete picture of the earthly life and character of our Lord and Saviour, in whom the whole fulness of the Godhead and of sinless Manhood dwell in perfect harmony. Each is invaluable and indispensable; each is unique in its kind; each has its peculiar character and mission corresponding to the talent, education, and vocation of the author, and the wants of his readers.

MATTHEW, writing in Palestine, and for *Jews*, and observing, in accordance with his former occupation and training, a rubrical and topical, rather than chronological, order, gives us the Gospel of the new Theocracy founded by Christ—the Lawgiver, Messiah, and King of the true Israel, who fulfilled all the prophecies of the old Dispensation. His is the fundamental Gospel, which stands related to the New Testament as the Pentateuch does to the Old. MARK, the companion of Peter, writing at Rome, and for warlike *Romans*, paints Christ, in fresh, graphic, and rapid sketches, as the mighty Son of God, the startling Wonder-Worker, the victorious Conqueror, and forms the connecting link between Matthew and Luke, or between the Jewish-Christian and the Gentile-Christian Evangelist. LUKE, an educated Hellenist, a humane physician, a pupil and friend of Paul, prepared, as the Evangelist of the Gentiles, chiefly for *Greek* readers, and in chronological order, the Gospel of universal humanity, where Christ appears as the sympathizing Friend of sinners, the healing Physician of all diseases, the tender Shepherd of the wandering sheep, the Author and Proclaimer of a free salvation for Gentiles and Samaritans as well as Jews. From JOHN, the trusted bosom-friend of the Saviour, the Benjamin among the twelve, and the surviving patriarch of the apostolic age, who could look back to the martyrdom of James, Peter, and Paul, and the destruction of Jerusalem, and look forward to the certain triumph of Christianity over the tottering idols of Paganism, we must naturally expect the ripest, as it was the last, composition of the gospel history, for the edification of the *Christian Church in all ages.*

The Gospel of John is the Gospel of Gospels, as the Epistle to the Romans is the Epistle of Epistles. It is the most remarkable as well as the most important literary production ever composed by man. It is a marvel even in the marvellous Book of books. All the literature of the world could not replace it. It is the most spiritual and ideal of Gospels. It introduces us into the Holy of Holies in the history of our Lord; it brings us, as it were, into His immediate presence, so that we behold face to face the true Shekinah, "the glory of the Only Begotten of the Father, full of grace and truth." It presents, in fairest harmony, the highest knowledge, and the deepest love, of Christ. It gives us the clearest view of His incarnate Divinity and His perfect Humanity. It sets Him forth as the Eternal Word, Who was the source of life from the beginning, and the organ of all the revelations of God to man; as the Fountain of living water that quenches the thirst of the soul; as the Light of the world that illuminates the darkness of sin and error; as the Resurrection and the Life that destroys the terror of death. It reflects the lustre of the Transfiguration on the Mount, yet subdued by the holy sadness of Gethsemane. It abounds in festive joy and gladness over the amazing love of God, but mixed with grief over the ingratitude and obtuseness of unbelieving men. It breathes the air of peace, and yet sounds at times like a peal of thunder from the other world; it soars boldly and majestically like the eagle towards the uncreated source of light, and yet hovers as gently as a dove over the earth; it is sublime as a seraph and simple as a child; high and serene as the heaven, deep and unfathomable as the sea. It is the plainest in speech and the profoundest in meaning. To it more than to any portion of the Scripture applies the familiar comparison of a river deep enough for the elephant to swim, with shallows for the lamb to wade. It is the Gospel of love, life, and light, the Gospel of the heart taken from the very heart of Christ, on which the beloved disciple leaned at the Last Supper. It is the type of the purest forms of mysticism. It has an irresistible charm for speculative and contemplative minds, and furnishes inexhaustible food for meditation and devotion. It is the Gospel of peace and Christian union, and a prophecy of that blessed future when all the discords of the Church militant on earth shall be solved in the harmony of the Church triumphant in heaven.

TESTIMONIES ON JOHN.

No wonder that this Gospel has challenged the enthusiastic love and admiration of great and good men in all ages and countries; and, on the other hand, provoked the utmost skill and ingenuity of the modern assailants of Christianity, who rightly feel that it is the strongest fortress of the Divine character of our Lord.

Let us hear some of the most striking testimonies of divines, philosophers, and poets, which tend at the same time to describe more fully its characteristic peculiarities.*

ORIGEN, the father of biblical exegesis, calls the fourth Gospel the main Gospel, and says that those only can comprehend it who lean on the bosom of Jesus, and there imbibe the spirit of John, just as he imbibed the spirit of Christ.†

CHRYSOSTOM, the ablest expounder and greatest pulpit orator of the Greek Church, extols, with all the ardor of his eloquence, the celestial tones of this Gospel: it is, he says, a voice of thunder reverberating through the whole earth; notwithstanding its all-conquering power, it does not utter a harsh sound, but is more love-bewitching and elevating in its influence than all the harmonies of music. Besides, it awakens the awe-inspiring consciousness, that it is pregnant with the most precious gifts of grace, which elevate those who appropriate them to themselves above the earthly pursuits of this life, and constitute them citizens of heaven and heirs of the blessedness of angels.‡

JEROME, the most learned of the Latin fathers, says: "John excels in the depths of divine mysteries." §

* Some of these testimonies were collected by Tholuck (*Com. on John*, Introduction, p. 19, Krauth's translation).
† *Commentaria in Ev. Ioa.*, (*Opera*, tom. IV. p. 6 ed. Delarue).
‡ Compare his first Homily on John, in the 8th volume of the Bened. ed. of the works of Chrysostom, pp. 2 sqq.
§ Catal. cap. 9.

AUGUSTINE, the greatest of all the fathers, after speaking of the differences of John and the Synoptists, and the incomparable sublimity of the Prologue, gives him the preference and says: "John did but pour forth the water of life which he himself had drunk in. For he does not relate the fact without good reason, that at the Last Supper the beloved disciple laid his head on the Lord's bosom. From this bosom his soul drank in secret. Then he revealed this secret communion to the world, that all nations might become partakers of the blessings of the Incarnation, Passion, and Resurrection."*

LUTHER speaks of the Gospel of John as being "the unique, tender, genuine, leading Gospel, that should be preferred by far to the others.† John records mainly the discourses of Christ in his own words, from which we learn truth and life as taught by himself. The rest dwell at length upon his works."

CALVIN appropriately designates it as the key that opens the way to a right understanding of the other three. This Gospel reveals the soul of Christ; the others seek rather to describe His body.‡

LESSING pronounces it, without qualification, to be the most important portion of the New Testament.

ERNESTI calls it "The heart of Christ."

HERDER enthusiastically exclaims: "Written by the hand of an angel!"

SCHLEIERMACHER, in his "*Weihnachtsfeier*," expresses his own preference for John's Gospel in the language of Edward, the third speaker at the festival: "The mystic among the four Evangelists communicates but little information about particular events, and does not even relate the actual birth of Christ, but eternal, child-like Christmas joys pervade his soul."

Commentators of recent date, such as LUECKE, OLSHAUSEN, THOLUCK, MEYER, ALFORD, GODET, and LANGE, share the same preference.

"The noble simplicity," says THOLUCK, "and the dim mystery of the narration, the tone of grief and longing, with the light of love shedding its tremulous beam on the whole—these impart to the Gospel of John a peculiar originality and charm, to which no parallel can be found." He also applies to it, in an elevated sense, the language of HAMANN in reference to CLAUDIUS: "Thy harp sends forth light ethereal sounds that float gently in the air, and fill our hearts with tender sadness, even after its strings have ceased to vibrate."

MEYER, the ablest grammatical exegete of the age, who is rather dry and jejune, and apparently indifferent to dogmatic results, but who, by a life-long study of the Word of God, gradually rose from rationalistic to an almost orthodox standpoint, and

* See the 36th *Tractate* of Augustine on John's Gospel, in the third tom. of the Bened. edition, fol. 543 and 544. As we find here the finest patristic appreciation of John, I shall give the original passage in full: "*In quatuor Evangeliis, vel potius quatuor libris unius Evangelii sanctus Johannes apostolus, non immerito secundum intelligentiam spiritalem aquilæ comparatus, altius multoque sublimius aliis tribus erexit prædicationem suam, et in ejus erectione etiam corda nostra erigi voluit. Nam celeri tres Evangelistæ, tanquam cum homine Domino in terra ambulabant, de divinitate ejus pauca dixerunt: istum autem quasi piguerit in terra ambulare, sicut ipso exordio sui sermonis intonuit, erexit se, non solum super terram et super omnem ambitum aëris et cœli, sed super omnem etiam exercitum Angelorum, omnemque constitutionem invisibilium potestatum, et pervenit ad eum per quem facta sunt omnia, dicendo, 'In principio erat Verbum, et Verbum erat apud Deum, et Deus erat Verbum: hoc erat in principio apud Deum. Omnia per ipsum facta sunt, et sine ipso factum est nihil.' Huic tantæ sublimitati principii etiam cetera congrua prædicavit, et de Domini divinitate quomodo nullus alius est locutus. Hoc ructabat quod biberat. Non enim sine causa de illo in isto ipso Evangelio narratur, quia et in convivio super pectus Domini discumbebat. De illo ergo pectore in secreto bibebat; sed quod in secreto bibit, in manifesto eructavit, ut perveniat ad omnes gentes non solum incarnatio Filii Dei, et passio, et resurrectio; sed etiam quid erat ante incarnationem Unicus Patri, Verbum Patris, coæternus generanti, æqualis ei a quo missus est; sed in ipsa missione minor factus, quo major esset Pater.*"

† "*Das einzige zarte rechte Haupt-Evangelion und den anderen dreien weit vorzuziehen und höher zu heben.*"—Luth.'s Preface to the N. T., in the earlier editions. The passage was afterwards (since 1539) omitted, probably from apprehension that the preference given to John above other books of the Bible might be misunderstood.

‡ In the introduction to his *Commentary on John*: "*Quum omnibus [Evangelistis] communiter propositum sit Christum ostendere, priores illi corpus, si ita loqui fas est, in medium proferunt, Joannes vero animam. Quamobrem dicere soleo, hoc Evangelium clavem esse, quæ aliis intelligendis januam aperiat.*"

marks this steady progress in the successive editions of his valuable commentary, endorses Luther's eulogy, and expresses the conviction that "the wonderful Gospel of John, with its fulness of grace, truth, peace, light, and life," is destined to contribute to a closer union of Christians.*

Dr. LANGE calls the fourth Gospel "the diamond among the Gospels which is most fully penetrated by the light of life, and which reflects the glory of the Godhead in flesh and blood, even in the crown of thorns." †

Dr. ISAAC DA COSTA, of Amsterdam, in a discriminating analysis of the peculiarities of the four Gospels, says of the fourth: "As John was the special object of his Master's choice, so is his Gospel a select and exquisite production. . . . It is a voice from heaven; it is the language of a seer. It is a Gospel from the height, and likewise from the depth. . . . We find in it something more than the artless and childlike simplicity of St. Matthew's narrative; more than the rapidity and terseness of St. Mark's record; more than the calm and flowing historical style of Luke. With that artlessness, and that terseness, and that calmness, there is here mingled a higher and more elevated tone—a tone derived from the monuments of the remotest sacred antiquity, as well as from the hidden depths of the most profound theology; a tone reminding us sometimes of the Mosaic account of creation, sometimes of the wise sayings of Solomon, sometimes akin even to the later theology of Jewish-Alexandrine philosophers." ‡

Dean ALFORD thus speaks of John: "The great Apostle of the Gentiles, amidst fightings without and fears within, built in his argumentative Epistles the outworks of that temple, of which his still greater colleague and successor was chosen noiselessly to complete, in his peaceful old age, the inner and holier places. And this, after all, ranging under it all secondary aims, we must call the great object of the Evangelist: to advance, purify from error, and strengthen that maturer Christian life of *knowledge*, which is the true development of the teaching of the Spirit in men, and which the latter part of the apostolic period witnessed in its full vitality. And this, by setting forth the Person of the Lord Jesus in all its fulness of grace and truth, in all its manifestation in the flesh by signs and by discourses, and its glorification by opposition and unbelief, through sufferings and death." §

Canon BROOKE FOSS WESTCOTT represents the Synoptical Gospels as the Gospel of the Infant Church, that of St. John as the Gospel of its maturity; the former as containing the wide experience of the many, the latter as embracing the deep mysteries treasured up by the one. "No writing," he continues, "combines greater simplicity with more profound depths. At first all seems clear in the childlike language which is so often the chosen vehicle of the treasures of Eastern meditation; and then again the utmost subtlety of Western thought is found to lie under abrupt and apparently fragmentary utterances. St. John wrote the Gospel of the world, resolving reason into intuition, and faith into sight." ‖

Bishop WORDSWORTH applies to the Gospel of John, as compared with the Synop-

* See the closing words to his preface to the fifth edition of his *Commentary on John* (1869). He adds that "the Lutheran Church (to which he belongs), born with a manifesto of war and grown up in fierce controversy, has been unable as yet to rise to the clear height and quiet perfection of this Gospel." But the same may be said of other Churches. The Moravians have, perhaps, more of the spirit of John than any other denomination.

† *Leben Jesu*, vol. iii., p. 539.

‡ *The Four Witnesses: being a Harmony of the Gospels on a new Principle.* Translated by David Dundas Scott. New York: 1855. pp. 229, 232. (Against Strauss.)

§ *The Greek Test.*, etc., Vol. I. 6th Ed. 1868. p. 61.

‖ *Introduction to the Study of the Gospels*, pp. 254, 255, 308 (Am.Ed., Boston, 1852).

tists the words of the marriage feast at Cana: "Thou hast kept the good wine until now" (John ii. 10).*

HENRY PARRY LIDDON: "St. John's Gospel is the most conspicuous written attestation to the Godhead of Him Whose claims upon mankind can hardly be surveyed without passion, whether it be the passion of adoring love, or the passion of vehement and determined enmity." †

Not only theologians, but profound philosophers also have been particularly fascinated by the Introduction (ch. i. 1–18), which may be regarded as a compendium of the highest philosophical wisdom. FICHTE, during the latter and more religious period of his life, and SCHELLING, in his *Philosophy of Revelation*, regard John as the typical representative of the perfect ideal church of the future. And this idea, already suggested by a mediæval monk, JOACHIM DE FLORIS, has taken root in the theological consciousness of the nineteenth century.‡

Finally, poets too have lavished their praises on this mysterious and wonderful production of the Apostolic age.

ADAM of ST. VICTOR, one of the greatest poets of the Latin Church, who died about 1192, describes John in one of the finest and most musical stanzas ever written in Latin or any other language:—

"Volat avis sine meta
Quo nec vates nec propheta
Evolavit altius:
Tam implenda, quam impleta,§
Nunquam vidit tot secreta
Purus homo purius." ‖

In another poem, on the four Evangelists, after praising Matthew, Mark, and Luke, Adam of St. Victor places John above them all:—

"Sed Joannes ala bina
Caritatis aquilina,
Forma fertur in divina
Puriori lumine." ¶

The pious and childlike German poet CLAUDIUS, of Wandsbeck, who remained faithful in an age of almost universal skepticism and apostasy, gives perhaps the best description of the Gospel of John in these words, which are conceived in the very spirit of the Evangelist:—

"Above all do I like to read the Gospel of John. There is something truly wonderful in it: twilight and night; and athwart flashes the vivid lightning. A soft evening sky, and behind the sky, in bodily form, the large full moon! Something so

* *The New Test.*, etc., Vol. I., p. 257, 5th Ed. 1866. Most of what Dr. Wordsworth, in the General Introduction, says of the characteristics of the four Gospels is a reproduction of patristic fancies which cannot stand the test of sober criticism.

† Bampton Lectures on *The Divinity of our Lord Jesus Christ*, 2d ed., Lond. and Oxf., 1868, p. 206.

‡ Comp. the closing section of my *History of the Apostolic Church*, p. 674.

§ *Implenda* refers to the Revelation, *impleta* to the Gospel.

‖ From the poem *De Joanne Evangelista*, commencing: *Verbum Dei Deo natum;* see Daniel's *Thesaurus hymnologicus*, tom. II., p. 166, and Mone's *Lat. Hymnen des Mittelalters*, III. 118. I append an English and a German version of this rare gem:—

"Bird of God! with boundless flight
Soaring far beyond the height
Of the bard or prophet old;
Truth fulfilled, and truth to be,—
Never purer mystery
Did a purer tongue unfold!"—(Dr. WASHBURN.)

"*Seht zum Licht den Adler fliegen,*
Höher als sonst nie gestiegen
Dichter noch Prophete war.
Niemals sah so tief Verhülltes,
Jetzt und künftig erst Erfülltes
Ein so reiner Mensch so klar."

¶ This poem commences *Jocundare, plebs fidelis,* and is given in full by Daniel, *Thesaurus hymnol.*, II. 84, translated by J. M. Neale, *Mediæval Hymns*, third ed., p. 106. The "double wing of love," means, of course, love to God and love to man.

"John, love's double wing devising,
Earth on eagle plumes despising,
To his God and Lord uprising,
Soars away in purer light." (John M. Neale.)

"But on twofold eagle pinion,
Wrought by love in her dominion,
John, a form divinely bright,
Upward soars in purer light."—(THOS. C. PORTER.)

Mone, vol. III., pp. 112 sqq., gives a number of other mediæval hymns on John which, however, are of inferior merit.

sad, so sublime, so full of presage that one can never weary of it. Every time I read John, it seems as if I could see him before me reclining on the bosom of his Master at the Last Supper—as if his angel were standing by my side with a lamp in his hand, and, when I come to particular passages, would clasp me in his arms and whisper a word in my ear. There is a great deal that I do not understand when I read; but I often feel as if John's meaning were floating before me at a distance; even when my eye lights on a dark place, I have nevertheless a presentiment of a grand and glorious sense that I shall some day understand. On this account I grasp eagerly at every new exposition of John's Gospel. But alas! the most of them only ruffle the evening clouds, and the bright moon behind them is left in peace." *

TRUTH OR FICTION?

Yet this very Gospel, which has exerted such an irresistible charm upon the purest and profoundest minds of all Christian ages, is now the main point of attack in the great conflict of modern skepticism with the old faith. This is no matter of surprise, any more than that Jesus Christ Himself, in the days of His flesh, should have provoked the malignity of the whole Jewish hierarchy, who charged Him with having an evil spirit, and at last nailed Him to the Cross—as a rebel, a false Messiah, and a blasphemer. The power of truth and life with which John bears testimony to the historical and ideal Christ, is the very reason of the intensity of interest on both sides of the controversy; it is as if Christ Himself lived His life over in the pages of His faithful biographer, and confronted there His enemies in person. Human nature is the same now as it was eighteen hundred years ago, and cannot remain neutral on the great question of Christ and His amazing claims upon our faith: it must either declare for Him or against Him, either accept or reject the offer of His salvation. And as He can no more be crucified in person, He is crucified in the Gospels by the modern Scribes and Pharisees and Sadducees.

In putting the case so strongly, I do not mean to deny the valuable learning, acumen, and a certain measure of honest earnestness in some of the negative critics of our age. There are among them skeptics of the order of Thomas, who loved and found the truth, as well as skeptics of the tribe of Pilate, who connived at the crucifixion of the Truth. The inquiring doubt of the former has a useful and important mission in the church, and has done good service in solving the problems connected with the origin, character, plan, and mutual relations of the Gospels.

A live Commentary in a live age must be written in full view of these modern attacks, and the new aspects and relations which old truths and facts have assumed. Reference direct and indirect to the present state of the controversy is as important and necessary in a critical work as the frank record of the bitter hostility of the Jewish leaders in the Gospels. The old and the new phases of opposition to the Christ in the flesh explain and illustrate each other.

I have no misgiving as to the ultimate result. I am as confident as I am of my own existence that the Gospel of John will come triumphant out of this fiery ordeal. The

* The quaint originality of this classical passage it is difficult to reproduce in English.
"*Am liebsten lese ich im Sanct Johannes. In ihm ist so etwas ganz Wunderbares—Dämmerung und Nacht, und durch sie hin der schnelle, zuckende Blitz! Ein sanftes Abendgewölk und hinter dem Gewölke der grosse, volle Mond leibhaftig! So etwas Schwermüthiges und Hohes und Ahnungsvolles, dass man's nicht satt werden kann. Es ist mir immer beim Lesen im Johannes, als ob ich ihn beim letzten Abendmahl an der Brust seines Meisters vor mir liegen sehe, als ob sein Engel mir's Licht halte und mir bei gewissen Stellen um den Hals fallen und etwas in's Ohr sagen wolle. Ich verstehe lange nicht alles, was ich lese, aber oft ist's doch, als schwebt' es fern vor mir, was Johannes meinte, und auch da, wo ich in einen ganz dunklen Ort hineinsehe, habe ich doch eine Vorempfindung von einem grossen herrlichen Sinn, den ich einmal verstehen werde. Und darum greife ich so gerne nach jeder neuen Erklärung des Evangelium Johannis. Zwar—die meisten kräuseln nur an dem Abendgewölke, und der Mond hinter ihm hat gute Ruhe.*"

old doctrinal opposition of the Alogi has long passed into history. Bretschneider's critical battery was soon silenced and spiked by the commander himself. The heavier artillery of Strauss, Baur, Renan, and their sympathizers has nearly spent its ammunition without effecting a single breach in this fortress. Indeed, the latest and wisest utterance from the Tübingen School on the Johannean question is the significant concession, that *the fundamental ideas of the fourth Gospel lie far beyond the horizon of the Church in the second century, and indeed of the whole Christian Church down to the present day.**

I accept this statement both as a just tribute of an able and honest opponent to the value of the Gospel, and as a confession of the entire failure of modern criticism to disprove its apostolic origin. *Verily, no man in the second century, no man in any subsequent age or section of the Church could have written, or could now write, such a work. More than this, no man in the first century could have written it but John the Apostle, and even John himself could not have written it without inspiration.*

To declare such a Gospel, which is admitted to reach the highest attainable or conceivable height of moral purity and sublimity, beyond which the Christian world has been unable to go to this day—to declare such a Gospel a conscious fiction, not to use the plain term, a literary forgery, of some obscure, unknown, and unnamable pseudo-John in the second century,† involves not only a psychological and literary impossibility, but also a moral monstrosity almost as great as the blasphemous charge of the Jewish hierarchy, that Christ Himself was an impostor and in league with the devil. The compromise-hypothesis, which divides it between truth and fiction, by admitting the historical truthfulness either of the discourses of Jesus,‡ or of the narrative portions,§ is set aside by the unmistakable unity in language and thought of the fourth Gospel, which is a work of instinctive literary art, complete and perfect in all its parts.

We are shut up to the choice either to adopt the whole as historical, or to reject the whole as an invention. Were the Gospel of John not a Gospel, but some secular story, it would, with half the evidence in its favor, be admitted as genuine by scholars without a dissenting voice. For it is better attested than any book of ancient Greece and Rome, or modern Germany and England. The unanimous testimony—heretical as well as orthodox—of antiquity reaching to the beginning of the second century, *i. e.*, almost to the lifetime of John, the language and style, ‖ the familiarity with Jewish nature and Palestine localities, the minute circumstantiality of account, the number of

* Prof. Holtzmann, of Heidelberg, in his article *Evangelium des Johannes*, in Schenkel's *Bibel-Lexikon*, vol. ii. (1869), p. 232, says of the Gospel of John: "*Dieses sinnlich-übersinnliche Evangelium ist durchgängig die kunst- und sinnvollste Verbindung von 'Wahrheit und Dichtung,' die wir kennen;*" and p. 234: "*Die grundlegendsten und weitreichendsten Gedanken des vierten Evangeliums liegen weit über die dem zweiten Jahrhundert und überhaupt der ganzen bisherigen Entwickelung der Kirche erreichbar gewesene Höhe hinaus.*"

† The hypothesis of a historical romance to illustrate the Logos doctrine. So, with various modifications, Baur, the leader of the Tübingen School (*Kritische Untersuchungen über die Evangelien*, 1847, etc.), Schwegler, Zeller, Köstlin, Hilgenfeld, Schenkel, Volkmar, Lang, Réville (1864), Scholten (1864), Keim (1867), J. J. Tayler (1867), S. Davidson (1868). Strauss originally (1835) applied to the Gospel of John his mythical theory of an *unconscious*, innocent poem; but the subsequent investigations of the Tübingen School convinced him that the only alternative here is between the orthodox historical view and Baur's hypothesis of *conscious invention* in the interest of a specific doctrinal and speculative tendency. In his new *Leben Jesu* (1864), p. 79, he says with regard to the Gospel of John: "*Hier hat sogar die Einmischung philosophischer Construction und bewusster Dichtung alle Wahrscheinlichkeit.*"

‡ The view of Weisse (1838), Freytag (1861), etc.

§ So Renan (comp. the 13th ed. of his *Life of Jesus*, 1867), and Weizsäcker (1864). Weizsäcker, however, who is Baur's successor in Tübingen, admits a considerable amount of historical substance also in the discourses of Jesus, and is a man of altogether different spirit from Renan.

‖ The style of John is altogether unique: it is a pure Hebrew soul in a pure Greek body. Thus I reconcile the apparently contradictory judgments of two of the most eminent orientalist scholars. "In its true spirit and afflatus," says Ewald, "no language can be more genuinely Hebrew than that of John." "His style," says Renan, "has nothing Hebrew, nothing Jewish, nothing Talmudic." Renan looks to the surface, Ewald to the foundation. The style of John has been carefully discussed by Luthardt, in the second section of his Introduction (I. pp. 21–69), and by Westcott, in his *Introduction to the Gospels* (pp. 264–281). Comp. also the remarks of Godet (II. p. 712, 713), who says: "*Dans le style de Jean, le vêtement seul est grec; le corps est hébreu.*"

graphic touches and incidental details which unmistakably betray an eye-witness, the express and solemn testimony of the writer to have witnessed the issue of blood and water from the pierced side of Jesus, and his indirect and delicate self-designation as the most favorite among the chosen Twelve, the high and lofty tone of the whole narrative, the perfect picture of the purest and holiest being that walked on the face of this earth—all point irresistibly to the conclusion that the fourth canonical Gospel is the composition of none other than the inspired Apostle whom Jesus loved, who leaned on His breast at the last supper, who stood at the cross and the open tomb, and who personally witnessed the greatest facts which ever occurred or ever will occur in the history of mankind.

COMMENTARY ON JOHN.

The preparation of the English edition of Dr. Lange's Commentary on John (from the third edition, revised and improved, 1868) was attended with unexpected difficulties and delays, which demand some explanation.

The work was first intrusted to the late Rev. EDWARD D. YEOMANS, D.D. From his rare ability and experience as a translator, and his admiring appreciation of Lange, he was admirably qualified for the difficult task; * but before he had half finished the first draft of a translation, he was called to his rest in the prime of his life and usefulness (at Orange, New Jersey, August 26, 1868), and left his manuscript as a sacred legacy in my hands. It is due to the memory of an esteemed and dearly beloved friend and co-laborer, who was one of the purest and noblest Christian gentlemen I ever knew, that I should insert his last letter to me on the subject:—

ORANGE, N. J., June 13, 1868.

MY DEAR DR. SCHAFF:—I have been again attacked with a return of the difficulty which caught me in the pulpit some four months ago. It has now shown itself distinctly mental, and has been more acute. Just four weeks ago it laid me up, and I have been unable till now to apply myself even to such a letter as this. I am strictly forbidden study for at least two months, and must then return to nothing beyond what my congregation requires, if I can return even to any good part of that.

Providence now plainly shows me that my work on Lange must cease. I suspected this, as I wrote you some months ago; but hated positively to abandon it. I must now, however, relieve myself entirely of all connection with it. And I send you herewith, by express, the original and your books you have lent me, and all my own manuscripts.

I feel sad over this failure. It has the look of an entire failure on my part. It has, however, a very different side, when I remember that, after assuming the work, Providence called me, in succession, to the organization of two new parishes—devolving far more pastoral work upon me than my continuance in my already formed parish at Trenton would have required. . . . .

This continual delay of John I have been continually hoping to cut short. I can now only redeem it by offering you the free use of these MSS. of mine, with not the slightest pecuniary claim, and with no appearance of my name in the concern. This I most cheerfully do, and pray you leniently to accept it. My MSS., I see, need revision, as you will see by the first bunch, which I revised and have considerably changed. I cannot do anything further to them in the way of revision. I must positively retire from *all* connection with this great, and to me most engaging work. I only hope you will be able so to shape your work that John can go into no other hands but *your own*.

I am obliged to write with effort, to *compose* a letter. But, my dear and inestimable friend, I could not fairly express my heart to you, with my best powers, not only over my apparently mortifying failure to fulfil this important and long-promised service, but over this termination of a long, and to me most pleasant and profitable association with you in the highest walks of theology; though *my* part has been that of a mere amanuensis, in another tongue, to your own brains and learning. I am only the more happy to think that this terminates only an association of the *letter*, and touches not our *personal* friendship and companionship in the least, nor our association in laboring for the propagation of the common truth as it is in Jesus.

I cannot say more, but must cut myself short with assuring you that, with all my heart,

I am, as ever, yours, E. D. YEOMANS.

It was a sad pleasure to me to prepare the neat manuscript of my departed friend for the press. I treated it with scrupulous regard to his memory, which I shall ever sacredly cherish, hoping for a blissful reunion in a better world.

After considerable delay, I happily secured the assistance of an unusually gifted lady, Miss EVELINA MOORE (a grand-daughter of Bishop Moore of Virginia), who, with

* Competent judges (such as Drs. Jos. A. Alexander, Hodge, Stowe, H. B. Smith, McClintock, Bunsen, etc.) had previously assigned to Dr. Yeomans the very first rank among translators of theological works from the German into pure, idiomatic English. A reviewer of my *Church History*, in the *British and Foreign Evangelical Quarterly Review*, London, April, 1868, pays him the following tribute: "In point of style and general structure there is nothing to indicate that the book is a translation from the German. Indeed in this respect it will stand a favorable comparison with the best English classics." Similar views were expressed on his translation of my *History of the Apostolic Church*, when first published in 1853.

womanly instinct and intuition, penetrated to the very heart of John and his commentator, and finished the translation from Chs. IX. to XXI. to my entire satisfaction.

In the Homiletical Department, from the tenth chapter to the close, I am also greatly indebted to the valuable aid of the Rev. Dr. CRAVEN, of Newark, who, with conscientious fidelity, selected the best thoughts and suggestions from the *Catena Patrum*, from Henry, Burkitt, Clarke, Ryle, Barnes, Owen, Stier, Krummacher, and other practical commentators, not already noticed by Lange. His additions are marked with his own name; they will be found in no way inferior to the corresponding selections of the German original, from Starke, Gossner, Gerlach, Schleiermacher, Heubner, etc., and help to make this department a complete thesaurus.

For the preparation of the Text, with the Critical Apparatus and the numerous additions to the Exegesis proper (enclosed in brackets), as well as for the final revision and editing of the whole volume, I am responsible myself. My endeavor has been to combine the most valuable results of ancient and modern, European and American labors on the fourth Gospel, and to make the Commentary permanently useful for study and reference.

The revision of the Authorized English Version was, of course, made directly from the Greek, and with constant reference to the latest critical sources, viz.: the eighth large edition of TISCHENDORF now in course of publication, TREGELLES (Luke and John, 1861), ALFORD (Gospels, 6th ed. 1868), and advanced sheets of WESTCOTT and HORT's forthcoming edition of the Greek Testament, which were kindly furnished to me by my friend Canon Westcott. In examining these critical editions of German and English scholars, I have gained the conviction that we are steadily approaching a pure and reliable text of the Greek Testament. Lachmann, following the hints of Bentley and Bengel, boldly opened the way by departing from the comparatively modern and unreliable "textus receptus," and substituting for it the oldest text that can be obtained from the uncial manuscripts, the oldest versions and the quotations of the ante-Nicene fathers. The discovery and publication of the Sinaitic code (*Aleph*) by Tischendorf, has given additional weight to the readings of the uncial MSS. (A. B. C. D. etc.). In the great majority of variations I find a remarkable agreement between the best German and English critics. The latter are almost entirely unknown even to the best German commentators. Lange, with sound critical judgment, follows chiefly Lachmann, but could not make use of the eighth edition of Tischendorf, whose first volume (containing the Gospels) was not completed till 1869, and presents many variations from his former editions.

In the Exegetical and Critical Department I have carefully compared and freely used (always with due credit) the latest editions of the best commentaries on John, especially MEYER (fifth edition of 1869, which has 684 pages to 586 of the fourth edition of 1861, and required constant rectification of Lange's frequent references to earlier editions), ALFORD (6th ed. 1868), and GODET (1865), who respectively represent the present state of German, English, and French research on the Johannean Gospel.* On the more important passages I have also examined ORIGEN (*Com. in Evang. Joh.*), AUGUSTINE (124 Tractates on the Gospel of John, Tom. III., Part II., pp. 290–826,

* The pleasure of daily spiritual communion with these distinguished scholars, during the preparation of this volume, was deepened by personal reminiscences which can never be effaced. On my last visit to Europe, in 1869, I spent some delightful days with Dr. Lange in Bonn, who is still in full vigor and unceasing activity; with Dr. Alford at the Deancry of Canterbury, who was called from his earthly labors before I finished my task; with Professor Godet at Neuchatel, with whom I studied and prayed at Berlin, when he was superintending the education of the present crown prince of Prussia, and heir to the new imperial crown of reunited and reconstructed Germany; and with the venerable Dr. Meyer, at Hannover, who devotes his whole time to new editions of his Commentary on the New Testament.

Bened. ed.), CHRYSOSTOM (88 Homilies on John, Tom. VIII., pp. 1–530, Bened. ed.), among the fathers; LUTHER and CALVIN, among the reformers; GROTIUS, BENGEL, OLSHAUSEN, DE WETTE-BRÜCKNER (5th ed. 1863), THOLUCK, HENGSTENBERG, LUTHARDT, STIER, WEBSTER and WILKINSON, WORDSWORTH (5th ed. 1866), BARNES, and OWEN, among more recent exegetes. The very elaborate Calvinistic commentary of LAMPE (1724), and the classical work of LÜCKE (3d ed., 1840), I had previously studied with care, when, in the first year of my academic career (1843), I wrote out a full course of lectures on the Gospel of John for my students in the University of Berlin. On all the principal passages I found myself in agreement with the views of my youth.

The American edition, then, is to a large extent a new work. It exceeds the German, which numbers only 427 pages (third edition), by more than one-third. It has not only 228 more pages, exclusive of the Preface, but each page, owing to the smaller type, contains two more lines (70 to 68). Add to this the fact that the whole Critical Apparatus (which is almost entirely new), and many of my exegetical notes are set in still smaller type; and it may be fairly said that the contents of this one volume, if leaded and printed in larger type, would fill four ordinary octavo volumes. I state this in justice to the publishers, who sell Lange's Commentary at so low a price, in proportion to the vast cost of manufacture, that only a large and steady sale can save them from serious loss.

It would have been a more easy, certainly a more agreeable, task to prepare, on the basis of my own lectures, and on a simpler plan, an original Commentary in unbroken composition, instead of improving, supplementing, and adapting a foreign work, with constant restraints thrown around me. I confess that Dr. Lange has often sorely tried my patience and defied my efforts to interpret his uncommon sense to the common sense of the English reader. But, with all his defects, if such they may be called, he has rare qualifications for sounding the mystic depths and and scaling the transcendent heights of John; and, in my humble judgment, he has dug more gold and silver from the mine of this Gospel, than any single commentator before him. He sees "the clear full-moon" behind the clouds, and where he does not see, he feels, divines, and adores. Every reader must admire his elaborate care, fertile genius, and lovely Johannean spirit.

Of the merits of my own additions others may judge. With all the minute labor bestowed upon it, the work is far from coming up to my own imperfect standard of a Commentary on this marvellous Gospel. At the end of my task I feel more strongly than ever that our best efforts to interpret the unfathomable depths of the words of the eternal Son of God, as recorded by His favorite disciple, are but the stammerings of a child. "Now we see through a glass, darkly," and know only "in part;" but the time will come when we shall see "face to face," and know "even as we are known." "It doth not yet appear what we shall be, but we know that, when He shall appear, we shall be like Him, for we shall see Him as He is."

One more volume remains to complete the American edition of the New Testament division of this *Bible-work.* The Commentary on the Revelation of John has recently appeared in German, and the English edition has been intrusted to able hands. A full Index of the whole work is also in course of preparation.

PHILIP SCHAFF.

BIBLE HOUSE, NEW YORK, May 1871.

[Shine graciously upon Thy Church, we beseech Thee, O Lord; that, being enlightened by the doctrine and filled with the mind of Thy blessed Apostle and Evangelist, Saint John, whom Jesus loved, it may come at last into Thy beatific presence, and enjoy the rewards of everlasting life; through Jesus Christ our Lord, who liveth and reigneth with Thee and the Holy Ghost, ever one God, world without end. Amen.—*Collect for St. John's Day, the second day after Christmas.*

[Volat avis sine meta
Quo nec vates nec propheta
Evolavit altius:
Tam implenda, quam impleta,
Nunquam vidit tot secreta
Purus homo purius.

Bird of God! with boundless flight
Soaring far beyond the height
Of the bard or prophet old;
Truth fulfilled, and truth to be,—
Never purer mystery
Did a purer tongue unfold!—]

THE GOSPEL ACCORDING TO JOHN;

OR,

THE GOSPEL OF THE ETERNAL IDEA OF THE HISTORY OF CHRIST,

OR OF HIS ETERNAL PERSONALITY, AND HIS KINGDOM OF LOVE, CONSIDERED AS THE REALITY AND FULFILMENT WHICH ALL SCRIPTURE AND THE WORLD SYMBOLIZE.

(JOHN'S SIGN: THE EAGLE.)

INTRODUCTION.

§ 1. JOHN, THE EVANGELIST AND APOSTLE, IN HIS PECULIAR CHARACTER AND LIFE.

On the name *Johanan*, God is gracious, or, God graciously gives, see the Commentary on *Matthew*, x. 2.* The character of the Evangelist and Apostle John, so peculiar in loftiness, idealness, richness, and depth, and yet clearly marked, cannot easily be described; though it seems easy to exhibit him in a sketch of his life from the New Testament authorities, and the statements of the fathers. The very difficulty is, to set forth duly the wonderful significance of all the historical features of his life, and to combine them in a true unit.

John, as a man, represents a firmness and unity of ideal turn, in which even inherent sinfulness veils itself without hypocrisy in the noble forms of devout zeal (Luke ix. 54), proud aspiration (Mark x. 35), and perhaps even courtly ease (John xviii. 16). As a Christian and an Apostle, he represents in the Church an apostolate of the heart and spirit of Jesus, in which he attracts even little catechumens with the patriarchal charms of kindliness; while he remains, even for the awakened and believing, veiled in a mysterious and ghostlike glimmer, in which he is often rather revered and praised, than heard through and studied out. To most every-day Christians he is too much of a Sunday nature for them to make themselves familiar with; and if his apostolic and churchly dignity did not shield him, scholars of the ordinary stamp would doubtless be inclined to consider him, for his great, heaven-high, and world-embracing conceptions, fantastic or visionary.

We may try to catch the transcendency, the idealness of his nature, by analogies. Somewhat thus: As Plato was related to Socrates, so is John to Christ. Or: The Evangelist John opens to us a deep, shadowy, presageful insight into infinity, like a night illumined by the

* [It is probable that the indirect self-designation of the Evangelist, "the disciple whom Jesus loved" (xiii. 23; xix. 25; xx. 2; xxi. 7, 20), is an ingenious interpretation of his name *John*, Ἰωάννης, יוֹחָנָן for יְהוֹחָנָן—i. e., *Jehovah is gracious* (comp. the Greek *Theodore*, and the German *Gotthold*, *Gottlieb*); for, according to the prologue, and chap. xii. 41, the Jehovah of the Old Testament, or God revealed, is the eternal Logos who became incarnate for our salvation. His name contained a prophecy which was fulfilled in his intimate relation to Christ.—P. S.]

moon (Asmus Claudius; see Tholuck's Introduction to his Commentary, p. 7 [Krauth's translation, p. 22]). Or, again, according to the ancient Church symbol of this Apostle: As the eagle soars against the sun, so John, in high flight of spirit, faces the sun of revelation in Christ (*e. g.*, Alcuin; see Credner's *Einleitung in das Neue Testament*, p. 57; Heubner, *Johannes*, p. 214). That John is most easily intelligible when taken as the contemplative disciple, in distinction from the practical disciple, the Apostle Peter, is palpable. The two apostles form the centre of the two halves of the apostolate, in which the operation of Christ shades itself off in the world; and from this point of view Andrew and the sons of Alpheus, James the Less, Simon Zelotes, Judas Lebbæus, and, as to natural talent, Judas Iscariot, range on the side of Peter; James the Elder, Philip, Thomas, Bartholomew-Nathanael, and Matthew, on the side of John. Our Evangelist is thus, in any case, balanced in his predominantly ideal tendency by the other side, as the Apostle Peter in his practical tendency is supplemented by his opposite.

But within this one sublime tendency itself there are opposites enough, which paraphrase this richest apostolic life. A repose of gaze, a predominance of insight, which, in the intensity of its light-like nature, easily springs into a lightning-flash; in other words, a serenity which manifests itself in the most glowing heartiness; a spiritual intuition which, with the most distinct logical consciousness, chooses the richest symbolical expression; an intellectual femineity of fervent surrender to the beloved central object of all its contemplations, displaying a masculine energy in the most copious organizing and formative works (Gospel, Epistles, Apocalypse); an originality which enriches itself with all the available material of religious learning (Logos-doctrine, Apocalyptics); a fervor of love which, in the keenest distinctions between light and darkness, proves its devoted personalness and its holiness; therefore a child-like and virgin-like nature, which unconsciously displays itself in an angelic majesty: all this pervaded with an unlimited depth of humility longing for salvation, and with a heroic faith, which, in assurance of consummation, soars above the already condemned world;—these are some of the antithetic features in which the character of John opens to us in the copiousness of his life.

And, like every predominantly ideal life, the life of John reveals itself most clearly in definite, more *actual* lines reflected from other characters. We prefer, therefore, to sketch his life by contrasts.

1. John and Salome. (See Matt. iv. 21; xx. 20; Mark xv. 40; xvi. 1; comp. Matt. xxvii. 56). John was the son of Zebedee, a fisherman of Galilee, residing we know not certainly whether at Bethsaida (Chrysostom, and others) or Capernaum (on this latter supposition, see Lücke, *Comment.*, p. 9). His mother was Salome, who no doubt was a sister of Mary, the mother of the Lord (John xix. 25; comp. Wieseler, *Studien und Kritiken*, 1840, iii. p. 648); and he himself, with his probably older brother James, was bred to his father's calling. The family has been styled a poor fishing family (Chrysostom); Lücke shows (p. 9) that it must have possessed some wealth. Zebedee had hired servants (Mark i. 20), and a partnership in business (Luke v. 10); his wife Salome was one of the women who supported the Lord from their means (Luke viii. 3), and embalmed his body; John himself owned a property (John xix. 27.) Whether this property, and his residence in Jerusalem, were the ground of his acquaintance in the house of the high-priest Caiaphas, cannot be determined. "Jerome unwarrantably inferred from that acquaintance that the family of John belonged to the better class."

Of his father Zebedee we know very little, yet enough. We may suppose that he consented to the discipleship of his sons, and probably (unless he died before Salome joined in the itinerancy of Jesus) to the discipleship of his wife. That "his mind seems not to have risen above the pursuit of earthly things" (Credner), is not necessarily to be inferred from his continuing at his nets. The family seems to have been fully of the sort who, familiar, in true Israelitish piety, with the Old Testament, were at that time living in quickened hope of the Messiah (Luke ii. 38). Salome especially shared this hope with womanlike surrender of soul. It is remarkable that the New Testament apocrypha, and the legends, relate the affinity of Salome and her family with the Lord, without knowing the true connection. Salome is said to have been now a daughter, now a sister, now a former wife of Joseph. She looks spiritually like a sister of Mary; noble of thought like her, she is more ambitious, more wilful, and therefore, on the other hand, more visionary (see Matt. xx. 20), though in spirit the true mother of a John and a James in cheerfulness of self-sacrifice (Luke viii. 3; xxiii. 55), and in that strength of attachment as a disciple, in which she remained steadfast under the cross. At the cross we lose sight of the noble woman (compare, however, Acts i. 14), who probably, with her sister Mary, lived a considerable time with her sons in Jerusalem in the house of John. We know not what part she may have had in John's coming so early into the school of his namesake, the Baptist. All the indications are, that she was the motherly fosterer of the great gifts of her sons, their guide on the path of the future toward the New Testament salvation.

How variously did the seer-like, expectant spirit of the women then on the sea of Galilee bear itself toward the New Testament future! The Mary in Nazareth becomes the chosen handmaid of the Lord; the Mary in Magdala lapses for a while, probably in wealthy circumstances, to a free-thinking, antinomian life of sensual love, misinterpreting the new time; Salome kindles in her sons the fire of a Messianic hope and search. Perhaps James, the more practical, was her favorite; John was her richer inheritance.

2. John and James. Probably James (*major*) was the older in relation to John as well as the other James, for he is always placed before John. Both were named, from their common traits, "sons of thunder" (Mark iii. 17; comp. the Comm. on *Matthew*, x. 2). It is simply inconceivable that the Lord, as Gurlitt thought (*Studien und Kritiken*, 1829, No. 4; comp. *Leben Jesu*, i. p. 281), should have given the two sons of Zebedee this name in pure censure. Though the well-known anger of the two brothers against a Samaritan city (Luke ix. 51), as is not at all improbable, gave occasion for this epithet, yet the Lord must have intended to denote and immortalize, not the sinfulness of His disciples, which was disappearing under the working of His Spirit, but only such a trait of character as was in itself capable of sanctification, though it had expressed itself sinfully here. Nathanael asks, in a sinful way: "Can any good thing come out of Nazareth?" Christ calls him, immediately after, a true Israelite, in whom is no guile. As in him a sinful haste in judgment was associated with noble uprightness, so, in the sons of thunder, that carnal zeal dwelt with an energy, a loftiness and decision of moral feeling, an exalted strength of character, which may utter itself in indignation like lightning. Theophylact referred the name to the thunder-like elevation and depth of their discourse (μεγαλοκήρυκες καὶ θεολογικώτατοι). Lücke remarks, that even the metaphorical sense of the Greek βροντᾶν is not quite suitable to this; still less the Aramaic רֶגֶשׁ (p. 17). But energy, grandeur, elevation of mind, according to the Old Testament import of thunder and storm, are, at all events, well expressed by this title. (See Ps. xxix.) That the name does not occur more frequently, is doubtless due to its being a collective name of both the brothers. But John gradually acquired a surname of his own: "the disciple whom Jesus loved;" the friend of Jesus in the most eminent sense, the bosom friend, who lay on His breast; hence, among the fathers, ἐπιστήθιος (Lücke, p. 14). And James had to be distinguished from the other James, as the son of Zebedee; and thus, in his case also, the surname remained unused. But he proved himself the spiritual brother of John on his entrance upon his discipleship (Matt. iv. 21); in the fiery zeal just mentioned (Luke ix. 51); in that well-known request of the sons of Zebedee, which was at the same time the request of their mother (Mark x. 35; Matt. xx. 20); and his superior character was recognized by the Lord, who made James, with Peter and John, in the select triad, a confidant of His highest mysteries (Matt. xvii. 1; xxvi. 27).

But if John takes precedence of him as the companion of Peter in the Lord's most special errands of symbolical prophetic meaning (Luke xxii. 8), and if afterwards, in the apostolic fortunes of the brothers, the greatest contrast appears which is to be found in the history of the apostles, there must have been also a contrast in the character of the two. We suppose that the lofty energy of soul in James received from his mother Salome a practical direction, and hastened to outward action; while John found his highest satisfaction in ideal action, developing and reproducing his impressions. Hence it was probably James in particular who, in the indignation against the Samaritan village, and in other cases, urged to action; while John was perhaps the one to ask the Lord: "Wilt thou that we command fire to come down from heaven?" And again, it was probably James in particular who forbade the exorcist casting out devils in the name of Jesus (Mark ix. 38), and who afterwards was foremost in the request for the first place in the kingdom of the Lord. We infer this from the fact that James the Elder seems at the first to have been, above all others, the leader or representative of the church at Jerusalem. At all events, it could not have been without reason that he was the first seized by Herod Agrippa I. in his persecution of the apostles (Acts xii. 1).

Thus the elder son of Zebedee was the first martyr among the apostles, while the younger was almost the last of the apostles (Simon Zelotes probably died later, about 107, a martyr's death) to be taken home, and, after a temporary exile, died a natural death, toward the end of the century. John, with his contemplative, stately, ideal mind, went angel-like through life. As he did not interfere directly and by main force with the world, he was little heeded by the world; though, by virtue of his hidden depth of life, he was doubtless a mighty lever of motion, an awakener of kindred spirits, even from the time he was a disciple of the Baptist.

The contrast between the two sons of Zebedee may also explain the fact that James the Elder is only once mentioned in the fourth Gospel, chap. xxi. 2. The Evangelist used only those materials of the gospel history which would completely present his ideal view. Notices of James lay in another direction. Even his mother John mentions only in circumlocution; and he speaks in the same indirect way of himself. (See John xx. 4; xxi. 7.)

3. John the Evangelist and John the Baptist. A John represents in the gospel history the deepest trend of the Old Testament, as it prepares for and points to the first advent of Christ (John i. 6); a John again represents the New Testament, which proceeds from Christ, as, in its deepest current, it prepares for the second coming of Christ in glory (John xxi.). *God is gracious*, is the name of the forerunner, who is greater than all the prophets; *God is gracious*, is the name of the disciple of Jesus who does not die. Believing hope of the Messiah made the younger son of Zebedee, even in youth, a disciple of John; believing certainty of the Messiah makes him one of the first to enter the discipleship of Christ (John i. 35); and that, at the words of the Baptist: "Behold the Lamb of God." Indeed, it is a characteristic, that the ideal Apostle has taken even the Baptist entirely on his evangelical side, leaving the severe preacher of the law and of repentance quite out of view. The difference between the treatment of the Baptist in the Synoptical Gospels and in John exactly corresponds with the difference in the portraiture of Christ. And yet it is the same Christ, the same John the Baptist, viewed on the side most congenial to this disciple.

The Old Testament John was to the New Testament John the voice of the gospel spirit of the Old Testament (chap. i. 23), the witness-bearer of God who pointed to Christ. In this spirit the disciple was joined to the master in a fellowship which embraced the strongest antithesis. In energy of moral indignation he could assuredly vie with the Baptist; and the words of John the Baptist: "He shall baptize you with fire," "He will burn up the chaff," might have been in his mind when he wished to baptize with fire and burn the Samaritan village.

But by degrees the mighty contrast appeared between the master senescent in spirit, legal, ascetic, austere, and practical, and the disciple eternally youthful, contemplative, joyful, festal, hovering over the earthly world. The christology of the Baptist ended in the historical Messiahship of Jesus of Nazareth, and His priestly atoning sufferings and kingly judging; the christology of the son of Zebedee transfigured heaven and earth into an emblem and copy of the universal Christ. And between the later disciples of John the Baptist and the theology of John the Divine, this contrast became a very chasm.

Nevertheless, both names doubtless have given the name John unlimited currency in

Christendom. Every encyclopædia testifies how many princes, scholars, and divines are graced with this name; and how many popes—sometimes, shamelessly enough, without a breath of the spirit of John—have chosen his name for their decoration.

4. John and Andrew. The fisherman's son John had gone with the fisherman Andrew from Bethsaida into the school of the Baptist on the Jordan. That Andrew was one of the foremost pioneering spirits among the apostles, is attested by the few traces of him in the gospel history, and by the legend. (*Leben Jesu*, ii. 2, p. 695; comp. Winer: *Andreas*). Andrew brought Simon Peter, his brother, to Jesus. It is possible that John had, in like manner, won over his brother James. At all events, both Andrew and John were men of pioneering, progressive mind. Hence they were admitted, with Peter and James, to the confidential eschatological discourse of Christ on the Mount of Olives (Mark xiii. 3). But they led off on different paths: the one on the path of missionary action, the other on the path of that knowledge which overcomes the world.

5. John and Judas Iscariot. If we can suppose that Judas the traitor had blinded most of the disciples by his Messianic enthusiasm, and was able often to carry them with him (*Leben Jesu*, ii. 2, p. 702; comp. p. 651 sqq.)—indeed, that he had probably been received into the circle upon the special intercession of the disciples in their blind confidence—John was the first to see through him (chap. vi. 71; xii. 6; xiii. 27). The silent depth of a solid enthusiasm and devotion finds itself instinctively repelled by the flaring fire of an impure ambition. And as Judas was the serpent which coiled himself upon the bosom of the Lord (John xiii. 18), John lay on the breast of Jesus as a chosen friend. Even he might often grieve Him (Luke ix. 54; Mark ix. 38; x. 35), and for a moment forsake Him, but he soon returns to His side (chap. xviii. 16), and, though not a confessor in word, as he was not yet required to be, he is a confessor in act, as he stands and waits with the mother of Jesus beneath the cross (chap. xix. 26).

6. John and Abraham, or, John the Friend of Jesus. As Abraham was distinguished above all the men of the Old Covenant by being called, in a special sense, a "friend of God" (James ii. 23), so John is honored above all the men of the New, as the friend of Jesus. And in both cases the reason of this eminence must have lain in an energy of personal knowledge or steadfast love in these friends of God and Christ, arising from a particular Divine election. Abraham was called by a personal God into a personal covenant, and, by his self-surrender to the personal God, his own personal life was transfigured and secured to him down to an endless posterity; for this personal love he gave up home and friends, and all things, and gained the promise of the Holy Land and an hereditary kingdom (Gen. xii. 1–7). So John resigned himself to the knowledge of the world-embracing, divine personality of Christ, with a devotion which cast the whole world into the shadow of Christ. In this contemplation of the personal Christ he acquired that peculiar radiance in which he appears as the friend of Christ. Judas loved Jesus for a while for the sake of the Messianic kingdom as he conceived it; the other disciples, on the path of their discipleship, loved Jesus and His kingdom; John found all in the person of Jesus: kingdom and redemption, Father and home.

Hence he is at first one of the disciples, in the general sense (John i.; Matt. iv.); then, one of the twelve (Matt. x.); then, one of the three (Matt. xvii.); then, one of the two (Luke xvii. 18); at last, the *one* who lies on the bosom of Jesus (John xiii. 23), to whom Jesus commits His mother at the cross (chap. xix.), to whom alone He promises a tarrying till He come again (chap. xxi.), and to whom, on the island of his exile, the Lord once more appears in personal majesty, long after His personal appearances among His people have ceased (Rev. i.).

7. John and Mary. That a special affinity of spirit existed between the mother and the friend of the Lord, might naturally be presumed, and is confirmed by the direction of Christ upon the cross. It would be contrary to all christological principles to suppose that Jesus, by that bequest, severed and abolished His human relation to His mother. The kingdom of glory glorifies human relations; it no more annuls them, than it abolishes the human nature of Christ himself. But the comfort of intimate friendship, which contributes to the

edification of His people, Christ appoints to these two sufferers. To Mary and John the form of Christ had become most copiously and most purely transfigured. Mary seems to have led, for a considerable time, a quiet life in communion of spirit with John in his house at Jerusalem (John xix. 27; see the article "Maria," in Winer). Both lived in joyful musing on the past, the present, and the future of the Lord. Without doubt they formed a most efficient support of the congregation at Jerusalem, which was the whole church at first; and Mary might well have had a mental part in the "one tender leading Gospel." *

John himself, indeed, was a predominantly feminine nature, if by that be understood the perfect receptivity and self-surrender which is proper to all religious feeling and exercises of faith. (See the article "John" in Herzog's *Encyclopædia*, by Ebrard.) But a feminine nature, in the stricter sense, he cannot be called. He was great not merely in receiving and feeling, but also in contemplative reproduction, statement, and imagination, though his statement and imagination were eminently ideal. More sublime compositions than the fourth Gospel and the Revelation cannot be conceived. This plastic, creative work, was by no means of the nature of secular art for being ideal. It produced awakening and edifying creations for the Church. But John also, in his way, labored practically, as much perhaps as Peter, only in a direction less striking to the eye.

8. John and Peter; or, John and the first half of the apostolic age. It is not correct to call Peter, without qualification, the first of the apostles. Peter and John mark the contrast in the position of the apostles between Christ and the world. John is the first on the side of the apostolate toward Christ; Peter, the first on the side toward the world, and in that view truly the first of the apostles in the stricter sense. If, therefore, John for the most part stands in lofty silence beside the speaking and acting Peter (Acts, chaps. iii., viii., and xv.), we should greatly err if we should take him for a mute or in any way passive figure, according to the measure of his silence. John had no talent for popularity; he was always too much the whole man for that (see the above-mentioned article of Ebrard), too directly exposed his inward views and movements; but it may well be supposed that, as a support, a spiritual guide, he exerted almost as determining an influence upon Peter, as Peter exerted upon the world and the Church. The indications of this we find, for example, in John, chaps. xviii., xx., and xxi. So far as Peter might still need human advice, he found his privy council in the house of John and Mary; though we need not attribute to this circumstance the fact that in the apostolic council at Jerusalem he stood so firmly for the freedom of faith (Acts xv.), while soon after, at Antioch, where he was without the guidance of John, he wavered once more, and should have found his support in Paul. We at last find John, however, in that council in Jerusalem (about the year 53 [50]), and find him, with Peter and James the Less, one of the three pillars of the church (Gal. ii.). If there was at that time any definite demarcation of the three several positions of those pillars in the Jewish mission, as there was between that mission as a whole and the Gentile mission of Paul, James, it seems to be certain, was the president of the mother-church at Jerusalem, Peter more especially devoted to the Hebrew Diaspora, John to the Hellenists, or the Jews and proselytes of Grecian education.

This explains the wavering of Peter at Antioch, and his journey to Babylon to the Jews resident there; and it explains the later residence of John in Asia Minor, and his doctrine of the Logos, which we regard as determined by his intercourse with Hellenistic Jews. This direction of John's labors rested upon the universal destination which Christ had assigned him (John xxi.).

Peter may be said to have laid the foundation of the Christian Church, as a historical martyr; John, as a spiritual martyr, to have embraced in his mind all the ages of the development of the Church; to form her ideal, mystical background; to move through the dark times of her conflicts and through her predominantly practical tendencies as the great unknown, notwithstanding the thousand Johns in Christendom; perpetuating himself espe-

* ["*Das eine zarte Hauptevangelium*," an expression of Luther applied to the Gospel of John.—P. S.]

cially in all the healthful mystical and contemplative theology, to break forth in the end of the days with his full spiritual operation, and present to the Lord, as a bride adorned for her husband, a John-like church, matured in spiritual life.

Thus, as Peter was the first of the apostles in their relation to the world, John was the first in their relation to Christ. The talent of Peter was ideally practical; that of John, practically ideal. Peter is the chief of the working, edifying, upbuilding spirits of the Church; John, the chief of the contemplative. In John, the basis of enthusiasm or devotion to Christ was not an inexhaustible impulse to do, but a deep, wondering celebration of the eternal fact and work of the perfection of Christ.* The fundamental characteristic of Peter was energetic heart; that of John, reposing heartiness. John's piety, therefore, like that of Peter, has the character of the highest purity. In his humility he goes, with great delicacy, even to the suppression of himself, his mother, and his brother James, in his Gospel; introducing himself merely as "a disciple" of Christ (i. 40), or as "the disciple whom Jesus loved" (xiii. 23); his mother Salome, only as sister of the mother of Jesus (xix. 25); and James the Elder but once, as son of Zebedee. In like manner, through the terrors of the world his heart goes almost equally undisturbed. In the house of the high-priest he stands upright beside the falling Peter. His love has the character of tender depth; his believing knowledge is an intuitive beholding, rising to lyric stateliness. The ideas of love, life, and light, hatred, death, and darkness, are the fundamental elements of his ideal conception of Christianity and the world. Hence, to him, the Logos, as the original unity of these three elements, is the groundwork—the glory (the δόξα), or the absolute manifestation (ἐπιφάνεια), the final goal of the revelation of God. Peter sees the glory of Christ chiefly in the mighty unfolding of the glory of His kingdom; John sees all the glory of the kingdom of Christ comprised in the single glory of His personal exaltation and His future appearing. But his contemplativeness is not an idle posture; it is the energy of faith; it therefore supplies a silent force which proves itself preëminently an inwardly purifying agency in the Church; and it therefore expresses itself in the strongest abhorrence of evil. Thus John clarifies the Christian doctrine, the body of believers, the Church. And as, therefore, the contemplative Apostle was called to enlarge and complete the New Testament in *all its constituent elements* [historical, didactic, and prophetic], so also the purifying Apostle was called to be longest at the head of the apostolic Church, (Lange's *Apost. Zeitalter*, i. p. 358; comp. *Leben Jesu*, i. p. 262; Schaff's *Hist. of the Apost. Church*, § 103, pp. 407–411.)

[9. John and Paul. As our author omits to contrast the beloved disciple who impressed *Christ's image* most deeply into the heart of the Church, with the great Apostle of the Gentiles, who *labored* more than all in word and work, we insert here the following, by way of supplement, from Schaff's *History of the Apostolic Church*, Amer. ed., p. 411: "John and Paul have depth of knowledge in common. They are the two apostles who have left us the most complete systems of doctrine. But they know in different ways. Paul, educated in the schools of the Pharisees, is an exceedingly acute thinker and an accomplished dialectician. He sets forth the doctrines of Christianity in a systematic scheme, proceeding from cause to effect, from the general to the particular, from premise to conclusion, with logical clearness and precision. He is a representative of genuine *scholasticism*, in the best sense of the term. John's knowledge is that of intuition and contemplation. He gazes with his whole soul upon the object before him, surveys all as in one picture, and thus presents the profoundest truths as an eye-witness, not by a course of logical demonstration, but immediately as they lie in reality before him. His knowledge of divine things is the deep insight of love, which ever fixes itself at the centre, and thence surveys all points of the circumference at once. He is the representative of all true *mysticism*. Both these apostles together

* [The difference between Peter and John in their relation to Christ is parallel with the difference between Martha and Mary. Both loved the Saviour with their whole heart, but the one showed it more by outward, busy action, the other by inward, quiet contemplation; the one loved Him in His official dignity as the Messiah, the other in His personal character as the fountain of spiritual life. As Grotius ingeniously suggests, Peter was more a friend of Christ (Christophilos, or Philochristos), John a friend of Jesus (Jesuphilos), his bosom friend.—P. S.]

meet all the demands of the mind thirsting for wisdom; of the keenly-dissecting understanding, as well as the speculative reason, which comprehends what is thus analyzed in its highest unity; of mediate reflection as well as immediate intuition. Paul and John, in their two grand systems, have laid the eternal foundations of all true theology and philosophy; and their writings, now after eighteen centuries of study, are still unfathomed."]

10. JOHN AND SIMON. After the Apostolic Council, John disappears from the New Testament history of the apostles. When Paul made his last visit to Jerusalem (about the year 59 or 60), he conferred only with James and the elders. John was away—at all events, not present with the others. And he could not yet have been in Ephesus when Paul, some years later (about 67), wrote thither to Timothy. To the question, where he may have been in the meantime, the traditions of the ancient Church give no answer (see Lücke, p. 23; my *Apost. Zeitalter*, ii. p. 420). If we suppose that, in his noiseless solicitude, he went to Peræa on the first symptoms of the Jewish war, and prepared the way for the settlement of the community in Pella, it is only a conjecture. But since John was the greatest seer among the Christians, the statement of Eusebius (iii. 5), that an oracle was imparted by revelation to the most approved of the Church, which directed the whole Christian people to emigrate from Jerusalem and seek a new abode in a city of Peræa called Pella; and the statement of Epiphanius, that an angel from heaven instructed the Christians to leave the capital (*De ponderibus et mensuris*, cap. 15), may naturally be referred above all to the outstripping prophetic gift of John. To this, add the presumption that John, even before taking his residence in Ephesus—that is, while preparing for the composition of his Gospel, which seems to have taken place, at least in part, before the destruction of Jerusalem (see below, and *Apost. Zeitalter*, ii. p. 420)—became familiar with Grecian modes of thought, as his Gospel shows. This familiarity he might have first gained in the Palestinian Decapolis, especially in Pella. Here the Jewish-Christian type of thought must have mingled with the Greek-Christian.

Pella therefore formed the natural bridge for the Apostle from Jerusalem to Ephesus, and probably he did not leave the congregation at Pella, to pass to Asia Minor, until it was firmly established.

We infer this course of things also from the harmonious correspondence in which the Jewish-Christian church at Pella (*Apost. Zeitalter*, ii. p. 263), under the direction of Simon, stood with the Gentile-Christian church of John at Ephesus. It is the fact, that the Jewish-Christian church in Pella, under the bishop Simon, stood in communion with the Gentile Christians. This appears, first, from the very fact of the flight of these Jewish Christians to Pella; they did not share the fanaticism of the Jews who went to destruction with their temple. Then, from the account of Hegesippus, that the aged Simon was martyred through the treachery of the Jewish-Christian heretics (Euseb. iii. 32). What they hated in Simon, could only be his more liberal, anti-Ebionistic position. Finally, from the account of Epiphanius and Sulpitius Severus, that "at the time that Hadrian prohibited the Jews from going to Ælia Capitolina, the Christians, in order that they might return to the Holy City, had put away every connection with the Jewish worship, and had confirmed this renunciation by choosing a Gentile bishop by the name of Mark." But certainly so great a freedom must have time to ripen; and this was afforded by the episcopate of Simon. It is further to be observed, that, according to the testimony of the monk Maximus, Aristo of Pella wrote an apology against the Jews; Clement of Alexandria attributed this apology to Luke (*Apost. Zeitalter*, ii. 464).

But if the church of Pella was in decided fellowship with the Gentile Christians, the church of Ephesus and Asia Minor, which in its main element was Gentile-Christian, was in equally decided fellowship with the Jewish Christians. In favor of this is, first of all, the strong affinity of the writings of John, especially of the Apocalypse (which most certainly belongs to Asia Minor), with the Old Testament, and with Old Testament images and modes of expression. Then it is a fact that John, with the Christians of Asia Minor, observed Easter according to the Jewish reckoning, and at the same time with the Jews; as is proved by the testimony of the bishop Polycrates in the Easter controversies (Euseb. iii. 31; v. 24).

Finally, it is well known that John had to contend as firmly in Ephesus against the Gentile-Christian Gnosticism, as Simon in Pella against the Jewish-Christian Ebionism. This his writings, and the testimony of the ancients, prove. (See the section on the Design of the Gospel, below.) His contest was, indeed, in part with the mixed forms of a Gnostic Ebionism, as represented by Cerinthus. As to the affinity of John with Judaism, Irenæus infers from the Acts, and from Gal. ii. 9, that, so long as he was in Jerusalem, John, with the other apostles, continued the strict (religious) observance of the Mosaic law (*Adv. Hæreses*, iii. 12). "This, however," observes Lücke (p. 19), "is to be very much qualified on account of the growing separation between the Jewish and Christian communities in Jerusalem."

But the degree of this separation, and the whole import of it, must be distinctly fixed. The apostles were severed from Judaism in principle by the death of Christ (Eph. ii. 15; Col. ii. 14; Acts xv.). By the real Passover, the Jewish Passover, as a type, was for them abolished; that is to say, the centre of communion in the Jewish religion was for them destroyed (John xix. 36). No element of Judaism could henceforth appear to the apostles necessary to salvation (Acts xv. 10, 11). But this did not require them to abandon the fellowship of the temple; the less, since, on the preaching of Peter (Acts ii.), a large Jewish-Christian congregation had formed itself about them. According to the law of the Spirit, they did not withdraw, but they suffered themselves to be thrust out. The gradations of this passive excommunication appear plainly in Acts v. 40; vii. 58; xii. 1, 2; xv.; to which add especially the execution of James the Just (see "James," in Winer). But if, nevertheless, the apostles supposed that circumcision might continue among the Jewish Christians, and if they even, according to Acts xv., made it the duty of the Gentile Christians to bind themselves to the so-called Noachic commandments, we must again insist, that these were not *religious conditions of the inward assurance of salvation, but ethical conditions of the outward fellowship of salvation, or of the communion between Jewish and Gentile Christians*, ecclesiastical, ethical dogmas, the formal obligation of which might vanish with the vanishing occasion of them (the prohibition of blood). The statement of Polycrates of Ephesus (Euseb. iii. 31; v. 24), that John, being of the family of the high-priest, continued, while an Apostle, to wear the high-priest's diadem (πέταλον) among the Jews, we consider, like the similar statement of Epiphanius respecting James the Just, (with Solomon Cyprian,) a symbolical mode of expressing the preëminent authority of John among the early Christians (Lücke, p. 20, note).

Thus we see the harmonious contrast which existed in the first half of the apostolic age between the churches of Jerusalem and Antioch under the leadership of Peter and Paul, and then of James and Paul, in the second half of the apostolic age, the most obscure period of the rise of the Church, the time of its sprouting in the field of the world like winter grain under the snow, propagating itself in the contrast of Pella and Ephesus under the apostolic episcopates of Simon and John.

How the residence of John in Ephesus is related to the Church tradition that Timothy was the first bishop of Ephesus (Euseb. iii. 14), cannot be accurately determined. If it be possible that Timothy continued to labor in Ephesus under the direction of John, it is, on the other hand, improbable that he should have died here as a martyr under Domitian (Niceph. iii. 14), while banishment only was inflicted upon John.

Two points in reference to the later life and the death of John remain to be particularly noted: the question of the time of his banishment to Patmos, and the testimonies respecting his great age and his end.

We consider the assumption that John was banished to Patmos under the reign of Domitian, established both by ancient testimonies and by modern researches. According to Irenæus (v. 30), John had his vision toward the end of the reign of Domitian. According to Clement of Alexandria (*Quis Dives salvus*, § 42, and in Euseb. iii. 23), John was recalled from the island of Patmos to Ephesus after the death of the tyrant. He does not, indeed, name the tyrant; but this indicates that the tradition was already quite established. Origen also appeals to a settled tradition (on Matt. xx. 22, 23). Eusebius (iii. 18, 23, Chronicon on the fourteenth year of Domitian) has explicitly fixed this tradition *under Domitian*. The variations from it begin with Epiphanius. They are divided between Claudius and Nero. The older rest on conjectures, the later in good part on dogmatic prejudice. Internal evidences: the picture of a later condition of the Church in the Apocalypse (*e. g.*, c. iii. 18, &c.) speaks likewise for the time of Domitian. Also a more general form of persecution than that under Nero. In a more extended induction, specially directed against Lücke, Hengstenberg (*Die Offenbarung des Johannes*, p. 2 sqq.) has vindicated anew the ancient tradition The composition of the Apocalypse accordingly falls in the years 95 and 96. Tertullian has supplemented the historical fact by the legend that John, before his banishment, was immersed in boiling oil at Rome, but came out unharmed.

There lies, then, probably a long interval between the first settlement of John in Ephesus and his banishment to Patmos. In this interval of great, silent ministry, the Johannean school and church bloomed in Ephesus and Asia Minor.

The death of John in Ephesus is attested by the Easter Epistle of the Bishop Polycrates of Ephesus, so early as the middle of the second century. According to Irenæus, he died in the reign of Trajan; therefore after the year 98. According to Jerome, he attained the age of one hundred years; according to Suidas, a hundred and twenty. The Chronicon Paschale says he had lived in Ephesus for nine years before his exile on Patmos, spent fifteen years in exile, lived twenty-six years after the exile, and died at the age of a hundred years and seven months, in the seventh year of the reign of Trajan. He must have been near a hundred years old; for Polycarp, who died about 170, and Papias, who died in 164, had been his disciples.

The Church tradition has preserved some significant incidents of his later life: (1.) Of his heroism in rescuing from robbers a youth who had been converted by him, and had afterwards apostatized (Euseb. iii. 23, after Clement of Alexandria); (2.) of his flight from a bath in which the heretic Cerinthus was (Iren., *Haers.* iii. 3, 28); (3.) of the raising of a dead man by his hand at Ephesus (Euseb. v. 18); (4.) of his play with a partridge, which he made the emblem of the blessing of recreation (Joh. Cassian, *Collat.* xxiv. 21); * (5.) of his last sermon: Little children, love one another (Hieron., *Comment. ad Galat.* vi.).

The statements of tradition have gathered embellishing legends of his miraculous burial and end, and even of his continuing alive, with reference to John xxi. 22: (1.) According to pseudo-Hippolytus, he did not die, but was translated, like Enoch and Elijah. (2.) Augustine tells the story, from apocrypha, that he caused his grave to be prepared while he yet lived, and laid himself in it, as in a bed, to die; and on the ground of the expression in John xxi., it was believed that he did not actually die, but only slept; his breathing moved the earth over his grave, and continually threw up a white powder from beneath. This last was reported, Augustine says, by trustworthy people. (3.) In the Middle Ages, and even in modern times, the saying has been widely spread, that he still lives. Lücke says: Certainly in his writings. Why not as much in his spiritual kin, and in the John-like mystical and mysterious background of the Church? (4.) The legend that God raised him from the grave, and preserved him for the last times, in which he was to bear witness to the truth, and, with Enoch and Elijah, resist Antichrist.

Polycrates called him a martyr (according to Euseb. iii. 31; v. 24); no doubt in the antique sense of a witness who persevered even unto death. Subsequently it was a trouble to Chrysostom and Augustine, that he was not a martyr in the literal sense. The early Church, on the contrary, celebrated his remaining always a stranger to sensual love, and extolled him as the virgin-like, παρθένιος, παρθένος, from Rev. xiv. 4.†

That John was a martyr and a virgin-like spirit in a higher sense than the legalistic

* [Prof. Plumptre, in his article on John in Smith's *Dictionary of the Bible*, i., p. 1107 (in Hackett's ed. p. 1423), is disposed to accept this tradition of Cassian, as illustrating the truth—

"He prayeth best who loveth best
All things both great and small."—P. S.].

† [Augustine calls him "*virgo mente et corpore.*" St. John may certainly be regarded as the highest male type of all moral chasity, as the Virgin Mary stands out as the model of female purity.—P. S.]

Church could conceive, is evinced by the whole character of his inner life. Who can tell what griefs a legalistic and formalistic tendency in the later apostolic age alone had already prepared for him (see the first of his three Epistles)? He has the promise, that he shall not die, but live till the Lord come, and doubtless come forth in some special way toward the end of the days, before the coming of the Lord;—which has given occasion to Schelling's profound construction of the three successive apostolic periods (the Petrine, the Pauline, and the Johannean). See my *Geschichte des apostolischen Zeitalters*, ii. p. 649, and Schaff's *Hist. of the Apostolic Church*, Amer. ed., pp. 674–678 [and Schaff's note to Lange on *Romans*, Amer. ed., pp. 1, 2].

There are named to us as immediate disciples of John, Papias (underrated by Eusebius), Ignatius of Antioch, and Polycarp (Euseb. iii. 22, 39; Iren. iii. 3; Euseb. v. 20 and 24). But with the rising importance of Irenæus, Hippolytus, and other representatives of the Asiatic Church in Italy, South France, and Britain, the importance of the school of John also must come more into view. It was the salt of the mediæval Church, and continues to prove itself a quickening element in theology and the Church, tarrying for a richer future (see the citations of Meyer, p. 4; my *Apost. Zeitalt.*, ii. p. 448; p. 466; p. 603; the article "John," by Ebrard, in Herzog's *Encyclopædia*; the same article in Winer's *Real-Lexikon* and in the Commentaries, &c.). For further sources for the biography of John, see especially Credner's *Einleitung*, p. 214 sqq. [The reader is also referred for biographical details to the article *John* in the English Bible Dictionaries of Smith (Hackett and Abbot's ed.), Kitto, and Fairbairn, and to Schaff's *Hist. of the Apost. Church*, §§ 99–108, pp. 395–430. On the legends respecting the Apostle, see Mrs. Jameson's *Sacred and Legendary Art*, i. 157–172, 5th ed.—P. S.]

§ 2. THE WRITINGS OF JOHN.

The writings preserved by the Church under the name of John, of the genuineness of which we must speak in the proper place, with all their diversity, corresponding to the diversity of their literary species, have so many and so important peculiar traits, and have these traits, too, so much in common, that, with a better developed taste in regard to biblical style, we shall be no more able to ascribe them to different authors, than to attribute the different masterpieces of one great painter to different masters.

The peculiarities of the matter of these writings are: (1.) The depth and fulness of the christological idea of Christ and His kingdom (*the Word*); (2.) The spiritual concentration of the depth and fulness of the Messianic life in the personality of the Lord, making heaven and earth a symbolism of Christianity, of its struggles and its triumphs (*Love*); (3.) The universalism of Christianity, grounded in God, embracing and shining through the world (*Life*); (4.) The festive spirit of the assurance of victory, wherein Christ in His imperial power destroys the works of the devil as works of falsehood and darkness (*Light*). Love, life, and light, in the sense of infinite fulness and personal distinctness, come forth with the Word, and destroy the kingdom of hatred, darkness, and death.

In reference to the first trait, compare John i. 1–3; 1 John i. 2; Rev. i. 5–8. For the second, see John i. 4, 14; 1 John iv. 8, 12; comp. chap. i. 7; Rev. i. 17, 18; comp. chap. v. 6. For the third, John v. 26; xi. 25; xiv. 6; 1 John i. 2; ii. 25; Rev. vii. 13; chap. xxi. For the fourth, John viii. 12; 1 John i. 7; Rev. xxi. 23. The views homogeneous, however, pervade all the writings of John; everywhere the divine Word, Love, Light, Life; the destruction of the destroyer of man, and of his manifestations, hatred, darkness, and death.

If it be objected that these traits appear also in the other apostolic authors, we most readily grant it in a certain sense; for John is not Christ, and has no new Christ. But in the proportions of his christology he is beyond even Paul, with reference to the first trait, in the *distinctly expressed* celebration of the Logos with God *in an ontological trinity*, his eternal existence *God-ward;* with reference to the second, in the fact that for him the personality of Christ is his history, not the converse, and of Christ not only as made man, but also as made flesh; with reference to the third, in his making Christ not only the creative and upholding force of the world, as in Paul (Col. i. 17), but also the inmost kernel, the gist, the truth of its life (John xv. 1); with reference to the fourth, in the fact that, with John, Christ not only in an ethical operation enlightens the world, and luminously judges and awakens it, but also is the ideal truth and reality of the world, reducing and exalting the whole real world to a transparent symbol of the eternal kingdom of light and love.*

To these peculiarities of the matter of the Johannean writings, their peculiarities of form correspond: (1.) The mighty unity of principle, ruling the whole representation—that is, the clearness and transparence of the theme, the motto of the books. (2.) The personal holding and shaping of all historical and didactic matters, to give their central, spiritual, hearty expression. (3.) The universal grandeur, sublimity, and organically pure structure of the compositions, and the richness of the elements embraced and organized by them. (4.) The lyric, festive diction, with the consequent directness of expression, the limited but pregnant fund of language, and the inimitable coloring, reminding only of the Song of Songs, and of the highest products of human poesy. On the diction of John, and his circle of words, see Credner, *Einleitung*, p. 222; Guericke, *Isagogik*, p. 205 [p. 213 in the 3d ed. of 1868].

Just this deep and beautiful monotony of the Johannean view and statement contains the reason, however, why the Johannean spirit unfolds itself in the copious variety of views and of forms. The trunk, rooted in a bottomless depth, strong in its solitary unity, spreads its palm-crown far out over the New Testament.

We have four Evangelists in the New Testament; John, the Evangelist who lay on Jesus' bosom, wrote the most profound and far-reaching Gospel, the fourth, and the complement of the other three.

The Apostle Paul left the richest treasure of Epistles; John, the Apostle and primitive presbyter of the Church, left a trilogy of Epistles, in which the deepest essence and the ideal order of the fellowship of the Church in Christ reflects itself for all ages.

The Evangelist Luke is, next to Paul and John, the most copious author of the New Testament (the Gospel of Luke and the Acts). Luke, in his exhibition of the life of Jesus, went back to the historical beginning of his childhood, and Luke's final historical goal was the Church in Rome; but the Gospel of John goes back into the depths of the Godhead, and the Apocalypse exhibits the entire history of the Church to its consummation in the new, eternal city of God (not in the eternal world, for the actual world must merge organically in the thoroughly personal city of God).

If we remember that the first three Evangelists wrote on special occasion, and that the Epistles of Paul were in reality not literary productions, but historical acts, John appears as preëminently *the author* of the New Testament, even more than Luke, and, as such, entirely fitted to appear for the holiness of the Bible. The language of Scripture is the word of spirit; in this language must the disciple who does not die especially speak.

Some have found a considerable difference between the Gospel and the Epistles of John. But here the unity in the diversity needs apology least of all.

But the contrast between the Gospel of John and the Apocalypse has been urged with very special emphasis. It has been said [by De Wette, Lücke, Bleek, and others] that John,

* [From Schaff's *History of the Apostolic Church*, p. 618: "John's theology is by no means so complete, or developed with such logical precision and argumentative ability, as that of Paul. It is sketched from immediate intuition, in extremely simple, artless, childlike form, in grand outlines, in few but colossal ideas and antitheses, such as light and darkness, truth and falsehood, spirit and flesh, love and hatred, life and death, Christ and Antichrist, children of God and children of the world. But John usually leaves us to imagine far more than his words directly express—an infinity lying behind, which we can better apprehend by faith, than grasp and fully measure with the understanding. And especially does he connect every thing with that idea of a theanthropic Redeemer, which had become part and parcel of his own soul; nor can he strongly and frequently enough assert the reality and glory of that which was to him, of all facts and experiences, the surest, the holiest, and the dearest. But with regard to its principle, and the point of view from which it is constructed, the doctrinal system of John is the highest and most ideal of all—the one toward which the others lead and in which they merge. It wonderfully combines mystic knowledge and love, contemplation and adoration, the profound wisdom and childlike simplicity, and is an anticipation, as it were, of that vision face to face, into which, according to Paul (1 Cor. xiii. 12; comp. 2 Cor. v. 7), our fragmentary knowledge, and faith itself, will finally pass."]

the author of the Gospel, cannot have written the Revelation. Minds like Luther and Göthe have measured and mismeasured their strength upon the Apocalypse. Then again it has been said [by Dr. Baur and the Tübingen school], John was the author of the Apocalypse, and therefore cannot have written the fourth Gospel. But in the end it has to be conceded that only one person, the author of the fourth Gospel, could have written the Apocalypse; and that, conversely, only one man, the author of the Apocalypse, can have been the writer of the Gospel. It is one thing to speak in the understanding [νοῦς], in reflective consciousness; another, to speak in the spirit [πνεῦμα], in the directness of an inspired frame (1 Cor. xiv. 15). The Gospel requires the Apocalypse, the Apocalypse presupposes the Gospel (see my *Vermischte Schriften*, vol. ii. p. 173, and Schaff, *Hist. of the Apost. Church*, § 107, pp. 422 ff.). The supposition of two authors, besides, is connected with Eusebius' old fiction of the presbyter John of Ephesus, which arose from a misinterpretation of Papias. (On this, comp. Guericke, *Die Hypothese von dem Presbyter Johannes, als Verfasser der Offenbarung*, Halle, 1831; my *Apost. Zeitalt.*, i. p. 215; Schaff, l. c. p. 421.)

On the relation of the fourth Gospel to the first three, the Synoptists, comp., in the vol. on *Matthew*, the Introduction to the New Testament, § 2, and the works cited there. The Epistles of John belong together to the division of Catholic Epistles. On the idea and the group of the Catholic Epistles, compare Guericke, p. 430 [p. 416 ff., 3d ed.].

In the Apocalypse the highest immediacy and directness—that of vision—is combined in the most wonderful manner with the highest sacred art—that of apocalyptic, traditional symbolism (see Lücke, *Einleitung in die Apoc.*). And in this view, we have in the form of this Apocalypse a sealing of the incarnation, an incarnation raised to the highest power; the intensely earnest seer-spirit becomes art in the purest sense; art in ghostly severity becomes the prophetess of the judgment and the glorification of the world.

To come to the contents: The writings of John form a trilogy. The Gospel, the Epistles, and the Apocalypse represent the evangelic founding, the organic shaping, and the eternal future of the Church; Christ who was, and is, and is to come.

But each unit has again a trilogical constitution. The Gospel testifies in the prologue the outgoing of Christ from eternity (chap. i. 1–18); in the body of it, His historical manifestation; in the epilogue (chap. xxi.), His future spiritual presence in the world, represented by the Petrine and Johannean type of Christianity and the Church.

As to the three Epistles: The second and third form corollaries to the first. The first sets forth the fellowship of believers in the love of Christ, in opposition to those who do not belong to them; the second speaks against the lax obliteration of the line of this fellowship, requiring the condition of the essential confession; the third reproves the harsh contracting of the line in fanatical stringency. We readily see that these two Epistles stand in regular sequence, and that the second could not be the third, nor the third the second.

The Apocalypse places itself at the beginning on the historical basis of the seven churches, and of the seven epistles which transform those churches into types of the future (chap. i.–iii.). Upon this the prophetic images of the future are unrolled. (After the seven churches, the seven seals, the seven trumpets, the seven thunders, the seven heads of Antichrist, the seven vials of wrath, then the consummation, as the total manifestation of the seven spirits at the beginning.) At the end, after the consummation of the judgment, appears the counterpart of the seven churches, the eternal city of God (chap. xxi.).

§ 3. THE GOSPEL OF JOHN, ITS CHARACTER AND IMPORT.

The Gospel of John is the Gospel of the real ideality of the life of Jesus and His eternal operation; the Gospel of the real ideality of Christianity; or, the Gospel of the ideal personality, therefore, of the glorification of all the ideal relations of the world and of life. In this view we may consider it (1.) in its intrinsic import; (2.) as the complement of the three Synoptical Gospels; (3.) as the antidote to the false, religious idealism and realism of its time; (4.) as the consummation of the gospel history and doctrine in general; as exhibiting the realization of all the types in the world; as the ideal transfiguration of all real relations of the world; as the Gospel of absolute personality, of the unity of idea and life.

1. THE GOSPEL IN ITSELF CONSIDERED.

(*a.*) *Its Character in General.*

The Christ of John has been called a "shadowy form" (*Nebelgestalt*). The truth is, that He comes into the purest light of personality; that the Gospel is, throughout, the most distinct biography of the most distinct character, though of a character which to the beclouded eye can appear cloudy on account of its ideal fulness, and on account of the delicacy and majesty of its outlines. The Gospel sets out from the manifestation of the personal God in his Logos (chap. i. 1–14); it ends in the personal epiphany of the glorified Christ. It places all antiquity, the entire ancient covenant, before our eyes in personal concentration in John the Baptist. The second personage, in whom the old covenant was in a still higher manner concentrated—Mary—remains for a while in the background (chap. i. 13, 14). She herself is represented by her Son, so far as the old covenant fulfils itself in Him (John i. 17). Likewise the life of the post-historical Christ to the end of the world is here represented by the antithesis of two persons: Peter and John (John xxi. 15–23), in their connection with the company of the Apostles represented by a number seven (John xxi. 2). Between this introduction and conclusion the Gospel places the biography of the historical Christ; and in distinct chronological order.

The first section extends to the first Passover, at which Christ openly appears as the great, anonymous Prophet (John i. 19–ii. 12). John has pointed the Jews to Jesus, and they have not known Him (chap. i. 19–28). Therefore Jesus, renouncing the name of Messiah, must reveal himself in His Messianic power. So He reveals himself at first to the first disciples (John i. 29–51), represented by Andrew, John (intimated, not named), Peter, Philip, Nathanael (Bartholomew). He reveals himself to them by His master-look into their inmost life, and His distinct exposure of it, by a prophetic reading of character in the miraculous power of Divine knowledge; the copy of the election of God himself. He reveals himself next to the pious in general at the marriage in Cana by His first miracle. The mother of Jesus becomes the personal expression of faith in the need of life, which He only can supply; the master of the feast becomes witness to the richness of life which He gives. With this the holy family is established, the first germ of the Church in purely personal outlines (chap. ii. 12).

The second section extends from the Passover of the year of Rome 781 (see Wieseler, *Chronologische Synopse*, p. 166) to the feast of Purim of 782 (see Winer, *Purimfest*, in the Spring, before the Passover), and relates the first public manifestations of the Lord (chap. ii. 13–iv. 54). Jesus reveals himself first to the people in the temple, then to Nicodemus by night, afterwards to the disciples of John the Baptist, then to the Samaritans, finally to the noblemen of the government of King Herod Antipas. The Jews find Him, in the purification of the temple, the most genuine of Jews, whom zeal for His Father's house threatens to consume; Nicodemus, the master of Israel, must do homage to Him as the divine Master; John the Baptist must utter his acknowledgment of the greater Baptizer; the Samaritans, represented by the woman of Samaria, learn to greet in Him the Messiah of the Jews, who makes an end of the old antagonism between Mount Moriah and Mount Gerizim; the royal official must recognize in Him a royal power which sends its saving behests afar.

The third section extends from the feast of Purim in 782 to the feast of Tabernacles in the same year, according to Wieseler, the 12th of October (chap. v. 1–vii. 9). The decisive struggle with guilt and need in Israel begins. The pool of Bethesda, with its angel-miracles in Jerusalem, heals no more; the cripple who has waited there thirty-eight years for help, and who represents the impotence of effete Judaism, Jesus heals on the Sabbath, and presents himself to the Jews, who would kill Him for the act, as the life-giving healer and the quick ener of the dead. The people faint on their pilgrimage to the Passover on Zion; Jesus feeds and satisfies the people with His miraculous bread, overcoming the anxieties of the natural view of things, which Philip, who calculates the great demand, and Andrew, who counts up the small store, mutually represent. And as He has avoided the persecutions of the Jews in Jerusalem who would kill Him, so the Jews of Galilee, who persecute Him with their sensuous homage, to make Him king, He escapes first on the mountain in the night, then upon the sea, in a miracle which here appears only as an incident (as an exertion of miraculous power, in which He flees from false disciples, and seeks the true), and then declares to them plainly that He comes not to give them bread outwardly, as Moses, but, in the sense of the spirit, He must be to them Himself the bread of life, the living food from heaven. By this He effects the beginning of a separation between His true and false disciples (chap. vi. 66–71). Thus is expressed the antagonism between Him and the world, in which even His brethren, as representatives of His discipleship in general, do not yet know themselves to be, and which determines Him to continue His course in sporadic manifestations (chap. vii. 1–9).

The fourth section extends from the feast of Tabernacles in the year 782 to the feast of the Dedication of the Temple in the same year, Dec. 20th, according to Wieseler (chap. vii. 10–x. 22). Jesus brings His controversy with the Jews to an issue.

(1.) In respect to His authority as a teacher (chap. vii. 15–18).

(2.) In respect to His miracle on the Sabbath (chap. vii. 19–24).

(3.) In respect to His extraction (chap. vii. 25–31).

(4.) In respect to His and their future (chap. vii. 32–36).

(5.) In respect to His relation to the temple solemnities, first the festival of the drawing of water from the well of Siloam (chap. vii. 37–53), then the torch-light celebration at the feast of Tabernacles (chap. viii. 1–11; 12–27).

(6.) In respect to the false hope of the Messiah (chap. viii. 28–59).

(7.) In respect to the true and false power of enlightenment for the world on Temple Hill (chap. ix.), presented in the healing of the man born blind by means of the water of Siloam.

(8.) In respect to the true and false claims to the pastorship of the people of God (chap. x. 1–21).

With this great contest He brings on the incipient separation between His friends and His enemies, the children of the light and the children of darkness.

The fifth section goes from the feast of the Dedication in 782 to the Passover of 783 (chap. x. 22–xii. 50). Jesus offers himself more distinctly to the Jews on their inquiry (probably for the second time to the authorities) as the true Messiah, the Son of God.

(1.) Appealing to His works (x. 22–31).

(2.) Appealing to the Old Testament (vers. 32–42), likewise by the sign of the raising of Lazarus, the great life-miracle among his friends, represented by the family of Bethany hard by the gates of Jerusalem (chap. xi. 1–45), and by that very step He draws on the final resolution of the Jews, represented by the high-priest Caiaphas, to kill Him (chap. xi. 46–57).

He prepares himself for death.

(1.) By the anointing in the family at Bethany, among whom He has proved himself the resurrection, in a circle in which the anointing disciple and the objecting traitor represent the part of His friends and His enemies in His death (chap. xii. 1–8).

(2.) By His triumphal entry into the city and the temple, where the homage of the Greeks fills Him with the presentiment of His death (chap. xii. 9–33).

(3.) By the last parting words with which He withdraws from the people (vers. 34–50).

The sixth section gives the history of the last Passover at large (chap. xiii. 1–xix. 42).

(1.) The feet-washing, as the symbolical purification of the disciples and the real example of the Lord, connected with the virtual expulsion of the traitor from the circle (chap. xiii. 1–30).

(2.) The parting discourses concerning the spiritual glorification of the Son of Man: *a.* Connected with the supper, His approaching departure, His denial by Peter (chap. xiii. 31–38); *b.* Pointing to His Father's house and the reunion beyond the grave, and answering

2

the questions of Thomas respecting the way, and of Philip respecting the goal (chap. xiv. 1–15); *c.* Promising, by the Comforter, full compensation for His departure from them in this world, and His own return and reunion with them in the fellowship of the Father through the Holy Ghost, and answering the question of Judas, why this revelation was given only to His own, and not to the world (chap. xiv. 16–31); *d.* The condition of the new death-spanning fellowship of the disciples with the Lord; He being the vine, they the branches. Their relation to the Lord. Their relation to the world (chap. xv. 1–xvi. 11); *e.* The preparation of the disciples for the impending distress and the ensuing time of joy (chap. xvi. 12–32); *f.* The glorification of the whole redeeming work of Christ, to the perfection of His Father's house amidst the dissolution of the ungodly world, in the prayer of Christ for the glorification of His person; or the high-priestly prayer (chap. xvii.).

(3.) Jesus, the Lord of glory, judged by the world (chap. xviii. 1–19, 42); *a.* Jesus, with the traitor Judas, and the hostile guard; their dismay before the majesty of Jesus; *b.* Jesus, and the carnal zeal of Peter, in contrast with the sublime calmness of the Lord; *c.* Jesus in the house of Annas, the two disciples in the hall; the serenity of the Lord; *d.* Jesus before Caiaphas; the fulfilled prophecy of the Lord; *e.* Jesus before Pilate; the judicial acts and struggles of Pilate; the royal dignity of Jesus; *f.* Jesus on the cross, the King of the Jews; *g.* The forsakenness of the dying Christ; *h.* His last word: "It is finished;" *i.* The miracle in His dead body; the miraculous awakening of silent friends to their discipleship.

The seventh section embraces the course of the feast of the Passover from the first to the second Lord's Day (chap. xx.). Christ risen makes himself known to His disciples, and makes them perfectly free from the wretchedness and unbelief of the world. Magdalene, Peter, and John, the disciples in general, the first fruits of the Spirit, and the mission of Christ. Thomas.

The histories of the last chapter have a typical, symbolical import, and, as an epilogue on the post-historical movement of Christ in the world, correspond to the prologue on His pre-historical movement in the world. That the life of Jesus is here set before us in the grandest outlines of personal life, is plain. The Gospel brings few personages before us, but these all have a general import besides their individual; they represent human nature and the world in their most diverse aspects. The personality of Christ, however, throws light on all, now to condemnation, now to salvation; and in and above the personality of Christ, the being and the movement of God himself becomes manifest to us in the threefold radiance of the Father, the Son, and the Comforter.

(*b.*) *The Ideality and Symbolism of the Gospel.*

Agreeably to the peculiarity of the Gospel of John, all the real persons, things, and circumstances in it are symbolically or allegorically transparent, being suffused with the light of the idea. John gives us not only a symbolism of the Old Testament word, of Old Testament institutions, histories, and persons; he gives us also the symbolism of nature, of antiquity, and of history, of personal life; hence the absolute symbolism, or the ideal import of all real existence in significant outlines. He thus goes far beyond the symbolism of Matthew, and of the Epistle to the Hebrews, and even of Paul.

As scriptural symbolism we adduce: chap. i. 1, with reference to Gen. i. 1 sqq.; ver. 11, with reference to Ex. ix.; ver. 23, with reference to Isa. xl. 3; ver. 27, with reference to Mal. iv. 5; ver. 29, with reference to Isa. liii. 7; ver. 51, with reference to Gen. xxviii. 12; chap. ii. 17, relating to Ps. lxix. 10; chap. iii. 13, to Dan. vii. 13; ver. 14, to Num. xxi. 8, 9; ver. 29, perhaps to Ps. xlv. 8, 10; chap. v. 39, 46, and chap. vii. 38, to Zech. xiv. 8 *et al.*; chap. viii. 17, to Deut. xvii. 6; xix. 15; ver. 44, to Gen. iii.; chap. x. 14, to Zech. xi. 7; chap. x. 34, to Ps. lxxxii. 6; chap. xii. 14, to Zech. ix. 9; ver. 38, to Isa. liii. 1; ver. 39–41, to Isa. vi. 1; chap. xvi. 32, to Zech. xiii. 7; chap. xvii. 12, to Ps. xl. 10; chap. xix. 24, to Ps. xxi. 19; chap. xix. 29, to Ps. lxix. 22; ver. 36, to Ex. xii. 46; ver. 37, to Zech. xii. 10.

That John accounts not only conscious verbal prophecies as symbolical utterances, is evinced by many of his citations. In him, the sense of the anticipation of the New Testament element in Old Testament types of mind and of things is especially developed. In the life of Christ, every important word of the Old Testament finds its purest expression, its final fulfilment. And the symbolism of Old Testament persons, institutions, and events, unfolds itself in equal richness. The whole Old Testament is concentrated in the prophecy of John (chap. i. 6). The ground-thought of the Old Testament is: Israel the people of God; the Evangelist declares forthwith that Christ has a new people, born of the Spirit, for His possession (chap. i. 11–13). The mysterious centre of the Old Testament system is the manifestation of the "glory of the Lord," the δόξα (Shekinah); the Evangelist declares that this glory has appeared essentially in Christ (chap. i. 14). The antithesis between the Old Testament and the New is fully drawn in the antithesis between Moses and Christ (chap. i. 17).

But Christ comes forth as the substance of the Old Testament itself, for He was before John the Baptist (chap. i. 15, 27). He is the Messiah of promise, not only baptized, but baptizing with the Holy Ghost (chap. i. 32, 41). Nathanael represents the true Israelite (ver. 47), even an Israel who should see without ceasing the angels of God ascending and descending (ver. 51; see Gen. xxviii. 12). And the temple of the Israelites is a symbol of the body of Christ (chap. ii. 19). Circumcision in connection with washing is a symbol of the second birth into the real kingdom of God, the counterpart of His typical kingdom (chap. iii. 5). The brazen serpent which Moses lifted up as a healing sign, is a symbol of Christ lifted up on the cross (chap. iii. 14). The typical nuptial relation between Jehovah and His people in the Old Testament, is a symbol of the relation between Christ and His Church (chap. iii. 29). Jacob's well in Sychem is a symbol of the inner life from the fountain of the peace of Christ (chap. iv. 10). Mount Zion is a symbol of the supremacy of spirit and truth wherein God should be worshipped (chap. iv. 23); the pool of Bethesda, with its angelic help, a symbol of the divine healing workings of Christ in His Church (chap. v.). The raging sea is an emblem of the raging voices of the people, above which Jesus walks, as the mountain is an emblem of the exaltation of His life of prayer above the world (chap. vi.). The manna of the wilderness is a symbol of Christ, the true bread of life, from heaven (chap. vi.). Circumcision in its old patriarchal import is a symbol of the higher restoration of man (chap. vii. 23). The water-drawing from the fountain of Siloam is a symbol of the outpouring of the Holy Ghost (chap. vii. 38, 39). The torch-display at the feast of Tabernacles, was a symbol of the enlightenment of the world which proceeds from Christ (chap. viii. 12). The prescription of the law concerning the validity of the testimony of two witnesses before the judgment-seat, is a symbol of the concurrent testimony of the divine consciousness (Christ) and the divine works which the Father performs (chap. viii. 17). The bondage of the Jews is an allegory of the bondage of sin (chap. viii. 32). Abraham's children after the flesh are only symbols of Abraham's true children (chap. viii. 39). The serpent in paradise is an allegory of Satan (chap. viii. 44). Abraham is a symbol of Christ (chap. viii. 56). The Old Testament sons of God (judges and kings) are symbols of the Son of God (chap. x. 34). So the Urim and Thummim, or, what is essentially the same, the judicial opinion of the high-priest Caiaphas, becomes an unconscious symbolical representation of the judicial decision of God, which turns the judgment of the world to salvation (chap. xi. 51). The Jewish festival salutation, Hosanna, is a symbol of the salutation of the Messiah (chap. xii. 13). The hardening of the people in the old covenant, is a typical foreboding of the complete hardening of Israel against Christ (chap. xii. 38). Therefore also the Paschal supper is become the symbol of the celebration of the death of Christ (chap. xiii.), as the killing of the Passover is the symbol of His death itself (chap. xix. 36). Friday, as the day of preparation, is a symbol of the toil of Jesus and of His being laid to rest (chap. xix. 30, 31). The great Sabbath is a symbol of His repose in the grave (ver. 31).

And it must especially be observed, further, that here all the great festivals of Israel, the Passover, the Purim, the feast of Tabernacles, the feast of the Dedication, and then the Passover again, become to the legal Israel days of darkening and hardening against the light and substance of all the festivals, the Messiah, and days of the glorifying of the Messiah to the believing Israel.

Among the symbolical personages of the Old Testament, Abraham and Moses, John and Mary, have special prominence.

The Old Testament symbolizing of the fourth Gospel rests, however, on a universal view, which makes all the finite a similitude of eternal substance in Christ and in His kingdom. The whole universe, nature and history, is a mirror-like work of the Logos (chap. i. 3); light and darkness is an emblem of the great antagonism between Christ, or the kingdom of God, and the kingdom of evil; birth, an emblem (in the way of antithesis) of regeneration (chap. i. 13); the pure manifestation of the world, an emblem of the holy Word (ver. 14); the dove, an emblem of the Holy Ghost (ver. 32); the dwelling of Christ, an emblem of fellowship with Him (ver. 39); the prejudice of Nathanael against the wretched Nazareth, an emblem of all prejudice in the world against the earthly origin and form of the life of the Spirit (chap. i.), like the dishonoring of a prophet in his own country (chap. iv. 44); the marriage, an emblem of the festivity of human life, which issues in sheer want (the water-pots), till Christ comes into the midst and turns the water into wine (chap. ii.); the wind, an emblem of the Spirit of God blowing where it listeth (chap. iii. 8); marriage, a symbol of the union of Christ with His people (chap. iii. 29). The living water in the sacred well of Jacob signifies the peace of Christ; earthly food, the spiritual nourishment of Christ; the fields white to the harvest, the field of Christ's mission; the sower and the reaper, the earlier and later laborers in the kingdom of God (chap. iv.). The earthly healing fountain signifies the silent healing agency of Christ in the world (chap. v.); earthly bread, the heavenly food in Christ which gives new life to the world (chap. vi.); the earthly day, with its hours, the working-day of Christ in the world (chaps. viii., ix.); the true shepherd, Christ the Good Shepherd; and the thief and the hireling, the false prophets and the faithless keepers of souls; the two-fold flock of a rich shepherd, the heathen and the Jewish worlds in their relation to redemption; the shepherd's voice, the call of Christ (chap. x.); the Greeks at the feast who inquire for the Lord, the heathen world drawing near; the perishing corn of wheat which brings forth much fruit, the death of the good, especially the death of Christ, with the fruits of His resurrection; the approaching evening, the declining of the day of grace (chap. xii.). The hospitable feet-washing is an emblem of love which humbly serves, especially of brotherly, cleansing admonition (chap. xiii.). The heavenly world, revealed in the starry sky of night, is an emblem of the Father's house (chap. xiv.). The vine and the branches are Christ and His kingdom; the fruitful branches, living disciples of Christ; the dead branches cut off and burning, apostate Christians in the judgment of fire (chap. xv.). The travailing woman in her pangs and her joy of motherhood, is an emblem of sorrowful Good-Friday and Jubilant Easter in the Church (chap. xvi.). The crossing of the brook Kedron, is the sign of decision (chap. xviii.).

The position of Christ toward Pilate is an enlightening of Rome by Christianity, as His position toward the Greeks (chap. xii. 20) is an enlightening of Greece. Christ in the crown of thorns and the purple robe is the royal manifestation of the suffering One. The superscription on the cross is a prophecy of the dominion of Christ in all the languages of the world. The draught of vinegar is the refreshment of the dying Christ from the side of the world; the blood and the water flowing from the side of Christ after His death, are the sign of His miraculous transformation (chap. xix.). The carefully-laid linen with the napkin in the tomb is a sign of the resurrection rest, peaceful in God; the breath of Christ and His breathing upon His disciples signify the communication of the Holy Ghost to His people (chap. xx.). The fish in the net betoken the apostles' converting the world (chap. xxi.).

(c.) *The Reality or Historic Energy of the Christological Ideas of the Gospel.*

As, in this Gospel, on the one hand, all that is real and historical bears reference to the ideal world, and has an ideal, universal significance, so, on the other hand, all the fundamental ideas of the kingdom of God take living form in the actual world. Out of the one ideal form of the eternal being of Christ, the Word, come forth the ground-forms of His revelation, to manifest Him in the world. In operation, His nature branches into life and light (chap. i. 4); His nature is love (chap. iii. 16; i. 17); His manifestation is glory (the δόξα).

Over against Him stands, however, the anti-ideal acting of the kingdom of evil, darkness; its nature, hatred; its operation, death (chap. viii. 44; xv. 25); the manifestation of its children involuntary self-condemnation and a going out and extinction in night (chap. xiii. 30).

The nature and movement of the life in love for the sinful world is grace; the nature and movement of light is truth. The light divides the children of light from the children of darkness, and this affects the ideal judgment manifesting itself in wrath (chap. iii. 36), as the basis of the judgment to come. The children of the light are children of truth and uprightness; the children of the darkness are children of falsehood (chap. iii.). Grace and truth, become personal in the glory of Christ, are the principle of the glorification of life (chap. ii.) and of the beginning of that glorification in regeneration (chap. iii.). In their personal appearance in Christ, they give peace of soul (chap. iv.), abolish sickness and death as a negative liberation of life (chap. v.), nourish the restored life with positive food (chap. vi.), bestow a life-awakening life in the Holy Ghost (chap. vii.). The truth leads to freedom in Christ, the counterpart of which is bondage (chap. viii.); to the living knowledge of Christ, the counterpart of which is blindness; to trustful and obedient following of Christ, the counterpart of which is apostasy (chap. x.).

To believers the grace of Christ unfolds itself as eternal life (chap. x. 28); to His friends, as the power of resurrection (chap. xi.); to the Gentiles, as the power of spiritual exaltation to the heavenly life (chap. xii. 24, 32; to the confidential circle of the disciples, as the most self-sacrificing love (chap. xiii.). This resurrection is accompanied with the judgment of unbelievers, whose unbelief discovers itself in steady aggravation (chaps. xi.–xiii.). The gracious truth initiates in all the mysteries of the kingdom of heaven: the mystery of the Father's house above (chap. xiv. 1–15); the mystery of heaven upon earth, constituted by the Holy Ghost (vers. 16–31); the mystery of the kingdom of heaven in this life and in the life to come (chap. xv. 1–17); and the mystery of the enmity of the world, and of the disciples victory over the world (chap. xv. 18–xvi. 12). This leads to the glorification of Christ: the promise of His glorification in the Spirit (chap. xvi. 12–33); the eve of His glorification in His sacerdotal prayer (chap. xvii.). The glorification of His passion, and of all the elements of His passion (chaps. xviii. and xix.). The glorification of the risen Christ among His own (chap. xx.), and through His own in the world (chap. xxi.).

(*d.*) *The Idealism and the Realism of the Gospel in the Unity of Personal Life.*

We have already remarked that we find the unity of the real and the ideal in personal life; hence the unity of this Gospel of the ideal history is in the history of personality. Therefore it is that personages, both good and bad, play so significant a part in the light of the personality of Christ, the image of the personality of God: On one side, John the Baptist, Mary, the disciples, Nicodemus, the man born blind, Mary of Bethany, Martha, Magdalene, Joseph of Arimathea, more especially Thomas, Peter, John; on the other, the Jews, an Annas, a Caiaphas, a Judas, a Pilate. How sharply and at the same time how delicately are all these life-figures marked, and how transparent their meaning!

With equal significance is the fermenting, the shaping, the separation of the parties for and against the Lord portrayed.

And hence the same may be said of the small selection of the miraculous acts of the Lord. It is in keeping with the character of this Gospel that the miracles of knowledge here stand out so prominently (chap. i. 42, 48; comp. ii. 25; ii. 19; iv. 17; vi. 70; xi. 11; xiii. 3; xvii. 12; xx. 27; xxi. 6; ver. 18; ver. 22). The first miraculous work of the Lord according to John stands, entirely in the spirit of the fourth Gospel, at the head: a miracle of the exaltation of life to heavenly festivity out of earthly need (chap. ii.); and it is suitably followed by the purification of the temple, as a chiefly moral miracle, foretokening the restoration of the temple in the raising up of the real temple (chap. ii.). The second sign of Jesus in Galilee is the performance of a cure at a distance, which the Lord sends before to His home as a speaking token of His approach. The first miracle in Judea, the healing of the cripple at the pool of Bethesda, is rendered specially significant by its being wrought at a medicinal fountain religiously sacred to the Jews, and wrought on the Sabbath—a doubly mortal offence to the "Jews"—that is, to the Pharisees and the priest party. The first miraculous feeding in the wilderness appears here in contrast with the solicitude of the disciples, as the miraculous provision of wine in contrast with the solicitude of the mother; and at the same time it marks the turning-point in the life of Jesus, where He strikes clear to the ground the false Messianic hopes of the people, to direct their mind to the eternal (chap. vi.). The second miracle of Christ in Jerusalem, the healing of the man born blind, again has a twofold offence for His enemies; the taking of the pool of Siloam, the sacred well of the temple, as an instrument, and the performance of the work again on the Sabbath, notwithstanding his adherents had been threatened with the ban. This miracle is intended to bring the issue nearer. But the final issue is brought on by the great public miracle of the raising of Lazarus in Bethany (chap. xi. 53). This raising the dead from the grave is the crown of all the miracles of Jesus, and the presage of His own resurrection, and of the resurrection of all the dead.

John has thus recorded few miracles; but by the manner of his record he has made them great life-pictures of the wonderful dominion of Christ in the province of personal life. And the great discourses of the Lord are likewise an exhibition of the realization of all the fundamental ideas of the kingdom of God in the province of personal life, in which He himself stands as the luminous centre.

2. THE GOSPEL AS THE COMPLEMENT OF THE SYNOPTICAL GOSPELS.

After this sketch, we must observe the relation of the fourth Gospel to the three preceding.

If it may be said of each of the Gospels, that it completes in its own way the other three, since the whole four set forth the infinite fulness of the life of Christ in its four grand forms (see *Leben Jesu*, i. p. 234; the vol. of this Comm. on *Matthew*, General Introduction, p. 24–26, Amer. ed.), this may evidently be said with special emphasis of the fourth. But beyond this, the relation of the fourth Gospel to the Synoptists as a whole must be distinguished. The supplemental effect is so important, that it was in various ways explained even by the earliest writers. Eusebius (iii. 24) relates the opinion of the ancients, that John intended to confirm and complete the three already existing Gospels. And in modern times he is regarded pre-eminently as the completer [by Ebrard, Ewald, Godet, Wordsworth, and many others].

That the fourth Gospel has this office in fact—that John might have been conscious of it—and that he had it in view as a thing desired, are probable in the nature of the case; but the highest and ultimate design of his writing lay far beyond. The independent, original character of the work, as well as his own declaration (chap. xx. 31), establish this. None the less stands it true, that we owe to the fourth Gospel not only some of the most weighty facts of the life of our Lord, as well as His most important discourses, but also the exhibition of His ministry from the very beginning, the extended accounts of His ministry in Judea, as well as an accurate chronological sequence of events, from which it is possible to construct a chronological view of the life of Jesus.

Of equal or greater importance with the *ex*tensive supplementing of the first three Gospels, is the *in*tensive, the communication of the deepest and highest self-revelations of the Lord, and the exhibition of the whole life of Jesus in the most exalted light of an ideal apostolic intuition, as celebrated from Clement of Alexandria (Euseb. vi. 14) to Luther ("the one true, tender, main Gospel;" see Lücke, i. p. 157), and made in recent times an occasion, with some, of extolling this Gospel as the only true one at the expense of the Synoptists (Gfrörer); with others, of holding the synoptical portraiture of Christ as exclusively the correct, historical view (Weisse).

Even in the relation between the fourth Gospel and the Synoptists as to statements of fact, some have endeavored to find such differences as to make this relation an argument now against the exact reliability of the Gospel statements, now against the genuineness of the fourth Gospel. We recur to this in our discussion of the genuineness.

Here it must only be remarked, that, with all the elevation of its view of Christ and His work, this Gospel does not transcend the three others in their estimate of the Divine character of Christ, nor present another, a more spiritual, or a less historical Christ. The fourth Gospel's portrait of Christ, as has been already elsewhere remarked, is still a Johannean Christ, not a Christian John, no picture of John's fancy in Christlike colors (see *Leben Jesu*, i. p. 177); for John has taken his representation not from his own life, but from the depths of the life of Christ, though in conformity with his own deep contemplative and ideal turn of mind. In his drawing, no mastering subjective conception rides over the objective Master, as, in the other Evangelists, no subjective incapacity falls short of representing the objective Master.

The truth is, Christ was and appeared so boundlessly rich, that four specifically different original minds with different receptivities were needed to set forth the fulness of His revelation in adequate leading forms, each of which is alone in its kind. And thus the fourth Gospel could not properly compensate either of the other three with us, though, as the Gospel of the full idealization of the real life of Jesus in the perfect personal life of love, it must evidently stand as the conclusion, the completion, and the crown of the Gospel books.

3. THE GOSPEL IN ITS ANTAGONISM TO GNOSTICISM AND EBIONISM.

This import of the Gospel of John with reference to the other three, expresses also its permanent relation to Gnosticism on the one hand, and to Ebionism on the other. Irenæus supposed (*Adv. Hær.* iii. 11, 1) that John composed his Gospel against the mischief of Gnosticism, particularly against Cerinthus and the Nicolaitans. Epiphanius (*Hær.* lviii. 12; lxix. 23) and Jerome (*De viris illust.* c. 9) added the Ebionites. The hypothesis of an antignostic aim is revived by modern scholars (Grotius, Michaelis, and others [Hug, Ebrard, Alford, Hengstenberg, Webster and Wilkinson, Wordsworth]. Meyer [p. 43, 5th ed.], on the contrary, observes, that the Evangelist nowhere betrays a polemic aim against the opinions of the time.

It is, however, with this *intrinsic* polemic character as with the *extrinsic* supplemental office of the Gospel. Though it was not properly the main object of the Evangelist, yet, in a time when the germs of Gnosticism and Ebionism so plainly appeared (see the later Epistles of Paul, the Second Epistle of Peter, and the Epistle of Jude), he could not but feel his Gospel to be an actual argument against both these extremes; and a twofold series of strong assertions unmistakably reminds us, on the one hand, of that allegorical, fantastic idealism which could not allow the Word, or the idea-life, to become flesh, because it assumed an essential antagonism between matter and spirit (chap. i. 3, 14; vi. 54, 55; xix. 34; xx. 20, 27); and, on the other hand, of that realistic spirit of "the Jews," which acknowledged no full revelation of the eternal light of the Godhead in this world (chap. i. 11, 14; v. 18; vi. 62, 63; x. 36; and *passim*).

And we may well suppose that the prophetic spirit of the Evangelist was fully aware that his Gospel would actually exert this two-edged power against all Gnostic idealism and all Ebionistic realism in all times. For this is its effect, constantly beginning anew, and ever more powerful the more the Gospel discloses itself; though the consciousness of the Evangelist, reposing in the personal believing contemplation of the person of Christ unfolding its life for the redemption and glorification of the world, soared eagle-like above the need of an anxious attention to extreme views which had been already in principle utterly transcended and left behind by the birth of Christ.

The Christian doctrine of personality has in our day, for the first time, come forward in theology with independent distinctness. In the mighty unfolding of it, to which the pantheistic idealism lately impelled the theological mind, and a materialistic realism now impels it, the importance of this Gospel also must rise, as the consummation of the evangelic history in the contemplation of the perfect, world-transforming, personal life. And with this will all just elements of the ideal in the world and in the Church, in science, art, and theology, be brought more and more into the true light, and instated in their real rights; as, on the other hand, under the blessing of this revelation of personality, the real also, the great fact and the little incident, the creature, and even matter, must maintain the ideal glow of significance. In this view the fourth Gospel will prove itself the Gospel for all the ideal that is misty and in love with itself, and for all the real that is dark and imprisoned within itself; * in a word, the Gospel of personality called to freedom in the personality of *Christ* and its personal work of love.

4. THE GOSPEL AS THE CONSUMMATION OF THE EVANGELIC HISTORY AND DOCTRINE.

Accordingly, the fourth Gospel, in its import with reference to the consummation of the gospel history and doctrine, appears to us (1.) as the specific Christian view of John, the pure reflection of the character of John; (2.) as the first writing of John, which, in its spiritual expression, is perfectly homogeneous with the rest; (3.) as the foundation of the Johannean type of doctrine; (4.) as the highest revelation of the life of Christ in the mirror of John's contemplation; (5.) as the first member of the completed apostolic form of doctrine in general; (6.) as the type of the future completion of the Christian doctrine, the Christian view of the world and of life.

On the import of the fourth Gospel, see Lücke, *Einleitung*, p. 153; the citations in Meyer, p. 4; Tholuck, *Einleitung*, p. 6 [Eng. ed., by Krauth, p. 11 sqq.]; *Leben Jesu*, i., p. 261 sqq.

The Gospel of John is much extolled and much abused, as the gospel of the Lord himself. The spiritual Gospel, said Clement of Alexandria; a mixture of heathenism, Judaism, and Christianity, said Evanson; the one true, tender, main Gospel, said Luther; a production without value or use for our time, said the Lutheran Superintendent Vogel in Wunsiedel (Lücke, p. 93); the heart of Christ (*pectus Christi*), said Ernesti; mystic, confused, tedious, a dissolving view, said others; least authenticated, decidedly spurious, mixed with Gnosticism, said the latest opponents; while, since Irenæus, it has remained, for the sons of the apostolic spirit, the crown of the apostolic Gospels.

§ 4. THE GENUINENESS OF THE FOURTH GOSPEL.

[The Gospel of John has never been seriously assailed in the Christian Church till the nineteenth century. The rejection by the Alogi, of the second century, was a consequence of their denial of the doctrine of the Divine Logos, and unsupported by any argument. The doubts of Evanson, 1792, Eckermann, 1796, Ballenstädt, 1812, and others, were superficial, and made no impression. But more recently it has become the chief battle-ground between the old faith and modern criticism as applied to the documents of primitive Christianity. The first respectable critical attempt to dispute the Johannean authorship, was made by Bretschneider, in his *Credibilia de evang. et epistolarum Johannis apostoli indole et origine*, 1820. Since then, its apostolic origin was positively denied with more or less show of argument by Strauss, 1835, Bruno Bauer, 1840, Lützelberger, 1840, F. C. Baur (the ablest and most formidable opponent of the Gospel), 1844, 1847, 1853, &c., and his followers of the Tübingen school (such as Zeller, Schwegler, Hilgenfeld, Volkmar, Lang), also by Schenkel, 1864, Scholten, 1865, and Keim, 1867. The composition was assigned by these writers to some anonymous author of the second century, though without any agreement as to the exact time. The author assumed the name of John to give apostolic sanction to his theological system, which, according to Baur, is the last and most ingenious attempt to reconcile the supposed antagonism of the Jewish-Christian or Petrine, and the Gentile-Christian or Pauline types of Chris-

* [Lange: *das Evangelium für alles getrübte, in sich selbst verliebte Ideale, wie für alles finstere, in sich selbst verfangene Reale.*]

tianity, and presents an artificial history as the symbolical vestment of ideas. Renan, like Weizsäcker (1864), denies only the genuineness of the discourses of Jesus, and admits the Johannean composition of the historical portions. He defends this position in a concluding essay to the thirteenth edition of his *Vie de Jésus*, 1867. See below, p. 31. Schenkel also, in his *Charakterbild Jesu* (1864, p. 32), admits a basis of Johannean traditions for the post-apostolic speculations of the fourth Gospel. But these inconsistencies are untenable, and must give way to the alternative of a whole truth or a whole fabrication. Strauss, in his new *Life of Jesus*, 1864, exchanges his former mythical hypothesis of unconscious poetic composition for Baur's hypothesis of conscious invention, as the *only* other alternative to the orthodox view, and thereby he shows his sound and clear sense. Keim, in his *Geschichte Jesu von Nazara* (Zürich, vol. i., 1867, pp. 146 ff., 167 ff.), with all his attempts to mediate between the traditional view and the Tübingen school, arrives at the same result, but traces the composition of John about fifty years higher than Baur. He represents it as the production of an anonymous genius, a liberal Jewish Christian of Asia Minor in the age of Trajan (100–117), *i. e.*, almost within the lifetime of John. To call such a pseudo-Johannean work by its right name—a literary forgery—is, according to Prof. Keim (p. 170), a sign of ignorance, or results from a rough nervous constitution! He even doubts that John ever was in Ephesus.—English and American divines so far have had too much reverence and common sense, or too little interest in such problems, to be affected to any considerable degree by the bold hypercriticism of the Continent. But quite recently, it has been reëchoed by some writers in the *Westminster Review*, more elaborately by J. J. Tayler, *Attempt to Ascertain the Character of the Fourth Gospel*, London, 1867, and by Dr. Samuel Davidson, in the new edition of his *Introduction to the Study of the New Testament, Critical, Exegetical, and Theological*, London, 1868, 2 vols., vol. ii. pp. 323 ff. and 357 ff. Dr. Davidson, a man of learning, but little judgment, who, in his first edition (1848, vol. i. p. 244 ff.), had vindicated the Johannean authorship of the fourth Gospel against the crude vagaries of Lützelberger, now openly advocates the subtle speculations of the Tübingen school, and assigns the composition of John to an anonymous writer about A. D. 150. "This great unknown" (as he calls the author, p. 449), "in departing from apostolic tradition, teaches us to rise above it. He has seized the spirit of Christ better than any apostle; and if, like him, we ascend through their material setting to ideas that bring us into close contact with the Divine ideal of purity to mankind, we shall have a faith superior to that which lives in the visible and miraculous." This is all idle illusion. An anonymous tract, entitled, "*Was St. John the Author of the Fourth Gospel?*" by a Layman, formerly Fellow of Trinity College, Cambridge, London (Longmans, Green & Co.), 1868, takes a similar view, and, after a superficial discussion of the alleged discrepancies between the Synoptists and the fourth Gospel, arrives at the conclusion that the latter is the invention of some unknown author of the second century, with the exception of those passages that are to be found in some one of the other Gospels. But the discrepancies between the antagonists of John are far more serious and fatal than the discrepancies between John and the Synoptists. In one thing only they agree: in rejecting the Johannean origin of the fourth Gospel, and ascribing this sublimest of all literary compositions to an unknown impostor, they make it the greatest mystery in the history of literature. All these attacks will pass away without being able to "pluck a single feather from the mighty wing of this Eagle," who sails serenely and majestically above the clouds, in full vision of the light of eternal truth.—P. S.]

On the historical testimony to the genuineness of the fourth Gospel, compare Lücke's *Commentary;* Luthardt, *Das Johannes-Evangelium;* Tholuck's *Commentary on John;* Tholuck's *Glaubwürdigkeit der evangelischen Geschichte;* Guericke, *Isagogik*, p. 179 [199 ff. in the third ed. of 1868—P. S.], Kirchhofer, *Geschichte des neutestamentlichen Kanons bis auf Hieronymus*, p. 142; the treatise of Schneider, *Die Aechtheit des johanneischen Evangeliums nach den äusseren Zeugnissen*, Berlin, 1854; Heubner, p. 212; and others.

The evidences of the authenticity of this Gospel begin properly in the New Testament itself; to wit, in John xxi. 24 (see Tholuck, *Glaubwürdigkeit* p. 276). This testimony is, indeed, without subscription, and has become a constituent of the thing to be attested; but it has force from the fact that it passed under the criticism of the early Church, and was acknowledged by it (see my *Leben Jesu*, i. p. 169). To this add the following consideration: The author of the Gospel does not, indeed, name himself; but he repeatedly speaks of the disciple whom Jesus loved, and is designated by the Gospel itself as this disciple, chap. xxi. 24. Of this disciple it is said, in chap. xiii. 25, that he lay on Jesus' bosom; and the ancients named John as this disciple who lay on Jesus' bosom (Tholuck, p. 6). Again, when the power to estimate the apostolic characters shall be further developed, it will undoubtedly be perceived that the Gospel of John, the Revelation, and the Epistles of John, stand or fall together (and they will *stand*), as the productions of one clearly distinct mind (see my *Vermischte Schriften*, vol. ii., p. 173 sqq.: "On the indissoluble connection between the individuality of the Apostle John and the individuality of the Apocalypse"). The relation of the two closing verses to the Gospel is to be treated hereafter. The words *καὶ οἴδαμεν, ὅτι ἀληθὴς ἐστιν ἡ μαρτυρία αὐτοῦ*, are undoubtedly to be considered in any case an addition, probably an interpolation of the Ephesian church.* We certainly cannot esteem it any glory to theology, to have made the Gospel and the Apocalypse mutually exclusive in regard to authenticity. (Lücke: Because the Gospel is Johannean, the Apocalypse cannot be; Baur, the reverse.)

So early as Ignatius, in his Epistle to the Romans, chap. vii., we find distinct allusions to the Gospel (Lücke, p. 43); and the fact that Papias does not name it, is accounted for by the predilection, extolled by himself, for oral tradition, which, in reference to John, he was permitted to enjoy. (See *Leben Jesu*, i. p. 151.) † Yet, according to Euseb. iii. 39, 8, Papias knew the First Epistle of John, and this [in view of the obvious and universally admitted identity of thought and style in the two compositions] constitutes him indirectly a witness

* [Comp. the *Exeg. Notes* on chap. xxi. 24, 25, and Abbot's addition to Smith's *Bible Dictionary*, ii. p. 1430. Abbot justly concludes: "The only plausible explanation of vers. 24 and 25 seems to be, that they are an attestation of the trustworthiness of the Gospel by those who first put it into general circulation—companions and friends of the author, and well known to those to whom it was communicated; and the only plausible account of the first 23 verses of the chapter is, that they are a supplementary addition" [or rather the Epilogue, corresponding to the Prologue, as Dr. Lange regards it], "which proceeded directly from the pen, or substantially from the dictation, of the author of the rest of the Gospel."—P. S.]

† [Dr. Lange omits to notice, in his third edition of 1868, some important data which have come to light since his second edition in 1862. We can now appeal to two or three *direct* and explicit testimonies of Papias in favor of the Gospel of John. These set aside the argument from his alleged *silence*, which has been recently urged by Strauss, Renan, Zeller, Hilgenfeld, Volkmar, and others, as a very dangerous argument against the apostolic origin of the same. (1.) The first is found in a Latin MS. of the Gospels in the Vatican Library, marked "Vat. Alex. No. 14," and dating apparently from the ninth century, where, in a prologue to the Gospel of John, the following remark occurs: "Evangelium iohannis manifestatum et datum est ecclesiis ab iohanne adhuc in corpore constituto, *sicut papias nomine hierapolitanus discipulus iohannis carus in exotericis* [no doubt an error of the copyist for *exegeticis*] *id est in extremis quinque libris* [*i. e.*, at the close of the fifth book of his lost λογίων κυριακῶν ἐξηγήσεις] *retulit*." This testimony (which is not invalidated by the additional improbable notice that John dictated his Gospel to Papias) was known already to Cardinal J. M. Thomasius, who entered it in his collections (*Opp. omnia*, Rom, 1747, tom. i. p. 344; comp. Aberle in the Roman Catholic *Quartalschrift* of Tübingen, 1864, pp. 1–47), but it attracted no attention until it was recently rediscovered in the Vatican Library, and brought to notice by the eminent Benedictine scholar, Cardinal Pitra, and Prof. Tischendorf, on his visit to Rome, March, 1866, who assigns the Prologue to a writer before the time of Jerome. (2.) The second testimony which was discovered by Aberle (*l. c.*) in a Proëmium to the Gospel of John in the Catena Patrum Græcorum, ed. by Corderius, is from an anonymous Greek commentator, who asserts that John, the Son of Thunder, dictated his Gospel to his disciple Papias of Hierapolis (τῷ ἑαυτοῦ μαθητῇ Παπίᾳ εὐβιώτῳ [probably for ἐπισκόπῳ] τῷ ἱεραπολίτῃ. Although this tradition may have no foundation in fact, it proves, nevertheless, the intimate connection of Papias with the Gospel of John in the opinion of the ancient Church. (3.) Finally, Irenæus, at the close of his work, *Adv. Haer.*, v. 36, §§ 1, 2, quotes a passage from John xiv. 2 in such connection with Papias, and other presbyters who had known John personally (*presbyteri qui Johannem discipulum Domini viderunt*), as to make it extremely probable that he quoted either from the work of Papias, or of the presbyters, who were still older and better witnesses.—On the other hand, we can make no use (as Dr. Wordsworth does for another purpose) of the fragment of "Papias" in an Oxford MS. (see Grabe, *Spicil.* ii. 34, 35; and Routh, *Reliquiæ Sacra*, vol. i. 16) on the four Marys (among whom he mentions "Mary Salome, the wife of Zebedæus, the mother of *John the Evangelist*"), for this passage is an extract from a Dictionary or Glossary of another Papias, of Lombard, in the twelfth century, as Hofstede de Groot (*Basilides*, &c., p, 112 f.) has conclusively proved from another copy of the *Lexicon Catholicum* of the mediæval Papias.—Comp. on these testimonies of Papias to the Gospel of John (which have escaped also the attention of Prof. Fisher and Mr. Abbot), the fourth revised and enlarged edition of Tischendorf, *Wann wurden unsere Evangelien geschrieben?* Leipzig, 1866, pp. 101–119, especially p. 118, and P. Hofstede de Groot, *Basilides*, &c., Leipzig, 1868, pp. 109–116. The latter closes his discussion with the remark: "Who knows what else may not yet be discovered? But, for the present, the facts adduced are sufficient to prove that Papias was acquainted with the fourth Gospel as a production of John."—P. S.]

also to the Gospel. In Polycarp, too, appear proofs of intimacy with John (see Tholuck, p. 25).*

If John, according to an established tradition, lived to the close of the first century, a living Gospel, we may be satisfied if we find even in the middle of the second century perfectly sure signs of the existence of his Gospel, as we do in the Logos-doctrine of Justin Martyr, though the Evangelist is not cited by name (since Justin wrote primarily for the West, where the fourth Gospel was as yet comparatively very little current).† On Justin's acquaintance with the fourth Gospel, see Ewald, *Jahrbücher*, 1852–'53, p. 186; Lücke, i. p. 44; Meyer, p. 4, and Tholuck, p. 27, with reference to Semisch's *Justin*, p. 188. [See also Weizsäcker, Tischendorf, Keim, and the article of Prof. Fisher above cited, *Essays*, p. 46 ff., and his addition to Smith's *Dictionary*, ii. p. 1433. Even the skeptical Keim, *Leben Jesu*, i. (1867) p. 138, admits that Justin knew the Gospel of John, and ridicules the absurd idea of a dependence of John on Justin.—P. S.].

These indications further appear in the fact that Tatian, a pupil of Justin, composed a work on the Gospels, entitled *Diatessaron* (διὰ τεσσάρων, one out of four, an expression looking back to the ἀπομνημονεύματα of his teacher), which could have had none but our four Gospels for its basis; that the Valentinians, toward the middle of the second century, knew the Gospel, since even the Valentinian Heracleon accompanied it with a commentary; and that the Montanists, in the second half of the second century, appealed to the promise of the Paraclete, which involves their familiarity with the Gospel of John.

Add to these the first new discovery, made by means of the close of the Clementine Homilies found by Dressel, that the author of it (perhaps about A. D. 160) knew the Gospel of John, and the second new discovery through the "Philosophoumena," edited by Miller [1851, and better by Duncker and Schneidewin, 1859.—P. S.], that even the Gnostic Basilides, a younger cotemporary of John, knew his Gospel (Tholuck, p. 28, with reference to the treatise of Jakobi, *Deutsche Zeitschrift*, 1851, p. 222).‡

The acquaintance of the Gnostic Valentine and of Marcion (first half of the second century) with this Gospel, has likewise become more and more certain. [Comp. Fisher, *l. c.* p. 59 ff., and especially Hofstede de Groot, *Basilides*, &c., pp. 90–106.—P. S.]

Nothing more can be desired than such a group of evidences, reaching back, some to the middle of the second century, some to the beginning of it.

But then, in the second half of the same century, Theophilus of Antioch (*Ad Autolyc.* ii. 22) and Irenæus (*Adv. Hæres.* iii. 1) appear as express witnesses for the authorship of John. They are followed by a series of the Church fathers, beginning with Clement of Alexandria, Tertullian, Origen, and Eusebius.

The peculiarity and elevation of the fourth Gospel passed among the ancients, with scattering exceptions, for a special seal of its apostolicity. Characteristically, the same circumstance had that weight with them which to the modern rationalistic criticism makes the Gospel preëminently suspicious, or rather gives this criticism occasion for its cavils.

In the history of this criticism we must distinguish two stages: First, the objections of

* [Polycarp, a disciple of John, quotes from 1 John iv. 3 the passage concerning the mark of Antichrist (*Ep. ad Philipp.*, c. 7).—P. S.]

† According to Volkmar (*Ueber Justin den Märtyrer und sein Verhältniss zu unserem Evangelium*, Zürich, 1853), it should of course be granted that Justin was ignorant of the fourth Gospel. John writes ἄνωθεν γεννηθῆναι, Justin ἀναγεννηθῆναι. But Justin was free from pedantry; and in Rome, where the Petrine term (1 Peter i. 3. 23) was familiar, did well to use it. [That Justin, Apol. i. 61, in quoting from memory (as was usual with him) the passage on regeneration, John iii. 3–5, uses ἀναγεννάω for γεννάω, and βασιλεία τῶν οὐρανῶν for βασ. τοῦ θεοῦ, is not strange if we consider that ἀναγεννάω, besides being found in a few MSS., had become the current term for regeneration; that the Synoptists use βασ. τῶν οὐρανῶν, and that the same inaccuracy in quoting this very passage occurs frequently in Irenæus, Eusebius, Chrysostom, and other fathers, as has been shown in a learned note by Abbot in his and Hackett's edition of Smith's *Dictionary of the Bible* (1869), ii. 1433. Even Jeremy Taylor once quotes the passage inaccurately thus: "Unless a man be born of water and the *Holy* Spirit, he cannot enter the kingdom of *heaven*."—P. S.]

‡ [On the important testimony of Basilides (A. D. 65–135) brought to light in 1851 with the discovery of the "Philosophumena" of Hippolytus, see the learned and able treatise of P. Hofstede de Groot, of Groningen, written first in Dutch, and then enlarged in German: *Basilides als erster Zeuge für Alter und Autorität N. T. Schriften, insbesondere des Johannesevangeliums*, Leipzig, 1868—P. S.].

the vulgar rationalism, which we may designate also as Ebionistic. The judgment of its critique runs thus: The Johannean Christ is not true enough to have been actual; the Synoptists alone portray the actual and true Christ. Then, the objections of the modern pantheistic rationalism, which may, in like manner, be called Gnostic. In its opinion, the Christ of the fourth Gospel is too true—that is, a too far developed idea of the ideal Christ—to have been actual. The two views agree in establishing a contradiction between the Synoptists and the fourth Gospel. To the first class belong the Alogi of the ancient day,* and, in our time, Evanson (1792), Eckermann, Schmidt, Bretschneider, and others (see Lücke, Comm. i. p. 89; Guericke, *Isagogik*, p. 188); to the second, Baur and his disciples. A party which forms a bridge between these opposites, finds in this Gospel some things too real, some too ideal, for the book to have been genuine (Strauss, Weisse).

It is remarkable, that Bruno Bauer [not to be confounded with F. C. Baur] makes the Gospel to have proceeded from the bosom of the orthodox, poetizing Church; Lützelberger, from the borders of the Church, from the hand of a Samaritan Christian; Hilgenfeld, from the bosom of the Valentinian Gnosis. How wanton the confusion of notions sometimes is which this negative criticism permits, is shown by the remark of Hilgenfeld, that we have to do with an age in which the idea of literary property was wholly wanting. Tholuck, on the contrary (p. 6), adduces evidences against literary frauds. And it must above all be borne in mind, that the instinctive moral idea, which abhors falsification, and the modern legal idea of literary property, are utterly different things.

For extended demonstration of the genuineness, we refer to the works already cited; to Credner, p. 261, and others; to the *Evangelienkritik* of Ebrard, p. 828 sqq.; the well-known critical apologetic treatises on the life of Jesus; the work of Ebrard, *Das Evangelium Johannis und die neueste Hypothese über seine Entstehung;* and Bleek, *Beiträge zur Evangelien-Kritik*, pp. 175 sqq.

[In addition to these works, the following more recent apologetic treatises on the Johannean question deserve special mention: Prof. Riggenbach (of Basle), on the *Testimonies for the Gospel of John*, Basle, 1865; Prof. Godet (of Neuchatel), *Examination of the Chief Questions of Criticism concerning John* (French and German), Zürich, 1866; Prof. Van Oosterzee (of Utrecht), *The Gospel of John*, four Lectures (Dutch and German), 1867 (English translation by Dr. J. F. Hurst, Edinburgh, 1869); the *fourth* revised and enlarged *German* edition of Tischendorf's valuable book on the *Origin of the Gospels* (*Wann wurden unsere Evangelien geschrieben?*) Leipzig, 1866. (English translation by W. L. Gage, Boston, 1868); Prof. Hofstede de Groot (Groningen), on the *Testimony of Basilides for the New Testament Books, especially the Gospel of John* (Dutch and German), Leipzig, 1868; Abbé Deramey, *Défense du quatrième évangile*, Paris, 1868. See also the Commentaries of Lücke, Tholuck, De Wette (the 5th edition by Brückner, 1863), Meyer, Luthardt, Bäumlein, Astié, Godet, and Holtzmann in Bunsen's *Bibelwerk*, vol. viii. (1866), pp. 56–77. The best English discussions of the Johannean question with reference to the attacks of the Tübingen school, are by Prof. George P. Fisher, of New Haven, *The Genuineness of the Fourth Gospel*, first published in the

* [From the account of Epiphanius, *Hæresis* L. *adv. Alogos*, which is almost the only source of our information on the Alogi (so called first by Epiphanius, as deniers of the Logos, with a sarcastic insinuation of their unreasonableness), it is not clear whether they rejected the divinity of Christ altogether, or simply John's doctrine of the Logos (i. 1–14). He says, indeed, that they denied the Gospel of John, καὶ τὸν ἐν αὐτῷ ἐν ἀρχῇ ὄντα θεὸν λόγον (*Hær.* liv. c. i.); but, on the other hand, he closely distinguishes them from the Ebionites, as well as from the Gnostics. They rejected both the Gospel and the Apocalypse, and absurdly ascribed these books to the Gnostic Cerinthus, a later contemporary of John. This very fact, however, proves that these books were regarded as ancient at the time of the Alogi, who flourished during the Montanist controversy, about 170, and furnishes a strong argument against the position of the Tübingen school which would put the composition of the Gospel of John down to the middle of the second century. Had the Alogi had any idea of its late origin, they would no doubt have turned it to account. According to Heinichen (*De Alogis, Theodotianis atque Artemonitis*, Leipzig, 1829), they rejected merely the Apocalypse, not the Gospel of John. But this is irreconcilable with the account of Epiphanius, who expressly says (*Hær.* l. c. 3), that if they had cast off the Apocalypse only, there might be some excuse in view of the obscurity of that book; but since they rejected all the writings of John, they showed clearly that they belonged to the antichrists spoken of, 1 John ii. 18. They tried to refute John with the Synoptists, but very feebly. They were also violently opposed to the Montanists, and denied the continuance of prophecy and miraculous gifts in the Church.—P. S.]

Bibliotheca Sacra for April, 1864, and then incorporated in his *Essays on the Supernatural Origin of Christianity*, New York, 1866, pp. 33–152 (comp. also his addition to Smith's large *Dictionary of the Bible*, vol. ii. pp. 1431–'37); and by H. B. Liddon, in the fifth of his Bampton *Lectures on the Divinity of Jesus Christ*, London, 2d ed., 1868, pp. 207 ff. For a complete list of the polemic and apologetic literature on John, see Meyer, *Comm.*, 5th ed. (1869), pp. 38–41; Ezra Abbot's addition to W. Smith's *Dictionary of the Bible*, vol. ii. (1869), pp. 1437–1439; and Dr. Hurst's Appendix to his English translation of Van Oosterzee's *Apologetic Lectures on John's Gospel*, Edinburgh (1869), pp. 241–246.—P. S.]

Here it may be suggested, that the criticism which denies the genuineness of the Gospel, annihilates itself most effectually by its own internal confusion and contradiction. The earlier rationalists make the Gospel of John an obscuration of historical Christianity; the later, an ideal amplification and provisional completion of it. According to one, John existed as a Jewish apostle, who is supposed, in a qualified sense, to have written the Apocalypse (Baur); according to another, the Apostle did not exist at all, at least as the author of the fourth Gospel, which was composed by a Samaritan toward the middle of the second century (Lützelberger). Thus, a Samaritan forged it, according to Lützelberger; the Christian community invented it, according to Bruno Bauer. According to Zeller, Valentinianism grew out of the conceptions of John; according to Hilgenfeld, the Gospel grew out of Valentinianism.

The objections which have been made against the Gospel may be classified as follows:

1. Supposed historical contradictions with the Synoptists.

(*a.*) The different festival journeys of the Lord in John, together with the many incidents peculiar to him. Explained by the difference in the character of the Gospels, and by the complemental position of the fourth.

(*b.*) The many omissions of John: the Lord's Supper, the agony in Gethsemane (with which the exhibition of the triumphant spirit of Christ in His sacerdotal prayer is supposed to be inconsistent). Explained by the fact that the place of the Supper is plainly enough marked (chap. xiii. 34), and that there is abundant cause for the strongest alternations of experience in the life of our Lord, and the actual occurrence of them in every Gospel by itself.

(*c.*) The dates of the last Passover and the death of Jesus. Compare, on this point, this Commentary on *Matthew*, Special Introd. to chs. xxvi. and xxvii.; my *Geschichte des apostol. Zeitalters*, i., p. 69; Tholuck, p. 38 ff. [also the Lit. on the Paschal controversy of the second century].

(*d.*) Supposed differences of minor importance. Accounted for by what has already been said; especially by the fact, to be emphasized, that the Evangelists have given Gospels, *i. e.*, religious, historico-ideal views, each his own, of the gospel history; not chronological pragmatic reports of events.

2. Pretended doctrinal differences between John and the Synoptists. The presumption that John was a Jewish Apostle, and therefore Judaistic, and that, consequently, he could not have written the Gospel, we pass; it falls with the Ebionite hypothesis of Baur. (Comp. Tholuck, p. 53.)

(*a.*) Jesus here speaks, in general, chiefly of His person. Answer: He speaks of His person also in the Synoptists; John differs from them only by collecting more especially the utterances of the self-consciousness of Jesus.

(*b.*) The speculative tone. But this is just what makes John John. Tholuck refers to the fact that Plato has written of Socrates in a higher tone than Xenophon (*Glaubwürdigkeit*, and Comm. [Krauth's translation, p. 30]). Heubner finds this doubtful (p. 213). The analogy would only be doubtful, if Tholuck had at the same time said that John has Johanneanly idealized the actual Christ, as Plato Platonically idealized Socrates (which Weisse holds). We can perfectly maintain the complete dependence of John's view of the objective Christ, and yet perceive that John, according to his subjective individuality, has apprehended just that which is most distinctive in the objective Christ. Heubner mistakes this truth, and would not admit the individuality of John as a factor (p. 213). He is right, however, in insisting that Christ was inexhaustibly rich, therefore endlessly manifold, in His self-revelation; citing Demosthenes as an analogy (note on p. 213).

(*c.*) The difference in the teaching of Christ. But there is enough that is Johannean in the Synoptists, on the eternal Godhead of Christ, His preëxistence, His sole relation to the Father (see Matt. ii. 15; iii. 3, 17; xi. 19 and 26–30; xvi. 16; xxvi. 64; xxviii. 18; Mark i. 2; ii. 28; xii. 35; xiii. 26; xvi. 19; Luke i. 16, 17; ver. 76; ii. 11, &c.,) and enough that is synoptical in John (chap. ii. 14; v. 19; vi. 3, &c.), to establish the result that the Christ of all four Gospels is the same, but that the particular calling of John was to hold forth especially the spiritual glory of Christ. If in this he has his own mode of representation, he need not be found "dissolving" because he is solemnly elevated, nor "inaccurate" because, as is proper to his solemn style, he soars above logical forms of transition. If, finally, Christ speaks in proverbs and parables only in His discourses to the multitude, and, even according to the Synoptists, had other discourses besides, the prevalence of the dialogue and the discourse in John argues genuineness, since it corresponds to the different nature of the occasions and circumstances.

3. The mutually exclusive authorship of the Gospel and the Apocalypse. According to Lücke, this does not indeed touch the genuineness of the Gospel; only, the Evangelist John cannot have written the Apocalypse, because he wrote the Gospel. According to Baur, on the contrary, he cannot have written the Gospel, because he wrote the Apocalypse.

We maintain that the Gospel and Apocalypse require each other. If it be first sufficiently considered (*a.*) that there is an essential difference between speaking ἐν τῷ νοΐ and ἐν τῷ πνεύματι, according to 1 Cor. xiv. 15; (*b.*) an essential difference between a historical and an apocalyptic, *poetico-symbolical* work;* (*c.*) that the Gospel of John has no special eschatology, as the others have; (*d.*) that the Apocalypse presupposes a kindred Gospel, especially the Evangelist and Apostle; (*e.*) that the Apocalypse evinces the same theological depth, the same fulness of ideas, the same universal view, as the Epistles of John and the fourth Gospel. After these considerations, we cannot help concluding, that all the books attributed to John can have been written only by one man; and that one, this unique John, with whose preeminent trait of contemplativeness in the Gospel and in the Apocalypse the contemplative character of the Johannean books is in perfect harmony.

4. Intrinsic difficulties which the Gospel is supposed to present. Particularly

(*a.*) The improbability that such discourses as those recorded by John should be retained by the memory. But this objection has never duly considered, that John could as well have put down his memorabilia at once during his intercourse with Jesus, as the many, of whom Luke speaks (Luke i. 1). Nor has it further put to the account, that the ways of memory are different, and that the memory of the loving worshipper is always tenacious of the words kindred to its spirit; and it has confounded the notions of a substantial and a verbal record. That Christ might receive a Johannean coloring in the representation of John, without being transformed from a Johannean Christ to a Christian John, is made perfectly clear by the analogy of the three Synoptists.

(*b.*) Wearying repetition and diffuseness. This objection becomes at once a self-accusation of the critics. The pregnant, the lyrically iterative, in the language of an inspired ideal intuition, presupposes yielding harmony and affinity of spirit.

§ 5. THE INTEGRITY OF THE GOSPEL.

The unity of character of the fourth Gospel, the whole incommunicable spirit of it, is so plain, that the hypothesis of the working over by a later hand of an original record by John (Weisse, *Die Evangelische Geschichte, et al.*), or of the filling out of such a record by interpolations (A. Schweizer, *Das Evangelium Johannis*), may be passed over (see *Leben Jesu*, i. p. 197; Luthardt, *Die Integrität*).†

* [The remark of Tholuck, p. 11, that "the Old Testament prophets speak not a whit more impure Hebrew than the prose-writers," mistakes the main point here at issue—to wit, the difference between the states of consciousness, in which a Hebrew at one time speaks pure Greek, at another, Hebraizes.]

† [Luthardt, in the first chapter of his able work: *Das Johanneische Evangelium nach seiner Eigenthümlichkeit ge-*

The genuineness of the 21st chapter of the Gospel remains to be specially considered. The words of John xx. 30 have been supposed to form the evident close of the Gospel; and then the 21st chapter itself has been thought to bear traces of spuriousness. Accordingly, many who have acknowledged and honored the Gospel, from Grotius to Lücke, and others, have declared against the genuineness of this chapter. (See the list in Meyer's *Comm.* [p. 571, 4th ed.]). On the contrary, the genuineness of it has been as decidedly vindicated, from Calovius to Guericke and Tholuck. According to Meyer, the chapter, excepting the last verse, is *a supplement* to the Gospel of John, which closes with the 31st verse of the 20th chapter. But a supplement can be only an appendix, as Meyer intends, in case the book itself is completed according to its plan. Now, a careful estimate of the total structure of the Gospel leads to a plan which constitutionally includes the 21st chapter. In this view we distinguish the Prologue, chap. i. 1–18, the historical Gospel, more strictly speaking, and the Epilogue, chap. xxi. The division of the Gospel, made and pursued in this volume, must justify this conception; and we here refer the reader thereto. Even most of the advocates of the genuineness, however, have more recently explained the 24th and 25th verses as a later addition; and again, Weitzel has declared against this (*Studien und Kritiken*, 1849, i. 1). We hold that, if the interpolation: "We know that his testimony is true," be an interpolation of the Ephesian church, the rest reveals the hand of the Evangelist himself; since ver. 24 looks back to chap. xx. 31, and the proverb in ver. 25, though termed by Meyer an *absurd exaggeration*, is entirely characteristic of John's contemplation.*

It is otherwise with the section, chap. viii. 1–11.† It is, in the first place, established, that the section is wanting in a series of the most important codices, B. L. T. X. Δ., to which certainly Cod. Sin., and probably A. and C., are to be added; and that a series of the oldest and most eminent fathers, from Origen downward, are entirely silent respecting this section. Add to this the fact that the section, at first view, does not improve, but impairs the connection of the Gospel. We ourselves have hitherto thought there were sufficient proofs that it belongs to the day of the great onsets of questionings which the Pharisees made upon the Lord on the Tuesday after the feast of Palms (see Lücke, ii. p. 243; Hitzig, *Ueber Johannes Markus*, p. 205; my *Leben Jesu*, ii. p. 952; p. 1222). From this apparent misplacement of the section, however, it would not necessarily follow that the passage itself is not apostolic; not even that it is not Johannean. Since the other Evangelists have described those onsets, it is improbable that the section should have come from them (as, for example, Hitzig places the passage in Mark, between chap. xii. 13–17 and vers. 18–27). On the contrary, it is more natural to suppose that this Gospel relic belongs to John, or, at all events, to the Johannean tradition in Ephesus. The codd. 1, 19, 20, put it at the close of the Gospel; codd. 69, 124, 346, put it after Luke xxi. 38. We might well suppose that the latter manuscripts are in the right as to the place of the incident, the former as to the authorship of the account. We think it suitable, however, to recur to the question in the Commentary on the section itself;

schildert und erklärt (Nürnberg, 1852, pp. 1–20), satisfactorily defends the integrity of the fourth Gospel against the views of Weisse and Schweizer, which may be regarded as exploded. But since that time the same error has been renewed in a modified form. Renan (*Vie de Jésus*, 1863) is disposed to regard the narrative portions of John as genuine and to acknowledge a historical substratum even in the discourses. He accepts as historical the belief in the resurrection of Lazarus, but turns it into a counterfeit miracle, the result of guilty collusion, which is certainly no better, but worse, than the German notion of a mythical poem, or a symbolical vestment of the idea of immortality. In the 13th edition of his *Vie de Jésus*, Paris, 1867, Renan enters for the first time into a discussion of the Johannean question. He distinguishes, in the Preface, four views on the subject: (1.) the orthodox, which holds fast to the whole Gospel of John as genuine; (2.) the middle position, which recognizes him as the first author, but admits that it has been brought into its present shape and form by his disciples; (3.) the critical, which derives it from a disciple of John about A. D. 100, and gives up the discourses, but admits a Johannean tradition in the historical portion; (4.) the second critical view, which regards the whole as a fiction or historical novel of the second century. He professes to hold the third view, and defends it in a concluding essay. Weizsäcker, who is Baur's successor in Tübingen, (in his *Untersuchungen über die evangel. Geschichte*, Gotha, 1864; comp. his notice of Renan in the *Jahrbücher für Deutsche Theologie*, for 1868, pp. 521 ff.), substantially agrees with Renan, and divides the authorship between John and one or more of his disciples, probably the elders at Ephesus.—P. S.]

* [Comp. the first foot-note on p. 26.—P. S.]

† [The genuineness of John viii. 1–11, or rather vii. 53–viii. 11, as also of chap. v. 4, with the last clause of ver. 3, is purely a question of textual criticism. See the *Textual Notes in loc.*—P. S.]

since, on a more accurate weighing of the critical and historical considerations, the section might decidedly maintain its existing position. (On the critical treatises relative to this section, compare Meyer, on chap. viii. [p. 320, 5th ed.]).

§ 6. SOURCES AND DESIGN OF THE GOSPEL.

The Gospel of John appears the most original of all the Gospels, in that it shows itself thoroughly independent of the Synoptical evangelical tradition while yet presupposing it, and confirming the essential substance of it. It manifestly rests on the personal memories of one of the earliest disciples of Jesus—the most profound and spiritual of all—on whom the Lord's exhibitions of himself impressed themselves in indelible lines.

That John early committed to writing in *memorabilia* the most important matters of his recollection, especially the Lord's discourses, we may well suppose, though these constituents of his Gospel continually became fresh again and clear by the suggestions of the promised Paraclete, which coöperated with his enthusiastic love for the Lord.

But since, by the direction of the dying Saviour, he was made the son of Mary, and Mary thenceforth lived with him in his house (see the article *Maria*, in Winer), and this little family, formed under the cross, could have had no more engaging matter of conversation than the memory of the Lord, we may doubtless ascribe to Mary a mental share in the gradual formation of this slowly maturing Gospel.

To the memories of the Apostle must be added the experiences of his life, especially the friendly and peaceful movements of his apostolic development. How he might thus have been led also to his peculiar shaping of his Logos doctrine, is suggested by Lücke's and other treatises on the Prologue.

To speak now of the design: The Gospel, like Christian worship, which is in this respect akin to art, and, like every thing belonging to the Christian Church, must have been produced primarily for its own sake, as the one spontaneous effusion of the lofty contemplations of the Evangelist. If this may be said even of the first Evangelists, and our school-theology must be charged with inquiring far too readily and too exclusively for an exterior design, while a due regard to the fervid spontaneity of the four Gospels might cure criticism of many prejudices of a lower conception;—all this is true in a very peculiar degree of the fourth Gospel. Contemplative minds like that of John must give expression to their experiences and views first of all for their own satisfaction; and if we have understood any thing of the nature of John, we cannot wonder that we find five productions of his hand, forming at bottom a trilogy of the evangelic, epistolary, and the apocalyptic character in the New Testament.

Yet, as the Christian cultus, with all its art-like character, by no means stops in the idea of mere exhibitive art, but builds itself out of the elements of eternally active truth, and aims with distinct purpose in efficient enthusiasm at edification, the Evangelists must as distinctly, and with still more distinct consciousness, have had their objective impulse and their practical design. And the Evangelist John has himself distinctly stated his first and his next practical design, chap. xx. 31. His immediate and decisive aim was neither to fight a heresy nor to complete the other Gospels. He knew too well that the positive statement of the life of Jesus, purely and fervidly given, was itself the most effective polemic (chap. iii. 19), and that a round, complete collection of the most significant points in the life of the Lord, set forth in orderly succession, would form the most fitting supplement (John xx. 31).

Nevertheless, this great apostolic presbyter-bishop of Ephesus could not have stood for half a century between the opposite germinant motions of Ebionism and Gnosticism, without writing his Gospel in the consciousness that it would practically transcend that antagonism, nor without, in this conviction, everywhere emphasizing the relevant anti-Ebionistic and anti-Gnostic points. The expressly polemic passages in his Epistles (comp. 1 John ii. 18, 22, 23; iv. 1 sqq., 2 John), as well as in the Revelation, particularly in the letters to the seven churches, give abundant proof that he was fully conscious of the historical and dogmatical points in his Gospel against the heresies of his time, and that he relied upon their operative force. And undoubtedly it was his Logos doctrine especially, in connection with the doctrine of the historical, personal Christ, which in the second century most effectively contributed to the victory of the Church over both Ebionism and Gnosticism. The doctrine of personality, concretely defined by the doctrine of the person of Christ, still ever operates as a two-edged sword against all Gnostic and Judaistic distortions of the truth. "With John, therefore, in his Gospel, the person of the Saviour is of supreme importance."

The consciousness of supplementing the first three Gospels, which at the time of the origin of John's Gospel had already gained a considerable currency among the Christians, was likewise natural. The Evangelist may even have been conscious of the twofold completion, internal and external, which he furnished; and in that case he surely intended to furnish it. But not in such sense as to be a theological or historical emendator.

When Clement of Alexandria (according to Euseb. vi. 14) remarks that the other Evangelists have delineated particularly the external history, giving us a εὐαγγέλιον σωματικόν; and the object of John was to give something higher, a εὐαγγέλιον πνευματικόν, he unites in one expression a partial truth, and a leaning of the Alexandrian turn of thought which must not be overlooked. Luther's dictum also, of the "one true, tender, leading Gospel," needs to be reduced to the most strictly qualified sense. All the Gospels are spiritual, pneumatic, each in its way; but the fourth Gospel is preëminently the Gospel of the real ideal personality of Christ, and as such, in the phrase of Ernesti, the heart of Christ (*pectus Christi*).

Clement further states that John wrote his Gospel at the request of his friends; likewise, the canon of Muratori, which Jerome ingeniously interpreted thus: that the bishops and churches of Asia Minor urged him to write his Gospel against the incipient heresies, and in it to make the divinity of Christ distinctly appear. But John hardly needed such a spur; he might at most have been hastened by it in the publication of the Gospel. The *historical* supplementing of the three Synoptists is made prominent, particularly by Eusebius (iii. 24) and Theodore of Mopsvestia (*Comment. in Joann.*). But if, beyond his delight in a more exact statement and essential enrichment of the Gospel history, John had been moved by the desire of an external supplementing of the records of his predecessors, the chronological points would have appeared still more clearly marked, and the array of facts and events much more copious. His object lay on a higher level than this; and so, indeed, did the object of the first three Evangelists themselves.

The modern criticism has come down so low as to represent John in his Gospel, according to Strauss, as aiming an indirect polemic against Peter; according to the anonymous Saxon work, "*Die Evangelien*," as intending to glorify himself and put himself in Peter's place; according to the Baur school, a fraudulent writer allowed himself to put forth, in the interest of an irenical tendency, a pseudo-Johannean Gospel!

§ 7. TIME AND PLACE OF THE COMPOSITION.

As to the time of the composition of the Gospel: It is the unanimous tradition of the ancients (Irenæus, Clement, Origen, &c.) that the fourth Gospel was the last written. We are also pointed probably in any case to the time of the Apostle's residence in Ephesus, which cannot yet have begun at the date of the Second Epistle to Timothy, because that Epistle shows no trace of John in Ephesus. This date, it is true, must vary according to the view taken respecting the time of Paul's death; we consider the traditional view well authenticated. For Ephesus as the place of composition, we have the authority of Irenæus, and, after him, many others.

According to Epiphanius, John wrote the Gospel at the age of ninety years; according to pseudographic traditions [Pseudo-Hippolytus *De XII. App.*], he wrote it on Patmos, and afterwards published it at Ephesus. Lücke supposes the Gospel to have been written between the seventh and the last decade of the first century, and says, only by way of conjecture, not before the eighth decade (p. 167). Guericke supposes [3d ed. p. 190] after the Apocalypse [between 80 and 90]. The first reason, however—viz., that the Gospel is written in purer Greek than the Apocalypse—amounts to nothing, since the Gospel was written ἐν νοΐ, the Apocalypse ἐν πνεύματι; that is, the former in the language of conscious communication with the culture of the world, the latter in the spontaneity of inspired expression in a native Hebrew; and as to the second reason, the relation of the Gospel to the Gnosis, &c., the beginnings of the Gnosis appear as early as the Pastoral Epistles. Meyer also supposes that the Gospel originated a considerable time after the destruction of Jerusalem, say about the year 80 (p. 41). He therewith assumes as probable, that the Gospel circulated for some time in a narrower circle of Ephesian friends, and was afterwards published more generally with the addition of the 21st chapter. This theory has nothing improbable, in so far as it takes the addition to be the finishing of the Gospel itself by the hand of John.

We take, as betokening a later origin, the publication of the raising of Lazarus (on the supposition that the first three Gospels omitted it out of regard for the still living family); and the account of Peter's use of the sword, with mention of his name, as well as the premonition of his martyrdom, chap. xxi. (see my *Apost. Zeitalt.*, ii. p. 419).

The question, however, arises, whether the passage (chap. v. 2) which speaks of the pool of Bethesda with its five porches as if still existing, does not indicate that Jerusalem was yet standing when John wrote the account (*Apost. Zeitalt.*, ii. p. 420). Lücke disputes this; and Guericke. The preterite ἦν, xi. 18; xviii. 1; xix. 41, proves, of course, nothing against the present tense, ἔστι, v. 2; for in those cases it refers to constant circumstances which must outlast the destruction of Jerusalem. Yet the pillars of Bethesda are not a perfectly firm support; since we might have here a previously written memorandum, or John might have been writing in a general view of Jerusalem as still standing. Withal, there is no similar indication of a later date; and as regards the reference to John's Greek, and to his familiarity with the theology of his time (the Logos doctrine), and with the incipient heresies, a few years are, in any case, enough to make him in these respects the author of the Gospel; and in Pella and in Decapolis there was material enough of Greek culture to bring him completely to his peculiar point of gospel view, which undoubtedly belongs to his residence in Ephesus.

That the Gospel belongs before the Apocalypse, and before the Epistles of John, and therefore, at all events, in the earliest part of his residence in Ephesus, seems to be especially indicated by its missionary leaning in chap. xx. 31.

It is matter of interest, that the critical Semler (like Tittmann) sought to make the fourth Gospel the first written of all; while his latest critical descendants put its origin in the middle of the second century. Another proof of the pretended infallibility of morbid criticism!

As to the original home of the Gospel: Not only tradition, but also the spiritual character, and its references, point decidedly to Ephesus.* The discourse of Paul to the elders of Ephesus, at Miletus, already indicates such antagonisms as the Gospel thrusts through in both directions at once; his Epistles to the Ephesians and the Colossians still more clearly indicate the same; and, finally, his Pastoral Epistles. The Gospel betokens a more advanced stage of these antagonisms, and a position of the Apostle's preaching between the opposite errors; the Epistles and the Revelation exhibit the third stage. Thus, with the place of the Gospel in time between the end of Paul and the end of John, its geographical place also is fixed. The Gospel presents to us the Apostle John in Ephesus, while the Epistles and the Apocalypse denote rather in Ephesus the bishop and prophet of the apostolic Church.

§ 8. SIGNIFICANCE AND MISSION OF JOHN, HIS SPIRIT, AND HIS WRITINGS.

The spirituality and subtilty, the ideality and pure mysticalness of John and his writings, throw the whole phenomenon into the background in proportion to the prevailing Petrine and Pauline character of the historical Church and her theology.

* [The unanimous tradition of the ancient Church concerning the labors of John in Asia Minor, which even the skeptical school of Baur left untouched, has been quite recently rejected by Dr. Keim in his *History of Jesus of Nazara*, vol. i. (1867) p. 161 ff., but ably defended by Dr. Steitz in the *Studien und Kritiken* for 1868, p. 487.—P. S.]

But, from the background, John has exerted in all ages the mightiest influence on the course of the Church. This influence is far from being fully appreciated. In the ancient Church it found a concrete embodiment in the Johannean school, whose import is yet further to be understood. Ignatius, Irenæus, Hippolytus, and others, are the earliest members of a spiritual family, which perpetuated itself in the British missionaries, in the Culdees, in the mediæval intellectual life of the Abbey of St. Gall.

In the Middle Age it was John who, in his writings, comforted and supported the Church, when, under the corruptions of the hierarchy, she was tempted to despair (see Gieseler, *Church History*, 2d vol. 2d part, p. 357, Germ. ed.). At the same time, it remains curious that the popes have not ventured to name themselves after Peter, but have freely called themselves after Paul and John. With the twenty-third John this self-judgment of an unsuspecting estrangement of spirit reached an extreme. The less they read John, the more they called themselves after his name in dark, deep reverence for the mysterious patron.

It cannot be wholly accidental that most of the forerunners of the Reformation bore the name of John; though even the Reformers, with all their deeper study of theology, have not yet quite reconciled themselves to the whole John, as we see from their posture toward the Apocalypse. And if, taking such a position as Paul took between Peter and John, they have introduced the transition to a Johannean age, the fact that the fourth Evangelist in particular has formed the rock of offence to modern criticism (comp. also Göthe's opinion of the Apocalypse), may nevertheless be a proof that we are as yet none too near that age. In any case, Schelling's construction of the three ages of the Christian Church will maintain its validity as an utterance of divinatory insight, which, of course, is exposed to much misinterpretation (comp. my *Apost. Zeitalt.*, ii. p. 650 [and the Amer. ed. of *Comm. on Romans*, pp. 1 and 2, note]); and it has long since been perceived that the Gospel of John forms the culmination of the evangelic history, as theology will more and more acknowledge that John's type of doctrine forms the consummation of the apostolic theology.

The saying among the disciples in the apostolic age must prove itself the truth in the higher sense: This disciple does not die!

§ 9. TOTAL VIEW OF THE GOSPEL HISTORY ACCORDING TO THE GOSPEL OF JOHN.

Since the Gospel of John forms the complement of the Synoptical Gospels in respect of regular chronological order, the historical view of the life of Jesus must be completed on the basis of John. We give the result of our labors in the following sketch:

Introduction: The Antecedent History of the Life of Christ.

The *eternal* antecedents of Christ. The Logos and His function; John i. 1–5. His history in the Old Covenant, represented by the testimony of John; vers. 6–13. The *temporal* antecedents of Jesus. Synoptists: Luke and Matthew. Luke: The genealogy of Jesus from Adam to Christ; chap. iii. 23–38. Matthew: The genealogy from Adam to Christ; chap. i. 1–17. Luke: The announcement of Jesus; Gabriel, Zachariah, Elizabeth, Mary, John; chap. i. 1–80. Matthew: The announcement; Mary and Joseph; chap. i. 18–25. Parallel to Luke i.

I. The Childhood of Jesus.

John: The birth of Christ, and the relation of His birth and operation to the natural birth; chap. i. 1–14. Luke: The journey to Bethlehem, and the birth of Jesus. The holy night, and the shepherds; chap. ii. 1–21. Matthew: The wise men from the East, and the flight into Egypt; chap. ii. 1–19. The presentation of Jesus in the temple, and the residence in Nazareth; Luke ii. 22–40; Matt. ii. 20–23. Jesus at twelve years of age; Luke ii. 41–52.

II. THE ANNOUNCEMENT OF CHRIST BY JOHN THE BAPTIST. THE MANIFESTATION OF CHRIST. FROM THE APPEARANCE OF THE BAPTIST TO THE FIRST PUBLIC ATTENDANCE OF CHRIST AT THE PASSOVER, 781 A. U. C. THE ACCREDITING OF CHRIST BY JOHN AND BY HIMSELF DOWN TO THE FIRST PASSOVER.

The testimony of the Baptist concerning Christ in general, connected with the baptism; John i. 15–18.—The baptism of Jesus at the Jordan in the parallels: Matt. iii. 1–17; Mark i. 1–11; Luke iii. 1–38.—The testimony of John concerning Jesus before the rulers of the Jews, that He is the Christ; John i. 19–28.—Parallels: The temptation; Matt. iv. 1–11; Mark i. 12, 13; Luke iv. 1–13.—The testimony of John concerning Jesus before His disciples. The first disciples of Jesus. The return of Jesus to Galilee. The marriage at Cana. The journey to Capernaum. The first public visit to the temple at the Passover in the year 781.

III. THE PUBLIC APPEARANCE OF CHRIST AMIDST THE ENTHUSIASTIC GREETINGS OF HIS PEOPLE. FROM THE PASSOVER OF 781 TO THE FEAST OF PURIM IN 782.

a. The First Ministry of Jesus in Judea, down to the Imprisonment of John the Baptist.

Sojourn in Jerusalem. Nicodemus. Baptizing in the country of Judea. The repeated testimony of John the Baptist; John i. 29–iii. 36.

b. The First Ministry of Jesus in Galilee.

The transfer of the ministry of Jesus to Galilee. Jesus in Samaria, and the Samaritan woman. The removal of the residence of Jesus from Nazareth to Capernaum. The healing of the son of an imperial officer; John iv. 1–54. Parallels: The return of Jesus to Galilee. Jesus thrust out of Nazareth; Luke iv. 16–31; Matt. iv. 12; xiii. 53; Mark i. 14–16.—Residence of Jesus in Capernaum, and ministry there. The demoniac in the synagogue; the mother-in-law of Peter; Peter's draught of fishes; the calling of the first disciples; Matt. iv. 12–22; viii. 14–17; Mark i. 14–38; iii. 9–12; Luke iv. 31–43 (44); v. 1–11.

c. The Three Great Missionary Tours of Jesus in Galilee. The Mountain Tour, the Sea Tour, the Tour through the Cities.

The first journey of Jesus through the country of Galilee (the mountain region). The sermon on the mount and in the plain. The healing of the leper; Matt. iv. 23–viii. 4; Mark i. 35–45; iii. 12, 13; Luke v. 12–16; vi. 12–49.—The return of Jesus from the tour of Galilee. The centurion at Capernaum. The followers. The second sermon on the sea. The voyage to Gadara, and the return; Matt viii. 5–13, 18–34; ix. 1; chap. xiii; Mark iv. 1–41; v. 1–21; Luke vii. 1–10; viii. 4–15, 22–39; ix. 57–62.—The return of Jesus from His journey to Gadara. The crowd. The paralytic. The calling of Matthew. Particular conflicts with the Pharisees and the disciples of John. A series of miracles; Matt. ix. 1–34; Mark ii. 1–22; v. 21–43; Luke v. 17–39; viii. 40–56.—The preparation for the third tour, through the coast cities. The selection of the twelve apostles. The instruction to the apostles; Matt. ix. 35–x. 42; xi. 1; Mark iii. 14–19; vi. 6–16; Luke vi. 12–16; ix. 1–6.—The journey of Jesus through the cities, and the apostles' going before. The woman who was a sinner. The fame of Jesus. The son of the widow of Nain; Matt. xi. 1; Mark vi. 12, 13; Luke vii. 11–17, 36–50; viii. 1–18.—The message of John the Baptist from prison; Matt. xi. 2–19; Luke vii. 18–35.

IV. THE TIME OF THE APPEARANCE AND DISAPPEARANCE OF JESUS UNDER THE PERSECUTIONS OF HIS ENEMIES; OR, HIS BANISHMENT AND FLIGHT-LIKE PILGRIMAGE. FROM THE FEAST OF PURIM IN 782 TO THE PALM-DAY BEFORE THE PASSOVER OF 783.

a. From the Feast of Purim to the Feast of Tabernacles, 782.

Jesus at the feast of Purim in Jerusalem. His conflict with the hierarchy, and their first attempt to institute capital process against Him; John v. The return of Jesus to Galilee. The account of the execution of John the Baptist. The first feeding of the multitude in the wilderness. Christ's walking on the sea; John vi. 1–21; Matt. xiv.; Mark vi. 14–56; Luke ix. 7–17.—Discourse of Jesus in the synagogue at Capernaum on the manna from heaven. His rebuke of chiliastic Messianic hopes in Galilee. The turning back of many of His followers; John vi. 22–71.—The Passover not attended by the Lord in the year of the persecution, and the occurrences connected therewith; John vi. 4; Luke x. 38–42; Matt. xv. 1, 2; comp. xxi. 1–3; xxvi. 18, 36; xxvii. 57.—The accusation of the Lord in reference to the plucking of the corn; Matt. xii. 1–8; Mark ii. 23–28; Luke vi. 1–5; John vii. 1.—The healing of the man with the withered hand; Matt. xii. 9–21; Mark iii. 1–6; Luke vi. 6–11.—The decisive public contest of the Lord with the Pharisees of Galilee. The healing of the deaf and dumb demoniac. The (second; comp. Matt. ix. 34) public culmination of the miraculous power of Jesus. Of the sin against the Holy Ghost. The second demand of a sign from heaven; comp. John ii. 18. The family of Jesus. The banquet in the house of the Pharisee. The crowd. Warning against the hypocrisy of the Pharisees, and against covetousness. The delivery of parables on the sea; Matt. xii. 22–50; xiii. 24–30, 33–58; Mark iii. 20–35; Luke viii. 18–21; xi. 14–54; chap. xii.—Accounts of persons returning from the feast concerning the unfortunate Galileans whom Pilate had slain in the temple; Luke xiii. 1–9.—The healing of the crooked woman: another miracle on the Sabbath; Luke xiii. 11–17.—The deputation from Jerusalem, taking the Lord to task for the free conduct of His disciples. The removal of Jesus: His wandering through the borders of Phœnicia and through Upper Galilee to Gaulonitis, on the other side the sea. The Canaanitish woman. The deaf and dumb. The second miraculous feeding. The crossing to the western coast of the sea of Galilee; Matt. xv.; Mark vii. 1–37; viii. 1–10.—Public hostility to Jesus at Magdala, and His return across the sea to the mountains of Gaulonitis. The healing of a blind man in the eastern Bethsaida. The confession of Peter, and his horror of the cross; Matt. xvi.; Mark viii. 11–ix. 1; Luke ix. 18–27.—The transfiguration; Matt. xvii. 1–13; Mark ix. 1–13; Luke ix. 28–36.—Healing of the lunatic; Matt. xvii. 14–21; Mark ix. 14–29; Luke ix. 37–45.—Homeward journey of Christ through Galilee, and His brethren's proposal that He join the pilgrimage to the feast of Tabernacles. Refusal of Jesus, and His secret ascent to Jerusalem, to appear there, not as a pilgrim, but as a Prophet; John vii. 1–10; Matt. xvii. 22, 23; Mark viii. 31, 32.

b. From the Feast of Tabernacles to the Feast of the Dedication in 782.

The sudden appearance of Jesus in the temple during the feast of Tabernacles. He accuses His enemies, before all the people, of seeking His life, and announces His departure; John vii. 10–36.—Jesus begins to announce the antagonism between the Old Testament symbolism of the temple and the reality of the New Testament salvation in Him. His testimony of the living fountain in opposition to the Pool of Siloam. Futility of the design of the Sanhedrin to imprison Him; John vii. 37–52.—Jesus the light of the world, in opposition to the lights and the torch festival in the temple; John viii. (1–11 *) 12–20.—The more distinct announcement of Jesus, that He intended to take His departure from the Jewish people; John viii. 21–30.—Flash of a chiliastic expectation among the people at Jerusalem. Dis-

* [See remarks on vers. 1-11 in the section on the Genuineness, and the passage in its place in the Commentary.]

course of Jesus on the distinction between the true freedom and the true bondage, and on the distinction between the faith of Abraham and the seeing of Christ; John viii. 31–59.—Healing of the man born blind; John ix.—Jesus gives the false shepherds of Israel the marks of the true shepherd, and presents himself as the True Shepherd, ready to lay down His life for His sheep; John ix. 40, 41–x. 1–21.—Last appearance of Jesus in Capernaum. Conduct of the disciples respecting the primacy; Matt. xvii. 24–xviii. 5; Mark ix. 33–37; Luke ix. 46–49.—Peril of offences; Matt. xviii. 6–11; Mark ix. 38–50; Luke xvii. 1, 2.—Departure of Jesus from Capernaum, and intimation of the apostasy of a great mass of His people; Luke xiii. 22–30.—Intrigues of the Pharisees; Luke xiii. 31–35.—Banquet in the house of a Pharisee. The dropsical man. Address of the Lord to the guests; Luke xiv. 1–24.—Multitude following Jesus on His departure. His warning to undecided followers; Matt. xix. 1, 2; Luke xiv. 25–35.—Reception of Publicans and sinners. Fellowship of the disciples of Christ. Parables; Matt. xviii. 12–35; Luke xv. 1–xvii. 10.—Hindrance to Jesus' journeying through Samaria; Luke ix. 51–62.—Sending of the seventy disciples, and the recurrence of Jesus to His labors in Galilee; Matt. xi. 20–30; Luke x. 1–16.—Journey of Jesus through the border country between Galilee and Samaria to Perea; Luke xvii. 11–19.—Return of the seventy. The narrow-hearted Scribe, and the good Samaritan; Luke x. 17–37.—Jesus' first sojourn in Perea, and His labors there; Matt. xix. 1, 2; Mark x. 1; Luke xvii. 20–xviii. 14.

c. From the Feast of Dedication in 782 *to the Palm-Day before the Passover in* 783.

Jesus at the feast of Dedication in Jerusalem. Last attempt of the Jews to make Jesus chime in with their chiliastic expectation; tempting Him; John x. 22–40.—Second and last sojourn of Jesus in Perea. Treatment of divorce; children brought to the Lord. The rich youth; John x. 40–42; Matt. xix. 3–xx. 16; Mark x. 2–32; Luke xviii. 15–30.—Raising of Lazarus in Bethany; John xi. 1–44.—Definite decree of the Sanhedrin to put Jesus to death, and secret sojourn of Jesus in Ephraim till His last pilgrimage to the Passover; John xi. 47–57.

V. The Decisive Yielding of Jesus to the Messianic Enthusiasm of His People. From the Palm Festival to the Feast of the Passover in the Year 783.

Journey of Jesus to Jericho, and His intercourse with the pilgrims to the Passover. Renewed announcement of His crucifixion. Ambition of the family of Zebedee. Healing of the blind men at Jericho. Zaccheus. Parable of the ten servants and the ten pounds intrusted to them; Matt. xx. 17–34; Mark x. 32–52; Luke xviii. 31–xix. 1–28. *Saturday:* Banquet in Bethany, and the anointing. Treason; John xii. 1–11; Matt. xxvi. 6–16; Mark xiv. 3–11; Luke xxii. 1–6. *Sunday:* Triumphal entrance of Jesus into Jerusalem; John xii. 9–18; Matt. xxi. 1–11; Mark xi. 1–11; Luke xix. 29–46. *Monday:* The great day of the Messianic dwelling and administration of Jesus in the temple. Cursing of the fig tree. Purifying of the temple. Keeping holy the temple. Exercise of His office of teacher, and miraculous cures, in the temple. The hosanna of the children, objection of the Pharisees, and Christ's vindication (the Greeks, and the voice from heaven; John xii. 19–36. See the passage in the Commentary. It is hard to fix the precise moment of the appearance of the Greeks); Matt. xxi. 12–22; Mark. xi. 12–19; Luke xix. 45–48. *Tuesday:* End of the Old Testament theocracy. The withered fig tree. Attempt of the Sanhedrin to crush the Lord by its authority. Consequent ironical temptations on the part of Pharisees, Sadducees, and Scribes. Great counter-question of Christ. Great discourse of the Lord against the Pharisees and Scribes. Woes against Jerusalem, and departure from the temple. The widow's mite; John xii. 37; Matt. xxi. 10–xxiv. 2; Mark xi. 20–xiii. 2; Luke xix. 47–xxi. 6. *Tuesday night, Wednesday:* Jesus looking back upon the temple from the Mount of Olives in the circle of His confidential disciples. Announcement of the judgment of God, the destruction of the Holy City and the temple, and the end of the world. Parables of the Ten Virgins and the Talents. The final judgment; Matt. xxiv. 3–xxv. 46; Mark xiii. 3–37; Luke xxi. 7–36. *Wednesday:* Retirement of Jesus into secresy. The Evangelist John's review of the ministry of the Lord; John xii. 37–50; Luke xxi. 37, 38.

VI. Treason of the People of Israel against their Messiah. The Decree of the High Council. The Paschal Lamb and the Supper. The Parting Discourses. The Passion, Death, and Burial of Jesus. From the Passover to the End of the Great Passover Sabbath.

Introduction to the passion of Jesus. Distinct announcement of Jesus, that He should suffer at the Passover. Contemporaneous decree of the Sanhedrin (two days before Easter, Tuesday evening, the day of the decisive rupture) to put Him to death, *but not at the Passover.* The ordering and preparation of the paschal supper; Matt. xxvi. 1–5; vers. 17–19; Mark xiv. 1, 2; vers. 12–16; Luke xxii. 1, 2; vers. 7–13.—The feet-washing. The paschal supper. Institution of the Holy Supper. Parting discourses of the Lord. Sacerdotal prayer. Exit to the Mount of Olives; John xiii.–xvii.; Matt. xxvi. 20–35; Mark xiv. 17–31; Luke xxii. 14–39.

a. Jesus in Gethsemane.

The struggle and victory in His inward passion; John xviii. 1–12, 13; Matt. xxvi. 36–46; Mark xiv. 32–42; Luke xxii. 39–46.—Jesus in Gethsemane before His enemies. The traitor. Free surrender of Jesus. Guarantee of the disciples, and their flight; Matt. xxvi. 47–56; Mark xiv. 43–52; Luke xxii. 47–53.

b. Jesus before the Spiritual Court (Sanhedrin).

Jesus before Annas and before Caiaphas. The false witnesses. Christ the true witness, with the confession that He is the Son of God. The denial of Peter, and his repentance. The first mocking of the Lord, and the final hearing; John xviii. 13–27; Matt. xxvi. 57–75; Mark xiv. 53–72; Luke xxii. 54–71.

c. Jesus before Pilate.

Leading of Jesus away to the Prætorium, and end of Judas; John xviii. 28; Matt. xxvii. 1–10; Mark xv. 1; Luke xxiii. 1.—Jesus before the secular tribunal. The threefold accusation of sedition, blasphemy, and treason. The three hearings: before Pilate, before Herod, and again before Pilate. The three great forebodings: the jealous tumult of the Sanhedrin; the dream of Pilate's wife; the saying, that Jesus is the Son of God. The three attempts at rescue: Barabbas; the scourging; the last remonstrance of Pilate. The three rejections of Christ on the part of the Jewish people: Christ offered with Barabbas; Christ declared innocent by Pilate's washing of his hands; Christ crowned with thorns. The hand-washing of the Gentile, the self-imprecation of the Jews. The three condemnations: delivery to the mercy of the people; to scourging; to death. Threefold mockery of the Lord: in His own raiment before the High Council; in white before Herod; in purple before Pilate. Sentence of death; John xviii. 28–xix. 16; Matt. xxvii. 11–31; Mark xv. 1–20; Luke xxiii. 1–25.

d. Jesus on Golgotha.

The leading of Jesus away to Golgotha; John xix. 16, 17; Matt. xxvii. 31–33; Mark xv. 20–22; Luke xxiii. 26–33.—The crucifixion. The seven last words. The signs of divinity. The signs of judgment, or the scoffing and the beginnings of trembling after the uproar. The signs of faith. The signs of turning; John xix. 17–30; Matt. xxvii. 33–56; Mark xv. 22–41; Luke xxiii. 33–49.

e. The Burial on Good-Friday Evening.

The new disciples. The old female disciples. The sepulchre. The burial; John xix. 31–42; Matt. xxvii. 57–66; Mark xv. 42–47; Luke xxiii. 50–56.

VII. The Resurrection, or the Glorification of the Lord.

a. The Resurrection and the Appearances of Jesus in Judea.

The resurrection, and the first announcement of it to Magdalene and the women; John xx. 1–18; Matt. xxviii. 1–10; Mark xvi. 1–11; Luke xxiv. 1–12.—Announcement of the resurrection of Jesus among His enemies; Matt. xxviii. 11–15.—The walk to Emmaus. Peter; Mark xvi. 12, 13; Luke xxiv. 13–35.—First appearance of Christ in the circle of the apostles on the first Sunday evening, ; John xx. 19–23; Mark xvi. 14; Luke xxiv. 36–44. Second appearance of Jesus on the second Sunday evening in the circle of the apostles. Thomas; John xx. 26–31.

b. The Appearances of Christ in Galilee.

First appearance of Jesus in Galilee in a company of apostles; John xxi. Second appearance of Jesus in the midst of a great company of disciples, as valedictory to the larger body of disciples in Galilee, or His people at large; Matt. xxviii. 16–20; Mark xvi. 15–18; Luke xxiv. 45–49. Comp. 1 Cor. xv. 6.

c. Last Appearance of Jesus in the Circle of His Apostles in Judea. The Ascension.

Walk to the Mount of Olives, and ascension; Mark xvi. 19, 20; Luke xxiv. 50–53. Comp. Acts i. 1–12.

d. The Spiritual Return and Eternal Presence of Christ in His Church.

Christ with His people alway, even to the end of the world; John xxi. 15–25; Matt. xxviii. 20; Mark xvi. 20; Luke xxiv. 51. Comp. Acts i. and ii.

Observation.—John unites his peculiar selection of facts for points of view, which distinguishes his arrangement of the Gospel, with the closest chronological sequence. With the Synoptists the interest in facts induces greater deviation from chronological order. In regard to Matthew and Mark, we refer to the Introductions. In our construction of the Gospel history, some of the greatest changes of chronological order occur in Luke. The shaping of facts in Luke proceeds from his interest to exhibit the whole life of Jesus as a wandering, which had its goal at Jerusalem, and which the Evangelist viewed as a teaching of salvation in facts and the acts of the Lord (see Acts x. 37, 38. Comp. my *Leben Jesu*, iii. p. 345 sqq.). Matthew exhibits the gospel fulfilments of the Old Testament in great stadia; Mark the victorious conflicts of the gospel; John presents general gospel views of the moral universe in the light of the person of Christ; Luke, the *gospel pilgrimages.* The pilgrimage of Mary forms the centre of the first chapter. The pilgrimage of the parents, and of Jesus at twelve years, to the temple, is the issue of the second. In the third, John is a pilgrim on the Jordan, and the people make pilgrimage to him; so at last does Jesus. The history of the temptation also (chap. iv.) stands here under the particular aspect of a caravan; hence probably the transposition of the second and third temptations. After this, Jesus journeys from His home in Nazareth to Capernaum. But in Capernaum He does not stay; the preaching and healing itinerancies through Galilee begin. In schools, on ships, at custom-stands, in harvest-fields, on mountains, the Lord unfolds the riches of His divine-human gentleness and kindness. The three pilgrimages through Galilee, also, Luke so transposes as to make the voyage to Gadara the close (chap. viii.). And then, in the ninth chapter, Jesus, in the calling of the twelve apostles, and in the transfiguration, prepares himself for the great pilgrimage to Jerusalem. The journey begins, the seventy disciples in advance. Now the Evangelist distinguishes for us the several parts of the journey of Jesus from Galilee to Jerusalem. These parts, put together without regard to chronological relations, form a grand panorama of the pilgrimage of the faithful in the kingdom of God, or a representation of saving truth in facts; chap. x. 38–xviii. 30. The end of the journey is the progress of Jesus to Jerusalem; chaps. xviii. 31–xix. 48. Here is most graphically painted the progress of Jesus over the Mount of Olives; and among the parables which the Lord now delivers in the temple, Luke gives prominence to that of the lord of a vineyard travelling into a far country; the disciples should flee to the mountains before the destruction of Jerusalem; they should lift up their heads in the last judgment, and escape all its terrors. The passage of Christ to Golgotha becomes, in Luke's hand, a significant pilgrimage amidst the lamentations of the daughters of Jerusalem. The female disciples, who ministered to the Lord and aided in His burial, are female Galilean pilgrims. Even one of the chief appearances of the risen Lord we find, in Luke, interwoven with a journey of the disciples from Jerusalem to Emmaus, and the ascension is the end of a pilgrimage of Jesus with His disciples to Bethany. With this principle of arrangement, on the basis, no doubt, of existing memorabilia (see Luke i. 1, and Schleiermacher's *Lukas*), Luke united the spirit of the Pauline type of doctrine in the form of Grecian culture; and in his human conception of the Divine kindliness and spiritual beauty of Christ he set points of gentleness, grace, compassion, foremost, especially in contrast with Pharisaic pride and self-righteousness. On these two subjects compare the admirable remarks [of Dr. Van Oosterzee] in the Introduction of the Commentary on Luke.

On the synoptical relations of the Gospel, should be further compared the Synopses of De Wette and Lücke, Tischendorf [Robinson, Strong], and others, and the modern works on the life of Jesus, especially that of Pressel. Also the *Harmony of the Gospels*, by Lex.

§ 10. FUNDAMENTAL IDEA AND DIVISION OF THE GOSPEL OF JOHN.

The fundamental idea of the Gospel is this: Christ, as the eternal, personal Word, is the personal basis of the world; its foundation of love, which branches into life and light, and the primal nature and form of which all things, by their symbolical formation, testify. Therefore also Christ, as the Life and Light of the world, breaks victoriously through the darkness of sin in the world, till He becomes incarnate, and thence, till His glorification, to redeem the world. And since the perfect glorification of Christ is the perfect redemption of the world, the operation of His redemption in the world must perfect itself in the glorifying of the world—that is, in His advent, which makes the world the Father's house. Accordingly, the whole Gospel falls into three parts: (1.) Concerning the pre-historical glory of Christ, or His pre-historical advent and His manifestation; the prologue, chap. i. 1–18; (2.) Concerning the historical glory of Christ, or His victory in conflict with the darkness; the gospel history in the strict sense; chap. i. 19–xx. 31; (3.) Concerning the post-historical glory of Christ over His Church, and in it, or His second advent; chap. xxi.

The subdivisions arrange themselves as follows:

I. The Prologue, Chap. i. 1–18.

1*st Section.*—Christ in His eternal essence and life, and His position between God and the world; vers. 1–5.

(1.) The personal Word (Christ) in His eternal essence and life as related to God; vers. 1, 2.
(2.) As related to the creation; ver. 3.
(3.) To the world and to mankind in their original constitution; ver. 4.
(4.) To the world in darkness; ver. 5.

2d Section.—The personal Light, or Christ, in His pre-historical advent in the world, especially in His Old Testament advent, testified by the Old Covenant as represented by John the Baptist.

(1.) The representative of the advent of Christ, John the Baptist; vers. 6–8.

(2.) The coming of Christ into the world as to its general groundwork and its historical development; ver. 9.

(3.) Relation of Christ to the world, and conduct of the world toward Him, or the general groundwork of His advent; ver. 10.

(4.) Relation of Christ to Israel, and conduct of Israel toward Him, or the imperfect, symbolical advent; ver. 11.

(5.) Gradual breaking forth of Christ into the world in the distinction of the elect from the less susceptible, constituted (*a.*) by faith, as the beginning of the real advent; ver. 12; (*b.*) by the sanctification of births, and birth from God. Development of the real advent; ver. 13.

3d Section.—Incarnation of the Logos. Appearance of the real Shekinah among the faithful; vers. 14–18.

(1.) Incarnation of the Logos, or the absolutely new birth. Appearance of the real Shekinah; ver. 14.

(2.) Testimony of John in general; ver. 15.

(3.) Experience of believers, or grace; ver. 16.

(4.) Antithesis between Moses and Christ, the law of the Old Testament and Christianity, in their authority and work; ver. 17.

(5.) Antithesis between the whole old world and Christ in their relation to God; ver. 18.

II. THE GOSPEL OF THE HISTORICAL MANIFESTATION OF CHRIST, OR HIS SELF-REVELATION AND HIS VICTORY IN CONFLICT WITH THE DARKNESS OF THE WORLD, Chap. i. 19–xx. 31.

1st Section.—Reception which Christ, the Light of the world, finds in His life of love among the men akin to the light, the elect; chap. i. 19–iv. 54.

(1.) John the Baptist and his public and repeated testimony concerning Christ (before the rulers of the Jews and his disciples); Jesus, accredited as the Christ, attested the Son of God, the eternal Lord, and the Lamb of God; vers. 19–34.

(2.) The disciples of John and the first disciples of Jesus. Jesus acknowledged as the Messiah, the King of Israel, who knows His Israelites, and also knows the "Jews;" signalized by miraculous discernment of spirits, personal characters becoming manifest in His personal light; vers. 35–51.

(3.) The kindred and friends of the Lord, and the first miracle of Jesus at Cana, as the earnest of the glorification of the world, and as the first manifestation of His glory. Christ transfiguring the earthly marriage feast into a symbol of the heavenly; chap. ii. 1–11.

(4.) Jesus the guest in Capernaum, and the pilgrim to the Passover. The purification of the temple, as a prelude of the redeeming purification of the world and reformation of the Church. Christ the true Temple. The sign of Christ: The destruction of the temple and the raising it again. The first spread of faith in Israel, and Christ the Knower of hearts; vers. 12–25.

(5.) Jesus in Jerusalem, and Nicodemus as a witness of the first powerful impression of Jesus on the Pharisees. The conversation of Christ with Nicodemus by night concerning the heavenly birth as the condition of entrance into the kingdom of God. Symbolism of the water, the wind, and the brazen serpent; chap. iii. 1–21.

(6.) Jesus in the Judean country, and the spread of His baptism, with the faith of the people. Last testimony of the Baptist concerning Christ; Christ the true Baptist.

The bridegroom of the Church, who comes from heaven (the real Song of songs); vers. 22–36.

(7.) Jesus at Jacob's well. The woman of Samaria. Christ the Fountain of Life, the Fountain of Peace. The white harvest-field, or the field of earth and the field of heaven. The sowers and the reapers. The faith of the Samaritans, a presage of the universal spread of the gospel; chap. iv. 1–42.

(8.) Residence of Jesus in Galilee, and believing Galileans in particular. The nobleman. The miracle of distant healing, as a second sign; vers. 43–54.

2d Section.—Open antagonism between Christ, as the Light of the world, and the elements of darkness in the world, especially in their proper representatives, unbelievers, but also in the better men, so far as they still belong to the world; chaps. v. 1–vii. 9.

(1.) The feast of the Jews and the Sabbath of the Jews, and their observance of it: killing Christ. The feast of Christ and the Sabbath of Christ, and His observance of it: raising the dead. Offence of the Judaists in Jerusalem at the Sabbath-healing of Jesus, and at His testimony concerning His freedom and His Divine origin (and besides, doubtless, at His outdoing the Pool of Bethesda). First assault upon the life of Jesus. Christ the true Fount of Healing (Pool of Bethesda), the Glorifier of the Sabbath by His saving work, the Raiser of the dead, the Life as the vital energy and healing of the world, accredited by John, by the Scriptures, by Moses. The true Messiah in the Father's name, and false messiahs; chap. v.

(2.) The Passover of the Jews, and the manna of the Jews. The Passover of Christ, ver. 62, and Christ the Manna from heaven. Miracle of feeding in the wilderness. Miracle of the flight and escape over the sea, wherein Christ withdraws himself from the chiliastic enthusiasm of earthly-minded admirers, and hastens to the help of His disciples. Decisive declaration of Christ. Offence of His Galilean admirers and many of His disciples at His refusing to give them bread in the sense of their chiliasm, and presenting himself in His Spirit with His flesh and blood as the Bread of Life; chap. vi. 1–65.

(3.) Apostasy of many disciples. Incipient treason in the circle of the twelve. Confession of Peter; vers. 66–71.

(4.) Approach of the feast of Tabernacles, and offence of even the brothers of Jesus at His refusing to go to it. Christ, the object of the world's hatred; Christ's time, and the time of the worldly mind; chap. vii. 1–9.

3d Section.—Ferment in the contest between the elements of light and darkness. Formation of parties, as a prelude to the maturing opposition between the children of light and the children of darkness; chaps. vii. 10–x. 21.

(1.) Fermentation and party division among the people in general. (*a.*) Christ, the Teacher and the One sent from God, in opposition to the human rabbinical office, and in agreement with Moses. His earthly descent, in opposition to descent from heaven. His opponents, who would kill Him, in contradiction with Moses. The Prophet of God, intending to return to God; vers. 10–36. (*b.*) Christ, as the Dispenser of the Spirit, the real Siloam with its water of life. Increasing ferment in the people; vers. 37–44.

(2.) Fermentation and parties in the High Council; vers. 45–53.

(3.) Christ, the Light of the world, the real fulfilment of the Jewish torch-light festivities, as against the pretended seers, the false lights, in Israel. The adulteress, and Christ's sentence. His ideal appearance into the court of the Jews, and the two witnesses. The judges shall come into judgment. A twofold lifting up of Christ at hand. Appearances of yielding, or a great vacillation toward faith; chap. viii. 1–30.

(4.) Christ the Liberator, as son of the house, in distinction from servants; the One sent from God, as against the agents of the devil; the Eternal, and the Hope of Abraham, as against the bodily seed of Abraham; or: the Liberator of Israel, the

Adversary of Satan, the Hope of Abraham. A great swinging from faith to unbelief. Attempted stoning; vers. 31–59.

(5.) Christ the Light of the world, over against the blind; healing of the man born blind on the Sabbath, with the symbolical coöperation of the temple spring of Siloam. The day of Christ, and Christ the Light of this day. The light of the blind, a judgment on the blindness of those who pretend to see. Symbolism of the light, the day, the day's work. The ban, or the incipient separation; chap. ix.

(6.) Christ the fulfilment of all symbolical shepherd life; the truth of the theocracy and the Church. (*a.*) The Door of the fold, as against the thieves. (*b.*) The True Shepherd, as against the hireling and the wolf. (*c.*) The Chief Shepherd of the great twofold flock. The symbolical communion and the real communion, or the symbolical and real ban.—The fermentation in its utmost intensity; chap. x. 1–21.

4th Section.—Separation between the friends and the enemies of Christ, the children of light and the children of darkness; chap. x. 22–xiii. 30.

(1.) Contrast between the unbelievers in Judea, who would kill the Lord, and the believers in Perea, with whom He finds refuge. Feast of the Dedication. Last collision between the false Messianic hope and the working of the true Messiah; quickly followed by stoning. The true and the false dedication of the temple. Christ the Son of God, the true realization of the deified or Messianic forms of the Old Covenant; chap. x. 22–42.

(2.) Contrast between the believing and unbelieving Jews of Judea and Jerusalem at the grave of Lazarus. Christ devoted to death in consequence of His raising of Lazarus from the dead. Symbolism of day's work, and of sleep. The resurrection of the dead; chap. xi. 1–57.

(3.) Contrast between fidelity and apostasy in the circle of the disciples themselves. The life-feast over Lazarus, the eve or fore-festival of the death of Jesus: the anointing; chap. xii. 1–8.

(4.) Contrast between the homage of the pious Jews and feast-pilgrims and the Chief Priests and their party, who consulted to destroy His friends also with the Lord. The Prince of Peace, and the palm-branches; vers. 9–17.

(5.) (*a.*) Contrast between the worshipful heathen Greeks from abroad and the majority of the Jewish people who fell away from Christ in unbelief, and occasioned His withdrawal into concealment. Symbolism of Hellenism, the Jewish Passover, the corn of wheat. Glorification through the suffering of death, or the spiritual self-sacrifice of Jesus in the temple; vers. 20–36. (*b.*) Contrast between self-hardened Israel, and the longing, susceptible world, or the retirement of Christ, and the Evangelist's review of His official ministry; vers. 37–50.

(6.) Return of Jesus from concealment, in love to His own. Division in the circle of the disciples themselves. Perplexity and trembling of the faithful. Exclusion of Judas. Christ's washing His disciples' feet an exaltation of ministering lordship: symbolism and establishment of brotherly discipline in the Church. Actual excision of the adversary from the discipleship of Jesus; chap. xiii. 1–30.

5th Section.—The Lord in the circle of His friends, the children of the light, opening and imparting to them the riches of His inner life, and thereby consecrating them vehicles and mediators of His own life, to enlighten and glorify the world, and unite this world and that which is to come; the heaven opened; chap. xiii. 31–xvii. 26.

(1.) The clearly pronounced opposition between this world and that which is to come, and its mediation through the new institution of Christ (the Holy Supper, as) the ordinance of brotherly love. Earnest greatness of this opposition, expressed in the announcement of Peter's denial. Glorification of Christ, and the New Covenant. The new commandment, the exaltation of the law, and of the opposition between the departure of Christ and the remaining of His people in the world; chap. xiii. 31–38.

(2.) Opening and revelation of heaven (the heavenly home), by the revelation of the heavenly Christ in the present world. The glorification of the world to come, which was to arise from His departure, and His union with His disciples in the Spirit. Under the starry heavens. Christ the Way to the Father's house; chap. xiv. 1–31.

(3.) Glorification of the present world. Brought about by the judgment, and by the abiding of the disciples in the love of Christ, and by their influence upon the world, for which He would send His Spirit upon them. Between the burning garden fires in the vale of Kedron. Christ the Vine. Exaltation of the noble plant, and its culture. Exaltation of friendship and joy. Proving of the spiritual life of the disciples against the hatred of the world. Victory of the Holy Ghost in them over the world. Development of Christianity through the Holy Ghost. The holy excommunicated state of the children of God; chap. xv. 1–xvi. 15.

(4.) Higher union of the eternal world and the present world in the New Testament Easter and Pentecost. Glorification of Christ through the Holy Ghost, and of the Father through Christ. The going and returning of the Lord. The watchword of the Church: "A little while." Symbolism of suffering, of birth-pangs, and birth-joys. Good-Friday sorrow and Easter joy in the life of the Lord and in the life of the Church; chap. xvi. 16–27.

(5.) Glorification of the departure of Christ by His glorious coming from the Father into the world; vers. 28–33.

(6.) The high-priestly intercourse of Christ for His own, a prayer for the glorification of His name even to the glorification of His people and the world, even to the disappearance of the world, as world, to the honor of the Father. Christ the Truth and Fulfilment of the Shekinah and all manifestations of God in the world, in His self-sacrifice for the world. Glorification of prayer, of mental crises, of sacrifice. The heavenly goal; chap. xvii.

6th Section.—The Lord in the circle of His enemies, as the light invaded by the darkness; the sublime Judge, or the personal Tribunal, when He is judged; triumphant in His outward surrender; carrying out judgment to the victory of light and salvation; chaps. xviii. and xix.

(1.) Christ as the Tribunal of the Light amidst the confused nocturnal quarrel of the world against and about His person; over against His betrayer, His arresters, His violent defender. The majesty of the Betrayed in contrast with the nothingness of the betrayer; voluntariness of the suffering in contrast with the powerlessness of the arresters; the reference to the decree of the Father in contrast with the unlawful help of Peter. The repudiation of the violent act of Peter, and the vanity and insignificance of employing violent means for spiritual ends; chap. xviii. 1–11.

(2.) Christ in contrast with Annas and Caiaphas. Clearness of the Lord, over against the inquisition of the high priest and the abuse from the servant. The two disciples in the high priest's palace, and the wavering, falling Peter; vers. 12–27.

(3.) Christ in contrast with Pilate. Conduct of Pilate in reference (*a.*) to the first charge, that Jesus was a malefactor; (*b.*) to the charge that Jesus aspired to be King of the Jews; (*c.*) to the charge that Jesus had made himself the Son of God. —Decided fall of Pilate, when Jesus was accused of being an insurgent against the Emperor.—Kingdom of Jesus in opposition to the kingdom of this world. Symbolism of the Roman Empire. Jesus King in the realm of Truth. Acquittal of Jesus. Choice of the murderer Barabbas. Jesus in the crown of thorns and the purple robe. Judgment of Jesus upon Pilate. Pilate conceals his defeat in the disguise of disdain. The sentence of death; chap. xviii. 28–xix. 16.

(4.) Christ on Golgotha, the Light of salvation, or the glorification of the curse of the old world. Christ the cross-bearer. The Crucified in the midst of crucified. The superscription: "The King of the Jews," a motto of contempt, turning itself into a motto of honor. The booty of the soldiers, also, a fulfilment of Scripture. The appointment of departing love. The last draught. The word of victory: "It is finished!" vers. 17–30.

(5.) Christ the glorification of death, Life in death itself. The corpse of Jesus, a dark, evil omen to His enemies, a mysterious resurrection-omen to His friends (a sign that He was the true paschal Lamb, and that something wonderful would come to pass in Him), a decisive reanimating omen to the undecided disciples. The honorable burial in the garden, and in the new rock-hewn sepulchre. Premonitions of the victory of Christ; vers. 31–42.

7th Section.—Accomplished victory of Christ over the world and the kingdom of darkness, and His manifestation in the circle of His own. Christ proves His victory by banishing the last remnants of darkness, of sadness and unbelief, from His people, and making them certain of His resurrection; chap. xx.

(1.) How the risen Lord, by the signs in the grave, prepares His disciples for the signs in His life; vers. 1–10.

(2.) How He turns the disconsolateness of Mary Magdalene into blessed peace, and makes her the messenger of the resurrection; vers. 11–18.

(3.) How Christ delivers the circle of the disciples from their old fear, and raises them by the breathing of His Spirit to the presentiment of their apostolic calling; vers. 19–23.

(4.) How Christ puts to shame the unbelief of Thomas, and turns the doubting disciple into the most joyful confessor; vers. 24–29.

(5.) Purpose of the facts of the Gospel: testimony concerning Christ, and life in His name; vers. 30, 31.

III. The Epilogue. The Post-Historical Work of Christ in the World, till its Perfect Glorification, or the Second Coming of Christ; Symbolically Presented in the Particular Portions of the History of the Resurrection, Chap. xxi.

(1.) The manifestation of the risen Saviour on the sea of Galilee as a type of the future relation and conduct of Christ with His apostolic Church in this world; vers. 1–14.

(2.) The continued working of Christ in His Church, represented by the office, the walk, and the martyrdom of Peter, or the fortunes of the Church in her predominantly official and external character; vers. 15–19.

(3.) The continued working of Christ in His Church, represented by the office, the spiritual life, and the patriarchal age of John; or the fortunes of the Church in her predominantly inward character, and her immortal spiritual life; vers. 20–23.

(4.) The testimony of John and the testimony of the Church. The endlessness of the gospel history; vers. 24, 25.

For other arrangements, see Luthardt's Commentary, "*Disposition and Construction*," p. 254.

§ 11. LITERATURE ON THE GOSPEL OF JOHN.

For the general exegetical works on the Bible, or on the New Testament, which embrace the Gospel of John, see the Introduction to the New Testament prefixed to the Gospel of Matthew in this Commentary; also, for the literature relating to the four Gospels, and for the general homiletical works.

The exegetical and homiletical literature relating to the Gospel of John by itself, may be found in Lilienthal, *Biblischer Archivarius*, Königsberg, 1745, p. 265 sqq.; Walch, *Biblioth. theol.*, 4th part, p. 646; Winer, *Handbuch der theol. Literatur*, i. p. 248; ii. p. 118 sqq.; Supplement, pp. 38, 175; Danz, *Universal-Wörterbuch der theol. Literatur*, p. 460, and Supplement, i. p. 54; Zimmer, *Handbibliothek der theol. Liter. des 19ten Jahrhunderts*, pp. 10, 69; Hertwig,

Tabellen zur Einleitung in's N. Test., Berlin, 1855, p. 19; Guericke, *Isagogik*, p. 169 [3d ed., pp. 188, 189]; Tholuck, *Commentary* [Amer. ed., p. 49].

The most notable expositors are: Among the fathers, Origen [*Commentaria in Evang. Joannis*], Chrysostom [*Homiliæ LXXXVIII in Joh. Evang.;* Engl. transl. in the Oxford *Library of the Fathers*, vols. xxviii. and xxxvi., 1848–'52; Cyrillus Alex., *Comment. in Ev. Joh.*], and Augustine [*Tractatus CXXIV in Joh. Evang.*, practical homilies, see *Opera*, Tom. iii., P. ii., pp. 290–826, ed. Bened., Paris, 1658; transl. in the *Library of the Fathers*, Oxford, 1848–'49, 2 vols.]; * of the Roman Catholic expositors, Erasmus, Maldonatus, Este, Cornelius a Lapide, and the recent Ad. Maier (1845, 2 vols.) [Messmer, 1860, Bisping, 1865]; of the Reformers, Luther, Melanchthon, Bucer, Calvin, Beza, Chemnitz [d. 1586], &c.; of the seventeenth century, J. Piscator [1613], Hunnius [d. 1603], Grotius [d. 1645], Cocceius [d. 1669]; of the eighteenth, Lampe (*Comm. in Evang. Joh.* [1st ed., Amsterdam, 1724–'26, 3 vols. 4to.; a work of immense erudition and Calvinistic orthodoxy]), Bengel (*Gnomon*); of the nineteenth, Lücke [1st ed., 1820–'24; 3d ed., 1840–'43, 3 vols.; an exegetical masterpiece], Olshausen [1st ed., 1832; 4th ed., by Ebrard, 1862; the English translation from an older edition], Baumgarten-Crusius [1843–'45], H. A. W. Meyer [1834; 5th ed., 1869], De Wette [1837; 5th ed., revised by Bruno Brückner, 1863, much enlarged and improved]; Tholuck [1827; 7th ed., 1857; Engl. translation by Ch. F. Krauth, Philad., 1859, from the 6th ed., with additions from the 7th]; Luthardt, *Das Johanneische Evangelium*, 2 parts, 1852. More recently has appeared: E. W. Hengstenberg, *Das Evangelium des heil. Johannes*, Berlin, 3 vols., 1861–'63 [2d ed., 1867 ff. Engl. translation, Edinburgh, 1865, 2 vols.—To these must be added: H. Ewald, *Die Johanneischen Schriften übersetzt und erklärt*, Gött., vol. i., 1861; W. Bäumlein, *Comm. über das Evang. d. Joh.*, Stuttgart, 1863 (grammatical and brief); C. H. A. von Burger, *Das Evang. nach Joh. deutsch erklärt*, Nördlingen, 1868; and the excellent French works of J. F. Astié, *Explication de l'évangile selon St. Jean*, Genève, 1864, and F. Godet, *Commentaire sur l'évangile de St. Jean*, Paris, 1865, 2 vols.—P. S.].

As practical expositions, Tholuck mentions O. v. Gerlach, N. T., 2 parts; Stier, *Reden Jesu*, 4th part; Fr. Besser, *Bibelstunden über das Evangelium Johannis* [1851, 4th ed., 1860]. To these we add: S. J. Baumgarten, *Auslegung des Evangeliums Johannis*, Halle, 1762; Mich. Wirth, *Das Evangelium des Johannes erläutert*, Ulm, 1829; Fickenscher, *Biblisch-praktische Auslegung des Evangeliums Johannis*, Nürnberg, 1831; Diedrich, *Das Evangelium Johannis*, Leipzig, 1859; Heubner, *Praktische Erklärung des N. T.*, vol. ii. The Homilies on the Gospel of John, delivered by Fr. Schleiermacher in 1823 and 1824, published by Sydow, in 2 parts, Berlin, 1837, are to be especially noted.

As to the separate portions of the Gospel: The 11th chapter has been treated in sermons by Fr. Wilhelm Jul. Schröder, first series, Elberfeld, 1853; various sections in the Bremen *Post*, by Dr. Mallet, vols. i. and ii.; Reichhelm, *Christus die rechte Speise und der rechte Trank*, sermons on chaps. iv.–vii., Frankfurt a. d. O., 1857; Schmieder, *Das hohepriesterliche Gebet unsers Herrn Jesu Christi*, 20 Meditations, Hamburg, Agency of the Rough House. Also the sermons: "*Wir sahen seine Herrlichkeit*," Berlin, 1853, treat in good part the Johannean text.

On the Evangelist and his Gospel there are: Herder, *Von Gottes Sohn, der Welt Heiland, nach Johannis Evangelium*, 1797; Kleuker, *Johannes, Petrus, und Paulus als Christologen*, Riga, 1785; K. M. L. Köster, *Der Apostel Johannes nach der Entstehung, Fortbildung, und Vollendung seines christlichen Lebens dargestellt*, Leipzig, 1838; Da Costa, *De Apost. Joh. en zijne Schriften*, 1831; Herwerden, *Het Evang. van Joh.*, 1851; also the article, "John the Apostle," by Dr. Ebrard, in Herzog's *Encyclopædia*, and the same article in Zeller's *Biblisches Wörterbuch für das christliche Volk*, Stuttgart, 1856.

On the Johannean type of doctrine, we have: Schmidt, *De theologia Joannis Apostoli*, ii. progr., Jena, 1801; Frommann, *Der Johanneische Lehrbegriff*, Leipzig, 1839; K. R. Köstlin, *Der Lehrbegriff des Evangeliums und der Briefe Johannis*, Berlin, 1843; Hilgenfeld, *Das Evangelium und die Briefe des Johannes*, Halle, 1849, in the spirit of the ultra criticism; Neander,

* [Comp. *Catena Aurea:* Commentary on the Four Gospels, collected out of the works of the Fathers, by S. Thomas Aquinas, fourth vol. St. John. Oxford, 1845.—P. S.]

Schaff, and Lange, in the doctrinal sections of their Histories of the Apostolic Age. [C. F. Schmid, *Bibl. Theol. des N. T.*, 2d ed., Stuttgart, 1859, pp. 588–617 (abridged translation by G. H. Venables, Edinburgh, 1870, pp. 519–552); E. Reuss, *Histoire de la théol. chrétienne*, Strasburg, 1860, ii., 369–600; Weiss, *Der johann. Lehrbegriff*, Berlin, 1862; Beyschlag, *Die Christologie des N. T.*, Berlin, 1866, pp. 65–107; van Oosterzee, *Theology of the New Test.*, transl. by M. J. Evans, London, 1870, pp. 372–415.—P. S.]

The apologetic literature on John has already been mentioned, pp. 28 f.

Poetical Literature: A. E. Fröhlich, the celebrated Swiss poet, *Das Evangelium St. Johannis, in Liedern*, Leipzig, 1835; A. Köttgen, *Lazarus*, a religious drama, in A. Köttgen's *Gedichte*, edited by me, Essen, 1839. [The poetical paraphrase of Nonnus, in Migne's *Patrol.*, Tom. xliii.; Adam of St. Victor, Poem on the Four Evangelists (*Jucundare, plebs fidelis*), and *De Joanne Evangelista*, in which the famous description occurs: *Volat avis sine meta*, &c. (in Daniel's *Thes. hymnol.*, Tom. ii., 166; in Mone's *Lat. Hymnen des Mittelalters*, iii., 118, and in Trench, *Sacred Latin Poetry*, p. 71). Bishop Ken has a long poem on St. John in his *Christian Year*, new ed., London, 1868, pp. 28 ff.—P. S.]

[English Literature on the Gospel of John.—The commentaries which cover the whole Bible, or the New Testament, have been mentioned in the American edition of *Matthew*, pp. 18, 19, and more fully in that of *Romans*, pp. 51, 52. Alford (*Greek Test.*, vol. i., ed. 6, 1868) is brief, critical, sound, and judicious; Wordsworth (5th ed., 1866) is reverent, patristic, fanciful, unequal, and avoiding rather than solving difficulties. Canon B. F. Westcott (who, in his *Introduction to the Study of the Gospels*, ch. v., very ably discusses the characteristics of the fourth Gospel) is preparing a work on John for the forthcoming "Speaker's Commentary." Besides, we have translations of Lücke, Olshausen, Tholuck, Stier, and Hengstenberg. A translation of Meyer is announced.—The special English literature on John is mostly of a popular and practical character. Hutcheson, *Exposition of John*, London, 1657 (highly spoken of by John J. Owen in his *Comm. on John*, p. iii.); Archbishop Sumner, *A Practical Exposition of the Gospel of St. John*, London, 1835; 3d ed., 1838; R. Anderson, do., London, 1841, 2 vols.; James Ford, *The Gospel of St. John Illustrated from Ancient and Modern Authors*, London, 1852; John Cumming, *Sabbath Evening Readings on St. John*, London, 1855; F. D. Maurice, *Discourses on the Gospel of St. John*, Cambridge, 1857; J. C. Ryle, *Practical Exposition of the Gospel of John*, London, 3 vols., 1868 ff.—America has produced several useful popular commentaries on the Gospels, including that on John, by Barnes, Jacobus, Ripley, Owen (new edition, 1866), Whedon, and others.—Of Albert Barnes' *Notes* on the Gospels, which are especially adapted for Sunday-schools, and have an immense circulation both in Great Britain and the United States, a revised edition appeared shortly before his death (1870).—Comp. the Literature supplied by Mr. Ezra Abbot to the article *John, Gospel of*, in Hackett's and Abbot's edition of Smith's *Dictionary of the Bible*, vol. ii. (1869), pp. 1437–'39. For special dissertations and sermons on single chapters and verses of John, see James Darling's *Cyclopædia Bibliographica*, i., pp. 1058–1166.—P. S.]

THE

GOSPEL ACCORDING TO JOHN.*

I.

THE PROLOGUE OF THE GOSPEL. THE ETERNAL PRE-EXISTENCE OF CHRIST. HIS UNIVERSAL RELATION TO THE WORLD AND MANKIND, AND HIS THEOCRATIC ADVENT IN ISRAEL; OR, THE (OLD TESTAMENT AND NEW TESTAMENT) INCARNATION OF THE LOGOS.

Chap. I. 1–18.

INTRODUCTORY THEOLOGICAL AND HOMILETIC OBSERVATIONS.

The Evangelists Matthew and Luke give us the history of the childhood of Jesus, and indicate His divine descent with few words in the miraculous story of His birth. But their eye in this is mainly upon the human or, in the narrower sense, historical antecedents of Jesus, his pedigree: Matthew, from a predominantly theocratic point of view, tracing the line to Abraham; Luke, from the more general human point of view, tracing it to Adam.†

As an offset to this exhibition of the human genealogy of Christ, John signalizes his eternal origin, as well as his eternal advent, in the eternal præ-existence of the divine, personal Logos. In the two relations together [the human and the divine], we see how the word of Micah concerning the Ruler out of Bethlehem, whose goings forth have been from of old, from everlasting, is fulfilled (Mi. v. 2).

John, therefore, has this in common with Mark, that he introduces Christ according to His human nature, in His historical maturity and preparation, after John the Baptist, His forerunner. With Matthew he shares the theocratic point of view (vers. 11, 12); with Luke, the universal (vers. 9, 10); but he rises above all in pointing out a Christological theocracy and universality of the incarnate Logos, which in its one manifestation embraces time and eternity, heaven and earth, and unites Deity and humanity.

The Johannean doctrine of the Logos has ever been regarded in the Christian church as one of the most mysterious and important points of doctrine. It ruled incipient theology in the doctrine of the Logos of God down to the beginning of the third century, down to Tertullian, and then exerted also the most decisive influence on the more definite doctrine of the Son of God. The mediæval theology knew better how to gaze at this great page of the Gospel, than to appreciate it, yet the mediæval mysticism was moved by the Johannean spirit (see Tholuck, p. 69). John Wessel, the greatest theologian of all the forerunners of the Reformation, restored the deeper apprehension of the Logos doctrine, and when our Reformers aimed at a more practical apprehension of Christology, this doctrine became thenceforth pre-eminently a treasure of the evangelical church, which the evangelical mystics in particular were at pains to unlock. The eighteenth century with its humanistic, critical tendency, lost the spirit of insight into the depths of the Johannean theology; yet at a time when the rationalists were disdaining it, speculative philosophers, like Schelling and Hegel, and great poets like Göthe, could not but recall its import, though without a clear apprehension.

The later evangelical theology has applied itself with appreciative spirit to the Johannean theology, and therefore to the prologue of this Gospel. Testimony of this we have in the sermons of Schleiermacher on the Gospel of John, and Lücke's Commentary on it, in which the treatise

* [Codd. Sin. and Vatic., the two oldest, have simply: κατὰ Ἰωάννην (B.—ανην). So Tischend. in the 8th ed. Later MSS. read εὐαγγ. κατὰ Ἰωάνν. (so Griesb., Lachm.), or τὸ κατὰ Ἰ. εὐαγγέλιον, or ἅγιον εὐαγγέλιον, *etc.*—P. S.]

† [Comp. Chrysostom: "The other evangelists begin with Christ's incarnation in time; St. John with his eternal generation." Augustine (*Tractatus* xxxvi. *in Johannis Evang.* c. 8, §1.): "The other three Evangelists walked as it were on earth with our Lord as Man (*tamquam cum homine Domino in terra ambulabant*) and said but little of his divinity. But John, as if he found it oppressive to walk on earth, opened his treatise so to speak with a peal of thunder. . . To the sublimity of this beginning all the rest corresponds, and he speaks of our Lord's divinity as no other." Godet, *Commentaire*, I p. 143: "*Chaque évangelist entre en matière de la manière la mieux appropriée à l'esprit de sa narration. Matthieu veut démontrer le droit de Jésus au trône théocratique: il commence par une généalogie. Marc rédige ses souvenirs: il se jette sans exorde in medium rem*, (*in medias res, or medias in res*, is the proper phrase). *Luc prétend écrire une histoire proprement dite: il rend compte dans son préambule de ses sources et de sa méthode.*"—P. S.]

on the prologue extends from p. 249 to p. 378, (vol. I). By the side of the modern depreciation of the Gospel of John on the part of some critics goes a mistaken realistic doctrine of the Logos in its great import in Hofmann (*Weissagung und Erfüllung*, p. 7), and Luthardt (pp. 280 sqq.) Exegesis can hardly make this Gospel more real, when it covers the depth by an abstractly realistic interpretation. What is said of the fourth evangelist, is true also of his doctrine of the Logos: It does not die.

The distinction between the divine *essence in itself*, and *its manifestation in its word*, is an attribute of the personality of God, and therefore this distinction continually comes out in the Holy Scriptures, which is the word of the personal God (Gen. i. 1; ver. 26, *etc.*).

This distinction appears still more clearly defined, after the primal revelation, obscured by sin, comes again into historical operation as a revelation of redemption. From this time, however, it unfolds itself in a two-fold form: there being, first, in the theocratic theology of the Old Testament, the distinction of Jehovah and the Angel of the Lord; then, in the universal theology of the Old Testament, the distinction of Jehovah and His wisdom as the principle of the creation and of Providence, and of the divine administration in Israel.

The manifestation of Jehovah in His Angel, (מַלְאַךְ יְהוָֹה) develops itself through three stages: the Angel being designated first as the Angel of the Lord (Gen. xvi. 7-9sqq.); then as the Presence, or the Angel of the Presence (Ex. xxxii. 34; comp. xxxiii. 14; Isa. lxiii. 9); finally as the Angel of the Covenant (Mal. iii. 1).

That this Angel is the theophanic præ-exhibition of the God-Man himself, is evident especially from the point of issue of this idea, where the Angel, as the Angel of the Covenant, plainly denotes the Messiah (Mal. *l. c.*); and the recent objections of Hofmann, Kurtz, and others, who make this person a created angel, are not sufficient to invalidate the church interpretation, and if they were, they would dissolve the central, inmost bond between the Old Testament and the New.

As the personal præ-manifestation of Christ in the theophanies of the Logos, the Angel of the Lord is also characterized by his standing in the closest connection with the honor or glory of God (Lu. ii. 9); in fact, being identified with it (Ex. xvi. 10; xxiv. 16). With this it is well worthy of notice, that where in the Old Testament Jehovah, or even the Angel of Jehovah, Maleach-Jehovah, is spoken of, He is called instead by the Jewish Targumists מֵימְרָא or even the Shekinah of Jehovah, *i. e.*, the manifestation of God letting itself down into his dwelling (see Tholuck, p. 62).

Now while in the Angel of the Lord we find predominantly the central direction of God, in His revelation, towards Israel and the incarnation expressed as *the personal putting forth of the Word*, we find in the notion of the *Wisdom distinct* from God, as the formative power of the divine word, chiefly the universal tendency of His revelation, or the connection of His historical revelation with its basis, His eternal, world-embracing, universal revelation. In this peculiar significance the divine Wisdom appears first in Job (ch. xxviii.; comp. Schlottmann, *Hiob*, p. 129). According to Proverbs, ch. viii., it is the mediator of the creation, and the personification of it comes nearest to a hypostasis in chap. ix. where it appears as the founder of the theocracy. Also in the apocryphal Book of Wisdom, it first, according to its universal field of revelation, forms the spirit of all life, and then, in a special attitude, as the spirit of the devout in Israel, comes into contrast with the folly of the heathen idolatry. It has here, under the influence of Alexandrian views, an idealistic form; in Sirach, on the contrary, from the universal sphere of the creation which belongs to it, it goes, in a restless search, over to the people of Israel, and fixes on Zion a permanent place, and its concentration is the Book of the Covenant, the Thorah (ch. xxiv. 25). Thus its last embodiment is the Book according to Baruch (iii. 37; iv. 1). The normal development of the notion proceeds between these extremes of an idealistic and a legal theory of revelation. The sound apprehension of the distinction we find again only on the threshold of the New Testament in the religious contemplations of Zachariah and of Mary (Lu. i.) and of John the Baptist. With these the N. T. revelations are most immediately connected.

We get, however, but a one-sided view of the development of the Old Testament idea of revelation, unless we bear in mind also its Messianic complement on the human side, *i. e.*, the development of the idea of the Messiah in the stricter sense. This likewise passes through three stages.

(1) The chosen family; (a) mankind, the seed of the woman, Gen. iii.; (b) the race, Semitic, Gen. ix.; (c) the people, Israel, and particularly the tribe of Judah, Gen. xii. 49.

(2) The chosen line: David and his son, collectively considered; the *typical* Messiah.

(3) The chosen individual, the *ideal* Messiah, Isa. ix. sqq.

Now, as the idea of the revelation of God works towards incarnation, so the idea of the Messiah strives towards union with the divine nature; and at the passage where the ideal Messiah comes to view, the union is effected; the Messiah is become the Angel of the Lord (Isa. lxi. 1 and 2), the Angel of the Lord is become the Messiah (Dan. vii. 13; Mal. iii. 1).

With this synthesis is given also the notion of the Son of God. This has likewise three stages in its development:

(1) The chosen family, Ex. iv. 22 sqq.

(2) The chosen royal line, 2 Sam. vii. 14.

(3) The chosen individual, the ideal Messiah, Ps. ii.; Isa. ix.

But since the development of revelation is based on the development of redemption and the idea of the former unfolds itself with the idea of the latter, so the Messiah, as personal revelation, is also personal Redeemer. As such he has (1) to fight and conquer; (2) to work and struggle; (3) to suffer, and in sinking to overcome. From this point of view the Son of God is the servant of God, Isa. liii.

The Solomonic and Apocryphal doctrine of the Wisdom became in Alexandria, in its contact with Platonism, the doctrine of the Logos, as Philo shaped it.

The Logos of Philo, however, is essentially different from that of John, though it agrees with that of John in its being the Mediator between God and the world. It is subordinate to Deity, it stands over the world merely as world-former, demiurge; it shades off pantheistically from the personal character to impersonality; it cannot become flesh; it is different from the Messiah, and the Messiah is only a divine appearance, which leads the devout Jews back to Palestine (see Dorner, *Entwicklungsgeschichte der Christologie*, Introduction, p. 49).

However doubtful it may be, that John was acquainted with the writings of Philo, the ideas of Philo were widely diffused in the second half of the first century among the Hellenistic Jews (for they were not a separate philosophy of Philo, but the religious philosophy of Hellenistic Judaism in general), as the angel-worshippers of Colosse prove; so with the system of Cerinthus; and undoubtedly the Evangelist came into intercourse and conflict with them. Nor must the position of the Evangelist towards the Alexandrian idea have been altogether hostile; for the current Logos-doctrine was not pure error; it was affiliative and abrasive, reformatory and evangelizing, to this fundamental idea of the Hellenistic Jews. And the Evangelist could be the more free to use the term *Logos* in its full emphasis, since he found it already recommended by the Old Testament, and still more distinctly by the Jewish theology. It was no doubt an ambiguity in Philo's mode of expression, that he transferred the Solomonic and Apocryphal notion of the *σοφία* into the notion of the Logos, in which the Word of God in the Old Testament, the מֵימְרָא of the Jewish theology, seemed to coincide with the *νοῦς* of Plato, which might easily be confounded with *λόγος*.

The Logos of John is related to that of Philo, as Paul's sermon at Athens to the inscription of the unknown God. John declared the true Logos, who is distinguished from that mixed figment of Old Testament theology and Greek speculation, in that He is equal with God, as the full expression of His being; is the absolute ground of the world, even of its matter; embosoms the universe as its active force, not as an emanating fountain of new emanations from God; is as much life, as light, in the highest sense, and therefore could come in the flesh, as Messiah, to accomplish the absolute redemption.

The Logos-doctrine, even in terms, runs throughout the writings of John (see 1 John i. 1; Rev. xix. 13); but in substance it pervades the New Testament, especially Paul (see Col. i. 15–19; Heb. i. 3; Matt. xi. 19; Luke xi. 49).

On the doctrine of the Logos and on John's Prologue comp. Lücke, I., p. 365 sqq. [translated by Dr. Noyes in the *Christian Examiner* for March and May, 1849.—P. S.]; Tholuck, I., p. 61; Meyer, p. 75 [pp. 58–67 in the 5th ed. of 1869.—P. S.]; Adalbert Maier, p. 115; Hölemann, *De Evangelii Joannei introitu, introitus Geneseos augustiore effigie*, Lips., 1855; Jordan Bucher, *Des Apostels Johannes Lehre vom Logos*, Schaffhausen, 1856.

[M. Stuart, *Examination of John*, i. 1–18, in the Andover *Bibliotheca Sacra* for 1850, pp. 281–327. Hengstenberg, *Com. on John*, 1866, vol. I., pp. 6 ff. (where the Old Test. roots of the Logos-doctrine are brought out in opposition to its derivation from Philo). F. Godet, *Considérationes générales sur le prologue*, in his *Com. on John*, 1864, vol. I., pp. 220–265. T. A. Philippi, *Der Eingang des Johannesevangeliums ausgelegt*, Stuttgart, 1867. Röhricht, *Zur Johanneischen Logoslehre*, in the Theol. *Studien und Kritiken* for 1868, pp. 299–315. H. P. Liddon, *Bampton Lectures on the Divinity of Christ*, London, 1867, Lecture Vth, pp. 310–411. Among English commentators, Alford, on John i. 1, gives a condensed summary of the investigations of Lücke, De Wette, Olshausen and Dorner on the Logos-doctrine.—P. S.]

[ADDITIONAL REMARKS ON THE PROLOGUE, vers. 1–18. The Prologue is a condensed statement of the results of John's contemplation and experience as a faithful witness of the life and work of Christ on earth, and furnishes the key that unlocks the true meaning of the following narrative. It contains the theme and leading ideas of the Gospel, the eternal substratum, as it were, of the temporal history of Jesus, and creates the impression that in approaching the gospel history the reader treads on holy ground; Jesus of Nazareth being none other than the eternal Son of God, in whom we must believe in order to have eternal life (comp. ch. xx. 31). The theme is the eternal Logos or personal Word that was with God and of divine essence from the beginning of beginnings, and at last became incarnate for the salvation of the world. The leading ideas are life and light, grace and truth, as emanating from and centering in the Logos. Starting with the divine genealogy or eternal divinity of Christ, the Evangelist presents, in a few bold outlines, the progress of revelation from the creation to the incarnation, a sort of miniature photograph of the history of preparation for Christ's coming in the flesh, and states the impression which His workings and personal appearance made upon the unbelieving world and the believing disciples. John the Baptist is mentioned as the representative of the Old Test. revelation, which directly prepared the way for the Christian dispensation.

We have here brought together the characteristic features of the fourth Gospel—its simplicity, sublimity, depth and ideality. We hear the sounds of thunder uttered by the "son of thunder." Every sentence, every word, is pregnant with meaning, and furnishes inexhaustible material for meditation and reflection. In the whole range of literature, ancient and modern, there is no passage or chapter that can at all compare with this Prologue. It is not poetic in form—yet, like the account of the creation in Genesis, to which it forms the New Testament pendant, it rises, by its calm dignity, simplicity and grandeur, to more than poetic beauty. The theme so far transcends the boundaries of time and sense, that the ordinary arts of rhetoric and poetry are struck with the silence of adoration and awe. "In pregnant fullness and purest simplicity," says the great scholar, Ewald (*Comm. on John*, p. 111), "the Prologue is unique," even in this unique Gospel.—The Prologue has ever exerted a mysterious and irresistible charm upon the profoundest thinkers, from Origen and Augustine down to Fichte, Schleiermacher and Schelling.*

As to the *division* of the Prologue, Dr. Lange, with Olshausen and Godet, divides it into three sections: (1) the præ-mundane or eternal being of the Logos, and His relation to God and the world, vers. 1–5; (2) His activity from the creation to the incarnation, especially in the Old Dispensation, vers. 6–13 (Godet, vers. 6-11). (3) His incarnation and activity in the Christian Church, vers. 14-18. Ewald (p. 113) adopts a similar view, but closes the first division with ver. 3. According to Meyer (in his fifth edition, p. 98), the Prologue represents the Logos—(1) as præ-existent in His *creative* activity (1-3); (2) as the Fountain of *light* to men (4-13); (3) in His *divine-human manifestation* (14-18); the last section returns to the first in identifying the λόγος ἐνσαρκος with the λόγος ἀσαρκος ("who is in the bosom of the Father"). Lücke, Alford and others make but two divisions: the eternal existence of the Logos, vers. 1-5, and His historic manifestation and working, vers. 6-18. Luthardt and Hengstenberg substitute for chronological sections three concentric cycles (1-5; 6-13; 14-18), of which each reproduces the same idea of the activity of the Logos, but under new aspects—the first in relation to God and the world at large, the second with special reference to John the Baptist and Jewish unbelief, the third with reference to the blessings which result to true believers.—There is evidently a progress of ideas from eternity to time, from the creation to the Old Testament dispensation, and to the incarnation, but more in the form of comprehensive intuition, which is peculiar to John, than of strict logical order, which was more congenial to the mind and training of Paul. For particulars, see below.—P. S.]

* [Even heathen philosophers and heretical Gnostics were captivated by the speculative depth of the Prologue. (Comp. Lampe, *Com.* Tom. I., 231 sq., 239 sqq.) Göthe, too, connects the deepest mental struggles of Faust with an attempt to fathom the depth of the first sentence of John:

"*Geschrieben steht: im Anfang war das* WORT!
Hier stock ich schon! Wer hilft mir weiter fort?
Ich kann das Wort so hoch unmöglich schätzen,
Ich muss es anders übersetzen,
Wenn ich vom Geiste recht erleuchtet bin:
Geschrieben steht: im Anfang war der SINN!
Bedenke wohl die erste Zeile,
Dass deine Feder sich nicht übereile!
Ist es der Sinn, der alles wirkt und schafft?
Es sollte stehn: im Anfang war die KRAFT!
Doch, auch indem ich dieses niederschreibe,
Schon warnt mich was, dass ich dabei nicht bleibe.
Mir hilft der Geist! Auf einmal seh ich Rath
Und schreib getrost: im Anfang war die THAT!"—P. S.]

FIRST SECTION.

Christ in His Eternal Essence and Existence, and His Position between God and the World.

CHAP. I. 1–5.

(1) THE WORD (CHRIST) IN HIS ETERNAL ESSENCE AND EXISTENCE IN RELATION TO GOD, VERS. 1 AND 2; (2) IN HIS RELATION TO THE CREATION, VER. 3; (3) IN HIS RELATION TO THE WORLD AND TO MAN, PARTICULARLY IN THEIR ORIGINAL CONSTITUTION, VER. 4; (4) IN HIS RELATION TO THE WORLD IN DARKNESS, VER. 5.

1 In the beginning was [in existence] the [personal, substantial] Word[1] [the Logos],
and the Word [the Logos] was with God [the Deity, the Godhead], and the Word
2 [the Logos] was God [Himself]. The same was [existed] in the beginning with God.
3 All things were made by [through] him; and without [except through] him was
4 not anything made [ἐγένετο],[2] that was [hath been] made [γέγονεν]. In him was
5 [is][3] life [pure life]; and the life was the light of men. And the light shineth in
[the] darkness; and the darkness comprehended [apprehended; LANGE: suppressed[4]]
it[5] not.[6]

TEXTUAL AND GRAMMATICAL.

[1] Ver. 1. [There is no doubt that *Word* (Vulg: *Verbum*; Luth.: *Wort*) is the only proper translation here of Λόγος (from λέγω), for John never uses it in another sense, and here he plainly alludes to the account of Genesis that God in the beginning made the world through His word. But in the Prologue and in two other passages (1 John i. 1, ὁ Λόγος τῆς ζωῆς, and Apoc. xix. 13, ὁ Λόγος τοῦ θεοῦ,—the passage 1 John v. 7 is spurious) he employs it in an altogether peculiar, *personal* sense to designate the præ-existent Christ, as is evident from ver. 14. The Greek favored this application, λόγος being masculine; and Ewald, boldly breaking through all usage, retains the masculine article in his German translation: *der* (instead of *das*) *Wort*. In classic Greek λόγος has the double signification: *word* and *reason*, *oratio* and *ratio*; the former being the primary meaning according to the etymology. Both are closely related; word or speech is the λόγος προφορικός, the outward reason or thought expressed; reason or thought is the λόγος ἐνδιάθετος, the inward speech. We cannot speak without the faculty of reason, nor think without words in our mind, whether uttered or not. Hence the Hebrew phrase: *to speak in his heart*=*to think*. When λόγος signifies *word*, it refers not to the formal part, the mere name or sound of a thing (like ῥῆμα, ἔπος, ὄνομα, *vox*, *vocabulum*), but to the material part, the thing itself, the thought as uttered, sometimes a whole discourse, *sermo*, or *treatise* (as in Acts i. 1). When it signifies *reason*, it may denote the subjective faculty, human or divine, which

produces speech (so in Heraklitus), and hence the derivative terms, λογίζεσθαι, λογισμός, λογικός, which are applied to rational functions; but more frequently, and in the Bible almost exclusively, it refers to an objective reason to be given of, or for, any thing. Comp. such phrases as πρὸς λόγον, κατὰ λόγον, *agreeable to reason, reasonable* (in Plato, also Acts xviii. 14—this comes nearest to the sense of reason as a faculty); παρὰ λόγον, *contrary to reason, improbable;* λόγον τινος ἔχειν, or ποιεῖσθαι, *rationem habere alicujus, to make account of*, and λόγον διδόναι (ἀπέχειν, παρέχειν) τινός, *to give a reason, an account of a thing* (comp. Acts xix. 40; 1 Pet. iii. 15); also λόγον αἰτεῖν περί τινος, λαμβάνειν ὑπέρ τινος, *to ask, to receive an account of a thing.* For the faculty of reason the N. T. always employs other terms, as πνεῦμα, νοῦς, καρδία, σοφία. Hence we must object, with Zezschwitz (*Profangräcität und Biblischer Sprachgeist*, 1859, p. 33), to the trias, νοῦς, λόγος, πνεῦμα, as set up by Delitzsch in his *Biblische Psychologie*, retained in the second ed., 1861, p. 176. For the theological meaning of Logos as here used, *see* the EXEG. NOTES.—P. S.]

[2] Ver. 3. Lachm. construes: οὐδὲ ἕν, ὁ γέγονεν, *etc.*, according to Codd. C.* D. L. *etc.* [Sin. D. *al.* read οὐδὲν ὅ γέγ.; but οὐδὲ ἕν (*ne unum quidem*, not even the ὕλη), is more emphatic.—P. S.]

[3] Ver. 4. D. *et al.* (Lachm.) read ζωή ἐστιν. An exegetical hypothesis, see John v. 11. [Sin. D. and Codd. ap. Orig. sustain ἐστίν, and are followed by Tischend. in his 8th ed., but ἦν is supported by A. B. C. E. F. L. O. *al.* Some MSS. and Versions connect the first sentence of ver. 4 with the last words of ver. 3, and punctuate ὁ γέγονε ἐν αὐτῷ (a phrase never used by John for *to be made by*), ζωὴ ἦν (the Valentinian Gnostics and Hilgenfeld); others put a comma after γέγονε (Clem. Alex., Orig., Lachm.),—a forced and untenable construction. See EXEG. NOTES.—P. S.]

[4] Ver. 5. [On the different translations and interpretations of καταλαμβάνειν see EXEG. NOTES.—P. S.]

[5] Ver. 5. Some authorities read αὐτόν [sc. λόγον, for αὐτό, sc. τὸ φῶς. See Tischend. ed. VIII.—P. S.].

[6] [The symmetrical, almost poetic, or rather superpoetic, beauty of the Prologue will appear more fully from the following arrangement of its simple, short, abrupt and pregnant sentences:

THE LOGOS AND GOD.

1. Ἐν ἀρχῇ ἦν ὁ Λόγος,
καὶ ὁ Λόγος ἦν πρὸς τὸν Θεόν,
καὶ Θεὸς ἦν ὁ Λόγος.
2. Οὗτος ἦν ἐν ἀρχῇ πρὸς τὸν Θεόν.

THE LOGOS AND THE WORLD.

3. Πάντα δι' αὐτοῦ ἐγένετο,
καὶ χωρὶς αὐτοῦ ἐγένετο οὐδὲ ἕν
ὁ γέγονεν.

THE LOGOS AND MANKIND.

4. Ἐν αὐτῷ ζωὴ ἦν,
καὶ ἡ ζωὴ ἦν τὸ φῶς τῶν ἀνθρώπων.

THE LOGOS AND SIN.

5. Καὶ τὸ φῶς ἐν τῇ σκοτίᾳ φαίνει,
καὶ ἡ σκοτία αὐτὸ οὐ κατέλαβεν.—P. S.]

EXEGETICAL AND CRITICAL.

[Vers. 1 and 2 contain the ante-mundane or præ-temporal history of the Logos, the mystery of the eternal, *immanent* relation of the Father and the Son before any revelation *ad extra*. This was a blessed relation of infinite knowledge and infinite love. It supplies the only answer we can give to the idle question, what God was doing before the creation of the world. Ver. 1 sets forth, in three brief sentences, three grand truths or divine oracles: the eternity of the Logos (*in the beginning was*), the personality of the Logos (*with God*), and the divinity of the Logos (*was God*); ver. 2 sums up these three ideas in one. The subject here touched lies far beyond human experience and comprehension; hence the extreme brevity with which the fact is simply stated in its quiet majesty. Yet these two lines give us more light than the thousands of words wasted by Philo, and the ancient and modern Gnostics and philosophers, on the transcendent mysteries of præ-mundane existence. Bengel calls the first verse "a peal of thunder from the Son of Thunder, a voice from heaven." Augustine (*Tract.* 36*th in Joh. Evang.* §. 1) beautifully says: "John, as if he found it oppressive to walk on earth, opened his treatise, so to speak, with a peal of thunder; he raised himself not merely above the earth and the whole compass of the air and heaven, but even above every host of angels and every order of invisible powers, and reached to Him by whom all things were made, saying: 'In the beginning was the Word,' *etc.* To the sublimity of this beginning all the rest corresponds, and he speaks of our Lord's divinity as no other."—P. S.]

Ver. 1. **In (the) beginning.** Ἐν ἀρχῇ, בְּרֵאשִׁית, Gen. i. 1. Comp. the Introductory Observations, and Hölemann: *De evangelii Joan. introitu.* Different explanations:—1. Cyril of Alex.: the "beginning" is God the Father.*—2. The Valentinian Gnostics (according to Irenæus I. 8, 5): a distinct divine hypothesis between the Father and the Logos.—3. Origen: The divine Wisdom (σοφία).†—4. Theodore of Mopsuestia, and others: eternity.‡—5. The Socinians [and some

* [So also Marheineke (*Dogm.* p. 134). The Son is indeed called ἡ ἀρχή, Rev. iii. 14, but not the Father. Philo and the Gnostics called the Logos ἀρχή, but the Father προαρχή, or abyss (comp. Jacob Böhm's *Urgrund, Abgrund*). Besides, the corresponding term to Λόγος is θεός, while "Father" requires "Son."—P. S.]

† [Origen (*Com. in Joan.*, in Delarue's ed. Tom. IV. p. 19) makes τὸ εἶναι ἐν ἀρχῇ to be identical with τὸ εἶναι ἐν πατρί, which would lead to Cyril's interpretation; but soon afterwards, p. 20, he explains that Christ was called the beginning because He is the Wisdom, and refers to Prov. viii. 22, where Wisdom says: "God made me the beginning of His ways—ἀρχὴν ὁδῶν αὐτοῦ εἰς ἔργα αὐτοῦ,"—a passage which figured very prominently in the Arian controversy.—P. S.]

‡ [So also Chrysostom (*In Joannem Hom.* II., ed. Montfaucon, Tom. VIII. p. 13): τὸ γὰρ, ἐν ἀρχῇ ἦν, οὐδὲν ἕτερόν ἐστιν, ἀλλ' ἢ τὸ εἶναι ἀεὶ δηλωτικὸν, καὶ ἀπείρως εἶναι. Of modern commentators, Olshausen adopts this view: "Not in the beginning of creation, but in the primitive beginning, the *Uranfang*, *i. e.*, from eternity." This is a correct inference (see below), but not directly expressed. We can only speak of a beginning of finite or created existence—the existence of God has neither beginning nor end. Liddon (*The Divinity of Christ*, 4th ed., 1869, p. 228) somewhat modifies this interpretation after Meyer, in referring בְּרֵאשִׁית, Gen. i. 1, to the initial moment of time itself, ἐν ἀρχῇ to the absolute conception of that which is anterior to, or rather independent of, time. Ewald: the first conceivable beginning.—P. S.]

modern Unitarians]: the beginning of the gospel (*in initio evangelii*). [In Acts xi. 15 the expression has this meaning, but here it is entirely inconsistent with ver. 3.—P. S.].—6. Meyer: [John parallelizes the beginning of his Gospel with that of Genesis, but] he raises the historical notion of *the beginning* which in Gen. i. 1 implies the beginning of time itself, to the absolute idea of *præ-temporalness* [or timelessness, *Vorzeitlichkeit*], as in Prov. viii. 23. [Here the Wisdom which is the same with the Logos, says: *πρὸ τοῦ αἰῶνος ἐθεμελίωσέν με, ἐν ἀρχῇ πρὸ τοῦ τὴν γῆν ποιῆσαι, κ. τ. λ.*, ('from everlasting, in the beginning, before the earth was made'); comp. John xvii. 5, *πρὸ τοῦ τὸν κόσμον εἶναι*; Eph. i. 4, *πρὸ καταβολῆς κόσμου*. Comp. also 1 John i. 1 and Apoc. iii. 14.—P. S.]. We find an advance of the notion of the beginning primarily only in *was* (*ἦν*), and in the relation subsequently stated of the Logos to the eternal God, which unquestionably still further elevates, indirectly, the idea of the *ἀρχή*. The *ἀρχή* itself must ever refer to the primal generation or rise of things.* But if in this *ἀρχή* the Logos already was (*ἦν*), then He was from eternity. [The same is said of God, Ps. xc. 2, who was before the mountains were brought forth, *etc.*, *i. e.* from everlasting]. The Logos was not merely existent, however, *in the beginning*, but was also the efficient principle, the *ἀρχή* of the *ἀρχή* (Col. i. 18). The *ἀρχή*, in itself and in its operation, dark, chaotic, was, in its idea and its principle, comprised in one single luminous word, which was the Logos. And when it is said, the Logos was in this *ἀρχή*, His eternal existence is already expressed, and His eternal position in the Godhead already indicated, thereby. The Evangelist says not: In the beginning *of the world*, because he would make *the beginning* perfectly absolute; but he pre-supposes the reference to the genesis of the world.†

Was.—Not *became* [*ἐγένετο*, comp. vers. 6 and 14] the Son of God, a *κτίσμα*, as Arianism taught. (Comp. Prov. viii. 23; Sirach xxiv. 3.) It cannot be said, He might have become, or been made, before the beginning; for becoming and beginning are inseparable.‡

[The words: *in the beginning was the Logos*, clearly *assert*, as the best commentators now admit, the *eternity* of the Logos, but they *imply* at the same time His *divinity*, which is afterwards formally stated in the third sentence: *was God.* Metaphysically we cannot separate eternity, *ab ante*, from divinity, or predicate eternity of any creature. Luther felt this when he said: "That which was before the world and before the creation of all creatures, must be God." On the basis of monotheism on which John stood, there is no room for a middle being between God and the creature. Before creation there was no time, for time itself is part of the world and was created with it. (*Mundus factus est cum tempore*, not *in tempore*). Before the world there was only God, and God is timeless or eternal. Hence the Arian proposition concerning Christ: There was a time (before creation) when He was not (*ἦν ποτε ὅτε οὐκ ἦν*), involves the metaphysical absurdity of putting time before the world, a créature before creation.—P. S.]

The Word.—[*ὁ Λόγος*, with reference to Gen. i. 3: God *said, etc.* The living, speaking Word from whom the creative, spoken words emanate.—P. S.] The Word absolute, the one whole, all-embracing, personal manifestation of life; hence without the qualification: the Logos of God. It certainly includes also the divine reason or consciousness; though in the Scriptural usage *λόγος* never denotes the reason itself, but only the matured expression of the reason, word, speech, as a whole, the personal spiritual essence of God made, in its whole fulness, objective to itself,* as its own perfect expression and image. And in this view the literal interpretation is entirely sufficient, but is supplied by the historical doctrine of the Logos (see above).

The exclusively verbal expositions, and the exclusively historical, are alike insufficient and incorrect: 1. the *verbal*, which explain *ὁ λόγος* as (*a*) *ὁ λεγόμενος*, the promised one (Valla, Beza, Ernesti, Tittmann, *etc.*); (*b*) *ὁ λέγων*, the speaking one (Mosheim, Storr, and others); (*c*) the gospel objectively considered, as the word of God: the subject of the gospel (*alloiosis!*), hence Christ, [so Hofmann, *Schriftbew.*, I., p. 109 ff.]; or, according to Luthardt: the word of God which in Christ (Heb. i. 1) was spoken to the world, and the content of which is Christ (see, on the contrary, Meyer, p. 45, [pp. 58 and 59 in the fifth ed. of 1869.—P. S.]); 2. the *historical*, which would make either the Palestinian doctrine of the Wisdom [*Σοφία*, חָכְמָה] with the Word of God [מֵימְרָא or דִּבּוּרָא] of the Targums, or the Alexandrian Philonic doctrine of the Logos, or both, the proper root of the scriptural idea. This root is to be found in the manifestation of the consciousness of Christ, as it reflected itself in the intuition of John himself; the his-

* [Hengstenberg quotes for this view Matth. xix. 4; John viii. 44, and other passages where *ἀρχή* likewise refers to the beginning of the world, or the creation. So also Brückner, Godet, *etc.*—P. S.]

† [Comp. Bengel *in loc.*: "*In eodem principio cœli et terræ et mundi* (ver. 10; Gen. i. 1) *jam erat Verbum sine ullo principio initiore suo. Ipsum Verbum est mere æternum: nam eodem modo Verbi ac Patris æternitas describitur.*" Alford: "These words, if they do not *assert*, at least *imply*, the eternal *præexistence* of the divine Word. For *ἐν ἀρχῇ ἦν* is not said of an *act done ἐν ἀρχῇ* (as in Gen. i. 1), but of a *state existing ἐν ἀρχῇ*, and therefore without beginning itself." Brückner (in the fifth ed. of De Wette): "If the Logos *was* in the beginning of things, it follows that He had a being before all being." Ewald: "The words, 'In the beginning,' *etc.*, mean first of all that the Logos actually existed before the world or that there never could be conceived a time in which He was not already." So also Godet. —P. S.]

‡ [Bengel: "Erat *Verbum, antequam mundus fieret.*" Alford: "The existence of an enduring and unlimited state of being, implied in *ἦν* (the indefinite past), is contrasted with *ἐγένετο* in ver. 3, and especially in ver. 14."—Meyer: "John reports historically, looking back from the later time of the incarnate Logos (ver. 14)." This is more correct than Olshausen's exposition of *ἦν* as designating "the enduring, timeless existence of the eternal presence;" this would require *ἐστί*, as in John viii. 58, *πρὶν Ἀβραὰμ γενέσθαι ἐγὼ εἰμί*. (Chrysostom likewise takes *ἦν* here as denoting *τὸ ἀΐδιον*, because it is used of God.) But all these commentators agree that the *was* of the divine Logos is clearly distinct from the *became* or *began to be* of the creature, ver. 3, of the man John, ver. 6, and of the human nature of Christ, ver. 14. John suggests the idea of an (eternal) generation of the Logos from the substance of the Father (comp. the term *μονογενὴς υἱός*, ver. 18, and *πρωτότοκος*, Col. i. 15, which differs widely from *πρωτόκτιστος* or *πρωτόπλαστος*), but not of the Arian doctrine of a creation of the Logos out of nothing. The Son must be as eternal as the Father, being as indispensable to the Fatherhood of God, as the Father is to the Sonship of the Logos.—P. S.]

* ["*Das persönliche geistige Wesen Gottes in absoluter Selbstobjectivirung.*"]

torical rise of the idea is due to the theological conceptions of the Old Testament (see above); and the expression itself was suggested by the Philonic doctrine of the Logos. Only this further discrimination must be observed: that the Philonic doctrine lays stress not on the word, but the reason, while John emphasizes the absolute, personal, perfect Word, the image of God, as the original of the world, the idea and life of the whole ἀρχή of things.

[EXCURSUS ON THE MEANING AND ORIGIN OF THE TERM LOGOS, AND THE RELATION OF JOHN TO PHILO.—The Logos doctrine of John is the fruitful germ of all the speculations of the ancient Church on the divinity of Christ, which resulted in the Nicene dogma of the homoousion or the co-equality of the Son with the Father. The *præ-existent* Logos is the central idea of the Prologue, as the *incarnate* Logos or God-*Man* is the subject of the historical part of the Gospel. The Christ of idea and the Christ of history are one and the same. Logos signifies here not an abstraction nor a personification simply, but a person, the same as in ver. 14, namely, Christ before His incarnation, the divine nature of Christ, the eternal Son of God. God has never been ἄλογος, or without the Logos, the Son is as eternal as the Father. John is the only writer of the New Testament who employs the term in this personal sense, as a designation of Christ, *viz.*, four times in the Prologue (i. 1, 14, "the Word" simply and absolutely), once in his first epistle (i. 1, "the Word of life"), and once in the Apocalypse (xix. 13, "the Word of God"), but in the last passage the whole divine-*human* person of Christ in His *exalted* state is so called.* There is an inherent propriety in this application of the term, especially in the Greek language, where λόγος is masculine, and where it has the double meaning of reason and speech.† Christ as to His divine nature bears the same relation to the hidden being of God, as the word does to thought. In the word of man his thought assumes shape and form and becomes clear to the mind, and through the same the thought is conveyed and made intelligent to others. So the Logos is the utterance, the reflection and counterpart of God, the organ of all revelation both with regard to Himself and to the world, *ad intra* and *ad extra.* God knows Himself in the Son, and through Him He makes Himself known to men. The Son has declared or revealed and interpreted God (ἐξηγήσατο θεόν, ver. 18; comp. Matt. xi. 27).

The idea of such a distinction in God is in various ways clearly taught in the Old Test. Even in the first verses of Genesis we have already an intimation of the Word and the Spirit as distinct from, and yet identical with, God. Personal intercourse with Christ in the flesh and the inspiration of the Holy Ghost convinced John that Jesus was indeed the Word and the Wisdom of God, the Angel of the Covenant, Jehovah revealed (xii. 41), the centre and organ of all revelations (comp. the Introductory Remarks of Dr. Lange). The same idea, but in different form, we meet in Matt. xi. 27; Heb. i. 3; Col. i. 15-19, *etc.* The term λόγος was suggested to John by Gen. i. 3, according to which God created the world through the *word* of His power, and by such passages as Ps. xxxiii. 6: "By the *word* of the Lord were the heavens made," where the LXX uses the very term λόγος for the Hebrew דבר, instead of the usual ῥῆμα. This seems to be sufficient to account for the form of expression, and hence many commentators (Hölemann, Weiss, Hengstenberg) deny all connection of John with the speculations of Philo of Alexandria. There is indeed no evidence that he read a line of the writings of this Jewish philosopher, who flourished about A. D. 40-50.

Yet, on the other hand, Philo was a profound representative thinker mediating between the O. T. religion and the Hellenic philosophy, and it is more than probable that some of his ideas had penetrated the intellectual atmosphere of the age before the composition of the fourth Gospel, especially in Asia Minor, where they stimulated the Gnostic speculations towards the close of the first and the beginning of the second centuries. Comp. the warnings of Paul, Acts xx. 29 ff.; 1 Tim. iv., the errorists of Colosse, and the heretical gnosis of Cerinthus, who came into conflict with John in Ephesus, and who, according to Theodoret, studied first in Egypt. Apollos also, the learned Jew, came from Alexandria to Ephesus (Acts xviii. 24). It no more detracts from the apostolic dignity that John should have borrowed a word from, or at least chosen it with tacit reference to, Philo for expressing an original idea, than the general fact that the apostles appropriated the whole Greek language, which Providence had especially prepared to be the organ of the truths of the gospel. And inasmuch as John uses the term without any explanation, as if it were already familiar to his readers, the assumption of a connection with Philo, however indirect and remote, becomes more probable. Such a connection is asserted by Lücke, De Wette, Brückner, Meyer, Lange, Delitzsch,* Alford, and others.

Philo's doctrine of the Logos, in its relation to that of John, has been thoroughly ventilated by recent German scholars (see the literature in Lücke's and in Meyer's Com. p. 61). I shall briefly state the result in addition to the excellent remarks of Dr. Lange (p. 51). Philo, on the basis of the Solomonic and Apocryphal doctrine of the Wisdom and the Word of God, and combining with it Platonic ideas, represents the Logos (the Nous of Plato) as the embodiment of all divine powers and ideas (the ἄγγελοι of the O. T., the δυνάμεις and ἰδέαι of Plato). He distinguishes between the λόγος ἐνδιάθετος, or the Logos inherent in God corresponding to the reason in man, and the λόγος προφορικός, or the Logos emanating from God, like the spoken word of man which reveals the thought. The former contains the ideal world (the νοητὸς κόσμος); the latter is the first begotten Son of God, the image of God, the Creator and Preserver, the Giver of

* [1 John v. 7 is spurious. Luke i. 20; Acts xx. 32; Heb. iv. 12, are no proper parallels.—P. S.]

† [On the grammatical sense of λόγος see TEXTUAL NOTE 1.]

* [*Bibl. Psychologie*, secd. ed., p. 178: "*Dass die Johanneische Logoslehre nicht ausser Beziehung zur philonischen steht, ist ein unläugbares Factum. Die apostolische Verkündigung verschmähte die bereits vom Alexandrinismus ausgeprägten Ideenformen nicht, sondern erfüllte sie mit dem durch die neutestamentliche Erfüllungsgeschichte dargereichten Inhalt.*"—P. S.]

life and light, the Mediator between God and the world, the second God,* also the Messiah, yet only in the ideal sense of a theophany, not as a concrete historical person.†

But with all the striking similarity of expression, there is a wide and fundamental difference between Philo and John. 1) Philo's view is obscured by dualistic and docetic admixtures, from which John is entirely free. 2) He wavers between a personal and impersonal conception of the Logos (Keferstein, Zeller, Lange), or rather he resolves the Logos after all into an impersonal summary of divine attributes (so Dorner, Niedner, Hölemann, Brückner, Meyer); while in John He appears as a divine hypostasis, distinct from, and yet co-essential with, God. 3) Philo has no room in his system for an incarnation of the Logos, which is the central idea of the Gospel of John. His doctrine is like a shadow which preceded the substance. It was a prophetic dream of the coming reality. Lange compares it to the altar of the unknown God, whom St. Paul made known to the Athenians. It helped to prepare deeper minds for the reception of the truth, while it also misled others into Gnostic aberrations. "The grand simplicity and clearness of the Prologue" (says Meyer, p. 63, note) "shows with what truly apostolic certainty John *experienced* the influence of the speculations of his age, and yet remained *master* over them, modifying, correcting and making them available for his ideas."

These ideas of Christ formed the basis of his belief long before he knew anything of these foreign speculations.‡ But he seems to have chosen a form of expression already current in the higher regions of thought for the purpose of meeting a false gnosis of speculation with the true gnosis of faith. For the airy fancies about the Logos, as the centre of all theophanies, he substitutes at the threshold of his Gospel the substantial reality by setting forth Christ as the revealed God: thus satisfying the speculative wants of the mind and directing misguided speculation into the path of truth. A clear and strong statement of the truth is always the best refutation of error.—P. S.]

And the Word.—The clause: "In the beginning was the Word," contains the whole theme. Now follows first the relation of the Logos to the eternal God, then, more at large, His relation to the temporal world.

Was with God.—[*πρὸς τὸν θεόν*, rather than *παρὰ τῷ θεῷ*, xvii. 5.] Properly: with God, as distinct from and over against Him, in direction towards Him, for Him [in inseparable nearness and closest intercommunion, comp. ver. 18, "towards the bosom of the Father."—P. S.].* There is a similar phraseology in Mark vi. 3, and elsewhere. On the antithesis in the eternal constitution of God, see above, and Prov. viii. 30; Wisdom ix. 4. The doctrine of the Holy Ghost also is implied in this expression of the motion or posture of the Logos towards God, as well as in the further designation of the Logos: He was God. Starke: We must take good heed that we do not connect with the particle "with" the notion of place or space. The word denotes the most intimate and divine sort of relation to another.†

And the Word was [not the world, which did not yet exist, ver. 3, hence not man, nor angel, nor any creature, but] **God.**‡—*Θεός* is the predicate, *λόγος* the subject;§ and in the Greek the predicate stands first, for the sake of emphasis. [Comp. iv. 24: *πνεῦμα ὁ Θεός*.—P. S.] God [in the strict sense of the term], of divine nature and kind, was the Logos. Meyer shows how the omission of the article [before *θεός*] was necessary, to distinguish the persons or subjects, *ὁ θεός* and *ὁ λόγος*; and how, therefore, this expression is not to be taken in the sense of the *θεός* without the article [*a* God], the subordinate *δεύτερος θεός*, in Philo [p. 66].‖ Likewise the translation in the adjective form: [= *θεῖος*], divine (Baumgarten-Crusius), would alter the idea. Tholuck cites Chemnitz: *θεός sine artic. essentialiter, cum artic. personaliter.* He refers also to Liebner: *Christol.* I., p. 165; the Letters of Lücke and Nitzsch, in the *Studien u. Kritiken*, 1840 and '41; Thomasius: *Christi Person.* II., § 40.

[*Θεός* without the article signifies divine essence, or the generic idea of God in distinction

---

* [ὁ πρεσβύτερος υἱὸς τοῦ πατρός, ὁ πρωτόγονος αὐτοῦ, εἰκὼν θεοῦ, ἄγγελος πρεσβύτατος, ἀρχάγγελος, the λόγος τομεύς, δημιουργὸς δἰ οὗ ὁ κόσμος κατεσκευάσθη, ὁ ἀρχέτυπος καὶ παράδειγμα τοῦ φωτός, ἀρχιερεύς, ἱκέτης, δεύτερος θεός, and similar terms which show how nearly Philo, in speaking of the Logos, approached the teaching of St. John, although in fact he was nearer the later Gnostic speculations about the æons. He also says of the Logos that he was neither unbegotten (ἀγέννητος), like God, nor begotten (γέννητος), like ourselves.—P. S.]

† [Lücke, Alford and others go too far when they say that Philo did not connect the Logos with Messianic ideas.—P. S.]

‡ [Meyer likewise distinctly asserts the independence of the *matter* of John's Logos-doctrine, which rests on the O. T. and the teaching of Christ and the Holy Spirit. He arrives, by a purely exegetical process, substantially at the orthodox view, and thus sums up the result of his exposition of ver. 1 (p. 64): "*Mithin ist nach Joh. unter* ὁ λόγος . . *nichts anderes zu verstehen als die vorzeitlich* (*vrgl. Paulus, Col.* I. 15 *ff.*) *in Gott immanente, zur Vollziehung des Schöpfungsactes aber hypostatisch aus Gott hervorgegangene und seitdem als schöpferisches, belebendes und erleuchtendes persönliches Princip auch in der geistigen Welt wirkende wesentliche Selbstoffenbarung Gottes, diesem selbst an Wesen und Herrlichkeit gleich* (*vrgl. Paulus Phil.* II. 6), *welche göttliche Selbstoffenbarung in dem Menschen Jesus leiblich erschienen ist und das Werk der Welterlösung vollzogen hat.*"—P. S.]

* [This sentence excludes Sabellianism, while the following declaration: "The Word was God," excludes Arianism.—Bengel: "*Ergo distinctus a Deo Patre.* πρός *denotat perpetuam quasi tendentiam Filii ad Patrem in unitate essentiæ. Erat apud Deum unice quia nil extra Deum tum erat.*" Meyer: "πρός *bezeichnet das Befindlichsein des Logos bei Gott im Gesichtspunkte des Verkehrs.*" Brückner: "παρά *hebt mehr die Räumlichkeit,* πρός *mehr die Zugehörigkeit des Beisammenseins hervor.*" Alford: "Both the inner substantial union, and the distinct personality of the λόγος are here asserted." Liddon (l. c. p. 229): "He is not merely παρὰ Θεῷ (John xvii. 5), along with God, but πρὸς τὸν Θεόν. This last proposition expresses, beyond the fact of co-existence or immanence, the more significant fact of perpetuated intercommunion. The face of the everlasting Word was ever *directed towards* the everlasting Father." Owen: "*With* signifies a continual cleaving or adherence to the object towards which the relation of union is expressed, the closest union, together with distinct and independent personality." Godet: "πρός *exprime la proximité, la présence, le rapprochement mutuel, la relation active, la communion personelle.*" He translates it, "*en relation avec Dieu.*"—P. S.]

† ["*Ubi amor, ibi trinitas.*" God being love, He must be triune, a loving Father, a beloved Son, and the union and communion of both, which is the Holy Spirit, the Spirit of love and communion.—P. S.]

‡ [Meyer observes here (p. 65): "There is something *majestic* in the growth of the record of the Logos in these three brief, grand sentences."—P. S.]

§ [Luther reverses the order, following closely the Greek: *Gott war das Wort.* So also the old English translation authorized by Henry VIII.—P. S.]

‖ [Philo calls the Logos θεός only by misapplication, ἐν καταχρήσει, as he says; and he calls Him ὁ δεύτερος θεός in the sense of a middle being between God and man.—P. S.]

from man and angel; as σάρξ, ver. 14, signifies the human essence or nature of the Logos. The article before ϑεός would here destroy the distinction of personality and confound the Son with the Father. The preceding sentence asserts the distinct hypothesis of the Logos, this His essential oneness with God. To conceive of an independent being existing from eternity, outside or external to the one God, and of a different substance (ἑτεροούσιος), would overthrow the fundamental truth of monotheism and the absoluteness of God. There can be but one divine being or substance.—P. S.]

Ver. 2. **The same was.**—The first proposition characterizes the subject alone; the second declares the personal distinction of the Logos from God absolute; the third expresses the essential unity and identity of the divine nature. The clauses form a solemn climax: the Logos the eternal ground of the world; the Logos the image-like expression of God; the Logos God. The sentence now following combines those three propositions in one: This Logos, which was God, **was in the beginning with God.** [The emphasis lies on οὑτος, *this* Logos who was Himself God, and no other Logos; and with οὑτος is contrasted πάντα, ver. 3, the whole creation without any exception was brought forth by this Logos. So Meyer.—P. S.] This completes the statement of the position of Christ within the Godhead; then follows His relation to the world.

Ver. 3. **All things were made through** [δι'] **him.**—[From the immanent Word, the λόγος ἐνδιάϑετος, John now proceeds to the revealed Word, the λόγος προφορικός. The first manifestation of the Logos *ad extra* is the creation.—P. S.] Gen. i. Col. i. 17; Heb. i. 2; Philo, *de Cherub.* I. 162.* [The Son is the instrumental cause, the Father the efficient cause, of the creation; comp. 1 Cor. viii. 6 and the difference between ἐκ and διά. The Son never works of Himself, but always as the revealer of the Father and the executor of His will.—P. S.] As the Evangelist means, that absolutely all that exists, not only in its form and totality, but also in its material and detail, was called into life by the Logos, π ά ν τ α, *all*, without the article, is more suitable [being more general and unlimited] than τὰ πάντα [which would mean a specific and definite totality, as in 1 Cor. v. 18. The Socinian interpretation: 'the *ethical* creation,' or 'all Christian graces and virtues,' is grammatically impossible.—P. S.]†

And without him.—Not merely an "emphatic *parallelismus antitheticus*" [comp. v. 20; x. 28; 1 John ii. 4, 27], though it is this primarily (see Meyer), but also a further direct statement of the negation contained in the previous clause. For Meyer [followed by Godet] in vain calls in question John's intention to exclude by this negative sentence (as Lücke, De Wette, Olshausen and others have observed*) the Platonic and Philonic doctrine of the timeless matter (ὕλη). The argument that, since ἐγένετο and γέγονεν denote only a becoming which is subsequent to creation, therefore the ὕλη would not be included, seems itself to rest upon the unconscious notion of a præ-temporal ὕλη. The only question should be, whether ὃ γέγονεν could be said of the ὕλη; especially since the Evangelist does not distinctly enter upon the idea of the ὕλη in itself considered, and doubtless for very good reasons. A proposition so distinctly antithetic was undoubtedly expressed also with antithetic intent, and it would imply downright ignorance in the Evangelist to suppose him unacquainted with this antithesis so universally familiar to the ancient world. We should likewise remember, with Tholuck, that the sentence contains, on the other hand, the antignostic thought, that the orders of spirits also were made by the Logos. For Col. ii. 18 shows that the germ of the Gnostic doctrine of æons was already known. Yet the strong οὐδὲ ἕν [*not even one thing, prorsus nihil,* stronger than οὐδέν, *nothing*] proves that the antihylic aim decidedly prevails. [There is great comfort in the idea that there is absolutely nothing in the wide world which is unknown to God, which does not owe its very existence to Him, and which must not ultimately obey His infinitely wise and holy will. Comp. Ewald *in loc.*—P. S.]

That hath been made.—Perfect: ὁ γ έ γ ο ν ε ν. All created existence. The connection of this clause with the following: "That which was made, in Him it was life (had its life in Him)," has been advocated from Clement of Alexandria down, by eminent fathers like Origen and Augustine, and by some codices and versions. But, besides the mass of the codices, Chrysostom and Jerome are against this connection. It must be rejected for the following considerations: (1) that such connection would require ἐστί instead of ἦν after γέγονεν (Meyer); (2) that it would destroy the absolute idea of the ζωή which is expected here (see 1 John i. 1); (3) that it would cause the derived life in the creatures to be designated as the light of men; (4) that it would confuse the idea of the essential life itself here, and make the word equivocal.* Clement of Alexandria may have been led by his philosophy to separate somewhat the sentence: οὐδὲ ἕν, ὃ γέγονεν; then many followed him for the sake of the apparent profundity of his combination. On Hilgenfeld's introduction of the Gnostic ζωή here, see the note in Meyer [p. 63].

Ver. 4. **In him was life.**—[ζωή, the true life, the divine, immortal life (comp. iii. 15, 16; vi. 27, 33, 35, 40, 47; Matth. vii. 14; xix. 16; Rom. ii. 7; v. 10, 17, 18, 21, and a great many passages), as distinct from βίος, the natural, mortal life (comp. the Greek in 1 John ii. 16; iii. 17; Mark xii. 44; Lu. viii. 14, 43; xv. 12, 21;

---

* [Philo justly distinguishes the efficient from the instrumental cause of the creation, the former he signifies by ὑφ' οὗ, the latter by δι' οὗ: . . τὸν θεὸν, ὑφ' οὗ (ὁ κόσμος) γέγονεν ὕλην δὲ, τὰ τέσσαρα στοιχεῖα, ἐξ ὧν συνεκράθη· ὄργανον δέ, λόγον θεοῦ, δι' οὗ κατεσκευάσθη. The Bible excludes the Platonic and Philonic doctrine of the ὕλη which is dualistic. It teaches that the world was made by God the Father (in answer to the question ὑφ' οὗ), through the Son (δι' οὗ), out of nothing (ἐξ οὗ), for His glory (δι' ὅ).—P. S.]

† [Meyer: "John *might* have written τὰ πάντα (with the article) as 1 Cor. viii. 6; Col. i. 16; but he *must* not; comp. Col. i. 17; John iii. 35, for his idea is: 'All,' in the unlimited sense; τὰ πάντα would express the idea: the totality of things existing." Comp. Godet. Bengel observes on πάντα: "*Grande verbum, quo mundus, i. e. universitas rerum factarum denotatur, ver.* 10."—P. S.]

* [Also Alford: "This addition is not merely a Hebrew parallelism, but a distinct denial of the eternity and uncreatedness of matter as held by the Gnostics. They set *matter*, as a separate existence, over against God, and made it the origin of evil:—but John excludes any such notion."—P. S.]

† [Godet justly remarks that ζωὴ εἶναι is too strong an expression for creatures instead of ζωὴν ἔχειν.—P. S.]

2 Tim. ii. 4).—P. S.] The translation: "was life," is based on the absence of the article (De Wette, Meyer). But in Greek the omission of the article makes less difference than in German [and English]. To say [in English]: In Him was life, may mean: some measure of life. In the Greek it means, at least in this connection: the fullness of life, all life (Philo: πηγὴ ζωῆς).* Hence Luther's translation: *war das Leben:* was *the* life, is best. Meyer justly rejects the restriction of the idea to the spiritual life [ζωὴ αἰώνιος] (Origen [Maldonatus, Lampe, Hengstenberg] and others), or to the physical (Baumgarten-Crusius), or to the ethical (*felicitas*, Kuinoel).† Nor is the life here to be at all divided into physical, moral and eternal. It is the creative life, the ultimate principle of life, which manifests itself in the operations of life in every province. This, however, excludes the thought that God called things into existence by an act of abstract, pure will in the Logos. The Word was as much an animating breath as it was a logical, luminous and enlightening volition. The life refers chiefly to the creative power and the power of manifestation, to the substance and the principles of things, as the light to their laws and forms; though primarily life and light still form a unity. Gerlach: "From creation he passes to preservation and providence, and ascribes these also to the Word, in virtue of the creative vital force dwelling in Him. All beings, however, not only stand in Him, but have their true, perfect life, attain their end, and enjoy the happiness and perfection designed for them, only in Him. Comp. on this full sense of life, eternal life, ch. iii. 16, 36," *etc.*

And the life [the article ἡ refers to the ζωή just mentioned] **was the light of men.**—John passes from the relation of the Logos to the world at large to His relation to men. Here life kindles up into light. As God the Father is in the absolute sense life (v. 26.: ὁ πατὴρ ἔχει ζωὴν ἐν ἑαυτῷ) and light (1 John i. 5: ὁ θεὸς φῶς ἐστι), so is the Son likewise. Light is a figurative expression for pure, divine truth, both intellectual and moral, in opposition to darkness (σκοτία), which includes error and sin. Christ is not φῶς simply, but τὸ φῶς, the only true light; comp. v. 9; viii. 12; ix. 5. All nations and languages use light, which is the vivifying and preserving principle of the world, as a fit image of the Deity. Christ is not simply *doctor veræ religionis* (Kuinoel), but is here represented as the general illuminator of the intellectual and moral universe even before His incarnation. He is the φωσφόρος, the original bringer and constant dispenser of light to all men.* Light and salvation are closely related; comp. Ps. xxvii. 1: "Jehovah is my light and my salvation;" comp. Isa. xlix. 6.—*In* the Logos *was* the life, and *this life is* the light. Observe, it is not said the Logos was the life. The personal God, the personal Logos, have not passed into the form of mere life, as Pantheism holds; branched out into extension and thought, as Spinoza has it; alienated Himself from Himself; emptied Himself of Himself, as idea, according to Hegel and the modern philosophy of nature. And as little has He, according to the abstract supernaturalistic notion, made a purely creature-life out of nothing. He has creatively revealed the life which was in Him, and has made it, as the vital spiritual ground of the creation, the light of men. We must, therefore, on the one hand, keep the continuity of His revelation: the Word, the life, the light; but on the other hand, observe the antithesis, which now appears between the life and the light, more exactly defined: nature and spirit. With the idea of the light, the Evangelist passes to mankind. It belongs therefore to the constitution of humanity to receive the life as light (see Rom. i. 20; John viii. 12), and in the light still ever to perceive the personal revelation of the personal Logos. The light is, unquestionably, the divine truth, ἀλήθεια (Meyer); not, however, primarily as *theoretical* and *practical*, but as ontological or essential, and formal, logical; then also, doubtless, as the truth of the origin of life (ideal, religious) and the end of it (ethical). Meyer most justly maintains that here is described the primal condition of mankind in paradise,† not primarily the subsequent revelation of the Logos as λόγος σπερματικός in the heathen world, or as the principle of revelation in Judaism. And that the operations of that primal relation were not subsequently broken off, though certainly they were broken, is declared by the next verse itself, which thus forms a complete parallel to Rom. i. 20.

Ver. 5. **And the light shineth.**—[Comp. Isa. ix. 1; Matth. iv. 16].—*i. e.*, it still shines, even now. The darkness which entered was not absolute. If the light here, as is certainly the case, becomes the subject (Meyer against Lücke), Lücke, in his interpretation: And as the light shines the Logos, is still right, in so far as the light, rightly known, must be known as the manifestation of the personal Logos. Since the darkness has not been able to destroy the life, it has also not been able to destroy the light in the life, and shining inalienably belongs to the light. **—It shineth.**—Present: denoting continuous activity from the beginning till now. But it does not follow that the enlightening agency of the incarnate Word (λόγος ἔνσαρκος) is meant as well as of the Word before the Incarnation (λόγος ἄσαρκος). For where the λόγος ἔνσαρκος is known,

* [Comp. Ps. xxxvi. 9: "With Thee is the fountain of life; in Thy light we see light;" LXX: πηγὴ ζωῆς. Comp. also John xi. 25: "I am the resurrection and the life (ἡ ζωή);" and 1 John i. 1, where Christ is called the (personal) Word of life, τῆς ζωῆς.—P. S.]

† [Olshausen, Brückner and Alford likewise take life in this comprehensive sense, that the Logos is the source of *all life* to the creature, not indeed ultimately, but mediately, comp. ver. 26; 1 John v. 11. So θάνατος, the opposite of ζωή, covers in John the physical and spiritual. Chrysostom (*Hom.* V., al. IV.) refers ζωή mainly to the power of creation and preservation, but also to the resurrection. According to Olshausen ζωή designates the only real absolute being, the ὄντως εἶναι, of Deity, in contrast with the relative existence of the creature. Luthardt and Brückner: "*Das in sich gesättigte, wahre Sein, welches zugleich die schöpferische Lebenskraft schlechthin ist ohne Unterscheidung des Physischen und Ethischen.*" Godet: "*la santé vitale dans sa vigueur la plus intacte, le developement normal de l' existence,*" *i. e.* life in its normal and healthy condition, whether physical, or intellectual and moral, or supernatural and eternal.—P. S.]

* [Chrysostom: οὐκ εἶπεν, ἦν τὸ φῶς τῶν Ἰουδαίων, ἀλλὰ καθόλου τῶν ἀνθρώπων.—P. S.]

† [Ver. 4 relates to the condition before, ver. 5 to the condition after, the fall. So already Bengel. Godet goes further, and discovers in *life* and *light* an allusion to the trees of life and knowledge in paradise. Ingenious, but not properly warranted by the text.—P. S.]

the σκοτία is taken away. The Logos, however, even for the heathen and unbelievers, is still constantly active in all the world as ἄσαρκος round about the revelations of the ἔνσαρκος. De Wette groundlessly takes the present as a historical present, referring to the activity of the light in the old covenant.*

In the darkness.—The entrance of the darkness as a hostile counterpart to the light, *i. e.*, the fall, is here presupposed; and it must be inferred that the primitive condition just described was not disturbed by any such darkness.†—**The darkness**, however, is not simply "the state in which man has not the Divine truth" (Meyer). As the light is truth, so the darkness is falsehood (John viii. 44), the positive perversion of the truth in delusion, and the σκοτία denotes the total manifestation of sin as a total manifestation of falsehood, in its hostile workings against the light, together with its substratum, the kingdom of darkness in mankind, *i. e.*, primarily in human nature, yet only in so far as human nature is submissive to and pleased with falsehood. We very much doubt whether John would have called mankind itself, as sinful, darkness.

Suppressed [?] it not.—[The aor. κατέλαβεν is used because John speaks of it as a historical fact.] Common interpretation: Comprehend [*begreifen*], understand (Luther [Eng. Vers., Alford, Wordsworth; but in this sense the *vox media* only is used, Acts iv. 13; x. 34.—P. S.]). (2) Meyer: apprehend [*ergreifen*], grasp. [So καταλαμβάνειν is used xii. 35: ἵνα μὴ σκοτία ὑμᾶς καταλάβῃ; Mark ix. 18; Rom. ix. 30; Phil. iii. 12 f.; 1 Cor. ix. 24. The reason why the darkness rejected the light is indicated in iii. 19 and Matth. xxiii. 37.—P. S.]‡ (3) hinder, suppress; Origen, Chrysostom and others (Lange, *Leben Jesu*, III., p. 554), recently Hölemann. Meyer is obliged to concede that this interpretation is grammatically correct§ (Herod. i. 46, 87, *etc.*); he calls it, however, false to the context. But an absolute negation of the penetrating activity of the light would be false to the context; for it would destroy the full meaning of both of the next verses and the whole Gospel. The Evangelist intends to declare the very advent of the Light in the history of the world, its breaking through all the obstructions of the ancient darkness, as it appeared continuously in the history of Abraham.

[This interpretation gives good sense, but disagrees with the connection and destroys the parallelism of vers. 5, 10, 11, which is quite obvious, although there is a difference in the choice of the verbs καταλαμβάνειν, γινώσκειν, and παραλαμβάνειν, as also in the object (ver. 5, αὐτό, sc. τὸ φῶς; ver. 10, 11, αὐτόν, sc. τὸν λόγον.)

Ver. 5. τὸ φῶς ἐν τῇ σκοτίᾳ φαίνει,
καὶ ἡ σκοτία αὐτὸ οὐ κατέλαβεν.
Ver. 10. ἐν τῷ κόσμῳ ἦν,
καὶ ὁ κόσμος αὐτὸν οὐκ ἔγνω.
Ver. 11. εἰς τὰ ἴδια ἦλθεν,
καὶ οἱ ἴδιοι αὐτὸν οὐ παρέλαβεν.

The Gentiles, as well as the Jews (οἱ ἴδιοι), rejected the preparatory revelations of the Logos. Comp. Rom. i. 20 ff. John speaks, of course, only of the mass, and himself makes exceptions (ver. 12). The meaning of καί here and vers. 10 and 11 is *and yet*, notwithstanding the light shining in the darkness. There is here a tone of sacred sadness, of holy grief, which must fill every serious Christian in view of the amazing ingratitude of the great majority of men to the boundless mercies of God.—P. S.]

DOCTRINAL AND ETHICAL.

[1. The Bible speaks of three creations—the first marks the beginning, the second the central and turning point, the third the end, of the history of the world. The O. T. opens with the natural creation, the N. T. with the moral creation or incarnation, and the Revelation closes with a description of the new heavens and the new earth, where nature and grace, the first and second creation, shall be completely harmonized, and the perfect beauty of the spirit shall be reflected in a glorious and immortal body. The first words of the Gospel of Matthew: *The book of generation*, or *genealogy, origin* (βίβλος γενέσεως=סֵפֶר תּוֹלְדוֹת), reminds one of the heading of the second account of creation in Genesis ii. 4 (אֵלֶּה תוֹלְדוֹת, Sept.: Αὕτη ἡ βίβλος γενέσεως οὐρανοῦ καὶ γῆς). The first words of the Gospel of John, *In the beginning* (ἐν ἀρχῇ), contain an unmistakable allusion to the first words in Genesis (i. 1, בְּרֵאשִׁית, Sept.: ἐν ἀρχῇ); and the third verse of the former: "All things were made by Him" (the personal *Word*), may serve as a commentary on the third verse of the latter: "God *said* (וַיֹּאמֶר), Let there be light! And there was light." The world was created by God the Father through God the Son. Comp. Ps. xxxiii. 6; Col. i. 16; Heb. i. 2; Rev. iv. 11.—P. S.]

2. [In LANGE, No. 1.] The fundamental cardinal ideas of this section are: The *personal God* (ὁ θεός); the *Word* or the *Logos* absolute, the *beginning*, the *rise of things*, the *life*, the *light, men*, the *darkness*, the *shining* of the light in the darkness, the *irrepressible breaking* of the light *through* the darkness: all belonging to the exhibition of the eternal advent of Christ. God is designated

* [Brückner likewise dissents here from De Wette. Alford: "This φαίνει is not merely the historical present, but describes the whole process of the light and life in the Eternal Word shining in this evil and dark world; both by the O. T. revelations, and by all the scattered fragments of light glittering among the thick darkness of heathendom." Hengstenberg, on the contrary (p. 33), denies all illumination of the heathen world as foreign to the mind of John, and explains that the Logos before the incarnation was *virtually* life and light, but did not *manifest* Himself as such before the incarnation, so that those who lived before Christ were excluded from life and light. But this would cut off even the saints of the O. T. Comp. against Hengstenberg ver. 9; Rom. i. 18-24; ii. 14, 15; Acts xiv. 16, 17; xvii. 27, 28.—P. S.]

† As the σκοτία is not introduced here in its historical origin, Hilgenfeld (with the Baur school generally) has sought here to make ultimate opposites out of the light and darkness. Thus is the Gnostic filth everywhere brought in, just where the evangelist would sweep it out, as here by the preceding οὐδὲ ἕν.

‡ [Meyer: "οὐ κατέλαβεν, *ergriff es nicht; nahm nicht Besitz davon; es ward von der Finsterniss nicht angeeignet. so dass sie dadurch licht geworden wäre; sie blieb ihm fern und fremd.*" Ewald (p. 121) takes the same view, and finds besides in οὐ κατέλαβεν the idea of guilt: "*und die Finsterniss dennoch ihrerseits ergriff es nicht, eignete es sich nicht an, wie sie doch hätte thun können und sollen.*"—P. S.]

§ [According to classic usage, but in the N. T. this meaning has no parallel. John would probably have used κατέχειν in this case, as Paul did, Rom. i. 18; 2 Thess. ii. 6, 7.—P. S.]

as personal by virtue of His Logos: the Logos, on His God-ward side, is designated as the full expression of the being of God in objective, personal correlation; in the Epistle to the Hebrews, the χαρακτήρ, c. i. 3; in Paul, the image, εἰκών, Col. i. 15. As the human word is the expression of the human mind, so the Word of God is the expression of His being, in focus-like central clearness and perfect concentration. But if, with reference to God, the Logos is single, He is, on the side toward the world, inexhaustibly rich and manifold, comprising the *whole ideal kingdom of divine love*, John xvii. 5; Eph. i. 4. The Logos, as the expressed life of God, is the eternal ground of the temporal world. The beginning gives the becoming, the becoming gives the world. The ultimate cause of the world's coming into being and continuing is the *creating* and *upholding* life in the Logos, as He contains the principles of life. The whole revelation of this life in the world was light for man, who was himself of the light, *i. e.*, it was a spiritual element for his spirit. Even the encroaching darkness could not extinguish this light. In the midst of the darkness it shines (the bright side of heathenism), and through the darkness it breaks (the Old Testament revelation).*

3. [2.] The passage before us contains the ultimate data of the New Testament doctrine of the *ontological Trinity*.† The Evangelist states an antithesis in the Godhead which refers primarily not to the world, but to God. The Logos *was* in the beginning; this is His eternity, which at once implies His deity. He was God, *i. e.*, not a subordinate kind of deity (Philo, and the subordinationists), which, in view of the Biblical monotheism, is simply a self-contradiction in terms; not to say that the absence of the article with θεός emphasizes just the "divine being" of the Logos. With the divinity of the Logos as distinct from God (the Father), the antithesis in the Godhead is established. And at the same time is signified the unity of the speaking God and the spoken, *i. e.*, the existence of the Spirit, which Schleiermacher (in his *Dogmatik*), misses in the passage. Considered as the unity of God with the Logos, it is contained in the term *Logos;* considered as the unity of the Logos with God, it is contained in the phrase πρὸς τὸν θεόν. Of the Spirit distinctly John had here no occasion to speak.* But if the whole essence of God was concentrated as an object to itself in the Word, the eternal perfection of the divine consciousness in luminous clearness, unity, and certitude, is thereby declared, against all notions of a creaturely development in an originally crude divine being. In the eternal Logos lies the idea of the eternal consciousness, as well as its eternal concentration and revelation to itself: the idea, therefore, of the eternal personality, which, in its power of self-revelation, is the Lord; in its distinction, love; in its unity, the Spirit.

It may now be asked, why there is nothing said of Father, Son and Holy Ghost, and whether the ancient and modern distinctions between the eternal Logos of God and the coming of the Logos to be Son first in the creation (Marcellus, and in some measure Urlsperger), are not well grounded. It is to be observed, however, that the distinction between eternity and temporalness in Scripture is not the same as with these theologians. According to Scripture, time is not excluded or cut off from eternity, but embraced and penetrated by it, so that Christ says: "Before Abraham was, I am." In the Logos is from eternity the essence of the Son, as in God is the essence of the Father, as in the relation of the two is the essence of the Spirit. The distinction of the two in our Evangelist, however, proceeded from his making an antithesis between the eternity which is before the world, and the eternity which, with the beginning of the world, enters into the world and comes under temporal conditions. If the eternity of God beyond the world be conceived in contrast with the world, the Son is called Logos; if it be conceived absolutely, the Logos is called the Son. And the church doctrine treats of the Godhead absolutely, as it is from eternity to eternity; therefore of the Son. The Son, as Logos, *is* from eternity; the Logos, as Son, passes from eternity into development, *i. e.*, into the unfolding of the glories of the divine nature. On the development of the church doctrine of the Logos, see Dorner's *Entwicklungsgeschichte, etc.* (*History of Christology*).

4. [3]. After the relation of the Logos to God follows first His *relation to the world*, as antithetic

* [Victor Strauss (*Das Kirchenjahr im Hause*, Heidelberg, 1845, p. 63) beautifully reproduces and expounds the Johannean idea of the Logos in his relation to God and the world:

" *Vor Anbeginn der Schöpfung und der Zeiten*
Ist Gottes Eingeborner ewiglich,
Die Fülle selbst von Gottes Wesenheiten,

Das ew'ge Du, in dem des Vaters Ich'
Des eignen Wesens Wesenheit besiegelt,
Den eignen Abgrund aufgedeckt in sich,

Die Hand die Gottes Tief' ihm selbst entriegelt,
Sein Wille selbst in anfangloser That,
Sein Abglanz, der ihm selbst sich wiederspiegelt.

Das Wort, das er in sich geboren hat
Zum wahren Sein, drin Fülle der Naturen
In's ungeschaffne Dasein ewig trat.

Da ist der Grund, aus dem die Weltenfluren
Hervorgesprosst zum Anbeginn der Zeit,
Als ew'ges Dasein ward zu Creaturen;

Und Lebensfüll' in reinster Seligkeit
Ging aus von Ihm in die Erschaffnen alle;
Es war nur Licht, war keine Dunkelheit."—P. S.]

† [German divines properly distinguish since Urlsperger (who invented, not the distinction, but the terminology) between the *ontological* and the *œconomical* Trinity, or the Trinity of *essence* and the Trinity of *revelation*. The ontological Trinity is the Trinity of the Divine being before and independent of the world, the inherent threefold distinction in God, who both as absolute intelligence and as absolute will or love, is to Himself an object of knowledge and of love, and yet self-identical in this distinction. We have an analogy in our human self-consciousness which implies a union of the knowing subject and the known object; and in human love there is also a trinity—the loving subject, the beloved object, and the union of the two. The œconomical Trinity is the Trinity of God manifested in the world in the work of Creation and Preservation (as God the Father), Redemption (as God the Son), and Regeneration and Sanctification (as God the Holy Ghost). The Bible generally speaks of the Trinity as revealed, but this itself justifies by inference the assumption of the internal Trinity, since God reveals Himself as He actually is. There can be no contradiction between His being and His manifestation.—P. S.]

* [The dispensation of the Spirit, His œconomical manifestation in the world with the whole fullness of His power, presupposed the atoning work and glorification of Christ, and did not appear before the day of Pentecost and the founding of the Christian Church. Comp. John vii. 39.—P. S.]

to the former. And the world is here viewed not as a finished cosmos, but in concrete totality: all things (πάντα); because the cosmos is properly the result and manifestation of the development of the things; τὸ πᾶν is the finished appearance of the πάντα, as the Logos is their original source; because it should be distinctly remembered that the Logos is not merely architect of the *form of the world* (the demiurge of Philo), but also the producer of the *material of the world*, or rather of the *life of the world*, which reduces its subordinate, elementary forms to the *material of the world*. The question whether the creation of the world is from eternity, or arose in time, proceeds from an obscurity respecting the relation between the ideas of eternity and time. To conceive the world as arising in eternity, before time, incurs the absurdity of supposing a world, consequently a development (*ein Werden*) without time (*i. e.*, also without rhythm or established succession). To conceive the world as arising in time, presupposes an existence of time before the world, *i. e.*, a time without world. Time is the world itself in its unfolding. The world, therefore, arose with time, and time with the world, but upon the basis of eternity, which but reveals itself in all time.

5. [4]. "*And without him was not any thing made*," Ps. xxxiii. 6. The absolutely dynamic view of the world; in opposition to *materialism*, which, in its anti-dynamic dealing, is the philosophy of the absolute impotence of the spirit, vexed with a remnant of spirit. In the statement that all things were made *by the Logos* (not out of Him, nor yet by Him as an *instrument*, but as *principle*), the creation is at the same time represented as a pure act of the eternal personality; in opposition to all theories of emanation. Both the doctrine of an eternal heterogeneous opposition between God or spirit and matter (pantheistic Dualism), and the doctrine of an eternal natural outflowing of all things from God (dualistic Pantheism), are here excluded (not to speak of the cabbalistic fancies concerning matter, as a shadow of God, a negation of God, which have emerged again even in our day). By the harmonious distinction in God, or His absolute personality, the discordant opposition in the world, the heathen view of the world, is denied. Gerlach: The *by* is not to be understood as if the Logos, the Word, were only the external architect; Paul expresses it: "*In him** were all things created," and adds: "*by him* and for him," Col. i. 16.

6. [5]. But the next words: "*In him was the life*," *etc.*, with equal decision, contradict *Deism*, which sees in the world only an act and work of a God entirely outside and remote.† The Logos is the life of the life, the operative, creative force, by which all things are. Yet the things have their life in Him, not He His life in the things. And the preservation of the world rests upon the same word as the creation, Heb. i. 3; John v. 17.—The points of unity between the creation and the preservation of the world, in which the creation establishes the preservation, and the preservation reaches back to the basis of the creation, are vital principles, out of which the vital laws evolve themselves, Gen. i. 11; xii. 21, 28. The life is, however, before the light, nature before spirit; though even the natural light, as the first step of the separating (and liberating) process of the life, is a prophecy of the spirit, which, being of the nature of light, finds its essential light in the manifestations of the Logos.

7. [6]. "*And the life was the light.*" An intimation of the antithesis between *spirit* and *nature*. In man the revelation life of the Logos has appeared in the world as light. Consciousness is the light of being. But the life was the light of men, not merely as the source of life, in that the human spirit has its origin in the Logos; but also as the element of life, in that the clearness of the spirit subsists only through the in-working of the Logos. Without Him the light in man becomes itself darkness (Matth. vi. 22),* and the spirit, the πνεῦμα, itself becomes unspiritual flesh. But if the life itself was the light of men, the creation must have been, to the pure man, a transparent symbol, a perfectly intelligible likeness of divine things (Rom. i. 20). And this thought is most gloriously carried out in the Gospel. Christ has made the light of men manifest in the life.

8. [7]. "*In the darkness.*" The Evangelist, writing as a Christian for Christians, can introduce the idea of darkness without further explanation, with no fear of being misunderstood. As he has not intended to give a cosmogony, so he considers it unnecessary here to treat of the beginning of sin. His subject is the Logos, who has appeared as the Christ. Accordingly he delineates first the eternal divine nature of the Logos and His congenial, friendly relations to the world and to mankind, and now comes to His *hostile* posture towards *sin*. And this he views in its deepest and most suggestive aspect, as an opposition of the light to the darkness. The sin which has come into the world is, above all things, darkness, self-darkening of the light of spiritual life in falsehood, John viii. 44. And this darkness is not the sinful spirits, but sin, as the obscuration of the life, including the life itself, so far as it becomes one with sin. Hence: "*shineth in the darkness;*" not *into* the darkness. This darkness, as such, can be only broken through, destroyed, by the light, not transformed into light. But in this the power of the light has been made manifest, that it has not ceased to shine even in the darkness of the heathen world. Nay, the deeper the darkness, the more wonderfully does the light scintillate through it in obstructed, colored radiance, in the motley mythologies, usages and philosophemes

* ['Εν αὐτῷ; inaccurately translated *by him* in the English Version, and thus not rightly distinguished from δι' αὐτοῦ at the close of the same verse.—E. D. Y.]

† [Göthe thus refutes Deism:

"What were a God who only from without
Upon his finger whirled the universe about?
'Tis his within itself to move the creature;
Nature in him to warm, himself in nature;
So that what in him lives and moves and is,
Shall ever feel some living breath of his."—P. S.]

* [More properly, without Him there were no light at all in man. In Matth. vi. 22 the Lord speaks rather of a perversion, confusion, doubling of the vision by the carnal will, so that the light within becomes distorted and a source of positive error, than of an absence of the light itself. Such light-darkness, or dark-light, like the *ignis fatuus*, is a "greater" darkness than simple darkness itself.—E. D. Y.]

of the heathen world, so far as they are symbolical and have an ideal substance: the *λόγος σπερματικός* [the word implanted, disseminated among men].* John defines the relation between sin and the continual working of good in the world exactly as Paul does in Rom. ii. 13 and 14.

9. [8]. "*Restrained it not.*" The sense is: prevented it not from breaking through. Intimating the entrance of a historical advent in the active faith of Abraham. The historical beginning of the religion of active faith. [See my objections to this interpretation, p. 59. *κατέλαβεν* rather means here *grasped, apprehended.*—P. S.]

HOMILETICAL AND PRACTICAL.

The life of Jesus Christ in time, the great disclosure respecting eternity: (1) Respecting His own eternal nature; (2) Respecting the personal being of God; (3) Respecting the origin of all things (particularly the antithesis of spirit and nature); (4) Respecting the nature and destiny of man; (5) Respecting the contest between the light and the darkness in the history of the world.—The word of Scripture concerning "the beginning:" (1) The Old Testament word in the New Testament light; (2) The New Testament word on the Old Testament basis.—The great beginning between eternity and time considered: (1) As the great distinction between eternity and time; (2) As the great union between eternity and time.—The three great words concerning Christ: In the beginning was the Word: (1) In the beginning was *the Word;* the divine nature of Christ; (2) In the beginning *was* the Word; the eternity of Christ; (3) *In the beginning* was the Word; the eternal operation and generation of Christ. Or, The Word was (1) Before the beginning (His relation to God); (2) For the beginning (His relation to the world); (3) In the beginning (His relation to things).—The Word which was in the beginning, a testimony (1) To the eternal Personality as the ground of all things; (2) To the eternal Spirit-Light as the law of all things; (3) To the eternal Love as the kernel of all things; (4) To the eternal life as the life of all things.—The Word in His exaltation over time: He (1) In the beginning founded all things; (2) In the middle executed all things; that He may (3) In the end judge all things.—The import of the Word in God, illustrated by the word in man: (1) The expression and mirror of the personal nature (of the spirit, the reason); (2) The expression and signal of personal act.—The Word, as the bloom of the tree of life; or the gospel, a witness of its own spiritual nature: (1) Of the Word as the seed of the tree of life; (2) Of the Word as the heart of the tree of life; (3) Of the fruit of the tree of life, or life eternal—the Word in redemption, a transfiguration of the Word in creation.—The glory in the beginning: (1) The prototypal primal glory of God; (2) The archetypal glory of the Word; (3) The typical glory of the creation; (4) The antitypical glory of man.—The light in its rise; or: (1) The radiance of God and eternity; (2) The dawn of the world and time.—*All things, etc.*, or the Christian doctrine of the creation: (1) The purification of the heathen doctrine (obviating the eternity of matter); (3) The deepening of the Jewish doctrine of the Shekinah (clearly pronouncing the personal life of love in God, as it enters into the world): (2) The glorification of the sound doctrine of scientific investigation (man the final cause of things, the God-Man the final cause of man); (4) The verdict of the Spirit respecting the derivation of the word from a non-spiritual source (materialism).—The Christian features in all things: (1) The *creaturely* instinct of dependence, as an impulse towards the upholding Word; (2) The *natural* self-unfolding instinct, as the impulse towards freedom (the liberty of the children of God, Rom. viii.); (3) The *cosmical, world-forming* instinct, as an impulse towards unity; (4) The *spiritual* [*æonic*] instinct, as the impulse to rise into the service of the Spirit.—The unity and the difference between life and light: (1) In the Son of God; (2) In the world; (3) In man; (4) In the Christian life.—The life a light of men: (1) In man (consciousness); (2) For man; the works of God as the signs and words of God (symbolism); (3) Respecting man; Christ the life of the life.—The life and light, or truth and reality, inseparable: (1) Without reality truth becomes a shadow; (2) Without truth reality becomes a lie.—The great darkness which has spread over the bright world of God: The darkness (1) of falsehood; (2) of hatred; (3) of death.—The light in contest with the darkness, or the progress of revelation in the world of sinners: (1) The light shining in the darkness (the shaded, colored light); (2) The light breaking through the darkness.—The eternal foundations of the advent of Christ.—The divine Life of Christ, the mark of all life: (1) The mark of the original glory of the world; (2) The mark of the deep corruption of the world; (3) The mark of the great redemption and glorification of the world.—The wisdom of the Apostles and the wisdom of their time (or, of the ancient world).—Parallel passages: Gen. i.: Ps. viii., xix. and civ.; Is. xl.; John xvii.; Rom. viii.; 1 Cor. xv.; Ephes. i.; Col. i.; 1 John i.; Rev. i., xxi. and xxii.

STARKE:—God has revealed even His divine constitution and the inmost secret of His nature.—The Eternal Word is now become also ours. Through this Word God speaks with us, and we speak with God. The eternal Word speaks in us, through us, to us, with us.—QUESNEL: The knowledge of the Son of God must be the first and the most excellent; without it all knowledge

* [Justin Martyr applied the Platonic view of the relation of the *νοῦς* to the *νοερόν* in man to the relation of the divine *λόγος* to the *σπέρμα λογικόν*, the human reason, and derived all the elements of truth which are scattered like seeds among the ancient heathen, from the influence of Christ before His incarnation. He recognized in the rational soul itself something closely related to the divine Logos, a germ or spark of the Reason of reasons, a *λόγος σπερματικός*, a *σπέρμα τοῦ λόγου ἔμφυτον*. He regarded the heathen sages as unconscious disciples of the Logos, as Christians before Christ, and compared Socrates to Abraham. *Apol.* II. §13: "Each man spoke well in proportion to the share he had of the spermatic divine word (*ἀπὸ μέρους τοῦ σπερματικοῦ θείου λόγου*), seeing what was related to it. Whatever things were rightly said among all men, are the property of us Christians. . . . All the [heathen] writers were able to see realities darkly through the seed of the implanted word that was in them (*διὰ τῆς ἐνούσης ἐμφύτου τοῦ λόγου σπορᾶς*)." Comp. ii. §8, where, speaking of the Stoics and the poets, he says that their moral teaching in part was admirable on account of the seed of reason implanted in every race of men, *διὰ τὸ ἔμφυτον παντὶ γένει ἀνθρώπων σπέρμα τοῦ λόγου*.—P. S.]

is nothing.—NOVA BIBL. TUB.: See how many proofs of the divinity of our Jesus. He is God, the eternal Word, from eternity, in the beginning, before all creatures, the Creator of all things, the origin of all life, the source of all light.—If the Word of God was in the beginning, it is certain, that He also will be in future to the end (LANGE). It is not said: the light was the life, but: the life was the light. The life is the source of the light, even in the kingdom of nature, *etc.* That no true illumination takes place, except the man is brought back by regeneration from spiritual death to spiritual life (ZEISIUS). Whose life Christ is, his light He is also.—No other darkness can withstand the light, but the darkness of man.

MOSHEIM: The person through whom God spoke to men, did not first arise when the world was made, but was already, that is, from eternity.—RIEGER: This confessedly great mystery of the manifestation of God in the flesh continues as a standard at all times set up, under which all gather, that are born of God, and which all that are of the world pass by.—LISCO: From the Word, as the light, proceeds all that is true and good in mankind.—GERLACH, after AUGUSTINE: Sin, not indeed consists, but manifests itself, in coming of nothing, and bringing man to nothing (eternal death).—BRAUNE: Thought is clear only in word: *He came.* This implies personality; the Personality, the Enlightener, came near to the Jewish people; in reference to men in general, it is said: He was.—Thus John, who lay on the bosom of the Lord, as the Lord is eternally with His Father, opens his view into the depths of the life of Jesus Christ from the beginning, till it rises into the heights of the same life in the bosom of the Father.

HEUBNER: The mystery of the incarnation of the Son of God: (1) The holiest, deepest of all mysteries, in virtue of the person; (2) The most beneficent of all; (3) The most certain of all.—SCHLEIERMACHER: What is it which meets us everywhere as truth, in all the utterances of the human mind, in all investigations, in all holy words of inspired men? Ever that which contains a hint of the redemption which was to come through Christ.

[SCHAFF: Vers. 1, 2. The transcendent glory of Christ. 1. His eternity (against Arianism): "*In the beginning was* the Word." 2. His distinct personality (against Sabellianism): "The Word was *with* (in intimate personal intercommunion with) God." 3. His essential divinity (against Socinianism and Rationalism): "And the Word was *God.*"—The fundamental importance of the doctrine of Christ's divinity: it is the corner-stone of the Christian system, the anchor of hope. Without it His passion and death have no force against sin and Satan, and we are still lost.]

[BURKITT: "Until we acknowledge the eternity and divinity of Christ, as well as of God the Father, we honor neither the Father nor the Son. There is this difference between natural things and supernatural. Natural things are first understood, and then believed; but supernatural mysteries must be first believed, and then will be better understood." (Pascal makes a similar remark.) "If we will first set reason on work, and believe no more than we can comprehend, this will hinder faith: but if after we have assented to gospel mysteries, we set reason on work, this will help faith."—HENGSTENBERG: "The Logos was God;" this is the magic formula that drives away all doubt, anxiety and fear from the Christian. If God be for us, who can be against us?—RYLE: If Christ is so great, how sinful must sin be from which He came to save us?]

[SCHAFF: Ver. 3. The creation is the work of the Father through the Son in the Holy Spirit. This is intimated Gen. i. 1–3: *God* (the Father) created . . . And the *Spirit* of God moved upon the face of the waters. And God *said* (the Word).—The Scripture doctrine of creation differs—1) from Pantheism, which teaches an eternal world and confounds God and the world; 2) from Dualism, or the eternity of matter antagonistic to God (Parseeism, Platonism, Gnosticism, Manichæism); 3) from the emanation theory; 4) from Deism, which asserts the creation, but separates it from the Creator; 5) from Materialism, which makes matter the mother of the spirit, and is alike degrading to God and man.—Sin was not made by God, but is a subsequent corruption or perversion of what was made good. Sin is no essence, no creature, but something negative, a false direction of the will.—Christ's part in the creation the basis of His redemption. Having made man, He had the deepest interest in him from the start.]

[SCHAFF: Vers. 4, 5. Christ, the source of all true life and light.—Out of Christ there is but death and darkness.—The antagonism of life and death, and the antagonism of light and darkness is not, 1) a metaphysical conflict (as in the Gnostic and Dualistic systems), but, 2) a moral conflict involving personal freedom and responsibility. It began in time and will end in time; life and light will conquer the field and swallow up death and darkness. 3. The antagonism culminates in God and Satan, in Christ and Anti-Christ, but goes on in every man. 4. It should fill us with holy grief, manly courage, and intense earnestness.]

[On the whole section. BENGEL: Vers. 1 and 2 refer to eternity, ver. 3 to creation, ver. 4 to the state of innocence, ver. 5 to the fall.—RYLE: Not a single word could be altered in the first five verses of John without opening the door to some heresy.—There are hidden depths in this passage which nothing but the light of eternity will ever fully reveal.—P. S.]

SECOND SECTION.

The personal Light, or Christ, in His pre-historical Presence in the World, especially in His Old Testament Advent, testified by the Old Covenant as it is represented by John the Baptist.

VERS. 6–13.

CONTENTS:

(1) THE REPRESENTATIVE OF THE COMING OF CHRIST, JOHN THE BAPTIST, VERS. 6–8. (2) THE COMING OF CHRIST INTO THE WORLD, IN ITS GENERAL GROUNDWORK AND ITS HISTORICAL GENESIS, VER. 9. (3) THE RELATION OF CHRIST TO THE WORLD AND THE CONDUCT OF THE WORLD TOWARDS HIM, OR THE GENERAL GROUNDWORK OF HIS ADVENT, VER. 10. (4) THE RELATION OF CHRIST TO ISRAEL, AND ISRAEL'S CONDUCT TOWARDS HIM, OR THE IMPERFECT, SYMBOLICAL ADVENT, VER. 11. (5) CHRIST'S GRADUAL BREAKING THROUGH IN THE WORLD IN THE CONTRAST OF THE ELECT TO THE LESS SUSCEPTIBLE, EMBODIED—(*a*) IN FAITH, AS THE BEGINNING OF THE REAL ADVENT, VER. 12; (*b*) IN THE CONSECRATION OF BIRTH AND THE BEING BORN OF GOD; THE DEVELOPMENT OF THE REAL ADVENT, VER. 13.

6 There was [became, arose][1] a man sent[2] from God, whose name *was* John.
7 The same came for a [*omit* a] witness [testimony, εἰς μαρτυρίαν], to bear witness of
8 the Light, that all *men* through him might believe. He was not that [the] Light,
9 but *was sent* [*came*, Lange: *he was*] to bear witness of that [the] Light. *That* was
the true Light, which lighteth every man, that cometh into the world. [The true
Light which lighteth (lighteneth, shineth upon) every man, was coming (ἦν ἐρχό-
10 μενον) into the world.][3] He [It] was in the world, and the world was made by
11 him [it], and the world knew him not [Lange: did not recognize it in him]. He
came unto his own [his own possessions or inheritance, τὰ ἴδια], and his own [his
12 own people, οἱ ἴδιοι][5] received him not. But as many as received him, to them
gave he power to become the sons [children, τέκνα] of God, *even* to them that
13 believe on [in] his name: Which [Who] were born, not of blood [bloods, ἐξ αἱμά-
των], nor of the [natural] will of the flesh, nor of the [moral] will of man, but of God.[6]

TEXTUAL AND GRAMMATICAL.

[1] Ver. 6. [The Greek here is ἐγένετο (*became*), which differs from ἦν (*was*), ver. 1, as the German *ward* (or *geworden*) does from *war*, but it cannot be well rendered in English. It is the antithesis between *temporal* or *created* existence which has a beginning, and implies previous non-existence, and *eternal* or *uncreated* existence, which has neither beginning nor end. The same distinction—John viii. 58: πρὶν Ἀβραὰμ γενέσθαι, ἐγώ εἰμι.—P. S.]

[2] Ver. 6. [ἀπεσταλμένος does not belong to ἐγένετο=ἀπεστάλη (Chrysostom, *Hom.* VI. p. 42, and Hengstenberg), but to ἄνθρωπος.—P. S.]

[3] Ver. 9. [So Lange. Ewald somewhat differently: *Ja das wahrhaftige Licht, welches jeden Menschen erleuchtet, kam stets in die Welt.* Others translate: *that was the true Light which, coming into the world, lighteth every man.* ἐρχόμενον may be connected with ἄνθρωπον (Vulg.: *hominem venientem*, Luth., E. V.), or better, with ἦν (Lange, Ewald). See the EXEG. NOTES. In the latter case a comma should be made after ἄνθρωπον, as is done by Tischendorf, eighth ed.—P. S.]

[4] Ver. 10. [δι' αὐτοῦ. Cod. ℵ* reads δι' αὐτόν, probably an error of the copyist.—P. S.]

[5] Ver. 11. [The E. V. obliterates the distinction between the neutral τὰ ἴδια, *das Seine*, his own things, possessions, inheritance, and the masculine οἱ ἴδιοι, *die Seinen*, his own people, servants, subjects.—P. S.]

[6] Ver. 13. The difficulty of the passage has occasioned the omission of οὐδὲ ἐκ θελ. σαρκ., in Cod. E. and others; and of οὐδὲ ἐκ θελ. ἀνθρ. in Cod. B. and others. Others, as Augustine, have transposed the clauses. [See Tischend. Oct. VIII. p. 743.]

EXEGETICAL AND CRITICAL.

Ver. 6. **There was a man.**—Ἐγένετο [*fiebat*], arose, came into being; not ἦν [*erat*], was, absolutely [comp. viii. 58, Greek. The Logos *was* from eternity, Abraham and John *began to be* in time.—P. S.]—Chrysostom: ἐγένετο ἀπεσταλμένος. The life of John, so to speak, was lost in his mission (see ver. 23; comp. Is. xl. 3).* The appearance of John in this place is striking, and has been variously interpreted (see Meyer).* In the introduction of the Baptist in this pas-

* [Hengstenberg adopts the construction of Chrysostom, which would have been more naturally expressed by ἀπεστάλη, and defends it by referring to Mal. iii. 1, 23: "Lo, *I am sending* my messenger," *etc.*, compared with the words of the Baptist, John iii. 28: ἀπεσταλμένος εἰμὶ ἔμπροσθεν αὐτοῦ. I prefer the usual connection of ἀπεσταλμένος with ἄνθρωπος.—P. S.]

* [The Baptist is mentioned in the Prologue to confirm the reality of the historical appearance of Christ: Brückner; as a brilliant exception from the terrible darkness spoken of ver. 5: Ewald; to explain the rejection of Christ by His own people, vers. 10, 11: Meyer; to introduce the historic manifestation of the Word: Alford. He is mentioned rather as the personal representative of the whole O. T. revelation in whom the law and the promise, Moses and Isaiah, were united and pointed directly to Christ. See Lange in the text.—P. S.]

sage we see a representation of the whole prophetic testimony concerning Christ in concentrated, personal form, after the manner of this Gospel. The Baptist was the final recapitulation of all prophetic voices concerning Christ. The Old Testament had two sides—a hidden and a visible. The hidden side was the rise of the genealogical life of Christ itself, His Christological advent; the visible side was the prophetic testimony concerning this advent. And as the verbal prophecy anticipated the real prophecy, in the nature of the case, so the fulfilment of the verbal prophecy in John preceded the fulfilment of the real prophecy in Christ. John therefore here stands in the right place, the auroral radiance of the essential Light; the great witness of the advent of Christ; the forerunner.

[**Whose name** (*was*) **John**, *i. e.*, *Jehovah is merciful*, from the Hebrew יוֹחָנָן for יְהוֹחָנָן, Ἰωάννης; comp. the Greek Θεόδωρος. This significant name was given to the forerunner of our Saviour by divine direction, Luke i. 13. The evangelist laid stress on his own name, and saw in it a symbol of his relation to Christ as the disciple "whom Jesus loved," xx. 2; xxi. 20. Comp. Lampe and Hengstenberg.—P. S.].

Ver. 7. **The same came for witness.**—*Testimony*: stronger here than preaching; stronger even than prophecy, as hitherto existing. John appeared first as a preacher, a preacher of repentance. But the preacher showed himself at the same time a prophet, announcing under divine impulse the approach of the Messianic kingdom. And then, in the miraculous manifestation at the baptism of Jesus, through the testimony of God, he became a witness of the person of Jesus of Nazareth, that He is the Messiah; so to speak, an apostle before the apostolate. As a prophet who, by divine commission, pointed to the Messiah, he completed the Old Testament prophecy in testimony. And for this testimony he was come. His mission rose into the office of forerunner. And even his martyrdom in the strict sense is in keeping. He sealed his preparatory preaching of repentance with his death (see ver. 33).

That [ἵνα, the aim of John's testimony] **all men through him might believe.**—"Through John, not through the Light (Grotius), or through Christ (Ewald):" Meyer.* In the divine purpose John was to lead over the faith of Israel to Christ.† This Christ also signifies chap. v. 33 [where he calls John "the burning and shining light," or candle rather, λύχνος, not φῶς.—P. S.] Through the unbelief of the Jews this gracious design failed; though in the truly devout, first of all in the noblest of John's own disciples (ver. 35 sqq.) it was fulfilled; through them in all believers.

Ver. 8. **He was not the light.**—[ἦν is emphatic and contrasted with μαρτυρήσῃ. The article before φῶς is likewise emphatic, the Light of the world, the Light of lights, comp. ὁ προφήτης, i. 29; ὁ ἄρτος, vi. 32 ff.—P. S.] This is certainly not said merely with reference to the unbelieving disciples of John.* But in the wider sense the nation itself was an unbelieving disciple of John, contenting itself with the brightness of the Baptist, instead of going through him to the true Light itself, ch. v. 35. So far, therefore, as it is implied that many, even the leaders, made the Baptist rather a hindrance than a help to faith, the words are written even against the disciples of John.

But (*he was*).—De Wette takes the ἀλλ' ἵνα, *but in order to*, imperatively; Lücke supplies ἦν, *was;* Meyer, ἦλθεν, *came*. Since the preceding verse strongly pronounces that the whole prophetic existence of John was intended to rise into a testimony for the Messiah, we give Lücke the preference: "He was, that he might bear witness." [So also Alford and Godet. Baümlein supplies ἐγένετο, γίνεται, "or the like;" which is not so strong. I prefer with Meyer to supply ἦλθε from ver. 7, since the phrase, εἶναι, ἵνα instead of εἶναι εἰς τό is quite unusual.—P. S.]

Ver. 9. **The true Light—was coming** [ἦν τὸ φῶς τὸ ἀληθινόν—ἐρχόμενον].—Various interpretations: (1) He (the Logos) or it (the Light) was the true Light; so the older expositors and Luther [E. V., which supplies τοῦτο before ἦν, *that* was the true light.—P. S.] But τὸ φῶς τὸ ἀληθινόν must be subject, not predicate; for in ver. 8 John was the subject. [So also Meyer.] (2) Ἐρχόμενον εἰς τὸν κόσμον (*coming into the world*) is connected with πάντα ἄνθρωπον (*every man*), not with ἦν (*was*); Origen [Syr., Euseb., Chrys., Cyril, Vulg., Aug.] and most of the ancients, Luther,† Calvin [E. V.], *etc.*, Hölemann, Meyer.‡ [This would make either ἄνθρωπον or ἐρχόμ. superfluous.] Meyer observes that it could not be connected with ἦν; for the Logos was already in the world when John appeared. But the Evangelist here evidently goes back to the entire relation of Christ to mankind, especially goes back to ver. 4. He had before

* [In the fifth edition of Meyer the reference to Ewald is omitted. In his Commentary, Ewald translates δι' αὐτοῦ *durch ihn*, without explaining whether *ihn* is meant of John or of Christ.—P. S.]

† [Ryle: "One of those texts which show the immense importance of the ministerial office through which the Holy Spirit is pleased to produce faith in man's heart.—P. S.]

* [Meyer denies the reference to the disciples of John entirely. Godet, on the contrary, defends it, and justly so, in view of i. 20; iii 25; and in view of the Gnostic sect of the Disciples of John in the second century, who held that John the Baptist was the true Messiah. (Clementis Rom. *Recognitiones* l. I. c. 54 and 60. Comp. the articles of Petermann, *Mendäer* and *Zabier*, in Herzog's *Encyclop.* Vols. IX. p. 318 and XVIII. p. 341.) Only we must not suppose either that John wrote expressly, or exclusively against this error. See Dr. Lange above.—P. S.]

† [In the first ed. Luther translated: "*Das war ein wahrhaftig Licht, welches alle Menschen erleuchtet durch seine Zukunft in die Welt*," *i. e.*, "which, coming into the world, lighteneth all men." In the later editions he followed the Vulgate.—P. S.]

‡ [Meyer, however, lays the emphasis on ἦν, *aderat*, which is put first, and translates: "*Vorhanden war das Licht das wahrhaftige, welches erleuchtet jeden Menschen, der in die Welt kommt*," *the true light was in existence, etc.* But there is no good reason why ἦν should be emphasized rather than ἀληθινόν, and then ἐν τῷ κόσμῳ ἦν, ver. 10, would be a repetition of ver. 9. The old usual interpretation is preferable to Meyer's, but both are to be rejected, because the phrase *to come into the world* for *to be born*, though Rabbinical (כָּל בָּאֵי בָעוֹלָם=all men), is not Scriptural, as applied to common men, but is reserved exclusively for the Messiah with the implied sense of præ-existence, iii. 19, 31; vi. 14; xi. 27; xii. 46; xviii. 37. Bengel: "*Apud Hebræos frequens est periphrasis hominis,* הבא בעולם VENIENS IN MUNDUM, *sed in N. T. et præcipue in hoc libro id de solo Christo dicitur, sublimi significatu.* ERAT *enim, ante etiam, quam* VENIRET."—P. S.]

spoken of the witness of the advent of Christ—now he depicts the advent itself. This is divided into two parts: (1) The relation of the coming Logos to man in general; (2) His relation to Israel. Hence we interpret: He was (from the beginning and in conflict with the darkness, ver. 5) coming, was on His advent to mankind. Therefore not (*a*) was come [ἦν ἐρχόμενον=ἐλθόν]: Schöttgen, *etc.;* (*b*) just came (when John appeared): De Wette, Lücke [Alford]; (*c*) future: was on the point of coming [*venturum erat*]: Tholuck; or (*d*) was destined to come: Luthardt; desired to come: Ewald;* nor (*e*) was coming then, in the time before His baptism: Hilgenfeld, who even here would mix Valentinian Gnosis into the anti-Gnostic Gospel;—but in a purely historical sense [=ἦλθε, *came*], instead of the imperfect: Bengel, Bleek, Köstlin [Hengstenberg, with reference to Mal. iii. 1]; and with the peculiar Johannean significance: He was continually coming, continually on his way.† Hence the participial form. The essence of this universal advent is to be recognized in the fact, that the Logos shines in every man in his religious and moral nature and experience, as the λόγος σπερματικός. That the expression "every man" needed not the addition: that cometh into the world, is evident. And the phrase: "to come into the world," is not used of the natural birth of an ordinary man, but is reserved for Christ.

[**Which lighteth (enlightens, illuminates) every man**—ὁ φωτίζει πάντα ἄνθρωπον.—There is much force in the singular. *Quisquis illuminatur, ab hac luce illuminatur* (Bengel). Different interpretations: 1. The light of reason and intelligence (Cyril of Alex.). Better: Both the intellectual and moral light (reason and conscience) given to all men, as distinct from the spiritual light of saving grace given to believers. The former is the basis of the latter.‡ 2. The inward spiritual light given to all (Quakers). 3. The light of grace given to believers only, or to every one to whom Christ was preached (Crosby). 4. Intellectual and spiritual light sufficient for the salvation of Jews and Gentiles, though the majority are so blinded by sin as not to see Him. "Christ enlightens all as far as in Him lies" (Chrysostom, *Hom.* VIII.). Christ gives sufficient light to every man to leave him without excuse, but not sufficient to save (Arrowsmith, Ryle).—Comp. III. 19: "light is come into the world;" xii. 46: "I am come a light into the world;" vi. 14: "that prophet that should come into the world;" xviii. 37.—P. S.]

The true [veritable, genuine] Light [τὸ φῶς τὸ ἀληθινόν].—The real, essential Light in distinction from the outward, cosmical light, which, nevertheless, is His token and symbol. (See Milton's *Paradise Lost:* the greeting to the light. Comp. chap. viii. 12; ix. 5.)

[There is a nice difference between ἀληθής (*wahr*), *true* in opposition to *false*, and ἀληθινός (*wahrhaftig*), *true* in opposition to *borrowed* or *imitated*. This difference is obliterated in the E. V. The one expresses the harmony between thought and reality, word and fact; the other implies a contrast between the perfect original and a copy more or less imperfect. Ἀληθινός is a favorite term with Plato and John to signify that which is genuine, archetypal, original, true to the idea. It occurs eight times in the Gospel, ten times in the Apocalypse, three times in the first Epistle of John, but elsewhere only five times in the N. T. In this passage it stands in contrast not so much to the cosmical light (Dr. Lange), as to the borrowed intellectual and moral light of the Baptist and other human teachers; comp. v. 35; Matth. v. 14, where believers generally as members of Christ are called the light of the world. It is *lumen illuminans*, as distinct from the *lumen illuminatum*.—P. S.]

Ver. 10. **It was in the world.**—Not pluperfect (Herder [Tholuck, Olsh.]); nor "in the person of Jesus, when John was testifying" (Meyer); but referring to His infinite presence in mankind (Baumgarten-Crusius). The repetitions of the idea of the *world* (κόσμος) are to be distinguished thus: In the first case the word combines the material and the moral world in one; in the second, it means the material or visible world alone, up to the roots of its moral conduct; in the third, the moral world alone, but considered as resting upon and representing the visible. Meyer well says: (1) The world *might* have known Him (constitutional affinity); (2) it *should* have known Him (according to His claim). [Comp. Rom. i. 19 ff., where Paul fully proves the guilt of Gentiles and Jews in rejecting the light of nature and the preparatory revelation of the O. T.—P. S.]

Knew him not.—The whole verse strictly reads: "*It* was in the world, and the world was made by *it* [or Him, δι' αὐτοῦ], and the world knew *Him* (αὐτόν) not." The change of gender is highly significant. In the light of the world, the world should have known the personal founder of the world, the Logos. The gradation in the three clauses is also expressed by the repetition of "and." The world of heathenism knew not *the light*, still less *Him*, the personal character of the light. It took the divine for something *impersonal*, and sought to heal the wrong by fragmentary *personifications*, its gods [the altar at Athens "to the unknown God," Acts xvii. 23.—P. S.]

Ver. 11. **He came unto his own house or inheritance** [τὰ ἴδια, comp. xvi. 32; xix. 27].—Here the discourse is no longer of the universal advent of Christ in the world (Corn. a Lapide, Kuinoel, *etc.*);* but of the theocratic advent

* [In his Commentary Ewald explains somewhat differently. He connects ver. 9 with ver. 4: *es kam damals immer in die Welt*, it was at that time always coming into the world, so that every mortal, if he would, might have been guided by the light.—P. S.]

† [Keim: "*er war in stetem Kommen in die Welt.*" Similarly Ewald, see preceding foot-note. ἦν ἐρχόμενον is stronger than ἦν, and implies a continued action, like the English, *was coming*, as distinct from *came*. Comp. ἦν βαπτίζων, ver. 28. Hengstenberg accounts for this circumlocution of the simpler imperf. by the emphasis laid on ἐρχόμενος as a term of the Messiah; comp. Matth. iii. 11: ὁ ὀπίσω μου ἐρχόμενος; xi. 3; John i. 15, 27, 30.—P. S.]

‡ [Comp. the lines of Göthe:

"*Wär' nicht das Auge sonnenhaft,*
Wie könnten wir das Licht erblicken?
Lebt' nicht in uns des Gottes eigne Kraft,
Wie könnt' uns Göttliches entzücken?"—P. S.]

* [There is no Scripture proof that ἴδια (*viz.*, δώματα, οἰκήματα) means the world, and ἴδιοι mankind in general; both expressions refer to Israel as the peculiar people of God, ἴδια to the nation as a whole, ἴδιοι to the individuals. George Campbell (on the Gospels), Alford and Barnes would understand τα ἴδια of Palestine or Judea, and οἱ ἴδιοι of its inhabitants.—P. S.].

in Israel (Erasmus, Calvin, *etc.*, Lücke, Meyer); yet of this advent considered as intended for mankind. Israel is God's own people in the special sense, Ex. xix. 5; Deut. vii. 6; Sirach xxiv. 7 ff. It is not, however, the historical New Testament coming of Christ in Israel, which is here spoken of. The expression *He came*, as denoting the historical moving of the Logos in the history of the world, determines us against the more general conception of the "own." Yet it must be kept well in mind, that in John particularly Israel stands not for itself alone, but as the medium for the entrance of Christ into the whole world. See chap. x. 16.

And his own people [οἱ ἴδιοι, comp. xiii. 1]—*i. e.*, the Jews. See Is. vi.; Matth. xiii.; John xii. 41; Acts vii.; xxviii. 25; Rom. ix. [The transfer of the relation of Jehovah to Israel as His peculiar people upon Christ, implies that, in the view of John, Christ was the Jehovah of the Old dispensation; comp. xii. 41; viii. 56.—P. S.]

[**Received him not**—οὐ παρέλαβον, stronger than οὐκ ἔγνω, which is said of the world in general, ver. 10. The fact that the Jews were the peculiar inheritance of Jehovah, doubled their guilt in rejecting the Messiah. Comp. the οὐκ ἠθελήσατε, Matth. xxiii. 37; also Isa. i. 3; Rom. x. 21; and John xii. 37. The negative expression here, as ver. 10 and ver. 5, reveals a holy grief on the part of John.* Remember the tears of pity which the Saviour shed over unbelieving Jerusalem.—P. S.]

Ver. 12. **But as many as received him**—[ὅσοι, *whosoever, whatsoever persons*, denotes the universality of Christ's benefit without distinction of race, nationality or condition.—P. S.] No contradiction of the preceding words. His own, His people, as a whole, received Him not, but individuals. See Gal. iii. and iv. The antithesis: οὐ παρέλαβον and ἔλαβον should be observed. The Jews should παραλαμβάνειν, take Him in addition to the Old Testament, receive Him in pursuance of the true traditions. This they did not. Thus others' receiving Him became the absolute λαμβάνειν, contrary to the outward, false tradition. Λαμβάνειν in John and Paul is a strong word, denoting the moral act of faith, comp. Rom. v. 11.

To them gave he power.—Opposed to the descent from Abraham and the relative sonship with God, of which the Jews boasted, John viii. Ἐξουσία is neither merely [the *possibility* (De Wette, Tholuck), nor the *ability* (Brückner, Heng., Godet),† nor] the *dignity* or *advantage*, (Erasmus, *etc.*), nor the *right*, or *privilege* (Meyer),* but the real power, the spiritual faculty (Lücke), and, at the same time, the real title. *Sonship* with God was *growing*, in its *formation-state*, in the Old Testament; there were only *incipient* sons of God, Gal. iv. 1, but there were such really, and progressively, according to the advancing inwardness and depth of the Old Testament faith. This sonship with God, too, is connected indeed with a *semen arcanum electorum et spiritualium* (contrary to Meyer, see ver. 9); but this must be understood neither in a Gnostic sense, nor in a Hegelian, but in a Johannean, John iii. 21. This incipient regeneration is also most certainly ethical, but not merely ethical; it is also substantial, though the antithesis between the eternal μονογενής and the regenerate τέκνα θεοῦ by all means remains perfect, even after the advance of the latter to υἱοὶ θεοῦ. The distinctions: ethical theogony in John (according to Hase), legal adoption in Paul; υἱοθεσία first appearing in the kingdom of the Messiah in the Synoptists (Meyer), are of little use; unless it may be said that John emphasizes the *ideal begetting*, Paul the *historical new creation*. The Messianic kingdom begins with the children of God, not they with it. [**To become**—γενέσθαι.—Christ *is* the eternal, only begotten Son of God by nature; men *become* children of God by regeneration or a celestial birth; comp. iii. 3; 1 John iii. 9; Gal. iii. 26; 1 Pet. i. 23. Alford thinks that τέκνα θεοῦ is a more comprehensive expression than υἱοὶ τ. θ., as it involves the whole generation and process of our spiritual life and our likeness to God (1 John v. 5–7), while the other brings out rather our adoption and hope of inheritance (Rom. viii. 14 ff.)—P. S.]

To them that believe in his name.—[Πιστεύουσιν, not πιστεύσασιν; faith being a continued act and habit of the children of God. Mark also the distinction between believing Christ, that He is, and believing *in* Christ, in His name, His revealed being, in His person, εἰς τὸ ὄνομα; the former is purely intellectual and historical, the latter is moral and implies trust in and appropriation of Christ as our Saviour. The same difference holds with regard to the existence of God, comp. James ii. 19: καὶ τὰ δαιμόνια πιστεύουσιν.—P. S.]—Not "ætiological" [*quippe qui credunt*, Meyer], but "explicative;" for faith is not the cause of the gift of Christ, but the organ, *causa instrumentalis* [the subjective condition]. The clause describes λαμβάνειν. Faith in the name of the Logos [εἰς τὸ ὄνομα αὐτοῦ] is faith in Christ, more definitely, in His name (Acts ii. 36; iii. 16; iv. 12); and this definiteness of faith, in the evangelical acknowledgment of the personal truth in Christ, makes it saving, makes it the medium of the saving power of Christ, because the name of Christ denotes the concentrated expression of His nature in His

---

* [Something of this feeling of sadness, in view of the ingratitude of the world to Christ, pervades the hymn of the noble Novalis:

Wenn alle untreu werden,
So bleib ich Der doch treu,"

especially the second stanza:

I could weep night and morning
That Thou hast died, and yet
So few will heed Thy warning,
So many Thee forget.
O loving and true-hearted,
How much for us didst Thou!
Yet is Thy fame departed,
And none regards it now.—P. S.]

† [Godet translates: "*elle (la Parole) les a mis en position de devenir enfants de Dieu*," and explains ἐξουσία to mean essentially the same with the Pauline υἱοθεσία, the filial relation to which man is restored by faith, yet not identical with regeneration, but a condition to it. "*Car Dieu ne peut communiquer sa propre vie par le πνεῦμα qu' à un homme avec qui il est reconcilié. . . . Mais une foie que l' adoption a eu lieu, la regénération doit suivre . . . et c 'est la le second privilège, resultant du premier, que saint Jean exprime dans ces mots: 'Devenir enfants de Dieu.'*" But the second is rather explanatory of the first (ἐξουσία).—P. S.]

* [In the fifth ed. Meyer explains: *er ermächtigte sie*, he empowered them. Comp. v. 27; xvii. 2.—P. S.]

gospel, in which truth and personal fact are one.* So the name of God is to be understood: the revelation of God as a personal introduction of Himself to us. So the devout of the old covenant believed in the name of the Logos, in the essential contents and subject of the Messianic promises, chap. ii. 23; iii. 18, *etc.*

Ver. 13. **Who were born, not of bloods.**—It is confusing to ask whether *οἵ* refers to *τέκνα ϑεοῦ* † or *πιστεύοντες*. The subject is in both cases the same. It is the *πιστεύοντες* in the historical sense who are spoken of. The Evangelist introduces the antithesis of the natural generation and regeneration, yet regarding the natural generation itself as advanced from the purely physical to the religiously consecrated theocratic generation. He first states the antithesis in general: *οὐκ ἐξ αἱμάτων, not of bloods.* Augustine explains the plural from the twofold sex of man and woman; ‡ Hölemann refers it to the successive begettings of the theocratic genealogy; Meyer finds that the plural is the same as the singular.§ We find in the plural a premonition of an ethical distinction of *αἵματα*. In ethical matters *αἷμα* and *αἷμα* are not one and the same. And this the succeeding climax proceeds to say. According to Augustine [Theophyl., Schott, Olshausen] and others, *θέλημα σαρκός* denotes woman in distinction from man (*ἀνδρός*). [This would require rather the disjunctive *οὔτε—οὔτε, neither—nor*, than the adjunctive *οὐδέ—οὐδέ, nor—nor yet;* besides *flesh* is never used synonymously with *woman.*—P. S.]‖ Mosheim distinguishes native Jews and proselytes; others, natural children and adopted (Starke);¶ Lücke takes *ἀνήρ* as no more than *ἄνθρωπος*;** Meyer regards the sentence as a rhetorical progress to greater definiteness: the term *σαρκός* referring to the sexual instinct, *ἀνδρός* to the procreative will of the man.†† If this distinction be followed up, we must come involuntarily upon the track of the true interpretation. The common sensual desire knows nothing of procreative will, yet it doubtless has its *ϑέλημα*. Baumgarten Crusius, therefore, rightly asserts that the progress is from the sensual to the most noble;* and we see here a progress from the sensual begettings of the heathen world to the theocratically consecrated begettings, which introduce a sacred theocratic genealogy (see Lange's *Leben Jesu* III. 558, and *Posit. Dogm.* pp. 514, 532). In this passage is reflected the Scripture doctrine of hereditary blessing. Of course the Evangelist tells us also that the consecrated births may indeed exhibit an approach to regeneration, and be the instrument of it, but that they are not able to effect it, and that regeneration, as a heavenly generation, forms a counterpart to the earthly.

[The difference between *αἵματα*, *σάρξ* and *ἀνήρ* is not very clear, but the conjunction *οὐδέ—οὐδέ* (*nor—nor yet*), as distinct from *οὔτε—οὔτε* (*neither—nor*, comp. Winer, p. 454 f., 7th ed.), indicates a rising climax from the general (*αἵματα*) to the particular, and here again from the lower and physical agency (*σάρξ*) to the higher and moral (*ἀνήρ*), although *θέλημα* is ascribed to both. In Matth. xvi. 17; 1 Cor. xv. 50; Eph. vi. 12; Gal. i. 16, *flesh and blood* together signify human nature in its weakness. In John iii. 6 we have the same contrast between the natural birth from the flesh, and the supernatural birth from the Spirit. The threefold denial of all human agency in regeneration gives emphasis to the affirmation of the divine agency, which is expressed by **but of God,** *ἀλλ' ἐκ ϑεοῦ.* This does not exclude mediate instrumentalities, through which, ordinarily, men are regenerated and converted. The affirmation may be analyzed so as to correspond to the three members of the negation: 1) *not of blood*, but *of the seed of God* (1 John iii. 9), which is the *word* of God (1 Pet. i. 23: *ἀναγεννημένοι . . . διὰ λόγου ζῶντος θεοῦ*; James i. 18: *ἀπεκύησεν ἡμᾶς λόγῳ ἀληθείας*); 2) *nor of the will of the flesh*, but *of the Spirit* (John iii. 6: *γεγεννημένον ἐκ τοῦ πνεύματος*); 3) nor yet *of the will of man*, but *of the will of God* (James i. 18: *βουληθεὶς ἀπεκύησεν ἡμᾶς ὁ θεός*; Eph. i. 5: *κατὰ τὴν εὐδοκίαν τοῦ ϑελήματος αὐτοῦ*). Bengel analyzes differently: 1) *ex cœlesti Patre;* 2) *ex amore divino;* 3) *ex Spiritu sancto.* Grace does not descend through the channel of nature in any form, but a new creative act of God is necessary in every regeneration. Barnes, in his notes on ver. 13, confounds regeneration with conversion. Regeneration is an act of God, and may take place in infancy (think of John the Baptist leaping in the mother's womb); conversion or change of mind (*μετάνοια*) is the act of man, by which, under the influence of the Holy Spirit, he turns, in conscious repentance and faith, from sin and Satan to God.—P. S.]

DOCTRINAL AND ETHICAL.

1. The fact that a man (John) was designated the messenger of God even, so to speak, in his origin, Luke i. 15 and 44, announced the coming of another, in whom no issue between birth and new birth should exist. Yet the distinction is as clear as the connection. John, *as man*, became the messenger of God; the Logos, as messenger of God, John iii. 31; 1 Cor. xv. 25, became man.

* [Arrowsmith, quoted by Ryle: "The word 'name' in the Scripture is often put for person. The receivers of Christ are said to believe on His name, because the direct object of their faith is the person of Christ. It is not the believing that Christ died for all, or for me, or for the elect, or any such proposition, that saveth. It is believing on Christ. The person, or name of Christ, is the object of faith."—P. S.]

† [So Meyer, *constructio κατὰ σύνεσιν*, as in 2 John 1; Philem. 10; Gal. iv. 19. But Lange is right.—P. S.]

‡ ["*Ex sanguinibus enim homines nascuntur maris et feminæ?*" *Tract.* II. § 14. Ewald translates the plural *aus Blut und Blut*, and explains: *durch blosse Misschung von Zeugungsstoffen.* Wordsworth: human commixtures.—P. S.]

§ [The plural usage of *αἷμα* in the sense of this passage occurs only in Euripides, *Ion* 705: *ἄλλων τραφεὶς ἀφ' αἱμάτων*, but often in the sense of *murder*, in the classics and in the LXX. See quotations in Meyer.—P. S.]

‖ [Augustine, *In Joh. Tract.* II. § 14, quotes Gen. ii. 22 and Eph. v. 28, 29 to show that *caro* may be used for *uxor;* but these passages (as also Jude 7) are not to the point. *Flesh* here means human nature, male and female. "What is born of the flesh is flesh," iii. 6.—P. S.]

¶ [So Albert Barnes; "*adopted* by a pious man." Without a shadow of proof. Ryle and Crosby refer "flesh" to man's *own*, and "man" to any *foreign* human agency. But this could have been much more clearly expressed.—P. S.]

** [So also Alford, who quotes, with Lücke, the Homeric *πατὴρ ἀνδρῶν τε θεῶν τε.* But Meyer denies that *ἀνήρ* is ever generalized into *ἄνθρωπος*, least of all here where the act of generation is spoken of.—P. S.]

†† [Similarly Godet: The will of the flesh is *la volonté dominée par l' imagination sensuelle*, the will of man *la volonté plus independante de la nature, la resolution virile.*—P. S.]

* [Nature (*αἵματα*), desire (*σάρξ*), will (*ἀνήρ*). But the difficulty is that *θέλημα* is used in the second as well as the third clause.—P. S.]

In John and Mary appear the two summits of the Old Testament spirit, the highest aspiration of human nature in the train of the Spirit of God; in Mary the summit of fervent, humble, receptive piety; in John the summit of energetic, prophetic piety in the official service of the law. Yet in them the higher spirit works from below upward under the drawing from above. In Christ the divine is before, and in Him the nisus is from above downward under the drawing of the human longing, the need of life and salvation below. The Baptist is strongly conscious of this distinction, Matth. iii. 11; Jno. iii. 31. And in accordance with this nature of Christ is the nature also of Christianity, the righteousness of faith in a righteous life.

2. *The same came for witness.* John the Baptist, the last, most distinct form of the Old Testament prophecy, and as such the witness of Christ in the history of the world, at the same time in his freedom from jealousy a witness to the Holy Ghost in the Old Testament. The death of John a martyrdom (witness-bearing) to his fidelity as forerunner.

3. Through John His noblest disciples came to believe, through them all succeeding disciples and Christians. (See Schleiermacher, *Predigten* I., p. 18.)

4. *He was not the Light.* An antithesis applying not only to the Old and New Testaments, but also to Christ, the fountain of light, and the Apostles and Christians, with the prophets, as receivers and bearers of the light.

5. *The true Light was coming.* The pre-Christian Advent. (1) Founded (*a*) in the nature of Christ: "The true Light, which lighteneth every man," *i. e.*, shines into him from within through the fundamental laws of personal, mental life, from without through nature and history; (*b*) in the nature of the world: Made by the Logos, standing by His presence. (2) Unfolding itself (a) *in a general invisible force:* The shining in the darkness, the lighting of every man; Christ's being in the world [primordial religion]; (*b*) *in historical theocratic form:* Education of Israel for His possession, and His coming to His own (the Old Testament religion in its development).

6. *Received Him not.* The obduracy, a self-estrangement, as well as a hostile bearing towards the admission of the yearning Householder. The obduracy of Israel in its historical development and completion; the great warning to the Christian world; warning, and alas, still more, Matth. xxiv. 38.

7. *That believe in His name.*—Respecting the name, see above in the exegesis of this passage. Appearance of the name of the Logos, in the more definite sense, with the Old Testament revelation (the Angel of the Lord and the Messiah). Faith in the objective Messiah was in the subject, *incipient* sonship. In the righteousness of faith lay a point of union between the word of God and the heart of man, a quickening germ of personal children of God, therefore the power to *become* sons. But this could be brought to decision and contemplation only by the historical appearance of Christ and by the redemption accomplished in Him. As the revelation of God strove from the first towards concentration in *the Name*, the making Himself personally, perfectly known, so true faith strives from the beginning after the concentrated receiving of a distinct personal life. Centripetal faith, living faith; centrifugal faith, dying or dead faith.

8. *Who were born not of blood.* The truth and the insufficiency of inherited privilege. The Biblical doctrine of covenant grace not yet duly received in the church. Its antagonism to the unchurchly conception of the relation between nature and spirit, and even to the Augustinian overstatement of original sin. Its antagonism to Pelagianism. (See *Posit. Dogmatik.*, p. 514 sqq.)

9. *But of God.* First the righteousness of faith present; then circumcision as the symbol of regeneration. The idea of real regeneration develops itself with the idea of the personal Messiah. Its development or genesis is reciprocal with that of repentance, faith, the experience of grace, in the saving process as it advances from the outward to the inward.

HOMILETICAL AND PRACTICAL.

John the Baptist, the Old Testament Evangelist of the Light. (1) In his mission and his name; (2) in his testimony and his work; (3) in his retirement and disappearance before the Light itself.—The Old Testament Advent of Christ: 1. In its ultimate basis (He was in the world); 2. in its historical manifestation (He came to His own); 3. in its earnest of victory (As many as received Him); 4. in its last attestation (There was a man).—John and Christ, or the personal manifestation of the saving Light: 1. John, the attester of the Light; 2. Christ, the attested Light.—The Old and New Testaments, one light of revelation: 1. The Old in the day-light of the New; 2. The New in the dawn-light of the Old.—John and Christ, or the kernel of revelation, personal life.—The Son of God as the nameless Name: 1. The namelessness of the name, (*a*) in the world in general, (*b*) in Israel in particular; 2. the name of the nameless, (*a*) in its silent development (He was in the world; He came), (*b*) in its great works.—The Advent of Christ in the world, mistaken and yet perceived: Mistaken (*a*) by the heathen, (*b*) by the Jews. Yet perceived (*a*) by the yearnings of the devout in all the world, (*b*) by the hope of the faithful in Israel.—The name of the Light, its complete personal revelation in Christ.—Christ the name: 1. The name of the life in the world; 2. the name of the light in mankind; 3. the name of the salvation in the children of God.—Those who are becoming believers, are becoming children of God.—The power to *become*, or the freedom of the spirit, the groundwork of the new birth and nature.—The being born of blood and born of God considered: 1. In their antagonism; 2. in their essential distinction; 3. in their congenial connection; 4. in the Mediator of their union.—He who believes in the pollution of birth according to the Scriptures, must believe also according to the Scriptures in the consecration of birth.—The beginnings of the regeneration in the Old Covenant, a fore-shadowing of the eternal new birth of Christ from heaven.

STARKE: Jesus alone had a fore-runner.—Like the aurora before the sun, so John, according to the word of prophecy, must bear himself before Christ.—HEDINGER: Teachers and all Christians are indeed lights also, in virtue of their divine calling, fellowship with God, and holy living, yet their main object is to bear witness of the light in Christ, to lead to it by precept and example.—O glorious nobility! to be born of God, His child and heir!—Behold, what manner of love! 1 John iii. 1.—OSIANDER: What is due to Christ alone, must not be attributed to any man.—The eternal light sends forth rays in the hearts of all men. He who is not enlightened, must ascribe it to himself and the dominion of darkness.—CANSTEIN: Noble family helps not to sonship and salvation, but only the being born anew of God.—MOSHEIM: Men in the state of nature are not children of God, and therefore have no right to salvation.

GERLACH, after Augustine: Corrupt men are called the world, because they love the world more than its Creator. By love we dwell in a thing with the heart, and we have therefore deserved to bear the name of that wherein we dwell by love.

HEUBNER: John must prepare the way for the reception of the Light.—The light must come gradually, else it blinds.—The nobility of the children of God is attained only through the Spirit, through birth from God, through a proper spiritual generation.

[Ver. 6. John the Baptist, the greatest of men before Christ, because he was nearest to Christ, and comprehended all the light of the preparatory revelations of Moses and the prophets.—Ver. 7. Every minister only a borrowed light to lead men to Christ, the true Light.—Ver. 8. Christ is the sun of the soul, the source of spiritual light, life and growth.—P. S.]

[Ver. 9. ARROWSMITH: Christ is the true Light: 1. The undeceiving Light, in opposition to all the false lights of the Gentiles; 2. The real Light, in opposition to ceremonial types and shadows; 3. The underived Light, in opposition to all borrowed light; 4. The supereminent Light, in opposition to all ordinary light.—Ver. 10. HENGSTENBERG: The creature should shout for joy, if its Creator comes to redeem it.—Ver. 11. It is disgraceful if the creature despises the creature; it is doubly disgraceful if the people of the Covenant despise the Lord of the Covenant.]

[Ver. 13. The new (celestial, divine) birth constitutes the true nobility of grace, as contrasted with the aristocracy of natural birth, the aristocracy of money, the aristocracy of merit, the aristocracy of fame.—Regeneration: 1. Its origin; 2. Its growth; 3. Its manifestation; 4. Its end (the final resurrection).—The children of God the salt of the earth, the light of the world, the benefactors of the race.—Comp. the admirable description of Christian life in the Epistle to Diognetus, ch. 5 and 6, composed soon after the Apostolic age. Christians in the world are there compared to the soul in the body: they are scattered through the world and dwell in the world, yet are not of the world; they are hated by the world, yet love and benefit it; they are imprisoned in the world, yet preserve it from corruption; they are sojourners in the perishing world, looking for an incorruptible dwelling in heaven.—P. S.]

THIRD SECTION.

The Incarnation of the Logos, the Appearance of the real Shekinah among the Faithful.

CHAP. I. 14–18.

(1) INCARNATION OF THE LOGOS, OR THE ABSOLUTELY NEW BIRTH. APPEARANCE OF THE REAL SHEKINAH, VER. 14. (2) TESTIMONY OF JOHN IN GENERAL, VER. 15. (3) EXPERIENCE OF BELIEVERS, OR GRACE, VER. 16. (4) ANTITHESIS BETWEEN MOSES AND CHRIST, THE LAW OF THE OLD TESTAMENT AND CHRISTIANITY, IN THEIR AUTHORITY AND WORK, VER. 17. (5) ANTITHESIS BETWEEN THE WHOLE OLD WORLD AND CHRIST IN THEIR RELATION TO GOD, VER. 18.

14 And the Word was made [became, ἐγένετο] flesh, and dwelt [sojourned, tabernacled, ἐσκήνωσεν] [1] among us, (and we beheld his glory [the real Shekinah], the glory
as of the [an] only-begotten of [from, παρά] the Father,) [*omit* parenthesis][2] full of
15 grace and truth. John bare [beareth][3] witness of him, and cried [crieth],[4] saying,
This was he of whom I spake [said], He that cometh after me [behind me] is pre-
16 ferred [hath come to be] before me; for he was before me [lit. first of me]. And [For][5]
of his fulness have all we received [did we all receive], and [even] grace for grace.
17 For the law was given by [through] Moses, (*but*) grace and truth came [came to pass]
18 by [through] Jesus Christ. No man hath seen God at any time [No one hath ever
seen God]; the only begotten Son [God],[6] which [who] is in [toward] the bosom

of the Father [of the nature of the Father and in his full confidence and service] he hath declared *him* [hath interpreted *all*].[7]

TEXTUAL AND GRAMMATICAL.

[1] Ver. 14. [Or, *pitched his tent;* Meyer, Ewald: *zeltete;* Godet: *a dressé sa tente.* The verb ἐσκήνωσεν (from σκηνή, *tent*), which John uses also of God's dwelling with His people on the new earth (Rev. xxi. 3), was chosen in allusion to the *Shekinah* (שְׁכִינָה, or שְׁכִינָא, a Rabbinical theological term from שָׁכַן, *to dwell*), *i. e.*, the indwelling or glorious presence of Jehovah in the holy of holies of the tabernacle and the temple, which typically pointed to the incarnation. This allusion is evident from the correspondence of the letters (Bengel: "*eædem literæ in* שְׁכִינָה *et* σκηνή"), and from the following ἐθεασάμεθα τὴν δόξαν αὐτοῦ. Comp. Ex. xxv. 8 (where Aquila, Symmachus and Theodotion translate שָׁכַנְתִּי by σκηνώσω); xl. 34; Lev. xxvi. 11, 12; Ezek. xxxvii. 27; Hagg. ii. 8; Apoc. vii. 15; xxi. 3. In the Apocryphal books the Shekinah was especially ascribed to the Sophia (Sir. xxiv. 8: ἐν Ἰακὼβ κατασκήνωσον), and the Logos. The humanity of Christ became the Shekinah of His divinity.—P. S.]

[2] Ver. 14.—[The parenthesis marked in this verse in the text. rec. appears to be, like the division of chapters and verses, only conventional; though it serves us the good purpose of showing the true reference of "full" (πλήρης) to "the Word" (ὁ λόγος) rather than to "glory" (δόξα), which could not be otherwise indicated in the English version. The clause itself is not properly parenthetical. See the Exegesis.—E. D. Y.]

[3] Ver. 15. [μαρτυρεῖ, present; the testimony of John goes on. Meyer: "*Vergegenwärtigung, als tönte das Zeugniss noch fort.*"—P. S.]

[4] Ver. 15. [The perfect κέκραγε likewise implies continuation of the action in its *effect.* Meyer: "*Das Perf. in gewöhnlicher, classischer, präsentischer Bedeutung.*" Alford: "the voice is still sounding." Κράζω (also used of Christ, vii. 28, 37; xii. 44) is an onomato-poëtic word, imitating the hoarse cry of the raven, like the German, *krächzen*, the English, *to croak;* here *to call aloud* with the confidence and solemnity of a herald. Bengel: "*Clamat Joh. cum fiducia et gaudio, uti magnum præconem decet.*"—P. S.]

[5] Ver. 16, in most codd. [א. B. C.* D. L. X], begins with ὅτι, instead of καί: *For* of his fulness, *etc.* Griesbach, Lachmann, Tischendorf. [Hengstenberg and Godet prefer καί, and conjecture that ὅτι was occasioned by the preceding and succeeding ὅτι.—P. S.]

[6] Ver. 18. B. C.* L. Codd. Sin. *et al.* read θεός for υἱός; probably from ver. 1. [So also Meyer.]

[This is the first important difference of reading which occurs in the Gospel of John, and which, on account of its theological character, deserves a fuller notice than it has received from Lange or any other commentator, except Alford, in his sixth edition. The ancient authorities are almost equally divided between θεός, the (an) Only-begotten *God*, and υἱός, the Only-begotten *Son.* A minor difference relates to the article which is omitted by most of the authorities favoring θεός. The reading θεός is supported by the two oldest MSS., the Sinaitic (which has ΘC, the usual abbreviation of θεός, *a prima manu*, but which, in this very verse, by omitting the words ὁ ὢν before εἰς τὸν κόλπον, betrays the carelessness of the transcriber), and the Vatican (both from the 4th century), also by C.* L.; the Syr. Peshito; Clemens Alex. (once or twice), Excerpta Theodoti (a full quotation), Epiphanius (three times), the Second Synod of Ancyra, Didymus of Alex. (twice). To this must be added that Gregory of Nyssa and other Greek fathers repeatedly call Christ ὁ μονογενὴς θεός, where they do not quote from John i. 18. The reading υἱός is favored by a larger number of manuscripts, A. (Cod. Alex. of the 5th cent.), C.*** (the Ephræm MS. corrected) X. Δ. and nearly all other MSS.; the Curetonian Syriac Vers., the Lat. Vers. (Itala and Vulgata); Tertullian (*Adv. Prax.* c. 15), who is older by at least 120 years than the oldest known MSS., Eusebius (in six passages, in one, however, with the significant addition ἡ μονογενὴς θεός after ὁ μονογενὴς υἱός, for which reason Tregelles claims him for θεός, though unjustly; see Abbot, *Bibl. Sacra*, 1861, p. 859), Athanasius (four times), Chrysostom (eight times), Ambrose, Augustine and other fathers, also the emperor Julian (twice). Hilary, in seven places, supports *Filius*, but in one (*De Trin.*, XII. 24) he reads "unigenitus *Deus* in sinu Patris." The evidence from Irenæus, Origen, Basil and Cyril of Alexandria is contradictory and uncertain. Irenæus, the oldest witness in this case (A. D. 170), quotes the passage three times, twice in favor of *Filius* (*Adv. hær.* IV. c. 20, § 6), or *Filius Dei* (III. 11, 6), once in favor of *Deus* (IV. 20, 11: "unigenitus *Deus*, qui est in sinu Patris, ipse enarravit"). Origen reads θεός twice (*In Joh.* Tom. II. c. 29; XXXII. c. 13, Opp. ed. Delarue IV. p. 89 and 433), υἱός once (*Contr. Cels.* l. II. c. 71, Opp. I. p. 440, in a full quotation), besides υἱὸς τοῦ θεοῦ once (*In Joh.* Tom. VI. 2, Opp. IV. 102, with a different reading, υἱὸς θεός), and *Unigenitus Dei Filius* once (in Rufinus' version of Com. on Cant. l. IV. Opp. III. 91). Cyril of Alexandria, as edited by Aubert, has υἱός three times, θεός four times, and favors the latter in his Commentary, as printed. For a fuller statement of patristic testimonies see an elaborate article of Ezra Abbot (the learned librarian of Harvard University) in the Andover *Bibliotheca Sacra* for Oct. 1861, pp. 840–872. I have verified several of his quotations. He has corrected many errors of former critics and disproved the assertion of Tregelles that θεός is "the ancient reading of the Fathers *generally.*" The authorities for υἱός cover a much larger territory than those for θεός, which seem to be almost confined to Egypt. For *internal* reasons, θεός, being the more difficult reading, has the preference, according to the usual canon; for μονογενής naturally suggested υἱός, while the designation of Christ as "*the only begotten God,*" stands isolated in the Bible. On the other hand, a change of the abridged form YC to ΘC, which is usual in the uncial MSS., was as easy as the change from the latter to the former. There is moreover an inherent propriety for the use of υἱός in connection with μονογενής and with the mention of the *Father;* while θεός is hardly in place immediately after θεόν at the beginning of the verse, and introduces a harshness without a parallel in the style of John. The Scripture argument for the Divinity of Christ is strong enough, even from the first verse of the Prologue, without the reading θεός in ver. 18. In view of all the data before us, I see no sufficient reason here to depart from the received text. Tregelles, Westcott and Hort adopt θεός (without the article); Abbot, Alford, Tischend. (ed. VIII.) retain υἱός. Lachmann likewise reads υἱός, but before the authorities in favor of θεός were fully known. Comp. on this subject, besides Tregelles and Tischend. (ed. VIII., Vol. I., p. 745), especially the article of Ezra Abbot already quoted, and a long note in the 6th ed. of Alford (pp. 689–691).—P. S.]

[7] Ver. 18. [On the meaning of ἐξηγήσατο see the last foot note, p. 78. Christ is the true Exegete or Expounder of God.—P. S.]

EXEGETICAL AND CRITICAL.

[Ver. 14 contains the central idea of the Prologue, the Gospel, and the system of Christianity, yea, the central idea of the whole history of the world; for ancient history before the incarnation was a preparation for Christ as the fulfilment of all types, prophecies and nobler aspirations of men; history after that event is subservient to the spread and triumph of Christianity till Christ be all in all. The theology of John is Christological throughout (comp. 1 John iv. 2, 3); that of Paul, in the Romans and Galatians, is anthropological and soteriological, but the Colossians and Philippians are likewise Christological, and in 1 Tim. iii. 16 Paul makes the incarnation the central fact of our religion. But the idea of the incarnation, the great mystery of godliness, should not be confined to the mere birth of Christ, but extended to His whole divine human life, death and resurrection; it is "God manifest in the flesh." Bengel discovers a threefold antithetic correspondence between vers. 1 and 4:

THE WORD

Was in the beginning	*became*
God	*flesh*
With God.	and dwelt *among us.*—P. S.]

Ver. 14. **And.**—This καί has been explained in very different ways: as equivalent, for exam-

ple, to γάρ (for)* or οὖν (therefore),† or as signifying the condition of Christ's becoming man. But it denotes an actual historical advance;‡ not, however, as De Wette takes it, upon ver. 9, but, as Lücke, upon ver. 11. First, the universal advent was spoken of; then the theocratical advent in the Old Testament; now, after indicating the transitional distinction of consecrated human birth and birth from God, which were continually approaching each other, the Evangelist comes to the point of incarnation, where birth and new or divine birth coincide.

The Word became flesh.—In this finishing sentence the subject is again named. Not a life only, or a light, from the Logos, was made flesh, but the whole Logos as Life and Light (see Col. i. 19; ii. 9). He became σάρξ; the strongest expression for becoming veritable man.

[This grand sentence: ὁ λόγος σὰρξ ἐγένετο, stands alone in the Bible; but the same idea in somewhat different forms of expression occurs repeatedly, *viz.:* 1 John iv. 2 (ἐν σαρκὶ ἐληλυθώς, Christ having come in the flesh); 1 Tim. iii. 16 (ἐφανερώθη ἐν σαρκί, God was manifested in the flesh); Rom. i. 3 (γενόμενος ἐκ σπέρματος Δαυεὶδ κατὰ σάρκα, born from the seed of David according to the flesh); viii. 3 (ἐν ὁμοιώματι σαρκὸς ἁμαρτίας, in the likeness of sinful flesh); Phil. ii. 7 (ἐν ὁμοιώματι ἀνθρώπων γενόμενος, being made in the likeness of men); Heb. ii. 14 (where it is said that Christ, like other men, partook of αἵματος καὶ σαρκός, of blood and flesh). *Flesh* (σάρξ) is a strong Hebraizing term (בָּשָׂר) for *human nature* in its weakness, frailty and mortality. Comp. the English, *mortal* (the German, *der Sterbliche*), for *man.* When used of man, the idea of *moral* weakness or sinfulness is also often implied, but not necessarily. In the passages where it is ascribed to Christ, sin must be excluded in view of the unanimous testimony of the Apostles to the sinlessness of Jesus. The term is more comprehensive than *body* (σῶμα), which is used in distinction from soul (ψυχή) and spirit (νοῦς or πνεῦμα), while *flesh* sometimes includes both; it is more concrete and emphatic than *man* (ἄνθρωπος), and expresses more strongly the infinite condescension of the Logos, the identity of His human nature with our own, and the universalness of His manhood. Yet it is as correct to speak of Christ's becoming *man* (ἐνανθρώπησις, *Menschwerdung*) as of His becoming *flesh* (ἐνσάρκωσις, *incarnatio, incarnation, Fleischwerdung*). The Logos assumed, not an individual man or a single human personality, but human nature into union with His præ-existent divine personality. He moreover assumed human nature, not apparently and transiently (according to the Gnostic Docetic view), but really and permanently; nor partially (as Apollinaris taught), but totally, with all its essential constituents as created by God, body, soul and spirit. For Christ everywhere appears as a full man (comp. viii. 40: "Ye seek to kill *me, a man* who," *etc.*), and He is emphatically called "the Son of Man;" John speaks expressly of the soul (ψυχή) of Christ, xii. 27, and of His spirit (πνεῦμα), xi. 33; xiii. 21; xix. 30; comp. Matth. xxvii. 50. In the O. T., too, *flesh* often includes the moral or spiritual nature of man, comp. Lev. xvii. 11; Deut. xii. 15; Job xii. 10. It is not the flesh as opposed to the *spirit,* that is here intended, but human nature, as distinct from the *divine.* The flesh is the outward tabernacle and the visible representative of the whole man to our senses.* Finally Christ assumed human nature, not in its primitive state of innocence, but in its fallen, suffering, mortal state, yet without sin (which does not originally and necessarily belong to man); for He came to save this fallen nature. He was subject to temptation, or temptable, and was perfected through suffering (Hebr. ii. 14-18; iv. 15), but He was neither σαρκικός (Rom. vii. 14), nor ψυκικός (1 Cor. ii. 14). He appeared not "in the flesh of sin," but only "in the *likeness* of the flesh of sin" (Rom. viii. 2). He bore all the consequences of sin without a share of personal sin and guilt. This amazing miracle of His love is best expressed by the term: The Logos became *flesh.*† Comp. 2 Cor. viii. 9: "Ye know the grace of our Lord Jesus Christ that, though He was rich, yet for your sakes He became poor, that ye by His poverty might become rich." At His second advent Christ will appear as man indeed, yet no more in the likeness of sinful flesh, nor in weakness and poverty, but in glory and immortality (comp. Heb. ix. 28, χωρὶς ἁμαρτίας). P. S.]

It imputes a Judaistic [and Apollinarian] nonsense to the Evangelist, to represent him as saying that the Logos took only the human σάρξ, and not a reasonable human soul (Praxeas, Köstlin, Zeller‡). The evidence of the contrary lies not only in the impossibility of conceiving a human σάρξ without ψυχή, and such a ψυχή without πνεῦμα (see Meyer, p. 65), but especially in the Old Testament usage of the term *flesh* to denote human nature (Is. xl.); to say nothing of John's express designation of the ψυχή of Christ in ch. xii. 27, and the πνεῦμα in ch. xi. 33; xiii. 21; xix. 30. But while the half-Baur school thus construes John's statement of the incarnation Judaistically, Hilgenfeld construes it Gnostically: giving Christ (according to the Valentinian system) a real σάρξ, indeed, but such as was exalted above material limitations. Meyer (against Frommann and others) contests without good reason the anti-Docetic force of this expres-

* [So Chrysostom, Theophyl., Grotius, Lampe.]

† [So Bleek.]

‡ [So Meyer: "*einfach die Rede fortführend, wie alle καί des Prologs.*" Here the copula carries the reader to the highest pinnacle of contemplation. So far we may say with Godet that it is emphatic, but cannot adopt his translation: *Yea, indeed.*—P. S.]

* [Apollinaris had no more right to appeal to this passage for his assertion that Christ had no rational soul, its place being supplied by the divine Logos, than he had a right to draw the same inference from all those passages where *man* is called *flesh.* On the Apollinarian Christology comp. my *Church History,* Vol. III., pp. 708 ff.—P. S.]

† [Some of the ablest commentators urge this point. Calvin: "*Eo usque se Filius Dei submisit, ut carnem istam tot miseriis obnoxiam susciperet.*" Hengstenberg, I. p. 49, quotes at length from Luther to the same effect, and says: "There is a wealth of comfort in this fact, a balm for the poor, terrified conscience." Ewald, p. 127, makes these striking remarks: "Of all the words which express human nature, John chooses the meanest and most contemptible, *viz.: flesh,* which, in the O. T., denotes the lower, perishing, corruptible part of man; but even this the Logos did not despise, and thus He became man in the fullest sense of the term."—P. S.]

‡ [The same view is ascribed to John by Pfleiderer in Hilgenfeld's *Zeitschrift* for 1866, p. 260, and by Scholten of Leyden.—P. S.]

sion; though certainly the main force of it is rather anti-Gnostic; for the incipient Gnosticism first asserted an external connection of *σάρξ* and *λόγος*, against which the verb *ἐγένετο* would be more emphatic than the substantive *σάρξ*.

With the idea of the *σάρξ* comes also the idea of passibility, but by no means the idea of any weakness of the flesh arising from sin; for Scripture recognizes the flesh in three stages: (1) pure in paradise; (2) weakened by sin; (3) sanctified by the Spirit; and the Logos could become flesh only in the latter sense.

All this carries in it the antithesis between His incarnation and His eternal, immaterial existence; yet neither in the sense of Pantheism, which makes His incarnation an accident (Baur), nor in the sense of the mediæval scholasticism, which sees in it, even as incarnation, a humiliation of the Logos even into an incongruous, heterogeneous nature. The historical humiliation of Christ coincides indeed with His historical incarnation; yet the two are to be distinguished.

The supernatural birth of Christ is unquestionably implied in this passage, in that the origin of Christ as God-Man stands in opposition to the natural births previously described, all which, as such, needed to be completed by the birth from God (contra Meyer).

[**Became**, *ἐγένετο*.—Not *was*, *ἦν*, as in ver. 1, nor *ἐγένετο ἄνθρωπος*, as is said of John, ver. 6, who had no existence before his birth, but the præ-existent, personal Logos became flesh.* Comp. LXX., Gen. ii. 7: *ἐγένετο ὁ ἄνθρωπος εἰς ψυχὴν ζῶσαν*. The word denotes a single and completed act. The Logos was not *converted* or *changed* into flesh, nor simply *associated* with flesh, but endued with human nature, which He assumed once for all into personal and perpetual union with Him.† The Logos was henceforth Christ Jesus, the *God-Man* (*θεάνθρωπος*), and this not only for a transient purpose, but He continues so forever.—P. S.]

Tabernacled among us.—God dwelt as Jehovah in Israel, hidden in the most holy place of the tabernacle (*σκηνή*); now in the Logos He has tabernacled (*ἐσκήνωσεν*) among the disciples in the midst of the people, thus making the disciples themselves His tabernacle.‡ (On *among us*, *ἐν ἡμῖν*, see ver. 16. The disciples and witnesses of Christ are meant, but as the central point of the people, and of all mankind). The expression evidently alludes to the Old Testament dwelling of God in Israel. The idea of that dwelling of Jehovah in the holy tabernacle (Ex. xxv. 8; xxix. 45) is enlarged even in the prophets (Is. iv. 5; lvii. 15). Now the Lord has taken His dwelling among His own people themselves. This reference is confirmed by what follows. "The Targums likewise represent the Word (מימרא) as the Shekinah (שכינא), and the Messiah as the manifestation of the latter" (Meyer).*

And we beheld his glory.—Meyer rightly maintains, against Lücke, De Wette and Tholuck, that this main thought cannot be read as a parenthesis. Such reading has been occasioned by the nominative *πλήρης*† *χάριτος*, at the close of the verse, referring to *λόγος*. According to Baumgarten-Crusius and Meyer [Brückner, Alford], this nominative refers, by a solecism, to *αὐτοῦ*, and serves to give more independent prominence to the descriptive clause. But the clause may also be read as a declaration prompted by the contemplation; *ἦν* being understood.‡

We beheld.—The beholding has faith for its organ; it is not a merely outward vision, still less merely inward; nor does it perceive the glory of Christ only in single miracles or in a transfiguration, but in His whole life (comp. 1 John i. 1). [*Θεάομαι* moreover is richer than *ὁράω*, and means properly to behold or contemplate with admiration and delight. John speaks here in the name of all the Apostles and eye-witnesses of the life of Christ. The plural adds force to the statement, as in xxi. 24; 1 John i. 1; 2 Pet. i. 16. Faith lifts the veil of Christ's humanity and worships His divine glory, while to unbelief He is a mere man. Hengstenberg refers to several passages from Isaiah (xl. 5; lxvi. 2, 18), in which the beholding of the glory of Jehovah is promised. John recognized Jehovah in the incarnate Logos (xii. 41).—P. S.]

His glory, *δόξα*, כָּבוֹד.—The real appearances of the divine glory in the Old Testament must be distinguished from its symbolical signs. Its signs are the cloud and tempest on Sinai, the pillar of smoke and the pillar of fire, the cherubim over the ark of the covenant in the most holy place. Its real manifestations are, from the nature of the Old Testament, transient, and given in visions; manifestations of the Angel of the Lord (see above), or of the Lord Himself attended by a host of angels, Dan. vii. The manifestation of the Angel of the Lord is, in its nature, connected with the manifestation of His glory. The later Jewish theology has designated these manifestations as the *Shekinah*.§ In Christ the Shekinah appears in full reality.

* [Bengel remarks that nowhere in the whole range of literature is the difference of the verbs *εἰμί* and *γίγνομαι* more studiously observed than in the Prologue of John.—P. S.]

† [Godet, p. 194, puts a strained view of the *κένωσις* into *ἐγένετο*, and makes it to mean that the Logos gave up His divine mode of existence.—P. S.]

‡ [Or rather the humanity of Christ. His body (comp. ii. 19, 21) was the *σκηνή*, the tabernacle, the temple of God, in which He revealed His presence, the fulness of His grace and truth. The Apostles and the believers generally (comp. ver. 12, *ὅσοι ἔλαβον αὐτόν*) are the spectators and worshippers in this sanctuary.—P. S.]

* [Hengstenberg: "The indwelling of God among His people, which is implied in the idea of the people of God, was merely a shadow of the temple, and has attained its full truth only in Christ." Bengel sees in the verb *σκηνόω* an allusion rather to the *transitory* abode of Christ on earth: "*habitavit, ut in tabernaculo, vere, nec diu, spectaculum sui præbens.*" So also Godet. But this is certainly not applicable to God's dwelling with His people on the new earth, Apoc. xxi. 3. Ewald, on the contrary, urges the idea of a longer abode, which is equally untenable. The Apostle has no reference to time, but to the reality of God's abode with man in His incarnate Son as compared with the shadowy indwelling in the old tabernacle and temple. This sojourning implies community of life, as to say: We have eaten together, slept under the same tent, travelled together.—P. S.]

† [This is the proper reading, while *πλήρη*, *plenam*, is conformed to *δόξαν*, *πλήρου*, *pleni*, to *αὐτοῦ*.—P. S.]

‡ [Winer, *Gramm.*, p. 524 (7th Germ. ed.), likewise regards the comprehensive *πλήρης χαρ. κ. ἀλ.* as grammatically independent, and refers to Phil. iii. 19; Mark xii. 40. Hengstenberg views these words as an abridged relative sentence: (*who is*) full, *etc.*; comp. Apoc. i. 5. But even this supplement is not necessary. Ewald, repeating the main subject, well translates: *Er, voll Gnade und Wahrheit.*—P. S.

§ [שְׁכִינָה or שְׁכִינָא (from שָׁכַן, *to dwell*) does not occur in the O. T. Scriptures, and signifies the glorious presence of God with His people. Buxtorf (*Lexicon Chald., Talmud. et Rabbin.*, ed. Bas. 1640, p. 2394) gives the following definition

[We must distinguish four stages of this glory: 1) the præ-existent divine glory of the Logos with the Father, xvii. 5; 2) the preparatory shadowy manifestation of His glory in the Old Testament, as seen by the prophetic eye of Isaiah, xii. 41; 3) its visible revelation in human form in the life and work of the *incarnate* Word, which shone from every miracle, ii. 11; 4) the final and perfect manifestation of His *divine-human* glory in eternity in which the believers will share, xvii. 24.—P. S.]

When Meyer, with Hofmann (*Schriftbew.* II. 1, p. 21), makes the incarnation of Christ itself equivalent to His humiliation, and so conceives even *theanthropic* existence as distinct from simple divine, he has no Scripture for it, either in ch. xii. 41; xvii. 5, 22, 24, or in Phil. ii. 6. Unquestionably the human *δόξα* of Christ in His earthly life was to be relatively conceived; but only (1) in that He entered into the historical conditions of humanity, especially into subjection to the law, (2) in that the life of the first man waited in Him for its completion in the higher, imperishable manifestation of the second.

The glory [emphatically repeated] **as of an only begotten** [*δ ό ξ α ν ὡ ς μ ο ν ο γ ε ν ο ῦ ς π α ρ ὰ π α τ ρ ό ς*].—A closer description of the *δόξα*. It was alone in its kind, and could be characterized only thus: as of the only begotten. The *ὡς* expresses literally not the reality (Euthym. Zigabenus: *ὄντως*), but in similitude, the idea of the only begotten, to which the appearance of Christ corresponded, while assuredly it first awakened that idea and brought it to view.* Only the *μ ο ν ο γ ε ν ή ς* could manifest Himself so (ch. i. 18; iii. 16, 18; 1 John iv. 9).† That John has the term from Christ Himself, is shown by ch. iii. 16, 18. Paul's *πρωτότοκος*, *first begotten* [Col. i. 15; Heb. i. 6], is a parallel. Both terms denote not only the trinitarian relation of the Son of God, but also His theanthropic relation. In the expression of John, however, the incommunicable relation of Christ to God predominates; in that of Paul, His incommunicable relation to the world. In the one, the ontological idea of the Trinity rules; in the other, the economic and soteriological. The notion of the *only begotten* is closely akin to that of the *beloved* (*ἀγαπητός*), not identical with it as Kuinoel holds. The word denotes indeed, according to Meyer, the *only* begotten; but it thereby makes Christ also the *peculiarly* begotten (Tholuck), who is the principle of all other births and regenerations.* The reference of *μονογενοῦς* to *δόξα* (Erasmus and others) is wholly without support.

From the Father [belongs to *μονογενοῦς*, not to *δόξαν*].—Origen: *ἐκ τῆς οὐσίας τοῦ πατρός*. His origin and issue is from the essence of the Father. His coming forth from the Father (ch. vi. 46; vii. 29; xvi. 27) does not exclude, however, His continuance in the heaven of the Father (ch. iii. 13; comp. ch. i. 18). His human relations do not supersede His divine.

Full of grace and truth.—Comp. ver. 17. The result of the beholding, uttered in an exclamation of astonishment, expressing the main forms in which the *δόξα* was seen in Him. He was full of grace and truth. Not only did He seem all grace and truth, but grace and truth seemed concentrated in Him. And this was His glory, for grace and truth are the main attributes of Jehovah in the Old Testament, since the Messianic spirit recognized Him as pre-eminently the God of redemption (חֶסֶד וֶאֱמֶת [in the LXX.: *πολυέλεος καὶ ἀληθινός*], Ex. xxxiv. 6; Ps. xxv. 10; xxxvi. 6). This reference to the Old Testament is groundlessly doubted by Meyer;* for though אֱמֶת denotes also faithfulness, yet faithfulness and truth are one in the divine nature; and the rendering of חֶסֶד by *ἔλεος* in the Septuagint decides nothing, since *ἔλεος* finds its more precise equivalent in רַחֲמִים. But Meyer well observes that *ἀλήθεια* answers to the light-nature (*φῶς*), *χάρις* to the life-nature (*ζωή*) of the Logos. Of course the life is as much concerned in the truth of Christ, as the light in the grace; the latter notions are more soteriologically concrete, than the former. Christ, as absolute redemption, was pure grace; as absolute revelation, pure truth. [Christ is the personal Truth, xiv. 6, and is in the Apoc. called the *ἀληθινός*, iii. 7; xix. 11, is whom there is a perfect har-

---

of it: *habitatio, cohabitatio. In specie dicitur de præsentia, gloria et majestate divina aut Divinitate, quando dicitur hominibus esse præsens, aut cum eis conversari, auxilio suo, gratia et salutari præsentia adesse. Communiter explicatur, gloria vel majestas divina, divinitas gloriosa.*" In the same sense John uses *σκηνή* in Apoc. xxi. 3: *ἰδοὺ ἡ σ κ η ν ὴ τοῦ θεοῦ μετὰ τῶν ἀνθρώπων, καὶ σ κ η ν ώ σ ε ι μετ' αὐτῶν, καὶ αὐτοὶ λαὸς αὐτοῦ ἔσονται, καὶ αὐτὸς ὁ θεὸς ἔσται μετ' αὐτῶν, θεὸς αὐτῶν.* (Comp. TEXT. NOTE, 1.)—P. S]

* ['Ως is also here a particle of comparison, not of confirmation (like the falsely so-called Hebrew כְּ *veritatis*); but the comparison here is not between similar things, but between the fact and the idea, the reality and the expectation: as might be expected from one that is the only begotten. Hence the absence of the article before *μονογενοῦ*. The reality is implied as the basis of the comparison (against Alford).—P. S.]

† [John alone uses *μονογενής* of Christ, namely, in the five passages above referred to. Besides, the term occurs four times of human sons, three times in Luke (vii. 12; viii. 42; ix. 38) and once in the Hebrews (xi. 17). The term is called figurative, but it is more correct to say that all earthly relationships of fathers and filial affection are a figure and reflection of the eternal Fatherhood of God and the eternal Sonship of Christ. Comp. Eph. iii. 14, 15: "The Father of our Lord Jesus Christ, from whom the whole family in heaven and earth is named." I hold with Lange that John learned the word directly from Christ. Lampe and Hengstenberg derive the appellation from Zech. xii. 10, where the Messiah is *compared* to an only begotten (יָחִיד):

"And they have looked unto me whom they pierced,
And they have mourned over it,
Like a mourning over *the only One*—(הַיָּחִיד, LXX.: *ἀγαπητόν*; Vulg.: *unigenitum*).
And they have been in bitterness for it,
Like a bitterness over *the first-born*—(הַבְּכוֹר, LXX.): *ἐπὶ τῷ πρωτοτόκῳ*.—P. S.]

* [The term refers back to *τέκνα θεοῦ*, ver. 12, and marks the difference between Christ and the believers: 1) He is the only Son in a sense in which there is no other; they are many; 2) He is Son from eternity; they become children in time; 3) He is Son by nature; they are made sons by grace and by adoption; 4) He is of the same essence with the Father; they are of a different substance; in other words, His is a metaphysical, primitive and co-essential, theirs only an ethical and derived, sonship. The idea of generation, as Meyer correctly remarks, is implied in the very term *μονογενής*. Origen explains *μονογενής*=*ἐκ τῆς οὐσίας τοῦ πατρός*. This leads logically to the Nicene dogma of the homoousia and the eternal generation, *i. e.*, the eternal communion of love between the Father and the Son. (Comp. John xvii. 24.) Luther says: God has many children, but only one only begotten Son, through whom all things and all other children were made. —P. S.]

† [But defended by Hengstenberg, who sees here a new proof for the identity of Christ with the revealed Jehovah of the O. T. Grace and truth appear here as personal attributes, as in Ex. xxxiv. 6; while in ver. 17, as in Mich. vii. 20, they appear as gifts which Christ bestows.—P. S.]

mony between appearance and reality, claim and being, promise and fulfilment.—P. S.]

Ver. 15. **John beareth witness of him.**—Having described the advent of Christ to its consummation in the incarnation, the Evangelist comes to the testimony of John concerning Christ. He first introduced John's mission to bear witness of Christ, ver. 6; now he comes to his actual testimony concerning Christ, and that as a testimony even to His præ-existence and His higher nature. Afterwards follows the testimony of the Baptist concerning the Messianic (ver. 19) and the soteriological (ver. 29 sqq.) character of Jesus.

Beareth witness.—Present. John's testimony is perpetually living, active and valid. Its continued validity in the present rests upon the past fact that he cried only in Israel, and uttered what he had to say of Christ (κέκραγε λέγων). Hence Christ could appeal to his testimony, ch. v. 33; Matth. xxi. 24. Κράζειν, elsewhere also, ch. vii. 28, 37, *etc.*, for loud public proclamation. There is no reason for taking the perfect in a present sense. [Comp. TEXT. NOTES 3 and 4.—P. S.]

This was he of whom I said.—Οὗτος ἦν. He it *was.* Not because John is conceived as speaking in the present. In the testimony of John two periods must be distinguished: before and after the baptism of Jesus. Before the baptism, he preached the Messiah in His higher characters, as approaching, but knew not yet the Messianic individual; after the baptism he could point to Jesus and say: *This was He*, of whom I declared that præ-existence. Thus this second stage of his testimony is here in hand.

He that cometh after me.—[Ὁ ὀπίσω μου ἐρχόμενος, ἔμπροσθέν μου γέγονεν. A pithy oxymoron exciting attention and reflection, repeated vers. 27 and 30, and probably suggested by the prophetic passage, Mal. iii. 2: "Lo, I am sending My messenger, and he hath prepared a way before Me." The following words, ὅτι πρῶτός μου ἦν, which must be referred to the præ-existence of Christ (comp. ἦν, vers. 1, 9, 10), not to the superiority of rank (which would require ἐστί), contain the clue to the enigmatic and paradoxical sentence. The meaning may be thus explained: My successor (in time) has become (or has come to be) my predecessor (in rank); for He is before me (even in time), being absolutely the first, *viz.:* the eternal Son of God; while I am only a man born in time and sent to prepare the way for Him.—P. S.]

"He that comes after me, has come before me." Meyer.* But it means: *was made, has become* (γέγονε) before me. John appeared before Christ as His fore-runner and herald; as to his progressive approach in His Old Testament advent, Christ was before him. *His coming forth* pervaded the Old Testament, and was the impelling power and cause of all prophecy, even the prophecy of John. And this earlier coming had its ground in His earlier (absolutely early, eternal) existence; hence ὅτι πρῶτός μου ἦν. These are, indeed, primarily antitheses of time. But the designation of the one coming after, as being before, implies at the same time a deeper and higher principle of life. According to Aristotle, the *posterius* in the real development is the *prius* in the idea or the value of the life. This is true of man in relation to the animal world, of the New Testament in relation to the Old, of Christ in relation to the Baptist. The ἐντιμότερός μου ἐστί of Chrysostom, therefore, is involved in the clause; while Meyer is right, against Lücke, Tholuck and others, in not taking this for its primary sense. The ἔμπροσθέν μου γέγονεν, of course, means not *was* before me (Luther and others), but: *has become* [or *come to be*] before me (against Meyer). Commentators have not been able to reconcile themselves to this γέγονεν, because they have not yet fairly reconciled themselves to the Old Testament incarnation of Christ. Hence Meyer: it is equal to προέρχεσθαι; Luthardt: He who at first came after me, as if He were my disciple, is since come before me, that is, become my master. Baumgarten-Crusius: of the ideal præ-existence of Christ in the divine counsels. This interpretation lies in the right direction, but misses the fact that the præ-existence of the Logos was personal and real, and that the ideal præ-existence of the God-Man was from the first dynamically real, the power of the creation, the central force and the core of the Old Testament (the "*root*" of Isaiah), and in Israel was in a continual process of incarnation, which was objectively represented beforehand in the Angel of the Lord.

For he was before me [ὅτι πρῶτός μου ἦν].—The eternal præ-existence of Christ is the ground of His theocratic manifestation. Here again Meyer [on account of the ἦν] emphasizes the temporal sense, against the reference of the πρῶτος to rank [which would require ἐστίν], contrary to Chrysostom, Erasmus [Beza, Calvin, Grotius] and many others. He would take the merely temporal conception (*i. e.*, the præ-existence of the Logos); hence πρῶτος in the sense of πρότερος. The comparative, however, could hardly stand here. Such præ-existence itself involves the higher, even divine dignity.*

Meyer justly holds, against Strauss [De Wette, Scholten] and others, that the Baptist could certainly have from Mal. iii. 1; Is. vi. 1 ff. and Dan. vii. 13 ff., the idea of the præ-existence of Christ, which even the Rabbins attested. [Besides, we must assume a special revelation given to John at the baptism of Christ, i. 33.—P. S.]

Ver. 16. **For** [text. rec.: **And**] **of his fulness did we all receive.**—Undoubtedly the testimony of the Baptist continued, as Origen,†

---

* ["*Der hinter mir her Kommende ist mir zuvorgekommen.*" Meyer, like Origen, takes both adverbs in a temporal (or rather local sense; time being represented here in the form of space). So does Hengstenberg: *Der nach mir kommt ist mir vorangegangen.* Godet: *Celui qui vient après moi, m'a précédé.* The objection to this interpretation is that it makes ὅτι πρῶτός μου ἦν a mere repetition. Hence most commentators (Chrys., Lücke, Thol., Olsh., De Wette, Alf.) refer ὀπίσω to time, and ἔμπροσθεν to rank. So also the E. V: "He that cometh after me is preferred (*i. e.*, is advanced) before me." John's preparatory office decreased before the rising glory of the Messiah. This interpretation saves the distinction of ἐγένετο, *has become*, and ἦν, *was*, so carefully observed throughout the Prologue; ἐγένετο must, of course, not be referred to the divine dignity of the Logos, which is eternal, but to the divine-human dignity of the incarnate Christ, which was acquired. Dr. Lange ingeniously combines the reference to time and that to rank in ἔμπροσθεν and πρῶτος.—P. S.]

* [John probably chose πρῶτος instead of πρότερος, to raise Christ above all comparison. He is absolutely the first, the Alpha and Omega. Hengstenberg, too, finds in the word the idea of absolute priority, which would have been weakened by the use of the comparative.—P. S.]

† [Origen (*In Evang. Joh.*, Tom. VI. 2, Vol. IV., p. 102) blames Heracleon, a Gnostic commentator on John, from the

Chrysostom [Erasmus, Luther, Mel.] and others take it. We adjust the ἡμεῖς πάντες by referring it to the Old Testament saints (ver. 12), and particularly to the prophets, whose line John closed.

From the fullness of Christ have we all drawn our supply, says the last of the prophets, and (even) grace for grace. The last, best, highest, which each one in the end received from His fulness, was grace. Thus the Old Testament experience of salvation looked to its completion in the New Testament. Comp. 1 Pet. i. 11, 12.*

Of his fulness.—See ver. 14, πλήρης [also Col. i. 19; ii. 9, according to which the whole fulness of the Godhead dwelled in Christ bodily; Eph. i. 23, where the church as the body of Christ is called "the fulness of Him that filleth all in all."—P. S.].—That the idea of the πλήρωμα does not necessarily originate in Gnostic soil (as Schwegler and others [of the Tübingen School] hold), to pass thence into a pseudo-Johannean Gospel, a more thorough knowledge of the history of religion might abundantly teach.† The heathen philosophy knows only an ideal pleroma as the basis of things; in the actual world all proceeds in broken emanations *in infinitum*, upon the premises of pantheism. But the idea of the real pleroma was an essential principle of the Old Testament religion and promise. In the Messiah the old piece-work was to become a whole, shadows were to become reality, revelation was to be finished. See Is. xi. 1; [comp. Heb. i. 1, 2.] Hence even Matthew, at the outset, speaks repeatedly of positive fulfilment, ch. ii., *etc.* Likewise all the Evangelists and Apostles in their way, Eph. i. 10; Col. ii. 9, 17; i. 19. The pleroma of Christ in the world corresponds with the pleroma of the Trinity in heaven; it is absolute revelation and religion concluded and consummated in His personality; and it is patent that this idea could be only borrowed by the Gnostics, to be altered and corrupted. The πλήρωμα of Christ is His fullness of being in its revelation, ontologically present, actively demonstrating itself. He had already partially opened Himself in the Old Testament, so that all the prophets might draw from Him. Comp. John x. 6 sqq.; 1 Pet. i. 11, 12.

And (even) grace for grace.—*And even;* not: and that, or: to wit.‡—*Grace for grace* [חֵן עַל חֵן, *gratiam super gratiam*]. Variously interpreted: (1) Starke: The grace of restoration, for the grace lost in paradise. (2) Chrysostom, Lampe, Paulus and others: The grace of the New Testament instead of or after that of the Old.* (3) Augustine: First justification, then eternal life.† (4) Bengel and most moderns: One grace after another [ever growing supplies of grace] from the fullness of Christ.‡—At the same time, however, the Baptist doubtless thought of the different developments of religious experience in the course of the Old Testament prophecy. Grace was continually assuming new forms. [This remark loses its force if ver. 16 gives the words of the Evangelist, not of the Baptist.—P. S.]

Ver. 17. **For the law,** *etc.*—[Antithetic demonstration of ver. 16.] The antithesis of the Old and New Testaments, as in Paul (Rom. vi. 14; vii. 3; Gal. iv. 4, *etc.*]. It must be remembered that both Apostles (and all the Apostles) recognize likewise the unity of the Old and New Testaments. This unity, even according to our text, is Christ Himself, and it is elsewhere in John [ch. viii. 56], as well as in Paul (Rom. iv. 4), represented by Abraham, or by promise and prophecy, also by the prophetic, typical side of the Mosaic law itself. The law, however, as law, constitutes the opposition of the Old Testament to the New. But the law is here placed in a twofold opposition to the New Testament. (1) As against grace, it is the binding commandment, which cannot give life, but by its demand of righteousness works the death of the sinner, either unto life in repentance, or unto death in the judgment, while it is incapable of giving life, expiating, justifying, sanctifying. Rom. vii.; 2 Cor. v.; Gal. iii. (2) As against truth or the reality of salvation and of the kingdom of God, it is first only type, prefiguration, symbol; and then, when the reality is come, shadow, Col. iii. 17; Heb. x. 1. Notice also the further anti-

---

middle of the second century, for terminating the testimony of the Baptist at the end of ver. 17, and makes it continue to the end of ver. 18.—P. S.]

* [I prefer, with Meyer, Tholuck, Hengstenberg, Alford, Godet, to ascribe this and the following verses to the Evangelist, on account of their specific Christian character, and on account of *we all* (comp. ver. 14, ἐθεασάμεθα). The Baptist, after all, belonged to the O. T. dispensation, though standing at the very threshold of the New, as Moses died of the kisses of Jehovah outside, yet in sight of, the holy land. John speaks in the name of the Apostles, ver. 14, in the name of all believers, ver. 16. Hence πάντες, which already pre-supposes the existence of the Christian Church.—P. S.]

† [The Gnostic *pleroma* is the ideal world, containing all the æons, *i. e.*, the divine powers and attributes, such as mind, reason, wisdom, truth, life, which gradually emanate from it in a certain order (according to Valentine, in pairs with sexual polarity, the νοῦς and ἀλήθεια, the λόγος and ζωή, the ἄνθρωπος and ἐκκλησία). Christ is only one of these æons. But according to John, Christ is the whole pleroma from which flow all the benefits of salvation and gifts of grace. Irenæus, *Adv. Hær.* III. 11, 1, argues from the Prologue of John against the Gnostic idea of the pleroma.—P. S.]

‡ [*Und zwar, nämlich, et même.* In this epexegetical sense καί is taken by Winer, *Gram.* p. 407, Meyer and Alford. Comp. Gal. vi. 16; Eph. vi. 18; Heb. xi. 17. But Lange's interpretation makes καί more forcible. It often means *also, even* (*eben, ja*). See Winer, p 408. Similarly Bengel: *omne quod ex ejus plenitudine accipiendum erat,* ET (SPECIATIM) *gratiam pro gratia.*—P. S.]

* [Chrysostom supports this view by ver. 17, where the law of Moses is *contrasted* with the grace of Christ; but for this very reason the law cannot be another kind of *grace*, and is never so called. Cyril and Euthymius Zigabenus likewise explain: τὴν καινὴν διαθήκην ἀντὶ τῆς παλαιᾶς.—P. S.]

† [Or rather *fides*, and *vita æterna*, as the free reward of faith. "*Quia ipsa fides gratia est,* says Augustine, *et vita æterna gratia est pro gratia.*" *Tract.* III. *in Joh.*, Tom. III., Pars. II., p. 308. The similar interpretation of St Bernard: *gratia gloriæ pro gratia militiæ*, is equally true and equally insufficient. The glory of the heavenly state is only the last link in this chain of divine grace.—P. S.]

‡ [This interpretation is also adopted by Lücke, Thol., Olsh., Mey., Hengstenb., Alf., Wordsw., and falls in most naturally with the idea of πλήρωμα, nor is it inconsistent with the fundamental meaning of ἀντί (grace exchanging with grace). It is an unbroken stream of grace from justification through the various stages of sanctification to life everlasting, every new wave taking the place of and overwhelming, though not superseding or destroying, the other. Ewald refers to the multiplicity of spiritual gifts (χαρίσματα) in the Apostolic Church, 1 Cor. xii.—xiv., but the ordinary graces and blessings must be included. 'Αντί does not always mean an exchange that supersedes one thing, but, like παρά and ἐπί, a succession. Bengel refers for a similar use of ἀντί to Æschylus, *Agam.*, and Chrysostom, *De sacerd.* VI. 13. Other examples are added by Lücke, Meyer and Alford. John might have said χάριν ἐπὶ χάριτι or χ. ἐπὶ χάριν (as Phil. ii. 27) instead of ἀντί, but it would not have expressed so strongly the overwhelming flow of grace upon grace. For the idea comp. Rom. v. 1 ff.; Gal. v. 22; Eph. v. 9.—P. S.]

thesis, that the law was *given, set forth, laid down* (ἐδόθη), as a lifeless statute; grace and truth *came, became* (ἐγένετο), unfolded themselves as life.*

Grace and truth.†—*Grace* as the complete New Testament grace of redemption, "in the distinct and solemn sense" [Meyer, p. 93], yet according to its historical progress, which began with Abraham's righteousness of faith, Gen. xv. 6.—*Truth*, as the full truth of life and the full life of truth, the reality and substance of salvation, in contrast with the shadow. [Redeeming *grace* is opposed to the condemnation, *truth* to the typical and shadowy character, of the law, of which Bengel says: *iram parans et umbram habens.*]

Came through Jesus Christ.—In the historical synthesis: JESUS CHRIST, who is here for the first time called by His full [historical] name [in harmony with the instinctively artistic arrangement of the Prologue],‡ the development of the grace also culminates in the absolutely efficient grace of redemption. But as Christ the Logos was from eternity, so also was the grace, as the power of the love and righteousness of God over the foreseen guilt of the world. Development is therefore no more to be ascribed to the grace in itself, than to the Logos in Himself; but the eternal grace, with the eternal Logos, entered into historical development towards incarnation, and the consummation: Christ in Jesus, was also the consummation of the grace. The thing here expressed, therefore, is the historical completion and operation of grace, not as a mere work of Christ (Clement of Alex.), or of God (Origen), but rather as the vital action of God in Christ. Dorschäus: "*ἐδόθη et ἐγένετο eleganter distinguuntur, Ebr.* III., *prius enim organicam causam, posterius, principalem notat.*" Yet leaving the Father the first principle.

Ver. 18. **No man hath seen God at any time.**—That these words also might have been spoken by John the Baptist, appears from ch. iii. 31, 32; and that they are to be actually attributed to him, from the fact that the Evangelist evidently distinguishes the testimony concerning Christ which, from ver. 15, the Baptist gave in general, and particularly among His disciples, from his next following testimony, ver. 19, before the rulers of the Jews.* Our verse, however, not only particularizes respecting the ἀλήθεια, ver. 17 (Meyer), but at the same time enlarges the preceding thoughts. Christ is so truly the fulfiller of grace and truth, that He stands in contrast not only to Moses, but also to the prophets and to the Baptist himself (see ch. iii. 31). No man hitherto has seen and revealed God in the sense in which He has seen and revealed Him. Christ, therefore, as fulfilment, is the first veritable revelation.—GOD is emphatically put first. God, in His interior essence, and in His fulness and full glory, no man hitherto hath seen.—NO MAN—*i. e.*, not only: not even Moses, but also: none of all the prophets, not even the Baptist.—SEEN (ἑώρακε). Not merely *perfecte cognovit* (Kuinoel); nor does the term refer to intuition without visions (Meyer); still less to such a seeing on the part of the Logos, as was suspended by His incarnation. For as to Christ's seeing of God, this was in its nature at once internal, intuitive beholding and external seeing. When the prophets beheld, they saw not with the outward eye; when they saw, they beheld not in the prophetic way; and all that they in their prophetic moments beheld, was piece-work, which they beheld in its symbolical image. In Christ the prophetic vision became one with the ordinary external vision. He saw in all the outward works of God His Spirit, His personal love; and what He saw in the Spirit, He saw not merely as idea, but as actual divine operation. To Him all sensible seeing was permanently a sublime seeing of the majesty of God, a blissful seeing of the love of the Father. And of this vision of Christ, though it was grounded in the eternity of the Logos, Brückner justly observes that it was not interrupted by the incarnation. See ch. iii. [The same perfect knowledge of God, Christ claims for Himself alone, Matth. xi. 27,—a passage which strongly proves the essential harmony of the Christ of the Synoptists with the Christ of John.—P. S.]

The only begotten Son [God]† who is on (or toward) the bosom of the Father.—With the præ-existence of the Logos before His incarnation, His co-existence during His incarnation, is so simply put, that we can find in these words nothing too high for the theology of the Baptist. [?] If the Baptist elsewhere called Him the One who baptized with the Holy Ghost and with fire (Matth. iii.), the Bridegroom of the church (John iii. 29), the One who cometh from heaven, in contrast with all prophets, he thereby designated Him also as the only begotten Son. We may then leave it entirely undecided, how far he actually understood the Sonship of Christ from Psalm cx. and other passages, and whether the term μονογενής does not belong rather to our Evangelist.—WHO IS ON THE BOSOM OF THE FATHER [ὁ ὢν εἰς τὸν κόλπον—not ἐν τῷ κόλπῳ—τοῦ πατρός. The preposition εἰς expresses a leaning on, or direction towards,

* [Bengel remarks here that no philosopher so accurately employs words and observes their distinctions as John, especially in this chapter, and explains the difference between ἐδόθη and ἐγένετο: "*Mosis non sua est lex, Christi sua est gratia et veritas.*" Alford, after De Wette, finds the reason of the contrast in the fact that the law as a positive enactment was narrow and circumscribed, and hence ἐδόθη, while grace is unlimited. But besides the idea of positive enactment, ἐδόθη implies also the divine origin and solemn promulgation of the law, while ἐγένετο indicates the free, spontaneous and abiding nature of grace. Moses may disappear, for the law was only given through him, but Christ with His grace abides forever. The law commands, the gospel gives; the law condemns, grace justifies; the law kills, grace makes alive. The highest mission of the law is to awaken a sense of sin and guilt, the need of redemption, and thus to lead to Christ.—P. S.]

† [The conjunction καί before *grace*, as Bengel remarks, is here elegantly omitted; for a "but" as well as an "and" was in place here.—P. S.]

‡ [Comp. here the remarks of Meyer and Godet. The latter says: "*C'est à ce moment du prologue que l'apôtre prononce pour la première fois le grand nom attendu depuis si long temps, Jésus-Christ. A mesure, que la divine histoire des misericordes de la Parole envers l'humanité se déroule à ses regards, ce spectacle lui inspire des termes toujours plus concrets, plus humains.*" First the Word, then Life and Light, then the Only Begotten of the Father, now Jesus Christ, who embraces all that was said of Him before.—P. S.]

* [I dissent from this view. *See* foot-notes on page 76.—P. S.]

† [On this remarkable difference of reading: ὁ μονογενὴς υἱός, generally abbreviated in ancient MSS. ΥC and (ὁ) μονογενὴς θεός or ΘC, *see* TEXTUAL NOTES (6).—P. S.]

the bosom of the Father, the union of motion and rest in the love of the Only Begotten to the Father.* Comp. the notes on πρὸς τὸν θεόν, ver. 1. The phrase *to be (leaning) on the bosom*, like the Latin, *in sinu* or *gremio esse, sedere*, and the German, *Schoosskind, bosom-child*, expresses a relation of the closest intimacy and tenderest affection. Compare what is said of the Wisdom (the Logos) in Prov. viii. 30: "Then I was near Him as one brought up with Him; and I was daily His delight, rejoicing always before Him." Bengel remarks: "*The bosom* here is divine, paternal, fruitful, mild, sweet, spiritual. Men are said to be in the loins (*in lumbis*) who are yet to be born; they are in the bosom (*in sinu*) who have been born. The Son was in the bosom of the Father, because He was never not-born (*non-natus*, ἀγέννητος). The highest unity, and the most intimate knowledge from immediate sight, is here signified."—P. S.].—Acccording to Hofmann† and Meyer, the Evangelist is speaking here, and speaking *of Christ exalted*. From this the εἰς τὸν κόλπον is supposed to explain itself as expressing the exaltation. But this would deprive the clause of all force, and reduce it to a pointless, self-neutralizing announcement. If it means: *The only-begotten Son*, who has now ascended to the bosom of the Father, who once preached to us when He was with us,—the relative clause, besides being unmeaning, would be inaccurate; it should read: Who is *again* in the bosom of the Father. The passage i. 50 does not prove that during the earthly life of Christ such an εἶναι εἰς τὸν κόλπον τοῦ πατρός did not belong to Him.‡ The antithesis between His being on earth (ch. i. 51) and His being in heaven (ch. iii. 13), between His being with the Father (ch. viii. 35), representing the Father (xiv. 9), and being one with the Father (x. 30), and His coming forth from the Father (xvi. 28), His being alone with the Father in His passion (xvi. 32), and His being forsaken by God (Matth. xxvii. 46), as well as between His glory (c. i. 14) and His being not yet glorified (vii. 39),—is to be explained neither by a dualistic separation between the consciousness of the Logos and the consciousness of Jesus, nor by a pantheistic admission of human limitations into the Logos (Thomasius), but by the alternation of Christ's moods between His self-subsistent relation to God and His self-imposed compassionate relation to the world, or between the predominance of self-limiting grace and that of heaven-embracing omnipotence; between the states of humiliation and exaltation in their essential principle and positive spirit. We therefore, with De Wette, take ὤν as a time-less present, and εἰς, after the analogy of the πρὸς τὸν θεόν in ver. 1, as expressing the eternal direction of the Son towards the Father. Lücke rightly refers the being in the bosom of the Father, or for the Father, to the incarnate Logos, as He here appears in the definite character of the only begotten Son. Following the common acceptation, Tholuck considers the figure as borrowed from the place of fellowship at table, at the right hand, ch. xiii. 23 [ἦν ἀνακείμενος . . . . ἐν τῷ κόλπῳ τοῦ Ἰησοῦ].* Meyer thinks this unsuitable, but refers the expression to the paternal embrace, Luke xvi. 22 [ἐν τοῖς κόλποις].† But the common acceptation is supported by the kindred expression of Christ, that He will come with the Father to His own, to make His abode with them, John xiv. 23; comp. Rev. iii. 20; xix. 9.

He hath, *etc.*—Ἐκεῖνος ["an epithet of excellency and of distance," as Bengel observes] is certainly very emphatic [He, and none else]; yet not as looking to the local superiority of heaven,‡ but to the majesty of the Son of God.

Interpreted.—Ἐξηγήσατο is hard to explain. Lücke refers it to the grace and truth which Christ has seen in God; Meyer, to the substance of His view of God; [the E. V. (which supplies: *Him*), Alford, Owen, Godet, to God Himself in the beginning of the verse.—P. S.] Lücke translates: He hath revealed it; De Wette: He hath proclaimed (declared) it, told it; Meyer: He hath explained, interpreted [*viz.*: the contents of His intuitions of God]. The New Testament parallels, Luke xxiv. 35; Acts xv. 12, 14, *etc.*, admit both renderings, but favor that of De Wette; the passage Lev. xiv. 57 (LXX.) seems rather to favor Meyer, especially since the word, in classic usage, is applied particularly to the explaining of divine things.§ As we attribute the word to the Baptist, we conceive that it contains an allusion to the obscure beginnings of revelation in the Old Testament. The Baptist has not understood the historical predictions of Jesus, but has no doubt recognized in Christ the key of the ancient time, the perfect interpretation of the rudiments of revelation. We therefore take ἐξηγήσατο absolutely, with respect to the old covenant. In virtue of His seeing of God He has cleared up the law in grace and truth, brought the Old Testament gloriously to light in the New. He has *brought* and *made* solution.

[This very verb argues against Dr. Lange's view of the authorship of ver. 18, which must be as-

* [Winer, *Gramm.*, p. 387 (7th ed.): *an den Busen (angelehnt), gegen den Busen hin.* Ewald translates *am Schoosse.*—P. S.]

† [*Schriftbeweis*, Vol. I., p. 120, sec. ed.: *der in den Schooss des Vaters hingegangen.* But Meyer gave this explanation before Hofmann, who also refers to him.—P. S.]

‡ [Hengstenberg, Brückner, Godet, Philippi likewise oppose Meyer's ungrammatical reference of the *present* participle ὤν to the *future* state of exaltation. The intimate communion between the Son and the Father was not interrupted or suspended by the incarnation. Christ, while on earth, was at the same time in heaven (iii. 13), not simply *de jure* (as Meyer, in the fifth edition, p. 95, explains it), but *de facto* in a most real, though mysterious sense. (Wordsworth is altogether too fanciful if he finds in ὁ ὤν an allusion to the peculiar name of Jehovah, *the Being, the ever Existing One.*)—P. S.]

* [So also Winer, Lücke, Gess, Ewald, Godet, Alford, Webster and Wilkinson.—P. S.]

† [So also Robinson (*Lex. sub* κόλπος), Owen (from the idea of embracing a friend and straining him to the bosom) and Hengstenberg, who besides refers to similar expressions, Deut. xiii. 7; xxviii. 36; Mich. vii. 5; Isaiah xl. 11.—P. S.]

‡ [As Meyer explains it in accordance with his reference of the passage to the state of exaltation in heaven.—P. S.]

§ [The words ἐξηγέομαι (properly *to lead out*, either in the sense of *taking the lead*, or of *bringing out, explaining* the hidden sense), ἐξήγησις, ἐξηγητής, are technical terms used by the classic writers of the interpretation of divine oracles, visions, mysteries, prodigies, laws and ceremonies, and hence properly applied by Christian writers to the exposition of the holy Scriptures. See the passages collected by Wetstein, p. 841, and the references in Meyer, p. 96. Lampe, who strictly adheres to this technical sense, like Meyer, supplies no object, and takes ἐξηγήσατο=ἐξηγητής ἐστιν, *interpres est*, as *regnat* without the object is equivalent to *rex est*, and *docet* to *doctor est*. The emphasis certainly lies on the verb rather than the object. *He has explained*, truly and fully, in His words and in His life; His instruction alone merits the name of an explanation; He is *the* Expounder of God and divine things.—P. S.]

cribed to the Evangelist. The Baptist never came into close personal intimacy with Christ, and died before He had fully revealed the counsel of God and the meaning of the Old Testament. But the Evangelist, in full view of the atoning death and glorious resurrection, could use this term in its most comprehensive sense. With it the Prologue returns to the beginning, and ἐξηγήσατο suggests the best reason why Christ is called the Logos, since He is the Revealer and Interpreter of the hidden being of the Godhead in all that relates to our salvation.—John puts the supreme dignity of Christ, as the eternal Word, the Author of the world, the Giver of life and light, the Fountain of grace and truth, the only and perfect Expounder of God, at the head of his Gospel, because without this dignity Christianity would sink to a position of merely relative superiority above other religions, instead of being the absolute and therefore final religion for all mankind. Luther observes on the Prologue: "These are indeed brief words, but they contain the whole Christian doctrine and life."—P. S.]

DOCTRINAL AND ETHICAL.

1. See the preceding exegesis.

2. *The Word was made flesh.* He *was* God, He *became* flesh. What He *was*, He was not merely in idea (Hegel), but in personal divine subsistency; what He became (ἐγένετο), He became not merely *in appearance* (Gnosticism), nor in a *partial* way (joining Himself to the flesh, or veiling Himself in it, according to Nestorianism, or depriving the flesh of its genuineness, and transforming it into a divine manifestation, according to Eutyches), nor only for a *particular need* and *purpose* (Anselm), but perfectly and forever. As Word, He was the full expression of the essence of the Godhead, and therefore was also *pure* eternal *being* and personal *life;* in His coming forth, He entered into veritable, integral human nature in its pure essence. The Word could not be changed by the flesh (contrary to modern attempts to carry change into the essence of God), but the flesh was to be perfected by the Word in His coming in it, carried *from conditional potentiality to determinate actuality*, made the glorified organ of the eternal Spirit. The prosecution of the doctrine of the *Communicatio idiomatum* lies not on the side of the divine nature, but on the side of the human.

As regards the doctrine of the incarnation, the Logos, as eternal Logos, became man, without change in Himself; that is to say, the incarnation was not occasioned by the sin of man. The doctrine of the flesh must, according to our passage, be so constructed that the flesh shall be as penetrable (and more) to the Spirit as to sin. The union between the divine and human natures is the great mystery of life, and to think of it rightly we must keep the distinction, that the divine *being* unfolds itself in a conscious way, like a work of art from a human mind, while the human *becoming* effects itself in an unconscious way, after the manner of the development of a plant. The pure contra-distinction appears in the work of art, which unfolds itself *synthetically*, subjecting to its service the material originally belonging to it, and the metamorphosis of the plant, which reveals spirit *analytically*, without attaining any power over itself. In the life of the natural man (in the pure sense of the term) nature predominates, but the spirit comes more and more to power (1 Cor. xv. 45); in the life of the spiritual man, who is from heaven, spiritual consciousness predominates, appropriating, pervading, and ruling the human organism. So the Logos, with the absolute *master power* of His essence as Logos, entered into human nature. He is not only voluntary in His incarnation in general; He is *voluntary* in each act of His human nature, *i. e.*, of His human self-limitation for the sake of a higher spontaneity. He is voluntarily born (Luke i. 26 sqq.), voluntarily a child (Luke ii. 51), voluntarily sleeps (Mark iv. 38), is voluntarily ignorant as to the day of judgment (Mark xiii. 32, 33), voluntarily suffers (Matth. xxvi. 53), voluntarily dies (John x. 18); but all in order that He may truly *live* (John v. 17; ix. 4), truly unfold Himself (John x. 15, 16; xii. 24), truly watch (Matth. xxvi. 38), truly know (Mark iii. 12), truly act and triumph (John xii. 12), and eternally live (John xvii.).

In other words, Christ entered into the entire life of man, sin excepted, to raise it to the second, higher life of glorified humanity. This opposition is illustrated by the suspensions of consciousness in our natural life itself; and before we decide respecting the divine mystery of the Logos entering into sleep, we must be clear respecting the human mystery of our own mind's sleeping. He *goes* to sleep. Weakness must be transfigured by freedom into rhythm, or determination of power. In the *ideal* incarnation of Christ, His *historical* incarnation, His subjection to law, is actually involved.

3. *And we beheld His glory.* The humiliation of Christ in the form of a servant did not hinder the Evangelist from seeing His glory. The omnipotence which, in the strength of love, puts limits upon itself (Matth. xxvi. 53, 54), is not entered into an *absolute* humiliation, but into a humiliation *to our human vision*, in order to reveal Himself in a higher glory. It remained κρύψις, inasmuch as it remained at every point free; it became κένωσις, inasmuch as it made earnest of the self-humiliation. But it did not leave its riches of power and honor behind in heaven; it yielded them up to the world, 2 Cor. viii. 9. The world had the honor of judging the universal Judge; it had the power to put omnipotence to death; the wisdom to judge concerning him; the omnipresence of the Roman empire to bring him down to Golgotha, the grave and Sheol; but it thereby only gained the power to judge itself, that it might be the medium of that revelation of omnipotence in the impotence of Christ whereby it was overcome, judged and reconciled. Full faith in the cross must feel that Christ has humbled Himself by surrender of Himself to the world, not in heavenly reservation towards the world, and that here has taken place on the full scale what occurs elsewhere on smaller scales, or here in one central fact what appears otherwise every where in history: God makes Himself weak, and stands, as bound, in His government, over against the freedom of the sinner, to let him feel in the judgment that physical power is nothing of itself, and that truth, righteousness and love are all.

4. Christ is the *Only Begotten* (μονογενής), inasmuch as He is the one Word, in whom all things were ideally and virtually included, in distinction from the universe in its development; He is the First Born (πρωτότοκος), inasmuch as He has entered, as a principle, into development.

5. *And of His fulness.* If John could bear witness of the præ-existence of Christ, he could also testify that the prophets had all drank of His fulness, and that their highest, fairest experience had been the experience of grace.

6. *Grace for grace.* The reciprocal forms of grace in the Old Testament, and in the whole history of the world.

7. The distinction between the Old and New Testaments: (1) Moses, the servant, serving; Christ, the Son and Lord, reigning in the obedience of the Father; (2) Given, laid down; come; (3) Law; grace and truth (see above).

HOMILETICAL AND PRACTICAL.

The combined testimony of the Old Testament John and the New to the incarnation of the Son of God: 1) The agreement of the two testimonies; 2) their difference; 3) their copiousness. —The Old Covenant and the New: 1) In contrast: Moses and Christ; 2) In harmony: John and Christ.—The Old Covenant in its relation to the New: 1) The advent of the New (Christ in the Old Testament); 2) the discipline for the New (Moses and the Law); 3) a shadow vanishing before the New ("No man hath seen God at any time").—Twofold testimony of the Baptist concerning Christ: 1) Concerning the near approach of Christ, whose person he yet knew not; 2) concerning Jesus, that He is the Christ.—The Incarnation for our salvation: 1) A great mystery in its nature ("the Word was made flesh"); 2) a historical fact in its demonstration ("dwelt among us"); 3) an assured sight of blessed eye-witnesses ("we beheld"); 4) a blessed experience of all believers ("full of grace and truth").—The consummation of revelation: 1) The revealing Word, which had appeared in the Angel of the Lord, now become man; 2) the glory of God above the most holy place, now bodily manifested in the dwellings of men; 3) the entranced vision of divine tokens, now become the blessed seeing of the divine glory; 4) the law transformed into the fulness of grace and truth.—"The Word was made flesh:" a gospel of the highest knowledge; being 1) a view of Christ; 2) the key of philosophy; 3) a prophecy for Christianity.—The announcement: The Word was made flesh: 1) a preaching of repentance (sin therefore does not belong to the flesh, Rom. viii. 3); 2) a preaching of faith. Our flesh should be transformed through the Word.—Christ has explained all: 1) The mysteries of the Old Testament; 2) the mysteries of humanity (the Word was made flesh); 3) the mysteries of nature (the Word entered into the process of growth); 4) the mysteries of God.

STARKE: O the mystery! God is become man; the Son of God the Father, a son of man; the Word, a child; the Life, a mortal man; the eternal Light is in the midst of darkness, Rom. ix. 5.—How deeply the Most High has abased Himself, and how gloriously the Humbled has exalted us.*—CANSTEIN: Christ has pitched His tent in our nature, that He might make His abode in each one of us, and He will still more gloriously pitch His tabernacle among men, and more peculiarly manifest His glory, Rev. xxi. 3, 11.—Jesus is ever, in His whole office, full of grace and truth. In His prophetical office He preaches [and actually presents] grace and truth; in His priestly office He procures them; in His kingly office He gives and maintains them.—Seest thou how the Word is made flesh? Give diligence that thou mayest be made like Him according to thy measure in glory.—ZEISIUS: Christ, the one inexhaustible fountain of all graces, from which all believers from the beginning have drawn.—CANSTEIN: The true use of grace received fits us for more grace, so that one grace becomes the reward of another, yet remains grace, Heb. x. 1. Christ is the end of all the Mosaic system of shadows, and in Him we have the substance itself, which the shadows only prefigured, Heb. x. 1; Col. ii. 17.—*Ibid.*: Grace and truth belong together. Where grace is, in the forgiveness of sins, there appears also the truth of a holy and upright nature in Christ. And where the latter fails, grace also is wanting.—HEDINGER: Christ a prophet and interpreter of the divine will.

MOSHEIM: The second word: "Truth" is contrasted with ceremonies. Moses set forth only types and shadows; the Saviour has preached [acted in His life] pure truth, the grace and love of God towards men without figure.—VON GERLACH: "He that cometh after me is preferred," *etc.* One of the many sacred enigmas in this Gospel, in which the literary sense gives a paradox to incite us to seek a higher.—From AUGUSTINE: The same God who gave the law, has also given grace; but this law He sent by His servant; with the grace He has Himself come down.—HEUBNER: This sentence ["the Word was made flesh"] contains all: (1) The divinity of Christ—He is the Logos; (2) His true humanity—He is made flesh. This dwelling denotes His true human life, and is a pledge of our future dwelling with Him.—There is no stopping, no limit, in grace, but ever new growth in insight, power, joy and peace.—SCHLEIERMACHER: *Grace for grace.* It is properly equivalent to grace in reward for grace; *i. e.*, for our receiving one grace from Him, another grace is in turn imparted.—Only the One who is from the Father, hath seen the Father (John vi. 46); only in Him and through Him can man know God the Father, and draw from His fulness grace and truth.

[SCHAFF: Ver. 14. The Incarnation the central truth of Christianity and of all religion: 1) The end of the reign of separation from God, or the reign of sin and death; 2) the beginning of the reign of union and communion with God, or the reign of righteousness and life.—The Incar-

* [Richard Crashaw (1646):

"Welcome to our wondering sight,
Eternity shut in a span!
Summer in winter! day in night!
Heaven in earth! and God in man!
Great Little One, whose glorious birth
Lifts earth to heaven, stoops heaven to earth."

Luther, in his Christmas hymn: "*Gelobet seist Du, Jesu Christ,*" commemorates the sublime contrasts of the transcending mystery of the incarnation.—P. S.]

nation: 1) Its *nature:* (*a*) not a change or conversion of the Godhead into flesh, but an assumption of manhood into abiding union with the second person of the Godhead; the two natures remaining distinct, yet inseparably united for ever; (*b*) not an assumption of a part of human nature, but of the whole, body, soul and spirit; Christ being perfect God and perfect Man in one person; (*c*) not an assumption of sin, but only of its consequences, in order to remove and destroy them; sin being no part of human nature as originally constituted, but a corruption of that nature by a foreign poison and an abuse of freedom. Christ was tempted, and suffered and died as we, but He never submitted to temptation; He "knew no sin," and remained "holy, harmless, undefiled, and separate from sinners." 2. Its *effects:* (*a*) the redemption of human nature, or of the whole race, from the curse and dominion of sin and death; (*b*) the elevation of human nature to abiding union with the Godhead. —*The Word became flesh:* 1) really and truly (against Gnosticism, docetism, Arianism); 2) totally and perfectly (against Apollinarianism); 3) undividedly and inseparably (against Nestorianism); 4) unmixedly, without confusion or absorption of substance (against Eutychianism and Monophysitism).—The incarnation the end and aim of all religion; for religion (*religio*, from *relegare*, to *rebind*, to *reunite*) implies: 1) an original union of man and God in the state of innocence; 2) a separation of the two by sin and death; 3) a reconciliation and reunion which was effected by the atonement of Christ.—The mystery of the incarnation reversely repeated in every true regeneration by which man becomes a child of God, a partaker of Christ's "divine nature," and a "new creature in Christ Jesus."]

[BURKITT, ver. 14: Christ's taking *flesh* implies that He took not only human nature, but all the weaknesses and infirmities of that nature also (sinful infirmities being excepted), such as hunger, thirst, weariness. As man, Christ has an experimental sense of our infirmities and wants; as God, He can supply them all.]

[M. HENRY (abridged) on ver. 16: As of old, God dwelt in the tabernacle of Moses, by the Shekinah, between the cherubim, so now He dwells in the human nature of Christ, the true Shekinah, the symbol of God's peculiar presence. And we are to address God through Christ, and from Him receive divine oracles. All believers receive from Christ's fulness; the greatest saints cannot live without Him, the weakest may live by Him. This excludes boasting and silences perplexing fear.—*Grace* is the good will of God towards us, and the good work of God in us. God's good will works the good work, and the good work qualifies for further tokens of His good will.—As the cistern receives from the fulness of the fountain, the branches from the root, and the air from the sun, so we receive grace from the fulness of Christ.—*Grace for grace* speaks the *freeness* of grace; the *abundance* of grace; the *promotion* of grace by grace; the *substitution* of the N. T. grace for the O. T. grace; the *augmentation* and *continuance* of grace; the *conformity* of grace in the saints to the grace that is in Christ, the saints being changed into the same heavenly image. (A combination of different interpretations of χάριν ἀντὶ χάριτος, which may do for a sermon, but not for exegesis.)]

[AUGUSTINE on ver. 17: The law threatened, not helped; commanded, not healed; showed, not took away, our feebleness. But it made ready for the physician, who was to come with grace and truth.—OLSHAUSEN: The law induces and elicits the consciousness of sin and the need of redemption; it only typifies the reality; the gospel actually communicates reality and power from above.]

[J. C. RYLE, ver. 18: After reading this Prologue, it is impossible to think too highly of Christ, or to give too much honor to Him. He is the meeting point between the Trinity and the sinner's soul. "He that honoreth not the Son, honoreth not the Father who sent Him" (John v. 23).—QUESNEL calls the Prologue, especially ver. 1, "the gospel of the holy Trinity." Our knowledge of this mystery of mysteries begins with the knowledge of the Son, who reveals and expounds to us the Father, and who is Himself revealed and applied to us by the Holy Spirit.—P. S.]

II.

THE GOSPEL OF THE HISTORICAL MANIFESTATION OF CHRIST, OR HIS SELF-REVELATION AND HIS VICTORY IN CONFLICT WITH THE DARKNESS OF THE WORLD.

CHAPTER I. 19—XX. 31.

FIRST SECTION.

The Reception which Christ, the Light of the World, finds in His Life of Love among the men akin to the Light, the Elect.

CHAP. I. 19—IV. 54.

I.

JOHN THE BAPTIST, AND HIS PUBLIC AND REPEATED TESTIMONY CONCERNING CHRIST. JESUS ACCREDITED AS THE CHRIST, ATTESTED THE SON OF GOD, THE ETERNAL LORD, AND THE LAMB OF GOD.

CHAP. I. 19-34.

(CH. I. 19-28: Pericope for the 4th Sunday in Advent.)

(1) TESTIMONY OF JOHN THE BAPTIST BEFORE THE RULERS OF THE JEWS. JESUS THE MESSIAH COMING AFTER THE BAPTIST, THE ETERNAL PRE-HISTORICAL AND SUPER-HISTORICAL LORD BEFORE HIM.

19 And this is the record [testimony] of John, when the Jews sent [to him][1] priests
20 and Levites from Jerusalem, to ask him, Who art thou? And he confessed, and
21 denied not; but [and he] confessed, I am not [Not I am][2] the Christ. And they
asked him, What then? Art thou Elias [Elijah]? And he saith, I am not. Art
22 thou that prophet? And he answered, No. Then[3] [in official demand] said they
unto him, Who art thou? that we may give an answer to them that sent us. What
23 sayest thou of thyself? He said, I am the voice of one crying in the wilderness,
Make straight the way of the Lord, as said [Isaiah] the prophet Esaias [ch. xl. 3].
24 And they[4] which were sent were of the Pharisees [And they had been sent by the
25 Pharisees]. And they asked him, and said unto him, Why baptizest thou then, if
thou be not that [the] Christ, nor[5] Elias [Elijah], neither[5] that [the] prophet?
26 John answered them, saying, I baptize with [in] water; but there standeth one
27 among you [in the midst of you there standeth one], whom ye know not: he it is[6]
[This is he] who coming after me, is preferred [taketh place, or, hath come to be]
28 before me, whose shoe's latchet I am not worthy to unloose. These things were done
in Bethabara [Bethany][7] beyond Jordan, where John was baptizing.

(2) TESTIMONY OF THE BAPTIST BEFORE HIS DISCIPLES. THE HISTORICAL LAMB OF GOD; UPON HIM THE DOVE.

29 The next day John [he][8] seeth Jesus coming unto him, and saith, Behold the
Lamb of God, which taketh away [taketh away by bearing, or, beareth away][9] the
30 sin of the world! This is he of whom I said, After me cometh a man which [who] is
31 preferred [taketh place, or, hath come to be] before me; for he was before me. And
I knew him not; but that he should be made manifest to Israel, therefore am I come
32 [for this cause came I] baptizing with [in] water.[10] And John bare record [witness],
saying, I saw the Spirit descending from heaven like[11] a dove, and it abode upon
33 him. And I knew him not: but he that sent me to baptize with [in] water, the
same said unto me, Upon whom thou shalt see the Spirit descending and remaining [abiding] on him, the same is he which [who] baptizeth with [in] the Holy

34 Ghost [Spirit]. And I saw [have seen, *ἑώρακα*,] and bare record [have borne witness, *μεμαρτύρηκα*] that this is the Son of God.

TEXTUAL AND GRAMMATICAL.

1 Ver. 19.—Codd. B. C*., Lachmann add πρὸς αὐτόν. Not decisive. [ℵ. C.³ L. *al.*, text. rec., Tischend., 8th ed., omit it. Alf., with Lachm., inserts it.—P. S.]

2 Ver. 20.—[ὅτι ἐγὼ οὐκ εἰμὶ ὁ χριστός is the reading of the best MSS., ℵ. A. B. C*., L. X., Orig., Chrys., Cyr., Lachm., Tisch. (VIII. ed.), Alf., instead of οὐκ εἰμὶ ἐγώ. The former reading emphasizes ἐγώ, *I for my part*, and implies that John knew another who was the Messiah, while the latter reading emphasizes the negation: It is *not* I who, *etc.*—P. S.]

3 Ver. 22.—The οὖν after εἶπον here is significant. Not, as by Lachmann according to B. C., to be omitted. [Cod. Sin. has it.]

4 Ver. 24.—Tischendorf, after several codd. (A.* B. C.* L.), omits the article before ἀπεσταλμένοι. As Origen supposed a second embassy, the omission may have arisen with him. [The Cod. Sinaiticus has a gap here, indicating the original presence of the article.—E. D. Y.]

5 Ver. 26.—A. B. C. L. [Cod. Sin.] read οὐδέ both times, instead of οὔτε. The latter is probably exegetically the more accurate particle.

6 Ver. 27.—The words αὐτός ἐστιν and ὃς ἔμπροσθέν μου γέγονεν are wanting in B. and C. [Cod. Sin.] and in Origen. Bracketed by Lachmann, omitted by Tischendorf [and Alford]. The Johannean style is in favor of the first words; the connection with ὁ ὀπίσω., *etc.*, is in favor of the others. Cod. A., *etc.*, and the similar expression in ver. 15, are in favor of both.

7 Ver. 29.—The Recepta reads Βηθαβαρᾶ, after Origen. Authorities decisive against it. [Comp. the note of Alford *in loc.*—P. S.]

8 Ver. 29.—Against the addition ὁ Ἰωάννης are A. B. C., *etc.* Meyer: "Beginning of a church lesson." [Cod. Sin., a gap.—E. D. Y.]

9 Ver. 28.—[The E. V. follows the Vulgate: *qui tollit.* The Gr. verb αἴρειν has the double meaning *to take up* (to bear the punishment of sin in order to expiate it, comp. Isa. liii.: *he bore our griefs and carried our sorrows*), and *to take away* (=ἀφαιρεῖν). Both may be combined (as is done by Olshausen) and expressed by the German verb *hinwegtragen, to bear away, to take away by taking upon one's self*, or to remove the penalty of sin by expiation: *See* the EXEG. NOTES. The present ὁ αἴρων is used in prophetic vision of the act of atonement as a present and continuous fact.—P. S.]

10 Ver. 31.—[Some authorities insert here and in ver. 33 the article τῷ before ὕδατι, "in the water (of Jordan) in which you see me baptize." Alford brackets, Tischend. (ed. VIII.) omits, Meyer (p. 112) defends it.—P. S.]

11 Ver. 32.—Most codd. read ὡς, not ὡσεί, which comes from Matth. iii. 16; Luke iii. 22.

EXEGETICAL AND CRITICAL.

[Now follows the historical narrative. The testimony of John the Baptist, and the call of the first disciples form the historical introduction or the portico of the public life of Christ. John omits the birth, early history and discourses of the Baptist, as being sufficiently known from the Synoptists, and confines himself to his testimony *after* the baptism (alluded to as a past fact in vers. 33, 34) and the temptation of Christ in the wilderness, when He stood already in the midst of the Jews (ver. 26). The testimony is threefold, 1) before the deputies of the Sanhedrin from Jerusalem (19-28); 2) a day afterwards, before a larger public and His disciples, as it would seem (29-34); 3) again a day afterwards, before two of His disciples, who now joined Jesus (35-37).—The examination of John the Baptist by the official messengers of the Sanhedrin, who had the supervision of the public teaching of religion among the Jews (Matth. xxi. 23), displays the prevalence and confusion of the Messianic expectations, and the hostility of the leaders of the hierarchy to the approaching new dispensation. The five questions of the priests represent a descending climax (the Messiah; Elijah; an anonymous prophet; why baptizest thou?); the short, laconic answers of the Baptist, in striking contrast, are rising from negation to affirmation, and turn the attention away from himself and towards Christ.—P. S.]

Ver. 19. **And this is.**—The gospel history itself begins with the testimony of John the Baptist. Comp. Matth. iii.; Mark i.; Luke iii. The question is whether the same testimony is meant here, as in ver. 15. Origen supposed this to be another testimony; Meyer thinks it the same. Evidently in ver. 15 a general testimony, with μαρτυρεῖ, is distinguished from a special, καὶ κέκραγε. This most public testimony concerning Jesus before the rulers is undoubtedly meant here. It is a definite pointing of the rulers of the Jews to the person of the Messiah, not related so distinctly by the Synoptists, but of the highest importance for the history of the temptation. *This:* αὕτη, the following [it is the predicate, ἡ μαρτυρία the subject. A *verbal* testimony is meant. *Record* now refers to *written* evidence. —P. S.]. Ὅτε points also to a particular event, which took place at a particular time. That this event must have followed the baptism of Jesus is clear;* because, according to vers. 31-33, it was that which gave the Baptist himself his first certainty respecting the person of Jesus; and this certainty he expresses here, vers. 26, 27. Likewise ver. 29. Olshausen, Baumgarten-Crusius, and others, place the baptism between the two testimonies, ver. 19 and ver. 29; Ewald, between ver. 31 and ver. 32; all against the testimony of the section before us. That John knew of the existence of the Messiah earlier, and with human reverence presumed that he found Him in the person of Jesus, Matth. iii. 14, is not inconsistent with his still needing a divine attestation. As regards the history of the temptation, its termination coincides with the present testimony; for Jesus, the next day, comes again behind the Baptist, and soon afterwards (not forty days after) returns to Galilee.

When the Jews from Jerusalem.—[The Synoptists, who wrote before the destruction of Jerusalem, seldom use the term *Jews* as distinct from *Christians* (Matthew five times, Mark seven times, Luke five times); John, who wrote after the destruction of Jerusalem and after the final separation of the Synagogue from the Christian

* [So also Lücke, De Wette, Meyer, Wieseler, Ebrard, Luthardt, Godet, Alford, *etc.* Bengel infers from this passage that the preaching of the Baptist began not long before the baptism of Jesus; otherwise the embassy would have been sent earlier. Alford argues that it was absolutely necessary to suppose that John should have delivered this testimony *often*, and under varying circumstances, first in the form given by Luke: ἔρχεται ὁ ἰσχυρ. μου κ. τ. λ., and *after* it in this form, οὗτος ἦν ὃν εἶπον, where his former testimony is distinctly referred to.—P. S.]

church, uses it very often (over seventy times in the Gospel and twice in the Apoc.).—P. S.] Ἰουδαῖοι, probably as yet primarily in the neutral sense, though already conceived as about to become a hostile body, on the way to apostasy from true Judaism in opposition to the Messiah. The conception is the historical one of the Jews as the theocratic people, as in ch. ii. 13; iii. 1; v. 1, then branching into a friendly one (ch. iv. 22; xviii. 33) and a hostile (ch. v. 10; vii. 1; viii. 31; x. 24, *etc.*), which in the sequel prevails. In the latter sense the term therefore denotes the Jews as Judaists. Meyer therefore is not perfectly accurate when he says: "John, in his writing, lets the Jews, as the old communion, from which the Christian has already entirely withdrawn, appear steadily in a hostile position to the Lord and His work, the ancient theocratic people as an opposition party to the church of God and its Head." The Jews do certainly appear in this character predominantly in John, and with good reason Meyer observes that this can furnish no argument against the genuineness of His Gospel (against Fischer and Hilgenfeld). The expression, *The Jews*, as he also remarks, varies according to the context; here it is the Jews from Jerusalem, the Sanhedrin.

Priests and Levites.—[The two classes of persons employed about the temple service, Josh. iii. 3. In the wider sense, *Levites* designates the descendants of Levi; in a narrower sense, as here, the subordinate officers of the Jewish hierarchy, as distinct from the priests of the family of Aaron.—P. S.] The Levites as an attendant body were designed, under certain circumstances, to arrest the Baptist, and at any rate to add state as a convoy of police, or to enhance the official dignity of the priests. It is a touch of historical accuracy.

Who art thou?—*i. e.*, in thy official, theocratic character. That they supposed He might lay claim to the Messiahship, is evident from the answer of John. They had official right, according to Deut. xviii. 21, to inquire into his character and his credentials as a prophet. They had occasion to do so in his baptism (ver. 25), not only because the baptism connected itself with the kingdom of Messiah (Ezek. xxxvi. 25; xxxvii. 23; Zech. xiii. 1), but also because the baptism was a declaration concerning the whole congregation of the people, that it was unclean (Hag. ii. 14), which could easily offend the pride of the Pharisees. Besides, the people were already inclined to take him for the Messiah, Luke iii. 15. According to ver. 24, the delegates were of the party of the Pharisees. These had probably moved in the Sanhedrin, that the deputation be sent, because the Messianic question was of much more importance to them than to the Sadducees, and because they, with their sensuous Messianic hopes, took the matter of the credentials of the Messiah more strictly in their more external sense.

Ver. 20. **And he confessed, and denied not.**—Should this mean only: He denied not his own real character? he confessed in this matter the truth? The double expression, positive and negative, would be rather strong for this. The question of the Sanhedrin set before him the temptation to declare himself the Christ. But in so doing he would have denied the Christ whom he already knew, and denied his own better, prophetic knowledge. We suppose, therefore, that his confessing and not denying in regard to himself imply at the same time his confessing and not denying in regard to Christ. This is indicated also by the emphatic order of the words: ἐγὼ οὐκ εἰμί, which is supported by the best authorities as against οὐκ εἰμὶ ἐγώ. Meyer: "*I for my part*," implying that he knows another, who *is* the Messiah.—The reserve of the Baptist towards the deputation shows the mighty prophet, who understood them. He leaves each successive development of his deposition to be drawn from him, till the moment for his testimony arrives. This mysterious bearing is no doubt intended also to humble and press the self-conceited spirit.

Ver. 21. **What then? Art thou Elijah?**—The question is a half inference. He who comes with such pretensions must be, if not the Messiah Himself, at least the Elijah who precedes Him. They refer to the Messianic prophecy, Mal. iv. 5. The pure sense of this prophecy, that an *ideal* Elijah should precede the Messiah, which John actually was (Luke i. 17; Matth. xi. 14; xvii. 10), had early become corrupted among the Jews, as is shown by the very translation of the passage in the Septuagint. Ἠλίαν τὸν Θεσβίτην (Elijah the Tishbite).* Thus these messengers understood the word entirely in a superstitious sense, taking it literally for the actual Elijah. Hence John answers categorically: **I am not** [not the Tishbite, whom you mean.]† But he adds no explanation; for this would have involved him in an exegetical controversy, and turned him from his main object, which was to testify of Christ.

Art thou the prophet?—The next question in the spirit of their theology; hence occurring immediately. The prophet, with the article; *the* well-known prophet; a personage in their Messianic theology presumed to be familiar. According to Chrysostom [Bengel], Lücke, Bleek, Meyer, [Alford], the prophet meant would be the one spoken of in Deut. xviii. 15;‡ but this we must certainly, with Hengstenberg and Tholuck, deny, for this prophecy was at least in Acts iii. 22; vii. 37 referred to the Messiah. It is a question whether the passages, John vi. 14; vii. 40, refer to the passage in Deuteronomy. From Matth. xvi. 14 it is sufficiently evident that an expectation of Jeremiah§ or some one of the prophets as the forerunner of the Messiah was cherished. Probably this expectation was connected with the doctrine of the woes

* [Chrysostom, Jerome, Augustine and other fathers distinguished two Elijahs, corresponding to the two advents of Christ, 1) a man of the spirit and power of Elijah, *i. e.*, John the Baptist; 2) Elijah the Tishbite, who shall precede as a herald the second or judicial coming of Christ. This view is adopted by Ryle, who thinks that John could not well have answered in the negative, if there is no literal fulfilment of Malachi's prophecy in prospect. Trench (*Studies in the Gospels*, p. 214) leaves the question undecided.—P. S.]

† [Bengel: *Omnia a se amolitur, ut Christum confiteatur et ad Christum redigat quærentes.* "He turns all from himself, that he may confess Christ and bring the inquirers to Christ." This expresses the true character and mission of the Baptist. Comp. iii. 30.—P. S.]

‡ [The absence of a name is urged in favor of this interpretation.—P. S.]

§ [Grotius, Kuinoel, Olsh. refer ὁ προφήτης to Jeremiah.—P. S.]

of the Messiah, that is, with what was known of the suffering Messiah. The wailing Jeremiah, or one of the later prophets of affliction, seemed better fitted for the fore-runner of the suffering Messiah, than the stern, judicial Elijah. The gradual shaping of this expectation of Jeremiah as a guardian angel in the theocratic day of suffering, appears in 2 Macc. ii. 7; xv. 13. This particular prophet, therefore, is meant, who should complete the forerunning office of Elijah, and probably precede him. This expectation also was here literally and superstitiously taken. Hence again: No!—the short answer *οὔ*. Luthardt quite falsely refers to the prophets in the second part of Isaiah (c. xl.). Against this see Meyer [p. 101, note].

Ver. 22. **Then said they unto him, Who art thou?**—Now they come out with the categorical official demand of an explanation. Yet we must notice that they do not yet say: Thou art unauthorized. They distinguish the prophetic appearance of the Baptist in general from his baptism. They wished primarily that he should explain himself concerning his prophetic mission. [Alford: "They ever ask about his *person:* he ever refers them to his *office*. He is no one—a voice merely: it is the work of God, the testimony to Christ, which is every thing. So the formalist ever in the church asks, *Who* is he? while the witness for Christ only exalts, only cares for Christ's work."—P. S.]

Ver. 23. **I am the voice of one crying.**—Is. xl. 3. As Christ, when He calls Himself the Son of Man, applied to Himself as Messiah a passage of prophecy which had been unnoticed and obscured by the Jewish Messianic theology, Dan. vii. 13, so did the Baptist when he called himself the voice of one crying in the wilderness. By this the same subject was meant, as by the Elijah of Malachi, but the passage had not been corrupted by a carnal interpretation, and was perfectly fitted to denote the unassuming spirit of the Baptist, who would be wholly absorbed in his mission to be a herald of the coming Messiah. The quotation is after the Septuagint, except *εὐθύνατε* instead of *ἑτοιμάσατε*. It appears from this passage that the Synoptists (Matth. iii. 3), following John's own declaration respecting himself, have applied that passage of the prophet in its direct intent to him.

Ver. 24. **Were of the Pharisees.**—This conveys primarily the explanation that they did not understand a Scripture for which they had no distinct exegetical tradition; at least they knew not how to apply the passage cited to John. Then, that they were disposed to allow the right to baptize only to one of the three persons named: the Messiah Himself and His two forerunners. Baptism was the symbol of the purification which should precede the Messianic kingdom. The tract Kiddushin says (see Tholuck): "Elijah comes, and will declare clean and unclean."

Ver. 26. **I baptize in water.**—In this answer Heracleon, and Lücke and De Wette after him, have missed the striking point. According to Meyer, John now explains himself more particularly respecting what he has said. To the question: Why baptizest thou? he answers: I baptize only with water; the baptism of the Spirit is reserved to the Messiah. To the reminder: Thou art not the Messiah, *etc.*, he answers: The Messiah is already in the midst of you, therefore is this baptism needful. The matter resolves itself simply into John's declaration: The Messiah is the proper Baptist of the prophets; and his implied assertion: Your interpretation of Ezek. xxxvi. 25 is false. But because this true Baptist is here, I with my water-baptism prepare for His baptizing with the Spirit. It is at the same time implied that it is rather the Messiah who accredits him, than he the Messiah. *In water*. See Matth. iii. 11.

But there standeth one among you.—If the *αὐτός ἐστιν* and the *ὃς ἔμπροσθέν μου γέγονεν* be omitted, as they are in Codd. B. C. L., the clause would proceed: One whom ye know not, cometh after me, *etc.* We retain these words, which are doubted by Tholuck and Meyer; because John in ver. 15 has noted this formula as the most public testimony of the Baptist.—**Whom ye know not.**—A reproof: Ye ought to have known him already: a hint: Ye must now learn to know him. The words: *Standeth*, or hath come, among you, can hardly refer only to the birth of Jesus in Bethlehem and His obscurity in Nazareth. They look to the baptism of Christ as the beginning of His public appearance. The objections of Baur and Baümlein to this are groundless.

Ver. 27. **He it is, who coming after me** [behind me].—See ver. 15.—**Whose shoe's string,** *etc.* [In the East, people wore only sandals, or the soles of a shoe, bound fast to the foot by strings]. See Matth. iii. 11. That is: Whom I am not worthy to serve as a slave. It is a parallel, or a concrete form, of the expression, ver. 15: *ὅτι πρῶτός μου ἦν*.

Ver. 28. **In Bethabara beyond Jordan.**—Rather **Bethany**, see the Textual Notes. But not the Bethany on the Mount of Olives, ch. xi. 18. The place seems to have been a ford on the further side of the Jordan in Peræa, not otherwise known under this name of Bethany. Origen explored that region, and found a Bethabara (see Judges vii. 24) about opposite Jericho. The conjecture of Possinus and Hug, that the name בֵּית אֳנִיָּה, *domus navis*, expresses the same as בֵּית עֲבָרָה, *domus transitus* (ford-house), is not invalidated by the suggestion (of Meyer) that this etymology does not suit Bethany on the Mount of Olives; for the name of Bethany might have arisen in different ways. Bolten and Paulus, by a period after *ἐγένετο*, made out the Bethany on the Mount of Olives; Kuinoel made the "beyond," this side; Baur invented the fiction that the author would make Jesus begin, as well as finish His ministry in Bethany.—The statement that the deputation received their answer from the Baptist at Bethany, beyond Jordan, leads to the inference that on their return through the wilderness they already came unintentionally into the neighborhood of Jesus at Jericho.

Ver. 29. **The next day John seeth Jesus coming unto him.**—The Evangelist finds the days now following so important that he enumerates them in order; the first, ver. 29; the second, ver. 35; the third, ver. 43. Hereupon

Luthardt observes, p. 76: The Evangelist begins and closes with a *week;* on the third day those disciples come to him, on the fourth Simon, and on the fifth Philip and Nathanael join the others, on the sixth Jesus is journeying with His disciples, on the seventh in Cana. If this exact reckoning of a week were designed (so that Jesus, according to Luthardt, would, as it were, keep a Sabbath in Cana), the fourth day would have to be made distinct, and the third (ch. ii.) marked as the seventh. It is much more natural to let the three days come so that the calling of Peter falls late in the evening of the day of ver. 35. The third day (ch. ii. 1) is, according to Origen, Baur and Meyer, the third from the day of ver. 43. Baur gives as a reason for this (which is a change from a former view of his) a silly fancy, that the six days should correspond to the six water-pots in ch. ii. Meyer better: If it were the third day from that of ver. 35, or the day following that of ver. 43, we should have τῇ ἐπαύριον again. Against his longer reckoning (ch. ii. 1: the third day from that of i. 43) we must, however, observe that the proper starting-point of the reckoning thus far is still the day of the accrediting of Jesus as the Messiah on the part of John. It is important to the Evangelist to set forth what a life from day to day was then begun. On the first day, the pointing of the disciples to Jesus; on the next, three or four disciples gained; on the day after, two more. If now we suppose that the third day is the same with the ἐπαύριον of ver. 43, or is reckoned from the accrediting of Jesus, ver. 19, this explains the fact that the marriage-feast had already continued nearly three days when Jesus arrived, and that the wine was exhausted. The line between the day in the wilderness and the day of ver. 43 still remains somewhat uncertain.—Our first date, ver. 29, denotes the day after that declaration of the Baptist to the deputation from Jerusalem, not *one of* the days following. Jesus returns from the temptation. The reason why He returns to John is not given; yet it is at hand. John must know that Jesus intended to disappoint the chiliastic Messianic hopes of the Jews. He must also bear witness of the course which Jesus intended to take; he must be guarded to the utmost against the vexation of imagining that Jesus would adopt a different course from what he might have expected in the Messiah accredited by him. And then this also was what led to John's transfer of his disciples to the discipleship of Jesus, though the outward attachment of the Baptist himself to Jesus was not to be expected.

Behold the Lamb of God.—The Baptist knew from three sources the appointment of the Messiah to suffering: (1) The experience of suffering by the pious, especially the prophets, as well as the import of the sacrificial types and the prophecies of the suffering Messiah. (2) The baptism of Christ, which indicated to him that Christ must bow under the servant-form of sinners, or which was an omen of His suffering, see Matth. iii. 14. (3) A decisive point, which has not been noticed: The Baptist has directed the deputation from Jerusalem to the Messiah, who was in the vicinity. He may therefore suppose that they have come to know him. And now he sees Christ coming back from the wilderness, alone, in earnest, solemn mood, with the expression of separation from the world. He could not have been a man of the Spirit, without having perceived in the Spirit that an adversity, or a sacrificial suffering of premonitory conflict, had taken place. This accounts also for his first exclamation being: Behold the Lamb of God!—and the supposition that the Evangelist has put his own knowledge into the mouth of the Baptist (Strauss, Weisse), loses all support. That the subsequent *human* wavering of the Baptist, Matth. xi. 3, is not inconsistent with his present *divine enlightenment and inspiration,* needs no explanation; the opposition between the divine and human elements is nowhere entirely transcended in the Old Testament prophets. And Matth. xi. 3 itself proves that John had till then depended with assurance upon Christ, and even then could not give Him up under temptation. The Baptist, says Meyer in explanation, had not a sudden flash of natural light, or a rising conviction, but a revelation. But sudden flashes produced by rising convictions can hardly be separated from revelations, unless we conceive the latter as immediate, magical effects. With a natural light we have nothing to do.

Now comes the question: What is meant by *the Lamb of God?* By the article it is designated as appointed, by the genitive as belonging to God, appointed for Him for a sacrifice, Is. liii.; Rev. v. 6; xiii. 8. The phrase implies also, selected by God. The question arises, however, whether the expression is to be referred to the paschal lamb (with Grotius, Lampe, Hofmann, Luthardt [Bengel, Olshausen, Hengstenberg], and others), to the sin-offering (with Baumgarten-Crusius and Meyer), or to the prophetic passage, Is. liii. 7 (with Chrysostom) [Origen, Cyril, Lücke, Thol., De Wette, Brückner, Meyer (5th ed.), Ewald]. For it is clear that we are not, with Herder, to suppose it a mere figure of a religiously devoted servant of God. We are evidently directed primarily to that passage of Is. liii.; for John had taken the description of his own mission from the second part of Isaiah, and the Messianic import of the passage named cannot be evaded (see. Lücke, I. p. 408 sqq.; Tholuck, p. 90; my *Leben Jesu,* II. p. 466), and the particular features suit. [To the same chapter in Isaiah reference is had Matth. viii. 17; Acts viii. 32; 1 Pet. ii. 22–25.—P. S.] The Septuagint reads ἀμνός for the Hebrew רָחֵל, ver. 7. It is said in ver. 10, He made "His soul an offering for sin," אָשָׁם. It is said of Him in ver. 4: "He hath borne (נָשָׂא, Sept. φέρει) our griefs." Specially important is ver. 11: "By his knowledge shall my righteous servant justify many; for he shall bear (יִסְבֹּל) their iniquities." And the bearing, in connection with the idea of the offering for sin and the vicarious expiation, involves the idea of taking away, carrying off; it is therefore of no account that the Baptist says αἴρειν, and the Septuagint φέρειν (see 1 John iii. 5), for it is the way of the Seventy to express the bearing of sin by φέρειν.* The interpreta-

* [Meyer (p. 108), on the contrary, takes αἴρειν here in the sense *to take away, to abolish,* but admits that this idea pre-

tions: *put away* (Kuinoel), *support* (Gabler), abstractly considered, deviate from the notion of atonement, though they are included in the concrete term *αἴρειν: suffer—endure—piacularly bear —take away and blot out.* Latterly the term has been emptied of its element of expiation again by Hofmann and Luthardt, and referred to the then beginning suffering of Christ through the sins of men in His human weakness, without reference to His death (see against this Meyer and Tholuck). Of course, on the other hand, the word of the Baptist is not to be referred, as a mature dogmatic perception, to the future death of Christ. Yet a germ-perception of the atoning virtue of the holy suffering even the ancient prophets had, Is. liii. And how powerfully the thought had seized the Baptist, appears from his naming sin (τὴν ἁμαρτίαν) in the singular,* as the burden which Christ has to bear, and besides as the sin *of the world.*—But if the prophet, Is. liii., evidently himself went back to the notion of the expiatory sacrifice, then the Baptist also did the same. Lambs were by preference taken for the sin-offering, Lev. v. 6; see Tholuck. Christ, as the Lamb appointed by God, is a sin-offering, which atones for the guilt of the world. The fact that men have made Him, over and above this, even a curse-bearer, and that under the direction of God, is not included in the idea before us, yet neither is it excluded by it. But as regards the further step backward, to the paschal lamb, which Justin Martyr, Clement of Alexandria, and others combined with the reference to Is. liii., it is contested by Tholuck and Meyer. Justly, so far as the paschal lamb in the stricter sense served as a meal of thank-offering; but unjustly, so far as the paschal lamb in the wider sense formed the root of the whole system of sacrifice, and pointed by the blood on the door-posts to the atoning offering, nay, even ran back to the curse-offering, the extermination of the Egyptian first-born.—Mark further the rapt manner in which the Baptist utters the great word: Behold the Lamb of God! The sequel shows that he speaks thus to his disciples.†

Ver. 30. **This is he of whom I said.**—Meyer properly observes: These words refer not to the testimony in vers. 26, 27, but to all that John had previously said of the coming Messiah. John had described the divine mark of the Messiah, before he knew the particular person; now he joyfully shows that he rightly described Him, and said none too much.

Ver. 31. **And I knew him not.**—(Not: Even I knew him not.)*—That is, I did not with divine certainty, by revelation, know Him;—though in his human feeling he reverenced Him in unrestrained foreboding (against Lücke, Ewald). Hence no contradiction to Matthew (against Strauss, Baur). But now he shows how he came to this knowledge. As he was to introduce the Messiah in official authentication, he must have a token from above. This was given him.

But that he should be made manifest.—The ultimate and highest object of his baptism did not exclude the tributary purposes of preparing a people for the Lord. According to the Jewish tradition in Justin (*Dial. cum Tryph.*, ch. viii.) the Messiah was to remain unknown [ἄγνωστος] till Elijah should anoint Him, and thereby make Him known to all [φανερόν πᾶσι ποιήσῃ].—**Baptizing in water** [ἐν (τῷ) ὕδατι].—"An humble description of himself in comparison with Him who baptizes with the Spirit." Meyer.

Ver. 32. **And John bare witness, saying.**—We might expect the mark of the Messiah given to John to come before his testimony, *i. e.*, ver. 33 before ver. 32. Hence Lücke and others read this verse as a parenthesis. But this exhibition of the testimony of John is in two parts. The Evangelist distinguishes the first exclamation of John respecting Christ as the Lamb of God from the then following testimony of the way in which he came to know Him. Thus we have to make a new paragraph at ver. 32. John bears witness of the way in which he came to know Jesus in His baptism as the Messiah.

I saw the Spirit descending.—Here we must (1) assert against Baur, that the Baptist is speaking of the actual event of the baptism; this is clear from the connection of ver. 32 with ver. 31; (2) dispute [Theodore of Mops.], Tholuck, [Alford] and others in the idea that the Baptist had the manifestation alone, and that it was an inward transaction, excluding externality (though not excluding all objective element). "Even the σωματικῷ εἴδει in Lu. iii. 22, cannot prove the outwardness of the phenomenon; for it rather expresses only the unusual fact that the dove served as the symbol of the Spirit." Tholuck. Against this are (1) the fact that the event was given by an inward voice to the Baptist as the token. On the supposition of mere inwardness the inward voice alone would have sufficed; at all events it must have come at the same time with the token. (2) The mention of the appearance of the Spirit, ὡς περιστερά, *as a dove.* Merely inwardly seen, this would be only an apparition, not a token. (3) Θεάομαι is used, as in ver. 14, of a seeing which is neither merely outward, nor yet merely inward. (4) The participation of Christ; according to the Synoptists, in the seeing of the phenomenon; to which must be added

---

supposes the idea of *bearing* (*Das Hinwegnehmen der Sünde von Seite des Lammes setzt das Aufsichnehmen derselben voraus*). Dr. Lange's view is more correct. In Isa. liii., to which also Meyer refers the passage, the idea of expiatory bearing (נָשָׂא, LXX.: φέρει, ἀνήνεγκε, ἀνοίσει) prevails. By assuming and bearing our sin, Christ has abolished it. His blood cleanseth from all sin, 1 John i. 7.—P. S.]

* [This, with the article, forcibly presents the sins of the race as one fact. Christ bore the whole. "Sin and the world," says Bengel, "are equally wide. In Isaiah liii. 6, 8, 12 the same singular number is used in the midst of plurals."—P. S.]

† [Comp. on this important and difficult passage Lücke, I. 401-416, and Alford, who likewise refers the Lamb of God to the prophetic announcement in Isa. liii. 7, where it is connected with the bearing and taking away of sin. But this does not set aside the fact that Christ was indeed the true Paschal Lamb slain for us, 1 Cor. v. 7. The passage is strangely misunderstood by the author of *Ecce Homo*, Ch. I., who endeavors to explain it from the 23d Psalm, as describing a state of quiet and happy repose under the protection of the Divine Shepherd. The exegesis is the poorest part of this book.—P. S.]

* [Κἀγώ, or as א. reads, καὶ ἐγώ. Alford explains: *I also*, like the rest of the people, had no certain knowledge of Him. But καὶ here reassumes ἐγώ, ver. 30, and continues the narrative. See Meyer. John knew Jesus far better than the people (Matth. iii. 14), but in comparison with his *divine* knowledge of inspiration received at the baptism of Christ, his former *human* knowledge of conjecture dwindled into ignorance.—P. S.]

the voice: "Thou art my beloved Son!"—showing that Christ was the centre of the whole appearance. (5) The analogy of the signs (rushing wind and tongues of fire) at the outpouring of the Holy Ghost on the day of Pentecost. See this Comm. on Matth. iii. 13—17; p. 77. Tholuck: "The point of comparison between the symbol (symbolical phenomenon, we should say) and the Spirit, Theodore of Mopsuestia takes to be the affectionate tenderness and attachment of the dove to men; Calvin, its gentleness; Neander, its tranquil flying; Baumgarten-Crusius, a motherly, brooding virtue, consecrating the water (Gen. i. 1); most, from Matth. x. 16, purity and innocence.* This last is certainly to be taken as the main point,† yet it is connected with the gentle, noiseless flight of this particular bird. In the Targum on Cant. ii. 12, the dove is regarded as the symbol of the Spirit of God." We suppose that the *phenomenon* and the *symbol* are to be distinguished; the *phenomenon* we take to have been a soft, hovering brightness, resembling the flashes from a dove floating down in the sunlight (Ps. lxviii. 13: "Yet shall ye be as the wings of a dove covered with silver, and her feathers with yellow gold;" see Acts ii. 3); and the *symbol*, no one virtue of the dove, but her virtues, as a type of spiritual life, which, as such, never consists in a single virtue (see Matth. x. 16); hence purity, loveliness, gentleness, friendliness towards men, and vital warmth. On the reference of the dove to the church see the Comm. on Matth. iii. 13–17; p. 78. Hence the "abiding upon him" [καὶ ἔμεινεν ἐπ' αὐτόν, ἐπί, with the accusative signifies the direction to—] is part of the sign; in the continuance of the radiance the Baptist received assurance that the Spirit abode upon Christ.

Misinterpretations of this event: (a) The Ebionitic: An impartation of the Spirit, beginning with the baptism. (b) The Gnostic: The Logos uniting Himself with the Man Jesus;—a view dragged in again by Hilgenfeld. (c) Baur: The λόγος and the πνεῦμα ἅγιον are, according to John's representation, identical.‡ *Attempted interpretations:* (1) Frommann: The preparation of the Logos for coming forth out of his immanent union with God: (2) Lücke, Neander, *etc.*: The awakening of the divine-human consciousness. (3) Hofmann, Luthardt: The impartation of official powers. (4) Baumgarten-Crusius, Tholuck: The impartation of the Spirit for transmission to mankind. (5) Meyer: Not an impartation to Jesus, but only an objective sign (σημεῖον) divinely granted to the spiritual intuition of the Baptist.

We find in this occurrence not merely the full development of Christ's consciousness of Himself personally as the God-Man, but also of the accompanying consciousness of His Messianic mission, as a calling, in particular, to self-humiliation in order to exaltation;—a development produced by a corresponding communication of the Holy Ghost without measure, which should make Him, in the course of His humiliation towards exaltation, the Baptist of the Spirit (*Geistestäufer*) for the whole world (see Is. xi.; Joel iii.; Matth. xxviii.) This consciousness is (1) that of being the Son of God, and (2) that of the divine good pleasure blessing the path of humiliation upon which in His baptism He entered.

Ver. 33. **And I knew him not.**—Looking back to the earlier stage, and strongly emphasizing the ignorance by the repetition. Then the Baptist tells us how the miraculous appearance became to him the sign. In the nature of the case, this mark must have been given him before the occurrence itself. The description of Christ as the true Baptist, the Baptizer with the Holy Ghost, corresponds with John's humble sense of the impotence of his own baptism of water.

Ver. 34. **And I have seen.**—In the *perfect.* Plainly this cannot be understood of a mere internal process.—**And have borne witness.**—Not: I consider myself as having now testified (De Wette); nor: I have testified and do now testify (Lücke). The Baptist undoubtedly looks back with joyful mind to the testimony which he bore before the rulers of the Jews. He has borne it, and that a plain, straight-forward testimony: *borne witness to this Man*, Jesus of Nazareth, and testified that He is not merely Messiah, but also the Son of God. As if he would say: *I have lived.* My mission is in its substance accomplished (see ch. iii. 29). Hence from that moment forth he points his disciples to Jesus.

DOCTRINAL AND ETHICAL.

1. *Who art thou?* Starke: "Whether this question (of the Sanhedrin) was put sincerely, or hypocritically and with evil intent, is uncertain; but the latter is more probable. Others, however, think the former, since there are no indications that the delegation was sent out of mere envy, or with the design of questioning his office. Causes of the embassy: (1) John's unusual sort of official work, in the wilderness preaching and baptizing, and the great gathering of the people to him. (2) The conviction, from many signs, that the time of the Messiah must be at hand. (3) The vehement longing of the Jewish people everywhere for the advent of the Messiah, especially by reason of their great oppression under the Roman power, *etc.*, because they hoped the Messiah would erect again their fallen commonwealth, and because they did not yet imagine that the kingdom of the Messiah would turn to the prejudice of their prestige. Furthermore they must either not have known the origin and family of John, or must have been entirely foolish to suppose the Messiah could be born of the tribe of Levi."

2. The two testimonies of the Baptist form the contents of this section: Christ *the Lord* (the Old Testament manifestation of God, the Angel of the Lord, Jehovah): (1) Christ the *Lamb of God* (the Servant of God); (2) Christ the *Son of God.*

3. From the first testimony it is evident that Christ was accredited by John in an entirely official manner; in the second we see how Christ

* [Augustine urges simplicity as the *tertium comparationis.* "The Holy Ghost," he says (as quoted by Wordsworth who does not refer to the place), "then manifested Himself as a Dove,—and, at the day of Pentecost, in tongues of fire: in order that we may learn to unite fervor with simplicity and to seek for both from the Holy Ghost."—P. S.]

† After the martyrdom of Polycarp a dove arose from the ashes of the martyr.

‡ [The last view is sufficiently refuted by σὰρξ ἐγένετο, which could never be said of the Spirit. Comp. Meyer, p. 115.—P. S.]

was accredited by John himself most distinctly by God. Likewise, that John points his disciples to Christ, and that every genuine fore-runner does the same, while the spurious fore-runners, the chief priests, keep their disciples to themselves.

4. On the import of the baptism of Jesus see the exegesis under ver. 32, and Com. on Matth. ch. iii. 13, p. 76.

5. Between the 28th and 29th verses falls the close of the history of the temptation of Jesus, and with it the settlement of His Messianic calling or, as Reinhard puts it, His plan. He comes out of the wilderness with the clear sense of His destiny and His willingness to become the Lamb of God. This then the prophetic Baptist perceives in His appearance through the Spirit.

6. It is noticeable that the temptation of John by the Sanhedrin, and that of the Lord by Satan, coincides in time. The Baptist says: I am not the Christ; Jesus says: I am not the Christ according to the perverted antichristian hopes of the hierarchy, according to the notion of the ungodly world.

7. Gerlach: "In the fact that he alone knew the Messiah, while the entire people and their rulers knew Him not, John would give them the credentials of his own prophetic mission."

8. The ultimate object of the mission of John the Baptist: To make Christ known by official attestation according to the Old Testament law before the rulers of the Jews, by a testimony of the New Testament Spirit among His disciples. Malachi pointed to John (Elijah), John points to Christ, and thus the Messianic prophecy converges at last to the distinctness of an index finger.

HOMILETICAL AND PRACTICAL.

See the Comm. on Matth. iii. 13-17; Mark i. 1-8; Luke iii. 1-22. The temptation of John and the temptation of Christ. The first and last temptation of John, and the first and last temptation of Christ.—*Who art thou?* or, the perfect ignorance of a hardened, formal spirituality before living spirits.—*No*, and again *no!* or, how the spirit of John refuses to suit the forms of the Pharisees.—The great two-fold testimony of the Baptist concerning Christ: (1) The same both in public and in the confidential circle; (2) varying in form: in its legal office before the Jewish rulers describing Christ as the eternal Lord, and in its spiritual office in the circle of disciples describing Christ as the Lamb of God.—The denials of John and the denials of Christ as against the current notions of Elijah and Christ, a proof that between the spirit of Holy Scripture itself and the exegesis of a traditional hierarchical theology there is an immense difference.—The lessons of the connection between John's humble knowledge of himself and his knowledge of Christ.—John, as a witness of his own knowledge of Christ, free and open, yet also wisely reserved (1) in reference to *what* he knew of Christ (speaking to the unsusceptible only of *the Lord*, to the susceptible, of the *Lamb of God*); (2) in reference to *how* he knew it: showing to the one company only that he knows Christ, to the other, how he came to know him.—The self-denial of John the true confession, as an example to us: (1) The true confession of Christ; (2) the true confession of himself.—John and the Pharisees, or the servant of the law of God and the men of human commandments (the man of the law and the men of traditions).—The Baptist, as God's prophet, consistent with himself, and therefore one thing to the Pharisees, another to his disciples.—The glory of Christ in the light of the human and the divine nature: (1) High as heaven above the Baptist; (2) one with the Father in the Holy Ghost.—The word: I have borne witness, is equivalent to: I have lived: (1) In the mouth of the Baptist; (2) in the mouth of the Lord (the "true witness"); (3) in the mouth of every believer.—*The Lamb and the Dove*, or, the sensible signs of the kingdom of heaven (1) in the lamb and in all silent, devout passiveness of nature; (2) in the dove and in all pure, beautiful joyousness of nature.—[The lamb, the pure and gentle beast of earth; the dove, the pure and gentle bird of heaven: Ps. lxxxv. 10, 11.]—Christ the Lamb of God, who bears the sins of the world: (1) bears; (2) bears with; (3) bears away.—The testimonies of the Baptist concerning Christ, at first apparently without effect, and afterwards of immeasurable, permanent power.—Christ the centre of all testimonies of God: (1) The inexhaustibly and strongly Attested; (2) the inexhaustible and true Witness.—*The Pericope*, vers. 19-28. The spiritual position of things at the advent of Christ in its permanent import: (1) The spiritual leaders of the people understand not the Baptist and know not Christ; (2) the Baptist preaches and testifies of Christ as a voice in the wilderness; (3) Christ fights out His victory in secret.—John a pure prophetic character, the standard of value between the Pharisees and Christ: (1) As compared with the Pharisees, grandly exalted; (2) as compared with Christ, small, even to the deepest self-humiliation.—The mysteriousness of the testimony of the Baptist: (1) The mysteriousness in the testimony itself; (2) the mysterious features in the attested One; (3) the mysterious intimation of his work.

STARKE:—Before persons whose candor and fear of God we should most trust, we are many a time most on our guard.—Wo to the city and to the country whose watchmen are blind.—CANSTEIN: Christians in general, and preachers in particular, should not arrogate to themselves what belongs to Christ, but point their hearers away from themselves and to Christ, to look for all their salvation from Him.—HEDINGER: No one may take to himself credit, or receive praise beyond due measure and contrary to humility, 2 Cor. x. 13.—In calling himself a voice, he not only hints that his preaching is from heaven, but also that in him nothing is to be honored save his voice, nay, that all he is, is, as it were, nothing but voice.—CANSTEIN: We have to do not with the person (humanly taken), but with the matter itself.—CRAMER: Spare neither friends nor foes to confess the truth.—Jesus is in the midst of us, though we see Him not.—OSIANDER: To the minister of the church it belongs to preach and to administer the sacraments, but Christ gives the increase, and pours out the Spirit.—ZEISIUS: A true teacher should, after the example of John, be *well instructed, authenticated, and established.*

GERLACH:—The decisive self-denial of John in his relation to Christ gave and still gives the greatest weight to his testimony. This self-denial was and still is, to unbelief, incomprehensible; in this, that a man could so clearly know his mission and its limits.—BRAUNE: Whom John had announced as coming with axe, winnowing-fan, and fire, Him he now commended as the Lamb of God which taketh away the sin of the world.

HEUBNER:—On the rights of the magistracy in regard to religion.—What privileges has the spiritual power?—The limits of obedience.—Who art thou? as it were the: Who is there? demanded of every one in the ministry of the kingdom of God.—Tycho Brahe's symbol: *Esse potius quam haberi.*—Christian self-valuation.—Persius: *Quem deus esse jussit, disce.*—Christian choice of calling.—Assurance of an eternal mission.—In John the testimony of the best and noblest of his time and of the ages before is set forth.—SCHLEIERMACHER: The baptism of John stood in a manner between the law and the Gospel.—John's testimony concerning Christ a type of ours.—COUARD: An evangelical preacher will and must bear witness only of Christ.—To what the question: *Who art thou?* would lead us, if put to ourselves.—RIEGER: John the model of an evangelical preacher.*

[SCHAFF:—*Behold the Lamb of God*, ver. 29 (repeated ver. 36). (1) The person who speaks: *John the Baptist*, in the name of the whole Old Testament, responded to by the experience of the Christian believer. (2) The person spoken of: Christ, (a) compared to a *lamb* for His innocence and purity ("a lamb without blemish and without spot," 1 Pet. i. 19), meekness, gentleness, and quiet submission, ("as a lamb led to the slaughter," Is. liii.); (b) called the Lamb foretold by the prophet Isaiah in that remarkable passage on the suffering Messiah, liii. 7. Comp. also the *paschal* lamb, the blood of which, being sprinkled on the door-post, saved the Israelites from the destroying angel (1 Cor. v. 7), and the lambs of the *daily* sacrifices, Ex. xxix. 38; (c) the Lamb *of God*, appointed and ordained by God from eternity, dedicated to God, and approved by God. (3) The office of Christ: to *bear*, and by bearing, *i. e.*, by His propitiatory sacrifice, *to take away the sin*, the accumulated mass of the sins, *of the world*, *i. e.*, of the entire human race (1 John ii. 12), consequently also *my* sins. (4) The exhortation *Behold*, with the eye of a living faith, which appropriates the atoning sacrifice of Christ.—AUGUSTINE: How weighty must be the blood of the Lamb, by whom the world was made, to turn the scale when weighed against the world.—OLSHAUSEN: The sacrificial lamb which bears the sin, also takes it away; there is no bearing of sin without removing the same.—RYLE: The Lamb of God has made atonement *sufficient* for all mankind, though *efficient* to none but believers.—MATTHEW HENRY: John was more industrious *to do* good than to *appear* great. Those speak best for Christ that say least of themselves, whose own works praise them, not their own lips.—*The same:* Secular learning, honor and power seldom dispose men's minds to the reception of divine light.—J. C. RYLE, (abridged): The greatest saints have always been men of John Baptist's spirit; "clothed with humility" (1 Pet. v. 5), not seeking their own honor, ever willing to decrease if Christ might only increase. Hence God has honored and exalted them (Luke xiv. 11).—Humility is the beginning of Christian graces.—The learned Pharisees are examples of the blindness of unconverted men.—Christ is "still standing" among multitudes who neither see, nor hear, nor believe. It will be better on the last day to never have been born, than to have had Christ "standing among us" without knowing Him.—P. S.]

* [Several commonplace extracts or mere repetitions and themes of sermons have been omitted in this section.—P. S.]

II.

THE DISCIPLES OF JOHN AND THE FIRST DISCIPLES OF JESUS. JESUS ACKNOWLEDGED AS THE MESSIAH, THE KING OF ISRAEL, WHO KNOWS HIS ISRAELITES, AND ALSO KNOWS "THE JEWS;" SIGNALIZED BY MIRACULOUS DISCERNMENT OF SPIRITS, PERSONAL CHARACTERS BECOMING MANIFEST IN HIS PERSONAL LIGHT.

CHAP. I. 35–52.

35 Again the next day after [*omit* after] John stood, and two of his disciples;
36 and looking [fastening his eye] upon Jesus as he walked, he saith, Behold the Lamb
37 of God! And the two disciples heard him speak, and they followed Jesus.
38 (39) Then [And] Jesus turned, and saw them following, and saith unto them[1] What
seek ye? They said unto him, Rabbi, (which is to say [which means], being inter-
39 (40) preted, Master), where dwellest [abidest] thou? He saith unto them, Come and
[ye shall] see![2] [Then][3] They came and saw where he dwelt [abode][4] and abode
[for their part] with him that day: [.] for [*omit* for][5] it was about the tenth hour.
40 (41) One of the two which [who] heard John speak, and followed him, was Andrew,

41 (42) Simon Peter's brother. He first[6] findeth his own brother Simon, and saith unto
him, We have found the Messias [Messiah], which is, being interpreted, the
42 (43) [*om.* the] Christ [Anointed]. And he brought him to Jesus. And [*om.*
And] when Jesus beheld him, he [Jesus looking on him] said, Thou art Simon
the Son of Jona [John][7] thou shalt be called Cephas, which is by interpreta-
43 (44) tion, A stone [Peter].[8] The day following [the next day][9] Jesus [he][10] would
go [ἠθέλησεν, intended, was minded, to go] forth into Galilee, and findeth Philip,
44 (45) and saith unto him, Follow me. Now Philip was of [from] Bethsaida, the
45 (46) city of Andrew and Peter. Philip findeth Nathanael, and saith unto him, We
have found him, of whom Moses in the law, and the prophets, did write, Jesus
46 (47) of Nazareth, the son of Joseph.[11] And Nathanael said unto him, Can there
47 (48) any good thing [have] come [εἶναι] out of Nazareth? Philip saith unto him,
Come and see. Jesus saw Nathanael coming to him, and saith of him, Behold
48 (49) an Israelite indeed, in whom is no guile! Nathanael saith unto him [answered
him], Whence knowest thou me? Jesus answered and said unto him, Before
that [*om.* that] Philip called thee, when thou wast under the fig tree, I saw
49 (50) thee. Nathanael answered and saith unto him, Rabbi, thou art the Son of
50 (51) God; thou art the King of Israel. Jesus answered and said unto him, Because
I said unto thee, I saw thee under the fig tree, believest thou? thou shalt see
51 (52) greater things than these. And he saith unto him, Verily, verily, I say unto you,
Hereafter[12] [*om.* hereafter or henceforth], ye shall see heaven open [opened],
and the angels of God ascending and descending upon the Son of man.[13]

TEXTUAL AND GRAMMATICAL.

1 Ver. 38.—[Lit.: *(And) Jesus having turned, and seen them following, saith to them.* δέ after στραφείς is omitted by Tischend. (VIII. ed.), but retained by Tregelles, Alford, Westcott.—Tischendorf, Alford and others divide ver. 38 into two, commencing ver. 38 with τί ζητεῖτε; hence the difference of verses to the end of the ch.—P. S.]

2 Ver. 39.—[The text. rec. reads ἴδετε, *see*, in conformity with ἔρχεσθε and with ver. 47: ἔρχου καὶ ἴδε. Meyer, Alford, Tregelles, Tischendorf, Westcott, adopt ὄψεσθε, which could be more easily changed into ἴδετε than substituted for it.—P. S.]

3 Ver. 39.—[Text. rec. omits οὖν, which is supported by ℵ. A. B. C. L., *etc.*. Tischendorf, Tregelles, Alford, Westc.—P. S.]

4 Ver. 38.—[Μένειν is used here and twice in ver. 39, and there is no need of varying the transl., as in the E. V.—P. S.]

5 Ver. 39.—[The best authorities omit δέ after ὥρα. There should be a full stop after *day*. If the δέ of text. rec. be retained, it should be translated *and* instead of *for*.—P. S.]

6 Ver. 41.—[The text. rec., πρῶτος, referring to Ἀνδρέας (he before any other), is supported by ℵ.* L. Epiph. Cyr., *etc.*, and adhered to by Meyer, Lange and Tischendorf (ed. VIII.), while Lachmann, Tregelles, Alford and Westcott, on the authority of ℵ.c A. B. M. Orig, give the preference to πρῶτον, which would mean (*adverbialiter*) either *first* (before he found another) or (assuming an error of the transcriber for πρωΐ) *early* (hence the Itala: *mane*). But the change of ς in ν is easily accounted for by the following τόν.—P. S.]

7 Ver. 42.—Cod. B. reads Ἰωάνου [other authorities, Ἰωάννου, with double ν], so Lachmann; Cod. L. 33, and some versions, Ἰωάννου. The same authorities give the same in ch. xxi. 15, 17, and besides codd. C. and D. interchange Ἰωάνου and Ἰωάννου. The Recepta [*Jona*, or better, *Jonas*] is supported primarily by Matth. xvi. 17, where all authorities read Ἰωνᾶ. Lücke observes: The less usual Ἰωνᾶ might easily be confounded with the Ἰωάνου or Ἰωάννου more current among the Greeks. Meyer supposes that John gave the form Ἰωάνης to the name, whence it became the more usual Ἰωάννης. [Cod. Sin. Tregelles, Tischendorf, Alford, Westcott and Hort read Ἰωάννου, or the same with one ν. Ἰωνᾶ is a correction from Matth. xvi. 17. Ewald, on the contrary, thinks that the reading *Johannes* here and ch. xxi. originated in a mistake. He reads σύ εἶ, *etc.* as a question: *Du bist Simon Jona's Sohn?*—P. S.]

8 Ver. 42.—[For information on the meaning of Cephas, Petros, Petra, *see* my long annotation to Lange on *Matthew* xvi. 17, p. 293, *Text. Note* 3.—P. S.]

9 Ver. 43.—[τῇ ἐπαύριον, as in vers. 35 and 29. The E. V. needlessly and carelessly varies here the translation three times: *the next day* (ver. 29), the *next day after* (35), *the day following* (43).—P. S.]

10 Ver. 43.—After ἠθέλησεν the Recepta has ὁ Ἰησοῦς. "Beginning of a church lesson." [Omitted by Tischend., Treg., Alf., Westc.—P. S.]

11 Ver. 45.—[Lit. *Jesus, the son of Joseph, the one from Nazareth* (or *who is from Nazareth*), or *Jesus, Joseph's son, from Nazareth*, Ἰησοῦν τὸν υἱὸν τοῦ Ἰωσὴφ τὸν ἀπὸ Ναζαρέτ.—P. S.]

12 Ver. 51.—The ἀπάρτι is wanting in Codd. [ℵ.] B. L., and in considerable versions; omitted in Tischendorf and Lachmann. [Treg., Alf., Westc. and H.] It was doubtless dropped because it seemed unsuitable to the words following, which were taken for actual angelic appearances. [On the other hand, it may have been inserted from Matth. xxvi. 64. Alford.—P. S.]

13 Ver. 51.—[The Engl. Vers., also the Greek text of Tregelles, and Westcott and Hort number but 51 verses, but the Vulgate, Lachmann, Tischendorf, Alford, Luther's Vers., Lange, *etc.*, number 52. The difference in the counting begins at ver. 38.—P. S.]

EXEGETICAL AND CRITICAL.

[THE GATHERING OF THE FIRST DISCIPLES OF JESUS, 35–52. The humble beginning of mighty results. The cradle of the Christian Church. This call in Judea on the banks of Jordan was merely a preliminary acquaintance, which John supplies from his personal experience, while the final call to the permanent discipleship, as related by the Synoptists (Matth. iv. 18 ff.; Mark i. 16 ff.; Luke v. 1 ff.), took place at a later date in Galilee. We must assume that these disciples (two of them at least, *viz.*, Andrew and John, were formerly disciples of the Baptist), after becoming acquainted with Jesus on the banks of Jordan, and accompanying Him to Galilee to witness the miracle at Cana, returned for a while to their occupation as fishermen (as they did after the resurrection, John xxi. 1 ff.), until, before His journey to the passover in Jerusalem, He called them to the Apostolate. The readiness with which they followed, and the confidence of Peter in the miraculous powers of Jesus (Luke v. 5), are more readily explained from the previous intercourse related by John. The section has two divisions: 1) The calling of Andrew and John, and, through Andrew, of Simon Peter, 35-43; 2) The calling of Philip, and, through him, of Nathanael, 44-52. Christ *finds* disciples, they *find* their friends, and report how they *have been found* by Christ and *have found* Him (vers. 41, 45). Bengel observes on εὑρίσκει (ver. 41): "With the festive freshness of those days beautifully corresponds the word *findeth*, which is used here more frequently than elsewhere." Trench appropriately calls this "the chapter of the Eurekas." Christ used no outward compulsion, held out no worldly inducements of any kind; it was simply the force of spiritual attraction which draws "the brave to the braver, the noble to the noblest of all."—P. S.]

Ver. 35. **Again the next day.**—[Τῇ ἐπαύριον πάλιν εἱστήκει Ἰωάννης.]—The day after the first testimony of John [ver. 29] or after the day of Christ's return from the wilderness, which followed the day of John's testimony concerning the Messiah before the Jewish rulers; to the Evangelist ever memorable. He counts these never to be forgotten days one by one. Upon the testimony of the first day the two disciples of John did not follow Jesus. They doubtless felt that this must involve departure from their old master. The next day was the day of their calling and decision.

And two of his disciples.—One was Andrew, we know from ver. 40 (see *Com. on Matthew* ch. x. 1-4); the other was certainly John. We judge thus from (1) John's manner of mentioning himself, either not at all, or indirectly (chs. xiii. 23; xviii. 15; xix. 26; xx. 3; xxi. 20); a manner which he seems to have extended also to his mother (xix. 25; comp. *Introduction*, p. 5), and to which we might cite analogies in Mark (ch. xiv. 51) and Luke (ch. xxiv. 18). 2) The giving of one name, suggesting a personal reserve in regard to the other. 3) The very lifelike character of the subsequent account. 4) The more distinct calling of the sons of Zebedee immediately after, with the sons of Jonas, on the sea of Galilee, Matth. iv. As the calling of the latter is introduced here, so is doubtless the calling of the former.

Ver. 36. **And looking upon Jesus.**—His eye rests upon him, is steadily and continuously directed towards him, ἐμβλέψας, see ver. 42, *et al.* [ver. 43; Mark x. 21; Luke xx. 17].

As he walked.—The day before, Jesus had returned to John out of the wilderness. Probably He then took leave of him, after coming to an understanding with him respecting their conduct towards each other. We may suppose that Jesus expects the transfer of the disciples of John. To-day He comes no more to John, but after an excursion returns to His abode. That He comes within sight of the Baptist, is wholly natural, yet at the same time designed.

Behold the Lamb of God.—As the disciples of John had yesterday heard the same word, and no doubt some explanation of it, no more than this repetition of the exclamation was now necessary, to cause these two disciples to go personally after the Lord; no more extended discourse (so Meyer, rightly, against Lücke and Tholuck. And of a multitude standing by, to whom he spoke in presence of the two, there is not a word).

Ver. 37. **And they followed Jesus** [with profound reverence and in expectation of great things].—The ἀκολουθεῖν being immediately repeated, must mean more than: went towards Him to see Him (Nonnus, Euthymius [Alf.]). They went towards him, in any case, with the thought of discipleship, though their decision to be disciples must have been afterwards wrought by Christ. Bengel: "*Primæ origines ecclesiæ Christianæ.*"

Ver. 38 (39). **What seek ye?**—Anticipating, yet meeting their seeking. That they are seeking, He acknowledges. But in the impersonal τί He couches a sort of testing. That they were now quite timid, as Euthymius Zigabenus proposes, is evident from their embarrassed answer. They do not express themselves directly respecting their seeking; yet they plainly say that they seek not *something* from Him, but *Himself.*

Rabbi, where abidest thou?—An acknowledgment that He was a master [a travelling Rabbi]; an intimation that they wish to speak with Him in quiet; an implication that He has a hospitable house [with a friend] near by; an inquiry, when they may meet Him there. John writes for Greeks, and therefore explains the term *Rabbi.*

Ver. 39 (40). **Come and ye shall see.***—An unmistakable allusion to the rabbinical formula of requiring one to convince himself: Come and see! (בא וראה, according to Buxtorf and Lightfoot), which Meyer groundlessly rejects. [*Come and see*, afterwards used by Philip, ver. 47 (48), in reply to the objection of Nathanael, occurs Ps. lxvi. 5 (6) with reference to the great works of God (לְכוּ וּרְאוּ, LXX.: δεῦτε καὶ ἴδετε τὰ ἔργα τοῦ θεοῦ); comp. ver. 16 (δεῦτε, ἀκούσατε, *Come and hear* . . and I will declare what He has done for my soul). It is often the wisest answer we can give to honest skeptics on matters of Christian faith. Bengel calls it *optimum remedium contra opiniones præconceptas.* Personal experience is the best test of the truth of Christianity, which, like the sun in heaven, can only be seen in its own light. It was Pascal, I believe, who said, that human things must be known to be loved, but divine things must be loved first before they can be known.—P. S.]

And abode with him.—Ἔμειναν receives its significant sense from the preceding ποῦ μένεις.

It was about the tenth hour.—[The first hour of his *Christian* life was indelibly fixed upon the memory of John, as a great and glorious turning point, as a transition from darkness to light.† Such days will be remembered in eter-

* [Ὄψεσθε instead of ἴδετε, see TEXT. NOTE 2. Ewald infers from the reading ὄψεσθε, without sufficient reason, that the place of lodging was at some distance.—P. S.]

† [Augustine: *Quam beatum diem duxerunt, quam beatam*

nity, when their fruits will fully appear.—P. S.] According to the Jewish computation, four o'clock in the afternoon; according to the Roman (from midnight to midnight), ten o'clock in the morning. The expression: *abode with Him that day* [*τὴν ἡμέραν ἐκείνην*], seems to favor the latter computation. For this are Rettig [*Studien und Kritiken*, 1830, p. 106 f.], Tholuck, Ebrard, Ewald.* For the Jewish, Lücke, Meyer, [Alford, Hengstenberg]. Decisive arguments for the Jewish are: 1) The Greeks of Asia Minor, for whom John wrote, had with the Jews the Babylonian reckoning, from sun-rise to sun-set. 2) The Romans also used the natural day besides the other computation. 3) In ch. iv. 6 the sixth hour is far more probably noon, than six o'clock in the morning or evening (see *Leben Jesu*, II., p. 474); in ch. iv. 52 the seventh hour is most probably the first hour after noon; ch. xi. 9 implies the Babylonian reckoning; and in ch. xix. 14 the sixth hour cannot be six o'clock in the morning, though to place it at noon causes difficulty (see *Comm. on Mark* xv. 25, and *Matth.* xxvii. 45). 4) Even of a late part of the afternoon it may be said in popular speech, that they abode with Him that day, especially if the conversation extended into the night. Reference of the hour to what follows further on (Hilgenfeld, Lichtenstein; see Meyer), is unwarranted.

Ver. 40 (41). **One was Andrew,** *etc.*—The form of the statement leads us to inquire after the other. Andrew is more particularly described as the brother of Simon Peter, on account of the subsequent distinction of Peter. He no doubt influenced the decision of John, as well as of Peter, and afterwards of Philip (who "was of the city of Andrew and Peter"). He appears again as mediator and pioneer in John xii. 22 (comp. Mark xiii. 3). On Andrew see *Matth.* on ch. x. 1-4, and the word in Winer [Smith, and other Bible Dictionaries].

Vers. 41 (42). **He first findeth.**—For this finding Luthardt supposes a separate day, without support from the text. The text in fact leads us to suppose that this finding occurred on the same day that the disciples were with Jesus (Meyer, against De Wette, *etc.*) We may easily imagine, too, that Andrew found his brother on returning in a common lodging-place. The supposition that the disciples then brought Peter to Jesus still on the same evening, is more difficult. But even this has a parallel in the nocturnal visit of Nicodemus, and it makes the whole procedure uncommonly animated, showing the intense excitement of the disciples. Meyer thinks the emphatic statement that Andrew is the first to find his own brother, an intimation even that John next found his brother James, and brought him to Jesus. John is silent about it, indeed, after the manner of his peculiar, delicate reserve respecting himself and his kindred (even the name of James does not occur in his Gospel); but the *πρῶτος* betrays it, and the Synoptical account confirms it, Mark i. 19. This opinion is certainly more strengthened by the *ἴδιον* (which is not merely possessive), than the opinion of De Wette and others, that the two together sought out Simon.

We have found the Messiah [*Εὑρήκαμεν τὸν Μεσσίαν*.—Bengel: "A great and joyful *εὕρηκα*, and expected by the world for about forty centuries."—P. S.]—"With the stress on the first word, implying a longing search": Meyer. And the name *Messiah*, used by the Aramaic-speaking disciple, the Evangelist interprets to his readers. [*Χριστός*, from *χρίω*, *to anoint.* The article is omitted because the author wishes simply to identify the two *words* מָשִׁיחַ and *χριστός*, not the two *titles*. See Meyer and Alford. Anointing with oil in the O. T. is a symbolical act that signifies the communication of the gifts of the Holy Spirit and the solemn consecration to the service of God. It was performed on the three officers of the theocracy, the kings, priests and prophets, especially the kings (comp. 1 Sam. x. 1; xvi. 13, 14); hence kings were called emphatically *the anointed*, or *the anointed of the Lord* (1 Sam. ii. 10, 35; xii. 3, 5; xvi. 6, 10; 2 Sam. i. 14, 16; xix. 21; Lament. iv. 20; Zech. iv. 14). The term in its fullest sense was applied to Him who should be endowed with the Holy Spirit without measure (Isa. xi.; comp. John i. 32, 33; iii. 34), realize the typical significance of the kingdom of Israel (Ps. ii. 2; Dan. ix. 25) and combine the offices of prophet, priest and king in His own person for ever. P. S.]

Vers. 42 (43). **Beheld him.**—*Ἐμβλέψας.* The penetrating look of the Lord, introducing one of those mental miracles of immediate discernment of characters which here follow in rapid succession, and of which the knowledge of Nathanael is especially signalized. Jesus is the knower of hearts, ch. ii. 25. It is characteristic that John first brings out this power of the Lord: in keeping with his Gospel of the ideal personality.

Thou art Simon.—This calling him by name is not necessarily through miraculous knowledge (Chrysost., Luthardt), for Andrew had introduced him to Jesus; but is doubtless intended to put Simon as the son of Jonas in contrast with Peter. שִׁמְעוֹן, *heard*, יוֹנָה, *dove*, כֵּיפָא, *rock*. The sense is: What thou art not, and canst not be, as Simon, son of Jonas,* but what thou art adapted to be, that shalt thou become. [Christ says not: "Thou *art* Cephas," as He says to Nathanael: "Thou *art* truly an Israelite," but

noctem! Quis est, qui nobis dicat, quæ audierint illi a Domino?—P. S.]

* [Ewald maintains that John at Ephesus followed the computation which now prevails with us, so that here and xix. 14 the hours before noon are meant, but in iv. 6 and iv. 52 the hours of the afternoon.—P. S.]

* [The allegorical interpretations of *Son of Jona* (*Jonas*) or *Barjona* (Matth. xvi. 17), based upon the characteristics of the dove, *viz.*, man of *purity*, or man of *weakness* (as contrasted with man of *rock*), *etc.*, have no proper foundation, since the received text Ἰωνᾶ (which is a correction from Matth. xvi. 17) must give way to the far better authenticated reading Ἰωάννης or Ἰωάνης (see TEXT. NOTES [7]). In John xxi. 15, 16, 17, according to the best critical authorities, Christ addresses Peter: Σίμων Ἰωάννου (*Johannis* in the Vulg.). In conformity with this reading, *Jona* or *Jonas* in *Barjona*, Matth. xvi. 17, must be regarded not as the name of the prophet Jonas (from יוֹנָה, *dove*) but as a contraction of *Joana* or *Jehoanan* (יְהוֹחָנָן), *John*, *i. e.*, Jehovah is merciful (comp. the German *Gottlieb*, the Greek *Theodore*). Hence *Barjona* would mean *son of grace* rather than *son of the dove*. I expressed this view in a note on *Matthew*, p. 295, and find it now confirmed by the authority of so good a Hebrew scholar as Hengstenberg, *Com. on John*, I. p. 111.—P. S.]

"thou *shalt be called* Peter." It was therefore a *prophecy* of the future work and position of Peter in history, as the Apostle who, above all others, laid the foundations of the church, among the Jews on the day of Pentecost, and among the Gentiles by the conversion of Cornelius. *Cephas* (כֵּיפָא), *Peter, Rock*, is a symbol of firmness; comp. the contrast of rocky and sandy foundation, Matth. vii. 24–26, and the promise of indestructibility given to the church as founded upon the rock, xvi. 18.—P. S.] On the more particular sense of the antithesis see *Comm. on Matth.*, xvi. 17 [and the notes in the Am. ed., pp. 292, 293, 295]; on the different calls, *Matth.* on ch. iv. 19, p. 93. In Matth. xvi. 18 this previous naming is evidently pre-supposed.* It is characteristic of Judaism as the religion of personal life, that persons were commonly designated by names significant of their peculiarities. See the citation in Tholuck. According to Tholuck the rock, the emblem of firmness, would refer to the choleric temperament of Peter. But none of all the temperaments suffices to describe a *concrete direction of character*. A recent assurance, that the name Peter refers not at all to his stamp of character, but entirely to the work of grace in him, can be accounted for only by want of insight into the nature of a charism.†

[THE CALLING OF PHILIP AND NATHANAEL, vers. 43–52. Comp. on this passage Archbishop Trench, *Studies in the Gospels*, N. Y. ed., 1867, pp. 66 ff.—P. S.]

Vers. 43 (44). **The next day Jesus . . . . to go forth.**—Had therefore not yet gone forth. Was intending to set out.—**And findeth Philip.**—He was by this circumstance again detained. The acquaintance may be accounted for by two facts. Philip had been also at the Jordan; probably, like others, a disciple of John. He was a townsman of Andrew and Peter, of Bethsaida (iv. 5; xii. 21), and perhaps just then on his way home.‡ Philip, one of the earliest apostles of the Lord. His characteristic, according to John vi. 5; xii. 21 sqq.; xiv. 8, seems to have been a striving after ocular evidence in the nobler sense, a buoyant and resolute advance to the object in view (see *Comm. on Matth.*, p. 183). Tradition, contrary to the fact of his earlier calling, has made him the disciple to whom Christ spoke the words in Matth. viii. 22 (Clement of Alex., *Strom.* III. 187). More probable is the tradition that he preached in Phrygia (Theodoret, Nicephorus), and died at Hierapolis (Euseb. III. 31, *etc.*) The accounts of his marriage and his daughters have confounded him with Philip the deacon, with whom he is in general frequently interchanged (see the art. in Winer and in Herzog's *Real Encycl.*)

Follow me.—This cannot mean merely: Join the journeying company [Alford]; yet neither is it the call to the Apostolic office. It is the invitation to discipleship, in the form of a travelling companionship. The rest of the interview (how Jesus knew Philip, and Philip knew the Lord) is not mentioned; only the decisive word of the call. Probably the Evangelist would tell us that the quick, active character of Philip did not need many circumstances. [Trench: "This '*Follow Me*' might seem at first sight no more than an invitation to accompany Him on that journey from the banks of Jordan to Galilee, on which He was just setting forward. It meant this (thus compare Matth. ix. 9; Luke v. 27); but at the same time how much more. It was an invitation to follow the blessed steps of His most holy life (Matth. xvi. 24; John viii. 12; xii. 26; xxi. 19; Rev. xiv. 4), to be a partaker at once of His cross and His crown. How much of this Philip may have understood at the moment it is impossible to say; but whether much or little, he is not disobedient to the heavenly calling."—P. S.]

Ver. 44 (45). [BETHSAIDA of Galilee was on the western shore of the lake of Galilee, not far from Capernaum and Chorazin, but like these two towns, it is entirely obliterated from the face of the earth, so that even the memory of its site has perished. Robinson (III. 359) places it a short distance north of *Khân Minyeh*, which he identifies with Capernaum; while other travellers, perhaps more correctly, find the ruins of Capernaum in *Tell Hûm.* Comp. Matth. xi. 20 and the notes in *Matthew*, pp. 210, 211.—It is remarkable that none of the Apostles was from Jerusalem, the capital of the nation. Christ Himself proceeded from an insignificant town and an humble carpenter-shop, and selected His Apostles from among the illiterate fishermen of Galilee. This is the way of God who made the world out of nothing. Comp. 1 Cor. i. 27.—P. S.]

Ver. 45 (46). **Philip findeth Nathanael** (Theodore, gift of God).—The same with Bartholomew (see the *Comm. on Matth.* p. 182), and, according to ch. xxi. 2, of Cana in Galilee.* He was probably, therefore, going in the same direction. The calling of Nathanael also is represented as occurring at the outset of the journey, not (as Ewald makes it) on nearing Cana. Nathanael seems also to be one of the devout (Luke ii. 38), who had been with John the Baptist; and Philip's having to find his friend (we find him afterwards paired with Nathanael, Matth. x. 3,

* [So also Meyer against Baur and Scholten: "In Matth. xvi. 18 the *former* bestowal of the new name on Simon is presupposed, confirmed and applied." In giving new names, Christ acts with the authority of Jehovah in the O. T. when He changed the name of Abram into Abraham, Jacob into Israel, *etc.* Comp. Hengstenberg.—P. S.]

† [On the character of Peter see Schaff's *History of the Apostolic Church*, N. Y. ed., pp. 348 ff.].

‡ [His name and other Greek names of native Jews (Peter, Stephen, Nicanor, Timon, comp. Acts vi. 5, *etc.*), and the use of the Greek by all the apostles prove the wide spread of the Greek language, manners, and customs since the conquest of Alexander the Great, which prepared the way for the spread of the gospel.—P. S.]

* [Double names were quite common in Palestine. The identity of *Nathanael* (נְתַנְאֵל=God gave, the gift of God) and *Bartholomew* (בַּר תַּלְמַי, *i. e.*, Son of Talmai) did not suggest itself to any of the fathers (Chrysostom and Augustine exclude Nathanael from the list of the Apostles), but is now (perhaps since Rupert of Deutz in the 12th century, as Trench supposes) almost generally admitted for the following reasons: 1) Nathanael is here in his vocation coördinated with Apostles., 2) After the resurrection he appears in the company of Apostles, some being mentioned before, some *after* him. John xxi. 1, 2. 3) John never names Bartholomew, the Synoptists never mention Nathanael. 4) Bartholomew is no proper name, but simply a *patronymicum*. 5) The Synoptists in the catalogues of the Apostles (Matth. x. 3; Mark iii. 18; Luke vi. 14), name Bartholomew in connection with Philip, with whom Nathanael is associated by John in our passage. Wordsworth denies the identity and approvingly quotes Augustine, who assigned as a reason why Nathanael was not called to the Apostolate, that he was probably a learned man skilled in the law. But this reason would exclude Paul likewise.—P. S.]

etc., except in Acts i. 13), may be explained by Nathanael's having forgotten himself in devout meditation apart under a fig-tree.

Of whom Moses in the law.—The promises in Genesis and Deut. xviii. 15, recognized as verbal and typical prophecies.—**Jesus of Nazareth, the son of Joseph.**—[Literally: Jesus the son of Joseph, of Nazareth.] The distinguishing of the person first by his father, then by his residence, was usual among the Jews. Utterly groundless is the inference from these words, that John knew nothing of the miraculous birth of Jesus (De Wette, Strauss); this would not follow, even though the words were those of John himself, instead of Philip. [John, as a faithful historian, reports not what Philip ought to have said and would have said from his subsequent higher knowledge, but what he actually did say in the twilight of his first acquaintance, and in accordance with the prevailing belief. The mystery of the supernatural conception was a pearl not to be thrown before the multitude who would have misunderstood and abused it. That John believed in it as well as the Synoptists, is evident from his exalted view of Christ as the sinless Saviour from sin, and may be inferred also (as Neander suggests) from i. 14 (the *eternal Word* became *flesh*, *i. e.*, man), as compared with iii. 6 (what is born of *flesh*, *i. e.*, of corrupt human nature, is *flesh*).—P. S.]

Ver. 46 (47). **Can there any good thing come out of Nazareth?**—[Not so much an objection, as an expression of astonishment and a question frankly but modestly put.—P. S.] Grounds of the prejudice: 1) Nazareth lay in Galilee (Ebrard); yet Nathanael himself was a Galilean. 2) Nazareth too small and insignificant to be the birth-place of the Messiah (Lücke and others). 3) The village was considered, as is evident from the τὶ ἀγαθόν, immoral (Meyer, with the remark that Luke iv. 16 sqq. also may agree with Nathanael's opinion). Yet, literally taken, the expression would be absurd: out of the worst town some morally good thing may come. Any good thing, therefore, must here mean: any thing excellent, any eminent person; and Nathanael's doubt of this must have arisen from the smallness and insignificance of the place in proportion to the greatness of the Messiah. [So also Alford.] Tholuck: The place has no celebrity [is not even named] either in the Old Testament or in Josephus, and seems to have always been but an insignificant market-town, as the etymology of נָצַר implies (Hengstenberg, *Christol.* II. p. 127; Clark's Engl. ed. II., p. 109). The pagan Julian contemptuously called Christ *the Galilean* [and the Christians *Galilæans*]; the Jews call Him הַנָּצְרִי to this day. On Nazareth and its situation see the *Comm. on Matth.* on ch. ii. 23, p. 64.*

Come and see.—The second time. [An echo of Christ's *Come and ye shall see*, ver. 39.] A watchword of the Christian faith.

Ver. 47 (48). **Behold truly an Israelite indeed, in whom is no guile.**—[Ἴδε, ἀληθῶς Ἰσραηλίτης (Tischendorf reads—είτης) ἐν ᾧ δόλος οὐκ ἔστιν.—Comp. Ps. xxxii. 2, LXX.: μακάριος ἀνὴρ, ᾧ οὐ μὴ λογίσηται κύριος ἁμαρτίαν, οὐδέ ἐστιν ἐν τῷ στόματι αὐτοῦ δόλος.]—The word of the Lord addressed not directly to Nathanael, but to others on his approach. *An Israelite indeed:* that is, not merely a Jew, but a Jew of the higher theocratic turn. [*Israelite* is the theocratic and the most honorable title of the descendants of Abraham, in commemoration of Jacob's glorious victory of prayer (Gen. xxxii. 28; Acts ii. 22; iii. 12; v. 34; xiii. 16; Rom. ix. 4, *etc.*). The Ishmaelite and the Edomite were Abraham's seed as well as the Jews, but not Israelites. That was the exclusive title of the people of the covenant. With many this title was indeed a mere name, or even a contradiction and reproach, as the title Christian (*i. e.*, follower of Christ) is with a multitude of Christians so-called. But Nathanael was not merely a carnal descendant of Jacob, an Israelite after the flesh, but an Israelite in spirit, a genuine son of that new Jacob or *Israel* who had in faith and prayer wrestled with God and prevailed. Probably he was engaged in meditation and prayer under the fig-tree, and thus truly a wrestler with God, like Israel of old. A reference to that event in the history of Jacob which gave rise to his new name (Gen. xxxii. 28; Hos. xii. 4), is as likely, as the reference to Jacob's ladder in ver. 51 (see below) is certain. Perhaps the scene took place on the very spot which tradition assigned for the wrestling of Jacob. This would give additional force to the passage. Comp. my *History of the Apostolic Church*, p. 388.—P. S.]

The reason why Nathanael is called a genuine Israelite, is his freedom from *falsehood.* In the Jewish nature there was much guile [as it was the characteristic fault of Jacob, the supplanter. —P. S.]; in the Israelite temper and the lively character it unfolded, there was no guile. [There is an allusion in the name to יָשָׁר, *straight, upright, righteous*, the very reverse of the meaning and natural characteristic of Jacob, comp. Numb. xxiii. 10.—P. S.] Meyer's reference of the expression to the description of Jacob in Gen. xxv. 27 [אִישׁ תָּם, LXX.: ἄπλαστος, Aquila: ἁπλοῦς Symmachus: ἄμωμος] is not of decisive importance. Christ perceived the man without guile by spiritual distant sight, as Discerner of the heart; an advance, therefore, on the miraculous knowledge of Peter.* The frankness with which Nathanael expressed his prejudice against Nazareth, quite agrees with the judgment of the Lord. [The guilelessness of Nathanael must not be pressed too far and identified with sinlessness; on the contrary, it implies a readiness to confess sin instead of hiding it (comp. Ps. xxxii. 1, 2). It furnished, as Trench remarks, a kindly soil in which all excellent graces will flourish,

* [Trench, l. c., p. 69, takes the question: "*Can there any good thing come out of Nazareth?*" as having the same sense with the later objection: "*Shall Christ come out of Galilee,*" instead of Bethlehem (John vii. 41, 42, 45), and finds in *any good thing* a reference mainly to the Messiah. Similarly Hengstenberg.—P. S.]

* [Trench, l. c. 73: "Christ read, as often as He needed to read, not merely the present thoughts, but also so much as He desired of the past histories, of those who came in contact with Him; and this He did not merely by that natural divination, that art of looking through countenances into souls, interpreting the inner life from the outward bearing, which all men in a greater or less degree possess, and He doubtless in the largest measure of all (Isa. xi. 3); but 'in his spirit' (Mark ii. 8), by the exercise of that divine power, which was always *in* Him, though not always active in Him. It was

but did not supersede the necessity of the divine seed, out of which alone they can spring. Augustine: "*Si dolus in illo non erat, sanabilem illum judicavit medicus, non sanum.*"—P. S.]

Ver. 48 (49). The question of Nathanael: **Whence knowest thou me?** [Πόθεν με γινώσκεις] is a new feature of the straightforward, clear character. He does not hypocritically decline the commendation; he does not proudly accept it; but he wishes to know whereon it is founded. He expresses himself evidently as surprised, but not as overcome; hence as yet without the title Rabbi. According to Jewish etiquette, no doubt, uncivil.

When thou wast under the fig-tree.—According to Meyer, Philip cannot have found him under the fig-tree (as the Greek fathers and Baumgarten-Crusius suppose), but in another place; neither the *πρὸ τοῦ φωνῆσαι*, nor the *ὄντα ὑπό, etc.*, would have force. But if the mood of Nathanael under the fig-tree was the characteristic thing, Philip might have even found him still there, without the significant element of the Lord's expression being invalidated thereby. Again, according to De Wette and Meyer, the word of Jesus is intended to indicate only a miraculous vision of the person of Nathanael (beyond the range of natural sight), not a look into the depth of his soul. But in this case Jesus would not have answered the question of Nathanael at all. Jesus must have seen something in the spiritual posture of Nathanael under the fig-tree, which marked the person as the Israelite without guile. "As the Talmud often speaks of Rabbins who pursued the study of the law in the shade of fig-trees, most persons think of a similar occupation here." Tholuck. According to Chrysostom and Luther, Nathanael was probably occupied with the very hope of the Messiah.

[Trench also remarks that our Lord must refer here to earnest prayer, some great mental struggle, or strong temptation which took place in Nathanael's soul while sitting under the fig-tree; for this of itself was a common occurrence among Israelites (1 Kings iv. 25; Mic. iv. 4; Zech. iii. 10). Wordsworth and Alford find in *ὑπό* with the accusative (*ὄντα ὑπὸ τὴν συκῆν* instead of *ὑπὸ τῇ συκῇ*) an indication of retirement to the fig-tree as well as concealment there,—probably for purposes of meditation and prayer. It implies: when thou wentest under the fig-tree and while thou wert there.—P. S.]

Vers. 49 (50). **Rabbi, thou art the Son of God.**—In joyful certainty Nathanael now gives threefold expression to his hitherto reserved acknowledgment. First, *Rabbi*, the title, for even this most just due he had not before paid; then, *Son of God*, because he showed the divine power of the Heart-Searcher to look upon the soul; then, *King of Israel*, that is Messiah. There is at the same time an extremely fine return of the commendation: An Israelite without guile; Thou art the King of the Israel without guile, that is, my King. Though the ideas Christ and Son of God have become more or less interchangeable, yet it makes a difference whether the confession of the Messiahship precedes that of the divinity, or the reverse. Nathanael reasons from the Son of God, who demonstrated Himself to him, to the Messiahship.

[The title *the Son of God*, was a rare designation of the Messiah, derived from Ps. ii. 5. 12 (comp. Isa. ix. 6), and is so used by Peter, Matth. xvi. 16, the disciples in the ship, xiv. 33, Martha, John xi. 27, and the high priest, Matth. xxvi. 63. It signifies the divine nature, as the titles *the Son of Man*, and *the Son of David*, signify the human nature of the Messiah. (See Excursus after ver. 52). This is evident from the hostile indignation of the Pharisees and Scribes at our Lord when He claimed to be the Son of God (John v. 18; x. 30–39). It is, of course, not to be supposed that Nathanael or any of the disciples had, during the earthly life of Christ, a clear insight into the full meaning and metaphysical depths of the expression, but their faith, based upon the glimpses of the O. T.* and the personal knowledge of our Lord, contained more than they were conscious of, and anticipated the dogma.—P. S.]

Vers. 50 (51). **Because I said unto thee—believest thou?**—Not properly a question; still less an intimation of censure for a defective ground of faith (De Wette); but an expression of surprise that he so joyfully believes, upon a single token. Hence, too, a greater is then promised him.

Vers. 51 (52). **Verily, verily.**—The Hebrew *Amen.* אָמֵן, from אָמַן, an adjective: *sure, true, faithful;* also used as a substantive and adverb. When a final word of devout acclamation, Deut. xxvii. 15-26; Ps. xli. 13; lxxxix. 52, or of religious confirmation of one's own word, Rom. ix. 5; xi. 36, it is a sentence: *Ratum sit, ita sit.* When an initial word, it is an adverbial protestation: *verissime, certissime;* put singly in Matth., ch. v. 18; xvi. 28 (Luke ix. 27 *ἀληθῶς*), and Luke. In John double: ch. iii. 3; v. 19; viii. 51; xii. 24; xiv. 12; xxi. 18. Substantively: *Amen*, 2 Cor. i. 20; *the Amen*, Rev. iii. 14.—That the Hebrew word was early familiar in Christian worship, is evident from the fact that John does not explain it. In modern times even a small sect has gathered upon the consecrated word, called the *Amen* church.† For the first time here, the word of the most solemn asseveration. "Only in John, and only in the mouth of Jesus, hence the more certainly authentic."

[The Synoptists use the single *Amen* more than 50, John the double—25 times, even in parallel passages, as Matth. xxvi. 21, 34; John xiii. 21, 38. Bengel explains the repetition in John from the fact that Christ spoke both in His and in the Father's name. Probably it is a more emphatic assertion of the superiority of Christ above all preceding prophets. The double Amen could

thus, for example, that He read the life-story of that Samaritan woman (John iv. 17, 18; comp. v. 14); where it is impossible to presume a previous acquaintance; it was thus far most probably in the instance before us."—P. S.]

* [Hengstenberg (I. 126): "The O. T. teaches most definitely that the King of Israel, the Messiah is exalted far above the human level. This doctrine is contained in the very Psalm, in which both designations of the Messiah, as King and as the Son of God, occur, Ps. ii. 6, 7, and from which these designations are derived."—P. S.]

† [There is a branch of rigid Mennonites in Pennsylvania who call themselves *Amish* or *Omish* (a corruption of *Amenites*), but this name is sometimes derived from a Swiss clergyman, Jacob Amen, in the 17th century, who had a dispute on minor points with another Mennonite, John Heisly.—P. S.]

with full propriety only be used by Him who is the personal truth (John xiv. 6), the Amen (Rev. iii. 14), the God of Truth (in Hebr. *Amen*, Isa. lxv. 16), and in whom all the promises of God are Yea and Amen (2 Cor. i. 19).—P. S.]

I say unto you: to the little company of disciples now already collected. [This formula "*I say unto you*" differs from the "*Thus saith the Lord*," as Christ differs from all the prophets: He is the truth itself and speaks with divine authority His own word; they are only witnesses of the truth and speak the Word of God in the name of God.—P. S.]

(Henceforth) ye shall see heaven opened.—[This prospect to the public life of Christ, and uninterrupted communion between heaven and earth in and through Him, is an eminently fit conclusion of this chapter. Whether we retain ἀπάρτι (ἀπ᾽ ἄρτι) or not, the beginning of His public ministry and the first recognition of His Messianic dignity is meant, as the starting-point of an unbroken communion between God and man, and an exchange of divine grace and human prayers. The *open heaven* is here, as in the baptism of Christ, a symbolical expression for the ever present help and grace of God (comp. Gen. xxviii. 10-17; Ezek. i. 1; Matth. iii. 16; Acts vii. 17; x. 11); while the *closed heavens* signify the absence of divine help or the impending judgment of God (comp. Isa. lxiv. 1). The participle ἀνεωγότα implies the act of opening, and the fact that before Christ the heaven was closed. Bengel: "*apertum, præteritum, proprie*, Matth. iii. 16, *et cum continuatione in posterum*," John iii. 13; Acts vii. 56; Apoc. xi. 12.—P. S.] The expression is evidently suggested by the word concerning the Israelite without guile, and the description of Christ as the King of Israel; and stands related to that dream of Jacob, in which his higher Israel-nature decisively came forth (Gen. xxviii. 12), though he did not receive the honorable title of Israel until a later time.* The first Israel saw heaven open, but only in dream, only for a while; the ascending and descending of the angels were assisted by a ladder; the Lord stood above the latter in the heavens; and the vision vanished away. Yet the living intercourse between heaven and earth, between God and man, had announced itself and opened in the old theocracy, and was now gloriously to complete itself. The expression can by no means be limited to actual appearances of angels in the life of Jesus [at His birth, in the garden of Gethsemane, at the resurrection and ascension] (Chrysostom and others), nor to His working of miracles (Storr); yet these points are not (according to Meyer) to be set aside, since they are phenomena peculiar to the New Testament intercourse between heaven and earth. On the other hand, the angels are no more to be reduced to personified divine powers (as by De Wette),* than the divine powers to angels (as by Hofmann).† Meyer rightly emphasizes the terms *henceforth* (ἀπάρτι) and *ye shall see* (ὄψεσθε); they show that it is the total Messianic revelation in its actual operation, which is spoken of, and that this is represented in figurative language. The expression, however, is not exactly *symbolical*, inasmuch as, in a spiritual sense, heaven is really opened, and the living personal intercourse between the Father and the Son also becomes manifest in manifold angelophanies, voices, and spiritual revelations. "The ἀναβαίνοντες stand first in the Old Testament also [Gen. xxviii. 12]; we might, as in fact Philo does (*De Somniis*, p. 642), think of the reciprocal actings of human wants and prayers and divine powers; but the former are never called messengers of God. More correctly: They return to heaven to receive new commissions." Tholuck. If we consider that Christ is the incarnate Angel of the Lord, we may refer the ascending unquestionably to His high-priestly intercessions, works, and sacrifice, the descending to the gradual unfolding of the riches of His kingly glory. Luther: "Now are heaven and earth become one thing, and it is just as if ye sat above, and the gentle angels ministered to you." Calvin: "*Quum prius nobis clausum esset regnum dei, vere in Christo apertum fuit, ... ut simus cives sanctorum et angelorum socii.*" For other explanations see Tholuck, p. 102.

[We must here dismiss the notions of space. The incarnate Son of God is the bond of union, the golden clasp between earth and heaven, the mediating centre of all intercourse with God. Where He is, there is heaven and there are the angels, who ascend from Him as the starting-point, and descend upon Him, as the termination-point. He spoke while He was on earth, otherwise we would expect the reverse order. From the incarnate Saviour as the Alpha and Omega, this spiritual communion with heaven proceeds upon all believers. Ryle weakens the force of the prediction by confining it to the time of the future advent; this is sufficiently refuted by *henceforth*.—P. S.]

Upon the Son of Man.—In John as well as in the Synoptists Christ designates Himself by this term. See *Comm. on Matth.* ch. viii. 20. "Undoubtedly the precedent in Daniel has suggested the language in the Revelation, ch. xiv. 14; i. 13, in which latter is also μετὰ τ. νεφελῶν; and those like passages, in which the Redeemer is mentioned as appearing ἐπὶ τ. νεφελῶν, ἐν δόξῃ, in His Messianic and judicial glory, Luke xxi. 27; Matth. xxvi. 64; xvi. 28; so, therefore, Chemnitz, with the joint conception of the *humilitas* taken from the passages in Ezekiel; Beza, Scholten, Lücke." Tholuck. Yet the fact that the Lord applied this name to Himself, and that

* [The allusion to Jacob's vision of the ladder is generally admitted by commentators. Augustine: *Cujus nomine te appellavi, ipsius somnium in te apparebit.* (Comp. his *Tract.* VII. *in Joh. Ev.*). Grotius: *Quod ibi in somnio vidit Israel, idem vigilans visurus dicitur verus Israelita.* Bengel: *Vidit tale quid Jacob*, Gen. xxviii. 12; *quanto magis Israelitæ veri in N. T.* Alford: "The words have a plain reference to the *ladder of Jacob*, and imply that what he then saw was now to receive its fulfilment: that He, the Son of Man, was the dwelling of God and the gate of heaven, and that *through* Him, and *on* Him in the first place, was to descend all communication of help and grace from above." Trench: "What Israel saw, the true '*Israelite*' shall behold the same; yea, what one saw but in a dream, the other shall behold in waking reality; and more and better even than this; for then God was a God far off; the Lord stood above the ladder and spoke from heaven; but now standing at its foot, He speaks as the Son of Man from earth, for now the Word has been made flesh; and the tabernacle of God is with men."—P. S.]

* [Or preachers of Christ, as Augustine explains *angels* in this passage (*Tract.* VII. § 23).—P. S.]

† [Hengstenberg likewise takes a comprehensive view of the passage, as including the angels proper and all other mediums of divine communication.—P. S.]

the people did not recognize it as a designation of the Messiah, John xii. 34, itself very plainly shows that the phrase was not current as a Messianic phrase of the Jewish theology, though after the example of Daniel the term itself appears in the book of Enoch and in IV. Esdras, as well as, among the Rabbins, the expression: "He that cometh in the clouds." The fact that the Apostles abstain from the phrase, Tholuck explains from Heb. ii. 6; that is, because the term referred to the humiliation of the Son of God. As to Hofmann's hypothesis (*Schriftbeweis*, II. p. 51) see Tholuck, p. 104. Hofmann lays stress on the point that the phrase in Daniel is not: The Son of man, but: One *like* a son of man. This manner of interpretation would require that the Old Testament prophecy everywhere have the New Testament idea and phraseology pure and simple, in order to have them at all. Strangely Tholuck thinks the tracing of the expression to Daniel excludes the interpretation proposed by Herder: Man κατ' ἐξοχήν, the pattern man; that according to this by a son of man must strictly be understood a man who shares the lot of actual mankind, as in Numb. xxiii. 19; Job xxv. 6. And why not? Christ, as the second man, the Son of mankind, 1 Cor. xv. 47, is as well in His suffering the heir of its judgment, as in His work the heir of its righteousness of faith, and assuredly for this very reason the Son of Man, the supernatural bloom of the race, because He is the Son of God. Luthardt too thinks this latter idea, which he likewise gives, must be vindicated against the derivation of the name from the book of Daniel. But the vision in Daniel must after all have an idea. And it is sufficiently clear why Jesus chose this particular term from Daniel to designate Himself.

[Excursus on the Meaning of the Title "The Son of Man."—The designation of Christ as *the Son of Man* (ὁ υἱὸς τοῦ ἀνθρώπου), occurs in this chapter, ver. 51 (52) for the first time, and in the mouth of Christ; while the corresponding title, *the Son of God* (ὁ υἱὸς τοῦ θεοῦ), occurs first ver. 49 (50), in the mouth of a disciple (Nathanael), but had been previously applied to Christ by God in His baptism (Matth. iii. 16), and by Satan, hypothetically, in the temptation (Matth. iv. 3, 6). The former is found about eighty, or, deducting the parallels, fifty-five times in the Gospels, and is only used by our Lord Himself, except in three cases, *viz.*, once by Stephen when he saw "the heavens opened, and the Son of Man standing on the right hand of God," Acts vii. 56 (in allusion probably to Matth. xxvi. 64), and twice by the apocalyptic seer, Rev. i. 13; xiv. 14, with obvious reference to Dan. vii. 13, 14. Bengel (on Matth. xvi. 13) urges the circumstance as very significant that Christ, during His earthly life, was never called *the Son of Man* by anybody but Himself. His followers called Him *the Son of David* (the Messiah), or *the Son of God*. The title *the Son of God* is used sometimes by Christ Himself, but mostly by the Apostles and Evangelists. Christ could use both designations with equal propriety, but He preferred the title of humility and condescension which identifies Him with the human race, while the Apostles chose the title of honor and dignity which exalts Him far above men. The one signifies in general the true humanity, the other the true divinity of Christ, both together give us the full idea of the *God-Man* (θεάνθρωπος). Both titles are generic. In both titles, when applied to Christ, the definite article is nearly always employed. He is not simply *a* son of man among other men, nor *a* son of God on a par with the children of God, but He is emphatically and in a unique sense *the* Son of Man, and *the* Son of God. The definite article is as significant in one case as in the other, and suggests a distinction as well as a resemblance.

The appellation *the Son of Man*, when used by Christ of Himself, cannot, like the corresponding Hebrew בֶּן־הָאָדָם or בֶּן־אָדָם, be simply a poetic designation of man in general, in which sense υἱὸς ἀνθρώπου (without the article) is used Hebr. ii. 6 (in a quotation, however, from the Messianic Ps. viii.), and υἱοὶ τῶν ἀνθρώπων, Eph. iii. 5. It cannot be supposed for a moment that Christ should have used this term so often of Himself as a mere circumlocution for the personal pronoun. Nobody speaks of himself in this way. In the Saviour's native dialect, the Syriac, *Bar nosho, the son of man*, is man generically; the filial part of the compound denotes the identity and purity of the generic idea. This leads to the correct interpretation, as above indicated.

Nor does the title, as many suppose (*e. g.*, Justin Martyr, Tertullian, De Wette, Tholuck), express exclusively the humiliation and condescension of Christ, but it denotes at the same time, and chiefly His elevation above the ordinary level, and the actualization, in Him and through Him, of the ideal standard of human nature under its moral and religious aspect, or in its relation to God, (Bengel,* Schleiermacher, Olshausen, Neander, Hengstenberg, Trench, Liddon,† Godet,‡ and others).

Christ Jesus is the centre of the unity of mankind, the recapitulation of humanity, as Paul profoundly indicates (Eph. i. 10), and as Irenæus taught. He is the true seed of the woman, the second Adam (Rom. v. and 1 Cor. xv.), who more than restored what the first Adam lost. He fulfils and closes the preceding, and controls the succeeding, history of our race. All men, even the best and the greatest, have their weaknesses and defects, and reflect only a fragment of the idea of humanity. Once in history, and once only, there was born a man who represents humanity in its purity without the demoniac adulteration

* [Bengel (Matth. xvi. 13): *Unus hic nempe homo est, quem Adamus, post lapsum, ex promissione expectavit pro tota sua progenie;* ὁ δεύτερος, *secundus, quem omnis prophetia V. T. indigitavit, qui totius generis humani jura et primogenituram sustinet, et cui uni quod humani nominis nos non pœniteat, debemus.* Comp. his whole note on Matth. xvi. 13, which Trench calls "a wonderful specimen of the close packing of matter the most interesting and the most important in his *Gnomon*."]

† [*Lectures on the Divinity of Christ*, 1868, p. 8: "The title Son of Man does not merely assert His real incorporation with our kind; it exalts Him infinitely above us all as the representative, the ideal, the pattern Man."]

‡ [*Com.* I. 340: "*Il se declarait non seulement un homme, un vrai homme, mais le rejeton par excellence de la race humaine, l'homme attendue, prévu, moralement nécessaire, le répresentant normal du type. . . Jésus trouve ainsi le moyen d'affirmer de lui-même tout ce qu'il y a de plus grand, tout en employant la forme la plus fraternelle et la plus humble. Son égalité parfaite avec nous s'exprime jusque dans le terme qui révèle sa supériorité absolue sur nous.*"]

of sin, and its universality without the limitations of race and nationality. Christ felt more humanly, spake more humanly, acted, suffered and died more humanly than any man before or since His coming. Every word and act of His appeals to universal human sympathies and calls out the moral affections of all without distinction of race, condition, and degree of culture. He is the only ἀληθινὸς ἄνθρωπος (as Philo called the Logos), the *Urbild*, the archetypal or model Man, the King of men, and "draws all men" to Him. He could not have been so perfect a man without being also divine.

This interpretation of the title *Son of Man*, suggested grammatically by the use of the definite article, is confirmed historically by the origin of the term, according to the usual acceptation, in Dan. vii. 13 f., where it signifies the Messiah in His heavenly glory, as the head of a universal and eternal kingdom,* and perhaps also in Ps. viii. where man is represented in his ideal destination with reference to the Messiah as the true and perfect head of humanity (comp. Rom. v. 12; 1 Cor. xv. 27; Hebr. i. 2-8). *The Son of David* was likewise a designation of the Messiah (Matth. ix. 27; xv. 22; xii. 23; xxi. 9; xxii. 41 ff.), but is not so significant, as it represents Christ only as the flower and crown of the house of David, not of the whole human family. Our view commends itself, moreover, at once as the most natural and significant, in such passages as, "Ye shall see the heaven open, and the angels of God ascending and descending upon the Son of Man" (John i. 51); "He that came down from heaven, even the Son of Man who is in heaven" (John vi. 53); "The Son of Man shall come in the glory of His Father;" "The Son of Man is come to save" (Matth. xviii. 11; comp. Luke xix. 10); "The Father hath given Him authority to execute judgment also, because He is the Son of Man" (John v. 27). Even those passages which are quoted for the opposite view, receive, in our interpretation, a greater force and beauty from the sublime contrast which places the voluntary condescension and humiliation of Christ in the most striking light, as when He says: "Foxes have holes, and birds of the air have nests; but the Son of Man hath not where to lay His head" (Luke ix. 58): or, "Whosoever will be chief among you, let him be your servant; even as the Son of Man came not to be ministered unto, but to minister, and to give His life a ransom for many" (Matth. xx. 27, 28). Thus the manhood of Christ, rising far above all ordinary manhood, though freely coming down to its lowest ranks, with the view to their elevation and redemption, is already the portal of His Godhood. Comp. my treatise on the *Person of Christ*, Boston, 1865, pp. 113 ff., from which I have transferred a few sentences. —P. S.]

* ["I saw in the night visions, and behold, *one* like the Son of Man—כְּבַר אֱנָשׁ, LXX: ὡς υἱὸς ἀνθρώπου, Vulg.: *quasi filius hominis*—came with the clouds of heaven, and came to the Ancient of days . . . and there was given Him dominion and glory and a kingdom, that all people, nations, and languages should serve Him," *etc.* Comp. the words of Christ, Matth. xxiv. 30 and xxvi. 64: "Hereafter ye shall see the Son of Man sitting on the right hand of power, and coming in the clouds of heaven." The allusion in the last two passages to the prophecy of Daniel can hardly be mistaken.]

DOCTRINAL AND ETHICAL.

1. The greatness of the Baptist and the majesty of Christ appear in John's pointing his disciples to Christ, and Christ's attaching the best of them immediately to Himself. In these disciples of John the spiritual perfection of the work of the Baptist is seen.

2. It is remarkable, that the first disciples of John who followed Christ, followed Him upon the repeated testimony of the Baptist: Behold the Lamb of God. The testimony to the præexistence and glory of Christ does not convince the rulers of the Jews; this testimony which shows a future full of suffering for Christ convinces the disciples of John who here come to view. This of itself shows that they can never have shared the entirely crude, sensuous hope of the Messiah, in its hard, unspiritual form; much as they were still involved in sensuous expectations of a nobler sort.

3. Coming to Christ is here illustrated in every way. Prophetic testimony, office, word, points to him. Then brother brings brother, friend brings friend, townsman brings townsman. One comes with another, and one after another.

4. These first disciples stand the decisive test-question, whether they seek something from Him, or seek Himself and all in Him. They seek Him, and when they exclaim: We have found the Messiah, they mean: We have found—absolutely.

5. In keeping with this prominence of the personality of Christ, He manifests His glory first in miracles of pure knowledge with the most varied insight into the dark depths of personal life. Thus in our text He sees through, in particular, Peter and Nathanael, and at the close of the chapter the Evangelist celebrates Him as the knower of hearts. So afterwards He reads Nicodemus, the woman of Samaria, Judas, the people, *etc.*

6. The manner in which the Evangelist John, with delicate modesty, has here interwoven the story of his own calling with the gospel history, reminds us of the similar manner of Matthew (ch. ix. 9); and these two analogies might lead us to presume that Mark (ch. xiv. 51, 52) and Luke (ch. xxiv. 13-35) have done likewise. See the exegesis, ver. 35. Christianity, in the light of the person of the Lord, brings to view and into play the worth and warrant of all the personages purified by Him. But evidently these great, sanctified delineators of the life of Jesus and the facts of redemption have wrought in with the utmost modesty their own names, for the most part only by hints in any part of their picture.

7. In this place Israel meets us in its purity, and doubtless is made prominent in its higher import, because the Evangelist sees himself further on compelled to exhibit Judaism so strongly in its hatred of the truth.

8. Christianity, an open heaven over open eyes, and a revelation of ever new and ever greater glories of the Lord, first in His life, then in His church, because divinity is become one with humanity in Christ, and this life communi-

cates itself through the Holy Ghost to believers.

HOMILETICAL AND PRACTICAL.

On both histories together (vers. 35-43 and 44-51). The exuberant beginning of the Church of Christ: *a.* Its going forth out of the Old Testament; *b.* Its rising into the New.—The Israel of the Old Covenant, and the Israel of the New.—The effect of the testimony of John: residing (1) in the perseverance (repetition) and emphasis of it; (2) in the matter of it (the Lamb of God).—Three unique days in the kingdom of God (the next day, *etc.*).—Christ the Lamb of God.—The coming of the disciples to Jesus, a type of our coming to Him.—How quickly Christ and His elect recognize and meet each other.—The spring seasons of the kingdom of heaven.—The unity and the diversity of the Lord's ways of calling His disciples.—"We have found!"—Working for the Lord.—Christ the heart-searcher.—The three great proofs of the Messiah: (1) From the Old Testament (Moses and the prophets, closed up by John the Baptist); (2) from Christ's representation of Himself; (3) from the experience of the disciples.

On the first history (vers. 35-43). The first two disciples of Jesus: John and Andrew.—The two decisive questions: What seek ye? and, Rabbi, where dwellest thou?—The invitation of Christ: "Come and see," in its permanent import.—The first word of the Lord and His last respecting Peter, according to the Gospel of John.—How the natural brotherhood becomes transfigured in the spiritual.

On the second history (44-51). Philip and Nathanael, or friendship in its relation to the kingdom of God: (1) Its destination for it; (2) its glorification in it.—Honorable prejudice, and how it is overcome by the facts of experience.—The word of the disciple: "Come and see;" an echo of the word of Jesus: "Come and see."—The preaching of Philip: (1) Infinitely difficult: the connection of the name of Messiah, of whom Moses in the law and the prophets did write, with Jesus of Nazareth, the son of Joseph; (2) perfectly decided: We have found Him! (3) Irresistibly confirmed: Come and see!—One of the rare commendatory words of Christ, on a most rare occasion: (1) Bestowed upon a man who spoke contemptuously of His birth-place; was prepossessed against Himself; had, immediately after an hour of earnest devotion, fallen again under a prejudice; (2) and bestowed for the very reason, that he was without guile.—"An Israelite without guile:" In all nations, as in all men, the essential permanent nature and destiny must be distinguished from the corruption of it (the true Israelite from the false Jew; the intellectual German from the dreamy German; the open, frank Frenchman from the insolent Frenchman, *etc.;* Peter the rock from Peter the shaken reed, *etc.*).—The threefold homage of Nathanael: (1) Rabbi (which he had owed from the first); (2) Son of God (which he had denied Him); (3) King of Israel (with which he submits to Him as an Israelite without guile).—Christianity an open heaven over the open eyes and hearts of believers.—The ascending and descending angels; or, the intercourse between heaven and earth, a reciprocity of personal vital functions between the Father and Christ, Christ and His people, the church triumphant and the church militant.—Open hearts, a foretokening of the open heaven (Christ's look into the soul of Nathanael, a foretokening of all the wonders of revelation).

STARKE: Preachers must repeat a thing often for the sake of those weak in faith.—QUESNEL: To enforce industriously the all-sufficient sacrifice of Jesus Christ, a main duty of the servant of God.—Here the Lord begins to collect a little church, to which John has given up his disciples.—Jesus calls and draws men to Himself; yet without violence.—ZEISIUS: Experience in spiritual things gives great certainty and firmness in faith.—Regenerate Christians acquire a new name, which no man knows.—OSIANDER: Every one who truly believes in Christ is a rock, against which all the gates of hell are powerless.—QUESNEL: Judge of divine things not by outward appearance, nor under human prejudice.—ZEISIUS: Uprightness is pleasing to the Lord, 1 Chron. xxix. 17.—The omnipresent eye of the Lord.—The opening of heaven the opening of a way whereby the heavenly riches course to the earth, and free way (access) is given from earth to heaven.—Relation of the descending and ascending to the humiliation and exaltation of Christ (?).—Christ the ladder to heaven.

BRAUNE: The voice of the preacher prepared the way for Him; in the company of the preacher He must find His first adherents.—The anticipating friendliness of Jesus.—The blessedness of a Christian is ungrudging, and would communicate itself to all the world.—But why the ascending (of the angels) first, the descending after? Because intercourse between heaven and earth is not now first beginning, but has already begun (above all the Angel of the Lord has come down in the flesh).—GERLACH: It seems that John the Baptist always spoke in short, weighty sentences, which he often repeated and deeply impressed.—The Son of God, the King of Israel, Ps. ii.—LISCO: Jesus finds disciples through the testimony of His herald (and here the first two); Jesus finds disciples through the testimony of those who have come to know Him (and here probably again two: Peter and James the elder); Jesus finds disciples through the immediate call of His own word (here the last two). Yet, in the wider sense, (1) the office of the herald, (2) the joint witness of the disciples, (3) the call of Jesus run through the whole formation of discipleship.—The best counsel against all errors: Come and see!—HEUBNER: The whole service of the teacher consists in pointing to Christ; no man can take the place of Christ, but human aid can help to find Him.—Jesus' turning, a powerful stroke on the heart; Jesus' look, an attracting power.—What seek ye? a question which Jesus puts to every one who comes to Him.—The open hearts went straight forward.—There is a great difference between mediate and immediate acquaintance with Jesus.—The more like Jesus, the more inexhaustible a man is.—The more one is conversant with Jesus, the more he finds in Him. In other men one is often disappointed; in Jesus every expectation is exceeded.—ALBER-

TINI: How does the Saviour enlist disciples?—SCHLEIERMACHER: The meeting of Christ and His disciples an example for us in forming earnest social relations.—The deepest corruption is the falsehood of man.—Through the Redeemer alone is made the bond between heaven and earth.

[Ver. 51 (52). LUTHER: When Christ became man and had entered on His ministerial office and begun to preach, then was the heaven opened, and remains open; and has from that time, since the baptism of Christ in the Jordan, never been shut, and never will be shut, although we do not see it with our bodily eyes. . . . . . . Christ says this: 'Ye are now heavenly citizens, and have your citizenship above in the heavenly Jerusalem, and are in communion with the holy angels, who shall without intermission ascend and descend about you.'—Archbishop TRENCH: The Lord would indicate by these wondrous words that He should henceforward be the middle point of a free intercourse, yea, of an uninterrupted communion, between God and man, that in Him should be the meeting place of heaven and of earth (Ephes. i. 10; Col. i. 19); which should be no longer two, as sin had made them, separated and estranged from one another, but one, now that righteousness had looked down from heaven, and truth had flourished out of the earth. And this, the glory of Christ, they, His disciples, should behold, and should understand, that they too, children of man, were by Him, the Son of Man, made citizens of a kingdom which, not excluding earth, embraced also heaven. From earth there should go up evermore supplications, aspirations, prayers,—and these by the ministration of angels (Rev. viii. 3, 4), if some still want a certain literal fulfilment;—from heaven there should evermore come down graces, blessings, gifts, aid to the faithful and punishment for them that would hurt them (Rev. viii. 5; Acts xii. 7, 23). Heaven and earth should henceforward be in continual interchange of these blessed angels,

'And earth be changed to heaven, and heaven to earth;
One kingdom, joy and union without end.'

—BONAVENTURA: The heavenly ladder was broken in Adam, and repaired in Christ.—There is a beautiful hymn on Jacob's ladder, as a symbol of communion with God, by Mrs. Sarah Flower Adams, 1848:

"Nearer, my God, to Thee."

—P. S.]

III.

THE KINDRED AND FRIENDS OF THE LORD, AND THE FIRST MIRACLE OF JESUS AT CANA, AS THE EARNEST OF THE GLORIFICATION OF THE WORLD, AND AS THE FIRST MANIFESTATION OF HIS GLORY. CHRIST TRANSFIGURING THE EARTHLY MARRIAGE FEAST INTO A SYMBOL OF THE HEAVENLY.

CHAP. II. 1–11.

(Pericope for 2d Sunday after Epiphany.)

1 And the third day there was a marriage [a marriage feast was held] in Cana of
2 Galilee; and the mother of Jesus was there: And both Jesus was called, and his
3 disciples, [and Jesus also was invited and his disciples] to the marriage. And
when they wanted wine [And wine having failed, or, when wine failed][1] the mother
4 of Jesus saith unto him, They have no wine. Jesus saith unto her, Woman, what
5 have I to do with thee?[2] mine hour is not yet come. His mother saith unto the
6 servants, Whatsoever he saith unto you, do it. And there were set there six water-
pots of stone, after the manner of the purifying of the Jews, containing two or three
7 firkins apiece. Jesus saith unto them, Fill the waterpots with water. And they
8 filled them up to the brim [top]. And he saith unto them, Draw out now, and
9 bear unto the governor [ruler] of the feast. And they bare *it*. When the ruler
of the feast had tasted the water that was made [had become, or, been made] wine,
and knew not whence it was, (but the servants which drew [who had drawn] the
10 water knew), the governor [ruler] of the feast called the bridegroom, And saith
unto him, Every man at the beginning doth set forth good wine, [setteth forth the
good wine first]; and when men have well drunk,[3] then[4] that which is worse; but
11 [*omit* but][5] thou hast kept the good wine until now. This[6] beginning of miracles
[signs, *τῶν σημείων*] did [wrought] Jesus in Cana of Galilee, and manifested forth his
glory [his transfiguring power, *τὴν δόξαν αὐτοῦ*]; and his disciples believed [the more]
on [in] him.

TEXTUAL AND GRAMMATICAL.

1 Ver. 3. [ὑστερήσαντος οἴνου. ὑστερέω, prop. *to be behind* (either in time, or in rank), had, in the later Greek, also the meaning: *to fail, to be wanting*; comp. Mark x. 21, ἕν σοι ὑστερεῖ.—P. S.]

2 Ver. 4. [Τί ἐμοὶ καὶ σοί, γύναι; lit.: *What to me and to thee, woman? i. e.*, What have I *in common* with thee? This elliptic phrase corresponds to the Hebrew מַה־לִּי וָלָךְ, and is a disclaimer of communion, Josh. xxii. 24; Judg. xi. 12; 2 Sam. xvi. 10; 1 Kings xvii. 18; 2 Kings iii. 13; Matth. viii. 29; xvii. 19; Mark i. 24; Luke viii. 28; also in classical Greek. It is not (like the somewhat similar English phrases: *Mind your business, This is none of your business*, and the German, *Das geht dich nichts an*) necessarily disrespectful, but may be used in a friendly sense, as is evident from Judg. xi. 12; 2 Sam. xvi. 10; Matth. viii. 29 (comp. also the similar phrase of the wife of Pilate, Matth. xxvii. 19: Μηδέν σοι καὶ τῷ δικαίῳ ἐκείνῳ); yet it always implies more or less of reproof, however slight. So it is taken here by the best commentators, as a gentle rebuke of untimely interference, though it was no doubt mitigated by the tone of speaking. The term γύναι is entirely respectful, and must always be where the true dignity of woman is felt and recognized; comp. John xix. 26; xx. 15. See the EXEG. NOTES.—P. S.]

3 Ver. 10. [ὅταν μεθυσθῶσιν, Vulg.: *cum inebriati fuerint*; Tyndal, Cranmer, Alford: *when men be (are) drunken*; Geneva, Rheims, A. V.: *when men have well drunk*; Am. Bible Union (Dr. Conant), Young, Owen: *when they have drunk freely*; Luther; *trunken worden sind*; De Wette, Stier: *trunken sind*; Μεθύσκομαι (Mid.), like the Hebrew שָׁכַר, means *to become drunk, to get drunk* (Luke xii. 45; Eph. v. 18; Rev. xvii. 2), but also *to drink freely*, and does not necessarily imply excess (Sept. Gen. xliii. 34; Hagg. i. 6; probably also Cant. v. 1: πίετε καί μεθύσθητε, ἀδελφοί). Comp. Beza, De Wette, Tholuck. At all events no unfavorable inference is to be drawn, as regards the present company, from this general proverbial remark of the ruler of the feast. Bengel briefly and pointedly: *Simpliciter recensetur oratio architriclini, et consuetudo etiam Judæorum: ebrietas non approbatur.* Meyer contends for the usual meaning of the verb and translates: *wenn sie berauscht geworden sind*, but likewise guards against this inference. Alford: "While there is no reason to press the ordinary meaning of μεθυσθῶσιν, so neither is there any to shrink from it, as uttered by the ἀρχιτρίκλινος." See EXEG. NOTES.—P. S.]

4 Ver. 10. Τότε is wanting in ℵ. B. L. Probably overlooked by reason of the τόν immediately following.

5 Ver. 10. [δέ after σὺ is omitted by Lachm., Tregelles, Alford and Tischend.—P. S.]

6 Ver. 11. [The art. τήν before ἀρχήν in the text. rec. is wanting in ℵ. A. B. L. and rejected by Lachm., Tischend., Treg., Alf., West. and Hort. Hence the proper translation is: *This wrought Jesus as a beginning of (His) signs*.—P. S.]

EXEGETICAL AND CRITICAL.

[Here we have the fulfilment of the promise made in the last verse of ch. i., and a startling proof of the presence of supernatural powers in the person of the Son of Man. Christ significantly began His public ministry with a miracle of *transformation*: His whole mission was to convert sinners into saints, to turn grief into joy, to elevate earth to heaven. It was moreover a miracle of festive *joy* and *gladness*, and of more than royal *munificence*; showing—in striking contrast to the Mosaic law of condemnation and the ascetic austerity and water-baptism of John, and in the presence of his former pupils—that the gospel is life and peace, a religion of true happiness. Christ relieves not only the present need, but provides also an abundant supply for all the future, enough and to spare for every one that thirsteth. It is equally significant that this miracle was performed in the bosom of a *family*: for the family is the first institution of God on earth, and the nursery of Church and State, where all moral reforms of society must begin. Christianity restored marriage and the family to their original purity, and elevated them to true dignity by abolishing polygamy, emancipating woman from slavish degradation, and by making the relation of husband and wife a type of the sacred union of Christ to His church.—The miracle of Cana, as it was the first in time, is also the greatest in character, next to the raising of Lazarus which was the last, and which exhibited Christ as the Conqueror of death and the Prince of life eternal. Both belong exclusively to the fourth Gospel, while the miraculous feeding of the multitude is reported by all.* The change of water into wine was a proper transubstantiation or qualitative transmutation of an elementary substance. It is not a creative act in the strict sense of the term; for God made the world out of nothing, Christ always operated upon existing substances. But it involves the same creative power, and is strictly above nature and above reason (not *against* them), and therefore incomprehensible. Yet after all it is not more beyond our present comprehension than the change of the rain from heaven into the juice of the grape, the growth of plants by the transmutation of inorganic matter into organic, and all those miracles of nature, which by their daily occurrence appear to us natural and common.*—Like many sayings of Christ, the miracle of Cana is a stumbling-block to the superficial reader, and seems to conflict with the ideal character of the Gospel of John. It is indeed a rebuke to a morbid asceticism and desponding legalism, to which even many good people are given. But it abounds in high moral significance and symbolic beauty. It is altogether unnecessary to resort to the modern figment of an essential difference of the wine of the Bible and usual wine. The wine which Christ made was no doubt pure, good wine, in the proper sense of the term. But to think it even *possible* that Christ might have encouraged immoderate use of wine or any kind of excess, proves a false posture of mind and utter disqualification to understand the miracle. The piety and sobriety of this God-fearing family, with the Son of God as their guest, was the basis of the miracle; in an intemperate circle it would never have been wrought at all. *Procul abeste profani!* To the pure all things are pure. See DOCTR. and ETH.—P. S.]

* [Godet, I. pp. 362 and 365, gives some good reasons why John alone relates this miracle of Cana. It seems to have dropped out of the synoptical tradition, together with the first acquaintance of the disciples recorded in ch. i. It is moreover the only miracle in which the mother of Jesus, who was intrusted to the care of John, prominently figures.—P. S.]

* [The great poet, Friedrich Rückert, says with as much truth as beauty:

"*Ein Wunder wird der Mensch empfangen und gezeugt;*
Ein Wunder lebt er, wird geboren und gesäugt;
Ein Wunder wächst er fort und sieht und fühlt sein Wunder;
Ein Wunder, dass er denkt, und was er denkt, ein Wunder.
Ein Wunder steht er da in aller Wunder Mitte,
Und Wunder gehn ihm vor und nach auf Tritt und Schritte,
An Wunder wird er so allmälig unwillkürlich
Gewöhnet, dass sie ihm erscheinen ganz natürlich.
Und wunderbar erscheint ihm Ungewohntes nur,
Der unverwundert sieht das Wunder der Natur."—P. S.]

Ver. 1. **And the third day**, [τῇ τρίτῃ ἡμέρᾳ].—Most probably identical [?] with the ἐπαύριον, ch. i. 43 (44). See the EXEG. *ad loc.* The marriage-feast had probably been nearly three days in progress, when Jesus, on His arrival, was invited to it. [The third day is probably to be reckoned from the last date mentioned, *i. e.*, Nathanael's calling, i. 43 (44), not from the day of John's testimony, i. 29, as Dr. Lange takes it, still less from the day of Christ's arrival in Cana (Ewald); for this was not yet spoken of. Bengel: *Tertio die post promissum datum*, i. 52. *Nunc ostenditur specimen.* The journey from Judæa to Galilee required two or three days, the distance in a direct line being over twenty hours. —P. S.]

In Cana of Galilee.—In the Galilean Cana; in distinction from another. (So ver. 11; ch. iv. 46; xxi. 2). [Or, rather, as the other Cana lies likewise in Galilee, τῆς Γαλιλαίας is merely a local notice of John for foreign readers, comp. i. 28; 44, and Hengstenberg *in loc.*—P. S.] Not *Kef'r Kenna*, but *Kâna el-Jelîl*, according to Robinson, III., p. 443. [Am. ed. of 1858, vol. II. pp. 346–'49.—P. S.] Galilee was originally only a district (גָּלִיל) of Upper Galilee, which was divided from Lower Galilee by a line running from Tiberias to Zabulon. Hence in the time of John there was, no doubt, a Galilee in the stricter, ancient sense, to be distinguished from a Galilee in the wider sense. This distinction is important in John iv. 45. The other Cana, from which ours is distinguished, has been sought now, according to Josephus (*Vita* xvii. 1) erroneously in Peræa, now in a Cana in the tribe of Asher (Josh. xix. 28), south-east of Tyre (Robinson III.: 657), which, "though also to be counted in Galilee, lay so much in the vicinity of Phenicia, as to justify the designation of our Cana as K. τῆς Γαλιλαίας," (Meyer). But that northernmost Cana also belonged to Galilee. We can allow this distinction only on the supposition that the region of Cana of Galilee was a Galilee in the narrow sense, in the most provincial terms. As Kef'r Kenna, which tradition has fixed as the Galilean Cana, lies some distance to the south, it might fall in the province of Lower Galilee, and might well form the antithesis. Ewald has made a Kanath, east of Jordan, the other Cana; which is scarcely to be mentioned. Cana lay on a round hill.

[The location of Cana is still under dispute. Dr. Robinson's view has been adopted by Ritter, Meyer, Alford, Trench, Lange, Renan. Trench (*On the Miracles*, p. 83) numbers this among "the most felicitous and most convincing of Robinson's slighter rectifications of the geography of Palestine." *Kâna el-Jelîl* (*i. e.*, Cana of Galilee) is a mere ruin about seven miles or nearly three hours N. ½ E. from Nazareth, and about three miles N. by E. of Sepphoris (Seffûrieh). *Kef'r* (*i. e.*, village) *Kenna*, is a small village about 4½ miles north-east of Nazareth, where the monks locate Cana, and where the remains of a Greek church and the house of St. Bartholomew are pointed out. Robinson's arguments in favor of *Kâna el-Jelîl* are the identity of name, and a notice from Marinus Sanutus about A. D. 1321. But Hepworth Dixon (*Holy Land*, 1865, I. 332) contends again for *Kef'r Kenna*, as he and Thomson (*The Land and the Book*) contend for *Tell Hûm*, as the site of Capernaum, against Robinson's conclusion in favor of *Khan Minyeh*. Hengstenberg and Godet likewise decide for Kef'r Kenna. Grove (in Smith's *Dictionary of the Bible*) and Hackett (in a supplementary note to the Am. ed.) leave the question of the situation of Cana doubtful. Although Cana has nearly disappeared, it will always be remembered in connection with the festivity of marriage and the happiness of the family. —P. S.]

And the mother of Jesus was there.—The mother of Jesus, John writes; not Mary. [John never names Mary, as he does not name himself nor his brother James, perhaps on account of his intimate connection with her in virtue of the dying injunction of the Saviour, xix. 26, 27. So Alford.—P. S.] Luthardt (with Hofmann and Lampe) holds (p. 420; comp. p. 116) that Jesus entirely dissolved the relation of son to Mary on the cross, with the word: "Woman, behold thy son!"*. John seems far from this, to speak mildly, rare exegesis. Jesus returned with His disciples to Galilee, their common home. They accompanied Him to Nazareth. But the mother of Jesus had gone to the wedding at Cana, which lay further north in the mountains. Probably they met in Nazareth with the invitation which occasioned their following the mother.

[The occasion was evidently a family gathering. Besides the mother of Jesus, His brothers were also present, ver. 12. It was a farewell (*un adieu royal*, as Godet says) to His earthly relations. He was now leaving the privacy and obscurity of family life to enter upon His public ministry, and marked the transition by an exhibition of His divine power which was well calculated to convince His brothers, sisters, and friends of His Messiahship, and to convert them into His spiritual relations.—P. S.]

Ver. 2. **And Jesus also was invited, and his disciples**, [*i. e.*, those five mentioned in ch. i., Andrew, Simon Peter, Philip, Nathanael, and John. The evangelist was therefore an eye-witness of the scene, and probably a relative of Jesus.—P. S.] Ἐκλήθη [is the historical past: *was bidden, invited*, and] cannot be taken as pluperfect. Where would the inviter have looked for the Lord on the Jordan? And there, too, He had as yet no disciples to be invited with Him. The invitation was rather an after-thought, and from this in part the lack of wine might be explained. Meyer supposes that the invitation was given in Cana itself. But people do not go in search of a member of a family at a feast; at all events this would amount to their inviting themselves. The fact that Nathanael was of Cana might increase the relations of the Lord to the house of friends with which His mother Mary seems to have been closely connected. It may certainly be inferred from this passage and ver.

* [Similarly Godet (I. 350): The address *woman*, xix. 26, signalizes the definite rupture of the earthly relation of mother and son, and here at Cana Mary felt for the first time the point of that sword which was to pierce her soul beneath the cross (Luke ii. 35). This is going too far. Christ never broke that relation, but from His twelfth year (Luke ii. 49), He subordinated it to His higher relation to His heavenly Father. Here John, the adopted son and guardian of Mary, writing long after her death, calls her the mother of Jesus.—P. S.]

12, that Joseph was no longer living. (Against Meyer, who unwarrantably cites ch. vi. 42).* Of a removal of Mary from Nazareth to Cana, Ewald speaks alone.†—If we reckon for the return to Cana, including the stoppage at the calling of Philip and Nathanael, as a three days' journey, Jesus, according to Origen's computation of the third day (from the day of ch. i. 43), would have arrived with His disciples in the evening of the first day of the feast. As a wedding generally lasted seven days (among the poorer people, indeed, only three, or even one; comp. Gen. xxix. 27; Judg. xiv. 14; Tob. ix. 12), the supply of wine with but moderate care, would hardly have been exhausted so soon. We are forced to conclude, therefore, that the Lord came with His disciples on one of the later days of the feast; and this works backward to the supposition that the third day dates from the testimony of John, as the day when Jesus was publicly and theocratically accredited as the Messiah in Israel.‡

[The presence of Christ with His mother and disciples, at a wedding-feast, and His performing His first miracle there, is a silent condemnation of monkish asceticism, and a recognition of the marriage relation as honorable and holy. Christianity is no flight from the world, but a transformation of the world, no annihilation of the order of nature, but the sanctification of it, no moroseness of spirit, but joy and gladness. It is the leaven which is to leaven the whole lump of society. But by turning water into wine and revealing His glory at the wedding-feast, Christ gave us an example how to conduct ourselves in society, that is to introduce a higher, nobler element, and to change the water of trifling, frivolous talk into the wine of instructive, profitable conversation. Trench observes: "We need not wonder to find the Lord of life at that festival; for He came to sanctify all life—its times of joy, as its times of sorrow; and all experience tells us, that it is times of gladness, such as this was now, which especially need such a sanctifying power, such a presence of the Lord. In times of sorrow, the sense of God's presence comes more naturally out: in these it is in danger to be forgotten. He was there, and by His presence there struck the key-note to the whole future tenor of His ministry."—P. S.]

Ver. 3. **And when wine failed,** [*Καὶ ὑστερήσαντος οἴνου*]. Gladly had the nuptial family, which undoubtedly belonged to the true waiting ones in Israel, improvised their invitation; but it seemed to fare ill for awhile, in having neglected the usual Jewish calculation. The less could their spirit turn to their mortification. Tholuck adduces the cheapness of wine in the East, to infer that the family was in limited circumstances. But even where wine is cheap, it is not always at hand in abundance, even for the wealthy. In any case the need here existing was not so much that of poverty as that of family honor, especially of festal feeling and joy. [It also reveals the temperance of the family.—P. S.]

They have no wine.—No *more* wine. According to Chrysostom and others, Mary speaks these words, because Jesus had already wrought miracles, and she expects one now. Contrary to ver. 11. According to Lücke, Jesus has already done extraordinary works in smaller circles, and so given rise to the expectation.* According to Bengel and Paulus, Mary would suggest to Him to depart with His disciples;† according to Meyer, to provide some remedy, "which in fact might have been done in the most natural way (by fetching more wine)"! Calvin thinks it a hush-word to the guests (perhaps a hint to go). Tholuck: "The object of Jesus' journey could not have remained unknown to Mary; if, according to the popular faith, she was considering the miracle the test of the Messiah, she might now request even the first exercise of the divine power." Nothing of all these intentions appears in the words. To *tell* the need is not necessarily to *apply* for help. So far as its form is concerned, the expression proves only, that the people let Mary know the lack, and that she told it to the Lord; rather giving up than asking help. Mary had probably a hundred times found in her family life, that the holy Child, during His growth, could tell what to do, when no one else could, though not exactly by miracle strictly so called.‡ A *confident expectation*, however, must have been couched in her complaint; this is evident from the answer of the Lord. She certainly meant, in general: Tell us what to do; and, if any one please, more specifically, according to Bengel: Bring the feast to a close; though in some other way than by an embarrassed departure.

[I take the words of Mary to be an indirect prayer and a modest hint to relieve the difficulty, like the message of the sisters of Lazarus: "Lord, behold, he whom Thou lovest, is sick," John xi. 3. Mary had good reason to expect that her divine Son, now after His solemn inauguration by the baptism in Jordan, and the gathering of His first disciples, would signalize His entrance upon public life by a miraculous demonstration of His Messianic dignity, and she was not shaken in her expectation by His apparent refusal, as is evident from her words in ver. 5 (see my note, p. 106). The announcement of the angel, the supernatural conception, and the whole conduct of Jesus must have long before convinced her of His Messiahship. Lampe properly regards these words as a monument of the faith, humility and modesty of Mary. Yet there was

* [Joseph is last mentioned, Luke ii., when Jesus was twelve years of age, and accompanied His parents to Jerusalem. He seems to have died before the public ministry of Christ.—P. S.]

† [Renan, *Vie de Jésus*, pp. 71, 72, adopts this conjecture.—P. S.]

‡ [Doubtful; comp. my note on ver. 1, p. 103.—P. S.]

* [So very nearly Stier and Alford.—P. S.]

† [It seems incredible that such a profoundly spiritual and ingenious commentator as Bengel should have anticipated even once the insipid rationalistic exegesis of Paulus of Heidelberg. And yet so it is in this case. "*Velim discedas, ut ceteri item discedant, antequam penuria patefiat.*" This would be kind to the family, but hardly respectful to Jesus. Bengel, however, adopts this view to deprive the answer of Jesus of all apparent harshness, and explains ὥρα, ver. 4, to mean *hora discedendi*, so as to say: This is not the hour of withdrawing, but the hour of assisting. Ebrard, in his ed. of Olshausen, agrees with Bengel.—P. S.]

‡ [Similarly Cocceius, as cited by Trench: Mary had always found Jesus a wise counsellor, and mentioned the want to Him merely that He might suggest some way of remedying it.—P. S.]

a defect, an untimely haste and improper interference, though from the best motives, with the Messianic prerogative of her divine Son. This is manifest from the reply of Jesus.—P. S.]

Ver. 4. **Jesus saith unto her,** *etc.*—The terms of Luther's version [identical with those of the English]: Woman, what have I to do with thee?* are much too strong. The phrase forms a scale, from the strongest rebuke to the gentlest refusal, according to the tone.

The address: *γύναι*, **Woman**, has no tinge of contempt. Augustus says to Cleopatra [the Queen of Egypt] in Dio: *Θάρσει, ὦ γύναι.*† So the address to Mary Magdalene, John xx. 15, *γύναι*, is plainly an expression of compassion. And, so, too, is John xix. 26 to be taken.

[In English the term *woman* is frequently used in a solemn and honorable sense, as embracing the characteristic traits of the womanly ideal, when we speak of *a good woman, a noble woman, a true woman, be a woman.* Christ calls His mother *woman* when on the cross He commited her with tender affection to the charge of His bosom disciple. He does not call her *mother*, because this would not suit here in connection with *τί ἐμοὶ καὶ σοί*, and because He had regard mainly to His Father, and subordinated all earthly relations to the heavenly and eternal. Comp. Matth. xii. 49, 50; Luke viii. 19; 2 Cor. v. 16. The period of His subjection to her as His earthly mother had ceased. Even in His twelfth year He answered to her remark: "Thy father (Joseph) and I," by "My Father" (in heaven), Luke ii. 48, 49. Calvin: *Sic ergo matrem Christus alloquitur, ut perpetuam et communem seculis omnibus doctrinam tradat, ne immodicus matris honor divinam suam gloriam obscuret.* Olshausen: "The Son had now become the *Lord* also of His mother, who could secure her own happiness only by believing obedience to Him."—P. S.]

The phrase *τί ἐμοὶ καὶ σοί*, What to me and to thee (in which *κοινόν* or the like is to be supplied), has not among the Hebrews (מַה־לִּי וָלָךְ), as in the classics, a repulsive, reprehensive sense, as Grotius shows, *ad* Matth. viii. 29. The expression is uttered in Jud. xi. 12; 2 Sam. xvi. 10, in friendliness. It readily consists with this, that Jesus would assert the elevation of His divine calling above natural relationship, as in Matth. xii. 50 (Tholuck). Ebrard: That is my matter; leave that to me. Hengstenberg: "*Was mir und dir, Weib?*" Literally correct, but not good German.

[As the interpretation of this passage, which derives its true light from Matth. xii. 46-50, has a bearing on the subject of Mariology and Mariolatry, I shall quote passages from ancient and modern commentators, who agree (against the Romish) in finding here a slight reproof of Mary for a certain improper interference or impatient haste. Irenæus (*Adv. hær.* l. III. c. 16, § 7): "The Lord, repelling Mary's unseasonable urgency (*Dominus, repellens ejus intempestivam festinationem*), said: "What have I to do with thee," *etc.* Chrysostom (*Hom.* XXI. *al.* XX. *in Joh.* Tom. VIII. p. 122): "She wished to gain glory through her child (*ἐβούλετο . . . . ἑαυτὴν λαμπροτέραν ποιῆσαι διὰ τοῦ παιδός*) . . . therefore Christ answered her with severity (*σφοδρότερον ἀπεκρίνατο λέγων, κ. τ. λ.*)." He adds: "Mary had not yet the proper opinion of Christ (*οὐδέπω γὰρ ἣ ἐχρῆν περὶ αὐτοῦ δόξαν εἶχεν*), but because she bare Him, she thought that, after the manner of other mothers, she might in all things command Him whom she ought to have worshipped and adored as her Lord. For this reason He gave this answer." Such passages are irreconcilable with the belief in the sinlessness of Mary. As the veneration of the Virgin increased from the time of the Nestorian controversy and the universal adoption of the *θεοτόκος*, such comments disappear. Even the Nestorianizing Theodoret, though quite full in his notes on the miracle of Cana, says not a word which might reflect in the least on Mary's conduct. But the reformers and nearly all the Protestant interpreters take the same view of the passage as the fathers. Olshausen says that the words *τί ἐμοί, etc.* necessarily imply reproof, although the rebuke is but gentle. Meyer: "Christ, in the consciousness of His higher wonder-working power and will, as one without a mother (*ἀμήτωρ*), repels the interference of womanly weakness, which here confronted Him, even in His mother." Hengstenberg: "It lies in the nature of the case that the phrase always implies censure." Godet agrees with Hengstenberg. Ewald: "He reproves her expectation with severe words." Trench: "There is more or less of reproof and repulse in these words;" but he adds very properly that any harshness of the reply was mitigated by the manner in which the Lord suffered a near compliance with the request to shine through the apparent refusal. Alford: "The answer of our Lord is beyond question one of reproof, and disclaimer of participation in the grounds on which the request was made." St. Bernard, Maldonatus and other Romanists try to escape the force of the *usus loquendi* by saying that Christ spoke those words not for Mary's, but for our sakes, to teach us that He performed His miracles not from regard to human relationship, but from love and regard to God's glory. Very true; but He taught Mary first, and taught us through her.—P. S.]

Mine hour is not yet come.—Euthym. Zigab.: The hour for working miracles. Ewald: Of my full sense of Messianic power. Lücke and others: For the revelation of my glory. Meyer: The juncture for help. [Trench: Till the wine is wholly exhausted. Flat.—P. S.]. According to Bruno Bauer, His hour must always mean the hour of His death.*—According to

* [*Weib, was habe ich mit dir zu schaffen?* Vulgate: *Quid mihi et tibi est?* French N. T.: *Qu 'y a-t-il entre moi et toi?* Comp. my Text, Note,[2] p. 102.—P. S.]

† [Dion Cassius, *Hist.* LI. 12: *θάρσει, ὦ γύναι, καὶ θυμὸν ἔχε ἀγαθόν*, "Take courage, O woman, and keep a good heart," or, "be of good cheer."—P. S.]

* [Similarly Alford: "My time, the time at which, from the Father's appointment and My own concurring will, I am to begin miraculous working, is not yet arrived: forestall it not." Probably Mary, like the Apostles before the pentecostal illumination, was not yet quite free from carnal conceptions of the Messianic Kingdom, as a temporal reign, and expected that He would establish it at the beginning of His ministry. Christ declined the form of her petition, but answered the real intent in a better way than she conceived. In other passages of John the hour of Christ means the hour of His death and glorification, vii. 30; xii. 23, 27; xiii. 1.—P. S.]

Tholuck, it is the ὥρα for the manifestation of His δόξα, as determined by the object of the miracle and the circle of witnesses. In this regard this scene seemed not so suitable as Jerusalem, yet the affectionate Son would also fain please His mother. Hence οὔπω refers to the precise moment. The right time of publicity, the right moment—two different ideas: His hour is His time for acting or suffering, as the Father appoints it to Him by the occasion and in His spirit, in distinction from the hour which is assigned Him by the opinion of men. Comp. John vii. 6; viii. 20; xiii. 1; Luke xxii. 53. The "*not yet*" opens the prospect of help to come at the right time.

Ver. 5. **Whatsoever he saith unto you.**—Meyer thinks she means, He will require your service, perhaps in bringing wine. Meyer says: Whatsoever He saith unto you, without qualification; yet doubtless with the presentiment that He might say something very strange and striking, at which they were in danger of being startled.

[These words reveal the unbounded faith of Mary in her Son, whose gentle rebuke did not discourage her, and a confident expectation of some miraculous help at the proper time. She seems to have anticipated even the manner, *viz.*, that it was to be brought about by the aid of the servants. She may have inferred from some previous hint of Christ not related here, or from the gentle manner with which He apparently refused her desire, with the qualifying οὔπω (*not yet*), His disposition to grant it. Precisely the same words: ὁ ἐὰν εἴπῃ ὑμῖν ποιήσατε (Gen. xli. 55, LXX.), Pharaoh, at the time of the famine, addressed to all Egypt with regard to Joseph. Hengstenberg thinks that this coincidence is scarcely accidental in view of the similarity of the occasion, and the typical character of Joseph.—P. S.]

Ver. 6. **There were set** [κείμεναι, *positæ*] **there six water-pots of stone** [ὑδρίαι λίθιναι, made of stone, stone-ware].—*There;* in the wedding-chamber, says Meyer. The washing of hands hardly took place in the wedding-chamber, rather in the court of the house. And the pots were too large for this, being doubtless not portable in the ordinary way: "large stone fonts" (Starke).—*Six* water-pots there were. Whether according to Jewish custom, can hardly be ascertained; at all events, the number, as symbolical, is the number of work, toil and need. See ch. xii. 1: six days before the passover Christ came to Bethany. Rev. ch. vi.: the opening of the first six seals. Ch. xiii. 18: the number of the beast, 666. Nork (*Etymol. Symbol. Mythol. Real-Wörterbuch*): "Six is threefold discord (Dyad), hence 666 is the number of Antichrist. On the evening of the sixth day of creation, according to the Rabbinical tradition, Satan was created at the same time with woman. The Cabbalistic book Sohar warns against the threefold six as the number of punishment. On its face this number bespeaks an accurate reporter.*

After the manner of the purifying [κατὰ τὸν καθαρισμὸν τῶν Ἰουδαίων]—The washing of hands and vessels before and after meals, Matth. xv. 2; Mark vii. 3. Probably the supply of water in them was already mostly consumed; at all events, they were emptied for their new use.

Containing two or three firkins apiece [χωροῦσαι ἀνὰ—not approximately, *circiter*, but in the distributive sense, *singulæ*, as in the E. V.—μετρητὰς δύο ἢ τρεῖς].—The Attic metretes was equal to the Hebrew בַּת (Joseph. *Antiq.* VIII. 2. 9), and twenty-one Würtemberg or thirty-three Berlin quarts [about nine gallons English; so that the word "firkin" in the E. V. is almost exact. Accordingly, if all the water was changed into wine (see below), the quantity of wine thus produced was 6 times 18 or 27 gallons, *i. e.*, from 108 to 162 gallons.—P. S.] The Roman *amphora* was also called metretes, and was still smaller than the Attic; the Syrian Babylonian, on the contrary, was larger. "In view of this (total) quantity of from 252 to 273 quarts [over 100 gallons], the miracle is styled by De Wette [and Strauss] a 'miracle for luxury' (*Luxuswunder*), and found offensive. The circumstances already cited (abundant supply for a poor family; an expression of benevolence) remove this difficulty; in the miraculous feeding also the quantity exceeds the bare necessity." Tholuck.* The truth of the miracle, however, forbids us at the outset to trespass upon the ground of the miraculous. Hence also we raise no question whether the water was made wine *after* it was drawn out, or *before*, in the pots themselves (Meyer, Tholuck).

Ver. 7. **Fill the water-pots.**—Not only is the water in the pots necessary, but also the obedience of faith. So also in the drawing. The pots being full, precludes all thoughts of the possibility of a natural process or a mixture. According to Meyer, this feature is intended to denote the abundance of the wine which Jesus produced; Gerlach [and Barnes] on the contrary: Only what was drawn became wine.

[The miracle took place between vers. 7 and 8, but its actual process lies wholly beyond the region of sense and imagination. The same may be said of the process of growth in nature; we see only the results. It is not stated whether the miracle took place in the water-pots or in the act of drawing, and whether the whole amount of

* [For other and more fanciful allegorical interpretations of the six water-pots and the firkins, see Augustine, *Tract. IX.*, and other fathers. Chrysostom remarks that the scarcity of water in Palestine made it necessary to keep always an abundant supply in vessels.—P. S.]

* [Against the profane view of Strauss, we must rather call the miracle a miracle of love and beneficence. Christ gave as a King, yea, with more than royal bounty. The benevolent design of the abundant supply is pressed by several commentators, down to Lange and Godet. Luther says: "Christ, having no gold or jewels to give to the poor couple, presented them good wine." Maldonatus: "Christ desired not only to relieve a present necessity, but that a quantity of wine might remain for the married persons to assist them in their poverty and to leave a lasting (?) memorial of the miracle." Calvin, Trench and Alford properly refer to the analogy of God's method of dealing in providing the most abundant supply in every vineyard and all over nature, that every man may prove his temperance and moderation, as Calvin says, *in media affluentia.* Barnes, in the interest of teetotalism, supposes that the Saviour only made as much wine as was necessary for the immediate want, and that the miracle was confined to the water actually drawn from the pots. If, as Barnes assumes, the wine was not intoxicating, there can be no objection to the large quantity of it; but even if it was (as all but a few recent American commentators hold), there is no reason whatever to suspect that any improper use was made of it in a company honored by the presence of the Purest of the pure, and the Holiest of the holy. Comp. my remarks on verse 7.—P. S.]

water was turned into wine or only so much of it as was drawn by the servants. But the former view is much more probable, yea, almost certain. It seems to be implied in the exact statement of the number and size of the vessels, ver. 6, in the order to *fill* them with water, and in the strict compliance of the servants who "filled them up *ἕως ἄνω*, to the *brim*," ver. 7. This view agrees also best with the object of the miracle as a manifestation of Christ's Divine glory, in imitation of the boundless munificence which God Himself displays from year to year in the plentiful harvests, that in the midst of plenty we should be temperate and grateful.—P. S.]*

Ver. 8. **Draw out now, and bear.**—Expressing full confidence that they would, in virtue of His word, draw wine and carry wine. **Unto the ruler (master) of the feast** [*τῷ ἀρχιτρικλίνῳ*, a word of late and rare occurrence, lit. the ruler of the *triclinium* or dining-room with three couches.—P. S.].—Not the superintendent of the guests, *συμποσίαρχος* [or *συμποσιάρχης*, *βασιλεύς*, *modimperator*, *magister*, or *rex convivii*, *arbiter bibendi*], whom the guests chose as their president (Xenoph. *Anab.* VI. 1. 30),† but the superintendent of the servants, who as such also tested the meats and drinks, as a taster.‡ Tholuck distinguishes the warden of the drinking from the warden of the table, and remarks that the presence of the latter does not necessarily yield the inference of wealth. He may have been of the friends of the family. At all events, a number of servants were present.—**And they bare it.**—Meyer: "But knew not that what they carried was wine." But they must have *believed* it to be; else we should be left to suppose a tone of mind in the people, which would ill correspond with the elevation of the miracle. The drawing and bearing by the servants was an act of faith, like the sitting down of the multitudes in the wilderness to receive the miraculous feeding.

Ver. 9. [**When the ruler . . . tasted** (*ἐγεύσατο*).—Here the Romish argument in favor of transubstantiation drawn from this miracle, breaks down. The water had been made wine in form as well as in substance; it looked like wine and tasted like the best of wine; but the pretended change of bread and wine in the Eucharist contradicts all the senses and is a complete delusion.—P. S.]

That had become wine.—Not: That it became (was made) wine. In the perfect [*had been made*, and consequently *was* now].

And knew not whence it was.—It at first seems to give a better sense, to make the parenthesis of the 9th verse, according to Meyer, begin not with these words, but with: *οἱ δὲ διάκονοι*, ending with *ὕδωρ*. Meyer observes that the construction continues with *οὐκ ᾔδει*, and this supplies the motive of the consequent *φωνεῖ τὸν νυμφίον*. But the ruler calls the bridegroom, not to ask whence he has the wine, but to remark to him that he has reversed the usual order of things with this supply of wine, which he seems to suppose the bridegroom has reserved. And John elsewhere begins a parenthesis with *καί*, as in 1 John i. 2. A decisive consideration might be this: If we put the *πόθεν* before the parenthesis, it indicates in the ruler the impression of the natural origin of the wine; in the parenthesis it emphatically expresses the thought of the Evangelist, that he knew not the miraculous origin of the wine. The *ἐστίν*, as in ch. i. 40, is the usual intermixing of direct description in dependent clauses (Winer, p. 239).

Called the bridegroom.—The wedding took place in the house of the bridegroom, and he gave the banquet. As to the custom here mentioned, there is little other evidence (see Lücke, p. 473). Wetstein: Pliny, *H. N.* XIV. 14. Cato, when he embarked for Spain, said of the rowers (*remiges*): *Qui etiam convivis alia* (referring to wine), *quam sibimet ipsis ministrant* ["who even give their guests other wine than they drink themselves, or bring it in as the banquet proceeds"]. Two other citations (from Martialis and Cassius) Lücke himself considers entirely unimportant. The passage, seems, however, to have some sense different from that commonly supposed, which gives a mild interpretation to *μεθύσκεσθαι*, *madere*, "have drunk enough" (Tholuck, after De Wette and others); on the contrary Meyer: When they are intoxicated. The softening of the word gives the idea of a dishonorable custom: first to give good wine, then, at the height of the feast to give poor. The custom meant is probably that universally dictated by moral instinct, of at last pouring water into the wine for those who are intoxicated, or giving no more, or even, where courtesy requires the offer to be continued, giving poor wine.* This custom the

* [Calvin on ver. 8: "*Mirum est, quod Christus, frugalitatis magister, vini et quidem præstantissimi magnam copiam largitur. Respondeo, quum nobis quotidie Deus largum vini proventum suppeditat, nostro vitio fieri si ejus benignitas irritamentum est luxuriæ: quin potius hæc temperantiæ nostræ vera est probatio, si in media affluentia, parci tamen et moderati sumus.*" Godet: "*Son premier sign miraculeux doit témoigner hautement de sa richesse et de sa munificence, et devenir pour les assistants le type de la plénitude de grâce et de force que le Fils unique apporte à la terre.*"—P. S.]

† [So Trench, Alford, Wordsworth. This view more easily explains the freedom of remonstrance on the part of the ruler of the feast, than if he had been a mere servant, and is supported by a passage in the apocryphal book, the Wisdom of Sirach, ch. 35 (*al.* 32), vers. 1, 2: "If thou be made the master (ἡγούμενος) of the feast, lift not thyself up, but be among them as one of the rest; take diligent care of them and sit down; and when thou hast done all thy office, take thy place, that thou mayest be merry with them, and receive a crown (στέφανον) for thy well ordering of the feast." This description suits far better the position of the Greek and Roman king of the feast from among the guests, than of the head-waiter from among the slaves. See the next note.—P. S.]

‡ [So Chrysostom, the older commentators, also Kuinoel, Meyer and others. It was the custom among the Greeks to intrust a particular slave with the arrangement of the table, the tasting and distribution of the wines, the trimming of the lamps, and the control of the other servants. This slave, who seems to have combined the offices of a butler and head-waiter, is called *triclinarches* (by Petronius), which is equivalent in meaning to ἀρχιτρίκλινος, also ἐφηστηκώς, τραπεζοποιός, τραπεζοκόμος (by Athenæus), and corresponds to the Roman *structor mensæ*. Athenæus, in his *Deipnosophists* (Banquet of the Learned), lib. IV. c. 70 (in Schweighäuser's ed. Tom. II. p. 162), gives a full description of the τραπεζοποιοί, *setters of the tables*, and quotes in illustration several passages from poets, among the rest these lines from Philemon:

'There is no need of long deliberation
About the kitchen, for the table-setter
Is bound to look to that; that is his office.'

Comp. also Walch: *De architriclino*, Jen. 1753 (which I have not seen), and Becker's *Charikles*, II. p. 252 (second ed. by Hermann, Leipz. 1854). But I have seen no evidence that the same custom prevailed among the Jews, while the other custom with regard to the king of the feast, seems to be substantiated by the passage quoted in the preceding note.—P. S.]

* [Alford differently: When a man has some kinds of wine choicer than others, he naturally produces the choicest to suit the most discriminating taste.—P. S.]

master of the feast applies to the case in hand, without expressing any judgment respecting the condition of the guests.* His "until now" refers only to a later period of the feast.—There is likewise a question, whether we must take the word, with Meyer, as a pleasantry, or, with Tholuck, as a half-jocular reproof. Lücke's hypothesis of an expression of surprise seems more fitting. Pleasantly as the words may have been spoken in the expression: "Thou hast kept the good wine until now," the ruler in any case conveys great astonishment. And strongly as this, on the one hand, attests the objective fact of the miracle, it as strongly, on the other hand, shows a special quality in this wine. The wine seemed to the ruler the good, in contrast with what had been used.

Ver. 11. **This wrought Jesus as a beginning of the signs** [Ταύτην ἐποίησε ἀρχὴν τῶν σημείων Ἰησοῦς].—Ἀρχή without the article, hence: This sign wrought Jesus as His first in Cana of Galilee. [It was not only the first miracle wrought by Jesus in Cana—for no other is reported as having been wrought there—but the first of all His miracles. This is conclusive against all the reports of the apocryphal Gospels to the contrary.—P. S.]—Scholastic fancies respecting the bridegroom and the bride by Bonaventura, *etc.*, see in Heubner, p. 235.

[**The signs**, τῶν σημείων. The N. T. employs three terms for the miracles or supernatural works of Christ, σημεῖον, δύναμις and τέρας, sometimes also ἔνδοξον, παράδοξον, θαυμάσιον. The word σημεῖον, the Hebrew *oth* (אוֹת), *signum*, has reference to the moral aim of the miracle as intended to exhibit the presence of the divine power, and to produce faith in it; it is "a kind of finger-post of God," as has been said. The term τέρας, *prodigium*, *wonder*, which is often combined with σημεῖον (iv. 18), expresses the subjective effect, the emotion of astonishment and amazement which the miracle produces; and hence it is used also of strange and startling phenomena in heaven and on earth. All miracles are signs and wonders, but not all signs and wonders are miracles.† The term δυνάμεις, *virtutes*, denotes the origin of miracles, as manifestations of divine power. The E. V. is by no means consistent in the translation of these words. Trench (*Synonyms of the N. T.*, Second Part, p. 204, Am. ed.) says: "It is to be regretted that in our Version this word (δυνάμεις) is translated now 'wonderful works' (Matth. vii. 22); now 'mighty works' (Matth. xi. 20; Luke x. 13); and still more frequently 'miracles' (Acts ii. 22; 1 Cor. xii. 10; Gal. iii. 5); in this last case giving such tautologies as 'miracles and wonders' (Acts ii. 22; Heb. ii. 4); and always causing something to be lost of the true energy of the word—pointing as it does to new *forces*, which have entered and are working in this world of ours. With this is closely connected the term μεγαλεῖα = *magnalia* (Luke i. 49), in which in like manner the miracles are contemplated as outcomings of the greatness of God's power."—**His glory.** The δόξα of the incarnate Logos, i. 14, by whom all things were made, and who transforms all things. The miracles of Christ are manifestations of *His own* glory, of His wonderful *person*, while the miracles performed by Moses and the prophets revealed not *their* glory, but the glory of Jehovah.—**And his disciples believed on him**, ἐπίστευσαν. This is a higher degree of faith than the one spoken of i. 35-52, which was initial and introductory, while now they were strengthened in their belief by this startling evidence of His divine Messianic power and dignity. Faith is a continuous growth, and every increase of faith is a new beginning of faith.—P. S.]

* [Godet better: "This word has a proverbial sense, and does not apply to the present company." *Text. Note* 3.—P. S.]

† [Lampe: *Eadem miracula dici possunt signa quatenus aliquid seu occultum seu futurum docent; et prodigia* (τέρατα), *quatenus aliquid extraordinarium, quod stuporem excitat, sistunt. Hinc sequitur signorum notionem latius patere, quam prodigiorum. Omnia prodigia sunt signa, quia in illum usum a Deo dispemsata, ut arcanum indicent. Sed omnia signa non sunt prodigia, quia ad signandum res cœlestes aliquando etiam res communes adhibentur.*—P. S.]

DOCTRINAL AND ETHICAL.

1. *John's accounts of the miracles.* We have already called attention to John's putting strongly forward the miracles of knowledge together with those of act; that is, the insight of the perfect personality into the dark recesses of personal life and of nature, in keeping with the character of this Gospel. As in ch. i. 38, 42, 43, 47 (comp. ch. ii. 25); iii. 21; iv. 17; v. 6; vi. 70; xi. 11; xiii. 3 and 38; xix. 11 and 28; xx. 27; xxi. 6, 17, 18, 22. The miracles in the development of the life of Jesus Himself, John rather takes for granted, after his general testimony concerning the δόξα of Jesus; particularly the miraculous birth (which, however, follows from ch. i. 13); the transfiguration (to which, however, ch. xii. 23 sqq.; xvii. look back, and which the voice from heaven, ch. xii. 28, in some measure repeats); and the ascension (which is announced in ch. xx. 17). Even the miracle of the glorification of Jesus at the baptism is here only related incidentally by the Baptist, ch. i. 32; the walking of Jesus on the sea is but briefly touched, ch. vi. 16; and the resurrection of the Lord the Evangelist presents mainly in its noblest bearings, as a victory over doubt, weak faith, and unbelief. On the other hand John intimates by the prominence he gives to the voice from heaven (ch. xii. 28) in the temple, that Christ was always very near, and drawing nearer, His estate of glorification; and in the account of the flowing of water and blood from the side of Jesus' body, he undoubtedly points to the mystery of the transformation in the body of Christ after His death (John xix. 34; comp. *Leben Jesu*, II., 3, p. 1608).

Now as regards the miraculous works in the stricter sense, John entirely omits the expulsions of devils. According to Meyer he significantly relates seven miracles of Jesus, "mentioning one of each of the main kinds, *viz.*, a transformation, ch. ii. 1; a healing of a fever, iv. 47; a healing of a cripple, v. 1; a feeding, vi. 4; a walking on the sea, vi. 16; a healing of the child, ix. 1; a raising of the dead, xi. 1."

We distinguish, in the first place, these miracles in the stricter sense from miracles in a wider sense, among which we count the purification of the temple (ch. ii.), the moral enchaining of the officers (ch. vii. 45), and like things, especially the miracles of knowledge. Furthermore, we distinguish the miracles in Galilee and those in Judea, insomuch as the miracles of Jesus have opposite effects in the two different spheres. After the first miracle in Galilee, His disciples believed on Him, ch. ii. 11; after the second He found faith in the imperial officer at Capernaum and in all his house, ch. iv. 53; after the third (wrought indeed on the east side of the sea, yet no doubt mostly on Galilean people), the people proposed to make Him king, ch. vi. 15; and the fourth could but enhance their reverence, ch. vi. 25. After the first miracle in Judea, on the contrary, which Jesus performed at the feast of Purim, healing a cripple whom the Jewish supernatural fountain and the angel had not healed, process was at once begun by the Jews against Him for excommunication and death, ch. v. 16; comp. vii. 32. After the second, the healing of the blind man at the feast of tabernacles, in which He brought the temple-fountain and the pool of Siloam into service, to show that He was the God of the temple, the ban was pronounced on His followers, and therefore doubtless upon Him at least in so far as He acknowledged His Messianic dignity, ch. ix. 22. Upon the third, the raising of Lazarus, the decree to put Him to death was passed by the Sanhedrin (ch. xi. 47), the edict for His apprehension was issued to the people (ver. 57), even the death of Lazarus was consulted (ch. xii. 10), and in the sequel, on the passover itself, Jesus was crucified. Thus Judaism celebrates its feasts, and opposes to the life-miracles of Christ plots of death, the sentence of death, and the death of the cross.

The miracles recorded by John we divide, according to their kinds into *three miracles of healing*: the healing of the man sick of a fever, of the cripple, of the blind man; *three miracles of the mastery and glorification of nature:* the miraculous supply of wine, the feeding, the miraculous draught of fishes, ch. xxi. (Christ walking on the sea, related without the addition of Peter's, belongs with the miracles of the unfolding of the life of Jesus Himself); finally *three symbolical miracles of the judicial majesty of Christ:* the purification of the temple (ch. ii.), which in its first performance was much more wonderful than in its repetition at the close of the life of Jesus; the moral enchaining of the officers, who were sent to arrest the Lord (ch. vii. 45; comp. ch. viii. 59; x. 39); and the striking down of the soldiers in Gethsemane with His word. The greatest of the miracles related by John is the raising of Lazarus from the dead, the premonition of the resurrection of Christ, the foretokening of the resurrection, the glorification, and the judgment of the whole world, the great development of miracle which begins with His resurrection.

2. *The first miracle of Jesus.* Not only in John, but in the Gospel history in general, the changing of the water into wine is the first miracle of Jesus. But as the first in John it has a peculiar significance. As the portal of the Gospel of the absolute transfiguration of the world by the glorious spiritual personality, and the redeeming operation of Christ, this miracle is the typical, symbolical token of the glorification of the world (see *Leben Jesu*, II., p. 479).

Explanations of this miracle:

(*a*) NATURAL [low rationalistic] explanations by Venturini, Paulus, Langsdorf, Gfrörer.* Paulus: A wedding joke; Jesus had caused a quantity of wine to be brought into the house and to be put, mixed with water, into the pots at the table. Gfrörer†: A wedding surprise-gift on the part of Mary (similarly Ammon).

(*b*) MYTHICAL. [A religious poem or legend unconsciously produced and honestly believed by the primitive Christian community as if it had actually occurred.—P. S.] Strauss: Mythical basis: the changing of bitter water into sweet, in Ex. xv. 23 ff.; 2 Kings ii. 19.‡ Weisse: A parable misunderstood.

(*c*) SYMBOLICAL [and fictitious, not historical]. Baur: A demonstration that the time had come when Jesus, the true Bridegroom, should lead off from the water of the provisional level of the Baptist to the wine of the higher Messianic glory.

(*d*) HISTORICAL. Various modifications.

(1) An *absolute* miracle of the [*immediate*] transformation of substance regardless of conditions; the older supernaturalism (Meyer even refuses to recognize any elevation of the spirit of the company).

(2) Historical in a still stricter sense, as a miracle admitting some *conditions; change of substance* under conditions; Augustine (*ipse fecit vinum in nuptiis, qui omni anno hoc facit in vitibus*),§ Chrysostom,‖ Olshausen: acceleration of a natural process (which, however, must have included an acceleration of an artificial process, and in this the main factor, the vine, was wanting. Objections of Strauss, Meyer).¶

* [Meyer justly calls this rationalistic explanation a frivolous transformation of history (*eine frivole Geschichtswandlung*).—P. S.]

† [This writer subsequently became a Roman Catholic and died as professor of history in the University of Freiburg. —P. S.]

‡ [Comp. against the mythical view the remarks of Godet, I. p. 364. Even Baur admits that the whole tenure of the narrative excludes the mythical interpretation. Renan touches this miracle but slightly.—P. S.]

§ [An abridged quotation (made first by Olshausen) from the beginning of Augustine's 8th *Tract. in Joh.* The same idea Augustine repeats in the 9th *Tract.* §1: "*Ipse est Deus, qui per universam creaturam quotidiana miracula facit, quæ hominibus non facilitate, sed assiduitate viluerunt. .... Sic aquam in vinum conversam quis non miretur, cum hoc annis omnibus Deus in vitibus faciat?*" And again, *Serm.* 123, c. 3: "*Quæ aqua erat, vinum factum viderunt homines et obstupuerunt. Quid aliud fit de pluvia per radicem vitis?*"—P. S.]

‖ [*Hom. in Joa.* xxii. (*al.* xxi.), Tom. VIII. p. 127 sq. Chrysostom remarks that there is a difference between changing the quality of an existing substance and creating the substance itself, and that the latter is much more wonderful, but the divine power the same. Christ shows in this miracle that He who changed water into wine in a moment, was the same who annually in the vineyards changes the rain through the root into wine, αὐτός ἐστιν ὁ ἐν τοῖς ἀμπέλοις τὸ ὕδωρ μεταβάλλων, καὶ τὸν ὑετὸν διὰ τῆς ῥίζης εἰς οἶνον τρέπων, ὅπερ ἐν τῷ φυτῷ διὰ πολλοῦ χρόνου γίνεται, τοῦτο ἀθρόον ἐν τῷ γάμῳ εἰργάσατο.—P. S.]

¶ [Olshausen first used this expressive term of an accelerated process of nature (*ein beschleunigter Naturprocess*) and applied it also to the miraculous feeding of the multitude. Strauss, in his *Leben Jesu*, endeavored to ridicule his view by an analysis of this process of *nature* and the accelerated process of *art* (*beschleunigter Kunstprocess*), which must be added in both cases, *viz.*, the gathering and crushing of the grapes, the action of the wine-press and the fermentation, in the making of wine, and the operations of the mower, miller and baker, in the making of bread. But Olshausen meant to assert only the similarity, not the identity, of the process, which in both cases passes our comprehension. Hase (in his *Life of Jesus*) and Trench (*Miracles*) adopt Augustine's and Olshausen's view, Trench with the judicious remark: "This analogy does not help us to understand what the Lord did now, but yet brings before us that in this He was working in the line

(3) *Change of accidents* under conditions. Neander: instances of mineral springs which have the taste of broth, intoxicating wines, *etc.* (instances from the classics in Lampe and Neander*). Meyer puts Tholuck also on this ground; but Tholuck at present says: "These are still no help towards understanding the miracle, inasmuch as the inorganic or hard matter of the mineral springs would only come in the place of the vegetable. (Yet Neander mentions those facts only as analogies, showing how water can be modified.) In that which gives the offence here—the change of substance—natural science, however, till very lately has believed, with its *generatio equivoca* (*i. e.*, the change of substance by changes of form—erroneously), and now chemistry would see everywhere only change of form (but through change of substance—again erroneously)."

(4) *Transfiguration of the substance in actu.* [Lange.] Tholuck states with strange incorrectness: "J. P. Lange (*Leben Jesu*, II. 1, p. 307) falls back upon the view that the elevated frame of mind in the master of the feast and in the guests caused the water to taste like wine." Meyer represents the thought more carefully, though he can make nothing of it. "In the element of an elevated frame of mind, to which the guests, like the disciples on the mount of the transfiguration, were raised, *the transfiguration took place.*" But I had even said: "Thus Christ transported to heaven a company of devout and submissive men, and gave them to drink from the mysterious fountain of His divine life-power" (*Leben Jesu*, II., p. 479). The operation of Christ, furthermore, I described as threefold: (*a*) The creative substitution of the wine, sympathetically communicated to the guests in their contemplation of Christ; (*b*) influence upon the drinkers through faith; (*c*) influence upon the element of the drink itself (p. 308). I cannot consider it an advance in exegesis, that Meyer comes to such an emphasizing of the change of substance as seems virtually to make the conditions of Augustine and others unsuitable; and that Tholuck appeals in fine to two systems of natural science which he himself considers false. As the abstract supernaturalism takes the simple, immediate change of substance for the gist of the miracle, I pointed to the central point of all miracles, and this among them, suggesting that all are rooted in the heavenly birth of Christ, and are conditioned upon the beginnings of regeneration, as the continuous development of the eternal central miracle, therefore also upon frames of the human heart. That such frames of heart existed here, is shown by the faith of the disciples, the confidence of Mary, the submissiveness of the drawers, the enthusiasm of the master of the feast. For this very reason, moreover, we have emphasized the act, in opposition to an abstract computation of the quantity of wine; as, for example, the Protestant orthodoxy emphasizes the presence of the body and blood of Christ in the substance of the act, in distinction from the magical representations of the body of Christ in the material substance (without deciding concerning the material left unemployed in the act; as Gerlach, for instance, see the exegesis on ver. 7). Then in the third place the analogy of similar instances of transfiguring mastery of nature was taken into account. Through the communion of the spirit of Christ the feedings become wonderful; through the communion of the spirit of Christ alone Peter walks on the water; in the hearts of the believing lay the conditions of the miracles of Christ throughout.

In thus tracing the miracle to its Christological centre, the principle of the glorification of the world, we suppose, however, that Christ here brought also a latent, mysterious susceptibility of the water to an instantaneous development, in which, with regard to the quantity, it must certainly be considered that the very filling of the water-pots was done at His word and in the obedience of faith. Thus the δόξα of Christ in His first self-manifestation is to us the main thing.*

(*e*) The miracle HISTORICAL, and at the same time of TYPICAL, SYMBOLICAL import:†

(1) Older expositors, Lampe, Baumgarten-Crusius, Luthardt: Exhibition of the contrast between the Old Testament and the New.‡

(2) Christ sets forth in the miracle at the same time the contrast of His new covenant with the severe ascetic spirit of the Baptist (Flatt, Olshausen).§

(3) Prefiguration of the communion of the Lord with His people on the height of the glorified world (*Leben Jesu*, pp. 307, 479).

(4) Hofmann, Luthardt (with a simultaneous reference to the ancient covenant): Prefiguration of the heavenly marriage-supper, Rev. xix. 9 (translation of the ideal conception just given (3) into realistic terms).

---

of His more ordinary workings which we see daily around us, the unnoticed miracles of every-day nature."—P. S.]

* [Athenæus and Theopompus, also Vitruvius, speak of springs of water which had the intoxicating properties of wine.—P. S.]

* [Dr. Lange, as appears from this defense of views previously expressed in his *Life of Jesus*, does not mean to deny the objective character of the miracle, but simply to bring it into organic connection with Christology and to insist upon a corresponding subjective condition and elevation of the witnesses, *i. e.*. upon faith on their part, as the medium of apprehension. The miracle itself consisted in a real change of the quality of one substance into that of another. And this must be guarded against any attempt, however ingenious and plausible, to explain it away. A miracle is a miracle, and passes our comprehension. I think it most probable and consistent with the tenor of the narrative that the change was effected in the water-pots, not in the act of drawing, or of drinking; and that consequently *all* the water was turned into wine, although only so much of it was *used* on the present occasion as was right and proper. Comp. my remarks on p. 106 f.—P. S.]

† [Dr. Lange might have mentioned here first the *allegorical* interpretations of Cyril, Augustine, Theodoret and other fathers, followed by Alcuin, Bernard and other mediæval divines. But they are very fanciful and almost worthless. Even the sober Theodoret makes the six water-pots to signify the five senses and the reason, Augustine six ages, *etc.*—P. S.]

‡ [So also Eusebius, Augustine, Bernard, Cornelius a Lapide ("*lex mosaica instar aquæ insipida et frigida—evangelium gratiæ quæ instar vini est generosa, sapida, ardens et efficax*"), Trench and many others. The first miracle of Moses is also often contrasted with the first miracle of Christ: Moses turned water into blood—characterizing the law as a ministration of death—Christ turned water into wine—the gospel being an administration of life and the bringer in of joy and gladness.—P. S.]

§ [Olshausen: The first disciples of Christ were all originally disciples of the Baptist. His manner of life—rigid, penitential austerity and solitary abode in the desert—naturally appeared to them the highest form of piety. What a contrast for them, when the Messiah, to whom the Baptist himself had pointed them, leads them first of all to a marriage. This contrast needed a reconciliation which was supplied by means of a miracle.—P. S.]

(5) De Wette: The distribution of wine a counterpart of the distribution of bread, and both together analogies of the Holy Supper (of which again Meyer finds nothing in the record. Comp. *Leben Jesu*, p. 310. On Hilgenfeld's explanation of it into a Gnostic element, comp. Meyer).

3. *The symbolical import of the miracle.* All the miracles of Jesus are to be considered as signs; that is, not merely facts, but also mirrors of the Christian idea, the Christian principle and its universal operation. But John has reason for marking this sign as the first which Jesus did, and as a manifestation of His glory. The description of it as a manifestation of His δόξα announces the wide symbolical significance of the miracle.

(*a*) The Old Testament pots of water, of purification, of statute, are changed into New Testament vessels of wine, vivification, free, festive life.

(*b*) The want, in which the feasts of the old, natural life end, is changed by the grace of Christ into the fountain of the higher joys of the kingdom of heaven.

(*c*) Mary, as the highest representative of the Old Testament faith, with the servants and the master of the feast, are changed into instruments of the manifestation of the New Testament glory of Christ.

(*d*) The earthly nuptials are changed into the basis of a higher festivity, the marriage of Christ with His own in their now established faith.

(*e*) The gift of the wine is made a token of the δόξα of Christ: which, as grace, converts all need into supply, and, as truth, gives every thing symbolical, even earthly wine, in heavenly reality (He Himself the real vine).

(*f*) The gift of wine a token of the Supper of Christ, as the constant type of the progressive glorification of life and its ultimate perfect glorification in the heavenly world.

[4. *The miracle of Cana and the Temperance question.* Albert Barnes (*in loc.*), in his zeal for total abstinence, labors to show, contrary to all exegetical tradition, that the wine which Jesus made and the wine generally used in Palestine was the *unfermented* juice of the grape, and hence without any alcoholic admixture, or intoxicating quality. Jacobus, in his Notes on John, takes the same view.* The arguments on this side are collected in a tract by the Rev. W. M. Thayer: *Communion Wine and Bible Temperance*, published by the American National Temperance Society, New York, 1869. But they are not convincing. The wine of the Bible was no doubt *pure* and *unadulterated*, and so far unlike that poisonous article which is frequently sold as wine in our days, especially in Northern countries; but it was genuine and real wine, and, like all wine in wine-growing countries, exhilarating, and, if used to excess, intoxicating. The grape, says an Italian proverb, has three fruits, pleasure, intoxication, and grief. Pure water is no doubt the safest and most wholesome beverage. Ἄριστον μὲν ὕδωρ, says Pindar, in his first ode. We honor zeal against the fearful scourge of intemperance; but even a good thing may be undone by being over-done. Total abstinence from wine, or from meat, or other things in themselves innocent and lawful, can be sufficiently defended as a moral duty under certain circumstances, on the ground of *expediency* and *charity*, from regard to our weak brethren or the good of the community at large. This is the position taken by Paul, 1 Cor. viii. 13; Rom. xiv. 13-23. Considerations of health, climate, nationality and condition of society must also be allowed due weight in this question. But to lay down the principle that the use of intoxicating drinks as a beverage is a sin *per se*, is to condemn the greater part of Christendom, to contradict the Bible, and to impeach Christ Himself, who drank wine (He was slanderously called a 'wine-bibber'), who made wine by a miracle, who instituted the holy communion under the symbols of bread and wine, and commands us to commemorate the shedding of His blood by drinking of the fruit of the vine until we shall drink it anew with Him in His Father's kingdom. There can be no higher and safer rule than the command and example of our Saviour; while, on the other hand, every principle of morals or rule of conduct which reflects on Him, *must* be unsound and mischievous.—P. S.]

* [Prof. M. W. Jacobus confidently asserts from his own observation: "The present wines of Jerusalem and Lebanon, as we tasted them, were commonly boiled and sweet, without intoxicating qualities. The boiling prevents the fermentation. Those were esteemed the best wines which were least strong." But other travellers assert just the reverse.—P.S.]

HOMILETICAL AND PRACTICAL.

The first miracle of Christ the speaking expression of His life and work: 1) Of His person, in which the earthly human nature becomes a heavenly (the essential, genuine vine, ch. xv. 1); 2) of the power of His love, which transforms the water of earthly need into the wine of heavenly joy (brings forth judgment unto victory, makes blessedness out of divine sorrow); 3) of His works, in which is everywhere reflected His main work of bringing to pass the new birth of mankind from the earthly kingdom into the heavenly; 4) of His last work, the glorification of the world.—The first miracle of Christ a prefiguring of His last.—A reflection of the first creation, in which the whole world, with all its estates, treasures and forms of life, came forth out of water (and the Spirit of God moved—brooded—upon the face of the waters).—The miracle at Cana, the unveiling of a threefold mystery: 1) The mystery of a glorifying power in Christ; 2) the germ of transformation in nature; 3) the conformation of human nature for heavenly life.—The first sign of Jesus a revelation of His glory.—The great transformations in the one transformation of water into wine: 1) The transformation of the formal company into a fellowship of love; 2) of the earthly marriage into a figure and token of the heavenly; 3) of need into abundance; 4) of dishonor into glory.—The first work of Christ a token of that which turned the ignominy of the cross into the glory of the resurrection (the feast would have ended in shame).—The least guests become the first.—Human feasts: 1) What they are by nature; 2) what they become by sin; 3) what they again become, and only become, by the grace of Christ.—Jesus and His disciples also bidden to the wedding; or: These guests 1) the best guests in general, 2) in particular, the best wedding-guests, 3) therefore also the best guests at the table of need.—Jesus and Mary; or, the position of the Lord towards His mother according to Scripture and history (in contrast with the position which the legend gives). Mary, in her domestic life, had probably not known Jesus as a worker of miracles (Luther's *Tischreden* ch. vii. § 12, p. 398; see Heubner, p. 240), but no doubt she had known Him as the little wonder-man, who knew a way in all domestic straits. —The hours of human judgment, and the hours of the Lord.—The water-pots of the Jewish ceremonial purification changed into wine-pots of Christian vivification (figure into reality, negative austerity into positive creative agency, want into satisfaction).—The good wine comes only with the word and blessing of Christ.—The wedding-blessing of Christ and the marriage-feast. —Christian marriage: 1) What it pre-supposes (friends of Jesus, susceptible, earnest); 2) What it brings (the blessing of Christ).—And manifested forth His glory, and His disciples believed on Him. (As at wedding-feasts often new betrothals arise, so here); Christ at this wedding becomes manifest as the Bridegroom, His disciples as the bride.—Christ the help of His friends in need.—The friendliness of God perfectly manifest in the friendliness of Christ.—Disgrace in matters of honor, one of the keenest troubles. Christ alone can relieve it.—The blessing of trouble.—The spiritual fruit of temporal want.—The glorification of the household by Christ, a beginning and foreshadowing of the glorification of the world: 1) The household a miniature of the world; 2) the Christian household the basis of the Christian world; 3) the household glorified by Christ, a prophecy of the glorified world.—The manifestation of His glory is the covering or neutralizing of our shame.—The human marriage-feast transformed into a type of the marriage-feast of Christ: 1) The festive beginning; 2) the interruption of failure; 3) the miraculous glory at the end; and this (*a*) in the life of Jesus, (*b*) in the history of the church, (*c*) at the end of time.

Starke:—*Nova Bibl. Tub.:* When we enter into the married state with Jesus, and invite Him to the wedding, blessing is to be expected; on the contrary, those marriages and weddings commonly do not prosper, at which Jesus is not present, but carnal motives, lust, and desire of honor or wealth prevail, 1 Cor. vii. 39.—Blessed the wedding, at which Jesus is a guest.—*Bibl. Wirt.:* The Lord Jesus made His appearance at a wedding, to honor the estate of marriage as His own (divine) ordinance, Rev. xix. 9; Hos. ii. 19.—How Jesus is invited. By what means He is driven away, and the devil invited.—Christians should come to each other's assistance in want, and if they themselves can do nothing, they should fly to God to create help.—Canstein: If Christ receives not dictation from His mother in His humiliation, how much less in His glory. —Mary pointing away from herself to Christ.—Majus: Mary was a sinner, therefore she cannot be a mediator.—God has a very different hour from that which we men have.—The conversations at Christian weddings (and festivals). —If we would have God work miracles in us, we must first be obedient to His word.—*On the drawing of the water* (ver. 8). *Bibl. Wirt.:* Without labor heaven will yield nothing.—First: Hands on (labor), then: Hands up (to receive the blessing).—The hearts which before were vessels of trouble, God makes afterwards vessels of the greatest joy.—Cramer: God lets no one to come to shame, who waits for Him.—God gives His gifts not sparingly, but in profusion.—Jesus transforms everything for the better, not for the worse. We should imitate Him in this, as far as possible, Ps. xxxiv. 8.—Chrysostom: Christ made not wine simply, but the best wine. —God keeps the best drink for His children for the most part for the last, many a time even for heaven.—The first miracle of Moses was the changing of water into blood, for the punishment of the Egyptians; the first miracle of Jesus was the changing of water into wine, for the comfort of the poor (contrast between the law and the gospel).—The first sign, but not the last.

Lisco:—We must not allow ourselves to be discouraged, if the help delays.—Gerlach: In the previous words Jesus had promised the reopening of an uninterrupted communication between heaven and earth, God and man, in the person of the Son of Man. Here He now confirms this promise by His first miracle, which, however, like all miraculous occurrences in this Gospel, is related as if not for its own sake, but as an emblem of a perpetual miracle, whereby the Saviour is continually acting directly upon the human race (and the world).—Though there is no greater authority on earth than that of father and mother, yet it is nothing when the word and work of God approach (Luther).—The world gives first the best it has, thereby entices, and therewith intoxicates; Christ always keeps the best till the last.—Heubner: Influence of Christianity on the married life.—Jesus participates in social enjoyments, in banquets; therefore the Christian may. Christ teaches us the true behaviour in such society.—Christianity would sanctify the social propensity.—The good and bad sides of our social life.—We should sanctify the bonds of consanguinity.—The [bad] proverb: *Ehestand, Wehestand:* Wedded state, woful state.—Pious, needy families are a special object of the providence of God, and should be a special object of Christian philanthropy.—Romanists would find here a proof of the intercession of Mary. We find here rather a refutation of it, Ps. xxxvi. 8.—Jesus the true giver of joys, awakener of life, reliever of cares (invert the order).—The glory of Jesus manifesting itself on His first appearance.—The conduct of Jesus a model for Christians in social life.—The wedding at Cana, the picture of a Christian marriage: (1) The beginning, holy and happy; (2) the progress, bringing need and care, which Christ, however, helps to bear; (3) the end, the seeing of the glory of Jesus.—Pischon: How can we build up the kingdom of God in our domestic life?—Rambach: The great value of domestic joys.—Harms: When need is greatest, God is nearest.—Schleiermacher: How, under the direction of God, the nobler element, instead of the common and low, usually gains the upper hand in human society.—Reinhard: The special care on which needy, but spiritually-minded Christian families may rely.—Draeseke: How Christians make wine out of water (a source of enjoyment out of everyday life).—Rautenberg: Jesus, the best family friend.—Mine hour is not yet come.

This word should quiet us 1) amidst the faults of the church; 2) amidst trouble in our houses; 3) amidst the conflict in our hearts.—HARLESS: Marks of the grace of Christ: 1) That Christ gives us the most precious for nothing; 2) makes a glorious thing out of a common; 3) gives the best last; 4) gives according to His own time, not according to our ideas.

[MATTHEW HENRY:—The curse of the law turns water into blood (Ex. iv. 9), common comforts into bitterness and terror; the blessing of the gospel turns water into wine. Christ's errand was to heighten and improve creature-comforts to all believers, and make them comforts indeed.—The transformation of the substance of water into a new form with all the qualities of wine, is a miracle; but the popish transubstantiation, the substance changed, the form and appearance remaining the same, is a monster.—Christ is often better than His words, but never worse. —Temperance, *per force*, is a thankless virtue; but if Providence gives us the delights of sense, and grace enables us to use them moderately, this is self-denial that is praiseworthy.—*And His disciples believed in Him.* Even the faith that is true, at first is but weak. The strongest men were once babes, so were the strongest Christians. —Christ Himself the greatest miracle.—P. S.]

[TRENCH (after AUGUSTINE, *Serm.* 123, ch. ii.): He who made wine out of water, might have made bread out of stones. But He will do nothing at the suggestion of Satan, though all at the suggestion of love.—TRENCH: The Lord a witness against the tendency of our indolent nature of giving up to the world or the devil any portion of life, which, in itself innocent, is capable of being drawn up into the higher world of holiness, as it is in danger of sinking down and coming under the law of the flesh and of the world.—Trench quotes in contrast Cyprian who says (*De hab. virg.* 3, 4): *Nuptiarum festa improba et convivia lasciva vitentur, quorum periculosa contagio est;* but Cyprian and Chrysostom warned against participation in marriage festivals which were essentially heathen; while Christ was in a God-fearing Jewish family, which was probably related to Him.—P. S.]

[Christians should never conform to the world, but always endeavor to transform it into the kingdom of Christ; but where the world is too strong for you, keep off, for the world might transform you.—*Thou hast kept the good wine until now.* Sin gives its best first: pleasure, riches, honors, *etc.*—its worst last: sorrow, poverty, disgrace, ruin. Christ on the contrary gives His followers first the cross, the race, the battle, but last the crown, the rest, and the glory.—The marriage-feast of Cana, a prelude and pledge of the marriage-supper of the Lamb in the kingdom of glory, Matth. xxvi. 29; Rev. xix. 8.—P. S.]

IV.

JESUS, THE GUEST IN CAPERNAUM, AND THE PILGRIM TO THE PASSOVER. THE PURIFICATION OF THE TEMPLE, AS A PRELUDE OF THE REDEEMING PURIFICATION OF THE WORLD AND REFORMATION OF THE CHURCH. CHRIST THE TRUE TEMPLE. THE SIGN OF CHRIST: THE DESTRUCTION OF THE TEMPLE AND THE RAISING IT AGAIN. THE FIRST SPREAD OF FAITH IN ISRAEL, AND CHRIST THE KNOWER OF HEARTS.

CHAP. II. 12–25.

12 After this he went down to Capernaum [Kapharnaum], he, and his mother, and
his[1] brethren [brothers],[2] and his disciples; and they continued there [and there they
abode, καὶ ἐκεῖ ἔμειναν][3] not many days.
13 And the Jews' passover [the passover of the Jews, τὸ πάσχα τῶν Ἰ.] was at hand
14 [or, near, ἐγγύς], and Jesus went up to Jerusalem, [.] And [he] found in the tem-
ple those that sold oxen, and sheep, and doves, and the changers of money [money-
15 changers] sitting [established]: And when he had made [having made, ποιήσας]
a scourge of small cords, he drove them [*omit* them] all out of the temple, and
[both] the sheep, and the oxen;[4] and poured out the changers' money[5] [the money of
16 the exchangers], and overthrew the tables; And said unto them that [to those who]
sold doves, Take these things hence; make not my Father's house a house of mer-
17 chandise [a market]. And his disciples remembered that it was [is] written, The
18 zeal of [for] thine house hath eaten me up [will eat me up].[6] (Ps. lxix. 9.) Then
answered the Jews [The Jews therefore answered] and said unto him, What sign
19 shewest thou unto us, seeing that thou doest these things? Jesus answered and
said unto them, Destroy this temple, and in three days I will raise it up [again].
20 Then said the Jews, Forty and six years was this temple in building, and wilt
21 thou rear [raise] it up in three days? But he spake of the temple of his body.

22 When therefore he was [had] risen from the dead, his disciples remembered that
he had said this unto them [*omit* unto them];[7] and they believed the Scripture, and
the word which Jesus had said [spoken].
23 Now when he was in Jerusalem at the passover in the feast day [at the feast, ἐν
τῇ ἑορτῇ], many believed in his name [ἐπίστευσαν, trusted in his name], when they
24 saw the miracles [his signs, αὐτοῦ τὰ σημεῖα] which he did [wrought]. But Jesus
did not commit himself unto them [οὐκ ἐπίστευεν αὐτὸν αὐτοῖς, did not trust himself
25 to them], because he knew all men, And needed not [had no need] that any [one]
should testify of [concerning] man; for he [himself, αὐτὸς] knew what was in
man.

TEXTUAL AND GRAMMATICAL.

[1] Ver. 12. [αὐτοῦ after οἱ ἀδελφοί, is omitted by B. L., Treg., Westcott and Hort, but supported by ℵ. A. al and retained by Tischend and Alf. (the latter in brackets). Westcott and Hort bracket καὶ οἱ μαθηταὶ αὐτοῦ. The false view about the ἀδελφοί of Christ may have had some influence on these variations.—P. S.]

[2] Ver. 12. [As "brethren" is now almost exclusively used in the spiritual sense, it is better to substitute "brothers," where, as here, kinsmen, *i. e.*, either cousins, or more probably half-brothers of Jesus, are intended. In the Scriptures the term denotes either (1) actual brotherhood, or (2) kinsmanship (cousins), or (3) common nationality, or (4) friendship and sympathy. Where there are no obvious objections, the first sense, being the most natural, must always be preferred, especially when the term, as here, occurs in connection with mother. See the EXEG. NOTES.—P. S.]

[3] Ver. 12. [The singular ἔμεινεν (instead of the plural ἔμειναν) in A. F. G. was occasioned by the preceding κατέβη and the succeeding ἀνέβη.—P. S.]

[4] Ver. 15. [The words τά τέ πρόβατα καὶ τοὺς βόας, "the sheep *as well as* the oxen," are merely epexegetical of πάντας (masc. on account of βόας), and imply that the φραγέλλιον was used on the beasts only, although it scared the men away likewise. The *them* and *and* of the E. V. convey a false impression.—P. S.]

[5] Ver. 15.—B. L. X., *etc.* [Alford, Tregelles] read: τὰ κέρματα [moneys, small change, instead of the singular, τὸ κέρμα (text rec., Tischend). Greek writers generally use the plural. The singular is here collective.—P. S.]

[6] Ver. 17.—The reading of the Recepta [κατέφαγε] is conformed to the Septuagint. The most important codd., particularly ℵ. A. B. R., besides Origen, *etc.*, read καταφάγεται [the future, contracted from καταφαγήσεται, *will consume me*, in the Sept. and the Apocrypha.—P. S.]

[7] Ver. 22.—The addition αὐτοῖς is very feebly accredited. [Omitted by all the modern critical ed.]

EXEGETICAL AND CRITICAL.

[The Messianic purification of the temple was the first, and, according to the Synoptists (Matth. xxi. 12, 13; Mark xi. 15-17; Luke xix. 45, 46), also the last public act of Christ in Jerusalem.* It very appropriately opens and closes His labors in the sanctuary of the theocracy. It was foretold by the prophet Malachi, iii. 1 ff., that immediately after the forerunner the Messiah Himself "shall suddenly come to His temple," for the purpose of cleansing it: "He shall purify the sons of Levi and purge them as gold and silver, that they may offer unto the Lord an offering in righteousness." The gross scandal in the Court of the Gentiles represented the general profanation and corruption of the theocracy (as Tetzel's and Samson's sale of indulgences revealed the secularization of the Latin Church in the 16th century). Christ commenced the reformation at the fountain-head, in Jerusalem and the temple where it was most needed. The expulsion was a judicial act of the Lord of the Sabbath and the temple. He acted here not simply as a prophet or Zealot, but as the Messiah, as the Son of God; and hence calls the temple the house of *His*, not *our*, Father (ver. 16). Some infidels have misrepresented it as an outburst of passion and an argument against the sinless perfection of Christ. But the result conclusively shows that it was an exhibition of superhuman power and majesty, which so overawed the profane traffickers, that, losing sight of their superiority in number and physical strength, they submitted at once, and without a murmur to the well deserved punishment.* Their bad conscience, which always makes men cowardly, and the conceded right of prophets like Elijah, to rebuke scandulous profanations of religion, would not sufficiently account for this complete victory. A similar instance is recorded, John xviii. 6, where Judas and his band of men and officers shrunk back and fell to the ground before the defenceless Jesus.—P. S.]

Ver. 12. **After this he went down** [κατέβη] **to Capernaum.**—No doubt not directly from Cana, but from Nazareth. Not that, as Meyer says, the brethren here mentioned were not with Him at the wedding (this is not necessarily to be inferred from the silence respecting them), but that Nazareth was still the residence of Jesus and of the family of Mary, who no doubt returned home before they all went together to Capernaum, that they might thence join the nearest festival caravan for Jerusalem. He went down from the hill country towards the sea, on the coast of which Capernaum lay. On Capernaum, see the *Matth.* at ch. iv. 13. [Am. ed. pp. 90, 91. The question of the site of Capernaum, or properly Kapharnaum (*i. e.*, the Village of Nahum), is still unsettled between the rival claims of *Tell Hûm* (*i. e.*, the hill of Nahum) and *Khân* (*i. e.*, lodging-place) *Minyeh* (with a near fountain called *Ain-et-Tin, i. e.*, the spring of the fig-tree), two heaps of ruins on the Western shore of the sea of Galilee about three miles apart. Robinson (*Researches* II. 403 ff.) and Porter (*Handbook of Syria*, II. 425) decide for Khân Minyeh, but Van de Velde, Ebrard, Thomson,

* [The double purgation of the temple is rightly defended by all the older commentators, and by Schleiermacher, Olshausen, Tholuck, Ebrard, Meyer, Lange, Hengstenberg, Godet, Alford. Among those who admit only one, Strauss, Baur and Schenkel defend the report of the Synoptists, while Lücke, De Wette, Ewald decide in favor of John].

* [Hieronymus: *Igneum quiddam et sidereum radiabat ex occulis ejus et divinitatis majestas lucebat in facie.* Comp. the remarks of Godet, I. p. 379, who attributes the effect chiefly to the imposing majesty of Christ's appearance, and the irresistible force of His consciousness of supernatural power.—P. S.]

and Dixon, for Tell Hûm, at the head of the Lake. For this view speaks the similarity of name. (Hûm is a mutilated נחום = ναούμ), and the far greater importance of the ruins. The English explorers, Captain Wilson and his associates, are reported to have discovered in 1866, among the ruins of Tell Hûm, a synagogue of elegant architecture dating from a time before the Christian era. See, besides Robinson, II. 403-405, the article *Capernaum*, by Grove, with the additional note of Hackett, in Smith's *Dictionary*, I. p. 382; the *Lond. Athenæum*, Feb. 24, and Mar. 31, 1866; and an essay of Prof. Ebrard in the *Studien and Kritiken*, for 1867, No. IV., pp. 723-740.—P. S.]

He, and his mother, and his brothers, and his disciples.—The singular (κατέβη) is explained by the fact that Jesus was the leader of the train. That the family had already settled in Capernaum (which, according to Ewald, is here stated, according to De Wette presupposed), is contradicted by the distinct indications that this removal did not take place till after the return of Jesus from Judea, and His appearance in Nazareth (Matth. iv. 13; Luke iv. 31; Jno. iv. 43); though Meyer maintains that there also the removal is neither intimated nor supposed. But no doubt the removal had already been virtually induced by the connection with the disciples from the sea. The brothers of Jesus are distinguished from the disciples. Even though now His brothers, James, Judas, and Simon, had been called to be disciples, which is not at all probable, a separate category had still to be made, because there were yet Joses and the sisters, Matth. xiii. 55, 56. And that they had already attached themselves to the company of Jesus, shows that the usual exaggerated and extreme pressing of the statement in John vii. 5 is false. See Hengstenberg: *Das Evang. Joh.*, I. p. 149 sqq.

[The gradual transition from Christ's private to His public life is here indicated. At Cana and at Capernaum His earthly relations are still with Him, but in the next verse He appears alone with His disciples or spiritual relatives. As to the vexed question of the brothers of Jesus, I have given my views in full in my German work on *James, the brother of Christ*, Berlin, 1842, and in a note on Matth. xiii. 55, pp. 256-260. Comp. also the notes on Matth. i. 25, and John vii. 3, 5. Meyer, Godet (I. 368 ff.), and Alford take ἀδελφοί here in the proper sense, as brothers, *i. e.*, sons of Joseph and Mary. Hengstenberg (*in loc.*) revives the R. Catholic cousin-theory which dates from Jerome in the 4th century, and owes its origin and spread mainly to an ascetic overestimate of the perpetual virginity of Mary, as expressed in the words of Augustine: *Maria mater esse potuit, mulier esse non potuit.* Dr. Lange's hypothesis is an ingenious, but somewhat artificial modification of this view, and assumes that Mary, though in the full sense the wife of Joseph, could bear no children after giving birth to the Messiah, and that the brethren of the Lord were both His cousins (as the sons of Clopas, a brother of Joseph, not as the sons of a supposed sister of Mary), and His foster-brothers (having been adopted, after the death of their father, into the holy family). To my mind the only alternative lies between the Epiphanian or old Greek view, which makes them elder sons of Joseph from a former marriage, and the view held by Tertullian and Helvidius, that they were younger children of Mary and Joseph, and so half-brothers of Jesus. Ancient tradition favors the former, an unprejudiced exegesis the latter view. Prof. J. B. Lightfoot, of Cambridge (in a learned excursus on Galatians, Lond., 1866, pp. 247-281, where much use is made of my book on James), elaborately defends the Epiphanian theory, mainly on account of John xix. 26, 27, which he regards as conclusive against the Helvidian hypothesis; but if this passage is allowed to decide the controversy, it overthrows also the Epiphanian theory. It receives its true light from the peculiar intimacy of Christ with John, and the fact that His brothers were still unbelievers when He entrusted His earthly mother to the care of His bosom disciple, who was probably also His cousin according to the flesh.—P. S.]

Not many days.—Depending solely on the preparation for the approaching passover, which Jesus attended in company with His disciples, v. 23. But that during these few days Jesus wrought miracles in Capernaum, must be inferred from Luke iv. 23.

Ver. 13. **And the passover of the Jews was at hand.**—On the passover see the *Matth.*, p. 459.

And Jesus went up.—Besides the attendance of Jesus at the feast when He was twelve years old, mentioned by Luke alone (ch. ii.), and the last attendance on the passover in the year 783, related by all the Evangelists, John gives the remaining occasions of this kind. Here the first attendance on the passover, in the year 781; then a visit to another feast, not named, most probably the feast of Purim of 782 [ch. v.]; then the feast of tabernacles [ch. vii.], and the feast of the dedication [ch. x. 22], in the same year. See the Introduction, § 8.

Ver. 14. **And found in the temple.**—In the fore-court of the temple. On the temple and the fore-court see the *Matth.* on ch. xxi. 12 [p. 375], and Winer, *sub. v.* Also Braune: *Das Evangelium von Jesus Christus*, p. 45. The first act of the Lord, in the confidential circle of susceptible disciples, was an act of positive glorification, coming into the place of the symbolical purification; His second act, in the bosom of the corrupted religious life of the people, was an act of negative purification, significant at the same time of His glorification. That this deed was looked upon by the better people as a miraculous sign also, and that besides this Jesus wrought other miracles in Jerusalem, may be inferred from ch. iii. 2. But John relates the purging of the temple alone as the first characteristic work, the signal-miracle of the Lord on His public appearance. To him the first cleansing of the temple was more important than the second. But the fact that John mentions only this cleansing at the opening of the Lord's official life, and the Synoptists mention only the similar act at its close, proves nothing against the truth of either or both the occurrences. See the *Matth.* on ch. xxi.

[The market in the Court of the Gentiles (the ἔξωθεν ἱερόν) was introduced, we know not when, from avaricious motives, in violation of the spirit of the law and to the serious injury of public worship, though it was no doubt justified or excused, as a convenience to foreign Jews for the purchase of sacrificial beasts, incense, oil, and the sacred shekel or double drachma in which the temple-tax had to be paid (Ex. xxx. 13). Similar conveniences and nuisances, markets, lotteries and fairs, are not seldom found in connection with Christian churches. The most striking analogy is the traffic in indulgences, which made the forgiveness of sin an article of merchandise and became the occasion (not the cause) of the Reformation in Germany and Switzerland.—P. S.]

Ver. 15. **He drove all out.**—Referring grammatically not to the animals, but to the men. But He drove the men out by raising the whip against their animals; precisely after the analogy of His method with the money-changers, whose tables He overthrew. To drive the men themselves, by themselves, from the temple, was not His design. Grotius: The whip, a symbol of the divine wrath.* Meyer rejects all typical import. Yet even about the whip of an actual ox-driver there is somewhat typical; and the whip in the hand of Christ is at least a type of the punitive, reformatory office of discipline in the theocracy and the church.

And poured out the money of the exchangers, and overthrew, *etc.* —That is, He first dashed upon the tables hither and thither and then overturned them. The right of free motion in the temple-space, where tables of money-changers did not belong.

Ver. 16. **Unto them that sold doves.**—Because the doves were in baskets, they must be *carried* away (Rosenmüller, Schweizer). His command now sufficed for this, after the dove-traders had seen His earnestness. Showing, that even the ox-traders also He had not driven out with the lash; and showing likewise that He intended no injury, else He would have let the doves go. De Wette: He dealt more gently with the dove-merchants, because the doves were bought by the poor. Stier: Because He saw in the dove the emblem of the Holy Ghost. Both groundless. The difference in the mode of expulsion arises simply from the nature of the articles: doves in baskets. That the dove-sellers came last, may have been determined by the modesty of their business, which generally makes also modest people. These people were doubtless not so much traders properly speaking, as they were poor farmers or farmers' boys. As to the doves being emblems, so were also the sheep and oxen.

My Father's house.—See Luke ii. 49.† The temple was still His Father's house, because He was still waiting for the repentance of the people. The moment He takes His departure from the temple on account of their obduracy, He calls it: Your house, given over to desolation, Matth. xxiii. 38. *Our* Father's, even a prophet might perhaps have said; *My* Father's, Jesus says in the consciousness of His divine dignity and authority; as it were betraying Himself, without their understanding immediately the full sense of His word. The Pharisees, however, have doubtless already reflected upon the word as very suspicious (see John x.).

A house of merchandize.—The term here is not so strong as at the second purification. It denotes the entire secularization of the system of worship. The term "den of thieves" [*σπήλειον λῃστῶν*], in Matth. xxi. 13, on the contrary, denotes the prophet-killing and spirit-killing fanaticism, into which this secularization at last ran out.

Ver. 17. **And his disciples remembered.**—Olshausen: After the resurrection. Meyer. [Godet, Alford], on the contrary, rightly: At the occurrence itself. The passage is Ps. lxix. 9, (10): "For the zeal of thine house hath eaten me up; and the reproaches of them that reproached thee are fallen upon me."* Whether the Psalm be by David (Tholuck; comp. v. 31; Ps. li.), or by Jeremiah (Hitzig, see v. 14?), or by some other theocratic sufferer, it belongs at all events, like Ps. xxii., to that class of typical passages, in which the passion of Christ miraculously reflects and foreshows itself. Hence also Peter, Acts. i. 20, applies to Judas the words of v. 25 ("Let their habitation be desolate"), and Paul applies the Psalm several times to the conduct of the Jews towards Jesus, Rom. xi. 9; xv. 3. When Bengel, Olshausen, *etc*, and Luthardt refer the words: hath eaten me up, to the death of Jesus,† and Meyer says, on the contrary, that the word is to be understood of the inward attrition of zeal (so that the disciples would mean, His zeal will yet consume Him from within), we may freely march over this difference of schools, and suppose (against Meyer) that the disciples, with anxious forebodings for the future of Christ, were smitten with the remembrance of that passage of the Psalm. For it is not necessary to suppose they had made out a clear idea of the sense of those words; any more than that Mary, with her words, meant: "Make wine!" or: "Go home!" The school always reaches after fully expressed ideas or thoughts; actual life has also vague presentiments, anxious forebodings, dim, confused ideas; that is, life is subject to the fundamental law of gradual development. That the disciples did not connect a distinct expectation of the death of Jesus with their application of the verse of the Psalm to this action of their Lord, is proved by ver. 22; after Ps. xxii. 6–8, *etc.*, they could not confine their thoughts to an exclusively internal self-attrition; probably they did not think of it at all in the Old Testament sense, though the metaphorical use of *ἐσθίειν* is clear, and consuming passions too (see Meyer, with a reference to Chrysostom, Lampe, Wolf) are not wholly excluded. But here for the first time met and struck them the conflict of the spirit of Christ with the spirit of the people, the terrible

---

* [So also Godet: a sign of authority and judgment. If Christ had intended physical punishment, the instrument would have been disproportionate to the end.—P. S.]

† [Alford: The coincidence with Luke ii. 49 is remarkable. By this expression thus publicly used, our Lord openly announces His Messiahship.—P. S.]

* [Sept.: Ὅτι ὁ ζῆλος τοῦ οἴκου σου κατέφαγέν με (Vulg.: *comedit me*), καὶ οἱ ὀνειδισμοὶ τῶν ὀνειδιζόντων σε ἐπέπεσον ἐπ' ἐμέ.—P. S.]

† ["The *καταφάγειν* spoken of in that passion Psalm, was the marring and wasting of the Saviour's frame by His zeal for God and God's Church, which resulted in the buffeting, the scourging, the Cross." Alford].

life-staking earnestness in the appearance of Christ, which threatened to bring incalculable dangers after it. We may no doubt further suppose that this remembrance indicates great apprehensiveness in the disciples respecting the Lord. Though the future καταφάγεται may occur in the sense of the present,* it does not follow that, according to Tholuck, it is to be read as present here. In this case the Evangelist might better have used the κατέφαγε of the Septuagint.

Ver. 18. **Then answered the Jews.**—'Απεκρίθησαν οὖν. Here the Jews already begin to appear in opposition to Jesus; accordingly the Pharisaic and Judaistic Jews are intended, particularly the rulers. They regarded the act of Christ as a reproach to their religious government; therefore their interruption was an answer. And from their spirit it was to be expected; hence οὖν.—**What sign shewest thou unto us?**—They did not see that the majestic and successful act itself was a great moral, theocratic sign, which accredited him; they intended therefore a sign after some magical, chiliastic sort. It should be noticed that they did not venture to dispute the theocratic propriety of the act itself. The right of zealotry against theocratic abuses was legalized in the example of Numb. xxv. 7; yet the prophets were accustomed to support great acts of zealotry by special miraculous signs, 1 Kings xviii. 23. The idea of such signs, however, particularly of the sign with which the Messiah should attest Himself, had gradually passed into the magical and monstrous. At all events, the challenge of a sign from heaven, Matth. xii. 38; xvi. 1, is here already put forth.

Ver. 19. **Destroy this temple.**—[One of those paradoxical and mysterious sayings which, though not understood at the time, stuck in the memory as seed thoughts for future sprouting.† Comp. Christ's word on the sign of Jonah, Matth. xii. 39, 40, in which He likewise mysteriously and typologically predicts His resurrection.—P. S.]—This is the sign which He would give them. The imperative is permissive. (Glassius: *est Imperat. pro Futuro permissive*).‡ The Jews took the words of Jesus in an entirely literal sense, as ver. 20 proves, yet hardly without design. From this conception gradually arose the malignant perversion, slander, and accusation: This fellow said, I am able to destroy the temple of God, and to build it in three days, Matth. xxvi. 61; Mark xiv. 58; comp. Acts vi. 13. This conception John corrects in ver. 21: **He spake of the temple of his body** [for His humanity]. The fathers universally acknowledge this interpretation. It has been supposed, He pointed to His body as He spoke.* Of this there is no indication.

Since Herder, Henke, and Paulus, down to Lücke [De Wette], Bleek, Ewald (see Meyer, *in loc.*), it has been suggested, on the contrary, that John misunderstood the Lord; that Christ spoke of the temple as the symbol of the Jewish system of religion.† Destroy this edifice of religion, and in three days, *i. e.*, in a short time, proverbially (with reference to Hos. vi. 2) represented by three days, I will set it up again renewed.

Kuinoel, Tholuck, Meyer, and many others‡ have maintained the correctness of John's interpretation. And with all reason; for an error of the Apostle and the whole company of disciples in respect to so important a word of the Lord is utterly inadmissible (see the several, not absolutely irrefragable arguments in Meyer).§

A third view adheres to John's interpretation, but holds likewise an element of truth in the second view, and puts them in connection. The temple on Zion was the symbolical dwelling of God; the body of Christ was the real dwelling of God [and hence more than the temple, comp. Matth. xii. 6].‖ The word of Christ, therefore, underneath its immediate reference to the external temple, has a deeper meaning: Destroy this temple and worship, as ye have already begun to do by your desecration,—destroy it entirely, by putting the Messiah to death, and in three days I will build it new, *i. e.*, not only rise from the dead, but also by the resurrection establish a new theocracy (Theodore of Mopsuestia, Olshausen, Lange, *Leben Jesu*, I., p. 200; simultaneously Ebrard, *Kritik*, p. 325; later, in similar manner, Luthardt).¶

* [So also Tholuck, Hengstenberg, Godet, but Meyer contends that καταφάγεται (=καταφαγήσεται) is only used in the sense of the future.—P. S.]

† [Renan (*Vie de Jésus*, p. 354) can see in this profound enigma of our Lord only "an imprudent word spoken in bad humor" ("*Un jour sa mauvaise humeur contre le temple lui arracha un mot imprudent*")! Godet, I. 387, well remarks: "*La méthode de Jésus est de jeter une énigme et de ne réceler la vérité qu'en la voilant sous un divin paradoxe, qui ne peut être compris qu'en changeant de cœur. C'est là un secret de la profonde pédagogie.*"—P. S.]

‡ [Meyer, with his usual and at times pedantic philological strictness, takes the imperative λύσατε as strictly *provocative*, and explains it from a painful excitement of feeling in view of the opposition already manifesting itself. But the apparent harshness is softened by the prophetic character of the word and the double reference to the temple and the person. John xiii. 27, where Christ calls upon Judas to do quickly what he intended to do, furnishes a parallel. If the fruit is once matured, it must fall.—P. S.]

* [So Bengel (*nutu gestuve*) and Meyer. But in the fifth ed., p. 144, note, M. gives up this reference. Such pointing would have been the solution of the riddle, contrary to its intention; but neither the Jews nor the disciples understood Him at the time. The Jews on this and the second purgation referred τὸν ναὸν τοῦτον to the temple, ver. 20; Matth. xxvi. 61; xxvii. 40. Meyer now assumes that Christ pointed to the temple (this temple before you), but meant His body as the antitype of the temple and the true dwelling of God, and thus put the image in the place of the thing typified, "*so dass diese scharfen lebendigen, ohne Auslegung hingeworfenen Bildzüge wie in einem Bilderräthsel eine symbolisch prophetische Vorhersagung seiner Auferstehung enthalten, wie Matth. xii. 39; xvi. 4.*"—P. S.]

† (See Heubner, p. 242. Henke was not the first to take this view, but Zinzendorf has it in his *Homil. über die Wundenlitanei*, p. 160.)

‡ [Olshausen, Stier, Brückner (*versus* De Wette), Alford, Godet.—P. S.]

§ [Meyer, pp. 145-147, raises seven objections against this view. It is plainly irreconcilable with apostolic inspiration. In my Lectures on the Gospel of John, written at Berlin, 1842, I find the remark: "It involves an immense presumption on the part of theologians of the nineteenth century, however respectable, if they imagine that they understand Christ better than His favorite disciple and bosom-friend to whom He revealed the future struggles and triumphs of His Kingdom." Alford also justly protests against such liberty of interpretation. For we have here not a chronological statement, but a doctrinal exposition of a most important declaration of Christ.—P. S.]

‖ [This idea John expresses in ἐσκήνωσεν, i. 14 (see notes on pp. 71, 73), and Paul when he says that the whole fulness of the Godhead dwelled in Christ bodily. Col. ii. 9.—P. S.]

¶ [Comp. also Hengstenberg, I. 165. He thinks that no justice can be done to this holy enigma which Christ proposed to the Jews, unless we recognize the essential identity of the temple, the appearance of Christ in the flesh and the church.

This combination is supported (1) by the actual connection. The crucifixion of Christ was the desecration, the spiritual dissolution of the temple, which must be followed by its outward destruction (see Matth. xxiii. 38; xxvii. 51), because the body of Christ was the real temple of God. (2) Christ, on this account, has repeatedly represented His death and resurrection as the one great sign which was to be given to the Jews instead of the required sign from heaven (John iii. 14; Matth. xii. 39; xvi. 4), and this sign too always connected with an antecedent Old Testament type. (3) A word concerning His death, without connection with an intelligible figure, would have assuredly been as yet wholly unintelligible to the Jews. (4) John gave the inmost and ultimate significance of the expression of Christ for the sole reason, that it was the main matter, and that the figurative sense was self-evident. (5) In Matth. xxvi. 61 Christ puts in the true explanation, ver. 64, immediately upon the false interpretation, besides perversion, of His utterance.

In three days, a round number, 1 Sam. xxx. 12; see the *Matth.* on chap. xii. 40, p. 226.

I will raise it up (again).—"It is only apparently contrary to John's explanation, that Christ, according to the New Testament doctrine, did not raise Himself, but was raised by the Father." Meyer. And besides, the resurrection of Jesus was in one view as much His own act [John x. 18; Rev. v. 5], as, in another view, the act of His Father, especially in its results, 1 Cor. xv. 57; Eph. iv. 8. That Jesus was already familiar with the thought of His death, appears from the conversation which soon followed, John iii. 14. The explanation of Athanasius, quoted by Tholuck, is an ingenious modified form of our third: With the putting to death of the body of Christ the Jewish system of types and shadows also is dissolved, and the real church thereby (by means of the resurrection) established.

Ver. 20. **Then said the Jews.**—With an *οὖν;* it was to be expected that they would finish their malicious misunderstanding consistently.—**Forty and six years.**—They mean the renovation and enlargement of the temple of Zerubbabel, which begun in the eighteenth year of Herod's reign, 20 B. C. (Joseph. *Antiq.* XV. 11, 1), and was finished under Herod Agrippa II. in A. D. 64 (Joseph. *Antiq.* XX. 9, 7). According to Wieseler, it appears, therefore, that in this computation of forty-six years since the work was begun, the passover of the year 781 is the occasion on which it is made (*Chronol. Synops.* p. 106).

Ver. 21. **The temple of his body.**—Genitiv. Apposit.

Ver. 22. **His disciples remembered that he had said this.**—This remembrance does not exclude former remindings; but the right remembrance came now with the right understanding of it. [Remarks like this impress upon the reports of the discourses of Christ the stamp of historical fidelity. A later falsifier would have made the reference to the resurrection much plainer.—P. S.]—**And they believed the Scripture.**—[Faith in Christ is the key to the understanding of the Scriptures of the O. T.; comp. vii. 38, 42; x. 35; xiii. 18. The singular τῇ γραφῇ indicates the unity and harmony of the canonical books from Genesis to Malachi, which, considering the great number of authors, the long period of time, and the variety of circumstances in and under which they were composed, is a strong evidence of their divine origin.—P. S.] Comp. Luke xxiv. 26: "Ought not Christ to have suffered these things," *etc.* As they now found the death of Christ foretold in the Old Testament, so they found also His glorification, which included His resurrection, Ps. xvi. 10; comp. Acts ii. 27; xiii. 35; 1 Pet. iii. 19; Ps. lxviii. 18; comp. Eph. iv. 8; Is. liii. 7; comp. Acts viii. 35. [Alford: "At first sight it appears difficult to fix on any passage in which the resurrection is directly announced: but with the deeper understanding of the Scriptures which the Holy Spirit gave to the Apostles and still gives to the Christian church, such prophecies as that in Ps. xvi. are recognized as belonging to Him in whom alone they are properly fulfilled: see also Hosea vi. 2." This is not satisfactory. The O. T. indeed does not expressly prophesy the resurrection, as a separate fact, but very often the exaltation and glorification of the Messiah after His humiliation and suffering, and this implies the resurrection, as the intervening link or the beginning of the exaltation itself. Hence we may count here in a wider sense, with Hengstenberg (I. 171), the prophecy of Shilo as a ruler, Gen. xlix. 10; Ps. cx., where the Messiah is represented as sitting at the right of God and ruling over all His enemies; Dan. vii. 13, 14, where He appears at the head of a universal Kingdom; Isa. liii., where, after His atoning death, He is raised to great glory; Zech. ix. 9, 10, where Zion's King appears first lowly and riding upon an ass, yea, as dying (comp. xii. 10; xiii. 7), but afterwards speaking peace to the heathen and having dominion from sea to sea and from the river to the ends of the earth; comp. also Isa. ix.; xi.; Mich. v.; Ps. xvi. It is quite in keeping with the character of prophecy to behold the various stages of the exaltation as one continuous panorama. It is under this view that the Scripture of the O. T. is said to have foretold the resurrection; Luke xxiv. 26 ("to enter into His *glory*"); John xx. 9; 1 Cor. xv. 4; 1 Pet. i. 11 ("the sufferings of Christ and the glory that should follow").—P. S.]

Ver. 23. **Now when he was in Jerusalem at the passover.**—The Evangelist thus distinguishes the stay of Jesus in Jerusalem during the passover from His first appearance there.—**On the feast.**—Meyer justly says, this addition is not intended to explain the term passover for Greek readers; that must have been done by ver. 13. The expression signifies participation in the celebration of the feast. We suppose the feast days themselves are set off against the day of His entrance. On the day of

of the N. T. He explains: "If ye once destroy the temple of my body, and with it this external temple, the symbol and pledge of the kingdom of God among you, I shall rebuild in three days the temple of My body and with it at the same time the substance of the eternal temple, the kingdom of God." The crucifixion of Christ involved as a necessary consequence the destruction of the temple and the O. T. worship; the resurrection of Christ the creation of the Christian church, and worship, of which the temple was the type and shadow. Godet explains: "Destroy this your temple, by killing Me, the Messiah."—P. S.]

the symbolical castigation He wrought other miracles, probably miracles of healing; and the first surprise of the Jews was followed by a demonstration of faith on the part of many attendants of the feast. **The signs.**—Evidently implying a multiplicity of signs, and such as determined those people to believe. He must therefore have done many miracles in Jerusalem.

Ver. 24. **Did not commit himself unto them.**—The second πιστεύειν ἑαυτόν is evidently connected with the first πιστεύειν. He believed not in their believing, to such a degree as to commit or deliver up Himself to them. Various interpretations: (1) He withheld His doctrine (Chrysostom, Kuinoel); (2) He did not yield Himself to personal intercourse with them (Meyer). Without doubt simply: He did not yet entrust Himself to them as the Messiah, did not offer Himself as the Messiah, though they seemed inclined to recognize Him as such. It is the Lord's determination, not to appear publicly under the title of Messiah; and He follows it henceforth till the triumphal entry into Jerusalem; in full accordance with Matth. iv. 1–11. **Because he.**—He Himself, in distinction from indirect knowledge through others. How He knew them all, is in part shown by what has preceded. He knew in general that the secular spirit predominated in them; but He also saw through each one, as He met him, with a divine physiognomic discernment. In both cases is intended not only the general prophetic illumination, but the penetrating spiritual eye of the God-Man.

Ver. 25. **And needed not.**—Explanatory of αὐτός in the previous clause.—**Of man.**—Of man as to his sinful nature in general, and of man in particular, as He encountered each individual.—**For he knew.**—The positive expression for: *He needed not.*—**What was in man.**—Not only the special, miraculous, physiognomic knowledge (Meyer cites ch. i. 48; iv. 18; vi. 61, 64; xi. 4, 14; xiii. 11; xxi. 17), but also the general knowledge of the constitution of human nature (John iii.), of the order of the universe (xix. 11), and of the situation of the Jewish people in particular. Result: In the familiar circle of His disciples Jesus manifested His glory; in public He preserved His mysterious anonymousness as to the Messianic office.

[Christ knows us better than we know ourselves. He sees the end from the beginning, we the beginning from the end. He, says Calvin, knows the roots of the tree, we know the tree only by its fruits.—P. S.]

DOCTRINAL AND ETHICAL.

1. *The different meanings of the two purifications of the temple.* According to Meyer, no essential difference should be perceived between the two acts. Yet the difference between the expressions "house of merchandize" in John, and "den of thieves" in the Synoptists, "the house of My Father" (ὁ οἶκος τοῦ πατρός μου) in John, and "My house" (ὁ οἶκός μου) in the Synoptists, as well as the greater rigor in the second case as described by Mark (not suffering any man to carry any vessel through the temple), is plain enough. According to Hofmann, Lichtenstein, and Luthardt, Christ in the Synoptists appears as a prophet to protect the place of prayer, in John as the Son to execute His domestic right. But this would lead to an entire reversal of the order of things in the self-manifestation of the Lord. The case is just the reverse. Christ performed the first cleansing of the temple, as an anonymous prophet in the right of zealotism and the right of a prophet (see the *Matth.* on xxi. 12, p. 376); the second, as the Lord of the temple, publicly introduced by the people to the holy city and temple as the Messiah.

2. *The body of Christ, the most real temple of God.* The crucifixion, the destruction of the temple in the strictest sense (Rom. ii. 22); the resurrection, the building of the eternal temple. Meaning of the sign: He who builds the eternal, essential temple, has power also to purge the symbolical. The truth, that Christ is perpetually building greater, more glorious the temple of God, which the sin of man demolishes. The centre of this truth is the death and resurrection of Christ; its first tokens, the fall of Adam and the first promise (the protevangelium), the flood and the rain-bow, *etc.*; its unfolding, the destruction of the theocracy and temple in Jerusalem, the rise of the church, the ruin of the mediæval church by the hierarchy, and its rebuilding in the Reformation, the inducing of the judgment of the world by anti-christianity, and the erection of a new heavens and a new earth. The wedding at Cana before the purification of the temple, the token of the transfiguration of the world before the judgment of the world.

3. *The first and second purifications of the temple:* when once the temple is made a house of merchandize (John ii.), it has also become in effect a den of robbers or of murderers, Matth. xxi. First the selling of indulgences, then persecution and reformation.

4. Christ entrusts Himself to no one in Jerusalem; *i. e.*, He does not as yet come on the stage in His office as Messiah. Comp. the *Com. on Matth.* on ch. iv.

5. The *supernatural knowledge of Christ*, the source of His miracles of knowledge, and in fact everywhere divine-human; *i. e.*, on the one hand not merely divine, nor on the other merely human, but both at once; divinely immediate, humanly exercised through means and organs.

HOMILETICAL AND PRACTICAL.

See Comm. on *Matthew*, on ch. xxi. 12–22, p. 377; *Mark*, on ch. xi. 12–26; *Luke*, on ch. xix. 41–48.—The visit of Jesus the youth to the temple, and the visit of the man matured for the execution of His Messianic office.—The first, second, and last solemn appearance of Jesus in the temple (the last, Matth. xxi.—xxiii.).—As the crucifixion of Christ completed the desecration of the temple, so the resurrection of Christ completed the restoration of the temple.—Out of His word of holiest zeal *for* the temple, they made a word of blasphemy and deadly sin *against* the temple.—The purification of the temple, the perpetual charter of reformation.—What sign shewest thou, *etc.?* The spiritual blindness which demands a sensible sign for the holiest sign of the Spirit.—How Judaism, by overdoing itself, falls back into heathenism, in asking a sign for the sense, when the sign of the Spirit gloriously stands forth.—So also the Judaism of legality in Christendom.—The scourge in the hand of Jesus, or the anger of personal gentleness itself. (1) The overpowering sign of the highest zeal (against sin); (2) the humbling sign of the highest majesty (against frivolity); (3) the ocular sign of the highest assurance (against doubt).—The Old Testament spirit in which the disciples viewed the matter, indicated by their word: The zeal of Thine house hath eaten me up; the New Testament watchword of Jesus: My meat is to do the will, *etc.*, John iv. 34.—To the temple of a Herod the hierarchs had even a right; in the temple of Christ they found themselves utterly out of place.—The token which Christ gives the Jews for the truth of His divine mission.—This token, the token also of reformation: Commit the utmost abominations in the temple, the more gloriously will the ruined temple be restored!—The conduct of the Jews on Christ's purifying of the temple, in its permanent import.—The destroyers of the temple would be its restorers, and the restorers must pass for destroyers.—From this first day of the public appearance of Christ, enmity calumniously laid up the word, which was to bring it to naught.—The Lord's great word concerning His end, at the beginning of His career.—The subsequent remembrance of Christ's words by His enemies, and the subsequent remembrance of them by His friends.—When He was at Jerusalem, many believed on Him; or, (1) festival believers, believers of festival seasons when things go grandly in the church; (2) yet festival times, also true birthdays of faith.—But Jesus did not commit Himself to them; or, secret disciples, and a secret Saviour (anonymous believers, and an anonymous Christ).—Christ, the knower of hearts.—The first sign of Christ in the pious house, and His first sign in the impious church.—The transformation of water into wine, and of the driver's whip into a beneficent sceptre (in contrast with those who have turned the sceptre into a whip).—Christ and the hierarchs with reference to the temple of God: (1) He purifies and sanctifies it, they would make its desecrated condition its holiness; (2) He gives a moral and religious sign of the Spirit, they demand a magical, sensuous sign to accredit it; (3) He gives them for a sign the prophecy that they will kill Him, and they make of it a mortal charge against Him; (4) He announces to them a new supernatural temple, and they harden themselves in their old system to their judgment.—The first public Easter festival of Jesus, a foretokening of His future and eternal Easter.—Christ's observance of the prescribed feasts the dawn of the free festivity of the gospel.—Christ at the feast: (1) As an Israelite, in the spirit of the patriarchs; (2) as a Jew, according to the law of Moses; (3) as a prophet, after the manner of the prophets (my Father's house not a house of merchandize, the court of the Gentiles not a cattle-market); (4) as the Christ, introducing and indicating the course of His life and work.—Holy zeal and unholy zeal in contrast in the purification of the temple.—The open, noble indignation of Jesus, and the impure malicious reserve of His opponents.—Jesus, here as in Cana, a man, and a sinless man.—The keeping holy the temple: (1) The house of God; (2) the body; (3) the church. The rising of the divine above the corruption and ruin of the human; the eternal divine token thereof, the luminous centre of all divine signs: the resurrection of Christ from the death of the cross.

STARKE: MAJUS: Though the word and works of God are not bound to place, yet it is right, after the example of Christ, to observe proprieties of place and time.—OSIANDER: Christ, the Lord of the law, submitted Himself to it, that He might redeem men from it.—CRAMER: Christ, not a secular king, but Lord of the temple; therefore He comes into the temple, and there begins His public function, Hag. ii. 3, 18.—HEDINGER: What has the abomination of usury to do in the temple of God? What the indulgence-monger in the sanctuary?—Ah, our churches to this day are sufficiently profaned by sinful garrulity, proud display of dress, *etc.* (even by unsanctified discourses).—*Nova Bibl. Tub.:* The abuses which have crept into the church must be scourged and banished. How much more must traditional abuses call forth our zeal! Hos. xii. 8; Zech. xiv. 21.—It is incumbent on all Christians, particularly on ministers, to be zealous for the house of God; yet should every one take good heed lest it be not according to knowledge.—OSIANDER: He who diligently pursues his calling, may fear no danger. The protection of God will be with him.—MAJUS: The works of God need no miraculous attestation. They shine so brightly upon the eye, that God and His divine glory may be sufficiently recognized in them.—HEDINGER: Unbelief demands miracles and signs.—ZEISIUS: Where we have to do with false, malicious men, we are not called upon to make the truth so clear and bright, to their greater condemnation (dark words for dark men).—A mind occupied only with the earthly, cannot perceive the mysteries of God.—Instruction often serves more for others in the future, than for those to whom it is given at the time.—*Ibid:* Fulfilment yields the best interpretation.—QUESNEL: Truth brings forth its fruits in their season.—*Ibid.:* Christian prudence requires that we do not lightly judge and condemn any, yet that we do not easily trust ourselves to any who present a good appearance.

GERLACH: "As Christ's kingdom is not a sword, how is it that He deals so hardly and harshly here with the priests of the temple, and concerns Himself with what properly belongs to the secular power? Because the Lord at that time stood between the Old Testament and the New, between what Moses had established in Israel, and what Christ was to establish after His death through His Holy Spirit and the preaching of the gospel; and He shows thereby that He is a Lord who holds both dispensations in His hand" (Luther).—LISCO: A picture of the reformation of a temple-desecration which had arisen from an abuse of Deut. xiv. 24–26.—HEUBNER: How much is contained in completely trusting one!—We must judge not, yet not hastily open and surrender ourselves to any. The more perfect and noble a man is, the more true and open (and yet the more is he, again, a higher mystery).—SCHLEIERMACHER: What a zeal for His Father's house did the Lord Himself sanctify, in doing that!—But there afterwards came a time, when even the Christian church was a house of merchandize.—Then He again gathered a whip; Luther, Zwingli, Calvin and all the reformers.—It was not the whip that effected what the Redeemer did, but the spiritual power, of which that was only a sign and seal.—Our failure to act in many cases as the Redeemer acted here, is the cause of many evils in the Christian church and in all human affairs. That one is always putting upon another the performance of works well-pleasing to God, and no one maintains a fresh and free consciousness of the power which God the Lord has given him, and does all he can do to promote truth and goodness and prevent wickedness,—this is the reason why so many disorders are daily renewed in the smaller and larger relations of men.—BESSER: The Saviour (because they stifle the voice of conscience) draws back from them, and veils in a holy riddle the sign which they demand, and which was intended to be given them as the sign of all signs, the proper sign of Christ.—From every defeat a victory unfolds to the church; from every shame a glory.—*When therefore He was risen, etc.* Chemnitz presents the disciples, in their relation to the discourse of Jesus to them, as an example for all Bible-readers: They should not at once despise and reject everything in the Holy Scriptures which they cannot at first glance understand; nor must they despair of understanding, if they cannot at once penetrate the deep mysteries of the word. For the Spirit of knowledge leads us into the truth by degrees.—Christ's power of trying spirits (Isa. xi. 3 comp. with 1 Sam. xvi. 7; 1 Tim. v. 22).

V.

JESUS IN JERUSALEM, AND NICODEMUS AS A WITNESS OF THE FIRST POWERFUL IMPRESSION OF JESUS UPON THE PHARISEES. THE CONVERSATION OF CHRIST WITH NICODEMUS BY NIGHT CONCERNING THE HEAVENLY BIRTH AS THE CONDITION OF ENTRANCE INTO THE KINGDOM OF GOD. SYMBOLISM OF WATER, WIND, AND THE BRAZEN SERPENT.

CHAP. III. 1–21.

(Chap. iii. 1–15, Gospel for Trinity Sunday; 16–21, Gospel for 2nd Pentecost).

1 [But][1] there was a man of the Pharisees, named Nicodemus, a ruler of the Jews:
2 The same came to Jesus [him][2] by night, and said unto him, Rabbi [Master], we
know that thou art a teacher come from God; for no man can do these miracles
3 that thou doest, except God be with him. Jesus answered and said unto him, Ve-
rily, verily, I say unto thee, Except a man be born[3] again [from above][4] he cannot
4 see the kingdom of God.[5] Nicodemus saith unto him, How can a man be born
when he is old? can he enter the second time into his mother's womb, and be born?
5 Jesus answered, Verily, verily, I say unto thee, Except a man be born of water
and *of* the [*omit* of the][6] Spirit, he cannot enter into the kingdom of God [of hea-
6 ven].[7] That which is [hath been] born of the flesh is flesh; and that which is
7 [hath been] born of the Spirit[8] is spirit. Marvel not that I said unto thee, Ye
8 must be born again [from above]. The wind[9] bloweth where it listeth [will], and
thou hearest the sound thereof, but canst not tell [knowest not, οὐκ οἶδας], whence it
cometh, and[10] whither it goeth; so is [*it with*] every one that is [hath been] born
9 of the Spirit. Nicodemus answered and said unto him, How can these things be?
10 Jesus answered and said unto him, Art thou a master [the teacher, ὁ διδάσκαλος] of
Israel, and knowest not these things?
11 Verily, verily, I say unto thee, We speak that we do know [that which we know]
and testify that [which] we have seen; and ye receive not our witness [testimony].
12 If I have told you earthly [human] things, and ye believe not, how shall ye believe,
13 if I tell you *of* [*omit* of] heavenly [divine] things?[11] And no man hath ascended
up to heaven, but he that came down from heaven, *even* the Son of Man which
14 [who] is in heaven. And as Moses lifted up the serpent in the wilderness [made it
a high signal for the surrounding wilderness], even so must the Son of man be lifted
15 up: That whosoever believeth in him[12] should [may] not perish, but [*omit* not pe-
rish but][13] have eternal life.

16 For God so loved the world, that he gave his only begotten Son, that whosoever
17 believeth in him should [might] not perish, but have everlasting life. For God
sent not his Son into the world to condemn [judge][14] the world; but that the
18 world through him might be saved. He that believeth on him is not condemned
[judged]; but he that believeth not is condemned [hath been judged] already, be-
19 cause he hath not believed in the name of the only begotten Son of God. And this
is the condemnation [judgment] that [the][15] light is come into the world, and men
20 loved [the] darkness rather than [the] light, because their deeds were evil.[16] For
every one that doeth evil hateth the light, neither cometh [and cometh not] to the
light, lest his deeds should be reproved [detested, discovered, shown to be punish-
21 able]. But he that doeth [the] truth cometh to the light, that his deeds may be
made manifest, that [for][17] they are wrought in God.

TEXTUAL AND GRAMMATICAL.

[1] Ver. 1. [δέ after ἦν seems to imply that Nicodemus was not one of those to whom Christ did not trust Himself, ii. 24; for He opened to him the profoundest secrets of the kingdom of God. It may be, however, merely continuative = and.—P. S.]

[2] Ver. 2.—The Recepta reads πρὸς τὸν Ἰησοῦν, against which there are decisive authorities, particularly A. B. "Beginning of a section and a lesson." Meyer.

[3] Ver. 3. [γεννάω means usually *to beget* (of the Father), Matth. i. 2 ff. and often; hence ὁ γεννήσας, the father; rarely *to bear, to bring forth* (of the mother), as Luke i. 57. God or the Holy Spirit produces the higher spiritual life; hence *begotten from above*, would perhaps better express the idea; comp. i. 13; 1 Cor. iv. 15; Philem. 10; 1 John ii. 29; iii. 9; iv. 7; v. 1, 4, 18; Heb. i. 5; v. 5.—P. S.]

[4] Ver. 3. [ἄνωθεν, מֵעַל, the reverse of κάτωθεν, and equivalent to ἐκ τοῦ οὐρανοῦ, *from heaven*, iii. 31; xix. 11, 23; Matth. xxvii. 51; Mark xv. 38; James i. 17; iii. 15, 17, or ἐκ θεοῦ, *from God*, comp. John i. 13; ἐκ τοῦ πνεύματος, iii. 6, 9, which may be taken as the true explication. If the temporal sense be preferred (in which Nicodemus misunderstands it, ver. 4); comp. Luke i. 3; Gal. iv. 9, it should be rendered *anew*, *afresh* (from the root, entirely new) rather than *again*. Tyndale: *boren a newe;* Cranmer: *boren from above;* Geneva: *begotten againe;* Rheims: *borne againe;* Conant: *born again;* Alford: *born anew*, with a marginal note: or, *from above;* Young: *from above;* Vulg.: *renatus fuerit denuo;* Luth.: *von neuem geboren werde;* Ewald: *von vorne an* (*i. e*, *ganz von neuem*) *geb. wird*. See the Exegesis.—P. S.]

[5] Ver. 3. [βασιλεία τοῦ θεοῦ only here and ver. 5 in John, but in xviii. 36 Christ speaks of *His* kingdom. The Synoptists use for it more frequently the term βασ. τῶν οὐρανῶν, which John never employs unless it be in ver. 5. (See note 7 below.—P. S.]

[6] Ver. 5. [The absence of the article both before ὕδατος and πνεύματος should be noticed. It gives to the two agents a generic character, and favors a more comprehensive interpretation of *water* than that which confines it to a particular kind of baptism, Jewish, Johannean, or Christian. See Exeg. Notes.—P. S.]

[7] Ver. 5. [Instead of the text. rec. βασ. τοῦ θεοῦ, which is retained by Tregelles, Alford, Westcott and Hort, and others, Tischendorf (ed. viii.) reads βασ. τῶν οὐρανῶν on the authority of א[1] and the still older Euseb., Orig., Hippol., Iren., and Just. M. Irenæus (*Fragm.* 35) quotes the passage literally thus: καθὼς καὶ ὁ κύριος ἔφη, ἐαν μή τις, κ. τ. λ., εἰς τ. βασ. τῶν οὐρανῶν. Justin M. (middle of the 2d cent.), *Apol.* I. c. 51 (ed. Otto, I. p. 144), cites less accurately from memory: Καὶ γαρ ὁ χριστὸς εἶπεν. Ἀν μὴ ἀναγεννηθῆτε (instead of ἐαν μή τις γεννηθῇ), οὐ μὴ εἰσέλθητε (instead of οὐ δύναται εἰσελθειν) εἰς τὴν βασιλείαν τῶν οὐρανῶν. Chrysostom also, in his homilies on John iii., reads several times βασ. τῶν οὐρανῶν. The change from this into the received reading may be traced to a desire to conform to ver. 3.—P. S.]

[8] Ver. 6. [Here and in ver. 8 the article is used before πνεύματος, and of course should be retained in the translation.—P. S.]

[9] Ver. 8. [The double meaning of the Greek πνεῦμα and the Hebrew רוּחַ, *wind* and *spirit*, suggested this analogy.—P. S.]

[10] Ver. 8.—Lachmann: ἤ ποῦ, *or where*, according to A., the Vulgate, and other versions, Armenian, Arabic, Syriac, and several of the fathers. The καί, therefore, arose probably from the need of a proverbial form of the sentence. [The usual reading καὶ ποῦ, *and* where (whither), is retained by Treg., Alf., Tischend. on the authority of א. B. L. T., *etc.*, also Ignatius *Ad Philad.* c. 7.—P. S.]

[11] Ver. 12. [Literally *the* earthly things—*the* heavenly things: τὰ ἐπίγεια—τὰ ἐπουράνια.—P. S.]

[12] Ver. 15.—Lachmann: ἐπ' αὐτόν, according to Cod. A.; Tischendorf: ἐν αὐτω, according to Cod. B. and others. Theodoret and Cod. L. read ἐπ' αὐτῷ; Meyer is for ἐν αὐτῷ, and proposes to connect this with ἔχῃ. Against this is the parallel v. 16. Probably the above variations are efforts of the catholic spirit to sharpen the idea of faith; εἰς αὐτόν being a more general conception.

[13] Ver. 15.—Μὴ ἀπόληται, ἀλλ' is wanting in [א] B. L. J., and many others. It is omitted by Tischendorf [Treg., Alf.], and put in brackets by Lachmann. It has probably been taken from ver. 16.

[14] Ver. 17. [Κρίνειν, *to judge*, is used, not κατακρίνειν, *to condemn*, here and ver. 18, and ἡ κρίσις, ver. 19. The E. V. is not consistent in the rendering of κρίνειν, κρίμα and κρίσις, using alternately *to judge, to condemn, to damn*, yet in the great majority of cases *to judge*. Κατακρίνειν is seventeen times translated *to condemn*, twice *to damn*.—P. S.]

[15] Ver. 19. [τὸ φῶς, the true personal Light, Christ, comp. i. 4, 5, 8, 9. The importance of the definite article is obvious. The E. V. retained it in ver. 20, but dropped it here—one of its innumerable inconsistencies.—P. S.]

[16] Ver. 19.—The order: αὐτῶν πονηρά [instead of πονηρὰ αὐτῶν].

[17] Ver. 21. [ὅτι assigns the reason for the preceding intention. See *Exeg.*—P. S.]

EXEGETICAL AND CRITICAL.

[This is one of the richest and most important sections of the Bible. The sixteenth verse alone contains the whole gospel in a nutshell, or "the Bible in miniature," and is worth more than all the wisdom of the world. The infinite love of the Father, the mission of His Son, the work of the Holy Spirit, the lost condition of man, the necessity of a new birth from above, faith in Christ as a condition of salvation, the kingdom of God, eternal life—all these fundamental doctrines are set forth by the unerring mouth of our Lord in this interview with a timid, yet earnest and anxious inquirer. The central idea of the passage is the new birth, which implies the total depravity of man and the work of divine grace. This great doctrine stands in the proper place at the beginning of Christ's ministry.

The first miracle of Christ was a miracle of transformation, His first public act in Jerusalem an act of reformation, His first discourse a discourse on regeneration. He is not satisfied with mere improvements of the old, but demands a new life, lays a new foundation. True religion in the soul begins with a personal conviction of sin and guilt, and of the necessity of a radical change. Without such a conviction all efforts to convert a man are in vain. The night discourse with Nicodemus is the *locus classicus* on the new birth, as the indispensable condition of admission into the kingdom of God. It occupies a position in the Gospel of John, similar to that which the Sermon on the Mount does in the Gospel of Matthew.

It is characteristic of the idealism and mysticism of John that in his Gospel he gives no account of the institution of the church* and the sacraments. But, anticipating the visible rite, he presents in ch. iii. the idea of the new birth, which is symbolized in Christian baptism, together with the idea of "the kingdom of God," which is the internal and abiding essence of the church. So in ch. vi. he gives the general idea of vital union with Christ, which underlies the sacrament of the Lord's Supper.

According to the Synoptists, Christ began His public ministry by preaching to the people: "The time is fulfilled, and the kingdom of God is at hand; repent ye (change your mind, μετανοεῖτε), and believe in the gospel" (Mark i. 15). According to John, He made, at the outset of His ministry, the same demand, first indirectly, and then directly (δεῖ ὑμᾶς, ver. 7), upon an individual, a man circumcised, orthodox, honest, unblemished, yea, of the highest rank, a member of the Supreme Council of the theocracy, even favorably disposed to Christ and almost ready to accept Him as the Messiah, in a word, a man endowed with every personal and official claim to membership of the Messianic kingdom, yet lacking one fundamental condition: a new birth from above. Christ answers not so much to the words, as to the thoughts of Nicodemus, penetrating his heart to the very core (ii. 25). With historical faithfulness, John does not state the result of the conversation, because it did not appear at once, but some time afterwards (vii. 50; xix. 39).

Regeneration (ἀναγέννησις, παλιγγενεσία) is a creative act of God the Holy Spirit, whereby a new spiritual life from above is implanted in man, through the means of grace, especially the preaching of the gospel; like the natural birth, it can occur but once. Conversion (μετάνοια, which must not be confounded with regeneration) is the corresponding subjective change of heart, whereby man, under the influence of the Spirit, in conscious repentance and faith, turns from the service of sin to the service of God; this may be repeated after a relapse. Regeneration, as to its origin and mode of operation, is a mystery like the natural generation and birth, but a mystery manifest in its effects to all who have spiritual eyes to see; it meets us as a fact in every true Christian, or child of God, who is as sure of the higher life of Christ in his own soul as he is of his natural existence. The difficulties in the exposition of this passage are mainly dogmatical, and arise from the relation of regeneration to baptism, *viz.*, whether *water* means baptism at all, and, if so, whether it refers to John's baptism, or the baptism of the disciples of Jesus, or, by anticipation, to Christian baptism (which did not appear till the day of Pentecost), or the general idea of baptism in its various forms as a historic preparation for Christian discipleship; and also from the question as to the necessity of baptism for salvation. These difficulties are fully discussed below.—P. S.]

Ver. 1. **There was a man.**—An important incident of the residence of Jesus in Jerusalem, exemplifying what has just been said, and introduced with the continuative δέ. [Comp. however, Text Note 1.—P. S.] Lücke [and Godet]: An example of the higher knowledge just mentioned; Tholuck: Of the weak faith just mentioned;* De Wette: A proof of vers. 23–25; Luthardt: Transition from the people to an individual; Ewald: Nicodemus an exception; Strauss: Added through desire to show a believer from the cultivated world; Baur: Nicodemus a typical figure: outwardly believing, inwardly unbelieving Judaism. (On the contrary Luthardt: He is in fact a genuine disciple in disguise, see Tholuck.) The views of Lücke and Tholuck do not exclude, but meet in, that of De Wette. An example, that is to say, at once of the weak faith to which Jesus cannot entrust Himself, and of His power to discern it. Yet John has especially selected this incident also on account of its great didactic importance, and as an example of the enthusiasm which Jesus at first awakened, extending even into the circle of the Pharisees.†

Nicodemus.—A current name, first with the Greeks, then with the Jews (נַקְדִּימוֹן, נַקְדֵּם; Lightfoot and Wetstein). Akin to Νικόλαος. Starke: "If the name be Hebrew, it is equivalent to *innocent blood* (נָקִי and דָּם), but if Greek, *conqueror of people* (the same as Nicolaus). As the Jews gave not only Hebrew, but Greek and Latin names also, to their children, both meanings at last met in Nicodemus." The gradual unfolding of his faith appears by stages in this place, ch. vii. 50 and ch. xix. 39. "Tradition adds that he afterwards, having publicly acknowledged the doctrine of Jesus, and having been baptized by Peter and John, was deposed from his office and banished from Jerusalem (Photius, *Biblioth.*, Cod. 171), but was supported in a country-seat by his kinsman Gamaliel, till his death." Winer. Thus tradition makes him again in an unworthy manner keep out of sight with his faith. The Talmud mentions also a Nicodemus, Son of Gorion, properly called Bunni, who was a disciple of Jesus, and survived the destruction of Jerusalem, whose family sank from wealth into great poverty (Delitzsch,

* [The term ἐκκλησία never occurs in John's Gospel and first Epistle, though repeatedly in his third Epistle, and in the Apocalypse. In the Gospel and first Epistle the ideal side of the church prevails, in the Apocalypse the real, empirical, because it is there represented in its historical conflict with the powers of darkness.]

* [So Hengstenberg, and Alford: One of the believers on account of Christ's miracles, ii. 23. Bengel: *Ex iis, de quibus c. ii. in fine; sed nonnihil melior multis.*—P. S.]

† Treatises on the section: Knapp, *Scripta varii arg.* I., p. 183 sqq; Fabricius, *Commentat.* Gott. 1825; Scholl, in Klaiber's *Studien* V. 1, p. 71: Jacobi, *Stud. und Krit.* 1835, 1. Hengstenberg, *Evang. Kirchen-Zeitung*, 1860, No. 49. [A large number of English tracts on Regeneration (mostly doctrinal and practical) are noticed in Malcom's *Theological Index* (Boston, 1869) pp. 396, 397.—P. S.]

(*Zeitschr. f. Luth. Theolog.* 1854, p. 643). The identity is not proved. Josephus also, *Antiq.* XIV. 3, 2, speaks of a Nicodemus, who was sent as a legate of the Maccabean Aristobulus to Pompey. The apocryphal literature has completed the biography of Nicodemus in a Gospel ascribed to him.*

The germ of a genuine faith had to contend in Nicodemus with regard for the polite world, thoughts of his station, fear of men, Pharisaic prejudice, but, on a foundation of sincerity, conscientiousness, rectitude, and a higher fidelity even to his office, issues victorious in courageous confession and joyful offerings; and the closing words of the conversation, ver. 21, are plainly enough a prediction of the Lord respecting him, after a reproof, ver. 20, of his stealthy coming in the night as a suspicious sign. Similar characters, though they probably did not all so decidedly come out, are described in ch. xii. 42.

A ruler of the Jews.—Member of the Sanhedrin [comp. Luke xxiii. 13; xxiv. 20; Acts xiii. 27], like Joseph of Arimathea, ch. vii. 50. Of the party of the Pharisees. [ἐκ τῶν φαρισαίων. This is not mentioned as derogatory. Hengstenberg remarks that the Pharisees were specially hostile to the doctrine of regeneration and resolved religion into a self-made holiness. But the Sadducees were even more opposed to spiritual religion. A Paul could proceed from the earnest Pharisees, but not from the frivolous and skeptical Sadducees.—P. S.]

Ver. 2. **By night.**†—That this is intended for a mark of weakness, is proved by ver. 20; and even by the particular mention of this circumstance itself, as well as by the very gradual appearing of his adhesion to Jesus.‡ Koppe puts him down as a hypocrite (see Lücke), who came to question the Lord with evil intent, and who feigned simplicity; Niemeyer, on the contrary, represents his shyness as a true caution. "He was an honorable character, rather slow of nature," says Meyer. Yet no doubt something more. An educated man of age, sitting as pupil to a young, untitled rabbi; a Pharisee, stepping free of the despotic and heresy-scenting spirit of his sect; a Sanhedrist, who soon ventures to oppose the fanaticism of the whole council; a prominent, serene-tempered, mature man of the world, who under the cross of the dead Jesus appears as a disciple, and in a costly burial-gift gives token of his unreserved and joyful devotion, and thus evinces that there were given to him and have continued with him, in his frigid school, a noble vigor of spirit, in his legal dignity a living yearning, in his high age a youthful striving, under all traditional prejudice a large ingenuousness, above all, under the whole system of Pharisaic show a sincere heart, and under all the rust of worldliness the metal of a turn for the faith and devotion of the Christian. Meyer justly observes, against De Wette and others, that the coming of Nicodemus by night does not imply that no disciples were present at the interview; and the directness, of the narrative, though bearing the Johannean stamp, leads us to supppose that John was a witness.

Rabbi, we know [οἴδαμεν].—First of all, Nicodemus accords to the Lord the dignity of Rabbi, denied to Him by many (ch. vii. 15); and this, considering the importance attached by the scribes to this title, is not without a favorable significance. This "we know" implies that he had kindred spirits in his circle, who acknowledged the high office of Jesus.* Yet the word shades off, in a somewhat politic sense, from a Pluralis excellentiæ into a suggestion of an indefinite prospect of recognition by the whole Sanhedrin.† It expresses also the self-sufficient scribe-spirit, and unconsciously betrays over-valuation of knowledge and under-valuation of faith.

A teacher come from God.—Acknowledgment of an indefinite prophetic character.‡—**For no man can do these miracles.**—Acknowledgment of a number of accredited, important miraculous signs [ταῦτα τὰ σημεῖα, *hæcce tanta signa*], which Jesus had done in Jerusalem, and which, in the judgment of Nicodemus, certified Him to be a new prophet of God. Miracle a test of a prophet, but under qualifications, Deut. xiii. 1; xviii. 20.

Except God be with him.—The miracle proves the supernatural power which stands by the worker. False miracles might be performed through Satanic agency, Ex. vii. But the character and greatness of the miracles of Jesus made it certain to Nicodemus that He wrought them in the power of God. And this involved the further inference that He was accredited by the miracles as a prophet sent from God. The ἔρχεσθαι is significant, ch. i. 6, 15.

Ver. 3. **Verily, verily, I say unto thee.**—One of the great cardinal truths of the kingdom of heaven, solemnly introduced. The answer consists of a series of antitheses: (1) The address of Rabbi is answered by an address without Rabbi; (2) the "we know" is met with "verily, verily, I say unto thee;" (3) the word: Thou art come from above, and therefore art a teacher (from the kingdom of God), is met by the word: A man must be even *born from above*, if he would so much as see the kingdom of God; (4) the sign is met by the kingdom of God itself. And this antithesis runs through all: Thou wouldst know that I am a prophet, but thou still lackest the qualifications for seeing who I am, and seeing in me the personal manifestation of the kingdom of God.

Various views of the relation of the answer of

* [The *Evangelium Nicodemi* comprises the *Acta Pilati* and the *Descensus Christi ad inferos*. See Tischendorf, *Evangelia Apocrypha*, Lips. 1853, pp. 203–412, where the whole is given in Greek and Latin.—P. S.]

† [Bengel remarks to νυκτός: "*Nunquam non recipit Christus ad se venientes.*"—P. S.]

‡ [Augustine: *Quamvis ad Jesum venerit, tamen quia nocte venit, adhuc de tenebris carnis suæ loquitur.* Hengstenberg: The night is mentioned as a symbol of the darkness of the mind of Nicodemus (xi. 10; xiii. 30). Better: He came in the dark from fear of public opinion. Yet he came, which is far better than not coming at all. The remark does not exclude company. John and other disciples of Christ were probably present at the interview. Ewald conjectures that also Nicodemus had some attendants with him.—P. S.]

* [Bengel: *Ego et mei similes, principes potius, quam Pharisæi*, xii. 42. *Huic plurali respondet pluralis*, ver. 7.—P. S.]

† [Comp. here the note of Alford. Stier thinks that Nicodemus, in using the plural, concealed his own conviction, so as to be able to draw back again if necessary. Rather far-fetched.—P. S.]

‡ [The word διδάσκαλος seems to imply a cautious inconsistency. The expected Messiah was a *king*, and never regarded "as a mere *teacher* till the days of modern Socinianism." Alford].

Jesus to the address of Nicodemus: (1) Intermediate talk omitted (Kuinoel and others). (2) Jesus would lead him from the faith of miracles to the faith which morally transforms (Augustine, De Wette). (3) Jesus is come not as a teacher, but for the moral transformation of the world (Baumgarten-Crusius). (4) Thou thinkest thou already seest a sign of the kingdom of God; no man can see the kingdom of God, unless he be born anew (Lightfoot, Lücke). (5) Meyer: The address of Nicodemus is interrupted by Christ, and must therefore be completed from this answer. Nicodemus intended to ask: What must I do, to enter into the kingdom of the Messiah? To this Christ here gives him the answer. But (*a*) the hypothesis of interruption is unsuitable; better, that of hesitation; best, that of polite, skilful waiting, as if to say: What more? (*b*) Nicodemus was as yet hardly so far advanced as to ask what Meyer puts into his mouth. The connection is probably this: Thou thinkest that I am *come* from God. But he who would even *see* the kingdom of God, must be more than this; he must be *born* from above; how much greater must be said of the Founder of the kingdom of God.

Jesus gave him to understand that he had not yet reached the forecourt of true knowledge. At least Christ's answer confronts the proud consciousness of the address with the humbling nature of truth. And when He requires the new birth from above as the condition of seeing the kingdom of God, He means, according to the analogy of the Jewish designation of proselytes as born again (Jeramoth fol. 62, *etc.*), primarily: Except a man come out from the old system, become a proselyte, publicly commit himself to a new position. And in birth from above the word demands a great transition. Nicodemus would privately assure Him of the adhesion of a party of the Pharisees, implying the presumption that he would attach himself to the old order of things. Jesus demands of him a proselytism wrought by God, a coming forth from the darkness of night and of the old party, if he would have any understanding at all of the kingdom of God which he himself announces. We may still suppose that John relates only the essential, salient words, and omits intervening details; the main progress of thought, however, he has undoubtedly given, though in the color of his own contemplation.

Except a man be born from above [Ἐὰν μή τις γεννηθῇ ἄνωθεν].* Various interpretations of ἄνωθεν: (1) Locally: from heaven (ἐκ τοῦ οὐρανοῦ); (2) temporally: afresh, from the very beginning (ἐξ ἀρχῆς). Both views are adduced by Chrysostom [who himself explains the word by παλιγγενεσία]. In favor of the latter, in the sense of *iterum, denuo*, are the Vulgate [Augustine], Luther [Calvin, Beza], Olshausen, Neander, Tholuck [Alford, Hengstenberg, Godet]. Against it are the verbal criticisms, that ἄνωθεν, taken temporally, means not *again*, but *from the beginning*, and that the rendering *again* has probably arisen under the influence of the expressions of Paul in Rom. xii. 2; Gal. vi. 15; Eph. iv. 23; Col. iii. 10; Tit. iii. 5; and of Pet. in 1 Pet. i. 23. For the *local* explanation are Origen and many others, down to Bengel [SUPERNE, *unde Filius hominis descendit*], Lücke, and Meyer [also De Wette, Robinson, Baur, Bäumlein, Weizsäcker, Owen, Wordsworth]. *From above*, in the sense of *from God*, ἐκ θεοῦ. This is further favored by the consideration "that John conceives regeneration not under the aspect of a second birth, but of a divine birth, ch. i. 13; 1 John ii. 29; iii. 9; iv. 7; v. 1." Meyer. The ideas of being born from above or of God and being born anew are, however, in substance interchangeable, and Tholuck's objections to Lücke, *etc.* [Krauth's trs., p. 114], are untenable.

[Often as the fact of regeneration appears in the N. T., the terms for it are rare, and not near as frequent as the terms μετάνοια and others, which signify the corresponding act of man in turning to God under the regenerating operation of the Holy Spirit. The verb ἄνωθεν γεννηθῆναι, *to be begotten*, or *born from above, i. e.*, from God, which is used twice in this ch. (vers. 6, 7), occurs nowhere else in the N. T. John also uses once *to be born of water and Spirit* (γεννηθῆναι ἐξ ὕδατος καὶ πνεύματος), ver. 5, and twice *to be born of the Spirit* (τὸ γεγεννημένον ἐκ τοῦ πνεύματος, ver. 6, ὁ γεγ. ἐκ τ. πν., ver. 8, without the *water*), but the more usual phrase with him is *to be begotten*, or *born of God* (γεννηθῆναι ἐκ θεοῦ), i. 13; 1 John ii. 19; iii. 9; iv. 7; v. 1, 4, 18. The verb ἀναγεννάομαι, *to be begotten*, or *born again*, occurs but once or twice, 1 Pet. i. 23 (ἀναγεγεννημένοι οὐκ ἐκ σπορᾶς φθαρτῆς ἀλλὰ ἀφθάρτου, διὰ λόγου ζῶντος θεοῦ); 1 Pet. i. 3 (ἀναγεννήσας ἡμᾶς εἰς ἐλπίδα); comp. James i. 18 (ἀπεκύησεν ἡμᾶς λόγῳ ἀληθείας). The noun ἀναγέννησις, *regeneration*, is not found at all in the N. T. (although often in the Greek fathers), but the analogous noun παλιγγενεσία occurs twice, once in connection with baptism, Tit. iii. 5 (ἔσωσεν ἡμᾶς διὰ λουτροῦ παλιγγενεσίας καὶ ἀνακαινώσεως πνεύματος ἁγίου), and once in a more comprehensive sense, with reference to the final resurrection and consummation of all things, Matth. xix. 28 (ἐν τῇ παλιγγενεσίᾳ, ὅταν κ. τ. λ.). Paul speaks of a *new creature* (καινὴ κτίσις) in Christ, 2 Cor. v. 17, and of the *new man* (καινὸς ἄνθρωπος), Eph. iv. 24. The Rabbinical theology had a very superficial conception of the new birth and confined it pretty much to the change in the *external* status of a proselyte to Judaism. Hence the comparative ignorance and perplexity of Nicodemus who, being a circumcised Jew, did not feel the need of such a radical change.—P. S.]

The kingdom of God.—The fact that the phrase "kingdom of God" occurs only here and in ver. 5, and nowhere else in John (except ch. xviii. 36, the βασιλεία Χριστοῦ, which Meyer has overlooked), not only proves, as Meyer rightly observes, the independent originality of this Gospel, but also characterizes John's view of Christianity. From his point of view John sees not the form of a universal kingdom, but the world transfigured in personal being. Lücke: John seems to have transformed the positive Jewish idea into the more abstract, and to the Greeks more intelligible formula of fellowship (κοινωνία,

* [Bengel: "*Sermo indefinitus, quem Nicodemus tamen recte ad se applicat, comp. ver.* 7, *vos.*" This passage was already quoted in the middle of the second century by Justin M. See Text. Note 7. The idea of some modern hyper-critics that the author of the Gospel should have borrowed from Justin is simply ridiculous.—P. S.]

1 John i. 3), the unity of believers with God and Christ. The essential elements of the idea of a kingdom, however, come out distinctly in chapters x. and xvii., and are fully developed in the Apocalypse. On the βασιλεία τοῦ θεοῦ see *Com. on Matthew* iii. 2, p. 69. [The kingdom of God is a deeper and more spiritual conception than the church, which is the earthly training school for the heavenly and everlasting kingdom. We could not with any propriety substitute here: "Except . . . he cannot see the *church*."—P. S.]

He cannot see.—Not even see; to say nothing of entering, being at home therein. Meyer disputes this interpretation; comp. εισελθεῖν, ver. 5. That entrance and experience go with the seeing, must of course be understood.

Ver. 4. **How can a man be born when he is old?**—Taken literally, this reply of Nicodemus supposes an absurdity. And so Meyer, after Strauss, would take it. He admits that a Jewish theologian must have been familiar with the Old Testament ideas of circumcision of the heart (Deut. xxx. 6; Jer. iv. 4), and a new heart and spirit (Ezek. xi. 19; xxxvi. 26; Ps. li. 10; lxxxvi. 11); yet Nicodemus may have been limited in other respects; and now on meeting Jesus, become really perplexed. We might rather suppose that the good-humored old man spoke, possibly even wittily, with a double meaning.* The first sentence may mean either: How can a Jewish Senator, an elder of the people, become a heathen proselyte? or: How can a physically old man, undergo new, fundamental, spiritual transformation? The second sentence would then illustrate this impossibility by a physical impossibility: Can he enter the second time into his mother's womb? The expositor must remember that the Orientals constantly express their thoughts in such similitudes. Meyer: "The ἄνωθεν he understood not as δεύτερον, but not at all." He assuredly did understand it as an equivalent of δεύτερον, for the total antithesis is evidently implied: ἄνωθεν γεννηθῆναι, ἐκ τῆς γῆς γεννηθῆναι. Then the idea of being born from above involves that of being born anew. Various interpretations. (1) A Jew is required to make himself the same as a proselyte (Wetstein, Knapp). (2) Luthardt: The beginning of a new spiritual life is not to be conceived without a new beginning of the natural. (This could not be said by one familiar with the Old Testament). (3) The demand is as unreasonable as that one should enter a second time into his mother's womb, *etc.* (Schweizer, Tholuck). (4) No one can turn in mature age into a different spiritual state (Schleiermacher, Baumgarten-Crusius). Besides the two antitheses here quoted—an old man required to make a new spiritual beginning, a Jewish elder to become a proselyte—the expression contains also the intimation that an old, matured stage of the Jewish spirit could not pass into a new and different youthful life. But we still suppose that Nicodemus employs the sensuous expression in innocent good-nature, to bring out vividly, with rabbinic art, the impossibility of the requirement of Jesus.

Ver. 5. **Born of water and Spirit** [γεννηθῇ ἐξ ὕδατος καὶ πνεύματος].—The next answer of Jesus has three noticeable features: (1) The imperturbable confidence expressed in the repetition; (2) The advance of the thought; the explanation of the birth from above as a being born *of water and Spirit;* (3) The entering into the kingdom of God, instead of seeing it. Whereupon further explanations follow, vers. 6, 7, and 8.

[Before giving the various interpretations, we shall briefly state our own view on this important and difficult passage. The key to it is furnished by the declaration of the Baptist that he baptized only with *water*, but Christ would baptize with the *Holy Ghost*, John i. 33 (βαπτίζειν ἐν ὕδατι—τὸ πνεῦμα); Matth. iii. 11, and by the passage of Paul where he connects Christian baptism, as "the *bath* of regeneration" (λουτρὸν παλιγγενεσίας) with "the renewal of the *Holy Ghost*" (ἀνακαίνωσις πνεύματος ἁγίου), and yet distinguishes both, Tit. iii. 5. Comp. also Eph. vi. 26 (καθαρίσας τῷ λουτρῷ τοῦ ὕδατος); 1 John v. 6 ("that came by *water* and blood," after which ℵ. B. insert καὶ πνεύματος, "not by water only, but by *water* and blood"); ver. 8 ("three that bear witness on earth, the Spirit, and the *water*, and the blood"). The term ὕδωρ then is closely related to, and yet clearly distinguished from, πνεῦμα, and in such connection always refers to *baptismal* water. It is water in its well known *symbolic* significance, as representing purification from sin by the cleansing blood of atonement. So water appears often already in the O. T., especially in Messianic passages. Ps. li. 2: "Wash me thoroughly from mine iniquity, and cleanse me from my sin." Isa. lii. 15: "So shall He sprinkle many nations." Ezek. xxxvi. 25: "Then will I sprinkle clean *water* upon you, and ye shall be clean;" to which is added, ver. 26, the promise of a new *spirit* and a new *heart*. Zech. xiii. 1: "In that day there shall be a *fountain* opened in the house of David and to the inhabitants of Jerusalem for sin and for uncleanness;" comp. xii. 10, where the outpouring of the *Spirit* of grace is promised at the coming of the Messiah. Nicodemus, though ignorant of Christian baptism, which did not appear till the day of Pentecost, was familiar with these passages, with Jewish lustrations, with the baptism of John unto repentance, probably also with the baptism of the disciples of Jesus (mentioned soon afterwards, John iii. 22; iv. 2), and the baptism of proselytes which Jewish tradition traces back to remote antiquity. The idea which underlies all these baptisms is essentially the same. We would therefore not confine ὕδωρ to any particular form of baptism, but (with Lange, see below, No. 5) extend it to all preparatory lustrations; nor would we refer it directly to the sacrament as an external act or rite, but (with Olshausen) to the *idea* rather of which the cleansing with water is the symbolic expression; just as in ch. vi. we have an exposition of the general *idea* of the holy communion before the *sacrament* was instituted in which it comes to its full embodiment. The idea underlying all forms of baptism, is the *forgiveness of sins* on condition of repentance. This is the *negative* part of regeneration, while

* [Godet finds in the words of Nicodemus no absurdity, but a good-natured irony, *une bonhomie un peu ironique.* This hardly suits the seriousness of the occasion. Nicodemus speaks comparatively. A moral new birth in an old man seems to him as impossible as a second natural birth.—P. S.]

the new life communicated by the Holy Spirit is the *positive* part, or regeneration proper. So Peter in his pentecostal sermon represents the matter when he calls upon his hearers: "Repent and be baptized in the name of Jesus Christ for the remission of sins, and ye shall receive the gift of the Holy Ghost" (Acts ii. 38). The chief matter is, of course, the positive part, the gift of the Holy Spirit, who is the efficient cause, the creative and vivifying agent of regeneration, and who alone can make the word and the sacrament effective. Hence the Spirit alone is mentioned vers. 6 and 8. The omission of water here is as significant, as the omission of baptism in the negative clause of Mark xvi. 16, where the condition of salvation and the reason of damnation are laid down. This is a sufficient hint that the necessity of water baptism to salvation is not absolute, but relative only. The penitent thief passed into paradise without water baptism. Cornelius was regenerated before he was baptized, and many martyrs in the early ages died for Christ before they had a chance to receive the sacrament. It is possible to have the substance without the form, the baptism of the Spirit, without the baptism of water; as it is quite common, on the other hand, to be baptized with water and have the Christian name without the Christian spirit and life. The Apostles themselves (except Paul) never received *Christian* baptism, for Christ Himself who alone could have administered it to them, did not baptize (iv. 2). In their case the pentecostal effusion of the Spirit was sufficient. We are bound to God's appointed means of grace, but God is free, and the Spirit "bloweth where it listeth."—P. S.]

Different interpretations of water.

(1) The water signifies [*Christian*] baptism (fathers, and older Lutheran divines, Meyer,* Tholuck, De Wette).† Baptism is λουτρόν παλιγγενεσίας as the means of cleansing, Tit. iii. 5; 1 Pet. iii. 21; Eph. v. 26; Heb. x. 22; 1 John v. 6, 8. With baptism the gift of the Holy Ghost is joined, Acts ii. 38. Tholuck: "The water is (ch. vii. 39) the symbol of the communication of the Spirit." Yet probably in another sense. Calvin's objection: The words would then have been unintelligible, because the baptism of Christ had not yet begun.‡ Strauss: This very thing proves a later insertion [a proleptic fiction] of the Evangelist.

(2) The older Reformed divines (except Beza, Aretius), also Arminians, Socinians: ὕδωρ is a *figurative* term *for the purifying power of the Spirit;* therefore ἓν διὰ δυοῖν.*

(3) Piscator, Grotius, Episcopius, Neander, Baumgarten-Crusius: the baptism of *John.*†

(4) Schweizer: the *proselyte* baptism, with: not only, but also—to be supplied.‡

(5) Baptism in the comprehensive sense as a theocratic historical lustration in its various phases according to the degree of the development of the kingdom of God. Thus the flood even is represented as a prototype of Christian baptism [1 Pet. iii. 20, 21]. Lücke alone brings

* [Meyer: Baptism is meant as the *causa medians*, the Holy Spirit as the *causa efficiens* of regeneration. He thinks that no other but Christian baptism can be meant because it is connected with the Holy Spirit.—P. S.]

† [So also Hengstenberg, Godet, Webster and Wilkinson, A. Barnes, Owen (who explains: *except ye receive the rite of Christian baptism*). Hooker, as quoted by Wordsworth, remarks: "Of all ancient writers there is not one to be named who ever expounded the text otherwise than as implying *external* baptism." Wordsworth, who follows the fathers into all their allegorical fancies, has a curious note here to show what an important part water occupies in the Gospel of John. Christ just came from the water, Christ turned water into wine, Christ presents Himself as the water of life (ch. iv.), Christ does nothing without water, *etc.*—P. S.]

‡ [True; but Nicodemus understood from the lustrations of the O. T. and the public baptism of John, the general idea of baptismal purification which culminated in Christian baptism; and besides Christ spoke not only to Nicodemus, but through him to all men and all ages. J. C. Ryle (of the evang. party of the Church of England), in his *Expository Thoughts* on John, urges six arguments against the usual interpretation, especially because the reference of water to baptism would imply the regenerate state of all the baptized and the absolute necessity of baptism for salvation. But this is reasoning from dogmatical inferences which are not justified either by the context or the analogy of Scripture. Christ clearly demands, besides baptism, the new birth of the Spirit, and lays the main stress on this (vers. 6, 8), as He does on faith, Mark xvi. 16, as the indispensable condition to salvation. See below.—P. S.]

* [Calvin: Of water, which is the purifying Spirit, so that water and Spirit mean the same thing, as Spirit and fire, Matth. iii. 11. Coccejus: *Gratia Dei, sordes et vitia abluens.* Lampe: *Obedientia Christi.* Grotius: *Spiritus aqueus, i. e., aquæ instar emendans.* But in view of the facts that John baptized, that Christ Himself was baptized, that His disciples (iv. 2) baptized in His name, it seems impossible to disconnect *water* from baptism. Calvin's interpretation arose from doctrinal opposition to the R. Catholic over-valuation of the sacrament, which must be guarded against in another way. Godet, of the Reformed Church of Switzerland, correctly remarks (I. 408): "*Il est impossible de ne pas prendre le mot eau dans son sens naturel et de ne pas l'appliquer au baptême.*"—P. S.]

† [This view is also held by Bengel, Hofmann, and Dean Alford; yet by the latter so as to allow for a wider application to *Christian* baptism, which certainly should not be excluded. After showing that ὕδωρ must mean *baptismal* water, Alford goes on to say: "This being then recognized, to *what does ὕδωρ refer?* At that time, two kinds of baptism were known: that of the *proselytes* by which they were received into Judaism,—and that of *John*, by which, as a preparatory rite, symbolizing repentance, the people were made ready for Him who was to baptize them with the Holy Ghost. But both these were significant of *one and the same truth;* that namely of the *entire cleansing of the man* for the new and spiritual life on which he was to enter, symbolized by water cleansing the outward person. Both were appointed means,—the one by the Jewish Church,—the other, stamping that first with approval, by God Himself,—towards their respective ends. John himself declared his baptism to be *incomplete*,—it was *only with water;* one was coming, who should baptize *with the Holy Ghost. That declaration of his is the key to the understanding of this verse.* Baptism, complete, with *water* and the *Spirit*, is the admission into the kingdom of God. Those who have received *the outward sign and the spiritual grace*, have entered into that kingdom. And this entrance was fully ministered to the disciples when the Spirit descended on them on the day of Pentecost. So that, as spoken to Nicodemus, these words referred him to the baptism of John, which probably (see Luke vii. 30) he had slighted. But they were *not only* spoken to him. The words of our Lord have in them life and meaning for all ages of His Church: and more especially these opening declarations of His ministry. He here unites together the two elements of a complete Baptism which were sundered in the words of the Baptist, ch. i. 33—in which united form He afterwards (Matth. xxviii. 19, 20; Mark xvi. 16) ordained it as a sacrament of His Church. Here He speaks of spiritual Baptism, as in ch. vi. of spiritual Communion, and in both places in connection with the outward conditions and media of these sacraments. It is observable that here, as ordinarily (with a special exception, Acts x. 44 ff.), the outward sign comes first, and then the spiritual grace, vouchsafed in and by means of it where duly received." The objection to a reference of ὕδωρ to John's baptism is, that Christ after manifesting Himself as the Messiah could not well have made the baptism of His forerunner a condition of admission to His kingdom. In this case He would have said at least οὐκ ἐξ ὕδατος μόνον, ἀλλὰ καί, *not only* of water, *but also* and chiefly of the Spirit.—P. S.]

‡ [This is entirely inapplicable to Nicodemus, who was a Jew in full communion. Besides it is not quite certain, although probable, that the Jewish proselyte baptism existed before Christ. Comp. Schneckenburger, *Ueber das Alter der jüd. Proselytentaufe und deren Zusammenhang mit dem johanneischen und christlichen Ritus*, and Herzog's *Encycl.*, vol. XII., p. 245.—P. S.]

forward the universal idea of baptism in its symbolical import. "Water is here, as in the baptism of John, the symbol of purification, of *μετάνοια*, of the essential but negative beginning of the being born of God." It is only to be observed, first, that a merely negative beginning is inconceivable; and secondly, that the *μετάνοια* in question is one which completes itself by entrance into a new, higher fellowship by means of the corresponding lustration. And this lustration, of course, was not yet before Nicodemus in the Christian form, but only in the form of the baptism of John. The word refers, therefore, *primarily to the baptism of John*. But to this, as the *lustration of its time*. The word found its fulfilment in the *Christian* baptism, which actually asserts its character as a dividing lustration between the old world and the new. The passage is therefore to be explained from the words of John: "I baptize with *water, etc.;*" except that Christ makes of the antithesis a synthesis. Concretely: One must become a divinely begotten proselyte, through the medium of discipleship under John and discipleship under Christ. It cannot be objected, that John's office is only temporary (against Meyer). As the transition is through the Old Testament into the New, so it is also through the person who closes the Old Testament to him who opens the New, to Christ. One must first become historically a Christian, receiving the lustration of Christian discipline; then, spiritually a Christian. As the condition of salvation, the two things are a concrete unit; the first not without the second, the second not without the first; yet the second, the baptism of the Spirit, the chief and decisive thing according to ver. 6.

Of water and Spirit.—The relation of the two.—Olshausen: The water denotes the soul purified in simple repentance, as the feminine principle, the Spirit, the masculine. (Is this a remnant of theosophy?)* Meyer: The passage shows the necessity of baptism to participation in the kingdom of the Messiah, but only to those passing over to Christianity, not to Christian children (for which he quotes, without warrant, 1 Cor. vii. 14). Tholuck: According to the Lutheran doctrine the communication of the Spirit is not *absolute*, but only *ordinarie* dependent on baptism. The *ἐκ*, according to the Lutheran doctrine, denotes the *causa materialis*, according to Musæus, *instrumentalis*. Tholuck himself proposes a middle view, making *ἐκ* denote the visible source, the operating cause. This, however, is not a middle view, but a still stronger form of the *causa materialis*. Unquestionably the *ἐκ* with *water* denotes the historical means, with *Spirit*, the vital.—The water is the predominantly negative medium of the birth, the Spirit, the predominantly positive. In general, the birth from water might be intelligible to the Israelite from his usual lustrations, and particularly from the promises in Is. i. 16; Mal. iii. 3; Jer. xxxiii. 8; Ezek. xxxvi. 25; and the birth from the Spirit, from circumcision, and such promises as Ezek. xxxvi. 26; Joel ii. 28; Zech. xii. 10.

* [Olshausen refers for illustration to the brooding of the Spirit of God over the waters of the deep in the first creation, which in a certain sense is repeated in every new birth; hence the regenerate is called a new creature, 2 Cor. v. 17.—P. S.]

He cannot enter.—Lücke: In the nature of the case *εἰσελθεῖν* must be the same as *ἰδεῖν*; that is, have a share in the presence of the kingdom of God. [So also Meyer]. Still *ἰδεῖν* denotes this rather in the aspect of perceiving as an object, *εἰσελθεῖν*, of entering into it. And this makes the expression a further development of the idea of the participation, corresponding to the further definition of the being born from above, as a being born of water and of the Spirit.

[It is from this expression mainly (*οὐ δύναται εἰσελθεῖν, etc.*), that the fathers inferred the doctrine of the absolute necessity of baptism for salvation, which is still taught in the symbols of the Greek, Roman, and Lutheran churches. Clement of Alexandria assumed that even the saints of the O. T. were baptized in hades before they could pass into heaven, and Augustine went so far as to exclude all unbaptized infants who die in infancy from heaven,—an inference against which all our nobler feelings instinctively rebel. Baptism no doubt is the ordinary and regular way to Christ's church, as circumcision was to the Jewish church. But on the other hand it has always been maintained by judicious divines in all churches, that it is not the want, but the contempt of the sacrament that condemns (*non defectus*, or *privatio, sed contemptus sacramenti damnat*), and that under certain conditions the baptism of *desire* (*baptismus flaminis*), and the baptism of *blood* in martyrdom (*baptismus sanguinis*), may be a full equivalent of baptism proper (*baptismus fluminis*). The omission of water in vers. 6 and 8, implies that the Holy Spirit may produce regeneration without baptism, as He undoubtedly did under the Jewish dispensation and in the case of Cornelius; while on the other hand the example of Simon Magus proves that baptism may take place without being accompanied by spiritual regeneration. The necessity of regeneration and faith to salvation is absolute, the necessity of baptism, or any thing else, is merely relative. Only unbelief, *i. e.*, the rejection of the gospel, with or without baptism, condemns. This is clearly taught, Mark xvi. 16: *ὁ δὲ ἀπιστήσας* (without the addition *καὶ μὴ βαπτισθεὶς*) *κατακριθήσεται*. Comp. my remarks on p. 127.—P. S.]

Ver. 6. **That which is born of the flesh.**—The *σάρξ* here is the designation of human nature in its sinful tendency, antithetic to spirit. Generally John uses *σάρξ* for human nature as a whole. He now, at the outset, views human nature as sinful *σάρξ* in contrast with the Spirit (ch. i. 13, and here). But that he can conceive it also as regenerate *σάρξ*, appears from ch. i. 14, and vi. 51 sqq. From this alone it follows, that he must have an idea of an original pure *σάρξ*; and this is evident also from ch. xvii. 2. *Σάρξ*, absolutely, therefore, is not "the material nature of man, ethically determined by sinful inclination of which it is the seat, with the principle of the sensuous life of the *ψυχή*" (Meyer). *Σάρξ* is here, as in ch. i. 13, the whole human nature, body, soul, and spirit, but under perverse dominion of the *σάρξ* in the narrower sense, in contrast with the ruling of the human spirit by the Spirit of God. The neuter stands for the personal, to make the expression as general as possible (Winer, p. 160). There is thus the same antithesis as in ch. i. 13. All men are flesh, in so far as they have proceeded from the natural, carnal generation, stand opposed to the kingdom of God, and need the birth from the Spirit. What, therefore, is born of the flesh is flesh, and would be flesh again, though a man could be born the second time of his mother. Besser says: "Not something in us is carnal, but everything" (see Flacius.)

That which is born of the Spirit.—The water in ver. 5 is omitted as less decisive, but is implied, especially in so far as the office of the water is to abnegate that which is sinful in the birth from the σάρξ in order to mediate the birth from the Spirit. The passage relates not only to a proceeding of the moral nature and life from the Spirit of God (Meyer), but to a transformation of the whole person himself by the operations of the Spirit.—**Is spirit.** That is: Is determined in its whole nature by the Spirit as its principle, growing towards entire spiritualization, as that which is born of the flesh is determined by the flesh as its principle, and in its abnormal development sinks into carnality, Rom. viii. 5. Evidently the whole sentence applies to the whole human race (not, as Kuinoel holds, to the Jews alone), and expresses: (1) The contrast between the old man and Christ as the Son of Man; (2) The contrast between the unregenerate and the regenerate (see Rom. v.). Meyer: "In the conclusions respectively, the substantives σάρξ and πνεῦμα stand significantly and strongly [comp. 1 John iv. 8] for the adjectives σαρκικός and πνευματικός, and are to be taken qualitatively."

Ver. 7. **Marvel not.**—The expression of Jesus reflects the astonishment of the aged hearer. His confusion seems to pass into waiting admiration. Christ then shows him why he should not wonder, by illustrating the spiritual mystery by a mystery of nature. With great force He here brings out the word: YE MUST, *etc.* Bengel: *Te et eos, quorum nomine locutus es.*

Ver. 8. **The wind bloweth where it listeth.**—The comparison of the one πνεῦμα with the other, as well as the verb πνεῖ, satisfies us that the subject here is the wind, not the Spirit, as Origen and Augustine took the word. Not alone the double sense of the word (πνεῦμα, רוּחַ), but the symbolical import of the wind also occasions the illustration of the spiritual case by the natural analogy. With John, concrete, graphic circumstances always reflect themselves in high thoughts; and thus we may suppose the figure here to have been furnished by a storm or roaring wind in the night. Now first comes the question: What does the figure say? Then: What does it mean? The wind in its blowing, the air in its motion, is a type of the Spirit, because it is in fact the element of the unity and union of the diversities of the earth. It bloweth *where it listeth.* The personification of the wind is suggested by its unconfined, apparently free motion, as unaccountable as original, personal will. *Where?* Meyer presents an example of ποῦ with a verb of motion; but here the *where* is emphatic, the place where the wind whistles and roars in its strength.

[There are three points of comparison between the wind and the Spirit in the work of regeneration: 1) the freedom and independence: ὅπου θέλει πνεῖ; 2) the irresistible effect: τὴν φωνὴν αὐτοῦ ἀκούεις; 3) the incomprehensibility: οὐκ οἶδας, both as to origin (πόθεν) and termination (ποῦ ὑπάγει). To these might be added a fourth analogy, which, however, is not stated in the text, *viz.*, the different degrees of power; the Holy Spirit acts now like the gentle breeze upon minds as tenderly constituted as John, Melanchthon, Zinzendorf, now like a sweeping storm or whirlwind upon characters as strong as Paul, Luther, Calvin, Knox. Hence the presumption and folly to make our own experience the measure and rule for all others. We should rather adore the wisdom and goodness of God in the variety of His operation.—P. S.]

And thou hearest the sound thereof, but canst not tell.—Though perfectly manifest, the deepest mystery. And first in reference to the WHENCE. Even if the general conditions of its origin be known, as they were only in part to the ancients (locality, season, heat, *etc.*), yet the particular actual conditions, and the precise origin of a given current, are not known. No more the *end* of the current, its particular actual effects. So with the Spirit, both as to its origin and its effects, in the matter of regeneration. The origin of the rustling wind of the new life-word of Christ, which stirs him, Nicodemus does not know. The wind comes down mysteriously through the Old Testament with ever increasing strength. Nicodemus has marked many things in the Old Testament, but not the rising motion of the Spirit. Still less knows he whither this mighty Spirit-current leads, out over Israel into the Gentile world, and out over the earth into the eternal heaven. Yet the Lord immediately gives to the figure a definite application. In whatever soul the Spirit of regeneration would act, there he is present all at once in his untrammelled power. The beginnings are a mystery. So the issues in the eternal life. This, too, Nicodemus did not yet know; how the Spirit had seized him, and whither it would go with him, 1 Cor. xv. 28. How some of the older theologians used this passage for the doctrine of *gratia irresistibilis,* while others denied this use of it, and how Calvin interpreted it, not for his system, but only as presenting the incomprehensible and mysterious in the work of the Spirit, see in Tholuck. The words concerning the wind and regeneration would evidently say: Regeneration is a thing which, both as to its origin and its goal, is a mystery of faith, but in its manifestation, especially under the preaching of the Gospel and under awakening miracles, is a mighty, unmistakable life. Faith as life is plain; life as faith is a mystery. The wind a type of divine operation; Xenoph. *Memorab.*, 4, 3, 14. Comp. Ps. cxxxv. 7; Eccles. xi. 5.

So is every one.—Popular phrase for: So is it with every one.

Ver. 9. **How can these things be?**—Luther: "Nicodemus becomes more foolish and gets no idea of the parable." Stier: "He now really asks, instead of contradicting." If the question be interpreted from the advance of the discourse of Jesus, it says far more, and the πῶς is not *hæsitantis,* as Grotius takes it. Nicodemus asks now with the wish that such a regeneration may be possible by a power which makes water and Spirit operative. Though the wind so mysteriously comes and goes, it yet has its sufficient cause; where lies the sufficient cause for the mysterious regeneration of water and the Spirit? The δύναται having been already treated, the emphasis now is not on it, but on πῶς.

Ver. 10. **Master of Israel, and knowest not these things?**—Not now a rebuke for want of faith in the power of the divine Spirit (Tholuck), but a reminder that he, as Master of Israel, ought to know the ground for the outpouring of the Spirit, to wit, the doctrine of Christ the Son of God, and His sufferings and His redeeming work.—**Master of Israel.** According to Scholl (see Lücke, I. p. 527) three men stood at the head of the Sanhedrin: The president (הַנָּשִׂיא), who was called, by eminence, the public *teacher* of the law; the vice-president, or *pater domus judicii, sive Synedrii* (אַב בֵּית דִּין); and the *wise man* (חָכָם), sitting on the left of the president. Now Nicodemus could hardly have been the president of the Sanhedrin; but he might have been "*the wise man.*" Yet, as Lücke remarks, this last office is doubtful, and the ideas of wise man, teacher, *etc.*, do not coincide. Lücke, after Erasmus: "*Ille doctor, cujus tam celebris est opinio.*" Nicodemus took the lead of those who desired to know concerning Jesus; so far he was the teacher of Israel. He wished to know what he was, and did not know that he was the Messiah, or what the Messiah was, as the basis of the sending of the Spirit and of regeneration. This he might know from Is. xi. and lxi.

Ver. 11. **Verily, verily, We speak that which we know.**—The introduction of another cardinal truth of the doctrine of Christ the Son of God, His sufferings and His work. An *intimation* that it is He himself, without the *declaration* that it is He. *That we do know.* The personal certitude of Christ meeting the ignorance of Nicodemus. A plural of personal dignity, veiled in the plural of the new Christian community. The plural, therefore, does not mean simply: (1) Christ and John the Baptist (Knapp, Luthardt); (2) Christ and the prophets (Luther, [Calvin], Tholuck); (3) Christ and God (Chrysostom, and others);* (4) Christ and the Holy Ghost (Bengel); (5) Men (Baumgarten-Crusius); (6) The universal Christian consciousness (Hilgenfeld); (7) Jesus alone (Meyer).† "We speak that which we know," has reference to the consciousness of Christ alone. "Testify that which we have seen," relates to Christ and his associates, the Baptist and the disciples, who recognized in him the glory of the Son of God, [Hengstenberg and Godet include the disciples in both plurals. Godet makes some good remarks here (I. p. 420), and says that the plural gives to the passage a festive rhythmical character in the consciousness of standing no more alone. It reminds one of Matth. xi. 25, where our Lord thanks His Father that He had revealed the mysteries of the kingdom to babes, while they are hid from the wise and prudent.—P. S.] Meyer refers ἑωράκαμεν to Christ's having seen with God in his præ-existence. But here the præ-existence and the life of Christ form a concrete unit.

* [Stier: The three Persons in the Holy Trinity. But ἑωράκαμεν suits neither God the Father nor the Holy Spirit.—P. S.]

† [Lücke, De Wette. So also Alford, but in a proverbial rather than rhetorical sense.—P. S.]

And ye receive not our witness.—The Sanhedrin had not admitted the testimony of John or the manifestation of Christ; Nicodemus himself acknowledged only the prophet in Him, and had objected to the doctrine of regeneration.

Ver. 12. **If I have told you earthly (human) things.**—Ἐπίγεια, in antithesis with ἐπουράνια. According to the context, the Lord evidently means by ἐπίγεια the doctrine of regeneration and its conditions, as He afterwards means by ἐπουράνια the doctrine of the Son of God, the suffering Christ, the redemption of the world. But why these terms? By ἐπίγεια we understand the truths and facts already having place on earth (ἐπίγειον, that which is found on earth),* by ἐπουράνια (ἐπουράνιον, that which is found in heaven),† new heavenly revelations and things. The doctrines of regeneration, of baptism, of the outpouring of the Holy Ghost, were more distinctly expressed in the Old Testament than the doctrine of their cause, the Son of God, *etc.*; they were in some sense already at home in Israel. For though the ἐπουράνια, before God and in idea, form the *prius*, and are the basis of the ἐπίγεια, yet here, as everywhere, the *posterius* comes to view before the *prius* in its whole, essential glory. It should be noticed that further on γῆ and οὐρανός come in the same sort of antithesis. In a theological point of view the ἐπίγεια might be compared with anthropological truths, the ἐπουράνια with the strictly theological, Christological, and soteriological.

Various interpretations.

(1) Luther, Beza, Grotius: The ἐπίγεια, are the preceding figurative expressions; therefore the ἐπουράνια, what they mean.

(2) Lücke: ἐπίγεια, synonymous with τὰ ἐν χερσίν, as in Wisd. ix. 16;‡ tangible things, lying near to men, at hand [easily understood]; those ἐν οὐρανοῖς, unsearchable, remote from men§ (Tholuck: the divine counsels).

(3) De Wette, Baumgarten-Crusius: Moral things, in which the man has a receptive activity, and heavenly things, in which he bears himself with receptive faith.‖

(4) Meyer, somewhat more uncertainly: What Jesus had hitherto presented, among other things the doctrine of regeneration, in distinction from what He would present in future, heavenly mysteries.¶

* [Comp. 1 Cor. xv. 40; 2 Cor. v. 1; Phil. ii. 10; iii. 19; James iii. 15; Sap. ix. 16.—P. S.]

† [Comp. Matth. xviii. 35; 1 Cor. xv. 40, 48; Eph. i. 3; Phil. ii. 10, *etc.*—P. S.]

‡ [A striking parallel: καὶ μόλις εἰκάζομεν τὰ ἐπὶ τῆς γῆς καὶ τὰ ἐν χερσὶν εὑρίσκομεν μετὰ πόνου, τὰ δὲ ἐν οὐρανοῖς τίς ἐξιχνίασε. But in this passage the earthly things belong to the order of nature, while in our passage the Lord distinguishes between earthly things and heavenly things in the sphere of religion and revelation.—P. S.]

§ [So also Reuss, *Hist. de la théol. chrét.*. t. II., p. 427. But ἐπουράνια never has this meaning.—P. S.]

‖ [Similarly Godet: *des choses dont vous pouvier constater en vous-mêmes la realité*, and on the other hand *les secrets du ciel qu'il faudra croire uniquement sur ma parole.*—P. S.]

¶ [Regeneration, says Meyer (5th ed. p. 162), though originating in heaven, takes place on earth and so far belongs to the category of the ἐπίγεια. He includes in this, however, all that Jesus had hitherto told the Jews (εἶπον ὑμῖν), as distinct from the ἐπουράνια, *i. e.*, the Messianic mysteries and *divine* counsels in regard to the redemption of the world. Hengstenberg essentially agrees with Meyer (I. 197). Alford takes the earthly and the heavenly things to mean the same mysteries. but viewed under two aspects, either as occurring on earth and among men, or as having their origin in the divine counsels.—P. S.]

(5) Lampe, more clearly: The earthly things, that which had hitherto been presented, because (*a*) the work of grace is wrought upon earth; (*b*) Israel had been already instructed concerning it under the economy of the law. The heavenly things, the new things which were to be presented concerning the heavenly origin of that work and the nature of the divine decree, *etc.*, as dark things, and for the most part remaining yet unknown.

How will ye believe, *etc.*—Expressing apprehension of finding Nicodemus still more obtuse to what he had yet to say. It should be observed that in both cases Nicodemus is regarded in his connection with the Jews. Just this connection makes it so hard for him to believe. The singular also should be noticed, which here comes in with great strength in contrast, with the previous plural: If I tell you,—introducing what follows.

Ver. 13. **And no man hath ascended.**—Now follows first the doctrine of the Son of God Himself, yet in deep, obscure hints corresponding to the indecision and incredulity of Nicodemus. The *καὶ* here must be noted at the outset. Olshausen makes it adversative (yet), Beza demonstrative (for), Baumgarten-Crusius concessive (indeed), Meyer continuative, that is unmeaning, Lücke corroborative of the preceding. Correctly, "And yet He alone can tell, ἐπουράνια, who is Himself ἐπουράνιος." That is: And yet you must be told heavenly things by Him who, being the heavenly One, is Himself the first subject of this revelation.

Next must be observed the three significant tenses: Perfect, ἀναβέβηκεν, aorist, καταβάς, and present, ὁ ὤν. Evidently, the first proposition is founded on the second, the second on the third; therefore, conversely the third is proved by the second, the second by the first. If now the whole amounts to: *The Son of Man hath ascended into heaven*, the perfect cannot be taken for future, referring to the future *adscensio* (Augustine, Bengel, and others); nor as denoting an ecstatic *raptus in cœlum*, according to the Socinians; nor tropically, for the immediate knowledge of divine things, which Christ as it were brings down from heaven (Beza, Lücke, referring to Prov. xxx. 4); still less does it say, according to Jansen, Meyer, Tholuck, and others: "*Nullus hominum in cœlo fuit, quod adscendendo fieri solet, ut ibi cœlestia contemplaretur, nisi;*" that is: No man hath been in heaven, but He, *etc.* This would reduce the matter to a mere assurance. From the miracles, which Nicodemus himself acknowledged, it should be concluded that Jesus has perfectly ascended to heaven, that is, in virtue of His moral perfection He is a new revelation, and that, the new one, which brings the kingdom of heaven down from heaven. And again from this should be inferred that He came from heaven, that is, has constitutionally a heavenly origin, became man from heaven. From this should further be inferred that He Himself in His incarnation continues one with God, in the presence of God, and thus in heaven. And from this root we pass back again. From the Godhead of Christ, and from the divine consciousness of Christ as the Son of Man, results His incarnation, and from this the new revelation which He, in virtue of His moral perfection, brings from heaven. Then the *οὐρανός* explains itself: "Lampe, in opposition to the doctrine of the *cœlum empyreum* of the Reformed theology: *Generatim cœlum est symbolum rerum omnium supra nos et extra conspectum nostrum in altum evectarum.* Corresponding to this is the Lutheran conception: *non τοπικῶς, sed τροπικῶς sumendum,* of the *status majestatis divinæ* (comp. Flacius, *Clavis*). Yet Quenstedt (III., p. 395) thinks that in the third ἐν οὐρανῷ the *status beatitudinis* is meant. It accords with John's use of language simply to suppose, according to rabbinic usage, a metonymic transfer of *οὐρανός*, the *sedes divina,* to God Himself; so ἐξ οὐρανοῦ ἐρχόμενος, ch. iii. 31; ἐκ τ. οὐρ. δεδόμενον, ch. iii. 27." Tholuck. Yet different elements are to be distinguished in the one conception: (1) The world of heavenly spiritual revelations; (2) the world of heavenly life, origin, centre, and goal; (3) the world of the heavenly glory of God, of the omnipresence. The idea of the *heaven* to which Christ ascends, and which expressly is to be conceived *τοπικῶς*, attaches itself to the second of these elements. Ὁ καταβάς, Hunnius and others: "*Descendit ratione divinæ naturæ, non quidem motu locali, sed humanæ naturæ assumtione, et voluntaria exinanitione.*" The ὁ ὤν was referred by the older theologians to the *omnipræsentia*, or the *status beatitudinis*. Erasmus, the Socinians, Semler, Luthardt quite gratuitously substitute an imperfect: ὃς ἦν. Nor does it denote, according to De Wette and Tholuck, the abiding, real manifestation of God in Christ; for the being of the Son of Man in God is to be distinguished from the being of God in Him.—*The Son of Man.* Intimating that those characteristics belong to the Messiah; that the Son of Man is the Messiah; and the Messiah is the Son of Man; without more particular explanation.*

Ver. 14. **And as Moses in the wilderness.**—The dark expression of the divinity of Christ and His Messiahship is followed by a dark expression of the appointment of the Messiah to suffering, and to exaltation through suffering. The connection (the *καὶ*) is variously taken. Meyer: The transition is "neither from the being able to communicate heavenly things to the being obliged to communicate them (Lücke), nor from the theoretical to the practical (De Wette), nor from word to fact (Olshausen), nor from enlightenment to salvation (Scholl), nor from present lack of faith to the future origin of it (Jacobi), nor from the subjective condition of the kingdom of God, regeneration, to the objective redemption (Tholuck), nor from the work of Christ to His person (Baumgarten-Crusius). Nor, we add, "from the ground for believing to the blessedness of him who believes" (Meyer himself). According to Tholuck, 7th ed., it is the transition to the communication of the ἐπουράνιον; which, however, he too evidently began in ver. 12. It is clearly

* [Alford remarks against the figurative explanation of this passage: "Hebrew metaphors are founded on deep insight into divine truth; these words in fact express the truths on which Hebrew metaphors are constructed." As uniting in Himself God who dwells in heaven, and man who dwells on earth, Christ was always both in heaven and on earth, the golden clasp of both. Augustine: *Ecce hic erat et in cœlo erat: hic erat in carne, in cœlo erat divinitate, natus de matre, non recedens a Patre.* Augustine adds that in some sense all true Christians partake of this double existence. *Tales fecit discipulos suos. Paulum audi apostolum dicentem, nostra autem conversatio in cœlis. Si homo Paulus apostolus ambulabat in carne in terra et conversabatur in cœlo, Deus cœli et terræ poterat esse et in cœlo et in terra.*—P. S.]

the transition from the Son of God to the work of redemption.

The serpent in the wilderness.—Christ attaches His doctrine to the event in Num. xxi. 8: Moses, at the command of God, set up a brazen serpent as a standard of salvation for those who were bitten by the fiery serpents in the camp.* Glossa ord.: "*Magistrum legis ad significationem legis invitat.*" Meyer recognizes only two points of comparison: (1) The lifting up of the brazen serpent, and of Jesus on the cross; (2) the being restored to health by looking on the serpent, and to eternal life, by faith in Christ. He unwarrantably rejects Bengel's further point: *Ut serpens ille fuit serpens sine veneno contra serpentes venenatos, sic Christus homo, homo sine peccato contra serpentem antiquum.* But we should go still farther. As the brazen serpent, the image of the deadly serpent, was changed into an image of the remedy, so Christ, the crucified, made in the likeness of the sinner (so Luther, Bengel, Olshausen, Jacobi, Stier, Lechler), of the deceiver of the people (Matth. xxvii. 63), of the false Christ and Antichrist (Matth. xii. 24; Jno. xviii. 33), a curse (Gal. iii. 13) and image of sin itself (2 Cor. v. 21), as if He were the very manifestation of the murderer of men (Jno. viii. 44), was made with His cross the sign of salvation, by looking upon which in faith men should be saved. The contrasts: Bad appearance, good reality; apparently poisonous, in reality wholesome; apparently overcome, made powerless, in fact victorious; lifted up apparently as a reproach, in fact as an honor. Ethical idea at the bottom of these paradoxes, and the same in both cases: Reconciliation with the image of the evil, and infinite calmness resulting therefrom through the believing look, through the πίστις. The serpent bites Him who is lifted up, who destroys it; sin has power over him who has not reconciled himself to the judgment of God, to the evil, as a remedy against the sin. The believing look upon the brazen serpent healed by calming and elevating the soul. Faith in the Crucified is the faith that Christ in the form of one condemned has transformed the judgment of God into deliverance, and the consequent, willingness to suffer the cross with Him. Wisd. xvi. 6: σύμβολον σωτηρίας.

Of course the ὑψωθῆναι primarily means a being lifted up under suffering and shame, not, as Paulus makes it, a being glorified outright; and it darkly points to the lifting up of malefactors on the post; yet the passages Jno. viii. 28; xii. 32 involve also glorification in the death of the cross. And this is also probably (as Lechler, Tholuck, and others think) included here. Hofmann wavers between the wholly opposite ideas of elevation for exhibition (*Weissagung und Erfüllung*, II. p. 143), and for putting away (*Schriftbeweis*, II. p. 198). Tholuck: "A word must have been used in the Aramaic, which admitted both conceptions; and this is the case with זקף (against Bleek's *Beiträge*, p. 231), which means in the later Chaldaic, as in the Hebrew, to 'set up,' in the Syriac, to 'crucify,' but also to 'lift up,' Targum Jer. iii. 2: וְקִיפִי עֵינָךְ." This secondary sense Bleek and, according to the impression of Hofmann (II., 1, 198), also Luthardt would make in fact the only one, excluding from the passage all reference to the cross, and taking it only as saying that Christ will be, not only as humble, but also as exalted, the object of faith. But both ch. viii. 28, and John's own interpretation, ch. xii. 33, put this out of the question. On the contrary the double sense is plainly suggested by the way in which Christ conceives His death as His essential δοξασμός (ch. xiii. 31, 32); according to the sentence of Hamann, "the cross is the star with the rays taken off." Tholuck's exposition: "The comparison primarily offered is: Ignominious elevation made saving to believers." The *ignominious*, however, does not come first in the image of the serpent, but the appearance of the hostile and destructive.

Even so must.—The preparation of this remedy rests upon the divine counsel (δεῖ, comp. Lu. xxiv. 46). It is evident also from this passage, that Christ was from the beginning conscious of the necessity of His dying for the salvation of mankind, and of dying an ignominious death under the condemnation of men (see ch. ii. 19), and that He from the beginning spoke of it; but at first only in mysterious hints. His unveiled utterances, especially to His disciples, came later. Lücke justly suggests that the *must* (δεῖ) does not say the death of Christ was rendered necessary by that type of the brazen serpent; still the lifting up of the serpent was made a type only because it really was a type, if not in the mind of the bitten Israelite, at least in the mind of the ordaining Spirit. In Moses, too, must have already flashed the presentiment that evil, the consequence of sin, must become the

*[Num. xxi. 8f: "And the Lord said unto Moses, Make thee a fiery serpent (שָׂרָף, Sept. ὄφιν χαλκοῦν, Vulg. *serpentem æneum*, brazen serpent) and set it upon a pole: and it shall come to pass, that every one that is bitten, when he looketh upon it, shall live. And Moses made a serpent of brass, and put it upon a pole, and it came to pass, that if a serpent had bitten any man, when he beheld the serpent of brass, he lived." Here we have two kinds of serpents, 1) the living, poisonous serpent whose bite is deadly—image of sin; 2) the dead, brazen serpent without the poison—a symbol of Christ and His salvation. He was made "in the likeness of sin," yet without sin. (Rom. viii. 3; 2 Cor. v. 21; 1 Pet. ii. 24). This furnishes the first point of comparison: the brazen serpent and Christ. The other two points are the elevation to the pole—to the cross, and the healing effect, which in the O. T. was physical and temporary, in the N. T. is spiritual and permanent. The Hebrew *saraph* is so called, from the red spots on its skin, or from the burning effect of its poison which is like a consuming fire; hence certain serpents were called by the Greeks πρηστῆρες and καύσωνες. Moses took not a living serpent, but a dead image of it, which had the appearance, but not the poison of a serpent, and acted as a healer instead of a destroyer. In Egyptian theology the serpent is the symbol of healing, and in Sap. xvi. 6, it is called σύμβολον σωτηρίας. In the Bible it is primarily the symbol of the devil, of sin and death, from Genesis down to the Apocalypse (xx. 2: τὸν ὄφιν τὸν ἀρχαῖον ὅς ἐστι διάβολος). The physiology of the serpent aids in understanding its agency in the fall. A. F. Krummacher (the father of the celebrated pulpit orator) gives the following unique and suggestive description of this mysterious reptile: "The serpent, a beast like to an embodied thunderbolt that has had its origin in the deepest night, parti-colored, painted like fire, as black and dark as night, its eyes like glowing sparks, its tongue black, yet cloven like a flame, its jaws a chasm of the unknown, its teeth fountains of venom, the sound of its mouth a hiss. Add to this the strange and wonderful motion, ever striving like a flash to quiver, and like an arrow to flee, were it not hindered by its bodily organization. It appears among the beasts like a condemned and fallen angel; in the heathen world of false gods, it hath found and still finds ever awe and adoration; its subtlety has become a byword, its name a naming of Satan, whilst the popular feeling, even now, as in all times past, connects a curse and exorcism with its appearance."—P. S.]

remedy for evil, the serpent's bite be healed by the serpent's image. The οὕτως here has peculiar force: expressing the feeling and contemplation of the infinite contrast between the glory of the Son of Man and His suffering on the cross.

Works: Buxtorf, *Dissertat.*, the treatise: *Historia. serpentis æneі;* Vitringa, *Observat.* I., 2, ch. 11; Rambach, *Geheimniss der ehernen Schlange;* Menken, *Ueber die eherne Schlange*, 1812. In Menken's Works, Bremen, 1858, Vol. VI., p. 353 sqq. [Erskine, on the *Brazen Serpent.*]

The serpent, primarily the type of the devil, is supposed to have been, in the form of the brazen serpent which was attached to the sacred banner of Israel (?), a figure of the sanctification of the human nature of Christ perfected on the cross, and thus the brazen serpent was a symbol of salvation. The fiery serpents in the wilderness, however, were primarily the form of a divine punishment, presented in a form elsewhere denoting sin. The elevated serpent-standard was thus the type of punishment lifted in the phantom of sin, and transformed into a means of salvation. This is the nature of the cross. The look at the cross, is a look at the curse-laden One, who is not a sinner, but a divine token of evil and penalty, and of the suffering of penalty, which is holy and therefore transformed into deliverance. Reconciliation *by the suffering of penalty* becomes in the believing heart reconciliation *with the suffering of penalty*, and so salvation. It may even be said: In the form of the cross, as in the form of the serpent, the distinction between damnable sin, which the sinner did not recognize, and wholesome punishment, healing evil, in which he would see his misfortune, is made perfect and clear; and faith means *purely* distinguishing between bad sin and good penalty or evil. Jacobi, *Stud. und Krit.*, 1835, p. 37; Lechler, *Stud. und Krit.*, 1854, p. 826.

[I add here the note of Alford: "The serpent is in Scripture symbolism, *the devil*,—from the historical temptation in Gen. iii. downwards. But *why* is the devil set forth by the *serpent?* How does the bite of the serpent operate? It *pervades with its poison the frame of its victim:* that frame *becomes poisoned:* and *death ensues.* So sin, *the poison of the devil*, being instilled into our nature, that nature has become σὰρξ ἁμαρτίας, a *poisoned nature*,—*a flesh of sin.* Now the brazen serpent was made *in the likeness of the serpents* which had bitten them. It represented to them the poison which had gone through their frames, and it was hung up there on the banner-staff, as a trophy, to show them that *for the poison, there was healing;*—that the plague had been overcome. In *it*, there was *no poison*, only the *likeness* of it. Now was not the Lord Jesus made ἐν ὁμοιώματι σαρκὸς ἁμαρτίας, Rom. viii. 3? Was not He made 'Sin for us, who knew no sin' (2 Cor. v. 21)? Did not He, on His cross, make an open show of and triumph over the Enemy, so that it was *as if the Enemy himself had been nailed to that cross* (Col. ii. 15)? Were not Sin and Death and Satan crucified, when *He was* crucified? ἐκεῖ μέν ἐπεὶ δι' ὄφεως ἡ βλάβη, δι' ὄφεως καὶ ἡ θεραπεία· ἐνταῦθα δὲ, ἐπεὶ δι' ἀνθρώπου ὁ θάνατος εἰσῆλθεν εἰς τὸν κόσμον, δι' ἀνθρώπου καὶ ἡ ζωὴ παρεγένετο. Euthym.—P. S.]

Ver. 15. **That whosoever believeth in him.**—Application of the figure. The look at the brazen serpent a type of faith. The thing there to be prevented, death; here, perdition. The thing there to be gained, healing; here, salvation, eternal life. Yet the theocratic looking at the brazen serpent was not without an internal element of faith; and so, on its part, the moral salvation has its external side; it is an infinite vital development from within outward. The ζωὴ αἰώνιος, the opposite of θάνατος and ἀπώλεια; beginning with the new life of faith and love, in the spirit; already manifesting itself in this world in the healthful issues of the spirit through the ψυχή and σῶμα as a real, substantial, not merely moral ζωή; completing itself in eternity and in the appearing of Christ as δόξα and ἀνάστασις. Ζωή in the essential sense, as life from God and participation of His life in Christ, in opposition to essential death in sin; αἰώνιος, not simply the eternity of duration and of the world to come, but the eternity of the transcendent presence of all times and places, according as to their divine purport at every point, as against the ἀπώλεια, in which the man is lost not only from God and from himself, but also from time and space, to go down without bottom and without end. The divine life, or the spiritual, embracing the depth and breadth of eternity. The *whosoever* must here already be noted. It marks the accessibleness of the salvation to all, its individual and universal character at once, as well as the moral nature of faith ("whosoever believeth in Him.")

Ver. 16. **For God so loved the world.**—The summing up of the several preceding doctrines in a total picture of the ἐπουράνια, after the analogy of ch. i. 14, and like passages. Christology here goes back to the basis of theology; soteriology unfolds itself to the *ordo salutis* and to eschatology. A gospel *in nuce*, like the sentences of 1 Tim. iii. 16, and others.

Through Erasmus (see Lücke, I. p. 543) the view has become current with later scholars, Kuinoel, Paulus, Tholuck, Olshausen, Maier, and others, that from ver. 16 the Evangelist continues the discussion on his own part. The disappearance of dialogue, the preterites ἠγάπησεν, ἦν, the term μονογενής peculiar to John, and the general character of the discourse, are taken to show this. But this hypothesis has been with good reason contradicted by Meyer [p. 168], Stier, Baumgarten-Crusius, and myself in the *Leben Jesu* ii. p. 508.* John's coloring is in fact admitted elsewhere; why not here? Lücke proposes a middle view. The conversation continues in ver. 16, narrated by John, but with the illustrative, amplifying hand of the narrator more free than before. But Kling has justly objected that this even would lead to an undistinguishable mingling of narration and reflec-

* [Also by Alford, *in loc.*, who well sums up the chief arguments. The Dean justly remarks, that it would give us a very mean idea of the honesty or reverence of the Evangelist to suppose him capable of attributing to his Master words and sentiments of his own invention. Of the two examples which are quoted on the other side, ch. i. 16 is not to the point, for the whole prologue is John's, and iii. 31 ff. is disputed, see notes there. In any case John could get such words and ideas only from his divine Master, and would not have ventured on expressing them without authority from Him.—P. S.]

tion. Against the breaking-off of the dialogue it is enough to remark, that there would be no close; in favor of the continuance of it, that all that follows is very specially appropriate for Nicodemus, and peculiarly the closing words in vers. 20 and 21. The disappearance of the form of the dialogue is expressive, showing that Nicodemus has become a willing hearer. Tholuck in support of his view cites ch. iii. 31, where it is thought still more necessary to assume a continuation by the Evangelist himself. But there, no more than here and in ch. i. 16–18 [?], can an unmarked interruption of the historical narrative be conceded.

Ver. 16 contains not merely a confirmative repetition of ver. 15 (Tholuck), but gathers the statements of ver. 13, 14, and 15 into one. Here each several word has the utmost weight. The **for** (γάρ) bases the two preceding statements, the Christological and the soteriological, upon the love of God. The **so** (οὕτως) is a resonance of the οὕτως in ver. 14. **Loved** (ἠγάπησεν) denotes infinite love as the motive, the purpose, and the act of redemption, or as love, grace, and mercy. **God** (Θεός), the Holy in His entire antagonism to the world, the Merciful in His entire yearning towards the world. **The World** (κόσμος) the world of man, founded on the world of God, now lost in worldliness. Against the Jewish particularism (with Lampe: *Universitas electorum*).* **His only begotten Son** (See note on ch. i. 14). [Here John learned the term μονογενής from Christ Himself.] Expresses the singular proof of love, 1 Jno. iv. 9; Rom. viii. 32; Heb. xi. 17. An allusion to Abraham's offering, Gen. xxii. 2.† At the same time transforming the designation Son of Man into Son of God. **Gave**. Combining the two ideas of the simple διδόναι (ἀπέστειλεν, 1 Jno. iv. 9; see here ver. 13 and 17) and διδόναι ὑπέρ (Lu. xxii. 19) or παραδιδόναι (Rom. viii. 32), which appears in ver. 14 and 15. Meyer properly remarks, ἔδωκεν contained more than ἀπέστειλεν, ver. 17 (which itself, however, in another aspect, contains a specific idea); but when he adds, that it denotes not specially a giving up to death, but the entire state of humiliation, we must observe (1) that the preceding words [ver. 15] refer to death, and (2) that Christ is given to the world not only in His humiliation, but also in His glory to all eternity. **That** (ἵνα) marks the sole object of the sending of Christ; **whosoever believeth** (πᾶς ὁ πιστεύων) expresses at once the universal offer of salvation and the condition of it; **might not perish** (μὴ ἀπόληται), &c., the salvation itself in its negative and positive infinity. The alternation of the aorist [ἀπόληται] and the present [ἔχῃ] not only denotes the being lost and being saved as already beginning in the present, but also expressing, like the aorist: *he gave*, the actual present existence of the Redeemer.

Ver. 17. **For God sent not his Son.**—A contradiction of the Jewish exclusivism was contained in ver. 16. Here it comes out more distinctly. Offsetting the lowly, suffering form of Christ in ver. 15, which is visible also through ver. 16, the kingly side of Christ in His work is here brought forward. Hence we have here *sent* instead of *given;* the *power to judge* is attributed to Him in reference to the *being lost*, and it is His *power to save* which secures for believers eternal life. It is asserted, however, that the *saving* of the world is the object of His mission, not the *judging*. According to the Jewish Christology (Bertholdt, *Christologie*, pp. 203 and 223) the Messiah was to come for judgment against the heathen. Carnal interpretations of Old Testament passages like Ps. ii. 9; Mal. iv. 1; comp. Matt. iii. 10, had led the exclusive Pharisaic spirit to this view. This decidedly bespeaks this verse as a continuation of the conversation with Nicodemus; yet the second τὸν κόσμον is not on this account to be specially referred merely to the *heathen* world (Lücke and Tholuck here are not accurately represented by Meyer). The statement, however, is negative enough in its expression of the Christian universalism over against the Jewish particularism. And not only "has the thrice pronounced κόσμος something solemn about it" (Meyer), but also something doctrinally decisive against that particularism. As regards the fact that Christ is nevertheless also Judge of the world, Tholuck puts this right: A damnatory judgment was to be only an incidental result of His advent, as also in Lu. xii. 51. Meyer distinguishes with more dogmatic clearness between the first advent of Christ to σωτηρία, which was not a coming to judgment, because, if this were to judgment, it would bring condemnation upon all; and the second advent to judgment against those who remain unbelieving, ch. v. 22, 27. Both views are right, but not sufficient. The first coming of Christ also brings a judgment with it (ver. 19), and the second has for its first feature the consummation of the σωτηρία, and the final judgment, as a judgment to condemnation, is only a revelation of the self-condemnation of the unbelieving, which began with their induration in unbelief. The difference between the Old and New Testament types of the Messiah is this: In the Old Testament the Judge becomes Redeemer by His judging (Is. x. 22; lxv. 8, &c.; a σπέρμα is saved); in the New the Redeemer becomes Judge by His redeeming. Acknowledgment of the need of redemption is voluntary self-judgment, repentance; rejection of redemption, unbelief, is the ideal, virtual judgment, which be-

* [To confine κόσμος to the *mundus electorum* (as is done by supralapsarian Calvinists, and the Swiss Formula Consensus), is to destroy the beauty and force of the passage which is to bring out the boundless love of God to all His creatures. God hates nothing that He has made, and Christ died for all, but the benefits of His death are available only to those who accept them by faith. *World* means in the Scriptures and in popular language 1) the whole universe; 2) the earth; 3) all men (so here); 4) the present order of things as distinct from the future world; 5) the ungodly world, in opposition to the kingdom of God, and as subject to Satan, who is called "the prince of this world" (John xii. 31). But it never means *the elect* or *the saints*, which would be just the reverse of the last mentioned signification. If it had this meaning here, Christ might have said: "God so loved the *world* . . . that the *world* (instead of *whosoever believeth*) might not perish." The universality of God's love and the all-sufficiency of Christ's atonement (which, however, must not be confounded with its actual *efficiency*) is most clearly taught here and in such passages as 1 Tim. ii. 4; 2 Pet. iii. 9; 1 John ii. 2 (which illustrates our passage): "He is the propitiation for our sins: and *not* for ours *only*, but *also* for the sins of the whole *world*."—P. S.]

† [So also Stier, Hengstenberg, and Alford. Nicodemus, in being reminded of Isaac's offering, was reminded of the love required, the substitution made, and the prophecy there uttered to Abraham, to which ἵνα πᾶς ὁ πιστεύων nearly corresponds. Comp. Heb. xi. 19; Gen. xxii. 16.—P. S.]

gins at once upon the manifestation of Christ [ch. xii. 48]; the establishing of the fact that the man has entirely alienated himself from the Redeemer and the redeemed, and cannot in any way have part in the final redemption, is the last judgment.

Ver. 18. **He that believeth on Him is not judged.**—New Testament transfiguration of the Old Testament doctrine of salvation by faith, Gen. xv.; Is. xxviii. 16; Hab. ii. 4. Manifestly these words again are perfectly fitted and designed to shake the Jewish views of Nicodemus. Pharisaic Judaism had perverted the principle: The believer is not judged, the unbeliever is judged,—into the principle: The Jew is not judged, he who is not a Jew is judged. So the Roman Catholic dogma: He who is within the pale of the Catholic faith, is saved; he who is not, is damned. Likewise the old Protestant formula: He who comes *in this life* into the sphere of the faith of the gospel, &c. Christ, on the contrary, makes salvation dependent on an individual, personal, living faith, and perdition on decided, obstinate personal unbelief. The believer is not judged because he as a sinner puts himself voluntarily under a spiritual judgment, and thereby receives the righteousness of faith for the perfecting of his life in the sphere of salvation.

The guilt of the unbeliever is strongly emphasized as a treble guilt: He has not accepted God in His Son. He has not received the Only Begotten, in whom all the value of faith, the fulness of the manifestation of God, is concentrated. Finally he has not believed in his name, *i. e.* in the developed knowledge of Christ as concentrated in the sphere of His Spirit. He *hath* not believed (perfect), *i. e.* he is fixed in unbelief, and in so much as he is fixed, the fact also is fixed that he has fallen under condemnation to meet the final judgment by the sheer unfoldings of his condemnation. The antithesis is put here with all its sharpness; but not as passing upon the given unbeliever the opinion that he is fixed in his unbelief. The ideal unbeliever is condemned *quia*, the actual unbeliever *quatenus*. Tholuck: "But ὅτι gives not the external ground on which the judgment rests (Chrysostom)—for neglect of the Son of God—but the way in which the condemnation is wrought." Yet it also gives the decisive ground; only the Son of God, in the case, is not to be conceived as external.

Ver. 19. **And this is the judgment.**—The tale now, *by its form, its choice of terms*, turns directly towards Nicodemus, to press him to a decision and bring him to the light. At the same time, as to its matter, it proceeds to the explanation of the immoral, damnable nature of unbelief, and to the intimation that the rulers of the Jews are already further gone in this unbelief than Nicodemus suspects. Thus they are already judged. The actual beginning of the virtual judgment of the world, which from Jerusalem is spreading through the world, working outward from within, runs parallel with the unfolding of faith, till the consummation in the day of glory.

That light is come into the world.—This belongs to the judgment, because it calls for the separation, κρίσις.

And men loved.—Particular signs of this, therefore, have already come to view [see above]. While Nicodemus can still fancy that the Sanhedrin is with him inclined to faith, Christ already sees the beginning of the end. Indeed the δεῖ in ver. 15 is connected with this. The aorist, therefore, does not imply that a later period is in mind.

The darkness rather.—Is the μᾶλλον *magis* or *potius?* Bengel, Tholuck ("because the φῶς, ch. i. 4, which man originally possessed, prevents him from entirely mistaking the ἀλήθεια in the light") say the former; Origen, Meyer, the latter: and no doubt rightly, because the Lord is speaking of the time of decision, at which the lesser love of the light passes into hatred of it, ver. 20. Before the critical manifestation of the light, it might mean *magis;* now it means *potius.* It is the decided choice of the evil, that is in view.—**Because their deeds.**—Αὐτῶν placed first is significant. Far more than: They had sin. Their whole bent was to do evil, hence they needed the cover of darkness for their evil deeds. See Matt. xxiii.

Ver. 20. **For every one that doeth evil.** Looking to those who persist in unbelief. Γάρ comes not to justify the preceding γάρ (Meyer), but to explain it and define the expression for the evil choice: ἠγάπησεν μᾶλλον. The doing evil (φαῦλα) denotes the law of the nature. The adjective denotes not only bad, cowardly, hateful, but also trifling, insignificant; and in antithesis to ver. 21 probably corrupt, false.—**Hateth the light.**—Comp. Rom. viii. 7. Unbelief is the root of impious conduct.—**Lest his deeds.**—The evil consciousness and intention of unbelief.—**Should be reproved.**—The ἔλεγχος, the exposure, the conviction, the condemnation of the deeds, shunned by him who, through pride and cowardice will not submit to the condemnation of shame, accept the judgment of the penitent spirit, nor renounce his false deeds. Thus he chooses the darkness, *i. e.* the dominion of delusion, falsehood, with sense of the falsehood. Luke iii. 7; John viii. 9; Eph. v. 11, 13.

Ver. 21. **But he that doeth the truth.**—A most suitable parting word for Nicodemus. If thou art and continuest to be honest, thou wilt yet come to the light. Thus a conditional promise. This, however, is the specific reference of the expression; the general truth is: The Lord gives good speed to the upright, Prov. ii. 7. *Doeth* THE *truth.*—Meyer: That which is really moral; Tholuck; Acting in the whole spirit of his life according to objective truth. The doing of the objective truth, however, is expressed by the coming to the light. Hence the references to subjective truth. He who inwardly loves sincerity shuns deceit, is faithful against himself, and acts in this spirit (is true to the inner light), has a leaning towards the light of revelation, towards faith; he feels himself attracted by the light as the false man feels himself repelled.—**That his deeds may be made manifest.**—Not that he would parade them, but that he would be made certain of his actions and his spirit in the full light of moral day. "The need of moral satisfaction in itself, and of the victory of the good over the world"

(Meyer).—**For they are wrought in God.**—This is the ground of his moral courage and striving after truth. So far as he has acted in sincere regard for the inner light, he has done his work in God. In other words, the drawing of the Father to the Son (ch. vi. 44, 45), the work of the *gratia præveniens*, is in it. The *for* does not mean at all, he is conscious that his deeds are wrought in God, but this direction of his doing is the unconscious ground of his courage. According to his best knowledge and conscience he has acted with inward trembling before the divine, therefore he cannot tremble before the objective light of God in the world. Calvin (with others) takes ver. 21 as set against ver. 20 only to show what the truth-loving man on the contrary would do (the ideal conception of the truth-loving man). In answer to this Tholuck: Then either all men would fall into the first class and no one would come to Christ, or the regenerate man must be intended. The Greek, Roman Catholic, and Arminian exegesis holds, according to Tholuck's concurring statement: The good conscience, which may present its strivings, weak as they are, before Christ, whatever of darkness is still about them, however, thereby receiving its κρίσις. Tholuck refers to John viii. 47; xviii. 37; vi. 44, 45; to a Synesius, to the rich young man, to the scribe, Mark xii. 34. Over against this he places another interpretation: The Protestant exegesis and Augustine found this sense contrary to the *analogia scripturæ*, according to which a *bonum spirituale* before regeneration is impossible. According to Augustine, Luther, Olshausen, Stier, the ποιεῖν τὴν ἀλ. therefore must mean: "to be upright, sincere." We cannot consider this interpretation clearly distinct from the other. It is plain that the doing of the truth here still cannot mean the doing of revealed truth. Such truth might be spoken of in the case of the Jews before Christ; hardly in the case of the Gentiles before Christ. And even though it be, the doing will be in both cases the doing of objective truth as it shines upon the consciousness. And to endeavor earnestly to conform to this truth would be, *to be upright, to act according to the best of one's knowledge and conscience.* The works which proceed from this are works done in God, *i. e.*, relatively good works, striving towards their perfection in God; comp. Rom. ii. 7. Thus the uprightness is not to be conceived without the fruit of such deeds, nor indeed the doing without the root of uprightness. *They are wrought in God.* The upright man works unconsciously under the influence of the *gratia præveniens*, or the Logos, and thus his works, having their starting point in God, will continually reach out towards their full manifestation in the light.

In these words Jesus seemed to say to Nicodemus: Thou art now come to Me in the night; thou wilt yet come to Me in the light; farewell, to meet again in the light.

DOCTRINAL AND ETHICAL.

[Comp. my introductory remarks, p. 122 f.—P. S.]

1. *The interview of Christ with Nicodemus by night.* Even a secret disciple Christ admits, if he be sincere, and therefore be tending towards openness. Proof in the history of Christianity: *Disciplina arcani*, Hugenots, *etc.* The contrast between a pure secrecy which works towards openness, and an openness which conceals itself in evil secrets. Regeneration itself, the subject of this nocturnal conversation, is a deep secret, which presses towards the most open manifestation in a consistent life and at the day of Christ.

2. *The unwavering certainty of Christ* towards Nicodemus is reflected in the posture of pure Christianity towards human hierarchy, tradition, rank, and policy. Nicodemus is better than his theology; in theology he is the type of a rationalizing supernaturalism; in character he is an inquiring child involved in the prejudices of old age.

3. Christianity is not merely a purer, newer life, but *life absolutely pure and new.* [Still less is Christianity mere *doctrine*, although doctrine is included in life. Luther explains ver. 3: "My teaching is not of doing and leaving undone, but of a radical change in the man, so that it is not new works done, but a new man to do them; not another life only, but another birth." Alford: "Our Lord replies, It is not learning, but life, that is wanted for the Messiah's kingdom; and life must begin by birth."—P. S.]

4. *Regeneration* is the fundamental *condition* of seeing and entering the kingdom of God.

5. Regeneration, a *birth from above.* See the exegesis, ver. 3. (1) The counterpart of the carnal birth (see Rom. v. 12 sqq.); (2) the glorification of pure natural birth as it would have been in paradise; (3) the fulfilment of the typical Old Testament regeneration, represented by circumcision; (4) the groundwork of the future great regeneration in the resurrection and *the* regeneration, the *palingenesia*, Matt. xix. 28.

6. The *media* or *elements* of *regeneration:* (1) The historical and symbolical: washing with water; (2) the active and real: the Spirit.—Of water and Spirit the first creation (Gen. i.); of water and Spirit the second and higher. [But in the first creation, the Spirit brooding over the waters; in the new, the water signifying and sealing the Spirit. In the old, the Spirit applying the water, moulding it to its purposes; in the new and higher, the water applying the Spirit.—E. D. Y.]

7. *Christian baptism:* (1) The glorification of water; (2) the fulfilment of the symbolical washings, the baptism of John, and the baptism of the disciples of Jesus: (3) the goal of the historical types, the flood and the passage of the Red Sea; (4) the fellowship of the baptism of Jesus with water in the Jordan; (5) the fellowship, the symbol and sacrament of the baptism of Jesus with blood (Rom. vi. 6); (6) a separation through Him and with Him out of the old world and from it.

8. The *Spirit* which accompanies baptism: (1) The glorification of the vital air, the blowing wind, the storm at night (as also of fire, Acts ii.; see Ps. civ. 4; Ezek. i. 4; xxxvii. 9; Dan. vii. 2; Hag. ii. 6); (2) the fulfilment of the symbolical and typical Spirit—breathings: inspirations, trances, visions, single words and works of the Spirit.

9. *Water and Spirit* inseparable in the groundwork of the kingdom of God. The word and the sacrament, accompanied by the quickening Spirit.

10. The birth of the new life a deep *mystery* and the most open *manifestation*, 1 Tim. iii. 16.

11. The *necessity* of being born again of water and the Spirit, and its *apparent impossibility*, v. 1–8. The *possibility*, the conditions and basis of it, v. 9–16. The basis of the regeneration to be realized on earth lies in the heavenly origin of Christ: His eternal, divine generation, and His heavenly, divine-human birth. This birth is consummated, as to its historical process, in His elevation on the Cross and His death upon the throne of glory, by His atoning death and His victory. And the basis and unity of both lies in the love of God and His giving of His Son for the redemption of the world.

12. The *earth*, in Scripture, the symbol of the theocracy, of divine institution and administration upon earth, of the historical tradition of salvation, Ps. xciii. 1; civ. 5; Rev. xiii. 11. As distinguished on the one hand from *the sea*, emblem of the swelling, formlessly moving life of the nations, Ps. xciii. 3; Dan. vii. 3; Rev. xiii. 1. On the other hand from *the heavens*, emblem of the future kingdom of heaven, the completed revelation of God, Is. lxiv. 1; Matth. iii. 16.

13. Christ *descending* and *ascending* between heaven and earth, because He *is* in heaven. On His eternal, divine-human constitution and office rest (*a*) His descending, His incarnation and humiliation, (*b*) His ascending and exaltation.

14. The *brazen serpent* the most obscure and the most pregnant mystery of the Old Testament typical system. See the exegesis, v. 14. Its connection with the symbolical use of the serpent in general in the Scriptures.

15. The condition of the appropriation of salvation, faith, and the consequent twofold operation of salvation: redemption and condemnation. Deciding for Christ by faith, secures redemption; deciding against Him by unbelief, begins condemnation (see 1 Cor. i. 18; 2 Cor. ii. 16; comp. Deut. xxx. 15).

16. The condition of susceptibility to faith: Sincerity, subjective truth, *i. e.*, obedience to the *gratia præveniens*. Inward falsehood the source of unbelief, a poison which perverts the form of faith itself into hypocrisy.

17. Yet sincerity or uprightness (Prov. ii. 7; Eccl. vii. 29; John i. 47) not to be confounded with proud bluntness or downrightness, which may very easily strike over into self-deceit and falsehood. Uprightness moreover, even in company with diffidence, and notwithstanding its timidity, in constant submission to the guidance of God, or through the obedience of truth, issues in the gladness of confession and the light. (Moses, Jeremiah, Calvin,* like Nicodemus, originally timid characters, but faithfully sincere.)

18. The Pharisee Nicodemus a fore-runner of the Pharisee Paul. [Both alike sincere, but very unlike in energy and decision.—P. S.]

19. *The Pericope for Trinity.** See Strauss [late court-preacher of the King of Prussia and Prof. at Berlin]: *Das evang. Kirchenjahr*, p. 279. Braune: This account is the gospel for Trinity. The feast arose upon this doctrine, not upon an eternal divine fact (—yet the triune God reveals Himself here through His act as triune God in the triune operation of the new birth—). The church feared that the people might be led by the Christmas festival in honor of the All-Merciful, the Easter festival in honor of the Conqueror of the power of darkness, and Pentecost in honor of the All-Sanctifying Spirit, to worship three Gods in the Father, the Son, and the Holy Ghost. (It no doubt had also a more joyful motive). Strauss distinguishes four periods of the Trinity festival. First period: The day of the feast not yet distinctly prominent. Second period: The trichotomy of the church year makes the feast the octave and appendix of Pentecost ("little Pentecost"). At first *Festum omnium sanctorum.* This festival Gregory III. or IV. transferred to the 1st November; the Sunday after Pentecost at first became again the Pentecostal octave, while in the East it continued to be All Saints' day. Third period: Formerly a Trinity festival had been celebrated on the last Sunday of the year; now this is transferred to the octave of Pentecost. Gradual development in the thirteenth and fourteenth centuries, in which the feast of Trinity becomes the prelude to *Corpus Christi.*† Fourth period: Protestant settlement of it as neither a prelude nor a close, but a festival for the opening of the second part of the church year, the Trinity season. On the changes of the pericopes, see Strauss, p. 282.

HOMILETICAL AND PRACTICAL.

See hints already given under the two former heads. What is true of every section of the Bible, is true in a peculiar degree of this: It is homiletically inexhaustible. Many a single verse forms a theme of itself; vers. 3, 5, 6, 16, *etc.*—If we would treat it in larger sections, we must first embrace the whole.

The sacred discourse of the Lord with Nicodemus by night concerning the sacred mysteries of God's night: (1) Concerning the divine night of regeneration in the soul; (2) by means of the divine night in the operation of means of grace; (3) on the basis of the divine night (*Weihnacht*, "holy night," as Christmas is called in the German) of the incarnation of Christ; (4) decided

* [Calvin says of himself (*Præf. ad Psalm.*): "*Ego qui natura timido, molli et pusillo animo me esse fateor,*" and he fairly trembled when Farel, as by divine authority, detained him in Geneva as his proper field of labor.—P. S.]

* [Trinity Sunday is the first Sunday after Pentecost or Whitsunday. It commemorates the mystery of the Holy Trinity, and closes the festival part of the Christian year. It is of Latin origin and cannot be clearly traced beyond the tenth century. The Greek church (from the times of Chrysostom) celebrates on the same Sunday the feast of all Saints and Martyrs (which in the Latin church falls on the first of November). The Lutheran and Episcopal churches have together with the other great festivals retained Trinity Sunday. The discourse with Nicodemus is the gospel for the day, because regeneration is the work of the Holy Spirit and the basis of Christian life.—P. S.]

† [The feast of transubstantiation, which, of course, is rejected by all Protestant churches. It is celebrated in the Roman church with unusually solemn processions on the first Thursday following Trinity Sunday (*feria quinta proxima post octavam pentecostes*), with reference to Maunday Thursday, as the day of the institution of the Eucharist. In German it is called *Fronleichnamsfest, i. e.*, the feast of the Lord's body.—P. S.]

by the divine night of the death and glorification of Christ; (5) all proceeding from the divine night of the purpose and love of God for the redemption of the world; and (6) unfolding its complete operation in the decision between the divine morning of eternal salvation, and the night of judgment.—The conversation of Christ with Nicodemus concerning the being born from above: (1) Concerning the necessity of it (in order to see the kingdom of God), vers. 1-4; (2) concerning the effecting of it (through water and the Spirit), vers. 5-8; (3) concerning the conditions precedent for the possibility of it; (*a*) objectively: the incarnation of the Son of God, His passion; both resting on the purpose of divine love; (*b*) subjectively: faith in the love of God in giving Christ; (4) concerning its decisive operation; (*a*) saving, negatively: deliverance from corruption, death, perdition; positively: the gift and possession of eternal life; (*b*) condemning: manifestation of the self-judgment and self-condemnation of unbelief.—Awaking to a Christian life of faith, a birth: (1) A regeneration, or second birth, as distinct from the first; (2) a birth from above, as the perfect, real birth for the eternal kingdom of God.—How Christian earthly things, the personal experiences of the Christian, are rooted in Christian heavenly things, the mysteries of God.—Water and wind, the fundamental elements of the first creation, emblems of the second.—Christianity the most hidden life, and at the same time the most manifest.—The conversion of Nicodemus, or Christ the Saviour even of the great of this world.—And the Saviour of an honest Pharisee.—The being born *from* heaven alone leads *to* heaven.—Twice, the number of life: (1) Twice to be born; (2) twice to die; (3) twice to live.—A ruler of the Jews and the King of the Jews, or the hierarch and the Lord.—The heavenly birth and the heavenly eye.—Water and the Spirit.—Wind and the Spirit.—The voice of the wind and the course of the wind.—The newly born: A breath of the Spirit, manifested by its sound.—The knowledge of Nicodemus and the knowledge of Christ.—The threefold relation of Christ to heaven: (1) The *inner* heaven; (2) the *upper* heaven; (3) the *open* heaven.—The serpent emblem, and the emblem of the Crucified.—The elevation in supreme judgment.—God *so* loved, *etc.*, (ver. 1) the infinite scale of the love of God.—Condemnation, despised salvation.—Unbelief, the second and irremediable fall.—Unbelief, sin in its desperate form, as the root, the sum, and the denial of sin. Unbelief once decided, judgment begins.—The false man and the sincere.—The shunning and the seeking of light. The works of the upright strive as shoots of light towards the light of day.

The Pericope for Trinity, vers. 1-15. The Father, the Son, and the Holy Ghost active and manifest in the work of regeneration.—The experience of the Christian an experience of the Holy Trinity; (1) Of the Spirit, in the virtue of the word and sacrament; (2) of the Son, in the virtue of the death and resurrection of Christ; (3) of the Father, in the virtue of manifested, world-embracing love.

The Pericope for 2. *Pentecost*, v. 16-21. The love of God for the world, the motive to the divine consummation of the world: (1) In the redeeming gift of the Son; (2) in the testing operation of the Spirit.—The redeeming motion of the love of God in its all-embracing majesty: (1) Comprehended in the gift of the Son, and therefore embracing the world (Jews, heathen, *etc.*); (2) directed to each lost individual, and to all, as a power of salvation; (3) embracing depth and height (death and life) to raise sinners from perdition to the eternal life of heaven; (4) a redeeming operation so decisive that, embracing heaven and hell, it is manifest both in the condemned and in the saved (in the one as love despised, in the other as love believed); (5) embracing beginning and end, manifest in a process of grace having its root in the election of grace passed upon all the children of truth (*gratia præveniens*), and its top shining in the light of eternal glory.—Christianity not in any wise a condemnation: (1) Neither in its source (the love of God), (2) nor in its design (the sending of Christ); (3) nor in its operation (the believer *is not* judged, the unbeliever *has* judged *himself*).—The *gift* of the Son a precursor of the *outpouring* of the Spirit.—The mysteries of darkness and the mysteries of light in the world, as all brought into day by the light of Christ.

STARKE: Examples of notable converts are worth recording, that the goodness of God may be magnified, and others may be encouraged. Those who sit in the highest ranks and the most honorable offices, should think more of their human misery than of their elevation and dignity in the world.—A man, though living in the most hardened condition (Pharisæism), may nevertheless be converted.—Rank, office, and fear often stand in the way of conversion; but happy they who value more the salvation of their souls, and overcome those hindrances.—MAJUS: Not all nocturnal meetings for edification are suspicious and to be forbidden.—Fear a great hindrance to goodness.—OSIANDER: The weak in faith must not be despised.—LANGE: The ground of the necessity of regeneration lies in the nature of God and of man.—The doctrine of regeneration must be diligently pressed, 1 Cor. ii. 14.—The scruples of scholars.—Tit. iii. 5.—1 Peter iii. 21.—The patience of Christ with the weakness of man, and His friendly care to remove all doubts and scruples, are a model for us, 1 John iii. 9; 2 Peter i. 4; Rom. viii. 5.—ZEISIUS: All that proceeds not from spiritual regeneration, be it never so pure and brilliant in its glitter, is nothing towards salvation, and cannot please God.—The nobility of the regenerate: raised to the highest ranks of heaven, Col. iii. 9, 10.—MAJUS: The senseless astonishment of unbelief is good for nothing, but before the sublimity of the divine mysteries one loves in reverence to wonder.—*The same:* The grace of the Holy Ghost is free, not bound either to means, persons, or times.—CANSTEIN: As often as we hear the wind, we ought to think of the mystery of regeneration, Job xxxvii. 9.—*Art thou a master, etc.* The true heart-theology is not always to be found among people of great titles and places.—*God so loved* (v. 16). So overflowingly and so intensely, and after this manner and in this order. The love of God the first and true source of all our blessedness.—Believers must, it is true, stand before the judgment, but they come not into judgment. —*Bibl. Wirt.*: Faith alone is the means of salvation; therefore unbelief is the sole cause of damnation.—The blame lies with men, Hos. xiii. 9.—HEDINGER, on the words: Every one that doeth evil: Wickedness shuns the light, yet it must come to the light.—ZEISIUS: Could the stones and beams of many a palace and dwelling speak, what abominations, wrought in secret, should we not hear! Yet that great day of judgment will make manifest every hidden thing, as truly as God is God.—OSIANDER: Many would rather in eternity be put to shame before God, angels, and the elect, than blush a moment before a few people in the world.

GERLACH: A chief point of corruption in the doctrine of the Pharisees of that day was their entirely outward conception of the law, and their consequent utter mistaking of the relation of man to God. The deep, sinful corruption of human nature and the necessity of a regeneration were to all purpose utterly hidden from them. If, therefore, they would partake of the salvation which Christ brings, they must clearly perceive the need of it.—At all events Nicodemus hoped to find out whether the kingdom of God was soon to appear; that he, in that case, was to have a share in that kingdom, he had no doubt.—Jesus shows him that the kingdom of God, which he was expecting as future and external to himself, was already inwardly present; but not yet for him, because this required an entire transformation and renewal of the mind. —The baptism with water was an emblem of repentance under the law, grief for sin; the baptism with the Spirit denotes the operation of the renewing, inwardly transforming power of the grace and truth of God in Christ Jesus. To the water baptism of John (which Jesus continued by His disciples), he therefore says, must be added the Spirit-baptism of the Messiah, which was promised by John himself.—Every force produces its like. If a man should even be bodily born a second time by an external miracle, he would remain the same.—The Spirit, the eternal, almighty, all-creating and all-renewing divine life which is in God and is God Himself, by partaking of which man, against and above nature, is renewed to holiness and to victory over the world and death.—Christ was begotten of the Holy Ghost, and those who believe in Him are children of God by the same Spirit. —The beginning of good works is the confession of evil works.

LISCO: Regeneration is necessary in part on account of the constitution of the spiritual kingdom to which the man is to belong, in part on account of the natural state in which the human heart is found, which is flesh (Luther's Marginal Note).—The two parts: Word and Spirit, belong together, as in wind the two things: sound and blowing.—Faith and unbelief as the inner ground of the opposite fates of men.—BRAUNE: Nicodemus came to Jesus by night. If not through cowardice, at least through delicate self-love and regard for his associates in rank and office. Yet he came, and had much to overcome: riches of earthly goods, riches of reputation and power, riches even of virtue and righteousness.—Gideon's act in the night, Jud. vi. 27.—2 Cor. v. 17. —Every soul has its determination either to rise to glorification in the clear light of the divine Spirit, or to sink into the perdition of the curse, and God would that every soul should be born again not of corruptible seed, but of incorruptible, by the word of God, which liveth and abideth forever, 1 Peter i. 23.—RIEGER: Christ leaves Nicodemus time to take root and bear fruit.

HEUBNER; *Noctes Christianæ* more than *Noctes Atticæ*.—The danger of worldly honor. He who stands high in the world, must be at unspeakable pains to become small and humble.—The miracles a legitimate ground of belief in the divine mission of Jesus.—Nicodemus here stood in the fore-court of conversion.—A man is always only one thing, ruled either by the flesh, or by the Spirit (there is, however, a stage of transition, Rom. vii). Nothing more astonishes and offends an unconverted man, than to say to him: Thou must be radically changed. The doctrine of the Father, the Son, and the Spirit, as the sum of Christianity: (1) God the Father, full of severity and love, has founded a kingdom for which man is destined; (2) for this fallen man needed regeneration by the Spirit; (3) this he now receives through Christ, by faith in Him.—Love of sin prepossesses against truth.—Here is to be found the Christian conception of those who are really *obscurantists*.—Often the opinion steals in, that the inward alone (that is, what is kept back, shut up,) makes the Christian. When Victorinus (so Augustine relates), deeply moved by reading the Holy Scriptures, said confidently to Simplicianus in Rome: "Know that I am already a Christian," and Simplicianus answered: "I will not believe it, nor count thee among the Christians, till I see thee in the church of Christ." Victorinus laughed and said: "Do the walls then make a Christian?" But afterwards, fearing Christ might not confess him, unless he confessed Christ, he suddenly came to Simplicianus and said: "*Eamus ad ecclesiam, Christianus volo fieri*" (August. *Conf.*, ch. 2, § 3, 4). Swift held his family worship with his servants in perfect secresy, merely to avoid suspicion of hypocrisy (see his *Life of Sheridan*). Learn to rise above the judgment of the world; be not ashamed of your better principles.

SCHLEIERMACHER: In every one the beginning of the divine working can no more be determined, than the end of it can be descried.—Even those whom we may compare to the master of Israel, have continued but too long in that which could be the property and benefit of only a particular age or a small part of the Christian Church; and they had not been able to rise above this narrow horizon, and view the work of grace in its whole grand compass; and just by reason of this, they have led believers astray. —Vers. 16–18: The great object of Christ's mission. He appeared among us as a (the) token (token and seal) of the love of God, the object of faith, the universal possession of all men.—BESSER, on the brazen serpent: Jesus the life of my life, Jesus the death of my death.—NITZSCH: The mystery of our spiritual regeneration: (1) The necessity of it; (2) the possibility of it; (3) the actuality of it.—HOSBACH: The new birth: (1) What is it? (2) How does it arise? (3) Whither does it lead?—O. V. GER-

LACH: The glorification of the triune God in the regeneration of man.—KLING: The being born of the Spirit, on the one hand manifest, on the other hidden as to its origin and end.

[BURKITT: 'Tis not enough that we be new-dressed, but we must be new-made, that is, thoroughly and universally changed, the will by renovation, the affections by sanctification, the life by reformation. We must be like God, or we can never live with Him. If we be not like Him in the temper of our minds on earth, we can never be happy in the enjoyment of Him in heaven; for heaven, which is a place of the greatest holiness, would be a place of the greatest uneasiness to an unregenerate and an unholy person; the contagion is universal, deep, and inward, therefore such must the change be. —The way and work of the Holy Spirit in the soul's regeneration, is oft-times very secret, and usually exceeding various. Various as to the *time*. Some are wrought upon in youth, others in old age. Various in His *methods* of working: Some are wrought upon by the corrosives of the law, others by lenitives of the gospel. Various in the *manner* of His working, and in the *means* by which He works: Upon some by a powerful ordinance, upon others by an awakening Providence. But the Spirit's work in all still the same, it produces likeness to God.—RYLE: What a feeble beginning a man may make in religion, and yet finally prove a strong Christian. Never despise the day of small things (Zech. iv. 10).—What a mighty change our Lord declares to be needful to salvation, and what a remarkable expression He uses in describing it.—A day will come when those who are not born again will wish that they had never been born at all.—AUGUSTINE (on ver. 15): The bite of the Serpent brought death; the death of Christ brings life. Look at the Serpent, that the Serpent may not harm you. Look at death that death may not hurt you. But at whose death? At the death of Him who is the Life. Death died in Christ, so that we may now say: "O death, where is thy sting," *etc.*—LUTHER: Henceforward, he who is condemned must not complain of Adam, and his inborn sin. The seed of the woman, promised by God to bruise the head of the serpent, is now come and has atoned for sin and taken away condemnation. But he must cry out against himself for not having accepted and believed in the Christ, the devil's head-bruiser and sin-strangler. If I do not believe the same, sin and condemnation must continue.—LAVATER (ver. 16): Jesus means one who creates joy and happiness. He who views Jesus otherwise than as a bringer of joy, the gospel as anything else but a message of joy, suffering as anything but a fountain of joy, knows neither God nor Christ nor the gospel. God is love, and love can only love. God is the living will of love. Love is pure joy and makes happy all who come in contact with it.—P. S.]

VI.

JESUS IN THE JUDEAN COUNTRY, AND THE SPREAD OF HIS BAPTISM, WITH THE FAITH OF THE PEOPLE. LAST TESTIMONY OF JOHN THE BAPTIST CONCERNING CHRIST. CHRIST THE TRUE BAPTIST. THE BRIDEGROOM OF THE CHURCH, WHO COMES FROM HEAVEN. (*The Real Song of Songs.*)

CHAP. III. 22–36.

22 After these things came Jesus and his disciples [came] into the land of Judea;
23 and there he tarried with them, and baptized. And John also was [still] baptizing
in Ænon near to [*omit* to] Salim, because there was much water there: and they
24, 25 came and were baptized. For John[1] was not yet cast into prison. Then there
arose a question between *some* of [on the part of] John's disciples and the Jews
26 [a Jew][2] about purifying [religious washing]. And they came unto John, and said
unto him, Rabbi, he that was with thee beyond [the] Jordan, to whom thou barest
[hast borne] witness [didst serve as a witness], behold the same baptizeth, and all
men come [are going] to him.
27 John answered and said, A man can receive nothing, except [unless] it be given
28 him from heaven. Ye yourselves bear me witness, that I said, I am not the Christ,
29 but that I am sent before him. He that hath the bride is the bridegroom: but the
friend of the bridegroom, which [who] standeth and heareth him rejoiceth greatly
[lit., rejoiceth with joy, χαρᾷ χαίρει] because of the bridegroom's voice: [.] this my
30 joy therefore is fulfilled [is made full, complete]. He must increase, but I must de-
31 crease. He that cometh from above is above all: he that is of the earth is earthly
[is of the earth],[3] and speaketh of the earth: he that cometh from heaven is above
32 all.[4] And [*omit* And][5] what he hath seen and heard, that he testifieth; and no
33 man receiveth his testimony [and his testimony no one receiveth]. He that
hath received his [his emphatic, αὐτοῦ τὴν μ.] testimony hath set to [*omit* to] his
34 seal that God is true. For he whom God hath [*omit* hath] sent speaketh the
words of God: for God [he][6] giveth not the Spirit by measure *unto him* [*omit unto*

35 *him*].[7] The Father loveth the Son, and hath given all things into his hand.
36 He that believeth on [in] the Son hath everlasting life: and he that believeth not
[disobeyeth, ὁ δὲ ἀπειθῶν] the Son shall not see life; but the wrath of God abideth
on him.

TEXTUAL AND GRAMMATICAL.

1 Ver. 23. [The art. ὁ before Ἰωάννης is wanting in ℵ. B. and omitted by Tischend., bracketed by Alf.—P. S.]

2 Ver. 25. [ἐγένετο οὖν ζήτησις ἐκ τῶν μαθητῶν Ἰωάννου μετὰ Ἰουδαίου. The singular is strongly sustained by ℵ.c A. B. L., *etc.*, and adopted by Tischend., Treg., Alf., W. and H., against the text. rec. Ἰουδαίων which is supported by ℵ.* G., *etc.* Meyer: *Der Plural bot sich mechanisch dar, viz.*, to conform to μαθητῶν.—P. S.]

3 Ver. 31. [ὁ ὢν ἐκ τῆς γῆς ἐκ τῆς γῆς ἐστίν, is apparently tautological, but the difference lies in the emphasis: to the origin of a man corresponds his character.—P. S.]

4 Ver. 31. [The second ἐπάνω πάντων ἐστίν is omitted by ℵ.* D. and Tischend. (ed. VIII), supported by ℵ.c A. B. L. and retained by Treg., Alf., Westc. and H. (in brackets), Meyer, Lange.—P. S.]

5 Ver. 32. [The καὶ is wanting in several codd., also in B. L. al. which retain the second ἐπάνω πάντων ἐστίν, and is omitted by Tischend., Alf., Treg., W. and H.—P. S.]

6 Ver. 34. Ὁ θεός is wanting in B. and in other considerable codd. [ℵ. C.[1] L., omitted by Tischend., Alf., *etc.*—P. S.]

7 Ver. 34. [The A. V., with many commentators, refers the passage to Christ, and hence supplies αὐτῷ. But the sentence is general in its character, hence the present δίδωσι. Christ had already received the fulness of the Spirit in baptism. —P. S.]

EXEGETICAL AND CRITICAL.

Ver. 22. **After these things.**—Μετὰ ταῦτα. Probably not only after the interview with Nicodemus (Meyer), but after all that is related of His stay in Jerusalem.

Into the land of Judea.—Judea here, of course, not in the wider sense of Palestine, but in the narrower sense, as distinguished from Samaria, Galilee, and Perea; Southern Palestine, on this side the Jordan, having Samaria on the north, the Jordan and the Dead Sea on the east, Idumea on the south, Philistia and the Mediterranean on the west. And here, too, not the province of Judea itself is meant, to which in fact Jerusalem especially belonged, but the Judean country; Ἰουδαία being here used adjectively [χώρα Ἰουδαία, Mark i. 5; Acts xvi. 1]. From the baptizing Meyer infers a sojourn on the Jordan towards the north-east.

And there he tarried with them.—From the time of His return to Samaria (probably about seeding time, see ch. iv. 35) we may infer that He continued in the Judean country from the month of March till perhaps November or December, at least half a year (see the place referred to).

And baptized.—According to ch. iv. 2 Jesus Himself did not baptize; but as John remarks this only in a passing and supplemental way, he evidently intends to designate this baptism as a baptism of Jesus Himself. [Virtually (according to the maxim: *quod quis per alium facit, id ipse fecisse dicitur*), but not literally; for the testimony of iv. 2 is explicit, that Jesus Himself did not baptize. His work was to preach and to baptize with the Holy Spirit; water baptism was a subordinate ministerial office, and could as well be performed by others. For the same reason Paul did not baptize except in a few cases, 1 Cor. i. 14-16. The baptism of the disciples of Jesus, which is only mentioned here and iv. 2, was still essentially the baptism of John, but it prepared the way for Christian baptism, which was instituted after the resurrection, Matt. xviii. 19, and first performed on the birth-day of the Christian Church, Acts ii. 41. Before Christ had finished His work on earth, the Holy Spirit was not yet in full regenerative operation (vii. 39), nor could baptismal water signify the cleansing blood of atonement (xix. 34; 1 John i. 7). This baptism then had a prophetic character, and was subsequently not repeated, but completed by the pentecostal baptism of the Spirit.—P. S.]

Ver. 23. **And John also was baptizing.**—This statement serves to explain what follows.—**In Aenon**; עֵינָן, עֵינוֹן, adjective of עַיִן, "place abounding in springs." Meyer makes out of it עַיִן יוֹן "dove-fountain," without arguing the matter. According to Eusebius and Jerome: [Onomasticon under *Aenon* and *Salem*] Aenon lay *in octavo lapide Scythopoleos ad meridiem juxta Salem et Jordanem;* and Salem: *in octavo lapide a Scythopoli in campo Vicus Salamias.* From this it is inferred that both places were in Samaria; which Epiphanius (*Hær.* lvii. 2) confirms.* This has been thought so inconsistent with our passage, that two places of similar names, Shilhim and Ain, which, according to Josh. xv. 32, lay on the southern border of Judea, have been substituted.† According to others the places in question might have lain in Judea hard by the Samaritan border (see Meyer). Robinson (III., p. 322) found a Salem near Nablus, remote from the Jordan. According to this it has been held improbable that Aenon was on the Jordan, and Lücke thinks it was a place of springs. We suppose that John might very probably have been baptizing temporarily on Samaritan ground. Elijah, his pro-

* [This view is held by Dr. Thomson (*The Land and the Book*, II., 176). He visited *Beisân* (Scythopolis) and the neighborhood, and represents the valley there as abounding in fountains and brooks and as one of the most fertile in Palestine; yet he found no traces of the name. "The lovely valley of Jezreel," he says, "irrigated by the Jalûd, and the Ghor Beisan below, watered in every part by many fertilizing streams, are capable of sustaining a little nation in and of themselves. Besides, Beisan is the natural highway from Bashan and the east to the sea-board at Haifa and Acre, and also to southern Palestine and Egypt. The Ghor once teemed with inhabitants, as is evident from ruined sites, and from tells too old for ruins, which are scattered over the plain. I took down their names as now known to the Arabs, but none of them have any historic significance. Of Salim and Enon, which must have been in the ghor at no great distance, I could hear nothing."—P. S.]

† [So also Hengstenberg, I., 224. The Alex. Codex of the Sept. renders the three names of places in Jos. xv., Σελεεὶμ καὶ Ἀὶν καὶ Ρεμμών. In Neh. xi. 29 the last two names are combined in En-rimmon. The southern country was very dry, a continuation of the Arabian desert. Hence the remark, "there was much water there," which would be rather superfluous if applied to a place in Galilee or on the banks of the Jordan, receives its full meaning. Yet this holds good also of Dr. Lange's view, who, with Robinson, locates Salem near Nablus.—P. S.]

totype, dwelt long with a Phenician widow; Elisha healed the Syrian Naaman by directing him to wash in the Jordan. John, on his appearance, preached: God is able of these stones to raise up children unto Abraham. If John was to execute his office as fore-runner of Christ in His universal character, he must have come to Samaria, and even to the Galilean court (see the direction of the angel, Luke i. 17 and 76). He might have had, moreover, special reasons for this. He could not give up his work, because he felt himself appointed to die in his official service; yet he wished also to give way to the Lord, and, not as compelled by events, but voluntarily, to decrease by the side of Him. This purpose would be exactly served by his retiring into a small place, and especially by his beginning to labor in Samaria. It is further noteworthy, that immediately after this Christ begins to teach in Samaria, though only in passing, and that the passage before us relates to the disciples of John who were involved in a controversy with a Jew concerning purification. If this Jew seems to have given the preference, as a Jew, to the baptism of Jesus, it is natural to suppose that he based his preference on the fact that Jesus was baptizing on Judean soil, John in Samaria. Enon at all events lay this side the Jordan. The objection that John was still baptizing in his old way, is solved by his calling. As to the objection that he was not baptizing "into Jesus," he had only to baptize into Christ; to point out the Christ in Jesus was the business of his testimony. Meyer remarks, against Bretschneider and others, that he did not baptize into Jesus because Jesus had not yet appeared at all as the Messiah. Yet John had designated Him as the Messiah, and now did so again with the utmost clearness. But his office as fore-runner had not ceased with a public appearance of Jesus as the Messiah.

There was much water.—This can be mentioned to define only the spot, not the region.

Ver. 24. **John was not yet thrown into prison.**—This, according to De Wette, Meyer, *etc.*, is intended to be a correction of the Synoptical tradition. But it is only a completion of it; for the Synoptists open the ministry of Jesus with His labors in Galilee, not because these were the "very beginning" (Tholuck), but because this was the current tradition, and because their method of construing the history, particularly with regard to the contrast between John and Christ, required it. At the time of the return of Christ from the country of Judea to Galilee in the winter of 781 John had been cast into prison, according to Mark i. 14; during his first great tour in Galilee He received the embassy from the Baptist in the spring of 782; after His return from the feast of Purim in March of 782, however, He received the intelligence of the execution of the Baptist, according to Matth. xiv. 12; comp. John vi. 1.

Ver. 25. **A question.**—Ζήτησις, disputation. Not with the Jews, but with a Jew. [See TEXTUAL NOTES.] The one Jew, who disputes with the disciples of John concerning *purification* (περὶ καθαρισμοῦ), that is, concerning the religious washing for purification, which must precede the kingdom of heaven [Ezek. xxxvi. 25; Zech. xiii. 1], or concerning the baptisms of John and Jesus as to their purifying virtue and Messianic validity, gives exegetical trouble. According to Tholuck the controversy was begun by disciples of John, and yet the Jew on his part contentiously extolled the baptism of Jesus, to provoke the disciples of John; in other words, with not the best design. This evil design is more strongly represented by Luthardt: An intent to make the Baptist untrue to his office, in order to operate the more effectually against Jesus. Chrysostom and Semler, on the contrary, have supposed that the Jew had been baptized by Jesus, which seems also implied in the complaint of John's disciples in the next verse. [The first sacramental controversy, and the forerunner of a good many.—P. S.]

Ver. 26. **He that was with thee, to whom thou hast borne witness.**—Jealousy is at the out-set betrayed by the avoidance of the name of Jesus (comp. Luke x. 37; xv. 30); then it is implied that Jesus had been at first Himself dependent on him, that is, as one baptized by him; though it is not asserted, as by the modern criticism, that He had been a pupil of John. *To whom thou barest witness, etc.* A reproach against John and Jesus at once ("behold, the same"). Yet expressed only in the tone, in the choice of words, while nothing is literally ventured beyond historical statement. But that they, themselves irritated, wished to provoke the Baptist to see in Jesus an unauthorized rival in the matter of baptism, no matter how much He may be in other respects, is manifest. Every expression, in this view, is pregnant. Even the words: "beyond Jordan," might imply that they had known better baptism-days on a better soil. Finally their displeasure expresses itself in the exaggeration: "all men come to Him." Nevertheless they cannot be considered decidedly hostile; they show an uncertainty, a wavering, in the issue of which the mass of John's disciples afterwards split into two branches, one friendly, the other hostile. The Baptist was to express himself on this distinction of *two baptismal communions existing together*.

Ver. 27. **A man can receive nothing** (take nothing upon himself).—A general principle of religion, applied to the kingdom of God. Gifts and positions in the kingdom of God rest upon the free grace and investiture of God Himself. Here lies the obligation of humility before God, reverence for the gifted, freedom from envy, modesty, self-respect. The form of the expression silences by its universality, the spirit of the expression purifies by its repression of human nature, its emphasizing of the divine. The reference of the maxim: (1) To the Baptist, according to many ancients and moderns (Lücke). Wetstein: *Non possum mihi arrogare et rapere, quæ deus non dedit.* (2) To Jesus; De Wette, Meyer: The greater ministry is given by God to Him. (3) To John and Jesus (Kuinöel, Luthardt; Tholuck doubtful). The last view is no doubt the true; for the maxim is the general superscription of the following contrasts: Christ and John; (1) Christ and the forerunner; (2) the Bridegroom and the Bridegroom's friend; (3) the increasing One, and the decreasing; (4) He who is from heaven, and he that is of the earth. God is above the distinction, and gives to each one his own.

Ver. 28. **Ye yourselves bear me witness.**—Ye yourselves, so jealous, bear witness to my modesty, in that ye recall how I bore witness to Him. **But that.**—'Αλλ' ὅτι seem only a transition to the discourse dependent on it (Meyer, Winer). Yet the expression might also point back to the Baptist's description of himself (ch. i. 23), with the sense; τοῦτό εἰμί, ὅτι ἀπ.—'Εκεῖνος refers to Jesus, of whom they had been speaking. De Wette.

Ver. 29. **He that hath the bride.**—The Old Testament theocratic figure of the marriage-union between Jehovah and His people, Is. liv. 5; Hos. ii. 19; and the Song of Songs, according to Bengel and Luthardt;* which Meyer doubts, because that book is not quoted in the New Testament; yet it is manifestly an example at least in favor of the view here mentioned.—This figure passed over to the relation between Christ and the renewed and adorned theocratic people, Eph. v. 32; Rev. xxi. 2, 9. He that hath the bride, is therefore he to whom *she* is given from above, and who is thereby distinguished as the supremely Gifted. He is the bridegroom (De Wette: Comp. the proverb: *Wer das Glück hat, führt die Braut heim*).—From him is here distinguished the **friend of the bridegroom**, a distinct personage in the Jewish wedding usage. Lücke: Φίλος τοῦ νυμφίου answers to the Hebrew שׁוֹשְׁבִין, in which, however, the ideas of φίλος τοῦ νυμφ. and παρανύμφιος or νυμφαγωγός are combined. According to the Hebrew custom, the Shoshben, a friend of the bridegroom, was a necessary mediator both in the formation and in the conclusion of the marriage. In behalf of his friend he made suit with the bride, and was the indispensable negotiator between the bride and bridegroom in relation to the wedding. At the wedding itself he was a chief manager of the feast, a necessary functionary at the inspection of the wedding-chamber, and even after the close of the marriage a mediator in misunderstandings and dissensions.—In a passage *Ketuvoth* (fol. 12, 1) it is expressly said: *Duos* שושבנים *constituebant, unum sponso, alterum sponsæ* (Schöttgen, *Horæ Hebr. et Talm.*). Another name is אָהָב (tr. *Sanhedrin* f. 27, 2). Doubtless John has especially in his eye the business of the wooing, to which he was appointed. And then besides his subordination to the bridegroom, and his unenvious service in relation to the bride, he expresses also the honor and satisfaction he has in his position.

Standeth and heareth him.—(1) Interpretation according to rabbinic passages: customary listening of the shoshbenim at the door (ἐπὶ τῇ θύρᾳ) of the bride-chamber. For the particulars see Lücke, I., p. 564. Probably only isolated apocryphal instances suggested by apocryphal accounts (Tobias. Something like it here and there perhaps in the history of Jesuitism and Herrnhutism). Hard to imagine as general custom. (2) Baumgarten-Crusius, Luthardt: He waits for him that is to come, and hears his voice as he approaches, bringing his bride home. Against this Meyer: The παρανύμφιος does not stand waiting for the bridegroom, but accompanies him on the way to the house of the bride. Such waiting is the part of the bride's-maid, Matth. xxv. 1. (3) Eckermann, Meyer: He stands at his service, waiting his bidding, and meantime rejoices in his conversation and gladness in general. (4) Tholuck: The conversation of the bridegroom with the bride preceding the wedding. (5) Lücke: The voice of the bridegroom has in the Old Testament almost the tone of a proverb, Jer. vii. 34; xvi. 9; xxv. 10. The friend stands at his side and hears the happy voice of the bridegroom. More accurately Grotius: עָמַד, *stare est ministrare, ut Genes.* xli. 46; *Deut.* i. 38; *Zach.* iii. 7: *audiens blandimenta ad sponsam. Vide Cant. Cantic.: Hæc est vox* φωνὴ νυμφίου. The reference is no doubt to affectionate and tender greetings to the bride, not commissions (Meyer: bidding) to the friend. The friend stands (back) and hears in silence how the bridegroom himself talks to the bride of his love, contrasted with his own business-like talking of it to her in urging the suit.

The voice of the bridegroom is therefore the New Testament words of love, the gospel of Christ, and that even in distinction from the now ceasing lispings of prophecy concerning the new covenant. De Wette also: Of the gladness of the bridegroom. When Tholuck observes that φωνή must not be referred to the rejoicings at the wedding, since the wedding begins later with the inauguration of the kingdom, and thus far only the conversation of the bridegroom is introduced, it must be remarked that the figure of the wedding is not intended to be pressed. According to the word of Christ, Matth. ix. 15, the wedding had already in one view begun with His appearance. In another view it began with His resurrection and the founding of the church, Matth. xxii. 9. In still another view it is to come at the second appearing of Christ, and meantime the Apostles are the wooers of the bride, 2 Cor. xi. 2; Rev. xxi. 19. These aspects might perhaps be distinguished by the three stages of going for and saluting the bride (the act primarily meant here), the wedding-feast, and the final nuptials; denoting the preaching of the gospel, the outpouring of the Holy Ghost and founding of the church, and the manifestation of the kingdom. Yet we cannot apply this distinction of periods to the words of the Baptist. To his prophetic view the wedding was begun.

Rejoiceth with joy.—Χαρᾷ χαίρει, see Luke xxii. 15, [and שׂוֹשׂ אָשִׂישׂ, Is. lxi. 10. A Hebraizing mode of intensification: pure joy, joy and joy only.—P. S.] The διά, as in 1 Thess. iii. 9, which is unusual, in place of the classical ἐπί, *etc.*, adds emphasis to the voice in itself. He finds that voice a compensation to his position. Contrast of this unenvious joy with the jealous tones of the disciples of John.

This my joy.—This his share in the wedding. **Hath been made full** (πεπλήρωται, perfect tense).—In the happy meeting of the bridegroom and bride in the house of the bride the wedding itself is, to him, as good as come. He has happily completed his task as wooer of the bride. He has done the work of his life. See the analogous perfect: μεμαρτύρηκα, and the exegesis, ch. i. 34. *Is fulfilled*, has become *perfect.*

* [Hengstenberg also (I. 232 f.) sees in the whole passage, and especially in the *voice* of the beloved, and the *friend* of the bridegroom, clear allusions to Cant. II. 8; V. 2.—P. S.]

Yet only in its kind, as the joy of the friend of the bridegroom; therefore to be distinguished from the perfection of the New Testament joy of faith, John xv. 11; xvi. 24; xvii. 13 (which places Meyer cites). He meant not by this the ceasing of his work, but the decreasing and diminishing of it before the increasing glory of the word and work of Christ.

Ver. 30. **He must increase.**—The true description of the relation between John and Christ, and between the Old Covenant and the New, in the primitive church, in the mediæval church, in this modern age, in the life of every evangelical community, and of every individual Christian. *Increase:* In labors, in authority, in disciples. *Decrease:* ἐλαττοῦσθαι, be diminished. Noble freedom from envy. An admonition to His disciples. St. John Baptist's day in the calendar, the longest day [June 24th], after which the days decrease; the birth-day of Christ [Dec. 25], one of the shortest, from which the days grow longer.

Ver. 31. **He that cometh from above is above all.**—The relation of the section now following to the preceding. Different views [of the authorship of vers. 31-36]: (1) A meditation of the Evangelist (Wetstein, Bengel, Kuinoel, Schott, Paulus, Olshausen, Tholuck, *etc.*), as supposed to be indicated by the John-like strain, an assumed contradiction between vers. 32 and 26, and the disappearance of all reference to the Baptist. Against this it is observed, that there is no break at any point, and the present in vers. 31 and 32 indicates the time of John the Baptist. (2) A middle view (Lücke, De Wette, Hofmann): The discourse of the Baptist is continued indeed, but the subjective reproduction of the Evangelist makes it almost a reflection of his own. (3) Continuation of the address of the Baptist, like vers. 16-18 in ch. i., and as in ch. iii. vers. 16-21 continue the discourse of Christ; my *Leben Jesu*, II., 2, p. 521, Ebrard, *Kritik*, p. 294; also Meyer, [p. 180];* the Johannean character and coloring being also admitted even here. The stately conclusion of the *prophetic* testimony of the Baptist concerning Christ is not at all inconsistent with his subsequent expression of *human* feeling, Matth. xi. According to Strauss and Weisse this passage in particular is supposed to prove, that the discourses in John are not historical, but composed by himself. From this passage then, on the contrary, a clear light may be shed upon the exquisite, far-reaching, teeming historical truth of the whole gospel.

'Ο ἄνωθεν ἐρχόμενος. Present, referring to the mission of Christ, which is just unfolding itself. See the testimonies of the Baptist concerning the divine dignity of Jesus, ch. i. 15-18; ver. 27; vers. 29, 34.—**Above all.**—With respect to Christ all men are put in the category of the need of salvation.

He that is of the earth, *etc.*—Not a tautology, but signalizing the difference of origin and of consequent quality. From the origin of the person, his nature appears, and from this his mode of speaking. But how could John say this of his testimony (Hofmann)? Tholuck argues: Therefore the Evangelist says this, not the Baptist. But the thing said must nevertheless be true, and then it might even better be said by the Baptist in his humility, than by the Evangelist respecting his former teacher. The Baptist himself therefore must have said it. The question is in what sense? We have a parallel at John i. 18. In full comparison with the full glory of Christ no one, not even of the prophets, nor the Baptist, has ever seen God; in this comparison every man, even of the prophets, the Baptist not excepted, is of the earth. Then does this mean: of the earth, in the sense of John i. 13; iii. 6, belonging to the old, sinful world as to his origin, therefore in his kind, therefore also in his speech, since, even as prophet, he can speak the divine but rarely, in fragments, and under the veil of figures; or in the sense of the ἐπίγεια as distinguished from the ἐπουράνια in ver. 12? Exegesis passes by this question, and treats the antithesis as if it had the sense of ch. iii. 6; the σάρξ in distinction from the πνεῦμα. We understand, however, by the earth (γῆ) primarily the old economy and Theocracy in distinction from the heaven (οὐρανός), whence the new revelation comes (see on ver. 12). With the idea of the old is then connected unquestionably the idea of the imperfect and defective. The antithesis of earthly and heavenly, or carnal and spiritual descent passes into the antithesis of the old and the new time, and this into the antithesis of mankind needing revelation and redemption, and the Redeemer. Moreover John speaks here of his human λαλεῖν, not of his prophetic εἰπεῖν, or this latter is reduced in his view to a minimum in his human λαλεῖν, in comparison with the divine μαρτυρεῖν of Christ, and it should be observed that John says: λαλεῖ ἐκ τῆς γῆς, not τὰ τῆς γῆς.

He that cometh from heaven.—A solemn repetition of the preceding, giving it the strong form of a dogmatical statement.

Ver. 32. **What he hath seen and heard.**—See ch. iii. 13; also i. 18. Meyer: In His præ-existence. Rather, in His whole living divine nature, in virtue of which His testifying is at every moment preceded by a having seen or a having heard. The seeing and hearing denotes not only the directness of His knowledge, but also the full reality, the total scope of it, identifying it with His bodily vision (*Leben Jesu* II., p. 518).

And no man receiveth his testimony.—According to the critics, in contradiction with ver. 26. Unquestionably a contradiction of the noble-minded master to his small-minded disciples. For them it was quite too much to see all running to Jesus; but to him it was quite too little; to him it was as nothing. A hyperbole, therefore, of grief and indignation. A rebuke to the disposition of his disciples; moreover, an admonition to them to go to Jesus, as in ch. i. 29. He could not send them away by force, because his school was a school of preparation, in which those only had become perfect, who went of their own will to Jesus. The Baptist qualifies his hyperbole (see similar expressions of the Evangelist, ch. i. 11; xii. 37) by what follows. Tholuck: "John reviews the history as a whole,

* [Alford likewise ascribes the last verses to the Baptist, and urges the inner coherence of the discourse itself, in which John explains to his disciples the reason why Christ must increase and throw his own dignity into the shade. —P. S.]

in the course of which the believers are a vanishing minority." John no doubt speaks here with the conduct of the Jews chiefly in view. See Rom. ix.

Vers. 33, 34. **He that hath received his testimony . . . . for God giveth not the Spirit by measure.**—Aorist: *ὁ λαβών*. And this doubtless with special reference to such disciples of John as had gone to Christ; commending them, and recommending imitation. **Hath set his seal,** hath sealed. A tropical term, denoting generally in the Old Testament fastening up, in the New rather complete authentication; affixing the signature of execution, ch. vi. 27; Rom. iv. 11, *etc.* In Christ the truth of God as revelation is completed, 2 Cor. i. 20; by the believing confession of Him this fact, that the truth of God has proved itself perfect, is attested, sealed. How far? The answer to this question depends on the right interpretation of the two following verses. (a) If v. 34 refer to Christ, the syllogism is this; Christ as the messenger of God speaks the words of God, because God has given to Him the Spirit not by measure, but in immeasurable fulness (Lücke, De Wette); he, therefore, who acknowledges the word of Christ to be true, acknowledges the word of God himself; he who believes not Christ, makes God a liar. (b) But the 34th verse may refer to the prophets, summed up and represented in John: The messenger of God speaks the words of God, for God gives his Spirit copiously enough for this; he, therefore, who accepts not Christ, denies, in the Fulfiller of the testimony of the prophets, the word of God also in that testimony itself, or rather he necessitates the inference, that God promised that the Messiah should come, and has not kept His word, or that in His different revelations He has contradicted Himself. (c) Then again these opposite interpretations may be modified. The first interpretation thus, according to Meyer: 'Whom God hath sent,' fits not every prophet, but Christ alone, according to ver. 31, in view of His mission from heaven. On the other hand, the *οὐ γὰρ ἐκ μέτρου*, expressing a general truth, should not be referred primarily to Christ; else *αὐτῷ* must have been added. The statement is, that God gives the Spirit in general not *ἐκ μέτρου*, but regardless of *μέτρον*, to one more, to another less, yet to every one enough for inspiration; whence it follows that Christ is the most richly endowed (*ἐκ* denoting the norm). Yet the more to one and less to another may be given in limited measure, and it is a preliminary question whether the *μέτρον* should mean a general *proportion* for all, or a *limited measure* for each individual. The passage in Vajikra rabba Sectio 15 (cited by Lücke and others): "*Etiam spiritus sanctus non habitavit super prophetas, nisi mensura quadam* (במשקל); *quidam enim librum unum, quidam duos vaticiniorum ediderunt*"—speaks not of a proportion, but of limited portions for different individuals. If now the expression be referred to the prophets, it cannot mean: God gives the Spirit immeasurably. If we would refer it directly to Christ, *αὐτῷ* is wanting. But we may take the expression as a motto of the New Testament age which has now opened. God now gives the Spirit, and gives it not according to a limited measure (Joel ii.; Acts ii.).—**Not by measure.** Gerlach: "Perhaps this is an allusion to the fact that the priests were only sprinkled with the anointing oil, while upon the head of the high-priest the whole of the oil was poured, Exod. xxix. 7; Ps. cxxxiii. 2." From this it is clear that He whom now pre-eminently God hath sent, Christ, speaketh *τὰ ῥήματα* (not only *ῥήματα*) *τοῦ θεοῦ*, *i. e.*, all the words of God, the entire revelation, which has hitherto been spoken only piecemeal (see ch. i. 17, 18; Heb. i. 1). This the believer seals. He attests it with the confidence of the confessor and martyr, as it is attested to him in his heart. The second interpretation is modified by referring the messenger of God [ver. 34] to the prophetic office, as represented by John, and then taking the sentence about the Spirit thus: In this day, wherein God gives the Messiah the fulness of the Spirit, the Baptist also has his share in the abundance (see the history of the Baptism of Jesus). Then with this John Christ is compared, as described in ver. 35. In favor of this antithesis are the facts, (1) that John here still appears as pre-eminently the *ἀπεσταλμένος*; [ch. i. 6], Christ as the *ἐρχόμενος*; (2) that it is said in ver. 34: *ὁ θεὸς ἀπέστειλεν*, in ver. 35; *ὁ πατὴρ ἀγαπᾷ*; (3) that here the *λαλεῖν* (not *εἰπεῖν*) of the *ῥήματα θεοῦ* is set against the fact that all things are given into the hands of Christ.

The result is, we find ourselves compelled to decide for the second explanation of the difficult passage: The last messenger, in virtue of his participation in the New Testament advent of the Spirit, speaks the prophetic words of God as such (in distinction from fact); the Son presents Himself as the fulfilment of these words in fact. He, therefore, who receives Him, seals that God in His prophetic words (spoken by the Baptist) is true. He who disavows Christ, disavows, therefore, His fore-runner also. A good disciple of John must become a disciple of Christ.

Ver. 35. **Loveth the Son.**—Emphatic: in singular manner. This love is the cause of the glorifying of the Son. *All things:* not to be qualified (Grotius: *Omnia mysteria regni*; Kuinoel: *Doctrinæ partes*). Matth. xi. 27; xxviii. 18; John xiii. 3.—**Into his hand.**—Strictly: *in his hand* [*ἐν τῇ χειρὶ αὐτοῦ*]. Pregnant diction: so into His hand, that they are in His hand (Winer, p. 385).

Ver. 36. **He that believeth in the Son.**—The Baptist concludes his prophetic preaching with the great alternative, which Christ also pronounces in ver. 18, and at His departure from the earth.—**Everlasting life,** see ver. 15. **Hath.**—It is noteworthy that this inwardness of the eternal life was already recognized by the Baptist.—**He who is not obedient in faith to the Son,** *ἀπειθῶν*; not: believeth not (Luther [and the E. V.]),* but is disobedient; meaning, however, as standing opposed to faith, the refusal of the obedience of faith. In faith lies the moral kernel of obedience veiled in love, peace, joy; hence *ὁ πιστεύων*. Out of unbelief disobedience, or even *ἀνομία*, as a moral worm comes forth openly; hence *ἀπειθῶν*. Meyer: "Disobedient to the Son, inasmuch as He requires faith." Right, but not enough. Tholuck:

*[Alford defends the E. V.: "ἀπειθῶν may mean *disbelieving*. Unbelief implies disobedience."—P. S.]

'Απειθεῖν alternates with ἀπιστεῖν, Rom. xi. 30.—**Shall not see life.**—With the everlasting life he fails of *life* in general; he shall not even see it, to say nothing of having it. **But the wrath of God.**—Neither punishment on the one hand, nor a holy passion on the other, but the righteousness of God combined with His veiled jealousy in its visitation of judgment, Rom. i. 18; Eph. ii. 3; Matth. iii. 7. **Abideth on him**; in proportion as his unbelief is incorrigible (strictly: abideth *towards* him; pressing more and more strongly *upon* him). The effect of the ὀργή is θάνατος. [The μένει implies, that we *are* by nature in a state of condemnation; comp. τέκνα φύσει ὀργῆς, Eph. ii. 3; John iii. 6.—P. S.]

A worthy closing word of the Old Testament; the last peal of the thunder of the law; the farewell of the Baptist. For what he afterwards says to Herod, he says as teacher, not as prophet; and the question with which he sends his disciples to Christ, is the question of a tempted, believing man.

DOCTRINAL AND ETHICAL.

1. *The first ministry of the Lord* in the Judean country, a counterpart of His last public ministry in the temple on Zion from the triumphal entry to the Tuesday evening (see *Com. on Matt.* on ch. xxi. 12-14, p. 379).; in that in the first case the hostility of the rulers of the Jews had not yet broken out, in the last case it seemed vanquished by the hosanna of a believing people. Hence here a preliminary baptizing finds place, there a teaching and healing in the temple. And the cessation of baptism in the Jewish country is a prelude of the final departure of Jesus from the temple (Matth. xxiii.)

2. The *baptizing of Jesus* through His disciples a connecting link between the New Testament baptism of the Spirit and the baptism of John, as John's baptism was a connecting link between the Old Testament washing and circumcision, and the baptism of Christ.

3. The *last prophetic testimony to Christ given by the Baptist* in his glory and in elevation above his last struggle [Matth. xi.]; the last flash, so to speak, of the Old Testament in the light of the New Testament itself, and a testimony to the higher glory of the New.

4. The symbol of the *intimate relation, the betrothal between Jehovah and His people* (Ps. xlv.; Song of Solomon; Is. liv.; lxii.; Ezek. xvi. 8; xxiii.; Hos. ii. 19) finds its fulfilment in the *bridal relations between Christ and the church* coming forth to meet Him. It belonged to the office of the Baptist to complete this prophecy in the most concrete vivid form. Christ on His part has taken up the word in the most varied applications, first to the disciples of John himself (Matth. ix. 15), and afterwards throughout the whole New Testament, 1 Cor. xi. 3; Eph. v. 23; Rev. xxi. 9. The love of the bride is the symbol of the life of the Spirit. Plato's Symposion is a heathen parallel to the Song of Solomon.

5. The perpetual force of the maxim: *He must increase, but I must decrease.*

6. So far as in him lay, John sent all his disciples forward to Christ, and pointed all the Jews to Him. Not only most of the Jews, however, but even many of John's disciples failed to come up to the word of the prophet, and fell under the condemnation pronounced by him. On the disciples of John see Gieseler, *Kirchengeschichte*, I., p. 69 [Edinb. ed. I., 58].

7. Both of the glory of Christ, and of the condemnation, John speaks in a more Old Testament way than Christ Himself (comp. vers. 35 and 13; vers. 36 and 18); quite in keeping with his mission. His last word is a last thunder-clap from Sinai and a last lightning-flash of Elijah, prophesying of the baptism of fire (Matth. iii.) and the flames of the judgment of the world (2 Pet. iii. 10).

HOMILETICAL AND PRACTICAL.

A series of separate themes in the sentences of the Baptist, vers. 27, 29, 30, 31 sqq.—The baptism of Jesus by the side of the baptism of John, the gradual transfer of the Old Testament order of things into the church of Christ.—Relation of the baptism of Jesus to the baptism of John: (1) Points in common; (2) points of difference.—The harmony between John and Christ, and the dissension between their disciples, the living type of a primeval and a constantly repeated history (see Gen. xiii. 7).—Two divided purification or reformation churches, to be united by being pointed from men to the Lord.—The jealousy of the disciples and the purity of the Master.—The last testimony of the Baptist concerning Christ, an expression at once of the highest, gentlest love and the mightiest wrath.—Christ the Bridegroom of the bride: (1) Adorned to be such by the election of God; (2) recognized as such by the greeting of the bride; (3) honored as such by the wooer and friend; (4) proved such by His fidelity and glory.—The word of the Baptist: He must increase, but I must decrease, in its application to the natural life (1) of the world, (2) of the church, (3) of the Christian.—Christ the Witness from heaven.—Faith in Christ, a sealing of all the words of God in the Old Testament. Truth is the unity of correlative opposites.—Without faith in the truth of God, we cannot perceive the unity in the great distinction between the Old Testament and the New.—With the New Testament the Jews lost also the truth of the Old.—With their acknowledgment of the Old Testament, Christians may also obscure the truth of the New.—The life of faith a moral life on a heavenly scale: (1) Faith, an obedience rising into free, blissful confidence, and veiled in it; (2) Unbelief, a moral disobedience (immorality) in naked, open deformity.—The wrath of God, the jealousy of rejected love, *i. e.*, a full tide of gracious operation, changed by the unbelief of the man himself into judgment. See Rom. ii. 5.—Jesus in the Judean country, or an effort in hope to lead the people of Israel over by gentle ways into the new covenant (comp. Gen. v. 5).—The two baptizers together.—Religious controversy in its bad and its good operation (the words of the disciples of John, and the words of their master).—The word of the disciples: All men come to Him, and the word of the master; No man receiveth His testimony.—Only what is given him from heaven can a man truly take to himself: (1) What he usurps is given him in wrath, and received to condemnation; (2) what is given to him is forever his own.—He that hath the bride is the bridegroom; or, the life of Christendom a testimony to Christ.—The wedding of the Son.—The friend of the bridegroom, in His behaviour, an example for guidance and warning, to bishops, ministers, divines.—The decreasing of the Baptist, his increase.—The man of the earth, and the Man from heaven above all.—The believer, a witness of God attested by God.—Christ the seal of the word of God, manifest in the burning seal of living Christian hearts, 2 Cor. i. 20; Rev. iii. 14.—The outpouring of the Spirit without measure.—The Father, the Son, the Spirit.—The last word of the Baptist concerning the Son: (1) What the Son *is;* (2) what He *has;* (3) what He *gives;* (4) what He *is worth* [vers. 34-36].

STARKE: *Nova Bibl. Tub.:* Premature zeal, envy, dependence on human authority, and self-interest: O how much harm they do!—CANSTEIN: Satan and his tools know too well how much depends on the unity of Christians; hence they take special pains to make schism of every kind among them, Gal. v. 20.—MAJUS: It is dangerous for hearers to flatter their teachers.—People must not hang with sinful passion upon a teacher who is renowned.—As the peace-makers are called the children of God, so the instigators of division are justly called children of the devil.—HEDINGER: The office of the preacher and its profitable success come from God.—We men have nothing from ourselves, but everything from heaven; therefore should we ascribe nothing to ourselves, but everything to God alone, and thank Him for it, 1 Cor. iv. 7.—OSIANDER: He who attempts high things, to which he is not called of God, spends all his care and labor in vain, and comes to shame at last, as the examples of Absalom, Theudas, Judas of Galilee, and others, prove, Sirach iii. 23.—HEDINGER: Let no man thrust himself into an office, without the will of God.—QUESNEL: Every calling, every grace (gift) has certain limits above which no man may elevate himself.—He who purely and steadfastly preaches Christ, may appeal to the testimony of his hearers.—A servant of the church, though in high office, has yet more cause to be humble than to be exalted.—Servants of God justly rejoice, when they can lead many souls to the Lord.—Moon and stars are lost when the sun rises; so with me, when the Sun of Righteousness appears.—HEDINGER: Christ, the Alpha and Omega, should be all; we instruments are nothing.—CANSTEIN: Because all ministers are men, their word must be tested by the doctrine of Christ.—Christ's testimony is the whole counsel of God for our salvation.—Christ spoke the word, or proclaimed the counsel of God, as the personal and independent Word of God.—MAJUS: The believer may verily be sure of his salvation, because he already has eternal life, though in the world he still is subject to much suffering.—CANSTEIN: Unbelief, the cause of condemnation, because it rejects the means by which the wrath of God might be averted.

GOSSNER: Eternal life is given to the believer from the hour he believes. He need not wait for it; he has it already here.—BRAUNE: As a man stands towards the Saviour, so stands he towards God and the gift of God, eternal life.—SCHLEIERMACHER: It is an old fault, which reappears continually in a multitude of forms, and even in the Christian church,—the strong disposition of men *to believe in a man.*—And how does God give from heaven, what He gives to a man? Surely not otherwise than through the man's own conduct and that of other men. So long then as our own conduct is in contradiction with the divine working, we should not console ourselves with the knowledge that a man can receive nothing except it be given him from heaven, but do our utmost to find out what and how much is given us from heaven.—That John must *decrease,* and the Lord *increase,*—this is the true relation between the old covenant and the new, between every imperfect worship of God, every other less firmly closed relation of men to Him, and that which is offered in Christ.—SCHENKEL: Our future welfare rests not on man, but on Christ: (1) Not on the word of man, but on the Gospel of Christ; (2) not on the work of man, but on the atoning work of Christ; (3) not on the name of man, but on the glorious name of Christ.

HEUBNER: True calling comes only from God, from Him alone success; the rise and fall of human names, success and failure, are matters of divine control.—(From ZINZENDORF): When souls depend on men, *etc.,* they are in most cases betrayed. Then when one such poor man comes to confusion, they are all confounded; when he is taken suddenly from them, they are all lost.—How rarely are men like John! Often the later exalt themselves over the earlier, pupils above masters; and how men envy, attack, belittle the greater merit! Men will not see others, especially their followers, outstrip them (true, alas, peculiarly of Germany, and to not the least extent of Evangelical theologians and clergymen).—*Hath set his seal:* Every believer is a living attestation of the true God himself. What honor, to confirm the truth of God to others!—God gives not the Spirit by measure. All, even the most gifted, are capable of growing in the Spirit *in infinitum.*—The guilt of rejecting divine grace leaves in the heart of the unbeliever nothing but the sense of an angry God. Conscience is the preacher of this wrath (yet the wrath manifests itself especially in swelling judgments against the unbeliever).

VII.

JESUS AT JACOB'S WELL. THE WOMAN OF SAMARIA. CHRIST THE FOUNTAIN OF LIFE, THE FOUNTAIN OF PEACE. THE WHITE HARVEST FIELD, OR THE FIELD OF EARTH AND THE FIELD OF HEAVEN. THE SOWERS AND THE REAPERS. THE FAITH OF THE SAMARITANS, A PRESAGE OF THE UNIVERSAL SPREAD OF THE GOSPEL.

Chap. IV. 1–42.

1 When therefore the Lord [Jesus][1] knew how [that] the Pharisees had heard that
2 Jesus made [makes] and baptized [baptizes] more disciples than John (Though
3 Jesus himself baptized not [did not baptize], but his disciples), He left Judea, and
4 departed again[2] into Galilee. And he must needs go through Samaria.
5 Then cometh he [He cometh, therefore] to a city of Samaria, which is [*omit* which
is] called Sychar, near to the parcel of ground [or piece of land] that Jacob gave to his
6 son Joseph. Now [And] Jacob's well [fountain][3] was there. Jesus therefore, be-
ing wearied with his journey, sat thus [simply sat down] on the well: [.] *and* [*omit*
and] it was about[4] the sixth hour.
7 There cometh a woman of Samaria to draw water: Jesus saith unto her, Give
8 me to drink.[5] (For his disciples were [had] gone away unto the city to buy meat
9 [food]). Then[6] saith the woman of Samaria [The Samaritan woman[7] saith] unto
him, How is it that thou, being a Jew, askest drink of me, which [who] am a wo-
man of Samaria [a Samaritan woman]? for the [*omit* the] Jews have no dealings
10 with the [*omit* the] Samaritans.[8] Jesus answered and said unto her, If thou knew-
est the gift of God, and who it is that saith to thee, Give me to drink; thou wouldst
11 have asked of him, and he would have given thee living water. The woman saith
unto him, Sir, thou hast nothing to draw with,[9] and the well is deep: from whence
12 then hast thou that [the] living water? Art thou greater than our father Jacob,
which [who] gave us the well, and drank thereof himself, and his children [sons],
13 and his cattle? Jesus answered and said unto her, Whosoever [Every one that]
14 drinketh [πᾶς ὁ πίνων] of this water shall [will] thirst again: But whosoever drink-
eth [whosoever shall drink, ὃς δ' ἂν πίῃ][10] of the water that I shall give him
shall [will] never thirst; but the water that I shall give him[11] shall be [be-
come, γενήσεται] in him a well [fountain] of water springing up into everlasting
15 life. The woman saith unto him, Sir, give me this water, that I thirst not [may
16 not thirst], neither [nor] come [all the way, διέρχωμαι] hither [ἐνθάδε] to draw. Jesus
17 [He][12] saith unto her, Go, call thy husband,[13] and come hither. The woman answered
and said, I have no husband [οὐκ ἔχω ἄνδρα]. Jesus said unto her, Thou hast well
said, I have no husband [A husband I have not, or, Husband I have none, ἄνδρα
18 οὐκ ἔχω]: For thou hast had five husbands; and he whom thou now hast is not thy
husband: in that saidst thou truly [in this thou hast spoken truly, or, truth, τοῦτο
19 ἀληθὲς εἴρηκας]. The woman saith unto him, Sir, I perceive that thou art a pro-
20 phet. Our fathers worshipped in [or, on] this mountain; and ye say, that in Jeru-
21 salem is the place where men ought to worship. Jesus saith unto her, Woman, be-
lieve me,[14] the [an] hour cometh [is coming], when ye shall neither in [or, on] this
22 mountain, nor yet [*omit* yet] at [in] Jerusalem, worship the Father. Ye worship
ye know not what [that which ye know not]: we know what we worship [we wor-
ship that which we know]; for [the] salvation[15] is [or, comes] of [from] the Jews.
23 But the [an] hour cometh [is coming], and now is, when the true worshippers shall
[will] worship the Father in spirit and in truth: for the Father seeketh such to
24 worship him [for also (καὶ γάρ) such worshippers the Father seeketh]. God is a
Spirit [is spirit]:[16] and they that worship him must worship *him* [*omit him*] in spi-
25 rit and in truth. The woman saith unto him, I know that Messias cometh, which
26 [who] is called Christ:[17] when he is come, he will tell us all things. Jesus saith
unto her, I that speak unto thee am *he*.
27 And upon this came his disciples, and marvelled that he talked with the [a] wo-
man:[18] yet no man [no one] said, What seekest thou? or, Why talkest thou with her?

28 The woman then left her water-pot, and went her way [went away] into the city,
29 and saith to the men, Come, see a man, which [who] told me all things that ever[19]
30 I did: is not [*omit* not][20] this the Christ? Then [*omit* Then][21] they went out of the
city, and came unto [to] him.
31 In the mean while his disciples prayed [asked] him, saying, Master [Rabbi], eat.
32 But he said unto them, I have meat [food] to eat that ye know not of.
33 Therefore said the disciples one to another, Hath any man brought him *aught* [any
34 thing] to eat? Jesus saith unto them, My meat [food] is to do[22] the will of him
35 that sent me, and to finish his work. Say not ye [Do ye not say], There are yet
four months [it is yet a four-month[23]], and *then* cometh [the] harvest? behold [Lo!]
I say unto you, Lift up your eyes, and look on the fields; for they are white already
36 to harvest [white for harvest already]. And [*omit* And][24] he that reapeth [the
reaper] receiveth wages, and gathereth fruit unto life eternal: that both he that
37 soweth and he that reapeth [the sower and the reaper] may rejoice together. And
[For, γάρ] herein [in this spiritual field] is that saying [fully] true, One soweth, and
38 another reapeth. I [have] sent you to reap that whereon ye [have] bestowed no
labour: other men [others have] laboured, and ye are [have] entered into their
labours.
39 And many of the Samaritans of that city believed on [in] him for the saying [be-
cause of the word, διὰ τὸν λόγον] of the woman, which [who] testified, He told me
40 all that ever I did. So when [When, therefore] the Samaritans were come [came]
unto him, they besought him that he would tarry with them [to abide with them]:
41 and he abode there two days. And many more believed because of his own [*omit*
42 own] word [διὰ τὸν λόγον αὐτοῦ]; And said unto the woman, Now we believe, not
[No longer do we believe] because of thy saying [story, διὰ τὴν σὴν λαλίαν]: for we
have heard *him* [*omit him*] ourselves, and know that this is indeed the Christ [*omit*
the Christ],[25] the Saviour of the world.

TEXTUAL AND GRAMMATICAL.

1 Ver. 1.—[ὁ Ἰησοῦς is supported by ℵ. D. A. Vulg. Syr., Tischend. (ed. VIII.); the text. rec. ὁ κύριος by A. B. C. *al.*, Treg., Alf., Westc. and Hort.—P. S.]

2 Ver. 3.—The πάλιν is doubtful, being wanting in Codd. A. E. F., *etc.*, many minuscules, and many versions among them. [Sustained by ℵ. B.2 C. D. *etc.*, Tischend., Alf.—P. S.]

3 Ver. 6.—[John uses, alternately, with good reason, πηγή (vers. 6, 14) and φρέαρ (11, 12); the Vulgate retains the distinction, rendering the former by *fons*, the latter by *puteus*. Augustine says: *omnis puteus fons, non omnis fons puteus.* Only such a spring as is not on the surface, but deep and low down, is called a well (comp. ver. 11: "the well is deep"). The Arabs make a similar distinction between *'ain* or fountain, which bubbles and gushes up at its source, and *beer* (*bîr*) or well, which is constructed by a shaft sunk deep into the earth, either built of stone or excavated in the solid rock. The A. V. obliterates the distinction. "Fountain" is a better rendering of πηγή, at least in connection with "springing," ver. 14.—P. S.]

4 Ver. 6.—A. B. C. *etc.*, ὡς. [Text. rec. ὡσεί with E. Chrys. Cyr.—P. S.]

5 Ver. 7.—On the writing error πῖν, comp. Meyer. [Text. rec.: πιεῖν, Tischend., Alf.: πεῖν, which is best supported. It is the infin. aor. of πίνω. Both forms are used, but the dissylabic πιεῖν is more correct. See the quotation from Herodian in the 8th ed. of Tischend.—P. S.]

6 Ver. 9.—[οὖν is omitted by Tischend. (VIII.) and Alford.—P. S.]

7 Ver. 9.—[ἡ γυνὴ ἡ Σαμαρεῖτις. In ver. 7 it is γυνὴ ἐκ τῆς Σαμαρείας. The country is meant, not the city of Samaria (Sebaste), which was two hours distant.—P. S.]

8 Ver. 9.—[The explanatory words: οὐ γὰρ συγχρῶνται Ἰουδαῖοι Σαμαρείταις, are omitted by Tischend. in his 8th ed., but retained by Lachm., Treg., Alf. Westcott and Hort include them in brackets. Meyer, Trench and most commentators take the words as an insertion of the Evangelist, but Lange ascribes them to the woman.—P. S.]

9 Ver. 11.—[Κύριε, οὔτε ἄντλημα ἔχεις. The ἄντλημα, *haustrum* (*hauritorium* in Augustine), *bucket* in most of the early E. V., is not the same with the ὑδρία or *water-pot* which the woman leaves behind in her zeal to communicate the good news to the people in town (ver. 28), but, another vessel, with a rope or stick to draw up the water from the well. Trench, quoting from Malan, says, it is "the situla [?] generally made of skin, with three cross sticks tied round the mouth to keep it open. It is let down by a rope of goat's hair, and may be seen lying on the curb stones of almost every well in the Holy Land." —P. S.]

10 Ver. 14.—["The ὁ πίνων sets forth the recurrence, the interrupted seasons, of the drinking of earthly water;—the ὃς δ' ἂν πίῃ—the *once having tasted*, and ever continuing in the increasing power, and living forth-flowing, of that life-long draught." Alford.—P. S.]

11 Ver. 14.—Lachmann has put the words: οὐ μὴ διψήσει εἰς τὸν αἰῶνα, ἀλλὰ τὸ ὕδωρ, ὃ δώσω αὐτῷ in brackets, because they are wanting in Cod. C., in Origen, and in several minuscules. These words, however, are sufficiently attested. Probably the omission has arisen through a confounding of the second αὐτῷ with the first. It should be further noted that there is a wavering between διψήσῃ and διψήσει. Most of the authorities (A. D. L.) are for διψήσει. [Wordsworth prefers the lect. rec. διψήσῃ (*shall* not thirst) as intimating that the believer shall be preserved from thirst by divine power. But διψήσει (*will* not thirst) is supported by ℵ. A. B. D. L. M., *etc.*, and adopted by Tischendorf, Alford, *etc.*—P. S.]

12 Ver. 16.—Ὁ Ἰησοῦς is wanting in B. C.* *etc.*

13 Ibid.—The order σου τὸν ἄνδρα in Cod. B., minuscules, and Origen, adopted by Tischendorf, has the advantage of stronger emphasis. [*Lect. rec.* τὸν ἄδρα σου.—P. S.]

14 Ver. 21.—[In the best authorities γύναι follows after the verb: *Believe me, woman.*—P. S.]

15 Ver. 22.—[ἡ σωτηρία, the promised salvation, the only salvation.—P. S.]

16 Ver. 24.—[Πνεῦμα, which in the original stands emphatically first, is here not the Holy Spirit as a distinct Person, but the spiritual, immaterial nature of God which is common to all persons of the Holy Trinity. Hence *spirit* should not be capitalized, as in the A. V. Nor should the indefinite article be retained. The meaning is: God is pure spirit, spirit in the highest, absolute sense, nothing but spirit. Comp. *God is light*, 1 John i. 5; *God is love*, 1 John iv. 8.—P. S.]

[17] Ver. 25.—[The words ὁ λεγόμενος χριστός are probably the words of the woman, not a parenthetical explanation of the Evangelist. Comp. ver. 29.—P. S.]

[18] Ver. 27.—[The insertion of the definite article by the A. V. shifts the astonishment from the sex to this particular woman, of whom the disciples knew nothing. See EXEG. NOTES.—P. S.]

[19] Ver. 29.—The ὅσα of the Recepta, after A. D., is more expressive and more probable than the ἅ of B. C., adopted by Tischendorf. The same in ver. 39. [ἁ is rather better sustained by ℵ. B. C.* Syr. Orig., and adopted by Tischend. ed. VIII. Alford reads ὅσα.—P. S.]

[20] Ver. 29.—[μήτι (and μή), as interrogative particle, presupposes a *negative* answer, or at least leaves the matter in doubt, like the German: *doch wohl nicht*, comp. Matth. vii. 9, 10; Luke vi. 39. The woman is afraid to trust her own great discovery, and therefore modestly asks in this doubting style.—P. S.]

[21] Ver. 30.—The οὖν of the Recepta is too feebly attested.

[22] Ver. 34.—The reading ἵνα ποιῶ (Tischend.) is better supported than ποιήσω (Lachm.), which has come from the succeeding τελειώσω.

[23] Ver. 35.—The reading of the Recepta: τετράμηνον would elucidate the well supported τετράμηνος. [The latter is the reading of the oldest uncial MSS. including ℵ. B., and adopted by Tischend. and Alf.—P. S.]

[24] Ver. 36.—Καὶ is wanting in Codd. B. C.* D. [Cod. Sin.—E. D. Y.], and others. Probably inserted to prevent the connecting of ἤδη (ver. 35) with what follows (ver. 36) as in Cod. A. and others. The ἤδη nevertheless belongs to ver. 35. [Tischendorf and others connect ἤδη with ver. 36.—P. S.]

[25] Ver. 42.—The addition of ὁ Χριστός in the Recepta [*after*: "the Saviour of the world;" the Engl. Vers., like Luther's, reverses the order.—E. D. Y.], supported by A. D., is made uncertain by B. C. [Cod. Sin.—E. D. Y.], Origen, Irenæus, and minuscules.

EXEGETICAL AND CRITICAL.

[In this section our Saviour, sitting on Jacob's well in weariness of body, yet with ever fresh sympathy for man, discourses on the water of eternal life with an ignorant, degraded, semi-heathenish, yet quick-witted, sprightly and susceptible woman, a sort of "Samaritan Magdalene,"* and teaches her the sublime truths of the true worship of God which broke down the partition wall between Jews and Gentiles. He saw, by super-natural intuition, the dark spots in her character, but also the deeper aspirations of her soul which had not been extinguished by a life of shame; and when she began to repent and believe, He unveiled to her the future of His kingdom, as He had not done to an orthodox Jew. This scene is in striking contrast with the one related in the third chapter, where He instructed a Jew of the highest respectability in Jerusalem on the mystery of regeneration and the divine counsel of redemption. Christianity touches the extremes of society: humbling the lofty, raising the lowly, saving both. Christ's intercourse with women, "the last at the cross and the earliest at the tomb," was marked by freedom from Jewish and Oriental contempt of the weaker sex (comp. ver. 27), by elevation above earthly passion, and a marvellous union of purity and frankness, dignity and tenderness. He approached them as a friend and brother, and yet as their Lord and Saviour, while they were irresistibly drawn towards Him with mingled feelings of affection and adoration. He dealt with them as one who condemned even an impure look (Matth. v. 28), and yet He permitted the sinful woman to wash His feet with tears of repentance (Luke vii. 37 ff.). He partook of the hospitality of practical, busy Martha, while gently reminding her of the better part which her contemplative sister Mary had chosen in reverently listening to His instruction (Luke x. 38 ff.), and comforted them both at the death of their brother (John xi.); He lent a sympathizing ear to the sorrows of travail and the joy of deliverance (John xvi. 21); He remembered His mother in the last agony on the cross (xix. 26, 27); and He appeared first in His resurrection glory to Mary Magdalene, out of whom He had cast seven devils.†

* [So Dr. Lange calls her.]

† [Comp. Guizot's remarks on this subject, quoted below, DOCTR. AND ETHIC. No. 6.—P. S.]

[The Samaritans, whether we regard them (with Gesenius and the majority of modern scholars) as the descendants of the remnants of the ten tribes and the heathen colonists introduced by the Assyrians, or (with Hengstenberg, Robinson, and the older writers) as pure heathen in descent, who afterwards adopted certain features of the Jewish religion, such as circumcision, the worship of Jehovah and the hopes of the Messiah (comp. note on ver. 4), were, at all events, in their religion, a mongrel people, at one time more Jewish, at another more heathenish, according to circumstances and policy, much given to deceit and lying, and more cordially hated by the Jews than the pure Gentiles. Christ broke the spell of this long nourished national prejudice. It is true, He forbade the disciples, in their early missionary labors, to go to the Samaritans (Matth. x. 5, 6), and this seems to be inconsistent with His own conduct as related in this chapter. But the prohibition was only temporary and well founded in the divine law of order and progress. The Apostles were first sent to the house of Israel; they must lay the foundation of Christianity in that soil which had been providentially prepared for centuries, before it could be successfully planted among Gentiles. At the same time Christ Himself, though in the days of His flesh "sent to the lost sheep of the house of Israel," incidentally and by prophetic anticipation, as it were, made an exception, not only in this case, but also in the case of the Syro-Phenician woman (Matth. xv. 21 ff.), and the heathen centurion of Capernaum (Matth. viii. 5 ff.); and, in the parable of the good Samaritan (Luke x. 30 ff.), He rebuked the pride and prejudice of the Jews with regard to that people. His favorable reception among them is confirmed by the report of Luke xvii. 11 ff., that of the ten lepers whom He healed on a journey through Samaria, only one returned thanks, and he a Samaritan, putting to shame the remaining nine, who were Jews.

[The discourse here told has all the artless simplicity, freshness, vivacity and truthfulness of historical reality. No one could have invented it. The portrait of the woman is remarkably life-like—every word and act is characteristic. The whole scenery remains to this day almost unchanged: Jacob's well, though partly in ruins; round about the waving harvests of a fertile and beautiful valley, with abundance of water; the mountains of Ebal and Gerizim; a heap of stones on the spot where the Samaritan temple stood; the flat roofs of the neighboring town, visible through olive trees; veiled women in oriental costume coming for water, bearing a stone pitcher on the head or the shoulder; the weary traveller thirsting for a refreshing drink; the old bigotry and hatred of race and religion still burning beneath the ashes. How often has this chapter been read since by Christian pilgrims on the very spot where the Saviour rested, with the irresistible impression that every word is true and adapted to the time and place, yet applicable to all times and places. Jacob's well is no more used, but the living spring of water which the Saviour first opened there to a poor, sinful, yet penitent woman, is as deep and fresh as ever, and will quench the thirst of souls to the end of time.

[On this visit of our Saviour, the seed was sown which, a few years afterwards, as He prophetically foresaw (ver. 35), grew up into a plentiful harvest and resulted in the conversion of the Samaritans, as related Acts viii. 5 ff., and this in turn prepared the way for the conversion of the Gentiles. From Samaria hailed Simon Magus with the first doctrinal corruptions of Christianity by the admixture of heathen notions, but also Justin Martyr, the fearless apologist, who was a native of that very Sychar or Flavia Neapolis, where Christ met the Samaritan woman. But of far greater consequence than the result related in the Acts, is the example here set by Christ for missionary operations, and the doctrines laid down for all ages.—P. S.]

See the Literature in Heubner, p. 269 *et al.;* NIEDHOFER: *Jesus und die Samariterin* (Homiletic Discourses), Augsburg, 1821. [Archbishop Trench: *Christ and the Samaritan Woman,* in his *Studies in the Gospels,* pp. 83-137. Dr. J. R. Macduff: *Noontide at Sychar; or the Story of Jacob's Well. A N. Test. chapter in Providence and grace.* N. York, 1869 (pp. 268).—P. S.]

Ver. 1. **When therefore the Lord [Jesus] knew.**—*The Lord,* for the first time in this Gospel.* Ἔγνω or γνούς no doubt has in John, after what he has previously said of Christ's immediate knowledge of men's hearts, a special signification when it relates to human thoughts and purposes connected with Christ.† Οὖν primarily looks back to the preceding account of the growing labors of Jesus; but it also points to the insight of Jesus into the spirit of the Pharisees, which was well understood, as natural means of knowledge are not excluded.

The Pharisees had heard.—Their hearing carries with it the idea of their having sought information, and keeping a jealous watch. Hence Jesus, it is true, avoids a premature hindrance to his labors, or, as Meyer says, a danger.‡ Yet this one motive, which John states, does not exclude another: that the Baptist was about this time cast into prison, after having labored last in Galilee, and that in answer to the special occasion thus arising for a confirming of hearts in that region, Christ appeared in the place of John in Galilee. Besides, enough for the present had been done for Judea. A third motive probably was, that Jesus had now determined for a while entirely to cease baptizing.

That Jesus made more disciples.—Literally: "makes and baptizes." The verbal quoting of what they had heard, expressed by the present tense, indicates a very definite or a very well known report. **More disciples than John.**—Jesus gave the Pharisaic spirit more to fear: His freer address; more public appearance in Jerusalem; His stronger influence; the purification of the temple: His higher authority; miracles; Himself accredited as the Messiah by John.

Ver. 2. **Though Jesus himself.**—Evidently a parenthesis, otherwise it would belong to what the Pharisees had heard.* The Evangelist does not correct the report (Meyer), for it was true; he only states the fact more precisely. The observation no doubt means not that it so happened, but that it was a rule, that Jesus Himself baptized not. Why? (1) Because the work of teaching was more important (1 Cor. i. 17, De Wette [Alford]); (2) because He would have had to baptize into Himself (Tertullian); (3) Bengel: "*Baptizare actio ministerialis est. . . . Christus baptizat Spiritu sancto.*" [So Godet, Trench. Godet: "*Il était le Seigneur, et il se réservait le baptême de l' Esprit.*"—P. S.] Nonnus follows this: the Lord baptizes not with water. Tertullian's explanation, too, has warrant. As Christ is the object of baptism, the centre of the new kingdom, He would obscure the idea of baptism, if He should not have the transition from the old system to the new, so far as the baptism was concerned, administered by others.†

Ver. 3. **He left Judea.**—At the same time giving up baptizing. Why? Because the imprisonment of the Baptist in the midst of the Jewish people had brought a ban of uncleanness again upon the whole congregation of Israel (see my *Leben Jesu,* II. 2, p. 515). This settled it, that a new baptism could proceed only from the baptism of blood, which at the same time would give it a deeper significance (as the final ideal consecration of death).

Departed again into Galilee.—As after He was baptized.

Ver. 4. **Through Samaria.**—Samaria lay between Judea and Galilee, and through this

* [But the reading is doubtful, see TEXT. NOTES. The term κύριος, as equivalent to Jehovah or Adonai in the O. T., is not near as often applied to Christ in the Gospels (comp. vi. 23, 34; xi. 2; xx. 28, *etc.*) as in the Epistles, because in its full sense it presupposes the elevation of Christ to glory. In the mouth of the Samaritan woman, ver. 11, and others not acquainted with the true character of Christ, it is simply a title of courtesy.—P. S.]

† [Meyer denies the supernatural character of ἔγνω here.—P. S.]

‡ [Against the artificial interpretation of this occurrence by Hofmann, *Schriftbeweis,* I. p. 168, see Meyer, p. 186, note (5th ed.). Withdrawal from danger, no less than firm courage in the face of martyrdom, is under circumstances a duty to God and the church, expressly enjoined by Christ, Matth. x. 23, and sanctioned by His example. Flight from cowardice is always contemptible, flight from fidelity to duty is compatible with unflinching courage. An humble retreat may at times imply more self-denial than proud and ambitious resistance.—P. S.]

* [Hence the use of *Jesus* instead of *He.*—P. S.]

† [Clement of Alex. and other fathers, in their over-estimate of water baptism, assumed, without any warrant from the text, that Jesus baptized at least Peter, who then baptized Andrew, *etc.* To the three reasons mentioned above for Christ's not administering baptism, Lightfoot adds a fourth, *viz.,* Because He would prevent all quarrels and jealousies which might have arisen if some had been baptized by Christ Himself and others only by His disciples. But the one sufficient reason is no doubt because water baptism is a ministerial act of secondary importance, and that Christ reserved to Himself instead the baptism with the Holy Ghost.—P. S.]

province, therefore, the usual route of pilgrimage also passed (Joseph. *Antiq.* XX. 6, 1).* The custom of scrupulous Jews, to make a circuit through Peræa, could have no force with Jesus; though afterwards the Samaritans themselves once occasioned His following it. But He then also had probably already come near the boundary of Samaria (see Maier, *Commentar.*, p. 328), Luke ix. 52. *Samaria*, שֹׁמְרוֹן; Chald. שָׁמְרַיִן, Ezra iv. 10, 17, primarily the name of a city. The city lay in the kingdom of the ten tribes in middle Palestine, on a mountain (Robinson [Germ. ed.] III. p. 365); built by Omri about 922 B. C., and made the seat of the kingdom of Israel (1 Kings xvi. 24, and elsewhere); a chief seat of the worship of Baal during the time of the apostasy, 1 Kings xvi. 31; as the capital of Ephraim, the counterpart of Jerusalem (Ezek. xvi. 46, and elsewhere). Shalmanezer conquered the city and filled it with colonists, 2 Kings xvii. 5 sqq. John Hyrcanus destroyed it, but it was soon rebuilt. Herod the Great, to whom Cæsar Augustus gave the city, beautified it, strengthened it, planted a colony of veterans in it, and named it *Sebaste* [*Augusta*, in honor of Augustus, Joseph. *Antiq.* XV. 8, 5]. The growth of Sichem [Neapolis] in the vicinity threw back the city to a hamlet, which still exists as Sebustieh, in ruins. From the city of Samaria (*Σαμάρεια*) the region of Middle Palestine gradually took its name, *Σαμαρεῖτις* (1 Macc. x. 30); it is a separate province in the time of the Syrian kings (also *Σαμαρίς*. *Σαμάρεια* in Josephus). The description which Josephus gives of the country, see in Winer under the word. Samaria appears more friendly than Judea, rich in vegetation and forest-clad hills. In the same article are the accounts of modern tourists respecting the city of Samaria.

By the *Samaritans*, שֹׁמְרוֹנִים, *Σαμαρεῖται*, *Σαμαρεῖς*, history understands the later post-exilian inhabitants of the country, the *Χουθαῖοι* (Joseph. *Antiq.* IX. 14, 3, *etc.*). According to the prevailing view, a mixed population grew up from the heathen colonists of Shalmanezer (and Esarhaddon, Ezra iv. 2) from Assyrian provinces (2 Kings xvii. 24), Babylon, Cuthah, Ava, Hameth, and Sepharvaim, and from the remnants of the Israelites. In the land of Israel they adopted the Israelite religion (2 Kings xvii. 25; Ezra vi. 21; Nehem. x. 28), and soon went so far as to call themselves the genuine offspring of Israel, or of the house of Joseph (Joseph. *Antiq.* XI. 8, 6). And now they would still be called Israelites, but not Jews. But as they presumed in pride to boast an Israelite descent, so too they often permitted themselves through policy utterly to deny this extraction, and give themselves out for Persians (Joseph. *Antiq.* XI. 9, 4) or Sidonians [*Ibid.* XI. 8, 6].

After Hottinger and others, Hengstenberg in particular [*Beiträge* I. 117; II. 3 sqq.] has wholly denied to the Samaritans any genealogical connection with the Jews. The document, 2 Kings xvii., mentions nothing, it is true, of remaining Israelites, and the Samaritans have often boasted that they were of heathen origin. This last fact, however, can signify nothing; for they likewise boasted, generally, that they were pure Jews (and the *ἀλλογενής*, Luke xvii. 18, evidently proves nothing). But it is said in 2 Kings xvii. 24, that the colonists were placed *in the cities;* so that the colonization was limited. Besides, the deportations of this kind in history, as Winer observes, are never radical. The Samaritans were also early distinguished from the heathen (1 Macc. iii. 10). Under Hezekiah (2 Chron. xxx. 6, 10) and under Josiah (2 Chron. xxxiv. 9) there were remnants of Israel in Ephraim and Manasseh. And Christ, as well as the Apostles after Him, considered the Samaritans a middle people between Jews and heathen, Acts i. 8; viii. 5. A predominance of heathen blood is assumed by many.

As might be expected of such a mixed people, adopting Judaism in an outward way, (1) they were not consistent in their national and religious spirit; they professed now to be Jews, now to be Gentiles, as their interest might require. Under Antiochus Epiphanes their temple was dedicated to Jupiter Hellenius. Heresy in the Christian church, which is mainly a mixture of Christianity with heathenism, takes its rise in the Christianity of Samaria.* (2) They attained no living development of their religious ideas; so that in their canon (the Pentateuch), their Messianic expectation, and their use of the law, they stopped where they began; whence they in many respects resembled the Sadducees (though the Sadducees had their abridged and stunted Judaism for having gone backwards with a negative criticism, the Samaritans for having gotten fast in the letter, and not gone forwards). (3) For this very reason, however, their Messianic hope remained more simple and pure. (4) After having been refused a share in the re-building of the temple in Jerusalem [Ezra iv. 1 sqq.] they fully reciprocated (first of all by hindering the building of the temple, Ezra iv. 4, and the subsequent strengthening of the city, Neh. iv. 1) the fanatical hatred of the Jews, who looked upon them as heretics, not as heathen [see Sir. L. 27]; and they built a temple of their own on Gerizim. According to Josephus, *Antiq.* XI. 8, 4, this took place in the time of Alexander the Great. Manasseh, brother of the Jewish high-priest Jaddus, had a heathen lady for his wife. The Jewish rulers demanded his circumcision; whereupon Sanballat induced him to renounce his membership in the Jewish religion, and built the temple on Gerizim, of which Manasseh became high-priest. According to Neh. xiii. 28, a son of the high-priest Joiada, not named, had married a daughter of Sanballat, and was excommunicated for it. We may suppose that the two accounts relate to the same case, and that the chronology of Josephus is here at fault, the case having occurred under Darius Nothus (see Winer, *Samaritaner*). On the further fortunes of the Samaritans, see Winer, l. c. (comp. *Com. on Matth.* x. 5, p. 185; *Leben Jesu* II. 2, p. 539).

Ver. 5. **To a city of Samaria, which is called Sychar** [lit. *drunken*].—Near to the city,

* [Hence *ἔδει*, which expresses a geographical necessity, if the *shortest* route was to be chosen. This necessity became a providential opportunity for doing good.—P. S.]

* [Simon Magus: See my *Geschichte des apostol. Zeitalters*, I. p. 301 ff; and the treatise: *Die Samariter und ihre Stellung in der Weltgeschichte von J. Grimm* (priest), Munich, 1854.]

into its vicinity: εἰς πόλιν. Συχάρ=*Shechem* or *Sichem* (שְׁכֶם), Gen. xxxiii. 18, *etc.;* Συχέμ, Sept., Acts vii. 16; also Σίκιμα; after the time of Christ, *Neapolis* [Joseph. *De bello Jud.* IV. 8, 1]; now *Nabulus* (Robinson, III. p. 336; Schubert, III. p. 136).*

Its general identity with Sichem is established by the particular statement that Jacob's well was near. But the name *Sychar* for *Sichem* is not otherwise known, apart from the statement in Wieseler, that in the Talmud occurs the name of a place עין מוכר, *well of the grave,* literally *of the purchased,* that is, of the purchased burial-ground. Hug also (*Einleitung* II. p. 218) supposes the name comes from Suchar, and denotes the place of burial where the bones of Joseph [Josh. xxiv. 32] and, according to the tradition common in the times of Jesus, of the twelve patriarchs of the children of Israel, were deposited. Acts vii. 15, 16. It is the prevailing presumption that Συχάρ is a popular Jewish nick-name, a contemptuous travesty of Sichem; with allusion, according to Reland, to Is. xxviii. 1, 7: Samaria the crown of pride of the drunkards in Ephraim, therefore the city of drunkards [שִׁכּוֹר, *drunkard*]; according to Lightfoot, alluding to שֶׁקֶר, heathenism as falsehood [Hab. ii. 18], therefore the city of deceit.† According to Hug and others, Sychar is to be distinguished from Sichem itself somewhat as a suburb, and then means the city of the sepulchre. This view is favored by the fact that both Schubert and Robinson put the ancient Sichem nearer Jacob's well, than the present town lies, and that at the time of Eusebius, Sychar and Sichem were distinguished as two places. Consequently the views of Reland and Lightfoot may well be dismissed as ingenious scholastic conjectures (especially since the first view would make the city of Samaria, not Sichem, a Sychar, and since the allusion to Habakkuk is quite too subtile), though it might be some relief to suppose, with Meyer, that John uses the name Sychar only as the vulgar name. Yet then we might have to admit ignorance in reference to the true name; which we could hardly do; still less admit that John made nick-names. The hypothesis of an interchange of the *liquidæ* (Tholuck) is also inconclusive. We abide, therefore, by the hypothesis that Sychar is distinguished as the city of the sepulchre from Sichem.* On the situation of Nablus between Gerizim and Ebal, see Schubert, Robinson, and others (comp. *Leben Jesu* II. 2, p. 525).

Near to the parcel of ground that Jacob, *etc.*—The basis of the tradition is Gen. xxxiii. 19. Jacob buys of the children of Hamor a field in Shechem on which to settle. The passage, Gen. xlviii. 22, is to be regarded as a prophecy; he would give Joseph a portion above his brethren, which he (in his posterity) would win (not had won; see Knobel on the passage) from the hand of the Amorites with his sword and bow. Finally, in Josh. xxiv. 32 it is said that the bones of Joseph were buried at Shechem in the parcel of ground which Jacob bought of the sons of Hamor, and the sons of Joseph received them (with the field) for an inheritance. The somewhat inaccurate version of the Sept. is of no importance at all to the estimate of the perfectly correct account (against Meyer).

Ver. 6. **Jacob's Well.**†—The well which Jacob, according to the Israelitish tradition, dug; which by this tradition was made highly sacred. It is thirty-five minutes from the present Nablus, sunk in rock to the depth of a hundred and five feet [now only about seventy-five feet.—P. S.], with a diameter of nine. Maundrell found fifteen feet of water in it; Robinson and others found it dry.‡

* [The old Hebrew *Shechem*, or *Sichem*, or *Sychar*, the Græco-Roman colony *Flavia Neapolis* (founded probably after the destruction of Jerusalem, by *Flavius* Vespasianus), and the modern Arabic *Nabulus*, or *Nablus* (*i. e.*, Neapolis), are substantially identical as to location, though probably a little apart from each other (see below) and must be sought in the narrow, fertile and beautiful valley between Mt. Ebal and Mt. Gerizim, which is much admired by modern travellers, as the Eden of Palestine. Dr. Robinson, who is by no means enthusiastic in his descriptions, says of Shechem: "It came upon us suddenly like a scene of enchantment. We saw nothing like it in all Palestine." The place figures very conspicuously in sacred history. At Sichem Abraham built his first altar in Canaan; there Jacob pitched his tent, buried the idols of his household, built the well and bought the tomb of Joseph; there Dinah was defiled by Shechem, the son of Hamor, prince of the country; there Joseph was sold by his brethren and found the last resting-place for his bones. After the conquest of Canaan under Joshua, Shechem was made a city of refuge and a centre of union to the tribes; under the judges it was the capital of the abortive kingdom of Abimelech; subsequently the capital of the kingdom of the ten tribes till Samaria deprived it of that honor; it continued during the exile and long afterwards the ecclesiastical metropolis of Samaria, the only temple of the Samaritan worship being close by on Mount Gerizim. The present city of Nabulus has, according to Dr. Robinson, about 8,000 inhabitants, all Mohammedans, except about 500 Jews and as many Greek Christians, with a bishop, who, however, resides in a convent at Jerusalem. Dr. Rosen (in the *Zeitschrift der M. D. Gesellschaft* for 1860, pp. 622-639, as quoted by the writer of the art. *Shechem* in Smith's *Dictionary*), estimates the population of Nabulus at about 5,000, among whom are 500 Greek Christians, 150 Samaritans, and a few Jews, the Mohammedans making up the bulk of inhabitants.—P. S.]

† [Or *Lietown*, *Lugstadt*. So also Hengstenberg (I. 244), Wordsworth, Trench: "St. John, by this turn of the word, which has brought it into closest connection with the Hebrew for a lie, declares at what rate he esteemed the Samaritan worship, declares by anticipation at what rate it was esteemed by his Lord."—P. S.]

* [Dr. Thomson, *The Land and the Book*, and others, likewise distinguish them for the reason that at Sichem (Nablus) there are delicious fountains of water which the Samaritan woman would hardly have left to draw from a well that is nearly two miles off. Bovet, of Neuchatel (*Voyage en Terre Sainte*, p. 363, as quoted by Godet) thinks he has discovered some ruins of Sichem in the midst of olive plantations between the present Nablus and the well of Jacob. "*Le nom meme de Naplouse,*" adds Godet, "*indique un nouvel emplacement; autrement la nouvelle ville eut conservé le nom de Sichem. Cette circonstance explique peut etre comment la femme Samaritaine venait chercher le l 'eau au puits de Jacob.*" This conjecture may be correct, but the narrative does not require it. The woman may have labored or dwelt near the well of Jacob, or put a special value on its sacred waters to induce her to go to special trouble. Porter, who identifies the two places, but assumes that the ancient Shechem was a much larger city than the present Nablous, says (*Handbook for Travellers in Syria and Palestine*, Part II., p. 342): "The mere fact of the well having been Jacob's would have brought numbers to it had the distance been twice as great. And even independent of its history, some little superiority in the quality of the water, such as we might expect in a deep well, would have attracted the Orientals, who are, and have always been, epicures in this element. There is a well called ez-Zenabîyeh, a mile or more outside St. Thomas' Gate, Damascus, to which numbers of the inhabitants send for their daily supply, though they have fountains and wells in their own houses far more abundant than ever existed in the city of Shechem."—P. S.]

† [The same is now called by the natives *Bir-Jakoub*. Renan, *Vie de Jésus*, p. 233.—P. S.]

‡ [It should be remembered, however, that Dr. Robinson visited the well in the middle of June. He remarks that "it was said usually to contain living water, and not merely to be filled by the rains." Jews, Samaritans, Christians and

Probably it was not the well nearest the city. The woman, however, might have had occasion to avoid the conversation of other women at other wells; perhaps for the same reason she chose the unusual hour of noon (other possible reasons, from Robinson, in *Leben Jesu*, II. 2, p. 526).

Sat thus [ἐκαθέζετο οὕτως, a graphic touch].—Simply sat. Probably indicating the absence of all constraint and reserve.* **About the sixth hour.**—According to the Jewish reckoning, noon. Meyer: "Never to be forgotten by John."

[The hour is probably also mentioned to bring more vividly to our mind the weariness of our Saviour at the heat of the midday sun, the burden and toil He suffered for us at the very moment He opened a fountain of refreshment to this poor thirsty woman and to us all. On the dates of John, see note on i. 39, p. 92 f. There are additional reasons for assuming that he reckoned here in the Jewish manner from sunrise to sunset. Otherwise he would have noted whether it was six in the morning (as Rettig assumes), or six in the evening (as Ebrard and Wordsworth hold). The former is too early to account for the fatigue of the Lord, the latter leaves no time for what follows, as the night sets in with little or no intervening twilight in Eastern countries. The conversation must have lasted at least half an hour, then the woman goes away to the city, tells her experience to the men, and they come to the well of Jacob; and yet after all this it must have been still daylight, to account for the words of Jesus: "Lift up your eyes and look on the fields" (ver. 35). Considering the oriental contempt for woman and the prejudice even of the disciples (ver. 27), a conversation with a woman late in the evening would have been even more unseemly than at noon-day. The fact that the woman was *alone* sufficiently explains that she came so early to draw water, instead of the evening as usual. The time of the year—it was at the end of December—permitted travelling till towards noon. Porter, in his excellent *Handbook for Travellers in Syria and Palestine*, ii. p. 341, takes the same view. "Christ probably came up the plain of Mukhna, and about noon reached the well." So also Macduff, p. 36.—P. S.]

Ver. 7. **A woman of Samaria.**—That is, of the country. The city of Sebaste was two hours [six miles] distant.* Tholuck remarks that the characteristic traits of this very highly individualized woman are indifference to higher interests and roguish frivolity.† But these are hardly individual traits; and these traits form hardly the whole outline of a deeply fallen character, who shows, however, a considerable versatility of mind and great energy, besides a deeper susceptibility under the veil of a bright, resolute nature. A sort of Samaritan Magdalene. With good reason Tholuck insists on the individuality of the woman against Strauss and Weisse. The striking invalidation of Baur's fiction respecting the design of this supposed fiction is likewise worthy of notice.

Give me to drink.—Points: (1) The truth of Christ's thirst; (2) the freedom of His intercourse,—with a Samaritan, and a woman; (3) the higher purpose of His words; (4) the mastery of the great Fisher of souls [Luke v. 10], in having the earthly given to Him in order to give the heavenly.‡

Ver. 8. **For his disciples.**—Immediate occasion: The disciples had gone to the city. Probably they also carried a vessel for drawing water (ἄντλημα, ver. 11) with them.§ **To buy**

Muhammedans all agree in this tradition respecting both Jacob's well and Joseph's tomb. Adjacent to the well are the ruins of an ancient church forming mounds of rubbish, among which Robinson discovered three granite columns. When last measured, the well was only about seventy-five feet deep. A portion of the vault has fallen in and completely covered up the mouth so that nothing can be seen but a shallow pit half filled with stones and rubbish. See Porter's *Handbook for Travellers in Syria and Palestine*, II., p. 341.

My friend, the Rev. W. W. Atterbury, who visited Jacob's well, April 7, 1866, kindly permits me to extract the following observations from his Journal, which confirm Dr. Robinson's account as to the present condition of the well:

"At the entrance of the Nablus valley we stopped to visit Jacob's Well. In the middle of a ploughed field, a low stone wall enclosed a ruined vault, through the broken arch of which we let ourselves down to its floor, where, almost entirely closed with fragments of stone, was the well. We could judge something of its depth by the fall of a stone, and thus ascertained that there is now no water in it. It is said to be 70 ft. deep, and is hewn out of the solid rock. Sitting on the fallen stones that covered the mouth of the well, I read the 4th chap. of John. A few rods N. W. is a small Moslem tomb, of stone, said to cover the grave of Joseph. The way up the vale to Nablus was charming. Gerizim and Ebal, bare of trees, and but scantily carpeted with vegetation, except near their bases, were at first so near each other that ordinary voices might shout audibly from one side to the other. The valley widened as we advanced. A recess occurs on each side, opposite the one to the other, like the transepts of a vast Cathedral in which it is easy to suppose respective divisions of the tribes were stationed when, the priest standing in the midst, the people responded to the blessings and the curses."—P. S.]

* [So Chrysostom and the Greek commentators: ἁπλῶς ὡς ἔτυχε, *just as it happened*, *i. e.*, on the ground or the stones surrounding the well; Grotius: *ut locus se obtulerat;* Bengel: *sine pompa* (to which he adds: *admirabilis popularitas vitæ Jesu*); Meyer: *so ohne weiteres*, *i. e.*, without ceremony and preparation; Wordsworth: *as any one among men.* But Erasmus, Beza, Winer, Stier, Hengstenberg, Webster and Wilkinson and Alford, refer οὕτως to κεκοπιακώς, *i. e.*, *sic nempe quia fatigatus*, *fatigued as He was, as a weary man would*, or *accordingly.* We might say (with Godet) that the word was inspired by the contrast to the unexpected task before Him. But Fritzsche and Meyer object that in this case οὕτως should precede ἐκάθεζετο, as in Acts xx. 11; xxvii. 17; to which may be added Hebr. vi. 15.—P. S.]

* [The Roman martyrology knows the name of the woman (Photina) and of her children. Augustine: "*Venit mulier ad puteum, et fontem quem non speravit, invenit.*" Trench: "To that same well she oftentimes may have come already, day by day, perhaps, during many a weary year of the past. And now she came once more, little guessing how different was to be the issue of this day's coming from that of all the days which had gone before . . . that in the midst of that and all the other weary toil, outward and inward, of this earthly life, she should have within herself a fountain of joy, springing up unto life eternal, should draw water with joy from unfailing wells of salvation."—P. S.]

† [Dr. Lange very properly objects to this low estimate of the Samaritan woman who, with all her vices, had some higher traits of character. Hengstenberg justly remarks (I. 254) that Jesus would hardly have entered into a conversation with her, if He had not discovered in her an open susceptibility to the truth.—P. S.]

‡ [The physical thirst introduced the deeper spiritual thirst. While appearing as the receiver of natural water, He was the giver of supernatural water and thirsted to communicate this to the woman. Somewhat differently Augustine: *Ille qui bibere quærebat, fidem ipsius mulieris sitiebat.* Trench observes in this request of Jesus, and the discourse to which it was the prelude, a threefold testimony against the narrow-heartedness of His age and people—against that of the Jew who hated the Samaritan, of the Rabbi who would have scorned such familiar intercourse with a woman (ver. 27), of the Pharisee who would have shrunk from this near contact with a sinner (Luke vii. 39).—P. S.]

§ [This is the usual interpretation, but the Saviour may have isolated Himself from His disciples in the spiritual in-

food.—Meyer: "The later [Rabbinical] tradition* would not have allowed this. But at that time the separation may not have been so rigid, especially for Galileans, whose route of pilgrimage passed through Samaria. Besides, Jesus was above the divisions of the people, Luke ix. 52."

Ver. 9. **How is it that thou, being a Jew, askest**, *etc.*—She recognizes Him in particular by His Jewish dialect and pronunciation [perhaps also from His Jewish physiognomy and the dress of a Rabbi]. Tholuck: The Samaritan tongue is between the Hebrew and the Aramaic. As Jesus Himself spoke Aramaic, this is not quite clear, and probably a medium between Western and Eastern Aramaic is meant.† More than one thing might surprise her: not only that a *Jew* spoke with her, and asked drink from her pitcher, but also that this *distinguished Jew* condescended to *ask* of her. In truth we might well suppose that she was moved with a feeling of her unworthiness in the dignified presence: He unconsciously defiles Himself on my pitcher; at least she hints at the difference between the man and the always less regarded woman. Though the national enmity could not wholly prevent her asking water in her turn (Tholuck), yet the breach was wide enough to make her feel the request of Jesus to be a great and free condescension. Then the expression of this feeling may easily have been accompanied or disguised by a certain humor giving vent to her national spirit, as she now, with her pitcher, seems to have the better of the stranger. The addition: **The Jews have no dealings**, *etc.*, is commonly taken as an explanatory note of the Evangelist. But in that case we should expect: The Jews and the Samaritans have no dealings with one another. The disdain being here ascribed to the Jew alone, the words no doubt belong to the woman's reply.

[The question of the woman illustrates the intensity and bitterness of sectarian bigotry and hatred as it then prevailed, and sets in stronger contrast the marvellous freedom of Christ from existing prejudices.‡ According to Dr. Robinson and others the ancient hatred is still kept up, and the remnant of Samaritans neither eat, nor drink, nor marry, nor associate with the Jews, but only trade with them. An experienced traveller says, apparently to the contrary: "Never yet, during many years' residence in Syria, and many a long day's travel, have I been refused a draught of water by a single individual of any sect or race. The Bedawy in the desert has shared with me the last drop in his water-skin. Yet the only reply of the woman to the weary traveller was, 'How is it that thou, being a Jew,'" *etc.* (Porter's *Handbook for Travellers in Syria and Palestine*, P. II., p. 342.) But this courtesy to strangers is not inconsistent with Dr. Robinson's statement, nor with our narrative, for the woman did not refuse a drink of water to Jesus, but only expressed her surprise at His asking her for it.—P. S.]

Ver. 10. **If thou knewest the gift of God.**—Tholuck: "This answer indicates that she, instead of hesitating, must have felt herself honored, and made haste." More pertinently Meyer: "Unquestionably Jesus immediately perceived the susceptibility of the woman; hence His leaving His own want, and entering upon a conversation so striking as to arouse the whole interest of the sanguine woman." She is surprised that He, the supposed haughty Jew, is the asker; the Lord brings out the opposite relation, that *she* is the needy one, *He* the possessor of the true fountain of satisfaction.

The gift of God: (1) The person of Jesus (Greek com., Erasmus). [Hengstenberg refers to iii. 16: "God *gave* His only begotten Son," and Isa. ix. 5: "to us a Son is *given*," as decisive proofs that Christ designated Himself "*the gift of God.*"] (2) The Holy Spirit [with reference to vii. 38, 39] (Augustine, *etc.*) (3) Correctly: The singular grace of God in the golden opportunity of this moment (Grotius and others).* [(4) Eternal life. So Lampe and Godet; vers. 13, 14; comp. Rom. vi. 23 where eternal life is styled "the gift of God" (χάρισμα, but here we have δῶρον); Rev. xxii. 17. (5) Living water, in anticipation of what immediately follows: "He would have given thee living water." So Stier and Trench. Alford regards this as the primary view, but combines with it the first three, like Dr. Yeomans in the preceding footnote.—P. S.]

terest of the woman in order to win the easier her repentance and confession of sin. (Cornelius a Lap. and Trench). Hengstenberg (I. 253) plausibly assumes that John remained with the Lord and heard the conversation which he so accurately and vividly records. He was afterwards with Peter delegated to Samaria, Acts viii. 14. But he may have learned the conversation from Jesus or from the woman after her conversion.—P. S.]

* [*Rasche ad Sota*, p. 515: "*Hominis Samaritani panem comedere aut vinum ejus bibere prohibitum (nefas) est.*" *Tanchuma* fol., 43, 1: "*Dicunt, qui edit frustum Samaritani, est ut edens carnem porci, et non proselytus fit Samaritanus in Israele, nec est ipsis pars in resurrectione mortuorum.*"]

† [Stier (*Reden Jesu*) thinks that the woman recognized the Jew rather by his dress (after the manner of the Rabbis), than by His softer dialect. If the Samaritans, like the Ephraimites of old (Judg. xii. 6) were still distinguished by lack of the full sibilant (*sh*) in their pronunciation, the words which Jesus probably used הַשְׁקִינִי נָא or תְּנִי לִי לִשְׁתּוֹת (*teni lishethoth*, Samaritan: *teni lisethoth*), were enough to indicate the nationality. In any case we may infer from the words of the woman that our Lord had nothing in His personal appearance, dress or manner to distinguish Him from other Jews, and to attract the superficial observer. Yet the spotless beauty and peace of His soul must have shone through His eye and the expression of His face. He had not the physiognomy of a sinner.—P. S.]

‡ [Ecclus. c. 25, 26: "There be two manner of nations which my heart abhorreth, and the third is no nation: they that sit upon the mountain of Samaria, and they that dwell among the Philistines, and that foolish people that dwell in Sichem."—P. S.]

* [Neither of these interpretations alone seems sufficient for this very full expression. The third is certainly the leading one, but it includes the others. The third itself, as here given, is too vague. The "singular grace of God in the opportunity of this moment" is, in particular, that God, so far from being beyond the reach of our requests, appears as a fellow-man asking a service from us. His taking such a place, to be kindly served of us for our joy and salvation is itself a gracious *gift of God*. In Jesus alone could this wonderful relation between God and man be established and offered; He alone is God-Man; "the gift of God" therefore includes the person of Jesus. And it includes a gift of *life* still in reserve for those who, knowing Christ, ask of Him; and *this* gift of God, waiting for our asking, is in substance the Holy Ghost. J. J. Owen: "The connection refers it evidently to the gift of living water, which was emphatically the gift of God bestowed through the agency of His Spirit." But a still more careful weighing of the context shows that it rather refers this "*gift of God*" to a gift which God had already given, than to one which He had yet to give; rather to the *actual gift* of His condescension, than to the *offered gift* of living water or the Holy Ghost.—E. D. Y.]

And who it is.—Unfolding the thought of the gift of God. **Thou** (σύ) **wouldest** (*already*) **have asked** (not: wouldest ask him, Luther) **of him.**—Expressing the greatness of her need, the greatness of His gift, the urgency her request would have; doubtless also her susceptibility. [Mark the difference between ὁ λέγων σοι which Christ uses of Himself, after the woman had naturally asked: πῶς σὺ παρ' ἐμοῦ αἰτεῖς (ver. 9), and σὺ ἂν ᾔτησας, which assigns at once to the woman a position of inferiority and dependence on Him, the possessor and giver of that living water. "There lies often," says Trench, "in little details like this an implicit assertion of the unique dignity of His person, which it is very interesting and not unimportant to trace."—P. S.]

He would have given thee living water. —מַיִם חַיִּים [Sept. ὕδωρ ζῶν] well-water.* Expressing at once the greatness of the gift and the readiness of the giving, in a figure drawn from *His own* request, but answering perfectly to her unsatisfied state of mind. The figures of Ps. xxxvi. 8; Jer. ii. 13; xvii. 13. The sense of the words, *living water*, explained in ver. 14. Various interpretations: (1) Baptism (Justin, Cyril [Cyprian, Ambrose]. But the water of Baptism is not water for drinking, which becomes a fountain in him who drinks it. (2) The evangelic doctrine. Grotius, similarly Meyer: The truth.† Shall a man then after that thirst no more? (3) Tarnow; *Gratia justificans*. Like most of the explanations, too dogmatically exclusive. (4) *Institutio salutaris* (Semler). (5) Lücke: Faith. (6) Olshausen: Life (ch. vi. 33). (7) The Holy Spirit, vii. 39 (Maldonatus, Bucer, [Webster and Wilkinson, Wordsworth] and others). The act of giving must no doubt be distinguished from the living water itself: The giving of the water is the gospel, the word of Christ; see ver. 26. The water itself, which quenches thirst, proves itself already operating when the woman sets her pitcher down, [ver. 28]: it is evidently *the inner-life* as the operation of the life of Christ, conceived predominantly under *the aspect of inward peace* (no longer thirsting), developing into regeneration, life in the Holy Ghost (the water's becoming a fountain) and perfection in blessedness (springing up into everlasting life). Tholuck: "The word of salvation the medium of a living power of the Spirit, ch. vii. 38; xi. 26." [Godet: Living water is the life eternal, which is Christ Himself living in the soul by the Holy Spirit. *Donner l'eau vive, c'est pour lui se communiquer lui-même; car la vie est identifiée avec son principe.*—P. S.]

Ver. 11. **Sir, thou hast nothing to draw with.**—*Sir.* A title of respect usual even at that time among men, ch. v. 7; vi. 34, *etc.* Used in the ordinary sense.* The spiritual conception was rendered difficult by the lack of the prophets among the Samaritans, and the want of knowledge of the prophetic metaphors (Tholuck). On this presumption the reply is not exactly "saucy" (Tholuck), but no doubt clearly thought, firm, savoring of national pride, exulting again in easy humor. *Thou hast nothing.* Exactly: Thou hast not *even* a vessel to draw with.† She evidently distinguishes between the water itself standing in the well, and the spring at the bottom of it. Thou hast not even a bucket, *i. e.*, thou canst not even reach down to the standing water. **And the well is deep.**—That is, even with the bucket thou couldest not come to the living spring.‡

Ver. 12. **Art thou greater.**—Σύ emphatic. Μείζων cannot mean nobler, of higher rank, as Meyer thinks; for noble lords, as such, are not exactly masters in water-drawing or well-digging. The question proceeds from a feeling that Jesus assumed some extraordinary character, that He claimed a spiritual power; perhaps claimed to be a prophet, like Moses, who could make a fountain of water by miracle. **Than our father Jacob.**—Expressing the national jealousy towards the Jew. The Samaritans traced their descent from Joseph [Joseph. *Antiq.*, viii. 14, 3; xi. 8, 6].

Who gave us the well.—This was a simple inference from the tradition that Jacob dug the well and left it to his posterity. The sense is: The patriarch himself knew not what better to give, and this sufficed for all the wants of his entire nomadic establishment. Meyer: "The woman treats the enigmatical word of Christ at first as Nicodemus does, ch. iii. 4, but more thoughtfully [considering the false conception of Nicodemus], and at the same time more pertly and with feminine readiness of speech." In her last word: θρέμματα, *cattle*, she finishes her carnal misapprehension of His spiritual words. [The mention of the *cattle* (which does not necessarily include the slaves, as sometimes on inscriptions (see Meyer, p. 192), completes at the same time the picture of the *nomadic* life of the patriarch. Stier is wrong therefore in regarding it as a falling off in the lofty language of the woman to descend from Jacob's sacred person to his cattle. There is in the question of the woman a slight resentment at the seeming intentional disregard of the venerable traditions and memorials of her people by which they connect-

* [As distinct from cistern water, or water of reservoirs, or stagnant water, comp. Gen. xxvi. 19; Lev. xiv. 5; Cant. iv. 5; Jer. ii. 13; the *vivi fontes* of the Romans. Then used metaphorically for spiritual blessings, truth, wisdom, even the Holy Spirit. On this double meaning rests the turn of the discourse from the earthly to the heavenly, and the point of comparison is the refreshing power and the satisfaction of thirst. Here the ὕδωρ ζῶν means, in the highest spiritual sense, fresh, springing, life-giving, self-renewing water from Him who is αὐτοζωή, life itself, and imparts life to all His followers (John i. 4; v. 40; Rev. vii. 17; xxi. 6; xxii. 1, 17] in fulfilment of the prophecy, Ezek. xlvii. 9: "Everything shall live whither the river cometh" (that issues from under the threshold of the house of God).—P. S.]

† [Meyer (5th ed.) agrees substantially with Calvin, who sees here *tota renovationis gratia*, and refers the living water to both *grace and truth* with reference to i. 14.—P. S.]

* [Yet κύριε is an advance on σὺ Ἰουδαῖος, ver. 8, and indicates a dawning sense of the dignity of the stranger. We infer this, however, more from the connection than from the word itself, for this is also used by Rebekah in addressing the servant of Abraham, Gen. xxiv. 18, and by Mary Magdalene in speaking to Jesus whom she mistook for the gardener, John xx. 15. Euthymius: κύριον αὐτὸν προσηγόρευσε, νομίσασα μέγαν εἶναι τινα.—P. S.]

† [Ἄντλημα is not to be confounded with ὑδρία, ver. 28. Comp. the TEXT. NOTES.—P. S.]

‡ [Or rather: Neither (οὔτε) hast thou a vessel to draw with, and (καί, instead of οὔτε, *nor*) the well is too deep (over a hundred feet) to get at it without such a vessel. There is a change of construction here, οὔτε—καί, instead of οὔτε—οὔτε (comp. the Latin *neque—et*), as John ver. 10, and often in the classics. Comp. Winer, p. 460 (7th ed.), and Jelf, § 775.—P. S.]

ed themselves with the patriarchal history. She had evidently a considerable degree of self-respect, national pride and interest in religious questions, and was a brave upholder of patriarchal succession.—P. S.]

Ver. 13. **Shall thirst again.**—[As Christ Himself did, physically, on this occasion, and when He exclaimed on the cross *διψῶ*.—P. S.]—The excellence of that well Jesus suffers to pass.* But in His view of the spiritual water, that has the fundamental defect of every earthly satisfaction: the partaker thirsts again. So it was with all the woman's enjoyment of life hitherto. [She had by successive draughts at the "broken cistern" of carnal lust only increased her thirst, and the sense of the utter vanity of all earthly pleasures]. **Shall never thirst.**—[Comp. vi. 35: "I am the bread of life: he that cometh to me shall not hunger; and he that believeth in Me shall never thirst." Apoc. vii. 16: "They shall hunger no more, neither thirst any more." xxi. 6: "I will give unto him that is athirst of the fountain of the water of life freely." Old Test. passages: Isa. lv. 1; xlix. 10.—P. S.] An opposite word: the sentence of Wisdom in [the apocryphal book of the son of] Sirach, xxiv. 21: "Those who drink of me (the Wisdom) shall thirst again" (Οἱ πίνοντές με, ἔτι διψήσουσι). Meyer, not clearly: "This figure rests on another aspect of the drinking, as viewed in its particular moments, not in the continuity constituted by them." Jesus *Christ* expresses the absolute satisfaction which is given in principle in the peace of the Christian life; Jesus *Sirach* describes the desire for further knowledge begotten by the first taste of wisdom. Not only is the object viewed on different sides; the object itself is in Sirach imperfectly conceived, with reference rather to quantity than quality. The Old Testament strives after life, the New strives in the life. What Sirach calls a thirsting again, Christ calls an everlasting springing up †

Shall be in him a fountain of water.‡—Not "after the negative operation the positive" (Meyer), for the quenching of the thirst is itself positive; but, after the elemental working of Christianity, coming point by point from without, as a *means*, its life as a *principle* continually reproducing and propagating itself as its own object. First *water drunken*, then *water welling up*: distinction of the catechumenate and the anointing of the Spirit. A fountain whose stream gushes into eternal life. The decisive word, spoken with the utmost confidence, stirring the soul of the hearer to its depths. The spiritual sense of the whole declaration of Christ appeared in every feature: (1) A water, after drinking which one thirsts no more; (2) a water drunken, which becomes a fountain; (3) a fountain which ever joyously flows (which can rarely be said of wells in the east); (4) a fountain which gushes into everlasting life. Here the spiritual sense was perfectly transparent. By the union of the divine Spirit with the human, the latter becomes an organ of the divine life, and therefore a self-supplying fountain of life. Calvin, in the interest of his doctrine, here emphasizes the thought that the life of the Spirit in the regenerate cannot dry up; Bengel, in the interest of his, that if a man thirst again, it lies not with the water, but with the man. [So also Alford.] Above this doctrinal antagonism stands the concrete unity of the life of faith sealed by the Spirit. Tholuck takes the thought that Christ assumes form in the believer; which does indeed describe the personal and objective side of spiritual life. He observes that some (Origen, Zwingle, and others) have been misled by the analogy of ch. vii. 38 to think here also of a flowing for the quickening of others. The woman, at all events, does soon come to quickening others, though the fundamental thought here of course is satisfaction for one's self.

In ἅλλεσθαι, applied to the fountain, are included (1) springing up from a hidden depth within; (2) incessant flow; (3) living, joyous, springing motion; (4) rhythmic life, continually increasing in a steady succession of living acts. That the fountain also, as a fountain, becomes more and more copious, is indicated by its streaming forth into *eternal life.* Comp. Sir. xxiv. 31.

It is a question, how *into everlasting life* (εἰς ζωὴν αἰώνιον) is to be interpreted. (1) Up into the heavenly life, like a fountain (Origen, Grotius, and others).* Tholuck objects that this substitutes οὐρανόν. (2) Redounding to eternal life; affording it (the word being referred to πηγή not to ἁλλομένου, Luthardt). This loses the figure. According to Jno. iii. 36, one might indeed take the sense to be, that the spiritual life passes into eternal life; as in Sir. xxiv. 43: My brook became a river, my river a sea." But there, as in Ezek. xlvii., the subject is the immeasurable objective unfolding of the revelation of salvation, or wisdom; here a subjective unfolding of saved life. Though this is eternal life, yet, to be complete, it must pour itself into the objective eternity (Olshausen: The eternal rests not, till it comes to eternity).† In view of

* [A dispute about the comparative greatness of Jacob could have led to no result, and is therefore wisely avoided, but the question, μὴ σύ μείζων εἶ, is virtually answered by what follows. If Jesus is the Messiah and the Giver of the water of eternal life, He is, of course, greater than Jacob, and all the patriarchs and prophets.—P. S.]

† [Bengel (with whom Alford agrees) reconciles the two passages thus: "*Sane aqua illa, quantum in se est, perennem habet virtutem; et ubi sitis recurrit, hominis, non aquæ defectus est: at aquæ elementaris potio sitim subinde ad aliquot tantummodo horas sedare valet.*" Olshausen sees in Sirach the negative expression of the same idea, *i. e.*, who drinks of the (essential, divine) Wisdom, is ever turned away from the temporal, and ever turned towards the eternal." The apocryphal writer looks upon revelation as a growth, Christ as something completed. Hengstenberg: There is always deep contentment in the believer's heart, though often concealed. (Calvin: *nunquam prorsus aridi*). Stier: Christ intensifies and reverses the more imperfect expression of the same truth in the O. T. Also the Christian must continue to drink of the water of life to the end. Drusius and Trench: He shall never thirst for any *other* water save this living water which Christ imparts.—P. S.]

‡ [Comp. Isa. xii. 3 ("with joy shall ye draw water out of the wells of salvation"); lv. 1; Cant. iv. 12 ("a spring shut up, a fountain sealed"); 15 ("a well of living waters and streams from Lebanon"); Apoc. xxii. 1.—P. S.]

* [Grotius: *Emphasis est in voce* SALIET. *Solent enim aquæ salire ad altitudinem suæ originis.* Trench: "These waters shall find their own level: they shall return to God whence they came. The water of life is borne upward by a supernatural impulse."—P. S.]

† [Comp. the lines of Albert Knapp (in his beautiful poem on the *Wurmlinger Capelle*, near Tübingen):

"*Was ewig ist will Ew'ges haben,*
Muss an dem Lebensstrom sich laben,
Der ungetrübt und unverhüllt
Vom Throne des Allmächt'gen quillt."—P. S.]

this, and in accordance with the figure, we understand by the words a flowing on of this well into the eternal life of perfect fellowship with God in the world to come. This eternal life is doubtless conceived in the figure as an ocean [into which all the rivers of life of individual believers empty at last]. The fountain leaps into eternal life (Meyer: ἅλλεσθαι εἰς, *to leap into*). The water drunk becomes a well, the well a fountain which incessantly flows into the ocean of eternal life.

As Jesus engages the stiffened Pharisaic spirit of Nicodemus by the free wind of the Spirit and its transforming power, so He enlists the restless, inconstant woman, whose thirst continually returned, by the offer of an endless satisfaction, which is at once an infinite tranquility and a perfect decision of effort, and soon passes into the enjoyment of the eternal life.

Ver. 15. **That I thirst not, neither come hither.**—The sigh of a poor, weary woman, in whom neediness and the burden of toil seem to form a contradiction to spiritual claims, though the sigh is disguised by the air of good humor. The last words betray, to be sure, a misapprehension of the spiritual sense of the words of Jesus. But about *her* meaning there remains uncertainty.

(1) She means, in all earnest, a miraculous water, which might have the effect described by Jesus (Maier, Meyer). Not readily conceivable. Of such water no one would wish to drink.

(2) She asks the water, in order to get behind the mystery. Lampe: *Tentare voluit audacula, quomodo præstita petitionis conditione, promissionem suam exsecutioni daturus esset.* This is not ironical, as Tholuck thinks. At least it is only half so; according to Lücke's interpretation: Her request is half sportive, half earnest.* Such water is inconceivable to her, but yet she wishes for what has become to her a dim appearance of a toilless life.

(3) Ironical talk. Lightfoot: *Verba irrisorie prolata longe apertius concipias, quam supplicatorie.* So also Tholuck.

(4) The presentiment of something higher which might do her good is awakened in her (Baumgarten-Crusius and my *Leben Jesu*, II. p. 529).† This is more probable, if we suppose that the woman had even journeyed to that sacred well in some sort of religious feeling under a troubled conscience, while there were other wells at least nearer the city of Sichem. Then, too, the third interpretation is accompanied with the view that Jesus breaks off, in order to take an entirely new method; and this involves the unintended, but hazardous presumption that the first method had failed. On the contrary, we suppose that the next word of the Lord was suggested by this request.

Ver. 16. **Call thy husband.**—(1) The husband was to have part in the saving gift, and so she was to be brought indirectly to confession of sin (Chrysostom, *etc.;* Lücke). (2) Christ would in this way lead her indirectly to a consciousness of her guilt (Calov., Neander, Tholuck, Stier, Luthardt). (3) He intended to give her a sign of His prophetic knowledge in the lower sphere of life, to gain her confidence for disclosures from the higher (Cyril, Schweizer; similarly Meyer). (4) Conformity to custom and to the idea of the law. Hitherto Jesus had influenced her after the manner of a missionary, as man with man. In her last request, expressing spiritual susceptibility, the woman came to the position of a catechumen. But, as a proselyte, she must not act without the knowledge of her husband. Meyer objects: The husband was in truth a paramour. True, they were not legally united. But the highest, most delicate social law lies somewhat deeper; she had given that man the rights of husband. If there was still a moral spark in the immoral connection, Christ had an eye to detect it. Even Stier and Tholuck have not been able to appropriate this interpretation. But it is connected on the one hand with the moral principle, Matth. iii. 15; on the other with the principles in Matth. x. 12; 1 Cor. vii. 15; xi. 10, and with all those principles which distinguish the Evangelical church from the Roman Catholic in the manner of making proselytes.

[I must dissent from this interpretation as assuming a relation and a duty which did not exist. The words of Christ: *Call thy husband,* opened the wound at the tender spot where the cure was to begin, and were the first step in granting the woman's request: *Give me to drink.* By a prophetic glance into her private life of shame, which, after five successive marriages, culminated in her present illegitimate relation, He at once effectually touched her conscience and challenged her faith in Him. Conviction of sin is the first indispensable condition of forgiveness, and is the beginning of conversion. She at once understood the intention, and her next word is a half confession of guilt, quickly followed by faith in the prophetic character of Christ.—P. S.]

Ver. 17. **I have no husband** [Οὐκ ἔχω ἄνδρα].—She feels the effect of the sudden turn. She is living in a settled, to all appearance exclusive, but illegal relation; and this causes her to deny the correctness of the Lord's address. This is the summit of her resistance,* and the master-hand of Christ must prove itself over her. *Call thy husband!* This might be a word of conjecture. She supposes this, and so ventures the denial, half true, and half false. Her denial is untrue in that she denies a fact of which she is perfectly aware; true, in that she places herself on the ground of the law, and judges by that. Then in this might be already couched a confession of sin, or even the vow: I renounce him, if I may thereby share thy instruction and thy promise. At all events, we may be sure of this: If she had hitherto answered pertly and ironically in a vulgar way, she would now have departed with her pitcher filled, under an ironical promise to call her husband. If, on the contrary, she had taken Jesus for a magician, from

* [So also Alford: "half in banter, half in earnest."—P. S.]

† [The address κύριε and the next word of Christ imply seriousness expressed with a simple-hearted naivete. The woman who had thirsted so long and found no satisfaction in sensual gratification, was still confused, but blindly longing after the water of life. So also Godet and Trench.—P. S.]

* [Yet at the same time the beginning of her conversion. It proved her sincerity. She dare not call the man with whom she lived, her husband, and thus by implication admitted her guilt. Her subsequent conduct shows that she was moving in the right direction. See Dr. L.'s remarks further on.—P. S.]

whom she might receive a magical water of life, she would have called her husband, and permitted him to be recognized as such. Thus her denial itself proves (1) that she is bound up by the word of Christ; (2) that she for an instant looks on her relation with new eyes; (3) that she deceives herself in attempting to deceive the Lord; (4) that the confession of her guilt is already almost upon her lips. By some expositors the woman is made far too jovial, saucy, spiritually obtuse, and even vulgar.

Thou hast well* said, husband I have not [*ἄνδρα οὐκ ἔχω*].—The emphasis is on *husband.* [Hence ἄνδρα here precedes, while, in the woman's answer, it follows the verb.—P. S.] The saying is commended as *proper.* This is true of her saying in its strict sense, but it has an irony intended to drive out the *reservatio mentalis*, the untruth lurking behind the true saying; and this it does even by the emphatic placing of the word husband: *Husband* I have none.†

Ver. 18. **For five husbands thou hast had.**—Some have concluded from the confession in ver. 29, that those former connections also had been illegitimate. [So Meyer.] Against this is the antithesis: Five husbands, and: Whom thou now hast, *etc.* Five marriages, therefore, had preceded, "of which at least some had been dissolved through the wantonness of the woman." Tholuck. Whether the fault lay in sensual wantonness (licentiousness in the narrower sense), or in an antinomian looseness of spirit, does not appear. With Magdalene the latter seems to have been the case; and it is to be considered, that in Samaria, as well as on the sea of Galilee, Greek views of the marriage relation might already have had an effect. "According to the Talmud, the Samaritans did not acknowledge the laws of divorce; probably referring not to the laxer Hillelian view current among the Jews, but only the more strictly Biblical view of Shammai, following Deut. xxiv. 1. Yet even according to this, it was not only adultery that divorced, but any כָּעוּר, as the Talmud calls it: uncovering of the arms, laying off the veil, and the like." Tholuck. Meyer supposes that she had not been faithful in one or more of her marriages, and was now a widow living with a paramour. But she might have been a divorced woman.‡

The extraordinary disclosure of the Lord. Different explanations:

(1) The hypothesis that Jesus had learned the history of the woman from others (Paulus, von Ammon, *etc.*). Simply contrary to the text.

(2) The disciples added what they afterwards learned (Schweizer). The supposition of a forgery needs no refutation.

(3) The mythical hypothesis, with reference to the five heathen nations which came to Samaria (2 Kings xvii. 24 sqq.; Joseph. *Antiq.* XIX. 14, 3: *πέντε ἔθνη—ἕκαστον ἴδιον θεὸν εἰς τὴν Σαμάρειαν κομίσαντες*).*

(4) A providentially ordered representation of the life of the Samaritan people by this woman: the woman is Samaria; the five husbands are five gods, *etc.*; Hengstenberg, *Beiträge* [*zur Einl. in's A. T.*, 3 vols., 1831–'39] II. p. 23 sqq.†

To this Meyer objects that in this case the husbands must be six; and Heracleon actually read six. This is disposed of by a more attentive examination of Hengstenberg's opinion. It may rather be observed that to the five nations, seven gods are reckoned, 2 Kings xvii. 30 sq. But the chief point is that an actual personal offence of the woman, as here described by the Lord, is the subject, and that the woman would assuredly have understood nothing of such a scholastic allusion of the Lord, if He had intended to make it; and of this there is not the slightest indication. At most, however, the woman would be only an *accidental allegory* of the history of her people, since the marriage law of the Samaritans was strict; and not at all an allegory in so far as Samaria had at the same time from five to seven gods, and these not merely instead of, but together with, Jehovah. [The woman had her five husbands in succession, and was not guilty of polygamy, consequently she could not represent the polytheism of the Samaritans.—P. S.]

(5) "Lange, *Leben Jesu* II. 2, p. 531, strangely says, that the psychical effect of the five husbands upon the woman had forced out traces in her appearance which Jesus perceived." So Meyer reports my view. This judgment might be expected from the author. Our reasons are still the same: 1. Every hair casts its shadow. Every marriage relation leaves its psychical mark; only in most cases our weak eyes do not see it. 2. There is a deep *communicatio idiomatum* in the life of the Lord. What He knew by His divine nature in a divine, immediate way, He at the same time knew in virtue of His human nature, in a human way through means. From the Christological point of view the old false scholastic alternative of merely divine or merely human is done away in reference to the life of Jesus.

[Dr. Lange here undoubtedly goes too far in the

* [*καλῶς*, *correctly*, *to the point* (*richtig*, *zutreffend*), as viii. 48; Matth. xv. 7; Luke xx. 39. In the next verse Christ says: *τοῦτο ἀληθὲς εἴρηκας*, she spoke the truth objectively (*ἀληθές*) in this one thing, but not truthfully (*ἀληθῶς*, subjectively), for she concealed her real guilt under the duplicity of *ἄνδρα ἔχειν*.—P. S.]

† [Meyer and Godet likewise find something of irony in the words of Jesus. There is no doubt that the partial assent to the answer of the woman implies a rebuke, but no dissimulation. He simply draws her out, with a firm and gentle hand, from the hiding-places of her shame to the open daylight. While admitting the literal truth, He detects the hidden falsehood, yet so kindly and mildly as to conceal the censure under an approval. There are, however, clear instances of the use of irony and sarcasm in the Bible, *e.g.*, in the epistles of Paul, and in Elijah's remark about the priests of Baal, 1 Kings xviii. 27.—P. S.]

‡ [The five were lawful husbands, and are distinguished from the sixth, who was not. Whether she had forsaken her former husbands, or been forsaken by them, or lost them by death, there was certainly more or less guilt and shame in such unseemly haste and inordinate desire, as there was in her present intimacy with a paramour.—P. S.]

* [The view of Strauss in the first ed. of his *Leben Jesu* (1835), Vol. I. p. 519, retained in the second, but abandoned in the third and fourth ed. (see ed. 4th, I. p. 541). He represents the story as an unconscious mytho-poetic fiction. Keim (*Geschichte Jesu von Nazara*, 1867, Vol. I., p. 116, footnote 3) changes the mythical interpretation into a symbolical, in the sense of a conscious invention of the Evangelist. This is still worse, but more consistent.—P. S.]

† [Repeated in his Commentary on John (1861) I. 262 ff. Hengstenberg, of course, differs from Strauss and Keim in that he considers the narrative strictly historical as well as allegorical. The coincidence with the fact recorded 2 Kings xvii. and by Josephus, is certainly remarkable, and the double meaning of *living water*, and *give me to drink*, *etc.* may be adduced in favor of this allegory. But when we attempt to carry it through, it breaks down. See below. Wordsworth, without mentioning Hengstenberg, has adopted the allegorical view; Lücke, Stier, Meyer and Trench reject it; Alford ignores it.—P. S.]

application of a true principle. It is, indeed, a fact that traits of character and habits, good and bad, especially pride, sensuality and intemperance, express themselves in the countenance and the eye, as the mirror of the soul.* But this is very different from the assumption that particular events and relations of the past life, such as the five marriages, leave each a distinct mark on the face which may be read, as the forester reads the age of the tree in the number of its rings. Such details of private history even Christ could not know, except from report, or by special revelation, or by His mysterious union with the divinity. The last is the only proper view we can take of the case in hand. Not that Christ was strictly omniscient in the state of humiliation (He Himself disclaimed this, Mark xiii. 32); but wherever it was needed for His mission of saving sinners and the interests of His Kingdom, He could, by an act of His will and in virtue of His vital and essential union with the omniscient Father, unlock the chambers of the past, or penetrate, by immediate intuition, to the inmost secrets of the human heart, and read the history which is indelibly recorded on the pages of memory (comp. ii. 25).—P. S.]

Ver. 19. **Sir, I perceive that thou art a prophet.**—1 Sam. ix. 9. She justly infers this from the miracle of knowledge. [The Samaritans regarded the Messiah mainly as a prophet, see below.] We must note the gradual growth of her respect: (1) Σύ, Ἰουδαῖος ὤν, ver. 9; (2) Κύριε, ver. 11; (3) Κύριε, δός μοι.—*At the same time a concession of her guilt, yet skilfully veiled.*

Ver. 20. **Our fathers worshipped.**—The caricaturing estimate of this personage represents her as everywhere frivolously bantering up to this point without intelligence or misgiving, and now also as putting this question to get away under its cover (De Wette and others, Schweizer, Ebrard, Tholuck). Christ would hardly have gone so far to no purpose with such worthlessness.† It may be going too far, to find in this sentence an expression of strong personal religious interest, as if: She perceives in Christ the searcher of hearts, perceives her guilt, and wishes to go to the holy place of forgiveness (Zwingli, Luthardt [Besser], and others). According to Chrysostom, Neander and others, an interest in objective religion at least was awakened in her. The case is probably to be thus conceived: Having indirectly owned her guilt, she cannot treat of it much further with the stranger. The need of religious atonement comes home. But with it comes the question: Where is the right place of atonement? And this question takes its precedence probably not merely from an external, superficial spirit, but rather from the preponderance of a reflective turn. In other words, she turns, not hypocritically, in embarrassment or silliness, to religious controversy, but, under a spiritual bias over-ruling her simple womanly feeling, to reflection. Probably also she had, through the same disposition, lost caste in Samaria, like Magdalene in Galilee (a homeless nature in Sichem, as on the sea of Galilee). Furthermore, she might hasten with this question, (1) because the opportunity of asking a prophet concerning it might not occur again; (2) because she could not but wish to agree in reference to religion and the place of worship with the prophetic man who inspired her with reverence, and who was privy to her guilt.

On this mountain.—Pointing to Gerizim, which was near. On Gerizim comp. v. Raumer, *Palästina*, p. 38; Winer, s. v.; and the books of travel.* But she does not say: We worship here, ye there; the antithesis is of another sort: Our fathers worshipped, and ye say. A decline of the Samaritan system of worship, and a sense of the weight of the Jewish protest in favor of Jerusalem, are expressed in the carefully chosen terms. At the same time, her having the religion of her fathers in any case contained an apology for her position.

Our fathers.—Down from the first Samaritans who were rejected by the Jews, and who, from being excommunicate, had become schismatic by setting up a temple on Gerizim.† Chrysostom, Kuinoel, and others, suppose she goes back in thought to Abraham and Jacob; but the antithetic ὑμεῖς contradicts this.‡ Even after the destruction of the temple by John Hyrcanus, the pinnacle of the temple continued to be the seat of the Samaritan worship (Joseph. *Antiq.* XVIII. 4, 1), and is so to this day (Robinson, III. p. 319). "Latterly the Turks have interposed hindrances." Tholuck.

It is very expressive, that the woman merely states the issue, without making a question, which place of worship is the true one. By making a question, she would have somewhat compromised her system, and at the same time disparaged the prophet's place of worship. Whether she meant anything by saying: *In Jerusalem* is the place, instead of: *On Mount Zion*, remains uncertain. She seems, at all events,

* [John Ruskin, the ablest English writer on æsthetics, in his work "*The True and the Beautiful in Nature, Art, Morals and Religion*" (Am. Sel. p. 27) has some good remarks on the effects of sin and vice upon the human face and figure. He speaks "of the terrible stamp of various degradations; features seamed with sickness, dimmed by sensuality, convulsed by passion, pinched by poverty, shadowed by sorrow, branded with remorse; bodies consumed with sloth, broken by labor, tortured by disease, dishonored in foul uses; intellects without power, hearts without hope, minds earthly and devilish; our bones full of the sin of our youth, the heaven revealing our iniquity, the earth rising up against us, the roots dried up beneath, and the branches cut off above; well for us only if, after beholding this our natural face in a glass, we desire not straightway to forget what manner of men we be."—P. S.]

† [Comp. the remarks of Hengstenberg and Godet in agreement with Lange.—P. S.]

* [Comp. also the very instructive article *Samaria*, by Petermann, in Herzog's *Real-Encyclopädie*, Vol. XIII. pp. 359-391. According to Petermann, who derived much of his information from a Samaritan high-priest, the Samaritans now believe what they probably believed in the days of Christ, that the top of Mount Gerizim was the seat of paradise, that from its dust Adam was formed, that from this holy mountain the rains descend to fertilize the earth. They still point out on that mountain the spot where Adam built his first altar, where Seth did the same, where the ark rested after the flood—for they identify Gerizim with Mount Ararat—, where Noah erected an altar after the flood, where Abraham offered Isaac, and where Jacob slept and saw the ladder which reached to heaven. All these and other important events they locate on the highest plateau of Gerizim, where there is now nothing but a forsaken mosque (l. c. p. 377).—P. S.]

† [So also Meyer, Alford: the ancestors of the schismatic Samaritans, the founders of the Samaritan worship, the builders of the temple on Gerizim.—P. S.]

‡ [Trench and Owen contend that a reference to the patriarchs, the common fathers of Jew and Samaritan, gives greater force to the woman's question who had called Jacob *our father* (ver. 11) and did her best to maintain her position against the Jewish strangers. But it should be remembered that she already recognized in Him a prophet.—P. S.]

proud of her holy mountain, as well as of her holy well. It might seem to favor the Samaritans, that Moses had designated Gerizim as the mountain of the benedictions of the law (Deut. xi. 29); in fact he seemed to appoint it distinctly as the seat of worship, according to Deut. xxvii. 4, where the Samaritan Pentateuch reads Gerizim instead of Ebal. On the other hand, Jerusalem had now a mighty representative in this prophet, who gave her, moreover, a strong impression of the dignity of the Jewish prophetic office.

Ver. 21. **Woman, believe me, an hour is coming.**—[Believe *Me*, not *us*. A more familiar and condescending phrase for *Verily, verily, I say unto thee*. Nowhere else used by Christ. —P. S.] Ἔρχεται ὥρα, a Johannean phrase, ch. v. 28, &c.—**Ye shall worship the Father:** pointing to a new, more inward mode of worship. [*Ye*, says Christ, not *we*, as an ordinary prophet would have done. He refers not only to the future conversion of the Samaritans (Meyer), but to all Christian ages. *The Father* indicates, as Grotius remarks, *suavitatem novi fœderis;* for the fatherhood of God is fully known and felt only in Christ, the only begotten Son, and the only Mediator between God and man.—P. S.] To speak of the "stupidity" of the woman on which Jesus wasted a sublime utterance, is utterly without foundation. The sublime utterance teaches the distinction between external and internal worship in a concrete form. The expression evidently contains primarily, in a gentle hint, a preferring of Jerusalem. The progressive grades of worship are: (1) Samaria, (2) Jerusalem, (3) Christianity. It cannot therefore be exactly asserted that Jesus evades a decision: still less that He puts Jews and Samaritans alike under mistake (Baumgarten-Crusius). But the greater prominence is given to the issue which puts Samaria and Jerusalem on one side, and the worship of God in spirit and in truth on the other. This is evident from the advent of Christianity in particular to the Samaritans. The negation of Samaria and Jerusalem only denies that prayer was to continue at all restricted to the places named; that is, it declares the abolition of external, legal cultus, both Samaritan and Jewish.* At the same time it marks the woman's question as one too little concerned with essential things.

Ver. 22. **Ye worship that which ye know not.**—The question concerning the *where* of worship could be resolved only by the *what*, and this again by the *how*. The neuter instead of *whom* is significant. Just because God is not truly known to them, He is a ὅ rather than a ὅς, more impersonal than personal. Meyer supposes that the neuter denotes God in His essence and substance; Lücke, that it denotes τὰ τοῦ θεοῦ, which does not suit the term προσκυνεῖν. De Wette: Ὅ refers to the act of προσκυνεῖν; ye worship, and therein do *what ye know not*. Brückner objects to the correctness of the sentence, that the Samaritans were monotheists. But there are different monotheisms. Tittmann and others explain: *Pro vestra ignorantia*. Tholuck (after Lücke): "The true knowledge is that which is shaped by the history of redemption; and the Samaritans who were limited to the Pentateuch for their sacred books, knew Jehovah, that is, the historical God of Israel, but partially." As a whole, in a living growth of knowledge, they almost knew Him not. This accounts also for the ὅτι.

We worship that which we know.—Designating the Jewish fellowship in its living unity, as represented in fact by Himself. [The ἡμεῖς in the mouth of Christ in relation to God, is without example; but is easily explained by the fact that here He speaks as a *Jew*, defending the Jewish worship as the true one against the Samaritan. Otherwise He always calls God *His* Father, and puts Himself, as the only begotten Son, in a unique and exclusive relation to Him. In vers. 23, 24 He drops the ἡμεῖς and speaks of the Christian worshippers in the third person.—P. S.]

For salvation is from the Jews.—[ἐστίν, the present, not ἔσται, for salvation was already at hand in the person of the Saviour.—P. S.] Σωτηρία: (1) Chrysostom, *et al.:* All benefits of salvation; (2) Erasmus: The prophetic knowledge of salvation; (3) The true Jews worship the God of continuous revelation. The proof of this lies in the fact that salvation breaks forth out of Judaism (*Leben Jesu*, II. p. 533). Similarly Tholuck, Meyer. In ἐκ τῶν (see Rom. ix. 4 ff.) are intimated (1) the personal issuing of salvation out of Judaism, (2) its inward connection with Judaism, (3) its distinction from it. The expression is an evidence that John names the Jews not in a hostile sense alone.

[By this declaration Christ sets the seal of His authority on the Jewish religion as a divine revelation to prepare mankind for His coming, and sets aside all other religions as false, or at best as groping in the dark after "the unknown God." This preparation by law, types, and prophecy, running back in unbroken succession to Abraham, and even to the very gates of paradise lost (Gen. iii. 14), forms one of the most convincing evidences of Christianity, as the final and perfect religion of mankind.—P. S.]

Ver. 23. **When the true worshippers.**—The hour *now is*. Christ was the centre of these worshippers, and about Him was gathering the discipleship of the true worship. The hour *is*, and the hour *cometh*. *The true:* the inward, whose prayer is truly prayer. The true worshippers are not so called for being beforehand worshippers in spirit and in truth (excepting Christ), but they are such as *become* so under the Christian revelation. [Οἱ ἀληθινοὶ προσκυνηταί are distinguished not only from hypocrites, but also from all worshippers before Christ, whose worship was necessarily imperfect.—P. S.]

In spirit and in truth.*—[The preposition ἐν signifies the element and the sphere in which worship moves.] This is the space-less place of prayer, in distinction from [and yet at the same time including both] *Gerizim* and *Jerusalem*. [Also πνεῦμα in opposition to *flesh* (σάρξ), ἀλήθεια in opposition to *falsehood* (ψεῦδος), both in opposition to mere forms and symbols

* [Meyer infers from οὔτε ἐν Ἱεροσολύμοις, that the modern doctrine of a restoration of the glory of Jerusalem is a chiliastic dream.—P. S.]

* [Cod. Sin. reads: ἐν πνεύματι ἀληθείας, in the Spirit of truth, probably referring πνεῦμα to the Holy Ghost.—P. S.]

(*σκιά* and *τύποι*).—P. S.] **In spirit**, as opposed to external, stiffened, and even carnally fanatical modes of worship; in the life of the spirit, the life of the human spirit moved by the Spirit of God (Rom. viii. 14, 16, 26).* The distinction itself shows that *πνεῦμα* here cannot denote the Holy Ghost (Luthardt, after the ancients); yet neither can it denote the human spirit as such by itself. This is doubtless in especial opposition to some fanatical, carnal devotion of the Samaritans. **In truth.**—Neither subjective truth of the man, sincerity, of itself (which is involved earlier in *ἀληθινοί*);† nor objective truth as such (which would mean in unity with God, or in the doctrine of God); but the opposite of a merely symbolical, formal, ritualistic worship; in real, actual religious life, *i. e.*, in a true interaction between the personal worshipper and the personal God, in a religious vitality of the worshipper worthy of the living God. This probably in especial opposition to the Jewish symbolical system of prayer. Athanasius, *et al.*: *Πνεῦμα* is the Holy Ghost; *ἀλήθεια*, the Son of God.‡ Augustine, *et al.*, with reference to the *place*: *In spiritu*, in distinction from space: *Foras eramus, intromissi sumus; in templo vis orare, in te ora.*§ Lücke, *et al.*: That which is akin to God in spirit, the sphere of true prayer. Calvin, *et al.* with reference to the *mode*: The *actio spiritualis* itself; Bucer, *et al.*: The posture of mind corresponding to the Spirit of God. We must not overlook the close connection of "spirit and truth" as in an ideal unity. It implies that one cannot exist without the other. The rendering with the article—in the Spirit, etc. [in Luther's V.]—is substantially not incorrect, yet it does not let the connection of the two things stand out strongly enough.

For such [*τοιούτους*, emphatically placed first] **worshippers the Father also** [*καὶ γάρ*, *nam et pater* (Vulg.), *denn auch*] **seeketh.**—On the part of the Father Himself this living prayer is sought, as on its own part it seeks the Father. *Such* He desires and requires; such He would have, and must have.—Interpretations: 1. The Father also, besides the Son [Besser]. 2. Also seeketh (referring the *καί* to *ζητεῖ*, which makes the antithesis not clear). 3. The Father also seeketh what these worshippers do (Meyer). More accurately: He seeketh for Himself such worshippers, as these worshippers seek for themselves such a God.

* [So also Godet: "*L 'esprit désigne ici cet élément le plus profond de l' âme humaine, par lequel elle est capable de communiquer avec le monde divin. C'est le siége du recueillement, le sanctuarie où se célèbre le vrai culte. Rom. i.* 9: *λατρεύω ἐν τῷ πνεύματί μου. Eph. vi.* 18: *προσεύχεσθαι ἐν πνεύματι. . . . Mais le πνεῦμα ἀνθρώπινον n'est qu'une simple virtualité. Il n'acquiert une énergie victorieuse, à l'égard des autres éléments de la vie humaine* [*σῶμα and ψυχή*], *qu'au contact de l'Esprit divin; et ce n'est que dans cette union qu'il réalise la vraie adoration, qui lui est attribuée dans notre text et dans les passages cités. Ce premier trait caractérise l'intensité du culte nouveau.*"—*P. S.*]

† [Comp. Ps. cxliv. 18 Sept.: *ἐγγὺς κύριος πᾶσιν τοῖς ἐπικαλουμένοις αὐτὸν ἐν ἀληθείᾳ*.]

‡ [With reference to John, xiv. 6, where Christ calls Himself "the Truth," *ἡ ἀλήθεια*. Basil (*De Spiritu Sancto*, 26), and Ambrose (*De Spiritu Sancto, iii.* 11, 81), and Bengel likewise see here the whole mystery of the Trinity. Bengel: *Pater adoratur in Spiritu Sancto et in veritate per Jesum Christum.* But in this case we should expect the article before *πνεῦμα* and *ἀλήθεια*.—P. S.]

§ [He adds: "*Sed prius esto templum Dei, quia ille in templo suo exaudiet orantem.*"—P. S.]

Ver. 24. **God is spirit.**—Emphasis on *πνεῦμα*.* The mode of prayer must correspond to the object of prayer. Hence it is now become the law of life for all worshippers, that they must worship God in spirit and in truth. Every other sort of praying is thereby done away, as well as, or in proportion as, the provisional system of religion. The mode of prayer is to be conformed to the mode of religion. God as the living Spirit, and as pure Spirit, is present to His worshippers, and He rejects an outward prayer or a false prayer from a carnal mind, as well as a symbolical prayer from a trammeled mind. God's being spirit was neither a thing already known, now emphasized (Hofmann, Meyer), nor a thing entirely new to the Old Testament (Köstlin, etc.). The Old Testament speaks of the Spirit of God, and intimates also the spirituality of God (Ex. xx. 4; Nu. xvi. 22; 1 Ki. viii.; Is. xxxi. 3), the New speaks of God as spirit; being in this matter also the finished revelation. Common prayers, liturgies, are not hereby forbidden; they may be regarded as the embodiment of the Christian spirit of prayer (Stier); but here is established the condition that this body be living, under perfect discipline, spiritual.

["God is spirit"; "God is light" (1 John i. 5); and "God is love" (1 John iv. 5), all from the pen of John, are the briefest and profoundest definitions, or divine oracles rather, concerning the nature of God, which can be found anywhere. The first refers mainly to His metaphysical, the second to His intellectual, the third to His moral essence; but, of course, the line cannot be so distinctly drawn. Light refers to purity and holiness as well as to truth. Although no metaphysician can exhaust these words, yet even the ignorant Samaritan woman could understand them sufficiently for all practical purposes, viz. that God, being a spiritual being, is not confined to Gerizim or Jerusalem or any other place, but is omnipresent, and can be worshipped everywhere. Trench applies to this passage the well-known saying, that the Scripture has depths for an elephant to swim in, and shallows for a lamb to wade,—a saying which seems to date from Gregory the Great (Preface to his *Com. on Job*: "*Divinus sermo . . . est fluvius planus et altus, in quo et agnus ambulet et elephas natet*"). Spirituality of Christian worship does, of course, not exclude forms, which are indispensable, as man consists of body as well as soul, but puts them in a subordinate position, as vehicles and aids of devotion, while formalism makes them substitutes for, or hindrances of, the inner service of the heart.—P. S.]

Ver. 25. **I know that Messiah cometh.**—Here, too, comes a decidedly incorrect esti-

* [Hence placed first in Greek: *πνεῦμα ὁ θεός*, comp. i. 1: *θεὸς ἦν ὁ λόγος*. The absence of the article indicates the generic character, the *essence* of the spirit here spoken of, not the *personality*. The same is the case with *θεός* i. 1. Hence the indefinite article of the E. V. (*a* Spirit) should be omitted. God is pure spirit, absolute spirit, in opposition to all materialistic and materializing conceptions. This clearly implies that the anthropomorphic expressions of the Bible must not be taken literally. Tertullian ascribed to God a body, corporeity, but perhaps he meant it in the sense of substance. Comp. an able article of Ackermann on *πνεῦμα, νοῦς, und Geist*, in the *Theol. Studien und Kritiken* for 1839, pp. 873-944.—P. S.]

mate of the woman in Tholuck: "The woman is not inclined to enter into so high matters, and therefore answers like Felix, Acts, xxiv. 25." Similarly, De Wette, Lücke, [Scott, Barnes]. Would Christ have revealed Himself as the Messiah to such a woman? Meyer better: "The woman is apprehended by the answer of Jesus, but does not as yet apprehend it, and appeals to the Messiah." Evidently the words of the wonderful Unknown quicken in her the Samaritan expectation of the Messiah. Even a presentiment that this might be the Messiah, may readily be imagined (Luthardt); and then her answer would have to be construed as a feeler for the true solution; perhaps as Lampe explains her words: "Give me this water." At all events, she now felt the old system to be shaken, and with a longing for the inner life, the longing for the Messiah awoke (see *Leben Jesu*, II. 2, 534).*

A. Maier (p. 344): "If the Messianic hope of the Samaritans, who acknowledged only the Pentateuch, based itself on Deut. xviii. 15, they must have expected in the Messiah chiefly a divine teacher, who like Moses, should make known to them the divine will, and lead them into hidden truths." The Samaritans expected the Messiah of old, and they expect Him to this day. "The latest on this subject is in the work of Barge's: *Les Samaritains de Naplouse*, 1855. They call Him הַשָּׁהֵב, or הַתָּהֵב, which Gesenius, *Anecdota Samarit.*, p. 65, *etc.*, [and Ewald] would interpret *conversor*, Hengstenberg [and Meyer], with greater probability, *restitutor*,† which the Samaritan priest in Barge's confirms." Tholuck. For other interpretations see the note in Tholuck, p. 150. The woman may have well known the Jewish term, and have chosen it instead of the Samaritan. According to V. Ammon, and others, the term [the explanation: *Who is called Christ*] is the Evangelist's;‡ which is very questionable, since he generally prefers to record the original expressions.

Ver. 26. **I am he** ['Εγώ εἰμι, *ego sum*, *viz.*, the Messiah].—The subject of ἐγώ εἰμι is to be supplied from the text. Thus He now voluntarily presents Himself to this sinful woman openly as the Messiah, as in the old covenant the angel appeared first to Hagar as angel of the Lord (Gen. xvi. 7), and as the risen Jesus appeared first to Magdalene. Among the Jews Jesus long avoided the name of Messiah,§ because its meaning was distorted by Chiliastic notions; the Samaritan idea of the Messiah was stunted, but not as yet encumbered with Chiliastic inferences, and therefore could here be introduced. [The Jews looked upon the Messiah as the *King* of Israel, and expected from Him first of all political changes (comp. John vi. 15): while the Samaritans, deriving their Messianic expectations chiefly from Deut. xviii. 15-19, regarded Him simply as a *prophet* or *teacher*, and were less liable to abuse this revelation for disturbing political purposes.—P. S.]

Ver. 27. **Marvelled that he talked with a woman.**—Not with this woman as such (Kuinoel), but with *a* woman, on the low level assigned her by the rabbinic views. Two considerations met here: 1. The Oriental custom which imposed rigid restriction on intercourse with the female sex: *Pirke Aboth* I. 5. "*Docuerunt Sapientes, ne multiplices colloquium cum muliere. Cum uxore dixerunt, quanto minus cum uxore alterius.*" (Lightfoot, Schöttgen.) 2. Rabbinical scholastic prejudice. "According to Jewish Rabbinical ideas the female sex was incapable of *religious* instruction." (Tholuck. It should doubtless be: *Rabbinical* instruction.)* **Yet no man said.**—Expressing reverence, and the acknowledgment that He might well establish a new and higher custom. An enlargement of their horizon. Comp. Luke x. 38. Τί ζητεῖς is hardly: What desirest Thou? (Meyer without connecting it with μετ' αὐτῆς.) Plainly the ζητεῖν, in distinction from λαλεῖν, is to discuss in rabbinical style; the latter meaning merely to talk (chat). Μέντοι in the New Testament is almost peculiar to John.

Ver. 28. **The woman then left her water-pot.**—"Now for the first time the force of the argument from His prophecy comes powerfully upon the woman, perhaps under the additional influence of an awakened conscience." Tholuck. Why: Now for the first time? and why: perhaps? "She forgets her work, as the Redeemer had forgotten His need." Luthardt: "Nicodemus went away silent and burdened; this woman hastens away in joyful certainty, with a burning heart, to be the herald of His name." And she calls now not her husband, but the whole city. [Meyer: "What a power of the decided awakening of a new life in this woman!" She has been justly regarded as a fit illustration of the proper work of the church, *viz.*, to be a witness of Christ, and thus to lead men to Him as the Saviour of the world.—P. S.]

Ver. 29. **Who told me all things that ever I have done.**—Under the sense of her guilt she thinks He has told her everything she had done, that is everything wrong. The testimony of an awakened conscience.† Unquestionably what Jesus said to her contained the sum of her particular transgressions. Besides this she had no doubt perceived by His look and tone, that He saw through her whole life. It may indicate still her legal spirit, that she speaks in the plural of her sins; yet she may also intend by this to magnify the wonderful vision of the prophet. The ὅσα, instead of ἅ, is full of emphasis.

Is this the Christ?—On the negative, doubtful element in the μήτι, comp. Meyer and Tholuck against Lücke (is He really the Messiah?) De Wette, however, suggests the analogous μήτι in Matth. xii. 23, which calls for an affirmative answer. Considering the boldness of the announcement, especially in presence of the authorities, the interrogative form is perfectly intelli-

* [Trench also (p. 123) sees in these words of the woman a cry of helplessness connected with a timid presentiment, such as she hardly dares own, much less ventures to utter: "Thou perhaps art He whom we look for."—P. S.]

† [Another Moses, Deut. xviii. 15.]

‡ [So also Trench; comp. i. 41; xi. 16; xx. 26; xxi. 2.]

§ [Comp. Matth. viii. 4; xvi. 20; xvii. 9; John ix. 31.]

* [The same contempt for woman we find among Christian monks, especially in the East, even such men as St. Anthony and Pachomius. Some church fathers are not free from it.—P. S.]

† [And the exaggeration of a lively womanly temper.—P. S.]

gible in the mouth of this poor outcast, and yet so shrewd and dexterous woman.* The more, that she passes over Christ's announcement of Himself, in order perhaps to take to herself somewhat of the honor of a glorious discovery. A sinful ambition may well still cleave to her confession of guilt which was more public than it was perfectly open. That she herself believes, or is inclined to believe, is evident from her extraordinary agitation, which impels her beyond all the bounds of reserve, bashfulness, and despised condition. Compare the woman who was a great sinner, and ventured into the house of the Pharisee, Luke vii. 37.

Vers. 31–33. **In the meanwhile.**—The woman was gone, the Samaritans had not yet come. The mistake of the disciples: "*Quid mirum, si mulier non intelligebat aquam? ecce discipuli nondum intelligunt escam.*" August. [*Tract.* xvi. 31.—P. S.].

Ver. 34. **My food is.**—A very intelligible figure. Not merely satisfaction, but nourishment and quickening. An opposite judgment of the disciples, c. 1. A parallel, Matth. iv. Ἵνα adds to the nature of the food (ὅτι) its suitableness to its purpose. The aorist τελειώσω denotes the act which completes the ποιεῖν.

Ver. 35. **There are yet four months.**—Τετράμηνος, sc. χρόνος. Harvest began in April [in the middle of Nisan], about Easter, and lasted till Pentecost. Four months run back to December. Seed-time itself fell in the beginning of November (the month Marcheshvan). The fields, therefore, were probably green; and the more piquant was the expression: The fields are white for the harvest. The figure follows the analogy of the food. The Lord, as represented by John, is perfectly consistent in His use of the earthly as the symbol of the heavenly. Probably the Samaritans were already coming through the green fields, and they were the fields white for harvest. The disciples saw the green seed-field, He saw the white harvest-field, and to this He wished to open their spiritual eye. Many have taken the four months proverbially: "*From seeding to harvest there are four months*" (so also in the Talmud); and in this view the passage would lose its chronological value,† and only denote in general some time before harvest (Lightfoot, Grotius, Lücke, *etc.*). Against this Meyer: The proverb does not elsewhere occur [nor is the seed-time mentioned]. After all there seems to be something proverbial about the expression. Yet it is suitable only at seed-time. It may then be an expression as well of joyful hope (*only* four months yet), as of waiting patience (*yet* four whole months). Lücke rightly chooses the latter sense. In the natural world we must wait yet four months; in the spiritual, it is already the time of harvest.

Yet this again may be understood in different ways. 1. In the natural world four months intervene between seeding and harvest; here a harvest follows immediately upon the sowing. Ver. 38 goes against this. 2. In the natural world it is now seeding time; in the spiritual the harvest time is opening. Chemnitz, Baur (Stier, Luthardt, Tholuck), and others find in the harvest not only the harvest of the Samaritans (Acts viii.), but also the harvest of the Gentiles.* But then where would be the previous sowing? Primarily the talk is only of a field *now* white for the harvest, though betokening, to be sure, all future harvest fields.

Ver. 36. **And he that reapeth,** *etc.*—The connection with the preceding is this: The field is white for harvest. Be reapers. Reaping in the spiritual field is full of promise. Tholuck: Christ thought of the conversion of far-off Gentiles. Then came the sad thought, that He Himself would not live to see it in this world; which relieved itself with the joyful thought that their joy would also be His. So De Wette, Meyer. In that case Christ would have mixed two figures; one representing Himself as already harvesting, another representing Him as sower. But harvest is the subject here, and the disciples are supposed to be reapers with Him. The sowing, therefore, *must* be sought at some previous time (Chrysostom: The prophets were the sowers). Even in Samaria spiritual seed had been sown by Moses and the Pentateuch, by Jewish teachers, last perhaps by John the Baptist (see iii. 23, p. 141 f.). As little can we accept the exposition of Meyer, Tholuck, and others, which makes the καί after μισθὸν λαμβάνειν only expletive: that is, he gathereth fruit unto eternal life. This again is simply contrary to the figure, which represents an employed reaper. Hunnius and Calov: The μισθός is the gracious reward, the *gradus gloriæ;* the καρπός is the converts. But since the wages of the reaper are represented as given in this world, over against the gathering of fruit unto eternal life, the primary idea is the immediate spiritual blessings and joys of the harvesters, the joy of spiritual harvest, the communion of the converts themselves. A different and further joy is that of carrying the fruit into heaven, to gladden there the sower who passed thither long before, and to have with Him a common and simultaneous (ὁμοῦ) rejoicing; a thing not possible in the kingdom of nature, but belonging to the kingdom of grace. The ζωὴ αἰώνιος is here again represented objectively, as above; there under the figure of the ocean (ver. 14), here under the figure of a garner (Lücke).

Ver. 37. **Herein is that saying fully true** [ἀληθινός, not ἀληθής].—The fundamental thought is the wonderfully great distance between seeding and harvest, in contrast with the wonderful fact that reaper and sower rejoice together in heaven. This, however, they can do only in heaven; in this world they are far, often very far, apart. Here, therefore, is the proverb fully true; here it reaches its proper truth; whereas in earthly life the sower is generally the reaper, and the proverb simply exaggerates into a general rule the exceptional fatality of the sower not living to

* [Meyer: The woman believes in the Messiahship of Jesus, but, carried away by the greatness of the discovery, she does not trust herself, and ventures only modestly and doubtingly to ask.—P. S.]

† [On the chronological value of the passage, which Alford denies, see Wieseler: *Chronol. Synopse,* p. 214 ff., and Robinson: *Harmony of the four Gospels in Greek,* p. 189. Christ must have tarried in Judea about eight months, from the preceding passover in April (ii. 13, 23) till December.—P. S.]

* [So also Meyer: Christ looked prophetically beyond the approaching Sycharites to the green fields of the whole humanity, for whose conversion He laid the foundation. Godet denies this general reference and confines the scene to an extemporized Samaritan harvest festival.—P. S.]

see the harvest time, or at least not himself receiving and enjoying his harvest. [The words of Joshua spoken to the tribes of Israel at Shechem: "I have given you a land for which ye did not labor (οὐκ ἐκοπιάσατε), and cities which ye built not," *etc.* Josh. xxiv. 13, form a striking parallel to this saying of our Lord uttered on the same spot, and perhaps with reference to it.—P. S.] Tholuck, after De Wette, incorrectly: Ἀληθινός may here mean only ἀληθής.* Then the proverb in its ordinary sense would be declared false. It has, however, some truth; but it does not sustain its truth throughout; as earthly things are not ἀληθινά, but only symbols of the infinite, though they all have their ἀληθές. And since in the spiritual sphere sowing and reaping seem often almost to coincide, we must not overlook the actual reference to the present case. Yet the ἐν γὰρ τούτῳ does not mean *in this instance*, but *in this matter*. Then, too, the proverb must here be a universal law. The crop in the kingdom of God ripens slowly.† The full harvest is the end of the world. The earliest seed was the word of God in paradise, or the earliest sowers were the earliest patriarchs. The kingdom of God is the mightiest realm of nature and history; and Christ is the root of nature in His slow growth towards His appearance in the middle, and again at the end of time. (On the proverb: Wetstein.)

Ver. 38. **I sent you to reap.**—Ἀπέστειλα (comp. chap. xvii. 18.) Hardly merely "in the sense of the prophetic future" (De Wette, Tholuck). They are not yet apostles by a distinct appointment; still they were already disciples to whom an apostolic commission is prospectively affixed. Hence thus: I have chosen you for apostles, or, to keep the figure, for laborers, to send you into the harvest-field. Ye are destined pre-eminently to reap a spiritual harvest which has been long preparing (so also Meyer). According to Meyer the ἄλλοι and αὐτῶν refer simply to Jesus, in the plural of category."‡ But Jesus here evidently sets Himself above the distinction of sowers and reapers as the Lord of the harvest (Olshausen, with reference to Matth. xxiii. 34). The older expositors [also Grotius, Bengel, Luthardt, Ewald] include at least the prophets [and John the Baptist] with Him. Bucer: even the heathen philosophers and their elements of truth. [Tholuck: All the preparatory organs of the economy of salvation.] The seed here in view, however, is not the seed of general culture and intelligence, but the seed of theocratic faith.

Others have labored. The painful labors and toils of the prophets. Their sowing was a sowing in tears. It should shame and encourage the disciples, that they so suddenly come into the great harvest of the history of the world, for which the grandest seeds-men have for centuries labored. This does not exclude either the relative harvest which exists at every stage of the kingdom of God, or again the great sowing in the work of the apostles; yet the sight of a present harvest predominates, as in Matth. ix. 38; especially here, that the disciples might feel reverence before the hidden work of God in the despised Samaritans, and believe in their susceptibility to conversion, as they were just now approaching. They could no more take offence at the labors of Jesus with the Samaritans, than at His helping the Canaanitish woman; here as there His leading of their spirit corresponds to His outward act.

Ver. 39. **And many of that city believed.**—These first believers, who were gathered by the word of the woman, are distinguished from the much greater company afterwards won by the word of Jesus (ver. 41). These believers are now come to Him (see ver. 30). [Olshausen: "If the Redeemer had been like any other man, His λόγος could have had no more weight than that of any other, and in support of His own cause, it would have been still less effective. But as the sun proves its existence and reality merely by the light and the animating warmth which it imparts: so Christ, as the Sun of the spiritual world, in all ages past, and to this day, has had but one witness for Himself, *viz.*, His own operation upon souls. By this one means He so entirely takes possession of every unprejudiced mind, that through the reception of His higher vital energies, it becomes to them experimentally certain that the salvation of the world rests in Him. Hence conceptions of the truth and doctrinal knowledge are not *principles* in the life of faith, but *effects* resulting from the reception of the spiritual element."—P. S.]

Ver. 40. The evangelist makes record that Jesus tarried two days teaching in the Samaritan city. [Orthodox Jews besought the Lord to depart from their coasts (Matth. viii. 34), took up stones against Him, and plotted for His overthrow (Matth. viii. 34; Luke iv. 29; xiii. 31, 32, *etc.*). Heretical Samaritans besought Him to tarry with them. The first became last, and the last first.—P. S.]

Ver. 41. **And many more believed,** *etc.*—From the great result, analogous to that in Judea, we infer a great work of Jesus, which however was, at least for the most part, a labor in word. [In these two days of incidental labor Jesus made more converts among the half-heathenish, yet less bigoted and prejudiced Samaritans, without working miracles, than in the preceding eight months of official work in word and signs among the Jews in Jerusalem. The harvest in Samaria was only an episode in the life of our Lord, and yet how rich in immediate results and future promise! His servants also often accomplish most in times and places where they least expect it. Not seldom the meaning of many years or a whole life is condensed into a few days or hours. No labor for the Lord, however, is in vain; if it bear not the proper fruit in this world, it will do so at the final harvest of history.—P. S.]

* [On the difference of ἀληθινός, *genuine*, and ἀληθής, *true*, see my note on I., 9, p. 66. Meyer: "*Die Fassung von* ἀληθινός *gleich* ἀληθής 2 *Pet. ii.* 22 (*De Wette, u. V.*) *ist ganz gegen die Johanneische Eigenthümlichkeit* (*auch xix.* 35)." ἐστιν is here = *applies*, comp. συμβέβηκεν, 2 Pet. ii. 22.—P. S.]

† ["*Habet Deus suas horas et moras.*" "God's mills grind slowly, but surely and finely."—P. S.]

‡ [In correspondence with ὑμεῖς, as it was ἄλλος—ἄλλος in the proverb. So also Lücke, Stier, Alford and Trench, who find here an antithesis not between two different companies of laborers—the prophets and the Apostles—but between Christ Himself and His Apostles, the Master and His servants.—P. S.]

Ver. 42. **And said unto the woman,**—Under the direct impression which Jesus made upon them, the indirect testimony of the woman certainly became to them a λαλιά; not as contemptuous, but as now appearing insignificant.* Meyer justly notices that John himself, as an impartial narrator, says of her word: τὸν λόγον. We must here take into account also the serenity of happy feeling, to understand that the expression has no malice, more than that of the governor of the feast: "Thou hast kept the good wine until now." (Comp. the remarkable expression in John viii. 43.)

We have heard him ourselves.—Found out by our hearing, so that we now know. [This is a higher order of faith connected with knowledge and personal experience ("come and see," i. 39, 46), while formerly it rested only on external authority. Difference of the Roman Catholic and the higher Evangelical Protestant conception of faith. Grotius: "*Notarunt veteres in hac Samaritidi ecclesiæ esse figuram, quæ nos adducit ad verbum divinum; nos verbo, maxime propter ipsius majestatem et sanctitatem, credimus.*"—P. S.]

That this is the Saviour of the world [Only here and 1 John iv. 14].—Tholuck doubtfully (after a doubtful expression of Lücke): "Whether the idea contained in ὁ σωτὴρ τοῦ κόσμου is lent to the people by the evangelist, is a question." But this puts in question the whole point of the great narrative. Meyer better: "A confession sufficiently intelligible as the fruit of the two days' instruction of Jesus, the more since the Samaritan Messianic faith was more accessible to a universality of salvation [see Gesenius, *De Samarit. Theol.*, p. 41 sqq.] than the Jewish with its concrete and rigorous particularism." As Samaritans they had peculiar reason to express themselves thus: Yea verily, He is not only a Messiah for the Jews, but also for us and the Gentiles; in Him the divided world again becomes one.†

The work of Jesus in Samaria laid the foundation for the subsequent conversion of that people under the Apostles, Acts viii.

DOCTRINAL AND ETHICAL.

1. Respecting the pretended contradiction between this history and Matth. x. 5 (Strauss, Bruno Bauer, and in part Weisse), it should be remarked that the case in Matthew is that of a special mission of the disciples in a particular direction towards Jerusalem, not of the general itinerancy of the Lord. And when He Himself gave out, in reference to His earthly office, that He was not sent but unto the lost sheep of the house of Israel [Matth. xv. 24], He referred to the divine law of His work, and did not exclude the Samaritans from an incidental share of His labors. It was consonant with the historical position of the Samaritans, with their susceptibility, with the directions of the Lord Himself (Acts i. 8), and with the subsequent spread of Christianity from Judea over Samaria and the Gentile world, that He already appeared for once among them; as, on the other hand, it was in conformity with the economy of His work, that this visit was only incidental, and not for a protracted ministry. Thus were the disciples exercised beforehand in the true order of preaching the gospel. Acts viii. 5 is supposed to have occasioned the mythical invention of the story before us; whereas that great conversion rather points to a historical preparation. Meyer justly calls attention to the perfect naturalness of the several features of the story, which could not have proceeded from a poetizing spirit. It may be added, that the several stumbling-blocks which have been found in it, such as the misapprehensions of the woman, are simply so many misapprehensions of criticism and exegesis. The remarkable directness of the representation also, in respect to season, locality, the individuality of the woman, rabbinical custom, *etc.*, must be noted. With Baur this history dissolves into a type: "The woman of Samaria, representing susceptible heathendom, readily opening itself to faith, and offering a wide field of harvest, the counterpart of Nicodemus, who is the type of unsusceptible Judaism." Neither rhyme nor reason, and a further proof of the legend-like fantasticism of a criticism past its crisis, in its last stage of consumption.

2. On the history of the hatred between the Jews and the Samaritans comp. Robinson, III., p. 339 sqq.; *Leben Jesu*, II., 2, p. 539.

3. On Hengstenberg's reference of the five husbands, *etc.*, to the five gods of old Samaria, see *Leben Jesu*, II., 2, p. 540. [Comp. my annotations on ver. 18. Hengstenberg's allegorical interpretation is at least more sensible than that of Augustine (*Tract.* xv. c. 19), who understands the five former husbands of the five senses, and explains the words, *Call thy husband*, to mean, *Apply thy reason*, by which thou must be governed, rather than by the bodily senses (*adhibe intellectum, per quem docearis, quo regaris*)! In another place he finds in the five husbands the five books of Moses, and in the sixth husband the Lord Himself, as if He said: Thou hast served the five books of Moses as five husbands; but now *he whom thou hast, i. e.*, whom thou hearest, *is not thy husband:* for thou dost not yet believe in him!—P. S.]

[3 b. Ver. 7. "*Give me to drink.*" So God introduces Himself to us for our salvation: He asks of us a service. He does this from the beginning, and puts our whole earthly life to us as a serving of Him. Our daily labor is at least required of us as a patient submission to His condemnation: "In the sweat of thy face," *etc.* And in His covenant of grace, as with

* [Calvin, Alford and others, take λαλιά here in the classical sense, *garrulous talk, babbling, gossip* (*Geschwätz Gerede*); but in later Greek (Polybius, Josephus, Sept., Apocrypha) it has no such slighting usage, certainly not in John, who ascribes it to Christ, viii. 43. It is equivalent to λόγος, ver. 39, but properly chosen from the standpoint of the speaking Samaritans, while John as reporter uses as aptly τὸν λόγον. Comp. Meyer on viii. 43 (p. 356). Trench remarks (p. 135): "This speech of her fellow-townsmen to the woman has nothing rude or offensive about it, rather, indeed the contrary: We set our own seals to the truth of thy report."—P. S.]

† [Comp here the remarks of Calvin and Trench, p. 136, to the same point. The historical character of the narrative is vindicated even in this circumstance that it puts the expression σωτὴρ τοῦ κόσμου, which nowhere else occurs in the Gospels, into the mouth, not of bigoted, particularistic Jews, but of Samaritans who had no exclusive claims and privileges and could accept salvation only on the same terms as the heathen. Trench thinks it likely that they may have found some ground for this belief in the prophecy of Shiloh, to whom "shall the gathering *of the people* be" (Gen. xlix. 10), which the Samaritans of old referred to the Messiah, while the modern Samaritans refer it to Solomon.—P. S.]

Israel, it is consecrated to be primarily a devout serving of Him with tithes and first-fruits. Our ministry to one another is also a giving Christ meat, or drink, or otherwise ministering to Him. Our constitutional unbelief, the enmity of the carnal mind against God, like the natural enmity of Samaritans to Jews, makes us skeptical that He should have any such dealing with us. But if we only *know* the gift of this wonderful reciprocity established between us and God in Christ,—if we have a heart for it—it opens the deepest fountains of devotion and prayer in our souls. It gives us a wonderful introduction to God! In other words, this sort of presentation of Himself to us lays the foundation of substantial religion in ourselves, and thus also opens the way for the richest gifts of everlasting life from God.—E. D. Y.]

4. As Jesus appears in chap. i. higher than John the Baptist, in chapter ii. higher than the temple, in chap. iii. higher than the rulers of the people, so here He appears greater than the sacred well of Jacob and its founder, as afterwards greater than the porches of Bethesda, the manna, the temple-light, the pool of Siloam, *etc.* And the superiority is at the same time antithetic: Christ is everything in truth (the ἀληθινός), in realized essence, which before Him was presented only in type. *Thus Christ is here the real antitype of the typical patriarchal well-diggers, in particular the patriarch Jacob;* hence His spiritual life is the real living water of a sacred well. To this main symbol of this chapter are attached the other symbols of the food, the harvest field, the Lord of the seed-field and harvest-field, the sowers, the reapers. In reference to each, see the exegesis.

5. As Christ makes light the symbol in manifold respects of His nature and life, so with the well, and water. Here He is evidently a giver of peace within one's self, as in chap. vii. He is a giver of the Spirit communicating itself to others, while in chap. v. He appears as the true well of healing. Thus the fountain of life is the fountain of peace, of healing, of the Spirit.

[6. *Jesus and women.* Jesus was never married, because He was the Son of *God* as well as the Son of Man, and because He represents *sinless* and *universal* humanity. Hence no *fallen* creature and no *single* daughter of Eve even without sin, if there were such, but only the whole church of the redeemed is fit to be His bride. Nevertheless He had much intercourse with women, and this, as well as His dealing with children, forms an interesting chapter in His life and an evidence of Christianity, especially if we contrast it with the radically different position which woman holds at the source of other religions and licentious mythologies. The subject has not yet received the attention it deserves. In addition to my introductory remarks (p. 150), I shall give the views of Guizot,* partly in opposition to Renan, the only writer of note, who, to his own discredit, has dared to cast a reflection on this relation so pure and Christlike. "The women," says Guizot, "seem irresistibly attracted toward Him, with hearts moved, imaginations struck by His manner of life, His precepts, His miracles, His language. He inspires them with feelings of tender respect and confiding admiration. The Canaanitish woman comes and addresses to Him a timid prayer for the healing of her daughter. The woman of Samaria listens to Him with eagerness, though she does not know Him: Mary seats herself at His feet, absorbed in reflections suggested by His words; and Martha proffers to Him the frank complaint that her sister assists her not, but leaves her unaided in the performance of her domestic duties. The sinner draws near to Him in tears, pouring upon His feet a rare perfume, and wiping them with her hair. The adulteress, hurried into His presence by those who wished to stone her, in accordance with the precepts of the Mosaic law, remains motionless in His presence, even after her accusers have withdrawn, waiting in silence what He is about to say. Jesus receives the homage, and listens to the prayers of all these women with the gentle gravity and impartial sympathy of a being superior and strange to earthly passion. Pure and inflexible interpreter of the Divine law, He knows and understands man's nature, and judges it with that equitable severity which nothing escapes, the excuse as little as the fault. Faith, sincerity, humanity, sorrow, repentance, touch Him without biasing the charity and the justice of His conclusions; and He expresses blame or announces pardon with the same calm serenity of authority, certain that His eye has read the depths of the heart to which His words will penetrate. In His relation with the women who approach Him, there is, in short, not the slightest trace of man; nowhere does the Godhead manifest itself more winningly and with greater purity. And when there is no longer any question of these particular relations and conversations, when Jesus has no longer before Him women suppliants and sinners, who are invoking His power or imploring His clemency: when it is with the position and the destiny of women in general that He is occupying Himself, He affirms and defends their claims and their dignity with a sympathy at once penetrating and severe. He knows that the happiness of mankind, as well as the moral position of women, depends essentially upon the married state; He makes of the sanctity of marriage a fundamental law of Christian religion and society; He pursues adultery even into the recesses of the human heart, the human thought; He forbids divorce; He says of men, 'Have ye not read, that He which made them at the beginning made them male and female? For this cause shall a man leave father and mother, and cleave to his wife: and they twain shall be one flesh. Wherefore they are no more twain, but one flesh. What therefore God hath joined together, let no man put asunder.' . . . . Signal and striking testimony to the progressive action of God upon the human race! Jesus Christ restores to the divine law of marriage the purity and the authority that Moses had not enjoined to the Hebrews 'because of the hardness of their hearts.'"—P. S.]

* [In the first volume of his *Meditations on the Essence of Christianity.* I quote from the English translation, N. Y., 1865, pp. 323 ff.]

HOMILETICAL AND PRACTICAL.

The retreat of Jesus from Judea to Galilee through Samaria, the first turning-point in His official life: 1. Motives (the Pharisees began to watch Him with hostile eye: the Baptist is imprisoned). 2. Character: Free consciousness (He retreats in free discretion, without fear; in holy discretion, hence: "the Lord knew"). 3. Rich results (beneficent sojourn in Samaria, beneficent results in Galilee). 4. Significancy (He ceases to baptize, tarries in Samaria on His return).—Symbolical import of baptismal water and drinking water in Christianity. (In ch. iii. Jesus *baptized* with water; in ch. iv. he passes to offer a living water to be drunk.)—The resting of the Lord on Jacob's well, a living emblem of the old patriarchal days and the new evangelistic time in one.—Christ in His human weakness and divine exaltation, (1) weary, and yet the rest of a weary soul; (2) thirsty, and yet a fountain; (3) hungry, and yet enjoying heavenly food, the Lord of the harvest-field; (4) left alone, yet in spirit surrounded with approaching nations.—Christ a Saviour even from the religious perversities of fanaticism.—Fanaticism in its inhumanity and its immoral conduct.—The woman of Samaria, or a Samaritan Magdalene.—The condescending pity of Jesus in the conversion of the woman of Samaria.—How the grace and love of Christ can break through all conventional restrictions, for being the new law of the Spirit: the restrictions (1) of the ancient religious separation, (2) of the ancient national separation, (3) of the old social custom (as to the separation of the sexes), (4) of the old contempt for the fallen.—How many prejudices that one little word of Jesus: Give me to drink, abolishes: 1. The prejudice of the ancients against the female sex; 2. The prejudice of statute against the fallen; 3. The prejudice of nationality; 4. The prejudice of religion.—The wisdom and gentleness of the Lord in winning souls: 1. The opening of the conversation (Give me to drink; a token of common life). 2. The progress of the conversation (*a.* objective salvation in a sensible emblem: *b.* subjective need of salvation). 3. The goal: Manifestation of Christ to a sinful, penitent heart.—The stages of the religious instruction of the Samaritan woman: 1. The missionary stage; 2. The catechetical stage; 3. The church stage (see the exegesis).—How Christ sent back as an evangelist into her city a woman who came out of it a notorious sinner.—The day of grace (If thou knewest.)—The life of the Lord, living water (spring-water) in distinction from the stale water of this world's life: 1. The latter provokes thirst, the former quenches thirst. 2. The one becomes foul, the other takes away foulness. 3. The one stands, in a marsh, the other gushes and flows. 4. The one sinks away, evaporates, the other becomes an eternal fountain.—Christ the life, as fountain of life.—The fountain of life, as a fountain of peace.—Jacob's well, the pool of Bethesda, the fountain of Siloam, emblems of the salvation in Christ.—The water of life, which Christ bestows: 1. A draught which becomes a fountain; 2. A fountain which becomes a stream; 3. A stream which runs into the ocean of eternal life, without losing itself therein. The crystal spring of truth (that may be likened to spring water) in contrast with the turbid water of vanity and sin (which may be likened to salt water and puddles and ponds).—The miraculous virtue of self-reproduction in the water and the bread which Christ bestows.—The thirst of life, and the satisfaction of it in Christ.—Sir, give me this water, or the unsatisfied longing of the poor, sinful heart: (1) Astray, deceived, debauched in sin; (2) led aright, purified, brought to itself by the awakening of repentance; (3) satisfied, transformed into blessed life by grace.—Call thy husband. Christ not only the knower of hearts, but also the knower of lives.—Christ aims at the conscience, to subdue the sinner.—The gradual awakening: 1. Awakening of reflection; 2. Awakening of conscience; 3. Awakening of faith.—The divine visitation in the hour when the dark human heart feels itself exposed and seen through by a heavenly eye.—The decision of Christ respecting the religious controversy between the Samaritans and the Jews, in its permanent typical import.—"Salvation comes from the Jews."—But while they quarrel on over the old issue, a new and higher point of unity is present.—The future of religion: Worship of God in spirit and in truth.—The Messiah's revelation of Himself for the woman of Samaria (compared with the self-presentation of the angel of the Lord to Hagar, of the risen Jesus to Magdalene).—The school which the disciples of Jesus went through in Samaria in reference (1) to the Samaritan woman, (2) to the Samaritans.—The marvelling of the disciples of Jesus at His talking with a woman, in conflict with their reverence.—The whole life discipline of the Christian an alternation of the spirit of captious and of reverential wonder.—The food of Jesus.—Heavenly remembering and reminding an earthly forgetting: 1. Christ forgets His earthly meat; 2. The woman forgets the earthen pitcher.—The difference between the Master and the disciples in their way of seeing: 1. The disciples still look upon the green growing fields (according to the earthly appearance); 2. The Master looks upon the white harvest fields (according to the spiritual reality).—The Samaritans on their way to Jesus, a sign of harvest;—a mission token.—The messengers of Christ not only sowers, but also reapers.—The miraculous relation between sowing and harvest in the kingdom of God: 1. The two infinitely far apart; 2. The two coincident.—The sowers and the reapers of the Lord: 1. How they for the most part do not know each other in this world. 2. How they rejoice with one another in the next.—The symbolism of the field (of the sown field and of the harvest field).—The double grounds of faith which the Samaritan had: 1. The account of the woman; 2. Acquaintance with Christ Himself.—The two days of the sojourn of Jesus in Samaria.—The dark side and the bright side of the Samaritan life: 1. Greater danger of the adulteration of Christianity with heathenism, than among the Jews; 2. Greater freedom from Jewish prejudice, and hence greater access for the word of faith.—The testimony of the Samaritans: This is indeed the Christ, the Saviour of the world: 1. A fruit, ripened (*a*) under the sense of contempt from the Jews, (*b*) under the sense of free grace on the part of the Lord; 2. A bud which fully unfolded in subsequent faith and under the preaching of the Apostles.

STARKE: Envy (with reference to the Pharisees).—(CRAMER): Christians should take care of themselves, Matth. x. 23.—(MAJUS): The dignity and virtue of the sacraments depends not on persons who administer them.—Christ seeks the salvation of all men by all means and at all times. —There is no land entirely void of monuments of grace even from its antiquity.—Christ, as true man, became weary.—If the Lord became weary for the good of His creatures, we should be incited to the patient endurance of the toilsomeness of our calling.—Man must also have his rest.—CANSTEIN: Direct the necessary rest to the glory of God.—A picture of the grace which anticipates us and fondly persuades us.—QUESNEL: Jesus voluntarily humbles Himself so far as to have need of His creatures, that we may not be ashamed to accept their help.—Thirst for the salvation of men was greater in Christ than bodily thirst for water.—Christianity consists not in secluding oneself and locking the room and sitting with the prayer book behind the stove; else the Lord would not have talked with the Samaritan woman. MAJUS: National hatred pernicious and sinful.—CANSTEIN: We should not withhold the general duties of humanity on account of difference in religion.—*The same:* An inordinate estimate of our ancestry may sometimes be a hinderance to salvation.—OSIANDER: No earthly refreshing and delights can satisfy the heart.—Thirst a great need;—those who once drink from this fountain of life furnish themselves against all thirst for the world.—He who is to be converted, must be brought to a knowledge of his sin.—CANSTEIN: Christ and His Spirit must disclose to a man his secret shame if they are to help him.—*Bibl. Wirt.:* Jesus looks especially upon one's conduct of his married life.—PISCATOR: In matters of religion and faith no one should appeal to fathers or ancestry, unless their doctrine be first proved from the word of God.—Prayer and worship depend not on time, place, posture, bending of knees or folding of hands, but upon spirit and truth.—Worship in spirit and in truth by no means supersedes outward worship.—CANSTEIN: The way of serving God must agree with the attributes of God.—MAJUS: If between contending parties there still is agreement or harmony in some points, one must not despise him, but endeavor as opportunity offers to turn it to edification.—OSIANDER: The true knowledge of Christ fills a man with heavenly joy.—HEDINGER: Grace, when it is vitally kindled in the soul, gives joy and alacrity.—*The same:* Doing the will of God should be to us above eating and drinking and every necessity.—QUESNEL: A great consolation for those in the church of God who labor much and see no fruit, that they are here assured that they shall lose nothing of their reward.—HEDINGER: He who continues to depend on man, attains not to divine certainty.—Christ a universal Saviour of the whole world, 1 Tim. iv. 10; Tit. ii. 11, 13.

GOSSNER: Where the true Christ comes, He first uncovers disgrace and shame, and then takes them away.—BRAUNE: This is the fixed order in the kingdom of God, which is above all time: that it reaches over centuries, and every generation reaps what the preceding sowed, and in turn must sow what the succeeding may reap.

GERLACH:—Every sensuous form of worship, even that ordained by God Himself, is a symbolical worship, and therefore reaches its truth only in the spiritual,—without which it would be a false worship.—"Wouldst thou have a high, a holy place? consecrate thyself inwardly a temple of God; for the temple of God is holy, which temple ye are, 1 Cor. iii. 17. Wouldst thou pray in a temple, pray in thyself; but become first thyself a temple of God, for He hears him who calls to Him out of His temple." (Augustine.)

HEUBNER: Jesus teaches us prudence, silent withdrawal; it is more illustrious than bold daring, challenge, resistance, and foolhardiness. —A blessing often still rests on old places.—The inward progress in the leading of souls.—"*There cometh a woman.*" How the steps of man are guided!—Request, an approach to the heart.—The gospel seems at first only to ask of the unconverted, but under this apparent asking the offer of the highest grace is covered.—The first apprehension of the soul by divine grace takes place so secretly and imperceptibly that the souls themselves do not at all suspect it.—Religious hatred the bitterest hatred among nations.—Jesus does not stop upon invidious partizan disputes.—He who begins to know Jesus, asks of Him, calls upon Him.—"The well is deep." How deep then is the well of Jesus from which the flock of God is refreshed!—The natural man resists the demand of radical renewal with the pretence that godly ancestors have surely been saved by their mode.—"Greater than our father Jacob?" This was her standard. How imperfect in comparison with Jesus.—God compels man to reflect, to come to the knowledge of Himself. —Through Christianity the whole earth is to become a temple of God. The heavenly Jerusalem has no temple (Rev. ch. xx. and xxi.).—Yet Christ does not teach syncretism. He compromises nothing of the truth.—The future in the germ already lies in the present.—Ver. 24. Jerome well applies this passage to pilgrimage.—Ver. 30. One coal kindles the others.—Eternal life equalizes all. In it all faithful laborers enjoy in common the fruit of the labor of all.—There is a faith at first hand and a faith at second hand. The latter must lead to the former, because the latter is not enough.—(From SCHLEIERMACHER: Why Christ did not baptize and why Paul acted in like manner, 1 Cor. i. 14; both, on the contrary, preached, whereas among us the authority to preach comes before the authority to administer the sacraments, Vol. I., p. 237).—It is certainly false for a man to say, he must not speak of such (spiritual) things in social life, because they would be too high and deep. For the earthly and the spiritual are not so separate. —In those hot and dry countries where water was scarce, thirst became a tormenting sensation, such as we cannot share.—Soon the time will come when ye shall not use some this word, some that word, to express a given Christian truth, but when men shall express themselves on the same subject in a manner in which controversy disappears.

[E. D. YEOMANS:—The Saviour, wearied with ages of pilgrimage among us and of forbearance towards our heartless service of Him, sits on the well—at the sources of earthly life, which we frequent and throng, to draw,—a well of really holy memory, consecrated by the draughts of the patriarch's faith,—and asks of us a drink, Himself the gift of God to us! If we but saw things so, what glad labors, what cheerful sufferings, what effectual prayers, what glorious hope, would make up our life!]

[SCHAFF:—Several idyllic scenes of Scripture, such as the meeting of Abraham's servant with Rebecca (Gen. xxiv.), Jacob's first interview with Rachel (Gen. xxix.), Moses' meeting with Zipporah in Midian (Ex. ii.), took place in the neighborhood of wells; but the most interesting and important event is that attached to Jacob's well.—"Few can see the literal wells of Palestine, all can visit the better fountain of salvation, all can gather around the true Shepherd, lie down on the green pasture of His love, and drink of the still waters" (MACDUFF).—Christ's divine-human dealing with women, as a friend and Saviour, securing both their affection and adoration—an evidence of Christianity.—Christ offering the same gospel to an ignorant, semi-heathenish woman, as to a learned, orthodox Pharisee (ch. iii.).—Christ's discourse with the Samaritan woman a proof of His condescending love. (CALVIN: *Mirum bonitatis ejus exemplum! Quid enim fuit in misera hac femina, ut ex scorto Filii Dei repente discipula fieret?*)—Christ's discourse with the Samaritan woman, in its effect, breaking down national and religious hatred and bigotry, and elevating woman to higher dignity.—Jewish and Samaritan bigotry continued in the sectarian quarrels of Christendom, contrary to the spirit of Christ. Catholics "have no dealings" with Protestants, nor Episcopalians with Presbyterians, Lutherans with Calvinists, Baptists with Pedobaptists, high churchmen with low churchmen, *etc.*—The weariness and thirst of Christ turned into an unfailing fountain of refreshment for a poor woman and for all thirsty souls.—A touching allusion to Christ's weariness in the *Dies iræ:*

"Quærens me *sedisti lassus*,*
Redemisti crucem passus:
Tantus labor non sit cassus."

Weary sat'st Thou seeking me,
Died'st, redeeming, on the tree,
Let such toil not fruitless be.

Christ's weariness, hunger and thirst—a proof of His true humanity, including our infirmities.—"When we are carried easily, let us think on the weariness of our Master" (HENRY).—The thirst of Christ's soul for the salvation of man.—'Christ weary *in* His work, but not *of* His work.'—Christ always more ready to give than we are to ask.—Christ, the great Fisher of man, as eager to catch a single soul, as a vast multitude.—The priceless value of a single soul in the view of Christ.—Christ the model of a practical teacher in commencing a most spiritual discourse in a most natural way, and rising from physical wants to the wants of the soul.—How to spiritualize and Christianize the events and occasions of every-day life.—Vers. 16–19. There is an avenue to every human heart.—Kindness often more effective than severity.—Reproof is most profitable when least provoking.—"Those who would win souls should make *the best* of them and *work* upon their *good-nature;* for if they make *the worst* of them, they certainly *exasperate* their *ill-nature*" (HENRY).—"Amongst all sins the sin of uncleanness lies heaviest upon the conscience; for no sin is so directly opposite to holiness; no sin quenches the Holy Spirit like this" (BURKITT).—Christ keeps a record of our sins.—Conviction of sin the first step to conversion.—Ver. 20. The right and wrong appeal to the fathers and to tradition.—Vers. 21–24. The spirituality of worship distinct: 1. from formalism and ritualism; 2. from intellectualism; 3. from fanatic spiritualism.—True and false spirituality.—"O for a mountain to pray on, thou criest, high and inaccessible, that I may be nearer to God, and God may hear me better, for He dwelleth on high. Yes, God dwelleth on high, but He hath respect to the humble. . . . Wouldest thou pray in the temple? pray in thyself; but first do thou become the temple of God" (ST. AUGUSTINE).—The right use and abuse of forms in worship.—Vers. 28–30. The Samaritan woman a specimen of unpretending and effectual lay-preaching. (Origen, who himself preached before his ordination to the priesthood, calls her "the apostle of the Samaritans.")—Vers. 41, 42. Two kinds of faith: faith resting on external authority or tradition (the woman's λαλιά), and faith resting on personal experience (αὐτοὶ ἀκηκόαμεν καὶ οἴδαμεν).—The Samaritan woman a picture of the church in leading men to Christ that they may see and know for themselves.]

* [Vulgate, John iv. 6: "Jesus *fatigatus* ex itinere, *sedebat* sic supra fontem."]

VIII.

RESIDENCE OF JESUS IN GALILEE, AND BELIEVING GALILEANS IN PARTICULAR. THE NOBLEMAN. THE MIRACLE OF DISTANT HEALING, AS A SECOND SIGN.

CHAP. IV. 43–54.

(Vers. 47–54. Gospel for 21st Sunday after Trinity.)

43 Now after [the, τάς][1] two days he departed thence, and went [*omit* and went][2]
44 into Galilee.[3] For Jesus himself testified, that a prophet hath no honor in his own
45 country. Then when [When therefore, ὅτε οὖν] he was come [he came, ἦλθε] into
Galilee, the Galileans received him, having seen all the things [*omit* the things] that
he did at Jerusalem at the feast: for they also went unto [to] the feast.
46 So Jesus [he][4] came again into Cana of Galilee, where he made the water
wine.
And there was a certain nobleman [a royal person or officer, τις βασιλικός],
47 whose son was sick [,] at Capernaum. When he heard [The same, having heard,
οὗτος ἀκούσας] that Jesus was [had] come out of Judea into Galilee, he went unto
him, and besought him that he would come down, and heal his son: for he was at
48 the point of death. Then said Jesus unto him, Except ye see signs and wonders,
49 ye will not believe. The nobleman saith unto him, Sir, come down ere my child
50 die. Jesus saith unto him, Go thy way; thy son liveth. And the man believed
the word that Jesus had spoken [spake, εἶπεν] unto him, and he [*omit* he] went his
51 way. And as he was now going down, his servants met him, and told *him* [brought
52 word],[5] saying, Thy son [his child, παῖς αὐτοῦ][6] liveth. Then [he] inquired he of
them the hour when he began to amend. And they said unto him, Yesterday
53 at the seventh hour the fever left him. So the father knew that it was at [in] the
same hour, in the [*omit* the] which Jesus said unto him, Thy son liveth: and
54 [. And he] himself believed, and his whole house. This is again the second miracle *that* Jesus did [This again, a second sign, wrought Jesus, τοῦτο πάλιν δεύτερον σημεῖον ἐποίησεν ὁ Ἰησ.], when he was [had] come out of Judea into Galilee.

TEXTUAL AND GRAMMATICAL.

[1] Ver. 43.—[The article refers, of course, to the δύο ἡμέρας in ver. 40.—P. S.]

[2] Ver. 43.—Codd. B. C. D. omit: καὶ ἀπῆλθεν; but A. supports the Recepta. Tischendorf omits the words. Meyer also rejects them. But it is evident that they have been omitted through failure to perceive their import. The Evangelist would distinguish between the departure for Galilee in the wider sense, and the removal to Upper Galilee, called by him simply Galilee, in the provincial sense. [The received text is in favor of Dr. Lange's interpretation of πατρίς, see EXEG. NOTES, but the latest editions reject καὶ ἀπῆλθεν on the authority of the oldest MSS. ℵ. B. C. D. Orig. Cyr.—P. S.]

[3] Ver. 43.—[Dr. Lange here inserts in small type the gloss: *from Lower Galilee to Upper*, thus anticipating his explanation of πατρίς, ver. 44. See the EXEG. NOTES.—P. S.]

[4] Ver. 46.—This ὁ Ἰησοῦς, wanting in most authorities, is added by the textus receptus.

[5] Ver. 51.—[Alford brackets καὶ ἀπήγγειλαν. Tischend. ed. VIII. reads καὶ ἤγγειλαν with ℵ. D. Westcott and Hort omit it.—P. S.]

[6] Ver. 51.—Lachmann: ὁ παῖς αὐτοῦ, after A. B. C. *etc.* [Tischend., Alf., Mey. likewise adopt ὁ παῖς αὐτοῦ for the easier lect. rec. ὁ παῖς σου, which may have been conformed to ὁ παῖς σου, ver. 50.—P. S.]

EXEGETICAL AND CRITICAL.

[The miraculous healing of the nobleman's son resembles the healing of the centurion's servant, Matth. viii. 5; Luke vii. 1, but must not be confounded with it (see the points of difference in the note on ver. 46). It was the second miracle which Christ wrought in Galilee (ver. 54); the first being the change of water into wine (ch. ii.). John relates a third miracle in Galilee, the feeding of the multitude, which is followed by a long discourse (ch. vi.), and three miracles in Judea, *viz.:* the healing of the cripple at the pool of Bethesda (v.), the healing of the blind (ix.), and the raising of Lazarus (xi.). He also relates three appearances of the risen Saviour (xxi. 14). Bengel (on ver. 54) notes this threefold trinity with the remark: "*Hæc nimirum Johannis methodus est, ut per ternarium incedat.*"—P. S.]

Ver. 43. **And went.**—The repetition: Ἐξῆλθεν ἐκεῖθεν, and καὶ ἀπῆλθεν, should be noted with reference to the next verse. See the Textual Notes (No. 2).

Ver. 44. **For Jesus himself testified.**—

Himself. Meyer: "Not only other people in reference to Him. For the matter itself, comp. Matth. xiii. 57; Mark vi. 4; Luke iv. 24." Tholuck better: "He had himself acknowledged the correctness of the popular proverb." [The proverb itself is based upon common experience and needs no explanation. "Familiarity breeds contempt," while "distance lends enchantment to the view." The Germans have a similar proverb: "This is not far off" (*Das ist nicht weit her*), *i. e.*, nothing uncommon. Many of the greatest men were despised or ignored in their native land or city, and made their renown or fortune in foreign lands. The only difficulty is in the logical connection as indicated by γάρ.—P. S.] The question is, how is the *for* (γάρ) to be explained? or how can He go to Galilee because a prophet hath no honor in his own country? for we should expect either the reverse, or *although* (καίπερ) instead of *for* (γάρ).* Answer:

1. Πατρίς [*patria*] is not the native *country* (*Vaterland*), but the native *city* (*Vaterstadt*), even in antithesis to the country of Galilee (Chrysostom, who understands it of Capernaum, Cyril, Erasmus, Calvin, *etc.*). Against this: The antithesis is not demonstrated.

[Nearly all who understand πατρίς of the native town, refer it, not to Capernaum (with Chrysostom and Euthymius Zig.), which is altogether out of the question, but to *Nazareth*, where Christ was not born, indeed, but raised, and where He lived to the time of His public ministry. (So Cyril Alex., Calvin, Grotius, Bengel, Olshausen, Hengstenberg, Bäumlein, Trench, on *Miracles*, p. 99, Wordsworth.) Nazareth in Galilee then is contrasted here with Galilee in general, as the city of Jerusalem is contrasted with the land of Judea, iii. 22. This view has a strong support in Luke iv. 24 (comp. Matth. xiii. 57; Mark vi. 4), where Christ says in the synagogue of Nazareth: "No prophet is accepted in his own country" (ἐν τῇ πατρίδι αὐτοῦ). This was soon shown by the action of the Nazaræans who "thrust Him out of the city and led Him to the brow of the hill, that they might cast Him down headlong" (ver. 29); while in Capernaum the people "were astonished at His doctrine" (ver. 32), and, as John relates, received Him well (iv. 45). John may have supposed this event to be already known from the other Gospels. The only objection to this view is, that *Galilee*, ver. 43, would naturally include Nazareth. It would be necessary to explain the γάρ from ver. 46: Christ went to Cana in Galilee (which lies north of Nazareth), without passing through His native place, for the reason mentioned. The choice lies between this interpretation and that of Dr. Lange (see below, No. 7), which comes nearest to it. All others are too far-fetched.—P. S.]

2. Πατρίς is Judea, since He was born in Bethlehem (Origen, Maldonatus, Schweizer, Ebrard [formerly], Baur). Against this: *a.* His acknowledged home was Nazareth, notwithstanding He was born in Bethlehem;† *b.* In Judea He had been well received by the people; *c.* The construction, that Judea was His country, as being the country of the prophets (Origen, Baur, Baumgarten-Crusius), would be unintelligible.

3. Judea is indeed meant to be understood as His πατρίς, but this just proves the unhistorical character of John's Gospel (Schwegler, Bruno Bauer; Schweizer: The unhistorical character of the ensuing narrative, which is to be considered an interpolation).

4. *For* means *namely, that is to say*, and relates not to what precedes, but to what follows. The sentence is a preliminary explanation of the fact that the Galileans did indeed this time receive Jesus well, but only on account of the miracles they had seen at their visit to the last passover in Jerusalem [which set them the fashion in their estimate of men and things, while the Samaritans believed in Him for His word without signs]. (So Lücke [III. ed.], De Wette, Tholuck.* Contrary to the spirit of the maxim, to the context (for a nobleman from Capernaum meets Him at the outset at Cana seeking help); and to the fact in general.

5. Christ went to Galilee just *because* He expected not to find acceptance there. (*a*) Brückner: To accept the conflict—which, however, was more threatening in Judea; (*b*) Hofmann, Luthardt [now also Ebrard]: Because He hoped [to avoid publicity and] to find rest and quiet in Galilee—in which, however, He would be disappointed. [Against both these views may be urged also that the text reports neither a conflict, nor a quiet retirement in Galilee, but a miracle of healing.—P. S.]

6. Meyer: "Πατρίς is not the native town, but the native country, *viz.*, *Galilee*, as is proved by vers. 43 and 45, and as usual with the Greeks since Homer. The words contain the reason why Jesus did not hesitate to return to Galilee, but the reason lies in the antithetic relation implied in ἐν τῇ πατρίδι. For if, as Jesus Himself testified, a prophet is without honor in his own country, he must earn it in another. And this Jesus had done in Jerusalem. He now brought with Him the honor of a prophet from a distance. Hence too He found acceptance with the Galileans, because they had seen His miracles in Jerusalem (ii. 23)."† Against this: *a.* Then the word must have stood at ch. iv. 1. But there another motive stands for His having now left Judea. *b.* The remark must have been, that He came already full of honor, because He had none to expect in Galilee. *c.* It must not have been known that He was ill-received in His own πατρίς, in the narrower sense, on this very return.

7. Πατρίς is *Lower* Galilee, to which Nazareth belonged. We believe we have found the full solution in the fact that now took place, the removal of Jesus from Nazareth, where He had been thrust out, to Capernaum, on the presumption that Capernaum belonged to Galilee in the narrower sense, *i. e.*, to *Upper* Galilee, to which Nazareth, in Lower Galilee, did not belong. This is supported (*a*) by the fact that the name Galilee in the narrower sense referred to Upper Galilee (see Forbiger, *Handbuch der alten Geographie*, II., p. 689); (*b*) by the statement of Jose-

* [Augustine, Tittmann, Kuinoel and Bloomfield take γάρ here in the sense of καίπερ, which is against all grammar.—P. S.]

† [Comp. John i. 46; ii. 1; vii. 3, 41, 52.—P. S.]

* [Dr. Lange mentions Olshausen after Tholuck. But in the third ed. of his Com., Olshausen refers πατρίς to Nazareth. Dean Alford adopts De Wette's view, but in his sixth edition he combines with it Luthardt's (see below, sub 5).—P. S.]

† [Godet pretty nearly agrees with Meyer.—P. S.]

phus, that Upper Galilee was separated from Lower Galilee by a line drawn from Tiberias to Zebulon [*De bello Jud.* III. 3, 1), which throws Nazareth into Lower Galilee. If now we consider that John writes with the living, popular view of Palestine thoroughly in his mind; that he knew of an unknown Bethany, a ferry-village on the other side of the Jordan, of an otherwise unknown Salim, near Ænon, of an elsewhere unknown Sychar, probably a suburb of Sichem, of the pool of Bethesda with its porches, of Solomon's Porch in the temple,—we may also conceive that John knows of a Galilee in the provincial sense, and that he can say without geographical reflection, Jesus went to Galilee, as the Swiss in Geneva says without reflection: I am going to Switzerland; the Pomeranian: I am going to Prussia. This is further favored by the expression in Luke iv. 31: He "came down from Nazareth to Capernaum, a city of Galilee;" against which it signifies nothing that Galilee sometimes occurs in John, especially in the mouth of another, in the wider sense. (See *Leben Jesu*, II. 2, p. 542.)

Ver. 45. **The Galileans received him.**—Received Him favorably. A general observation concerning His acceptance in Upper Galilee, particularly in Cana, Bethsaida, Capernaum, *etc.* They received Him; antithetic to an implied rejection. **Having seen all the things that he did.**—No ignoring of His earlier miracles in Cana and Capernaum. It was to the Galileans a new and higher attestation, that Jesus had made a great impression even in Jerusalem with His signs. It was their countryman who had purified the temple, and filled the holy city with wonder.

Ver. 46. **So Jesus came again.**—What means this *οὖν, so?* The first time Jesus had gone on from Nazareth to Cana. And now He again went first to Nazareth. And if He wished to go thence to Galilee, we might expect He would proceed first to His friends in Cana. In Cana He seems to have tarried several days; at all events the βασιλικός comes hither for Him.

And there was a certain nobleman [royal officer, βασιλικός**].**—An officer of Herod Antipas, the tetrarch (whom the common people considered and called a king, Matt. xiv. 1, 9),* The title βασιλικός combines civil and military dignity; hence some have taken this βασιλικός to be identical with the centurion of Capernaum (Irenæus, Semler, Strauss, Baumgarten-Crusius).

The office, the sick boy, the distant healing, are similar features.

On the other side are these differences:

1. The time; here before the removal of Jesus to Capernaum, there long after it.

2. The place of Christ at the time; here Cana, there the vicinity of Capernaum.

3. The characters; here excited, weak, feebly believing, there calm, confident, strong of faith.

Other differences, by themselves considered, might be more easily wiped away: The υἱός here, the δοῦλος there (a distinction, however, which is not resolved by the common παῖς: here the boy is a small boy, a child (ver. 49), there a stout youth); there a Gentile, here a miracle-believer, probably a Jew. Yet these with the foregoing strengthen the difference. But the most decisive diversity is in the judgment of the Lord. The faith of the centurion He commends with admiration; the faith of the nobleman He must first subject to a trial. [Chrysostom, Trench, Alford: The weak faith of the nobleman is strengthened, while the humility of the centurion is honored.]

Accordingly this miracle has been in fact by most expositors (from Origen down) made distinct from the other.*

Ver. 48. **Except ye see signs and wonders.**—Shall have seen. Ye must first have seen these, before ye come to faith. The stress does not lie decidedly on ἴδητε (Storr), thus censuring the request to go with him. The man's answer does not agree with this; and ἴδητε must then have stood first. Still the ἴδητε is not without significance; as is indicated by the fact that we here have for the first time in John σημεῖα καὶ τέρατα, whereas hitherto he has spoken only of σημεῖα. *And wonders* (τέρατα) must be emphasized. But the less therefore can we suppose a general reproof of the Galileans, with reference to ver. 45 (Meyer); for it was the way of Jesus Himself to lead through faith in miracles to faith in the word, John x. 38; xiv. 11; xv. 24. Christ, therefore, reproves not the faith in miracles in itself (Eckermann), but the craving for miracles or miracle-mania. He intimates besides, that there is a higher grade of faith than that which rests on the seeing of miracles; as appears more distinctly afterwards, in John xiv. 11; xx. 29. He designates the petitioner and those like him as a class of people who are not set beforehand towards the kingdom of God, but have yet to be brought to faith by signs and wonders (τέρατα); of course presupposing a sensuous spirit with a weak readiness to believe, passion for miracles, personal interest in the miracle (signs and wonders for yourselves), and an inordinate desire for seeing, 1 Cor. i. 22. We must, however, consider that the reproof is not intended for a rejection, but for discipline, to hush the excitement of the man, and recall him to his inward spirit. Yet the palliation of Maldonatus [Rom. Cath.] is too strong: That the words contain no censure, but only a declaration of the spiritual *infirmity* of the people now proved by a fact.

Ver. 49. **Sir, come down ere,** *etc.*—The man proves not strong enough, indeed, to take the reproof of Christ, but it is enough that he does not feel wounded and repulsed, and that he persists and grows more urgent in his prayer. The utterance of a father's love in trouble and anguish: My child is dying; as in Jairus, the Canaanitish mother, and the father of the demoniac under the mount of transfiguration. This distress of love makes him a believer.

Ver. 50. **Go thy way; thy son liveth.**—

* [Some identify this nobleman with Chuza, Herod's steward, whose wife Joanna was among the followers and supporters of Jesus, Luke viii. 3. A mere conjecture.—P. S.]

* Among those who have identified the two, Strauss and others would give the preference for accurate narration to Matthew, Gfrörer and Ewald to John. With Weisse again it is "a misapprehension of a parable." According to Baur the doctrinal import of the story of Nicodemus and of that of the woman of Samaria is here combined in a third story, teaching: How faith in miracles comes by means of faith in word, and consequently is in reality only such. In other words two critical legends are supposed to be combined in a third, and the Jewish councillor and the Samaritan woman become in this phantasy the Galilean nobleman!

Not only the word of miraculous help, but at the same time also the second and decisive test. He must believe and go at the word. And the man believed the word; he stood the test.

Explanation of the miracle:

1. Paulus makes of it a medical prognostication after the account of the sickness given by the father: comp. also Ammon.

2. Others have supposed the operation of a magnetic healing power (Olshausen, Krabbe, *etc.*).

3. Meyer, on the other hand: By his *will.* This is of course the main thing, as in the doctrine of creation. God created the world by His will. But if we conceive the will of God abstractly, and exclude all co-operation of His vital force, we are ultra-supernaturalistic (and perhaps ultra-Reformed). The will of Christ is unquestionably the main thing, but it does not work abstractly; without a vital force proceeding from Him (comp. Mark v. 30) the thing is not apprehended, though the magnetic healing virtue affords only the natural analogy or form for it. Even the miracle of immediate knowledge comes into the account, inasmuch as Christ wrought only where He saw the Father work, John v. 19. And the same instant, in which this saving life-ray flies into the heart of the father, it flies also into the heart of his distant son. For how near this father now was to his son in his inward communication, Jesus alone knew.

Ver. 52. **Then he inquired of them.**—The fact alone did not satisfy him; he wished to trace it to its cause. That is, he leaned towards faith. "Not self-interest merely, but a religious interest also in the case, is guiding him." Tholuck. And then it appeared, (1) that the son suddenly recovered, and (2) at the hour when Jesus spoke the word. **Yesterday at the seventh hour.**—According to the Jewish division of the day this could perhaps have been said in the evening of the same day, after six o'clock. The healing took place soon after noon, and probably the father set out immediately for home. According to our reckoning of the day, a night must have intervened; which would give a strange length of time for a distance of some eight or ten hours, and Lampe adjusts by supposing that the man, in his firm faith, did not travel *festinans*, while De Wette thinks it strange that he stopped over night on the way. But the meeting of the servants might very well have occurred the next morning, without the journey having been slow.

Ver. 53. **And he himself believed, and his whole house.**—It is palpably the rule, that, with the father, the family also become believers (Acts x. 44; xvi. 15, 32); but here the Evangelist calls particular attention to it by his expression. The members of the family had seen the sudden recovery, but had not heard the word of the Saviour.

Ver. 54. **This sign Jesus wrought as the second,** *etc.* Πάλιν is not to be connected with δεύτερον, nor to be referred to ἐποίησεν by itself, but to the statement that Jesus had returned from Judea to Galilee. Jesus had meantime done many other miracles, even in Capernaum; this miracle marks His second return to Galilee, as the miracle at Cana had marked the first. He brought healing with Him at once, and it went out from Him even in distant results.

DOCTRINAL AND ETHICAL.

1. In regard to the spirit in which Jesus just now comes to Upper Galilee and performs this miracle, it must be observed that according to Luke iv. 14 sqq.; Matth. xiii. 53 sqq., He had just been thrust out from His city Nazareth. See *Leben Jesu*, II. 2, p. 541. Experiences of this kind could in Him produce only an increase of His manifestations of love to those who were susceptible.

2. As the first miracle of *distant* operation this incident bears a close relation to the healing of the servant of the centurion at Capernaum and of the daughter of the Canaanitish woman. In the mysterious manifestation of the divine power of Christ, we must still not neglect the human media, which here lay in the inward connection of an anxious father's heart with the dying child. As in fact the help of God owns the human intercession. The spiritual roads, streets and paths which human love, distress, and prayer have to make for the divine help in the invisible world, can only glorify the freedom, truth, and miraculous power of this help, as a power which is at the same time the power of a personal Spirit and love, *i. e.*, not abstractly working in a void, but as divine life applied to the human.

3. As the Lord in the case of the Samaritan woman rebuked superstitious trust in a place of pilgrimage, so here He reproves superstitious trust in visible miracles.

HOMILETICAL AND PRACTICAL.

After the two days. The great days of grace, in which the Lord visits us, are numbered, and swiftly pass away.—*Jesus departed thence.* The itinerancy of Jesus a clear expression of His inner life: (1) of His Israelite fidelity to duty; (2) of His heavenly calling; (3) of His love; (4) of His holy Spirit.—The rapid change of time and place in the life of Jesus a token of His unworldly pilgrim nature.—How the Lord learned and sealed in its highest sense the universal human experience that a prophet has no honor in his own country, in order to make of it a holy maxim of life.—Want of esteem at home, the prophet's signal to travel.—The closed door a waymark for the Lord and His disciples to go on to the open door.—A good word finds its place.—It is no question, *Whether* there be in the world persons susceptible to thy mission; the only question is, *Where* they are (whether here or far away; whether in the present or in the future); and herein is much to be unlearned and to be learned by the heart of youthful Christian enthusiasm.—How the divine fire of Christ was always only inflamed by the coldness of men.—The two works of Jesus in Cana, the transformation of water and the distant healing, as conspicuous tokens of His heavenly nature: 1. The first, so to speak, leads up into heaven. 2. The second as it were comes down from heaven.—How the nobleman of Capernaum learns to believe. This nobleman compared with the centurion of Capernaum (resemblances, differences, see above).—The deliberation of Jesus with the nobleman, a mark of the elevation of His spirit; (1) Of His freedom from obsequiousness and respect of persons; (2) of His wise reserve and loving compliance.—Except *ye* see signs and wonders. Or, the distinction between true and false resting of faith on miracles.—Also a distinction between the true and the false miracle.—The marks of each (faith and miracle).—Except *ye*. Or, the connection between worldly-minded unbelief and worldly-minded superstition in the polite world (at that time the court of Herod).—Yet a nobler germ may lie in the miracle-craving form of faith. (The question is, which is the germ, and which the shell.)—The testing of faith, which the nobleman stands: 1. How he is tested (*a*) in his humility by a stern word which might wound the pride of a nobleman; (*b*) in his faith, by being required to trust a word. 2. How he stands the test: (*a*) in his persistent prayer he passes the test of the humility of his faith; (*b*) in his confident departure at the word of Jesus he proves the power of his faith.—Only the faith, which is itself a miracle of God can receive the miraculous help of God.—Faith in the divine help must be directed above all to the divine in the help.—How the Lord in granting refuses and in refusing grants.—His refusing, a higher granting.—Necessity and love as handmaids of faith.—Comparison of the nobleman with the Canaanitish woman.—The father and his sick child.—How the upright man in approaching Jesus becomes at once smaller and greater: 1. The nobleman is smaller in his going than in his coming, in that he is humbly satisfied with the healing word of Jesus, and no longer desires that he should go down with him. 2. He is greater in his going than in his coming, in that he returns full of confidence in the word of Jesus. The majesty in trusting the promise of Christ, the power, out of which the greatness in the confidence of the believer grows. Out of the Amen of Christ the Amen of the believer. The divine education of the sensuous believing of miracles into believing of the word: (1) In this incident, (2) in the church, (3) in the life of the individual Christian.—The health-message of Christ and the health-messenger of the servants; or, how the health-messages of heaven by far precede the health-messages of earth.—The echo of the divine word of Christ: Thy son liveth! in the mouth of the servants: Thy son liveth!—The dull echo of earth, and the clear echo of heaven.—The hard ascent and the glad descent in the journey of the nobleman.—Yesterday at the seventh hour; or, in the proper hour the help comes home with power.—Mark the great hours (of extremity, of prayer, of miraculous help).—Remember those hours, and believe!—The distress of the whole house must become also the faith of the whole (this may be said of the family, of the church, of mankind).—The faith wrought by the miracle at the moment must make itself good in the moral expansion of faith. 1. Through the whole life, 2. Through the whole house.—How the sickness of a child may become the salvation of a whole house; may, under His management, serve to glorify the Lord.—The connection between the faith of the father and the germ of faith in the heart of the child.—He prayed for the healing of his child, and obtained healing for himself and his whole house.—The Lord comes announced by the forerunning miraculous help.—The healing work of Christ in His presence and at a distance: (1) At a distance even when it is in His presence; (2) in His presence even when it is at a distance (susceptible hearts are near to Him, and He is near to them).—Jesus always peculiarly rich when He comes from Judea to Galilee: 1. From enemies to friends; 2. From the great to the small; 3. From the proud to the poor.

STARKE: The bad manners of men in esteeming nothing which is common and always before their eyes, but highly esteeming what is strange and rare.—Every one is bound, indeed, to serve his own country; but if his own country despise him, any place which receives him is his country.—HEDINGER: Jesus comes again (when He has once retired apparently in vexation).—God has a holy seed even among the great. All men, whatever their station, are subject to need and sickness.—*The same:* Trouble gives feet, humbles pride, teaches prayer.—LANGE: To seek Jesus under special distress is indeed good and needful, but it is better that one should not wait so long, but knowing his sin and misery should in spirit be near to Jesus.—OSIANDER: Parents should interest themselves both bodily and spiritually for their children.—The bodily sickness of children troubles Christian parents; what an affliction, when they lie sick in soul! Christ comes always at the right time with His help.—*Bibl. Wirt.:* Christ rejects not those who are weak in faith, but takes pains, that their faith may grow.—*Nova Bibl. Tub.:* Faith is [seems] shameless and cannot be rebuffed.—OSIANDER: It is well to persevere in prayer, but not prescribe the manner or time of help.—Faith has not only grand, but also swift results: almost every hour some form of divine help meets the believer.—As the master, so the servant; good governing makes good domestics.—CANSTEIN: When we duly reflect, not an hour passes in which God does not show us good.—OSIANDER: Christ's followers must not be weary of wandering far on earth and doing good in all places.—The more a country has seen and heard of Christ, the heavier judgment will it receive, if it believe not.—RIEGER: Much of the teaching and wholesome direction of God comes to us through our children, and what concerns their life and death, their success and hindrances, goes to our heart.—All depends on whether a man will.

BESSER: It is a wonderfully beautiful example of growing faith, that we have in this nobleman. Methinks John expresses his own joyful surprise, when he pictures to us the suddenly stilled and satisfied man: The man believed the word that Jesus had spoken unto him, and he went his way.

HEUBNER: By the sickness of children God disciplines the parents themselves.—Though he was at the court of Herod (at least as a servant), yet he went to Jesus.—Domestic troubles should drive us to Jesus.—The true sense is: Except ye *see* signs and wonders. The emphasis lies on *see* [yet τέρατα also is not unmeaning].—There is a secret inclination [a universal passion of the world] for miracles: 1. Desire for special extraordinary fortune to befall us, while we do not exert ourselves to obtain that which satisfies. 2. Waiting for extraordinary help in exigency, when we will not earnestly use the right means. 3. Desire for extraordinary fruits of our labor, when we will not sow, hoping in faith. 4. Desire of extraordinary violent assistance when we wish to get rid of faults, while we ourselves do not lift a hand. 5. Desire or expectation of honor, *etc.*, while yet we have done or sacrificed nothing at all for the glory of God.—The word of Jesus holds good for us in every conflict and every strait; Go thy way, and believe!—Hours of deliverance in human life: —The more thou searchest, the more plain will the moments of the divine deliverance be to thee. —*And he believed.* This faith was more than the preceding; it attained to faith in Jesus the Saviour.—This faith was the fruit of trial. For this God sends distress.—The Christian father, as priest in his own house.—(Whitefield): The head of a family has three offices (prophet, priest, king: "the last he does not so easily forget"). —The nobleman as an example of gradual progress in faith.

Draeseke: The new house: 1. It has a new attitude outwardly. 2. It has a new manner of spirit. (These two are reversible).—Greiling: To our sufferings we owe the most precious experiences of our life.—Goldhorn: Consolatory reflections on the moral influence of sickness.—Grueneisen: Concerning the growth of faith: 1. Need is its rise; bodily need, less than spiritual. 2. Trust is its second stage; and it must be directed less to the bodily than to the spiritual. 3. Experience is the third stage; experience more of spiritual than of bodily help.—Kniewel: The three stages of faith: 1. Its childhood, the stage of seeking miracle. 2. Its youth, the stage of receiving miracle. 3. Its manhood, the stage of the power of miracle.—Reinhard: How weighty should be to us the thought, that distress is often our guide to truth. —Schulz: How trial and trouble lead men to the fellowship of Jesus Christ.—Bachmann: The Christian calls the Saviour to his sick: 1. He calls Him. 2. In due time. 3. In the right spirit. 4. With the most blessed result.—Lisco: The house of the Christian, when God visits it with trouble: The trouble (1) unites the members in tenderer love, (2) directs their hearts more trustfully to the Lord, (3) awakens them to importunate prayer and intercession, (4) produces at last a joyful and thankful faith.—Kaempfe: The humility and the persistence of the nobleman.—Ahlfeld: The blessing of trial. —Beck: The exigence, the test, the victory, of faith.—Rautenberg: The hard condition of the Christian at the sick-bed of his darlings.

[Alford: This miracle is a notable instance of our Lord "not quenching the smoking flax," just as His reproof of the Samaritan woman was of His "not breaking the bruised reed." The little spark of faith in the breast of this nobleman is by Him lit up into a clear and enduring flame for the light and comfort of himself and his house. —Wordsworth: Our Lord would not *go down* at the desire of the *nobleman* to heal his *son*, but He offered to go down to heal the *servant* of the *centurion* (Matt. viii. 7). He thus teaches us, that what is lofty in man's sight, is low in His eyes, and the reverse.—There are degrees in faith (ver. 53) as in other virtues.—Ryle: The lessons of this miracle: 1. The rich have afflictions as well as the poor. 2. Sickness and death come to the young as well as the old. 3. What benefits affliction can confer on the soul. 4. Christ's word is as good as Christ's presence.—P. S.]

SECOND SECTION.

Open Antagonism between Christ, as the Light of the World, and the Elements of Darkness in the World, especially in their proper Representatives, Unbelievers, but also in the Better Men, so far as They still belong to the World.

Chap. V. 1—VII. 9.

I.

THE FEAST OF THE JEWS AND THE SABBATH OF THE JEWS, AND THEIR OBSERVANCE OF IT: KILLING CHRIST. THE FEAST OF CHRIST AND THE SABBATH OF CHRIST, AND HIS OBSERVANCE OF IT: RAISING THE DEAD. OFFENCE OF THE JUDAISTS IN JERUSALEM AT THE SABBATH-HEALING OF JESUS, AND AT HIS TESTIMONY CONCERNING HIS FREEDOM AND HIS DIVINE ORIGIN (AND BESIDES, DOUBTLESS, AT HIS OUTDOING THE POOL OF BETHESDA). FIRST ASSAULT UPON THE LIFE OF JESUS. CHRIST THE TRUE FOUNT OF HEALING (POOL OF BETHESDA), THE GLORIFIER OF THE SABBATH BY HIS SAVING WORK, THE RAISER OF THE DEAD, THE LIFE AS THE VITAL ENERGY AND HEALING OF THE WORLD, ACCREDITED BY JOHN, BY THE SCRIPTURES, BY MOSES. THE TRUE MESSIAH IN THE FATHER'S NAME, AND FALSE MESSIAHS.

Chap. V.

1. The Healing.

1 After this [these things, μετὰ ταῦτα, not τοῦτο] there was a feast[1] of the Jews; and
2 Jesus went up to Jerusalem. Now there is at Jerusalem by the sheep *market*
[sheep *gate*][2] a pool, which is called in the Hebrew tongue [in Hebrew, Ἑβραϊστί]

3 Bethesda,[3] having five porches. In these lay a great [*omit* great][4] multitude of
impotent folk [of the sick, or diseased persons], of [*omit* of] blind, halt [lame],
4 withered, waiting for the moving of the water. For an angel went down at a cer-
tain season into the pool, and troubled the water: whosoever then first after the
troubling of the water stepped in was made whole of whatsoever disease he had.
5 [*Omit* all from waiting to had.][5] And a certain man was there, which had an infirmity
6 [who had been in his infirmity][6] thirty and eight years. When Jesus saw him lie,
and knew that he had been now [already] a long time *in that case*,[7] he saith unto
7 him, Wilt [Desirest] thou [to] be made whole? The impotent [sick] man an-
swered him, Sir,[8] I have no man, when the water is troubled, to put me [carry me
quickly, cast me] into the pool: but while I am coming, another steppeth [goeth]
8, 9 down before me. Jesus saith unto him, Rise, take up thy bed, and walk. And
immediately the man was made whole, and took up his bed, and walked.

2. THE OFFENCE AT THE HEALING ON THE SABBATH.

10 And on the same [on that] day was the sabbath.[9] The Jews therefore said unto
him that was cured, It is the sabbath day [*omit* day]; it is not lawful for thee to
11 carry *thy* bed [to take up the bed]. He answered them, He that made me whole,
12 the same said unto me, Take up thy bed, and walk. Then[10] asked they [They
asked] him, What man is that which [Who is the man that] said unto thee, Take
13 up thy bed, [*omit* thy bed][11] and walk? And [But] he that was healed[12] wist
[knew] not who it was: for Jesus had conveyed himself away [withdrawn him-
14 self], a multitude [or crowd] being in *that* [the] place. Afterward Jesus findeth
him in the temple, and said unto him, Behold, thou art made whole: sin no more,
15 lest a [some, τι] worse thing come unto thee [befall thee]. The man departed, and
told[13] the Jews that it was Jesus, which [who] had made him whole.

3. THE ACCUSATION, A TWOFOLD ACCUSATION, AND THE VINDICATION OF JESUS CONCERNING HIS WORKING ON THE SABBATH, AND CONCERNING HIS CLAIM TO BE THE SON OF GOD.

16 And therefore did the Jews persecute Jesus [And for this cause the Jews per-
secuted (judicially arraigned) Jesus], and sought to slay him [*omit* and sought to
slay him],[14] because he had done these things on the sabbath day [*omit* day].
17 But Jesus answered them, My Father worketh hitherto [is working unceasingly
18 even until now, or, up to this time] and I work [am working]. Therefore the Jews
sought the more to kill him, because he not only had broken [broke, ἔλυεν] the
sabbath [according to their opinion], but said also that God was his Father [but also
called God his own Father, πατέρα ἴδιον], making himself equal with God.
19 Then answered Jesus [to this second accusation] and said unto them, Verily, verily,
I say unto you, The Son can do nothing of himself, but what he seeth the Father do
[doing, ποιοῦντα]: for what things soever he doeth, these things also doeth the Son
20 likewise [in like manner]. For the Father loveth the Son, and sheweth him all
things that [which he] himself doeth: and he will shew him greater works than
these, [and greater works than these will he show him],[15] that ye may marvel.

4. THE SAVING OPERATION OF THE SON, HIS QUICKENING IN GENERAL.

21 For as the Father raiseth up the dead, and quickeneth *them;* even so the Son
22 quickeneth whom he will. For the Father judgeth no man [Neither doth the
Father judge any one], but hath committed all [the entire] judgment unto the Son:
23 That all *men* should [may] honour the Son, even [*omit* even] as they honour the
Father. He that honoureth not the Son honoureth not the Father which hath sent
24 [who sent] him.—Verily, verily, I say unto you, He that heareth my word, and be-
lieveth on him that sent me hath everlasting life, and shall not come [cometh not,
οὐκ ἔρχεται] into condemnation [judgment, κρίσιν]; but is passed from [hath passed
out of][16] death unto [into, εἰς] life.—

5. THE SPIRITUAL RAISING OF THE DEAD NOW IMMEDIATELY BEGINNING.

25 Verily, verily, I say unto you, The hour is coming, and now is, when the dead
26 shall hear the voice of the Son of God; and they that hear shall live. For as the
Father hath life in himself; so hath he given [gave he] to the Son [also] to have

27 life in himself; And hath given [he gave] him authority to execute judgment also
[*omit* also][17] because he is the [a] Son of man.[18]

6. THE FUTURE RAISING OF THE DEAD.

28 Marvel not at this: for the [an] hour is coming, in the [*omit* the] which all that
29 are in the graves shall hear his voice, And shall come forth; they that have done
good, unto the [a] resurrection of life; and they that have done evil, unto the [a]
resurrection of damnation [judgment, κρίσεως].
30 I can of mine own self [of myself] do nothing; as I hear [the actual sentence of
God], I judge; and my judgment is just; because I seek not mine own will, but
the will of the Father [him][19] which hath sent [who sent] me.

7. TESTIMONY OF JESUS.

31 If I [myself] bear witness of [concerning] myself, my witness is [according to law
32 of testimony] not true. There is another that beareth witness of [concerning] me;
and I know that the witness which he witnesseth of [concerning] me is true.

8. TESTIMONY OF JOHN THE BAPTIST.

33 Ye [have] sent [ἀπεστάλκατε] unto John, and he bare [hath borne] witness [μεμαρ-
34 τύρηκεν] unto the truth. But I receive not testimony [authentication] from [a]
man.[20] But these things I say [I speak openly of this matter], that ye [who know of the
35 circumstances] might [may] be saved. He was a [the] burning and a shining light
[lamp][21]: and ye were willing for a season [a little while, an hour, πρὸς ὥραν] to
rejoice in his light.[22]

9. TESTIMONY OF THE FATHER IN THE WORKS OF JESUS AND IN THE SCRIPTURES.

36 But I have greater witness than *that* of John[23]: for the works which the Father
hath given me to finish, the same works that I do [the very works or, the works
themselves which I am doing], bear witness of me, that the Father hath sent me.
37 And the Father himself,[24] which hath sent [who sent] me, hath borne witness of
me.[25] Ye have neither heard his voice at any time, nor seen [spiritually] his shape.
38 And ye have not his word [Old Testament word] abiding [with living power] in you;
39 for whom he [himself] hath [*omit* hath] sent, him ye believe not. Search [Ye do
search][26] the Scriptures; for [because] in them [in the several books and letters] ye
40 think ye have eternal life: and they are they which testify of me. And [yet] ye
will not come to me; that ye might [may] have life [the life of those Scriptures them-
selves].

10. INCAPACITY OF THE JEWS TO KNOW THE TRUE MESSIAH, AND THEIR DISPOSITION TO RECEIVE FALSE MESSIAHS IN SPITE OF THE TESTIMONY OF MOSES, WHOSE ACCUSATION THEY INCUR.

41 I receive not [do not appropriate to myself] honour [glory, δόξαν] from men.[27]
42 But I know you, that ye have not the love of God in you [are not inwardly directed
43 towards God]. I am [have] come in my Father's name, and ye receive me not: if
44 another shall come in his own name, him ye will receive. How can ye believe,
which [who] receive honour [glory] one of another, and seek not the honour that
45 *cometh* from God only [the glory that is from the only God, or, from him who alone
is God]?[28] Do not think that I will [shall] accuse you to the Father: there is *one*
46 that accuseth you, *even* Moses, in whom ye trust [ye hope, or, have placed your
hope, ἠλπίκατε]. For had ye believed [if ye believed] Moses, ye would have be-
47 lieved [ye would believe] me; for he wrote of me. But if ye believe not his [not
even *his*] writings, how shall [will] ye believe[29] my words?

TEXTUAL AND GRAMMATICAL.

[1] Ver. 1.—The reading ἡ ἑορτή is after Codd. C. E. F. L. (also Cod. Sin.). It probably arose from an effort to make the feast the chief feast of the Jews, the passover. [Tischendorf, ed. viii., influenced mainly by ℵ., reads ἡ ἑορτή, but Lachm., Alf., Treg., Westcott and Hort omit the definite art. with A. B. D. G. K. Orig. The article has some bearing on the question whether the great feast of the passover, or a subordinate feast is meant; yet it is not absolutely conclusive; for in Hebrew a noun before the genitive is made definitive by prefixing the article, not to the noun itself, but to the genitive, and the same is the case in the Sept. (Deut. xvi. 13; 2 Ki. xviii. 15) and in some passages of the N. T., as Matth. xii. 24; Luke ii.

4; Acts viii. 5. Comp. Winer, who quotes also examples from the classics, p. 119 f. (Thayer's transl., p. 126). Tholuck remarks: "Were the article genuine, we would be compelled to regard the chief festival, that is the Passover, as the one meant. If it is not genuine, the Passover *may* be meant, but so also may some other feast."—P. S.]

[2] Ver. 2.—[Sheep *gate* is the marginal reading of the E. V. *πύλη* is usually supplied to *ἐπὶ τῇ προβατικῇ*.—P. S.]

[3] Ver. 2.—[Different spellings of this name—*Βηθεσδά*, *Βηθσαιδά*, *Βηθζαθά*. There are also different readings for *ἐπιλεγομένη*, sc. *λεγομένη* and *τὸ λεγόμενον*. Tischendorf prefers the last, which is supported by Cod. Sin.* The lect. rec. *ἐπιλεγομένη*, *zu*benamt, *sur*named, would imply that the pool had another proper name, perhaps *the Sheep's Pool.* The Vulgate connects *κολυμβήθρᾳ* (dative) with *προβατικῇ* and translates: "*Est autem Jerosolymis probatica piscina, quæ cognominatur hebraice Bethsaida.*" *Ἑβραϊστί* refers to the prevailing Aramaic which was spoken by the Jews after their return from the exile. It proves incidentally the Greek composition of the Gospel.—P. S.]

[4] Ver. 3.—[*Πολύ* is wanting in B. C. D. L., *etc.* [and Cod. Sin.]; put in brackets by Lachmann; rejected by Tischendorf.

[5] Vers. 3, 4.—Omissions: (1) The words: "Waiting for the moving of the water," and ver. 4, are wanting in B. C.*, *etc.* [also in the Cod. Sin.—Y.]; (2) the words: "waiting for the moving of the water," in A. L.; (3) the 4th verse alone, in D. See further below. [Tischendorf (ed. viii.), Alford (ed. vi.), Tregelles, Westcott and Hort omit the last clause of ver. 3 (*ἐκδεχομένων τὴν τοῦ ὕδατος κίνησιν*), and the whole of ver. 4 (*Ἄγγελος* to *νοσήματι*). Lachmann retains here the text. rec., which is backed by the authority of Tertullian (*De Bapt.*, ch. 5), an authority much older than the oldest MSS. But it is not easy to account for the omission of the clause (its legendary character was certainly not objectionable to the fathers, translators and transcribers). The large number of *ἅπαξ λεγόμενα*—*κίνησιν*, *ταραχή*, *δήποτε*, *νόσημα*—also speak against it. It was probably a very ancient marginal gloss suggested by the popular belief in order to explain the assemblage of the sick, ver. 4, and the answer in ver. 7, which implies that belief. Its omission saves some trouble to the commentator by relieving John from the superstition of the Jews in regard to the healing water. Comp., however, the EXEG. NOTES.—P. S.]

[6] Ver. 5.—[The best authorities read *α ὐ τ ο ῦ*, after *ἐν τῇ ἀσθενείᾳ*. The meaning is: he had been sick for 38 years. *ἔχων* belongs to *τριάκοντα καὶ ὀκτὼ ἔτη*, (as the accusative of the time, comp. John viii. 57; xi. 17), not to *ἐν τῇ ἀσθ. αὐτοῦ* =*ἀσθενῶς ἔχων*.—P. S.]

[7] Ver. 6.—[Or, *in that condition*, or, *sick; ὅτι πολὺν ἤδη χρόνον ἔχει*, sc. *ἐν ἀσθενείᾳ*, ver. 5. Alford, in his revision, retains the rendering of the A. V. Noyes: "that he had been for a long time *diseased*." Version of the Am. Bible Union: "that he had been already a long time *thus*."—P. S.]

[8] Ver. 7.—[*Κύριε* is here, as in iv. 11, simply a title of courtesy to a stranger, and hence correctly translated, *Sir*, instead of *Lord*.—P. S.]

[9] Ver. 10.—[*ἦν δὲ σάββατον ἐν ἐκείνῃ τῇ ἡμέρᾳ*. Alford: "Now on that day was the sabbath." Noyes: "And that day was the sabbath." Young: "It was a sabbath on that day."—P. S.]

[10] Ver. 12.—[The *οὖν* of the text. rec. after *ἠρώτησαν* is sustained by A. C., bracketed by Tregelles, omitted by ℵ. B. D. Alf., Tischend.—P. S.]

[11] Ver. 12.—*Τὸν κράββατόν σου* is wanting in ℵ. B. C.* L., omitted by Tischendorf. With the omission the expression is more significant, as the addition contains something palliative.

[12] Ver. 13.—[Tischend. reads *ὁ δὲ ἀσθενῶν*, *the diseased man*, (from ver. 7), but *ἰαθείς*, *the healed man* is supported by ℵ. A. B. C., *et al.*, Vulg. (*curatus*), Lachm., Treg., Alf.—P. S.]

[13] Ver. 15.—Waverings between *ἀνήγγειλε*, A. B., Recepta, Lachmann; *ἀπήγγειλε*, D. K., *etc.*; *εἶπεν*, C. L., *etc.* [Cod. Sin.—Y.]. The first reading is at once the most exact and the most suitable. [Tischend. reads *εἶπεν*, Treg., Alf., Westcott and Hort.: *ἀνήγγειλεν*.—P. S.]

[14] Ver. 16.—The words [of the text. rec.]: *καὶ ἐζήτουν αὐτὸν ἀποκτεῖναι*, are wanting in ℵ. B. C. D. L., *etc.*, the Vulgate, *etc.* Probably occasioned by the *μᾶλλον*, *etc.*, ver. 18.

[15] Ver. 20.—[*Μείζονα* is emphatically put first.—P. S.]

[16] Ver. 24.—[So *μεταβέβηκε ἐκ* is translated by Alford, Noyes, and Conant. Luther: *hindurchgedrungen;* Lange: *hinübergegangen.*—P. S.]

[17] Ver. 27.—[The *καί* before *κρίσιν* is omitted by Tischend., Alf., *etc.*—P. S.]

[18] Ver. 27.—[Here *υἱὸς ἀνθρώπου*, without the article, as also Apoc. i. 13; xiv. 14 (with reference to Dan. vii. 13); but in other passages where it is applied to Christ in the full, ideal sense, we have *ὁ υἱὸς τοῦ ἀνθρώπου*. See the EXEG. NOTES, and Excursus on I. 52, p. 98.—P. S.]

[19] Ver. 30.—The addition of *πατρός* is feebly supported.

[20] Ver. 34.—[Or, *Yet the witness which I receive is not from man*, *ἐγὼ δὲ οὐ παρὰ ἀνθρωπου τὴν μαρτυρίαν λαμβάνω*.—P. S.]

[21] Ver. 35.—[*ὁ λύχνος* (not *φῶς*, comp. i. 8) *ὁ καιόμενος καὶ φαίνων*. Alford: *He was the lamp that burneth and shineth.* Lange inserts the gloss: "the signal-light of the Messiah, illuminating also the Messiah and the way to Him."—P. S.]

[22] Ver. 35.—[Lange inserts these comments: Ye were willing (*ye liked*) for a little while to rejoice (*exult, revel*) in his (*own*) light (*as summer flies*).—P. S.]

[23] Ver. 36.—[Alford: *But the testimony I have is greater than John.*—P. S.]

[24] Ver. 37.—Tischendorf, after B. L., *ἐκεῖνος*. [So also the Cod. Sin.—Y.]

[25] Ibid.—Cod. D., *μαρτυρεῖ*.

[26] Ver. 39.—*Ἐρευνᾶτε* is taken as the indicative mood by Cyril, Erasmus, Beza, Bengel, Olsh., De Wette, Meyer, Godet, Lange; as the imperative by Chrysostom, Augustin, Grotius, Tholuck, Ewald, Hengstenberg, Alford. See EXEG. NOTES.—P. S.]

[27] Ver. 41.—A. K., *et al.*, *ἀνθρώπου*, *a man;* B. D. [Cod. Sin.—Y.], and many others, *ἀνθρώπων*.

[28] Ver. 44.—[*τὴν δόξαν τὴν παρὰ τοῦ μόνου θεοῦ*, the only God, in exclusion of all the idols of the natural heart; comp. John xvii. 3: *ὁ μόνος ἀληθινὸς θεός*. The rendering of the A. V. would require *μόνον*, or *μόνου* after *θεοῦ*, Matth. iv. 4; xii. 4; xvii. 8. Alford: "The words *from the only God*, are very important because they form the point of passage to the next verses, in which the Jews are accused of not believing the *writings of Moses*, the very pith and kernel of which was the *unity of God* and *the having no other gods but Him*."—P. S.]

[29] Ver. 47.—D. G. S. Δ., Origen [Lange]: *πιστεύσητε* [*credatis*, ℵ. A. L., *etc.*, Vulg., Treg., Tischend., Alf.: *πιστεύσετε*, *credetis*. B. V. Iren. *etc.*, Westcott and Hort. *πιστεύετε*, *creditis*.—P. S.]

EXEGETICAL AND CRITICAL.

[PRELIMINARY REMARKS.—The healing of a helpless and hopeless cripple at the House of Mercy is the first miracle of Jesus in Judea related by John, although He had performed signs there before, which are only alluded to, ii. 23; iii. 2. It forms the basis of a lengthy and most important Christological discourse, which opens the conflict of Jesus with the unbelieving Jewish hierarchy, and reveals the contrast between His positive fulfilment of the spirit of the law and their negative observance of its letter, as also between His living theism and their abstract monotheism. His doing good on the Sabbath was made the ground of a charge of Sabbath-breaking, and His claim to be in a peculiar sense the Son of God was construed as blasphemy deserving of death. Christ here proclaims all those grand truths, which John had announced in the Prologue. He reveals Himself as one with the Father, who never ceases doing good, as the Lord of the Sabbath, as the Giver of life, as the Raiser of the dead, and the Judge of the world, and claims divine honor. He supports these astounding claims, which no mere man could make without being guilty of blasphemy or madness, by the united testimony of John the Baptist, of God the Father through His works, and of the O. T. Scriptures, and drives this threefold testimony with terrible earnestness into the conscience of the Jews. He then traces their unbelief to the secret chambers of their self-seeking hearts, and completely turns the tables by presenting their own Moses, in whom they boastfully put their hope, as their accuser for not following his lead to Christ, to whom he pointed in all his writings. Thus the mouths of these hypocritical worshippers of the letter and enemies of the spirit and aim of the law were stopped, but their hearts continued in opposition and longed for an opportunity to carry out their bloody design. The significance of this discourse is well brought out by Dr. Lange in his analysis (see the headings) and in the Doctrinal remarks. Comp. also my concluding note on ver. 47.—P. S.]

Ver. 1. **After these things.**—On the distinction between μετὰ ταῦτα and μετὰ τοῦτο, see Lücke on this passage.* Here closes the first great ministry of Jesus in Galilee (see *Leben Jesu*, II., 2, pp. 556–745).

A [The] **feast of the Jews.**—[Which feast? This point is still under dispute, but the controversy is now narrowed down to a choice between the Passover and the Purim. The decision has a bearing on the chronology of the gospel history. If the feast here spoken of be the Passover, then our Lord's public labors continued during three and a half years, since John notes three other passovers as falling within His ministry, ii. 13; vi. 4; xii. 1 and xiii. 1. If not, then the time must in all probability be reduced to two and a half years. On the bearing of the definite article on the question, and the various readings, see Text. Notes.—P. S.] Meyer: "Which feast is meant, appears with certainty from ch. iv. 35; comp. vi. 4. For ch. iv. 35 was spoken in the month of December; and from ch. vi. 4 it appears that the passover was nigh at hand; hence the feast here intended must be one falling between December and the passover, and this is no other than the *feast of Purim*, which was celebrated on the 14th and 15th of Adar (Esth. ix. 21 ff.), that is, in March [one month before the passover], in memory of the deliverance of the nation from the massacre projected by Haman. So Keppler, [who first suggested this view], d'Outrein, Hug, Olshausen, Wieseler, Neander,† Krabbe, Anger, Lange, Maier and many others."‡ Meyer justly adds: The feast is not designated, because it was a minor festival, whereas the greater feasts are named by John: not only the passover, but also the σκηνοπηγία, vii. 2, and the ἐγκαίνια, x. 22.

[The chief objections to this view are: 1. The feast of Purim was no temple feast, and required no journey to Jerusalem. But Christ may have attended this feast as He attended other festivals (vii. 2; x. 22) without legal obligation, merely for the purpose of doing good. 2. The Purim was never celebrated as a Sabbath. But the Sabbath spoken of, ver. 9, may have preceded or succeeded the feast.—P. S.]

Other views of the feast: (1) The *passover:* Irenæus,* Luther, and many more;† (2) *Pentecost:* Cyril [Chrysostom, Calvin], Bengel, *etc.;* (3) the feast of *tabernacles:* Cocceius, Ebrard [Ewald]; (4) the feast of *dedication:* Petavius; (5) a feast which cannot be determined: Lücke, De Wette, [Brückner], Luthardt, Tholuck (7th ed.)‡

The feast of Purim [יְמֵי הַפּוּרִים, or simply פּוּרִים, *lot*, from the Persian], Esth. ix. 24, 26; ἡ Μαρδοχαϊκὴ ἡμέρα, 2 Macc. xv. 36; Joseph. *Antiq.* xi. 6, 13. On the 13th of Adar a fast preceded the feast; in the festival itself the book of Esther (called מְגִלָּה by eminence) was read in the synagogues. As a popular festival it was distinguished, like the feasts of tabernacles, and dedication, by universal rejoicings. Fanaticism in the people naturally sought to make it a festival of triumph over the Gentiles (subsequently over the Christians also). And on this account was this particular feast of Purim so pre-eminently *the feast of the Jews* (with the article), and the article in the Cod. Sinait. in this place cannot be made to speak exclusively, as Hengstenberg proposes, for the passover.§ We must no doubt mark a difference between the simple expression, *feast*, and the expression: *feast of the Jews.*

Ver. 2. **Now there is at Jerusalem.**—The ἔστι has been interpreted with reference to the porches, as indicating that, at the time of the composition of this passage, Jerusalem had not been destroyed. On this see the Introduction. Eusebius writes in his *Onomast.* s. v. Βηζαθά: καὶ νῦν δείκνυται [but he does not mention the locality]. Yet the ἔστι may also be attributed to rhetorical vivacity.

By the sheep gate.—'Επὶ τῇ προβατικῇ sc. πύλῃ.‖ According to Nehemiah's topography of the restored city it was what is now Stephen's gate in the north-east quarter of the city, leading out over Kidron to Gethsemane and the Mount of Olives (Bâb Sitty Merijam, 'Gate

* [Lücke makes μ. τοῦτο (ii. 12; xi. 7, 11; xix. 28) to signify the immediate, μ. ταῦτα (iii. 22; vi. 1; vii. 1) the mediate succession. Tholuck and Alford assent, Meyer and Hengstenberg object. The latter occurs uniformly in the Apocalypse, usually in the Gospel of John, comp. ver. 14, which speaks rather against the distinction. But in this case at all events some interval must have elapsed since the last verse of ch. iv., and much matter must be inserted from the Synoptists between ch. iv. and v.—P. S.]

† [Neander (*Leben Jesu*, 6 ed., 1862, p. 280), upon the whole, decides rather in favor of the passover, and should be transferred.—P. S.]

‡ [So also Stier, Bäumlein, Godet.—P. S.]

* [Who makes it the second passover of our Lord's ministry, *Adv. hær.* ii. 22, 3 (I. 357 ed. Stieren): "*Et post hæc iterum secunda vice ascendit in diem festum paschæ in Hierusalem, quando paralyticum curavit.*" But Irenæus had an interest to lengthen Christ's ministry, for two reasons which he brings out in this very connection. 1. Because he believed that Christ passed through all stages of human life to save them all, consequently He became also "*senior in senioribus, ut sit perfectus magister in omnibus, non solum secundum expositionem veritatis, sed et secundum ætatem, sanctificans simul et seniores*" (II. ch. 22, § 4, p. 358); 2. Because he inferred from the question of the Jews, John viii. 57, that Jesus was not yet, but nearly fifty years of age at the time (II. 22, 6, p. 360). This somewhat weakens this testimony, which is pressed too much by Robinson and others.—P. S.]

† [So also Grotius, Lightfoot, Hengstenberg, Neander, and Robinson.—P. S.]

‡ [Alford also, after giving, from Lücke, a brief statement of the different views on this much controverted point, expresses his opinion that "we cannot with any probability gather what feast it was." In this case, of course, the elaborate chronological argument based upon a definite view of the feast here spoken of, falls to the ground. On the chronological bearing of the interpretation see Robinson, *Gr. Harmony of the Gospels*, p. 190 ff.—P. S.]

§ [Comp. on the force of the article my addition to the first Text. Note.—P. S.]

‖ [שַׁעַר הַצֹּאן, *porta gregis*, mentioned Neh. iii. 1, 32; xii. 39. Meyer, however, with the Vulgate, Theodore of Mopsu. and Nonnus, connect προβατικῇ with κολυμβήθρᾳ (reading this as dative): "There was at the sheep pool the so called Bethesda." Eusebius and Jerome speak of a προβατικὴ κολυμβήτρα, *probatica piscina.* Comp. the Text. Notes.—P. S.]

of My Lady Mary;' also 'Gate of the Tribes,' or 'Porta vallis Josaphat.' Comp. Winer, Art. *Jerusalem*, I. p. 548; Krafft, *Die Topographie Jerusalems*, p. 148; Robinson, I. p. 386; II. 74, 136, 148; Von Raumer, *Paläst.* p. 255. [If the Pool of Bethesda is identical with the Fountain of the Virgin (see below), the Sheep Gate cannot well have been St. Stephen's Gate, which is too far off.—P. S.]

A pool, which is called in Hebrew Bethesda.—בֵּית חִסְדָא, *house of kindness, grace, gentleness, house of mercy.* Tholuck: Institution of charity, *Charité.* **Five porches.**—Tobler (*Denkblätter von Jerusalem*, 1853, p. 62): So late as the fifth century five porches were still shown. According to his (medical) hypothesis there were five arched compartments for the separation of the patients. Tholuck: Colonnades, porticoes, to shelter the patients from wind and rain; probably the rear one having a wall. Theodore of Mopsuestia imagined one central hall (probably inclosing the pool), and four halls on the circumference of it (perhaps crosswise); this would have been, at all events, the most convenient arrangement for the sick. The outer portions must doubtless have been protected on more than one side.

As to the location of the pool, there is on the outer side of the gate of Stephen a small fish-pond or reservoir, and inside the gate the very large, deep reservoir, to which the name of Bethesda is usually given; probably without foundation.* It is perfectly dry, and on the bed of it grow large trees, the tops of which do not even reach to the level of the street. In this pool Robinson sees the remains of an old trench which belonged to the fortress of Antonia. He supposes, on the other hand, that the *Fountain of the Virgin* † may have been the pool of Bethesda. Robinson says [Am. ed. of 1856, vol. I. p. 337]:

"On the west side of the valley of Jehoshaphat about twelve hundred feet northward from the rocky point at the mouth of the Tyropœon, [or the valley of the Cheesmongers] is situated the fountain of the Virgin Mary; called by the natives' *'Ain um ed-Deraj*, Mother of Steps. In speaking of Siloam I have already brought into view the singular fact, that there is no historical notice later than Josephus, which can be applied to this fountain, before near the close of the fifteenth century, and have also mentioned the more modern hypothesis, which regards it as the *fountain* of Siloam, in distinction from the pool of that name. Others have held it to be the Gihon, the Rogel, and the Dragon-well of Scripture; so that in fact it has been taken alternately for every one of the fountains, which anciently existed at Jerusalem. It is unquestionably an ancient work; indeed there is nothing in or around the Holy City, which bears more distinctly the traces of high antiquity. I have already alluded to the reasons which make it not improbable, that this was the 'King's Pool' of Nehemiah, and the 'Pool of Solomon' mentioned by Josephus, near which the wall of the city passed, as it ran northwards from Siloam along the Valley of Jehoshaphat to the eastern side of the temple." This spring is connected with the well of Siloam by a passage [of about 2 feet wide, 1750 feet long, and cut through the solid rock], through which Robinson and his companions [for the first time] laboriously passed.* "The water in both these fountains, he relates [I. p. 340], is the same; notwithstanding travellers have pronounced that of Siloam to be bad, and that of the upper fountain to be good. We drank of it often in both places. It has a peculiar taste, sweetish and very slightly brackish, but not at all disagreeable. Later in the season, when the water is low, it is said to become more brackish and unpleasant. It is the common water used by the people of Kefr Selwân. We did not learn that it is regarded as medicinal, or particularly good for the eyes, as is reported by travellers; though it is not improbable that such a popular belief may exist." At the upper fountain (the Fountain of the Virgin) Robinson observed a sudden bubbling up of the water from under the lower step. "In less than five minutes it had risen to the basin nearly or quite a foot; and we could hear it gurgling off through the interior passage. In ten minutes more it had ceased to flow, and the water in the basin was again reduced to its former level. . . . Meanwhile a woman of Kefr Selwân came to wash at the fountain. She was accustomed to frequent the place every day; and from her we learned, that the flowing of the water occurs at irregular intervals; sometimes two or three times a day, and sometimes in summer once in two or three days. She said, she had seen the fountain dry, and men and flocks, dependent upon it, gathered around and suffering from thirst; when all at once the water would begin to boil up from under the steps, and (as she said) from the bottom in the interior part, and flow off in a copious stream." [I. p. 342].

[For these reasons Dr. Robinson merely suggests, without expressing a definite conviction himself (I. p. 343), that this Fountain of the Virgin may have been Bethesda, the same with the "King's Pool" of Nehemiah and the "Solomon's Pool" of Josephus. T. Tobler, during frequent visits to the Fountain of the Virgin in the winter of 1845, early in the morning and late in the evening, confirms the observations of Robinson as to its intermittent character which bring it into striking resemblance with the Pool of Bethesda. Neander (*Leben Jesu*, p. 282), and Tholuck (*in loc.*) are inclined to Robinson's view.

* [Robinson, I. 330, says that there is not the slightest evidence that can identify the present *Bethesda*, or *Sheep Pool*, or, as the natives call it, *Birket Israîl*, with the Bethesda of the N. T. Eusebius and Jerome indeed speak of a *Piscina Probatica* shown in their day as Bethesda, but give no hint as to its situation. Robinson derives the tradition from the fact that St. Stephen's gate, owing to its proximity, was erroneously held to be the ancient Sheep gate.—P. S.]

† [So called because the Virgin Mary is said to have frequented this fountain before her purification in order to wash the linen of the infant Saviour. See Robinson, I. 337. According to another explanation, mentioned by Porter (*Handbook of Syria and Pal.* I., p. 139), the water of this fountain was a grand test for women accused of adultery; the innocent drank harmlessly; but the guilty no sooner tasted than they died. When the Virgin Mary was accused, she submitted to the ordeal, and thus established her innocence. Hence a name it was long known by—the fountain of accused women. —P. S.]

* [Since that time Lieutenant Charles Warren, of the Palestine Exploration Society, in Dec. 1867, likewise made his way with great difficulty through that winding rock-cut passage, entering from the Siloam end. His measurements differ 42 ft. from those of Dr. Robinson, but, considering the length of the Virgin's Fount, they nearly agree.—P. S.]

Tholuck, who frequently visited the springs of Kissingen in Bavaria, speaks of a gaseous spring of this kind in Kissingen, which after a rushing sound *about* the same time every day commences to bubble and is most efficacious at the very time the gas is making its escape. Comp. also an article on the miracle of Bethesda by Macdonald, in the Andover *Bibliotheca Sacra*, for Jan. 1870, pp. 108 ff. According to Wolcot and Tobler, the water of the Fountain of the Virgin and the Pool of Siloam, as well as that of the many fountains of the Mosque of Omar, proceeds from a living spring beneath the altar of the temple.* This spring was, as Dean Stanley says, (*Sinai and Palestine*, new ed., Lond. 1866, p. 181), 'the treasure of Jerusalem,' its support through its numerous sieges—the '*fons perennis aquæ*' of Tacitus (Tac. *Hist.* v. 12)—the source of Milton's

> 'Brook that flowed
> Hard by the oracle of God.'

But more than this, it was the image which entered into the very heart of the prophetical idea of Jerusalem. 'There is a river (a perennial river), the streams whereof shall make glad the city of God, the holy place of the tabernacle of the Most High' (Ps. xlvi. 4). 'All my fresh springs shall be in thee' (Ps. lxxxvii. 7). 'Draw water out of the wells of salvation' (Isa. xii. 3). In Ezekiel's vision (Ezek. xlvii. 1-5) the thought is expanded into a vast cataract flowing out through the Temple-rock eastward and westward into the ravines of Hinnom and Kedron, till they swell into a mighty river, fertilizing the desert of the Dead Sea. And with still greater distinctness the thought appears again, and for the last time, in the discourse, when in the courts of the Temple, 'in the last day, that great day of the feast (of Tabernacles), Jesus stood and cried, saying, If any man thirst, let him come unto Me, . . . out of his belly shall flow rivers of living water' (John vii. 37, 38)."—P. S.]

Other hypotheses see in Meyer [who, however, thinks that the exact situation of Bethesda, cannot be fixed with certainty; see p. 219]. What leaves the theory of Robinson in need of further investigation is the assumption that here, contrary to the usual order, the bathing pool or fish pool must have been placed above, and the spring below on the same fountain stream or flume. This difficulty may be obviated by distinguishing between the point of the spring itself and a bathing pool situated somewhat aside. But the distance of the Fountain of the Virgin from the Sheep Gate invalidates Robinson's theory. [Or rather it may invalidate the identity of the Sheep Gate with St. Stephen's Gate, which is of more modern origin.†—P. S.]

It is more probable that, according to Krafft (*Topographie Jerus.* p. 176), the now dry Struthion pool in the church of St. Anna was the pool of Bethesda. "To attribute the healing virtue of the water, which, according to Eusebius, was of a red tinge, and was perhaps impregnated with mineral substance, to the sacrificial blood from the temple, and to derive the name from אַשְׁדָּא,* *effusio* (Calvin, Arret., and others, after Eusebius), is unfounded, and contrary to ver. 7. The usual interpretation of the name is found even in the Peshito." (Meyer). "Struthion is an alkali. This alkali, together with particles of iron, mixed with the water, may have given it its red color and medicinal effect." (Krafft).

Ver. 3. **Blind, lame, withered.**— Three kinds of sick folks [τῶν ἀσθενούντων] are specified: The *blind* first; comp. ch. ix.; the *lame*, those disabled in their limbs; the *withered*, those who were fallen away, emaciated, consumptive, (comp. Matth. xii. 10; Luke vi. 6, 8). [Also paralytics, as this man was, to judge from his lameness and the κράββατος *paralyticorum*, Mark ii. 4; Acts ix. 33.—P. S.]

Waiting for the moving of the water.— See the textual note above. On this passage together with the next verse, criticism has four theories:

1. All is spurious; a later interpolation of the popular belief for the explanation of ver. 7. This is favored by (a) the omission of the whole *locus* in B. C.,* 157, 314, and in the Coptic and Sahidic V.;† (b) the many variations in the several expressions, see Tischendorf; (c) the many ἅπαξ λεγόμενα, as κίνησις, ταραχή, *etc.*; (d) the stamp of popular tradition upon the statement; (e) "If the passage were genuine, it would not have been omitted." Lücke, Olshausen, Tischendorf, Meyer. [Tregelles, Alford, Westcott and Hort.—P. S.]

2. The whole doubtful passage is genuine. (a) In favor of the close of ver. 3, Cod. D., *etc.*; in favor ver. 4, Cod. A., *etc.* Tertullian,‡ the Peshito.

* [The recent excavations of the Palestine Exploration Society have not yet established such a connection, but make it very probable. In Oct. 1867 they discovered a sloping rock-cut passage above the Fountain of the Virgin leading N. E. by E. 8 ft. wide and from 10 to 12 ft. deep. See the account of Lieut. Warren at a meeting of the Society held at London, June 11, 1868. in the Reports of the Society, and the maps published with them.—P. S.]

† [Porter, *Handbook of Syria and Palestine*, I. p. 140, likewise doubts Robinson's theory, and supposes that the Fountain of the Virgin is identical with the *King's Pool* mentioned by Nehemiah ii. 14, 15, and called by Josephus Solomon's Reservoir, situated between the Fountain of Siloam and the Southern side of the Temple. Robinson suggests the identity of the Fountain of the Virgin with the King's Pool (I. p. 343). Grove (Art. Bethesda in Smith's *Bible Dictionary*), urges against Robinson's view the confined size of the Fountain of the Virgin, and the difficulty of finding room for the five porches. But there might have been some artificially constructed basin in connection with this spring which has perished. Grove defends the traditional view of the identity of Bethesda with the large reservoir called the *Birket Israil*, within the walls of the city, close by the St. Stephen's gate, and under the North-East wall of the Haram area. But there is not the slightest indication that this dry fosse, full of weeds and rubbish, ever could have been an intermittent spring. So far the greater probability is in favor of Robinson's conjecture. It is to be hoped that the labors of the Exploration Society will before long settle this disputed point. —P. S.]

* [Meyer (p. 220) writes אַשְׁדָּא. The word does not occur in the O. T., but אֶשֶׁד does, Num. xxi. 15, "at the effusion of the brooks."—P. S.]

† [To these must be added the testimony of Cod. Sinaiticus, which reads thus:

(ver. 3) τωνασθενουντων
τυφλων
χωλων
ξηρων
(ver. 5) ηνδετισανθρωπος.

The chasm here does not indicate an omission, but probably the co-ordination of τυφλῶν, χωλῶν and ξηρῶν, as specifications of the various classes of disease implied in the general term τῶν ἀσθενούντων.—P. S.]

‡ [*De baptismo*, ch. 5, ed. Œhler, vol. I., p. 615: "*Piscinam Bethsaidam angelus interveniens commovebat: observabant qui valetudinem querebantur. Nam si quis prævenerat de-*

(b) The insertion could not well be accounted for, Baumgarten-Crusius, Brückner,* Lachmann, [Reuss, Lange, Hengstenberg].

3. The close of ver. 3, ἐκδεχ.—κίνησιν, is genuine, ver. 4, a later addition. This is favored by (a) the omission in D., where the close of ver. 3 remains; (b) the consideration that without this passage ver. 7 would be unintelligible. Ewald, Tholuck, [Godet].

4. The close of ver. 3 is spurious, ver. 4 is genuine; being more strongly supported by A. C.* So Hofmann.

It is of great weight, (1) that Tertullian stands so early a witness for the whole text. He ought not to be estimated here according to his realistic view elsewhere, but as reporting a document which was sacred to him. † (2) that ver. 7 would be in fact unintelligible without ver. 4. (3) that ver. 4 is more strongly attested than the close of ver. 3, particularly by Codex A. (4) that the close of ver. 3 might have been carried away with ver. 4, when the latter was omitted. (5) that the silence of Origen leaves us to suppose that the Alexandrian school found the passage offensive for its realism.

On the other hand ver. 4 cannot be sustained (a) by Hofmann's doctrine of angels, which makes angels the agents in all second causes, or natural phenomena; (b) by Tholuck's observation that John himself would no doubt have explained that natural phenomenon, as the Christian and the general religious popular opinion explained it in the second century, especially after what the Apocalypse says of the angel of the waters and of fire (ch. xvi. 5; xiv. 18). The Revelation, like the book of Daniel, is a symbolical book.

The matter is no doubt to be thus explained: According to the Jewish popular conception there was a personal angel who produced the moving of the water. John found the conception and admitted it in his narrative, translating in his own mind the personal angel into a symbolical angel, or a distinct divine operation, *i. e.*, in reference to such facts, for in a higher sphere he well knew the personal angels. He could leave the reader to adjust the passage according to ch. i. 51.‡

Ver. 4. **Troubled the water.**—According to Wolcott an Arabian substituted for the angel in the fountain of the Virgin "the convolutions of a dragon at the bottom." Tholuck, p. 161. [The common legend is that a great dragon lies within the intermittent Fountain of the Virgin; when he is awake, he stops the water; but when he sleeps, it flows. See Robinson, I. p. 342; Porter. I., 140.—P. S.]

First after the troubling.—The popular religious idea of the periodical moments of healing efficacy in the spring.

Ver. 5. **Thirty-eight years** [τριάκοντα καὶ ὀκτὼ ἔτη ἔχων ἐν τῇ ἀσθενείᾳ αὐτοῦ].—It is a question whether ἔχων is to be referred to the thirty-eight years, or to ἐν τῇ ἀσθ. [that is, whether the exact expression is, he had so many years in his infirmity, = ἔχων τριάκοντα κ. ὀ. ἔ., or had his infirmity for so many years = ἀσθενῶς ἔχων]. The usage of John is in favor of the former (ver. 6; ch. viii. 57; xi. 17; comp. Lücke, II. p. 25). He had lived thirty-eight years in his impotency. [He had been sick thirty-eight years—not at Bethesda all that time. The long disease makes the cure appear all the greater. Hengstenberg allegorizes here again, and discovers in the sick man of Bethesda a symbol of the Jewish nation, and in the thirty-eight years of his sickness a symbol of the thirty-eight years which Israel spent under the bane in the wilderness (I. 300 f.). So also Wordsworth *in loc.*—P. S.]

Ver. 6. **And knew.**—Γνούς; when He perceived. We cannot venture to assert, with Meyer, that this does not intend supernatural knowledge. A natural medium there might have been; the insight into the whole situation partook of the supernatural. The indefinite πολὺν χρόνον also indicates this. [So also Hengstenberg, Godet and Alford.—P. S.]

Desirest thou to be made whole?—Meyer: "The question is asked to excite the attention and expectation of the suffering man. Paulus falsely: The man had been a malicious beggar, who represented himself as sick; wherefore Jesus asked him with reproving emphasis, Desirest thou to be made whole? Art thou in earnest? Similarly Ammon; whereas Lange takes him only for a man of faint will, whose slumbering energy of will Christ here aroused again (?); of which the text gives as little sign, as that the question was intended for the whole people of whom this invalid was a type (Luthardt)." But the following points are clearly implied in the narrative, as Meyer himself must admit: (1) that in this miracle of healing alone an *unasked offer* occurs, though in ch. ix. there is an unasked healing (yet every honest beggar virtually asks the greatest possible alms); (2) that, besides, the man always allows himself to be anticipated by all others, though he is still able feebly to walk; (3) that he complains in a feeble manner without point; (4) that he lets his benefactor slip away, without learning his name, or even eagerly asking it, and then, against the Jews, appeals only to the command of Jesus; (5) that he receives from Jesus in the temple a warning, which implied a fickle character; (6) that immediately after his recognition of Jesus he goes to the Jews and gives the name of his miraculous healer, though he must have observed their evil designs. All this is in the text. Yet malevolence properly so called cannot be asserted. His continuance at the pool of Bethesda leads us to recognize in his indolence a spark of spiritual patience; in his helpless and forlorn condition

scendere illuc, queri post lavacrum desinebat." But Tertullian does not give this as a quotation from John. He may have found it as a gloss on the margin of a copy of the Text. —P. S.]

* [*Formerly*, but in the last edition of De Wette, Brückner rejects the whole passage.—P. S.]

† [But comp. the preceding footnote, p. 182 f.—P. S.]

‡ [Hengstenberg, I. 293 ff. defends ver. 4, as being in entire harmony with the Scripture idea of the living God, who clothes the lilies, who feeds the birds, who rides in the storm, and uses winds and flames as messengers (Ps. civ. 4; Hebr. i. 7). He refers especially also to the angel of the waters, Apoc. xvi. 5, as a parallel to the angel moving the water of Bethesda. Bengel says: *Circa balnea frequens θεῖον, aliquid divinæ opis est.* Very true, but the Divine power and goodness in the healing waters makes itself felt not supernaturally by angels, but through the laws and agencies of nature, and not exceptionally, but uniformly. I prefer, with Tischendorf, Meyer and the best English critics, to omit the whole passage.—P. S.]

he appears a very peculiar object of sympathy; his visiting the temple seems to bespeak a sense of gratitude; even in his giving of the name of Jesus a mistaken obedience, may have had a share; but exegesis cannot make him a valiant confessor. [The question of Jesus, addressed to the cripple's desire for health, was a proof of sympathy with his sufferings, and kindled a spark of hope when on the brink of despair, and thus naturally prepared the way for his cure.—P. S.]

Ver. 7. **Another goeth down before me.**—Meyer: "The brief motion must be conceived as limited to *a particular point* of the pool, so that only one at a time can receive the benefit." But there is nothing of this in the text; and motion in a pool cannot possibly be confined to a particular point. Rather might the stairs have been constructed on the presumption that only one bather would receive healing. In ver. 4 Meyer, without warrant, sees the apocryphal expression of a superstitious popular opinion. [Alford: "The man's answer implies the popular belief, which the spurious but useful insertion in vers. 3, 4 expresses."—P. S.]

Ver. 8. **Rise, take up thy bed,*and walk.**—Three words of power in one wonderful work, or even three thunder strokes of the might of the divine healing will, which awaken at once the faint will and the worn-out energy of the deceased man. The words of healing addressed to the paralytic in Matth. ix., are similar indeed, in Mark (ch. ii.) the very same, yet they have here a different import; they are intended to give threefold vividness to the outward visibility of the power of Jesus in proof of His invisible work of grace on the heart of the sufferer. The criticism of Strauss and Weisse, which can make of this story a legendary exaggeration of the healing of that paralytic, shows more than mere indifference to place, time, and circumstances, and all connected with them; it confounds a true heroic faith with the most weak-minded inclination to faith, and a man who causes his friends to break through the roof with a man, who can find no one even to put him into the water. Critical opinions of this sort themselves lie like blind, lame, and withered about the pool of Bethesda. [Against Baur and Hilgenfeld see Meyer, p. 221 f.]

Ver. 9. **And on that day was the Sabbath.**—A twofold scruple might arise, one against the healing, another against the carrying. In reference to the healing, the principle universally prevailed: "All danger or preservation of life removes the Sabbath restrictions" (*Omne dubium vitæ pellit Sabbatum*); though this principle was so encumbered with casuistic distinctions and exceptions that in most cases it was not possible for the laity duly to distinguish the lawful and the unlawful, the forbidden and the allowed (Lücke, ii., p. 29). So too the carrying of articles on the Sabbath is, according to the Talmud, not indeed absolutely forbidden, but was at most allowed only under many restrictions; for one thing it could not be done on the open street (see Tholuck).

Ver. 10. **The Jews.**—[Not the people, but those in authority who misrepresented the people in their rejection of Christ]. In such cases the matter goes quickly through fanatics, informers, and subordinates to the chiefs. Here the hierarchical chiefs already seem to speak; according to Meyer and Tholuck, the Sanhedrists. Yet it is possible that the matter only gradually reached them. At first they attack only the man himself for his carrying, which was the most palpable.

Ver. 11. **He that made me whole.**—Beyond the word ἐκεῖνος, no trace again of individual energy appears in the answer, nothing but historical statement. Unquestionably the words seem to say: One who made me whole, a wonder-worker, must certainly have had the right to heal me. Hence Meyer: They savor of defiance; Tholuck: The man puts the authority of the Wonder-worker as in ch. ix. 30 against theirs. But the character of the blind man in ch. ix. is at least an entirely different one from this. That man makes bold to draw inferences, this one does not, and the sentence before us, according to the connection, may be taken as well for an excusing of himself by the strange injunction of the strange man, as for anything else. At all events this man seems not to make head against the Jews. It must be remembered, too, that he could not otherwise designate Jesus, since he did not know His name.

Ver. 12. **Who is the man that?**—Not only is the contemptuous expression *the Man** characteristic, but also the fact that they seem entirely to ignore the miraculous healing itself. [They do not ask: '*Who is he that healed thee?*' but they carefully bring out the unfavorable side of what had taken place, as malicious persons always do.—Alford.]

Ver. 13 f. **And he that was healed knew not.**—Bengel's apology: "*Grabbato ferendo intentus et judaica interpellatione districtus,*" says less than the rest of the verse itself, **for Jesus had withdrawn himself.** † Meyer incorrectly: He withdrew "when this collision with the Jews arose." This would be at least a very equivocal course, to forsake one who was attacked on His account; this Jesus never did. He turned aside because a multitude was there, whose demonstrations He wished to avoid; perhaps the treatment of this invalid also required it.

Ver. 14. **Jesus findeth him in the temple.**—Chrysostom, Tholuck, Meyer: The healing made a religious impression upon him. Yet the evangelist seems intentionally to imply that this meeting did not immediately follow; he writes μετὰ ταῦτα, not μετὰ τοῦτο.‡ And the address of Christ to him does not indicate a man thoroughly possessed with gratitude. **Sin no more, lest,** *etc.*—An unusually earnest injunction upon one whom He had healed, notwithstanding He finds him in the temple. Hence, too, it cannot be supposed that no more is intended here than merely

* [Κράββατος, Lat. *grabbatus*, used only by late writers, is a *small couch*, a mat or rug, or a cloak, which might easily be carried about.—P. S.]

* [Meyer quotes Ast, *Lex. Plat.* I., p. 178 for this contemptuous use of ὁ ἄνθρωπος.—P. S.]

† [ἐξένευσεν, not from ἐκνέω, *enatavit, emersit*, "He *emerged* from the waves of the crowd and reappeared in the quiet harbor of the Temple," as Wordsworth fancifully explains, but from ἐκνεύω, *turned aside;* He spoke the healing words and passed on unobserved.—P. S.]

‡ [But the distinction between μετὰ ταῦτα and μετὰ τοῦτο is made doubtful by this very passage and the uniform use of μετὰ ταῦτα in the Apocalypse. Comp. note on ver. 1.—P. S.]

the general connection of sin with evil (Iren. *Adv. hær.*, V. 15; Bucer, Calov, Neander). This interpretation on the contrary, is no doubt a false application of John ix. 3. Here a special connection between a particular kind of sin and the particular disease must have existed, according to Chrysostom, Bullinger, Meyer, and others. Neither the special sin nor the special disease is known; which magnifies the penetrating knowledge of the Lord.* But a sin which produced disease thirty-eight years before, may be designated in general even in an old man as a sin of youth. **Lest something worse befall thee.**—Bengel: "*Gravius quiddam quam infirmitas 38 annorum.*" [Trench: The χεῖρον τι "gives us an awful glimpse of the severity of God's judgments." Comp. Matt. xii. 45.]

Ver. 15. **The man departed.**—Strictly: *Then departed the man; ὁ ἄνθρωπος.* Chrysostom concludes that it was not ingratitude which moved him to this; that he had spoken before the Jews not of carrying his bed, but of that which they cared least to hear: *that Jesus had healed him.* This apology falls, when we consider his former declaration. There he described the unknown man by the words, He that made me whole. For this reason he now says in giving his information: He that made me whole is Jesus. Meyer explains: the motive is neither malice (Schleiermacher, Lange [incorrect citation; Comp. *Leben Jesu*, II. p. 769], Paulus, *etc.*), nor gratitude wishing to get Jesus acknowledged among the Jews (Cyril, Chrysostom), nor obedience to the rulers (Bengel, Lücke, De Wette, Luthardt), but his authority (Jesus) is to him forthwith higher than that of the Sanhedrists, and he braves them with it. (Thus this man would be a hero, while Nicodemus is supposed to be hampered.) According to Tholuck the man is somewhat stupid and without suspicion of the rulers. Probably he added to weakness of heart and ignorance a fear of the Jews, in which he sought to shield himself from their reproach without perceiving that he might be prejudicing. It is worthy of notice, that they probably let his case drop, while the blind man in chap. ix. they in the end excommunicate; that here in fact they even base upon the statement of this man a process against Jesus.

Ver. 16. **For this cause the Jews persecuted Jesus.**—What follows evidently refers to a trial (Lampe, Rosenmüller, Kuinoel; against Meyer [and Alford]; comp. Luke xxi. 12, διώκειν used of judicial process), though the terms are so chosen as at the same time to express the continuance of the persecutions after the failure of the process. Probably Jesus was arraigned before the little Sanhedrin. Winer: "There were smaller colleges of this name (Sanhedrin, the little Sanhedrin), consisting of twenty-three counsellors (according to *Sanhedrin*, 1, 6) in every Palestinean city which numbered more than one hundred and twenty inhabitants; in Jerusalem even two (*Sanhedr.* 11, 2)." But of these, as also of the courts of three, to which the cognizance and punishment of lighter offences pertained, Josephus knows nothing; whereas he mentions a court of seven (*Antiq.* iv. 8, 14) in the provincial cities, which always had among its members two from the tribe of Levi (Matt. v. 21; x. 17). The variations in the form of the little Sanhedrin amount, however, to nothing; enough that it existed.

Because he did* these things; ταῦτα.—They craftily combine the two charges: (1) the healing of the invalid on the Sabbath, and (2) the commanding him to carry his bed, in the single indictment for breaking the Sabbath in various ways: thus covering the main fact that He had wrought a miracle. Concerning the restriction of healing by the Sabbath regulations of the Pharisees, see above on ver. 9.

[**On the Sabbath**, ἐν σαββάτῳ.—This was the cause of offence and brings out, in connection with ver. 17, the difference between the then prevailing Jewish and the Christian idea of Sabbath observance. The former is negative and slavish, the latter positive and free. The Pharisees scrupulously adhered to the *letter* of the fourth commandment as far as it *forbid* any (common) work, and hedged it around with all sorts of hair-splitting distinctions and rabbinical restrictions, but they violated its *spirit* which demands the positive *sanctification* of the Sabbath by doing good. The rest of the Sabbath is not the rest of idleness or mere cessation from labor, else God Himself who is always at work (ver. 17), would be a Sabbath-breaker as well as Christ. It is rather rest in God, a rest from ordinary work in order to a higher and holier activity for the glory of God and the good of man. We must cease from *our* earthly work, that God may do *His* heavenly work in and through us. The Sabbath law, like the whole law, is truly fulfilled by love to God and love to man. Christ refutes the false conception of Sabbath rest, as a mere cessation from labor, in various ways, now by the example of David eating the show-bread, now by the example of the priests working in the temple, now by the readiness of the Jews to deliver an ox out of a pit on the Sabbath. Here He takes higher ground and claims equality with the Father who never ceases doing good. God's rest after creation was not a rest of sleep or inaction, but a rest of joy in the completion of His work and of benediction of His creatures. "God *blessed* the seventh day and *sanctified* it." (Gen. ii. 3). His strictly *creative* activity ceased with the Hexaëmeron, but his world-*preserving* and *governing*, as well as His *redeeming* activity continues without interruption, and this is properly His Sabbath, combining the highest action with the deepest repose. In the case of man while on earth abstinence from the distracting multiplicity of secular labor and toil is only the necessary condition for attending to his spiritual interests. Acts of worship and acts of charity are proper works for the Christian Sabbath, and are refreshing rest to body and soul, carrying in themselves their own exceeding great reward. The eternal Sabbath of God's people will be unbroken rest in worship and love, as Augustine says, at the close of his *Civitas Dei*: "There we shall rest and see, see and love, love and praise."

*[This is as striking an instance of the penetrating look of our Lord into the inner recesses of man's heart, as His knowledge of the history of the Samaritan woman.—P. S.]

*[Not *had done* (E. V.). The imperfect ἐποίει seems to imply the malignant charge of *repeated* or *habitual* Sabbath-breaking. Comp. Godet *in loc.*—P. S.]

Christ never violated the fourth or any other commandment of God, in its true divine meaning and intent, but fulfilled it by doctrine and example (Matt. v. 17). He emancipated us from the slavery of the negative, superstitious and hypocritical sabbatarianism of the Pharisees, and set us an example of the true positive observance of the Sabbath, by doing good; the Sabbath being made *for man* (Mark ii. 27), *i. e.*, for his temporal and eternal benefit. This was its purpose when God instituted it, together with the marriage relation, in the state of man's innocence, and this Christ has restored, as He restored the marriage relation to its original purity. The commentators pass too slightly over this point, and some of them misconstrue Christ's and Paul's opposition to the Jewish sabbatarianism of that age into a violation or abrogation of the fourth commandment.* Trench, in his work on *Miracles*, p. 206 (Am. ed.), has some good remarks on ver. 16, which I shall transfer here:

"'*The Jews*,' not here the multitude, but some among the spiritual heads of the nation, whom it is very noticeable that St. John continually characterizes by this name, (i. 19; vii. 1; ix. 22; xviii. 12, 14;) find fault with the man for carrying his bed in obedience to Christ's command, their reason being because '*the same day*' on which the miracle was accomplished '*was the Sabbath;*' and the carrying of any burden was one of the expressly prohibited works of that day. Here, indeed, they had apparently an Old Testament ground to go upon, and an interpretation of the Mosaic law from the lips of a prophet, to justify their interference, and the offence which they took. But the man's bearing of his bed was not a work by itself; it was merely the corollary, or indeed the concluding act of his healing, that by which he should make proof himself, and give testimony to others of its reality. It was lawful to heal on the Sabbath day; it was lawful then to do that which was immediately involved in and directly followed on the healing. And here lay ultimately the true controversy between Christ and His adversaries, namely, whether it was most lawful to do good on that day, or to leave it undone (Luke vi. 9). Starting from the unlawfulness of leaving good undone, He asserted that He was its true keeper, keeping it as God kept it, with the highest beneficent activity, which in His Father's case, as in His own, was identical with deepest rest,—and not, as they accused Him of being, its breaker. It was because He Himself had 'done those things' (see ver. 16), that the Jews persecuted Him, and not for bidding the man to bear his bed, which was a mere accident and consequence involved in what He himself had wrought."—P. S.]

Ver. 17. **My Father worketh until now** [ἕως ἄρτι, "*inde a creatione sine intervallo sabbati*," Bengel], **and I work also.**—A difficult answer. It undoubtedly asserts (1) Christ's exaltation above the Sabbath law, like Mark ii. 28; (2) the conformity of His working to the law of the Sabbath, in other words His fulfilling of the Sabbath law, Matt. xii. 12; (3) the relation of the working of God to His own working as its pattern, ver. 20; (4) *His working out from God* and *with God*, which makes their charge a charge against God Himself, ver. 19. The last idea has special emphasis. According to Strauss the sentence is Alexandrian. [Philo of Alexandria, in his Treatise on the *Allegories of the Sacred Laws*, chap. vii. says with regard to the institution of the Sabbath after creation: "God never ceases to work (*ποιῶν ὁ θεὸς οὐδέποτε παύεται*), but when He appears to do so, He is only beginning the creation of something else; as being not only the Creator, but also the Father of everything which exists."—P. S.] But Alexandrianism explained only the law of the Sabbath by the eternal working of God. There is a distinction between the creative work of God at the beginning which originates the world, and looks like human effort, and His subsequent festive working in the created world. This way of God, working on the Sabbath the works of the Spirit, works of relief and love, in incessant divine agility, as it manifests itself in the objective world, must manifest itself also in the Son. According to Tholuck, modern expositors (Grotius, Lücke) stop with the idea that human activity is allowed on the Sabbath. We substitute: Divine activity.

According to Luthardt the words are uttered with reference to the future Sabbath: First the working of the Father, then that of the Son, then that of the Holy Spirit. A correct idea, but not here in place, for according to our text the Father and the Son work simultaneously and together. Meyer: "The subject is not the preserving and governing of the world in general, but the continued activity of God for the salvation of mankind in spite of His Sabbath resting after the creation" (Gen. ii. 1-3). But this is in fact the work of preserving and governing, *providentia*. Olshausen and De Wette explain: the working of God is rest and activity together, and so it is in Christ. Meyer on the contrary: of rest and contemplation there is not a word. The subject, however, is a divine working which as such is also repose, combining at once activity and festive contemplation. Grotius: It is a relation of imitation. Meyer denies this, contrary to ver. 19; it is only the necessary correlation of volition and execution. The Father's having the initiative brings in the element of imitation which by no means exhausts the idea of co-operation (so as to reduce it to a mere working side by side after the same manner, as of one God with another). On Hilgenfeld's discovery of the demiurge, see Meyer [p. 223 f., 5th ed.].

[Godet compares with this ver. Luke ii. 49, and justly remarks that it virtually contains the whole following discourse. It asserts the mysterious union of Christ with God, which Christ had already expressed in His twelfth year to His parents. It is rightly understood by the Jews (ver. 18), though wrongly construed by

*[So also Reuss, against whom Godet, II., p. 26, justly remarks that Christ's condition as a Jew, and His mission as the Jewish Messiah, forbid that He should ever, during His earthly life, have violated any of the Divine commandments, in their proper sense, which it was His sacred duty strictly to fulfil. Ewald, the great oriental scholar, is perfectly correct in saying (on John, p. 205), that Christ in ver. 17, mortally hit the Sabbath laws as they were then understood and carried out, but not the true sense of the primitive Sabbath and the fourth commandment, which forbid not higher work, but only the ordinary work of week days.—P. S.]

them into blasphemy, since they saw in Him a mere man. It is at the same time the most triumphant refutation of the charge of Sabbath-breaking. What a sublime apology this! In charging Me, He says to His adversaries, with breaking the law of God, you charge the Lawgiver, my Father, with breaking His own law: for my activity continually and in each moment corresponds to His. Owen remarks on this verse: "There is not the shadow of a doubt, that Jesus did here claim, and intended to claim, absolute equality with the Father. What is here most logically inferred, is distinctly stated, John i. 1; Col. i. 15-17; Heb. i. 2, 3."—P. S.]

Ver. 18. **The Jews sought the more to kill him**, *etc.*—The one complex charge (of Sabbath-breaking) now becomes two, and the second is the greater. He has ascribed to Himself a singular relation to God. By this He is supposed to have blasphemed God and incurred the death of the blasphemer, Lev. xxiv. 16 (Bengel: "*Id misere pro blasphemia habuerunt*"). They had already hated Him unto death on the first charge, but a prosecution for death they could not easily under the circumstances make out of the Sabbath-breaking, and in their second charge their real intention becomes also the formal one of finding Him guilty of death. Hence *nunc amplius*, to interpret the μᾶλλον [Bengel], is more suitable than the *magis* of Meyer. *Amplius* means not only *insuper*, but also *appertius.* Tholuck incorrectly: the murderous wish still remains *informata.* The matter still depended on the inquisition only in so far as the pretended blasphemy seemed to be not sufficiently established by Christ's expression: *My Father.* "The name of father, except in the much disputed passage, Job xxxiv. 36, and in Ps. lxxxix. 26 where it is descriptive, is not used in the Old Testament as a personal name. In the Apocrypha the individual use of the word first begins to develop itself, Wisd. xiv. 3; Sir. xxiii. 1, 4. Otherwise God is only in the national (theocratic) sense Father of the people, and even in the use of the term in this sense there still appears in the century after Christ a certain reserve, *etc.* Thus this specific calling of God his Father (comp. ἴδιος, Rom. viii. 32) must have been very striking in his mouth." Tholuck.

[The Jews correctly understood ὁ πατήρ μου (instead of ἡμῶν) to assert a *peculiar* and *exclusive* fatherhood (πατέρα ἴδιον, *patrem proprium*) in relation to Jesus such as no mere man could claim, and a peculiar sonship of Jesus such as raised Him above all the children of God and made Him equal in essence with God. (Comp. the μονογενὴς υἱός of John and the ἴδιος υἱός of Paul, Rom. viii. 32). But regarding Jesus as a mere man, and evidently a man in His sound senses, the Jews charged Him with blasphemy. This is inevitable from their premises. The only logical alternative is: Christ was either a blasphemer, or equal with God. Comp. x. 33. Alford remarks: "The Jews understood His words to mean nothing short of *peculiar personal Sonship*, and thus equality of nature with God. And that this their understanding was the right one, the discourse testifies. All might in one sense, and the Jews did in a closer sense, call God *their*, or *our*, *Father;* but they at once said that the individual use of 'MY FATHER' by Jesus had a totally distinct, and in their view a blasphemous meaning: this latter especially, because He thus made God a participator in His crime of breaking the Sabbath. Thus we obtain from the adversaries of the faith a most important statement of one of its highest and holiest doctrines." Augustine says (Tract. 17): "*Ecce intelligunt Judæi, quod non intelligunt Ariani.*"—P. S.]

Ver. 19. **The Son can do nothing of himself, but what he seeth the Father doing**,* *etc.*—introduced with **Verily, verily**; thus opening a new truth. He retracts nothing that He has said, but now, that the question of the Messiah comes up, plants Himself on general ground, and speaks alternately now objectively of the Son and the Father, ver. 19-23; ver. 25-29, now subjectively of Himself and the Father, ver. 24; ver. 30-47. *By this changing of the grammatical person, with the perfect identity of the real person, so that the objective sentences assert universal Christological relations, and the subjective His relation to the Jewish rulers,*—by this master stroke of self-vindication, not noticed by expositors, He sustains His wisdom, without prejudicing in the least the steadfastness of His confession, and He puts their inquisition in the issue utterly to shame (or makes it a *mandatum de supersedendo*). Luther: "A beautiful *excusatio*, making the matter worse." Tholuck: "Jesus strengthens that which gave offence." But the turn, with which He does this ought not to be overlooked. The time of His unveiled revelation of Himself as the Messiah was the time of His death: *this was not yet come.* On the different views of the fathers as to the ensuing discussion, whether it presents the revelation of the Father to the Son in the internal trinitarian aspect, or in the economic, see Tholuck, p. 165. Tholuck remarks (p. 97): "In the Gospels, as in Paul, the predicate υἱός is not to be understood of the λόγος ἄσαρκος, but of the ἔνσαρκος (Nitzsch, *System*, § 83; Hofmann, *Schriftbeweis*, I., p. 173): yet like the Pauline, the Johannean view also regards the Incarnate Word in continuity with the λόγος ἄσαρκος, and hence applies to Him what is said of the former." It is to be observed that the opposition between eternity and time is not so abstractly carried out in the Scriptures, as in scholastic theology.

Can do nothing,† nothing at all, denotes not

*[Bengel's remarks on this verse are worth quoting: "ἀφ' ἑαυτοῦ οὐδέν; *Hoc gloriæ est, non imperfectionis . . . . Hæc ex intimo sensu unitatis naturalis et amorosæ cum Patre profecta sunt. Defendit Dominus, quod fecerat opus in sabbato, Patris sui exemplo, a quo non discedut. Sic de Spiritu Sancto, xvi.* 13, *ubi etiam simillimum huic loco sequitur antitheton. At diabolus ex propriis loquitur, viii.* 44, *et falsi doctoris est in* SUO *nomine venire et ex* SUO *corde loqui aut facere, V.* 43." Godet directs attention to the naivete of the form of this sentence as contrasted with its sublimity. Jesus speaks of His intimate relation with the infinite Jehovah as of the simplest thing in the world. It is the saying of the child of twelve years: "I must be about my Father's business," elevated to the highest key.—P. S.]

†[Οὐ δύναται is here a moral, not metaphysical, inability, and such an inability which is absolute unwillingness, and hence identical with the highest moral ability. So perfect freedom is the highest ability to do good, or negatively expressed, the absolute inability or unwillingness to do wrong, hence identical with moral necessity. Christ's assertion, therefore, that He can do nothing independently of the Father, far from indicating imperfection, implies the highest moral perfection. Godet: "*Tout est moral dans cette relation. Le non-pouvoir dont il s'agit ici n'est que le côté négatif de l'amor filial.*"—P. S.]

only the dependence of the Son on the Father in His working, the negative side of obedience, nor only His imitation of the Father, the formal side of obedience, but also His working at the motion of the Father. The Father is the limit or the law, the Father is the example, and the Father is also the motive, the impulse of His action. The action of the Son is at every point begotten by the action of the Father. The negative side of the obedience of Christ consists in His being unable to do anything *of Himself;* the positive side consists in His *seeing*, His intuitive perception of the initiative of the Father (βλέπειν, comp. chap. viii. 38, and ἀκούειν, chap. xvi. 13). [Meyer: "In ἀφ' ἑαυτοῦ we must not find a distinction between the human and the divine will (Beyschlag), nor an indistinct and one-sided reference to the human element in Christ (De Wette), but the *whole divine-human subject*, the *incarnate Logos*, with whom there can be no *ascitas agendi*, no self-determination independent of the Father; otherwise He would be exclusively divine or exclusively human. Hence there is here no contradiction with the Prologue."—P. S.]

[**In like manner**, ὁμοίως, excludes the idea of imitation and the analogy of master and servant, or teacher and pupil; it points to the equality of the Son with the Father. The Son does the same things with the same power and in the same manner. He is as the Nicene Creed has it, "God of God," "very God of very God."—P. S.] The human analogy of the child doing like the father, is here only distantly alluded to; the main thing is the original priority of the Father even in the Trinity, a point which the Greek church rightly asserts, but falsely exaggerates. [A priority of office and dignity, but not of substance, for this is the same in the three Persons of the Trinity. —P. S.]

Ver. 20. **For the Father loveth the Son.** —Not merely the ethical foundation of what precedes (Meyer), but more than all the substantial.* The term φιλεῖν [which always expresses the *affection* of love] is more personal or individual [and tender] than the more general ethical term ἀγαπᾶν. This φιλεῖν with respect to the Son not merely proceeds from the eternal relation of the Father to the Son, it is the foundation of this relation itself.

And it manifests itself in the Father's *showing the Son all things*.† The *showing* of the Father answers to the *seeing* of the Son. It is the absolute self-revelation of God in His acting, in its teleological working. The Son sees the Father in all His works, and sees what He intends by the works. And the Father shows Him in all things Himself and His works, and therein impels the Son to carry out and finish those works in redemption and judgment. The seer has momentary visions, *shown* him by the Lord (Rev. i. 1; iv. 1); in Christ the whole view of the world is an insight of the working of God, in which spiritual intuition and sensible vision are one. Christ moves in this living symbolism of the infinite, which in its essential elements the fourth Gospel opens to us; He hears and understands all the words of God, He sees and knows all the signs of God, and His total view of things concentrates itself in the guiding ἐντολή of the interior aim and spirit of His life.

And greater works than these will he show him.—[The theme of all that follows to ver. 30. Comp. here the striking parallel, xiv. 12: "Verily, verily, I say unto you, He that believeth in Me, the works that I do shall he do also; and greater works than these (μείζονα τούτων) shall he do; because I go unto the Father."—P. S.] Tholuck: "Here appears for the first time that use of ἔργα which is peculiar to John's reports of the discourses of Christ. In John Christ designates as ἔργον, for the fulfilment of which He came, the *communication of life* to the world (chap. iv. 34, xvii. 4); all actual operations for this object he calls ἔργα, such as the miracles (chap. x. 32, 38; xv. 24; ix. 4), and His ordinary labors for salvation, as here. It is further to be considered that just these ἔργα here named were proofs of the Messiah, for the doctrine of the Messiah and raiser of the dead, in its external positive shell, the people possessed." The greater works of which Christ here speaks, lie in the same line with the work which Christ has just performed. The fundamental thought is the restoration of a life mortally damaged. The Father restores impotent life by healing springs, miraculous remedies, angels of health: Thus He is the example to the Son. But He also shows Him to what purpose He has now appointed Him Saviour. And with the first, the further greater works, the quickenings of the dead, are announced, for He must finish His work, ver. 36.

That ye may marvel.—Faith they might withhold, astonishment He will compel. [ἵνα expresses not only the result, but the (divine) intention.—P. S.] They suppressed and dissembled the impression which the miracles at the pool of Bethesda had made, and ignored the miracle itself. To this His expression refers, Ye shall at last break out in astonishment [of shame]. Calvin: "*Oblique ingratitudinem perstringit, quod illud tam splendidum virtutis Dei specimen contemserant.*" *Ye.* Meyer: "The [unbelieving] hearers;" Tholuck: "The present unbelieving generation, viewed in identity with the future, as in chap. vi. 62; Matt. xxiii. 39." Yet the present hearers form the foreground (see Matt. xxvi. 64).

[Godet, II., p. 35, regards vers. 19 and 20 as the most remarkable Christological passages in the N. T., and ably defends against Reuss their agreement with the ideas of the prologue.— P. S.]

Vers. 21–29. **As the Father raiseth up the dead,** *etc.*—Ver. 21-23 collect in a unity the total quickening working of the Son of God, *spiritual* and *bodily*, including the spiritual and bodily judgment, yet with special reference to his historical evangelic working at that time. (So also Luthardt and Tholuck). Ver. 24 is the first personal address and practical application. Then vers. 25-27 treat of the spiritual quickening and judging of men by the Son. Vers. 28, 29 refer to the quickening and judging as completed in the body. Finally vers. 31-47 are again personal address and application. [This view of the

*[In the note on the preceding verse, however. Meyer (p. 226) distinctly asserts that the union of the Son to the Father is metaphysical as well as moral.—P. S.]

†[Bengel: *Qui amat, nil celat.*—P. S.]

passage as progressing from the general to the particular, and from the moral or spiritual resurrection in this life to the general resurrection of the body in the life to come, was indicated by Augustin (though not consistently), and is held (though with various modifications) by Calvin, Lampe, Lücke, Tholuck, Olsh., De Wette, Meyer, Hengstenb., Godet, Alford, Wordsworth.—P. S.]

Various constructions:

1. Most suppose that in ver. 21-27 the subject is only the *moral* operation of Christ in general; in ver. 28 and 29 the *real universal* raising of the dead is added as the consummation. This division is the prevailing one (Calvin, Jansen, Lampe, Lücke, [Meyer], *etc.*)

2. Even in ver. 28, 29 the *moral* resurrection *alone* is to be understood (the Gnostics, Eckermann, Ammon, Schweizer, Baumgarten-Crusius [Reuss].

3. The whole passage, ver. 21-29 is to be understood (especially in opposition to the Gnostics) of the *bodily* resurrection, and the judgment *in the strict sense* (Tertullian, Chrysostom), *etc.*, (Erasmus, *etc.* Schott, Kuinoel, *etc.**)

Against this go (1) the manifold features of an operation already beginning and pre-eminently spiritual ("*ye* may marvel," ver. 20, *etc.*); (2) the distinctly different characterizing of the resurrection proper in ver. 27, 28.

It is a question whether the distinction between the first and second resurrection, Rev. xx. 5, 6 (the disputing of which in Hengstenberg's exposition of the Revelation has great weight, it seems, with Tholuck), is also to be found intimated here. Olshausen thought he found the intimation of it in ver. 25; but the expression *and now is*, contradicts this. The first resurrection, however, though it may not be literally expressed here, is nevertheless here fully implied in the gradualness of the resurrection. In other words, a resurrection which proceeds by organic unfolding from within outward, and from the centre of humanity to the circumference, must give us to expect a distinction between the first fruits of the resurrection and the universal final manifestation of the resurrection power, (see 1 Cor. xv. 22-24).

Ver. 21. **As the Father raiseth up the dead.**—It is a question how this is to be understood: whether improperly of quickenings and restorations in the general sense (Deut. xxxii. 39; 1 Sam. ii. 6) according to the earlier books of the Old Testament; or of the future work of resurrection according to the later books, especially the Apocrypha (2 Macc. vii.) [Job xiii. 2; Sap. xvi. 13], or of an omnipresent motion of reviving in the whole province of the working of the Father in general. Undoubtedly the last is meant. Raising up, quickening, bodily and spiritual, spiritual and bodily, is a fundamental tendency of the government of the Father in nature, history, and theocracy. Hence the tokens of His quickening agency in His healing agency, of outward quickening through inward and the reverse, and the constant development of strong and stronger facts, like the teaching by facts in the Old Testament, Rom. iv. 17. Meyer: "Ἐγείρει καὶ ζωοποιεῖ might be expected in the reverse order (as in Eph. ii. 5, 6)." The bodily healing itself, however, serves to awaken spiritual life, and in general the first raising up must precede the quickening, in order to lead to the last, most proper raising. Tholuck: "Ἐγείρειν gives the negative idea of the abolition of death, ζωοποιεῖν, the positive."

Even so the Son quickeneth [ζωοποιεῖ].—As the redeeming and judging consummator, the finisher of the work of the Father. Ζωοποιεῖν here involves ἐγείρειν; yet the idea of the spiritual quickening, as the decisive one, predominates. Meyer would have only spiritual awakening asserted in the οὓς θέλει, Tholuck justly finds bodily also; by which again are meant not simply the particular raisings of dead persons by Jesus. The present tense denotes at the same time the particular case (*that* present) and the law (*all* present). **Whom he will.**—Calvin: Referring to His purpose. Meyer: Referring to faith, ver. 24. We refer οὓς θέλει to the tribunal of the Jews which would restrain Him in that work. He asks not for your judgment for that is no judgment of God; it is not ye that administer the judgment of the Father, but the Son. This explains the connection with what follows. [Alford refers *whom He will*, not to any selection out of mankind, nor to the Jewish prejudice that their nation alone should rise from the dead, but rightly makes it to mean, that in every instance where *His will is to vivify*, the result invariably follows. So also Bengel: "*Nunquam ejus voluntatem destituit effectus.*" Ewald refers θέλει to God, which is unnatural.—P. S.]

Ver. 22. **For neither* doth the Father judge any one.**—Explanations of the connection: 1. In the full power of the Son to quicken *whom He will*, His power to judge is already manifest (Lücke, De Wette, Meyer). 2. Not the θέλειν, but the ζωοποιεῖν is corroborated, and this by the fact that the Son is Judge. He who is the Judge, must also be the quickener (Luthardt, Tholuck). 3. Assuredly, however, the θέλει is confirmed, as the unlimited freedom of the Son to spread life in the region of death; though the connection of the ideas of *quickening* and *judging* remains to be considered. Those who, according to their hierarchical statutes, would hinder the Son in His raising and quickening, thereby set themselves up to judge the world already, so far as in them lies, and condemn it to death. And further their judgment against the Son is a sentence of condemnation against the world. But only as an unauthorized

*[So most of the older expositors, also Beza, Grotius, Bengel, Bäumlein, Ewald, Owen. Against this view Meyer (p. 223) raises six objections, *viz.* 1) ἵνα ὑμεῖς θαυμάζητε, ver. 20, which represents the hearers as continuous witnesses; 2) οὓς θέλει which must be understood ethically; 3) ἵνα πάντες τιμῶσι, 23, which implies the divine purpose of a continuous effect commencing in this world; 4) ἐκ τοῦ θανάτου which cannot be understood of physical death; 5) νῦν ἐστιν and οἱ ἀκούσαντες clearly refer to the present spiritual quickening; 6) the literal resurrection ver. 28 f., is distinguished as something greater and future from the former.—P. S.]

*[The οὐδέ is generally overlooked by commentators, and entirely omitted by the E. V. Meyer explains: *For not even the Father* judges any man, to whom by universal consent judgment belongs; consequently it depends entirely upon the Son, and the οὓς θέλει is all right. Comp. on οὐδέ vii. 5; viii. 42; xxi. 25. Alford explains: As the Father does not Himself, by His own proper act, *vivify* any, but commits all quickening power to the Son: so it is with judgment also.—P. S.]

encroachment upon the judgment which the Father has committed to the Son. That is to say, the judgment and the last day are not now immediately to follow upon the sin and death of the old world, but the universal ministration of grace, quickening, and salvation intervenes, and unbelief towards the Son alone forms the inner judgment, and brings on the last day. Κρίνειν here is condemnation [pronouncing sentence of spiritual death] (chap. iii. 17; v. 24, 27, 29) in distinction from ζωοποιεῖν.—The whole judgment, not "the whole condemning" (Meyer), but the total work of judging, in which acquitting is included. **Committed to the Son.**—The new, the gospel economy of salvation; the representation of the Father by the Son—for the glorifying of the Father in the Son.

Ver. 23. **That all men may honor the Son.***—Teleology of the divine administration. The Father manifests Himself in the acts of the Son, because He manifests Himself in the being of the Son. And the acts of the Son unfold themselves in the total works of salvation and judgment, to the end that the Son may be honored and glorified as the Father, in order that the Father may be glorified in Him. **He that honoreth not the Son,** *etc.*—Spoken most especially against the Sanhedrists.

[Ver. 23 is another argument for the divinity of Christ from His own mouth. Τιμᾶν does not necessarily imply acts of worship (προσκυνεῖν), but it expresses the sentiment of religious reverence from which worship flows. And as Christ claims precisely the same honor (καθώς) as is due to the Father, He puts Himself on such a footing of equality with Him as implies unity of essence; since monotheism is very jealous of the honor of Jehovah, as the only being entitled to the worship of the creature. There can be no two rival Gods. The worship of the Son is so far from interfering with the worship of the Father, that there can be no true worship of the Father without the worship of the Son. The Fatherhood of God is an unreal abstraction without the co-eternal Sonship of Christ. Comp. with this passage John xx. 28; Phil. ii. 10.—P. S.]

Ver. 24. **He that heareth my word.**—Here is the first of the pregnant turns from the third person to the first, which we have pointed out above. Still more emphatic is the introduction of Christ's reference to Himself by the *Verily, verily.* Expositors so entirely overlook this turning point of Christ's description of Himself in His discourse that Tholuck here remarks: "The view is now directed to the commencement of the quickening process of time, ver. 24 *in abstracto*, ver. 25 in the historical development." Rather is verse 24 the practical application of what precedes, and verse 25 the beginning of the distinction between the period of the spiritual resurrection and the epoch of the bodily. The *hearing* of the word of Jesus is put in the closest relation to the believing on the God that sent Him; the two are distinct, the two are one. A man cannot *truly hear* Him, without believing in God; believing in God depends upon a man's hearing Christ. This gives the counter statement, John xii. 47. Such an one *has* eternal life. Thus the operation of the word of Christ in believers is the act of imparting life, of quickening (see 1 Pet. i. 23; James i. 18). The result of this quickening to eternal life is: He *comes not into condemnation*, and that because conversely he *has passed* from the state of a condemned one into *life, i. e.*, from internal, essential death into internal, essential life.* The death internally accomplished must pass through the judgment into death externally accomplished, the pains of damnation; the internally accomplished life transforms the judgment itself to an entrance into life, chap. viii. 51. But not without effort, not without a transition does this great change take place. This most prodigious effort, bringing to pass the greatest work of God, is performed in the most silent passive way: Hearing the word of Jesus, believing the God in Him and above Him.

Ver. 25. **Verily, verily—an hour is coming** (see chap. iv. 23)—Second change of the grammatical person. Objective talk again concerning the Son. At first only concerning the spiritual resurrection, vers. 25, 26. The hour which is one day to come, *already is* [νῦν ἐστιν]. In other words, these hours are in one another, coherent, because the things in hand are eternal. The whole resurrection exists in germ in the life of Jesus and His quickening work. The antithesis is, the hour as coming, the apostolic and New Testament period till the second advent, and the hour as already present, the time of the earthly ministry of Jesus. The awakening of mankind to new life virtually began with His earthly work; it developed itself on the day of Pentecost. Reference to the particular instances of His bodily raising of the dead, as well as to Matt. xxvii. 52 (Olshausen), is not by this cut off (against Meyer); for in those signs the spiritual awakening power of Christ is manifest; but the primary subject is the spiritual awakening of men, for which the physical not only *morally*, but even *dynamically* and *organically*, prepares.—**The dead** [οἱ νεκροί], therefore, are the spiritually dead (Matt. viii. 22.)

His voice [τῆς φωνῆς τοῦ υἱοῦ τοῦ θεοῦ].—The word of Christ figuratively represented, or rather designated as an awakening call in its total effect upon spirit and body together. And also φωνή for the sake of the succeeding antithesis. Precise antithesis: οἱ νεκροὶ ἀκούσονται τῆς φωνῆς, and οἱ ἀκούσαντες. All the dead must hear the word of the Son, but unbelievers stop with the hearing of the φωνή (see chap. xii. 28; Acts ix. 17; comp. chap. xxii. 9; xxvi. 14). The others, on the contrary, are persons who have simply heard, actually heard. He, therefore, who has heard, shall live; for the call of Christ is a call of creative life and a summons to life eternal. Meyer: If the passage be referred to bodily resurrection, the οἱ ἀκούσαντες is, on account of the article, utterly inexplicable.

*[Bengel observes to τιμῶσι: "*vel libenter, judicium effugientes per fidem, vel inviti, judicis iram sentientes.*" But a *voluntary* homage is meant here, as the following ὁ μὴ τιμῶν τὸν υἱόν shows. But those who refuse this honor to the Son, will, by their damnation, negatively and reluctantly glorify the Son. Comp. Phil. ii. 10, 11.—P. S.]

*[Note the present tense ἔχει, *has*, already, not *shall have*, spiritual *life*, and the corresponding perfect μεταβέβηκεν, *has passed* from the death of unbelief and sin to the life of faith and righteousness. Of the unbelievers it is said likewise in the perfect ἤδη κέκριται, *he is already judged*. Partly from Bengel.—P. S.]

On the attempts to adjust this to that interpretation, see Meyer (p. 232). [Alford also regards *οἱ*, "*they* who have heard it" or "hear it" (not ἀκούσαντες merely, "having heard it"), as conclusive in favor of *spiritual* awakening in this verse. Godet says that the article divides the dead into two classes, those who hear, and those who having ears, yet hear not (xii. 40). He sees in ver. 25 a reproduction of the thought of ver. 24 under a more dramatic and solemn form, the images being borrowed from the future physical resurrection to paint the spiritual resurrection. Christ appears here as the only living one in a world of spiritual death and desolation. Comp. the magnificent vision of the dry bones made alive by the breath of Jehovah, Ezek. xxxviii.—P. S.]

Ver. 26. **As the Father hath life in himself, even so gave he to the Son also to have life in himself.**—The Son in his incarnation, (comp. chap. x. 18), or the λόγος ἔνσαρκος; but on the ground of His essential nature as λόγος ἄσαρκος. Tholuck: "If the emphasis lay on ἐν ἑαυτῷ, to give prominence to the self-subsistence of the life, this assertion would be in contradiction to ἔδωκε; it must therefore be assumed that ἔχειν ἐν ἑαυτῷ only serves to express more emphatically in the Johannean idiom the idea of possession, as in chap. v. 42; vi. 53, *etc.* Comp. the formula μένοντα ἔχειν." But after all the emphasis does evidently lie on the repeated ἐν ἑαυτῷ, and the thing spoken of is not a thing which Christ has in common with Christians, but a thing which He has in common with the Father. Between the primal originalness which pertains to the Father (to be carefully distinguished from the aseity or self-subsistence of the triune God, which pertains to all three persons), and the permanent possession of life, which is communicated to believers, lies yet the great mystery, that Christ is in Himself the second personal principle of all life. Euthym. Zigabenus: πηγάζει. He has an essential, absolute power of regeneration, not only for Himself, but also for the life of the world.

[Ἔδωκε refers to a historical fact, the incarnation, and τῷ υἱῷ to the God-*Man*, the Saviour of the world. But this communication of life to the incarnate Son is itself only the temporal manifestation of an eternal self-communication of life by the Father to the pre-existent Son; and οὕτως implies an underlying equality of essence. To have life in Himself just as the Father has it in Himself, and to be an independent source of life to others, cannot be said of any creature or mere man. We all live and move and have our being in God, and are absolutely depending on Him. The Nicene doctrine of the eternal generation of the Son by the Father is not a mere idea, but a fact, as the eternal subordination of the Son to the Father is a fact. Both are acts of divine love, the one of the Father to the Son, the other of the Son to the Father. By the generation the Father gives eternally His own self-existing independent life, *i. e.*, His all to the Son, by His subordination the Son gives Himself to the Father. "To give all, to return all, this is love. God is love. He loves divinely, and is beloved divinely."—P. S.]

Ver. 27. **And gave him authority to execute judgment, because he is Son of man** [Καὶ ἐξουσίαν ἔδωκεν αὐτῷ κρίσιν ποιεῖν, ὅτι υἱὸς ἀνθρώπου ἐστίν].—Besides the power of life which the Father gave Him as Son of God, and from which proceeds the activity before mentioned, the Father gave Him the power of judgment also, because He is Son of man. We must note the distinction. And since assuredly the ideal judgment has been presented as a corollary of the saving and quickening work of Christ, the full power of judging in general, and of the solemn final judgment in particular, is here intended. This last is grounded especially in the fact that Christ is *Son of man*, as in particular the vicarious position and work of Christ in justification are grounded in the same.

Account must be made of the fact that in this passage alone υἱὸς ἀνθρώπου stands without the article.* Different explanations:

1. The omission is unimportant, and the expression means here as elsewhere: the *Messiah* (Lightfoot, Lücke, *etc.*) Against this is the fact that the Son of Man with the article denotes the Messiah, and therefore the Son of God, and that as such He has been already here introduced. Of course the Son of Man is the Son of God in an undivided human identity; but here His being man is emphasized by itself as a new point.

2. Because He is *man* (Luther, Jansen, *etc.*, Meyer). And how is He made Judge on this account?

(*a*) Luther, *etc.*, De Wette [Reuss]: "The judgment is to take place with human publicity, therefore the Judge must be visible as man."

(*b*) Bucer, *etc.*: "He humbled Himself to be made man, therefore as man He is glorified."

(*c*) Wetstein, Stier: "Man is to be judged by the lowliest, most loving man," Heb. ii. 17, 18.

(*d*) Este, Meyer: "Because He is man, and would not have had the authority to judge, if it had not been given to Him" (merely, therefore, to make room for the "*given*").

(*e*) Tholuck: "Because He is incarnate Redeemer, the judging also is given to Him in this redemption itself.

(*f*) The idea is no doubt a juridical principle: because He is to judge men, therefore He must have not only knowledge of man, but also a human experience. As *Son* of man, thus embodying the ideal of human life, He *is the standard* of the judgment, and virtually the judgment itself; as Son of *man*, He has the whole experience of humanity, sin excepted (which is no pure experience), and as He, in that He has been tempted, is able to succor them that are tempted, He is able also to judge them that are tempted.†

[By His incarnation Christ has so identified Himself with all the interests of humanity, as its Head and Saviour, that humanity belongs to Him: it is for Him to redeem, to save, to make alive, to judge, to condemn. The final resurrection and judgment are only the completion of the pro-

*[ὁ υἱὸς τοῦ ἀνθρώπου in the Synoptists and John i. 52; iii. 13 f.; vi. 27, 53, 62; vii. 28, *etc.*; υἱὸς ἀνθρώπου only here, and with ὅμοιον, Apoc. i. 13; xiv. 14, in allusion to Dan. vii. 13. Comp. the Excursus on this designation of Christ, p. 98 f.—P. S.]

†The false construction, which connects the words with what follows: Because He is man, marvel not, *etc.* (Peshito, Chrysostom, Paulus, and others), need only be mentioned.

cess commenced in His becoming man for us, and for our salvation. Alford explains: Man is to be judged by Man,—by that Man whom God has appointed, who is the inclusive Head of humanity, and to whom mankind, and man's *world*, pertain by right of covenant-purchase. Jacobus (*Notes on John*): This is the kindest arrangement, 1) because as mediator He must have the most tender regard for man; 2) because as man He would sympathize with us, as to all our temptations; 3) as God-Man He would have a fellow-feeling with us as well as with God.—P. S.]

Ver. 28. [**Marvel not at this.** Bengel: "They are great things which He spake all along from ver. 21, and worthy of marvel; but greater and more marvellous are the things which follow: *τοῦτο, this*, is to be referred to what goes before. Jesus knew the feeling of wonder which had been just now raised in the mind of the Jews."—P. S.] **In which all that are in the graves.**—[Verses 28 and 29 evidently refer to the future general resurrection; hence *πάντες οἱ ἐν τοῖς μνημείοις*, and hence also the omission of the words, *καὶ νῦν ἐστιν*, Christ rises now to the last and highest mediatoral act of His *ἐξουσία*.—P. S.]—The expression, *in the graves*, is to be taken *strictly*, *i. e.*, of those who are bodily dead, yet not *literally*: of those only that are buried. It is not, however, the dust of the dead that is intended any more than it is the risen themselves (Tholuck), when it is said they shall hear His voice, but the souls of the dead on the way to resurrection. Their being in the graves signifies their need of entire reclothing or new embodiment in the day of the appearance of Christ. The subject here is evidently the general resurrection (1 Cor. xv.), which excludes neither the first resurrection (Rev. xx.), nor the gradual, organic reclothing (2 Cor. v.). The distinguishing of those who have done good and those who have done evil, proves that the subject here cannot be the spiritually dead; and to the same effect is the expression: that are in the graves. Comp. Isa. xxvi. 19; Ezek. xxxvii. 12; Dan. xii. 2.

[**Shall hear his voice.**—1 Thess. iv. 16: "The Lord Himself shall descend from heaven with a shout, with the voice of the archangel and with the trump of God." Comp. 1 Cor. xv. 52. The same voice, which ye hear this very moment for your spiritual resurrection, shall summon your dead bodies from the tomb for the final resurrection, and I shall award them, according to their deeds, eternal life, or eternal woe. Comp. the third stanza of the terrific *Dies Iræ*:

Tuba mirum spargens sonum,
Per sepulchra regionum,
Coget omnes ante thronum.

"Wondrous sound the Trumpet flingeth,
Through earth's sepulchre it ringeth,
All before the Throne it bringeth."—P. S.]

Ver. 29. **They that have done good** [lit. **the good** *τὰ ἀγαθά* and **the evil**, *τὰ φαῦλα*. The article gives the terms an absolute meaning.—Comp. Rom. ii. 7; Matth. vii. 21; xxv. 31, sqq. also John iii. 20, on the difference between *ποιεῖν* applied to good, and *πράσσειν* to evil]. At the last day righteousness of faith must have ripened into righteousness of life, and all will have had opportunity to make it their own, 1 Peter iii. 19; iv. 6. **Unto a resurrection of life** [*εἰς ἀνάστασιν ζωῆς*].—1. Meyer: "A resurrection to life locally conceived, *i. e.*, a resurrection, the essential result of which is life, that is, the life in the kingdom of Messiah." 2 Macc. vii. 14 [*ἀνάστασις εἰς ζωήν*; Dan. xii. 2]. 2. Tholuck (after Luthardt): "After the pregnant sense in which the promise of the *ἀνάστασις* occurs in chap. vi. 40, 44, 54, it seems more correct to translate: life-resurrection, and damnation-resurrection, indicating that in this act the *ζωή* and the *κρίσις* respectively reach their summit." No doubt correct. The one class come forth into the resurrection of life, into the final perfect manifestation of life; the other, into the final perfect manifestation of condemnation. This includes the first interpretation in the strongest form of expression. That Christ is here standing before a Jewish tribunal, is indicated by His bringing out in ever mightier prominence the thought of the divine judgment committed to Him. [**Unto the resurrection of judgment,** *εἰς ἀνάστασιν κρίσεως*.—A resurrection from death temporal to death eternal. Who can realize the awful idea! The resurrection of the wicked is expressly taught Dan. xii. 2; Acts xxiv. 15 (*ἀνάστασις νεκρῶν, δικαίων τε καὶ ἀδίκων*), and implied Matth. x. 28, (*ψυχὴν καὶ σῶμα ἀπολέσαι ἐν γεέννῃ*); xxv. 34 ff.; Rev. xx. 5.—P. S.]

Ver. 30. **I can of mine own self do nothing.**—Having asserted so great things concerning the Son, Jesus again speaks of Himself in the first person. Thus we have not here (and in ver. 31) a new train of thought according to John's mode of connecting ideas (Tholuck), but the second turn of the discourse into self-assertion and personal application (other misapprehensions of the connection, see in Meyer, p. 237.) The portion ver. 30-39 treats of the true Messianism, the witnesses to it, and the unbelief which receives not the testimony. The portion verses 41-47 treats of the false Messianism, which runs finally into anti-Messianism. *I can do nothing, etc.* See ver. 19.

As I hear.—Denoting in the form of sensible perception absolute, sensible, spiritual knowledge. A *hearing*, in the sense of perfect moral, teleological perception of the divine will, as previously a *seeing* in the sense of perfect intellectual perception of things in principle. The words at the same time assert the Saviour's knowledge of the men's condemnation of themselves. **Because I seek not mine own will.**—Because He perpetually sacrifies Himself, He can judge the world in execution of the will of His Father, who sent Him. The *paternity* points to His origin, the *sending*, to His object.

Ver. 31. **If I bear witness of myself, my witness is not true.**—A man's testimony in his own cause is not received; it must be supported by the attestation of another: the oath. A human tribunal requires at least two witnesses, Nu. xxxv. 30; John viii. 16, 17.* Yet

*[According to the usual rule of law. *Chetub.* f. xxiii. 2: *Testibus de se ipsis non credunt.* Christ argues here hypothetically: If My testimony concerning Myself could be independent and separated from that of the Father, it would be false according to the law of testimony. In John viii. 13-16 the *other side* of the same argument is presented: Christ *does* in fact bear witness of Himself, but as He is the Logos of God, the organ of the Father, His testimony is the testimony of the Father in and through Him, and therefore true. "*Though* I

not the number of witnesses, but the nature and quality of the witness, is the thing here emphasized by the Lord. The attester must be distinct from the one attested. This is the human rule. In theocratic terms: A prophet without divine attestation, or even the Messiah without the same, would be a contradiction. "The precise principle is, that the individual does not testify to himself, and thus separate himself from the universal, but that one testifies for another, and then on the highest scale he who is other to the Son, the Father, testifies to the Son. Chap. viii. 14 seems to contradict this. But: (1) In the law of judicial testimony a person's testimony respecting himself has its place; (2) particularly in regard to a fact of personal consciousness; (3) in case of a testimony which has the testimony of the Father associated with it.

Ver. 32. **There is another.**—The sequel shows that this ἄλλος is the Father. [So Cyr., Aug., Beza, Beng., Lücke, Thol., Olsh., Luthardt, Hengstenb., Brückner, Meyer, Godet, Alford. It cannot be John the Baptist (Chrys., Erasm., Grot., De Wette, Ewald), on account of ver. 34, 36, where Christ presents His testimony as unnecessary, and assigns it a subordinate value as compared with that of the Father. "The reason why our Lord mentions John is not 'as ascending from the lesser witness to the greater,' but purposely to remove the idea that He meant him only or principally by these words, and to set his testimony in its proper place: then at ver. 36 He returns again to the ἄλλος μαρτ. περὶ ἐμοῦ." (Alford.) **I know that,** *etc.* This, as Meyer observes, is too strong and solemn for the testimony of the Baptist. "It is the Son's testimony to the Father's truth," comp. vii. 28, 29; viii. 26, 55.—P. S.]

Ver. 33, 34. **Ye sent unto John.**—Reminding them of the fact which the evangelist relates in chap. i. 19. Towards the end of His pilgrimage also, Matth. xxi. 25, He again reverts to this. At the same time hinting what follows farther on. This leads to the more precise explanation of the words: **I receive not testimony from man** (Ver. 34). That is, not: I reject it (Tholuck), or, do not make use of it (Beza), or, do not catch at it (De Wette), but: *I do not need it for Myself, and do not make account of it,* as necessary to support my public appearance as Messiah.* I expect my attestation in a higher testimony, in the testimony of the Father. John was a witness with whom, as the completer of the Old Testament, they must from their point of view be satisfied; but Jesus cannot satisfy Himself with this testimony; as founder of the New Testament, He must have a new and higher. **But these things I say, that ye may be saved.**—[Not for *My* benefit, for I do not need this human testimony, having a divine one, which is all sufficient, but for *your* salvation. Bengel: *Vestra res agitur.*—P. S.] He reminds them of that testimony, because for them it was valid, and contempt of it would be an undoing of the old covenant, and would bring perdition upon them.

Ver. 35. **He was the lamp burning** (or, **lighted**) **and shining.** ['Εκεῖνος ἦν ὁ λύχνος ὁ καιόμενος καὶ φαίνων. "What a glorious phenomenon was he, and how little have you appreciated him!" Meyer.] He *was.* John has retired. He was in prison at the time of the Lord's return to Galilee (chap. iv. 44; Matth. iv. 12), and was soon after beheaded (chap. vi. 1; comp. Matth. xiv. 13). [So also Stier and Alford.—P. S.] Jesus therefore considered his imprisonment as the end of his course.

The lamp. With the article.* The appointed lamp of the advent of the Messiah, burning and shining. Interpretations: 1. Bengel: Elijah, with reference to Sir. xlviii. 1: "Then stood up Elijah the prophet like a fire, and his word burned like a **lamp.**"† 2. Luthardt: The figure of the one who carries a light before the coming bridegroom. The rejoicing just afterwards mentioned, which might be probably the performance of a wedding dance in the torch-light, might be decisive for this view. But the one who holds the torch is not the torch itself. The general figure in Luke i. 76 (Meyer) is not quite satisfactory.‡ It must be observed, that the manifestation of Jehovah is always preceeded by a token of light and fire. The indication of this appears even in Genesis, chap. iii. 24; xv. 17. Then the burning bush becomes the token of the manifestation of Jehovah, Ex. iii. 2; afterwards the pillar of fire, Ex. xiii. The permanent typical symbol of the manifestation of God in Israel was the candle-stick in the temple; its complement being the fire upon the altar. In the prophetic vision the manifestation of Jehovah is announced and marked by a token of light and fire combined (Ezek. i. 13); by light and fire the advent of the Messiah is heralded and proclaimed, Zech. xiv. 7; Mal. iii. 2. All those tokens of light and fire meet in the Baptist. He is the flame-signal of the Messiah, the last Old Testament form of the pillar of fire and of the candle-stick in the temple; therefore *the lamp,* at once flaming and shining. The figure of the lamp (λύχνος) was current (2 Sam. xxi. 17; 2 Peter i. 19; Rev. xxi. 23).

Burning and shining. Meyer disputes the opinion that these words denote two peculiarities of John: fiery zeal and illumination; since the two belong together.§ And yet the two are also to be distinguised. It was the sin of the

---

bear witness of Myself, yet My witness is true, for I know whence I came: . . . *Yet* if I judge, My judgment is true, for I am not alone, but I and the Father that sent me."—P. S.]

*[λαμβάνειν τ. μαρτυρίαν, as in iii. 11, 32, to *receive,* to *accept,* but here as *testimony* (not in the sense of *believing*). See Meyer, p. 238.—P. S.]

*[Omitted, as often, in the E. V., which also translates λύχνος *light* (γῶς), instead of *lamp,* and thus brings this passage needlessly in conflict with i. 8: οὐκ ἦν ἐκεῖνος τὸ φῶς; ἀλλ' ἵνα μαρτυρήσῃ περὶ τοῦ φωτός. John was, indeed, *a* light, but only in a subordinate sense, a derived light, a light *lighted,* not *lighting,* and hence ἐν τῷ φωτὶ αὐτοῦ is spoken of in the next clause in the sense of the predicate, not the noun.—P. S.]

†[Καὶ ἀνέστη 'Ηλίας προφήτης ὡς πῦρ, καὶ ὁ λόγος αὐτοῦ ὡς λαμπὰς ἐκαίετο. Stier and Alford think that this passage may be referred to here, and gave rise to a common way of speaking of Elijah, as certain Rabbis were called "the candle of the law."—P. S.]

‡[Meyer: The article signifies the particular lamp which was to appear in John as the forerunner of the Messiah whose mission was to teach the people the knowledge of the Messianic salvation, δοῦναι γνῶσιν σωτηρίας τῷ λαῷ αὐτοῦ, Luke i. 76 f. Lange goes deeper, as usual, where he differs from Meyer. De Wette takes the article as meaning "the lamp which was to lead you.'"—P. S.]

§[Meyer quotes in support, Luke xii. 35: οἱ λύχνοι καιόμενοι; Rev. iv. 5; λαμπάδες πυρὸς καιόμεναι, but in both cases φαινόμενοι is omitted. According to Alford φαίνων sets forth the *derived* and *transitory* nature of John's light.—P. S.]

Jews, that they were not warned by the burning of John and so made his shining a mere transitory appearance.

And ye were willing.—Ἠθελήσατε. Bringing out the sinful caprice in which they made the earnest light a passing festival torch for a joyous throng or dance. Respecting the enthusiastic concourse on the appearance of the Baptist, see Matth. iii. 5. Out of this came, instead of the *μετάνοια* which John preached, an *ἀγαλλιασθῆναι*. We might think here of the dancing of gnats in the twilight, or a swarm of flies around a lamp; but more natural is the thought of a joyous dance approaching with a festive torch. **For a while.**—Πρὸς ὥραν belongs according to Bengel, to *ἠθελήσατε*, according to Meyer, to *ἀγαλλιασθῆναι*; but the two things are not to be separated. To their fickle *ἐθέλειν* it belonged to make to themselves out of the earnest preacher of repentance, an entertaining event of the day. **In his light.**—They made the *λύχνος* itself for awhile the *light*, *φῶς*, of which it was to be only the harbinger. Comp. Matth. xi. 16. Furthermore they endeavored to find a bright entertaining side to the earnestness of his preaching of repentance, and hence at last forsook him, because he was too earnest for them.

Ver. 36. **Greater witness.**—Μείζω τοῦ Ἰωάννου, instead of *τῆς μαρτυρίας τοῦ Ἰωάννου*. *Constructio compendiaria.* **For the works which the Father hath,** *etc.*—The testimony of His miracles is the testimony of His Father Himself, because the Father hath given Him the works. **To finish.**—The idea of consummation again; description of Christianity. **That the Father hath sent me.**—The end (*τὸ τέλος*) points back to the beginning, the *ἀρχή*, the sending, which, in its eternity, becomes a perfect: *ἀπέσταλκε*, chap. iii. 34.

Ver. 37. **And the Father himself . . . hath borne witness of me.**—It is a question whether a new and different testimony from that of the works (ver. 36) is here introduced. 1. This *is* the testimony of the works (Augustine, Grotius, Bauer, Neander, Stier, *etc.*). 2. The testimony of God at the baptism of Christ (Chrysostom, Bengel, Paulus).* 3. The witness in the spirit of the believer, the drawing of the Father (De Wette [Alford], Baumgarten-Crusius, Tholuck; but wavering). 4. The testimony which God has given in His word, in the Scriptures of the Old Testament, to His Son (Cyril, Nonnus, *etc.*, Bede, Calvin, Lücke, Meyer). Unquestionably this last interpretation is established by the perfect *μεμαρτύρηκε*, as well as by the ensuing discussion on the Holy Scriptures. Evidently, however, Christ combines the outward word with the inward word in the spirit; and He means not the abstract letter of the Scripture, but the concrete, living Old Testament revelation as a unity of word and spirit (see vers. 37, 38). The third and fourth interpretations, therefore, must be combined. This is the direct, strongly pronounced testimony of the Father.

Ye have neither heard his voice at any time, nor seen his shape.—Christ denotes the soul, the inner life, the truth of the Old Testament revelation. This consisted in the hearing of the voices of God, the word of revelation given in vision, and seeing the emblems of God, His *δόξα* (the Angel of the Lord), by the true believers of the ancient covenant, particularly by the prophets. From this life of revelation, *i. e.*, from the spirit and truth of the Old Testament, these persons were so alienated that Jesus could say to them: Ye have never heard even one of His voices (one living tone of His voice), never seen a single form of His manifestation (a glimmer of His living revelation). And this He could say to them with perfect assurance, because they did not perceive the voice of God even in the word of Christ (comp. Heb. i. 1), because they did not see even the angel of the Lord in His incarnation, as He stood before their eyes, John xiv. 9. In this reproof it is implied that the process of revelations by visions, out of which the Holy Scripture as a document proceded, must in some sense repeat itself in the inward *awakening* (hearing) and *illumination* (seeing) of the true reader (*Leben Jesu*, III., p. 598). Hence also the conjunctive *οὔτε, οὔτε*, is followed by *καὶ οὐ*. The result of such an awakened hearing and enlightened seeing is the abiding of the word, as a new life and vision, in the believing heart (*λόγος μένων ἐν ὑμῖν*). That is, the *φωνή* and the *εἶδος* go together in the one effect and efficient power of the *λόγος μένων*.

Different interpretations: 1. The voice at the baptism (Chrysostom, Lampe, Bengel; Lücke on the contrary: We should then expect *τὴν φωνήν*). 2. Jesus concedes in His words some objection which the Jews would have made (Euthymius Zigab., Kuinoel, Paulus; a characteristically rabbinical interpretation). Similarly Baumgarten-Crusius: "Never before has this direct exhibition of God been made, as it now is." 3. Cyril, Theophylact: Jesus denies to them all direct apprehension of the Old Testament revelations (Lücke: "then Jesus must have spoken of their fathers"). 4. A reproof that they had no eye nor ear for the direct testimonies of God in His—the Messiah's—appearance and work (Lücke). But this comes in the succeeding demonstrative words: For whom He hath sent, Him ye believe not. 5. A metaphorical interpretation (still more definite than in Lücke): "*Metaphoricæ sunt locutiones, quibus in summa docere vult, alienos esse prorsus a Dei notitia. Nam sicuti vultu et sermone homines se patefaciunt, ita Deus vocem ad nos suam Prophetarum voce emittit, et in sacramentis quasi visibilem formam induit, unde cognosci pro modulo nostro queat. Verum qui eum in viva sua effigie non agnoscit, satis hoc ipso prodit, nullum se numen colere, nisi quod ipse fabricarit* (2 Cor. iii. 14)." Calvin. Similarly Luthardt: "*Φωνή* and *εἶδος* are not to be referred to particular symbolical revelations in the Old Testament, such as Isaiah's and Jeremiah's hearing the *φωνή* of God, and Ezekiel's and Daniel's seeing his *εἶδος* in the Spirit; but to the total revelation recorded in the Old Testament, as God's exhibition Himself." So Meyer also, except that he includes theophanies and visions. And to just these, in their symbolical import, the whole matter comes.

Ver. 38. **And ye have not his word abiding in you**—[*καὶ τὸν λόγον αὐτοῦ οὐκ ἔχετε μένοντα ἐν ὑμῖν.*] A Johannean phrase, 1 John ii. 14. Meyer: "You lack a

* [This interpretation is excluded by the addition, *at any time.*—P. S.]

permanent inward appropriation of His word."* Not the revelation of God in the conscience (Olshausen,† Frommann), but the living, especially the Messianic word of God as the seed of the knowledge of Christ. **For whom he sent him ye believe not.**—The fact that they did not recognize and accept in Christ the perfect revelation, the φωνή and εἶδος, of God, proves that they had not understood the intimations of this revelation in the Old Testament; that they had not the Old Testament living in them; that they were deaf and blind to the word of God in the Holy Scriptures as a direct testimony to the Son (see Isa. vi. 6; Matth. xiii. 14; John xii. 40; Acts xxviii. 26; Rom. xi. 8; 2 Cor. iii. 14). The ὃν ἀπέστ. is emphasized by being placed first, and made yet more prominent by τούτῳ ὑμεῖς. [Grotius: *Quomodo mandata regis discet, qui legatum excludit.* With the messenger of God they necessarily also rejected His message.—P. S.]

Ver. 39. **Ye search the Scriptures.**—Meyer: "That ἐρευνᾶτε is indicative (Cyril, Erasmus, Casaubon, Beza, Bengel, and many moderns, including Kuinoel, Lücke, Olshausen, Klee, De Wette, Maier,‡ *etc.*), not *imperative* (Chrysostom, Augustine, Theophylact, Euthymius Zigab., Luther, Calvin, *etc.*, Paulus, Baumgarten-Crusius, Hofmann, Luthardt,§ *etc.*), is shown by the context, to which an imperative would be foreign matter, particularly out of harmony with the correlative καὶ οὐ θέλετε. Comp. also Lechler in the *Studien und Kritiken*, 1854, p. 795." Comp. 2 Cor. iii. As the Jews, in their way, searched the Scriptures very diligently (see Tholuck, p. 175), the sentence, if imperative, must have specified and strongly emphasized the right mode of search.

[Grammatically, ἐρευνᾶτε may be imperative: *search*, or indicative: *ye search.* It is not easy to decide between the two interpretations. The former has, by Luther's German V. and by the A. E. V., become the current interpretation in the Protestant, as it was in the old Greek Church, and is often (by an *a fortiori* application to the *New* Testament) popularly used as an argument against Romanists. It is favored by the following considerations: 1) The position of ἐρευνᾶτε *before* τὰς γραφάς, which, however, is by no means conclusive. 2) The omission of ὑμεῖς before ἐρευνᾶτε, comp. ὑμεῖς before the indicative δοκεῖτε. 3) The consent of the Greek fathers, with the important exception, however, of Cyril of Alexandria. 4) The intrinsic improbability that Christ should have spoken in any way reproachfully of the study of the Scriptures. (Hengstenberg discovers a far fetched allusion to Isa. xxxiv. 16: "Seek ye out of the book of the Lord," a passage which is omitted in the Sept.)—Yet these arguments are in themselves insufficient, and must give way, in my judgment, to the one consideration that the connection and natural sense of the passage as a whole requires the indicative. The Saviour exposes the inconsistency, blindness and perverseness of the Jews in searching the letter of the Scriptures, and imagining to have eternal life in them, and yet refusing to believe in Him to whom these very Scriptures bear witness, and who alone can give to them that life which they vainly sought in the killing letter instead of the vivifying spirit. Thus by their unbelief the very book of God which they professed to honor, became their accuser, and a savor of death to them. Had He intended to *exhort* the Jews to search the Scriptures, He would not have continued: "for *in* them ye *think*, or, *imagine* to have (ὑμεῖς δοκεῖτε ἔχειν) eternal life," but: "*through* them ye *have* (ἔχετε) or rather, *shall have, shall find*, eternal life;" nor would He have added: "*And* they are they which testify of Me," but "*for;*" this being the reason why they should study the Scriptures. He would also probably have defined the verb as to the spirit and manner of searching the Scriptures; for the Jews *did* search them nicely and diligently, although by no means in the best way. The more natural interpretation, therefore, is this: "*Ye do* (indeed) *search the Scriptures* (not τὸν λόγον θεοῦ, but τὰς γραφάς, the letter of the several written books of the Old Testament), *for in them* (not *through* them, as a mere means to get at the living word of God) *ye imagine to have eternal life; and they are they which testify of Me. And* (yet—how inconsistent, how preposterous!) *ye are not willing to come to Me that ye might have* (that eternal) *life.* Ἐρευνάω is the very word which the Sanhedrists used of the study of the Scriptures, vii. 52, when they told Nicodemus: "Search (ἐρεύνησον), and see that no prophet has arisen out of Galilee."* The Pharisees studied the Old Testament as they kept the Sabbath, and Christ rectified their study by pointing out the Christ in the Bible, as He rebuked their Sabbath keeping by doing works of mercy on the Sabbath day. They knew the shell of the Bible and ignored the kernel within. They searched minutely, pedantically and superstitiously the *letter*, but had no sympathy with the indwelling *soul.* They idolized the *written book*, while they resisted the *living word* contained therein (comp. ver. 38). Such bibliolatry led them away from Christ, while the true study of Moses and the prophets leads to Christ, as the fulfiller of the law and the promise. The O. T. promises life, not to the mere reader and searcher, but to the *doer*, of the law: "Ye shall therefore *keep* my statutes and my judgments: which if a man *do*, he shall live in them" (Lev. xviii. 5). The Rabbis said: "He who *acquires the words* of the law, acquires for himself eternal life (*Qui acquirit sibi verba legis, is acquirit sibi vitam eternam*)." The unbelieving Jews search the Old Testament to this day in the same spirit and with the same result; their minds are blinded, and the vail is upon

*[Meyer puts only a comma after ver. 37. John might have continued: οὔτε τὸν λόγον, *etc.*, but by using καί, and connecting the negation with the verb (οὐκ ἔχετε) instead of the particle (οὔτε), he lays greater stress on the new charge against the Jews.—P. S.]

†[Olshausen: According to John the word of the eternal God speaks or sounds in the mind of every man. Sin has diminished, but not destroyed his susceptibility to truth. Without something analogous in the mind, man cannot perceive the things of God. It is the same as the "light in thee," Matt. vi. 23. But Lange's interpretation (the same as Meyer's) is preferable.—P. S.]

‡[Also Henry, Doddridge, Barnes, Brückner, and Godet. —P. S.]

§[The imperative is also preferred by Maldonatus (R. C.), Cornelius a Lap. (R. C.), Grotius, and, among recent commentators, by Stier, Tholuck, Ewald (p. 218), Hengstenberg (who refers to Isa. xxxiv. 16), Bäumlein, Alford, Wordsworth (wavering), Owen, Jacobus.—P. S.]

*[Hence Luthardt is all wrong in ascribing to ἐρευνᾶτε here a profounder meaning.—P. S.]

their heart (2 Cor. iii. 14, 15). In like manner the New Testament is a sealed book to thousands of its readers and students within the Christian church, who either superstitiously, like the Jews, or skeptically, like the rationalists, stick to the mere outside of the Bible, and ignore or oppose the Christ within. Christ is the life and light of the whole Bible, its Alpha and Omega, and the only key that unlocks its mysteries to the believing mind. Comp. the remarks on ver. 46.—P. S.]

For in them ye think ye have.—*Thinking*, or *imagining* (δοκεῖτε) in opposition to *believing* or *knowing* [and *thinking to have* in opposition *to actual having;* comp. ver. 45, and chap. viii. 54 ὑμεῖς λέγετε], imply in the first instance ignorance, but here error also; therefore a censure (contrary to Meyer); for the sense is not: Ye think that eternal life is communicated to you through the Scriptures, but: Ye think to have eternal life in the Scriptures themselves (the plural is significant), *in their mere outward letter*, and to have it as an external possession *outside of yourselves* in their *objective existence;* thus clearly designating that Rabbinism, which for the *Word of God made man* substitutes the *Word of God made book* (see Sir. xxiv. 23 [ταῦτα πάντα βίβλος διαθήκης θεοῦ ὑψίστου]; comp. H. Richter: *Die evang. und röm. Kirchenlehre*, Barmen, 1844, p. 47.)*

And they are they [καὶ ἐκεῖναί εἰσιν].—Καί emphatic. [*Just they, these very Scriptures* which ye search. The copula brings out the absurdity of coupling contradictory things. Ye search the Scriptures which testify of Me, *and* ye reject Me; ye seek life, *and* ye will not come to Me who alone can give you life.—P. S.] **Which testify of me.**—The participle εἰσιν αἱ μαρτυροῦσαί means strictly: they are the testifiers of me, *i. e.*, their proper nature and office is to bear witness of me. [The Old Testament was to Christ a mirror which reflected His own image.]

Ver. 40. **And ye will not.**†—The Scriptures point to Christ; but they will not come from the Scriptures to Him, that they might have life. The αἰώνιος seems designedly omitted. They think they already have the ζωὴ αἰώνιος in the letter of their Scriptures; but they must come to Christ before they can have any life at all. Of course the life meant is the ζωὴ αἰώνιος, but here great stress falls on its very conditions and incipiency. Bengel: *Propius in Christo, quam in Scripturis vita habetur.* [Οὐ θέλετε implies the voluntary character, and hence the moral guilt of unbelief, comp. Matth. xxiii. 37.‡ The end of the discourse uncovers the secret motive of this unbelief, namely the self-seeking ambition of the heart. Reason may be more easily convinced of the truth of Christianity than the will may be subdued to the obedience of Christ. The springs of belief and unbelief are in the heart rather than the head. "Keep thy heart with all diligence, for out of it are the issues of life," Prov. iv. 23.—P. S.]

Ver. 41. **Glory from men.**—Glory. Mere honor, especially in John, cannot be intended by the word δόξα. It is the δόξα of the Messiah. This Christ declares He will not receive, or appropriate, from human sources. The connection is: The Father testifies of Me in the Scripture; I must leave all to Him, as He glorifies Me; I cannot be glorified by the testimony of John in his ministry among you. That Jesus intended to prevent the charge of injured ambition (Luthardt, Meyer), is hardly to be supposed.

Ver. 42. **But I know you.**—[Ἔγνωκα, perfect. Bengel: *Cognitos vos habeo; hoc radio penetrat corda auditorum.* He knew them from their past history and from their conduct towards Him.—P. S.] With His sure discernment, that their heart is not directed towards God, He cannot and will not expect that His δόξα will be prepared for Him by the Sanhedrin, or by Judaism in general. The reason why they did not know, and honor Him, was that they did not love God. **Ye have not the love of God in you.**—They had none of that spirituality which is earnestly directed towards God and eternal things. Τὴν ἀγάπην: the love which is required by the law, as its sum and substance, or even that which is awakened by the promise. **In you.**—Ἐν ἑαυτοῖς [in your own hearts]. They have this love in their holy Scriptures, *outside of themselves*, in the holy medium of revelation, as they have eternal life outside of themselves;—they themselves are full of worldliness.

Ver. 43. **In my Father's name.**—The very fact that He is come in the name of His Father, that He has predicated nothing of Himself, that He has executed the mission of the Father, done the works of the Father, answered to the testimony of the Father in the Old Testament, that He has even avoided the oft falsified name of Messiah, is the reason why they do not receive Him.

If another shall come in his own name.—We might doubt whether the Lord does not intend to say: under the assumed name of Messiah in some specifically shaped form. But the man coming in his own name is, in any case, a false Messiah (Meyer, against Luthardt); for he comes, (1) with no commission from the Father, but of his own ambitious impulse; (2) not with the works of the Father, but with self-chosen deceptions; (3) not for the glory of the Father, but for his own; (4) not in agreement with the holy Scriptures, but with a false Messianic idea. Meyer: "He will find acceptance, because he satisfies the opposite of the love of God, *self-love* (by promise of earthly glory, *etc.*). A distinct prediction of false Messiahs. See Matth. xxiv. 24. According to Schudt: *Jüdische Merkwürdigkeiten*, 6, 27, 30 (in Bengel), sixty-four such de-

---

*[Rothe (*Studien und Kritiken*, 1860, p. 67) and Weiss (*Johan. Lehrbegriff*, p. 106), likewise maintain that δοκεῖτε implies a censure of the excessive Rabbinical over-estimate of the letter of the Bible. This view is strengthened by the emphatic ὑμεῖς, *ye on your part*, and the obvious sense of δοκεῖτε in verse 45. I suggest also that ἐν αὐταῖς is significantly chosen instead of δι' αὐτῶν, as if the written Scriptures were the eternal life itself, while they are only the record of life and the witness of Christ. Meyer rejects this interpretation, as being inconsistent with the high veneration of Christ for the Scriptures; but He is simply protesting (and that in the wisest and most guarded manner) against the abuse and perversion of the Scriptures, just as He protests against the Jewish perversion of the Sabbath. Meyer admits, however, that there is an opposition here to real ἔχειν ζωήν, which Christ could not say of the Jews, as they rejected the Christ of the Scriptures.—P. S.]

†[Ewald reads this as a question. But it is stronger as an assertion.—P. S.]

‡[Alford: "The words *ye are not willing* to come, here set forth strikingly the *freedom of the will*, on which the unbeliever's condemnation rests: see chap. iii. 19."—P. S.]

ceivers have been counted since the time of Christ." Since then many new ones have doubtless been added. (See the periodical: *Dibre Emeth*, Breslau, 1853 and 1854, and the note in Heubner, p. 304.) Tholuck, without sufficient reason, disputes the reference of the passage to false Messiahs, and refers it only to the false prophets, who came in their own name, and always found more followers than the true. Yet all appealed to a divine commission. Those who came in their own name, did so in opposition to the true Messiah; and this method is always pseudo-Christian and anti-Christian at the same time. Meanwhile the false prophets of the ancient time were but fore-runners of the pseudo-Messianic manifestations of the New Testament age; and such future manifestations the Lord evidently has in view.* **Him ye will receive.** Affinity of the ungodly mind, more explicitly declared in John xii. 43.

Ver. 44. **Who receive glory one from another.**—Not merely honor, but here again *δόξα*, with reference to the specific honor of Messiah: Messianic honors. Messianic dignities are both accorded and accepted in a hierarchical system from human, sinful motives, ambition, favor and the like. **And seek not the glory that cometh from the only God.**—Here evidently the *δόξα* is the divine pleasure, as conferring honor and glory on the believer; the *δόξα θεοῦ* of Paul in Rom. iii. 23. *From the only God, παρὰ τοῦ μόνου θεοῦ.* Grotius, De Wette [E. V., Godet]: From God only; making the adjective rather adverbial. Meyer and Tholuck [Alford], on the contrary, take *μόνος* after the analogy of John xvii. 3: *'Ο μόνος ἀληθινὸς θεός*; 1 Tim. vi. 15: *'Ο μόνος δυνάστης.* It was the deepest reproach to Jews, who gloried in the worship of the one God, that they recognized so various, and even human, sources of the *δόξα*, as really to be *polytheistic* in their conduct. These creature lights, in which the lustre is not recognized as radiance from the centre of light and honor in the only God, but which are made by men of men,—these form a disguised and subtle polytheism, a heathenism within a Judaistic hierarchical system.

Ver. 45. **Do not think that I shall accuse you.**—[Christ's office is not to accuse, but to judge.] Referring, no doubt, to the accusations which they brought against Him and the human trial upon which they put Him. Before their court He has assumed more and more the mien of a majestic judge. He has finally represented them as contradicting the testimony of God, as anti-Christs, pagans. They are disarmed by the authority and power of His words, and discharge Him. Now, so far as He is concerned, He proposes to discharge them. He will not accuse them to the Father, but another, says He, will accuse you, **even Moses, in whom ye hope** [*ἠλπίκατε*, have set your hope, comp. 2 Cor. i. 10]. This is the last, the mightest stroke.† That very Moses on whom they set their hope, will accuse them, and put their hope to shame. Not exactly the Holy Scriptures (Tholuck), but Moses himself, in his spirit, as the representative of the legal basis of the Holy Scriptures. If they rightly searched the Scriptures, they would find Christ and only Christ in the Old Testament, even in the books of Moses alone; but they find Moses in them, and only Moses, only law even in the prophets, and on this omnipresent Moses, whose all the Scriptures are in their view (see ver. 47), that is, on the legal element of the Holy Scriptures, they placed their self-righteous confidence. Through Moses they sought to be heirs of the Messianic kingdom; Christ Himself was to appear as a second Moses (*nova lex*). But Moses, says He, is the very one who will accuse you. Not so much that the law pronounces the curse on those who deal in the works of the law, as that Moses, both in single passages (Deut. xviii. 15), and in his whole law, especially in the types, wrote of Christ. Bengel: *Scripsit nusquam non.* [Comp. further remarks sub. ver. 46.—P. S.] Where and how accuse? In all judgments of conscience as well as in all the historical judgments of Israel the real Moses, the spirit of the law, accuses them for their unbelief even unto the end of the world. Not, therefore, for unbelief of particular prophecies, "as even De Wette thinks, but because the religious spirit of his law deposes so strong a testimony in favor of Him who, by His whole appearance, proves that He is the fulfilment of it." Tholuck.

Ver. 46. **For if ye believed Moses, ye would believe me.**—*True law-Jews are true faith-Jews.* The same applies to Christianity. [Every true Jew who follows the teachings of the Old Testament revelation, becomes naturally a Christian, as was the case with the apostles and primitive disciples, but every bad Jew instinctively rejects the gospel, because the Old and New Testaments are the revelation of one and the same God, the Old being a preparation for the New, the New the fulfilment of the Old. "*Novum Testamentum in Vetere latet, Vetus Test. in Novo patet.*" The agreement of Moses and Christ is also the underlying thought of the whole sermon on the Mount; Matthew and John are the disciples of one Master.—P. S.]

[**For of me he wrote,** *περὶ γὰρ ἐμοῦ*—emphatically placed first—*ἐκεῖνος ἔγραψεν.*—Moses wrote of Christ, as the seed of the woman that shall bruise the serpent's head (Gen. iii.), as the seed of Abraham by which all the nations of the earth shall be blessed (Gen. xii. ff.), as the Shiloh unto whom shall be the gathering of the people (Gen. xlix.), as the Star out of Jacob, and the Sceptre that shall rise out of Israel (Numb. xxiv. 17), as the great Prophet whom God will raise up, and unto whom the Jews should hearken (Deut. xviii.). Moreover, the moral law of Moses, by revealing the holy will of God and setting up a standard of human righteousness in conformity with that will, awakens a knowledge of sin and guilt (Rom. iii. 20; vii. 7), and thus serves as a school-master to bring us to Christ (Gal. iii. 24). Finally, the ritual law and all the ceremonies of Mosaic worship were typical of the Christian dispensation

*[Some of the fathers, and recently also Alford, refer the passage to the anti-Christ who shall appear in the latter days, 2 Thess. ii. 8-12.—P. S.]

†[Bengel: "*Maxime aptus ad conclusionem.*" Godet: "*Sa parole prend une forme dramatique et saisissante. . . . Il se trouvera que celui dont vous me reproche de transgresser la loi, témoignera pour moi, tandis qu' il s'élevera contre vous, ses zélateurs. Quel renversement de toutes leurs notions.*"—P. S.]

(Col. ii. 17), as the healing serpent in the wilderness pointed to Christ on the cross (Numb. xxi. 9; John iii. 14). This is a most important testimony, from the unerring mouth of Christ, to the Messianic character and aim of the whole Mosaic dispensation, and to the Mosaic origin of the Pentateuch. Comp. Luke xxiv. 44; Rom. x. 5.—P. S.]

Ver. 47. **But if ye believe not his writings, how shall you believe my words?**—Twofold antithesis [Moses and Christ—Moses' writings and Christ's words]. First, as the stronger, ἐκείνου—ἐμοῖς. Not as if Moses were more credible than Christ. But he is easier for beginners, and only through him do men get to Christ. This antithesis does not, as Meyer thinks, exclude the second. The Sanhedrists, like the Rabbins in general, officially concerned themselves simply with the writings; the words of Christ they heard only by the way.* They had sought to prosecute Him according to the Sabbath law of Moses; He declares that they are apostates from Moses. But as they postpone their judgment, He postpones His.

[The discourse ends, as Meyer says, with a question "of hopelessness," I prefer to say, holy sadness. Yet after all there is implied in this question a tender appeal of that infinite love which would again and again gather the children of Jerusalem together, even as a hen gathereth her chickens under her wings, though they would not (Matth. xxiii. 37).—This whole discourse is one of the most remarkable in the New Testament. Nowhere else does Christ so fully explain His relation to His Father. It is not metaphysical, but the simple expression of His filial consciousness. With the utmost naturalness and almost childlike simplicity He utters the sublimest truths concerning His official dependence on, and essential oneness with, the Father.° This relation the Nicene Creed has briefly and clearly expressed by calling Christ "Light of Light, God of God, very God of very God." What can we mortals do but reverently listen to these astounding disclosures of the mysterious union of the Saviour of the world with the infinite God! And how terrific is the force of the argument against the blind and dead leaders of the Jews, especially when, at the close, He pursues them to their own territory and takes away the very foundation from under their feet by calling the grand figure of their liberator and lawgiver in whom they placed their hope, from the grave, and changing their pretended advocate into their accuser! The whole discourse is so characteristic, grand, pointed and telling, that the idea of an invention is utterly preposterous. Even Strauss and Renan dare not deny its essential genuineness, though they insist upon its Johannean coloring. "*Le thème*," says Renan of the Johannean discourses in general (*Vie de Jésus*), "*peut n'être pas sans quelque authenticité; mais dans l'exécution, la fantaisie de l'artiste se donne pleine carrière.*" But John first became conformed in his mind to Christ before he conformed Christ to his mode of thought and speech, so that his theology is a faithful reflection of the theology of Christ. It would take no less than another superhuman Jesus to invent such a Jesus as the one exhibited by this plain fisherman of Galilee. The historical reality is the only sensible solution of the problem.—P. S.]

* [Alford insists on the antithesis of γράμματα and ῥήματα. "Men give greater weight to what is written and published than to mere words of mouth;—and ye in particular give greater honor to Moses than Me: if then ye believe not what he has written, which comes down to you hallowed by the reverence of ages,—how can you believe the words uttered by Me, to whom you are hostile? But this is not all: Moses leads to Christ; if then ye reject the *means*, how shall ye reach the end?"—P. S.]

DOCTRINAL AND ETHICAL.

1. The advancing *opposition* of the darkness to the light of the world, in its most diverse forms.

2. Christ, the *quickening life*, is the central thought of chapters iv.–vii. In the fourth chapter He presents Himself as the refreshment of life, the fountain of peace; in the fifth, as the fountain of healing, the healing quickener of the sick and the dead, even to resurrection; in the sixth, as the sustaining and nourishing bread of life; in the seventh, as the hidden, mysterious spirit-life, whence the fresh fountain-life of the spirit flows. After this the idea of *light* comes forward. In the eighth chapter Christ is the preserving, enlightening light, the day of the world; in the ninth, the awakening, quickening light, the light-star of the world, by which the blind receive sight, and those who profess to see, become blind; in the tenth, the shepherd through life to death; in the eleventh, the resurrection from death to eternal life; in the twelfth, the transfigurer of death into the seed of full and glorious life.

3. As the fourth chapter presents Christianity in contrast with sacred antiquities (Jacob's well), and with the places and services of the temple in the ancient time, so this fifth chapter unfolds it in contrast with ancient miraculous localities and curative resorts.

4. The very first public attendance of Christ at a feast had been followed by a hostile demonstration of the Jews; and this second one brings them already to the commencement of capital process against Him. This *contrast* of the *feasts of the Jews* and the *feasts of Christ* runs through the whole fourth Gospel; the former preparing death for Christ, the latter quickening the world with miracles of life. A contrast which reminds us of *autos-da fe*,* Maundy Thursday=bulls, and Saint Bartholomew nights on the one hand, and the true evangelical festivals of the faith on the other.

5. The man healed at the pool of Bethesda is not only parallel, but also in some respects a contrast, to the man healed at the pool of Siloam. The most important point of contrast is the indolence and sleepiness of the one and the brightness and energy of the other. But just this makes the former case the more suitable type of the general resurrection. The re-animating principle in Christ raises up not only living believers, but also in the last day the most lifeless unbelievers; though a whole age intervene between the first and the general resurrection.

6. The *fountain of Bethesda* an example of

* [The inquisitorial "acts of the faith," it will be remembered, were usually celebrated on some church festival.—E. D. Y.]

earthly sources of healing, a symbol of the divine source; the pool and hall of Bethesda an example of watering-places, hospitals, *etc.*, a symbol of the theocracy; the hall of Bethesda, visited by Christ, a representative of the church, the dispensary of divine grace in the sinful world.

7. *The Sabbath of the Jews and the Sabbath of Christ.* Christ here gives the deepest warrant for the higher Sabbath work, in opposition to a dead Sabbath rest. God's creating, and God's working in His creation, are different things. And the most important works of God in His Sabbath are His festal works of love for the restoration of man. So with this festal Sabbath work of Christ. The Sabbath of the Christian should follow the example. [Comp. Exeg. Notes on ver. 16.—P. S.]

8. The *two accusations* brought against Jesus before the Jewish court mark the two positive fundamental motives of the persecution of Him, which come out stronger and stronger in the progress of the Gospel history. The first is His offending against their statutes, particularly their Sabbath laws; the second is His manifestation of Himself (as Son of God), offending against their deistic theology. But we must not overlook two corresponding negative motives: (1) Their anger at His refusal to embrace and yield Himself to their chiliasm; (2) their envy at His greatness and consideration with the people. These different motives may be reduced to the single motive of the offence He gave their hierarchical malignity. This offence was (1) objective; a statutory offence, both (*a*) ecclesiastical, with reference to the Sabbath, and (*b*) theological, with reference to the doctrine of the unity of God. The offence was (2) subjective; an official offence, in that (*a*) He does not fall in with their ideas, is not a Messiah to suit their worldly ambition, and (*b*) He eclipses them before the people, rousing their envy. The opposition may also be expressed in Johannean terms, as the hostility of darkness to light (of lie to truth), of hatred to love, of death to life.

9. The *self-offence* of Christ before the judgment-seat, in respect to its wisdom, which is especially striking in the interchange of the third and first persons, is a master-stroke, eclipsing all human rhetoric. In respect to its matter, it is the divine depth of the doctrine of the organic nature and process of the resurrection, from its origin in Christ, through the awakening and quickening wrought by Him, to the full regeneration of the world; the organic difference and contrast also between the first resurrection and the second being indicated thereby. In respect of its issue or effect, the discourse marks a victory, after which the Jewish court drops the action, but does not abandon it.

10. The *discourse* of Christ speaks of the Father in His deepest nature and work: as being life in and of Himself and giving life; of the nature of the Son as corresponding to the essence and operation of the Father; and of this in particular, as bringing with it a corresponding moral administration. The discourse then exalts the economy of the Son as an administration of saving quickening (a time of grace), which suspends the old judgment, and presents the new judgment of the Son purely as a condemnation to be left unquickened by the Son. It presents the healing work of Christ as a basis and presage of the awakening of the dead, the spiritual awaking as the introduction and beginning of the bodily; and it exhibits this last in its double aspect of the consummation of life and the consummation of damnation. It declares the final purpose of the judgment: The glorifying of the Son for the glory of the Father. Next it treats of the great testimonies which accredit this mission of Christ: The testimony of a historical office (John); the testimony of the Father in miracles, and in the holy Scriptures; and in particular the testimony of Moses. Finally it holds up the contempt of these witnesses as punishing itself by preventing the man, misled and obstructed by the false witnesses of human ambition, from perceiving the witness of the Holy Ghost, and so deprives him of all witnesses of power and blessing, and plunges him through unbelief into condemnation. "The re-awakening of the dead of Israel in the time of the Messiah had been predicted by Isaiah (xxvi. 19) and Ezekiel (xxxvii.); and the general resurrection of the righteous and the wicked, by Daniel (xii. 2), pointing, in immediate connection, to the Messiah intrusted with the judgment of the world; comp. Ps. ii. 8; cx. 6; Is. xlv. 23, 24; lxvi. 23, 24; Joel iii. 1; Mal. iii. 2. But as the kingdom of God among Israel had to begin inwardly, before it could appear in outward glory, so the resurrection of the dead and the judgment; he alone who is spiritually quickened has the pledge, and the beginning, of the bodily resurrection to life; by faith or by unbelief each one already pronounces his own sentence, chap. iii. 18. In token of the spiritual and the future bodily resurrection, and of the unity of the two, Jesus at that time raised dead persons to life," *etc.* Gerlach.

11. The *quickening work of Christ.* He who would hinder Him in it, passes judgment, because he closes the day and the work of grace. But Christ does not suffer Himself to be hindered, because the Father, with His quickening power, gives Him commission to perfect His quickening. This judging is the reverse side (the medium) of His quickening. In proportion as He cannot and does not quicken, condemnation exists; either *still* exists, or exists *anew*.

12. The *different witnesses of Christ.* If the testimony of the Baptist here seems subordinate to the testimony of the Scriptures, it is not his testimony as such, but only his testimony by itself, in distinction from the entire testimony of the Old Testament, of which his is the completion.

13. Christ, in picturing the Jews thinking they have eternal life in their sacred books, characterizes every *false estimate of ecclesiasticism* or the *objective church.* The general perversion of this spirit is objectivism, a person's alienating his religion from himself, and thinking he has his life as an external treasure in ecclesiastical objects and means; whether the mere outside, the letter, of the holy Scriptures, or the mere elements of the sacraments, or the mere official processes of church discipline. The essence of this objectivistic churchliness is lifelessness, unspiritual-

ness, residing first in the spiritually dead persons, and thence making the objects dead likewise. The objectivism of the Jews had a double form. They thought they had their life in the Scriptures, and in their traditional theology, or the traditions of the elders. Christ intimates the second point, but gives the prominence to the first, because the Scriptures have, besides the letter that kills, a spirit that quickens; and because this spirit is their true life, in which they testify of Christ. The same sort of exaltation of the legal canonical authority of the Bible over the living revelation of God in voices and visions, and especially in Christ, shows itself in various ways even in the Protestant theology. The true ground, however, is not the opposite extreme of a subjectivism which loosens off from the Scriptures, but a subjective spirit of faith which inwardly unites itself with the testimony of holy Writ.

14. The crown of the address of Jesus in this judicial hearing is the gradually developed idea of the essential judgment, in which Moses himself, to whom Christ's accusers appeal against Him, will appear against them as their accuser.

HOMILETICAL AND PRACTICAL.

In proportion as Christ, the Light and the Life, attracts kindred, susceptible souls, He repels the haters of light.—The awaking and the working of the powers of darkness in Israel against the Lord.—Christ's act of healing in the little Bethesda (house of grace), and His discourse of the great Bethesda of the Father and the Son.—The reflection of the legalistic spirit of the Jews in the capital action which they brought against Christ: 1. They are scandalized by His entrance into the emblematical "house of mercy" with a substantial work of mercy (eclipsing the medicinal bubbling and the angel). 2. They charge against Him His festal work of charity on the Sabbath as a labor deserving of death, and as a bad example. 3. On the feast of Purim, the feast of the reversed lot (which gave safety to the Jews and destruction to the heathen, reversing what seemed to be decreed), they made a sinner's lot of new life the lot of death for him. 4. His vindication, appealing to the example of his Father, they turn into a second and a heavier accusation. 5. When they cannot condemn Him, and are speechless, they turn their nonsuit into a reservation to persecute Him the more steadily. —On the feast-day, which the people are keeping with merry-making, Christ visits the hospital. —The most helpless of all attracts most Christ's attention.—As the hand of justice touches the highest haughtiness, the hand of mercy touches the lowest misery.—The sufferer says: "I have no man;" and the Saviour stands by him.—The pool of Bethesda a type of favored localities in a religious community in which the highest miraculous aid has not yet appeared. The miraculous aid is (1) enigmatical (an angel troubling the water); (2) occasional (at a certain season); (3) extremely limited (to the one who steps in first;) (4) to many unavailable (the impotent). — Irresolution and impotence, the worst part of any malady (in melancholy, hypochondria, *etc.*): 1. It is itself disease. 2. It aggravates the other disease. 3. It hinders the cure. 4. It can make the cure uncertain again ("lest a worse thing come unto thee").—Christ takes even the honest wish of a man of faint faith, for faith.—As here Christ's word of power puts an impotent man upon his feet, so in the general resurrection it sets the universe upon its feet.—The cripple at the pool of Bethesda, compared with the blind man sent to the fountain of Siloam, John ix.—"He that made me whole, the same said unto me, Take up thy bed, and walk." The feeblest confesssion, still a confession.—If it is lawful to be made whole, it must be lawful to go home with the bed.—The first word of Christ to the impotent man in Bethesda, and His second word to the healed man in the temple. — Christ's self-defence (see Doctrinal Thoughts, No. 9).—"My Father worketh." The difference between a festal, divine working and an unlawful, human laboring.—The working of God in the medicinal spring (or well of health) an emblem of the saving operation of God in general. 1. In its forms: *a.* The saving operation of the Father in the kingdom of nature. *b.* The saving operation of Christ in the kingdom of grace. 2. In its stages: *a.* Christ's miraculous healing and raising of dead in general. *b.* The spiritual awakening and the organic unfolding of salvation in the New Testament dispensation. *c.* The finished work of salvation in the general resurrection.—The Lord's highest justification made a capital charge against Him.—Ver. 19: Christianity the second, the spiritualized and glorified creation. 1. Christ the image of the Father; 2. His word the spirit of the creation; 3. His work the copy of the works of the Father.—The Son's inability to do any thing of Himself, a paraphrase of His omnipotence to do whatever the Father does. — The Father's speaking and showing to the Son, an out-flowing of His love. — The Son's hearing and doing, a proving of His reciprocal love.—The perfect harmony of Christ's moral conduct with His essential nature.—"And He will show Him greater works than these." The works of healing a fore-shadowing of the miracle of the resurrection.—The Son unrestricted in His quickening work ("quickeneth whom He will"); or, Christ's ministration of grace amenable to no limitations: 1. To no abridgment of its day. 2. To no contraction of its field. 3. To no diminution of its wonders.—Every opposition to the saving work of Christ a condemnatory judgment, which would make (call in, administer) the judgment day itself.—The Father has committed judgment to the Son; implying: *a.* Every condemnation of the old dispensation, before the Son judged, is removed (it is a day of grace). *b.* The Son's judging is but the consequence and the reverse of His quickening (the manifestation of the self-condemnation of unbelievers).—The design of the merciful judgeship of Christ: 1. To glorify the Son above all (Phil. ii. 6-11). 2. To glorify the Father through the Son.—Only as men honor Christ as Son, do they honor God as Father.—Only in personal homage to Christ does the brightness of the personal divine Being disclose itself to man (the personal essence is known through the essentially personal manifestation).—Verse 24: "Verily, verily, *etc.* The sure way to the highest salvation for all. 1. The way: *a.* Hearing Christ's word. *b.* Believing God in His sending of Christ. 2. The salvation: *a. Having* everlasting life. *b.* Coming not into condemnation. *c.* Being passed from death unto life.—The utmost passiveness of submission to God through Christ, the highest action.—All in the foundation of the Christian life has been already done, when any decisive beginning is made in the manifestation.—"The hour is coming, and now is." All the future is included in the present of Christianity. This is true (1) in the history of Christ, (2) in the history of the church, (3) in the individual Christian.—In one hour of the eternal life all hours of the eternal future lie in germ.—The spiritual resurrection as the ground-work and the genesis of the universal resurrection.—All *must* hear the voice of Christ; but only those who hear aright, shall live.—The resurrection of all bodies must follow as by natural necessity from the operations of Christ, but the resurrection of hearts depends on voluntary faith, which Christ does not force.—Christ the dispenser of life, in the special sense, as Son of God.—Christ the judge, in the special sense, as Son of Man. And yet at once life-giver and judge in both relations.—Christ's power to have life in Himself (see above).—"Marvel not" (comp. ver. 20); or, the most extraordinary manifestations of Christianity yet impend.—"The hour is coming in which all." It is coming, (1) as the hour of the great trumpet which all must hear; (2) as the judgment-day of pure light, in which all must appear; (3) as the millennial summer, which brings everything to maturity.—Those who come forth on the day of the resurrection: 1. What all have in common (all come forth under the operation of Christ's power; all must hear the voice of His power, follow its call). 2. How they differ and separate (in their relations to the operation of the grace and Spirit of Christ). *a.* The result of the manifestation: Some have done good according to the principles of the kingdom of God, have sealed their faith by works of love; the others have done evil, have sealed their unbelief in obduracy. *b.* The reward: The two classes come severally to the resurrection, the complete development, of the sentence which is in them.—Verse 30: The judgment of Christ, a judgment of the Father also.—The witnesses who accredit the Lord: 1. He does not begin with His own testimony (but leaves this to follow other testimonies, without which it could not have its full weight). 2. He does not rest upon the official testimony of John, which ought to have satisfied the Jews, but could not satisfy Him (and so to this day He rests not on the official testimony of the church, though to men this must suffice for the beginning). 3. But He appeals to the testimony of the Father in His works (miracles of power) and in the Holy Scriptures (miracles of prophetic knowledge).—Verse 32: Christ sure of His divine credentials.—The misconduct of the Jews towards John the Baptist a presage of their misconduct towards the Lord: 1. Of John's solemn mission (preaching repentance) they made a pleasant entertainment; and, conversely, of the glad tidings of Christ they made a tragic offence. 2. They separated John's light from his fire, that they might dance with the visionary hope of an outwardly glorious Messianic kingdom; and in Christ they despised the light, that they might harden themselves in the fire of His love. 3. In the fickleness of their enthusiasm they soon gave John over to the caprice of Herod; and with the same fickleness they delivered the Lord to Pilate.—The misconduct of the spirit of the world and the spirit of the age towards the messengers of God.—Christ still attested, and more and more attested, by the words of Scripture and tokens of life.—Marks of dead and false faith: 1. It adheres to the means of revelation (Scriptures, tradition, church, sacraments, ministry), and has no sense for their living origin, the personal God. 2. It adheres to the forms of those means, and has no heart to receive the personal centre of them, Jesus Christ, with His word. 3. It adheres to the particulars of the forms (the letters of the Scripture), and imagines it has *eternal* life in them, while it is full of antipathy to Christ and the life itself. Or: 1. It has a Scripture and tradition of revelation, and no quickening power of it in the Spirit of the living God. 2. It has holy Scriptures, but no holy Scripture, the centre of which is the living Christ. 3. It thinks it has eternal life outside of itself in the means of grace, while it bears enmity to the life of the spirit in Christ, the very life itself.—This dead faith alienates itself more and more (1) from the Father, the source of revelation, (2) from the living Christ, the word of revelation, (3) from the life of the Spirit, the life of revelation.—Men cannot have eternal life merely outside of themselves, in external church privileges.—Even the Holy Scripture should not be exalted, in a legal spirit, above the living Christ.—A man's study of Scripture must be vivified by the study of his own heart.—Faith, when merely external, may turn itself upon any means of revelation: (1) Turn from personal life to things, (2) from the inner life, the spirit, to the outer form, (3) from the centre of the life to the details of its exhibition.—The moral causes of dead faith: 1. Want of sense for the divine spiritual glory of Christ, for the purity of His life and the revelation of the Father in Him. 2. Morbid sensitiveness to the false spiritual glory (honor) of men. 3. Ambitious desire to take part in the mutual glorification of men; or, the want of that simplicity which constitute the true responsiveness to God through Christ, arising from the ambition of the heart, which is a false responsiveness to the honor of men.—Aversion to God and propensity to deify the world and self, the fundamental characteristic of sin and of heathenism, and the root of the perversion of the (theocratic and ecclesiastical) disposition to believe.—The condemnation of the false, legalistic faith: 1. It misses salvation in Christ, and falls over to false prophets and false Messiahs, and to anti-Christ at last. 2. It loses the honor which is from God, and comes to shame before the world itself. 3. It finds its heaviest condemnation in the law of the Lord itself, which it hypocritically professes to honor.—Unbelief, the soul of a dead and empty legalistic faith.—The spirit of legalism is much more completely condemned and overthrown by its own illegality (its lawlessness) than by Christianity.—Before the eyes of the world this spirit is put to confusion by the law, especially by the fundamental laws of humanity as laid down by Moses, far in advance of the judgment-day.—Christ in His first judicial appearance, and in His last.

STARKE: *Nova Bibl. Tub.:* The example of Christ in attending public worship at every opportunity, even though He had no need of it.—*Ibid.:* What is the world but a hospital, the abode of the bodily and spiritually sick?—ZEISIUS: The world a very Bethesda.—MAJUS: Hospitals, asylums for poor and sick are most justly established and maintained.—*Ibid.:* From the wells of charity flow many healing waters.—The movings of the heavenly water of healing are not under our control, yet that we may expect and wait for them is itself a mercy.—ZEISIUS: Look into the mirror of this most wretched and patient sufferer, thou who art so discontented and impatient under sufferings hardly as many days, or even hours, protracted, as this man's infirmity was years!—HEDINGER: Patience, the best thing.—Tedious infirmities, veritable trials of patience.—QUESNEL: The more we are deprived of human help, the better right we have to hope for the help of God.—MAJUS: Jesus looks graciously upon those at whom the proud world casts not a glance. Follow His example.—To visit and help the sick, a large part of love.—By questions God encourages our faith.—Though men cannot or will not help, yet God stands by with sure mercy.—*Nova Bibl. Tub.:* When Jesus speaks, it is done, *etc.* Ps. xxxiii. 9.—ZEISIUS: Help comes at last.—HEDINGER: Hypocrites strain out gnats.—QUESNEL: A servant of Christ, upon a noble achievement, must not wait for the applause of the people, but withdraw himself.—CANSTEIN: All temporal benefits should promote our conversion.—HEDINGER: If God take one cross off thee, be not sure another and greater may not be laid upon thee.—We must never take holiday from good works.—CANSTEIN: The honor which the children of God have from God their Father, and from their sonship, is always an eye-sore to the ungodly.—If Jesus, our Head, is all life, we His faithful members are perfectly certain also to live forever.—MAJUS: God testifies in us and of us by the divine works which He performs in and through us.—On ver. 35. ZEISIUS: As a burning light, while lighting others, consumes itself, so Christian teachers should sacrifice themselves in the service of God and their fellowmen.—How rarely are light and heat found together!—QUESNEL: When a light arises in the church, it immediately gives forth a brightness in which people are glad; but this lasts not long.—Ver. 38: And His word ye have, indeed, in books, in schools, and on lips, and outwardly hold it high, but have it not abiding in you.—Ver. 39: Even from the Old Testament Christ may be known.—He who departs from Christ, flies before life.—Teachers must seek not their own honor, but the salvation of men.—He who does not obediently receive the word of God, has no love for God.—MAJUS: It is by no means a mark of true doctrine, that it and its teachers are eagerly received by the multitude.—Ambition not only corrupts the desires, but also as it were, bewitches the judgment and sensibilities, so that in religion the man never yields to, but always resists, the light and truth.—Ambition is with many the cause of their hardening themselves against the preaching of the gospel.—A Christian, after the example of Christ, must not accuse the enemies of the truth to God, but pray for them.—QUESNEL: Christ the key of the Old Testament.—The cavillers are mightily refuted on their own ground.—The appeal of the Son of God Himself to the written word should quicken in us the deepest reverence for the Holy Scriptures.

BRAUNE: If God rested as the Jews would have men rest on the Sabbath, no sun would rise, no flower would bloom.

HEUBNER: Jesus never (as a rule) let a feast go by without visiting Jerusalem: (1) To fulfil the duty of an Israelite; (2) to use the opportunity of preaching the word not only before the inhabitants of Jerusalem, but before all Israel, and before strangers; (3) to testify the truth there to the leaders at a time when He might appear before them without their venturing to lay hands on Him. — Evangelical clergymen also should use the high Christian festivals with conscientious fidelity, (1) because it may be expected that the Spirit of God will then be specially active; (2) because souls are then in more solemn mood than at other times; (3) because at least many will be present then, who at other times are not. At such festivals it is disclosed, of what manner of spirit a preacher is.*—Bethesda, *i. e.*, asylum, hospital, an emblem of the Christian church (primarily an emblem of the theocratic church of the law).—Jesus did not avoid such sad sights, the retreats of the diseased. In fact He was the physician.—There is a true waiting for divine help: waiting for that which God alone can do; but there is also a false waiting: waiting for that which we ourselves should do, or for the removal of that which should not hinder us at all.—Ver. 4: This and the whole passage would be a grand text for sermons at watering places, where it is rarely heard.—*The angel.* Even nature has invisible spiritual forces for her own secret spring. All proceeds from the spiritual world.—The judgment of a great physician, that a man cannot be a thorough theologian unless he also understand nature, nor a thorough naturalist unless he be also a theologian.—The healing powers in the kingdom of nature, emblems of the healing powers in the kingdom of grace.—*Troubled the water.* The first operation of the Spirit of God upon the soul seems even to be a troubling, disquieting; all is stirred up in the soul, the bottom of the heart is shaken up; but by that very means new energies are excited, life is quickened, and clearness comes.—*Whosoever then first, etc.* Watch the time!—*Wilt thou?* Jesus would have our earnest will.—*Rise!* The word of Jesus has power; what He commands, He gives.—True and false observance of the Sabbath.—God's working is eternal: He is the living God, He is the absolute life, and this life is love. This flows forth without interruption forever.—The thought of the living God, the highest stimulus to work.—Unbelievers will *marvel* with terror and to

*[This observation is truly German, and scarcely applicable to America where church festivals are little esteemed, while the weekly Lord's Day is the more strictly observed. Of late, however, the observance of Christmas, Good Friday, and Easter has made much progress.—P. S.]

condemnations, believers with joy and triumph in their glory.—Unwillingness in spite of the most pressing invitations is the cause of the misery of men.—(Luther:) In more secular callings, positions, and talents, it is less pernicious to be proud and ambitious, but in theology to be arrogant, haughty, and ambitious, does the utmost mischief.

BESSER: (Brenz:) Wilt thou be made whole? So the Lord asks us in all our troubles, whether we would be delivered.—(Chemnitz:) The Lord speaks to the Jews exactly as if I should say to the Papists: It is not I, but the very fathers whose authority you allege in support of your superstition, that will accuse you of ungodliness. Or as if we should say to the pope: It is not we that accuse or condemn thee, but Christ Himself whose vicar thou callest thyself, Peter whose successor thou claimest to be, Paul whose sword thou pretendest to carry; these are they that accuse thee. (And Mary as surely impeaches mariolatry, as every true saint the distribution of the honor of Christ among the saints.)

SCHLEIERMACHER: How could it have been that so many refused to accept the Redeemer? There is *unbelief* on the one hand, *irresolution* on the other, and the two, in their innermost and deepest root, are one and the same. If man can come to a firm resolution to forsake the earthly and strive for the heavenly, the eye of the Spirit will soon open in him, enabling him to seek and to find the true fountain of healing whence eternal life proceeds.—We have life not in ourselves, but from Him and through Him.

[SCHAFF: Ver. 1. Christ went up to Jerusalem at a feast: 1. Because it was a divine ordinance, and to teach us to attend religious assemblies (Heb. x. 25); 2. Because it was an opportunity for doing good. (From HENRY.)—When Christ came to Jerusalem, He visited not the palaces, but the hospitals, for He came to save the sick and wounded. (The same.)—Vers. 2-4. Nature has provided remedies, men must provide hospitals.—How many are the afflictions in this world, how full of complaints, and what a multitude of impotent folks! (The same.)—The earth is a great Bethesda. (SCOTT.)—The fathers, and the high Anglican, WORDSWORTH, regard the healing pool of Bethesda stirred by an angel, as a figure of baptismal water to which all mankind is invited, and whose virtue is never exhausted. But Christ healed the cripple simply by His word, ver. 8.—MATTHEW HENRY calls Bethesda a type of Christ, who is the *fountain opened.*—ALBERT BARNES indulges in remarks against the frivolous amusements of modern watering places, where more than anywhere else men should be grateful for the goodness of God.—Ver. 8. *Rise, take up thy bed and walk.* Christ first gives, and then commands, He imparts the strength to do His will. Augustine: "Give what Thou commandest, and command what Thou wilt." (*Da quod jubes, et jube quod vis. Conf.* x. 29. This sentence was especially offensive to Pelagius, as it was directly opposed to his view of the inherent moral ability of man.)—Ver. 9. The day of rest was chosen by Christ as the fittest season for Divine acts of mercy. Thus He fulfilled the law and showed His oneness with the Father. God rested on that day from all His works of creation; but on that Day of rest He specially works in doing acts of mercy to the souls of His creatures in public worship. (WORDSWORTH.)—Ver 14. Jesus escapes from the crowd; but finds us and is found by us in the temple. God is seen in solitude. (WORDSWORTH.) — They who are healed from sickness should seek the sanctuary of God, and give Him thanks for His mercy. (ALBERT BARNES.)—*Sin no more, lest a worse thing, etc.* The doom of apostates is a worse thing than thirty-eight years' lameness. (HENRY.) — From the healing of the sick at Bethesda we learn 1. What misery sin has brought into the world; 2. How great is the mercy and compassion of Christ; 3. That recovery from sickness should impress us with the determination to sin no more, lest a worse thing happen to us. (RYLE.)—Ver. 17. What would become of the Sabbath unless God worked on the Sabbath? (BENGEL.)—Christ speaks here as God who makes His sun to rise and His rain to fall, and clothes the grass of the field on the seventh day as well as on the other six. (CHRYSOSTOM.)—The law of the Sabbath is a law of a Being who never rests from doing good. (THEOPHYLACT.)—The Jews, understanding the law of the Sabbath in a carnal sense, imagined that God was wearied by the labor of the creation, and was resting from fatigue. As He works always without labor, so Christ. (WORDSWORTH.)—Jesus did not deny the obligation of the Sabbath law, but explained its constitution. The solemnities of the Sabbath were and are necessary to restore the human spirit, distracted by the diversity of earthly affairs, to the oneness of the Divine Being, but Christ, who ever reposed in this unity, observed a perpetual Sabbath, like the Father, and no activity could distract Him. (OLSHAUSEN.)—Christ nowhere sets aside the obligation of the fourth commandment, but places it on the right foundation, and shows us that works of necessity and mercy are no breach of the commandment. The error and danger of the present age is the opposite of the Jews. The experience of eighteen centuries proves that vital religion cannot flourish without the Sabbath. (RYLE.)—Ver. 19. If the Son does the same things as the Father, and in the same manner, then let the Jew be silenced, the Christian believe, the heretic be convinced; the Son is equal with the Father. (AUGUSTINE.)—This is the strongest possible assertion of equality. If the Son does all that the Father does, then like Him, He must be almighty, omniscient, all-present and infinite in every perfection; in other words, He must be God. (BARNES.)—Ver. 21-29. That form of Man which was once judged will judge all men. He who once stood before the judge will sit as Judge of all. He who was once falsely condemned as guilty, will justly condemn the guilty. Christ will be seen by the good and the wicked; God by the good alone. (AUGUSTINE.) *All that are in the graves* (ver. 28), whether in costly sepulchres or with monuments of marble, or in lonely deserts, whether in the catacombs, or in the depths of the sea, whether their bodies have been embalmed, or burned to ashes and scattered to the winds of heaven, *all* must appear before the Judge "of tremendous majesty" for a final settlement of the accounts of this earthly life.—The immortality of the soul without faith in Christ, is only an immortality of misery.—Live always in view of the judgment to come, and prepare for it in time:

"*Quid sum miser tunc dicturus,*
Quem patronum rogaturus,
Quum vix justus sit securus.

Recordare, Jesu pie,
Quod sum causa tuæ viæ;
Ne me perdas illa die!" (From the *Dies Iræ.*)

Wretched man, what shall I plead,
Who for me will intercede,
When the righteous mercy need?

Recollect, good Lord, I pray,
I have caused Thy bitter way;
Don't forget me on that Day!

[Ver. 38–40. Different modes of searching the Scriptures, the one purely critical and heartless, mechanical, dwelling on the outside, confined to the letter, excluding the spirit, leading away from Christ; the other spiritual, experimental, penetrating to the marrow, leading to Christ. The former mode may be either hyper-orthodox and superstitious, as with the Pharisees and Rabbinical Jews, or rationalistic and skeptical, as with the Sadducees and many nominally Christian commentators. — The Old Testament an unbroken testimony to Christ. So He read it, so we ought to read it.—HENRY: "Christ is the treasure hid in the field of the Scriptures, the water in their wells."—ALFORD: "The command[?] to the Jews to search the Scriptures, applies even more strongly to Christians; who are yet, like them, in danger of idolizing a mere written book, believing that *in the Bible* they have eternal life, and missing the personal knowledge of Him of whom the Scriptures testify."—42. *I know you.* Christ knows men better than they know themselves, and than their neighbors and friends know them.—Ver. 44. Worldly ambition a great hindrance to faith. (HENRY.)—Ver. 46. Moses leads to Christ, the law is a school for the gospel (Gal. iii. 24).—]

II.

THE PASSOVER OF THE JEWS, AND THE MANNA OF THE JEWS. THE PASSOVER OF CHRIST, AND CHRIST THE MANNA FROM HEAVEN. MIRACLE OF FEEDING IN THE WILDERNESS. MIRACLE OF THE FLIGHT AND ESCAPE OVER THE SEA, WHEREIN CHRIST WITHDRAWS HIMSELF FROM THE CHILIASTIC ENTHUSIASM OF EARTHLY-MINDED ADMIRERS, AND HASTENS TO THE HELP OF HIS DISCIPLES. DECISIVE DECLARATION OF CHRIST. OFFENCE OF HIS GALILEAN ADMIRERS AND MANY OF HIS DISCIPLES AT HIS REFUSING TO GIVE THEM BREAD IN THE SENSE OF THEIR CHILIASM, AND PRESENTING HIMSELF IN HIS SPIRIT WITH HIS FLESH AND BLOOD AS THE BREAD OF LIFE.

CHAPTER VI. 1–65.

(Vers. 1–15, Pericope for Lætare Sunday. Parallels: Matth. xiv.; Mark vi. 14–56; Luke ix. 7–17; John vi. 1–21.)

1. THE MIRACULOUS FEEDING.

1 After these things Jesus went over the sea of Galilee, which is *the sea* of Tiberias.
2 And a great multitude followed him, because they saw[1] his [the][2] miracles which
3 he did on them that were diseased. And Jesus went up into a [the] mountain, and
4 there he sat with his disciples. And the passover, a [the] feast [ἡ ἑορτή] of the Jews,
5 was nigh. When Jesus then lifted up *his* [the] eyes, and saw a great company come
[coming] unto him, he saith unto Philip, Whence shall [are we to][3] we buy bread
6 that these may eat? And [But] this he said to prove him [proving him, πειράζων
7 αὐτόν]: for he himself knew what he would do [was going to do]. Philip answered
him, Two hundred penny-worth [denāries'-worth][4] of bread is not sufficient for them,
8 that every one of them [each one][5] may take a little. One of his disciples, Andrew,
9 Simon Peter's brother, saith unto him, There is a [one][6] lad here, which [who]
10 hath five barley-loaves, and two small fishes: but what are they among so many?
And [*omit* And][7] Jesus said, Make the men sit [lie] down. Now there was much
11 grass in the place. So the men sat [lay] down[8] in number about five thousand.
And Jesus [therefore][9] took the loaves: and when he had given thanks, he distributed (to the disciples, and the disciples)[10] to them that were set [were lying]
12 down; and likewise [in like manner] of the fishes, as much as they would [desired].
When they were filled, he said unto his disciples, Gather up the fragments that
13 remain [over], that nothing [may] be lost. Therefore [So] they gathered *them* together, and filled twelve baskets with the [*omit* the] fragments of the five barley-loaves, which remained over and above unto them that had eaten.

2. THE MIRACULOUS WITHDRAWAL OVER THE SEA.

14 Then those [the] men, when they had seen [seeing] the miracle [sign] that Jesus
[he][11] did, said, This is of a truth [truly, ἀληθῶς] that [the, ὁ] Prophet that should
15 come [is coming, or, is to come] into the world. When Jesus therefore perceived
[Jesus therefore, knowing] that they would come and take him by force, to make
him a king, he departed [withdrew] again[12] into a [the] mountain himself alone.
16 And [But] when even was now come [when evening came], his disciples went
17 down unto the sea [or, lake][13] and entered into a ship, and went [having entered
a ship, they were going] over the sea toward Capernaum. And it was now dark
18 [darkness had now come on], and Jesus was not [yet][14] come to them. And the
sea arose by reason of a great wind that blew [And as a strong wind was blowing,
19 the sea began to rise]. So when [When therefore] they had rowed [in vain] about
five and twenty or thirty furlongs, they see [behold] Jesus walking on the sea, and
20 drawing nigh unto the ship: and they were afraid. But he saith unto them, It is
I; be not afraid.
21 Then they willingly received him [they were willing to take him][15] into the ship:
and immediately the ship was at the land whither they went [were going].

3. DECISIVE DECLARATION OF CHRIST, AND OFFENCE OF MANY DISCIPLES.

22 The day following, when [*omit* when][16] the people which stood on the other side
of the sea saw[17] that there was none [no] other boat there, save that one [but one],
whereinto his disciples were entered [*omit* whereinto his disciples were entered],[18] and
that Jesus went not with his disciples into the boat, but that his disciples were gone
[went] away alone [so that they for a time supposed that Jesus was still somewhere in their
23 vicinity]; (Howbeit [And though the disciples had been seen to go away without Jesus]
there came other boats [among which they might have returned] from Tiberias nigh
unto [near] the place where they did eat [ate the] bread, after that [when] the
24 Lord had given thanks:)[19] When the people therefore saw [at last perceived] that
Jesus was not there, neither his disciples, they also[20] took shipping [they them-
selves[21] entered into the boats] and came to Capernaum, seeking for Jesus.
25 And when they had found him on the other side of the sea, they said unto him,
26 Rabbi, when camest thou hither? Jesus answered them and said, Verily, verily,
I say unto you, Ye seek me, not because ye saw the [*omit* the] miracles [signs], but
because ye did eat [ate] of the loaves, and were filled.
27 Labour not [Work not, Busy not yourselves] for the meat [food] which perisheth,
but for that meat [the food] which endureth unto everlasting life, which the Son of
man shall give [giveth][22] unto you: for him hath God the Father sealed [for him
hath the Father sealed, even God].
28 Then said they unto him, What shall we do, that we might [may] work the
29 works of God? Jesus answered and said unto them, This is the work of God, that
30 ye believe on him whom he hath [*omit* hath] sent. They said therefore unto him,
What sign showest [doest] thou then, that we may see, and believe thee? what
31 dost thou work? Our fathers did eat [ate] manna in the desert [wilderness]; as
it is written, 'He gave them bread from heaven to eat.' [Ps. lxxviii. 24.]
32 Then said Jesus unto them, Verily, verily, I say unto you, Moses gave you not
that [the] bread from heaven; but my Father giveth you the true bread from
33 heaven. For the bread of God is he [that] which cometh down from heaven, and
34 giveth life unto the world. Then said they unto him, Lord, evermore give us this
bread.
35 And[23] Jesus [therefore] said unto them, I am the bread of life: he that cometh
to me, shall never [not][24] hunger; and he that believeth on me, shall never thirst.
36 But I said unto you, That ye also [*omit* also] have [even] seen me,[25] and believe
37 not. All that the Father giveth me, shall [will] come to me; and him that cometh
38 to me, I will in no wise cast out. For I came down [have, or, am come down,
καταβέβηκα] from heaven, not to do mine own will, but the will of him that sent me.
39 And this is the Father's will which hath sent me [the will of him that sent me],[26]
that of all which he hath given me, I should lose nothing, but should raise it up

40 again at the last day. And [For][27] this is the will of him that sent me [the will
of my Father],[28] that every one which seeth [who looketh on] the Son, and be-
lieveth on [in] him, may [should] have everlasting life: and I will [and that I
should] raise him up at the last day.
41 The Jews then [therefore] murmured at him, because he said, I am the bread
42 which came down from heaven. And they said, Is not this Jesus, the son of Joseph,
whose father and mother we know? how is it then that he saith [how then doth
43 this man say],[29] I came [have come] down from heaven? Jesus therefore answered
44 and said unto them, Murmur not among yourselves. No man [no one] can come
to me, except the Father which hath sent [who sent] me draw him: and I will
45 [shall] raise him up at the last day. It is written in the prophets, 'And they shall
be all taught of God' (Isa. liv. 13). Every man therefore[30] that hath heard, and
hath learned of the Father [or, that heareth from the Father and learneth],[31]
46 cometh unto me. Not that any man [one] hath seen the Father, save he which is
47 of God [but he who is from God], he hath seen the Father. Verily, verily, I say
48 unto you, He that believeth on me[32] hath everlasting life. I am that [the] bread of
49 life. Your fathers did eat [ate the] manna in the wilderness, and are dead [died].
50 This is the bread which cometh down from heaven, that a man may eat thereof,
51 and not die. I am the living bread which came down from heaven: if any man
[one] eat of this [of my] bread,[33] he shall live forever: and the bread that I will give
is my flesh, which I will give[34] for the life of the world.—
52 The Jews therefore strove [contended] among themselves, saying, How can this
53 man give us *his* flesh to eat? Then Jesus said unto them, Verily, verily, I say
unto you, Except [Unless] ye eat the flesh of the Son of man, and drink his
54 blood, ye have no life in you. Whoso [He that] eateth my flesh, and drinketh
55 my blood, hath eternal life; and I will [shall] raise him up at the last day. For
my flesh is meat indeed [true food, *ἀληθὴς βρῶσις*],[35] and my blood is drink indeed
56 [true drink, *ἀληθὴς πόσις*]. He that eateth my flesh, and drinketh my blood,
57 dwelleth in me, and I in him. As the living Father hath [*omit* hath] sent me, and
I live by [by reason of, or, because of] the Father: [even] so he that eateth me, even
58 he shall live by [by reason of] me. This is that [the] bread which came down
from heaven: not as your [the] fathers did eat [ate] manna,[36] and are dead [died]:
he that eateth of this bread shall [will] live forever.
59 These things said he in the synagogue, as he taught [while teaching] in Caper-
naum.
60 Many therefore of his disciples [themselves], when they heard *this*, said, This is an
61 hard saying [This saying is hard];[37] who can hear it? When Jesus knew [But Je-
sus knowing] in himself that his disciples murmured at it [were murmuring at this],
62 he said unto them, Doth this offend you? *What* and if ye shall see [What then
if ye should behold] the Son of man ascend up [ascending, *ἀναβαίνοντα*] where he was
63 before? It is the Spirit that quickeneth [giveth life]; the flesh profiteth nothing:[38]
the words that I speak [have spoken, *λελάληκα*][39] unto you, *they* [*omit* they] are
64 spirit, and *they* [*omit* they] are life. But there are some of you that believe not.
For Jesus knew from the beginning who they were that believed not, and who
65 [it was, *τίς ἐστιν*, that] should betray him. And he said, Therefore said I unto
you [For this cause I have told you], that no man can come unto me except it
were [be] given unto him of my Father.

TEXTUAL AND GRAMMATICAL.

[1] Ver. 2.—[Two readings, but the same sense, *ἐθεώρουν* and *ἑώρων*. John uses *ὁρᾶν* only in the perfect. See Tischend. and the crit. Note of Meyer.—P. S.]

[2] Ver. 2.—*αὐτοῦ* is wanting in the principal MSS.

[3] Ver. 5.—The subjunctive aorist *ἀγοράσωμεν* [instead of the indicative future of the Recepta, *ἀγοράσομεν*] is established by A. B. D. [Cod. Sin.], *etc.*

[4] Ver. 7.—[*διακοσίων δηναρίων ἄρτοι.* *Denarius* is a Roman silver coin, at first equal to ten asses (hence the name), afterwards increased to sixteen, and equivalent to the Greek *drachm.* From the parable of the laborers in the vineyard it would seem that a denarius was then the ordinary pay for a day's labor, Matt. xx. 2. Its value was about equal to 7 English pence, or 15 American cents. The E. V. should have retained the Latin term, as the Evangelists did in Greek, or it should have rendered it *shilling*, rather than *penny*, which is too far below the value.—P. S.]

[5] Ver. 7.—[The rec. inserts *αὐτῶν* after *ἕκαστος*. Omitted by א. A. B. L., and the recent edd.—P. S.]

[6] Ver. 9.—The *ἕν* [of the Recepta: *a single lad*], omitted by B. D. L., might have more easily dropped out [after the preceding *παιδάρι—ον*] than crept in. It is wanting also in the Cod. Sin., thrown out by Tischend., bracketed by Lachm. and Alford.—P. S.]

[7] Ver. 10.—[The rec. inserts *δέ* after *εἶπεν*, without good authority.—P. S.]

[8] Ver. 10.—[The verbs *ἀναπίπτω* (f. *ἀναπεσοῦμαι*, aor. 2. *ἀνέπεσον*) and *ἀνάκειμαι* signify in the N. T. the ancient custom of *reclining* at table, upon the couch or triclinium, which was usually higher than the low table. The English equivalent is *to sit at table* or *at meat*. In this case they lay upon the ground. Mark and Luke describe the manner. See Mark vi. 39-40.—P. S.]

[9] Ver. 11.—[*οὖν*, *therefore*, is much better supported than *δέ* of the *text. rec.*, and is adopted by Lachm., Tischend., Alf. (Lange, in his version, follows here the *text. rec.*, but usually the readings of Lachm. Probably an oversight.)—P. S.]

[10] Ver. 11.—The words: "*the disciples, and the disciples to*" [*τοῖς μαθηταῖς, οἱ δέ μαθηταί*, text. rec.], are wanting in A. B. L. [and in the Cod. Sin.], *etc.*, and in almost all the Versions. They have been supplied from Matt. xiv. 19.

[11] Ver. 14.—[The text. rec. inserts *ὁ Ἰησοῦς* after *σημεῖον*,—beginning a church lesson, omitted by the critical editors.—P. S.]

[12] Ver. 15.—*Πάλιν* (omitted by Tischendorf), with reference to ver. 3, is sufficiently supported by A. B. D. [In the 8th crit. ed., Tischendorf has restored *πάλιν*, probably influenced by Cod. Sin. He also now reads *φεύγει* instead of the usual *ἀνεχώρησεν* with the remark that the latter is a correction from Matthew, and *φεύγει* was thrown out as not being consistent with the dignity of Jesus. *Certe φεύγει alienissimum est a correctore.*—P. S.]

[13] Ver. 16.—[Dr. Lange puts a period here, and several editions of the Greek a semicolon, instead of the comma of the Recepta.—E. D. Y.]

[14] Ver. 17.—The reading *οὔπω*, *not yet*, in B. D. L., *etc.*, and in the Versions and the fathers [and Cod. Sin., instead of the *οὐκ* of the *rec.*] adopted by Lachmann [Tischend., Alf.], is hardly an explanatory gloss (Meyer), but was more probably dropped on account of its difficulty. See the Exegesis.

[15] Ver. 21.—[Cod. Sin. reads *ἦλθον* for *ἤθελον*. See the Exeget. Notes.—P. S.]

[16] Ver. 22.—[This "when" is simply an anticipation of the *ὅτε* at the beginning of ver. 24. It is the English Version's solution of the grammatical difficulty of the whole sentence, ver. 22-24. The Vulgate and Luther avoid the difficulty by following the reading *εἶδον* or *εἶδεν*, instead of the participle *ἰδὼν* (see below). Lange's ingenious construction I have not attempted to represent in the text. It will be found in full in the Exegesis. But the substance of it may be carried along in the very words of the English Version, as I have indicated.—E. D. Y.]

[17] Ibid.—Cod. A. [B. L.], Chrysostom, the Versions, Lachmann [Tischend., Alf.] read *εἶδον*; D. [ℵ.]: *εἶδεν*. A grammatical conjecture. [Meyer defends the text. rec. *ἰδών*, and says that the definite tense was inserted to ease the grammatical structure.—P. S.]

[18] Ibid.—The words *ἐκεῖνο εἰς ὃ ἐνέβησαν οἱ μαθηταὶ αὐτοῦ* [text. rec., ℵ.* D.] are wanting in A. B. L., the Vulgate and the Itala, and appear as an elucidation with many variations. [Omitted by Lachm., Tischend., Alf.]

[19] Ver. 23.—[The parenthesis of this verse in the Text. Rec. is removed by Dr. Lange, or rather is extended to the whole passage from *ὁ ἑστηκὼς πέραν τ. θ.*, ver. 22, to the end of ver. 23. See his construction in the Exegesis. Meyer entirely obliterates the parenthesis.—E. D. Y.]

[20] Ver. 24.—The *καὶ* before *αὐτοί* is lacking in the best MSS. [and in Cod. Sin.].

[21] Ibid.—[Αὐτοὶ.]

[22] Ver. 27.—[For the future *δώσει* Cod. ℵ. D. Syr., Chrys. and Tischend. (ed. viii.) read the present *δίδωσιν*.—P. S.]

[23] Ver. 35.—[Text. rec., inserts *δέ*, *and*, after *εἶπεν*, ℵ. D. Tischend. *οὖν*. Omitted by B. L. T., Alf.—P. S.]

[24] Ver. 35.—[The E. V. connects *πώποτε* with *οὐ μὴ πεινάσῃ* as well as with *οὐ μὴ διψήσει*.—P. S.]

[25] Ver. 36.—The *με*, wanting in Cod. A., bracketed by Lachmann, is sufficiently attested. [It is wanting in the Cod. Sin., and omitted by Tischend., but retained by Alford. Lange translates *καί* in this verse correctly *sogar*, *even*.—P. S.]

[26] Ver. 39.—According to the best Codd. *πατρός* is an addition. [In the Cod. Sin. the whole clause *Τοῦτο—πατρός* is wanting (*homœotel.*)—E. D. Y.]

[27] Ver. 40.—*Γάρ*, according to A. B. C., *etc.* [and Cod. Sin.], instead of the *δέ* of the Recepta.

[28] Ibid.—Most Codd., B. C. D. [Cod. Sin.], *etc.*, Clement and other fathers, and some versions read *πατρός μου*, instead of the Recepta *πέμψαντός με*. A third reading, M. Δ., *etc.*, *πέμψαντος πατρός*, aims to adjust the two. The *text. rec.* comes from verse 39.

[29] Ver. 42.—The second *οὗτος* has several MSS. against it, but could have more easily dropped out than crept in. [The Cod. Sin. has the *οὗτος*, and reads: *οὗτος λέγει· Ἐγώ ἐκ*, instead of the *text. rec.*: *λέγει οὗτος· Ὅτι ἐκ*—E. D. Y.]

[30] Ver. 45.—*Οὖν*, *therefore*, after *πᾶς* is not sufficiently supported.

[31] Ibid.—The readings *ἀκούσας* and *ἀκούων* are both strongly attested; the former somewhat the more strongly, while the latter is favored by the probability that the tense of *μαθών* following would react. [The Cod. Sin. has *ἀκούσας*.—E. D. Y.]

[32] Ver. 47.—[The words *εἰς ἐμέ* are omitted by ℵ. B. and other ancient MSS., and by Tischend., but inserted by other MSS. and the Versions, and retained by Lachm., bracketed by Alf.—P. S.]

[33] Ver. 51.—[Tischend., ed. viii., reads with Cod. Sin., *etc.*, *ἐκ τοῦ ἐμοῦ ἄρτου* (Hil. *ex meo pane*; Cypr. *de meo pane*), instead of *ἐκ τούτου τοῦ ἄρτου* with B. C. L. The latter looks like a correction.—P. S.]

[34] Ver. 51.—On the omission of these words: *which I will give*,—in Codd. B. C. L. D., *etc.*, see the Exegesis. [In the Cod. Sin. the whole clause: *ἣν ἐγὼ—κόσμου ζωῆς*, is wanting.—E. D. Y.]

[35] Ver. 55.—Lachmann and Tischendorf read *ἀληθής* [*true*] both times (according to B. C. K. L., *etc.*) instead of *ἀληθῶς* [*truly, indeed*]; the latter is probably explanatory, since *ἀληθινή* (Cyril, Chrysostom) is the word to be expected. [Tregelles, Alford, Westcott and Hort unanimously adopt *ἀληθής*. So also Tischend., 8th ed., Meyer, 5th ed., and Lange, who renders: *wahrhafte*, *i.e.*, real, substantial, *Speise*, *Trank*. Cod. Sin. has here several corrections which Tischendorf notes: "ℵ* *ab αληθως priore ad posterius transiluit; ℵ*[c] *supplevit omissa ac bis αληθης dedit, nisi quod alterum* (a.[cb]?) *rursus in αληθως mutatum.*"—P. S.]

[36] Ver. 58.—The omission of the *ὑμῶν* by important MSS., B. C. L., *etc.* (adopted by Lachmann and Tischendorf), may be due to theological reasons. Likewise the omission of *τὸ μάννα* in C. T., *etc.* (adopted by Tischendorf). The former reading is supported by D., *etc.*, the latter by B. [The Cod. Sin. lacks both *ὑμῶν* and *τὸ μάννα*. Tischend., 8th ed., Tregelles, Alford, Westcott and Hort do the same, and read simply: *καθὼς ἔφαγον οἱ πατέρες καὶ ἀπέθανον*, *as the fathers ate and died*.—P. S.]

[37] Ver. 60.—[Tischend., Alf., *etc.*, read: *σκληρός ἐστιν ὁ λόγος οὗτος*, which is supported by ℵ. B. C. D., *etc.*, against the text. rec. which puts *οὗτος* before *ὁ λόγος*.—P. S.]

[38] Ver. 63. [Lange inserts after *flesh* the gloss: *as such, separately considered*, and after *nothing*: *doeth nothing towards it.* See Exeg.—P. S.]

[39] Ver. 63.—The perfect *λελάληκα* is supported by decisive authorities, B. C. [Cod. Sin., Tischend., Alf., *etc.*]. The Recepta [*λαλῶ*] generalizes the word.

1. THE MIRACULOUS FEEDING.

EXEGETICAL AND CRITICAL.

See the parallels in Matthew, Mark, and Luke, and the comments in the first two vols.

[The double miracle of the feeding of the multitude, and the stilling of the tempest, is the only miracle which John has in common with all the Synoptists (Luke alone omits the stilling of the tempest). But he relates it chiefly as the occasion and basis of a lengthy discourse of Jesus, which is omitted by the other evangelists, and which brings out the symbolical meaning of the miraculous feeding. He represents Himself here as the Bread of Life, as in the 4th chap. He exhibits Himself as the Water of Life. Thousands upon thousands in all ages and countries of the world have satisfied their spiritual hunger by feeding on Him, and yet He remains to this day, and will remain to the end of time the same inexhaustible source of supply. The miraculous feeding bears also a striking resemblance to the miracle of the change of water into wine in chap. ii. The nearness of the typical paschal feast (vi. 4,) gives the discourse a bearing on the great paschal sacrifice of the Lamb of God for the life of the world.

Chap. vi. develops the national unbelief or false belief in the people of Galilee, as chap. v. reveals the national unbelief of the leaders in Judea; but both chapters bring out the crisis. Alford says: "In chap. v. Christ is the *Son of God*, testified to by the Father, received by faith, rejected by unblief; here He is the *Son of Man*, the incarnate Life of the World, and the unbelief of the Jews and His own disciples is set in strong contrast with the feeding on Him as the Bread of Life." But He is this Bread of Life by virtue of His descent from heaven, as the incarnate Son of God, and by sacrificing His flesh and blood, *i. e.*, His whole human life on earth, in holy obedience and atoning suffering for the life of the world. The discourse of the sixth chap. bears the same relation to the Lord's Supper as the discourse with Nicodemus (chap. iii.) does to baptism, *i. e.*, it expresses the *general idea* which precedes and underlies the sacramental rite as subsequently instituted. See remarks on ver. 27 and the *Excursus* at the close of the Exeg. Notes.—P. S.]

The history of the miracle. The time, place, and essential features are those of the first of the two miraculous feedings which Jesus performed (Matt. xiv. 13; Mark vi. 30; Luke. ix. 10. See the Comm. on *Matt.*). The historical connection of it in John is not, as Meyer asserts [p. 249], different from that in the synoptical Gospels. In John the miracle is preceded by a voyage over the sea to the eastern side from the vicinity of Tiberias, and followed by the miraculous walking upon the sea. In Matthew also Jesus "departed by ship into a desert place," because Herod had executed John and was curious to see Jesus; and the feeding is followed by the walking on the sea. In Mark it is further specified that the sending out of the twelve, in other words Christ's setting out towards Jerusalem (to the feast of Purim), had occurred shortly before, and that the apostles had just gathered themselves together again to Jesus. The order is exactly the same in Luke, though Luke gives not the walking on the sea.—The single external difference, therefore, in regard to the cause of the voyage is, that John gives the attempts to ensnare Jesus in Jerusalem as the cause of *His return to Galilee*, and the synoptical Evangelists mention the more immediate occasion of *His going over the lake*, to wit: Herod's intention to bring Jesus before him. The two motives are manifestly akin, and might easily coëxist. See Com. on *Matt.*, chap. xiv.

Ver. 1. **After these things Jesus went away over the sea of Galilee.**—[Μετὰ ταῦτα, *i. e.*, after the transactions related in chap. v. Christ probably returned to Galilee soon after the feast of Purim (chap. v. 1), which took place in March, and performed this miracle between the feast of Purim and the next passover, which was celebrated a month later, but which Jesus did not attend for the reason mentioned in chap. vii. 1. He continued in Galilee till the feast of Tabernacles, which occurred in October, and which He attended (vii. 1, 2, 10). This gives us seven consecutive months in Galilee during this year, including the last month of the first and six months of the second (or, third, according to the view taken of the ἑορτή in v. 1, *see* remarks there) of our Lord's public ministry. John relates in chap. vi. only the most salient events of this period, and takes much for granted and well understood from other sources.—P. S.]

Ἀπῆλθεν is not to be referred, as by Baumgarten and Meyer, to the departure of Jesus from *Jerusalem.** After the return of Jesus to Galilee, which of course took place very soon after the feast of Purim, since Jesus was no longer safe in Judea, one more circumstance came in, which the synoptical Evangelists record (see *Leben Jesu*, II. 2, p. 779). Yet Tholuck groundlessly supposes a long intervening ministry in Galilee, because the passover came not long after the feast of Purim, and the passover was now just at hand (ver. 4).† Meyer disputes the view of Brückner and earlier interpreters, that the ἀπῆλθεν must be referred to some place in Galilee, and the view of Paulus, that the genitive, τῆς Τιβερ., indicates that He crossed the sea from Tiberias;‡ following chap. v. 1, the phrase must amount to: ἀπολιπὼν Ἱεροσόλυμα ἦλθε πέραν. This is undoubtedly right so far as it represents the crossing of the sea as occasioned by the experiences in Jerusalem; and John also calls the sea of Galilee in chap. xxi. 1, θάλασσα τῆς Τιβεριάδος, after the manner of the Greeks (λίμνη Τιβερίς, Pausan. v. 7, 3). But in the verse before us the first designation, τῆς Γαλιλαίας, certainly was not necessary in addition to the second; for any one would understand the second, though it differed from the expression of the synoptical Evangelists (Matt. iv. 18). The second designation, therefore, must be taken as an additional specification.§ Thus large seas often have particular names from particular districts on their coasts; the *Bodensee* is also the *Lake of Constance*, and the *Vierwaldstätter See*, or *Lake of the Four Forest Cantons, the Lake of Lucerne.* After all is said, the Evangelist of course does not intend to make the Lord embark at Jerusalem. And the interest which Herod Antipas was just now taking in the appearance of Christ, and the Lord's own rapid escape, as well as the straggling ships from Tiberias mentioned immediately after (ver. 23), imply that Christ embarked from the part of the coast about Tiberias. Respecting the lake, see note on *Matthew* iv. 18.‖

---

*[Meyer arbitrarily supplies: "having left Jerusalem." All older commentators, as also Brückner, Hengstenberg, Godet, refer ἀπῆλθεν to Capernaum or some other place in *Galilee.* Alford, agreeing with Lücke, says that ἀπῆλθεν ὁ Ἰησ. πέραν τῆς θαλάσσης, if connected with the preceding discourse, would be unintelligible, and can only be understood by the fragmentary (?) character of John's Gospel as relates to mere narration, and the well known fact being presupposed, that His ministry principally took place in Galilee.—P. S.]

†[Ewald, with his usual oracular self-assurance, as if he had been present at the composition of the Gospel of John, asserts that by a sad accident a whole sheet (he does not specify the precise number of chapters and verses) between chap. v. and vi., was lost before the Gospel came into general circulation. *Die Johanneischen Schriften*, I., p. 221.—P. S.]

‡[This would require ἀπό or ἐκ Τιβεριάδος.—P. S.]

§[Τιβεριάδος is a geographical genitive, inserted for the easier understanding of Gentile readers (comp. xxi. 1), who knew the lake best by that name (Pausan. v. 7, 3; *αὐτὸς οἶδα Ἰόρδανον λίμνην Τιβερίδα ὀνομαζομένην διοδεύοντα*), though Matthew and Mark always call it θαλ. τῆς Γαλιλαίας, Luke once (v. 1), λίμνη Γεννησαρέτ, Josephus (*De bello Jud.*, iii. 10. 8, *etc.*), usually Γεννησάρ or Γεννησαρῖτις. Hence the Vulg. and Beza correctly translate: "mare Galilææ, *quod est Tiberiadis;*" so also the E. V.—P. S.]

‖[Dr. Robinson (*Lex.* sub Γεννησαρέτ, p. 141) thus describes the sea of Tiberias: "It is about 12 miles long, and 5 or six broad, and is still celebrated for the purity and salubrity of

We must further consider that if Jesus, returning from Jerusalem, wished to pass as soon as possible over the sea, He must rather sail from the region of Tiberias, than from Capernaum.

Respecting the eastern coast (Matt. chap. xiv.) comp. von Raumer's *Palästina*, p. 60 and 205 sqq. "The ancient Bashan, about the time of Christ, embraced five provinces: Gaulanitis, Trachonitis, Auranitis, Batanæa, and Ituræa. Gaulanitis corresponded nearly to the present Tsholan, and lay between the upper Jordan, the sea of Tiberias, and the lower Mandhur." The eastern shores of the sea (chalk, interspersed with basalt) rise to a height of from eight hundred to a thousand feet, and spread into a table-land cut up with wadys; the western mountains are about half as high. The eastern coast was an asylum for the Lord on account of its solitude, and on account of its being under the jurisdiction of Philip, a son of Herod the Great, and a mild prince, who after his father's death had become tetrarch of Batenæa, Gaulanitis, Trachonitis, and Paneas. He died childless at Julias, A. D. 34, and his dominions were attached to the province of Syria (not to be confounded with the Philip whose wife Herodias was married to Herod Antipas; see on Matt. chap. xiv).

Tiberias.—A city in Galilee, and in the most beautiful part of it, on the western shore of the lake, south of the middle, on a narrow plain (Joseph. *Antiq.* xix. 8, 1; xviii. 2, 3), a then modern, Herodian city of Palestine, adorned with a royal palace and a race-course, inhabited mostly by heathens, named by Herod Antipas in honor of the emperor Tiberius. Herod seems to have usually resided here; and this, according to Bachiene, was the reason why Jesus never visited this city. From Herod Antipas to the accession of Herod Agrippa II., it was the capital of the province. Fishing and lake transportation were the chief employment of the inhabitants. After the dissolution of the Jewish state, for several centuries, it was the seat of a renowned Jewish school (Lightfoot), and one of the four sacred cities of the Jews. In the vicinity, at the village of Emmaus, were warm baths (sulphur, salt, iron; medicinal). Some, without sufficient reason, identify the place with Cinneroth (Josh. xix. 35, belonging to the tribe of Naphtali), with Hammath (Ibid.), and with Rakkath (Ibid.). Now *Tabaria*, with about three thousand inhabitants, Jews. An earthquake in the year 1837. See Von Schubert III., 233, Robinson III., 500. [Boston ed. of 1856, vol. II., 380-394. Robinson describes the present town, called in Arabic *Tŭbarîyeh*, as "the most mean and miserable place" in Palestine, "a picture of disgusting filth and frightful wretchedness." It suffered much from an earthquake in 1837, when about 700 persons died out of a population of 2500.—P. S.]

Ver. 2. **And a great multitude followed him.**—It seems not to be a multitude which has just now gathered (ἠκολούθει); it possibly consisted in part of the remnants of the Galilean caravan returning from the feast of Purim, but certainly for the most part of the beginnings of the Passover caravan; without doubt Galileans. Many might have attached themselves to the returning disciples, who also wrought miracles. Yet the text implies that new miracles of the Lord, performed on the western shore, were the particular attraction.

Ver. 3. **Into the mountain.**—This standing phrase is accounted for (1) by the character of the Palestinian landscape, affording everywhere heights on which Christ could withdraw from intercourse with the people in the plain; (2) by the Lord's habit of retiring upon a mountain; (3) by a symbolical view which has insensibly connected itself with this habit: taking the solitude of a high mountain for the stillness of prayer. The region is more particularly stated by Luke (chap. ix. 10); it was near the eastern Bethsaida in Gaulanitis.

Ver. 4. **And the passover, the feast of the Jews, was nigh.**—*The* feast, *i. e.*, the principal feast. The passover of the same year, 782. Lücke groundlessly supposes that Jesus attended this feast. The absence from the principal feasts was nothing inconceivable, as may be inferred from the questions in chap. vii. 11 and xi. 56. (Paulus, contrary to the usage of the language, ii. 13; xii. 2., *etc.*, renders: *not long past.*) [The nearness of the passover accounts for the multitude of people ready for a journey to Jerusalem, and suggested in part the subject of the following discourse on the sacrifice of Christ's life for the life of the world, which was typically foreshadowed in the Jewish passover.—P. S.]

Ver. 5. **A great company come unto him.**—Meyer: "It was a *new* company [pilgrims to the festival], not that of ver. 2, which had followed Him on His way to the sea." The contrary is plainly stated by the synoptical Gospels, Matt. xiv. 13; Mark vi. 33; Luke ix. 11. According to Lampe, Bruno Bauer, Baur, and Luthardt [Hengstenberg], the subsequent discourse of Jesus concerning the eating of His blood relates to the passover, and reveals the antitype of that type. Meyer disputes this, because the discourse lacks the slightest hint of it. Some hint, however, lies in the very choice of the striking terms and in the subsequent words of institution.

To Philip.—To this disciple the question must have been a peculiar test. See the note on chap. i. 45. It is possible, however, that Philip was the one who first solicited the Lord to send the people away, Matt. xiv. 15.—According to Bengel, Philip had charge of the *res alimentaria.* Meyer urges against this that Judas was the treasurer [xiii. 29], which is not a sufficient reason; with better reason he refers also to the individuality of Philip, as exhibited in chap. xiv. 8, which, however, he calls *verstandesmässig* [jejune and calculating, and somewhat skeptical, like Thomas. Chrysostom also infers from xix. 8, that Philip was weaker in faith or tardier in spiritual apprehension than the rest. Alford takes the circumstance as simple matter of fact, implying perhaps that he was nearest the Lord at the mo-

its waters, and the abundance of its fish. It presents, indeed, a beautiful sheet of limpid water in a deep depressed basin, with a continuous wall of hills on the sides; but the hills are rounded and tame; and although after the rainy season the verdure of the grass and herbage gives them a pleasing aspect, yet later in the year they become naked and dreary. Its position exposes it to gusts of wind." Comp. his *Researches*, Boston ed. of 1856, Vol. II., 380, 386, 415-417.—P. S.]

ment.—P. S.] John's omission of the circumstance that Jesus had previously been teaching this multitude and healing their sick (see on *Matt.*), making the Lord ask immediately: "**Whence shall we buy bread** [ἀγοράσωμεν, *conjunct. deliberat.*]?" is of course only an abridgment of the history sustained by many examples (see ver. 1; Lücke, Neander), not a *difference*, as Meyer holds, nor a sign of defective testimony, according to Baur. By the circumstance that Andrew had already made the acquaintance of a baker's errand boy, or bread vender in the caravan, John himself indicates that the scene did not occur abruptly. Also by the aorists. [John represents the Lord as first suggesting the question how to feed the multitude; the Synoptists relate that the disciples came to the Lord and asked Him to dismiss the multitude from this desert place into the villages where they might buy themselves food. John's narrative is abridged. But in every important point the agreement is complete. See the remarks of Alford *in loc.*—P. S.]

Ver. 6. **To prove him.**—Plainly a test of faith; which Meyer without reason denies, and then himself confirms; Philip must be more ready to experience the power of faith. But it was also a test of love which the disciples stood better than the test of faith. [**For he himself knew.**—Jesus did not need the counsel of Philip.—P. S.]

Ver. 7. **Two hundred denaries' worth.**—A hundred denaries were equivalent to about fourteen dollars and a half. Comp. on Mark vi. 37. Grotius supposes, this was the contents of the treasury. John represents it as the prompt calculation of the quick-minded Philip. The representation in Mark is not inconsistent with this; yet seems to imply that the disciples are ready to apply all their fund to the feeding of the people. Yet, according to Philip, even the high estimate of two hundred denaries would not suffice.

Ver. 8. **Andrew . . . saith unto him.**—Here again, as in chap. xii. 22, Andrew appears near Philip and in like manner in an act of friendly interest and assistance.—Andrew seems to be a master in mediation and advice, John i. 40 sqq., and xii. 22. On that other occasion also he supplements Philip. But why is it said: "*One of His disciples?*" Wassenbergh considers the apparently superfluous and disturbing words to be a gloss. But John intends to mark that it was one of the disciples who first, though with trembling heart, directed his eye to that little store with which Jesus wrought the miracle.

Ver. 9. **There is one here.** Παιδάριον ἕν. One little boy; one young slave; one little apprentice.* The last, most likely a bread vender or sutler accompanying the caravan. The sense is: there is only one little trader here, and he has only so much.

Barley-loaves. — The food of the poorer classes. *Tr. Pesachim* [fol. III. 2]: "Rabbi Johannan said the barley is fine. He was answered: say this to horses and asses [*nuntia hoc equis et asinis*]." **Two small fishes.**—'Οψάριον [Lat. *opsonium*], a diminutive of ὄψον [from ὀπτάω, or ἕψω, *to cook, to roast*], any thing cooked or roasted, to go as a relish with bread (προσφάγιον): generally fish [little fish], as here. [Of later Greek usage. In the New Testament ὀψάριον is peculiar to John who employs it five times (vi. 9, 11; xx. 9, 10, 13). The Synoptists use here the word ἰχθύες.—P. S.]

Ver. 10. **Much grass in the place.**—A mark of the eastern spring about the time of the passover.* [After the rainy season.]—**The men.** Constituting, no doubt, according to the idea of the festival caravans, the great mass. They appear here as heads of families, around whom in many cases women and children were grouped. [οἱ ἄνδρες, a touch of accuracy; the *men alone* were arranged in companies and numbered, while the women and children were served promiscuously. (See Meyer and Alford *in loc.*) According to Mark the multitude reclined on the green pasture ground by parties or in groups of hundreds and fifties. They probably formed two semicircles, an outer semicircle of 30 hundreds, and an inner semicircle of 40 fifties. A wise symmetrical arrangement for the easy and just distribution of the food.—P. S.]

Ver. 11. **Given thanks.**—Matt. xiv. 19. According to the best authorities, the distribution by the disciples, which is in the Textus Rec. supplied here from Matthew, is left by John to be supposed. See the TEXTUAL NOTE.

[Εὐχαριστήσας, for which the other Evangelists use εὐλογεῖν, is in accordance with the blessing or grace of the father of a Jewish family at meals, and has here a special bearing on the miracle. John describes the distribution (διέδωκε τοῖς ἀνακειμένοις) as being the act of Christ, without, however, excluding the intervention of the disciples as mentioned by Matthew, Mark and Luke. Verse 11 is the place for the miracle, but the exact moment and manner of its performance eludes the grasp of the senses. It must have taken place immediately after the prayer of Christ as He distributed the bread through the apostles to the eaters. The evangelists show their good sense in omitting a description of what is indescribable. Augustine's and Olshausen's ingenious idea of a divinely hastened process of *nature* (to which must be added an accelerated process of *art*, or the combined labors of the reaper, miller and baker, by which wheat or barley is changed into bread) does not help the understanding of the matter, and has only the value of an analogy. We cannot conceive, philosophically, of supernaturally, yet visibly growing loaves, and of supernaturally growing or multiplying fishes. A miracle, like the primitive creation, can only be apprehended by faith, which is the organ of the supernatural. It is, indeed, not a strictly creative act by which things non-existing are called into existence, for a miracle is always performed on matter already existing, but it is as great and difficult as a creative act, and is produced by the same divine power which,

* [Wordsworth: *One* person, and he a *child;* and he has only five loaves, and they of *barley;* and two fishes, and they *small.* Then Dr. W. goes on allegorizing about the elements of the sacrament.—P. S.]

* [Wordsworth: A beautiful figure of the 'green pasture' (Ps. xxiii.), in which Christ feeds His people in the ministry of His word and sacraments, where He prepares a table for them in the wilderness. This may do for homiletical application.—P. S.]

in one case, originates nature, and, in the other, acts from above and beyond nature upon (not against) nature. Comp. my notes on the miracle at Cana, chap. ii., pp. 106 f., 109 f., and the notes on *Matthew* pp. 267.—P. S.]

Ver. 12. The *gathering of the fragments* here appears as directed by the Lord. [A lesson of economy, which is consistent with the greatest liberality. "Make all you can, save all you can, give all you can." κλάσματα (from κλάω, *to break*, as *fragments* from *frango*), *broken pieces*, not *crumbs*. More fragments were left than the original supply of five loaves, which would not have filled five baskets.—P. S.]

Ver. 13. **Filled twelve baskets with the fragments.**—[Probable reference to the twelve apostles, each of whom gathered the fragments and brought his basket full. *Basket*, the ordinary furniture of a travelling Jew for carrying his food. Some commentators refer the number to the twelve tribes of Israel as the type of the church which is fed by the bread of life to the end of time.—P. S.] Meyer urges that the twelve baskets were filled *only* with the fragments of the *bread*, and adds: Mark, vi. 43, states otherwise. Yet he would conceive the miracle only as a *creative* act, which operates here on quantity, as it operated on quality in the changing of the water into wine.

DOCTRINAL AND ETHICAL.

1. On the miracle and the different explanations of it, see the Com. on *Matt.*, chap. xiv. [Am. ed., pp. 266, 268, where the *rationalistic*, the *mythical*, the *symbolic*, and the *orthodox* views of the miracle are fully noticed. Comp. also my remarks on ver. 11 (p. 210), and Prof. van Oosterzee in the Com. on *Luke*, p. 146.—P. S.] Not simply "a miracle of satisfying would Lange consider it," as Tholuck inaccurately states. [Dr. Lange admits an actual increase of the substance and nourishing quality of the bread by a power which went forth from the Logos, but assumes at the same time a modal or mystic medium in a corresponding moral and religious disposition awakened by Christ among the eaters, so that it was a heavenly feast of the soul as well as a literal meal for the body. See his remarks below, and in *Matthew*, p. 267, also his *Leben Jesu*, III. p. 786, where he says: "Christ fed the people with His bread, His faith, His divine power and the blessing of His love."—P. S.] Meyer: "A creative act." But we have here, by all means, a miracle of the Son, the Redeemer, not an absolutely creative act [*ex nihilo*]. If we know what *creative* is, we also know that all the days of creation were applied to it, till there was first the herb, not to say bread; therefore (1) a miracle of the increase of force in the element of divine power; then (2) of the increase of substance in the element of love; the whole being (3) a miracle of the heavenly kingdom, in which one fares very ill if he leaves the heart out of account.

2. In John this miracle gains a peculiar significance from its relation to the miracle of the turning of water into wine. *Wine and bread.* It receives further light from the history which follows.

[3. The miracle of the miraculous feeding an illustration of the truth that Christ is the *bread of eternal life* to His people in the "desert place" of this world, on their journey to the "feast" of the heavenly Jerusalem. In this spiritual sense the miracle is continued from day to day. On its relation to the Lord's Supper, see the Excursus at the close of the Exegesis of this passage.—P. S.]

HOMILETICAL AND PRACTICAL.

See the Com. on Matthew, Mark, and Luke, on this passage.

Jesus hastens from the tribunal of the Jews away beyond the sea into the mountain of God. —So the pious heart has a right to betake itself, from the pain which legalistic jealousy has ready for it in human schools and temples, to the great temple of God. (But to find refuge and elevation in nature is one thing, and to run wild in nature is another.)—Over the sea and upon the mountain: the great, bold course of Christ: In His life; in history; in the leading of His people. — The passover-feast, the passover-journey, and the passover-sermon of Christ before the passover of the Jews; the Lord ever in advance of His people. (The whole chapter.)—The trial of Philip's faith.—What he saw, and what he did not see.—The character of Philip.—The arithmetic of Philip and the arithmetic of the Lord.—In the reckoning of men there is always a deficit, in the reckoning of Christ there is always a surplus.—How the Lord has led His apostles to interest themselves even in the bodily wants of men.—How He has trained His ministers and messengers to care also for the poor and sick.—The sentiment of Andrew, compared with the sentiment of Philip. (The one would begin with much, the other seems at least inclined to begin with little.)—How in a Christian consultation we gradually come nearer the right.—The little bread vender; Christ founds His great miracle on a small, every day incident.—"Make the men sit (lie) down:" a word of perpetual application.—When once a Christian people sit down together in peace and quietness, then the Lord works His wonders.—So He still works His miracle when the people sit down at His bidding (in the church, at the holy Supper, *etc.*). —Christ's giving of thanks, the seal of His confidence.—The wonder-working table-blessing of Christ.—The divine miracles of faith at the supper in the desert.—The miraculous feeding; miraculous 1, in the sitting down of the people at the bidding of Christ; 2, in the thanksgiving of Christ before the feeding; 3, in the distribution and breaking of the bread according to the appetite of all; 4, in the satisfaction of all; 5, in the surplus (more at the end than at the beginning).—Even the superfluity of God we should carefully economize.—The effect of the miraculous feeding on those who were fed: 1. Their true interpretation (that this is that Prophet, *i. e.*, the Messiah); 2, their false application of it (desiring to make Him a king to their mind). —The Lord must withdraw Himself as often from the homage of men, as from their persecution.—Christ escaped to the mountain, and He alone: 1, the humble One, who offers up to the Father His miracle-working blessing; 2, the self-possessed One, whom no fanaticism of men excites; 3, the exalted One, above the ambition of the world; 4, the holy One, who mingles not His affairs with human doings.—"They would make him a king:" in the midst of this temptation, in which nobles fall by thousands, He stands erect, because *He is the King.*

STARKE: HEDINGER: God uses all sorts of means, most rarely curiosity, for the conversion of sinners.—The nearer a feast, the more the children of God seek to dress their hearts for Him; they keep the feast in honor of Him.—Jesus is so high that He can overlook all His children, and can know what each one wants.—CRAMER: The Lord cares for all, and is kind even to the unthankful.—*Nova Bibl. Tub.:* It is the weakness of our unbelieving heart, that, in our necessities, we always consider only their greatness and the slenderness of the means of relief, and not the infinite wisdom, power, and goodness of God. If we have possessions, we have heart; but lack of money brings lack of faith.—QUESNEL: We sin as well when we think that God will pass by the ordinary means of His providence as when we limit the providence of God to outward means.—ZEISIUS: Christ can make bread in the desert, and abundance in want.—CANSTEIN: Whenever we eat, we ought to pray and thank God.—CRAMER: Every creature, and therefore food, is sanctified by prayer and the word of God, 1 Tim. iv. 5.—Happy are those ministers of the word who receive from the Lord what they deliver to their hearers.—He to whom God intrusts temporal blessings, should not keep them to himself, but share them with others.—To eat and be filled, is the blessing of God; and to eat and not be filled, is His curse, Hag. i. 16.—OSIANDER: The common mass is unintelligent; now it will exalt one to heaven, and soon after it will thrust the same one down to hell. Let no one intrust himself to the favor of the multitude.—HEDINGER: In the beginning of illumination, in the first glow, a man usually falls to extravagant undertakings, not according to the rule of divine prudence.—ZEISIUS: Flee, according to the example of thy Saviour, from that which the world, with its carnal mind, holds high, and seek that which is above. — GOSSNER: Jesus purposely caused the bread to pass through the hands of the disciples, that *they* might grasp it in their hands, who in their unbelief had seen it to be too little.

BRAUNE: The creative power of God which every year makes much grow from little, the harvest from the seed, even to superabundance, here also works. As it wrought in the beginning of the world, and works yearly in secret, here it comes forth openly.—The gathering frugality, which saves at the right time, belongs to the art of beneficence.—Jesus is the Redeemer from the sin which man loves, from the devil in whom man does not believe, from the death of which man does not think, from the hell which man does not fear; therefore He is not a Redeemer for all. Were He but a Redeemer from hunger and from labor for a living (by means of material abundance), then He would be acceptable to all. The people wished to make Him a king; He was to be their work; they wished to have their hand in everything, even where they did not understand, and nothing should have honor which they did not give,—not even Jesus, the Prophet, the Messiah.—LISCO: Philip and Andrew both looked at the visible; the one at the insufficient money, the other at the insufficient food.

HEUBNER: The power of Jesus to draw men to Himself. The power to do good draws more than the power to punish.—Unbelief everywhere looks at the small means and the feeble power. But God can accomplish much with little.—The purpose and the wonderful help of God are ever revealing themselves to the astonishment and shame of unbelief.—Jesus has regard for order and division, by means of orderly arrangement the multitude was easily viewed. So everywhere in the kingdom of God. Men are divided, every one in his place.—In the hand of Jesus everything becomes blessing.—The disciples were hodmen of Jesus; and so are we.—To cover political plans under the cloak of religion, is scandalous abuse of religion. — The Christian should strive to keep clear of worldly distinction.—Ver. 1–15, the pericope for *Lætare* Sunday. *How Jesus performs His miracles:* 1. With holy design. 2. In love, only to relieve the actual stress of want and suffering. 3. With divine power. 4. With quietness and dignity. 5. With earnest precaution.

SCHLEIERMACHER: The Lord even feeds and nourishes those who truly gather round Him.—DRAESEKE: It is not we that make Him king, but He that makes us kings, because citizens in His kingdom.—REINHARD: Thoughts on the constancy with which Jesus holds to the great end of His life.—MARHEINEKE: The Christian in solitude.—GREILING: We should learn from Jesus to do much with little.—SCHULTZ: On the earthly blessing which God diffuses among men. SCHUDEROFF: The earthly mind always miscalculates.—LISCO: The gospel for the day, a history of the feeding, seems to have been appointed for this Sunday* not so much on account of the incidental remark that "the passover, a feast of the Jews, was nigh," as because Jesus was called by the people, whom He had miraculously fed, "the Prophet that should come into the world;" for it is plainly the design of the last three Sundays of Lent to hold before us the threefold office of our Mediator, the suffering Jesus, as Christ: Prophet, Priest, and King.—*Ibid:* In Christ is full satisfaction for us.—The behaviour of Jesus towards weak and insincere friends: 1. He condescended to the necessities of their weakness. 2. He avoided their well-meant, but impure homage.—BACHMANN: How urgently the Lenten season invites us take the bread of life.—AHLFELD: The Lord makes everything come out gloriously: (1) Where man is at his wits' end, (2) God goes right on.—KRAUSSOLD: Our daily bread a guide-board to heaven—*Ibid.:* How faithfully the Lord cares for His people.—RAUTENBERG: The eating of the bread from heaven: (1) How it is performed; (2) how much it includes.—*Ibid.:* Christ's kingdom is not of this world: This (1) brings Him suffering in this world; (2) draws my heart from this world;

* [The Fourth Sunday in Lent.—E. D. Y.]

(3) remains my comfort, when all things fail.—HARLESS: The need, which receives the blessing of the Lord: 1. The need. 2. The testing. 3. The confirming. 4. The blessing.—RAUTENBERG: The miracle at the table of the Lord: 1. The love which prepares the table. 2. The food, which it offers. 3. The satisfaction which it gives.—JASPIS: Jesus, ever the helper of the poor.—J. J. RAMBACH: The victory of faith in the exigencies of life.—AHLFELD: How goes it with the Christian who goes with Christ? 1. He cleaves to his Lord, and forsakes Him not. 2. The Lord may hide from him His face for the time, till 3. He at last breaks to him the bread of grace.—WIESMANN: The miraculous feeding shows us that Christ has for His people: (1) A warm heart; (2) a clear eye; (3) an open hand.—*See the next section.*

[HILARY: There is no catching by eye or touch the miraculous operation; it only remains for us to believe that God can do all things (consistent with His nature and character).—AUGUSTINE (*Tract. in Joh.* 24; *Serm.* 130, 1): Christ multiplied in His hands the five loaves, just as He produces harvest out of a few grains: there was a power in His hands; and those five loaves were seeds, not indeed committed to earth, but multiplied by Him who made the earth. (The same idea is revived by Olshausen, but the comparison is only serviceable as a remote analogy. See the Exegesis.)—TRENCH: Here is a miracle of creative accretion, by which Christ proclaimed Himself the bread of the world, the inexhausted and inexhaustible source of all life for the spiritual needs of hungering souls in all ages.—The twelve baskets, an apt symbol of Divine love which after all its out-goings upon others, abides itself far richer. Comp. 2 Kings iv. 1–7; Prov. xi. 24: "There is that scattereth, and yet increaseth."—Analogies of this miracle: the manna in the wilderness; the multiplying of the widow's cruse of oil and her barrel of meal by Elijah, 1 Kings xvii. 16; Elisha satisfying a hundred men with twenty loaves of barley, 2 Kings iv. 42–44.—RYLE: Learn from this miracle: 1) Christ's almighty power; 2) a lesson about the office of ministers—to receive humbly and to distribute faithfully what Christ provides and blesses; 3) the sufficiency of the gospel for the wants of mankind.—P. S.]

2. THE MIRACULOUS WITHDRAWAL OVER THE SEA. VI. 14–21.

EXEGETICAL AND CRITICAL.

See the parallels in Matthew xiv. 22–33; and Mark vi. 45–56. [Omitted by Luke. Alford: "An important and interesting question arises, Why is this miracle here inserted by St. John? That he ever inserts for the mere purpose of narration, I cannot believe. The reason seems to me to be this: to give to the Twelve, in the prospect of so apparently strange a discourse respecting His Body, a view of the truth respecting that Body, that it and the things said of it were not to be understood in a gross corporeal, but in a supernatural and spiritual sense. And their very terror and reassurance, tended to impress that confidence in Him which kept them firm, when many left Him, ver. 66."—P. S.]

Ver. 14. **The Prophet that is to come.**—This denotes here not the fore-runner, but the Messiah, referring to Deut. xviii. 15; as is proved (1) by the addition: "that should come into the world;" (2) by the inclination to make Him a king.

Ver. 15. **Take him by force.**—Carry Him forcibly into their circle, and conduct Him in triumph—*in order to make Him a king;* as festival pilgrims, lead Him to Zion in triumphal procession. The arbitrary, confused, and premature idea of the subsequent triumphal entry.

He withdrew again into the mountain. The πάλιν denotes not only return to the mountain, but also a second withdrawal of Himself from the pressure of the people. He sought solitude, to escape the people; but this of course does not exclude His sanctifying the solitude by prayer.

Ver. 16. **And when evening came.**—It would not appear from ver. 17, but it certainly does from the parallels, that this was the "second evening," *i. e.*, the later even-tide, from the decline of the day till night.

Ver. 17. **Having entered a ship.**—The ἐμβάντες before ἤρχοντο is hardly intended to repeat once more that they had already gone to sea which had been said in ver. 16, but to express that, after embarking, they took an involuntary course, driven by a fearful storm. See Com. on Matthew and Mark on the passage. According to Mark the disciples were to go before the Lord in the direction of Bethsaida. This must mean the eastern Bethsaida, not the western, because the return itself was to Capernaum; therefore a coast-wise passage northerly is intended. Christ wished to embark in a solitary place, unseen by the people. The storm intervened; the disciples were driven out into the midst of the sea. Then Jesus came to them on the sea; *i. e.*, He met them as a helper in their distress under a *contrary* wind; not merely went after them as they were driving with a *favorable* wind. [Dr. Thomson (*The Land and the Book*, II. p. 30) maintains, in opposition to the usual view, that there was but *one* Bethsaida, and that it was situated at the entrance of the Jordan into the lake, a few miles north-east of Tell Hûm, the supposed present site of Capernaum. The disciples would naturally sail from the southeast *toward* Bethsaida in order to reach Capernaum.—P. S.]

And Jesus had not yet come to them.—As the disciples were not expecting Jesus to walk on the sea, the "yet" has been found troublesome, and has been dropped. But the sentence means: They had not yet been able to take up Jesus according to the original plan of the voyage. [See TEXT. NOTES.]

Ver. 18. **And the sea began to rise.**—An explanation of their misfortune. We repeat: A violent gale, by which they would have come immediately twenty or thirty furlongs westward, could not have been to them a contrary wind, if they had intended to go westward without Jesus.

Ver. 19. **Five and twenty or thirty furlongs.**—The lake was forty stadii wide (Joseph. *De Bell. Jud.* III., 10, 11).* The indefinite mea-

* [According to Robinson, the lake is about twelve English miles long, and five or six broad.—P. S.]

sure is very graphic; it reflects the situation: Darkness and an angry sea, in which accurate measurement of distance was impossible at the time. Matthew says "the midst" of the sea, xiv. 24; denoting, however, an earlier moment, when Jesus was still on the shore. John marks the later moment, at which the disciples saw the Lord. The στάδιον is a Greek measure (Luther: *Feldweg*, furlong). Eight stadia made a Roman mile. A stadium is the fortieth part of a geographical or German mile [a little less than an eighth of an English mile, and nearly equal to the English furlong; so that the twenty-five or thirty stadia would come between three and four miles.—E. D. Y.]. Of the full two leagues' breadth of the lake the ship had therefore already passed a league and a quarter or a league and a half.

They behold Jesus.—Graphic present. **And they were afraid.**—Moderate expression of a powerful feeling. Compare the synoptical Evangelists. So little had they expected His coming to them in this way.

Ver. 21. **Then they desired to receive him.**—They still desired to take Him into the ship; that is, they still stood to their purpose. In the effort to take up the Lord on the eastern shore, the ship had already gone nearly to the western. The Evangelist finds it superfluous to state that the Lord now embarked, and sailed the small remaining distance with the disciples. He likewise passes over the falling of the wind.

According to the usual view of the event, in which Jesus *went after* the disciples, instead of *meeting them*, the expression of John is very hard to be explained. And here again Meyer (after the example of Lücke and De Wette) brings out a collision with the synoptical Evangelists. "They wished to take Him into the ship, and immediately (before they carried out the ἐθέλειν) the ship was at the land." He seems even to introduce here a wondrous agency of Jesus bringing the ship *immediately* to land, notwithstanding its distance of five or ten stadia and the "*surging*" of the sea. "An unfortunate attempt at harmony [it is then said by Meyer, p. 255, 5th ed.]: *They willingly received Him* (Beza, Grotius, Kuinoel, Ammon, and many others; see against it Winer, p. 436); which is not helped by the assumed antithesis of a *previous unwillingness* (Ebrard, Tholuck)." The sentence says simply this: They were still occupied with the effort to take Him up on the eastern coast, when by this miraculous intervention of Christ they at once reached the western side.

The ὑ π ῆ γ ο ν, in the versions and expositions, to a great extent fails of its full force. It often denotes a secret, skilful or mysterious removal, escape, or disappearance. And so especially here, where the Lord was put upon extreme deliberation, and could properly use a miracle to rid Him of the multitude. If they still followed Him in spite of all, we must consider that certainly all could not follow Him in the boats which had come from Tiberias, and that Christ still found it necessary in the synagogue at Capernaum to put off the people by meeting them sternly and with the boldest declarations.

DOCTRINAL AND ETHICAL.

1. The culmination of the enthusiasm of the Galilean populace for Jesus is here brought out, and by John alone, with great distinctness. The great popular mass, a host of five thousand chiliastically excited men, would violently lift a Messianic standard with Him and for Him. But because Jesus cannot yield Himself to this project, the culmination of their enthusiasm is at the same time its turning-point.

2. In respect to the miracle of Christ's walking on the sea, compare the Com. on Matthew and Mark.

HOMILETICAL AND PRACTICAL.

The misinterpretation of the divine sign of Christ by the perverseness of earthly-minded men.—They draw from the sign a correct conclusion (a true doctrine) and a false application (a false moral).—So with orthodox faith a false (ecclesiastical or secular) morality is often associated.—The flight of Jesus before the revolutionary design of the people: It occasions (1) His retiring in solitude to the mountain; (2) His sending the disciples before Him with the ship; (3) His hastening in the night, ghostlike, over the sea.—Jesus on the mountain above the political designs of men; He alone: 1. He alone the free One, who is more a king than any prince of earth. 2. He alone the clear-sighted One, who sees far above all craftiness of policy. 3. He alone the silent but decisive Disposer of all things.—The flight from the sedition and tumult: 1. The flight of Christianity (Christ). 2. The flight of the Church (the ship).—The disciples in the ship, driven from east to west, a foreshadowing of the fortunes of the church.—The miracle of the walking on the sea, as to its holy motives: Occasioned (1) by a holy flight; (2) by a holy solicitude. — Christ's superiority to nature.—Christ the sea-king (He, not Mary, the true *Stella Maris*).—Christ as master of the water—the helper in perils of the sea (not the holy Nepomuc).—Christ the helper in perils of water and of fire.—While they were wishing to take Him up on the eastern shore, they were ready to land on the western.—The hour when the Church becomes perfectly joyful in the presence of her Lord in this world, is the hour when she lands on the shore of the other.—How the Lord suddenly puts an end to the reverses of His people.—Every new necessity of the Christian, a new revelation of the glory of Christ. Every new necessity of man, a new revelation of the miraculous help of God.—Perils of the night; perils of storm; perils of the sea. Sufferings from night, from storm, and from sea; Christ, the Deliverer.

Starke: God's wonders among them that go down to the sea in ships. Ps. cvii. 23.—Prov. xxx. 19.—Wisd. xiv. 3.—Be not troubled when thou must journey from one place to another, *etc.* The goal is all rest.—Comest thou into a dark night of tribulation, *etc.*: Jesus is there.—The perils of one's calling.—Good fortune is followed again by ill; but to believers all is for the best.—Canstein: Christ lets His people come almost to extremity, but then loses not a moment.

—In our troubles we commonly set God before us in a different character from the true; as an object of terror.—ZEISIUS: What a mighty hero is thy Saviour and mine!—QUESNEL: Christ's word and presence make everything good and tranquil again.—CRAMER: Christ has more ways of helping than one.—ZEISIUS: Thus the saints come through great storms and trouble to the haven of eternal peace and safety.—GOSSNER: When Christ is in the ship, the ship receives more help from Him than He from it. So is everything which we call the service of God more profitable to the servant than to the Lord whom he serves.—HEUBNER: Distance, mountain, and sea cannot separate Him from His.—SCHLEIERMACHER: We see here at first a certain dependence on an immediate and bodily presence, which is always united with a certain want of faith in the spiritual, and of a sense of spiritual power and agency.—SCHENKEL: How do we stand towards Christ? (1) So as to have Him flee from us? (2) Or so as to have Him come to us?

[WORDSWORTH: Ver. 20. "*I am* ('Εγώ εἰμι), the Ever-living One, Jehovah, the Author of Life. I am always at hand and never pass by you, therefore be not afraid, but trust in Me. Our Lord allows us to be in trial and danger, to struggle in the storm, to endure for a long time, in order that our patience and perseverance and faith may be proved, and that we may resort to Him who alone can save us. We are often in darkness and in storms, and the devil and evil men assail and affright us: but let us listen to Christ's voice, 'Εγώ εἰμι, μὴ φοβεῖσθε, and when human help fails, then divine aid will come. Terrors pass by, but Christ never passes by. He ever says, 'It is I.' I am He who always *am*, who ever remain; therefore have faith in Me. And if we are rowing in the Apostolic Ship of the Church, doing our duty there in our respective callings, and if we desire to receive Christ into the Ship, He will not only quell the storm, but give us a fair breeze, and we shall soon be at the harbor where we would be—the calm harbor of heavenly peace. They who are in the Ship, and are rowing in the storm; they who labor in the Church, and continue in good works to the end, will receive Christ, and will at length arrive at the waveless haven of everlasting life."—A fine Greek poem of Anatolius on Christ in the tempest, translated by J. M. Neale: "Fierce was the wild billow" (see Schaff's *Christ in Song*, p. 451).—P. S.]

3. DECISIVE DECLARATION OF CHRIST, AND OFFENCE OF MANY DISCIPLES.

VI. 22–65.

EXEGETICAL AND CRITICAL.

[After a brief historical introduction, ver. 22–25, John gives that wonderful discourse which unfolds the symbolic meaning of the miraculous feeding of the multitude, namely, the grand truth that Christ is the Bread of everlasting life, which alone can satisfy the spiritual wants of men. It may be divided into four parts, each of which is introduced by an act of the audience and determined by their moral attitude. 1) The first part is introduced by a simple question of the Jews: "When and how didst Thou come hither?" It exhorts them not to busy themselves about perishing food, but to seek food which endures *forever*, and which the *Son of Man* alone can give, vers. 25–35. 2) The Jews asking for this imperishable bread, Jesus declares *Himself to be the Bread of life* that came down from heaven, vers. 35–40. 3) The Jews murmured at this extraordinary claim; whereupon Jesus repeats the assertion with the additional idea, that *His flesh which He was to give for the life of the world*, is that Bread of life, vers. 41–51. 4) This causes not only surprise but offence and contention among the Jews (ver. 52), but Jesus, instead of modifying and explaining, declares in still stronger language that *eating His flesh and drinking His blood*, *i. e.*, a living appropriation of His person and sacrifice is the *indispensable condition of spiritual life* reaching forward to the resurrection of the body, vers. 52–58. 5) The rest, from vers. 59–65, describes the crisis produced by this discourse and furnishes at the same time, in ver. 63, the key to the proper understanding of the same.*—The authenticity of this discourse is sufficiently guaranteed by its perfect originality, sublimity, and offensiveness to carnal sense, as well as its adaptation to the situation and the miracle performed. No writer could have invented such ideas and dreamed of putting them into the mouth of Jesus. Nor could any *mere* man in his sane mind set forth his own flesh and blood as the life of the world. We are shut up here to the conclusion of the divinity of Christ. As to the difficulty of the discourse, we must always keep in mind that Christ spoke for all ages, and that history furnishes the evidence of the wisdom and universal applicability of His teaching. The disciples and the hearers were prepared for it by the two preceding miracles which raised them, so to say, to a supernatural state. The sacramental interpretation will be discussed below in an Excursus.—P. S.]

Vers. 22–24. The construction of these verses is a matter of great difficulty. [Such complicated sentences are exceedingly rare in John. Two other instances occur in chap. xiii. 1, and 1 John i. 1 ff. In this case the parenthetical and involved construction is, as Alford remarks, characteristic of the minute care with which the evangelist will account for every circumstance which is essential to his purpose in the narration.—P. S.] De Wette: "As regards the construction, the sentence is interrupted by the parenthesis of ver. 23, and resumed in ver. 24 (ὅτε οὖν εἶδεν=ἰδών, ver. 22), except that while ἰδών, ver. 22, relates to the circumstances under which the departure of Jesus seemed impossible, and the resumptive ὅτε—εἶδεν expresses the certainty nevertheless reached, that he was no longer there." Meyer: "The construction resumes ὁ ὄχλος, the subject of the whole, with ὅτε οὖν εἶδεν ὁ ὄχλος, ver. 24; and ver. 23 is a parenthesis which prepares the way for the following apodosis. The participial sentence ἰδὼν, ὅτι to ἀπῆλθον is subordinated to ἑστηκὼς πέραν τ. θαλ., and explains what made the people linger there and stand again the next day in the same place: They thought Jesus must still be on the eastern side of the sea, since no other ship

* [For a somewhat similar division see Godet, II. 97.]

had been there except the one in which the disciples had gone away alone, ver. 22, and even the *disciples* might again be there, since other boats had come from Tiberias, in which they might have returned." [Somewhat modified in ed. 5th, p. 256.—P. S.] We suppose that here, as often elsewhere in the New Testament a supposed clumsiness and irregularity of expression arises in the sphere of exegesis from our overlooking the conciseness resulting from the vividness of the oriental style. The present passage may be elucidated by the remark that Christ made His escape from the people with extreme deliberation and care, and that the people pursued Him with intense expectation; and the sentence takes this shape: *And immediately* the ship (in which they were escaping) was at the land whither they were going (for escape from the people); the day following the people (also) which stood (still remained standing, like a wall) on the other side of the sea, because they saw (in the first place) that there was none other boat there, save that one, and that Jesus went not with His disciples into that, but that His disciples were gone away alone (whence it seemed to follow, that Jesus was still in the neighborhood); but (in the second place) that other boats had come from Tiberias nigh unto the place where they had eaten bread by the power of the Lord's thanksgiving (boats in which the disciples also might have returned). When the people therefore, *etc.*

Ver. 24. **They themselves entered into the boats.**—Took those boats which had come from Tiberias. As these vessels are called πλοιάρια [*small* boats], and besides were probably not very numerous, having accidentally arrived, it is not to be supposed that the whole five thousand came across.* Tholuck supposes that the festival-pilgrims would have left, probably finding it necessary to go immediately on to the temple at Jerusalem. This mistakes the point of their extreme excitement. The αὐτοί is not antithetic to a previous passive behaviour of the people (Meyer), but to their wrong supposition that the disciples had been in the ships, and had returned by them. They sought the Lord in the place of His residence, Capernaum.

Ver. 25. **On the other side of the lake.**—With reference to the eastern point of departure. According to ver. 59, they find Him in the synagogue at Capernaum. Meyer correctly: "The πέραν τ. θάλ. is intended to suggest that the object of their *wonder* was their finding him on the *western* side." **When camest thou?**—[Π ό τ ε ὧ δ ε γ έ γ ο ν α ς; In Greek this implies the double question of *when* and *how*, as Bengel remarks: *Quæstio de tempore includit quæstionem de modo. When* didst Thou come hither? and *how* didst Thou get here (perf. γέγονας) so unexpectedly, like a ghost?—P. S.] The question *how* seemed the more natural. Yet they appear to suppose immediately that He went round the sea, or crossed at some other point. They ask, when He arrived just here. Meyer thinks they suspected some miracle, and Jesus did not enter into their curious question; but the passage leads rather to the opposite inference. The Lord must expect, not that they had been led by the feeding to think of the walking on the sea, but undoubtedly that they expected of Him so much of the miraculous as to make the question of *when* superfluous. This triviality is the very thing that betrays the sensuous confusion of their enthusiasm itself.

Ver. 26. **Verily, verily, I say unto you, Ye seek me.**—The term here is particularly strong, because it emphasizes a severe personal judgment. Considering this strength of the expression, the interpretation of the correlatives οὐχ'—ἀλλ' by *non tam—quam*, in Kuinoel and others, entirely obliterates the thought. **Not because ye saw the miracles.**—Lücke explains the plural by the healing of sick before the feeding (see the other Evangelists); Meyer groundlessly rejects this, observing that the antithesis is simply the eating of the loaves; that the plural is a plural of category, and goes no further than the feeding. But if they had waited for the kingdom of God as true believers in the Messiah, they would have perceived the spiritual glory in all the miracles. On the contrary, the sensuous expectations of the Messiah fastened selfishly on the eating of the loaves. (Comp. Matt. iv. 3, 4.)

Ver. 27. **Work not for the food.**—We think the first word must be emphasized. It is aimed at the chiliastic inclination to laziness in the enjoyment of miraculous food, and resembles the word of Paul in 2 Thess. iii. 11, 12. But the injunction immediately takes a turn designed to lead their mind to the essential point. Direct your labor not to the food which perisheth, but, *etc.*—The radical meaning of ἐργάζεσθε it is difficult here to preserve in its precise force; and yet we are led to do so by the spirit of the transaction. Luther: *wirket, work, produce;* De Wette: *erwirket, work out;* Van Ess: *mühet euch, trouble yourselves.* Luther also translates ἐργαζόμενος, Eph. iv. 28, by *schaffen, work.* There is a double oxymoron or paradox: (1) that they should not labor for the perishable food, which is the very thing they must get by working; (2) that they should labor for the heavenly food, which is not to be earned by labor. The solution lies (1) in the position of the exclamation: *Labor,* at the beginning of the sentence: Be earnest workers; (2) in the addition of the next words to elucidate the first. Work not for the earthly food, which perisheth; even work for daily bread should not aim at mere material support and sensual enjoyment, but at the eternal in the temporal; (3) in the doing away of all thought of human production in matters of faith by the further words: "Which the Son of Man shall give unto you."—**The food that perisheth**; or rather, which spoils, corrupts. Earthly nourishment enjoyed in idleness, without sanctification of the Spirit, is not merely *perishable.* This word is too weak for ἀπολλυμένην (comp. Matt. ix. 17: οἱ ἀσκοὶ ἀπολοῦνται); the food goes to destruction, and with it the man who seeks his life in it. It therefore leaves not only hunger, but also loathing (Num. xxi. 5, in regard to the manna). Decaying food loses not only (1) its efficiency, but (2) its healthful nature, and (3) its very nature itself. On the contrary food which endureth unto everlasting life has (1) eternal efficiency; (2) eternal fresh-

* [Strauss unnecessarily creates this difficulty.—P. S.]

ness; (3) eternal durability.—The difference between this and the water which quenches thirst, chap. iv. 14. That passage concerns the life of Christ refreshing, quickening, and satisfying the soul; this describes the life of Christ refreshing, nourishing, and supporting the whole being of the man.—**Everlasting life**;—viewed here in the main as an outward object, but including the internal operation of it.

Which the Son of man shall give unto you.—Undoubtedly based on the figure of laborer and employer, as in chap. iv. 36, and in the parable of the laborers in the vineyard, Matt. xx. 1 sqq. In His service they must work only for the eternal food, and this He would *give* them. And as the eternal food can come from God alone, He declares that He is sealed as steward of the Father; appointed and accredited with commission and seal (σφραγίζειν also denotes confirmation, appointment with a seal). He is sealed (accredited in particular by the miraculous feeding as a sign) as the Son of His Father's house, commissioned or sent from God. He thus seems to appoint them as laborers of God; and hence the question that follows.

Ver. 28. **What shall we do, that we might work the works of God?**—They seem ready to consent to the requirement of Christ. They wish to be in a general sense the servants of God, and do His work. But that their spirit in the matter is rather chiliastic than moral (Meyer) is shown (1) by their asking about *works* in the plural; (2) by their stress on *their doing*. The case is like that in John viii. 30: an apparent or conditional readiness, arising from chiliastic misconception. Not exactly a merely moral legalness of mind, though it includes this. Two interpretations: 1. The works which God *requires*, has commanded (De Wette, Tholuck). [Alford: the works well pleasing to God, comp. 1 Cor. xv. 58.—P. S.] 2. The works which God *produces* (Herder, Schleiermacher). The former interpretation is true to the mind of the people.

Ver. 29. **This is the work of God, that ye believe in him whom he sent.**—Jesus meets the plural with the singular,* and their proposal to *do* with the demand of *faith* in Him whom God sent. The connection of ideas is close: As servants of God they must yield themselves with unreserved confidence to the messenger of God; through Him alone do they become capable of doing anything, ver. 50; xvii. 3; 1 John iv. 17. Bullinger, Beza: Faith is called a work *per mimesin*. Tholuck, on the other hand: Faith is itself a work. It is the decisive work of the man, in which resides the decisive work of God. [Mark the distinction between believing Christ, which is simply an intellectual assent to an historical fact and which may be ascribed to demons and infidels, and believing *in* Christ as an object of confidence and hope, which implies vital union with Him. This is both a work of Divine grace and the highest work of man. Godet finds here the germ of the whole Pauline theology and also the bond of union between Paul and James. Faith is the greatest act of freedom towards God; for by it he gives himself, and more man cannot do. In this sense James opposes works to a faith which is nothing but an intellectual belief; and in an analogous sense Paul opposes active living faith to dead works of mere outward observance. The faith of Paul is in fact the work of James, *i. e.*, the work of God. Schleiermacher calls this passage the clearest and most significant declaration that all eternal life proceeds from nothing else than faith in Christ.—P. S.]

Ver. 30. **What signs shewest thou then?**—*i. e.:* To prove that Thou art the one sent of God? For that He professed Himself to be this messenger, is evident from what He had said. The term Messiah is indeed not used, but it is implied. Some have considered the question strange, because the people had just yesterday been miraculously fed. Grotius supposed it to be put by persons who had not been present at that feeding; the negative critics found in it a contradiction of the preceding account (Bruno Bauer, and others): De Wette considers the conversation as having no reference to the feeding. But we must bear in mind, that the people presumed that Jesus, if He were the Messiah, must have accepted their acclamation and their proclamation of His royalty; and that, instead of doing so, He had, to their great chagrin, eluded their design. They therefore demanded that He more satisfactorily attest Himself than He did by that feeding. A sign from heaven they probably did not, like the Sanhedrists and Pharisees, intend; but no doubt a perpetual miraculous supply of bread under the new kingdom now to be set up. This is indicated by the explanatory addition: "What dost Thou *work?*" τί ἐργάζῃ. What dost Thou produce? Ironically pointed at His demand that they should work. The chiliastic Messiah must take the lead of all the people as the greatest master-workman. The expression is doubly antithetic: putting *His working* against theirs, and especially putting a *working* in testimony of His Messiahship against His declaration of it.

Ver. 31. **Our fathers did eat manna.**—Meyer: "The questioners, after being miraculously filled with earthly bread, rise in their miracle-seeking, and demand bread from heaven, such as God gave by Moses." What they wanted was, no doubt, primarily continuance; though not this alone. The thought is: If Moses perpetually fed his people with bread from heaven, it is too little that the Messiah, the greater than Moses, should give His people only one transient miraculous meal, and as it were put them off with that. He ought to introduce the Messianic kingdom by giving every day a miraculous supply, and that by all means finer than barley loaves, superior manna. Comp. Matt. iv. 3.

As it is written, He gave them bread from heaven. (Ex. xvi. 4; Ps. lxxviii. 24; cv. 40). Meyer: The Jews considered the manna the greatest of miracles.* As Moses was the type of the Messiah (Schöttgen, *Horæ Talm.*, II., p. 475), a new manna was expected from the Messiah Himself: "*Redemptor prior descendere fecit pro iis Manna; sic et redemptor posterior*

* [So Bengel: "*Jesus singularem numerum opponit plurali Judæorum, qui dixerant, opera Dei*, ver. 28." Alford: "Because there is but this one work, properly speaking, and all the rest are wrapt up in it."—P. S.]

* [Josephus called it θεῖον καὶ παράδοξον βρῶμα.]

descendere faciet Manna." *Midras Coheleth.* Fol. 86, 4. (Lightfoot, Schöttgen, Wetstein.)

The *manna* (מָן), which miraculously furnished the Israelites in the Arabian desert [for forty years] the means of support, Ex. xvi.; Num. xi., *etc.*, fell during the night, and in the morning lay as dew upon the earth, Ex. xvi. 14, in small grains (like coriander-seed, Ex. xvi. 31), sweet, like honey, to the taste. It had to be gathered [every day except the Sabbath] before the sun rose, or it melted, ver. 21. "The quantity divided daily to each person, Ex. xvi. 16, Thenius (*Althebräische Masse*) estimates at somewhat over two Dresden quarts" [about three English quarts.—P. S.]. On the well-known oriental (medicinal) manna of natural history, see Winer, *sub v.* This appears even in southern Europe on various trees and shrubs; then in the east (manna-ash, oriental oak, especially the sweet-thorn), likewise tarfa-bush; abundant in Arabia, particularly in the vicinity of Sinai. A resinous exudation, resembling sugar, appearing sometimes spontaneously, sometimes through incisions made by insects or by men; appearing specifically on leaves and twigs. Several travellers assure us that in the east the manna falls as dew from the air. Even in this case a vegetable origin must be presumed. Our idea of the miraculous manna must be formed after the analogy of the Egyptian plagues: A natural phenomenon miraculously increased in an extraordinary manner by the power of God for a special purpose.* At present scarcely six hundred-weight are gathered on the peninsula of Petræa in the most favorable years.—According to Chrysostom and others the manna came from the atmosphere, and so from just below the real heaven.

Ver. 32. **It is not Moses** [οὐ before Μωυσῆς] **that gave you the bread from heaven.**—Introduced with a: *Verily, verily.* Not questioning the miraculousness of the manna (Paulus), but denying that the manna of Moses was from the real heaven, and was real manna. The question is not of a manna in an ideal sense, but of the *real, true* manna. Tholuck: "The negation is to be taken not absolutely, but only relatively." It is relative, of course, considering the affinity of the symbol to the substance; but it is also absolute considering the infinite difference between them. According to Meyer the words "*from heaven*" in both cases (and in ver. 31) relate not to the bread (for then the phrase would be τὸν ἐκ τ. οὐρ.), but to δέδωκεν and δίδωσιν; and "in like manner in Ex. xvi. 4, מִן הַשָּׁמַיִם belongs not to לֶחֶם, but to מַמְטִיר." But we must not forget that the nature of the bread is described with the source of it: Bread of heaven, Ps. lxxxviii. 24; cv. 40. Just on account of the former of these two passages, to which the words before us refer, and where the Septuagint has ἄρτον οὐρανοῦ, Tholuck, not without reason, prefers the usual interpretation.

[**My Father giveth you;** δίδωσιν, now and always, opposed to δέδωκεν, which is said of Moses. Bengel: *Jam aderat panis*, ver. 33.—P. S.] **The true bread from heaven.**—[ἀληθινός, *genuine, veritable, essential*, as opposed to derived, borrowed, imperfect, while ἀληθής, *true*, is opposed to *false*. Comp. note on i. 9, p. 66.—P. S.] Exactly parallel with the *true* light (chap. i. 9); the *true* vine (xv. 1); and to the same class of expressions: the *true* well of water, the *true* medicinal fountain, the *true* shepherd, *etc.*, substantially belong.

Ver. 33. **For the bread of God is that which cometh down from heaven.**—The decisive declaration by way of a description of the bread of God; ὁ καταβαίνων referring to ἄρτος, not to Christ (against Paulus, Olshausen).* Without this bread there is no substantial life, and no substantial nourishment of life. [**Unto the world,** *i. e.*, all mankind; in opposition to the Jewish particularism which boasted in the manna as a national miracle. Bengel: *Non modo uni populo, uni ætati, ut manna cibavit unum populum unius ætatis.*—P. S.]

Ver. 34. **Lord, evermore give us this bread.**—Comp. the request of the woman in chap. iv. 15. The people presume that Christ is the agent of the Father's gift. Interpretations: 1. Dim suspicion of the higher gift [perhaps the heavenly manna which, according to the Rabbis, is prepared for the just in heaven; comp. Rev. ii. 17] (Lücke, Tholuck, and others). 2. They think the bread something material, separate from Christ (De Wette, Meyer, [Godet]). And in any case their prayer is more decidedly sensuous and chiliastically perverted, than the prayer of the woman of Samaria. [Some take the prayer as an irony based on incredulity as to the possibility of such bread. Not warranted.—P. S.]

Ver. 35. **I** ['Εγώ] **am the bread of life.**—[Transition from the indirect to the direct form of speech, as in ver. 30, and a categoric answer to the request of the Jews: "Give us this bread," together with the indication of the way how to get it. Here is this bread before you, and all you have to do is to come unto Me. I am the bread, and faith is the work or the means of getting it.—P. S.] Most emphatic and decisive

* [Others regard the Scripture manna as wholly miraculous, and not in any respect a product of nature. So the writer of the article *Manna* in Smith's *Dictionary of the Bible*, who thus sets forth the difference between the natural and this supernatural manna: "The natural products of the Arabian deserts and other oriental regions, which bear the name of manna, have not the qualities or uses ascribed to the manna of Scripture. They are all condiments or medicines rather than food, stimulating or purgative rather than nutritious; they are produced only three or four months in the year, from May to August, and not all the year round; they come only in small quantities, never affording anything like 15,000,000 of pounds a week, which must have been requisite for the subsistence of the whole Israelitish camp, since each man had an omer (or three English quarts) a day, and that for forty years; they can be kept for a long time, and do not become useless in a day or two; they are just as liable to deteriorate on the Sabbath as on any other day: nor does a double quantity fall on the day preceding the Sabbath; nor would natural products cease at once and for ever, as the manna is represented as ceasing in the book of Joshua."—P. S.]

* [Alford: "The words ὁ καταβ . . . are the predicate of ὁ ἄρτος, and do not apply, in the construction of this verse, to Christ personally, however truly they apply to Him in fact. The E. V. is here wrong: it should be, *The bread of God is* THAT (not HE) *which cometh, etc.* Not till ver. 35 does Jesus first say, '*I am* the bread of life.' The manna is still kept in view, and the present participle, here used in reference to the manna, is dropped when the Lord Himself is spoken of." The note of Wordsworth on ver. 33 is a curious specimen of the wild allegorizing of this learned and devout patristic and Anglican antiquarian. He sees here everywhere allusions to the sacrament. Even the meaning of the word *Manna*, "what is it," is made to indicate the wonderful double nature of Christ and the mystery of His presence in the eucharist.—P. S.]

assertion. Still stronger than that in chap. iv. 26, since it was more open to contradiction; though here it is not the profession of Himself as the Messiah by name. (Philo, *Allegor. legis*, lib. III.: λόγος θεοῦ ψυχῆς τροφή.)—**He that cometh to me.**—Is willing to believe, and uses the means of faith that he may believe. Conversion in its Christian aspect. Not, as Meyer makes it, only a different phrase for πιστεύων.* According to Meyer the expression: "Shall never thirst," is a confusion of the figure, and anticipates the drinking of the blood of Christ, which follows. But it is rather an introduction to Christ's further declaration of Himself. As faith is developed, it brings, besides the *impartation* and *sustenance* of the spiritual life, the *satisfaction* also of having drunk. It is less natural to make this addition, with Lücke [and Alford], a description of the excellence of the heavenly bread over the manna [which was no sooner given, than the people began to be tormented with thirst and murmured against Moses, Ex. xvii., 1 ff.—P. S.]

Ver. 36. **But I said unto you.**—He said this to them not, as Lücke and De Wette have it, at chap. v. 37; for there He was speaking to the Sanhedrists in Jerusalem; but, as Grotius [Bengel] Luthardt and others, [Stier, Olsh., Hengstenberg, Godet] make it, at verse 26; though He there said it to them in other words. [Christ quotes Himself here, as He often quotes the Old Testament, more after the spirit than after the letter.] According to Euthymius Zigabenus [and Alford] the Lord refers to some utterance not recorded; according to Meyer it means: *I will have said* [εἶπον=*dictum velim*] *to you just now;* which it *can* mean,† as to the letter, but *must* not mean here. **That ye have even seen me.**—They have already seen Him in a Messianic function at the feeding, and yet did not see the sign in His miracle, and so did not truly see *Him*. So near were they to salvation; but they lacked faith. A paraphrase of ver. 26. [The two καί are correlative and bring out the glaring contrast of the two facts of even seeing the Son of God in His glory, and yet not believing in Him.—P. S.]

Ver. 37. **All that the Father giveth me.**‡—As to the connection: The judgment just uttered is true of the body of those who were before Him. It is not intended to exclude the thought that there were some among them, whom the Father had given to Him. It is, therefore, not in absolute antithesis to what precedes (as Meyer makes it). **All.** Neuter. The strongest expression of totality, as in chap. iii. 6, [*totam quasi massam*, as Bengel has it; comp. also xvii. 2, where πᾶν is likewise used of persons in this emphatic sense of totality.—P. S.]* **That the Father giveth me.** [The same as whom the Father *draws*, ver. 44.—P. S.] Not only the *gratia præveniens*, operating through nature and history, conscience and law, (comp. ver. 44), but also the effectual call to salvation—the *gratia convertens*—itself, is the work of the Father. The conversion, the coming to Jesus, is the answer to the call. Tholuck: It runs through the Gospel of John as a fundamental view, that all attraction towards Christ presupposes an affinity in the person for Christ, and then this affinity is the operation of the Father; and so here the unsusceptibility of the people is traced to this want of inward affinity. The phrase δίδοσθαι παρὰ τοῦ πατρός is also in chap. x. 29; xvii. 2, 6; comp. in the Old Testament, Is. viii. 18: "I and the children whom the Lord hath given me." The Predestinarians refer this passage to the eternal election [Augustine, Beza], the Arminians to the *gratia generalis*, the ability to believe [Grotius: *pietatis studium*], the Socinians to the *probitas*, natural honesty and love of truth, *etc.* We consider that in the "*giveth*" the three elements of election, predestination (fore-ordination), and calling are combined, Rom. viii. 29. But undoubtedly fore-ordination is very especially intended. [**Shall come unto me,** πρὸς ἐμὲ ἥξει. By an act of faith. Comp. the following τὸν ἐρχόμενον. Godet distinguishes ἥξει from ἐλεύσεται, and explains it: *will arrive at Me*, will not suffer shipwreck, but infallibly attain the goal. He calls the usual interpretation tautological, in as much as the gift consists in the coming, but this is not correct; the δίδωσι is the act of God, and the ἔρχεσθαι the act of man, *i. e.*, faith in actual motion towards Christ.—P. S.]

And him that cometh to me, I will in no wise cast out.—Every one who *comes* to Him is *welcome*. The only criterion is the coming or the not coming; no matter what the previous condition or guiltiness; the coming bespeaks the will of the Father, which it is the office of Christ to fulfil. [Οὐ μὴ ἐκβάλω ἔξω does not refer to Christ's office as Judge at the resurrection, but to the present order of grace, and is a litotes, *i. e.*, it expresses in a negative form more strongly the readiness of Christ to receive with open arms of love every one that comes to Him.—P. S.]

Ver. 38. **For I came down from heaven,** *etc.*—Expressing the complete condescension and humiliation in the estate of the Redeemer. But how could His will be different from the Father's?

* [So also Godet: "*Les deux termes, venir et croire, expriment, avec et sans figure, une seule et meme idée: le joyeux et confiant empressement avec lequel le cœur affamé et pressé de besoins spirituels s'empare de l'aliment céleste qui lui est présenté en Jésus Christ.*" *Coming* to Christ is faith indeed, yet not in repose as mere trust and confidence, or as a state of mind, but in active exercise and motion from the service of sin to the service of Christ; comp. 37, 44, 45, 65; vii. 37, 38.—P. S.]

† [In classical usage (see Kühner, II., § 443, 1, and Hermann *Ad Viger.*, p. 746) but not in New Testament unless it be the εἶπον in John xi. 42.—P. S.]

‡ [Yet the absence of a connecting particle seems to indicate a pause of reflection intervening between the preceding reproof (οὐ πιστεύετε), and the following description of the true children of God.—P. S.]

* [Bengel's observation on πᾶν is longer than is usual with this epigrammatic commentator, but well worth quoting: "A most weighty word, and, in comparing with it those things which follow, most worthy of consideration; for, in the discourses of Jesus Christ, what the Father hath given to the Son Himself, that is termed, both in the singular number and neuter gender, *all* (*omne*): those who come to *the Son* Himself, are described in the masculine gender, or even the plural number, *every one* (*omnis*), or *they* (*illi*). The Father hath given to the Son, as it were, the whole mass, in order that all whom He hath given, may be a *unit* (*unum*): that *whole* (*universum*) the Son evolves individually (one by one), in the execution of the Divine plan. Hence that expression, chap. xvii. 2, *that* ALL which (πᾶν ὅ, *omne quod*) THOU HAST GIVEN *Him*, HE SHOULD GIVE THEM (αὐτοῖς, *eis*) *eternal life*. In the Greek style of the New Testament, especially of John, wheresoever fastidious minds would say the construction was a solecism, an elegance truly divine, which to the Hebrews never seemed harsh, is usually found to lie beneath. That remark especially holds good of this passage."—P. S.]

The ideal will of the Son of man, in and of itself, must continually press towards the perfecting of the world and of life, and therefore legitimately lead to judgment. But in the spirit of redemption Christ continually directs this current of rightful judgment by the counsel of that redemption which is in operation till the end of the world; and this is His humiliation to the death of the cross, and this His patience, in the majesty of His exaltation.

Ver. 39. **And this is the will of him that sent me** [according to the correct reading instead of **the Father's will**] **that of all which he hath given me.**—The decree of redemption. Hence the perfect: *Which He hath given me.* Spoken not from a point of view in the future (as Meyer says); nor with reference to election, but with with reference to the perseverance of the divine purpose of salvation, to which the perseverance of the patience of Christ and the perseverance of believers correspond (see Rom. viii. 29 ff.). **I should lose nothing.**—Let nothing be lost by breaking off before the final decision of persistent unbelief in every case. **But should raise it up.**—Evidently meaning the resurrection to life. The Son is not only to continue, but to carry to its blessed consummation the work of resurrection. It is not, therefore, the day of death (Reuss),* nor specifically the first resurrection (Meyer), which is intended. **The last day,** ἐσχάτῃ ἡμέρᾳ.—The period of judgment and resurrection from the second coming of Christ to the general resurrection, Rev. xx.

[The resurrection of the body is the culmination of the redeeming work beyond which there is no more danger. Bengel: *Hic finis est, ultra quem periculum nullum. Citeriora omnia præstat Salvator.* This "blessed refrain," as Meyer calls it, is three times repeated, vers. 40, 44, 54; comp. x. 28; xvii. 12; xviii. 9. What stronger assurance of final resurrection to life everlasting can the believer have than this solemnly repeated assurance from the unerring mouth of the Saviour: "I shall raise him up on the last day." But true faith is no carnal confidence, it is always united with true humility. The more we trust in Christ, the less we trust in ourselves. All is safe if we look to Christ, all is lost, if we look to ourselves alone. Christians should pray as if all depended upon God, and watch and work as if all depended upon themselves.—P. S.]

Ver. 40. **That every one that seeth the Son.**—A stronger putting of the gracious will of God in its final intent. Hence again naming the Son in the third person. What John said to his disciples, Jesus now says openly to the Jews: Faith in the Son has everlasting life. Who the Son is, He gives them to know by declaring that He will raise up these believers.

Ver. 41. **The Jews therefore murmured at him.**—A new section of the affair, occasioned by the Jews' taking decisive offence at the preceding discourse. The οὖν is again very definitive. The verb γογγύζω, of itself, denotes neither, on the one hand, a whispering, nor, on the other, a grumbling or fault-finding; but the murmuring is here the expression of fault-finding, and is made by the context ("among yourselves," and by the antagonism ("at Him") synonymous with it.—**The Jews.** In the ὄχλος itself the Jewish element was aroused (De Wette); but no doubt the Pharisaic members of that synagogue are here especially concerned; and even Judas, whose very name is Jew, here seems to have already become soured (see ver. 64).

The bread which came down from heaven.—This declaration transcended their idea of the Messiah; and that in it which, unconsciously, most offended them was its offer of a suffering or self-sacrificing Messiah. Hence the Lord afterwards brought this out with special prominence. But they seized the declaration in another aspect. When, without directly claiming it, He indicated His divine sonship by saying that He came down from heaven, they considered Him as contradicting His known origin. A sensuous, narrow, literalistic apprehension.

Ver. 42. **Is not this Jesus.**—The οὗτος, primarily, strongly demonstrative. The same person, of whom we know that He sprang from Nazareth and rose to be a Rabbi, pretends to have come down from heaven. This contrast and the skepticism of the people add a contemptuous tone to the pronoun. **The son of Joseph.**—These words do not imply that both the parents were still living (Meyer), but that the people considered both (whom they once *knew*) to be His parents. Of Joseph, whom the tradition represents as advanced in years at the time of his marriage to Mary, we have no trace in the Gospels after the childhood of Jesus (comp. Matt. xiii. 55). [John introduces here the Jews as speaking from their own stand-point. They, of course, knew nothing of the mystery of the supernatural conception, and would not have appreciated it, if Jesus had corrected them. This was a truth for the initiated, and was not revealed even to the disciples before they were fully convinced that Christ was the Son of God. —P. S.]

Ver. 43. **Murmur not among yourselves.**—Jesus intended not to draw out their thoughts, but goes on to expose their defect.

Ver. 44. **No man can come to me.***—Here: *reach* Me; in particular: reach an understanding of My nature, apprehend the Spirit in the flesh, Deity in humanity, the Son of God in the Nazarene. **Except the Father draw him.**—Ἑλκύειν denotes all sorts of *drawing*, from violence to *persuasion* or *invitation*. But *persons* can be drawn only according to the laws of personal life. Hence this is not to be taken in a high predestinarian sense (Calvin: It is false and impious to say *non nisi volentes trahi;*† Beza: *Volu-*

* [Against this false interpretation of Reuss (*Hist. de la théol. Chrétienne*, II. p. 462), comp. Godet II. p. 114.—P. S.]

* [In ver. 37 Christ had declared that the totality (πᾶν which is to be taken collectively as of one integral whole) of those whom the Father giveth Him, shall come to Him; in ver. 44 He declares that no one can come in any other way except by the drawing of the Father. The effect follows in every case from a certain cause, but this effect will follow from no other cause.—P. S.]

† [Calvin, however, says before (*ad loc.*) that the efficient motion of the Holy Spirit first makes unwilling men willing ("*homines ex nolentibus et invitis reddit voluntarios*"). So also Augustine who expressly says that faith is inseparable from will (*credere non potest nisi volens*), and: "*Non ut homines, quod fieri non potest, nolentes credant, sed ut volentes ex nolentibus fiant.*" He quotes from Virgil: *trahit sua quemque voluptas*, to show that the drawing is that of choice not of

mus, quia datum est, ut velimus; Aretius: *Hic ostendit Christus veram causam murmuris esse quod non sint electi*). Yet on the other hand the force of the added clause, denoting a figurative, vital constraint, subduing by the bias of want, of desire, of hope, of mind, must not be abated. The *drawing of the Father* is the point at which election and fore-ordination become calling (the *vocatio efficax*), represented as entirely the work of the Father. Meyer: "The ἑλκύειν is the mode of the διδόναι, an internal pressing and leading to Christ by the operation of divine grace (Jer. xxx. 3, *Sept.*), though not impairing human freedom." The element of calling is added through the word of Christ. Hence: **The Father who sent Me.** As sent of the Father, He executes the Father's work and word. The congruence of the objective work of salvation and the subjective operation of salvation in the individual.

['Ελκύειν (or ἕλκω, fut. ἕλξω, which is preferred to ἑλκύσω by the Attic writers), *to draw, to drag, to force*, almost always implies force or violence, as when it is used of wrestling, bending the bow, stretching the sail, or when a net is drawn to the land, a ship into the sea, the body of an animal or a prisoner is dragged along, or a culprit is drawn before the tribunal (comp. John xviii. 10; xxi. 6, 11; Acts xvi. 19, and the classical Dictionaries, also Meyer, p. 266). It is certainly much stronger than δίδωσι, ver. 37, and implies active or passive resistance, or obstructions to be removed. Here and in xii. 32, it does, of course, not mean physical or moral compulsion, for faith is in its very nature voluntary, and *coming to Christ* is equivalent to *believing in Him;* but it clearly expresses the mighty moral power of the infinite love of the Father who so orders and overrules the affairs of life and so acts upon our hearts, that we give up at last our natural aversion to holiness, and willingly, cheerfully and thankfully embrace the Saviour as the gift of gifts for our salvation. The natural inability of man to come to Christ, however, is not physical nor intellectual, but moral and spiritual; it is an unwillingness. No change of mental organization, no new faculty is required, but a radical change of the heart and will. This is effected by the Holy Ghost, but the providential drawing of the Father prepares the way for it.—P. S.]

Ver. 45. **It is written in the prophets,** *etc.*—[This verse explains what kind of drawing was meant in the preceding verse, *viz.*, by divine illumination of the mind and heart.] *Prophets, i. e.*, the division of the Holy Scriptures called the *Prophets*. Yet the phrase is no doubt intended to assert that the particular passage, Is. liv. 13, (quoted freely from the Sept.), is found in substance throughout the prophets (which Tholuck calls in question; comp. Isa. xi.; Jer. xxxi. 33; Joel iii. 1). **Taught of God.**—Taught by God; the genitive with the participle denoting the agent. The promises of universal illumination in the time of the Messiah. In the prophet the point of the passage quoted lies in the "**all**" in contrast with the isolated enlightenment under the Old Testament. And here, too, this universality is not denied, though it is to be limited to all believers. The children of the Messianic time are the "all" from the fact that an inward, immediate divine illumination gives them faith in the word spoken by Christ. Cyril, Ammonius, and the older Lutheran expositors: Taught of God, *per vocem evangelicam;* the mystics: by the Spirit working with the outward word, by the inner light; Clericus, Delitzsch, and others: by the prevenient grace.—It is the calling provided for by election and fore-ordination; but it is this calling considered inwardly, as the operation of the Father by the Spirit;—an operation distinct from the spiritual life which proceeds from the Son, but not separate from it. Effectual calling, on its intellectual side: the enlightening of the mind.

Every man that hath learned of the Father.—According to the reading ἀκούων, we suppose the hearing the Father is to be conceived as continuous. As soon as the *having learned* is thereby effected, the man, as one *taught of God*, comes to Christ. The reference is of course to the whole discipline of the Father, which proceeds from His election; but it is to this (1) as becoming manifest in the effectual calling, and (2) as therein reaching its goal. Hence it is not the elect simply in view of this election (Beza), that are intended; still less the elect in a predestinarian sense.

Ver. 46. **Not that any one hath seen the Father.**—Explaining, that those who are taught of God in the Messianic age, still have need of the Messiah. Different interpretations: (1) The Lord would contrast His true seeing of God with that of Moses (Cyril, Erasmus). (2) He would forestall the spiritualistic view, that the inward manifestation of God supersedes the historical Christ (Calovius, Lampe). (3) He would mark a difference in degree and kind of revelation (Bengel: *Videre interius est, quam audire;* Tholuck). The third interpretation does not, as Tholuck thinks, set aside the second. The *same* fact, that the historical Christ is the positive fulfilment of all previous revelation and knowledge of God, and is therefore indispensable, is expressed in a different way; but all such facts as that He is Reconciler, King, Redeemer, are rooted in the fact that, being the Son, He is, in His perfect vision of God, the absolute Prophet (comp. chap. i. 18). **Save he who is of God.**—The full divine nature was necessary to the full view of God.

Ver. 47. **He that believeth on me hath everlasting life.**—Here again it must be observed, (1) that Christ has put His previous Messianic statements in a general form, not in the first person, but that He connects His soteriological statement, His declaration of salvation, directly with His person; and (2) that He asseverates: *Verily, verily.* This is, therefore, Christ's positive offer of Himself as the personal Saviour; and now follows the declaration.

compulsion. Calvin expressly guards in this connection against the abuse of his doctrine. "They are madmen," he says ad. ver. 40, "who seek their own salvation or that of others in the labyrinth of predestination, not keeping the way of faith which is proposed to them. . . . Since God has elected us to this very end that we believe, we destroy the election if we set aside faith (*tolle fidem, et mutila erit electio*) . . . If God calls us effectually to faith in Christ, it is of the same force to us, as if by an engraved seal He confirmed His decree concerning our salvation. For the testimony of the Spirit is nothing else but the sealing of our adoption. To every man, therefore, his faith is a sufficient attestation of God's eternal predestination, so that it is impious and an insult to the testimony of the Holy Spirit to search beyond it."—P. S.]

[Mark the present tense *hath* (ἔχει), not *shall have*. Eternal life is not confined to the future world, but is ever present and becomes ours as soon as we lay hold of Christ who *is* eternal life Himself. The resurrection of the body is only the full bloom of what has begun here. Mark also that *faith*, and nothing else, is laid down here, and in this whole discourse (comp. ver. 40; iii. 15, 16,) as the condition of eternal life. The eating of Christ's flesh and the drinking of His blood, to be consistent with this, is only a stronger form of expressing the same idea of a real personal appropriation of Christ by faith. This refutes all forms of ecclesiasticism which throw any kind of obstruction between the soul and Christ, as an essential condition of salvation, whether it be the authority of pope or council or creed or system of theology, or the intercession of saints, or good works of our own. Salvation depends solely and exclusively upon personal union with Christ: all other things, however important in their place, are subordinate to this. *Without faith in Christ there can be no salvation* for any sinner: this is the exclusiveness of the gospel; but *with faith in Christ there is salvation* for all of whatever sect or name: this is its charity.—P. S.]

Ver. 48. **I am the bread of life.**—Tholuck (like Meyer), on vers. 47-51: "After repelling the objection of the Jews, Jesus returns to His former theme in vers. 32-40, and in the first place repeats the same thought." We find here not a return, but an advance, carrying the thought forward from the person of Christ to His historical work. This appears from what follows. "Of *the* life." Referring to the preceding promise of eternal life. "Τῆς ζωῆς. *Genitiv. qual. and effectus.*" Or probably, conversely, the genitive of form or mode of existence. [That is, not: "the bread which has the quality and effect of life, the bread which is and which gives life;" but: "the life which is bread; the life existing and offered in the form of bread, and operating as bread."—E. D. Y.] Previously the bread was the subject, with various predicates (the person); now the bread becomes an attribute of the life (the giving and the effect of the person). *The life as bread*, not the bread as life. That Jesus is the life, follows from vers. 46 and 47. This thought is expanded further on.

Ver. 49. **Your fathers did eat manna.**—The manna gave no abiding life, because it was not essential life.

Ver. 50. **This is the bread.**—By this the bread may be known as the true bread: that it comes down from heaven for the purpose and to the effect that whosoever eateth of it shall not die; or, more precisely: It cometh down from heaven, in order that men may eat of it (the ἵνα affecting this first clause), and that he who eateth of it may not die. The definition of the true bread by its origin, its design, and its effects. The μὴ ἀποθάνῃ is more exactly expressed in the κἂν ἀποθάνῃ of chap. xi. 25.

Ver. 51. **I am the living bread.**—I am the bread living. The life is now the logical subject. The Vulgate: *Ego sum panis vivus* (,) *qui de cœlo descendi;* the bread living, who [1st pers.] have come down from heaven.

If any man eat of this bread.—Because Christ is the living bread, He offers Himself as bread, and communicates by the eating of this bread a living forever. Christ, therefore, now distinguishes Himself as life from the bread of life as a gift.

And the bread that I will give.—No longer: The bread which I *am*. The καί—δέ, [*atque etiam*] is to be noted [*i. e.*, καὶ ὁ ἄρτος δέ, ὃν ἐγ. δ.: "And the bread, now, which I will give."] See Tholuck.* **Is my flesh.**—The bodily, finite, historical form of Christ, which He yields up for the world in His death, and thus gives to the world for its nourishment, chap. ii. 19; iii. 14. Not only the sacrifice of Christ in His atoning death to procure the eternal life of the world (Meyer), but also the renewal and transformation of the world by its participation of the sacrificed life of Christ; as, in chap. ii. 19 and iii. 14, death and resurrection are combined. It seems strange that the second ἣν ἐγὼ δώσω [after ἡ σάρξ μου ἐστίν] should be wanting in Codd. B. C. D. L. T. [and א.], the Itala, the Vulgate, and three times in Origen; so as to be stricken out by Lachmann and Tischendorf [Tregelles, Alford, Westcott and Hort.—P. S.] Tholuck accordingly says, with Meyer: "A pregnance like this: The bread which I will give, is my flesh, *for the life of the world*,—would be as contrary to the style of John as the repetition ἣν ἐγὼ δώσω is agreeable to it." And he conjectures: "The omission may have been caused by the preceding δώσω." But the addition, too, may very easily have been made for doctrinal elucidation, to make the sentence point more distinctly to the atoning death. If, therefore, we let the above manuscripts decide, the death and resurrection are united; the point of the sacrificial death by itself is not yet so distinctly brought out in this place; and this seems more congruous with chap. iii. 14 (and with the conception of the Jews in the sequel). Therefore: *My flesh for the life of the world.* The manifestation in the flesh is necessary to the full life. The flesh of Christ will be the life of the world. That is, the giving up of His flesh in death and the distribution of His flesh in the resurrection will be the life of the world. Yet in the giving up of His flesh, His sacrificial death is mainly intended, and in the eating of it, faith in the atonement; and as this element in the conception is to be distinguished, on the one hand, from the fact that Christ is the bread in His person, in His historical life itself, so, on the other hand, it is to be distinguished from the fact that He, in His flesh and blood, prepares His life, glorified through death, for a eucharistic meal for the world.

Ver. 52. **The Jews therefore strove among themselves.**—Here a dispute arises concerning the sense in which the Lord could give men His flesh for the life of the world. And this dispute is described as a dispute of the Jews. Yet it is not a question of the interpretation of Christ's word, but of the offensiveness of it, which here sets the Jews at strife. The skeptics and cavillers lead, saying: **How can this man,** *etc.* They seem

* [Tholuck says: καί—δέ designates a more detailed statement, as in John i. 3, or a correction, as in xv. 27. Zwingli (as quoted by Tholuck), "*Dixi diu me panem esse vitæ, sed nondum quo facto id fiat, hoc jam aperiam.*" Δέ introduces here something of special importance. Comp. Meyer *in loc.*—P. S.]

disposed to charge the word with an abominable meaning, taking it literally.

Ver. 53. **Unless ye eat the flesh of the Son of man, and drink his blood.**—Jesus recedes not for the offense, but with a *verily, verily*, He goes further, and now divides the flesh into *flesh* and *blood*, and to the eating adds *drinking*, which He had first introduced at ver. 35.

Mark further: (1) This truth, enforced with *verily, verily*, is now expressed in *four different forms;* four times the Lord speaks of eating and drinking His flesh and blood. (2) The first time in a conditional injunction on the Jews with reference to the Messiah, in the negative form of threatening: "Unless ye eat, *etc.*, ye have no life in you." The second time in a positive statement referring to Jesus Himself, in the form of promise. The third time, in a statement of the nature and substantial effect of the flesh and blood of Christ, on which the preceding practical alternative is founded: "For my flesh is meat indeed," *etc.* The fourth time, in explication of all these three propositions: "He dwelleth in Me, and I in him."

For the interpretation, we must remember that elsewhere *flesh* (σάρξ), by itself, denotes *human nature* in its full concrete manifestation (John iii. 6); hence the *flesh* (σάρξ) of Christ, likewise, is the manhood of Christ, His personal human nature. But *flesh and blood* (σὰρξ καὶ αἷμα) elsewhere denotes inherited nature; in Peter (Matt. xvi. 17), for example, his old, hereditary Jewish nature, with its associations and views; in Paul (Gal. i. 16), his Pharisaic descent, spirit, and associations; in Christians (1 Cor. xv. 50), the mortal, earthly nature and form, received from natural birth, which cannot inherit the kingdom of God. Accordingly *the flesh and blood of Christ* are the peculiar descent and nature of Christ in historical manifestation; *the historical Christ.* As the flesh and blood of historical mankind are reduced to the material and nutriment of its culture and development, its humanity; so the flesh and blood of the historical Christ are given to be the nutriment of mankind's higher spiritual life, its divinity. And when the partaking of His flesh and blood is made the indispensable condition of salvation, the meaning is: The life of man proceeds only from the life of Christ completed in death; only by Christ's actual person being made the especial vital element of mankind, the nourishment and refreshment of the real life of man,—by this means alone does man receive true life.

The four sentences of this passage may be arranged in the following system:

(1) The flesh and blood of Christ are really the food and drink of man; *i. e.*, the sacrifice and the participation of the actual, divine-human Christ are for mankind the only escape from death, and the only way to the higher, spiritual life.

(2) Because nothing but the full reception of the historical Christ can effect full communion with Him, consisting in the believer's dwelling in Christ (justification), and Christ's dwelling in the believer (sanctification).

(3) Therefore he that eats, takes the nutriment of eternal life, which works in him to resurrection.

(4) He who takes not this nourishment, has no true life, and can attain to none.

Note: (1) the phrase *flesh and blood* (σὰρξ καὶ αἷμα) in our passage differs from *body and blood* (σῶμα καὶ αἷμα) in the words of institution of the holy Supper: the former applying to the whole historical, self-sacrificing Christ, the latter simply to His individual person just coming forth from the sacrifice. (2) In the preparation of the σὰρξ καὶ αἷμα for food, the life, death, and resurrection of Christ are blended in one, the leading element being the death; as in σῶμα καὶ αἷμα the two are blended under the leading aspect of the new life.—Tholuck: "The addition of αἷμα to σάρξ abates nothing from the notion (Matt. xvi. 7; Eph. vi. 11; 1 Cor. xv. 20), but only expresses still more definitely, that is, by its two main constituents, the sensible human nature." This, therefore, in its earthly manifestation (vers. 50 and 58), is to be spiritually received, and ver. 50, continuing to qualify the succeeding verses, shows that it is to be received especially in its atoning death, to which also the αἷμα may perhaps particularly point. The addition of αἷμα, however, denotes primarily the *generic* life in the *individualized* σάρξ. The flesh and blood of Christ are the historical Christ in His entire connection with God and man (as the "Son of God and of Mary"), as made by His death the eucharistic meal of the world;—certainly, therefore, a new point, with death as the most prominent aspect. [It should be added that the *blood* of Christ in the New Testament always signifies His atoning death for the sins of the world, comp. Rom. iii. 25; Col. i. 14, 20; Hebr. ix. 14, 20; x. 10; 1 Pet. i. 2, 19; 1 John i. 7; Rev. i. 5. It must refer to the same sacrifice here, and *flesh* must be interpreted accordingly. *Flesh and blood* are the whole human life of Christ as offered on the cross for the propitiation of the sins of the world, and thus become the fountain of life for all believers.—P. S.]

VARIOUS INTERPRETATIONS:

1. The atoning death of Christ: Augustine,* Luther, Melanchthon, Calvin, Beza, [Grotius, Calov.] Lücke, and many other modern expositors (see Meyer).†

2. The entire human manifestation of Christ including His death (Paulus, Frommann, De Wette, *etc.*)

3. The deeper self-communication of Jesus, faith eating and drinking in the human nature of Jesus the life of God (Hofmann, *Schriftbeweis*, [II. 2, p. 245 ff.]. "Not the giving of His flesh, but His flesh itself Jesus calls food." (Delitzsch).

4. A prophetic discourse in anticipation of the Lord's Supper (Chrysostom, most of the fathers [Cyril, Theophyl., Euth. Zigab., Cyprian, Hilarius, perhaps also Augustine, but see p. 228,] and Roman Catholics [Klee, Maier], Calixtus [a moderate Lutheran, strongly opposed by the high Lutheran Calovius], Zinzendorf, Bengel, Michaelis, Scheibel, Olshausen, Kling, *etc.*, Kahnis,‡ Luthardt [Wordsworth]; according to

* [On Augustine's interpretation see note in the Excursus below, p. 228.—P. S.]

† [Meyer (p. 270) adds to the above names, as favoring this view, Tholuck, Neander, Jul. Müller, Lange, Ebrard, Keim, Weiss, Ewald, Kahnis, Godet. But Lange, Ewald, Kahnis, Hengstenberg and Godet should be classed with No. 6 below. —P. S.]

‡ [In his work on the Lord's Supper, p. 104 ff., but later, in his Dogmatics, Vol. I. p. 624, Kahnis denies that John vi. re-

Heubner, the Reformed Church [he should say the Reformed theology] with the exception of Calvin).

5. A mythical discourse here anticipating the Lord's Supper, as John iii. anticipates baptism. (The negative critics, Bretschneider, Strauss, Baur, *etc.*).

6. The Lord does not speak here of the Supper itself, but expresses the idea on which the Supper is founded. (Here Meyer names Olshausen, Kling, Lange).

As to the first interpretation: Unquestionably the atoning death is in view, but in connection with its antecedent (the historical fact of Christ) and its effect (the historical gospel).

As to the second: The subject is no longer only the living person of Christ itself, but that which it will yield by its sacrifice of itself.

As to the third: The further pressing of the words themselves takes us to the very mode by which the life of Jesus is changed into the food and drink of mankind (death).

As to the fourth: The Lord's Supper itself cannot be the subject. (Heubner quotes the Lutheran church as denying this hypothesis, especially Luther. Yet it is plain from the foregoing that this exegetical antagonism is not confessional.) (*a*) The discourse would anticipate too much, and be unintelligible. (*b*) Ver. 53 would teach the absolute necessity of taking the communion rather than of evangelical saving faith. ("Even the Lutherans consider the Supper not *absolute* but only *ordinarie* necessary.") (*c*) The expression σὰρξ καὶ αἷμα is not equivalent to σῶμα καὶ αἷμα. (*d*) A *manducatio spiritualis* is here intended; for the partaker is assured of eternal life, which is only conditionally the case in the *fruitio oralis*. (*e*) The eating here described is perpetual.

As to the fifth: It is disposed of with the assumptions of that school of criticism in the Introduction. (The σάρκα φαγεῖν of Ignatius and Justin can prove nothing. It has its origin here.)

As to the sixth: As the specific ordinance of baptism is, in chap. iii., lodged in germ in the general idea of baptism as already known to history, so the specific ordinance of the Lord's Supper is here present in germ under the general idea and historical forms of the evening meal.

The hearers of Jesus were on their way to eat the paschal lamb; He says to them: Ye must eat Me, the real paschal lamb now offered in the history of the world. This then unquestionably contains a prophecy of the holy Supper, though it is not the Supper itself that is directly described.—*The emphasizing of the person is the decisive point. Personal reception of the historical person of Christ in its communication and sacrifice of itself (through the medium of the word and sacrament) is the fundamental condition of personal eternal life.*

Respecting the copious literature of this section, see Tholuck: Meyer [p. 273]. The dissertations of Kling, Müller,* Tischendorf [*De Christo pane vitæ*, 1839], the works on the Lord's Supper by Ebrard, Kahnis, Lindner, [Rückert, Nevin], Dieckhoff, the Excursus of Lücke,* *etc.*, are of mark.

Vers. 53, 54. **Unless ye eat** [φάγητε] . . . **and drink**. . . . **He that eateth** [τρώγων] **my flesh and drinketh my blood.**—*Eating* and *drinking* denotes full, actual faith, full, actual appropriation by faith. According to Hofmann, faith is not the thing directly in view, but is presupposed. The reception here meant is distinct from faith.† Against this see vers. 40 and 47, and the many passages in which the πιστεύειν is represented as the sole condition of the ζωὴ αἰώνιος. Τρώγειν [*to gnaw, to crack, to chew*, repeated four times, 54, 56-58.—P. S.], though in its general meaning equivalent to φαγεῖν, is a stronger expression (De Wette, *et al.*, against Tholuck);‡ and to it πίνειν is added. The tropical phrase is interpreted not so well by Eph. iii. 17 and Sir. xxiv. 21, as by the institution of the paschal lamb, and from the eating and the manna from which the discourse started. It is the strongest assertion of the personal aspect of salvation. **In you**, ἐν ἑαυτοῖς; *see* chap. v. 26.

Ver. 55. **My flesh is true food** [ἀληθής βρῶσις].—Ἀληθής is better attested than ἀληθῶς. [See TEXT. NOTES.] Tholuck considers it the antithesis of the real to the pretended, and disputes the sense ἀληθινός [*genuine, veritable*] (Origen, Lücke, *etc.*). *Rightly, if it be understood that the ἀληθινός, as opposed to the symbol (in this case, e. g., the manna), is strengthened to ἀληθής, and the symbol falls to nonentity and falsehood, the moment men put the symbol against the reality for which it stands.*§ **And my blood,**

fers *directly* to the Lord's Supper, and explains the eating and drinking to be identical with believing for the reason that the same effect is made dependent on both, *viz.*, eternal life. He should be classed with No. 6.—P. S.]

* [Latin dissertations on the difference between Luther's and Calvin's views on the Lord's Supper, 1853, now reproduced in German by Dr. Jul. Müller, of Halle, in his *Dogmatische Abhandlungen*, just published, Bremen, 1870, pp. 404-467.—P. S.]

* [In the second Excursus to the second edition of his Commentary on John (which is omitted in the third edition), and in the third edition, Vol. II., pp. 149-159.—P. S.]

† [Alford likewise makes this distinction, which is not sustained by the context. He says: "*What* is eating and drinking? Clearly not *merely faith*; for faith answers to the *hand reached forth for the food*,—but is *not the act of eating*. Faith is a *necessary condition* of the act: so that we can hardly say with Augustine, '*crede, et manducasti*;' but *crede et manducabis*. Inasmuch as faith will necessarily in its energizing lead to this partaking, we sometimes incorrectly say that it *is* faith: but for strict accuracy this is not enough. To eat the flesh of Christ, is to realize, *in our inward life, the mystery of His Body now in heaven,—to digest and assimilate our own portion in that Body*. To drink His Blood is *to realize, in our inward life, the mystery of His satisfaction for sin,—to digest and assimilate our own portion in that satisfaction, the outpouring of that Blood*. And both these definitions may be gathered into one, which is: The eating of His Flesh and drinking of His Blood import the making to ourselves and using as *objectively real*, those two great Truths of our Redemption in Him, of which our faith subjectively convinces us. And of this realizing of faith He has been pleased to appoint certain symbols in the Holy Communion, which He has commanded to be received; to signify to us the spiritual process, and to assist us towards it."—P. S.]

‡ [Meyer thinks that the change implies no intention of a stronger expression, since τρώγειν καὶ πίειν is used Matt. xxiv. 38 (τρώγοντες καὶ πίνοντες), by Demosthenes, Plutarch and Polybius without perceptible difference from φαγεῖν or ἐσθίειν. Τρώγων expresses the present of φαγών, which must be either τρώγων or ἐσθίων. So also Alford: The real sense is that by the very act of inward realization the possession of eternal life is certified. Wordsworth on the other hand presses the difference and, in fanciful sacramentarian exaggeration, says that τρώγειν presents the climax of the difficulty, and shows the need of coming to Christ in the holy communion with devout cravings and earnest longings of a famished soul for heavenly food.—P. S.]

§ [Meyer: ἀληθής expresses in opposition to mere appearance the *actual reality* (1 John ii. 27; Acts xii. 9), which the Jews could not comprehend, ver. 52. Alford: "ἀληθής is here not=ἡ ἀληθινή, nor is the sense, '*My flesh is the true meat*,' etc., but '*My flesh is true meat*,' *i. e.*, really *to be eaten*, which they doubted. Thus ἀληθῶς is a gloss, which falls short of the depth of the adjective. This verse is decisive *etc.*—"The life of the flesh is in the blood," says Lev. xvii. 11. Here it is said, in ver. 63: "It is the Spirit that quickeneth;" and in 1 Cor. xv. 45. If, now, as we have said on ver. 53, the flesh denotes rather the individualized nature of man, and the blood rather the general, then the blood of Christ also bears a reference to His generic life as Christ in distinction from His flesh, His personal manifestation in history. The connecting notion between His blood and His flesh is His life. We must eat His distinct historical form in believing, historical contemplation, but His life we must drink in spiritual contemplation and in the appropriation of fervent faith.

Ver. 56. **Dwelleth in me, and I in him.**—A Johannean phrase (chap. xv. 4; xvii. 23; 1 John iii. 24; iv. 16). Denoting personal community of life with Christ in its two correlative fundamental forms which appear singly in Paul: We in Christ, is the first (Gal. ii. 17); Christ in us, the second (Gal. ii. 20). From this effect of the heavenly food the reception of it may be more precisely defined: The vital appropriation of the whole person of Christ. This is not a *unio mystica* (Meyer, Tholück) in the stricter theological sense, though the living faith contains the basis for it. That an effect like this cannot be claimed for the reception of the Lord's Supper in and of itself, is plain. Yet the reception of the holy communion is the most efficient and copious medium, and the appointed seal; the believing participation is the highest specific act and form of this vital communion; and for this reason the unbelieving participation forms the most violent collision with this vital communion to judgment.

Ver. 57. **And I live by the Father.**—Here also the vital correlation is the main thing; Christ lives in the Father; that is, by the contemplation of the living, almighty Father, who is life absolute, and pure life, Christ is living and is sent by the Father. The Father lives in Him; that is, Christ has His own life by the Father's living in Him for the Father's sake, *i. e.*, He lives *for the Father.* (Διά with the accusative denotes not the *cause:* by the Father,* and hardly *the ground:* because the Father has life;† but the entire purpose and direction. "The Father will and must have such, He seeks such," chap. iv. 23. Angelus Silesius: "I am as much to Him as He is to me"). **So he . . . shall live by me.**—Here the eating is again the eating of Christ Himself. He to whom it is the nourishment of His life to sink Himself in the personal presence of Christ, as Christ has sunk Himself in the contemplation of the Father,—he is sent forth by the life of Christ, and lives for Him, as Christ is sent forth by the life of the Father, and lives for the Father. ("He shall divide the spoil with the strong" [German version: "He shall have the strong for a prey"]. Is. liii.

Ver. 58. **This is that bread.** Conclusion of the whole matter. As Christ had passed from the bread which He in Himself presents, to the bread which He gives, He here returns to the bread which He Himself is. Yet not merely in the same sense as before is He now Himself the bread. There it was Christ in His historical manifestation; here it is the eternal Christ, by the eternal intuition (τρώγων) of whom we live forever.

Ver. 59. **These things said he in the synagogue, as he taught in Capernaum.**—A historical note, accounting, in particular, for the fact that not only the Judaistic spirit in the popular mass which followed Him, but also many of His old adherents and disciples in Capernaum itself took offence at His words. From this locality of His discourse the sensuous construction of the eating of the body of Christ has been styled a *Capernaitic* eating.

Ver. 60. **Many therefore of his disciples, when they heard this.**—Many of His adherents in Capernaum and the vicinity. Μαθηταί in the wider sense. See the woe of Christ on Capernaum, Bethsaida, and Chorazin, Matt. xi. 20 ff. **Hard**; σκληρός, harsh, stern, rigorous; opposed to μαλακός, soft, tender, gentle. דְּבַר־עֶצֶב, Prov. xv. 1. Hard to *solve*, hard to *do*, hard to *bear*. The interpretation is contained in the next words: Who can hear it? *i. e.*, bear it. Hence not: *hard to understand* (Chrysostom, Grotius, Olshausen). According to Tholuck and others: *presumptuous*, for its making life depend on a scandalous eating of His flesh and blood (on man-eating). De Wette (Kuinoel, Meyer): Because they would not admit the thought of the death of the Messiah; not because they understood literally the eating of His flesh (Augustine, Grotius, Lücke). Unquestionably in the sequel, the suffering Messiah and His death on the cross were, as Meyer observes, the standing and specific σκάνδαλον of the Jews (chap. xii. 34; 1 Cor. i. 23). This interpretation is further commended by the fact that on this occasion Judas seems to have conceived his first aversion. Yet the succeeding utterance of the Lord gives a still more distinct clew. Formally, they certainly stumbled at the idea of eating flesh and drinking blood, in consequence of their Jewish laws of purity in reference to such acts and in reference to the abomination of human sacrifice. But then, materially, the thought of His sacrifice for their salvation which shone out intelligibly enough, was most certainly hard to them. They sought the Messianic kingdom in a rain of miraculous manna and other blessings from heaven; He would have them find everything in His own person, and even in the sacrificial suffering of that person. And the more repugnant to them the suggestion of this idea, the more they inclined to stick to the letter in which it was expressed, and to find it hard.

Ver. 61. **Knew in himself.**—'Εν ἑαυτῷ. Bengel's *sine indicio externo* is too strong. There were indications, no doubt, of their aversions; but He also knew how to interpret them as the searcher of hearts. **Doth this offend you?** Σκανδαλίζει. The Jewish idea of offence, σκάνδαλον; *i. e.*, the taking offence or occasion of falling (see σκάνδαλον, מוֹקֵשׁ *et* מִכְשׁוֹל in Bretschneider;

against all explaining away or metaphorizing the passage. Food and drink are not here mere metaphors;—rather are our common material food and drink mere shadows and imperfect types of this only real reception of refreshment and nourishment into being." Godet: "*L'adverbe* (ἀληθῶς) *ou l'adjectif* (ἀληθής) *exprime la pleine réalité de la communication vitale opérée par ces éléments.*"—P. S.]

* [*Per Patrem*, as the fountain of life. So Beza, De Wette, Alford, *etc.*—P. S.]

† [As Meyer takes it: *wegen des Vaters, d. i. weil Mein Vater der lebendige ist.* He quotes Plat. *Conv.*, p. 203, E.: ἀναβιώσκεται διὰ τὴν τοῦ πατρὸς φύσιν.—P. S.]

(comp. Rom. ix. 33; 1 Cor. i. 23; Gal. v. 11; 1 Pet. ii. 8).

Ver. 62. **What and if ye shall see the Son of man ascending where he was before?**—*Aposiopesis* [from ἀπο-σιωπᾶν, to be silent]. That the form of the broken sentence may be completed by *What shall ye say then?* (τί ἐρεῖτε; according to Euthym. Zig., Kuinoel, and others) is groundlessly disputed by Meyer. The only question is whether the meaning then would be: *shall ye then still take offence?* (ἔτι τότε σκανδαλισθήσεσθε;) or *shall ye then not be more offended?* (οὐχὶ μᾶλλον σκανδαλισθήσεσθε;) Opposite interpretations:

1. Meyer, after De Wette: The ἀναβαίνειν, *etc.*, denotes the dying of Jesus (comp. chap. vii. 33; xiii. 3; xvi. 5, 28),* and to the beholders, who saw only this humble, ignominious fact of the death of Jesus, this amounted to the highest offence (so Beza, Semler, *etc.;* the οὖν also is adduced in support).

2. Olshausen [Hengstenberg, Godet, Alford] and others, after the expositors of the ancient church: 'Αναβαίνειν denotes (as in chap. xx. 17) the ascension of Christ, and with this, or with His exaltation, offence must cease. Thus the question is: Will ye then still be offended? Augustine, *et al.*: Then will a deeper insight into the φαγεῖν τὴν σάρκα come.† Calvin: Then will the offence which they took at His sensuous manifestation, be done away. Lyser: Then, by His glorification, the glorification of His flesh for food will also be provided for. Luthardt: The glorified state of existence will take the place of the fleshly.

Meyer groundlessly urges, that the ascension, as a *visible* occurrence, is not attested by any *apostle*,‡ and in the unapostolical accounts § none but disciples in the narrower sense are mentioned as eye-witnesses.‖ The fact itself was nevertheless a visible one.

Meanwhile it is doubtless no more the ascension exclusively which is here in view, than it was exclusively the atoning death a little while ago. There the death includes the life and the exaltation; here the exaltation includes the death, chaps. iii. and xii. But it is evidently the exaltation viewed especially as produced by the Spirit, of which the next verse speaks. Hence in the same general sense as in Matt. xxvi. 64. It must also be considered, that Christ throughout gives to the Jews not only His death, but with it also carefully His resurrection, for a sign (Jno. ii. 19; Matt. xii. 39, and xvi. 3, the sign of Jonah). The resurrection destroyed the offence of the cross itself for the believing; and therefore for such it does away also the offensive word. *At the same time it glorified the personal life of Jesus by the outpouring of the Holy Ghost for the world's believing participation.* Nevertheless the Judaists continued to be offended, and perhaps for this reason the word of Christ remained an aposiopesis. [ὅπου ἦν τὸ πρότερον clearly implies the pre-existence of Christ; comp. i. 1; viii. 58; xvii. 5, 24; Col. i. 17; Rev. i. 8.—P. S.]

Ver. 63. **It is the Spirit that maketh alive, the flesh profiteth nothing.**—[Christ does not say *My* Spirit (τὸ πνεῦμα μου), and *My* flesh (ἡ σάρξ μου); the sentence is general and contains a hermeneutical canon which applies not only to this, but to all the discourses of Christ, and the proper mode of apprehending and appropriating Him. It must not be understood so as to conflict with the preceding declaration concerning His flesh. The flesh *without* the Spirit, or the flesh as mere matter and materially eaten, is worthless; but the flesh *with* the Spirit is worth much, most of all the flesh which the Logos assumed for our salvation (i. 14) and which He sacrificed on the cross for the sins of the world.—P. S.] Interpretations:

1. Of the holy Supper: spiritual participation [πνεῦμα], as opposed to Capernaitic or material [σάρξ]. So Tertullian, Augustine,* Rupert v. Deutz, Calvin, [Grotius] Olshausen, Kahnis [*Lehre vom Abendmahl*, p. 122]: "That which imparts to the eater of My flesh the virtue of eternal life, is not the flesh as such, but the Spirit."

2. The Spirit is put for the spiritual apprehension of the word of Christ, the body representing the carnal apprehension (Chrysostom and many others, Lampe).

3. The πνεῦμα is the human soul, which animates the body (Beza, Fritzsche).

4. Not His bodily manifestation, the approaching dissolution of which was so offensive to them, but His Spirit is the life-giving thing. His bodily substance merely of itself profits nothing towards the ζωοποιεῖν. Under the figure of physical life, in which the spirit animates the flesh, Christ expresses the truth that the historical side both of His *life* and of His *word*, needs to be animated and glorified by His Spirit. This they should and might see clearly in His very words. The substantives assert: They are *pure spirit, pure life.*

How Luther and Zwingle contended over the sense of these words, see in Heubner, p. 321 sqq. Zwingle appealed to these words against the Lutheran doctrine of the Lord's Supper†; Luther

---

* [Comp. also the ὑψωθῆναι ἐκ τῆς γῆς, xii. 32. To make this interpretation at all plausible, the ἀναβαίνειν ὅπου ἦν τὸ πρότερον must be understood from the standpoint of Jesus whose death was a return to the heaven whence He descended, and to the glory which He had before the foundation of the world, comp. xvii. 5. But the hearers could not have understood ἀναβαίνειν in this sense.—P. S.]

† [Aug.: *Certe vel tunc videbitis, quia non eo modo, quo putatis, erogat corpus suum; certe vel tunc intelligetis, quia gratia ejus non consumitur morsibus.* Harless and Stier: Then you will understand that, and how my glorified heavenly humanity and corporeity can be food and drink. But this would make Christ speak of a *future* act. Meyer remarks against Harless: The *glorified* body of Christ is, as *flesh and blood, inconceivable* (1 Cor. xv. 49 f.)—P. S.]

‡ [Comp. against this assertion of Meyer John iii. 13; xx. 17, where the ascension is clearly alluded to. Usually Jesus speaks of His death in John as a going to the Father or to Him that sent Me, vii. 33; xiii. 3; xiv. 12, 28; xvi. 5, 28; xvii. 11, 13.—P. S.]

§ [Mark xvi. 19; Luke xxiv. 51; Acts i. 9.—P. S.]

‖ [But Christ may have addressed here some of the apostles. Hengstenberg says, the witnesses of the resurrection were the representatives of all the disciples.—P. S.]

* [Aug. *Tract. in Joh.* 27, § 13 (*Opera* III., 503): *Caro non prodest quidquam quomodo illi intellexerunt . . . quomodo in cadavere dilaniatur, aut in macello venditur, non quomodo spiritu vegetatur . . . Accedat spiritus ad carnem, quomodo accedit caritas ad scientiam, et prodest plurimum. Nam si caro nihil prodesset, Verbum caro non fieret, ut inhabitaret in nobis.* Similarly Bengel: *Caro mera nil prodest: qualem scil. Judæi putabant esse carnem illam, de qua loquebatur Jesus. Loquitur sub conditione eaque impossibili, si sola caro esset . . . Caro est vehiculum virtutis divinæ omnis vivificantis, in Christo et in credentibus: et Christus, carne mortificatus, spiritu vivificatus, virtutem suam maxime exseruit,* 1 *Pet. iii.* 18; *John xii.* 24; *xvi.* 7.—P. S.]

† [He and Œcolampadius regarded ver. 63 as a *ferreus murus* of their doctrine of the Lord's Supper; yet Zwingli, like the other reformers, did not directly understand the passage, vers. 51–58, of the sacrament.—P. S.]

distinguished *the* flesh and *My* flesh, and explained "the flesh" as the carnal, corrupt mind of man. The verse no more supports Zwingle against a bodily presence of Christ, than it speaks, according to Luther's interpretation, of the corrupt flesh of the sinner.

Ver. 64. **For Jesus knew from the beginning.**—Ἐξ ἀρχῆς means not, metaphysically from the beginning of all things (Theophylact), nor from the beginning of His acquaintance with each one (De Wette, Tholuck), nor from the beginning of His collecting of the disciples around Him, or the beginning of His Messianic ministry (Meyer; comp. chap. xvi. 4; xv. 27), nor from the very murmuring (too special: Chrysostom, Bengel), but from the first secret germs of unbelief. So also He knew His betrayer from the beginning. [On Judas see note to ver. 71.]

Ver. 65. **Therefore said I unto you, that no man can come unto me.**—That is, He expressly gives them again to understand that He had spoken that sentence not as a mere theoretical proposition, but with reference to the faith and the unbelief towards Him which was forming itself in particular persons.

[EXCURSUS ON THE SACRAMENTAL INTERPRETATION OF THIS DISCOURSE.—The relation of the passage, vers. 51–58, to the Lord's Supper involves two questions: 1. Whether the FLESH and *blood* (σὰρξ καὶ αἷμα) of Christ here spoken of, are the same as His broken BODY and shed *blood* (σῶμα καὶ αἷμα) in the words of institution of that sacred ordinance (Matt. xxvi. 26-28 and parallel passages), or the *living humanity* of Christ (comp. the meaning of σάρξ in John i. 14, and the note there); 2. Whether *eating* and *drinking* (τρώγειν or ἐσθίειν* and πίνειν) signify, literally, *sacramental* fruition (*manducatio oralis*), or, figuratively, the *spiritual* appropriation of Christ by *faith*. If the discourse had been preceded by the institution of the sacrament a reference to it could not be mistaken; but as it was spoken long before the institution of this ordinance, and to hearers who as yet knew nothing of it, such a reference is made doubtful. This doubt is strengthened, first by the use of the term *flesh* instead of *body;* secondly by the substitution of *Me, i. e.*, the living Person of Christ (ver. 57 ὁ τρώγων με, comp. the ἐγώ in 35, 40, 51) for His *flesh* and *blood*, as the object of appropriation; and thirdly and mainly by the fact that Christ presents here the eating of His flesh not as a *future*, but a *present* act, and as the essential *condition* of spiritual and everlasting *life*, which, if understood sacramentally, would cut off from the possession of this life not only the disciples present on that occasion, but also all the saints of the old dispensation and the large number of Christians who die before they receive the holy communion (infants, children, death-bed converts, Quakers, and all unconfirmed persons). If participation in the Lord's Supper were a necessary prerequisite of salvation, Christ would undoubtedly have said so when He instituted the ordinance. But throughout the Gospels, and especially in this discourse (comp. vers. 40, 47), He makes *faith* the only condition of eternal life. He first exhibits Himself as the bread of life, and promises eternal life to every one who eats this bread, *i. e.*, who believes in Him. He then holds out the very same promise to all those who eat His flesh and drink His blood, which, consequently, must be essentially the same act as believing. The discourse, therefore, clearly refers to a broader and deeper fact which precedes and underlies the sacrament, and of which the sacrament is a significant sign and seal, *viz.*, *personal union of the believing soul with Christ, and a living appropriation of His atoning sacrifice.* This union culminates in the celebration of the Lord's Supper and is strengthened by it; and *so far* the discourse had, in the mind of Christ who looked at the time forward to His death (ver. 51: "My flesh which I shall give for the life of the world," comp. vers. 60 and 70), a prospective bearing on the perpetual memorial of His sacrifice, and may be applied to it indirectly, but not directly, or in a narrow and exclusive sacramentarian sense. We must distinguish between a *spiritual* manducation of Christ by faith, and a *sacramental* manducation; the former alone is essential to everlasting life, and is the proper subject of the discourse. John omits an account of the institution both of baptism and the Lord's Supper, which was known to his readers from the gospel tradition and the Synoptists, but he gives those profound discourses of Christ which explain the spiritual meaning of the sacraments, namely the idea of regeneration which is signed and sealed in baptism (chap. iii.), and the idea of personal communion with Him, which is celebrated in the Lord's Supper (chap. vi.). This suggests a very important doctrinal inference, *viz.*, that the spiritual reality of regeneration and union with Christ is not so bound to the external sacramental sign that it cannot be enjoyed without it. *We* must obey God's ordinances, but *God* is free, and we should bless whom He blesses. High sacramentarianism is contrary to the teaching of Christ according to St. John.

As to the history of interpretation we may distinguish three views:

1. The discourse has no bearing either direct or indirect on the sacrament of the Lord's Supper. So Tertullian, Clement of Alex., Origen, Basil among the fathers, Cardinal Cajetan, Ferus and Jansen among Roman Catholics, Luther, Melanchthon, Calov, Lücke, Tholuck (wavering) among the Lutherans, Calvin, Zwingli (doubtful), Beza, Bullinger, Grotius, Cocceius, Lampe (tom. II., 258 sq.), Hammond, Whitby, Barnes, Turner, Owen, Ryle among the Reformed, Paulus, Schulz, De Wette among the rationalists.

2. It refers, by prophetic anticipation, directly and exclusively to the Lord's Supper. This interpretation has consistently led to the introduction of infant communion in the early Catholic and in the Greek church. So Chrysostom, Cyril, Theophylact among the fathers, the Schoolmen and Roman Catholic expositors with a few ex-

* [John uses here τρώγειν four times, φαγεῖν once; Matthew, Mark and Luke, in the words of institution, use φαγεῖν only, (which is employed as the second aorist of ἐσθίειν from an obsolete φάγω). On the peculiar meaning of τρώγειν, *manducare*, see note on ver. 54. It cannot be essentially different here from φαγεῖν, since John uses the latter, ver. 53, in the same sense.]

ceptions, Calixtus, Zinzendorf, Scheibel, Knapp among Lutherans, Wordsworth among Anglicans, Bretschneider, Strauss and Baur among the Skeptics.

3. It refers directly to the spiritual life-union of the soul with the Saviour by faith, and indirectly or inferentially to the sacramental celebration of this union in the holy Supper. So Augustine (perhaps),* Bengel, Doddridge, Kling, Olshausen, Stier, Lange, Luthardt, Alford, Godet.†

It cannot be said that the question has a denominational or sectarian interest. The sacramental interpretation has been both opposed and defended by divines of all confessions and in the interest of every theory of the Lord's Supper, the Roman, the Lutheran, the Calvinistic, and the Zwinglian. The Romanists (Cardinal Wiseman, *e. g.*, who wrote an elaborate treatise on John vi.) urge the literal meaning of the very strong language used repeatedly and without explanation by our Lord, as an argument for the dogma of transubstantiation; and even Tholuck is of the opinion that the Catholics have the advantage of the argument if the discourse be understood of the sacrament. But it seems to me that both transubstantiation and consubstantiation are clearly excluded 1) by the canon of interpretation laid down in ver. 63; 2) by the declaration of our Lord concerning the *effect* of the fruition of His body and blood which is in all cases eternal life, vers. 54, 56, 57, 58; while Romanists and (symbolical) Lutherans agree in teaching that *unbelievers* as well as believers may sacramentally eat the very body and drink the very blood of Christ, the one unto *judgment*, the others unto *life*. No such distinction has any foundation in this passage, but is at war with it.† Moreover the Romish withdrawal of the cup from the laity is (as was already urged by the Hussites) incompatible with vers. 54-56 where the drinking of Christ's blood is made as essential as the eating of His body. As far as the discourse bears a sacramental interpretation at all, it favors the Reformed theory. But by this I mean not the now widely-prevailing Zwinglian view, which is hardly compatible with the strong and mysterious language of our Lord, but the Calvinistic, which acknowledges the mystery of a spiritual real presence and a communication of the vital power of Christ's humanity (σάρξ) to the believer by the Holy Spirit.—P. S.]

DOCTRINAL AND ETHICAL.

1. See the exegesis itself, particularly on vers. 31 and 32 ff.; and ver. 52 ff. [And the Excursus above.—P. S.]

2. Christ, the life of the world is, as the bread of life, *the necessary means of life for* the awakening, quickening, and strengthening of men to a personal eternal life. Salvation is not in out-

* [I say *perhaps*, for Augustine is not clear and is sometimes (*e. g.*, by Meyer) quoted in favor of the first, more frequently in favor of the second interpretation. In his *Tract.* 26 *in Joh. Evang.* § 15 (ed. Bened. III. 500) he says, in expounding this passage, that the sacrament of the body and blood of Christ is received by some *ad vitam*, by others *ad exitium* (1 Cor. xi. 29), but he adds: *res vero ipsa cujus sacramentum est, omni homini ad vitam, nulli ad exitium, quicunque ejus particeps fuerit.* Comp. § 18 in the same homily (III. 501): *Qui non manet in Christo et in quo non manet Christus, procul dubio nec manducat* (some MSS. insert here *spiritualiter*,—evidently a Romish correction) *carnem ejus, nec bibit ejus sanguinem, licet carnaliter et visibiliter premat dentibus sacramentum corporis et sanguinis Christi.* In commenting on ver. 29 (*Tract.* 25, § 12, Tom. III. 489) he identifies the eating with believing: *Crede et manducasti.* At all events, Augustine cannot be quoted in favor of either transubstantiation or consubstantiation. Comp. on his doctrine on the eucharist my Church History, Vol. II. pp. 498 f.—P. S.]

† [This third view which I have defended myself in the text, was first clearly brought out by that profound, acute and devout commentator, Bengel, in his *Gnomon* on ver. 51, where he says: "Jesus purposely framed His words so skilfully that immediately at that time, and at all times subsequently they would indeed apply in their strict literal sense to the spiritual enjoyment of Himself (*de spirituali fruitione sui*); and yet that afterwards the same words should, by consequence, be appropriate to express the most august mystery of the Holy Supper when that should be instituted. For He applied to the Holy Supper the thing itself which is set forth in this discourse; and of so great moment is this sacrament, that it may be readily thought possible, that Jesus, as He foretold the treachery of Judas at ver. 71, and His own death in this verse, so also foretold, one year before the institution of the Holy Supper, concerning which He most surely thought within Himself whilst speaking these words: and with this object in order that the disciples might afterwards remember His prediction. The whole of these words concerning His flesh and blood have in view the passion of Jesus Christ, and along with it the Holy Supper. Hence arises the separate mention of *one flesh* and of *the blood* so invariably; for in His passion the blood was drawn out of His body, and the Lamb was thus slain." The same view is substantially held by Olshausen, who says: "The Saviour could indeed not with propriety speak of a *rite* before it was instituted, so that nobody could understand Him; but He might touch the *idea*, out of which the rite subsequently grew. This idea is that Jesus is the principle of life and nutriment to the new, regenerate man, not only for his soul and spirit, but also for his glorified body" (which, according to Olshausen is prepared here in germ to appear in full bloom at the final resurrection). Kahnis (*Luth. Dogmatik*, Vol. I., p. 625): "The discourse of Christ, John vi., does not treat directly of the Lord's Supper, but of faith which unites us in living union with Christ. But He purposely veiled this faith in the image of eating and drinking His flesh and blood in order to express the mysterious idea embodied in the Holy Supper, just as John iii. 5 expresses the idea of baptism." Alford says: "The question whether there is here any reference to the ordinance of the Lord's Supper, has been inaccurately put. When cleared of inaccuracy in terms, it will mean, *Is the subject here dwelt upon the same as that which is set forth in the ordinance of the Lord's Supper?* And of this there can surely be no doubt. To the *ordinance itself*, there is here *no reference*; nor *could* there well have been any. But the spiritual verity which underlies the ordinance is one and the same with that here insisted on; and so considered, the discourse is, as generally treated, most important towards a right understanding of the ordinance." Webster and Wilkinson: "What our Lord said at this time He afterwards expressed in a permanent form by the sacrament of His Body and Blood. He is not here alluding to that sacrament; but what He here teaches, and what He afterwards taught by it, are the same." Godet (II. p. 135): "This mystery of our perfect union with the person of Christ (Eph. v. 30–32) which in this discourse is expressed in *words* (*en paroles*), is precisely the same which Jesus desired to express by an act (*par un acte*) in the rite of the holy Supper. It is not necessary to say that in this discourse He alluded to the holy Supper; but we must say that the holy Supper and this discourse refer to one and the same idea, expressed here by a metaphor, there by an emblem. Hence in the institution of the Supper, holding and breaking one piece of bread, He used the term σῶμα, *body*, which as an organism corresponds to the broken bread; in the discourse at Capernaum where He treats only of nourishment in adaptation to the miraculous multiplication of loaves of bread, He represents His body more as *substance* (σάρξ) than as an organism. This perfect propriety of terms proves the originality and authenticity of the two forms."]

* [Luther, Melancthon and the orthodox Lutherans of the 17th century felt this, and for this reason (not, as Tholuck thinks, from fear of transubstantiation) they repudiated the sacramental interpretation altogether. Luther says: "Eating in this passage means believing: he who believeth, eateth and drinketh Christ." Melanchthon: "I do not understand this discourse as referring to the Lord's Supper or the ceremonial manducation, but as the words of Christ which preceded above were about faith, whereby we believe that God's wrath was propitiated by the death of His Son, who offered His body and shed His blood for us,—so I understand all the rest of the same faith." This interpretation was sanctioned by the Form of Concord, p. 743. When Calixtus came out in favor of the sacramental interpretation, he was charged with heresy by Calovius of Wittenberg.]

ward enjoyment and outward things, but in the heavenly life of the Spirit (antithesis of the heavenly and earthly mind); the striving after heavenly things consists not in legal, perfunctory works, but in the inward, single, personal, divine work of faith (antithesis of the spiritual and the legal nature); life consists not in the *doing* of spiritual *things* as such, but in the person of Christ Himself (antithesis of personal and perfunctory Christianity). The personal life, however, manifests itself (1) in the total, undivided consciousness (*Christ Himself*), (2) in its giving of itself (*His flesh*), (3) in its impartation of life (*flesh and blood*).

The *Spirit* (chap. iii.) brings the heavenly birth to life; the *well of life* (chap. iv.) gives the first thing in regeneration, the refreshment of the soul thirsting for life with the peace of God; the *healing waters of life* (chap. v.) give the restoration of the life from disease and death (spiritual and bodily); the *bread of life*, the heavenly manna (chap. vi.), gives an eternal, substantial existence.

By the idea of the personal life of Christ all personal relations are glorified. (1.) Calling becomes a laboring in the service of God. (2.) Labor becomes a production of heavenly food. (3.) Bread becomes the person of Christ, the flesh and blood of Christ; eating and drinking become a real corporeo-spiritual participation and receiving into one's self of the highest life. Hearing is a hearing of the voice of God, which invites to this feast; seeing is the perfect knowledge of intuition.

This chapter thus contains the symbolism of bread, of industrial calling, of labor, of eating and drinking, of hearing and seeing; the symbolism of the whole life of sense in its central relation to the personal life and to the highest personality.

3. Laboring in manifold divided earthly works for earthly food in the service of the world has the perishing of the life itself, with the perishing of the meat, for its reward (Gal. vi. 8; 1 John ii. 17); but the working of the one divine work in the service of God, faith in Christ, has the heavenly manna for its reward. He who is intent upon partaking of the supreme person, comes to the delight of personal, eternal existence in the kingdom of God.

4. The exaltation of the *manna* of the desert as a symbol of the real manna. Without this real manna the life of man is a breadless desert in the strictest sense. The marks of the bread of God: (1.) It must come down (not fall down) from heaven: be Spirit-life, personal life, divine life. (2.) It must give life to the world. Not merely give respite to physical life now and then, but first awaken, then sustain and renew, personal life forever.

5. *Earthly* interest in Christ and in Christianity in distinction from *heavenly*. The *chiliastic* spirit in opposition to the spirit of the *kingdom*.

6. It is remarkable how this discourse of Jesus not only kindled *strife* among the Jews, but has also fed the controversy of different confessions [denominations] in the evangelical church. Controversies over the doctrine of *predestination* have hung upon the words of vers. 37, 44, 64, and 65; and upon the words of vers. 53 sqq., and 63 sqq., controversies over the *holy Supper*. The middle age has transmitted to the evangelical church a far too meagre doctrine of spiritual personality; else would the doctrine of *personality* be found to yield the higher synthesis of the Reformed and the Lutheran doctrines both on *predestination* and the *Lord's Supper*.

Without the personal drawing of the Father no coming to Christ is conceivable; but the Father, too, draws only in a personal way, *i. e.*, under the form of freedom. Hence in vers. 44 and 45 divine determination and human freedom are linked together.

Without the appropriation of the entire historical personality of Christ, spirit and body, no full, saving partaking of the redemption purchased by Christ is conceivable; but in this partaking every medium of redemption is conditioned through the life and the Spirit of the Redeemer. Hence, on the one hand, we are required, with a fourfold emphasis, to eat and to drink the flesh and the blood of Christ, and on the other, we hear the strong condition: "It is the Spirit that quickeneth; the flesh profiteth nothing."

7. *Honest striving*, the unconscious drawing of God to *holy living*.

8. *Whispering* and *murmuring*, the indication of narrow-minded offence at the word of truth.

9. The mark of those who are *truly taught of God:* They pass (1) from the old world [paganism] into the Old Testament, (2) from the Old Testament into the New, (3) through the New Testament into a new world.

10. He that *believeth* on me hath (1) life, (2) eternal life.

11. Christ *the bread of life* in the three stages of the manifestation of His life: (1) In His person and history. (2) In His "flesh," or "His giving Himself a sacrifice," whereby He is transformed from the curse of the world and the burnt-offering and expiation of God into a pure and entire thank-offering of believing man. (3) Therefore is His "flesh and blood," wherein He makes His historically finished life, by historical ordinances, the life of the world. The first stage represents the true bread itself; the second, the preparation of it for eating; the third, its being perfectly ready for believing participation: flesh and blood.

And then there are also three stages in the partaking of Christ: (1) The putting of confidence in Him as personally the source of life. (2) Firm faith in the life which is in His sacrificial death. (3) The ideal communion, which on the one hand receives the life of Christ in spirit and body through His historical ordinances, the summit of which is the Lord's Supper, and which, on the other hand, ever refers the actual world more and more to Christ, and makes it, in labor and in enjoyment, the manifestation of Christ. The Christian must first of all eat the flesh and blood of Christ, in order at last to eat this flesh and blood in all things.

12. The four great words concerning *the flesh and blood of Christ*, confirmed with the "Verily, verily." (1) Ver. 53. The want of this eating and drinking of the flesh and blood of Christ is the want and loss of life (even of one's own, personal life; "No life in you"). (2) Ver. 54. The eating and drinking of the flesh and blood

of Christ yield eternal life even now, and resurrection hereafter. (3) Ver. 55. The first reason: His flesh and blood are the real staff of life (meat and drink). (4) Ver. 56. The highest reason: The partaking of His flesh and blood is the condition of community of life with Him ("dwelleth in Me, and I in Him"). *The transfiguration of the passover, of the paschal lamb, of the paschal feast of the Jews.*

13. The living of Christ in God is not only the *root*, but also the *type* of the living of believers in Christ. So surely as God is the source of life, Christ, as the pure revelation of God, is the focus of the life in the world. But so surely as Christ is this focus, he who refers his life and his world to Christ, and Christ to his life and his world, stands in the kingdom of eternal life.

14. The most comforting and most glorious of all the words of Christ a *hard* saying to the Jewish mind.

15. The transfiguration of the *humiliation* of Christ and of its blessings by His *exaltation*. Christian morality, the union of spirit and nature in Christ. The organization of the Spirit (sacraments and church); the spiritualizing of the organization (the natural life of man), till God shall be all in all.

16. "It is the *Spirit* that quickeneth," *etc.*, hold true (1) in our natural life, (2) of the word of Christ, (3) of the historical manifestation of Christ, (4) of the sacraments, particularly of the Supper of the Lord. The revelation of the Spirit glorifies the Lord as the life of the world, which makes the new world the body of Christ, wherein everything is bread of life for all.

17. It is the problem of faith, and of theology, to carry out *the synthesis of Spirit and flesh* in the right way, (1) in regard to the relation between God and the world in general, taking the world not, indeed, as the body of God, yet doubtless as a revelation of Him; (2) in regard to the word of Holy Scripture; (3) in regard to the person of Christ; (4) in regard to the ordinances of Christ, the church, and especially the sacrament of the Supper. The first step in this process is the simple, direct recognition of the actual manifestation of Spirit and flesh in concrete unity. This simple recognition, under the symbolical primitive religion, sees God revealed in the world; under the religion of revelation in general, it sees the Spirit of God revealed in the theocracy and the Scriptures; in the apostolic Christianity, it sees the Son of God in the several miracles of His life; in the primitive church, the unity of the Spirit of Christ and His ordinances.

Yet the consciousness of a distinction and antithesis between the Spirit and the flesh is everywhere present. And because the earthly mind, along this whole line, is inclined to lose the sense of this opposition, and because, in the mass of men, it does actually lose it, the strong distinction becomes a necessity ("It is the Spirit that quickeneth; the flesh profiteth nothing").

The Old Testament distinguishes between God and the world in opposition to heathenism. Christ distinguishes between the living revelation and outward theocracy and the letter of Scripture, in opposition to Judaism. The Antiochian criticism and the mediæval mysticism distinguish between the spiritual personality of Christ and its several relations and manifestations, against the traditional exegesis. The Reformation distinguishes between the spirit of the true church and its external form; and between the substance and the form of the sacrament.

But these distinctions look to the restoration of the true union. Christ exhibits the true union of God and the world both in His person and in His consciousness (the incarnation of God): Christian theology works out the known synthesis between revelation and Scripture (the word of God in its organic life); sacred criticism aims at a view of the gospel history whose heart and pulse is the personal Christ (religious history is not documentary); evangelical dogmatics seizes the kernel of the true church in the visible church (ideal tradition is not external tradition), and in place of the mediæval identification of grace and the external sacramental performance it puts, in the Lutheran view which is more fervent for the union, the *organic* synthesis, and in the Reformed [Calvinistic] view which is more careful of the distinction, the *symbolical* synthesis (inseparableness of word and sacrament).

Hence it follows that the dangers of the Lutheran view lie in the direction of confusion, and the dangers of the Reformed view in the direction of separation; and that therefore the two views themselves can have their safest operation only in living synthesis. And the true union, the third and highest step, consists in the recognition of the Spirit as in relation to the flesh, (1) the sole power, (2) a transforming, renewing power, (3) a glorifying power, taking on itself the flesh as its transparent crystal-like organ. Hence, also, Christ here points on to exaltation.

18. Jesus, the *heart-searcher* in reference, above all, to the faint germs of faith and unbelief.

HOMILETICAL AND PRACTICAL.

See the Doctrinal and Ethical reflections.

The flight of Jesus over the sea, and His discourse in the synagogue at Capernaum, a continuation of His victory over the tempter in the wilderness, Matt. iv.—The decisive and divisive discourse of the Lord concerning salvation in personal life-union with Himself.—Those who seek salvation in impersonal Christian things with an impersonal conduct, cannot find salvation in the person of the Lord with personal faith.—The hoping of the mere mind in Christ is vain: 1. Vain both in its naked form of earthly-mindedness and selfishness and in its sanctimonious dress of chiliastic enthusiasm. 2. Vain both in its standing and lingering (on the eastern side of the sea), and in its haste and running (to the western shore). 3. Vain whether in its effort to magnify Christianity in secular style (to make Christ king of bread), or in its effort to belittle it according to a worldly standard (to deny its heavenly descent and its heavenly nucleus, the atonement). 4. Vain in its desire to alter Christianity, instead of itself becoming altered by it. Conclusion: Vain, *i. e.*, ruinous.—The true servants and workmen of God, and the true work of God.—The demand of the sensuous and legalistic way of thinking, that Christ should in an Old Testament manner go beyond the Old Testament: Christ should surpass Moses: 1. In miracles of outward benefit ("What dost thou work?"). 2. In requirements of eternal law ("What shall we do?"). 3. In terror of external judgment (as king of the Jews ruling over the heathen). — Verily, verily, not Moses, but the Father in heaven, gives the bread of God.—Christ *is* the bread of God in His personal divine life, vers. 32-40: (1) The typical and the true bread of God, vers. 32, 33. (2) The false and the true appetite for this bread, vers. 34-38. (3) The liberating and quickening operation of this bread, vers. 39, 40.—Christ *gives* the bread of life in His giving up of His flesh in His atoning death, vers. 41-51: (1) He gives it not to the murmurers, but to them that are drawn and taught of the Father, vers. 41-47. (2) He gives with it the full partaking of eternal life, vers. 48-50. (3) He gives it in giving Himself, ver. 51. (4) He gives it in giving His flesh for the life of the world, ver. 51.—Christ *institutes the meal of life* in making His flesh and blood a feast of thank-offering to the world, vers. 52-59: (1) The offence at the words concerning the flesh of Christ, ver. 52. (2) The heightening of the offence by the fourfold assertion concerning the flesh and blood of Christ, vers. 53-56. (3) The ground of this assertion: the life of Christ in the Father, ver. 57. (4) The conclusion of this assertion, vers. 58, 59.—Christ transfigures the meal of life into a meal of the Spirit, vers. 60-65: (1) By His exaltation, ver. 62. (2) By the sending of the Spirit, ver. 63. (3) By His word, ver. 63. (4) By the excision of unbelievers, ver. 64.

On single sentences: Ver. 25. To these Jews the second miracle of Jesus (the walking on the sea) remains a close secret, because they do not recognize the divine sign in the first (the breaking of bread).—Ver. 26. "Verily, verily, ye seek Me," *etc.* They have seen not the miraculous sign in the feeding, but only the feeding in the miraculous sign.—Thus they are a type of all false friends of religion, who seek not the kingdom of heaven in earthly advantages, but only earthly advantages in the kingdom of heaven.—Ver. 27. Christ, who has not where to lay His head, intrusted by God with the official seal which makes Him steward for the whole world.—Vers. 28, 29. The legalistic Christian *thinks he can do works* which earn for him the blessing of God; whereas the gospel requires a work in which God is the agent: faith.—Faith is a work of man from God, with God, for God; and for this very reason as much the work of God as it is the highest, freest work of man. The miraculous feeding the seal and sealing of the divine steward.—Ver. 30. Ingratitude towards the Lord: how it always forgets the past sign from God, and demands a new one.—Ver. 31. How an earthly mind can pervert even the Scripture.—The true bread from heaven can be given to us not by man, but by God alone (the Father of our Lord Jesus Christ).—Ver. 33. Marks of the bread of God: 1. It comes down from heaven. 2. It gives life to the world.—Ver. 34. "Lord, evermore give us," *etc.*: the vain prayer, to the very face of the Lord: 1. Because it recognizes not the Giver in the bread. 2. Because it recognizes not the bread of life in the Giver.—Ver. 35. The answer of Jesus aims to disclose their spirit (1) by insisting on the figure, the representation of the bread in His person; (2) by enlarging the figure: bread for hunger and thirst; (3) by explaining the figure: Come to me, believe on me.—Christianity the truth and the true sanctification of eating: 1. Making faith an eating. 2. Making eating faith.—Ver. 36. The incapacity of the earthly-minded man to see into the mystery of the divine life. One can see Jesus, the church, her reformers, her great spirits, with the eye, without seeing the spirit, or the glory of the personal life.—They will see and believe *things*, but they have not seen nor believed His *person*.—Ver. 37. It needs a stirring of the personal life of love descending from God, to see the glory of the personal life in Christ.—Christ draws all divinely chosen and kindred ones into His kingdom, since (1) all that the Father gives Him, come to Him, and (2) none who come to Him, does He cast out.—Ver. 38. *Him that cometh, etc.* He casts out none, because He judges men not by the perfection of their life, but by the dispositions, affinities, and beginnings of it.—As the Spirit attaches Himself everywhere to the work of the Son (chap. xiv. 26; xvi. 13), so the Son everywhere to the work of the Father,—Christ aspires not, according to His own will, to an ideal position of life for Himself, but enters, according to the will of His Father, into the historical duty of life. His will is of heavenly purity, and yet His life is a continual sacrifice of His will.—Vers. 38-40. The gracious will of the Father: 1. In regard to the Redeemer. 2. In regard to those to be redeemed and those redeemed. 3. In regard to the way of redemption.—The purpose of the Father in Christ: 1. What it forbids (ver. 39: "lose nothing"). 2. What it enjoins (ver. 40).—Thus He is in both views the bread of life: 1. Redeeming from death. 2. Imparting eternal life.—The unfolding of personal life in redemption: 1. In the first phase of redemption (in ver. 39) personality is but feebly developed; the needy life is spoken of (in the neuter), which is in danger of being lost; in the next phase (in ver. 40), we have no longer the mere rescue from destruction, but the conferring of the highest life; and here personality comes clearly to view. 2. In the first case redemption has to do with lost men in the mass; in the second, with individuals. 3. There the redeemed one is comparatively passive; here he is an active person, turned to the Redeemer, finding life in the beholding of His life. 4. There redemption bears chiefly the impress of divine predestination; here it takes that of human freedom.—The gracious operations of Christ go on to glorious completion in the last day.—The greatness of the promise of a new, infinite fulness and freshness of life at the end of the world.—How often the Lord points forward to the completion of His work at the last day.—Ver. 41. "The Jews then murmured:" The characteristics of the illiberal partisan spirit: 1. They murmured. 2. They murmured to one another. 3. They murmured against the Lord and His word.—Ver. 42. The old and ever new offence at the words of Christ respecting His heavenly origin: 1. Because He is from Nazareth, He cannot be from heaven. 2. Because He is the Son of Man, He cannot be the Son of God.—The sinful world's condemnation of itself in its sundering of the divine and human natures in Christ.—The deceptions of vulgar conceit in matters of the Spirit. 1. The people think they know Him, because they know His parents. 2. They think they know His origin, because they know His foster-father. 3. They think they know His mother, because they know her poverty and lowliness. Comp. chap. vii. 27; Matt. xiii. 55.—Vers. 43, 44. "Murmur not among yourselves:" the drawing of partisan spirit a drawing of the earth, against the drawing of the Father from heaven.—The drawing of the Father to the Son.—Ver. 45. As one must first be a believer, to become a true disciple of God, so must one, in another view, be first taught of God, in order to become a believer.—Ver. 46. The revealing of God, as it was the peculiar property of Christ, is above every experience of God in sinful men. Comp. chap. i. 18.—We begin the new life by hearing an obscure word (see Gen. xii. 1); He has seen from eternity the face of the Father.—Ver. 47. "He that believeth on me, hath," *etc.*

Ver. 48. Christ the bread of life: (1) The bread as life. (2) The life as bread: (*a*) the true manna; therefore (*b*) the bread of God, bread of heaven, bread of life.—The true bread to be known especially by the fact that it gives itself.—It is the nature of a loving personality, to give itself.—He gives Himself, as the Father has given Him.—He gives His only life to death, to awaken the world out of death to life. While He was dead, the life of the world hung on the single seed and glowing spark of His life, which broke forth for the resurrection and re-animation of the world.—Ver. 52. They wonder that they should eat His flesh; then He speaks of eating His flesh and blood.—Christ the true paschal lamb (1 Cor. v. 7).

Vers. 53-56. The four great asseverations of the Lord concerning the eating of His flesh and the drinking of His blood. See above.—The appropriation of the historical personality of Christ in its vital, heavenly operation by means of Christ's historical ordinance.—How Christ still gives Himself even now in His flesh and blood, in His full human form and His entire heavenly nature, to be eaten by men.—How the eating of the flesh and blood of Christ is effected: 1. Through His word, particularly His history. 2. Through His sacraments, particularly the sacrament of His body and blood.—In ourselves also Christianity must in a holy sense, become flesh and blood.—How Christ does away the opposition between the spiritual and the bodily in His kingdom: 1. Corporealizing the spiritual (word in sacrament, gospel in church). 2. Spiritualizing the bodily (members into instruments of righteousness, the world into His Father's house).—Ver. 57. As Christ lives by the Father, we should live by Him.—He who lives in Christ, stands at the focus of eternal rejuvenation.—Ver. 58. All who have lived only under the law and in symbols, have eaten manna and are dead. Most have died under heavy judgments, Heb. iii. 17. Comp. the history of the mediæval church (*Corpus Christi*, festivals, battle-fields, the plague).—Ver. 59. The wonderful sermon of Christ on the bread of life delivered in the synagogue of the Jews at Capernaum.—Ver. 60. The grandest living word of Christ, a hard saying to the Jewish mind.—Ver. 61. Offence at the word of salvation.—Ver. 62. How that which is dark and enigmatical in the humiliation of Christ is cleared up by His exaltation.—Ver. 63. "It is the Spirit," *etc.*—Ver. 64. The words of Christ as spirit and life, and as a type of His whole administration. The spirit and life hidden from unbelievers, even when they gush with spirituality and vitality.—Christ knows the beginnings of unbelief as well as of faith.

Starke. Ver. 26. Hedinger: Self-interest may lurk under the holiest works.—Zeisius: O how subtle a poison is selfishness!—Ver. 29. Quesnel: The great work of God in us is the work of a living faith which works by love.—Ver. 32. Majus: Christ the most precious gift of God, in which and with which are given to us all things. Rom. viii. 32.—Ver. 33. Quesnel: O Bread of God, thou art life indeed, true life, eternal life, life of body and of soul, life not of one people only, but of all nations!—Ver. 35. Canstein: Not only in His person is Christ the life, but from Him life goes forth to all men; natural life, since He is the Word of the Father, Gen. i. 3; Acts xvii. 28; the life of righteousness in His believing ones before the judgment seat of God, Rom. viii. 10; spiritual life in regeneration, 1 Peter i. 23; and eternal life, inasmuch as all the glory of believers not only comes from Him, but also consists in their partaking of Him and in His being all in all to them.—Osiander: No temporal possessions and bodily pleasure can truly satisfy and quicken the heart; nothing but Christ.—Ver. 37. Quesnel: Pastors after the example of the chief Shepherd, should receive all whom God sends to them, and labor for their salvation.—So surely as Christ did not suffer in vain, so surely shall no penitent be cast out.—Jesus not only does not cast out a penitent sinner, but will also lead him into His inmost sanctuary.—Ver. 39. Rom. viii. 31. What belongs to Christ, though esteemed lost in the eye of the world, is not therefore lost in truth; in the resurrection of the dead all shall come together again in universal joy.—Ver. 41. Here we find the counterpart of the murmuring of the Israelites in the wilderness, where they were fed with manna. Here the Jews murmur against the true manna.—Hedinger: Reason stumbles at divine teaching, 1 Cor. i. 18, 23, 24.—Ver. 42. Jesus, subjected to great contempt. If thou, dear Christian, art now thought meanly of, thou art like the Saviour, and thou shalt be honored for it forever.—Ver. 44. The drawing of God is not a drawing by force, yet it is a drawing with power. Augustine: "*Ramum ostendis ovi et trahis illam. Nuces puero demonstrantur, et trahitur, etc.. Trahit sua quemque voluptas. Quomodo non traheret revelatus Christus a patre. Ergo tractio illa non fit violenter sed mediate.*" Phil. ii. 13.—Ver. 45. Zeisius: Every one who comes to Christ by faith is taught of God.—Hearing, learning of the Father, and coming, are intimately joined together.—The Holy Ghost teaches in experience as in His own school.—Ver. 47. The spiritual life of faith is a beginning of the eternal life which consists in vision.—Ver. 48. If thou art full of the most costly dainties, and hast not eaten of the bread of life, thou wilt soon be hungry enough, and must be hungry forever.—Ver. 49. Ver. 31 has "*our* Father;" here the *our* is changed with design into "*your*."—He means by it not all the fathers; for the believing received a spiritual food (1 Cor. x. 3); but the unbelieving whose footsteps they were following, Matt. xxiii. 32: 1 Cor. x. 5.—If we do not rightly use the riches of God's goodness, we incur the heavier judgment.—Ver. 57. LAMPE: The power which gives heavenly food to the inward man, must be applied to walking in the way of the Lord, and earnestly carrying forward His work.—GOSSNER: The weightiest and highest truths, which most quicken and comfort the faithful, confound the ungodly.

BRAUNE: The sacrament, which did not exist till after the institution, is not intended here; but, as in the conversation with Nicodemus we have the *idea* of baptism, so here we have the *idea* of the Lord's Supper.—Before His resurrection His Spirit was hidden under the flesh; but since the resurrection the Spirit so pervades and advances the flesh that it now can make good everything He here says of it. So may it be said of our eye: What is hidden in the little bit of flesh? (Then follows a contrast between the living eye and the dead.)—LISCO: 1. Jesus enjoins laboring for the imperishable meat, Vers. 25-31. (a) He rebukes the earthly mind, vers. 25, 26; (b) He exhorts to labor for the imperishable food, ver. 27; (c) He points out that the labor is faith, vers. 28, 29. 2. Jesus Himself is the true bread of life (vers. 30, 31), vers. 32-40, *etc.*—GERLACH: All earthly food only nourishes here below the perishable life, and perishes with it; but as the man whom it is given to nourish, does not perish, it points to and produces hunger for an imperishable food for his immortal spirit.—The manna was primarily only an earthly food, etc.; though it was certainly an emblem of the nourishing, fostering faithfulness of God, a pledge of grace, a sacrament in a certain sense, 1 Cor. x. 3. However since it primarily nourished only the body, while in virtue of the nature of this nourishing it gave food to the spirit, *etc.*, Christ could contrast it with the true bread of heaven.—On ver. 37 (LUTHER): This is spoken after the manner of the Scriptures, which, where they deny, do in the very strongest manner assert; when Christ says: "I will in nowise cast out," it is as if He said: I will receive with joy; and this depicts as well His willing and hearty obedience to the Father, as His most precious love.—The word *flesh* in the New Testament is never equivalent to the word *body*. The former signifies primarily the mass, the substance, of which the earthly body distinctively consists; the latter, the skilfully constructed whole.—This discourse also explains the double form of the Holy Supper, and shows how those who withhold the cup from the laity, deprive them of their free personal communion with Christ (the spiritual priesthood, 1 Pet. ii. 5, 9; Rev. i. 6), and so far as in them lies, reduce the laity to a general mass of Christian people governed by a few full members of the Lord.

HEUBNER: False love to Jesus may be (1) sensuous, sentimental; (2) selfish; (3) hypocritical; (4) ostentatious, ambitious.—The earthly mind and love to Jesus are absolutely incompatible.—Contrast between Moses and Christ.—Moses could not communicate inward spiritual life.—Ver. 36. O, to think of the theologians who have been occupied for years with the New Testament, yet have no love to Jesus,—what ossified hack souls * they must be!—The nearer Christ comes to the heart, the more life, love, light.—Ver. 37. The gospel of Christ is a message of salvation to all.—Ver. 43. Unbelief has infectious power.—Ver. 45. A more particular explanation of the drawing. Being taught of God. The phrase *eating and drinking* frequent among the Jews for spiritual enjoyment (see Lightfoot, *etc.*)—BESSER, Ver. 30: They degrade the "believe on him," to a "believe thee."—Vers. 38-40. Chemnitz calls attention to the terms in this discourse, *seeing* (ver. 36), *beholding* [the "seeing" of ver. 40], *believing*, and *eating and drinking*,—as denoting so many steps of faith: 1. Historical knowledge (*notitia*). 2. Hearty assent (*assensus*) 3. Trusting (*fiducia*). 4. Personal appropriation (*applicatio*). SCHLEIERMACHER: They were quite mistaken in looking upon the manna miracle of Moses as one which had been to their fathers a ground of faith in the mission of Moses. The first thing with which the Lord consoles Himself, (over their unbelief), is His great, indomitable long-suffering.—The Lord's invitation to vital union with Him.

[Christ the source of spiritual and eternal life. 1. Natural life in the plant, the animal, and in man; its character, pleasures, miseries, vanity and death; 2. Spiritual life, its origin, character, development, and final consummation in the resurrection to glory everlasting. AUGUSTINE (*Tract. in Joh.* xxvi. 13. Tom. iii. 499): *O sacramentum pietatis, o signum unitatis, o vinculum caritatis! Qui vult vivere, habet ubi vivat, habet unde vivat. Accedat, credat, incorporetur ut vivificetur.—Ibid.* (iii. 501): *Hoc est ergo manducare illam escam, et illum bibere potum, in Christo manere, et illum manentem in se habere.* (Ver. 57.)—BURKITT (Vers. 51-59). Carnal persons put a carnal sense upon Christ's spiritual words, and so occasion their own stumbling.—Learn, 1. That the Lord Jesus Christ is the true spiritual food for all believers; 2. That those and those only who feed upon Him by faith, shall obtain a life of grace and glory from Him.—*Ibid.* If the passage be understood of the sacramental eating and drinking (which Burkitt rejects), then woe to the Church of Rome for denying the cup to the laity.—As meat is turned into the eater's substance, so believers and Christ become one; and by feeding on Him, *i. e.*, by believing on Him, there follows a mutual inhabitation; Christ dwells in them, and they in Him.—P. S.]

* [*Verknöcherte Handwerksseelen.*]

III.

APOSTACY OF MANY DISCIPLES. INCIPIENT TREASON IN THE CIRCLE OF THE TWELVE. CONFESSION OF PETER.

Chapter VI. 66-71.

66 From that time [upon this][1] many of His disciples went back, and walked no
67 more with him. Then [Therefore] said Jesus unto the twelve, Will ye also [do ye
68 also wish to] go away? Then [*omit* Then][2] Simon Peter answered him, Lord, to
69 whom shall we go [go away, ἀπελευσόμεθα]? thou hast the [*omit* the] words of eternal life. And we believe and are sure [we have believed and have known] that
70 thou art that Christ [the Christ],[3] the Son of the living God [the Holy One of God].[4] Jesus answered them, Have not I chosen you twelve, [Did I not choose
71 you the twelve?] and one of you is a devil? [!] He spake of Judas Iscariot the son of Simon [Judas, the son of Simon Iscariot][5]: for he it was [it was he] that should [was about to] betray him, being[6] one of the twelve.

TEXTUAL AND GRAMMATICAL.

[1] Ver. 66.—['Εκ τούτου is causal, and expresses, according to Lange and Meyer, the reason, not the time. Alford and Godet combine the temporal and causal meaning. Alford translates: *Upon this.* Noyes and Conant: *From this time.*—P. S.]

[2] Ver. 68.—[The οὖν of the text. rec. is omitted by the best authorities.—P. S.]

[3] Ver. 69.—[The text. rec. inserts from Matt. xvi. 16 ὁ Χριστός, which is wanting in the oldest sources, and is omitted by critical editors.—The original text is simply, ὅτι σὺ εἶ ὁ ἅγιος τοῦ θεοῦ, *that thou art the Holy one of God*. This, however, is equivalent to *Christ* or the promised *Messiah*.—P. S.]

[4] Ver. 69.—Codd. B. C.* D. L., *etc.*, Griesbach, Lachmann, and Tischendorf, read ὁ ἅγιος τοῦ θεοῦ. The Recepta conforms to Matt. xvi. 16. [Cod. Sin. supports the ὁ ἅγ. τ. θ., which also appears to have been a characteristic phrase with Peter; comp. Acts ii. 27, 31; iii. 14; iv. 27, 30.—E. D. Y.]

[5] Ver. 71.—The reading 'Ισκαριώτου is here supported by B. C. G. L. (Lachmann, Tischendorf), against 'Ισκαριώτην. Also at c. xiii. 26, by decisive authorities. On the other hand at c. xiv. 22, after the treasonable decision, Judas himself is distinguished as 'Ισκαριώτης. This evinces a historical delicacy, which Meyer misses when he proposes to read 'Ισκαριώτης in all the places on the strength of c. xiv. 22. [Stier and Theile adopt 'Ισκαριώτην in this place and in xiii. 26; while the Cod. Sin. has in the latter case 'Ισκαριώτου, belonging to Σίμωνος, and in our passage ἀπὸ καρυώτου, also referring to Σ.—E. D. Y.]

[6] Ver. 71.—[The ὢν of the text. rec. after εἷς is wanting in the best authorities and probably inserted from Mark xiv. 43.—P. S.]

EXEGETICAL AND CRITICAL.

Ver. 66. **Upon this many of his disciples.**—'Εκ τούτου. (1) From this moment (Lücke, De Wette). (2) Meyer, more correctly, according to c. xix. 12: On account of this discourse, "which disappointed their carnal Messianic hopes." And in addition had become the strongest positive offence.

Went back; εἰς τὰ ὀπίσω.—Comp. c. xviii. 6; xx. 14.

Ver. 67. **Will ye also,** *etc.*—So Luther, Baumgarten-Crusius [and the English version], not accurately. Rather, "But *ye* will not go away, will ye?"* Expressing confidence mingled with suspicion in reference to the traitor. Giving occasion for a voluntary decision. [The Lord asked the question in order to test their faithfulness, to elicit their confession, and to attach them more closely to Himself, but not, as Alford suggests, for His own comfort and encouragement; for as He knew the future treason of Judas (vers. 64, 71), so He foresaw also the faithfulness of the eleven. In this place, John first mentions the Twelve, without a word about their previous calling,—a clear proof that he took for granted a general knowledge of the gospel history.—P. S.]

* [Μὴ καὶ ὑμεῖς θέλετε ὑπάγειν. The interrogative μή looks to a negative answer (*doch nicht?*) comp. vii. 31; xxi. 5; Rom. iii. 5, *etc.* and Winer's *Gr.* p. 476. Godet, discarding this rule, wrongly explains: *Si vous le voulez, vous pouvez aller.*—P. S.]

Ver. 68. **To whom shall we go.**—So also Luther's version. More accurately: To whom shall we go over, go away from Thee? Meyer: ἀπελευσόμεθα, future, ever go away. [Denying the future possibility.—P. S.] No second Messiah will appear. [Augustin: *Da nobis alterum Te*]. Prelude to the confession of Peter in Matt. xvi. 16. [Peter quickly, resolutely and emphatically speaks and acts here as elsewhere in the name of the Twelve. He is the mouth-piece of the apostolic college. This gives him a certain primacy and priority down to the day of Pentecost and the calling of Paul, who was the independent head of Gentile Christianity by Christ's own appointment. The Romish Church turns the temporary and personal primacy of Peter into a permanent and official supremacy of the Bishop of Rome. This, and the identifying of the church of Rome with the Kingdom of Christ, is the πρῶτον ψεῦδος, the fundamental error and the fundamental sin of the papacy.—P. S.]

Words of eternal life. And we.—The objective and subjective grounds of cleaving to Him. Words which come forth from, possess, and lead to, eternal life. See ver. 63.—**And we**: [καὶ ἡμεῖς] the answer of faith to the object of faith. Not excluding, of course, the other "antithesis to the deserters." (Meyer.)

[Ver. 69. **And we have believed and have**

known.—The perfect: πεπιστεύκαμεν καὶ ἐγνώκαμεν, expresses the completed action and permanent result: assured faith and firm knowledge. *Fides præcedit intellectum*, "faith precedes knowledge." This Augustinian and Anselmic maxim (which Schleiermacher also adopted; see the motto of his *Dogmatics*) may be derived from the order of πίστις and γνῶσις in this verse.* But the reverse maxim: *Intellectus præcedit fidem* (Abelard), is also true, though not in a rationalistic sense, and is supported by the order, John x. 38 (*that ye may know and believe*) and 1 John v. 13. We must first be made acquainted with Christ before we can believe in Him ("faith comes by hearing," Rom. x. 17), but we must believe in Christ in order to attain an experimental and saving knowledge of Him. Faith itself is an intellectual as well as a moral and spiritual act.—P. S.]

The Holy One of God [see TEXTUAL NOTES.] The One consecrated by and for God. Comp. x. 36; Mark i. 24; Luke iv. 34; Acts iv. 27; Rev. iii. 7. [The coincidence of the original text with the testimony of the demoniacs (Mark i. 26), who with ghostlike intuition perceived the higher character of Jesus, is remarkable.—P. S.] More indefinite designation of the Messiah. The full, matured confession, born of the Spirit, we find first in Matt. xvi.;—a fact mistaken by Weisse, when he makes this passage a variation of that in the Synoptical account.† Peter's answering here in this complete way for all the twelve could not be entirely of the Spirit, [as the later confession Matt. xvi. was]. It unconsciously served to sustain Judas in his false and cold self-command, and to cover the aversion which was in him at the very time; and thus it gave occasion for the severe words of Jesus.

Ver. 70. **Did I not choose you the twelve?**—A more definite exposition of the words of ver. 67. Meyer: "Not the language of reflection, but of sudden pain over the tragic result, in contrast with that joyful confession which Peter was convinced he could give in the name of all." It probably refers not to the "tragic result," but to the moral alienation, the germ of apostasy, which from this time forth developed itself in Judas. The distribution of the emphasis is very significant. "I" is first; then "you;" then "the twelve." I, as the Holy One of God; have chosen you, to the highest honors.

And now the fearful contrast: **One of you is a devil!**‡—Interpretations: An informer (Theophylact, [DeWette]); an adversary or betrayer (Kuinöl, Lücke, *et al.*); devil, devilish, of a diabolical nature (Meyer).§ In New Testament designations, however, an ideal meaning is always lodged; the word is not a mere *nomen;* as Matt. xiii. 39; Rev. xii. 10 prove. And this is the more sure to be the case in this figurative designation. In Matt. xvi. 23 the term "Satan" is chosen, because Jesus intends to describe a tempter instigated by the devil; so here also "devil" denotes an actual traducer instigated by the devil. We must by all means abide by the term. The expression: "sons, or children of the devil," (ch. viii. 44; 1 John iii. 10), is not so strong. The mention of the number twelve shows that the brothers of the Lord also were by this time in the circle. [? See below, p. 241.—P. S.]

Ver. 71. **He spoke of Judas.**—That is, He meant him. See the Textual Notes. On Judas Iscariot see the Com. on *Matthew*, ch. x. [p. 182.] Not to be confounded with the other Judas (son of James), ch. xiv. 22.

For it was he that was about to betray him.—Ἤμελλεν is hard to translate. *Traditurus erat.** The betrayal germinated in him from this time forth. Meyer, groundlessly: "Not that he was already meditating the betrayal, (see, on the contrary, ch. xiii. 2), but that the betrayal was the divinely appointed result." Ch. xiii. 2 speaks of the final resolution; this passage of the first swerving of the temper and inclination. **One of the twelve.**—Showing up the monstrous, diabolical character of this incipient infidelity. The silence of Judas is in keeping with his character. It now firmly lodges the seed. On the Lord's choosing of Judas see Meyer [p. 285, 5th ed. See also the Literature quoted below in DOCTR. and ETHICAL No. 3.—P. S.]

[The CALL OF JUDAS is only one of the innumerable mysteries in God's moral government, which no system of philosophy can solve at all, and which even Christianity solves but in part, reserving the final answer for a higher expansion of our faculties in another world. It involves the whole problem of the relation of God to the origin of sin, and the relation of His foreknowledge and foreordination to the free agency of man. The question why Christ called and received Judas into the circle of His chosen twelve, is more dogmatical than exegetical, yet cannot be passed by unnoticed. It admits of three answers, none of which, however, is entirely satisfactory:

1. Christ elected Judas an apostle, not indeed for the very purpose that he might become a traitor (which no sensible divine ever asserted, at least not directly); but that, through his treason, as an *incidental* condition or a necessary means, the Scriptures might be fulfilled (comp. John xiii. 18; xvii. 12), and the redemption of the world be accomplished. So Augustine (*electi undecim ad opus probationis, electus unus ad opus tentationis*), supralapsarian Calvinists, also Daub who (in his speculative treatise: *Judas Iscariot*) represents the traitor as an incarnate devil, predestinated to exhibit wickedness in its worst form in contrast with the highest manifestation of goodness in Christ. This view, although it contains an element of truth, seems after all to involve our blessed Lord in some kind of responsibility for the darkest crime ever committed.

* [So Bengel: *Fidem sequitur cognitio*, 2 *Pet. i.* 5. *Perversi sunt qui cognitionem prius postulant.*—P. S.]

† [Meyer justly remarks against Weisse that in the nature of the case a confession that filled the hearts of the apostles, must have been repeated on similar occasions.—P. S.]

‡ [The interrogation stops with τοὺς δώδεκα, and what follows is an exclamation of holy sadness. So Meyer and Lange. Alford follows the wrong punctuation of the A. V.—P. S.]

§ [So also Alford, and rightly, for Christ had in view the treason of Judas which was inspired by the Evil One. The strong term corresponds to the profound indignation at the hypocrisy of the traitor who covered himself under the confession of Peter.—P. S.]

* [It is more than the mere future (Alford), and yet not quite as strong as *intended;* it represents the future as an accomplished fact, the germ of which was already in existence at the time, and was detected by the penetrating eye of Christ.—P. S.]

2. Jesus foresaw the financial and administrative abilities of Judas (comp. xii. 6; xiii. 29), which might have become of great use to the apostolic church, but not his thievish and treacherous tendencies, which developed themselves afterwards, and He elected him solely for the former. This explanation is rather rationalistic and incompatible with the prophetic foresight of Christ, as well as the express remark of John ᾔδει ἐξ ἀρχῆς, ver. 64, and vers. 70, 71.

3. Jesus knew the whole original character of Judas from the beginning, before it was properly developed, and elected him in the hope that the good qualities and tendencies would, under the influence of His teaching, ultimately acquire the mastery over the bad. So Meyer, Park and many others. This implies that Jesus was mistaken, if not in His judgment at the time, at least in His expectation, and is likewise at war with His perfect knowledge of the human heart.

Alford despairs of solving the difficulty. Wordsworth and other English commentators pass it by in modest or prudent silence.

I must add that the fall of Judas does not necessarily interfere with the doctrine of the perseverance of saints. For by his election is evidently meant the external historical call to the apostleship which was confined to the twelve, (ὑμᾶς τοὺς δώδεκα ἐξελεξάμην, ver. 70), not the eternal election of the Father and the drawing of the Father to the Son, which applies to all true disciples who persevere to the end. (Rom. viii. 28 ff.; John x. 28, 29; xiii. 18). With this important distinction we may endorse Bengel's remark: "There is therefore a *certain kind of election* from which man may fall away (*Est igitur aliqua electio ex qua aliquis potest excidere*)," but we must add: there is another kind of election which is as certain and unchangeable as God.—P. S.]

DOCTRINAL AND ETHICAL.

1. The *turning-point* in the life of Jesus which John here brings to view is of the highest importance in the history. It accounts for the falling away of the majority of the Galilean followers of Jesus, and that in a way perfectly agreeable to the Galilean character, which was inclined to boisterous insurrectionary projects. Because Jesus refused Himself to the fanatical proposal of these people to make Him a king, and demanded in stringent terms an inward, submissive faith in His person, instead of an outward hoping for the things of an earthly kingdom, many began to fall back.

2. Undoubtedly also the first disaffection now formed itself in the mind of *Judas;* since after the explanation of Jesus, he must have felt that he had been deceived in his glowing expectations. How little the disciples in general noticed this, appears from the protestation of Peter. Yet, besides the all-seeing eye of Christ, the feeling of John seems also to have caught an impression of this alienation. (See *Leben Jesu*, II. p. 609.)

3. On the *calling* [and *character*] of *Judas*, comp. *Matthew*, p. 183; Meyer *in loco* [5th ed. p. 285]; Lücke II. p. 182. [Also Schaff's treatise on the *Sin against the Holy Ghost* (Halle, 1841), pp. 35 ff., the article *Judas* in Winer and in Smith, especially the analysis by Prof. Park of Andover in Hackett's edition of Smith, Vol. II. pp. 1495-1503.—P. S.]

4. The *protestation of Peter* forms a beautiful contrast to the sullen silence of Judas, in whose apostasy three periods are to be marked: 1. The beginning of alienation from this time forth; 2. The thought of betrayal and the dalliance with it after the anointing in Bethany; 3. The full purpose and the execution of it after the passover. And yet the beautiful contrast is not perfect, because Peter indiscreetly and without misgiving answered for the whole company, including Judas himself. Even the grand sentence: "Thou hast the words of eternal life,"—does not fully reach the deep meaning of Jesus in His discourse, if it refers to it. The word of the disciple falls something short of the self-presentation of the Master. The confession in Matt. xvi. 16 is an expression of purer and riper faith. Hence Jesus answers here with the stern word: "One of you is a devil," while after that other confession he blesses him. Even in the latter case it is true, that the sharp rebuke, "Get thee behind me, Satan,"—follows the benediction; for in that case also the divine enthusiasm of faith had not yet matured in Peter into a firm spirit of faith; Peter was not yet free from all sympathy with Judas in chiliastic ambition.

5. It is not to be supposed that the disciples in general received any definite idea as to whom the Lord meant. Least of all do they seem to have fixed on Judas, who, on the contrary, appears from the account of the anointing at Bethany in Matthew and Mark to have enjoyed high consideration among them. That Judas felt himself in some way hit, is very probable; and also that John was led to suspect who the forbidding fellow disciple was (see John's account of the anointing). The stern word of Christ must therefore have burdened the minds of the disciples as a heavy riddle, giving them continuous warning, even amidst the great successes of His subsequent ministry.

The turn we here mark in the history of Jesus now comes fully to view in His subsequent conduct as depicted in the next chapter.

HOMILETICAL AND PRACTICAL.

The first apostasy from Christ in its solemn and typical import: 1. Its motives; 2. Its extent; 3. Its consequences.—The majestic calmness of the Lord in the apostasy of false disciples, as revealed in His stern dealing with those who remain.—The deep grief of the Lord visible even through His free and tranquil conduct, 1. His calmness: He begs not, flatters not, makes no terms; He remains sure of Himself and of His word. 2. His grief: He sees a danger to all His disciples; seems even to miss hearing the fair words of Peter; declares with a shudder that one of the chosen twelve is a devil.—The first apostasy, the first sifting of the hosts of Christ's disciples, 1 Jno. ii. 19.—However great the apostasy may be, it never can be universal.—The stages of apostasy: 1. Retention of the earthly mind in discipleship, Matt. xiii. 5. 2. Development of unbelief, of rupture with Christ. 3. The actual apostasy itself.—Apostasy: a total view of the mournful thing: 1. Its main features in the gospel history. 2. Its preludes in the Old Testament history. 3. Its development in the history of the Christian church. 4. Its final form as depicted in the prophecies of the Bible. The affinity of the apostasy in Galilee with the hostility in Judea.—The apostasy of the Jews a prelude to the traitorous apostasy of Judas.—The malignant silence of Judas a bad sign.—Falsehood of the diabolical nature.

"Nothing more grimly holds thee back
Than falsehood of thy being."

—The silence of Judas and the out-speaking of Peter.—The striking contrast in the circle of the twelve: Peter and Judas: 1. Honest loyalty and false adherence. 2. Fresh, clear openness and dark obduracy. 3. Happy confession and unhappy reserve.—Peter, Judas and John.—The declaration of Peter in its light and shade.—"Lord, to whom shall we go?"—We must continue with Jesus our Lord, because (1) no other Christ will come; (2) no one will bring a better word; (3) there remains no other faith; (4) there remains no brighter knowledge.—The solemnity and dread with which Jesus answered the declarations of Peter.—The fearful contrast: To be chosen to a higher service than angels, and to prove a devil.—The terrible omen, that from among the twelve arose a traitor to the Lord, and a betrayer of the Lord Himself.—The depravity germinates slowly, but ripens rapidly to judgment. —The second turn in the life of Jesus (in Galilee), compared with the first (in Judea).—Because Christ presented Himself to His disciples as the bread of eternal life, many feared they should starve, and fell away.—They wish only things, things, things (worldly things, spiritual things, ecclesiastical things), and so come not to personal life in the beholding and partaking of the glorious personality of Christ.—As a man's ideal is, so is he: he who wishes only idols and stocks, is like idols and stocks; he who wishes only creatures and things, is himself but creature and thing; and this leads to apostasy. [comp. Ps. cxv. 8.—Tr.]—Hence apostasy is from Christianity to Judaism, from gospel to law.—It needs courage to trust oneself to Christ, the focus of life, and let the world go; but a believing courage which the Lord gives to him who asks.

Starke: Quesnel: A preacher may lose his hearers through no fault of his own.—Majus: As Jesus unkindly thrust no one away, so He will forcibly retain none. Let those go who wish not to stay. He who forsakes Christ, the Life, follows Satan to death.—Canstein: Christ needed none, but no one can do without Him.—It often fares with faithful teachers as with Christ (in the history here before us).—There is hardly a company, but the devil finds one or another in it.—Preachers may certainly rebuke the sins of their hearers, yet with care that they call no one by name; for this embitters without edifying.—In unbelievers Satan so nestles, that they themselves are as it were the devil. Eph. ii. 2.—Trouble thyself not and doubt not for the truth of the gospel, when one of the most distinguished ministers becomes a Mameluke and proves faithless to Christ.—Osiander: Even those who are adorned with excellent gifts, may still forfeit the grace of God.—Beware of presumptuous security! False brethren give more pain to the faithful servants of God, than open enemies.—Bengel: Christ is concerned not for the number, but for the purity of His disciples.—Gossner, on ver. 67: By this He would show that He forces no one, but would have all voluntary disciples.—Heubner: There is a gross apostasy from Jesus; this is rare; but there is also a subtle apostasy, which is the more frequent.—The voluntary departure of spurious disciples is no loss, but a gain.—Ver. 67: Jesus pours out His whole heart in this question, His sorrow and His love.—He still puts this question continually to all believers (*i. e.* in every solemn test) for the trial of their fidelity.—Upon the least likelihood that Jesus might doubt their fidelity, Peter breaks out the louder; so the Christian will attach himself the more fervently to Jesus at the faintest trace of apostasy.—*Have believed and known.* A hint that the believing, child-like posture of mind must precede the attainment of knowledge.—Jesus still knows all the faithful and the faithless ("The Lord knoweth them that are His").—Christ bore with Judas; the hardest test of His love. Bear cheerfully with men, in whom thou canst not find thyself.—Not to be upright towards the most upright One, betrays a wicked heart. The richest grace of intercourse with the most holy One can turn to perdition with a wicked heart. Judas went out of the school of Jesus far worse than he went in. —Besser: Unbelief towards this single article (the eating and drinking of His flesh and blood) brought on a complete renunciation of Christ. [More accurately: Offence at being required to find all salvation in His whole self-sacrifice and self-imparting person itself, led them to separate from His person. Offence also at the last utterance of Jesus, ver. 65, which runs as a companion thought through the whole discourse, must in some way come into the account. As the doctrine of the divine person of Christ and its impartation of perfect life through a sacrificial death which made it a sacrificial meal was an offence to them, so was the doctrine of a distinction made by a gracious spiritual drawing of God between the small election of the spiritual Israel and the mass of the theocratic Israelitish church.]—Judas represents what is befallen to the Jewish people as a whole. How immeasurably deep must be the grief of love, that what was intended for Israel's salvation became its hardening! He chose Judas. He turned upon him the full earnestness of His saving love, and He endured that one of the twelve should do the service of the devil to Him, that the Scripture might be fulfilled, xvii. 12; Ps. cix.—Schenkel: Why we are resolved not to go away from Jesus Christ. We answer, with Peter, to the question of the Lord: 1. Whither would we go? 2. The Lord has the words of eternal life. 3. We have believed and known that He is Christ, the Son of the living God.

[Themes for discourses: The sifting power of truth. The sin of backsliding (ver. 66).—Peter the Confessor.—The first and fundamental Christian confession.—Christ, the best of teachers, the truest friend, the only refuge of the sinner.

—Words of everlasting life.—Christ and Peter. —Christ and Judas.—It is better, with Peter in regard to Judas, to err on the side of charity than severity of judgment.—Christ, the purest of the pure, and the holiest of the holy, bore the traitor in His company to the close of His public ministry! What self-denial, what condescending mercy, what a rebuke to our intolerance and pride. —The mercy and severity of Christ in dealing with Judas.—The unknown sufferings of Christ in foreseeing the betrayal of one, and the treason of another disciple.—Peter called "Satan" for his human weakness (Matt. xvi. 23), Judas, a "devil" for his lurking treason.—Christ's wisdom and mercy in withholding the name of Judas, while giving him a clear hint of his danger.—A hypocrite may for a long while deceive all men, but he cannot deceive Christ.—Judas an involuntary instrument for the greatest good.—The overruling power and wisdom of God.—Christ, the true prophet of human nature who knows and reveals the secrets of the heart.—P. S.]

IV.

APPROACH OF THE FEAST OF TABERNACLES, AND OFFENCE OF EVEN THE BRETHREN OF JESUS AT HIS REFUSAL TO GO TO IT. CHRIST'S TIME AND THE TIME OF THE WORLDLY MIND. CHRIST THE OBJECT OF THE WORLD'S HATRED.

Ch. VII. 1–9.

[And][1] After these things[2] Jesus walked in Galilee: for he would not walk in
2 Jewry[3] [Judæa], because the Jews sought to kill him. Now the Jews' feast of taber-
3 nacles was at hand. His brethren [brothers][4] therefore said unto him, Depart
hence, and go into Judea, that thy disciples also [thine adherents in that country,
4 especially in Jerusalem] may see the [thy] works that thou doest. For *there is* no
man that doeth anything in secret, and he himself [For no one doeth anything in se-
cret and yet himself] seeketh to be known openly. If thou do [doest] these things,
5 shew thyself to the world. (For neither did his brethren believe in him.) [For even
6 his brothers did not believe in him.] Then[5] Jesus said [saith] unto them, My time is
7 not yet come: but your time is always ready. The world cannot hate you; but me
it hateth, because I testify of it, that the works thereof are evil. Go ye up unto
8 this[6] [the] feast; I go not up yet unto this feast; for my time is not yet[7] full [fully]
9 come. When he had said these words unto them[8] he abode *still* [remained] in
Galilee.

TEXTUAL AND GRAMMATICAL.

[1] Ver. 1.—Καί is omitted by ℵ* and ℵ^cb. C.[2] D. text. rec. Tisch. (ed. VIII.), inserted by ℵ^ca (but erased). B. C.* L. X. and other uncial MSS. Lachm. Treg. Alf. Westcott & Hort.—P. S.]

[2] Ver. 1.—The μετὰ ταῦτα immediately follows the καί in [ℵ.] B. C. D. G. K., *etc.* [In the text. rec. it follows after ὁ Ἰησοῦς.—P. S.]

[3] Ver. 1.—[*Jewry* is antiquated. The E. V. uses it twice in the N. T. (Luke xxiii. 5), in all other passages *Judæa.*—P. S.]

[4] Ver. 3.—[On the meaning of ἀδελφοί, see Text. Notes on II. 12, p. 114.—P. S.].

[5] Ver. 6.—[Οὖν, *therefore*, is wanting in ℵ.* D. and omitted by Tischend., but retained with ℵ.^c B. L. *etc.*, by Lachm. Alf., *etc.*—P. S.]

[6] Ver. 8.—This first ταύτην is wanting in B. D., *etc.*, and is omitted by Lachmann and Tischendorf.

[7] Ver. 8.—"Elz., Lachmann: οὔπω, *not yet;* supported, too, by the preponderance of Codd. (only D. K. M. [ℵ] and three minuscules have οὐκ); but against the weight of versions, most of which, including Vulgata and Itala, read οὐκ. Of the fathers, Epiphanius, Cyril, Chrysostom, and many others, have οὐκ. Porphyry found οὐκ in Jerome, and drew from it the charge of fickleness against Jesus. Just to avoid this offence οὔπω was introduced." Meyer. [Lange adopts, with Meyer, οὐκ, (*not*, instead of οὔπω, *not yet.* So also Cod. Sin., Tischend. ed. VIII.) Alf., Treg., while Lachm. and Westcott and Hort retain οὔπω.—P. S.]

[8] Ver. 9.—Tischendorf reads αὐτός instead of αὐτοῖς after some undecisive Codd. [The Cod. Sin. D. Vulg. (*ipse*) support αὐτός.—P. S.]

EXEGETICAL AND CRITICAL.

"According to Baur this seventh chapter goes to show how the dialectics (criticism?) into which unbelief enters, is only its own dialectical (critical?) refutation." Meyer.

Ver. 1. **And after these things Jesus walked.**—After the occurrences and discourses in Galilee in ch. vi.; a new general date succeeding the μετὰ ταῦτα of ch. vi. 1. The festival caravan had proposed to take possession of Him and make Him a king. But He had completely delivered Himself from them, and went not with them to the passover. Nor did He join the next train, which went up to the feast of tabernacles. The words "walked in Galilee," therefore, mean, as their primary antithesis, that He went not up with the caravan to the feast [passover, vi. 4] next following. John mentions only the second antithesis: that He could not walk in Judea, without peril of death. If He had now at once gone about publicly in Judea, and remained there, He would have too seriously embarrassed His exit. In Judea, the main theatre of His ministry, He no longer had room to work; He still had room in Galilee. And His isolated and sudden appearance and His ministry in Judea hereafter take place only under the protection of secresy, or of Galilean and Perean friends and adherents, as well as individual disciples in Judea. The proximate period of the walking in Galilee is from the feast of Purim to the feast of tabernacles of the year 782 (A. D. 29), from the month Adar to the month Tisri. (Wieseler: from the 19th March to about the 12th October.)

In this period of Galilean itinerancy fall the charges of heresy against Jesus in Galilee and His contests with the hostile Pharisees there, Matt. xii.; most of His parables or sermons on the sea, Matt. xiii. (Matt. xiv. dates the beginning); His interview with the deputation from Jerusalem, and the great gathering on the mountain, which followed, Matt. xv.; the last contest with Pharisean power in Galilee, the retirement of the Lord and His transfiguration, Matt. xvi. and xvii. 21 (not ch. xv. to xviii., as Meyer gives it.)

Ver. 2. **The feast . . . was at hand.**—The second occasion and demand to go with a festival caravan, which Jesus declined. Though He went to Jerusalem, He did so not in the full publicity of the festival pilgrimage, nor in the capacity of a festival pilgrim.

Feast of tabernacles.—חַג הַסֻּכּוֹת, σκηνοπηγία in Josephus, σκηναί in Philo.* The third of the great festivals of the Jews (Passover, Pentecost or Weeks, Tabernacles); celebrated in the seventh month or Tisri (in October), for seven days from the 15th, in memory of the dwelling of the Israelites in tabernacles or tents on their journey through the wilderness, and in thanksgiving for the harvest now, with the fruit and grape gathering, entirely finished. Thus: Passover: deliverance from the destroying angel and from Egypt, beginning of harvest; Pentecost: completion of grain-harvest, thanksgiving feast of first-fruits, no doubt also in celebration of some point of the theocratic history (Maimonides: the giving of the law on Sinai); Tabernacles: feast of the wandering and of vintage. It is to be remembered that the eighth day of this feast (23d Tisri) was kept by the Jews as the feast of the joy of the law. The feast of tabernacles formed at the same time the counterpart to the great penitential feast of the day of atonement which occurred five days before, as a sort of preparation for the feast of joy. The feast was distinguished by its grand offerings, as well as its joyful tone; so that it was called by Josephus "the holiest and greatest of the feasts." [*Antiqu.* viii. 4, 1: ἑορτὴ ἁγιωτάτη καὶ μεγίστη.—P. S.] People lived in tents formed of live branches of trees, on roofs, in streets, on open grounds; they carried boughs of fruit, noble, handsome fruits, especially branches of palms and citrons, in their hands, and had merry banquets. The feast of tabernacles had so joyous an appearance that Plutarch could think it a feast of Bacchus. But it is a mistake to try to trace the Israelitish festivals of events of theocratic history to original festivals of nature. As Israelitish feasts they must be primarily historical. They may have attached themselves, however, to existing popular feasts of Asia, absorbing and spiritualizing them, as was confessedly done by Christian festivals [Christmas, Easter, *etc.*] in reference to existing feasts of heathenism (comp. *Leben Jesu*, II. p. 941). Attendance on these festivals in Jerusalem was binding upon the male portion of Israel (Deut. xvi. 16). Respecting the particular practices of the feast of tabernacles, see below.

Ver. 3. **His brothers therefore said unto him.**—According to Matt. xiii. 55 these were James, Joses, Simon and Judas. A disposition on their part to act as guardians and advisers to Jesus appears again, and prominently in Mark iii. 21. But they as surely mean well with their counsel here, as they meant in that other case to act in faithful solicitude for Him. Euthymius Zigabenus [also Luther], attributed to them a malicious design (to draw Him into the hands of the Jews), because their unbelief is afterwards mentioned. The speech of His brethren refers to the fact that Jesus did not go to the late passover that in general he seems to wish to avoid Judea, and that, by going about on the mountains and the sea, He makes even His residence in Galilee a half-concealed one. They propose that He should appear publicly in Judea and accredit Himself as the Messiah before His adherents there. Evidently the echo of the spirit of ch. vi. 15. They were right in assuming that a Messiah could not complete His legitimation of Himself and His work outside of Judea and Jerusalem; they were wrong and frivolous (1) in beginning to think lightly of His quiet ministry in Galilee; (2) in still hoping that by a public appearance in Jerusalem, He might carry the nation with Him, and become a Messiah glorious after an Old Testament sort; (3) in not submitting themselves to His wisdom and His self-determining course of action. And herein chiefly lay their unbelief.

Vers. 3, 4. How important the brothers of Jesus thought it, that He should change His field, appears from the twofold expression: **Depart hence and go into Judæa, that thy disciples also may see thy works,** *etc.* μετάβηθι ἐντεῦθεν, καὶ ὕπαγε, κ. τ. λ. In this view we are to understand by the disciples who were to see His works, all His adherents in the land of Judea; chiefly the influential ones in Jerusalem, but not these alone. In contrast with such an appearance His Galilean work, particularly His quiet itinerancy and His withdrawal to the Phenician borders, to the highlands of the Jordan, and across the sea, seems to them an incongruous working **in secret** (ver. 4). And it presents to them the contradiction of His proposing to be a public personage with a secret ministry. (On the misinterpretations of ἐν κρυπτῷ, by Baumgarten-Crusius, Brückner, and Luthardt, see Meyer.) Not the least thing which pertains to the authentication of a public character, does such an one perform in secret; much less does he waste such (great) works (ταῦτα) on an obscure region. The εἰ ["if Thou doest these

* [On the σκηνοπηγία or ἑορτὴ τῶν σκηνῶν (from σκηνή and πήγνυμι, *lit.* a booth-pitching, tent-pitching) comp. Lev. xxiii.; Deut. xvi.; Josephus, *Antiqu.*, iii. 10, 4; iv. 8, 12; viii. 4, 1; Ewald, *Jewish Archæol.*, p. 481 f.; Keil, *Arch.* I, § 85, and the respective articles in Winer, Smith, Kitto, Fairbairn. —P. S.]

things"] is not intended to throw doubt on the works; it denotes the logical premise. (Meyer, against Lücke, *etc.*)

Ver. 5. Then when John remarks: **For even his brothers did not believe in him,** it is entirely gratuitous to make of this, as has been done, a disbelief of His Messiahship itself common to all the brothers, and to infer that the brothers of the Lord, James, Judas and Simon, must be distinguished from the apostles of the Lord, James, Judas and Simon, whom He had chosen before the feast of Purim (Matt. x.) See Com. on *Matthew* on ch. x. and xii. 46 ff., (comp. *Mark,* at ch. iii. 30; *Matt.* xiii. 55).; *Leben Jesu,* II., p. 139 sqq., and 926; Herzog's *Real-Encyklop.*, Art. *Jakobus, der Bruder des Herrn.* It is plain from the connection that the unbelief of these brothers of the Lord was a *want of confidence* in Him of the same sort, at the worst, as that of Mary in Mark iii. 31, of Peter in Matt. xvi. 22, and of Thomas in Jno. xx. 25; that is, while believing in His Messiahship, they lacked in the perfect yielding of a believing obedience, and assumed to prescribe to Him from their own judgment; but they were not unbelieving in the sense in which Caiaphas and the Jewish people were. Tenaciously as the Ebionistic Clementine tradition, distinguishing between the three apostolic brothers of the Lord and the three apostles, James, the son of Alpheus, Judas, and Simon, endeavors to maintain itself, it will not ultimately withstand, with its half-dogmatical, half critical prejudice, the sense of Scripture and the primitive church tradition. [I dissent from this view. See my remarks below on ver. 9, p. 241. The theory here opposed is certainly older and exegetically more natural, than the cousin-theory, which cannot be traced beyond Jerome in the fourth century,* and which owes its popularity far more to an ascetic over-estimate of the perpetual virginity of Mary (and Joseph) than to exegetical or critical arguments. It is clearly irreconcilable with the whole tenor of this passage, as I shall presently show.—P. S.]

Ver. 6. **My time is not yet come.**—Interpretations: 1. The time for Me to go to the feast (Jansen, *et al.*); 2. The time to show Myself openly to the world (as they had demanded in ver. 4, Lücke, *et al.*); 3. The time of my passion (Chrysostom, *et al.*). The first interpretation is connected with the second, the second with the third. His first public entrance into Jerusalem was the entrance in the procession with palms; by that He showed Himself publicly to the world, and by that also He brought on His own death. Hence: My time for going to the feast to manifest Myself to the world. His words, therefore, referred primarily to the time of journeying, but in connection with the deeper meaning. The connection lies in the fact that *His fixed time* (καιρός), like *His hour* (ch. ii. 4), denotes the time *ordained and appointed to Him by God* for His public appearance, in distinction from the hours arbitrarily chosen by other men.

Hence the other words: **But your time is always ready**; describing the free, arbitrary disposal of times which sinful men make; with primary reference to their travelling, but with respect also to the safety with which they may show themselves to the world, with which they do not yet stand, like Him, in full and pure antagonism, ver. 7. An intimation of their want of decided faith.

Ver. 7. **The world cannot hate you.**—The world considered as unbelieving, in its antagonism to the Lord. It can no more take the internally complete attitude of mortal enmity towards you, than ye have thus far taken this attitude toward its spirit. All chiliastic kinds of faith, (*e.g.* in the church of the middle ages) have an element akin to the world and open to its sympathy. **But me it hateth.**—The entire antagonism brought into play by His testimony against the world.

Ver. 8. **Go ye up unto this feast.**—This is, after the ritual manner of the Israelitish law, as pilgrims in the festival caravan, to participate in the exercises of the feast.

I go not up (yet) unto this feast.—Interpretations with reference to ver. 10: [omitting the "yet."]

1. The hostile interpretation of Porphyry, that Jesus proved Himself fickle (Jerome, *Contra Pel.*)

2. Bruno Bauer's modification: The Evangelist entangles himself in contradiction in his narrative (see Lücke, p. 193; kindred constructions by F. Chr. Baur, *etc.*, see in Meyer.)

3. Meyer: "Jesus might *alter* His plan without being inconsistent, especially since the motive of this change of purpose is not patent. He also changed His purpose with the Canaanitish woman (Matt. xv. 26 sqq.)." But He no more changed it there, than here. The entrance of a new motive, must at least have been intimated.

4. The reading οὔπω [which is omitted by some of the oldest MSS., but inserted by others and by the early Versions.—P. S.] or to the same purpose, the emphasizing of the *present* ἀναβαίνω, inserting a νῦν in thought (Chrysostom, Lücke, and others). Of the same class is the restricting of the οὐκ by the οὔπω following (De Wette and others).

5. Emphasizing of *feast*, ἑορτή; Cyril: οὐκ οὕτως ἑορτάζων. He took no part ritually in the festal train or the festal scenes, (*Leben Jesu,* II. p. 927; Ebrard and others). In favor of this is the ensuing: οὐ φανερῶς, ἀλλ' ὡς ἐν κρυπτῷ.

6. The explanation: Not with the caravan (Bengel, Ewald, Luthardt), is properly only one part of the preceding interpretation. It is emphatically said, moreover: "unto *this* feast;" Jesus thus already announcing in a manner His intended decisive observance of the next passover. A glance at that last feast we see in the words: "*For my time,*" *&c.*

Ver. 9. **He remained in Galilee.**—That is, He let the train pass on, and perhaps His brothers with it.

[Remarks on the Brothers of Jesus.—The family dispute which John relates in this section from personal knowledge, with the simplicity and

*[The passage of Papias about the four Marys, published by Grabe and Routh from a Bodleian MS., (No. 2397), which Mill, Wordsworth, and two writers in Smith's *Dictionary* (sub. *Brothers* and *James*) have uncritically quoted in favor of the cousin-theory, is not from the Papias of the second century, but from a mediæval namesake of the bishop of Hierapolis and author of a dictionary. Comp. Lightfoot Com. on *Galatians*, 2d ed., 1866, p. 265 f. Lightfoot asserts and proves that the Hieronymian hypothesis is a pure conjecture unsupported by any previous traditional sanction.—P. S.]

frankness of a genuine historian, gives us an insight into the domestic trials of our Saviour. The unbelief of His *brothers* need not surprise us any more than the unbelief of the Nazarenes generally, according to the sentence: "A prophet has no honor in his own country" (comp. note on iv. 44). Not unfrequently the nearest relatives throw more obstacles in the way to God's children than strangers. Christ entered into the condition of fallen humanity with all its daily troubles, temptations and miseries. The unbelief and misconduct of His brothers must have been to Him a deep source of grief and a school of patience and forbearance in order that, being tempted even as we are in all things, He might become a merciful High Priest able and willing to sympathize with His followers in passing through similar experiences. (Heb. ii. 17, 18; v. 7, 8).

But the full significance of this passage depends upon the proper view of *the brothers of Jesus*. And here I must again dissent from the cousin-theory of Jerome, advocated in a modified form by Dr. Lange, which assumes that these brothers were only distant relatives of Jesus, and that three of them, James, Simon and Jude (*i. e.*, all but Joses or Joseph), were identical with the three apostles of that name. I regard this passage (with Meyer, Godet, Alford, Lightfoot) as one of the strongest arguments in favor of the more natural view that the brothers of Jesus were really members of the holy family and under the care of Joseph and Mary in whose company they constantly appear.*

1. It is perfectly plain that John here, as in ii. 12 and in harmony with the Synoptists, also with Acts i. 13, 14, and 1 Cor. ix. 5, distinguishes the brothers of Christ from the apostles. The brothers themselves make this distinction in ver. 3, "That thy disciples also," *etc.*, on which Bengel remarks: *Eo ipso ostendunt se non esse discipulos.*

2. But what is more conclusive, John represents here the brothers as *unbelievers*, and as using irreverent, presumptuous and ironical language against our Lord. This is absolutely incompatible with the assumption that they were apostles, especially after the sifting process described in ch. vi., and the noble confession of Peter in the name of all (vi. 67, 68). I readily admit that the brothers were not unbelievers in the sense of the hostile Jews or indifferent pagans, but they certainly were not *believers* in a sense in which we must suppose all apostles (with the exception perhaps of Judas Iscariot) to have been almost from their first acquaintance with Jesus, and as John expressly says that they were even as early as the miracle at Cana, ii. 11; comp. ver. 22; xvi. 17; xvii. 8. How, in the name of consistency, could he say that the apostles *believed in Him* (*ἐπίστευσαν εἰς αὐτόν*), and afterwards, that His brothers, including at least three of the apostles, *did not believe in him*, *οὐδὲ οἱ ἀδελφοὶ αὐτοῦ ἐπίστευον*—mark the imperfect which denotes continued and habitual unbelief, in distinction from a momentary act as expressed by the aorist—(*ἐπίστευσαν*)? Why did he not avoid such flat contradiction by the qualifying words: *some* of His brothers, or by using a milder term than unbelief?† John recognizes indeed different degrees of belief (comp. ii. 23; iv. 39; viii. 31; xii. 42), and different degrees of unbelief, but he never confounds the sharp lines which, in his system especially, distinguish belief from unbelief, light from darkness, truth from falsehood. Moreover the language used by the brothers on this occasion, however mildly we may explain it, is very unbecoming, and strongly contrasts with the profound reverence shown by the apostles to our Lord on every occasion, even where they could not understand or appreciate His conduct (comp. John iv. 27).

3. Finally our Lord Himself here characterizes His brothers as men of the world whom the world cannot hate (ver. 7); while He says the very reverse of His apostles, xv. 18 f. comp. Matt. x. 5 ff., 22, 40 ff.

We infer then that all the four brothers of Jesus were distinct from the apostles, and were not converted till after the resurrection. James, it would seem, became a believer in consequence of a special manifestation of the risen Lord, 1 Cor. xv. 7. They first appear among the disciples, Acts i. 14.

As to the other question, whether the brothers of Jesus were *older* brothers of Jesus from a former, otherwise unknown marriage of Joseph (the old Greek tradition defended by Epiphanius), or *younger* children of *Mary* and Joseph (the view held by Tertullian and Helvidius, and denounced first by Jerome as heretical and profane because of its conflict with the prevalent ascetic belief in the perpetual virginity of Mary), our passage gives no decisive answer. The patronizing tone assumed by the brothers towards Jesus on this occasion seems to favor the former view, but may be found also with younger brothers. Comp. the fuller discussion of this whole question in my notes on *Matthew*, pp. 256-260, also on Matt. i. 25 and John ii. 12. (p. 115 of this vol.)—P. S.]

DOCTRINAL AND ETHICAL.

1. The heavenly *precaution* with which Jesus guarded His life from a premature end, that He might sacrifice it with full effect at the right hour, forms a contrast with the heedless *boldness* with which His brothers would push Him upon the stage of the most glaring publicity; and a contrast with the many premature sacrifices which occur in the lives of worldly heroes and even of Christian missionaries and martyrs. The life of the believer must be in spirit offered up to God at all times; but the actual sacrifice of it must be put with all decision under the law of Christian wisdom. No one should prematurely squander his life; every one should, in the holiest sense, "sell it at the highest possible price." But for His wise reserve, the life of the Lord would perhaps have fallen before the hatred of Judaism in the very first year of His ministry; certainly at the feast of Purim in the spring of

* [This was my conviction nearly thirty years ago when I first carefully examined this vexed question in my German treatise on *James the Brother of the Lord*. Berlin, 1842.]

† [For a refutation of the various attempts to weaken the force of *οὐκ ἐπίστευον*, see my treatise on *James, etc.* pp. 51 ff. In John vi. 64, the *μαθηταὶ οἱ οὐ πιστεύουσι* are clearly distinguished from the twelve, and they forsook the Lord (66), while the apostles remained (68). In Luke xii. 28, the disciples are called "men of little faith," but this is very different from unbelief. The *γενεὰ ἄπιστος*, Matt. xvii. 17, refers to a particular fact and a single act, not to a state of mind or tendency. The question, John xvi. 31, *ἄρτι πιστεύετε* (if it be a question), can in no way contradict the *πεπιστεύκατε* in ver. 27 and the *ἐπίστευσαν*, xvii. 8.]

the second year. A ministry of about three years in the midst of Pharisaic Judea could be secured to Jesus only by His heavenly wisdom.

2. The subsequent *appearance* of Christ at the feast of tabernacles does not contradict this caution. It is an act of consummate psychological mastery. By this oft-repeated sudden appearance, He places Himself as an astounding wonder before His enemies; they themselves are restrained by fear, or at least their servants, and they do not venture to seize Him. They are disarmed not only by the personal impression of Jesus, but also by fear of the powerful popular following which He had, particularly of the fighting Galileans. Not till the continuous stay of Christ among them at the last passover could they carry out a definite plan against Him.

3. It agrees with the nature of human restlessness that the same *brothers* of the Lord, who with His mother sought to rescue Him some time before from the press of Galilean enemies through fear (Mark iii., Matt. xii.), now sought in recklessness to press Him upon the theatre of decision. Apart from the fact that such extremes beget and account for each other, the experience which the brothers of Jesus had had of the uselessness of their fear and of the security of Jesus amidst the strongest probabilities of danger, might urge them now to the utmost risk in His behalf.

4. Jesus, in respect to His *time* and *place* is subject to the individual direction (ἐντολή) of His Father. Thus His time at every point is a point of eternity, and His being in every place is a being in heaven. The contrast between the Divine discernment of His time and His hour [in the life of Jesus] and the arbitrary caprice of men in the use of times and hours.

5. The notion of the *world* which the brothers of Jesus express, differs greatly from the notion expressed by Christ. Judas Lebbæus recurs to this favorable idea of the world in ch. xiv. 22. The brothers of Jesus vaguely see a world ready to receive Christ with open arms; Christ sees through a world disposed to kill Him. Undoubtedly Christ Himself also distinguishes between the world as the object of the Divine love (ch. iii. 16), and the world in its decided ungodliness and unbelief.

6. Christ's word: *The world cannot hate you*, expresses the truth that there is no deeper, more incisive opposition than that between a godly mind and a worldly mind, faith and unbelief. The world's hatred comes out completely only in opposition to that which is divine.

7. There is an infinite difference between the delicate precision of the Lord's form of expression and a made-up *reservatio mentalis.* But for this reason the words of Christ, and especially His expression here: *I go not up to this feast*, are also exposed to the ready abuse of men. The abuse is not due to ambiguities on His part, but to the want of discrimination on the part of His expounders. Else it would have been easily seen that between a public Messianic progress of Jesus to the ceremonial observance of a feast, and an incidental appearance of the anonymous prophet at the feast, the difference is wide.

HOMILETICAL AND PRACTICAL.

See under the previous head.

The quiet walking of Jesus in Galilee a token also of His glory.—A token of His prudence, His foresight, His wisdom, in His spirit of self-sacrifice.—How Jesus by wisdom preserved and spared His official life till the right, decisive moment, though it was forfeited to death from the first.—The most splendid and joyous feast of the Jews no allurement to the Lord, but an object of holy solicitude and dread.—The want of the obedience of faith in the enthusiastic zeal of faith in the brothers of Jesus.—The contrast between Christ's knowledge of the world and His brothers' knowledge of it.—Marks of the worldly element in the belief of the Messiah.—The word of Jesus to His brothers: vers. 6-8.—The declaration in vers. 6 and 7;—the several words of vers. 6-8.—"No guile found in His mouth," or, Jesus, even in the pure and precise form of His words, hard to understand by the ordinary way of thinking.—The sharp precision of the words of Jesus a reflection of the perfect clearness of His mind.—The lesson of the divine peace in the Lord's quiet tarrying at home while His brothers go to the brilliant feast.—We also must be able to stay at home.—With what a different eye from that of His brothers did Christ look upon the glories of the world and even of the Jewish people of God (or "church").

STARKE: Hasten not after suffering: it will come soon enough.—CRAMER: Let every one look well to himself in his office that he may long serve the church of God.—Christians still celebrate their feast of tabernacles when they heartily praise God for His shelter and defence.—HEDINGER: Let no one lord it over the wisdom of God.—CANSTEIN: Follow not the voice which urges thee to seek a great name and become renowned in the world. The sole voice of self-love often leads a minister to leave a place where he may do much good, and move to another where he can do none.—Kindred are most commonly the ones who obstruct the godly.—*Bibl. Wirt.:* A true Christian heart desires not to distinguish itself; the more secret, the happier.—God does everything exactly at the right time, but men do much out of season.—One hawk does not pick out another's eyes; he who accommodates himself to the world, will be loved by it.—The friendship of the world, Jas. iv. 4.—CANSTEIN: It bespeaks humility and prudence for a man to wait God's time, keeping himself quiet till it come; this does not conflict with the joyousness of faith, which afterwards goes joyfully forward when it perceives its time.—GOSSNER: I guide myself by the hour-glass of my Father; ye can go according to your pleasure; ye may say what ye will, ye will never be arraigned for it; but I must walk cautiously, that I may not wantonly encounter my suffering. He who follows his own will, who does everything out of his own head, and *never consults the divine moment*,—his time is always ready. But he who loves God, lets all his moments depend on the will and indication of God.—BRAUNE: Even though they (the brothers) hastened forward to the feast, they after all remained behind.—They who are forward with outward worship, do not therefore worship the Lord in spirit and in truth. With the boisterous (Is. v. 19) the Redeemer can have no fellowship. —It is trying indeed to be left alone with one's Christianity in a good cause, but it is better to be alone than to burden one's self with precarious companions who rather corrupt than improve. (RIEGER).—Circumspection and prudence best become the boldest.—GERLACH: Such an appearance as ye demand would draw upon me not splendor and honor, but death and ruin.

HEUBNER: The world is still challenging: Show thyself, come out, make thyself known to the great rulers, recommend thyself by writings and the like.—BESSER: *Their* time did not coincide with *His* time. It is the peculiar glory of believers, that in all their actions, God's time is also theirs.—The more one sees the extraordinary mind develop itself under the common limitations of life, the harder he finds the acknowledgment of it.

THIRD SECTION.

Ferment in the Contest between the Elements of Light and Darkness. Formation of Parties, as a Prelude to the full Opposition between the Children of Light and the Children of Darkness.

CHAPTER VII. 10—X. 21.

I.

FERMENTATION AND PARTY DIVISION AMONG THE PEOPLE IN GENERAL.

(*a*) CHRIST, THE TEACHER AND THE ONE SENT FROM GOD, IN OPPOSITION TO THE HUMAN RABBINICAL OFFICE, AND IN AGREEMENT WITH MOSES. HIS EARTHLY DESCENT IN OPPOSITION TO DESCENT FROM HEAVEN. HIS OPPONENTS, WHO WISHED TO KILL HIM, IN CONTRADICTION WITH MOSES, THE PROPHET OF GOD, INTENDING TO RETURN TO GOD.

CHAP. VII. 10-36.

10 But when his brethren [brothers] were [had] gone up [to the feast][1] then went
he also [he also went] up unto the feast, not openly [as a festal pilgrim], but as it
11 were in secret [as a private person, a non-participant spectator]. Then the Jews [The
Jews therefore] sought him at the feast, and said, Where is he [that man, ἐκεῖνος]?
12 And there was much murmuring among the people [the multitudes, ἐν τοῖς ὄχλοις]
concerning him: for some said, He is a good man: [but][2] others said, Nay; but he
13 deceiveth the people [the multitude, τὸν ὄχλον]. Howbeit, no man spake [Yet no
one spoke] openly of him, for fear of the Jews.
14 Now about the midst of the feast, Jesus went up into the temple and taught.
15 And [Then][3] the Jews marvelled, saying, How knoweth this man letters, having
never learned [been schooled as a Rabbi].
16 Jesus [therefore][4] answered them, and said, My doctrine is not mine, but his that
17 sent me. If any man [one] will do his will [is willing, desirous, anxious to do his
will, θέλῃ τὸ θέλημα αὐτοῦ],[5] he shall know of [concerning] the doctrine, whether
it be of [is from] God, or *whether* I [in my doctrine] speak [make words, λαλῶ] of
18 [from] myself. He that speaketh of [from] himself, seeketh his own glory: but
he that seeketh his glory [the glory of Him] that sent him, the same is true,
19 and no unrighteousness [*i. e.* no transgression of the law, see ver. 21] is in him. Did
not Moses give you the law, [?] *and yet* none of you keepeth the law? [!][6] Why
go ye about [Why do you seek] to kill me?
20 The people [multitude—not the rulers] answered and said, Thou hast a devil
[a demon, δαιμόνιον, a spirit of melancholy]: who goeth about [seeketh] to kill thee?
21 Jesus answered and said unto them, I have done one work, and ye all marvel
22 [on account of it].[7] Moses therefore [on this account, for this cause, see note 7]
gave unto you [the] circumcision (not because [that] it is of [from] Moses, but of
23 [from] the fathers;) and ye on the Sabbath-day [*omit* day] circumcise a man. If
a man on the Sabbath-day [*omit* day] receive circumcision that the law of Moses
should [may] not be broken; are ye angry at me, because I have made a man every
whit whole on the Sabbath-day [because I have made sound, or, restored to health a
whole man, ὅλον ἄνθρωπον (*i. e.* the entire body of a man, not only a single member as in

24 circumcision) on a Sabbath]? Judge not according to the [*omit* the] appearance,
but judge righteous judgment.
25 Then said some of them of Jerusalem, Is not this he whom they seek to kill?
26 But [And] lo, he speaketh boldly, and they say nothing unto him. Do the rulers
27 know indeed[8] that this is the very [*omit* very, see note 8] Christ. Howbeit, we know
this man [Still, as to this man, we know], whence he is: but when [the] Christ
cometh, no man knoweth whence he is.
28 Then [Therefore] cried Jesus in the temple, as he taught, saying [teaching in
the temple and saying], Ye both know me, and ye know whence I am: and I am
29 not come of myself, but he that sent me is true, whom ye know not. But[9] I know
him; for I am from him, and he hath sent me.
30 Then [Therefore] they sought to take [seize] him: but [and yet][10] no man [one]
31 laid hands on him, because his hour was [had] not yet come. And many of the
people [But of the multitude many][11] believed on him, and said,[12] When Christ
cometh, will he do[13] more miracles [signs] than these[14] which this *man* hath done?
32 The Pharisees heard that the people murmured such things [heard the multitude
murmuring these things] concerning him: and the Pharisees and the chief priests
[the chief priests and the Pharisees][15] sent officers to take [seize] him.
33 Then said Jesus [Jesus therefore said] unto them, Yet a little while am I with
34 you, and *then* I go unto him that sent me. Ye shall [will] seek me, and shall
[will] not find *me* [me]:[16] and where I [then] am, *thither* [*omit* thither] ye cannot
come.
35 Then said the Jews [The Jews therefore said] among themselves, Whither will
he [this man] go, that we shall not find him? will he go unto the dispersed [the
36 Diaspora] among the Gentiles [Greeks] and teach the Gentiles [Greeks]? What
manner of saying is this [What is this word] that he said, Ye shall [will] seek me,
and shall [will] not find *me* [me]:[16] and where I am, *thither* [*omit* thither] ye cannot come.

TEXTUAL AND GRAMMATICAL.

[1] Ver. 10.—[The text. rec. transfers εἰς τὴν ἑορτήν after ἀνέβη. But the position indicated in brackets is maintained by ℵ. B. K. L., *etc.*, and the best critics.—P. S.]

[2] Ver. 12.—Δέ after ἄλλοι is wanting in [ℵ] D. G. F., *etc.*, and in Tischendorf. [Inserted in B. L., Alf., W. and H.—P. S.]

[3] Ver. 15.—Lachmann and Tischendorf: οὖν instead of καί, after many authorities. Also after ἀπεκρ., ver. 16.

[4] Ver. 16.—[The οὖν, which is wanting in the text. rec. and ignored by Lange, is well supported by ℵ. B. T., *etc.* Alf., W. and H., *etc.*—P. S.]

[5] Ver. 17.—[The E. V. disregards the θέλῃ, and the implied harmony of man's will with God's will, and might convey the idea that the mere performance of God's commandments will lead men to a knowledge of Christ, which is not necessarily the case. Comp. Alf. *in loc.*—P. S.]

[6] Ver. 19.—[The interrogation mark should be put after the first τὸν νόμον. The question is followed by a categorical charge. So Lachm., Tischend., Meyer, Lange.—P. S.]

[7] Vers. 21 and 22.—[Dr. Lange not only connects the διὰ τοῦτο with θαυμάζετε instead of δέδωκεν, but divides the verses between τοῦτο and Μωϋσ. The latter is not done even by some editors who connect the διὰ τοῦτο grammatically with the preceding verse; but of course it should be done. The Cod. Sin. lacks the δ. τ. altogether, and reads: θαυμάζετε Ὁ Μωϋσ. —E. D. Y.]

[8] Ver. 26.—Ἀληθῶς, in most MSS., B. D. K. L., *etc.*, occurs only once, and that before ἔγνωσαν, Tischendorf. Yet it is probable that the second ἀληθ. has been dropped on account of the striking repetition, which, however, is very expressive and significant.

[9] Ver. 29.—[Text. rec. with ℵ. D. insert δέ after ἐγώ, B. T., Vulg., Tert., Orig., Alf., W. and H. omit it.—P. S.]

[10] Ver. 30.—[Καί here, as in vers. 13, 28 and often in John, adds an *opposite* thought=*atque, und doch, and yet.* Comp. Hartung, *Partikellehre*, I. p. 147 f. Meyer on ver. 28: "Pronounce *and* emphatically, and imagine a dash after it."—P. S.]

[11] Ver. 31.—Ἐκ τοῦ ὄχλου δέ πολλοί, Lachmann, Tischendorf, [Alf., W. and H., with B. K. L., *etc.* This position puts the ὄχλος in stronger contrast to the subject of ἐζήτουν, ver. 30, and is preferable to the πολ. δ. ἐκ. τ. ὄχλ. of the Rec., which is backed here by ℵ. D.—P. S.]

[12] Ibid.—Ὅτι [after ἔλεγον] before ὁ Χρ. ὅταν, is lacking in B. D. L., *etc.*, and Lachmann [and Cod. Sin.]

[13] Ibid.—Instead of μήτι [text. rec.] Lachmann and Tischendorf [Alf., W. and H.] read μή [*doch nicht*].

[14] Ibid.—The τούτων must be considered an explanatory addition. [Lachmann, Tischendorf, Alford, *etc.*, omit it on the authority of the uncial MSS.—P. S.]

[15] Ver. 32.—[Οἱ ἀρχιερεῖς καὶ οἱ φαρισαῖοι is sustained by the uncial MSS. against the reverse order of the text. rec.—P. S.]

[16] Ver. 34.—[The second με here and ver. 36 is omitted by the text. rec., and hence italicised in the E. V., but sustained by B. T. X.—P. S.]

EXEGETICAL AND CRITICAL.

Ver. 10. **Had gone up.**—The ἀνέβησαν is pluperfect.

Ibid. **Not openly.**—That is, not in the festal train, not as a festal pilgrim; but not: by another road, De Wette, *etc.* (On the Docetism which Baur and Hilgenfeld would find in the words, see Meyer.)—**But as it were in secret.**—This expression denotes a solitary journey, a quiet stay near Jerusalem (perhaps in Bethany), and a subsequent appearance at the feast not incognito, and not in the character of a festal pilgrim, but in the capacity of a prophet coming forth out of concealment to the feast, to point out the insufficiency of the festal symbols in contrast with their real fulfilment in His person. And because He did so appear it is said ὡς, "*as it were* in secret." This was the character in which He went up, not in which He continued. Meyer is incorrect in saying that this was the final departure of Jesus from Galilee. The present departure of Jesus from Galilee was entirely private; the final departure took place under a great convoy (Matt. xix. 1, 2; Mark x. 1; *Leben Jesu*, p. 928). More below, at ch. x. 22.

Ver. 11. **The Jews therefore sought him at the feast.**—According to ver. 13 the hostile Jews are, of course, primarily intended here. They thought to continue unto death the persecution opened against Jesus in ch. v. Hence also the expression ἐκεῖνος, "Where is that man?"

Vers. 12, 13. **And there was much murmuring.**—An expressive designation of the ferment in the popular mass, and the powerful working of the hostile rulers upon the sentiment of the people. In the division of opinion the friends of Jesus express themselves with timid reserve: **He is a good man** (ἀγαθός), kind, benevolent. According to the New Testament usage (see Matt. xx. 15; Rom. v. 7), the term no doubt means something more than "honest, a man of honor" (Meyer); though the attenuation of the confession of Jesus in the period of rationalism could go so far that some one wrote a pamphlet: *Jesus and His Disciples were honest People.* The confession is evidently suppressed also here. The others more boldly speak out their opposite opinion: **He deceiveth the people.**

But that the more favorable public opinion concerning Him was already under the terrorism of the hostile party spirit, is told us by the addition: **Yet no one** [*i. e.* of the friendly part] **spoke openly of him, for fear of the Jews**—According to Meyer this last verse includes literally all. "Even the hostile ones were afraid, because, so long as those (the hierarchy) had not yet *officially* decided, a *reversion* of their sentiment was conceivable. A faithful picture of bad, Jesuitical domination of the people." The οὐδείς μέντοι will certainly have a meaning; though the opinion, "He deceiveth the people," was open enough. The distinction between λέγειν and λαλεῖν must be observed here. Persons on both sides were expressing themselves in a scanty λέγειν; yet did not come to a λαλεῖν παῤῥησίᾳ, a full, free, talk, concerning Him, because any expression of acknowledgment could easily be communicated by heresy-hunters, and because an unfavorable opinion also might easily have something contrary to form. The bondage of conscience was such that no one ventured to utter fully the thoughts of his heart, before the hierarchy had spoken.

Ver. 14. **The midst of the feast.**—In a seven or eight days' feast three or four days were now past, and it became clear that He did not intend this time to take part in the observance. If Jesus had come earlier to the place, it is more probable that He lodged in the vicinity than in Jerusalem itself. See above, on ver. 10.

Up into the temple.—It might seem as if by this step He passed from extreme caution to extreme boldness. But even by this new manner of appearance He proves Himself the great Master in the knowledge of men. From this time forth He could safely appear in Judea and Galilee only by suddenly entering a great assembly of the people, and working there. The spirit of reverence for Him, which animated the people, still for a time shielded Him in these situations from His enemies. Thus He made the crown or halo of the popular assembly His faithful guard, so long as the better Messianic spirit of the people recognized in Him the Son of David. He was adorned in the presence of His enemies with the wreath of popular veneration, till this wreath too was torn and withered by the poisonous breath of their enmity. (*Leben Jesu*, II., p. 932).

And taught.—From the subsequent narrative we may suppose that His teaching related to the feast of tabernacles. So, in ch. ii., His teaching connected itself with the symbolical import of the temple, which He was then for the first time officially visiting; His conversation with the theocratic Nicodemus on the need of real regeneration in order to pass from the old theocracy to the new kingdom of heaven connected itself with the proselyte baptism; His conversation with the Samaritan woman took its turn from the holy wells in Israel; His discourse in ch. v., from the medicinal spring and the healing; and even in His Galilean discourse in ch. vi. there is a manifest reference to the approaching passover in Jerusalem.

Ver. 15. **How knoweth this man letters** [γράμματα οἶδεν].—First are heard the voices of the adversaries of Jesus. Their first objection is founded on the fact that He is not a promoted Rabbi; the second (ver. 27) on His origin.—**The Jews** here are evidently the Judaists, and probably, judging from their expressions, scribes, Rabbis. They [the hierarchical opponents, probably members of the Sanhedrin, as in xi. 13.—P. S.] **marvelled**; they cannot deny that He knows the books and has the gift of teaching; but, full of envy, school-bigotry and statutory zeal, they fall upon the circumstance that He *has not studied* [μὴ μεμαθηκώς], and is not a regular graduate of the Rabbinical schools. The γράμματα without ἱερά (2 Tim. iii. 15) denotes not the Holy Scriptures (ἡ γραφή, according to the Peshito, Luther, Grotius), but literature, the field of learning (in the Vulgate, *litteræ*, see Acts xxvi. 24).* The passage is "important against the attempts, ancient and modern, to trace the wisdom of Jesus to human education" (Meyer). The words evidently grope in confusion half way between acknowledgment and denial of His wisdom. But the stress lies not on the concession, but on the questioning. Though He seems to know books, yet there must be some deception about it, since He has not studied and advanced in the regular prescribed way. A young school-enthusiast trusts not his eyes, trusts not his ears, trusts not even his enthusiasm and his intellectual gain, when he meets a teacher who has the prejudice of the school against him; the old school-enthusiast is at once fully decided in his prejudice by the absence of school-endorsement. The point at which the

* [As in the English phrase: A man of *letters*. Yet here it means chiefly *Scripture-learning*, almost the only kind of learning known among the Jews.—P. S.]

teaching of Jesus came most in contact with Jewish learning, was the relation of His symbolical interpretation to the Jewish allegorizing (of the Old Testament and its types). It was indeed a relation as between a melon and a gourd; but the appearance of similarity must have struck the eyes of these people more than the difference. Yet, after their manner, regardless of the actual teaching of Jesus, they fell upon His want of legitimation. His doctrine is not *delivered* as the sacred *tradition of the schools*, not *systematized* according to the *rules and practice of the school*, not *legalized* as the production *of a graduate*.

[This testimony of enemies to a fact well known to them, strongly confirms what we otherwise know or must conjecture concerning Christ's education, or rather the absence in His case of the ordinary ways and means by which other men receive their knowledge. He was neither school-taught (ἀλλο-δίδακτος), nor self-taught (αὐτο-δίδακτος), nor even God-taught (θεο-δίδακτος, like inspired prophets) in the *usual* sense of these terms. No doubt He learned from His mother, He went to the Synagogue, He heard and read the Scriptures, He studied nature and man, and the Holy Ghost descended upon Him at the baptism in Jordan; yet the secret fountain of His knowledge of God and man must be found in His mysterious and unique relation to the Father and derived from direct intuition into the living fountain of truth in God. He was and continued to be the only begotten Son in the bosom of the Father who explained Him to us as no philosopher or prophet could do. I quote an appropriate passage from my book on the *Person of Christ*, p. 34 ff.: "Christ spent His youth in poverty and manual labor, in the obscurity of a carpenter's shop; far away from universities, academies, libraries, and literary or polished society; without any help, as far as we know, except the parental care, the daily wonders of nature, the Old Testament Scriptures, the weekly Sabbath services of the Synagogue at Nazareth (Luke iv. 16), the annual festivals in the Temple of Jerusalem (Luke ii. 42 ff.) and the secret intercourse of His soul with God, His heavenly Father. . . . . Christ can be ranked neither with the school-trained, nor with the self-trained or self-made men; if by the latter we understand, as we must, those who, without the regular aid of *living* teachers, yet with the same educational *means*, such as books, the observation of men and things, and the intense application of their mental faculties attained to vigor of intellect, and wealth of scholarship,—like Shakspeare, Jacob Bœhme, Benjamin Franklin, and others. All the attempts to bring Jesus into contact with Egyptian wisdom, or the Essenic theosophy, or other sources of learning, are without a shadow of proof, and explain nothing after all. He never quotes from books, except the Old Testament. He never refers to secular history, poetry, rhetoric, mathematics, astronomy, foreign languages, natural sciences, or any of those branches of knowledge which make up human learning and literature. He confined Himself strictly to religion. But, from that centre, He shed light over the whole world of man and nature. In this department, unlike all other great men, even the prophets and the apostles, He was absolutely original and independent. He taught the world as one who had learned nothing from it, and was under no obligation to it. He speaks from divine intuition, as one who not only *knows* the truth, but *is* the truth; and with an authority that commands absolute submission, or provokes rebellion, but can never be passed by with contempt or indifference."—P. S.]

Ver. 16. **My doctrine** (or, **teaching**) **is not mine.**—That is, I am no self-taught man in such a sense as to be an upstart and pretender; there is another in whose school I have regularly advanced. With cutting irony He off-sets His teaching against their Rabbinical teaching (both as to form and matter); His authority, the Father, against their authorities, the old Rabbinical masters. The first "My" therefore denotes His discourse (His system, the school He teaches); the second, His authority (the school He has learned in). Meyer: "Οὐκ—ἀλλά here also is not equivalent to *tam—quam* (Wolf, *etc.*), but is absolutely exclusive." Hardly "absolutely," but only so far as His person is regarded in its human aspect. Tholuck: "His human personality is viewed abstractly by itself, as in ch. v. 31; viii. 16." The primary distinction is between the Son sent, who both in word and act executes the ἐντολή of the Father, who speaks what He hears of the Father, and does what the Father shows Him,—between this person and the Father Himself. And He so far views His personality abstractly by itself as He yields to their idea of an independent human person distinct from God.

But his that sent me.—That is, it is not only directly the doctrine of God, but also more than doctrine, the direct message of God to you, a doctrine of the most decisive words of life.

Ver. 17. **If any one is willing to do his will** [ἐάν τις θέλῃ τὸ θέλημα αὐτοῦ ποιεῖν].—The indispensable condition for understanding the doctrine of Christ. We must be truly turned towards God, in order to recognize the divine, which proceeds from God, as divine. And more particularly, we must be earnestly bent upon the divine in practice, if we would know it in theory as doctrine. Man's moral θέλειν of the moral θέλημα of God is the condition of man's intellectual γινώσκειν of the intelligible διδαχή of God. Without the earnestness of doing there is no truth in our knowing; and like cannot know like without a like bent of soul. Plato, *Lys.*: Ὅτι τὸ ὅμοιον τῷ ὁμοίῳ ἀνάγκη ἀεὶ φίλον εἶναι. Comp. Matt. x. 40-42. This condition of willingness to do, that is, of practical effort, has its root in the doing of the truth, or moral sincerity (ch. iii. 21), and develops into the love of God (ch. v. 42). The point cannot be *the doing* of the will of God, as against sinners and beginners in knowledge; it is only the θέλειν (which, of course, is the beginning of the doing according to the best of one's knowledge and conscience, in the form of *trying*; Rom. vii.). Meyer: "The θέλῃ is not redundant (Wolf, Lösner, and many others), but is the very *nerve* of the matter; in θέλῃ—θέλημα the *suavis harmonia* (Bengel) has been noticed."

His will: 1. The Old Testament revelation (Chrysostom, *et al.*). 2. The demand of faith in

Christ (Augustine, Luther, *etc.*); or at least 3. In His doctrine (Semler, *etc.*). 4. Tholuck: "Still further from the truth is the interpretation which makes it even a requirement of faith for proof." 5. Willing obedience to God in general (Lücke, Meyer).

It is a proposition which, in its universality, certainly refers not merely to believers of revelation; but which, on the other hand, has in view a universal revelation of the divine will. Therefore: He who strives to do the will of God according to the best knowledge he can get on his level of knowledge. This holds even for the heathen; but for the Jews it has special regard to the Old Testament revelation of the will of God (see ch. v. 38), and now for Christians to the fully developed Christian principles of life; always, however, putting the chief stress on full inward earnestness of moral endeavor (θέλῃ). Meyer: "This passage accordingly contains undoubtedly the *testimonium internum*, but not in the ordinary theological sense, as applying to persons already believers, but as applying to persons not yet believers, when the divine doctrine addresses them." The *testimonium internum*, upon candid consideration, leads on from the subjective *testimonium* of calm conviction, as well as of unsatisfied doubt and longing, into the objective *testimonium Spiritus Sancti*, which by all means is promised in the γνώσεται περί, κ. τ. λ. It is false to ask whether, in the conflict in Rom. vii. 7, the unconverted man, abstractly viewed, or the converted, is the subject; and it is equally false to introduce this division here. The subject is the actual living elect in their motion towards God under the drawing of His grace.*

He shall know concerning the doctrine, *etc.*—The γνώσεται is emphatic. He shall have not only assurance of faith, but living certainty of discernment. And if the demand was universal, so is the promise in the first instance: "He shall know concerning the doctrine," indefinitely, of every sort of religious doctrine, whether, and how far, it be from God. But from this the other thing immediately follows: He shall know whether Jesus only speaks (λαλῶ) on His own authority (as an uncalled, self-taught individual), or whether, on the contrary, His word be not absolutely *the doctrine* (from God). Cameron is right, therefore, in making a distinction here between the moral demand and the theoretical doctrine (which Tholuck disputes); only the theoretical doctrine of Christ is as far from being merely theoretical, as an inward ethical bent or *nisus* is from being merely practical or in the ordinary sense moral. See ch. iii. 12.

Ver. 18. **He that speaketh from himself seeketh his own glory,** *etc.*—The proof that He does not speak from Himself. The mark of one who speaks from himself is ambition; he would glorify himself. He, therefore, who would not glorify himself, but God, speaks not from himself; he is true. The direct applying of the proof Christ leaves to themselves. The argument, however, has not an abstract, syllogistic form; it is enriched by a term of life. In the first place a second proof is inserted into the first. If the person sent seeks only the honor of the prince or lord who sends him, his message is to be trusted; he is true. And he is true, because no unrighteousness, no unfaithful conduct appears in his message. It may be depended upon, that what he says his master has said to him. Freedom from all assumption bespeaks the real teacher; if he had received nothing to teach, he could not possibly have taught. Personal disinterestedness bespeaks the commissioned agent; if he had received nothing to deliver, he would not have appeared. And freedom from all assumption and self-interest evince themselves in the undivided energy with which the one sent seeks the honor of the master who sends him. This therefore constitutes the difference between a false Messiah and the true. The motive and the centre of gravity of the false Messiah lie in self-glorification; those of Christ lie in the glorification of the Father, to whom He attributes everything He says and does.

Thus He has proved that He is true in His doctrine; even intellectually true, because there is no moral obliquity in Him, no self-seeking or unfaithfulness to the throne which sends Him. As in men the intellectual knowing of the truth comes as the reward of moral endeavor, so in Christ the truth of His doctrine is founded in the righteousness of His life. Ἀδικία, therefore, is not equivalent here to ψεῦδος (Grotius, *et al.*); though connected with it, inasmuch as ἀδικία would produce ψεῦδος. Self-seeking darkens knowledge.

Ver. 19. **Did not Moses give you the law?**—The sudden transition of Jesus here from the defensive to the offensive has led to the hypothesis of an intermediate conversation (Kuinoel) or act between vers. 18 and 19; for which there is really no ground at all. We must remember: 1. That since the feast of Purim, at which "the Jews" had already begun capital process against Him, Jesus had not met them, but had on their account avoided Judea, and now re-encountered them for the first time. 2. That all their "assaults and negations" (Meyer), including their last attack on His *right to teach*, covered the design of bringing Him to a capital conviction. 3. That it perfectly accorded with the openness and wisdom of Jesus to draw out their hidden plan, and to make it a subject of talk before all the people in the temple. *The only protection against secret adversaries is to expose their designs with the most relentless publicity.* 4. That Christ has already in fact introduced the offensive by the last words of the defensive: "There is no unrighteousness in him" (as they had charged on the ground of the Sabbath cure).—**Moses,** quoting their highest authority.—**Give you the law.**—Of course the law in general; for he who breaks one commandment transgresses the whole law. It is not specifically the prohibition of murder (Nonnus), nor Sabbath law (Kuinoel), which is intended here by "the law." But that the rebuke does particularly refer to the prohibition of killing, is shown by what follows.

And yet none of you keepeth the law.—A general address. Because there is in you no true striving to do the will of God, ye cannot know My divine mission. And how truly this is the case with you in general (the "*none*" representing the spirit of the people and its general

* [Just the position denoted by the *covenant*. The historical covenant, the field of the *gratia præveniens*.—E. D. Y.]

aim) appears from the fact that ye (the [hierarchical] Judaists in the first instance) seek to kill Me. Yet the people are unconsciously implicated and included in this charge, because the high-handed conduct of the hierarchs has its occasion in the mental indolence of the laity. The people must know that they hate Him and "persecute Him without cause."

Ver. 20. **The multitude answered and said,** *etc.*—The [hierarchical] Judaists are speechless under the charge of Christ, because they consider it dangerous to have their plan so soon canvassed before the people. Their silence is a malicious reserve, like that of Judas in ch. vi. 70. The people, however, take the accusation to themselves, thinking it wholly unfounded. As "they of Jerusalem," who speak in ver. 25, very well knew of the project, which had already become notorious in Jerusalem, it must be the festal pilgrims who speak here, who were still far not only from the design announced, but even from any knowledge of it.

Thou hast a demon [δαιμόνιον].—The term here is figurative, drawn from the belief in demoniacal possession. It was probably a proverbial expression in this general sense, especially to denote gloominess, melancholy, laboring under jealous, brooding suspicions. So it was compassionately said of John the Baptist: "He hath a demon" (Matt. xi. 18). Men pitied a man otherwise so able and devout. Here also the reply seems to be not malicious [Hengstenberg and older commentators], but rather sympathizing. "Not an expression of malice, but of surprise that a man who could teach so finely, could think of a thing which they considered morally impossible and a mere hallucination" (Meyer). But the same expression in ch. viii. 48 and x. 20 is shown by the connection to be evil-minded. Chrysostom and others take the ὄχλος to be the *rulers*, and their question to be a dissimulation. This obliterates the true sense of the transaction.

Ver. 21. **And said unto them, I have done one work.**—Jesus, continuing His train of thought, advances as clearly beyond the reply of the people as He did in ch. vi. 70 beyond the answer of Peter. His piercing and foreseeing knowledge contrasts with a stupidity which sets up against it, and which considers Jesus in this case even smitten with a pitiable delusion. It is not an inaccuracy (Tholuck) that John represents the ὄχλος [the multitude] as answering the Lord. Christ intends to bring before the ὄχλος the malicious inquisitorial conduct of the hierarchy. The ὄχλος must be made privy to the secret affair and shown their unconscious complicity in the wickedness.

The **one work** is the healing on the Sabbath, ch. v. 2. (Olshausen needlessly inserts here the subsequent murderous designs). The Lord cannot here mean that He has done only one miracle in Jerusalem (see Jno. iii. 1). The antithesis lies in the καὶ πάντες θαυμ. It is not the miracle, but the work that here bears the stress; and it is not wonder at a miracle that is meant, but surprise at *one* work, though not terror, as Chrysostom and others have it. And in the surprise of all an indignation (Grotius) on the part of many is also unquestionably implied. Offence at that work had therefore spread at least very generally in Jerusalem and among the people. And their morbid condition was manifest in the very fact that they all stared and made an ado over one act of a man who abounded with divine works. The supposed spot upon the one work threatens to eclipse in their view all that has ever filled them with wonder. And even this spot is only in their own vision.

Ye all marvel.—The διὰ τοῦτο is referred by Theophylact, *etc.*, Lücke, [Olsh., De Wette, Stier, Hengstenberg, Ewald, Godet] *etc.*, to the clause preceding (θαυμ.); by Chrysostom, Luther [Grot., Bengel, Luthardt, Meyer, Alford] and others to the clause following.* But in the latter connection it has been considered by some redundant, by others elliptical (ye ought therefore to know). Meyer has attempted another explanation, which Tholuck considers "tortured."†

Ver. 22. **(For this cause) Moses gave unto you the** (rite of) **circumcision**, *etc.*—Jesus now proves to them from their own law that it is good to heal a sick man on the Sabbath. Moses *ordained circumcision* for you. Parenthesis: Yet he did not introduce it as strictly a Mosaic law, but confirmed it as a patriarchal law (coming down from the fathers, that is to say, a fundamental religious law of the Abrahamic covenant of promise, Gen. xvii.) And this patriarchal Mosaic law so outweighs the mere Sabbath-law, that ye not only may, but must circumcise a man on the Sabbath, when the prescribed day (the eighth day, Lu. ii. 21; Rabbinical passages in Lightfoot; Rabbinical maxim: *Circumcisio pellit Sabbatum*) falls on a Sabbath. The reason of this higher superiority of the patriarchal law lies in the design of circumcision, to make the man partially (in a symbolical sense) whole. But if this is so, how much more is the Sabbath-law suspended (in the legal point of view suspended, in the higher view fulfilled) by the eternal law of God which enjoins the healing of a man wholly diseased; enjoins it even in legal form in the commandment: Thou shalt not kill.

Christ thus sets forth three sorts of laws: (1) Eternal principles of humanity, as enacted formally in the decalogue; among which is the law not to destroy life, but to preserve it, to heal. (2) Patriarchal fundamental laws of theocratic civilization; among which belongs circumcision. (3) Mosaic law in the narrower sense.

To this last class belongs, not indeed that Sabbath-law which is the safe-guard of human nature with its need of rest (the *humane and moral* Sabbath [grounded in the very constitution of man, and hence dating from creation]), yet doubtless the *symbolical and ritual* Sabbath with its prohibition of every kind of work as a symbol of the legal theocracy. If, therefore, these Mosaic ordinances must be suspended by patri-

* [Cod. Sin.* omits διὰ τοῦτο altogether, and so does Tischendorf in the 8th ed. He reads ὁ Μωϋσῆς with the article. The phrase διὰ τοῦτο in John usually stands at the beginning, not at the close of a sentence, comp. v. 16, 18; vi. 65; viii. 47; x. 17; Rev. xvii. 7.—P. S.]

† [In ed. 5 (p. 301) Meyer connects διὰ τοῦτο with the following οὐχ ὅτι (as Bengel), and explains: Moses on this account gave you circumcision, not because it is from Moses, but because it is from the fathers (the patriarchs). Similarly Alford in the 6th ed.—P. S.]

archal practice, how much more by the primal laws of God. But just so far as they are suspended in the spirit of the law, they are only raised out of a prescribed symbolical meaning to their real truth; they are *fulfilled*. The Sabbath is fulfilled by doing good, by healing men (Matt. xii. 12); circumcision is fulfilled by regeneration, according to the commandment: "Thou shalt not covet," as it is written on the heart by faith as a law of the Spirit.

The observation that circumcision **"is of the fathers,"** has been interpreted by Euthymius Zig. and others as depreciating circumcision by showing it to be not a Mosaic institution. "It might rather express the superiority of circumcision, by virtue of its higher antiquity (and by virtue of its more fundamental character). Then the gradation is very piquantly expressed by Bucer: 'Ye rank the *fathers* above the law, I the *Father*'" (Tholuck).—Circumcision had its origin not in Moses (ἐκ τοῦ Μ.), but in the fathers (ἐκ τῶν πατ.).

Ver. 23. **If a man on the Sabbath receive circumcision, that,** *etc.*—Circumcision is emphatic, in antithesis with the healing of the whole man in the next clause; hence placed [in the Greek] at the beginning of the sentence.—It is wrong to weaken the ἵνα μή so as to read: *without* breaking the law (Bengel, *et al.*). It is just by circumcising a man on the Sabbath, if that be the eighth day, that violation or nullification of the law is to be prevented. The *idea* in the prescription of the eighth day is that the circumcision should be performed as early as possible, the earlier the better. The higher import of the patriarchal ordinance appears also in the fact that what are called the Noachic commandments continued for a time to be *morally* binding in the Christian church, while the specifically Mosaic law, even in regard to circumcision, became extinct as a religious statute (Acts xv.) Hence, too, the parallel cited by Luthardt from Gal. iii. 17, which subordinates the law to the promise, is not without force. Meyer thinks it is; and Tholuck (p. 216) here again fails to see the precedence given to the patriarchal dispensation, as brought out even by Lampe. He thinks that if that had been intended, the words would have been: ἵνα μὴ λυθῇ ἡ ἐντολὴ τῶν πατέρων, that the statement is therefore inserted simply as matter of history. But the law of Moses had sanctioned anew even the usage of the patriarchs, and had soared above specific camp regulations.

Are ye angry at me because I have restored a whole man to health?—The ὅλος is emphatic in antithesis with περιτομή, which was the healing of a single member. Purport of the antithesis:

1. Wounding and healing (Kling, *Stud. u. Kritik.*, 1836). This is against the notion of the particular healing, or of an argument *a minori ad majus*. Likewise unsuitable is the reference, by Lampe, *etc.*, to the subsequent healing of the wound of circumcision.

2. The legal observance of circumcision, and the real mercy of the miraculous cure (Grotius).

3. "Circumcision was a sanitary measure, purifying and securing against disease. If ye perform on a Sabbath the wholesome act of circumcision, which after all pertains only to *one* member, I will have a still better right to heal an entire man on a Sabbath. (*Philo De circumcisione*, ed. Mangey, Tom. II. Michaelis *Mos. Recht*, 4, § 186, particularly the article '*Beschneidung*' [Circumcision] in Winer)." Lücke.*

4. Meyer: The sanitary purpose did not lie in the law, but in the religious notion of the people; the circumcision was performed only with a view to making the person pure and holy.† (Tholuck also is of Meyer's opinion. But of a "sacramental healing of the single member" one can hardly form an idea, though Kurtz is for it. Sensual lust has its seat in the heart. Of more account is the argument of the Rabbi Eliezer quoted by Tholuck, and similar to the reasoning here in question). In support of this Meyer quotes the later sentiment from Bammidbar: "*Præputium est vitium in corpore;*" *vitium in corpore*, however, is put away, not by *purification*, but by a *surgical* or *medical* operation; *i. e.*, the removal of it is an act of healing. And this must be intended; for circumcision in the symbolical sense also made the *whole* man pure and holy. The literal surgical healing of a part, therefore, which symbolically purified the whole man, is the thing intended. It is manifest that a symbolical act performed on a man in this form must be founded in a presumed need of physical healing, however temporary, local, or peculiar to antiquity this might be (the Lord puts Himself at His adversaries' point of view, as in the Synoptical Gospels, Matt. xii. 12, *etc.*); which is also true of the Jewish "laws of purity and purification."

5. We have still to mention the antithesis of a healing performed only on the flesh (σάρξ), and a healing extending to the whole man, body and soul (Euthymius, Bengel, Stier, *etc.*). This antithesis does not come into view here, although the miraculous cures of the Lord did extend even to the soul. In truth the bodily circumcision also was intended to be the means of circumcision of the heart.

Ver. 24. **Judge not according to appearance** [κατ' ὄψιν].—1. Augustine, *etc.:* Not according to the person, but according to the fact. 2. Melanchthon, *etc.:* Not according to the outward form of the work, but according to its motives. 3. Not according to the startling appearance of things, but with a righteous and true judgment, which is expressed in the gradations of the ordinances, and executed in the actual healing of that sufferer.

Vers. 25, 26. **Some of them of Jerusalem.**—These are better instructed than the ὄχλος; they openly avow that the rulers have laid a plan to kill Jesus; yet cautiously, without directly naming them. The repetition of ἀληθῶς shows that they demanded in the Messiah qualifications which they did not find in Jesus. They seem, as an ultra party, to be solicitous even over the circumspection of the rulers, and to treat it with irony. They follow their ironical expression with their own judgment, which breathes the haughtiness of the citizens of a hierarchical capital. As the Rabbis reproach the Lord with

*[Similarly Alford: The distinction is between circumcision which purified only part of a man, and that perfect and entire healing which the Lord bestowed on the cripple.—P. S.]

†[According to Meyer (5th ed. p. 303] the antithesis is between the healing of a single *member* of the body, and the *whole* body (but not body *and soul*).—P. S.]

His lack of a regular education and graduation, these Jerusalemites cast up against Him His mean extraction.

Ver. 27. **Whence he is.**—This, no doubt, refers both to the despised town of Nazareth and to the family of the carpenter; not, however, by contrast with Bethlehem, as in ver. 42, but by contrast with the purely supramundane or mysterious origin which was claimed for the Messiah. Meyer's restriction of the "whence" to the father and mother is arbitrary, and proceeds from a confounding of the different views here expressed.

As to the origin of the view that men should not know whence the Messiah is, there are different opinions.

1. Lücke [Alford] and others, referring to Justin Martyr (*Dialog. cum Tryph.*): According to the Jewish view the Messiah should be ἀγνωστος, even unknown to Himself, until Elijah should have anointed Him. Against this Tholuck, after Meyer: In that case the earthly πόθεν of Christ would doubtless be known, but not His Messiahship. This dismisses the passage in question too cheaply; for a man who does not himself know whence he is till he is anointed, must have something mysterious about his origin.

2. Tholuck: From Dan. vii. 13 they expected a sudden heavenly manifestation of the Messiah who, according to one of the various popular notions, lived in a secret place or in paradise (Targum Jonathan, Mic. iv. 8; Gfrörer, *Jahrh. des Heils*, II., p. 223). It must be remembered that Daniel's doctrine of the Son of Man was but little known. On the contrary educated people in Jerusalem might very easily be familiar with Alexandrian ideas (as in cultivated regions gleanings of spiritualistic and rationalistic literature combine in various ways with reigning orthodoxy), and Philo taught (*De exsecrat.* 8) that the Messiah in the restoration of the people would appear and go before them as an ὄψις. Such people, too, can make up a view *ex tempore*, for the sake of an impudent denial; and the demand that for every opinion a previous origin must be shown, refutes itself as a scholastic pedantry. At all events these Jerusalemites think that Jesus ought to have at least as noble an extraction as themselves.

Ver. 28. **Therefore Jesus cried, teaching in the temple, and saying.**—We do not think, with Meyer, that He raised His voice to a *shout*. The upstart loses confidence, when His origin is spoken of; Jesus purposely enters very emphatically into what they say of His origin. Even in the temple among the throng of people He makes no reserve. It is not without an ironical accordance that He takes up their own arrogant word (τοῦτον οἴδαμεν, which is with them quite equivalent to knowing πόθεν ἐστιν).

Ye both know me, and ye know whence I am.—He makes a difference, however, between *Himself* and His *origin*, because the latter implied in their view the utmost meanness, in His view His supreme dignity.

Different interpretations:

1. Grotius, Lampe, and others take the words *interrogatively* (know ye me? *etc.*).

2. Calvin, Lücke, *etc.*, ironically.

3. Chrysostom and others, as charging them that they did certainly know His divine person and origin, but denied them.

4. Meyer (after De Wette), as a concession: "The people really had this knowledge." But that they had with it nothing, and less than nothing, even an obstacle towards the knowledge of Himself, Christ asserts by the ironical tone of His words, when He says: Ye both know Me (by rote) and ye know (by rote) whence I am.*

And yet I am not come from myself.—*Καί* is emphatic and adversative: *And yet* I am not come, *etc.* These words briefly designate His higher nature, which these adversaries do not know. An ordinary extraction elevates itself only by ambition, which comes from itself and has no higher descent at all; Christ is, in the first place, simply come, and in the second place not from Himself. This introduces the declaration of His descent from God.

But he that sent me is true.—The ἀληθινός is variously explained. 1. In the sense of ἀληθής, a true person, *verus*, one who speaks the truth (Luther, Grotius). 2. A reliable person, *firmus, verax* (Chrysostom, Lampe), ch. viii. 26. 3. A real, genuine person, fulfilling the idea (Lücke, Tholuck, 7th ed.). 4. As used absolutely, for the true, essential God (Olshausen, Kling); against which Meyer observes that ἀληθινός, without a particular subject, forms no definite idea. But certainly we have a particular subject in ὁ πέμψας με. Still we stop with the idea of the real, the living One. The Jews, in their legalistic spirit, live only in symbols, figures, marks of distinction; the Jews of Jerusalem, doubly so: they have a typical, painted religion, painted sins, painted forgiveness, a painted nobility of lineage, a painted God. The real, living God, who has sent the real living Christ, they do not know.†

Ver. 29. **But I know him.**—Intensely significant contrast to their ignorance. Founded both on (1) real, ideal descent from Him, and on (2) formal, historical commission from Him.

Ver. 30. **Then they sought to seize him.**—As the Jerusalemites previously named show themselves Judaists in the strictest sense, it is unnecessary here to think of Jews distinct from them. **Because his hour had not yet come.**—John gives the ultimate and highest reason why they could not take Him, passing over secondary causes, like fear of the people and political considerations.

* [Alford: "It has been questioned whether these words are to be taken ironically, interrogatively, or affirmatively. I incline to the last view for this reason: obviously no very high degree of knowledge *whence He was*, is implied, for they knew not Him that sent Him; see also ch. viii. 14, 19, and therefore could not know *whence He was*, in this sense. The answer is made *in their own sense:*—they knew that He was from Nazareth in Galilee, see ver. 41,—and probably that He was called the son of Joseph. In this sense they knew *whence He was*, but further than this they knew not."—P. S.]

† [Alford: "The matter here impressed on them is the *genuineness*, the *reality* of the fact: that Jesus *was sent*, and *there was one who sent Him*, though they knew Him not, and consequently knew not πόθεν ἐστίν. The nearest English word would be *real:* but this would not convey the meaning perspicuously to the ordinary mind;—perhaps the E. V. *true* is better, provided it be explained to mean *objectively*, not *subjectively*, true: *really existent*, not '*truthful*' which it may be questioned whether the word ἀληθίνος will bear, although it is so maintained by Euthym., Cyril, Chrys., Theophylact, Lampe, Baumgarten-Crusius, Tholuck, and many others."—P. S.]

Ver. 31. **And many of the people believed in him.**—A mark of the increasing ferment in the people, working towards separation. This believing in Him undoubtedly means faith in the Messiah, not merely in a prophet or a messenger of God; yet we must distinguish between their faith and their timid confession. Hence the words: "When Christ cometh, will He do," *etc.*—are to be taken not simply as referring to the doubt of the opposing party (Meyer), but as double-minded. Hence the mention of a "murmuring" further on. That the people regard the miracles as Messianic credentials, accords with the expectation of the Messiah.

Ver. 32. **The Pharisees heard.**—Pharisees by themselves alone hear the sly murmuring of the people, which betrays an inclination to acknowledge Jesus as the Messiah. They then get the chief priests to join with them in ordering the official arrest of Jesus. The officers who are sent to take Jesus are to be distinguished from the Jerusalemite Judaists before mentioned as wishing to take Him. Under a despotic system the absolutist party of the people are always in advance of the absolutist government: more royalist than the absolute king, more papist than the pope. There was no need of the Sanhedrin being just now assembled (as at the moment at which the chapter closes). An acting authority which could issue hierarchical warrants, was permanent in the chief priests; and the process for the healing at the pool of Bethesda was here still pending.

Ver. 33. **Jesus therefore said unto them, yet a little while,** *etc.*—To whom? 1. Euthymius Zig.: To the officers. 2. Tholuck: To those Pharisees who gave the information. 3. Meyer: To the whole assembly, but with the chief priests mainly in view. As the officers at first enter the assembly of hearers clandestinely, waiting the proper moment to secure Jesus, and Jesus knows their design, He speaks these words primarily to them; for He fixes them, and they feel themselves hit; while the multitude take His words to themselves. The sentence has evidently a more special and a more general sense. The words: "*Yet a little while I am with you,*"—uttered with majestic emphasis, mean primarily to the officers: Ye must let Me freely speak a little longer here! (see Luke xiii. 32, 33); and then also to the assembly: My work among you draws to a close. The words "*And then I go to Him that sent Me,*" mean primarily: I then withdraw into the protection of a mightier One, who has sent Me in a power different from that in which ye are sent; in the more general sense: I go home to God. The words "*Ye will seek Me, and not find Me*" (ver. 24), were likewise capable of a special and a general interpretation, but in all these cases the two meanings lay in the same line, so that the more general included the special. This explains the conduct of the officers, and their expression, in ver. 46.

I go unto him that sent me.—According to Paulus and Meyer this would be an addition of John's because according to ver. 35 Jesus could not have said definitely whither He was going. But His first expression was made enigmatical to the Jews by the second. *To go to God* does not necessarily mean to them to die; still less, more definitely, to go to heaven. *The Christian heaven of the blessed is first disclosed by the parting discourses of Christ and His ascension.* It would have been most natural to them to think of the paradise in Sheol. But if they did suspect this, they did not dwell upon it, because they could not themselves renounce the hope of going into Abraham's bosom. And hence perhaps the remote evasive conjecture: "*Will He go . . among the Greeks,*" *etc.* This explanation is confirmed by ch. viii. 22, where the evasion is still more malicious than here. The expression of Christ, therefore, is a dark hint of an unknown ποῦ (Lücke), the import of which they might feel, but not understand (Luthardt).

Ver. 34. **Ye will seek me, and not find (me).**—Comp. ch. viii. 21; xiii. 33. Interpretations:

1. A hostile seeking (Origen, Grotius, *etc.*) This applies only in the immediate reference of the words to the officers.

2. A seeking of the Redeemer for redemption, too late. Two sorts of turning to Him: (a) After the *terminus peremptorius gratiæ* (Augustine, *et al.*); which, however, can be known in fact only by the cessation of that seeking. (b) With a false, Esau-like repentance, which only trembles before the *damnum peccati* (Calvin).

3. A seeking for the saving Messiah, whom in My person ye have rejected, especially in the catastrophe of Jerusalem [Luke xx. 16ff.; xix. 43] (Chrysostom, Lampe [Hengstenberg] *etc.*).

4. "And that, Himself, the rejected Jesus, not the Messiah in general." Meyer.*

Jesus, however, is found of those who seek. When it is said; "Seek, and ye shall find," it is implied that seeking without finding proves a *vitium* in the seeking; though we cannot, with Maldonatus and others, consider the seeking to be placed here merely for an aggravation of the not finding, as if the Lord would say, by a Hebraism: Ye shall be utterly unable to find Me, Ps. x. 15; xxxvii. 10; Isai. xli. 12. The mere inability to find itself points back to a kind of seeking; and seeking is the emphatic thing in ch. viii. 21; xiii. 33; but a false seeking, in which Israel has continued through all the centuries since. Of the mass the word is spoken, and to the mass Jesus speaks; individuals, therefore, who turned, even though in a mass, to Jesus after the destruction of Jerusalem, are exceptions, and do not here come into view. That mass of the Jews has incessantly sought its delivering Messiah, but (1) in another person, (2) in a secular majesty, (3) in the spirit of legal religion, and (4) with earthly, political, revolutionary prospects.

And where I am.—"To explain the present εἰμί, metaphysically, like Augustine: *Nec dicit, ubi ero, sed ubi sum; semper enim erat, quo fuerat rediturus* (ch. iii. 13),—there is no reason; like ὑπάγω, it is the present of vivid representation." Tholuck. The thought that His heaven is not merely local, but also inward, and that He therefore is always at His goal, is not entirely out of sight, though undoubtedly His estate of glory is chiefly in view.

* [Still others: My bodily presence will be withdrawn from you; I shall be personally in a place inaccessible to you. So Alford.—P. S.]

Ver. 35. **The Jews therefore said among themselves.**—The mocking malice of their reply (in vain questioned by Meyer) rises in a climax of three clauses: 1. Whither will He go, that we might not follow Him? (into Paradise?) 2. Will He seek His fortune among the Jewish dispersion among the Gentiles, with the less orthodox, less respectable and intelligent Jews? 3. Or will He even teach the Greeks (to whom, indeed, judging from His conduct towards the law and His liberal utterance, He seems rather to belong than to us)? But what they say in mockery, must fulfil itself in truth; they prophesy like Caiaphas (ch. xi. 50, 51) and Pilate (ch. xix. 19).—**Unto the dispersed among the Greeks.**—The διασπορά (dispersion, *abstract. pro concret.*) τῶν Ἑλλήνων (genitive of remoter relation), not the dispersed Gentiles (Chrysostom), or Hellenists or Greek Jews (Scaliger), but, according to specific usage (Jas. i. 1; 1 Pet. i. 1), the Jews dispersed in the Gentile world.

Ver. 36. **What is this saying that he said?**—Indicating that they cannot get away from this saying. They seem to feel the dark, fearful mystery in the words, but are inclined to persuade themselves that it is sheer nonsense.

DOCTRINAL AND ETHICAL.

1. See the preceding exegesis.

2. The *whispering concerning Jesus from fear of the Jews* is a type of the whole spirit of hierarchy in the Church, and absolutism in the State, with its tyranny over opinion and conscience, its censorship, heresy-hunting, and inquisition; and an example of the fact that under such systems the enemies of the truth always venture to speak rather more boldly than its friends.

3. The *appearance of Jesus at the first feast of the Jews* (the passover of 781) was a *reformation* of it. His appearance at the *second* (Purim of 782) was a *completing of it.* His appearance at the *third* (the feast of tabernacles of 782) was a *contrast* or *counterpart* to it. (Even His being sent to the people and His going forth to the Father seem to allude to the sending of Moses to their fathers and the pilgrimage of those fathers through the wilderness to Canaan, which they were celebrating.) His appearance at the *fourth* (feast of the dedication, 782) is the *following up of this contrast.* His appearance at the *last passover* (783) was the *fulfilling* of the typical feast of the passover with the *reality*, the *abolition* of it thereby.

4. The two *reproaches* which the Jews cast upon the Lord, and His answers, in their permanent import. The reproach of *Rabbinism* that He was not regularly educated, and His answer that He was not self-taught, but taught of God. The reproach of the court *aristocracy* that He was of mean birth, and His appeal to the fact that His person and His mission are a mystery of heavenly descent; carrying with it the intimation that, as the Messenger of God, He bears the dignity of God Himself.

5. The *test* of true doctrine, of the true course of study in order to come to the knowledge of the truth, and of the true capacity to judge of doctrine, vers. 16-18. Tradition and originality. The tracing of the wisdom of Christ to the schools of the Essenes or other educational institutions, is also a soulless Rabbinism, which is perfectly blinded to the original resources of His mind.

6. *The public appearance of Christ and the unveiling of the secret designs of His hierarchical adversaries* before the people, a parallel to His turning to the people in Galilee (Matt. xv. 10), a permanent type and a spiritual rule, followed in appeals from the pope to a general council, from the general council under trammels to the Christian people; and yet especially different from all democratic solicitation of the people, Christ treats the laity as accomplices of the hierarchy. The mental indolence of the former supports the mental tyranny of the latter.

7. Heubner: "How is it possible that after so strong and plain a declaration of Jesus, men should continually persist in thrusting human means of education upon Him, as Ammon, for example, does (*Fortbildung des Christenthums zur Weltreligion*, I. p. 220). Comp. Storr's explanation in Flatt's *Magazin*, I. p. 107 sqq.; IV. p. 220; Süsskind: *In welchem Sinn hat Jesus die Göttlichkeit seiner Lehre behauptet?* p. 25-47; Weber's Programme: *Interpretatio judicii, quod Jesus Joh.* vii. 14-18 *de sua ipsius doctrina tulisse legitur*, Wittenb., 1797."

8. *Circumcision* as healing; or, the symbolical ordinances in Israel founded on real conditions of life at the time. Gradation of ordinances. Jewish fundamental articles. A hint of the eternal fundamental laws of religious and moral life.

9. *Earthly, historical descent and heavenly, personal originality.* Contrast of a polite world lost in symbolical mummery, usage, conventionalism, titles, and privileges, and a real, personal life coming from God and standing in God's word and Spirit, vers. 27, 29.

10. The Jews of Jerusalem sought to take Jesus,—the ultra-hierarchical and ultra-imperial party, which always in its fanatical zeal outdoes the hierarchical and absolutist government.

11. The various Christological systems of the Jews in this chapter (vers. 15, 27, 42), a type of the deep and confused divisions of opinion under an apparently uniting constitution.

12. The officers and their arrest by the word of Jesus, a single point in the line of Christ's ethico-psychological miracles. See Jno. ii. Discussion of the miracles.

13. The expression of Christ concerning His going to Him that sent Him, the first gleam of the Christian doctrine of heaven.

14. *Ye will seek Me and will not find Me.* A great prophecy of Christ respecting the tragic retribution of the Jewish people. Seek and not find. To seek salvation and not find it, is the lot of a world lost in vanity; to seek and not find the Messiah, the lot of wretched Israel sunk in the vanity of the letter and of chiliastic worldliness. An ultimate rectification of the false seeking into the true seeking and finding, is not forbidden. See Rom. chs. ix. and xi.

HOMILETICAL AND PRACTICAL.

See the previous heads.

Even in the Lord's wise distinction between His brethren's legal observance of the feast and

His own voluntary appearance at the feast (as the personal truth of the feast), no guile is found in His mouth, 1 Pet. ii. 22.—The wonderful wisdom with which Christ prolonged His life more than a year (from the feast of Purim in ch. v.) after it had fallen under the deadly hostility of the Jews.—The ferment of popular opinion concerning the Lord in Jerusalem, a token of the approaching separation between His friends and enemies.—Fear of the Jews, or of the despotism of the letter an ancient and modern hindrance to faith and knowledge.—The gospel's victorious piercing of the old Jewish hierarchy, a presage of its ever fresh piercing of all hierarchical incrustations.—The fear of man in the adherents of Jesus, over against the fearlessness in Himself.—The example of Jesus in relying on the utmost publicity against the secret plottings of a wicked party spirit.—In the midst of the feast, in the midst of the temple, the Lord appears—appears yet for a long while, though both seem already fallen into the possession of His enemies.—The lion-like spirit of the Lord, in which He seeks His lion enemy in His den: 1. Proved (*a*) by this incident; (*b*) by His previous going into the wilderness; (*c*) by His subsequent surrender to the judgment of the high council. 2. Again proved in the life of His apostles and in the course of the Church (the apostles in Jerusalem, Peter in Babylon, Paul in Rome, missions to the heathen).—The wisdom of the Lord in bringing before the people the secret design of the Jewish court to kill Him.—The offence of Jewish pride at the Lord's call to teach: 1. The phases of it; (*a*) Rabbinical offence at His want of a Rabbinical education; (*b*) Offence of metropolitan people at His obscure birth. 2. Its self-contradiction in its expression: (*a*) He knows letters; (*b*) He speaks boldly, though they seek to kill Him. 3. Christ's declaration in the face of it; (*a*) As to His school and His doctrine; (*b*) As to His origin.—The alliance of ecclesiastical and secular party spirit against the Lord.*—The fanaticism of the hierarchical party, always in excess of the fanaticism of the hierarchical authorities.—The words of Jesus concerning the heavenly tradition of His doctrine. 1. It is not a word of man (of human invention), but a message of God, of eternal and heavenly origin. 2. It attests itself by the fact that *whosoever desires to do the will of God* must find in this doctrine the goal of his effort. 3. It attests the Lord who teaches it, by its looking solely to the glorifying of God, and thereby proving the freedom of Jesus from human ambition and human self-deception.—*If any man will do His will, etc.;* or: Christ the goal of all really sincere, devout striving.—Sincerity of will, the first and last condition of true knowledge.—The mark of a genuine witness of God, ver. 18.—The true purity of doctrine dependent on the purity of the mind in its endeavors; or, the word of truth dependent on the truth of the word.—*Why go ye about to kill Me?* So Christ ever turns His defence into attack.—How He unveils to the people the fearful thought of murder against the Messiah, which is germinating in them while yet they themselves think not of it.—"Thou hast a devil (demon);" so unbelief has at all times represented the Lord's stern, cutting insight into human corruption as a morbid, melancholy conceit of His own mind.—They charge Him now with bright heedlessness, now with gloomy, demoniacal despondency or madness, because they understand not His holy mind.—Jesus often taken for crazy.—How far are the words of Jesus in ver. 21 an answer to the charge in ver. 20? They had taken offence at His work; that is the beginning of the hatred of Christ, which afterwards developed into the murder of Christ.—Christ's vindication of His healing on the Sabbath by appeal to the circumcision which was lawful on the Sabbath.—They condemned themselves in their judgment of Jesus: 1. They vexed themselves over *one* work of the Lord on the Sabbath, while in circumcision they continually performed works on the Sabbath. 2. They broke the Sabbath for the sake of a slight necessity, while they charged the Lord's healing of a whole sufferer as a transgression.—Law contends with law, knowledge with knowledge, letter with letter, when they are not interpreted and reconciled by the Spirit.—Christ, like Paul, overpowered the Jews with their own weapons, with their own art of Rabbinical logic.—Why Jesus did not openly reveal to the people who were troubled over His descent, the mystery of His miraculous human birth and His eternal divine nature.—How He represents the law of circumcision as a law of healing.—How He discloses as the kernel of it, a law of love, of mercy, of liberty.—"Judge not according to appearance;" or, judging according to the letter a judging according to exterior looks.—The proud contempt with which the people of quality in Jerusalem express themselves respecting the Lord, in its spiritual imbecility: (1) More fanatical than the Jewish authorities; (2) more ignorant in regard to Christ's descent than the people; (3) wholly incapable of appreciating His spiritual greatness.—The mocking wit of the polite adversaries of the Lord in union with gross ignorance.—The testimony of Christ concerning His heavenly origin hardens the proud.—The divine origin of the doctrine of Christ in its connection with the divine origin of His being.—How imagined greatness is embittered and enraged before the evidences of true greatness.—*They sought to take Him: but no man, etc.*—Impotence of the adversary against the Lord: 1. His impotence in the most diverse designs (they sought to take Him themselves, they sought to take Him through instruments). 2. Its impotence in the presence of true power: (*a*) of the faithful adherents of Christ; (*b*) of the Lord Himself; (*c*) of the overruling of God (His hour not yet come). 3. His impotence fully displayed just when His hour is come, when it *seems* almighty.—With the enmity of unbelief ripens also the heroism of faith, vers. 30, 31.—The first decided attempt of the Jewish rulers upon the life of the Lord, brought on by the whispering of the people that He was the Christ.—This first attempt at the feast of tabernacles in the autumn related to the last attempt at the passover of the next year. The exalted words of Christ to the people, addressed to the servants of the chief priests in particular, vers. 33-36: 1. An expres-

*[A recent example: Napoleon III. and Pope Pius IX.—P. S.]

sion of His security in the full presentiment of His insecurity. 2. The language of simplicity, and yet of double meaning. 3. To the Jews an occasion of mockery, and yet at the same time a momentous riddle.

Yet a little while am I with you (ver. 33): the great importance of the *little while:* 1. The period of grace. 2. The year of grace. 3. The day of grace. 4. The hour of grace.—The death of the Lord and of His people, a voluntary going home.—Killed at last, and yet even thereby escaped from His murderers.—How the Jews cannot get away from the word of Jesus: "Ye shall seek Me," *etc.*—The divergent paths which separate the Lord from His despisers: 1. The path upward. 2. The path downward.—Christ perfectly inaccessible to His adversaries: 1. They seek Him and do not find Him. 2. They find Him, and bind Him, and have Him not. 3. They nail Him up, and bury Him, and seal the stone, and keep Him not.—Acts xxvi. 7. The tragical hope of Israel for the Messiah: 1. How noble in its truth. 2. How vain in its perversion. 3. How prophetic in spite of its delusion.

STARKE: God knows the true and better time to appear and help.—That neither He nor His apostles were instructed by men, shows the heavenly origin of His doctrine.—CRAMER: In Christ are hidden all treasures of wisdom; but we must go the ordinary way, go to school, study, ask, *etc.*, that we also may be wise.—*His that sent me:* 1. Because it [His doctrine] contains the whole counsel and pleasure of the Father, Jno. vi. 39, 40. 2. Because it was in substance one with Moses and the prophets, through whom the Father had spoken, Heb. i. 1. 3. Because Christ was filled with the Spirit of the Father, ch. xvii. 8. 4. Because His doctrine aimed at the glory of the Father.—ZEISIUS: The test of orthodox and righteous teachers: 1. Their being able to say with Christ in some measure and truth: My doctrine is not mine, but, *etc.;* taking their doctrine not from their own reason, but from the holy, revealed word of God. 2. Their seeking therein not their own glory, but the glory of God and of Christ, and directing everything towards this purpose of glorifying the name of God. Hearers also are bound on their part to obey them, on peril of their salvation.—*If any man will, etc.* As much as to say: I appeal to the experience of all the devout.—MAJUS: He who uses not the word of God with the true purpose of learning and doing it, will not be sure of its divinity.—In divine and spiritual things we must believe no one absolutely (blindly), but try every one's doctrine, whether it be of God, or whether the man speak of himself.—HEDINGER: Many are ever learning, and yet cannot come to the knowledge of the truth. Why? They hear much, and do it not.—QUESNEL: A preacher must seek not his own glory, but only God's.—MAJUS: He whose words and works aim only to honor God, is faithful and true, and worthy to be believed.—It is good to remind people of their evil deeds, and convince them of them: perchance some will lay it to heart and be converted, Mark ii. 27.—*Nova Bibl. Tub.:* It is a sure mark of envy and malice, when a man censures in others, and condemns others for, what he does himself.—*Ibid.:* Whence come so many uncharitable, false judgments of our neighbor's conduct? From our not seeing to the bottom of the heart, *etc.*—ZEISIUS: How can preconceived opinions but blind us, and prevent our true understanding of the Scriptures?—To the pretentious and fine-talking, who boast so much of their knowledge, we must show that they lack the best.—*Ibid.:* Satan with his tools cannot hurt a hair, without the will of God.—QUESNEL: Simplicity and humility open the heart to divine truth, but pride and boastfulness close it.—When Christians are persecuted, open-hearted confessors are commonly very few; men keep themselves so concealed, that the confession of Christ is rather a murmuring than a true confessing.—Shame, that in spiritual things carnal means are thought of, and the power of the Spirit is opposed by the arm of secular authority.—HEDINGER: The season of grace lasts not forever: follow its drawing!—CANSTEIN: It is but a little while that the pious are in the world; afterwards they will be forever separated from it by death. Therefore they can for the little time bear a little from the wicked world.—QUESNEL: The death of believers is a return to their Father.—MAJUS: In heaven there is peace for all trouble and rest from all labor.—What the world says in mockery will often prove true to its hurt.

VON GERLACH: A sublime disposition would enable them to know divine things.—This is still the proper way to attain to the knowledge of the divine origin and matter of Christianity; to follow with the heart all traces of the divine, and thus with honest purpose to endeavor to do what God requires.—Jesus implicated the whole people, because He made all responsible for these purposes and acts of the rulers; without the consent of the people, the rulers, even afterwards, could not have put Jesus to death.—Penetrate to the spirit of my words, and contradictions resolve themselves!

LISCO: Obedience to Jesus leads to experience of the divine virtues of His doctrine and His gospel (Rom. i. 16), of which there are three, corresponding to the three principal faculties of the human spirit: power to enlighten (mind), to sanctify (will), to bless (heart). (From PASCAL). Human things we must know in order to love (only conditionally true), divine we must love in order to know.—The Jews know indeed the true God, but they knew Him not as the true and real (they knew Him not truly in His true nature).—The lost opportunity of grace cannot be regained.—BRAUNE: Therefore not the doing of the will of God, but even before that, the *will* to do the will of God, enables one to experience the truth of Christ's assertion that His doctrine is of God. If thou only hast the will, art decided in thy wish, to do the will of God as thou knowest it from conscience, nature, education, Scripture,—this leaning of will and heart to the will of God gives (as a condition) the knowledge of the truth.—Ambition makes a man dull and unsusceptible to knowledge.

GOSSNER: *Where is He?* might one often ask in bustling church-solemnities, or in learned, flowery sermons. Where is *He*, the chief person?—*There was much murmuring among the people concerning Him.*—So Christ and His truth must be canvassed by perverse opinions. This is so to this day.—How men must avoid speaking evil of any other, but speak as much evil as possible of Jesus.—Christ comes forth at the right moment.—The world calls it learning and education, only when one has passed through many classes in a school; of another way of learning it knows nothing.—The doctrine of Jesus puts us already in heaven, and thereby evinces clearly and visibly enough its divine origin.—Those who must uphold the letter of the law, and form, and would banish the Spirit from it, most sadly break the law and the form.

HEUBNER: Humanly speaking, Jesus was an uneducated man, but He towers infinitely above all the educated.—*If any man will, etc.* Without religious need, without longing for God and salvation, no conviction of the truth of Christianity, no faith in Christ, is possible. To the conscience all proofs must appeal.—And it follows—which few think of—that this declaration of Jesus contains rebuke and condemnation of the strongest kind: He who cannot be convinced of the divinity of the doctrine of Jesus, *etc.*, has no earnestness in regard to his salvation. The proposition of Christ is universal; here the *universio logica* holds.—Ambition is a betrayer of a calling not divine, of a self-commissioned prophet, Deut. xviii. 15.—*Thou hast a devil.* How those who now so impudently clear themselves, soon after convict themselves of falsehood; for the people loudly demanded His death.—Wickedness, enmity, always judges according to appearances. Righteous judgment is only with the friends of God.—All religion is indifferentism, when men govern themselves in it by the authority of rulers; this is contrary to the principle of Protestantism. —*But I know Him.* The heart of the believer is an inaccessible sanctuary, from which the world cannot tear out the consciousness of salvation.—SCHLEIERMACHER: *Having never learned.* Literally taken, this is certainly false; for from the beginning of our Lord's life the history informs us that He increased in wisdom, which means that He *learned.* They think there were at that time particular institutions, *etc.* In such a school the Lord had not learned.—We also can make a distinction between what is brought into our souls by others and developed from their own power, and what in them is the gift of the Spirit of God.—Unless man hears the voice of the divine will, he cannot know whether the doctrine of Christ is of God or not.—There is no more dangerous enemy of the true welfare of man, of the pure salvation which we have in Christ, than spiritual pride.

(b) CHRIST AS THE DISPENSER OF THE SPIRIT, THE REAL SILOAM WITH ITS WATER OF LIFE. INCREASING FERMENT IN THE PEOPLE.

Ch. VII. 37-44.

37 [Now][1] In the last day, that [the] great *day* of the feast, Jesus stood and cried,
38 saying, If any man [any one] thirst, let him come unto me, and drink. He that
believeth on [in] me, as the Scripture hath said, out of his belly [body][2] shall flow
39 rivers of living water. (But this spake he of the Spirit, which they that believe[3]
on [in] him should [were about to] receive, for the Holy Ghost [the Spirit] was
40 not yet *given*, [*omit given*][4] because that [*omit* that] Jesus was not yet glorified.)
Many[5] [some] of the people [multitude] therefore, when they heard this saying
41 [these words],[6] said, Of a truth this is the Prophet [This is truly the Prophet.]
42 Others said, This is the Christ. But [*omit* But] some [Others][7] said, Shall Christ
come out of Galilee [Doth the Christ then come from Galilee]? Hath not the
Scripture said, That [the] Christ cometh of [from] the seed of David, and out of
the town of Bethlehem [from Bethlehem, the town][8] where David was?
43 So there was a division among the people [the multitude] because of him. And
44 some of them would have taken him [wished to seize him]; but no man [one]
laid hands on him.

TEXTUAL AND GRAMMATICAL.

[1] Ver. 37.—[The δέ after ἐν is not without force, and should not have been omitted in the E. V.—P. S.]

[2] Ver. 38.—[ἐκ τῆς κοιλίας αὐτοῦ. Alford and Conant retain the strong term of the A. V. Noyes translates: *from within him;* Luther and Lange: *body.* Κοιλία properly means *belly, abdomen, bowels, stomach,* as the receptacle of food, but tropically also, in Hellenistic usage, the *inward parts,* the *inner man,* the *heart* (καρδία; comp. the Lat. *viscera*), and so it is taken here by Chrysostom and others. The LXX. often interchange κοιλία and καρδία. See the EXEG.—P. S.]

[3] Ver. 39.—Lachmann [Alford] reads πιστεύσαντες [those who believed] instead of πιστεύοντες, on the authority of B. L. T. [ℵ. D. rel. Tischend.: πιστεύοντες.—P. S.]

[4] Ver. 39.—Ἅγιον [*Holy* before *Spirit*] is omitted by Lachmann and Tischendorf, after the Vulgate, Itala, most versions K. T. As B. D. and others have the word, we may suppose the omission of ἅγιον to have been occasioned by doctrinal con-

siderations, which, however, have rather made the passage more difficult than easier. Δεδομένον [given] which Lachmann, after Cod. B., retains, stands less firm. [Both ἅγιον and δεδομένον are wanting in Cod. Sin. which simply reads οὔπω γὰρ ἦν πνεῦμα (without the article). So Tischendorf in the 8th ed. Alford omits δεδομένον and retains ἅγιον, but puts it in brackets. Westcott and Hort put [ἅγιον] δεδομένον on the margin.—P. S.]

5 Ver. 40.—Ἐκ τοῦ ὄχλου οὖν ἀκούσαντες. The πολλοὶ [text. rec.] or τινὲς [explanatory] are dropped, according to B. D. L. T. &c.

6 Ver. 40.—Τῶν λόγων, Lachmann, Tischendorf, according to [א] B. D. E. G. &c. [Cod. Sin., Tischend., Alf.: τῶν λόγων τούτων, Lat. *hos sermones, verba illa, hæc verba*. The text. rec. reads τὸν λόγον.—P. S.]

7 Ver. 41.—Instead of ἄλλοι δὲ, Lachmann has οἱ δὲ, after B. L., *etc.* [Tischend. after Cod. Sin.: ἄλλοι—ἄλλοι without δέ.—P. S.]

8 Ver. 42.—[This is the position of the Greek, ἀπὸ Βηθλ. τῆς κώμης ὅπου.—P. S.]

EXEGETICAL AND CRITICAL.

Ver. 37. **In the last day.**—Meyer: "As the eighth day (the 22d Tisri according to Lev. xxiii. 34; Numb. xxix. 35; Neh. viii. 18) was reckoned in with the seven days of the feast proper, and as, *Succah*, fol. 48, 1, the last day (אחרון) of the feast is the eighth, John certainly meant this day and not the seventh (Theoph., Buxtorf, Bengel, Reland, Paulus, Ammon); especially as it was customary at a later period to speak of an eight days' celebration of the feast of tabernacles (2 Macc. x. 6; Joseph. *Ant.* III. 10, 4; *Gem. Eruvin.* 40, 2; *Midr. Kohel.* 118, 3). To this corresponds, too, the translation ἐξόδιον (finale of the feast), by which the Septuagint expresses the designation of the eighth day, עֲצֶרֶת [solemn assembly] in Lev. xxiii. 36; Num. xxix. 35; Neh. viii. 18. Comp. Ewald, *Alterthümer*, p. 481." Tholuck: "A general jubilee (Plutarch calls it a Bacchanal) and splendid ceremonies of many kinds took place at this feast, so that the Rabbis were accustomed to say: He who has not seen these festivities, knows not what jubilee is. See H. Majus: *Diss. de haustu aquarum.*"

[Alford takes the same view as to the day, and then tries to solve the difficulty which attaches to it. "The *eighth* day seems here to be meant, and the *last of the feast* to be popularly used. But a difficulty attends this view. Our Lord certainly seems to allude here to the custom which prevailed during the seven days of the feast, of a priest bringing water in a golden vessel from the pool of Siloam with a jubilant procession to the temple, standing on the altar and pouring it out there, together with wine, while meantime the Hallel (Ps. cxiii.–cxviii.) was sung. This practice was by some supposed —as the dwelling in tabernacles represented their life in the desert of old—to refer to the striking of the rock by Moses:—by others, to the rain, for which they then prayed, for the seed of the ensuing year:—by the elder Rabbis (Maimonides, cited by Stier, iv. 331, ed. 2), to Isa. xii. 3, and the effusion of the Holy Spirit in the days of the Messiah. But it was universally agreed (with the single exception of the testimony of R. Juda Hakkadosh, quoted in the tract *Succa*, which itself distinctly asserts the contrary), that on the eighth day this ceremony did *not take* place. Now, out of this difficulty I would extract what I believe to be the right interpretation. It *was* the eighth day, and the pouring of water *did not* take place. But is therefore (as Lücke will have it) all allusion to the ceremony excluded? I think not: nay, I believe it is the more natural. For seven days the ceremony had been performed, and the Hallel sung. On the eighth day the Hallel was sung, but the outpouring of the water did not take place: '*desideraverunt aliquid.*' '*Then Jesus stood and cried,' etc.* Was not this the most natural time? Was it not probable that He would have said it at a time, rather even than while the ceremony itself was going on?" This accords with the view taken by Lange (see below and DOCTR. AND ETHICAL No. 1), but Wordsworth, Owen and others defend the usual opinion that on the eighth day as well as on those preceding, and with louder and more general expressions of joy, the priest brought forth, in a golden vessel, water from the spring of Siloam, and poured it upon the altar, and that Jesus at that very time proffered the water of life to all who would come unto Him and drink.—P. S.]

The *last* day of the feast of tabernacles was an especially high day, being the close of the feast (as well as of the festal season of the year), and being a Sabbath, a day on which the congregation assembled according to the law (Lev. xxiii. 36), and which was therefore distinguished by a special sacrificial ritual. But one thing the day lacked, which distinguished the other days. On each of the seven preceding days, in the morning, occurred the festal water-drawing. A priest drew water daily with a large golden pitcher (holding about two pints and a half) from the spring of Siloam on the temple hill, brought it into the temple, and poured it out mingled with sacrificial wine, into two perforated dishes at the altar. The ceremony was accompanied with the sound of cymbals and trumpets, and the singing of the words of Isa. xii. 3, which Rabbi Jonathan paraphrased: "With joy shall ye receive the new doctrine from the chosen righteous." This was the celebration of the miraculous springs which God opened for the people on their pilgrimage through the wilderness. But because the eighth day marked the entrance into Canaan, the water-drawing ceased. On this day the springs of the promised land gave their waters to the people; an emblem of the streams of spiritual blessing which Jehovah had promised to His people. To this symbolical performance the words of Jesus on the last day of the feast evidently refer (*Leben Jesu*, III. p. 619). It is of no account that, according to Rabbi Juda, the pouring out of the water took place on the eighth day also. This was probably a later supplement, if the statement is not an error.

The great day [τῇ μεγάλῃ].—That is, especially great in comparison with the other days.* See the preceding remarks. Philo also [*De Septenaris* II. 298] observes that it was the close of the yearly feasts; *i. e.* of the three great feasts, not of all.

Cried, saying.—Jesus had not hitherto so

* [Meyer: The μεγαλότης of the eighth day consisted just in this, that it brought the great feast to a solemn close.]

openly presented Himself as the personal object of a saving faith.

If any one thirst [*i. e.* **whosoever thirsts**] **let him come to me and drink.**—See the observations on ver. 37. The reference of this preaching of salvation under the promise of a miraculous draught and fountain of water to the water-drawing is groundlessly considered by Meyer to be dubious. It agrees entirely with the character of the fourth Gospel, in which Jesus presents Himself in the most varied ways as the fulfilment of the Old Testament symbols. The spiritual import of the water-drawing appears in Isa. xii. 3 ["with joy shall ye draw water out of the wells of salvation"]. This water-drawing must be distinguished from the devotional water-drawing on days of humiliation and fasting, 1 Sam. vii. 6.

[The invitation first given to the Samaritan woman at Jacob's well, is here extended to all the people on the great feast in Jerusalem. The N. T. closes with a similar offer of the water of life (Rev. xxii. 17). There is an inner thirst as there is an inner man, and the former is deeper and stronger than the thirst of the body, and can only be satisfied from the fountain of life in Christ. "Under the imagery of one thirsting for water, which everywhere, and especially in countries like Palestine where the want of water is so frequently experienced, would be well understood, our Lord proffers to all such persons that which will forever satisfy the longings of the soul and give it permanent rest." Owen. "An allusion to the water drawn in a golden vase from the pool of Siloam and poured on the altar in the temple . . . as a memorial of the water from the rock smitten in the wilderness, and typical of the living water of the Spirit from the true Rock (1 Cor. x. 4)." Wordsworth.—P. S.]

Ver. 38. **He that believeth* in me,** *etc.*—Explaining the expression: "Come unto me and drink."—**As the scripture hath said.**—These words are not to be connected with ὁ πιστεύων, as if the meaning were: "He who according to the scripture believeth in Me" (Chrysostom, Calovius, and others). An ἐστι may be understood. Meyer: 'Ο πιστεύων is *nominat. absol.* The question then is, what words of Scripture the Lord means. The expression [which follows: "out of his body shall flow rivers of living water"] does not occur literally in the Old Testament; so that Whiston and others took up the idea that it was from some canonical or apocryphal sources now lost. Against this are (1) the usage of the New Testament, (2) the general reference to "the scripture," which, as such, seems to be intended to point rather to a promise running through the Old Testament than to any particular passage (see Isa. xliv. 3; lv. 1; especially lviii. 11; Ezek. xlvii. 1 ff.; Joel ii. 23; Zech. xiii. 1; xiv. 8). Olshausen fixes particularly on those passages which promise a flowing forth of living water from the temple, the believer being considered as a living temple.* And undoubtedly Christ at least would as surely have Himself considered the true temple-fountain, as He in ch. ii. presented Himself as the true temple. The notions of the temple (ch. ii.) and the fountain (ch. iv.) here run together. The question is whether the believer also will himself be a temple-spring. See the next paragraph.

Out of his belly (body).—'Εκ τῆς κοιλίας αὐτοῦ. That κοιλία (בֶּטֶן) may denote in Hebrew usage the inward part, the heart, is proved by Prov. xx. 27, and similar passages (see Bretschneider's Lexicon); hence Chrysostom [his successors] and others have taken κοιλία as equivalent to καρδία. [Augustine: the inner man, the heart's conscience.—P. S.] The only question is, why the Lord chose the strong term. Meyer [p. 312] thinks it should be strictly understood of the abdomen [*Bauchhöhle*, as the receptacle of water taken into a man], and then this should be taken figuratively. His body shall give forth living water as a stream of a fountain (through the mouth!); without the figure, the divine grace and truth which the believer has taken from the fulness of Christ into his inner life, remains not shut up within himself; but imparts itself in overflowing abundance to others. This rendering accounts for the striking expression κοιλία no better than that of Chrysostom. Κοιλία, in the wider sense denotes any belly-like cavity [the belly of the sea, of a mountain, of a large vessel, *etc.*]. If we keep in view the symbolical reference to the "water-feast," we may refer the expression to the belly of the temple hill (Gieseler [in the *Studien und Kritiken*, 1829, p. 138 f.]; see Lücke, II. p. 229), and also to the body of the great golden pitcher with which the priest drew the water (Bengel). We have previously (*Leben Jesu*, II., p. 945) given the former interpretation.† But as Christ Himself is the parallel of the temple hill with the spring of Siloam, so the believing Christian is well represented by the golden pitcher with which the priest drew the water; at least this enters into the choice of the expression.‡ The

* ['Ο πιστεύων is an emphatic absolute nominative. The predicate is not expressed, but implied in the words ποταμοί . . . ῥεύσουσιν. Such irregularity is not unfrequent in the best Greek classics. It is intended to give greater prominence to the noun, hence to the necessity of faith. Similar instances John vi. 39 (πᾶν); xvii. 2; Acts vii. 40; Apoc. ii. 26 (ὁ νικῶν—δώσω αὐτῷ); iii. 12, 21; comp. Buttmann, *Neutestamentl. Grammatik*, p. 325.—P. S.]

* [The most remarkable and appropriate of these passages are Ezek. xlvii. 1-12, where *rivers* are prophetically described as issuing *from under the threshold of the temple eastward* (ver. 1), and making alive and healing all that is touched by them (ver. 9); Zech. xiv. 8: "And it shall be in that day, that living waters shall go out from Jerusalem" (ἐξελεύσεται ὕδωρ ζῶν ἐξ 'Ιερουσαλήμ); and Isa. lviii. 11, where Jehovah promises the thirsty to satisfy his soul in drought and to make him "like a watered garden, and like a spring of water, whose waters fail not." To these prophetic words the quotation applies in a free and comprehensive way, and the characteristic ἐκ τῆς κοιλίας αὐτοῦ is an interpretation in application to the individual believer. Compare here also the remarks on p. 182 in regard to the fact made almost certain by recent researches that there was a living spring beneath the altar of the temple, from which all the fountains of Jerusalem were fed, the source of the "Brook that flowed hard by the oracles of God,"—the "perennial river the streams whereof shall make glad the city of God" (Ps. xlvi. 4).—P. S.]

† [So also Olshausen: The believer is here represented as a living temple. Alford: The temple was symbolic of the Body of the Lord (see ch. ii. 21); and the Spirit which dwells in and flows forth from His people also, who are made like unto Him, Gal. iv. 6; Rom. viii. 9; 1 Cor. iii. 6.—P. S.]

‡ [This interpretation seems rather far-fetched. The cavity of a *small* vessel is hardly designated by *belly*. Besides the Christian is not only an instrument, but a living member, of Christ, and Christ Himself is in him. Godet's reference to the rock in the wilderness, which Moses smote, so that ἐκ τ. κοιλίας αὐτοῦ corresponds to מִמֶּנּוּ, Ex. xvii. 6, is still more artificial.—P. S.]

meaning is: The whole Christian is a vessel of grace emptied of vanity, filled with the Spirit. Of course the pitcher of itself yields no stream of living water; but this is just the miracle of the true life, that, being drunk (ch. iv. 10) or drawn in faith (as in our passage), it becomes a flowing fountain of living water. To refer the ἐκ τῆς κοιλίας αὐτοῦ to Christ (Hahn: *Theologie des Neuen Testaments*, I. p. 229 [and Gess: *Person Christi*, p. 166]), jars with the context, especially ver. 39. The living water is explained below.

[**Shall flow rivers of living water.**—Ποταμοί is put first in the original to emphasize the abundance. Chrysostom comments on the plural: "*Rivers*, not *river*, to show the copious and overflowing power of grace: and *living water*, *i. e.* always moving; for when the grace of the Spirit has entered into and settled in the mind, it flows freer than any fountain, and neither fails, nor empties, nor stagnates. The wisdom of Stephen, the tongue of Peter, the strength of Paul, are evidences of this. Nothing hindered them; but, like impetuous torrents, they went on, carrying everything along with them."—P. S.]

Ver. 39. **But this spoke he of the Spirit which they that believe in him were about to receive.**—[An explanatory remark of the Evangelist similar to the one in ii. 21. Important for apostolic exegesis. Otherwise the Evangelists never insert their own views or feelings to interrupt the flow of the objective narration which speaks best for itself.—P. S.].—According to Lightfoot the Rabbins also considered the water-pouring or libation of the feast of tabernacles as the outpouring of the divine Spirit (*haustio Spiritus Sancti*). [Comp. the prophetic predictions of the Messianic outpouring of the Spirit, Joel iii. 1; Isa. xxxii. 15; xliv. 3; Ezek. xxxvi. 25; xxxix. 29].

According to Lücke (II. p. 230) the "living water" is intended to mean as much as "eternal life" [iv. 10, 14], but not the Holy Spirit; and John's exposition may be indeed "*epexegetically* correct, but is not *exegetically* accurate."* His arguments are: (1) "The outflowing, ῥεύσουσιν ἐκ, is not a receiving (λαμβάνειν)." But the receiving is everywhere identical with *faith*, and the Spirit, which the believers received, also in fact flowed forth. (2) "The ῥεύσουσιν cannot be an absolute future, excluding the present." But neither has the gospel history made the outpouring of the Holy Ghost so; for before this, in fact, a certain miraculous power already flowed forth from the apostles [comp. also xx. 22]. (3) "Olshausen, it is true, observes that even in the New Testament the Spirit is conceived under the figure of water, as the description of the Spirit as 'poured out,' Acts x. 45; Tit. iii. 6, clearly shows. But how comes it, that the corresponding emblem of water is never expressly used in the New Testament for the Holy Ghost. We have ὕδωρ τῆς ζωῆς, but never ὕδωρ τοῦ πνεύματος." This is accounted for by the fact that the symbol arose from the contrast, so vivid to Palestinians, between the stagnant water of cisterns and the living water of springs. The *legal* system gave a certain measure of life, like cistern water, which did not propagate itself, and easily corrupted. The *gospel* dispensation of faith gave the water of life, which like a fountain replenished itself, increased, and was always fresh. And this was the Spirit. Lücke says: "The essential affinity of the expressions ζωὴ αἰώνιος and πνεῦμα is undeniable." Here, however, is more than *affinity;* the two expressions denote the same life of the Spirit, only under different aspects.

Meyer rightly adduces for the correctness of the Evangelist's explanation the strength of the term ποταμοί (to which ῥεύσουσι may be added). But when he goes on to remark, that John does not consider the Holy Ghost Himself to be meant by the *living water*, but only says of the whole declaration, that Jesus meant it of the Holy Ghost, leaving the Christian mind to conceive the Spirit as the *Agens*, as the impelling power of the stream of living water,—he runs substantially into Lücke's interpretation.

We have only to distinguish between the Spirit of the life, as the cause, and the life of the Spirit, as the effect; carefully remembering that the cause and the effect are here not physically separate, but penetrate each other. Assuredly the words of Jesus speak directly of the operation of the Holy Ghost. The Spirit is a self-supplying spring.

On the doctrine of the Spirit of God in the Old Testament and of the Holy Ghost in the New, comp. the biblical and dogmatic theologies; Spirit is the uniting formative principle of visible life. So the air, the symbolical spirit of the earth; so the spirit in man. And the Spirit of God is, in the first place, the uniting life and formative principle of the creation (Gen. i. 2; Ps. xxxiii. 6); then, of the life of the creature, and in particular of man (Gen. vi. 3; Ps. civ. 29, 30); then, of the theocracy (Num. xi. 25, *etc.*). Subsequently the promise of a new kingdom (see the Prophets). So in the New Testament, the one life and formative principle of the life of Jesus, of the body of disciples, of the New Testament Church, of the new world.

For the (Holy) Ghost was not yet [οὔπω γὰρ ἦν πνεῦμα (ἅγιον).*—For the

* [Alford justly remarks that it is lamentable to see such an able and generally right-minded commentator as Lücke carping at the interpretation of an apostle, especially John, who of all men had the deepest insight into the wonderful analogies of spiritual things. The difficulties raised by Lücke rest in his own misapprehension. John does not say that the promise of our Lord was a prophecy of *what happened* on the day of Pentecost, but of the *Spirit* which the believers were about to receive. The *water of life* after all is the life of the *Spirit*, for the "Spirit is life" and "the mind of the Spirit is life." Rom. viii. 6, 10. The communication of eternal life always implies the gift of the Spirit of Christ.—P. S.]

* [The ἦν can, of course, not refer to the essential or personal *existence* and previous *operation* of the Spirit, who is coëternal with the Father and the Son, who manifested Himself in the creation (Gen. i. 3; Ps. xxxiii. 6) and through the whole O. T. economy, as the organizing, preserving, enlightening, regenerating and sanctifying principle (Gen. vi. 3; Ex. xxxi. 3; Ps. li.; civ., *etc.*), who inspired Moses and the prophets (Num. xi. 25; 1 Sam. x. 19, 26; Isa. lxi. 1; 2 Pet. i. 21), who overshadowed Mary at the conception of Christ (Matt. i. 20; Luke i. 35), who descended upon Him without measure at the baptism in Jordan (John i. 32, 33; iii. 35), but to the *presence* and *working* of the Spirit as the Spirit of *Christ* with the fulness of the accomplished redemption in the Christian Church, or to the dispensation of the Spirit, which, according to the promise of Christ (John xiv.-xvi.), commenced after His resurrection and ascension, on the day of Pentecost.

reasons above given we keep the ἅγιον. The Spirit was already always present; the Spirit of God had evidenced Himself even in the Old Testament; but the revelation of God as Holy Ghost was not yet given. In the glorification of Christ the Spirit of God first came to view as the Holy in the specific New Testament sense. The ἦν is therefore emphatic; He was not yet present and manifest upon earth to men. The addition [δεδομένον, *given*, in the E. V.] in cod. B. (Lachmann) seems to be a gloss explanatory of the difficult term. ' Christ was conceived, indeed, by the Holy Ghost, and anointed with the fulness of the Spirit; but this was as yet a mystery to the world; the Holy Ghost could not come into the world till after the ascension of Christ, John xvi. 7. Hofmann (*Schriftbeweis* I., p. 196): "The outpouring of the Spirit was the demonstration of His super-mundane nature"—and of His *intra-mundane* existence; the appropriation of His perfect form of life and vital operation to the world (comp. Acts xix. 2).—"The Macedonians were unwarranted in applying this passage against the personality of the Holy Ghost. It is *metonymia causæ pro effectu.*" Heubner. (Or also: *metonymia existentiæ pro revelatione*).

[**Because Jesus was not yet glorified** (ἐδοξάσθη).—By the atoning death, resurrection and ascension of Jesus to the right hand of God the Father, from whence He promised to send and did send the Spirit, as the Spirit of the gospel redemption. In promising this Spirit, Christ expressly said that He must withdraw His visible presence from the disciples and return to the Father before the Comforter could come (xvi. 7). The previous working of the Spirit under the old dispensation was preparatory, prophetic, fragmentary and transitory, like the manifestations of the Logos before the Incarnation. On the day of Pentecost the Spirit took up His abode in the Church and in individual believers, as an immanent and permanent principle, as the Spirit of the God-Man and Saviour, as the Spirit of adoption, as the Spirit of truth and holiness, who reveals and glorifies Christ in the hearts of believers, as Christ revealed and glorified the Father, and abides with them forever.—P. S.]

Vers. 40, 41. **When they heard the sayings** [instead of **this saying**].—The reading: "heard *the sayings*," has the weight of authorities. The total impression of Christ's utterances at the feast is therefore intended. The "*heard*" is emphatic: those of the people who listened to Him with earnestness (ἀκούσαντες τῶν λόγων), said, *etc*.—**Of a truth this is the Prophet**.—Meyer groundlessly says, this means the prophet who was to precede the Messiah, not the Messiah Himself; and yet it means the person promised in Deut. xviii. 15. That is, these people are all agreed that Jesus is the Prophet in general. After this, however, they divide. Some are decided, others are not. The ἀκούσαντες separate into ἄλλοι, ἄλλοι. The former declare outright, that He is the Prophet of Deut. xviii. 15; He is the Messiah. The latter, who would admit Him to be the Prophet, the forerunner of the Messiah according to the Jewish theology, have a difficulty—the supposed Galilean origin of Christ. The birth of Christ in Bethlehem was unknown to them. John considers it superfluous to show up their error, and hence De Wette has gratuitously inferred that John himself did not know that Christ was born in Bethlehem.* John well knew that the conditions of faith had to lie higher and deeper than such a circumstance. Minds which sincerely yield themselves to the impression of Christ, could easily learn His origin, and so be delivered from their error.

Ver. 42. **Hath not the scripture**.—Isa. xi. 1; Jer. xxiii. 5; Mic. v. 1.—**Where David was**.—1 Sam. xvi.

Ver. 43. **So there was a division**.—This division or violent split among those who accorded recognition to the Lord in different degrees, must be distinguished from the division between all those who were friendly to Him and the enemies, of whom ver. 44 at once goes on to speak, or the analogous divisions in ch. ix. 16 and x. 18. There were at first but a few among the people, who made common cause with the hostile Pharisees. See below.

Ver. 44. **And some of them**.—That is, not of the two preceding classes, but of the people who heard His words. As ἐξ αὐτῶν stands after ἤθελον, it is even a question whether the words should not be ἐξ ἑαυτῶν: would have taken Him of themselves, on their own responsibility. De Wette thinks they might have wished to rally the intimidated officers. But the probability is that the officers, as a secret police, as under-sheriffs, had mingled with the people; for no point is mentioned, at which they showed themselves openly; and such an arrangement would correspond with the scrupulous caution of the Sanhedrists. These hostile people, therefore, felt an impulse to open the summary process of zealotism against Jesus.—**But no man laid hands on him**.—They were still fettered by the counsel of God, on the one hand, the fear of the adherents of Jesus, on the other, an involuntary awe. And that the servants of the Sanhedrin did not venture to seize the Lord, we first learn in the next section.

DOCTRINAL AND ETHICAL.

1. It yields an incongruous conception, to suppose (with Tholuck and the older expositors,) that Jesus stood and proclaimed aloud the words of vers. 37 and 38, while the priest was carrying that holy water through the fore-court, and the people were giving themselves up entirely to

' The readings δεδομένον, δοθέν, ἐπ' αὐτοῖς, are all superfluous glosses to guard against a misunderstanding. If anything is to be supplied to ἦν, it should rather be *present* (*aderat*), or *working* (ἐνεργοῦν), or *in the believers* (ἐν πιστεύουσι) from the preceding.—P. S.]

* [Alford: "The mention of the question about Bethlehem seems to me rather to corroborate our belief that the Evangelist was well aware how the fact stood, than (De Wette) to imply that he was ignorant of it. That no more remarks are appended, is natural; John had one great design in writing his Gospel, and does not allow it to be interfered with by explanations of matters otherwise known. Besides . . . if John knew nothing of the birth at Bethlehem, and yet the mother of the Lord lived with him, the inference must be that *she* knew nothing of it,—in other words, that it never happened." Owen argues from this passage in favor of the importance of the genealogical tables of Matthew and Luke to answer Jewish objections like these against the acknowledgment of Jesus as the Messiah.—P. S.]

their jubilations over this symbol. Just then He would have announced that in Him was offered in reality what was there signified in symbol. So public an assault upon the temple-worship, as should assume even the appearance of a vehement rivalry, cannot be expected of the Lord. On the contrary, the eighth day, with its lack of the festal water-drawing, must have brought with it to the attendant people a sense of want, to which Jesus addressed His call with good effect. At that moment, when the symbolical lights of a legally inefficient religion were burning low and going out, the evangelical substance of the symbols appears. The points which determine the symbolical utterance of the Lord are these: (1) The water-drawing was a symbol of spiritual blessing. The redeemed of Israel, on their second return to Canaan, were to draw water on the way with joy out of the wells of salvation, Is. xi. 12; xii. 3. (2) Siloam was situated, indeed, on the temple-hill, but it rose not in the temple itself, but outside of it, at the foot of the holy mountain. So the true spirit of life was lacking in the sacerdotal worship of the temple; it appeared most in the prophetic office, symbolized by the fountain of Siloam in Is. viii. 6. (3) Hence the prophets foretold the future priesthood and worship of the Spirit under the figure of a stream issuing from the temple, Ezek. xlvii.; Joel iii. 18. All Jerusalem was to become full of fountains, Zech. xiv. 8; in fact the whole people was to be like a watered garden, and like a spring of water, Is. lviii. 11. (4) The eighth day of the feast of tabernacles, in its symbolical place, denoted the time of this gushing life of the Spirit; hence it was primarily a day of expectation, of longing, of prayer for the outpouring of the Holy Ghost (see *Leben Jesu*, II. p. 942). This is the Lord's opportunity. In Him the miraculous fountain of the eighth day, for the breaking forth of which from the temple they hoped, was given to the people.

2. *Out of his belly*. Tholuck: "Luthardt's observation, that 'even the corporeal nature was to be an abode of the Holy Ghost,'—is irrelevant." Yet this is, in fact, involved in the idea of regeneration, of the inner man, of the members made instruments of righteousness (see *Leben Jesu*, II. 945: "Their new human nature itself will become the ground whence these springs of water shall issue"). *Rivers of living water*. While in chap. iv. 14, the self-replenishing of the inner life is promised, here the impartation of new life appears in its tendency to issue into the world as a stream for the refreshing of others. Comp. Tholuck, p. 224.

3. On the relation between the Holy Ghost and eternal life, comp. the Exegetical and Critical remarks on ver. 39.

4. *For the Holy Ghost was not yet* (*given*). In what sense? since even in the Old Testament the Spirit of God, as the Holy Spirit, inspired the prophets, 2 Pet. i. 21, and was the principle of life in the devout, Is. lxiii. 10, 11; Ps. li. 12; cxliii. 10. That the prophets of the Old Testament were conscious of a difference between the measure of the Spirit vouchsafed to them and the New Testament revelation of the Spirit, is shown just by the Old Testament predictions of the streams of living water (see above); of the effusion of the Spirit (Joel iii. 1); of the anointing of the Messiah with the sevenfold Spirit of God (Is. xi. 2; lxi. 1); and of the Spirit of the inward law, or of regeneration (Jer. xxxi. 33; Ezek. xxxvi. 26). Tholuck: "The majority of ancient and modern commentators consider the difference only *quantitative* (one of degree). Chrysostom: *Ἤμελλε τὸ πνεῦμα ἐκχεῖσθαι δαψιλῶς, etc.* Chrysostom, however, gives a *qualitative* difference (difference in kind (?) not in the *πνεῦμα* itself, but in the aim of its operations: Εἶ*χον μὲν οἱ παλαιοὶ πνεῦμα αὐτοί, ἄλλοις δὲ οὐ παρεῖχον.* Such a difference in the *πνεῦμα* itself Augustine points out, in the fact that the Christian impartation of the Spirit was connected with miraculous gifts; so Maldonatus, the Lutheran expositors Tarnow, Hunnius, Gerhard, *Loci*, I., 308, Lyser, Calovius, Meyer." Evidently this would not prove much; for the Old Testament prophets also wrought miracles. Brenz, in singularly arbitrary style: "Not till after Pentecost did the preaching *de remissione peccatorum* go forth, which was in the strict sense the *opus Spiritus*."—This is, after all, of the centre of the thing, though not the whole thing. On the contrary Luthardt regards as the qualitative difference that which is indicated in Rom. viii. 15 and 2 Tim. i. 7: "The Holy Ghost was not yet in His office; the old preaching and law were still in force." That is, correctly, it was not yet the economy of the Holy Ghost. "Cocceius also, in opposition to the identification of the economies which was current in his time, presses this distinction of the *tempus promissionis et consummationis. Equidem puto, hic evidentissime dici, adeo multum interesse inter tempus, quod antecessit glorificationem Christi et id, quod consecutum est*," *etc.* P. 226.—The complete exhibition of Christ and His work in history was the *objective* condition precedent of the outpouring of the Holy Ghost; the complete spiritual susceptibility of the disciples, as matter of history, and in them the susceptibility of the world, was the *subjective* condition. Not until all the elements of the life of Christ and of His redeeming agency had appeared in objective and subjective reality, could the Spirit of the life of Christ enter into believers, and become the Spirit of believers. And not till then could it become manifest and begin an economy of its own as the Holy Ghost, who has His life personally in Himself (*Leben Jesu*, II. 2, 946). The absolute exaltation of Christ *above* the world was the condition of His absolute sinking *within* the world, which made Him the principle of the new life in believers; this first brought into full manifestation that glory of the Holy Ghost which is a new form, and the third form of the personality of God, and at the same time a wholly gracious operation (*gratia applicatrix*). Yet this blessing of the life of Jesus must be distinguished from His personality itself, and the Spirit imparted to believers is not to be considered, as it is by Tholuck, "the Son of man Himself transfigured into Spirit."

5. Important as it is that the dispensation of the Spirit be duly appreciated, it is wrong to talk, as the Montanists, the Franciscan Spiritualists, the Anabaptists, and Hegel do, of a separate age or kingdom of the Holy Ghost, supposed to lie beyond the kingdom of the Son.

6. The divisions among the disciples of Jesus themselves, of which the Evangelist tells us, are intimated also in Matthew (chap. xvi. 14). In them is reflected the much larger division which was germinating between the friends and the enemies of Christ, and which is the main thing in the section before us. Lücke's supposition that the ostensible objection that Jesus was not from Bethlehem, whence the Messiah ought to come, was made in particular by the scribes among the people, is gratuitous. But it could not enter into the Lord's plan, to work upon the people with the testimony of His birth in Bethlehem; because His way was, to leave the popular notion of the Messiah quite aside, and to have His Messiahship recognized from His spirit and His work.

7. Here at last a knot of fanatical enemies of Jesus, who would fain seize Him, comes to light in a marked manner among the people themselves. It was the murderous intent of which Jesus had before testified: "Ye seek to kill Me." They fain would, they well might; but involuntary reverence for the Lord, fear from above, and fear of the people, still restrained them.

HOMILETICAL AND PRACTICAL.

Jesus at the feast of His people: 1. At the beginning: staying out of sight. 2. In the middle: appearing and teaching. 3. At the close: standing and calling aloud.—The last day of the feast, the most glorious.—As the hours of grace decline, Christ sounds His gracious call the louder.—How majestically Christ will stand at the last day of the feast of the world, and how loud His call will be then.—Christ the true end of all feasts.—Christ the truth and substance of every sacred feast.—Even of that feast.—As the need of salvation is a thirst, so faith is a drinking (a refreshment) in the highest and holiest sense.—Thirst, as a prophetical pointing: (1) to spiritual thirst; (2) to the spiritual refreshment of salvation; (3) to the destination of the man to be a fountain of life to others.—The call of Christ at the feast of water-pouring: 1. His invitation. 2. His promise.—The measure of the supply which Christ gives to the believer's thirst: 1. The believer himself shall drink. 2. Out of his belly shall flow streams of living water (he shall give drink to many).—As Christians are to be lights through the light of Christ, and shepherds through the staff of Christ, so they are to be fountains of life through Christ, the fountain of salvation.—"*Out of his belly* (body):" Even our bodily nature is to be sanctified as a vessel of the Spirit (from mouth and hand, eye and footsteps, it should trickle and stream with blessing).—The promise of the new life a promise of the Spirit.—"*The Holy Ghost was not yet:*" 1. The declaration. 2. Its import for us.—How the outpouring of the Holy Ghost was dependent on the exaltation of Christ: 1. The world must first be perfectly reconciled, before it can be sanctified. 2. Christ must first transcend sensuous limitation in time and space, before He can communicate Himself to all everywhere according to His essential life. 3. Christ must first be fully the Lord of glory, before He can glorify Himself through the Spirit in all hearts.—In Him the world was offered up to God; therefore through Him God could enter into the world.—All parts of His redemptive manifestation were completed; therefore the Spirit of the whole could come forth.—When the manifestation of the Father was completed, it was followed by the manifestation of the Son. When the manifestation of the Son was finished, it was followed by the manifestation of the Holy Ghost; while yet this itself was a glorifying of the Son, and of the Father through the Son.—The glory of the dispensation of the Holy Ghost.—The different effects of the words of Christ.—The division over the words of Christ.—The division between the friends and enemies of Christ shades off among His adherents themselves (ver. 41), and among His enemies (ver. 44).—The hand of God overruling the hands of the enemies of Christ: 1. A hand of omnipotence (they can do *nothing*, so long as He restrains). 2. A hand of wisdom (they can do no harm, when He lets them loose). 3. A hand of faithfulness (they must serve His people, when He lets them prevail). 4. A hand of triumph (they must destroy their own work, and judge themselves).

STARKE: What it is to thirst. To long after righteousness and salvation, Matt. v. 3; Rev. xxii. 17, *etc.*—*Nova Bibl. Tub.:* We can most nobly keep our feast-days by coming to Jesus.—MAJUS: The wells of salvation are open to all men who are like dry ground.—QUESNEL: In vain do we seek to satisfy our desires and quench our thirst among created things; we only thirst the more, with a thirst unquenchable, till we come to Christ.—According to the breadth and depth of the vessel of our faith will be our portion of the water.—"Rivers," a type of overflow, Is. xlviii. 18; lxvi. 12.—MAJUS: True faith is like a copious fountain; it cannot restrain itself from gushing forth in holy love.—HEDINGER: Christianity spreads; it is fain to communicate itself by holy conversation, testimonies of disapproval, patience, *etc.*—CRAMER: The world will never be of one mind concerning Christ; and yet amid a multitude of divisions the true church and the true religion can easily be maintained.—He who loves and seeks the truth, finds it. But he who contemptuously asks, What is truth? falls into error.—QUESNEL: We have not so much to fear from the evil will of men, as from our own.—*Ibid.:* Blessed is he who is in the hand of God, whom no fleshly arm of man can hurt.—It is the method of antichrist always to use force.—OSIANDER: God upholds those who follow their calling in spite of all the rage and bluster of enemies, till they have finished their course.

BRAUNE: "If any man thirst, let him come unto me, and drink." Faith has three constituents: Longing for the satisfaction of the most stringent wants; turning of the heart to the Saviour who helps; and reception of that which He offers, and which exactly meets the longing.—From Him, from His personality as sanctified by faith, rivers of living water, active, vigorous quickenings in rich abundance overflow to others. The believer came with *thirst*, with the feeling of want; and he sends forth *rivers*.

GERLACH: While John records the grand words of the yearning invitation and mighty promise, he feels how far they were from being fulfilled to any disciple who came to the Lord at the time he spoke them; and that the day of the outpouring of the Holy Ghost was but the beginning of their true fulfilment.

HEUBNER: PFENNINGER: Every good thing in the world must be longed for, thirsted for; else it is not a good.—BENGEL: Nothing but thirst, yet sincere thirst, is needed. To him who has a true thirst, nothing is of so great account as the satisfaction of it. Without Christ everything is dry and barren: everything should drive and draw us to Him.—The believer is not only to receive vital force for himself, but also to become a fountain of life for others.—The Spirit of God is a fulness, out of which we are to impart to others.—When Christians can give but little, they prove thereby that they themselves have not much of the Spirit.—What comes from the Spirit tastes, so to speak, like fresh spring-water, not flat like water which has grown stale in a vessel.—We lack in faith, therefore lack in the Spirit.—Discord commonly arises wherever Jesus and the gospel attack men.—Thorough inquiry and thorough knowledge would have solved the doubt and discord. The authors of divisions and schisms are swelling smatterers, who have no true knowledge of the Scriptures.

SCHLEIERMACHER: We see everywhere, that the Redeemer of the old, to which His people ever persist in adhering, points them at every opportunity to the new.—But what else was the fruit which the life of the Lord was to bring forth, than just this: that the fulness of the Godhead which dwelt in Him, should pass thence to the community of believers, the whole congregation of the Lord.—BESSER: There is a doubleness in the nature of the church [and of every believer]: like Abraham, she is *blessed* and she is a *blessing* (Gen. xii. 2).—She is both at once: a garden and a "fountain of gardens" (Song of Sol. iv. 15, 16).

II.

FERMENTATION AND PARTIES IN THE HIGH COUNCIL.

CHAP. VII. 45–53.

45 Then came the officers [The officers therefore came] to the chief priests and
Pharisees; and they said unto them, Why have ye not brought [did ye not bring]
46, 47 him? The officers answered, Never man spake [spoke] like this man.[1] Then[2]
48 answered them the Pharisees, Are ye also deceived [led astray]? Have any of
49 the rulers, or of the Pharisees believed on [in] him?[3] But this people [this
multitude, rabble][4] who knoweth not the law[5] are cursed.[6]
50 Nicodemus saith unto them (he that [formerly][7] came to Jesus by night [*omit*
51 by night],[8] being one of them,) Doth our law judge *any* [a] man before it hear
52 him [unless it first hear from him], and know [learn] what he doeth? They
answered and said unto him, Art thou also of [from] Galilee? Search, and look
[see]: for out of Galilee ariseth[9] no prophet.
53 *And every man went*[10] *unto his own house.*[11]

TEXTUAL AND GRAMMATICAL.

[1] Ver. 46.—[Codd. ℵ.[3a] B. L. T., *etc.*, Origen, *etc.*, Lachmann, Tischendorf (in former edd.), Westcott and Hort. read only: ἐλάλ. οὕτως ἄνθρωπος, *never man spoke thus*, omitting ὡς οὗτος ὁ ἄνθρ., *like this man*. Tregelles and Alford retain the last words, but in brackets. Tischendorf, in his eighth ed., adopts the reading of ℵ.* in this form: ὡς οὗτος λαλεῖ ὁ ἄνθρωπος. Omission is more easily accounted for (by *homœotel.*) than insertion. Meyer and Lange retain the clause.—P. S.]

[2] Ver. 47.—[The οὖν of the text. rec. after ἀπεκρίθησαν is sustained by B. T. Vulg., but omitted by ℵ. D. Alf. Tischend.—P. S.]

[3] Ver. 48.—[According to the more lively order of the Greek: *Hath any of the rulers believed in Him, or of the Pharisees?*—P. S.]

[4] Ver. 49.—[Ὄχλος, *multitude* (*Pöbelhaufe*), is here used evidently with great contempt, not only to designate the persons, but to indicate their character.—P. S.]

[5] Ibid.—[Some put a comma after νόμον, some a semicolon, the English V. has no stop. Dr. Lange, in his rendering of the text, adopts the semicolon, and construes thus: "But only this rabble who know nothing of the law (believe in Him); cursed are they!" Meyer also makes ἐπάρατοί εἰσι! an exclamation. The whole sentence is certainly a passionate outburst of the rabbinical *rabies theologica*, but no decree of excommunication (Kuinoel) which was inapplicable to the mass of the people.—P. S.]

[6] Ibid.—Instead of ἐπικατάρατοι, Lachmann and Tischendorf, after [ℵ.] B. T., Origen, *etc.*, read ἐπάρατοι.

[7] Ver. 50.—[Πρότερον, according to B. L. T. and others, Lachmann, Alford. But Tischendorf, ed. viii., with Cod. Sin.* (*prima manu*) omits the clause ὁ ἐλθὼν νυκτὸς πρὸς αὐτὸν πρότερον, and reads simply: Λέγει Νικόδημος πρὸς αὐτούς. Lachm., Alf., Mey. retain the clause with the exception of νυκτός; comp. xix. 39.—P. S.]

[8] Ibid.—Νυκτός is only in minuscules [and in ℵ.*]; supplied from ch. iii.

[9] Ver. 52.—Codd. B. D. K. S. [ℵ. Vulg.] read ἐγείρεται. So Lachmann, Tischendorf [Alford]. The Coptic and Sahidic versions have even the future. Meyer: "An inverted attempt to correct a historical error." Yet ἐγήγερται [text. rec.] seems not sufficiently accredited. It makes no material difference in the sense of the passage; because the word "search" points to the past.

[10] Ver. 53.—The reading ἐπορεύθη is preferable to the reading ἐπορεύθησαν in D. M. S.

[11] Ver. 53.—[This verse is usually connected with the following section, viii. 1-11, and subject to the same critical doubts (see *Text. and Gram.* in ch. viii.); hence I have italicized it.—P. S.]

EXEGETICAL AND CRITICAL.

Ver. 45. **Then came the officers,** [οἱ ὑπηρέται].—The inference is: As, in general, no one ventured to lay hands on Jesus, so, in particular, the officers did not.

To the chief priests and Pharisees.—The latter without the article. The two are here viewed in the Sanhedrin as a unit.

Ver. 46. **Like this man.**—A well-founded addition, expressive of surprise and astonishment. Augustine: "*Cujus vita est fulgur, ejus verba tonitrua.*"

Ver. 47. **Are ye also deceived?**—Even ye officers of the supreme spiritual college?

Ver. 48. In this view the continuation is characteristic: **Have any of the rulers,** *etc.*—For them the authority and example of the rulers must be everything. We should not fail to notice that the testimony of the officers makes not the slightest wholesome impression upon the rulers; or rather, it extremely disturbs and excites them.

Or of the Pharisees.—As if they added this out of an evil conscience. Lest ye should not trust your governors alone, see how the whole great orthodox, aristocratic Jewish party is against Him! How inaccurate they are in both points, is immediately afterwards proved by the example of Nicodemus.

Ver. 49. **But this multitude.**—As heroes let themselves out before their valets, so the hierarchical rulers with their ecclesiastical servants. The venerable fathers give themselves up to a fit of rage, and curse. They curse the people intrusted to them; they curse the devout among the people. But their curse is at the same time a threat of excommunication. This is, however, a cunning means of intimidating the officers, and of seducing them to exalt themselves likewise in hierarchical haughtiness above the people.

Who knoweth not the law.—What genuine hierarchs always think, judge, and *in fact expect* of the people in all cases—a laic ignorance—that in special cases they cast up against them as a reproach. These are here on the way to put Christ to death, as they pretend according to law, as a false prophet, while the people are on the way to acknowledge Christ as the Messiah.

Are cursed.—Not a formula of excommunication (Kuinoel), but an intimation that the ban is impending, which in ch. ix. 22 is hypothetically decreed against the followers of Jesus. The threat is intentionally equivocal. The emphasis assists in this: *The people who know nothing, i. e.*, so far as they know nothing, *of the law;* or, what is the same, who acknowledge Jesus to be the Messiah. To put the people in general under the ban, could not enter the mind of the chief priests. "The hierarchical insolence and theological self-conceit here bears a genuine historical character (comp. Gfrörer, *Das Jahrhundert des Heils*, 1 Abthlg. p. 240). The Sanhedrists and the bigoted party of the Pharisees would pass for the supreme authority as to the truth. The common people were called עַם הָאָרֶץ, even שֶׁקֶץ, *vermin;* even among the nobler sentences in *Pirke Aboth*, 2, 5, it is said: 'The illiterate man is not godly.'" Tholuck. The Talmudists went so far in their folly as to assert that none but the learned would rise from the dead. See Lücke II. p. 339.

[The aristocratic contempt of the people is found everywhere in Church and State. The pride of priestcraft, kingcraft, and schoolcraft is deeply seated in the human heart. The *rabies theologorum* also reappears in all Christian churches and sects in times of heated controversy (*e. g.*, the trinitarian, Christological, and sacramentarian controversies in the fourth, fifth, sixteenth and seventeenth centuries). Theological passions are the deepest and strongest, as religious wars (think of the Thirty Years' War) are the fiercest.—P. S.]

Vers. 50, 51. **Nicodemus saith unto them.**—The ground seems more and more to sway under their feet. First the officers spoke in favor of Jesus. Now a colleague does so. It is noted that he had come to Jesus, though he was a member of their Christ-hating body. His words are the first public utterance of his courage to testify, though couched only in an impartial admonition from a judicial point of view. Yet they are not without an edge. The other members had cast up to the people their want of knowledge of the law; Nicodemus reminds their fanatical zeal, that it is conducting itself illegally in condemning the accused under passionate prejudice without a hearing. This was contrary to the law, Ex. xxiii. 1 (against false accusation); Deut. i. 16; xix. 15 (the insufficiency of a single witness). They have assured the officers that no one of the rulers or Pharisees believes in Jesus; he intimates the possibility of this being untrue, at least as concerns himself.—**Doth our law judge a man, unless,** *etc.*—Does the law do as ye do? This is an ordinance of the law: First hearing, then judgment. The law itself is here designated as the authority which is to hear the case; and probably with a purpose. Nicodemus wishes to bring out the objective nature of a pure judgment.

Ver. 52. **Art thou also from Galilee?**—A contemptuous designation of the followers of Jesus; for most of them were from Galilee.* The angry humor of the council is not calmed but only further inflamed. A striking picture of fanaticism. Calmness and gentleness, admonition of truth and righteousness, admonition of the word of God itself,—all inflame it, because its zeal (being carnal) includes just the suppression of the sense of truth, the sense of justice, and reverence for the word of God, and is on the path of a wilful diabolical blindness and hardness. —**From Galilee.**—Mockery and threat combined: We should take thee for a countryman and follower of the Galilean, and not for our honorable colleague. "Galilee was despised for its remoteness from the centre of Jewish culture—'The Galilean is a blockhead,' says the Talmud authority—and for its mixture of heathen population."

Search, and see: for out of Galilee ariseth no prophet.—These words again are characteristic of the blind, rushing unconscionable zeal, which despises everything divine and human [and does violence to history]. Not only Jonah, but Elijah of Thisbe also, and [perhaps] Hosea and Nahum were of Galilee. Tholuck:

*[Julian the Apostate, in the fourth century, contemptuously called Christ "the Galilean," and the Christians "Galileans."—P. S.]

"It is possible, however, that they followed a divergent tradition respecting the origin of the former two prophets." [Comp. Winer, Herzog, Smith, *etc. sub* Elias and Jonas.] Heubner: "According to the tradition Elijah and Elisha, Hosea and Amos were Galileans; it is certain that Nahum and Jonah were. In Tiberias even a seminary was (afterwards) founded, in which were renowned Rabbins like Hakkadosh, *etc.* The Talmud also came from that quarter, so that the Jews now are ashamed of this proverb (see Olearius: *Jesus the true Messiah*, p. 223)."

This gross error, the modern skeptical criticism (since the time of Bretschneider) has absurdly endeavored to use as a mark of the spuriousness of the fourth Gospel. How could the Sanhedrists, with their Scriptural learning, blunder in such fashion? But how often has this criticism held the Gospels responsible for the violent blindness of fanaticism, for the mistakes of Herod, for the stupidity of the devil himself. We must not fail to notice, besides this feature of unconscious or intentional falsification of history in the mouth of the Sanhedrists, the other fact that they make an utterly irreligious point when they say: "Out of Galilee ariseth no prophet." They deny, in the first place, the Galilean Israel, and in the second place, the freedom of God; and in particular the promise in Isa. ix. 1, 2. To these add the third reproach, that they take not the slightest pains to ascertain the real origin of Jesus.

Ver. 53. **And every man went**, *etc.*—This is usually connected with the first section of ch. viii. But it is a closing word, of great significance, intended to say that the Sanhedrin, after an unsuccessful attempt against the life of Jesus, found themselves compelled to separate and go home, without having accomplished their purpose. For the idea that the words refer to the return of the festal pilgrims, is unworthy of notice. Probably the Sanhedrists were in full session, expecting that Jesus would be brought before them for their condemnation. If this was so, this breaking up of their session was the more mortifying.

DOCTRINAL AND ETHICAL.

1. The two methods which the members of the council adopted with their officers and with their colleague Nicodemus, a type of obdurate *hierarchical fanaticism* in its fundamental features: (1) Perfect insensibility to the voice of truth and the dictates of conscience, and a corresponding perfectly fixed prejudice. (2) Haughtiness, rising even to crazy contempt of the people and of an entire division of the country, joined with crafty fawning upon subordinates. (3) Abusive vulgarity, arraying itself in the robe of sacerdotal and judicial dignity in execution of the judgment of God (cursing excommunicators). (4) Browbeating rejection and derision of impartial judgment, joined with impudent, intentional, or half-intentional perversion and falsification of historical fact. Bringing the voice of justice under suspicion of being a prejudiced partisan voice inflamed by partisan hatred. (5) Perpetual frustrations alternating with orders of arrogance.

2. Even in a circle so degenerate as this the Lord has His witnesses. The officers shame their superiors. The minority of one or two voices (Nicodemus, Joseph of Arimathea) outweighs the large majority of fanatical prejudice, and yet a while delays the judgment of God over the high council.

3. *Nicodemus.* The voice of impartiality and justice in defence of Christ, a prelude of the act and confession of faith.

4. As the Sanhedrin appeals to the Pharisean party as an authority, so the officers refer to their experience, and Nicodemus appeals to the law.

5. "*Never man spake like this man:*" the testimony of the bailiffs to the superhuman power of the word of Jesus. The victory of His word over the official order of His enemies.*

6. After victoriously withstanding the Jewish taunt, that the Christians were Galileans, and Christ was a Nazarene, Christianity afterwards again triumphs over the heathen taunt (of Celsus), that it was a vulgar religion.

7. The falsification of fact by the chief priests, continued in Matt. xxviii. 13. The Talmudic imitation of this example. Similar frauds of the mediæval hierarchy [*e. g.* the Pseudo-Isidorian Decretals].

HOMILETICAL AND PRACTICAL.

An hour of helplessness, as an hour of visitation: 1. In itself considered: (*a*) The helplessness. Unmanageable officers. Opposing colleagues. Impotent adjournment. (*b*) The call to repentance in this situation. *The officers:* "Never man spake," *etc.* Even ye yourselves and the Pharisees speak not like Him. His word is mightier than your order over us. *Nicodemus:* Ye condemn the people as not knowing the law, and ye yourselves despise the precepts of the law. (*c*) The impenitency in the helplessness: in the utterance to the officers, in the utterance to Nicodemus. By these their helplessness becomes a deeper inquisition and advising with hell. 2. As a historical type. Similar occurrences in the history of Christian martyrdom, and in the persecution of the Reformation.—The portrait of fanaticism. Contemptuous and fawning towards men. Hypocritical and cursing. Casting suspicion and lying. Threatening and taking cowardly refuge. Helpless and obstinate to the last.—Carnal zeal degenerates. It sinks gradually from intentional ignoring and falsification into actual ignorance. It condemns itself with every word: "Are ye also deceived?" *etc.*—They went home to their houses, but Christ went to the Mount of Olives. They went, to recover themselves in the selfish comfort of their estates; He prepared Himself for self-sacrifice.—Witnesses of the truth in the camp of Christ's enemies.—The testimony of the officers concerning the words of Christ: 1. As their own

* [Involuntary witnesses of the innocence or even divinity of Christ, and the truth of the Gospel: Pontius Pilate and his wife, the centurion under the cross, Judas the traitor, Tacitus (in his account of the Neronian persecution), Celsus, Lucian, Porphyry, J. J. Rousseau, Napoleon, Strauss, Renan, *etc.* A collection of such testimonies to the character of Christ from the mouth or pen of enemies or skeptics see in the Appendix to my book on the *Person of Christ*, Boston and New York, 1865.—P. S.]

excuse. 2. As an accusation against their superiors. 3. As a glorification of the superhuman innocence of Jesus.—According to the divine appointment, spiritual and temporal despots in the end fail of instruments.—The passive resistance of the officers.—The double measure of the Jewish rulers: 1. To the sound popular judgment of the officers they oppose the authority of their party faith. 2. To the sound regard of Nicodemus for authority, appealing to law, they oppose the grossest popular judgment.—"Have any of the Pharisees believed on Him?" A despotic ecclesiastical government supports itself upon a despotic party.—"Out of Galilee ariseth no prophet." Falsifications of sacred history: (*a*) The Talmud. (*b*) The mediæval tradition (Pseudo-Isidorian Decretals, *etc.*).

Nicodemus: the silent, sure advances of a true disciple of Jesus: 1. A timid but honest inquirer after truth (ch. iii.). 2. A calm but decided advocate of justice (ch. vii.). 3. A heroic confessor of the Lord, bringing his grateful offerings (ch. xix.).—How Nicodemus meets their boastful bluster with the words of calmness and justice: (1) The boast, that no ruler believes in Jesus. (2) The boast, that they were zealous for the law.—Carnal zeal runs deeper and deeper into blindness and obduracy: 1. To shameless reviling of the justice it professes to administer. (2) To shameless denial of the truth and history, for which it imagines itself contending.—"And every man went unto his own house." Most of them went from a wandering assembly to a wandering house and a wandering heart, not to commune with the Lord upon their beds.—How differently they went home: 1. The enemies. 2. Nicodemus.—They went home, but Christ went unto the Mount of Olives.

Starke: Canstein: So the wise God deals with His enemies in the dispensation of grace: He often makes friends among their own people, children, households and servants; and therein the masters may see and should see the finger of God.—Zeisius: No man, however great he may be in the world, is to be obeyed contrary to the word of God and a good conscience.—Quesnel: Those who issue unjust commands from the necessity and demand of their office, without knowing the unrighteousness which pervades them, are not so far from the kingdom of God as those who issue the same from envy, hatred, or other wicked affections.—Zeisius: Unlettered, honest simplicity is much better fitted to know the truth of God, than the swelling, conceited wisdom of the schools.—Hedinger: O wonderful power of a word, which can stop deluded hearts in the current of their wickedness, and convert them. Acts ix. 5, 6.—Even the means which are intended for an utterly base end, God can turn to the wholesome use of souls.—*Bibl. Wirt.*: How strangely God works with His enemies; how He makes their schemes miscarry, and confuses the game so curiously that often those who are commissioned to do evil, are compelled to do well to a good man. Num. xxiii. 11; Prov. xvi. 7.—Masters ought to set their servants a good example for imitation, but they are often so ungodly that they rather lead them astray than aright. O what will become of them!—Majus: True conversion and confession of the truth the world calls delusion. Matt. xxvii. 63; 2 Cor. vi. 8.—Quesnel: The world is so corrupt that it even hates those who will not join with it in persecuting the good.—Hedinger: Diabolical pride! Fear of men is less than nothing in matters of faith. Poor souls, which have no other rule of faith than the decrees of blind bishops, *etc.* The worst is when the state policy prescribes rules of faith.—Shame on the teachers of the law that they have left the people in such ignorance.—Lampe: It is a very small thing to be cursed by men who are themselves under the curse, when God blesses.—Majus: One man may set himself against a whole wicked assembly if only he is equipped with the whole word and Spirit of God.—Zeisius: God still always has His own even among apostate masses.

Braune: *Have any of the rulers believed on Him?* In the haughty exaltation of their own persons there lies a frightful contempt of others.—This is Pharisaism, which holds the external knowledge of the letter and the law of the Scripture, or theology, above religion.—*Art thou also of Galilee?* As a disgrace they add the falsehood: Search, and look, *etc.*—The fiendish joy that no ruler or Pharisee had believed in Jesus, here comes to nought.

Heubner: The humblest servants shame their masters. Those who are sent to take Jesus are themselves taken. The rulers could here see the finger of God. The Lord reigned in the midst of His enemies. To be deceived here means, to give honor to the truth. So living, simple Christians are always considered deceived.—The judgment of men is set up as the rule of faith: Courts, colleges are to decide concerning the truth. But the truth has not always been laid down by them, as we have seen in the councils.—The first trace of the gentle and timid announcement of adhesion to Jesus. Nicodemus merely insists on fair dealing with Jesus: It is unjust to begin the *Processus ab executione.*—The opponents of revelation act substantially like these Pharisees. They begin with this: There is no revelation, and can be none; whereas they ought to suppose and investigate at least the possibility of a true revelation.—No tribunals have proceeded more unrighteously than spiritual tribunals.

Gossner: They freely confess against their masters, in whose pay they were and whose song therefore (according to the way of the world) they should have sung—it was not the sound which so struck the people, as if He spoke vehemently, thundered and lightened; but a divine authority always lay in His gentle address. His word, in fact His very presence, struck as lightning to the heart. In this no man could speak like Him.

Schleiermacher (the officers): This is the first beginning. The ground must first be laid in the soul in a holy awe before the doctrine and the person of the Lord.

[The preaching of the gospel sometimes restrains the violence of the hand when it works no change in the heart.—When Christ appeared, the great ones of the world not only refused to believe in Him, but boasted of their unbelief as an argument of their wisdom.—Great in honor and wise in understanding, are a sweet couple, but seldom seen together.—There is no wisdom, nor understanding, nor counsel against the Lord. (From Burkitt.)—Nicodemus an example of the slow but sure work of grace, from the timid seeking of the Lord by night to this manly confession. —Different ways to the same Christ, short and long, direct and circuitous.—Even in high places Christ may have friends of whom we know nothing.—Majorities in counsel may be wrong as well as minorities.—One man with God on his side is stronger than any majority.—One little word spoken in season may avert a persecution. —P. S.]

III.

CHRIST, THE LIGHT OF THE WORLD, THE REAL FULFILMENT OF THE JEWISH TORCH-LIGHT FESTIVITIES, AS AGAINST THE PRETENDED SEERS, THE FALSE LIGHTS, IN ISRAEL. THE ADULTERESS, AND CHRIST'S SENTENCE. HIS IDEAL APPEARANCE AT THE COURT OF THE JEWS, AND THE TWO WITNESSES. THE JUDGES SHALL COME INTO JUDGMENT. A TWOFOLD LIFTING UP OF CHRIST AT HAND. APPEARANCES OF YIELDING; OR, A GREAT VACILLATION TOWARDS FAITH.

Chap. (VII. 53) VIII. 1-30.

Chap. VII. 53. *And every man went unto his own house.* [;]
Chap. VIII. 1, 2 [*But*][1] *Jesus went unto the mount of Olives: And early in the morning he came again into the temple, and all the people*[2] *came unto him; and he sat down*
3 *and taught them.*[3] *And the Scribes and* [*the*] *Pharisees brought unto him a woman*
4 *taken in adultery* [or *in sin*],[4] *and when they had set her in the midst, They say unto him*
[*The priests say unto him, tempting him that they might have to accuse him*],[5] *Master,*
5 *this woman was taken*[6] *in adultery, in the very act. Now Moses in the law commanded*
6 *us, that such should be stoned: but what* [*what then*] *sayest thou? This they said,*
tempting him, that they might have to accuse him.[7] *But Jesus stooped down, and with*
his finger, wrote on the ground, as though he heard them not [*omit as though he*
7 *heard them not*].[8] *So* [*But*] *when they continued asking him, he lifted up himself,*
and said unto them, He that is without sin among you, let him first cast [*be the*
8 *first to cast*] *a stone at her. And again he stooped down, and wrote* [*with his*
9 *finger*][9] *on the ground. And they which heard it being convicted by their own conscience* [*And when they heard this, they*], *went out one by one, beginning at* [*with*]
the eldest [or, *elders*, ἀπὸ τῶν πρεσβυτέρων], *even unto the last:*[10] *and Jesus was left*
10 *alone, and the woman standing in the midst. When Jesus had lifted up himself,*
and saw none but the woman [*omit and saw none but the woman*],[11] *he said unto*
her, Woman,[12] *where are those thine accusers?* [*where are they?*][13] *hath no man con-*
11 *demned thee?* [*Did no one condemn thee?*] *She said, No man* [*no one*], *Lord.*
And Jesus [*he*] *said unto her, Neither do I condemn thee: go, and* [*henceforth*][14]
sin no more.

* * * * * * * * * * *

12 Then spake Jesus [Jesus therefore spoke] again unto them [see chap. vii. 37 sqq.],
saying, I am the light of the world: he that followeth me shall not walk in [the][15]
13 darkness, but shall have the light of life. The Pharisees therefore said unto him,
14 Thou bearest record [witness] of thyself; thy record [witness] is not true. Jesus
answered and said unto them, Though I bear record [witness] of myself, *yet* [*omit*
yet] my record [witness] is true: for I know whence I came, and whither I go: but
15 ye cannot tell [know not] whence I come, and [or][16] whither I go. Ye judge after
16 the flesh, I judge no man. And yet if I judge [But even if I myself judge], my
17 judgment is true:[17] for I am not alone, but I and the Father that sent me. It is
also [Moreover, it is] written in your law, that the testimony of two men is true.
18 I am one that bear [he who beareth] witness of myself; and the Father that sent
me, beareth witness of me. Then said they [They said therefore] unto him, Where
19 is thy Father? Jesus answered, Ye neither know [neither] me, nor my Father:
if ye had known me, ye should have known [would know] my Father also.

20 These words spake Jesus [he][18] in the treasury, as he taught [while teaching] in
the temple: and no man [no one] laid hands on him, for his hour was [had] not
yet come.
21 Then said Jesus again [Again therefore he said] unto them, I go my way [I go
away], and ye shall [will] seek me [in vain], and shall [will] die in your sins [sin]:
22 whither I go, ye cannot come. Then [Therefore] said the Jews, Will he kill him-
23 self? because he saith, Whither I go, ye cannot come. And he said to them, Ye
are from beneath; I am from above; ye are of this world; I am not of this world.
24 I said therefore unto you, that ye shall [will] die in your sins: for if ye believe not
25 that I am *he*, ye shall [will] die in your sins. Then [Therefore] said they unto
him, Who art thou? And Jesus saith unto them, Even *the same* that I said unto
you from the beginning [For the beginning; or, To begin with (*I am*) that which
26 I even say to you].[19] I have many things to say, and to judge of you [before I fully
express myself concerning myself]: but he that sent me, is true; and I speak[20] to the
27 world those things which I have heard of him [what I heard from him]. They
28 understood not that he spake [spoke] to them of the Father. Then [Therefore]
said Jesus unto them, When ye have lifted up the Son of man, then shall [will]
ye know that I am *he*, and *that* I do nothing of myself, but as my[21] Father
29 hath taught me, I speak these things. And he that sent me is with me: the
Father [he][22] hath not left me alone; for I do always those [the] things that
please him.
30 As he spake [spoke] these words, many believed on [in] him.

TEXTUAL AND GRAMMATICAL.

[The whole section concerning the adulteress, from chap. vii. 53 to viii. 11, is omitted as spurious, or bracketted as doubtful by the critical editors of the Gr. Test. Hence I have italicized the E. V. to distinguish it from the undisputed text. (The same course should be pursued with Mark xvi. 9 ff.) Without anticipating the very full and judicious discussion of the genuineness by Dr. Lange in the EXEG. AND CRIT. below, I shall only state the chief authorities for both opinions, and the conclusion to which I have attained:

1. The section is defended as genuine by Augustine (who comments on it in *Tract.* xxxiii., and suggests, in another place, *De conj. adult.*, II. 7, that it was thrown out of the text by enemies or weak believers from fear that it might encourage their wives to infidelity), Mill, Whitby, Fabricius, Lampe, Maldonatus, Corn. a Lapide, Bengel, Michaelis, Storr, Kuinoel, Hug (R. C.), Scholz, Klee, Maier (R. C.), Horne, Owen, Webster and Wilkinson, Wieseler, Ebrard, Stier, Lange.

2. It is rejected as an interpolation (though not on that account as untrue) by Erasmus, Calvin (?), Beza, Grotius, Wetstein, Semler, Paulus, Knapp, Lücke, Tholuck, Olshausen, Bleek, De Wette, Baur, Reuss, Luthardt, Meyer, Ewald, Hengstenberg (who regards it as an apocryphal fiction of some strongly anti-Jewish Christian of the second century), Godet, Wordsworth (?), Scrivener. So also Lachmann, Tischendorf, Tregelles, Alford, Wescott and Hort.

The *prevailing critical* evidence, though mostly negative (especially from the Eastern Church), is *against* the passage, the *moral* evidence *for* it; in other words, it seems to be no original part of John's *written* Gospel, but the record of an *actual event*, which probably happened about the time indicated by its position in the 8th chapter. The story could not have been invented, the less so as it runs contrary to the ascetic and legalistic tendency of the ancient church which could not appreciate it. It is eminently Christ-like and full of comfort to penitent outcasts. It breathes the Saviour's spirit of holy mercy which condemns the sin and saves the sinner. It is a parallel to the parable of the prodigal, the story of Mary Magdalene and that of the Samaritan woman, and agrees with many express declarations of Christ that He came not to condemn, but to save the lost (John iii. 17; xii. 47; Luke ix. 56; xix. 10; comp. John v. 14; Luke vii. 37 ff.). His refusal to act as judge in the case, has a parallel in a similar case related by Luke xii. 13–15. The conduct of the Scribes and Pharisees in trying Jesus with ensnaring questions is characteristic and sustained by many examples of the synoptical Gospels. Calvin, who is disposed to reject it, admits that it "contains nothing contrary to the apostolic spirit." Meyer (p. 321), while disowning its Johannean origin, says: "It entirely agrees with the tone of the Synoptical Gospels, and betrays not the least indication of a dogmatic or ecclesiastical reason which might account for its later invention." It is moreover so manifestly original, and has so many positive witnesses in its favor, especially in the Western church, that it may be regarded as a genuine relic of the primitive evangelical tradition which was handed down in various recensions, but treated with great caution from fear of abuse in a licentious age, until in the second, certainly in the third, century it found its way into many copies of the Gospel of John. (Comp. Meyer.) Some older critics supposed that it is the same story as that which Papias (perhaps from the mouth of John) related of "a woman taken in *many sins*" (ἐπὶ πολλαῖς ἁμαρτίαις, not one ἁμαρτία, as in our case), and which was contained in "the Gospel of the Hebrews" (Euseb. *H. E.*, III. 39); but this Judaizing Gospel would hardly have given currency to a story so strongly anti-Jewish. Alford suggests that John himself may have, in this solitary case, incorporated a portion of the current *oral* tradition into his narrative; Wordsworth and others, that John delivered the story *orally*, and that another hand wrote it first on the margin from which it afterwards passed into the text. But these are mere conjectures.

The number of readings is unusually large. There are two main recensions, that of the received text (from which the E. V. is made), that of Cod. D. (*Cod. Bezæ*) which is somewhat abridged; both are given with the *lectiones variantes* by Tischendorf, ed. VIII., I. pp. 830-836, and Tregelles, p. 417. To these may be added a third and more lengthy recension of other MSS. differing from those on which the received text is founded (see Griesbach and Wordsworth, p. 309).

For the critical details, the reader is referred to Dr. Lange's discussion below, Lücke's *Com.*, Vol. II., pp. 243-279; Meyer, pp. 320-323; Tregelles on the *Text of the Gr. Test.*, pp. 236-243; Tischendorf (ed. VIII.), Bloomfield's *Recensio Synoptica*, Alford (ed. VI.), and Wordsworth.—P. S.]

[1] Ver. 1.—[Δέ, unquestioned in the original, does not appear in the English Version.]

[2] Ver. 2.—Codd. G. S. U., ὄχλος; not decisive against λαός.

[3] Ibid.—[Cod. D. omits the words of the text. rec. καὶ καθίσας ἐδίδασκεν αὐτούς. Not decisive.]

[4] Ver. 3.—Cod. D.: ἐπὶ ἁμαρτίᾳ γυναῖκα εἰλ. [instead of ἐν μοιχείᾳ]. Euphony.

[5] Ver. 4.—[The insertion is from Cod. D.: λέγουσιν αὐτῷ ἐκπειράζοντες αὐτὸν οἱ ἱερεῖς, ἵνα ἔχωσιν κατηγορείαν αὐτοῦ. The text. rec. omits these words here, but has them in ver. 6. Cod. M. has them at the close of ver. 11.—P. S.]

[6] Ver. 6.—[Different readings and spellings: κατειλήφθη (aor. I., with *augmentum* for κατελήφθη, as εἴληφα stands instead of the unusual λέληφα, see Winer, p. 69), κατελήφθη, κατείληπται, εἴληπται, κατειλημμένην, καταληφθεῖσαν.—P. S.]

[7] Ver. 6.—[This clause must be omitted here, if it is inserted with Cod. D. in ver. 4.—P. S.]

[8] Ibid.—In E. G. K., μὴ προσποιούμενος is added. In others, καὶ προσπ. Both exegetical.

[9] Ver. 8.—[The rec. omits here τῷ δακτύλῳ, which Cod. D. supplies. Cod. U. and others have the strange addition: ἑνὸς ἑκάστου αὐτῶν τὰς ἁμαρτίας.—P. S.]

[10] Ver. 9.—E. G. H., *etc.*, omit ἕως τῶν ἐσχάτων; D. and others: ὥστε πάντας ἐξελθεῖν. [Alford in his version adopts the reading of Cod. D.: "But each of the *Jews* went out, beginning with the elders, *so that all went out.*"—P. S.]

[11] Ver. 10.—Καὶ to γυναικός (*and seeing none but the woman*), is wanting in D. M. S.

[12] Ibid.—Ἡ γυνή wanting in D. E. F., *etc.*

[13] Ver. 10.—[Ποῦ εἰσιν; So Cod. D., *etc.* The text. rec. inserts ἐκεῖνοι οἱ κατήγοροί σου.—P. S.]

[14] Ver. 11.—[The text. rec. reads καί, but Cod. D. ἀπὸ τοῦ νῦν which is more forcible.—P. S.]

[15] Ver. 12.—Instead of περιπατήσει, Lachmann and Tischendorf, after Codd. B. C. K. T. have περιπατήσῃ.

[16] Ver. 14.—Codd. D. K. T. and many others read ἤ. The καὶ probably comes from the preceding sentence, [Codd. Sin., καὶ.]

[17] Ver. 16.—B. D. L., *etc.*, ἀληθινή. So Lachmann, Tischendorf [Alford. Cod. Sin. supports here the text. rec., ἀληθής.]

[18] Ver. 20.—The ὁ Ἰησοῦς interpolated after ἐλάλησεν.

[19] Ver. 25.—[On this difficult passage and its many interpretations, see the EXEG. AND CRIT. Alford renders τὴν ἀρχὴν ὅτι καὶ λαλῶ ὑμῖν: *In very deed* (or *essentially*), *that which I also speak* (*discourse*) *unto you.* Noyes: *In the first place, I am just that which I speak to you.* Am. B. U. (Conant): *That which I also say to you from the beginning.* Lange: *Furs. Erste das, was ich auch euch sage* (*sagen mag*).—P. S.]

[20] Ver. 26.—B. D. K., Lachmann, Tischendorf: λαλῶ, instead of λέγω. [Cod. Sin., λαλῶ.]

[21] Ver. 28.—Μου, an interpolation, according to many authorities [Cod. Sin. among them].

[22] Ver. 29.—According to B. D. L., *etc.*, ὁ πατήρ should be dropped. [Cod. Sin. has it, but instead of μετ' ἐμοῦ ἐστίν· οὐκ ἀφῆκέ με μόνον, reads οὐκ ἀφῆκέ με μόνον· μετ' ἐμοῦ ἐστίν.]

A. CHAPTER VIII. 1–11.

[CHRIST AND THE ADULTERESS, AND THEIR ACCUSERS.]

EXEGETICAL AND CRITICAL.

DISCUSSION OF THE GENUINENESS OF THIS SECTION.—The difficulty of handling the question of the genuineness of this section, we have already indicated in the Introduction [p. 31]; and we have there indicated also the present state of the question. Four points are to be considered: 1. The authorities. 2. The condition of the text. 3. The historical connection of the occurrence. 4. The connection of the section with what precedes and what follows.

1. "Griesbach and Schultz give a list of more than a hundred manuscripts in which the pericope appears.* Among them are D. G. H. K. M. U.† Jerome, in his day, asserts that the pericope appears in many Greek manuscripts,‡ and some scholia appeal to ἀρχαῖα ἀντίγραφα," *etc.* Lücke. On the contrary, "the majuscules B. C. L. T. do not contain the passage;§ neither do the older manuscripts of the Peshito, nor the Nestorian manuscripts; and it is certain that it was not translated into Syriac till the sixth century. Of the manuscripts of the Philoxenian version, in which it occurs, some have it only on the margin, and others have it in the text with the note that it is not everywhere found. So in most manuscripts of the Coptic version, and in the Arabic version which was based upon the Coptic, we seek it in vain. Of the manuscripts of the Armenian version, some have it not, others have it at the end of the Gospel. In the Sahidic and Gothic versions it is also wanting. Among the fathers, the Greek expositors Origen, Cyril of Alexandria, Chrysostom, Nonnus, Theophylact, entirely omit the pericope, and seem to know nothing of it. So the *Catenæ*, both published and unpublished. Euthymius expounds it, as a προσθήκη which is not without use.‖ The current mention and use of the pericope in the Latin church begins with Ambrose and Augustine." Ibid. "Furthermore, several manuscripts in Griesbach contain the passage, but add either the sign of rejection nor of interpolation. Others put the passage at the end of the Gospel; others again, after chap. vii. 36, or viii. 12; still others place it after Luke xxi. It not rarely appears in the manuscripts mutilated." Ibid.

This position of the authorities presents a great critical problem, which at best makes the section in its present place suspicious; especially when we consider that Origen has not the passage, that Tertullian and Cyprian, when they write on subjects which would bring it in, do not mention it, and that the older manuscripts of the Peshito are without it.

2. The condition of the text. This is the sorest side of the passage. Reading disputes reading. Compare Griesbach, Lachmann, Tischendorf.* "We have three very different texts,—an unheard-of case in the Gospel of John. Besides the received text, Griesbach gives two others: first the text of Cod. D., secondly one compiled from other manuscripts." Lücke. This diversity seems unaccountable, unless a traditional apostolic relic (oral or in Hebrew, or preserved in substance with free variations) was scattered through different copies before it resulted in this passage.

[To this unusual number of variations must be added the entire diversity from the narrative style of John, which Meyer and Alford regard as the most weighty argument *against* the passage. Here belong the terms ὄρθρον, πᾶς ὁ λαός, οἱ γραμματεῖς καὶ οἱ φαρ., ἐπιμένειν, ἀναμάρτητος, καταλείπεσθαι, κατακρίνειν, which are not otherwise used by John, the absence of his usual οὖν which occurs but once in this passage, while δέ is here found eleven times. Hengstenberg misses also the "mystic twilight" which is characteristic of John's style. Upon the whole, the style is more like that of the Synoptists. Tischendorf (ed. VIII. p. 829) says categorically: "*Locum de adultera non ab Johanne scriptum esse certissimum est.*"—P. S.]

3. The historical connection of this with other occurrences in the Gospel.

A. In this respect many doubts have been raised, which must, of course, be carefully weighed.

* [Wordsworth (p. 309) says that it is found in more than 300 cursive MSS.—P. S.]

† [Also E. F. S., but in E. the passage is marked with asterisks in the margin, in S. with obeli. Ten cursive copies put it at the end of John, some insert it at the end of Luke xxi.—P. S.]

‡ ["*In multis et Græcis et Latinis codicibus; Adv. Pelag.*, II. 17. It should also be added that most of the copies of the Itala and Vulgata contain the section.—P. S.]

§ [To which must be added Cod. Sin. Tischendorf (I., p. 826) enumerates the following uncial MSS. as witnesses against the section: א. A. B. C. L. T. X. Δ.; but A. and C. are here defective, and L. and Δ. have an empty space, though not sufficient for the whole passage.—P. S.]

‖ [Euthymius remarks that the pericope from vii. 53 to viii. 12 παρὰ τοῖς ἀκριβέσιν ἀντιγράφοις ἢ οὐχ εὕρηται, ἢ ὠβέλισται. Διὸ φαίνονται παρέγγραπτα καὶ προσθήκη.—P. S.]

* [Also Tregelles, Alford and Wordsworth. Godet (II., 199) says: *Un vari text apostolique n' a jamais été exposé à des altérations si considérable.*—P. S.]

(*a*) That chap. vii. 53 refers to Sanhedrists returning to their houses, not to festal pilgrims returning to their homes, is obvious. This, however, yields a very suitable connection. They had expected Christ to be brought before their bar, and now were compelled—to go home disappointed and divided.

(*b*) The statement in chap. viii. 1, that Jesus went unto the mount of Olives. It is thought that this method of securing Himself against the snares of His enemies was not employed by Jesus till the time of the last passover. Yet the fact that this was necessary is here evident enough; for the Sanhedrin was seeking to arrest Him. Lücke's reasoning (p. 255) overlooks this point.

(*c*) Chap. viii. 2: "All the people came unto Him." Even if the great day of the feast, on which Jesus made His last appearance, was the eighth, there would be nothing to prevent all the people who did not immediately leave Jerusalem, from assembling the next day in the temple.

(*d*) The Scribes, γραμματεῖς, who do not elsewhere appear in John, are strange here.* Their appearance here, however, is in keeping with the immediately succeeding fact that a question of the law comes up; the strangeness of it is not decisive. Other differences of expression are less important (see Lücke, p. 257).

(*e*) It seems not clear whether the Scribes appear as witnesses, or as accusers, or as judges. Plainly as accusers, or as judges who would refer their decision, in irony, to the tribunal of Jesus; not as zealots, according to Wetstein.

(*f*) There is no mention of the adulterer (Lev. xx. 10; Deut. xxii. 22, 24). This signifies nothing at all.

(*g*) According to the Rabbins the legal punishment of adultery was strangulation (Lücke, p. 259). On this point Michaelis has justly denied the authority of the Talmud, and has asserted, on a comparison of Ex. xxxi. 14; xxxv. 2 with Nu. xv. 32-35, that the formula *put to death*, generally means stoned. Besides, strangulation is frequently used first only as an alleviation of the prescribed penalty, as in the burning in the middle ages.

(*h*) But what temptation was there in the question? Chiefly the fact that Jesus had not yet officially declared Himself Messiah, while He nevertheless was largely acknowledged as such among the people, and seemed Himself to give occasion for such recognition. The procedure with the adulteress was, therefore, in its very form, a temptation to Him to declare Himself concerning His authority (with reference to Moses). Then in the matter of the case lay a further temptation, to wit, in the conflict between the so-called commandment of the law on the one hand, and the prevailing milder practice and the known gentleness of Christ on the other. To this question, however, we must return.

B. But now the apparently strange features are offset by a number, which speak for the genuineness of the narrative.

(*a*) The feast of tabernacles was pre-eminently a joyous popular feast of the Jews; it was celebrated in the good time of the year; such a sin as the one here narrated, might easily occur.

(*b*) The writing of Jesus on the ground is so peculiar a feature, that it would hardly have been fabricated.

(*c*) The same may be said of His challenge; "He that is without sin among you," *etc.*, and of His closing word to the woman.

[(*d*) the peculiarity of the whole incident, as presenting to the Lord a case of actual sin on its direct merits, is in its favor. Such an incident might be said to meet a want, or at least to fill a place of its own, in the gospel history. And if such an incident occurred at all, John would be the Evangelist most likely to notice and record it; since he is the one to record the somewhat kindred issue raised by the disciples over the man born blind, chap. ix. With so many cases of actual human misery, and of general sinfulness, brought before the Lord for His treatment, "whether in pretence or in truth," and with various hypothetical cases of conscience put to Him, it would seem suitable that we should have one case of actual and flagrant crime.—E. D. Y.]

Nothing, therefore, can be adduced against the details of the story or its connection with other facts of the Gospels; it is even a question, whether there are not special data in its favor.

4. As to the connection of the section with the preceding and following portions of the Gospel: It is clear that the story of the adulteress in this place not only introduces no disturbance, but even serves to elucidate the discourse of Christ in chap. viii. 12 sqq. The woman had walked in darkness; her judges had admitted that they found themselves in darkness in regard to the disposal of this case; but for the very purpose of making an assault of the power of darkness upon the Lord with their captious question. This connection does not exclude a further reference to the temple-lights and the torch-light festivities in the celebration of the feast of tabernacles.

One of the principal questions is the question of internal criticism: Is it conceivable that the Jewish rulers would so early make a captious attack upon the Lord by an ironical concession of His Messiahship? We must here, in the first place, remember that the enemies of Jesus at the last passover made a whole round, a very storm, of such assaults upon Jesus (*Leben Jesu*, II. 3, p. 1218). The situation there was this: They first endeavored, by their authority, to confound Him before the people in the temple-enclosure with the question, by what power He thus appeared; but He baffled them with counter-questions. He maintained His position before the people, and seemed unimpeachable; while they were impotent. Then they had recourse to craft; they ironically assumed that He was the Messiah, in order to catch Him in entangling questions. It is now asked, Is it conceivable, that they had already attempted this trick before? In the Synoptical Gospels there could be no mention of this, because they relate only the last attendance of Jesus at a feast. But in John we should expect earlier attacks of the same sort to be mentioned, if any had occurred. A decisive preliminary question, however, is this: How came the Jewish rulers to their diabolical irony

* [John names the Pharisees twenty times,—four times in connection with the *chief priests*, but never with the *Scribes* as here.—P. S.]

and the ensnaring questions which proceeded from it? The history answers: by the sense of impotence which came with the perception that with force and authority they accomplished nothing.

This condition already existed here at the feast of tabernacles, when even the officers who had been sent to take Jesus, returned paralyzed by His word and unsuccessful, and when a division began to appear even in the Sanhedrin itself. The impotent embarrassment of force was there, and with it the devilish counsel of craft.

Accordingly this maneuvre was thrice repeated; first at the feast of tabernacles as recorded in this section; then at the feast of dedication in the winter, as recorded in chap. x. 24; finally at the last passover, when these tempting proposals became so thick, that we may well infer the rulers of the Jews had accustomed themselves to it by former practice. Of course in this first instance their assumption of His Messiahship is very equivocal; it does not reach the full measure of its insolence till the last passover.

But the same condition of things which brought the rulers of the Jews to this stratagem—that is, the previous failure of their forcible attempt,—led Jesus, for the purpose of security, to withdraw for the night to the mount of Olives. He would therefore be here just in the right place according to chap. viii. 1.

That the gospel history thus gains much in life-like development, connected progress, is palpable. And at the same time the exhibition of the Jewish feasts in their religious and moral degeneracy becomes more complete. We have already observed that, in the view of John, the tragic dissolution of Judaism in the gradual completion of the murderous design of the Jews against Christ at their successive feasts. This is the one side; the other is the religious and moral decay of the people themselves, which comes to light at the great feasts. At the passover, the great passover of the Jews, this decay manifests itself in the transfer of the whole traffic in sacrificial animals and money into the temple itself, chap. ii. At the feast of Purim, the feast of brotherhood and deliverance, it shows itself in the leaving of the sick without attendance, help, or sympathy in their Bethesda, chap. v. The feast of tabernacles, the great feast of popular thanksgiving and joy, appears defiled by licentiousness, scenes of adultery, and partizan, temporizing policy among the Pharisees (who here let the guilty *man* run free), chap. viii., while the blind brother is left to beggary and Pharisaic alms, chap. ix., against the law of Deut. xv. 4. The feast of dedication, chap. x. 22, seems not distinguished by any similar mark of corruption, unless it is symbolical that the storm of winter blows through Spirit-forsaken halls which the Spirit of Christ alone still quickens, and that the multitude of the people, who at other times always gathered to protect the Lord, have fled before wind and weather, so that the Jews can suddenly surround Him, and at last propose to bury him under a heap of stones in the middle of the very court of the temple.

Internal evidence, therefore, speaks decidedly for this, as the proper place for the section in hand. If the alternative is, either that the tradition of the early church for definite reasons partially overlooked and then dropped this section, or that it inserted the passage here as an ancient relic of Ephesian tradition from John,—the former theory is not more difficult than the latter. Indeed the prevalence of the ascetic spirit in the church might almost make the omission of a larger section of this character more probable than insertion. We observe a late interpolation of a few words in 1 John v. 7 and 8. We consider the passage, 2 Pet. i. 20 to iii. 2, an interpolation, but entirely taken in substance from the Epistle of Jude (*Apostol. Zeitalter*, I., p. 155). On the other hand, the conclusion of Mark, chap. xvi. 9, seems to afford an example of omission rather than of interpolation. Now it is easy to imagine that the centuries of ascetic austerity, from the end of the second century to the end of the fourth, might scruple to read in public this passage, in which the guilt of adultery *seemed* to be so leniently dealt with.

We must, therefore, by all means consider any words of the fathers which speak of such a scruple. Ambrose: *Profecto si quis ea auribus otiosis accipiat, erroris incentivum erroris incurrit* [*quum legit . . . adulteræ absolutionem. Lubrica igitur ad lapsum via*] (*Apol. Davidis posterior*, chap. i.). Augustine: *Hoc infidelium sensus exhorret, ita ut nonnulli modicæ vel potius inimici veræ fidei, credo, metuentes peccandi impunitatem dari mulieribus suis, illud quod de adulteræ indulgentia Dominus fecit, auferrent de codicibus suis, quasi permissionem peccandi tribuerit, qui dixit: "Deinceps noli peccare"* (*De adulterinis conjugiis*, II. 7). Nicon [from the 10th century in Coteler. *Patr. Apost.*, I. 238]: The Armenians expunged the pericope from their version: *βλαβερὰν εἶναι λέγοντες τοῖς πολλοῖς τὴν τοιαύτην ἀκρόασιν* (see Lücke, p. 249). Augustine's declaration we have only to change from one of pastoral animadversion to one of historical criticism. The scruple was begotten not of the interested unbelief of some individual husbands, but of the ascetic, weak faith of a legalistic age. (Against this Lücke, p. 248 and 252, can bring nothing that amounts to more than assertion.)*

It may be supposed that the disuse of the passage passed through different stages. 1. The narrative stood in its place, but was left standing and passed over in the public readings, or in discussions of the question of marriage. The ascetic Tertullian could form a very suitable predecessor to Cyprian in such a step, and Origen an equally suitable predecessor to others. 2. Next, perhaps, the pericope began to undergo improvement by other readings (*e. g.*, Cod. D, *ἐπὶ ἁμαρτίᾳ* instead of *ἐν μοιχείᾳ*), and especially abbreviation. 3. Some transcribers then went further, and transferred the pericope to the end of the Gospel as an appendix. 4. This led to the last stage of entire omission. But now the codices

* [Wordsworth also urges this point, especially the severe discipline of the Eastern church towards adultery. According to Bingham (*Antiqu.* XVI., chap. 11), S. Basil's Canons prescribe fifteen years' penance for adultery, the Council of Ancyra seven years', the Council of Eliberis (in Spain) five years' for a single act, and ten if repeated. Webster and Wilkinson: "The views of the fathers of the nature and objects of Christ's mission, and of the distinction between the covenants of the law and the gospel, were imperfect and limited . . . If the story appeared improbable, from moral considerations, to expositors of the third and fourth century, it would appear far more so, on the same grounds, to those of the seventh and eighth."—P. S.]

which had kept the pericope reacted. The passage came to be inserted again in various places, either where we have it now, or after chap. vii. 36, or after chap. viii. 12, or, with the view of combining this temptation with those of the last passover, after Luke xxi. In this process some accepted it with a mark of addition or even of rejection. From this twofold procedure the critical confusion in regard to this section resulted.

In any case the passage is an apostolic relic.*

But another thing in favor of the genuineness of it is the *πάλιν οὖν αὐτοῖς ἐλάλησεν ὁ Ἰησοῦς*, chap. viii. 12, and the *εἶπεν οὖν πάλιν αὐτοῖς*, ver. 21. The words in viii. 21 literally refer to the words of vii. 34. It is harder to see the reference of the first *πάλιν*, if we have to take in the idea; "I am the light of the world." The Lord, however, already implied this to them in chap. v. 35, 36 sqq. John was a light, and yet only a witness to Christ who was appointed for their deliverance, ver. 40. Apart from this, the terms of chap. viii. 12: "Then spake Jesus again unto them,"—must be taken absolutely, meaning simply that He addressed them again. In other words: by their attack upon His life they had, in all reason, already brought His intercourse with them to a close. But then, chap. viii. 1-11, they had apparently relented, and though He knew that their question was put to Him in malicious hypocrisy, yet He let it pass in the official form which it assumed before the people. He was committed to the people, after this recognition of the rulers, to resume intercourse with them; but that He might soon say to them once more, that He shall forsake them and give them up. Thus the two occurrences of *πάλιν* in chap. viii. form, in our view, a distinct demand for the section concerning the adulteress.

As to the opponents, as well as the advocates, of the genuineness of this passage, compare Lücke, p. 243, and Meyer [p. 320-323, 5th ed.].

Ver. 1. **Jesus went unto the mount of Olives.**—This retirement for the night to the mount of Olives (Gethsemane or Bethany) was caused by the direct demonstration of the Sanhedrin against the freedom and life of Jesus. At the same time it forms a significant counterpart to the words: "Every man went unto his own house." To them everything, meantime, remained in the old way; but not to Him, for He saw further. During His last residence in Jerusalem this method of spending the night in the mount of Olives appears as a fixed rule, Luke xxi. 37.

Ver. 2. **And early in the morning.**—Ὄρθρου. John writes elsewhere *πρωΐ* (chap. xviii. 28; xx. 1; *πρωΐα*, chap. xxi. 4), Luke, on the contrary, *ὄρθρου*. It is to be observed here, however, that the term *ὄρθρου* denotes more precisely the dawn of morning, and that it is intended to denote just this time. **And all the people.**—Πᾶς ὁ λαός. If John elsewhere prefers *ὁ ὄχλος*, *the multitude*, or *οἱ ὄχλοι*, *the multitudes*, we must consider that He here intends to signalize the gathering of the whole remaining mass of festal pilgrims to Jesus in the temple. The same may be said respecting the *καθίσας ἐδίδασκ. αὐτ.* [which is not used by John]; He again set Himself right down among them, as if He wished to begin again, after He had provisionally foiled the attack of the Sanhedrists. That the *γραμματεῖς*, the *scribes*, are here named, though not elsewhere, arises from the fact that a question of scriptural law comes up in the sequel. And the frequently recurring *δέ*, too, instead of the Johannean *οὖν*, has an internal reason in the great series of unexpected incidents which here begins. That Jesus goes to the mount of Olives, is accounted for by the beginning of the hostile machinations, ver. 1. That He returns to the temple in spite of the persecution (ver. 2), is due to the fact that the scribes and Pharisees now make as if they would acknowledge Him (ver. 3), though they mean only to tempt Him, ver. 6. The like may be said of most of the subsequent occurrences thus introduced. Only the great accumulation of the *δέ* seems certainly strange; but in these unusual turns there was less occasion for an *οὖν*.

Ver. 3. **And the scribes and Pharisees brought unto him**, *etc.*—Certainly not as a distinct act of zealotry (Wetstein); nor as a formal deputation of the Sanhedrin. Probably it is the committee of a particular synagogue-court, with which on the one hand the zealots who had taken the woman in her crime, leagued themselves as witnesses, and which, on the other hand, acts in concert with the Sanhedrin. The case was just now brought before a Jewish court; it is thought well fitted to be made a trap for the Lord, by an ironical concession, for reasons above-mentioned, that He is the one to decide it. The party cannot be described as "not official" (Meyer), because in that case it could not have deferred its judgment to the Lord. As the death-penalty was involved, the Sanhedrin must have been in concert.

Ver. 5. **Taken in the very act.**—Ἐπαυτοφώρῳ, *i. e.*, *ἐπὶ* [*ἐπ'*] *αὐτοφώρῳ*, *in ipso furto.** "The man, who was likewise liable to death (Lev. xx. 10; Deut. xxii. 24), might have escaped." Meyer. Though stoning, according to Deut. xxii. 23, 24, was ordered for the particular case in which a betrothed bride yielded herself to unchastity (because she was regarded as already the wife of her spouse), it does not follow that this guilty woman must have been a betrothed *bride* (Meyer), since in the passage referred to the death-penalty uniformly appointed for adulteresses (Lev. xx. 10; Deut. xxii. 22) seems only to be more particularly described (Michaelis, Tholuck, Ewald, and others). The sentence of the Talmud: *Filia Israelitæ si adultera, cum nupta, strangulanda, cum desponsata, lapidanda*, on the one hand cannot be decisive for that period, on the other may only mean a modification of the general penalty of stoning for a *nupta*.

Ver. 6. **Tempting him.**—That this means a malicious temptation, not innocent questioning (Olshausen), the clear sense of the term in other places proves. But wherein consisted the precarious alternative, which was to entangle Him? Interpretations: 1. The antagonism between the

* See *Leben Jesu*, II., p. 952; Hitzig, *Ueber Joh. Mark.*, p. 208 sqq.; and Meyer's designation of it as an "apocryphal document" is therefore extremely unbecoming. [In his fifth edition (p. 320), Meyer does not call it so, but rather "*ein aus der apostolischen Zeit herrührendes Schriftstück, eine uralte Reliquie evangelischer Geschichte.*"—P. S.]

* [Also the adjective *αὐτόφωρος*, *caught in the very theft*, and generally *in the very act.*—P. S.]

Roman criminal law, which did not punish adultery with death, and the law of Moses. Their expectation was that He would declare Himself for Moses against the Roman law, and then they would accuse Him to the Romans. Hence the σὺ οὖν τί λέγεις, ver. 5. A plan, therefore, similar to that of the question about tribute-money, Matt. xxii. (Schulthess, Meyer). It is nothing against this, as Lücke thinks, that the criminal law of the Romans in the provinces did not override the peculiar customs or ordinances of the respective peoples. But this interpretation is, no doubt, opposed by the fact that a declaration of the woman's being worthy of death might be joined with a reference of the plaintiffs to the legal court, besides the fact that they would either have to execute the penalty themselves, or, as informers against Jesus, openly violate the precept of Moses.

2. The issue lay between the traditional tribunal of the people and the supposed new tribunal of the Messiah: the question being, whether Jesus would leave the decision to the ordinary course, or would at once take it upon Himself. Undoubtedly this was a leading point in the temptation; this gave the temptation its form (see above); but it was not the whole of it (Baumgarten-Crusius, *et al.*).

3. The alternative was the old, strict letter of the law, and the looser popular practice which had gained prevalence, which no longer visited adultery with death; hence the question of a judicial process or none at all (Ebrard). But with this alternative in full view their question would have condemned themselves. The popular practice had a sort of indulgent tradition on its side.

4. The alternative was the Mosaic law literally applied and the known gentleness of Christ. A negative answer would appear, therefore, as in contradiction with Moses; an affirmative answer, as in contradiction with Himself (Augustine, Erasmus, Luther, and others). A modification of this view is, that they certainly expected the lenient decision, in order to charge Him with opposition to Moses (Euthymius, Bengel, Neander, *et al.*). This modification increases the tangling dilemma. But this was not simply an issue between the rigor of Moses and the mildness of Christ; it had reference to the old legislation of Moses and the new reformation of the law by Christ as opposed to the traditional practice of the Jews. If He had simply affirmed the Mosaic letter, He would have invaded the rabbinical tradition and practice, the existing order of things, the popular opinion and feeling concerning Himself; they would have turned the tradition against Him. If He had affirmed the popular practice, they would have turned the letter of Scripture against Him. But they wished above all things to find out whether He would venture, with Messianic authority, to lay down a new law. On another interpretation, by Dick (*Stud. und Krit.*, 1832), and Baur's view, see Meyer.

And with his finger wrote* on the ground.†—Some manuscripts, such as E. K., add μὴ προσποιούμενος [*dissimulans*], others καὶ προσποιούμενος [*simulans*]; that is, according to Lücke, in the one case: not merely feigning; in the other: only feigning. Manifestly exegetical additions. According to the correct interpretation of Euthymius Zigabenus, the whole act of stooping down and writing on the ground was symbolical, and was meant to express inattention to the questioners before Him. Lücke: "This gesture was familiar to antiquity as a representation of deep musing, perplexity or languor of mind;" see the examples in Lücke, p. 269, note 1, where Wetstein also is quoted. It is, therefore, contrary to the spirit of the text to ask what Jesus might have written (Michaelis: the answer: "As it is written" Bede: the sentence in ver. 7; conjectures in Wolf and Lampe).*

If we ask, why Jesus does not here enter upon the question, as He did in like cases at the last passover,—it is not enough to answer, that He would not interfere in civil matters (Matt. xxii.; Lu. xii. 13 sq., Meyer), or that He would intimate that the question was too malicious to deserve an answer (Luthardt). We have rather to consider that He has not yet received His distinct introduction as Messiah in Jerusalem by the public hosanna, and now abstains from any official offer of Himself as Messiah, and indeed intends not to appear at all as Messiah, according to their idea. Therefore, as this matter is still in suspense, He also leaves His position towards their question in suspense; He neither rejects nor accepts it. But He certainly does already assume the expression of a calm majesty which is not pleased to have its leisure and recreation intruded upon with a street scandal. If they really take Him for the Messiah, they must consent to this.

Ver. 7. He that is without sin among you, *etc.*†—The test just named, they stand. They continue in their questioning. Hence He now gives them the New Testament decision,

* [κατέγραφεν or ἔγραφεν, a descriptive imperfect, *He kept writing*.—P. S.]

† [This minute circumstance Hengstenberg considers as a mark of fiction unworthy of Christ; Meyer, Stier and Alford, correctly as a mark of originality. The hypocritical malignant questioners well deserved this contemptuous treatment. Writing or figuring on the ground may indicate ennui or distraction of mind or embarrassment or deep reflection or intentional indifference to what is going on. The last case is the only one that is applicable to Jesus, and the gesture here has the same meaning as His words, Matt. xxii. 18: *Why tempt ye me, ye hypocrites?* (Comp. also Luke xii. 14.) This disregard and rebuke implied in the act itself, is the thing essential, not the words or signs written; else they would have been recorded. It is therefore idle to ask what He wrote on the ground.—P. S.]

* [Some MSS. add after the word κατέγραφεν (ver. 8): *the sins of every one of them.* Wordsworth: An emblem that the law which He Himself had given, had been written on earthly and stony hearts. Very fanciful. Lightfoot and Besser: the curses written by the priest against unfaithful women, Num. v. 17. Augustine and others: reference to Jer. xvii. 13: "They that depart from me shall be written in the earth." Wolf and Lampe, like Bede, conjecture that He wrote the sentence in ver. 7; Godet: the sentence of the judge which must be written. But Christ evidently did not wish to listen to them or to act as judge, and when asked the second time, He did not answer their question about the woman, but reminded them of their own sins.—P. S.]

† [Owen remarks on this verse: "This is one of the most profound and searching remarks to be found in the whole gospel. 'Who are you that you should be so clamorous for the meting out of punishment to this woman? Have you no sins of your own to be repented of? Is it your appropriate task to sit in judgment upon your fellow-men, as though you yourselves were perfect and deputed of God to do this? Look to your own hearts, inspect your own conduct in the light of God's law (Matt. v. 28, 32), and be less solicitous in respect to the exact degree or kind of punishment to be meted out to your fellow-men.'"—P. S.]

"Without sin." As ἀναμάρτητος, *sinless*, occurs only this once in the New Testament (though frequently in classic usage), it cannot be made into an inconsistency with the style of John. How is the word "*without* sin," to be understood?

1. Erasmus, Zuingle, Calvin, Baur, Hase [Owen] make it absolute sinlessness. Hase therefore thinks that the answer is a proof of the apocryphal nature of the section; so do Paulus and Baur, since the demand that only sinless men alone should act as judges and pronounce sentence, is utterly inadmissible.

2. Meyer [p. 330], after Lücke: "Whether He means freedom from the *possibility* of fault (of error or of sin), like Plato in *Pol.* I. p. 339 B., or freedom from *actual* fault [comp. γυνὴ ἀναμάρτητος, Herod. v. 39]; and likewise, whether He means this latter in *general* (2 Macc. viii. 4), or in respect to a *particular category* or *species* of sin (2 Macc. xii. 42; Deut. xxix. 19), is to be decided solely by the context. And here freedom from sin must be understood, not indeed of *adultery* specifically, because Jesus could not presume this of the whole hierarchy even in view of all their moral corruption; but of *unchastity*, because one guilty of this stands in question and before the eyes of all as an actual opposite of ἀναμάρτητος [sinless one]. Compare ἁμαρτωλός, Lu. vii. 37. Ἁμαρτάνειν, Jacobs' *ad Anthol.* X., p. 111; and in chap. v. 14, in μηκέτι ἁμάρτατε, a specific sort of sinning is meant; and the same injunction given in ver. 11 to the adulteress, is the authentic commentary on this ἀναμάρτητος." So De Wette also, and Tholuck [and Alford]. Yet Lücke (and De Wette likewise) takes in addition the moral point of view: Jesus would not trench upon the office of civil justice; He looked at the case solely in its moral aspect and with reference to the βασιλεία τοῦ θεοῦ (Luther: "Therefore we have preaching in the kingdom of Christ, and when this preaching comes, it supersedes swords, judge, and all").

The question is: In what relation did Christ place Christian morality to the theocratic civil law of Moses? And here it must be remembered that, with the Pharisees, the idea of being a sinner, and of being without sin, had reference to the law. *Publicans and sinners* are such as are fallen under Levitical discipline, liable to excommunication. But now the Levitical discipline was, according to the spirit of the law, so ideal that, strictly taken, it made every one necessarily unclean (see Hag. ii. 12 sqq.; our Comm. on Matt. chap. iii.). And this is most especially true with regard to sexual impurities and offences. The law, therefore, in its full ideal consistency, could not be carried out; and the mitigations of it in practice partook not only, on the one hand, of laxity, but, on the other, of moral earnestness, which must scorn to apply the law with hypocritical rigor in particular cases, when it could not apply it consistently in all. (Luther and Zwingle had scruples about the discipline of church law in similar consistency.) Christ, therefore, by His word, approves the prevalent leniency, but at the same time leads His hearers back to the principle of the ideal stringency.

His expression means, in the first place: Whosoever among you knows himself to be Levitically clean, particularly in respect of sexual defilements and unchastity, let him begin the execution of the penalty upon the woman. It presumes that no one will venture to proceed, and the conscience of the accusers must sanction this judgment. Then, secondly, in this actual impossibility of restoring the Mosaic rigorism is couched the deeper moral principle, that, in the Christian point of view, any condemnation of a guilty person by a host of accusers and judges who deem themselves guiltless, must be abandoned. For it must be considered that the legal condemnation presupposed this guiltlessness, and, at the same time that theocratic penalty of death stood for damnation (the cutting off of its soul from its people). Christ could no longer recognize either the innocence of those supposed to be clean, nor the liability of the culprit to damnation (which in fact the Mosaic system had only aimed to exhibit symbolically). The Old Testament had now unfolded itself into the New, which laid down on the one hand, the liability of all, even of human judges, to damnation, and on the other hand, the capacity of all even of the fallen, for salvation.

This, however, in the third place, does not supersede human acquittal and condemnation; it only shows that they must proceed upon a new basis (sympathy of the sentence with the sinner) and caution against hasty and over-stringent judgment). How, far, then, this principle should allow the civil punishment of seduced or infatuated women, Christ leaves to the future, but intimates that, on the part of severity, stringency and pride, there is a motive equally ready to hold the culprit to punishment. It was itself a death-penalty, that the adulteress was socially outlawed and condemned.

It must further be considered how singularly Christ distributes His decision between Himself and the appellants or Jewish court. He states the principle, that is the vital idea of the law; but they are left to apply it according to their best knowledge and conscience: First judge themselves, then others.

Let him be the first to cast a stone at her [not the first stone; βαλέτω, not only permission, but command].—According to Deut. xvii. 7, the witnesses were to cast the first stone. But here the first one means him who will have the courage to condemn as being himself innocent.—According to the Rabbins the first blow struck the breast, often with fatal effect.

Ver. 8. **And again he stooped down.**—The Prophet, the Messiah, had solved His problem and returned to His rest, and represented His leisure in symbolical recreation, that they may understand that it now rests with them to act, that is, in the first place to condemn themselves. *He* is discharged of the matter. And as He has previously not looked nor glanced at the woman in her conscience of guilt, so He now does the same with them. Jerome: He would give them room to make their escape. [Inconsistent with ver. 6.]

Ver. 9. [**They went out**, ἐξήρχοντο, descriptive imperfect.—**One by one**, εἷς καθ' εἷς, or εἱς καθεἱς (instead of καθ' ἕνα). A later Greek formula.—The preposition is here adverbial. Comp. Mark xiv. 19; Rom. xii. 5; Acts.

xxi. 21; the Hebrew לְאַחַר אַחֵר, and Winer, p. 234.—P. S.].—**Being convicted by their own conscience.**—Tholuck: "It is historically attested, that at that time many prominent Rabbins were living in adultery." Wagenseil on the *Sota*, p. 525. And some of them must have feared that when He should lift up Himself again, they might hear something further, which would be still less pleasant (Musculus).

Beginning at the eldest.*—Fritzsche and others construe so as to make ἀρξάμ. ἀπὸ τ. πρεσβυτέρ. substantially a parenthesis; the main statement being, that they went out even to the last; this being more particularly described by the parenthesis; the eldest made the beginning. Winer and Tholuck: They went out, the eldest leading off; and the ἕως τ. ἐσχ. is a breviloquent addition. The former interpretation seems clearer; and in many manuscripts this last addition is wanting. The eldest went out first, partly because of a guilty conscience, partly because they were the more shrewd. Is not πρεσβύτεροι here an official name? This is at least probable, because the group is a judicial one; hence Lücke, De Wette and others take it of rank. Meyer (and Tholuck, 7th ed.), on the contrary: This is not yielded by the contrast; there would then be no proper antithesis; it is a phrase: from the first to the last. But from the oldest to the last is no antithesis. On the contrary, a sufficiently clear antithesis is: from the elders (of the synagogue) to the last, *i. e.* the servants, 1 Cor. iv. 9. The expression: *to the last*, might, however, have been afterwards added, to destroy the definiteness of the term *elders*, which perhaps might have given the section a wrong and offensive bearing in the Christian congregations.

["They went out—what else could they do? Not stop there, with the people gazing alternately at them, and at the finger moving to and fro on the ground! They retreat, but observe how orderly they do it. The Evangelist is careful to inform us that they 'went out, one by one, beginning at the eldest, even unto the last.' Perhaps they hung back for a moment, no one disposed to go first, lest he should thereby seem to betray himself the greatest sinner in the lot. So, to avoid suspicion, they will depart in the order of age. As well-bred men, they give precedence to seniority, the younger bowing out the elder.—'Not before you, sir, reverend Doctor—Rabbi Eliezer, Rabbi Jehudi,' *etc.* They leave; the people staring after them: their long robes and broad phylacteries not quite so imposing as when they came in. They are gone. The court has adjourned. There has been an adjudication, not precisely that for which the court was called. There has been a conviction not of the accused, but of the accusers, and they, self-convicted, not daring to look the Judge in the face, who could see them through and through."—From a sermon of Dr. Mühlenberg on the *Woman and her Accusers.* N. Y., 1867.—P. S.]

Left alone, and the woman.—Only the band of accusers had gotten away; the disciples and the people who were looking on could remain. But that the woman remained standing as if bound, and did not withdraw, seems to show what an impression Jesus made upon her conscience. She stood, as if bound to His judgment-seat.

Ver. 10. **Hath no man condemned thee?**—The οὐδείς is emphatic; but so is the *condemn*, κατακρίνω [not found elsewhere in John]. It denotes the *sententia damnatoria* of theocratic judgment, a sentence of death considered at the same time as a religious reprobation. Meyer remarks that since these people came asking advice, the vote of each one is the only thing intended. But in asking advice they wished to refer to the Lord a judicial sentence, which He referred back to them, and this is therefore the thing in question. Hence it is neither, on the one hand, the actual "stoning" (Wolf) which is meant, nor on the other hand a mere moral condemnation (Tholuck), nor any dismissal of the reference (Meyer).* The people had left the decision to Him, though in irony; and they did the same again, when He in a conditional way cast the decision back upon them. When He now says: if they have desisted from their condemnation, *I also condemn thee not*,—unquestionably He means this in the New Testament sense, as in ch. iii. 17; Matt. xviii. 11. But in this case her acquittal is included in His decision, so far as He interprets the tacit practical verdict of her accusers. This is proved by His next words. This withholding of moral *condemnation* is, however, no withholding of moral *judgment*. Augustine (*Tract.* 33): *Quid est Domine? faves ergo peccatis? Non plane ita. Attende, quod sequitur: 'vade, deinceps jam noli peccare.' Ergo et Dominus damnavit, sed peccatum, non hominem.*" [Ambrose: *Emendavit ream, non crimen absolvit.*—P. S.]

DOCTRINAL AND ETHICAL.

1. See the exegesis particularly on verses 1, 2, 6, 7, *etc.*

2. If the section of the adulteress can be restored to the credit of genuineness, it materially *enriches* the history of the life of Jesus. A systematic view of the progress of the persecution of Jesus by the Sanhedrin commends the theory of its genuineness according to the rules of internal criticism. It would be natural, that the temptation of Jesus which proceeded upon the ironical assumption that He was the Messiah, should form a series and climax. And the conduct of Jesus perfectly accords with the existing state of the Messianic question, on account of His official position towards the question whether He was the Messiah.

3. The *conduct of Christ* in this situation exhibits majestic elevation, calmness, prudence, wisdom, and boldness.

4. The only mention of Jesus' *writing;* and that in the sand of the earth, no one knows what. His usual form of writing was a writing of the law of the Spirit in hearts with the flame of His word.

* [Or as Lange below explains πρεσβύτεροι from the *elders*, the *presbyters* of the synagogue.—P. S.]

* [In his fifth edition, p. 332, Meyer says on οὐδὲ ἐγώ σε κατακρ.: "This is not a sentence of *forgiveness*, like Matt. ix. 2; Luke vii. 48, nor yet a mere *refusal of jurisdiction*, . . . but a *reversal of the condemnation*, in the consciousness of His Messianic mission, which was not to condemn, but to seek and to save the lost, iii. 17; xii. 47; Matt. xviii. 18."—P. S.]

5. *He that is without sin among you:* (1) Acknowledgment of the Mosaic law in their view. Stone her if you please; she has deserved death according to the law of Moses. (2) Assertion of His New Testament ground. But first judge yourselves. Stone her not till one without sin be found who may begin the stoning. (3) Indication of the relation between the Old Testament and New Testament points of view. Christ declares the principle and spirit of the law of Moses. Then they may act according to their best knowledge and conscience. It must not be forgotten that the death penalty according to the letter of the Jewish law was at the same time a reprobation.

The Roman church considers Christ a second Moses, a new law-giver; and according to her He must have given a stricter law of marriage. But with a properly religious legislation a ministry of death also is connected (2 Cor. iii.). And of those who in this view insist on remaining under the law, the words of the apostle in Gal. iii. 10 hold good.

6. On the other hand, here in the group of accusers and judges are fulfilled the words of 1 Pet. iv. 17: "The time is come that judgment must begin at the house of God."

7. Christ can transform the tribunal of the legalists into an asylum of criminals, into a means of repentance and of the call of grace.

8. The New Testament gentleness the source of a New Testament severity in questions of moral conduct.

HOMILETICAL AND PRACTICAL.

The retirement of Christ to the Mount of Olives outside the city of Jerusalem, an example for the persecuted company of believers.—The first temptation of Christ by a show of recognition on the part of the rulers of the Jews.—This temptation compared with the other (subsequent) ones.—The adulteress: or, a life-like and warning scene from the joyous ecclesiastical and popular festivals of Israel.—The law of marriage a favorite question of the Pharisees.—Conjugal infidelities a measure of the spiritual decay of popular life.—The diabolical craft, which would make the show of a holy zeal for the law a snare for the Lord.—Analysis of the temptation: (1) Crafty plotting. Apparent homage was to impose upon them all. (2) Malicious assault they aim not at the execution of the woman, but at the execution of the Lord. (3) Heartless, cruel procedure. The woman, in a form of judicial process no longer practised, was to be sacrificed as a means to an end. (4) Shameless law question. They sought to make either zeal for Moses or an approval of their own tradition and custom a capital charge against the Lord. (5) Unsuspecting blindness. They know not how soon their double judgment against the woman and against the Lord is to be turned into a judgment against themselves. (6) The most headstrong obduracy. Though in their conscience convinced of their unworthiness to condemn the woman they still do not perceive their sin against the Lord.

The conduct of the Lord towards His tempters: 1. Their hypocritical homage to the Messiah He meets with the calm, stately action of Messianic majesty (He stooped down, *etc.*). 2. Their tempting of His Spirit He meets with the searching of their conscience. 3. Their Pharisaic question concerning the highest grade of punishment He meets with the question of the gospel concerning the innocent judge. 4. Their judgment was to work death and damnation; His judgment aims at deliverance and salvation. 5. They come as accusers and judges, they go as condemned. 6. They intended to destroy a holy one; He rescues a lost sinner.—Or: 1. His silence a condemnation of their craft and excited passion. 2. His stooping and looking down a condemnation of their shameless treatment of the woman's shame. 3. His writing, a mysterious action, pointing to the wicked mysteries of their life.—Christ and the Pharisees compared as judges of the adulteress: (1) With respect to rigor. Their rigor is an uncharitable delight in the damnation of the sinner after gross outward sins. His rigor delights in salvation, and presses on their conscience with a wholesome condemnation of the Spirit. (2) In respect to gentleness. Their gentleness is carnal laxity which encourages sin. His gentleness is overpowering grace which destroys sin.—Christ is not a new Moses, but the Redeemer from sin by the law of the Spirit.—The position which Christ takes toward civil legislators and judges: (1) He stands distinct from them, in that He makes no civil laws. (2) He stands in connection with them, in that He furnishes them the law of the Spirit, the fundamental principles for their legal administration.—The glorification of the ancient light and law in the new covenant: (1) The perfection of rigor. The perfect knowledge of sins recognizes all as worthy of death and perdition. (2) The perfection of gentleness. The full gracious perception of faith recognizes all as called to the salvation of the children of God. (3) The perfection of administration. The decided life of the Spirit fixes the standard of law and discipline between the perfect rigor and the perfect gentleness.—The judgment of Christ a word of terror for the guilty consciences on both sides: (1) The woman must tremble under the words: "Let him be the first to cast a stone at her." (2) The accusers under the words: "He that is without sin among you" (*i. e.* he that is not himself worthy of death).

The guilty woman before the judgment seat of Christ: (1) How she stands bound to the judgment seat, till He has spoken. (2) How she is released with a Saviour's word: *Sin no more.*—The Christian spiritual care of released criminals, particularly of penitent fallen ones.—The silence of the woman an intelligible language of penitence to the Lord.—The judgment of the Pharisees in the light and judgment of Christ.

STARKE: *Nova. Bibl. Tub.:* The wickedness of the ungodly knows how to abuse even the law, the punishment of faults, the best and holiest things. Shame, that stupidity and silliness undertake to tempt wisdom itself. It does not become teachers and preachers to try to have one foot in the pulpit and the other in the council chamber.—HEDINGER: Thou hypocrite, look into thine own bosom.—Though no magistracy can be without sin it should nevertheless not be chargeable with the sins which it must visit with bodily punishment upon others. Magistrates ought to be honest persons who fear God, Ex. xviii. 21.—QUESNEL: Prudence and love require that we should give persons an opportunity to withdraw, without ado and disgrace, from a bad cause, into which their passsion has seduced them.—ZEISIUS: What a mighty, and in truth irresistible witness is the conscience of man! Thus must they themselves come to shame who seek to put others, especially faithful teachers, to shame; treachery comes home to him that forges it.—Preachers must be no doubt earnest and zealous with great sinners, but not with gross harshness, for this does not improve and edify. —HEDINGER: The pulpit should not meddle in secular affairs, and much less should the secular order meddle with spiritual matters.—CANSTEIN: If any one is rescued from the hands of justice, he should be diligently exhorted not to abuse his deliverance, but prove his gratitude to God and men.

GERLACH: The answer of Jesus puts their cunning to shame, without infringing the law, justice, or love.—At the same time His sentence guards the woman against despair by pointing at the sinfulness of all. He does not extenuate the sin of the adulteress; but He hints at inward sin which puts one further from God than gross outward transgressions.—To drive these hypocrites away needs only a word of the Lord which strikes the heart like a hammer that grinds the rock.—Now Jesus could exercise His saving office. He forgives her the sin, *etc.*—This implies not the slightest disapproval of legal punishments. [But it no doubt does imply a Christian principle for the criticism and reformation of civil punishments].

BRAUNE: Early in the morning, with much watchfulness, Jesus was in the temple, the place where He loved to labor all the day. The thought of His approaching death and the various impressions of His work upon different hearts; it seems as if this doubled His zeal.—The sins which in Christendom also attach to Sundays and feast-days.—The previous evening that session against the Redeemer had been held; then (during the night) this case comes. How natural the thought, that Jesus might be caught by means of it. And now the Pharisees and scribes are in concert, *etc.*—She says: "Lord;" she feels the majesty of Jesus, and this implies that she certainly condemns herself, Matt. xxi. 31.—Deliverance from the hand of civil justice is not yet deliverance from the almighty hand of the holy God.—Jesus with His meekness showed a greater judicial earnestness than the severest condemnation to death can express.

HEUBNER: *Unto the Mount of Olives.* John gives a hint that Jesus is approaching the time of His passion.—Ver. 3. "*But* the Scribes and Pharisees" [instead of the Eng. Vers. *And*], intimates the contrast: these scribes had spent the night in working out new plans against Jesus.—(The woman). To all her shame, to her fear of death which already took hold of her soul, was now added the eye of the pure and Holy One who judged without respect of persons.—It is no good fortune to remain undiscovered in transgressions.—The heavy guilt and shame of adultery are evident from all laws of antiquity against it (and also the evil of that neglect, oppression and improper use of woman, which have been gradually done away with by Christianity alone).—Men may be zealous for the divine law with evil hearts.—Worldlings and hypocrites have a passion for bringing good people into perplexity with entangling questions. But Jesus shows us the way of Christian wisdom to escape the snares of men.—Thunder from a clear sky could not have so terrified the sinners as the word of the Lord, which must have smitten them with the fear that He knew their secret sins.—Cicero *Ad Verrem* III. exord.: *Vis corruptorem vel adulterum accusare? Providendum diligenter, ne in tua vita vestigium libidinis appareat. Etenim non est ferendus accusator is, qui quod in altero vitium reprehendit, in eo ipso deprehenditur.* —The wonderful power of conscience even in hypocrites.—*No man, Lord:* It sounds like a sigh of anguish, shame and faith.—Christ's office is not to condemn, but to show mercy and redeem.—We should never uncharitably bring the secret sins of our neighbor into the light.—Despair not of improving those who have fallen very low.—GOSSNER: He went *early* to His work; the people came *early* to hear Him. *Early* let our souls be given to Him, for He comes *early* into His temple, the heart.—O poor men, let the stones lie which ye would cast at your fellow-sinners and fellow-pilgrims on this earth.—BESSER (after BENGEL): Your names are written in the earth, Jer. xvii. 1, 13.—(From LUTHER): They fancy that the stones are looking at them and it seemed long to them before they could find a hole and get to the doors.—The difference between the Pharisees and the woman: They, convicted by their conscience, get away from Jesus; she, convicted by her conscience, stays by Jesus.—The two were left alone: Misery and commiseration (*miseria et misericordia*, pitiableness and pity), says Augustine.—What malice prompted the Pharisees to do, was made to drive a lost sheep into the arms of the good shepherd.

[SCHAFF: A suitable text for the Midnight Mission and at the dedication of Magdalene asylums, but to be wisely and cautiously handled. See an excellent sermon on the text by Dr. MUHLENBERG, of St. Luke's Hospital, preached and published in New York, 1867.—The startling contrast: a woman guilty of a most heinous crime and exposed to public ignominy worse than death, confronted with the Purest of the pure, who condemned even an impure look as adultery in germ.—Christ acts here not as an avenging judge, whose duty is to administer the law, but as a merciful Saviour and Sovereign with the privilege of pardoning. So He acted towards the Samaritan woman and Mary Magdalene.—He does not make light of sins against the seventh commandment, but, in His parting word: "Sin no more," He recognizes the enormity of the woman's guilt and exhorts her to break off from all sin (not adultery only) at once and forever.—The wisdom of our Saviour in avoiding the snare of the Pharisees and rebuking their conscience, and His tender and holy mercy in dealing with the poor woman.—

The heartless cruelty of modern society in turning the seduced adulteress over to perpetual infamy, while winking at the greater crime of the seducing adulterer.—Christ metes out the same truth and justice to great and small, respectable and disreputable alike. "He reverses the judgment of the world which casts the stone of infamy at the ruined and leaves the author of the ruin unharmed."—Social respectability was the shield of the character of the Pharisees and Scribes, and yet their spiritual pride, hypocrisy and secret unchastities made them more guilty in the eyes of the Lord than the open shame of the poor woman at whom they were ready to cast stones. "The publicans and the harlots go into the kingdom of God before you," Matt. xxi. 31, 32.—(From MUHLENBERG): The service of the Midnight Mission is to approach fallen women in the spirit of the Saviour, "with the voice of brotherly and sisterly concern; to let them feel that they are not utterly friendless; to address them with unaffected sympathy; to whisper in the ear words of the one true Friend; to be Christ's missionaries to them by night, like Himself seeking the lost in a benighted world: this is no dark mission, but a mission of blessed light, illumined of heaven, cheered too with the light of penitence and gratitude."]

B. CHAP. VIII. 12-30.

[CHRIST, THE LIGHT OF THE WORLD.]

EXEGETICAL AND CRITICAL.

Ver. 12. **Again therefore Jesus spoke to them** [πάλιν οὖν αὐτοῖς ἐλάλησεν ὁ Ἰησοῦς].—The connection varies according as the section on the adulteress is regarded as in its true place or interpolated.

On the supposition of its interpolation Meyer construes thus (and Lücke): "After the Sanhedrin had failed in their attempt to get possession of Jesus, and had become divided among themselves, as is related in ch. vii. 45-52, Jesus was able, in consequence of this miscarriage of the plan of His enemies (οὖν), to appear again and speak to the assembly in the temple." The πάλιν is supposed to show that the time of the discourse is one of the days following the day of the feast. De Wette, on the contrary, supposes that John has not intended to preserve closely the thread of the history. Tholuck considers it impossible to decide whether the discourse was delivered on the last day of the feast or after it. He says: "If the pericope is genuine, this exclamation must have occurred some hours later." Rather, a whole night and some hours later.

If the section be genuine, the words following are connected with the affair of the adulteress (Cocceius, Bengel). We have given this connection the preference. In view of the remarks that the repeated πάλιν in ver. 12 and ver. 21 is quite unmeaning without this section, for Jesus has not been interrupted by the history ch. vii. 45-52; only the evangelist has interrupted himself by communicating some things which preceded behind the scenes. But the official state of things after the production of the adulteress must have been essentially changed. The rulers who threatened to take Jesus, and occasioned His saying, I shall soon go away from you,—have given Him an involuntary token of acknowledgment before the people; now He has the field again for a time, and can speak once more. The transactions following took place, accordingly, after the scene just preceding, on the day after the last day of the feast.

I am the light of the world.—Opinions as to the occasion of this figurative utterance: 1. Sunrise, or sunset. But the former was long past, and the latter had not yet come; and Jesus appears here not as antitype of the sun, as in ch. ix. 5, but as the essential light, the light of the night. 2. The reading of the section Isa. xlii.; since the "light of the Gentiles" (φῶς ἐθνῶν) of ver. 6 is equivalent to the "light of the world" (φῶς τοῦ κόσμου) of this place, and designates the Messiah. Jesus, accordingly, here addresses Himself to the hope of the light of Israel and the Gentiles (Luke ii. 32; John i. 4, 9). Against this it has been observed that the reading of Scripture lessons belonged to the synagogues, not to the temple; even the temple-synagogue, which Vitringa adduces, was not in the temple itself (Lücke, p. 283). 3. The torch-feast, or the illumination at the feast of tabernacles. In the court of the women stood great golden candelabras, which were lit on the evening of the first day of the feast, and spread their light over all Jerusalem, while by the men a torch-light dance with music and singing was performed before these candelabras (see Winer, *Laubhüttenfest*. These lights are not to be confounded with the large golden lamps in the sanctuary). According to Maimonides this illumination took place also on the other evenings of the festival. Even apart from this, the exhausted lamps in the women's court, or in the treasury-hall where Jesus according to ver. 20 was speaking, would on the day after the feast as distinctly suggest the symbolical transitory illumination of Jerusalem, as the eighth day of the feast would suggest the cessation of the symbolical streams of water; and this gave the Lord the same occasion for describing Himself as the true enlightener of the night, which the previous day had given for presenting Himself as the opener of the true fountain (Wetstein, Paulus, Olshausen; see *Leben Jesu*, II., p. 955). Opinions which lack a full appreciation of John's symbolization, like Meyer's, lose their weight by that very lack; though according to them we must take not the torch-light part of the feast, but, with Hug, the sight of the candelabras, as the occasion of our Lord's expression. Of course the Messianic prophecies in Is. xlii. 6; Mal. iv. 2; Lu. ii., as well as the rabbinical figures (Lightfoot, p. 1041), assisted this application. But beyond doubt the illumination was specifically an emblem of the pillar fire which had accompanied Israel at the time of its pilgrimage in the wilderness and its dwelling in tabernacles; therefore also an emblem of the later manifestation of the δόξα of the Lord, the idea of the Shekinah (see Is. iv. 5). To this was further added, as the immediate occasion, the fact that the adulterous woman had fallen into darkness, and that the tempters of Jesus had come and gone away in spiritual darkness.

The light of the world. Κόσμος is here, as

in xvii. 11, and elsewhere, the world of humanity in its obscuration. The true light, which enlightens the human night, the antitype of the temple light and of all lamps and night lights, is the personal truth and purity, which enlightens and sanctifies, or delivers from walking in religious and moral darkness. The substance or New Testament fulfilment of the pillar of fire.

Shall in no wise walk in the darkness [οὐ μὴ περιπατήσῃ ἐν τῇ σκοτίᾳ].—According to the reading περιπατήσῃ,* this is assuring: He shall surely not walk. A stronger expression of the assurance which is implied in the light of Christ; not to be understood as a demand, for this is precluded by the words: He that followeth Me. *Darkness;* the sphere of error, of delusion, of blindness. A fundamental conception of John.

Shall have the light of life.—Σκοτία, the fear of death, had literally brought the adulteress to the verge of bodily death itself. Hence the light of life is here not the life as light, but the light as life, as giving, securing, and sustaining the true life. *He shall have* it for a sure possession of his own, for the following of Christ by faith causes an enlightenment from Him which proves itself as a living light, the life turning into light, the light turning into life, a fountain of life; as the water which He gives becomes a fountain within.

Ver. 13. **Thy witness is not true.**—The Pharisees who were present rejected the great utterance of Jesus respecting Himself, "but, prudently enough avoiding the matter of it, they dispute its formal validity." Meyer. In reference to the matter of it they perhaps felt half bound by the preceding hypocritical act of homage on the part of their fellows. Jesus Himself also seemed to them to have formerly, chap. v. 31, suggested to them this rule which they now stated. But (says Lücke) the case is different. Matters of conscience, of the inmost sense of God and of divine things must be juged of otherwise than matters of outward experience. As God can only reveal and bear witness to Himself (ὁ δὲ θεὸς αὐτὸς ἑαυτῷ ἀξιόπιστος μάρτυς, says Chrysostom), so the divine life and light in the world are only their own evidence. "*Lumen,*" says Augustine, "*et alia demonstrat et se ipsum. Testimonium sibi perhibet lux, aperit sanos oculos, et sibi ipsa testis est.*" Yet the times differ. Christ must be first accredited and introduced by the Father on the testimony of Scripture and miracle; afterwards His own testimony of Himself is valid. The connection also in that place and in this is very different. There Christ professed Himself the awakener of the dead, and as such the Father had accredited Him by the miraculous raising of the sick. Here He presents Himself as the sure guide through the darkness of this world to the true life, and His credential in this character must be the certitude of His own conviction. The proof of the truth of this conviction lies in the fact that He is clear respecting the course of His own life, His origin and His goal, and this proof He soon states further on. [Comp. my note on ch. v. 31, p. 192.—P. S.]

* [The rec. reads περιπατήσει, with D. E. *al.*, but περιπατήσῃ is supported by ℵ. B. F. G., *etc.* Orig., and adopted by Lachmann, Tischendorf and Alford.—P. S.]

Ver. 14. **Though I bear witness of myself,** *etc.*—Even when I am in this situation, as I am just now. He hereby intimates, that in other respects He quotes also another witness (the Father), as immediately afterwards in ver. 17.

For I know whence I came.—The clear consciousness of His origin and appointment on the one hand, and of His destination on the other (His ἀρχή and His τέλος), gives Him also a clear knowledge of His path, clearness respecting His own way and His guidance of others. He comes from the Father and goes to the Father (chap. xvi. 28). Therefore He reveals the Father and is the way to the Father. Or He *is* in His essence pure person, He goes to the perfection of His personality, therefore He is in His holy personal conduct the quickener and restorer of erring souls to personal life.

But ye know not [ὑμεῖς δὲ οὐκ οἴδατε] **whence I come, and whither I go.**—In the former case the aorist (ἦλθον), now the present (ἔρχομαι, ὑπάγω). They could not know whence He had come, but they ought to have seen whence He still at present came, to wit, that He was sent by God. And from His appearance they might then have inferred His origin. No more did they know whence He was going, though they fully intended to put Him to death; that is, they did not know that by the sacrifice of His life in death He would rise to glory. The reading: *or* [ἤ instead of καί, *and*] whither I go, is improbable, because the knowledge of Christ's end depends upon the knowledge of His spiritual origin. Grotius accounts for Christ's testifying of Himself from His being sent of God: "*Legationis injunctæ conscius est is, cui injuncta est, reliqui ab ipso hoc debent discere.*" A true point, but not the whole thought. Coccejus observes that no other man knows whence He comes and whither He goes, and in this respect Christ stands above others, and may testify of Himself. Unquestionably His clear divine-human consciousness was the bright star of salvation in the night of the world.

Ver. 15. **Ye judge according to the flesh** [κατὰ τὴν σάρκα].—Tholuck (after De Wette): "The loose and floating progression of ideas looks as if the ideas were inaccurately reproduced." Hardly! The train of thought is similar to that at chap. vii. 24; except that here the emphasis falls on the *judging itself.* Ye *already judge* persons and actions according to the flesh, according to their outward, finite appearance, and according to finite standards (κατ' ὄψιν, vii. 24). He means, therefore, primarily, judging by a false outward standard, but, in connection with it, judging by a false inward estimate (so Chrysostom, De Wette: after a carnal, selfish manner). Ye judge (condemn) the internal character of the Son of Man from His humble form; **I judge** (condemn) **no person.** Meyer justly observes that the addition: *according to the flesh,* is not to be here supplied (as Augustine and others would have it; Lücke: as ye do), but the κρίνειν is emphatic in the sense of κατακρίνειν. This is supported by the turn in ver. 16. The sentence, however, probably includes a reference to their theocratic judicial office, which in the affair of the adulteress had shown a thirst for reprobation, while His office consists not only in not judging, but in delivering and saving. Hence modifications of the sentence: *I judge no one. Now* (νῦν, Augustine and others) is not untrue to the sense, but superfluous. So is the explanation: I have no pleasure in judging (De Wette). The maxim of Christ, however, is founded of course on the fact that He distinguishes between the original nature or essential constitution of persons and their caricature in sin (which Meyer disputes). It is just this which makes Him Redeemer.

Ver. 16. **But even if I myself judge.**—Meyer supposes that this also means *condemn*, and that the Lord would say that there are "exceptions to that maxim of not judging." But the exceptions would destroy the positiveness of the previous sentence. He judgeth no man (unfavorably), but He does judge in general, and in the special sense judges in condemnation of sin in every man. Thus in His decision respecting the adulteress and her accusers He judged. Thus He judges or forms His estimate of them and of Himself. But all His judging is κρίσις ἀληθινή (see the critical notes), the real, essential estimation (of persons), discrimination (of sinner and sin), and separation (of believer and unbeliever). The *ground* of this judgment, of His being thus true, is that the Father by the actual course of things executes these same decisions, separations, and judgments, which the spirit of Christ passes.

Ver. 17. **In your law.**—From this turn it clearly appears that Christ was including judgment respecting Himself. After He has declared that His own testimony is alone sufficient for the declaration that He is the light of the world, He returns to the assurance that after all He is not limited to His own testimony, but has the Father also for a witness. In *your* law, *i. e.*, in the law in which ye make your boast, and the very letter of which also binds you; not in the law which is nothing to Me (whether in the *antinomian* interpretation of Schweizer, or the *doctrinal* interpretation of De Wette). Comp. chap. v. 39; vii. 22; viii. 5, 45-47; x. 35.—Tholuck: In this way of speaking of the νόμος we must by no means fail to perceive a characteristic of John.—**The testimony of two men is true.** A free quotation from Deut. xvii. 6. *Two men* is emphatic.

Ver. 18. **I am he who beareth witness,** *etc.*—He produces two significant witnesses: *His own consciousness* and the power of *the Father* working with Him. Paulus would take the ἐγώ to mean: I, as one who knows Himself; Olshausen: I, as Son of God. But it means also in particular: I, as the one sent by the Father. That which makes two witnesses valid in law, is the agreement of two consciences in a public declaration under oath. And if there may be two false witnesses it must be one of those abnormal, horrible exceptions for which human society cannot provide. But when the power of God in the miracles of Christ and His word in the Old Testament agree with the word of Jesus, it is a harmony of testimonies, in which the testimony of the Father Himself joined with the testimony of Him whom He has sent must be acknowledged.

Ver. 19. **Where is thy Father?**—An intentional misapprehension and malicious mockery. Therefore no doubt also a feint, as if they were inquiring after a human father of Jesus (Augustine, and others); the use of ποῦ instead of τίς is not against this. The Pharisees well knew that God is invisible; if their question had referred to God, it must have been: Where then does God, Thy Father, testify of Thee? They seem, in mockery, to look about for a human father of Jesus as His witness. This reference of the word to a human father does not necessarily involve, as Tholuck thinks, the calumnious intimation that He was a bastard (Cyril); for the thing in hand is not any exact information concerning His birth, but the presentation of His Father as a witness. Yet the irony might possibly have gone even to this wicked extent.

If ye had known me, *etc.*—Because they did not and would not perceive the divine Spirit in the words and life of Jesus, they were blind to the Spirit of God in His miracles, as well as to the testimony of God concerning Him in the Scriptures; and this proved that they did not know God Himself any more than they knew Jesus. Comp. chap. xiv. 9.

Ver. 20. **In the treasury.**—Ἐν τῷ γαζοφυλακίῳ. We must in the first place distinguish between the treasury-hall, the γαζοφυλάκιον, which was in the court of the women (*i. e.*, the court beyond which the women did not venture, but where the men also stopped or passed, see Mark xii. 41), and the treasure-chambers of the temple, γαζοφυλάκια. Then we must again distinguish between the more special term γαζοφυλάκιον, applied to the thirteen chests, and the same term in its more general application to the whole hall of the chests, which was also called γαζοφυλάκιον, (see Tholuck, p. 241, where Meyer's translation: *at* the money chests,—is also set aside). The evangelist names this locality, because it was the most public, here everybody deposited his temple gifts. The locality gives the bold words of Christ concerning Himself and concerning the Pharisees their full force; yet "*no one laid hands on Him, for His hour had not yet come,*" chap. vii. 30. "The refrain of the history with an air of triumph." Meyer.

Ver. 21. **Again therefore he said to them, I go away, and ye will seek me, and will die in your sin** [ἐν τῇ ἁμαρτίᾳ ὑμῶν ἀποθανεῖσθε].—As He had said before, chap. vii. 33. Not a new discourse, placed by Ewald and Meyer, contrary to the usual view, on one of the subsequent days. It seems unnecessary to assume (with Tholuck) a special occasion for this discourse; for the occasion in the preceding mockery of the Pharisees stands out strongly enough (hence the οὖν). The mockery of unbelief stands entirely on a line with persecution; mockery therefore is here to the Lord a new signal of approaching death, as persecution was at chap. vii. 34. But for this reason He here declares still more strongly than He did there, both His freedom in His death and their condemnation. In the former case: *Ye will not find me;* now: *Ye will die in your sin.* The *seeking* again denotes the seeking of the Messiah amidst the impending judgments; not a penitent seeking of the Redeemer, but a fanatical chiliastic seeking of a political deliverer. Hence without any finding of Christ. And the not finding is, positively, a dying in sin. Lücke: The thing meant is natural dying in the state of sin, not a dying on account of sin or by reason of sin. But the former idea cannot here be kept apart from the latter. The sins are their sins as a whole, sealed by their unbelief and their murderous spirit towards the Messiah; the dying is dying in the whole sense of the word: perishing in woe, irremediable death, utter ruin in this world and in that which is to come; and lastly the persons meant are the people as a whole, deceivers and deceived. But as the ὑμεῖς does not mean every single Jew, so the sin of obduracy is not foretold of all, nor the prospect of death extended to hopeless damnation in every case. Only the sin and death of the nation as a body are without limit.

The extension of the condemnation into the future world Jesus declares in the words: "*Whither I go, ye cannot come.*" As they now could not spiritually reach Him, so hereafter even as suppliants they could not reach Him on the throne of His glory nor beyond in His heaven. A distinct opposite of hell is not to be thought of (as Meyer holds); a place of punishment is no doubt at least implied.

Ver. 22. **Will he kill himself?**—Formerly He said: "*Where I am;*" now he says: "*Whither I go.*" Hence they now (the Jews in the Judaistic sense) give their mockery another and a more biting form. "The irony of chap. vii. 35, rises to impudent sarcasm." Tholuck. They assume that He spoke of His death; and as He called this a ὑπάγειν, they mock, because they have no conception of the element of voluntary departure in the violence of death: "Will He kill Himself?" They think He has set Himself far above them in saying that they could not reach Him; they revenge themselves by suggesting that He will sink far below them. An orthodox Jew, they would say, utterly abhors suicide. According to Josephus, *De Bello Jud.* III. 8, 5, the self-murderer goes to the σκοτιώτερος ᾅδης. Thus, according to the orthodox Jewish doctrine, to which the Pharisees bore allegiance, the suicide falls to the lowest hell of Hades, and is separated by a great gulf from Abraham's bosom (Luke xvi. 26), into which they hoped to go. Concerning a peculiar interpretation of Origen, see Lücke, p. 207: [that Jesus would kill Himself, and so go to the place and punishment of suicides, to which the Jews could not go, because *their* sin did not subject them to it.—Tr.]

Ver. 23. **Ye are from beneath; I am from above.**—Jesus meets their mockery with a calm assertion which turns the point of it against themselves. For *from beneath* hardly means here merely *from the earth* (Meyer), as in chap. iii. 31; but, as in viii. 44, it denotes the diabolical nature which they have shown, and by virtue of which they belong to that dark nether world. They therefore could go thither, where they are spiritually at home; He could not, since He is *from above*, from heaven (chap. iii. 3). The antithesis in these words is that of hades and heaven, says Origen; in the moral sense, says Stier; on the contrary Tholuck, with Meyer, makes the antithesis heaven and earth. But the parallel κόσμος οὗτος does not prove this; for that expression denotes not the visible world in itself, but the old bad nature of the world.

The more obscure first sentence He explains by the second: **Ye are of this world.**—Κόσμος οὗτος, also, according to the Jewish Christology, denoted pre-eminently the ancient heathen world, which was to come into condemnation. **I am not of this world.** Therefore in spirit and life belonging to the αἰὼν ὁ μέλλων, the new and higher world. The former antithesis denotes the *principle of the life;* the latter, the *sphere of life* corresponding.

Ver. 24. **I said therefore unto you, that ye will die in your sins.**—That is to say, the words: "ye will die in your sins," and the words: "ye are of this world," or "from beneath," are equivalent. Their being from beneath as to the principle of their life is the reason why they will die in their sins (Crell. Other views of the connection see in Tholuck). Meyer: "Observe that in this repetition of the denunciation the emphasis, which in ver. 21 lay upon *in your sins*, falls upon **will die**, and thus the perdition itself comes into the foreground, which can be averted only by conversion to faith."

Yet they must not understand Him that they are in a fatalistic sense from *beneath*, or of this world, and therefore cannot but die in their sins. Hence He adds the condition: **If ye believe not that I am He.** There is, therefore, no lack of clearness in the connection (as Tholuck supposes). The expression: "*that I am He,*" is mysteriously delivered, without mention of the predicate. Meyer: "To wit, the Messiah, the self-evident predicate." But the matter was not so simple; otherwise Christ would have previously named Himself the Messiah. And this He would not do, because their conception of the Messiah was distorted. They must, therefore, step by step perceive and believe that He is what He professed to be: the one sent of the Father, the Son of Man, the Quickener, the Light of the world; last: the one from above. They must believe in Him according to His words and His deeds; His higher existence, His real being, which stood before their eyes, and the real nature of which they criticised away, they must believe; not till then could they receive the word that He was the Messiah. The predicate is, therefore, the representation of Himself which Jesus gives in the context. According to Hofmann (*Schriftbeweis*, I. 62), an imitation of the Old Testament אֲנִי הוּא. Undoubtedly correct in the view that both here and there the self-evidencing living presence of the divine person must be above all things acknowledged without prejudice.

This mysterious import of the word is indicated also by the question of the Jews: "*Who art thou?*" (ver. 25). They wished to draw the last decisive word from Him. The answer of Jesus which follows speaks to the same point. Luther takes the σὺ τίς εἶ as contemptuous; so does Meyer. But it is rather a sly question, to decoy or force Jesus to an avowal. Comp. chap. x. 24. If we compare the expression ὅτι ἐγώ εἰμι with that in ch. vii. 39: οὔπω γὰρ ἦν πνεῦμα ἅγιον,—we might naturally translate: that I am here. That He is *present as* He is *present* in the fulness of His divine-human life, —this they must believe and apprehend before they will rightly apprehend Him as the Messiah.

Ver. 25. **Even the same that I said unto you from the beginning.** [So the E. V. renders τὴν ἀρχὴν ὅ τι καὶ λαλῶ ὑμῖν,

Comp. TEXT. NOTES.—P. S.].—This passage has been a *crux interpretum*, because the progressive unfolding of the idea of the Messiah by Christ in His presentation of Himself has not been appreciated. The interpretation depends not merely on the sense of τὴν ἀρχήν, but also on that of the expression ὅ τι καὶ λαλῶ ὑμῖν.

[To state the points more fully, the interpretation depends: 1) On the construction of the whole sentence—whether it be interrogative, or exclamatory, or declarative; 2) on the sense of τὴν ἀρχήν, whether it be taken substantively (*principium, the beginning, the Logos*), or adverbially (*in the beginning, from the beginning, first of all, to start with*, or *omnino, generally*); 3) on the ambiguity of ὅτι (conjunct.) and ὅ, τι (relative); 4) on the meaning of λαλῶ as distinct from λέγω; 5) on the proper force of καί. I remark in the premises that we must take τὴν ἀρχήν adverbially, and write ὅ, τι, since ὅτι (*quoniam, quia*) gives no good sense.—P. S.]

1. Constructions which take the sentence as a question.

(*a*) Cyril, Chrysostom, Matthæi, Lücke (more or less equivalent): Why do I even speak to you at all? [*Cur vero omnino vobiscum loquor? cur frustra vobiscum disputo?*—P. S.] (Comp. x. 25). This is grammatically possible, for τὴν ἀρχήν can mean *omnino* (in certain circumstances), and ὅ, τι can mean *why*. But such a sentence would be contradicted by Christ's going on to speak, and it would be too "empty" (Meyer).

[With this agrees in sense Ewald's explanation, with this difference that he takes the sentence as an indignant *exclamation*: That I should have to speak to you at all! (*Dass ich auch überhaupt zu euch rede!*) But this leaves the position of τὴν ἀρχήν before ὅτι (as Ewald writes instead of ὅ, τι) unexplained.—P. S.]

(*b*) Meyer (and Hilgenfeld): What I originally (from the first) say to you, that do ye ask? or (Do you ask), what I have long been telling you? The objection to this is that Christ had from the first *not* presented Himself as Messiah. Besides, there is no: Do ye ask?—in the sentence.

2. Constructions which connect with this sentence the πολλὰ ἔχω following [ver. 26, and put only a comma, instead of a period, after λαλῶ ὑμῖν]. Some manuscripts, Bengel, Olshausen. Hofmann: "For the first, for the present, since He is engaged in speaking to them, He has many reproving and condemning things to say to them." This would be an entire evasion of the question they had put.*

3. Constructions which take the sentence as a declaration.

(*a*) Augustine (similarly Bede, Rupert, Lampe, Fritzche): *Principium* (the Logos, the Word) *me credite, quia* (ὅτι) *et loquor vobis, i. e. quia humilis propter vos factus ad ista verba descendi.* [Wordsworth: "I am what I am also declaring to you, *the Beginning*;" comp. Rev. xxi. 6, ἡ ἀρχὴ καὶ τὸ τέλος.—P. S.] Untenable both in point of grammar and of fact; τὴν ἀρχήν is adverbial, and Jesus could not present Himself to these adversaries as the divine Logos. [A reference to the Logos would require λέγω instead of λαλῶ.—P. S.]

(*b*) Calvin, Beza, Grotius, Baumgarten-Crusius, Tholuck: "I am* what I told you in the beginning (and tell you until now)." But (1) He had not given them from the beginning a definite description of Himself; (2) τὴν ἀρχήν ought not to stand first; not to say that we ought rather to have ἐλάλησα [instead of λαλῶ].

(*c*) Luthardt: "From the beginning I am, that [ὅτι] I may even speak to you." Obscure, and in part incorrect; for Jesus did not exist merely to speak to the Jews (see Meyer).

(*d*) Bretschneider: "At the outset I declared concerning Myself what I say also now." But there is no λελάληκα.

(*e*) De Wette: "*First of all*, or above all, I am what I even say to you."† Luther: "I am your preacher; if ye first believe this, ye will also know by experience who I am, and in no other way." (Ammon: He is to be known, above all things, from His words). But, in the first place, τὴν ἀρχήν must mean *for the first thing*, to begin with; and secondly, Christ says not that they must know Him from His words, but He refers to accounts which He actually gave of Himself.

(*f*) Winer: "I am *wholly* such as I represent Myself in My words." See the grammatical objection against *wholly* in Meyer.

(*g*) "To begin with, for the first, I am that which I even say to you;" or, "First of all, I am the very thing I am declaring unto you." Erasmus, Bucer, Grotius,‡ *et al.*, *Leben Jesu*, II., 963, Brückner.§ For the first thing, they must receive with confidence His descriptions of Himself as the fountain of life, the light of the world, *etc.*, which He openly and familiarly talks (λαλῶ) to them; then they will come to a full knowledge of His character; for all depends on their ceasing to determine His character by their crude notion of the Messiah, ceasing to require in Him such a Messiah as they have imagined, and beginning to determine their ideas of the Messiah from His revelation of Himself, and to correct and spiritualize them accordingly. When Tholuck objects that, upon this interpretation, Jesus would be drawing them first to a lower view of Himself, and afterwards to a higher, he is mistaken; for the issue here is between a designation of Him-

*[Baümlein: "If we must take the question: Who art thou? as expressing contempt and wonder that Jesus should venture to say: Ye shall die in your sins,—the reply: τὴν ἀρχὴν—ὅ τι καὶ λαλῶ ὑμῖν—πολλὰ ἔχω περὶ ὑμ. λαλ. κ. κρ. is perfectly suitable: Assuredly (from the first, in general) I have—what I am doing also now—many things to say," *etc.*—E. D. Y.]

*['Εγώ εἰμι is supplied from the preceding question of the Jews: σὺ τίς εἶ;—P. S.]

†[*Von vorne herein (vor allen Dingen) bin ich, was ich auch zu euch rede; i. e.*, I am in fact what I say; I must be known from My speeches. Alford professes to follow this interpretation of De Wette as expanded by Stier, but translates somewhat differently: "*Essentially* (τὴν ἀρχήν, traced up to its principle, generally), *that which I also discourse unto you*; or, *in very deed, that same which I speak unto you.* He is the Logos—His discourses are the revelation of Himself. . . When Moses asked the name of God, *I am that which I am*, was the mysterious answer; . . . but when God manifest in the flesh is asked the same question, it is: I am that which I SPEAK.'" Profound and true in itself; but hardly an interpretation of the text in hand. The question, in all its circumstances and its spirit, is *not* the same as that of Moses: and a hidden reference to Λόγος would produce λέγω rather than λαλῶ.—P. S.]

‡[Grotius: *Primum hoc sum quod et dico vobis* (*i. e., lux mundi*) = πρῶτον μὲν ὅ, τι καὶ λέγω ὑμῖν.—P. S.]

§[Brückner, ed. 5th, does not materially differ from De Wette, except that he rejects his rendering of τὴν ἀρχήν by *above all things* (*vor allen Dingen*), and translates: *to begin with* (*von vorne herein*).—Godet translates: (I am) *Precisely* what I tell you (no more or less).—P. S.]

self by the New Testament *thing* that He is, and a designation of Himself by the theocratic *name*, which in its rabbinical form had to be regenerated by the New Testament spirit, and the course of thought is not from lower to higher, but from the more general to the more specific.

Ver. 26. **I have many things to say and to judge of you.**—Περὶ ὑμῶν is emphatic. Because He has so much to say and to judge of them, so much to clear up with them, He cannot go on to the final, decisive declaration concerning Himself. It must first be still more clearly brought out, what *they* are, and where *they* stand. Tholuck, therefore, groundlessly remarks, quoting an opinion of Maldonatus: "This expression also disturbs the clearness of the course of thought." The opinion, of course, has in view also what follows.

But he that sent me is true.—'Αλλά is difficult. Meyer, with Apollinaris: πολλὰ ἔχων λέγειν περὶ ὑμῶν, σιγῶ. So Euthymius and others. Better Lücke, Tholuck and others, after older expositors: However much I have to judge concerning you, My κρίσις is still ἀληθής. Yet this sentiment is to be modified. It grieves Him that He has so much to judge of them; yet it must be so; God, who hath sent Him, is *true*. God judges in act according to truth, and Christ, the interpreter of His essential words which He hears of Him through the facts and through the showing of the Spirit, must do the same in speech. The ἀλλά, therefore, forms an adversative (missed in this view by Meyer) to the πολλά ἔχω. According to Chrysostom the apodosis would mean: But I limit Myself to speaking τὰ πρὸς σωτηρίαν, οὐ τὰ πρὸς ἔλεγχον. Meyer: He has things to say to the world, other than the worthlessness of His enemies. But in this view God would rather be referred to as gracious, than as true. And Christ would not appeal to His duty to speak what He hears (comp. ch. v. 30).

Ver. 27. **They understood not.**—Different conceptions: (1) 'Ω τῆς ἀγνοίας, Chrysostom. (2) Strange and improbable that they did not understand, De Wette. (3) The beginning of a new discourse with other hearers, Baumgarten-Crusius, Meyer. (4) A moral obtuseness, and refusal of acknowledgment, Lücke. So Stier and Tholuck: hardness of heart.—The failure to understand was due, on the contrary, to their suspecting a secret behind the expression: *He that sent Me*, on account of their greedy chiliastic hope of a Messiah. For as Messiah in their sense Christ would have still been welcome to them. This introduces what follows.

Ver. 28. **When ye have lifted up the Son of man.**—It is now their turn to be tempted by Jesus, though in a holy mind. Jesus apparently yields to their vagueness of mind with a term of many meanings; hence the οὖν. The sense is: lifted up on the cross, as in ch. iii. 14; but it carries also the thought that this shameful lifting up would be the means of His real exaltation (Calvin, *et al.*), which comes more strongly to light in ch. xii. 32. Now His hearers understand it to mean: When ye have acknowledged the Son of Man as Messiah, and proclaimed Him in political form.—**Then shall ye know that I am he.**—Some willingly, in the outpouring of the Holy Ghost; others against their will, in the destruction of Jerusalem, *etc.* (comp. ch. vi. 62, a passage which is elucidated by this. On the different interpretations of the *knowing*, see Tholuck). They take it thus: Then shall ye perceive how I manifest and prove Myself the Messiah after your mind.—**And that I do nothing of myself.**—('Απ' ἐμαυτοῦ comes under ὅτι, and is not, as Lampe takes it, a new proposition). That is: That I do not of My own will and ambition usurp the honor and glory of Messiah. They understand it: That I, for secret reasons, do not come forward on my own responsibility, but abide the result.—**But speak these things as the Father taught me.**—His action is according to the instruction of the Father, primarily a testifying, speaking (therefore not a completing, according to Bengel and De Wette: λαλῶ completed by ποιῶ, ποιῶ by λαλῶ); and this very thing includes self-command in the matter of a decisive Messianic profession. Just this reserve leads Him into the difficult position, in which He seems to stand alone, and yet is not alone. He manifests Himself and conceals Himself as the Father instructs Him. See the history of the temptation. Now His hearers take it that the divine arrangement requires the Messiah to let the Messianic people take the initiative in His elevation.

Ver. 29. **And he that sent me is with me.**—The Messiah's trust to the arrangement of the Father in the trying course assigned Him. But in the progress of their misapprehension they must take Him as expressing His confidence of happy success in His Messianic enterprise with the help of God.—**He hath not left me alone.**—Pointing to the help of God which He has hitherto received, and which is secured to Him by the co-working of the divine purpose throughout the government of the world with His work, as well as with His Spirit, and by the co-working of His dominion with the Father. But they probably think of the silent preparation of extraordinary succor.

For I always do the things that are pleasing to him.—(Not: As appears from the fact that I do, *etc.*, Maldonatus. The assistance of the Father is to be distinguished from the essential unity of the Father with the Son, and reciprocates the obedience of Jesus.) In His unconditional obedience He has the seal of His unconditional confidence. But they may imagine: He has already introduced and arranged everything according to the direction of God.

Ver. 30. **As he spoke these words, many believed in him.**—In the simplest historical sense: Became disciples, came forward as followers and confessors of Him. What kind of faith this was, the sequel must teach, and Jesus Himself took care that the faith which arose out of chiliastic misconstructions should soon be tested and set right. Tholuck: "Πιστεύειν is here used for a faith which arises certainly not from miracles, but from the word; by force of the imposing power of His testimony concerning Himself; a faith, however, which was but superficial, for it did not find in the words of Jesus ῥήματα τῆς ζωῆς. They stand upon the footing of the disciples mentioned in ch. vi. 66; hence μένειν is required of them." The main thing required is submission to the word of Christ, renunciation of their carnal expectations, and a clearing and spiritualizing of their faith.

Failure to observe the misconstructions traced above has occasioned much confusion over the words of Jesus immediately following, and over the relapse of many or most of these disciples, which follows soon upon them.

DOCTRINAL AND ETHICAL.

1. As Christ is the *source of life* under different aspects: source of satisfaction, source of healing, source of quickening and inspiration, —so He is *the light* also under different aspects: the star by night which prevents wandering in darkness, the sun by day which brings with it the works of the day and opens the eye to the day, ch. ix. Here He is the star or lamp of the night, the true pillar of fire, which is set to lighten from Mount Zion the holy city and the world. Suggested by the illumination at the feast of tabernacles. "Next to the water-drawing and libation, this illumination was the leading feature of the festivities. As the drawing and pouring of the water typified the fulness of salvation which abode in Jerusalem and flowed forth thence, so these lights typified the enlightening of the world from the mountain of the Lord, Mic. iv. 2; Isa. ii. 2; lx. 3, 5; lv. 5; Zech. xiv. 7, 17. After the manner of His former interpretation of the water-drawing Jesus points here to that illumination. It was in Him that that prophetic festivity found its fulfilment: the light of the Gentiles, Isa. xlii. 6; xlix. 6; ix. 1, 2. He who follows Him, follows no flitting, earthly glimmer, which first flashes up, and then leaves the darkness only the more dismal: His light is a light of life, a light which in itself is life." Gerlach.

2. The consciousness of Christ is the star of night, the sun of day. He is sure of His origin (from the Father), of His destination (to the Father), and therefore of His way (with the Father), and can therefore offer Himself with absolute certitude and confidence as the guide of life to the people who are wandering in darkness. "Though I bear witness of Myself, yet My witness is true." Consciousness attested by conscience is the basis of all certitude (Luther, Descartes, Kant, Schleiermacher). Christ's divine self-consciousness is the starting-point of all divine certitude. Augustine: A light shows itself, as well as other things. You light a lamp, for example, to look for a garment, and the burning lamp helps you find it; but do you also light a lamp to look for a burning lamp?

3. The assault of the men of the letter on the testimony of Christ concerning Himself, a type of the battle between dead tradition and living faith.

4. The world's way of *judging*, and Christ's way: (1) The world judges of the nature of the person after the flesh (subjectively, with a carnal judgment, and objectively, from the mere appearance); Christ judges not the nature of the person, but his guilt. (2) The world forestalls the judgment of God, and, midway, condemns Christ to the cross; Christ pronounces the judgment of God, and the actual judgment He does not execute till the end of the world.

5. Christ's appeal to the testimony of His Father, and the mockery of the Jews; the fact, and the mistaking and denial, of the original Life. "It is remarkable how, in the words: *in your law* (of which ye are so proud), Jesus takes issue with them, and indeed, as it were quits them." Gerlach. "Had not God from eternity come out of a rigid, self-imprisoned *unity*, and revealed Himself as second person in the Son, *etc.*, He had not been able to redeem the human race, nor even therefore, to reveal, demonstrate Himself to it in His full truth." *Ibid.*

[5½. The significant expression: "the Father is with Me," is a counterpart of: "The Word was with God," in ch. i. 1. From eternity the Son was with the Father; in time the Father is with the Son. This personal distinction of the Father and the Son from each other is the stronger rather than the weaker, for that other: "The Word was God," which stands by its side, and which has a parallel here in ver. 19: "If ye had known Me, ye should have known My Father also." It is impossible to do justice to its significance, without the doctrine of the essential, eternal trinity of the Godhead; and this doctrine may be said to be contained in this combination of mysterious words. Augustine, in the *Catena*: "Blush, thou Sabellian; our Lord doth not say, I am the Father, and I the self-same person am the Son; but *I am not alone, because the Father is with Me.*"—E. D. Y.]

6. The suicidal world suspects Christ and Christianity of a suicidal intent. Character of suicide on the part of the Lord. *From beneath*: the contrast of suicide, which is from beneath, and self-sacrifice, which is from above.

[6½. Here the Lord says: "I am from above;" "ye neither know Me, nor My Father;" "ye cannot tell whence I come, and whither I go." He had said before, ch. vii. 28: "Ye both know Me, and know whence I am." This apparent contradiction only reflects in His free, spontaneous utterance the perfect harmony and unity of real deity and *real humanity* (against Docetism and Apollinarianism) in Him. And yet His having a really earthly, human origin, as well as a really divine, was not the same as being *from beneath* and *of this world*. *This world* "lieth in the wicked one."—E. D. Y.]

7. Christ reveals Himself in the spirit by veiling Himself in the flesh. "The teaching of Christ is not something outside of Him or added to Him; He Himself is all teacher, all revelation; His doctrine is Himself." Gerlach.

[7½. "The Being who sent Jesus into the world, was in such close companionship with Him, that He shared with Him, so to speak, all the opprobrium and hostility with which His mission was met, and would be present to His aid in every danger. . . . It should ever be borne in mind that this obedience of the Son, although strictly predicable of Him only in His Messianic office, is to be regarded as proceeding from His essential unity with the Father; else, as Olshausen well remarks, . . . it would depend for its perpetuity upon the fidelity of the Son. . . . It is based upon those immutable relations of companionship springing from the essential unity of the Father and Son, and referred to so emphatically in the preceding words, *is with me.*" J. J. Owen.—E. D. Y.]

8. The *chiliastic* elements in the life of Jewish people: *a.* During the life of Jesus, in Galilee (John vi.), in Judea (John viii.); *b.* After the ascension of the Lord, (1) at the time of founding of the church, Acts vi. 7; (2) before the death of James the Just. See his biography.

9. It is not right to presume that the rulers of the Jews would have absolutely closed themselves beforehand against the impression of the Messiahship of Jesus. On the contrary they were thoroughly disposed from the beginning, under certain conditions, to acknowledge Him as Messiah; *viz.*, if He would meet their idea of Messiah (see Matt. iv.) This accounts for the alternate attractions and the repulsions, which John exhibits to us in the boldest contrast, ch. iii.; chs. viii. and x. Even in the revilings against Christ on the cross the craving for a chiliastic Messiah may be perceived (Matt. xxvii. 42; see *Leben Jesu*, II. 3, p. 1562). This explains again the Lord's reservation of His name of Messiah, which He positively refused to have publicly proclaimed by the people until the Palm-Sunday, and to which He Himself did not confess until the hour of His condemnation before the high council.

10. In the miraculous gliding of Christ out of the hands of His enemies, both here and often elsewhere, Luthardt rightly sees a presage of the resurrection of Christ, by which He perfectly transported Himself from the violence of His foes.

HOMILETICAL AND PRACTICAL.

See the Doctrinal and Ethical points.—Christ the true pillar of fire to His people: 1. He gives light upon the world of sin. 2. He gives light through the world of nature. 3. He gives light to His believing followers.—Christ the light of the world in His saving work for those who follow Him: 1. The Light of the world. 2. The followers of the light. 3. The saving effect: (*a*) They shall not walk in darkness. (*b*) They shall have the light of life.—The star of heaven in the night of earth.—The morning star, which guides out of the night of death into the day of life.—The light of life: 1. The light as life. The effect of the enlightening of the understanding is the quickening of the heart. 2. The life as light. Quickening is enlightenment. —The true light and the true life are one.—Redemption by the light of life from walking in the night.—Christ the light of the world: 1. In the sureness of His course. 2. In that which His work begins with: not judging, not destroying, but quickening. 3. In that which His work ends with: separating by the effects of light, judging according to the fact, separating dead and living. 4. In that which His work both begins and ends with: the revealing of the real God, of the Father in His working, His quickening, His judging.

The Jews' judging after the flesh, a judgment against themselves: 1. It is a judgment of the carnal mind, of passion, on the revelations of the Spirit. 2. It is a judgment according to outward appearance and pedigree on the wonders of the new life. 3. It is a carnal condemnation of the divine gentleness which could rescue from damnation.—Prejudice, a way to condemnation.—The Jewish students of God, in the treasury of God, unmasked as ignorant despisers of God.—The manifest Father of Christ, a hidden God to His adversaries.—How Christ can charge spiritual ignorance upon His adversaries at the height of their power (in the treasury). Men of the letter have the treasury of God, and not the knowledge of God.

The fearful word of Christ concerning His departure: 1. The horrible misinterpretation of it. 2. Its true meaning.—Suicide elucidated by the conversation of Christ with the Jews.—Self-killing and self-sacrifice; or, the death from beneath, and the life from above.—To be from beneath, and to be from above.—How Christ would be known according to His own representation of Himself, and not according to the preconceived opinions of the world: 1. According to the Old Testament, not according to the Jewish schools. 2. According to the New Testament, not according to mediæval tradition. 3. According to His divine glory, not according to our human notion. —Legitimate steps in the revelation of Christ to us.—Before the world would come to a decision concerning Christ, it must have the judgment of Christ concerning Himself.—Ver. 26. The judgment of Christ concerning the world unavoidable: 1. As a testimony to the real government of God. 2. As a testimony to His true view of things.—The words of Christ concerning His elevation, as they are misinterpreted by the ear of the Jews. —The power of the Spirit in these words of the Lord: (*a*) His confidence that His elevation on the cross will be the lowest depth of His path to His heavenly exaltation. (*b*) The mercy with which He still gives His enemies the prospect of knowing their salvation by His death and resurrection. (*c*) The clear prediction of the effect of the preaching of the cross in the New Testament dispensation.—The twofold knowing that Jesus is the Lord, as produced by His twofold elevation (the knowing which believers have, and that which unbelievers have).

The word of Christ: *I am not* (left) *alone:* 1. The sense of the expression: The Father is with Him through the whole course of His sufferings (Gethsemane). 2. The confidence of it: Notwithstanding He was soon to be forsaken by all the world and apparently by God Himself. 3. The foundation of the confidence: for I do always those things, *etc.*

Those who believe from misunderstanding.—The form of enthusiastic belief, which can immediately turn into the bitterest unbelief.—Misunderstanding of the word of God: 1. Its forms. 2. Its causes. 3. Its marks. 4. Its solution. 5. Its consequences.

Starke: Lange: The illumination of the understanding always inseparably connected with the sanctification of the will. On life depends light or use of eyes.—Teachers should always lead their hearers from the earthly to the spiritual.—Hedinger: He who follows Christ never misses the right way; always with will-o'-the-wisps! Is. xi. 3, 4.—God, who is (αὐτόπιστος) the truth itself, can testify of Himself, and all men, though they be but liars, must believe His testimony.—If the Father and the Son testify the very same thing, how strong, how invincible is the testimony!—Stiff-necked enemies of the truth deride what they do not and will not understand, and when they can go no further, they start something ridiculous.—(In the treasury.) God wonderfully protects faithful teachers and confessors of His word.—QUESNEL: Jesus says nothing but what the Father bids Him say; therefore should His ministers also preach nothing but what they have learned of Him, Rom. xv. 18.—Ver. 28. ZEISIUS: The prophecies of God will never be more truly and fully understood than in their fulfilment.—O how many Christians do not know Christ before they have crucified Him with their sins!

BRAUNE: "Shall not walk in darkness," in unholiness, in sin. It is manifestly a fundamental truth that mind and will belong together; neither can be corrupted or improved without the other; and enlightenment and sanctification ever play into one another. At the same time, looking at the preceding occurrences, the Lord seems to intend to guard His dealing with the fallen woman against all abuses. He does not let sin prevail.—Does not the sun bear witness even to its own existence? Set it aside, if you can.—Jesus alone knew both whence He came and whither He went; His adversaries knew neither.—Contend not with blasphemers over God, but over noble life.—The cross is the knot in which humiliation and exaltation are entwined. In the cross the deepest humiliation ended; in the cross exaltation began.

HEUBNER: Some light a man will always follow; the question is whether he will choose the right one. Criterion: The following of Jesus casts out all uncertain, restless groping.—There are only two ways: that of the darkness, and that of the light.—The test of true illumination is that it gives life.—Bearing witness to one's self by no means absolutely inadmissible.—The believer also knows the source and the goal of his life.—How little would the hostile Jews have suspected that this Jesus, their antagonist, would soon be exalted at the right hand of God. So the children of the world suspect not the speedy glorification of the godly whom they despise.—Ver. 19; comp. v. 37. The knowing of the Father and the knowing of the Son are inseparable.—*I go my way.* Our enjoyment of the means of grace has its day.—*Ye shall seek Me.* The time is sure to come when the man shall know those through whom God would have saved him: children their father, *etc.*—*Ye cannot come.* Heaven inaccessible to the assaults of the wicked.—*From beneath, etc.* Between the worldly-minded and the heavenly-minded there is as great a distance (and an abyss) as between heaven and earth.—The enemies of the good cause must involuntarily promote it.

SCHLEIERMACHER: Walking in the light, walking in the truth.—If our faith in the Lord rested on any human testimony, He could not be that on which we might build the full certainty of our salvation. We must cease to be of this world: then we can believe that He is that.—The Lord leaves not alone those who are joined with the Redeemer.—BESSER: Zech. xiv. 7: "At evening time it shall be light."—If Christ is the light of the world, the world without Him is darkness. — What a cutting contradiction: The *treasury of God* surrounded by a *God*-forsaken people, whose offerings were as heartless as the coin clinking in the chest.—Heb. xii. 3.—Christ, and Christians with Him, go above, to heaven, because they are come down from above; but the servants of sin and of the devil go down, because they are from beneath.

[MATT. HENRY: Ver. 12. *He that followeth Me.* It is not enough to look at this light, and to gaze upon it; but we must follow it, believe in it, walk in it,—for it is a light to our feet, not our eyes only.—Ver. 26: *I have many things to say, etc.* 1. Whatever discoveries of sin are made to us, He that searcheth the heart hath still more to judge of us, 1 John iii. 30. 2. How much soever God reckons with sinners in this world, there is still a farther reckoning yet behind, Deut. xxxii. 34. 3. Let us not be forward to say all we can say, even against the worst of men; we may have many things to say by way of censure, which yet it is better to leave unsaid, for what is it to us?—E. D. Y.]

IV.

CHRIST THE LIBERATOR, AS SON OF THE HOUSE IN OPPOSITION TO SERVANTS; THE ONE SENT FROM GOD, AS AGAINST THE AGENTS OF THE DEVIL; THE ETERNAL AND THE HOPE OF ABRAHAM AS AGAINST THE BODILY SEED OF ABRAHAM. OR: THE LIBERATOR OF ISRAEL, THE ADVERSARY OF SATAN, THE HOPE OF ABRAHAM. A GREAT SWINGING FROM FAITH TO UNBELIEF. ATTEMPTED STONING.

CHAP. VIII. 31–59.

(Vers. 46–59, the Pericope for *Judica* Sunday.)

31 Then said Jesus [Jesus therefore said] to those Jews which believed on him [who
had believed him]. If ye continue in my word, *then* are ye [ye are] my[1] disciples
32 indeed; And ye shall [will] know the truth, and the truth shall [will] make you
33 free. They answered him, We be [are] Abraham's seed, and were never in bond-
34 age to any man: how sayest thou, Ye shall [will] be made free? Jesus answered
them, Verily, verily, I say unto you, Whosoever committeth sin is the servant [a

35 bondman, a slave] of sin.[2] And the servant [the bondman] abideth not in the house
36 for ever: *but* [*omit* but] the Son [son] abideth ever.[3] If the Son therefore shall
37 make you [If then the Son make you] free, ye shall [will] be free indeed. I know
that ye are Abraham's seed; but ye seek to kill me, because my word hath no place
38 [maketh no progress] in you. I speak that which I have seen with my [the]
39 Father: and ye [likewise][4] do that which ye have seen with your father.[5] They
answered and said unto him, Abraham is our father. Jesus saith unto them, If
40 ye were [are][6] Abraham's children, ye would[7] do the works of Abraham. But now
ye seek to kill me, a man that hath told you [spoken to you] the truth, which I
41 have heard of [I heard from] God: this [the like of this] did not Abraham. Ye do
the deeds [works] of your father. Then said they [They said] to him, We be [were]
42 not born of fornication; we have one Father, *even* God. Jesus said unto them, If
God were your Father, ye would love me: for I proceeded forth and came [am
43 come] from God; [for] neither came I of myself, but he sent me. Why do ye not
44 understand my speech? *even* because[8] ye cannot hear my word. Ye are of *your*
father [of the father who is] the devil, and the lusts of your father ye will [ye desire to] do: he was a murderer from the beginning, and abode not [doth not stand]
in the truth, because there is no truth in him. When he[9] speaketh a lie, he speaketh of his own [from his own nature]: for [because] he is a liar, and the father of
45 it [thereof]. And [But] because I tell *you* [speak] the truth, ye believe me not.
46 Which of you convinceth [convicteth] me of sin? And [*omit* And] if I say the
47 truth, why do ye not believe me? He that is of God heareth God's words: ye
therefore hear *them* not [for this cause ye do not hear], because ye are not of God.
48 Then answered the Jews [The Jews answered], and said unto him, Say we not
49 well that thou art a Samaritan, and hast a devil [demon]? Jesus answered, I have
50 not a devil [demon]; but I honour my Father, and ye do dishonour me. And
51 [But] I seek not mine own glory: there is one that seeketh and judgeth. Verily,
verily, I say unto you, If a man keep my saying [my word][10] he shall [will]
never see death.
52 Then[11] said the Jews unto him, Now we know that thou hast a devil [demon].
Abraham is dead [died], and the prophets; and thou sayest, If a man keep my saying
53 [my word], he shall [will] never taste of death. Art thou greater than our father
Abraham, which is dead [who died]? and the prophets are dead [the prophets also
54 died]: whom makest thou [dost thou make] thyself? Jesus answered, If I honour
[glorify][12] myself my honour [glory] is nothing: it is my Father that honoureth
55 [glorifieth] me; of whom ye say, that he is your [our][13] God: Yet ye have not
known him; but I know him: and if I should say, I know him not, I shall [should]
56 be a liar like unto you: but I know him, and keep his saying [word]. Your[14]
father Abraham rejoiced to see [that he should see, ἵνα ἴδῃ] my day: and he saw
57 *it*, and was glad. Then said the Jews [The Jews therefore said] unto him, Thou art
58 not yet fifty[15] years old, and hast thou seen[16] Abraham? Jesus said unto them,
Verily, verily, I say unto you, Before Abraham was [was made, or, born, *γενέσθαι*]
I am [*εἰμί*].
59 Then took they up [Therefore they took up] stones to cast at him: but Jesus
hid himself, and went out of the temple, going through the midst of them, and
so passed by [*omit* going—by].[16]

TEXTUAL AND GRAMMATICAL.

[1] Ver. 31.—[Cod. Sin. omits the *μου*, so generalizing the idea of *disciple*.—E. D. Y.]

[2] Ver. 34.—*Τῆς ἁμαρτίας* is wanting in Cod. D., Iren., Hil., *etc.* [Cod. Sin., with most of the leading authorities, has it]. The omission has been caused by the general expression ὁ δὲ δοῦλος following.

[3] Ver. 35.—[This whole clause *ὁ υἱὸς—αἰῶνα* is wanting in Cod. Sin. Otherwise it is unquestioned. The omission is probably an effort to strip the ὁ δὲ δοῦλος, ver. 34, of that generalness which seemed to others to require the omission of the *τῆς ἁμαρτίας* before it.—E. D. Y.]

[4] Ver. 38.—[*οὖν* after *ὑμεῖς* is disputed in the Greek text, and should be translated *therefore* or *accordingly* or *likewise* or *by the same rule*. Meyer: "*In οὖν liegt eine schmerzliche Ironie*."—P. S.]

[5] Ver. 38.—Instead of ὃ *ἑωράκατε παρὰ τῷ πατρὶ ὑμῶν*, we should read, according to decisive authorities (B. C. K.): *ἃ ἠκούσατε παρὰ τοῦ πατρός*. [An ironical allusion to the devil.] *Μου* and *ὑμῶν* are probably exegetical interpolations. [Lachmann, Tischendorf, and Alford omit them. ℵ. D. have them. They also support Lachmann and Tischendorf in reading *ἃ ἐγώ* instead of *ἐγὼ ὃ*, in the first clause. But in the second it reads: *ἃ ἑωράκατε παρὰ τοῦ πατρός*. Nothing in the nature of the case would seem to require *ἠκούσατε* here rather than the *ἑωράκ.* which is used of Christ in His relation to the Father; for in ver. 40 the *hearing* is applied to Christ, and in ver. 41 the *seeing* is implied in the case of the Jews.—Y.]

[6] Ver. 39.—B. D. L. [ℵ] *ἐστε*, [instead of *ἦτε*, *were*, text. rec.] to which, however, the *ἐποιεῖτε* does not correspond. [Meyer: "The apparent want of grammatical correspondence between the two members has occasioned the change now of *ἐστε* into

ἦτε, now of ἐποιεῖτε into ποιεῖτε (Vulg., Aug.)." Meyer, with Griesbach and Lachmann, prefers ἐστε, and is supported by Cod. Sin.—Y.]

[7] Ibid.—The ἂν is not sufficiently accredited.

[8] Ver. 43.—[Dr. Lange translates this as belonging to the question, not as an answer; takes ὅτι=ὥστε: "Why do ye not understand my speech, so that ye cannot hear my word?" See the Exegesis.—Y.]

[9] Ver. 44.—[The reading ὃς ἂν is untenable.]

[10] Ver. 51.—Τὸν ἐμὸν λόγον. The reading τὸν λόγον τὸν ἐμόν is exegetical. [Lachmann and Tischendorf read τὸν ἐμὸν λόγον, and Meyer thinks the balance of authority in favor of that reading. Hahn, Stier and Theile, *etc.*, prefer the other, and Cod. Sin. supports it. Cod. Sin. also has the weaker futures τηρήσει and θεωρήσει, instead of the subjunctives τηρήσῃ and θεωρήσῃ. But in ver. 52 it agrees with all the great authorities in γεύσηται, against the future γεύσεται of the Text. Rec.—Y.]

[11] Ver. 52.—[Cod. Sin. supports Lachmann and Tischendorf in omitting οὖν.—Y.]

[12] Ver. 54.—According to B. C.* D. [Cod. Sin.], *etc.*, δοξάσω. [Rec.: δοξάζω.]

[13] Ibid.—[The Recepta, and therefore the English Version, are supported by the Cod. Sin.: ὑμῶν, but A. B.[2] C. al. read ἡμῶν, direct discourse. J. J. Owen: "Some critics connect" the succeeding clause with this, "and translate *of whom ye say 'he is our God,' and know him not.* But this presents less forcibly the contrast between their arrogant claims and real ignorance of God." The conjunction is simply καί. The main contrast also would seem to lie between the Jews' ignorance and Christ's knowledge of God.—Y.]

[14] Ver. 56.—The authorities waver between ἡμῶν (*our* father) and ὑμῶν (*your* father). The first reading is more probable. [There is probably a mistake here. Lachmann indeed quotes Origen in favor of ἡμῶν, but Tischendorf, Tregelles, Alford, Westcott and Hort mention no such reading in this verse, while in ver. 55 the authorities are divided between θεὸς ὑμῶν and θεὸς ἡμῶν.—P. S.]

[15] Ver. 57.—The reading τεσσαράκοντα in Chrysostom and others is exegetical.

[16] Ibid.—[Cod. Sin.[1] ἑώρακεν σε; *hath Abraham seen thee?* to conform their question to Christ's assertion, ver. 56.—Y.]

[17] Ver. 59.—The words from διελθών to the end are wanting in B. D., Vulgate, and seem to have been transferred from Luke iv. 30 by way of exegesis. [Wanting also in Cod. Sin.—Y.]

EXEGETICAL AND CRITICAL.

[The last discourse had made an impression on many, and brought them to the door of a superficial discipleship (ver. 30), while yet their heart was full of prejudice. These half converts the Lord now addresses and warns them not to be satisfied with a passing excitement of feeling, but to become true and steady disciples. Then they would know the truth, and the truth would give them true freedom from the degrading bondage of sin and error. Knowledge appears here as the fruit of faith, and freedom as the fruit of knowledge. This earnest exhortation brings out the latent hatred of the Jews, whereupon the Lord, with fearful severity, exposes the diabolical nature of their opposition to Him, while He at the same time reveals His divine nature as the destroyer of death and the One who was before Abraham was born. This address, in the lively form of dialogue, unites the character of a testimony concerning Himself and a judgment of the Jews, and rises to the summit of moral force.—P. S.]

Ver. 31. **If ye continue in my word.**—That is, here, not merely: continue to believe, but believe according to the spirit of the word, and in obedience to the word, which He spoke. Working towards an exposure of their misapprehension of His words—**Ye are my disciples indeed.**—This, therefore, must first appear. [There is a latent antithesis between πεπιστευκότας and μαθηταί. It was one thing to believe in Jesus, quite another to be disciples, *learners.* The one could be a momentary impulse; the other required constant study and obedience?] True discipleship is the condition and guaranty of their knowing the truth; and then this knowledge carries the blessing, that the truth should make them free. Freedom is the very thing they were bent upon all along; but a political, theocratic freedom, as pictured by a chiliastic mind. Christ opens to them the prospect of a higher freedom which, if they should be true disciples, they would owe to the liberating effect of the truth, the living knowledge of God; He opens the prospect of freedom from sin.

Ver. 32. **Ye shall know the truth more and more.** [Hengstenberg: "A difference of degree of knowledge is put in the form of knowledge itself as opposed to ignorance, because in comparison with future attainments of knowledge in the path of fidelity, the present knowledge would be quite insignificant. The truth is not merely something thought; it has taken flesh and blood in Christ, who says, *I am the truth.* By a deeper and deeper knowing of Christ they would know also the truth, after which, as after freedom, every man who is not utterly lost has a deep constitutional longing, and this living truth would make them free from the bondage of sin and error; while the truth considered merely as a thought of the mind would be utterly powerless. The same liberating effect which is here ascribed to the truth, is in ver. 36 ascribed to Christ."—E. D. Y.]

[**The truth will make you free,** ἡ ἀλήθεια ἐλευθερώσει ὑμᾶς. Comp. ver. 36: "If the Son make you free, ye will be free indeed," ὄντως ἐλεύθεροι. Christ associates liberty always with the truth, which He is Himself, and presents the truth as the cause, and liberty as the effect. So also Paul speaks of liberty always in this positive, highest and noblest sense, liberty in Christ, the glorious liberty of the children of God, liberty from the bondage of sin and error, comp. Rom. viii. 21; 2 Cor. iii. 17; Gal. ii. 4; v. 1, 13; Jas. i. 25; 1 Pet. ii. 12. Man is truly free when he is released from abnormal foreign restraints and moves in harmony with the mind and will of God as his proper element. "*Deo servire vera libertas est.*"—P. S.]

Ver. 33. **They answered him, We are Abraham's seed** (or; **offspring**).—Here comes the turning-point. Christ has openly told them that He would redeem them spiritually from sin by the truth, and in this sense make them free; and now they see their misapprehension of His former words. But in bitter vexation they plunge into a new mistake, supposing that Christ had their political bondage in view, and would require them to console themselves under their political oppression with the enjoyment of spiritual truth. Hence, instead of explaining: Thou shouldst free us from the domination of the Romans, they explain with insulted pride, that they are already free; they have never been any man's slaves. This answer contains (1) an unbelieving denial of their spiritual servitude; for they studiously avoid the spiritual meaning of the words of Jesus; (2) a revolutionary, chiliastic protest against the idea that they acknowledged the dominion of the Romans, or that they could, as the words of Jesus implied, console themselves under it with spiritual elevation. This breaks again the scarcely formed union with Christ. This sharp contrast in the same Jews between a great demonstration of submission to Jesus and a hostility ready to stone Him,—this reaction of sentiment, coming the moment they were undeceived concerning their chiliastic expectations, appears repeatedly in the Gospel of John in significant gradations. It has already come distinctly to view chap. vi. 30 (comp. ver. 15); and in chap. x. 31 (comp. ver. 24) it is still more glaring than here.

If these historical points are not duly considered, it must seem strange that the same Jews who had just believed in a mass, should so soon relapse into the bitterest unbelief. Hence many have supposed that here other Jews of the mass, quite distinct from those believing ones, now come forward and take up the conversation (Augustine, Calovius, *etc.*, Lücke *et al.*). Tholuck: "It is far more likely that the same adversaries who have hitherto been in view, the 'Ἰουδαῖοι, are the subject of ἀπεκρίθησαν. Before the believing hearers speak, some of the rulers interpose, to repel the supposed slander upon the whole people." This would imply an inaccuracy of expression. On the contrary, according to the narrative of the evangelist, they are manifestly the same to whom Jesus had spoken, and ἀπεκρίθησαν cannot be translated: *it was answered.* Justly, therefore, Chrysostom, Maldonatus, Bengel, and others, have taken them to be the same. Chrysostom gave the sufficient interpretation: Κατέπεσεν εὐθέως αὐτῶν ἡ διάνοια· τοῦτο δὲ γέγονεν ἀπὸ τοῦ πρὸς τὰ κοσμικὰ ἐπτοῆσθαι. ["Their belief immediately gave way; and that because of their eagerness after worldly things."] It seems transparent (1) that Jesus in His reply, ver. 34, to those who speak in ver. 33, simply pursues the discourse He had begun in vers. 31, 32; and (2) that His suggestion of the need of being made free, ver. 32, was *intended* to test the sincerity, or provoke the latent insincerity, of the faith of the persons of vers. 30, 31. Contrary to Dr. Tholuck's remark above, the evangelist has here very accurately designated the interlocutors, ver. 31, as Jesus and those Jews who believed on Him. Meyer suggests that "the πολλοί, ver. 30, are many among the *hearers in general;* among these 'many' were some *hierarchical Jews,* and to *these* Jesus speaks in ver. 31." There probably was this difference among the believing many; but it is hardly in John's view here. Hengstenberg, who agrees on this point with Tholuck, thinks "John was quite too much intent upon reality than to ascribe faith to such murderous enemies of Christ as these, on the ground of a mere fleeting emotion." But this very consideration might work the other way: the Evangelist would take even a transient and impure faith for what it is worth as faith for the time. This great relapse from a flash of faith into deepened darkness of unbelief may be just the "reality" on which John is intent. [Of recent expositors Olshausen, Meyer, Stier, Alford, Ellicott ("*Life of Christ*"), J. J. Owen, and others, take the same view with Dr. Lange.—E. D. Y.]

Ibid. **We are Abraham's seed.**—These words are put as the foundation of what follows: **And were never in bondage** (never yielded ourselves as bond-servants). Because they were Abraham's seed (on the strength of many Old Testament passages like Gen. xxii. 17; xvii. 16), they claimed, according to Jewish theology, not only freedom, but even dominion over the nations. As πώποτε includes the whole past, these words can only mean: Often as we have been under oppression (under Egyptians, Babylonians, Syrians), we have never acknowledged any oppressor as master, but have always submitted only from necessity, reserving our right to freedom, and striving after it. This reservation carried the spirit and design of revolution, and afterwards, in the Jewish war, acted it out in the Zealots and Sicarii (Joseph. *De bello Jud.*, vii. 8, 6).

This extremely simple state of the case many interpreters have lost sight of, failing to distinguish between a bondage *de facto* and a bondage *de jure;* hence a list of mistaken explanations (specified by Tholuck, p. 250). Tholuck, referring to my *Leben Jesu*, II. 2, 968: "They were as far from *acknowledging* subjection to Rome, as modern Rome is from acknowledging secular relations which contradict its hierarchical consciousness." "Only as a domination *de facto*, and not *de jure*, does even Josephus represent to them the Roman domination, on the prudential principle of yielding to superior force (*De bello Jud.* v. 9, 3). And to this day it stands among the fifteen benedictions which should be said every morning: 'Blessed art Thou, that Thou hast not made me a slave.' *Schülchan Aruch. tr. Orach Chajim*, fol. 10, ch. 3. The meanest laborer who is of the seed of Abraham, is like a king, says the Talmud."*

Ver. 34. **Whosoever committeth sin** [π ᾶ ς ὁ π ο ι ῶ ν τ ὴ ν ἁ μ α ρ τ ί α ν, living in the practice of sin], **is a slave of sin.**—A solemn declaration, enforced with: *Verily, verily.* In these words Jesus utterly expels the political question from His scope. He states first the principle, then the application. The *committing* of sin is to be taken with emphasis; He whose tendency and habit is to commit sin;† which may be applied in a wide sense to every man born of the flesh (Rom. vii. 14), in the narrower sense to the evil propension of the earthly-minded (ch. iii. 20; 1 Jno. iii. 8). He is the servant, the slave, of sin; fallen into the worst conceivable bondage, or rather the only real bondage; the man being even at heart a slave,

* [Meyer's interpretation that the Jews here in an excited state of mind, confine their view to their own time, and then make earnest of the show of freedom allowed them by the Romans (Joseph. vi. 6, 2), by no means excludes Dr. Lange's, which Meyer thinks unnecessary. Indeed the constitutional and traditional temper of the Jews, as Lange here finely analyzes it, would be just the source of such excited exaggeration as Dr. Meyer finds in these words. And conversely, Lange's view might well include Meyer's; for the Jews are here not so much stating a refined political doctrine, as venting a passionate jealousy supported by it. Nor need even the still less qualified view of Dr. J. J. Owen be left out: "to refer their reply to the loose and inconsiderate manner of speaking which characterizes persons in a state of high excitement, such as that into which these persons were thrown by the answer of Jesus." Y.]

† [Comp. Matt. viii. 23, ἐργαζόμενος τὴν ἁμαρτίαν.]

whereas in other sorts of servitude the man may himself be free within, though in outward bonds. And the application was obvious. Jesus implied that they, not only for being born of the flesh, but for being carnally-minded and practically hostile to the truth, committed sin. The hint that they were therefore in the hardest slavery, and in the utmost need of liberation by the truth which they despised, the Lord in the sequel turns gradually into a decided opinion. Comp. Rom. vi. 17; vii. 14, ff. "Analogous instances from the classics see in Wetstein; from Philo, in Lösner, p. 149." Meyer. ["The mere moral sentiment of which this is the moral expression, was common among the Greek and Roman philosophers." Alford.—P. S.]

Ver. 35. **And the bondman abideth not in the house for ever.**—The thought takes its turn from the legal relations of civil life. The bond-servant is not an organic member of the household, has no inheritance, and can be expelled or sold, Gen. xxi. 10; Gal. iv. 30. According to the law of Moses the Hebrew servant must be set free in the seventh year, if he desire; but even if he wishes to remain servant of the house, he does not thereby become a member of the family, Ex. xxi. 1 ff. To this legal status of the servant, however, as not a permanent member of the household, Jesus gives an allegorical meaning. And in so doing He goes upon a presumption, where expositors readily incline to see a jump. He who is the servant of sin, is, under the dispensation of the law, an involuntary subject of the law; therefore a slave of the letter; and he who is such a slave of the letter, is a slave of sin. Paul also goes on this presumption in Gal. iii. 10. The slave of the letter, therefore, being a slave of sin, abides not in the house of God, the theocracy. The application is obvious: In the kingdom of God there have been hitherto children and servants (Gal. iii. 22; iv. 1); the servants at this time are the unbelieving Jews; they are one day driven out (Matt. viii. 12; Rom. ix. 31; Gal. iv. 30). Not all Israel, but only the unbelieving portion; of these, who treat the law as a mere statute, a slavery to the letter, which corresponds with the bondage of sin, it is declared that they hold no relation of affinity and sonship to the master of the house. The reference of the servant to Moses, propounded by Chrysostom and Euthymius, belongs to a different train of thought and a different aspect of the servant, Heb. iii. 5.* *The house;* typically denoting the royal family of the Lord, the household of God, Ps. xxiii. 6; xxvii. 4.

The son abideth forever [*viz.*, in the house.]—He is by blood one with the house and heir of the house. This point of law is also a similitude, expressing the perpetual dwelling and ruling of Christ in the kingdom of God. As the son is spoken of in the singular, the word cannot be taken to imply a class of men who are morally and religiously free. And in fact the children of the house themselves, under the Old Testament economy, not having attained their maturity, are put under the same law with the proper alien slaves.*

[The contrast is here between bondage to sin and a freedom to which even the *children* of the house of God could attain only in a new stage, a manhood, of spiritual life; and into this new stage of full-grown sonship they, and much more those who had let themselves down into *servitude*, could come only in Christ, *the* Son of God. There *were no sons*, whose position would afford, except prospectively, a *general maxim* of the kind here before us. Even the children differed not yet from servants, though they were not servants of sin. While, therefore, the word *son* not *directly* denoting Christ, but being used generically, might properly be printed both here and in the verse following without a capital, Dr. J. J. Owen's remark upon it in this verse is unwarrantable, and in the next inconsistent: "The word *son* improperly commences with a capital in our common version, as though it referred to the Son of God. It stands here opposed to *servant*, and is generically put for all those born to a state of freedom, and consequently heirs to the paternal inheritance and privileges. In the next verse the word *Son* is properly capitalized."—E. D. Y.]

Ver. 36. **If then the Son make you free.**†—A new legal principle is here again presupposed by this expression. The son can give servants their freedom; and he can receive them to membership in the house, as adopted brothers, and to participation in his inheritance. The spiritual application which Jesus makes of this principle stops with the first point. The house of God has its son; and this son must make the servants in the house of God free, before any true freedom can be spoken of among you.

Note, that He speaks primarily only of the son of the house, not of the Son of God, and that He does not designate Himself as the son (comp. ch. v). But His meaning, that He is the son of the house, and as such the Son of God, the only one who is spiritually free and can give spiritual freedom, stands out clearly enough. The sentence is so framed, that it may be taken as containing at once the condition of the true freedom for Israel, a prophecy concerning the believing portion of Israel, and a warning and threatening for the unbelieving portion.

Ye will be free indeed [ὄντως ἐλεύθεροι].—As opposed to their visionary, fanatical effort after external, political freedom in their spiritual bondage. Without the *real* freedom they could neither attain, nor maintain, nor enjoy the outward; while the inward freedom must ultimately bring about the outward. The fact that the son appears as the liberator, instead of the lord of the house himself, agrees with the figure; all depends in this case on what he is willing to do in regard to his hereditary right in the servants. Comp. ch. x. 26; 27.

Ver. 37. **I know that ye are Abraham's seed; but ye seek to kill me.**—The acknow-

* [Alford, with Bengel, Stier, Ebrard, assumes here a reference to Ishmael and Isaac, the bond and the free sons of the same Abraham, but the bondwoman and her son are cast out. Meyer objects; the sentence being general.—P. S.]

* [Meyer: "ὁ υἱος μένει εἰς τ. αἰῶνα, namely, ἐν τ. ῇ οἰκίᾳ—is likewise a general sentence, but with the intended *application* of the ὁ υἱός to *Christ*, who as the Son of *God* forever retains His position and power in the house of God, *i. e.* in the theocracy, comp. Heb. iii. ff."—P. S.]

† [Grotius: "*Tribuitur hic filio quod modo* (ver. 32) VERITATI, *quia eam profert filius.*"—P. S.]

ledgment of their claim to natural descent from Abraham serves only to strengthen the reproof that follows. What a contrast: Abraham's seed, murderers of Christ! Christ can charge them with seeking to kill Him: (1) because they are already turned into an apostasy from Him, which cannot stop short of deadly enmity; (2) because they are impelled by the chiliastic idea of Christ, which leads in the end to the crucifixion of Christ; (3) because they go back to the hierarchical opposition, which has already determined His death.

Because my word maketh no progress in you.—*Χωρεῖν*: to make way, go through, encompass. Metaphorically: to come to something, to succeed, to make progress. The last meaning is the most probable here. These adversaries are the persons in view; hence *ἐν ὑμῖν* cannot mean *among you* (does not take effect: Luther; has no success: Lücke). *In you:* (*a*) Finds no room, gains no ground in you. Origen, Chrysostom, Beza, *et al.* Meyer says, it cannot mean this; Tholuck favors this meaning; and Origen and Chrysostom ought to have known the admissible use of the word. Yet this thought must then be reduced to: (*b*) Finds no entrance into you (Nonnus, Grotius, Luthardt, Tholuck). But then the accusative [or *εἰς ὑμᾶς*] would be expected. Better, therefore, De Dieu and Meyer: It makes no progress in you. It does not thrive in you. This, in fact, Christ has just had experience of with them. They have first misunderstood His word, then loose hold of it again. This then turns into an opposition, which by the strength of its spirit and its reaction ("he that is not with Me," &c.) must pass into deadly enmity.

Ver. 38. **I speak what I have seen with the (my) Father.**—The contrast between Him and them is threefold: 1. My Father, your father (though the verbal antithesis here is critically doubtful; see the TEXT. AND GRAM. NOTES.) 2. He acts according to what He has clearly seen with His Father; they act according to what they have indistinctly heard from their father (and a further antithesis between the perfect *ἑώρακα* and the aorist *ἠκούσατε*.) Yet to limit *ἑώρακα*, with Meyer, to the pre-existent state of Christ, is partial.* 3. His way towards them is to speak openly (*λαλῶ*) what He has known to be the will and decree of the Father; they, on the contrary, true to the manner of their father, even in moral concerns, go right on to malicious dealing. ("In *οὖν* there is a sad irony."—Meyer.) It is the contrast, therefore, of a moral parentage, a moral instruction, a moral way, which in Christ issues in a purely spiritual witness-bearing, and one which in the Jews issues in a fanatical, murderous falling upon Christ. He speaks God's judgment respecting them; they put Him on Satanic trial for death. The other result of Christ's seeing: His doing what He sees His Father do, does not here come into view. His doing is all a doing good, and for this a susceptibility is prerequisite. But to His adversaries He says how it stands with them before the law and judgment of God. Who His Father is, and who is theirs, they must for the present forebode. Meyer: "He means, however, the devil, whose children in the *ethical* view they are, whereas He is in the metaphysical view and in reality the Son of God." But the ethical view is also included. On the one hand, clear impression, free compliance, calm declaration; on the other, dark, sullen impulse, forced obedience, malignant practice. "*Ποιεῖτε*: constant conduct; including the seeking to kill, but not exclusively denoting that." Meyer.

Ver. 39. **Abraham is our father.**—The distinction between true children of Abraham and spurious children who therefore, as to their moral nature, must have another father, Christ has introduced by the foregoing sentence. They suspect the stinging point of His distinction; hence their proud assertion, which calls forth the Lord's denial: **If ye were Abraham's children.** In the spiritual sense [children in moral character and habits, as distinct from *seed* or mere natural descent, ver. 37.—P. S.] **Ye would do the works of Abraham,** works of faith, above all the work of faith. [*τέκνα* and *ἔργα* are correlative.] Abraham had a longing for the coming of Christ, ver. 56. "Just as Paul does in Rom. ix. 8, Jesus here distinguishes the ethical posterity as *τέκνα* from the physical as *σπέρμα*." Tholuck. [So also Meyer and Alford. —P. S.] *Σπέρμα*, *seed*, is rather used to designate Abraham's posterity as a unit, Gal. iii. 16.

Ver. 40. **But now ye seek to kill me.**—The very opposite of Abraham's spirit. The Lord does not yet characterize their murderous plot as a killing of the Christ; this alone condemns them, that they wished to kill in Him a *man*, and a man *who had spoken to them the truth*, who did nothing more but told the truth which He had *heard from God*, and therefore stood as a prophet.* The counterpart is Abraham with his benevolent spirit in general, with his homage for Melchizedek, and with his sparing of Isaac when God interposed.

[**A man,** *ἄνθρωπον*, with reference to *παρὰ τοῦ θεοῦ*. This self-designation of Christ as a man, a human being, implies all that is essential to our nature. It occurs nowhere else, but instead of it the frequent title *the Son of Man*, with the definite article, which at the same time elevates Him above the *ordinary* level of humanity, *λελάληκα*, the *first* person, according to Greek rule, see Buttmann, *N. T. Gr.* p. 241. **This did not Abraham.** Litotes, *ἐποίησε*, *fecit* (not *fecisset*), a statement of fact all the more stinging. A reference to Abraham's treatment of the Angel of Jehovah, Gen. xviii. (Lampe, Hengstenberg), is not clear.—P. S.]

Ver. 41. **Ye do the works of your father.** —Thus much is now perfectly manifest: They have, in respect to moral character, some other father than Abraham, who is exactly the opposite of them in spirit. The deeds of that father they do; that is, they do according to his deeds, and they do according to his bidding; they do his deeds in his service.

* [Dr. Lange, it will be observed, adopts the reading: Ye do that which ye *heard* with your father. See the TEXT. NOTE. This reading seems, indeed, to be doubtful. But *παρὰ τοῦ πατρός* here (*from* your father), in distinction from the *π. τῷ πατρί* (*with* my Father) in the former clause, is less doubtful, and warrants substantially Dr. Lange's second antithesis.—Y.]

* [Godet: "*Remarque la gradation:* 1, *Faire mourir un homme;* 2, *un homme organe de la* VERITE; 3, *de la vérité qui vient de* DIEU."—P. S.]

We were not born of fornication.—They seem to suspect the spiritual intent of Christ's words, yet they avoid it by at first standing upon the literal interpretation of them, that they may then immediately save themselves by a bold spring to the spiritual. In the first instance, therefore, they say: We are not bastards fathered upon Abraham, but genuine offspring of Abraham (bastards were excluded from the congregation, Deut. xxiii. 2). But they intend thereby at the same time to say; We are not idolaters (Grotius, Lampe, Lücke); as is evident from their next words: **We have one Father, God.**—Their genuine descent from Abraham, is supposed to involve their having God for their Father, in the spiritual sense; and when they speak of Him as the *one* Father, the ἕνα is also emphatic.

Accordingly they intend to say: *We* (ἡμεῖς, with proud emphasis) are not like the heathen, who are born of whoredom, in apostasy from God (Hosea ii. 4; [Ezek. xx. 30; Is. lvii. 3]), and have many gods for their spiritual fathers (as they charged especially the Samaritans); bodily and spiritually we are free from the reproach of adulterous birth.* Children of Abraham, children of God, Deut. xxxii. 6; Is. lxiii. 16; Mal. ii. 10; Rom. iv. 16; Gal. iv. 23. The position: God is our father, is therefore in no opposition to the paternity of Abraham. The reference of Euthymius Zigabenus to the contrast of Isaac and Ishmael is unwarrantable. [For the Jews would not call Abraham's connection with Hagar one of πορνεία, which implies several fathers, but one mother.] It is obvious that with their appeal to the fatherhood of God they wish to crowd Jesus from His position; whether they at the same time intended an allusion to the birth of Jesus (Wetstein and others) is doubtful. In their monotheistic pride they could boast of being the children of God, even while the accusations of the prophets, that Israel was of Gentile whoredom (Ezek. xvi. 3; see Tholuck, p. 254), were in their mind; and we already know how little the Jewish fanaticism felt bound by the Scriptures.

Ver. 42. **If God were your father, ye would love me.**—Emphatic: Ye would have (long ago) learned to love Me;† that is, being kindred in spirit and life. Luthardt: This would be the ethical test. From the fact, therefore, that they do not love Him [the Son of God, the Beloved of the Father], He can infer with certainty their ungodly mind and nature. Proof: **For I** (ἐγώ) **proceeded forth and am come from God.**—His consciousness is the clear mirror, the true standard. He is certain (1) that He proceeded forth in His essence and in His personality from God, ontologically and ethically; (2) that also, in His appearance and mission among them, in His coming like a prophet to them, He came from God.* But again, He is certain of this because *He came not of Himself, i. e.* because He knew Himself to be pure from all egotistic motives (love of pleasure, love of honor, love of power; see the history of the temptation, Matt. iv.); and because He was conscious of *being sent by God, i. e.* of being actuated by divine motives. Nothing but this alternative was conceivable: from Himself, or from God, (chap. vii. 18, 28); no third origin (Meyer) is supposable.

Ver. 43. **Why do ye not understand my speech?**—Λαλιά, in distinction from λόγος; the personal language, the mode of speech, the familiar tone and sound of the words, in distinction from their meaning [xii. 48: ὁ λόγος ὃν ἐλάλησα; comp. Phil. i. 14; Heb. xiii. 7]. From its original idea of *talk, babble,* λαλιά† here preserves the element of vividness, warmth, familiarity. It is the φωνή, the tone of spirituality and tone of love in the shepherd-voice of Christ.‡ They are so far from recognizing this "loving tone," that they are incapable of even listening to the substance of His words with a pure, undistracted, spiritual ear. Fanaticism is characterized by "false hearing and words;" primarily by false hearing. Our Lord means *unprejudiced,* kindly-disposed hearing and attention; something more therefore, even here, than the general power to understand, which is expressed by γινώσκετε, and, in the first instance, something less than the willing hearing which is the beginning of faith itself. To take λαλιά and λόγος as equivalent, and to lay stress on ἀκούειν, and make it the condition precedent to γινώσκειν (as Origen and others do), in the first place ignores the distinction of the two meanings of λέγειν and λαλεῖν, which distinctly runs through this Gospel, and in the second place it overlooks the language: οὐ δύνασθε ἀκούειν. The point here is an ability to hear the λόγος, to which the recognition of the λαλιά is the condition precedent. We therefore, with Calvin, take the ὅτι as inferential, equivalent to ὥστε, not with Luther as meaning *for.* Manifestly δύνασθε is to be understood ethically, not, with Hilgenfeld, in a Gnostic, fatalistic sense (see Tholuck). The lively emotion in the painful interrogatory utterance of these words introduced the solemn declaration following.

Ver. 44. **Ye are of the father who is the devil.**—[Of the (spiritual or moral) fatherhood or paternity of the devil, ἐκ τοῦ πατρὸς τοῦ

* [Meyer denies all reference to idolatry, as defended by Lange with Lampe, Lücke, De Wette, Tholuck, Stier, Hengstenberg, Bäumlein, Alford. Bengel aptly characterizes this objection of the Jews as a *novus importunitatis Judaicæ paroxysmus.*—P. S.]

† [Dr. Lange presses the imperfect ἠγαπᾶτε, but this is conditioned by the ἦν in the protasis, and is better rendered: *Ye would love Me,* than: *Ye would have loved Me.* The sentence belongs to the fourth class of hypothetical sentences mentioned by Winer, p. 273 and 285, where the condition of the protasis is supposed not to exist: in these cases εἰ is used with the imperf. indic., and followed in the apodosis by a præterit with the same force; comp. ver. 39: εἰ τέκνα τοῦ Ἀβρ. ἦτε, τὰ ἔργα τοῦ Ἀβρ. ἐποιεῖτε, "*if ye were Abraham's children, ye would do the works of Abraham;*" John v. 46: εἰ γὰρ ἐπιστεύετε Μωϋσῇ, ἐπιστεύετε ἂν ἐμοί, *if ye believed Moses, ye would believe Me;* ix. 41: εἰ τυφλοὶ ἦτε, οὐκ ἂν εἴχετε ἁμαρτίαν, "*if ye were blind, ye would not have sin;*" xv. 19: εἰ ἐκ τοῦ κόσμου ἦτε, ὁ κόσμος ἂν τὸ ἴδιον ἐφίλει, "*if ye were of the world, the world would love its own;*" xviii. 36; Luke vii. 39: εἰ ἦν προφήτης, ἐγίνωσκεν ἄν, "*if he were a prophet, he would know,*" *etc.*—P. S.]

* [Meyer refers ἐξῆλθον to Christ's incarnation, and ἥκω to His presence. It is the result of ἐξῆλθον, and still belonging to ἐκ τ. θεοῦ.—P. S.]

† [In classical Greek, but in Hellenistic Greek and with later writers it often is *sermo, speech,* without any contemptuous meaning. λαλιά refers to the delivery or manner and form, λόγος to the matter or substance, of His discourses.—P. S.]

‡ [Alford: "The *spiritual idiom* in which He spoke, and which can only be spiritually understood."—P. S.]

διαβόλου. This is the most important doctrinal statement of Christ concerning the devil, teaching soberly and solemnly without figure of speech: (1) the objective personality of the devil; (2) his agency in the fall of the human race, and his connection with the whole history of sin as the father of murder and falsehood; (3) his own apostasy from a previous normal state in which he was created; (4) the connection of bad men with the devil.—ὑμεῖς with great emphasis, ye who boastfully claim to be lineal children of Abraham and spiritual children of God, *are children of* His great adversary, *the devil.* τοῦ διαβόλου is in apposition to πατρός.—P. S.] Not: Of the father of devils (plural τῶν διαβόλων: Grotius); nor the Gnostic absurdity: "of the father of the devil" [the demiurge], that is the God of the Jews [Hilgenfeld, Volkmar]; also not: "of *your* father, the devil" (Lücke, [De Wette, E. V., Alford,* Wordsworth]); but: "of a father who is the devil" (Meyer). The idea is clearly confined to ethical fatherhood by the placing of *father* first; so that John could not have written simply ἐκ τοῦ διαβόλου. **And the lusts** [τὰς ἐπιθυμίας τοῦ πατρός ὑμῶν θέλετε ποιεῖν]—Plural; primarily meaning not merely thirst for blood [but this is included]. According to Matt. iv., these are of three main classes [love of pleasure, love of honor, love of power.—P. S.]. These lusts of the devil are the main springs of the life of his like-minded children, who, with their captive propensity, desire (θέλετε) to do them.†

He was a murderer [*lit.* **a manslayer**] **from the beginning** [ἀνθρωποκτόνος ἀπ' ἀρχῆς].—With special reference to their hatred of the Messiah issuing in blood-thirstiness and falsehood, hardened adherence to delusion and calumnious persecution of the truth and the evilness of it. The devil was a murderer of men from the very *beginning* (not of his existence, but) of human history (comp. Matt. xix. 4, where ἀρχή likewise stands for the beginning of human history).‡ How so? Different interpretations.

(1) The devil is a murderer as the author of the fall of Adam, by which death came on man (Gen. iii.; Rom. v. 12). So Origen, Chrysostom, Augustine, and most in modern times. [Schleierm., Thol., Olsh., Luth., Meyer, Ewald, Hengstenb., Godet, Alford, Wordsworth.—P. S.] This interpretation is supported by the expression: "from the beginning;" and by Wisd. of Sol. ii. 24; Rev. xii. 9; xx. 2;§ comp. also *Ev. Nicod.:* where the devil is called ἡ τοῦ θανάτου ἀρχή [and ἡ ῥίζα τῆς ἁμαρτίας, the beginning of death, and the root of sin.—P. S.]

(2) As the author of Cain's murder of his brother. Cyril, Nitzsch, Lücke, and others. [So also De Wette, Kling, Reuss, Bäumlein, Owen. The arguments for this interpretation are its appropriateness in view of the design of the literal murder of Christ entertained by the Jews, and especially the apparent parallel passage, 1 John iii. 12: "Cain was of the wicked one (*i. e.* a child of the devil, like other sinners, 1 John iii. 8) and slew his brother," comp. ver. 15: "Whosoever hateth his brother is a murderer." But neither here nor in Gen. iv. is the Satanic agency in the murder of Abel expressly mentioned, as it is in the history of temptation (Gen. iii.), although it stands out prominently in the Bible as the first glaring consequence of the fall and as the type of bloodshed and violence that have since in unbroken succession desecrated the earth (comp. besides 1 John iii. 12, also Matt. xxiii. 35; Luke xi. 51; Jude 11). Moreover, Cain's deed itself presupposes the previous agency of the devil, when by the successful temptation of our first parents, he introduced first spiritual and then temporal murder and death into the world. The fall is the "beginning" of history, and of universal significance as the virtual fall of the whole race, and the fruitful source of sin in general and murder in particular. There the devil, in the shape of a serpent, proved himself both a murderer and a liar, as he is here described. To it therefore the passage must chiefly refer. 1 John iii. 8 (ὁ ποιῶν τὴν ἁμαρτίαν ἐκ τοῦ διαβόλου ἐστιν, ὅτι ἀπ' ἀρχῆς ὁ διάβολος ἁμαρτάνει) which all commentators refer to the history of the fall, is the real parallel to our passage, and not 1 John iii. 12.—P. S.]

(3) He is quite generally described as a murderer, without any special reference. Baumgarten-Crusius, Brückner.

(4) Evidently the thing intended is the murderous work of Satan in all history, aiming to complete itself in the killing of Christ, but having signalized itself in the beginning in the temptation of man and the lie against God, which afterwards bore their full fruit in Cain's murder of his brother (Theodoret, Heracleon, Euthymius).

We therefore consider that there is properly no question here between Adam and Cain, 1 Jno. iii. 15, 16. Yet the chief stress plainly lies on the temptation of Adam; for the devil, by his spiritual murder of man, brought man himself also to murder; and he is described pre-eminently as a liar. From that "beginning" he was a murderer of man from time to time.

And doeth not stand [οὐχ ἕστηκεν] **in the truth**.—Interpretations:

(1) He did not continue in the truth. Augustine (Vulg.: *stetit*), Luther, Martensen [*Dogmatik*, § 108], Delitzsch [*Psychol.* p. 62]. This makes the word refer to the fall of the devil according to 2 Pet. ii. 4; Jude ver. 6. Against this interpretation see Lücke and Meyer. It would require the pluperfect εἱστήκει, *stood.* The perfect ἕστηκα means, *I have placed myself, I stand* [comp. John i. 26; iii. 39; Matt. xii. 47; xx. 6, etc.]

(2) He does not stand in the truth. He has

* [Alford defends the rendering of the E. V. on account of the definite article before πατρός. But Meyer objects that this would require ὑμεῖς ἐκ τοῦ ὑμῶν πατρός.—P. S.]

† [The force of θέλετε, *ye are willing, ready, desirous, ye love, to do*, is obliterated in the E. V. Comp. on this use of θέλειν ch. vi. 21; Acts x. 10; Phil. ii. 13; Philem. ver. 14. Alford: "It indicates, as in ver. 40, the freedom of the human will, as the foundation of the condemnation of the sinner." Godet: "*Le verb* θέλετε *est contraire à l'idée d'une dépendance fataliste que Hilgenfeld attribue à Jean; il exprime l'assentiment volontaire, l'abondance de sympathie, avec laquelle ils se mettent a l'œuvre pour satisfaire les appetits de leur père.*"—P. S.]

‡ [ἀρχή is relative and must be defined by the connection, here by ἀνθρωποκτόνος which implies the existence of man.—P. S.]

§ [Add Heb. ii. 14, where Satan is called the prince of death, ὁ ἔχων τὸ κράτος τοῦ θανάτου. The rabbinical writings prove that the agency of the devil in the fall was the universal belief of the Jews.—P. S.]

taken no stand and he holds no ground in it. In an emphatic sense he does not take a position; he has not honorably planted himself and valiantly stood. Euthymius: Οὐκ ἐμμένει, ἀναπαύεται; Lücke: "He is perpetually in the act of apostasy from the truth." De Wette, Meyer: "Falsehood is the sphere in which he stands; in it he is in his proper element, in it he has his station." Correct, except that there can be no *standing* or *fixedness*, and no station in falsehood. Perpetual restlessness and going to and fro are his element, Job ii. 2. Hence he is the spirit or devil of endless toil, and the number of his representative, as antichrist, is 666 (Rev. xiii. 18). Compare the description of Lokke, his deceptions and his flights, in the Scandinavian mythology. He denies his own existence, as he denies all truth and reality.* But he is the perpetual rover, because he is the deceiver.

[The passage then does not teach expressly the *fall* of the devil, but it *presupposes* it. ἑστηκεν has the force of the *present* and indicates the permanent character of the devil, but this status is the result of an act of a previous apostacy, as much as the sinful state of man is brought about by the fall of Adam. God made all things, without exception, through the Logos (i. 3), and made the rational beings, both men and angels, pure and sinless, yet liable to temptation and fall. As to the *time* of the creation and fall of Satan and the bad angels, the Scriptures give us no light.—P. S.]

Because there is no truth in him.—Because falsehood is in him as the maxim of his life, he is in falsehood; because he keeps no position with himself, he keeps no position in reality. As he deceives himself, so he deceives the world. For internal truth is the centre of gravity which causes a moral being in the sphere of truth to stand firm as a pillar in the world. [Mark the absence of the article before ἀλήθεια, *subjective* truth, truthfulness, while in the preceding clause ἀλήθεια has the article and means *objective* truth, the truth of God. Comp. De Wette and Meyer.—P. S.]

When he speaketh [λαλῇ] **a lie.**—[τὸ ψεῦδος is generic, but the English language requires here the indefinite article, while it retains the definite article in the phrase "to speak *the* truth." See Alford *in loc.*—P. S.] Through the devil falsehood comes to its manifestation, through his familiar way, his persuasion, his whispering, his insinuation (λαλεῖν). But then he always **speaketh of his own** [ἐκ τῶν ἰδίων λαλεῖ, out of his own resources], from his own nature; himself revealing his own truthless and loveless mind ("The devil has a half-charred heart"); revealing himself to his own condemnation, Matt. xii. 34 [ἐκ τοῦ περισσεύματος τῆς καρδίας τὸ στόμα λαλεῖ]. His ἴδια are to be taken ethically. Yet the description of a lie as that which is the devil's *own*, includes the idea that it originates from his *own will*, and that, being only for his own sake, it remained a thing of his *own*, having no ground in the foundation of truth, in God.

For he is a liar and the father thereof [ὅτι ψεύστης ἐστὶν καὶ ὁ πατὴρ αὐτοῦ].—That which he says proceeds indeed from within himself, and what he is within himself as devil, in his ἴδιον of Satanic egoism, that he puts forth continually in his own work and in the work of his child as *its father*. Different interpretations of πατὴρ αὐτοῦ:

(1) The father of *the lie*, τοῦ ψεύδους, Origen, Euthymius, *et al.*, Lücke. [With reference to the first lie recorded in history, by which the devil seduced Eve: "Ye shall not surely die," Gen. iii. 4.—P. S.] Observe, on the contrary, that Christ intends to speak here not merely of the author of the lie, but also concretely of the father of the liars, to whom he returns. Therefore,

(2) Father of *the liar* [τοῦ ψεύστου = τῶν ψευστῶν. Consequently he is your father, and ye are his children, see beginning of the verse—ψεύστης being singular the pronoun αὐτῶν is attracted into the singular αὐτοῦ.—P. S.] Bengel, Baumgarten-Crusius, Luthardt, Meyer [Tholuck, Stier, Alford, Hengstenberg]. Then we must of course take ψεύστης first as a general predicate of the wicked personality. The devil is a liar in himself, and is father of the liar in abominable self-propagation through the delusion of the children of wickedness (2 Thes. ii.)

The ancient Gnostic [and Manichean] interpretation, taking the demiurge as father of the devil, re-applied to the Gospel by Hilgenfeld [and Volkmar], is disposed of by Meyer [p. 359].* Meyer justly observes that in this passage the fall of the devil is presupposed; but it is by no means presupposed that the devil always was wicked (Hilgenfeld and others). It should be added that this description of the devil always suggests the causes of his fall: selfishness, falsehood, envy, hatred. The devil, the beginner of wickedness, 1 Jno. iii. 8, 12; the founder of wickedness, the spirit of the wicked. In the temptation of Adam (Wisd. ii. 24; Heb. ii. 14; Rev. xii. 9)† as well as in Cain's fratricide, that twofold nature of selfishness showed itself: hatred of truth and love of murder, which culminated in the crucifixion of Christ.‡ There is, however, here no opposition of *formal* truth and *formal* falsehood, but the full extent of both ideas

* [Mephistopheles, in Göthe's *Faust*, characterizes himself as the persistent denier and enemy of all existence:

> *Ich bin der Geist der stets verneint,*
> *Und das mit Recht, denn was entsteht,*
> *Ist werth, dass es zu Grunde geht.*
> *D'rum besser wär's, dass nichts entstünde.*
> *So ist denn alles, was ihr Sünde,*
> *Zerstörung, kurz, das Böse nennt,*
> *Mein eigentliches Element.*—P. S.]

* [This interpretation refers αὐτοῦ to the devil and πατήρ to the demiurge: "He (the devil) is a liar, and his father (the demiurge) also;" or, "He is a liar like his father" (hence the old reading ὡς and καθὼς καί instead of καί). This translation would require αὐτός before ψεύστης, and implies the unscriptural doctrine that the devil has a father. Another interpretation even more absurd and untenable is that of so sensible and learned a man as Bishop Middleton who, according to Alford *in loc.*, proposed this rendering of the passage: "When (any of you) speaks that which is false, he speaks after the manner of his kindred (ἐκ τῶν ἰδίων!), for he is a liar, and so also is his father," *i. e.* the devil. Middleton stumbled at the article before πατήρ, which on the contrary is emphatic and necessary. There is but one father of lies and liars, that is the devil. The kingdom of darkness is a monarchy as well as the kingdom of light.—P. S.]

† Comp. the passage from *Sohar Chadash:* "The children of that old serpent who has slain Adam and all his posterity." Tholuck, p. 257 [Krauth's trans. p. 236].

‡ [In the midst of this sentence the translation of my dear, departed friend, Dr. Yeomans, was interrupted by disease, never to be resumed. *Vale—pia anima!*—P. S.]

is kept in view (Luthardt, Tholuck); this is evident from the nature of the completed opposition itself, when speaking the truth turns life itself into truth, and in like manner lying makes life itself a lie. So the external murder of Abel which Satan effected through Cain is inconceivable without the spiritual murder performed in Adam, which became the cause of the literal murder.

Ver. 45. **But I—because I speak the truth, ye believe me not.**—The *ἐγὼ δέ* is forcibly put first, not so much in opposition to the devil (Tholuck, Meyer), as in opposition to the Jews as the spiritual children of the devil. After telling them what *they are*, the last word of the explanation, what *He is*, hovers on His lips. Jesus characterizes His Ego to the extent of their present need: (1) He is the witness or the prophet of truth, in opposition to the arch-liar and his children; 2) The sinless one, in opposition to their lust of murder, intending to kill Him; 3) Coming from God, with the word of God, in opposition to their diabolic nature. This however is the great obstacle of His full self-revelation, or rather the Messianic designation of His full self-revelation, that in their hardened lying disposition they are opposed to His spirit of truth; that they do not believe Him for the very reason of His telling them the truth. [Alford: "This implies a charge of wilful striving against known and recognized truth."] Euthymius [filling up the context]: *εἰ μὲν ἔλεγον ψεῦδος, ἐπιστεύσατέ μοι ἄν, ὡς τὸ ἴδιον τοῦ πατρὸς ὑμῶν λέγοντι* [If I should speak a lie, you would believe Me as speaking what properly belongs to your father].

Ver. 46. **Which of you convicteth me of sin?** [*τίς ἐξ ὑμῶν ἐλέγχει με περὶ ἁμαρτίας.*]—Different explanations of sin.

1) Because the truth in speaking is previously mentioned, *ἁμαρτία* must here mean *error* or intellectual defect. Origenes, Cyril, Erasmus and others. Against this speaks *a*) that *ἁμαρτία* in the New Testament throughout designates *sin*, and even with the classics it does not mean *error*, *deceit*, unless with a defining addition, *e. g.*, *τῆς γνώμης*. [Comp. Meyer, p. 360 f.—P. S.] *b*) Jesus would in this case make the examination of truth an object of intellectual reflection, we might say, of theological disputation, while otherwise He represents it as a moral and religious process. *c*) The truth of His word is authenticated by the truthfulness and sinlessness of His life, see chap. vii. 17, 18.

2) Sin in speech, *untruth, falsehood.* Melancthon, Calvin [false doctrine], Hofmann ["*Sünde des Wortes*"], Tholuck. Against this: Either this interpretation amounts to the same as the first, or it must include the idea of intentional delusion, of sinful and wicked speech, or all this together ("wicked delusion," Fritzsche, Baumgarten-Crusius). But for this the expression is too general.

3) *Sin*, the *moral* offence. [This is the uniform usage of *ἁμαρτία* in the New Testament.—P. S.] Lücke, Stier, Luthardt,* *etc.* Jesus speaks from the fundamental conception that the intellectual life is inseparably connected with the ethical (Ullmann, *Sinlessness of Jesus*, p. 99). There is no reason in this explanation (with Tholuck) to miss a "connecting link," or to assume a defect in the narrative. Meantime this declaration is also differently interpreted: *a*) The sinless one is the purest and safest organ of the perception and communication of truth (Lücke), or the knowledge of the truth rests upon purity of the will (De Wette). *b*) Meyer against this: this would be discursive, or at least imply that Jesus acquired the knowledge of the truth in the discursive way, and only in His human state, while, according to John especially, He knew the truth by intuition and from His preexistent state, and in His earthly state by virtue of His unbroken communion with God. His reasoning is: If I am without sin—and none of you can prove the contrary—I am also without error, consequently I say the truth, and ye, on your part have no reason to disbelieve Me. But Jesus could exhibit His morally pure self-consciousness only by His life. Hence *c*) the word is to be understood according to the historical connection of the reproach of theocratic sin. They tried to make Him a sinner in the sense of the Jewish regulation with regard to excommunication, but they do not venture to accuse Him publicly, still less can they convict Him. But this consciousness of His legal irreproachableness implies at the same time the consciousness of the moral infallibility of His life and the sinlessness of His character and being, as He on His part recognizes no *merely legal* righteousness. Our expression is therefore certainly a solemn declaration of the Lord in regard to His sinlessness, which indeed is indirectly implied also in other testimonies concerning Himself, as for instance in ver. 29. The circumstance, that the divine-human sinlessness of Christ had to develop and prove itself in a human way, affords no reason to call it (with Meyer) *relative* in opposition to the *absolute* sinlessness of God according to Heb. v. 8.

[This is a most important passage, teaching clearly the sinlessness, or (to use the positive term) the moral perfection, of Christ. He here presents Himself as the living impersonation of holiness and truth in inseparable union, in opposition to the devil as the author and instigator of sin and error. The sinlessness of Jesus is implied in His whole mission and character as the Saviour of sinners from sin and death; for the least transgression or moral defect would have annihilated His fitness to redeem and to judge. It is confirmed by the unanimous testimony of John the Baptist (Matt. iii. 14; John i. 15; iii. 31), and the apostles (Acts iii. 14; 1 Pet. i. 19; ii. 22; iii. 18; 2 Cor. v. 21; 1 John ii. 29; iii. 5, 7; Heb. iv. 15; vii. 26). Christ

*[So also Meyer, Alford, Webster and Wilkinson, Owen. (Wordsworth says nothing of this important verse.) I quote the remarks of Alford, which are to the point: "*ἁμαρτία* here is strictly sin: not '*error in argument*,' or '*falsehood*.' These two latter meanings are found in classical Greek, but never in the New Testament or LXX. And besides, they would introduce in this most solemn part of our Lord's discourse a vapid tautology. The question is an appeal to His *sinlessness of life*, as evident to them all,—as a pledge for His truthfulness of word: which word asserted, be it remembered, that *He was sent from God*. And when we recollect that He who challenges men to convict Him of sin, never would have upheld *outward* spotlessness merely (see Matt. xxiii. 26–28), the words amount to a declaration of His absolute sinlessness, in thought, word, and deed."—P. S.]

challenged His enemies to convict Him of sin, in the absolute certainty of freedom from sin. This agrees with His whole conduct, with the entire absence of everything like repentance or regret in His life. He never asked God forgiveness for any thought or word or deed of His; He stood far above the need of regeneration, conversion or reform. No other man could ask such a question as this without obvious hypocrisy or a degree of self-deception bordering on madness itself, while from the mouth of Jesus we hear it without surprise, as the unanswerable self-vindication of one who always speaks the truth, who is the Truth itself, and is beyond the reach of impeachment or suspicion. If Jesus had been a sinner, He must have been conscious of it like all other sinners, and could not have thus challenged His enemies, and conducted Himself throughout on the assumption of entire personal freedom from sin without a degree of hypocrisy which would be the greatest moral monstrosity ever conceived and absolutely irreconcilable with any principle of virtue. But if Christ was truly sinless, He forms an absolute exception to a universal rule and stands out the greatest moral miracle in midst of a fallen and ruined world, challenging our belief in all His astounding claims concerning His divine origin, character and mission.—The sinlessness of Jesus must not be confounded with the sinlessness of God: it is the sinlessness of the *man* Jesus, which implied, during His earthly life, peccability (the possibility of sinning, *posse-peccare*), temptability and actual temptation, while the sinlessness of God is an eternal attribute above the reach of conflict. If we view Christ merely in His human nature, we may say that His sinlessness was at first relative (*impeccabilitas minor, posse non peccare*) and, like Adam's innocence in paradise, liable to fall (though such fall was made impossible by the indwelling divine Logos); nevertheless it was complete at every stage of His life in accordance with the character of each, *i. e.*, He was sinless and perfect as a child, perfect as a boy, perfect as a youth, and perfect as a man; there being different degrees of perfection. Sinless holiness grew with Him, and, by successfully overcoming temptation in all its forms, it became absolute impeccability or impossibility of sinning (*impeccabilitas major, non posse peccare*). Hence it is said that He *learned* obedience, Heb. v. 8.—The historical fact of the sinlessness of Jesus overthrows the pantheistic notion of the necessity of sin for the moral development of man.—P. S.]

Ver. 46. **I speak the truth, why do ye not believe me.**—Luther co-ordinates this word with the former; Christ asking the reason why they did not believe in Him, since they could censure neither His *life* nor His *doctrine.* My life is pure, for none of you can convict Me of sin, My doctrine also, for I tell you nothing but the truth. But εἰ δὲ ἀλήθειαν λέγω cannot be co-ordinate to the question. The connection is rather this: Sinlessness is the truth of life; he who acts out the truth in a blameless life, must be admitted also to speak the truth and to be worthy of faith. Purity of life guarantees purity of doctrine, as *vice versa*, James iii. 2.

Ver. 47. **He that is of God heareth God's word.**—A syllogism; but not with this conclusion: I now speak God's words (De Wette), but: you are not of God. That Jesus speaks the word of God is pre-supposed in the foregoing. An attentive hearing and reception of the word of God is meant. This is conditioned by being from God, by moral relationship with God; for only kindred can know kindred. The being of God has above been more particularly characterized as a being drawn by God (chap. vi. 44), being taught by Him (ver. 45), as showing itself by doing truth in God, chap. iii. 21.

Explanations of *he that is of God* (ὁ ὢν ἐκ τοῦ θεοῦ): *a*) *of divine essence* and *origin*, in the dualistic, Manichean sense of two originally different classes of men (Hilgenfeld); *b*) *elect, predestinated* (Augustine, Piscator); *c*) *born again* (Lutheran and recent Reformed interpreters). In reference to the third interpretation it is to be assumed, that to be of God and to manifest it by hearing His word, is the beginning of the new birth; in reference to the second, that hereby true election comes to light, in reference to the first, that the antagonism between the children of God and the children of the devil is not metaphysical or ontological, but ethical, and is so defined in the New Testament, especially in John. On both sides self-determination is pre-supposed, but a direction and change of life is hereby expressed, which on the one side appears more and more as freedom and resemblance to God, on the other as demoniacal slavery (See vers. 24, 34).

Ver. 48. **Thou art a Samaritan, and hast a demon.**—Malicious refusal of, and reply to, His reproach. A *Samaritan* is doubless the designation of a heretic; but also with the secondary meaning of a spurious origin (from a mongrel nation), and an adversary of orthodox Judaism. (Paulus).* "*Samaritan*" is meant to be a retort to His reproach: "You are no spiritual children of Abraham." But His reproach: "You are of the devil," they answer with the insult: "*Thou hast a demon,*" here in the more definite sense of being possessed of a Satanic spirit. To His two ethical reproaches they oppose two insults, by which they expect triumphantly to silence Him. Hence the self-complacent expression: οὐ καλῶς λέγομεν ἡμεῖς; Are we not right? Did we not hit it? The form of the expression betrays, that they do not utter these words for the first time. Perhaps the reproach: "Thou art a Samaritan," was hinted at already in ver. 19; at all events the other reproach: "Thou hast a demon," in a milder form, was made by the people on a previous occasion (chap. vii. 20); but here we must remember the fact, that the Pharisees had already formerly slanderously charged Him with casting out devils through Beelzebub, the prince of the devils (Matt. ix. 34; comp. x. 25; xii. 24). It is significant that in their view demoniacal possession and a voluntary demoniacal working are the same thing, or rather that they consider the former condition the higher degree of devilish life.

Ver. 49. **I have not a demon.**—Jesus, with sublime self-control and calmness, ignores the first reproach (especially as He cannot recognize the designation of *Samaritan* either as a title of abuse or a verdict of rejection, "because He had already believers among the Samaritans,

* [So also Meyer: *ein ketzerischer Widersacher des reinen Gottesvolkes.*]

and He therefore did not hesitate in the parable of the good Samaritan to represent Himself under the symbol of a Samaritan." Lampe). Yet He answers this reproach, while answering the second. He does this first with a simple refusal or protest, but then by the positive declaration: **I honor my Father.** This furnishes at the same time the counter-proof that He is no Samaritan and has no demon. No Samaritan: He proves it by word and life that God is His Father; not a demon: He proves it, that He is not possessed of a dark spirit, but full of the Spirit of the Father, and glorifying Him. This explains the character of their reproaches: they insult and blaspheme; they insult in Him the representative of God's glory, therefore indirectly the glory of God itself. With this wickedness the matter cannot rest, because God reigns as the God of truth and righteousness. His *τιμή* obscured by their *ἀτιμάζειν*, must face them in higher brilliancy as *δόξα*. But it is not His business to aspire to this *δόξα* arbitrarily (chap. v. 41); He leaves this to the Father with the confidence: that as surely as He seeks the *δόξα* of His Father, so surely will the Father, by His guidance, seek His. He knows that this is even a constant direction of the divine guidance; God is in this respect *ὁ ζητῶν*, and brings the case to a decision as *ὁ κρίνων*, in opposition to those who restrain the truth.

Ver. 51. **If a man keep my saying, he will never see death.**—The announcement of God's judgment, includes the announcement of death. This announcement Jesus could not make unconditionally to a Jewish audience, for 1) there might be some among them and there were some who really kept His word; and 2) He could not yet withdraw from His adversaries the invitation to salvation; 3) the thought of the terrible judgment always awakened in Him an impulse of pity and mercy (comp. Matt. xxiii. 27). It is therefore incorrect to assume (with Calvin, De Wette) that these words after a pause were addressed to believers only, or to connect them (with Lücke) with ver. 31, instead of ver. 50. Meyer justly points out the antithesis to the reference to the judgment. His word will carry the believers safely through judgment and death, or rather beyond judgment and death, as the Christians afterwards really experienced at the destruction of Jerusalem. Generally the expression is equal to the similar one: to hear the word, to remain in the word; yet in this keeping the probation in trials and dangers of apostasy is especially emphasized in the *κρίσις* (Matt. xiii. 21; John xv. 20; xvii. 6). **He will never see death** (not: he will not die for ever); a promise, that his life shall pass entirely safe through the whole succession of judgments, and will not see death even in the final judgment.

Ver. 52. **Now we know that thou hast a demon.**—The answer of blind enmity to His enticing call of mercy. If they understand the word of Jesus of His natural death, it is probably an intentional misunderstanding in order to escape the force of His thoughts. They argue thus: He who promises to others bodily immortality, must Himself possess it in a still higher degree. But since Abraham and the Prophets died, it is a senseless and demoniacal self-exaltation if you claim for yourself freedom from death. It seems to be a characteristic part of their speech when they say: *Now we know that Thou hast, etc., i. e.,* Now at last we know positively what we have before accused you of; and when they further change *τόν ἐμὸν λόγον* (ver. 51) into *τὸν λόγον μου* (ver. 52), and the expression *οὐ μὴ θεωρήσῃ* into: *οὐ μὴ γεύσηται,* though the latter expression is also used by the Lord in a different connection, Matt. xvi. 28. The *γεύεσθαι* is a usual expression among the Rabbins (Schöttgen, Wetstein), probably not merely in general a picture of experience, but a figure of the drinking from the cup of death; in any case it denotes ironically the antithesis to every enjoyment of life. While the expression: *not to see death,* denotes the *objective* side of the believer's experience, according to which death is changed into a metamorphosis of life, the phrase: *not to taste death,* means the *subjective* emancipation from the guilty sinner's dread and horror of death.

Ver. 53. **Whom dost thou make thyself?**—With more than half-feigned shudder before the word of self-exaltation, which He is about to utter, they manifest at the same time a demoniacal curiosity to know the last word of His self-designation. Thus the form of the excited questions is explained by the mixture of their fanatical and chiliastic emotions.

Ver. 54. **If I glorify myself, my glory is nothing.**—At first a protest against the reproach of self-exaltation. He makes nothing of Himself from His own will, but suffers Himself to become everything through the guidance of God. He does not answer their question directly, because every word referring to the true greatness of His *δόξα* would only be to them unintelligible and cause error and offence. The full majesty of the divine-human Son of God must as a new fact be accompanied by the new idea, a new name, Phil. ii. 9. The accomplishment of this fact, however, belongs to the government of the Father. Therefore He cannot arbitrarily anticipate His glorification, without contradicting His real *δόξα*, which is just a fruit of self-humiliation and perfect patience, Phil. ii. 6. But for this very reason the Father is active as the one *that glorifieth Him* (*ὁ δοξάζων με*), of whom they say *that He is their God* (*ὅτι θεὸς ἡμῶν ἐστιν*). To them it is the strongest reproach, that He is the same, whom they with spiritual pride point out as their God, and which is true in a historical, though not in a spiritual sense, to their own condemnation. The whole force of the contrast between their and His knowledge of God lies in this, that He can say: it is My Father, who glorifies Me, the same one whom you unjustly call your God, as you do not even know Him. That they do not know Him, they prove by their not recognizing His revelation in Christ, and their persecuting and insulting Him unto death.

Ver. 55. **Ye know him not, but I know him.**—Commentators are apt to ignore the contrast between the *οὐκ ἐγνώκατε αὐτόν* and the threefold *οἶδα αὐτόν* [see, however, Meyer, footnote, p. 366]. In any case it means: you have not even indirectly made His acquaintance, but I have made His acquaintance directly; I have looked at Him and know Him by intention. We choose from the different shades of the idea, the expression: *I know Him.*—**I should be a liar like you.** The child-like expression of the sublime self-consciousness of Christ. Were He to deny this unique and constant experience of God as His Father (Matt. xi. 27), He would, if this were possible, through mistaken and cowardly modesty become a liar like them. They are liars and hypocrites while pretending to know God (comp. ver. 44); He would fall into the opposite kind of hypocrisy, if He were to deny His consciousness.—The addition: **But I know him and keep his word,** is an ultimatum, a declaration of war against the whole hell: the word of God confided to Him, which is one with His own consciousness, He will not permit to be torn out of His heart by the storm of the cross.

Ver. 56. **Abraham your father* rejoiced that He should see** [ἠγαλλιάσατο ἵνα ἴδῃ]. The object of His joy is represented as its purpose and aim. Abraham rejoiced, that he should see, and that he might see. His belief in the word of promise (Gen. xv. 4; xvii. 17; xviii. 10) was the cause of his joy,—this the reason of the rejuvenating of his life, and this again the condition of his patriarchal paternity, Heb. xi. 11, 12; comp. John i. 13. The birth of Isaac was mediated by inspiration of faith (Rom. iv. 19; Gal. iv. 23), and is therefore a type of that complete inspiration of faith, with which the Virgin conceived the promised Saviour by the overshadowing power of the Holy Ghost. The laughing of Abraham, Gen. xvii. 17, forms only an incident in this cheerful elevation of life, and so far as it is connected with a doubt of Abraham, it can be only regarded as a symbol of rejoicing, not, according to Philo, as a pure expression of his hope.†

That he should see my day.—The expression of all the immeasurable hopes of Abraham united in their central point of aim. The hope for the heir—for the heirs—for the inheritance (Heb. xi.) was a hope whose aim and centre appeared on the day of the Divine Heir who embraces all other heirs and the whole inheritance. The *day* of Christ is therefore also the whole time of the New Testament, as it reaches beyond the last day into the eternal day of His glory. "Not the passion-time (Chrysostom),‡ not the time of the parusia (Bengel), not the birth-day (Schleusner),§ but the time of the appearance of Christ, as in the plural, Luke xvii. 23, in the singular, ver. 24." Tholuck. On the worthlessness of the hypothetical shape of the sentence with the Socinians, see Lücke and Tholuck, p. 267. In reference to a similar longing of the theocratic pious kings, see Luke x. 24. The connection with the previous: 1) Chrysostom, Calvin: *Ille me absentem desideravit, vos præsentem aspernamini.* 2) De Wette: Now Jesus really places Himself above Abraham, by representing Himself as the object of Abraham's highest desire. 3) Baumgarten-Crusius: As the Giver of life He could raise Himself above Abraham, for Abraham himself had in joyful anticipation expected and received life from Him. "Origen also finds in the εἶδεν καὶ ἐχάρη a definite refutation of the 'Αβρ. ἀπέθανε," maintained by the Jews (Tholuck). In answering their question whether He was greater than Abraham who had died, Christ asserts two points: 1) Abraham did not die in their cheerless sense of death; 2) He did not raise Himself above Abraham, but Abraham subordinated himself to Him; comp. the parallel word on David, Matt. xxii. 45.

And he saw it and rejoiced.—Different explanations:

1) He foresaw the day of Christ in faith [on the ground of the Messianic promises made to him during his earthly life, Gen. xii.; xv.; xvii.; xviii.; xxii.; Rom. iv.; Gal. iii. 6 ff.—P. S.] So Calvin, Melanchthon and older Protestant commentators [also Bengel: *Vidit diem. Christi, qui in semine, quod stellarum instar futurum erat, sidus maximum est et fulgidissimum.*—P. S.].

2) He saw it in types: the three angels [one of them being the Logos, Gen. xviii.; so Hengstenberg], especially the sacrifice of Isaac [as foreshadowing the vicarious death and resurrection of Christ]. So Chrysostom, Theophyl., Roman commentators, Erasmus, Grotius.

3) In prophetical vision. So Jerome, Olshausen [who refers to Isaiah's vision of the glory of Christ, xii. 41], *etc.*

4) In the celebration of the birth and meaning of Isaac. Hofmann. [So also Wordsworth, fancifully: The name *Isaac* (*laughing*), Gen. xvii. 17, had a reference to the ἀγαλλίασις of Abraham; for in Isaac, the promised seed, he had a vision of Christ, in whom all rejoice.—P. S.]

5) *Visio in limbo patrum.* Este, *etc.**

6) As one living in paradise in the other world [comp. Luke xvi. 22, 25], like the angels, 1 Pet. i. 12; Moses and Elijah on the mount of transfiguration, Matt. xvii. 4; Luke ix. 31. So Origen [Lampe], Lücke, De Wette [Meyer, Stier, Luthardt, Alford, Bäumlein, Godet] and different others.† Doubtless the proper sense: therefore His living Abraham in opposition to their dead one. [Abraham saw the day of Christ as an actual witness from the higher world, like the angels

* [Dr. Lange reads *our* father, and adds the remark: "*Our* father is here full of meaning." But he seems to have had in view ver. 54, where the authorities are divided between θεὸς ἡμῶν (*oratio directa*) and θ. ὑμῶν. In ver. 56 the text. rec. ὁ πατὴρ ὑμῶν, is adopted by Lachmann, Tischendorf, Tregelles and Alford, and ἡμῶν is not even mentioned by them in their apparatus of variations (except by Lachmann). As to the meaning, '*your* father' is rather more forcible with reference to ver. 39, and shows the antagonism of their claim with the true spirit of Abraham.—P. S.]

† [See the passage in Lücke, p. 363, likewise a similar passage from the Sohar.]

‡ [In the offering of Isaac as a type of the vicarious sacrifice on the cross. So also Theophylact and Wordsworth.—P. S.]

§ [So also Meyer (p. 366, note), who insists that the singular ἡ ἡμέρα ἡ ἐμή means the specific day of the birth of Christ when ὁ λόγος σὰρξ ἐγένετο. But, "the day" of Christ is no more to be contracted in this way, than the day of grace, and the day of judgment.—P. S.]

* [The *limbus patrum*, like the *limbus infantum*, is one of the border regions of Sheol or Hades in the supernatural geography of Romanism; it was the abode of the Old Testament saints before Christ, but when He descended into Hades and proclaimed the redemption and deliverance to them, they were transferred to heaven. The *limbus patrum*, therefore, is empty now, while the *limbus infantum* is still the receptacle of all unbaptized children who die in infancy and are excluded from heaven, yet not actually suffering the pain of damnation.—P. S.]

† [Meyer, p. 368, quotes from the apocryphal fiction of the *Testamentum Levi*, p. 586 sq., where it is said after the Messiah Himself opens the gates of Paradise and feeds the believers from the tree of life: then *will Abraham rejoice* (τότε ἀγαλλιάσεται 'Αβρ.), and Isaac and Jacob, and I, shall be glad and all the saints shall put on gladness.—P. S.]

who sang the anthem over the plains of Bethlehem.—P. S.]

And rejoiced.—Indication of changes in the realm of death, wrought by the appearance of Christ.* The calm joy of the blessed, ἐχάρη, in opposition to the excited joy of anxious desire, ἠγαλλιάσατο. According to rabbinical traditions God showed to Abraham in prophetic vision the building, the destruction and re-construction of the temple, and even the succession of empires (see Lücke, the note on p. 363). These traditions represent the dark shadow of the light which the word of Christ casts into Hades.

Ver. 57. **Thou art not yet fifty years old.**—The sensual, half imbecile and half malicious and intentional misunderstanding grows more and more in its folly. "The fiftieth year was the full age of a man, Numb. iv. 3." Tholuck: From this passage arose the misunderstanding of Irenæus that Jesus had gone through all the ages of human life. [Irenæus inferred from this passage that Jesus was not quite, but nearly fifty years of age, *Adv. hær.* II. 22, § 6 (ed. Stieren I. p. 360). E. V. Bunsen (a son of the celebrated statesman and scholar) defends this view, and infers from John ii. 20 f., that Christ was forty-six years of age (*The Hidden Wisdom of Christ*, Lond. 1865, II. p. 461 ff.). Keim also is inclined to extend the earthly life of Christ to forty years, but confines His public ministry to one year and a few months, (*Geschichtl. Christus*, p. 235, *Gesch. Jesu von Nazara*, I. 469 f. note). It is obvious that no clear inference as to the age of our Lord can be drawn from this indefinite estimate of the Jews, and Irenæus was influenced by a dogmatic consideration, *viz.*, that Christ must have passed through all the stages of human life, including old age (*senior in senioribus*), in order to redeem them all. But the idea of declining life is incompatible with the true idea of the Saviour. He died and lives for ever in the memory of His people in the unbroken vigor of early manhood.—P. S.]

Ver. 58. **Verily, verily . . . Before Abraham became I am.**† Over against the completely hardened stupidity of spiritual death flashes up the perfect mystery of eternal life. Γενέσθαι not "was" (Tholuck [De Wette, Ewald,]), or "born" (Erasmus), but "became" (Augustine); the antithesis of the created and the eternal, which implies at the same time the antithesis of the temporal and the eternal. Εἰμί expresses the pre-existence (after the fathers), yet not only as the divine pre-existence, but that which reflects itself in Christ's divine-human consciousness of eternity and extends to the present and the future as well as the past, or that form of existence which makes Him the Alpha and the Omega, the Beginning and the End. He is the propelling principle and centre of the times. We distinguish, therefore, a threefold mode of existence: 1) The divine, timeless or pre-temporal existence of the Logos; 2) the divine-human principial existence of the Logos as the foundation of humanity and the world; 3) the divine-human existence of the coming and appearing Christ through the succession of times. This implies at the same time the ethical elevation of the feeling of eternity above the times. The principial and dynamic pre-existence must be understood in a sense analogous to the pre-existence of Christ before John, ch. i. 15, 17. To the Jews this sense was most obvious: Abraham's existence presupposes Mine, not Mine that of Abraham; he depends for his very existence on Me, not I on him. We have then here again a revelation of His essential Messianic consciousness, His primitive feeling of eternity over and above all time. Comp. ch. vi. 63; viii. 25, 42; xiii. 3; xvi. 28; xvii. 5.

Socinus explains according to his system: *Antequam Abraham fiat Abraham, i. e., pater multorum gentium, ego sum Messias, lux mundi.* The interpretation of Baumgarten-Crusius: "I was in the predestination of God," does not suffice, but is not incorrect, as Tholuck thinks; it denotes the principial aspect of pre-existence. In a similar sense the Rabbins boasted that Israel and the laws existed before the world.

[The passage most clearly teaches the essential and personal pre-existence of Christ before Abraham, in other words, before the world (xvii. 5), and before time (i. 1), which was made with the world, and implies His *eternity*, and consequently His *deity*, for God alone is eternal. This the Jews well understood, and hence they raised stones to punish the supposed blasphemer. The same doctrine is taught, ch. i. 1, 18; vi. 62; xvii. 5; Col. i. 17; Heb. i. 2. All attempts of ancient and modern Socinians and Rationalists to explain away the pre-existence, or to turn it into a merely ideal pre-existence in the mind and will of God (which would constitute no difference between Christ and Abraham), are "little better than dishonest quibbles" (Alford). I add Meyer's explanation which is clear and satisfactory. "Before Abraham *became* (*ward*, not *war*), *I am;* older than Abraham's becoming, is my being. Since Abraham had not pre-existed, but by his birth *came into existence*, the verb γενέσθαι is used, while εἰμί denotes *being as such* (*das Sein an sich*), which in the case of Christ who, according to His divine essence, was before time itself, does not include a previous γενέσθαι or coming into existence. Comp. i. 1, 6, and Chrysostom. The present tense denotes that which *continues* from the past, *i. e.*, here from the pre-temporal existence (i. 1; xvii. 5). Comp. LXX., Ps. xc. 2; Jer. i. 5. But the ἐγώ εἰμι is neither an *ideal* existence (De Wette) nor the *Messianic* existence (Scholten), and must not be found in the *counsel of God* (Sam. Crell, Grotius, Paulus, Baumgarten-Crusius), which is made impossible by the *present* tense; nor is it (with Beyschlag) to be conceived of as the existence of the real *image of God*, nor is the expression a *momentary* vision of prophetic elevation (Weizsäcker), but it essentially corresponds with Christ's permanent consciousness of per-

*[The descent of Christ into the region of the departed spirits changed the gloom of the Old Testament Sheol into the light of the New Testament Paradise; Luke xxiii. 43; Hebr. xi. 39, 40.—P. S.]

†[The E. V. (*Before Abraham* WAS, *I am*) obliterates the important distinction between γενέσθαι, *to become, to begin to be, to be born, to be made*, which can be said of creatures only, and εἶναι, *to be*, which applies to the uncreated God as well. This distinction clearly appears already in the Prologue where the Evangelist predicates the ἐστί and ἦν of the eternal existence of the Logos, ἐγένετο of the man John; comp. ch. i. 1, 6 and the notes there. The present "*I am*," for "*I was*," should also be noticed. It denotes His perpetual divine existence independent of all time. "He identifies Himself with Jehovah." See Chrysostom.—P. S.]

sonal pre-existence which in John meets us everywhere. Comp. ch. xvii. 5; vi. 46, 62. It is not an intuitive retrospective *conclusion* (*Rückschluss*), but a retrospective *look* (*Rückblick*) of the consciousness of Jesus." In other words, Christ did not, in a moment of higher inspiration, *infer* that He existed before Abraham and the world (Beyschlag), but He calmly declared His knowledge and conviction, or revealed His personal consciousness concerning His superhuman origin and pre-temporal existence.—P. S.]

Ver. 59. **Then took they up stones.**—The clear sound of the word concerning His eternity sounds to the Jews like blasphemy. They get ready, therefore, to execute theocratic judgment as zealots of the law (comp. x. 31). A summary stoning in the temple is related by Josephus, *Antiq.* xvii. 9, 3. "The stones were probably the building-stones in the vestibule, see Lightfoot, p. 1048 (Meyer)." Considering the frequent attempts of the Jews to stone Jesus, it must appear the more providential, that He nevertheless found His death on the cross, and the more divine that He foresaw it with certainty.

But Jesus hid himself (withdrew Himself), ἐκρύβη. A vanishing out of sight (ἄφαντος γίνεσθαι), as in Luke xxiv. 31 (Augustine, Luthardt [Wordsworth]), is hardly to be thought of; to become invisible is not a withdrawal, a hiding, and Jesus was not yet transfigured. He hid Himself while disappearing among the multitude of the people, especially His adherents. Therefore also not quite so ἀνθρωπίνως, as if He had fled (Chrysost.). The doubtful addition: διελθών, *etc.* [see Text. Notes], does not express a miraculous disappearance, but rather that He secured His safety in virtue of His majesty, just by breaking through the midst of the group of His enemies. Meyer, therefore, has no good reason to say that this occurrence is quite different from the one related, Luke iv. 30. The conjecture of a docetic view (Hilgenfeld, Baur) is arbitrarily put in. Also in these details we see how the crisis thickens and the storm is gathering.

DOCTRINAL AND ETHICAL.

1. The grand decisive turning point in the position of the Jews in Jerusalem towards the Lord, or the falling away from the beginnings of faith, a consequence of His exposition of *true discipleship* (in antithesis to false): (1) Real faith, true orthodoxy: continuance in His word, faithful obedience in contrast to arbitrary perversion of His word. (2) The fruit of faith, true philosophy: knowledge and recognition of divine truth in antithesis to the delusions of error. (3) The blessing of truth: true freedom, liberation from the service of sin, in antithesis to a spurious freedom or mock freedom, contemning the spiritual conditions of external freedom. The *truth* shall make you free. Afterwards: the Son maketh free. Truth is *personal* in Christ, Christ is *universal* in truth. Truth is the light, freedom the might of life. Truth is the enlightenment of the reason, liberty the redemption of the will. Truth is the harmony of the contrasts of life, having its central point in the life and work of Christ, its source in God, its rays in all fragments of knowledge: liberty the harmony of man in his true self-destination in accordance with his abilities and the reality of God. Truth corresponds to revelation, liberty to redemption.

2. *Causes of the falling away:* (1) Pride (Abraham's seed); (2) self-delusion ("not slaves"); (3) carnal aspirations (outward rebellion); (4) evil fellowship, or party spirit ("we, we," *etc.*).

3. Antithesis of true *freedom* and true *servitude.*—Servitude: (1) Beginning of servitude (the commission of sin); (2) state of servitude (the slave of sin); (3) result (only an unfree bond servant in the house of God, over whom expulsion is impending).—The servant (also the servile spirit) abideth not in the house of God (in the communion of the kingdom) forever. This has been first fulfilled in the case of unbelieving Israel.

4. The Son of the house, as the real *Freeman*, also the true *Liberator.*

5. The contrast between *Christ* and His *adversaries:* (1) In disposition. He estimates them impartially (Abraham's seed); He woos them with His word. They, on the other hand, do not suffer His word to spring up in them, therefore hatred to Christ buds within them (they change the savor of life unto life into a savor of death unto death). (2) In the impulses of life. The Father of Christ, the father of the Jews; the seeing of Christ, the hearing of the Jews; the witnessing of Christ, the doing of the Jews. (3) In conduct: Israelitish, anti-Israelitish ("if Abraham were your father"); prophetic ("a man that telleth you the truth"), murderously anti-prophetic ("ye seek to kill Me"); divine-human, anti-Christian. (4) In origin: Of God, of the devil.

6. "*I am from above.*" This answer to the intimation: He is about to descend far below as a suicide, contains the idea of His ascent. To the Jews death was in general a going downward. In the Old Testament the germ of the opposite hope was implanted. Gen. v. 24; xxviii. 12, in the holy mountain-ascents of Moses (Ex. xix.; Deut. xxxiv. 4), in Elijah's ascension to heaven, in expressions such as Prov. xv. 24. Christ here makes the idea of the heavenly abode appear more clearly (comp. chap. vii. 34); at a later period, chap. xiv., He reveals it openly to His disciples in order to confirm it by His ascension.

7. The doctrine of Jesus concerning the *devil.* See the Exegetical Notes. Comp. Com. on Matt. iv. 1; xii. 26 [pp. 81, 223, Am. ed.]. Comp. the *Dogmatik* of the author (*Die Lehre vom Teufel*).

8. *Characteristics of the devil and his children:* (1) Lusts, passions; (2) murder, hate; (3) falsehood; (4) contagion and seduction. Starke: "A seed is figuratively ascribed to the devil, Gen. iii. 15. By this are commonly understood not only the fallen angels but also all malignant sinners (1 John iii. 10; Matt. xiii. 38, 39); partly because the first origin of the evil was the first sin of the devil, partly because all wicked people fulfil his will with filial obedience and hence bear his image. Διάβολος means properly a slanderer, calumniator, because Satan is (1) a slanderer who belies (slanders) and defames God to men (Gen. iii. 3, 5), in that he suggests to believers hard thoughts of God, and tells them that He is angry with them, whilst in reality He is reconciled to them through Christ, but persuades the wicked that God is favorable to them and un-

mindful of their iniquities. He also accuses and calumniates men to God, Job i. 9; Rev. xii. 17. (2) An adversary of Christ and the faithful, Gen. iii. 15; Zech. iii. 1; 1 Pet. v. 8; Rev. xii. 9. (3) A deceiver and seducer of men, 2 Cor. xi. 3, 14, *etc.;* he is the chief seducer, and then also all evil spirits who are under him as their head."

9. The *Sinlessness of Jesus.* Comp. Ullmann, *The Sinlessness of Jesus* [7th ed., 1863] and Schaff on the *Person of Christ*—[Germ. ed. Gotha, 1865, revised ed. New York, 1870, Engl. ed. Boston, 1865, pp. 50 ff. The sinlessness of Jesus is strongly asserted even by divines who are by no means orthodox, (Schleiermacher, Hase, Keim, Bushnell) and has been assailed only by a few writers of any note (such as Strauss, Pecaut, Theo. Parker, Renan), and even these are forced to admit that He made a nearer approach to moral perfection than any other man. But the only logical alternative is between absolute sinlessness or absolute hypocrisy; and to admit the former is virtually to admit the whole Christian system.—P. S.]

10. *Unbelief* the uniform characteristic of the devilish mind: (1) Unbelief of the truth of Christ *because* it is truth, (2) because it is the effluence of His holiness, (3) because it is divine. Or (1) the lack of a sense of truth, proneness to falsehood, (2) the want of appreciation of the purity of life, (3) the lack of affinity to God, of obedience to the voice of God in the breast.

11. "A *Samaritan.*"—The insulting and abusive retort to the calm sentence of truth contains the life-picture of *fanaticism,* which has first boldly chicaned (ver. 13), then quibbled and sneered (ver. 19), after this uttered taunts (ver. 22); then with eager longing for a chiliastic mystery and mystical proceeding has drawn Him out (ver. 25), and worshipped Him (ver. 30). Turning round again it grows rancorous (ver. 33), boasts (ver. 39), and arrogantly and abusively contradicts (ver. 41). Here it stands in its fullest development. It slanders while it reviles and reviles as it slanders.

12. The wonderful proof of Christ's *self-command, patience* and *freedom of spirit* exhibited throughout the chapter. His frankness, His prudence, His wisdom, His incorruptibleness (vers. 30, 31), the most diverse virtues of the Lord prove superior to the most difficult situation and the severest temptations. From the midst of the solemnly moving serenity with which He proclaims judgment, His mercy bursts forth again as a flaming beacon of deliverance, ver. 51. The declaration in ver. 51 reverts to that contained in ver. 31.

13. *Christ and Abraham* in antithesis to the previously depicted relation of the Jews to Abraham. On the feeling of life and the feeling of death. Between *the doctrine of the pre-existence of Christ* and the doctrine of the anticipatory joy of Abraham in the Messiah and his celebration of the Messianic day in the other world, there exists the closest connection; similarly, the comfortless speech of the Jews with regard to the death of Abraham and the prophets is connected with their witless estimation of the duration of the life of Christ. (And thus the Evangelical Church was reproached with her three centuries and the Evangelical Alliance with its three decennaries under the misapprehension of the eternity of the Evangel and the primitiveness of the fellowship of faith.)

14. *Abraham's* exultation in this world, Abraham's joy in the other world, or the excited celebration (of the Messianic day) of the mortal, and the calm, peaceful celebration of the glorified one. The anticipatory joy of the ancients was not without painful longing, their longing not devoid of rapturous glimpses of the future.

15. Isaac, the son of faith, also in this a type of Christ, who was conceived by the Holy Ghost, born of Mary, the Virgin.

16. Christ's proffer of everlasting life answered by the Jews with an attempt to stone and kill Him.

17. As Christ ever more gloriously escaped from the Jews, thus too shall the Church of Christ in her evangelical confession and spiritual life ever more gloriously escape the persecutions of the legalists.

HOMILETICAL AND PRACTICAL.

The uprightness of Christ.—How the Lord by His heavenly uprightness gradually enchains the true disciples, gradually alienates the false ones (see John iii. 6; ix. 1).—How He does not captivate the false disciples: 1. Will not captivate them; 2. cannot captivate them.—The true profitable conduct of disciples towards the word of Jesus: 1. The conduct; (*a*) to suffer themselves to be kept by the word (to continue in it, the obedience of faith, ver. 31); (*b*) to keep the word in temptation as a guiding star through the darkness of judgments (the loyalty of faith, ver. 51). 2. Whereunto this is profitable: knowledge of the truth and freedom from sin (life in brightness and freedom from death).—Continuance in the word of Jesus the condition of true spirit-life: 1. Of true knowledge of God, 2. of true moral freedom.—Through truth to freedom.—Through inner freedom to outer freedom.—The false confidence of legal saints in their freedom (religious, ecclesiastical, political freedom): 1. They are enslaved outwardly by the world (the Jews by Rome); 2. enslaved at home by the letter of the law; 3. enslaved within and without by sin.—Domestic right in the house of God: 1. The Son, 2. the bond-servants, 3. the freedmen.—The true children of Abraham, Rom. iv.—Where the word of Christ can not grow in the heart, enmity against Christ flourishes, ver. 37.—How man can by spiritual pride turn inherited blessings, even ecclesiastical ones, into a curse (as here the boast about being Abraham's seed).—*The prudence of Christ* in antithesis to the temerity of sinners, ver. 38: 1. He speaks that which He has seen of God. 2. The evil that they have faintly heard, they do.—The trial of the Jews, instituted by the Lord, as to whether they are genuine heirs of the spirit and faith of Abraham: 1. The trial, (*a*) after the works of Abraham, (*b*) after their susceptibility of God's words. 2. The result, ver. 44.

Abraham's seed (consecrated children of God by circumcision; called regenerate), and yet of their father the devil. So, too, one may be called a Christian, an evangelical Christian, etc., and yet be of one's father, the devil.—

The devil a person who, by murder and lying

continually, calls in question his personality and all personality.—Christ's severe words concerning the devil (here, Matt. xiii., Matt. iv. and elsewhere).—The fundamental traits of the devilish nature. How they are embraced in the ONE fundamental trait of unbelief (or of apostasy).—Falsehood and hate cognate: 1. Falsehood a murder of truth, of ideal reality. 2. Murder falsehood against life (denial of God, of love, sullying of the right).—How all threads of human falsehood and hatred and murder unite in the murder of Christ, the crucifixion.—How love and loyalty to all truth shine inseparable and pristine in the Crucified One.—The majesty of Jesus in His testimony to the devil and his children, etc. 44.—Hatred of truth.—Unbelief as a hatred of truth resting upon the love of sin.

THE GOSPEL FOR JUDICA [fifth Sunday in Lent], vers. 46–59.—The two-fold judgment in the separation between Christ and His adversaries: 1. The false judgment of the world, resulting in the justification of Christ; 2. Christ's true judgment of the world, that shall lead to the justification of sinners.—Christ, the Prophet of everlasting life, considered in relation to the prophets of death: 1. Wherefore He is the Prophet of life, and why they are prophets of death. (a) He is the Holy One, the Sinless One, the publisher of the Word of God, and Himself the Word; existing from eternity, in respect of His essence—as respects His works, the Saviour of life, in time; (b) they are the sinners, enemies of the word, lost in temporalness, killing life with the fatal letter. 2. How He proclaims everlasting life, but they can preach of nothing but death. (a) Of His eternal life, of the eternal life of Abraham; (b) they of the death of Abraham and the Prophets. 3. How He offers them eternal life (ver. 5), whilst they, in return, wish to kill Him, ver. 59. 4. How He is proved to be the Ever-Living One, while they have gone the way of death, vers. 54, 55.—As error is connected with sin, so is truth with innocence and righteousness.

The sinlessness of Jesus corroborated by challenging the testimony of His enemies.—The testimony of the world and of Christ's enemies to the innocence of Jesus (Pilate, Judas, the high-priests and elders themselves, Matt. xxvii. 43).—The innocence of Christ in respect of its complete revelation: 1. Founded upon divine impeccability, 2. approved in human sinlessness. —The voice of Jesus, from the mere fact of its being the voice of the Holy Man, should receive the consideration of the whole world. 1. In its uniqueness, 2. in its credibility, 3. in its revelations.—He that is of God heareth God's words. —Ver. 48. The answer of the Jews a historically stereotype reply of the spirit of the law to the preaching of the gospel.—How religious testimony is turned into invectives in the mouth of fanaticism, ver. 48.—The calmness of the Lord in contrast to the railing excitement of His enemies.—Peter imitates Him in this composure (Acts ii.); so likewise do all faithful witnesses for the truth.—The cry of grief with which the Lord again offers salvation even to self-hardeners and blasphemers.—The New Testament word of everlasting life decried as a word of the devil by the false servants of the Old Testament.

Ver. 55. *And if I should say.* The fidelity of the Lord to truth in the faithfulness of His self-consciousness and knowledge of God.—Ver. 57. The length of true life, 1. measured by earthly-mindedness, 2. measured by godly-mindedness.—The Jews as accountants and reckoners opposed to the Lord and His numbers.—How the everlasting TO-DAY of the Father (Ps. ii.) is re-echoed in the everlasting I AM of the Son.—Ver. 59. The ever repeated and ever vain attempt of Christ's enemies to stone Him.—They were able in the end to crucify Him and they thus contributed to His glorification, but to consign Him to oblivion beneath a heap of stones was beyond their power.—How Christ always passes gloriously through the midst of His enemies.

STARKE: It is not enough to make a good beginning in Christianity if one do not end well (continue and persevere).—*Make free*, Rom. vi. 18; Gal. v. 1; 1 Pet. ii. 16. From the bondage of sin, ver. 34, and of eternal death, ver. 51; Luke i. 77; by remission of guilt and punishment and by communication of the Spirit of adoption and of faith.—That only is real and sound truth which can sanctify and save.—OSIANDER: Believers are not free from external servitude and civil burdens; their freedom is far more glorious, for they are free from sin, death, the devil and hell, and can bid defiance to all enemies, Rom. vi. 22.—ZEISIUS: Of what avail is it to have pious parents and ancestors, and not to be pious ourselves? To be of noble blood, but ignoble in soul, &c.—*Ibid.*: Oh wretched liberty whose companion is thraldom under sin and the devil!—CANSTEIN: If sin but play the master and have dominion over a man, it obtains right and might to plunge him into sundry and greater sins.—He who will be forever with God must not be a slave but a son; and this is the highest good, this is true felicity—to dwell in the house of the Lord forever. Ps. xxiii. 6.—ZEISIUS: Priceless liberty of the children of God; but beware that thou abuse not such liberty by making it an occasion of security!—Ver. 41. The sinner who is forever vindicating himself does but entangle himself the more.—It is the way of the flesh to be always intent upon evasions.—*Nova Bibl. Tub.*: He who loves not Jesus is not born of God but of the devil.—Jesus proceeded from the Father to seek us; should not we then go forth from ourselves and the whole world to meet Him?—The CAN NOT ver. 43: A wicked, unruly will lay at the bottom of this.—ZEISIUS: Execrable as falsehood is because it is the offspring of the devil, just so base is it, alas! But O insolvent nobility of liars!—*Ibid.*: It is the old way of the world to love and to hearken to the devil's lies, hypocrisy and flattery rather than truth.—As long as man can not endure truth he is incapable of faith.—Ver. 46. Against him who can ground his defence upon a good conscience the harshest invectives and abuse of his enemies will accomplish nothing.—A Christian is bound to appeal to his good conscience when his enemies revile and slander him without a cause.—Ver. 47. ZEISIUS: Infallible test of those who belong to God: who truly love God's word, &c. —When wicked men are convinced of their wickedness and have nothing to answer, they resort to abuse, invective, and calumny, Acts vi. 10, 11. —LAMPE: To call upright witnesses for the truth heretics and enthusiasts, moreover to persecute them, and to boast of one's own orthodoxy on the other hand—are characteristics of antichristian spirits, 1 Pet. iii. 9.—Ver. 49. The more we honor God, the more the world will dishonor us. But courage! God will honor us in return.—Perverse world! It honors what is despicable, and despises what is honorable.—Ver. 50. It is honor enough for believers that they are the children of God. God, moreover, will defend them.—The godly find what they do not seek, but the wicked attain not that for which they strive.—Ver. 52. The wicked trample the most precious promises under foot and draw only poison from the fairest flowers of the divine word.—CRAMER: The devil is a sophist.—Ver. 54. Vanity and folly make a great boast of themselves! Consider the Saviour and follow His example.—Ver. 56. The most pious parents often leave descendants who do not possess their faith, piety and virtue.—Believers see what is invisible, and believe that which is incredible, and rejoice with all their hearts.—Christians existed before the birth of Christ and were saved through Him, Heb. xiii. 8.—CANSTEIN: Truth always comes off conqueror.

GERLACH: The truth, the revelation in Christ, 1 John i. 6, 8; ii. 21; Heb. x. 26. This truth makes free, for only that being is free that develops in accordance with its God-created nature.—The first sinner in God's creation, the devil, fell from the truth; he fell out of God, as the eternal source and vital element of all created beings. Thus he became a living contradiction in himself, a lie.—Ver. 47; 1 John v. 20.—Recognize Him they would not, refute Him they could not, therefore they reviled Him.—Ver. 52. All the Jews at that time believed that the Messiah would raise the dead and judge the world, even in the carnal, literal sense; hence the language of Jesus might well have excited their astonishment if they had not been inclined to receive Him as the Messiah: bitter enmity however prompted their treatment of His words, and the utter contempt which they entertained for Him is visible in their reply. (Be it observed only that they were also offended because He asserted His possession of this power without publicly presenting Himself as the Messiah.)—He strengthens the impression of mysterious majesty about His person, in that He, by virtue of His glance into the higher spirit-world, affirms that of Abraham which a mere man could not know.

BRAUNE: Continuance, 1 John ii. 28.—Blessed is he that endureth unto the end.—A real delirium of liberty had seized the Jews.—Bondage, 2 Pet. ii. 19.—Emancipation, Rom. viii. 2.—When a man takes offence at the expression of Jesus, he is not in harmony with the thoughts and mind of Jesus.—The evil will is the tool of Satan, the true devilish momentum.—Thus the devil's nature is not naturally evil; but wickedness made it evil. It is not I that is evil but egotism. Without the *I* there were no love in which *I* learns *thou* and says *we*.—"To his haughtiness humility is servility, dependence on God slavery; to his false serpent-wisdom simplicity and honesty seem stupidity, and his egotism holds love to be foolish sensibility; his pride finds contrition, repentance and petitions for mercy an insufferable humiliation. The struggle for autocratic likeness to God delusively causes his aspirations and efforts to seem grand to him, his non-subjection to God sublime" (Sartorius).—There is cause for fear when he deceives and lies rather than when he rages.—Why did they say fifty years old? The fiftieth year is the close of manhood, and hence formed the period of the Levites' time of service. Jesus was not as old as this, but they mention this age, as though they magnanimously granted more than could be demanded, in order to give an appearance of absurdity to His language.

HEUBNER: Christ distinguishes between real and false, firm and wavering disciples.—The slave of sin does not so much as know that he lacks freedom. One does not perceive that until one begins to see clearly. That is already the beginning of freedom.—Man is blinded by many things so that he thinks himself perfectly free. Here it is a religious species of pride of ancestry, &c. But besides family pride there are a number of other considerations which exert a delusive power: external refinement, rank, authority, proficiency in business, commendation, a varnish of morality, art, science.—Why servant? when he says: it is my own will. Answer: Because the sinner never can say that his choice is the result of full and sober-minded conviction. He is reproved by conscience.—God will have no slaves, no unwilling servants by compulsion and for hire; He wants children, free, loving children. Their supreme right is: to abide in the Father's house.—Man's destiny: either adoption into the paternal house of God or exclusion from it.—The Son has broken the chains forged by Satan. He is the Redeemer of the human race.—Fictitious freedom.—The remembrance of pious ancestors should be a mighty impulse to good.—Christ has a unique speech.—The devil abode not. Hence the earliest fathers of the Church called the devil an apostate (ἀποστάτης).—Apostasy from truth leads to the entire loss of truth. Be it observed, moreover, that as early as in the apocryphal *Predicatio Pauli* the sinlessness of Jesus is denied.—Good men can be understood only by the like-minded. Christ teaches us equanimity in reference to worldly honor.—What is true honor?—The difference between honor with God and honor with the world.—That no slander can strip us of our true honor.—Ver. 52. The words of Christ seem presumptuous because virtue often has the appearance of presumption. He who is morally good really makes the highest claims without immodesty or presumption; on the other hand presumption is to be found in the world.—Living among wicked and perverse people the severest trial of holy men.—What strengthens the pious in this life? 1. The consciousness of their lofty and intimate fellowship with the devout of all ages; 2. The prospect of everlasting blessedness, from eternity prepared for believers, through Christ.

GOSSNER: The world falsely declares itself free when it is over head and ears in slavery.—This is the tyranny of the devil, which he exercises over natural men to such an extent, that Paul rightly calls him the god of this world, who hath his work in the children of unbelief, Eph. ii. 2; 2 Cor. iv. 4.—From the Son of God all the children of God derive their birth, their life, their freedom, their redemption, their right of sonship and heirship.—What He is, that He also communicates to His people and makes them kings, prophets and priests. They have the honor of bearing His unction, seal and name.—Infidels believe the devil, while denying his existence.*—A man may try himself whether he be a child of God or of the devil.—Lying is his proper character.—Christ would not die in the temple because He was to be sacrificed not alone for the Jewish nation, but for the whole world; for this another altar was requisite, whereon He might be offered up in the sight of all the world, as upon Golgotha.—What a judgment, to cast out Jesus! What a void in the heart, the temple of the Church, where Jesus must hide Himself and give way to blind zeal, pride, ambition, falsehood, selfishness—before all which He must flee!

SCHLEIERMACHER: Their belief (vers. 30 and 31) was in itself utterly imperfect, because expectations were mingled with it which did not correspond with the real purpose of God, that He would accomplish in Christ. Now so long as these expectations exist, it is possible that when a man begins to doubt their truth and yet still clings to them at heart, he will forsake the faith. But just that clinging of the heart to something incompatible with true and living faith in the Redeemer is at the same time a *non-continuance in His word* and a cherishing of another word in the heart, 2 Cor. iii. 15.—There is no other way for us all to be filled and penetrated with the truth than by gazing into His holy image and suffering ourselves to be purified through Him from all falseness.

BESSER: Ver. 32. Something of this was known also to the heathen; Cicero says: The wise man alone is free. But they comprehended the nature neither of divine wisdom nor of divine liberty.—No thraldom, says Seneca, is worse than the thraldom of the passions. Plato calls the infamous lusts the hardest tyrants. Epictetus says: Liberty is the name of virtue, slavery the name of vice. The Brahmin sages call the natural state of man: "Bondage."—SCHMALZ: The rage for heretical accusation: 1. It makes invectives take the place of convincing arguments; 2. it craftily distorts the plainest utterances of others; 3. it casts suspicion on the heart of others; 4. to combat them it grasps at unlawful and violent means.—RAMBACH: Jesus the sublimest pattern of meekness.—J. C. E. SCHWARZ: Falsehood: 1. in respect to its nature (apostasy from God, rebellion against His kingdom, pollution of His image in ourselves and others); 2. in respect to its fruits (self-belying, mischief, impulse to new sin).—J. MUELLER: The holiness of Jesus Christ is proof of the truth of His testimony about His divine dignity.—SCHNUR: Why truth is so hated: 1. Because it sees too deeply; 2. because it speaks too openly; 3. because it judges too severely.—RAUTENBERG: Truth and its lot upon earth: 1. It is rejected but does not keep silence; 2. it is reviled but wearies not; 3. it is persecuted but does not succumb.

* [A free rendering of the German: *Sie glauben* IHM (*dem Teufel*), *ohne* IHN (*den T.*) *zu glauben.*—P. S.]

V.

CHRIST THE LIGHT OF THE WORLD OVER AGAINST THE BLIND. THE HEALING ON THE SABBATH OF THE MAN WHO WAS BORN BLIND, WITH THE SYMBOLICAL CO-OPERATION OF THE TEMPLE-SPRING OF SILOAM. THE DAY OF CHRIST, AND CHRIST THE LIGHT OF THAT DAY. THE LIGHT OF THE BLIND A JUDGMENT OF BLINDNESS ON THOSE WHO IMAGINE THEY SEE. SYMBOLISM OF LIGHT, OF DAY, OF DAY'S WORKS. (ALL LIGHT OF THE SUN SHOULD BE USED, AFTER THE EXAMPLE AND SPIRIT OF CHRIST, TO PRODUCE LIGHT; HENCE TOO ALL EFFORTS OF CULTURE A SYMBOLICAL CREATION OF LIGHT, POINTING TO HIM WHO CREATES LIGHT IN THE REAL SENSE OF THE TERM.) THE EXCOMMUNICATION, OR THE GERMINANT SEPARATION.

CHAP. IX.

1 And as *Jesus* [he] passed [was passing] by, he saw a man which was [*omit* which
2 was] blind from *his* birth. And his disciples asked him, saying, Master [Rabbi],
who did sin [who sinned], this man, or his parents, that he was born [should be
born] blind?
3 Jesus answered, Neither hath this man sinned [Neither did this man sin] nor his
4 parents: but that the works of God should be made manifest in him. I [We][1]
must work the works of him that sent me, while it is day: the night cometh, when
5 no man can work. As long as I am in the world, I am the light of the world.
6 When he had thus spoken, he spat on the ground, and made clay of the spittle,
7 and anointed the eyes of the blind man with the clay.[2] And said unto him, Go,
wash in the pool of Siloam, (which is by interpretation, Sent). He went his way

8 [away], therefore, and washed, and came seeing. The neighbours, therefore, and
they which before had seen him that he was blind [who had before observed him
because he was a beggar][3] said, Is not this he that sat and begged [sitteth and beg-
9 geth]? Some said, This is he: others *said*, [said, Nay, but,][4] He is like him: *but*
10 [*omit* but] he said, I am *he*. Therefore said they unto him, How were thine eyes
11 opened? He answered and said [*omit* and said], A man that is called Jesus made
clay, and anointed mine eyes, and said unto me, Go to the pool of [*omit* the pool of][5]
Siloam, and wash: and I went and washed, and I received sight [I went therefore
12 (οὖν) and washed and received sight]. Then said they [They said] unto him,
13 Where is he [that man, ἐκεῖνος]? He said [saith, λέγει], I know not. They brought
14 [bring] to the Pharisees him that aforetime [before, once] was blind. And it was the
sabbath day [it was sabbath on the day][6] when Jesus made the clay, and opened
15 his eyes. Then again [Again therefore] the Pharisees also asked him how he had
received [he received] his sight. He said unto them, He put clay upon mine eyes,
16 and I washed, and do see. Therefore said some of the Pharisees, This man is not
of [from][7] God, because he keepeth not the sabbath day [*omit* day]. Others said,
How can a man that is a sinner do such miracles [signs]? And there was a divi-
17 sion among them. They say [therefore][8] unto the blind man again, What sayest
thou of him, that [because, or, seeing that, or, for having opened] he hath opened
thine eyes? He said, He is a prophet.
18 But the Jews [The Jews therefore] did not believe concerning him, that he had
been blind and received sight, until they called the parents of him that had re-
19 ceived his sight. And they asked them, saying, Is this your son, who ye say was
20 born blind? how then doth he now see? His parents answered[9] them [*omit* them]
21 and said, We know that this is our son, and that he was born blind: But by what
means he now seeth, we know not; or who hath opened [who opened] his eyes, we
know not: he is of age; ask him [ask him: he is of age]: he shall [will] speak
22 for himself. These *words* spake his parents [These things his parents said] because
they feared the Jews: for the Jews had agreed already that if any man did con-
fess that he was Christ [should acknowledge him as Christ], he should be put out
23 of the synagogue [excommunicated]. Therefore said his parents [For this reason
his parents said], He is of age; ask him.
24 Then again called they [So they called the second time] the man that was
[had been] blind and said unto him, Give God the praise [Give glory to God]; we
25 know that this man is a sinner. He [therefore] answered and said [*omit* and said],[10]
Whether he be a sinner *or no* [whether he is a sinner], I know not: one thing I
26 know, that, whereas I was blind, now I see [that I, a blind man, now see]. Then[11]
said they to him again[12] [They therefore said to him], What did he do to thee?
27 how opened he thine eyes? He answered them, I have told you already, and ye
did not hear: wherefore [why] would ye hear *it* again? will [would] ye also be
28 [become] his disciples? Then [*omit* Then] they reviled him and said,[13] Thou art
29 his disciple; but we are Moses' disciples. We know that God spake [hath spoken]
unto Moses: *as for* this *fellow* [but as for this man], we know not from [*omit* from]
30 whence he is. The man answered and said unto them, Why herein is a marvellous
thing, that ye know not from [*omit* from] whence he is, and *yet* he hath opened [he
31 opened] mine eyes. Now [*omit* Now] we know that God heareth not sinners; but
if any man be a worshipper of God, and doeth [do] his will, him he heareth.
32 Since the world began was it not heard [it was never heard] that any man opened
33 the eyes of one that was born blind. If this man were not of [from] God he could
34 do nothing. They answered and said unto him, Thou wast altogether [wholly,
ὅλος] born in sins, and dost thou teach us? And they cast him out [not simply from
the place where they were, but from the synagogue=excommunicated him].
35 Jesus heard that they had cast him out; and when he had [*omit* had] found him
he said unto him, Dost thou believe on [in] the Son of God [the Son of Man]?[14]
36 He answered and said, Who [And who] is he, Lord, that I might [may] believe on
37 [in] him? And [*omit* And] Jesus said unto him, Thou hast both seen him, and it
38 is he that talketh with thee. And he said, Lord, I believe [I believe, Lord]. And
39 he worshipped him. And Jesus said, For judgment I am come [I came] into this

world, that they which [who] see not might see; and that they which [who] see
might be made [might become] blind.
40 And *some* of the Pharisees which [who] were with him heard these words, and
41 said unto him, Are we [also] blind also? Jesus said unto them, If ye were blind,
ye should have no sin [ye should not have sin]; but now ye say, We see; [.] there-
fore [*omit* therefore][15] your sin remaineth.

TEXTUAL AND GRAMMATICAL.

[1] Ver. 4.—Instead of the first ἐμέ, B. D. L., the Coptic and other translations read: ἡμᾶς. The idea presented by the passage furnishes us with the motive for the dissimilarity between ἡμᾶς δέ and πέμψαντός με; this dissimilarity, however, was doubtless the cause of the two words' being made the same—several Codd. wrote ἐμέ at the beginning also, whilst Cod. L., the Coptic and other translations placed ἡμᾶς in the second place likewise. [The first ἡμᾶς is probably genuine, the second a correction occasioned by it. Cod. Sin.* sustains ἡμᾶς in both clauses. Alford reads ἐμέ and μέ, Tischend. (ed. viii.) ἡμᾶς twice.—P. S.]

[2] Ver. 6.—According to Codd. [Sin.] A. B. C.,** *etc.*: αὐτοῦ τὸν πηλόν, *His clay* (paste), the earth-ointment prepared by Him. Tischendorf omits τοῦ τυφλοῦ, in accordance with the not decisive testimony of [Sin.] B. L. [Tischend. reads in ed. viii.: ἐπέχρισεν αὐτοῦ τὸν πηλὸν ἐπὶ τοὺς ὀφθαλμούς. So also Alford (ed. vi.), and Westcott and Hort, except that the latter, with B. C.[1] adopt ἐπέθηκεν (*put, spread*), instead of ἐπέχρισεν. Lange, Meyer and Ewald retain τοῦ τυφλοῦ. *He spread His clay upon the eyes* (of the blind man). Noyes translates: *He anointed his eyes with the clay*; Alford in his N. T.: *He spread* (but in the text of his Com. he reads ἐπέχρισεν, *anointed*) *the clay upon his eyes*; Lange: *Er schmierte seinen* (*den von ihm gemachten*) *Teig auf die Augen des Blinden*; Ewald: *Er strich diesen Brei auf die Augen des Blinden.*—P. S.]

[3] Ver. 8.—[The true reading is προσκαίτης, *beggar*, instead of the τυφλός, *blind*, of the text. rec., and is sustained by ℵ. A. B. C.[1] D., *etc.*—P. S.]

[4] Ver. 9.—[ἔλεγον, οὐχί, ἀλλ' (ℵ. B. C., *etc.*), for the text. rec. which omits these words.—P. S.]

[5] Ver. 11.—Εἰς τὸν Σιλωάμ B. D. L. X. [Also Iren. and Cod. Sin. The text. rec. τὴν κολυμβήθραν τοῦ, after Cod. A. and Vulgate is explanatory.—P. S.]

[6] Ver. 14.—Instead of ὅτε we should read, according to B. L. X. [Sin.] and several translations: ἐν ᾗ ἡμέρᾳ.

[7] Ver. 17.—B. D., *etc.*, Lachmann, Tischendorf: οὐκ ἔστιν οὗτος παρὰ θεοῦ ὁ ἄνθρωπος.

[8] Ver. 16.—Lachmann supplies οὖν, in accordance with A. B. D. [Cod. Sin., Tischend., Alf.—P. S.]

[9] Ver. 20.—According to Lachmann, the οὖν after ἀπεκρ. is not to be expected here, upon consideration of the subject-matter, and is supported by B. only. Similarly the δέ in Cod. A., *etc.*, and the αὐτοῖς seem to be additions, against which are B. L. X., *etc.*

[10] Ver. 25.—The καὶ εἶπεν [text. rec.] is omitted according to Lachmann and Tischendorf by reason of [Sin.] A. B. D., *etc.*

[11] Ver. 26.—According to Codd. B. D. K., *etc.*, οὖν. [Text. rec. δέ.—P. S.]

[12] Ver. 26.—Πάλιν [text. rec.] omitted by many Codd. [Sin.[1] B. D.] in opposition to Cod. A. [Sin.[3a]], *etc.*, was perhaps left out on account of a misapprehensive assumption of a collision with the πάλιν of ver. 15. That πάλιν, however, has reference to the preceding question of the people.

[13] Ver. 28.—The construction has the power of making the following words which they uttered, to be looked upon as the substance of their revilings. This seemed inadequate and probably occasioned the reading: οἱ δὲ ἔλεγον in D. L., *etc.*

[14] Ver. 35.—Codd. B. D. and the Ethiopian translation read: τοῦ ἀνθρώπου, because Jesus was wont thus to designate Himself. [This reading is sustained by Cod. Sin. and adopted by Tischend., ed. viii., and Westcott and Hort.—P. S.]

[15] Ver. 41.—The οὖν before ἁμαρτία is wanting in [Sin.] B. D. K. L., *etc.*

EXEGETICAL AND CRITICAL.

[The account of the blind man and the miracle wrought on him, with its consequences, is uncommonly life-like, full of circumstantiality and characteristic details which could not have been invented, and clearly show that the writer was an eye-witness of the scene. All attempts of modern skeptics to turn the miracle into a medical cure of inflammation of the eyes (Ammon), or to explain it from a misunderstanding of ver. 39 (Weisse), or from a mythical imitation of the healing of Naaman, 2 Ki. v. 10 (Strauss), or from dogmatic design (Baur), are baseless and exploded conjectures. Comp. Meyer, p. 391, 5th ed.—P. S.]

Ver. 1. **And in passing by** (καὶ παράγων). This history is evidently connected [by καί] in respect to time and place with the preceding chapter [with ἐξῆλθεν ἐκ τοῦ ἱεροῦ, viii. 59]. As regards time, it was the day after the close of the Feast of Tabernacles, and that a Sabbath, ver. 14. See Lev. xxiii. 39. As for the place, Jesus had just quitted the temple, and we are most probably to imagine the blind beggar as seated at the entrance to the temple (comp. Acts iii. 2). De Wette cannot reconcile this peaceful occurrence with the scene of violence, chap. viii. 59;* but it is precisely in this secure deportment of Jesus, and in His halt after the moment of the most imminent peril of death, and while He was still in the vicinity of danger, that we should recognize the Lord and Master. Hence we refer the παράγων (comp. Mark ii. 14), not to the beggar, but to Jesus Himself. It is obviously the participle of the preceding, even though doubtful παρῆγεν οὕτως. While He is in the act of passing by the last frequenters of the temple, the blind beggar meets His eye at the door, and the fact of His pausing to look at Him is revealed by the question of His disciples.

[**A man blind from his birth**, ἐκ γενετῆς = ἐκ κοιλίας μητρός, Acts iii. 2. Possibly the beggar himself proclaimed the fact of his *native* blindness as giving additional force to his appeal for alms. It makes the miracle all the greater, and places it beyond the reach of an extraordinary medical cure (Ammon and other rationalists), but does not warrant the extravagant notion of some fathers (Irenæus, Theodorus Mopsu., Nonnus) that Jesus *created* the eyes out of the πηλός, as God made the first man out of clay. According to Luthardt, the blind man represents the "world," to which Christ turned after being rejected by the Jews; but this does not follow from ver. 5, "I am the Light of the world," for the emphasis lies on *light*, and the *world* embraces the whole of humanity, Jews and Gentiles.—P. S.]

Ver. 2. **Rabbi, who sinned?** The motive for this question on the part of the disciples could, in their present situation, scarcely be dogmatical interest, being, as they were, just reunited to the Master after His escape from sto-

* [So also Lücke and Alford; while Olshausen, Meyer, Stier and Trench (on the *Miracles*, p. 233) side with Lange as to the date.—P. S.]

ning. We suppose that they wish to induce the Lord to pass by the man as unworthy of His self-sacrificing interest, in order that He may hasten on; and that hence their question, uttered on the spur of the moment, derives a decided Pharisaical coloring from the popular notion. According to Euth. Zigabenus they suppose neither to be the case. Admitting this, the question itself would fall to the ground. The disciples take for granted that this blindness was caused only by sin;* the question is merely as to the dilemma: this man or his parents? † The latter supposition was the proximate one, in accordance with the Pharisaical explication of Ex. xx. 5 (Lightfoot, p. 1048). Nevertheless, the disciples give the first place to the more remote question: whether this man himself sinned. Beza, Grotius and others have accounted for the expression by the belief in the transmigration of souls. This belief, however, could not have been entertained by orthodox Jews, even though it may subsequently appear among the Cabalists (see *Comm. on Matth.*, chap. xiv. 2, p. 272, Am. ed.). Cyril, De Wette and others mention, in explanation of the question, the belief in the pre-existence of souls (in accordance with Wisdom of Solomon, viii. 20); but neither was this a national tenet of orthodox Jews, although it had forced an entrance from Platonism into Alexandrian Jewish theology.‡ The view that most naturally suggests itself is, that the man may already have sinned in the womb, as an embryo, by evil affections. The distinction between nobler and baser vital motions in the embryonic state is also intimated by Scripture, Luke i. 41, 44. Rabbinism has with reference to Gen. xxv. 22 [the struggle between Jacob and Esau in the mother's womb] further matured this idea (Lightfoot, *Sanhedrin*, fol. 91, 2, *etc.*). An obscure idea of pre-existence may have occurred to the disciples, who were here fashioning a question from reminiscences, together with this notion of embryonic guilt. The conception of Lampe, Luthardt, *etc.*: has he sinned, or, as this is inconceivable, *etc.*, is not in accordance with the text. Tholuck's supposition after Camero: they thought that he might in anticipation have been branded as a sinner [for *predestinated sin* to be committed hereafter], is certainly not altogether clear (Meyer), [and without analogy in the Scriptures]. Von Gerlach speaks doubtfully in this connection of a punishment that precedes sin; and just as one-sidedly of how the work of divine grace has swallowed up avenging justice; while according to Heubner it is simply a question of the recognition of the fact that there are also unmerited sufferings (*i. e.*, of sinful men, who yet have not directly brought the suffering upon themselves).

Ver. 3. **Neither did this man sin nor his parents.** There is no question of their sinfulness in other respects, but Christ knows that no sin, either of this blind man or of his parents, was the cause of his being born blind.—**But that** (ἀλλ' ἵνα); namely, to this end was he born blind [τυφλὸς ἐγεννήθη]. The ultimate object of evil, as of things in general, is the glorification of God in the salvation of men; the glorification of God is however more definitely a glorification through the works of Christ, which are God's own works. Here, too, God should be glorified in the salvation of the man who was born blind. It is incorrect to suppose that the question of the disciples first directed the attention of Jesus to the unfortunate man. This view is contradicted by the preceding εἶδεν.

[Trench's remarks on this verse (*Miracles*, p. 238 f.) are appropriate: "The Lord neither denies their [the parents'] sin, nor his: all that He does is to turn away His disciples from that most harmful practice of diving down with cruel surmises into the secrets of other men's lives, and, like the friends of Job, guessing for them hidden sins in explanation of their unusual sufferings. This blindness, He would say, is the chastening of no *particular* sin on his own part, or on his parents'. Seek, therefore, neither here nor there the cause of his calamity; but see what nobler explanation the evil in the world, and this evil in particular, is capable of receiving. The purpose of the life-long blindness of this man is *that the works of God should be made manifest in him*, and that through it and its removal the grace and glory of God might be magnified. We must not, indeed, understand our Lord's declaration as though this man was used merely as a *means*, visited with this blindness to the end that the power of God might be manifested to others in its removal. The manifestation of the works of God has here a wider reach, and embraces the lasting weal of the man himself . . . it includes their manifestation *to* him and *in* him" [as well as *on* him]. Comp. John xi. 4; Rom. v. 30; ix. 17; xi. 25, 32, 33.—P. S.]

Ver. 4. **We** [not **I**] **must work.** See the TEXTUAL NOTES. According to Kuinoel, Jesus designed to meet the scruples entertained by the disciples as to the propriety of the healing on the Sabbath, which He was about to undertake. It is more probable that with this saying He encounters their urgent entreaties to hasten away from the dangerous position. Hence, with the "*we*," He holds *them* fast also to the place where it is their duty to remain, and reveals to them that in the future *they*, as the prosecutors of His work, must stand firm in similar situations; with a view to which destiny they are now being exercised.—**Who sent me.** Not: Who sent *us*. The works of God are comprehended in His

* [This is the meaning of ἵνα, which is τελικῶς (not merely ἐκβατικῶς) and expresses the merited consequence according to the divine *intention*.—P. S.]

† [So also Meyer, while Euthymius Zig., Ebrard and Hengstenberg put into the question the meaning: *Neither* one *nor* the other can be possible in this case; Stier: this man, or—this being out of the question—his parents; Alford and others: the question was vaguely asked without any strict application to the case in hand, merely taking it for granted that *some sin* must have led to the blindness. The disciples held the popular Jewish opinion that *every* evil must be the punishment for a *particular* sin. This is decidedly denied by Christ here, and Luke xiii. 9 ff. The *general* connection of sin as the cause, and evil as the result, is undoubtedly taught in the Bible from the first introduction of sin, Gen. iii. But since sin is in the world, evil in particular cases may be a school of *discipline* of God's love, as the misfortunes of Job, the blindness of Tobit, Paul's thorn in the flesh, and the many trials and troubles to which the children of God are often more subject in this life than the ungodly; for "whom the Lord loveth, He chastiseth" (Hebr. xii. 6; Prov. iii. 12; Rev. iii. 19).—P. S.]

‡ [Pre-existence was taught by Philo, the Essenes and Cabalists. See Grimm, Comm. on Sap., p. 177 f., and Bruch, *Doctrine of the Pre-existence of the Soul* (Strassburg, 1859), p. 22, (translated in *Bibliotheca Sacra* for 1863, pp. 681 ff). See Meyer *in loc.* Stier, however, doubts the applicability of the passage, Wisdom viii. 19, 20.—P. S.]

work, for which He alone is *sent;* in the carrying out of His work in individual works His disciples are to be participators with Him.

As long as it is day; the night is coming. The antithesis of day and night is the antithesis of the time of His life and activity in opposition to the period of His passion and death; uttered in anticipation of His approaching death, yet in the assurance that at present no mortal peril threatens Him. Similarly the contrast of *day* and *night* is significant of the contrast of *life* and *death* in the classics, especially in Homer (see Meyer). In the Rabbins: "*Pirke Aboth,* II. 19; 'R. Tarphon spake: The day is short; the work is great; the Master presseth.'" Tholuck. Hence the interpretation of Chrysostom and others with reference to the αἰὼν οὗτος and μέλλων is incorrect. Paulus quite tritely explains: Broad-daylight was requisite for cures effected upon the eyes! The day-time of the day's work of Christ was at the same time a day-time of redemption, of visitation for Israel, which terminated with His night, *viz.:* His death (see ver. 5). Only we must not convert this relative antithesis into an absolute one by the declaration: now is the time of grace, afterwards the time of darkness; thus Olshausen, after earlier exegetes (Grotius and others), too strongly defined the contrast. Luthardt: The presence of Christ in the world is the time of the event of redemption; His subsequent separation from the world the time solely of the appropriation of redemption;* this interpretation comes nearer the mark, and yet Meyer, not without foundation, quotes against it John xvi. 7, 15, 26; xiv. 26 and other passages, according to which the death of Jesus was the condition of greater enlightenment. The figure of the day's work is here the decisive one. Every man has for his day's work his one day by which he must profit; when his night comes he can work no more. So too must Christ perform His great, single, and yet universal, official historical day's work, conditional upon His earthly pilgrimage.

Ver. 5. **While I am in the world.**—We suppose that Christ here compares Himself to the sun, the light of day, as chap. viii. to the pillar of fire, the light of the night. This assumption is founded on the preceding antithesis; *day, night.* Accordingly the ὅταν will mean *quamdiu* (Vulgate and many others), but not *quandoquidem* (Zwingle, Lampe, Lücke), or: [*quando*] *at the time when* (Meyer). The sun, throughout the day, as long as it is in the world, is the light of the world. The sun, however, opens and enlightens only the eyes of the seeing; Christ, as the real Sun, opens and enlightens the eyes of the blind likewise. And along with this is expressed the fact that He is the Sun of the world in a spiritual sense. The ὅταν, however, in its figurative sense, denotes the antithesis between the personal presence of Christ in the world and His departure from the world, after which He does not indeed cease to be the light of the world (for the operations of the Paraclete are His), but He no longer works corporeo-spiritually as light, but spiritually, until at the last day the great solstice returns with the day of resurrection. The figure of the sun, which in its day illuminates everything, is the strong expression of His assurance that He will enlighten the eyes of the blind man.

Ver. 6. **He spat.**—The whole conduct of Jesus is manifestly expressive of strong intentionality, and this must first receive our consideration. As the pursuers are close behind Him, and the disciples in a state of anxious tension, it seems to Him that His primary concern must be to give proof of His tranquillity by calmly remaining on the ground. Moreover, as His adversaries accounted Him guilty of antagonism to the law of Jehovah in His previous healing on the Sabbath, chap. v., they should now see that the God of their temple is His co-agent on the Sabbath, since the temple-waters of Siloam are brought into co-operation: a fundamental motive, this, which exegesis has omitted to notice (see *Leben Jesu,* III., p. 635). Furthermore, as the blind man does not yet know Him, and at first is *en rapport* with Him only through the tone of His voice, the life of faith must of course be developed within him by a gradual process, as in the case of the blind man at Bethsaida (Mark viii. 23; comp. Mark vii. 33).

With reference to the use of external means, the three factors: the saliva, the clay, the spring of Siloam, and also the unity of the entire act must be distinguished. Respecting the employment of *saliva* comp. the analogous cases Mark vii. and chap. viii. (See *Com. in loc.*).* On the sanativeness of *clay* in diseases of the eyes see Tholuck's quotation from Serenus Samonicus:† "*Si tumor insolitus typho se tollat inani, Turgentes oculos vili circumline cœno;*" and Lightfoot. On the virtue of the waters of *Siloam* see above the Exegetical Notes on the pool of Bethesda (chap. v.) and Robinson II., p. 155.

In discussing the destination of the elements here employed in Christ's *one* act of healing, we have to distinguish the idea of their *material* or *medicinal,* their *organic* or *instrumental,* their *ethical* and their *allegorical* destination. That the external elements in their combination had, as ancient remedies, no *medicinal* power to give sight to the man who was born blind, is evident. But that they were the better fitted to be *organical* bearers of the miraculous power of Christ, *i. e.,* conductors of it (Nonnus: πηλὸς φαεσφόρος; Olshausen and others), because they were moreover accounted medicinal, is all the more obvious since the question is here of the saliva of Christ and of a salve that He made with His own hand. But since the receptive faith in the miracle must correspond with the positive miraculous power, the alternative is misapprehended when Tholuck and Meyer will set aside the *psychologico-ethical* consideration (Chrysostom, Calvin and others) of the awakening of faith by the use of these in the case of the man who was born blind. In the instances given in the Old Testament also

* [Or, as Luthardt also expresses the antithesis, *Heilsgeschichte and Heilsaneignung,* or the *day* is the time of Christ's *Weltgegenwart* (presence in the world), the night the time of His *Weltgeschiedenheit* (absence from the world).—P. S.]

* [In the two accounts of Tacitus (*Hist.* iv. 8) and Sueton. (*Vesp.* ch. vii.) of the restoring of a blind man to sight by the emperor Vespasian, the use of *saliva jejuna* is recorded. Pliny (*Hist. Nat.,* xxviii. 7) mentions it as a usual remedy in cases of disorders of the eyes. See Wetstein's note, p. 902.—P. S.]

† [A physician in the time of Caracalla who wrote a poem on medicine in hexameter.—P. S.]

(2 Kings iv. 41; chap. v. 12; Isa. xxxviii. 21) the organic operation of the miracle-worker is to be grasped conjunctively with the awakening of the psychologico-ethical receptivity. The *allegorical* interpretation (Luthardt on the anointing with clay: he who will see must become blind; after some Church fathers) is the most remote; on the mythical interpretation of Strauss, Baur, *etc.*, see Meyer [p. 378.]

Ver. 7. **Go, wash.**—It is a question here whether the asyndeton would not be better composed of three members than of two. The latter (go, wash thyself *into* the pool) is of course explained by the custom of the language. Tholuck: νίψαι εἰς pregnant, either including the entering into the water or expressive only of the dipping into it. Winer, p. 369 [387].—**In the pool of Siloam.**—The spring, Isa. viii. 6; the pool, Neh. iii. 15. Its situation see above, chap. v. Meyer: "Re-discovered by Robinson (II., p. 142 ff. [Am. ed. of 1856, vol. I., pp. 338 ff.]), after Josephus, at the mouth of the Valley of Tyropœum on the south-east side of Zion. See Tobler, *The Fountain of Siloam and the Mount of Olives*, 1852, p. 1 ff.; Rödiger in Gesen. *Thes.* III. p. 1416; Ritter, *Erdkunde*, XVI. p. 446 ff. [Comp. my annotations with regard to the latest researches, on pp. 181 ff. Alford, at the close of his vol. on the Gospels, p. 923 f., gives a communication of a correspondent on the supposed identity of Siloam with the pool of Bethesda. Robinson has discovered, and Tobler and Warren have confirmed the connection of the intermittent Fountain of the Virgin (probably the pool of Bethesda) with the Fountain of Siloam, and both were probably connected with a fountain beneath the temple, which remains to be proven by further exploration.—P. S.]—**The pool of Siloam.**—The chief reference of this is not to the district of Siloam (as Tholuck has it, referring to Luke xiii. 4; Joseph. *De bello Jud.* ii. 16, 2; vi. 7, 2); but it is especially the Siloah-pool of Siloah-*spring* which is again mentioned in the following. Tholuck's explanation of the sending to this pool—for the purpose of purification—is too bald, as is also the design ascribed by Meyer: in order that the healing power of the clay ointment might have the necessary time for operation. Concerning the more direct purpose see the note to the preceding verse. As regards the sanative element of the water we can as little reject it (Meyer: the rabbinical traces of a healing power resident in the water point to the organs of digestion, see Schöttgen) as attach any particular credit to it; at all events it assisted in forming a foothold for the faith of the blind man.*

Which is, when translated, One Sent.—The designation שִׁילוֹחַ (Greek in the Sept. and in Josephus Σιλωάμ) signifies: the **sending** [*missio* sc. *aquarum*], probably with reference to the fact that the temple-mount sends forth its spring-water. The question is, how far this word may become synonymous with שָׁלוּחַ **sent**, [*missus*], or **the sent.** According to Hitzig the form is derived from שָׁלוּחַ as יִלּוֹד from יָלוּד, and John has correctly translated: ἀπεσταλμένος (*Com.* on Isa. viii. 6, p. 97. For particulars see Tholuck, p. 327). According to Bengel, Meyer and others the evangelist referred the name to the blind man who was sent to the spring. An unfounded typology, unsupported by the context. This fountain, in that it is called the *Sent*, is the type of Him who in John continually designates Himself as the real Sent One, the type of Christ (Theophylact, Erasmus, Calvin [Ebrard, Luthardt, Hengstenb., Brückner, Godet, Trench, Alford, Wordsworth] and others). It is remarkable how this pregnant symbolism has perplexed the commentators. Wassenbergh and others are inclined to consider the parenthesis (after the Syrian and the Persian translation) a gloss; Lücke also (p. 381) will not be "persuaded" that the parenthesis is Johannean; Meyer pleads in extenuation the "far more striking example" of a "typical etymologizing," Gal. iv. 25.

He went away therefore.—As there is no mention of any leader it seems certainly to be indicated that a faint dawning of sight had already begun.* Of course we are not to imagine that the anointing of the eyes glued them together; the release of the visive faculty may also have been preceded by a clairvoyant disposition. Compare the fine description of the restoration to sight of blind Œdipus in Sophocles. But as this trait is at all events not brought forward, it cannot be insisted upon as a certainty (comp. Tholuck with reference to Neander: "although we may also think that there was a guide").—**And returned.**—Not in particular to Jesus, but from the spring and to his family (ver. 8).

Ver. 8. **The neighbors therefore.**—Now follows an account of what further befell the blind man; so minute, distinct and true to life is this narration that we are at liberty to suppose the Evangelist had it from the very lips of him who was blind and healed (see Tholuck, Meyer).

Ver. 11. **A man that is called Jesus.**—He is therefore not acquainted with the Messianic character of Jesus; he, however, emphasizes the name of *Jesus.* He has immediately noticed the significant name, which was not the case with the impotent man of Bethesda (chap. v.). The form of his already budding faith in the prophetic dignity and divine mission of Jesus declares itself in vers. 17 and 33; he as yet does not know Him as the Messiah, ver. 35.

I received sight.—Ἀναβλέπειν means to look *up*, to see *again.* Meyer maintains against Lücke's explanation: *I looked up* (Mark xvi. 4, *etc.*), the: *I received sight again;* for this there is no ground in vers. 15 and 18, although the explanation of Grotius: *nec male recipere quis dicitur, quod communiter tributum humanæ naturæ ipsi abfuit*, is ingenious.

Ver. 13. **They bring to the Pharisees the whilom blind man.**—Doubtless the Pharisees in a peculiar sense are meant; hence in their magisterial capacity and as enemies of Jesus;

* [The typical reference of the waters of Siloam to the cleansing and healing water of baptism (Ambrose, Jerome, Calovius, and even Trench), is unsuitable.—P. S.]

* [This conjecture is unnecessary; blind beggars generally have a guide, and I have known three blind men (one a music teacher, another a preacher), who without aid could find any familiar locality within a considerable distance.—P. S.]

this is proved also by what follows. For to regard it as signifying the Pharisees in general "as a corporation" (Meyer) is historically inaccurate. Neither is there any ground for the assumption that they had led him before the Pharisees on account of the healing on the Sabbath, because they believed the transgression of the law should be reported. On the contrary, the clause: **him that once was blind,** indicates that they considered it their duty to bring the miracle to the cognizance of the theocratic court (see Tholuck). It is only after the introductory clause: it was the Sabbath, that the stumbling-block appears among the Pharisees. If these Pharisees did at all events form a judicial court (comp. the Pharisees chap. vii. 47; xi. 46), since, as subsequently appears, they call a judicial inquiry and execute an act of excommunication, the question arises, whether it was the great Sanhedrin itself (Tholuck), or a minor Sanhedrin (Lücke); of the latter there were two in Jerusalem; these small Sanhedrins, as synagogue-courts consisting of 23 assessors, settled minor lawsuits in the Jewish cities. The latter supposition is the more probable, in accordance with hierarchical discipline; yet doubtless the small Sanhedrins in Jerusalem were closely connected with the great Sanhedrin, especially in matters that concerned the Person of Jesus. Tholuck alleges in support of his position, that the great Sanhedrin alone wielded the power of excommunication from the congregation of Israel. But the grade of the ban incurred by the healed blind man is not mentioned, and in minor degrees the right of excommunicating was possessed by the small Sanhedrins as well. Lücke assumes that the leading before the Pharisees took place after the Sabbath, as, according to the Talmud, on the Sabbath and on feast-days no causes were tried; Tholuck thinks it probable that sessions were held on the Sabbath also; he supposes only "that no writing was done." At all events, such Sabbath sessions were extraordinary, and members of the Sanhedrin themselves took the initiative in them; therefore in this case we are safe in supposing that the presentation occurred after the Sabbath.

Ver. 14. **And it was Sabbath on the day when Jesus.**—"A rabbinical statute specially prohibits the spreading of saliva on the eyes on the Sabbath. Maimonides, *Schabb.* 21. If this ordinance was not yet extant or sanctioned, still the general law was in force which forbade all healing on the Sabbath except in cases where life was imperiled (Schöttgen and Wetstein *ad Matt.* xii. 9)." Meyer. Hence stress is laid upon the fact that Jesus made clay on that day.

Ver. 15. **Again therefore the Pharisees also asked him how he received his sight.**—It is characteristic of them that they pass over the miracle itself, *that* he has received sight, and inquire at once as to the *manner how*, because the latter is the point to which the accusation of heresy against Jesus must attach itself.

He put clay (a paste), *etc.*—Meyer justly draws attention to the circumstance that the man relates only what he has himself felt, and hence does not mention the saliva; so before ver. 11.

Ver. 16. **This man is not from God because he keepeth not the Sabbath.**—Characteristic hyperbaton, by which the name of God is brought forward first with hypocritical reverence, and then a contemptuous emphasis is laid upon: *this man. Because he keepeth not the Sabbath,* see note on ver. 14. **Others said, How can a man that is a sinner do such signs?** The disparaging inference was drawn only by a portion of the tribunal; by the majority, it is true. From the mention of a greater division in this forum it seems to result that it was an association other than the great Sanhedrin.* Be it observed, that these more conscientious judges express themselves timidly through fear of the others, but yet go so far as to declare that the miracle performed by Jesus proves that He is not a sinner.

Ver. 17. **What sayest thou** [σύ is emphatic] **of him, because,** etc.—John introduces this statement with the characteristic οὖν again. It was to be expected that they would resort to artifices. For the evangelist is again speaking of the dominant party in this court. So explain Apollinaris and others: it is the *hostile* party which is here spoken of; Chrysostom on the contrary, erroneously: it is the *friendly* party; Meyer and others: *all* are included. It is patent, however, that the conduct of the suit is in the hands of the predominant hostile party. But of course the examination takes place in the name of the whole body. As regarded the fact itself, they had no further hold on the clear-headed and firm man. Hence they inquire what conclusion he has reached with respect to the miracle-worker,—what opinion he has formed of Him—in order from this dogmatical point to unsettle him and betray him into some other statement. From the question of faith they design to unsettle him in the question of fact, as the hierarchy once did with the Jansenists in France.

He is a prophet.—The straight-forward, decided and intelligent character of the man appears still more distinctly here. May we call him "uncouth" also (Tholuck)? Instead of that he manifests good humor, acuteness and ready wit. [These attributes, especially a cheerful temper, I have frequently found in blind persons. Kindly nature often compensates for so great a calamity as the loss of an organ.—P. S.]

Ver. 18. **The Jews therefore did not believe.**—That the hostile party is here designated by the name of Jews, by no means proves that in this place it first re-appears in active operation (Meyer). It characterizes them, however, as Jews, or unbelievers, that they now, having heard the confession of the man, issuing from the fact, do not believe, *i. e. will not* believe the fact itself. This does not mean that they consider the whole account, for example, of the making of clay by the Lord, a lie; but they pretend that some fraud may exist. John again intimates by the expressive οὖν that their unbelief and mistrust originate in their fanaticism. In the first place, they evidently desired to reproach Jesus with a violation of the Sabbath. But in this they were thwarted by the great miracle which weighed heavily in the balance.

* [Yet even in the great Sanhedrin there were men like Nicodemus (viii. 50) Joseph of Arimathea (Luke xxiii. 50), and possibly Gamaliel (Acts v. 34 ff.), who might have asked this question concerning Jesus.—P. S.]

Therefore they now hope to accuse Him of a spiritual deception and, at the same time, of violating the Sabbath.—**Until they called the parents.** Meyer explains; Then they believed. Tholuck on the contrary: This does not result from the ἕως ὅτου. Of course it follows only, that they must now let pass the judicially protested statement of the man, whether they believed it or not.

Ver. 19. **Is this your son?**—The *one* question progessively subdivides itself into three questions [put in strict legal formality: 1. Is this your son? 2. Was he born blind? 3. How did he recover his sight?—P. S.]. They, however, hasten on to the third query, because in it is concentrated the weight of their fanatical passion, or because by intimidating the parents, they hope to be able to weaken the testimony of the son.

Ver. 21. **But by what means he now seeth, we know not.**—The first and second questions are successively answered by the parents simply in the affirmative. The third question they evade. Yet they hint that they have heard of One who has opened his eyes. On this point the son must speak for himself. The whole reply is characteristic of parents who are honest and sensible, but at the same time timidly and selfishly cautious. Something of their son's intellectual humor is perceptible in their answer, which however especially testifies to their pride that their son has wit enough to give them correct information with regard to the last question. The thrice repeated *αὐτός* [*αὐτοῦ ἡμεῖς—αὐτόν—αὐτός*] is in the highest degree significant. On the one hand, it tells of their confidence in their son, but on the other hand also of their fear. That they thereby jeopardize him, or leave him in the lurch, is truly a selfish trait. They lack strength to prove their gratitude for the healing of their son by uniting their testimony to his, although they clearly indicate by the tartness and touchiness of their reply that they are thoroughly observant of the bad intentions of the inquisitors.

Ver. 22. **For the Jews had already agreed,** *etc.*—A public and formal decree or act (Tholuck) can not as yet be intended, else they must now have brought the cause of Jesus to an immediate termination; a mere agreement of private individuals (Meyer) would, however, be saying too little. Doubtless the subject in question is a regulation, made by the Jews in Jerusalem, concerning excommunication from the synagogue. Such a regulation directly became known to the people and served to intimidate the spirits of the undecided. The *ἵνα* gives the interest of excommunication as a motive for the regulation. This determination probably coincided with the resolution to have the Lord taken, chap. vii.

He should be put out of the synagogue [be excommunicated.]—Tholuck: "The word *ἀποσυνάγωγος* has led to researches into the nature of the Jewish law; of these the latest (for example, Rüetschi in Herzog's *Encykl.*) still refer to the old authorities, to Drusius, Lightfoot; the subject has been more thoroughly investigated in Gildemeister's *Blendwerk des Rationalismus*, 1841.* According to this the Mischna does not recognize several grades of excommunication;* it knows of but *one*, the נִדּוּי, in pursuance of which the excommunicated person was not permitted to shave or wash or to enter other than an outer hall of the temple. The duration of this was dependent upon the contrition of the person. Excommunication was inflicted by the President of the great Sanhedrin. Opinions differ with regard to the biblical expression *ἀποσυνάγωγος γίνεσθαι*, as to whether it means simply exclusion from divine worship in the synagogue of a single congregation (Vitringa, *De Synagog. vet.*, p. 741; Witsius, *Miscellanea*, ii. p. 49), or exclusion from the קָהָל, the united congregation (Selden, *De Synedr.* i. 7). But the former appeared merely as a substitute, when the temple was no longer in existence. Moreover the recognition of Jesus as the Messiah was such an offence that nothing can be intended save exclusion from the great congregation."

The matter, however, is scarcely decided so simply. Evangelical history demonstrates that this man suffered a species of excommunication which did not prevent him from going about with impunity, while Jesus came under a ban with which a trial resulting in death was connected. The idea of the *ἀνάθεμα* (Rom. ix. 3) or *ἀνάθεμα, μαρὰν ἀθά* (1 Cor. xvi. 22) is manifestly derived from circumstances connected with the synagogue and denotes an excommunication symbolically expressive of reprobation, the Cherem of the Old Testament. On the other hand, we know that unclean persons and lepers (these from levitical reasons, as also from ethical reasons "publicans and sinners") were excluded from the full right of communion in a way which could scarcely have amounted to Cherem. Thus from two to three degrees of excommunication are faintly traced in the Holy Scriptures themselves, and three grades of excommunication are certainly intimated by the words of Christ also: in danger of (the synagogue's) judgment, in danger of the council (Sanhedrin), in danger of hell fire (Matt. v. 22). The first degree, as it appears in rabbinical tradition (*Niddu*), may be designated a congregational course of discipline. The second degree is ecclesiastical or rather theocratico-political (*Cherem*); the third hierarchico-criminal (*Schamatha*). The fact that the Mischna treats of excommunication in its more limited sense only, might be thus explained: the Jews had in its time lost all right of conducting religious criminal proceedings or executing the *Cherem*, whilst on the other hand, in the absence of a religious centre, the disciplinary congregational proceeding might coincide with the ecclesiastical in the limited sense of the latter term. The subsequent distinct, rabbinical development of several grades of excommunication (see Winer, *s. v.* Bann) must at all events be grounded on ancient tradition. In this connection be it observed that a purely disciplinary course of pro-

* [The last work was occasioned by a controversy between the celebrated Dr. F. W. Krummacher and the rationalistic preacher Paniel, in consequence of a sermon of the former preached in Bremen, on the Anathema of Paul, Gal. i. 8.—P. S.]

* [Three according to the older view; 1. to be shut out from the synagogue for thirty days; 2, the repetition of this exclusion accompanied by an anathema or curse; 3, final exclusion.—P. S.]

ceeding is no longer spoken of, while the *Cherem* in Elias Levita is in its turn intensified by the idea of *Schamatha*. Analogous to the latter is the solemn form of the great excommunication accompanied by curses in the Church of the middle ages.*

Ver. 24. **Then they called the second time the man,** *etc.*—The rigor of the judicial procedure appears from the fact that they caused the man who had been healed to go away or step out during the examination of his parents. As they do not attain their purpose with them, they summon him again.—**Give glory to God.** As regards the *expression*, this is a solemn charge to tell the truth, which he might possibly have concealed hitherto (Jos. vii. 19); as regards the *intention*, it is an insinuation that he should make a statement such as they desired; hence in reality it is blasphemous hypocrisy, meaning as much as this: give the hierarchy the glory, and lie or play the hypocrite. So they seek to influence his evidence by the previous statement of their opinion.

Ver. 25. **Whether he is a sinner I know not. One thing I know.**—The dogma of the hierarchical dignitaries he is content respectfully to leave undecided. But he will not be dissuaded from his actual experience. He knows full well too, what light his experience throws upon the dogma whereby they support their accusation of heresy.

Ver. 26. **To him again: What did he to thee?**—They at first endeavored to make the healed man the accuser of Jesus on the score of a violation of the Sabbath, then on the ground of spiritual deception. They now despair, in view of the firmness of the man, of making away with the miracle itself, that Jesus had wrought. They return therefore to the *how*, to the accusation of breaking the Sabbath, in order to make that a means of working upon the man. Their evidently malicious examination, however, fills the man with scorn, and he mingles irony with the expression of his displeasure.

Ver. 27. **Are ye also desirous to become his disciples?**—Chrysostom: He thus presents himself (with the *καί*) as the disciple of Jesus. But he utters the words principally with reference to all the disciples of Jesus, of whom he has heard. Plainly perceiving their intention to stamp him also as the disciple of Jesus if his testimony does not accord with their wishes, he makes use of the ironical and withal defensive expression not without a presentiment of his own destiny.

Ver. 28. **They reviled him.**—At first gravely, craftily, calmly, now passionately, meanly they press upon him. To call him the disciple of Jesus delights them as if it were some vile aspersion; and the accusation seems to them true, because he has allowed himself to be healed by Him on the Sabbath, bears witness to this fact and believes Him to be a prophet,—or, because he will not turn liar to please them. The antithesis: *Jesus' disciple, Moses' disciples*, relates here to the pretended violation of the Sabbath, in the guilt of which he seems to have participated, and to their zeal for the sanctity of the Sabbath. Qualification of the antithesis by the antithesis: Moses, Jesus. Moses characterized as a prophet, Jesus as an antithesis to Moses, a suspected person, concerning whom they reserve their final opinion. Yet a sting lies in the expression: we know not whence. From some quarter He had extraordinary power; this his dealings with the blind man demonstrated; now if this power was not from above, the man on whom the cure had been performed would be distressed by the thought that he had been healed by demoniacal agency.

Vers. 30, 31. **With respect to him, this is marvellous, to wit,** *etc.*—We do not translate *ἐν τούτῳ: in this matter, herein*, but: *in respect to this one*, namely Jesus, previously the subject; and we render the *γάρ* not by: *truly*, but by: *namely*. They have ambiguously declared: we know not how it is with *that fellow;* he is a mystery to us. He rejoins ironically: *certainly that is wonderful as far as He is concerned.* And now comes the strange thing: they, fathers in Israel, know not whence He is, and yet He is a man of God and a prophet, who has opened his eyes. The expression doubtless bears the twofold signification that now his spiritual eyes are beginning to be opened. And he then appeals to their common creed: **Now we know that God heareth not sinners,** (ver. 31). Job xxvii. 9; xxxv. 13; Ps. cix. 7; Prov. xv. 19. But a miracle is a hearing of prayer (ch. xi. 41; Mark vii. 34), consequently Jesus must be free from their reproach; He is of necessity no sinner, but in favor with God.—**But if any be a God-fearing man,** *etc.*—First, therefore, comes the testimony to the innocence and piety of Jesus, and then the enthusiastic testimony to His unique prophetic glory bursts forth.

Vers. 32, 33. **Since the world began it was never heard,** *etc.*—Hereby, in accordance with his subjective sense of the greatness of the miracle experienced by himself, he not indistinctly elevates Jesus above all the prophets, and even above Abraham and Moses, whom they had exalted as judges over Him. Finally, reverting to what had gone before, he says appeasingly: **If this man were not from God** (as a prophet), **he could do nothing.**—He would likewise be unable to disquiet you.

Ver. 34. **Thou wast born wholly in sins.**—These Pharisees assume from the beginning that his being born blind is a punishment for sin; now however they cast upon him the additional reproach of being *ὅλος* (not simply *ὅλως*) born in sins,—intimating, namely, that as a heretic he was not only physically blind and maimed, but that his soul shared the defects of his body. With haughty emphasis: *thou*, born *thus, thou* wilt *teach* us?

Cast him out.—The external turning of the man out (of the hall of judgment) was doubtless here symbolical, a corroboration of the excommunication, the casting out נִדַּח, נָדָח = *ἐκβάλλειν ἔξω*, ch. vi. 37; xii. 31, which preceded. The excommunication is indeed with malicious wit prefaced by the words: thou wast *on every side* born in sins (comp. also ver. 35), and is denied by Meyer without valid reason.

Ver. 35. **Dost thou believe on the Son of God** [**Son of Man?**—See TEXT. NOTES.—

* [Comp. the Excursus on *Anathema* in my ed. of *Romans* pp. 302 ff.—P. S.]

P. S.] After Jesus has heard that by his steadfast testimony he has earned the disgrace of excommunication, He can reveal to him by His question the faith that he ignorantly possesses. According to Meyer, Jesus makes the assumption that he has confessed the Messiah before the tribunal; and Meyer also states that this conclusion is "virtually" correct. Jesus only assumes that the man has believingly recognized the living God in *His* miraculous deed, and has maintained this belief in temptation without being aware of what faith nominally comprehends. It is precisely the question of Jesus that gives him this fulfilment and sealing. Meyer asserts that not the metaphysical but solely the theocratical signification of *the Son of God* is to be understood in this place. The theocratical signification was, however, not exclusive; its background was formed by the "metaphysical" acceptation of the title.

Ver. 36. **And who is it, Lord, that I may believe in him?** *etc.*, ((ἵνα).—He is ready to take Jesus' word for it. That is: he credits Jesus in an unlimited sense, and in this trust of his lies the presentiment that Jesus Himself is the Son of God;—the germ of his faith in Him.

Ver. 37. **Thou hast both seen him,** *etc.*—The animated question is followed by an animated answer from Jesus, hence beginning with καί (see ch. xiv. 22; Mark x. 26). Thou hast seen Him. Tholuck construes the word ὁρᾶν in a general sense, with reference to experience, namely, even to their first meeting; Meyer as having reference to the present seeing: *thou hast a view of Him.* But with this the rendering of the *καί—καί, as well*—as *also*—does not correspond. The seeing really seems to contain also an allusion to his spiritual *receiving of sight,* (Lücke). Indeed thou hast already seen Him, and—He it is that speaketh with thee. Manifestly, a turn is given to the expression. The true antithesis would be: thou hast perceived Him, and He hath given thee sight, or: thou hast seen Him and dost see Him now.

Ver. 38. **I believe, Lord.**—*Lord* in a loftier sense here than in ver. 36 (Bengel). The προσκυνεῖν denotes adoring worship.

Ver. 39. **For judgment I came,** *etc.*—The kneeling man has sealed his excommunication by his act of adoring homage and, knowing as yet little of fellow-disciples, finds himself in a unique and isolated position, confronting, with Jesus only, the mighty hierarchy. Jesus appreciates the state of the case. He reveals to him that he is entering into a congregation of the seeing, that the hierarchs who condemn him stand over against him as blind men, and that *He* Himself, Jesus, is the destined cause of this separation. The oxymoron at the same time utters the decree that he has become possessed of spiritual sight, that he is illuminated inwardly as well as physically. The motive is the contrast between the Pharisees, learned in the Scriptures, hardening themselves in spiritual blindness in presence of His light, and the ignorant blind beggar who receives sight through His light; this contrast is presented in the light of divine appointment (see Matt. xi. 25). *The judgment* is not a judgment of damnation (Euthym., Olshausen), for it refers also to the blind who obtain sight. It is the judgment of active sentencing and retributive separation between those who are in need of light and those who shun it; of course for the latter this severance is the beginning of the judgment of damnation, while to the former it is the commencement of bliss. The contrast between *those that see not,* who receive sight, and the converse, is ingeniously apprehended by Bucer and Neander in an intellectual and a physical sense, *i. e.,* typically, not simply allegorically. The spiritually blind do not see well physically until with spiritual sight they receive also true bodily sight. Those possessed of spiritual sight, being primarily discerners of Old Testament truth, but who subsequently delude themselves in their self-conceit, become through their obduracy intellectually and physically blind in presence of the Messiah. Christ particularly addresses this saying to the blind man; but it is also loudly and solemnly uttered for the disciples and all that are about Him.

Ver. 40. **Some of the Pharisees who were with him.**—Faithless former disciples (Chrysostom), more favorably disposed ones (Calvin), spies from Jerusalem (Tholuck, Meyer). According to Matt. xii. 30 and other passages, the εἶναι μετ' αὐτοῦ seems to denote a relation of discipleship. Probably a remnant of pharisaically-minded followers is meant, who stand to Him in such wise as the people, Luke xviii. 9; comp. John x. 19, 20. Judas, as the last Pharisee, did not desert Him until after this.

Are we also blind?—They cannot mean this in the physical sense (as Chrysostom and others explain); neither can they understand it with reference to those who have become blind (Hunnius, Stier), but with reference to the intellectually blind who must receive sight. They deny, therefore, that they, as blind men, have received sight, or are yet to receive it, *i. e.,* they assail the principle laid down by the Lord, and establish a third class consisting of men originally possessing sight and ever becoming more clear-sighted. This attack upon His antithesis calls forth the piercing words of Jesus.

Ver. 41. **If ye were blind ye would not have sin.**—It is questionable whether blindness is to be taken in the same sense here as ver. 38, οἱ μὴ βλέποντες, *i. e.,* whether it denotes those who need light. Or: *if ye considered yourselves blind.* Thus interpret with reference to the: **ye say: we see,** Augustine, Calvin, Meyer, Stier. Tholuck is undecided. Augustine: "*Quia dicendo: 'videmus,' medicum non quæritis, in cecitate vestra remanetis.*" On the other hand Chrysostom, Zwingli, *etc.*, Lücke, Neander [Alford] discover in the expression the recognition of a certain superiority. Tholuck: It cannot be denied that the position of the scribes towards the fountain of the saving knowledge of the Redeemer is regarded as an advantage (Luke xi. 52; John iii. 10); and thus Matt. xi. 25 they are called συνετοί not merely inasmuch as they thus look upon themselves, but as men who really were so in comparison with the ὄχλος ἀγράμματος. So too in the practical field, where the δίκαιοι are confronted with the ἁμαρτωλοί, the δίκαιοι are in very truth relatively righteous and the ἁμαρτωλοί gross sinners, publicans, Matt. ix., comp. the elder brother, Luke xv.; certainly, however, the former are also such as *think themselves endowed with a sufficiency in possessing this δικαιοσύνη and σύνεσις.* The recollection of this parallel has induced many commentators to see in the words εἰ τυφλοὶ ἦτε the recognition of a certain pre-eminence. "If ye were indeed utterly incapable of perceiving what is divine," or better: "if a certain insight into the truth of salvation were not granted you;" De Wette: "if ye were ignorant, erring, —with the accessory idea of susceptibility,—the imputation of sin would be on a smaller scale." —We also assume that Christ here attributes to them a certain degree of sight. It is the gleam of a better, objective, Old Testament knowledge which they are consciously converting into a false, unbelieving knowledge, *i. e.* into the blindness of self-infatuation. Hence the advantage of Old Testament knowledge itself (as of legal righteousness itself) can not be meant. Certainly, however, self-conceit in the possession of this knowledge is meant; the vain-gloriousness that turns the Old Testament dawn into a dazzling brightness, legal righteousness into self-righteousness (=impenitence), and represses the consciousness within them that in the presence of the broad day they are still blind, *i. e.* in need of New Testament illumination.

Between Chrysostom and Augustine there is then no real antithesis. If a man is to acknowledge himself to be blind (Augustine), there must needs be a relative gleam of light (Chrysostom); if he prematurely deem that he possesses sight, he *abuses* this very glimmering of light with *evil consciousness,* making himself then totally blind. But forasmuch as the emphasis lies upon this *evil consciousness,* both interpretations are one-sided. If ye knew not that ye falsify yourselves, ye would through sincerity arrive at self-knowledge, and your sin (with the guilt the sin also) would be taken from you. But as, on the contrary, ye *pretend* against your better consciousness that *ye see* and that ye have always possessed sight, ye, with your need of light as with the light that has arisen upon you, fall into blindness and your sin remaineth (because the guilt remains). Thus in the *saying,* there is a dissembling, whereby they contradict their own deepest consciousness. Self-blinding results in self-hardening on the part of the intellect. Hence: if ye did not in reality know better how it is with you, *etc.;* but now ye haughtily dissemble, *etc.* This undoubtedly: your eyes are in some faint degree illuminated, but just sufficiently to render you entirely blind.

DOCTRINAL AND ETHICAL.

1. "That of which Dr. Paulus regretted the absence in the tales of the miracles, a *thorough investigation,* is in this instance present in the form of a judicial examination on the part of the most embittered antagonists." Tholuck.

2. The fact that in all cases *evil* is in a general sense connected with *sin,* had at an early period been individualized by natural Phariseeism; this is to be found among Gentiles as well as among Jews. Gentiles and Jews agreed in the disposition to see in the misfortune of an individual the punishment of his sin, in the wretch a man hateful to God (comp. Acts xxviii. 4), or at least to regard his affliction as a curse entailed upon him by the sin of his parents. It is indeed in many instances impossible to mistake the immediate connection between sin and punishment in the life of an individual; neither can we shut our eyes to the fact that parents are frequently to blame for the misery of their offspring. That Jesus did not unconditionally reject this reference, the following passages demonstrate: Matt. ix. 2; John v. 14; Luke xxiii. 28. Nevertheless He does here reject the *Pharisaical* rule that in all cases *extraordinary* sufferings may be immediately traced to *extraordinary* sins,—a rule already contradicted by the book of Job. Luke xiii. 1. He likewise repudiates the judicial condemnation of afflicted sinners by sinners as yet unvisited by God, whether the guilt of the former be more or less apparent. The thing, however, most abhorrent to Him is the perverted view men take of misfortune and suffering in themselves, as though they were as bad as sin, nay, as if they were in the strictest sense of the word, evil itself, conducing to the perdition of souls, Matt. v. 10, 11; Luke xv. 16, 17; Matt. xvi. 24; the present passage. Consistent Phariseeism saw in the lowliness of Jesus His unworthiness, in His defencelessness His guilt, and, after having crucified Him, in His cross His curse, whilst Jesus recognized therein His own glorification and the salvation of the world.

3. The declaration of Jesus: "Neither this man hath sinned, nor his parents," opens to us a glimpse of the profoundest depths of life. There might still be a genealogical cause for the malady,—a cause, however, far remote and contained in the guilt of generations long since dead. But at the same time He teaches us to meditate upon the clear teleology, the removal of evil to the glory of God, rather than ponder over the particular causality of individual evil.

4. *That the works of God might be made manifest in him* (ver. 3). A clear and Christological teleology of evil, as also of the permission of sin. The old world of evil, debased by sin, is destined to be destroyed* by the new wonder-world of Christ; similarly, the centre of evils, sin itself, is to be destroyed by the wonder of His life as the centre of His miracles.

5. The works of *Christ* the very works of *God* (ver. 4).

6. *Christ's day* is the day of the world, from which proceeds all the day-light of the world until the last day (vers. 4, 5). The *day's work of Christ* is the day's work of the world, the source of all New Testament days' works until the last day. The *night* of His death-time is the termination of His work; it contains for unbelievers the principle and germ of the Last Judgment and the night of eternity.

7. The *history of the man* who was born *blind* is the portrait or type of the great and sudden conversion of an upright man; the portrait of a simple, wise, cheerful, vigorous and valiant manner of belief; the portrait of a leading from belief in the living God of miracles to the Personal Christ; the portrait of a Jewish inquisition, as

* [The verb *aufheben* is here used (as often in the Hegelian philosophy) in the double or triple sense of *tollere, conservare, elevare; e. g.* childhood is *aufgehoben*—abolished, preserved and elevated—in manhood.—P. S.]

of the impotence of hierarchic excommunication.

8. Christ is the real Sun-light of the world (ver. 5), as His work is the real day's work in this Sun-light. Christ, in co-operation with the sacred temple-water of Siloam, appears as the real Shiloah and temple-fount itself. Christ has come into the intellectual world for judgment, to transform the seeing into blind men and to endow with sight those who are blind. The distinction in this fact between human guilt and divine dispensation in judgment is to be observed; similarly the distinction between the Christological purpose (the operation of Christ) and the final design (the glory of God).

9. The brook of *Siloam* was the true temple-spring at the foot of the temple-mount, outside of the sanctuary; hence at an early period it was a symbol of prophetic spiritual blessing, the fulfilment of which symbol has appeared in the Messiah. See Isa. viii. 6.

10. The discouraged *disciples* of Jesus, who had at this time in Jerusalem hoped for His glorification within the precincts of the temple—see John vii.—and were now obliged to accompany Him in His flight from the temple to escape the stoning, stood in need of special encouragement. This was afforded them in the healing of the blind man, whose confession might even put them to shame. Here too we see how in every situation Jesus above all things restores to His dejected people first courage, confidence, and therewith presence of mind and true composure.

11. It is remarkable that the Pharisees do not directly prosecute Jesus Himself on account of this Sabbath-day healing. Probably because He called the temple-spring of Siloam into co-operation.

HOMILETICAL AND PRACTICAL.

The history of the man who was born blind: 1. The miracle or the power of the love of Christ; 2. the trial or the power of upright simplicity and gratitude; 3. the issue or the victory of faith over the strongest temptation; 4. the profound interpretation and lofty signification of the event.—The question of the disciples, 1. with regard to its purport, 2. with regard to the motives which prompted it.—The answer of Jesus to the question of the disciples—in the most general sense all sufferings are to this end: God will glorify Himself in the sufferers.—The obscure causes of human sufferings often evade our glance, but the divine purpose is ever clear. —Above all things we should keep in sight the divine purpose and our duty in view of it.—Christ the real Light of the world: 1. hence a creative Light, not only luminous but illumining (the Light of the blind); 2. hence likewise the Day of the world, Light and Life; 3. hence, too, the Accomplisher of the great day's work of the world.—The exhortations of God to the day's work of Christ: 1. The day's work (as type, archetype, copy); 2. the warnings (of day, of night).—Christ the Light of our day's work.—The irrecoverable day of our life.—The Lord, the Giver of light and life when Himself in peril of death.—The beggars at the temple-gates (comp. Acts iii.).—The night cometh, *etc.*—Christ, the Healer, in His employment of natural remedies: 1. He does not need them; 2. He uses them for the sake of the one who is to be healed; 3. He consecrates them as the foretokens of Christian therapeutics.—Christ the Light of heaven, and earth's Fountain of salvation.—He the real Siloam, or all good is of God's sending: 1. The typical embassador, the spring; 2. the real Embassador; 3. the embassadors sent in His likeness and after His example (His disciples).—How the Pharisees do not consider the *what* in the miracle of Jesus, but the *how*. A characteristic of the Pharisaic spirit.

Parallels and antitheses: The man who was born blind and the impotent man (John v.).—The blind man and the Pharisees.—The blind man and those who were favorably disposed in that tribunal.—The blind man and his parents.—The blind man and his neighbors.—Good intentions and their evil consequences.—Character of the laity and spirit of Protestantism in our history.—The power of moral indignation.—The blind beggar transformed into a clear-sighted preacher before the Jewish tribunal.—The prudence as well as heroic courage in the confession of the man who was born blind.—The power of facts.—The victory of personal, spiritual experience over traditional ordinances.—One thing I know.

Characteristics of the hierarchical spirit of persecution: 1. Malevolent examination; 2. hypocritical exhortation; 3. anathematization. How impotent when opposed to the bravery of a faithful soul!

The development of the blind man's faith instructs us as to the nature of true faith: 1. The heart before the head; 2. trust before knowledge; 3. the thing before the name; 4. acting and confessing before worshipping.—Darkness a result of misused light.—Obduracy a result of perverted awakening.—Falsehood turns light into blindness, as sincerity changes blindness into the beginning of sight.—The conversion of the faint gleam of light into a blinding glare the cause of fatal darkness.—When the morning comes, the birds of day that could not see during the night, obtain sight; on the other hand, the night birds, which can see in the absence of daylight, become blind.—These have light enough to see and hate the darkness, to long for and love the light and to be enabled to see in it; the others have light enough to see the light, to hate it and to be blinded by it.

STARKE: ZEISIUS: As Christ omitted not to do good, even in the heat of persecution; so too should we after His example, *etc.*—The benignity of Christ always anticipates men and affords them more effectual help than they in their penury can desire.—Happy is he who, seeing a wretch, takes pity on him.—A blind man a poor man.—ZEISIUS: Brother, be not over hasty in pronouncing judgment on the misfortune of thy neighbor!—How fortunate it is for many a one that he is lame, *etc.;* he is thus saved from hell. —God knows how to make use of our infirmities for the glory of His name.—With Christ we must be attentive to the signal and purpose of God in His service, that we may neglect nothing.—HEDINGER: Time and opportunity to do good. Grasp them and lay up none for the morrow. —ZEISIUS: To every man God has appointed the limit of his activity and labor; this goal is soon attained.—BIBL. WIRT.: Now or never!—*The same:* The works of God often seem strange to our eyes, nay, utterly foolish and preposterous;—but how gloriously is His purpose accomplished!—CANSTEIN: The more speedily a man grasps and executes the word of Christ, the more quickly and powerfully he experiences His help.—*The same:* The manifold speeches and opinions of men concerning the actions of God serve to make these the better and the more widely known.—OSIANDER: The ordinance of God, to care for the poor.—CANSTEIN: When a man is enlightened by the Holy Ghost, he becomes so changed that even his acquaintances and friends do not know him.—*The same:* It is a good thing to tell of the misery from which we have been delivered and of the loving-kindness that God has shown us.—*Ver.* 15. In this answer: Simplicity, truth, frank avowal.—ZEISIUS: True miracles, the more they are investigated, the more they are recognized and shine forth, whilst, on the contrary, in false miracles the more apparent does the deceit become.—*Ver.* 22. HEDINGER: It is a sin and a shame to fear men more than God.—*Ver.* 26. O how sorely the wicked often strive to fell a child of God! but their attempts are fruitless.—If enemies of the truth are unable to gain their point, they grow bitter and wrathful and begin to curse and revile.—ZEISIUS: Despised simplicity baffles the superiors (rulers) in Israel.—He rightly confesses Christ, who, for His name's sake, gladly suffers himself to be cast out by the wicked.—ZEISIUS: They who for confession of the truth are rejected and accursed by the world, are graciously looked upon by Christ and blessed by Him with a larger measure of divine light, *etc.*—HEDINGER: How speedy is the operation of grace in a willing soul!—BIBL. WIRT.: Faith has its steps.—ZEISIUS: Faith in Christ, the Son of God, is no frigid approbation, but such a fervent affection and stirring of the soul, that the whole heart together with all the remaining powers of the man are forcibly impressed into the service of Him on whom he believes.—CRAMER: No punishment more fearful than privation of sight.—*The same:* The first step towards help is the acknowledgment of sin.—ZEISIUS: Hypocrites are always the wisest and most sharp-sighted in their own eyes, even though they are in very deed blinder than bats.

BRAUNE: Do not ponder over the origin of evil; work with helpful, divine love! How repulsive is the appearance of a blind eye, unavailable for sight; how glorious the clear lustre of the friendly eye in the upright man! Equally repulsive is the blinded man whose inner eye is destroyed by evil lusts, and equally glorious is the recognition of a clear enlightened spirit.—GOSSNER: When a man is delivered from his spiritual blindness, people say: Is not this he who formerly did thus and so? In this way they testify to his reformation. But for them it is a shame.—A man whose heart has been enlightened by Jesus and changed by His grace can not be recognized any more.—Thus it is to this day: Pharisees cling to the form and reject Him for whose sake the form is, and to whom the form is to lead. They hold to the letter which kills them and with the form and the letter strike dead the life of the spirit, although the letter should be a receptacle, a vessel of the spirit.—"They cast him out." But he is not at all offended at this; on the contrary, it was a happy thing for him, for they did but cast him out of their hypocrisy.—Blessed proscription, that separates us from connexion with blind and malicious men and brings us nearer to Christ.—He who proscribes believers, proscribes not them, but himself.

SCHLEIERMACHER: But what are the works of God in this connection? None other than the manifestation of love in all human misery. For love is the strength of God and whatsoever proceeds from it is the work of God.—Yes, God has given man eyes to know Him; the intellectual ability is there, but it is opened and awakened only by Him who has come to change darkness into light.—It is in order that the works of God should be made manifest that God has permitted the human race to sit in darkness.—The parents of the *blind man.* Here we see one of the sad instances of the consequences of handling anything that appertains to faith, to the innermost sanctuary of man's conviction, with outward violence, for the purpose either of disseminating or crushing it.

HEUBNER: See examples of remarkable blind men, Didymus,* Milton,† *etc.* [Add: Homer, Prescott, the American historian.—P. S.]—The want

* [Didymus, the last distinguished teacher of the Alexandrian School of theology, a follower of Origen. He wrote several commentaries and an able work on the Holy Ghost, and died at a great age in 395. St. Anthony, the father of monks, once told him: Do not mourn over the loss of those eyes with which even flies can see, but rejoice in the possession of those spiritual eyes with which angels in heaven see the mysteries of God.—P. S.]

† [Milton repeatedly alludes to his blindness, *e. g.*, in Sonnet XIX. commencing:

> "When I consider how my life is spent
> Ere half my days, in this dark world and wide,
> And that one talent which is death to hide,
> Lodged with me useless, though my soul more bent
> To serve therewith my Maker," *etc.*

In the third Canto of *Paradise Lost* he hails in the sublimest strains the holy light, and mourns its loss to him:

> . . . . . . "Thee I revisit safe,
> And feel thy sov'reign vital lamp; but thou
> Revisit'st not these eyes, that roll in vain
> To find thy piercing ray, and find no dawn."

I add the following most touching and eloquent allusions of the great poet to his terrible affliction:

> . . . . "Thus with the year
> Seasons return; but not to me returns
> Day, or the sweet approach of ev'n or morn,
> Or sight of vernal bloom, or summer's rose,
> Or flocks, or herds, or human face divine;
> But cloud instead, and ever-during dark
> Surrounds me, from the cheerful ways of men
> Cut off, and for the Book of knowledge fair
> Presented with a universal blank
> Of Nature's works to me expunged and razed,
> And Wisdom at one entrance quite shut out."

* * * * * * * * * *

> "O dark, dark, dark, amid the blaze of noon;
> Irrevocably dark! total eclipse,
> Without all hope of day!"

* * * * * * * * * *

> . . . . . "These eyes,
> Bereft of light, their seeing have forgot;
> Nor to their idle orbs doth sight appear
> Of sun, or moon, or star, throughout the year,
> Or man, or woman. Yet I argue not
> Against Heaven's hand and will, nor bate a jot
> Of heart or hope; but still bear up, and steer
> Right onward."

There is also a beautiful poem on Milton's blindness by Miss E. Lloyd, in which this passage occurs:

> "On my bended knee
> I recognize Thy purpose clearly shown;
> My vision Thou hast dimmed, that I may see
> Thyself, Thyself alone."—P. S.]

of the external sense is said to sharpen the inner one.—It is the duty of gratitude to bear witness to our Saviour even before His enemies.—The parents of the blind man a type of all who, in order to escape the enmity of the world, draw back from the fellowship of the children of God. —False zeal for the old (here Moses) blinds men. —Simple-minded laymen have a sounder eye, a more correct judgment than false proud scholars and theologians.—BESSER: Christ hastens with rapid and ever more rapid steps in the career of blessing in which He with His servants is at work.—Their cursing is before God nought but blessing.—It was the misfortune of Israel that he was wise in his own eyes (Is. v. 21) and thought himself clean and whole (Prov. xxx. 12).

VI.

CHRIST THE FULFILMENT OF ALL SYMBOLICAL PASTORAL LIFE; THE TRUTH OF THE THEOCRACY AND THE CHURCH. *a*) THE DOOR OF THE FOLD IN ANTITHESIS TO THE THIEVES; *b*) THE FAITHFUL SHEPHERD IN ANTITHESIS TO THE HIRELING AND THE WOLF; *c*) THE CHIEF SHEPHERD OF THE GREAT DOUBLE FLOCK. (REFERENCE OF THE DOOR OF THE FOLD TO THE EXCOMMUNICATION, CHAP. IX. 35. CHARACTERISTICS OF FALSE SHEPHERDS, THIEVES AND MURDERERS. CHARACTERISTICS OF THE GOOD SHEPHERD. CHRIST, THEREFORE, NOT ONLY THE HIGHER REALITY OF THE EARTHLY, BUT ALSO THE TRUTH AND FULFILMENT OF THE SPIRITUAL PASTORAL OFFICE IN ISRAEL AND THE CHURCH, IN CONTRAST TO THE FEARFUL PERVERSIONS OF THE SYMBOLICAL OFFICE.) THE SYMBOLICAL COMMUNION AND THE REAL COMMUNION, OR SYMBOLICAL EXCOMMUNICATION AND REAL EXCOMMUNICATION.—THE COMMOTION AND DISAGREEMENT AMONG THE JEWS AT THEIR UTMOST HEIGHT.

CHAP. X. 1–21.

(Vers. 1-11 pericope for Tuesday in Whitsun-week; vers. 12-16 pericope for Misericordias Domini.)

1 Verily, verily, I say unto you, He that entereth not by [through] the door into
the sheepfold, but climbeth up some other way, the same is a thief and a robber.
2 But he that entereth in by [through] the door is the [*omit* the] shepherd of the
3 sheep. To him the porter openeth; and the sheep hear [give heed to] his voice:
4 and he calleth[1] his own sheep by name, and leadeth them out. And when he put-
teth forth his own sheep [when he hath put forth all his own],[2] he goeth before
5 them, and the sheep follow him: for [because] they know his voice. And [But]
a stranger will they [they will] not follow,[3] but will flee from him; for [because]
they know not the voice of strangers.
6 This parable spake Jesus [Jesus spoke] unto them; but they understood not
what things they were which he spake [spoke] unto them.
7 Then said Jesus unto them again [Jesus therefore said],[4] Verily, verily, I say
8 unto you, I am the door of the sheep. All that ever [All those who] came before
me [or, instead of me, ἦλθον πρὸ ἐμοῦ][5] are thieves and robbers: but the sheep did
9 not hear them. I am the door; by [through] me if any man enter in, he shall
10 [will] be saved, and shall [will] go in and out, and [will] find pasture. The thief
cometh not, but for [*omit* for] to steal, and to kill, and to destroy: I am come
[I came] that they might [may] have life, and that they might have *it* more abun-
dantly [may have abundance].
11 I am the good shepherd: the good shepherd giveth [layeth down][6] his life for
12 the sheep. But he that is an hireling, and not the [a] shepherd, whose own the
sheep are not [nor the owner of the sheep], seeth the wolf coming, and leaveth the
sheep, and fleeth; and the wolf catcheth [teareth] them, and scattereth the sheep.[7]
13, 14 The hireling fleeth,[8] because he is an hireling, and careth not for the sheep. I
am the good shepherd, and know my *sheep*, and am known of mine [and they know
15 me[9] even as]. As [as] the Father knoweth me, even so know I [and I know, κἀγώ] the
16 Father: and I lay down my life for the sheep. And other sheep I have, which
are not of this fold: them also I must bring, and they shall [will] hear my voice;
and there shall be [will become] one fold [flock, ποίμνη, not αὐλή, comp. ver. 16], *and*
17 [*omit* and] one shepherd. Therefore [On this account, for this reason] doth my
[the] Father love me, because I lay down my life, that I might [may] take it again.

18 No man [No one] taketh it from me, but I lay it down of myself. I have power
to lay it down, and I have power to take it again. This commandment[10] have I
received of my Father.
19, 20 There was a division therefore again among the Jews for these sayings. And
many of them said, He hath a devil [demon], and is mad; why hear ye him?
21 Others said, These are not the words of him [of one] that hath a devil [demon].
Can a devil [demon] open the eyes of the blind?

TEXTUAL AND GRAMMATICAL.

[1] Ver. 3.—Φωνεῖ, in accordance with A. B. D. L. [X., Sin., Lachm., Tischend., Alf.], *etc.*, instead of καλεῖ [text. rec.]. The former verb better corresponds with the figure. The sheep, as sheep, are not influenced by an understanding of the call, but by its warm, accustomed tone.

[2] Ver. 4.—Τὰ ἴδια πάντα a more expressive reading than the received text, in accordance with B. D. L. X. [Sin.], *etc.*, Lachmann, Tischendorf. [Alford: The text. rec. reads καί at the beginning, and τὰ ἴδια πρόβατα, *his own sheep*, mechanically changing πάντα into πρόβατα.—P. S.]

[3] Ver. 5.—In accordance with vastly preponderant authorities, A. B. D., *etc.*, ἀκολουθήσουσιν instead of θήσωσιν. [The usual conjunct. was substituted for the indicat. and is sustained by Cod. Sin., which in this case agrees with the text. rec.—P. S.]

[4] Ver. 7.—[The text. rec. inserts αὐτοῖς with D, against preponderating testimony, πάλιν is better supported, but omitted by ℵ.* Tischend., ed. viii., reads simply εἶπεν οὖν ὁ Ἰησοῦς. Alf. retains πάλιν.—P. S.]

[5] Ver. 8.—Πάντες is wanting in D., *etc.*, on account of the difficulty of the passage, and πρὸ ἐμοῦ in E. F. and some others, because the passage could be turned against the Old Testament by the Gnostics. See De Wette on the passage. [Tischendorf, ed. 8, omits πρὸ ἐμοῦ in accordance with ℵ.* E. F. G., *etc.*; Alf., Westcott and Hort retain it, and explain its omission, with De Wette, Meyer and Lange, from the fear of the Gnostic and Manichæan misuse of the passage against the O. T. On the different translations of πρὸ ἐμοῦ—*before me*, *instead of me*, *without regard to me*, *etc.*—see the EXEG.—P. S.]

[6] Ver. 11.—[τίθησιν, *layeth down*, is preferred by Tischend., Alf., W. and H. to δίδωσιν, *giveth*.—P. S.]

[7] Ver. 12.—[The last τὰ πρόβατα is omitted by ℵ. B. D. L., Tischend., W. and H., bracketed by Lachm., Alf., defended by Meyer and Lange, who regards it as "indispensable for the expression of the idea that the wolf is indeed able to make individual sheep his prey, but not the flock as a whole which he can only scatter."—P. S.]

[8] Ver. 13.—The words: ὁ δὲ μισθωτὸς φεύγει, *the hireling fleeth*, might appear to be a superfluous repetition or might be omitted; on this account they are wanting in B. D. L. Sin. (Tischendorf). They however serve as an introduction to the characterization of the hireling.

[9] Ver. 14.—Instead of γινώσκομαι ὑπὸ τῶν ἐμῶν [text. rec.], B. D. L. [Cod. Sin.], *etc.*, read γινώσκουσίν με τὰ ἐμά. So Lachmann, Tischendorf. Meyer justly remarks (following De Wette): This active turn is in conformation to the following.

[10] Ver. 18.—[Lange renders ἐντολήν rather freely: *Lebensgesetz*, *law of life*; Noyes: *charge*.—P. S.]

EXEGETICAL AND CRITICAL.*

[The parabolic discourse of ch. x. is closely connected with the preceding miracle and suggested by the tyrannical and cruel conduct of the Pharisees—the blind guides and false shepherds—towards the blind man who had been restored to sight by Jesus—the Light of the world and the true Shepherd. It was no doubt spoken before the same audience, as may be inferred not only from the uninterrupted connection, but also from the express reference to the preceding miracle in ver. 21. We have here a divine pastoral taken from everyday life in Palestine and addressed mainly to ministers of the gospel. With the whole subject should be carefully compared the Old Testament descriptions of the false shepherds and the true Shepherd of Israel with prophetic reference to the Messiah, in Ezek. xxxiv.; Jer. xxiii. 1-6; Zech. xi. 4-17. To these may be added, as a remoter parallel, the incomparable Ps. xxiii. which represents the Lord as the good Shepherd of the individual believer, who feeds and guides and protects him throughout life, and even through the dark valley of death.†—John omits the parables which form such a prominent and characteristic part of Christ's teaching in the Synoptists (comp. especially Matt. xiii.), but he gives two parabolic discourses or parabolic allegories, extended similes (called παροιμία, x. 6), one on the *Good Shepherd* (ch. x.), and on the *True Vine* (ch. xv.), which are not found in the other Gospels. A *parable* (παραβολή, from παραβάλλω, a comparison, a similitude), in the strict technical sense derived from the synoptical parables, is a poetic narrative taken from real life for the illustration of a higher truth relating to the kingdom of heaven, which is reflected in, and symbolized by, the world of nature. As a *conscious* fiction, the parable differs from the *myth*, and the *legend*, which are *unconsciously* produced and believed as an actual fact (as children invent stories without doubting the reality); as a *truthful* picture of *real* life for the illustration of *spiritual* truth, it differs from the *fable*, which rests on admitted *impossibilities* (as animals thinking, speaking and acting like rational men), and serves the purpose of inculcating the lower maxims of *worldly* wisdom and prudence. John's parables are extended allegories rather than parables; they present no narrative or completed picture, but simply one figure, either a man (the shepherd in relation to his flock), or an object of nature (the vine in relation to its branches), as a symbolic illustration of the character and relation which Christ sustains to His true disciples.* Christ stands out here expressly as the object and meaning of the parable. In the parable before us we must distinguish two acts: in the one Christ appears as the *Door* of access to the church and to God,

* Comp. Chr. Fr. Fritzsche: *Commentatio de Jesu janua ovium, eodemque pastore.* In *Fritzschiorum Opuscula.* [Vorretzsch: *Dissert. de Joh.* x. Altenb., 1838].

† [Comp. also the description of eastern shepherd life in Dr. Thomson's *The Land and the Book* (New York, 1859), vol. I., p. 301 ff., which tends to confirm and illustrate many particulars in this parable].

* [Similar brief parabolic allegories we find also in the Synoptists, Matt. ix. 37, 38; xxiv. 43-45; Luke xv. 4, 5; xvii. 7-9. John never uses παραβολή, which occurs nearly fifty times in the Synoptists and twice in the Hebrews, but παροιμία four times, *viz.*, x. 6 (*parable* in the E. V.); xvi. 25, 29 [rendered *proverbs*]. Literally, παροιμία [from παρά and οἶμος, *way*, *course*] means a by-word, an out of the way discourse, hence a figurative, enigmatic, pregnant speech, a dark saying [in opposition to παῤῥησίᾳ λαλεῖν]; then also, and, like the Hebrew *maschal*, a sententious maxim, proverb or also parable in the usual sense.—P. S.]

vers. 1-10; in the other as the true *Shepherd* of the flock, vers. 11-18.* A similar blending of images we find in Heb. ix. and x., where Christ is set forth both as the priest and the sacrifice, as the offerer and the offering (ix. 12; x. 19). Bengel says: *Christus est ostium et pastor et omnia.*—P. S.]

Our section closes the period of undecided fluctuations and fermentations in the nation. It is not merely a continuation of the word of the preceding chapter (as Meyer, Tholuck, Besser suppose); in that *light* is the fundamental idea, in this the *shepherd* is the leading thought. The conversion of the man who was born blind to Christ and his excommunication by the Pharisees (it appears from this chapter also, that they acted as an official forum) induce the Lord to exhibit in His own person the truth and fulfilment of the earthly as of the spiritual pastoral office, and in believers on Him the truth and fulfilment of the theocratic communion. Hence, this discourse ripens the disagreement among the people to a point necessarily resulting in separation. The scene is undoubtedly unchanged, the auditors are the same, but there is no reason why we should on this account, in pursuance of the example of Meyer [to which Alford assents], begin the chapter with chap. ix. 35. Even vers. 40 and 41 belong to the close of the foregoing chapter.

This figurative speech is in form a *flowing parabolical discourse* (παροιμία, together with παραβολή to be comprehended in the Hebrew מָשָׁל; according to Quinctilian: *fabella brevior*, as the saying, chap. xv. 1), and not a completed similitude (a parable). There is no foundation for the assumption of Strauss, that what was originally a parable was transposed by the hand of the evangelist into this more fluent form, especially as flowing parabolic discourses are to be found in the Synoptists also. Tholuck after Wilke (*Rhetorik* [p. 109],): "It has the character of an *allegory*, which exhibits a *relation* and is technically significant in all its features, not that of a *parable*, the scope of which is the application of the fundamental thought." Allegories and parables form, however, no true antithesis. See Comm. on *Matthew*, chap. XIII.

Vers. 1-9. FIRST PARABOLIC DISCOURSE.—Christ the Door of the fold for the true shepherds of the communion in antithesis to thieves and slaughterers. Introduced by the solemn formula, **Verily, verily.**—Certain knowledge of the true church-discipline in antithesis to that exercised by the hierarchy.

Ver. 1. **He that entereth not through the door,** *etc.*—A figure borrowed from oriental pastoral life. The *sheep* needing protection and guidance, but, at the same time, submissive and gentle, pressing closely to its fellows in such wise as to form a flock, knowing and following its leader, symbolizes the pious, believing soul;† the *flock* is a symbol of the Church;* the *shepherd*, entering by the door, symbolizes the ministry in the Church (Ps. c. 3; xcv. 7; lxxvii. 20); the *fold* (גְּדֵרָה, αὐλή, *aula*), *i. e.*, an uncovered space, surrounded by a low wall and affording protection to the flock at night—is a symbol of the fenced-in and inclosed theocracy (φραγμός, Matt. xxi. 33); the *door* itself, as the necessary entrance to the fold, is the symbol of Christ. For the further features consult the sequel. The ENTERING in [εἰσερχόμενος] is brought forward as the leading thought in antithesis to the *climbing up* [ἀναβαίνων]. By itself it denotes authorized entrance with right purposes. Each, however, is characterized by the addition: THROUGH THE DOOR. There should be no doubt as to the meaning of this, after the explanation of Christ, ver. 7, in reference to the Pharisees who did not understand Him, ver. 6: I AM THE DOOR.

The interpretation of the door as signifying the Holy Scriptures (Chrysostom, [Theophyl., Euth.-Zigab.] Ammon), is connected with the false discrimination of the parabolic discourses, in accordance with which the similitude changes as early as ver. 8 or 9; Tholuck approves of this discrimination. Patristic expositors since Augustine have therefore rightly comprehended the expression as having reference to the institution of the ministry by Christ; they were wrong only in limiting it to the historic Christ and the New Testament ministry. Luthardt wishes us to understand by the door, simply, the way ordained by God, without further definition, in contradiction to ver. 7. Tholuck, assenting to the opinion of Luthardt: *the right, divinely ordained entrance*, by which devoted love to the sheep is meant. De Wette: Only in HIS truth, in HIS way can one arrive at the condition of a true shepherd of the faithful. Approximately correct. But why is Christ spoken of in the Old Testament, and why is He in an especial manner the subject of this Gospel throughout? Christ is the *principle* of the Theocracy, the *fundamental idea, fundamental impulse* and *goal* of the Old Testament church of God, and hence the principle of every theocratico-official vocation from the beginning. Thus, He is the Door of the fold. He who enters not by Abrahamic faith in the promise, or through the spirit of revelation and in accordance with that, upon a theocratic office, has not entered into the fold through the door. Even Meyer says: Christ Himself is the door,—with the wonted, chiliastic reference, however, to the "future members of the Messianic Kingdom."†

Climbeth up some other way [ἀναβαίνων ἀλλαχόθεν].—Climbeth over from some other side [than the one indicated by the door], in order to

*[Dr. Lange resolves it into three parables, by dividing the second act into two (ver. 16). Christ the Shepherd in relation to the sheep, and Christ the Arch-shepherd of Jews and Gentiles. Godet, less appropriately: First Parable: the shepherd (in general), 1-6; Second Par.: the door, 7-10; Third Par.: the Good Shepherd, 11-18.—P. S.]

†[Augustine, Lampe, and Meyer correctly confine the sheep to the elect, or the true believer. Alford: "The *sheep* throughout this parable are not the mingled multitude of good and bad; but the *real* sheep, the faithful, who *are*, what all in the fold *should be*. The false sheep (the *goats* rather, Matt. xxv. 32) do not appear; for it is not the character of the *flock*, but that of the *shepherd*, and the relation between him and the sheep, which is here prominent."—P. S.]

*[That is the community of believers in the church; while the church as an organized institution (the theocracy in the Old, the visible church in the New economy), is represented by the *fold*, the αὐλὴ τῶν προβάτων. See below.—P. S.]

†[Meyer quotes in illustration Ignatius *Ad. Philad.* c 9, where Christ is called θύρα τοῦ πατρός, and Pastor Hermæ *Sim.* ix. 12, to which may be added iii. 9: "As no one can enter into a city but by its gate, so no one can enter into the kingdom of God but by the name of the Son of God." The reference of the door to Christ is settled by the text itself (ver. 7) and should not be disputed, as Melanchthon says: "*Ipse textus addit imagini interpretationem qua contenti simus.*"—P.S.]

get in over the wall or over the hedge. The "OTHER WHENCE [ἀλλαχόθεν, like the old classical ἄλλοθεν]," chiefly indicates the other place; it denotes likewise, however, the comer from some other direction, the stranger, who does not belong to the fold. Significant of the untheocratic mind, *i. e.*, disbelief of the promise, and of untheocratic motives (according to Matt. iv. cupidity and sensuality, ambition, lust of power). The climbing over may denote a human, vain striving in scriptural learning, legalistic zeal, *etc.*, in antithesis to the way of the Spirit.

The same is a thief and a robber.* The false way is in itself indicative of treacherous designs. The λῃστής, *robber*, is not simply a climactic augmentation (Meyer); neither is it a downright murderer. But the robber readily becomes a murderer if he meet with resistance, and the sheep-robber in the like case becomes a slaughterer (in this respect also the translation: MURDERER is incorrect, since it is a question of sheep). In the explanation, ver. 10, the thief is the leading idea; it is divided, however, into the stealing thief and the rapacious slaughterer and destroyer. Thus, false officials become thieves to those souls that submit themselves to them and confide in them, and worriers of those that maintain their independent faith, as chap. ix. of the blind man whom they excommunicated. The antithesis presented by these thieves and true shepherds is of course (after Tholuck) the antithesis of selfishness (Ezek. xxxiv. 8) and love (Jer. xxiii. 4).

Ver. 2. **Is a shepherd of the sheep.**—[ποιμήν without the article, in the generic sense, while in vers. 11, 12, 14 where it refers specifically to Christ, the article is used three times. The E. V. misses this difference by translating in all cases "*the* shepherd," while Luther is equally inaccurate in using uniformly the indefinite article: "*ein* (guter) Hirte." In the first part of the parable, vers. 1-10, Christ appears as the *Door;* in the second as the *Shepherd.* He is indeed both, but the figures must not be mixed in the same picture.—P. S.] Only he who has become a shepherd through faith in the promise or through Christ, has a loving shepherd's heart. The form of his entrance upon the office must have been pure, in accordance with his pure motive, and he will prove himself a shepherd. This TRUE shepherd does but form a contrast to the robber; he is not yet, as the GOOD Shepherd, placed in antithesis to the hireling, or as the head Shepherd (ver. 16) to the under shepherds.

Ver. 3. **To him the porter [ὁ θυρωρός] openeth.**—The porter watches in the night-time within the fold, and in the morning thrusts aside the bolt for the shepherd when he announces himself. Meyer (after Lücke, De Wette and others): "Ὁ θυρωρός is requisite to complete the picture of the lawful entering in, and is not designed for special exegesis; hence it is not taken into consideration again ver. 7. It is, therefore, not to be interpreted either as referring to GOD (Maldonat, Bengel [Tholuck, Ewald, Hengstenberg, with reference to vi. 44 f.]), or to the HOLY SPIRIT, Acts xiii. 2 (Theodor., Heracl., Rupert, Aret., Cornel. a Lap. and several others), or to CHRIST (Cyrill, Augustine), or to MOSES (Chrysost., Theod. Mopsuest. and several others)." Tholuck interprets it as signifying THE FATHER, in accordance with chap. vi. 44, 45. But as the porter is within, in the fold, we must undoubtedly, with Stier, apprehend the Holy Spirit in this feature of the parable, although qualified as the Spirit of the church; this view is contested by Luthardt without sufficient grounds.*

And the sheep [τὰ πρόβατα] give heed to his voice, and he calleth his own sheep [τὰ ἴδια πρόβατα] by name.—The article τὰ πρόβατα is to be observed. According to most expositors, these are ALL the sheep of the fold, and are identical with the ἴδια πρόβατα. [Bengel, Luthardt, Hengstenberg, *etc.*—P. S.] This view is impugned by the fact that nothing is said of the πρόβατα in general, but that they hear his voice; the ἴδια, however, he calls *by name.*† According to Bengel, these ἴδια are distinguished from the great mass of the sheep by their special need. Meyer considers it necessary to make use of the circumstance that one fold often afforded shelter at night to several flocks, whose shepherds, coming every morning, were known to all the sheep. On the other hand, the ἴδια are the sheep belonging to the particular flock of the shepherd in question. It is, however, an unfree dependence [of Meyer] upon an archæological note to pretend to discover in this passage a portrayal of the driving together of a plurality of flocks, when the figure has reference to the unitous Old Testament Theocracy. The second misapplication of an archæological comment, according to which it was customary for the shepherds to give names to the sheep (Pricæus on our passage), consists in the idea that the shepherd must call out all the sheep of his flock by their names (indulge in a very minute roll-call). The statement that the sheep hear his voice forms part of the ideal background of the figure, for in the enclosure of the Old Testament Theocracy there are some that are not true sheep, and these do not give ear to the voice of the shepherd (comp. the Prophets and Galatians, chaps. iii. and iv.). But from the real sheep, *i. e.*, the susceptible in general, Christ further distinguishes the ἴδια πρόβατα, that the shepherd calls by name; the *favorite* sheep, the *elect* in a stricter sense (*Leben Jesu*, II., p. 995); in the symbol of pastoral life the bell-wethers which precede the flock and are followed by it.‡

---

* [Comp. ver. 8, where the same persons are meant by κλέπται καὶ λῃσταί, *viz.*, the anti-messianic (Jewish) and anti-christian hierarchy, especially the Pharisees and their successors in the Christian church. In the Synoptists Christ speaks of them with equal severity; comp. Matt. xxiii. 13; Mark xii. 38-40; Luke xii. 2.—P. S.]

* [Alford agrees with Lange and Stier in referring the θυρωρός especially to the Holy Spirit. In the parallel passages, however, which he quotes, Acts xiv. 27 (how *God* had opened the door of faith to the Gentiles); 1 Cor. xvi. 9 (no agent mentioned); 2 Cor. ii. 12; Col. iv. 3 (that *God* would open unto us a door), there is no specific reference to the Holy Spirit, except in Acts xiii. 2, which he omits. Godet understands the porter of John the Baptist (comp. i. 7), but this would confine the parable to the Old Testament theocracy, while it is equally applicable to the Christian church. Webster and Wilkinson: θυρωρός, as in Mark xiii. 34, signifies a minister, one who has charge of the house of God.—P.S.]

† [κατ᾽ ὄνομα, distributively, *each by its own name*, not simply ὀνομαστί, or ὀνόματι, or ἐπ᾽ ὀνόματος. It denotes Christ's individual interest in each soul. On the eastern custom to name sheep, individually, as we give names to horses and dogs, see the quotation in the next note.—P. S.]

‡ [In favor of this interpretation may be quoted the follow-

Meyer controverts this view in the text and ratifies it in the note (against Luthardt) in these words [p. 395]: "Only the ἴδια does the shepherd call by name." The idea of the figure is very clear: among the sheep there are some that are on terms of closest intimacy with the shepherd; these he calls by name, and because these follow him, he is followed by the whole flock. But τὰ πρόβατα, the others in the fold, do not here come under further consideration.

Ver. 4. **And when he hath put forth** [ἐκβάλῃ] **all his own** [τὰ ἴδια πάντα, according to the true reading, instead of τὰ ἴδια πρόβατα, *his own sheep*.—P. S.] These come at his call. He LAYS HOLD OF THEM and brings them out through the door. Comp. Acts x. An intimation of the exode of the faithful from the old theocracy. He brings forth all the elect (see the reading πάντα), leaves not one behind.

['Εκβάλλειν illustrates the energetic mode of ἐξαγαγεῖν, and is appropriate to the employment of a shepherd who "drives" and "turns out" the sheep to pasture. It implies that the sheep hesitate and linger behind, and must be almost forced out of the enclosure. Dr. Lange first discovered in this passage an allusion to the approaching violent secession of the Christian church from the Jewish theocracy, although Luther already intimated that Christian freedom from legal bondage and judgment was here hinted at. It is supported by the term ἐκβάλλειν, by the true reading, πάντα, but especially by the preceding historical situation, the excommunication of the blind man, ix. 34, the threatening decree of the excommunication of Jesus with all His disciples (ix. 22) and the deadly hostility of the Jewish leaders, which made an ultimate violent rupture inevitable. Meyer objects without reason, but Godet adopts and expands Lange's view, although he connects it more with ἐξάγει (ver. 3) than ἐκβάλῃ (ver. 4). "*Jésus*, he says (II. 280), *caractérize par ces mots une situation historique déterminée. Le moment est venu pour lui d'emmener son propre troupeau hors de la théocratie, dévouée à la ruine*," *etc.*—P. S.]

Ver. 5. **But a stranger.**—The communion represented in vers. 4 and 5, is delineated in respect of its *exclusive* nature. By the stranger only the false prophets can here be understood, until the time of the pseudo-Messiahs.*

[**They will not follow, but will flee from him.** The future οὐ μὴ ἀκολουθήσουσιν (the true reading instead of ἀκολουθήσωσιν), and φεύξονται is taken by Lampe as prophetic, pointing to the *cathedra Mosis plane deserenda*, by Meyer simply as indicating the consequence.—This whole picture of vers. 4 and 5 is drawn from real life, and is to this day illustrated every day on the hills and plains of Palestine and Syria. Thomson, *The Land and the Book*, I. p. 301: "I never ride over these hills, clothed with flocks, without meditating upon this delightful theme. Our Saviour says of the good shepherd, 'When he putteth forth his own sheep, he goeth before them, and the sheep follow him.' . . . This is true to the letter. They are so tame and so trained that they *follow* their keeper with the utmost docility. He leads them forth from the fold, or from their houses in the villages, just where he pleases. Any one that wanders is sure to get into trouble. The shepherd calls sharply from time to time to remind them of his presence. They know his voice, and follow on; but, if a stranger call, they stop short, lift up their heads in alarm, and if it is repeated, they turn and flee, because they know not the voice of the stranger. This is not the fanciful costume of a parable; it is a simple fact."—P. S.]

Vers. 6, 7. **This parable spoke Jesus unto them,** *etc.*—Παροιμία [not=παραβολή], any discourse deviating from (παρά) the common way (οἶμος). See above [and Meyer and Alford *in loc.*]. What has been said is totally incomprehensible to the Pharisees, in consequence of the idea entertained by them of their office; hence follows the direct explanation of Christ, see above. Tholuck remarks: The not understanding is not to be taken in a merely literal sense, any more than chap. viii. 27; it means rather a state of being sealed up against that truth, which would affirm that they are not the true leaders of the people. Nevertheless it is here a question of an inability to understand, resting upon that evil basis, not simply of the *unwillingness to understand*.—**The door to the sheep,** *i. e.*, here, the door of the shepherds; not yet primarily that of the sheep (Chrysostom, Lampe). [Ver. 7. **I am the door of the sheep.** An expansion of the parabolic allegory and the key to its understanding. 'Εγώ, emphatic. τῶν προβάτων, not *to* the sheep (Lange and Meyer who thinks that ver. 1 requires this interpretation), but *for* the sheep, *i.e.*, the door through which both the sheep and the shepherds (spoken of vers. 1-5 in distinction from *the* one true arch-shepherd, mentioned afterwards, ver. 11) must pass into the fold of the church of God (Chrysostom, Lampe, Hengstenberg, Godet, Alford, *etc.*).—P. S.]

Ver. 8. **All who came instead of me,** ἦλθον πρὸ ἐμοῦ.—The expression is obscured by the failing to abide strictly by the figure, *i. e.*, the DOOR. In the first place, then, the meaning is: all who πρὸ τῆς θύρας ἦλθον. With the first idea of passing by the door, this other is connected: the setting of themselves up for the door, *i. e.*, all who came claiming rule over the conscience, as spiritual lords, instead of the Lord who is the Spirit. The time of their coming is undoubtedly indicated to be already past by the ἦλθον, not, however, by the πρό, forasmuch as the positive πρό does not coincide with the temporal one. Hence we must not only re-

---

ing remarks from Dr. W. W. Thomson, *The Land and the Book* (N. Y., 1859), vol. I., p. 302: "Some sheep always keep near the shepherd, and are his special favorites. Each of them has a name, to which it answers joyfully, and the kind shepherd is ever distributing to such choice portions which he gathers for that purpose. These are the contented, happy ones. They are in no danger of getting lost or into mischief, nor do wild beasts or thieves come near them. The great body, however, are mere worldlings, intent upon their own pleasures or selfish interests. They run from bush to bush, searching for variety or delicacies, and only now and then lift their heads to see where the shepherd is, or rather, where the general flock is, lest they get so far away as to occasion remark in their little community, or rebuke from their keeper. Others again are restless and discontented, jumping into every body's field, climbing into bushes, and even into leaning trees, whence they often fall and break their limbs. These cost the good shepherd incessant trouble. Then there are others incurably reckless, who stray far away, and are often utterly lost."—P. S.]

* [So also Alford: ἀλλότριος is not the shepherd of another section of the flock, but an *alien:* the λῃστής of ver. 1.—P. S.]

ject the interpretation of this passage as an anti-judaistic utterance against Moses and the Prophets (Hilgenfeld*), but also the temporal construction of Meyer: the hierarchic, especially the Pharisaic opposition preceded Him.† John the Baptist also came before Him, as did all the Prophets. The explanations of Camerarius: *præter me* (*sine me, me neglecto*), of Calov: *before me* (*antequam mitterentur*, instead of *after me*), of Tittmann, Schleussner: ὑπέρ, *loco*, *in the place of*, are correct; they are, however, imperfect and liable to misapprehension, since all the prophets came in a certain sense *loco Christi*. The *instead* of our text at once expresses the substitution of some one for Christ, the denial of Christ, the claim to absolute Messianic authority. And at the same time emphasis is given to the ἦλθον. They came as though the Messiah were come; there was no room left for Him (Jerome, Augustine, *etc.*). As a matter of course, they were false Messiahs, though without bearing that name. It is not necessary that we should confine our thought to those who were false Messiahs in the stricter sense of the term (Chrysostom, Grotius and many others), since the majority of these did not make their appearance until after Christ. Every hierarch prior to Christ was PSEUDO-MESSIANIC in proportion as he was ANTI-CHRISTIAN, for pseudo-christianity involves anti-christianity, and the converse is also true. To covet rule over the conscience of men is pseudo-christian. Be it further observed that the thieves and robbers who climb over the wall, appear in this verse with the assumption of a higher power. They stand no longer in their naked selfishness; they lay claim to positive importance, and that not merely as shepherds, but as the Door itself. Thus, the hierarchs had just been attempting to exercise conscience-rule over the man who was born blind.

But the sheep did not heed them. Only those who were like-minded with them became their followers. But the true sheep remained constant to the good Shepherd.

Vers. 9, 10. **I am the door; if any one enter in through me.**—Conclusion of the antithesis.—**Enter in through me, he will be saved**; *i. e.*, he shall find deliverance in the theocratic communion. The fence of the fold saves from destruction; so also does entrance into the true fastness of the church THROUGH CHRIST.—**He will go in**, *i. e.*, in the truth of the Old Testament he shall subordinate himself to the Law.—**He will go out**; *i. e.*, he shall find in the fulfilment of the Old Testament, in Christ, the liberty of the New Testament faith.—**And will find pasture.** He who goes out through the door shall reach the true pasturage of faith, knowledge, peace. Already a new parabolical discourse announces itself: the true shepherd does indeed find the pasture for his sheep in the first place, but he also finds it for himself as a sheep (Augustine, Stier and others). Opposed to him stands the thief who arbitrarily makes a false door for himself, and finally himself counterfeits the door. He comes but, on the one hand, to steal, *i. e.*, to rule over souls, and, on the other hand, to slay, *i. e.*, to cast out spirits; in the one case, however, as in the other, to destroy.

The following words: **I came that they may have life, and that they may have abundance** (περισσόν), constitute the transition to the next parable. Two considerations here claim our attention. First, they are for the first time to receive true life; secondly, together with true life they are to receive abundance of true food (green meadows, fresh water-springs). [Comp. John i. 1: "Of His fulness have we all received grace for grace." The English Version (with the Vulg., Chrysostom, Grotius, *etc.*), renders περισσόν "more abundantly," but this would require περισσότερον.—P. S.]

Ver. 11. **I am the good shepherd.** Second parabolic discourse. Antithesis of the good Shepherd and the hireling, on the one hand; on the other hand, of the good Shepherd and the wolf, vers. 11-15. I, Ἐγώ, emphatically repeated. As THE Shepherd (with the article), He is the true, real Shepherd, in antithesis to symbolical shepherds in the field and symbolical shepherds in the legal office (Heb. xiii. 20: ὁ ποιμὴν ὁ μέγας); as THE GOOD Shepherd (ὁ καλός*). He is the ideal of the shepherd (Ps. xxiii.; Is. xl. 11; Ezek. xxxiv. 11) in antithesis to bad shepherds (Ezek. xxxvii.; Zech. xi.; Jer. xxiii.), who first appeared in the form of the thief, and now branch out into the figures of the HIRELING and the WOLF. That this is at the same time indicative of the *promised* Shepherd, Ezek. xxxiv. 23; xxxvii. 24, results from the foregoing passages, especially the: "I came," "they came in my position." "Comp. Tr. *Berachoth*, fol. lv. 1: Three things God Himself proclaims; famine, plenty and a פרנס טוב, *i. e.*, a good shepherd or head of the congregation; פרנסים טובים of Moses and David in Vitringa, *Syn. Vet.*, p. 636. As the leading consideration in the idea of the shepherd, sacrificing love for his sheep is brought forward in Heb. xiii. 20." Tholuck.

Layeth down his life for the sheep.—Τιθέναι τὴν ψυχήν, a Johannean expression (ch. xiii. 37; xv. 13; 1 John iii. 16). If we keep the figure in mind, this is here expressive neither of the sacrificial death, nor of the payment of a ransom for the slave, but of the heroic risking of life in combat with the wolf. The ὑπέρ, then, is here synonymous with ἀντί. The shepherd dies that the flock may be saved. [Alford: "These words are here not so much a prophecy, as a declaration, implying, however, that which ver. 15 asserts explicitly."—P. S.]

Ver. 12. **But he that is an hireling** [μισ-

* [And the anti-Jewish Gnostics and Manichæans, who used this passage as an argument against the Old Testament.—P. S.]

† [So also Bengel (who presses εἰσί as indicating living opponents) and Lücke. Dean Alford likewise takes πρό in the sense of *time*, but includes in those false predecessors all the followers of the devil (comp. viii. 44), who was the first thief that clomb into God's fold. His was the first attempt to lead human nature before Christ came. Wordsworth lays the stress on ἦλθον, *came* (*i. e.*, in their own name), as opposed to being *sent*; but such a distinction is artificial and is set aside by the fact that Christ says of Himself ἐγὼ ἦλθον, ver. 10. Still others limit πάντες to false Messiahs and false prophets before Christ.—P. S.]

* [Καλός, *fair*, *beautiful*, often in the moral sense, *good*, comp. the Attic καλὸς ἀγαθός in opposition to πονηρός, κακός. Here it is almost identical with ἀληθινός, *genuine*, as set over against the imperfect, the inadequate; the model shepherd. Comp. i. 9; vi. 32; xv. 1 (I am the true, genuine, ideal Vine).—P. S.]

ϑωτός].—He is characterized by two things: 1. he is not a real shepherd to the sheep, but a hired servant,—he has no affection for the sheep; 2. the sheep are not his own, are not united to him by appropriation and cannot confide in him. The inner vital bond is wanting on both sides. Characteristic of the Pharisaic leaders of the people. **Whose own the sheep are not**, does not denote the "owner," but the own shepherd. In this very thing consisted the guilt of the hierarchical hirelings, that they constituted themselves "owners" of the flock. And in this very way also they became *hirelings*, *i. e.* under-shepherds, to whom the dishonestly increased wages were the principal thing, while they of course as hirelings had also the predicate of the official situation. [Christ sees here, prophetically, the long list of those selfish teachers who make merchandise of the ministry for filthy lucre and hate the cross, from the apostolic age (Gal. vi. 12; Phil. iii. 18) down to the present.—P. S.]

He beholdeth the wolf coming.*—That he perceives him while yet at a distance, is expressive of his fear, not of his watchfulness; this fear is manifested by his withdrawal at first to a place of security (ἀφίησι τὰ προβ.), and then by his downright flight (φεύγει). The wolf comes from without, from the wilderness; he is, however, connected with the hireling by the fact of his being an alien to the flock and by his treachery towards it. He has been interpreted as symbolizing *the devil* (Euthymius and others, Olshausen), heretics (Augustine and others), "every anti-theocratic power" (Lücke); "every anti-Messianic power, whose ruling principle, however, as such, is contained in the devil" (Meyer). According to Matt. vii. 15 and Acts xx. 29, wolves may also make their appearance in an official or pseudo-prophetic form. In such case, however, according to the first passage, they have disguised themselves in sheep's clothing. The declared wolf is the enemy of the flock, displaying his enmity openly and boldly, while the apostasy of the hireling is still cloaked in cowardly friendship; hence the wolf is the antichristian adversary of the Church, as heretic or persecutor,—in any case the instrument of Satan (comp. the Wolf in Northern Mythology).

The wolf ravisheth them and scattereth.—Twofold pernicious effect. Individual sheep are ravished and torn to pieces, *i. e.* individual souls are destroyed, but the flock as a whole, the Church, is confused and scattered.

Ver. 13. **The hireling fleeth, because he is an hireling,** *etc.*—No repetition, but the explanation of the flight. As a hireling, he is solely and selfishly interested in pasturing himself; he has not the welfare of the sheep at heart. It is questionable in what degree this figure is illustrated by the conduct of the Jewish shepherds of that time. They did not seem to be wanting in bravery; at first they acted like ravening wolves towards Christ, the Good Shepherd, and in the Jewish war they conducted themselves in a similar manner towards the Romans. The point illustrated by the figure is this: *The hireling vanishes* at the appearance of danger. There are two classes of shepherds to be found when destruction overtakes a church; the one class is composed of *cowards* who are secretly faithless, the other of *bold* and open apostates. It is, however, the *cowardice* of the former that enables the *boldness* of the latter class to excite consternation in the church. Such hirelings composed a good part of the Sanhedrin, and were especially numerous among the Scribes in the time of Jesus (John xii. 42); they possessed a consciousness of the truth of Christ but no heart for it, and they delivered up the Good Shepherd to the wolf.

Ver. 14. **I am the good shepherd. I know my own,** *etc.*—Explicit interpretation of the parabolic discourse just unfolded, as ver. 7. The proof of this character: *I know them that are Mine*, and the fact of the indissoluble connection with the flock, with true believers, whom the Father has given Him, here expressed by the relation of *mutual acquaintance.* True, this knowing does not mean *loving;* but it is still an emphatic expression by which a loving knowledge is implied. It is the expression of the personal, divine cognition of kindred personalities. The grace of Christ is such a cognition of His own on His part; faith, on the other hand, is a corresponding cognition of Christ on their part.

Ver. 15. **Even as the Father knoweth me.**—[Belongs to the preceding verse. The E. V. wrongly treats this as an independent sentence.—P. S.] In the personal, spiritual communion of the Father with Christ, and of Christ with the Father, the mutual relationship between Christ and the faithful is rooted. The "as" denotes the similarity of manner as also of kind, inasmuch as the life imparted by Christ to His people is a divine one. A chief motive for the comparison, however, is that the cognition on the part of Christ is the cause of His recognition by believers in return, as the cognition of the Father is the foundation for the corresponding cognition of Christ (comp. chap. xiv. 20; xv. 10; xvii. 8, 21; 1 John v. 1; Matt. xxv. 40). Tholuck: "The γινώσκειν τὰ ἐμά corresponds with the καλεῖν κατ' ὄνομα, the γινώσκομαι with the οἴδασι τὴν φωνὴν αὐτοῦ."—**And I lay down my life.**—Expression and measure of the strength of His love towards His people. But the salvation of the heathen also is to be effected by His death (see chap. xi. 52; xii. 24; Eph. ii. 14; Heb. xiii. 20). Thus this thought leads to the following. Τίϑημι. "Near and certain future," Meyer.

Ver. 16. **And other sheep I have.** [Other *sheep*, not another *fold;* for they are scattered throughout the world (xi. 52), while there is but *one* kingdom of Christ into which they will all ultimately be gathered, and to which they already belong in the counsel and love of God and His Son. Salvation comes from the Jews, but passes over to the Gentiles.—P. S.] Christ the chief Shepherd as Shepherd of the double flock of believers from the Jews and the Gentiles, ver. 16. The Jews resident out of Palestine (Paulus) are not meant, for they too belonged to the unitous Jewish fold; it is the heathen to whom Christ

* [In the East the shepherds are well armed to defend their flock against fierce wolves, leopards, and panthers who prowl about the wild wadies and frequently attack the sheep in the very presence of the shepherd. And when the thief and the robber come, the faithful shepherd has often to risk his life for the flock. Dr. Thomson says (I. 302): "I have seen more than one case in which he had literally to lay it down in the contest."—P. S.]

refers; they are not to be thought of as existing in a fold (De Wette), although subject to the guidance of God in another way (chap. xi. 52; Acts xiv. 16). The heathen are His sheep in the manner stipulated, even as the Jews, *i. e.* those who hear His voice, who follow the drawing of the Father. Of these Christ says: *I have them* (ἔχω) with divine confidence. He *must* lead them (δεῖ); it is the decree of His Father's love and of His own love. That He shall bring them into the fold of Israel (Tholuck), is not implied by the ἀγαγεῖν, which "means neither *adducere*, *bring* (Vulgate, Luther, Beza, Lutthardt [Hengstenb. Godet]), nor συναγαγεῖν (Euthymius, Casaubon and others), but to lead as a shepherd." Meyer. Bengel: "*Non opus est illis solum mutare.*" Yet the form: ἀγαγεῖν certainly indicates that the imminent *manifest* leading of these sheep is a continuation of a *secret* leading, previously begun (*gratia præveniens*). Christ saw the restriction of His ministry to Israel (Matt. x. 5) abolished with His death (Matt. xxi. 43; chap. xxviii.) As the exalted Christ He was made manifest as the Shepherd of the nations.

And they shall hear my voice.—Christ's confidence in His mission to the Gentiles presupposes at the same time an assurance of their destination to salvation and of the divine guidance of grace exercised over them. They are already sheep, not merely proleptically speaking (Meyer), for the idea of the sheep which gives heed to the voice of the shepherd, and the idea of the regenerate child of God are not one and the same. The sheep is a symbol of the man who hears the voice of Christ; hence, he is shown to be a sheep by his *calling*, while regeneration occurs but in company with justification.

One shepherd, one flock [μία ποίμνη, εἷς ποιμήν].*—The asyndeton betokens the closer connection of the two members. On an analogous utterance of Zeno in Plutarch† (*Alex.*, chap. vi.), see Tholuck. The two flocks become one flock by means of the one Shepherd, in Him; not by entrance into the αὐλή of the Jews. On the contrary, the subject recently under consideration has been the leading of the Jewish flock out of the αὐλή to pasturage. Tholuck: "Since the Old Testament and the New Testament kingdom of God is but ONE kingdom, the latter being merely an outgrowth of the former, the Gentiles' reception into it is pictured as a leading unto Zion (Is. ii. 3; Zech. xiv. 17), by Paul as a grafting into the trunk of the good olive-tree and, similarly, in this passage as a reception into the αὐλή of Israel." See, against this view, the note to ver. 16. In connection with the unity of the Old and the New Testament kingdom of God, we must, however, not overlook the antithesis between the typical Old Testament theocracy and the real New Testament kingdom of heaven. See Dan. vii. 14. The latter does not issue from the former, but the former goes before the latter shadow-wise. Christ is the principle of the kingdom of heaven; He is, therefore, also the principle of the unity of the two flocks, Rom. xi. 25. Inner relation to Christ being the grand point here, this promise has been fulfilled from the beginning of Christianity (one church); but, hence, it must also receive at last its perfect fulfilment in appearance. [Christ is, as Bengel remarks on εἷς ποιμήν, always the one Shepherd by *right*, but He is to become so (γενήσεται) more and more in *fact*. So it may be said, the unity of Christ's flock exists *virtually* from the beginning and need not be created, but must be progressively *realized* and *manifested* in the world. The unity of the church, like its catholicity and holiness, are in a steady process of growth towards perfection. "It has not yet appeared what we shall be." The nearer Christians draw to Christ, the more they will be united to each other. It is a shallow exegesis to say that this word of Christ was completely fulfilled in the union of Jewish and Gentile believers in the apostolic church. It was indeed fulfilled then; comp. Eph. ii. 11-22, which is a good commentary on the passage; but it is also in ever-expanding fulfilment, and, like His sacerdotal prayer for the unity of all believers, it reaches as a precious promise far beyond the present to the gathering in of the fulness of the Gentiles and such a glorious unity and harmony of believers as the world has never seen yet. Meyer says correctly: "The fulfilment of the sentence began with the apostolic conversion of the Gentiles; but it progresses and will only be complete with Rom. xi. 25 f."—P. S.]

Ver. 17. **On this account doth the Father love me.**—The freedom of Christ's self-sacrifice, vers. 17 and 18. Various conceptions. 1. Διὰ τοῦτο—ὅτι significatively refers to the following: "By this doth the love of my Father appear, that I lay down My life only to take it again" (Bucer, Stier). This view may seem to be upheld by the fact that the love of the Father precedes the work of redemption, and is manifest in the exaltation of Christ. But the love which from eternity has flowed from Father to Son, the love modified by their Trinitarian relation, does not exclude a love to the God-Man, called forth by His historic accomplishment of the work of redemption, and by His moral conduct on earth. Comp. John viii. 29; Phil. ii. 9. Hence 2. Meyer: Διὰ τοῦτο—ὅτι is to be understood as in all passages in John (chap. v. 16, 18; viii. 47; xii. 18, 39; 1 John iii. 1): on this account, because namely,—so that διὰ τοῦτο refers to the words preceding, and ὅτι introduces an exposition of διὰ τοῦτο. Consequently: "therefore, on account of this my pastoral relation of which I have been speaking (down to ver. 16), doth My Father love Me, because namely, I (ἐγώ with the emphasis of self-appointment, see ver. 18) lay down My life," *etc.* Manifestly, the whole thought is contained in vers. 15 and 16 also, for the resurrection of Christ must of course precede the taking possession of the "other sheep" from the heathen-world.

Even the conclusion, **in order that I may take it again** (ἵνα πάλιν λάβω αὐτήν), is variously understood. 1. It denotes the *simple consequence* of the sacrifice of Christ expressed in the preceding clause (Theod. of Mopsuest., and

* [Alford: "The μία ποίμνη is remarkable—not μία αὐλή, *as characteristically, but erroneously rendered in the E. V.*: not *one fold*, but *one flock*; no one exclusive enclosure of an outward church,—but one flock, all knowing the one shepherd and known of Him." The E. V. followed the Vulgate (*ovile*), Cranmer's and the Geneva Bible.—P. S.]

† [Of a union of all men ὥσπερ ἀγέλης συννόμου νόμῳ κοινῷ συντρεφομένης. A stoic dream that can only be realized by Christianity.—P. S.]

many others); 2. it indicates the condition (*hac lege ut*, Calvin, De Wette); 3. the subjective purpose of Christ: because thus only could be fulfilled the ultimate design of the pastoral office ver. 16 (Stier, Meyer); 4. the divine appointment of the aim; namely, in order to take it again, in accordance with the purpose of God, 1 Cor. i. 14; vii. 29; Rom. viii. 17. This taking again, also, is comprehended in the divine *ἐντολὴ τοῦ πατρός*, ver. 18. Tholuck. Since the obedience of Christ is here represented as the object of the love of God, *ἵνα* must undoubtedly be understood as referring to the purpose of Christ; this purpose, however, is not merely subjective, but corresponds with the *ἐντολή* of the Father, which again, is an *ἐντολή of personal life;* this has, not without reason, been urged by Calvin and De Wette.

The sense then is this: therefore doth My Father love Me, because I, dying, render a sacrificial obedience whose principle and motive is *infinite trust* in the resurrection of My personal life in the fellowship of His absolute personality; because I do not die despairingly, with the idea of annihilation, but in the assurance that I shall thus obtain the full revelation of life; or because I fall into the ground like a grain of wheat, in order to bear much fruit. In this victorious reliance on the new life in death contained in His sacrifice, Christ is the delight of the Father, as, in a similar spirit, the Christian is well-pleasing to God in Christ (see Is. liii. 12; Luke ii. 14; Matt. iii. 17; chap. xvii. 5; John xii. 28; chap. xvii. 1). "If the Father love the Son for this reason, this love contains also His love to the world, in the sense of chap. iii. 16. Calvin: *amorem unigenito debitum ad nos velut ad finalem causam refert.*" Tholuck.

Ver. 18. **No one taketh it from me.**—As on many other occasions Christ has here, by the solemn asseveration of His voluntary self-sacrifice, precluded any misconstruction of His death, as if He had succumbed to the hostile power of the world involuntarily and contrary to His expectations.*—**I have power to lay it down, and I have power to take it again.** Different interpretations of *ἐξουσία*.

1. Ancient dogmatical opinion: the power of the Son of God, the power of the divine nature to render the human nature quiescent in death, and to rouse it again. Tholuck: "Like ch. xiv. 13 a *dictum probans* for the *non posse mori* of the Redeemer (Quenstädt, III. p. 420, also according to Beck, *Christl. Lehrwissenschaft*, II. p. 513 and 517). But it is not the intrinsic, physical necessity of death that is denied, but the compulsive force of circumstances, as *οὐδείς* shows. Nothing is meant but what is contained in Matt. xxvi. 53. Comp. John xiv. 30. Mortality, as also Luther rightly acknowledges, is to be imputed to Christ, inasmuch as He took upon Himself *sin-infected* [?] humanity; see my [Tholuck's] Commentary on Romans vi. 9."

2. Meyer: "The authorization, in the first place of His self-sacrifice and secondly of His reassumption of life, resting in the divine *ἐντολή*." Probably a not altogether correct resumption of the views of Lücke and De Wette.

3. Lücke: "If the Father have *given* to the Son to have life in Himself (ch. v. 26), He has also *given* Him power to take it again. If that power be essentially a moral one, so too is this. But holy, moral power is at the same time always a power over nature. Forasmuch as Christ freely died as the Holy One, He likewise had power over death, but as a power in which the power of the Father is always present as absolute cause."—There, however, the definite distinction: *in Himself*, ch. v. 26, is not adhered to.

4. Tholuck: "The human *πνεῦμα* of Christ did not die; His self-activity, gaining still greater freedom by His death, penetrates the bodily organ and admits it to the process of spiritualization; thus, according to ch. v., Christ proceeds in the case of believers. Again, in ch. ii. 19 it is the Son who effects His own resurrection."

5. A separation of the divine and the human nature is unseasonable here. It was in His divine-human nature that Christ had life, as the principle of immortality and revivification, in Himself, *i. e.*, in personal principial independence, though it was communicated by the Father. In this life-power, as the Man of spirit from heaven (1 Cor. xv. 45), He could pass immediately, by transformation, from the first earthly form of existence into the second heavenly one. But He also had power to let His pure and holy body assume the death-form of natural humanity (not by a quiescence of its immortality, but by suffering the natural conditions of death, by humbling Himself as a man even to die as men do). He might die, but He could not see corruption; for He had power to take His life again, *i. e.*, to cause the transformatory energy reposing in His spirit, now modified into a resurrective energy, to operate within His organism from which life had been expelled. This fact is a re-animation on the part of the Father, since the physical conditions of life, the omnipresent healing powers of God in nature, forthwith meet the spirit returning to life; it is a spontaneous resurrection, because, at the actual life-call of the Father, Christ from the other world performs the wonder of His self-quickening. [Comp. ch. ix. 19; xi. 25, *ἐγώ εἰμι ἡ ἀνάστασις*; 1 Pet. iii. 19, *ζωοποιηθεὶς πνεύματι.*]

This commandment, *i. e.*, this known, universal law of life. Christ never has but *one* law of life, for holy life is perfect simplicity. This *ἐντολή* is the voice of God in unison with His situation and His consciousness. It has a peculiar form for each moment, chap. xii. 49. Here, however, He has sketched it in respect of its ground-plan. It is the fundamental plan foretokened in the leading of all Old Testament saints through suffering to glory and reflected in the lives of all the faithful. This *ἐντολή* has reference not merely to dying (Chrysostom), nor is it to be understood simply as a promise of new life (many of the ancients); it embraces both considerations, their indissoluble connexion being precisely the main point.

Vers. 19-21. **There was a division there-**

* [Olshausen: "Ver. 18 shows that neither a compulsory decree of the Father, nor the power of the Evil One occasioned the death of the Son, but that it resulted only from the inward impulse of the love of Christ. . . This view sets aside many objections derived from the argument that God, as love, could not deliver the Son to death. The death of Christ is the pure effluence of boundless love, which thus displays its very essence in the sublimest form."—P. S.]

fore again.—The definite presentation of the characteristic features of Christ's redemptive work again occasions a division among the Jews, vers. 19-21; a division which is to be regarded as the final and most serious one, the foretoken of approaching separations. Be it observed that this division occurs among the "Jews" (not in the ὄχλος), *i. e.*, among the Pharisaic hearers with whom the Lord's last discussion was, chap. ix. 40. Πάλιν refers to chap. ix. 16.

The last words of Christ had indeed the effect of embittering and hardening the majority still more. They now advance the opinion: **He hath a demon,** *etc.;* still they dare not say it to His face. They propose, however, to treat Him as a madman and pay no more attention to Him. On the other hand, the friendly minority seem to be intimidated in this instance also. It is patent that they are themselves impressed by the *words* of Jesus ("*these words are not the words,*" *etc.*); but the only argument that they think will tell upon their adversaries is: **Can a demon open the eyes of the blind?** Meyer: The miracle seemed to them too great to have been performed by such agency, although it results from Matt. xii. 24, that in former times even beneficent miracles may have been ascribed to demons. That passage, however, does not present a view prevalent among the Jews; it merely demonstrates that the spirit of blasphemy ventured to put an evil construction upon all the miracles of Jesus.

DOCTRINAL AND ETHICAL.

1. Symbolism of the Theocracy, the Church and the Christian Pastorate. *Christ the Door of the Fold, i. e.*, the fundamental condition of a true pastoral life for all time.

A. First Parable: *His relation to the shepherds: He is the principle, the spirit and the goal of the pastoral office.* They are either real shepherds, or, with the appearance of shepherds, thieves and murderers. *a.* Characteristics of genuine shepherds: In respect of their relation to Christ, to the porter, to the sheep. (They know the sheep; the sheep know them. They lead them out of the fold to the pasture, from forms into life.) *b.* Characteristics of false shepherds: In relation to Christ, to the porter, to the sheep. *Pseudo-Christianity* in the broader sense of the term: (1) Before the appearance of Christ. (2) After the appearance of Christ.

B. Second Parable: *His relation to the sheep* (to which the shepherds also belong). *He the Good Shepherd, the Arch-Shepherd.* Property of the Good Shepherd. Antithesis: the hireling and the wolf. False shepherds in collusion with declared enemies. Pseudo-Christianity in its transition to Anti-Christianity.

C. Third Parable: *Christ the Head-Shepherd. The other* sheep and their union with the sheep of the fold. The end: One Shepherd and One Flock. The condition: the sacrificial death of Jesus. The freedom of His self-sacrifice. The three periods of the divine pastoral office on earth; *a. Christ the spirit and root of the pastoral office.* Applied pre-eminently to the Old Testament time. *b. Christ the Arch-Shepherd.* Appearance, life and work of Jesus. *c. Christ the Head-Shepherd.* The New Testament Church.

2. The dechristianized official life. How the thief gradually branches out into the hireling and the wolf. The thief and the robber. The render and scatterer. How he neither knows, nor will know, any door of the fold, either for ingress or egress. How he at last vanishes from the scene, and there is but One Shepherd, One Flock. When the right motive is absent, there are always false motives (egotistical worldly ones); where the true means of entrance are not, there are always false ones (simony in the fullest sense); where true pastoral labor is not, a destructive influence over the flock invariably takes its place.

3. Christ the Door of the Fold or Old Testament Theocracy: (1) For protection from without during the night-time, (2) for removal to the pasture in the New Testament morning.

4. Church-life at the core a personal relation: (1) The Shepherd and the favorite sheep and the sheep in general; (2) the sheep which understand His call,—which at least know Him by the tone of His voice.

5. Decisive mark of the true shepherd: Love to the sheep, faithfulness, devotion to them unto death. The death of the Arch-Shepherd, the preservation of the sheep.

6. The end: One Shepherd, One Flock.

7. The mystery of the resurrective power in the dying Christ.

8. The opinion of enemies touching the shepherd's call of the Lord. The disagreement between friends and enemies progressing towards separation.—See, moreover, in reference to particular details,—for example the doctrine of excommunication—the above Exegetical Notes.

HOMILETICAL AND PRACTICAL.

Trial of the excommunication or ban-decree of the Pharisees on the part of the Lord—Trial of the spiritual administration of office by the symbol of pastoral life.—Earthly pastoral affairs an image of spiritual pastoral affairs.—The three parables of Christ concerning the marks of genuine shepherds: 1. They are called through the pastoral spirit of Christ (by Him, in Him, to Him); 2, they are themselves sheep in Him, the Arch-shepherd; 3, they rejoice at the union of the divided flock, the scattered sheep.—Christ's conception of the pastoral office.

The first parable, or Christ the Door of the fold. 1. What the passing by imports: *a*, denial of the door; *b*, an arbitrary climbing in; *c*, denial of the sheep; *d*, stealing, strangling, destroying. 2. What the going in through the door imports; *a*. recognition of the door and the porter; *b*, a calling of the sheep; *c*, a leading of them out to the pasture; *d*, the proving one's self to be a shepherd in the pasture also.—The voice of the shepherd and the voice of the stranger—What Christ understands by the *voice* of the *pastor*.—The door to the church and the door to the hearts (to the fold and to the sheep) *one*.—The cordial understanding between shepherd and flock.

The second parable, or Christ the Good Shepherd. 1. His pastoral aim, ver. 10; 2. His pastoral mind, ver. 11; 3. His pastoral zeal. He removes the hireling, opposes the wolf, vers. 12, 13; 4. His pastoral joy, vers. 14, 15.—The hireling and the wolf in the flock of Christ: 1. In respect of their contrast; 2. in respect of their connection.—The sheep are His: 1. By original nature; 2. by divine appointment; 3. by virtue of His self-sacrificing fidelity.—The Good Shepherd knows His own: 1. By their attraction to Him; 2. by their tractableness.

The third parable: "And other sheep I have." 1. Sheep without a fold, without pasture, without shepherds, and yet His sheep, or the wonders of *gratia præveniens.* 2. Attested as sheep; *a,* by His destination to die for them and to be exalted to glory in order to lead them; *b,* by the fact that they know His voice; *c,* by their becoming under Him, the Shepherd, One Flock with the former sheep.—"And there shall be *one* flock, *one* Shepherd."—The death of the faithful Shepherd, the revelation of the divine pastoral fields; 1. The sign of true shepherds and true sheep; 2, the salvation of the flock; 3, their union under the *one* Shepherd's staff of Christ.—The word of Christ: One Shepherd, one flock; 1. How it has already been invisibly fulfilled; 2. how its fulfilment shall one day be fully visible; 3. how it is continually being fulfilled more and more in great signs.—The One Shepherd is Christ alone, as believers alone constitute the One Flock.—The freedom in the self-sacrifice of Christ: 1. As a power of love; 2, as a power of life; 3, as a power of hope.—The mark of genuine, pious submission to God unto death, is the hope of resurrection.—True joyfulness in sacrifice is always at the same time an assurance of resurrection.—The death of Christ the consummation of the good-will of God to mankind in Him.—The death of Christ the unique great deed, 1 John iv. 9.—The communion of God a kingdom of personal life.—How the word of Christ concerning His faithfulness as a Shepherd itself severs the true members of His flock from His enemies (the prelude to the final future separation of sheep and goats).

Starke: The church (Theocracy) resembles a sheep-pen (a fold): 1. Unity of the sheep; 2. goats among them, hypocrites; 3. protection from cold, thieves, robbers; 4. of mean appearance; 5. in wildernesses yet fruitful places, (or rather in solitary but grassy pastures). Considered significant of separation from the world; riches of the Word of God, *etc.,* (Ezek. xxxiv. 1; Jer. xxiii. 1; Matt. ix. 36; Is. xl. 11; i. 23; Hos. vi. 9, *etc.*)—Zeisius: The mask must finally be torn away from unfaithful shepherds, wicked teachers.—The door of faith, of the mouth, of heaven, *etc.*. All such doors must be opened to us by the Holy Ghost.—Shepherds and sheep are together; preachers must not sunder themselves from their hearers.—Canstein: In all ages a true though invisible church has existed, which has not listened to seducers, but has followed Christ only.—Quesnel: We never know better what is meant by good shepherds and hirelings, than in times of persecution.—Men may flee not only in body, but also in spirit.—False prophets called dumb dogs, Is. lvi. 10; Ezek. xiii. 5,—who, as shepherds, assume a very bold front, and yet flee when they should stand.—Zeisius: O gracious, cordial and blessed acquaintance of Christ and believers!—Who would count his life too dear when the honor and will of Christ demands it? Christ affords all men at all times, and in all places, an opportunity of becoming sheep of His flock.

Braune: Ps. lxxviii. 72; Ezek. xxxiv.—A hireling gradually becomes a thief and a murderer because he has not a shepherd's heart.—Gossner: Where do the thieves climb in? How do they enter upon the office of teachers, into the churches? Ambition and avarice, *etc.*—The harmony existing between Christ and the Holy Ghost.—They flee from him (the sheep from the stranger). They do not in addition, however, use violence towards him.—Hence the world's lamentations over the obscurity of the Bible: The porter does not open to them because they are not sheep. But why do the simple understand? Because they are sheep.

Heubner: "He that entereth not in at the door." General import: He who does not enter upon his work as a teacher in the open way, pointed out by God Himself. Special import: He who fails to enter upon the office of a teacher through the Messiah whom God has ordained, with faith in Him, in His strength and in fellowship with Him,—"But climbeth in some other way." The general meaning of this is: He who seeks to gain access to the people and to obtain office and authority with them by unlawful means, without inward calling and with carnal views.—A soul-murderer is far more horrible than a body-murderer.—False preaching, wolf's preaching, as Luther calls it.—Poor fools, who seek to press into hearts by their strength, art or clamor.—Sheep, souls who already feel drawn to the Saviour, soon obtain a right discernment.—*He calleth His sheep by name.* In this see the special care of souls.—One's life is more edifying than one's doctrine.—Ver. 6. How many thousands of hirelings have read this text without noticing how it touches them.—*On the first pericope,* vers. 1-11: Comparison of false teachers and Christ.—How shall Christians learn to distinguish misleaders from true leaders?—The Good Shepherd. Love will run some risk.—The wolf. The devil and men resembling Satan.—An evil spirit has supplanted the old public spirit of faith.—The extent of the love of Christ.—Such a great, wide-embracing heart is proof of the wide-embracing spirit.—If we grow more like Jesus our hearts also expand.—In Christ is the *centrum unitatis* of the churches.—*On the second pericope,* vers. 11-21 (Misericordias): The mutual fidelity of Jesus, the Good Shepherd, and His flock.—Ver. 18. The death of Jesus a voluntary self-surrender.

Schleiermacher: Those who are able to promote the outward prosperity of men should make use of this excellent gift; but they should neither believe themselves nor persuade others that they thereby give men the right and the true.—(Faithful following of Jesus:) The bond of faithfulness which has held the little troop of believers together through all seasons of disgrace and persecution.—Marheineke: The invisible rule of Christ over all human souls.—Höpfner: What relation does the Reformation sustain to the promise of the Lord: There shall be one flock and One Shepherd?—Burk: The acquaintanceship between Christ and believers. — Rautenberg: The dispersion of the flock of Christ.—Arndt; The Good Shepherd knows His sheep: 1, By their faith; 2, by the Holy Ghost; 3, by the renewal of their lives; 4, by prayer.—Florey:

In the pastoral office of the Lord the glory of His divine love is revealed.—AHLFELD: The Good Shepherd and His flock.

[CRAVEN: Christ the *author* and *finisher* of our faith: 1. the shepherd who *seeks* the *unfolded* sheep and *guides* them (ver. 16); 2. through Himself, the *door;* 3. to Himself, the governing, nourishing and protecting Shepherd.—Christ the *door*, denoting—1, His *authority* to admit and shut out; 2. His *sacrifice*, Heb. x. 19, 20.—Vers. 19-21. The division occasioned by the revelation of unpleasant or mysterious truth. Unbelief ignores miracles because of difficulties; faith ignores difficulties because of miracles.—From CHRYSOSTOM: Ver. 1. The Scriptures the *door;* they 1. admit to knowledge of God; 2. protect the sheep; 3, shut out wolves; 4, bar entrance to heretics.—(Our Lord calls *Himself* the *door*, ver. 7: He is the *door* as He introduces us to the Father, but the Scriptures are a manifestation of Christ, and in certain respects they are what He is.—E. R. C.)—*Some other way* (ver. 1); the commandments and traditions of the Scribes and Pharisees.—From AUGUSTINE: Christ a *lowly* door—he who enters through Him must be lowly, the proud climb up *some other way.*—Ver. 3. He *leadeth them out*, implies that He looses the chains of their sins that they may follow Him.—Ver. 6. Our Lord: 1. *feeds* by plain words; 2. *exercises* by obscure.—Vers. 5, 8. The *times* (before and after the advent) different; the *faith*, the same.—Ver. 8. By *going in, i. e.*, by *faith*, they have life; by *going out, i. e.*, by *death*, they have life more abundantly.—Vers. 7, 9. How does He enter by Himself? We enter by *the door* because we preach Christ, He preaches Himself.—Ver. 11. The *good* Shepherd; 1. not because He gave His life, but 2. because He gave His life *for the sheep*, 1 Cor. xiii. 3.—Ver. 18. He shows His natural death was the consequence; 1. not of sin in Him, but 2. of His own will, as to the (1) why, (2) when, (3) how.—From THEOPHYLACT: Ver. 3. The Holy Spirit the *porter*, by whom; 1. the Scriptures are unlocked; 2. the truth revealed.—Ver. 10. The *thief* is the devil, who 1. *steals* by wicked thoughts; 2. *kills* by the assent of the mind to them; 3. *destroys* by acts.—Ver. 14. The *good* Shepherd *knows* His sheep (and *is known* by them.—E. R. C.), because He is so attractive to them.—From GREGORY: Ver. 9. *Shall go in, i. e.*, to faith; *shall go out, i. e.*, to sight; *find pasture, i. e.*, in eternal fulness.—Ver. 11. He, 1. did what He bade; 2. set the example of what He commanded.—Vers. 12, 13. An *hireling* holds the place of a shepherd, but 1. seeks not the gain of the sheep; 2. pants after the good things of earth; 3. rejoices in the pride of station. The hireling flees; 1. not by changing place, but 2. by withholding consolation. The hireling does not face danger, lest he should lose what he loves. Whether one be a shepherd or an hireling cannot be told for certain except in time of trial.—Ver. 15. By my love for my sheep, I show how much I love my Father.—From ALCUIN: Ver. 18. The WORD does not receive a commandment by word, but contains in Himself all His Father's commandments.—From MELANCHTHON: Ver. 4. A picture of a true pastor; he shall 1. be saved himself; 2. go into intimate communion with God; 3. go forth furnished with gifts and be useful in the church; 4. find food and refreshment for his own soul.—From MUSCULUS: Ver. 9. Our Lord does not say; 1. if any learned, or righteous, or noble, or rich, or Jewish man, but 2. if *any* man.—Ver. 12. Churches cannot keep together without (faithful) pastors, the wolf *scattereth* them.—From M. HENRY: The similitude is borrowed from the custom of the country; similitudes should be taken from those things which are familiar, that the things of God be not clouded by that which should clear them.—The industry of the wicked to do mischief should shame us out of slothfulness and cowardice in the service of God (ver. 1).—The rightful owner enters in by the door as one having authority (ver. 2).—Good men have the good qualities of sheep; 1. harmless, 2. meek, 3. patient, 4. useful, 5. tractable to the Shepherd, 6. sociable, 7. much used in sacrifice.—The *good* Shepherd 1. knows His own sheep, 2. calls each one by name, 3. marks them, 4. leads them out to pasture, 5. makes them feed and rest, 6. speaks comfortably to them, 7. guards them, 8. guides them by going before.—Christ's *explication* of the parable; whatever difficulties there may be in the sayings of Jesus, we shall find Him willing to explain, if we be willing to understand; one scripture expounds another.—Though it may be a solecism in rhetoric to make the same person to be both the *door* and the *shepherd*, it is no solecism in divinity to make Christ have His authority from Himself—*Himself to enter by His own blood* into *the holy place.*—Christ the *door*, 1. a door *shut*, to keep out thieves and robbers, 2. a door *open*, for passage and communication—(1) by Him we have our first admission into the flock, (2) by Him we go in and out in religious conversation, (3) by Him God visits and communicates with the church, (4) by Him we are at last admitted into heaven.—The *mischievous* design of the thief; the *gracious* design of the shepherd—(1) to give life to the sheep, (2) to give His life for the sheep.—A description of *bad* shepherds—1. their *bad principles* (as hirelings), (1) the wealth of the world their chief good, (2) the work of their place the least of their care; 2. their *bad practices* the effect of bad principles, (1) they *desert* the flock when danger threatens, (2)(they *rob* when in apparent safety. E. R. C.)—The acquaintance of Christ with those hereafter to be of His flock (ver. 16); Observe 1. the eye Christ had to the Gentiles, 2. the purposes of His grace concerning them ("*them also I must bring*"): (*a*) *the necessity of their case* required it, (*b*) the necessity *of His own engagements* required it; 3. The blessed effect of His purpose, (*a*) *they shall* hear *my voice*—not only shall my voice be heard *among* them but *by* them, (*b*) *there shall be one fold* (flock) *and one Shepherd*—Jews and Gentiles (all classes) being united to Christ, unite in Him.—Christ takes off the offence of the cross by four considerations (vers. 17, 18), the laying down of His life was 1. in order to His receiving it again, 2. the condition of His exaltation—*therefore doth My Father love Me*, 3. voluntary, 4. by order and appointment of the Father.—Better that men should be *divided* about the doctrine of Christ than *united* in the service of sin (ver. 19).—From BURKITT: *He calleth His own sheep by name* (ver. 5)—this denotes, 1. a special love He bears them, 2. a special care He has over them, 3. a particular acquaintance with them.—*He goeth before them* (ver. 4), He treads out those steps which they take in their way towards heaven.—He does not say all that were *sent* before Me, but all that *came* before Me (ver. 8).—The properties of a *good* shepherd—1. to know all his flock, 2. to take care of them, 3. to lay down his life for them, 4. to take care for increasing his fold (ver. 16).—From BESSER: Ver. 14, *Am known of Mine;* a rebuke of those doubters who in voluntary humility refuse to be sure of their salvation.—From STIER: I. Concerning the true and false shepherd *generally* in order to a transition to Christ Himself, who is in the *fullest* sense the Shepherd: 1. the *fundamental* difference, *i. e.* the *entering in* to the fold through the right *door* (vers. 1, 2); 2. the difference *as to result*, the *true* shepherd, (1) is admitted by the porter, (2) is acknowledged by the sheep, (3) leads them out going before, (4) they follow—the *stranger*, they (1) follow not, (2) flee from (vers. 3-5). II. The medium of *transition* concerning Christ as the *door:* 1. to the sheep *for all under-shepherds* (vers. 7, 8), 2. more comprehensively, *of the shepherds and the sheep* (ver. 9). III. The *true* and *good* shepherd in the sole and supreme sense, 1. in *contrast* with the *enemy* and his *servants*, with (1) the *thief* (ver. 10), (2) the *hireling* and the *wolf* (vers. 11-13), 3. *independently* (vers. 14-18).—Ver. 3. *Preaching* is the *calling* of individuals, and finds its consummation in *the special care of souls;* the *leading out* requires the *going before* of the shepherd in *life* and *example.*—Ver. 14. *My sheep—mine*, a plain indication that there are *false sheep* [? *goats* rather according to Scripture language] as well as *false shepherds.*—From RYLE: The use of a parable to convey *indirectly* a severe rebuke. Ver. 2. If we would know the value of a man's ministry we must ask—Where is the *door?* does he bring forward Christ and give Him His rightful place?—Ver. 3. The character of a *true* shepherd shown, 1. the porter knows by his manner of approach that he is a friend, 2. the sheep recognize his voice, 3. he calls each sheep by its own name, 4. he leads the sheep out to pasture.—Vers. 4, 5. A spiritual instinct in believers which generally enables them to distinguish between *true* and *false* teaching, 1 John ii. 20.—Ver. 6. *They understood not;* if Christ was not understood, His ministers cannot wonder that they are often misunderstood.—Ver. 9. *Go in and out* is a Hebraism, 1. implying a habit of using a dwelling as a *home*, 2. expressing the *habitual* and *happy* intercourse of a believer with Christ.—Vers. 11-13. The great secret of a useful and Christ-like ministry is to love men's souls; he that is a minister merely to get a living, or to have an honorable position, is the hireling of the verses. The *true* pastor's first care is for his sheep; the *false* pastor's first thought is for himself.—Ver. 14. Christ *knows* all His believing people; He knows 1. their names, 2. their families, 3. their dwelling-places, 4. circumstances, 5. private history, 6. experience, 7. trials.—Ver. 16. One *flock* (ποίμνη not αὐλή); there is only "One Holy Catholic Church," but there are many various visible churches.—From BARNES: Vers. 1, 2. The only way of entering the Church is by the Lord Jesus, *i. e.* by, 1. believing on Him, 2. obeying His commandments.—Ver. 10. *Life—more abundantly;* they shall have, 1. not merely life, *i. e.* bare *existence*, but 2. all those superadded things which are needful to make life blessed and happy (both *here* and *hereafter*. E. R. C.)—Ver. 21. The preaching of Jesus always produced effect—it made bitter enemies, or decided friends. Not the fault of the gospel that there are divisions, but of the unbelief and mad passions of men.—From OWEN: Ver. 5. *The blessings* promised are twofold, 1. *perfect safety* (shall go in and out), 2. *abundance* of pasturage.—Ver. 15. *I lay down My life;* the *consequence* and *illustration* of His love.—Ver. 18. The fact that Christ's death was *voluntary* shows that it was *necessary.*—From WEBSTER and WILKINSON: Ver. 9. There is no door between the soul and Christ.—Ver. 16. Eph. ii. 11-22 a perfect commentary on the passage.]

FOURTH SECTION.

The separation between the friends and foes of Christ, the children of light and the children of darkness.

CHAPTERS X. 22—XIII. 30.

I.

ANTITHESIS BETWEEN THE UNBELIEVERS IN JUDEA, WHO WISH TO KILL THE LORD, AND THE BELIEVERS IN PEREA, AMONG WHOM HE FINDS REFUGE. THE FEAST OF THE DEDICATION OF THE TEMPLE. THE FINAL CONFLICT BETWEEN THE FALSE MESSIANIC HOPE AND THE TRUE MESSIANIC WORK; FOLLOWED SPEEDILY BY THE STONING. THE TRUE AND THE FALSE DEDICATION OF THE TEMPLE. CHRIST THE SON OF GOD. THE ACTUAL REALIZATION OF THE DIVINE AND MESSIANIC FORMS OF THE OLD COVENANT.

CHAP. X. 22-42.

22 And it was at Jerusalem the feast of the dedication [Then the feast of the dedi-
23 cation occurred at Jerusalem], and [*omit* and] it [It] was winter [,]. And Jesus
24 walked [was walking, περιεπάτει] in the temple in Solomon's porch. Then came
the Jews round about him, and said unto him, How long dost thou make us to
doubt [agitate our souls, hold our minds in suspense]? If thou be [art] the Christ,

25 tell us plainly [frankly]. Jesus answered them, I told you [spoke to you], and ye
believed [believe][1] not: the works that I do in my Father's name, they [these] bear
26 witness of me. But [Nevertheless] ye believe not, because [for, γάρ] ye are not of
27 my sheep, as I said unto you.[2] My sheep hear [heed] my voice, and I know them,
28 and they follow me: And I give unto them eternal life; and they shall never perish,
neither shall any *man* [and no one shall] pluck [tear] them out of my hand.
29 My Father, which gave *them* me [who hath given *them* to me], is greater [some-
thing greater, μεῖζον] than all,[3] and no man [no one] is able to pluck [tear] *them*
30 [*anything* (*at all*)] out of my Father's hand. I and *my* [the] Father are one
[Ἐγὼ καὶ ὁ Πατὴρ ἕν ἐσμεν].
31 Then the Jews [The Jews therefore] took up stones again to [in order to, ἵνα] stone
32 him. Jesus answered them, Many good works have I shewed you from my [the]
33 Father; for which of those [these] works do ye stone me? The Jews answered
him, saying, [*omit* saying].[4] For a good work we stone thee not; [,] but for blas-
34 phemy; and because that [*omit* that] thou, being a man, makest thyself God. Je-
sus answered them, Is it not written in your law, 'I said, Ye are gods?' (Ps. lxxxii.
35 6). If he called them gods, unto whom the word of God came, and the Scripture
36 cannot be broken [made void], Say ye of him, whom the Father hath [*omit* hath]
sanctified, and sent into the world, 'Thou blasphemest;' because I said, I am the
37, 38 Son of God? If I do not the works of my Father, believe me not. But if I
do [them], though ye believe not me, believe the works; that ye may know, and
believe [understand],[5] that the Father *is* in me, and I in him [in the Father].[6]
39 Therefore they sought again to take [seize] him; but [and] he escaped [passed
40 out, went forth, ἐξῆλθεν] out of their hand, And went away again beyond [the]
Jordan into [to] the place where John at first baptized [was baptizing]; and there
41 he abode. And many resorted [came] unto him, and said, John did no miracle
[John indeed wrought no sign]: but all things that John spake [said] of this
42 man were true. And many believed on [in] him there.

TEXTUAL AND GRAMMATICAL.

[1] Ver. 25.—[Tischend., Alf., *etc.*, read οὐ πιστεύετε instead of οὐκ ἐπιστεύσατε.—P. S.]

[2] Ver. 26.—Καθὼς εἶπον ὑμῖν probably erroneously considered a superfluous addition, on which account it is wanting in Codd., B. K. L., *etc.* [It is wanting also in Cod. Sin., omitted by Tischend., bracketed by Alford.—P. S.]

[3] Ver. 29.—[The received text reads: ὁ πατήρ μου ὃς δέδωκέ μοι, μείζων πάντων ἐστί, *the Father who hath given* (them) *to me is greater than all;* but the best authorities omit μόυ, and read ὃ for ὃς, and μεῖζόν for μείζων. Tert.: *Pater quod mihi dedit, majus est omnibus.* So Tischendorf: ὁ πατὴρ ὃ δεδωκέν μοι πάντων μεῖζόν ἐστιν, *that which the Father hath given me is greater than all.* But this gives no good sense. The neuter μεῖζον was no doubt the original reading, but as transcribers did not understand it as belonging to πατήρ, they changed ὃς into the neuter. Restoring ὃς, we get the sense: "*The Father* (or, *My Father*, if we retain μου) *who hath given* (them) *to me, is something greater* (*a greater power*) *than all.*" On the different readings see the apparatus in Tischend., ed. 8.—P. S.]

[4] Ver. 33.—λέγοντες must be dropped in accordance with preponderant authorities. [λέγοντες is omitted in Sin., A. B. K. L., *etc.;* it occurs in D. E. G. H., *etc.*]

[5] Ver. 38.—Meyer, in company with Lachmann and Tischendorf [Alford], prefers the reading: ἵνα γνῶτε καὶ γινώσκητε [*learn and know*, or, *know and understand*], in accordance with B. L. X., supposing the γινώσκητε, on account of a failure to comprehend it, to have been changed into πιστεύσητε [*believe*]. But manifestly the *lect. recepta* might at an earlier period have appeared strange to minds of the Alexandrian school. Yet its sense, notwithstanding the objections raised against it, is rich and pertinent.

[6] Ver. 38.—Instead of ἐν αὐτῷ, B. D. L. [Sin.], *etc.*, most versions, *etc.*, read ἐν τῷ πατρί.

EXEGETICAL AND CRITICAL.

[Lücke introduces this *Discourse at the Feast of Dedication*, vers. 22–42, with the remark: "The conflict thickens, the issue looms up with certainty, the great hour approaches swiftly." The section is remarkable for one of the strongest assertions of Jesus concerning His dynamic and essential oneness with, and personal distinction from, God the Father, ver. 30.—P. S.]

Ver. 22. **The feast of the dedication of the temple.**—Christ, after His appearance at the Feast of Tabernacles, returned to Galilee (*Leben Jesu*, vol. II. p. 1004), in order to prepare the great body of His disciples for the last decisive journey to Jerusalem. The proof of this is given above. According to the testimony of the Synoptists, Jesus was followed at His final departure from Galilee by great multitudes that accompanied Him through Peræa, whereas the greatest secresy had been observed on the occasion of His journey to the Feast of Tabernacles.* The charge of "harmonistic hypothesis," made against this assumption, is utterly without weight; πάλιν, ver. 40, assuredly has reference to the presupposition that Jesus had before sojourned in Peræa. Tholück alleges, in opposition to the view of Paulus, Ebrard, P. Lange and Neander, that the feast of the dedication of the temple *might* be celebrated out of Jerusa-

* [The same view of a new visit to Jerusalem is taken by Neander, Ebrard, Luthardt, Godet, Alford; while Meyer, Wieseler, Hengstenberg, Ewald and Owen assume that Jesus during the two months intervening between the feast of Tabernacles and that of the Dedication remained at or in the neighborhood of Jerusalem. The words ἐν τοῖς Ἱερουσ. favor Dr. Lange's view and seem to indicate a previous absence from the city.—P. S.]

lem; it, however, by no means follows that it *must* be celebrated out of that city. The evangelical history is made to exhibit a strange anomaly by the supposition that Jesus passed two entire months (between the Feast of Tabernacles and that of the Dedication of the Temple) in Jerusalem, without leaving any traces or reminiscences of His stay. This journey to the Feast of the Dedication may be regarded as an episode in the journey to the last Passover,—the latter journey being begun with full decision of purpose *as openly and at as early a period* as possible.

The Feast of the Dedication of the Temple was by no means so insignificant; it must, from its nature, draw the Israelite, and hence the Lord individually to the temple, so long as He had not come to a positive rupture with the temple. It was the feast of renovation (חֲנֻכָּה, ἐγκαίνια) instituted by Judas Maccabæus (1 Macc. iv 36; 2 Macc. x. 6; Joseph. *Antiqu.* x. 7, 6 [xii. 7, 7]) in commemoration of the purification and fresh dedication of the temple after its profanation by Antiochus Epiphanes; it was the type of the Christian festival of church dedication (which is also called ἐγκαίνια). The celebration lasted eight days, commencing with the 25th of the month Kislev (the middle of December); its jubilant pageantry resembled that of the Feast of Tabernacles; there was especially a general illumination of the city, and hence the feast was also called τὰ φῶτα, while from its fundamental idea it derived the name of ἡμέραι ἐγκαινισμοῦ τοῦ θυσιαστηρίου.

At Jerusalem.—Even if there was a general observance of the feast throughout the country, its centre was of course the temple.*

It was winter (-weather).—As this remark is designed as an explanation of what follows, it is not to be regarded (with Lücke [Meyer, Alford]) as merely denoting the wintry season, in order thus to explain [to Greek readers] why Jesus walked in a porch of the temple, particularly as the temple was ordinarily the constant resort of Jesus when He was in Jerusalem. The raw wintry weather is at the same time indicated (Matt. xvi. 3, Clericus, Lampe), very probably in explanation of the circumstance that Jesus was, for the instant, not encircled and protected by the customary throngs of faithful followers, when the Jews suddenly surrounded Him.†

Ver. 23. **In Solomon's porch** [arcade, colonnade].—The στοὰ Σολομῶνος (Acts iii. 11) was according to tradition incorporated into the new temple buildings as a venerable remnant of the temple of Solomon (Josephus *Antiqu.* xx. 9, 7). It was situated on the eastern side of the temple-porch (στοὰ ἀνατολική in Josephus). Exegetes direct attention to the trace of eye-witness-ship in this remark (comp. ch. viii. 20).‡

[In the same place the apostles afterwards wrought miracles and proclaimed the gospel of Christ, Acts iii. 11; v. 12. Large portions of massive masonry, evidently belonging to the early ages of the temple, are still found on the temple area. Dr. Robinson (*Researches*, Am. ed., 1856, vol. I. p. 289), after describing these ruins, says: "The former temple was destroyed by fire, which would not affect these foundations; nor is it probable that a feeble colony of returning exiles could have accomplished works like these. There seems, therefore, little room for hesitation in referring them back to the days of Solomon, or rather of his successors, who, according to Josephus, built up here immense walls, 'immovable for all time' (ἀκινήτους τῷ παντὶ χρόνῳ, *Antiq.* xv. 11, 3). Ages upon ages have since rolled away, yet these foundations still endure, and are immovable as at the beginning. Nor is there aught in the present physical condition of these remains, to prevent them from continuing so long as the world shall last. It was the temple of the living God; and, like the everlasting hills on which it stood, its foundations were laid for all time."—P. S.]

Ver. 24. **Then came the Jews around him** [lit. **gathered around him in a circle**, ἐκύκλωσαν αὐτόν].—It is manifest that Jesus is at this time destitute of adherents,—a situation of which the hostile Jews promptly take advantage.* He finds Himself unawares encircled by them. He must, however, have had His reasons for permitting the arrival of this moment. Here again are things spoken, by which their most secret thoughts are laid bare and exposed to the illumination of the word of Christ. As a matter of course, these Jews are Pharisees; the position assumed by them and Jesus' answer to them, ver. 26, prove that they are likewise members of the Sanhedrin.

How long dost thou agitate our soul? [Ἕως πότε τὴν ψυχὴν ἡμῶν αἴρεις;]—Not: how long dost Thou take possession of our hearts, but, how long dost Thou raise us up, excite us, how long dost Thou hold our souls in suspense? See the illustrations from the Classics and Josephus in Meyer. [In Josephus ψυχὴν αἴρειν means *to uplift the soul, to raise the courage* (*Antiq.* iii. 2, 3; iii. 5, 1), but it has also the more general sense *to excite the soul* (=μετεωρίζειν), which in this case was done by Messianic expectations.—P. S.]

If thou art the Christ.—The usual explanation, that they design from the first hypocritically to draw from Him some expression whereupon they may ground His condemnation, leaves unnoticed the ardent longing of the Jews for a temporal Messiah after their own heart,—a longing which occupies a conspicuous place in the gospel history. Hypocrisy certainly is at work, but only inasmuch as they have a presentiment that He will not answer their chiliastic cravings. There is then a visionary longing as well as a fanatical irony in their question (comp. chap.

* [The temple was soon to be profaned again and to be destroyed by the Romans. But Christ raised His own body, and with it the indestructible temple of the true worship of God. Hooker and Wordsworth infer from the feasts of Dedication and of Purim the lawfulness of appointing religious festivals by *human* authority.—P. S.]

† [Wordsworth has a long note here on the supposed spiritual signification of this remark (χειμὼν ἦν) and the inner sympathy between the world of nature and the world of grace. But it is imposition rather than exposition.—P. S.]

‡ [So Meyer: "The indication of this specific locality belongs to the traces of eye-witness-ship (*Augenzeugenschaft*), which impressed such events indelibly upon the memory of the author." But he objects to the far-fetched view of Thiersch and Luthardt, that by walking in Solomon's porch Christ intended symbolically to set forth the unity of the O. and N. covenant.—P. S.]

* [" How grateful," says Bengel, "would their approach have been to the Saviour, had they approached in faith."—P. S.]

viii.) The feast of the dedication was the festival of Judas Maccabæus who had driven the heathenish Syrians out of Jerusalem. *On that day did the Jews wish more ardently than ever that a new Maccabee or Hammerer might arise and beat down the Romans.*

Ver. 25. **I have spoken to you.**—The εἶπον ὑμῖν must not be translated: I have told you so. For that would be an unmistakable affirmative, and would at once present to them the alternative either of paying Him homage as the Messiah, or of seizing and trying Him as a false prophet. The εἶπον might indeed be considered to have a positive reference to the foregoing εἰπὲ ἡμῖν παῤῥησίᾳ: "I have (plainly) told you, but," *etc.** Christ subsequently, however, sets forth His desire to be first acknowledged by them in the works that He does in the Father's name (not in the official Messianic name). Therefore we read: "I have spoken to you—and ye believe not—: the works," *etc.*,—*i. e.* I have given you a token of what I am. This answer is not really evasive, for it is Christ's will to be known as the Messiah by what He is to them, and not by their Messianic idea in what He is. According to Meyer Jesus had already told them many times that He was the Messiah, though not so directly as He had told the Samaritan woman. But the tragical part of this history and the proof of how far a would-be orthodox theology may depart from the living word of God, is contained in the very fact that it was necessary for Him to lock up His Messianic name from them in His own heart, until the moment (Matt. xxvi. 64) when their fanatical Messianic conception condemns Him to the cross.

Ver. 26. **For ye are not of my sheep.**—A statement of the reason of their unbelief. Ye do not recognize Me in My word and work, and, not knowing Me, ye do not subordinate yourselves to Me and trust in My guidance; on the contrary, ye desire a Messiah, that he may be the subservient tool of your passions.—**As I said unto you.**—The omission (see the Text. Notes) was probably occasioned by the fact that no verbal declaration to this effect is to be found. Such a declaration is, however, conveyed in intention by the parables of the Good Shepherd, ch. x. Hence we must not with Euthymius and others refer these words to the subsequent discourse of Jesus. And so much the less, since entirely new considerations are therein presented to us: 1. that the sheep follow the Shepherd, 2. that He gives His sheep eternal life, *etc.* Neither can any importance be attached to the doubts of Strauss and others concerning the probability of the assumption that Jesus is reminding His hearers of a parabolical discourse uttered by Him two months before; and Meyer justly observes that it was not characteristic of Jesus to repeat His more lengthy discourses.

Vers. 27-29. **My sheep hear my voice,** *etc.*—Bengel: "*Tria sententiarum paria, quorum singula et ovium fidem et pastoris bonitatem exprimunt per correlata.*" But we apprehend the three correlative members somewhat differently, always placing the Shepherd before the sheep. In advance, however, comes the saying which embraces the whole: *the sheep that are Mine, they hear My voice* [τὰ πρόβατα τὰ ἐμὰ τῆς φωνῆς μου ἀκούουσιν]. The unfolding of this personal connection: a. *I know them* [κἀγὼ γινώσκω αὐτά]: *and they follow Me* [καὶ ἀκολουθοῦσίν μοι]; b. *I give unto them eternal life; and they shall never perish* [κἀγὼ δίδωμι αὐτοῖς ζωὴν αἰώνιον, καὶ οὐ μὴ ἀπόλωνται εἰς τὸν αἰῶνα]; c. *none shall tear them out of My hand* [οὐχ ἁρπάσει τις αὐτὰ ἐκ τῆς χειρός μου]: *the Father gave them to Me, and He is greater than all: none can tear them out of the Father's hand.*

In this arrangement of the propositions, Christ is the Shepherd, the principle of the relationship; with His personal conduct the conduct and relationship of the flock correspond. The first proposition (*a*) declares the foundation and condition of salvation; the second proposition (*b*) declares the blessing, internally and externally considered: because Christ gives them eternal life, they shall never perish in the terrors of eternity, death and judgment. The third proposition (*c*) is descriptive of the absolute protection which they enjoy. It has reference to the former word concerning the wolf. Exegesis, however, should not overlook the fact that the Jews at that time beheld the wolf in the Roman power which threatened destruction to their nation. If, then, Jesus means to say that the spiritual safety of believers, as the Church of Christ, should be secured in His hand, so too He says that in the hand of the Father who is exalted above every power of this world, they should at the same time be preserved from destructive oppression on the part of the Roman temporal power. Therefore, what the Jews in carnal and fanatical excitement sought in vain in their Messiah, they should really and truly find in Christ.

According to Augustine and Calvin, Christ's words declare the doctrine of the grace of final perseverance; Tholuck agrees, but insists upon the condition which Augustinian and Calvinistic divines imply, that the marks of a true sheep must be discoverable in them that are kept, and that according to 1 John ii. 19, the apostate is regarded as not really belonging to the Church, because of his failure to comply with the condition of walking in the light. Meyer, on the other hand, remarks in accordance with the Lutheran belief, that the possibility of falling away is not excluded by the words of Christ. What is excluded is, above all things, the confounding of different stages: he who is awakened may fall away as an awakened man; he who is sealed is sealed. A dispute upon this subject, without distinction of the different stages, is a battle of words.*

* [So most commentators, referring to such passages as v. 19: viii. 36, 56, 58; x. 1, *etc.* Yet He did not *expressly* and *directly* reveal His Messiahship to the people, as He did to the Samaritan woman and to the blind man; the chief proof was His Messianic *works*, v. 36, and here.—P. S.]

* [Vers. 27-29 characterize the true sheep of Christ with a glorious promise as to their future, and draw a clear line of demarcation between His true disciples and the unbelieving and persecuting Jews, as well as all that are merely nominal Christians. 1. *Subjective* marks: (*a*) "They hear My voice;" the receptive side, faith. (*b*) "They follow Me;" the active side, love, obedience. 2. *Objective* marks: (*a*) "I know them;" this knowledge implies recognition of the sheep by Christ and corresponds to their faith. (*b*) I give unto them eternal life (δίδωμι, even now in this world). This life is eternal both intensively and extensively, and implies (*aa*) "that they shall never perish;" lit. "they shall not at all," in no wise

Ver. 30. **I and the Father are one.**—This grand saying of Jesus serves primarily as a proof of the preceding statement; hence its primary signification is: I and the Father are one in the work of salvation. The heart of the Shepherd corresponds with the nature of the sheep, which nature the Father created by His *gratia prœveniens.* The Shepherd's call of grace corresponds with the divine vocation in them. His eternal life that He puts into their hearts, corresponds with the destiny prepared for them by God,—that they shall never perish. His spiritual preservation corresponds with the historical preservation ordained by God: the triumphant Church of Christ is the triumphant Kingdom of God. But this *soteriological* oneness of Father and Son in work and government is at the same time expressive of their *ontological* oneness in power and substance. This saying, therefore, has not a mere soteriological reference to the oneness of the *hand* or the oneness in *power*, as set forth in this syllogism: (*a*) No man can pluck them out of My Father's hand; (*b*) I and My Father are one; (*c*) consequently no man can pluck them out of My hand. (Chrysostom, Calvin, and others, Lücke). It is rather the unity of the whole parallel, "the co-operation of Father and Son in the whole economy of salvation." Tholuck after Tertullian and others; comp. 1 Cor. iii. 8. "In the Arian controversies Alexander, Athanasius and many others made use of this passage against the Arians as a *dictum probans*, declaring it to mean the *unitas naturæ* of the Logos and the Father, while the Arians on the other hand held that it signified the *consensus voluntatis.* The interpretation of the Socinians, who regarded it as signifying the *unitas voluntatis et potestatis*, was not indeed rejected by the representatives of the Church, but the latter considered the *unitas naturæ* to be implied by the *unitas potentiæ.* See Gerhard I. p. 252, Lyser and others. Even Calvin—although on this account accused by Hunnius of a *scelus*—brought forward this argument. The point treated of by this saying is, in fact, not the Trinitarian relationship, but the relation of the Incarnate One to the Father." Tholuck. Meyer is also of this opinion.* In upholding this view, however, they overlook these facts: 1. That the economical Trinity [of revelation] points back to the ontological Trinity [of essence]; 2. that the Jews apprehend this expression ontologically, and hence accuse Christ of blasphemy against God; 3. that Christ does not correct their ontological conception of His meaning, but favors it, and in conclusion, as they fully believe, confirms it, ver. 38.

[The neuter ἕν denotes, according to the connection and for the purpose of the argument, unity of *will* and *power*, which rests on the unity of *essence* or *nature;* for power is one of the divine attributes which are not outside of the divine essence, but constitute it. Even if we confine ἕν to dynamic unity, we have here one of the strongest arguments for the strict divinity of Christ. It is implied even more in ἐσμεν than in ἕν. No creature could possibly thus associate himself in one common plural with God Almighty without shocking blasphemy or downright madness. In this brief sentence we have, as Augustine and Bengel observe, a refutation both of Arianism and Sabellianism; ἕν refutes the former by asserting the dynamic (and, by implication, the essential) unity of the Father and the Son, Ἐγώ καὶ ὁ πατήρ and ἐσμεν refute the latter by asserting the personal distinction. Sabellianism would require the masculine εἷς instead of the neuter, and this would be inconsistent with ἐσμεν and the self-conscious Ἐγώ.†—P. S.]

(οὐ μή, double negation) "perish for ever" (εἰς τὸν αἰῶνα); (*bb*) that "no one" (no wolf, no robber, no hireling, no enemy) "can tear them out of the hand," (*i. e.* the possession and protecting power) of Christ; for to tear them out of His hand would be to tear them out of the hand of His Father, who is greater (μεῖζον, neuter, something greater, a greater power) than all (πάντων) the enemies and opposing forces, singly or combined; since Christ and the Father are one in power because they are one in essence (ver. 30). Reduced to a syllogism the argument is this: No one can tear My sheep from the hand of My Father, God Almighty; I and My Father are one; consequently no one can tear them out of My hand. This is the strongest possible assurance of the faithfulness of Christ to His chosen followers and a protection on His part that will prevail over all opposition, including the devil and his host. We have no right to weaken the language by arbitrary insertions and qualifications in the interest of a particular system of theology or sect. It will not do for instance to exempt sin from the opposing forces (πάντων), for, as Hengstenberg *in loc.* well remarks, this would deprive Christ's promise of its chief weight and comfort, since we require first of all a guarantee against ourselves; sin being our greatest enemy.—There is therefore a kind of election which implies the grace of perseverance to the end and which can in no way be defeated. This is taught not only here, but also in ch. iv. 14; vi. 37, 39, 40, 44, 45; xvii. 2, 9, 10; 1 John ii. 19; iii. 9; v. 18; Rom. viii. 28-39; Eph. i. 4 ff. 13, 14; 2 Tim. ii. 13, 19; 1 Cor. i. 8, 9, *etc.* On the other hand the Scriptures are full of exhortation and warning addressed to believers against the danger of unfaithfulness and apostasy (Heb. vi. 4 ff.; x. 35; Gal. v. 4, *etc.*), which are strengthened by not a few examples (Adam and Eve, David, Solomon, Peter, *etc.*) The apparent contradiction between these passages involves the great problem of the relation of God's sovereignty to man's freedom, which we are unable fully to solve theoretically in our present limited state of knowledge. Practically there is no serious difficulty among true Christians, who are all agreed that their ultimate salvation depends entirely on the power and grace of God, and implies faithful perseverance on their part. Looking to Christ, we are perfectly safe, looking to ourselves, we are surrounded by danger. Genuine faith and trust in God always implies distrust in ourselves, but controls and overrules it by constant prayer and watchfulness. Paul puts both together, Phil. ii, 12, 13: "Work out your own salvation with fear and trembling; for it is God who worketh in you both to will and to work for His good pleasure." Pious Lutherans and Methodists pray like Calvinists, as if all depended on God, and pious Calvinists work like Arminians, as if all depended on themselves. Theologically at war, they are devotionally agreed, and, forgetting the doctrinal antagonisms of their great hymnists in the days of their flesh, they unite all over the world in singing the hymns of Paul Gerhardt and Tersteegen, Toplady and Wesley, as if they had been of one creed. I discussed the question here involved more at length in my treatise on the *Sin against the Holy Ghost* (Halle, 1841) pp. 103-125. Alford and Wordsworth, perhaps from aversion to Calvinism, do not enter into an exegesis of this passage. Owen *in loc.* says: "The doctrine of the saints' perseverance in holiness is here most expressly taught. If one of the elect should finally perish, it would not only falsify the declaration here made by Christ, but would be a violation of the compact between the Father and the Son (see vi. 37), and contrary to the expressly declared will of the Father (vi. 39, 40). Yet this great truth, which so illustrates the sovereign mercy of God through Jesus Christ, and which is the only sure foundation upon which the believer rests his hope of eternal life, must not be abused to justify any laxity of effort on his part to make his calling and election sure, by a life of prayer and holy living, such as becometh the disciples of Christ."—P. S.]

* [Meyer understands ἕν ἐσμεν of the *dynamic* union, or union of *power*, and rejects both the Arian and Socinian interpretation of *moral* union, and the orthodox interpretation of *essential* union, but he admits that, especially in the theological system of John, the essential union, the homoousia, though not required here for the argument, is the presupposed basis of the dynamic union. See p. 409 f. (5th ed.) —P. S.]

† [The best commentators (with the exception of Calvin who understands the passage *de consensu cum Patre*), support the interpretation given in the text, as the following quota-

Ver. 31. **Took up stones again.**—Again as ch. viii. 59 and for a similar cause. The arrival of the decisive turning-point in their wavering mood is again induced by Christ's asseveration concerning His divine nature. They have no use for such a Messiah who contradicts their consciousness, that has become unitarian.—They have already caught up stones and raised them high in air (ἐβάστασαν); nevertheless the word of Jesus fetters their arm. It is the counteraction of the might of His Spirit; no doubt assisted, however, by the want of a literal formula, upon the strength of which they might securely bring Him to trial. His words are everywhere peculiar to Himself, the Man of the Spirit, and they are forever in doubt as to whether they have rightly understood Him. But the matter with which they think they can reproach Him, they subsequently declare.

Ver. 32. **Many good works have I shewed you from my Father.**—*Jesus answers them;* that is, He replies to their sign-language. He has thoroughly understood them in their malice, but designates them as incomprehensible, in accordance with their own consciences to which He appeals. Καλὰ ἔργα, 1. Works of love: Baumg.-Crusius; 2. *præclara opera*, excellent works: Meyer; 3. irreproachable works: Luthardt. Special importance attaches to the ἔργον itself. The ἔργον ἐκ τοῦ πατρός is a miracle. Similarly, the ἔδειξα without doubt contains the idea of sign-giving. Καλόν is indicative of moral beauty, beneficence.—**For which of these works do ye stone me?** The ironicalness of this expression is unmistakable and invites an elucidation of biblical irony in general (comp. 2 Cor. xii. 13. A principal passage is Ps. ii.). At the foundation, however, of this ironical speech lies the deeper meaning that He, in all His words and works, is but the representative of the Father; so that their every assault upon Him is a declaration of war against God Himself. Furthermore these words seem to assume 1. that capital punishment should not be inflicted on account of a word; 2. that it should be inflicted on account of a work, only inasmuch as that work is proved to be deserving of death. Execution should be preceded by a regular trial. Above all things we should fix our eyes upon the sublime composure of Jesus as manifested by His ironical speech in this condition of affairs.

Ver. 33. **For blasphemy, and because thou, being a man, makest thyself God.**—It is questioned whether the following καὶ ὅτι σύ, *etc.*, is simply an explanation; according to Meyer: "For blasphemy and that because." The καί would then be superfluous. They reproach Him with two things: first, that He places God on a par with Himself—and this they call blasphemy; secondly, that He makes Himself God—and in this they think they recognize the false prophet; although both ideas undoubtedly play into each other.

Ver. 34. **Is it not written in your law, I said ye are gods?**—In your law (see ch. viii. 17), a reference to Ps. lxxxii. 6. According to Tholuck and Ewald the psalm does not refer to angels or foreign princes but to unjust theocratic judges. אֱלֹהִים, Ex. xxi. 6; xxii. 28 (comp. 2 Chron. xix. 5-7). "Moses uses it in a collective sense—Sept. τὸ κριτήριον τοῦ θεοῦ; here in the Psalm it is a personal appellation of individuals; in parallel with θεοί is υἱοὶ ὑψίστου." Tholuck.—**I said,** εἶπα. Ewald explains this: I thought ye were. Tholuck thinks it has reference to the institution of Moses; according to the subsequent explanation of the Lord, the expression refers to the fact that the λόγος τοῦ θεοῦ came to them,—that they were called to their office by the word of God. Full of meaning, then, is the idea of Cyril who considers the passage as significant of the λόγος ἄσαρκος; and that of Theodor-Mopsuest. (and Olshausen) who take it to mean the word of God's revelations to the judges. In opposition to this Tholuck remarks that revelations were attributed only to the Law-giver as judge. This latter view is, however, contrary to the Old Testament: every judge in the time of the judges was called by a λόγος θεοῦ; David and Solomon were so called and every royal or priestly Mashiach was assumed to have received such a call, inasmuch as he did at least receive it through the typical anointing. A principal consideration is this: the theocratical callings came by the Angel of the Lord, *i. e.*, by Christ in the Old Testament, the λόγος ἄσαρκος, and hence those who were called received the name of Elohim.

Ver. 35. **If he called them gods.**—Conclusion: *a minori ad majus.* In what respect: 1. from those blameworthy judges and their lofty title—to Christ (Bengel, Lücke); 2. from those who derived their dignity from the Mosaic institution, to Him whom God hath sanctified (Gerhard, Tholuck); 3. from those to whom the λόγος τοῦ θεοῦ did but come, to Him whom God sanctified and sent into the world, *i. e.*, whom He has actually made His λόγος to the world; the Logos-nature of Christ is here implied though not expressed (Cyril, *etc.*). This last we hold to be the only correct conception, the only one satisfactory to the Old Testament Christology.

[Alford: "The argument is *a minori ad majus.* If in any sense they could be called *gods,*—how much more properly He, whom, *etc.* They were

---

tions from different ages and churches will show. Euthymius Zigabenus: ἓν κατὰ δύναμιν, ἤγουν ταὐτοδύναμοι; εἰ δὲ ἓν κατὰ δύναμιν, ἓν ἄρα καὶ κατὰ τὴν θεότητα καὶ οὐσίαν καὶ φύσιν. Bengel: "*Unum sumus non solum voluntatis consensu, sed unitate potentiæ, adeoque naturæ. Nam omnipotentia est attributum naturale.*" Godet (II. 307): "*Ce pluriel* 'NOUS SOMMES,' *ne serait-il pas un blasphème dans la bouche d'une créature? Le ministre d'état qui se permit un jour de dire: Le roi et moi, nous. . . . provoqua le rire de tout le Parlement; que mériterait la créature qui oserait dire: 'Moi et Dieu, nous.'* . . ." Alford: "One in *essence* primarily, but therefore also one in *working*, and *power* and in *will*. This certainly is implied in the words, and so the Jews understood them, ver. 33." Comp. also the long notes of Webster and Wilkinson, and Wordsworth *in loc.*—Two objections are raised against the orthodox interpretation: (1) The reply of Jesus, vers. 34-36; but this is evidently an *argumentum a fortiori.* See below. (2) The passages, John xviii. 11, 21, where Christ applies the same language to the unity of believers among themselves and with Him: "that they may be one as we," and "that they also in us may be one." But the imperfection of the copy does not prove the imperfection of the original; and then the union of believers with Christ is really more than a moral union, it is a vital union, a community of life. Godet (II. p. 307): "*L'union de Jésus et des fidèles n'est point un simple accord de volonté*, c'est *une action consubstantielle. L'incarnation a fondé entre Jésus et nous un rapport de nature tellement complet, qu'il embrasse notre personalité tout entière, physique et morale.*" Compare also Hengstenberg *in loc.*—P. S.]

only officially so *called*, only λεγόμενοι θεοί—but He, the only One, sealed and hallowed by the Father, and sent into the world (the aorists refer to the time of the Incarnation), is essentially θεός, inasmuch as He is υἱὸς τοῦ θεοῦ. The deeper aim of this argument is, to show them that the idea of *man and God being one*, was not alien from their Old Testament spirit, but set forth there in types and shadows of Him, the real God-Man."—P. S.]

And the Scripture cannot be broken; λυθῆναι, Matt. v. 19; John v. 18; vii. 23. Be made invalid, subverted. Meyer: "The *auctoritas normativa et judicialis* of the Scripture cannot be done away with. Note here the idea of the unity of the Scriptures." This practical sense of the Scripture certainly prevails here, although it is founded upon the inspiration of the sacred writings. (Gaussen, Stier). Inspiration is undoubtedly modifiable, though not by the distinction of important and "unimportant" words.

[Webster and Wilkinson: "This remark proves that the *terms* in which God made His revelation to man were regarded by our Lord as Divinely inspired; that the form as well as the substance of Scripture is given by inspiration of God, for His argument here is founded upon the mode of expression adopted by the sacred writers." Godet: "The expression shows the boundless confidence with which the Scripture word inspired Jesus."—P. S.]

Ver. 36. **Whom the Father hath sanctified,** *etc.*—Interpretations: 1. Melanchthon and others: the *unctio* with divine gifts and attributes; 2. Tholuck: consecration to the Messianic office, one with the σφραγίζειν, ch. vi. 27, *etc.* (?). The meaning, in accordance with the idea of sanctification, is as follows: He has taken Him out from the world in order to appropriate Him to the world; *i. e.*, He has made Him the God-Man, the new Man, the wonder of the new life, and has also accredited Him to you by His sinlessness and miraculous works. This is spoken in antithesis to the typical sanctification, or consecration to office, enjoyed by the Old Testament judges or messiahs. They were *consecrated* by men, by means of outward anointing or calling; He is *consecrated* by the Father, by the anointing of the Spirit and the attestation of works. This circumstance, then, contains the strongest intimation that He is in truth the Messiah, and at the same time furnishes the most conclusive evidence that He is no *typical* Messiah, but *the real Messiah.*

I am the Son of God.—Christ's reasoning receives additional force from the antithesis between the real dignities and the titles. In respect of the dignities He proceeds *a minori ad majus;* in respect of the title *a majore ad minus* (*gods, Son of God*),—*i. e.*, at least according to the literal expression as apprehended by them. This expression is also an explanation of the words: I and My Father are one. The conclusion, ver. 38, proves that the υἱὸς θεοῦ might, in accordance with rationalistic interpretation, be primarily understood as a mere official name.

Ver. 37. **If I do not the works.**—The works of Christ are the Father's works as new works, creative works, such as He can do only in oneness with the Father, ch. ix. 3.—**Believe me not.**—A conditional absolution from belief; at once real and ironical.

Ver. 38. **And ye believe not me** (might not—are not able to believe).—Distinction of a gradation in faith. They cannot, perchance, soar up to the direct view of His personality. This flight of faith is not allotted to every one. But they *are* able and are morally bound to set foot upon the first step of faith: to recognize the divinity of His mission by His works. Hence they will derive the *knowledge* that Christ stands in the closest communion with God, and thus a higher *belief* in His personality will be produced in them. There would hardly be an immediate *knowledge* on their part of His divine personality; and this also is unfavorable to the reading quoted above and recommended by Meyer [see TEXT. NOTES].

That the Father is in me.—This is not the full import of that oneness with the Father, declared by Christ, ver. 30, but the living manifestation of it in His works; if they would not harden themselves, they would be in a condition believingly to take knowledge of that revelation, and their further progress in faith would be assured. In a sense, then, the *περιχώρησις essentialis* is but intimated here.* Christ in His character as the Redeemer is in the Father by submersion, contemplation, by the seeing of His works; the Father is in Christ by revelation, appearance, co-operation in the works of Christ.

Ver. 39. **Again to take him.**—(See ch. viii. 30, 32). This denotes a milder ebullition of their rage in comparison with their previous attempt to stone Him. The apparently obscurer and more indefinite saying of Christ seemed to demand a preliminary trial.

And he escaped out of their hands.—"Something in this of a miraculous nature (a rendering of Himself invisible), although assumed by many ancient exegetes and still by Baumg.-Crusius and Luthardt, is not intimated by John." Meyer. But John has just shown that Christ was able so to impress His enemies as to render them powerless.

Ver. 40. **Again beyond the Jordan.**—Peræa. See Note on ver. 22. In thus doing He has not given up the people, but He withdraws into a region of greater susceptibility. He was still bound to the last trial, as to whether the dynamical power of His friends would overcome that of His enemies or succumb to it, when the whole nation should be assembled at the Paschal Feast. He remained in that place from the time of the feast of the dedication until His journey to Bethany.

Ver. 41. **And many resorted unto him.**—Bengel: *Fructus posthumus officii Johannis.* But we must not overlook the fact that Christ had before sojourned in Peræa and worked there.—**John did no miracle.**—Nevertheless he is attested by Christ Himself in what he said of Him.

* [The patristic and scholastic terms περιχώρησις (from περιχωρέω, *to circulate, to go about*), ἐνύπαρξις, *inexistentia, inhabitatio, intercommunio, circumincessio* (also *circuminsessio*), are intended to express the reciprocal indwelling and vital communion of the Persons of the Trinity. The doctrine is based upon such passages as: "I am in the Father and the Father in Me;" "The Father that dwelleth in Me," John xiv. 10, 11.—P. S.]

And thus his testimony to Christ lives again and continues working to the furtherance of faith.

STARKE: The different dedications of the Jewish temple: 1. Under Solomon, 1 Kings viii. 2; 2. under Hezekiah, 2 Chron. xxix. 17, 19; 3. by Zerubbabel, Ezra vi. 16; 4. by Judas Maccabæus, 1 Macc. iv. 41; 2 Macc. x. 1; 5. in the time of Herod. Joseph. *Antiqu.* xv.

DOCTRINAL AND ETHICAL.

1. See the EXEG. NOTES vers. 24-30 and ver. 34.

2. The longing of the Jews for a Messiah in its relation to the temptation of Jesus in the wilderness, to ch. vi. 15, and to similar moments in the evangelical history.

3. The temptation of Christ by the Jews, in connection with the temptation, ch. viii. 1-11, and the temptation in the history of the Passion.

4. Christ here also evades their Messianic idea in order, on the other hand, to establish His own.—*The life of Christ the ideal realization of Maccabæan heroism and of the new Dedication of the Temple.*

5. The sheep of Christ, or the germs of the New Testament biblical doctrine of election, predestination and vocation, Rom. viii. 29.

6. "*I and the Father are one.*" (Ver. 30). The soteriological foreground, the ontological background of this word. The distinction of Person: *We;* the oneness of substance: *One.*

[Comp. the EXEG. NOTES.—Wordsworth *in loc.:* "*We are one.* Listen to both words '*are*' and '*one.*' The word '*are*' delivers you from the heresy of Sabellius; the word '*one*' ('*unum*') delivers you from that of Arius. (Aug.). Sail thou in the midst, between the Scylla of the one and the Charybdis of the other. Christians framed a *new word*, '*Homoousion Patris* (*consubstantial with the Father*), against the impiety of Arianism; but they did not coin a *new thing* by a new word. For the *doctrine* of the Homoousion is contained in our Lord's own words,—'I and My Father are *one*'—'*unum,*' *one substance* (Aug. *Tract.* xcvii. See also Aug. *Serm.* 139). And there were Christians in *fact*, before the *name* 'Christians,' was given to believers at Antioch. (Acts xi. 26). The same remark applies to the words '*Trinity*,' Θεοτόκος, and some others; against which exceptions have been made by some in modern times. It has been objected by Socinians and others, that these words of Christ do not signify oneness of *substance*, because our Lord used a similar expression when speaking of His disciples, in His prayer,—*ἵνα πάντες ἓν ὦσιν, καθὼς σὺ, πάτερ, ἐν ἐμοὶ, κἀγὼ ἐν σοὶ, ἵνα καὶ αὐτοὶ ἐν ἡμῖν ἓν ὦσιν*, xvii. 21; comp. vers. 22, 23. That language of Christ does indeed prove that the Father and the Son are not the same *person;* and so it is valid against the Sabellian heresy. But it does not show that they are not consubstantial. It is a *comparison;* and things compared are not identical. It contains a prayer, that all believers may be one in heart and will, as the Persons of the Trinity are; that by virtue of Christ's Incarnation, by which He became Emmanuel,—God with us, God manifest in the flesh, or, as He there expresses it, *ἐγὼ ἐν αὐτοῖς* (xvii. 23, 26)—they may be united in the One Godhead. Indeed that language proves the consubstantiality of the Three Persons. *Men* are not different natures from each other; they are all of one blood (Acts xvii. 26), of one substance,—being all from Adam and Eve. If the Son is inferior in nature to the Father, and different in substance from Him, the comparison could not have been made. The consubstantiality of all men, with a diversity of persons in each individual, and their union in God, is an apt illustration, as far as human things can be, of the true doctrine of the One Nature and Plurality of Persons in the Godhead."—OWEN: "Some refer this unity to one of purpose merely. But the context refers to *power*, as the attribute of the Father specially referred to. This shows that unity of power, rather than unity of purpose, is here predicated of the Father and Son. But a oneness of power—which with God is omnipotent power—involves the idea of a unity of being or essence, and shows that the Father and Son are essentially one. But even if a unity of will and purpose only is meant in the unity here spoken of, does not an absolute oneness in this respect presuppose essential unity? In either case, whether unity of power or purpose be intended, the passage teaches most clearly an essential unity of the Father and Son. The manifest design of the declaration is to prevent any misconception which arises from the fact, that the sheep are spoken of as being in the hand of both the Father and the Son. The question might arise, how, at one and the same time, they could be in the hand of two distinct beings, each so powerful that none could pluck them from their hand. The answer, simple, concise, and unmistakable, is that these Persons are one and the same in essence; and that so united are they in their essential being, that whoever claims the protection and care of one, has an equal demand upon that of the other. Hence there was nothing strange in the assertion, that the sheep were in His hand, and also in that of His Father. That this is the great argument of the passage, seems too plain to be for a moment questioned. To claim that a mere unity of will and purpose, aside from an essential unity of being, meets the requisitions of this declaration, when considered in relation to the context so clear and well defined, is as absurd as to say that two persons may have distinct and personal possession of a thing at one and the same time, merely because there exists between them a unity of will and purpose. That essential unity is here intended is clear, not only, as we have shown, from the scope of the passage, which requires something more than oneness of purpose, but also from the following context, and especially ver. 38, where the mutual indwelling of the Father and Son is expressly declared, in terms which admit of no other interpretation, than as referring to the mysterious and ineffable union taught so clearly in the passage before us. The numeral *one* is the Greek neuter, the idea of essence and not of personality being predominant. Had the masculine form been employed, it would have been *I and My Father are one person*, which would involve an untruth and an absurdity."—P. S.]

7. *The authority of Holy Scripture.* Be it observed that Christ by His quotation also reminded the unjust judges who stood opposed to Him of the threat in the Psalm cited: *ye shall die.*

8. Foretokens of the doctrine of the divinity of Christ in the Old Testament. Whom the Father hath sanctified, *i. e.*, really consecrated by the anointing of the Spirit (after Ps. ii.), in antithesis to the typical consecrations under the Old Covenant.

9. *The majestic escapes and flights of Christ.*

HOMILETICAL AND PRACTICAL.

The Jewish dedication of the temple: 1. In respect of its noble destination, 2. in respect of its degeneracy, 3. in respect of its terrible end in our text.—The degeneration of Christian church dedications. Its gradation: 1. The church is glorified more than Christ its Lord; 2. the festival is more a cause of rejoicing than the church; 3. attempts are finally made to cast out the Lord as the disturber of this joy.—Nevertheless, church dedication, as the birth-day feast of individual congregations of the Reformation, has the qualities of a delightful festival.—Christ suddenly surrounded by enemies in Solomon's porch: provocative of a query as to the whereabouts of His friends.—Hindrances of Christians from the public assembling around the Lord, a measure of their fervor and faithfulness: 1. Wind and weather; 2. amusements; 3. contagious example.—Enemies around! The ever fresh experience of the always victorious Christ.—How long dost thou make us to doubt? or the wicked, temptatious ambiguity of the Jews' question: 1. The old and fading desire that He might become a Christ in their sense; 2. the ever new and ever higher blazing enmity unto death.—Christ's presence of mind at the moment when He sees Himself surrounded by enemies: 1. In His cautious and yet decided reply to their question, vers. 25-28; 2. in the calm and triumphant answer and threat, vers. 31, 32; 3. in the profound and yet clear response to their charge of heresy, vers. 34-38; 4. in the majestic answer in deed to their attempt, vers. 39, 40.—The import of Christ's answer, ver. 25 ff.: I am not a Christ in your sense, but the Christ in the name of the Father. —They do not know the Shepherd because they are not His sheep.—The word of Christ concerning His sheep a presentation of their cordial reciprocal conduct: 1. He is their Shepherd; they hear His voice; 2. He knows them; they follow Him; 3. He gives them eternal life; they do not perish; 4. He keeps them securely in His hand; they rest safely through Him in the Father's hand.—The great word of Christ: I and the Father are one—how it holds good: 1. Of His work of redemption in the life of His people and in the world; 2. of His redemptive impulse and His consciousness; 3. of His divine essence in the eternity of God.—"Ye are gods," or the presages in the Old Testament of the doctrine of the divinity of Christ.—"The Scripture cannot be broken." In particular not in its testimony to Christ. Christ sanctified by the Father; this, to a comprehender of the Old Testament, presented the following meaning: consecrated and anointed by the Holy Ghost as the real Messiah, in accordance with Ps. ii.; Is. lxi. 1.

The fearful contradictions in the conduct of fanatical passion: 1. First flattering, hypocritical questions, then murderous threats and assaults; 2. first the stoning, then the accusation; 3. first the charge of blasphemy, then the proposal of investigation (wished to take Him).—The charge of blasphemy brought against the Lord by the Jews, on account of the holy revelation of His divine consciousness of being one with the Father.

The three great vouchers for the divinity of Christ: 1. The Scriptures; 2. His works; 3. the direct impression of His personality.—The separation between the friends and enemies of Christ.

The retreat of Christ into Peræa a prelude to the flight of the Christians into Peræa before the destruction of Jerusalem.—Peræa, or the mountain sanctuaries of the Church of Christ (in the Piedmontese mountains, the mountains of Bohemia, the Cevennes, the Scottish hills, the mountains of Switzerland.—But principally in spiritual hill-countries, or in a popular life in which the heights of spirituality and the depths of simplicity and humility are united).—The believers of Peræa, or how John's work revives, glorified, in the work of Christ.—The flights of Christ lay the foundation for the refuge of sinners.

Starke: *Nova. Bibl. Tub.*: Church dedication an old but abused custom.—Zeisius: A Christian can, in pursuance of his Saviour's example, with a good conscience observe those festivals which, though instituted by men, have a single aim to the glory of God and the edification of the Church.—Quesnel: The walks of our Saviour are not idle ones, *etc.*—The concourse of many men even to a holy place is not invariably an indication of zeal for learning.—As Christ proved by His works that He is the Messiah and Son of God, so shouldest thou prove by thy works that thou art a Christian and a child of God.—Zeisius: Believers may be entirely certain of the divine favor and of their salvation in this world and the next, Rom. viii. 31-39.—Cramer: Steadfastness in the faith does not rest in human strength, but we are by the grace of God preserved unto salvation.—The hand of the Father is God's omnipotence.—*Ibid.*: The Father is one Person, the Son is another, and yet Father and Son are not divided but are one in substance. See the mystery of the Holy Trinity.—Holy Scripture is the sword wherewith we may strike our adversaries.—On ver. 35. Magistrates are indued by God Himself with a lofty title; hence they must not be despised, but honored.—Majus: Christ goes from one place to another with His Gospel.—*Ibid.*: Yet truth triumphs finally.—Zeisius: Godly meditation upon the strange and wonderful things that formerly came to pass in this or that place, may be a powerful incentive to repentance and faith.

Gerlach: He and the Father are not εἷς, one Person, but ἕν, one divine Being.—Lisco: Since He (the Father) is greater, mightier than all, than all hostile powers, Christ's friends are *safe* under the protection and guidance of the Almighty, nay, safe under the protection of both (Father and Son).—It is only malefactors that are usually persecuted; why then do ye persecute Me, who have conferred only benefits upon you?—Braune: He believes the *works*, who through them experiences suggestions and presentiments of the divine in Jesus; he believes

Jesus, who knows that God is truly in Him.—GOSSNER: *If Thou be Christ, tell us plainly.*—*Ye are not of My sheep:* ye are *in* the Church, but not *of* the Church.—*I know My sheep.* The whole world may judge them as it will; He knows what to think of them.—*My sheep follow Me.* It is the magnet of love, that draws and drives, voluntarily on both sides.—ETERNAL LIFE.—Who can resist the hand of the Almighty or despoil it of anything? How sweetly and securely, then, may we repose in His hand!—The salvation of the chosen sheep of Christ stands firm, for 1. they belong to Christ, from whom no violence can ravish anything; 2. they are the gift of the Father, a gift of infinite love, presented by Him to His Son; 3. they are an irrevocable gift that can never be taken back; 4. they are the gift of a Father who is mightier and greater than all creatures.—To their stony reply He makes a right loving rejoinder.—As they caught up stones, He once more laid hold of their hearts.—Can it be wondered at, that the holiest truths we preach are railed at as errors and fanaticism, when Jesus Christ Himself was treated as a blasphemer because He spake the truth?—On ver. 37. A ghostly-man must be ghostly-minded, a Christian must have the mind of Christ, a child of God must be godly-minded; they must lead lives spiritual, Christian, and worthy of God, or make no professions so to live.—*He escaped out of their hands*, but they shall not escape Him.—He stays as long as He can,—until they begin stoning Him, until He finds everything walled up and petrified.

HEUBNER: The Church is permitted [within proper limits] to institute festivals in commemoration of great benefits from the Lord (Festival of the Reformation; Days of Prayer and Humiliation, of Thanksgiving).—Ver. 23. He who here walked in a porch was more than all the Peripatetics and Stoics.—Jesus reveals Himself only to still and deep souls.—Many scoff at the figure: "Sheep, Flock of Jesus." O were they but sensible of the warmth and tenderness of that love which chose the figure!—A believer must lose his faith in Jesus before he can be torn away from Him.—The enemy can disperse and scatter outward societies but not the confederation of hearts. — Ver. 33. They themselves were the blasphemers.—Ver. 41. *John did no miracles.* In this very thing Jesus was to have the preeminence over John. — Ver. 42. Thus John's preaching is working even to this day.

SCHLEIERMACHER: Art thou the Christ? No doubt they said as did others: Never man did such miracles before, *etc.;* but because they found in Him no food for their carnal natures, no encouragement for their lust of outward distinctions among men, their souls were kept in suspense: they wavered and fluctuated between faith and unbelief,—nothing firm took form in them. Hence *they demanded only the letter and hoped for good from it.* (All their fanatical claims, however, were attached to the letter; they held that if Jesus were the Messiah, He must be a Messiah in their sense of the term, *opposed as that sense was to the divine Word*).—But why did the Redeemer keep from them this trifling gift of the letter? In the first place, He would permit nothing to turn Him from the path on which He had once entered; secondly, the time was approaching when (at a formal trial) the Lord should hear this same question from those who, as the spiritual superiors of the people, deriving their superiority from the gradual conformation of time, had a right to demand of Him the decisive letter. So for that occasion He reserved it. Then that letter, being in the right place, also possessed the highest fulness of *spirit* and *life.*

[CRAVEN: From CHRYSOSTOM: Ver. 30. *I and My Father are one;* this is added that we may not suppose that the Father protects while *He* is too weak to do so.—Vers. 34, 35. Our Lord did not correct the Jews as if they misunderstood His speech, but confirmed and defended it in the very sense in which they had taken it.—Vers. 39, 40. Christ after discoursing on some high truth commonly retired immediately, to give time to the fury of the people to abate.—From AUGUSTINE: Vers. 27-29. Of these sheep, 1. the *wolf* robbeth none, 2. the *thief* taketh none, 3. the *robber* killeth none.—Ver. 30. *We* are *one;* what *He* is, that am *I*, in respect of *essence*, not of *relation.*—Vers. 34, 35. If men by partaking of the word of God are made gods, much more is the Word, of which they partake, God.—From THEOPHYLACT: Ver. 41. Our Lord often brings His people into solitary places, thus ridding them of the society of the unbelieving, for their furtherance in the faith.—Christ departs from Jerusalem, *i. e., the Jewish people*, and goes to a place where are springs of water, *i. e., the Gentile church* [?].—From ALCUIN: *They follow Me*—1. *here*, by walking in gentleness and innocence, 2. *hereafter*, by entering into the joys of eternal life.—From ZELLER: Ver. 27. Hear *My voice;* one may hear the *words* of the Lord without submitting to His *voice;* the *voice* of the Lord is the spiritually quickening influence of His words upon the heart.—From BURKITT: Ver. 24. The subtlety of Christ's enemies, expressing earnest desire for information that they might entrap.—Ver. 25. The wisdom and caution of Jesus: He, 1. (refuses a direct answer, E. R. C.), 2. refers to His miracles.—Ver. 26. The true cause of infidelity, 1. not obscurity of doctrine, but 2. not having the properties of Christ's sheep.—Ver. 27. All Christ's sheep follow Him in His, 1. doctrine, 2. example.—Ver. 28. *Eternal life* is, 1. the portion of Christ's sheep, 2. the gift of Christ, 3. *now* given to the sheep, in (1) purchase, (2) promise, (3) first fruits.—Ver. 32. Such was the perfect innocence of Christ that He dared appeal to the consciences of His most inveterate adversaries.—From HENRY: If Wisdom's sayings appear doubtful, the fault is not in the *object*, but in the *eye.*—Vers. 24, 25. The Jews pretended that they only *doubted*, Christ declared that they *did not believe; skepticism* in religion is no better than *infidelity.*—Ver. 26. *Ye are not of My sheep, i. e.*, ye are not 1. *disposed* to be My followers, 2. *designed* to be My followers.—Vers. 27-29. Jesus described concerning His sheep, their—1. *gracious disposition*, they (1) hear His voice, (2) follow Him; 2. *happy state*, He (1) takes cognizance of them, (2) has provided happiness for them (*a*) eternal life, (*b*) freely bestowed, (3) has undertaken for their *security* and *preservation.*—Ver. 37. Christ does not require a blind and implicit faith, nor an assent to His divine mission further than He gave proof of it.—Ver. 39. The *flight* of Jesus, 1. not an inglorious retreat, but 2. a glorious retirement. He *escaped*, 1. not because He was afraid to suffer, but 2. because His hour was not come, ch. viii. 30.—Ver. 40. Though persecutors may drive Christ and His gospel out of *their city*, they cannot drive Him or it out of *the world*.—Ver. 41. The result of John's ministry after his death; the success of the word preached not confined to the life of the preacher. —Ver. 42. Where the preaching of *repentance* has had success, there the preaching of gospel-grace is most likely to be prosperous.—From BARNES: Ver. 29. It is implied that God will so control *all* other *beings* and *things* as that they shall be safe.—Vers. 28, 29. We are taught concerning Christians that—1. they are given by the Father to Christ, 2. Christ gives to them *eternal life, i. e.*, (1) *procures* by His *death* and *intercession*, and (2) *imparts* by His Spirit, that religion which results in eternal life, 3. both the Father and the Son are pledged to keep them, 4. there is no power in man or devil to defeat Christ's purpose.—Vers. 39-42. The opposition of the wicked resulted in the increased success of the cause they persecuted.—From RYLE: Ver. 26. "*My* sheep" indicates the close connection between Christ and believers; they are His, 1. by gift from the Father, 2. by purchase, 3. by choice and calling, 4. by their own consent.—Believers are called *sheep*, because they are, 1. helpless and dependent on their Shepherd, 2. harmless, 3. foolish and liable to go astray [?].—Ver. 27. Christ *knows* His people with, 1. approbation, 2. interest, 3. affection.—Ver. 28. Christ, 1. often withholds worldly prosperity, 2. never fails to give *eternal life, i. e.*, (1) grace, (2) peace, (3) glory.—Ver. 35. The high honor Christ puts on the Scriptures.—Vers. 37, 38. The importance Christ attached to His miracles.]

II.

ANTITHESIS BETWEEN THE BELIEVING AND THE UNBELIEVING JEWS OF JUDEA AND JERUSALEM AT THE GRAVE OF LAZARUS. CHRIST, IN CONSEQUENCE OF HIS RAISING OF LAZARUS FROM THE DEAD, HIMSELF DEVOTED TO DEATH. SYMBOLISM OF DAY'S WORK AND OF SLEEP. THE RESURRECTION FROM THE DEAD.

CHAP. XI. 1—57.

A. *Christ's death-bringing journey to Bethany to raise His friend from the dead. Symbolism of day-life and night-life. Symbolism of sleep.*

(VERS. 1—16.)

1 Now [But] a certain *man* was sick, *named* Lazarus, of [from] Bethany, the town
2 of Mary and her sister Martha. (It was *that* [the] Mary which [who afterwards]
anointed the Lord with ointment, and wiped his feet with her hair, whose brother
3 Lazarus was sick.) Therefore his sisters sent unto him, saying, Lord, behold he
4 whom thou lovest is sick. When Jesus heard *that*, he said [And Jesus hearing it,
said], This sickness is not unto death, but for the glory of God, that the Son of
God might [may] be glorified thereby.
5, 6 Now Jesus loved Martha, and her sister, and Lazarus. When he had heard
therefore [When therefore he heard] that he was sick, he abode two days still in
the same place where he was [he then remained in the place where he was, two
7 days]. Then after that saith he [Then after this he saith] to *his* [the] disciples, Let
8 us go into Judea again. *His* [The] disciples say unto him, Master, the Jews of late
sought [just now were seeking, νῦν ἐζήτουν] to stone thee; and goest thou thither
9 again? Jesus answered, Are there not twelve hours in the day? If any man
10 walk in the day, he stumbleth not, because he seeth the light of this world. But
11 if a man walk in the night, he stumbleth, because there is no light in him. These
things said he: and after that [this] he saith unto them, our friend Lazarus sleep-
12 eth [hath fallen asleep]; but I go that I may awake him out of sleep. Then said
his disciples [The disciples therefore said to him][1], Lord, if he sleep [hath fallen
13 asleep] he shall do well [become whole, recover][2]. Howbeit Jesus spake [But
Jesus had spoken] of his death: but they thought that he had spoken of taking
of rest in sleep [he was speaking of the rest of sleep, περὶ τῆς κοιμήσεως τοῦ ὕπνου][3].
14 Then [Then therefore, τότε οὖν] said Jesus unto them plainly, Lazarus is dead.
15 And I am glad for your sakes that I was not there, to the intent ye may believe;
16 nevertheless let us go unto him. Then said Thomas, which [who] is called Didy-
mus [*i. e.* twin child], unto his fellow-disciples, Let us also go, that we may die
with him.

TEXTUAL AND GRAMMATICAL.

[1] Ver. 12.—Lachmann αὐτῷ οἱ μαθηταί in accordance with Codd. D. K.; Tischendorf simply αὐτῷ in accordance with Cod. A. *etc.*; according to Meyer, the latter might be the original reading. [In ed. viii. Tischend. reads, with Cod. Sin.: εἶπον οὖν αὐτῷ οἱ μαθηταί. (Cod. Sin. εἶπαν). So also Westcott and Hort. Alford brackets οἱ μαθηταί, but retains αὐτῷ.—P. S.]

[2] Ver. 12.—[Lange inserts the gloss: without our making a perilous journey thither.—P. S.]

[3] Ver. 13.—[Or "of the taking of rest in sleep," or "of taking rest in sleep."—P. S.]

EXEGETICAL AND CRITICAL.

In the raising of Lazarus from the dead, the most stupendous of the revivifying (quickening) miracles of Jesus, we see at once the ultimate occasion of His death, and the first foreshadowing of His resurrection. Bayle relates of Spinoza [the Jewish philosopher]: "*On m'a assuré qu'il disait à ses amis, que s'il eût pu se persuader la résurrection de Lazare, il aurait brisé en pièces tout son système et aurait embrassé sans répugnance la foi ordinaire des chrétiens.*" [*Dict.* art. *Spinoza*].*

The special plea of modern criticism against the reality of this miracle is the silence of the Synoptists. This fact may be explained: 1. By the character of the Gospels, each one of which being a particular view of the life of Jesus, uses only such historical matter as suits its total; 2. by historical circumstances which made it seem advisable to the Synoptists, who wrote earlier, to omit from their records the history of the family of Bethany, probably in order to avoid attracting to it the attention of Jewish fanatics in Jerusalem (see *Leben Jesu*, II. 2, p. 1132);† 3. by the preponderance of Galilean tradition in the Synoptists, which may well be connected with the fact that a great portion of this tradition was derived from narratives of the life of Jesus addressed by the earlier disciples of Galilee to the later disciples at Jerusalem. We have proof in the writings of the Synoptists that they were well aware of the frequent sojourn of Jesus at Jerusalem; Matt. xxiii. 37; Luke x. 38.‡

* ["I have been assured that he would say to his friends: If he could have convinced himself of the resurrection of Lazarus, he would have dashed to pieces his entire system [of pantheism] and embraced without repugnance the common faith of Christians." This is sound reasoning. If Christ could raise the dead to life, it was an easy task for Him to heal the sick, and to command the powers of nature, and He must have been truly the Son of God. This miracle was a fulfilment of what He said concerning His person as the Fountain of life, and a prophecy of His resurrection. It contains, as then for the family of Lazarus, the disciples and friends of Jesus, so now and for all time, the most solid comfort, and effectually disperses the gloom and terror of the grave.—P. S.]

† [According to tradition (Epiph. *Hær.* 66) Lazarus lived thirty years after his resurrection and died sixty years old. But the Gospels were probably written after the year 60. Epiphanius, Grotius, Herder, Olshausen, Bäumlein, Godet and Wordsworth agree with Lange in explaining the silence of the Synoptists from a prudential regard to the surviving family of Lazarus, but Meyer (ed. 5th, p. 439) and Alford (*Proleg.*, p. 15) reject this supposition, because such concealment was alien from the spirit and character of the Evangelists, and because the Gospels and Epistles were at first not published to the world at large, but to believing communities. Meyer explains the omission from the plan of the Synoptists who confined themselves to the Galilean activity of Jesus till His solemn entry into Jerusalem (Matt. xxi. and parallels), while John, omitting the Galilean miracles of the raising of the daughter of Jairus and the widow's son from the dead, describes the resurrection miracle which took place in Judea.—P. S.]

‡ [Cyril remarks that the resurrection of Lazarus furnishes the true explanation of the plaudits and hosannas of our Lord's triumphal entry into Jerusalem as described by the Synoptists.—P. S.]

[The narrative is divided into three parts: (1) The preparation, which is ruled by the idea of death, 1-16; (2) The raising of Lazarus, or the triumph of life over death, 17-44; (3) The effect, (*a*) the positive effect: confirmation of the faith of the disciples, 45; (*b*) the negative effect: exciting the opposition of the Sanhedrin to deadly hatred, 47-57.—The miracle carries its own evidence to every fair and unprejudiced mind. But as the performance of it was a moral test to the Jews, so is its narrative to the readers and critics: a savor of life and a source of comfort to believers, a stumbling-block to unbelievers. There are four false theories, opposed to the true one: 1. The RATIONALISTIC view of a raising from a trance, in spite of the ἤδη ὄζει, ver. 39! (Paulus, Gabler, Ammon, Kern, Schweizer, modified by Gfrörer and Weisse). 2. The MYTHICAL hypothesis of an unconscious poem of the primitive Christian fancy. (Strauss, in his large "Life of Jesus," while in his new *Leben Jesu*, p. 476 ff., he represents the historic Lazarus of John as a free fiction of the fourth Evangelist based upon the parabolic Lazarus of Luke.) 3. The theory of a conscious SYMBOLICAL OR ALLEGORICAL representation of the death-conquering glory of Christ and His disciples. (Baur, Weizsäcker). 4. The infamous hypothesis of a downright IMPOSTURE or pious fraud, an intrigue of the family of Bethany, to which Jesus lent Himself as an instrument with the view to make an impression upon the unbelieving Jews. (Renan, *Vie de Jésus*, p. 359 f.). All these theories owe their origin to a disbelief in the supernatural. They neutralize each other and explain nothing at all. The only alternative is: historic truth, or dishonest fiction. The historic truth is abundantly attested by the simplicity, vivacity and circumstantiality of the narrative, the four days in the tomb (ver. 39), and the good sense and moral honesty—to say the very least—of Lazarus and his sisters, the Evangelist and Christ Himself.—P. S.]

Ver. 1. **But there was a certain man sick.**—The δέ indicates that Jesus' stay in Peræa was terminated by the sickness and death of Lazarus.

Lazarus, from Bethany.—The designation of Lazarus: *from* Bethany [ἀπό, like ἐκ, denotes descent, or, as here, residence], as also the designation of Bethany, as **the town of Mary and Martha her sister** (comp. ch. i. 44), presupposes the acquaintance of the readers with the family of Bethany, and places Mary, as the most prominent personality of the group, in the foreground. After her, mention is made of Martha, as her sister; after both, Bethany is designated; after Bethany, Lazarus.

BETHANY on the Mount of Olives, distinct from the Bethany beyond Jordan, in the environs of which Jesus is now, probably, again abiding (see ch. i. 28), is distant three-quarters of an hour [about two miles] from Jerusalem, in a south-easterly direction, on the other [eastern] side of the Mount of Olives, over whose southern portion the road leads. From its situation on the declivity of the mountain, Simonis thus construes it: בֵּית עֲנִיָּה, *locus depressionis, Low Borough, Valley Borough;* with more probability, however, Lightfoot, Reland and others hold that it derives its name from its date-palms: בֵּית הִינֵי, *locus dactylorum, House of Dates, Date Borough* (see the palm-entry, Matt. xxi.).* In the history of the Passion, Bethany appears as a peaceful refuge for the Lord from hostile Jerusalem; Matt. xxi. 17; xxvi. 6, *etc.*†

[Bethany is never mentioned in the Old Testament or the Apocrypha, and is known to us only from the New Testament, but possesses an unusual charm as the place where more than in any other Jesus loved to dwell and to enjoy domestic life. There was a house of peace with three children of peace, where the Prince of Peace went in and out as a friend. There He received the hospitable attentions of busy Martha, and commended the contemplative Mary (Luke x. 38 ff.); there He performed His greatest miracle on their brother Lazarus, and proved Himself to be the Resurrection and the Life; there Mary anointed Him against the day of His burial; from Bethany He commenced His triumphant entry into Jerusalem; to Bethany He resorted for the rest of the night during the few days before His crucifixion; and near this village He loved so well, He ascended to heaven. At present it is a poor, wretched mountain hamlet of some twenty families, and is called, from Lazarus, *El-Azarîyeh* (by Robinson) or *El-Lazarieh* (according to Lord Lindsay and Stanley); the traditional sites of the house and tomb of Lazarus are still shown. Stanley and Grove give a very unfavorable account; but Bonar and Lindsay describe the *situation* of Bethany, as viewed from a distance, as "remarkably beautiful," "the perfection of retirement and repose," "of seclusion and lovely peace." It is no doubt with Bethany as with Jerusalem and Palestine generally: it is a mere shadow of the past, a scene of desolation and death; yet not without traces of former glory, and not without hope of a future resurrection.—P. S.]

Ver. 2. **It was the Mary who** (afterwards) **anointed the Lord with ointment,** *etc.*—John supposes the history of the anointing to be familiar through the evangelical tradition; and this trait shows the vividness and copiousness of that tradition and at the same time the historical character of this Gospel. In the next chapter he proceeds to relate the history of the anointing itself [as required by the course of his narrative]. The evangelist designs here to bring into view the friendly relation existing between Jesus and the brother and sisters of Bethany, in explanation of the following history. Comp. Com. on *Matthew*, chap. xxvi.; *Luke*, chap. x. Touching the vast difference between Mary of Bethany and the great sinner or Mary Magdalene, comp. the Art. *Maria Magdalena* in Herzog's *Real-Encyklopædia* [vol. ix. p. 102 ff.].* On the character of the two sisters comp. the Com. on *Luke*, chap. x.† Hengstenberg's romance founded upon the story of the family of Bethany, is well known.

[Hengstenberg devotes twenty-six pages of his Commentary on John (vol. ii. pp. 198-224) to prove that Lazarus of Bethany whom the Lord raised from the dead, is none other than the poor Lazarus of the parable, and that Mary of Bethany is the same with the unnamed sinner who washed the Saviour's feet with her tears of repentance (Luke vii. 36 ff.) and with Mary Magdalene (Luke viii. 2). In the former he is original; in the latter he follows the tradition of the Latin church which identified the two or three Marys, down to recent times when it was rightly opposed by several Roman Catholic as well as Protestant divines. Out of the scattered hints of the Gospels Hengstenberg, with more ingenuity than sound judgment and good taste, weaves the following religious novel, which is worthy of a place in a Romish legendary. Mary, originally of Magdala, a village on the western coast of the lake of Galilee, near the city of Tiberias, led a disreputable life, but was converted to Christ, who expelled from her seven devils, *i. e.*, her wild passions, and gave her rest and peace. She clung to Him with boundless devotion and followed Him on His journeys in Galilee (Luke viii. 2) and to Judea. While the Lord labored

* [Stanley (*Sinai and Pal.*, p. 144) agrees with this last derivation, but admits that even then the palm tree was probably rarely found on the high land in Palestine. The olive and fig now only remain. Arnold (art. *Bethania* in Herzog's *Encycl.*, II. p. 116) derives the name from the Chaldee or Aramæan בֵּית עֲנִיָא, *domus miseri, House of the afflicted* (comp. Buxt. *Lex. Chald.* col. 631 sq.). Origen and Theophylact call it οἶκος ὑπακοῆς, as if related to עָנָה, *respondit, exaudivit, i. e.*, where the prayer of the needy is heard and answered.—P. S.]

† With respect to the Bethany of the present day, see Notes on *Matt.*, ch. xxi.; Art. B. in Winer [Smith, Kitto and others], the books of Eastern travel; the legends on Lazarus see in Thilo, *Cod. Apocr.*, p. 711; Fabric. *Cod. Apocr.*, III., p. 475. On the name of Lazarus see Com. on *Luke* xvi. 20 [p. 254, Am. Ed., also art. Lazarus in Smith's *Dict.*—P. S.]

* [The Roman tradition (since Tertullian, *De pudic.* 11), contrary to its usual habit of multiplying scriptural personalities, identifies Mary of Bethany with Mary of Magdala and the unnamed sinful woman who anointed the Saviour's feet (Luke vii. 37 ff.), although Irenæus, Origen and Chrysostom clearly distinguish them. To account for the difference of locality, it was arbitrarily assumed that Mary of Bethany in Judea had a country-seat at Magdala in Galilee. But the anointing recorded by Luke (vii.), differs as to time, place and character from the anointing in Bethany (Matt. xxvi.; Mark xiv.; John xii.). The superstitious Pope Gregory I. gave his sanction to this hypothesis of the identity of the three Marys, so that it even passed into the service of the Roman Breviary for July 22d and several mediæval hymns, *e. g.*, one *de S. Maria Magdalena* (in Daniel's *Thesaurus hymnol.* tom. I. p. 221):

> "*Lauda, mater ecclesia,*
> *Lauda Christi clementiam,*
> *Qui septem purgat vitia*
> *Per septiformem gratiam.*
>
> "*Maria, soror Lazari,*
> *Quæ tot commisit crimina,*
> *Ab ipsa fauce tartari*
> *Redit ad vitæ limina,*" *etc.*

Comp. other hymns on Mary Magdalene in Mone, *Lat. Hymnen des Mittelalters*, vol. II. pp. 415-425. On all points of exegesis and criticism the Romish traditions are worth very little or nothing at all.—P. S.]

† [Martha represents the active, practical, Mary the contemplative, passive, type of piety. They are related to each other as Peter and John among the apostles. Romish asceticism has perverted Mary into a nun and abused the eulogy of the Lord, Luke x. 42 ("Mary hath chosen the good part") for an overestimate of monastic seclusion from the world and its daily duties.—P. S.]

in and around Jerusalem she resided at Bethany in the house or country-seat of her sister Martha, who had married a rich but low-minded Pharisee, Simon the Leper. Here she anointed the Lord and wiped His feet with the tears of repentance, six days before His passion (Luke vii., which is assumed to be the same with the scene described John xii.) Her brother Lazarus, after a similar life of dissipation and consequent poverty, resorted also to the protection of Martha and lived off the parsimonious charity of his brother-in-law. He is the beggar at the gate of "the rich man who was clothed in purple and fine linen and fared sumptuously every day" (Luke xvi. 19 ff.). He died, was buried, and carried to Abraham's bosom, but was raised again by Christ, to which an allusion may be found in the parable (ver. 31, "though one rose from the dead"). Mary and Lazarus were so dearly loved by Him, not on account of their virtuous and lovely character, but as striking examples of the power of redeeming grace. They illustrate His saying that it is easier for publicans and sinners to enter the kingdom than for righteous Pharisees.—The grounds for this strange combination are the identity of names (Lazarus of the parable—the only name mentioned in any parable of the New Testament—and Lazarus of Bethany; Mary Magdalene and Mary of Bethany), and the similarity of the anointing scene related by Luke, ch. vii. 36 ff., and the one described by John, ch. xii. 3, as well as Matthew, ch. xxii. 3 ff.; and Mark xiv. 3. But the differences of locality (Magdala and Bethany), of time (the beginning and the close of Christ's ministry), and of circumstances, in the anointing scenes, are sufficient to neutralize the superficial appearance of identity. Besides, there are strong arguments against Hengstenberg's hypothesis. 1. Luke's Gospel which is constructed on the chronological order (i. 3), can not be charged with such a glaring chronological mistake, as to place the anointing of Christ in Bethany in the first year of Christ's ministry, when according to Matthew, Mark and John it occurred only six days before His passion and had special reference to His near burial. 2. Luke, in introducing Mary of Bethany in ch. x. 39, gives no intimation that she was the unnamed sinner of ch. vii. or the Mary Magdalene whom he had already honorably mentioned in ch. viii. 2; nor does John give any hint of such identity when he introduces Mary Magdalene in ch. xix. 25. To explain this fact, Hengstenberg (p. 208) resorts to the far-fetched conjecture of intentional concealment of the identity from family considerations and apprehensions of abuse. 3. If Lazarus lived in miserable dependence on a mean brother-in-law, it would have been cruel to call him back from Paradise. 4. There is an intrinsic improbability, as urged already by Origen and Chrysostom, that Jesus should have selected for His special friendship persons whose former lives were stained by gross impurity.—The view of Hengstenberg has been generally rejected by German commentators, but Bishop Wordsworth (on John xi. 1), without mentioning his name, seems to adopt it as far as the identity of the Lazarus of the parable and the Lazarus of the miracle is concerned. He finds in the parable a prophecy of the miracle, in the latter a fulfilment of the former. Godet (II. 320) aptly says of Hengstenberg's dissertation that it only proves the facility with which a man of learning and acumen can prove any thing he *wants* to prove.—But while we must utterly reject the identification of the two Lazaruses, it is quite possible that the Lazarus of John xi. was either a son or a brother-in-law of Simon the Pharisee. An article in Smith's *Dict.* (vol. II., p. 1614) identifies him with the young and rich ruler who came to Jesus and was loved by Him, Matt. xix.; Mark x.; Luke xviii. 8, but this conjecture is without proof and contrary to the chronological order of events. The traditions concerning the later life of Lazarus and his labors in Marseilles, where he is said to have founded a church and suffered martyrdom, are worthless. The ecclesiastical applications of the name of Lazarus (*Knights of St. Lazarus, lazaretto, lazar-house, lazzarone*) are derived from the Lazarus of the parable and connected with the etymology (Lazarus=לֹא עֵזֶר, *auxilio destitutus, no help, helpless,* or better=לְעָזָר, abridged from אֶלְעָזָר, *Eliazar, Deus auxilium,* the German *Gotthilf*). The *Lazarists*, a French Society of missionary priests, were named after Lazarus of Bethany (from the College of St. Lazarus in Paris which they acquired in 1632).—P. S.]

Ver. 3. **Lord, behold, he whom Thou lovest is sick.**—If we read in these words the indirect expression of a *positive entreaty* that Jesus would come, possibly we overlook the situation of the parties. It is as evident to the sisters in Bethany as to the disciples that imminent peril of death threatens the Lord in Jerusalem and its surrounding country. We are not warranted in assuming that they rated the sickness of their brother higher than the deadly peril impending over Jesus. In fact, in their very appreciation of His danger we read the explanation of their tender message in its delicate historicalness. They give emphasis to their communication thus: *whom Thou lovest;* it is the expression of an ardent, heart-felt desire wherewith they inform Him of what may happen. [ὃν φιλεῖς is more solicitous of help than the mere name, and yet more modest than "who loves Thee," or the designation of "friend," as the Lord in His condescending love calls Lazarus, ver. 11.—P. S.]

Ver. 4. **Jesus hearing it said** [εἶπεν] **This sickness,** *etc.*—[Alford: "The only right understanding of this answer, and our Lord's whole proceeding here is,—*that He knew and foresaw all from the first,*—as well the termination of Lazarus's sickness and his being raised again, as the part which this miracle would bear in bringing about the close of His own ministry."—P. S.] In the lack of ἀπεκρίνατο (replied) there is no warrant for the assumption that these words did not form part of a message sent to the sisters, although they were addressed to the disciples also. It was, in reality, His prophetic utterance concerning the entire sickness.—**Is not unto death** [πρὸς θάνατον].—The expression was an ambiguous one and involved a trial of faith for the sisters. They might thus understand it: The sickness will not result in death, will not be fatal; and to this interpretation the rest of the sentence might seem to point: **for the glory of God,** *etc.* From these words it was possible to draw the inference that Jesus would at all events preserve Lazarus from death; perhaps by an exercise of healing power from afar. But this was not His meaning. The certainty and the necessity of the death of Lazarus were manifest to Him from the beginning; He foreknew also that He should raise him from the dead. In this sense, therefore, we are to understand His words: The end and aim of this sickness is not death, but the glorification of God by a raising of the dead, which shall also glorify the Son of God.* Therein lay a trial of faith for the sisters (Brenz, Neander). A human instrumentality in order to the divine awakening of the dead was also thus ordained. The sick man and his sisters waited hopefully for the Lord even until the coming of death; then, if they would not be perplexed by the promise of Jesus (see ver. 40), on which their hopes were based, they must take refuge in the mysterious expression: to the glory of God. Not only does the text afford no ground for the supposition that a second message concerning the further progress of the malady was sent to the Lord, informing Him of the incorrectness of His favorable opinion (Paulus, Neander), but such a supposition is directly contrary to the text (see ver. 14).—**That the Son of God may be glorified thereby.**—This was the purpose of God. Not that God should be glorified by the glorification of Christ (Meyer), but that the glorifying of God through the miracle wrought in His name should also glorify the Son of God,—and this in a striking manner, in the presence of a great multitude and in the vicinity of Jerusalem. They who accused Him of working miracles by the power of Satan, should be witnesses to this astounding miracle, performed by Him after a solemn invocation of that God, whom they called their God and as the blasphemer of whom they denounced Him. It is noteworthy that after this fact He is no more charged with having a demon and working miracles by the assistance of Beelzebub. Christ's prayer to God at the grave of Lazarus was, however, introduced by the sending of the man who was born blind to the pool of Siloam, that being the property of the temple and of the God of the temple.

Ver. 5. **Now Jesus loved Martha, and her sister, and Lazarus.**—[*and—and*: happy family! Bengel.]—Reference of these words: 1. De Wette: Explanatory of ver. 3; 2. Meyer: explanatory of the consoling assurance contained in ver. 4; 3. Baumgarten-Crusius: preparatory to ver. 6. "Although He loved them all, He tarried." Why is Martha here the prominent person and Mary simply designated as *her sister?* Martha stood in peculiar need of a still greater trial of faith, of purification from her petty cares; and in order to these results, death must be felt in all its terrors and deliverance in all its rapture. In this sense Jesus loved her. Thus the connection with ver. 6 might also be expressed by a "*therefore,*" *etc.*

* [Alford: "It need hardly be remarked, with Olshausen and Trench, that the glorifying of the Son of God in Lazarus *himself* is subordinately implied. Men are not mere tools, but temples of God." Comp. ver. 15, *that ye may believe.*—P. S.]

But since the evangelist has not specified this connection more positively, room is left for both conjectures ("although" and "therefore"). The expression ἠγάπα, not ἐφίλει (as ver. 3), may not have been chosen solely "on account of the therewith mentioned sisters" (Meyer), but also on account of the loftily severe conduct of the love of Christ. [ἀγαπᾶν may be used of divine love, but φιλεῖν expresses human love and the personal relation of friendship. The relation of Jesus to the female sex exhibits a tenderness truly human with a purity and dignity truly divine. Comp. the remarks on p. 167.—P. S.]

Ver. 6. **When therefore he heard that he was sick, then (at that time), indeed, he remained two days.**—Τότε μέν [*tum quidem*, omitted in the E. V.]. The μέν leads us to expect a δέ after ἔπειτα, which has, however, been omitted in order that the conclusion of the sentence might appear independently in all its significance. Explanation of the delay of Jesus:

1. In order to test the faith of the interested parties (Olshausen after the ancients). This motive cannot be rejected as "inhuman arbitrariness" (Meyer). It was undoubtedly influential, although not exclusively so.

2. Jesus was detained in Peræa by important business (Lücke [Neander, Tholuck] and others.) Here, without doubt, we have the grand motive and the foundation of the previously mentioned one, for it would have been an utter impossibility for Jesus to remain two days away from Bethany in *inactivity.* Meyer objects to this explanation on the ground that nothing of the kind is stated in the text. But it is implied everywhere that Jesus was never inactive and that He had days' works, times (καιροί) and hours, appointed Him by God.

3. Meyer [and Alford]: The motive is indicated ver. 4: the glorification of God through the miracle. This was undoubtedly a final and supreme motive, one, however, that never stands alone; it is invariably associated with concrete, moral motives. Assuming this to be the sole motive, the delay of two days was totally unnecessary, since Lazarus had already been dead a long time.

Bretschneider and his followers have based their arguments against the authenticity of the history itself upon this delay, which they did not comprehend. We must further beware of the false idea that Jesus first suffered Lazarus to die, and then went to raise him from the dead. As Lazarus had already lain in the grave four days, when Jesus arrived at Bethany, he would (assuming the distance to have been a day's journey) have been two days in the grave, if Jesus had set out for Bethany immediately upon receiving the message. Hence He caused no fruitless waiting by the bedside of the sick man. The sisters had deferred sending the message to Jesus until Lazarus was at the point of death, because they knew the danger attending the return of the Saviour to Judea. *So fine a historical trait cannot have been invented.*

Two days.—On the great activity of Jesus in Peræa see the Com. on *Matthew.* He was to depart from a province in which there were many that believed on Him.

Ver. 7. **Let us go again into Judea** (from Peræa), *etc.*—He does not say, to Bethany. To

Judea, "to the land of unbelief and deadly enmity."* The πάλιν is doubtless indicative of the fact that Jesus had previously journeyed with the disciples from Peræa to Judea, to attend the feast of the consecration of the temple.

Ver. 8. **But just now† the Jews were seeking to stone Thee.**—Dissuading, in view of the obvious peril of death. In this connection the form of the message sent by the sisters is to be explained. These words, as well as ver. 16, prove that the disciples were not apprehensive as to their own safety merely, but that the Lord was the principal subject of their anxiety.

Ver. 9. **Are there not** (fully) **twelve hours,** *etc.?*—"In Palestine, where the days are of nearly equal duration, they are divided, the whole year through, into twelve hours." Gerlach.‡ Jesus probably uttered these words in the early morning, in view of the rising sun,§ just as the day was beginning; in like manner the words: I must work as long as it is day (ch. ix. 4), were spoken in face of the setting sun. In the first place, this was not said to allay the apprehensions of the disciples on their own account (Chrysostom, Neander); it had reference to the life-journey of the Lord Himself: Christ employs, however, such general terms, that the words are applicable to the life-journey of the disciples also. Under the figure of the *day*, the idea of the *life-day* of the individual and of the *day's work* appointed him is again presented, as in ch. ix. 4 f. Here, however, the God-given, fully meted out day of life is the main point. If there the meaning be: I must work with speed, for My day draweth near its close—there is but little time remaining—the twelve hours will soon be over; so here the signification is: I can still work without peril of death,—I can still make the journey thither,—My twelve hours are not yet at an end. The determination of the day to twelve hours has led Grotius and others to this explanation: Are there not *only* twelve hours—contrary to the sense of the figure, which portions out the *one* day into twelve assured sections. Lyra and Luther have discerned in the twelve hours the image of the changing moods of men: "the hearts of the Jews are fickle." This is at all events an import of minor weight and prominency. Entirely arbitrary and gratuitous is the interpretation of Augustine; according to him, the twelve hours are the twelve apostles, who must follow the Lord as the hours follow the sun.

But now arises the question, whether, by the twelve hours, Jesus intended to express simply His present safety from mortal peril, or whether He would intimate at the same time that, in the future, death was inevitably prepared for Him; that a time of suffering and death was impending, when He must desist from active work. That we are to understand Him as having reference to both facts, the subsequent sentence proves: *but if any man walk in the night, etc.* The one consideration does not exclude the other; on the contrary they form together a higher unity. To walk and to work as long as the assured day of life lasts, but after that, to rest, and not by wilful working in the night of suffering and death, to plunge into danger and ruin,—such is the teaching of the outward life-regimen, prescribed to us in the distinction of day and night.

But again, the expression, and particularly the "stumbling in the night" points to a still higher antithesis: as the day was made to symbolize the day of life, so the day of life becomes the symbol of duty and of heavenly light in divinely appointed duty; and the evening and night of life are an image of the darkness outside of duty. This was especially applicable to the disciples. Now, when the day of life was still assured to them, they would willingly have abstained from walking and working; but when the Saviour's night of suffering arrived, then they desired to walk and to act. Judas walked, stumbled, and fell into bottomless perdition; Peter walked, and fell after the most perilous fashion. I walk in the day, and as long as the day lasts, in perfect security; take care that ye do not now desire prematurely to rest, and then, at an unseasonable time, when the night has come, to walk.

Meyer admits only the former apprehension: "The working time appointed Me by God has not yet passed away; so long as this lasts, no man can prevail against Me; but when it has expired, I shall fall into the hands of My enemies, just as he who walks at night stumbles, because he is destitute of light" (and thus Apollinaris, Jansen [Maldonatus, Corn. a Lapide] and others). Tholuck apprehends in this the symbol of working as predominant over that of walking, with reference to the περιπατεῖν, which undoubtedly implies such an idea, because now the work of Jesus was a walking to Bethany; nevertheless, this is not the prevailing view; to warrant its adoption as such, another verb would be requisite. With the primary figure of the day of life, Lücke, after Melanchthon, has rightly connected the figure of the day of duty. Luthardt: "He who moves within the bounds of duty, does not stumble, makes no false steps, for the light of the world, *i. e.* the will of God, enlightens him; but he who walks, *i. e.* is active, outside of the limits of his vocation, will err in what he does, since not the will of God but his own pleasure is his guide." And still further, beyond even this second figure, has the spiritual interpretation of this saying been carried out. Chrysostom and others: The walking by day is that blameless conduct, wherein one has nought to fear; Erasmus and others: It is fellowship with Christ; De Wette: It is a pure, guiltless, clear course of action;—the twelve hours being the ways and means of activity, the night, deficiency in wisdom and integrity. All these considerations, however, are included in a just perception of the antithesis of day and night.

The great law of *physical* life: the day-time for walking and working, the night-time for resting and sleeping, is a symbol of the law of *moral*

* [Luthardt, Godet and Gumlich discover the same design in πάλιν. But it corresponds rather to the πάλιν πέραν τοῦ Ἰορδάνου in ch. x. 40.—P. S.]

† [νῦν with the imperfect ἐζήτουν refers to the recent past as being still present, x. 31. Kühner II. p. 385.—P. S.]

‡ [Alford thinks that the twelve-hour division was probably borrowed from Babylon, and refutes the view of Townson and others, that John adopts the so-called Asiatic method of reckoning time: see on ch. i. 40; iv. 6.—P. S.]

§ [So also Gumlich and Godet.—P. S.]

life: during the whole day of life to fulfil with joyous and fearless activity the whole duty, and then, in the night of suffering and death, to submit calmly to God's providence, and rest and cease from labor in Him. But this law of *moral* life is conditioned by that of *religious* life: to work in the day of the light of God and Christ; not in the night of self-will, whereby we should prepare for ourselves a fall into perdition. And thus this thought also is indicated: that a false prolongation of life by evasion of duty is the immediate preparation for a night, in which one must of necessity stumble and fall; while a resigned and passive demeanor in the divinely appointed night of death becomes a walking in a loftier sense, a going to the Father (*Leben Jesu*, II. 2, p. 1118). Still this is but the result of the ethical idea, not the immediate sense of the figure itself.

Twelve, brought forward with emphasis, signifying, objectively, life full-measured, rich, with its manifold appointments; subjectively, Christ's joyful assurance of life.

If any man walk.—The living man a walker and worker, a pilgrim and workman of God.—**In the day.**—The present day a symbol of the day of life, which, together with its day's task, is appointed to man.—**He stumbleth not.**—As men run against objects at night. He does not stumble upon an occasion of his death.—**For he seeth.**—The light shines upon him so that he avoids the stumbling-blocks that obstruct his road even in the day-time. Thus, in a moral sense, man sees in the light of his calling the dangers which he can and should avoid, without being obliged to abandon his vocation.

But if any man walk in the night.—The exceptions to the law of physical life (nocturnal working and walking) do not here come under consideration. Such is the rule in the physical life:—a rule which obtains in a still greater degree in the moral life. A self-seeking excitement—tumultuous living—of life prepares for itself death in the twilight of suffering, and destruction in the night of death. As Jesus has no desire to walk=work in the night, this remark is intended especially for the disciples.—**He stumbleth.**—See the account of the disciples in the history of the Passion.—**The light is not in him.**—No day-light from heaven, no light in the eyes; this holds good both in a physical and in a symbolical sense. The weakening of the antithesis of day and night to *tempus opportunum* and *inopportunum* (Morus, Paulus, *etc.*) is not incorrect but altogether insufficient.

Ver. 11. **And after this.**—After the tranquilizing words a pause.

Our friend Lazarus.—Thus Christ was acquainted with his sickness, with the hour of his death and the nature of it, by virtue of His divine-human consciousness. OUR FRIEND. An expression of hearty love and fellowship, in which they also do and should share. [Bengel notices the kind condescenion with which our Lord shares His friendship with the disciples. Only twice more does Christ call men by the endearing name of *friends*, *viz.*, the apostles, ch. xv. 14, 15; Luke xii. 4. Figuratively John the Baptist called himself a friend of Christ (ch. iii. 29). Abraham is called a "friend of God" (James ii. 23; comp. 2 Chr. xx. 7; Isa. xli. 8), but more in the passive sense; the favorite of God.—P. S.]

Hath fallen asleep.—This expression is not selected simply in view of the approaching awakening. Comp. Matt. ix. 24; 1 Thess. iv. 13. It is the kinship of sleep and physical death, that Christ here proclaims. Sleep is the periodical death on earth; death is the final sleep for earth in the period of its present existence;—sleep is the concentration of outward life to the interior, in the nocturnal consciousness and vegetation of the body; death is the concentration and internalization of life in the transit of the soul to another state of existence.—**But I go.**—The confidence of the Lord in His mission.

[Bengel: "Death, in the language of heaven, is the sleep of the pious, but the disciples did not here understand His language. The freedom of the divine language is incomparable; but men's dullness often degrades Scripture to our sadder mode of speaking. Comp. Matt. xvi. 11." The scriptural designation of death as a sleep from which the pious awakes in the glorious morning of eternity (Matt. ix. 24; xxvii. 52; Acts vii. 59; xiii. 36; 1 Cor. xv. 6; 1 Thes. iv. 13; Rev. xiv. 13), furnishes no basis for the false doctrine of the sleep or unconscious condition of the soul from death till resurrection (*psychopannychia*), against which Calvin wrote his first theological treatise. The life union of the believer with Christ can not be suspended or lost in the darkness of unconsciousness; on the contrary, it passes through death to a higher degree of clearness and joy, being translated into the immediate presence of the Lord, although it does not attain to its perfect maturity till the time of the general resurrection, when the whole body of Christ, and consequently every member of it, will be fully grown.—P. S.]

Ver. 12. **He shall be restored** (be saved).—*i. e.* recover by means of sleep as a health-bringing crisis. Their misapprehension of the Lord's words and their application of them to bodily sleep have a psychological connection with their repugnance to the journey to Bethany. According to Bengel and Luthardt, they thought that the sleep had been produced by the agency of Jesus while yet absent (to which the πορεύομαι is considered to refer); according to Ebrard, that a cure had already been effected by the same agency (after ver. 4). The text affords no ground for either assumption.—**Of the rest of the sleep.**—Of the rest of dream-life; *i. e.*, of real sleep in antithesis to the sleep of death.

Ver. 14. **Plainly: Lazarus is dead.**—Παῤῥησίᾳ, here, without circumlocution, vers. 10, 24.

Ver. 15. **I am glad for your sakes.**—He is glad that *He was not there.* This does not mean, glad that He was not there to see Lazarus die, because his death might have raised doubts in the minds of the disciples (Paulus; against this construction Bengel remarks, that none ever died in presence of the Prince of Life),—but glad because now the greater miracle of a raising of the dead should take the place of a healing of the sick. He rejoices—not at his death—but in anticipation of the sign from God.—**That ye may believe**.—[The subjective intent with regard to the disciples themselves; the objective intent being the glory of God, ver. 4.—P. S.] With reference to their still weak faith, and to the trials of faith which they are about to encounter. Meyer: "Every new step of faith is in measure a new believing." Comp. chap. ii. 11.—**But let us depart**.—The ἀλλά terminates the conversation in order to the departure, as ch. xiv. 31.

Ver. 16. **Then said Thomas.**—תְּאוֹם=תָּאמָא [Aramaic] corresponding to the Greek Δίδυμος [*Didymus*], *twin*.* In the Gospels (Matt. x. 3; Mark iii. 18; Luke vi. 15) he is mentioned in connection with Matthew, in the Acts (i. 13) with Philip. He was probably a Galilean, as he is mentioned John xxi. 2 together with the Galilean fisher-apostles. Tradition has made him a veritable twin and bestowed the name of Lysia on his sister. In yet another relation he was pronounced a twin. According to Eusebius, *H. E.* I. 13, 5, he was called Judas; he is also designated in the *Acta Thomæ*, and has doubtless in this way been confounded with Judas, "the brother of Jesus." Tradition assigns Antioch as his birth-place, states that as an apostle he preached Christianity among the Parthians and that he was buried at Edessa. According to later authority (as early, however, as Gregory of Nazianzen) he made an apostolic journey to India and there, after the latest tradition, suffered martyrdom. Apocryphal literature has appended his name to an *Evangelium Thomæ* and the *Acta Thomæ*.

His characteristics are vividly portrayed in the sayings preserved by St. John; thus here chap. xi. 16; xiv. 5; xx. 24 (xxi. 2). In ecclesiastical tradition he is one-sidedly designated as skeptical, from his conduct in the moment of temptation. For various delineations of his character see the Art. *Thomas* in Winer. According to Winer, he had a bias towards the visible and comprehensible; he was, above all things, desirous of seeing clearly and was then rashly, even violently, decided. According to Tholuck, he united a mind inclining to doubt and despondency with intense acuteness of sensibility. From the passages cited it would appear that his doubting was the result of profound earnestness approaching to melancholy, and allied to a yearning after truth; hence, he became the critical spirit of the circle of apostles;—and hence, too, he displays the utmost decision in living in conformity to his convictions (see *Leben Jesu*, II. 2, p. 697; Com. on *Matthew*, p. 183).

Ver. 16. **Let us also depart that we may die with Him.**—With reference to Jesus [Meyer, Alford], not to Lazarus (Ewald, following Grotius). Thomas foresees, as he believes, that Jesus is going to His death and is ready to die with Him. Weak faith, strong love; an unequal relationship which is thus explained: a vigorous germ of faith, reflected in his not yet purified and glorified love to Jesus; a weak, dull development of faith, held in check by the carefulness of his hitherto empirical view of the world.

[It is the language of mingled melancholy, resignation and courage, controlled by love to Christ. It is in full accordance with the character of Thomas as it appears on other occasions, ch. xiv. 5; xx. 5 ff. He is ever inclined to take the dark view, but deeply attached to his Lord, and ready to die with and for Him. He represents the honest, earnest and noble skeptics, who do not hold fast to the Invisible as if they saw Him, who require tangible evidence before they believe, but who submit to the evidence when presented, and exclaim before the risen Saviour: My Lord and my God!—P. S.]

* [Hengstenberg fancies that Christ gave Thomas this name to designate his double nature and vacillation between unbelief and faith, and refers for this to Gen. xxv. 23 f.! Christ did not thus brand His disciples; the names He gave (to Peter and the sons of Zebedee) were names of honor.—P. S.]

DOCTRINAL AND ETHICAL.

1. *The raising of Lazarus, the death of the Lord.* Christ as dying for the resurrection of the world.

2. The *three dead-awakenings* of Christ in their gradation: The child on its death-bed,—the youth on his bier,—the man in his grave; the awakening in the hushed circle of friends,—in presence of a funeral procession of acquaintances,—in the midst of the Jews.

3. How the opinion of Jesus concerning the *sickness* of Lazarus applies in a *broader* sense to every sickness, considered with reference to its final aim, and so in a peculiar sense to the sickness of the believer.

4. The *love* of the Lord to His friends is holy, and therefore manifoldly and inscrutably deep and mysterious in its manifestation, like the providence of God itself.

5. The *delay* and *haste* of Jesus.

6. *Symbolism of day-life* and *night-life.* The duty of the day is the day of the duty. This is applicable to the day of life as well as to the individual day.

7. *Symbolism of sleep.* Christ has changed death into sleep; but as the death of His people is sleep, so is the spiritual sleep of unbelievers death.

8. The noble and therefore open *doubt* of *Thomas* in antithesis to the wicked, secret and reserved doubting of *Judas*.

9. The mysterious *rapport* of spirit and life between the praying Christ in Peræa and the praying household in Bethany.

HOMILETICAL AND PRACTICAL.

[LITERATURE: On the raising of Lazarus see the numerous and valuable notes of DR. MALLET on John, ch. xi. and xii. in the "*Bremer Post,*" from the close of the year 1857 to the year 1859. Similarly John xi. Sermons on the eleventh chapter of St. John's Gospel by DR. SCHROEDER, Pastor at Elberfeld, 1853. As also the list of books in HEUBNER, p. 389. *Historie von Lazaro*, by SUTELLIUS, Wittenberg, 1543; JOH. ARND'S *Lazarus redivivus*, Jena 1620; BALTHASAR MUENTER, Public Lectures on the discourses of Jesus, *etc.*, ninth volume, 1793; LILIENTHAL, *Predigten über die Auferweckung des Lazarus*, 1764; EWALD, *Lazarus*, Berlin 1790; HERDER, *Homilies*, No. 19; SEILER, *Pastoral-Theologie*, II. p. 93-101; HANSTEIN, *Erinnerungen an Jesu*, vierte Fortsetzung; WICHELHAUS;

Weg zur Ruhe; BOURDALOUE, *Sermon, etc.;* MASSILLON, FOURNIER, *Bethanien*, Berlin, 1837; THEREMIN, *Predigten*, III. no. 8; W. HUELSEMANN, *die Geschichte der Auferweckung des Lazarus*, Leipzig, 1835. [GUMLICH, in the *Studien und Kritiken*, 1862, pp. 65 ff., 248 ff.; TRENCH, *Notes on the Miracles*, pp. 312 ff. See also a large list of English sermons, lectures and practical treatises on John xi. in DARLING'S *Cyclopædia Bibliographica*, vol. I., pp. 1115 ff.—P. S.]

THE THREE SECTIONS from vers. 1-57 together, as a homiletical trilogy: 1. The journey of Jesus to Bethany to the grave of His dead friend, or the journey into peril of death, in order to the raising of the dead; 2. the miracle at Bethany, or the raising of the dead in the face of mortal enemies; 3. the message from Bethany, or the death-fate impending over the Lord in consequence of the message of the Prince of Life.—"Now there was one sick," or how the distress of His people draws the Lord unto them: 1. down from heaven into human misery; 2. over the Jordan into peril of death; 3. forever back from the rest of heaven into the conflict of earth; 4. in the future, from the throne of glory to the judgment-seat.

OUR SECTION, vers. 1-16. The pious household of the sick man.—The fellowship of a believing family: 1. a relationship of blood and spirit; 2. fellowship of suffering and triumph.—The imperishable glory and blessedness of the names of the just. How they shine eternally in the light of the love of Jesus.—"That the Son of God may be glorified thereby." Or how Christ has always in the highest sense made a virtue of necessity: 1. Of oppression, deliverance; 2. of danger, a triumph; 3. of temptation, a victory; 4. of misery, redemption; 5. of death, a festival of resurrection.—Brothers and sisters after the flesh, as spiritually kindred in Scripture and history.—The message from Bethany: 1. How strong; 2. how tender.—Christ, the Master, over against His people: 1. They call and He tarries; 2. they dissuade and He goes.—Christ's heavenly knowledge of the earthly circumstances of His people.—"Let us go again into Judea." Or Christ returns in spite of His enemies.—The twelve hours of the day, or life-time and life's duty in their indissoluble unity: 1. The certainty of life within the bounds of duty. The servant of God does not die until his work is performed. 2. The sacredness of duty within the bounds of life.—Day and night in relation to the life of duty; 1. Within, day; 2. without, night.—The order of the antithesis between day and night, an image of the antithesis between life-time and death. (Now—work, then—rest).—The inverters of this order, who pass their time in idleness now, shall then incur fearful pains.—Our friend Lazarus sleepeth. How this is applicable to every departed believer: our friend sleeps.—This also is true: the Awakener is already on the way.—The misunderstanding of the disciples.—"Let us go!" Or the same words in their twofold meaning: 1. In the mouth of Christ; 2. in the mouth of Thomas.—The three expressions of doubt proceeding from Thomas and the victory of his faith. A. The expressions of doubt: 1. A doubt as to the victory of life; 2. a doubt as to the way to heaven (chap. xiv.); 3. a doubt as to the certainty of the resurrection (chap. xx). B. The victory of his faith. 1. Prepared by his ardent love to Jesus and to the brethren (chap. xi.); 2. introduced by his longing desire for a higher disclosure (chap. xiv.); 3. decided by his joy at the manifestation of the Risen One (chap. xx.)

STARKE: MAJUS: In distress and misery we should dispatch sighs and tears as our messengers to Christ, and remind Him of our covenant that we have made with Him.—ZEISIUS: Not to the physician of the body, as is the general custom; but to Christ, the omnipotent Physician of soul and body should the sick first of all resort. Ps. cxxxiii. 1.—CRAMER: We pray well when we ground our petitions on the love of Christ, that is, on His love to us, not on ours to Him.—HEDINGER: To be sick and to be a dear child of God go well together.—When we pray, we must not limit the Lord in respect to time and method.—QUESNEL: God's manner of regarding sickness and prayer for the sick often differs materially from that of praying relatives and friends. He is concerned for His honor and the eternal salvation of the sufferer, Rom. viii. 28; Phil. i. 20.—HEDINGER: Help is oftentimes delayed, only that deliverance may be all the more glorious.—QUESNEL: God sometimes denies us a small favor, that He may show us a greater one.—There is no believer who is not at times forced to cry out: O Lord, how long! Ps. xiii.; Matt. xxvii. 46.—MAJUS: Jesus does not forget His own, although it sometimes seems as if He did; before they are aware, He is with them.—When God calls a man to venture something, he must shun no danger.—They who seek to escape the cross are never at a loss for excuses.—HEDINGER: Death a sleep, Is. xxvi. 19; lvii. 2.—The ways of the Lord, which apparently militate against faith, must often serve to strengthen it.—*Ibid.:* It is well, if thou be ready to go with Christ unto death.

BRAUNE: In no narrative is the Lord's fulness of love more clearly and richly revealed, and nowhere is the heart of the Redeemer more fully unveiled to us.—Ver. 4. Honor, therefore, the Christian, and ye honor God; the two things are inseparably connected.—Ver. 14. Jesus rejoiced when men wept;·He may likewise be angry, when men are glad.

GERLACH: The dead man was not a stranger to Him, like the young man of Nain and the daughter of Jairus (although it is a question, whether these were essentially strangers to Him), but he believed on Him.—In all such cases Jesus proceeds in precisely the same manner as divine Providence, which generally affords relief in the most wonderful ways only when the utmost need is reached. Thus, forsooth, dares no human helper act, who holds not the issues in his power.—When God carries the torch before us and bids us follow, we may courageously advance, even though menaced on all sides by death.

GOSSNER: The Church of Jesus resembles this house, where Jesus stopped. It has Marys, clinging with ardent devotion to the Lord; it has Marthas, active and fruitful in good works; it has Lazaruses, sick or even dead (better: it has suffering and dying members), but who are healed and raised up by the word of Jesus.—Love and a cross; man cannot make the two rhyme, but it is thus that God always rhymes. HEUBNER: We can distinguish a three-fold love in Jesus: 1. Towards all men; 2. towards believers on Him; 3. towards individuals; a peculiar friendship for them, as here for this family, and for John.—Happy the household, the hearts of whose members love to Jesus unites.—One of the three was sick; the others suffer with him.—The sickness of loved ones is a means of strengthening and intensifying the bonds of love.—"Lazarus, by his weakness and death, assists in the accomplishment of a greater and more glorious work than if he had personally preached in all the world." (Sutellius.)—Before God all the discord of suffering humanity is already melted into harmony.—*Habet Dominus suas horas et moras.*—As sleep is the withdrawal of life inwards, for the gathering of new strength, so likewise is death, *etc.*

SCHLEIERMACHER: But two houses are mentioned in which Jesus was peculiarly at home; one was the house of Peter (Matt. viii. 14), when He began to dwell at Capernaum and as often as He abode there afterwards; the other is the house of Lazarus and his sisters at Bethany, in the vicinity of Jerusalem. (The third is doubtless the country-house of Gethsemane, the fourth the house in Jerusalem, where He kept the Passover; but a veil hangs over the respective families.)—We may be right in believing that He would not leave this region (Peræa) so suddenly, without saying farewell to those that believed on Him, leaving with them yet other sound words of doctrine and establishing more firmly their faith and love;—all this He must do before He could depart thence with a good conscience and tranquil heart.—From the raising of Lazarus they were to derive the hope that the promise, so frequently heard by them and so deeply graven on their hearts, should in like manner be fulfilled in the case of the Lord.

SCHRÖDER: The brother and sisters of Bethany; Lazarus, Martha, Mary. Was it not, perhaps, a step-ladder of spiritual life? Well, if we take Lazarus for the beginning, Martha may be our point of transit, but Mary ever our aim and end.—Vers. 3-5. The love of the Lord a tabernacle of God among men. The outer court (ver. 3), the Holy Place (ver. 4), the Holy of Holies (ver. 5).—Vers. 6-10. The way of Jesus: He acts in darkness, He walks in light.—Vers. 11-13. The death of His friends a sleep. They fall asleep, they rest, they awake.

[CRAVEN: From AUGUSTINE: Ver. 4. *This death* itself was not unto death, but to give occasion for a miracle; whereby men might be brought to believe in Christ, and so escape eternal death.—Vers. 11-14. To our *Lord*, he was *sleeping;* to *men*, who could not raise him again, he was *dead.*—From CHRYSOSTOM: Ver. 3. They *sent*, not *went*, partly—1. from their great faith in Him; 2. because their sorrow kept them at home.—Ver. 5. We are instructed not to be sad if sickness falls upon good men, and friends of God.—Vers. 9, 10. The upright need fear no evil, the wicked only have cause for fear: Or, If any one seeth this world's light, he is safe; much more he who is with Me.—From THEOPHYLACT: Ver. 15. *I am glad for your sakes*, for—1. had I been there I should have only *cured a sick man;* but 2. having been absent, I shall now *raise a dead man.*—From BRENTIUS: Ver. 3. The message is like all true prayer; it does not consist in much speaking and fine sentences.—From LAVATER: Ver. 6. Jesus proposed to help them in His own way, that is *as God.*—From M. HENRY: Ver. 2. Extraordinary acts of piety, will not only find acceptance with Christ, but will gain reputation in the church, Matt. xxvi. 13.—Ver. 3. *His sisters sent unto Him;* though God knows all our wants, He would know them *from us*, and is honored by our laying them before Him.—*He whom Thou lovest*—not, *he who loveth Thee;* our greatest encouragements in prayer are fetched from God Himself, and from His grace.—Note 1. there are some followers of Jesus for whom He hath a special kindness, chap. xiii. 23; 2. it is no new thing for those whom Christ loves to be sick; 3. it is a great comfort (blessing) when we are sick, to have those about us who will pray for us; 4. we have great encouragement in our prayers for the sick, if we have reason to believe that they are such as Christ loves.—Ver. 4. The afflictions of saints are designed for *the glory of God; The Son of God is glorified thereby*, as His wisdom, power and goodness are glorified—1. in *supporting* the sufferers; 2. in *relieving* them; (3. in ordering their sorrows for their welfare. E. R. C.)—Ver. 6. It is not said, He loved them, and *yet* He lingered; but, He loved them and *therefore* He lingered: He *lovingly* delayed—1. that He might *try* the sisters, and through trial, bless; 2. that He might have opportunity for doing more for Lazarus (and his sisters) than for any others.—God hath gracious intentions even in seeming delays, Isa. xlix. 13, 14; liv. 7, 8.—Ver. 7. When Christ knew they were brought to the last extremity (ver. 14) He said—*Let us go into Judea;* Christ will arise in favor of His people when *the set time* is come, and the *worst* time is commonly the *set* time—*man's extremity is God's opportunity.*—*Let us go;* Christ never brings His people into any peril without accompanying them in it.—Vers. 7, 8. Christ's gracious purpose of revisiting persecuting Judea, and the wonder of the disciples thereat; His ways in passing by offences, are above our ways.—Vers. 9, 10. Christ shows—1. the comfort and satisfaction of walking in the path of duty; 2. the pain and peril of not walking in this path.—Christ ever walked *in the day;* and so shall we, if we follow His steps.—Ver. 11. *Our friend Lazarus sleepeth:* see here how Christ calls—1. a believer, *friend;* 2. a believer's death, *sleep.*—Note 1. there is a covenant of friendship between Christ and believers; 2. those whom Christ owns as *His* friends, all His disciples should take as *theirs* (*our* friend); 3. death does not break the bond of friendship.—A Christian when he dies does but *sleep;* he—1. rests from the labors of the day past; 2. is being refreshed for the next morning.—Ver. 13. How carefully the evangelist corrects the mistake of the disciples; those who speak in an unknown tongue, or use similitudes, should learn to explain themselves.—Ver. 14. Christ takes cognizance of the death of His saints, for it is *precious in His sight*, Ps. cxvi. 15.—Ver. 15. *Let us go unto* him—not, unto his *sisters;* death, which separates from all other friends, cannot separate us from Christ.—Ver. 16. Let us go that we may die with *Him, i. e.* with Christ (?); Thomas here—1. recognizes the danger of following Christ; 2. expresses a gracious readiness to die with Him; 3. manifests a zealous desire to bring his fellow disciples to a similar readiness. —From BURKITT: Ver. 4. *God* is glorified when *His Son* is glorified.—Vers. 9, 10. Learn—1. Every man has his working time assigned him by God in this world; 2. whilst this time is unexpired he shall not be disabled (for the performance of *the work given him.*—E. R. C.), he shall not die; 3. every man has his *night* in which he must expect *to stumble, i. e. to die.*—Ver. 15. *To the intent ye may believe;* the faith of the strongest —1. needs confirmation; 2. is capable of increase. —From SCOTT: Vers. 1-5. Those families in which love and peace abound are highly favored; but they whom Jesus loves and by whom He is beloved, are most happy.—Ver. 1. Jesus did not come to preserve His people from affliction; but —1. to save them from sin and the wrath to come; 2. to convert sorrows and temporal death into means of completing that salvation.—Vers. 1-6. We cannot judge of Christ's love to us by outward dispensations.—From ALFORD: Ver. 4. The glorifying of the Son of God in Lazarus *himself* is subordinately implied; men are not mere *tools,* but *temples,* of God.—From STIER: Ver. 4. The *indefinite answer* of Jesus—1. includes a consolation which dispels the fear of death as to the issue; but 2. leaves "*this sickness*" to itself, to run its appointed course.—The resurrection of Lazarus, the comprehensive concluding symbol of all the miracles exhibiting the glory of God in Christ.—From BARNES: Vers. 3-5. *Whom Thou lovest;* this shows that—1. *peculiar* attachments are lawful to Christians; 2. those friendships are peculiarly lovely which are tempered and sweetened with the spirit of Christ.—Vers. 11-14. The word *sleep* is applied to *death*—1. because of the resemblance between them; 2. to intimate that death will not be final. —From WILLIAMS: Ver. 15. Instead of raising up Lazarus from sickness, as they whom He loved had desired, they are all by this miracle to be raised up, together with Lazarus, unto the life of Faith, which will never die.—From A PLAIN COMMENTARY (Oxford): Ver. 6. "To faithful suppliants there is no better sign than for their prayers not to be soon answered, for it is a pledge of greater good in store."—From RYLE: It was meet that the victory of Bethany should closely precede the crucifixion at Calvary.—Ver. 1. How much in life hinges upon little events, and especially on illness; sickness is one of God's great ordinances.—Ver. 2. The good deeds of all saints are recorded in God's book of remembrance.—Ver. 3. The humble and respectful confidence of the message.—Ver. 5. Jesus loves all who have grace, though their temperaments differ—*Marthas* as well as *Marys.*—Ver. 6. Christ knows best when to do anything for His people.—The pain of a *few* was permitted for the benefit of *the whole Church.*—Ver. 8. How strange and unwise our Lord's plans sometimes appear to His short-sighted people.—Ver. 15. Jesus does not say, *I am glad Lazarus is dead;* but, *I am glad I was not there:* we may not rejoice in *the death* of Christians, but we may rejoice in *the circumstances* attending their deaths, and *the glory redounding to Christ* and the *benefit accruing* to saints from them.—Ver. 16. The *despondency* of Thomas; a man may have notable weaknesses of Christian character, and yet be a disciple of Christ. — From OWEN: Ver. 10. Spiritual light is as necessary to the spiritual traveler, as the natural sun is to one who walks on the earth.]

B. *The raising of Lazarus. The trial and victory of faith at the open grave. The heart of Jesus. The glory of the God of Israel and the glory of Jesus united in a glorious work, for a sign for the Jews from Jerusalem.*

(VERS. 17-44.)

17 Then when Jesus came, he found that he had *lain* [been] in the grave four days
18 already.[1] Now Bethany was nigh unto [near] Jerusalem, about fifteen furlongs
19 off: And [But][2] many of the Jews came [had come, ἐληλύθεισαν] to Martha and
Mary,[3] to comfort them concerning their brother [the brother, π. τοῦ ἀδελφοῦ].[4]
20 Then Martha, as soon as she heard that Jesus was coming, went and met him
[when she heard that Jesus was coming, went to meet him]: but Mary sat *still*
21 [*omit still*] in the house. Then said Martha unto Jesus, Lord, if thou hadst
22 been here, my brother had not died.[5] But I know, that even now [And even
now I know that][6] whatsoever thou wilt [mayest] ask of God, God will give *it*
23 thee [will give to thee]. Jesus saith to her, Thy brother shall [will] rise again.
24 Martha saith unto him, I know that he shall [will] rise again in the resurrection

25 [of all] at the last day. Jesus said unto her, I am the resurrection, and the life:
he that believeth in me, though he were dead [should die], yet shall he [he will]
26 live: And whosoever [every one that] liveth and believeth in me shall never die
27 [lit. will not die for ever, οὐ μὴ ἀποθάνῃ εἰς τὸν αἰῶνα]. Believest thou this? She saith
unto him, Yea, Lord: I believe [have believed, become a believer][7] that thou art the
28 Christ, the Son of God, which should come [who cometh] into the world. And
when she had so said [having said this] she went her way [away] and called Mary
her sister secretly, saying, The Master is come [is here, πάρεστι], and calleth for
29 [*omit* for] thee. As soon as she heard *that* [*it*], she arose quickly, and came[8] unto
30 him. Now Jesus was [had] not yet come into the town, but was [still] in that
31 [the] place where Martha [had] met him. The Jews then [therefore] which [who]
were with her in the house, and comforted [were comforting, παραμυθούμενοι] her,
when they saw Mary, that she [saw that Mary] rose up hastily and went out, followed
her, saying, She goeth unto the grave [thinking[9] that she was going to the tomb]
32 to weep there. Then when Mary was come where Jesus was, and saw him [Mary
therefore, when she came . . . seeing him, or, as soon as she saw him], she fell
down at his feet, saying unto him, Lord, if thou hadst been here, my brother had
33 not died [comp. vers. 21, 22]. When Jesus therefore saw her weeping, and the Jews
also weeping which [who] came with her, he groaned [ἐνεβριμήσατο, was deeply
and indignantly moved, stirred up[10]] in the [his] spirit, and was troubled [troubled
34 himself, ἐτάραξεν ἑαυτόν], And said, Where have ye laid him? They say unto
him, Lord, come and see.
35 Jesus wept.
36, 37 Then said the Jews, Behold how he loved him! And [But] some of them said,
Could not this man, which [he who] opened the eyes of the blind [man, τοῦ τυφλοῦ,
38 see chap. ix.] have caused that even this man should not have died [die]? Jesus
therefore again groaning in [deeply moved within] himself cometh to the grave
39 [tomb]. It was a cave, and a stone lay upon it [against it]. Jesus said [saith]
Take ye [*omit* ye] away the stone. Martha, the sister of him that was dead,[11]
saith unto him, Lord, by this time he stinketh:[12] for he hath been *dead* four days
40 [he hath his four days]. Jesus saith unto her, Said I not [Did I not say] unto
thee, that, if thou wouldest [*omit* wouldest] believe, thou shouldest [shall] see the
glory of God?
41 Then they took away the stone *from the place* where the dead was laid [*omit from
the place* where the dead was laid].[13] And Jesus lifted up *his* [the] eyes [to heaven,
42 or upward, ἄνω] and said, Father, I thank thee that thou hast heard me. And
[Yet] I knew that thou hearest me always: but because of the people [for the sake
of the multitude] which stand by [around] I said *it*, that they may [might] be-
43 lieve that thou hast sent [didst send] me. And when he thus had [had thus]
spoken, he cried [out] with a loud voice, Lazarus, come forth.
44 And he that was dead [the dead man] came forth, bound hand and foot with
graveclothes; and his face was bound about with a napkin. Jesus saith unto
them, Loose him, and let him go.

TEXTUAL AND GRAMMATICAL.

[1] Ver. 17.—[Tischendorf omits ἤδη (*already*), on the authority of A.* D., *etc.*; but Alford, Westcott and Hort retain it with B. C.[1]—P. S.]

[2] Ver. 19.—Lachmann, Tischendorf, [Alford, Westcott and Hort] read: πολλοὶ δέ, instead of καὶ πολλοί, in accordance with important authorities. [ℵ. B. C. D. L. X., *etc.*]

[3] Ver. 19.—Lachmann [Alford, Westc. and H.], in accordance with B. C. L. [also Cod. Sin.] read: πρὸς τὴν M., *etc.* [The text. rec. and Tischend., ed. 8th, read πρὸς τὰς περὶ M., *to those who were around Martha and Mary.* The allusion seems to be to the custom of a *company* of comforters collecting themselves around mourners. The expression is foreign to the N. T. See Exeg.—P. S.]

[4] Ver. 19.—Tischendorf omits αὐτῶν in accordance with the B. D. L. [So also Cod. Sin., Alford, Westc. & H.—P. S.]

[5] Ver. 21.—Different placings of the words. Tischendorf: οὐκ ἂν ὁ ἀδελφός μου ἐτεθνήκει. [So formerly; but in his 8th crit. ed. 1869, Tischendorf gives—οὐκ ἂν ἀπέθανεν ὁ ἀδελφός μου. Ἀπέθ. is in accordance with ver. 32, supported by Cod. Sin. B. C.* D. K. L. X. II., *etc.*, and is also adopted by Westcott & Hort; while Alford prefers ἐτεθνήκει, *would have died.*—P. S.].

[6] Ver. 22.—Ἀλλά is wanting in B. C., *etc.* [The proper reading is καὶ νῦν, and is now preferred by Tischend., Alf. to ἀλλὰ καὶ νῦν.—P. S.]

[7] Ver. 27.—[πεπίστευκα is the proper reading adopted by all the critical editors; πιστεύω is poorly supported.—P. S.]

[8] Ver. 29.—[Tischendorf, ed. 8th, reads ἐγείρεται and ἔρχεται, but Alford, Westcott and Hort retain the reading of the text. rec. ἠγέρθη and ἤρχετο, which is sustained by Cod. Sin. and B. The historical present is more lively, but may be an emendation.—P. S.]

[9] Ver. 31.—[Δόξαντες is abundantly sustained by ℵ. B. C.* D. L. X. Verss., and now generally adopted instead of the λέγοντες of the text. rec.—P. S.]

[10] Ver. 33.—[It is perhaps impossible to find a precise equivalent in English for the Greek ἐμβριμάομαι in the sense in which it is used here and in ver. 38. See the EXEG., pp. 352 f.—P. S.]

[11] Ver. 39.—Τετελευτηκότος established by A. B. C.* Sin., *etc.*, against the τεθνηκότος of the Recepta.

[12] Ver. 39.—[The Saxon *stinketh* for ὄζει is no doubt a repulsive term for a repulsive thing, but for this reason also more expressive than *is offensive* (Noyes, Conant and others) or similar modern substitutes.—P. S.]

[13] Ver. 41.—In accordance with B. C.* Sin. and others, the sentence: οὗ ἦν ὁ τεθνηκὼς κείμενος must be omitted.

EXEGETICAL AND CRITICAL.

Ver. 17. **Four days already.**—Jesus comes into the vicinity of the place and learns that Lazarus has already been buried four days. The journey from Peræa to Bethany is estimated at ten hours,—a day's journey. One day, therefore, is consumed by His journey, two days by His stay in Peræa after the receipt of the message, and still another day by the journey of the messenger. Hence it results that Lazarus, who, in conformity to the Jewish custom, was buried on the day of his death, died shortly after the departure of the messenger, or while he was preparing to depart. The first and last days enter into the computation as parts of days. And so, when Lazarus died, his sisters must have known, with perfect certainty, that their messenger had not yet reached the Lord, or, at all events, that Jesus could not so soon be with them. They could not, therefore, with the feeling common to humanity, attribute the death of Lazarus to any delay on the part of Jesus; on the contrary, it is far more probable that they reproached themselves with delay in despatching the messenger. But this very trait, like their timid message, finds its explanation in the condition of affairs; they were well aware of the peril involved in His coming. Be it also observed that plain-spoken Martha says: "If Thou hadst been here, my brother had not died,"—and not: "If Thou hadst come sooner."

Ver. 18. **About fifteen furlongs** (stadia) **off** [ὡς ἀπὸ σταδίων δεκαπέντε].—A stadium (στάδιος and in the classics also στάδιον) a distance of 125 paces. The fifteen stadia about three-quarters of an hour [about two miles]. Ancient construction (Tholuck): Trajection of the preposition ἀπό, which relates to Jerusalem. In opposition to this, Winer, [p. 518]: The ἀπό designates the locality beyond the fifteen stadia, and is to be considered as referring to the stadia. The latter construction seems far-fetched.* The short distance is mentioned in order to account for the presence in Bethany of so many Jews from Jerusalem. The use of the preterite (Bethany *was*) is to be explained by its connection with the historical narrative.

Ver. 19. **Many of the Jews,**—*i. e.* not necessarily members of the Sanhedrin (ver. 46), but people of Pharisaic or Judaistic views. Possibly they wished to regain this family in the absence of Jesus, whose friendship for them may have been known. However, many of the kindred of the family may have been among these Jews and we have no grounds for representing all who came to condole with them as miserable comforters.

* [Buttmann, *N. T. Gr.*, p. 133, derives this peculiar position of ἀπό and πρό in indications of space and time from the influence of the Latin. Comp. John xii. 1, πρὸ ἓξ ἡμερῶν τοῦ πάσχα; xxi. 8; Apoc. xiv. 20.—P. S.]

To Martha and Mary. Πρὸς τὰς περὶ Μ. κ. Μ. Properly, to the two sisters, with the persons about them. According to later Greek usage it might be indicative simply of the two sisters. "But the New Testament contains no instance of its use in this sense and there is here an especial *decorum* in the expression, since those who came to them were *men.* It reveals, moreover, an establishment of the better class." (Meyer).* But the more obvious and definite allusion is, probably, to the company of mourners and wailing women.

To comfort them.—The conventional condolences and consolations lasted seven days, according to 1 Sam. xxxi. 13; 1 Chron. x. 12; Maimonides, *De luctu*, cap. xiii.; Lightfoot [pp. 107 sqq.], and others.

Ver. 20. **Then Martha, when she heard,** *etc.*—She appears as mistress of the house and receives the message. She goes without delay to meet the Lord and does not first communicate the news to Mary; ver. 28 also leads us to suppose that such was the case (Meyer in opposition to Tholuck).—**But Mary sat in the** (interior of the) **house**; "because, according to Geier, *De luctu Hebr.* [pp. 210 sqq.] and others, it was the custom to be seated in receiving condolences," or "sitting was a part of the mourning rite with the Greeks and Hebrews." But certainly not for this reason alone. The different conduct of the two sisters in our Gospel is in perfect accordance with the characters in Luke x. 38-42. [This agreement between two Gospels so widely different is no small proof of the historical character of the two sisters. Both loved our Lord, but Martha was more active, practical, demonstrative; Mary contemplative, pensive and quiet, but moved in the deep. Martha as soon as she hears of the Lord's approach, hastens to Him. Mary does the same afterwards (ver. 29), but speaks less and feels more. We have a precise analogy in the difference between Peter and John.—P. S.]

Ver. 21. **Lord, if Thou hadst been here** [εἰ ἦς ὧδε, not the language of reproach, but of regret].—Meyer translates: If Thou *wert* here,—not abiding in distant Peræa. That would mean: if this were Thy constant place of abode. This would convey an excellent sense if Bethany had ever been the permanent dwelling-place of Christ; this, however, was not the case.—**My brother would not have died.**—Strongly expressed: ἐτεθνήκει. [On the different readings see TEXT. NOTE 5.—P. S.]

Ver. 22. **And even now** [καὶ νῦν without ἀλλά] **I know that**, *etc.*—She still retains this assurance. She gives strong expression to her confidence: 1. *Whatever Thou mayest ask God,* 2. *God will give it to Thee*—in the original, the

* [Alford almost verbally copies this note from Meyer. We have good reason to infer from several indications that the family of Bethany was "one of large hospitality and acquaintance." Comp. ch. xii. 3, 5 and note.—P. S.]

"give" [δώσει σοι] takes precedence of the rest —; 3. the name of God twice mentioned. Certainly an indirect expression of the boldest hope, to which she dares not verbally give utterance—a hope, namely, of the raising of the dead man. The sisters at Bethany were acquainted with the raising of the daughter of Jairus and of the youth at Nain. Martha also remembered the promise (ver. 4) contained in the message of Jesus (Tholuck, Meyer). Hence not simply: if Thou wilt implore consolation (Rosenmüller), or: that Lazarus may not be cast away (Euthymius), or only an assurance: nevertheless, I consider Thee a favorite of God (Paulus). We must not, however, convert this indefinite and sifting expression into a confident expectation of the raising of the dead man,—as results also from the words: **whatever Thou mayest ask.**

[This is the only place where αἰτεῖσθαι is used of Jesus as praying to God, instead of ἐρωτᾶν, παρακαλεῖν, προσεύχεσθαι, δεῖσθαι, comp. Luke xxii. 32; John xiv. 16; xvi. 26; xvii. 9, 15, 20. Bengel calls *αἰτεῖσθαι, verbum minus dignum;* it is certainly more human and implies a state of dependence and need. It is, however, as Meyer remarks, in keeping with the deep excitement of Martha and her as yet imperfect knowledge of the superhuman relation of Christ to the Father. —P. S.]

Ver. 23. **Thy brother will rise again.**—A grand promise, though corresponding with the indefinite hope in being indefinitely worded; not: I will *now* raise him up. She might understand Him as referring to the general future resurrection. And besides, specific faith in the raising of the dead must issue from a general faith in their resurrection. It was an ambiguous expression, designed for the trial and development of her faith.*

Ver. 24. **I know that he will rise again,** *etc.*—Her meaning is obvious: I acquiesce in that, but I hope for something more. Her words are expressive not merely of a sad resignation, but of an indirect query—she is feeling her way (De Wette).

Vers. 25, 26. **I am the resurrection.**—[This is evidently the central idea of this chapter: Christ the Resurrection of the dead, and the Life of the living. The following miracle is the practical proof of what He is in His own person and a pledge of what He will do on the last day. To Himself (ἐγώ), therefore, He first directs the weak faith of Martha; from the future resurrection and the dead brother she was to look to the present (εἰμί), ever-living and life-giving Saviour. The general resurrection of the dead is only a manifestation of the moral power of the person that stood before her. What sublimity and what comfort in this testimony of Christ concerning Himself! Who can measure the effect which it produces from day to day in countless chambers of mourning and before open graves all over the Christian world!—*Resurrection* is put first, in opposition to the present power of death which is to be overcome; Resurrection is Life itself in conflict with, and victory over, death, it is the Death of death, the triumph over decay and dissolution swallowing up mortality in life. (Luther has forcibly described the marvellous duel between Life and Death on the cross, in an Easter hymn, where the passage occurs: "*Wie ein Tod den andern frass; Ein Spott aus dem Tod ist worden.*") *Life* comprehends spiritual as well as physical life, life eternal of body and soul. Christ is the Victor of death and the grave, because He is the Prince of life in this absolute sense. In the words following the first clause is an explanation and application of the term *Resurrection*, the second of the term *Life*. I am the *Resurrection: he that believeth in Me, though he have died, will live* (will be raised up again). I am the *Life: whoever liveth and believeth in Me will never die* (will live forever in unbroken life-union with Me, the Prince of life).—P. S.]

I [and no other], *i. e.*, the future resurrection is not an impersonal fate that is to take place at some future time, but a personal effect proceeding from Me who am present with you. It is even now present and active in Me.—**And the life.**—Life in the absolute sense, in its power to awaken spirit and body. Hence, as well the principle of resurrection (Hunnius, Luthardt), as its essence and result (Meyer). As the vital principle of the resurrection, He exerts a purely quickening influence, which branches into two forms: *a. He who believes on Him, if he have died* [ἀποθάνῃ, past], *shall live*, shall continue to live, shall rise again; *b. he who is still living*, who through belief on Him becomes truly alive, *shall never die, i. e.* shall not become a prey to death and the sense of mortality.* The life of Christ is the author of the resurrection in a two-fold sense; it is the root of the waking of the physically dead, because it is the power which effects the moral awakening,—the power which rouses into spiritual life. They that live in Him shall not die; and the dead are not dead, but live again. In both cases, undoubtedly, the saying has reference to the same believer; the two propositions do not resolve themselves, as ancient commentators declare, into the parallel: "for *dead* believers I am the resurrection, for *living* ones the *remedium mortis*." It is true, however, that the two propositions indicate, after Euthymius and others, the two-fold point of view; whether one be already dead (Lazarus) or still living (Martha, Mary). In both cases, the *spirituo*-physical or whole life-agency of Christ is meant. The dead rise spiritually and corporeally to the new life of the resurrection. The living are not swallowed up in the death of the

* [So also Meyer, and Alford who remarks that *ἀναστήσεται* is pedagogically used to lead on to the requisite faith in her mind, and doubts whether it *could* be used of a recall into *human* life. Hengstenberg refers the word *mainly* to the final resurrection, and *subordinately* to the translation to Paradise, which he includes in the *first* resurrection (Apoc. xx. 5 ?); but Lazarus must have been already in Paradise (comp. *to-day* in Luke xxiii. 43).—P. S.]

* [The phrase *οὐ μή—εἰς τὸν αἰῶνα*, ver. 26, is in itself ambiguous and may mean either *not forever*, or *never*. The first and literal rendering would give a very plain sense: *He that liveth* (physically) *and believeth in Me, will not die* (physically) *for ever*, *i. e.* will be raised again. But in all other passages in which the same phrase occurs (ch. iv. 14; viii. 51, 52; x. 28; xiii. 8; 1 Cor. viii. 13), it is equivalent to *never*, like the Hebrew לֹא־לְעוֹלָם (Ps. lv. 22; Prov. x. 30), with an emphasis on the negation: *surely not, in no wise, by no means* (see Winer, p. 407, on the force of the double negation in Greek). We must then suppose that Christ in ver. 26 either spoke of *spiritual* death, or overlooked *physical* death as a vanishing transition to real and eternal life.—P. S.]

world either spiritually or bodily (inasmuch as they transport with them the germ or the concrete body of the resurrection).

Therefore we are not to attach a merely spiritual meaning to the two propositions, just because Jesus is speaking of faith,—as, for instance: he that believeth on Me shall rise again spiritually, and he that hath received life shall retain it for ever; which would, *implicite*, involve the idea of the resurrection (Calvin). Neither is the first sentence to be referred to the resurrection of the body and the second to that of the spirit (Lampe, Olshausen, Stier). Comp. chap. vi. 51; viii. 56.*

Believest thou this?—Christ had said: *Every one* that liveth and believeth, and had thus laid down a general rule. Now comes the application of it to her. If she believes this, she believes on Him.

Ver. 27. **I have believed that Thou art the Christ, the Son of God.**—It is apparent that Martha does not thoroughly comprehend the grand thoughts in the words of the Lord; she, however, takes for granted that He is designating Himself as the Raiser of believers from the dead, and perceives that this is involved in a belief on the Messiah. She therefore utters a joyful confession of her faith in Him,—Ἐγὼ πεπίστευκα, with emphasis. She does not believe this now for the first time; she has already become a believer, being convinced *a.* that He is the *Christ*, *b.* as the Christ *the Son of God;* she believes in the full sense of the term, not simply in accordance with the theocratic idea of belief (Meyer), although she has not yet attained to a developed Johannean knowledge; *c. that cometh* [ὁ ἐρχόμενος] *into the world* (Present), that is: Who is even now continually engaged in the unfolding of His Messianic glory and work. Observe the truthfulness of Martha, which will not permit her to repeat Christ's expressions word for word, but moulds her confession into conformity with the measure of her faith. And yet this is enough. Confessions differing in outward form or expression may agree internally and in substance.

Ver. 28. **And when she had so said, she went away.**—Martha knows enough for the moment. With womanly instinct (such as especially belongs to her practical nature) she does not enter upon a deeper investigation of the great thoughts of Jesus; sufficient for her is the practical thought, that He meets her boldest hopes with the assurance that the resurrection is not merely a *distant resurrection-time*, but rather a *present resurrection-power* resident in His person. **And called Mary, her sister, secretly.**† —On account of the Jews who were present. It appears that Mary was still sitting in the interior of the house, surrounded by the Jews. Therefore Martha called her *secretly*,—λάθρᾳ, a word, no doubt, indicative of a whisper: therefore she simply said: **the Master is here**— which Mary well understood; and therefore: **He calleth thee.** She was to go out to Him. The prudence of Jesus, who remained standing outside, is met by the prudence of Martha; common fear, however, is not to be attributed to either. He must remove His disciples from the influence of the Jews; and they, by going out to Him, must make confession of their faith in Him. It was, moreover, the rule of the Lord to avoid making a parade of His miracles, though He did, on this occasion, finally welcome the *eventual* notice of the Jews. Remarkable consonance of human prudence and divine assurance. We must not suppose that Martha simply gathered the mandate: *He calleth thee*, from the expectations that Jesus excited in her own breast (Chrysostom, Tholuck [Brückner, Stier]); she tells of a behest of Jesus (Lücke, Meyer).*

Ver. 29. **As soon as she heard that.**— Mary, as the more important personality, now steps into the fore-ground, although Martha, as we see from ver. 39, again makes one of the group.

Ver. 30. **Now Jesus was not yet**, *etc.*— See note to ver. 28. Jesus might have been assured from the circumstances of the case, that there were Jews in the house of mourning; it was needless for Martha to apprise Him (after Meyer) of the fact.

Ver. 31. **The Jews . . . . followed her, thinking that she was going to the tomb to weep there.**—It was a custom much practised among the Jews and Greeks, to sit down and mourn by the graves of their dead (Wetstein, on this passage; Geier, *De luctu Hebr.*). They therefore went with her, doubtless regarding the scene of mourning which they expected to witness, as a ceremony that had to be performed in compliance with Oriental custom. Even in these points the false way of the ancient world, which gratified its feelings by a common lamentation over the dead, stands contrasted with the truth of life, which demands solitude for its grief. Of course the too great isolation of mourners is to be guarded against as much as the other extreme.

Ver. 32. **Mary . . . fell down at His feet.** —The first stroke of character which distinguishes her from Martha. The second is, that she says nothing further than: **Lord, if Thou hadst been here, my brother had not died.** While Martha added to these words: *and even now I know, etc.* (ver. 22), Mary bursts into tears. Martha may at first strike us as the one who possesses the greater joy in believing, but Mary is the more human and warm in her feelings, and there is more of devotion in the expression of her faith. Her kneeling posture and her tears are more eloquent than the words of Martha. The saying that both utter, constitutes a precious trait from life. They made this remark to each other over and over again at the

* [Comp. Godet *in loc.* (II. 333), who justly says that it is impossible here to separate the moral and the physical sense in the words *resurrection* and *life*. I subjoin the remarks of Trench (*Miracles*, p. 322) on this glorious declaration: "*I am the Resurrection and the Life;* the true Life, the true Resurrection; the everlasting triumphs over death, they are *in Me* —no distant things, as thou spakest of now, to find place at the end of the world; no things separate or separable from Me, as thou spakest of lately, when thou desiredst that I should ask of another that which I possess evermore in Myself. In Me is victory over the grave, in Me is life eternal: by faith in Me that becomes yours which makes death not to be death, but only the transition to a higher life."—P. S.]

† [Alford: "Her calling her sister is characteristic of one who (Luke x. 40) had not been much habituated herself to listen to His instructions, but knew this to be the delight of Mary. Besides this, she evidently has hopes raised, though of a very faint and indefinite kind. προσδοκήσασά τι ἀγαθὸν ἀπὸ τῶν λόγων αὐτοῦ (Euthymius.")—]

* [So also correctly Alford and Godet.—P. S.]

death-bed of Lazarus: *if He were here,* etc. Bengel: "*Ex quo colligi potest, hunc earum fuisse sermonem ante fratris obitum: utinam adesset Dominus Jesus!*"

Ver. 33. **He was vehemently (indignantly, angrily) affected (stirred up) in (his) spirit and troubled himself** [ἐνεβριμήσατο τῷ πνεύματι καὶ ἐτάραξεν ἑαυτόν.—Comp. ver. 38 ἐμβριμώμενος ἐν ἑαυτῷ, but also the weeping between, ἐδάκρυσεν, ver. 35. Note first of all the perfect participation of the Lord in our natural feelings and His sympathy with our sorrows (Heb. ii. 17; iv. 15), in opposition to the stoic apathy, yet at the same time His perfect control over passion and grief and its violent outbreak.—P. S.]—He was deeply perturbed in spirit. The ἐνεβριμήσατο τῷ πνεύματι (see Matt. ix. 30; Mark i. 43; xiv. 5) makes the passage one of exceeding difficulty. The affection here depicted is explained in three ways: 1. as anger, 2. as grief, 3. as a general affection of the mind, in which there is a combination of different emotions.*

1. Of ANGER. "βριμάομαι with all its compounds has in the classics as well as in the fathers of the Church (and the Byzantines) the signification: *to snort* (of horses), *to mutter* (of Hecate), *to express anger, to threaten angrily.*"† But again, anger is variously understood:

a. He was angry, in respect of His divine nature, with His human spirit (πνεῦμα) in its passionate emotion (πάθος). So Origen, Chrysostom [Cyril, Theophylact, Euthymius Zigab.], recently Merz [Alford]. This conception is doubly untenable: in the first place, it condemns the human sentiment of grief; and secondly, it creates a conflict in the consciousness of the Lord. [It is also inconsistent with the act of weeping, which follows, ver. 35, and with the parallel expression ἐν ἑαυτῷ,—*in Himself,* ver. 38, which proves that τῷ πνεύματι cannot be the *object,* but must be the *sphere* of the emotion=*in His spirit.*—P. S.]* Hilgenfeld and others fall upon the same interpretation, with a different conception of it, in imputing a gnostic Christology to this Gospel.

b. He was angry at the power of sin and death (Augustine, Erasmus and others, Luthardt).† Not to be excluded, but too abstract by itself.

c. At the unbelief of the Jews [Erasmus, Scholten, Wordsworth], and also the sisters (Theodor of Mopsueste, Lampe [Kuinoel], Wichelhaus]). But the sisters were *not* unbelieving.

d. That He was unable to avert the death of Lazarus (De Wette). This would be impious and is contrary to the connection.

e. At the misconception of His enemies and the want of comprehension displayed by His friends (Brückner). There was, at the moment, no special occasion for such a feeling.

f. At the mingling of the hypocritical tears [crocodile tears] of the Jews with the true tears of Mary (Meyer). Against this, comp. ver. 45 ["Many of the Jews . . . *believed* in Him"].‡

g. This description of anger has, in the interest of negative criticism, been caricatured by Strauss and others.

2. Of GRIEF. In the passages, Matt. ix. 30;

---

* [Lange translates: *regte sich tief auf im Geiste, stirred Himself up in His spirit;* Noyes and Alford: *was greatly moved in His spirit.* The E. V. *groaned in spirit,* expresses more the feeling of grief and pain than of indignation and wrath (though Trench on *Miracles,* p. 325, strangely asserts the very reverse); comp. 2 Cor. v. 4: "We that are in this tabernacle do *groan,* being burdened." Webster defines *groaning:* "to give forth a low, moaning sound, to utter a mournful voice, as in pain and sorrow," and says nothing of anger. The E. V. translates the verb in four different ways: *to charge straitly,* Matt. ix. 30; Mark i. 43; *to murmur,* Mark xiv. 5; *to groan,* John xi. 33, 38.—P. S.]

† [So the Vulgate: *infremuit spiritu;* Luther: *Er ergrimmete im Geiste, was wroth at, moved with indignation.* βριμάομαι and ἐμβριμάομαι (from the root βρέμω, *to rush, to roar,* φριμάω, *fremo, to roar, to bluster;* comp. βρίμη, *anger,* βριμώ, *The Angered,* a name of Persephone or Hecate), when not used of uttering a sound (snorting, murmuring), always express an emotion of *anger* or *indignation,* and are equivalent to ὀργίζεσθαι and ἀπειλεῖν. Passow and Pape know no other meaning. Gumlich has abundantly proved it in the *Studien und Kritiken* for 1862, pp. 260-269. Sophocles, in his Lexicon of Byzantine Greek (Boston, 1870, p. 453), gives the meaning *to be greatly moved,* but without any authority except the two passages in John xi., which are under dispute. Meyer confidently asserts (p. 431): "*Nie anders als vom heftigen* ZORN (violent anger) *wird* βριμάομαι *und* ἐμβριμάομαι, *wo es nicht das eigentliche Schnauben oder Brummen* (*Aesch. Sept.* 461, *Luc. Necym.* 20) *bezeichnet, bei Griechen,* LXX. *und im* N. T. (Matt. ix. 30; Mark i. 43; xiv. 5) *gebraucht.* S. Gumlich, p. 265 f." Hengstenberg agrees: "*Es ist längst festgestellt, dass* ἐμβριμᾶσθαι *keinen anderen Affect bezeichnen kann als den des heftigen Zornes.*" Alford: "ἐμβριμάομαι can bear but one meaning, that of *indignor* ('*infremuit,*' Vulg.),—the expression of *indignation* and *rebuke,* not of *sorrow.*" Trench (p. 325): "It is nothing but the difficulty of finding a satisfactory object for the indignation of the Lord, which has caused so many modern commentators to desert this explanation, and make the word simply and merely an expression of grief and anguish of spirit. Lampe and Kuinoel defend the right explanation; and Lange (*Theol. Studien und Kritiken,* 1836, p. 714 sq.) has many beautiful remarks in an essay wherein he seeks to unite both meanings." Godet: "*Il est généralement reconnu, à cette heure, que le terme* ἐμβριμᾶσθαι (*de* βριμάζειν, *hennir, rugir*) *ne peut désigner qu'un frémissement d'indignation.*" But all this does not yet settle the precise meaning in this verse. See below. The verb is generally transitive and constructed with the dative of the person or thing against which the angry feeling or rebuke is directed; but here and in ver. 38 it is used intransitively; πνεύματι being not the *dat. obj.,* but the *dat. instrum.* or *loci.*—P. S.]

* [The Greek interpreters usually take τῷ πνεύματι=τῷ πάθει (as dative of the *object*), but Cyril refers it (as *instrumental* dative) to the Holy Ghost or the divine nature of Christ, by which He indignantly rebuked His rising human sympathy. (ἐμβριμᾶται τῷ πνεύματι, τουτέστι τῇ δυνάμει τοῦ ἁγίου πνεύματος ἐπιπλήττει τρόπον τινὰ τῇ ἰδίᾳ σαρκί.) In a milder form Dean Alford renews the Greek interpretation without its stoic repulsiveness. He thinks that Jesus, with the tears of sympathy already rising and overcoming His speech, *checked them so as to be able to speak the words following.* He considers this self-restraint as merely physical, requiring indeed an act of the will, and a self-troubling, but implying no deliberate disapproval of the rising emotion which immediately after is suffered to prevail. Webster and Wilkinson likewise explain ἐνεβριμήσατο of a violent repression of emotion. But this is clearly refuted by the explanatory ἐτάραξεν ἑαυτόν, and by the fact that Jesus did shed tears immediately afterwards. His effort at self-restraint then would have failed, which is incredible.—P. S.]

† [According to Augustine, Cornelius a Lap., Olshausen, Trench and Gumlich, Christ was indignant at *death as the wages of sin;* according to Nic. Lyra, Melanchthon, Ebrard, Luthardt and Hengstenberg, at the *power of death,* the terrible foe of the human race, who dared here to confront and threaten his great Conqueror. Nic. Lyra: *Fremitus Christi procedebat ex indignatione ejus contra diabolum, per cujus suggestionem mors intravit in mundum, quam erat cito debellaturus.* To the same effect is Luthardt's remark (II. p. 217): "*Ueber den Tod und den der des Todes Gewalt hat, Seinen Gegner von Anfang an, ergrimmte Er, dass er Ihm solches angerichtet, so in Seinen nächsten Kreis gedrungen und so Ihm Selbst wie drohend entgegengetreten war. Und das Ergrimmen Jesu ist wie ein Gegendrohen, das sich in der Auferweckung dann versinnbildlichte. Es sind gleichsam die ersten gegenseitigen Ankündigungen des letsten äussersten Kampfes.*" Comp. my notes to Lange's view below.—P. S.]

‡ [Meyer urges the preceding words ὡς εἶδεν αὐτὴν κλαίουσαν—καὶ τοὺς Ἰουδαίους κλαίοντας, as indicating this contrast and cause of the indignation; but this is not applicable to the second use of the verb in ver. 38, although ver. 37 clearly shows that the indignation must have had some reference to the unbelief of the Jews.—P. S.]

23

Mark i. 43, anger is out of the question. Tholuck: "This verb is equally comprehensive with the corresponding German '*grimmen*,' *i. e.* originally, an inward convulsive emotion of anger, grief, *etc.* Hence Luther renders: *Er ergrimmete*, which he himself explains by σπλαγχνίζεται."* Yet Tholuck observes that the signification of *grief* is not supported by usage, but only by analogy.† In favor of this view are—Nonnus, Buzer, Grotius and others, Lücke.‡ Tholuck, in the early editions of his Commentary, and Ewald: an emotion of great strength, analogous to the στενάζειν τῷ πνεύματι of Jesus, Mark vii. 34 (comp. Mark viii. 12).§

3. A GENERAL AFFECTION of the spirit, in which different sentiments combine and alternate.‖ This construction is supported: (1) by the choice of the expression, since the Evangelists are familiar with other terms for the definite emotion either of anger or of grief; (2) by the addition: τῷ πνεύματι. The nature of the *spirit* renders it impossible for any single *psychical* emotion to rule within it; the spirit is the all-embracing unity of the many-parted life of the soul.¶ (3) By the psychological experience, that when the soul is in a state of intense excitement, it is seized at once by the most diverse emotions (see the quotation from Göthe's *Iphigenie:* "*Es wälzet sich ein Rad von Freud' und Schmerz durch meine Seele*"—"A wheel of joy and grief revolveth through my soul."—*Leben Jesu*, p. 1125). (4) By the situation. The weeping of Mary could excite nought but the most heart-felt sympathy. But the tears of the better sort among the Jews were mingled with the tears of the unbelieving. A scene of human lamentation over death presented itself—sympathy in view of the power of death was aroused. Jesus had not to bar out this sympathy; still it was necessary that He should stand on His guard against it—and rouse Himself in indignation against it. Thus His emotion was converted into an ecstatic anticipation of victory. I had at first chosen the expression: *Er schütterte sich—He convulsed—agitated Himself.* It is significant of violent agitation. But the one upon which I finally settled seems preferable: *Er regte sich tief auf, He stirred Himself up from the deep.* He moved Himself in the spirit to such a degree that the disciples perceived His agitation in His bodily appearance,—hence: *He convulsed Himself; He billowed up,—He surged up.* A divine storm of the spirit [*ein Gottesgewitter des Geistes*] passed through His breast, under which His human nature quaked. The *fremere* invariably arises out of the depths.

[It is not inconsistent with this interpretation of Dr. Lange, if we emphasize *sin* and *death* as the chief *object* of Christ's mingled emotion and commotion. In this heart-rending scene of mourning: the grave of the departed friend, the broken hearts of the beloved sisters, and the tears of their sympathizers, Jesus saw a miniature photograph of the world of human suffering caused by the terrible curse of sin; all the graves and all the mourners passed in endless procession before His vision; He felt the combined misery and woe of the human family ("*der Menschheit ganzer Jammer fasste Ihn an*"); He was moved at once with holy indignation at sin which caused all this dreadful desolation, and with tender sympathy for the sufferers, which latter feeling found vent in tears.—**And troubled (shook) himself, ἐτάραξεν ἑαυτόν.** This is not quite the same with the passive form ἐταράχθη τῷ πνεύματι, which is used on a similar occasion, John xiii. 21, but it expresses the external manifestation of the inward commotion by a voluntary act. Hengstenberg (II. 261): "Jesus excites Himself for the energetic conflict with Death, the evil enemy of mankind." Comp. Meyer, Luthardt, Godet, *in loc.* Augustine, Bengel and Wordsworth derive from the expression the inference that Christ's affections were not *passions*, but voluntary emotions (*voluntariæ commotiones*), which He had entirely in His power, and that the emotion here spoken of was therefore orderly, rational, full of dignity and directed to proper ends.—P. S.]

Ver. 34. **Where have ye laid him?**—Manifestly, the impulse to work the miracle is completed by what has been going on in His inner life.—**Come and see.**—The answerers—Martha and Mary.

Ver. 35. **Jesus wept** ['Εδάκρυσεν ὁ 'Ιησ.].—Two little words: a whole verse, of infinite value. Significant and pertinent verse-division. On the way to the grave, Jesus weeps. After He has troubled Himself in spirit and has made good His stand against all sympathy with Jewish lamentations for the dead, He is at liberty to give Himself up to His fellow-feeling with the sisters; the tear follows His passion, as a summer rain succeeds the thunder-storm. The objection, that Jesus could not weep if He had a real presentiment of the miracle that He was about to perform, carries with it a doubt as to the compatibility of the divine and the human nature; it is also contradicted by human experience itself.* Not only the succession of feelings, but likewise the truth and disinterestedness of feeling, are explained by a fact, in accordance

* [As now used, however, *ergrimmen* always signifies in German violent emotion of anger, indignation.—P. S.]

† [Tholuck and Lücke refer to βριμάσσω, *to shake with petulance*, βράσσω, *to ferment* (intransitive), and *to shake violently* (transitive), also to the Hebrew זָעַף.—P. S.]

‡ [Among American commentators, Owen takes this view: A deep feeling of grief, and not a rebuking of such a feeling.—P. S.]

§ [Ewald (*Com.* I. 323) translates: *Er erbrauste im Geiste und erschütterte sich*, and explains that Jesus, like a hero of old, like a Jacob, gathering up the deepest powers of his mind, went forth to the conflict and in the conflict burst out in tears. Comp. Ewald's *Life of Christ*, p. 486.—P. S.]

‖ [Dr. Lange has more fully demonstrated this comprehensive interpretation in a treatise on the words: ἐνεβριμήσατο τῷ πνεύματι, in his *Miscellaneous Writings*, vol. iv. pp. 194 ff. (originally published in the *Theological Studies and Criticisms* for 1836); comp. also his *Leben Jesu*, II. 2, p. 1125. Tholuck (7th edition) substantially adopts Lange's interpretation: "We shall, then, include a feeling of horror also. *etc.* Hence we assume κινεῖσθαι to be the established philological signification, as one of the most ancient commentators, the translator of the Peshito has done."]

¶ [Meyer thinks that John might as well have written τῇ ψυχῇ (xii. 27); Godet (II. 329) distinguishes πνεῦμα as the seat of religious, ψυχή as the seat of natural emotions. There is certainly a difference. Here and xiii. 21, when speaking of the treason of Judas, and Mark viii. 12, Jesus was moved in the *spirit;* while when speaking of His approaching passion He says: "My *soul* is troubled," John xii. 27.—P. S.]

* [Neander: "The sympathizing physician in the midst of a family drowned in grief—will not his tears flow with theirs, though he knows that he has the power of giving immediate relief?"—P. S.]

with which the deepest grief may invade the mind when it is occupied with the anticipation of joy, and *vice versâ;* nay, more;—these opposite emotions may even succeed each other with the rapidity of lightning, like a "wheel of fire" in swift revolution. "Chrysologus supposed that Jesus wept for joy; Isodorus Pelus., because the raising of Lazarus would summon him from repose back to the unrest of life (this was the decision even of the *Concilium Toletanum*) *etc.* All these explanations of the fathers of the Church are utterly unnatural." HEUBNER.

[This sentence is the shortest, and yet one of the most significant verses in the Bible. It stands by itself unconnected by any particle with what precedes or what follows. It describes what was seen, and intimates what was felt. Jesus knew that He would shortly raise Lazarus, but in true sympathy He opened His heart to the *present* grief which opened to Him a picture of the universal desolations of the king of terrors; and with a sympathizing heart, not with a heart of stone, He raised the friend to life again. He felt and acted like a man before He gave a proof of His divine power; so He slept just before He stilled the storm (Matt. viii. 24). But His grief was moderate. *Δακρύειν* signifies a gentle weeping, the expression of a calm and tender grief; it differs from *κλαίειν*, the crying and wailing of the sisters and their friends, ver. 33, which implies "not only the shedding of tears, but also every external expression of grief" (Robinson, sub. *κλαίω*). It is remarkable that the very Gospel which most clearly reveals the divinity of Christ, notices this truly human trait of His character. As far as we are informed, Jesus wept or shed tears on three occasions: tears of tender friendship and silent grief at the grave of Lazarus (*ἐδάκρυσεν*); tears of bitter sorrow and loud lamentation over unbelieving Jerusalem in view of the approaching judgment, Luke xix. 41 (*ἔκλαυσεν*); and bloody tears of agony and sacerdotal intercession in Gethsemane when He bore the burden of the sins of all mankind and wrestled with the powers of darkness, Luke xxii. 44 (comp. Heb. v. 7, *μετὰ κραυγῆς ἰσχυρᾶς καὶ δακρύων*). The eternal Son of God in tears! What a sublime contrast; what a proof of His true humanity, condescending love and tender sympathy. How near He is brought in His tears to every mourner. How far more natural, lovely and attractive is a weeping Saviour than a cold, heartless, unfeeling stoic!* By His conduct at the grave He has sanctified tears of sympathy, provided only we sorrow not immoderately as those who have no hope (1 Thes. iv. 13). His tears over Jerusalem and in Gethsemane should call forth our tears of repentance and gratitude. —P. S.]

Vers. 36, 37. **Behold how he loved him.**—This even the Jews could see, without comprehending the full significance of His tears. It is certainly the intention of the evangelist to distinguish these kindly disposed Jews from the others who thus express themselves: **Could not he who opened the eyes of the blind man,** *etc.* (ver. 37). According to Chrysostom and most of the ancients, as also Luthardt and Meyer, this speech has something of malice in it;* according to Lücke, Tholuck and others, it is well meant. The idea of malice is supported by 1. the manifest intention to spread abroad an accusation against Jesus, to the effect that He was either unable (want of power) or unwilling (want of love) to avert this death; 2. the circumstance that their words occasion again the convulsive self-agitation of the Lord, and, so to speak, constrain Him to brace Himself anew in the spirit. 3. Here, as in ver. 46, John distinguishes the malicious Jews from those of the better sort by *τινὲς δέ*. ["John seldom uses *δέ* as a mere copula, but generally as *but*, see vers. 46, 49, 51." Alford]. Hence arises the conjecture that they, starting from the assumption of the powerlessness of Jesus in this case, are desirous to cast a shadow of doubt even upon the healing of the blind man (Meyer). Still less is it to be expected that these citizens of Jerusalem should cite the previous raisings of the dead in Galilee (Strauss) rather than the healing of the blind man, which last was an event of recent occurrence in Jerusalem, still fresh in the memory of all,—an occasion of admiration to some, and to others of Pharisaical offence.† Their words are the cause of fresh agitation on the part of the Lord, now, however, He is stirred not only in spirit but in Himself, *i. e.* the emotion is felt in the *soul-life* also.

Ver. 38. **To the tomb. It was a cave.**—[An indication of the comparative wealth of Lazarus and his sisters that they had a family vault, such as is here implied. The poor were buried in common places. The large concourse of mourners from Jerusalem, and the very costly ointment with which Mary anointed the feet of our Lord (xii. 3), lead to the same conclusion.—P. S.] On the Israelitish graves see Com. on *Matt.* chap. xxvii.‡ On the grave of Lazarus,

* [After the appearance of Christianity, the heathen notions about the rightfulness of human affections underwent a silent revolution, and the rigor of Stoicism was broken. Comp. the beautiful passage in Juvenal, *Sat.* 15, quoted by Trench:

. . . . *Molissima corda*
Humano generi dare se natura fatetur,
Quæ lacrymas dedit: hæc nostri pars optima
sensûs.—P. S.]

* [Alford and Godet take the same view. The second emotion of indignation (*πάλιν ἐμβριμώμενος ἐν ἑαυτῷ*, ver. 38) seems to have been provoked, partly at least, by this exhibition of unbelief, as the *οὖν* indicates.—P. S.]

† [Trench, Alford and Godet rightly regard it as a mark of historical accuracy that these dwellers in Jerusalem should refer to a miracle performed there and still fresh in their memory rather than to the former raisings of the dead in distant Galilee, which they probably may have heard of, but naturally would not thoroughly credit on mere rumor. Says Trench: "A maker up of the narrative from later and insecure traditions would inevitably have fallen upon those miracles of a like kind, as arguments of the power of Jesus to have accomplished this." Comp. the pointed remarks of Godet (II. 342) against Strauss.—P. S.]

‡ [Also the art. *Gräber* in Winer's *R. W. B.*, art. *Tomb* in Smith's *B. D.* (Hackett and Abbott's ed., vol. iv. pp. 3277 ff.), Robinson, *Researches*, I. pp. 349 ff., and Capt. C. W. Wilson, *Remains of Tombs in Palestine* (in Quarterly Statement of the Palest. Exploration Soc., Lond. 1869). The Jewish sepulchres were out of town, away from the living, and either natural caverns or artificial, excavated by man's labor from the rock, with recesses in the sides, wherein the bodies were laid, occasionally with chambers one above another, and closed by a door or a great stone to prevent the numerous jackals and beasts of prey from tearing the bodies. Many of these tombs still remain. Robinson, I. p. 352: "The numerous sepulchres which skirt the valleys on the north, east, and south of Jerusalem, exhibit for the most part one general mode of construction. A doorway in the perpendicular face of the rock, usually small and without orna-

which is said still to exist, see the books of travel (Robinson, II. p. 310).*—**And a stone lay upon** [or **against**] **it.**—Ἐπέκειτο may mean: *upon* or *before*, according as the grave is to be conceived of as a perpendicular vault (such were entered by means of steps), or as a horizontal one. That the tradition makes it a perpendicular sepulchre is not conclusive proof that it was so; yet the expression ἄρατε τὸν λίθον, seems also to testify in favor of a perpendicular grave. In Matt. xxviii. 2 the term is ἀπεκύλιτε.†

Ver. 39. **Lord, by this time he stinketh** [ἤδη ὄζει].—The fearful reality of the grave, in which her brother has lain four days, disturbs the practical woman and shakes her faith. She thinks a scandal may result from the bursting forth of the odor of corruption,—especially in the presence of so many people from Jerusalem. For it follows from the reason she assigns for her remark, that she does not already perceive this odor: **for he hath been dead four days.** [Lit. *he is now the fourth day* (*viz.* as a dead man), τεταρταῖος *quatriduanus*, an adjective marking succession of days, but used only proverbially, like δευτεραῖος, τριταῖος. δωδεκαταῖος.—P. S.]‡ "It is a proverb in the Talmud and the Targum, that corruption sets in the third day after death" (Tholuck after Wetstein). As "*the sister of the dead man*" [ἡ ἀδελφὴ τοῦ τετελευκότος] she shudders at the thought of seeing her brother in a putrefying state, of witnessing the exposure of that countenance upon which corruption had already set its seal. We cannot, from the words of Martha, draw the inference that a previous embalming of the body by wrapping spices about it, had not taken place; the customary anointing might, however, have been deferred by the sisters, because, almost unconsciously to themselves, a spark of hope was smouldering within them, as they anxiously expected the coming of Jesus. Hence, likewise, Mary had saved the precious ointment of spikenard. There is no more foundation for the statement that at this particular moment Martha, influenced by the utterances of Jesus, vers. 23-26, had merged her hope of a special raising of Lazarus in a higher stretch of faith (Meyer), than there is ground for questioning the momentary tottering of her hope (Tholuck). This only can be said: she is so agitated by the fear lest her brother appear as a putrefying corpse, that she is unmindful for the instant of the duty of submission to the word of Christ, and delays the execution of His command.

Ver. 40. **Did I not tell thee?**—Not only the words, ver. 25, but the whole of His sayings from ver. 4.—**The glory of God** appears at such time as He reveals Himself in His wonder-working might. Manifestly, therefore, they had faith in the words of Jesus as they took the stone away (41).

Ver. 41. **Jesus lifted up His eyes to heaven.**—We have already adverted to the grand aim of this form of the miraculous healing of Jesus. The Jews in Jerusalem are to see in a great sign, not only the miraculous power of Jesus but also His connection with their God in the working of this miracle. Hence the unreserved outpouring of the prayer. But the prayer is a thanksgiving: **I thank thee.** He is confident of being heard, and this presupposes earlier prayers.* So that when He says: **I knew that thou hearest me always,** an intimation is given us of an uninterrupted life of prayer, a continual union, in prayer, of the will of Jesus with the will of the Father—a union resulting in the continual working with Him of God's omnipotence. Thus Christ accomplishes His miracles as the God-Man; not in pure divinity, or as a super-human God, without the Father (see ch. v. 19, 26; vi. 6), nor in simple humanity amidst sporadic entreaties.†

At the same time this saying introduces the following utterance: **but because of the multitude standing around,** *etc.*—Those who, like Baur, have inferred from these words that the prayer of Jesus is debased to a mock-prayer have failed to comprehend the grand idea of it.‡

---

ment, leads to one or more small chambers excavated from the rock, and commonly upon the same level with the door. Very rarely are the chambers lower than the doors. The walls in general are plainly hewn; and there are occasionally, though not always, niches or resting-places for the dead bodies. In order to obtain a perpendicular face for the doorway, advantage was sometimes taken of a former quarry; or an angle was cut in the rock with a tomb in each face; or a square niche or area was hewn out in a ledge, and then tombs excavated in all three of its sides. All these expedients are seen particularly in the northern part of the valley of Jehoshaphat, and near the tombs of the Judges. Many of the doorways and fronts of the tombs along this valley are now broken away, leaving the whole of the interior exposed."—P. S.]

* [Robinson (vol. I. p. 432, Am. ed.) says: "The monks, as a matter of course, show the house of Mary and Martha, that of Simon the leper, and the sepulchre of Lazarus. The latter is a deep vault like a cellar, excavated in the lime-stone rock in the middle of the village, to which there is a descent by twenty-six steps. It is hardly necessary to remark, that there is not the slightest probability of its ever having been the tomb of Lazarus. The form is not that of the ancient sepulchres; nor does its position accord with the narrative of the New Testament, which implies that the tomb was not in the town."—P. S.]

† [Meyer leaves it undecided whether ἐπί here is to be rendered *upon* or *against*, *before*, the cave: "ἐπέκ. ἐπ' αὐτῷ *kann auch heissen:* ER LAG DARAN, DAVOR (*vgl. Homer*, *Od.* vi. 19: θύραι δ' ἐπέκειντο), *so dass ein horizontaler Eingang gedacht sein würde. Zu entscheiden ist nicht.*"—P. S.]

‡ [Olshausen, Luthardt and Trench agree with Lange that the words ἤδη ὄζει, which were spoken *before* the opening of the tomb, indicate only the *conjecture* of Martha, which was erroneous, and assume that He who sees the end from the beginning watched over the body of Lazarus in His providence that it should not hasten to corruption. But the fathers (*e.g.* Augustine: *resuscitavit putenten*), Calvin (*alios Christus suscitavit, sed nunc in putrido cadavere potentiam suam exserit*), Stier, Owen, Alford and Wordsworth take the judgment of Martha as a statement of a sensible *fact*, on the ground that the very act of death is the beginning of decomposition, and that there is no more monstrosity in the raising of a decaying corpse than in the restoration of the withered hand. Godet also is of this opinion: "*Il est plus naturel de voir dans ces mots l'expression d'un fait positif et dont elle a fait elle-même l'experience.*" As an expression of fact it has been turned to apologetic account against the hypothesis of a mere trance or swoon; but the miracle is sufficiently attested without this by the veracity of Christ and of John.—P. S.]

* [So also Meyer and Alford. Others suppose that petition and thanksgiving coincided (Merz, Tholuck), still others that Jesus thanked in anticipation of the miracle as if it was already an accomplished fact (Godet, comp. Hengstenberg).—P. S.]

† [Trench (p. 330): "The power (of working miracles) was most truly His own, not indeed in disconnection from the Father, for what He saw the Father do, that only He did; but in this, His oneness with the Father, there lay the uninterrupted power of doing these mighty works. . . . The thanks *to* God were an acknowledgment that the power was *from* God."—P. S.]

‡ [Baur calls the prayer a *Scheingebet*, Weisse a *Schaugebet*, conceived by the evangelist in the apologetic interest for the divinity of Christ (Strauss, Scholten). Such impious nonsense arises from utter ignorance of the singular intimacy

In presence of the Jews of Jerusalem, Jesus calls upon their God as His Father, and is heard.* Thus Moses, in pursuance of God's instructions, produces his credentials as the ambassador of the God of Israel, before his nation and before Pharaoh (Ex. iv. 3 ff; chap. vii. 9); and thus Elijah on Mount Carmel, before the priests of Baal and the backsliding people, petitions the God of Israel for the decisive sign from heaven which shall corroborate the truth of the Israelitish faith, 1 Kings xviii. 36 ff. For this cause, the design of this prayer is so distinctly emphasized: **that they might believe that Thou didst send Me.**—That prayer may not have a reflexive reference to the hearers of it, is a tenet which finds prayer only in pantheistic moods; it would, if consistently acted upon, abolish the idea of motherly, ecclesiastical, judicial prayer (the oath), of prayer offered in performing miracles and of prayer generally.

Ver. 43. **Lazarus, come forth!**—Properly: Lazarus, hither! forth! [δεῦρο ἔξω, without a verb, *huc foras! Ici, dehors!* The simple grandeur, brevity and force of this resurrection call corresponds with the mighty effect, and may be compared to the sublime passage in Genesis: *Let there be light! And there was light.* Cyril calls it θεοπρεπὲς καὶ βασιλικὸν κέλευσμα.—P. S.] According to Origen [and Chrysostom] the moment of awakening preceded the thanksgiving of Jesus and the call merely occasioned the forthcoming of the recipient of new life. But, manifestly, the loud call with a powerful voice and majestic utterance should itself be recognized as the moment of awakening.†

Ver. 44. **Bound hand and foot with grave-clothes.**—Since the dead man was so wrapped up, even his face being covered, there happened, according to Basilius (θαύμαζε θαῦμα ἐν θαύματι), Chrysostom and many others, Lampe, Stier, a miracle within a miracle,—namely, that Lazarus was able to go forth in spite of his wrappings.‡ Others, again, have assumed that he was wrapped about after the fashion of the Egyptians, his hands and feet being bandaged separately (Olshausen, De Wette). Lücke supposes him to have been wrapped from head to foot so closely that his freedom of motion was not impeded.§ From our passage the windings certainly seem to have been partial; whether they were applied in the Egyptian style or not. Such might also have been the idea of the sisters, particularly as the ceremonies of anointing and interment had not yet been completed. But it is obvious that the miracle of new life might be carried out in a miraculous walking, similar to somnambulism. And indeed it was necessary that the forthcomer should be disencumbered of his wrappings, in order that he might move with perfect freedom,—in accordance with the words of Jesus: **Loose him and let him go.**—*i. e.* go home independent of aid. We cannot adopt the inference of Grotius; he holds that Christ did not accompany him: *ne quasi in triumphum ducere videretur.*

[The terms ἄφετε ὑπάγειν, as Godet observes, have a triumphant tone, like the order to the cripple: "Take up thy bed and walk" (ch. v. 8). Trench: "St. John here breaks off the narrative of the miracle itself, leaving us to imagine their joy, who thus beyond all expectation received back their dead from the grave; a joy, which was well nigh theirs alone, among all the mourners of all times,

> 'Who to the verge have followed those they love
> And on the insuperable threshold stand,
> With cherished names its speechless calm reprove,
> And stretch in the abyss their ungrasped hand.'

He leaves this, and passes on to show us the historic significance of this miracle in the development of the Lord's earthly history, the permitted link which it formed in the chain of those events, which were to end, according to the determinate decree and counsel of God, in the atoning death of the Son of God upon the cross." —P. S.]

DOCTRINAL AND ETHICAL.

1. *Christ the Resurrection and the Life*, the principle of the future resurrection:

a. The foretokens of the principle: the miracles of transformation and the histories of raisings from the dead in the Old Testament, and the raisings of the dead effected by Jesus.

b. The appearance of the principle in the revivifying life and spiritual resurrection of Christ.

c. The operations of the principle until the first resurrection and until the general resurrection.

2. *Faith* in Christ, the Son of God, embraces the resurrection.

3. The *mysterious, holy affections* in the life of the Lord. The sensational life in the spirit or the innermost and highest emotion, within which all feelings revolve;—supreme compassion for the misery of men, supreme indignation at the unbelief of the world. The Lord's bracing of Himself against all sympathy with ungodly sorrow, while at the same time fully sympathizing with the godly sorrow of men.

4. THE RAISING OF LAZARUS.

Different *interpretations:* (1) Lazarus was *apparently* dead (Paulus, Ammon, Schweizer and others); (2) the account a myth (Strauss); either a misunderstanding of a conversation concerning the resurrection, held with the two women of Bethany on the occasion of the death of Lazarus (Weisse); or a remodelling of the story of the raising of the young man at Nain (Gfrörer); or a dogmatico-allegorical representation of the

---

between Christ and the Father, which is so often asserted in this Gospel (ch. v. 19-21, 36, 37; viii. 16, 18, 29, 42; x. 25, 30, 38) and illustrated on this occasion. By virtue of this intimacy He, the only Begotten, never addressed God as "*our* Father," but as "*My* Father" or "Father" simply, and stood in *constant* communication with Him so that His prayers assumed, as it were, the character of reflection and mutual consultation, and were *always* answered.—P. S.]

* [So also Godet: "*En rendant grâces à Dieu devant tout le peuple avant de faire le miracle, Jésus met positivement Dieu en part dans l'œuvre qui va se faire; cette œuvre devient par là celle de Dieu même. Jehovah, le Dieu d'Israel, sera désormais le garant de sa mission,—ou le complice de son imposture.*"—P. S.]

† [So also Hilary (*nullo intervallo vocis et vitæ*), Meyer, Alford, Trench. So in the general resurrection the dead will come forth from their graves when they hear the quickening *voice* of the Son of Man, ch. v. 28, 29; comp. the "shout," 1 Thes. iv. 16; and "the last trump," 1 Cor. xv. 52.—P. S.]

‡ [Also Augustine: *processit ille* VINCTUS: *non ergo pedibus propriis, sed virtute producentis.*]

§ [So also Meyer, Trench, Owen. Alford is uncertain.—P. S.]

δόξα of Christ (Baur).*—At the grave of Lazarus modern skeptical criticism manifestly celebrates its own dissolution—every man tells a different story.

Omission of the history in the Synoptists: (1) The synoptists were not acquainted with it (Lücke and others). (2) It lay beyond the circle of their statements (Meyer). (3) It was omitted out of consideration for the family of Bethany (Herder, Schulthess, Olshausen, Lange, *Leben Jesu,* II. 2, p. 1133). Meyer assures us that this last explanation runs counter to the mind and spirit of that first age of Christianity (he should say rather: to the spiritual bravado of the Montanists and Circumcellians). Comp. John xii. 10.

Instrumentalities of the miracle. a. The general one: Christ the resurrection and the life, the principle of raisings, quickenings, of the dead. *b. The special one:* Christ, now entertaining a presentiment of His own death and resurrection. It was necessary that Jerusalem and the Supreme Council should behold a sign of His glory beaming very near to them; this robbed them of all excuse. *c. The most special one:* The faith of the sisters and of Lazarus, and the expectation of all,—especially of the dying man,—that Jesus would come and manifest His power and willingness to help; an expectation which Lazarus preserved in death, as Jesus Himself carried down to death His confidence in His own resurrection (see my *Leben Jesu,* II. 2, p. 327 and 1127 ff.).

The form of the miracle: A prayer for the hearing of the God of Israel, as a testimony to the Lord in the face of Jerusalem.

Its import: The crown of His raisings from the dead, the presage of His resurrection, the first flashing of His δόξα from the Mount of Olives over Jerusalem.

5. "As regards the *moral application,* there is no need for allegorical interpretation such as is found in Jerome, Augustine, Bourdaloue, H. Martin, *etc.* This allegorical interpretation is obviously without historical foundation; it is unnatural,—and to make Lazarus, the friend of Jesus, the type of a sinner utterly dead and even stinking,—is also unseemly." HEUBNER.

HOMILETICAL AND PRACTICAL.

The raising of Lazarus as the most glorious of the revivifying miracles of Jesus: 1. In respect of the peculiar circumstances attending it in comparison with the previous raisings of the dead; 2. in respect of its intrinsic significance, as demonstrating that Christ is the Resurrection and the Life, or as a demonstration of His glory; 3. in respect of its decisive effects.—Or: the raising of Lazarus in respect of its essential features: 1. The introductory conversation; 2. the walk to the grave; 3. the prayer of thanksgiving; 4. the awakening call; 5. the appearance of the dead man; 6. the effect of his resurrection.—The arrival of Jesus on the fourth day after the burial of Lazarus. Or: Jesus, coming as a Saviour, never comes too late.—How the banished and fugitive Jesus from Peræa and those haughty scorners of Him, the Jews from Jerusalem, meet again at the grave of Lazarus.—The different kinds of condolence on the death of a member of a family: 1. The condolence of the world in general; 2. the ceremonious condolence of Pharisees; 3. the hearty condolence of relatives and friends; 4. the heavenly condolence of Christ.—Christ waiting before the village, or the divine power of Christ in His human weakness,—the type of the Christian life.—The greatest precaution combined with the most joyful anticipation of victory.—Martha and Mary at the grave of Lazarus. Comparison of the two, 1. At their first meeting with Jesus (Luke x. 38), 2. at the second here, 3. at the third in the history of the anointing.—The saying of both: *Lord, if Thou hadst been here, etc.*—The *if* of mourners in view of the dead. *If* this and that had happened: 1. In what degree *sinful?* As an expression of grief that will not be reconciled to the dispensation of God. 2. In what degree *warranted?* As an expression of pain investigating the causes of the suffering. 3. In what degree *salutary?* As an expression of humiliation before God on account of actual neglect.—The trial of faith imposed upon Martha.—The deliverance of Martha from petty household cares by means of the deep distress and mighty aid.—Christ the Resurrection and the Life: 1. What this means: *a.* the Life unto resurrection; *b.* the Resurrection unto life. 2. What this signifies to believers: *a.* to the dead; *b.* to the living.—Believest thou this?—The confession of Martha in reply to the question of Christ touching her faith.—How Martha here already subordinates herself to Mary, whom she before desired to tutor (she takes a still more subordinate position in the history of the anointing,—serving silently).—"The Master is here:" 1. The Master is here 2. and calleth thee.—The presageful visit to the grave, prelusive to the most presageful visit to the grave of Jesus.—The weeping of Mary and the weeping of the Jews: 1. In itself; the external similarity, the internal diversity; 2. in its signification: thus voices mingle in the songs of the sanctuary, tears in our houses, different spirits in the company of Jesus.—The twice-repeated convulsion of Jesus in spirit: 1. The occasion, 2. the mood, 3. the fruit.—The sensational life of Jesus.—The heart of Jesus in its full revelation: 1. In the full revelation of its love, 2. of its holiness, 3. of its divine power.—How the Lord Himself must guard His temper before His great work.—The moving and yet so salutary sight of the grave.—Our graves.—In their relation to the grave of Christ.—The temptation of Martha.—The prayer of thanksgiving and its signification: 1. In relation to the Lord: reliance on God; 2. with reference to the Jews: a miracle in fellowship with their God, as a testimony against them and to them; 3. in relation to the mourners: the divine consecration of their human joy.—The call of Christ three ghostly words, instinct with vital power: 1. The name, 2. to Christ, 3. forth.—The voice of Christ.—The infinitely significative and comprehensive nature of the human voice.—The unique heaven-tone (the peal of love and lightning-flash of life) in the voice of Christ.—The decidedness of Christ in all His

* [Dr. Lange omits the disgraceful explanation of Renan, who here resorts to the theory of a downright imposture. See above, p. 339.—P. S.]

vital traits,—even in His voice.—The appearance of the living man in the garments of the grave, a type of the new life of the Christian in the old vestments of death.—What is expressed by the words: "Loose him and let him go": 1. How the adoring amazement of the chronicler is lost in silence; 2. how Christ gives Lazarus credit for full vital strength; 3. how He diverts attention from Himself to him who has been raised up.—The three evangelical stories of Bethany.

STARKE: CANSTEIN: Jesus comes soon enough because He always brings salvation with Him, though to us He often seems to come too late.—HEDINGER: Everything is possible to the power of God: it quickens physically and spiritually those who have lain in the grave for an hour or for a thousand years,—who have sinned for a long or for a short time.—To comfort the mourning is a part of godliness.—QUESNEL: We comfort one who has lost his brother by death, and have little or no compassion for him who has lost his God.—OSIANDER: See how faith wrestles and battles with unbelief!—God is rich above all who call on Him and can do infinitely more than we ask.—BIBL. WIRT.: The greatest consolation of Christians in all kinds of misery and so in peril of death, is the resurrection of the dead, 1 Cor. xv. 54; Heb. ii. 14.—He who believes not on Christ is dead ere he dies.—Ver. 28. Ah, how fitting it is for one friend to call the other to Christ!—It is often better to preach Christ in secret than to proclaim Him publicly.—Ver. 29. HEDINGER: Love tarrieth not.—Ver. 31. ZEISIUS: Those whose hearts are very heavy—and particularly those that are sorely tempted—should not be left alone.—Ver. 32. CANSTEIN: A believing knowledge of Jesus worketh holy reverence toward Him and deep humility.—The misery of men moves Jesus' pity. We too, after His example, should pity the wretched.—ZEISIUS: We may weep and lament for them that are asleep in Jesus,—but with moderation; and we may comfort ourselves, on the other hand, with the future, joyful resurrection, 1 Thes. iv. 13, 18.—Ver. 35. Thus He wept over Jerusalem (Luke xix. 41) and in the garden of Gethsemane, Heb. v. 7. He first gives a sign of His true humanity and then of His divinity.—Ver. 41. *Ibid.*: Learn here from Jesus, when thou art about anything of importance, not to enter upon it without prayer.—Ver. 43. OSIANDER: A testimony to the divine majesty of Christ.—Ver. 45. QUESNEL: It is good for us to visit pious people; sometimes our salvation depends thereon.—GERLACH: Jesus begins here, as He often does, with words purposely mysterious and sifting; they sound like a general consolation uttered in view of the future resurrection.—It was the grand aim of Jesus in many of His discourses to exhibit the unity of the spiritual and bodily resurrection; He therefore raised up the bodies of the dead.—The resurrection of the wicked is not a true resurrection, but the second death.—He calls the dead as He would a living man, as God calls that which is not as though it were, Rom. iv. 17.

LISCO, ver. 33: The affections of believers have not the mastery over them; they are not passions.—BRAUNE: Mourning has a good name in the Old Testament; Abraham, Isaac and Jacob mourned. And Paul writes (Rom. xii. 15): "Rejoice with them that do rejoice, and weep with them that weep." Comp. Phil. ii. 27.—From the God of all comfort cometh the gift of consolation.—Ver. 27. In *this* belief is contained her all. Lest her defective conception should deprive her of the enjoyment of salvation.—Mary, ver. 32. Not another word,—only tears; they speak louder.—*He was convulsed, etc.* What a glorious glimpse of the great heart of Jesus John gives us here!—Scripture mentions eight persons who were raised from the dead: the son of the widow of Sarepta, by means of Elijah (1 Kings, xvii. 22), the son of the Shunamitess by Elisha (2 Kings, iv. 35), a dead man who was cast into the grave of Elisha (2 Kings, xiii. 21), the young man of Nain (Luke vii. 15), the daughter of Jairus (Matt. ix. 25), Lazarus, Tabitha by Peter (Acts ix. 40), Eutychus by Paul (Acts xx. 9).—GOSSNER, ver. 17. Yet He never fails to come.—No Christian dies.—It is true a child of God may outwardly suffer all manner of things,—but that is to be sick; that is not death.—*Mary.* She arose, not to go to the dead, but to Him who was her life.—Mary spoke in the same tone that her sister used. For it is customary for one thing to infect another. One man may discourage and dishearten another.—Another time He said on a similar occasion: Weep not! Namely, for the consolation of the widow of Nain. But here He weeps Himself. By His tears 1. He heals (hallows) ours, 2. He wipes them away.—The mighty voice of the Saviour a type of His almighty grace.

HEUBNER: The longer faith is obliged to wait, the stronger faith grows by waiting and trial,—the more glorious is the help afforded (Wichelhaus).—Ver. 24. A general belief in a certain truth is indeed of no avail. This does not touch a man. It must become a faith personally applied to and personally concerning us.—"Believest thou this?" A proof-question for every one.—"The inner relationship of the heart to Jesus must remain a secret to the world, although we should freely confess Jesus" (Wichelhaus).—The Master calleth *thee.* It is a question of personal relationship.—Ver. 29. Who may delay when Jesus calls him?—What divine strength human tears possess!—Ver. 43. The voice that we now hear is the authoritative word of the Awakener of the Dead, who hath the keys of hell and of death.—Like a spirit Lazarus comes forth, that at the sight of him all may be seized with trembling and awe, as they think of the invisible world thus brought near to them.—The dead man vouchsafes no narrative to our ears. "He had nought to say in words of this earth" (Herder).—SCHLEIERMACHER: The Jews. Such sympathy in the common incidents of life as is manifested even by men who do not share our feelings in regard to the things which are most important and which we have most at heart, should not be condemned by us as devoid of sincerity.—The grief that locks itself up within itself is selfish, inasmuch as it separates a man from connection with his brethren.—That which can rise so high (to God), that which is capable of such communion with the universal fountain of life, is also removed beyond the power of death. If thou believe, thou shalt see the glory of God.

MALLET: Jesus' wrath and tears.—Tears are not only the signs of love, interest, grief; they are also infallible signs of human impotence and weakness. Thus tears here reveal His holy love, but they conceal His might and glory.—She called the grave the place of corruption,—the Lord calls it the place of glory.—The Jews. There is a power in the rays of the sun. They wake the vital germ within the grain of corn and call a new, beautiful and manifold life into being. But the same sun-beam draws poisonous vapors out of bogs and morasses. It summons life from the one,—death from the other.

[CRAVEN: From ORIGEN: Ver. 41. *Then they took away the stone;* Some delay had arisen; it is best to let nothing come between the commands of Jesus and doing them.—*Jesus lifted up His eyes:* We should pray after Christ's pattern—lift up the eyes of our heart above present things in memory, in thought, in intention.——From HILARY: Vers. 41, 42. Christ's prayer did not benefit Himself, but our faith; He did not want help, but we want instruction.——From AUGUSTINE: Ver. 22. Martha does not say, Bring my brother to life again, but *I know whatsoever Thou wilt ask, God will give it Thee—i. e.,* what Thou wilt do is for Thy judgment and not for my presumption to determine.—Ver. 25. *He that believeth in Me:* Faith is the life of the soul.—Ver. 34. *Where have ye laid him?* He knew, but He asked to try the faith of His people.—Ver. 35. *Jesus wept:* Wherefore did He weep, but to teach men to weep?—Ver. 39. *Take ye away the stone:* Mystically, Take away the burden of the law, proclaim grace. [?]——From CHRYSOSTOM: Vers. 20, 28. Martha does not take her sister with her because she would speak with Christ alone; when her hopes had been raised by Him she called Mary.—Ver. 29. In her devotions to (trust in?) her Master, she had no time to think of her afflictions.—Vers. 35-38. That He *wept* and *groaned* are mentioned to show the reality of His human nature.——From BEDE: Vers. 32, 33. Mary did not say so much as Martha, she could not speak for weeping, (but her *tears* were as effective as the *words* of her sister.—E. R. C.)——From ALCUIN: Ver. 17. Our Lord delayed for *four days* that the resurrection of Lazarus might be the more glorious.—Ver. 25. I am the Resurrection, because I am the Life.—Ver. 26. Jesus knew that she believed, but sought a confession unto salvation.—Ver. 35. *Jesus wept* because He was the fountain of pity.—Vers. 43, 44. Christ *awakes,* because His power it is which quickens inwardly; the disciples *loose,* because by the ministry they who are quickened are absolved, [?] (*through* the ministry they are delivered from the bondage of sin.—E. R. C.)——From THEOPHYLACT: Ver. 28. *The Master is come and calleth for thee:* the *presence* of Christ in itself a call.—Vers. 33-35. He *groaned—wept:* Jesus sometimes gave His human nature free vent, sometimes He restrained it: He acted thus—1. to prove that He is very man; 2. to teach us the due measure of joy and grief—the *absence* of sympathy and sorrow is brutal, the *excess* is womanly [better: heathenish.—P. S.]—Ver. 43. *He cried with a loud voice*—the symbol of that trumpet which will sound at the general resurrection.——From BURKITT: Vers. 21, 22-38. *Faith* and *infirmity* mixed together: *faith,* in Martha's firm persuasion of Christ's power; *infirmity,* in her limiting Him as to *place* and *time.*—Ver. 23. Christ's meek answer to Martha's passionate discourse.—Ver. 30. The earnestness of Christ to finish His work—He went to the grave before entering the house.—Ver. 35. *Jesus wept* partly *from* compassion, partly *for* example—1. *from* compassion, (1) to *humanity* debased by sin to death, (2) to *Lazarus* whom He was about to bring back to a sinful and suffering world, ((3) to the sorrowing sisters.—E. R. C.); 2. *for example,* to bring tears from us—(1) at the sight of others' woes, (2) at the graves of our friends.—Ver. 39. *Take ye away the stone:* Our hands must do their utmost before Christ will help.—Ver. 43. Our Lord did not say *Lazarus, revive,* as to one dead; but *Come forth,* teaching us that they are alive to Him who are dead to us.——From M. HENRY: Ver. 17. *When Jesus came:* Promised salvations though they often come *slowly,* always come *surely.*—Ver. 19. The home of Martha and Mary a house of mourning.—Grace will keep sorrow from the *heart* (chap. xiv. 1) not from the *house.*—Where there are *mourners,* there ought to be *comforters.*—They comforted them *concerning their brother,* speaking (probably), 1. of the good name he had left behind; 2. of the happy state to which he had gone.—Ver. 20. The different temperaments of Martha and Mary, as manifested by their different conduct.—Ver. 21. *If Thou hadst been here:* We are apt to add to our troubles by fancying what *might have been.*—Ver. 22. When we know not what in *particular* to ask, let us in *general* refer ourselves to God. When we know not what to pray for, the Great Intercessor knows and is never refused.—Ver. 23. The comforting answer of Jesus. *Thy brother shall rise again,* directing Martha's thoughts forward to what *shall be.*—Vers. 25, 26. Note 1. The sovereign power of Christ, *I am the Resurrection and the Life;* 2. the promise of the new Covenant, (1) what it is, *life* (*a*) for the *body, a blessed resurrection,* (*b*) for the *soul, a blessed immortality,* (2) to whom made, *believers in Him.*—Ver. 27. Martha's *Creed;* observe 1. The *guide* of her faith, *the word of Christ;* 2. The *ground* of her faith, *the authority of Christ;* 3. The *matter* of her faith, *that* Christ *was* (1) THE CHRIST—the *anointed One,* (2) *The Son of God,* (3) *The One who should come, ὁ ἐρχόμενος.*—Vers. 29-31. The (gracious) *haste* of Mary; she did not consult 1. the decorum of her mourning, 2. her neighbours.—Vers. 29-32. Mary's abounding love for Christ; though He had seemed unkind in His delay she takes it not amiss.—Vers. 31-33. The Jews who followed Mary led to Christ by the beholding of the miracle; it is good to cleave to Christ's friends in their sorrows, for thereby we may come to know Him better.—Ver. 33. The *tears* of Mary; the tears of devout affection have a loud, prevailing voice with Christ.—*He was troubled, i. e., He troubled Himself;* He was voluntary both in His *passion* and His *compassion.*—Ver. 35. *Jesus wept,* showing that He was *a man of sorrows and acquainted with grief.*—Vers. 39, 40. Martha's (momentary) distrust, and Christ's gentle reproof and re-assurance.—Ver. 41. The prayer of Christ teaches us in praying—1. to call God, *Father;* 2. in our prayers to praise Him.—Ver. 42. The objects of His *public* thanksgiving—1. to obviate the (possible) objections of His enemies that He wrought miracles by *charms* or the power of Satan; 2. to corroborate the faith of His friends.—Ver. 43. *Loud voice*—1. *significant* of the power put forth; 2. *typical* of other works of resurrection—(1) of the *gospel call,* (2) of the Archangel's trumpet at the last day.—Ver. 44. The miracle was wrought—1. *speedily,* 2. *perfectly,* 3. with the additional miracle, that Lazarus *came forth* though *bound* hand and foot.——From SCOTT: Ver. 41. We cannot raise the spiritually dead, but we should remove the stones and the grave clothes.——From STIER: Ver. 21. *Lord, if Thou hadst been here;* thus does man look back with *if* in all his heavy trials.—Ver. 22. Martha at this point a heroine in faith, but only for a moment.—Ver. 24. The implied dissatisfaction of the bereaved one with the mere promise of a resurrection at the last day—("*Half-faith* always does what Martha here does." DRAESEKE).—Ver. 25. I am the Resurrection —1. *because* I am the Life; 2. *as* I am the Life —in the same most intrinsically true, and already prevailing, sense.—Vers. 25, 26. He that believeth in Me shall receive a life which death cannot invade. When the *living* bury *His living* nothing should be heard but resurrection joy. —Ver. 33. *He groaned in the spirit* (*ἐνεβριμήσατο τῷ πνεύματι*): The *sorrow* of Jesus on account of sin, and His *wrath* against death.—Ver. 44. *Loose him:* The relics of the (spiritual) grave are (in the case of the spiritually quickened) to be removed, by the Lord's appointment, through the ministry of men.——From BARNES: Ver. 26. *Believest thou this?* The time of affliction a favorable period to try ourselves whether we have faith.—Ver. 28. *The Master:* A title which Jesus claimed for Himself, Matt. xxiii. 8, 10.—Ver. 35. *Jesus wept:* Learn—1. that the most tender friendship is not inconsistent with the most pure religion; 2. that it is right to sympathize with the afflicted; 3. that sorrow at the death of friends is right; 4. the tenderness of the character of Jesus.—Ver. 40. *The glory of God:* The power and goodness displayed in the resurrection.——From MELVILLE: Ver. 25. *I am the Resurrection and the Life;* Christ the cause and the origin of the immortality of our bodies and our souls.——From HALL: Ver. 28. *Secretly* for fear of the unbelieving Jews: Christianity doth not bid us abate anything of our wariness. ——From A PLAIN COMMENTARY (Oxf.): Ver. 20. The blessedness of Martha in going forth to meet her Lord.—Ver. 30. By His remaining without the town, the whole body of friends brought to Him (and to the beholding of the miracle.—E. R. C.)——From HUTCHESON: Ver. 24. Men believe great things that are *far off,* when their faith proves weak in a less matter of *present* trial.——From WILLIAMS: Vers. 33-41. God created man by a word, without effort; but recalls him to life not without many groans and tears and intercessions.——From RYLE: Vers. 20-27. To know how much grace believers have, we must see them in trouble.—Ver. 21. A strange mixture of emotions—1. reproachful passion; 2. love; 3. faith; 4. unbelief.—Ver. 24. *General* faith is easier than *particular.*—Ver. 31. Those who came to comfort, themselves blessed.—Vers. 33-35. He *saw* weeping and He wept (as the consequence of His real humanity); He still retains His human nature.—Ver. 36. *Behold how He loved him!* Of all graces, love most arrests the attention and influences the opinion of the world. —Ver. 40. *Said I not unto thee:* The best believers need reminding of Christ's sayings.——From OWEN: Vers. 25, 26. *He that believeth in Me, etc.:* Our Lord's commentary on the preceding words, *I am the Resurrection and the Life.*

Vers. 41, 42. The duty of *public thanksgiving* for gracious answers to prayer*—1. that God may be glorified by the one benefited before others; 2. that others may be led to glorify Him.]

* [Is not the address recorded in these verses simply a *thanksgiving* spoken in respect of a previously offered *private prayer?* Is it not probable that the prayer was being offered during the period of delay beyond Jordan, throughout the travel to Bethany, and in the *groanings* at the sepulchre?—E. R. C.]

C. *Two-fold result of the raising of Lazarus. The believing Jews. The obdurate ones as betrayers. The high-priestly prophecy, or the extinction of the ancient Urim and Thummim. Demoniacal policy and Divine counsel. Jesus now in the wilderness of Ephraim, as He was in the wilderness at the beginning of His ministry.*

(VERS. 45-57.)

45 Then many [Many therefore] of the Jews which came [who had come][1] to Mary,
46 and had seen the things which Jesus [what he] did, believed on [in] him. But
some of them went their ways [went away] to the Pharisees, and told them what
things [*omit* things] Jesus had done.
47 Then [Therefore] gathered the chief priests and the Pharisees a council [the
Council, or, the Sanhedrin][2] and said, What do we [shall we do, or, are we to do]?
48 for this man doeth [worketh] many miracles [signs]. If we let him thus alone [thus
go on], all *men* [*omit men*] will believe on [in] him; and the Romans shall [will]

49 come and take away both our place and nation. And [a certain] one of them,
named [*omit named*] Caiaphas, being the [*omit* the] high priest that same [*omit*
50 same] year, said unto them, Ye know nothing at all, Nor [do ye] consider that
it is expedient for us [for you],[3] that one man should die for the people, and that
51 the whole nation perish not [and not the whole nation perish]. And this spake
he [he spoke] not of [from] himself: but being high priest that year, he prophe-
sied [gave the high-priestly prophetic decision] that Jesus should [was about to] die
52 for that [the] nation; And not for that [the] nation only, but that also he should
[that he might also] gather together in [into] one [body, or, people] the children of
God that were [are] scattered abroad.
53 Then [Therefore] from that day forth they took counsel together[4] for [*omit* for]
54 to put him to death. Jesus therefore walked no more [longer] openly [freely]
among the Jews; but went [departed] thence unto a [into the] country near to
[*omit* to] the wilderness, unto a city called Ephraim, and there continued [so-
55 journed, abode] with his [the] disciples. And [Now] the Jews' passover [the pass-
over of the Jews] was nigh at hand [*omit* nigh, or, at hand]: and many went out
56 of the country up to Jerusalem before the passover, to purify themselves. Then
sought they [They sought therefore] for Jesus, and spake [said] among themselves,
as they stood in the temple, What think ye, that he will not come to the feast?
57 Now both [*omit* both][5] the chief priests and the Pharisees had given a command-
ment [issued commandments or, ordered],[6] that, if any man [any one] knew where
he were [was], he should shew *it* [give information, or, make it known], that they
might take [seize] him.

TEXTUAL AND GRAMMATICAL.

[1] Ver. 45.—[Οἱ ἐλθόντες is the true reading, supported by Origen, and adopted by Alford, Tischendorf, *etc.*, instead of τῶν ἐλθόντων of Cod. D.—P. S.]

[2] Ver. 47.—[συνέδριον means the Sanhedrin, the great council of the Jews. See EXEG.—P. S.]

[3] Ver. 50.—[Tischendorf (ed. 1869), Alford, Westcott and Hort read ὑμῖν in accordance with B. D. L, *etc.*, instead of ἡμῖν. Lange follows here the text. rec.—P. S.]

[4] Ver. 53.—[Tischendorf supplies συνεβουλεύσαντο by ἐβουλεύσαντο in accordance with Sin. B. D.—P. S.]

[5] Ver. 57.—καὶ is omitted by Lachmann and Tischendorf in accordance with many Codd. Yet it is recommended by Cod. D. and others, and was perhaps omitted because men failed to recognize the great intensification of the persecution of Jesus expressed in this mandate. Since the decree in question must be disseminated throughout the land, we also consider the reading ἐντολάς, in accordance with B. M., *etc.*, to be correct. [The first καί after δεδώκεισαν, which in the E. V. is rendered *both*, must be rejected on the authority of ℵ. A. B. K. L. M. U. X., Alford, Tischendorf, Westcott and Hort.—P. S.]

[6] Ver. 57.—[The singular ἐντολήν of the text. rec. as a correction (because but one is mentioned) must be set aside for the plural ἐντολάς, *orders*, on the authority of Cod. Sin. and B., *etc.*—P. S.]

EXEGETICAL AND CRITICAL.

Ver. 45. **Many of the Jews therefore.**—A new split in the Pharisaical party in Jerusalem itself. The important effect of the raising of Lazarus is observable in the fact that many of these Jews became believers. Some, however, of those who witnessed the miracle at Bethany, separate from the believing portion and confirm themselves in their obduracy, giving notice of the event to the Pharisees, *i. e.*, here, the hostile members of the Sanhedrin. Origen held these individuals to be friends of Jesus, whose intentions in giving the information were good. On the other hand the view of Euthymius, who regarded them as malevolents, is the one generally entertained. According to Euthymius, they denounced Him as a sorcerer (γοέτης); according to Theophylact, as a sacrilegious person, who had disinterred a corpse. These hypotheses overlook the possibility that the hardened denunciators held the same opinion to which Caiaphas gives utterance ver. 50, and considered Jesus to be merely a dangerous man. And thus their notification is apprehended by the generality of people. Meyer impugns the assumption of hostile intention on the part of these men; it is οἱ ἐλθόντες [who had come], says he,—not τῶν ἐλθόντων [the reading of D. and text. rec.—P. S.] But in this construction the evangelist would say, that the Jews who came to Bethany constituted a plurality of the whole body of Jews. The better plan would be, perhaps, to distinguish among the spectators friends of Mary, sharers of her sentiments; these had come to Mary and were θεασάμενοι. The Jews were well aware of the deadly enmity of the Pharisees towards Jesus; if these informants had been friends, they must have witnessed for Jesus with heroic martyr-courage, and they would have secured a firm and conspicuous station in the evangelical history.

Ver. 47. **The high priests and the Pharisees therefore assembled the Sanhedrin.**—See Comm. on *Matthew*, chap. v. p. 113, Am. Ed.; Winer, Art. *Synedrium.*

1. The NAME: συνέδριον, talmudic: סַנְהֶדְרִין, *Sanhedrin.**

* [*Sanhedrin* is more accurate than *Sanhedrim*, though this is more frequently used (even by Alford). The rabbinical attempts to trace it to a Hebrew root are futile (see Buxtorf, *sub verb.*); it is formed from the Greek συνέδριον (σύνεδρος, ἕδρα), a sitting together, an assembly, a council. Winer's article is more scholarly than the article *Sanhedrim* in Smith's *Dictionary of the Bible.* Lange has conveniently brought together all the necessary information on the subject.—P. S.]

2. Signification: the supreme, theocratico-hierarchical Court of the Jews, resident at Jerusalem.

3. Composition and organization. It consisted of seventy-one members forming three classes (chief priests, elders, scribes). At that time it was composed of Pharisaic and Sadducean elements (Caiaphas, the high-priest, belonged to the Sadducean party). The Sanhedrin had a president (הַנָּשִׂיא), ordinarily the high-priest, who was assisted by a vice-president (אַב בֵּית דִּין). There is not sufficient proof that a third functionary, styled חָכָם, stood at the left of the high-priest (Vitringa).

4. Sessions. *Extraordinary:* in urgent cases at the house of the high-priest. *Ordinary:* held daily (with the exception of the Sabbath and feast days), of old in a session room adjoining the temple, called *Gazith*, but in later times (from a period of forty years before the destruction of the temple) in places near the temple-mount.

5. Matters coming under the cognizance of this court as a forum: Matters concerning a whole tribe, a false prophet, the high-priest, or an arbitrary war, or blasphemy.

6. Punitory power. Formerly: Infliction of capital punishment (stoning, burning, beheading, hanging); later: excommunication and recommendation for capital punishment.

7. Administration. Connection with the minor courts; highest court of appeal from these; intercourse with them through surrogates and apparitors.

8. Extent of authority: Legislation, administration, justice.

9. History. According to the Talmudists this court originated in the institution of Moses, Num. xi. 24. That, probably, was but prelusive. So, too, the supreme court of Jehoshaphat, 2 Chron. xix. 8. Increased importance of this institution after the exile. The *γερουσία* in the time of the Seleucidæ (2 Macc. i. 10); the first decided mention at the time of Antipater and Herod (Joseph. *Antiqu.*, xiv. 9, 4). A session of the Sanhedrin is called.

What shall we do [or, **What are we to do**, *ποιοῦμεν*]?—The indicative, *i. e.*, something *must* be done.—**For this man.**—Implacable hatred. They no longer protest against the many signs of Jesus; but nevertheless they contemptuously say: *this man.* Doubtless the expression—*many miracles*, is also intended to obliterate the simple recognition of the grand raising of the dead. At the same time an expression of fear that He would perform yet other miracles.

Ver. 48. **If we let Him thus alone.**—The policy of fear and anti-christianity. It is a *wicked* and *empty* fear that all will believe on Him; a *wicked* and *empty* fear that thence troubles will arise that will cause the Romans to invade the country; a *wicked* and *empty* fear that they will then make an end of the Jewish commonwealth. There is, moreover, in each one of these considerations a co-operative element of falsehood; hence it is likewise a trebly hypocritical fear. And a fear, in sooth, which thinks itself justified by its motives, in carrying on hostile proceedings against a prophet of God, a doer of many miracles. In fine, a fear that occasions the very mischief it considers itself bound mischievously to avert. Weisse and Strauss have regarded this hierarchical portrait as an improbable one. Analogies at once suggest themselves; for instance, Ultramontanism confounds the Reformation with Anabaptism, Socialism, Communism, Antichristianity,—and is itself the parent of those very things which it seeks to foist upon the other.

They will take away both our place and nation [*καὶ τὸν τόπον καὶ τὸ ἔθνος*]. *᾿Αροῦσιν* according to Euthymius and many others, *ἀπολέσουσιν*, according to Nonnus and others: they will wrest from us; this certainly is more in accordance with their egotistical sentiment which considers everything lost when the hierarchical rule is gone. Tholuck is in favor of: annihilate,—because Judea was already a Roman province. But the hierarchy still exercised rule. *Our*, *ἡμῶν*. Meyer: placed first, with the emphasis of egotism. *Τὸν τόπον* variously construed: 1. *As the temple*, as the central sanctuary (Origen, Lücke [De Wette, Hengstenberg] and others, after Acts vi. 13; 2 Macc. v. 19); 2. as the country, "*Land und Leute*" [Luther] country and people—(Bengel, Luthardt, and others);* 3. as the holy city [the seat of the Sanhedrin and the whole hierarchy], in favor of which, 2 Macc. iii. 18, 30. Chrysostom, Meyer.† Be it observed that the temple with the holy mountain and the holy city form a concrete unit, as the residence of the theocratical hierarchy. However, the expression is also an unconscious prophecy, like the subsequent remark of Caiaphas.

Ver. 49. **And a certain one of them, Caiaphas.** *Καϊάφας.* See *Comm. on Matt.* chap. xxvi. 3. Also Luke iii. 2. It must be observed that the Sadducees, to whom Caiaphas belonged, have already begun to take part in the hostility against Jesus; having probably long despised Him, their active enmity is doubtless excited by the raising of Lazarus. They now, in the person of Caiaphas, take the foremost rank in the persecution; subsequently we see them for a time take the lead even of the Pharisees in hostility towards the Christian Church (Acts iv. 1, 2).

Being high-priest that year [*τοῦ ἐνιαυτοῦ ἐκείνου*]. Different interpretations:

1. Bretschneider, Strauss [Schenkel, Scholten]: It is the erroneous idea that the high-priestly office changed hands from year to year. [But whoever was the writer of this Gospel, he shows sufficient familiarity with Jewish customs and localities throughout, to manifest that he was incapable of making such a mistake.—P. S.]

2. Baur: The Pseudo-John supposed Caiaphas and Hannas to have discharged the office alternately [very arbitrary].

3. Tholuck: "The repetition of *τ. ἐνιαυτοῦ ἐκ.* vers. 49, 51; ch. xviii. 13 cannot be understood otherwise than thus: namely, that the high-priest who once in the year offered the joint sacrifice for the people (Heb. ix. 7), must himself declare that in that year *a greater and more universal joint sacrifice should be offered.*" Yet John himself refers the saying not to the high-

* [Alford: *Our local habitation* and national existence.—P. S.]

† [So also Grotius, Ewald, Bäumlein, Godet.—P. S.]

priestly, but to the prophetic position of the high-priest.

4. Lücke: In that *memorable* year, the *death-year* of the Redeemer, Caiaphas was at the head of affairs (and the Evangelist deemed it superfluous to add to the mention of this fact a reference to the duration of the office).* This suffices; yet the expression undoubtedly contains also an intimation to the effect, that the high-priestly-office was debased at that time by the frequent alternations it sustained. See *Leben Jesu*.

Ye know nothing at all. Οὐκ οὐδέν. As he is aware that he is giving utterance to the inmost wishes of the greater part of them, he can, with an appearance of righteous indignation, revile them, without apprehending the taking of much offence.

Ver. 50. **Nor consider that it is expedient** [συμφέρει] **for us**—*us* of the Sanhedrin†—**that one man should die for the people** [ἵνα—according to divine purpose—εἷς ἄνθρωπος ἀποθάνῃ ὑπὲρ τοῦ λαοῦ, **and not the whole nation perish,** καὶ μὴ ὅλον τὸ ἔθνος ἀπόληται. Thus the Jewish priesthood expired with an unconscious and unwilling prophecy of Christ's atoning death, which it typically foreshadowed. Stier and Luthardt see in this a sublime irony of a most special Providence in the very centre of the world's history.—P. S.] The ὑπέρ, *in commodum, for the benefit,* becomes also an ἀντί, *instead of,* in consequence of the concluding clause: "*and that not the whole nation* (λαός, the whole mass of the people) *perish.*"‡ "Analogous sentences are collected by Schöttgen and Wetstein." The devilishness of this pseudo-political maxim as conceived by Caiaphas, is contained in the idea that Jesus shall be a *guiltless* and *involuntary* sacrifice to secure the good of the nation. This diabolical notion causes the proposition to assume, in this sense, an ultra-heathenish, superstitious and lying aspect. It is the completed idea of the most revolting heathen Moloch-sacrifices, into which Israel lapses when at the very acme of its legalistic zeal for putatively pure Judaism. See *Leben Jesu* II., 2, p. 1138.

Ver. 51. **But being high-priest that year, he prophesied**—*i. e.*, unconsciously to himself, the wicked decree, as *he* apprehended it, had the significancy of an official prediction, and, as such, a higher sense. Various interpretations:

1. In the sense of בַּת־קוֹל (De Wette). There is undoubtedly something of a kindred nature in the *Bath Kol;* yet that is here insufficient, and it belongs to another sphere. See Herzog's *Real-Encyklopædie* [I. 719].§

2. An involuntary prophecy, like that of old, contained in the involuntary blessing of Balaam (Lücke, Tholuck).* The cases are certainly allied; they differ, however, in that in the case of Balaam, a distinction must be made between his common consciousness and his inspired mood (wherefore his words of blessing are not susceptible of a double interpretation, as is his character), while in Caiaphas we have to distinguish between his consciousness and the unconscious expression, mirroring a higher truth, and hence bearing a double meaning.

3. A sentence in accordance with the appointment of the high-priest, to prophesy by the Urim and Thummim, *i. e.*, to utter the decision assignable to divine causality. *Leben Jesu* II., 2, p. 1137. [So also Alford. This view is confirmed by the repetition of the phrase ἀρχιερεὺς ὢν τοῦ ἐν. ἐκ. But this reference to the Urim and Thummim does not exclude the second view.—P. S.] "The high-priest," says Meyer, "was considered in ancient Israelitish times as the bearer of the divine oracle, the organ of divine revelation (Ewald, *Antiquities*, p. 385 sq.), which he obtained by examination of the Urim and Thummim (Ex. xxviii. 30; Lev. xxvii. 21). It is true that this examination was discontinued in later times (Joseph. *Ant.* III., 8, 9)—the high-priestly office being in all things shorn of its glory; yet even in the prophetic age there still existed a belief in the prophethood of the high-priest (Hos. iii. 4); we find also in Josephus *Antiq.* VI., 6, 3, the ancient high-priesthood represented as the bearer of the oracle," *etc.*, [p. 444 *f.*, 5th ed.] The high-priest was not the organ of divine *revelation*, but of divine *decision;* for the people whose king was God, must be able in all cases to have the mandate of its King. Now the decision was, if auspicious (as Philo,† idealizing the priest, represents him as a prophet), a prophecy of blessing; but if the high-priest was an unenlightened man, his oracle became the utterance of a curse. The decision might also, in itself, be the fountain sometimes of fortune, sometimes of misfortune. But even in the latter case there was attached to it the blessing of a divine judgment, that brought deliverance to the pious (rabbinical passages of unconscious predictions in Schöttgen).

* [So also Meyer and Alford. Comp. xviii. 13, where the expression is repeated.—P. S.]

† [Lange follows Lachmann in reading ἡμῖν. But the true reading is ὑμῖν, *for you*, see TEXT. NOTES.—P. S.]

‡ [There is here a slight mistake, as will be seen by referring to the Greek text. Caiaphas uses λαός in the first, and ἔθνος in the last clause. Meyer distinguishes between ἔθνος, the people as a *nation*, and λαός, the people as a political or theocratic society. Or, to speak more accurately, λαός usually signifies the *chosen* people (Matth. i. 21; ii. 4, 6, *etc.*), ἔθνος, a nation among the nations (comp. below ver. 52 οὐχ ὑπὲρ τοῦ ἔθνους μόνον); Matth. xxiv. 7, "nation against nation;" xxv. 32, "*all* nations," *etc.*). Yet λαός is also used for a great crowd or multitude, like ὄχλος, John viii. 2; Luke xxiii. 27, "a great company of people," *etc.*—P. S.]

§ [The Talmudic term, *Bath Kol*, lit., "the daughter of the voice," means the echo of a heavenly voice of revelation, or a divine oracle which the Rabbins imagined to receive, or which they were accustomed to derive from accidental circumstances and lots. It arose after the extinction of the prophecy and is a bastard substitute for it. John would not use of this the verb ἐπροφήτευσεν.—P. S.]

* [So also Trench and Wordsworth. Similar instances of involuntary prophets or witnesses to the truth we have in Pharaoh, Saul, Nebuchadnezzar, Pilate. God uses bad men as well as good ones for His own ends; He can speak wisdom even through the mouth of an ass, and confound the philosophers. Trench says: "There is no difficulty in such *unconscious* prophecies as this evidently is. How many prophecies of the like kind,—most of them, it is true, rather in act than in word, meet us in the whole history of the crucifixion! What was the title over our blessed Lord, 'Jesus of Nazareth, the King of the Jews,' but another such scornful and contemptuous, yet most veritable prophecy? Or what again the robe and the homage, the sceptre and the crown? And in the typical rehearsals of the great and final catastrophe in the drama of God's providence, how many Nimrods and Pharaohs, antichrists that do not quite come to the birth, have prophetic parts allotted to them, which they play out, unknowing what they do; for such is the divine irony; so, in a very deep sense of the words,

'*Ludit in humanis divina potentia rebus.*'"—P. S.]

† [*De creat. princ.* II., p. 367.]

That Jesus was about to die [ἤμελλεν ἀποθνήσκειν]. Ὅτι. The subsequent observation is not merely a pious reflection of John, as Lücke represents it; it is declaratory of the decisive providence of God, which caused the wicked decree to be so worded that it must express at the same time, unconsciously to the speaker, a *divine* sense, containing the real doctrine of salvation,—the doctrine of the redemption of man by the death of Jesus. **To die for the nation.**—The ὑπὲρ τοῦ λαοῦ (ver. 50), with its hierarchico-national sound, is here changed, in accordance with the last words of Caiaphas, into ὑπὲρ τοῦ ἔθνους.

Ver. 52. **And not for the nation only, but that he might also gather together into one [people] the children of God that are scattered abroad.**—Christian universalism, conditional, however, upon divine ordinance, as defined in the Bible, and upon human faith.—[Ver. 52 is an addition of the Evangelist to the unconscious prophecy of Caiaphas to prevent a limitation of the benefits of Christ's death; comp. 1 John ii. 2: "He is the propitiation for our sins; not for ours only, but also for the sins of the whole world."] *The children of God.* Interpretations:

1. The future children of God. [Among the heathen. Prophetic and proleptic, like x. 16]. (Euthymius [ὡς μέλλοντα γενέσθαι], Meyer [Alford, Trench: Those who should hereafter become His children. So also Calvin, in a predestinarian sense (to which Meyer assents): *Filios ergo Dei, etiam antequam vocentur, ab electione æstimat.*—P. S.]

2. Children of God, who are longing for Christ (Messner [Tholuck, Luthardt, Godet]).

3. Children of God by nature, who are such without first becoming so through Christ (Hilgenfeld [contrary to i. 12; iii. 3, 6, *etc.*])

4. The children of God generally, among the Jews,—they being in reality scattered by the hierarchy, jealous for the λαός,—as among the heathen, whose religious men have been scattered abroad since the building of the tower of Babel. The antithesis is: dying for the *nation* as a *unit;* dying in order to the gathering of the people of God from all places whither they have been scattered. The fundamental idea is the bringing together (this expression does not refer to place) of all the children of God into *one, i. e.,* into *one nation,* in antithesis to the λαός of Caiaphas. Comp. Ephes. ii. 14. In that passage the fundamental idea is the union of believing Jews and Gentiles, as ch. x. 16; here the fundamental thought is the union of the scattered sheep. Caiaphas said: the nation is perishing—therefore He must die; John says: He, doubtless, has by His death created the true, real λαός. Christ is the union of this people.

Ver. 53. **From that day forth** they held assemblies of their council, having in view His death: meetings for the murder of Christ. Before this time inferior courts, as well as the Sanhedrin itself, have *occasionally* sought to bring about His death (chh. v. and viii.); before now, individual Pharisees have sought to thrust Him aside by means of their standing tribunal of zealotism (chh. ix. and x.); before this, too, His adherents have been threatened with excommunication,—have been actually excommunicated (ch. ix.) Now the question how He shall be put to death, becomes a settled and ever recurring subject of debate in the Sanhedrin. It is clear that Jesus has long been considered by them as under the ban; apparently, fear of the people has deterred them from inflicting public and formal excommunication upon Him, although this is involved in the mandate issued subsequently to this session.

Ver. 54. **To a city called Ephraim.**—Jesus can no longer appear openly among the people without exposing Himself to the danger of being seized and prematurely sacrificed. It only remains to Him to reflect upon the true way of sacrifice. For this purpose He retires to the city of Ephraim, a small place, whence He can easily withdraw into the wilderness for security and contemplation.—**Into the country.**—The country in antithesis to Jerusalem.—**Into a region near the wilderness.**—Ἔρημος generally denotes the wilderness of Judea. In reality, however, it is a uniform desert tract between Jerusalem or the hill-country of Judea and the valley of the Jordan; its centre is formed by the wilderness of Judea between Jerusalem and the Dead Sea, to the right of the brook of Kidron; this wilderness is continued southwards in the deserts of Engeddi, Siph and Maon, and northwards in those of Tekoa, Jericho (with Mt. Quarantania) and Ephraim, which last appears as the northern extension of the whole desert region of Judea. Thus it was, in effect, *one* wilderness in which Christ dwelt at the beginning and the close of the years of His ministry. Ephraim was probably situated not far from Bethel, since it is several times associated with Bethel in historical events and records. With regard to the site of Bethel, it is Robinson's belief that he recognized it in the ruins of Beitîn (*Biblical Researches,* II., p. 127 [Am. ed., vol. I., p. 449]). "Bethel," he remarks, "was a border city between Benjamin and Ephraim; at first assigned to Benjamin, but conquered and afterwards retained by Ephraim. According to Eusebius and Jerome, it lay twelve Roman miles from Jerusalem, on the right or east of the road leading to Sichem or Neapolis (Nâbulus). From Beitîn to el-Bîreh we found the distance to be forty-five minutes, and from Bîreh to Jerusalem three hours, with horses." In an easterly direction, not far from Bethel, Robinson passed the night at the village of Taiyibeh. "Here the proximity of the wilderness was plainly discernible." In particular, there is here a rocky valley, "overgrown with furzy plants and sage, interspersed with the fragrant Zaeter." For a description of the desert itself see Robinson. The village of Taiyibeh is considered by some to be identical with the ancient Ephraim [the same with Ophrah (Josh. xviii. 23; 1 Sam. xiii. 17) and Ephron (2 Chr. xiii. 17) of the Old Testament. So besides Robinson, Van de Velde and Stanley. The latter says (*Sinai and Palestine,* p. 210): 'Further still, the dark conical hill of Taiyibeh, with its village perched aloft, like those of the Apennines, the probable representative of Ophrah of Benjamin, in later times 'the city called *Ephraim,*' to which our Lord retired, 'near to the wilderness,' after the raising of Lazarus."—P. S.]

Since Jesus was now resolved to repair to Jerusalem with the next Galilean and Peræan paschal caravan, *i. e.* since but *one* step remained for Him, to surrender Himself publicly to the Messianic hope entertained by the pious among the people and now purified by Him,—possessing a distinct foresight, however, of the death resulting upon this step, accompanied by the succumbing of the party of believers to the hierarchical party—(see *Leben Jesu* II. p. 1140)—Ephraim was the place exactly fitted for a temporary sojourn. Hence He could at need withdraw into the desert; here He could collect His disciples and prepare them for the last journey (see *Comm. on Matthew*, p. 360, Am. Ed.); here He could join either the caravan coming across Samaria to Bethel or the one passing through Jericho on its way from Peræa (see Tholuck, p. 316). Comp. Jos. xv. 61; xvi. 1; xviii. 22; 2 Kings ii. It was in the vicinity of Jericho, according to the Synoptists, that Jesus attached Himself to the festive train from Peræa, having, it is probable, previously received His friends from the Galilean company that passed through Samaria.

Ver. 55. **And the passover of the Jews was at hand.** The nearness of this feast occasioned many to go out of the Jewish country (χώρα not simply that region, as Bengel supposes, but the *country* in contrast to Jerusalem) beforehand up to Jerusalem, because they had to purify themselves (Lightfoot) before the feast, by means of the prescribed sacrifices and ablutions (Num. ix. 6; 2 Chron. xxx. 17 ff.).

Ver. 56. **They sought therefore for Jesus.** We gather from this, in the first place, how eagerly all the people were expecting the appearance of Jesus at the feast. They had hoped to find Him already in Jerusalem. Hence, then, it likewise follows that no special reference is had to people from the country about Ephraim. We therefore translate the ὅτι οὐ μὴ ἔλθῃ: *that He will not come* (with Meyer), but not: *that He has not come* (Vulgate and others). Some appear to take it for granted from the condition of things that He will not come, while others question this decision. Manifestly, it is like a sort of betting whether He will come or not. The occasion of this conduct was the mandate of the high-priest, which had been spread abroad throughout the land by means of special orders of the Sanhedrin (see the Textual note) and in accordance with which every one who knew of the abode of Jesus, was bound to give information of it. This mandate —a kind of interdict—of course presupposes excommunication. There seems to have been at that time not a single traitor among the peasants and dwellers in the deserts of Ephraim. Subsequently, however, this decree formed a point for Judas to fasten on. He probably silenced his conscience at first with the cry, that he must be an "obedient son" of the hierarchical Church, or a "loyal subject" of the spiritual authorities. The decree may be regarded as the result of the session ver. 47 (comp. ver. 53, Meyer). The anteposition of δεδώκεισαν, with reference to the decree, is emphatic. We must observe that this edict was at all events designed as an interdict,—a fact of special importance to the friends of Jesus; no one should receive Him into his house without giving information of Him, *i. e.* without hostility to Him. In all probability the command was issued with a particular view to the family of Lazarus. See Chap. xii. 10.

DOCTRINAL AND ETHICAL.

1. It has been early demonstrated by John in the history of Nicodemus, that a sincere law-zealot, Jew and Pharisee may believe and be saved. Here he gives prominence to the fact that many Jews believed after witnessing the raising of Lazarus. And this was the second great spiritual miracle connected with the external mighty miracle of the raising of Lazarus: with one impulse many Jews believed on Him. Some, indeed, of those who at first were overpowered by the grand fact, may probably have apostatized. At all events, there was a remnant of unbelievers. To these the savor of life unto life did here become literally a savor of death unto death.

2. The Jews who go from Bethany, from the grave of Lazarus, to the Pharisees, to show them what Jesus has done, are thus become precursors of Judas; in a general sense, types of apostates. They all come—from Bethany; they all go—to the Pharisees; they all, with hostile intent, report what Jesus has done.

3. The council of blood. The policy of fear. It occasions what it means to avert. The policy of timidity became a policy of intimidation, terrorism. Probably the rough words of Caiaphas to his colleagues were further serviceable in terroristically beating down any attempt on the part of the friends of Jesus, Nicodemus and Joseph of Arimathea, to dwell upon His many miracles (comp. Gerlach on this passage). It is not likely that these men had any share in the subsequent determined deliberations of the Council of Blood. Once they expressed their positive disapprobation (see Luke xxiii. 51), probably on this very occasion. To this the minute account of this session is no doubt attributable.

4. On the road of ultra-Judaism the Jews have relapsed into the worst heathenism. Pursuant to the counsel of Caiaphas, they relapsed, as regards their intentions, into the Moloch-sacrifice. After the destruction of Jerusalem, at the conquest of Massada, into the suicidal despair of the Hindus (Josephus, *De bello jud.*, VII.; chh. VIII., IX.); with their Talmud into a mythology which, in comparison with that of Greece and Rome, is utterly odious. Thus, too, Christian Judaism [Romanism] usually relapses into the most abominable heathenism.

5. Even Caiaphas, then, has with tolerable plainness set forth the maxim: the end justifies the means.

6. The extinction of the Old Testament office of high-priestly prophecy in the sentence of Caiaphas. Caiaphas must unconsciously sketch the principal features of Christian dogmatics and soteriology. The fearful double meaning of his speech with regard to his intention and the meaning of the Spirit. What it proves: 1. Prov. xvi. 1:* Man is master of his intention; that is his own; not so, however, the full import

* [Luther's translation reads differently from our English version, *viz:* "Man indeed proposeth in his heart, but from the Lord cometh what the tongue shall speak."]

of his words. In the domain of speech the coöperating and counteracting rule of divine providence begins. 2. The symbolical ministry becomes, even in its ungodly tendency, an unconscious prophecy of the real ministry of the Spirit; the false, official high-priest a prophet of the true High Priest and His sacrifice. In what relation do these types stand to the former typism? They are types moulded by the irony of divine dispensation from the elements of human perversity. The school of truth is perfected in the *mouth* of these wicked priests, while the school of falsehood is perfected in their *heart.* Hence they are able to blaspheme with words of prayer, to prophesy with words of demoniacal policy. Caiaphas prophesied. "Roman Catholics apply this to popes; popes, though wicked, might still be the organs of truth, as Stolberg remarks in his History of the Religion of Jesus. Our church teaches only—that the Word of God and the Sacraments retain their own virtue even when administered by unregenerate preachers." Heubner. But here also a relative soundness of the Church as a body must be assumable.

7. The Urim and Thummim are likewise expressive of the truth that decision and resolution are needful in all cases, while, on the other hand, endless vacillation is the greatest evil. Therefore God hardens Pharaoh's heart with the view of expediting matters, and Judas also receives the command, "What thou doest, do quickly." The temporal hardening of the people of Israel, however, was designed to prevent their eternal obduracy, Rom. ix.-xi.

8. The work of Christ, regarded by His enemies as a scattering and destroying of the ancient people of God, resulted in the creation of a new and real people of God, gathered from abroad.

9. Christ in the wilderness at the beginning and the end of His career. In the beginning He resolved not to appear publicly under the title of the Messiah, to avoid the Messianic conception of His nation. Now the time had come for Him to issue from the desert for the purpose of surrendering Himself to the Messianic faith of His people, in the state of purification to which He had brought it.

10. Christ the subject of interest and conversation with all the people, while they are occupied with services of ordinances and legal works of purification. How is this? An ultra-montane mind cannot rid itself of the thought of the Evangelical Confession; moreover, the friends of Jesus are present in the camp of legality.

11. The mandate of the Supreme Council: the interdict. Men should show where Christ was. Soon He showed Himself and afterwards all Christian church-steeples pointed upwards to Him. And thus Luther is no longer hidden in the Wartburg, but is everywhere proclaiming himself to the hierarchy.

HOMILETICAL AND PRACTICAL.

The decisive effect of the raising of Lazarus.—Bethany and its quiet family the starting point of the decision: 1. The starting point of the positive separation between the friends and the enemies of Jesus; 2. of the palm-entry; 3. of Judas, as 4. of the faithful anointing of the dying Christ.—Sincere consciences are liberated from dead ordinances by facts of life.—The "some" also believed that Jesus had raised Lazarus; they believed it and trembled with fear and rage. Comp. James ii. 19.—Even the new life of Lazarus to some a savor of death unto death.—And thus every important awakening is a soul-danger (of offence) for those whose attitude towards the truth is a false one.—Treachery a main-spring of unbelief.—The conference of the Supreme Council about the raising of Lazarus: 1. The wicked lack of counsel of some; 2. the hellish counsel of the high-priest; 3. the silenced voice of the pious counselors (Nicodemus, Joseph of Arimathea); 4. the heavenly counsel of divine Providence.—How selfish fear ever brings on by its superstitious proceedings the very trouble it would avert by arbitrary acts (the parents of Œdipus).—He who thinks to escape some fate by wicked ways of his own choosing, incurs the doom he flees.—The Supreme Council also prophesied in its own fashion,—like the high-priest; the former conversely, Caiaphas unconsciously.—The recognition of the works of Christ uttered by the Supreme Council: He doeth many signs.—The saying of Caiaphas in its twofold sense.—The irony of divine Providence as exercised over human perversity, Ps. ii. 4.—The ministry of the letter a type of the ministry of the spirit; thus, too, unconsciously, official—things and words are manifoldly typical.—Christ, by His death, the Rescuer of the ancient people, the Creator of a new people.—They would kill Him because He made alive.—This the main reproach that the slaying ordinance has to make against vitalizing faith.—How the Supreme Council has become a standing court of inquisition against Christ.—Jesus, outlawed and banished, in the wilderness.—The Jews who have repaired to Jerusalem, do not converse about their Jewish rites and ceremonies, but about Christ.—The conjectures (bets), as to whether He will dare come or not.—The champion of God; and Israel with Philistinish thoughts concerning Him.—The Jewish edict and interdict, ver. 57.—How all the world fulfils this commandment: 1. How enemies show where Christ is; 2. friends.—How Christ gives information concerning Himself. See Matt. xxvi. 64.—How far the edict was ineffectual or rather accomplished the reverse of its design.

STARKE, HEDINGER: How wise worldly-minded people and knavish men think themselves, when they imagine that they are able to quench the word and kingdom of Christ by their false, famous strokes of state!—CRAMER: It is possible even for councils and assemblies of the learned to err.—It is never well to make church matters affairs of state.—ZEISIUS: The Jews thought that if they did but put Christ out of the way, their repose and prosperity would be lastingly secured, and it was thus that they lost both their temporal and spiritual good things.—BIBL. WIRT.: God often punishes the wicked with calamities which they thought they had averted.—CANSTEIN: It is almost a daily occurrence for men to plunge into disaster while essaying to ward off some imaginary evil.—*Ibid.*: It is the way of worldly-minded politicians to measure all things by the standard of profit and gain, not by that of truth, righteousness and justice; and this, while in most cases the prosperity of the country is declared to be the grand reason for such a course, though in reality they are actuated by nothing but selfishness.—OSIANDER: The false church is cruel and blood-thirsty.—O happy country, that receives the Son of God in His persecution!

GERLACH: "That He should die instead of the whole nation, a cleanse-offering, as it were, to avert the ruin that else would threaten the entire nation.—It seems that superstition was mingled with the unbelief of the Sadducee, or that he feigned it while in company with the Pharisees. (Not the Sadducees, however, but the Essenes, were at variance with the old system of sacrifices).—Not merely for the Jews whom Caiaphas meant, but also that He should gather God's elect into His flock from among the heathen, whilst this wicked high-priest believed that the dispersion of His followers would be the natural accompaniment of His death. (Quite right. This, however, is the first antithesis present to the mind of the evangelist: In the sense of Caiaphas the meaning is: if Christ die, the Jewish nation lives, in the ordinary sense,—while the higher sense of the ambiguous expression was; if Christ die, the nation lives as a redeemed people, and thus a great nation is formed from the scattered children of God).—LISCO: The decision of Caiaphas, *that the end justifies the means*, that necessity is here an excuse for injustice.—They feel that *one* must fall: the kingdom of purity and truth, or the kingdom of falsehood and hypocrisy; and this last, in their avaricious lust of dominion, they desire to save.

GOSSNER: They are forced to say it themselves: *this man doeth many miracles.* This is true, to be sure,—*but*—of what consequence is a single man? (thinks Caiaphas) it is the *many*, to whom regard is due. The world cares nothing for the small ones of the earth; it thinks: what if they be unjustly dealt with, so long as the others are satisfied?—Ver. 55. To His last hour He was a faithful church-goer and observer of religion. If He for once missed a feast-day, the people immediately inquired: where is He?—Ver. 57. They wished to prepare themselves a festive joy, and to do God a service by slaying His Son at the Passover.—*He should show it.* An obedient son of the devil was Judas, who conscientiously obeyed this command of hell and delivered Jesus into their hands. "The church hath commanded it." Thus Judas might (fain would) think.

HEUBNER: The assembly should have met for the recognition of Jesus. It was the duty of the Supreme Council to be the first to accept Jesus and to call upon the nation to accept Him. But from this very college proceeded the rejection of Jesus. The power of self-interest, and avarice, make men blind to the strongest proofs of divine power,—deaf to the voice of God.—Vers. 49, 50. How are the weal of the masses and the right of the individual to be united? Impure state-craft never discovers the right means for accomplishing such a result.—The same words have an entirely different sense in the mouth of the wicked and the meaning of the Holy Ghost.—Ver. 54. This concealment of Jesus also belonged to His state of humiliation. The Light that lightened all men must withdraw itself.—Often it was a hidden country, valley, that received Christ's faithful ones until the wrath of the enemy was overpast.

SCHLEIERMACHER: Evil should be overcome only by good. But to do evil that good may come is the grossest perversity and the worst depravity into which man can fall.—Involuntarily he prophesied, and in uttering the counsel of human depravity, he declared at the same time the counsel of eternal wisdom and love,—the counsel of Him who gave His Son for us while we were yet sinners.

BESSER, ver. 46: They went their way to the Pharisees who were a net spread, Hos. v. 1.—Once, on the threshold of the Promised land, Israel was blessed through the prediction of a prophet who would fain have cursed; him the strength of the Lord overpowered, putting words into his mouth which confirmed the promise made to the Patriarchs and renewed through Moses, Num. xxiii. 24. Thus Caiaphas, willing to curse, must now, a second Balaam, on the threshold of the New Covenant, pronounce a blessing upon the true Israel, confirming the prediction of the law and the prophets concerning the expiatory death of the Lamb (see, however, the note to ver. 51).—"Caiaphas and Pilate condemned Jesus, but both must testify of Him in words exceeding the sense which they consciously attached to them; here Caiaphas witnesses to the *high-priestly* death of Christ,—there Pilate testifies to His *kingdom*, in the superscription of the cross" (BENGEL).—John reads the names of many scattered ones already written in God's heart as children; he gazes with opened eyes into the holy mission movement of the whole reconciled world, *which movement shall not end* until all that the Father hath given the Son are *brought together.*

[CRAVEN: From ORIGEN: Ver. 47. This speech an evidence of their *audacity and blindness.*—Ver. 51. Not every one who prophesies is a prophet, as not every one who does a just action is just.—Ver. 54. *Jesus therefore walked no more openly among the Jews:* It is praiseworthy when struggles are at hand (pressed upon us) not to avoid confession or refuse to suffer; and it is no less praiseworthy to avoid giving occasion for such trial. If we do not avoid our persecutor, when we have the opportunity (without sin), we make ourselves responsible for his offence.——From GREGORY: Vers. 50–53. That which human cruelty executed against Him, He turned to the purposes of His mercy.——From AUGUSTINE: Vers. 47, 48. They were afraid of losing temporal things and thought not of eternal life, and thus they lost both.—Ver. 54. He would show by example that believers do not sin by retiring from the sight of persecutors.——From CHRYSOSTOM: Ver. 51. The power of the Holy Ghost in drawing forth a prophecy from a wicked man.—The virtue of a (divinely appointed) office.—Ver. 56. His enemies made the *feast* time, the time of His death.——From ALCUIN: Ver. 56. Men may seek Jesus with bad intent.——From THEOPHYLACT: Vers. 55-57. While engaged in *purifications* they were plotting our Lord's death.——From BURKITT: Vers. 45, 46. The different effects produced by this miracle.—Ver. 48. Opposers of Christ color their enmity with specious pretences.—Ver. 50. A most wicked speech: as a *judge* he regarded not what was *lawful* but as a politician consented to what was (apparently) *expedient*.—It is unlawful to (strive to) promote the greatest national good by unlawful means.—Ver. 51. It is consistent with the holiness of God to make use of the worst of men in declaring His will.—Ver. 53. The baneful effects of evil counsel, especially from leading men.——From M. HENRY: Ver. 47. The witness of the Sanhedrin for Christ.—Ver. 48. The success of the gospel the dread of its adversaries. When men lose piety they lose courage. Pretended fears are often the color of malicious designs.—Vers. 49, 50. Carnal policy commonly sets up *reasons of state* in opposition to rules of justice.—That calamity which we seek to escape by sin, we take the most effectual course to bring upon us.—*That the welfare of communities is to be preferred before that of individuals*, is a true or false maxim as it may be employed; it is *expedient* and *honorable* for an *individual* to hazard his life for his country, but it is *devilish* for *rulers* to put an innocent man to death under color of consulting the public safety.—Ver. 51. Caiaphas *prophesied*—1. God often employs wicked men as His instruments; 2. prophecy in the mouth is no infallible evidence of grace in the heart.—Vers. 51, 52. The enlargement of the Evangelist on the prophecy; teaching—1. *for whom* Christ died, (1) the Jews, (2) *the children* of God scattered abroad, (*a*) then living, (*b*) throughout all time; 2. *the purpose* of His death concerning these, *to gather them together in one*.—Christ's dying is—1. the great *attractive* of our hearts; 2. the great *centre* of our unity, (1) by the merit of His death recommending all in *one* to the favor of God, (2) by the *motive* of His death drawing each to the love of every other.—Ver. 53. Evil men confirm themselves and one another in ill practices by conference.—Ver. 57. It is an aggravation of the sins of rulers when they make their subjects the instruments of their unrighteousness.——From SCOTT: Vers. 47-57. No devices of man can derange the purposes of God; whilst hypocrites and worldlings pursue their own projects, Christ still communes with His disciples (ver. 54) and orders all things for His own glory and their salvation.——From BARNES: Vers. 50, 51. God may—1. *fulfill* the words of the wicked in a way they do not intend; 2. make their wicked plots the means of accomplishing His purposes.——From A PLAIN COMMENTARY (Oxford): Ver. 51. The unworthiness of the *individual* does not affect the sanctity of *his office*.——From RYLE: Ver. 46. Seeing miracles will not necessarily convert souls, Luke xvi. 31.—Vers. 47-57. The power of unbelief; ecclesiastical rulers are often the foremost enemies of the gospel. Ver. 50. What is *morally wrong* can never be *politically right*.—Ver. 53. The conclusions of great ecclesiastical councils are sometimes wicked.—Ver. 54. Christ *retires* Himself for a season before His last great work; it is well to get alone and be still, before we undertake any great work for God.—Ver. 55. What importance bad men sometimes attach to outward ceremonial. The religion which expends itself in zeal for outward formalities is worthless.——From OWEN: Ver. 52. *Gathered in one, i. e.*, into *one* spiritual nation or people.

[Vers. 47-50. The blinding power of hate.—Ver. 54. Christ never acted *recklessly* nor in *bravado*, nor in the spirit of one *seeking martyrdom;* He hid Himself from danger when duty did not require exposure.]

III.

ANTITHESIS BETWEEN FAITHFULNESS AND APOSTASY IN THE CIRCLE OF DISCIPLES ITSELF. THE LIFE-FEAST OVER LAZARUS AN ANTICIPATORY CELEBRATION OF THE DEATH OF JESUS. THE ANOINTING (OF THE MESSIAH, AT THE BEGINNING OF THE SIX DAYS' WORK OF HIS PASSION, THE NEW SIX DAYS' WORK FOR THE REDEMPTION AND GLORIFICATION OF THE WORLD).

CHAP. XII. 1—8.

(Matt. xxvi. 6-16; Mark xiv. 3-11; Luke xxii. 3-6.)

1 Then Jesus [therefore], six days before the passover, came to Bethany, where
Lazarus was which [who] had been dead,[1] whom he [Jesus][2] raised from the dead.
2 There they made him a supper [dinner];[3] and Martha served: but Lazarus was
3 one of them that sat [reclined] at the table with him. Then took Mary a pound
of ointment of [pure] spikenard, very costly, and anointed the feet of Jesus, and
wiped [dried][4] his feet with her hair; and the house was filled with the odour of
4 the ointment. Then saith [Judas Iscariot] one of his disciples, Judas Iscariot,
Simon's *son* [*omit* Simon's *son*],[5] which should betray him [who was about to be-
5 tray him], Why was not this ointment sold for three hundred pence [denâries],[6]
6 and given to the poor? This [however] he said, not that [because] he cared for
the poor; but because he was a thief, and had the bag [kept the purse], and bare

7 [laid hold of, took away] what was put therein. Then said Jesus, Let her alone;
against the day of my burying hath she kept this [Suffer her that she may keep
8 this for (or, until) the day of my burial].[7] For the poor always ye have [ye have
always] with you; but me ye have not always.[8]

TEXTUAL AND GRAMMATICAL.

[1] Ver. 1.—[In Cod. Sin. B. L. X. ὁ τεθνηκώς is wanting, on which account Lachmann and Alford have bracketed the words, and Tischendorf, Westcott and Hort have omitted them. Probably this purposely significant term was employed as expressive of the fact that a man who had lately been dead did, by means of the miracle of Christ, appear as one of the guests at the feast. It is, however, superfluous, the fact being sufficiently indicated without it.—P. S.]

[2] Ver. 1.—[Tischendorf, Alford, *etc.*, read 'Ιησοῦς in accordance with Sin. A. B. D. E. G., *etc.* The text. rec. omits it. —P. S.]

[3] Ver. 2.—[δεῖπνον should perhaps be better translated *dinner* or *feast*, than *supper*, for it was the chief meal of the Jews, as also of the Greeks and Romans, taken after the work and heat of the day early in the evening and often prolonged into the night. ἄριστον is *breakfast, lunch.*—P. S.]

[4] Ver. 3.—[ἐκμάσσω or ἐκμάττω, *to wipe off, to wipe dry*, in poets and later prose writers, for the Attic ἀπομόργνυμι and ἐξομόργνυμι.—P. S.]

[5] Ver. 4.—Instead of 'Ιούδας Σίμωνος 'Ισκαριώτης in accordance with Codd. A. Q. and the Recepta, Tischendorf simply reads 'Ισκαρ. in accordance with Cod. B. and several minuscules. Σίμωνος appears doubtful, being now become superfluous. Omitted also from the Sin. [Tischendorf, ed. 8, Alford, Westcott and Hort read Ιοῦδας ὁ 'Ισκαριώτης, without Σίμωνος.—P. S.]

[6] Ver. 6.—[A δηνάριον (Lat. *denarius*=10 asses), a Roman coin, is equal to the Attic drachma, about 15 or 17 cents of our money. Three hundred *denarii* therefore are about £9 16s. sterling, or from 45 to 50 Am. dollars. The E. V. gives a very false idea of the value of this ointment. *Dimes* or *shillings* (in the New York sense) would come nearer.—P. S.]

[7] Ver. 7.—Instead of εἰς τὴν ἡμέραν τοῦ ἐνταφιασμοῦ τετήρηκεν [*hath kept*] αὐτό (comp. Mark xiv. 8), Lachmann and Tischendorf [Alford, Westcott and Hort] read in accordance with ℵ. B. D. K. L. and others, Vulgate and other translations and Fathers: ἵνα εἰς τὴν ἡμέραν τοῦ ἐνταφιασμοῦ τηρήσῃ [*may keep*]. The Sin. likewise.

[8] Ver. 8.—The eighth verse is wanting in Cod. D. "and might be suspected of having been introduced from Matt. xxvi. 11; Mark xiv. 7, if it came before ἄφες, and the characteristic order of the words were the same as in the Synoptists (πάντοτε first)." Meyer. Here, however, the complete preponderance of Codd. is alone decisive in favor of the verse. [Tischendorf, ed. 8, Alford and Westcott and Hort retain it.—P. S.]

EXEGETICAL AND CRITICAL.

Ver. 1. **Jesus therefore came.**—The οὖν is certainly not designed merely to resume the story of Jesus (Meyer); neither does it declare simply that Jesus went consciously and freely to meet death (Luthardt). It is preparatory to the fact that Jesus Himself showed Himself to the Sanhedrists in the most public manner. The edict commanding that information should be given of the hidden Jesus, was answered by Him with the palm-entry. (Starke, from harmonistic interest, supposes two anointings in Bethany, one at the house of Simon, two days before the Passover, the other at the house of Lazarus, six days before the Passover.)

Six days before the Passover.*—See *Comm. on Matt.*, ch. XXVI. [Am. ed., p. 454 ff., and Robinson's *Harmony*, pp. 207 and 212 ff.—P. S.] The 15th of Nisan was the dying day of Jesus, a Friday; six days before, therefore, was the Sabbath (the 9th of Nisan). We learn here that a day intervened between the departure of Jesus from Ephraim (and Jericho) and the palm-entry on Sunday; this day is passed over by the Synoptists, who place the palm-entry in immediate connection with the departure from Jericho. In accordance with the more exact statement of John, we must suppose that Jesus left Jericho on Friday, in company with the festive caravan, and arrived in the neighborhood of the Mount of Olives. Here they rested during the Sabbath. On the evening of that day, after the legal Sabbath time, the meal was prepared for Him at which the anointing occurred.*

Upon the difference which Meyer and others pretend to discover between John and the Synoptists see the *Comm. on Matthew;* see the same on the motives which induced the Synoptists to transpose chronologically the story of the anointing, and make it introductory to the history of the Passion.

Meyer reckons with Ewald from the 14th back to the 8th of Nisan; he also asserts, however, that it was a Sabbath, in accordance with the false assumption that Jesus died on the 14th of Nisan, and yet on a Friday. Grotius, Tholuck, Wieseler and others fix upon Friday, because the law regulating a Sabbath day's journey forbids the arrival in Bethany on the Sabbath. Hence, according to Tholuck, the feast was on Friday evening. But certainly the caravan of pilgrims to the feast might be encamped on the Sabbath around the Mount of Olives, and thus extend itself into the vicinity of Bethany. Theophylact and Lücke are in favor of the 9th Nisan. Others reckon it to have been Sunday (De Wette) others Monday (Baur). The matter is confused by prejudice respecting the difference between John and the Synoptists, and by the different ways of reckoning,—from the 14th or 15th Nisan. (Upon the calculation of this date see Jacobi, *Stud. u. Kritik.* 1838, No. 4; Wieseler, *Chronol.*, p. 377; Wichelhaus, *Leidensgeschichte*, p. 147.)

The *trajectio verborum* πρὸ ἓξ ἡμερῶν instead of ἓξ ἡμέραις πρό seems to have been made for the

* [πρὸ ἓξ ἡμερῶν τοῦ πάσχα, instead of ἓξ ἡμέραις πρὸ τοῦ πάσχα, is no Latinism (*ante six dies*, instead of *six dies ante pascha*), but very frequent in later Greek writers (Philo, Josephus, Plutarch, Appian, *etc.*), see Winer, p. 518 f., 7th ed. The same combination is formed with μετά, and in local specifications, comp. ch. xi. 18, ὡς ἀπὸ σταδίων δεκαπέντε. Greswell (as quoted by Alford) defines the expression to be *exclusive* of the period named as the limit *ad quem* or *a quo* (according as πρό or μετά may be used), but *inclusive* of the day or month or year of the occurrence specified.—P. S.]

* [Wordsworth: "This Supper at Bethany was probably on the Sabbath before His death. It was on a Sabbath—*the* Sabbath before *that great* Sabbath, on which Christ *rested* in the grave and fulfilled the Sabbath, and prepared the grave as a place of rest for all who pass from this life in His faith and fear." He also allegorizes on the meaning of Bethany, a house of passage, as prefiguring the passage to the spiritual banquet in Paradise.—P. S.]

sake of emphasis: perchance, before the great six days' work or Hexaëmeron of this passover.

Where Lazarus was.—Made prominent as a continual living sign of the glory of Jesus; also in particular as a motive for the anointing of Mary, for the palm-entry, and for the hatred of the Sanhedrin.

Ver. 2. **There they made Him a dinner (feast).**—See the parallel passages in Matthew and Mark. The Jews were fond of giving entertainments at the close of the Sabbath. The following points in John's statement are characteristic:

1. The representation of the feast as a festive celebration of the raising of Lazarus in the circle of the brother and sisters of Bethany.

2. The distinct delineation of the three,—Lazarus sits with the guests; he is therefore perfectly well; Martha serves at table, in accordance with her way, and as hostess; Mary glorifies the feast by the extraordinary anointing.

3. The manner of the anointing. "A vase of precious ointment," says Matthew; "of pure, precious nard," says Mark; "a pound of ointment of pure precious nard," says John (comp. the precise mention of the one hundred pounds of spices, ch. xix. 39, and other precise accounts; for instance, ch. xxi. 11). According to Matthew, she anoints the head of Jesus; likewise according to Mark,—breaking the flask, however; according to Matthew, she pours it on his head, —so, too, according to Mark; John gives prominence to the fact that she anointed the feet of Jesus and dried them with her hair. Manifestly this latter item does not exclude the former ones; to John, however, this strong expression of adoration and devotion is the main point.

The trait reported by John reminds us of the anointing of the feet of Jesus by the great sinner; from this similarity, as well as from the name of Simon in Luke, some have taken occasion, utterly without ground, to identify this history with that related by Luke ch. vii. 37 ff. Furthermore John mentions that the house was filled with the odor of the ointment.

4. John, who gives the most explicit account of the act of Mary, pursues the same course with regard to the censure encountered by that act. According to Matthew, *the disciples* were angry, —according to Mark, *some* had indignation,—according to John, *one* of the disciples, *Judas*, Simon's son, the Iscariot, lifted up his voice. It is John alone, too, who distinctly characterizes Judas as a *thief*. We arrive at the conclusion that the murmuring originated with Judas, that it infected some of the disciples; but that the disciples generally were, by their silence, more or less concerned in this sin. John seems best to have understood Mary who, in her feeling, was in advance of the entire circle of disciples. On the other hand, John omits the promise for Mary, that her deed should be proclaimed in all the world; he mentions, however, the exceedingly significant saying: she hath kept the ointment for this day.

Ver. 3. **A pound.***—According to Olshausen, this unwonted measure of ointment employed by her was an expression of love; Meyer corrects him: she did not anoint *with* the pound, but *from* it. But John writes,—she took the pound and the house was filled with the odor; Mark writes that she broke the vase. Had not the anointing in its heroic measure given rise to the appearance of prodigality, Judas would hardly have ventured to speak, and would have still less met with assent among the disciples. "Who knows whether it was a Roman or a Greek pound? And the ancient Greek pound was but half as large as the Roman pound, while that, again, does not equal our pound." Braune. Comp. *Comm. on Matthew*. p. 463, Am. Ed.

Anointed the feet.—"The anointing of the *head* at feasts was a customary thing, and might have been passed over by the Evangelist in order to mention the unusual demonstration of love for which the remainder of the ointment might be employed. To wash the feet with tepid water, and then to anoint them with costly oil, is mentioned in the Talmud *tr. Menachoth* as a duty of maid-servants." Tholuck. Braune gives prominence to the fact, that the anointing of the feet was also particularly noticeable to John, since he reclined by the side of Jesus and the anointing of the feet took place close behind him.

Ver. 5. **For three hundred denâries** [*i. e.*, between forty-five and fifty dollars gold. See TEXT. NOTE 6.—P. S.]. See *Comm. on Matthew*. The precise estimation is characteristic. Indicative of the wealth of the family. [Utterly inconsistent with Hengstenberg's hypothesis of the identity of the historic Lazarus with the poor Lazarus of the parable.—P. S.]

Ver. 6. **He kept the purse**, γλωσσόκομον, cash repository.* Luther, significantly and expressively: *the purse* (*Beutel*). The common cash-box, made up by male and female disciples (Luke viii. 3), to supply the common wants. Alms for the poor likewise (ch. xiii. 29) were of course taken from this coffer. This keeping of the cash must have been connected with a corresponding talent possessed by Judas; that talent, however, was, in its turn, connected with the temptation that made him a thief; and thus a connection exists between his chiliastic views of the kingdom of Christ and the despondency which led him to turn traitor (see *Comm. on Matthew*, ch. x.). He proved himself a thief by his management of the coffer. *He laid hold* of what was put therein. He put aside for himself a portion of what others offered. Βαστάζειν may mean: *he bore, kept* (*portabat*) what was donated (Vulgate, Luther, Lücke, *etc.*, Luthardt), [De Wette, Alford, Ebrard, Hengstenberg, Ewald, Godet], and *he bore away, stole* (*auferebat*), he abstracted the deposits (Origen, Nonnus and others, Meyer). Stress has been laid upon the article, as opposed to the latter view. It is inconceivable that Judas should have purloined everything. Be it observed that βα-

* [The Greek λίτρα, the Latin *libra, a pound*, was adopted into the Aramaic, and is found in the Rabbinical writings as equivalent to a *mina* (see Friedlieb, *Archäol. der Leidensgesch.*, p. 33, quoted by Alford). The Roman *libra* was divided into 12 ounces, and was equivalent to nearly 12 ounces avoirdupois.—P. S.]

* [Lit., a tongue-box (from γλῶσσα and κομέω) or reed-case for keeping the tongues or mouth-pieces of pipes and flutes; then any kind of chest, or box, or pouch, or purse for money. Found only in late writers. Mark the striking contrast between the money-box of Judas and the alabaster box of Mary, his thirty pieces of silver and her three hundred denâries, his love of money and her liberality, his hypocritical profession of concern for the poor and her noble deed for the Lord, his wretched end and her blessed memory throughout the Christian world to the end of time.—P. S.]

στάζειν also means *to lay hold of, to touch, to handle.** We adopt this intermediate signification: he laid violent hands on the money and especially on the alms. His lusting after the three hundred denâries renders him not simply heartless towards Mary's beautiful act, but it also makes him a hypocrite.

With reference to the apparent singularity of his being intrusted by Jesus with the purse, the following considerations are to be pondered:

1. The common purse itself, doubtless, did not acquire considerable importance before the final departure from Galilee; 2. the appointment of the cashier was probably a general determination of the disciples rather than a matter with which Christ particularly concerned Himself. Compare the institution of deacons, Acts. vi. 3. 3. The disciples must learn by experience that their reliance upon the brilliant talent of Judas —in accordance with this trust, doubtless, he was introduced by their intercession into the circle of the apostles (see *Comm. on Matthew*)—was even in this point premature. 4. Jesus committed the bag to him, not indeed to deprive him of all excuse for his treason (Chrysostom and others), but He committed it to him having respect to his destiny, and because such a character might better be cured by confidence than by mistrust. 5. We are guilty of a wondrous over-estimation of the cashiership in relation to the apostolic dignity, if we think that a man intrusted with the former is beset with greater difficulties than one upon whom the latter is conferred. The Lord in a measure intrusted Judas with Himself and His life; it was a small thing for Him to commit the money-bag to his keeping. So the grand question would again be: wherefore He called him (hereupon comp. *Leben Jesu*, II., p. 693 and 700). Since Jesus could venture to have Judas for His apostle, He might well risk having him for His cashier. 6. The history, it is probable, was also intended to be expressive of the standard by which the purse was here estimated in relation to higher good things, and it should be a significant warning to the Church not to reckon upon the security of an accumulation of external church-property.

Ver. 7. **That she may keep this** [τηρήσῃ, spoken proleptically, and therefore, like all similar expressions of our Lord, somewhat enigmatically] **for the day of my burial.**—See the TEXTUAL NOTES. We do not understand the reading of Lachmann as Meyer does: *Let her alone that she may* (not give this oil, a portion of which she has just used to anoint My feet, to the poor, but) *keep it for the day of My embalming.* Meyer means, namely, on the actual day of burial. In this we can detect nought of the "odor of the ointment." The sense is: Permit her *to keep* the ointment (which she might already have used at the burial of Lazarus and which would not keep well in thy bag) for the day of My burial (which is now ideally present with the outbreak of thy malignity). In this we, at the same time, read the declaration that she, though without being clearly conscious of His approaching death, did entertain a foreboding presentiment of it and offered this great sacrifice of love as her farewell to Him. Baumgarten-Crusius: Suffer her, that she may have kept; Luthardt: that she has reserved. These explanations too are grammatically proper in the sense: leave her this, do not grudge her this, —that she has kept it and is even now saving it from your bag for the anointing of My body unto death. We are of opinion that the τηρεῖν also contains an allusion to the infidelity of Judas; a reference which, as well as the numerous authorities, recommends this reading; and we deny the need for the explanation that the reading originated in the necessity for meeting the objection urging the later occurrence of the embalming (Lücke.)

Ver. 8. **For the poor,** *etc.* See *Com. on Matthew* on the same passage.

* [Meyer, while substantially agreeing with Lange, objects that βαστάζειν means *to seize* only in the literal sense of ψηλαφᾶν (Suidas).—P. S.]

DOCTRINAL AND ETHICAL.

1. See the *Comm. on Matthew* and *Mark. The anointing of the Messiah, the Anointed One,* previous to His public procession as the Messiah and entry into Jerusalem: (1) By whom anointed? The Christ by a grateful, presageful Christian woman. (2) Wherewith anointed? With flowing ointment, with precious balm, the offering of devoted love. (3) How anointed? On the head and feet. The hair which adorned the head of His disciple, appropriated to His service. (4) Whereunto anointed? To His high-priestly sacrificial death as the completion of His life-work (to the six days' work of His Passion, as the preliminary condition of His Sabbath). With a foreboding presentiment, half consciously, half unconsciously, well known to the Spirit of God.

2. *The six days before the Passover* (until the death of Jesus) the six days of Christ's great toil and labor. Comp. Isa. lxiii. 1 ff. and the symbolism of the number six in ch. ii. 6.

3. *The post-celebration of the raising of Lazarus* at the same time the pre-celebration of the death of Jesus. This connection makes the death of Jesus appear in a peculiar sense a sacrifice for His friends and His friend in Bethany.

4. *The festive celebration of the Bethanian family* in honor of the Lord a symbol of the feasts of the living communion in the Church, and of the heavenly feast.

5. The involuntary similarity in the anointing of the *great disciple* and that of the *great sinner* [Luke vii. 36.—P. S.] The contrast and its equalization. The disciple as a sinner,—the sinner as a disciple,—at the feet of Jesus.—If the washing of a pilgrim's feet denoted the termination of the little journey of a day, so the anointing of the feet of Jesus with oil might be indicative of the end of His glorious life-pilgrimage. Thus too did the great sinner anoint the feet of Jesus, wetting them with her tears—those feet which had drawn near to rescue her. But in our anointing there is a predominant reference forwards, to the death of Jesus, in accordance with His explanation.

6. The *contrast* between the heavenly offering and life-portrait of *Mary* and the hellish malice and death-portrait of *Judas.* Faith's half-conscious presentiment of the death of Jesus and of its import, within the breast of Mary. The

already half-conscious thought of the betrayal to death in the soul of Judas. The evangelic hearty acquiescence of Mary in the Passion of Christ. The anti-christian self-will of Judas in his obduracy. The deed of the innermost heart and the words of the outermost hypocrisy. Over against the first ripe Christian woman stands the first ripe anti-christ. Heaven and hell in their manifestations drawn up in close opposition.

7. The *silence* of *Mary*, the *speech* of *Jesus*.

8. Christ suffers no sort of hypocrisy to obtain dominion in His Church; neither hypocrisy of prayer nor of fasting, nor humanistic eleemosynary hypocrisy.

9. The doctrine of Judas is at bottom self-destroying. If every one should sell the precious ointment, in order to give it to the poor, it would be rendered *worthless*. Judas must therefore assume: the ointment is too good for Christ; it is for people of higher rank, or the moment is not one of sufficient importance. Pauperism.

10. Antithesis between the fixed affairs and exercises in the kingdom of God and the unique, irrecoverable moments; and the subordination of the former to the latter.

11. An evangelic flash of light, illuminating the subject of church-property, the temptations of administration and the dangers of an increase of property in the common treasury (see Acts v. 1).

12. The gradual hardening of Judas at the two feasts of the glory and grace of Christ. Great operations of grace are succeeded in false minds by a great reaction of wickedness.

HOMILETICAL AND PRACTICAL.

In what way Jesus, upon the edict of the Sanhedrin commanding that information should be given against Him, Himself appears by making the palm-entry into Jerusalem.—The six work-days or Passion-days of Christ until Easter.—The feast at Bethany or the trio (Lazarus and his sisters) in three different meetings with the Lord: 1. The visit of Jesus: Lazarus probably at his business, Martha serving, Mary learning at Jesus' feet [Luke x.]. 2. The return of Jesus: Lazarus in the grave, Martha busy about the grave of Lazarus, Mary with her tears at the feet of Jesus [John xi.]. 3. The departure of Jesus: Lazarus at the table, participating in the feast, Martha the festive hostess, Mary with the costly ointment at Jesus' feet [John xii.]. Or: 1. The school of the word; 2. the battle-ground of distress; 3. the feast of salvation.—The festival in Bethany compared with the festival of the Lord's Supper. Agreement, difference.—The house was filled with the odor of the ointment.—The anointing in its signification: 1. The expression of the most heartfelt gratitude, 2. of the most solemn veneration and homage, 3. of the deepest humility, 4. of the most devoted love, 5. of the holiest sorrow, 6. of the boldest confidence.—How Mary by her spirit of sacrifice manifests her budding courage in the face of the cross and death.—The discipless, a ripe Christian heart, uncomprehended even in the circle of the disciples, and in advance of most of the disciples.—Mary and Judas.—The two in their participation in the death of Jesus.—Self-denial, in its heavenly brilliance, over against selfishness, in hellish darkness.—The connection of fanaticism and avarice in the soul of Judas (after the prelude of Balaam).—How the secrets of hell come to light face to face with the secrets of heaven.—The Lord's defence of Mary in its eternal signification: 1. A defence of a festive spirit in opposition to hypocritical sadness, 2. of great love-offerings in opposition to a hypocritical reckoning, 3. of holy spending (prodigality) in opposition to a hypocritical pauperism.—The perception of the unique moments of life.—The censure of Judas, merely as a rude disturbance of the feast, immoral and reprehensible; on the other hand, the reproof of Christ gentle, mild, in accordance with the festive spirit and intelligible in its hidden sharpness to the disturber of the peace alone.—The separation between Christ and the poor made by Judas, was opposed to the spirit of Christ (see Matt. xxv. 35). For: 1. In the true veneration of Christ consists the most effectual caring for the poor; 2. true care for the poor ministers to Christ in the poor.—While, therefore, Christ accedes to the separation of Judas, He at the same time pronounces His judgment upon the false, externalized care of the poor. (Externalized poverty itself is forever at your heels; it is inexterminable; but Christ, meanwhile, is vanishing from you).—The contradiction in the censure of Judas. If Christ should not be anointed with the precious ointment, who then should? People of rank? Manifestly, the Lord has grown small and poor in his sight, and the polite world rich and great.—The offence of Judas: 1. The fair, festive joy augments his gloom, 2. the celebration of the honor of Jesus his envy, 3. the princely munificence his avarice, 4. the mild reproof his exasperation against Him, 5. the heavenly calmness with which Jesus saw through him the dark self-confusion in which he surrendered himself to the influences of Satan.—The false antithesis which Judas makes between Christ and the poor: 1. It asperses the Lord; 2. it asperses poverty.—A prelude to pauperism.—The judgment upon this pauperism: 1. It loses the Christ; 2. it retains the poor.—How the spirit of Christ is victorious over the disturbances of the feast.

Starke: Zeisius: Though Christ gave place for a time to the rage of His enemies, He, nevertheless, returns in accordance with His divine vocation; duty, therefore, must not be abandoned by a teacher or by any Christian on account of danger.—Hedinger: Love spares no expense.—Canstein: All Christ's friends, when they have been awakened by Him, sup with Him in the kingdom of grace (Rev. iii. 20), and when He shall have aroused them from bodily death at the last day, they shall sit with Him at His table in the kingdom of glory, Luke xvi. 22; xxii. 30.—That which is spent on Christ is not wasted but well employed.—Cramer: Even in extreme persecution God does not leave His own without comfort and refreshment.—A friend of Christ gladly lays out all that he has, even to the very choicest of his possessions, in testimony of his love to his Saviour.—Nothing more shameful than ingratitude.—ZEISIUS: Hypocrites always find something to censure in the works and conduct of honest Christians.—*Ibid.:* Judas is a true type of wicked church-patrons, directors, managers of ecclesiastical estates, who, under cover of all sorts of specious reasons, secure to themselves the funds, benefices and revenues and do not restore them).—Christ espouses the cause of His people and defends them faithfully.—PISCATOR: Men, impelled by the Holy Ghost, frequently perform an important action without comprehending its significance.

BRAUNE: What a feast was that where the noble Simon, gratefully rejoicing in his health, was host; Lazarus, the visible trophy of life's triumph over death; friend Martha, personating business-like alacrity, is the waitress; but where Mary, as thoughtful love, brings precious oil, and Jesus, the Son of God, going to a death upon the cross, appears as guest, to refresh Himself on the way! *Here is a table prepared for Him in the presence of His enemies, and His head is anointed with oil,* Ps. xxiii. 5. —To John, Bethany is as *one* house, and families friendly to Jesus (the house of Simon the leper, the house of Lazarus and his sisters) are as *one* family.—1 Tim. vi. 10.—Like Mary, prevent death, that death may not prevent thee and cut off thine opportunity.—GOSSNER: *Mary.* With her what was outward proceeded from within, as it always should be.—The odor of her ointment, *etc.* How the glorious odor of the gospel fills all Christendom, and particularly the house of a heart that receives it.—Judas betrayed that he would rather have money in his purse than his Saviour in his heart.—Yes, to such lengths do abuses go that the thief, avarice, covetousness, the devil, steals into the apostolic college.—Ointments were preserved among the household treasures until burial.—It is true that we have Jesus always with us in the poor, but His presence with us is not always to be felt. Therefore when He discloses Himself so perceptibly, as if we saw Him, as if He were corporeally and visibly present, we must profit by this occasion and not forsake Him for the sake of outside works that can be performed at another time.

SCHLEIERMACHER: The human kindliness and pleasantness of the Redeemer.—As Christians, who have become what they are by the death of the Lord, death itself must remain a something continually present to us all. But gladsomeness of heart is just what turns even the continual thought of death into something that does not annoy us in the cheerful moments of social life. —MALLET: The odor of the ointment. Thus the house had suddenly become the very opposite of the grave (there a savor of mould,—here a savor of life).—The days of glory and the cross in Jerusalem stand in the closest connection with the occurrences in Bethany.

[CRAVEN: From AUGUSTINE: Ver. 6. Judas was already a thief, and followed our Lord in *body,* not in *heart:* wherein we are taught the duty of tolerating wicked men in the Church (for a season.—E. R. C.)—It is not surprising that Judas who was accustomed to steal money from the bag, should betray our Lord for money.—In the person of Judas are represented the wicked in the Church.——From ALCUIN: Ver. 1. As the time approached in which our Lord had resolved to suffer, He approached the place He had chosen for the scene of His suffering.—Ver. 2. The Lord's Supper is the faith of the Church working by love.—Martha *serveth,* whenever a believing soul devotes itself to the worship of the Lord.—Lazarus is one of them that sit at table when those who have been raised from the death of sin, rejoice together with the righteous, in the presence of truth, and are fed with the gifts of heavenly grace.——From BURKITT: Ver. 1. Our Lord's example teaches us that although we are bound by all lawful means to preserve ourselves from the violence of persecutors, yet when God's time for our suffering is come we ought to set our faces cheerfully toward it.—Ver. 3. When strong love prevails in the heart nothing is adjudged too dear for Christ.—Vers. 4-6. How does a *covetous* heart think every thing too good for Christ.—Vers. 5-7. Men may, through ignorance or prejudice, censure those actions which God commends.——From M. HENRY: Ver. 1. As there is a time when we are allowed to shift for our own preservation, so there is a time when we are called to jeopard our lives for God.—Ver. 2. *Martha served:* Our Lord had formerly reproved her for being *troubled with much serving,* she did not therefore leave off all *serving* as some who being reproved for one extreme run into another. —Better a *waiter* at Christ's table than a *guest* at the table of a prince.—*Lazarus—sat at the table with Him:* Those whom Christ has *raised up* to a spiritual life, are made *to sit together with Him,* Eph. ii. 6.—Ver. 3. The act of Mary manifested a *love*—1. *generous,* 2. *condescending* (self-humbling), 3. *believing.*—God's *Anointed* (Messiah) should be our *Anointed*—with the ointment of our best affections (and service). Honors done to Christ are to God and men an offering of a *sweet smelling savor.*—Ver. 4. It is possible for the worst of men to lurk under the disguise of the best profession.—Vers. 4, 5. Coldness of love to Christ in professors of religion is a sad presage of final apostasy.—Ver. 5. Here is—1. a *foul iniquity* gilded over with a specious pretence; 2. *worldly wisdom* passing censure on *pious zeal;* 3. *charity to the poor* made a color for opposing an act of piety to Christ.—Many excuse themselves for *laying out* in charity, under pretence of *laying up* for charity.—Proud men think all *ill advised* who do not *advise with them.*—Ver. 6. *Judas the purse-bearer:* Strong *inclinations* to sin *within,* are often furnished with strong *temptations* to sin *without.*—*He was a thief:* The reigning love of money is *heart-theft,* as much as anger and revenge are *heart-murder.*—Judas who betrayed his trust, soon after betrayed his Master. —Ver. 7. *Against the day of My burying hath she kept this:* Providence often *so* affords opportunity to Christians that the expressions of their pious zeal prove to be more *seasonable* and *beautiful* than any foresight of their own could make them.—Ver. 8. The good which may be done *at any time,* ought to give way to that which cannot be done but *just now.*——From STIER: Vers. 4, 5. The censure of Judas echoed by the other Apostles (see Matt. xxvi. 8, 9; Mark xiv. 4; also the *ye* of ver. 8): 1. "Censure infects like a plague;" 2. Could we but know the wicked origin of many of the judgments which we thoughtlessly echo, the Judas-heart from which springs many of the current criticisms of books and things (and men)—how should we recoil from them!—An example of those views and judgments which have their foundation in the *principle of utilitarianism* falsely applied—1. to the wounding of pious hearts; 2. to the damage of that justifiable *cultus* which, (1) aims worthily to express the sentiments of reverence and love, (2) is in itself productive of highest blessing.—An example of—1. the "cold judgments passed upon the virtuous emotions of warm hearts;" 2. the more or less conscious or unconscious censures of the artless outgoings of honest feelings; 3. the narrow-minded criticism of others according to our own mind and temper; 4. that slavish spirit which metes out all good works by rigid rule.—Vers. 7, 8 (see also Matt. xxvi. 10-13; Mark xiv. 6-9). Christ's *affectionate* and *sympathetic* justification of the *wounded* Mary;—1. He surpasses the blame of the disciples by His own instant praise and consolation; 2. Behold the moral *æsthetics* in the estimation of human acts which He teaches and requires—He commends the *deed* as deriving its value from the state of the soul thereby expressed; 3. He corrects the errors of human judgment as to what is great and noble in human works—the *greatness of the result* gives them not their value, but the *intention;* 4. Observe the deepest ground of His verdict—*she hath done it* UNTO ME (Matt. and Mark)—love for Him (for God) the first, and most essential regulating measure of all good and lovely works.—Be confident, misunderstood soul—He knows thee and thy purpose; even if His disciples blame, He will justify thee both now and hereafter.—Ver. 7. The *beautiful work* (*καλὸν ἔργον*) of love elevated, interpreted and glorified into a *prophetic act;* Jesus establishes from its *providential significance* its *moral propriety.* (?)—Ver. 8. No *agragrian law* can abolish the poverty which is ever being reproduced; we must, indeed, *give* with the wisdom of charity, but without hoping that *giving* will make poverty cease. ——From BARNES: Ver. 6. *He was a thief and had the bag:* Every man is tried according to his native propensity—the *object* of trial is to bring out a man's native character.—Vers. 4-6. Learn that—1. it is no new thing for members of the Church to be covetous; 2. *such* members will be those who complain of the great waste in spreading the gospel; 3. this passion will work all evil in a Church (even the betrayal of our Lord, Ver. 4).—— From WILLIAMS: Vers. 3-5. Observe the nature of the action selected by our Lord as the one above all others that should receive an earthly memorial (Matt. xxvi. 13); it was—1. wrought in a *private room;* 2. an expression of loving, reverential *thanksgiving;* 3. not to please men, but for the simple purpose of doing honor to Jesus.—Ver. 5. But for the reproof of Judas the costliness of Mary's offering had not been known and honored—the evil eye (and tongue) of the wicked serves to do honor to God's servants.——From A PLAIN COMMENTARY (Oxford): Ver. 3. Can we wonder at the *love* of Mary? Lazarus was at the table!—Vers. 2, 3. Christ at the table with the Leper who was cleansed (Matt. xxvi. 6) and with the dead man whom He had raised to life—a figure of His Church when he who is cleansed and he who is raised from the death of sin, sit with Christ, and eat and drink in His kingdom which is filled with the odor of His Death.—(*Altered* from WILLIAMS).—Vers. 5-7. The offering of Mary *the most expensive* she could procure: Our Lord's commendation is—1. the abiding warrant for munificence on every similar occasion; 2. the perpetual rebuke of those who think that anything is good enough for the House of God, while they deny themselves in no luxury at home. — Ver. 6. Christ suffered Judas to remain amongst the Apostles—teaching us not to look for a Church (or a ministry) where *all* shall be saints.—Ver. 8. The *poor* always with the Church, in order that His people may always show them kindness for His sake.——From RYLE: Ver. 2. The *supper* a type of the marriage supper of the Lamb.—Ver. 5. A specimen of the way in which wicked men often try to *depreciate* a good action, by suggesting that something better might have been done.—Ver. 6. Multitudes, like Judas, excuse themselves from one class of duties by pretended zeal for others—they compensate neglecting Christ's cause by affecting concern for the poor.—It is the successors of Mary and not of Judas who really care for the poor.—*He was a thief*, and yet an Apostle—*privileges* alone convert nobody.—A man may go far in Christian profession without inward grace. — Ver. 7. Christians do not always know the full meaning of what they do—God uses them as His *instruments.*—Ver. 8. The existence of pauperism is no proof that States are ill governed or that Churches are not doing their duty.—Relieving the poor is not so important a work as doing honor to Christ. (During His absence from us is He not honored by our ministering to the poor (Matt. xxv. 40, 45)?—E. R. C.)—Ver. 8. *Me ye have not always:* These words overthrow the Romish doctrine of transubstantiation.——From OWEN: Vers. 4, 5 (in connection with Matt. xxvi. 8; Mark xiv. 4). How pernicious, even upon good men, may be the example and influence of one, who with apparently charitable motive decries the benevolence that would surrender all for Christ.—The Evangelist does not seek to cover up the disgrace brought upon the family of Christ by having cherished so long in its number this bad man: it is thus (by their honesty) that the sacred writers manifest the truthfulness of their statements.—Ver. 8. The inference is clear that it is a Christian duty to relieve the wants of the poor.]

IV.

ANTITHESIS BETWEEN THE HOMAGE OF PIOUS JEWS AND FESTAL PILGRIMS, AND THE HIGH-PRIESTS WITH THEIR ADHERENTS, WHO DESIRE TO DESTROY THE LORD'S FRIENDS AS WELL AS HIMSELF. THE PRINCE OF PEACE AND THE PALM-BRANCHES.

(VERS. 9–19.)

(Matt. xxi. 1-11; Mark xi. 1-10; Luke xix. 29-44.)

9 Much people[1] of the Jews therefore knew [learned] that he was there: and they
came [thither] not for Jesus' sake [on account of Jesus] only, but that they might
10 see Lazarus also, whom he had raised from the dead; But the chief priests con-
11 sulted that they might put Lazarus also to death. Because that by reason of him
[For on his account] many of the Jews went away, and believed on [were going
away and believing in] Jesus.
12 On the next day much people that were [had] come to the feast, when they heard
13 [hearing] that Jesus was coming to Jerusalem, Took [the] branches of [the] palm
trees, and went forth to meet him, and cried, Hosanna: Blessed *is* the King of
Israel that cometh in the name of the Lord [Blessed *is* he that cometh in the name
14 of the Lord, even (*καί*) the king of Israel].[2] And [But] Jesus, when he had found
15 [having found] a young ass, sat [set himself] thereon; as it is written, Fear not,
daughter of Zion: behold, thy King cometh, sitting on an ass's colt. [Zech. ix. 9.]
16 These things[3] understood not his disciples [his disciples did not understand] at
the first: but when Jesus was glorified, then [they] remembered they that these
17 things were written of him, and *that* they had done these things unto him. The
people [multitude] therefore that was with him when[4] he called Lazarus out of his
18 [the] grave [tomb], and raised him from the dead, bare record [bore witness]. For
this cause [On this account] the people [multitude] also met him, for that [because]
19 they heard that he had done this miracle [wrought this sign]. The Pharisees
therefore said among themselves, Perceive ye how ye prevail nothing? [Ye see
that ye accomplish, or, effect nothing:][5] behold, the world[6] is gone [has run
away] after him.

TEXTUAL AND GRAMMATICAL.

[1] Ver. 9.—[Noyes translates ὄχλος πολύς, *the great multitude*, Conant: *a great multitude*. Alford retains the A. V.]

[2] Ver. 13.—Lachmann in accordance with D. K. X., Origen, *etc.*: ὁ βασ. Since even B. L., *etc.*, read: καὶ ὁ βασ., the omission of the article seems unfounded. [The reading καὶ ὁ before βασιλεὺς is adopted by Tischendorf in ed. 8, Alf., Westc. and H., and supported by ℵ* *et* cd B. L. Q., *etc.*—P. S.]

[3] Ver. 16.—[Lachmann in accordance with A. D., *etc.*, inserts δέ; Tischendorf, Alf., W. and H. omit it by authority of ℵ. B. L. Q., *etc.*—P. S.]

[4] Ver. 17.—For ὅτι B. [?] D. E.* K. L., Lachmann, Tischendorf [formerly]; for ὅτε A. E.** G. M., and many others. Since ἐμαρτύρει receives additional weight, the eye-witnesship greater emphasis by ὅτε, and the preponderance of Codd. is in favor of it, this reading seems preferable. [Tischendorf, ed. 8, for *contextual* reasons, prefers ὅτι; although he affirms that not only ℵ. A. E.² G. H. M. Q., *etc.*, but also B., give ὅτε, which is adopted by Alford, Westcott and Hort. If we read ὅτι, the translation would be: *The multitude that was with him bore witness that he called Lazarus out of the tomb, and raised him from the dead.*—P. S.]

[5] Ver. 19.—[*Viz.*, with our cautious, undecided, hesitating policy. Bengel: *Approbant Caiphæ consilium* (xi. 50). The sentence is generally taken as an interrogation (also by Lange and Alford); but it seems to be more forcible as a direct assertion.—P. S.]

[6] Ver. 19.—[Or, the *whole* world. In D. L. Q. X., ὅλος is inserted; Tisch. omits it, in accordance with ℵ. A. B. Γ. Δ. Λ. Π., *etc.*—P. S.]

EXEGETICAL AND CRITICAL.

See the *Commentary on Matthew*, ch. xxi.; on *Mark* x.; on *Luke* xix. It has been shown there that there are no actual differences (the existence of which is claimed by Meyer and others) between the narrative of John and the accounts of the Synoptists, irrespective of the fact that the latter have in effect blended the two halves of the journey, from Jericho to Bethany, and from Bethany to Jerusalem, into *one* journey, without mentioning the intervening rest. Consequently a double entry (Paulus, Schleiermacher) is still less conceivable: on these points comp. the construction of the facts in *Matthew* [p. 368, 371].

Ver. 9. **A great multitude of the Jews.**—The Jews in the national sense (especially the inhabitants of Jerusalem, as the word is generally understood) were, at the same time, most of them Jews in the Pharisaic sense, and here also John understands the expression in this latter sense, not, however, necessarily of "the Jewish opposition" (Meyer [and Alford]). The raising of Lazarus had created a great sensation among these Jews in Jerusalem; it had inclined many of them to believe, so that the whole party of the Pharisees seemed about to go over to Christ, ver. 19.

They came thither.—All the people streamed forth to Bethany. Some already believed, and wished above all things to see Jesus again; others were desirous of seeing Lazarus, *i. e.*, they were on the high road to faith. This pilgrimaging began as early as Saturday evening, see ver. 12.

Ver. 10. **But the high-priests took counsel.**—The state of matters seemed so desperate to the high-priests (Caiaphas, Hannas and the innermost circle of chief-priestly intimates in the Sanhedrin) that they consulted together as to how they might make away with Lazarus also, the living memorial of the miraculous power of Jesus. The consequence of the counsel of blood: 'It is expedient that *one* man should die,' thus begins to make itself manifest. It ever demands more blood, as is proved by the history of the hierarchy. Upon similar, secret murderous plots see Acts xxiii. 12; xxv. 3. Of course, as Lampe remarks, the Sadducean party, of which Caiaphas was a member, were specially interested in putting Lazarus aside, he being a living witness to the truth of the resurrection. Comp. Acts iv. 1, 2.

Ver. 11. **Many of the Jews were going away;** *ὑπῆγον*.—Lampe and others: They apostatized. Meyer combats this interpretation. The apostasy is indeed merely a consequence of their going away to Bethany; nevertheless it is intimated.

Ver. 12. **On the next day.**—On Sunday morning. See *Comm. on Matthew.* Here, too, the diversity between John and the Synoptists continues; John mentions that part of the palm-procession which issues from Jerusalem, while the Synoptists give prominence to the portion accompanying Jesus, *i. e.*, the Galilean. Since the same story is here told us by the Synoptists and by John, it becomes very evident that it was John's intention to supplement their accounts. However, the Synoptists themselves distinguish between a part of the procession that preceded Jesus, and a part that followed Him. By the former attendants those seem to be meant who set out from Jerusalem intending to bring Jesus into the city. John, on the other hand, likewise discriminates between two divisions (vers. 17 and 18),—citizens of Jerusalem and festal pilgrims who are already in Jerusalem.

A great multitude that had come to the feast, hearing, *etc.*—Believing pilgrims to the feast, already present in Jerusalem. Be it observed that, according to John, the Hosanna movement, the solemn proclamation of Jesus as the Messiah, originates with these festal pilgrims. Jerusalem herself seems to receive the Lord as her King. According to Tholuck, these were Galilean pilgrims; this is contradicted by the fact that the Galilean festive train is just approaching from Peræa; but a considerable portion of the Galilean pilgrims may have already entered Jerusalem or its environs, and may thus turn back to join in escorting Jesus. The acclamation, according to Ps. cxviii. 25, 26, "where the Messiah is greeted as coming *ἐν ὀνόματι κυρίου*. A reception such as is allotted to kings and conquerors, 1 Macc. xiii. 51; 2 Macc. x. 7." Tholuck.

Ver. 13. **They took the branches of the palm-trees** [*τὰ βαΐα τῶν φοινίκων*].*—A lively view of the well-known palm-trees, which then, as the reporter vividly reminds us, stood on the road leading from the city to Bethany. This notice is wanting in Luke; Matthew mentions only branches of the trees; Mark speaks of things strewed in the way; we are indebted to John alone for the precise information; and therewith for the terms: *Palm-Sunday*, *Palm-entry*, and the symbolism of the palm-branch. "As the pomegranate tree is the symbol of the secretly flowing fulness of blessing, so, on the other hand, the palm-tree represents the overflowing horn of plenty and is the symbol of all fulness of strength and outward prosperity: thy stature is like to the palm-tree, thy breast like clusters of dates, Sol. Song vii. 7. Hence Tamar† a favorite name for women, Gen. xxxviii. 6; 2 Sam. xiii. 1; xiv. 27. Hence the palm has from ancient times been regarded as the escutcheon and sign of Israel. Coins of the times of the Maccabees have on one side the palm, and on the other a vine branch as tokens of the land. Also on the medals of the Emperor Titus, struck at his command in countless numbers from the spoil of Jerusalem and distributed among the Roman army, the 'Captive Judah' is portrayed as a woman sitting under a palm-tree." (*Bibl. Naturgesch.*, publ. at Calw., p. 343.) By the biblical palm we are generally to understand the date palm. Elim, the camp of the seventy palm-trees, Ex. xv. 27; Num. xxiii. 9; the palm-branches at the feast of tabernacles, Lev. xxiii. 40; Jericho, the city of palms, Deut. xxxiv. 3; Jud. i. 16; the righteous a flourishing palm-tree, Ps. xcii. 13; Sulamith, Sol. Song vii. 8. According to these stages of the symbol it is expressive of refreshment, blessing, festival, new life or victory; 1 Macc. xiii. 51 a sign of victory.

Hosanna.‡ Matthew: "Hosanna to the Son of David! Blessed is he that cometh in the name of the Lord; Hosanna in the highest!" Mark: "Hosanna! Blessed is He that cometh in the name of the Lord: Blessed be the kingdom of our father David, that cometh in the name of the Lord! Hosanna in the highest!" Luke: "Blessed be the king that cometh in the name of the Lord! Peace in heaven and glory in the highest!" Here (as in the account of the resurrection) the variations more decidedly attest the reality of this scene of intense excitement than would a uniform account. It is the liturgy of ecstatic life. Some cry thus, others thus; each evangelist reports in accordance with his own hear-

* [The article *τῶν* (not *τά*), which is omitted in the E.V., indicates, as Lange and Meyer explain, that the palm-trees were on the road, or perhaps that the custom was usual at such festivities (Alford).—P. S.]

† [תָּמָר, the palm-tree.—P. S.]

‡ [Ὡσαννά, from the Hebrew, means *σῶσον δή*, *save now*, and is originally a formula of supplication, but conventionally one of triumphant acclamation and joyful greeting to a deliverer.—P. S.]

ing or that of witnesses. Be it observed that in John the Hosanna precedes the mention of the ass's colt, while in the Synoptists it is subsequent to that. Naturally, because the Hosanna with which, as with the watch-word of the day, the festal pilgrims from Jerusalem approach, is not communicated until later to the festal train from Galilee and Peræa. In this the new disciples are in advance of the old ones; hence too more rapturous.

Vers. 14-16. **And Jesus having found a young ass,** *etc.* See *Comm. on Matthew:* the quotation Zech. ix. 9. Freely cited. That upon which alone the evangelist lays stress, is the contrast between the devout homage paid to Jesus, and His humble equipment, mounted upon a young ass (ὀνάριον),—found, as it were, by accident,—together with the prediction concerning this fact in the prophet. Hence he also gives prominence to the circumstance that the disciples did not then understand this fulfilment of prophecy. Hence the highly emphatic, thrice repeated ταῦτα, "*these things,*" ver. 16. That the fulfilment of the prophecy was directed by God and not by men, is expressed by the first and the third ταῦτα. Exactly so men did unto Him, and even the disciples did not so much as understand it. Even if Jesus was conscious of the fulfilment of that prophecy, the unsuspicious co-operation of men proves it to have been the dispensation of God. At a later stage of enlightenment the import of this moment was revealed to the disciples also. And here it cannot be merely the fulfilment of a type which is spoken of. It is the fulfilment of a prediction concerning the Messiah; in a typico-symbolical form, doubtless, *i. e.*, the prophet has predicted the entrance of the Messiah in insignificant equipment; but to him the ride upon the ass's colt was typically the symbol of the gentle and humble accoutrement of the Prince of Peace,—*i. e.*, the investment of his prediction.

Ver. 17. **The multitude therefore . . . bore witness.**—An antiphony is formed between the eye-witnesses of the raising of Lazarus (inhabitants of Jerusalem, of Bethany, and others) and the people who have come, as believers, from Jerusalem to meet Him. This antiphony is likewise indicated in Mark (where in our translation we read: and they that went before and they that followed). Luke, too, has indicated that the disciples who formed the escort of Jesus praised Him on account of His wondrous deeds. Here John supplements; he informs us that the raising of Lazarus was the leading motive for the ascriptions of praise to Jesus in the Palm-procession. This motive was passed over by the Synoptists for the same reason which induced them to pass over the raising of Lazarus itself.

Ver. 19. **The Pharisees therefore said.**—According to Chrysostom, thus spoke the secret friends among the Pharisees. But it is manifestly the language of despairing rage. Comp. the similar expression of displeasure on the part of John's disciples, chap. iii. 26. They reproach each other for not having taken more energetic measures. In the great movement they, as they hyperbolically express themselves in their excitement and fear, believe they already see the apostasy of the whole nation from the hierarchical party. This moment of despair on the part of the Pharisees is the corresponding contrast to the triumphal procession of Christ. But that Christ better understood the import of this procession is proved not only by His weeping in the midst of the triumphal entry, according to Luke, but also in the subsequent portrayal of the mood of Jesus by John himself.

DOCTRINAL AND ETHICAL.

1. See *Comm. on Matthew, Mark, Luke,* on the Palm-entry.

2. As Jesus, at the beginning of His ministry, issued from the wilderness resolved to avoid, during His official pilgrimage, the unpurified Messianic name among His people,—connected, as it was, with all false Messianic hopes,—in order, by His actual self-revelation in prophetic anonymousness, to purify the Messianic hope of His nation, and the Messianic conception,—so now He has come forth from the wilderness with the determination of surrendering Himself to the purified Messianic faith of His disciples in the nation, *i. e.*, to the nation itself, in respect of its present festive enthusiasm. In both cases He acts, according to the command (ἐντολή) of the Father, in perfect obedience; according to the principle of truth, as personal Wisdom, in perfect freedom. But He foreknows the event; He knows that in the fluctuations of dynamical moods in His nation the curse shall at first outweigh the blessing, or the demoniacal spirit that came to Him as a tempter in the wilderness, according to Matt. iv., shall circumvent and overpower the heavenly enthusiasm with which He has inspired His people; that He consequently shall be betrayed, that He goes to meet His sacrificial death, but that then, when the propitiatory effect of His death has been manifested in His resurrection, the blessing shall preponderate over the curse, for His people as well as for the whole world. And thus the Palm-procession has a twofold import. In reference to the Lord, it is the free surrender to His people, in His real Messianic dignity, unto death, and, therewith, the free surrender to the disposition of the law itself—a veiled type of His sacrificial procession to Golgotha; hence, also, the symbolical pre-celebration of His Easter passage, in the resurrection, back to the Mount of Olives, and up to the Throne of glory, of His triumphant entry into the world and His kingly appearing to judgment. But in reference to the world itself, it is the surrender to a legal enthusiasm of His people, which cannot protect Him from death, but changes to treachery, and His surrender to the people of true believers, with which surrender His real glorification in the world begins. In the former relation we have to distinguish the extolled Christ who became the Crucified One, and the crucified Christ who became the Risen One; in the latter relation the symbolic Hosanna of those who were under the temporary influence of a spirit of enthusiasm, and the real Hosanna of the children of the Spirit.

3. In the celebration of the raising of Lazarus by the Palm-entry is concentrated the celebration of the whole official pilgrimage of Christ,

particularly in His thaumaturgic activity. See Luke xix. 37.

4. To the symbolism of sacred springs and mountains is annexed the symbolism of trees which are especially hallowed. The fig-tree, under which Nathanael sat, the symbol of peace, of calm life and of quiet contemplativeness (chap. i. 48), is here joined by the palm-tree, the symbol of blessing and victory, of peace, of kingly state and royal grandeur and glory; subsequently, however, chap. xv. 1 ff., the symbol of the vine is set forth in detail: see Friedreich, *Symbolik und Mythologie der Natur*, Würzburg, 1859, p. 332: the Palm-tree.

5. "Thus Zechariah, in one of his visions (chap. ix. 9), describes the Messiah, in wretchedness and lowliness approaching His people. That this—and not the *bringing of peace*—is the meaning of this symbol—has been convincingly shown by Hengstenberg (*Christologie des A. T.* on the passage, iii. 1. Second edition). Christ designs by facts to recall this prophecy; the young ass's colt in the prophet forms a climax to *ὄνος* (Ewald, Hengstenberg), and as this (*ὄνος*) presents to our view what is already contained in עָנִי, not gentleness, but *lowliness*, so the colt is expressive of the same in a higher degree. Seeing that John omits not only the significative predicates צַדִּיק, נוֹשָׁע, but also the *πραΰς* of the Septuagint and of Matthew, the simple riding upon this colt must have been significant enough,—namely, as a symbol of lowliness,—for great men and kings ride only upon horses." Tholuck.

To this we have to remark: (1) the idea of lowliness as condescension is not necessarily connected with wretchedness; (2) in Zechariah the symbol of humility is evidently a symbol, at the same time, of gentleness and peace, vers. 9, 10. (3) If John, therefore, pretended to see in His mounting of this animal merely a sign of lowliness, then would Matthew's interpretation of the prophet be more correct than his. (4) But this is the more out of the question since, according to John, the people that wish to glorify the Lord, put Him upon the young ass. In accordance with the she-ass of Balaam, we should see in the ass a symbol of the presageful in the irrational creation. In Friedreich's *Symbolik und Mythologie der Natur* are various interpretations without result. Here we have to do with the ass merely as the beast of peace.

6. John too intimates, with *εὑρών*, that the choice of the ass' colt proceeded from Jesus. But he lays special stress on the fact that the people, not thinking of that prophecy, did thus with Him; thus he emphasizes the providential direction of the event, which took care that the prophecy should be fulfilled, consciously to the Lord, but unconsciously to the disciples and the people.

7. The great contrast. The victorious kingdom of Christ seemed to have arisen, the whole nation was apparently going over to Him with Hosannas; the hostile party was in despair. Then the treachery of Judas brought the fearful turning. But what explanation is to be found for the treachery of Judas in the present posture of affairs? Judas saw that Jesus did not *utilize* the triumphal entry for the founding of a worldly kingdom, and he now gave up His cause for lost. Exactly the opposite to this contrast is formed by the triumph of enemies after the crucifixion of Christ. Hell is jubilant, Christ dies, His disciples fear. And now Nicodemus and Joseph desert the Sanhedrin and go over to Christ, as Judas, after the Palm-entry, forsook the company of the disciples and went over to the enemy. Appearances, therefore, are not decisive in the situations of the kingdom of God. Exalted moments of triumph are admonitory to extreme prudence; on the other hand, the greatest calamities are accompanied by the announcement of an approaching wondrous festival in honor of the victory of divine help and wisdom.

HOMILETICAL AND PRACTICAL.

See *Comm. on Matthew, Mark, Luke.*—The great movement and meeting between Bethany and Jerusalem, or the Communion of the Gospel and the Communion of the Law: 1. Jerusalem comes to Bethany; 2. Bethany comes to Jerusalem.—Christ's great victory over the Jews a sign of eternal promise.—*To kill Lazarus also*, or the consequence of violence in the domain of the spirit and faith.—The Palm-entry according to John. 1. Its cause (vers. 9–11); 2. its form (vers. 12–18); 3. its effect, ver. 19.—Antithesis of life and death in the story of Lazarus: 1. In contemplating the life-miracle of the Prince of Life susceptible hearts become alive; alive to such a degree that all Israel seems to quicken; 2. the mortal hatred of dead Pharisee hearts towards Christ seeks to kill Lazarus also, and with the breath of death breathes upon the people (even upon the flock of disciples, especially Judas).—The scattering of palm-branches, or triumphal homage to the Victor: 1. As Victor and King in the kingdom of the Spirit, in the believing heart, the believing people, the whole world receptive of salvation; 2. as Victor over, and Destroyer of, the kingdom of darkness in the heart, in the church, in the world (here and hereafter); 3. as Victor and Conqueror with the spoils of victory (His are souls entirely; His the people of the peoples—their marrow).—The world in its destiny as the new heaven and the new earth.—As Sunday precedes the week-day, so the Palm-entry precedes the last great work of Christ: 1. As a refreshment for the work; 2. as the survey of the work; 3. as the warranty for the success of the work.—The Hosanna of the people of Jerusalem: 1. In the old time (Ps. cxviii. 26); 2. on Palm Sunday; 3. at Pentecost; 4. in the time of the Reformation.—The riding-beast of Balaam and the riding-beast of Christ, a sign: 1. How dumb nature, (*a*) loudly contradicts all false prophets, and (*b*) is wiser than they. 2. How it is (*a*) serviceable to the King of truth, and (*b*) is rendered worthy and consecrate by Him.—The important, minute fulfilments of ancient prophecies in the life of the Lord.—The Spirit of Christ in the Old Testament specially glorified by the prophecy under our consideration: 1. The prophet knew in spirit the wonderful humility and meekness of Christ; 2. he saw in spirit a people, spiritual enough not to be offended in a Prince of Peace on the ass's colt.—The grand antiphony on the Mount of Olives, or the greetings and counter-greetings in the kingdom of faith: 1. From heart to heart; 2. from congregation to congregation; 3. from church to church; 4. from world to world (from star to star, or between heaven and earth).—The Pharisees' hour of despair: 1. Why they despair (on account of the triumphs of Christ); 2. how they despair (they lose head after having lost heart, and dispute among themselves); 3. who comes to their aid in their despair (Satan and treacherous disciples); 4. whereunto that helps them (into ever deeper despair).—The kingdom of darkness, the shadowy foil of the kingdom of light.—*Ye see that ye prevail nothing, etc.*, or how the hierarchy prophesies concerning its own downfall; 1. In vain all our plots; 2. all the world sides with Him.—Behold, thy King cometh unto thee.—*He cometh;* 1. *He* cometh; 2. He *cometh.*

Starke, Quesnel:—Only Satan's spirit, yea, Satanic envy, would fain destroy the works of the Spirit of God.—Miracles arouse human hearts, but they do not convert; that belongs to the word of the Lord, Luke xvi. 29.—*Ibid.:* Jesus leaves to the kings of earth their magnificence which they need as a cloak for their weakness. Humility and lowliness are the best adornments of a King who is fighting only against pride, and who wills to triumph over sin and death.—Cramer: In the school of Christianity there is much to be learned and remembered, even though it be not yet understood; for we do not believe *because* we understand, but *that* we may finally understand.—Zeisius: Believers increase in the knowledge of Christ and in understanding of the Holy Scriptures.—Canstein: As a general thing, the fulfilment of prophecies first exhibits their true meaning.—Hedinger: We should praise God's work and the grace of Him who hath called us to His wonderful light.—Zeisius: Christ, His honor and doctrine, must be boldly confessed, even though His enemies be like to "burst" with envy and malice.—Honor to whom honor is due.—Cramer: Envy does not injure Christ, but His enemies themselves.—The whole world runneth after Christ, is still the language of the wicked; O that it might soon come to pass in the greatest fulness!

Lisco: The manner of His entry showed Him to be not an earthly prince, but a King of Peace. —Ver. 16. Braune: Thus what seemed lost for the present has become a blessing for the future. —Palm branches are true peace branches. The palm is verily the noblest tree; it is ever reaching upwards, without lavishing its strength in side-branches, and it proves itself of the utmost utility in leaf, fruit and wood.—Yet there was a little band of believers hidden in unbelieving Jerusalem; some of the seven thousand of God, whom Elijah saw not, came forth.—Gossner: *Wished to kill* Lazarus. This is the religion of Caiaphas and Herod. It spares nothing. Everything that is feared must be thrust out of the way.—Instead of reporting Him to the magistrates, as they were commanded to do, ch. xi. 57, they bring Him as their King.—Jesus always finds more faith and love among the people than among those who hold themselves above the people.—The state of our King consists in simplicity and lowliness. He comes with such condescension that even the meanest need not fear but may gather confidence.—All wrath is put away; He is all meekness and goodness.—*Behold, the whole world, etc.* O that this would come to pass today! Truly, it is written, Gen. xlix. 10.

Heubner:—Those that were healed or raised by Jesus were standing witnesses to His glory.—Jesus accepted applause; He knew it to be the road to shame. And He then endured shame as having the prospect of eternal glory.—Schenkel: How Christ as a King is continually coming to His people: 1. What Christ as the coming King brings us; 2. what we as His people should bring Him.—Besser: *Ye see that ye prevail nothing;* behold, the world runneth after Him. Even in this angry speech somewhat of a prophecy lies hidden, and that which we are about to read is a prelude to the fulfilment of this prophecy.

[Craven: From Augustine: Ver. 9. Curiosity brought them, not love.—Ver. 10. O blind rage! as if the Lord could raise the *dead*, and not raise the *slain.*—Vers. 12, 13. See how great was the fruit of His preaching, and how large a flock of the lost sheep of the house of Israel heard the voice of their Shepherd.—Vers. 13-15. Christ was not the king of Israel, to exact tribute and command armies, but to direct souls and bring them to the kingdom of Heaven.—For Christ to be king of Israel was a condescension, not an elevation—a sign of His pity, not an increase of His power.—From Chrysostom: Ver. 13. This is what more than any thing made men believe in Christ, *viz.*, the assurance, that He was not opposed to God, that He came from the Father.—From Bede: Vers. 13-15. Christ does not lose His divinity when He teaches us (by example) humility.—From Burkitt: Ver. 9. It was the *sin* of many that they flocked after Christ rather out of *curiosity* than *conscience.*—Vers. 10, 11. Such as have received special favor from Christ must expect to be made the butt of malicious enemies.—Nothing so enrages the enemies of Christ as the enlargement of His kingdom.—Vers. 14, 15. That it might appear that Christ's kingdom was not of this world He abandons all outward magnificence.—Ver. 19. In the day of Christ's greatest solemnity there will be some who will neither rejoice themselves nor endure that others should.——From M. Henry: Ver. 9. *Much people came not for Jesus sake* only: yet they came to see *Jesus*—there are some in whose affections Christ will have an interest in spite of all the attempts of His enemies to misrepresent Him.—Ver. 10. The *consultation* of the Chief-priests a sign that they neither *feared God* nor *regarded man.*—Vers. 12, 13. Those who have a true veneration for Christ will neither be ashamed nor afraid to own Him before men.—Those that met Him, were they *that were come to the feast;* the more regard men have to God and religion in general, the better disposed they will be to entertain Christ. —Tidings of the approach of Christ and His kingdom should awaken us to consider the work of *the day*, that it may be done in the day.—The *palm-branch* was—1. a symbol of triumph; 2. carried as a part of the ceremonial of the feast of Tabernacles—its use on this occasion intimates that all the feasts, especially that of Tabernacles, pointed to Christ's gospel. (It *may* have been so in the purpose of God. E. R. C.)—Ver. 13. The language employed was that of Psalm cxviii. 25, 26; high thoughts of Christ are best expressed in Scripture words.—Thus must every one bid Christ welcome into his heart—we must *praise* Him, and be *well pleased* in Him.—Ver. 14.—This was—1. *More of state* than *He* used to take—showing that, though His followers should be willing to take up with mean things, yet it is allowed them to use the inferior creatures; 2. *Less of state* than the great ones of earth usually affect—manifesting that His kingdom was not of this world.—Ver. 16. See—1. the imperfection of the disciples in their *infant* state; 2. their improvement in their *adult* state.—The Scripture is often fulfilled by the agency of those who have no thought of Scripture in what they do.—There are many excellent things both in the Word and Providence of God which disciples do not at first understand.—It becomes Christians when they are grown to maturity in knowledge frequently to reflect upon the weakness of their beginning.—Such an admirable harmony there is between the *Word* and *works* of God that the remembrance of what is *written* will enable us to understand what is *done*, and the observation of what is *done* will help us to understand what is *written*.—Ver. 17. They who wish well to Christ's kingdom should proclaim what they know.—Vers. 17-19. This miracle reserved for one of the last that it might confirm those that went before, just before His sufferings; Christ's works were not only *well done*, but *well timed*.—Ver. 19. They who oppose Christ will be made to see that they prevail nothing.——From SCOTT: Ver. 10. There is nothing so wicked and infatuated that men who have engaged in persecution, will not attempt to escape defeat.——From BARNES: Ver. 10. When men are determined not to believe the gospel, there is no end to the crimes to which they are driven.——From A PLAIN COMMENTARY (Oxford): Ver. 10. Notice the rapid *growth* of sin. Vers. 12-15. Royal even in its lowliness is the mysterious pageant!——From RYLE: Vers. 9-11. People will think for themselves when God's truth comes into a land.—Ver. 13. From "Hosanna" to "Crucify Him," there was an interval of only a few days! Nothing so soon caught up as a popular applause.—Ver. 16. Men may be true Christians and yet very ignorant on some points.—In estimating others we must make great allowance for early training and association.]

V *a*.

ANTITHESIS BETWEEN THE GENTILE GREEKS FROM ABROAD WHO DO HOMAGE TO CHRIST, AND THE MAJORITY OF THE JEWISH PEOPLE THAT FALL AWAY FROM CHRIST IN UNBELIEF AND OCCASION HIS RETURN INTO CONCEALMENT. SYMBOLISM OF THE JEWISH PASCHAL-FEAST, OF HELLENISM, OF THE GRAIN OF WHEAT. THE GLORIFICATION BY SUFFERING AND DEATH, OR THE SPIRITUAL SELF-SACRIFICE OF CHRIST IN THE TEMPLE.

VERS. 20—36.

(Chap. xii. 24-26. Laurentius-Pericope; vers. 31-36. Elevation of the Cross.)

20 And [But] there were certain Greeks [Ἕλληνες, Gentile Greeks, not Ἑλληνισταί, Greek
Jews] among them that [those who] came up [made pilgrimage up to Jerusalem] to
21 worship at the feast. The same [These] came therefore to Philip, which [who] was
of [from] Bethsaida of Galilee, and desired [asked] him, saying, Sir, we would see
22 [wish, or, desire to see] Jesus. Philip cometh and telleth Andrew: and again [*omit*
23 and again][1] Andrew [cometh] and Philip [, and they] tell Jesus. And [But] Jesus
answered them, saying, The hour is [hath] come, that the Son of man should be glori-
24 fied. Verily, verily, I say unto you, Except a corn [the grain] of wheat fall into the
ground and die, it abideth alone [isolated, by itself alone]: but if it die, it bringeth
25 forth much fruit. He that loveth his life [his own soul, τὴν ψυχὴν αὐτοῦ][2] shall lose it;
and he that hateth his life [his own soul] in this world shall [will] keep it unto life
26 [ζωήν] eternal. If any man [any one would] serve me, let him follow me; and where
I am, there shall [will] also my servant be: if [ἐάν without καί][3] any man [any one
27 shall] serve me, him will *my* [the] Father honour. Now is my soul troubled; and
what shall I say? Father, save me from this hour: [!][4] but [But] for this cause[5]
28 came I unto [I came to] this hour. Father, glorify thy name. [!] Then came there
a voice from heaven, *saying* [*omit saying*], I have both glorified *it*, and will glorify
it again.
29 The people [multitude] therefore that stood by, and heard *it*, said that it thun-
dered: others said, An angel spake [hath spoken, λελάληκεν] to him.
30 Jesus answered and said, This voice came not because of me [for my sake, δι' ἐμέ],

31 but for your sakes [δι' ὑμᾶς]. Now is the judgment of this world: now shall [will]
32 the prince of this world be cast out. And I, if I [shall][6] be lifted up from the
33 earth, will [shall] draw all *men* unto me [myself, πρὸς ἐμαυτόν]. This he said,
signifying what death he should die [by what manner of death he was about to die,
34 or, what kind of death he was to die]. The people [multitude, therefore, οὖν] answered him, We have heard out of the law that [the] Christ abideth for ever: and
how sayest thou [how then dost thou say], The Son of man must be lifted up? who
35 is this Son of man? Then Jesus [Jesus therefore] said unto them, Yet a little
while is the light with you [within you].[7] Walk while [as][8] ye have the light, lest
darkness come upon you [that darkness may not overtake you, ἵνα μὴ σκοτία ὑμᾶς
καταλάβῃ]: for [and] he that walketh in [the] darkness knoweth not whither he
36 goeth. While ye have [the] light, believe in the light, that ye may be the children
of light [become sons of light, ἵνα υἱοὶ φωτὸς γένησθε].

These things spake [spoke] Jesus, and departed, and did hide [and, having departed, he hid, or, withdrew] himself from them.

TEXTUAL AND GRAMMATICAL.

[1] Ver. 22.—Instead of καὶ πάλιν, *etc.* [text. rec.], Lachmann and Tischendorf read ἔρχεται 'Ανδρέας καὶ Φίλιππος, καὶ λέγουσιν, in accordance with Cod. Sin., A. B. L., *etc.*

[2] Ver. 25.—[ψυχή, *soul* (distinct from πνεῦμα, spirit) should be distinguished here from ζωή, *life*, and be translated as in ver. 27. Lange renders: *sein Eigenleben*, his *self-life*. See the Exeg. Notes.—P. S.]

[3] Ver. 26. [The text. rec. with A. Γ. Δ., *etc.*, inserts καί before the second ἐάν; in ℵ. B. D. L. X. Lat. Syr., *etc.*, καί is omitted, which agrees with the E. V. In Luther's Vers. the καί is translated, but Lange omits it.—P. S.]

[4] Ver. 27. [Lange (with Chrysostom, Grotius, Lampe, Thol., Ewald, Godet) takes the words πάτερ, σῶσόν με ἐκ τῆς ὥρας ταύτης, *interrogatively*, as if we had here a reflective monologue, instead of an address to the Father. In this case a colon must be put after *say*, and an interrogation mark after *hour*. So also Lachmann in his Greek Testament. But I take the words (with the E. V., Meyer, Alford, *etc.*,) as a veritable prayer which corresponds to the prayer in Gethsemane, Matt. xxvi. 39, and the Messianic prayers in the Psalms: "My soul is troubled, Lord, help me" (Ps. vi. 3, 4; xxv. 17; xl. 12, 13; lxix. 1).—P. S.]

[5] Ver. 27.—[Lange inserts after *this cause* the gloss: *in order to be troubled*. But the meaning of δια τοῦτο is disputed. See Exeg. and Crit.—P. S.]

[6] Ver. 32.—[The rendering of ἐάν by *when* (ὅταν) instead of *if*, is inaccurate. It does not *necessarily* imply doubt. Herrmann (*Vig.*, p. 832) explains the phrase ἐὰν τοῦτο γένηται, thus: *Sumo hoc fieri, et potest omnino fieri, sed utrum vero futurum sit necne, experientia cognoscam.* I cannot quite agree with the note of Alford: "The Lord Jesus, though knowing all this, yet in the weakness of His humanity, puts Himself into this seeming doubt, 'if it is so to be;' comp. Matt. xxvi. 42." I would say rather that the stress is laid on ἑλκύσω as a *certain fact*, and ἐὰν ὑψωθῶ expresses, in a conditional form, the necessary antecedent condition. Just so ἐάν is used in John xiv. 3: ἐὰν πορευθῶ καὶ ἑτοιμάσω τόπον ὑμῖν, πάλιν ἔρχομαι, κ. τ. λ.—P. S.]

[7] Ver. 35.—Instead of μεθ' ὑμῶν [*with you*, text. rec. with A., Chrys., Cyr.,] should be read ἐν ὑμῖν, *within you*, in accordance with ℵ. B. D. K. L., *etc.*—P. S.]

[8] Ver. 35.—The reading ὡς instead of ἕως [text. rec.] has the overwhelming authority of A. B. D. L., *etc.*, in its favor, Lachmann, Tischendorf [Alford]. So likewise, ver. 36. The close of ver. 36 also recommends ὡς, rather than ἕως, since Jesus departs with this very word.

EXEGETICAL AND CRITICAL.

Ver. 20. **Certain Greeks** ["Ελληνες].*—By these we are 1. not to understand (after Semler and Baumgarten-Crusius [Calvin, Ewald],) Jews who spoke Greek [Hellenists]; this view is contradicted by the name, comp. ch. vii. 35, the whole scene and the deduction of Christ, vers. 23 and 32,—the reference to the universal extension of His ministry. 2. Not perfect or pure heathen (after Chrysostom, Euthymius, Schweizer), against which interpretation ἀναβαίνοντες† militates,—but, as this very word proves, 3. *proselytes of the gate* [half Jews, or Judaizing pagans], like the treasurer, Acts viii. 27. See *Comm. on Acts* [p. 155, Am. ed.]. "If they were from Galilee, which was partly inhabited by Gentiles, we might imagine them to have been previously acquainted with Philip; yet (Grecianized) Syrians inhabited the country from Lebanon to Lake Tiberias (Josephus, *De bello Jud.*, III. 4, 5); Peræa had Greek cities (Joseph. *Antiq.*, XVI. 11, 4), *etc.* Philip's consultation with Andrew must be attributed to the unusualness of seeing the Master hold intercourse with Gentiles (Matt. x. 5)—for the uncircumcised proselytes of the gate were still so considered—(Acts x.)." Tholuck. On this we remark that it is not altogether probable that these Gentiles were from Galilee, or from any part of Canaan, because in that case they might easily have had an earlier opportunity of seeing Jesus. Furthermore, Jesus had already had dealings with the Gentile captain at Capernaum, and the Canaanitish woman; the disciples, however, might for reasons of policy, hesitate for a while before bringing the Lord, after He had just been proclaimed King of Israel, into contact with Gentiles, in the sight of all the Jews. For, doubtless, the scene occurred within the area of the temple, *i. e.*, the porch. Perhaps Jesus was, by the mediation of His disciples, to be called back into the court of the Gentiles. This locality is supported by 1. the testimony of the Synoptists, that in the days subsequent to the Palm-entry Jesus abode continually in the temple; 2. the character of these Gentile visitors to the temple; 3. the concourse of people, ver. 29. (Contrary to all indications Michaelis and others have shifted the scene to Bethany; Baur places it "in the idea of the author!") As to the day, the thirty-sixth verse

* [Bengel: *Præludium regni Dei a judæis ad gentes transituri.*]

† [The present *indicates habitual* pilgrimage to Jerusalem. P. S.]

seems to indicate that it was the last of the three days of Jesus' stay in the temple, *i. e.*, Tuesday (see DOCTRINAL AND ETHICAL NOTES, No. 1).

[These God-fearing Greeks, who (in their groping after "the unknown God," embraced the monotheism and the Messianic hopes of the Jews, without being circumcised) belonged to the church invisible, to the children of God scattered among the heathen, x. 16; xi. 52, and were the forerunners of the Gentile converts. Stier: "These men from the West at the end of the life of Jesus, set forth the same as the Magi from the East at its beginning; but they come to the *cross* of the King, as those to His *cradle*." We find such chosen outsiders under the Old Testament, as Melchisedek, Jethro, Job, Ruth, king Hiram, the queen of Sheba, Naaman the Syrian. Augustine, exclusive as was his system, yet adduces the case of Job as an example of genuine piety outside of the visible theocracy, and infers from it that among other nations also there were persons "*qui secundum Deum vixerunt eique placuerunt, pertinentes ad spiritualem Jerusalem*" (*De civit. Dei* xviii. 47).—P. S.]

Ver. 21. **These therefore came to Philip.**—Philip might be accidentally in the court of the Gentiles, and hence, as the first of the disciples who was forthcoming, be charged with the communication of their request to the Lord. It is still remarkable, however, that both Philip and Andrew had Greek names and, according to tradition, their labors were likewise in part among the Greeks.

Sir, we wish to see Jesus.—[*Κύριε*, not in the higher sense, yet with reverence]. The expression of their desire is threefold: 1. The solicitation; 2. the respectful manner of addressing even the disciple of the celebrated Master; 3. the strong and yet modest expression of the wish. *To see* can here mean nothing less than: *to speak with*. (Goldhorn: They wished to propose to Him that He should go to the Hellenists. A misapprehension of the proselytes and also of the situation. Brückner: They wished merely to see Him. Too literal). As proselytes of the gate they shared Israel's hope and the enthusiastic feelings of the people.

Ver. 22. **Philip cometh and telleth Andrew.**—Meyer: Philip was of a deliberate disposition.* The other characteristics of Philip are in no wise indicative of a deliberate man. The case was of sufficient importance, as an official question, for two disciples, and Mark iii. 18 we find these two in close contact; John vi. 7, 8, however, they even act in concert, as in this place, and in measure, likewise, in "foreign affairs."—**Andrew cometh and,** *etc.*—Andrew seems to take the lead.

Ver. 23. **And Jesus answered them.**—The following discourse is framed so decidedly for the Greeks that we cannot assume their request to have been denied by Jesus (Ewald [Hengstenberg, Godet]),—such a proceeding would, moreover, be unprecedented; neither can we hold that the admission of the Gentiles had been resolved upon, but that the voice from heaven changed the scene (Meyer). De Wette thought the answer unsuitable. Tholuck, in accordance with the usual conception, supposes the meeting between Jesus and the Greeks to have preceded this discourse; Luthardt: the disciples had given Jesus occasion to speak in presence of the Greeks. The scene certainly seems to have changed; either the Greeks must have immediately followed the two disciples to Jesus, or else Jesus directly accompanied the disciples to the Greeks. He seems to have intentionally avoided addressing Himself particularly to the Greeks, preferring to discourse in their presence to the circle of disciples, with special reference to them and their desire. For at this moment and in this place it was of the utmost importance that He should withhold from His enemies every pretext for reproach.

Ver. 23. **The hour is come.**—From the visit of the Gentiles Jesus deduces the preparation of His mission for the Gentiles, *i. e.*, His resurrection. From the nearness of the period when the bounds which have encompassed Him shall be removed, and His ministry be rendered a universal one, He infers His imminent death. Universalness and resurrection are for Him reciprocal ideas; universalness and preceding death are for Him inseparably connected, ch. x. 15, 16; ch. xvii. And so this saying also again recalls the barrier which hinders Him from surrendering Himself to full communion with the Greeks. But the decisive hour which is to conduct Him across this barrier is at hand; it announces itself in this petition. The hour, however, is not His hour of death by itself, but that together with the hour of His departure out of this world. The two are comprehended in one, as in the idea of exaltation, vers. 32, 34, and ch. iii. 14. Thus Christ saw in the Samaritans (ch. iv.) and in the Gentile centurion (Matth. viii. 11) a distant indication of the future approach of the believing Gentiles; here the future of the believing Gentile world, the future of its access to Him, is before Him in its nearest representatives as an incipient present (comp. ch. xiii. 31).

Be it observed that here it is the *glorification* of the **Son of Man** that is spoken of, not simply that of the Son of God, as ch. xi. 4. The glorification of the Son of Man is the exaltation of Christ in His human nature above death (a transit from the first stage of human life to the second), above the limits of the servant to the boundless liberty of the lord; above a qualified working by individual words and signs to unqualified activity through the Spirit. It is a development of His inner wealth, according to ver. 24; a personal lifting up, according to ver. 32; a local, but at the same time a universal one, according to ver. 33. For the Greeks, whom we conceive to have been true Hellenes, a peculiar significance attached to the announcement that Christ as the Son of Man should be manifested in His glory. This glorification presupposes a suffering of death, in accordance with a law of nature (ver. 24) and in accordance with an ethical law obtaining in this world, ver. 25.

Ver. 24. **Except the grain of wheat fall into the ground and die,** *etc.* [*ἐὰν μὴ ὁ κόκκος τοῦ σίτου πεσὼν εἰς τὴν γὴν ἀποθάνῃ, αὐτὸς μόνος μένει*].—First oxymoron. A fundamental truth is again announced with **verily, verily.** We assume the subsequent

* [So also Bengel: *cum sodali, audet*, when associated with a companion, Philip makes bold and does it.—P. S.]

words to have been intended to correct the Greek view of the world, just as those contained in ch. xviii. 36 are applicable to the ideas entertained by the Romans. Human nature does not attain in this world a true and essentially beautiful appearance by the aid of poetry and art; but it arrives at the true and the beautiful by passing through death into a new life (see 1 John iii. 2). The grain of wheat here symbolizes the new life which must proceed from death in order to appear in its richness, its fruit. Hence the thought is no mere elucidation of the preceding sentence. It advances from the idea of the personal glory of Christ in the new life (the glorification of His human nature) to the idea of His glorification in the universal Church. Thus even nature protests against the Hellenic fear of death, against the Hellenic isolation of the personality in the outward individuality. In the way of death, not only does the single grain of wheat develop into many, but these many, as fruit for nourishment and new seed, appear as an infinite power, a universal life. It is evident that this symbolism of the grain of wheat is indirectly illustrative of simple death in the physical nature itself. This death, however, is in particular a symbolism of the ethical, sacrificial death. [Alford: "The symbolism here lies at the root of that in ch. vi., where Christ is the BREAD *of life*."]

Ver. 25. **He that loveth his own life** [Lange translates: *Eigenleben;* better: **his own soul,** ὁ φιλῶν τὴν ψυχὴν αὐτοῦ], *etc.*—Comp. Matth. x. 39; xvi. 25; Luke ix. 24; xvii. 33. This is the watch-word of Christ, and it should be that of His people also, Matth. x. 38, 1 John ii. 6. The egoism that clings to the outward life of appearance, and lives for that, loses its true life which is conditional on surrender to God; the spirit of sacrifice which does not cleave to its life of self, nay, which hates it in its old form in this old world, *i. e.*, joyfully sacrifices it, the sooner the better, and even hates it, if it be about to become a hindrance—regains it unto a higher, eternal life. That ψυχή must here mean *soul* in our conception of the word, does not result (as Meyer maintains) from the distinction made between ψυχή and ζωή (αἰώνιος); for the latter is expressive not simply of an endless duration of natural life, but of divine life. The declaration Matth. xvi. 25 ["for whosoever will save his life, τὴν ψυχὴν αὐτοῦ, shall lose it," *etc.*] is undoubtedly intended as the rationale of the foregoing ἀπαρνησάσθω ἑαυτόν, and hence it is proved that ψυχή means "self" as well as "life" (Tholuck).* But the reason of this is that the false love of life is one with, and has its root in, false self-love. With the life of self the selfishness of the soul, the false self, must be sacrificed; thus with the life in God, in the true self, new life also is gained. But the point in question is the sacrifice of *life*, since the opposite is *death*. On the μισεῖν comp. Luke xiv. 26. Augustine; "*Magna et mira sententia, quemadmodum sit hominis in animam suam amor ut pereat, odium ne pereat; si male amaveris, tunc odisti, si bene oderis, tunc amasti.*"—**Unto life eternal.**—First promise.

Ver. 26. **Follow me.**—Indicative of the way of suffering and death so readily forgotten by the disciples, as they witness the fresh homage rendered him by the Greeks; a way which Hellenic worldly-mindedness in particular must henceforth tread.

And where I am, there, *etc.*—Not simply on the same road (Luthardt); that is expressed in the preceding sentence; nor only in the Parousia (Meyer), but first in the state of humiliation, of death, then in the state and land of δόξα, beyond death,—the idea of the raising of the servant being thus involved (see ch. vi. 39, 44, 54; xvii. 24; 2 Tim. ii. 11, 12). Second promise.

Him will the Father honour [τιμήσει].—Third promise. The Father Himself will esteem him as a personality connected with Himself and exalted above death.

Ver. 27. **Now is my soul troubled** [Νῦν ἡ ψυχή μου τετάρακται].*—The agitation of soul experienced by Jesus has been already introduced by the whole train of thought from ver. 24. Primarily, indeed, Jesus fixed His eye upon the great goal of the death-road; now the road itself engages His attention. Another thing the Greeks must learn by His example, *viz.*, neither to be fanatically enthusiastic about the conditions of death, nor to turn away their eyes from them in cowardly dread. He therefore gives free utterance to His emotion. This change of mood is, however, not unlooked for in the life of the Lord. In the perfect life of the spirit the most blissful moods pass, in the sublimest transition of feeling, into the saddest. Thus in the Palm-entry (Luke xix. 41), thus here, thus after the high-priestly prayer, thus at the Supper, ch. xiii. 31. On the other hand, the saddest moods likewise pass into the most blissful. Thus at the departure from Galilee (Matt. xi. 25), thus at the Supper (ch. xiii. 31), thus in Gethsemane (John xviii. 15 ff.), thus on the Cross (see *Comm. on Matthew*, ch. xi. 25; comp. Luke xii. 49, 50). The difference between the ἡ ψυχή μου τετάρακται and the ἐτάραξεν ἑαυτόν, ch. xi. 33, does not lie in the antithesis of πνεῦμα and ψυχή (as Olshausen affirms; since the latter passage does not treat of a ταράσσεσθαι τῷ πνεύματι), but in the fact that there the psychico-corporeal agitation is an effect of His indignation in spirit, an act of His spirit (Origen: τὸ πάθος ἦν ἐρχόμενον τῇ ἐπικρατείᾳ τοῦ πνεύματος), while here it is an affection of suffering inflicted upon Him by the objective situation. It is the horror of death which the contemplation of death brings upon the inward life of feeling. The soul may and must be thus troubled,—prepared, as it were, for its death; but not so the καρδία (ch. xiv. 1, 27). So then, the subject under consideration is neither the trichotomy nor the dichotomy, body and soul (Tholuck), but the antithesis of passive and actual consciousness, or of the life of feeling and the will. The thought of death moves Him as the law of His death, as of the death of all His followers who must be baptized with His baptism into His death. And doubtless this, rightly understood, is a feeling of divine wrath, not as confronting Jesus within

* [Alford: "The word *soul* (or, *life*) is not really in a double sense: as the wheat-corn retains its identity, though it die, so the soul: so that the two senses are in their depth but one. Notice that the *soul* involves the *life* in both cases, and must not be taken in the present acceptation of that term."] P. S.]

* [Bengel: *concurrebat horror mortis et ardor obedientiæ.*]

His conscience, but as perceived by Jesus in the law of death governing sinful humanity, to which law He has submitted Himself. A "momentary abhorrence of the pains of death, induced by human weakness" (Meyer), must be out of the question, inasmuch as abhorrence involves an active inclination of the will. We might with equal truth talk of an innocent abhorrence of suffering or the cross. (Beza, Calov, Calvin: *Mortem, quam subibat, horroris plenam esse oportuit, quia satisfactione pro nobis perfungi non poterat, quin horribile dei judicium sensu suo apprehenderet.*) Schleiermacher gives special prominence to the thought, that to Jesus the coming of the Hellenes was attended with the full presentiment of the fact that His people would reject Him, and that the salvation of the Gentiles was conditional upon the great judgment on the Jews. That was the great tragic grief of Paul also (Rom. ix.; comp. 2 Cor. xii. 7). We have seen how, also in Gethsemane, Christ's sufferings were especially grievous to him as a being betrayed and delivered up (see Comm. on *Matthew*, ch. xx. 17; Note 3).

And what shall I say? *etc.* — [On the punctuation compare the TEXTUAL NOTE.—P. S.]. It is difficult to suppose with Euthymius [ἀπορούμενος ἀπὸ τῆς ἀγωνίας] and others (Lücke, Meyer, *etc.*, even Calvin [Alford]), that Jesus is uncertain what to pray for; that in this uncertainty He at first prays: **Father, save me from this hour**; but then, in the subsequent words, retracts "this momentary wish of a human abhorrence of death." In opposition to this view: 1. the assumption of such an *uncertainty* on the part of Jesus is not justified by Rom. viii. 26; 2. the presentation of such a retracted wish would be explained neither by the words, Heb. v. 7, nor by the prayer in Gethsemane; 3. the idea of a self-correction is inappropriately applied to Jesus. We prefer, therefore, the interrogative explanation with most Greek exegetes and Erasmus (Lampe, Tholuck [Ewald, Godet], *etc.*), the interrogative interpretation of πάτερ, *etc.* After Jesus has revealed His quaking heart to His auditors He can also show them how He works off the affection, that they in like situations may behave similarly. They too should accord to grief its sacred right. We cannot discover that such a reflection is incongruous with this mood replete with emotion, as Meyer maintains. Comp. ch. xi. 42. They may thus see that He stands at the junction of two ways. What shall I say? He asks them. Hence the subsequent words are part of the question. Would you advise Me to give utterance to My feeling in these words: Father, save Me? *etc.*

From this hour.—Meyer: "The hour of suffering is made present to His mind as if He had actually entered into it." But He has indeed actually entered it, for here as little as in Gethsemane is He speaking of the hour of external death in itself alone (comp. Comm. on *Matthew*). It is the convulsion itself in its deathlike might. In Gethsemane, when He was similarly and yet more powerfully affected, He could conceal Himself in some measure from His most intimate friends; it humiliates Him to be obliged to stand here before representatives of the Gentile world who are to greet in Him the King of Glory, in this sad figure. [?] But He is directly able to reconcile Himself to this juncture, and with the question there begins already His elevation above the nameless grief which has come upon Him from the historical world.

But for this cause I came into this hour. —[*But:* Christ controls and corrects the natural shrinking of His true humanity from the horrors of death by the consideration that He came to this world for the very purpose of enduring death for the redemption of the world. To do full justice to the deep commotion of our Lord on this occasion and in Gethsemane of which this was a foretaste, we must keep in view the vicarious nature of His passion by which He bore the sins of the whole world.—P. S.] *For this cause* [διὰ τοῦτο], not that by My mortal sufferings Thy name may be glorified (Lücke, Meyer), but in order to be thus troubled, and in order to appear before you in this commotion. He knows: 1. that grief itself has its holy aim, and 2. that the humiliation in His grief, like every one of His humiliations (see the Baptism, the conflict in Gethsemane), is connected with a glorification, to the glorification of the Father. And because in His grief He has just sacrificed Himself to the Father, He can now pray as follows.*

Ver. 28. **Father, glorify Thy name** [δόξασόν σου τὸ ὄνομα].—The σου emphatically comes first, yet not in antithesis to an "egotistical" reference of the preceding prayer [Meyer]. It expresses the idea: it is *Thy* cause and for *Thine* honor that there should be a compensation for this humiliation also. Whereby is the Father to glorify His name: 1. Greek exegetes [and Alford]: by His death (Comp. chap. xxi. 18); 2. Bengel: *quovis impendio mei;* 3. Tholuck: by the bearing of fruit, ver. 34; chap. xv. 8. The most obvious explanation is: by the issue of this mood itself. By this the name of the Father, *i. e.*, the one God of revelation, must be glorified in presence of the Greeks in particular. And this purpose was served by the heavenly voice, in and for itself, irrespective of its purport; a form of revelation exactly suited to the exigencies of the Gentile disciples.

Then came there a voice from heaven. —The evangelist, in writing οὖν here, expresses the assurance of his faith. The answer to Christ's prayer could not fail. We must first distinguish the VOICE *itself* from its PURPORT, because the voice, in the abstract, was a glorification at once of the Father and the Son. INTERPRETATIONS OF THIS WONDER:

1. "Since Spencer many (Paulus, Kuinoel, Lücke, *etc.*) have apprehended this heavenly voice to be the Jewish *Bath-Kol* (בַּת קוֹל, *daughter of a voice*), and this has been regarded as a voice issuing from a peal of thunder—according to modern rationalistic interpretation (as in his time

* [This interpretation of διὰ τοῦτο (to *endure this suffering*) is also defended by Grotius, De Wette, Luthardt, Ebrard, Godet, Hengstenberg, Wordsworth. Olshausen supplies: *that the world may be saved*, which is not sustained by the connection, but results necessarily from the atoning death of Christ. Alford, with Lampe and Stier, supplies: ἵνα σωθῶ ἐκ τῆς ὥρας ταύτης, I came to this hour for the very purpose that I might be delivered from it, or that, by going into and exhausting this hour, I might pass to My glorification. But this interpretation is not very clear, and would in consistency require the interrogative punctuation of the preceding clause, which Alford opposes.—P. S.]

Maimonides) the subjective interpretation of a peal of thunder on the part of Jesus and His disciples." Tholuck. However "the *Bath-Kol* itself cannot be traced to a peal of thunder, and how much less the voice mentioned here, where the narrator expressly excluded the idea of thunder" (the same). Still it is remarkable that by the Bath-Kol a derivative voice is to be understood, one developed from another, the echo of a voice, a voice in the second power, *i. e.*, the transformation of an apparently fortuitous sound into a spirit-voice by the interpretation of the Spirit conformably to the situation (comp. Tholuck on this passage; Lübkert *Stud. u. Krit.*, 1835, III.; Herzog's *Real-Encyklopædie: Bath-Kol*).

2. A voice actually issuing from heaven, considered by John as an objective occurrence.

a. Acoustic. The voice sounds directly over Christ's head; hence those who stand at some distance from Him perceive only a heavenly talking, those still further removed, but a sound as of thunder (ancient commentators). But in the case of *purely* objective sounds as loud as thunder, even those at a distance must have understood the words as well. Untenable, likewise, is the interpretation which affirms that the σαρκικοί soon forgot the more exact impression of what they had heard (Chrysostom).

b. Resembling thunder, so that the precise words sounding through these tones were unperceived by the insusceptible (Meyer). There is a lack of clearness in this reasoning in the case of a purely objective voice, for in such case perception would depend upon the acuteness of the hearing, not upon the degrees of spiritual susceptibility.

c. Of an angelic nature, mediated by angelic ministry (Hofmann). Apart from the arbitrary interpretation of an intensified doctrine of angels, this would afford not the slightest explanation of the voice.

d. A *spirituo-corporeal* [a spiritual and celestial, yet audible] voice, which was understood more or less according to the corresponding frame of mind (Tholuck; my *Leben Jesu*, II., p. 1207).*

Manifestly, the voice now heard by Jesus is entirely analogous to the voice at His baptism (see Comm. on *Matthew*, the baptism of Jesus, and at His transfiguration (see Comm. on *Matthew*, the Transfiguration). Its distinguishing point is the circumstance of its sounding here openly above the temple, in the hearing of all the people and of the Greek proselytes, and the trait of its striking even the insusceptible with the force of a sound like thunder, ringing upon the ears of the more susceptible with a beauty of tone which they can liken only to angelic voices, while Jesus, and with Him doubtless the most intimate of His disciples, perceive the perfectly distinct expression of the words which even contain an antithesis. Just this latter trait of a twofold gradation converts the event into a revelation concerning the nature of celestial voices. In the voice heard by Samuel, and not by Eli (see the note in Tholuck, p. 333), the subjective, ecstatic condition of the voice was clearly conspicuous, as in the case of the two angels seen by Mary Magdalene, and not by the disciples, this contrast became apparent in reference to miraculous visions. In the history of Paul there is a proportional, simple gradation between Paul himself, who sees the Christ within the shining light and hears the word of His voice, and the attendants who perceive only the brilliant light and the sound (see *Apostol. Zeitalter*, II., p. 115). But here a twofold gradation appears: the hearing of Christ and His intimate friends, the hearing of the people, the hearing of others. The ecstatic conditions of such a hearing are clearly manifest, Acts ix. 7; comp. chap. xxii. 9. The condition upon which an apprehension of the voice by those not standing in the centre of revelation (as here Christ; Acts ix., Paul) depends, is spiritual connection, fellowship of feeling,—sympathy; this results especially from the *rapport* between Christ and the Baptist at the baptism in Jordan. But the objectivity of the voice which proceeds from the living God is proved by sensuous evidence which it creates and procures. Tholuck: "Voices from heaven, as in this place, are found also, Dan. iv. 31; 1 Kings xix. 11, 12; Matt. iii. 17; xvii. 5; Acts ix. 7; x. 13; Rev. i. 10; iv. 5, where we read of φωναί together with βρονταί;—on this Züllich: articulate sounds contrasted with the inarticulate thunderings."

Purport *of the voice:* **I have glorified it, and will glorify it again** [Καὶ ἐδόξασα καὶ πάλιν δοξάσω. Πάλιν is no mere repetition, but an intensification of the glorification]. Meyer makes the first sentence of the voice refer to the works of Jesus hitherto, the second to the impending glorification through death to δόξα. Taking into consideration the antithesis, chap. x., and the existing state of matters, we assume that the consummated glorification of the name of God refers to His revelation in Israel, closing of course in the labors of Christ, and the new glorification of His name to the impending revelation of God in the Gentile world, this of course being conditioned by the death and resurrection of Jesus.

Ver. 29. **The multitude therefore,** *etc.* Perception *of the voice.* 1. The comprehension of it was probably not confined to Jesus, but was shared by His disciples, or by some chosen ones among them. 2. For the surrounding people the voice had a tone like thunder. Is this expressive simply of the third degree of susceptibility? Perchance it contains also an intimation of the judgment impending over the people of Israel. 3. To this hearing the hearing of others seems to form an antithesis. Those hear a voice of thunder; they, on the other hand, angelic speech. Is it not possible that by these others the Greek proselytes are meant? Such a thing is not positively expressed. Be it observed, however, that it is these very men whom Jesus seems to answer in the subsequent speech. At all events, their attitude towards the people is that of a more susceptible minority.

* [So also the ancients, and, among modern commentators, Olshausen, Kling, Stier, Meyer, Luthardt, Godet, Alford. Lange mentions only incidentally (sub. 1) the rationalistic interpretation of actual thunder and no more (Paulus, Kuinöl, Ammon, *etc.*). Hengstenberg (II., p. 320 ff.), otherwise so uncompromisingly *anti*-rationalistic, likewise assumes natural thunder which was identical with "the voice from heaven," and through which God spoke to Christ. But then it could not have been mistaken by some for the voice of an angel. It was clearly a supernatural phenomenon, a spiritual manifestation from the spiritual world, clothed in a symbolic form, an articulate sound from heaven, miraculously uttered, heard by all, but variously interpreted according to the degree of spiritual susceptibility.—P. S.]

Ver. 30. **This voice came not** [was not audibly uttered] **for my sake, but for yours.**—The disciples were really no longer in need of this attestation of Jesus. Neither was it needed by that portion of the people that believed on Him on account of the raising of Lazarus. From the words immediately following it seems to be spoken with special reference to the Greeks. Hence He continues:

Ver. 31. **Now is the judgment of this world,** *etc.*—The Jewish world is assuredly included; the words, however, relate pre-eminently to the heathen world. Therefore Satan is spoken of as **the prince of this world** who is now being cast out. The words are explanatory of the heavenly voice: *I will glorify it again.* Judgment was also now proclaimed to the world. It proclaimed itself with His woful feeling of death; it was put in execution by His death, made manifest by His resurrection, published and appropriated to the world by His Holy Spirit (chap. xvi. 11). The judgment upon the world should, however, be the world's salvation; a judgment in which it was judged but as an ungodly world, its prince (2 Cor. iv. 4; Eph. ii. 2; chap. vi. 12) being cast out of it and Christ in his stead assuming the sovereignty over it. In the rabbins, Satan, as regent of the heathen world, bears the name; *Prince of the world* * (according to Lightfoot, Schöttgen and Eisenmenger. Delitzsch, *Bibl. Psychologie*, p. 44). The expulsion from heaven (Luke x. 18) is not again meant here. Satan had penetrated into the Paradise of the first man when he tempted the first of the human race; when he tempted Christ in the wilderness he had ventured into heaven itself (the heaven of spiritual life) as a tempter. With the victory of Christ over Satan in the wilderness, the latter fell from heaven like lightning; and upon this transaction rested the victories of Jesus' disciples over demons in Israel (see *Leben Jesu*, II., 3, p. 1070; III., p. 428). Now Satan is likewise cast out of the world, the *κόσμος οὗτος, i. e.*, the old pre-Messianic and non-Messianic world—with special reference to the Gentile world whose highest *cosmical* formation is the very Hellenism that is confronting Him. Satan's empire over the world is shattered with the death and resurrection of Jesus. He is indeed still tarrying and working over the earth (Eph. ii. 2); here he retains his Ἔξω, the air and wind regions of the human world as far as it is not yet spiritual, whence he reacts upon the church of Christ. Subsequently he is cast upon *the earth* (Rev. xii. 9), *i. e.*, he possesses himself of traditional, ancient ordinances, now deadened —lifeless. But in time to come he is also cast out of the earth into the bottomless pit, Rev. xx. Thus this saying opens up a perspective of the final judgment, whilst Hilgenfeld has pretended to discover in it a negation of the last judgment (together with other favorite gnostic ideas).

Ver. 32. **And I, if I shall be lifted up** [*κἀγὼ ἐὰν ὑψωθῶ ἐκ τῆς γῆς*]. See chap. iii. 14; viii. 28. As in those passages both events are understood by the lifting up; the lifting up upon the cross and the lifting up upon the heavenly throne; in this place, pre-eminently the latter.* This double meaning of the word (Erasmus, Tholuck, *etc.*), is disallowed here by Meyer; he particularly denies that there is any reference to the crucifixion (the Fathers, most of the ancients, Kling, Frommann), maintaining that the *ἐκ τῆς γῆς* conflicts with such an interpretation, though indeed it is that of John himself. However, the crucifixion itself in its inward essence was an exaltation of Christ above the earth. With the dethroning of Satan, the dark usurper in the world, the enthroning of Jesus corresponds; hence: "*And I.*" With the breaking of the Satanic principle and the power of the spirits of darkness by the expiatory and redemptive death of Christ, the full power of the Christian spirit releases itself; then comes the Holy Ghost, ch. vii. 39; xiv. 26 ff.

Will draw all men unto Myself [*πάντας ἑλκύσω πρὸς ἐμαυτόν*].—**All** is referred: 1. by Chrysostom, Cyril, Calvin, Lampe, to the antithesis of Jews and Gentiles, after ch. x. 16; 2. by Lutheran theologians to all who hear the preaching of the Gospel and do not resist the drawing of Christ; 3. by individual Reformed theologians to the elect; 4. Meyer: without restriction.† We suppose it to be indicative of the totality of the nations in antithesis to the firstlings of the Greeks who have here inquired after Him; similarly: *I will draw them* forms a contrast to the *announcement sent* by these individuals. It is the attraction of the cross,—its medium the preaching of the crucified One,—made effectual by His Spirit, which draws the nations to baptism and death with Him, and to new life. But the *ἑλκύειν* of the Son does not here assume the place of the *ἑλκύειν* on the part of the Father, ch. vi. 44 (Tholuck); for the drawing of the Son is the *gratia convertens* in *vocation* which joins the drawing of the Father in the *gratia præveniens* or *fore-ordination.* All must experience the powerful drawing of calling grace; yet it is a drawing without moral compulsion because it is a drawing of free love calling unto freedom. The emphasis contained in *πρὸς ἐμαυτόν* (comp. ch. xiv. 3) signifies of course: *to Myself.* They will not stay with Philip or Andrew, or require the mediation of a Jewish or priestly church.‡

Ver. 33. **Signifying what kind of death he was to die** [*ποίῳ θανάτῳ ἤμελλεν ἀποθ-*

* [שַׂר הָעוֹלָם. Paul calls Satan ὁ θεὸς τοῦ κόσμου τούτου, 2 Cor. iv. 4, ὁ ἄρχων τῆς ἐξουσίας τοῦ ἀέρος, Eph. ii. 2.—P. S.]

* [The deepest humiliation of Christ is at the same time His highest exaltation; His crown of thorns is His crown of glory. The double meaning of ὑψωθῆναι is in keeping with John, comp. ii. 19; iii. 3; iv. 10; xi. 51. Alford: The Saviour crucified, is in fact the Saviour glorified; so that the exalting to God's right hand is set forth by that uplifting on the cross. —P. S.]

† [Some infer from πάντας the apocatastasis or final restoration of all men. But in all such passages *all* must be explained in accordance with other passages where *faith* is expressly laid down as the indispensable *condition* of salvation. Chrysostom finds in ἑλκύω an intimation of deliverance from the chains of Satan. It rather implies the strong and irresistible power of Christ's love. This attraction of the cross is one of the richest themes for effective evangelical sermons. See the HOMILETICAL Department.—P. S.]

‡ [I add the note of Alford on ἑλκύω: "by the diffusion of the Spirit in the church: manifested in the preaching of the Word mediately, and the pleading of the Spirit immediately. Before the glorification of Christ, the Father drew men to the Son (vi. 44), but now the Son Himself to Himself. Then it was, 'no man can come except the Father draw him;' now the Son draws *all.* And, to *Himself*, as thus uplifted, thus exalted;—the great object of faith; see ch. xi. 52."—P. S.]

νήσκειν].—Not simply a Johannean interpretation (Meyer) or a mere hint perchance (Tholuck). For the death of the cross was not only objectively the condition of the lifting up of Christ; it is also subjectively the strongest and the single decisive attraction to the exalted Christ (*ποῖος θάνατος!*).

Ver. 34. **That the Christ abideth forever** [ὁ Χριστὸς μένει εἰς τὸν αἰῶνα].—A people is spoken of that recognizes the Christ in Jesus. They have heard out of the *law* [ἐκ τοῦ νόμου], *i. e.*, by the reading, as well as by the explanation of the Holy Scriptures generally, that the Messiah should *abide forever.* This conception was occasioned in them by passages such as Ps. cx. 4; Isa. ix. 7, and the like. According to Meyer also Dan. vii. 13. But with this last passage in their minds, Christ's being lifted up from the earth could not have appeared strange to them, for there the Son of Man is brought to the Ancient of Days before whom His kingdom is given to Him. Neither was that passage popularly supposed to refer to the Messiah. According to Meyer it was likewise from the Danielic passage that they took the expression: *the Son of Man,* and put it into His mouth; such an explanation of their use of the term is entirely unnecessary since Jesus has just entitled Himself the Son of Man (see ver. 23)—(although even Tholuck can remark, in opposition to Luthardt, that this reference to Christ's words is too remote).* Neither is it alone the distinction of the earthly and the spiritual Messianic hope which here comes under consideration, even though an elucidation is found in the fact that Jonathan translates the אֲבִי־עַד, Isa. ix. 6, precisely as the people express themselves: "He that abideth forever, the Messiah;" the Septuagint, however, has it: *πατὴρ τοῦ μέλλοντος αἰῶνος.*" Tholuck. But the people, as also the disciples, lack as yet all discrimination between the first and the second coming of Christ. They imagine that if the Messiah had but come (with the breaking forth of the "Messianic travail-pangs," perchance) the Kingdom of Glory would at once be ushered in with His residence at Jerusalem. At this they first stumbled,—that their Christ should be removed again from the earth, like Enoch and Elijah. But manifestly at this also, that He has again exchanged the name of Messiah for the designation of the Son of Man. And hence they ask: who is this Son of Man? Meyer considers their meaning to be: Who is this anti-Scriptural Son of Man who is not to abide in accordance with Daniel, but is to be lifted up from the earth? Thus too Tholuck. But in that case they would not ask: who is this Son of Man? but, how does that agree with the Son of Man? The first offence, namely at His being lifted up, concerns the *spiritual* and *heavenly* side of the Messianic picture set up by Christ; the second concerns that universality in the idea of the *Son of Man,* which they doubtless feel. The Greeks, evidently, have again excited their Jewish jealousy, manifested on a former occasion, ch. vii. 35. Especially prominent in the response of the people is this practical trait; their carnal Messianic hope prevents them from having the slightest suspicion of what is impending over the Messiah, and hence also over them in their relation to Him during the next days. To this the answer of Christ has reference.

Ver. 35. **Yet a little while is the light among you.**—[τὸ φῶς refers to Christ Himself; see ch. i. 4, 5, 7, 8; vii. 33; viii. 12; ix. 4, 5.—P. S.] Jesus does not enter upon a theological disquisition with the view of convincing them of their error in stumbling at His sayings, because the reason of their stumbling lies in their want of obedience to His word, in their lack of true surrender to the light. In the path of this surrender they should be freed from stumbling. Thus He practically lays hold of them in the centre, the conscience. They have not the slightest suspicion or presentiment of what awaits Him and them. Therefore: **Walk as ye have the light** (ὡς stronger than ἕως),* in accordance with the fact that the light is about being taken from you, unless, by submissive faith, ye appropriate it permanently to yourselves as inward light.

That darkness may not overtake you, [ἵνα μὴ σκοτία ὑμᾶς καταλάβῃ].—Namely unprepared, and so to your destruction. The great night of temptation came upon them on the day of crucifixion, and to those who confronted it unsuspiciously, with their outward Messianic hope, it likewise became an inward night of apostasy and ruin.

He that walketh in the darkness.—He that *acts* then, *walks* then (comp. ch. xi. 10). This *περιπατεῖν* is expressive of the fault by which outward darkness is converted into inward obscurity.—**Knoweth not whither he goeth.**—The figure drawn from outside life is strikingly demonstrative of the fate of the Jews. They knew not whither they went—into perdition, into dispersion to the ends of the world, into the curse of judgment until the end of time. Antithesis to Christ's going to the sure goal of glory.

Ver. 36. **Believe in the light that,** *etc.*—Faith here especially conditional upon obedience. The stumbling of these believers on the Messiah proved that they had not yet true faith in the sense of submissive obedience. The walk should be in conformance to the light, *i. e.*, with trust in the light.—**That ye may become** [not **be**] **sons of light** [ἵνα υἱοὶ φωτὸς γένησθε. It is by believing in the light that men become sons of light]. Then should the inward light of illumination conduct them safely through the outer darkness, Luke xvi. 8. It is most fitting that these should be the last words of Christ to the believing portion of the people. Nothing but trust in that light which had risen upon them in Him, could lead them safely through the fearful night of trial.

And He departed and hid Himself from them [καὶ ἀπελθὼν ἐκρύβη ἀπ' αὐτῶν].—This moment coincides, as regards the main point, with the departure from the temple described by the Synoptists (see *Comm. on Matthew,* p. 415, Am. Ed.) Meyer [and Alford]: "Pro-

* [Alford refers to the still remoter passage in the discourse with Nicodemus, ch. iii. 14, and "perhaps in the other parts of Christ's teaching which have not been recorded." The reference to ver. 23 ἵνα δοξασθῇ ὁ υἱὸς τοῦ ἀνθρώπου, is sufficient.—P. S.]

* [Alford: ὡς, *as,* not exactly "*while*" (E. V.): walk, according to your present state of privilege in possessing light: which indeed can only be done *while it is with you.*—P. S.]

bably to Bethany [Luke xxi. 37], in order to spend the last days of His life, before the coming of His hour, in the circle of the disciples." These last days of His life amounted at the utmost to two. On Tuesday evening Christ left the temple; on Thursday, towards evening, He returned to Jerusalem to celebrate the Passover.

DOCTRINAL AND ETHICAL.

1. John's description of the close of the public ministry of Christ forms a most important supplement to the description of the same given by the Synoptists, Matth. xxiii. 39; Mark xiii. 1; Luke xxi. 38. They depict pre-eminently the departure of Jesus from the hostile portion of the people (with the exception of Luke, whose account in this respect is less definite), while John delineates His departure from the more friendly portion. But if we regard the Palm-entry as the introduction to this history, then John has supplemented an account not only of the immediate occasion of the Palm-procession, but also of the grand acme of it,—the coming of the Greeks and the glorification of Jesus by the voice from heaven within the precincts of the temple itself. In accordance with this presentation of the subject, we should conjecture that the introduction of the Greeks took place on the great, festive Monday when Christ displayed His glory in the temple undisturbed (see *Leben Jesu*, III., 1, p. 1200). It were possible so to incorporate these words (descriptive of His stay in the temple) with the Johannean account, that we should find in the ἀπελθών ver. 36 an intimation of the farewell discourse of Jesus, Matth. xxiii. together with the preceding great contests on the Tuesday. But since the denunciatory discourse, at all events, which Matthew records as pronounced against the Pharisees by Jesus, was followed by His still longer stay in the temple over against the treasury, according to Mark and Luke,—since Matthew is induced by the *order of affairs* to alter the historical sequence, not so, however, John,—since, furthermore, the definite announcement, in the temple, of His speedy death, nay, the very presentiment of death which has already entered His soul, seem to presuppose His final, open rupture with the Hierarchs on the great day of contest, Tuesday,—we now assume this conference of Jesus with the Hellenes, the glorification consequent upon it, and His charge to the people, to be significant of the last grand sunbeam which His presence shed on Mount Zion; the very reference to the remnant of day-light still illumining the nation is apparently indicative of the decline of this, the last day of His public ministry. These proselytes of the gate remind one involuntarily of the tradition (protested against indeed) that Luke was one of the seventy disciples. Comp. Luke xxiv. 13 ff.

2. The last facts recorded by John do not present the motive for Christ's departure from the people and the temple as distinctly as do those related by the Synoptists; nevertheless, the cause is intimated by the final question of the people that recognize Him as the Messiah. They have not the faintest foreboding of the state of matters, and even their lofty enthusiasm of the day of Palms begins to be obscured again by Judaistic expectations. This exhibition of the mind of the multitude seems to the evangelist sufficiently expressive; but he too subjoins his explanation in his epilogue on the public ministry of Jesus and the motive for His retirement.

3. Remarkable is the glorious, threefold climax with which, according to John, the public ministry of Jesus closes: 1. The anointing of Jesus in Bethany before His official Messianic entry into Jerusalem; 2. the Palm-entry itself, originating particularly with festal pilgrims going forth to Bethany out of Jerusalem; contrasted with this, the despair of the Supreme Council; 3. the announcement of the Greeks, and the glorification of Jesus through the voice from heaven, upon Mount Zion itself, in the hearing of the whole nation,—together with the proclamation from His own mouth of His redemptive death, His glorification for all nations, and the universal Gospel.

4. Christ's last words of farewell to the people on the temple-mount a gentle warning, according to John, and yet also an earnest explanation of Jewish stumblings. Therefore did Jesus return no answer to these stumblings themselves. Obedience from the heart unto truth alone can free from the prejudices of tradition.

5. At the moment of the consummated apostasy of the sacerdotal party from the Christ on Zion, the first Gentiles most significantly made their public appearance as His disciples. The hypothesis of Sepp assuming them to have been a deputation sent to Jesus by king Abgarus of Edessa, after the well-known account of apocryphal sound in Eusebius, cannot avail to enrich this event.

6. THE HELLENES. A literal fulfilment of the predictions of the prophets, especially of Is. ii.; also a fulfilment of the type contained in the history of the wise men from the East. A foretoken of the ensuing conversion of the proselytes of the gate, then of the Gentile world itself.

7. The pure historical truth, the clear picture of the situation in the intercession of the disciples Philip and Andrew.

8. THE HOUR. To the Lord the presentiment of His death is connected with the presentiment of His glorification. Be it observed that John regards even the humiliation of Jesus unto death as a particular form of Christ's exaltation, and that not simply in the ironical sense of the being lifted up upon the cross. It is the perfect exaltation of Jesus in His love, to the perfect glorification of the grace of God.

9. Stier very ingeniously remarks: "For this He now appeals—not to the testimony of the prophets, but to a secretly prophetic mystery of nature (as a proof also that His discourse is aimed at the Greeks as well as the Jews) which yet on the instant shines transfigured in His mouth." *Symbolism of the grain of wheat.* See Note on ver. 24. The word concerning the grain of wheat has a threefold reference: (1) It declares a universal law of life: *a death-like metamorphosis*, as a condition whereon depends the renewal of life, is a type of the fundamental law in the kingdom of God, which law provides that we by a priestly surrender of our own wills to the will of God do obtain new kingly life in God. (2) The law of life of sinful humanity; in God's kingdom

of this earth real death is a condition of the transition from the old life to the new; a symbol of the propitiatory sacrificial death of Christ for the reconciliation and glorification of the world; likewise of the death of thank-offering in which believers die with Christ in order to walk with Him in new life. (3) In the most special sense, the law of life of the regeneration of Hellenism, whose peculiar essence consists in a fleeing from death and the cross in the embellishment of the present life (*Leben Jesu,* II. p. 1203; III. p. 665).* The Greek's aim is levelled at beauty of appearance. Even these Greeks, religious though they be, betray themselves with the expression: "*We wish to see Jesus.*" Essentially eternal youth, beauty and glory in the new world are attained by the Christian only through death.

Hence the butterfly alone does not suffice for a symbol of immortality; the symbol of the grain of wheat must be added to it. The butterfly symbolizes the capacity of man for a paradisaical, death-like metamorphosis which yet is not dead and is merely a symbol of an individual renewal; the grain of wheat symbolizes the renewal of life through death,—and that a renewal which is at once its infinite enrichment and extension, and its glorification in spirit. Jesus did not indeed see corruption, but He drew very near to it; and thus it is, at bottom, with the grain of wheat; it passes through the semblance of corruption, but, in respect of its innermost kernel, its life leaps out from corruption into the metamorphosis of the butterfly, just, as on the other hand, the butterfly must strip itself of a corruptible something—the dead pupa. Christ has glorified both forms of transit from the old to the new life. Moreover all the chief moments in the life of Christ are prefigured in the history of the grain of wheat: Christmas, Good Friday, Easter, Ascension, Whitsuntide.

10. The two oxymora, vers. 24, 25; the three promises, vers. 24-26. See the EXEGETICAL and CRITICAL NOTES.

11. Ver. 27. The first presentiment of the death of Jesus in the temple a fulfilment of the foretoken of His baptism, the announcement of His baptism of suffering (Luke xii. 50); again, a foretoken of the mortal conflict of His soul in Gethsemane, the sure prophecy of His death; crowned, therefore, as a great moment in the pathway of His humiliations, with a glorification,—like the baptism, like the announcement of His sufferings (Matt. xvi. 21 by the transfiguration chap. xvii. 1), like His conflict in Gethsemane, like His death. We have too mean an idea of the emotional life of Jesus if we refer these moods to a fear of death. See EXEGETICAL and CRITICAL NOTES on ver. 23 and the conclusion of that on the first clause of ver. 27. The present moment denotes nothing less than the mental self-sacrifice of Jesus in the temple.

12. The voice within the precincts of the temple. See EXEGETICAL and CRITICAL NOTES.

13. Ver. 31. The DIFFERENT STAGES in the SUBJECTION of SATAN, the prince of this world. See EXEGETICAL and CRITICAL NOTES. The death of Jesus a judgment, glorified by the Spirit. See John xvi. 1. The foundation and beginning of the separation between Satan and the world; 2. the foundation and beginning of the separation between believers and unbelievers; 3. the foundation and beginning of the union of all the godly. "The anabaptists cited this verse (31) among others as a proof that the powers that be are not of divine ordinance. See the refutation in Gerhard, *Loci theol.* 13, p. 260." HEUBNER.

14. Ver. 35. WHO IS THIS SON OF MAN? It was as little their desire to find the doctrine of the Son of Man in their Christology, as to discover in it the doctrine of the Son of God. They would have no true Son of Man, no Redeemer revealing divinity in the perfection of manhood and humanity, no suffering Messiah; they wanted an orientally superhuman and godlike Son of David, displaying the perfect and exact medium of a divinity broken through humanity, of a humanity broken through divinity;—the ideal of all benumbed orthodoxistic systems, a rigid, everlasting symbol of the God-Man, which should be the central point of the rigid symbolism of the kingdom of God, beyond which symbolism they desired never to pass. (See *Leben Jesu,* III. p. 608.)

15. Vers. 35, 36. The gentle and impressive farewell words of Jesus to the believing portion of the people in the evening of His public ministry. But once more should He re-appear as a prisoner among the people; like a setting sun, to shed upon them for the last time the radiance of His life. (*Ibid.* p. 668.)

HOMILETICAL AND PRACTICAL.

See the DOCTRINAL NOTES.—The Greek proselytes, or Judaism a leading of the Gentiles to Christianity: 1. In the historical sense; 2. in the spiritual sense.—The advance of the Gentiles at the recession of the Jews in the history of the kingdom of God: 1. Historical; 2. typical.—The last discourse of Jesus in the temple for the benefit of the Greeks, compared with the last discourse of Jesus in the temple for the benefit of the Jews (according to Matthew).—The two signs in the meeting of Jesus with the Greeks within the temple limits: 1. The sign seen by Jesus in the appearance of the Greeks: a sign of decision, a sign of death, a sign of life. And that in accordance with the Old Testament and the law of the spirit. 2. The sign given by the Father to the people about Jesus.—How the Lord was troubled also by grief at the impending rejection of His nation when He saw the coming of the Gentiles (see the conclusion of the note on the first clause of ver. 27).—The humiliation and glorification of Jesus in the temple an image —a reflection—of His whole life (especially of the baptism, the transfiguration, His soul-passion in Gethsemane, His death).—The great

* [Comp. the beautiful verses of Nic. Lenau (from Savonarola's Christmas sermon):

"*Die Künste der Hellenen kannten*
Nicht den Erlöser und sein Licht.
D'rum scherzten sie so gern und nannten
Des Schmerzes tiefsten Abgrund nicht.

Dass sie am Schmerz, den sie zu trösten
Nicht wusste, mild vorüberführt,
Erkenn' ich als der Zauber grössten,
Womit uns die Antike rührt."—P. S.]

change in the great emotional life of the Lord: 1. How often it appears (see note on first clause of ver. 27); 2. what it denotes: the strength, extent, earnestness, buoyancy and holiness of His spirit.—Even the humiliation of Christ already an exaltation of Him, or the beginning of the full revelation of the glory of His inner life: 1. In His obedience; 2. in His confidence; 3. in His love.—Made specially prominent by John as a precursory exaltation.—The anticipatory solemnization of the Christian sacrificial feast upon the eve of the Jewish one.—Christ and the Greeks (Christianity and Hellenism): 1. The application of the Greeks: *a.* Courteous form (through Philip and Andrew); *b.* purport: we would *see* Jesus. 2. The word concerning the *grain of wheat.* Concerning the life of this world; concerning the following of Christ.—Messianic traits in our history: 1. The *teaching* Christ (vers. 24-26); 2. the *high-priestly* Christ (vers. 27, 28, first half); 3. the *royal* Christ (vers. 28-32); 4. the wholly *undivided* Christ (vers. 33-36).—The saying concerning the grain of wheat and the succeeding sayings: 1. A sermon on salvation, as a word concerning Christ; 2. a sermon on repentance, as a word for us; 3. a sermon of consolation, as a word concerning suffering and dying Christians.—The Christian life in three decisive traits: 1. In the three truths concerning the grain of wheat, life, service; 2. in the three demands of Christ; 3. in the three promises.—The soul-passion of Jesus in the temple a foretoken of His soul-passion in Gethsemane.—The self-sacrifice of Christ in the temple: 1. Its occasion: the announcement of the Gentiles; 2. its form: assumption of the feeling of death; by anticipation, therefore, of death itself; 3. its result: the voice, the future of Christ.—The three voices from heaven in attestation of the Lord: 1. By Jordan; 2, on the Mount of Transfiguration; 3. in the temple.—The prospect of death and of glory as *one* undivided prospect with Jesus. The import of this to the Christian.—The two stumbling-blocks to the believing Jews in the word and life of the Lord: 1. His removal to heaven unto divine glory; 2. His humanity and devotion to mankind.—The farewell words of Jesus to the better portion of the Jews like the solemn, tender, parting gleam of the sinking sun.

STARKE: It was not without the special providence of God that so great a multitude of strangers from the Gentiles were at Jerusalem in those days;—to the end, namely, that in this way the truth of the revealed glory of Christ might, through approved witnesses, not from the Jews alone, but also from the Gentiles, be published and corroborated throughout the world.—LAMPE: This desire (of the Greeks) typified the fulfilment of the prophecies in which it was predicted that the nations should cleave unto Him (Christ), Gen. xlix. 10; Hag. ii. 7, 8.—O shame, that heathen who have not God's word, outstrip Christians in inquiring after Christ, though these latter call themselves after His name!—(Philip and Andrew.) Preachers must agree in this, the leading of souls to Christ.—Ver. 24. ZEISIUS: Christ's death is the world's life.—HEDINGER: He who would live in Christ must first die unto flesh and sin.—Ver. 25. *Ibid.:* Much lost to gain a thousand-fold more.—ZEISIUS: How many servants Christ hath and yet so few true and constant followers!—Ver. 27. Soul, if thou be not cheerful and joyous, but, on the contrary, sad and dejected, look upon thy Saviour,—He in His infirmities was as thou art; courage! as He conquered, thou too shalt conquer in Him.—*Ibid.:* No better remedy for all suffering, nay, for death itself, than fervent prayer after the example of Christ.—OSIANDER: Even the cross and tribulation add fresh glory to the name of God; therefore we also should take such upon us with thorough willingness.—Ver. 29. LAMPE: O how diverse are the hearers of the Gospel!—Ver. 30. (The voice of God.) CANSTEIN: We must take for granted that we too are concerned in everything that it says.—Ver. 31. Heb. ii. 14.—Ver. 32. CRAMER: Christ is the true magnet that draweth us after itself.—Ver. 35. HEDINGER: To-day, to-day is certain,—to-morrow is uncertain.—ZEISIUS: The greater the light was, the thicker the darkness of wrath fallen upon the despisers of grace.—Am I too a child of light?—GERLACH: Jesus warns His disciples likewise not to surrender themselves now to earthly hopes of a carnal glory; He indeed is going to His glorification, but the way lies through death and resurrection.—The goal of suffering and death,—that of Christ and hence His people's also,—is glorification.—MY SOUL IS TROUBLED. To the end that He may the more decisively counteract the carnal hopes of His disciples, He openly announces the state of His feelings.—THE VOICE. As, at the conclusion of the Old Covenant, Moses spake and God answered him aloud (Ex. xix. 19), so the New Covenant is here solemnly concluded before all the people, the Son offering Himself to the Father and the Father accepting His sacrifice.—THE PRINCE OF THIS WORLD. It stands to reason that this is no denial of the devil's power to tempt the people of Christ after His exaltation; as little do the words of Jesus: "It is finished," declare that there are no more-battles to be fought by Christ and His Church. But the power of the prince of this world has now become impotency in respect to the faithful; individual Christians, as well as the Church of the Lord as a body, are now in faith on Christ sure of their ultimate victory.—He had striven to subdue the carnal transport of joy by the mention of His mortal sufferings (ver. 24), and seeks with equal earnestness to show that His death itself, His deepest humiliation, would constitute the strongest centre of attraction for the hearts of men. Hence in this instance the double meaning attaching to the term "lifted up" is expressive of the following facts: His deepest humiliation should be His very exaltation,—the most horrid shame His highest honor; and so afterwards in the incidents attendant upon His death everything significantly came to pass after this fashion (purple, crown, chap. xix. 2; kingly title, chap. xix. 19-22), which very circumstances are mentioned by John with peculiar emphasis.—LISCO: Fruits of the death of Jesus.—The true and only way to serve Christ is to follow Him.—To the impenitent the Gospel is thunder; to him who thirsts for salvation it is an angel; to him on whom salvation has been bestowed, it is Jesus Himself and His heavenly Father.—By means of the Redeemer's passion and death, judgment is passed upon the world.

BRAUNE: This scene constitutes most truly the close of Christ's public ministry. Gentiles approach Jesus, divining that they behold in Him the Light of the Gentiles, whilst His nation rejects Him; here a divine voice attests Him in Jerusalem at the close of His ministry, as by Jordan at its beginning; and before the conflict, He is stirred with a sense of victory.—He speaks here, as at the commencement of the high-priestly prayer, John xvii. 1.—IT ABIDETH ALONE. It doth not increase; no slender verdant stalk, no rich ear is given it, wherewith to rejoice in the brightness of the sun, and to make glad the eyes of the world.—Seed-time and harvest, suffering and glory are mated for Himself and His people. —The glimpse of the rich harvest ensuing from the seed of His death, draws His soul into that conflict, whose first traces are perceptible in His lamentation, Luke xii. 50, and whose culmination is reached in Gethsemane. The Baptist cried: "Behold the Lamb of God!" This title was given to Christ, not simply under the cross, but from the beginning; and thus, side by side with the assurance of victory, the anguish of conflict threaded His life. Divine life did not stifle or abolish human feeling; and this must needs struggle against the sufferings which were pressing upon Him,—against death. (? But doubtless the struggle consisted 1. in His working off His emotion, and in His submission, 2. in His resurrection.) Jesus was the *original* man, not an *unnatural* man; not *dis*-humanized, but the *ideal* of *pure* human nature. His grief was the misery of all who despised Him, *etc.*—Follow Him. He requires the act of obedience.—FATHER, GLORIFY, *etc.* That was a sublime moment on earth, in perfect unison with that heaven, whence a voice resounded.—Are there not, then, organs of perception for the higher regimen of the world? Ephes. v. 8.——GOSSNER: Thus He gives death an entirely different form. It is, namely, nothing but a passage; the goal is glorification.—AND WHERE I AM. Where Christ stayeth, there do we stay also.—Thus it is betwixt the Saviour and the soul. He comes to us with truth, and we go to meet Him with our faith.-Ver. 37. Gone is gone. One trembles when one sees His blind people upon the very verge of losing the light for ever because it loves darkness so much.

HEUBNER, ver. 23: Everywhere the future opens wider to the God-fearing man than to the common eye.—THE HOUR. Jesus calls the whole period of His final suffering an hour; it was the great hour for the world, when, by His passion and death, the liberty and life of mankind were obtained; He suffered the natal pangs of the whole world in order that He might bring a new world into being.—The missionary discourse of James is glorious: *The attractive power of the cross of Christ*, Nuremberg, 1820.—Josephus can not depict in colors dark enough the confusion, the anarchy, into which everything lapsed in the Jewish nation. This was the consequence of the rejection of Jesus.—Any enlightenment that fails to lead to a new and holy life is no true enlightenment.

SCHLEIERMACHER: On the grain of wheat, reference to John xvi. 7, 14; xiii. 34.—We know that it is only His redeeming and sanctifying love, diffusing itself amongst us and taking root within ourselves, from which depends the fruit that He shall bear.—We should know and love no other honor than that which comes to us from God, the Father of our Lord Jesus Christ and of us.—It is still true that we can enter into the kingdom of God only through tribulation.—His soul could not but be troubled by the reflection that the very greatest and most glorious event, the salvation of the human race, should not be brought about without the deepest ruin (of the Jewish nation, in particular),—that heavenly light should force a way for itself only by a hard conflict with the darkness. It is the same sorrow that filled Him when He gazed upon Jerusalem and said: "Jerusalem, Jerusalem," *etc.*; the same sorrow that He would fain have communicated to others when He said: "Daughters of Jerusalem, weep not," *etc.* And this sorrow —that the word of life could not come unto the Gentiles except after the Jews had rejected Himself, the Prince of life—was natural to His soul at the moment when Greeks desired to see Him. —We too should keep fast hold of the maxim, *that for this cause we are come into every hour*, namely, that the alone-wise counsel of God may be executed in us and through us, that all things may be fulfilled whereby the glorification of Him whom God has sent for our salvation may be accomplished.—"*Glorify Thy name.*" In this every wish of ours should centre. To us also the name of the Most High should be glorified in His ways. —In our speculations let us ever hold fast that which is far greater than speculation,—namely, that we walk in the light and believe on the light.

BESSER: The glorification of the Son of Man comprehends three things: 1. the perfection of His obedience in the sacrifice of His love; 2. exaltation to the glory proper to Him; 3. the exhibition of His name as that of the Saviour of mankind, the gathering of a holy church, the outpouring of the Holy Spirit.——BENGEL: "A son of thunder (Mark iii. 17) is well able to hear voices of thunder (Rev. iv. 5; x. 3). The saying of the Lord: 'now is judgment passed upon the world,' was deeply graven on his soul."—RICHTER: The mission to the Gentiles is a glorification of Christ. —The Father does but see how one is affected towards His Son whom He would have us resemble. —First one walks by the light, then one believes in it, and thus one becomes a child of light.

[CRAVEN: From AUGUSTINE: Vers. 20, 21. Lo! the *Jews* (some of them) wish to *kill* Him, the *Gentiles* to *see* Him.—Behold them of the circumcision (some of them, ver. 13), and them of the uncircumcision, once so wide apart, coming together in one faith of Christ.—Ver. 23. Christ took occasion from this request of *some* Gentiles to see Him, to announce the approaching *fulness* of the Gentiles.—Ver. 24. That *grain* of wheat was He; to be *mortified* in the unbelief of the Jews, to be *multiplied* in the faith of the Gentiles (and in the subsequent faith of the Jews also. E. R. C.)—Ver. 26. They *serve* Christ, who seek not their own things but the things of Christ, *i. e.*, who *follow* Him—love Him for His own sake and think it a rich reward to be with Him. —Ver. 27. *Now is my soul troubled:* Thou of Thy love wast of Thine own will troubled to console those who are troubled through the infirmity of nature, that the members of Thy body perish not in despair.—Ver. 31. There is a judgment, not of *condemnation*, but of *selection*, which is the one here meant—the *selection* of His own redeemed. —*Now shall the Prince of this world be cast out:* The devil never ceases to tempt believers; but it is one thing to *reign within*, another to *lay siege from without.*—Vers. 32-35. The Jews understood that our Lord spoke of His own death; it was not wisdom imparted, but conscience disturbed, which disclosed the meaning of His words.—Ver. 36. When He hid Himself, He consulted our weakness —He did not derogate from His own power.—— From CHRYSOSTOM: Ver. 26. *Where I am, there shall also my servant be;* death shall be followed by resurrection.—What greater honor can an adopted son receive than to be where the *Only Son* is?—Vers. 27-33. As He draws near to the cross His human nature appears—Christ had a body free from *sin*, but not from *natural infirmities.*—Ver. 22. The Father draws (ch. vi. 44) by the Son Who draws.—*I will draw*, He says, as if men were in the grasp of some tyrant from whom they could not extricate themselves.——From BEDE: Ver. 24. He Himself, of the seed of the Patriarchs, was sown in the field of this world, that by dying, He might rise again with increase; He died *alone*, He rose again with *many*.—— From THEOPHYLACT: Ver. 25. It were harsh to say that a man should *hate* his soul, so He adds, *in this world, i. e.*, for a particular time, not forever.

[From BURKITT: Vers. 33, 34. Jesus arms His disciples against the scandal of the cross, by showing the great benefit that would result from His death—1. (to Himself—He was to be glorified, E. R. C.) 2. to all mankind.—As corn *unsown* never increases, but if sown brings forth a crop; so if Christ had not died He would have had no Church, whereas His death made Him fructify.—Observe how plainly our Lord dealt with His followers.—Ver. 25. The surest way to attain *eternal* life is to lay down our *temporal* life when the glory of Christ requires it.—Ver. 26. If any man profess himself to be My servant, let his conversation correspond with his profession.—All that will be Christ's servants must be His *followers, i. e.*, they must—1. obey His doctrine; 2. imitate His example.—Christ's servants must not expect better usage than their Master received.—God will crown the fidelity of Christ's servants with the highest honor.—Vers. 27, 28. Their *trouble* is no *sin;* Christianity does not make men senseless.—The fear of death, especially when accompanied with apprehension of the wrath of God, is most perplexing and soul-amazing.—Vers. 31, 32. The double effects of Christ's death—1. the judgment of this world; 2. the drawing all men unto Him.—Learn that—1. Satan is the Prince of this world, not by *right* but by usurpation; 2. this usurper will not quit his possession unless he be cast out; 3. Christ by His death has cast him out.—There is a twofold lifting up of Christ—1. *ignominious*, when He was hung upon the cross; 2. *glorious*, in the preaching of the gospel: *meritoriously* by His death, *instrumentally* by the preaching of His gospel, He draws all men unto Himself.—All persons are naturally unwilling to come to Christ, they must be *drawn.*—All men are not *effectually* drawn to Christ, but by the preaching of the gospel they are called (so drawn) as to render those who do not come inexcusable.—Ver. 35. Note—1. A *privilege* enjoyed, *the light is with you*, (1) a *personal* light, Christ, (2) a *doctrinal* light, the gospel; these brought with them the *light* (*a*) of *knowledge* answering our darkness of *ignorance*, (*b*) of *holiness* answering our darkness of *sin*, (*c*) of *joy* answering our darkness of *misery;* 2. The *time* of enjoying this privilege limited, *yet a little while is the light with you;* 3. A duty enjoined, *walk whilst ye have the light, i. e.*, walk according to—(1) the *precepts* of the gospel, (2) its *privileges*, (3) its *supplies of grace*, (4) its *hopes:* 4. A *danger* threatened to neglecters, *lest darkness come upon you*, a darkness of (1) judicial blindness, (2) error, (3) horror and despair, (4) the blackness of darkness forever.——From M. HENRY: Vers. 20-22. The Greeks having a desire to see Christ were industrious to use the proper means; they that would have the knowledge of Christ must seek it.—They made their application to one of the disciples; they that would see Christ by faith must (should) apply themselves to His ministers.—It is good to know those who know the Lord.—Ver. 25. Behold—1. the *fatal* consequence of an inordinate love of life; 2. the *blessed* recompense of a holy contempt of life.—Our *life in this world* includes all the enjoyments of our present state; these we must *hate, i. e.*—1. *despise* them as vain, 2. *dread* the temptations that are in them, 3. *cheerfully part* with them when they come in competition with the service of Christ.—Ver. 26. The Greeks desired to *see Jesus;* He lets them know that it was not enough to *see* Him, they must *serve* Him.—Christ fixes for His servants both their *work* and their *wages:* 1. their *work*, to attend—(1) *His motions—let him follow Me*, (2) *His repose—where I am, let my servant be*, (*a*) in the *assemblies of the saints*, (*b*) in *heaven* in thought and affection: 2. their *wages*, they shall be—(1) happy with Him; (2) honored by His Father.— Ver. 27. Trouble of soul sometimes (often) follows great enlargement of spirit.—Note—1. The *sin* of our souls was the *trouble* of His soul; 2. The trouble of *His* soul was designed to ease the trouble of *our* souls.—Holy mourning is—1. consistent with *spiritual* joy; 2. the way to eternal joy.—*What shall I say:* He speaks *like one at a loss;* He was in all points tempted like as we are.— When our souls are troubled we must take heed of speaking unadvisedly, and debate with ourselves *what we shall say.*—It is the *duty* and *interest* of troubled souls to pray to God, and in prayer to eye Him as a *Father.*—Prayer against trouble may consist with *patience* and *submission.*— He calls His suffering *this hour*, intimating that the time of suffering was—1. a *set* time, 2. a *short* time.—*For this cause came I unto this hour;* it should reconcile us to our darkest hours that we were all along designed for them.—Ver. 28. Father, *glorify Thy name;* here is—1. More than bare submission, a *consecration of His sufferings to the glory of God;* 2. A *mediatorial* word—a *tender* of His sufferings as satisfaction for the wrong done the Father's glory by our sin.—What God *has done* for His own glory, is an encouragement to us to expect what He will yet farther do.—

Ver. 29. *God speaketh once, yea twice, yet man perceiveth it not*, Job xxxiii. 14.—Ver. 30. The supports granted to our Lord in His sufferings were *for our sakes.*—Vers. 31, 32. Two things designed by the death of Christ—1. that Satan should be conquered; 2. that souls should be converted.—Christ's death *the judgment of this world*, a judgment—1. of *discovery* and *distinction;* 2. of *absolution* to the chosen ones; 3. of *condemnation* against the powers of darkness.—Satan is here styled the *Prince of this world*, because he rules over the men of the world by the things of the world.—Christ *reconciling* the world to God by the merit of His death, broke the *power of death* and cast out Satan as a *destroyer;* Christ, *reducing* the world to God by the doctrine of His cross, broke the *power of sin*, and cast out Satan as a *deceiver.*—The bruising of Christ's heel was the breaking of the serpent's head, Gen. iii. 15.—Ver. 32. Christ *all in all* in the conversion of a soul—1. it is Christ who draws; 2. it is to Christ we are drawn.—He does not *drive*, but *draws.*—Ver. 34. Great knowledge in the *letter* of the Scripture may be abused to serve the cause of infidelity.—In the doctrine of Christ there are *paradoxes* which to men of corrupt minds are *stones of stumbling.*—Christ's *dying*, was as consistent with His *abiding forever*, as the setting (eclipse) of the sun is with its perpetuity.—Ver. 35. The Jews had *the light;* they had—1. Christ's bodily presence; 2. His preaching; 3. His miracles.—It is good for us to consider what *a little while* we have the light.—*Walk while ye have the light;* as travellers who make the best of their way *forward.*—Our life is but *a day* and we have *a day's journey* to go.—The best time of walking is while we have the light.—*Lest darkness come;* lest you lose your opportunities.—The sad condition of those who have sinned away their day of grace—they know not *where* they go nor *whither* they go.—Ver. 36. They that believe in the light *shall be children of light*—1. sons of God, Who is *light;* 2. heirs of Heaven, which is *light.* —*Jesus departed and hid Himself:* He justly removes the means of grace from those that quarrel with them.——From Scott: Vers. 20, 21. They who are nearest the means of grace often ripen fastest for vengeance, whilst sinners come from afar to inquire after Christ.—Ver. 31. In the death of Christ *faith* beholds the world judged, Satan vanquished, his slaves liberated, and his work destroyed.—Vers. 34-36. An obedient faith is better suited to our condition than disputatious speculations.

[From Stier: Vers. 23-36. The Lord's *last public* declaration concerning His death.—Vers. 20, 21. *We would see Jesus*, a great missionary text; the *Greeks* (Ἕλληνες) were *heathens* (?)—unconsciously they speak in the name of the world of heathenism, the highest desire of which in all times has this for its goal—to find and know *a Jesus.*—Ver. 24. The Greeks were to behold the Cross succeeding the triumphant entry—He presents beforehand the solution of the mystery, He explains in brief His (philosophic) *system.*—Not only *prophecy* in Israel, and the *presentiments* of the heathen world, but *Nature* also speaks of the mystery of a *redeeming death.*—The inmost kernel of the *seed* and *harvest* parables.—*Wheat* is specified, partly because it is the most *precious* grain, partly because it more effectually than any other perishes in pushing forward the almost invisible germ, (partly because the most productive).—The germ of St. Paul's resurrection doctrine in 1 Cor. xv.—Ver. 25. That which holds good of Christ in its peculiar sense, is a type for us and is fulfilled in us to a similar victory and blessedness.—Ver. 26. *Where I am, there shall or should also My servant be:* Both an *added condition* and a *promise.*—What shall be done to the man whom the Blessed and Only Potentate, the King of all kings, the Creator of the universe, the *Father* of Jesus Christ, delighteth to honor!—Vers. 27, 28. A prelude to Gethsemane—the *lamentation*, the *petition*, the *resignation.*—All the typical appeals and supplications of the Psalms reach in the lips of our Lord their *Messianic meaning.*—The *two opposites* pressed hard upon Him, perfectly *combined* but *separated in utterance*—the cry (desire) for help and (spirit of) submission.—The entering into *this hour* is the being brought out of it, the *suffering* is the *deliverance* (?).—Ver. 28. The glorification is not of the Father Himself but of His *Name*—of the revelation of Himself in the *Son of Man* (see ver. 23).—Ver. 28. The *three* accrediting voices from heaven—at the *beginning*, the *middle*, the *end* of the Messiah's course—all in relation to the assumption on His part of His *destiny of death.*—Ver. 29. "Before men will see (hear) and believe in God they will resort to all kinds of imaginations of thunder and angels." Hamann.—Ver. 31. Our dogmatic theology has much to do before full justice will be done to *all* the relations of the mystery of the Cross—the revelation of love, the vindication of right, the reconciliation between the world and God, the mortification of sin in the flesh, the abolition of death, *the breaking down of Satan's power.*—The ungodly world is in a certain sense *judged* in its prince, even while it is *saved.*—The casting out of Satan goes on from age to age down to the final victory.—Ver. 33. *What death* (ποίῳ θανάτῳ) comprehensively expresses all that our Lord had said concerning the *significance*, the *power*, and the *fruit* of His death.—Vers. 32, 33. "*The attraction of the Cross.*" (James, of Birmingham). —I will draw them *unto Me*, through the *Cross*—*first*, to Me *on the Cross; ultimately*, away from earth into heavenly places.—*Before* the glorification of Christ, the Father draws to the Son; *afterwards* the *Son Himself* draws immediately.—Does not the Lord actually *draw* all men?—*drawing* is no *enforcement.*—*Children of light* is not a mere Hebraism—a new *race* (γενεά) was to be born of the light.

[From A Plain Commentary (Oxford): Ver. 24. The whole World is but one mighty Parable to which the Gospel supplies the clue.—Ver. 27. The Humanity of our Lord—*Soul* as well as Body—becomes more and more apparent as His Cross draws nearer in sight.—Ver. 35. Men walk in darkness *because the god of this world hath blinded their minds*, 2 Cor. iv. 4; the light is around them, the darkness is *to* them and *within* them. ——From Barnes: Ver. 26. *Let him follow Me*, *i. e.*, 1. imitate Me; 2. do what I do; 3. bear what I bear; 4. love what I love.——From Ryle: Ver. 24. The *death* of Christ the *life* of the world. —Death is the way to spiritual life and glory.—

"By *abiding alone* Christ meant that if He did not die, He would be *alone* in Heaven with the Father and the elect Angels, but without any of the sons of men." (GILL.)—Ver. 25. The object of Jesus in thus speaking—1. to prevent His disciples from looking for good things in this world; 2. to teach them that like Him they must sacrifice much in the hope of glory in the world to come.—Ver. 26. However little we know of the life to come we do know that we shall be *with Christ.*—Honor from men, Christians may not have; honor from the Father shall make amends for all.—The clearest (and most blessed) conception we can form of Heaven is *being with Christ and receiving honor from God.*—Never did Jesus keep back the *Cross,* or bribe men to follow Him by promising temporal comfort or happiness.—Ver. 27. The possibility of much inward conflict without sin.—The weight of the world's imputed sin laid on our Lord's soul.—"By Thine *unknown* sufferings, good Lord, deliver us." (LITANY of the GREEK CHURCH).—"*What shall I say?* is the language of highest perplexity and anxiety; the Lord found deliverance in prayer." (ROLLOCK).—Ver. 28. *Glorify Thy Name*—the highest, greatest thing we can ask God to do.—Ver. 31. Satan is a vanquished enemy.—Ver. 32. "The passion of Christ began to draw souls at once, as in the case of the penitent thief and the centurion." (EUTHYMIUS).—Ver. 34. A half knowledge of Scripture will account for a large portion of mistakes in religion.—Vers. 35, 36. The duty of using present opportunities.——From OWEN: Ver. 25. The import of the mask of discipleship well understood by the early Christians when a profession of Christ was attended with fearful persecution.—Self-sacrifice and a readiness to sacrifice all things for Christ now demanded.—Ver. 26. A beautiful correspondence between the words *follow Me* and the promise of attainment to the presence of our Lord in His glorified state.—Ver. 32. *All* of every nation—both Jew and Gentile.—*Unto Me*—to the state of dominion and glory to which He was raised.—From WHEDON: Ver. 31. The Cross is the test and discriminator of the responsible character and final destiny of the race—the *Cross* becomes a *throne of judgment.*]

V *b*.

ANTITHESIS BETWEEN SELF-HARDENING ISRAEL AND THE WORLD, THAT BOTH STANDS IN NEED OF SALVATION AND IS READY TO RECEIVE IT,—OR THE WITHDRAWAL OF CHRIST AND THE EVANGELIST'S REVIEW OF HIS OFFICIAL LABORS.

(CHAP. XII. 37–50.)

37 But though he had done so many miracles [had wrought so many, or, so great
38 signs][1] before them, yet they believed not on [in] him: That the saying of Esaias
[Isaiah] the prophet might be fulfilled, which he spake, 'Lord, who hath believed
our report? and to whom hath the arm of the Lord been revealed' [Isaiah liii. 1]?
39 Therefore [On this account, or, For this cause] they could not believe, because that
40 [*omit* that] Esaias [Isaiah] said again, 'He hath blinded their eyes, and hardened[2]
their heart; that they should not see with *their* eyes, nor [and] understand with
41 *their* heart, and be converted [turn themselves],[3] and I should heal[4] them.' These
things said Esaias [Isaiah], when [because][5] he saw his glory, and spake [he
42 spoke][6] of him. Nevertheless among the chief rulers also [Yet even of the rulers]
many believed on [in] him; but because of the Pharisees they did not confess him
43 [*omit* him], lest they should be put out of the synagogue [excommunicated]. For
they loved the praise [glory] of men more than [rather than at all][7] the praise
[glory] of God.
44 [But] Jesus cried [aloud] and said, He that believeth on [in] me, believeth not
45 on [in] me, but on [in] him that sent me. And he that seeth [beholdeth] me seeth
46 [beholdeth] him that sent me. I am come a [*omit* a, *ins.* as] light into the world,
that whosoever [every one that] believeth on [in] me should not abide in [remain
47 in the] darkness. And if any man hear my words, and believe [keep *them*][8] not
48 I judge him not: for I came not to judge the world, but to save the world. He
that rejecteth me, and receiveth not my words, hath one that judgeth him [his
judge (with him)]: the word that I have spoken, the same shall [will] judge him
49 in the last day. For [Because] I have not spoken of [from] myself; but the
Father which [who] sent me, he gave me a [*omit* a] commandment, what I should

50 say, and what I should speak. And I know that his commandment is life everlasting: whatsoever I speak therefore, even as the Father said [hath said unto me, εἴρηκέν μοι], so I speak.

TEXTUAL AND GRAMMATICAL.

1 Ver. 37.—[Τοσαῦτα may be understood of magnitude: *so great, such* (comp. Matt. viii. 10; Luke vii. 9; Rev. xviii. 17; Gal. iii. 4), or of multitude: *so many* (Matt. xv. 33; John vi. 9; xiv. 9; xxi. 11). Lücke and De Wette decide for the former, Meyer and Alford for the latter. Lange translates *such.*—P. S.]

2 Ver. 40.—[Tischendorf gives ἐπώρωσεν, instead of the πεπώρωκεν of Lach., in accordance with A. B.* K. L. X., *etc.*, and also ℵ. II., as amended from ἐπηρώτησεν.]

3 Ver. 40.—[Tischendorf and Alford give στραφῶσιν in accordance with ℵ. B. D.; the text. rec. reads ἐπιστραφῶσι according to A. D.2 E. F., *etc.*]

4 Ver. 40.—The Future ἰάσομαι is to be preferred to the Subjunctive ἰάσωμαι, in accordance with the decided preponderance of authorities, Lachmann, Tischendorf. [ℵ. A. B. D., *etc.*]

5 Ver. 41.—Ὅτι [*because*] is to be adopted in the place of ὅτε [*when*, text. rec., E. V.] in accordance with [ℵ.] A. B. L., *etc.*, Lachmann, Tischendorf [Alford, Westcott and Hort].

6 Ver. 41.—[See Exegetical Notes].

7 Ver. 43.—[See Exegetical Notes].

8 Ver. 47.—Καὶ μὴ φυλάξῃ instead of καὶ μὴ πιστεύσῃ, in accordance with Codd. [ℵ.] A. B. K. [L. M.], *etc.*, Lachmann Tischendorf [Alford, Westcott and Hort]. Jesus goes away after uttering this saying. [ℵ. T. Δ. Λ. and Verss. give ἕως, in this verse; in ver. 36, ℵ. B. D. L. give ὡς.—P. S.]

EXEGETICAL AND CRITICAL.

The entire section is an epilogue of the Evangelist on the public ministry of Jesus and its result in the Israelitish nation; a result already announced by the lamentation, chap. i. 11. Even the concluding words from ver. 44 are to be regarded throughout as an epilogue (according to Coccejus and many others, Lücke, Tholuck, Olshausen, Meyer).

We reject therefore as unfounded 1. the supposition of Chrysostom and all the ancients (among the moderns Kling), that Jesus once more addressed the people publicly in these words; 2. the modification of this hypothesis in Lampe and Bengel, who affirm that on His departure from the temple, in the very act of withdrawal from the Jews, He shouted out these words to them from afar; 3. the conjecture of Besser and Luthardt, who hold that He uttered these remarks respecting the Jews in the presence of the disciples; 4. finally, the fancy of De Wette, who supposes these reminiscences to have grown under the hand of the Evangelist into a regular discourse—one, however, not delivered by Jesus. The main support of assumptions of this kind has been found in the ἔκραξε καὶ εἶπεν, ver. 44. But the first word is employed by John in the sense of loud, public declarations (chap. i. 15; vii. 28, 37), and does not necessarily signify a shout from a distance, or a final, vehement outcry. And as for the aorists, it is not necessary to regard them, with Tholuck, as resumptive Pluperfects. On the contrary, the whole is a *résumé en gros* of the life of Jesus, in which summary the account of the unbelief and obduracy of the great mass of the Jewish people and its rulers is contrasted with the account of Christ's holy testimony to Himself.

Ver. 37. **But though He had done such,** *etc.*—Τοσαῦτα, Lücke, De Wette: So *great;* Meyer, Tholuck: so *many,* so too the E. V. Its proper signification is: such signs as those He did; hence the nature of the signs itself determines whether so *great* or so *many* should be understood. The passages chap. vi. 9; xiv. 9; xxii. 11 certainly seem, as Meyer remarks, to be in favor of the interpretation: so *many;* yet the generalness of the term is doubtless indicative of quality as well.

Yet they did not believe in Him.—In disobedience to the purpose of God in the signs, and to the divine attestation of Jesus.

Ver. 38. **That the word** [ὁ λόγος] **of Isaiah,** *etc.*—"It is in the very presence of unbelief and of hinderances cast in the way of the kingdom of God that both Jesus and the apostles most frequently appeal to the word of prophecy. For prophecy exhibits the divine ὡρισμένον (comp. Luke xxii. 22 with Matt. xxvi. 24), while it demonstrates the fact that even these seeming contradictions in history must be co-included in the divine counsel, chap. xiii. 19; xvii. 2." Tholuck. The passage is Is. liii. 1 according to the Septuagint. According to Meyer, Jesus is introduced in this passage as addressing God, κύριε. According to Luthardt, it is a lament of the Evangelist and of those like-minded with him, and ἀκοή means the message that we actually receive from Jesus. If, however, we adhere to the context, it is the lament of the prophet, in his own name and that of his colleagues, over his time. But the emphasis is upon the words: that it **might be fulfilled.**—Herewith, undoubtedly, the lament of the prophet becomes indirectly, and as a type, the lament of Christ (comp. Ps. xxii. 1). The prophets might lament over two things: 1. That men did not believingly receive their ἀκοή (the message heard by them—the prophets—or the message which penetrated the ears of the hearers); and 2. that men did not suffer their prophetic wonders whereby they made plain the arm of the Lord, *i. e.*, interpreted the great deeds of God, to be the means of revealing to them these deeds in their significance. All this unbelief which opposed itself to them as an incipient hardening, is now fulfilled in the perfect obduracy manifested by the Jews towards Jesus: towards His preaching and His revelation of the arm of the Lord in His miracles (by the arm of the Lord, Augustine and others incorrectly apprehend Christ Himself); hence the lament of the prophets is also fulfilled in the words of Jesus and His people. The saying is most significantly chosen from the beginning of the prophecy about the suffering Messiah, Is. liii. The hardening began to be accomplished in the face of the sufferings of the prophets; its fulfilment is completed in the crucifixion of Christ on the part of the Jews and in the rejection of the Crucified and Risen One.

Ver. 39. **On this account they could not believe, because Isaiah said again.**—According to Meyer διὰ τοῦτο—ὅτι, *therefore*, on this account, has reference to what has gone before, *i. e.* the saying of ver. 38 contains the ground for the saying ver. 40. On the other hand, according to Theophylact and many others, also Tholuck and Luthardt, διὰ τοῦτο is preparative;—it announces the cause, *i. e.* the inability to believe of ver. 39 explains why they did not believe according to ver. 38. This interpretation seems to be supported by the sequence of the dicta; first Is. liii. 1, then Is. vi. 10, and Tholuck remarks: "After the fact of their unbelief is declared, the reason of it is assigned in the fate of hardening decreed them by God." But their divinely decreed destiny, as a judicial infliction, presupposes their guilt in voluntarily choosing unbelief, as it is also remarked by Tholuck: "The fact that the guilt of the parties involved is not excluded in such an *actus judicialis Dei* in the Scriptural sense, is most plainly set forth by the history of Pharaoh, in which it is said in six places: he hardened himself, and in six others: God hardened him." Moreover it is not necessary to regard Is. liii. as the thought-sequence of Is. vi.; with regard to *facts* the train of ideas may be inverted, and thus it is doubtless here. Fast upon the οὐκ ἐπίστευσαν follows the οὐκ ἠδύναντο πιστεύειν as a judgment. Undoubtedly, therefore, διὰ τοῦτο is to be explained in accordance with Meyer. As in the prophet the preaching of the prophet was the object by means of which the judgment of hardening should be brought upon Israel, so in the evangelical history it was the manifestation of Jesus by word and deed. That which might and should have been a savor of life to the Jews, became a savor of death to them; and herein was accomplished their judgment of hardening. As the most speaking type of this judgment the passage Is. vi. 9, 10 is repeatedly cited: Matt. xiii. 14; Acts xxviii. 26; Rom. xi. 8 (comp. Luke ii. 34).

The quotation from Is. vi. 9, 10 varies from the letter of the original text, but in a way that is agreeable to its sense. There the prophet is commissioned to occasion obduracy by his preaching; here it is said, by way of historical report: He hath hardened them. *I. e.* the secondary or instrumental cause mentioned by Isaiah is omitted by the Evangelist, because in the latter, Christ, in accordance with ver. 41, is at once the secondary cause and the author of this hardness. According to Isaiah, God is the author or efficient cause, in His revealed form, His δόξα; according to John, Christ is the author, in His divine glory, as the Christ of the Old Testament. Hence there is no foundation in the text for the assertion of Meyer (and Tholuck) that not Christ, but God, is to be understood as the subject; the interpretation of Morus and others who consider the nation itself as the subject, likewise does violence to the text. According to Meyer, on the other hand, Christ is, in the sense of the Evangelist, the speaker in Isaiah, God the hardener, while ἰάσομαι has reference to Christ. The assumption that the hardener cannot also be the healer, is a groundless one. According to Tholuck ἰάσομαι should also be referred to God, having, as a negligence in expression, remained in the first person; Grotius and others, and Luthardt are correct in considering the whole as referring to Christ. The "negligence" is, however, conscious breviloquence; to be supplemented is: and as it is further written, That I should heal them. This turn, however, has its foundation in the fact that the negation of καὶ ἰάσομαι, *etc.* is not to lapse into the historical past like the items of the hardening, and that there is present to the mind of the Evangelist a distinction between Christ as the retributive God of revelation and the historical Saviour.

Ver. 41. **These things said Isaiah because** [ὅτι] **he saw his glory.**—Meyer: "According to Is. vi. 1, it was indeed the glory of *God* that was seen by the prophet (God sitting upon His throne, attended by seraphim, *etc.*); in accordance with the idea of the Logos, however, the theophanies are appearances of the Logos." Rather, the Logos who is about becoming incarnate, is Himself one with the δόξα of the Father, although this again in the abstract is distinguished from the δόξα of Christ (comp. Heb. i. 3); and hence too the δόξα of God is one with the Angel of the Presence (see Luke ii. 9), although Christ again has also His divine-human δόξα. His essential estate is the μορφὴ θεοῦ. The seeing of Christ on the part of the prophet was not cognitive (Origen), but visionary (Tholuck). Vatablus and others have, in opposition to the context, referred αὐτοῦ to God.—**And he** (not dependent upon ὅτι, the prophet) **spoke of Him.**

[Alford: "Αὐτοῦ *of Christ*. The Evangelist is giving his judgment,—having had his understanding opened (Luke xxiv. 45) to understand the Scriptures,—*that the passage in Isaiah is spoken of Christ*. And, indeed, strictly considered, the glory which Isaiah saw *could only* be that of the Son, who is the ἀπαύγασμα τῆς δόξης of the Father, whom no eye hath seen."—Wordsworth: "The Evangelist here says that Esaias (Is. vi. 1-9) saw the glory of the *Son*. St. Paul says (Acts xxviii. 25) that he heard the words of the *Holy Spirit*. There is one glory, therefore, of the Holy Trinity: and the glory of the Father is the glory of the Son, and is the glory of the Holy Ghost. (Theoph.) The glory of the Ever-blessed *Trinity* appeared to Isaiah, when he heard the Angelic *Holy, Holy, Holy* (Is. vi. 3); and the glory of the Trinity is here called the glory of Christ, because Christ is God. (*Cyril*).—There is a remarkable resemblance to this passage in the Book of Revelation (Rev. iv. 8-11), compared with Rev. v. 12-14, where the glory ascribed to the *Holy Trinity*, and the worship paid to the Holy Trinity, is ascribed and paid to *Christ;* and is therefore a clear evidence of His Divinity." —P. S.]

Ver. 42. **Yet even of the rulers many believed in him.**—The Evangelist limits and explains the preceding sentence. In relating that many even of the rulers (Sanhedrists) believed on Christ, he cannot mean such people as Nicodemus and Joseph of Arimathea (Meyer). We must appreciate the fact that John distinguishes between the wider sense of the word "believe" (chap. viii. 30) and its more limited sense (chap. vii. 5; xx. 27). Manifestly, it is belief in the wider sense of the term, inward historical recognition ("almost faith"), that is here meant. The Evangelist then proceeds to explain how it happened that the great commotion and awakening in the nation did not ripen into a great conversion.

But because of the Pharisees they did not confess (*it* or *him*), *etc.*—The counteraction of Pharisaism in its broadest sense is meant. They did not confess, did not come forward with the confession of their belief, for fear of *excommunication.* But excommunication seemed so frightful to them because they loved honor among men better than any (ἤπερ emphatically) honor with God. This means in the first place objectively the honor which men bestow by their recognition, in contrast to the honor given by God. This signification is, however, not exclusive of the subjective sense in which we interpret that honor of men to be of a human kind, but the honor of God of a divine sort, 2 Macc. xiv. 42; Rom. iii. 23.

Ver. 44. **But Jesus cried aloud and said.**—A perfect antithesis to the honor-seeking partyism of the Jews, which was the cause of their unbelief, is now presented to us by the Evangelist in Jesus' testimony to Himself, as the expression of His mental disposition or mind. *In the first place, the setting forth of the person of Christ was free from ambition; it was a setting forth of the glory of God.* He sought singly and alone the glory of God. Belief in Him should be a belief in the living God to the same extent as if it were no belief in Christ, *i. e.* as if belief in His human, individual appearance were fully merged in the divine glory of revelation of which He was the Mediator. And thus, also, in correspondence with the above, His appearance should be to those who saw Him the image of the appearance of the Father who sent Him.

So, moreover, the sending of Him was free from selfish aims; being designed purely for the salvation of those to whom He was sent. Being, as Light that came into the world, in principle purely a shining of God, so He was, in respect of His aim, absolutely the deliverance of believers from darkness, ver. 46.

Further, therefore, the operation of Christ was likewise purely and exclusively of a redeeming species without admixture of a condemning agency. This shining unto salvation and deliverance from darkness is in so great and exclusive a degree the aim of His mission that He is able to say: he that shall have heard My word and not have kept it (which will be proved at the Day of Judgment) shall not be judged by Me. *I. e.* He came solely and alone (in His one appearance as the Saviour of the world) *to save.* But the word of God which the unbeliever has not kept, but which holds him fast in the evil consciousness of his unbelief; the consciousness within him of the divine mission that he has slighted—that shall judge him at the last day (the ἐσχάτη ἡμέρα, comp. chap. vi. 39, 40).

And this is then, finally, purely and absolutely a judgment of God, devoid of any humanly turbid, individual admixture, because He has not spoken of Himself, but entirely in accordance with the ἐντολή of God by which He was conducted;—and that, as it regards the purport (the εἰπεῖν) of what He said, as well as the form, the human treatment and argument (the λαλεῖν). The ἐντολή, however, is not simply the commission laid upon Him at His sending; it is God's law for Him—a law continually in operation, fitting itself to each moment; it is the voice of God within Him ("an individual court of appeal"). But as this life-law of the speech of Christ is principally a commandment of God, so it is, in regard to its end and aim, eternal life; *i. e.* it contains, imparts, is productive of, eternal life; it develops into eternal life in the obedience of faith. And Christ, being fully conscious that He stands, with every word, between the God who has commissioned Him and the eternal life of the soul, says nothing in false selfism, but gives utterance to all things as the Father has told them to Him. *I. e.* even in expression, His word is thoroughly in accordance with God. So Christ could testify of His works that they were pure from all self-seeking and selfism, as though He vanished out of each one; disappearing first as a principle, in presence of the causal all-agency of the personal God, and then theologically before the aim of bringing salvation to souls as the perfect Mediator. This is one side of the divine-human revelation—and this, as a clear mirror, is contrasted by John with the sombre picture of that ambitious, selfish, utterly falsified party righteousness which rejected the Lord. In contemplating this we may not overlook the other side, namely, that this pure revelation of God was accomplished by the very perfection and perfect distinctness of the human individuality of Christ.

DOCTRINAL AND ETHICAL.

1. The pause between the end of the prophetic and the beginning of the high-priestly ministry of Christ, is marked by the Evangelist with an epilogue, which excites the certain expectation that the close of the second half of the Gospel will also be furnished with its epilogue, as a conclusion to the entire Gospel and also as a companion piece to the prologue (see the Introduction and chap. xxi.)

2. Had Jesus been simply a Prophet, His work would have been accomplished with the announcement of judgment made by Him within the temple after the rulers of the people had tempted Him and hardened themselves against Him within that building (see Comm. on *Matt.* p. 418, *etc.* Am. Ed.). But the bond of fellowship with His nation, the bond of high-priestly compassion, now drew Him forth again from His concealment to the hour of the Paschal sacrifice.

3. *The grief* of the disciple that Israel hardened himself in face of the full and perfect unfolding of the life of the prophetic Christ, ver. 37..

4. *The pacification* of the Evangelist in submissive contemplation of God's word and providence, vers. 38-41. Analogous is the *lament* of the Prophet and *his pacification* in which the Evangelist merges himself.

5. *The lament of the Prophet* (Is. liii.) abstractly considered. The unbelief of the Jews in the time of Isaiah impenitently opposed itself to the preaching of the prophets as well as to the arm of the Lord,—His wonders and signs of judgment. Hence the prophet saw in the sufferings

of the prophethood the type of the suffering servant of God, the Messiah. And hence the greatest of the Evangelists, in passing to the sufferings of Christ, reverts to that lament of the greatest of the prophets. He knows that lamentation to have had its perfect fulfilment in the face of the sufferings of Christ and in those sufferings. Isaiah, in prophetic spirit, saw the beginnings of unbelief of the Messianic promise, the beginnings of impenitence and obduracy, the beginnings of the suffering prophethood and of judgment accelerated by the preaching,—and depicted the future in advance; John witnessed the fulfilment of all this in the life of Jesus.

6. *Unbelief*, as an *unwillingness to believe*, was punished even in Isaiah's time with the *inability to believe*, the judgment of obduracy. It is the solicitous operation of the word of God which, with a holy and even healing purpose, drives the beginnings of judgment towards their completion. The Evangelist, like the Prophet, becomes tranquillized in adoring this judgment.

7. The Evangelist, with equal meaning, explains the unbelief of the Jews, which brought about the sufferings of Christ, by the introduction to Is. liii., and the judgment of impenitence upon the Jews by the vision Is. vi. Consequent upon the judgment of impenitence was the destruction of the city, the climax of which was reached by the burning of the temple; Isaiah himself had seen the temple totter at the revelation of the glory of Christ, the house being filled with smoke at the appearance of the seraphim. Hence these are doubtless symbolical angels of fiery judgment, as, in like manner, the cherubim are symbolical angels of divine providence under its historical veil, in great storms especially; an explanation certainly more obvious than the usual interpretation of שָׂרָף.

8. Christ, in the Old Testament, the manifestation of the δόξα of God, as also the Angel of the Presence (see Notes on ch. i. 14).

9. But the Evangelist is also necessitated to assign the human, ethical reason for that divine judgment in the unbelief of his nation. He therefore repeatedly gives prominence to the *inclination* to believe, found not only in the greater part of the people but also in many of its rulers. It is a fact of the highest significance that fear of the Pharisees, of the enmity of the Pharisaic party against Christ, was the ruin of everything and prepared for the nation its tragic fate. It is a statement of startling gravity that all the causes of the general apostasy were concentrated in the one sin of fear; and that the different phases of fear: the fear of man, the fear of spectres, the fear of shame and suffering, were concentrated in the one form: the fear of Pharisaic excommunication. Such fearful ruin can the dominion of a Pharisaic terrorism effect. This has been again demonstrated by the history of the Reformation. And the true courage of belief and conviction is as holy and replete with blessing as that fear, in spite of all its pretended holiness, is fatal and damnable. The emotion of fear was, however, grounded on the impulse of ambition, slavish devotion to the honor of Jewish patriotism, irreproachable orthodoxy, Pharisaic righteousness. Yet the ultimate reason of this wordly ambition in hypocritico-spiritual apparel, was the lack of a knowledge and sense of honor with God, the lack of true, inward spiritual life and of a prayerful spirit,—spiritual lethargy, spiritual death under the mask of the most fiery life.

10. In contrast to the gloomy picture of fatal and damnable ambition presented by Pharisaic Judaism, which denied the honor of God in Christ and finally blasphemed it and covered it with shame on the cross, appears the *bright image of the mind and self-presentation of Christ.* He sought nothing for Himself, with human selfism and selfishness, but made His life a pure sacrifice for the glory of God and the salvation of the world. So it is with His personality: it is the pure ideality of His essence as the manifestation of God, ver. 44. Thus with the sending of Him: it is the pure ideality of His appearance: the glorification of the manifestation of God, ver. 45. With His aim: it is the pure ideality of the transfiguration of the substantial world, of the enlightenment of the darkened world of sin, ver. 46. With His operation: it is the pure ideality of redemption, ver. 47. With the judicial operation of His word: it is the pure ideality of His coming to judgment, ver. 48. So it is with the motive, the aim and even the expression of His word, *i. e.* the pure ideality of His obedience, life and conduct even to the expression of His word itself, vers. 49, 50.

11. We may sum up this résumé of the self-presentation of Jesus in these words: Jesus was the pure, perfect, divine-human hypostasis; transparent as crystal in respect of the motive of His life, the manifestation of the Father, hence pure devotion, in His love, to that portion of the world that will receive salvation,—the pure outpouring of eternal life. He was, however, just this complete personality because His presentation by the Father was equally distinct with His own presentation of the Father; *i. e.* He was the complete divine-human individuality, the complete character. And He gave proof of His perfect personality as well as of His perfect individuality because He, in perfect subjectivity, continually transformed the general ἐντολή into the momentary ἐντολή of His consciousness, or kept the will of God in unison with His own will. (Comp. *Leben Jesu*, II. p. 1292.)

HOMILETICAL AND PRACTICAL.

The Evangelist's retrospect of the public ministry of Christ and its apparently frustrated result.—This retrospect in the light of prophecy.—*Yet* they believed not. The *yet* of unbelievers and the *yet* of believers, Ps. lxxiii. 1: 1. An antithesis in which the reality of human freedom is expressed; 2. the glory of divine judgment and divine grace; 3. decision for eternity; 4. a contrast, as betwixt heaven and hell.—The shocking obduracy of the Jewish nation in view of Christ's full, divine revelation of life.—How unbelief is changed from guilt to judgment: 1. Unwillingness to believe, as a crime demanding judgment; 2. inability to believe, as the judgment upon the crime.—The fault contained in the unbelief of the Jews a warning to all times.—The form of their fault: 1. Fear the cause of their unbelief; *a.* as a fear of excommunication; *b.* of excommunication by the Pharisees. 2. Ambition the foundation of their fear· a morbid delight in the fame of piety, righteousness, orthodoxy, *etc.* 3. The want of knowledge, of spiritual life and of a sense of God's honor the foundation of their morbid ambition.—The frightful effects of a Pharisaic ordinance of excommunication: 1. As displayed in our history; 2. in the history of the middle ages; 3. as resulting from the very nature of such an ordinance.—The curse of the fear of man, especially in matters of faith.—The ultimate and deepest cause of all evil the want of a sense of God's glory, Rom. i. 21.—Unholy party spirit in its fatal effects: 1. Characteristics of such party spirit: mutual belying, deception, exciting, fettering. 2. The fatal effects; *a.* fear; *b.* denial; *c.* universal ruin.—The rarity and gloriousness of true frankness in the service of truth.—Christ the Glory of God in the Old Testament.—That the Jews despised the glory which God gives, was manifest in that they despised Christ, who, in His righteousness, revealed the glory of God.—*Jesus cried aloud.* The solemn protestation of Jesus against the charge of having arrogated to Himself a peculiar glory as a false prophet.—The gloriously effulgent picture of the life of Jesus, who rejoiced in sacrifice, contrasted with the selfishness of His contemporaries: 1. They sought their own profit, honor, life, *etc.;* He lived but for the cause of God. 2. They, therefore, were slavishly dependent one upon another; He stood free in God. 3. They, under the mask of zeal for the glory of God, sought to mar and obliterate the radiant image of His glory; Christ glorified the honor of God and His mercy to His enemies by His perfect joyfulness in meeting shame.—Christ the pure manifestation of God: 1. In His essence; 2. in His aim; 3. in His work; 4. in His word. —Christ the pure manifestation of God in the clear distinctness of His personal nature.—What distinguishes Christ's testimony to Himself from all self-praise: 1. His remounting unreservedly to the source of His life, the Father; 2. His single aiming at His life's goal, the salvation of the world.—How the unbeliever is unable to rid himself of the despised word of salvation, bearing it with him, as an inward judgment, to the Last Day, which day shall convert it into an outward judgment also.—The Last Day a revelation of inward judgment.—Christ's clear law of life an admonition to us to make our darkened life-law clear.—Christ's law of life as the law of His freedom.—The Evangelist's retrospect of the prophetic work of Christ a proof that His high-priestly and kingly work was yet to follow.—The deep grief and the sublime pacification of Prophet and Apostle (Isaiah, John) in regarding the unbelief of their times.

Starke, Canstein: What happens, happens not because it has been foretold, but it was foretold because God foresaw that it would happen. —The truth of righteous and divine obduration. —Ver. 42. Hedinger: Blessed is the man to whom the world, with all her rags of honor, is crucified, and who holds her to be worth no more than a thief on the gallows, Gal. iv. 16.—Cramer: True, unfeigned belief must always be in harmony with a man's confession.—Quesnel: Stand we in whatsoever circumstances or situation we may, we are on no account to attach ourselves to them; we must place our dependence on nothing that men can deprive us of, if we desire to obtain and keep that which God alone can give.—Canstein: Christ always appeals to the Father when defending Himself against His enemies. So may faithful servants of the word, finding themselves in contempt and adversity, trust in the ministry which they have received from God.—Ver. 46. The sun is a fair light; Christ, the Sun of Righteousness, many thousand times fairer.—Ver. 47. A loyal servant of the Word is sent only to bring salvation.—Ver. 48. Quesnel: It is never permitted to the servants of Christ to avenge themselves on the despisers of their preaching; it is God's word; at the right time He will judge such conduct.

Gerlach: The guilt of the Jews assumed such magnitude in that they were not only inwardly estranged from Jesus and His revelation, but also, when, by the most glorious miracles, Jesus supported that highest proof (see chap. vii. 17), they yet turned away from Him.—The discourse from ver. 44 is not a single one; in order to show the inexcusableness of Jewish unbelief John subjoins a summary of the Lord's discourses; many reminiscences of former speeches. With ver. 44 comp. ch. vii. 16; v. 19; viii. 42.—With ver. 44 ch. viii. 19; xiv. 10; chap. i.—With ver. 46 chap. i. 5; viii. 12; xii. 35.—With vers. 47 and 48 chap. iii. 17; v. 45, *etc.*—With ver. 49 chap. viii. 28, 38.—With ver. 50 chap. vi. 39, 40; x. 11.—His revelation was nothing but light, life and love.

Braune: Elisha did twelve miracles, Elijah fewer still, and if we reckon up all the miracles of the prophets we find that seventy-four were performed by them; those of Moses are estimated at seventy-six. But although John chronicles but seven, he remarks, chap. xxi. 25, that the world would not contain the books that would have to be written if all the deeds of Jesus should be detailed. (Interesting from a theological point of view; homiletically a quantitative numeration of all the miracles would be unadvisable. As to the Number Seven of John the case is of course quite different). *And yet they believed not on Him.* Awful *yet!*—In sins of conscience the beginning is to fear and flee.—Without confession, faith soon wanes and its light threatens to become extinct.

Gossner: We fear the excommunication of men, but not the excommunication of God, of Christ.—This fear of an unrighteous excommunication may plunge us into eternal perdition, into the eternal excommunication of God.—It is possible for a soul to be saved without external communion with the Church, without sacraments administered by priests, if it be unrighteously shut out from them.—Let us therefore fear nothing but excommunication from Christ in our hearts, nothing but separation from the love of Christ.—Faith is the name of the way that leads from darkness into light.—Ver. 48. The hearing of God's word is never without result; a man cannot remain neutral with regard to it; it is either, or—friend or foe—grace or judgment.—Ver. 50. He preaches with exceeding joyfulness who speaks nothing from himself; when it is His (God's) word and not the preacher's babble or work of art.

HEUBNER: The secret, inward conviction of the divine mission of Jesus makes him so much the more culpable who is ashamed of acknowledging such a conviction.—The confession of the gospel, the confession of Jesus, is of particular worth in times when it involves shame.—How many dangers and hinderances to free confession there are in high positions! The fear of men, and ambition are the mightiest impediments to outspoken belief.—*Pharisees.* Entire parties may exert an influence in the repression and hinderance of the gospel.—To reject Jesus is to reject God.—His judging at some future day shall not be partial, as on account of personal injuries inflicted by unbelievers. The unbeliever will be condemned by his own conscience. Unbelief bears its judge within itself.—Christ left no particle of His duty undone. So it was no fault of His if men would not believe.

SCHLEIERMACHER: There is but *one* honor—and that is the honor which is in God's sight; there is but *one* fear which does not debase men—and that is the fear that says: How should I do this great wickedness and sin against God? But we do commit sin against God and His Spirit, if we seal up within our hearts what we in their inmost depths account as truth, and put a bar to its outgoing and further operation. For as common property and possession the Lord has endowed us with all spiritual gifts.—Some are of opinion that it was the general design of the Lord to turn aside the belief of mankind in great measure from His own person and direct it towards Him who sent Him; others think: All the faith that He demands must be directed to Him and His person alone. Let us avoid the one and the other extreme, whilst we combine the two, for such was the Redeemer's intention.—In view of His Passion and Death saith the Redeemer: I know that His commandment is life everlasting.

BESSER: Perhaps the expression that so frequently and emphatically recurs in the discourses of the Lord, to the effect, namely, that God had *sent* Him, should also serve to designate Him as the *Angel* (Ambassador) of the Lord in the Scriptures of the Old Testament.—STIER: John knows no other true and full belief than that which makes confession.

[CRAVEN: From AUGUSTINE: Ver. 38. It is evident that *the arm of the Lord* is the Son of God Himself.—Vers. 37, 38. God predicted the unbelief of the Jews but did not cause it; He does not compel men to sin because He knows they will sin.—Vers. 39, 40. If any ask why they *could* not, I answer, Because they *would* not—it is the fault of the human will that they *could* not. They well deserved this—God *hardens* and *blinds* a man by forsaking and not supporting him.—Vers. 42, 43. As their faith grew, their love of human praise grew still more, and outstripped it.—Vers. 44, 45. He signifies that He is more than He appears to be.—We believe an Apostle, but we do not believe *in* an Apostle.—Ver. 46. He saith to His disciples, *Ye are the light of the world,* but He does not say, *Ye are come a light into the world that whosoever believeth in you, etc.;* All saints are lights but they are so by faith [reflection] because they are enlightened by Him.—Ver. 47. *I judge Him not, i. e.* not *now; now* is the time of *mercy, afterward* will be the time of *judgment.*—Ver. 49. He Himself is the Word which the Father speaketh.——From CHRYSOSTOM: Vers. 37, 38. The prophets had predicted this very unbelief, and He came [amongst other intents] that it might be made manifest.—*That* is expressive not of the cause but of the event; they did not disbelieve because Isaiah said they would, Esaias said they would because they would.—Ver. 39. *Could not,* a common form of speech among ourselves; we say, *I cannot love such a man,* meaning only a vehement will.—Vers. 39, 40. He does not leave us except we wish Him; we begin to forsake first.—As it is not the fault of the sun that it hurts weak eyes, so neither is God to blame for punishing those who do not attend to His words.—Ver. 43. The praise [glory] of God is publicly to confess Christ; the praise [glory] of men is to glory in earthly things.—Ver. 47. I am not the cause of his judgment, but he is himself by despising My words.—Ver. 48. That this (vers. 46, 47) might not serve to encourage sloth, He warns of a terrible judgment about to come.——From LITANY of the CHURCH OF ENGLAND: Vers. 37-40. "From all hardness of heart, and contempt of Thy Word and commandment, good Lord, deliver us."

[From BURKITT: Vers. 38-41. The reference is to Is. vi. 3; whence a clear argument for Christ's divinity may be drawn.—Ver. 37. Let not the ministers of Christ be discouraged at their want of success, when they consider the small success of our Lord's own ministry.—Ver. 38. Isaiah's complaint of the small success of his preaching, a prophecy of the like success that Christ and His ministers should have under the gospel.—The gospel in all ages has met with more that rejected it than have savingly entertained it.—Vers. 38, 40. When men close their eyes *wilfully,* it is just with God to close their eyes *judicially.*—The infidelity of a people is to be resolved into the perverseness of their own wills, and not to any judicial blindness wrought by God upon them *antecedent* to their own sin.—God's act of hardening was consequential upon their sinning.—Ver. 42. Even in times and places where infidelity most prevails, the ministry of the word shall not be altogether without fruit.—Fear of men has kept many from believing on Christ, and more from confessing Him.—Ver. 43. They valued applause from men, more than God's approving them; no greater snare to draw persons from duty than an inordinate love of their own reputation.—How often is the applause of men preferred before the commendation of God.—Ver. 45. We do not see Christ aright unless we see Him to be truly God.—The Father is not to be seen but in the Son.—Ver. 46. The dreadful judgment denounced by Christ against all unbelievers.—Vers. 46, 47. Learn—1. Christ and His doctrine inseparable; 2. rejecters of Christ and His doctrine shall not escape the judgment of Christ at the last day; 3. were there no other witness against rejecters, the word preached would be sufficient.—The word preached is now the rule of *living,* hereafter it shall be the rule of *judging.*

[From M. HENRY: Vers. 37-41. The honor done to our Lord by the Old Testament prophets.—Two things said concerning untractable Israel

—1. they *did not* believe; 2. they *could not* believe.—*They could not believe* because—1. they *would* not, a *moral* impotency like that of one accustomed to do evil, Jer. xiii. 23; 2. God had *blinded their eyes*, God is not the author of sin and yet, (1) a righteous hand of God sometimes to be acknowledged in the *blindness* of those who persist in sin as punishment for preceding resistance, (2) *judicial blindness* is threatened against those who *wilfully* persist in wickedness.—Vers. 42, 43. Many professed more kindness for Christ than they had, these had more than they were willing to profess.—A struggle between their *convictions* and *corruptions*.—There are more good people than we think there are—some are better than they seem.—The *power of the world* in smothering convictions.—Observe concerning these believers—1. *wherein they failed*—in not confessing Christ; 2. *what they feared*—disgrace and damage; 3. *the ground of* their fear—they loved the praise of men more than the praise of God.—Love of the praise of men—1. as a *by-end* in that which is *good*, will make a man a *hypocrite* where religion is in fashion; 2. as a *principle* in that which is evil, will make one an *apostate* where religion is in disgrace.—Ver. 44. Jesus *cried* [aloud] and said: this intimates His *boldness* and *earnestness* in speaking.—Vers. 44-46. The *privileges* and *dignities* of those that believe, they are brought into—1. an *honorable acquaintance* with God; 2. a *comfortable enjoyment* of themselves.—Vers. 47, 48. The peril of those that believe not; observe—1. who they are whose unbelief is here condemned—those who *hear* and believe not; 2. the constructive malignity of their unbelief—a *rejection* of Christ; 3. the forbearance of Jesus toward them; 4. their certain judgment at the great day.—Vers. 49, 50. The *authority* of Christ—1. His *commission* from the Father; 2. the *design* of that commission—life everlasting; 3. His own observance of the instructions thereof.—Our Lord *learned* obedience Himself before He taught it to us.—Those who disobey Christ despise everlasting life.

[From Doddridge: Vers. 42, 43. Strange infatuation! that the human mind should be capable of believing that there is a God, and yet of preferring the creature before Him.—From Scott: Vers. 42, 43. That will not be accounted true faith which does not overcome [worldly] ambition, and induce its possessors to confess Christ before His enemies.—*Chief Rulers* are especially in danger of prevaricating.—From A. Clarke—Vers. 42, 43. Many persons are liberal in their condemnation of the Jews who are probably committing the same sort of transgression under circumstances which heighten their iniquity.—It is possible for a man to credit the four Evangelists [the entire Bible] and yet live and die an *infidel* so far as his own salvation is concerned.

[From Stier: Vers. 39, 40. The predicted *judicial hardening* [of the Jews] in the fulfilment of which, unbelief itself becomes only a new sign [to us] in proof.—The *guilt* of unbelief rested solely with Israel —Vers. 37-43. Of the *unbelieving* there are, according to St. John, *two classes*—1. the unsusceptible and hardened; 2. those who *confess not* in spite of their [imperfect] *belief*—He knows no other *genuine* and *perfect* faith than that which confesses.—Ver. 50. The commission *is*, in its ground and aim, according to its design and indwelling power, *life everlasting* for all who believe.

[From A Plain Commentary (Oxford): Ver. 46. It is evidently implied that He found all the world in darkness.——From Barnes: Ver. 37. The Jews did not believe as a *nation*.—Vers. 42, 43. *True* faith is *active*—it overcomes the fear of man, it prompts to self-denying duties.—Ver. 48. *Hath one that judgeth him:* He will carry his own condemnation with him, *his own conscience* will condemn him.—Learn that—1. a guilty conscience needs no accuser; 2. the words of Christ will be remembered by the rejecter; 3. this [rejection] will be the source of his condemnation; 4. the conscience of the sinner will *concur* with the sentence of Christ in the great day; 5. the word that Christ has spoken will be that by which the sinner will be judged in the last day.—Ver. 50. *His commandment is life everlasting, i. e.* the *cause* or *source* of everlasting life.—The [one] reason of the earnestness and fidelity of Jesus—He saw that eternal life depended on faithful preaching.—Every minister should have a deep and abiding conviction that he delivers a message connected with the eternal welfare of his hearers; under the influence of this belief he should preach fearlessly.—The *close* of the *public* ministry of Christ; such a close as all His ministers should desire to make.

[From Ryle: Ver. 37. Where there is the greatest quantity of *the form of religion*, there is often the greatest proportion of *formality* and *unbelief*.—Ver. 38. It is a singular fact that the very chapter which the Jews have been most unwilling to believe should begin with the question—*Who hath believed our report?*—If the Jews had not been unbelieving, the Scriptures would have been untrue.—"Darkness does not blind men so much as light, unless God renews the mind by His Spirit." [Rollock.]—Remark how *seeing*, *understanding*, *being converted*, and *being healed*, are linked together.—Ver. 42. *Many of the Chief Rulers believed:* their faith was only of the *head* and not of the *heart*—they were cowards.—Ver. 43. The same miserable motive is still ruining myriads of souls.—"They were not willing to part with their great places in the magistracy." [Poole.]—Ver. 48. There will be a resurrection of all faithful servants at the last day.

[From Owen: Ver. 40. He hath *blinded*—*hardened;* this He did *mediately* or by the instrumentality of the truth; the indirect agency of truth *when resisted* to render the soul insensible to divine love is equally certain and dreadful in its results as though the effect were produced by a direct agency upon the heart.—Ver. 50. *His commandment* contains in itself the germ and principle of eternal life, and when received into the soul results in everlasting salvation.

[From Whedon: Ver. 40. Although God was the unwilling cause of their blindness, it was their wicked will that gave to the cause its effect.—Their perverse will transformed His mercy into judgment; his means of softening into results of hardening—thus does the same sun that melts the wax harden the clay.—Ver. 42. A type fulfilled in nearly every age of advancement and beneficent resolution.—Ver. 50. God's divine, authoritative word implanted within our soul *is* eternal life in its very element and essence.]

VI.

THE RETURN OF JESUS FROM CONCEALMENT, IN LOVE TO HIS OWN. THE SEPARATION IN THE CIRCLE OF DISCIPLES ITSELF. THE ABASHMENT AND AGITATION OF THE FAITHFUL. THE SEPARATION AND WITHDRAWAL OF JUDAS. THE FOOT-WASHING OF CHRIST A GLORIFICATION OF HOSPITALITY, AS OF MINISTERING MASTERSHIP. SYMBOLISM AND FOUNDATION OF BROTHERLY DISCIPLINE IN THE CHURCH. THE DYNAMICAL SEPARATION OF THE ADVERSARY FROM THE DISCIPLESHIP OF JESUS.

Chap. XIII. 1–30.

(Comp. Matt. xxvi. 17–35; Mark xiv. 12–31; Luke xxii. 7–38; vers. 1–15 Pericope for Maundy-Thursday).

1 Now [but] before the feast of the passover, when Jesus knew [Jesus knowing]
that his hour was come [coming][1] that he should depart out of this world unto the
Father, having loved his own which were (who remained behind) in the world, he
2 [*omit* he] loved them unto the end. And supper being ended [the meal being
about to begin, or, having begun][2] the devil having now [already, ἤδη] put into the
heart of Judas Iscariot, Simon's *son*, to betray him [put into the heart, *i. e.*, sug-
3 gested that Judas Iscariot, the son of Simon, should betray him]; [3]Jesus [He][4]
knowing that the Father had given [him, αὐτῷ] all things into his hands, and that
he was come [came forth, ἐξῆλθεν] from God, and went [was going, ὑπάγει] to God;
4 He riseth from supper [the meal],[5] and laid [layeth] aside his garments [the outer
5 or, upper garment];[6] and took a towel and girded himself. After that [thereupon
or, then] he poureth water into a [the] basin, and [and he] began to wash the disci-
6 ples' feet, and to wipe *them* with the towel wherewith he was girded. Then cometh
he [so he cometh] to Simon Peter: [,] and Peter [he] saith unto him, Lord, dost
7 thou wash my feet? Jesus answered and said unto him, What I do thou knowest
8 not now; but thou shalt know [wilt learn, understand] hereafter. Peter saith unto
him, Thou shalt never [Never shalt thou] wash my feet. Jesus answered him, if I
9 wash thee not, thou hast no part with [in] me. Simon Peter saith unto him, Lord,
10 not my feet only, but also *my* [the] hands, and *my* [the] head. Jesus saith to him,
He that is washed [hath been bathed] needeth not save to wash *his* [the] feet [need-
eth not to wash himself (save his feet)],[7] but is clean every whit [wholly, entirely
11 clean]: and ye are clean, but not all. For he knew who should [was about to] be-
tray him; therefore [for this reason] said he, Ye are not all clean.
12 So after he had washed their feet, and had taken his garments [upper
garment] and was set [had sat][8] down again, he said unto them, Know [Un-
13 derstand] ye what I have done to you? Ye call me Master [the Teacher] and
14 [the] Lord: and ye say well; for *so* I am. If I then, *your* [the] Lord and Master
[the Teacher], have washed your feet; ye also ought to wash one another's feet.
15 For I have given you an example, that ye [also] should do as I have done to you.
16 Verily, verily, I say unto you, The [A] servant is not greater than his lord; nei-
ther he that is sent [nor one sent] greater than he that sent [the one sending] him.
17 If ye know these things, happy [blessed] are ye if ye do them [the same].
18 I speak not of you all: I know whom I have chosen [I chose]: but (*thus it is*)
that the Scripture may be fulfilled, "He that eateth bread with me hath lifted up[9]
19 his heel against me." (Ps. xli. 9). Now [From henceforth] I tell you before it
come [hath come to pass], that, when it is [hath] come to pass, ye may believe that
20 I am *he*. [He, the Messiah indicated in Psalm xli. 9]. Verily, verily, I say unto you,
He that receiveth whomsoever I send receiveth me; and [but] he that receiveth
me receiveth him that sent me.
21 When Jesus had thus said, he [Having said this, Jesus] was troubled in spirit,
and testified, and said, Verily, verily, I say unto you, that one of you shall [will]

22 betray me. Then [*omit* then][10] the disciples looked one on another [at one another]
23 doubting [being uncertain (ἀπορούμενοι)] of whom he spake. Now[11] there was lean-
ing [reclining at the table] on [in] Jesus' bosom one of his disciples, whom Jesus
24 loved. Simon Peter therefore beckoned [beckoneth, maketh a sign, νεύει] to him,
that he should ask who it should be of whom he spake [and saith to him, say, who
25 is it of whom he speaketh]?[12] He then [But he][13] lying [leaning back (thus), ἀνα-
26 πεσὼν (οὕτως)] on Jesus' breast saith unto him, Lord, who is it? Jesus [therefore]
answered, He it is to whom I shall give a sop, when I have dipped *it* [for whom I
shall dip the sop (morsel) and give it to him].[14] And when he had dipped the
sop he gave *it* [Having therefore dipped the sop, he taketh and giveth it] to Judas
27 Iscariot, *the son* of Simon [to Judas, the son of Simon Iscariot].[15] And after the
sop Satan entered into him. Then [Therefore] said Jesus unto him, That [What]
thou doest, do quickly.
28 Now [But] no man [no one of those reclining] at the table knew [understood]
29 for what intent he spake [said] this unto him. For some *of them* thought, because
Judas had the bag [kept the purse] that Jesus had [*omit* had] said unto him, Buy
those things that we have need of against [Buy what we need for] the feast; or,
30 that he should give something to the poor. He then, having received the sop, went
immediately out; and [but] it was night.

TEXTUAL AND GRAMMATICAL.

[1] Ver. 1.—In accordance with Codd. A. B. K. Sin. and others, Lachmann, Tischendorf, we should read ἦλθεν, not ἐλήλυθεν. "The Perfect resulted from the recollection of chap. xii. 25." Meyer. [Alford, Tregelles and Westcott and Hort likewise read ἦλθεν, *came, was coming*.—P. S.]

[2] Ver. 2.—B. L. X. Sin., *etc.*; γινομένου instead of γενομένου; a momentous difference. [Lachmann and Alford read γενομένου (*cum cœna facta sit*), but Tregelles, Tischend. ed. 8th, Westcott and Hort give the preference to γινομένου (*cum cœna fieretur*), which is supported by ℵ. B. Origen. Noyes and Conant translate: *supper being served;* Alford: *when supper was begun.* The E. V. (*supper being ended*) is inconsistent with ver. 12, where the Saviour placed Himself again at the table, and with ver. 26, where the meal is still going on. The aorist crept in as the more usual form in disregard of the chronology.—P. S.]

[3] Ver. 2.—The reading ἵνα παραδοῖ αὐτὸν Ἰούδας Σίμωνος Ἰσκαριώτης, in accordance with B. L. M. X. Sin., Copt., Arm., Vulgate, *etc*, received by Tischendorf, affirmed by Meyer to be the correct one, is not entitled to prevail against the reading given by A. D., *etc.*, Lachmann [which is the text. rec. followed by the E. V.: εἰς τὴν καρδίαν Ἰούδα Σίμωνος Ἰσκαριώτου ἵνα παραδῷ (Lachm. παραδοῖ) αὐτόν]. Meyer interprets the above reading: *When the devil had already made his plot* (*taken it into his own heart*) *that Judas should betray Him,* and remarks that this reading was early (so early as Origen) misunderstood to be an account of the seduction of Judas by the devil. Fear was, however, probably entertained that fatalism might find a support in the *Recepta,* and thus originated a conjecture which, however, without its being remarked, must necessarily have a far more fatalistic effect. [The preponderance of authority is in favor of the more difficult reading: εἰς τὴν καρδίαν ἵνα παραδοῖ αὐτὸν Ἰούδας Σ. Ἰσκ., which is adopted by Tregelles, Alford, Tischend., ed. 8th, Westcott and Hort. The text. rec. looks like a rearrangement to escape the difficulty of construction. The subjunctive form παραδοῖ is unusual in the New Testament, but sustained by ℵ. B. D.[1] The text. rec. reads παραδῷ.—P. S.]

[4] Ver. 3.—The words ὁ Ἰησοῦς are wanting in B. D. L. X. Sin., *etc.* Cod. A. and others give them. They might easily have been omitted because they seemed unnecessary in the already involved sentence.

[5] Ver. 4.—[Lange inserts the gloss after *the meal:* "which should now begin, and is hindered by the circumstance that no one performs the hospitable rite of foot-washing." See Exeg.—P. S.]

[6] Ver. 4.—[Lange: *das Oberkleid.* Τὰ ἱμάτια may mean the outer and inner garment, or, as here, and often simply the outer garment, *mantle, pallium* (different from the tunic or χιτών, and worn over it), which was wrapped around the body or fastened about the shoulders, and was often laid aside, comp. Matt. xxi. 7, 8; Acts vii. 58; xxii. 20. There is no necessity to suppose that Jesus literally divested Himself as the basest of slaves.—P. S.]

[7] Ver. 10.—[Tischendorf, ed. 8th, (1869), omits, in accordance with Orig. and Cod. Sin., ἢ τοὺς πόδας, which he gave in the ed. of 1859 in accordance with A. C.^{3} E.* G., *etc.*; Lachmann, Tregelles and Alford retain εἰ μὴ τοὺς πόδας, in accordance with B. C.* K. L., *etc.*; Westcott and Hort put it in brackets. Meyer explains the omission from the following καθ. ὅλος. If we read simply οὐκ ἔχει χρείαν νίψασθαι, we would have to translate: *hath no need to wash himself.*—P. S.]

[8] Ver. 12.—Tischendorf: καὶ ἀνέπεσεν in accordance with Codd. [ℵ.] B. C.,* *etc.* In favor of καί are also A. L. and others. [The text. rec. omits the second καί and reads ἀναπεσών.—P. S.]

[9] Ver. 18.—[Instead of ἐπῆρεν (B. C. D. L. Lachm. Treg. Alf., Westcott and Hort), Tischendorf, ed. 8th, reads ἐπῆρκεν with ℵ. A. U. Π.—P. S.]

[10] Ver. 22.—[Tischendorf, Alford, Westcott and Hort omit οὖν in accordance with ℵ.^{c} B. C.; Lachmann gives it according to ℵ.* A. D. L., *etc.* Tregelles retains it, but in brackets. Its insertion is easier accounted for than its omission.—P. S.]

[11] Ver. 23.—[Tischendorf, Tregelles, Alf., Westcott and Hort, omit δέ in accordance with B. C.* L.; Lachmann gives it according to ℵ. A. C.^{2} D., *etc.*]

[12] Ver. 24.—[Codd. [ℵ.] B. C. [I.], L. X. Vulgate and Origen read καὶ λέγει αὐτῷ· εἰπέ τίς ἐστιν, περὶ οὗ λέγει. The reading πυθέσιθαί τίς ἂν εἴη [text. rec.] seems modeled after ver. 25.—[The latter reading has the authority of A. D. Γ. Δ. Λ. Π.; but the former is adopted by Treg., Alf., Tischend., Westcott and Hort.—P. S.]

[13] Ver. 25.—The δέ, omitted by Tischendorf [Treg., Alf., Westcott and Hort] in accordance with [ℵ.] B. C., retained by Lachmann, in accordance with A. E. F. G., manifestly places the conduct of John in a certain antithesis to the expression of Peter. The οὖν in Codd. D. L. M., seems to be exegetical, *i. e.*, it explains how Peter intended his speech; Say, *etc.*, *i. e.*, ask the Master.

[14] Ver. 26.—The reading in Tischendorf in accordance with B. C. L., *etc.*: βάψω τὸ ψωμίον καὶ δώσω αὐτῷ obliterates the more exact sense. The first ἐμβάψας [βάψας with ℵ.] in Lachmann, in accordance with A. D. K. seems to be conformed from βάψας in accordance with the second ἐμβάψας which is in its right place. [βάψας οὖν in accordance with ℵ. B. C. L.; καὶ ἐμβάψας with A. Γ. Δ. Λ. X. Π.,^{2} *etc.* Tregelles, Alford, Tischend., ed. 8, and Westcott and Hort agree in reading: ᾧ ἐγὼ βάψω τὸ ψωμίον καὶ δώσω αὐτῷ—*for whom I shall dip the sop and give it to him.* Lachmann's reading ᾧ ἐγὼ ἐμβάψας τὸ ψωμίον ἐπιδώσω, and the reading of the text. rec.: ᾧ ἐγὼ βάψας τὸ ψωμίον ἐπιδώσω, which is preferred by Lange, requires the translation *to whom, having dipped the sop, I shall give it,* or, *for whom I shall dip the sop and to whom I shall give it.*—P. S.]

[15] Ver. 26.—[The correct reading is Ἰούδᾳ Σίμωνος Ἰσκαριώτου, according to ℵ. B. C. L. M., *etc.*, Tischend., Alf., Treg., Westcott and Hort., over against Ἰσκαριώτῃ of the text rec., which is conformed to vi. 70.—P. S.]

EXEGETICAL AND CRITICAL.

[Here begins the third main part of the gospel of John setting forth the glorification of Christ as the suffering High Priest and the victorious King. It is subdivided into three sections. The first treats of His private glorification in the midst of His disciples; the foot-washing, the parting discourses and the sacerdotal prayer, chs. xiii.-xvii.; the second His public glorification in His passion and death, chs. xviii. and xix.; the third His full glorification in His resurrection and reappearance among His disciples as the pledge of His abiding presence to the end of time, chs. xx. and xxi. With ch. xiii. we approach the Holy of holies in the earthly life of our Lord. Having completed His prophetic office and public ministry, He spent the evening before His crucifixion in the quiet circle of His disciples and friends, and poured out before them His heart, in full view of the sacrifice on the cross by which He was shortly to show in fact His boundless love to them and to the whole world. Such an evening occurred but once in the world's history: the fullness of eternity itself was condensed into a few fleeting moments. The farewell words of our Lord, chs. xiii. 31–xvii. 26, stand alone even in the Book of books. The nearest approach to them we may find in the parting song and blessing of Moses (Deut. xxxii. and xxxiii.), and the farewell address of Paul to the elders of Ephesus (Acts xx. 17 ff.). A more remote parallel is the prophetic picture in the second part of Isaiah, the prince and evangelist among the prophets, especially ch. liii., where the Messiah is represented as a man of sorrows who bore our griefs and carried our sorrows, who was wounded for our transgressions and bruised for our iniquities. The last words of our Lord to His own combine the deepest emotion with serene repose; they are solemn, weighty and affecting beyond description; they seem to sound directly from heaven, and they lift the reader high above time and space. We have here more than words, we have things, verities, acts of infinite love going out from God and going into the hearts of men. The main idea is: I in the Father, the Father in Me; I in the believers, the believers in Me, sharing My glory; or, as Bengel puts it: I came from My Father in heaven, I fulfilled His will on earth, I now return to My Father. ("*Veni a Patre, fui in mundo, vado ad Patrem*"). No disciple was so well qualified to apprehend, preserve and record these farewell words, as the bosom friend of Jesus who, during their delivery, reclined on His breast and heard the beatings of His heart. He omits an account of the institution of the Lord's Supper, as being already sufficiently known from the other Gospels, but these discourses, as also those in chs. iv. and vi., are full of the ideas of vital union with Christ and the communion of saints, which the sacrament symbolizes. In the same way John omits the form of baptism, but unfolds the underlying idea of regeneration (ch. iii.). Comp. on these wonderful chapters the introductory remarks of Dr. Lange below on ch. xiii. 31 and ch. xvii.*—P. S.]

On the hypotheses of modern criticism (Bretschneider, Strauss, Baur, *etc.*), concerning the history of the foot-washing, see Meyer [p. 492]. On the relation of the Johannean account of the farewell-repast of Jesus to that found in the Synoptists, comp. Comm. on *Matthew*, chap. xxvi. [Am. ed. p. 454 ff., where the English literature on this difficult question of chronology with many additional remarks is supplied.—P. S.]. After that general examination it will here suffice for us to render prominent once more the agreement between John and the Synoptists in those particular passages in which it is disputed. Thus here vers. 1-4; ver. 27; chap. xviii. 28; chap. xix. 31.

Bynäus, Wichelhaus (*History of the Passion*) and Röpe (1856) hold that the repast of the foot-washing was not identical with the feast of the Passover. This view, is, indeed, not tenable in its separation of the two repasts;—there is, however, some truth in it, inasmuch as two divisions in the Last Supper are to be definitely distinguished, of which divisions the Synoptists portray preëminently the second, *i. e.* the institution of the Lord's Supper, while John brings into relief the first section, *i. e.* the Jewish paschal feast,—that which has been transformed into the typical Christian love-feasts. That the Christian Agape, in its distinction from the Lord's Supper and yet in conjunction with the same, was already existent at the time when John wrote his Gospel, is evident from 1 Cor. xi. 17 ff., *etc.;* Jude ver. 12; 2 Pet. ii. 13; probably also from Acts ii. 42, 46; vi. 2. That, moreover, the Agape preceded the celebration of the Supper in the Apostolic Church, is evidenced by 1 Cor. xi. 20, 21 and by the fact that down to Augustine's time the African Church retained the custom of holding a common feast in the Church on Maundy Thursday, previous to the reception of the Lord's Supper; this was the case long after the ordinary Agapes had been separated from the Lord's Supper. (There was doubtless, however, a more decided separation of the Love Feast and the Communion in the Western than in the Eastern Church).

Now if in John's time the Agape already existed in the stead of the Paschal feast, we can readily comprehend that the term ἀγαπᾶν,—an expression which of itself signifies: to testify love,—might have a double meaning in the mouth of John, and thus imply: He showed them His love by the Agape. The mysterious expression of the Evangelist seems to contain still more of design when we consider that τὸ τέλος was likewise indicative of the religious ceremony, the celebration of initiation. The scarce translatable word: *unto the end, unto the decision He loved*

* [The remarks of Ewald, *Johann. Schriften*, I. p. 344 ff., are also worth reading. "What Christ discussed," he says, "with the Twelve in these hours, our Apostle describes here with a vivacity and quiet flow of composition which even surpasses all his former reports of the discourses of Christ, but which after all is doubtless only a weak attempt to fully reproduce the infinite glow of holy love and divine earnestness with which Christ addressed to them His earthly farewell." This is rather a left-handed compliment to John, but it will do for Ewald, who, in his own way, is an enthusiastic admirer of the fourth Gospel and with the intuition of genius looks often deeper into its meaning than many an orthodox commentator. On p. 359 he characterizes these parting discourses as "the greatest and most wonderful" piece of composition.—P. S.]

them (or: His love to them brought on His end together with its [His love's] completion; or, as Zinzendorf has it: He loved Himself to death, brought on death by loving), contains for Christian Greek readers the assonance of the thought: He gave them the Agape in anticipation of the Christian festival of initiation, of Christian initiation into the fellowship of His death by the Lord's Supper.

Since Christ desired to develop the Passover into the New Testament form of the Supper, it was quite significant that He so ordered the feast that the Passover itself took place before the beginning of the 15th Nisan and only the Supper fell into the full feast. Therefore He came early with the disciples to Jerusalem and commenced the celebration before the turning-point of the two days, *i.e.* before six o'clock on the evening of the 14th Nisan; so early was it that the conclusion of the Paschal feast or original Agape was reached before six o'clock, or, at all events, just about that hour. This simple supposition removes all difficulties, especially when it is observed that in those days the accuracy of our measurement of time had no existence.

Ver. 1. **But before the feast of the passover,** *etc.* [*Πρὸ δὲ τῆς ἑορτῆς τοῦ πάσχα, εἰδὼς ὁ Ἰησοῦς ὅτι ἦλθεν αὐτοῦ ἡ ὥρα ἵνα μεταβῇ ἐκ τοῦ κόσμου τούτου πρὸς τὸν πατέρα, ἀγαπήσας τοὺς ἰδίους τοὺς ἐν τῷ κόσμῳ, εἰς τέλος ἠγάπησεν αὐτούς.*]* Different constructions:

1. The first sentence continues to the close ver. 5 [or rather ver. 4—P. S.] and the apodosis begins with the words ver. 4: "He rose from supper" (Griesbach, Matthäi [Bleek, Ebrard, Westcott and Hort] and others). If we make it the evening before the festal eve, or the evening of the 13th Nisan and allow of no pause, the history is continued uninterruptedly through the night until the end of chap. xvii., and the crucifixion follows the next day, on the 14th, still before the feast. This assumption is contradicted by *a.* the exceedingly difficult construction (comp. chap. vi. 22); *b.* the different sense of *εἰδώς*, vers. 1 and 3; the distinction is entirely blotted out if we consider the second *εἰδώς* a repetition of the first, and the words: *εἰς τέλος*, *etc.* a parenthesis. (Bleek: Before the feast, when Jesus knew that His hour was come to depart out of this world unto the Father, having loved His own who were in the world—He did love them unto the end—, when a repast was spread, *etc.*). The Evangelist had in view a *twofold* great antithesis redounding to the glorification of the Lord. The first (ver. 1) glorifies especially His love, whereby in the love-feast itself He revealed His love to the disciples unto the consummation; the second (vers. 2-4) especially glorifies His humility, in which He washed the disciples' feet, although He knew, of Himself, that the Father was already tendering omnipotence to Him and that the Satanic betrayer was amongst the disciples. These two specifically different considerations cannot be mingled without obliterating the sense of the entire passage. *c.* The formal ending of the sentence ver. 1 is equally clear.

2. The first sentence comes to a conclusion with the first verse (Vulgate, Luther, Lücke, Lachmann, *etc.* [Ewald, Hengstenberg, Godet]). Still there are various conceptions:

a. Kling, Luthardt and others connect *πρὸ τῆς ἑορτῆς*, *etc.* with *εἰδώς*: *when Jesus knew before the feast of the passover.* But this would render the designation of the time unmeaning.

b. Application of the *πρὸ τῆς*, *etc.* to *ἀγαπήσας* (Wieseler, Tholuck) in this sense: *having even before the feast, in His consciousness of His approaching departure* (chap. xii. 23), *loved His own, He loved them more than ever at the end.* In connection with this, Tholuck observes, that it is impossible to interpret *ἠγάπησεν αὐτούς* with Lücke: *He gave them a proof of His love*, and he maintains that it indicates merely a loving frame of mind. But certainly it may mean a loving mood manifesting itself by a sign. And this admitted, the loving mood relapses into the proof of love.

c. Application of *πρὸ τῆς* to the entire history. Meyer thinks that if it had been the eve of the feast (the evening of the 14th Nisan) John must have written: *τῇ πρώτῃ τῶν ἀζύμων*. The chronological turning-point seems to be obscured in this place by the fear of "Harmonistics." *Τῇ πρώτῃ τῶν ἀζύμων* and *πρὸ τῆς ἑορτῆς* are the self-same thing. We make *πρὸ τῆς*, *etc.* relate to the mysterious and significant *εἰς τέλος ἠγάπησεν αὐτούς*. But before the feast He came forward again (contrast to what has gone before). Then He carried His love to the *τέλος*. The completed expression of His love brought along with it the completion of His life. In particular, namely, He manifested at the love-feast the humility of His love.

Jesus, knowing [*εἰδὼς ὁ Ἰησ.*].—The *δέ* [after *πρό* at the beginning of the verse] is of great moment here, serving also as an elucidation. Jesus had withdrawn Himself. *But* before the beginning of the feast He was again drawn forth by the consciousness that His hour was come, and by His love to His own, and now He loved them so that the end, or the crisis, was the result. The love-feast brought the crisis. And so, even though the primary reference of the words of the first verse is to the disciples, they also relate to the great mass of His own in the world. He came back and carried out His work of love to the end. He loved Himself to His end, to death, for the paschal feast brought on the decision of the betrayer and hence His death. *Ἠγάπησεν*, therefore, has reference undoubtedly to the whole love-feast, and the like is true of *πρὸ τῆς ἑορτῆς*. Before the paschal evening had fully begun, Judas went out into the night; with his departure *τὸ τέλος* was decided; Jesus' act of love had induced the decision. But the more definite date was the leaving of Bethany for Jerusalem: that was the expression of His love by which the end was occasioned. The reference of the words *ἀγαπήσας τοὺς ἰδίους* to the foregoing: to depart unto the Father, after He had loved (Meyer), is void of meaning; but the interpretation: "He rendered them the last testimony of His love," likewise withholds from *εἰς τέλος* its rights.

* [Lachmann, Tischendorf (ed. 8th), Tregelles and Alford agree in making a stop after *αὐτούς*. But Westcott and Hort, with Griesbach, Matthæi, Scholz, put *ἀγαπήσας—αὐτούς* in parenthesis and close the sentence with ver. 4.—P. S.]

Ver. 2. **And when the meal had begun, or, supper being served** [καὶ δείπνου γινομένου].—The introduction of δεῖπνον without an article is explained by the fact that John has already indicated the nature of the δεῖπνον by the ἠγάπησεν in the first verse. "It seems unfavorable to the idea that it was the paschal meal (Wichelhaus), but as ἀπὸ δείπνου, ἐπὶ δεῖπνον ἰέναι mean: after the repast, to go to table, so δείπνου γινομένου does not mean: when *a* meal took place, but it signifies *when the meal took place* or *was about to take place*, to wit, the repast of this day, and that was the festive meal." Tholuck. Should we even read γενομένου (see the TEXTUAL NOTES), it would not mean: after the repast was over (Luther, Hofmann [E. V.]), but after it had already begun. According to Meyer and many others this meal was not the supper; John, they say, assumes that to be already known to his readers (it having been celebrated on the same evening). Hence, according to Meyer the paschal meal is omitted. According to Baur it is omitted because the author of the Gospel chap. vi. connected it with the second paschal feast of Jesus; according to Strauss the Evangelist knew nothing of the Supper. [According to Schenkel John intended to guard against ascribing a *magical* effect to the Lord's Supper, and to prevent sacramental controversies. But this could have been done more effectually by plain instruction.—P. S.]

The meal having begun, or, being served.—That is, they had already reclined, vers. 4, 12. [Not *being ended*, as in the E. V. See TEXTUAL NOTES.—P. S.]

The devil having already put it into the heart of Judas [τοῦ διαβόλου ἤδη βεβληκότος εἰς τὴν καρδίαν]—The explanation of Meyer, *when the devil had already made his plot* [had put it into *his* heart], is untenable (see TEXTUAL NOTES).* Strange indeed it would be if the *heart* of the devil were the subject of this announcement, independently of the fact that after all there would be little sense in the statement: the devil had resolved within himself, *etc.* As if such a thing were dependent on the resolve of the devil. The condition of affairs is this: the devil had sown the thought, the ἐπιθυμία, of betrayal in Judas' heart; the wicked *counsel* becomes a firm decree only in ver. 27. It is true that, according to Matthew, Judas had previously been to the high-priests and negotiated with them; this fact, however, does not preclude subsequent waverings and conflicts on the part of the unhappy man. Now while the first antithesis was general in its character and referred to the whole love-feast, this second antithesis is special and has reference to the humility of the love of Jesus which found expression in the washing of the disciples' feet. Yet the words: *the devil having, etc.*, are to be primarily referred as a supplement to the foregoing, in this sense: the brooding treason in the breast of Judas did not hinder the Lord from causing the repast to commence. Perhaps, however, it is likewise intended that the words should mark out Judas as the chief author of the dispute which arose among the disciples on this occasion as to their respective ranks,—a dispute chronicled by Luke. No doubt the unwillingness of each one of the disciples to take upon himself the office of the foot-washing was one of the modes in which their contentious spirit manifested itself (Luke xxii. 24, 27; ancient exegetes; *Leben Jesu*, II. p. 1314). Euthymius Zigabenus sees in the mention of Judas a trait illustrative of the long-suffering of Jesus; the truth of this view Meyer groundlessly denies.

Ver. 3. **Jesus, knowing.**—Albeit He had the presentiment of His glory; namely 1. the presentiment of His elevation to divine power; 2. of His perfected mission resting upon His descent from the Father; 3. of His imminent elevation to the throne of glory.

Ver. 4. **He riseth from supper.**—The contrast of His service with the presentiment of His lofty dignity. He rises to perform the foot-washing. Since this was ordinarily done by slaves previous to the commencement of the meal, in the absence of a slave the duty naturally devolved upon the humblest of the circle. In this assumption lay the *fuse* that kindled the disciples' last strife for preëminence. At all events the dispute recounted by Luke appears to have been in part the occasion of the foot-washing. According to Strauss, De Wette, Meyer and others this is not the place for that dispute. It was, however, natural for it to break out more than once, and we should be attributing too great a piece of inaccuracy to Luke, were we to imagine that his placing of it in the history of the Supper was altogether erroneous. According to Meyer and Tholuck no such cause was requisite to induce Jesus to wash the disciples' feet; they maintain that the act was a purely symbolical one. But this is in opposition to the realism of the life of Jesus and commingles the Old and New Testaments. Symbolism set forth in ceremonies is of the Old Testament. Wichelhaus discovers in the foot-washing an indication that the entertainment was no paschal feast, since, if it had been, the host must have assumed the duty. As contradictory to this view we cannot, with Tholuck, cite Luke vii. 44, affirming that the washing of the feet was not always practiced. The omission of it there is reprehended. Manifestly, the very absence of the host proves that it was the time of the celebration of the Passover. On the evening of the 13th Nisan the host might have charged himself with the foot-washing; on the evening of the 14th Nisan he was obliged to eat in company with his family-circle as the father of the house and was thus prevented from performing the rite in question. For he did not sup with the circle of disciples; here the position of father of the family belonged to Jesus.

Layeth aside His outer garment [τὰ ἱμάτια. Bengel: *eas vestes, quæ lotionem impedirent.*—P. S.]—The prompt and joyous alacrity of the Lord is picturesquely delineated by the rapid succession of the several sentences in designation of the several acts. The fact of His girding Himself contrasts with the expectation that others should have done it for Him.

Ver. 5. **Into the wash-basin** [τὸν νιπτῆρα].—Into the one appointed which stood there. [Grotius: *Nihil ministerii omittit.*] From

* [Alford calls it "wholly unworthy of a scholar and simply absurd." He explains βεβληκότος, *etc. suggested, proposed*, viz., to the mind of Judas.—P. S.]

this trait as well as from the expression: *He girded Himself*, we perceive that the foot-washing was anticipated and had been left undone in default of a servant, or a disciple willing to discharge the office.

And He began [*καὶ ἤρξατο*].—It undoubtedly seems to follow from the relation of ver. 5 to ver. 6, that He had already washed the feet of other disciples when He came to Peter (Meyer), because the whole proceeding is already described ver. 5. But He seems too to have come soon to Peter, since the latter interrupted His work as He was beginning. It would also be contrary to the inversion of orders of rank in the foot-washing if Jesus had begun with a disciple who was in a certain respect the first. Augustine and many Catholic exegetes make Peter the first; Chrysostom and others, on the contrary, conceive Judas to have been the first.

Ver. 6. **Dost thou wash my feet?**—According to Tholuck (with reference to Chrysost.), this is a refusal *from reverence*, only after the reproof of Jesus becoming a refusal *from self-will*. Yet the unmistakable reverence is lacking in a true sense of the extraordinariness and spiritual significance of the action,—is lacking in full submission; thus a germ of self-will lent its influence even here. At all events Peter applied to the action of Jesus the same rule of outward rank, which effectually hindered the introduction into his own mind of the idea that *he* should wash the feet of his fellow-disciples.

Ver. 7. **Thou knowest not now, but thou wilt know hereafter** [*σὺ οὐκ οἶδας ἄρτι, γνώσῃ δὲ μετὰ ταῦτα*].—The antithesis of *σύ*, *μου* is sternly met by the antithesis of *ἐγώ* and *σύ*. According to Chrysostom and others, also Tholuck [Hengstenberg, Ewald], *μετὰ ταῦτα* is indicative of subsequent enlightenment [after the day of Pentecost]; according to Luthardt it means: in eternity; according to De Wette and Meyer, the explanation ver. 12 ff. That explanation is doubtless intended in the first instance, not, however, to the exclusion of a progressive experience or knowledge in Christian illumination. Calvin: *Quavis scientia doctior hæc ignorantiæ species* (*est*), *cum Domino concedimus, ut supra nos sapiat.*

Ver. 8. **Peter saith unto Him, Never shalt Thou wash my feet** [*οὐ μὴ . . . εἰς τὸν αἰῶνα*].—Again the self-will of the apostle develops into open contradiction and disobedience,—as on the occasion when Jesus announced that He was about to tread the path of suffering, Matt. xvi. 22. The connection between the two passages is discoverable, on the one hand, in the great attachment and reverence which Peter entertained for the Lord; but, on the other hand, also, in his cleaving to the external glory and sovereignty of Christ and in coveting a share thereof for himself. Christ now began practically with His self-humiliation to turn Peter's moral view of the world upside down; Peter, meanwhile, instead of divining the blessing of the cross enfolded in this act, struggled with anxious forebodings against its pricks. Christ's washing of the disciples' feet was an affair utterly repugnant to his soul. Never; properly—to eternity, into the æon; *εἰς τὸν αἰῶνα*.

If I wash thee not.—In this case too Jesus must give utterance to a threat, as in Matt. xvi. 23, before Peter's strong self-will is brought into subjection. This strong self-will is indicated in the further history of Peter and likewise by the words of Jesus John xxi. 18. Hence the saying of Jesus was true, primarily, in the literal sense; not, indeed, in the sense ascribed to it by Peter, viz., If I do not corporeally cleanse thy feet,—but: if thou accept not my service of love in this washing of thy feet. Peter, had he persistently refused, would have put an end to the relationship between disciple and Master. The entire relationship was made dependent on this single point. No fortuitous thought was thereby involved, but a symbolico-typical act. Insomuch as this is true, Peter's resistance was, in the first place, a negation of the act of religion symbolized by Christ; in the second place, a refusal to have his life purified by the Lord; a fatal protestation,—this latter—against that spiritual foot-washing, for example, which was apportioned him chap. xxi. and without which he could have had no part in Christ; his resistance was, finally, a revolt against that ordinance obtaining in the kingdom,—the law of ministering love and humility in the Church of Christ;—a revolt which would in no wise have fitted him for his place as the first pioneer of that kingdom.

Thou hast no part with Me [*οὐκ ἔχεις μέρος μετ' ἐμοῦ*].*—Matt. xxiv. 51, *etc.* (אֵת חֵלֶק עִם, חֵלֶק) *i. e.* in the same kingdom and the same glory of the kingdom, they being founded on loving and serving. According to Maldonatus and others, the menace contains a renouncement of personal friendship; according to Grotius an announcement of the loss of eternal life; according to Bengel, Luthardt and others it signifies: no part in my cleansing. The latter explanation is, however, not demanded, as Tholuck thinks it is, by the ethical and symbolical sense of the washing (in so far as this sense is presupposed, which is certainly to be assumed). The outward washing is accompanied by that which is inward, *i. e.* moral purification; from this, however, the future blessing must be distinguished. Baptism is attended by the renunciation of sin, but the blessing of it is communion with Christ and Christians in this present world; the Lord's Supper is attended by the sealing of reconciliation and the communication of the new life of Christ: but its future blessing is communion with Christ and with Christians in the resurrection. The view represented by Bengel, Luthardt and Tholuck might be designated as one-sided or ultra-Reformed.

Ver. 9. **But also my hands and my head.**—An utterance prompted by the agitation and entire subjection of the disciple. Not for all the world would he lose the fellowship of Jesus. He would be washed by Him as a child; he offers to Him all the uncovered portions of his body: his hands, his feet, his head. A trace of *dictatorialness* is, however, still visible in this act of submission; a fact connected with his apprehension of the action of Christ; he still regards it in too great measure as an outward or legal thing and does not yet fully perceive the simple,

* [The corresponding classical phrase would be *οὐκ ἔχεις* or *μετέχεις μέρος μου*.—P. S.]

spiritual symbolicalness which appertains to it when viewed in accordance with the idea of Christ. Hence *a third reprimand* is necessary, albeit one of dispassionate mildness.

Ver. 10. **He that hath bathed, needeth not to wash himself.**—Not a shade of doubt (as, for instance, by Tholuck) should be cast on the fact that Jesus primarily proclaims a law of the Jewish ordinances relative to purification (Michaelis, *etc.*). But this ordinance consisted not in the custom of bathing before each meal (Wetstein), and then again washing the feet, defiled by the going forth to the meal, or washing the feet again separately on account of their pollution by the bath-water itself (Beza). Rather, the bathing is indicative of the *greater* and *rarer* purification,—the foot-washing of the *minor* and *daily* one, such as was requisite each time that the traveller paused for rest or refreshment. Provided, therefore, that a man had seasonably bathed himself in conformity to the ordinance, he needed, on such an occasion as the present one, nought save to wash his feet. Jesus, then, declares in the first place, on Peter's demanding a bath for his whole body, that he must content himself with the washing of his feet, in accordance with the law which regulated this custom. But at the same time He pronounces the spiritual law of life in conformity to which He would wash the feet of His people spiritually and symbolically. Ye are bathed in the spiritual sense and thus clean in general (although not all of you); hence ye need, in this sense, but the washing of your feet.

What is the meaning of this? A distinction must here be made between the signification of the saying as a rule of Christian ethics, and as the rule of an ecclesiastical ordinance. *Relative to the former.* Origen: they were clean in general through baptism;* it was obligatory merely that the inferior parts, the affections, should be purified. Theod., Herak.: Clean by means of the *doctrine;* their feet must be consecrated to the apostleship. Chrysost.: Clean through the *word* (chap. xv. 3); the washing of their feet signified that they had still to learn *humility*. The latter interpretation is doubtless the true one. As disciples, they had received, in the fellowship and the Word of Christ, the principle of their general purification or regeneration; but they must, by the shaming example of their Lord and Master, be cleansed from ambition and other sins which had clung to their feet, their endeavorings, in their pilgrimage as disciples.

The maxim generalized reads thus for Christians; Justification must be followed by sanctification or daily repentance (evangelical theologians). Connected with this is the symbolical interpretation with reference to the *ecclesiastical* ordinance in Cyprian, Aug. and others: "They were clean through baptism, and had need but of the *Sacramentum pœnitentiæ.*" Only not in a legal sense. The manner in which Christ made the love-feast with the foot-washing a purificative preparation for the Supper, is a vivid type for the evangelical, ecclesiastical ordinance, in accordance with which a purificative, disciplinary preparation or confession precedes the celebration of the Lord's Supper. It is not altogether clear how Tholuck, after De Wette, Lücke (so too Meyer) can protest against the universal, symbolical significance, originally intended, of Christ's words; for together with the primary signification of the act for the disciples, its second universal, Christian, moral signification is established; and the latter contains likewise the ecclesiastical ordinance in embryo. Be it observed, furthermore, *that the declaration relative to the needs of the disciples must by no means be confounded with the enforcement of the example of Jesus upon the disciples* (vers. 14, 15), although the second consideration corresponds with the first.

And ye are clean.—Application of His words to the disciples.—**But not all.**—A hint at the traitor. Since he does not stand in the communion of Jesus and His word, or, figuratively speaking, is not bathed, the foot-washing is vain in his case. "Such further comments on our passage as impute to it a polemical tendency against Peter, in spite of chap. i. 42; vi. 68, *etc.* (Strauss, Schwegler, Baur, Hilgenf.), and even credit Peter with the demand for an Ebionite lavation of the whole body (Hilgenf.), are pure fabrications." Meyer.

Ver. 12. **Know ye what I have done to you.**—Namely, the meaning and significance of it. Herewith begins the introduction to the explanation.

Ver. 13. **The Teacher and the Lord** [*ὁ διδάσκαλος καὶ ὁ κύριος**].—מַר and רַבִּי were likewise the titles given by the Rabbins' scholars to their masters (Lightfoot and others). With the relation of the Master, who was also the Lord (in a theoretico-practical school), corresponded the relation of the disciples, who were also servants.

Ver. 14. **If I then,** *etc.*—If your Lord has performed for you this service of a slave, ye must do likewise to one another. *One another.* Much more should ye, in conformity to your natural coördination, discharge for one another this lowly office of self-denying love. But since the disciples were to be under a life-long obligation to self-abasement in humble love, this act of Christ must also suggest to their minds the spiritual fact of His having ever thus served them in a spiritual sense. The sign of His self-humiliation hitherto in slavery to legal ordinances should thus be to them a presage of His impending self-humiliation unto the death of the slave. And so neither had the Lord in mind the outward copying of His action, but rather the spiritual imitation of it. This imitation in the service of love and humility is to consist, however, specifically in a mutual foot-washing, *i. e.*, in efforts for the purification and emancipation of our brother from the sin that cleaves to him. If we would show our brother the right way and lead him in it as we should, we must do it in the spirit of humility, of subordination in self-denying love; thus done, it is an act of the greatest self-denial. Reprehension or reproof adminis-

* [The reference of ὁ λελουμένος to baptism as the "bath of regeneration (Tit. iii. 5; Eph. v. 26)," is also defended by Theodor. Mopsv., Augustine, Erasmus, Olshausen, Ewald, Hengstenberg, Godet, Wordsworth, but wholly denied by Meyer, who, like Lange, sees the purifying element in the *word*, as in chap. xv. 3.—P. S.]

* [The nominative of the title, after verbs of designation; see Winer, p. 172, 7th ed., and Buttman, *N. T. Gr.*, p. 132.—P. S.]

tered from the high horse or throne is no foot-washing.

Hence it is remarkable that the literal foot-washing gradually gained ground as a ceremony in the church at a time when the spiritual foot-washing receded more and more before hierarchical pride, lust of power and austerity (See the Article *Fusswaschung*, by H. Merz in Herzog's *Real-Encyklopädie*, with reference to Bingham, IV. 394). It follows from Augustine's *Epistol.*, 118 *ad Januarium*, that it was in use during his time, though without definite appointment of the day. Bernard of Clairvaux desired to convert the customary Catholic ceremony into a sacrament; without success. Catholic argumentation for the tradition of this rite does not sufficiently discriminate between the ancient custom of hospitality (1 Tim. v. 10), which of course extends forward into Christian times, and the rise of the Catholic ceremony. On Maundy-Thursday Catholic monarchs and the pope symbolically practise it upon twelve poor old men. Upon this Bengel sarcastically comments thus: "*Magis admirandus foret pontifex, Unius regis, quam duodecim pauperum pedes, seria humilitate, lavans.*" Luther counsels the substitution of a bath for the poor men when they really stand in need of one. Yet we cannot avoid recalling the beautiful saying of Claudius touching ceremonies that have become void: "they are little flags, floating above the surface of the waters and showing *where a richly freighted ship hath sunk.*" In the communion of the Moravians the governors of the choir decide as to the practice. The sacramental character of the foot-washing has found an advocate in Fr. Böhmer (*Stud. u. Kritiken*, fourth number, 1850). Tholuck.*

The frequent recurrence of evangelical theologians to this view overlooks these facts:

1. That the Lord desired a *reciprocal foot-washing of all the faithful*, not a one-sided one of inferiors by superiors.

2. That He elevated His foot-washing into a *unique* symbol, expressly substituting for His people the *ethical explanation* and application.

3. That the foot-washing as a sacrament would be a sacrament devoid of any definite word of promise; a circumstance which would, of course, alter the whole idea of a sacrament.

4. That the ecclesiastical consideration of the moral exaction of the Lord is fulfilled in the evangelical preparation or confession.

5. That the foot-washing as a sacrament would constitute a pendant to the Lord's Supper, as the sacrament of sanctification, equally marring with the Catholic confession or absolution in *its* relation to the Lord's Supper. Irrespective of the fact that the outward foot-washing is too climatic in its nature and too closely connected with the difference between sandals and shoes, to be adapted for a universal rite. In many places it is more necessary *to shoe* the feet; in the Polar regions *to warm* them.

The commandment of the Lord; ye shall wash each other's feet, is indicative of the duty of humbly and lovingly helping our neighbor in his daily repentance; with equal distinctness does the necessity for washing the feet set forth the necessity for accepting the assistance of others in our daily repentance. "Humbly to labor for the purification of others" (Meyer, Luthardt).

Ver. 15. **For I have given you an example.**—Now an example is intended not to be outwardly counterfeited, but to prompt to ethical imitation.

Ver. 16. **A servant is not greater,** *etc.*—Comp. chap. xv. 20; Matt. x. 24; Luke vi. 40. With a "*verily, verily*" the humility and self-denial of ministering love here enforces the axiom according to which the servant should look upon himself as being at least as lowly as his master. Well did the Lord foresee the great temptations and errors connected with clerical self-upliftment in His church. See Matt. xx. 25; xxiv. 49.

Ver. 17. **Blessed are ye if ye do them.**—"In conclusion yet another reference to the great gulf that is wont to lie between insight and practice with regard to this very commandment." Tholuck. As with regard to all commandments; here, however, it is particularly damnable. This is a saying spoken by the Lord as if in anticipation of the ceremony of foot-washing. For the ceremony is at all events an expression of intelligence. Suggestive of the "*servus servorum.*" The non-performance of knowledge, then, is in like manner followed by unblessedness. A knowing without doing, *i. e.*, without moral realization in spirit and life, is creative of a shadowy doing in abortive ceremony; in many respects the ceremony may be regarded as the visible type of knowledge that falls short of performance.

Ver. 18. **Not of you all.**—*A second stronger* allusion to Judas. See ver. 10. Tholuck: "According to general interpretation, ver. 18 is connected with ver. 17: a fulfilment of this ministering love is not to be expected from you all. Since this thought, however, does not fit into the connection of the subsequent remarks, we must assume that reference is had to ver. 10,—a looseness which fails to appear surprising in the Johannean style." Yet even here John is sufficiently precise. Meyer, after ancient exegetes (Augustine: *est inter vos, qui non erit beatus, neque faciet ea*), more pertinently refers ver. 18 to the beatitude, ver. 17. The two verses are even implicative of a sharp antithesis: there is one who, instead of washing the feet of his fellow-disciples, ventures to trample his Master under foot. The contrast to faithful, humble, ministering love towards fellow-disciples is found in false, haughty, seditious treason to the Lord and Master.

I know whom I chose.—This sentence—ἐγὼ οἶδα οὓς [Tischend., Alf.: τίνας] ἐξελεξάμην—is differently explained:

1. The emphasis is upon ἐκλέγεσθαι. Election *ad salutem* is meant, either in accordance with the Calvinistic doctrine of decree, or with reference to foreknowledge, agreeably to the teaching of the Lutheran communion. "*Non omnes ad apostolatum electi ad beatitudinem electi sunt*" (Gerhard). Tholuck gives a slightly different explanation: "I know whom I have *really* chosen; thus in 1 John ii. 19 the signification is: 'those who have fallen away from us were—not *really* of us." Yet another interpretation has been attached to this: I know whom *I* have chosen, *i. e.* of My own accord, not at the instigation and intercession of the circle of disciples. But there is no

*[The sect of the Tunkers in Pennsylvania are strenuous advocates of foot-washing.—P. S.]

second ἐγώ to support this. The passage chap. vi. 70 is, however, contradictory of the method of explanation noted above. In this place, as in the former passage, a distinction must be made between the *eternal election of God* and the *historical election of Christ.* That Christ acknowledges having in the historical sense chosen Judas, is proved by the following: "he that eateth My bread." Hence

2. Οἶδα must be emphasized. I know them; I fathom them all and discriminate between them; thus I know even the wretch. The same idea is presented as in chap. vi. 70; it is but developed. But then, according to Meyer, the idea proceeds thus: ἀλλ' with the supplement of ἐξελέξαμεν αὐτούς, *etc.*: but I have made the selection in the service of that divine destiny conformably to which the Scripture had to be fulfilled.* An exceedingly hazardous and fatalistic supplement. Meyer here also fails to discriminate betwen the moment of the calling of Judas and that moment of his germinant apostasy, John vi. 70. [Οὐκ ἐγὼ ὑμᾶς τοὺς δώδεκα ἐξελεξάμην; καὶ ἐξ ὑμῶν εἷς διάβολός ἐστιν].

But—that the Scripture may be fulfilled.—This *but* contrasts the allusion to the apostasy of Judas, prophesied by the Scripture, with the painful fact that Christ sees through His chosen ones and perceives a traitor among them. It is the ever-recurring antithesis of the human, moral grief of Jesus over unbelief, apostasy, and His religious elevation and pacification in view of that divine providence which directs all things; a mode of pacification in which He has been followed by the apostles and by all Christians of all ages (see chap. xii. 38). Hence the connection of ἀλλ' with τρώγων (whereby ἵνα ἡ γρ. would be resolved into a parenthetic proposition, Semler, Kuinoel) is contrary to analogy (comp. chap. xix. 28, 36). To be supplied is "this happened" (see 1 Cor. ii. 9).†

The Scripture: Ps. xli. 9. A free citation [differing from the Hebrew and the Sept.] without any material alteration of the sense. The expression: *My bread* is changed into: **bread with me.**‡ It was not Christ's intention to represent Himself as the bread-provider of Judas in a literal sense; David, to whom the description is more applicable than to Jeremiah (Hitzig), might with truth thus speak of *his* betrayer. But in a higher sense Judas did indeed eat His bread, subsisting, as he did, upon the blessing of His society. But what Jesus desires to throw into relief is the contrast between the malicious plot of the traitor and the unbounded confidence that prevailed in his familiar association with Judas at the table. This prophecy manifestly belongs to the spiritual types [and was fulfilled in an analogous experience of a higher order]; even that experience of shameful treason allotted to David, the typical Mashiah, must finally, in accordance with divine judgment, be fulfilled in that highest imaginable treason of Judas to the real Messiah. The choice of the passage was likewise suggested by the meal.—**He hath (already) lifted up his heel against me.***—The figure represents a fellow who, having turned his back, makes off with a sudden act of cunning and brutal malice; it cannot be expressive of the throwing of the foot under in wrestling [πτερνίζειν]. We need not enlarge upon the truth that the prophecy of the Scripture is in this instance as little proclamatory of a fatalistic destiny as in similar cases, since the prophecy should be regarded as the ideal consequence of the facts, although it does historically precede them.

Ver. 19. **From henceforth I tell you** [ἀπ' ἄρτι, now, from this time], *etc.*—He intimates that He will tell them repeatedly, and gives His reason for so doing.—**That I am he** [ὅτι ἐγώ εἰμι] has here more of explicitness than chap. viii. 24, to which Tholuck refers. The very Person is meant to whom that passage in the Psalms typically points. When the treachery of Judas stalked forth in all its horridness, the disciples (whose faith might have been shaken by the success of that treachery, Meyer) stood in special need of comfort; this was afforded them when they contemplated the fulfilled word and sentence of God.†

Ver. 20. **He that receiveth whomsoever,** *etc.*—Comp. Matt. x. 40. The original fitness of the saying in this place is confirmed by the preceding: **verily, verily** (notwithstanding that Kuinoel and Lücke consider the words as a gloss derived from Matthew, and that Lampe [Hengstenberg] and others annex them to ver. 16). The connection is resident in the fact that Jesus intends to contrast the future glory of His faithful ones with the picture of the miserable traitor, for the consolation and comfort of those (Melanchthon and others), and for a mirror to the traitor; in connection with the antithesis between those whom He has historically chosen and those, from among these historically chosen ones, whom He will send in the might of the Spirit (between disciples and apostles). They shall be endued with such dignity, they shall communicate such blessing, as though He came Himself; nay, as though, mediately through Him, God Himself came. This dignity is still more powerfully represented in its spiritual ex-

* [Meyer emphasizes ἐγώ, *I for my part*, in distinction from the *divine* intention (ἀλλ ἵνα), which required that Judas should be included among the chosen. Similarly Alford, who thus states the connection: It might be supposed that this treachery has come upon Me unawares; but it is not so: I know whom I have selected (*viz.*, the whole twelve, vi. 70, not only eleven, as Stier, with reference to xv. 16 assumes): but this has been done by the determinate counsel and foreknowledge of God, declared in the Scriptures.—P. S.]

† [Most commentators supply τοῦτο γέγονε after ἀλλά. Meyer, on the contrary, supplies ἐξελεξάμην αὐτούς: *aber ich habe die Auswahl im Dienste des göttlichen Verhängnisses vollzogen, nach welchem die Schrift erfüllt werden musste.* This sounds rather fatalistic, as Lange charges.—P. S.]

‡ [Cod. ℵ. A. D. Vulg. read: ὁ τρώγων μετ' ἐμοῦ τὸν ἄρτον, B. C. L.: μου τὸν ἄρτον. The Hebrew: אוֹכֵל לַחְמִי; the Sept.: ἄρτους μου; the Vulg.: *panes meos.* Wordsworth falsely refers this to the eating of the sacramental bread. This would be incompatible with the reading μετ' ἐμοῦ, and besides Judas left before the institution of the Eucharist (see below). Augustine says: The eleven disciples ate the Lord who is the bread (*panem Dominum*), Judas the bread of the Lord (*panem Domini*).—P. S.]

* [The præter. ἐπῆρεν (from ἐπαίρω, *to lift up*, the figure being taken from a vicious horse kicking from behind), represents the treason of Judas as an accomplished act. Instead of ἐπῆρεν ἐπ' ἐμὲ τὴν πτέρναν αὐτοῦ, the Sept. reads less expressively: ἐμεγάλυνεν ἐπ' ἐμὲ πτερνισμόν, and the Vulg.: *magnificavit super me supplantationem.* Bengel remarks: *Congruit hic sermo imprimis ad lotionem* PEDUM, *et ad morem veterum discumbentium ad* PANEM *edendum.*—P. S.]

† [As Meyer well expresses it: *Durch die Vorhersagung wird, was* ZWEIFELS*grund hütte werden können,* GLAUBENS*grund.*—P. S.]

altedness by being portrayed in the light of the receivers of apostles, *i. e.* of the faithful. By means of them Christ shall appear, God shall be made manifest, throughout the world. And thus the contrast between treason and apostolic worth is also expressed (Hilgenfeld, see Acts ii. 17, 18). According to Calvin Christ means to say: the wickedness of some few who are guilty of unworthy conduct in the apostolic office does not impair the dignity of that office—a conclusion which results but indirectly from this passage and which is but conditionally correct; according to Zwingle, He designs to dissuade the others from imitating the apostasy of Judas;—but of their eventual fidelity He was assured (see ver. 10). [Alford: The saying sets forth the dignity of that office from which Judas was about to fall; and the consideration of this dignity, as contrasted with the sad announcement just to be made, leads on to the ἐταράχθη τῷ πν. of the next verse. Meyer connects ver. 20 with ἵνα πιστεύσητε, ver. 19, *i. e.* to confirm you in this faith, I say to you, etc.—P. S.]

Ver. 21. **One of you will betray me.**—On the relation of John to the Synoptists comp. *Comm. on Matthew* [p. 469 Am. Ed.]; Tholuck, p. 347. In the 21st verse we find the first intimation of the Lord's Supper, together with the beginning of the history relative to the disclosure of the betrayer. Comp. Matt. xxvi. 21. That the conflict here undergone by Jesus [ἐταράχθη τῷ πνεύματι, comp. ch. xi. 33; xii. 27] extended far deeper than that recorded John xi. 33, and that it was not merely "physical compassion," results from the fact that He is here represented not as being stirred up in spirit so that He troubles Himself outwardly, but as being troubled in the spirit itself. The inmost life of His human spirit was invaded by horror at the unprecedented fact of His approaching and imminent betrayal; the sight of the crafty one and of his connection with the circle of disciples, most of whom were without suspicion of his guilt and had trusted implicitly to his fidelity, tempted Him to despise the whole race of mankind and tended to produce in Him an exasperation of spirit which He must summon all His energies to resist. His victory was comprised in the open proclamation, characterized by John both as a testimony and a declaration [ἐμαρτύρησεν καὶ εἶπεν]: *One of you will betray Me.* Strong emphasis is placed, in the first instance, upon the "*one of you.*" The Lord must bring into view the entire accompliceship of the disciples simultaneously with the immeasurable iniquity of the disciple. Such is His object; the saying may not be regarded as barely expressive of "His grief-stirred soul." The horror of spirit from which Christ here frees Himself can not be lightly compared with an emotion of grief having its seat in the soul.

Ver. 22. **Then the disciples looked one on another,** *etc.*—See the Synoptists: they were troubled. They inquire of each other and of the Lord, saying: surely it is not I?

Ver. 23. **On Jesus' bosom** [ἐν τῷ κόλπῳ τοῦ Ἰησοῦ].—Κόλπος, the bellying of the garment over the girdle [Luke vi. 38; Pliny, *Ep.* iv. 22], the bosom, the lap; ethically defined, the breast. They reclined [on divans or couches] in a half sitting posture, facing the low table, the left elbow resting upon the pillow, the feet outward [behind], and the right hand free. So that the person who sat to the right of another seemed to lean upon his breast. (Hardly, however, in accordance with Lightfoot [p. 1095 s. v.] and others, did "the back of his head come into contact with His breast," because in that case the other would have been unable to reach the table with his right hand). The purposed omission of the name proves this person spoken of to have been John; comp. ch. xix. 26; xx. 2; xxi. 7, 20. The traditional name of John: ὁ ἐπιστήθιος. See the Introduction.—**Whom Jesus loved.** In a special sense; hence designative of friendship. Here for the first time do we meet with this ["nameless and yet so expressive"] self-designation, induced by "the hallowed moment, never to be forgotten by him." [Words of Meyer *in loc.* Bengel: "*Optabilius est amari ab Jesu, quam nomine proprio celebrari. Est tamen hoc loco notatio ipsius nominis proprii* (*uti Luc. ii.* 11; *Apoc.* i. 1)." Besides Bengel, Hengstenberg also and Godet discover in the designation ὃν ἠγάπα ὁ Ἰησοῦς a periphrase of the name of John="Jehovah is merciful," *Gotthold.* Godet adds (II. 446) that for this reason Jesus gave to John no new name, as He did to Peter, being content to sanction the significant name which involved as it were a prophecy of his relation to Jesus. Meyer objects on the ground that Ἰησοῦς is used, not κύριος. But see ch. xii. 41.—P. S.]

Ver. 24. **Simon Peter, therefore, beckoneth to this man.**—They were, then, not sitting by each other. The reading: "*and saith unto Him: Say, who is it of whom He speaketh?*" (see the TEXTUAL NOTES) is to be preferred; insomuch the more since it is more vividly characteristic of Peter. Peter, with his usual impetuosity, presupposes that John already knows. And, without doubt, John had a distinct presentiment of the facts of the case, without, however, allowing himself prematurely to declare his suspicion. See ch. vi. 70. The whole disturbance among the disciples is indicative of an anxious whispering, murmuring, or speaking in an under-tone. In this and similar traits, Baur and others pretended to discover an indication of the intention of giving Peter an inferior position in comparison with John; whereupon, see Meyer [p. 493, foot-note]. It is the perverted fancy of a humanly cunning, egotistical pragmatism that seeks to foist the like base motives of its own invention upon every passage of the Holy Scriptures.

Ver. 25. **Leaning back on the bosom of Jesus.**—Illustrative. Indicative of a low and familiar questioning. [John, who was before reclining on the *bosom* (ἐν τῷ κόλπῳ, ver. 23) of Jesus, now moved his head more closely to His *breast* (ἐπὶ τὸ στῆθος) and whispered the question into His ear; ἐπιπεσών, *having fallen upon, thrown himself upon,* is better supported than ἀναπεσών (although ἀναπίπτω is the usual verb for reclining at table, see notes in Tischend. ed. 8th), and indicates a lively movement corresponding to the excited state of feeling.—P. S.].

Ver. 26. **He it is to whom I shall give the sop.**—*I. e.* whose turn it is that I should give him the morsel. In the first place, we must remove the prejudice denying that the paschal meal is here spoken of; such, for instance, is

Meyer's view. Then the question arises as to what moment of the paschal meal is intended. As regards the order of the Passover (see *Comm. on Matthew*, p. 469, *etc.*), it is a question whether we are to understand by the *morsel* [τὸ ψωμίον] presented, a morsel of the bitter herbs which were partaken of after the first cup, or the morsel of blessed bread distributed by the householder subsequently to the second cup. According to Tholuck, a sop of the bitter herbs wrapped together might also be called *ψωμίον*. Contradictory to this, however, is the fact that the herbs were not handed round, but that several dipped in the dish at the same time. On account of this latter circumstance Tholuck opines that the ὁ ἐμβάψας in Matthew, spoken with reference to Judas, cannot be conceived to apply to anything but the herbs. But doubtless a weightier meaning attaches to the trait that Judas dipped his hand also into the dish. According to Matthew, Jesus says: *he that dippeth his hand with Me in the dish;* similarly Mark; according to Luke, to whom we owe the greatest number of psychological traits, He even exclaims: *But lo! the hand of My betrayer is with Me on the table.* Hence we persist in regarding this trait—*viz.*, that Judas thrust his hand into the dish simultaneously with the Lord—as an arbitrary movement of his hand in violation of the rite, by which movement his evil conscience betrayed itself (see *Comm. on Mark*, p. 140, Am. Ed.) Hence, too, the token in the Synoptists coincides perfectly with the token in John. It was the presentation of the morsel of bread subsequently to the second cup.

Three things are now conceivable:

First supposition. That Judas received the consecrated bread and, shortly after, the consecrated cup likewise. This, however, is flatly contradicted by the account of John. After the sop Satan entered into him and he went out into the night. It is simply inconceivable that the presentation of the cup took place prior to this movement of Judas; irrespective of the consideration that John would have mentioned such an item. This statement is not invalidated by the different sequence which Luke, in conformity to his view of the facts, observes, if we only rightly understand the construction of Luke. It is doubtless to be apprehended thus. He designs, in the first place, Luke xxii. 15-20, to set before us a picture of the sacred transaction, inclusive of *the celebration of the Passover as well as the Lord's Supper.* Then he reverts to the Lord's dealings with individual disciples on this occasion (vers. 21-38)—and, again, not chronologically, for he first disposes of the betrayer, then recounts the contention of the disciples relative to their respective ranks and, finally, relates the warning of Simon. The story proceeds in its order from the worst disciple to the one of most repute, him who after his conversion is to strengthen his brethren. The account of Matthew and Mark makes the institution of the Lord's Supper succeed the putting aside of the traitor.

Second supposition. Judas did not receive the cup, but he did receive the consecrated bread. It is true that Luke is not here to be taken into consideration in respect of chronology; but John speaks of a sop dispensed by Christ. However, not only are Matthew and Mark against the view now under examination,—albeit simply by giving the precedence to the positive unmasking of the traitor,—but also John, inasmuch as it is not until after the purification of the circle of disciples by the withdrawal of Judas, that he pictures the Lord as yielding Himself up, in entire trustfulness, to communion with the disciples.

Third supposition. Judas did not participate at all in the Lord's Supper. In favor of this: *a.* the destination of the love-feast, to purify the circle of disciples; *b.* the great contrast made by John between the celebration prior to the departure of Judas and after it; *c.* the account of Matthew and Mark. But hence it will result that, after the distribution of the paschal loaf, when Jesus handed Judas the bread with the words: *this is the bread of affliction, etc.*, and after which Judas withdrew, Jesus paused in order then to begin the distribution of the bread for His Supper. It would even be conceivable that Judas was the first and last who received the morsel of the paschal loaf as such: the bread of affliction.

Give the sop when I have dipped it.—According to Meyer, this act was merely a sign for John, whose query was prompted not by curiosity but by affection. Taking this view of the matter, the act would certainly be a somewhat surprising one,—and thanks for an elucidation of the moment are due to the harmony of the Evangelists. Judas, in imitation of the other disciples, asked, at about this time: *is it I?* and Jesus answered him: *thou sayest it.* We are doubtless to conceive of the words: *he it is*, as spoken in a tone sufficiently loud for Judas to hear them;—the betrayer must have sat near Christ since his hand reached the dish. Then, upon his shameless question, followed the direct announcement of Jesus. (On Strauss' preference of Luke, and Weisse's of Mark, see Meyer [p. 494]. Weisse psychologically maltreats the entire narrative of John as a fiction growing out of ver. 18).

Ver. 27. **And after the sop.**—That is, after the reception of the same, he took his resolve,—made up his mind—τότε. [*Then, at that moment;* marking with graphic power and pathos the horrible moment of Satan's entering into the heart of the traitor and taking full possession of him. When Satan entered *into* Judas, εἰσῆλθεν, Judas went *out*, ἐξῆλθεν, from the company of Christ into the darkness of crime and despair.—P. S.] John specifies three periods in the development of the iniquity of Judas; these may be severally designated as the period of the treacherous bent or disposition of mind (ch. vi. 70); as the period of the thought of betrayal (ch. xiii. 2; comp. ch. xii. 1, *etc.*); and as the period of the resolve of betrayal (in this place). He now resigned his will entirely to the will of Satan, becoming the devil's slavish tool. Meyer disputes the interpretation of Theodore of Mopsueste who holds that the consummate hardening of Judas is meant [τὴν κύρωσιν τῶν καταθυμίων τῷ διαβόλῳ λογισμῶν]. But what other designation could the ethical side of the present transaction possibly receive? The only thing is, that the expression is not sufficiently strong for the historical import of the moment; in respect of that, he became the complete tool of the enemy of Christ in the midst of a posture of affairs the like of which was never seen again. The confounding of the condition of Judas with the state of actual demoniacs (Meyer) must, however, not be ascribed to John. Neither should too great stress be laid upon the distinction of Bengel: *post offulam, non cum offula;* as if the matter of the greatest importance were to guard against the imputation of a magical effect to the sop. In this connection Tholuck remarks that he far rather became an organ of Satan "in consequence of perceiving that he was known and therewith (with the bestowal of the sop) branded." Notwithstanding all this, his hardening did accompany his reception of Christ's last token of love; it was of course no *magical* result, but an *ethical* one. Thus unworthy communicants eat and drink judgment—condemnation—to themselves, and perfect hardening can, as a general thing, take place only in connection with the full operation of the gospel. The unmasking of the traitor was so gentle, so gradual as to allow time enough for repentance; the branding was accomplished by Judas himself, when he arose after the sop and went out. Even at the words: *What thou wilt do, do quickly*, most of the disciples were ignorant as to how matters stood with him.

What thou doest (wouldest do, art about to do), do quickly [*ὁ ποιεῖς, ποίησον τάχιον, lit.*, **more quickly, right soon**].—Ποιεῖς, art on the point of doing. See ver. 6. The comparative [*τάχιον*] is not only augmentative in reference to the time, but also mitigative in reference to the command.* Thou art already doing it, without any word of Mine; and so be quick about it, and not so lurkingly slow. In point of fact this saying is declaratory of the true expression for the divine judgment of obduracy, in the whole world and to all time. The command in all these judgments is never: do quickly what thou art not yet intending to do, but invariably: *what thou wilt do*, what thou hast already begun to do, do *more speedily*. Those who have really resolved upon evil are, by such circumstances as God has ordained, driven to their goal as in a storm;—and there is a holy reason for this: 1. It is the final attempt at deliverance; if a single spark of resisting power remain, it may be kindled under the pressure of outward decision, whilst it will assuredly expire if a more lingering course be pursued. 2. It is the vital law of what is holy to purify itself, by a crisis, from admixture with such elements of obduracy. 3. The later judgment is, the more fatal it is; although in this case it was fatal enough already. 4. The freedom of divine providence is therein manifested; it knows itself to be in no wise jeopardized by such acts of rebellion.

Therefore the imperative is undoubtedly not permissive in this passage (Grotius and others). And therefore, also, we must likewise take into consideration as a motive the desire of Jesus to be freed from the irksome proximity of the traitor (Ambrose, Lücke). We can not overlook the fact that Jesus invokes the decision for His own sake also (not simply, however, in order that He might accomplish His ὥρα).

But the main consideration for the Lord is the independent purpose which the departing of Judas is designed to accomplish, *viz.:* 1. His holy separation from the wicked one, in the form of a voluntary self-destination on the part of the latter; 2. the purification of the circle of disciples from the dangerous and infective member; 3. the restoration of a confidential circle in which He may open His whole heart. Tholuck: "Now such a reason for desiring his departure is contained in the necessity for expressing before the circle of disciples the feelings that have been awakened in Him by that decision. It is the wondrous prerogative of Supreme Causality to celebrate the loftiest triumphs over the very blackest of individual deeds, in that these, entering into that objective connection which worldly events sustain to each other, issue in something entirely at variance with the end that they were humanly designed to accomplish, Acts iv. 27. But this triumph over evil that is to be converted into a means of good, cannot be expressed in presence of the evil-doer himself, previous to the performance of his deed, without, by such expression, assuming for the evil-doer the character of a solicitation to evil. Rom. iii. 7."

[I add the explanation of Alford on this difficult passage, who agrees substantially with Meyer: "These words are not to be evaded, as being *permissive* (Grotius), or *dismissive* (Chrysostom). They are alike the sayings of God to Balaam, Num. xxii. 20, and of our Lord to the Pharisees, Matt. xxiii. 32. The *course of sinful action is presupposed*, and the command to go on is but the echo of that mysterious appointment by which the sinner in the exercise of his own corrupted will becomes the instrument of the purposes of God. Thus it is not, ὅ, or εἴ τι, ποιήσεις, but ὃ ποιεῖς—'*that which thou art doing*, hast just now fully determined to put in present action, *do more quickly* than thou seemest willing,'—or perhaps better, 'than thou wouldst otherwise have done.'"—Godet: "*La parole de Jésus à Judas n'est point une simple permission; c'est un ordre. On a réproché à Jésus d'avoir poussé Judas dans l'abîme, en lui parlant de la sorte. Mais Jésus ne le ménage plus, précisément parce qu'il n'y a plus de retour possible pour lui.*"—P. S.]

Ver. 28. **Now no one of those reclining at the table understood,** *etc.*—Preceding observations show that John tacitly excepts himself (Bengel and others). He also qualifies this verse by ver. 29. It was at least impossible for him to share the following conjectures. But his remark proves that even now the circle of disciples as a body did not definitely regard Judas as the traitor.

Ver. 29. [**Because Judas kept the purse.** See note on ch. xii. 6].* **What we have need of for the feast.**—Judas was cashier. Meyer observes: "No necessaries for the feast,

* [Meyer: "The comparative expresses the idea: *hasten your deed.* So often θᾶσσον in Homer."—P. S.]

* [Wordsworth (after Augustine) makes here the practical remark: "Here is the primitive form of a church fund, and thence we learn that when Christ commanded us not to be careful about to-morrow, He did not forbid us to possess money, but He forbade us to serve God in the hope of gaining it, or to forsake righteousness for fear of losing it."—P. S.]

therefore, had as yet been purchased." But it was hardly customary for people to buy necessaries for the eight days' feast *all at once.* This trait, generally cited in favor of the view which defers the beginning of the paschal feast until the evening of the following day, is in reality most decidedly opposed to it (see *Matthew*). No one could pitch upon the idea that the command: *Make haste*, had reference to the making of purchases, if the whole of the next day might be thus employed. So also Tholuck, p. 351. But it is hardly to be supposed that the close of this feast was not until "the tenth hour of the evening." The foot-washing had commenced before six o'clock and the distribution of bread after the second cup occurred about in the beginning of the feast. "And as regards the legal permission to make purchases after the beginning of a feast, we will confine ourselves to the mention of what follows: That the killing, baking and cooking of food for the feast was allowed on the 15th of Nisan is proved by Ex. xii. 16,—to which passage no exceptions are made even by Rabbinical expounders (Jarchi, Aben Ezra, particularly R. Levi); moreover, according to Luke xxiii. 56, purchases were also made; nay, even on the Sabbath, which was still more strictly observed than the feast days, not only almsgiving, but also the making of purchases, upon certain conditions (as for instance, buying on pledge), was permitted (*tr. Schabbat*)." Tholuck. —**Or, that he should give something to the poor.**—Special aid was afforded to the poor in the way of assisting them to procure necessities for the feast.

Ver. 30. **He, then, having received the sop, went out immediately** [ἐξῆλθεν, comp. the εἰσῆλθεν, ver. 27].—The fact of Judas' immediate departure is brought out by John, as though with the view of precluding any misunderstanding; hence it is impossible to suppose that the former participated further in the festive meal. The circumstance is likewise expressive of the full decision of the traitor.

But it was night [ἦν δὲ νύξ].—The *but* is indicative of an antithesis. It was, indeed, rather late to buy provisions for the feast or to give alms to the poor; night had stolen unobserved upon the deeply agitated circle; but still another truth is intimated; viz. that Judas went out into a spiritual night to accomplish the work of darkness. See chap. xii. 35; Luke xxii. 53. [So also Origen, Olshausen, Stier, *etc.* There is certainly something awful in this termination, and its brevity makes it all the more impressive (Meyer). The event had so deeply engraven itself on the mind of John that he remembered the hour. Similar indications of his retentive memory see in chs. i. 40; vi. 59; viii. 20; x. 23. The "night" does not imply that Judas was present at the Lord's Supper (Wordsworth); the contrary may be inferred from ἀγόρασον, ver. 29. The institution of the eucharist took place *after* ver. 30. See note on ver. 26, and Meyer, p. 500. This is now pretty generally admitted among the best commentators. The presence of the traitor would have most seriously disturbed that holy feast of love, and would cut off the right of discipline and excommunication so necessary for the purity and dignity of Christ's church.—P. S.]

DOCTRINAL AND ETHICAL.

1. Love to His own was the motive for the adherence of Jesus to His nation until death, even after that nation had rejected Him. This fundamental motive is at the same time explained by the second and secondary one,—His faithfulness to the law, which made Him at the appointed time keep the paschal feast in Jerusalem. The great difficulties occasioned by the beginning of the 13th chapter are particularly induced by the insertion of the Evangelist's closing reflections, contained in chap. xii. 37-50, in the midst of the grand antithesis contemplated by him. Now this is the form of said antithesis: Jesus, after having spoken His last words of exhortation to the people, departed and hid Himself from them (chap. xii. 37). *But before the feast of the passover He issued forth again* (albeit not amongst the people); *warned by a consciousness that the great hour was come when He should go home to the Father, and impelled by His love to His own whom He left in the world, He gave these a sign of His love, namely His death; by this at once attaining to His own consummation in love and to His end by love.* On the relation of the love-feast, which He celebrates with the disciples, to the passover of the Synoptists, see the introductory note.

2. From the demands of custom as well as from indications in Luke, it results that the FOOT-WASHING was no mere symbol, manufactured by the Lord, but a symbolical example shaped by the force of circumstances. See the closing note to ver. 5. As a symbolical example it can not be a sacrament; it may well be, however, the introduction to a sacrament, that is, to the Lord's Supper. The fulfilment of the foot-washing appears again in a truly evangelic discipline, preparation, and confessional ordinance as a solemnity to be observed previous to the Lord's Supper. This is demonstrated by the fact that Christ, by His foot-washing and love-feast, separated Judas from the communion of the disciples, without employment of legal compulsion, and also instructed the disciples themselves relative to their spiritual standing and reproved them, with a view to purifying, warning and arming them. See ver. 22. But the symbol of the ecclesiastical ordinance is at the same time expressive, as an ethical example, of the two fundamental requisites of Christian sanctification: 1. We should be ready to have our feet washed by the brethren in the name of the Lord,—to accept reproof, instruction, correction from them; 2. we should be ready, as circumstances may require, to perform this service of love in all humility for the brethren. To this must be added, however, the maxim that should be our guide: that the latter, rightly exercised and practised, is still more an act of self-denying love and humility than the former.

3. The washing of the feet, to be effectual, must have been preceded by a *bathing of the entire body, i. e.* baptismal grace and the substantiation and moral actualization of baptism, as the theocratico-social regeneration, in PERSONAL REGENERATION. The disciples in general were benefited by the foot-washing, while in the case of Judas it accelerated the judgment of obduracy.

4. Not only did Christ draw forth the New Testament Flower of the Lord's Supper from the covering which enwrapped it, but He likewise metamorphosed the covering itself—the Passover—into something in keeping with the New Testament by transfiguring it to the CHRISTIAN AGAPE. The discontinuance of the Agape in the Church is productive of a heavy loss of blessing; a loss which, at the utmost need, does but begin to be supplied by Christian union festivals. Still less are our charitable institutions the full and lively expression of that brotherly fellowship in life which is shared by differing Christian ranks.

5. The two great antitheses: Christ, already parted from the world, is drawn back into the world by love to His own, in order that He may give them a last proof of His love, which proof grows into that exhibited in His death itself; Christ, entertaining the presentiment of His omnipotence and confronting disciples within whose circle there nestles, in the person of the betrayer, the canker-worm of Satanic treason, washes the disciples' feet.—Jesus, girded for the foot-washing and washing those feet that have already hastened to the Pharisees to shed His blood, a living warning against those who fancy that they have established a Church, whether Novatian or Donatistic in its form, within whose pale none but saints are found.—The foot-washing the presage of His humiliation unto the death on the cross (Hilgenfeld).

6. Yet the washing of feet, conducted with the holy and startling earnestness employed by Him towards this circle, is, in an equal degree, the living archetype for the spirit in which the sanctuary should be cleansed, and the Christian communion protected by an evangelically severe and free discipline, dealing not in legal thunders, but endued with power to make men quake.

7. THE PORTRAIT OF JUDAS. The stages of his growing obduracy John delineates with a master-hand. See note to ver. 27.

8. THE PICTURE OF THE DISCIPLES. The fact of their not perceiving that Judas was the traitor, even when the end was near, is a proof of the strength of the prejudice entertained by them in favor of his talents and his promising deportment. (See the history of the anointing in the Synoptists; Com. on *Matthew*, p. 463, Am. Ed.)

9. THE PORTRAIT OF PETER. *Before the Lord's Supper.* Piety, love to the Lord, heroic humor, are traits not to be mistaken, but self-will, dictatorialness, eccentricity are likewise unmistakable; self-exaltation, proud modesty that would fain pass for humility. *After the Lord's Supper.* Over-estimation of his spiritual strength, of his joyfulness in confession and death. In both cases a stiff-necked inclination to refuse the full obedience of faith to Christ's words "in order that he may have his say." In this respect also Peter, before his conversion, was symbolical. He repeatedly needed the sternest threats of the Lord and yet he came to himself only when the cock (*gallus*) proclaimed most fearful judgment upon him. Three times did he deny before the cock crowed.

10. THE PORTRAIT OF JOHN, the friend of Jesus: 1. *He reposed on His breast;* 2. not a word, not a gesture, not a mood of the Heavenly Friend escaped him; 3. *he shared* with Him the deep emotions of His soul in grief and horror at evil, in the anticipation of glory; *he saw in His light.*

11. The position of the LORD'S SUPPER in our chapter. See note to ver. 26. On the different hypotheses see Meyer [p. 500 f.]; Paulus and others, after ver. 30; Lücke and others, between vers. 33, 34; Neander and others, after ver. 32; Olshausen, after ver. 38; Sieffert, before the foot-washing; Bengel, Kern, Wichelhaus, after chap. xiv. 31. (These assume Jesus to have at that time just set out for Jerusalem, in order to celebrate the paschal meal.) Meyer: At all events not until after the departure of Judas. See the next Section, ver. 34.

12. On the question as to *whether Judas participated in the Lord's Supper,* see note to ver. 26; Comm. on *Matthew*, chap. xxvi.—Tholuck: "Unquestionably the ancient Church in general conceived of the ψωμίον (Vulg.: *panis*) as the sacramental bread; this view was likewise entertained by the Lutheran Church. The *Form. Conc. Art.* vii. alleges the example of Judas as a precedent for the partaking of the body and blood of Christ by *unbelievers.* That view is at present, however, generally abandoned;—even by Kahnis, *Abendmahl*, p. 10. Comp. the historical part in Bynäus, *De morte Christi*, I. p. 344 f." Comp. Wichelhaus, *Leidensgeschichte*, p. 256 ff.

13. "*What thou doest, do quickly.*" The true formula of the judgment of impenitence. See note to conclusion of ver. 27.

HOMILETICAL AND PRACTICAL.

How the love of Christ to His own in the world decided Him to issue forth from His concealment upon the path of suffering.—How He transformed the paschal feast into a love-feast.—The Passover, as a feast of triumph over the darkness of Egypt, changed into a feast of triumph over the Prince of darkness and his tool.—How, with the revelation of His love at His last love-feast, the Lord accomplished in spirit the journey of His life.—After the example of Christ to depart blessing others.—The beginning of a threefold celebration of love on Christ's part: 1. The passover and love-feast as a feast of parting and death; 2. the Supper as a feast of reconciliation and life; 3. the farewell-discourses as a feast of spirit and knowledge.—The manifestation of Christ's love to His own at the last repast: 1. *The perfect faithfulness* and *devotion* of His love: the return of the defunct Prophet to life, that He may suffer (the transition from the Prophetic to the High-priestly Work. "Until the end"). 2. *The profound humility* of His love (the Foot-washing). 3. *The severity and divine decision* of His love (towards Peter). 4. *The masterhood and animating power* of His love (an example for the disciples). 5. *The fondness* of His love (John, the confidential communication). 6. *The holiness* of His love (the grief and horror excited in Him by Judas; the separation of the latter through the power of the Spirit).—The Foot-washing: 1. as an instructive custom (hospitality); 2. as a beginning of the redemptive self-humiliation of Christ (the Father of the family discharges a slave's office);

3, as an ecclesiastical symbol (preparation or confession); 4. as an example for the Christian life (to suffer one's own feet to be washed; to wash the feet of others).—The purification of the circle of disciples by the foot-washing: 1. The shaming of the whole body of disciples. 2. The correction of Peter. 3. The separation of Judas.—How confidently Christ knew His hour: 1. The hour of glorious home-going as the hour of painful departure. 2. The hour of His death-journey as the hour of His exode to the Father.—The picture of Jesus, girded in readiness to serve as a slave in the circle of disciples: 1. How gracious, free, brisk and serene: a picture of *free* love. 2. What a contrast to His heavenly glory: a picture of the *humblest* love. 3. How entirely expressive of His holy feeling: a picture of *saving* and *awakening* love.—Heaven and hell arrayed against each other for spiritual combat at the paschal meal: 1. The lineaments of hell in the conduct of Judas (reserve, subtleness, gloom, hate, rebellion, despair; which things are one with Satan, the murderer of mankind, the murderer of Christ). 2. The lineaments of heaven in the conduct of Jesus (openness, faithfulness, brightness, love, humility, peace; which things are one with God, the Saviour of mankind, filled with grief and horror at the traitor himself).—The wonderful self-denial in the foot-washing of the Lord: 1. the Master washes the disciples' feet; 2. the Heir of omnipotence performs this service for a circle harboring the betrayer.—Peter's self-will: 1. In his refusal; 2. in his compliance.—Return of these characteristics of Peter's in ecclesiastical time.—The stern word of the Lord to Peter (ver. 8): 1. In its literal sense, or the necessity of obedience; 2. in its figurative sense, or the necessity of sanctification.—How Christ in dealing with Peter, who in his self-will is desirous of laying down the law, gives a legal expression to His Gospel itself.—As the eye of Christ once pierced through His circle of disciples, so His penetrating glance scans His whole Church for evermore. (The Lord knoweth His own.)—The example of Jesus: 1. Wherein appearing; 2. how authoritative (as a law of life for the disciples); 3. of what exclusive (clerical pride, hierarchicalness, an undisciplined condition of His Church); 4. what it requires (humility to perform the heaviest services of love; alacrity in accepting them).—Vers. 16, 17. See above.—It is easier to set forth Christianity symbolically and ecclesiastically, than to practise it morally and humanely.—True symbols should be changed into real life; not life itself into arbitrarily manufactured symbols.—The heavenly wisdom of Christ; how it unites the most careful forbearance with the holiest openness in the gradual unveiling of the traitor.—The word of Scripture concerning the traitor, the everlasting label, the brand of all traitorous ingratitude—especially in unbelief or apostasy from Christ, or from evangelic truth.—The startling contrast between the figure of Judas and the glorious destiny and dignity of the apostles (vers. 19, 20).—The lofty signification of the expression: "Jesus was troubled in spirit;" or how Jesus then, in the midst of the circle of disciples, victoriously fought out His spiritual combat with Satan: 1. The temptation of the evil spirit to scorn of mankind, hatred of mankind, doubt as to the healableness of the human heart, as to God's ruling hand. 2. The victory: A victory of the God-filled *Son of Man* over the Satan-ruled hireling of the legal hierarchy: a victory of trust over despair, of humility over pride, of love over hate, of life over death. 3. The circumstances; this conflict not distinctly known to the disciples, yet felt by them with grisly discomfort.—So it is with the spiritual conflict that Christ carries on His church with Satanic spirits.—The fearful but deserved excitement of the circle of disciples at the awful disclosure of Christ.—At the revelation of the enemy of Jesus, it is the disciple's duty and honor to call himself Jesus' friend (ver. 23).—The sop, a type and expression of the opposite effects of the Gospel.—The presentation of the sop a final, unavailing warning to the conscience of Judas: 1. The final one: *a.* Had there been a spark of honesty in him, he would now have confessed. *b.* Had there been a spark of repentance in him, he would not have tasted the sop amidst these signs. 2. Unavailing: *a.* By the sign that it was he, he became thoroughly exasperated to hatred and turned the bit of blessing into a serpent's bite. *b.* He still continued his falsehood and hypocrisy before the circle of disciples after being unmasked before the eyes of Jesus and the nearest witnesses.—"What thou doest," *etc.* See above. The reserve of Judas a fundamental feature of his ruin. Reserve and pious reticence (see the conduct of John in antithesis to the conduct of Judas): 1. The former shuts his heart to heaven and opens it to hell. 2. The other shuts his heart to the world and hell, and keeps it open for the Lord and His people.—The decision of the wicked a laceration of the inmost life.—The going of Judas out into the night. 1. Into the beginning night. (His sun of peace has set upon him.) 2. Into the midnight. (The fellowship of the wicked awaits him for the work of darkness.) 3. Into eternal night. (Endless despair.)

STARKE: ZEISIUS: The death of the faithful is a going out of the world to the heavenly Father.—The spiritual birth of believers is *of* God, their life *in accordance with* God, their departure out of the world *to* God. Well is it for those who have an experimental knowledge of this and comfort themselves with the thought of it, 1 John v. 19.—A Christian shows politeness to friends and enemies, and renders loving services to both.—HEDINGER: Humility, precious possession.—See that thou come not with an unwashed, *i. e.*, impenitent heart to the table of the Lord.—ZEISIUS: Untimely humility, uncourteous courtesy, unwise wisdom, that refuses obedience to Christ.—It befitteth us always to obey Jesus; but always to know why this or that is done is no part of ours: neither doth it behoove us to wish to know all.—Believers do not know, in time, all of God's workings within them in the grace of sanctification, and how blessedly He is conducting them even when He seems to them to be leading them through misery,—but in a blissful eternity they shall fully know these things and gloriously praise Him.—Ver. 8. It is an abuse of good breeding to set fine manners in opposition to the ways of the kingdom of God. Christ cannot endure that. — Untimely and excessive complimenting is inconsistent with Christianity.—We must tell even our good friends of their faults, Ps. cxli. 5.—Happy is he who here accepts reproof for his sins.—Ver. 9. HEDINGER: Exercises in humility, originating in our own heads, are worthless, like all other self-chosen works.—We must not lay down rules to God in any particular.—Ver. 10. We are, in truth, all washed, but not all clean. The visible Church is, and will continue to be, a mixed mass.—If Christ washed the feet of Judas, His betrayer, oughtest not thou likewise to love thine enemy and do him good? Matt. v. 44.—Many a man has an enemy in his household, and is ignorant of the same.—OSIANDER: Those who preserve the intention of sinning are not clean in the sight of God.—Ver. 15. Pastors and preachers must be exemplars for their flocks.—Ver. 16. Let our earthly rank be high or low, we are but servants of Jesus, and hence may not refrain from rendering every loving service that has need of us, 1 Pet. ii. 16, 17.—QUESNEL: The bare knowledge of God's commandments avails men nothing, but only causes them to be judged the more rigorously.—Ver. 18. The making of bad distinctions is sinful, but the making of good distinctions is Christian.—CANSTEIN: The fulfilment of divine prophecies a grand corroboration of our faith.—OSIANDER: O shameful ingratitude!—That the good are often so shamefully rewarded for many benefits.—Ver. 19. HEDINGER: Time opens many truths, as in temporal, so in divine mysteries.—Ver. 20. Wherein the reception of a servant of God consists.—CANSTEIN: Righteous servants of the divine Word may derive strong consolation from a contemplation of the lofty dignity of their office, and may, by such contemplation, arouse their souls to action.—QUESNEL: The union of Christ with His members is so complete that He receives the good done to them.—Consolation for faithful servants of God,—that some do good to them, even permitting their ministry to be fruitful in them.—HEDINGER: The righteous are not at a loss for signs of the common destruction of a church as well as of the hastening of a soul to ruin.—ZEISIUS: If Christ was so bitterly distressed in spirit at the devilish wickedness of Judas, how is it possible that God should be the cause of the sin and damnation of a single man?—ZEISIUS: Christ did not make His betrayer known at once; He knocked at his soul ever and anon to incite him to repentance.—CRAMER: Christ washed the feet of His betrayer, suffered him at the feast of the paschal lamb, Himself gave him the sop, endured his kiss in the Garden. Learn by this great and unspeakable example of the love, meekness and patience of Jesus, to love *thine* enemies also, and to recompense evil with good.—Ver. 27. HALL: The wicked spirit generally takes occasion to fall upon us with an access of zeal when we have been the recipients of some divine gift.—ZEISIUS: He who deserts God is deserted by Him in return, and he who will not be ruled by His Spirit is given over to the power of the Evil One.—No vice opens the door wider to the devil, who was the first hypocrite, than hypocrisy.—Ver. 30. Satan grants his worshippers no rest; they dare not delay to do evil.—He who withdraws from Christ, the true Light, and loses the light of grace, will assuredly fall into the thickest darkness.—QUESNEL: When the wicked man does evil in the night, the night that he bears within his own heart, is far blacker than that which he chooses for his work of darkness.

HEUBNER: Jesus always knew His time, *i. e.*, what was to be done. He even knew the time of His death.—It is a divinely illumined glance that teaches us rightly to know the time, *i. e.*, God's peculiar purpose with us at a certain time.—Jesus teaches us the duty of setting all our affairs in order before death, of bestowing every proof of love on our dear ones that it is possible for us to give.—At parting, all love's yearnings awake, even though they may have slumbered a little before.—This love, what hate, what falseness and ingratitude were opposed to it.—The nearer thou feelest thyself to God, the more humility have thou.—Spiritually He is ever thus descending and washing us clean.—Jesus' humility is an enigma to the disciples. In like manner the lowly conduct of the righteous is ofttimes surprising to the unconverted.—Ver. 8. He whom Jesus does not sanctify, has no fellowship with Him.—Ver. 9. We must learn true moderation in our zeal and obedience.—Ver. 10. They were clean in Christ; in faith in Him. Judas lacked this faith.—Ver. 13. MASTER=Whose word we believe; LORD=Whose commands we should obey.—*The foot-washing.* It is a customary rite in a few cathedral cities only; in Vienna, for instance, where, on Maundy-Thursday, the emperor washes the feet of twelve aged men. Zinzendorf reckoned it among the sacramental acts, but not among the sacraments. We do not interpret it literally.—The imitation of the act of Christ in spirit: to render services of love that are somewhat burdensome, such as nursing the sick, *etc.*—How glaringly it contrasts with Christ's act when the so-called Holy Father (the pope) suffers his foot to be kissed.—Sad incongruity between knowing and doing.—Ver. 18. Christ's word holds good with regard to many of His servants who eat His bread.—Ver. 21. None can inflict more sorrow upon the heart of Jesus than unfaithful, false disciples.—Ver. 22. The disciples were dismayed: 1. It was a grief and a shame to have such an one in the midst of them; 2. each one was reminded of the danger to his own heart; 3. they must needs stand in dread of such a sad issue to the fate of Jesus.—The most anxious condition for a pious soul: When it becomes uncertain as to its perseverance and state of grace.—It is possible that Judas perceived himself to be discovered when he took the sop and was put into a certain rage by the fact. (Be it observed that it was only at the reception of the sop, or the manner of its reception, that his decision was formed and he was designated as the traitor.)—Ver. 27. *Quod dubitas, ne feceris.* Timorous delay excites the suspicion of wrong.

GOSSNER: Ver. 8. So politeness turns to incivility.—Peter's fault consisted in his liking always to have his own way.—Ver. 9. But Peter now errs on the other side and will not be satisfied with what Jesus here purposed.—Now we want to do (or suffer) too little,—now too much.—The feet that walk upon earth are continually gathering some particles of earth, and intercourse with the world imperceptibly contracts something from the world.—Peter did not here recline next to Christ: John was nearer to the Lord. From this we see that love has the primacy in the Church of Christ. It may ask questions, and it receives answers, about things that Peter does not know of, and of which it must be the means of his hearing when he desires to know them.—*What thou doest.* Do but quickly accomplish the work of iniquity, that I also may be able perfectly to reveal the work of My grace, the wonders of My love.

GERLACH: How he (John) is always most anxious to exhibit the soul, the spiritual meaning, of things that were already sufficiently familiar to all his readers through the other Gospels and oral tradition. As he, therefore, makes no mention of the institution of holy baptism, but touches upon the internal process of regeneration whose sacrament it is (chap. iii.), so, in like manner, he is silent about the institution of the Lord's Supper, the sacrament of continual and intimate communion with the Saviour, dwelling, by preference, on a former occasion upon the partaking of His flesh and blood (chap. vi.), and now upon the invisible yet genuine union of Jesus with His disciples, and of the disciples among each other in Him.—The world wills His death, and He and the Father will it also. But now that He is dead to the world and will no more manifest Himself to it (chap. xiv. 17, *etc.*)—*i. e.* before His death—He lives entirely in His own. (Conjecture) Jesus first washed the traitor and then came to Peter.—*No part with Me.* He who does not recognize true greatness and dignity in love that humbly serves, is no disciple of Christ's. Coloss. iii. 13.—(Augustine:) He lay on the breast (in the lap) of Jesus. For what is meant by the lap or breast save the part that is hidden?

LISCO: How close Judas was to Jesus; how far removed from Judas was Jesus soon after! He in glory and Judas in perdition.—Jesus the Revealer of hearts.—BRAUNE: Ver. 6. Modesty is praiseworthy; but obedience is still more so. Peter was terrified at his unworthiness in the sight of the holy Saviour, as on that occasion in the ship when he said (Luke v. 8): *Lord, depart, etc.* His speech bears a resemblance to that of the Baptist, Matt. iii. 13. But not all brave words are always seasonable. (We must not fail to observe, however, that in this case the turning-point with Peter was his unreadiness to be reconciled to the spiritual humiliation of Christ and to what of necessity followed—his own self-humiliation.)—The temperament (mental constitution) of Peter did not willingly listen to promises of future knowledge.—2 Pet. i. 5.—Ver. 8. Recalls chap. vi. 53. Applicable to Judas is the saying of Peter, 2 Pet. ii. 20.—Ver. 12. Jesus sought to strip them of pride by means of a child that He placed amidst them (Matt. xviii.), by the parable of the envious laborers, by the repulsion of the sons of Zebedee; He must now make another similar attempt (yet not simply as an attempt). (Herder:) Christianity gained rule only by ministering to all. The noblest bears sway only by understanding how to minister to many,—if it be possible, to all.—Christ walks majestical in lowliness. Follow Him. Trust Him in all dark matters, in all enigmas of Gospel history and of life.—STIER: When it is necessary, love lays its own shoulder to the wheel; it does not rest satisfied with contributing its two pence for the care of the sick and the poor. It willingly performs *burdensome, unusual, despised, nay, loathsome* services, to use Dräseke's expression. But yet the real, spiritual work of foot-washing in the sense of Jesus' words, ver. 10, is described Gal. vi. 1 and 2.—Luther says justly: Now, therefore, this example of foot-washing is particularly meant for those who are in ecclesiastical offices.—Ver. 20. (Rieger.) He inspires them with courage again in view of their future ministry, for it would please the devil to divest all Christ's servants of authority. When some Judas is set up by him, he would fain have men look upon the eleven others as in no whit better; he would be glad if they themselves thought: We are disgraced; no one will put any faith in us now; our whole order is made to stink. But no! the Lord's: Verily, verily, *etc.*, interposes; He can justify us by proving that we are sent from Him.—See GODET (*the Foot-washing*). In the "*Stimmen der Kirche*," Langenberg, 1852 (p. 214).

[CRAVEN: From ORIGEN: Ver. 3. *The Father had given all things into His hands, i. e.* into His power, for His hands hold all things; or, to Him, for His work.—Ver. 5. Even they who sup with Jesus need a certain washing, not indeed of the top parts of the body, *i. e. the soul*, but its lower parts which cleave necessarily to earth.—Vers. 6-9. Peter often appears in Scripture as hasty in putting forth his own ideas of what is right and expedient.—An instance that a man may say a thing with a good intention, and yet ignorantly to his hurt.—As Peter did not see his own good, our Lord did not suffer his wish to be fulfilled.—Ver. 10. Christ washes their feet after they are clean, showing that grace goes beyond necessity.—Ver. 14. It is not necessary for one who wishes to do all the commandments of Jesus, *literally* to perform the act of washing feet—this is merely an act of custom, and the custom is now nearly dropped.—This spiritual washing of the feet is done *primarily* by Jesus Himself, *secondarily* by His disciples.—Ver. 23. *Whom Jesus loved:* this has a peculiar meaning, viz. that John was admitted to a knowledge of the more secret mysteries of the Word. (?)—Ver. 27. At first Satan did not enter into Judas, but only put it into his heart to betray his Master; let us beware that Satan thrust not any of his darts into our heart, for if he do, he watches till he gets an entrance there himself.

[From AUGUSTINE: Ver. 1. All was now to take place in reality of which the first passover was a type.—We perform a most wholesome journey or *pass-over* when we pass over from the devil to Christ, from this unstable world to His sure kingdom.—*Unto the end, i. e.* that they themselves too might pass out of this world, by love, unto Him their head; for what is *unto the end*, but unto Christ?—Vers. 4, 5. *He laid aside His garments* when, being in the form of God He emptied Himself; He *girded* Himself *with a towel*, when He took upon Him the form of a servant; *He poured water into a basin*, when He shed His blood on the earth with which He washed away the filth of their sins; *He wiped them with the towel*, when with the flesh wherewith He was clothed

He established the steps of the Evangelists—the whole of His passion [humiliation] was our cleansing.—Ver. 12. Let us confess our faults one to another, forgive one another's faults, pray for one another's faults—thus we shall wash one another's feet.—Ver. 29. *Judas had the bag:* the first institution of ecclesiastical property; our Lord shows that His commandment not to think of the morrow does not mean that the saints should never save money.

[From CHRYSOSTOM: Ver. 1. By His *departure* He means His *death*—being so near leaving His disciples, He shows more love for them; He left undone nothing which one who greatly loved should do.—Ver. 7. How useful a lesson of humility it teaches thee.—Ver. 29. How was it that He who forbade scrip, and staff, and money carried bags for the relief of the poor? It was to show thee that even those who are crucified to the world ought to attend to this duty.—Ver. 30. *It was night* showing the impetuosity of Judas.

[From BEDE: Vers. 13, 14. Our Lord first *did* a thing, then *taught* it.—Ver. 17. To know what is good and not to do it, tendeth not to happiness, but to condemnation.——From ALCUIN: Ver. 12. When, at our redemption we were changed by the shedding of His blood, He took again His garments rising from the grave, and clothed in the same body ascended into heaven and sitteth on the right hand of the Father.

[From BURKITT: Ver. 1. Christ chose the time of the Passover to suffer in, that He might prove Himself to be the substance of that type. —Ver. 2. Can we wonder to find friends unfaithful, when our Saviour had a traitor in His own house?—It is no uncommon thing for the vilest sins to be acted by the most eminent professors of religion.—The devil, being a spirit, has a quick access to our spirits and can instil his suggestions into them.—Vers. 4, 5. The most amazing instance of self-denial, for our *encouragement* and *example.*—We ought to be ready to perform the lowest offices of love and service toward one another.—Vers. 6-8. A sinful humility to refuse the offered favors of Christ because we are unworthy to receive them.—Though we are not worthy of *Christ,* and of His *love;* yet Christ is worthy of *us,* and of our *faith.*—The servants of God themselves often cannot understand, *at present,* the dealings of God with them, yet there will come a time for the clearing of them.—Christ washeth all that have an interest in Him both from guilt and pollution.—Ver. 10. All *justified* persons are in God's account *clean.*—The holiest saints, whilst in this world of sin and temptation, do need a daily washing by repentance.—Ver. 17. The necessity of—1. *knowledge* in order to *practice;* 2. *practice* in order to happiness.—Ver. 18. How many are there who by *profession* lift up their *hand unto Christ,* yet who by *treason* lift up their *heel against* Him.—Ver. 20. Christ and the Father account the respect paid to faithful ministers as paid to themselves.—Ver. 21. It is the duty of Christians not rashly to judge one another; but to hope the best of others, and to fear the worst of themselves.—It is possible for secret wickedness to lurk in the *hearts* of those in whose *conduct* nothing has appeared to give a just suspicion.—Ver. 30. Judas went immediately out, *and it was night:* what a warmth and zeal in the devil's cause.—Men given over by God and possessed of Satan are unwearied in sin. . .

[From M. HENRY: Vers. 1-17. A wise man will not do a thing that looks *odd* and *unusual* but for very good reasons: Christ acted thus that He might—1. testify His love to His disciples (vers. 12); 2. give an instance of His voluntary humility (vers. 3-5); 3. signify to them spiritual washing (vers. 6-11); 4. set them an example (vers. 12-17).—Ver. 1. Our Lord has a people in the world that are *His own* by,—1. gift from the Father; 2. costly purchase; 3. His setting them apart for Himself; 4. their own devotion to Him as a peculiar people.—His own, not *things* (τὰ ἴδια) as cattle which are transferable, but *persons* (τοὺς ἰδίους) as a man's wife and children to whom he stands in a constant relation.—*Having loved His own . . He loved them unto the end:* He *did* love them with a love of *good-will* [benevolence] when He gave Himself for their redemption; He *does* love them with a love of *complacency* when He admits them into communion with Himself.—Those whom He loves, He loves *unto the end; i. e.* 1. with an *everlasting* love; 2. unto *perfection,* He *will perfect that which concerneth them.*—Vers. 4, 5. Christ's love was *condescending.*—The disciples had just before shown the weakness of their love by grudging the ointment that was poured on His head, yet now He gives this proof of His love to them; our infirmities are foils to His kindnesses and set them off.—Ver. 2. The treason of Judas traced to its *original.*—Those that would be conformable to Christ must keep their minds low in the midst of advancements.—Vers. 4, 5. Nothing is below us which may be serviceable to God's glory and the good of our brethren.—Many will do *mean* things to curry favor with superiors, they rise by stooping and climb by cringing; but for Christ to do this to *His disciples,* could be no act of policy or complaisance, but pure humility.—*He riseth from supper;* learn—1. Not to reckon it a disturbance to be called from our meal to do God or our brother a real service—Christ would not leave His *preaching* to oblige His nearest relations (Mark iii. 33), but left His *supper* to show His love to His disciples; 2. Not to be over nice about our meat.—*He laid aside His garments and took a towel;* we must address ourselves to duty as those who are resolved not to *take state,* but to *take pains.*—Vers. 7, 8. Subsequent providences explain preceding ones.—We must let Christ take His own way, both in ordinances and providences, and we shall find in the issue it was *the best way.* —In the refusal of Peter there was—1. A *show of humility;* 2. A *real contradiction* of the will of Jesus.—Christ's answer—1. A severe caution against disobedience; or, 2. A declaration of the necessity of spiritual washing.—Ver. 10. The evidence of a justified state may be clouded, but the charter of it is not taken away.—It should be the daily care of those who are in a justified state to cleanse themselves from daily defilement. —*Ye are clean, but not all:* many have *the sign,* but not the thing signified.—Ver. 12. He adjourned the explication till He had finished the transaction—1. to try their submission; 2. to finish the riddle before He unriddled it.—It is the will of Christ that *sacramental signs* should be *explained.*—Ver. 13. *Master and Lord.*—1. He is *Master and Lord* that He may be Redeemer and Saviour; 2. It becomes us thus to call Him; George Herbert when he mentioned the name of Christ used to add *my Master*, and thus wrote:

"How sweetly doth *my Master* sound, MY MASTER!
As ambergris leaves a rich scent unto the taster,
So do these words—a sweet content, an oriental fragrancy
—MY MASTER."

Vers. 14, 15 with 4, 5. A parable to the eye, our Master thereby teaching us—1. An humble *condescension;* 2. A condescension to be *serviceable;* 3. A serviceableness to the *sanctification* one of another.—What a good teacher Christ was, teaching by *example* as well as *doctrine.*—When we see our Master *serving* we cannot but see how ill it becomes us to be *domineering.* —Ver. 17. Most people think, Happy are they that *rise* and *rule;* Christ saith, Happy are they that *stoop* and *obey.*—Nothing is better known than that we should be *humble*, and yet how little is seen of true humility; most *know* for *others*, few *do* for *themselves.*—Ver. 18. They that are *chosen*—1. Christ Himself chose; 2. Are known to Him.—All that *eat bread* with Christ are not His disciples indeed.—Judas *lifted up his heel* against Christ—1. *forsook* Him, *turned his back* upon Him; 2. *despised* Him, shook off the dust of his feet; 3. *spurned* at Him.—Ver. 20. Judas *had been* sent—they that *received* him, and perhaps had been converted and edified by his preaching, were never the worse when he afterward proved a traitor.—Though some by entertaining strangers have entertained robbers yet we must still be hospitable; the abuses put upon our charity will neither justify uncharitableness nor lose us our reward.—Ver. 21. Christ is not the author of sin, yet this sin of Judas He—1. *foresaw;* 2. *foretold.*—The *sins* of Christians are the *grief* of Christ.—Ver. 22. Christ *perplexed* His disciples for a time that He might—1. *humble* them; 2. *prove* them; 3. *excite* in them a *jealousy of themselves;* 4. *excite* indignation at the baseness of Judas.—Ver. 23. There are some of His disciples, whom Christ lays in His bosom, who have more free and intimate communion with Him than others.—Vers. 23, 24. It is good to engage for ourselves the prayers of those that *lie in Christ's bosom.*—They who lie *in Christ's bosom* may often be reminded of something that will be profitable by those who lie at *His feet.*—Ver. 25. Though John whispered in Christ's ear, yet he called Him *Lord; familiarity* did not lessen *respect.*—Ver. 26. Our Lord indicated the traitor by *a sop;* we must not be *outrageous* against those whom we know to be *malicious* against us —*if thine enemy hunger feed him.*—Ver. 27. *After the sop Satan entered* into him; many are made worse by Christ's bounties.—Ver. 28. The disciples did not suspect that Jesus spoke to Judas as the traitor; it is an *excusable* dulness in Christians not to be sharp-sighted in their censures. —Christ's disciples were so well taught *to love one another*, that they could not readily learn to suspect.—*Give something to the poor:* Learn that 1. our Lord, though He lived on alms (Luke viii. 3) yet gave alms; 2. the time of a religious feast is a proper time for charity.—Ver. 30. Withdrawing from the communion of the faithful is commonly the first *overt act* of a backslider, the beginning of an *apostasy.*

[From SCOTT: Vers. 1-11. Neither the deepest abasement, nor the highest exaltation, rendered our Redeemer for a moment inattentive to the concerns of His disciples.—Vers. 18-30. If professed disciples and ministers be found unfaithful, let us not be discouraged; the Scripture hath foretold that thus it must be.—As some are more near to Him than others, we should not *envy* their privilege but use their friendship. From A. CLARK: Vers. 1-17. It was the common custom of our Lord to pass from things sensible and temporal to those which were spiritual and eternal: He was a consummate philosopher, every subject appears grand and noble in His hands.—Ver. 16. Christ has *ennobled* the acts of humility by practising them Himself.—Ver. 17. "*Sacred knowledge* and *devotedness to God* are the means whereby a man can arrive at *beatitude.*" [Institutes of MENU].

[From STIER: Vers. 1-30. If the history of the *Passion* is the Holy of Holies in the New Covenant, St. John opens to us the very Ark of the Covenant in the heart of the incarnate Saviour.—Vers. 4, 5. For thy sake, O sinner, I have laid by the garment of My glory, have girded Myself with the napkin of the flesh, to pour out My blood as a cleansing bath for thee —*as thy God and thy Servant.*—Ver. 13. The Master is *believed*, the Lord is *obeyed.*—Ver. 14. The mutual feet-washing embraces the whole *collective* duties of Christian charity among Christ's disciples.—Love is humility, it delights to *serve* the necessities as well of body as of soul. —Ver. 30. It was *night* in the soul of Judas; *night* in a broad circle around Judas—in the hearts of many, condensed and mighty *darkness; nevertheless* [therefore?] Jesus goes on to speak the words of light and life which have approved their full meaning in the overcoming and extinction of all darkness.

[From A PLAIN COMMENTARY (Oxford): Ver. 1. The disciples, on the eve of orphanhood, were objects of His compassion indeed!—Ver. 17. The *knowledge* of religion is worthless, apart from the practice of it.—Ver. 20. Our Lord spreads over the ministrations of His ministers the awful sanction of His own special presence.—Ver. 26. Does it not follow from this portion of the narrative that while John was reclining on one side of our Lord, *Judas must have been reclining on the other?*—Ver. 27. After the sop Satan entered into him:—The warning, evermore, of the unworthy communicant.—Ver. 29. Judas, the *Almoner* of Christ.—The contrast between the traitor's *outer* and *inner* life.—Vers. 1-29. Ministers of Christ "following their Divine Master in their earnest search for souls, are to leave none, no, not even the most abandoned untried by their hand; even Judas was washed." (Rev. T. T. CARTER).——From BARNES: Ver. 2. Satan *can* tempt no one unless there is some inclination of the mind. [? See ver. 30, p. 458.]—Ver. 23. "The highest honor that can be conferred on any man is to say that *Jesus loved Him.*" (ROBERT HALL.)

[From KRUMMACHER: Vers. 4, 5. O great and significant symbol! O powerful exposition of the words, "I came not to be ministered unto but to minister."—Vers. 6-8. Even to this day we hear it said—"*For the honor* of Christ, I cannot believe that He receives sinners, as such, without any thing further." If you wish to *honor* Jesus, do so by submitting to His word.—Ver. 9. Excellent, but not altogether correct; Simon now oversteps the line to the *right*, as he had before transgressed to the *left*.—Ver. 10. When a Christian is overtaken by a fault, he has no need of an entirely new transformation, but only of a *cleansing;* he must let his feet be washed.—Vers. 14, 15. Acts of *love* never *degrade*, however menial they may be.—Vers. 8-14. Christ Himself must first wash us before we can wash the feet of any in the sense intended by Him.—Vers. 18-30. The heathen world is ignorant of a Judas, such a monster matures only in the sphere of Christianity.—The Lord appointed Judas the receiver and almoner in His circle, and assuredly for no other reason than that He perceived he was the fittest.

[From OWEN: Ver. 1. The whole economy of redemption is made up of most signal developments of Christ's love for His chosen.—Vers. 4, 5. Our Lord in view of the foregoing strife of the disciples for precedence (Luke xxii. 24) performed this ablution. (?)—Ver. 14. "The Pope would do a more remarkable thing if, in unfeigned humility, he washed the feet of one king, than he does in washing the feet of twelve poor men." (BENGEL.)—Ver. 17. "The recognition of such a duty, is a much more easy matter than the putting it in practice." (ALFORD.)——From WHEDON: Ver. 8. Peter in his presumptuous humility is *utterly disobedient.—I know whom I have chosen:* He knew, of the entire twelve, the fidelity of most and the treason of one.—Ver. 30. The son of *night* goes through the darkness of night on his errand of treason (darkness).

[Vers. 3-5. The act of Jesus one of *self-humiliation*, but not expressive of *humility;* humility is *a readiness of mind to take a low place because of conscious weakness or unworthiness;* self-humiliation is an act which may spring from humility, or it may be, as in the case of Jesus, conscious greatness stooping to beneficial service.—He washed the feet of *all*, Judas included, teaching us that we are not to look for certain evidence of piety before performing fraternal service.—A manifestation of what is involved in true *Lordship*—viz.: *service*.—Ver. 9. The submitting to being washed often a greater test of humility than the washing of others.]

FIFTH SECTION.

The Lord in the circle of His friends, the children of light; how He discloses and communicates to them the riches of His inner life, thereby consecrating them as bearers and ministers of His own life, with a view to the enlightenment and transfiguration of the world, and the union of the present and the hereafter.—Disclosure of Heaven (and explanations relative to the Heavenly life).

CHAP. XIII. 31—CHAP. XVII. 26.

SYNOPTICAL VIEW.

The farewell discourses of Jesus, as recorded by John, contain the most mysterious and most holy of all the sayings through which He manifested Himself to His own. They form the spiritual ante-celebration of His own glorification and that of His people in the new celestial life opened up by His death and resurrection. Distinction must be made between historical periods and those embracing different divisions of the subject-matter; there exists, however, an exact correspondence in the march of the two. The total is the walk to the Mount of Olives and the revelation of heaven or the new heavenly home, high above the old Sheol of the dead.

FIRST PERIOD. From the end of the paschal meal, or the departure of Judas, to the end of the Supper. Starting-point of the meditation: *the Supper;* how it *reveals* the gulf that intervenes between the heavenly home that Christ discloses and whither He is going; but also *transfigures* the same, supplying Christ's presence to the disciples, who sojourn on this earthly shore, until the time when they shall be ripe for heaven and at liberty to follow the Lord as martyrs (ver. 36). Martyrdom the fairest, ripest fruit of the Lord's Supper. Therefore: the task and goal of personal life in that Kingdom of glory, to found which Christ leaves this world, chap. xiii. 31-38.

SECOND PERIOD. From the close of the Supper to the departure for the Mount of Olives. On stepping forth beneath the starry sky. Starting-point of the meditation: the going forth into the dark world, and the contemplation of the nocturnal heavens. Revelation of the heavens situate beyond the gulf. Exposition of heaven, or the Father's House, as the goal of Christ and His people.

1. *Christ as the Way to the goal;* in the truth and life of His personal essence standing surety for the goal, in spite of the contradiction of outward agencies which reveal an apparently aimless and pathless vista of misery and death (Thomas).

2. *Christ as the Goal of the way*, or the spiritual and heavenly theophany, in antithesis to the sensual and earthly theophany; or as the personal Christ, through whom the personal Father manifests Himself, and who, through the Holy Ghost, founds the fellowship of personal, heavenly life (ver. 20; Philip).

3. *Christ, on His return, at once the Goal and the Way.* How, in the communion of His people, He establishes the hidden heaven upon earth, as the Kingdom of the Spirit and of Love in antithesis to the ungodliness of the world (Judas Lebbæus).

4. *The departure for the Passion as a departure for heaven*, or the parting salutation as a pledge of greeting at a speedily ensuing meeting.

The one warranty for the heaven beyond this world—which warranty is given us through the heavenly Christ present in the world—branches out into various manifestations: (1) Of the heavenly Christ; (2) of the heavenly Father; (3) of the heavenly Spirit or other Paraclete; (4) of the heavenly and personal life and operation of Christians.

First promise of the Holy Ghost as the Spirit of Christ and the Church generally, ver. 16. Second promise of the Holy Ghost as the Spirit of evangelic knowledge and of enlightenment, ver. 26. Chap. xiv.

Third Period. The walk from the city to the brook Kedron. *Vineyards and nocturnal garden-fires on either side* (see below). Starting-point of the meditation: the sight of the vineyards, of the cleansed vines and the burning branches. Glorification of this earthly shore; or the heavenly life upon earth, in the history of the Kingdom of Love or the Vine of God; in the judgment executed upon dead branches, and in the fruit-bearing—love's blessing—of living ones.

1. Divine *establishment* and *cultivation* of the heavenly *Vine* upon earth, or the establishment of the heavenly Kingdom of Love—a kingdom rich in joy. The fiery judgment upon dead branches; the purification of living ones; or the destiny of the Vine (chap. xv. 1-8).

2. *The fruit-bearing* of disciples in their life of love (vers. 9-17).

3. *Verification of love* in opposition to the hatred of the world, or the *defensive* conduct of the disciples of Jesus (ver. 18 to chap. xvi. 6).

4. *Consummation of love* in the fellowship of the Holy Ghost who convinces and conquers the world by the judgment of the Spirit, or the *offensive* conduct of disciples, chap. xvi. 7-11. Revelation of the future, together with the development of Christianity, vers. 12-15.

Third promise of the Holy Ghost as the Spirit of martyr-faithfulness, chap. xv. 26. Fourth promise of the Holy Ghost as the Spirit of victorious might that overcometh the world, chap. xvi. 8-11. Fifth promise of the Holy Ghost as the Spirit of apostolic development and apocalyptic revelation of the future, chap. xvi. 12-15.

Fourth Period. Towards the end of the way. Conclusion of communications, and promise of future disclosures through the Holy Ghost. Starting-point of the meditation: The approach to the goal. Transfiguration of the union betwixt this world and the world beyond, in the new, heavenly life.

1. Promise of the revelation of the new and second heavenly life in the resurrection of Christ, vers. 16-22.

2. Promise of a new meeting, when He of the further shore shall hold intercourse with them who are still remaining on this side of the gulf, vers. 23, 24.

3. Promise of life in the Spirit, vers. 25-27.

4. The flash of light from the Spirit, apportioned to the disciples even now in surveying the life of Jesus, vers. 28-31.

5. Christ's consciousness of victory, His assurance of new life, as a legacy of consolation for His people, vers. 32, 33. Chap. xvi. 12-33.

Fifth Period. Before the crossing of the brook Kedron, the black brook in the gloomy vale. *Period of final decision.*

Development of Christ's consciousness of victory in His high-priestly prayer for the transfiguration of the personal Kingdom of Love, or House of the Father, in this world and the next, through the sanctification or sacrifice of Christ, the redemption of mankind:

1. For the glorification of the Son, vers. 1-8;

2. For the glorification of His people, vers. 9-19;

3. For the glorification of all future believers until the disappearance of the world before the glory of the Son and of His heaven, vers. 20-24;

4. The perfect glorification of the Father, in conformity to His righteousness; the foundation of said glorification having already been laid by the Son, vers. 25, 26. Or, the prayer for the perfection of the Kingdom of Love unto the absolute Epiphany, Rev. xxi.; Tit. ii. 13; 1 John ii. 28; iii. 2. Chap. xvii.

Synopsis. *First Period:* Antithesis between heaven and earth; *Second Period:* Heaven and its vouchers on earth; *Third Period:* Establishment and development of heaven on earth; *Fourth Period:* Internal union of heaven and earth; *Fifth Period:* The perfect appearing.

On the farewell discourses of Jesus see Luther's *Sermons* of the year 1538, vol. viii. [ed. Walch]. Matthesius: Luther said this was the best book he had written. G. Lehr: *De sublimitate sermonum Jesu Christi*, John xiii.-xvi., Göttingen, 1774. Stark: *Paraphr. et Comment. in Ev. Joh.* xiii.-xvii., Jena, 1814. An extensive catalogue of separate treatises see in Lilienthal's *Bibl. Archivar*, p. 321; Danz, *Universalwörterbuch der theolog. Literatur*, p. 466, *etc.* On the sacerdotal prayer see below chap. xvii. [Comp. also our introductory remarks on ch. xiii. 1, p. 405.—P. S.]

I.

STRONG ANTITHESIS BETWEEN THIS PRESENT WORLD AND THE WORLD BEYOND; ALSO THE LINK BETWEEN THEM FORMED BY THE NEW INSTITUTION OF CHRIST (THE LORD'S SUPPER, AS THE COMMANDMENT OF BROTHERLY LOVE). GRAVE MAGNITUDE OF THIS ANTITHESIS, EXPRESSED IN THE ANNOUNCEMENT OF PETER'S DENIAL. THE GLORIFICATION OF CHRIST; AND THE NEW COVENANT. THE NEW COMMANDMENT AS THE TRANSFIGURATION OF THE LAW AND LIKEWISE OF THE ANTITHESIS BETWEEN CHRIST'S VISIBLE EXISTENCE IN THE WORLD BEYOND AND THE SOJOURN OF HIS PEOPLE IN THIS PRESENT WORLD.

CHAP. XIII. 31–38.

(Matt. xxvi. 26-35; Mark xiv. 22-31; Luke xxii. 31-38.)

31 Therefore,[1] when he [Judas] was [had] gone out, Jesus said,
32 Now is the Son of man glorified, and God is glorified in him. If God be [is]
glorified in him,[2] God shall [will] also glorify him in himself, and shall [will]
33 straightway [immediately] glorify him. Little children [τεκνία], yet a little while
[only a little while longer] I am with you. Ye shall [will] seek me; and [,] as I
34 said unto the Jews, Whither I go, ye cannot come; so now I say to you. A new
commandment I give unto you, That [in order that, ἵνα] ye love one another;
35 [even] as I have loved you, [in order] that ye also love one another. By this shall
[will] all *men* know [perceive] that ye are my [ἐμοί] disciples, if ye have love one
to another.
36 Simon Peter said [saith, λέγει] unto him, Lord, whither goest thou? Jesus an-
swered him [*omit* him],[3] Whither I go, thou canst not follow me now; but thou
37 shalt [wilt] follow me[4] afterwards. Peter said [saith] unto him, Lord, why cannot
38 I follow thee now? I will lay down my life for thy sake [for thee]. Jesus an-
swered [answereth][5] him, Wilt thou lay down thy life for my sake [for me]?
Verily, verily, I say unto thee, The cock shall not crow [will not have crowed],[6]
till [before] thou hast denied[7] me thrice.

TEXTUAL AND GRAMMATICAL.

[1] Ver. 31.—[Tischendorf, Alf. and W. & H. give ὅτε οὖν, in accordance with ℵ. B. C. D. L. X.; οὖν is omitted in A. E. H. K., *etc.*, and those ed. who wrongly join ὅτε ἐξῆλθεν to ver. 30.—P. S.]

[2] Ver. 32.—The words εἰ ὁ θεὸς ἐδοξάσθη ἐν αὐτῷ are wanting in [ℵ.*] B. C. D., *etc.* Probably the repetition was regarded as superfluous. [They occur in ℵ.c A. C.2 T. Δ., *etc.*, they are retained by Tischend., omitted by Westc. and H., bracketed by Alf. The omission may have been occasioned by the similar endings of this and preceding clauses.—P. S.]

[3] Ver. 36.—[Tischendorf, Alford, Westcott and Hort omit αὐτῷ (text. rec.), in accordance with B. C.* L.; it occurs, however, in ℵ. A. C.3 D., *etc.*—P. S.]

[4] Ver. 36.—The μοι is wanting in [ℵ.] B. C.* L. X., Vulgate, *etc.* [It occurs in A. C.3 D., *etc.*, text. rec., but is omitted by Tischend., Alf., Westc. and Hort.—P. S.]

[5] Ver. 38.—[Instead of ἀπεκρίθη the best authorities read ἀποκρίνεται, in accordance with ℵ. B. C. L. X., *etc.*—P. S.]

[6] Ver. 38.—Φωνήσῃ, against φωνήσει, has very strong authority. [It is so given ℵ. A. B. G., *etc.* and in the best crit. ed.—P. S.]

[7] Ver. 38.—The reading ἀρνήσῃ decidedly preponderant over against the (synoptic) composite [ἀπαρνήσῃ]. A milder term. [The former occurs in B. D. L. X.; the latter in ℵ. A. C. T. Δ., *etc.*—P. S.]

EXEGETICAL AND CRITICAL.

Ver. 31. **Now when he had gone out.**—Chrysostom and others connect this sentence with the foregoing: "but it was night when he went out." Not only the οὖν, but also the emphatic pause introduced by the word νύξ, and the strong contrast between the preceding and the ensuing Sect. are declarative against this view.

Now is the Son of Man glorified [ἐδοξάσθη].—This is not merely a proleptical announcement on the part of Jesus of approaching triumph [Meyer, Alford, *etc.*]. It is the celebration of an actual triumph. *In spirit* He has already vanquished the kingdom of darkness. His victory succeeded to His perturbation of spirit at the sight of Judas, and was gained on this wise: By the operation of His Spirit in perfect consistency with His truth, love and patience as opposed to the utmost falseness, embitterment and irritation, He, as the Christ, sundered Antichrist from the communion of the faithful through the mere exercise of His personal might. The victory gained by Him in spirit over Judas, is a victory over Satan himself and over those worldly temptations whose nature partakes of the spirit of Iscariot (see *Leben Jesu*, II., p. 1327; III., p. 675). This victory lays the foundation for the victory in His psychical life (Gethsemane) and for that in His physical life (Golgotha): in view of this fact He is already glorified in principle.

Ver. 32. **If God is glorified in Him.**—Antithesis to the Son of Man. It was while conserving to the uttermost His purely human nature that He, as the Son of Man, overcame Judas; but, as this Son of Man, He was also the instrument of God, chap. v. 19; 2 Cor. v. 19. It is effectual to the glory of God Himself that evil,—the whole kingdom of Antichrist—is, in respect of its principle, overcome in so purely human a manner now, and that it shall henceforth be thus overcome throughout the world.

God will also glorify Him in Himself.—As God is glorified in the heart of Christ and in His victorious conduct, being therein set forth as the omnipotence of the Spirit, He shall also glorify Christ in Himself; *i.e.*, He shall glorify the almighty spiritual power of the Son in His (the Father's) divine providence, in His peculiar domain, the sphere, the revelation of the Father—and that especially in that world and from that world whither Christ is now returning. Ἐν ἑαυτῷ has been interpreted by Chrysostom and Ammon as equivalent to διά. Such an interpretation does away with the antithesis. In like manner the antithesis is weakened by the explanation of Cocceius: Since God was glorified, the Son also was glorified. Augustine and many others interpret the passage as referring to the exaltation: "*ita scilicet, ut natura humana, quæ a verbo æterno suscepta est, etiam immortali æternitate donetur.*" Tholuck refers to Phil. ii. 9: "The exaltation of the Son, which, in accordance with the representation of Paul, is the μισθός for His humiliation." Meyer: By the return to the fellowship of God, out of which He went forth. From this point of view ἐν ἑαυτῷ needs defining. The existence of Christ was an existence in God, not alone from the time of His ascension, but from the moment of His death, inasmuch as He was removed from this present world. For this world His personal *life* was now hidden in God's providence, but His personal *essence* issued forth again, clear and distinct, from the providence of God, simultaneously with the resurrection and the sending of the Spirit; an essence now glorified in divine spiritual might, and destined to be ever more and more glorified until His appearing. See Col. iii. 3. Hence the expression: *in Him*, has been in course of fulfilment ever since the death of Christ.

And shall immediately.—The second καί introduces the modifying word, εὐθύς, from which it follows that the glorification of Christ in God shall take place immediately.

Ver. 33. **Little children, but yet a little while (a little longer).**—After the stern dismissal of the traitor He is at liberty to unbosom Himself to the disciples and to reveal to them the love and grief that stir His heart at parting from them. Here for the first time we find the tender "little children," τεκνία. With them too, however, He has to deal earnestly (see Comm. on *Luke*). He designs teaching them not to set their hearts upon following Him to death now. [Alford: "τεκνία—*here only* used by Christ (comp., however, παιδία, chap. xxi. 5)—affectingly expresses not only His brotherly, but fatherly love (Isa. ix. 6) for His own, and at the same time their immature and weak state, now about to be left without Him." The same term of endearment, τεκνία, *little children, dear children*, is used once by Paul, Gal. iv. 19, and seven times by John, the disciple of love, in his Epistle. According to Jerome the last exhortation of the aged John to his congregation in Ephesus was simply this: "Little children, love one another," because this comprehended the whole of practical Christianity.—P. S.]

Ye cannot come.—As I said unto the Jews, chap. vii. 34; viii. 21, 24. He now says the same thing to them; although in another sense [and without the threatening addition: "and ye will not find Me, and ye will die in your sins." The ζητεῖν of the unbelieving Jews is the vain looking for a deliverer after rejecting the true Messiah, the ζητεῖν of the disciples is the seeking of faith and love.—P. S.]. What He says to them *now* [ἄρτι, emphatically put last, as vers. 7, 37; xvi. 12.—P. S.] is binding only *for the present*. *For the present* they cannot follow Him to heaven. From the two propositions: ye will miss Me, and: ye cannot follow Me now, the following results.*

Ver. 34. **A new commandment I give unto you** [ἐντολὴν καινὴν δίδωμι ὑμῖν].—Manifestly, the new commandment is to supply His [visible] presence to them for a time, until they come to Him again. Different interpretations, premising, in every case, that the corollary: ἵνα ἀγαπᾶτε ἀλλήλους, *etc.*, contains the substance of the new commandment. The consideration that the commandment of neighborly love is not a *new* but an *old* one, (Lev. xix. 18; Matt. v. 43 ff.; xix. 19; xxii. 39), has led some to ascribe an *intensive* sense to the adjective *new*, and others to take it in an *altered* sense.

1. The INTENSIVE sense [new in *degree*].

(*a*.) One is not to love his neighbor simply as himself [ὡς ἑαυτόν], but more than himself [ὑπὲρ ἑαυτόν] (Cyril, Theod. Mopsueste [Theophyl., Euthym. Zigab.; among modern commentators, especially Knapp, *Scripta var. arg.*, p. 369 sqq.] *etc.*). Without regard to other objections to the view, the idea of it is not clear. [Christ, Matt. xxii. 39, 40, and Paul, Rom. xiii. 9, adopt the Old Testament commandment, "Love thy neighbor *as thyself*," *without addition*, as the second great commandment which is like unto the first, "Thou shalt love the Lord thy God," *etc.* The ὡς ἑαυτόν is the highest measure of love and does not exclude, but includes *the* self-denial even to the sacrifice of life for our neighbor. Finally καθώς does not indicate the degree, but the kind of love.—P. S.].

(*b*.) One should love his neighbor as Christ has loved His people. The following ἠγάπησα is modificative of καινή (Chrysostom, Tholuck).†

* [Similarly Stier and Alford connect vers. 33 and 34: Ye will be left on earth, when I go to heaven; but, unlike the Jews, ye will seek Me and find Me in the way of love to Me and to one another, forming a united body, the church, in which all will recognize My presence among you as My disciples.—P. S.]

† [So also Wordsworth who, however, combines with this interpretation that of Augustine (*renewing*), see below, 2 f.

Against this view it has been objected (by De Wette) that the modifying clause does not apply to what precedes, but to that which follows it. A main consideration against the view just set forth is that it represents the most involved commandment as being given, without any instructions as to the manner of its fulfilment.

(*c.*) It is the new commandment of Christian brotherly love as distinguished from a general love to our neighbor. Grotius, Kölbing, *Stud. u. Krit.*, 1845; and similarly Luthardt, [Ebrard, Brückner, Bäumlein, Hengstenberg, Godet]. Meyer: "The novelty lies in the *impulsive power* of love; the love of Christ, as experienced by us, should be this impellent. Thus the commandment, old in itself, is endowed with new explicitness, *viz.*, the love ἐν Χριστῷ." Here the fact is overlooked, that a commandment with which we are experimentally conversant and which is instinct with motive power, is no longer a mere commandment, but an inwardly impellent principle. Therefore,

(*d.*) The principle of the new life brought by Christ (De Wette). Meyer: That, indeed, is the new ἐντολή, but it is not so stated here. In that respect, then, Meyer's own interpretation would be refuted.

(*e.*) The removal of the bounds which, in the Old Testament, inclosed neighborly love within national limits (Köstlin, Hilgenfeld). This has already been done, Matt. v. 44, inasmuch as Christ there finds in the Old Testament commandment itself the germ of His commandment of neighborly love, in antithesis to the ordinance of the scribes.

2. ALTERED sense:

(*a.*) *Præceptum illustre* (Hackspan, [Hammond], Wolf).

(*b.*) *Mandatum ultimum* (Heumann).

(*c.*) The most recent (Nonnus; ὀπλοτέρην).

(*d.*) One always new (Olshausen:) never growing old, ever fresh [=ἀεὶ καινή].

(*e.*) A renewed one (Irenæus, Jansen) [Calvin, Maldonatus, Schöttgen].

(*f.*) A renewing [regenerating] one (Augustine), [Wordsworth].

(*g.*) An unexpected one (Semler: unexpected after the strife touching rank, Luke xxii. 24 ff.).

[(*h.*) The καινότης of this commandment consists in its *simplicity* and *unicity* (?) Alford. Similarly Owen: "a love unique, simple, self-renewing and ever fresh." The same applies to the old commandment.—P. S.]

3. We adhere to the view which we have previously set forth, *viz.*, that the ἐντολὴ καινή, is indicative of the *institution of the Lord's Supper* (*Leben Jesu*, II., p. 1330; III., 681); and Meyer's wondering note of exclamation we accept as a sign of affirmation.* That Christ did not intend His precepts to be taken in the sense of outward laws, is a fact which the whole of the New Testament warrants us in assuming. But He did found institutions for His Church: the Lord's Supper, Baptism, the ministry, *etc.*, all centering in the Lord's Supper. Of that Christ says: τὸ αἱμά μου τῆς καινῆς διαθήκης (Matt. xxvi. 28; Mark xiv. 24), or, also, ἡ καινὴ διαθήκη (Luke xxii. 20). If διαθήκη and ἐντολή be thoroughly kindred ideas, the former is converted into the latter by the words: "Do this in remembrance of Me;" "Ye *shall* show forth," *etc.*; if there be but *one* new διαθήκη, but *one* new ἐντολή, the one necessarily coincides with the other.

Moreover, it is just in *this place* that we should expect John to mention the Lord's Supper. Tholuck: "The institution of the Lord's Supper, omitted by John—on account of its being sufficiently well known by tradition—would here (ver. 34) find the place best befitting it. That Supper is not only a memorial feast of the Departing One (1 Cor. xi. 25), but a feast of union with His disciples in love *until He comes*, Rev. iii. 20; 1 Cor. xi. 26. In like manner it is a feast wherein His cherished ones are mutually united, 1 Cor. x. 17."—Attention should likewise be directed to the ἠγάπησα; on which word Meyer: "For Jesus perceives Himself to be at the end of His work of loving self-surrender." This was undoubtedly the case at the institution of the Lord's Supper, and it can be explained only by a reference to that institution.

In order that [ἵνα] **ye may love one another,** *etc.*—Agreeably to the foregoing explanation, these words do not constitute the *substance* of the new commandment, but the ethical *purpose* of it. The Lord's Supper is to be the channel for the conveyance of light, impulse and strength for such a brotherly love. Two-fold construction:

1. The sentence: καθὼς ἠγάπησα, *etc.*, is a parallel sentence to the preceding one (Beza, De Wette and others). Καθώς, *etc.*, is emphatically put first: "As I have loved you—that ye so love one another." Meyer remarks with reason: This does not correspond with the simple Johannean style.

2. The sentence: καθὼς ἠγάπησα, *etc.*, is the apodosis to the preceding clause, and contains that which shall ensure compliance with the admonition: ye shall love one another. Meyer: "In order that ye may love one another, in accordance with My having loved you, in order that ye, on your part, might love one another." This would make the last clause either tautological or oblique. The love of Jesus would be modified solely in accordance with its purpose of exciting love, and it would be accordingly required that the disciples' love should exhibit a similar mode.

We come back to No. 1, with a different apprehension of it, however: The new institution is founded in order that the disciples may love one another; [its foundation being] in conformity to the fact that Christ has loved His people in order that they may love one another. That is: The Lord's Supper is the sacrament by which

Similarly Webster and Wilkinson: "This love was to resemble His love to them in manner and degree (καθώς, κ. τ. λ.), and therefore must be grounded on their spiritual relationship to each other in Him."—P. S.]

* [In his fifth edition, Meyer has no "wondering note of exclamation," but objects to Dr. Lange's reference of ἐντολή to the institution of the Lord's Supper, that it is not indicated in the connection, and is contrary to the parallel passage, 1 John ii. 8. But it should be remembered that these words were spoken at the very time when the Lord's Supper in connection with the Agape was instituted and commanded to be observed to the second advent as a perpetual commemoration of Christ's dying love. Neander, Ammon and Ebrard put the institution after ver. 32; Tholuck at ver. 34. Lange makes the ἐντολὴ καινή itself the καινὴ διαθήκη, the love-feast of which Christ says: "Do this in remembrance of Me." This view is certainly ingenious and plausible, and allows ἵνα its full force.—P. S.]

the καθὼς of His sacrificial death is brought home to the minds of His people; the ethical fruit that would spring from that death itself, *viz.*, a company of believers living in the fellowship of brotherly love—shall now be realized by the Supper as the lively representation of His sacrificial death, and the substitute for His presence.

Ver. 35. **By this will all know (perceive).**—Mutual brotherly love the distinctive mark of Christians, 1 John iii. 10; Neander's *Denkwürdigkeiten*, I., p. 97; G. Arnold, *Abbildung der ersten Christen*, Vol. III. Tholuck: "The heathen were wont to exclaim with astonishment: 'Behold how these Christians love one another, and how they are ready to die for one another.' * One Minucius Felix, the heathen, says of the Christians: 'They love each other before knowing each other;' and Lucian (in *Peregrinus*) sneeringly remarks: 'Their law-giver has persuaded them that they are all brethren.' "

Ver. 36. **Lord, whither goest thou?**—Peter finds a thorn in the saying of Jesus (ver. 33), of whose prick he cannot yet rid himself. Jesus, therefore, meets the true idea of his question with the answer: Thither thou canst not follow Me now. He thus makes an application of the general sentence (ver. 33) to him; comforting him, however, with the obscure intimation of his martyrdom, as He pacified the sons of Zebedee, Matt. xx. 23 (comp. John xxi. 18). By δύνασαι Tholuck apprehends simply the subjective impossibility in Peter, whereas, on the other hand, he conceives δύνασθε to be declarative of an objective impossibility. In both cases, however, an objective and a subjective import correspond. The disciples were no more *ordained* to pass through death immediately with Christ than they were *ripe* for such a journey. [The words ἀκολουθήσεις (μοι is doubtful, see TEXTUAL NOTES) ὕστερον, are probably an allusion to the crucifixion of Peter, comp. ch. xxi. 18, 19.—P. S.]†

Ver. 37. **Why can I not follow thee now? I will lay down my life for thee.**—It is clear to him that the going is to be through death. But not only does he undertake to die *after the example* of the Master; he even protests that he will lay down his life *for Him*.‡

Ver. 38. Jesus answers in view of these facts and puts Peter to the blush. He uses the asseveration: *Verily, verily*. Lay down thy life for Me! Thou wilt not so much as confess Me. On the contrary, thou wilt deny Me. And that three times. And this will come to pass directly, before the cock hath crowed, before the ensuing morning. Peter again stood in need of strong and emphatic words.

As regards the time of this conversation with Peter, Luke's account agrees with that of our Evangelist, while it supplies additional items (chap. xxii. 31-34). Matthew and Mark are induced to record the conversation after the departure of Jesus from the place where He celebrated the Passover to the Mount of Olives, by their desire to superordinate the more general declaration made by Jesus to all His disciples, to the effect that they should all be offended that night because of Him. This declaration might also very readily occasion Peter once more to avouch his faithful devotion.

DOCTRINAL AND ETHICAL.

1. The exultant breathing again of Jesus after the departure of Judas: (*a*) *A presage* of the reviving and shining of the Church at the Last Day, Matt. xiii. 43; Luke xxi. 28; (*b*) *a sign expressive of the great victory of His Spirit* in the spiritual combat with treason in the circle of disciples,—with Judas as the representative of Satan; (*c*) a *symbolical sign* for His Church, teaching her how she shall conquer the anti-Christian Adversary and finally expel him by a dynamical censure; all this she shall do (after the example of the Son of Man) in simple humanity, a state which God, in the person of His Son, has hallowed, and with whose conditions He has complied. Similarly, an intimation that we should solemnly rejoice at the open desertion of false brethren and members rather than be vexed at the same.

2. The *contrast* of the pure Son of Man, the representative of God's honor, and the false friend who, from an historical point of view, became the tool of a Hierarchy possessing hearts hardened against Christ, or, regarded from an ethical stand-point, delivered himself up to be the tool of Satan.

3. *Glorification* is the revelation of internal spiritual power in the untrammeled appearance and activity of its life;—hence, appearance in conformity to the idea,—the real and perfect beauty, a representation of spiritual sovereignty in the unobstructed glory of life. The Father glorified through Christ. The highest victory of love over hate, of faithfulness over falseness, of humility over pride, of a repose of soul over excitement and self-perturbation, of brightness over demoniacal gloom, is the highest verification of the glory of the personal Son of Man, the central Hypostasis Himself, and, at the same time, the perfect glorification of the personal God, the Father, who has given such power to His Son and, through Him, to His children. *The glorifying of the Son of Man in God.* In and from

* [From a well-known passage in Tertullian's *Apologeticus*, c. 39. He adds: "Yea, verily this must strike them (the heathen); for they hate each other, and are rather ready to kill one another. And even that we call each other brethren, seems to them suspicious for no other reason than that among them all expressions of kindred are only feigned. We are even your brethren in virtue of the common nature, which is the mother of us all; though ye, as evil brethren, deny your human nature. But how much more justly are those called and considered brethren, who acknowledge the one God as their Father; who have received the one Spirit of holiness; who have awaked from the same darkness of uncertainty to the light of the same truth?" Comp. my Church History, Vol. I., p. 336 ff., N. Y. ed.—P. S.]

† [The question of Peter κύριε, ποῦ ὑπάγεις; *Domine, quo vadis?* has furnished the name to a church outside the city of Rome, on the spot where, according to the legend, Peter having from love of life escaped from prison, was confronted by the appearance of Christ, and asked Him: "Lord, whither goest Thou?" The Lord replied: "I go to Rome, to be crucified again," whereupon the disciple returned to his prison and cheerfully suffered martyrdom on the cross. *Si non e vero, e ben trovato.*—P. S.]

‡ [Augustine: Peter imagined that he could precede his guide. Presumptuous supposition! It was necessary that Christ should first lay down His life for the salvation of Peter, before Peter could be able to lay down his life for the gospel of Christ. But when Christ had died for Peter and redeemed him by His own blood, and had risen from the dead, then Peter was able to follow Christ, even to the cross.—P. S.]

the other world God glorifies Christ's personality as the absolutely dynamical principle which retains its grasp of itself even in death, which breaks through all the bonds of death, soars above the highest heavens, comprehends in its personality the depths of the Spirit and pours them out over all flesh; in order to draw all mankind up into the Kingdom of personal life and love and, in and along with mankind, to glorify the world into the Father's House.

4. The tender saying of Christ at His departure, *Little children, etc.*, echoing in the words of His disciple; 1 John ii. 1; chap. iii. 18. The chasm betwixt this world and the world to come disclosed, and closed, or glorified, by the Lord's Supper.

5. Christ no new Law-giver, because He has comprehended all of His commandments: (*a*) In the institution of love which is His sacrament accompanied by His word, or (*b*) in the gift of His Spirit; two principal phases of the same blessing.

6. If the *Lord's Supper* be intended to supply to us the *presence* of Christ, because He works and manifests Himself dynamically through it, how can the self-same thing be declared of the *Comforter*, chap. xiv. 16? For the reason that the office of the Comforter bears altogether upon the heritage left by Christ to His people, the institutions established by Him in word and sacrament; and only in the fellowship of the Holy Ghost has the proclamation of the death of Christ by word and sacrament its full truth.

7. The unsuspicious *self-confidence of Peter* a great warning to the Church and a foretoken of her history.

8. How Christ, by the celebration of the Love-feast and the Supper, has prepared His disciples for the new and great revelation of the heavenly Paradise, of heaven, and of the living connection between heaven and earth which He is to establish by means of them.

9. The divine assurance of Christ in view of the treason of Judas and the denial of Peter, an assurance of the absolute victory of Divine Providence over all the contradictions of evil; of the triumph of truth and righteousness over wickedness; of the triumph of love and grace over needy sinners.

HOMILETICAL AND PRACTICAL.

Christ's triumphant joy consequent upon the departure of the traitor.—The Lord's subsequent aloneness with His disciples a type of the purified, heavenly Church: 1. in respect of the cordial intimacy; 2. the high festivity; 3. the rich revelation of love and life; 4. the glorious disclosures; 5. the presageful glimpse of eternity—in this communion.—What the Lord discourses of with His disciples after Judas has gone out: 1. Not another word does He say of Judas himself, let alone a harsh one; 2. but He talks of God's triumphant over-ruling of his dark deeds. —*Now is the Son of Man glorified.* A blissful sense of victory is felt in the disburdened breast, after the weightiest of oppressions and the hottest of conflicts (ver. 21).—Judas goeth out to betray His Master, and Christ trembleth not—except for joy.—He looketh not upon that which is being done by men who have conspired together against Him, but upon what God doeth.—And therein also should the evangelical Church recognize and follow His example.—The mutual glorification of the Father and the Son. See ch. xvii.: 1. How the Son of Man has glorified His God as the Friend of man in holy humanity. 2. How God glorifies the Son of Man as the Son of God in holy and divine sovereignty.—*Dear little children.* The sensations of the Lord in anticipation of His departure: 1. of grief; 2. of bliss; 3. of apprehension; 4. of good confidence.—Or: The horror and joy of Christ at the departure of Judas, in comparison with the mild grief with which He now departs from the disciples.—The intimation of Christ relative to His entrance into heaven: 1. He is now going thither; 2. the Jews, *as Jews*, can *never* come thither; 3. the disciples cannot *now* come thither.—A decided indication of our need to ripen for heaven by a Christian life.—Christ's bequest to His people upon His departure, or the new commandment.—The Holy Supper the new life-law of Christ's Church.—The Supper of the Church her fundamental law: 1. the sum of her institutions (Word, Baptism, Discipline, *etc.*); 2. the sum of her teaching; 3. the sum of her moral admonitions.—Love, the mark of Christians.—The interruption of Christ's leave-taking with His disciples by the overweening protestations of Peter: 1. Once more a self-willed contradicting of Jesus' words, and that after the foot-washing and the Supper; 2. the utterance of a stout vow of fidelity, a vow which the Lord foresaw would turn to denial.—Comparison of Judas and Peter at this moment: 1. Similar features: The former, out in the night, prostitutes himself to the enemy in determined apostasy; the latter, within the circle of disciples, lays claim to a fidelity for which he has not the strength. 2. The difference: In that case embitterment, in this love to the Lord; Yonder the utmost falseness, here sincerity and open outspokenness.—There is always a capability of redemption in the sincere man.—The sad certitude of Jesus touching the imminent denial of Peter, set in the calm assurance of the certain victory of grace.

STARKE, ver. 31: A wise teacher giveth not that which is holy unto the dogs, nor casteth the pearls of the divine word before swine, Matt. vii. 6; 2 Tim. ii. 15.—CANSTEIN: All the sufferings of true Christians end in their glorification; nay, they are themselves a glory to them.—ZEISIUS: In all tribulations the best course to be pursued is to fix the eye of faith immovably upon the promised, future glory.—Even in the midst of suffering, as in the deepest humiliation and in death itself, the most admirable beams of glory shine forth.—ZEISIUS: Christ's glory is our glory also, for to this end (also) was He glorified, that He might bring us to everlasting radiance and glory.—A blissful death is the way to the eternal glory of God's children in heaven. —Ver. 34: — HEDINGER: Try thyself. Much love, much Christianity.—1 Pet. i. 22.—ZEISIUS: As the brethren of a fleshly order have their particular insignia, so love is the badge of spiritual brethren, or faithful Christians. He who has not this, has forfeited his order.—Ver. 36.—QUESNEL: God has His hours. What we cannot do at *one* time, He causes us to perform at *another*.—Ver. 37.—HEDINGER: Even in good hearts there is sometimes more presumption than strength, Phil. ii. 13.—Christ must die for Peter before Peter can die for Christ.—Beware, therefore, of relying upon thyself. Everything must come of Christ's Spirit and death.—Ver. 38. We should not reject or disown our brethren on account of their many infirmities, but bear with them, in the confident hope of their renewal and purification, 1 Cor. x. 12.—God sometimes lets His saints stumble and fall, so that the ruin latent in them may become right patent to them.

HEUBNER: *Now.* With the treason of Judas, Jesus looked upon His death as determined (the proximate sense of the "now," however, is, that His victory *was* already decided), as good as accomplished and, by consequence, His glorification was the same.—Ver. 32. A man is deserving of glory in proportion to what he himself has done and sacrificed for the glory of God.—He who makes that glory his first aim, may confidently hope that God will glorify him. How were the apostles glorified!—Ver. 36. An assurance that an honest man grows in strength for duty, in the strength of spiritual life.

GOSSNER: On ver. 30. The devil is a stormy master; he demands to be served with speed, and he leaves a man no time to bethink himself. Away with thee quickly! Be off! he cries.—Ver. 33. The way I go is as yet too rough for you (and the goal is still too high for you).—Throughout the world Christians should be known by *love*. Each reverences that grace in another, which the other honors in him.—On ver. 37. Human nature is so arrogant. It thinks itself able to outrun grace, until, having started in the race and stumbling, as in Peter's case, pride dies at last.——GERLACH: By the word *glorify* we are to understand the revelation of the divine power and glory. The divine glory is God's manifest, almighty, holy love.—This *one another* (ver. 34) deserves our special consideration.—In these last parting discourses Jesus is no longer speaking of the world, (? See chap. xvi. 8, *etc.*), but of His people only; therefore not of the love that sacrifices itself for another without meeting with any return from that other; but of the love existing in the mutual relationship of true disciples. It is the duty of these *to strive for a unity* like that of the Father and Son (chap. xvii. 21), and to manifest this unity before the world, that the world may know that Jesus was sent from God. This brotherly love is, in its nature, one and the same with a universal love; it differs, however, in expression.—Ver. 36. In this annexed allusion to the future martyr's death which Peter should suffer, there is contained a word of comfort that afterwards had the power to raise him up, when bitter grief at his deep fall brought him nigh unto despair. Comp. Luke xxii. 32.——LISCO: *I will lay down my life.* Thus he spoke with a lively consciousness of his sincere love and hearty attachment to Jesus; but, blinded with regard to his weakness, he gave himself credit for more moral strength and firmness of faith than he possessed.——BRAUNE, ver. 31. An exultant cry of victory in the night in which He was betrayed.—God is glorified in Christ through suffering and death, and Christ is glorified in God through the (resurrection,) ascension into heaven and the exaltation to the right hand of the majesty of the Father.—*Little children*, 1 Pet. i. 23.—*And as I said unto the Jews.* But with what a difference here. Here the sharp words are wanting, that were aimed at the Jews; but the perverse rejoinders are missing likewise (John vii. 34; viii. 21).—A Christian destitute of this brotherly love, is like sounding brass or a tinkling cymbal.—Peter proves that a man is always better than his bad, but worse than his good, moods.

RICHTER: Ver. 37. That Peter did not, in the exercise of faith and obedience, keep silence, was the inward beginning of his fall.

STIER: Ver. 34. If the καινὴ διαθήκη, spoken of in the institution of the Lord's Supper, have reference to Ex. xxiv. 8, comp. Jer. xxxi. 31, then doubtless the ἐντολὴ καινή stands in closest connection with the διαθήκη. For the making of laws is the necessary accompaniment to a covenant.—*As I have loved you.* In Christ, a man like us, the first perfect fulfilment of the law now stands before us as a living decalogue; but when faith petitions, strength to love in like manner issues forth from His perfectness and flows *into us*, Eph. v. 1, 2.—It has been falsely said Peter's denial was *thrice* predicted; here, in accordance with Luke, in accordance with Matthew and Mark. Truer and more significant would be the statement that Peter thrice protested against such a catastrophe.—NITZSCH: It results of itself that those who love one another, are but practising and preparing themselves to extend their love outside of their own circle into the whole world.

[CRAVEN: From ORIGEN: Vers. 31, 32. It is the glory of the *Man* which is here meant; Christ at His death glorified God, *making peace by the blood of His cross*—thus the Son of Man was glorified, and *God glorified in Him.*—The word *glory* is here used in a different sense from that which some pagans attach to it, who defined *glory* to be *the collected praises of many;* the mind when it ascends above material things and spiritually sees God, is *deified*, and of this spiritual glory the visible glory on the face of Moses is a figure.—The whole of the Father's glory shines upon the Son; of this glory He hath made all who know Him partakers.—Ver. 33. *Little children* He says, for their souls were yet in infancy.—Ver. 33. To *seek* Jesus, is to seek the Word, wisdom, righteousness, truth, all which is Christ.—As if He said, I say it to *you* but with the addition of *now* (ver. 36); the Jews would never be able to follow Him, but the disciples were unable only for a little while.——From AUGUSTINE: Ver. 31. The *unclean* went out, the *clean* remained with the cleanser; thus will it be when the tares are separated from the wheat.—Ver. 34. He teaches them how to fit themselves to follow Him.—Ver. 36. He checks the *forwardness* of Peter but does not destroy his *hope;* nay, He confirms it.—Be not lifted up with presumption, thou canst not *now;* be not cast down with despair, *thou shalt follow me afterwards.*—Ver. 37. Peter knew his great desire, his strength he knew not.——From CHRYSOSTOM: Ver. 34. *As I have loved you;* My love has not been the payment of something owing to you, but had its beginning on My side.—Ver. 38. Thou (Peter) shalt know by experience that thy love is nothing, unless thou be enabled from above.——From BEDE: Vers. 36-38. Should any one fall, let the example of Peter save him from despair.

[From BURKITT: Ver. 33. *Little children;* intimating the tender affection He bears His disciples.—*Whither I go ye cannot come;* till our work be done, whither Christ is gone we cannot come.—Ver. 34. A *new* commandment because, urged from a *new motive*, and enforced by a *new example.*—Ver. 35. Christ will have His disciples known by their profound affection to each other.—One of the best evidences we can have of our vital relation to Christ, is a hearty love toward fellow. Christians.—Ver. 36. Though disciples shall certainly follow their Lord, they must patiently wait His time and finish His work.—Vers. 37, 38. The holiest of men knows not his own strength till temptation brings him to the trial.—None are so near falling as those who are most confident of their own standing.——From M. HENRY: From ver. 31, to the end of chap. xiv. Christ's *table-talk* with His disciples; teaching us to make conversation at table serviceable to religion.—Ver. 31. Christ did not begin this discourse till Judas had gone out; the presence of wicked people often a hindrance to good discourse.—Vers. 31, 32. Christ gives three comforting assurances concerning *His sufferings*—1. That HE should be *glorified in them*, by (1) obtaining a *glorious victory* over Satan, (2) working out a *glorious deliverance* for His people, (3) giving a *glorious example* of self-denial and patience; 2. That GOD THE FATHER should be *glorified in them*—those sufferings were, (1) the *satisfaction* of the Father's *justice*, (2) the *manifestation* of the Father's *holiness* and *mercy;* 3. That HE HIMSELF should be greatly *glorified after them*, in consideration of the glorification of the Father *by them* (ver. 32).—In the *exaltation* of Christ there was a *regard* had *to* His (self-) humiliation, and a *reward* given *for* it; those who mind *the business of glorifying God* shall have the happiness of being *glorified with Him.*—Ver. 33. The words *little children* do not declare so much their *weakness*, as His *tenderness and compassion.*—The declaration *Whither I go ye cannot come* suggests—1. *high* thoughts of Him, 2. *low* thoughts of themselves.—They could not follow Him to His *cross*, for they had not (then) courage; they could not follow Him to His *crown*, for they had not a sufficiency of their own, nor was their work yet *finished.*—Vers. 34, 35. He urges the great duty of *mutual love* by three arguments—1. The *command* of their Master; 2. The *example* of their Saviour; 3. The *reputation of their profession.*—*Brotherly love* is the *badge* of Christ's disciples, by this—1. *He* knows them, 2. *others* (the world) know them.—The *true honor* of Christ's disciples to excel in brotherly love.—Ver. 36. Peter's *curiosity* and the *check* given to it.—Believers must not expect to be glorified as soon as they are effectually called—there is a wilderness between the Red Sea and Canaan.—Vers. 37, 38. Peter's (*self-*) *confidence* and the *check* given to that.—Peter was *inconsiderate* but not *insincere;* we are apt to think we can do *anything*, but without Christ we can do *nothing.*—It is good for us to *shame ourselves* out of our *presumptuous* confidence; shall a bruised reed set up for a pillar, or a sickly child undertake to be a champion?—Christ not only foresaw that Judas would betray Him, but that Peter would deny Him; He knows not only the *wickedness of sinners*, but the *weakness of Saints.*—The most *secure* are commonly the least *safe.*——From SCOTT: Ver. 34. Alas! the commandment to *love one another as Christ has loved us* is still *new* and *strange* to most professed Christians.——From A. CLARK: Ver. 31. Now it fully appears (is about to appear) that I am the Person appointed to redeem a lost world by My blood.—Ver. 34. Christ *more* than fulfilled the Mosaic precept; He not only loved His neighbor *as* Himself, but He loved him *more* than Himself—His commandment was strictly *new.*—Vers. 36, 38. We should *will*, and then look to God for *power* to execute.——From STIER: Ver. 31. A cry of exultation in the night in which *He was betrayed.*—The first glorification is the beginning and ground of *that* which follows as its consummation.—In His *humiliation* He is *exalted*, in this darkness of shame does His glory beam forth, from Golgotha go forth those attracting energies which are to wrest from Satan the world of mankind.—The glorification of God in the suffering and dying Son of man embraces—1. when we *look into it*, the self-offering of God in the *person of this* Son of man as a great and solitary fact; 2. when we *look back*, the shining forth of God in *human nature* generally, as the longed for goal of all aspiration and effort; 3. when we *look forward*, the *representation and offering* of God to humanity as the object of faith and love.—The purest *honor of God* shines forth in the deepest *dishonor* of this *Son of Man.*—All is human and all is Divine; the *Ecce Homo* is changed to the eye of faith into—*Behold thy God!*—Ver. 32. The Lord speaks of a *twofold* glorification—1. He is made perfect through suffering; 2. the glorification of the Son of Man in God.—Ver. 34. A *new* commandment—1. in the simplicity and plainness of the *expression;* 2. in the perfection of the *new*, now first existing, *type;* 3. in the *power of fulfilment* which flows from this *life-giving type;* 4. and consequently, in the *abiding, living newness* of this commandment.—Ver. 37. Peter (*a little child,* ver. 33;) would be a *man* before the time!——From A PLAIN COMMENTARY (Oxford); Ver. 34. The commandment called *new* because destined to become *the great law of the new creation.*—From BARNES: Vers. 34, 35. This commandment to be a *badge* of discipleship; it was called *new* because—1. it had never before been made that by which any class of men had been distinguished; 2. of *the extent* to which it was to be carried.——From OWEN: Ver. 35. As a historical fact there has been no feature of Christianity exemplified in the life of believers, so potent in overcoming opposition as their mutual love.——From WHEDON: Vers. 36-38. Enough there was of a downfall to neutralize the pride of Peter, but his subsequent recovery evinced the earnestness of his profession.]

II.

HEAVEN (THE HEAVENLY HOME) THROWN OPEN AND REVEALED BY THE REVELATION OF THE HEAVENLY CHRIST IN THIS PRESENT WORLD. GLORIFICATION OF THE WORLD BEYOND, RESULTANT UPON HIS GOING AWAY AND HIS UNION WITH THE DISCIPLES IN THE SPIRIT. UNDERNEATH THE STARRY HEAVENS. CHRIST THE WAY TO THE FATHER'S HOUSE. (THE MANIFESTATION OF THE FATHER (AND OF HEAVEN) IN THE VISIBLE WORLD. THE COMMUNION OF THE SPIRIT AS THE ENTRANCE TO THE FATHER'S HOUSE, OR AS THE TABERNACLE AND FORETOKEN OF THE HEAVENLY HOME. THOMAS, PHILIP, JUDAS LEBBÆUS, OR: 1. THE PERSONAL CHRIST, AS OPPOSED TO THE MENACING ACTUALITY OF THINGS, AND TO DOUBT; 2. THE SPIRITUAL MANIFESTATION OF GOD, IN OPPOSITION TO A VISIBLE APPEARANCE AND TO SENSUOUS PREJUDICE; 3. THE CHURCH OF THE LORD IN OPPOSITION TO THE WORLD AND TO WORLDLY MESSIANIC IDEALS).

CHAP. XIV. 1–31.

(Vers. 1-14, Gospel for St. Philip and St. James' Day; vers. 23-31 for Whit-Sunday.)

1 Let not your heart be troubled: ye [*omit* ye] believe in God, believe also in me
2 [Have faith in God, and have faith in me].[1] In my Father's house are many mansions: if *it were* not *so*, I would have told you. [For, ὅτι] I go to prepare a place for you. [Lange: If it were not so, would I then have said to you, I go to prepare
3 a place for you?][2] And if [Lange: Even though] I go and prepare[3] a place for you, I will [*omit* will] come [ἔρχομαι] again, and [will] receive [παραλήμψομαι]
4 you unto myself; that where I am, *there* [*omit there*] ye may be also. And whither I go ye know, and the way ye know [And ye know the way whither I go, καὶ ὅπου ἐγὼ ὑπάγω οἴδατε τὴν ὁδόν].[4]
5 Thomas saith unto him, Lord, we know not whither thou goest; and how can
6 [should] we know the way?[5] Jesus saith unto him, I am the way, [and] the
7 truth, and the life: no man cometh unto the Father, but by [through] me. If ye had known me, ye should [would] have known[6] my Father also: and from henceforth ye know him, and have seen him.
8 Philip saith unto him, Lord, shew us the Father [visibly], and it sufficeth us [we
9 shall be satisfied]. Jesus saith unto him, Have I been so long time with you, and yet hast thou not known me [dost thou not know me], Philip? he that hath seen me hath seen the Father; and how sayest thou *then* [*omit then*], Shew us the
10 Father? Believest thou not that I am in the Father, and the Father [is] in me? the words that I speak[7] unto you I speak not of myself: but the Father that dwelleth in me, he doeth the works [the Father, abiding in me, doeth his
11 works].[8] Believe me that I *am* in the Father, and the Father in me: or else [but
12 if not] believe me[9] for the very works' sake. Verily, verily, I say unto you, He that believeth on me, the works that I do shall he do also; and [even] greater *works* [*omit works*] than these shall he do; because [for] I go unto my [the][10]
13 Father. And whatsoever ye shall ask[11] in my name, that will I do, that the Father
14 may be glorified in the Son. If ye shall ask anything in my name, I will do *it*.[12]
15, 16 If ye love me, keep my commandments. And I will [shall] pray the Father, and he shall [will] give you another Comforter [Paraclete[13]], that he may abide
17 [be][14] with you for ever; *Even* [*omit Even*] the Spirit of truth; whom the world cannot receive, because [for] it seeth [beholdeth] him not, neither knoweth him: but[15] ye know him; for [because] he dwelleth [abideth] with you, and shall be
18 [will be][16] in you. I will [shall] not leave you comfortless [orphans]: I will
19 [shall] come to you. Yet a little while, and the world seeth [beholdeth] me no
20 more; but ye see [behold] me: because [for] I live, [and] ye shall live also.—At that day ye shall [will] know that I *am* in my Father, and ye in me, and I in you.

21 He that hath [possesseth] my commandments, and keepeth them, he it is that
loveth me; and [but] he that loveth me shall [will] be loved of my Father, and
I will [shall] love him, and will [shall] manifest myself to him.
22 Judas saith unto him, not Iscariot, Lord, how[17] is it that thou wilt manifest thy-
23 self unto us, and not unto the world? Jesus answered and said unto him, If a man
[any one] love me, he will keep my words [word]: and my Father will love him,
24 and we will [shall] come unto him, and make our abode with him. He that
loveth me not keepeth not my sayings [words]: and the word which ye hear is
not mine, but the Father's which [who] sent me.
25 These things have I spoken unto you, being *yet* present [while yet abiding, or,
26 tarrying] with you. But the Comforter, *which is* [But the Paraclete, *even*] the Holy
Ghost, whom the [my][18] Father will send in my name, he shall [will] teach
you all things, and bring all things to your remembrance, whatsoever [which]
27 I have said unto you. Peace I leave with you, my peace I give unto you: not
as the world giveth, give I unto you. Let not your heart be troubled, neither
28 let it be afraid. Ye have heard how [that] I said unto you, I go away, and
come *again* [*omit again*] unto you. If ye loved me, ye would rejoice [ye
would have rejoiced, ἐχάρητε] because [that] I said [*omit* I said[19]], I go unto the
29 Father: for my [the][20] Father is greater than I. And now I have told you be-
30 fore it come to pass, that, when it is come to pass, ye might [may] believe. Here-
after I will [shall] not talk much [*add* more] with you: for the prince of this
[the][21] world cometh, and hath nothing in me [and of me there belongeth to him nothing
31 at all]. But that the world may know that I love the Father; and as the Father
gave me commandment [commanded me], even so [thus] I do. Arise, let us go
hence.

TEXTUAL AND GRAMMATICAL.

1 Ver. 1.—[Or, "Trust (confide) in God, trust also in Me." The sentence admits of four interpretations and translations, as πιστεύετε may be taken both times in the imperative, or both times in the indicative, or once in the imperative, and once in the indicative sense. Hence: 1. "Believe in God, believe also in Me" (Cyril, Nonnus, Theophyl., Euthym. Zigab., Lampe, Bengel, Whitby, Doddridge, Lücke, De Wette, Meyer, Stier, Alford, Hengstenberg, Godet); 2. "*Ye* believe in God, *ye* believe also in Me" (Luther in his trans.); 3. "Believe in God, and (then) *ye* will also believe in Me" (Olshausen, Lange); 4. "*Ye* believe in God, (therefore) believe also in Me;" *Creditis in Deum, et in Me credite* (Vulg., Aug., Erasmus, Beza, Engl. Ver., Grotius). I take πιστεύετε in both clauses as Imperative. See the EXEG.—P. S.]

2 Ver. 2.—[Ὅτι in accordance with ℵ. A. B. C.* D. K., Lachmann, Tischend., Alford, *etc.* The omission in the text. rec. arose from its being taken as the mere ὅτι *recitantis* and hence as unnecessary. It may be taken as the ὅτι *recitantis* with Lange who connects ὅτι πορεύομαι with εἶπον ἂν ὑμῖν, or in the sense *because, for*. See EXEG.—P. S.]

3 Ver. 3.—Καὶ ἑτοιμάσω. Lachmann, in accordance with A. B. E. G., *etc.*, omits καὶ. Tischendorf retains it in accordance with Codd. [ℵ.] C. I. L., the Vulgate and Itala. [Tischendorf, Ed. viii., claims B. as supporting the latter reading.] The former reading seems to have arisen from the idea that ἑτοιμάσω, as a promise, must be attracted to the subsequent πάλιν ἔρχομαι, *etc.* The corollary, however, is designed to limit Christ's going away and remaining in the other world. Codd. D. M., *etc.* read ἑτοιμάσαι in accordance with the foregoing.

4 Ver. 4.—Codd. B. C.* Sin., *etc.*, Tischendorf [Alford, Westcott and H.] read οἴδατε τὴν ὁδόν instead of οἴδατε, καὶ τὴν ὁδόν οἴδατε in accordance with A. D., *etc.* Meyer favors the former reading: "and whither I go, ye know the way." Ver. 5 he declares to be in favor of this reading. This passage indeed seems at first declarative for the Recepta, since it makes a decided distinction between the goal and the way. Nevertheless we must give the preference to the former reading, it being the more difficult and also according significantly with the context. [The καί and second οἴδατε of the text. rec. is explanatory according to ver. 5.—P. S.]

5 Ver. 5.—Lachmann and Tischendorf, in accordance with Codd. B. C.* D., Versions, *etc.* read οἴδαμεν τὴν ὁδόν instead of δυνάμεθα τὴν ὁδὸν εἰδέναι. The Recepta is explanatory [sustained by (ℵ.) A. C.[2] (K.) L., *etc.*]

6 Ver. 7.—Ἐγνώκειτε ἂν is opposed to ᾔδειτε ἂν by strong authorities, A. E. G., *etc.* [Tischendorf, Ed. viii., reads ἐγνώκατε, instead of ἐγνώκειτε, and γνώσεσθε (*cognoscetis*) for ᾔδειτε, with Cod. Sin. and D.* The other reading is supported by A. B. C. D.[2] L. N. Q. X., *etc.*, Lachm., Tischend., ed. 7th, Alford.—P. S.]

7 Ver. 10.—[Tischend., Alf., *etc.* read λέγω (with B. L. N. X.), the text. rec. λαλῶ (with ℵ. A. Q., *etc.*); D. aeth. λελάληκα, perhaps from vi. 63.—P. S.]

8 Ver. 10.—[According to the reading ὁ δὲ πατὴρ ὁ ἐν ἐμοὶ μένων ποιεῖ τὰ ἔργα αὐτοῦ, which is supported by ℵ. B. D. and adopted by Tischendorf, ed. viii. The text. rec. inserts αὐτός before ποιεῖ and omits αὐτοῦ, *he himself doeth the works;* so Lachm. and Tischend., ed. vii., in accordance with A. Q. Γ. Δ. Λ. Π., *etc.*—P. S.]

9 Ver. 11.—[Tischendorf, Ed. viii., omits μοι in accordance with ℵ. D. L.; Lachmann and Alford give it with A. B. Q., *etc.*—P. S.]

10 Ver. 12.—Μου is omitted in accordance with decisive authorities, [*viz.* ℵ. A. B. D. L. Q. X. Π.]

11 Ver. 13.—[Tischendorf gives αἰτήσητε in accordance with ℵ. A. D. L. X.; Cod. B. reads αἰτῆτε.—P. S.]

12 Ver. 14.—This verse is wanting in X. and a few Minuscles and Versions. Omitted probably on account of its similarity to ver. 13. [Tischendorf, Ed. viii. and Lachmann read αἰτήσητέ με in accordance with ℵ. B. E. H., *etc.*; Tischendorf in Ed. vii. omitted με with A. D. G. K., *etc.* So does Alford, ed. vi.—P. S.]

13 Ver. 16.—[On the different renderings of παράκλητος, *Paraclete*, *Comforter*, *Helper*, *Advocate*, *Representative*, see the EXEG. NOT. The English rendering *Comforter*, which corresponds to Luther's *Tröster*, is derived from Wicliff, who often uses it in the sense of the Latin *comfortari*, so as to combine the idea of help and strength with that of consolation. See Archdeacon Hare, *Mission of the Comforter*, vol. ii. j. a. and Alford *in loc.*—P. S.]

14 Ver. 16.—Instead of μένῃ according to Cod. [A.] D., in conformity to ver. 17 [ℵ.] B. L. Q. X. S. Lachmann, Tischendorf [Alford, *etc.*] decide in favor of ᾖ.

15 Ver. 17.—[Tischendorf and Alford omit δέ after ὑμεῖς, in accordance with ℵ. B. Q.; Lachmann gives it with A. D. L. X., *etc.*—P. S.]

16 Ver. 17.—The Future ἔσται, in accordance with [ℵ.] A. [D.[2] L.] Q. Tischendorf, in opposition to ἐστί [*is*] B. D. Lachmann [Alford], is recommended by the very μένει which precedes it as a Present (E. G. K.) instead of a Future (Vulgate).

[17] Ver. 22.—[Tischendorf reads καὶ τί in accordance with ℵ. G. H. K., *etc.*; Lachmann omits καὶ with A. B. D. E. L. X.—P. S.]

[18] Ver. 26.—[The μου is supported only by D. Π.[2] and a few inferior authorities.—P. S.]

[19] Ver. 28.—Εἶπον is omitted in accordance with Cod. [ℵ.] A. B. D. K., *etc.* A repetition from the foregoing.

[20] Ver. 28.—[The μου is omitted by Tischendorf, Ed. viii., in accordance with ℵ.[ca] A. B. D.,* *etc.*; Griesbach and Lachmann give it with ℵ.* D.[2] Γ. Δ., *etc.*]

[21] Ver. 30.—Τούτου is omitted in accordance with [ℵ.] A. B. D. [g. r.], *etc.* An explanatory addition.

EXEGETICAL AND CRITICAL.

[These discourses were spoken *after* the Lord's Supper, which took place, according to Lange and Tholuck, at ch. xiii. 34. A pause intervened between the close of the last and the beginning of this chapter. When Peter was "humbled and silent" (Lücke), and the other disciples sadly moved by what they had just heard of the treason of Judas, the denial of Peter and the departure of their beloved Lord and Master, He addressed to them these opening words of cheer which, coming from *His* lips with all the thrilling solemnities of the night preceding the crucifixion, have an immeasurable power of comfort and consolation in seasons of deepest distress and on the very borders of despair. The parting discourses have already been characterized at the beginning of ch. xiii. and on xiii. 31; but the beautiful remarks of Olshausen may here be added: "We come, finally," he says, "to that portion of the evangelical history, which we may with propriety call its *Holy of Holies.* Our Evangelist, like a consecrated priest, alone opens to us the view into this sanctuary. This is composed of the last moments spent by the Lord in the midst of His disciples before His passion, when words full of heavenly thought flowed from His sacred lips. All that His heart which glowed with love had yet to say to His friends, was compressed into this short season. At first the interview with the disciples took the form of conversation; sitting at table they talked together familiarly. But when (xiv. 31) the repast was finished, the language of Christ assumed a loftier strain; the disciples assembled around their Master, listened to the words of life and seldom spoke a word (only xvi. 17, 29). At length in the Redeemer's sublime intercessory prayer, His full soul was poured forth in express petitions to His heavenly Father on behalf of those who were His own. Meanwhile, His discourse retained the form of free communication, in which no marks of designed arrangement are to be discovered, as would be the case with a formal oration.—It is a peculiarity of these last chapters, that they treat almost exclusively of the most profound relations—as that of the Son to the Father, and of both to the Spirit, that of the Christ to the Church, of the Church to the world, and so forth. Moreover, a considerable portion of these sublime communications surpassed the point of view to which the disciples had at that time attained; hence the Redeemer frequently repeats the same sentiments in order to impress them more deeply upon their minds; and, on account of what they still did not understand, He points them to the Holy Spirit, who would remind them of all His sayings, and lead them into the whole truth (xiv. 26)."—P. S.]

Ver. 1. **Let not your heart be troubled** [affrighted, μὴ ταρασσέσθω ὑμῶν ἡ καρδία].—The spirit, the soul, may be troubled (see chap. xi. 33; xiii. 21); not so the *heart*, as the organ and symbol of trust. This encouragement has reference not simply to what He has told them about the approaching denial of Him (Chrysost., *etc.*), but, in the first place, to the announcement of His departure and to the decree uttered by Him (De Wette and others), to the effect that they could not follow Him. Taking this decree in its concrete sense, however, there comes into consideration as well the saying concerning the denial of Peter,—a saying which revealed a perspective full of danger to all the disciples. The prospect of the denial of faith's goal in the high and invisible world which lay beyond them, was a prospect calculated to startle them, even when apprehended in the most general sense.

Trust in God, and (then) ye (will) trust in me [or rather: *Have faith in God, and have faith in Me,* πιστεύετε (Imperative) εἰς τὸν θεὸν, καὶ εἰς ἐμὲ πιστεύετε (Imperative). See the TEXTUAL NOTES.—P. S.]—Πιστεύειν does not here mean *belief* in the general sense of that term (in which sense they had belief), but in its special sense—*trust: trust directed to God,* and trust *directed to Christ.* Hence we translate: *trust in;* namely, in God who is on high; in Me when I ascend on high. This sets aside:

1. The interpretation: '*ye* believe in God, believe also in Me.' With the first verb in the Indicative, the second in the Imperative (Vulg., Erasm. and others [E. V.]).

2. '*If* ye believe in God (as if it were εἰ πιστ.), ye believe also in Me' (Luther).* With the verb each time in the Indicative.

3. According to Cyril, Lücke, De Wette and others [Meyer, Alford, Godet], both expressions are in the Imperative: 'Rely on God and rely also on Me.' We do not think, however, that Christ can thus make two separate trusts. We might, perhaps, more reasonably expect: 'Rely on Me; in so doing ye rely also on God,'—in analogy with the saying ver. 6. But here Christ's ascension to heaven must be presupposed, as resulting from the fact that the Father in heaven is the goal towards whom that ascension tends. Therefore: Trust in God; in so doing ye do also trust in Me (εἰς, expressive of the direction of this trust to heaven and to the One who is about ascending into heaven).

Tholuck: "Even Erasmus observes that ver. 1 may be apprehended in four ways, according as πιστεύετε is assumed to be both times in the Indicative, the sense of an hypothesis being attached to the word at its first occurrence (Aug., Luth.), or taking the latter as Indicative and as a consequence of the former (Grot., Olsh. and others), or the former as Indicative and the second as Imperative (Vulg.), or, after the example of most of the church fathers, both as in the Imperative." For the reasons cited above,

* [In his translation, but not in his Commentary on chh xiv., xvi., where he follows the translation of the Vulgate, see no. 1.—P. S.]

we agree with Grotius in holding the first πιστεύετε to be in the Imperative mood,—attaching to it the sense of trust, however—and the second to be consecutive to the first.

[I prefer to read πιστεύετε both times *imperatively*, as in ver. 11, because this agrees best with the preceding imperative, μὴ ταρασσέσθω, and with the fresh, direct, hortatory character of the address. The other interpretations introduce a reflective tone. Our Lord exhorts and encourages the disciples to dismiss all trouble from their hearts and to exercise full trust and confidence (πιστεύετε, emphatically first and last) in God, who has in reserve for them many mansions in heaven, and consequently also to trust in Christ, who is one with the Father and is going to prepare a place for them; faith in God and faith in Christ are inseparable (hence εἰς ἐμέ is placed before the second πιστεύετε), and the glorification of the Son is a glorification of the Father in the Son; comp. xiii. 31, 32, with which this passage is closely connected. In claiming the same trust and reliance on Himself as on the Father, Christ makes Himself equal with God, as in ch. v. 17 and 23. Hence there is here no *addition* of faith in Christ to faith in God (as Olshausen objects), nor a transfer of our trust from its proper object to another, but simply the concentration of our trust in the unseen God—who out of Christ is a mere abstraction—upon the incarnate Son, in whom this trust becomes real and effective.—P. S.]

Ver. 2. **In my Father's house** [ἐν τῇ οἰκίᾳ τοῦ πατρός μου μοναὶ πολλαί εἰσιν. Mark the simple, childlike, cheering character of this address to dear children (τεκνία, xiii. 33): the touching ideas of Father, house, home, peaceful and durable rest, room enough for all in heaven.—P. S.] The house of the Father is the real temple of God, as opposed to the typical temple or house of the Father (chap. ii. 16), which they are now cast out of, having taken their leave of it as Jews. According to Meyer [p. 505], this house is "not heaven *in general*, but the particular *dwelling-place* of the divine δόξα in heaven, the place of His glorious throne (Ps. ii. 4; xxxiii. 13 ff.; Is. lxiii. 15, *etc.*), considered as the heavenly sanctuary (Is. lvii. 15), according to the analogy of the temple at Jerusalem as the οἶκος τοῦ πατρός on earth (John ii. 16)." But not in vain is it written: Our Father *in the heavens* (Matt. vi. 9); Christ came down *from heaven* (John iii. 13); ascended *into heaven* (Acts i. 11); is set on the throne of the Majesty *in the heavens* (Heb. viii. 1); the inheritance of Christians is reserved for them *in the heavens* (1 Pet. i. 4). Therefore even if the throne of God be denominated the central point in the heavens or the highest point above the heavens, still the heavens themselves are not excluded from being His house, for there is a distinction between the seat or throne in a house and the house itself; and this irrespective of the fact that heaven is also simply called His throne, Is. lxvi. 1. We assume, moreover, that we are not required to make a spiritualistic separation between God's heaven and the starry universe, and that the aspect of the starry heavens is a figure to us of the heavenly mansions, even though it be true that all stars are not to be regarded as heavenly places. (See my book: *The Land of Glory*.* Kurtz, *Bible and Astronomy;* also my *Leben Jesu*, II. p. 1349.) And so it is most probable that Jesus spoke these words to the disciples as they were leaving the Passover room, pointing, as He uttered them, up to the starry sky. [According to xiv. 31, they seem to have been still in the room, but see Lange's notes on the passage.—P. S.] Henceforth they, like Him, were strangers on earth, having no abiding place: at this moment He disclosed heaven to their view and gave them a promise of the many dwelling-places in the Father's house. Hence the significant choice of the expression: μονή, a place of rest, a lodging.

[The term μοναί, which in the N. T. occurs only here and ver. 23, is derived from μένω, *to abide*, and hence implies the idea of abode, rest, stability, home (comp. μένουσαν πόλιν, Heb. xiii. 14; the σκηναὶ αἰώνιοι, Luke xvi. 9, and the οἰκοδομὴν ἐκ θεοῦ, the οἰκία ἀχειροποίητος αἰώνιος ἐν τοῖς οὐρανοῖς, 2 Cor. v. 1). The E. V. *mansion*, from *mansio*, *manere*, μένειν (introduced by Tyndale), here and in old English means dwelling-house, not, as in modern usage, manor-house, palace. Christ probably alludes to the temple, His Father's house on earth (ch. ii. 16; Rev. iii. 12; comp. Luke ii. 49) with its numerous chambers (1 Kings vi. 5, 6, 10), perhaps also to the vast oriental palaces with apartments for all the princes and courtiers. Heaven is not only a *state*, which commences already here on earth with the presence of Christ in the soul and the possession of everlasting life by faith in Him, but also a *place*, from which Christ descended and to which He ascended, and where He, with the Father and the Spirit, dwells among saints and angels, patriarchs and prophets (Luke xiii. 28), in the fulness of His majesty and glory. Philosophy and astronomy are unable to define the *locality* of this spiritual heaven, it is a matter of

* [This little book of Dr. Lange, *Das Land der Herrlichkeit*, appeared first in a series of articles in Hengstenberg's '*Evangelical Church Gazette*,' and then separately, Mörs 1838. It is an argument for the Scripture idea of heaven against the astronomical objections, and abounds in beautiful poetic passages. I shall quote but two: "It is certain that there must be SOME PLACE in the upper worlds where the beauties and wonders of God's works are illuminated to the highest transparency by His power and holy majesty; where the combination of lovely manifestations, as seen from radiant summits, the enraptured gaze into the quiet valleys of universal creation, and the streams of light which flow through them, must move the spirits of the blest in the mightiest manner, to cry out: HOLY! HOLY! HOLY!—And there is the holiest place in the great Temple! It is there, because there divine manifestations fill all spirits with a feeling of His holiness. But still rather, because there He reveals Himself through holy spirits, and through the holiest one of all, even Jesus Himself!"—"Seek not to persuade us that all those vast regions are destitute of inhabitants. Seek not to persuade the pilgrim, wandering through the darkness, that yon cottage, whence a hospitable light streams forth to greet him, is without an inhabitant. So on us there shimmers from above, light out of 'many mansions.' It is a city of God that beams upon us, whose golden streets stretch forth into remotest infinitude. We see not its furthest battlements; its nearest ones *do* meet our gaze. And when we consider that light from there is thousands of years in reaching us, and that, starting from a remoter point, it is millions of years on its way, we may well call the city of the Living God an 'Eternal City.' Its radiance beams mightily upon our bodily vision if we do but step forth into the starry night: Its glory and higher nature have been made evident by science. But to the believer alone do the heavens disclose themselves as the Fatherland and Heritage of the Blessed. Unto Christians it is said: 'Ye are come unto the City of the Living God,' and 'in my Father's House are many mansions.'" P. 62.—P. S.]

pure faith, yet most real, even more so than this changing earth; for earth is but the footstool of God and derives its value from the life and light of the supernatural world above, around and within us. The Jewish Rabbis distinguished two heavens (comp. Deut. x. 14, the "heaven and the heaven of heavens"), or seven heavens (severally called *velum, expansum, nubes, habitaculum, habitatio, sedes fixa, araboth*; see Wetstein on 2 Cor. xii. 2). St. Paul speaks of the third heaven (2 Cor. xii. 2), which by some commentators is placed beyond the atmospheric and the starry heavens; but heaven may be much nearer than is generally supposed. According to the Apocalypse, the many heavenly mansions here spoken of are after all not the final but the intermediate resting-places of the saints till the general resurrection when the heavenly Jerusalem will descend upon the new, glorified earth, and God will dwell with His people for ever, Rev. xxi. 1 ff.; 2 Pet. iii. 13. Then heaven and earth will be one; earth being changed to heaven and heaven to earth, "one kingdom, joy and union without end."—P. S.]

Many mansions. Tholuck: "In the *multiplicity* of the μοναί the fathers discovered a diversity of grades; thus Clemens Alex., *etc.*, also Stier, Lange, *etc.* The context, however, does not indicate any difference of degrees, but simply the multiplicity of the dwellings." But if this multiplicity were merely quantitative and not qualitative as well, the expression: there is room enough, would suffice. Of course the words convey this meaning too, in accordance with Luther's saying: "If the devil with his tyrants hunt you out of the world, ye shall still have room enough." [Wordsworth agrees with Lange as to different degrees of felicity in the same blessed eternity. But Meyer, Godet and Alford confine πολλαί to the number: mansions enough for each and all, ἱκαναὶ δέξασθαι καὶ ὑμᾶς (Euthym. Zig.). The idea of degrees of dignity and blessedness in heaven corresponding to the degrees of perfection, though perhaps not implied in the word *many* here, is certainly scriptural, comp. 1 Cor. xv. 41, and has always been admitted in the Church. No envy or jealousy will arise from disparity of glory, for, as Augustine says, the unity of love will reign in all. —P. S.]*

If it were not so, would I have told you: I go to prepare a place for you? [This is Lange's construction, which differs from the English V. Comp. TEXTUAL NOTES and see below.—P. S.] Various constructions:

1. The fathers, Erasm., Luther and others [Maldonatus, Bengel, Ebrard], Hofmann: "*If it were not so, I would say to you: I go to prepare a place for you.*" [These interpreters refer εἶπον ἂν ὑμῖν to the following: ὅτι πορεύομαι. Lange does the same, but makes the sentence a question.—P. S.] Meyer thinks that ver. 3 is decisive against this supposition; according to that verse Jesus actually goes and prepares a place. But it would not be the only passage in which John presents a relative antithesis in the form of an absolute one. (See chap. i. 11, 12.) A more powerful consideration against the view is, that the work of Christ joins on to the work of the Father, re-organizing the creation but not extending it (*Leben Jesu*, II. p. 1350).

2. Laurent. Valla, Beza, Calvin, Lücke, Tholuck and many others have placed a period after εἶπον ἂν ὑμῖν. "*If it were not so, I would have told you.*"* The expression of Christ's veracity might recommend this reading, if the idea of the heavenly dwellings had been already diffused among the disciples. But this was not the case: hitherto they had had but the idea of Sheol, with its two grand divisions: Paradise and the place of punishment [Gehenna]. Hence it would have been superfluous for Christ to deny the truth of an idea which as yet they had not entertained.

3. We, therefore, adopt the interrogative apprehension of the words: "*would I then, etc.?*" (Mosheim, Ernesti, Beck); yet not in the sense of the Present: **would I tell you?** against which Meyer cites the aorist εἶπον, but: **would I have told you?** (Ewald). He has really told them this, though not literally, any more than He said to the Jews—chap. x. 14—: Ye are not My sheep (comp. ver. 26); for instance chap. viii. 22; comp. chap. xiii. 33; chap. x. 4, 11; vers. 28, 29; chap. xii. 26. So, then, He has told them before this, that He is going to another world where He has destined abiding-places for them near Himself. It is His intention now to develop this germ of revelation in the most glorious disclosures concerning heaven. The μονή is there already, by Christ, and above all by His making Himself the centre of it, it shall be converted into a fitting τόπος for them and all believers. For ἑτοιμάσαι τόπον does not mean: to create the place as a place, but: to arrange it as a habitable place. [Comp. 2 Pet. i. 11: "An entrance shall be richly ministered unto you into the eternal kingdom of our Lord;" 2 Cor. v. 1, "a building from God, a dwelling not made with hands, eternal in the heavens." Alford quotes here from the *Te Deum*: "When Thou hadst overcome the sharpness of death, Thou didst open the Kingdom of Heaven to all believers." Christ *prepared* a heavenly home for His disciples by His atoning death, resurrection and ascension; but considering that the heavenly mansions are merely intermistic abodes, the term may perhaps also refer to the building up of the

* [A very singular and painful abuse of this passage on the many mansions was made by Göthe in his old age (1823) when, in a letter to Countess Auguste Bernstorf-Stolberg who, as a friend and correspondent of his youth, had most delicately and touchingly entreated him to attend to the salvation of his soul, he coldly replied: "Let us dismiss all fears about the future. In our Father's kingdom are many provinces, and since He has prepared for us such a delightful abode in this world, He will no doubt take good care of both of us in the other world; perhaps we may there succeed also, what we failed to do heretofore, to become acquainted with each other face to face and to love each other all the more deeply. Remember me in undisturbed faithfulness."—P. S.]

* [So also the Eng. V., Grotius, Olshausen, De Wette, Meyer, Alford, Lachmann, Tischendorf (in their punctuation), Hengstenberg, Godet. In this case εἰ δὲ μή, εἶπον ἂν ὑμῖν is parenthetical, and ὅτι πορεύομαι, *for I go, etc.*, begins a new sentence which confirms (ὅτι) the assurance: "In My Father's house are many mansions;" the ἑτοιμάζειν τόπον implies μονὰς πολλάς. The parenthetical assurance, "if it were not so, I would have told you," agrees with the childlike simplicity of the discourse and is calculated to beget implicit confidence, comp. ch. xvi. 4. Upon the whole I prefer this interpretation and would retain the English Version, except that it omits *for* (ὅτι) before "*I go.*" Lange's interrogative interpretation is open to the objection that no such words as πορεύομαι ἑτοιμάσαι τόπον ὑμῖν, are recorded in the previous chapters of John.—P. S.]

heavenly Jerusalem, which is ultimately to descend upon the new earth. On πορεύομαι Augustine and Wordsworth remark: "Christ sets out on a journey, to prepare a place for us. Let Him depart; let Him ascend, and not be visible to the bodily eye; let Him be hidden from it, that thus He may be seen by the eye of faith; and being so seen, may be desired; and being desired, may be possessed for ever; the desire of our love is the preparation of our house in heaven."—P. S.]

Ver. 3. **And though I go.**—Here stress is laid upon the going away. To prepare for them the place in the inheritance of glory, He must, indeed, first leave them. But the going away is to be counterbalanced by His coming again to take them to Himself. [Meyer: καὶ ἐάν, not κ. ὅταν. Jesus does not intend to indicate the *time* of His return, but the *consequence* of His departure. The πορεύεσθαι κ. ἑτοιμάσαι are the antecedent facts which, once accomplished, result in the πάλιν ἔρχομαι. The nearness or distance of this return is left undecided by ἐάν.—P. S.]

I come again [πάλιν ἔρχομαι].—Three different interpretations:

1. As referring to the παρουσία of Christ on the last day (Origen, Calvin, Lampe, Meyer, Hofmann [also Luthardt, Brückner, Ewald]). On which Meyer: It is the idea of the imminent Parousia, an idea appearing also in John, though with less prominence. [Meyer refers to ch. v. 28 ff.; xxi. 22; 1 John ii. 28.—P. S.] This view is contradicted (*a*) by the erroneousness of the supposition that the disciples (or Christ Himself) conceived of the Parousia as so imminent, in a chronological sense. (*b*) By the fact that in the true Parousia there is to take place, not a re-union between Christ and His people in heaven (where Christ is), but a re-union on earth (where the Church is; see Rev. chap. xiv. and xx.); while here the disclosures made concern the heaven beyond this life, not the earth with its future destiny of glorification. (*c*) By the circumstance that the Present ἔρχομαι denotes a right speedy return of Christ, thus being adapted to console these disciples at their separation from Christ and in the sufferings inflicted upon them through persecution.

2. Christ's coming again to His people, through His Spirit, and their reception into the full and holy spiritual fellowship of the glorified Christ, in accordance with ver. 18 (Lücke, Neander [Godet], *etc.*). But that this spiritual re-union is not the precise thing intended by the passage, though con-supposed or pre-supposed, results from the fact that Christ is here speaking of coming to fetch them to a goal whose locality is determined.

3. The words are indicative of a coming of Jesus for the purpose of receiving the disciples into heaven by means of a blissful death (Grotius, Knapp, Baumg.-Crusius, Nitzsch [Reuss, Tholuck, Hengstenberg] and others). Against this view Meyer remarks: "It is in opposition to these words (comp. vers. 21, 22) and to the manner in which other portions of the New Testament speak of the coming of Christ; death truly transports the apostles and martyrs to Christ (2 Cor. v. 8; Phil. i. 23; Acts vii. 59), but nowhere is it said of Christ that He comes and takes them to Himself. Except in the Paraclete of whom John treats, Christ *comes* only in His glory at the Parousia." Against this we would remind our readers that the parable of Lazarus mentions a calling for and carrying away of pious souls (Luke xvi. 22). There, indeed, the coming of angels is still the temporary substitute for Christ's coming Himself. But when dying Stephen prays: "Lord Jesus, receive my spirit" (Acts vii. 58), he takes it for granted that the Lord is coming to meet his parting spirit; for this cause he saw Jesus beforehand, already standing, *i. e.* having arisen from His throne, on the point of receiving or fetching him (ver. 55). Further, unless we are willing to affirm that the saying of Christ, John xxi. 22, has not been fulfilled, there is no way in which we can understand it except as referring to His coming to John in death, to take him away with Him. Dying believers also (not "Apostles and Martyrs," only) are in Jesus' hand (chap. x. 28). But, without doubt, this coming of Jesus to believers in death is connected with His spiritual and yet personal coming to them in life, in Word and Sacrament, and in the Holy Ghost (chap. xvii. 23; Rev. i. 8; chap. iii. 20) and, similarly, it points to the last coming of Christ (Stier, and my *Leben Jesu*, II. p. 1351). Tholuck: "It only remains to explain ἔρχομαι agreeably to Biblical usage, according to which the word to come, to visit, פקד, is employed to express every revelation of the Lord, every manifestation of His power, whether for good or evil, comp. vers. 18, 23, 30; Matt. x. 23; xxvi. 64, and in Revelation whose whole theme is the ἔρχεσθαι of the Lord."

[Alford *in loc.*, with Stier and Lange, takes a comprehensive 'perspective' view of the coming again of our Lord from the resurrection of Christ to the final judgment. "This ἔρχομαι is *begun* (ver. 18) in His resurrection—*carried on* (ver. 23) in the *spiritual life* (xvi. 22 ff.), the making *them* ready for the place prepared;—*further advanced* when each by death is fetched away to be with Him (Phil. i. 23); *fully completed* at His coming in glory, when they shall for ever be with Him (1 Thess. iv. 17) in the perfected resurrection state."—P. S.]

Ver. 4. **And whither I go.**—See the TEXT. note. According to the Recepta Christ says to them: "Ye know the goal whither I go, and so ye also know the way." This reading seems to be confirmed by ver. 5, since Thomas too distinguishes between the goal and the way. But the connection rests upon the contrast of Christ's spiritual view to the sensual view which Thomas takes of the matter. Christ means to say: because ye know the way to the place to which I am going, ye also know the goal. Thomas, on the other hand, says: because we know not the goal, neither do we know the way. For here the subject of discourse is not simply the Father's house, or the Father generally, as the goal of Christ (ver. 2, to which Tholuck refers), but that place in the hereafter, the place of Christ's glory. The way should be their guide to an inference concerning the goal. Interpretation of the *way:* 1. The Passion and death of Christ (Luther, Grotius and others, Luthardt. Tholuck "the way of denial," chap. xiii. 36; xii. 24, 26). 2. Christ Himself, in accordance with ver.

6 (De Wette, Meyer). Christ most undoubtedly; Christ, however, in His motion; consequently the view presented in No. 1 is equally to be held here, in accordance with ver. 3 (Tittmann, Knapp). The expression is not anacoluthical; it is a specimen of breviloquence. *And whither I* (ἐγώ, emphatic) *go, thither ye know the way.* Christ is the living way for Himself and His people to δόξα with the Father.

Ver. 5. **Thomas saith unto Him: Lord, we know not.**—This was perfectly correct, supposing the goal to be inwardly and outwardly determined. Here the way or direction is known only by the goal. Grotius: *Quodsi ignoretur, quæ sit meta, non potest via sub ratione viæ concipi.* But this reflection is an accessory consideration merely; the main point is the oppressive sense of obscurity, of uncertainty with regard to the goal—uncertainty arising from their imperfect apprehension of their Lord and Master.

Ver. 6. **Jesus saith unto him: I am the way.**—The answer of Jesus is not intended to divert the over-forward curiosity of Thomas, as Calvin supposes. ("*In re magis necessaria insistit.*"*) Thomas has declared that he does not know the way to that goal of Christ, because he is ignorant of the goal itself. Jesus answers, very pertinently: *I am the way;* only for Him the way means something different from the idea which it conveys to the mind of Thomas. The contrast is, however, not that which exists between an exterior way and a spiritual one; it is a contrast between a local, dead, external way and a dynamical, living way, with which latter, incontrovertibly, the attribute of spirituality is bound up. Since *the way* is the main idea, it follows: 1. that the words: **the truth and the life** [καὶ ἡ ἀλήθεια καὶ ἡ ζωή], are explicative (the truth as well as the life), primarily of this way, *i. e.* for this reason: because He is absolutely truth and life; 2. that, on the other hand, the words: **No one cometh unto the Father but by Me,** are an applicative circumscription. The significative summing up of Augustine: *vera via vitæ* [the true way of life], is inadmissible, for it fuses into one the three definitions. Neither may they be apprehended as three co-ordinate definitions as (1) in respect of time; Luther: the beginning, the middle and the end on the ladder to heaven; (2) in respect of effects, Grotius: *exemplum, doctor, dator vitæ æternæ.* On the contrary, *the way* is the whole idea, metaphorically presented (De Wette, my *Leben Jesu*, p. 1353, Tholuck). We must further guard against conceiving of the way as the bare, objective means of salvation (Meyer, Tholuck); it is the objective and effectual means of coming to δόξα with the Father through salvation (redemption and glorification comprehended together in the predominant idea of glorification). But He is the way in an absolute sense because, in His own coming from the Father and going to the Father, He is *absolute motion* (the pioneer) and in His going first and bringing to the Father, He is the *absolute motor.* (A warranted double reference in Augustine, Lampe and others, misconstrued by Tholuck as an irrelevancy; Heb. ix. 12.)

* [Not *consistit*, as the original reads in 2d and 3d ed. A typographical error.—P. S.]

But now, to enter into particulars, Christ is the truth of this way, the clear manifestation of it, because He is, in general, the truth or manifestation of God; and He is the life of this way, the animating motive power by which we come to the Father, because He is, in general, life. This life is, indeed, ζωὴ αἰώνιος; it is, however, in part conceived of more generally, in part differently applied. The difficult conception of life presents for observation these items: the powers of development, appearance and action. If we turn truth into the metaphorical expression: light, then light and life appear side by side as exponents of the way,—that being identical with love, and, similarly, our transport past hate and its exponents, darkness and death.

No man cometh unto the Father.—"'And so, when a man is saved, the Lord Christ must have a hand in the work,' says Luther, rightly citing these words against Zwingli, who makes a Theseus, a Socrates, to be saved even without Christ." Thus Tholuck; inexactly, however; proof should have been adduced that Zwingli expressly taught the possibility of being saved in the other world *without Christ*, and that Luther, on the other hand, advanced the doctrine of salvation in the other world through Christ. De Wette observes: "the exclusive principle, to the effect, namely, that no man cometh unto the Father but by Christ, is mitigated in reference to those who are ignorant of Him as the historical Messiah, by the fact that He is also the eternal, ideal Logos." More definitely stated: that He is also the eternal Christ and High-priest. (See 1 Pet. iii. 19; iv. 6.)

Ver. 7. **If ye had known Me.**—In accordance with the antithesis: known *the Father*, the emphasis falls thus: known *Me*, not upon ἐγνώκ. It is not His intention utterly to deny their knowledge of His personality; what grieves Him, is that they have as yet not recognized in Him the absolute way to the absolute goal, *i. e.* the living, heavenly image of the heavenly Father,—an image coming from heaven and going to heaven. In a knowledge of the eternal, divine-human personality of Christ they would also have obtained a view of the personal Father and His love-kingdom in heaven—a kingdom elevated above all transitory things.—**And from henceforth.**—The sharp contrast: ye have not known the Father, and from henceforth ye know Him, is somewhat striking; hence it has been the subject of various interpretations: 1. The *terminus a quo* is imminent in the future; it is the time of the communication of the Spirit (Chrysost., Lücke and others; the explanation of Kuinoel and others, who apprehend the verbs as though they were in the Future tense, is but another phase of the above). 2. The statement is hypothetical: from henceforth, I hope (De Wette). 3. The *from henceforth* is indicative of the beginning of appropriation, comp. chap. xv. 3 (Tholuck). 4. From henceforth, "after My having told you, ver. 6, what I am" (Meyer).—The *from henceforth* denotes that method just now to be disclosed by Him, and which He desired sharply to define, by which they were to arrive at a knowledge of the Father and the Father's House—the method of faith, namely. Doubtless, however, the ἀρτι at the same time embraces the confirmation of this method by the whole grand period of Christ's death and resurrection, whereby, according to Rom. i. 4, He was demonstrated to be the Son of God and thus at once made the Surety and the Heir of the Father in heaven. The *καί* is expressive of both contrast and connection.—**Ye have seen Him.**—Said of the intuitive glance of faith.

Ver. 8. **Philip saith unto Him: Lord, show us,** *etc.*—As the seeming contradictions of reality darken the glimpse which Thomas' faith might have of things spiritual, so Philip, in like manner, looks for the confirmation of faith by sight; comp. chap. i. 46; vi. 5. According to De Wette, Tholuck, Meyer: he demands that Jesus effect a theophany, in accordance with Mal. iii. 1; as Ex. xxxiii. 18. The main point is this: accepting Christ's words: *ye have seen Him,* in their literal sense, he requires that Jesus should occasion an appearing of the Father *outside of Christ;* a sign in the heaven, perhaps, rather than a theophany. Luther: "he flutters up into the clouds." He declares his faith by assuming Jesus to be capable of producing such a vision; his failing to perceive the manifestation of the Father in Christ, however, proves that faith to be but small.—**And it sufficeth us.**—*I. e.* in accordance with the context: it suffices to render us certain of the goal above us or beyond us, and to make us journey towards it with a brave heart; or, to cause us to abandon the expectations we have hitherto entertained and to embrace the new hope.

Ver. 9. **And thou hast not known Me.**—For so long time I have appeared among you and hast *thou* not *known* the nature of My appearing? Not alone from the "words and works," but from the whole personality of Christ he should have recognized His heavenly origin, which did, indeed, display itself in word and work.

Ver. 10. **I am in the Father, and the Father in Me.**—See chap. x. 38. There the order is inverted, and with reason. The Father is in Christ in virtue of His Father-revelation in the works of Christ. Christ is in the Father in virtue of His Son-revelation in His words. The Jews were to ascend from a belief in His works and mission to a belief in His words and individual personality. But the disciples began with a belief in His word and they have not to *ascend* to a belief in His works, but to advance to a discrimination between the manifestation of the Father in Him through His works and His being in the Father with His word. Though Christ even speaks His word according to the Father's commission (chap. xii. 50), there is still this distinction: that the words are His most individual, personal life-revelation, while in the works the most special concurrence of the Father's government is, consciously to Christ, manifested in the creation and the human world. We may not wipe out this contrast with De Wette: "The words that I speak to you, I speak not of Myself, and the works that I do, I do not of Myself, but the Father who is in Me teacheth Me the words and doeth the works." Neither does there occur a climactic progression (as Theoph. and Lücke pretend): not only are the words God's words, but the works also are God's works. As little are the works here intended as a proof that Christ does not speak the words of Himself (Grot., Fritzsche, Meyer). Least of all are the works to be apprehended as effects of the word as, "the office of teaching" (Aug., Nösselt); nor are we to assume with Tholuck the existence of an "incongruence of contrasts peculiar to the Johannean style." Even the words Christ speaks not of Himself; as the Son He utters them from the depths of the Father; as it respects them, however, the initiative lies within Himself, while for the works the initiative is in the Father who permanently dwells in Him (*μένων*). Words and works are the property of both Father and Son; the words, however, are preëminently and primarily the Son's, the works preëminently and primarily the Father's.

Ver. 11. **Believe me for the very works' sake** [*διὰ τὰ ἔργα αὐτὰ πιστεύετέ μοι*].—Jesus here turns to the disciples as a body. For as Thomas' doubt was, more or less, the doubt of all, so the like was the case with the scruple of Philip. The explanation of the verse results from the foregoing. As disciples of Jesus, they ought first to believe that He was in the Father and then to know that the Father was in Him. If ye are not able to do this,—it is His intention to say to them in a few sharp words,—why then go to work the other way: begin with the works (in the way pointed out to the Jews, chap. x. 38) and, through a belief in the divinity of My works, arrive at a belief in the divinity of My person.

Ver. 12. **Verily, verily, I say unto you, he that believeth in me, the works that I do he shall do also,** *etc.*—Now follows, undoubtedly, a new series of consolations. Not only shall *they* be united to *Him,* but also He to them (Tholuck). The further progress of the discourse, however, must correspond with the principal thought, according to which His earthly appearance shall cease to veil from them the heavenly house of the Father. *The disclosure of which we speak, consists in the revelation of that personal, heavenly life which issues from His person as its centre. Verily, verily,* therefore it is written, *he that believeth on Me, i. e.* on the *divine personality* of Christ Himself, *the works that I do, shall he do also, and greater works than these. I. e.:* Through this faith there shall be developed in that man likewise such a mighty, personal spirit-life that works shall be the necessary outflowings of the life-spring of personality, which, originating in Christ, wells up within his breast; the heavenly state shall be unfolded to him on earth and become his surety for the *heavenly home,* which last should be regarded as the perfect revelation and realization of the personal kingdom of love founded by Christ in this world.—**He that believeth on Me.**—Not simply applicable "to the disciples of Jesus" in the strictest sense (Meyer). Still the "*believeth on Me,*" is emphatic. Bengel: *qui Christo de se loquenti credit, i. e.* he that believes on Himself, His personality (see ver. 11).—**The works that I do he shall also do himself.**—Expressive of the essential relationship or homogeneousness existing between the works of believers and the works of Christ; of the eternal progress of Christ's wonder-works through the world by means of Christianity,

And (even) greater than these shall he do [*καὶ μείζονα τούτων ποιήσει*].—The *καί* is climactic: *And even.* Tholuck: "Ancient writers believe this greaterness [*μειζονότης*] of the *ἔργα* to consist: 1. In their numerical superiority; 2. in their local extension beyond Judea; 3. in the more striking signs, such as the healing by the shadow of Peter, Acts v. (Theod., Herakl.).* Origen: In the victories which believers obtain, through faith, over the world, the flesh and the devil. Augustine: In the results of the preached word in the heathen world. Ch. iv. 38 He had, with prophetic glance, declared that others would reap what He had sowed; ch. xv. 26, 27, and, indirectly, ch. viii. 28; xii. 32 are likewise indicative of the greater efficacy of the Messiah through the medium of the apostolic testimony." Be it observed in this connection that even here, ver. 14, it is Christ that will do these greater works; the disciples, through their prayers in His name, in fellowship with Him, are to be but the instruments through which He acts, chap. xv. 16; xvi. 28; comp. Acts iii. 6; xvi. 18. Luther: "For He took but a little corner for Himself, to preach and to work miracles in, and but a little time; whereas the apostles and their followers have spread themselves through the whole world." Manifestly, Christ has in view the greatness of the development of His wondrous works throughout the Christian ages until the glorification of the world. [Alford: "This word *μείζονα τούτων* is not to be evaded (so as to=*πλείονα*, Lampe), but taken in its full strict sense. And the key to its meaning will be found chap. i. 51; v. 20. The works which Jesus did, His Apostles also did,—*scil.*, raising the dead, *etc.*;—greater works than those they did,—not in degree, but in kind: spiritual works; under the dispensation of the Spirit, which had not yet come in. But they did them, not as separate from Him: but in Him, and by Him; and so (ch. v. 21) *He* is said so to do them. The work which He did by Peter's sermon, Acts ii., was one of these *μείζονα τούτων*,—the first-fruits of the unspeakable gift. This union of them with and in Him is expressed here by *τὰ ἔργα ἃ ἐγὼ ποιῶ, κἀκεῖνος ποιήσει*." "He has sown, we reap; and the harvest is greater than the seed-time." Stier. Godet (ii. 472) refers the *μείζονα* to the communication of spiritual life which is superior to the healing of the body. "*Le terme plus grand ne désigne pas des miracles plus prodigieux, mais des miracles d'une nature plus excellente.*"—P. S.]

For I am going to the Father, and whatever ye shall ask, *etc.* [*ὅτι ἐγὼ πρὸς τὸν πατέρα (μου) πορεύομαι, καὶ ὅ, τι ἂν αἰτήσητε*].—Rationale of the preceding and, in the abstract, astonishing clause. Various interpretations: 1. The *πορεύομαι* forms the foundation for the idea that they are to do the miracles in His stead, because of His retirement from the scene (Chrysostom, Theophylact and many others [A. V.]); 2. because He goes *to the Father, i. e.* to glory with the Father and will thence work in them in His might (Luther, Baumg.-Crusius, Luthardt and others). In the first case a period follows *πορεύομαι*; in the second a comma. 3. The two considerations are not to be sundered. His going to the Father (*ἐγώ* is emphasized), as well as His being with the Father, is the reason for their doing *greater* miracles (Grotius, Lücke and others). When this view of the matter is taken, *πορεύομαι* is connected with the following sentence by a colon (Knapp, Griesbach, Lachmann, Tischendorf). Both items are more directly emphasized in chap. xvi. 7, in accordance with which our passage is to be explained.

Ver. 13. **Shall ask in My name.**—Exposition of the import of His going to the Father, in reference to their destiny to work miracles. Invocation of God in the name of Jesus, in order to any *τὶ* in the way of works of redemption or glorification; that is, in order to the working of miracles. Their power of prayer is to have no other limit than *His name.* A name is objectively the revelation of any subject,—subjectively, *experience of it;* the *signature* of its consciousness stamped upon the consciousness of others. The name of the heavenward-ascending Jesus is the Elijah-mantle left by Him to His people on the earth: the sign of the living revelation and knowledge of His essence, in which His essence, fully concentrated, works. His name, viewed by faith, is the continual working of His essence, or, rather, of His personality: the element of His personal self-revelation in the experience of His people; hence *a.* His word or cognizance, *b.* His Spirit or mind, *c.* His works, His institutions and instigations, *d.* His aim. In a word: the communion of His Spirit. There are various interpretations which form different parts of the one just given: 1. Bearing upon the principle. Chrysostom: Amidst the invocation of the name of Christ (formal); Augustine; In the name of Him who is called *Salvator* (*non contra salutem nostram*);* 2. Bearing upon the medium. Melanchthon: *Me agnito;* Luther: With faith in Me; Calov: *Per meritum meum.* 3. Bearing upon the end; Erasmus: *In gloriam Christi.* Or upon the furtherance of the end; De Wette: In accordance with My mind, and in My cause.† If we desire to sum up all in one, No. 2, setting forth the medium, seems best fitted for our purpose: in faith, knowing and confessing Christ; hence, briefly, *ἐν Χριστῷ, ἐν κυρίῳ* (Lücke), only with a more objective and teleological modification. Manifestly, the prevailing thought is the end purposed; hence the predominance of the idea: *as ambassadors of Christ, the Son of God,* by virtue of His *δόξα.* See chap. xv. 16; xvi. 23. Tholuck: "When even finite good things are prayed for in accordance with the mind of Christ, they are desired only as means to the final end, Matt. vi. 33. As, however, this may be attained by other means, the *cardo desiderii* is fulfilled even when specific requests are denied" (Augustine). Nevertheless, the ideal side of prayer, its perfect, prophetic nature, is here as-

* [Wordsworth refers also to the healing power of Paul's handkerchiefs (Acts xix. 12) and the speaking in new tongues. Comp. Mark xvi. 17 ff. But, as Meyer justly says, such a mechanical measurement of the greatness of miracles is entirely foreign to the New Testament. The true commentary on the *μείζονα ἔργα* is found in the Acts and especially the labors of Paul.—P. S.]

* [Similarly Wordsworth: in submission to My will, and conducive to your own salvation and to God's glory.—P. S.]

† [So Alford: "in union with Me, as being Mine, manifesting forth Jesus as the Son of God."—P. S.]

sumed, and, such being the case, the ὅ, τι is fulfilled in the τοῦτο.

That will I do [τοῦτο ποιήσω].—Stress falls upon τοῦτο; the ἐγώ, expressed in conjunction with πορεύομαι, is absent here. He will do precisely that for which they pray, and in such a manner, besides, that *their* doing in the matter shall be vindicated,—their believing, individual personality.

That the Father may be glorified.—The end is the δόξα; modified, the δόξα of the Father; still more explicitly defined, the δόξα of the Father in the Son. Hence results, also, the modification of prayer in the name of Jesus as prayer in the δόξα of the name of the Son of God, in the name of the glorified Christ.

Ver. 14. **If ye shall ask anything** [τι] **in My name, I will do it** [ἐγώ—emphatic—ποιήσω].—Ver. 14 appears, at first sight, to be a recapitulative repetition of the foregoing (Euthymius); Bengel, however, very justly gives prominence to the ἐγώ. Here the definite ὅ, τι, or the thing (this simply τι) is no longer emphasized; but stress is laid upon the asking in the name of Jesus,—the mind, the communion of spirit with Him, and, to correspond with this, upon His doing, as *His* doing. According to the preceding verse, He does it *upon* the request of the disciples; here He does it *through* their request, *Himself*, again. At the same time ver. 14 forms an introduction to vers. 15 and 16. See chap. xvi. 23. In the latter passage the doing is ascribed to the Father. But the Father operates through the Son. Here we see the *instrumentality*, there the final causality.

Ver. 15. **If ye love me, keep my commandments** [ἐὰν ἀγαπᾶτέ με, τὰς ἐντολὰς τὰς ἐμὰς τηρήσατε].—Jesus proceeds to explain more fully how the disciples are to attain to the doing of the greater works in His name. The first condition is, however, an assumption as well; to the effect, namely, that they love Him. Thence it will follow that they will keep His commandments, embraced, as these are, in the *one* commandment of fellowship. If they thus stand in the fellowship of prayer (see Acts ii. 1, ὁμοθυμαδὸν ἐπὶ τὸ αὐτό), the Holy Ghost shall, at Christ's intercession, be given them. Tholuck: "With John, love is no mere blissfulness of feeling; it is *oneness of will* with the beloved, ver. 21; chap. xv. 14; 1 John iii. 18. It is love which makes men susceptible of the communication of the Paraclete; the κόσμος cannot receive Him." A loving contemplation of Christ's personality is the bond of fellowship of disciples,—that which makes them a collective personality—and in this fellowship they may become the organ of the personal manifestation of the Holy Ghost.

Ver. 16. **And I will entreat the Father** [καὶ ἐγω ἐρωτήσω τὸν πατέρα].—Christ here makes choice of the term ἐρωτᾶν, not αἰτεῖν, as before, in reference to the disciples. Expressive of a more intimate, free and homogeneous relation. In chap. xvi. 26, on the contrary, He says: οὐ λέγω, ὅτι ἐρωτήσω. Tholuck, setting aside Calov's explanation: *non solus, sed vobiscum rogabo*, remarks: "He is there speaking of the time when they, in possession of the Spirit whose mediation is here promised, shall be able themselves to pray acceptably in that Spirit."

And he shall give you another representative, or, **helper** [καὶ ἄλλον παράκλητον δώσει ὑμῖν].—Here the great promise of the παράκλητος, to speak more accurately, the ἄλλος παράκλητος, makes its appearance; the promise of the Holy Ghost, spoken of under this name by John only, chap. xiv. 26; xv. 26; xvi. 7.* The word itself is never met with in the New Testament except in the writings of John, yet the designation: ἄλλος παράκλητος, announces that it may be applied to Christ also.

[The designation of the Holy Ghost, as *another* Paraclete, who would supply Christ's own place in His absence, implies that the Lord Himself is the *first* Paraclete; and this is confirmed by 1 John ii. 1, where "Jesus Christ the righteous" is called παράκλητος πρὸς τὸν πατέρα. This allusion is lost to the readers of our English version. I quote here beforehand the excellent interpretation of Calvin *in loc.*: "The name *Paraclete* is here applied to Christ as well as to the Spirit, and properly: for it is the common office of each to console and encourage us and to preserve us by their defence. Christ was their patron as long as He lived in the world; He then committed them to the guidance and protection of the Spirit. If any one asks whether we are not to-day under the guardianship of Christ, the answer is easy: Christ is a perpetual Guardian, but not visibly. As long as He walked on earth, He appeared openly as their Guardian (*patronus*); now He preserves us by His Spirit. He calls the Spirit *another* (sc. *paracletum*) in view of the distinction which we observe in the blessings proceeding from each. It was the appropriate work of Christ, by expiating the sins of the world to appease the anger of God, to redeem men from death, to obtain righteousness and life. It is the office of the Spirit, to make us partakers of Christ Himself, as well as of all His blessings." The designation *Paraclete, advocate* (as already Irenæus, *Adv. hær.* III. 17, and also Grotius observed), implies an antithesis to the *accuser*, the κατήγορος τῶν ἀδελφῶν, as the Spirit of evil is called, Rev. xii. 10. Comp. on this whole passage the excellent remarks of the late Archdeacon Hare on *The Mission of the Comforter* (a series of Sermons on John xvi. 7-11, preached before the University of Cambridge, 1840, with long notes which are by far the most important part of the book), 2d ed. 1850, Boston reprint 1854, pp. 348 ff.—P. S.]

* [Παράκλητος occurs five times in the N. T., four times in the Gospel of John, as a designation of the Holy Spirit, and once in the first Ep. of John, as applied to Christ. It is always translated by the E. V. *comforter* (following Wiclif), except 1 John ii. 1, where it is rendered *advocate* (after the Vulgate). In the Gospel the Vulgate retains the Greek with a slight change of *Paracletus* into *Paraclitus*; the long Greek η being turned into the short Latin *i*, as in *Kyrie eleison.* The R. C. Rhemish Version which is constructed on the convenient, but very slavish and un-English system "of taking the words of the Vulgate, chipping off the Latin, and tacking on English terminations," gives *paraclete* in all the four passages of the Gospel, and *advocate* in the Epistle, like the Vulgate. Archdeacon Hare observes (*Mission of the Comforter*, p. 349), that to avoid confusion the Greek word might have been anglicized (as *baptism, apostle, bishop, deacon, etc.*), but that this would have obscured our perception of the meaning and, by severing it from its etymological associations, deprived it of a portion of its power.—P. S.]

1. As to the PHILOLOGICAL meaning, Meyer says: "The παράκλητος is, according to classical Greek usage, one who is summoned to help; in particular, an *advocate* (*advocatus*), one who manages another's cause, or an *intercessor*. With this the talmudic פְּרַקְלִיט agrees. See Buxtorf, *Lexicon Talm.*, p. 1843, and in general Wetstein on our passage and Düsterdieck on 1 John ii. 1." [It should be added, however, that in our passage, as also in Philo *De opific. mundi*, p. 4, and in the Ep. of the church of Vienne, c. 5, ap. Euseb. v. 2 (both quoted by Knapp and Meyer, p. 515), παράκλητος must not be taken in the narrow sense of a legal advocate or pleader (for which the Greeks generally use the terms σύνδικος and συνήγορος), but in the more general sense of *counsellor*, *helper*, *patron*. On the philological meaning Knapp has a valuable dissertation *De Spiritu S. et Christo paracletis*, in his *Scripta varii arg*. I. pp. 115 sqq. He shows that the Greek παράκλητος and the Latin *advocatus*, answer more nearly to our general term *counsel* whose office is to advise, direct and support rather than to plead. It is the work of the Holy Spirit, not only to plead for the disciples, but also to plead in them, to direct them in all their ways, to give them mouth and wisdom, to fulfil the part of a higher conscience, to sustain, comfort and cheer them in all their trials and to lead them to heaven. Hence the English word *Advocate*, which relates more exclusively to the pleading of a cause, is no full equivalent to παράκλητος, and does not cover the whole extent of the office of the Spirit. The idea of *Comforter* must be added to it. A Comforter is a *spiritual* Helper. Unfortunately we have no single word coëxtensive in signification. See below sub. 2. —P. S.]

II. INTERPRETATIONS:

1. Conformably to the idea of the *advocatus* in its wider sense: *assistant*, *helper*, *etc.*, Tertullian, Augustine,* Calvin,† Lampe, most of the moderns. [I add under this head the names of Melancthon, Beza, Grotius, Wetstein, Bengel, Knapp, Lücke, Tholuck, De Wette (*Beistand*), Hengstenberg (*Fürsprecher*), Godet (*défenseur*), Hammond, Pierson, Webster and Wilkinson.—P. S.]

2. *Comforter*, *consolator* [in accordance with the Hellenistic use of παρακαλεῖν and παράκλησις], Origen, Chrysostom, Theophylact [Cyril, Euthymius Zigab.], Jerome‡ [Erasmus], Luther§ [Maldonatus, Jansen] and others [A. E. V.]. Against this Meyer says (according to the note in Lücke, p. 608): "It rests upon an unphilological confusion of the word with παρακλήτωρ (Sept., Job xvi. 2) in Aquila and Theodotus."‖ Nevertheless, we may safely give the Greek exegetes, who are by preference on this side, credit for having said something philologically justifiable. That, however, *in point of fact*, the word 1 John ii. 1 cannot mean *comforter*, but only *mediator*, *representative*, *helper*, and that here also there is no immediate question of comforting, is manifest.

[The term *Comforter*, as used in this and the 16th ch. of John by our E. V., in harmony with the Hellenistic use of παρακαλεῖν and παράκλησις, with all the Greek commentators and Luther (*Tröster*), carries with it so many sacred associations and expresses such an important part of the office of the Holy Spirit (comp. the παράκλησις τοῦ ἁγίου πνεύματος, Acts ix. 31), that it seems almost sacrilege to exchange it for another; and hence Archdeacon Hare and Dean Alford, while admitting that *Advocate* (in the wider sense above explained) is the strict etymological meaning of παράκλητος, which satisfies 1 John ii. 1, yet retain the E. V. and combine the idea of *help* and *strength* with that of *consolation* in the term.* Olshausen does the same among German commentators.† We should remember that the English word *Comforter* originally means not only *Consoler*, as now, but primarily also *Strengthener* and *Supporter*, agreeably to its derivation from the Latin *confortari*, to strengthen, which, though scarcely found in classical Latin, is common in the Vulgate, and was frequently used in its Latin sense by Wiclif, *e. g.* Luke xxii. 43; Acts ix. 19; 1 Cor. xvi. 13; Phil. iv. 13. In this sense it falls in with the connection and object of our Lord, which was, not merely to comfort the disciples for the loss of His visible presence, but mainly to strengthen their hearts. Dr. Lange, as will be seen below, likewise takes a broader but somewhat different view and combines in παράκλητος the idea of *Helper* (*Beistand*) with that of *Mediator* (*Vermittler*), and hence translates it *Representative* (*Vertreter*).—P. S.]

3. *Teacher*, Theod. of Mopsueste [Ernesti, *Opusc.* p. 215], Hofmann (*Schriftbeweis*, II. 2, p. 17), Luthardt [also Campbell who inappropriately translates *Monitor*.—P. S.]. This view has less to support it than either of the others.

In reference to No. 1, explanations are again divided:

a. Ancient exegetes explain *advocatus* as equivalent to *causæ patronus*, *orator*, against which view Lücke observes: "this would suit 1 John ii. 1, but not the passages of the Gospel."

b. It was Knapp who, supported by the usage of the term, in pure Greek writers as well as in Jewish ones availing themselves of the language, also in the writings of the Rabbins who have adopted the Greek word (פְּרַקְלִיט), *etc.*, demonstrated that the word originally possessed the general signification of a *helper* [*Beistand*]. "The office of helper as performed by the Holy Ghost

* [So in his 74th Tractate on John; but in the 94th, Augustine combines the interpretation *Advocate* with that of *Comforter*; both terms being equivalent to the Greek *paraclete*. See the quotation in Hare, p. 352 f.—P. S.]

† [The same may be said of Calvin; see his interpretation quoted p. 440.—P. S.]

‡ [In the Vulgate Jerome, as already observed, retains the Greek *Paraclitum* (Paracletum). Some MSS. of the Itala give *advocatum*.—P. S.]

§ [Luther translates *Tröster*, *Comforter*, but explains *Advocate*.—P. S.]

‖ [Meyer, in a footnote, p. 515, urges against this meaning the *passive* form παράκλητος, instead of the *active* παρακλητικός (Plat. *Republ.* p. 524 D.), in accordance with ἐπικλητικός ἀνακλητικός, *etc.* But it should be remembered that in the N. T. παρακαλέω does not mean *to call for*, but always *to exhort* or *to comfort*.—P. S.]

* [Wordsworth goes beyond these limits and makes παράκλητος to mean Sanctifier, Teacher, Comforter, Exhorter, Inspirer, Counsellor, Guide, *etc.*, all in one.—P. S.]

† [Olshausen remarks *in loc.*, that the original meaning, *advocatus*, *called to aid*, is lost in the more general idea of *helper*, *assistant*, *comforter*; that this idea suits admirably the connection in all passages where the word is applied to the Holy Spirit, but that *advocate* is better suited in 1 John ii. 1 where it is used of Christ.—P. S.]

consists of directing and leading to the truth, testifying and reminding, teaching and glorifying." Against this view, it must be observed: (*a*) Christ arrives at the idea of the ἄλλος παράκλ. through the promise: "What ye shall ask in My name, I will do." He will mediate with God for His accomplishment of their work. Thus He is the Mediator, 1 John. ii. 1. (*b*) The ἄλλος παράκλ. is described as "the Spirit of truth;" as such He is the Mediator through whose instrumentality believers are made one with the Father in Christ; He transports them into Christ, thus making them certain and glad of the operations of God. Without doubt, then, He is a *helper*, but it is because He is a *mediator* (see Rom. viii. 26, 27); *i. e.* since He conducts their cause before God, He conducts it before the world; (not *vice versâ*).

III. DOGMATICAL question. Tholuck: "The representative of the departing One is called, in these discourses, παράκλ. (rather ἄλλος παράκλ.); again, πνεῦμα τῆς ἀληθείας here and in chap. xv. 26; xvi. 13,—not immediately ὅτι ἀξιόπιστος ἔσται (Chrysostom), but on account of His being the Mediator of the theocratic and practical truth which, according to ver. 9, is Christ Himself; again, according to ver. 26, He is called πνεῦμα ἅγιον and, according to an expression peculiar to Luke, δύναμις τοῦ ὑψίστου, Luke xxiv. 49; i. 35; Acts i. 8. He is called ἄλλος, for it is not Christ according to His historical appearing. Yet again it is also Christ Himself: ver. 18; that which, according to chap. xvi. 25; xvii. 26 (γνωρίσω), is declared to them by Christ, is, according to chap. xvi. 14, to be declared to them by the Spirit, for He shall take of His (Christ's). These declarations lead us to the belief that, in John, by this πνεῦμα we must understand Christ, glorified into a spirit. The view setting forth this πνεῦμα as a 'self, distinct from Christ' has lately been revived by Olshausen, Meyer, Schmid, *Theologie des Neuen Testaments*, I. p. 108; Brückner, p. 230; Hofmann, I. p. 165. No arguments but those of Quenstädt have been brought forward in favor of it." It is strange that Tholuck will admit neither the expression ἄλλος παράκλ., nor the μεθ' ὑμῶν, nor the masculine ἐκεῖνος, nor the διδάξει, λαλήσει, *etc.*, as a proof that the Spirit is designated as another self, although he fully grants the hypostatizing of the Holy Ghost in the dogmatical conception of the Divinity. But if in this point dogmatics are to find their support in Paul, not in John, the latter is thrust into a false position, unsustained by the fact that *he* has given the deepest conception of the doctrinal system of the New Testament. That Christ alternately speaks of the coming of the Holy Spirit and of His own return, does not justify the expression by which the πνεῦμα is in this instance declared to be "Christ glorified into a spirit;" it is an expression inadmissible in any case,—Christ being, indeed, glorified *in* the Spirit and *through* the Spirit, but not *into* a spirit.* We might almost as well say that the Father is, according to ver. 9, glorified into Christ. We have seen that the two expressions; *I in the Father, the Father in Me* (chap. x. 38; xiv. 10), do not mean the same thing. The former is indicative of the personality of Christ, the other of the personality of the Father as manifested in Christ. Precisely in the same way do the expressions: *ye in Me, and I in you*, ver. 20, differ. By the translation of Christ's personality into the disciples, they are translated into Him as personalities; but that whereby they, being translated into Christ, are made *one* personality with Christ, is that very ἄλλος and ἐκεῖνος, the personality of the Holy Ghost. For the Holy Ghost Himself shall not only be *in them*, but also *with them*, ver. 17. Inasmuch as He is in them, Christ Himself is with them; inasmuch as He is with them, He is the ἄλλος παράκλ. and Christ is in them. That is, the fellowship rests, in individuals, upon the manifestation of the glorified Christ; individuals rest, as Christ's fellowship, upon the revelation of the Holy Ghost. Hence we may likewise expect the two ideas: in what degree Christ, in the Holy Ghost, is with them, and in what degree the Holy Ghost, in Christ, is with them, to branch out and divide when we ponder over them. First, then, the discourse turns upon this point: *Christ comes to them again, the Holy Ghost being in them*, vers. 18-31. The second point discussed is this: *they shall be in Christ, the Holy Ghost being with them*, chap. xv. 1 to chap. xvi. 15. The conclusion embraces both items in the promise of the resurrection, chap. xvi. 16-33.

That he may be with you for ever [ἵνα μεθ' ὑμῶν ᾖ εἰς τὸν αἰῶνα].—See the TEXTUAL NOTES. Observe, moreover, the μεθ' ὑμῶν, in accordance with the preceding elucidation. The εἰς τὸν αἰῶνα is explained by Meyer as having reference to the αἰὼν μέλλων. But doubtless such a fact would be more definitely expressed.

Ver. 17. **The Spirit of truth** [τὸ πνεῦμα τῆς ἀληθείας].—The Holy Ghost is the living, personal, divine unity of complete revelation and, as such, the Spirit of truth (see chap. xv. 26; xvi. 13). He is the Spirit of truth, inasmuch as He makes objective truth subjective in believers, in order to the knowledge of truth. Objectively He is the Spirit of God (Rom. viii. 14), and God Himself (Acts v.); the Spirit of the Father (Matt. x. 20); the Spirit of Christ (Rom. viii. 9); the Spirit of the Lord (2 Cor. iii. 17), the Holy Spirit (Acts ii.). Subjectively He is the Spirit of *truth*, the Spirit of wisdom and revelation (Eph. i. 17), the Spirit of power, of love and of a sound mind (2 Tim. i. 7), the Spirit of adoption, of prayer (Rom. viii. 15), the Spirit of sanctification (Rom. i. 4), of life (Rom. viii. 10), of meekness (1 Cor. iv. 21), of comfort (Acts ix. 31), of glory (1 Pet. iv. 14), of sealing, of the earnest of eternal life (Eph. i. 13, 14), of all Christian charismata (1 Cor. xii. 4). As the Spirit of truth, the Holy Ghost applies to believers the full truth of the perfect revelation of God in Christ.

Whom the world cannot receive [ὃ ὁ κόσμος οὐ δύναται λαβεῖν].—The world as world. Why not? 1. **It does not see him** [ὅτι οὐ θεωρεῖ αὐτό] in His manifestations, because it lacks the eye of faith. It does

* [Meyer also (p. 516) calls Tholuck's idea that the Paraclete is *der zu Geist verklärte Christus*, obscure, unjohannean and unbiblical. Comp. 1 Cor. iii. 17. Against a similar confounding of the Logos with the Spirit by Reuss, see Godet II. p. 480.—P. S.]

not even see the One God above the world, much less, the oneness of His manifestations in the world. And hence 2. **it does not know him** [*οὐδὲ γινώσκει αὐτό*]. It lacks experience of the Holy Ghost, 1 Cor. ii. 14.—**But ye know him** [*ὑμεῖς δὲ γινώσκετε αὐτό*]. The imminent future is already truly present, inasmuch as they have commenced to recognize the Holy Ghost in the manifestations of Christ, Matt. xvi. 17. They are already beginning to have an experimental knowledge of Him. Nevertheless, the full expression is indicative of a future, near at hand. *Proof*: **He remaineth with you, and will be in you** [*ὅτι παρ' ὑμῖν μένει* καὶ ἐν ὑμῖν ἔσται*]. He will not relinquish (Present) His activity among them (see Luke xxii. 32), until He comes with all His influences to dwell in them. Meyer correctly: Since "His abode is in the midst of them, in the Christian communion." It is necessary to add, however: since He will maintain His uninterrupted activity *amongst you* until He comes to be fully revealed *in you*. Not until then, indeed, will He in full measure be with them and abide with them as the Holy Ghost. The one Future *ἔσται*, *will be*, is contradictory of Meyer's assumption: namely, that the Present *γινώσκετε* should be taken as absolute, without respect to any set time.

Ver. 18. **I leave you not as orphans behind Me. I come to you** [*οὐκ ἀφήσω ὑμᾶς ὀρφανούς, ἔρχομαι πρὸς ὑμᾶς*. The rendering of Tyndale and the A. V., *comfortless*, may have been chosen with reference to the *Comforter*, but is no translation of *ὀρφανούς* and impairs the force and beauty of the original. Wiclif has *fadirless*. The marginal reading *orphans* ought to have been inserted in the text.—P. S.] See Mark xii. 19. The *τεκνία*, chap. xiii. 33, an expression of *πατρικὴ εὐσπλαγχνία* (Euthymius Zigabenus): *I come unto you*, the Present. [Not *will come*, as in the A. V. which follows the Vulgate: *veniam*.—P. S.] A connecting *γάρ* would do away with the pure antithesis.† I go not away from you in the sense of leaving you orphans; on the contrary, it is now that I do truly come unto you. In what respect is this true?

1. It is not to be understood as signifying Christ's Parousia in the abstract (Augustine, Beda, *etc.*, Luthardt, Hofmann; against which vers. 19, 20 ff.), although this glorious coming of Christ continues until the Parousia.

2. Nor the manifestations subsequent to the resurrection (the Greek exegetes: Origen, Chrysostom, *etc.*, Rupert, Grotius [Ewald, who however spiritualizes and idealizes the resurrection]). Against this view too vers. 20, 21, 23; chap. xvi. 16, 22, 23 are cited. Hence

3. Christ's spiritual coming through the Paraclete is intended (Calvin, Lücke and most of the moderns [Olshausen, Tholuck, Meyer, Bäumlein, Godet]).

4. We, however, uphold the explanation, according to which Christ had in view both His corporeal and His spiritual return (Luther, Beza, Lampe and De Wette [also Ebrard and Hengstenberg]); for His spiritual return was conditioned upon His first returning in the body—upon His resurrection as the consummation of His revelation (without Easter no Pentecost). There is no double meaning in this interpretation, forasmuch as the manifestations of the Risen One were assisted by the operation of the Spirit and the pouring out of the Holy Ghost was the means of perfectly revealing the Risen and Glorified One. Tholuck remarks on the opposite side, that the seeing again, spoken of chap. xvi. 16, is conditioned upon His going to the Father. True, but it was on His way to the Father that He saw them again, John xx. Tholuck's assertion of the identity of the returning Christ and the before-mentioned *ἄλλος παράκλ.* is of a piece with the disregard of the contrast: *being with you* and *being in you*, or the contrast between the *παράκλ.* and the *ἄλλος παράκλ.*

Ver. 19. **Yet a little while**, *etc.* [*Ἔτι μικρόν*, sc. *ἐστι*].—*Μικρὸν, καὶ*; כִּמְעַט ו. See chap. xiii. 33 [xvi. 16; Heb. x. 37; Hos. i. 4]. From now until the moment when He was removed from the world by death, less than twenty-four hours elapsed.—**But ye see Me.** Tholuck: Not "ye shall see Me again," but: "your eyes shall be opened to perceive Me." Against this be it observed that the same verb (*θεωρεῖν*) is used to express the not-seeing of the world. Beyond a doubt, the imminent seeing of the Risen One with the bodily eye is meant; a sight destined for the disciples but denied to the world. The second little *μικρόν*, from the death to the resurrection of Christ, is swallowed up in the first *μικρόν*. The fact that this *θεωρεῖν* of the disciples passes into the spiritual, eternal contemplation of Christ, does not militate against the bodily seeing of Him to begin with. The subsequent sentence is expressly indicative of this bodily seeing again: "for I live," *etc.* This seeing of Christ is to be brought about by the life of Christ.—**For I live, and ye also shall live** [*ὅτι ἐγὼ ζῶ, καὶ ὑμεῖς ζήσεσθε*. The reason of the preceding *θεωρεῖτέ με*. Not: "*Because* I live, ye shall live also," Beza, A. V., Godet.—P. S.] The antithesis of Present and Future supports the exegesis. The Present: *I live*, is expressive of His divine vital power, outlasting death (see ch. v.) ch. xii.; Rev. i. 18).* Luther: "He is the Person whom death could not devour, though, as it regards His bodily life, it did indeed kill Him." But His thus living, as the God-Man, mighty in life, is at the same time indicative of His living again in the resurrection,—a fact proved by the promise: *ye shall live.* For Christ's life has, by His death and resurrection, become the principle of the new life of His people, Rom. vi. 8; Eph. i. 19, 20. The one-sided interpretations of these words as having reference to the resurrection,—interpretations quoted by Meyer—(Grotius: Ye shall see Me really *alive* [*non spectrum*], and ye yourselves shall survive in the midst of the dangers imminent upon you; or Theophylact: Ye shall be as

* [The absolute present, not the future *μενεῖ*, *manebit* (Vulg.). Comp. Meyer *in loc.*—P. S.]

† [Meyer explains the omission of a connecting particle from the deep emotion.—P. S.]

* [Bengel: *Non modo* VIVAM, *sed* VIVO; Apoc. i. 18. VIVETIS, *futurum; nam vita fidelium sequitur vitam Jesu; et non ex se, sed ex illo vivunt*; vi. 57. Meyer's note on this passage is excellent. On these assuring words of Christ Schleiermacher, in the touching funeral discourse of his only son Nathanael, despairing of all philosophical arguments for the immortality of the soul, firmly placed his hope and trust for a future life.—P. S.]

men who have received new life; or Augustine: Ye shall rise at the last day) do no detriment to the general application of the saying to the resurrection.

Ver. 20. **At that day ye shall know** [Ἐν ἐκείνῃ τῇ ἡμέρᾳ γνώσεσθε ὑμεῖς, ὅτι ἐγὼ ἐν τῷ πατρί μου καὶ ὑμεῖς ἐν ἐμοὶ κἀγὼ ἐν ὑμῖν].—Various interpretations: 1. Reference to the resurrection (see the next note); 2. Meyer: "its historical fulfilment was the day of Pentecost;" 3. Luthardt: the day of the Parousia; 4. De Wette: *in that time.* Be it observed that the day of the resurrection became for them not only the continually returning day of the Lord, or Sunday, but also *the day* κατ' ἐξοχήν, the new Day of their life. Ye will know **that I am in the Father.**—*I. e.* ye will recognize My divine personality. It means more than the words: the Father in Me.—**And ye in Me.** *I. e.* personalities who have attained unto new life, who are in Christ through the Holy Ghost because Christ is in them (**I in you**) by means of His glorified personality, the spirit of His glorified life. See note to ver. 16.

Ver. 21. **He that hath my commandments.** [Ὁ ἔχων τὰς ἐντολάς μου καὶ τηρῶν αὐτάς, ἐκεῖνός ἐστιν ὁ ἀγαπῶν με].—The ὁ ἔχων is emphatic, significant of that inward appropriation whereby the words of Christ are become the νόμος τοῦ πνεύματος. The proof of this living *possession* will be the *keeping* of His commandments. And that shall be the mark of *love* to Jesus. Now love to Jesus is that whereupon an experience of the Father's love is conditioned [ἀγαπηθήσεται ὑπὸ τοῦ πατρός μου]; and that, again, is proved by the sending of the Holy Ghost. But the sending of the Holy Ghost is, at the same time, an act of Christ's love towards the believer; an act in which He manifests Himself to the believer as the heavenly Christ [καὶ ἐγὼ ἀγαπήσω αὐτόν καὶ ἐμφανίσω αὐτῷ ἐμαυτόν]. Hence the discourse neither bears solely upon the appearings of the Risen One (Grotius), nor has it a general reference to the Parousia considered in the abstract (Luthardt). It is this manifestation of Christ through the Holy Ghost which, to Philip and the disciples generally, is to supply and overbalance the wonted, actual, visible presence of Christ.

Ver. 22. **Judas, not Iscariot.** οὐχ ὁ Ἰσκαριώτης. To be distinguished from that traitor. The reader was indeed aware of the departure of the traitor, according to ch. xiii. 30, as also that he could not (according to Bengel) again be present. It was not John's desire on this occasion to give utterance to his "profound abhorrence" of the traitor [Meyer, Alford]; willingly, however, did he bring into view the contrast between that malicious Judas who despaired of Christ's cause, and this other Judas, replete with enthusiasm and energy, even now conceiving of his Lord as one certain of victory, for whom the conquest of the world—and that too in a material sense—was reserved.—*Thaddeus* or *Lebbeus* according to Matt. x. 3; Luke vi. 16 (see Comm. on *Matt.* p. 182, Am. Ed.). It is, then, one of the brothers of the Lord (Comm. on *Matt.* p. 256 ff. Am. Ed.; my *Apost. Zeitalter*, p. 189) and, as the brother of James the son of Alpheus, the author of the epistle of Jude. His name (the courageous or stout-hearted) as well as his participation in the scene, Mark iii. 21, in the challenge, John vii. 3 and the character of his epistle, give him the appearance of a peculiarly energetic and courageous nature. These characteristics perfectly correspond with the question in our chapter; the query is expressive of his expectation that Jesus would manifest Himself to the world. In this saying there echoes once more with sufficient distinctness the demand (ch. vii. 3) that Jesus should labor openly in Jerusalem (*Leben Jesu* II. p. 149 and 1360). The ecclesiastical tradition respecting Judas Thaddeus or Lebbeus, see in Winer under that art.: *Apostol. Zeitalter* II. p. 407.

How is it that Thou wilt manifest Thyself, *etc.?* Τί γέγονεν, What has happened? what is the reason? *I. e.* in spite of all the threats and persecutions of Thine enemies, there seemeth to me as yet no sufficient reason for this holding back. This courage may in part rest upon the expectation that the Messiah, if He manifest Himself at all, must manifest Himself to the whole world in His judicial glory; a view which Tholuck upholds by the citation of Dillmann on the Book of *Enoch*, chap. xxx. Christ's answer, however, renders it more probable that Judas entertained the hope that the whole world would pay Him homage if He should manifest Himself in full.

Ver. 23. **If a man love Me, he will,** *etc.* [(Ἐάν τις ἀγαπᾷ με, τὸν λόγον μου τηρήσει). Bengel: τὸν λόγον μου, *sermonem meum. Sermo unus est, in hoc versu, respectu fidelium; sermones plures* (τοὺς λόγους μου), *respectu infidelium, qui discerpunt*, ver. 24.—P. S.] In the following reply Jesus sketches the contrast between His people and the world, assigning such contrast as the reason which renders it impossible for Him to manifest Himself to the world or to make His abode in it. Be it observed that Jesus has inverted the similarly sounding words in ver. 21. There it is: "he that hath My commandments and keepeth them, he it is that loveth Me;" here: "if any man love Me, he will keep My word." There must be some good reason for this antithesis. The proof of the *inner* life, in antithesis to the *visible world*, must itself be visible; for this cause ver. 21 the keeping of the commandments is mentioned first as an evidence of love. The proof of the *divine* life, however, in antithesis to the ungodly life of the world, must be love for Christ, since the world can *counterfeit* the inner life and the keeping of the commandments. In the one case, the proof of the *subjective* truth of the religious life, *i. e.* the antithesis to *sensuality*, suffices; in the other, Christ treats of the proof of the *objective* truth of the religious life, *i. e.* of the antithesis to *demoniacalness.* Ascetics may have some inner life, and yet may subjectively belong to the world; but believers in justification, they being truly in Christ, do not belong to the world. Thus, love to Christ is the foundation. It keeps His word as His objective portrait and law. The believer, pursuing this course, is well-pleasing to the Father. Therefore, the Father comes to him with the Son (by means of the Holy Ghost, the Paraclete). For the manifestation of Christ is this: the glorification of the Father through the Son,—of the Son with the Father through the Holy Ghost. The Father will manifest Himself through the Son, the Son through the Holy Ghost. They make their abode *with him* [μονὴν παρ' αὐτῷ ποιήσομεν], not merely *in* him; *i. e.* they found a community, a place where the Triune God manifests Himself—which community forms a contrast to the world. The παρ' αὐτῷ does not mean: *in his dwelling.* The Spirit is not only *in* the faithful, but *with* them as well; He forms a fellowship of believers, the Church. Thus He builds the spiritual house for an individual. The dwelling with him presupposes a dwelling in him. (We may quote as a curiosity the explanation of Semler and Less: Christ and the disciples shall come unto the Father and make their abode with Him). New Testament realization of the tabernacling of God amongst His people, Lev. xxvi. 11; prophesied Ezek. xxxvii. 26 and *in loc.* The real Shekina.

Ver. 24. **He that loveth Me not** [Ὁ μὴ ἀγαπῶν με τοὺς λόγους μου οὐ τηρεῖ]. —*Characteristic* of the world. The world, as an ungodly world, loves itself; its tendency is not centripetal but centrifugal; hence it loves not Christ. Hence it keeps not Christ's word as a living word, for the reason that it lacks the bond that should hold it and Christ together—namely, the Spirit. Now in failing to keep Christ's word it also fails to keep the Father's word which He has sent into the world with Christ [καὶ ὁ λόγος ὃν ἀκούετε, οὐκ ἔστιν ἐμός, ἀλλὰ τοῦ πέμψαντός με πατρός]. And thus the preliminary condition on which depends the manifestation of God to the world, is wanting; that condition is the medium and focus of His word.

Ver. 25. **These things I have spoken unto you.** [Ταῦτα λελάληκα ὑμῖν παρ' ὑμῖν μένων].—*I. e.* thus much of the heavenly life on earth as the sign of the heavenly home that awaits you beyond this world. Thus much ye can understand now through My words. At some future time, however, the Paraclete shall make it all perfectly clear to you (see chap. xvi. 12). Ταῦτα λελάληκα. Perfect. I have spoken it, it shall be certain.

Ver. 26. **But the Paraclete,** *etc.* [ὁ δὲ παράκλητος, τὸ πνεῦμα τὸ ἅγιον ὃ πέμψει ὁ πατὴρ ἐν τῷ ὀνόματί μου, ἐκεῖνος ὑμᾶς διδάξει τὰ πάντα καὶ ὑπομνήσει ὑμᾶς πάντα, ἃ εἶπον ὑμῖν].—The designation of the Paraclete is more definite. The different predicates are summed up together: the Paraclete—the Holy Ghost—whom the Father sends—in the name of Jesus. Different interpretations of the ἐν τῷ ὀνόματί μου: 1. Grotius (Lücke and others): At My intercession (*in meam gratiam,* with reference to ver. 14). 2. Euthymius Zigabenus and others: *Instead of Me, i. e.* not, as Meyer explains: He will send Him instead of My sending Him, but: He will send Him as the representative of Me in My character of Ambassador. 3. Meyer: So that the name of Jesus is the sphere containing the divine purpose and will which are to be accomplished by the sending. The object of God's intent and design is the name of Jesus. Since the name is the subjective knowledge of an objective manifestation, the sense is: in the knowledge of Christ, perfected through the perfect manifestation of Christ,—in the glorified Christ,—in His inclination towards the Church, in the Church's inclination towards Him, a bias effected by love to Him and by the keeping of His word. Luther: Here the emphatic words are: *in My name* and: *what I have said unto you.*

He will teach you all things and bring all things to your remembrance.—The proximate reference is to the subject of chap. xiv., the heavenly home, the heavenly goal. But, together with His teachings on this head, He is to be the means of imparting all fulness of Christian knowledge regarding the whole plan of salvation (πάντα). The first promise embraces the whole Christian science of salvation, progressing, as it does, *in infinitum;* the second its inalienable principial basis: that which Christ has said. It is not specifically new truths that the Holy Ghost will teach; not specifically supplementary ones (traditions in the Romish sense), still less such as shall take the place of those taught by Christ (as the fanatics and enthusiasts would have it), or correct and contradict these (according to Rationalism). His teaching shall consist in reminding men of the word of Christ, in giving them a subjective understanding of the same. In performing this His office, He shall unfetter the word—break down the barriers of individualization, parable, misunderstanding—thus causing it to develop into an ever-living organism of doctrine, the specific soul and character of which does, nevertheless, remain the word of Christ. The first πάντα says that every one of Christ's words shall attain its full development; hence it refers to the infinite import or capability of development belonging to His words. The second πάντα declares that none of the words of Christ shall be lost, that they all, as items of His doctrine, shall become operative. The interpretation of Grotius, according to which ἃ εἶπον ὑμῖν extends even to the first πάντα, has the effect of confusing the parallels and intrenching upon the independence of the Spirit. The meaning is not: everything that I have told you, He shall teach you and remind you of,—but: He shall teach you all things, whilst He brings all things that I have told you, to your remembrance. The καί is explicative.

[The work of the Spirit is the appropriation of Christ to the believer. "*Dicente Filio,*" says Augustine, "*verba capimus, docente Spiritu eadem verba intelligimus.*" Objectively all is done by Christ, subjectively the same work is done or applied every day by the Spirit. The fulfilment of this promise of the Holy Spirit to the Apostles, who was to guide them into the whole truth and give them the right understanding of Christ's teaching, guarantees their inspiration, sufficiency and authority as witnesses of our Lord, and is abundantly testified by their writings, which carry in themselves their own best evidence, as the shining sun proves his existence to all but the blind. The πάντα furnishes a strong argument for the *completeness* of the New Testament revelation and against the Romish doctrine of ecclesiastical tradition, in the sense of an additional and co-ordinate source and rule of faith. For two of the most important dogmas of modern

Romanism—the sinlessness of Mary and the infallibility of the pope—there is not the faintest trace in the apostolic writings.—P. S.]

Ver. 27. **A peace I leave with you** [*Εἰρήνην ἀφίημι ὑμῖν, εἰρήνην τὴν ἐμὴν δίδωμι ὑμῖν*].—According to Luther (Neander and others) this is the farewell-greeting of Christ to His people (comp. 1 Pet. v. 14; 3 John ver. 14). Luther: "These are last words, as of one who, on the eve of departure, says good night or invokes a blessing." Tholuck remarks, against this view, that Christ is not going away from them, but that they are going with Him (ver. 31), and that in this case the corresponding phrase could not mean *εἰρ. ἀφιέναι*, but only *διδόναι* or *λέγειν*. And so *ἀφιέναι* (still according to Tholuck) should be taken in the sense of leaving behind, namely, as a parting gift, and it is the peace of reconciliation that Jesus speaks of. But this deeper meaning offers no obstacle to the belief that to the concrete fact of His departure He affixes His peace as a parting greeting. The Hebrew greeting was perfectly adapted to express this union of the highest with the trivial. And as certainly as the saying of the Risen One: *Peace be with you* (John xx. 19, 21), is the customary salutation and yet, at the same time, the announcement of the resurrection peace, just so certainly is the leaving of peace here at once the higher farewell greeting of Jesus and a real gift of peace. But there is nothing contradictious in the fact that parting friends may bid each other good-bye, perchance more than once, and still walk a little way together. It is here that the subject we have been considering—*viz.*, the going of Jesus to heaven, in order to the preparation of the place for His disciples—is brought to a conclusion. The term *ἀφίημι* is explained by the too slightly estimated *δίδωμι*. Thus the Hebrew שָׁלוֹם, prosperity, peace (go in peace, לֵךְ לְשָׁלוֹם, 1 Sam. i. 17, *etc.*; Mark v. 34, *etc.*; see the farewell salutations Eph. vi. 23 [1 Pet. v. 14; 3 John ver. 13]), in this place certainly *peace of soul* likewise; this interpretation is disputed by Meyer.*—**My peace** (peace-greeting) **I give unto you** [*εἰρήνην τὴν ἐμὴν δίδωμι ὑμῖν*].—We question the generally assumed identity of this saying with the foregoing one: "*A* peace (*εἰρήνην*) I leave unto you." On the contrary, the emphasis: "*My* peace" (*τὴν ἐμήν*) is of itself indicative of an antithesis. It is the intention of Jesus to declare in the strongest manner possible that His greeting on seeing them again shall follow fast upon His parting salutation, and that He will not present to them that full peace-greeting which is His specific property until, meeting them again, He salutes them, bringing His perfect and entire peace. With *a* peace I left you; with *My* peace I am with you again. I leave you a peace for a support; it is sufficient to keep you upright; My full peace I will give unto you. The most lively construction of the words: *after a little while*, ver. 19.

Not as the world giveth [*οὐ καθὼς ὁ κόσμος δίδωσι, ἐγὼ δίδωμι ὑμῖν*].—The proposition is, undoubtedly, a general one; not for this reason, however, should its application to the world's empty forms of greeting (Grotius, Bengel and others) be denied (De Wette, Meyer, Tholuck).* In the world also the manner of salutation on going and coming is connected with the manner of *giving*. The world gives as it greets, *i. e.* in a vain and empty way, 1 John ii. 17. Having just recognized an antithesis in the words of Christ: "I leave you a peace" at parting, "I give you *My* peace" at our new union, it readily occurs to us to meditate upon the inverted conduct of the world. At the start the world with its greetings promises golden mountains; coldly and heartlessly it takes leave of its servants and prepares them an end full of terrors. It fared literally thus with Judas. *Christ makes a warm and comforting farewell-greeting the forerunner of the beatific salutation which shall accompany the eternal meeting.*

Let not your heart be troubled, nor let it be afraid [*μὴ ταρασσέσθω ὑμῶν ἡ καρδία μηδὲ δειλιάτω*].—Repetition of the exhortation ver. 1; hence the indication of a concluded meditation. The annexed *δειλιάτω* (which is found in this place only in the New Testament)† proves that He views the trembling more as a natural emotion that might seize them at the thought of a hopeless parting, while in uttering the *δειλιάτω* His mind is contemplating the danger of a cowardly course of conduct proceeding from that emotion.

Ver. 28. **Said unto you**, *etc.* [*ἠκούσατε ὅτι ἐγὼ εἶπον ὑμῖν· ὑπάγω καὶ ἔρχομαι πρὸς ὑμᾶς*].—See ver. 2. At the same time, however, the words: **I go away and I come to you**, are doubtless explanatory of the farewell just uttered: "peace," *etc.*, "My peace," *etc.* Neither does the proposition mean simply: "I go away and come again," *etc.*, but, "by going away, I come to you more truly than ever;" as results from what follows.—**If ye loved Me** [*εἰ ἠγαπᾶτέ με*].—Of *perfect* love that casteth out fear (1 John iv. 18. He makes *their* love to *Him* a motive of comfort to *them*. They loved Him, but not spiritually enough, else they would have rejoiced at the prospect of His abiding spiritual presence. Bengel: *Amor parit gaudium; per se, et quia servat verbum Christi lætissima omnia aperiens*, "Love begets joy, both of itself, and because it keeps the word of Christ, which opens all the most joyful prospects."—P. S.]—**Ye would have rejoiced** (*ἐχάρητε* (not the Imperf. *ἐχαίρετε*) *ἂν ὅτι πορεύομαι πρὸς τὸν πατέρα*).—He does not mean: in that case ye would not be in the least affected by

* [In the fifth edition (p. 524) where Meyer takes *εἰρήνη* indeed in the most general sense of *prosperity*, like the Hebrew *Shalom* but so as to include "the peace of redemption or reconciliation with God as the first essential element."—P. S.]

* [Bengel: "*In salutationibus inanibus vel beneficiis duntaxat externis, cor non attingentibus, et cum præsentia, conspectu ac vita mortali desinentibus.*" (Comp. the English proverb, "Out of sight, out of mind."). "*Mundus ita dat, ut mos eripiat, non relinquit.*" Alford and Godet likewise refer the *καθώς* to the *manner of giving*, rather than the unreality and emptiness of the world's peace. But Meyer thinks a reference to the empty formulas of worldly greeting entirely out of place in the solemnity of this moment. Lange has the right view here.—P. S.]

† [But often in the Sept. For *δειλιάω* the classics use *ἀποδειλιάω*. *δειλός*, *timid*, *fearful*, occurs Matt. viii. 26; Mark iv. 40; Rev. xxi. 8, *δειλιά*, *timidity*, 2 Tim. i. 7. Bengel refers *ταρασσέσθω*, *ne turbetur*, to the *intrinsic*, *δειλιάτω*, *ne formidet*, to the *extrinsic* fear.—P. S.]

grief at parting from Me (comp. ch. xvi. 21), but, the joy of faith would preponderate. The thing in My difficult journey that would appear pre-eminent to your eyes would be My triumphal home-going to the Father. Hence: "**because I said unto you, I go unto the Father,**" *i.e.*, because I have put such a cheering interpretation upon My going away from you.—**For the Father is greater than I** (ὅτι ὁ πατήρ μείζων μου ἐστίν).—*A.* We have first to consider this proposition in the abstract, and then in its relation (ὅτι) to what precedes it.

1. *Theological* elucidations [in the essential or metaphysical sense]: *a.* The Arians regarded the declaration as a proof-text for their system.

[The Arians inferred from this passage that Christ is a creature of the Father, though existing before the world. The same interpretation has been revived by the Socinians, Unitarians and Rationalists, who deny also the preëxistence of Christ, which the Arians admitted. But this gives no intelligible sense at all. On the contrary, the words imply (as even Meyer freely admits, p. 526) the homoousia or divine nature of Christ. If a mere man or creature says: "God is greater than I," he talks blasphemous nonsense almost as much as if he said: "I am equal with God." Comp. also the remarks of Godet (II., 490): "*Cette parole suppose chez celui qui la prononce, le sentiment le plus vif de sa participation à la divinité.*"—P. S.]

b. Athanasius, Gregory of Nazianzum [Hilary, Euthym. Zigab.] and others, in modern times Olshausen,* considered it expressive of the ἀγεννησία of the Father in antithesis to the begottenness or eternal generation of the Son.

[On the Arian controversy concerning this passage see Suicer, *Thesaur.*, II., pp. 1368 sq., and Bull's *Defens. Fid. Nic.*, sect. 4. To escape the Arian inference it would have been better to refer the μειζονότης of the Father to His *official* superiority. The Nicene orthodoxy admitted a certain subordination of the Son to the Father, as to *dignity* or *office*, but not as to *essence* or *substance*, which is the same; there being but *one* God. But this passage has no reference to the essence or nature at all, but to the state or condition; for the superiority of essence which exists always and everywhere, could be no reason why the disciples should rejoice at the approaching departure of Christ to the Father. Hence no inference unfavorable to the orthodox doctrine of the homoousia can be drawn from it. Calvin clearly, with his usual tact, saw this, and gives substantially the right interpretation, which I may anticipate here (see ii. b.): "*Varie detortus fuit hic locus. Ariani ut Christum probarent quendam secundarium esse Deum, objiciebant minorem esse Patre. Patres orthodoxi, ut tali calumniæ ansam præciderent, dicebant hoc debere ad naturam humanam referri. Atqui ut impie hoc testimonio abusi sunt Ariani, ita nec recta, nec consentanea fuit patrum solutio. Hic enim neque de humana Christi natura, neque de æterna ejus divinitate sermo habetur, sed pro infirmitatis nostræ captu se medium inter nos et Deum constituit.*"—P. S.]

2. *Christological* explanations:

a. The superiority of the Father has reference to the *human* nature of Christ, because it is in this alone that He *goes* to the Father (Hunnius, J. Gerhard). [Comp. the Athanasian Creed: "equal to the Father as touching His Godhead; and inferior to the Father as touching His manhood." So also Webster and Wilkinson. Wordsworth: "Christ is speaking of *going* which cannot be predicated of God. My Father is greater than I am in that nature which *goes* to Him." This interpretation implies a mere platitude. Who need be told that the human nature is inferior to the divine? It also assumes an abstract separation of the two natures in Christ, which constitute one life. The speaking and acting *Ego* of Christ is His divine-human person, and the nature is the organ through which He acts.—P. S.]

b. Reference is had to Christ's state of humiliation (*status exinanitionis*, Luther, Calvin, Luthardt).

[This interpretation is also defended by Cyril, Melanchthon, Beza, Bengel, De Wette, Brückner, Stier, Alford, Barnes, Owen, *etc.* Christ spoke these words as the battling and suffering Messiah from His state of humiliation, which was to cease with His departure to the Father; and it is His prospective exaltation to glory and bliss which ought to have been an occasion for rejoicing to His disciples. There is no force in Meyer's objection that God is greater than Christ even in His *exalted* state (xvii. 5; 1 Cor. xv. 27 f.; Phil. ii. 9-11), as He was greater than the preëxistent Logos (John i. 1-3). He refers the μειζονότης of the Father to His superior *power*: "As My Father is greater, especially mightier, than I, My departure to Him will be an elevation to greater power and activity, to the victory over the world, to higher union with Him, hence a matter of rejoicing for those who love Me."—P. S.]

c. It refers to both the above-mentioned considerations ["humanity in its state of lowliness"] (Calov, Quenstädt, Tholuck, Augustine: "*quia naturæ humanæ gratulandum est eo, quod sic assumta est a verbo unigenito, ut immortalis constitueretur in cœlo*").

3. We must grasp at once the theological import and the Christological one, for there is a good reason why the *Son* of God became man and humbled Himself,—not the *Father*. Theologically considered, the Father is greater than the Son, as the first principle, *in respect of order* or *succession*, by whom the Son was established, both being perfectly equal in substance. Hence it follows that He is greater in *substance* also than Christ in His human nature, and above all, greater in regard to the *rule* or *power* which He exercises, than is Christ in His humiliation. And it is upon this latter circumstance that the stress here lies. [So also Meyer, see above.—P. S.] Christ, in going to the Father as to the One greater than He, enters into the joint possession of His greatness and majesty, without, however, thereby destroying the subordination of order (see ver. 16; ch. xvii. 3, 5; 1 Cor. xv. 27; Phil. ii. 9-11; 1 Cor. iii. 23; xi. 3). The characteri-

* [Olshausen explains: "The Son is born of the essence of the Father, but not inversely the Father from the Son: hence the Father is the cause (*der Grund*) of the Son, but the Son is not the cause of the Father. The Son proceeding thus from the Father (xiii. 3) there was necessarily in Him a desire to return to the Father, as every being is attracted to its source; accordingly the return to the Father was the satisfaction of the desire felt by the Son after His source, and this relation is indicated by the words μείζων μου ἐστίν." But the essential relation is eternal and hence unchangeable.—P. S.]

zation of the theological import as the "absolute monotheism of the New Testament," by Meyer, in connection with Lücke, is liable to misapprehension and fails to afford, in any case, a sufficient explanation.

B. We now consider the relation of this proposition to the preceding ἐχάρητε ἄν. **For** (ὅτι) the *Father*. Why should the disciples be glad of His going to the Father?

1. On account of His exaltation to δόξα and blessedness (Cyrill, Olshausen, Tholuck).

2. On account of the more powerful protection which He should thenceforth be able to bestow upon the disciples (Theophylact, Lücke and others).

3. On account of Jesus' exaltation to greater power and activity (Meyer).

4. Because the going away of Jesus was His own exaltation and was likewise of benefit to them (Luther, Bengel, Lampe).

It is as little possible to separate Jesus' exaltation to glory from His exaltation to power as to separate His own exaltation from the exaltation of His disciples; nevertheless, their love should first view His exaltation, passing on, however, as the context admonishes, from a glance at that in the abstract to the consideration that it is through His exaltation alone that He shall become in very deed their own.

Ver. 29. **And now I have told you.**—As is frequently His custom He emphatically states that He tells them such and such things beforehand, in order that, when His predictions are fulfilled, they *may believe.* Thus prophecy is, like miracles, a proof of the divine power and presence (Isa. xli. 22-26). It is impossible that the bare prediction of the death of Jesus can here be meant; it is the announcement of His exaltation by means of His death, resurrection and ascension. These facts, in which they saw Christ's prediction fulfilled, made perfect their faith. In this sense, therefore, it is written here also: "*that ye might believe.*" (See Chap. xx. 31).

Ver. 30. **Hereafter I shall not talk much with you** (οὐκ ἔτι πολλὰ λαλήσω μεθ' ὑμῶν).—A presentiment of departure, an introduction to the start which He was about proposing.—**For the prince,** *etc.* (ἔρχεται γὰρ ὁ τοῦ κόσμου ἄρχων).—See chap. xii. 31. A reference of the mood of Jesus to the preparations against Him that are going on in Jerusalem. In spirit He is aware that His enemies are now making ready to advance against Him; and in them He sees the tools of Satan; hence: "the prince of this world cometh," ch. xiii. 27.—**And hath nothing in Me** (καὶ ἐν ἐμοὶ οὐκ ἔχει οὐδέν).—The ἐν ἐμοί antithesis to the prince of this world. He comes as the prince of this world's power, of this world's fear, of death and corruption, to claim a power over Me, Heb. ii. 14. *Καὶ ἐν ἐμοί, etc.* Various constructions:

1. *He can, or is able* to, do nothing to Me; he cannot inflict death upon Me; of My own free will I suffer it (Chrysostom, Kuinoel).

2. *He finds nothing* in Me; no accusation against Me (Origen).

3. *He possesses* nothing in Me (Cyril, Augustine: *peccatum, cui debetur mortis supplicium;* Grotius, Meyer more generally: in Me he *possesses* nothing, as owning his sway). [Meyer thinks that the sinlessness (Augustine: "*in Me non habet quidquam, nullum omnino scilicet peccatum*") is not directly *expressed* in the passage, but necessarily *implied* as the causal condition, since only when Christ was free from sin, Satan had no hold on Him and no power over Him. Alford similarly: "no point of appliance whereon to fasten his attack."—P. S.]

4. Tholuck: He has *no claim on Me* (*nihil juris*). Submission on Christ's part was, therefore, voluntary; comp. chap. xix. 11 (so too De Wette, Hofmann and others).

The words certainly declare not only Jesus' sinlessness but also His freedom from death. They are a repetition of Jesus' solemn protestation of His freedom,—a protestation aimed against the idea which represents Him as of necessity succumbing to the irresistible fate of sinful men (see ch. x. 18; xii. 24; xiii. 19). At the same time the saying contains an intimation to the effect that Satan, possessing, as he does, not a single fibre or hair of Him in an ethical sense, shall likewise fail to retain a single fibre or hair of Him in a physical sense. But the fact that he now, in accordance with the counsel of God, is coming upon Him, is implied in the emphasis that rests upon the expression: *he cometh* (comp. Luke xxii. 53).

Ver. 31. **But that the world may know,** *etc.*—Expressive of His willingness to become a sacrifice. The root is love to the Father; the proof, obedience to the Father; the consequence: the departure, not so much in order to go obstinately to meet the enemy, but rather, in pursuance of God's guidance, to await him at the place of prayer, in Gethsemane. *That the world.* Bengel: "*Ut mundus desinat mundus esse et patris in me bene placitum agnoscat salutariter.*" That, in His personal submission to the personal Father, the kingdom of grace, love, personal life, may dawn upon the world, for a judgment upon its unrightful prince and in order to the freeing of it from that false tyranny which he exercises through the fear of death. That the world may know that love is stronger than death (comp. Sol. Song viii. 6: "strong as death").

Arise, let us depart.—The mighty saying prompted by a holy emotion finds expression not in two only, but in three asyndetical exhortations: ἐγείρεσθε—ἄγωμεν—ἐντεῦθεν. Various explanations of the item:

1. Jesus, accompanied by the disciples, proceeds to a secure place where He uttered chh. xv., xvi., xvii. (Chrysostom, Theophylact and others);—unsupported.

2. Still less tenable: hitherto Jesus had been outside of the city; He was but now about departing for Jerusalem to keep the Passover (Bengel, Wichelhaus [Röper]).

3. Jesus, too full of the matters which were still pressing upon His heart, spoke, still standing in the room where they had eaten the supper, chh. xv., xvi., xvii. (Knapp, Lücke, Tholuck, Meyer, [Calvin, Olshausen, Bleek, Brückner, Ewald, Alford, Owen], *etc.*). And this after the three powerful exhortations to depart?

4. The following (chh. xv.-xvii.) was spoken by Him on the road (Luther, Grotius, Lampe,

Lange, *Leben Jesu* II., p. 1347 [Ebrard, Barnes, Webster and Wilkinson, Wordsworth] and others). Meyer [Alford and Owen] in opposition to this view: The thing is psychologically improbable. Psychologically improbable indeed would be the supposition that Jesus did not discourse to the disciples of the most momentous matters even when they were upon the road to their destination. Walking and standing still and walking again is the very expression of a mind stirred by great things.

5. On the hypercritical remarks of De Wette (who identifies the ἐγείρεσθε, ἄγωμεν, Matt. xxvi. 46, with that of our text), Strauss, Weisse, Baur, Hilgenfeld, see Meyer [p. 529].

DOCTRINAL AND ETHICAL.

1. The farewell discourses of the Lord have not been sufficiently valued for what they are: namely, the *new revelation* of Christ concerning *heaven.* Until these discourses were delivered, the theocratic belief of Israel was acquainted only with *Sheol,* and with the antithesis of a paradise and a place of punishment (gehenna) in Sheol. See Luke xvi. 22 ff. The doctrine of paradise was of course the germ of the doctrine of the heavenly home, and even the Old Testament contained sundry dark intimations of the latter in the translation of Enoch, the ascension of Elijah, the description of heaven as the throne of God and the habitation of His holy angels, and the hope of the faithful for a closer union with God, in sayings such as Prov. xv. 24; Eccl. xii. 7. But it was reserved for Christ to throw heaven open, in the first instance by His *word* in the farewell-discourses, and, secondly, by His *act* in the ascension itself. Hence the farewell-discourses substantially contain a theology of Christ's ascension. The doctrine of heaven was, however, not intelligible to believing human hearts until the disciples were forced to learn experimentally that the earthly world was no longer a resting-place for the Lord and for them; that they were cast out of the world. When the world cast them out and its doors shut to behind them, there opened to them the gates of heaven. Understanding the ethical import of the going down of the sun and the gathering night, they could also comprehend the symbolical sign of the starry heavens, the Father's great open house. And even now they were enabled to grasp and hold fast this hope only through the imminence of Christ's ascension into heaven. But the revelation concerning heaven as the *place and land* of glory could and should not be the exchange of a new sensuous expectation for an old one; together with the *local* heaven Christ disclosed the *dynamical* heaven to their view—destined, this latter, to be developed in the new life upon earth as a personal kingdom of love; founded by the revelation of His personality, by the manifestation of the personal Father and the glorification, by means of the personality of the Holy Ghost, of the personal love-life of God as the foundation of the personal kingdom of love in which they are, which they are to maintain *against* the hate of the world, and which they are to spread through the world. In the second life of the second Man who is from heaven, in the resurrection of Christ, heaven was made manifest on earth (comp. 1 Cor. xv. 21, 22, 47; John xvi. 21); through the Paraclete as the Spirit of glory, of δόξα, the disciples were translated into the fellowship of this heavenly state (Phil. iii. 20).

2. The *startling effect* produced upon the disciple of Christ when this present world is darkened for him by the cross, and sets upon him or casts him out. Then he is comforted by the watch-word which bids him put his trust in the Christ who ascendeth to heaven and in the Father who is in heaven. The *soul* may be troubled at this transition; but not the *heart* (vers. 1, 27).

3. *Trust in God; in so doing, etc.* Become thorough Israelites, for thus ye shall also become Christians. We can go still further and say: become thorough Catholics and then ye will also be Evangelical Christians.

4. Man, having as a sinner lost his power over the earth and being chained by an autochthonic consciousness to particular climes and countries, had, in still greater measure, lost the bent or drawing of his astral or heavenly citizenship; his way led not upwards toward the stars, but downwards to the earth. Christ has restored us our heavenly citizenship (Heb. ix.). The words of Christ: *In My Father's house, etc.*, do not, indeed, contain any new astronomical system, but they do prove His view of the world and of heaven to have been infinitely elevated above that of His time.

5. The three sayings inculcating *faith in the heavenly home:* the saying addressed to Thomas, the saying addressed to Philip, the saying addressed to Judas Lebbæus. Or our heavenly home is sure to us in spite *of the contradiction* of an outward reality full of distress and death, in spite *of the want* of phenomena evident to the senses, in spite *of the denial of the hostile world,* which even by its hate, as the germ and sign of hell, must testify of love, as the seed and sign of heaven. See above.

6. Meyer on ver. 3 [p. 507, footnote]: "It is incorrect to affirm that the *idea of reward* is utterly wanting in John. (Thus Weiss in the *Deutsch. Zeitschr.*, 1853, pp. 325, 388 and in his *Petrin. Lehrbegr.*, 1855, p. 55 ff.) As Christ asks for eternal glory for Himself as a reward, chap. xvii. 4 ff., so in like manner does He promise it to the disciples as their reward. See chap. xvii. 24; xii. 25. Under this head we should also class the promise of ἰδεῖν τὴν βασ., τοῦ θεοῦ, chap. iii. 3, 5, and of the raising up at the last day, chap. v. 28 ff.; vi. 40, 54. Comp. 1 John iii. 2, 3, where the future glorification and union with Christ is expressly designated as the subject of the ἐλπίς; as also 2 John 8, where the term μισθὸν πλήρη is used and must be understood as referring to eternal bliss (see Düsterdieck, II. p. 505)."—Upon all which we must observe, that in John especially, the term *reward* cannot be apprehended in its legal sense; it is to be construed, in conformity to the kingdom of love, as a loving recompense, bestowed, it is true, in accordance with justice.

7. Christ *the living Way, the pledge of the goal.* Christianity the absolutely dynamical view of the world. The personal, God-filled heart and es-

sence of Christ becomes surety for the existence and unclosure of the personal, *i. e.* eternal and spiritually glorious world. Christ's heart the absolute *dynamis* of the eternal places and times, 1 Pet. i. 4. Christ the absolute Way, because He is the Truth,—the principle, medium and aim of all connection, all that is *lasting* in the world—perfect reality; and because He is the Life,—the complete manifestation of the highest appearance and beauty from the deepest ground: all-animating Life and Love.

8. *If ye had known Me.* The mystery of Christ's personality, the medium of the manifestation of God and of the manifestation of the personal kingdom.

9. The *greater works* of Christianity, a continual miracle in the world, to result in the wonderful metamorphosis of the world at the consummation of all things, and in its transfiguration into the world of the Spirit.

10. *The evidence of Philip and the evidence of Christ.* Philip still sees in things power over persons; the Lord sees in personality power over things. On the Paraclete see note to ver. 16, in reference to Tholuck, p. 364 [and Hare's *Mission of the Comforter.*—P. S.]

11. Similarly see note on the distinction between the manifestation of Christ in the Father and that of the Father in Christ. Analogously, the being of believers in Christ—justification—is distinguished from Christ's being in believers—sanctification.

12. The promise that His people shall *see Him again*, ver. 19, is inclusive of the resurrection, together with the entire future manifestation of Christ in His word and Spirit here, in His paternal house beyond this world, until the time of His great Epiphany. Hence it is wrong to contrast, as Meyer does (p. 400), Christ's paracletic coming again with His resurrection; and, similarly, to suppose it to result from the Johannean version that Christ did not so definitely predict His resurrection (except in such hints as are contained in chap. ii. 19; x. 17) as the Synoptists report Him to have done.

13. The manifestation of Christ in its relation to the world, according to the view of Judas Lebbeus and according to Christ's view. Love to Christ, as the tendency of the Spirit in the Church to the centre of life, is the fundamental condition, the medium of the manifestation of His personality; the world as world, on the other hand, is, in its centrifugal tendency, bent upon vanity, upon impersonal things. In this medium Christ cannot manifest Himself to it.

14. The doctrine of the *procession of the Holy Ghost*, according to ver. 26, stands, in a manner, betwixt the assertion of the Oriental and that of the Occidental Church. See the history of dogmas. The former Church with reason insists upon the priority of the Father as first principle; the latter, with equal reason, gives prominence to the autonomy of spiritual life which the Son too possesses and of which intimation is given here: "in My name."

15. On ver. 26. The Spirit is related, as Spirit, to a specific vital cause by which He is necessitated. The wind, as the symbolical Spirit, cannot be conceived of without the earth; the spirit of man cannot be conceived of without the substratum of a man. Spirit is the concentrated, conscious unity of a definite life. So the Spirit of God is the unity of the manifestations of the essence of God; the Holy Spirit the unity of the complete manifestation of the Father and Son, by which unity God has fully made manifest His antithesis to the world, in order thus fully to communicate Himself to the world. But because the essence of God is actual to its very foundation, the Holy Ghost also, as the Spirit of the complete manifestation of God, appears as a *particular third form of the personality of God*, and is free in Himself, like the Father and the Son. The life of the Spirit becomes a fountain of life in men's spirits. This truth has been misinterpreted by the Montanists, Manichees, the spiritualistic Franciscans and other enthusiasts of the Middle Ages, the Anabaptists and the philosophers of the school of Hegel, inasmuch as all these distinguish, more or less definitely, three kingdoms,—the kingdom of the Father, that of the Son, and that of the Holy Ghost. And the Catholic doctrine of ecclesiastical tradition adds to the kingdom of the Son a kingdom of the Spirit, to the administration of which the Hierarchy pretends. This forms the other extreme to the Spirit's sphere of manifestation according to the doctrine of the Quakers. *The Holy Ghost is related just as purely and entirely to the Son as the Son is to the Father.*—The infiniteness of the Christian spiritual life, the eternal nature of it, is expressed in the calling of the Spirit who has been given to the believer, now the Spirit of *truth*, now the Spirit of *knowledge*, of *strength*, *etc.* There is always denoted an infinite plenitude—self-begetting like a fountain—of this divine life of truth, knowledge, *etc.*

16. Christ's *farewell-greeting* a pledge for the *greeting of a future meeting.* Thus the Lord comforteth His people.

17. The *prophecies* in their fulfilment are miracles of God's Spirit, in order to the awakening, quickening and confirming of faith.

18. Christ's *repeated protest* against the misinterpretation of His *death-way*,—against the conception of it as a blind, inevitable fate or a sign of the world's superiority; in connection with the asseveration of His freedom in submitting to the will of His Father. In this free submission His high-priesthood is perfected; the Priest is the Sacrifice and the Sacrifice is the Priest Himself.

HOMILETICAL AND PRACTICAL.

The word of the Lord to His disciples: "Let not your heart be troubled!" or how He encourages them on their entrance upon the night of sorrows: 1. By the admonition to submissive and unconditional trust (ver. 1). 2. By the opening up of a view of the high and heavenly home (ver. 2). 3. By His going before and coming again (vers. 2 and 3). 4. By the explanations and promises whereby He removes all their scruples and doubts (the scruple of Thomas, of Philip, of Judas Lebbeus). 5. By the gift of His peace as a pledge of a speedy and joyful return (ver. 27 ff.).—The rise of the heavenly Paradise upon Christ's earthly night of passion: 1. The Paradise a heavenly one, better than the lost Paradise on earth. 2. Its rise, brought on by Christ's exode into the night of Passion, in company with His disciples. 3. Christ the Revealer and Perfecter of it, and the Guide to it.—Discovery of the new celestial realm of life above the old subterranean kingdom of the dead.—The glorification of the human life through Christ, at the same time the glorification of the creation. He hath brought life and immortality to light. First an inner life for God's paternal house, then a paternal house of God for that inner life.—The heavenly heart revealed and unlocked the heavenly home.—Christ has *dis*closed and *un*closed heaven: 1. He was the bearer of disclosures concerning it; 2. the opener of a way into it.—Christ has pledged His word to His people that there is an heavenly inheritance for them.—He makes all things ready for the heavenly life: 1. The place for His people, 2. His people for the place.—The Christian's way to earthly woe, the way to the Father's house in heaven. Heaven our Father-house: 1. The Father of the house; 2. the house of the Father.—Our journey to the Father's house: 1. The goal of our way; 2. the way to our goal.—The many mansions in the Father's house: 1. Many mansions, one Father-house. In all one Father, one Son and Heir, one inheritance for one throng of children. 2. One Father-house, many mansions. Room enough for many inhabitants. 3. The mansions, habitable, *resting-places, abiding-places*. 4. The mansions manifold, for every one a special home in the one eternal citadel of God.—The heavenly mansions: 1. In what respect prepared from the beginning; 2. in what respect receiving additional preparation through the ascension of Christ; 3. in what respect undergoing an eternal process of glorification.—The unshakable assurance of Christ with regard to the heavenly Fatherland.—The home-country of Christians where the glorified Christ is.—Christ's disclosures in regard to the way to heaven. (See above).—The doubt of Thomas.

The saying of Christ: *I am the way:* 1. He is the way, as the truth of the way;—the living, personal motion to the Father because He is truth itself; 2. He is the way, as the life of the way;—the victorious mover to the Father because He is life in general.—Christ the way in His divine-human personality: 1. God's way to man. Therefore 2. man's way to God.—Christ's personality as a pledge of the heavenly home: 1. As the truth of the heavenly life; 2. as the life of heavenly truth.—No way to the Father except through the Son.—He who knows nothing of the life beyond, knows nothing of it for this reason—because he is ignorant of the kernel of this present life.—The Lord's discourse with Philip.—The personal life of Christ the substantial appearance in the midst of the seemingness of the world.—The manifestation of the Father in the figure of the Son.—Christ the image of God, Heb. i. 3.—Different ways of knowing the one way of truth: 1. The knowledge of elect disciples, a cognition of the Father in the Son by means of the cognition of the Son in the Father, or a comprehension of Christ's works by Christ's word. 2. The way of the majority: or the cognition of the Son in the Father by the Father in the Son, *i. e.* comprehension of the word through a comprehension of the works. *The greater works*, or how the wonders of Christ are developing in the wonders of Christianity until the great wonder of His appearing.—How Christ's miracles are perennial in His works.—Greater works, *i. e.* the increasingly glorious unfolding of Christ's work in His people.—As Christ Himself has been glorified by the Holy Ghost, so the wonders of Christ have been glorified through the wonders of the Holy Spirit.

For I go to the Father. Christ's power rendered boundless by His going to the Father, the Fountain of power.—Prayer in the name of Jesus the channel for the performance of Christ's works.—The sighs of the Christian heart as the prophecy and origin of the triumphs of the Christian hand.—The longing of Christians and the blessing of Christ encounter one another.—An ever purer praying in His name results in an ever richer doing in His strength.

The Holy Spirit as the other Comforter, not Christ's substitute but His presence.—The promise of the other Comforter (Mediator).—The Holy Ghost promised to Christians as, above all, the Spirit of truth.—The world, as world, is not capable of receiving the Holy Ghost: 1. It does not see Him, therefore it does not know Him; 2. it does not know Him, therefore it does not receive Him.—The world with all its spirit yet without the (Holy) Spirit: 1. Its spirits lack the Spirit (the true Spirit); 2. its spirit lacks spirits (its inspiration does not attain to great personal spirit-life).—The Holy Ghost, like Christ, a stranger to the world.—Always an intimate of Christians, always a stranger to the world.—The disciples of Jesus become the intimates of His Spirit.—Christians never orphans.—Christianity a living in the coming of Christ: 1. He lives, therefore His people shall live. 2. He comes, therefore His people shall see Him.

The grand saying: *Yet a little while:* 1. Yet a little while and He will be here with us (as Comforter, as Quickener, Gladdener, Helper-through) with wonders of refreshment. 2. Yet a little while and we shall be yonder with Him.—After Gethsemane and Golgotha, in sooth,—but still after a little.—Through trouble and death, and yet after a little. (Rom. viii. 18.)—*At that day*, ver. 20. The new day of a three-fold lustre: 1. That of the Resurrection, 2. of the Ascension, 3. of the outpouring of the Spirit.—Isa. xxx. 26; lx. 19.—The resurrection time as the triumphal celebration of the personal life: 1. Of Christ, 2. of His own, 3. of the hearts that they, in His strength, shall awaken to personal life.—Upon what conditions do we become recipients of the manifestation of the living Christ? (See ver. 23.)

Christ's discourse with Judas Lebbeus.—The gloomy views of Thomas, the wavering views of Philip, and the cheerful views of Judas.—Judas' faith in the piety of the world not free from worldly-mindedness.—The difference and contrast between Jesus' disciples and the world: First mark: Love to Jesus; no love. Second mark: The keeping of Christ's word; the failing to keep it. Third mark: Experience of how the Father, together with the Son, takes up His dwelling with His own. The Father's staying away from the despisers of the Son.—Only where Christ's radiant image is extant in His word, is this radiant image filled with the power of His life.—Christ having covered up the great abyss between earth and heaven, discloses the great abyss between the company of the faithful and the world.

The Holy Ghost as the teacher of Christ's word: 1. How He brings to mind all things; 2. how He develops all things.—The Holy Ghost as a Reminder: 1. Who unlocks the penetralia of revelation for the Christian, 2. the penetralia of the Christian for revelation.—The inner life as a being reminded, or a calling to mind.—The mark of the true Christian spirit, unison with Christ and His word.

The peace-greeting of Christ His gift of peace.—The farewell-greeting of Christ the pledge for the greeting of a reunion.—How Christ greets us so differently from the world: 1. At coming, 2. at parting.—Christ's going away itself a mightier coming again to His own.—The gain of the faithful in Christ's going home to the Father.—How, in the hour of temptation, the heart's peace should stand firm in the midst of all and any grief of soul.—Christ's prophecies concerning His death and glorification, a fountain of faith for His people.—The protestation of Christ ver. 30.—The prince of this world cometh, or Christ's enemies a host of Satan.—He hath nothing in Me: He possesses none of Me. 2. He shall seize none of Me. 3. He shall retain none of Me.—Everything of Christ's belongs to the light, even His body. This fact decides His future: 1. His going home to the land of light. 2. His return in the power of light.—Christ's joyfulness in sacrifice (ver. 31): 1. Its purpose (that the world), 2. its impulse (love to the Father), 3. its act (obedience), 4. its expression (the exhortation to departure).—The eternal authoritativeness, as applying to Christ's people, of His charge to depart: 1. Arise! 2. Let us go! 3. Away from this place!

Gospel for Whitsunday vers. 23-31.—The promise of the Holy Ghost as an answer to the question of Judas: 1. The magnitude of that promise, 2. its certainty to the disciples of Jesus, 3. its seclusion against the world.—For whom is the promise of the Holy Ghost? 1. Not for the world, as world, but only for the disciples. 2. Not for the disciples alone, but for the whole world which, as world, is at once to be destroyed, and, in the susceptible, elevated and preserved.—The coming of the Holy Ghost: 1. The stipulation of it: a contrast between the disciples who love the Lord, and the world. 2. Form of it: a contrast between the condition of those who are anointed with the Spirit and the condition of immature disciples. 3. The effect of it: a contrast between the true peace of the Lord and the false peace of the world. 4. The aim of it: a contrast between victorious departure out of the world and the destruction of the world.—The development of the Christian life by means of the Holy Ghost: 1. Love to Jesus (vers. 23, 24). 2. Enlightenment (ver. 26). 3. Peace (ver. 27). 4. Joy. 5. Victory and perfection (ver. 31).

Starke: Luther: Whom the devil tries to terrify and dispirit, Christ comforts; but whom the devil lulls into security, and emboldens, Christ terrifies.—Jer. xvii. 9.—Hedinger: Faith, the best weapon of defence against all fear.—"In My Father's house:" in heaven, in the which house I am no servant but a son.—Canstein: O blessed friendship and fellowship of Christ with His faithful ones! His heart doth so hang upon them that He is not able, as it were, to dwell in heaven if He have not them with Him.—Zeisius: When the world will no longer put up with thee, remember His house.—On ver. 5. Luther: It is laudable for a man to perceive his ignorance in divine things.—On ver. 6. Rev. i. 8.—*Ibid.*: A Christian is a man who forthwith commences to go out of this life to heaven.—Hedinger: Through Christ we look into the divine nature.—Canstein on ver. 11: If *Christ* did not will that men should believe *Him* without works, still more does it behoove *Christians* to show in deed and in works how it is that *they* desire to be accounted of.—On ver. 13. Learn to pray aright.—On ver. 15. 1 Cor. xvi. 22.—Zeisius: If thou desire to know whether thou truly love Christ, ask thy conscience whether thou be leading a life of genuine and daily repentance, *etc.*—If thou grieve not the Holy Spirit with sins, He will not depart from thee, but will guide and lead thee into life.—Osiander on ver. 17: The bad Spirit is a lying spirit who seduces men, making them trifling and deceitful; but the Spirit of Christ is a Spirit of truth who brings forth truth and makes men true so that they take pleasure in the truth.—Ver. 18. Hedinger: Made sorrowful and yet beloved.—Luther: Christendom has this consoling promise in common.—On ver. 19. No matter how thyself and thine art, thy splendor and thy cleverness may be seen; yet a little while, and the world shall see thee no more.—On ver. 20. Hedinger: The cross and experience open both the eyes and the understanding.—O mysterious bliss of the faithful! They are united to Christ as Christ is to the Father.—Ver. 21. Zeisius: To love Christ is not merely to *know* His commandments, but to *keep* them.—Be solicitous of this manifestation of Jesus, O soul! more than of all in the world beside.—Ver. 23. Luther: Christ intends to say: This is the reason why I will not reveal Myself to the world; it is so mad-brained and foolish as to presume to lecture and tutor Me as to how I ought to rule. It should hear Me and learn of Me; but it thinks itself too clever for that and undertakes to dictate to Me how I should act.—Despise not the meanest human being that loves Jesus; meet such with reverence; his soul is a dwelling-place of the triune God.—Cramer: Precious guests, God the Father, Son and Holy Ghost; these come to us; not as to a wedding or on a visit, but to dwell in us—and so we are the temple of God.—Hedinger: Listen! Christ's word thou must *keep*, not simply *know*. Should'st thou say: that I will not do, that I cannot do, then thou must suffer us to dispute thy Christianity. Yet even keeping is not (necessarily) fulfilling.—Ver. 26. Cramer: The office of the Holy Ghost is implied in His name (and in His different names).—Zeisius: How will the Holy Ghost adorn His dwelling and fill it with light, comfort, righteousness, peace, joy.—Faithful teachers must first suffer themselves to be instructed and reminded by the Holy Ghost before they teach their hearers.—ZEISIUS: True love rejoiceth at the prosperity of the beloved. Why then, O Christian heart, dost thou mourn so bitterly at the departure of those who have shut their eyes upon this atrocious world and fallen asleep in Christ?—Ver. 30. Dost thou hear, worldling? thy prince is the devil.—As Satan has no power over Christ, neither has he power over those who are justified through the blood of Christ.—Ver. 31. The faith, the love and the patience of true Christians must shine in the eyes of the world. —CANSTEIN: All our actions must originate in faith in, and love to, God; their aim must be His glory, and the rule of them His will.—Be comforted, dear Christian, in thy misery; thou art suffering in accordance with thy heavenly Father's will. He will end thy sufferings in His own good time and will order them to the accomplishment of some good purpose.—NOV. BIBL. TUB.: What is the true Christian's pilgrimage? After the example of Jesus, it is a continual going hence and a continual hasting to the heavenly Father.

GERLACH: 1. Of Christ's going to the Father and the way to be pursued. 2. Of the Comforter, the Holy Ghost, in whom Christ comes to His people again in greater glory. 3. The setting out to suffer.—Now did the disciples more and more clearly understand that their Master was really about going away from them, and their faces reflected their fear and anxiety—emotions which had been heightened by His last words to Peter. Therefore it is that the succeeding discourse is preëminently comforting in its nature. —Jesus does not merely point out the way,—He *is* the Way; He does not simply guide to life,—He *is* the Life. The Way itself carries the man who enters upon it and continues in it, to the goal; the Truth lights him so that he cannot stray; the Life imbues him with strength in which he walks without growing weary.—This demand of Philip shows that the disciples still imagined the Father to be *with* Him, not *in* Him. —*The greater works.* Jesus had sowed, they were to reap (chap. iv. 38); before the whole work of redemption was finished, Jesus' works on the earth, His teaching, His working of miracles, His guiding and speeding of His people, could not but be (appear) small in comparison with the mighty works of the apostles, to whom the Holy Ghost more than supplied the visible presence of Jesus, glorifying Jesus and His cross for them, throwing open to them the doors of the heathen world, and giving them, through the word of reconciliation, multitudes for a spoil and the strong for a prey.—(LUTHER). Who is this "I?" He assumes to Himself all the power and strength of the divine majesty and seizes everything in a mass:—"Whatsoever ye ask, without exception."—Judas probably understood the "manifestation" to mean an outward one. —He hath no power over Me. In order that, even at His death, they might not believe that the prince of this world had conquered Him, He told them so clearly that He went of His own free will to the Cross.—LISCO. Vers. 1-14. The departing Redeemer comforts His disciples in view of their imminent separation.—Vers. 15-31. The departing Redeemer promises the Holy Ghost to His people and comforts them.

BRAUNE: To believers, death is in very truth a going home; their life a journey home. The Jews were gathered to their Fathers,—Christians go hence to the Father.—*The disciples, Thomas, etc.* How honestly they speak out their hearts; not one utters a false Yea.—Thomas: This reminds one of the verse of the natural man: "I live, I know not for how long; I die, I know not how soon; I go, I know not whither; how can I be so cheerful?"—In our earthly speech we say: The wayfarer *makes a* way, but in the spiritual tongue the Way makes the wayfarer. —The prophecy Isa. xxv. 8 is fulfilled in Christ. —*The greater works.* When He had completed the reconciliation, a free, familiar and living intercourse was opened between God and man, and streams of power from on high could now discharge themselves unchecked into the hearts of men.—(HERDER). He opens (says He) a clear and lightsome way. The assurance with which Christ declares this, makes heaven and earth one, as it were.—(BENGEL:) Truth makes all the virtues in us true; otherwise there would be false knowledge, false faith, false love, false hope.—Beginning with this passage (ver. 17), Christ makes a distinction between the world and His people, such as does not elsewhere appear in His addresses. Pentecost, however, confirmed this distinction and made it manifest. The Christian cannot be distinguished from the world if he has not yet celebrated His Pentecost. —The Holy Ghost. The longer we have Him, the better we have Him, the better we know Him, until finally He comes to be in us.—Thomas, Philip, and the faithful Judas speak; the more intelligent, profounder and greater disciples John, Peter, James, keep silence.—He says in the face of death: I live and ye shall live also. —*Peace be with you.* The heart is free from everything that is hostile to God; there is no latent love of the world, no want of trust in the spirit. Perfect concord of heart is where Christ and His peace are.

HEUBNER: It is the duty of the Christian to be courageous, undaunted and composed so long as Christ is with him.—We hear after what fashion the Son speaks, as one perfectly at home and able to find His way about in the house of the Father—more familiar with it than all the astronomers who scarcely descry the visible covering, the threshold of that heavenly house. —*Many mansions.* Many as regards number and kind: different in glory and blessedness.—So long as there are stars in the heavens, there shall not be wanting witnesses to a higher world. Comp. Daub, *Der Sternenhimmel mit Christlichem Auge zur Erhebung des Herzens betrachtet*, Essen, 1836.—There is already assigned us through Christ a place in heaven. What consolation does this afford in poverty, persecution and death. The reply of Basil to the question of the Arian emperor Valens, as to where he would remain in the face of his persecutions: *Aut sub cœlo, aut in cœlo.*—Urban, the deputy of Cajetan, to Luther: Where wilt thou abide then? Luther: Under heaven.—A saying of Frederick the Magnanimous (p. 427, note). Must not the Christian be homesick for his heavenly Fatherland? "Knowest thou the land?"—Ver. 3. Christ's going hence by the way of His cross and passion served,—through His appearing in the presence of God (Heb. ix. 24), through the offering of His blood in the Holy Place or the presentation of the sufficient reconciliation made by Him,—to purchase for us our re-adoption into heaven. It is to Him we owe our heavenly citizenship.—Ver. 3. Perfect union with Christ.—No heaven without Christ.—On ver. 23. We can surrender ourselves only to one who meets us with a trustful heart.—Ver. 26. Every one longs to be *spirituel* (a play upon words: *Alles will Geist haben, Geist* in the sense of *ésprit, wit*). Why do not men seek the true Spirit which is with Christ?—Whoso does not become a doctor in this school (of the Holy Spirit), is no true doctor.—What is true clearing up? What Christ makes clear, glorifies.—Ver. 28. Nothing against the divine nature of Christ can be deduced from this passage, even should we be unprepared to regard, as Basil does, the very fact of Jesus' instituting a comparison between Himself and the Father, as a proof of the Son's equality in substance with the Father. (Basil says, namely: none but things of a like nature can be compared,—angels with angels, men with men, *etc.*).—*The prince of this world.* Of course he thought it conducive to his highest interest to see Jesus, the Holy One, the Founder of the kingdom of God, covered with opprobrium as the greatest criminal,—and all under the pretence of justice.

GOSSNER: The Saviour had in His humiliation, never exactly declared (out and out) who He was. Therefore it was difficult for people who were to see him hanging for several hours on the cross between two murderers, to believe in His divinity.—*The Father's House.* No fear that there will not be room enough there.—No bridge nor path is there, leading from earth to heaven, from time to eternity, from this world to God, and stretching as far as Christ who did come from heaven and go to heaven. All other bridges break; all other roads fail thee just where they ought to begin,—namely, in death.—Philip here asked a question which has puzzled the brains of the wisest men of all ages—namely, as to what God is and how we may know Him.—Ver. 16. In this verse the Triune is clear as the sun.—Ver. 18. It is not: ye shall have a shadow, a conception, a thought of Me; no,—I am coming to you. Our soul doth live, our whole heart laugheth, when He revealeth Himself to us,—Christ, our salvation.—*At that day.* At the Easter day, which comes to every Christian when Christ rises within him and begins to live—at the day of manifestation.—Without Christ it is not possible to know Christ, without God it is impossible to know God. This saying: "I will reveal Myself unto him," must be fulfilled for each man or he knows nothing truly of Christ and has no living God.—On ver. 23. Scripture ascribes to the inner man all the senses of the outer man. Taste and see that the Lord is good, Ps. xxxiv. 8.—When the body is dead, the soul continues to be a living substance. This is a proof of the substantiality of spiritual experience in the heart.—Ver. 30. Against this, Christ's innocence, the devil has dashed his horns to pieces; it has broken his neck for him.—Ver. 31. Up, up! away! to suffer with Him; ye must not be taking your repose.

STIER: The first chapter (xiv.) manifestly takes for its starting-point *faith* in God as existent in Christ; the special subject of the second is the *love* of those who are united in Him and through Him; finally, the third contains (for the exercise of *hope*, we may say) the most minute announcement of all that is to result from and succeed *the departure of Jesus.*—RICHTER (Luther): So long as *we* are not ready, the *habitations* are not prepared for us, though in themselves they are prepared.

SCHLEIERMACHER: He requires faith in God and faith in Himself, as something which indeed seems to be two things—things, however, so inseparably united as to be actually one and the same.—That which we do in faith on the Lord, is a work of the Son; and when this work is promoted by the government which the Father exercises in the world, the Father is glorified in the Son.—Only he who holds fast that in My life which, as commandment, doctrine, or promise—for they are all one—has become an eternal, divine word of love and grace to men, *etc.*,—only he it is who loveth Me.—*My peace.* This peace resteth upon love, and love expelleth all fear.—BESSER: On ver. 1. Be of good courage, Deut. xxxi. 6, 7. But a greater than Joshua is here.—On the "other Comforter." The ancient Church advisedly took the Gospels for four Sundays of the glorious time between Easter and Pentecost from these three chapters of John.—Heaven the true archetype of the Old Testament temple. Heb. chh. viii.-xii.

ON THE PENTECOSTAL PERICOPE. GENZKEN: Concerning the glorious Pentecostal gifts which the Lord hath promised us.—BACHMANN: The Christian a temple of God, of the Holy Ghost.—RAMBACH: The victory of Christianity over the world.—HAGENBACH: The peace of God as the most precious legacy of our Lord, the most glorious gift of the Holy Ghost.—FLOREY: The kingdom of the Holy Ghost. A kingdom of love, truth, peace.—The peace of the world, and the peace of the Lord.

[CRAVEN: From HILARY (*De Trin.* vii. 9): Ver. 6. He who is the *Way* cannot lead us astray; He who is the *Truth* cannot deceive us; He who is the *Life* will not desert us in the darkness of death.—Ver. 9. He does not mean the sight of the bodily eye; the Father is seen in the Son by the incommunicable likeness of birth.—Vers. 9, 10. That the Father *dwells in* the Son shows that He is not solitary; that the Father *works* by the Son, shows that He is not different or alien.——From AUGUSTINE: Vers. 1-4. Our Lord consoles His disciples, who would be naturally troubled at the idea of His death, by assuring them of His divinity.—As the disciples were afraid for themselves when *Peter* had been told that he would deny his Lord, He adds *In My Father's house, etc.*, to assure them that they might with confidence look forward to dwelling with Him.—*Many mansions, i. e.* many degrees of dignity corresponding to people's deserts.—Vers. 5-7. The disciples *knew not* what they *did know.*—*I am the Way, whereby* thou wouldest go; *the Truth, whereto* thou wouldest go; *the Life, in which* thou wouldest abide.—Walk by *the Man*, and thou wilt arrive at God.—Ver. 8. To the joy of beholding His [the Father's] face nothing could be added.—Ver. 9. When two persons are very much alike, we say, If you have seen the one you have seen the other.—Ver. 10. Spiritual vision is the reward of faith, vouchsafed to minds purified by faith.—Ver. 12. *Greater works;* they afterwards converted the Gentiles to the faith.—Ver. 13. Why, then, do we often see believers asking and not receiving? Whatsoever we ask for that would hinder our salvation, we do not [truly] ask *in our Saviour's name.*—Whenever we ask any thing to the disadvantage of our *salvation,* He shows Himself our *Saviour* by not granting.—What we ask for is [often] *deferred,* not *denied.*—Ver. 17. The *world, i. e.* those who love the world, cannot receive the Holy Spirit; *unrighteousness* cannot become *righteous.*—The *world* cannot receive Him, *because it seeth Him not;* the love of the world hath not invisible [*i. e.* spiritual] eyes to see that which can be seen only invisibly [spiritually].—Ver. 19. *A little while;* that which seems long to men, is short to God.—Ver. 21. He that hath them in *mind* and keepeth them in *life;* he that hath them in *words* and keepeth them in *works;* he that hath them by *hearing* and keepeth them by *doing;* he that hath them by *doing* and keepeth them by *persevering, he it is that loveth Me.*—*Love* must be shown by *works,* or it is a mere barren name.—*Now* He loves us so only that we *believe, then* He will love us so that we shall *see; now,* we love by *believing* that which we *shall see; then,* we shall love by *seeing* that which we *have believed.*—Vers. 22-24. Love distinguishes the Saints from the world: it maketh men to be of one mind in an house; in which house the Father and the Son take up Their abode; Who give that love to those to whom in the end They will manifest Themselves.—*We will come unto him:* They *come* to us in that we *go* to Them; They *come* by *succouring,* we *go* by *obeying;* They *come* by *enlightening,* we *go* by *contemplating;* They come by *filling,* we *go* by *holding:* so Their manifestation is not *external* but *inward;* Their abode is not *transitory* but *eternal.*—The abode He promised them *hereafter* (ver. 3) is altogether different from that of which He now speaks; the one is *spiritual and inward,* the other *outward and perceptible to the bodily senses.*—Ver. 26. The Son *speaks,* the Spirit *teaches;* when the Son *speaks* we *take in* the words, when the Spirit *teaches* we *understand* those words.—*Bring to your remembrance, i. e. suggest;* every wholesome hint to *remember* is of the grace of the Spirit.—Ver. 27. He left no peace in *this world,* in which we conquer the enemy; He shall give us peace in the world to come, when we shall reign without an enemy.—This peace is *Himself,* both when we believe that He is, and when we shall see Him as He is.—His peace is such peace as He has Himself.—There is a peace which is serenity of thought, tranquillity of mind, simplicity of heart, the bond of love, the fellowship of charity; none will be able to come to the inheritance of the Lord, who do not observe this testament of peace.—Ver. 28. In that He was *Man,* He *went;* in that He was God, He *stayed.*——From CHRYSOSTOM: Ver. 9. *He that hath seen Me hath seen the Father:* A man cannot see the substance of gold in silver, one nature cannot be made apparent by another.—Ver. 16. *Another Comforter:* The word *another* shows the distinct personality of the Spirit; the word *Paraclete* (Comforter) His consubstantiality.—They were made to wait some time for this gift (*the Comforter*) in order that they might feel the want of it, and so be the more grateful when it came.—Ver. 19. *Because I live ye shall live also:* The death of the cross shall not separate you from Me forever, but only hide Me from you for a moment.—Ver. 27. External *peace* is often even hurtful, rather than profitable to those who enjoy it.——From GREGORY: Ver. 23. If thou wouldest *prove* thy *love, show* thy *works.*—Into some hearts He *cometh,* but not *to make His abode.*—In proportion as a man's love rests upon lower things is he removed from heavenly love.—To the love of our Maker, let the tongue, mind, life bear witness.—Ver. 26. Unless the Spirit be present to the mind of the hearer, the word of the teacher is vain.—The invisible Spirit *suggests,* not because He takes a lower place in teaching, but because He teaches secretly.——From ALCUIN: Ver. 21. By love, and the observance of His commandments *that* will be perfected in us which He has begun, *viz.* that we should be in Him and He in us.——From THEOPHYLACT: Ver. 6. When thou art engaged in the *practical,* He is made thy *way;* when in the *contemplative,* He is made thy *truth;* and to the *practical* and *contemplative* is joined *life,* for we should both act and contemplate with reference to the world to come.—Ver. 21. As if He had said, Ye think that by sorrowing for My death ye prove your affection, but I esteem the keeping of My commandments the evidence of love.—Ver. 26. The Spirit was to *teach* what Christ had forborne to tell His disciples because they were not able to bear it; He was to *bring to remembrance* what Christ had told and they had failed to remember.——From BURKITT: Ver. 1. The holiest of God's children subject to disquieting fears.—Christ's remedy for fear, *viz.* faith in God and in Himself.—Vers. 3-4. Christ's arguments of consolation in view of His departure.—Ver. 6. As though Christ had said—I am the author of the way that leadeth unto life, the teacher of the truth that directs to it, the giver of the life that is obtained by walking in it.—Ver. 8. Much ignorance may consist with saving grace.—Vers. 13, 14. Our Lord assures His disciples that whatever comforts they enjoyed by His presence, they should obtain by their prayers.—To pray in the name of Christ is—1. to look unto Christ as having purchased for us this privilege; 2. to pray in the strength of Christ; 3. to pray in respect of the present mediation of Christ.—The promise is doubled for the confirmation of it.—Ver. 15. Christ requires an obedient love, and loving obedience.—Not *waiters,* but *workers* are the best servants. [We often *work* by *waiting.*—E. R. C.]—The surest evidence of *love* to Christ is obedience.—Ver. 16. The office of the Holy Spirit—a *Comforter* [Paraclete], *i. e.* an *Advocate,* an *Encourager,* a *Consoler.*—Ver. 18. Christ does not say, I will not *suffer* you to be comfortless, but I will not *leave* you so.—Ver. 19. *Because I live ye shall live also.*—While there is vital sap in the root you that are branches shall not wither and die.—Ver. 21. Christ teaches—1. the necessity of knowledge in order to practice; 2. the necessity of practice in order to happiness.—*I will manifest Myself:* Obedient Christians shall not only enjoy the *benefit* of Christ's love, but also the *sense* thereof.—We may as rationally think to nourish our bodies with poison, as to enjoy the manifestation of Christ's love in a way of sin.—Ver. 23. *Make our abode* denotes—1. the *sweet and intimate fellowship* between God and the obedient; 2. the *perpetuity* thereof.—Ver. 26. The great Comforter, the special Teacher—He teaches, 1. condescendingly; 2. efficaciously; 3. plainly; 4. unerringly.—The Spirit the *Remembrancer*, He teaches nothing but what Christ Himself taught.—Ver. 27. The world may wish [in words] *peace*, yet never intend it; or they may wish it and not be able to give it; but Christ's peace is real and effectual: The *world's* peace is freedom from outward trouble; Christ's peace is deliverance from inward guilt, which though it does not give exemption from troubles, affords—1. a sanctified improvement of them; 2. an assurance of deliverance out of them.—Ver. 28. True love to Christ will make us rejoice in His advancement, though it be to our own disadvantage.——From M. Henry: Ver. 1. Christ knows our souls in adversity.—Let not your heart be *troubled*—He does not say let them not be *saddened*, but let them not be disquieted: Let not your *heart* be troubled—keep the *heart* with all diligence: Let not *your* heart be troubled—*you* that are My chosen, redeemed, sanctified ones.—Ver. 2. A particular declaration as to what we must trust God for—*viz. heaven*—Heaven will make amends for all.—Heaven is—1. a *house*, not a tent; 2. a *Father's* house, *My* Father's and therefore *our* Father's; 3. a place of *mansions;* (1) *distinct* dwellings; (2) *durable* dwellings; 4. a place of *many* mansions—for there are (1) *many* sons to be brought to glory, [(2) many *classes* of sons]. —*If it were not so I would have told you.*—The *assurance* of heaven, built upon—1. the veracity of His word; 2. the sincerity of His affection.—Ver. 3. The belief of Christ's second coming an excellent preservative against trouble of heart, Phil. iv. 5, James v. 8.—The coming of Christ is in order to our gathering together unto Him, 2 Thess. ii. 1.—The quintessence of heaven's happiness is being with Christ, ch. xvii. 24.—Ver. 4. Christ having set heaven before His disciples as the *end*, here shows them Himself as *the way* to it. —Ver. 6. The *nature* of Christ's mediation, He is—1. the *way*, the *highway*, Is. xxxv. 9—(1) *His own* way, Heb. ix. 12; (2) *our way;* 2. the *truth*, as opposed to—(1) *figure*, (2) *error*, (3) *deception;* 3. the *life*—we are alive unto God only in and through Jesus Christ, Rom. vi. 11.—*The way, the truth and the life*, He is—1. the *beginning*, *middle* and *end*, in Him we must *set out, go on* and *finish;* 2. as the *truth* the *guide* of our way, as the *life* the *end* of it; 3. the *true* and *living* way, there is truth and life *in* it as well as *at the end* of it; 4. the *only true* way to life.—*No man cometh unto the Father but by Me*—the *necessity* of Christ's mediation.—Ver. 9. He reproves Philip for—1. not improving his acquaintance with Him as he might have done; 2. his infirmity in the prayer made—we know not what we should pray for as we ought, Rom. viii. 26, and often ask amiss, James iv. 3.—All that saw Christ by faith saw the Father in Him; the Father's—1. *wisdom* in His doctrine; 2. *power* in His miracles; 3. *holiness* in His purity; 4. *grace* in His acts of grace.—Vers. 10, 11. Christ's miracles proofs of His divine mission, not only for the conviction of infidels but for the confirmation of disciples. —Vers. 13, 14. In prayer—1. humility prescribed, ye shall *ask;* 2. liberty allowed, ask *anything.*—*In My name*—1. to plead His merit; 2. to aim at His glory.—Ver. 16. The *Comforter* the great New Testament promise.—Ver. 17. Christ is the truth, and He is the Spirit of Christ. —Speak to the children of this world of the operations of the Spirit and you are as a barbarian.—The experiences of the Saints are the explications of the promises: Paradoxes to others are axioms to them. — Vers. 18–24. The departure of Christ neither *total* nor *final.*— Union with Christ the *life* and *felicity* of believers. —Ver. 19. *Because I live ye shall live also.* The life of Christians is bound up in the life of Christ.—Ver. 20. *At that day* you shall know *perfectly* what now you see through a glass *darkly.*—Vers. 21-24. Note—1. The *duty* of those who claim the *dignity* of being disciples; 2. the *dignity* of those who do the *duty* of disciples.— The returns for love—those who love shall have— 1. The Father's love; 2. Christ's love; 3. the comfort of that love.—*I will manifest Myself.*— Christ's manifestation of Himself to His disciples—1. is done in a *distinguishing* way to *them* and not to *the world;* 2. is justly marvellous in our eyes.—Ver. 23. God will be with *obedient believers* as at His *home.*—Vers. 25-27. With two things Christ here comforts believers, that they should be—1. Under *the tuition of His Spirit;* 2. Under *the influence of His peace.*—Ver. 26. He shall teach you all things, as a Spirit—1. of *wisdom;* 2. of *revelation.*—Ver. 27. *Peace I leave with you, etc.;* observe—1. the legacy bequeathed, *viz.: peace*, which is here put for all good; 2. to whom it is bequeathed—to His disciples; 3. the manner in which it is left—*not as the world giveth;* 4. the use that should be made of it—to prevent *trouble* and *fear.*—Ver. 28. Many that love Christ let their love run in a wrong channel; they think they must be in continual pain because of Him, whereas they should rejoice in Him.

[From Stier: Ver. 1. The already existing faith in God must be the *ground* of faith in Christ; and, on the other hand, the *perfect* faith in God is to be the *result* of faith in Christ.—Ver. 2. *House is home*, where one abides, to which he belongs, to which he has a right; still more—it is a firm, secure building, provided for all kinds of need.—Many *mansions*—the household character of the abodes; *many* mansions—intimating degrees and distinctions in blessedness.—Ver. 3. *His coming again and receiving* embraces the whole of His influence, drawing, setting free (ch. xii. 32; viii. 35, 36), beginning with the resurrection and ending in His final manifestation.— Ver. 5. When any one *in due time*, after the Word and Spirit of Christ have long spoken to him, *opposes* his "*we know not*," then becomes he the *unbelieving* Thomas who *will* not know and believe; but a genuine Thomas *asks for the way* in deep earnestness, and will not be long without a perfect understanding.—Ver. 6. Christ is as—1.

Man, the *way* which offers itself to all men; 2. *God*, absolute, independent *truth;* 3. *God-Man*, the *life*, that is the fountain of life springing from Him and received by us.—"Yea, Thou art the goal and Thou art also the way: so is a stream goal and way at once: I will bend my energies to go thither where the stream pours itself into the sea, thither where the Son sits at the right hand of the Father; and to reach it I will commit myself to the stream which is my way, and not only a way which *guides* me, but a way also which *bears* me: thus come I to Thee through Thyself, Thou *guidest* me and *bearest* me at once." (THEREMIN).—Ver. 8. Previous to the true "my Lord and my God" there was no greater honor given to Christ, or higher power ascribed to Him than in this *Lord show us the Father.—It sufficeth us;* to see God is blessedness.—Ver. 9. Christ is the *visibility* of the *Invisible*, as far as, and in such a way as, He may be seen.—Ver. 10. *Believest thou?* That is still the *humbling* question of the Lord which rebukes the presumption of every aspiring Philip *in life*, as it is the *consoling* question which alleviates the sorrow of every downcast Martha at *the grave.*—His *words* are no other than *works*, and His *works* are speaking and testifying *words.* —Vers. 11-24. The transition from *believing* to *loving;* from *believing* primarily as the reliance and subjection of knowledge, to *loving* as not merely the *fruit* of faith but as already the *living germ* of the true and living trust of a person on a person—*as the affiance of the heart.*—Ver. 12. He sowed, we reap—and the harvest is indeed *greater* than the seed.—*I go*—to death, indeed, but thereby *to the Father;* away from you, indeed, but thereby the more spiritually and effectually to unite Myself with you.—Vers. 13, 14. Let your *faith* in *My Person* become *prayer* in *My name.* To pray in the name of Jesus is—1. to mention Him in connection with the thing asked for, *appealing to* (*depending upon*) *Him;* 2. to pray actually *in the Person of Christ*, that is, as standing in His place; 3. to ask for nothing but what is *according to His mind, in His interest;* 4. to call immediately upon the name of Him, who is with the one praying by the Spirit at the same time that He is above with the Father.—Ver. 16. Christ is Himself the one Paraclete, and by His side with like personality stands the *other.*—The acts of the three Persons—asking, giving, abiding.—*Paraclete*—one who performs all that which a *Counsel* or *Representative*, being at the same time an *Adviser*, can perform for us.—Ver. 17. The Spirit brings to us the Truth—that is the truth concerning ourselves, the will of God toward us, the *way* of return to God through Christ; He shows, glorifies, *opens* to us this *way* as *truth* and *life*, so that we *know* what follows in ver. 20.—The world *cannot* receive Him, because to receive Him requires *susceptibility.*—The beginning and ground of all *knowing* is an internal true *beholding.*—Ver. 18. I will not leave you *orphans;* they are His little children, ch. xiii. 33.—Ver. 19. *Because I live ye shall live also;* there is *no* other guarantee for our personal continuance in the integrity of our being than *the personality of Christ*—all other arguments and hopes of immortality are like shadows and vapor before the light and power of this living word.—Ver. 21. *I will manifest Myself to him;* beyond this, promise has nothing greater or higher for man. (Is not the promise of ver. 3 greater—*I will come again and receive you unto Myself?*—E. R. C.).—Ver. 23. This first loving, which is the point of decision on our part, is the essential germ of life in living faith. —Learn better what *love* is, ye zealots, and make the banner of love to the Lord, the sole banner of His Church!—*My Father will love him, etc.*—the rewarding love for such as thus love (obediently) in full communion or manifestation.—As sin dwells in our hearts as a home, so does the new love which casts it out.—Ver. 26. On account of our weakness or our sinfulness, we forget the most familiar words just where they should be remembered, and there is always need that one should stand behind us ready to pronounce our duty in our ears.—Let us not scorn in relation to babes in the school of Christ the receiving and the keeping of even the word not understood.—Ver. 27. *Peace;* the whole *salvation* of man, his *re-establishment* into final perfect external and internal *well-being.*—"In the Hebrew this little word *peace* means nothing else but *thriving* and prospering" (LUTHER).—*My* peace; the peace which—1. I Myself have, 2. I alone can give, 3. I can give only through fellowship with Myself.—*Not as the world giveth;* public peace is not to be trusted, still less the world's peace of heart.—The peace of God in Christ is higher than all understanding; higher than all *words* about it, and deeper than all *consciousness* of it.—Ver. 28. They would rejoice at His departure *if they loved Him* aright; their love is not yet *disinterested* enough.—"Up! up! let us go forth to suffering and the fulfilment of the Divine will! Thus does the Lord arouse them, and carry them with Him into His contest, that they may be His followers in the way of suffering." (BERLENB. BIBEL).

[From BARNES. Vers. 2, 3. The universe is the dwelling-place of My Father; in that vast abode *earth* is one mansion, *heaven* is another; it should not be a matter of grief when we are called to pass from one part of this vast habitation to another.—I am about to leave you; but shall still be in the same habitation with you, performing an important work for you.—Ver. 7. *if ye had known Me:* they had not a *full* and *accurate* knowledge of His character and designs. —Ver. 13. *In My name, i. e. on My account;* if a man who has money in a bank authorizes us to draw it, we do it *in his name.*—Ver. 15. The evidence that a child loves his parents is his being willing without hesitation, gainsaying, or murmuring, to do all they require him to do.—Ver. 16. The *other* Comforter, a compensation for Christ's absence; it is the office of the Spirit —*To furnish to all Christians the instruction and consolation which would be given by the personal presence of Jesus.* Ch. xvi. 14.—Ver. 19. *Ye shall live also;* learn that—1. The life of the Christian depends on Christ; 2. The fact that Jesus lives is a pledge that all who believe in Him shall be saved.—Ver. 21. Religion is love.—Ver. 23. *We will come unto him* with the manifestation of pardon, peace of conscience, and joy in the Holy Ghost.—*Make our abode, i. e.* manifest ourselves in no *temporary* way.—Ver.

26. Bring all things *to your remembrance;* the Spirit will—1. *Remind* you of My sayings; 2. Teach you *the meaning* of them.—Ver. 27. *Not as the world giveth*—1. Not as the objects which men commonly pursue; 2. Not as the men of the world give; 3. Not as systems of philosophy and false religion give; 4. My peace is such as meets all the wants of the soul, silences the alarms of conscience, is fixed amid all external changes, and will abide forever.—Ver. 30. *Hath nothing in Me;* there is in Me no principle or feeling that accords with his, and nothing therefore by which he can prevail; temptation has only power because there are some principles *of evil* (?) in us which accord with the designs of the tempter. (How then could *holy* Adam have been tempted to a fall ?—E. R. C.)

[Vers. 13, 14. True faith, wrought by the Spirit, *cannot* unconditionally ask for anything not in accordance with the will of God; many say: If we had faith we could obtain such a (supposed) blessing for the asking—whereas if our minds were enlightened and purified by true faith we might not regard it as a blessing.]

III.

GLORIFICATION OF THIS PRESENT WORLD. BROUGHT ABOUT BY MEANS OF JUDGMENT, BY THE CONTINUING OF THE DISCIPLES IN THE LOVE OF CHRIST, AND BY THEIR INFLUENCE UPON THE WORLD, IN ORDER TO WHICH HE WILL SEND THEM HIS SPIRIT. AMID THE BURNING VINEYARD-FIRES IN THE VALLEY OF KIDRON. CHRIST THE VINE. GLORIFICATION OF THE NOBLE PLANT, AND OF HUSBANDRY. GLORIFICATION OF FRIENDSHIP AND JOY. THE HOLY EXCOMMUNICATEDNESS (BANISHMENT) OF THE CHILDREN OF GOD. CONFIRMATION OF THEIR SPIRITUAL LIFE IN FACE OF THE HATRED OF THE WORLD. THE HOLY SPIRIT'S VICTORY IN THEM OVER THE WORLD. DEVELOPMENT OF CHRISTIANITY THROUGH THE HOLY SPIRIT.

Chap. XV. 1.—Chap. XVI. 15.

(Pericope for Exaudi Sunday chap. xv. 26–chap. xvi. 4; chap. xvi. 5-15 Pericope for Cantate Sunday).

1. *The love of Jesus as the source of love to Him* (Vers. 1-10).

1, 2 I am the true vine,[1] and my Father is the husbandman. Every branch in
me that beareth not fruit he taketh away [αἴρει, cutteth off]: and every *branch* that
beareth fruit, he purgeth [καθαίρει, cutteth partially, pruneth, cleanseth] it, that it
3 may bring forth [bear] more fruit. Now ye are clean through [Ye are clean al-
4 ready because of, by reason of] the word which I have spoken unto you. Abide
in me, and I in you. As the branch cannot bear fruit of itself, except it abide in
5 the vine; no more [so neither] can ye, except ye abide in me. I am the vine, ye
are the branches. He that abideth in me, and I in him, the same bringeth forth
6 [beareth] much fruit; for without [apart from] me ye can do nothing. If a man
[any one] abide not in me, he is cast forth as a [the] branch, and is withered; and
men [they] gather them, and cast *them* into the fire,[2] and they are burned [they
7 burn (quickly and readily). If ye abide in me, and my words abide in you, ye shall
[may][3] ask what [whatsoever] ye will, and it shall [will] be done unto you.
8 Herein [Therein] is my Father glorified, that ye bear much fruit; so shall ye be
[and ye will become (thus for the first time truly)[4]] my disciples.
9 As the Father hath loved me, so [thus also] have I loved you: continue [abide]
10 ye in my love. If ye keep my commandments, ye shall [will] abide in my love;
even as I have kept my Father's commandments, and abide in his love.

2. *Joy* (Vers. 11-17).

11 These things have I spoken unto you, that my joy might remain [may be][5] in
12 you, and *that* your joy might be full [may be made full, filled up]. This is my
13 commandment, That ye love one another, as I have [*omit* have] loved you. Greater
love hath no man [no one] than this, that a man [he] lay down his life for his

14, 15 friends. Ye are my friends, if ye do whatsoever [what][6] I command you. Hence-
forth I call you not [No longer do I call you] servants; for the servant knoweth
not what his lord doeth: but I have called you friends; for all things that I have
heard of [which I heard from] my Father I have [*omit* have] made known unto you.
16 Ye have not chosen me, but I have chosen you [Ye did not choose me, but I chose
you], and ordained [appointed] you, that ye should [may] go and bring forth [bear]
fruit, and *that* your fruit should [may] remain; [in order] that whatsoever ye shall
17 ask of the Father in my name, he may give it you. These things I command you,
[in order] that ye [may] love one another.

3. *Steadfastness in view of the hatred of the world* (Vers. 18-25).

18 If the world hate you, ye [*omit* ye] know that it [hath] hated me before *it hated*
19 [*omit it hated*] you.[7] If ye were of the world, the world would love his [its] own
[in you]; but because ye are not of the world, but I have chosen you out of the
20 world, therefore the world hateth you. Remember the word that I said unto you,
The servant is not greater than his lord. If they have [*omit* have] persecuted
me, they will also persecute you; if they have kept my saying [if they kept my
21 word] they will keep yours also. But all these things will they do unto you[8] for my
22 name's sake, because they know not him that sent me. If I had not come and
spoken unto them, they had not had sin [would have no sin[9]]; but now they have
23 no cloak [pretext, excuse] for their sin. He that hateth me hateth my Father
24 also. If I had not done among them the works which none [no] other man
did,[10] they had not had [they would have no] sin: but now have they [they have]
25 both seen and hated both me and my Father. But *this cometh to pass*, that [But in
order that] the word might [may] be fulfilled that is written in their law, They
hated me without a cause (Ps. xxxv. 19; lxix. 4).

4. *Promise of the Holy Ghost as the strength of martyrdom* (Ver. 26 to Chap. xvi. 6).

26 But[11] when the Comforter [Paraclete] is come, whom I will [shall] send unto you
from the Father, *even* [*omit even*] the Spirit of truth, which [who] proceedeth from
27 the Father, he shall testify [will bear witness, μαρτυρήσει] of me: And ye also shall
bear witness [But ye also bear witness, or, are witnesses, καὶ ὑμεῖς δὲ μαρτυρεῖτε][12]
XVI. 1 because [for] ye have been [are] with me from the beginning. These
things have I spoken unto you, that ye should [may] not be offended [fall
2 through offence]. They shall [will] put you out of the synagogues [excommunicate
you]: yea the time [hour] cometh, that whosoever [when every man that] killeth
you will think that he doeth God service [a sacrificial service, or, that he is offer-
3 ing service to God]. And these things will they do unto you [*omit* unto you],[13] be-
cause they have not known the Father, nor me [they neither know the Father nor
4 me]. But these things have I told you [But I have spoken these things unto you],
that when the time shall come [when the (their)[14] hour cometh], ye may remember
that I told you of them [ye may remember them as I told you, or, ye may remem-
ber that I myself told you *of them*].[15] And these things I said not unto you [I told
5 you not] at the beginning, because I was with you. But now I go my way [ὑπάγω,
see ver. 7] to him that sent me; and none of you asketh me, Whither goest thou?
6 But [Yet] because I have said these things unto you, sorrow hath filled your heart.

5. *The Holy Ghost as the strength of the victory over the world* (Vers. 7-11).

7 Nevertheless [But] I tell you the truth; It is expedient for you that I go away
[depart, ἀπέλθω]; for if I go not away [do not depart], the Comforter [the Para-
clete] will not come unto you; but if I depart [go, shall have gone, πορευθῶ],[16] I
8 will send him unto you. And when he is come, he will reprove the world of sin,
and of righteousness, and of judgment [he will convince and convict the world, or,
bring conviction to the world concerning, or, in regard to sin, and to righteousness,
and to judgment, ἐλέγξει τὸν κόσμον περὶ ἁμαρτίας καὶ περὶ δικαιοσύνης καὶ περὶ κρίσεως].[17]
9 Of [In regard to] sin (that it is rooted and essentially consists in the fact), because

10 [that[18]] they believe not on me; Of [In regard to] righteousness (that it becomes
manifest in the fact), because [that] I (glorified) go to my [the] Father, and ye see
11 me no more (whereby grace and judgment are indicated); Of [In regard to] judgment,
because [that] the prince of this world is [hath been] judged (in the work of redemption).

6. *Promise of the Holy Ghost as the Spirit of the glorification of Christ, and the revelation of the future.* (Vers. 12-15.)

12, 13 I have yet many things to say unto you, but ye cannot bear them now. How-
beit [But] when he, the Spirit of truth is come, he will guide you into all truth [all
the truth, or, the whole truth, *εἰς τὴν ἀλήθειαν πᾶσαν*[19]]: for he shall [will] not speak
of [from] himself; but whatsoever he shall hear [he heareth],[20] *that* shall he speak
[he will speak about]: and he will shew you [tell you, proclaim to you] things to
14 come. He shall [will] glorify me: for he shall receive of mine [he will take of
what is mine, *ἐκ τοῦ ἐμοῦ λήμψεται*], and shall shew [will tell, proclaim] *it* unto you.
15 All things that the Father hath are mine: therefore said I [for this cause I said],
that he shall take of mine [he taketh of what is mine, *ἐκ τοῦ ἐμοῦ λαμβάνει*],[21] and
shall shew [will tell, proclaim] *it* unto you.

TEXTUAL AND GRAMMATICAL.

[1] Ver. 1.—[Dr. Lange translates ἡ ἄμπελος ἡ ἀληθινή, "*der wesentliche Weinstock*," the *essential* vine, and inserts the gloss: "*Wurzel und Stamm des persönlichen Liebesreichs*," root and stem of the personal love-kingdom. We have no precise equivalent in English for ἀληθινός, *wahrhaftig*, *veritable*, to distinguish it from ἀληθής, *true*. Ἀληθινός, *verus*, is *true* in the sense of true to the idea, genuine, primitive, essential, as distinct from what is derived, copied, typical, shadowy and more or less imperfect: while ἀληθής, *verax*, is true in opposition to false. Christ is the true, veritable, perfect Light, Bread, Shepherd, Vine, in distinction from all reflected light, *etc.*, as well as in opposition to false light, *etc.* See the remarks on ch. i. 9; vi. 32, and Trench's *Synonyms of the New Testament*, § 8. Our *true* has both meanings and is therefore retained by most translators.—P. S.]

[2] Ver. 6.—With the article τὸ πῦρ, in accordance with Codd. A. G. K. Sin., *etc.*, Tischendorf; the Recepta and Lachmann, in accordance with B. D., *etc.*, have πῦρ without the article. The passage is not, as Meyer thinks, to be estimated in accordance with Mark ix. 22, as here a particular fire is in view. See the exegesis.

[3] Ver. 7.—The Aorist αἰτήσασθε, in accordance with A. B. D., *etc.*; Lachmann, Tischendorf, instead of the Future αἰτήσεσθε. [Codd. ℵ. E. G. H., *etc.*, have the latter reading].

[4] Ver. 8.—The reading γενήσεσθε [ℵ.] A. E. G., *etc.*, Tischendorf, was probably changed into γένησθε (Codd. B. D. L., *etc.*, Lachmann) on account of the strangeness of the expression. Also in accordance with the φέρητε (Meyer).

[5] Ver. 11.—In accordance with Codd. A. B. D., *etc.*, Vulgate, Lachmann, Tischendorf, ᾖ instead of μείνῃ. [Cod. ℵ. gives the latter. Tregelles, Tischend., ed. 8th, Alford, Westcott and Hort, following A. B. D., agree in reading ᾖ.—P. S.]

[6] Ver. 14.—The 15th verse seems to favor the Recepta ὅσα (Cod. A., *etc.*) more than the ἅ (Codd. B. D. Sin., *etc.*) received by Lachmann and Tischendorf. [Tischendorf, in ed. 1859, gives ὅ, in accordance with what he declares to be the reading of B.; in ed. 8, he gives ἅ.]

[7] Ver. 18.—[Tischendorf, Ed. 8, in accordance with ℵ.* D., *etc.*, reads: γινώσκετε ὅτι ἐμὲ πρῶτον (without ὑμῶν) μεμίσηκεν, but Tregelles, Alford, Westcott and Hort retain ὑμῶν, which is sufficiently supported by ℵ.c A. B. L. N. X., *etc.*—P. S.]

[8] Ver. 21.—In accordance with Codd. [ℵ.a] B. D.* L., *etc.*, Lachmann, Tischendorf [Alford, *etc.*], we should read εἰς ὑμᾶς instead of ὑμῖν [text. rec.]

[9] Ver. 22.—[Or lit.: *would not have sin*, ἁμαρτίαν οὐκ εἴχοσαν. The Alexandrian form εἴχοσαν for εἶχον is sustained by ℵ. B. L. N.* II., Orig., Cyr., and adopted by Lachm., Tischend., Treg., Alf., Westc. and H. So also in ver. 24. Meyer (p. 530) objects for the reason that the Alexandrian form is established only in one passage, Rom. iii. 13, in a quotation from the Sept. (ἐδολιοῦσαν). Buttmann (as quoted by Meyer) conjectures that εἴχοσαν arose from the original εἶχον ἄν, but of ἄν there is no trace in the critical authorities, nor is it necessary.—P. S.]

[10] Ver. 24.—[Lange, Lachm., Tischend., ed. 8, Alf., Treg., read ἐποίησεν *did*, in accordance with ℵ. A. B. D., *etc.*, instead of the lect. rec. πεποίηκεν, *has done*.—P. S.]

[11] Ver. 26.—[Tischendorf, Ed. 8, omits δὲ, in accordance with ℵ. B. Δ., *etc.* Alford brackets it.—P. S.]

[12] Ver. 27.—[δέ after ὑμεῖς is omitted by D., Vulg., Syr., but retained by Tischend., Alf., *etc.*—μαρτυρεῖτε, on account of καί .. δέ, and the reason ὅτι κ. τ. λ., must be taken as indicative, not as imperative, which is too abrupt.—P. S.]

[13] Ch. xvi. ver. 3.—Ὑμῖν is omitted in accordance with decisive authorities. [Codd. A. B. Γ. Δ., *etc.*, omit; ℵ. D. L., *etc.*, give it.]

[14] Ver. 4.—The ἡ ὥρα αὐτῶν [*their* hour] in Lachmann in accordance with A. B., *etc.*, seems to be occasioned by the second αὐτῶν, which probably originally stood before μνημονεύητε (Meyer). [ℵ. D., *etc.*, Tischend., ed. 8, omit αὐτῶν, Alford, Westcott and Hort retain it.—P. S.]

[15] Ver. 4.—[Some MSS. omit the second αὐτῶν, others ὑμῖν. See the apparatus in Tischend., ed. 8, who reads μνημονεύητε αὐτῶν, ὅτι ἐγὼ εἶπον ὑμῖν.—P. S.]

[16] Ver. 7.—[The E. V. reverses the distinction between ἀπέλθω, to *depart* (from earth), and πορεύομαι, to *go* (to heaven). The one here signifies the starting point, the other the goal, of Christ's journey; as Bengel, with his usual sagacity, suggests: "ἀπέλθω, πορευθῶ, *abiero, profectus ero. Differunt verba; illud terminum a quo, hoc terminum ad quem magis spectat.*" In German the difference is well rendered by De Wette and Lange: *weggehen, hingehen.*—P. S.]

[17] Ver. 8.—[The E. V. *reprove* is certainly too weak for ἐλέγξει, which implies both a *convincing* unto salvation and a *convicting* unto condemnation. See the Exeg. Notes, and the remarks of Meyer (p. 551), who likewise ascribes to the ἔλεγξις the double aim of conversion (1 Cor. xiv. 24 f.) and condemnation (Acts xxiv. 25; Rom. xi. 7 ff.), in opposition to Erasmus, De Wette, *etc.*, who confine it to the latter. The first example of the ἔλεγξις of the Spirit as effected through the apostles, is the pentecostal sermon of Peter, Acts ii. and its double effect. Webster and Wilkinson: "ἐλέγξει means (1) convince by proof, (2) convict, (3) reprove or rebuke . . . The passage is to be interpreted by the preaching of the apostles, or rather, of the Spirit by them (Matt. x. 20). In their discourses, recorded in the Acts, these three objects are the most prominent: (1) Christ the only Saviour, and rejection of Him fatal and damning sin. (2) Righteousness or justification, through the exaltation and intercession of Christ. (3) The kingdom of Christ, instead of Satan's, now, and to be perfected in the final judgment."—P. S.]

[18] Ver. 8.—[I have given in this verse the translation of Lange with his explanatory insertions. He takes ὅτι in the demonstrative sense (=τοῦτο ὅ, τι), as pointing out the object of the preceding words. Alford and Noyes retain the A. V. *because* (ὅτι, causal=διὰ τοῦτο ὅ, τι). It can also be rendered "in that," or "inasmuch as" (ὅτι=εἰς ἐκεῖνο ὅτι, ii. 18; ix. 17; xi. 51). See the Exeg. Notes.—P. S.]

[19] Ver. 13.—The reading εἰς τὴν ἀλήθειαν πᾶσαν in Codd. A. B., Origen, *etc.*, Lachmann. [Tischendorf reads ἐν τῇ ἀληθείᾳ πάσῃ (which is more common after ὁδηγέω), in accordance with ℵ. D. L., Bas., Epiph., Tert., Nov., Hil. The text.

rec.: *εἰς πᾶσαν τὴν ἀλήθειαν.* Tregelles, Alford, Westc. and Hort agree with Lachm. and Lange in reading *εἰς τὴν ἀλήθειαν πᾶσαν.*—P. S.]

[20] Ver. 13. [The text. rec. reads *ἀκούσῃ*; Tischendorf, ed. of 1859, Tregelles, Alford, Westc. and H., give *ἀκούσει* in accordance with B. D. E*.; Tischend., in ed. 8, gives *ἀκούει* with ℵ. L. Lange translates: *hath heard* (historical transmission.)—P. S.]

[21] Ver. 15. In accordance with Codd. A. B., Lachmann, Tischendorf *λαμβάνει* instead of the Recepta *λήψεται.* [ℵ.[c] A. have the latter reading (or rather *λήμψεται*), but *λαμβάνει* is better supported, and adopted by Tischend., ed. 8th, Treg., Alf., Westc. and H.—P. S.]

EXEGETICAL AND CRITICAL.

[The parabolic discourse or allegory of the Vine and the Branches is the second of the two *παροιμίαι* recorded in the Gospel of John; the other being the parable of the Good Shepherd, ch. x. See the remarks p. 317 f. It illustrates, under the figure of the noblest of fruit-bearing plants, the precious truth of the organic life-union of Christ with believers: He is the only source of their spiritual life and fruitfulness; they live in Him and of Him; and apart from Him they must inevitably wither and die, like the branches cut off from the parent stem, although they may retain for a little while a deceitful greenness and appearance of life. The same truth is set forth by Paul under the similitude of the head and the members, Eph. v. 30; Col. i. 23; ii. 19; Rom. xii. 5; 1 Cor. x. 17; xii. 20, 27. In Archbishop Trench's *Studies on the Gospels*, pp. 273-286, there is a suggestive exegetical essay on vers. 1-6.—P. S.]

Ver. 1. **I am the true vine,** *etc.* [*Ἐγώ εἰμι ἡ ἄμπελος ἡ ἀληθινή, καὶ ὁ πατήρ μου ὁ γεωργός ἐστι*].—The new meditation takes for granted a preceding pause; the figure chosen by the Lord presupposes a particular inducement to its selection. Various conjectures as to the inducement:

1. It was presented by the golden vine on the door of the temple (Josephus *Ant.* xv. 11, 3; *De bello Jud.* v. 5, 4), viewed during a stay in the temple (Jerome, Rosenmüller), or seen from a distance in the moonlight (Lampe). [This golden vine was one of the chief ornaments of Herod's temple and no doubt a symbol of the theocracy which is called 'a noble vine' (Jer. ii. 21; comp. Isa. v. 1 ff.; Ezek. xix. 10 ff.; Ps. lxxx. 8-19); yet Christ would scarcely set Himself over against a dead image of man's workmanship.—P. S.]

2. The sight of the wine-cup at the Lord's supper (see Matt. xxvi. 28; Grotius, Nösselt, Meyer). [Ewald, Trench. The communion wine, the *γέννημα τοῦ ἀμπέλου* (Matt. xxvi. 28), which He had declared to be the symbol of His blood shed for the remission of sins, presented undoubtedly the nearest motive for this discourse on the closest union between Christ and His people, which is embodied in the sacrament of union with Christ and His people. Yet this does not exclude an external occasion such as is suggested by Lange, *sub* 6.—P. S.]

3. A vine which, from the house, had shot its tendrils into the guest-chamber (Knapp, Tholuck).

4. The view of vineyards reposing outside in the full moon (Storr).

5. Only the mental recollection of the Old Testament figure (Is. v. 1; Jer. ii. 21; Ezek. xv. 2; xix. 10; Ps. lxxx. 8; Lücke, Baumg.-Crusius. [Alford who, however, combines with this the second conjecture] considered as relating to Christ and the disciples who were about Him (Hofmann).

6. The walk down to Kedron through the vineyards (Lampe, Lange) [in his *Leben Jesu*, followed by Godet (II. 406), who supposes that Christ, seeing a vine with branches, stopped on the way, gathered His disciples around Him and spoke this parable.—P. S.]

We, however, in upholding this latter view, proceed from the supposition that there were burning along the sides of the valley of Kedron nocturnal vineyard-fires,—for the burning of the cut-off branches is a principal point of consideration. It was 1. the time of year for the vineyard-fires, 2. for the cleansing of the vine, 3. for the burning of the offal from the Paschal lamb; this last was strictly commanded (Ex. xii. 10; Num. ix. 12) and might easily have been performed in connection with the duties appertaining to vine-dressing (see *Leben Jesu* II. 3, p. 1425). The Easter-fires which the Gallic and British Churches caused to be kindled in the night following Maundy-Thursday, point to the celebration of the Lord's Supper as obtaining in Asia Minor and, through this, back to the Jewish Paschal-fires.

Jesus' discourse concerning the vine is neither an allegory nor a parable, but a parabolic discourse, and that a symbolical one (see chap. x.).

The *essential* Vine, not the "real." [Comp. on *ἀληθινός* the first TEXTUAL NOTE.—P. S.] That which the earthly vine is figuratively as a symbol, that which the people of Israel was as a type (Ps. lxxx. 8; Jer. ii. 21), Christ is in radical essentiality; He is the trunk-root and stem of the kingdom of love, of its invigorating and inspiriting fruit and effect: festive joy doth the vine represent in an earthly figure, more a child of the heavenly sun than of earthly soil. [The comparison with the O. T. theocracy (defended also by Ebrard and Hengstenberg who find in *ἀληθινή* an *antithesis* to the *unfruitful* vine of the Jewish theocracy) is not so natural here, since Christ represents *Himself*, and not His Church, as the true Vine, *i. e.* the reality of the idea which is figuratively represented in the natural vine.—P. S.]

Ye the branches [*ὑμεῖς τὰ κλήματα*, ver. 5.—P. S.] 1. Christ the principle of discipleship, bearing and quickening all through His Spirit; 2. they an organic whole with Him, through the communion of His Spirit.

The husbandman. [*γεωργός*, the owner of the vineyard as well as the laborer, is a more dignified term than *ἀμπελουργός*, *i. e.* the vine-dresser or actual cultivator of the vine. King Uzziah is called *γεωργός*, 2 Chr. xxvi. 10, and the leaders of the Jewish theocracy *γεωργοί*, Matt. xxi. 31-41. Trench: "Not that the *γεωργός* need be assumed to 'purge' or prune only by the hand of others. The labor of the vineyard is exactly of that lighter kind, in which the proprietor might be well pleased himself to take a share." Wordsworth: "He tills our hearts with the ploughshare of His word, and scatters the seeds of His precepts there, and sends us the dew and rain of the Spirit, that He may reap the fruits of holiness."—P. S.] God's rule over the world is 1. a personal government; 2. a teleological government: establishment, culture, perfection of the kingdom of love; 3. a government exercised upon Christ as the centre of the world and upon His disciples as His organs; a strict and wise government corresponding with the noble nature of the Vine; a government realizing the destiny of the Vine, partly through a cutting off of the useless, partly through a pruning of the serviceable, branches (judgments and purifyings). [Arians used this passage, as implying that the Son was a creature and entirely subordinated to the Father. But Christ calls Himself the true Vine, not in His eternal divine nature, but in His historical mediatorial character and work. Augustine: *Quamvis autem Christus vitis non esset, nisi homo esset, tamen istam gratiam palmitibus non præberet, nisi etiam Deus esset.*—P. S.]

Ver. 2. **Every branch in me that beareth not fruit, he taketh away** [Πᾶν κλῆμα ἐν ἐμοὶ μὴ φέρον καρπόν, αἴρει αὐτό].—*In Me;* namely in organic intimacy, ἐν ἐμοί.* Antithesis of the non-fruit-bearing and fruit-bearing branches. The circumstance that the fruit-bearing branches are not placed in the fore-ground, is indicative of the occasion which suggested the figure: the view of the vineyard-fires. The ground of unfruitfulness is declared in the following, ver. 4. The natural degeneracy of the proud shoots (Luther) which are not governed by the noble impulse of the vine, but are common, useless wood, is made a figure of the moral misconduct of such of Christ's members as stand in the external connection of discipleship, without, however, remaining internally connected with Him. [The fruits of the Spirit are enumerated Gal. v. 22.—P. S.]

Every (branch) that beareth fruit, he pruneth (cleanseth) it [καθαίρει αὐτό].—Seeming to attack *their* lives also with the knife, as is indicated by the similarity of sound: *αἴρει, καθαίρει.*† The purgings here mentioned are to be referred to the providences of the Father. Chrysostom calls them πειρασμοί; Augustine: *castigationes dei* ("*sunt emendatoriæ, non interfectoriæ*"). [Bengel: *afflictiointerna et externa;* Trench and others refer the purging to the whole process of sanctification which includes temptations and afflictions.—P. S.] The purging itself is not, indeed, accomplished without the co-operation of the internal judgment of the Spirit (Gal ii. 19); here, however, Christ has in view those divine judgments, such as overtook the disciples in the Passion-night.—**That it may bear more fruit** [ἵνα καρπὸν πλείονα φέρῃ].—The relation between Christ and His disciples is here indicated in such general terms as to render it impossible for the branches to denote only the Apostles, or the fruits official fruits merely. The general fruits of spiritual fellowship with Christ, particularly as fruits of love, constitute the meaning. Such fruits were, doubtless, to make their first appearance as results of the ministry of the Apostles, there being, indeed no true official fruits independent of the fruits of their labors.

Ver. 3. **Ye are clean already** [Ἤδη ὑμεῖς καθαροί ἐστε, clean by virtue of your connection with the root and stem, and yet in need of being cleansed as branches, ver. 2 (καθαίρει); *mundi atque mundandi . . quis enim in hac vita sic mundus, ut non sit magis magisque mundandus?* (Augustine). Clean objectively, as being justified in Christ, in need of cleansing subjectively, as to sanctification.—P. S.]—See chap. xiii. 10. It is a question whether the idea presented is that of men *already* purified in antithesis to those whose purification is yet *future* (Meyer), or that of an *internal principial* purification, which they already possess, in antithesis to the *external* purification which they still lack and must now receive (*Leben Jesu,* Tholuck). We regard the latter antithesis as the one intended and agreeing with the context.—The noble vine-branch is clean in respect of its inward vitality, but, nevertheless, it must be purged from wild outgrowths, shoots and appendicles. The purifying word of Jesus that made the disciples clean from within (see chap. vi. 57), must be supplemented from without by the Father's school of suffering; the latter, however, was not to *give* them the principle of purity, but to *strengthen* it and free it from the danger of degeneration. In this school of suffering their purification must be rendered complete through their abiding in Him.

[**By reason of the word which I have spoken to you,** διὰ τὸν λόγον—διά indicates the ground or reason, as vi. 57. The living word of Christ received by faith into the heart and dwelling there (comp. ver. 7, τὰ ῥήματά μου ἐν ὑμῖν μείνοντα) is the principle of regeneration and purification (xvii. 17; James i. 18; 1 Pet. i. 23; Eph. v. 26). It is not said *by reason of baptism;* the apostles were not baptized (except with the preparatory baptism of John), and regeneration is possible still without water baptism, which receives its force and efficacy only from the word and power of the Spirit present with it and working through it. Augustine who otherwise, as most of the fathers, has an exaggerated view of the efficacy and necessity of water baptism, remarks: "Why did He not say: 'Ye are clean by baptism?' Because it is the word which cleanses in the water. Take away the word, and what is the water? Add the word to the element, and it becomes a sacrament. Whence is this power of the water that it touches the body and the heart is cleansed? Whence, but because the word operates not merely in being spoken, but in being believed."—P. S.]

* [Trench emphasizes the ἐν ἐμοί. "All infants baptized into Christ are in Him; planted together in the likeness of His death, but it remains for themselves to determine whether by believing and obeying they shall make the potential blessings of this position actually their own; whether that fellowship with Christ, which has been so freely given to them, shall unfold itself into the new creation."—P. S.]

† [Bengel: "*suavis rhythmus.*" Yet no more than a rhythm, for καθαίρω is not derived from αἴρω (which would require καταίρω), but is a technical term for pruning or cleansing a vine or tree of useless branches. But there is a connection between καθαίρειν and καθαρός: we are purified by being pruned. "Cleanliness and fruitfulness," says Bengel, "mutually assist one another." The two πὰν κλῆμα are absolute nominatives emphatically placed first, as i. 12; vi. 39; xvii. 2.—P. S.]

Ver. 4. **Abide in Me and I in you** [*Μείνατε ἐν ἐμοί, κἀγὼ ἐν ὑμῖν*].—Not "on Me" (Meyer) but "in Me," *i. e.* in the true internal vital connection of spiritual communion with Christ. The abiding in Him is the condition whereon depends His ability to abide in them. The interpretation: "Take heed that I may abide in you" (Grotius), likewise converts the promise into a condition, and that the one already declared: "Abide in Me." [Meyer supplies to *κἀγὼ ἐν ὑμῖν*, with Lange, *μενῶ*, *I shall abide;* but Bengel, Godet, Trench supply, with Grotius, *μείνω*, *I abide.* Bengel: *Facite ut maneatis in me, et ut ego maneam in vobis.* Trench: "*Take heed* that ye abide in Me, and that I abide in you." This is supported by ver. 7 (*μείνῃ*), but it is grammatically less natural than the usual interpretation, which makes the second clause a promise.—P. S.]

As the branch cannot bear fruit of itself [*καθὼς τὸ κλῆμα οὐ δύναται καρπὸν φέρειν ἀφ' ἑαυτοῦ*].—The thing treated of here is, manifestly, the abiding of the branch as a *noble branch in* the vine, not merely as a *shoot on* the vine. This is the condition of fruit-bearing. The same law applies to the disciples: **so neither can ye** [*οὕτως οὐδὲ ὑμεῖς, ἐὰν μὴ ἐν ἐμοὶ μένητε*].—It is no question here of the natural inability of the old man (Augustine), but of the simple organic dependence of the believer on Christ; though with this dependence, the effect of such inability, or the constant danger of turning into a proud shoot again, is taken for granted also. The sort of synergism expressed under the supposition of abiding in Christ is explained by the figure itself; nothing without Him, everything in connection with Him. This is fulfilled, in the case of the branch, in organic vitality; in the case of the disciples, in free personality.

Ver. 5. **I am the Vine, ye are the branches** [*Ἐγώ εἰμι ἡ ἄμπελος, ὑμεῖς τὰ κλήματα*].—The positive antithesis to the negative declaration ver. 4. At the same time, however, an emphasizing of the organic contrast: I the Vine=principle; ye the branches=organs entirely conditional upon the Vine and dependent upon it.—**And I in him**, *abide*, namely.—**For apart from Me.**—Without fellowship with Me [*χωρὶς ἐμοῦ*=*χωρισθέντες ἀπ' ἐμοῦ*, *separate from* Me, which is more than *without Me.*—P. S.]—**Ye can do nothing** [*οὐ δύνασθε ποιεῖν οὐδέν*].—Properly, ye cannot be productive and creative as vine-branches. Hence, Christ is speaking of specifically Christian labors and achievements. Christian vital activity is entirely dependent upon vital communion with Christ. Even such noble things as precede conversion are, so far as they are noble, done in the truth of the Logos (Olshausen); but it is only through communion with the Christ of history that a man attains to the performance of Christian acts, new works, deeds of faith, God-like deeds,—or, in fine, that a man brings forth fruit. Luther: "He doth not here speak of a natural or worldly life and conduct, but of fruits of the Gospel."

[The passage plainly asserts the total spiritual inability and unfruitfulness of man without vital connection with Christ, and so far is a strong proof-text for Augustinian and against Pelagian views. Augustine says that Christ spoke thus "*ut responderet futuro Pelagio.*" Calvin: "*Non tantum co-operantis suæ gratiæ auxilium hic commendat, sed nos penitus privat omni virtute nisi quam suppeditat ipse nobis.*" Yet the passage has frequently been applied without proper discrimination. Christ speaks here not of natural morality and civil righteousness, which has nothing to do with man's salvation, but of spiritual righteousness and fruits of the gospel; nor does He speak of unconverted men, but of Christians who even *after* their conversion are in constant need of His grace for the performance of any Christian work. Christ is the beginning, middle and end of spiritual life; we can do nothing without Him, but much, yea, every thing with Him. Trench says: "It is a poor and inadequate interpretation of the words 'Without Me' to make them to mean, 'Ye can do nothing *until* ye are in Me and have My grace.' It is rather, '*After* ye are in Me, ye can even then accomplish nothing except ye draw life and strength from Me. . . . From first to last it is I that must work in and through you.' We have a warning here to the regenerate man that he never seek to do aught of himself; not a declaration that the unregenerate is unable to do aught."—P. S.]

Ver. 6. **If any one abide not in Me** [*ἐὰν μή τις μένῃ ἐν ἐμοί*].—Properly, shall not have abode.—**He is cast forth** [*ἐβλήθη ἔξω ὡς τὸ κλῆμα καὶ ἐξαράνθη, καὶ συνάγουσιν αὐτὰ καὶ εἰς τὸ πῦρ βάλλουσιν, καὶ καίεται*].—*I. e. already* cast forth (or cast out, *ἔξω*, *viz.* from the vineyard, *i. e.* the true Church), like *the* branch [*τὸ κλῆμα*, sc. *τὸ ἄχρηστον* (Euthym.), the useless branch.—P. S.] The article, as well as what follows, very distinctly intimates that Jesus and His disciples are viewing the burning up of withered branches. He is cast forth and is withered, and is now, in company with other similar branches, gathered for the fire. Interpretations of the Aorists [*ἐβλήθη* and *ἐξαράνθη*]:

1. As is the custom (Grotius);
2. They have a Future signification (Kuinoel, Baumg.-Crusius);
3. They are expressive of what is immediately to happen: very soon, *etc.* (Beza, Lücke, *etc.*);*
4. The events described are things past as viewed in presence of the Last Day. The fire, therefore, meaning the fire of the final judgment (Meyer).†

But we should not permit our interpretation to be biased by this allusion to the last fiery judgment, since fiery judgments manifold in their nature precede that final one, and every trial is directly converted into a fiery judgment to him who has not stood the test, Mal. iii. 3; Matt. iii. 12. Therefore the Aorists are indicative of time past, because the things which they denote are viewed from the stand-point of judgments already present in time. When we see branches gathered together and blazing up, we know that these

* [So also Winer, Tholuck, De Wette, Luthardt, Hengstenberg, Wordsworth.—P. S.]

† [Meyer (p. 535) refers to Heb. vi. 8; x. 27. So also Alford: "The aorists I take with Meyer as a consequence of the whole being spoken by our Lord as if the great day were come: hence also the presents, *βάλλουσιν* and *καίεται*." Alford regards this verse as "a most important testimony against supra-lapsarian error, showing us that *falling from grace* is possible, and pointing out the steps of the fall."—P. S.]

were withered because they were cut off, and they were cut off because they had not abode *in the* vine. Jesus is induced to select this tense: 1. by the sight of the burning branches; 2. by proximate reference to Judas who but now is being gathered up together with the withered branches of the Sanhedrin. Hence the *fire* is, primarily, only a prelude to the fire of Gehenna, though, at the same time, it points towards it; and the *gatherers** are all divinely ordained instruments of judgment, and not merely the angels at the end of the world, Matt. xiii. 41 (xxiv. 31; Rev. xix. 24); see Ps. civ. 4. Similarly Tholuck in reference to Heb. vi. 8.

And they burn [καὶ καίεται, sc. τὰ κλήματα].—Emphatic. Like dry brush they flame up quickly and are speedily consumed. Indicative of the conspicuous, rapid and shocking ruin of apostates, or, in general, of dead members of Christ.

[*They burn*, is more graphic and terrible than the E. V., *they are burned;* comp. the Pass. part. καιόμενος, *burning*, *flaming*, and Ezek. xv. 45, where it is said of the wood of the vine-tree:

'Lo, to the fire it hath been given for fuel,
Its two ends have the fire eaten,
And its midst has been scorched!'

Bengel: "*Magna vi positum eximia cum majestate.*" Trench: "All which is here expressed or implied, of 'the fire' (Matt. iii. 10), 'the flame' (Luke xvi. 24), 'the flaming fire' (2 Thes. i. 8), 'the furnace of fire' (Matt. xiii. 42, 50), 'the gehenna of fire' (Matt. v. 22; Mark ix. 43), 'the lake of fire' (Rev. xx. 15; xxi. 8), 'the everlasting fire' (Matt. xxv. 41; Jude 7), with all the secrets of anguish which words like these, if there be any truth in words, *must* involve, demands rather to be trembled at than needs to be expounded."—P. S.]

Ver. 7. **If ye abide in Me,** *etc.* [Ἐὰν μείνητε ἐν ἐμοὶ καὶ τὰ ῥήματά μου ἐν ὑμῖν μείνῃ, ὃ ἐὰν θέλητε αἰτήσασθε (imperative, which some MSS. have changed into the future tense αἰτήσεσθε), καὶ γενήσεται ὑμῖν]. The shocking judgment of the withered branches inspires them with the ardent wish that they may be preserved from a like catastrophe. The Lord's answer anticipates the expression of this wish. Ye shall not only be preserved, but the most glorious gain shall accrue to you; but ye must pray aright. But in order to pray aright, ye must retain my words within you,—and for this end, again, ye must steadfastly continue in the true fellowship of love with Me, 1 John v. 14.—**What ye will** (ὃ ἐὰν θέλητε, emphatically put first).—*I. e.* not in the sense of arbitrary choice, but in the way of love and of Christ's word [or "in the way of God's will and as tending to πολὺν καρπὸν φέρειν" (Alford)]. In this direction (in His name) no request which they may venture, can be too bold. How far did their deliverance and exaltation by means of the night of the Passion exceed all that they could ask or understand! [They who abide in Christ, can only pray in conformity or at least in entire submission to His will, and for things which tend to His glory and the salvation of souls. Such prayers *must* be heard, as to their true spiritual intent, although very often they are heard at a time and in a manner which differs widely from our short-sighted vision. God sometimes hears the substance of our prayers best by denying their form. On prayer in Christ's name, see notes on chap. xiv. 13 f.—P. S.]

Ver. 8. **Therein is My Father glorified** [Ἐν τούτῳ ἐδοξάσθη ὁ πατήρ μου).—We agree with Meyer in considering ἐν τούτῳ as relating not to the ἵνα following it (Lücke), but to the verse preceding it: "by this granting of prayer, conceded to the fulfilling of the condition,—the μένειν ἐν ἐμοί."* The first object to be accomplished by the granting of the disciples' prayers is the glorification of the Father, in pursuance of the glorification of the Son,—the latter being accomplished subsequently to the effusion of the Holy Ghost upon the disciples. This, the Father's glorification, should, however, react upon the disciples, causing them to bear much fruit and to become, more thoroughly than ever, the disciples of Jesus. The bearing of much fruit was not to be the means of their entering into new discipleship with Him; the two things were to appear simultaneously.—**So shall ye grow up to be true disciples to Me.**—[καὶ γενήσεσθε (Codd. Sin. and A., text. rec., Tischend. viii., Mey., *etc.*), or γένησθε (B. D., *etc.*, Lachm., Treg., Alf., Westcott and Hort) ἐμοὶ μαθηταί.—P. S.]. It is most fitting to interpret γενήσεσθε as a consecutive promise, not as a further demand; hence it is independent of ἵνα. [This is preferable. Γενήσεσθε expresses the results of πολὺν καρπὸν (φέρειν) with the additional idea of a gradual process of growth. Discipleship of Christ is the beginning and the end, or, as Bengel has it, the foundation and top (*fundamentum et fastigium*), of Christianity. Μαθηταί here is, of course, pregnant, such as are worthy of Me and worthy of the name of *Christians* which means followers or imitators of Christ.—P. S.]

Ver. 9. **As My Father hath loved Me.** [Καθὼς ἠγάπησέν με ὁ πατήρ, κἀγὼ ὑμᾶς ἠγάπησα].—The apodosis commences, not at μείνατε (Grotius) but at κἀγώ, as is demonstrated by the distinction ver. 10. Aside from this fact, the construction of Grotius would certainly afford a good sense. According as My Father hath loved Me, *i. e.* in accordance with the mystery of the Trinity,—and as I have loved you, *i. e.* in accordance with the mystery of redemption. *Continue in My love* [μείνατε ἐν τῇ ἀγάπῃ τῇ ἐμῇ]. Thus the whole weight would rest in the modification of the *continuing*. The continuing, however, has already been the subject of discourse; this continuing in Christ is modified here as a continuing *in His love*. It is a question whether the Aorists are employed because Jesus is standing upon the boundary of His life and looking back (Meyer), or whether the meaning of the expression is not: recognized in love, conceived a love for, as, similarly, the

* [The subjects in συνάγουσιν and βάλλουσιν. In the image they are the servants of the vineyard, in the application the instruments of God generally in the execution of His judgments, but especially the angel reapers.—P. S.]

* [Comp. ἐν τούτῳ, ch. iv. 37; xvi. 30, where it likewise has a retrospective reference, while vi. 39 may be quoted for the prospective reference, which is also adopted by Alford and Barnes. But Lange and Meyer are right, for ἵνα is not=ὅτι, and in its proper teleological sense it would here convey the wrong idea that God is glorified by the *intention* (instead of the actual *fact*) of bearing fruit.—P. S.]

term πεπίστευκα means: I have become a believer. We take the latter for granted; in this view of the case, the Aorists mark the love of God and Jesus as an accomplished fact, not simply from the boundary of Jesus' life, but from the whole future of the disciples. In the glorification of Jesus they should contemplate the fact of the Father's love to the Son; also, however, the measure of the Son's love to them—a love which was analogously to glorify them. They must continue, must take root in the contemplation of this love; their regeneration, their fruits, their discipleship, shall all spring from their thus abiding (*i. e.* it shall be the source of their justification). The ἀγάπη ἡ ἐμή not love to Jesus (Grotius and others), though grammatically the expression might have this signification, but the love of Jesus to them, as is proved by the foregoing (ver. 11 ἡ χαρὰ ἡ ἐμή). Love *to* Jesus is here, as throughout the section, expressed by the *continuing in Him.*

Ver. 10. **If ye keep My commandments.**—The commandments of Jesus are, in this place as elsewhere, the provisions that He has made for the spiritual regulation of men's lives: precepts, promises, instructions, consolations and warnings in a mass. The warmth and sincerity of vital communion is conditioned by fidelity in "will-oneness" (Tholuck). But, again, the singleness of our view of the life of Christ is conditioned by our faithful perception of His word in detail. True unity is conditioned by the plenitude of manifoldness, true synthesis by analysis, fidelity in great things by fidelity in small things.—**Even as I have kept My Father's commandments.**—The obedience of Jesus even to the death upon the cross; the conservation of the love the Father bore His human form and conduct.

Ver. 11. **These things have I spoken unto you.**—Now follows the section bearing upon the joy that the new life in brotherly love and friendship with Jesus brings. The discourse upon the love of Christ was to be the means of developing joy within them. Thus it is written of the fruit of the Spirit, Gal. v. 22: *love, joy.*—**That My joy might be in you** [ἵνα ἡ χαρὰ ἡ ἐμὴ ἐν ὑμῖν ᾖ. Observe the collocation of ἡ ἐμή and ἐν ὑμῖν].—Interpretations:

1. My joy in you [*mea de vobis lætitia*] (χαίρειν ἐν; Augustine, Lampe: the joy inspired by His viewing their life as pictured in predestination,—which joy was always perfect). That I may rejoice in you,—that ye may be a cause and subject for my joy (Luthardt).

2. Your joy over Me [*gaudium vestrum de me*] (Euth. Zigab., Grotius, Piscator; over Christ's merit).

3. That the joyfulness occasioned by Me may be in you (Calvin, De Wette).

4. The joy experienced by Christ Himself, the joy of His own Spirit (Cyril, Lücke, Meyer [Alford]). Doubtless this is the meaning of the passage. The holy joyfulness of Christ, the untrammeled, glad upsoaring of His soul in the midst of all His tribulations shall, through the Spirit, by means of the communication and awakening of love, devolve upon the disciples themselves (see 1 John iii. 21; iv. 17; Gosp. xvi. 22; Phil. ii. 17; iv. 4 and many passages in the epistles of St. Paul). It is impossible to maintain the distinction of a joy that Christ *tastes in Himself* (Chrysostom, Bengel), and of one which He *occasions* (Calvin, Hofmann, Tholuck); for Christ communicates to, and *occasions* in, His people precisely that which He *possesses* in Himself. That, moreover, Christ's joy itself was first made humanly complete in His exaltation and communication of salvation to the world, is certainly a fact to be insisted upon, in accordance with Chrysostom and Bengel, although they specialize individual considerations too much. From the following it also results that Christ's joy in the redeemed is likewise particularly treated of. "And good pleasure in men."—**In you,** *i. e.* as a new and resident vital principle. They have not this perfect joyfulness yet; it must come to them from Christ; and for this reason also the reading ᾖ is better than μείνῃ.—**And your joy may be made perfect** [καὶ ἡ χαρὰ ὑμῶν πληρωθῇ].—Man's natural impulse to joy has, even in the disciples, already developed into the beginnings of a sacred joy; these beginnings are, however, as yet imperfect; through Christ's joy, their joy shall be made complete ["uplifted and ennobled even to fulness—to the extreme of their capability and satisfaction" (Alford)]. And, again, the joy shall be *theirs*, existing under a peculiar phase in each one. For the dominion of Christ's personality in the hearts of His people does not destroy, but quicken, develop and glorify their own personality, 1 John i. 4; 2 John 12.

Ver. 12. **This is My commandment, That ye love one another.**—Christ does not here pass to another exhortation (Tholuck, Meyer); He does but declare the vital law whose aim is the perfection of their joy. It must be grounded on His love, developed in mutual brotherly love. As the 14th chapter is an exposition of the words chap. xiii. 33: "whither I go, ye cannot come,"—*i. e.* an exposition of the heaven beyond this present world, so here the exposition of the saying chap. xiii. 34 appears as the full explanation of the heaven upon earth treated of in chap. xv.: that earthly heaven, with its heavenly joy, is to be revealed in mutual brotherly love. This ἐντολή is the sum of the ἐντολαί ver. 10; comp. Rom. xiii. 8.—**As I have loved you.**—*I. e.* first qualitatively: as personalities destined for salvation they must love one another *sub specie æterni;* for only such loving constitutes true love; thus doing, however, they will always be quantitatively approaching the true sacrificial joyfulness of His love.

Ver. 13. **Greater love hath no man than this,** *etc.* [Μείζονα ταύτης ἀγάπην οὐδεὶς ἔχει, ἵνα τις τὴν ψυχὴν αὐτοῦ θῇ ὑπὲρ τῶν φίλων αὐτοῦ].—Difficulty is here occasioned by the ἵνα, and the different construction of this leads to a different interpretation of the verse. The ordinary explanation considers it an exposition of ταύτης. This makes the whole verse a generalized description of the love of Christ. "A greater love than I bear to you hath no man, namely, that he layeth down his life for his friends." Meyer, on the other hand, maintains that ἵνα is expressive of purpose even in this place; he interprets thus: Greater love than My love to you hath no man:

the divine purpose (ἵνα) which My love is destined to accomplish, is, that a man shall surrender his life for his friends. Opposed to this view is, however, the grammatical objection that ἵνα would then in reality be the beginning of a new sentence; another objection is the logical one that the love of Christ would then be cited merely as an example. Moreover, in the subsequent verse the Lord calls the disciples *His* friends, after having given utterance to the idea of a man's dying for his friends. Hence we must doubtless assume, with De Wette, that ἀγάπη, in conjunction with its meaning of love, contains the idea of an impulse of the will, a law;* and in like manner we must accept the supposition of Lücke, that the case of a sacrificing of life is put to express the ideal of love. The proper meaning of the saying is this: greater love hath no man than that which goes to the point of causing him to lay down his life for his friends. It is a picture of the love of Christ—generalized, however, because this love, after the pattern of Christ, should be to His people a law of their lives, and because foretokens of this love may make their appearance in the realm of the noble, even amongst the unchristianized of mankind.

Yet another interpretation were this: a love, great like this, hath no man beside,—in order that *One* there might be to give proof of such by laying down His life, *etc.* The dearth of love in all others renders the great love-sacrifice of the One necessary. Still, it is the intention of Christ to represent His self-sacrificing love as a pattern for the disciples, and therefore the usual interpretation seems advisable.

The passage Rom. v. 6 is apparently acquainted with a still higher degree of love. But dying for men who *have been* sinners and enemies is a dying for men who *shall be* friends; Christ dies for sinners who are to be friends; or, again, He dies in a *special* sense for sinners who have already become friends, in a *general* sense for friends who are still sinners. Be it observed, moreover, that He is not delineating His death under its unique form of an expiatory death, but under its *representative* form as a death of self-sacrificing friendly love.

Ver. 14. **Ye are My friends** [ὑμεῖς φίλοι μου ἐστέ, ἐὰν ποιῆτε ἃ ἐγὼ ἐντέλλομαι ὑμῖν].—Christ, with these words, applies the general proposition of the preceding verse to His relation to the disciples. I look upon you as friends for whom I die; but ye too must prove yourselves My friends by doing after My commandment, *i. e.* loving one another according to the degree set forth by My sacrificial love, in so far as that is designed as a pattern for you. And hence the idea of φίλοι is not merely that of "passive recipients of love"—and indeed the word must always, from the nature of the case, mean something more than that.

Ver. 15. **Now no more—servants.**—Neither did He officially call them servants before, but they were such in accordance with the conception of Rabbinical discipleship, and but a short time previous to this He had expressly brought out this characteristic of their relation. This is now at an end; but their emancipation and conversion into freedmen does not estrange them from Him; on the contrary, it elevates them into the category of friends. As, however, the idea of disciple is connected with that of servant, so the condition of friends is implicative of that of apostles. What Christ understands by the term friends, He explains by the antithesis of servants. A distinction must undoubtedly be made between the stricter and the broader sense of friend as well as of servant. Friends though they were before (Luke xii. 4; John xi. 11), from this time forth they become such in a higher sense; and though now ceasing to be His servants in a legal sense, yet, in the sense of free obedience, they do now become servants of His more truly than ever (ver. 20; Acts iv. 29; Rom. i. 1, *etc.*); just as the Son of God was, as such, also the Servant of God κατ' ἐξοχήν. In what respect, then, do they cease to be His servants in the former sense?

The servant knoweth not what his lord doeth; but I have called you friends, *etc.*—The servant executes the individual orders of his master but is not privy to the whole idea which informs his government; moreover he executes the individual order simply as under authority, without being in full unison with it, because it is not instilled into him as an idea and a motive,—and in respect of this fact, it is his master that does such and such things through him; still less does he understand what his master does personally, or through the medium of other servants. He, with his unfree individual performances, does not understand the free doings of his lord, Rom. vii. 15. The friend, on the other hand, is the confidant of the thought of his friend and exerts himself in harmony with him. And so the exaltation of the disciples from Christ's service to friendship is accomplished by His confiding to them the fundamental idea of His life, His sacrificial death of love in accordance with the loving counsel of God; it was by this confidence that He sought to arouse them to a loving activity that should rejoice in sacrifice. They are initiated into His foundation of the personal kingdom of love and consecrated to assist in the extension of the same.—And in this respect He has made known to them *all* (πάντα) that He has heard from the Father,—not *extensively* (see chap. xvi. 12), but *intensively;* in the Father's *counsel of love* all lies enfolded. Lücke makes this distinction: All that I have heard that was meant to be communicated to you; Meyer distinguishes the will of salvation and the *further* instructions connected with it. The distinction between a principle and its development is also intimated, Eph. i. 17 ff. Be it observed that also in Luke xii. 4 as well as in John xi. 11, the name of friend is placed in connection with joyfulness in death. Friendship with Christ is co-partnery in His loving, self-sacrificing dying-courage in the strength of the thought of self-sacrificing love.

Ver. 16. **Ye did not choose Me,** *etc.* [Οὐχ ὑμεῖς με ἐξελέξασθε, ἀλλ' ἐγὼ ἐξελεξάμην ὑμᾶς, κ. τ. λ. "A wholesome memento after the lofty things He had just said

* [Similarly Godet: "ἵνα *conserve la notion de but: 'le plus haut point auquel puisse aspirer l'amour dans cette relation, est,'*" *etc.* Alford rejects the idea of *will* and takes ἵνα simply=*scilicet ut.*—P. S.]

about their mutual indwelling, and the unreservedness of the friendship they had been admitted to" (David Brown).—P. S.]—Though sharers with Him in the perfect vital fellowship of joy, though placed on an equal footing with Him as friends, their relation is still not one of caprice and individual extravagance. For the principle of their friendship is not resident in them, but in His love. He has chosen them to be His friends,—not out of an abstract liking for their individuality, but in the light of the moral destiny of their personality. The election of Christ is not identical with the election to the kingdom on the part of God, in the Pauline sense (Augustine and others), though, in respect to these faithful disciples, the former election is pre-suppositive of the latter; the choosing spoken of by Christ is the election to the apostolic office (see chap. vi. 70; xiii. 18); in a more general sense it is here expressive of Christ's election of any and all of His disciples to render friendly service to Him as co-workers in His kingdom of love (Euth. Zig., Luthardt).

And appointed you.—This ἔθηκα ὑμᾶς presents with greater distinctness the idea of the apostolic calling. The election to friendship is, viewed from the stand-point of their moral destiny, a now still more settled calling or ordination to apostolic labors (τιθέναι, 1 Cor. xii. 28; 1 Tim. i. 12, *etc.*) Hence not: I have *planted* you (Chrysostom and others); this interpretation does not correspond with the preceding figure of the branches and still less does it harmonize with the following ἵνα ὑπάγητε. To suit this interpretation of ἔθηκα, the latter words were constrained to mean the reaching forth of plants (Chrysostom and others). They are expressive of the forth-going of the disciples by virtue of their mission as apostles (Meyer, Tholuck); at the same time, however, they imply a personal laboring, carried on in independent life (Luther, Lücke, *etc.*)—Meyer, without grounds, denies that this is the case. The repetition of ὑμᾶς countenances the view we have just set forth. Hence it results, however, that an oxymoron is contained in the antithesis ἔθηκα ὑμᾶς, ἵνα ὑμεῖς ὑπάγητε. I have set you right firmly in your place, in order that ye might sally forth right independently and travel far and wide, knowing no bounds. In the farewell discourses the item of the ordination, like a series of similar Preterites, is expressive of the imminent sending of the Comforter as a fact already determined; and thus we may regard the whole matter of the farewell discourses as a pre-celebration of the Pentecostal festival.

And that your fruit may remain.—Their institution into the *fellowship of His love* should result in their going forth under *the impulse of love;* this going forth should be followed by their bringing forth fruit, their *work and ministry of love.* This fruit, again, in its virtue of keeping and being propagated everlastingly, should be demonstrated to be a *foundation* imperishable, established by *love.* Undoubtedly the fruit is to remain unto eternal life (chap. iv. 36; Tholuck, Meyer); but here the proximate idea is the remaining of the apostolic fruit in the world and in face of the world,—as results from the following.

That whatsoever ye shall ask of the Father [ἵνα ὅ τι ἂν αἰτήσητε τὸν πατέρα ἐν τῷ ὀνόματί μου, δῷ ὑμῖν].—The Lord having previously made the bearing of fruit in work dependent upon prayer (vers. 7, 8), Lücke, Tholuck, Meyer, infer that the second ἵνα is here not co-ordinate with the first, but subordinate to it, whilst Chrysostom and others deem that the hearing of prayer is here declared to be the fruit of faithful activity. It is, however, possible that a good reason exists for the change in the succession of these two considerations. As prayer must precede work, so work, again, must become the basis of a more extended, bolder asking. This is what Christ has in view, He being upon the point of setting His disciples, with their work of love and fellowship of love, in array against the entire hatred of the whole world.

Ver. 17. **That ye may love one another** [ἵνα ἀγαπᾶτε ἀλλήλους].—With these words the Lord sums up the fundamental thought presented vers. 11-17 in one concluding utterance. Everything that He has told them of His perfect joy, His friendship, His election and their calling, is intended to become to them a vital law of mutual love. Brotherly love, concord, unity—are to form the close-banded fellowship of the disciples of Jesus, in which fellowship they may confront the hatred of the world and vanquish it.

Ver. 18. **If the world hate you** [Εἰ ὁ κόσμος ὑμᾶς μισεῖ.]—Saying concerning the hatred of the world and their *defensive* attitude towards it, reaching from vers. 18-27, in its more extended bearing, to chap. xvi. 6.—**Know that it hath hated Me before you** [γινώσκετε —imperative, not indicative—ὅτι ἐμὲ πρῶτον ὑμῶν μεμίσηκεν].—Me as the first, in advance of you. Before (above) you all. Together with its reference to time, the expression is indicative of causality and comparison: Me first, Me most; Me as the predecessor for whose sake it hateth you. Tholuck: "The superlative comprehends the comparative" (see chap. xiii. 16; Matt. x. 24; 1 Pet. ii. 21; iv. 12; 1 John iii. 13, 14).

Ver. 19. **If ye were of the world** [Εἰ ἐκ τοῦ κόσμου ἦτε].—"The five times repeated κόσμος is solemn" (Meyer). It is at the same time a strong emphasizing of the idea. Mankind is a world in its sympathy in sin, in the ungodly tendency in which individuals, as personalities, are dissolved. As a world, they hate believers; their individual antipathy to Christianity results from that sympathy with ungodliness wherein they stand.

Ver. 20. **The servant is not greater,** *etc.*—Chap. xiii. 16; comp. Matt. x. 24.

If they persecuted Me.—The hypothetical εἰ is exceedingly apodictical here. It expresses in a concrete manner the certainty of the fact that they, as disciples of Christ, must experience the same treatment at the hands of the world which Christ has met with. They must, therefore, be able to see by Christ what fate is awaiting them, since the life of Christ is the same in Christ and in them, and since the world, for its part, continues the same, as world. The first "if," then, reveals to them the positive prospect of persecution; the second tells them how scant a hope they need entertain of a contrary course of proceeding. It is inadmissible to apprehend τηρεῖν, as do Bengel and others, in the sense of: *to lurk for.* That, on the other hand, it contains an element of irony (Grotius), is not inconsistent with the gravity of the discourse; and neither is it inconsistent with the strength of the negation, that the second clause leaves them a ray of hope in regard to some with whom they may have to do (Olshausen, Baumg.-Crusius), since the subject here is not the world, but individual men.

Ver. 21. **But all these things will they do unto you,** *etc.*—The reference is to the first clause, that prophetic of persecution. Consolatory explanation of persecution: Worldly men persecute the disciples for Christ's name's sake, just as they persecute Christ because they have turned away from God who sent Him. Hence it follows that the persecuted have their Christ and God Himself on their side (see chap. viii. 19; xvi. 3). The name of Christ, in accordance with the full extent of its meaning, is the confession of the disciples. Now this name is odious to the children of the world for the reason that the originator of it, the Father, is unknown to them. The first clause is declarative of the world's guilt, the second of at least so much palliation of its guilt as to leave hope for its conversion; yet but in part.

Ver. 22. **If I had not come and spoken unto them, they would have no sin** [comparatively]. [*Εἰ μὴ ἦλθον καὶ ἐλάλησα αὐτοῖς, ἁμαρτίαν οὐκ εἴχοσαν* (Alexandrian form for *εἶχον*)].—This is expressive of the depth of His origin, the glory of His being, the holiness of His mission.—*And spoken to them* (*ἐλάλησα*). This is expressive of the perfect familiarity, clearness, fulness, warmth and condescension appertaining to the revelation He has made of Himself and of God. They would not have sin. *I. e.* in respect to this sin, they would be relatively sinless, guiltless. Unbelief, "the new and deeper fall," John iii. 16. Meyer seeks in vain to put a distinction between unbelief (Bengel and others) and hatred of the name of Jesus.

No pretext or excuse [*νῦν δὲ πρόφασιν οὐκ ἔχουσιν περὶ τῆς ἁμαρτίας αὐτῶν*].—*I. e.* every attempt at an apology comes to nought. It melts away in face of the revelations of judgment. Had Jesus not come, or not yet come, they would still be under the πάρεσις (Rom. iii. 25) of the olden time; now their sin has become guilt, has become a new παράβασις. The objection to this view, urged by De Wette: *As a matter of course they would not have fallen into this sin without the coming of Christ,* overlooks the indicated graduation of sin; in changing the hatred of Christ into a hatred of the divine cause, he mistakes the spirit of *this* Gospel in particular,—John's special characteristic being the merging of things in persons. As little is Tholuck (with Meyer) in the right in contesting that this new guilt is not the sin of unbelief *in specie* (in opposition to Augustine: *hoc est peccatum quo tenentur cuncta peccata, quod unusquisque, si non habet, dimittuntur ei peccata;* similarly Zwingli, Luther, Stier, Luthardt). The citations chap. viii. 21, 34; ix. 41 also speak of sins of self-blinding, which are identical with unbelief.—**But now they have no pretext.**—It can not be inferred from this that the heathen, to whom Christ has not yet spoken, are guiltless; such a supposition is the less tenable from the fact that the crucifixion perpetrated upon Christ by the Jews must be regarded as an act of the whole world. What does result from the passage is, not that they incur a lesser (damnation) punishment (Augustine), but that decision in regard to them is still reserved until the time of their own decision. If damnation be made dependent upon the antithesis to a *revelatio universalis, facta ab initio mundi* (Cyril, Melanchthon), the natural inference must be that that *revelatio* might have been sufficient even for salvation.

Ver. 23. **He that hateth Me, hateth My Father also.**—In the face of Christ, want of knowledge of the unknown God who sent Him (ver. 21) develops into hatred of the Father whom they do know. The unbelieving Jew, like the unbelieving Gentile, turns in hostility against the idea of the living, personal God of revelation,—and that in the face of Christ's works, though they be referred in a special manner to the Father.

Ver. 24. **Not done among them the works.**—Climactic gradation of the guilt of unbelievers in accordance with the distinction of degrees of faith: ch. v. 36; x. 37; xiv. 11.

Ver. 25. **The word that is written.**—The frequently recurring exaltation of Christ's spirit to a state of calm acquiescence in the providence of God (particularly that exercised over the Messiah), as portrayed centuries before in Holy Writ. The word is found Ps. xxxv. 19; lxix. 4; in neither case as a verbal prophecy, but as a mental type. They have cast (חִנָּם) their hatred upon Me without a reason, without a cause. *I. e.* not ironically: they faithfully follow what is in their law (De Wette), but: as a judgment upon them, there must be a fulfilment of what is written in their Law,—*i. e.* in their Holy Scriptures which they read with blinded eyes,—concerning their hatred of Messianic piety. The broader sense of νόμος is the one intended, as chap. x. 34. Αὐτῶν as ch. viii. 17; x. 34; it upbraids them with the fact that the same Scripture wherein they do continually read, as in their own, has sketched their portraits with so sure a touch (see ch. v. 45; 2 Cor. iii. 13).

Ver. 26. **But when the Paraclete is come,** *etc.* [*Ὅταν (δὲ) ἔλθῃ ὁ παράκλητος*].*—Promise of the Holy Ghost as the strength of their martyrdom in the world, ch. xv. 26 to xvi. 6.—If left to their own resources, they would succumb to the hatred of the world and be overcome of evil; but the Holy Ghost shall victoriously meet this hatred and, unmoved, bear testimony to Christ. Repeated promise of the Holy Ghost. Ch. xiv. 16 ff. He is first promised as the Spirit of faith and of the living knowledge of Christ. (See ver. 26). Here He is promised as the Spirit of steadfast testimony for Christ. Ch. xvi. 7 as the Spirit of the world-overcoming strength of the gospel. Ch. xvi. 13 as the Spirit of Christ's glorification and of the

* [Lange translates παράκλ. throughout *Vertreter, Representative.* See the Exeg. Notes on ch. xiv. 16, p. 440 f.—P. S.]

future until the consummation. It is declared in the promise that the Son *asks* the Father, and the Father sends the Spirit; whilst here the Son sends [ὃν ἐγὼ πέμψω] the Spirit who *proceedeth from the Father* [ὁ παρὰ τοῦ πατρὸς ἐκπορεύεται]. For it is only through the intercession of the Son that they receive the Spirit as the Spirit of prayer, and they then know that not only the Father sends the Spirit, but the Son sends Him too. Moreover, the glorification of Christ in the knowledge of believers is pre-eminently a work of the Father; the maintenance of the witness of Christ in the world is a work that He, the faithful Witness (Rev. iii. 14), continues through the Holy Ghost.

Upon the disagreement of the Greek and Latin Churches in respect to the procession of the Spirit, comp. the history of doctrinal theology and the notes upon chap. xiv. 16. To the Father, doubtless, belongs the honor of being the first ἀρχή from which the Son Himself proceeds; but since the Holy Ghost is at the same time the Spirit of the Son, unto whom (the Son) it is also given to have life in Himself, the διὰ τοῦ υἱοῦ (ἐκ τοῦ πατρός) of the Greek theology is not sufficient.

As it regards the ἐκπορεύεται, most of the Lutheran [and Greek] exegetes (also Lücke, Olshausen) understand it as having a *theological* reference to the trinitarian relations of the Spirit; Beza, Cocceius, Lampe, *etc.*, apprehend it *soteriologically* as identical with the being sent.* But if we decline to assume the existence of any tautology in our passage, the *soteriological* πέμπεσθαι may be referred to its *theological* basis, the proceeding from the Father; though the proceeding from the Father is also practically designed as an intimation of the Holy Ghost's invincible power of truth and witness.† Hence emphatically ἐκεῖνος [as opposed to the world, which hates Christ. Observe also the masculine, though τὸ πνεῦμα .. ὅ is neuter. An additional indication of the *personality* of the Holy Ghost, as distinct from a mere power or influence. His testimony is personal, and distinguished from the personal testimony of the disciples, ὑμεῖς δὲ μαρτυρεῖτε.—P. S.]

Will bear witness of Me [μαρτυρήσει περὶ ἐμοῦ].—"Of My person, My work," [Meyer]; according to the context, however, more particularly of Him as the Vine, of the personal life of love, and of His love.

[This is one of the principal proof-texts for the doctrine of the Holy Trinity. Both the essential identity and the personal distinction of the Father (παρὰ τοῦ πατρός), of the Son (ἐγὼ πέμψω—περὶ ἐμοῦ), and of the Holy Spirit (ἔλθῃ ὁ παράκλητος . . . ἐκπορεύεται . . . ἐκεῖνος μαρτυρήσει) are very clearly stated, especially when compared with xiv. 16, 18, 26; xvi. 7, 13; xx. 22. Our passage is also the *locus classicus* for the technical word "*procession*" of the Holy Ghost. The noun ἐκπόρευσις, *processio*, nowhere occurs in the New Testament, and belongs to the ecclesiastical language, but it is legitimately formed from the verb ἐκπορεύομαι, which is here (and here alone) used of the Holy Ghost and denotes the characteristic individuality (ἰδιότης, *proprietas, character hypostaticus*) of the person (not the essence, which is the same in all Persons) of the Holy Spirit, as Sonship or eternal Generation γεννησία, γέννησις, *generatio, filiatio*) is the propriety of the Son, unbegotten Paternity(*paternitas*, ἀγεννησία) the propriety of the Father. The Nicene orthodoxy refers the procession of the Spirit to the eternal, metaphysical procession from the Father. Christ speaks here no doubt mainly of the Trinity of *revelation* and of the *historic* mission of the Holy Ghost in the Christian Church and in believers (comp. ch. xx. 22; Rom. viii. 9; 1 Cor. ii. 10, 11; 2 Cor. iii. 17, *etc.*). Yet it is significant that while He speaks of His sending of the Spirit in the future tense (πέμψω), He speaks of the procession of the Spirit from the Father in the present (ἐκπορεύεται), as if He intended to intimate a *permanent* relation of the Spirit to the Father. The effusion of the Holy Spirit on the day of Pentecost is the historic manifestation of His eternal procession from the Father, and bears a similar relation to the latter as the incarnation of Christ does to the eternal generation. At all events we have a right to deduce the œconomical Trinity from the ontological or immanent Trinity; the former is the revelation of the latter; for God manifests Himself as He is (or, as Godet, II. 514, well expresses it: "*Les faits de la révélation reposent sur les relations trinitaires. Ils en sont comme les reflets.*"). Comp. Lange above. —As to the difference between the Greek and Latin churches on the subject of the procession of the Spirit, Beza, Meyer, Alford and others deny that our passage can be used either in favor of the Greek formula διὰ τοῦ υἱοῦ ἐκ τοῦ πατρός, or the Latin clause *filioque;* Godet maintains that the passage teaches both the homoousia and the subordination of the Son. Dr. Lange briefly intimates the true view. The original Niceno-Constantinopolitan Creed affirms the procession of the Holy Ghost from the Father not with an *exclusive* intent, but rather in opposition to the Pneumatomachi; and in this sense it is that Athanasius, Basil, the two Gregories maintain it; some Greek fathers, as Epiphanius, Cyril of Alexandria, expressly teach the procession of the Spirit from the Son as well as the Father; while Theodore of Mopsueste, Theodoret and the later Greek church maintain the *exclusive* procession from the Father alone. The Latin doctrine of the procession of the Spirit from the Son as well as the Father, is logically derived from the dogma of the homoousia, or the essential unity of the Father and the Son, and is exegetically based on the words ὃν ἐγὼ πέμψω in our passage, and πέμψω ch. xvi. 7, compared with John xiv. 26 ὃ πέμψει ὁ πατὴρ ἐν τῷ ὀνόματί μου. Augustine refers also to John xx.

* [So also Luthardt, Alford, Webster and Wilkinson, who understand the whole of the œconomical Trinity, or the Trinity of revelation. Luthardt (II., 335): "The words must be understood *historically*, and not metaphysically, of the immanent relation of subsistence, or in the sense of Gnostic emanation. For the expression, παρὰ τοῦ πατρὸς ἐκπορεύεται, is parallel to the other, ὃν ἐγὼ πέμψω παρὰ τοῦ πατρός. He is with the Father, and comes from the Father. The present tense (πορεύεται) does not express the timeless nature of the Spirit, but is determined by πέμψω." So also Meyer (p. 545): "The Spirit *proceeds* if He is *sent.*"—P. S.]

† [Stier likewise regards the first clause (ὃν ἐγω πέμψω) as spoken œconomically of the office of the Spirit in the Church, the second clause (ἐκπορεύεται) as referring to the ontological or essential relation of the Spirit to the Holy Trinity. Godet entirely agrees with Lange (II., 513), and emphasizes the difference in the *future*, πέμψω, and the *present*, ἐκπορεύεται.—P. S.]

22, where Christ breathes the Holy Ghost on His disciples (*De trinit.* IV., c. 20; *Tract. in Joh.* 99, § 9); but after all he makes the Spirit proceed *mainly* from the Father (*de patre* PRINCIPALITER, see *De trinit.* XV. 26; *Serm.* 71, c. 16; comp. Gangauf: *Des h. Aug. specul. Lehre von Gott dem Dreieinigen*, Augsb., 1866, p. 371). Dr. Waterland (*Works*, vol. III., p. 237 f.) thus briefly and clearly sums up this controversy: "The Greeks and Latins have had many and tedious disputes about the *procession.* One thing is observable, that though the *ancients* appealed to by both parties, have often said that the Holy Ghost proceeds *from the Father,* without mentioning the *Son,* yet they never said that He proceeded from the Father *alone;* so that the modern Greeks have certainly innovated in that article in *expression* at least, if not in real sense and meaning. As to the Latins, they have this to plead, that none of the ancients ever condemned their doctrine; that many of them have expressly asserted it; that the oriental churches themselves rather condemn their taking upon them to add anything to a creed formed in a *general Council,* than the *doctrine* itself; that those Greek churches that charge their doctrine as heresy, yet are forced to admit much the same thing, only in different words; and that Scripture itself is plain, that the Holy Ghost proceeds at least *by the Son,* if not *from Him;* which yet amounts to the same thing."—P. S.]

Ver. 27. **But ye also bear witness** [**or are witnesses,** καὶ ὑμεῖς δὲ μαρτυρεῖτε,—the present indicating their past and present experience, as the foundation of their future testimony; hence not *ye shall bear* (μαρτυρήσετε), E. V. Hofmann takes μαρτυρεῖτε in the imperative, which is abrupt and contrary to καὶ—δέ, *atque vos etiam.*—P. S.].—It is their constant duty to testify of Him from this time forth, *i. e.* to the same degree in which the coming of the Spirit, an event which is to take place after a little while, is realized in this anticipatory festival. *The reason:*—for—**because ye are with Me from the beginning** [ὅτι ἀπ' ἀρχῆς μετ' ἐμοῦ ἐστέ,—the present ἐστέ indicates the relation as continuing; hence not *have been,* E. V. ἀπ' ἀρχῆς, relatively, from the beginning of the Lord's ministry,—an important qualification of the apostles as witnesses (comp. Acts i. 21, 22; x. 40, 41; xiii. 31), which in the case of Paul was made up by a direct call of the exalted Saviour.—P. S.].—Comp. Acts i. 21. How are the testimony of the Holy Ghost and the testimony of the disciples distinguished?

1. The Holy Ghost shall testify by miracles, in particular by the Pentecostal miracle, by the conversion of the masses; the Apostles by the word (Theod., Mopsueste, Gerhard, *al.*).

2. The two sides of the unitous testimony of the Apostles are mentioned in company with one another (Augustine; see Acts v. 32; xv. 28). Similarly

3. The testimony borne by the Holy Ghost within the Apostles and designed especially for them; the testimony of the Apostles through the Holy Ghost—a testimony addressed to the world (Luthardt).

4. The *testimonium divinum,* through the power of the divine word, and the *testimonium historicum,* founded upon the fact that the Apostles were eye-witnesses of Jesus (Luke i. 1; Acts i. 8; Lücke, p. 646). Meyer [p. 545]: "One testimony; with a distinction, however, in respect of its two actual factors (comp. Acts i. 8; Rom. viii. 16; ix. 1) as Acts v. 32; comp. also chap. xv. 28." [Similarly Webster and Wilkinson: "The Spirit's testimony, as distinguished from theirs, consisted in their inspired utterances concerning the nature, office, and work of Christ, attested by the miracles which the Spirit enabled them to perform (Matt. x. 20; John xvi. 8, 14); also in His action upon others besides themselves. Their additional testimony—'and moreover ye'—consisted in their attestation of the facts of His life, death, and resurrection." Alford: "The witness is one and the same—the Spirit will witness in and by them." The historical witness of the apostles forms "the *human* side of this great testimony of the Spirit of truth, and OF WHICH OUR INSPIRED GOSPELS ARE THE SUMMARY; the *divine* side being His own indwelling testimony in the life and heart of every believer in all time. But both are given by the *self-same* SPIRIT;—neither of them inconsistent with, nor superseding the other."—P.S.]

Along with the last-mentioned interpretation, in particular, the following thought demands our consideration: the personality of the Holy Ghost is not, in the Montanistic sense, to convert the disciples into involuntary, mechanical organs; on the contrary, under His influence their personal life shall attain its full development, so that they too do now stand forth as personal witnesses (μάρτυρες) in accordance with their own peculiar historical and spiritual experience. [Godet makes a similar remark.—P. S.]. Μαρτυρεῖτε is not the Imperative (Hofmann), but the Indicative, for the entire passage bears the character of a sure promise.

CHAPTER XVI. 1–15.

Chap. xvi. ver. 1. **These things have I spoken unto you.**—Ταῦτα: Another recapitulation, this time of the contents of vers. 18-25, in order to the introduction of a new idea; like ch. xv. 17; xv. 11.—**That ye may not be offended** [ἵνα μὴ σκανδαλισθῆτε], *i. e.* that ye may not be disconcerted by coming in contact with the sufferings attendant upon the world's persecution, and be made to fall from the faith, but may, rather, steadfastly approve yourselves martyrs. See Matt. v. 29; xiii. 21; xviii. 7. Christ is discoursing of the danger of becoming offended in the future; His glance pierces beyond the offence that they shall take at Him in the impending night; He reverts to it, however, ch. xvi. 32.

Ver. 2. **They will put you out of the synagogues** [**or they will excommunicate you,** ἀποσυναγώγους ποιήσουσιν ὑμᾶς].—He now reveals to them, by fundamental traits, the operations of the world's hatred, announced to them by Him. First comes excommunication. See ch. ix. 22 [and xii. 42]. Jewish persecutions are meant; as a type, however, of the whole mass of declarations of excommunication and outlawry to be levelled against His followers. **Yea, and an hour cometh** [ἀλλ' ἔρχεται ὥρα].—In the form of an antithesis, ἀλλά [*at, yea and*] gives exceeding prominence to the following climax to the persecutions. [It introduces the contrast of a much more grievous, even bloody persecution; comp. 2 Cor. i. 9; vii. 11; Phil. iii. 8.—P. S.]. Lücke: They were also to experience the *bloody* fanaticism of the world at the hands of Jews and Gentiles. He Himself fell a sacrifice to the same, as, did later, Stephen, Acts vi. 8, *etc.*; 2 Cor. i. 9; 1 Cor. iv. 13.—**That every one.**—ἵνα lays stress upon the destiny of that hour. [Or, as Meyer expresses it, "that which shall happen in the ὥρα, is regarded as the *object of its coming*; comp. xii. 23."—P. S.].—**Will think that he doeth God sacrificial service** [ἵνα πᾶς ὁ ἀποκτείνας ὑμᾶς δόξῃ λατρείαν προσφέρειν τῷ θεῷ].—Serve God by offering unto Him a sacrifice.—λατρεία in the sense of worship, service rendered to the Deity [comp. Rom. xii. 1; Heb. ix. 1, 6, *etc.*]. The performance of the curse-sacrifice, *Cherem*, as the last and highest form of excommunication, was looked upon as a religious act. That the idea of a *Cherem* is present in this place is proved by the expression προσφέρειν, a term which Lücke seems not precisely to understand, whilst Meyer observes: "This axiom of Jewish fanaticism is well known: "*omnis effundens sanguinem improborum æqualis est illi, qui sacrificium facit.* Bammidbar Rabba, f. 329." Comp. Matt. x. Τῷ θεῷ "is primarily expressive of Jewish fanaticism: Gentile fanaticism, however, was substantially the same." Lücke. The Gentile world also was acquainted with the curse-offering and performed it in manifold ways. See 1 Cor. iv. 12.

Ver. 3. **And these things will they do unto you.**—This verse contains 1. consolation for the disciples in regard to their persecutions —conveyed in the intimation that these persecutions will not arise on account of anything in the disciples themselves; this involves the presupposition of their normal behaviour. 2. The thought is suggested that the persecutors will overweeningly imagine themselves to be raised above the disciples on the platform of intelligent judges and defenders of the truth, whilst in reality they are grovelling in the most lamentable darkness.

Ver. 4. **But I have spoken these things unto you.**—According to Lücke, ἀλλά is an explanation: notwithstanding that nothing else can be expected, I have, *etc.* But it has just been necessary for Him to inform them that these very things *must be* expected. Meyer interprets the ἀλλά as a breaking off. But enough: these things (thus much) have I told you beforehand, *etc.* [So also Alford]. A later recollection of the prophetic fore-announcements shall serve to strengthen faith,—faith in the trustworthiness of the Lord as well as in the divinely normal course of things, see chap. xiii. 19. Hence correctly Tholuck (after Cyril, Gerhard): But, so little is it My intention to affright you with these things, that I have told you of them only in order that, *etc.*

I told you not from the beginning.—In what respect do the words: **Because I was with you,** serve as an elucidation? 1. So that I could comfort you (Aug., Lücke). Against this view it may be said: they were then not in need of comfort. 2. The hatred of the world touched Me alone (Chrysostom, Luth., Meyer, *etc.*). 3. Because ye were then too weak to bear such sayings (Erasmus, Calvin). 4. Because He now promises them the help of the Spirit, He can also tell them of suffering (Bengel, Tholuck). The meaning may be simply this: because I thus had it in My power to tell you at any time and had neither inclination nor need to tell you something painful and oppressive too soon; now, however, for the reason assigned, I am obliged to tell you, in order that ye may not be astonished at experiencing sufferings, of whose coming I have forewarned you. Further motives, as, for instance, forbearance towards their hitherto gradual development, *etc.*, are not excluded by the above. But according to the Synoptists, Christ foretold such sufferings to the disciples at a much earlier time (Matt. v. 10 ff.; x. 16 ff.; xxiv. 9). Deliverances upon this diversity:

1. Here φοβερώτερα ἐκείνων are announced (Euthymius, Chrysostom).

2. Christ before spoke *minus aperte* (Grotius, Bengel).

3. Now He proclaims the cause of the world's hatred (Lampe).

4. As a farewell-word the revelation was a new one (Luthardt). [So also Alford: in reference to His immediate departure.—P. S.]

5. Earlier intimations of a more general and less definite character are reported by the Synoptists in agreement with later and more definite ones (Meyer).

6. Those earlier predictions probably belong to the time when Jesus delivered His last discourses (Beza, Maldonatus).

7. The expression here recorded by John can hardly be justified (De Wette).

8. Tholuck: Those utterances were of an isolated cast; Christ has here more expressly declared the principial position of the disciples. This view must be illustrated more in detail: (1) in the Sermon on the Mount, Matt. v. 10, the prediction is couched in such general terms that the disciples might apprehend it as referring to a participation in transient "throes of the Messiah," soon to be succeeded by the appearance of the kingdom of God. (2) In the Apostolic Instructions, Matt. x., the momentary predictions are, in accordance with the ideal order of things, amplified through later additions. Even to the adoption of the eschatological items. (3) The eschatological sayings, Matt. xxiv., were uttered but a day or two previously; hence they coincide ideally with our date.

Ver. 5. **But now I go** [ὑπάγω] **to Him that sent Me.**—The motive for His present full enlightenment of them with regard to their future, in order that, together with what is sad, He may tell them the most gladdening things.—**And none of you asketh Me**—This seems to be at variance with ch. xiii. 36; xiv. 5. The sense, however, is as follows: ye give yourselves up to the sad thought that I go *away* and make no inquiries as to the glad thought: *whither*, namely, to the Father. Calvin: "*Audito meo discessu expavescitis, neque enim reputatis, quo discedam, vel in quem finem.*"* They cling to the ruins,

* [So also Alford: None of you inquires into the *nature* (ποῦ being emphatic) of My departure, so as to appear

of their old expectations with regard to the Messiah's kingdom and are afraid to venture a leap into the new views of life, however urgently the solemn mood of the Lord presses them thereto.

Ver. 6. **Sorrow hath filled your heart.**—Sorrow and only sorrow. Verse 6 is explanatory of the mild reproach ver. 5,—none asketh Me: *whither?* They do the opposite; they linger at the fact of His departure and its immediate and sad results, as revealed to them by Him; they stay at the ὑπάγω, not at the πρὸς τὸν πέμψαντα. The course of ideas, therefore, is perfectly clear; De Wette and Lücke are under some misapprehension when they fain would improve it by reading ver. 6 before καὶ οὐδείς. Even the construction of Olshausen seems to be superfluous; he introduces a period and pause after πέμψ. με and makes ver. 6 follow as a question.

Vers. 7-11. The Holy Ghost as the strength of their victory over the world.

[This whole passage (7-12), relating to the mission of the Holy Ghost, is unmeaning and incomprehensible to the carnal mind, but unspeakably precious and comforting to the spiritual; it touches on the deepest questions of doctrine, and on the practical discipline of our hearts and lives. With a few great strokes, as Olshausen remarks, Christ depicts all and every part of the ministry of the Holy Ghost in the world, His operation on individuals as well as the mass, on believers and unbelievers alike. Comp. here the remarks on pp. 440 f., and the Critical Notes to the five Sermons of Julius Charles Hare (late Archdeacon of Lewis and Rector of Hertsmonceux) on John xvi. 7-11, entitled: *The Mission of the Comforter* (2d ed., republ. Boston, 1854). These notes betray a rare familiarity with patristic and German exegesis, and contain by far the ablest and fullest exposition of our passage in the English language; yet they are wholly unknown to continental commentators and are ignored even by Wordsworth.—P. S.]

Ver. 7. **But I tell you the truth,** *etc.*—Prominence given to the cheering results of His departure, as also to that departure itself. [*But, ἀλλά, notwithstanding, nevertheless,* refers to the λύπη in ver. 6.—P. S.]. *I tell you; ἐγώ* [*I myself,* in opposition to ὑμεῖς, the sorrowing disciples (5, 6), and in the consciousness of personal ability to remove their sorrow by sending the Comforter.—P. S.].—**It is expedient for you that I** [for My part] **should go away** [συμφέρει ὑμῖν ἵνα (expressing the divine necessity and intention), ἐγὼ ἀπέλθω (depart from this world, leave you).—P. S.] Ἵνα marks the fact of His going away, considered with regard to the purposes destined to be accomplished by it.

[With this passage should be compared ch. vii. 39 and the notes pp. 258 f. The sending of the Spirit to men as the Spirit of redemption and adoption, presupposes the offering of the atoning sacrifice, the glorification of Christ's humanity and His elevation to His mediatorial throne. Συμφέρει ὑμῖν, *it is profitable, expedient for you* (comp. 2 Cor. viii. 18; 1 Cor. vi. 12), indicates that the post-pentecostal dispensation of the Spirit who makes us partakers of the whole fulness of Christ and His completed redemption, is higher and more blessed than the dispensation of the Son in the state of His humiliation, as this was higher than the dispensation of the Father before Christ's advent. Christ's departure, in itself considered, without the consequent sending of the Paraclete mentioned in the last clause of this verse, would be the greatest calamity that could have befallen the disciples. For there never was any communion upon earth that could at all be compared in blessedness with their daily intercourse with their Lord and Master, who was dearer to them than life itself. But they lived then more in sight than in faith, and depended too much on His visible presence and His human form, like children upon the presence of their parents. They had to lose Christ as a mere man in order to find Him again as God exalted on His heavenly throne, from which He might send them His Spirit as it never had been sent before, establish His kingdom and convert through them the whole world. The book of Acts proves what they gained in independence and self-government, in strength and endurance of faith by the withdrawal of Christ's visible presence. Archdeacon Hare (Note C., p. 234) ingeniously turns this passage against the Church of Rome, which has indeed preserved the true confession of Christ against all Christological heresies, but has been unable to recognize how it was expedient for Christ to go away: "She has never been content, unless she could get something present, a vicar, images, outward works, actual sacrifices, with priests to offer them up, real flesh and real blood. She chose rather to defy the evidence of the senses, than not to have an object of sense." She has, as Augustine (*Serm.* 270, quoted by Hare, p. 232) says of Peter, "loved the Lord Jesus Christ as a man loves man, as the carnal loves the carnal, not as the spiritual loves true Majesty."—P. S.]

For if I go not away, *etc.* [ἐὰν γὰρ (ἐγὼ) μὴ ἀπέλθω (*depart, leave you*), ὁ παράκλητος οὐκ ἐλεύσεται πρὸς ὑμᾶς, ἐὰν δὲ πορευθῶ (*go* to My Father), πέμψω αὐτὸν πρὸς ὑμᾶς].—Explanation see in Doctr. and Ethical No. 15. Augustine: "*Si alimenta, quibus vos alui, non subtraxero, solidum cibum non esurietis.*" The expression here becomes sublime; it is indued with ghostly severity and heroic boldness.

Ver. 8. **And when He is come,** *etc.* [καὶ ἐλθὼν ἐκεῖνος].—Solemn and triumphant exaltation of spirit, and proclamation. The witness of the Spirit, announced chap. xv. 26, is now, in accordance with its subject-matter, power and effect, declared to be a threefold *victory* over the world. Mention is not made of the disciples for the simple reason that, as bearers of the Spirit, they seem to vanish utterly from sight in His glory. [Godet, II. 519: "*Voici la description de la victoire morale que, par l'organe des disciples, le Saint Esprit remportera sur le monde. Le discours de saint Pierre à la Pentecôte et ses effets sont le meilleur commentaire de cette promesse.*"—P. S.]

He will convict* the world [ἐλέγξει

anxious to know what advantages are to be derived from it. —P. S.]

* [The E. V. translates *reprove* (Luther: *strafen*), but gives in the margin *convince*, which is much better. See Text. Notes, and the exegesis below.—P. S.]

τὸν κόσμον περὶ ἁμαρτίας, κ. τ. λ.].—By His testimony. The *ἐλέγχειν* of the Holy Ghost is variously construed:

1. In the sense of a judgment. Chrysostom: They shall not do such things unreproved; on the contrary, sentence shall be passed upon them; similarly Theophylact [Erasmus, Wetzel] and others. De Wette: "The idea of judgment is conclusive." A one-sided and abstract upholding of the punitory consideration; in opposition also to the idea of conviction, which in the forum itself is distinct from the passing of sentence, as is the latter, again, from the infliction of punishment. The *κρίσις* here spoken of is the judgment upon the devil. [The patristic interpretation *to reprove, strafen*, conveys a very inadequate description of the work of the Spirit, and gives no clear sense when applied to *righteousness* and *judgment*.—P. S.]

2. A convicting, a bringing to a consciousness of the truth, in such wise that decision must ensue, resulting either in faith or in impenitence (Calvin, Lampe, Bengel, Lücke, *etc*).

Exposition No. 1 must not be confounded with the doctrine of the Holy Ghost's disciplinary office (Tholuck), in accordance with which Luther's translation: *strafen*, discipline, reprove, likewise conveys an excellent meaning.* The operation of the Holy Ghost is never external but always internal; His testification addresses itself to the human consciousness,—never to the intellectual consciousness alone, but invariably to the moral consciousness as well, the conscience. And inasmuch as this is true, the world, in being convicted, is always reproved as well, through the judgment of the Spirit. Now the power of Christ's saying is involved in the idea that the Holy Ghost, as the Paraclete of the persecuted Apostles, turns the tables upon their adversaries,—reverently be it said; He prosecutes the persecuting world, brings it to judgment, and, in its totality as world, as sinner, convicts it. Thus, with checkless superiority, He executes an ideal judgment upon the whole world. The conversion of the world, or its confirmation in impenitence, is a result resting not solely in the impressions of the Holy Ghost, but in the diverse reactions of men, some turning to belief, others hardening themselves in unbelief. Under this all-powerful *ἔλεγχος*, however, the world, as an ungodly world, advances towards its dissolution; after the accomplishment of the *ἔλεγχος* it no longer exists. (See chap. xvii. 23; 1 John ii. 17). The meaning, therefore, is as follows: He shall reprovingly convince—convict—the world in His judgment, and, by convicting it, occasion its disintegration into the two portions of the saved and the judged, neither of which is any longer a world. (See ch. iii. 20; viii. 46; 1 Cor. xiv. 24). *The conviction of the world ensues in three acts.*

Be it observed that the point of view taken by Christ in describing the following events, is that of the consummation of the things predicted; hence He employs the Present tense.* On the three themes see Tholuck, p. 384.

['Ελέγχειν in Homer and earlier Greek authors means chiefly *to rebuke, to reprove, to reproach;* so also in Luke iii. 19; 1 Tim. v. 20; Tit. i. 13; Rev. iii. 19. But in the phraseology of the courts of justice and of the schools the verb expresses demonstration, conviction and refutation of an opponent by fair and conclusive arguments. "In *ἐλέγχειν*," says Lücke, "is always implied the refutation, the overcoming of an error, wrong,—by the truth and the right." So the word is used Matt. xviii. 15; Tit. i. 9; James ii. 9 (*ἐλεγχόμενοι ὑπὸ τοῦ νόμου ὡς παραβάται*); John viii. 9 (*ὑπὸ τῆς συνειδήσεως ἐλεγχόμενοι, being convicted by their conscience*); viii. 46 (*τίς ἐξ ὑμῶν ἐλέγχει με περὶ ἁμαρτίας, which of you convicteth Me of sin?*). The last passage comes nearest to our own. The *ἔλεγξις* here meant is a *conviction* (*Ueberführung*), by which the sinner is proved to be such and becomes conscious of his sin and guilt, is "pricked to the heart" and "smitten in conscience" (comp. Acts ii. 37), and brought to a crisis that he will either sincerely repent and be converted (1 Cor. xiv. 24), or harden his heart and bring upon him condemnation (Acts xxiv. 25; Rom. xi. 7 ff.). The divine intention of this convicting agency is the salvation of the sinner; for the Holy Spirit, like Christ Himself, was sent not to condemn the world, but to save it (comp. John iii. 17). This view of *ἐλέγχειν* is substantially held by Calvin and Beza, who translate it *convincere*, Lampe, Bengel (*arguet*), Lücke, Olshausen, Tholuck, Stier, Meyer, Hare (l. c. p. 355 ff.), Alford, Wordsworth, Barnes ("convince men that they are sinners and cause them to *feel* this"), Godet (*convaincre de tort ou d'erreur, ici à la foi de l'un et de l'autre*).—**The world**, *ὁ κόσμος*, is the object of the Spirit's convicting agency and must not be confined to the Jews or to the heathen or to the ungodly, but be extended to all

* [This reproving and punitive action of the Holy Spirit is only the negative side of the *ἐλέγχειν* here spoken of; the positive side is the salutary action, which leads to godly repentance and conversion. Luther describes the *Strafamt* with his usual force. See the eloquent passage admirably translated by Hare, l. c. p. 357 f. The following is a specimen: "Christ gives here His apostles and the preachers of the gospel the highest authority upon earth, that they must rebuke the world with their preaching, and that all men must for God's sake be subject to their preaching, and must suffer themselves to be rebuked by it, if they would receive God's grace and be saved. Verily, this is a vast grasp in a word, and the beginning of a war which was to be great and arduous, that these few mean, poor beggars, the Apostles, are to stir up the whole world, and to bring it upon their shoulders. For what is meant by the world? Not one or two of their fellows; but all emperors, kings, princes, and whatever is noble, rich, great and learned, wise, or anything upon earth; all these are to be rebuked by their preaching, as being ignorant, unrighteous, and condemned before God, with all their wisdom, righteousness, and power, which they hitherto had had and made boast of.—The world cries out furiously, when this sermon begins, that it is a mischievous, intolerable sermon, producing dissension and confusion, giving rise to disobedience, insurrection, tumult. And we cannot wonder at these complaints; for it is a vexatious matter, that the preachers should take upon themselves to reprove all, without distinction, and should allow none to be just and good before God. Who can deem it right or reasonable that this sermon should breed such a hubbub, and bring about changes and innovations so that the whole former religion and worship, with so many beautiful ceremonies of such long standing, should be despised, and should fall? And the most vexatious thing of all is, that they who undertake the work of rebuking, are not high and mighty, learned or otherwise eminent men, but poor, mean, unknown, despised fishermen, and such folks as everybody would class with beggars and vagabonds."—P. S.]

* [Hare, p. 65: "That which was to be effected by His Spirit in the Church during the whole course of ages down to the end of the world, He concentrates, as it were, into a single point of space, and a single moment of time; even as our eye, with the help of distance, concentrates a world into a star."—P. S.]

men (comp. John iii. 16; xii. 31) who come under the influence of the Spirit and the preaching of the gospel. Calvin: "The term *world* comprehends those who were to be truly converted to Christ, as well as hypocrites and reprobates. For the Spirit reproves men through the preaching of the gospel in two ways. Some are seriously impressed, so that they willingly humble themselves, willingly subscribe to the sentence by which they are condemned. Others, although they are convicted and cannot escape from the position of a criminal, yet do not heartily yield, nor submit themselves to the authority and dictation of the Holy Spirit; nay, rather being constrained they inwardly fret, and in their perplexity cease not to cherish obstinacy of mind." Calvin aptly quotes, in illustration, 1 Cor. xiv. 24-5: "If all prophesy, and there come in an unbeliever or an ignorant man, he is convinced (ἐλέγχεται) by all, he is judged by all; and thus are the secrets of his heart made manifest; and so, falling down on his face, he will worship God and declare that God is truly in you." Godet: "*Si le monde est l'objet de la répréhension du Saint-Espirit c'est donc encore dans un but de salut.*"—The threefold objects of the conviction are *sin*, which belongs to men, *righteousness*, which belongs to Christ, *judgment*, which is executed on Satan by the overthrow of his kingdom and the establishment of Christ's kingdom. He who is convicted of sin, passes over either to the righteousness of Christ, or to the judgment of Satan (see Bengel). The triple ὅτι defines the substance and ground of the triple ἔλεγχος, and is=εἰς ἐκεῖνο ὅτι, *in that, inasmuch as* (comp. ii. 18; ix. 17; xi. 51). The omission of the article before the three nouns gives them the widest sense. The natural man has some slight perception of sin, righteousness, and judgment, as is evident from the writings of the heathen and infidels, and the penal codes of all nations; but it is only the Spirit of God who, appealing to the inner law of our conscience, and unfolding the higher law of God, especially the atoning sacrifice and divine-human fullness of Christ, leads us to a living, practical knowledge and personal conviction of these three facts, and traces them to their fountain-head and culminating point—sin to *unbelief*, righteousness to *Christ*, and judgment to *Satan*. Moreover, the natural man, with all his knowledge of sin, cannot get rid of its power. The great aim of the Spirit is to deliver man from his sin and from the judgment to come, and to make him partaker of the righteousness of Christ. The actual proof of this threefold work of the Spirit is found in the Acts of the Apostles, who were His organs, and is daily repeated in the history of the Church throughout the world; for the Spirit's convictive work goes on in unbroken succession wherever the gospel is preached, producing everywhere the same effects unto condemnation and salvation, and will go on to the end of time, as long as there is a world to be converted. There is, however, another work of the Spirit, which is not touched upon here, the work of the *sanctification* of those who have come out of the κόσμος. Our Lord speaks here of the great help of His disciples in their warfare with the world and in laying the foundations of Christianity. Within the Church the blessed gifts and graces of the Spirit, love, joy, peace, gentleness, goodness, *etc.* (Gal. v. 22, 23; 1 Cor. xii.-xiv.; Rom. xii.), will necessarily manifest themselves.—As to the interpretation of this profound and comprehensive passage there is a substantial agreement among orthodox commentators, yet with characteristic differences of theological schools and creeds. See the details below.—P. S.]

Ver. 9. **With respect to sin** [περί—concerning, on the subject of, in respect to—ἁμαρτίας].—Act the first.—**That they believe not on Me.**—ὅτι explicative: *inasmuch as*. Interpretations:

1. He will discover to them the sin they commit in not believing on Me (Euthymius Zigab., Lücke;—"He will convince them that their unbelief is sin, is wrong," Meyer).* But to the truth of this interpretation it were requisite that unbelief should be the object—not sin. And, moreover, the thought would not be a particularly comprehensive one. But above all, the view is subverted by the circumstance that the three terms: *sin, righteousness, judgment*, are mentioned with perfect universality, and unconditionally, in accordance with the universal operation of the Spirit.

Therefore, 2. The passage has reference to sin simply, which, as the Holy Ghost shall convince the world, consists in, is rooted in, in its different phases comprehended in, and, finally, made manifest in, their not believing on Me (Apollinar., Calvin [*qualis in se sit hominum natura*], De Wette [also Wetzel and Godet]. Only De Wette's construction of the case is obscure; he opines that the Saviour's words have reference solely to the unbelief of the impenitent as contrasted with believers, according to John iii. 36. That unbelief is not prior, but subsequent, to the act of ἔλεγξις. It is sin too, beyond a doubt; sin, however, of a particular kind, since it is unpardonable. Believers themselves do not attain unto faith without, through the medium of the conviction of the Spirit, perceiving the identity of their sin with the unbelief hitherto cherished by them. *The rejection of Christ is the central appearance of all the sins of all the world; light is thrown thereupon by the spiritual manifestation of Christ's divine exaltedness above all the world.* The old world makes a distinction between sin and unbelief, and even ventures to consider the latter a very meritorious thing; on that point, the views of the world shall be subverted by the Holy Ghost.

[Bengel: "*Infidelitas est confluens peccatorum omnium et omnibus pejor.*" Alford: "This unbelief is not a mere want of historical faith,—but unbelief in its very root,—the want of a personal and living recognition of Jesus as the Lord (1 Cor. xii. 3) which, wherever the Spirit has opened His commission by the planting of the visible church, is *the condemning sin* of the world." On this point Luther, in his usual forcible and graphic style, makes some remarks which show how much deeper he penetrated into the marrow of the Scriptures on the doctrines of sin and grace and the depths of faith and unbelief than the fathers,

* [Similarly Chrysostom, Theophylact, Grotius, Hammond, who refer at the same to signs and wonders and other external proofs as the principal means by which men are to be convinced of the sin of their unbelief.—P. S.]

not excluding even Chrysostom and Augustine. "The unbelief spoken of in the text," says Luther, "is not merely that which is planted by Adam in man's nature, but plainly this, that men believe not in Christ, that is, when the gospel of Christ is preached, in order that we may confess our sins, and through Christ seek and obtain grace. For when Christ came, the sin of Adam and of the whole human race, namely, their previous unbelief and disobedience, was taken away before God by Christ's sufferings and death; and He built a new heaven of grace and forgiveness; so that the sin, which we have inherited from Adam, shall no longer keep us under God's wrath and condemnation, if we believe in this Saviour. And henceforward he who is condemned must not complain of Adam and of his inborn sin: for this Seed of the woman, promised by God to bruise the head of the serpent, is now come, and has atoned for this sin, and taken away condemnation. But he must cry out against himself, for not having accepted or believed in this Christ, the devil's head-bruiser and sin-strangler. Thus every man's danger rests with himself; and it is his own fault if he is condemned; not because he is a sinner through the sin of Adam, and deserving of condemnation by reason of his former unbelief; but because he will not accept this Saviour Christ, who takes away our sin and condemnation. True it is indeed, that Adam has condemned us all, inasmuch as he brought us along with him into sin and under the power of the devil. But now that Christ, the second Adam, is come, born without sin, and has taken away sin, it cannot longer condemn me if I believe in Him; but I shall be delivered from it through Him and be saved. If, on the other hand, I do not believe, the same sin and condemnation must continue; because He who is to deliver me from it, is not taken hold of: nay, it will be a doubly great and heavy sin and condemnation, that I will not believe in this dear Saviour, by whom I might be helped, nor accept His redemption. Thus all our salvation and condemnation depend now upon this, whether we believe in Christ or no. A judgment has at length gone forth which closes heaven against all such as have not, and will not receive, this faith in Christ. For this unbelief retains all sin, so that it cannot obtain forgiveness, even as faith removes all sin. And hence without this faith everything is and continues sinful and condemnable, even in the best life and the best works which a man can perform; which although in themselves they are praiseworthy and commended by God, yet are corrupted by unbelief, so that on account thereof they cannot please God; even as in faith all the works and life of a Christian are pleasing to God. In fine, without Christ everything is condemned and lost; in Christ everything is good and blessed; so that even sin, which continues in our flesh and blood, being inherited from Adam, can no longer hurt or condemn us."—I add Olshausen's explanation, which well agrees with the foregoing extract: "In the first place the Spirit makes sin manifest, not however in its outward character,—in this respect the Law awakens the knowledge of sin (Rom. iii. 20),—but in its inward deep root. Now this is nothing else than unbelief, which we may call the mother of all sinful actions: but unbelief itself is, in its most glaring form, unbelief in the Incarnate Christ. The inability of recognizing this purest manifestation of the Divinity implies utter blindness." Stier and Hare may also be profitably consulted on this passage.—P. S.]

Ver. 10. **With respect to righteousness** [περὶ δικαιοσύνης*].—Act the second. Here, again, righteousness simply is manifested. *Christ's exaltation to the throne of glory is the central appearance of God's righteousness; we say, of God's righteousness in Christ, God's righteousness in His providence, God's righteousness in believers, in the conscience of unbelievers even,—an appearance illuminated by the spiritual manifestation of Christ's world-reconciling and glorifying operations.*

Meyer thinks that "things of entirely diverse natures are mingled together" in these words (*Leben Jesu*, II., 1385).† So Paul might seem to him to mingle things of different natures, Rom. iii. 26, but the δικαιοσύνη θεοῦ is but one.

1. By Chrysostom, Beza, *etc.*, Lücke, Meyer, the passage is construed to mean the *righteousness of Christ* ("guiltlessness," which is too weak a term in this connection); comp. 1 Tim. iii. 16.‡ This view, Tholuck thinks, is untenable in

* [The Rhemish version, as usual, follows here the Vulgate and translates *justice* (*justitia*), on which Hare (p. 371) makes the following instructive observations: "The Latin word is more appropriate here than in many other cases: though even here the corresponding Saxon word better expresses the vital principle dwelling and working in the soul; while the Latin, in conformity to the predominant character of the language, and of the nation whose image that language reflects, relates rather to outward acts and conduct. The difference is analogous to that which we find in the translations of the sixth beatitude, where, instead of *the pure in heart*, the Rhemish Version is led by the Vulgate, *beati mundo corde*, to put '*Blessed are the clean of heart.*' I trust it is neither unjust nor fanciful to look upon these two words as in some measure symbolical of the distinctive characters of the Reformed churches and of that of Rome, that is to say, so far as each answers to its peculiar principle and idea. The former seek *purity*, and cannot be satisfied without it, and therefore are always oppressed with a deep consciousness of impurity; the latter aim at *cleanness*, which may be attained in a high degree, and by means of outward acts. So may *justice*; but *righteousness* is unattainable. I do not mean that the Romish Church is altogether regardless of *purity* and *righteousness*, or the Reformed of *cleanness* and *justice*. Specific distinctions are seldom absolute, but relative, and are formed by the predominance of one or other of the constitutive elements, by the development of that which had been latent, the coming forward of that which had been kept in the background, the superiority of that which had been subordinate. Neither are the cleanness and justice inculcated by the Church of Rome irrespective of purity and righteousness; nor are the purity and righteousness, the ideas of which were the beacon stars of the Reformation, irrespective of cleanness and justice. Indeed it would be utterly impossible for either to exist without some admixture of the other. But the error, which is the caricature and corruption of each church, and has evermore lifted up its head therein, marks its tendency by its main danger: and this in the Church of Rome has been the proneness to Pelagianism, in the Reformed Churches the aptness to run into Antinomianism. Our modern impugners and revilers of the Reformation have never duly recognized these main distinctions between the two great branches, into which the Western Church since that event has been divided. Hence they have gone blindly astray in their judgments upon each, blaming and praising inconsiderately and irrelevantly, nay, at times blaming where they ought to have praised, and praising where they ought to have blamed, even as in their own theology they want to turn back the hands of the world's great clock, and to pull down to cleanness and justice, to rudiments of outward acts and observances,—*touch not, taste not, handle not*,—instead of urging and helping us to that inward *purity* and *righteousness*, which we are to seek from the Comforter, and which He alone can give."—P. S.]

† [Omitted in the fifth edition of Meyer.—P. S.]

‡ [So also Maldonatus, Bengel, Olshausen, Barnes, Bäumlein, Godet, Owen.—P. S.]

the absence of a μου in connection with δικαιοσύνη; in addition to this objection, we would state that "the going to the Father" and "the seeing Christ no more," must receive their share of consideration.

2. By Cyril, Augustine, Calvin, Luther, Gerlach, Stier, it is interpreted as significant of the *righteousness that comes of faith*, in the Pauline sense.* Controverted by Tholuck on the ground that in the writings of Paul δικαιοσύνη is the central idea, but in those of John that position is occupied by ζωή. Hence he thinks to interpret the word in accordance with the Johannean usage exemplified elsewhere (1 John ii. 29; iii. 7, 10), as indicative of moral purity or "*Rechtbeschaffenheit*" (*righteous nature*, to use the abortive term that has sprung up of late). But if we consider that the moral purity of Christ is infinitely positive, that it is the moral purity not of a child, but of the Lord of glory, we find that this exposition coincides with No. 1; irrespective of the fact that the lack of μου might with equal justice be complained of here.—Besides, the word is introduced entirely without limitation. The old world pronounced the Lord a sinner (chap. ix. 24); in His crucifixion it set Him forth as sin itself, as the enemy of man κατ' ἐξοχήν, and treated Him as such;—the Holy Ghost will subvert the world's old views in reference to Christ and, together with these, its views of the righteousness of God and the human life itself.

The expression, **and ye see Me no more** [καὶ οὐκέτι θεωρεῖτέ με], is interpreted by Meyer as an affectionate participation in the disciples' grief at their parting—an idea utterly incongruous with the context. It is likewise in accordance with righteousness that Christ, in His exaltation, is removed from the sinful world until His appearance in judgment; hence His kingdom this side of eternity must be a kingdom of the cross, and the world can reach Him only through faith.† The full glory of righteousness is still in the hereafter with Christ, and not until the Last Day shall it *appear*.

[The explanation of δικαιοσύνη has caused more difficulty than that of ἁμαρτία. Commentators are divided, as has already been stated, on the question whether δικαιοσύνη here means the *personal* and *inherent* righteousness of Christ (as maintained by the ancient Greek and the majority of modern exegetes), or the *communicated, justifying* righteousness apprehended by faith (as vigorously advocated by the reformers and recently by Stier). Dr. Lange rightly sides with the former view, but gives it, in his own original way, the most comprehensive meaning, in accordance with his exposition of the δικαιοσύνη θεοῦ in Rom. i. 17; iii. 26. (Comp. my annotations in the Comm. on *Rom.*, pp. 74 f., 134 ff). To me it is very clear that the personal righteousness or absolute sinless perfection of Christ is meant, and not justification by faith (although this, of course, rests on the former), for the following reasons: 1. δικαιοσύνη is plainly the opposite to ἁμαρτία, and *Christ* is the subject of "righteousness," as the *world* is the subject of "sin." (Stier and Alford, who take δικ. in the sense of justification of the sinner, consistently make κόσμος the subject not only of ἁμαρτίας but also of δικαιοσύνης and κρίσεως, which is unnatural). The absolute holiness of Christ is the only full and proper antithesis to the sin of the world, which centres in unbelief, as the mother of sins from Adam's disobedience down to the rejection of Christ in our day. 2. The explanatory ὅτι πρὸς τὸν πατέρα, *etc.*, refers to *Christ*, not to us, and gives the proof of *His* righteousness, not ours. It was by the triumphant exaltation of Christ to the right hand of the Father and His invisible reign, that He, who had been sent to death as a "sinner," yea as a blasphemer and impostor (John xviii. 30; ix. 24), was vindicated by God Himself and demonstrated by the testimony of the Paraclete, through the apostles, as the δίκαιος, the pure and holy one (comp. Acts ii. 33 ff.; iii. 14; vi. 52; Rom. i. 4; 1 Pet. iii. 18; 1 John ii. 1, 29; iii. 7). The other interpretation would require the mention of Christ's expiatory death (comp. vi. 51; xvii. 19), as the explanatory ground of justification, rather than His exaltation to glory. 3. John uses δικαιοσύνη always in its proper sense of *righteousness* (1 John ii. 29; iii. 7, 10; Rev. xix. 11), not of *justification*, which corresponds to the Greek δικαίωσις—a term unknown to John's vocabulary. 4. He expresses the Pauline idea of justification in opposition to condemnation not so much in its legal as in its moral aspects and in connection with its effects upon the soul by the familiar phrase: "He that believeth on Christ, hath *eternal life*" (ch. iii. 16; iv. 14; v. 24; vi. 27, 40, 47; xii. 50; 1 John ii. 25; v. 11, 13).—It is perfectly true, however, that according to John as well as Paul, Christ's righteousness becomes *our* righteousness by *faith*. Christ is *the Lord our Righteousness.* He did not come down to lead a holy life for Himself, for He was holy from eternity, but for our benefit, that we may become partakers of His righteousness, and so also sharers of His exaltation to the Father in glory. It is in this way that Archdeacon Hare, Dean Alford, and Bishop Words-

* [In this sense: The Spirit convinces the world also of the necessity of justification for the sinner (so that κόσμος would be the subject of δικαιοσύνης as well as of ἁμαρτίας); for after my atoning death I go to the Father and will work invisibly for you. This is substantially also the interpretation of Erasmus, Melanchthon, Lampe, Donne, Storr, Hengstenberg, Alford. Its chief representative is Luther, the almost inspired teacher of justification by faith. See the rich and full extracts given from him in fresh, racy Saxon English by Hare, pp. 441 ff., which are true in themselves and in opposition to Romish work-righteousness, and yet miss the proper sense of our passage. Ebrard adopts the same interpretation in the modified sense: the righteousness which the world ought to have, but has not. But in this case, as Meyer justly objects, the ἔλεγξις περὶ δικαιοσύνης would substantially amount to the same thing as the ἔλεγξις περὶ ἁμαρτίας.—P. S.]

† [Hare, p. 139: "In that Christ went to the Father, He gave the most certain demonstration of His righteousness. In that we see Him no more, He renders it easier for us to make His righteousness ours. Were He still living upon earth, were He walking about before our eyes, it would not be so. . . . So long as He continued with His disciples, they lived by sight, rather than by faith. Sight, as belonging to the world of sense, partakes of its frailties and imperfections. To put forth all its power, faith must be purely and wholly faith. It is so even with the human objects of faith and love. So long as they continue in the flesh, our faith in them, our love for them is imperfect. The infirmities of the flesh cleave to it. Their corruption must put on incorruption, —they must be transfigured by death,—they must pass away from this world of sight,—we must see them no more;—then may our faith and love towards them become pure and holy and heavenly and imperishable. When our love springs from the root of faith, then alone may it hope to blossom through eternity."—P. S.]

worth endeavor to combine the two interpretations. "If the conviction of righteousness," says Hare (p. 135 f.), "which the Spirit works in us, were merely the conviction of God's righteousness, or of Christ's, we could only fall to the ground with awestruck, palsied hearts: we could no more venture to look upon Christ, than the naked eye can look upon the sun. But when we are thoroughly convinced that Christ's righteousness is our righteousness, the righteousness which He purposes to bestow upon mankind,—that He came to fulfil all righteousness, not for His own sake but for ours, in order that He might give us all that we lack out of His exceeding abundance,—then indeed a bright ray of joy and comfort darts through the heart, startling the frost-bound waters out of their yearlong sleep. Then the soul, which before was a wilderness and a solitary place, solitary, because God was far from it,—yea, the barren desert of the heart rejoices and blossoms like the rose. All its hidden powers, all its suppressed feelings, so long smothered by the unresisted blasts of the world, unfold like the rose-leaves before the Sun of Righteousness; and each and all are filled and transpierced with its gladdening, beautifying light." Comp. also the note of Alford, who closely follows Stier.—P. S.]

Ver. 11. **With respect to judgment,** *etc.* [*περὶ δὲ κρίσεως, ὅτι ὁ ἄρχων τοῦ κόσμου τούτου κέκριται*].—Act the third. Elucidation of the judgment. The prince of this world appears therein as judged. *The judgment executed upon the devil through the death and resurrection of Christ, is the central appearance of all God's judgments in the history of the world until the end of the world; an appearance fully illuminated by means of the spiritual manifestation of the cross, or the accursed tree,—to which Satan brought Christ,—as the sign of victory.* Thus the Holy Ghost subverts the old view of the world, which made misfortune and the cross a sign of reprobation, but held the momentarily successful issue of Satanic plots to be a sign of the favor "of heaven." To that principiary judgment, consummated on the cross, the victory over the tempter in the wilderness (Matt. iv.), and that over the traitor in the midst of the disciples (chap. xiii. 30), were introductory: it must, however, as the consummation, be distinguished from those. This principiary consummated judgment has been in process of development throughout the world's history ever since the time of Christ and shall become evident on that day when the world is judged.

[For a full and able practical exposition of this conviction of judgment see Hare's fourth Sermon (pp. 162 ff.) and his ample notes. Luther is quite in his element here, when, in his bold, defiant, triumphant tone, he carries on as it were the word of God, and applies it to his own times. "Christ," says he, "here speaks very grandly and boldly. Not only, He says, shall all emperors, kings, princes, or others, who rage against God's word, be condemned along with their judgment, but the prince of this world himself, who has more might and strength in his little finger than all the world together. And the gospel shall not only be judge over flesh and blood, nay, not only over some of Satan's angels or devils, but over the prince himself, who has the whole world mightily in his hands, and is the all-wisest, mightiest and thereto the all-fiercest enemy of God and His Christians, so that everything which is great, mighty and wicked among men is nothing in comparison with him. . . . Therefore it behooves us not to dread or care for their judgment and condemnation, because we hear that it shall not harm us, but is already powerless, being condemned by God's contrary judgment, so that they shall not work or effect anything against us, however fiercely they rage against us with their condemnation, persecution and murder, but must finally and forever remain under condemnation, which is passed against them both by God, and by us who judge after and by His word. And Christendom shall maintain the supreme judgment, and shall abide, as it has done hitherto, in spite of the devil and the world." This is the same spirit that breathes in Luther's "*Ein' feste Burg.*"—P. S.]

Vers. 12-15. The Holy Ghost as the Spirit of the development of Christianity, and of the revelation of the future.

Ver. 12. **I have yet many things to say unto you, but ye cannot bear them now.** [*Ἔτι πολλὰ ἔχω λέγειν ὑμῖν, ἀλλ' οὐ δύνασθε βαστάζειν ἄρτι*].—Ye cannot bear them now. *Βαστάζειν.* Cannot bear them mentally; *i. e.* in the first place, ye are intellectually unable to comprehend them; doubtless, however, it also means, ye are morally incapable of supporting them. What is Jesus' meaning? Interpretations:

1. New articles of doctrine are intended. Tradition and its dogmas. Roman Catholic exegetes, Meyer also in measure. The latter does not pretend that the *πολλά* are specified, but he too conceives of the relation of new to old as *additional* ("for neither can we imagine the oral instruction of the *Apostles* to be fully set down in their Epistles"); he does not consider the new as an organic development of the old.

2. Sufferings to be endured by the disciples.

3. New forms of truth, in itself already familiar. Thomas Aquinas: "*Non nova fidei mysteria, sed novo tantum modo (sc. altiori) docebit.*"

4. New developments and applications of truth already known. Ancient Protestant interpretation, Lücke.

5. The entire ecclesiastical development of doctrine. Hegelian exegetes. Against this view Tholuck remarks: "The latter extension is manifestly in opposition to the context. Doubtless the promises made to the *apostolic* disciples, including those contained in the Sermon on the Mount and in Matt. x., must admit of an application to the disciples generally;—they can, however, only *relatively* be thus applied; even Hofmann, II., 2, 245 ff., says in reality nothing more than this. Now the persons here addressed are none other than those *μάρτυρες ἀπ' ἀρχῆς*, chap. xv. 27, those to whom chap. xvii. 18 applies, for whom He prays first, chap. xvii. 9, reserving His petitions for other believers on Him until later, ver. 20." Against the "development view" see Tholuck still further, p. 387. We agree with him in thinking that reference is not again had to the general development of Christian doctrine; that having already been treated of in chap. xiv. 26. Tholuck, with justice,

directs attention to the expression: *τὰ ἐρχόμενα ἀναγγελεῖ*; the term *ἀναγγελεῖ*, be it observed, occurs three times in succession.

Hence 6. Christ has in view the apocalyptic disclosures of apostolic Christianity in its more developed stage; revelations, for instance, concerning the perfect emancipation of Christianity from Judaism, Acts x., set forth also in the life of St. Paul, Eph. iii. 8, 9; preëminently those eschatological revelations reposing upon evangelical premises, which appear in the Revelation of St. John, in the Epistles to the Thessalonians, Rom. xi. 25; 1 Tim. iv. 1. Thus Albertus M.: "*Non solum futura in tempore, sed magis æterna, ad quorum amorem inflammabunt.*" Tholuck. The *æterna* are not to be excluded, we admit; the *ultima*, however, occupy the foreground of the picture. Of course these proclamations of things to come are principially contained in the communications hitherto made to the disciples, especially in the eschatological discourses of the Lord. Nevertheless, the theocratic and apocalyptic revelations as subsequently received by the Apostles (Acts x.; 2 Thess. ii.; the Apocalypse), constituted new matter in the development of the kingdom of God, never before revealed with such distinctness.

Ver. 13. **But when He, the Spirit of truth, is come, He will guide you into the whole (full) truth.** [*Ὅταν δὲ ἔλθῃ ἐκεῖνος, τὸ πνεῦμα τῆς ἀληθείας, ὁδηγήσει ὑμᾶς εἰς τὴν ἀλήθειαν πᾶσαν*].—See the TEXTUAL NOTES. Lachmann's reading suits the apocalyptic items of apostolic experience far better than does that of Tischendorf: *ἐν τῇ ἀληθείᾳ πάσῃ*. The emphatic position of *πᾶσα* is indicative of the new points of revelation.—On *The Spirit of truth*, see chap. xiv. 17.

[Rightly understood, this important passage proves the sufficiency of the Scriptures. The *πᾶσαν* after *τ. ἀλ.* expresses the truth in its completeness or totality; comp. ver. 22: *τὴν κρίσιν πᾶσαν*. The article is important: *the whole truth, the full truth.* The A. V. (*into all truth*), and all the preceding E. Versions, as also Luther in his G. V. (*in alle Wahrheit*, instead of *die ganze* or *volle Wahrheit*), miss the sense of the original by omitting the article. It is not omniscience or any kind of speculative or scientific truth which is promised, but the full knowledge of living, practical truth as it is in *Christ*, and as it relates to our soul's *salvation.* The Bible is not a universal encyclopædia of knowledge, but an infallible guide of religious faith and moral practice. Luther corrects his faulty translation in his comments. "This truth," he says, "which the Holy Spirit is to teach them, is not such a doctrine and knowledge as reason of itself can understand and hit upon . . . for the Holy Spirit and Christ's Church do not concern themselves with things which are subject to man's understanding and which belong to this temporal life and to worldly rule . . . but treat of far other matters, how God's children are to be begotten out of sin and death unto righteousness and everlasting life, how God's kingdom is to be established and the kingdom of hell to be destroyed, how we are to fight against the devil and to overcome him, how to cheer, strengthen and uphold faith, so that a man shall continue alive in the midst of death, and even under the consciousness of sin shall preserve a good conscience and the grace of God." Alford: "*All the truth, viz.* on those points alluded to in ver. 12. . . . The Lord had told them *the truth* and *nothing but the truth*, in spiritual things, but not yet *the whole truth*, because they could not bear it. This the Spirit should lead them into, open the way to it, and unfold it by degrees. No promise of universal knowledge, nor of infallibility, is hereby conveyed; but a promise to them and us, that the Holy Spirit shall teach and lead us, not as children, under tutors and governors of legal and imperfect knowledge, but as sons (Gal. iv. 6), making known to us the whole truth of God. This was in a special manner fulfilled to *them*, as set to be the founders and teachers of the churches."—Yet in a certain sense, the Spirit of God alone can lead us *into all truth*, even in temporal and human things, since the love of truth is inseparable from the love of God, and the perfect knowledge of truth from the knowledge of God, which comes from the Spirit of God, the true illuminator of the human intellect darkened and distorted by sin and its bosom companion, error. See some excellent remarks on this passage by Hare, l. c. Note B., pp. 224 ff.—P. S.]

For He shall not speak of Himself. [*Οὐ γὰρ λαλήσει ἀφ' ἑαυτοῦ, ἀλλ' ὅσα ἂν ἀκούει (ἀκούσῃ) λαλήσει, καὶ τὰ ἐρχόμενα ἀναγγελεῖ ὑμῖν*].—See above ch. xiv. 26. Luther: "Thus He imposeth a limit and measure (a basis and principle) to the preaching of the Holy Ghost Himself; He is to preach nothing new, nothing other than Christ and His Word;—to the end that we might have a sure sign, a certain test, whereby to judge false spirits." Thus the Spirit is conditioned by the Son, as the Son is by the Father, ch. v. 19.

Whatsoever He hath heard [heareth; on the different readings, *ἀκούει, ἀκούσῃ, ἀκούσει*, see TEXT. NOTES.—P. S.].—*I. e.* such historical things as He, as the Spirit of believers and of the Church, has heard from Christ, either directly or indirectly: 1. Heard from Christ (Olshausen, Kling, *etc.*); 2. from God (Meyer); 3. from both (Luthardt [Alford, Godet]). A hearing from God on the part of the Spirit, a hearing independent of history, is not a clear idea at all; it would, moreover, set the revelation of the Spirit, as a separate one, by the side of that of the Son.—**Things to come.**—See notes on ver. 12. [*Τὰ ἐρχόμενα* are especially the eschatological doctrines scattered through the Acts and the Epistles and most fully in the Apocalypse; see Rev. i. 1; xxii. 6, 20.—P. S.]

[Ver. 14. **He will glorify me,** *ἐκεῖνος ἐμὲ δοξάσει*.—The Son reveals and glorifies the Father, the Spirit reveals and glorifies the Son. *ἐκεῖνος* is emphatic and clearly implies, as this whole discourse does, the personality of the Holy Spirit. *ἐμέ* is also emphatic. The Spirit alone gives us a living knowledge of Christ as our Lord and Saviour, and makes us partakers of His very life and all His benefits. The sole aim of the Son is to glorify the Father, the sole aim of the Spirit to glorify the Son. A mysterious rivalry, so to speak, of divine love, whose very essence is to do all for the beloved. How much more should man's sole aim and end be to glorify God.—P. S.]

For He will take of what is Mine [ὅτι ἐκ τοῦ ἐμοῦ λήμψεται καὶ ἀναγγελεῖ ὑμῖν].—This, too, in reference to what the Spirit shall proclaim. Everything that shall appear until the arrival of the great Epiphany, is not only actually enclosed in Christ, but also germinally expressed in His word. [Alford: "This verse is decisive against all additions and pretended revelations subsequent to and besides Christ; it being the work of the Spirit to testify and to declare *the things of Christ*, not anything new and beyond Him. And this declaration is coincident with inward advance in the likeness and image of Christ (2 Cor. iii. 17, 18), not with a mere external development." Comp. also Wordsworth *in loc.*—P. S.]

Ver. 15. **All things that the Father hath,** *etc.* [Πάντα ὅσα ἔχει ὁ πατήρ, ἐμά ἐστιν· διὰ τοῦτο εἶπον ὑμῖν ὅτι ἐκ τοῦ ἐμοῦ λαμβάνει καὶ ἀναγγελεῖ ὑμῖν].—As the entire ante-Christian revelation of the Father, through the medium of the creation and the Old Testament, is embraced in Christ (Col. ii. 3, 9; 2 Cor. i. 20), so Christ is also the source of the entire post-Christian development of the new world until the Epiphany, together with all the revelations concerning that advent. *Jesus Christ, the same yesterday, to-day, and forever,* Heb. xiii. 8.

[Here again, as in ch. xv. 26, we have an incidental, but all the more convincing argument for the Trinity, both in its internal relation, as a living intercommunion and interpenetration of Father, Son, and Spirit in self-communicating infinite love, and in its external, self-revealing action upon the world for its salvation. The essential unity of Father, Son, and Spirit is implied in πάντα—ἐμά ἐστιν and ἐκ τοῦ ἐμοῦ, the tri-personality is clearly taught in the verbs ἔχει of the Father, εἶπον of the Son, λαμβάνει and ἀναγγελεῖ of the Spirit. Christ distinguishes Himself both from the Father and from the Spirit, and yet claims the whole fulness of the Father (πάντα ὅσα ἔχει), as His own (comp. Col. ii. 3), and communicates His fulness to the Spirit. The unlimited πάντα reveals His consciousness of the astounding grandeur of His person and mediatorial work. At the same time we must infer from this passage a certain subordination, not indeed of essence (for this is one and the same, and is incapable of division or multiplication), but of dignity and office; for the Son derives His life from the Father (comp. ch. v. 26 ἔδωκεν τ. υἱῷ ζωὴν ἔχειν ἐν ἑαυτῷ), and the Spirit takes and receives His fulness from the Son. The present λαμβάνει (the true reading against λήψεται of Elz., which is a correction from ver. 14) indicates a standing relation and permanent function, which necessarily precedes the future ἀναγγελεῖ and refers, like the future δοξάσει and λήμψεται, ver. 14, to the economical Trinity, the pentecostal and post-pentecostal action of the Spirit in His relation to the exalted Saviour and to the Church. Calvin correctly: "*Hic non tam de arcana et intrinseca, ut sic loquar, potentia disserit quam de injuncto sibi erga nos officio. Denique suas divitias prædicat, ut nos ad fruendum invitet.*" Olshausen: "This passage has special importance for the proper conception of the Scripture doctrine of the Trinity (comp. Matt. xxviii. 19), in that it clearly exhibits the *living, interexistence* of Father, Son and Spirit, and is equally opposed to the Arian subordination and to a mechanical, wooden, though orthodox co-ordination of the persons of the trias." Meyer explains the whole passage: "I have a full right to designate the *divine* truth which He (the Spirit) will reveal as *My* property, for all which the *Father* has, *i. e.*, according to the context, *the whole possession of the truth of the Father* (*der gesammte Wahrheitsbesitz des Vaters*) belongs to *Me* as the Son who was in intuitive communion with the Father (i. 18), who came out from the Father (viii. 42), who am consecrated (x. 36) and sent to fulfil His work, who also continually live and move in the Father and the Father in Me (xvii. 10). Observe the emphatic and comprehensive πάντα ὅσα, as the major proposition to the conclusion from the general to the particular; hence the less to be restricted to the announcement of the *future* (with Grotius and Hengstenberg)." Alford: "This verse contains the plainest proof by inference of the orthodox doctrine of the Trinity."—P. S.]

DOCTRINAL AND ETHICAL.

1. The first subject which has engaged our attention is the relation which the disciples sustain to the departure of the Lord, chap. xiii. In reference to this the καινὴ ἐντολή is given them. Then follows an intimation of relation to the Lord in heaven. In view of that, they have received the promise of the Holy Ghost; first as the Spirit of Christ and the Church in general, subsequently as the Spirit of knowledge and enlightenment, chap. xiv. By means of this Spirit they are to abide in Christ, like the branches in the vine, in order to the production of true fruit. In order, first, to the production of brotherly love, the specific fruit of Christianity. This brings us to a consideration of the mutual relationship of the disciples, and, further, to their attitude towards the ungodly hatred of the world. In view of this latter, the Holy Ghost is promised them, as the Spirit of martyr faithfulness, chap. xv. 26-xvi. 6. After which, their relation to the divine destiny of the world is treated of. In order to the realization of this, the Spirit of victorious strength, mighty to the overcoming of the world, is promised them, chap xvi. 7-11. Finally, the discourse turns upon their relation to the development of Christianity in the world and the development of the world in Christianity, a process to continue until the consummation of all things. In reference to this last-named relationship, they receive the promise of the Spirit of apocalyptical annunciation, chap. xvi. 12-16. It is then promised them that they shall celebrate a new life in spiritual communion with Christ, chap. xvi. 17-27; and in conclusion the Lord bestows upon them a momentary foretaste of the Pentecostal feast, with a view to strengthening them for His departure, chap xvi. 28-33.

2. Chapter xv. contains a dissertation upon the glorification of this present life through its conversion into an heavenly one, by means of

that spiritual fellowship with the heavenly Christ which is enjoyed by the disciples here. This heavenly life shall be revealed in a two-fold manner: (1) by the cordial brotherly love and fellowship of Christians; (2) by the fact that they, by their spiritual life, excite the hatred of the whole ungodly world, yet manfully stand their ground against it and overcome it with the testimony of Christ, in the strength of the Holy Spirit.

3. CHRIST THE REAL VINE. *Earthly things mere shadows and similitudes of heavenly realities.*—The most prominent symbols of Israel in the Old Testament are the palm tree (see Ps. xcii. 12), the olive tree (Jer. xi. 16), and especially the vine, or the vineyard (see Gen. xlix. 11; Is. v. 1 and the New Testament parallels; Jer. ii. 21; Ezek. xvii. 6, 7, 8, *etc.*). The vine, first cultivated and improved by Noah, though he was not the first to drink of its fruit (Matt. xxiv. 38; see *Calwer Naturgeschichte*), was especially fitted to be the symbol of Israel by the contrast of its insignificant appearance and its fine and generous nature (baseness and dignity); by the contrast of its immense need of culture and training and its generous fruit which not only refreshes, but inspirits man; by the contrast of its useless, dead wood and the fulness of blessing which waits upon its living branches; by the fair shade of its magnificent leaves, the sweet perfume of its delicate blossoms, the healthful, even healing refreshment of its generous clusters, the festive effect of its juice and its wine upon the human intellect and heart (Ps. civ.); by the contrast of its natural tendency to put forth its strength in luxuriant branches and its tendency when under cultivation, to bear rich fruit; finally, by the contrast of its misgrowth as evidenced by sour, wild grapes and its thriftiness as evinced in sweet, ripe clusters. But being the symbol of Israel, it is also, together with Israel itself, the symbol of the New Testament kingdom of God. Hence Christ is the real Vine in respect of His connection with mankind, in particular, the believing portion of mankind, the Theocracy, the kingdom of God, the Church. In this figure there appears the true idea of the universe, and particularly of the kingdom of God. It is a noble plant; hence it demands the care which we perceive to have been exercised by divine Providence in the history of the world, and it is destined to bring to maturity the precious fruit of refreshment to the human heart, the fruit of the divine and blessed life of love, the fruit of heavenly, festal mirth and joy attendant upon that life. But the simile, as enlarged upon in the text, will be our best informant as to the manifold relations of the life of Christ, adumbrated in the symbol of the vine. Believers are regarded as the branches, in respect of their close connection with the Lord. Their need of suffering finds a parallel in the demand of the branches for the pruning knife. Their remaining in the Vine is considered as a remaining in it, not in respect of the external connection of the wood simply, but in respect of the internal connection consisting in the fruit-bearing impulse; in view of this latter connection, the wild wood on the vine itself is degenerate and must needs be lopped off. Finally, the exceeding combustibility of the withered branches which have been cut off, is taken into consideration. See the EXEGETICAL NOTE.

It is worthy of remark still further, that the figure of the Vine has not the following for its meaning alone: viz. the Father hath planted Christ in mankind; its full sense is this: He hath made Him the foundation of mankind and the world; He hath made Him the principle and the centre of them. It is apparent at once that the parable has a special bearing upon the contrast of the disciples who have remained faithful, and Judas.

The figure of the Vine and the Branches is supplemented in reference to other of Christ's relations to His people, by the symbols of the Shepherd and the Flock, the Head and the Members, the Corner-stone and the Stones built upon it, the Bridegroom and the Bride.

4. *Without Me ye can do nothing.* The Christian life is so entirely dependent upon Christ, so entirely and organically dependent, that a man can accomplish nothing Christ-like and God-like without the most cordial connection with Christ. We might go still further and affirm: without the Logos no man can do anything at all, not so much as exist (Heb. i. 3); but here we are speaking of a doing of the Vine. And as, on the one hand, this doing is purely dependent on Christ, so, on the other hand, it is an organic co-living, co-working with the Vine, not a mere efficiency through mechanical impulsion. The passage is, in truth, utterly subversive of the views entertained by Pelagius; at the same time, however, it does not confirm the Augustine doctrine in its extravagances.

5. *Love* is the source of the Vine and its history. The love of the Father to the Son appears in the figure of the Vine-tiller who hath planted the Vine and tendeth it; the love of the Son to the disciples is revealed in His appropriation of them to Himself as His branches and His communication to them of His heart's life. They must prove themselves to be true branches by fruits of love. Christ now adds warnings to the consolations hitherto presented by Him.

6. *But as the fire of the grape is evinced by its producing a joyous enthusiasm, so the fire of Christ's love is manifested in the joy of His Holy Spirit; and it is designed to be manifested as the spirit of joy in and through the disciples also,* vers. 11-17. First as a mutual brotherly love. It is conjointly only that the single clusters, the single branches, make the wine of joy.

7. *Abide in My love.*—*I. e.*, continue to experience and contemplate My love. This is the idea of justification by faith. It is conditional upon the keeping of Christ's commandments, *i. e.* obedience to His word. The justification of the disciples, ver. 9, rests in the righteousness of Christ, ver. 10. They develop in perfect joy, or in the life of the Holy Ghost and the fruits of brotherly love. See Note on clause 2 of ver. 10.

8. Love, as joy in personal life (a prototype of that rapture which is the effect of the vine, Ps. civ.), is exercised in the centering of a man's aspirations upon the living of a life in the Spirit, hence, also, upon the perfect joy of a mind fully conscious of fellowship with God and Christ,

and of the possession of eternal life in the kingdom of love.

9. The farewell discourses a foretaste of the Pentecostal feast. See Note on ver. 15.

10. Servant and friend. See Notes on vers. 14 and 15.

11. Love being the gravitation of hearts and minds, in personal conduct, towards the centre of all personal life, it is thence evidenced that it is a fundamental characteristic of the world to *hate*, for, as an ungodly world, it gravitates, with a perverted force, toward the finite, toward things impersonal or unsubstantial, out into darkness and into the midst of death. Hate stands in the centre of evil betwixt falsehood and death, just as love occupies the centre of good between light and life. And as these last three characteristics are the fundamental traits of Christ, so, in like manner, the first three are the characteristics of the Prince of this world (John viii. 44) and, hence, of the world itself. Now if its peculiar propensity be to hate, it is natural that this propensity, diametrically opposed as it is to the Spirit of Christ, should first attain to full development by feeding upon Him and then spend itself upon the disciples.

12. The consummation of sin, in view of the word of Christ, ver. 22. Unbelief the second fall.

13. *Promise of the Holy Ghost* (see Note to ver. 26). The disciples have need of Him: (1) that they may not be overcome by the hatred of the world; (2) that they may overcome the world with the Spirit of love.

14. The shame and sufferings of Christ fraught, for His disciples, with the peril of becoming offended at Him; a peril made manifest in its full magnitude by the night of passion; rendered impotent, however, as far as His people were concerned, by His warning proclamation. See Note to chap. xvi., ver. 1.

15. *Christ must needs go away, in order that the Holy Ghost might come.* His departure was not necessary, as some might think, simply because He had to send Him, for He was perfectly able to summon Him hither while Himself still abiding in this world; it was necessary that His disciples should, from viewing Him with the eye of sense, come to look upon Him with the eye of the spirit; that they should pass from a contemplation of separate details of His life to the view of it as a total. He must be completely withdrawn from them, in order to become fully alive in them and to be formed in them. They must first despair utterly of His external glory, before His inward and eternal glory could arise upon them.—They must be completely submerged in the depths of their inner selves, in order that they might be fully translated into Him. See *Leben Jesu*, II. 1379.

16. The *personality* of the Holy Spirit. The three great operations of the Holy Ghost at His coming. See Notes on vers. 8-11.

17. The work of the Holy Ghost in its relation to the work of Christ. See Notes on vers. 12, 13. On the theological distinction of four offices of the Holy Ghost see works on doctrinal theology.

HOMILETICAL AND PRACTICAL.

Christ's parable of the Vine, and its interpretation: 1. As expressive of the Christian's cordial, vital fellowship with Christ; 2. of his faithful fellowship of love with the brethren; 3. of his firm fellowship of salvation with the hating world; 4. of his victorious spiritual fellowship with the Holy Ghost.—Heavenly things not symbols of earthly things, but the converse.—How does Christ found His heaven upon earth?—Saying concerning the Vine: 1. The Vinedresser and His ministry; 2. the Vine and its operations; 3. the branches and their work; 4. the fruit and its effect.—The genuine and the false branches, or the difference between a merely extrinsic connection with Christ and a lively connection, grounded within, at the same time that it is outwardly evident.—The solemn position of the Christian in the figure of the branch: 1. Dependence upon Christ is the condition of his life (without Me, *etc.*); 2. he must be purged by the Father's knife (ver. 2); 3. he may lapse from his connection with the Vine and go to destruction (may run wild, be lopped off, cast away, dried up, gathered, burnt); 4. he must evidence his branchhood by the noblest fruit.—The solemn and glorious position of the Christian in the figure of the branch: 1. The solemn position: see the foregoing remarks; 2. the glorious position: *a.* a planting of God, an object upon which God's eye ever rests; *b.* one with Christ in a historical and spiritual connection; a partaker in His salvation and His Spirit; *c.* one with all the faithful in the communion of salvation and the Spirit; *d.* destined to refresh and rejuvenate the fainting world in her sickness and hour of death.—The wine of love is designed to inspire the world, worn out with hatred, with new vigor.—The great and decisive difference between true and false branches: 1. The outward semblance of similarity (or the semblance of superiority on the part of the wild shoots); 2. the inward difference: *a.* these spend themselves in the finest and most precious fruit, those in the most useless wood; *b.* these kindle a beautiful fire of life, those are consumed in the flame of death.—As the vine is more a child of the heavenly sun than of the earthly soil, so is the Christian.

The abiding in Christ: 1. Whereby conditioned: the keeping of His commandments, *i. e.* the preservation of His word in the obedience of faith; 2. Wherein consisting: in abiding in the contemplation and experience of His love; 3. How blessed: with the blessing of the word, with the blessing of prayer, with the blessing of the work, of joy, of the Spirit.—Christ's love to His people, the model for their brotherly love: 1. The greatness of His love (in laying down His life); 2. the cordiality and intimacy of His love (friends); 3. the freedom of His love (chosen you); 4. the holiness of His love (established you that ye might bring forth fruit).—It is only in the faithful exercise of brotherly love that Christians overcome the hatred of the world.—The attitude of Christians towards the hatred of the world: 1. They think on the experience of the Lord (clear view); 2. on their vocation (valiant imitation); 3. on the guilt of the world (steadfastness in being hated without a cause); 4. on the Holy Ghost's office as Witness (faithful martyrdom).—The world's hatred of witnesses of the Gospel: 1. A hatred of Christ; 2. a hatred of the Father; 3. a suicidal hatred of the cause of her own life.—The flight of the world before the power of personal life: 1. From the truth of it (Pantheism); 2. from the demonstration of it (unbelief of the Gospel); 3. from the founding of it (turning away from the love-kingdom of Christianity).—The witness-ship of the faithful in the witness-strength of the Holy Ghost: 1. This witness-ship calls for this witness-strength; 2. this witness-strength demands this witness-ship. —The Lord's warning against offence at His shame and cross.—The excommunication and outlawry to which the world sentences the witnesses of Jesus: 1. In a (brutal or polished) secular form; 2. in ecclesiastical form; 3. in a sectarian form.—That ye may remember, ver. 4.

Christ's home-going in its two-fold effect upon the disciples: 1. In its deeply distressing effect upon their natural feeling; 2. in its highly exalting effect upon their life of faith.—The departure of the first Comforter, the arrival of the second.—Why must it be that Christ must go away? See the DOCT. and ETH. NOTES.—The infinitely quiet and secret, and yet all-powerful, victorious entry of the Holy Ghost into the world.—His office 1. In the world: an office of attesting, convincing, reproving and judging; 2. In the Church: an office of guiding, explaining, revealing, and of glorifying Christ.

The convincing and convicting of the world: 1. In respect of its subject: *a.* of the one sin in which all sins are embraced; *b.* of the one righteousness wherein all righteousness is manifested and fulfilled; *c.* of the one judgment in which all judgments are decided and grounded. 2. In respect of its effect: the convincement of men's opinions, minds, consciences, hearts.

How the Holy Ghost leads the children of truth into all truth: 1. He leads them, not away from Christ (roving, visionary spirits), but unto Christ (Spirit of the Church); 2. He adheres to gospel words and facts and explains them (whatsoever He shall hear); 3. He unfolds what there is of a prophetic nature in Christian truth—the love of the future; 4. He glorifies the Christ to come in the present of the Church's life.—The Holy Ghost as the Mediator of the perfect community of possessions existing between Christ and Christians.—How He conducts them into the whole inheritance of God, ver. 15.

On the Gospel for the Sunday after Ascension Day, chap. xv. 26-xvi. 4. Pray for the coming of the Spirit when the hatred of the world arrays itself against you.—For this hottest of temptations, God affords help by the sending of the Holy Spirit.—The martyrdom of Christians begins simultaneously with the true Christianity of the Spirit.—The coming of the Holy Ghost considered with reference to the riches of His names: 1. The (other) Mediator; 2. the (other) Helper; 3. the (other) Awakener; 4. the (other) Comforter.—The marvellous coming of the Comforter: 1. How it adds new sufferings to the old ones (the sufferings of the martyrs); 2. how it transforms the old sufferings together with the new ones into joy.—The martyrdom of true Christianity and the inquisition of false.—The ban of the sanctuary and the ban of fanaticism. —The cross of patience and the cross as the standard of persecution (crusades against the Albigenses and Waldenses).—The horrible festivals of faith of religious persecutions (*autos-da-fe*: in a broader sense "festivals of faith").—The perseverant patience of the Saints.

On the Gospel for the Fourth Sunday after Easter, chap xvi. 5-15. The sending of the Holy Ghost: 1. Dependent upon a painful condition (the departure of Christ); 2. glorious in its intrinsic value (victory over the world); 3. heavenly in its aim (the communion of the Holy Ghost, the glorification of Christ, the communion of goods with the Father).—As all the sad moments in the life of Jesus have been changed into joyful ones, so it is with His departure: 1. How this holds good with regard to all the earlier moments (His birth in poverty, His pilgrimage under the form of a servant, His death on the cross); 2. and how it is specially applicable to His going home through the medium of His departure from earth.—The Ascension, viewed under its two-fold aspect: 1. Wrapped in the gloom of Good Friday,—one with Good Friday; 2. bathed in the light of Easter and Pentecost,—one with Easter and Pentecost.—Christ's going away—or not until Christ went away, did He come to us in His most glorious form.—How the Lord meets His disciples' extreme depression (which does not so much as venture the question: Whither goest Thou?) with the loftiest elevation of His spirit (the word: It is expedient for you).—Weaning of the babes of the Spirit, ver. 7.—Wonderful relation between Christ and the Holy Ghost: 1. Christ must go in order that the Spirit may come; 2. the Spirit is not permitted to speak of Himself, to the end that Christ may remain.—The office of the Comforter an office of reproving: 1. True reproof as a comforting; 2. true consolation as a reproving. —The operations of the Spirit: 1. In the world (vers. 8-11); 2. in the Church (vers. 12-15).

STARKE: ZEISIUS: Just as a vine-dresser treateth his vine, doth the Heavenly Father deal with the Lord Christ in His bitter afflictions, and He dealeth even thus, in measure, with all His faithful people.—LUTHER: God is a Master who possesseth the art of making things that are meant for our hindrance and injury turn to our advancement and profit; whatsoever would kill us, must conduce to our life; whatsoever would plunge us into sin and condemn us, must aid in strengthening our faith and hope, in adding power to our prayer, and bounty to the answering of it.—HEDINGER: If God lay not the knife to the vine, its strength is consumed in useless shoots.—The word of the gospel the blessed means of bringing men to a condition of purification.—ZEISIUS: O the dignity, O the glory, of being a branch on the living Vine!—Love and obedience are bound up together.—CANSTEIN: The love of God, of Christ and of a Christian maketh a three-fold cord that never can be broken.—O inexpressible felicity, to be exalted to the friendship of God!—HEDINGER: Christ will have no forced selection of men, no soldiers by compulsion, no timorous slaves, but children, brethren, friends.—CANSTEIN: The dignity of being God's friend, James ii. 3. Rom. viii. 15. —The gospel does not make slaves, but freemen, children, heirs.—On ver. 16. Grace doth in all things anticipate us.—1 Pet. ii. 12, 16.—Blessed is the man whom God loveth, though the whole world hate him.—A Christian is a cross-bearer.—The member must conform to the example of the Head.—Ver. 23. That which is done to the Lord Jesus and His members, be it good or evil, is done unto God Himself.—Ver. 24. The greater unbelief, the heavier damnation. — LUTHER: There is no vice and no wickedness to which the world is so inimical as to the name of Christ and His gospel.—Ver. 27. A Christian should bear witness to Christ by word and by confession, by his life and walk, and by suffering, and that with a single view to God's honor.—On chap. xvi. 1; Luke viii. 13.—ZEISIUS: As Cain persecuted Abel, so the false Church still persecutes the true, so misbelievers still persecute true believers, hypocrites and mouth-Christians those who are Christians in sincerity, Gal. iv. 29.—Ver. 5. *Ibid.:* The whole Christian life a constant going to the Father.—Ver. 8. HEDINGER: The Spirit is not idle.—ZEISIUS: Everything, from the highest to the lowest, is subject to the Holy Ghost in His office of Reprover.—The reproving office of the Holy Ghost is as necessary to men as salt is to meat.—Ver. 9. Unbelief is a sin such as reason knows nothing of; the Holy Ghost must make it manifest.—Unbelief a cause of all sin, distress and misery in time and eternity.—Ver. 12. CANSTEIN: Faithful preachers must, in the execution of their office, have regard to the condition of their hearers, that they may discover what they are able to comprehend.

HEUBNER: Spiritual strength flows from Christ into believers as really as sap from the stem penetrates into the branches.—The Father, the efficient cause of the entire redemptive provision in Christ; He hath set and planted and tended Christ.—Pruning is painful; it is effected by grievous trials, but it is good and salutary, more blessed than to be lopped off and cast away.—Ver. 6. If it is a sad and menaceful thing to see one's physical strength declining, and sensibly to draw nearer dissolution, what must spiritual consumption and decay be.—Ver. 7. Steadfast abiding in Jesus: Jesus calls it the hearing of prayer, because everything in a man who has a living religion, turns to prayer—his thoughts, *etc.*—Jesus' friendship the reward of the faithful.—Ver. 15. A notable test of friendship—not to be making many presents, but to open the heart, to give that; that is more than to bestow all riches. —My openness towards another is a decisive mark of the confidence that I place in him. Jesus revealed to the apostles whatsoever He had heard from the Father; His most sacred thoughts, emotions, sentiments, therefore—the whole counsel of God.—Vers. 1-16. The cordial and intimate connection of Jesus with His people.—Vers. 17-27. An exhortation to patience even amidst persecutions.—Ver. 17. The very *commands* of Jesus are love.—It is a great consolation for a persecuted, hated Christian to know that he has a like fate with Jesus. There is then, thus teaches Christ, a hatred towards Him, an antipathy to His person. To imagine that these were possible only in the case of personal acquaintance with Jesus, would be to judge superficially. Hate has an intellectual spring in intellectual beings; to this day there exists hatred toward Jesus.—Ver. 27. *And ye also shall bear witness.* This passage is manifestly discriminative of a double testimony of the Apostles: a divine and a human testimony (inspired testimony and that founded upon what had come under their own observation).—Chap. xvi. 1, 2. A description of the sufferings of the first confessors of Christ, in particular, the martyrs (in the note, p. 457); *a register of the histories of the martyrs.*—Are religious persecutions to be laid to the charge of Christianity? No.—Religion, the supreme good, is exposed to the utmost abuse; to the danger of being made a cloak for malice and hate and the shedding of blood.—*Gospel for the Sunday after Ascension Day.* Chap. xv. 26-xvi. 4.—How Christ has been glorified in His Apostles. The call of the ancient martyrs to the later Christian world.—Chap. xvi. 6. There is a true and a false grief at separation from our friends.—Vers. 5-15. The divine enlightenment of the Apostles a fruit of Christ's departure.—Brotherly correction a duty of love. —The ministry of reproof of Christian teachers.

GERLACH: The glorification of God centres in the prosperity of the Church of Christ.—The redeemed disciple is Jesus' friend, without thereby ceasing to be His servant (*that* he is then, however, in a higher sense).—Chap. xvi. *He will not speak of Himself.*—These words are an irrefragable testimony to the personality of the Holy Ghost.

BRAUNE: Everything that one friend can say to another concerning the spirit of the Christian Church, concerning the harmony in which she must live, her purity of morals, activity in love and increasing illumination, concerning the confidence which she must needs possess, and her separation from the wrong, is here uttered in the trustful tone of parting love (Herder).—Purification is not effected without pain; even vine-branches are said "to bleed," when they are pruned.—Only let no breach be made in the bond of peace through vain glory or wrangling; else will prayer in Jesus' name be hindered, everything will become worm-eaten and go to destruction (Rieger).—On Chap. xvi. 2.—Ver. 7. *It is expedient for you that I go away.* A saying of wondrous magnitude.—The Spirit's work in regard to the world is comprised in the threefold operation of impressing her with a consciousness of *sin*, a consciousness of *the holiness of Christ*, the Redeemer from all sin, a consciousness of *the impotence of the Wicked One;* a conviction of the latter fact is adverse to the establishment of the devil's kingdom.

GOSSNER, ver. 2: Something must show itself; faithfulness must be evidenced; otherwise, if there be no result at all, a heavy judgment of God ensues.—Persecutors of Christians do not themselves constitute the vine-dresser; they are but pruning-knives; God is the Vine-dresser who guides the knife and casts it into the fire when it has entirely served His purpose (after Luther).—Ver. 3. *Through the word;* The branches derive their holiness (purity) from the

Vine.—Everywhere are all things ascribed to the word; not alone purification, as in this passage, but 1 Pet. i. 23 regeneration, Jas. i. 18, 21 the whole of salvation.—Ver. 4. This, the spiritual indwelling of Christ in us, is all-important.—Ver. 20. Either we must not profess to be servants of Christ, or we must put up with His cross. A good servant will not sit in the chimney-corner whilst his master's life is in jeopardy.—Ver. 24. Men do not care to have the name of haters of God, enemies of God; yet nevertheless, they put that name in practice in their works.—Vers. 26, 27. There are in the Church two inseparable witnesses for Jesus Christ: His Spirit and His word.—Chap. xvi. 2. This *hour*, when it is thought to be a species of religious service to persecute the truth and the witnesses for the truth,—this hour *is come; it is*, and it shall cease only with the end of the world. —Since the rise of the Spanish Inquisition, it has burnt, from the year 1481 to 1808, no less than 34,358 Christians in person and 10,049 in effigy, *etc.*—Unbelief. And so this or that thing is not the sin that damns thee. The Holy Ghost says: *this* is the sin,—that thou believest not on Jesus; this condemns thee.—Ver. 13. Such is the double office of the Holy Ghost: first He reproves and corrects, then He leads and guides, as a mother does her child.—All parties and sects, all speakers and gabblers, insist upon it that they have the Holy Ghost, and consequently demand that belief should be accorded to their words. But if we grasp for support these words of Jesus, we can repel them all, *etc.* Do but compare what they say with the word of Christ.

SCHLEIERMACHER: *Concerning the purifying—purging—of the branches.* The Lord has shown us in these words the uninterrupted progress of the Christian Church in purification, presupposing, at the same time, its continual development.—*Clean for the word's sake;* It is the whole connection of His words, a connection discoverable, of course, in every individual word of His.—The word was the only means by which He could unite men to Himself, just as it is our sole power of communication with each other. —If we would not be involved in the destiny of being sundered from connection with the divine and higher life, and of being profitable only through the ashes that remain of us—if we would not have it so, then must this be the great rule of our whole life: *without me ye can do nothing.*—The Lord here abolishes all those distinctions, so often made by men, between things spiritual and secular, things temporal and eternal. In whatever sphere of life we may be, our work, if done without Christ, is nothing; and its nothingness shall ever become more and more manifest. There is no strength or fruitfulness in aught without Him.—*The Comforter in His stead.* In all who believe on the name of the Lord, the strength of truth is to become a life and a continual activity, proper and peculiar to themselves. For this cause His bodily, personal presence must be withdrawn, to the end that, with the help and through the strength of the divine Spirit, all things that Christ had given them might develop into a peculiar (personal) life,—a life independently self-communicative and filling the whole human world with the same blessing.

BESSER: If the devil's ill-will were the only thing needful, he would soon lay his knife to our throats and stifle us with his manure and the stench of it. But God taketh him in his hand and saith: Devil, I know well that thou art a murderer and miscreant, but I will make such use of thee as I will; thou shalt be but My pruning-knife; the world and all that cleaveth unto thee shall be dung for My beloved vineyard, that it may prosper and improve (Luther).—If thou wilt not suffer the evil to be taken away from thee, thou wilt have to suffer thyself to be taken away (Bengel).—*To abide*—that is the whole. Constancy, says Bernard, is the king's daughter, the sum of the virtues and the perfection of them, *etc.* But what an affable and friendly command is this of His: *Abide in Me.*—The vine may live without the branches, and, instead of one that is cut off, may put forth three fresh ones, but the branch can not live without the vine.—Casting away, drying up, gathering, throwing into the fire, burning, are the five degrees of that judgment whose execution is dependent upon the long-suffering of God.—John is the faithful minister of the Comforter in the three grand departments of the latter: through his *Gospel* he reproves [convicts] the world concerning sin, righteousness and judgment, through his *Epistles* he guides it into all truth, through his *Revelation* he proclaims things to come.

On the Gospel for the Sunday after Ascension Day, chap. xv. 26–xvi. 24. SCHULTZ: What should be the conduct of the true Christian when experiencing the world's enmity to the kingdom of God.—RAMBACH: The persecutions of Christianity as a loud-tongued testimony to its worth.—GRUENEISEN: That our testimony and that of the Spirit belong together.—FLOREY: How edifying for us the memory of the martyrs of the first centuries of Christianity.—MUELLENSIEFEN (*Zeugnisse von Christo*, 1st collection, p. 101): Testimony to Christ: 1. How the Holy Ghost testifies of Christ; 2. how we, through the Holy Ghost, should testify of Christ.—KAPFF: The promise of the Holy Ghost: 1. How definitely bestowed by the Lord; 2. how much needed by us; 3. to whom fulfilled.—AHLFELD: The Holy Ghost is to testify of Christ, 1. in us; 2. through us.—STIER: The Holy Ghost's testimony to Christ: 1. How necessary for the world it was and is; 2. how it has really existed in the Church throughout all ages; 3. how it may and ought to be given through us also.—STEINHOFER: The government which, from His throne, the Lord Jesus exercises amongst men on earth: He leads us, 1. by His Spirit; 2. amidst the contradictions of the world; 3. to the glory of Himself and His Father.

On the Gospel for the Fourth Sunday after Easter, Chap. xvi. 5-15. DRAESEKE: Let not your heart be full of mourning.—HOSSBACH: The Redeemer's glorification in us through the Holy Ghost. —REINHARD: That God's Spirit reproves the world in our days just as emphatically as He ever did.—GÖRWITZ: What is requisite to make us regard our departure from the world as a going home to the Father?—W. HOFFMANN ("*Ruf zum Herrn*"): The Holy Ghost *testifies* of

Jesus; that is the beginning of His ministry to the world; He *glorifies* Jesus; that is the end and aim of His ministry to the believer.—STEINHOFER: The three principal things in which the Holy Ghost's operation and work upon the hearts of men appear. He labors at man's heart for the purpose of convincing him, 1. on account of sin, 2. on account of righteousness, 3. on account of judgment.—FUCHS: What consolation have we at the departure of our loved ones who have fallen asleep in the Lord?—AHLFELD: Rejoice ye at the arrival of the Comforter: 1. Rejoice, for the sake of Him who sendeth Him; 2. rejoice for the sake of what He doeth.—HEUBNER: The vocation of every true Christian, to reprove the world: 1. What is demanded by this vocation; 2. what binds us to it; 3. what renders us fit for it.—BURK: Want of faith in Jesus (Christ) the greatest, nay, the one only sin.—RAUTENBERG: *It is good for you that I go away;* A strong word of consolation: 1. from the mouth of the Redeemer; 2. from the mouths of departing redeemed ones.—*Ibid.:* That we are still unable to bear as much as the Lord hath to say to us.—HARLESS: The Holy Ghost's testimony against the world, at once reproof and comfort.

[CRAVEN: From HILARY: Ch. xv. vers. 1, 2. The *useless* and deceitful branches He cuts down for burning.—By pruning the branches we make the tree shoot out the more.—Ch. xvi. ver. 15. This unity hath no diversity; nor doth it matter from whom the thing is received, since that which is given by the Father is counted also as given by the Son.——From AUGUSTINE: Ch. xv. ver. 1. He says this as being the Head of the Church, of which we are the members, the Man Christ Jesus; for the vine and the branches are of the same nature.—Ver. 2. God's culture consists in extirpating all the seeds of wickedness from our hearts; in opening our hearts to the plough of His Word; in sowing in us the seeds of His commandments; in waiting for the fruits of piety; [and in pruning.]—*Every* branch; who is there so clean that he cannot be more and more changed? He cleanseth the clean, *i. e.* the fruitful, that the cleaner they be, the more fruitful they may be.—Ver. 3. Christ performs the part of the *husbandman* as well as of the *vine.*—Ver. 4. *Abide in Me and I in you*—not they in Him *as* He in them; the branches do not confer any advantage upon the vine, but receive their support from it.—*As the branch cannot bear fruit of itself, etc.* Great display of grace! He strengtheneth the hearts of the humble, stoppeth the mouth of the proud.—He who thinks he bears fruit in himself is not in the vine; he who is not in the vine is not in Christ; he who is not in Christ is not a Christian.—Ver. 5. *Without Me ye can do nothing;* He does not say, Ye can do *little.* —*Much fruit;* Christ, though He would not be the vine, except He were man, yet could not give this grace to the branches, except He were God. —Ver. 6. The branches are as contemptible, if they abide not in the vine, as they are glorious, if they abide.—One of the two, the branches must be in—either the vine or the fire.—Ver. 7. His words abide in us, when we *do* what He has *commanded,* and *love* what He has *promised.*—When His words abide in the *memory,* and are not found in the *life,* the branch is not accounted to be *in* the vine.—So far as we abide in the Saviour we cannot *will* anything that is foreign to our salvation.—Ver. 9. *As the Father hath loved Me, etc.;* This is the source of our good works,—they proceed from faith which worketh by love; but we could not love unless we were first loved.—The grace of a Mediator is expressed here.—Ver. 10. These words do not declare whence love arises, but how it is shown.—Ver. 11. What is Christ's joy in us, but that He deigns to rejoice on our account? And what is our joy, which He says shall be full, but to have fellowship with Him? He had perfect joy *on our* account, when He rejoiced in foreknowing and predestinating us; but that joy was not *in* us, because then we did not exist: it began to be *in* us when He called us. And this joy we rightly call our own, this joy wherewith we shall be blessed; which is begun in the faith of them who are born again, and shall be fulfilled in the reward of them who rise again.—Ver. 12. Where then love is, what can be wanting? Where it is not, what can profit?—This love is distinguished from men's love to each other as men, by the words, *as I have loved* you.—To what end did Christ love us but that we should reign with Him? —Vers. 13-15. Great condescension! Though to keep his Lord's commandments is only what a good *servant* is obliged to do, yet, if they do so, He calls them His *friends.*—Shall we therefore cease to be *servants* as soon as ever we are *good servants?* There are two kinds of servitude, as there are two kinds of fear. There is a fear which perfect love casteth out; which also hath in it a servitude, which will be cast out together with the fear. And there is another, a pure [filial] fear [and with it a filial servitude] which remaineth for ever.—Ver. 16. Ineffable grace! For what were we before Christ had chosen us, but wicked and lost?—He does not choose the good; but those, whom He hath chosen, He makes good.—Ver. 17. Love is this fruit (Gal. v. 22).—Vers. 18-21. Thou refusest to be in the body, if thou art not willing with the Head, to endure the hatred of the world.—Our Lord, in exhorting His servants to bear patiently the hatred of the world, proposes to them an example than which there can be no better and higher one, *viz.,* Himself.—Ver. 21. *For My name's sake; i. e. in you* they will hate *Me, in you* persecute *Me, your* word they will not keep because it is *Mine.* —Ver. 22. By *sin* here He means not every sin, but a certain great sin, which includes all, and which alone hinders the remission of other sins, *viz. unbelief.*—Vers. 23, 24. How could they hate one whom they did not know (ver. 21)? If the Jews were asked whether they loved God, they would reply that they did love Him, not intending to lie, but only being mistaken in so saying [through mistake as to His real character]. For how could they who hated the Truth, love the Father of Truth? They did not know that the Truth was born of God the Father, and therefore they did not know the Father Himself. Thus they both hated, and also knew not, the Father. —Ver. 25. A man hates *without a cause* who seeks no advantage from his hatred; thus the ungodly hate God.—Vers. 26, 27. The Holy Spirit by His testimony made others testify; taking away fear from the friends of Christ, and converting the hatred of His enemies into love.—Ch. xvi. ver. 4. *These things have I told you, that when the time shall come, ye may remember, etc.* The night of the Jews was not permitted to mix with or darken the day of the Christians.—Ver. 7. Christ departing in the body, not the Holy Ghost only, but the Father and the Son, came spiritually.—Ver. 9. It makes a great difference whether one believes *in* Christ, or only that He *is* Christ; for that He *was* Christ even the devils believed; but he believes *in* Christ, who both hopes in Christ and loves Christ. —Ver. 11. Satan is judged in that he is cast out; or, that he is destined irrevocably for the punishment of eternal fire.—Ver. 13. The Holy Spirit both teaches believers now all the spiritual things they are capable of receiving, and also kindles in their hearts a desire to know more.

[From CHRYSOSTOM: Ch. xv. ver. 2. By *fruit* is meant *life, i. e.* that no one can be in Him without good works.—Vers. 4, 5. Having said that they were *clean through the word which He had spoken,* He now teaches them that they must do their part.—*Without Me ye can do nothing;* the Son contributes no less than the Father to the help of the disciples.—Ver. 6. *Cast forth as a branch; i. e.* shall not benefit by the care of the husbandman: *is withered, i. e.* shall lose all that it desires from the root, all that supports its life, and shall die.—Ver. 8. He now shows that they themselves (true disciples) should be invincible, *bringing forth much fruit.*—Ver 11. As if He had said, If sorrow fall upon you I will take it away, so that ye shall rejoice in the end.—Ver. 15. All things, *i. e.* that they ought to hear.—Ver. 17. *These things* (vers. 13-15) *I command you that ye love one another;* I have said this (these things) not by way of reproach, but to induce you to *love one another.*—Ver. 18. As if to say, I know it is a hard trial, but ye will endure it, for My sake.—Ver. 19. He consoles them still farther by telling them, the hatred of the world would be an evidence of their goodness, so that they ought rather to grieve if they were loved by the world.—Vers. 19-21. Ye must not be disturbed at having to share My sufferings, for ye are not better than I.—Ver. 26. He calls Him not the *Holy Spirit* but the *Spirit of Truth,* to show the perfect faith that is due to Him.—Ch. xvi. ver. 7. *Nevertheless I tell you the truth, etc.*, as if He had said, Though your grief be ever so great, ye must hear how it is profitable for you that I go away.—— From GREGORY: Chap. xv. ver. 12. When all our Lord's sacred discourses are full of His commandments, why does He give the special commandment respecting love, if it is not that every commandment teaches love, and all precepts are one? As all the boughs of a tree proceed from one root, so all the virtues are produced from one love; nor hath the branch, *i. e.*, the good work, any life, except it abide in the root of love.—Vers. 12-15. The highest, the only proof of love is to love our adversary, as did the Truth Himself.—Our Lord came to die for His enemies, but He says that He is going to lay down His life for His friends, to show us that by loving, we are able to gain over our enemies, so that they who persecute us are by anticipation our friends.—Whoso in time of tranquillity will not give up his *time* unto God, how in persecution shall he give up his *soul?*—Ver. 19. The dispraise of the perverse is our praise.—He proves himself no friend to God who pleases His enemy; and He whose soul is in subjection to the Truth, will have to contend with the enemies of that Truth.—Chap. xvi. ver. 7. As if He said, If I withdraw not My body from your eyes I cannot lead you to the understanding of the Invisible, through the Comforting Spirit.——From ALCUIN: Chap. xv. vers. 4-7. All the fruit of good works proceeds from this root.—He Who hath delivered us by His grace, also carries us onward by His help.—*He that abideth in Me,* by believing, obeying, persevering, *and I in Him,* by enlightening, assisting, giving perseverance, *the same,* and none other, bringeth *forth much fruit.*——From THEOPHYLACT: Chap. xv. ver. 8. The *fruit* of the Apostles are the Gentiles.—Ver. 15. As if He had said, The servant knoweth not the counsels of his Lord; but since I esteem you friends, I have communicated My secrets unto you.——From DIDYMUS: Chap. xv. ver. 26. The Holy Spirit He calls the Comforter, a name taken from His office, which is not only to relieve the sorrows of the faithful, but to fill them with unspeakable joy.—Chap. xvi. vers. 13, 14. The Holy Ghost would lead them by His teaching and discipline into all truth, transferring them from the dead letter to the quickening Spirit, in whom alone all Scripture truth resides.

[From BURKITT: Chap. xv. vers. 1, 2. The *vine* doth most fitly symbolize Christ in His office for, and relation to, His people—1. As being weak, mean and small in outward appearance; 2. As being plentifully fruitful of sweet fruit; 3. In that the fruit thereof is *pressed* that it may be drink unto men; 4. As being the root from which all the branches derive their nourishment and fruitfulness.—The Father is *the husbandman,* He—1. ingrafts all the branches into this vine; 2. takes notice what store of fruit every branch brings forth; 3. daily tends His vineyard that it may bring forth fruit abundantly.—There are two sorts of branches, some fruitful, others unfruitful; some are branches only by external profession [mechanical connection], others by real implantation [ingrafting].—The true touchstone whereby to discern one sort of branches from another, is not by the fair leaves of profession [not by connection with the church], but by the substantial proofs [fruits] of a holy conversation.—In the most fruitful branches there remains much corruption to be purged out.—The Husbandman's hand manages the pruning knife of affliction; He had rather see His vine *bleed* than *be barren.*—Such branches as, after all the Husbandman's care, remain unfruitful, shall be finally cut off and cast away, as was Judas.—*He purgeth it,* by His word and Spirit, by ordinances and providences, by mercies and actions [afflictions].—Ver. 3. Now *are ye clean;* such as are justified and [partially] sanctified, are in Christ's account *clean* notwithstanding their many spots.—*Through the word;* the *word* of Christ is the *instrumental* cause of a believer's cleansing.—Ver. 4. Abide in Me, and *I in you;* abide in Me, not only by an outward profession, but by a real and fiducial adherence, and I will abide in you by the influences of My Spirit.—The union between Christ and His members is mutual.—Believers themselves, without daily dependence on Christ and constant communications of grace from Him, can do nothing.—Ver. 6. Such as have had a long standing in God's vineyard, and contented themselves with a withered profession, are in danger of having God's blasting added to their barrenness.—Ver. 7. Observe here—1. A glorious privilege declared, *ye shall ask what ye will and it shall be done unto you;* 2. The condition of this privilege, *If ye abide in Me and My words abide in you.*—Ver. 8. Our Lord here exhorts His followers to a holy fruitfulness by a double argument—1. One drawn from the glory of God; 2. The other from their own advantage, *so shall ye be My disciples, i. e.* hereby ye shall have evidence and prove yourselves to be My disciples.—Ver. 9. What a comparison is here! As *the Father hath loved Me* so *have I loved you!* This love is—1. real; 2. operative; 3. eternal; 4. immutable.—*Continue ye in My love;* it should be the care of every Christian to preserve the sweet sense and inward diffusion of Christ's love in his own soul.—Ver. 10. As our obedience to Christ is the best evidence of our love to Him, so it is the best means to preserve us in the sense and assurance of His love to us.—Ver. 11. Our Lord declares the reasons of His urging fruitfulness on His disciples—1. *That His joy might remain in them, i. e.* that the joy He had in their holiness might remain with Him; 2. *That their joy* in Him *might be full,* this arises from the former.—Ver. 12. Christ's love unto believers is both an *obligation* unto mutual love, and a *pattern* for it.—Ver. 13. Christ's love in laying down His life for His people a matchless love.—Ver. 14. Christ invites His people to obedience by the honorable title of friends.—*Ye are My friends, etc.*—1. Actively, you will manifest yourselves to be My friends; 2. Passively, I will declare Myself to be your friend.—Learn 1. How condescending is the love of Christ—He calls His servants, friends; 2. How glorious the believer's relation to Christ; 3. How grateful [excellent] is obedience to Christ; 4. Our conformity to Christ consists, not so much in imitation of what He did, as in obedience to what He prescribed—some of His *actions* are *inimitable,* but all His *commands* are *obeyable;* 5. Nothing short of obedience will evidence the truth of our relation to Christ.—Ver. 15. *Henceforth I call you not servants, i. e.* not *mere* servants, not that they were to be exempted from obedience.—All Christ's disciples are His *servants;* and all His servants are His *friends,* in regard of intimate communion and tender usage.—After His resurrection He called them *brethren,* chap. xx. 17; the dignity of believers is a growing dignity—the longer they follow Christ, the higher privileges are accorded them.—Vers. 17-21. With what frequency and importunity our Lord pressed the duty of mutual love upon His disciples; from this learn—1. The great importance of the duty; 2. The great averseness of our hearts to its performance.—The argument our Saviour uses to press His disciples to mutual love, *viz.,* that the world would hate them.—The considerations propounded by Christ to comfort His disciples under the world's hatred—1. His own usage by the world; 2. This hatred is evidence that they are not of the world; 3. Their relation to Him as servants to a master; 4. The goodness of the cause for which they suffer, *viz.,* Christ's name's sake.—Ver. 19. *Ye are not of the world, but I have chosen you out of the world;* 1. The children of God, though *in* the world, are not *of* the world either in *Spirit* or *conversation;* 2. The difference between them and worldlings is of God's making.—Ver. 21. *For My name's sake;* the great quarrel of the world against the disciples of Christ, whatever may be pretended, is for *the Name of Christ.*—Ver. 22. Sins of ignorance are, as it were, no sins, compared with those committed against light.—Sins committed against gospel light are of aggravated guilt, as against the very remedy.—The gospel, where it is plainly preached, takes away all excuse from sinners.—Vers. 23-25. Let men pretend to never so much respect for God, yet if they hate Christ and despise His gospel, they are haters of God.—The miracles wrought by Christ surpassed all others in number, kind, and manner.—Chap. xvi. ver. 1. All afflictions are so trying that the best of Christians have need to be guarded against them lest they should be offended.—Ver. 2. The being under one trial will not shelter from another.—Ver. 3. Ignorance of the Father and the Son the ground of the world's hatred against Christians.—Ver. 4. Christ is so tender of His disciples, that He will not put them under the hardness of suffering until they be prepared for it.—Ver. 7. *It is expedient for you that I go away, etc.* The presence of the Holy Spirit *with* us is a greater comfort and advantage, than the presence of Christ in the flesh *amongst* us.—Vers. 8-14. Our Lord declares the advantages that would redound by the coming of the Comforter—1. To the world, vers. 8-11; 2. To the Apostles, ver. 13; To Himself, ver. 14.—Ver. 9. *Of sin, i. e.,* of their sinful state and nature, of the large extent of sin, and particularly of the sin of unbelief.—Ver. 10. *Of righteousness, i. e.,* of the insufficiency of all human righteousness, or (and) of a complete and perfect righteousness in Me imputable to sinners for their perfect justification.—*Because I go to My Father and ye see Me no more;* as though He had said—Hereby you may be satisfied that by My active and passive obedience [righteousness] I have fully satisfied my Father's justice for you, and you shall never be charged or condemned; because, when I go to heaven, I shall abide there in glory with My Father, and never be sent back again—*ye shall see me no more*—as I must have been, had anything been omitted by Me.—Ver. 11. *Of judgment, i. e.,* that Jesus is both Lord and Christ, that He had power to judge Satan, the prince of the world, and that He did by His death put down the kingdom of darkness.

[From M. HENRY: Chap. xv. There are four words to which our Lord's discourse in this chapter may be reduced: 1. Fruit, vers. 1-8; 2. Love, vers. 9-17; 3. Hatred, vers. 18-25; 4. The Comforter, vers. 26, 27.—Vers. 1-8. Christ discourses concerning the *fruit,* which His disciples were to *bring forth,* under the similitude of a *vine;* observe—I. The *doctrine* of this similitude: that—1. Christ is (1) the *vine, i. e., (a) planted,* not spontaneous, (*b*) having an unpromising outside, (*c*) a spreading plant, (*d*) whose fruit honors God and cheers man, (2) the *true* vine, as opposed to (*a*) counterfeit, (*b*) type; 2. Believers are the *branches, i. e.*, (1) *supported* by the unseen root, (2) many, (3) yet meeting in one root, (4) insufficient to stand (and be fruitful) of themselves; 3. The Father is the *husbandman, i. e.*, (1) the proprietor, (2) the *land-worker*, γεωργός, though the earth is the Lord's, it yields Him no fruit unless He *work* it, (3) *the* husbandman, having care of the *vine* and all the *branches*, by *planting, watering*, [*pruning*], and [thus] *giving the increase*. II. The *duties* taught us by this similitude—1. To *bring forth fruit;* this duty is urged by (1) the doom of the unfruitful, ver. 2; (2) the promise made to the fruitful, ver. 2 [increased culture in order to increased fruitfulness]; (3) the duty of showing forth the power of the benefits they have received, ver. 3; (4) the glory that will redound to God, ver. 8; (5) the comfort and honor that will come to ourselves, ver. 8, *so shall ye be my disciples;* 2. *To abide in Christ* in order to fruitfulness, consider (1) the duty *to abide in Christ* by faith, (2) the *necessity* of so doing in order to fruitfulness, vers. 4, 5; (3) the fatal consequence of forsaking Christ, ver. 6; (4) the blessed privilege of those who abide in Him, ver. 7.—Ver. 2. Farther fruitfulness is the blessed reward of former fruitfulness.—The purging of fruitful branches is the care and work of the great Husbandman, for His own glory.—Ver. 3. There is a cleansing virtue in the Word, as it works grace and works out corruption.—Ver. 4. The knot of the branch abides in the vine, and the sap of the vine abides in the branch, and so there is a constant communication between them.—Ver. 5. We depend upon Christ, not only as the *vine* upon the *wall* for support, but as the *branch* on the *root* for sap. —Ver. 6. *Withered;* They that bear no *fruit*, after a while will bear no *leaves.*—*Fire* is the fittest place for *withered* branches, for they are *good* for nothing else.—Ver. 7. See here—1. How our *union* with Christ is maintained, *by the Word;* 2. How our communion with Him is maintained, *by prayer.*—They that abide in Christ as their heart's delight, shall have through Christ their heart's desire.—If we *abide in Christ* and *His Word in us*, two things are promised—1, that we will not ask for anything but what is proper to be done for us; 2, that we shall have an answer of peace to all our prayers.—Ver. 8. The fruitfulness of all Christians is to the glory of God—1, By their good works many are brought to glorify God; [2. Good works manifest the beauty of His law, and the power of His gospel.—E. R. C.].—Vers. 9-17. Christ who is *Love* itself discourses concerning a fourfold love,—I. The *Father's love* to Him, He tells us that—1. The Father did love Him (ver. 9); 2. That He *abode* in His Father's love (ver. 10); 3. That He thus abode *because* He kept His Father's law (ver. 10). II. *His own love* to His disciples, though He *leaves* them He *loves* them: Observe—1. The *pattern* of this love, *as the Father hath loved Me, etc.;* 2. The *proofs* and *products* of this love, which are (1) His laying down His life for them (ver. 13), (2) His taking them into a covenant of friendship (vers. 14, 15), (3) His freeness in communicating His mind to them (ver. 15), (4) His *choosing* and *ordaining* them to be the prime instruments of His glory in the world (ver. 16). III. The *disciples' love* to Him, this is enjoined in view of His love to them; He exhorts them to—1. *Continue* in His love, *i. e.*, keep up their love; 2. *Evidence* their love by keeping His commandments. IV. The *disciples' love one to another;* this is (ver. 12)—1. Recommended by Christ's pattern; 2. Required by His precept. —Ver. 9. A strange expression of the condescending grace of Christ! *As* the Father loved Him who was most worthy, *so* He loved them who were most unworthy.—Ver. 10. Ye shall *abide* in My love, *as a dwelling-place.*—Ver. 13. This is the love wherewith Christ hath loved us, He is our ἀντίψυχος—*Bail for us*, body for body, life for life, though He knew our insolvency and foresaw how dear the engagement would cost Him.—The excellency of the love of Christ beyond all other love; others have *laid down* (passively) their lives, Christ *gave up* (actively) His. —Ver. 16. The treasure of the gospel was committed to the disciples that it might be—1. propagated; 2. perpetuated.—Those whom Christ ordains *should* and *shall* be fruitful.—*Whatever ye shall ask, etc.* Three things set forth for our encouragement in prayer—1. That we have a God to go to who is a Father; 2. That we have a good name to go in; 3. That an answer in peace is promised.—Vers. 18-25. Christ discourses concerning *hatred:* Observe—I. Who they are that *hate, viz., the world, i. e.*, the children of *this* world as distinguished from the children of God, called *the world* as indicating their —1. number, 2. confederacy, 3. spirit. II. Who they are that *are hated*—1. The disciples of Christ; 2. Christ Himself; 3. God the Father (vers. 23, 24).—Ver. 19. Whom Christ blesseth, the world curseth; the favorites of Heaven have never been the darlings of the world.—Ver. 20. The fruits of the world's hatred—1. persecution; 2. rejection of doctrine.—Vers. 19-21. The *causes* of the world's hatred against Christians—1. They do not belong to it; 2. They belong to Christ, *for my name's sake;* 3. Its ignorance of God.—Ver. 22. Observe—1. The excuse they have who have not the gospel; 2. The aggravated guilt of those who reject the gospel.—Vers. 23, 34. In hating Christ the world hates God; *deists* are in effect *atheists.*—Ver. 25. Enmity to Christ is unreasonable.—Vers. 26, 27. Christ speaks of the Comforter, promising—I. That He should maintain Christ's cause in the world notwithstanding all opposition. II. That the Apostles by His assistance should have the honor of being Christ's witnesses.—Ver. 26. The Spirit is spoken of as —1. A *Person;* 2. A *divine* Person *proceeding from* the Father.—The offices of the Spirit—1. One implied in His title *Comforter* or *Advocate;* 2. Witnessing for Christ.—Ver. 27. The Spirit's working is not to supersede, but to engage and encourage ours.—They are best able to preach Christ that have themselves been with Him; ministers must first learn Christ and then preach Him.—Chap. xvi. Christ by His words—I. *Wounds*, vers. 1-6: II. *Heals* by the assurances that He—1. Would send them the Comforter (vers. 7-15); 2. Would visit them again at His resurrection (vers. 16-22); 3. Would secure to them an answer of peace to all their prayers (vers. 23-27); 4. Was now returning to His Father (vers. 28-32); 5. By virtue of His victory over the world would give them peace in Himself.—Vers. 1-6. Christ dealt faithfully with His disciples when He sent them forth, for *He told them the worst* of it, that they might sit down and count the cost.—Ver. 1. The disciples of Christ are apt to be *offended at the* cross.—Our Lord by giving notice of trouble, designed to prevent its being a surprise; *Being forewarned we are forearmed.* —Ver. 2. Behold two swords drawn against the followers of Jesus, that of—1. Ecclesiastical censure; 2. Civil power.—Many a good truth has been branded with an anathema, and many a child of God delivered to Satan. God's people have suffered the greatest hardships from *conscientious* persecutors.—Ver. 3. The true reason of the world's enmity to Christians, *because they have not known the Father nor Me:* Note—1. Many that pretend to know God are ignorant of Him; 2. They that are ignorant of Christ cannot have any right knowledge of God.—Ver. 4. When sufferings come it will be of use to remember that Christ has told us of them.—As Christ in His sufferings had, so we in ours should have, an eye to the *fulfilling of the Scriptures.*—Vers. 5, 6. As though He had said, Instead of inquiring after that which will comfort, you pore upon that which looks melancholy.—An humble believing inquiry into the design and tendency of the darkest dispensations would help to reconcile us to them.—It is the common *fault* and *folly* of melancholy Christians to dwell only on the dark side of the cloud.—Nothing is a greater prejudice to our joy in God, than *the love of the world.*—Ver. 7. *It is expedient, etc.*—1. Those things often seem *grievous* that are really *expedient;* 2. Jesus is always for that which is *most expedient* for us. —The glorified Redeemer is not unmindful of His Church on earth—though He *departs,* He sends the *Comforter;* nay, He departs that He *may* send Him.—Ver. 8. *Convincing* work is the Spirit's work.—The *Comforter* begins His work by convincing—first opens the wound, and then applies the remedy.—Ver. 9. The Spirit convinces of *Sin,* its—1. fact; 2. folly; 3. filth; 4. fountain—*corrupt nature;* 5, fruit—*death.*—He fastens especially on the sin of *unbelief* as—1. The great *reigning* sin; 2. The great *ruining* sin; 3. That which is at the bottom of all sin.—Ver. 10. *Of righteousness, i. e.,* Christ's righteousness—1. His *personal* righteousness; 2. His righteousness communicated to us *for our justification.*—Christ's *ascension* is the great argument proper to convince men of this righteousness; if He had left any part of His work unfinished He had been sent back again.—Ver. 11. *Of judgment, because the Prince of this world is judged;* the devil was *judged,* was discovered to be a great deceiver and destroyer; judgment was entered against him and in part executed; he was *cast out*—1. from the heathen world, when his oracles were silenced and his altars deserted; 2. from the bodies of men *in Christ's name;* 3. from the souls of people by the grace of God working with the gospel of Christ; 4. *as lightning from heaven.*—A good argument wherewith the Spirit convinces of *judgment*—1. Of inherent holiness and sanctification, Matt. xii. 18; 2. of a new and better dispensation of things; 3. of the power and dominion of the Lord Jesus (Isa. xlii. 1-4); 4. of the final *day of judgment.*—Vers. 12-15. See what a teacher Christ is! None like Him for—1. copiousness; 2. compassion.—Vers. 13-15. The Spirit promised—1. To guide the apostles; 2. To glorify Christ.—To *guide,* taking care—1. That they should not miss their way; 2. That they should not come short of their end.—*Into all truth*—into —1. The whole truth; 2. Nothing but the truth. —The Spirit glorified Christ—1. By His coming; 2. By leading the disciples into the truth.

[From PRESIDENT EDWARDS: Chap. xvi. ver. 9. *Of sin, etc.* The greatest sin in the world is sin against the Gospel, contempt of and opposition to Christ; and the greatest evidence of man's sin is his ill treatment of Christ, His Gospel and followers.—Ver. 10. *Of righteousness, etc.* Christ's ascension was the brightest evidence that He had suffered wrongfully; it confirmed the righteousness of His words, doctrines, design in coming into the world, and promises.—Ver. 11. *Of judgment, etc.* It is the greatest evidence of Christ's might and kingly power to overcome and dethrone Satan; and the greatest manifestation of His high judicial authority to judge and condemn this great rebel, and to execute vengeance upon him.——From SCOTT: Chap. xv. ver. 1. The union of the divine and human nature in Christ, and the fulness of the Spirit in Him, resemble the *root* of the vine, deriving the fertilizing juices from a rich soil; and His mediatorial work, like the *stem,* conveys these to all believers.—Vers. 1, 2. As professed Christians, we *appear* to belong to this vine; but woe to them who have no other union than what consists in notions, sacraments, and forms.—Ver. 9. *As the Father hath loved Me, so, etc.* No love of man to his dearest *friend* ever was comparable to His love to us, when *strangers* and *enemies.*—Vers. 18-20. We cannot experience worse usage than our Master met with; and we ought not to be offended or grow weary of well-doing, if we meet with no better.—Chap. xvi. vers. 2, 3. How fallacious the opinion that God will accept every man who is *sincere* in his religion, whatever that religion may be.—Humble docility, implicit belief of Scripture, and a disposition unreservedly to do the will of God, are essential to *godly sincerity.*—Vers. 6, 7. Our hearts are often filled with sorrow at events highly advantageous.—Vers. 8, 12. *Sin, righteousness, and Judgment;* On these subjects all who would be honored as instruments in converting sinners, should be frequent, copious, alarming, encouraging, distinguishing; but in matters less essential they would do well, after the example of Christ, not to press them on their hearers before they *are able to bear* them.——From A PLAIN COMMENTARY (Oxford): Chap. xv. vers. 1, 2. *The vine* is a tree which not only admits of pruning, but whose very productiveness depends on the judicious use of the pruning-knife.—Delightful is it to find writers about the Grape-Vine, who had nothing less in view than the illustration of the Gospel, becoming our instructors in such passages as the following;—"It is hardly possible to plant a Vine in any situation in which it will not thrive . . . The truth is that the roots of the Vine possess an extraordinary power of adapting themselves to any situation in which they may be planted, provided it be a dry one. They will ramble in every direction in search of food, and extract nourishment from sources apparently the most barren. In short, they are the best caterers that can possibly be imagined; for they will grow, and even thrive luxuriantly, where almost every other description of plant or tree would inevitably starve. . . . *Pruning* and *Training* are so closely connected together, that they almost constitute one operation. In *pruning* a Vine, regard must be had to the manner in which it is afterwards to be *trained;* and, in *training* it, the position of the branches must, in a great measure, be regulated by the mode in which it has previously been *pruned.* . . . The *old wood* of a Vine is not only of no use, but is a positive injury to the fertility of the plant. . . . The sole object in view in pruning a Vine is to increase its fertility. . . . Although by pruning a Vine its fertility is increased, its existence is no doubt thereby shortened (?). The severing of a healthy branch from any tree is, without doubt, doing an act of violence to it; the effects of which are only overcome by the superior strength of the vegetative powers of its roots." (CLEMENT HOARE on the Cultivation of the Grape-Vine).—Ver. 5. *And I in him;* The branch bears fruit, not because it abideth in the Vine, but because *in it the Vine abideth.*—Ver. 12. Love ye one another even unto death, as even unto death I have loved you.—Ver. 15. *The servant knoweth not what his Lord doeth;* "It is not necessary that he should! The *common soldier* is neither expected nor permitted to know the plans of the commander." (ROBERT SCOTT).—Ver. 22. "He meaneth they had no color of plea, nothing to pretend by way of excuse." (SAUNDERSON).—Ver. 24. Without effort, by a mere word, He showed that all creation was obedient to His will; from Him, as from an inexhaustible fountain, flowed forth healing virtue equal to the needs of all.—Chap. xvi. ver. 7. What must be the value of that great blessing which was given to them, which is given to us, to compensate for the loss of His visible presence!—Ver. 8. "He shall so bring home to the world its own *sin,* My perfect *righteousness,* God's coming *judgment,* shall so *convince* it of these, that it shall be obliged itself to acknowledge them." (TRENCH).—Ver. 9. Under one great head of *unbelief* the guilt of the world is gathered up and comprised; *unbelief* is therefore a sin of the heart, not a mere error of the understanding: a *fault* not a *misfortune.*—Ver. 15. "Our God is One, or rather very Oneness, and mere Unity, having nothing but itself in itself, and not consisting (as all things do beside God) of many things. In which essential Unity of God, a Trinity personal nevertheless subsisteth, after a manner far exceeding the possibility of man's conceit. The works which outwardly are of God, they are of such sort in Him being One, that each Person (in the Divine Unity) hath in them somewhat peculiar and proper. For being Three, and they all subsisting in the essence of One Deity, *from* the Father, *by* the Son, *through* the Spirit, all things are. That which the Son doth hear of the Father, and which the Spirit doth receive of the Father and the Son, the same we have at the hands of the Spirit as being the last, and therefore the nearest unto us in order, although in power the same with the second and the first." (HOOKER.)

[From STIER: Chap. xv., vers. 1-6. Our Lord's language in reference to *the Vine and its branches* is connected by a three-fold foundation with the whole system of the sacred language of figures—1. *Nature* in itself; 2. The *prophetic phraseology* which interprets nature; 3. The recently instituted *Supper.*—"Since God was constrained to give His vineyard up to ruin, He separated for Himself this Vine, and designed it to be a beginning from which a great increase should take its rise." (LUTHARDT).—*Bread* and *wine* are correlated as the flesh and blood in man's personality; hence Christ is the bread of life, *the corn of wheat* in the general, inasmuch as from His *body* and *life* the Church is nourished, but as He gives His *life* to death for that purpose, and in His *blood* makes us especially partakers thereof, He is also the *Vine.* The juice of the grape, the juice of stem and branches generally which is to be glorified, as it were, into a spirituous energy, is, according to the profound phraseology of Scripture, the *blood* and *life* of the noble plant. [This "has its classical analogies in the αἷμα βοτρύων of Ach. Tatius, the *sanguis terræ* of Pliny, the *rivarum frigidus sanguis* of Cassiodorus."] Ver. 1. *The* true *Vine:* The Vine in nature is only a figure and symbol pointing to Me.—Vers. 1, 2. He explains that all the sufferings which both He and they should encounter are no other than (the manifestation of) the diligent care and watchfulness which a vine-dresser bestows upon the vine and its branches.—Vers. 1, 2. They are "Christians" (branches) who have the *Word and Sacraments,* but receive them in vain; and to these the preacher should earnestly apply this saying! They are indeed planted in the vineyard like that fig-tree, Luke xiii. 6—even grafted for a beginning into the Vine.—The *fruit* which the Vine-dresser desires is, in its general principle, only the consummation and ripening of our own regeneration; as the cluster, so to speak, is the glorified form and manifestation of the virtue of the branch.—Every thing here goes strangely against appearances! An inexperienced person might say, For what purpose is this crooked and unsightly tree in this beautiful garden? [And why] the unpitying cutting away of so many shoots seemingly so green and healthy?—*EVERY branch that beareth fruit, He purgeth, etc.:* Purging is applied without respect of person, sparing none, according to the vine-dressing rule which aims at fruit, and the utmost possible fruit.—Ver. 3. "That which is clean bears fruit; that which bears fruit becomes also (more) clean." (HILLER).—All the cultivation and care of disciplining grace is efficient only on the condition of our receiving and faithfully keeping His *word;* Christ, the Vine, at once begins by His word to cleanse, and thus is *Himself* the Vine-dresser.—Vers. 4, 5. *On Me* has become *in Me* inasmuch as the connection of the shoots with the stem is no mere *joining on,* but there is a participation of the same juice flowing from one into the other.—So act by your abiding *that* I, as I gladly would, may abide in you.—Without our abiding in Him, there is no abiding of the Lord in us; as without our receiving Him there is no such coming as ends in His indwelling.—"The question here is not of *external doing,* and general influence upon men, but of the holy power to save ourselves and others, through deliverance from sin and death." (SCHMIEDER).—Leaves and sour grapes are not *fruit.*—Ver. 6. Our Lord indicates "the stages of *apostasy* and *rejection*" (ZELLER)—1. The solitary ground (apostasy), *if a man abideth not in Me;* 2. the *five* stages of judgment, the accomplishment of which begins in time, is fulfilled in eternity—(1) casting forth (the *appearance of life* continuing), (2) withering (the *appearance of life* departed), (3) gathering, (4) casting into the fire, (5) burning.—Concerning the damned *the present* (καίεται) may always be used; they *burn*, or feed the fire.—Ver. 7. Only those who wilfully forsake Me can ever thus burn; only apart from Me ye can do nothing and fall to ruin, *In Me* ye can do all things!—If His *words* remain in us, His *prayer* pre-eminently remains in us.—Ver. 8. "This means not only that our works appear in the world honorable as good fruit, but that they are carried up to heaven and offered to God, so that He accepts them as His especial honor and highest service" (LUTHER).—Those may take courage whose *light* the people will not regard.—"Therein, that *ye bring forth much fruit*, is My *Father* glorified, and *I* shall have in you genuine disciples who will do *Me* honor." (KLING.)—Vers. 9, 10. The *common life*, which from the vine-stock pervades the branches and produces their precious clusters, is *love.* Love is the first root-principle in God, the first living germ in us; and *perfect love, as* God loves, is also the last ripe fruit.—We can think of nothing beyond this, nothing greater to be promised than that the love, in which the Father and the Son through the Spirit are eternally one, shall be poured out also in us.—All *love*, like all righteousness, is livingly imputed, communicated, and implanted in us at once, from the Father through Christ.—In Christ the eternal love of the Father appears as the sole, abiding, impulsive principle of all His life and suffering, of all His acts and of all His love.—Ver. 11. *My joy* is pre-eminently the joy which He Himself has, but then immediately the words *might remain in you* makes it the joy which He gives.—*Your joy* is by no means only their joy, 'joy in Him and in His work,' but the gladness in God which flowed from Him into them.—Vers. 12, 13. Our Lord graciously condescends so deeply to a comparison with our human relations, that He, as it were, leaves out of sight for a time the all-embracing, and in the solitary sense *atoning*, character of His death. "The Lord does not speak (primarily) of the redeeming design of His death, but of that point in great love which we may recognize and imitate." (RICHTER).—Jesus calls even sinners and enemies, whom He desires to save, His *friends*, inasmuch and because He is first their friend. "The love wherewith, according to St. Paul, He dieth for *sinners*, is at the same time the love whereby, according to St. John, He maketh the disciples His *friends.* He dies for sinners only because in the fulness of His love He regards them as friends." (LUECKE).—Ver. 15. The proof of the relation of friendship is that *open, confidential, unrestrained* communion, the typical expressions of which are found—in Abraham's case, Gen. xviii. 17—that of Moses, Ex. xxxiii. 11—of the pious generally, Ps. xxv. 14; Prov. iii. 32, *etc.*—Ver. 16. Though the Lord calls us *friends*, this does not imply an equality; He calls His followers afterwards even *brethren*, but they all the more reverently call Him only their Lord and their God.—The love between us began with Me and not with you.—*Ordained* (ἔθηκα) *you, etc.* The *branches* become elevated, as it were, themselves into new *vines* of the second degree, since the Lord *sets* them to bear fruit.—"He who is *united with* Christ, obtains thereby the true *independence*, and stands before God as a personality pervaded by Christ." (FIKENSCHER).—I have planted and appointed you that ye should bring forth fruit, *that is*, that ye should secure fruit by your effectual prayer.—Ver. 17. By all these My discourses and commandments I would specially point you to that one (commandment) which I would confirm in your hearts, *that ye love one another!*—Vers. 17, 18. There is need that ye should be all the more closely united in My love, *for* the world hateth you.—Ver. 18. The most conscientious and tender Christian is the most likely to fall into the temptation of seeking the cause of the world's hatred solely in himself, of thinking that if he were perfect in goodness, love, humility, and meekness, the evil of the world must needs be overcome; and this might lead to a false compliance: Against *such* trouble and temptation the Lord arms us beforehand: "If the most holy love upon earth found no better return, if He did not succeed, if He could not in His wisdom avoid hatred when it arose against Him, all the more fiercely as His pure love more brightly beamed upon it—how could *we* hope altogether to escape this hatred?—or do we vainly imagine that we can surpass the love and prudence of our Lord?" (DIETZ.).—The world *cannot* love you, it *must* hate you *as* it hates *Me!*—Ver. 19. This world would not indeed love *you* (for it cannot truly love at all!)—but *its own in you.*—"Although worldly men often quarrel fiercely, which is one of the characteristics of corrupt nature, Tit. iii. 3, yet these enmities are only about particular conflicting interests: *in the great essentials there is always a perfect accord among them.*" (LAMPE).—The *I* has a twofold emphasis: as to the *world*, its hatred is reduced to hatred against Himself; as to the *disciples* it is impressed upon them that He alone is the origin of their new life.—*Therefore, etc.* The hatred of the world becomes to us a precious *note* (sign) that we are His—not indeed the first and only mark: as the *second* note it neither begins our test nor must we seek it or wish it; but *if*, alas, it incessantly comes, *then* it is time to comfort ourselves in the reflection that the love of the world would be a sad condemnation; Luke vi. 26; Gal. i. 10; Jas. iv. 4, *etc.*—Ver. 20. The *consolation* has an undertone of *demand*, that they should rejoice and feel themselves honored in being counted worthy to suffer as He suffered.—"It belongs to the *perfection* of a disciple, who would be as his Master, that he should encounter the hatred of the world." (BRAUNE).—The general tolerance of a tolerant world is always grazing the limits of its liberality; when the *I have chosen you out of the world* is obtruded upon them in all its earnestness, then begins their exclusion, their ban, their rage.—*If they have kept, etc.* Let not their hatred cause you to keep back this word; and also, Oppose the world with your word *alone*, do nothing more, for the rest suffer patiently as I have suffered.—Ver. 21. This sin is practical, persevering, opposing *unbelief*.—Ver. 22. "Ignorance would be otherwise an excuse"—but *here* it is in the fullest sense *inexcusable*.—Sin enough they have; but *all their sin* would have been forgiven and taken away through Christ, if they had received Him in faith.—Ver. 23. One of the many consequences that result from the unity of the Father and the Son; he that seeth Me, seeth—he that believeth in Me, believeth in—he that loveth Me, loveth—he that *hateth* Me, *hateth —the Father!*—He that *can* hate Jesus, the manifestation of God in the flesh, *must* bear in himself hatred to God.—Ver. 24. "My works, *Me*, and the Father, in them—to *see* and yet to *hate;* these two irreconcilables are reconciled by a God-hating world!" (LUECKE.)—Ver. 25. The last *solace for* the hatred to Christ which the God-hating world exhibits, lies in the counsel of the divine wisdom which foretold all this.—"In sin there is neither reason nor righteousness" (BERLENB. BIBEL).—"Hatred without cause is worse than idolatry or blood-guiltiness." (TALM. JOMA.)—Vers. 26, 27. While the Spirit previously testifies of Christ to the disciples themselves, and then *through* them to the world, He becomes at the same time a Counsellor, Helper, Intercessor, Representative, *for* the disciples.—*How* will He testify and *what?* He will not *immediately* (by any *personal* manifestation as the Son) bear witness, but *in* and *through you:* further, He will testify that which ye have already seen in Me, that which ye have already heard of Me—nothing besides, essentially different or new.—Then *shall ye* actually *bear witness;* and more, then will your testimony be the testimony of the Spirit, who will make you infallible *in this vocation and function.*—Not *a speculative idea*, but *a historical fact*, is the ground-work of the world's salvation.—We (of the present day) *first* livingly experience and receive, through the New Testament Scriptures, the life, deeds, and sayings of our Lord, as eye and ear witnesses of the second degree; *then* we also *wait* humbly for power from on high; and *then* it is our obligation and right to testify with power and success what *we* have seen and heard in historical conviction and living experience.—Chap. xvi. vers. 1, 2. It has been said that *excommunication* is a greater evil than bodily persecution, yet the Lord does not here so regard (present) it: he who is strong in the truth may suffer that truth to be called a lie without being much aggrieved; but to our weakness, and our unsinful natural love of life, the death of martyrdom must ever be the crown of patience and endurance.—O that unhappy *thinking*, into which the hatred of unbelief may be blinded and hardened, while it seeks to justify itself before God!—Ver. 3. Even the true Church should and must *cast out*, for the sake of truth and love; but it belongs to the false synagogue to treat those differing in faith with hatred which reaches unto persecution, and putting to death as *λατρεία*.—It becomes us to mourn over our blind persecutors, and, like Stephen, to continue the Lord's own intercession for those who know not what they do.—Ver. 5. We should never be too idle or too sorrowful to investigate and inquire from the impulse of faith and love, and with an eager desire for saving knowledge.—Ver. 6. The same disciples afterwards, when the risen Lord ascended to heaven, returned to Jerusalem with great joy, without any sorrow for the separation (Luke xxiv. 52).—"Under this gentle rebuke there lies a tacit consolation. While He accuses their negligence in not putting the question, *Whither goest Thou*, He gives them their own excuse, that their omission was due to excess of sorrow." (LAMPE.)—"The Lord knoweth our frame, and of what stuff we are made. And of this we can remind Him, Heb. iv. 15." (BERLENB. BIBEL.)—Ver. 7. In precise opposition to the disciples' view, that to *Him*, the pure and holy One, death would be no suffering or ruin, but *their* irreparable loss, the Lord points, in silent contrast, to the fact that to *Him* the departure to the Father through the death of a sinner, for sin's sake, would indeed be very bitter (ch. xii. 27)—but all the more does He turn it into an *it is expedient for you.* Thus speaks the love that looks not at its own.—The primary thought which, in the analogy of human relations generally, finds here its grandest application, is—that only after the withdrawal of the sensible presence of a teacher and master, his abiding and influential spirit is truly set free and penetrates our being.—"Before He went away,(the Christ after the flesh),the Christ after the Spirit could not come. When the former vanished, the latter appeared." (DRAESEKE.)—In all fellowship with the sufferings of Christ, which might seem to us to be His going away from us, the Comforter repeats to us His prototypic word of consolation—*It is expedient for you!*—Ver. 8. "The Apostles were to *convince* the unbelieving and hating world, *maintain their right* against it, and *conquer* it by the truth they testified." (ŒTINGER.)—The sentiment, so often misunderstood and perverted, that the world's history is the world's judgment, has its truth in this working and judging of the Spirit, this final preparation for the judgment to be revealed, which, again, must tarry for its consummation until that personal appearance of the Son to which the Spirit points the Church.—"The *reproof*, that is, the bringing to view of our own unrighteousness, could not be without a gracious revelation and offer of the true righteousness; even the judgment is exhibited before the world only *in order, where possible, to turn its thought to Him*, who frees all who believe from condemnation. (SCHLEIERMACHER.)—The *reproving* office necessarily precedes the *comforting.* The Paraclete does not, properly speaking, perform "a strange work, before He comes to *His own* work, that of comforting, and preaching grace." (LUTHER.)—In the three great words *ἁμαρτία, δικαιοσύνη, κρίσις*, the Lord names the three all-embracing, essential elements of truth and its whole procedure. Not until the Holy Ghost has explained these words, does the world know what *sin*, *righteousness* and *judgment* are.—The production of an experimental and perfect knowledge of these three words is the office of the *Spirit* alone, and that *as* Spirit,—by the mediation, indeed, of the word and the work, yet only so far as these are made *inwardly* efficient in the heart and conscience.—Ver. 9. The *ὅτι* gives us the *thing signified* in sin, righteousness, judgment, tells us what kind of sin, righteousness and decision of judgment, He means.—The Lord means first specifically the sin of *unbelief.* This is no mere error, but the foundation and crown, the fruit and kernel, the true essential substance of all *sin* of the evil will.—"The Holy Ghost reproves the world of *lying* when it pretends that its unbelief is *honest doubt, etc.*" (RICHTER's *Hausbibel*).—The reproof of unbelief is at once a *proffer of faith* (and) an offer of all strength and grace requisite in order to it.—Ver. 10. "The Holy Ghost convinces the world of *righteousness:* partly, that it *must necessarily have* a righteousness; partly, that it cannot find that righteousness in itself; partly, that it should seek such righteousness *in Christ.*" (RIEGER.)—The ὑπάγειν denotes here, as in ver. 7, a ministering, obtaining, *redeeming* departure.—The *not seeing* must refer to *faith* in the Invisible. The righteousness of Christ, *to be laid hold of* in faith, is thus arrayed against the sin of unbelief.—Ver. 11. Even the Holy Ghost (who was to do away with all accommodations and strip off all Jewish embellishments of the truth) does not put an end to the teaching concerning a *Devil*, but rather begins it anew.—The great cause is lost by the enemy of God, the author of all sin and unrighteousness, the blinder of men's minds into unbelief of a Saviour; and it is *won for the world,* in which he has no longer either power or right.—The *future* judgment to which the world is proceeding, under the deciding testimony of the Spirit, is founded on the judgment which has been already *accomplished* through the departure of Jesus, and which is *presented* to the minds of men by the Holy Ghost.—The Spirit's ἔλεγχος separates mankind into two classes, each consisting of three sorts of men. Among those who accept this ἔλεγχος, we distinguish the *penitent* who acknowledge their *sin*, the *believing* who are justified in Christ, the *holy* who are perfectly delivered from Satan's power in the full accomplishment of their sanctification. Among those who persistently oppose, there are the abiding *sinners, unbelievers, condemned.*—Satan is *either* condemned to our advantage if we lay hold on *righteousness, or* we remain with him in condemnation if we continue as the world in *sin.*—*Will ye then* be, and be forever, the Devil's? Will ye be condemned with him?—The three-fold office of the Holy Ghost has a corresponsive reference to the prophetical, high-priestly, and judicial offices of Christ.—Ver. 12. Ye cannot *bear* it, is a more gracious and stronger expression than if He had said, Ye cannot *receive* it. The Lord considers the weakness of their oppressed minds. A further development and exposition of these great things would have altogether *weighed them down,* without the understanding which the Spirit should first bring.—Prematurely to pour out to people the whole truth, is not only *useless*, but *it is also positively hurtful.*—Ver. 13. The living teaching of the Spirit is a guidance and leading into truth, in more senses than one. First, because it must assuredly presuppose, bring with it, require, a constantly corresponding practical obedience,—hence bringing no more to the inner and true understanding than the life is ripe for and fully willing to be guided by. "The Spirit will *lead,* the Christian must therefore *walk with* Him." (BRAUNE). Then, secondly, the Spirit gives, as we see in the case of the Apostles, His solutions and explanations according to the *need* and the *occasion* (Matt. x. 19, 20)—just as in part at least the laws of Moses were given according to the emergencies which required them. "In the activity of his vocation a man attains the region of truth," says BRAUNE. Thus, while the *leading into* of itself indicates a *gradualness,* in opposition to the mechanical and childish notion that the Apostles at one bound were established in all truth on the day of Pentecost, we have to seek the reason and the measure of this gradualness, both externally and internally; partly, in the internal ripening and progress of the Apostles themselves in their own sanctification, with which their knowledge keeps pace—and partly in the stages of the way in which their vocation as witnesses led them through the world.—"If the Holy Ghost may not speak of Himself, and out of Himself—O Preacher! how canst thou draw thy preaching out of *thyself,* out of *thine head* (or even *heart*)?" (GOSSNER.)—Let nothing of thy preaching and testimony come from thine own mere impulse and will to know and to teach, before the Spirit hath taught and impelled thee!—Ver. 14. The glorification of Jesus Christ will be consummated before His disciples and in them, only by the Holy Ghost. *He shall glorify Me*—in this the Lord names the inmost centre of the whole truth, around which the periphery of its manifold development revolves; as also the most decisive test for every spirit of lying.—"What preaches Jesus, and leads to faith in Him, is of the Holy Ghost. For as the Son speaketh of the Father and glorifieth the Father, even so speaketh the Holy Ghost of the Son and *glorifieth the Son.*" (LUTHER).—"The full harmonious close of all the words of Jesus is *Spirit;* the testimony of Jesus is the kernel and spirit of all the prophets." (ŒTINGER.)—The Holy Ghost *testifies* of Jesus (ch. xv. 26)—this is the beginning of His office in the world; He *glorifies* Jesus—that is the goal and end of His office in believers.—The glorification of Christ *before us* must coincide with the appropriating establishment of His image *in us.*—There is no other receiving of this glorifying light, no other living growing and becoming perfect in it than that which takes place according to 2 Cor. iii. 17, 18.—Ver. 15. The honor of the *Father* could not be left without its positive expression; we have found this pervading all these farewell discourses, but the Trinitarian expression and winding up of all culminates in this passage.—Thus, there is opened to us a glimpse into the living blessed bond of love in receiving and giving in the eternal ground of the triune essence of the Godhead.—"This is the circle; round and complete; all Three, Father, Son, and Holy Ghost in one eternal Divine nature:—thus the Holy Ghost is Himself true God, without any difference, only that He hath it both from the Father and the Son." (LUTHER).

[From BARNES: Chap. xv. 1. Christ really and truly gives what is emblematically represented by a vine.—A *vine* yields proper juice and nourishment to all the branches, whether these be large or small.—Ver. 2. *Every branch in Me;* Every one that is a true follower of Me—that is united to Me by faith—and that truly derives grace and strength from Me, as the branch does from the vine.—It is a union of friendship, of love, and of dependence; a union of weakness with strength; of imperfection with perfection; of a dying nature with a living Saviour; of a lost sinner with an unchanging Friend and Redeemer. It is the most tender and interesting of all relations; but not more *mysterious* or more *physical* than the union of parent and child, of husband and wife (Eph. v. 23), or friend and friend.—*He taketh away:* The vine-dresser cuts it off; God removes such in various ways: 1. By the discipline of the church; 2. By suffering them to fall into temptation; 3. By persecution and tribulation, by the deceitfulness of riches, and by the cares of the world. (Matt. xiii. 21, 22), by suffering the man to be placed in such circumstances as Judas, Achan, and Ananias were—such as to show what *they were*—to bring their characters *fairly out*, and to let it be *seen* that they had no true love to God; 4. By death.—To *bear fruit* is to show by our lives that we are under the influence of the religion of Christ; and that that religion produces in us its appropriate effects.—Ver. 4. Live a life of dependence on Me, and obey My doctrines, imitate My example, and constantly exercise faith in Me.—Ver. 5. We see hence, 1. That to Christ is due all the praise for all the good works the Christian performs; 2. That they will perform good works just in proportion as they feel their dependence on Him, and look to Him; 3. That the reason why others fail of being holy is because they are unwilling to look to Him and seek grace and strength from Him who alone is able to give it.—Ver. 8. *Bear much fruit:* Abound in good works; be faithful, zealous, humble, devoted, always abounding in the works of the Lord. This honors God, 1. Because it shows the excellence of His law which requires it; 2. Because it shows the power of His gospel, and His grace that can overcome the evil propensities of the heart, and *produce* it; 3. Because the Christian is restored to the divine image, and it shows how excellent is the character after which they are formed.—The Saviour says those who bear MUCH *fruit* are they who are His disciples.—No one should take comfort in the belief that he is a Christian who does not aim to do *much* good.—Ver. 9. *So have I loved you:* Not to the same degree, but with the same *kind* of love—deep, tender, unchanging; love prompting to self-denials, toils, and sacrifices to secure their welfare.—A strong reason why *we* should continue in His love, 1. Because the love which He shows for us is unchanging; 2. It is the love of our best Friend—love whose strength was expressed by toils, and groans, and blood; 3. As He is unchanging in the *character* and *strength* of His affection, so should *we* be—thus only can we properly express our gratitude, thus only show that we are His true friends; 4. Our happiness here, and for ever, depends altogether on our *continuing* in the love of Christ.—Ver. 16. *Bring forth fruit:* This is the great end for which Christians are chosen.—*Your fruit should remain:* This probably means, 1. That the *effect* of their labors should be *permanent* on mankind; 2. That their labor should be *unremitted*.—He that *expects* or *desires* to grow weary and cease to serve Christ, has never yet put on the Christian armor, or known anything of the grace of God.—Ver. 19. *If ye were of the world:* If you were actuated by the principles of the world—if, like them, you were vain, sensual, given to pleasure, wealth, ambition, they would not oppose you.—Ver. 22. We may understand this as teaching, 1. That they would not have been guilty of this *kind* of sin; 2. They would not have been guilty of the same *degree* of sin.—Chap. xvi. ver. 1. Learn, 1. That if Christians were left to themselves, they would fall away and perish; 2. That God affords means and helps *beforehand* to keep them in the path of duty; 3. That the instructions of the Bible and the help of the Holy Spirit, are all granted to keep them from apostasy; 4. That Jesus, beforehand, *secured* the fidelity, and made certain the continuance in faith, of His apostles—seeing all their dangers, and knowing all their enemies; and, in like manner, we should be persuaded that "He is able to keep that which we commit to Him against that day." 2 Tim. i. 12.—Ver. 7. *It is expedient for you, etc.;* 1. By His departure, His death, and ascension—by having these great *facts* before their eyes—they would be led by the Holy Spirit to see more clearly the design of His coming than they would by His presence; 2. While on the earth the Lord Jesus could be bodily present but in one place at one time; 3. It was an evident arrangement in the great plan of redemption, that each of the Persons of the Trinity should perform a part; 4. It was to be expected that far more signal success would attend the preaching of the gospel when the atonement was actually made, than before.—Vers. 8-11. Here is presented a condensed and most striking view of the work of the Holy Spirit.

[From OWEN: Chap. xv. 6. There is no true branch of the Vine that does not bear *some* fruit.—Those who have no living connection with Christ, represented by *abiding in Him*, are to be cut off eventually even from the outward and visible connection with His body, and cast forth.—Ver. 7. The word of Christ is His own presence: where that dwells and forms the rule of conduct, He dwells.—*Ye shall ask what ye will, etc.* This is not a promise, as some absurdly suppose, that every request made by Christ's disciples shall be granted; but that such petitions as result from His indwelling word, and are therefore in accordance with the mind of the Spirit, shall be heard and answered.—Ver. 8. We should be cautious not to refer the bearing of fruit to the external results only which crown a life of activity in the service of Christ; the main reference is to the growth of grace in the soul, the fruits of the Spirit (Gal. v. 22, 23).—*So shall ye be, etc.* The condition of discipleship in the school of Christ.—Ver. 9. The connection between Christ and His followers is one of love, having the same characteristics as that which subsists between the Father and Son.—Ver. 10. Not only is obedience the proof of true discipleship, but it is here declared to be the very means of indissolubly uniting the soul to Christ.—Ver. 16. The verb rendered *have chosen*, literally signifies, *to choose out for one's self, i. e.* for one's own use, or in accordance with one's own pleasure; hence it signifies a choice with the idea of *favor, approval* and *love*.—*Ye have not chosen Me:*

No one ever chooses Jesus in this evangelical sense of the word, until inclined thereto by the sovereign purpose and grace of God through Jesus Christ.—*Should go and bring forth fruit:* A picturesque expression denoting living energy and activity, a going forth under a profound sense of responsibility; and an addressing of one's self with all one's powers to the service assigned one.—Ver. 19. It is only in opposition to truth, and in hatred to the followers of Jesus, that the men of the world are united, and it is in reference to this hatred to everything that is good, that the world is said to love its own.—Ver. 24. Miracles must be connected with a holy life and true words, to have any power and significancy (as being from God).—Ver. 26. *Comforting* is an important function of the Spirit's office, though it constitutes but a small portion of His work as the Helper and Guardian of the saints on earth.—The preposition in *from the Father* implies that the original abode of the Spirit was *with* God.—Chap. xvi. 1. *Offended,* "Hindered by stumbling-blocks such as are mentioned in the next verse." (CROSBY.)—Ver. 10. "The world's only possible righteousness is in the grasping of the unseen and ascended Christ, and they will be convinced of that by God's Spirit either to salvation or damnation." (CROSBY.)—Ver. 14. *He shall glorify Me,* announces the great object of the Spirit's mission; as all that He reveals has reference to Christ, so in the fulness and clearness of His revelation is Christ glorified, 2 Cor. iv. 6.]

IV.

HIGHER UNION OF THE FARTHER AND THE HITHER WORLD AT THE NEW TESTAMENT EASTER AND PENTECOST. GLORIFICATION OF CHRIST THROUGH THE HOLY GHOST AND OF THE FATHER THROUGH CHRIST. THE GOING AND COMING AGAIN OF THE LORD. THE CHURCH'S WATCHWORD: A LITTLE WHILE. SYMBOLISM OF SORROW, OF NATAL PANGS AND JOYS. GOOD-FRIDAY GRIEF AND EASTER JOY IN THE LIFE OF THE LORD AND THE LIFE OF THE CHURCH.

CHAP. XVI. 16–27.

(Pericope for Jubilate Sunday, vers. 16-23; Rogate, vers. 23-30).

16 A little while, and ye shall not see me [and ye no longer[1] behold me, *οὐκέτι θεω-
ρεῖτέ με*]: and again, a little while, and ye shall [will] see me [*ὄψεσθέ με*], because
17 I go to the Father.[2] Then [Therefore] said *some* of his disciples among themselves
[to one another, *πρὸς ἀλλήλους*], What is this that he saith unto us, A little while,
and ye shall not see me [behold me not]: and again, a little while, and ye shall
18 [will] see me: and, Because I go to the Father? They said therefore, What is
this that he saith, A little while? we cannot tell what he saith [we know not what
19 he is speaking of, *οὐκ οἴδαμεν τί λαλεῖ*].[3] Now[4] Jesus knew that they were desirous
to ask him, and said unto them, Do ye inquire among yourselves of [Do ye inquire
of this among yourselves, *περὶ τούτου ζητεῖτε μετ' ἀλλήλων ὅτι*] that I said, A little
while, and ye shall not see me [and ye behold me not], and again, a little while,
20 and ye shall [will] see me? Verily, verily, I say unto you, That ye shall [will]
weep and lament, but the world shall [will] rejoice; and [*omit* and][5] ye shall [will]
21 be sorrowful, but your sorrow shall [will] be turned into joy. A woman when she
is in travail hath sorrow, because her hour is come: but as soon as she is delivered
of the child, she remembereth no more the anguish, for joy that a man is born into
22 the world. And ye now therefore [So ye also now] have[6] sorrow: but I will [shall]
see you again, and your heart shall [will] rejoice, and your joy no man [no one]
23 taketh [will take, *ἀρεῖ*,[7]] from you. And in that day ye shall [will] ask me nothing.
Verily, verily, I say unto you, Whatsoever ye shall ask the Father in my
name [If ye will ask the Father anything],[8] he will give *it* you [in my name].
24 Hitherto have ye [ye have] asked nothing in my name: ask, and ye shall [will]
receive, that your joy may be [made] full.

* * * * * * * * *

25 These things have I spoken unto you in proverbs [parables, *παροιμίαις*: but[9] the
time cometh [the hour is coming] when I shall no more speak unto you in proverbs
[parables], but I shall show [tell] you plainly of [concerning, about] the Father.
26 At [In] that day ye shall [will] ask in my name: and I say not unto you [I do not
27 tell you] that I will [shall] pray the Father for you: For the Father himself loveth
you, because ye have loved me, and have believed that I came out [forth] from
God [from the Father].[10]

TEXTUAL AND GRAMMATICAL.

[1] Ver. 16.—[The text. rec. reads οὐ, *not;* but οὐκέτι, *no longer*, is supported by ℵ. B. D. L., Orig., Vulg., Syr., *etc.*, and adopted by Lachmann, Tischend. (ed. viii., against οὐ of his former edd.), Tregelles, Alford, Westcott and Hort. Lange follows it, and says, in opposition to Meyer, who considers οὐκέτι an interpretation from ver. 10 and xiv. 19, that it agrees better with the contrast between θεωρεῖτε and ὄψεσθε.—P. S.]

[2] Ver. 16.—[The words ὅτι (ἐγὼ) ὑπάγω πρὸς τὸν πατέρα in the received text are supported by A. and retained by Lachmann and Lange (who accounts for their omission on the ground of their seeming inconsistency with ὄψεσθέ με), but they are wanting in ℵ. B. D. L., Orig., *etc.*, and dropped by Tischend., Alford, Treg., Westc. and H. It looks as if they were inserted to suit ver. 17.—P. S.]

[3] Ver. 18.—[On minor differences of reading in vers. 17 and 18 see Alf. and Tischend. ed. viii.—P. S.]

[4] Ver. 19.—[Lange with Lachm. retains οὖν (after ἔγνω) which is backed by A. and suits the Johannean style, but Tregelles, Alf., Tischend., W. and H. omit it in accordance with ℵ. B. D. L.—P. S.]

[5] Ver. 20.—[δέ, *but*, before λυπηθήσεσθε is omitted by Lange in accordance with ℵ.[1] B. D. L., Tischend. (ed. viii., against his former edd.), Alf., *etc.* It marks a contrast which has already been presented.—P. S.]

[6] Ver. 22.—[ἔχετε is supported by ℵ.* B. C., *etc.*, and adopted by Lange, Tregelles, Alf., Tischend., Westcott and H.; the future ἕξετε, which Lachmann prefers with A. D. L. and ℵ.[c], seems conformed to the fut. in ver. 20. Meyer, on the contrary, thinks that ἔχετε is conformed to ἔχει in ver. 21 and to νῦν.—P. S.]

[7] Ver. 22.—[The rec. αἴρει, *taketh*, is supported by ℵ. A. C. D.[2], L., approved by Lange, Tischend. (viii.); the future ἀρεῖ, *will take*, is adopted by Lachm., Alford, Tregelles, Westcott and Hort, in accordance with B. D., Vulg., Orig.—P. S.]

[8] Ver. 23.—[ἄν τι, *si quid*, *if anything*, is the correct reading, adopted by Tischend., Alf., *etc.*, in accordance with B. C. D. L., *etc.*, instead of the rec. ὅσα ἄν. The best authorities put ἐν τῷ ὀνόματί μου after δώσει ὑμῖν, not before (as the text. rec. does). Christ is the medium of all communication between the Father and the believer.—P. S.]

[9] Ver. 25.—[ἀλλ', *but*, is omitted by Tischend. and Alford, but retained by Lange with Lachmann on the authority of A. C.[3] D. He claims also B., but B. as well as ℵ., according to Tischend. ed. viii., sustain the omission.—P. S.]

[10] Ver. 27.—[The text. rec. and Tischend. ed. viii. read θεοῦ (from ch. xiii. 3) with ℵ.* A. C.[3], *etc.*, but ℵ.[ca] B. C.* D. L. X., Syr., *etc.*, Lachm., Lange, Tregelles, Alford, Westcott and Hort give the preference to πατρός.—P. S.]

EXEGETICAL AND CRITICAL.

[Olshausen states the connection thus: Before the Spirit can fulfil His blessed work, a painful separation is necessary. But the μικρόν suggests a more natural connection: The promised coming of the Comforter with His disclosures of the whole truth, spoken of vers. 13-15, is near at hand. The Lord now speaks of His speedy withdrawal with its joyful effect after a brief season of mourning. The mode of expression is purposely enigmatical, to stimulate the disciples. θεωρεῖτε and ὄψεσθε are not co-ordinate; the former refers to the bodily, the latter chiefly, though not exclusively, to the spiritual vision on the day of Pentecost, which, however, goes on to its final completion at the parousia. Comp. ch. xiv. 19.—P. S.]

Ver. 16. **A little while.**—The determination of time is not the same as chap. xiv. 19. In the latter passage the term is one reaching from the night of Maundy Thursday to Easter Day; in the present chapter the one little period is resolved into two small or lesser ones (after a sacred *divide et impera*, we might say). The first "*little while*" reaches to the death upon the cross; it amounts, therefore, to about one day; the second extends from that death to the resurrection, and, hence, amounts again to one day.—**And ye will no more behold Me** [καὶ οὐκέτι θεωρεῖτέ με].—According to Meyer, reference is not had to the resurrection in this place either, but to the spiritual viewing of Christ in the activity of the Paraclete. To accord with this view, the not seeing for a little while must likewise be merely spiritual. Better Tholuck: With still more directness than in chap. xiv. 19, our thoughts are led to Christ's resurrection, on the occasion of which His disciples did see Him again. [Ebrard, Hengstenberg, Ewald, Weiss likewise refer ὄψεσθε to the resurrection, but this seems inconsistent with ver. 23: "In that day ye shall ask Me nothing," comp. with Acts i. 6, 7, where the disciples did ask the Lord concerning the time of the establishment of His kingdom. Alford assumes in all these prophecies a perspective of continually unfolding fulfilments; the ὄψεσθε *began to be fulfilled* at the resurrection of Christ, then received its *main fulfilment* at the day of Pentecost, and shall have its final completion at the great return of the Lord hereafter.—P. S.]—**For I go away to the Father.**—I go away, not to abide in Sheol. Because I go to the realm of life, I can also soon manifest Myself again; manifest Myself *here* and *thence,—there* and *in the future.* After a little while, ye shall continually be seeing Me again and seeing Me more thoroughly than ye have ever yet seen Me; ye shall *view* Me with the eyes of the spirit and of living knowledge, because I am with the Father in the kingdom of life, as He that liveth.—And thus, together with the resurrection, there is embraced the entire manifestation of Christ through future ages until His coming;—a manifestation whose principle is contained in His resurrection. Luthardt: In the transient return of the Risen One they are to see a pledge of the Parousia (an opinion which Meyer groundlessly combats). On the genuineness of the words: *for I go, etc.*, see the TEXTUAL NOTES.

Ver. 17. **What is this whereof He saith: a little while** (τὸ μικρόν)?—The excitement and mutual questionings of the disciples in regard to the mysterious saying of the Master, are themselves of a somewhat mysterious nature. They passed by the first μικρόν, chap. xiv. 19, without stumbling. In the first place, the double μικρόν seems to stagger them. Formerly He said: "*A little while, and the world will behold Me no more; ye, however, will behold Me;*"—now He says: "*A little while, and ye will not behold Me.*" But He goes on to declare further: "*and again a little while, and ye will see Me,*" *i. e.* view Me in a more glorious way. And as a reason for all this is assigned His going to the Father.—**Now behold Me no more.**—This seemed to denote His death; **now view Me again**;—and this to be indicative of His glorious appearing to judgment. Should the first ensue, in what respect could the second be? or the second, then wherefore the first? And, assuming the second, how was it possible for them to view Him better than they had done before, if He went to the Father? Thus, they have a foreboding of the greatest, the most mysterious changes, but the greatest mystery of all to them is still that all these things are to happen in a short space; here, we must observe, they make their final stand, *viz.*, at the stress borne by τὸ μικρόν. And it is upon this, in accordance with the purpose of the Lord, that the accent *should* now fall; it is here that they *should* stand still. The pain of parting, just pressed upon them by Him in its full greatness and startling, trying power, must now be viewed by them from the other side, as a suffering, sharp but short, no longer analogous to the agony of death, in the natural world, but, rather, to the anguish of travail, as a swift transition from the depths of woe to the heights of joy. As to how the apostles, and with them all Christians, have learned this saying, see the DOCTRINAL and ETHICAL NOTES.

Ver. 19. **Now Jesus was aware.**—See chap. vi. 61. It was His desire to lead them to this point; He now offers them an explanation, the magnitude and certainty of which are introduced by a: **verily, verily.**

Ver. 20. **Weep and lament** [κλαύσετε καὶ θρηνήσετε ὑμεῖς].—The intensity of the anguish imminent upon them, vividly portrayed. The **ye will** is placed, in indication of their great contrast to the world, immediately before the words: **The world will rejoice** [ὁ δὲ κόσμος χαρήσεται].—The weeping and lamenting has for its subject, together with the death of the Lord, the apparent downfall of the hopes they had built upon the imminent kingdom of God and redemption of Israel.—**ye will be sorrowful** [ὑμεῖς λυπηθήσεσθε], emphatically: plunged in sorrow.* The expression is partly characteristic of the depth of their desolation, partly introductory to the second antithesis and, hence, descriptive of the measure of their joy. Not alone shall, for them, joy follow upon sadness; their joy shall grow out of their sadness, sadness **shall be changed into joy**; consequently, the bottomless depth of their sorrow shall be the heavenly measure of their joy. Their dying with Christ was the condition of new life with Him. [Alford: εἰς χαρὰν γενήσεται, not merely changed *for* joy, but changed *into*, so as itself to become—so that the very matter of grief shall become matter of joy; as Christ's cross of shame has become the glory of the Christian, Gal. vi. 14.—P. S.]

Ver. 21. **The [A] woman, when she is in travail** [ἡ γυνὴ ὅταν τίκτῃ, λύπην ἔχει. Mark this touching proof of the Saviour's sympathy with suffering humanity and woman's deepest trial (Gen. iii. 16).—P. S.] *The woman* [ἡ γυνή]. This is the universal rule; hence the definite article.† When she is about to be delivered or to give birth, she hath sorrow. Not alone physical pangs or throes, but likewise mental pressure, solicitude and anguish.—**Her hour** [ἡ ὥρα αὐτῆς, her (appointed) time]. For woman the fateful hour of tribulation.—**But when she is delivered of the child** [ὅταν δὲ γεννήσῃ τὸ παιδίον—not necessarily masculine (*puer*), but indefinite]. The anguish is forgotten—merged in the joy that a human being is born into the world. This is the rapturous thought of maternity. The child is a human being (ἄνθρωπος), a mystery of personal, infinite life. See Gen. iv. 1.—**Into the world** [ὅτι ἐγεννήθη ἄνθρωπος εἰς τὸν κόσμον]. Not into the natural life only: into the Cosmos and for it; in order to the full development and moulding of it.—In the Old Testament also, the pangs of a travailing woman are used as a symbol of that grief which is turned into joy, Is. xxi. 3; xxvi. 17; xxxvii. 3; lxvi. 7; Hos. xiii. 13.

Ver. 22. **And ye now therefore have sorrow.**—Explanation of the symbol, for the immediate comprehension and need of the disciples. Ye are like a travailing woman, in your sorrow; soon ye will also rejoice exceedingly. At this Meyer stops, in antithesis to older and more extended interpretations. Even Tholuck observes: "in the case of the disciples, the *subject* of their sorrow did indeed turn into a *subject* for their joy; their joy—we may say—was the recompense of their anguish; it was not, however, born of their anguish." Against this view we will cite the remark of Lücke: "The death-hour of Jesus was for the disciples the natal hour of new life." Thus, not in the change of the *subject* alone did the joy lie, but in the change of *their condition*, as well; only by the death of their old view of the world and by their fundamental renunciation of it, their dying with Christ, did they become capable of understanding the import of His resurrection and of rejoicing over that resurrection as they should." Prominence is given to this thought by Tholuck also. And exegesis is justified, on this point, in passing beyond the proximate application of the figure in accordance with the practical needs of the disciples at that time. Most undoubtedly, the death of Christ is, according to Apollinaris, Chrysostom, Olshausen and others, the agonizing travail of humanity, from which labor the God-Man issues, glorified, to the eternal joy of the whole body of mankind.* De Wette's remark: "the living Christ is subjectively the offspring of the mental productivity of the disciples," is

* [Alford: "Λυπηθήσεσθε goes deeper than the wailing and weeping before: and plainly shows that the whole does not *only* refer to the grief while the Lord was in the tomb, but to the grief continually manifesting itself in the course and conflict of the Christian, which is turned into joy by the advancing work of the Spirit of Christ:—and, in the completion of the sense, to the grief and widowhood of the Church during her present state, which will be turned into joy at the coming of her Lord." David Brown: "At the same time the sorrow of the widowed Church in the absence of her Lord in the heavens, and her transport at His personal return are certainly here expressed."—P. S.]

† [In the German, as in the Greek lang., the definite article is generic; but the *use* of the article in Greek and in German corresponds, in this case, to its *omission* in English; comp. ὁ δοῦλος, xv. 15.—P. S.]

* [Olshausen: "Hence the proper import of the figure seems to be, that the Death of Jesus Christ was as it were an anguish of birth belonging to all Humanity (*ein schmerzvoller Geburtsact der ganzen Menschheit*) in which the perfect man was born into the world; and in this very birth of the new man lies the spring of eternal joy, never to be lost, for all, inasmuch as through Him and His power the renovation of the whole is rendered possible." Alford adopts this view, and applies the same to every Christian who is planted in the likeness of Christ. His passing from sorrow to joy—till "Christ be formed in him," is this birth of pain. "And the whole Church, the Spouse of Christ—nay, even the whole Creation, συνωδίνει, till the number of the elect be accomplished, and the eternal joy brought in. And thus the meaning which Luthardt insists on as against the above remarks of Olshausen, *viz. the new birth of the Church*, is in inner truth the same as his."—P. S.]

open to misapprehension, for this reason, if for none other, *viz.* that mental productivity is an attribute of man, and not of woman. According to Luthardt, the subject treated of is the new birth of the Church, her transition to a state of glorification, an occurrence simultaneous with Christ's coming to the Church.* This view would completely obliterate the words: a little while, as well as the reference to Christ. Upon this fact, however, we must insist: namely, that man is perfectly born to the world only in his second, heavenly state of existence, in the resurrection, and that, inasmuch as this is conceded, before the resurrection of Christ no human being had been fully born into the world, whilst with Christ's resurrection, the birth of One Man into the world did at once make manifest this new world, and involve the co-geniture of the new humanity for this new world (with Christ dead, risen, transplanted into the heavenly existence). And thus, again, He was born of the travail-pangs of the Theocracy, the whole of the old humanity in its higher tendency, its longing for salvation; these pangs truly centered in His heart; at the same time, however, they thrilled through the members of believers and became the mortal agony of their old view of the world. (See Is. xxvi. 17; lxvi. 9; 1 Cor. xv. 47; Rev. xii. 1.)

Your heart will rejoice.—Meyer considers this as relative to the communication of the Paraclete, in opposition to the just view of most commentators, who assume it to have reference to the resurrection.—**And this your joy—no man will take from you.** It is the beginning of the eternal life in the heavenly existence, in which heaven and earth are intrinsically united.

Ver. 23. **And in that day ye will ask nothing of Me.**—This is the great, endless day, beginning in their souls with the beaming of the Easter Day. The day when they shall see Christ personally again and gaze upon Him spiritually. This seeing again includes the fact that the living Christ is then born in the disciples (De Wette); but this, the subjective festalness of the day is conditioned upon the objective dawn of the day of Christ. The glory of this festal day is depicted: 1. in the assurance that the disciples will ask the Lord nothing—an intimation of the enlightenment of the Spirit; 2. that, in the Spirit of sonship, they shall acceptably pray in Jesus' name, with perfect certainty of a hearing and of the reception of miraculous power; 3. that, thus praying, they shall have an entrance into the spiritual life of consummate joy. The Lord explains the first promise by the announcement that they shall at that time enjoy unbounded spiritual intercourse with Him which condition of affairs existing, He will unreservedly reveal divine things to them. The second and third promises He explains by telling them that they shall experience the Father's love in direct communion with Him. Hence it is the day of full, heavenly communion with the triune God, the Holy Ghost, the Son and the Father.

Ask—inquire of—Me nothing.—Chrysostom and others interpret ἐρωτᾶν as expressive of requesting. According to Johannean usage it might bear this meaning. And we should be forced thus to interpret it, if, from vers. 23-27, there were presented but a succession of fresh items in the promise. In that case, this first proposition would contain the general promise: on that day ye shall have nothing more to desire, to request, but shall experience the fullest content, for, first, ye shall have the hearing of your prayers granted you in My name, *etc.* But in ver. 25 the promise of ver. 23 οὐκ ἐρωτήσετε, is, from the stand-point of the future, further explained; similarly, vers. 26 and 27 are explanatory of the promise of ver. 23: Whatsoever ye shall ask—petition—the Father for, *etc.*—Accordingly, the meaning is: Ye shall in that day ask—inquire of—Me nothing. That is, their immature disciplehood and pupilage—that condition in which they were continually becoming astonished or startled at something, and were consequently led into many questionings (for instance chap. xiv. and chap. xvi. 17), failing, however, to put the true and decisive question (chap. xvi. 5)—shall come to an end and be replaced by the higher condition of enlightenment. The condition of enlightenment is a condition of ever-living revelation—revelation suited to all the true needs of the intellectual spirit, 1 John ii. 20.

Ver. 23. **If ye will entreat the Father for anything.**—Introduced by a **verily, verily.** Hence, it is upon the following promise that the principal weight lies. Christ divides their wants into intellectual and practical ones, the need of complete revelation and that of finished redemption; in laying particular stress upon the latter, He brings out the fact that the new life of knowledge is conditioned by the new life of prayer in the practical appropriation of salvation. We consider the reading ἄν τι to be established not only by the Codd. (see the Note), but also by the consideration that the principal emphasis should here rest upon *the filial invocation of the Father*, a circumstance unconsidered in Meyer's decision for ὅ τι ἄν after Cod. A.

He will give it you in My name.—[Notice here the right reading.—P. S.] See John xiv. 26. Just as the name of Christ, as the living view of His personal manifestation, and the experience of His salvation, is the medium of their prayer (a fact presupposed in the invocation of God as the Father, namely, the Father of Christ in the first instance), so a hearing on the part of the Father is allotted them through the name of the Son, *i. e.* the unfolding of the fulness of blessing, the divine power in His manifestation, His salvation and purpose. The name of Jesus, therefore, is not merely the "motive," but also the medium. The clearer, objective radiance of Christ's manifestation is the means by which God endows believers with more abundant power of prayer and more bountiful answers to it.

Ver. 24. **Hitherto ye have asked for**

* [Comp. Wordsworth *in loc.* (after Augustine): "In a secondary and wider sense, the Church in this world is the woman in travail; she is in travail with souls for the new birth to grace and glory (Gal. iv. 19). She groans in the pangs of parturition even till the great day of Regeneration, the day of the glorious reappearing of Christ, and the general resurrection and new birth to immortality (Rom. viii. 22). Then humanity will cast off its grave-clothes, and be glorified for ever with Christ."—P. S.]

nothing.—Not simply for the reason that they lacked divine illumination (Meyer), or because Christ Himself was not yet perfected (Hofmann), but because they prayed, as yet, with the reservations of their old view of the world, their old Messianic hope, not in that submission to the Messianic name of Christ and to His work, to which they should attain by means of the cross. **That your joy may be made full.**—See ver. 22 and chap. xv. 11. Glorious condition of the blessed spirit-life. Also an ultimate end of the life of prayer (ἵνα). Christ's exhortation to prayer manifestly has for its aim Pentecostal prayer for the Holy Spirit as the Mediator of that joy which should be their portion in the unanimity of love. Unanimity of prayer (Acts ii.) is the yearning of love. Unanimity in the Holy Ghost is the fulfilling of love, and that is the experience of heaven upon earth.

Ver. 25. **These things have I spoken unto you in parabolic discourses** [ἐν παροιμίαις].—The course through which the disciples, as unripe scholars, have hitherto been passing, with Christ for their Teacher, is here brought to a conclusion; hence it is that He contrasts the accommodative method which He has hitherto employed, with the system of instruction that He intends pursuing in future. The proximate reference of ταῦτα is, we admit, to the last discourse upon the saying, *a little while* (ver. 17), and, in particular, to the parabolic word concerning the travailing woman. But we must not (as does Meyer) limit its application to the above; the incorrectness of such limitation is proved by the plural ἐν παροιμίαις, itself (Tholuck). Even the reference of the word to all those matters of which Christ has hitherto been speaking, inclusive of His discourse concerning the Vine (Luthardt), fails to do full justice to this summary. The moment of the close of the Teachership till now exercised by Christ in the circle of disciples, could not remain without a designation of deep significance. Jesus characterizes the entire method which He has hitherto pursued amongst the disciples, as a speaking ἐν παροιμίᾳ. If it was necessary that He should speak much to the people in parables or complete similitudes, whilst to the disciples His deliverances were direct (Matt. xiii.), He still had been compelled until now to speak to the latter also *in figurative expressions* [see Notes on chap. x. 6 and xv. 1, pp. 317 and 461]. Be it observed in this connection that even the figureless saying remains a dark and simile-like conception to the unenlightened, while to the enlightened man the very concretest figure is illuminated by the idea of the Spirit (see the Revelation).*

But the hour cometh.—There shall be a great hour in that great Easter-Sunday of renewed meeting and of the Spirit,—an hour when the boundaries and wrappings of Christ's teachership, His revelation, shall fall. The Lord illustrates this new stand-point in a concrete manner, by repeating the two promises vers. 23 and 24.

But . . . . plainly—openly—without concealment—with freedom of speech—free-spokenly (παῤῥησίᾳ). As a substantive, παῤῥησία is sometimes subjective (perfect frankness), sometimes objective (perfect openness and freedom from concealment); and, the one signification being inconceivable without the other, it is, as a general thing, susceptible of both interpretations at once. These remarks are likewise applicable to the adverb in question, formed by the Dative of the substantive. It means—the objective sense predominating—: without reserve, with plainness, directness. According as Christ institutes a contrast between His whole future speaking in the Spirit and His speaking hitherto, it is assumable that He has in mind, in the first instance, the last parabolic saying concerning the travailing woman, at the same time intending, however, to characterize His whole style of speech hitherto, and, in antithesis to that, the new style in future employed by Him.

Ver. 26. **In that day ye will ask.**—Present petitions. From the complete manifestation of Christ through the Spirit, a manifestation realized, for them, in their enlightenment, there shall issue, as the product of the full knowledge-life, the true prayer-life in the name of Jesus. Worthy of note is the distinction: αἰτήσεσθε, ἐρωτήσω. [Bengel: *Cognitio parit orationem.* Lücke: "The more knowledge, the more prayer in the name of Jesus." Alford: "The approaching the Father through Him shall be a characteristic of their higher state under the dispensation of the Spirit."—P. S.]—**And I do not say unto you.** According to Aretius, Grotius and others, this is an intimation to the effect that Jesus *will* also pray for them: *I will not so much as mention that, etc.* According to Lücke and others, on the other hand, it is declarative of the directness of prayer to the Father,—a directness removing the necessity for intercession.* According to Meyer, this offers no contradiction to chap. xiv. 16; xvii. 19, for the reason that those passages treat of the intercessions of Christ previous to the time of the Paraclete. But yet John had received the Paraclete when he wrote 1 John ii. 1 (comp. Heb. vii. 25; Rom. viii. 34), a fact to which Meyer himself recurs later. The intercession of Christ for believers anointed with the Spirit, has, however, a different character. It is no longer a mediation whereby immediateness must be effected, but one by which it is carried to perfection; consequently, a mediation continually merged more and more in immediateness. His intercession has reference then to the development of reconciliation into sanctification. Also, this is the sense of our passage: even though I shall pray the Father for you, it will not be as though the necessity were upon Me of procuring you the favor of the Father, or the Spirit of son-

* [So also Alford: παροιμία, properly, a *proverb*:—but implying generally in Scriptural and oriental usage something dark and enigmatical; see especially Sir. vi. 35; viii. 8; xxxix. 3; xlvii. 17; '*in dictis tectioribus*,' Bengel. This is true of the whole discourse—and of the discourses of the Lord in general, as they must then have seemed to them, before the Holy Spirit furnished the key to their meaning. Olshausen remarks that all human speech is a παροιμία, only able to hint at, not to express fully, the things of God; and that the Lord contrasts the use of this weak and insufficient medium with the inward teaching of the Holy Spirit which is a real imparting of the divine nature and life.—P. S.]

* [So also Alford: "Christ is setting in the strongest light their reconciliation and access to the Father."—P. S.]

ship; on the contrary, ye shall learn that the Father Himself doth love you and communicate Himself unto you.

Ver. 27. **For He Himself, the Father loveth you.**—*I. e.* not: "without My intercessory mediation" (Meyer), but with the Holy Ghost the love of the Father doth also directly manifest itself unto you. The Christian life alternates between moods when, on the one hand, life's immediateness in God, on the other hand, its mediation through Christ, is felt; this immediateness being, however, modified by the fact of its existence in the name of Christ, and this mediation also appearing in the glorification effected by the Spirit. The Present denotes the proximity of the communication of the Spirit, or, rather, the already beginning ante-celebration of this communication as that of the Spirit of sonship, Rom. viii. 15; Gal. iv. 6.—**Because ye have loved Me.** "Because *ye are they* (ὑμεῖς emphasized) who have loved Me." Meyer. Love to Christ in faith in His name is the medium through which believers experience the Father's love or the consolation of their sonship.—**And have believed that I came forth from the Father** (see chap. viii. 42). This decided belief in the divine personality of Christ is the foundation and the proof of their love for Christ. For in the disciples, faith was not developed as another and secondary thing, from love to Jesus, but germinant faith, in the form of loving devotion, unfolded into this, faith's knowledge. The Perfects denote the festalness of the moment, which was anticipative of the Pentecostal time. That Christ regards the belief in His wondrous outgoing from the Father as the basis for the consummation of faith in Him, is evidenced by the following.

V.

GLORIFICATION OF CHRIST'S HOME-GOING THROUGH HIS GLORIOUS COMING INTO THE WORLD FROM THE FATHER. (PRE-CELEBRATION OF THE DAY OF PENTECOST IN A PRECURSORY PENTECOSTAL MOMENT OF THE DISCIPLES. THE FIRST RAY OF THE COMING ENLIGHTENMENT OF THE DISCIPLES.)

CHAP. XVI. 28–33.

28 I came forth from[1] the Father, and am come into the world: again, I leave the
29 world, and go to the Father. His disciples said unto him, Lo, now speakest thou
30 plainly [ἐν παῤῥησίᾳ], and speakest no proverb [parable]. Now are we sure [we
know, οἴδαμεν] that thou knowest [οἶδας] all things, and needest not that any man
31 should ask thee: by this we believe that thou camest forth from God. Jesus
32 answered them, Do ye now believe? [Now ye do believe.][2] Behold, the [an]
hour cometh, yea, is now [*omit* now][3] come, that ye shall [will] be scattered [Zech.
xiii. 7] every man [every one] to his own, and shall [will] leave me alone; and
yet I am not alone, because the Father is with me.
33 These things I have spoken unto you, that in me ye might [may] have peace.
In the world ye shall have [ye have, ἔχετε][4] tribulation: but be of good cheer; I
have overcome the world.

TEXTUAL AND GRAMMATICAL.

[1] Ver. 28.—Codd. B. C. L. X., Lachmann, Tischendorf read ἐκ; Cod. A. [C.[2] text. rec.], *etc.* παρά, which might be a dogmatical modification [or a repetition of the παρά in ver. 27].

[2] Ver. 32.—Νῦν [text. rec.] is wanting in ℵ. A. B. C.[1]

[3] Ver. 31.—[I read ἄρτι πιστεύετε not as a question, but, with Luther, Lange, Meyer, Stier, Alford, Godet, as a concession (comp. ver. 27; xvii. 8). Christ recognizes the present faith of the disciples, but shows how weak it was. *Now* (ἄρτι is emphatic) ye believe, but how soon will your faith be shaken! So also Godet: "*Maintenant, vous croyez, il est vrai; mais bientôt, que ferez-vous!*"—P. S.]

[4] Ver. 33.—The ἕξετε [*ye will have*] which Lachmann gives in accordance with B. D., has not sufficient authority to sustain it against ἔχετε [*ye have*, which is supported by ℵ. A. B. C., *etc.*—P. S.]

EXEGETICAL AND CRITICAL.

Ver. 28. **I came forth from the Father and am come into the world** ['Εξῆλθον ἐκ τοῦ πατρὸς καὶ ἐλήλυθα εἰς τὸν κόσμον· πάλιν ἀφίημι τὸν κόσμον καὶ πορεύομαι πρὸς τὸν πατέρα. Bengel: "*Recapitulationem maximam habet hic versus.*" Meyer: "A simple, grand summary of His whole personal life." Mark the symmetry of the four clauses: ἐξῆλθον, ἐλήλυθα, ἀφίημι, πορεύομαι, humiliation and incarnation, death and exaltation.—P. S.]—Solemnly Christ throws the individual elements of His discourse into a concentric expression, one representative of the unity of the whole picture of His life and, hence, declarative to the disciples of the cause of His going back to the Father in an extraordinary manner. He was, namely, obliged so to return because He had come forth from the Father thus wonderfully. The one half of His life, the way from heaven to earth, in faith surveyed by the disciples, demands the other half. The words of Jesus thus give them, for the first time, a clear view of His entire life, and, together with this bestowment, convey to them a ray of the pentecostal Spirit. For enlightenment through the Holy Ghost is, concretely taken, one with the survey and unitous view of the life of Jesus in its totality.

Ver. 29. **Lo, now speakest Thou plainly** [Ἴδε, νῦν ἐν παῤῥησίᾳ λαλεῖς, καὶ παροιμίαν οὐδεμίαν λέγεις].—*Behold, i. e.* with astonishment do they perceive that He even now speaks to them in this new way. We cannot subscribe to Lücke's and Tholuck's unconditional approval of the words of Augustine: *illi usque adeo non intelligunt, ut nec saltem se non intelligere intelligant.** Christ Himself recognizes that some great thing is *now* going on within them, ver. 31. They do but make the mistake of regarding this momentary view enjoyed by them in the radiance of *one* beam of the promised Spirit, as the beginning of an uninterrupted enlightenment and festival of the Spirit. *Now*, say they with emphasis, *now* Thou speakest plainly; even *now* do we perceive that Thou art able to anticipate by Thy disclosure every question that we might still have desired to ask Thee.

Ver. 30. **Now we know**, *etc.*—That they really understood Christ's saying, in respect of its fundamental thought, is proved by the declaration: **by reason of this we believe** [ἐν τούτῳ—*propter hoc*—πιστεύομεν ὅτι ἀπὸ θεοῦ ἐξῆλθες].—*I. e.* from the belief that Thou didst personally and miraculously come forth from God, faith draweth the deduction and reconcileth us to the fact that Thou wilt in like manner go to the Father. Ἐν τούτῳ (*propter hoc*), therefore, does not mean: on account of this that Thou hast just imparted to us, we do now believe that Thou camest forth from the Father,—but—in accordance with the words of Jesus—: supported by this conviction that Thou didst come forth from the Father, we believe the rest also. The first half of Thy life doth explain to us the second. And thus is also Meyer's interpretation set aside: they confess to have found a new and special reason for positiveness in their existent belief in the divine origin of Christ. [Meyer makes ὅτι dependent on πιστεύομεν and indicative of the *object* (not the *ground*) of faith.—P. S.]

Ver. 31. **Ye do now believe** [Ἄρτι πιστεύετε. Comp. ver. 27, πεπιστεύκατε ὅτι, *etc.*, and xvii. 8, ἐπίστευσαν ὅτι, *etc.*—P. S.]—In reading the sentence as a question, with Euthym. Zigab., Olshausen and others,* we should overlook the fact that Christ actually acknowledges the upsoaring of their faith,—a fact evidenced by the very restriction that follows. Lücke dubiously declares against the reading of the proposition as a question; Meyer is more decided in his recognition of the concession therein expressed;† Bengel takes said concession in too unconditional a sense: *nunc habeo, quod volui et volo;* opposed to the latter view are the restrictive ἄρτι and the subsequent words of Christ. [Bengel takes the following words as intended to strengthen the faith of the disciples against the gathering storm.—P. S.]

Ver. 32. **Behold, the hour cometh.**—Not the hour when your faith shall cease (see Luke xxii. 32), but the hour when it shall fail to stand the test,—when, therefore, it shall be characterized as an enthusiasm or rapture. The impulse and inspiration of faith must mature into the settled mind of faith.—**It is already come** [ἐλήλυθεν], saith the Lord, with a presentiment of the approaching crisis.—**That ye will be scattered** [ἵνα σκορπισθῆτε ἕκαστος εἰς τὰ ἴδια], with ἵνα; this is the destiny of the hour. See Matt. xxvi. 31; Zech. xiii. 7. [The passage of the prophet Zechariah, from which the σκορπισθῆτε of our text is taken is more fully quoted by Matthew and reads thus: "Awake, O sword against My Shepherd, and against the man that is My fellow" (My associate, My equal, nearest kinsman=the Messiah), "saith the Lord of hosts: smite the Shepherd, and the sheep shall be scattered" (the dispersion of the disciples at the crucifixion, and then of the Jewish nation), "and I will turn My hand upon the little ones" (the humble followers of Christ, the poor of the flock). Comp. the Notes in Com. on Matthew, p. 478.—P. S.]—**To his own business** or interests. We would not translate εἰς τὰ ἴδια: to his own property or home.‡ Comp. Is. liii. 6. A man's peculiar possessions were no hindrance to the κοινωνία, but the latter *was* shaken by the circumstance of every man's seeking safety in his own way.—**And leave Me alone** [κἀμὲ μόνον ἀφῆτε]. To this degree shall their faith waver.—*Going one's own way*, and *leaving Christ alone*, are reciprocal ideas. [This allusion implies a rebuke, most gently and lovingly expressed, but all the more deeply and humbly to be felt afterwards by the disciples. As a man, Christ was keenly alive to the law of sympathy, and their temporary desertion in the hour of need, when a friend proves to be a friend indeed, must have wounded Him to the quick; but the absence of human help was more than made up by the constant presence of His heavenly Father, and in the clear consciousness of this presence, He soared calmly and serenely over

* ["They so little understand Him as not even to understand that they did not understand; for they were as babes (*parvuli enim erant*)." Similarly Lampe: "They are annoyed that they should be accounted by their Master as unskilful and in need of another Teacher. . . And thus they go so far as to contradict Christ and dispute His plain words, and deny that He was speaking enigmatically to them." This is too strong. The disciples caught a glimpse at the truth and hastily inferred that the pentecostal time had already come for the ἐν παῤῥησίᾳ λαλεῖν. Calvin: *Exultant ante tempus perinde acsi quis nummo uno aureo divitem se putaret.* The stress lies on νῦν, as contrasted with the future λαλήσω and ἀπαγγελῶ, ver. 25.—P. S.]

* [Also Calvin, E. V., De Wette, Tischendorf, Hengstenberg, Ewald; comp. i. 51; xiii. 38; xx. 29.—P. S.]

† [So also Bengel, Stier, Alford, Godet. See TEXTUAL NOTE [3].—P. S.]

‡ [So Meyer: *Seine eigene Aufenthaltstätte;* Godet: *dans leur domicile.* The sense depends on the connection: in ch. xix. 27 τὰ ἴδια means John's home; while in ch. i. 11 it means the Jewish people. Here we are to understand more generally their own ways and interests which the disciples had left before in order to follow Christ; comp. Luke xviii. 28, where Peter says: ἡμεῖς ἀφήκαμεν πάντα καὶ ἠκολουθήσαμέν σοι. So also Bengel and Alford.—P. S.]

the clouds of loneliness caused by the unfaithfulness of men.—P. S.]

And (yet) I am not alone. [καί—adversative, *and yet*, an emphatic and pathetic use of καί, accompanied by a pause and unexpectedly introducing the opposite, as often in John (see Meyer and Alford)—οὐκ εἰμὶ μόνος, ὅτι ὁ πατὴρ μετ' ἐμοῦ ἐστιν.—P. S.] One of the sublimest and profoundest sayings. He will remain confident of the counsel, guidance, approval and presence of His Father and will preserve this confidence even throughout the darkest moment (Eli, Eli, *etc.*). [The exclamation on the cross, Matt. xxvii. 46, proceeded from a momentary *feeling* of desertion by the Father, with an underlying *faith* in His presence; hence He addressed Him still as *His* God, and His will continued subject to Him, as in the agony of Gethsemane. Comp. the Notes on *Matthew*, p. 526.—P. S.]

Ver. 33. **These things have I spoken,** *etc.*—[The concluding farewell word of these farewell discourses, revealing the deepest tenderness and suavity of affection, and indicating the one object: to give them His peace in this evil world, with courage and strength to overcome the world on the ground of His own triumph which He sees already completed.—P. S.] The reference of ταῦτα is not necessarily to the last ταῦτα alone; it refers to the whole of the farewell-discourses. We must recollect that the denial of Peter, and the disciples' inability to follow the Lord, form the starting-point of these discourses. To this thought, the occasion of the farewell-discourses, He has now, at their conclusion, returned. In their despondency they shall be preserved from despair.—**That in Me ye may have peace** [ἵνα ἐν ἐμοὶ εἰρήνην ἔχητε]. In antithesis to the tribulation prepared for them by the world. *In Me:* Luther: In My word; Tholuck: In vital communion with Me (after Gerhard, Lampe).* We may not apprehend the antithesis in as purely objective a sense as attaches to it when applied to the ripened Christian; it has its subjective side as well. Through faith in His word and through the keeping of the same, they were in Christ to an extent that sufficed for the preservation of their peace; but also in the world still, to an extent that necessitated their endurance of a tribulation perilous to their souls. This was their final departure out of the world to full communion with Him. Hence there was need for the exhortation: be of good cheer, and for the subsequent high-priestly, intercessory prayer.

[On εἰρήνη comp. notes on ch. xiv. 27; on θλῖψις, xvi. 21; xv. 18 ff. *Peace* embraces all that constitutes rest, contentment and true happiness of heart on the basis of the Christian salvation and vital union with Christ. *Tribulation* is both persecution from without and distress from within. The happiness of Christians in this life is subject to frequent interruptions and disturbances from their own remaining infirmities and sins as well as from an ungodly world. Yet deep down at the bottom peace continues to reign, however much the surface of the ocean of life may be agitated by wind and storm.—P. S.]

But be of good cheer [ἀλλὰ θαρσεῖτε].—The strengthening of their weakness in their impending tribulation. [A living commentary of this θαρσεῖτε is especially the apostle Paul; comp. Rom. viii. 37; 2 Cor. ii. 14; iv. 7 ff.; vi. 4 ff.; xii. 9; his speech before Felix and Festus, *etc.* (Meyer).—P. S.]—**I have overcome the world.** [ἐγὼ νενίκηκα τὸν κόσμον, "not only *before* you, but *for* you, that ye may be able to do the same;" comp. 1 John v. 4, 5. 'Εγώ—I, not you—is emphatic and gives prominence to that unique personality, whose victory secures all subsequent victories and makes His church indestructible.—P. S.] In the spirit of the farewell-discourses, this is the anticipatory celebration of His victory, or the perfect assurance of victory, expressed in an anticipatory celebration. It was the more proper, however, for this future event to be expressed in the Perfect tense for the reason that His whole course hitherto had been a victory over the world. The threefold victory over its *lust*, in particular, was decided in the story of the temptation in the wilderness (Matt. iv.); the first of the three great victories over the *anguish* of the world was decided in the triumph over Judas (see chap. xiii. 31). These were the pledge of the full accomplishment of His victory. *Be of good cheer, i. e.* this victory shall also conduct them past the tribulation which is in the world. This joyfulness of believers, in reliance on the victory of Christ, first displays itself in the life of the apostles (see Rom. viii.; 1 John v. 4, *etc.*)

[With a cheering shout of victory Christ closes His farewell-discourses to the disciples; but this was an anticipation of faith, which was to be realized by the omnipotent power of God; and hence, going forth to the last and decisive conflict with the prince of darkness, He pours out His heart in prayer to the Father for Himself, His disciples, and the whole future congregation of believers. See next chapter.—P. S.]

DOCTRINAL AND ETHICAL.

(On Chap. xvi. 16-33.)

1. In the preceding section Christ clearly distinguishes His presence with the disciples from the future presence of the Holy Ghost with them. But now He reveals to them the prospect of *Himself* speedily being *with them* again in a new form. By this can be meant, in the first instance, nothing else than the Resurrection, with its manifestations; that, however, is at the same time a symbol and pledge of the general fact of their future meeting;—of their meeting by means of viewing Christ in spirit, of their meeting on the way to the Father and in the Father's House, and of their meeting in the Parousia. With the Holy Ghost He Himself shall re-appear to them in His glory. The new day of Christ is but one day, and also the eternal seeing of Him again in faith is essentially one seeing.

2. *A little while* [ver. 16]. The one and the other μικρόν are symbolical of the alternation of Good Friday and Easter periods in the Church; an alternation regularly continuing until the day of Christ's appearing. The Apostles studied

* [So also Meyer: "Living and moving in Me." Comp. xv. 7. "This presupposes the return from the scattering in ver. 32,—the branches again gathered in the Vine" (Alford).—P. S.]

this μικρόν their whole lives long; but when proclaiming, as they did, ever and anon, during the tribulations of the early Church: the Lord cometh quickly, it is the last time, the last hour, they announced a *religious* date, established through the fellowship of the Christian spirit with the Spirit of God and Christ, before whom a thousand years are as one day and one day as a thousand years (2 Pet. iii. 8); and it is a decided mistake of modern exegetes to be continually regarding this *religious* date of a lofty, apostolic view of the world, as a *chronological* date of chiliastic error. The same Paul who, in a religious sense, proclaimed: "The Lord cometh quickly" (1 Thess.), in the second Epistle to the Thessalonians opposed the chronological misunderstanding by the declaration: The Lord cometh not so soon; and the same John who wrote the words: "It is the last hour" (1 John ii. 18), did in Revelation likewise depict the grand succession of the ages until the appearing of Christ.

3. Ver. 20. *The distress of the disciples, the joy of the world.* And the joy of the disciples? Here the Lord has not carried out the parallel, for the joy of the disciples is to be the Evangel for the world, and only to the impenitent portion of the world shall it be an occasion of lamentation. Hence homilists, in completing the second antithesis also, are but conditionally correct. Only the impenitent world with its distressful lamentations, forms a contrast to the joy of the disciples.

4. [Ver. 21.] *The sufferings of Christ were the birth-pangs of the Theocracy*, which made themselves felt in the disciples, the true children of the Theocracy. Christ's resurrection, however, was, in reality, *the birth of the eternal man* into the eternal world, simultaneously with which birth the *new mankind*, as a whole, was born into the world. When He died, the great work of God was finished; when He rose, the eternal God-Man was perfected. With Him the Church, the new mankind, was born. On this birth see Rev. xii. 1; on the First-born, Col. i. 18; on the congenitive humanity, Col. iii. 1. Comp. the note on Cl. 1 of ver. 22, p. 497.

5. Ver. 22. All Christianity is an *alternation of mourning and joy*, as the natural life is an alternation of joy and sorrow; parting grief and joy of meeting, in the highest sense. Joy not to be taken away. An alternation in spiritual, as in natural things, but in an inverse order.

6. *Verily, verily, etc.* (ver. 23): the solemnly asseverated, absolute hearableness of prayer in that degree in which it is prayer; and His *Amen* a prophecy of a hearing, spoken by the Spirit of prayer.

7. The Christian life is a spiritual life in which inquiries and researches are transformed into entreaties and experiences, ver. 24. That great day of New Testament spiritual life is a day when men shall live in the communion of the Father, the Son and the Holy Ghost, a day when men shall walk in the manifestation of heaven upon earth. See notes to ver. 23.

8. Perfect joy, and life in the Spirit are one. An exhortation to Pentecostal prayer. See note to last clause of ver. 24.

9. [Ver. 25.] To a man in an unenlightened state, every discourse, even one which in a direct manner presents ideas to the mind, becomes a *parabolic* speech; to a man in a condition of enlightenment, every discourse, even the figurative, parabolical one, becomes an undraped word of revelation; just as the unconverted man has, in addition to the [Mosaic] Law another Law in the Gospel, while the converted man finds, added to his Gospel, another Gospel in the Law. Law and symbol are the indivisible forms of revelation for the pious of tender age; the law for the heart and conscience, the symbol for the understanding; whereas, on the other hand, the Gospel and spiritual speech are the inseparable forms of revelation for the believer who has attained to maturity; see note to ver. 25. Life in the Spirit is a life in the ever new revelation, in the everlasting Gospel, Rev. xiv. 6.

10. [Ver. 26.] In the life of the faithful, Christ's intercession coincides with the immediate prayer of the Holy Spirit within the heart (Rom. viii. 26), in which latter prayer the manifestations of the Father's love are announced.

11. [Ver. 28.] The one half of the life of Christ,—namely, His personal coming, as the Son of God, from the Father—is the key to the other half—His going, in divine glory, to the Father.

12. [Vers. 29, 30.] The disciples, in obtaining from the Lord their first general view of His entire life and course, also experienced a foretaste of the Holy Spirit. For the Holy Spirit is the divine life in its central unity. Hence the first illumination touching the life of Christ and of all the divine manifestations in general, completed in the ascension, is the instrumentality for the reception of the Holy Ghost; as the anointing of the Holy Ghost is the instrumentality for the full, undivided view of the life of Jesus in its unity. The unit is needful and unity indispensable. This is so much a law of life, that always with the dismemberment of the patchwork of knowledge, life takes its departure, but with its centralization, life is evolved. For this cause, poly-history is an inanimate, true science a living, thing. For this cause, legality through ordinances is lost in death, while from central saving faith it develops an abundant life in God-like virtues. Even the pantheistic feeling of all-oneness (*Alleinsgefühl*) displays a rich shimmering of spirit; but a shimmering as false as pantheism itself, in its antagonism to personality. We do not doubt that the disciples had, in that moment, a glimpse of Pentecost.

13. This glimpse was, however, the last moment of their pre-Pentecostal enthusiasm. Enthusiasm is the blossom of the new life—a blossom, in prophetic times, so gloriously unfolding in the prophetic word. But enthusiasm must first pass through mortal suffering, to the end that it may set into fruit, into fire-proof disposition of mind. Such trial, therefore, was now imminent even upon the disciples, according to ver. 32.

14. Ver. 33. Christ's *peace* in the faithful on earth, is heaven upon earth. They have this peace in Him; in the world they have anguish. What is yet wanting to the fulness of peace, shall be supplied by the courage and confidence inspired by the thought that He has overcome the world. Peace is made entire by cheerful confi-

dence, as salvation through patience, Rom. viii. 25; see 1 John v. 4.

15. Christ *alone*, and yet *not alone* in His hour of suffering. See note to last clause of ver. 32.

16. The farewell-discourses of Jesus: discourses speaking *peace, warning, consolation, victory.* Ver. 33.

HOMILETICAL AND PRACTICAL.

(On vers. 16-33.)

How heaven and earth are now through Christ already made one in reality, with a view to their one day becoming one in actual manifestation also.—The great word of the Lord: *a little while;* 1. A little while and ye shall not see Me; 2. a little while and ye see Me again.—How we, in company with the disciples, have to make a life-long study of the words: a little while.—Alternation betwixt Good Friday and Easter periods: 1. In the life of Christ, 2. in that of the Church, 3. in that of the individual Christian, 4. in that of the whole present age of the world.—The history of the natural birth of man, a symbol of the history of the higher life.—Christ, as the First-born from the dead, is the First-born for the kingdom of everlasting life.—The blossom of the highest heavens in the low, earthly world.—The brightest day (ver. 23), preceded by the darkest hour (ver. 32).—The Christian life as the joy of fresh seeing: 1. The seeing of Christ again, perfect joy; 2. perfect joy a pledge of all Christian re-seeing, ver. 22.—And on that day: 1. Easter-day as Sunday, 2. Sunday as Easter-day.—The new and great God's Day of the Resurrection: 1. One day as a thousand years; 2. a thousand years as one day.—How all our questioning and searching should terminate in faithful prayer, ver. 23.—Acceptable prayer, vers. 23, 24.—Prayer in the name of Jesus.—The distinction of parabolic speech and spiritual speech: 1. In the word of revelation; 2. in the word of the Church; 3. in the ear of the Christian.—Tokens of salvation in fidelity to Jesus: 1. Prayer urged in His name guarantees us His intercession; 2. love to Him is our guaranty that the Father loves us; 3. the belief that He has come unto us from the Father is our guaranty that He has gone for us to the Father; 4. the word that He has spoken unto us is our guaranty that He will tell us all things.—The blissful moment of the disciples a foretoken of their darkest hour.—Even though the congregation be scattered, Christ standeth firm on the battle-ground.—Christ alone and not alone.—How Christ hath armed His people for their warfare, ver. 33.

The Christian's peace in the tribulation of the world: 1. How the peace of Christ and tribulation in the world demand one another; 2. the peace of Christ a source of tribulation in the world; 3. tribulation in the world a token of the peace of Christ.—The peace of Christ as a victory over the tribulation in the world: 1. How, as peace in Christ, it calls forth tribulation in the world; 2. how, as peace through Christ, it inspires courage and cheerfulness, and exalts a man above the tribulation of the world.

On the Pericope Jubilate (Gospel for the Third Sunday after Easter), vers. 16–23. Christianity, as the highest vicissitude betwixt sorrow and joy, contrasted with the worldly life as the highest vicissitude of joy and sorrow.—The word of the Lord, *a little while:* 1. An enigma to the disciples (vers. 16-19); 2. a prophetic type in the mouth of the Lord (vers. 19-22); 3. a blissful contemplation and experience in the new life of the children of His Spirit.—The natal hour of the natural man a type of the natal hour of the kingdom of God: 1. Symbol of the woman; 2. symbol of the child.—Every human being a token of the change between sadness and joy in the kingdom of God: 1. With anguish expected and born; 2. jubilantly received and welcomed into life.—The winning of life from out the peril of death: 1. In the natural life; 2. in the spiritual life.—Out of supreme renunciation the fulfilment of all desires, ver. 23.—The weeping and lamenting of the godly,—how it is changed into filial entreaties, proffered with heavenly confidence.—In the way of Christ all lost, all gained.—The heaviest hour (ver. 21), the womb of the most glorious day (ver. 23).—The word of the Pericope: *Be joyful!*

On the Pericope Rogate (Gospel for the Fifth Sunday after Easter), vers. 23-30. The new life of the faithful in the day of salvation: 1. A new speaking of believers to the Lord (ask nothing, ask in the name of Jesus); 2. a new speaking of the Lord to believers (not through parables, but through the immediate word of the Spirit); 3. a new order of conversation (He anticipates all their questions with His answers).—*The day of salvation:* 1. A day of blissful silence in view of the revelation of Christ (ver. 23); 2. a day of blissful prayer in view of the revelation of the Father (ver. 26).—The new life a praying in the name of Jesus: 1. A new craving, in contemplating His heavenly personality, for the full manifestation of the personal kingdom; 2. a new praying, trusting in the victorious right of His personality; 3. a new striving in the strength emanating from His personality.—The old and the new order of things in the Kingdom of God: 1. A communion of disciples, a communion of apostles (ver. 23); 2. a praying in general, an asking in His name; 3. an asking for the renunciation of all things; an asking for the granting of all things; 4. a parabolic word, a word of spirit and knowledge; 5. the consciousness of human love to the Lord, the consciousness of being divinely loved by the Father; 6. belief in the mission of Christ, belief in the life of Christ as perfected in the humiliation and exaltation.—How Christ's discourse concerning the Pentecostal time procured for the disciples the first blissful ante-celebration of that Pentecostal time.—The word of the Pericope: *Pray!*

STARKE: Of the disciples' state of mourning and rejoicing.—HEDINGER: Our tribulation is temporal, 2 Cor. iv. 17; Is. liv. 7; Ps. xxx. 5.—Men are always desiring to know how it shall fare with them in the world; here they are informed: They shall experience a constant alternation of joy and sorrow.—Men often do not understand the best consolation, it being, for the most part, enveloped in what appears to them the greatest cross.—CRAMER: It is a vexatious order of things in this world, that the godly weep, and the wicked laugh, believers mourn, and sinners rejoice, Job xxi. 7; Jer. xii. 1; Ps. lxxiii. 3.

But there shall follow a different alternation in which all will be reversed.—The best cometh last.—Woman is saved through child-bearing, if she abide in the faith, 1 Tim. ii. 15.—If the physical birth be so hard, what must the spiritual be!—O blissful pains, blessed labor! 2 Cor. xii. 10.—Worldly joy is unstable, and an evil hour sweepeth all away, but the joy of eternal life hath no end, 1 Pet. i. 4.—On ver. 26. Teachers particularly, as also other Christians, must accommodate themselves to the weak as much as is possible, and deal with them according to their simplicity, if they desire that their labor should not be in vain among them.—HEDINGER: God leads from one glory to another, until the face of Christ is fully uncovered.—There is still much of the knowledge of God, our heavenly Father, in arrears to us; but what we do not learn here, we shall certainly know in heaven.—As wine issues from grapes when they are pressed, and as spices, when bruised, give forth a powerful odor, so the tribulation of believers beareth glorious fruits, Eph. vi. 13.—Nowhere in the world is there rest for a child of God, but (everywhere) anguish only; in Christ, however, his Redeemer, he finds peace.

LISCO: The spiritual (and not simply spiritual) re-seeing, *i. e.* the new spiritual fellowship with Jesus, is for His people the *ground* of an indestructible joy.—GERLACH: The death of Christ, with all its effects upon His people, was the birth-pain of the new man upon earth; from His death there issued forth a new mankind unto the resurrection.—The joy which at that time sprang up, was an imperishable one, for the new man was, through Christ's resurrection, born forever, *i. e.* the redemption, with its infinite, eternal results, might not cease, but must grow into infinitude. The last words (ye shall ask me nothing) are to be understood similarly to Jer. xxxi. 34. The condition upon which ye then, after the Holy Ghost has led you into the whole truth (ver. 13), shall enter, sustains the same relation to your present one that the condition of a mature and intelligent man bears to that of a child, who must frame a separate question with regard to each thing, because he is ignorant of the centre and connection of the whole.—The whole, full meaning of the name of Jesus was first explained to them by His death and glorification.—In the filial relationship itself, the free love of the Father is sovereign, so that in that relationship we have free access to Him.—BRAUNE: Jesus does not say: a child; He says,—that a *man* is born—a man, still undeveloped, yet present, with all his hopeful powers, dispositions and destinies, in the child. The very pangs pierced the spring of out-gushing joy.—Tears are oft-times the dew-drops on the grass and the flower, by which names man is designated, Is. xl. 7; chap. xxvi. 17; lxvi. 7; Jer. iv. 31.—Every affliction (religiously applied), is a birth, in which the new man, or some gracious addition to the new man, is born.—Where religion is, there is prayer; but as the one varies, so also does the other. In Homer the Priest is called a Pray-er.

HEUBNER: The application of this saying to parting and meeting is very obvious and almost worn out. But the saying is deeper. It is the key to the knowledge of divine Providence.—(In sooth, the highest meeting of blessed spirits in the kingdom of Christ has the most perfect depth and is a final aim of Providence.)—The words: "A little while," contain much consolation for those who are in bodily distress, poverty, sickness,—for those who sorrow, *etc.*—The impatient man, indeed, would fain object: that is no *μικρόν*—it is a *μακρόν*.—Why does God part good men?—Hear His word, 1. Thou mourner; 2. thou child of fortune; 3. thou presumptuous sinner, 4. thou faithful and godly Christian!—We should regard the thought of the future meeting not simply as a joyous one, but also as a thought full of solemnity and warning. For many a one the re-seeing of others will be fearful.—Our spiritual life, also, is subject to vicissitudes. At one time we see Christ; at another we see Him not. The Christian's art is *patiently to wait.*—Vers. 17, 18. God's ways are often dark sayings to us also. The joy of the world is a brief joy, the suffering of the just is a brief suffering.—The recollection of sufferings endured out of love to, and for the sake of, God, is that which gives sanctity and dignity to joy.—Ver. 21. This simile reveals the tender interest which Jesus felt in mother-woes and mother-joys. Hence it must be refreshing to sensitive and pious mothers. Jesus bestowed a glance upon them. (Veith.)—Worldly joy and the dead Christ; spiritual joy and the living Christ.—Vigorous pangs are an indication of vigorous births; it is so also in spiritual things.—(Fenneberg): The children of God have three kinds of birthdays: 1. The natural one. Then they weep; their kinsmen rejoice. 2. The new birth. Then, also, do they often weep piteously; the angels in heaven rejoice. 3. The day of death (celebrated among the martyrs in the ancient Church as a birth-day). Their end is not without tears and woe, but after that an eternal rejoicing begins.

Jubilate-Pericope. [Vers. 16-23.] HEUBNER: The grief of the Apostles at their separation from Jesus: 1. Description (source, effects). 2. Application.—The tender love of Jesus for His weak, mourning disciples.—*Of prayer in Jesus' name:* No Christian prayer remains unheard.—Kant would not pray; but in his last hours he folded his hands. Spinoza could not pray, and wept because he could not.—Ability to pray is a sure indication of our own inner life, of our Christian condition. When we pray and learn to pray in Christ's name, there begins a new period in our life.—Prayer makes the spirit serene.—Ver. 25. (Luther): His words were dark and recondite to the disciples; it was as if He spoke with them in an unknown tongue; for as yet they had no experience of what He told them and knew not what sort of a kingdom Christ would establish. Hence, in accordance with the judgment of Jesus, an entirely new life-period must set in at such time as we begin to pray in Jesus' name, nay, to call upon Himself.—In the same sense in which He now leaves the world—personally, therefore—He had come forth from God.—Ver. 30. *Now we know, etc.* Whence did they know this? Because Jesus could thus read their hearts.

Rogate-Pericope. [23-30.] HEUBNER: Spirit of Christian prayer.—Close connection of our praying with our whole Christian piety.—Prayer the breath of spiritual life.—Doubts as to the blessing of prayer.—Causes of the non-hearing of prayer.—Prayer as the highest honor.—Ver. 32. When thou art deserted of all, fear not, so God but be with thee.—Who stands with Christ, and cleaves to Him, takes part in His victory.

GOSSNER: The humble and ingenuous man, failing to understand some passage in God's word, asks and learns; the proud and disingenuous man takes occasion thereat to despise or reject that word.—Ver. 19. Jesus advances to meet those who honestly desire truth and helps them out of their doubts. He anticipates their questions.—All is brought forth in anguish.—*He* was taken from them then (at His ascension); not so *joy*, Luke xxiv. 52.—Since that time they do ever see Him in spirit; He is at home with them; they are His house and His dwelling-place, John xiv. 23; Heb. iii.—There is a saying that people who have seen spectres are never glad any more, so long as they live. One who has seen Him can never grow sad. It is a privilege of God's children to pray to the Father in Jesus' name. —This promise: Whatsoever ye shall ask in My name, *etc.*, presupposes that our hearts and minds are in harmony with the Saviour.—Ver. 27. Men have such sorry thoughts about the Father, as if He were a hard man, with whom a legion of intercessors must speak for us and constrain and compel Him, as it were. But the Son of the Father tells a very different tale about Him.—Ver. 28. Thus must we too leave the world, if we would approach the Father.—His eternal outgoing, or birth from the Father, His coming and being born in the flesh as Man, His regeneration (birth of glorification)—by means of His death, resurrection and ascension—unto an everlasting, divine-human life in glory, are three births worthy of our wonder and admiration and constraining our worship.

SCHLEIERMACHER: The glorifying of the Lord forms part of the essential and imperishable work of the Holy Ghost.—The form of the Redeemer is set up for all ages in imperishable glory within the souls of the faithful, through the work of the Spirit whom He has poured out upon His Church.—*The Father loveth you because, etc.* The Father loveth us in the Son and will also be loved only in the Son.—*I am not alone.* He would comfort us with this truth,—that though we, *from weakness*, should leave Him alone, He yet is not alone, but His Father is with Him.—How could we derive comfort from the thought that the Lord has overcome the world, if we were not assured that He has overcome the world in our hearts.

BESSER: The final aim of all God's dealings with Christians, especially of all our experience in prayer, is this: "*that our joy may be perfected.*" *Not seeing* occasions sorrow, *seeing* occasions joy. It is a blessed thing that back of the *little while* of *sorrowful not seeing*, so soon over and gone, there lies a future of *joyful seeing* which shall never pass away.—*The seeing again:* The *Pentecostal* coming and seeing forms the central point, that of *Easter* is preparatory thereto, that of the last day is its completion.—And thus did the ancient Church understand the matter, for she has taken the Gospels for the four Sundays from *Jubilate* to *Exaudi* all out of the farewell-discourse in which Easter and Pentecost tones ring out together.—His speech is triply incomprehensible to them: in the first place, they know not what sort of a seeing shall succeed the not seeing; in the second place, they meditate fruitlessly upon the marvellous *because* ("because I go to the Father") and are unable to lay hold on the glorious fruit of His departure; lastly and thirdly (this they purposely thrust forward as particularly enigmatical), the hasty alternation between seeing and not seeing, the little while, they regard as wonderful exceedingly.—The sigh of St. Bernard: O thou little, *little while*, how long thou art! And the still more ancient sigh of David: Lord, how long! (Ps. vi. 3; xiii. 1, 2; lxxxix. 47).—We must have patience if we would arrive at the true *Jubilate.* — Ps. xxx. 11.—Is. xxvi. 17-20.—In those forty hours of travail the disciples wept and wailed as if there were on earth none but sinners godlessly laughing in their sin and sinners helplessly weeping over their sin (Stier).—"There is none whom the heavenly Father calleth *Benjamin* (son of my right hand), whom the Church, his mother, hath not first called *Benoni* (son of my sorrows)" (J. Gerhard). —Rev. xii.—John xx. 20, comp. with Luke xxiv. 52.—A white sheet (*carte blanche*), says Spener, subscribed beneath with His holy name, to be filled in above by ourselves with our petitions. —"If *I* do not deserve that my prayer should be heard, nevertheless *Christ*, in whose name I offer the same, doth abundantly deserve a hearing." (Luther).—If ever a request is denied us, it is because it is out of tune with the grand petition: Grant us but salvation.—"Whoso saith 'Our Father,' doth embrace in this one prayer the forgiveness of sins, justification, sanctification, redemption, sonship and heirship to God, brotherhood with the Only-begotten One, and the whole plenitude of the gifts of the Holy Spirit" (Chrysostom).—Vers. 26, 27. How should He not love those who become one with Him in the love of the Beloved?—"Threefold is the way which Christ trod for the salvation of the children of men: The way of love (from heaven to earth), the way of obedience (unto the death on the cross), the way of glory (return to the Father").—J. Gerhard. (According to ver. 28, however, the way is a twofold one.)—*Ye shall be scattered*, Zech. xiii. 7; Matt. xxvi. 31.—*The Father is with me.* John Huss comforted himself with this saying in his lonely dungeon.—Ver. 33. It is the peace of Shiloh (Gen. xlix. 9, 10; Is. ix. 6, 7; Rev. v. 5), of the celestial Solomon, Song viii. 10.—"Peace in Christ is that on which all Christian essence reposes. This peace shall have no end in time, but is itself the end of all our holy endeavors" (Augustine).—In order that we might have peace in Him, did the Lord speak these things. *His* word brings us peace.—Peace must triumph over anguish.—"'Tis *won!* 'Tis *won!* He crieth; danger and trouble are over. We need not struggle and war. All is done already. The world, death and the devil lie vanquished and prostrate; heaven, righteousness and life are victorious" (Luther).*

* [Here follow a number of themes for sermons, which are omitted.—P. S.]

[CRAVEN: From AUGUSTINE: Vers. 16-22. The bringing forth is compared to sorrow, the birth to joy, which is especially true in the birth of a boy.—*And your joy no man taketh from you:* their joy is Christ.—Nor yet in this bringing forth of joy, are we entirely without joy to lighten our sorrow, but, as the Apostle saith, we *rejoice in hope:* for even the woman, to whom we are compared, rejoiceth more for her future offspring, than she sorrows for her present pain.—Ver. 23. The word *whatsoever*, must not be understood to mean *anything*, but *something* which with reference to obtaining the life of blessedness is *not nothing*. That is not sought in the Saviour's name, which is sought to the hindering of our salvation; for by, *in My name*, must be understood not the mere sound of the syllables, but that which is rightly signified by that sound. He who holds any notion concerning Christ, which should not be held, does not ask in His name. But he who thinks rightly of Him, asks in His name, and receives *what* he asks, if it be not against his eternal salvation: he receives *when* it is right he should receive; for some things are only denied at present in order to be granted at a more suitable time.—Ver. 24. This *full joy* is not carnal, but spiritual, and it will be *full* when it is so great that nothing can be added to it.—And this is that full joy, than which nothing can be greater, viz. to enjoy God, the Trinity, in the image of Whom we are made.—Ver. 26. *At that day ye shall ask in My name:* What shall we have to ask for in a future life, when all our desires shall be satisfied? Asking implies the want of something.—Ver. 30. He asked questions of men not in order to learn Himself, but to teach them.—Ver. 31. He reminds them of their weak tender age in respect of the inner man.

[From CHRYSOSTOM: Ver. 21. He shows that sorrow brings forth joy, short sorrow infinite joy, by an example from nature; *A woman when she is in travail hath sorrow, etc.*—By this example He also intimates that He loosens the chains of death, and creates men anew.—Ver. 28. It was consolatory to them to hear of His resurrection, and how He came from God, and went to God: the one was a proof that their faith in Him was not vain; the other that they would still be under His protection.

[From GREGORY: Ver. 33. As if He said, Have Me within you to comfort you, because you will have the world without you.—From BEDE: Ver. 21. As a man is said to be born when he comes out of his mother's womb into the light of day, so may he be said to be born who from out of the prison of the body, is raised to the light eternal.—From ALCUIN: Ver. 20. This speech of our Lord's is applicable to all believers who strive through present tears and afflictions to attain to the joys eternal. While the righteous weep, the world rejoiceth; for having no hope of the joys to come, all its delight is in the present.—Ver. 21. The *woman* is the holy Church, who is fruitful in good works, and brings forth spiritual children unto God.—As a woman rejoiceth when a man is born into the world, so the Church is filled with exultation when the faithful are born into life eternal.—From THEOPHYLACT: Ver. 24. For when your prayers shall be fully answered, then will your gladness be greatest.—Ver. 27. The Father loves you, because ye have loved Me; when therefore ye fall from My love, ye will straightway fall from the Father's love.

[From BURKITT: Vers. 16-22. How unreasonable it is to arrogate to man's understanding a power to comprehend spiritual mysteries, yea, to understand the plainest truths, till Christ enlightens the understanding.—Ver. 20. The different effects which Christ's absence should have upon the world, and upon His disciples.—Ver. 22. The joy of the saints may be interrupted, it shall never be totally extinguished.—Ver. 23. To pray in the name of Christ, is, 1. To look up to Christ, as having purchased for us this privilege; 2. To pray in the strength of Christ, by the assistance of His grace, and the help of His Spirit; 3. To pray by faith in the virtue of Christ's mediation and intercession.—Ver. 25. The clearest truths will be but dark mysteries, even to disciples themselves, till the Holy Spirit enlightens their understandings.—Ver. 30. The knowledge and experience of Christ's *omniscience*, may and ought fully to confirm us in the belief of His Deity.—Ver. 32. God was with Christ, and will be with Christians in a suffering hour, in His *essential* presence, in His *gracious and supporting* presence.—Ver. 33. Hence learn, 1. That the disciples of Christ in this world must expect and look for trouble; 2. The remedy provided by Christ against this malady: *In Me ye shall have peace.* Christ's blood has purchased peace for them, His word has promised it to them, and His Spirit seals it up to their souls.—*I have overcome the world*, I have taken the sting out of every cross, the venom out of every arrow.

[From M. HENRY: Ver. 16. It is good to consider how near to a period our seasons of grace are, that we may be quickened to improve them while they are continued.—*The Spirit's* coming was Christ's visit to His disciples, not a transient, but a permanent one, and such a visit as abundantly retrieved the sight of Him.—Thus we may say of our ministers and Christian friends, *Yet a little while, and we shall not see them.* It is but a *good night* to them whom we hope to see with *joy in the morning.*—Ver. 18. The darkness of *ignorance* and the darkness of *melancholy* commonly increase and thicken one another; mistakes cause griefs, and then griefs confirm mistakes.—Though we cannot fully solve every difficulty we meet with in scripture, yet we must not *therefore* throw it by, but revolve what we cannot explain, and wait *till God shall reveal even this unto us.*—Ver. 19. The knots we cannot untie, we must bring to Him who alone can give an understanding.—Christ takes cognizance of pious desires, though they be not as yet offered up.—This intimates to us who they are that Christ will teach: 1. The *humble* that confess their ignorance. 2. The *diligent* that use the means they have.—Ver. 20. Believers have joy or sorrow, according as they have or have not a sight of Christ.—*The disciples were sorrowful and yet always rejoicing* (2 Cor. vi. 10); had sorrowful lives, and yet joyful hearts.—Vers. 21, 22. Applicable to all the faithful followers of the Lamb, and describes the common case of Christians—1. Their condition and disposition are both mournful; sorrows are their lot, and seriousness is their temper. 2. *The world*, at the same time, goes away with all the mirth. 3. Spiritual mourning will shortly be turned into eternal rejoicing.—The sorrows of Christ's disciples in this world are like travailing pains, sure and sharp, but not to last long, and in order to a joyful product.—Christ's withdrawings are just cause of grief to His disciples. When the sun sets, the sunflower will hang the head.—Three things recommend the joy: 1. The cause of it; *I will see you again.* 2. The cordialness of it; *Your heart shall rejoice.* 3. The continuance of it; *Your joy no man taketh from you.*—Note—1. Christ will graciously return to those that wait for Him, though *for a small moment* He has seemed *to forsake them*, Isa. liv. 7. 2. Christ's returns are returns of joy to all His disciples.—Joy in *the heart* is solid, secret, sweet, sure.—Vers. 23-27. An answer to their askings is here promised, for their further comfort. Now there are two ways of asking, asking by way of *inquiry*, that is the asking of the *ignorant;* and asking by way of *request*, and that is the asking of the *indigent.* Christ here speaks of both—1. By way of *inquiry*, they should not need to ask. 2. By way of *request*, they should ask nothing in vain.—The promise itself is incomparably rich and sweet; the golden sceptre is here held out to us, with this word, *What is thy petition, and it shall be granted?*—We are here taught *how* to seek; *we must ask the Father in Christ's name.—Perfect fruition* is reserved for the land of our *rest; asking* and *receiving* are the comfort of the land of our *pilgrimage.*—Ver. 24. Here is an invitation to them to petition. It is thought sufficient if great men *permit* addresses, but Christ *calls upon* us to petition.—Vers. 26, 27. Here are the grounds upon which they might hope to speed, which are summed up in short by the Apostle (1 John ii. 1). *We have an Advocate with the Father*—1. We have an *Advocate;* 2. We have to do with a *Father.*—Ver. 27. The character of Christ's disciples; they love Him, because they *believe He came out from God.*—See what advantage Christ's faithful disciples have,—the Father loves them, and that because they love Christ.—Believers, who love Christ, ought to know that God loves them, and therefore to come boldly to Him as children to a loving Father.—Vers. 28-33. Two things Christ here comforts His disciples with: 1. An assurance that, though He was leaving the world, He was returning to His Father; 2. A promise of peace *in Him*, by virtue of His victory over the world.—Vers. 29, 30. Two things they improved in by this saying (ver. 28): 1. In knowledge, *Lo, now Thou speakest plainly ;* 2. In faith, *Now we are sure.*—When Christ is pleased to *speak plainly* to our souls, and to bring us with open face to behold His glory, we have reason to rejoice in it.—Observe—1. The *matter* of their faith; *We believe that Thou camest forth from God;* 2. The *motive* of their faith — His omniscience. — Those know Christ *best*, that know Him by *experience.*—These words, *and needest not that any man should ask Thee*, may speak either: 1. Christ's *aptness* to teach; or, 2. His *ability* to teach.—The best of teachers can only answer what is *spoken*, but Christ can answer what is *thought.*—Vers. 31, 32. As far as there is *inconstancy* in our faith, there is cause to question the *sincerity* of it, and to ask, "Do we indeed believe?"—Ver. 32. Many a good cause, when it is distressed by its enemies, is deserted by its friends.—If we at any time find our friends unkind to us, let us remember that Christ's were so to Him.—Those will not dare to suffer for their religion, that *seek their own things* more than the *things of Christ.*—Even *then*, when we are taking the *comfort* of our *graces*, it is good to be reminded of our *danger* from our *corruptions.*—A little time may produce great changes, both *concerning* us and *in* us.—*Yet I am not alone, because the Father is with Me.* A privilege common to all believers, by virtue of their union with Christ—1. When solitude is their *choice;* 2. When solitude is their *affliction.*—While we have God's favorable presence with us, we are happy, and ought to be easy, though all the world forsake us.—Ver. 33. It has been the lot of Christ's disciples to have more or less tribulation in this world. Men persecute them because they are *so good*, and God corrects them because they are *no better.*—In the midst of the tribulations of this world, it is the duty and interest of Christ's disciples to be of good cheer.—Never was there such a conqueror of the world as Christ was, and we ought to be encouraged by it; 1. Because Christ has overcome the world *before us;* 2. He has conquered it *for us*, as the Captain of our salvation.

[From A PLAIN COMMENTARY (Oxford): Ver. 16. He shows that on His *departure* depended His *mysterious presence.*—Vers. 29, 30. Faith admits of degrees; and one of the periods is here marked when the disciples made a clear advance in this heavenly grace.—Ver. 33. It was not the object of the present Divine Discourse to gratify curiosity, or to solve doubts (for *that* was reserved for the Holy Ghost); but to administer heavenly consolation.

[From STIER: Vers. 16-24. There is, as for Himself the breaking through death into life, so for the disciples a deeply penetrating, fundamental *change from sorrow to joy.*—As this *way of the disciples through sorrow to joy* between the cross and the resurrection of our Lord was already for themselves something preparatory and typical, it becomes to us a type of the way which *all His future disciples* have also to pass through;—a way through that godly sorrow which at first distinguishes them fully from the world, into the joy of faith, and life in the Holy Ghost.—Ver. 20. This rejoicing of the world is the keenest sword to weakness and unbelief, as well as to the true dependence of the sorrowful disciples trusting in God (Ps. xlii. 10).—The sorrow is *itself* to *become* joy; it is not merely to be lost in, or exchanged for, joy, but the subject and ground of the sorrow becomes the subject and ground of the joy. The cross of our Lord is glorified into an eternal consolation; *out of* the sorrow at the cross and the sepulchre, because in it there was the believing and loving seeking of the Crucified, *is born* their joy in the Living, Risen One.—Those who weep, bear already the precious seed which rises again into sheaves of joy—"on the flood of tears we float out of ruin."—Ver. 21. Under the cross of their Lord the disciples learned to *sorrow for sin*, as they had never been taught before. They saw and they tasted with Christ, as far as in them lay, *the sin of the world*, and they saw, moreover, *their own sin* in it.—The way from sorrow to joy was to the first disciples as the pangs of birth for the outburst of resurrection-gladness. None of us appropriates, in true personal experience, the joy of Easter and Pentecost until the passion-sorrow has first prepared the way.—Ver. 22. "One feast followed another after the passion, in which *they had sorrow:* at the resurrection He *saw them again*, but (*we* would add) *they saw not Him yet* in full clearness, they had not their full joy through fear of the Jews; first at the ascension, when they saw Him go to the Father (βλεπόντων αὐτῶν, Acts i. 9), *their hearts rejoiced;* but this also would have vanished as a beautiful dream if the Comforter had not assured them at Pentecost that *no man should take from them their joy.*" (BECK.)—The last fulfilment of this promise reaches forward to the end of the church's victory, and this joy of the heart is the contrast of the world's joy turned into mourning (Is. lxv. 13, 14).—The world which, with or without Christ, would evade the thought of sin and death, the deepest ground of all sorrow, can secure its joy only by the dissipation of its inmost nature, and by becoming deaf to its voice. Therefore its joy is *loud*, while yet *silent* joy is alone genuine and profound.—The world is satisfied without satisfaction.—We lose not the heart's peace in the midst of all the tribulation which may befall.—The root and principle and strength of their joy cannot be touched, however afflictions may come.—The child-bearing woman is (further) the Church through the Spirit within her.—As the sum of all: Every disciple of Jesus through his entire life, the Church of Christ as a whole down to the end of the days, learns and experiences in the cross of Christ that true sorrow which genders *joy*, receives and enjoys *this* as the fruit of the resurrection and Pentecost in a progressive measure ever approaching perfection—until the great Day dawns, which will be followed by no night. Ver. 23. In the eternal glory, which will be the final issue of all temporal adversity, all our past doubts will be solved, all our complaints silenced, and *all our questioning answered* for ever.—Vers. 23, 24. Now, in the bright hope of that great day, *ask and pray as ye have never done before!*—As in the Old Testament way of holiness the problem had ever been to learn better how to *pray*, so also *we* have in the practice of prayer in the name of Jesus the only way of progress toward perfect holiness, knowledge and joy of heart. All the discourses, exhortations, encouragements of our Lord, find their ultimate aim in directing us to perfect prayer.—Ask, so shall ye *receive!* Many, alas, who only half pray, and do not urge their knocking even to pressing in, cannot afterward *receive* even what they have prayed for! But persistent prayer "obtains for me the blessing that I can receive, and appropriates that which the Father gives,—actually obtains the hand which enables me to lay hold of and receive the heavenly gifts." (RIEGER.)—Ver. 26. The state of perfection which knows no need is not *yet;* there is still the asking, and yet it is the *same* day. We seal every prayer with a doxology reaching forth, in confident and tranquil trust, toward the future eternity; and thus it is already the *same day* in the light of which we ask and receive the answer.—Ver. 27. This word most decisively overturns that false notion concerning the redemption which attributes to the Father *a wrath* which is to be extinguished, and not also that *reconciling love* which from eternity needed not first to be propitiated.—Christians who believe, to whom Christ has revealed this in all its clearness, cannot too often be reminded of this; "think not too little of the love wherewith *ye* are loved!" Not merely has the Father Himself already loved them as He loves all the world and every creature, but He loves *them* with that *especial* love which He bears to those in whom He finds Christ's word, and through faith in it Christ Himself, who stand before Him clothed in the garment of the righteousness of His Son.—Ver. 28. *To what end* did He come into the world, but to become the Saviour of sinners? Again, *to what end* and *in what way* does He return to the Father, but that He may accomplish eternal redemption through death, and diffuse from on high the fruits of His redeeming work?—Vers. 31, 32. It is true that ye do believe, but how soon will my passion make manifest your real and great weakness!—Ver. 32. "Whosoever well ponders this, will hold firm his faith though the world shake, nor will the defection of all others overturn his confidence; we do not render God His full honor, unless He alone is felt to be sufficient to us." (CALVIN.)—Ver. 33. In these last words He "condenses the sum of the instruction which He had ministered to the disciples at the last supper." (NITZSCH.)—Tribulation is certainly not alone "the violence and enmity of the world, which causes grief and anxiety to the disciples." For all this would not interrupt our peace, if the persecution did not meet with and excite weakness of faith, and the temptation sinful desire, *in us.* We must call to mind the θλῖψις of the woman in child-birth, a tribulation *from within* and *of herself.*—*Who is he*, where is there one, that overcometh the world, *except he that believeth* that Jesus is the Son of God? "In Him all overcome who rejoice to be the world overcome by Him." (NITZSCH).

[From BARNES: Ver. 20. The apparent triumphs of the wicked, though they may produce grief at present in the minds of Christians, will be yet overruled for their good.—Ver. 31. When we feel strong in the faith, we should examine ourselves. It may be that we are deceived; and it may be that God may even then be preparing trials for us that will shake our faith to its foundation.—Ver. 32. Pain is alleviated, and suffering made more tolerable by the presence and sympathy of friends; *He* died forsaken.—It matters little who else forsakes us, if God be with us in the hour of pain and of death.—The Christian can die, saying, I am not alone, because the Father is with me.—Ver. 33. The world is a vanquished enemy. Satan is an humbled foe. And all that believers have to do is to put their trust in the Captain of their salvation, putting on the whole armor of God.——From OWEN: Ver. 30. There was doubtless much darkness and error in their mind, much unbelief and sin yet to be eradicated from their heart; but yet their words were sincere, their love deep and tender, and their faith, imperfect as it was compared with its power after their baptism of the Spirit, embraced all His declaration.—Ver. 32. God the Father did not leave His beloved Son to enter *alone* upon His great redemptive work, but was with Him through all the scenes of His bitter agony. [The Father was ever with the Son; but was not His presence hidden from the *consciousness* of Jesus in the last hour, when He exclaimed, *My God, why hast Thou forsaken Me?*—E. R. C.]. Ver. 33. Here is the ground of all faith, confidence, and hope; only as the soul rests in Jesus, can it attain to that spiritual *peace* which is the foretaste of blessedness above.]

THE HIGH-PRIESTLY, INTERCESSORY PRAYER OF CHRIST ON BEHALF OF HIS PEOPLE. A PRAYER FOR THE GLORIFICATION OF HIS NAME EVEN TO THE GLORIFICATION OF HIS PEOPLE AND THE WORLD, OR UNTIL THE VANISHMENT OF THE WORLD AS WORLD. CHRIST, IN HIS SELF-SACRIFICE FOR THE WORLD, THE TRUTH AND FULFILMENT OF THE SHEKINA AND ALL THE MANIFESTATIONS OF GOD IN THE WORLD. GLORIFICATION OF PRAYER, OF DECISIVE CONFLICTS OF SPIRIT, OF SACRIFICE. THE HEAVENLY GOAL.

CHAP. XVII.

1 These words spake[1] Jesus, and lifted up his eyes to heaven and said [and having lifted
up . . . he said],[2] Father, the hour is come; glorify thy Son, that thy [the] Son also [omit
2 also] may glorify thee: As [According as] thou hast given him [gavest him, ἔδωκας]
power over all flesh, that he should give eternal life to as many as thou hast given
him [that whatsoever, or, all which thou hast given him, he might give to them life
3 eternal, ἵνα πᾶν ὃ δέδωκας αὐτῷ, δώσει αὐτοῖς ζωὴν αἰώνιον]. And this is life eternal [the
eternal life, ἡ αἰώνιος ζωή], that they might know[3] thee the only true God, and Jesus
4 Christ, whom thou hast sent [didst send]: I have glorified [I glorified, ἐδόξασα] thee
on the earth: I have finished [having finished, or, by finishing, τελειώσας][4] the work
5 which thou gavest [hast given, δέδωκας] me to do. And now, O Father, glorify thou
me with thine own self with the glory which I had with thee before the world was.[5]

* * * * * * * * * * * * * *

6 I have manifested [I manifested] thy name unto the men which [whom] thou
gavest me out of the world: thine they were, and thou gavest[6] them [unto] me;
7 and they have kept thy word. Now they have known [they know][7] that all things
8 whatsoever [*even* as many as] thou hast given me are of [from] thee. For I have
given unto them the words which thou gavest me; and they have received *them*, and
have known [they received them and knew][8] surely that I came out [forth] from thee,
9 and they have believed [and believed] that thou didst send me. I pray for them: I
pray not for the world, but for them which [those whom] thou hast given me; for they
10 are thine. And all mine [all things that are mine, τὰ ἐμὰ πάντα, neut.] are thine, and
11 thine are mine; and I am [have been] glorified in them. And now [*omit* now] I am
no more [longer] in the world, but [and, καί] these are in the world, and I come [am
coming] to thee. Holy Father, keep through thine own name those whom [keep them
in thy name which ἐν τῷ ὀνόματί σου ᾧ][9] thou hast given me, that they may be one
12 [even] as we *are* [*omit are*]. While I was with them in the world [*omit* in the
world][10] I kept them in thy name: those that thou gavest me I have kept [I
kept them—ἐτήρουν—in thy name which[11] thou hast given me, and guarded,
watched over—ἐφύλαξα—them], and none [not one] of them is lost, but the son of
13 perdition; that the Scripture might [may] be fulfilled. And [But] now come I
[I am coming] to thee; and these things I speak in the world, that they might
14 [may] have my joy fulfilled [made full] in themselves. I have given [δέδωκα] them
thy word; and the world hath hated [hated, ἐμίσησεν] them, because they are not
15 of the world, even as I am not of the world. I pray not that thou shouldest take
them out of the world, but that thou shouldest keep them from the evil [the evil
16 one, ἐκ τοῦ πονηροῦ]. They are not of the world, even as I am not of the world.
17, 18 Sanctify them through thy[12] truth [in the truth]: thy word is truth. As thou
hast sent [didst send] me into the world, even so have [*omit* even so have] I also sent
19 [or, even so I sent] them into the world. And for their sakes [or, for them, in their

behalf] I sanctify myself [mine own self], that they also might [may] be sanctified
through [in] the truth.

* * * * * * * * * * * * * * * *

20 Neither pray I for these alone [Yet not for these alone do I pray], but for them
also which shall believe [but also for those who believe, τῶν πιστευόντων][13] on [in] me
21 through their word; That they all may [may all] be one; as thou, Father, *art* in me,
and I in thee, that they also may be one[14] in us: that the world may believe that thou
22 hast sent [didst send] me. And the glory which thou gavest [hast given, δέδωκας] me I
23 have given [δέδωκα] them; that they may be one, even as we are one: I in them, and
thou in me, that they may be made perfect in [perfected into, τετελειωμένοι εἰς] one;
and [*omit* and[15]] that the world may know that thou hast sent [didst send] me, and
hast loved [didst love, or, lovedst] them, as thou hast loved [didst love, or, lovedst]
24 me. Father, I will that they also, whom [that what[16]] thou hast given me,[17] be
with me where I am; that they may behold my glory, which thou hast given me:
for thou lovedst me before the foundation of the world.
25 O [*omit* O] righteous Father,[18] [and (yet), καί[19]] the world hath not known thee
[knew thee not]: but I have known [knew] thee, and these have known [knew] that
26 thou hast sent [didst send] me. And I have declared [I made known] unto them
thy name, and will declare *it* [make it known]; that the love wherewith thou hast
loved [didst love, or, lovedst] me may be in them, and I in them.

TEXTUAL AND GRAMMATICAL.

[1] Ver. 1.—[Cod. A. B. C. D. E., *etc.*, Tischend., Treg., Alf, Westc. and H., read ἐλάλησεν, Cod. Sin. λελάληκεν, *had spoken*, which Noyes follows in his translation: "When Jesus had thus spoken."—P. S.]

[2] Ver. 1.—[ℵ. B., *etc.*, Lachm., Treg., Tischend., Alford, *etc.*, read ἐπάρας without καί, instead of the text. rec.: ἐπῆρεν. . . . καί.—P. S.]

[3] Ver. 3.—The ἵνα γινώσκουσιν (A. D. G. L., *etc.*, Tischendorf) probably not merely an ancient error in transcription (Meyer), but also a dogmatical correction. Ἵνα γινώσκωσι seems at the same time to denote the impulse of a striving after the perfect knowledge of God and Christ, characterizing such impulse as the beginning of eternal blessedness. [Tischend., ed. VIII., and Tregelles read γινώσκουσιν, but Lachm., Alford, Westcott and Hort, read γινώσκωσιν, which is supported by ℵ. B. C. X., Orig., and adopted also by Lange in his version: "*dass sie dich müssen erkennen.*" Alford and Noyes translate "*to know*," Conant: "*that they know.*"—P. S.]

[4] Ver. 4.—[The text. rec. reads ἐτελείωσα with D., Vulg.; but ℵ. A. B. C. L., *etc.*, and the best modern authorities read τελειώσας, which explains ἐδόξασα.—P. S.]

[5] Ver. 5.—[Instead of πρὸ τοῦ τὸν κόσμον εἶναι παρὰ σοί, Cod. D. reads γενέσθαι.—P. S.]

[6] Ver. 6.—[For the second δέδωκας, *thou hast given* (C. L., Orig., *etc.*, Alford), I prefer ἔδωκας, *gavest*, which is supported by ℵ. A. B. D. K, and adopted by Tregelles, Tischend., Westcott and Hort.—P. S.]

[7] Ver 7.—[ἔγνωκαν is best sustained by (A.) B. C. D., *etc.*, Lach., Tisch., Treg., Alf., Westc. Cod. Sin. reads ἔγνων. U. X. ἔγνωσαν.—P. S.]

[8] Ver. 8.—Καὶ ἔγνωσαν is wanting in A. D., Sin.,* Itala; it is bracketed by Lachmann, and by Meyer regarded as a gloss. It, however, has a decided reference to chap. xvi. 30. Codd. B. [C. L.], *etc.*, Hilary, support it. [Alford, Tregelles, Tischend. ed., viii., Westcott and Hort retain it.—P. S.]

[9] Ver. 11.—The reading ᾧ [referring to ὄνομα] instead of οὓς [referring to αὐτούς], rests upon A. B. C. [ℵ.], *etc.*, and is decisively established by the Codd. [ᾧ is adopted by Treg., Alf., Tischend., W. and H. See the Exeg.—P. S.]

[10] Ver. 12.—Ἐν τῷ κόσμῳ is wanting in B. C.* D. L., Sin., *etc.* With reason rejected by Lachmann and Tischendorf.

[11] Ver. 12.—Codd. B. L., *etc.*, read ᾧ δέδωκάς μοι καὶ ἐφύλαξα. Thence arises the reading in Tischendorf: "I kept them in Thy name which Thou hast given me, and I have watched or guarded them." Codd. A. D., *etc.*, are against said reading. [Treg., Alf., Tischend. ed. viii., W. and H., read also in ver. 12 ᾧ, instead of the οὓς of the text. rec.—P. S.]

[12] Ver. 17.—Σου is to be rejected in accordance with A. B. C.,* *etc.*, (Lachmann).

[13] Ver. 20.—In accordance with A. B. C. D., Sin., *etc.*, πιστευόντων instead of [text. rec.] πιστευσόντων. [All critical edit. read πιστευόντων.—P. S.]

[14] Ver. 21.—Ἓν is wanting in Codd. B. C.* D., *etc.*, in the Itala, *etc.*, in Hilary (Tischendorf). Ἓν is supported by Cod., A., Origen and, very decidedly, by the subsequent sentence. The world can see that Christians are one, but it cannot see that they are in God. [Cod. Sin. sustains the text. rec., but all the latest critical editions except Lachm., drop ἕν.—P. S.].

[15] Ver. 23.—The καί before ἵνα should be omitted. [So all the crit. edd.]

[16] Ver. 24.—Tischendorf reads ὅ in accordance with Codd. B. D., Lachmann οὓς in accordance with Cod., A., *etc.* This reading of the Recepta is sanctioned by Cyprian and Hilary. [ὅ is also sustained by Cod. Sin., and adopted by Alford, Tregelles, Tischend., Westcott and Hort. "The neuter has a peculiar solemnity uniting the whole church together as *one gift* of the Father to the Son" (Alford). In this case we should translate: "I will that *what* thou hast given me (ὅ δέδωκάς μοι), even they (κἀκεῖνοι) may be with me," *etc.*; or "As to that which thou hast given me, I will that they also be with me," *etc.*—P. S.]

[17] Ver. 24.—We retain the reading δέδωκας in accordance with the weightiest Codd. [instead of ἔδωκας. The E. V. is by no means consistent in the rendering of the tenses, and repeatedly confounds the aor. and perf. in this ch.—P. S.]

[18] Ver. 25.—[πατήρ: A. B.; πάτερ: ℵ. C. D. L.—P. S.]

[19] Ver. 25.—[καί is omitted in D. and Vulg., but sustained by the best authorities. On its meaning see the Exeg. Alford, like the E. V., ignores it in the translation; Meyer translates: *und gleichwohl* (*and yet*); Lange: *ja doch.*—P. S.]

EXEGETICAL AND CRITICAL.

[Introductory Remarks.—The seventeenth chapter, the simplest, and yet the deepest and sublimest in the whole Bible,* contains the *sacerdotal* or *high-priestly* prayer of our Lord, so called because He here intercedes for His people and enters upon His function as the High-Priest in offering His own life as a perfect sacrifice for the sins of the whole world.* Dr. Lange (see

* [Bengel: "*Quis non gaudeat, hæc perscripta exstare, quæ cum Patre locutus est Jesus? Hoc caput in tota Scriptura est verbis facillimum, sensibus profundissimum.*"—P. S.]

* [*Precatio sacerdotalis* or *summi sacerdotis*, first used in the sixteenth century by a Lutheran divine (Chytræus). Godet: "*On a appelé cette prière sacerdotale. C'est bien, en effet, ici l'acte du souverain sacrificateur de l'humanité, qui fait off-*

DOCTR. AND ETHIC. below) justly claims for it also a *prophetical* and *kingly* character. There are several prayers of Jesus recorded in the New Testament: the model prayer for His disciples (Matt. vi. 13), brief thanksgivings (Matt. xi. 25, 26; John vi. 11; xi. 41, 42); the petition in Gethsemane (Matt. xxvi. 39; comp. the similar petition John xii. 2); and the exclamation on the cross: "Father, forgive them," "Eli Eli," "Father, into Thy hands." The sacerdotal prayer, spoken in the stillness of the night, under the starry heavens, before the wondering disciples, in view of the approaching consummation of His work, for Himself, His apostles, and His Church to the end of time, is peculiarly His own, the inspiration of His grand mission, and could be uttered only by Christ, and even by Christ only once in the world's history, as the atonement could occur but once, but its effect vibrates through all ages. It is not so much the petition of an inferior, or dependent suppliant, as the communion of an equal, and a solemn declaration of His will concerning those whom He came to save. While praying to the Father He teaches the apostles (Bengel: *orat Patrem, simulque discipulos docet*).* He prays as the mighty Intercessor and Mediator standing between earth and heaven, looking backward and forward, and comprehending all His present and future disciples in one holy and perfect fellowship with Himself and the eternal Father. The words are as clear and calm as a mirror, but the sentiments as deep and glowing as God's fathomless love to man, and all efforts to exhaust them are in vain. See the quotation below *sub* B.—P. S.]

A. The time of the High-priestly prayer of Jesus. It is indicated with the going forth over the brook Kedron [xviii. 1]. The crossing of the brook Kedron was the act and sign of final decision. It is not necessary to understand the going forth as a going forth from the Supper-room, for the precincts of the city probably extended, in single residences, down into the valley.

B. Worth of the prayer. The highest estimation was accorded it by ancient theologians. Luther: "It is, verily, an exceeding fervent, hearty prayer; a prayer wherein He discovereth, both unto us and to the Father, the abysses of His heart and poureth forth its treasures."† Spener, according to Canstein (*Spener's Leben*, p. 146), would never preach on this chapter; he declared that a true understanding of it mounted above the ordinary degree of faith which the Lord is wont to communicate to His people on their pilgrimage. The evening before his death, however, he caused it to be read to him three times in succession.‡ Chytræus called it *precatio summi sacerdotis*. Similarly, Melanchthon (see Lücke, II., p. 692),* Lampe, Bengel [see quotation on p. 511], Herder and others have expressed their admiration of the prayer.

[Barnes: "It is perhaps the most sublime composition to be found anywhere." Owen: "It is Christ's almighty *fiat*, addressed to the Father, as Him from whom He came forth, and as the one that had covenanted to save and bless all who by the drawing of His ineffable love had come to Jesus." Tholuck: "If in any human speech divinity is manifest, and sublimity is joined to condescending humility, it is in this prayer." De Wette: "Here all the parting discourses are summed up and raised to the highest pitch of thought and feeling. It is beyond a doubt the sublimest part of the evangelical tradition, the pure expression of Christ's lofty consciousness and peace of God (*unstreitig das Erhabenste was uns die evang. Ueberlieferung aufbewahrt hat, der reine Ausdruck von Jesu hohem Gottesbewusstsein und Gottesfrieden*)." This testimony has all the more weight on account of the skeptical tendency of De Wette. Luthardt (II., 354): "Neither in the Scripture nor in the literature of any nation can there be found a composition which in simplicity and depth, in grandeur and fervor may be compared to this prayer. It could not be invented, but could proceed only from such a consciousness as the one which speaks here. But it could be preserved and reproduced by a personality so wholly devoted and conformed to the personality of Jesus as the Evangelist." Ewald (p. 386 f.): "A prayer such as the world never heard nor could hear . . . For Himself He has little to ask (vers. 1-5), but as soon as His word takes the character of an intercession for His own (6-26), it becomes an irresistible stream of the most fervent love. . . Sentence rushes upon sentence with wonderful power, yet the repose is never disturbed." Meyer (p. 587) calls it "the noblest and purest pearl of devotion in the New Testament (*die edelste und reinste Perle der Andacht im N. T.*)."—P. S.]

Bretschneider, on the other hand, has opened the way for the most unfavorable opinions of modern, negative criticism. He calls it an "*Oratio frigida, dogmatica, metaphysica.*"

[Rationalists and the advocates of the mythical and legendary hypothesis of the life of our Lord can do nothing with this prayer. Renan (*Vie de Jésus*, p. 275, 12th ed.) disposes of all the parting discourses, ch. xiii.–xvii., in a short footnote, categorically declaring that they cannot be historical, but must be a free fiction of John in his own language. So also Strauss, Weisse, Baur, Scholten. Such a view, which stands and falls with the whole fiction-theory of the Johannean discourses of Christ, is not only revolting to all religious feeling, but plainly incompatible with the depth and height, the tenderness and

---

rande à Dieu et de lui-même et de tout son peuple présent et futur." Hengstenberg derives this designation, rather arbitrarily, from the Aaronic benediction, Lev. ix. 22; Num. vi. 22 ff.—P. S.]

* [Comp. also Lampe: "*Confirmatio et conservatio discipulorum scopus primarius harum precum erat.*" Schmieder (*Das hohepriesterl. Gebet*, 48): "His speech was not only an outpouring of His heart towards the Father, but at the same time a well considered self-exhibiting work for the disciples."—P. S.]

† [Luther adds: "Plain and simple in sound, it yet is so deep, rich and broad that no one can fathom it." Luther's exposition of ch. xvii. was composed in 1534.—P. S.]

‡ [So did John Knox, who never feared the face of man, but bowed, like a child, before the will and word of God. In his last sickness he directed his wife and his secretary "that one of them should every day read to him, with a distinct voice, the seventeenth chapter of the Gospel according to John, the fifty-third of Isaiah, and a chapter of the Epistle to the Ephesians. This was punctually complied with during the whole time of his sickness." Th. M'Crie, *Life of John Knox* (Philada. ed. 1845), p. 332.—P. S.]

* [Melanchthon says: "*Digniorem nec sanctiorem nec fructuosiorem, nec magis patheticam vocem in cœlo ac terra unquam auditam fuisse quam hanc ipsius Filii Dei precationem.*" Zanchius (quoted by Lampe, III., p. 358): "*Plena est maximis consolationibus.*"—P. S.]

fervor of this prayer. If John, or whoever was the author of the Gospel, invented it, he must have been conscious of his own fiction and intention of deceiving the reader. That a person in such a frame of mind and heart could produce such a prayer as this, is a psychological and moral impossibility. That the prayer, as the discourses of Christ generally, was not only translated from the Hebrew into the Greek, but freely reproduced in John's mind, and received his peculiar coloring, may be admitted without impairing the faithfulness as to the thoughts and spirit, especially if we take into consideration that the Paraclete reminded the apostles of Christ's words and opened to them their full meaning (ch. xiv. 26; xv. 26; xvi. 13, 14). Godet (II., 367) justly remarks against Reuss, that the internal miracle of a faithful reproduction of the long discourses of Christ is less inexplicable than the artificial composition or fiction of such a master-piece.—P. S.]

C. Historical truth of the prayer and its relation to the agony in Gethsemane. The modern criticism of Bretschneider, Strauss, Baur pretends to discover a contradiction between the triumphant mood of Jesus in this prayer and His dejection in Gethsemane. This rests partly on the false assumption that in Gethsemane Christ petitioned for the averting of His death. See, in opposition to this view, Comm. on *Matthew* [p. 481, Am. Ed.] Since there can be no question of a change of resolve, but only of a change of mood, we have simply to recognize the profundity and gloriousness of Jesus' psychical life in the great contrasts presented by His mental frames. [Sudden transitions of feeling belong to human nature, and cannot appear strange in Christ who was peculiarly sensitive and sympathetic, yet in all these changing moods retained equilibrium and self-control, comp. ch. xi. 33 ff. On the apparent inconsistency between the calmness and repose of the sacerdotal prayer and the subsequent agony in the garden, which was but the anticipation of the sufferings of the cross, comp. also the sensible remarks of Meyer, p. 588, Hengstenberg, III. 143, and Godet, II. 507 f.—P. S.]

D. But *why* did not John append the psychical combat of Jesus in Gethsemane to this prayer? A presentation of that was, like a presentation of the Supper, foreign to his plan, and the omission must be justified by that plan. The victory of Jesus, in His spiritual sorrow, over Judas (chap. xiii. 31), involved the victory in Gethsemane, as also His victory on the cross. Moreover, John had related the prelude consisting of the suffering of Jesus in the circle of disciples, and the scene in the Temple-precincts (chap. xii. 27), and could assume the Church's familiarity with the conflict in Gethsemane, to which familiarity Heb. v. 7 also bears testimony. [Besides Christ Himself points to the agony, ch. xiv. 30, in the words: "The prince of this world cometh, and hath nothing in Me."—P. S.]

E. Symbolism of the prayer: With eyes upraised to heaven. An evidence that He seeks His home above, where the Father is. The observation that, in an astronomical sense, there is no above or beneath, is a worthless one here. Heaven, as the place where the Divine glory is manifested, constitutes the *above*, in antithesis to earth. Christ prays aloud, in order to the consolation and elevation of the disciples, for here, too, the rule holds good, that the human reference and design of prayer does not vitiate its directness and subjectivity. See chap. xi. 42. Augustine: *Tanti magistri non solum sermocinatio ad ipsos, sed etiam oratio pro ipsis discipulorum est ædificatio.*

F. Progression of the Prayer:

1. Christ first prays for His own glorification, vers. 1-5.

2. Then for the preservation of His disciples, vers. 6-19.

3. Finally for the congregation of believers, which they are to lead to Him; for their unity and perfection in the kingdom of glory, that the whole world may believe through them, may attain unto knowledge and, as world, vanish out of existence, vers. 20-24.

4. The conclusion sums up the whole in the thought that Christ's love in the disciples shall become the full presence of Christ in the world. [The connecting idea of the three parts is the work of God, as accomplished by Christ, carried on by the apostles, and to be completed in the church, to the glory of God.—P. S.]

Ver. 1. **These words spake Jesus and having lifted up His eyes,** *etc.* [*Ταῦτα ἐλάλησε ὁ Ἰησοῦς, καὶ ἐπάρας τοὺς ὀφθαλμοὺς αὐτοῦ εἰς τὸν οὐρανὸν εἶπε.* The double *καί* (*text. rec.*) is not carelessness (De Wette), but solemn circumstantiality of expression (Meyer). But *ἐπάρας* without *καί* is better authenticated than *ἐπῆρεν* with *καί*.—P. S.].—With this expression the Evangelist connects the prayer of Jesus with the farewell discourses, making it the sealing of the same. Prayer the blossom of holy speech; meditation the root of prayer. [Christ prayed aloud, partly from the strength of emotion which seeks utterance in speech, partly for the benefit of His disciples (ver. 13), that He might lift them up to the throne of grace and reveal to them and to the church the love and sympathy of His heart. Such reflection, especially in a prayer of intercession for others, is quite consistent with the deepest spirit of devotion (comp. on ch. xi. 42). The occasion made an indelible impression on the mind of John, who depicts here also the gesture and heavenward look of the praying Lord.—P. S.]

To heaven.—Calvin: *Quia cœlorum conspectus nos admonet, supra omnes creaturas longe eminere deum.* See the beginning of "*Our Father.*" We could not absolutely infer from this remark by itself, that Jesus offered up His prayer in the open air, as Rupert and others affirm. Since that fact, however, is otherwise established, the expression gains in significance.

[In prayer the eye of faith is always instinctively directed to heaven, as heaven is everywhere open, and angels are ascending and descending. Heaven is the abode of the Hearer of prayer and Giver of every good gift. Every prayer of faith is a spiritual ascension. Christ addresses God here as "*Father,*" *πάτερ*, simply, six times in this prayer, not "*Our* Father," as in the Lord's Prayer, which is intended for the disciples, nor "*My* Father," where He prays for Himself only. Bengel: "*Talis simplicitas appellationis ante omnes decuit Filium Dei.*" He is the Only Begotten Son of *His* Father, we the common children of *our* Father (comp. John xx. 17). The name of Father is the most endearing under which we can know and address God, and which calls out all our feelings of filial trust and gratitude. Christ probably used the Aramean word אַבָּא, *Abba*, which passed into the devotional vocabulary of Christians, Rom. viii. 15; Gal. iv. 6.—P. S.]

The hour is come [*ἐλήλυθεν ἡ ὥρα*].—The great, unique hour of decision by death and resurrection, which are inseparable; the hour whose aim and consummation is the glorification [xii. 23; xiii. 1, 32].

Glorify Thy Son [*δόξασόν σου τὸν υἱόν*—*σου* placed first to give force to the petition which, being the prayer of the Only Begotten Son, can not be refused—*ἵνα* (*καὶ*) *ὁ υἱός* (*σου*) *δοξάσῃ σέ*.—P. S.]. *δόξασον*, conduct Him into the state of *δόξα*, of glory. See ver. 5. This glorification of the Son was fulfilled in the Resurrection and Ascension, the "unbounding" of Christ; similarly, the thence-issuing glorification of the Father was fulfilled through the outpouring of the Holy Ghost and the establishment of the Church and of the gospel ministry. The interpretation of Didymus [De Wette, Reuss]: Manifest Me to them who know Me not, is expressive of but one consideration: the effect of Christ's exaltation. "The communication to mankind of the true consciousness of God" (Baur) is, apprehended monotheistically, a glorification of the Father. [Stier: "These words are a proof that the Son is equal to the Father as touching His Godhead. What creature could stand before his Creator and say, 'Glorify Thou me, that I may glorify Thee?'"—The Son glorifies the Father, not by adding to His glory, but by making it known to men through the Holy Spirit, who makes known and thus glorifies the Son.—P. S.]

Ver. 2. **According as Thou gavest Him,** *etc.* [*Καθὼς ἔδωκας αὐτῷ ἐξουσίαν πάσης σαρκός*].*—The *power over all flesh*, received by Christ, in His divine-human person, from God [xiii. 3], and in spirit exercised by Him through His spiritual victory, is the measure and index of His hope of glorification. The infinite power of His personality over mankind, the infinite verification of that power in the self-humiliation of His love, shall be the measure of His infinite glorification.—**Over all flesh** [*πάσης σαρκός*].—An Old Testament expression [*col basar*=all mankind], not found elsewhere in John. A solemn emphasizing of the universalism of His destination for the whole human race; the designation applied to mankind is significant not only of its antithesis to the spiritual life of Christ, but also of its susceptibility of salvation. This power over all flesh is expressive, therefore, of the magnitude of His expectations with regard to the spread of His gospel. See Phil. ii. 6 ff.

That all which Thou hast given Him, to them He should give, *etc.* [*ἵνα πᾶν ὃ δέδωκας αὐτῷ, δώσῃ* (al. *δώσει*) *αὐτοῖς ζωὴν αἰώνιον*].—A select number is not here meant by this; the peculiar expression (*πᾶν, αὐτοῖς*) brings out the fact that the Father has given Him a great, unitous collectivity in the creation;—a mass limbing and sundering into individual members, as men, successively exercising, and departing in, faith, come into possession of eternal life. The collective mass of created beings, souls destined for salvation, is necessarily broken up into individual members, for every man must *singly* attain to saving faith; this individualization, however, is but conducive to a higher unity. See ver. 21. His glorification is, it is true, an end in itself; nevertheless, it also aims at the bliss of believing humanity; and the one design is inseparable from the other. The design of the creation of the world is the glorification of God and Christ in the blessedness of men; such, likewise, is the design of the redemption. The Father is to be glorified by the diffusion of salvation in Christ, the dissemination of eternal life.

Ver. 3. **Now this is the eternal life** [*αὕτη δέ ἐστιν ἡ αἰώνιος ζωή*].—*Ζωὴ αἰώνιος*, see ch. i. 4; iii. 16, 36. According to the Prologue, the Logos appears in the fundamental forms of light, life, and love; and His absolute life (1 Tim. vi. 19) is communicated to believers, through the Holy Ghost, as the fundamental impulse and might of eternal life. Life is an appearing from within outwards, in the form of self-development; eternal life is an eternal self-rejuvenating and appearing; it is life in the eternity of God, inclusive of all times and spaces; the eternity of God in the power of life; an unobstructed self-developing beyond the æons. *The believer has the unity of eternity in the manifoldness of life and the manifoldness of life in the unity of eternity.** "If we define life as the undisturbed self-development of the idea implanted in the being, the term signifies, subjectively, self-gratification, bliss,—objectively, the glorification of the finite life in the divine." Tholuck. Chap. xv. 1-3. *This is, αὕτη δέ ἐστιν.* Not metonymically: *hoc modo paratur* (Beza, *etc.*), but by way of explanation: herein it consists, in respect of its principle.

That they must know Thee [*ἵνα γινώσκωσί* (*γινώσκουσί*) *σέ τὸν μόνον ἀληθινὸν θεὸν*—the distinctive truth of the O. T.—*καὶ ὃν ἀπέστειλας Ἰησοῦν Χριστόν*—the distinctive truth of the N. T.]. *ἵνα.* Eternal life at the same time an eternal, unobstructed striving, or further striving, toward a goal continually attained and as continually set afresh.† See the Textual Notes. The tendency toward the knowledge of God is not distinct and separate from that toward the knowledge of Christ; they are in reality one; the essential, true tendency of man. To this bias there is an *objective* and a *subjective* definitiveness.

I. The *objective.* Meyer after Lücke: A (confessionally distinct) summary of belief in antithesis to the polytheistic (*τ. μόνον ἀληθ. θεόν*), and Jewish *κόσμος* (which latter rejected Jesus as the Messiah). The distinction of the true God and His Ambassador emphasizes the personality of God and Christ, and lays stress upon the

* [Ewald begins a new sentence with *καθώς*, which is concluded in ver. 4, so that ver. 3 is parenthesis. Against this construction see Meyer.—P. S.]

* [Webster and Wilkinson: "As elsewhere, so here most especially, it is important to notice that *ζωή* in this connexion does not mean merely *conscious existence*, nor *αἰώνιος* merely *endless duration*; but by *ζ. αἰών.* is signified 'the life belonging to eternity,' the highest *kind* and *state* of being of which the creation is capable."—P. S.]

† [Godet: *ἵνα est mis au lieu de ὅτι, parce que la connaissance est présentée comme un but à atteindre.*—P. S.]

knowledge of it as the condition of life and development for the human personality (in opposition to Pantheism). The objective definitiveness of the expression requires that Christ should speak of Himself in the third person; He subsequently returns to ἐγώ.—**The only true God** [τὸν μόνον ἀληθινὸν θεόν, comp. μόνος σοφὸς θ., Rom. xvi. 27; μόνος ὅσιος κύριος, Rev. xv. 4.—P. S.]. The only *essential*, real God;—ἀληθινός in antithesis to the unreal, symbolical and mythical gods of the world, not of the Gentile world alone, but also of later Judaism in its estrangement from the faith of revelation, 1 John v. 20; Rev. v. 7; 1 Thess. i. 9. It is the God of revelation in Christ, the God and Father of our Lord Jesus Christ, Eph. i. 3; not in antithesis to the Old Testament idea of God or to the idea of Christ, but in antithesis to all false and obscured belief in God; hence God as He reveals Himself in Christ, distinct as to His divine consciousness and distinguished from Christ.—**And Him whom Thou hast sent, Jesus Christ.** Tholuck: Not Moses, not a prophet, could have been named in this co-ordination, by the side of God, but He only who could say: "he that seeth Me, seeth the Father." Calvin: *Sensus est, Deum mediatore tantum interposito cognosci.* At the same time, however, the modification of God's and Christ's personality must be observed. Where God is rightly known, He is known as the μόνος ἀληθινός; where Jesus is rightly known as the Sent of God, He is known as the Χριστός. In opposition to this, Tholuck says: According to the Christological view, the Father is not known *along with* the Messiah, but *in* Him, chap. x. 38; xiv. 7, 8; viii. 19. But it is just in the distinction of the two personalities that true knowledge of God in Christ is consummated.

Several explanations present themselves:

(1) Augustine, Ambrose [Hilary] and others: As though it were written: *Ut te et, quem misisti, Jesum Christum, cognoscant solum verum deum.** This is contrary to the text, though from the distinction of Christ from God the Arians and Socinians draw an unjust inference against the divine nature of Christ, the knowledge of God being indissolubly connected with the knowledge of Christ.

(2) The two terms are *nomina propria* in undivided unity (Tholuck, Luthardt).† In such case, however, too great a portion of the weight of the passage would be transferred from the objective to the subjective side, the knowing.

(3) Τὸν μόνον, *etc.* is predicate to σε, Χριστός is predicate to: "Whom Thou hast sent," Jesus (Clerikus, Nösselt and others).‡

(4) Χριστός is the subject; the predicate is contained in ὃν ἀπέστειλας (De Wette).

The last two interpretations lay too great stress upon the ideal on the objective side. We must not apprehend the modifications as predicates, declarative of doctrine, but as definitions, explanatory of the nature of Father and Son, or definitive *nomina appellativa.*

II. *Subjective definitiveness of the sentence.* "The schools, after the precedent of Augustine, held γινώσκειν to be a proof of the *beatitudo intuitiva æternitatis;* in the Hegelian period it was considered to prove the dignity of speculative science. But even Greek exegesis recognizes the practical value of the term; Cyril: τὴν ἐν ἔργοις πίστιν, Calov.: *notitia practica,* better: experimental knowledge. See chap. vi. 19." Tholuck. Still, we cannot overlook the fact that the whole experience of faith is teleologically leveled at its consummation in contemplative knowledge (Matt. v. 8; 1 Cor. xiii. 12). John recognizes no knowledge that is not practical, but also no practice whose aim is not seeing. The term *knowing* is so centrally poised between *believing* and *seeing,* as to embrace both, as well as mark the transition from the first to the second.*

Ver. 4. **I glorified Thee on the earth** [ἐγώ σε ἐδόξασα ἐπὶ τῆς γῆς, τὸ ἔργον τελειώσας (rec. ἐτελείωσα). The aorists are proleptical and should not be rendered as perfects as in the E. V.—P. S.]—Foundation of the foregoing petition. This not in the sense of urging His claims to being glorified by the Father on the score of legal merit, but in a sense that presents Him as intimating that, by His glorification of the Father, He has prepared the moment of His own glorification, and that He may now expect such glorification as a recompense agreeable to the fundamental law of the kingdom of love and righteousness. In ver. 1 He modified the succession thus: Father, glorify the Son, that the Son may glorify Thee; now He says: I glorified *Thee,* now do Thou glorify *the Son.* To avoid a mingling of the conceptions, we must admit the question to be here of a *preliminary* glorification of the Father through the Son. And this is Christ's meaning; He says: I glorified Thee *on the earth,* and in elucidation of these words He adds: I have finished the work, *etc.* In His doctrine and life He had manifested the Father conformably to the grace and truth of the latter, chap. i. 17. He could lay this work before the Father as finished and complete. Augustine and Gerhard understand by these words the sacrifice of Christ's death, of which He speaks, say they, as from the stand-

* [This would require in Greek: ἵνα γιν. σε κ. Ἰησ. Χρ. ὃν ἀπέστ., τὸν μόνον ἀληθινὸν θεόν. The fathers adopted this forced interpretation to escape the Arian conclusion that Christ was of a different and created substance, and subordinate to the Father. But the juxtaposition of Christ with the Father in connection with all that follows (comp. ἡμεῖς ἕν, ver. 22), is quite inconsistent with Arianism and Socinianism. God is here called ἀληθινός, not in distinction from His Son, but from idols and quasi-divinities. Christ, as to His divine nature, is Himself called ὁ ἀληθινὸς θεός, 1 John v. 22. Alford: "I do not scruple to use and preach on this verse (John xvii. 3) as a plain proof of the co-equality of the Lord Jesus in the Godhead."—P. S.]

† [So also the E. V., Lücke, ed. III., Godet, Alford, and most English commentators. Comp. ch. i. 17; 1 John i. 3, 7, and especially the Pauline epistles where Ἰησοῦς Χριστός is the usual designation of the divine-human Mediator.—P. S.]

‡ [So also Lücke, ed. II., Meyer and Ewald. But then we would expect the article before χριστόν, as in all the eighteen passages of John where χριστός occurs without Ἰησοῦς, except ch. ix. 22 (ὁμολογήσῃ χριστόν). Meyer thinks that Christ prayed in Hebrew, יֵשׁוּעַ הַמָּשִׁיחַ, but this is by no means certain, and would not affect Greek usage. Comp. also 1 John ii. 22; iv. 3; v. 1, 6; 2 John 9, and the later writers, *e.g.* Hegesippus in Euseb. H. E. II. 23: ὅτι Ἰησοῦς ἐστὶν ὁ χριστός. . . . . κινδυνεύει πᾶς ὁ λαὸς Ἰησοῦν τὸν χριστὸν προσδοκᾶν. Moreover, the predicate under which Christ is to be known, is already expressed by ὃν ἀπέστειλας.—P. S.]

* [Godet: "*L' écriture prend toujours le mot* CONNAITRE *dans un sens plus profond. Quand il s' agit du rapport de deux personnes, ce mot désigne la parfaite intuition que chacune a de l' être moral de l' autre, leur rencontre dans le même milieu lumineux.*"—P. S.]

point of its consummation. "Most commentators, even Grotius, at least consider it (the death-sacrifice) to be jointly included by prolepsis; Socinian exegesis alone absolutely excludes it. The fact that vers. 6-9 speak exclusively of Christ's doctrinal ministry is not decisive in favor of such exclusion." Tholuck. It is more decisive, however, that Christ here reckons His death as comprising one point in the *Father's* glorification of the *Son*. Hence it is doubtless in the more limited sense that He has been speaking of the work which the Father has commanded Him *to do;* in a sense similar to that of the words: I must work as long as it is day; the night cometh, *etc.*, chap. ix. 4. Now, however, this work is brought to a conclusion; He makes His high-priestly offering of Himself and seals *that* with His Passion. The Passion comes under consideration as the conclusion of His obedient doing. See also the καὶ νῦν δόξασον μὲ σύ.

Ver. 5. **And now glorify Me, Thou, Father, with Thyself** [καὶ νῦν δόξασόν με σύ, πάτερ, παρὰ σεαυτῷ τῇ δόξῃ ᾗ εἶχον].*—Although the mortal suffering of Jesus should indirectly conduce to the glorification of the Father (see ver. 1), it must be primarily a glorification of the Son; His glorification by death, resurrection and ascension. Christ henceforth conducts Himself *passively;* the Father assumes the active. *With Thyself, i. e.* not simply in heaven, but in His submissive resignation to God, in His going to the Father, in His being in God (Col. iii. 3), in antithesis to His life in the world hitherto. He has glorified the Father in this world and from this world; the Father is to glorify Him in the other world and from the other world. [παρά denotes closest proximity and equality with personal distinction, "with Thyself as Thy fellow;" comp. i. 2.—P. S.]

With the radiance of glorification [τῇ δόξῃ, **the glory**].—It is the *real* glory which Christ, as the Son of God and the λόγος, possessed, as the medium of the world, before the existence of the world; at once the *ideal* radiance of glorification which He then, as the future divine-human Lord of glory, had in the view of God, and the *ideo-real* radiance of glorification of His eternal nascency and advent from the beginning. For Christ in His glorification, did not merely receive *back* that which He once possessed in the μορφῇ θεοῦ (Phil. ii. 6; John i. 1); He also *newly* received a glory destined Him from the beginning and from the beginning in embryo, as the ideo-real fundamental impulse of the world (see the Prologue). Accordingly, the interpretation which apprehends this δόξα ideally alone, as significant of the *destinatio divina* (the Socinians, Grotius, Baumg.-Crus.), is inadequate; and inadequate is also the view which would limit the reference of the words to a re-reception of the original real glory (Meyer after some ancients). Be it observed that the future divine-human glory was assured to the Son along with His eternal Logos-glory. It is a question how the δόξα which, according to John i. 14, He manifested even in the state of humiliation, must be distinguished from that other δόξα. The divine *highness* or *majesty* consists in the limitless, unobstructed self-manifestation of God in *omnipotence* and *omnipresence* or in *creative working and appearing;* the divine *lowliness*, or self-divestment of Christ, consists in a self-limitation within the divinely appointed limits of judgment and suffering,—limits actualized in the counter-operations of the world against the Holy One; this self-limitation is carried to *impotence*, as the antithesis to *omnipotence*, and to *death*, as the antithesis to *omnipresence:*—only, however, that it may thus be all the more gloriously manifested in the δόξα of grace and truth. First, omnipotence and omnipresence stood forth, limitless, and grace and truth were, as yet, hidden; then grace and truth advanced; so boundless these, that omnipotence and omnipresence appeared to vanish behind them. The new condition of Christ, however, will consist in the glorifying of His grace into omnipotence, and of His truth into omnipresence, or of His self-divestment into majesty. Dogmatically defined: At first, alone the "physical" attributes of God are, in the Logos, exhibited in the creation of the world. In the redemption of the world, the "ethical" attributes are exhibited in the self-humiliation of Christ. In the glorification of the world, the "ethical" and "physical" attributes are to shine united, as a manifestation of the majesty of Christ. And so the new glory of Christ shall be an eternal synthesis of the *gloria mediatoria* (which Lampe considers as the sole meaning of the text) and the primordial majesty (Heb. i. 3); this latter, however, must not be described as the quality "by which God is God," unless we are prepared to understand by it the glory of God as the sum of all His attributes.

Ver. 6. **I manifested Thy name to the men,** *etc.* [ἐφανέρωσά σου τὸ ὄνομα τοῖς ἀνθρώποις οὓς ἔδωκάς μοι ἐκ τοῦ κόσμου]. Here begins the intercession for the disciples. He introduces it with a rationale; they are not simply worthy of His intercession; God's eyes must be fastened upon them as bearers of His name and Christ's work. The great work of manifestation must in them be protected and secured.—**Manifested Thy name.**—Such, in one word, was Christ's work hitherto. The name of God, its specific self-manifestation in the Son, and, with that name, the God of Christ, the personal, heavenly Father, was distinctly manifested to men by the word, work, and life of Christ. The *prophetic* office of Christ is completed in an absolute manifestation of God. Though the disciples were not yet enlightened to gaze into this revelation, it, nevertheless, was finished, as regarded its objective elements.—**The men whom Thou gavest me.**—[οὓς ἔδωκάς μοι ἐκ τοῦ κόσμου]. The disciples (see vers. 8, 11, and chap. xvi. 30). God gave them to Him through His election, through the attraction drawing them to the Son, and through the power of His calling.

* [Alford has a good note here: "Notice the correlation, which Meyer has pointed out, between ἐγώ σε before, and με σύ now. The same Person (ἐγώ) who had with the Father glory before the world, also glorified the Father in the world, and prays to be again received into that glory. *A decisive proof of the unity of the Person of Christ,* in His three estates of eternal præ-existence in glory, humiliation in the flesh, and glorification in the Resurrection-Body. This direct testimony to the eternal præ-existence of the Son of God has been evaded by the Socinian and also the Arminian interpreters by rendering εἶχον—'habebam *destinatione tua*,' Grot., Wetstein."—P. S.]

Christ then defines the process of development exhibited in their conversion:—

1. **Thine they were.** [σοὶ ἦσαν]. Not merely in the general sense in which all things belong to God (Cyril), but as Israelites without guile (see chap. i. 47; iii. 21); *per fidem Veteris Test.* (Bengel.)

2. **Thou gavest them to Me.**—[καὶ ἐμοὶ αὐτοὺς ἔδωκας]. The before-mentioned considerations of this giving became manifest and realized in the calling, chap. x. 27.

3. **And they have kept Thy word.** [καὶ τὸν λόγον σου τετήρηκαν]. Though it is still necessary that they should be sifted, they have stood the main test, and have not suffered themselves to be entangled in the apostasy of Judas. To Christ's eyes, they do already issue victorious out of temptation (see chap. viii. 51).

4. **Now they know that all,** *etc.* [νῦν ἔγνωκαν (Alexandrian form for ἐγνώκασιν) ὅτι πάντα, κ. τ. λ.]. Their fidelity has been rewarded by the beginnings of a higher faith-knowledge, or cognition of faith, as they have already testified. See chap. xvi. 30. Their knowledge is the knowledge that everything which has been given to Christ, *i. e.*, His doctrine (De Wette), and particularly His work (Luthardt), is of God; *i. e.*, they know God in Christ. They know the words of Christ to be divine by the works, the works by the words; the latter method Christ brings out with special prominence (as the higher way of knowledge, see above, chap. xiv. 11), in order to explain how they have attained to their faith-knowledge. They have received in faith Christ's words which He gave them. From this *trust* in the divine words *confided* to them by Him, there has sprung a true cognition of the *divine nature of Christ* (**they truly knew that I am come forth from Thee**, ver. 8), and thereby a belief in His divine mission to the world, in which mission theirs should now be rooted, has been mediated (**they believed that Thou didst send Me**). The Aorists [ἔγνωσαν and ἐπίστευσαν] jointly serve as an elucidation of the Perfect: νῦν ἔγνωκαν.—Such are the reasons why He prays for them.

[Ver. 8. **For I have given them the words which Thou gavest me,** ὅτι τὰ ῥήματα ἃ ἔδωκάς (*gavest;* so A. B. C. D.) Lachm., Tischend., Alf., Westc. *versus* δέδωκάς, *hast given*, which is supported by ℵ. L. X. and text. rec.) μοι, δέδωκα αὐτοῖς. "On the truth of this saying stands the whole fabric of creeds and doctrines. It is the ground of authority to the preacher, of assurance to the believer, of existence to the church. It is the source from which the perpetual stream of Christian teaching flows. All our testimonies, instructions, exhortations, derive their first origin and continuous power, from the fact that the Father has given to the Son, the Son has given to His servants, the words of truth and life." Bernard, *Progress of Doctrine in the N. T.* (1867) p. 25.—P. S.]

Ver. 9. **I pray (am praying) for them; I pray not (am not praying) for the world,** *etc.*—[ἐγὼ περὶ αὐτῶν ἐρωτῶ· οὐ περὶ τοῦ κόσμου ἐρωτῶ, ἀλλὰ περὶ ὧν δέδωκάς μοι, ὅτι σοί εἰσιν]. The grand stress of this intercession is contained, 1. In the ἐγώ; 2. in the fact that the proposition, *I pray for them*, is first simply laid down, then 3. negatively expressed: *not for the world;* 4. positively expressed: *but for them;* the motives assigned being: *they have been given Me by Thee*, and *they are Thine.* The expression: *not for the world*, is doubtless of *dogmatic* moment (which Meyer denies); it is, however, destitute of a *predestinarian* import (Calvin, Lampe; *pro quibus Christus non orat, pro iis non satisfecit*, and others; see ver. 20; Matt. v. 44; Luke xxiii. 34)."* It is significant of the *purely dynamical* view of the world and arrangement of the Gospel. By means of this dynamical principle, first concentrated in Christ and henceforth to be concentrated in His apostles, the world, as world, is to be clean done away with. Christ does not work by a fire of sparks, sprinkling them incidentally, one here and one there; His working is a concentrated central fire of absolute, *positive* resurrective force, which fire takes hold of the world in the centre of her receptive susceptibility, in order to her transformation. It is the strict vital law of the concentration of the divine power of the Gospel, archetypally declared in the calling and isolation of Abraham, typically set forth in the separation of Israel, and still continuing in the regulations which Christ has made for the development of His church (see Acts i. 4, 8). But the expression of Christ does not bear simply an *ideo-dogmatical* emphasis; it has, resulting from the ideo-dogmatical, also an *affectionate* emphasis: I pray, above all things, for these, who are Thine as the *fruit* of the Old Testament, and Mine as the firstlings of the New Testament; similarly, the expression has a *religious* force: the δόξα of Thy name is concerned; that δόξα is henceforth entrusted to them; it must be secured in them, must, through them, become universal in the world as the principle of the world's glorification. This expression of supreme entreaty, however,

* [Calvin (like Augustine, Luther, and Melanchthon) expresses himself moderately, and cannot be quoted in favor of the supralapsarian doctrine of a limited atonement, but rather held that Christ's atonement, though *efficient* only for the elect, is yet intrinsically *sufficient* for all. Lampe's explanation is much more harsh, and concludes with the revolting words: *Dum Jesus eos ab intercessione sua excludit, declarat, se eorum sacerdotem non esse adeoque mortem pro iis non obiturum. Tantum aberat, ut pro iis orare deberet, ut potius eorum interitum expetat omnesque dirus in illos pronunciet.* Among modern commentators Hengstenberg defends this interpretation; he refers to 1 John v. 16 (ἔστιν ἁμαρτία πρὸς θάνατον, οὐ περὶ ἐκείνης λέγω ἵνα ἐρωτήσῃ), as a parallel, and distinguishes between the susceptible world, which is an object of intercession (John i. 29; iii. 17; iv. 42), and the anti-Christian world which cannot receive the truth (xiv. 17), and which is as little an object of intercession as the ἄρχων τοῦ κόσμου, but rather of the curses of God (Ps. lxxix. 10; Acts vi. 10). Then he quotes Luther, who says: "How squares His refusal to pray for the world with His teaching us, Matt. v. 44, that we are to pray even for our enemies? This is in brief the answer: to pray for the world and not to pray for the world must both be right and good. For soon after He says Himself: '*Neither pray I for these alone, but for them also who shall believe on Me through their word.*' These very persons must yet be of the world, He must therefore pray for the world for the sake of those *who are yet to come forth from the world.* St. Paul was certainly of the world, when he persecuted and killed Christians, yet St. Stephen prayed for him and he was converted. Thus, too, Christ Himself prayed on the cross (Luke xxiii. 34). It is thus true that He prayed for the world, and does not pray for the world; but this is the distinction: In the same way and in the same degree in which Christ prays for them that are His, He does not pray for the world."—P. S.]

is simultaneously the expression of confidence: in them Thy divine work and Mine shall be made secure in the world.

[Bengel, Meyer, Stier, Luthardt, Alford, *etc.* explain in substance: I am not praying for the world *now and in this manner* (*hoo loco, tempore, et his verbis*), but I shall do so afterwards, vers. 20, 21. But this appears somewhat trivial, and does not give the exclusion the full force. The words οὐ περὶ τοῦ κόσμου ἐρωτῶ, are intended to justify and to emphasize the intercession of Christ for His own. The whole sacerdotal prayer is not offered for the outside world at all but only for His disciples, first for those whom He had already called out of the world (6-19) and then for those who should hereafter come out of the world and believe in Him (περὶ τῶν πιστευόντων, ver. 20 *ff.*). The world appears, even in vers. 20, 21, 23, not as an object of intercession, but as a hostile force, against which He asks the protection of the Father. Yet by the preservation and perfection of Christ's church in holiness and unity, which is the direct object of this prayer, the world itself is at last to be brought to believe in the divine mission of the Son, ἵνα ὁ κόσμος πιστεύῃ ὅτι σύ με ἀπέστειλας, vers. 21, 23. Hence the exclusion of the world is not absolute (in the sense of supralapsarian commentators), but relative. On proper occasions Christ *did* pray for the ungodly world, even His murderers ("Father forgive them," Luke xxiii. 34, adding, however, as a motive not, as here, "they have known," ver. 11, but on the contrary, "they know *not* what they do"); and He especially commands us to pray for our enemies (Matt. v. 44), as Stephen prayed for the persecuting Saul (Acts vii. 60). For Christians we should pray that God may preserve them from the world and the devil, for the ungodly world, that it may cease to be worldly and believe in Christ.—P. S.]

Ver. 10. **All things that are Mine are Thine.**—[τὰ ἐμὰ πάντα σά ἐστιν, καὶ τὰ σὰ ἐμά. The E. V. "All Mine is Thine" may be understood of *persons* only, while all *things*, the Godhead itself included, are meant. Comp. Alford.—P. S.] He gives prominence to the worth possessed by the disciples as the objects of His intercession. As Christ's property, they are the property of God; as God's property, they are the property of Christ; and since He is glorified in them, the δόξα of Christ, which is the δόξα of God, must be protected in them.

Ver. 11. **And I am (henceforth) no more in the world** [καὶ οὐκέτι εἰμὶ ἐν τῷ κόσμῳ]. This is the motive for His urgent, provident petition. He is departing out of the world, they remain in the world and so will be needing special protection. The words: **and I come to Thee** [κἀγὼ πρὸς σὲ ἔρχομαι], cannot be regarded as a mere repetition of the declaration: "I am no more," *etc.* On the contrary, the position and task of the disciples in the world shall be assured by Christ's coming to the Father with His intercession. In the first place, the *going away* of Christ is expressed, as perilous for the disciples who remain here; and, secondly, His *going home* is intimated, as the indemnification for the disciples, whose position and task are here.

Hence the apostrophe: **Holy Father** [πάτερ ἅγιε]. *God is to be the holy Father to Christians in this world when Christ has gone away.** God, in His holiness, is entirely separated from the unholy world, in order that He may belong entirely to the world that is to be sanctified: so, the Holy. He is the holy Father (ver. 11) of the Son who sanctifies Himself for His own, *i. e.*, goes away from both them and the world, in order to be entirely devoted to them and, through them, to the world (ver. 19), that they too may in this sense be sanctified in His truth, ver. 17. The petition itself: **keep them in** [better than *through of.*—E. V.] **Thy name,** *etc.* [τήρησον αὐτοὺς ἐν τῷ ὀνόματί σου.] In the revelation for Christian knowledge, as in Christian knowledge of revelation,—in that consciousness of God which Christ entertained.

Which (whom) Thou, *etc.* [ᾧ (οὓς) δέδωκάς μοι.] The reading ᾧ (see Text. Notes) is by Meyer and others, supported by Cod. D., considered to stand by attraction for ὅ and to relate to the name of God [ἐν τῷ ὀνόματί σου]. We must acknowledge that we have difficulty in reading: "Thou hast given me Thy name,"—the name of the Father and that of the Son not being mingled. From this difficulty the Recepta [which reads οὕς, *whom*] has doubtless arisen. We, therefore, prefer to read ᾧ as *Dativ. instrum.* [*by which*], in perfect accordance with the sense of vers. 6 and 12, and interpret the passage thus: through My manifesting Thy name unto them, in Mine office as Thine Ambassador, they did believe on Me and are thus become Mine. On the glorification of the Father through Christ as His Ambassador, through whom the Father operated, the glorification of the Son is founded. Since, however, the instrumental construction is scantily supported and a stronger expression might be expected for it, we suffer the interpretation given in the translation [*den, which*] to stand, only explaining the term: which Thou hast *given* Me, by: which Thou, with Thy revelation, hast *confided* to Me.

[Stier says that ᾧ can bear no proper meaning. One feels tempted with Bengel and Godet to read ὅ, and to refer this not to ὄνομα, but to the disciples, as equivalent to οὕς, just as in ver. 2, πᾶν ὃ δέδωκας—αὐτοῖς), and ver. 24, if ὅ be the proper reading there. But ὅ is very poorly supported, though it may more easily have been changed by mistake into ᾧ, than into οὕς. The reading of the text. rec. (sustained by D.[2] and Vulg.) is no doubt the easiest and falls in best with the style and general sentiment of John, comp. vers. 6, 9. But inasmuch as ᾧ has all the weight of external testimony (א. A. B. C., Syr., *etc.*) and is adopted by the best critical editors (Lachmann, Tregelles, Alford, Tischendorf, Westcott), we must give it the preference. The *name* must mean the essential revelation which the Father made to the Son, and the Son to the world (Luthardt), or rather the peculiar attribute of *Saviour, Jehovah our Righteousness.* (Alford and Wordsworth). There is, it is true, no strict parallel passage where God is said to have given *His* name to His Son, but an approach to it, Ex. xxiii. 21: "My name is in Him," *viz.*, the angel of the covenant; comp. Is. ix. 6; Jer. xxiii. 6, and especially Phil. ii. 9,

* [What a blasphemous profanation to call a mortal, sinful man, like the pope, "holy father!"—P. S.]

10, "God hath given Him a name (*ὄνομα*, but not *His* name) above every name, that at the name of *Jesus* every knee should bow."—P. S.]

The motive of the prayer is: whom Thou hast given Me. As the name of the Father is given Him for the disciples, so the disciples are given Him for the name (the Gospel of the New Covenant is for the called of the Old Covenant in the wider sense, and contrariwise). Purpose of the prayer: *ἵνα ὦσιν ἕν*. Meyer makes the *ἵνα* relate to *ὃ δέδωκάς μοι*, instead of to *τήρησον*, as is usual. The latter reference, however, is the more obvious one, for the full development of the unity of believers arrives as the fruit of their conservation. It is a question of consummate oneness (see ver. 22).

That they may be one as we [*ἵνα ὦσιν ἓν καθὼς ἡμεῖς*]. Throughout the high-priestly prayer, Christ brings into view the *oneness* of the disciples as the mark of their matured discipleship: the sign that they are one in the name of the Father of Christ. The living, known name of God has this unifying power. As it is the bond of union between the Father and Son, it is, in like manner, to be the bond of union among the disciples. In the true, living consciousness of God is the divine life of love, the unity of divine revelation and human religion, the unity of human faith and the unity of human ethics, Eph. iv. 6. [Alford: "The oneness here is not merely harmony of will or of love,—as some have interpreted it, and then tried to weaken the Oneness of the Godhead by the *καθώς*,—but oneness by the indwelling of the Spirit of Christ, the gift of the covenant (1 Cor. vi. 17), and ultimately oneness of nature, 2 Pet. i. 4, where the *ἐπαγγέλματα δεδώρηται* answers to the *ὄνομα ὃ δέδωκάς μοι* here." Godet: "*Les mots* COMME NOUS *signifient que, comme c'est par la possession de l'essence divine que le Père et le Fils sont un, c'est par la commune connaissance de cette essence (le nom) que les disciples peuvènt aussi rester un et être individuellement gardés.*" Yet the community of the spiritual life derived from Christ, must be added to the community of knowledge.—P. S.]

Ver. 12. **While I was with them** (in the world) [*ὅτε ἤμην μετ' αὐτῶν*]. Further explication of the words, ver. 11.—**I kept them** [*ἐφύλαξα*]. 'Εγώ with emphasis. Held them fast in Thy name. Their natural inclination tended ever out of the bounds constituted by the consciousness of God and by Christ's view of the world; His faithfulness held them fast within these limits, and, as souls given Him by the Father (see the TEXTUAL NOTE), He watched over them faithfully. Φυλάσσειν is an intensified expression of His vigilant care over them. He guarded them as the faithful Shepherd of the souls entrusted Him by the Father.—**And none of them perished except the son of perdition** [*καὶ οὐδεὶς ἐξ αὐτῶν ἀπώλετο εἰ μὴ ὁ υἱὸς τῆς ἀπωλείας*. Christ does not say, "*I lost none*" (comp. ch. xviii. 9, where no exception is made). "Judas lost himself." Even after the betrayal he might have been saved if he had in true penitence fled to the cross.—P. S.] Not simply a painful recalling of the traitor (Tholuck), but also the account-rendering of a faithful and good conscience concerning Judas, and, as such, appropriate at this moment.* **The son of perdition**.—A Hebrew expression:† the property of perdition, the prey of perdition, comp. chap. xii. 36; Matt. xiii. 12. But the specific child of perdition, in whom the *ἀπώλεια* (see Matt. vii. 13) of the Jews was concentrated, was also the instrument of perdition (see 2 Thess. ii. 10).—**That the Scripture might be fulfilled** [*ἵνα ἡ γραφὴ πληρωθῇ*]. Here, as in chap. xii. 38; xiii. 18, consolation is found in contemplating the decree of divine judgment. It was, however, not fated that Judas should become a child of perdition, but that, as such, he should be lost from the circle of disciples in accordance with the righteous judgment of God.‡

What passage of Scripture is here intended? According to Lücke and Meyer [Godet], Ps. xli. 10, on account of the citation of that passage, chap. xiii. 18; according to Euthymius Zigabenus, Ps. cix. 8 (see Acts i. 20); according to Kuinoel the whole mass of prophecies relative to the death of Jesus. We are of opinion that the passage Is. lvii. 12 is the one meant (see *Leben Jesu* II., p. 1412). It should be noted that the passage Ps. xli. 10 was already fulfilled in the occurrence referred to chap. xiii. 18. But Is. lvii. 12, 13 treats specifically, in typical prophecy, of the perdition of the destroyer.

Ver. 13. **To Thee, and speak these things** [*νῦν δὲ πρός σε ἔρχομαι, καὶ ταῦτα λαλῶ ἐν τῷ κόσμῳ*]. *I. e.*, I can no longer watch over them, as I have done hitherto, in visible, individual intercourse. Henceforth something else must guard them. But what shall this be? His joy shall become perfect in them, and shall be their guard. His joy is that complete consciousness of God which is to be imparted to them by the Holy Ghost, as the source of the most untrammeled vital movement in their spirits (see chap. xvi.). *I speak these things*,—I now, being still in the world and heard by them as well as by Thee, do confidentially carry this petition before Thee, that, *etc. I. e.*, not simply: Through My intercession they shall be assured of Thy protection and hence be filled with perfect gladness,—but rather: My intercession shall awaken the spirit of prayer in them and open their hearts for the reception of the Holy Spirit of perfect joy, for whom I am suing on their behalf. And if Thou *keep* them thus, by the bestowal of the Spirit of joy, He will *watch* over them as I have done until now.

---

* [So also Godet: "*Par le mot fils de perdition, et par l'allusion qu'il fait à la prophétie, Jésus veut uniquement dégager sa propre responsabilité, et nullement atténuer celle de Judas.*" —P. S.]

† [בֶּן מָוֶת, *υἱὸς θανάτου* (1 Sam. xxvi. 16); *υἱὸς γεέννης* (Matt. xxiii. 15); 'Αβαδδών (Rev. ix. 11, the name of the angel of the abyss, in Greek, *ἀπολλύων*, *Destroyer*); *τέκνα ὀργῆς* (Eph. ii. 3); *τέκνα κατάρας* (2 Pet. ii. 14). The "man of sin" is also called "the son of perdition," 2 Thess. ii. 3. The same term is applied to Satan in the *Evang. Nicodemi*, c. 20.—P. S.]

‡ [Wordsworth: "He perished *in order that the Scripture might be fulfilled*. But the Scripture would not have been written by God, unless God had foreseen that he would perish. And this divine Prescience, though it foreknew and foretold that he would perish, did not in any way *cause* him to perish. Why then was this Scripture written? In order that even his perishing might be an evidence of God's foresight; and so the traitor himself, even in the hands of Satan, and betraying Christ, might be a witness of the truth, even by his perishing; and Judas, 'the Son of Perdition,' might still even in his perdition, be an Apostle of the Son of God."—P. S.]

Ver. 14. **I have given them Thy word** [Ἐγὼ δέδωκα αὐτοῖς τὸν λόγον σου]. The prayer for the preservation of the disciples now divides itself into two petitions; the one is for their negative protection from the Evil One in the world, the other for their positive sanctification in the truth. First the negative portion, the protection, is discussed. Christ having given them His word, they are taken from the world and hence are become, equally with Himself, objects of the world's hatred. The ungodly consciousness of the world gravitates outwards into the impersonal; consequently the divine consciousness of Christ and His people, gravitating, in its impulse of faith and love, toward the absolute personality of God, is odious to the world. The antithesis: I, and: the world, contains the most concise expression of this fact. The world hateth them, properly: hath conceived a hatred for them (ἐμίσησεν αὐτούς). Luther: The world's hatred is the true livery of Christians, which they wear on earth.

Ver. 15. **I pray not that Thou,** *etc.* [οὐκ ἐρωτῶ ἵνα ἄρῃς αὐτοὺς ἐκ τοῦ κόσμου, ἀλλ']. The petition regarding the protection of the disciples from the world, likewise divides itself into two parts, a negative and a positive. They are to remain in the world, but are to be preserved from the world. Luther: "What I want is not that they also should pass out of the world with Me, for I have still more to accomplish by means of them; they must increase My little flock."—**That Thou shouldst take them out of the world,** *i. e.*, neither by actual death nor by ascetic mortifications. Christ has here rejected monkery also, as a form of life unsuited to His disciples, they having attained their majority. They are to be *in* the world, but not *of* the world. The petition runs thus: **that Thou shouldst keep them from the Evil One.** The question as to whether ἐκ τοῦ πονηροῦ is to be construed as neuter [*the evil.*—E. V.] or as denoting Satan [*the Evil One*], is decided by Olshausen, Baumg.-Crusius in the former, by Lücke and Meyer [Alford] in the latter sense with reference to "the Prince of this world," chap. xii., ver. 31; xiv. 30; xvi. 11, and to 1 John ii. 13, 14; iii. 12; v. 18, 19. If we add to these chapters viii. 44, we find that John merges the whole world in personal relations, as regards evil also; the world, as world, lies in the Wicked One; it has its pole in Satan; this is in conformity to the purely dynamical view of the world. The expression τηρεῖν ἐκ, Revelation iii. 10.

Ver. 16. **They are not of the world** [ἐκ τοῦ κόσμου οὐκ εἰσὶν καθὼς ἐγὼ οὐκ εἰμὶ ἐκ τοῦ κόσμου]. Motive for the following positive petition. They no longer have their vital principle in the world, but, like Christ and through Him, in the Father; therefore He prays that they may be perfected, in accordance with this their divine birth and kind.

Sanctify them in the truth [ἁγίασον αὐτοὺς ἐν τῇ ἀληθείᾳ, as the element in which the ἁγιάζειν takes place]. Explanations:

1. Chrysostom, Euthymius [Lücke, Godet, Wordsworth]: Make them holy *through* [ἐν instrumental, as in the E. V.] the gift of the Holy Ghost, and by true doctrine.

2. Luther: Adverbially construing *in the truth:* Make them *truly* [ἀληθῶς] holy [in distinction from the present *imperfect* holiness.—Hengstenberg. Against this is the article, and still more the following ὁ λόγος, *etc.*—P. S.]

3. Erasmus, Calvin: Take them away from the fellowship of the world.

4. Theophylact, Lampe: Separate them for the office of the ministry.

The phrase, *That they also may be sanctified* (ver. 19), must be defined pursuant to the holiness of God, ver. 11, and the self-sanctification of Christ, ver. 19. Now God is holy in withdrawing Himself from the ungodly world, in order to reveal Himself in a godly, kingly-priestly people, Lev. xi. 44, 45; 1 Pet. iii. 16. In conformity thereto, Christ sanctifies Himself; He departs out of the world in His self-humiliation, in order to enter into the world in His majesty. On the basis of this fact, the disciples are to be sanctified, the word of God in them, through the Holy Ghost within them, being converted into perfect truth, *i. e.* into a unitous light, a principially developing luminous and vital view and vital power, ever emancipating them more completely from the world in order to conduct them into the world, as emancipators, with the gospel. The expression ἐν τῇ is generally apprehended as denoting instrumentality: *By means of* or *by virtue of* the truth; Meyer, on the other hand, maintains it to mean: That He would furnish them, in this their vital sphere of truth, with holy *consecration, i. e.* inspiration, illumination, through the Holy Ghost. This view, however, brings the holy consecration into dubious antithesis to the truth. Doubtless the word, already possessed by the disciples, must be supplemented by the Holy Ghost with His consecration, but it is to the end that the word may for them be rendered living truth, at once the vital sphere and the instrument of their sanctification. Now Apostolic sanctification is always both moral and official sanctification. The further thought-sequence, however, proves that the official sanctification should be emphasized in this place.

The rationale of the petition follows: **Thy word is truth.** [ὁ λόγος ὁ σὸς ἀλήθειά ἐστι. Cod. B. reads ἡ, *the* truth, but all other authorities omit the article.—P. S.] Truth, this time without the article, as predicate of the word. The word of God is, in the abstract, pure truth, a lively word, the source of light and the light-impulse to perfect enlightenment; and so, what it is in itself, it must become in the disciples. See chap. iv. 24; xviii. 37; 1 John v. 16; 2 John 1 ff.

Vers. 18 and 19 contain the further assignment of motives for the whole intercession of Christ on behalf of the disciples.—**As Thou didst send Me** [καθὼς ἐμὲ ἀπέστειλας εἰς τὸν κόσμον]. First motive of the entire petition: that God would keep and sanctify the disciples. He is the great, unitous Messenger of God, in whom God's whole apostolate to the world is contained and who has been really consecrated for it by God (chap. x. 36); from Him they now are to become apostles, who, being divinely consecrated to His apostolate, ramify and go forth with the same into all the world. See chap. xv. 9; xx. 21; 2 Cor. v. 20. The Aorist ἀπέστειλα corresponds in part with the proleptical character of the high-priestly

Prayer,—as from the stand-point of that consummation of which He is in spirit assured,—in part with the fact that the commissioning of the disciples had its beginning simultaneously with their calling (Matt. x.), although this commissioning, graded hitherto, was to continue in gradual development until its perfection, chap. xx. 21; Matt. xxviii. 19; Acts i. and ii. The *καθὼς ἐμέ* is placed first as the basis and degree of the mission of the disciples.

Ver. 19. **And for them I sanctify Myself** [*καὶ ὑπὲρ αὐτῶν ἐγὼ ἁγιάζω ἐμαυτόν, ἵνα, κ. τ. λ.* The sense of *καὶ* here is: And, to make their sanctification (ver. 17) possible, I sanctify Myself. Mark the difference between the active *ἁγιάζω* and the passive *ἡγιασμένοι* and between *ἐγὼ—ἐμαυτόν* and *αὐτοί*=Christ sanctifies Himself by His inherent holiness, Christians are sanctified by another power.—P. S.] The specific, high-priestly element of the intercession as the concluding motive. Christ is already sanctified by the Father (chap. x. 36), in coming into the world; He now sanctifies Himself unto the Father, in leaving the world and, by His death, going unto the Father on behalf of His disciples, in order to lay the foundation for their sanctification. Christ sanctifies Himself for His people. The death of Jesus was a sacrificial death of self-sacrificing love for the benefit of His people; a death that as an expiatory death rendered them capable of sanctification through the Spirit, as a death of self-sacrificing love called them to a consecration unto the same love-life in the world. The expression *ἁγιάζειν* (הִקְדִּישׁ) is a customary term for the offering of a sacrifice in the Old Testament, Deut. xv. 19 ff.; 2 Sam. viii. 11; Rom. xv. 16.

Various interpretations:

1. *'Αγιάζειν* denotes the same thing in both sentences:

a. I sacrifice Myself for them that they may be truly consecrate to present themselves a sacrifice, Rom. xii. 1 (Chrysostom);*

b. That they also may be consecrated to sacrificial brotherly love (Olshausen and others).

Against these interpretations Tholuck cites the passive form of the second sentence; this form, however, is explained by the nature of the case, especially by the fact that the second sanctification (that of the disciples) is designated as the result of the first (the self-sanctification of Christ).

c. The official consecration of Christ is to result in the official consecration of the disciples (Heumann, Semler and others). The Present tense is unfavorable to this view.

d. There takes place a sanctification even on the part of Christ, inasmuch as the stripping off of the *σάρξ* is a being taken away from the world's fellowship (Luthardt).† Against this view Tholuck justly remarks: This is neither biblical nor correct. Nevertheless, the intimation of a sound thought is contained therein.

e. Christ's consecration to His holy deed of love is to have for its result the corresponding consecration of the disciples (De Wette). Correct as an item of the whole.

2. *'Αγιάζειν* is diverse in both sentences: I consecrate Myself to death, that they may be sanctified in the truth or, truly;

a. To righteousness in faith (Luther);

b. To *obedientia nova* (Calvin, Lampe).

Here, also, we must securely grasp the two imports of the conception: "to sanctify." Christ sanctifies Himself, in the negative sense, in that by His sacrificial death He separates Himself utterly from the world, is crucified to the world and goes unto God; positively, in that He thereby gains the power to come again into the world in the power of the Holy Ghost. He sanctifies Himself negatively for His people in that He presents His life for them as an expiation for their guilt; positively, in that, by this highest love-offering, He exercises a quickening reflex-influence over them and *establishes a principle of suffering out of which their martyr-sufferings shall develop, as do their works out of His works*, Col. i. 24. Thereby the disciples are said to be negatively sanctified, in that they recognize their crucifixion to the world (Gal. ii. 19) and present their lives unto God as a thank-offering; positively, in that, as peace-messengers, they proclaim the gospel to the world in a self-sacrificing love that stops not short of a martyr's death. This sanctifiedness (*Geheiligtsein*) in the self-sanctification of Christ (*ἵνα ὦσιν ἡγιασμένοι*) must be distinguished, as synonymous with justification by faith, as 1 Pet. i. 2, from the moral self-sanctifying and becoming sanctified that results from justification.

May be sanctified in truth [*ἵνα καὶ αὐτοὶ ὦσιν ἡγιασμένοι ἐν ἀληθείᾳ*]. Two explanations:

1. The term *in truth* is *adverbial* and means *truly* sanctified, *ἀληθῶς* (Chrysostom, Beza, Calvin, Bengel, Meyer):

a. In antithesis to the Jewish consecration, the *sanctimonia cæremonialis* (ancient exegetes [and Godet]);

b. The eminent consecration in antithesis to every other *ἁγιότης* in human relations (Meyer). There is, however, in Scripture no conception of *ἁγιότης* other than the Old Testament typical, and the New Testament real, idea.

2. *'Εν ἀληθείᾳ* is to be construed substantively; in truth=in the truth, as ver. 17 (Erasmus after some ancients, Bucer, Lücke [Olshausen, De Wette, Brückner, Ewald], *etc.*). In opposition to this view Meyer remarks: "In that case the article could not be dispensed with; advocates of this view in vain appeal to chap. i. 14; iv. 24;—the word must be interpreted in accordance with 3 John 1." But even in the latter passage its interpretation is doubtful. The lack of the article is explained by the fact that the *ἀλήθεια* is not to be conceived of here as an independent cause, but as the medium or element of the effect emanating from Christ. In that Christ sanctifies Himself, His disciples are sanctified in the blessing of truth that proceeds

* [Chrysostom takes *ἁγιάζ. ἐμ.* in the sense of *προσφέρω σοὶ θυσίαν*, I offer Myself as an oblation, as a holy victim to Thee. Christ is both priest and sacrifice. Heb. ix. 14; Eph. v. 2. So also Meyer: "*die thatsächliche Weihe, welche Christus, indem Er Sich durch Seinen Tod Gott zum Opfer darbringt, an Sich Selbst vollzieht.*"—P. S.]

† [Similarly Godet: Christ has a human nature with human inclinations, of which He was constantly making a holy offering of obedience to God to be completed in death, comp. Heb. ix. 14. "*Sa vie entière reçoit ainsi le sceau d'une consécration croissante, qui abutit enfin à l'entière immolation.*"—P. S.]

from Him. His expiatory power is the element of truth that pours forth from Him in His Spirit, in order to present them as sanctified persons. The fact that they are at the same time truly consecrated thereby, in antithesis to Old Testament priestly consecration, needs no comment.

Ver. 20. **Yet not for these alone do I pray.** [Οὐ περὶ τούτων δὲ ἐρωτῶ μόνον, ἀλλὰ καὶ περὶ τῶν πιστευόντων διὰ τοῦ λόγου αὐτῶν εἰς ἐμέ, ἵνα πάντες].—Now follows the intercession for future believers. "The view expands in space and, ver. 24, also in time." Tholuck. Since ver. 24 treats of the being of believers with Christ in glory, the glimpse afforded is into extended space as well. Time and space go on mutually expanding until the supreme consummation. The present πιστευόντων (see TEXTUAL NOTES), is a vivid realization of the future. The subject of His petition is not introduced by ἵνα (according to Grotius and others); that rather denotes the purpose, the aim, as ver. 11. Consequently, the subject of the intercession is the same as before: that in the world they may be preserved from the Wicked One and may be sanctified in the truth. Here too, however, the aim is their oneness.

Ver. 21. **That they all may be one according as,** *etc.* [ἵνα πάντες ἓν ὦσιν, καθὼς σύ, πάτερ, ἐν ἐμοὶ κἀγὼ ἐν σοί].—Thus, in this place, also, unity is the goal to be attained. Explanations:

1. Origen: The final aim, *Deus omnia in omnibus*, 1 Cor. xv. 28. But of this there is just now no question, as ver. 21 [last clause, ἵνα ὁ κόσμος πιστεύσῃ] proves. The remaining world has yet to be won by this unity which, doubtless, we are to understand as the unity of believers.

Hence, 2. The ancient exegetes: The unity of Christians in faith and love, as Acts iv. 32; Eph. iv. 4. In these things, then, shall the unity of Christians first appear, conditioned by their being crucified to the world and presenting themselves, a sacrifice of love, to the Lord.

According as Thou, Father, (art) in Me and I in Thee.—So utterly should Christians be bound one to another and united. The Arians thence inferred that the unity between Father and Son was likewise merely a moral one. Orthodox believers rejected this view with the comment that the text did not turn upon *sameness*, but upon *similarity*. With more correctness some commentators (Cyril, Hilary, a few Lutheran theologians) have remarked that the unity of *Christians* is not a *merely moral* one either. Unity in the one Holy Ghost, who is the same in all, is indeed more than moral unity. Since John starts from the presupposition of a purely personal, dynamical view of the world, along with this very oneness of persons, their characteristic self-distinction is brought to completion, *i. e.*, this oneness is precisely the opposite of a pantheistic obliteration of personal distinctions. And Christ gives utterance to this truth in setting up His oneness with the Father, as the type. They are just as decidedly distinct one from the other as they are One. In accordance with this, Their oneness, therefore, Christians are to become one in individuals and confessions. *Where there is no Christian distinction of character, there is no true union. Uniformity is the negation of unity.* On the other hand, the making of distinctions and the distinctions themselves between believers are elementary, raw, bad, if they do not serve to promote unity.

That they also may themselves be (one) in us. [ἵνα καὶ αὐτοὶ ἐν ἡμῖν (ἓν) ὦσιν].—The design of the preservation of the faithful was: 1. The unity of all; 2. a unity such as the unity between Father and Son; now 3. unity in the unity of the Father and Son.* The design is triply intensified: 1. All one; 2. one as We; 3. one in Us. This is the unity of vital fellowship with God, through the Holy Ghost in faith, through connection with the glorified Christ in the sacrament, through personal union with the Triune in the *unio mystica*. Irenæus, v. 1: *Filius dei propter immensam dilectionem factus est, quod nos sumus, ut nos perficeret, quod est ipse.* Augustine *De civit. dei* ix. 15: *Beatus et beatificus Deus, factus particeps humanitatis nostræ, compendium præbuit participandæ divinitatis suæ.* The overstepping of the human limitation of this assimilation to the Divinity, in the doctrine of deification, advanced by the medieval mystics [Master Eckart, Ruysbroek, Tauler, Suso, *etc.*] may not be controverted by laying too great stress upon the temporal and creaturely nature of man, but by the absolute dependence of the life of the branches on their connection with the Vine [ch. xv. 1 *ff.*]

That the world may believe. [ἵνα ὁ κόσμος πιστεύσῃ ὅτι σύ με ἀπέστειλας].—The Church, as the blessed congregation of confession and worship, or the communion of saints, is an end to herself; but she is also a means to an end as an institution of healing for immature believers and, especially, as a mission-community for the world. Hence the second ἵνα, the more remote design. The belief that the Father has sent Christ is characterized in ver. 8 as the true believingness of the disciples. The meaning of our passage is, therefore,—that the world may attain unto faith. Ver. 9 must be explained accordingly. True, immediate prayer for Christians is true, immediate prayer for the world.

[This verse and ver. 23 are the classical passages on Christian union, or the communion of saints. The following points seem to be implied in the text. 1. Christian union presupposes the *vital union* of believers with Christ (περὶ τῶν πιστευόντων εἰς ἐμέ), and is conditioned by it. 2. It is a reflection of the union which subsists between the Father and the Son (καθὼς σὺ πατὴρ ἐν ἐμοὶ κἀγὼ ἐν σοί), consequently not merely a *moral* union of sympathy, but a community of *spiritual life*; all partaking of the life of Christ, as the branches of the vine (comp. ch. xv.). 3. It *centres* in *Christ* and the *Father* who are one (ἵνα ἐν ἡμῖν ὦσιν). Christ is the divine harmony of all human discords, and Christians are one among each other just in proportion as they are one with Him. There is no intimation whatever of a visible centre of unity on earth (such as Rome claims to be), or of a particular form of

* [Godet one-sidedly presses the last: "*Il ne s'agit donc pas ici, comme on le croit souvent, de l'unité des chrétiens entre eux, mais de celle du corps des croyants avec Christ et, par lui, avec Dieu. Le Seigneur voit se former autour des apôtres, par leur prédication, un vaste cercle de croyants, qui sera son corps.*" Lange's more comprehensive view is in accordance with the text.—P. S.]

government (such as episcopacy or presbytery), or form of worship, as a necessary condition of such union, or means of its promotion. There was considerable difference in the apostolic age between the Jewish-Christian and the Gentile-Christian type of Christianity, between the doctrinal system of Paul and of James, *etc.*, and yet there was essential unity and harmony. 4. Hence Christian union is *free* and implies the greatest *variety* (but no contradictions) of types and phases of Christian life. Christian union and Christian liberty are not contradictory, but complementary and mutually sustaining forces (comp. ch. viii. 36; Rom. viii. 2; Gal. v. 1). 5. The unity must *manifest* itself in some outward form, so that the world may perceive it and be impressed by it (ἵνα ὁ κόσμος πιστεύσῃ). This was the case already in the apostolic church, Acts ii. 47; iv. 32, and in the times of persecution, when the heathen used to exclaim: "How these Christians love one another, and how they are ready to die for one another." Even among the sectarian strifes the spiritual union of Christians has never been lost; and it will deepen and expand, and be fully realized at last, like all the other attributes of the church (catholicity and holiness, *etc.*), with the glorification of the body of believers (ἵνα ὦσι τετελειωμένοι εἰς ἕν, ver. 23, ἵνα θεωρῶσιν τὴν δόξαν ἐμήν, ver. 24). "Corporeality," says Œtinger, "is the end of God's ways." To promote the union for which our Saviour so fervently prayed, is the duty and privilege of every Christian.—I quote in addition the note of the late Dean Alford who had liberal and enlightened views on this subject: "This unity has its true and only *ground* in faith in Christ through the word of God as delivered by the apostles; and is therefore not the mere outward uniformity, nor can such uniformity produce it. At the same time, its effects are to be real and visible, such that the world may see them."—P. S.]

Ver. 22. **The glory which Thou gavest me, I have,** *etc.* [κἀγὼ τὴν δόξαν, ἣν ἔδωκάς μοι, δέδωκα αὐτοῖς, ἵνα ὦσιν ἕν.]—The glory which the Father has given Christ, is the state of glorification (see ver. 5). This glory, *i. e.*, full fellowship in His glorified state (see Rom. viii. 17), Christ gave His disciples by giving them the principle of future glory in His word which was about to be glorified by the Spirit of glory (1 Pet. iv. 14). Baumg. Crusius explains the *given* as *destinare.* Meyer's interpretation amounts to the same thing, although he combats the view in rejecting the reference of the passage *to the glory of the inner life* (Olshausen), *to filiation* (Bengel), *love* (Calvin), *grace and truth* (Luthardt). It is more correct to deny its reference to the gloriousness of the apostolic office in doctrine and the working of miracles (Chrysostom), though all believers have their modest portion even of that. This word of the Spirit, with which the Spirit comes, is the bond of union and peace, and is designed to be this bond. Therefore: *that they may be one as We, etc.*, Eph. iv. 4

Ver. 23. **I in them, and Thou in Me, that,** *etc.* [ἐγὼ ἐν αὐτοῖς καὶ σὺ ἐν ἐμοί, ἵνα ὦσιν τετελειωμένοι εἰς ἕν, κ. τ. λ.]—"Appositional explication of ἡμεῖς; not isolated, not a new proposition," *etc.* Meyer. God's life in Christ through the Holy Spirit founds the ever richer life of Christ in believers; this founds their ripening to man's stature, to perfection (Eph. iv. 13); this brings with it their unity; this, finally, is instrumental towards the *full* conversion of the world, when it not only knows the Christ (does not simply believe), but also knows living Christians in their dignity: *and didst love them, as Thou didst love Me.*

Ver. 24. **That which (they whom) Thou hast given Me, I will,** *etc.* [πατήρ, ὅ—comprehending all believers as one gift of the Father to the Son (text. rec. οὕς)—δέδωκάς μοι, θέλω ἵνα ὅπου εἰμὶ ἐγώ, κἀκεῖνοι ὦσιν μετ' ἐμοῦ, ἵνα θεωρῶσιν τὴν δόξαν τὴν ἐμήν, ἣν δέδωκάς μοι, ὅτι, κ. τ. λ.]—The declaration θέλω must certainly not be referred to the following ἵνα; it is absolute. Since He has not now to ask for that which the Father has already given Him, θέλω is neither a prayer (Kuinoel), nor a desire (Beza, *etc.*), nor a petitioning in the consciousness of His ἐξουσία (Meyer), which would contain a certain contradiction, but the familiar communication of His wish from this time to assume possession of that which has been given Him. I will have them, *i. e.*, have them with Me, those whom Thou hast given Me, *i. e.*, with the ascension of Christ, the goal of perfected believers should be with Him in heaven (see chap. xiv. 1 ff.) [The θέλω (*volo*, not *velim*, which is too weak, comp. Mark vi. 25; x. 35) and the corresponding verses have, as it were, the solemn tone of a testamentary act. Bengel: *Rogat Jesus cum jure, et postulat cum fiducia, ut Filius, non ut servus.* Alford: θέλω is an expression of will, founded on acknowledged right; comp. διατίθεμαι, Luke xxii. 29.—P. S.]

That where I am, *etc.* Not the subject matter of a petition, but the consequence of a familiar expression of will. Be it observed that the prayer of Christ from this point does not issue in a human doxology of God, but in a divine dialogue with the Father. In the presentiment of His heavenly stand-point, He takes possession of them as objects bestowed by the Father. 1. They shall be with Him, where He is, in heaven (Meyer says here again: in the Parousia); 2. they shall see His glory which the Father has given Him. Of course this includes a participation in the same (Meyer; see Rom. viii. 18, 29). This latter admission, however, not to the preclusion of the fact that the beholding of Christ's glory does especially constitute their bliss (Olshausen). Luther: We should let this utterance be our soul's pillow and bed of down, and with joyful heart resort thereunto when the sweet hour of rest is at hand.—**Because Thou didst love Me** (comp. ver. 5). [ὅτι ἠγάπησάς με πρὸ καταβολῆς κόσμου].—Here, without doubt, as in ver. 5, the subject treated of is not simply the divine, but the divine-human δόξα of Christ in His state of exaltation; and, correspondingly, it is not a question merely of the trinitarian love of the Father for the Son, but of the eternal complacency of God in Christ in anticipation of His good conduct, in which complacency God appointed Him this state of exaltation. (Meyer). Comp. Eph. i. 19; Phil. ii. 6 ff.

Ver. 25. **Righteous Father!** [πάτερ δίκαιε,

καὶ ὁ κόσμος. See TEXT. NOTE.] Two difficulties present themselves here; first the accosting of the Father with *δίκαιε*, secondly the *καί* before *ὁ κόσμος*. Δίκαιος appears again in John as a predicate of God, 1 John i. 19. It there denotes a graciously recompensing righteousness. For our passage, however, the preceding saying, chap. xvi. 10, is decisive: *In respect of righteousness, that I go to the Father*. It is agreeable to the righteousness of God and Christ that a separation should be made betwixt the perfected Christ and this present world in its blindness,—that Christ should be exalted to heaven. For the world has not known God, either in His general revelation through nature and history, or in the mission of Christ; neither does it know Him now in the judgment wherein it is judged of God even whilst it judges His Christ, whereby Christ consequently bears the judgment of the world. Christ, however, even as Man, has known Him in His whole revelation; finally, He has known and understood Him in the present coming upon Him of the judgment of retributive justice. Therefore He confides in that righteousness as one that rewards also, that shall translate Him to heaven. But because the disciples also have known that He was sent from God, and thereby have begun to know the righteousness of God, they too belong on His side; after they have performed His work in the world, they must come to Him into His heaven. "The work of divine (and divine-human) holiness (ver. 11) would otherwise fail of its final consummation and manifestation" (Meyer). The manifestation of pure holiness shall be sealed in the manifestation of pure righteousness. But because Christ confides Himself to the Father in His punitively retributive righteousness, He likewise trusts Him in His remunerative righteousness; this latter, in establishing the antithesis between heaven and earth, becomes in its turn a divider.

Hence the antithesis: *καί, δέ*,—differently interpreted by different commentators:

1. As forming an antithesis to what precedes: Righteous Father, Thou art righteous, Thou givest such good things, *and yet* the world hath, *etc.* (Chrysostom, Meyer, Luthardt).

2. As drawing a deduction from the foregoing in a predestinarian sense: *Quia justus es, ideo te non cognovit mundus* (after Augustine, Lampe).

3. As announcing a subsequent antithesis: On the one side, on the other side (Heumann, Lücke, Tholuck). This grammatical construction of *καί, δέ* is combated by Meyer,—with reason justified by Tholuck. Yet we

4. Hold the antithesis to be not yet adjusted by the preceding view. He glances back upon the former antithesis: *Thou didst love Me before the foundation of the world*. This contrast of the eternal Christ to the upright world constitutes the first motive for His exaltation above the world. To it there is now added the second corresponding contrast, that the sinful world has also not known the righteous Father, whilst He has known Him thoroughly.

Ver. 26. **And I made known to them Thy name** [*καὶ ἐγνώρισα αὐτοῖς τὸ ὄνομά σου καὶ γνωρίσω, ἵνα, κ. τ. λ.*].—The first motive for the elevation of believers to a participation in His heavenly glory, was that they had believed in Christ's mission from God. This is continued in the second, *viz.*, that He has made known unto them the Father's name and will still make it known until the perfect revelation of it in glory. To these the third is added: **the love of God for the Son must also be in them**, *Christ Himself being thereby in them*, (through the Holy Ghost) [*ἵνα ἡ ἀγάπη, ἣν ἠγάπησάς με, ἐν αὐτοῖς ᾖ κἀγὼ ἐν αὐτοῖς*]. That is, they must be utterly lifted up to Christ in order to be perfected in the communion of the Triune God, the Father, the Son and the Holy Ghost (see 2 Pet. i. 4). Luther: That we may know the Father's heart, *now* set before us through the Word, *afterwards*, in *that* life, to be openly beheld.

[*Κἀγὼ ἐν αὐτοῖς*, **I in them**, with all the fulness of My love and the Father's love: this is the last and most appropriate word of this sublime prayer, and as Stier says, "a better seal than any doxology or Amen." The prayer was richly answered in the experience of the apostles; nothing could separate them from the love of Christ (Rom. viii. 39), and Christ ever remained with them and in them by His Spirit, and will remain with believers to the end, their strength and comfort and peace.—P. S.]

DOCTRINAL AND ETHICAL.

1. On the high valuation set upon this Prayer in the Church, see the Introductory Remarks. Comp. Heubner, p. 482; Besser, on John, chap. xvii. As prominent works upon the seventeenth chapter,—works important at once for their bearing upon doctrinal ground-questions, and upon homiletics, we must mention: Freylinghausen, *The Sacerdotal Prayer of our blessed Saviour Jesus Christ; twenty-six public Meditations upon it, as contained in the seventeenth chapter of St. John*. Halle, 1719. Again: *The Sacerdotal Prayer of our Lord Jesus Christ, twenty Meditations*, by Dr. Schmieder, Hamburg, Agency of the Rough House, 1848. Meditations of great worth, preceded also by an exceedingly momentous treatise upon theosophy and its relation to theology and orthodoxy. A full list of older theological and homiletical writings, see in Lilienthal's *Bibl. Archivarius der heil. Schriften Neuen Testaments*, p. 335. Among the works here mentioned, A. H. Francke's *Meditations upon the Sacerdotal Prayer* are worthy of note; also I. I. Ulrich in Zurich: *The Spiritual Aaron* (48 Sermons). [A long list of English sermons and treatises on John xvii. see in Darling's *Cyclop. Bibl.*, I. 1147 ff. A. W. Tyler gives the Greek text with a critical digest and translation in the Andover *Biblioth. Sacra* for April, 1871, pp. 323–333.—P. S.]

2. The High-priestly Prayer is *high-priestly* not merely because of its being the *intercession* of Christ for His entire kingdom of God, but also on account of its consummation of the sacrifice of Christ, His offering up of Himself, vers. 5, 13, and especially ver. 19. At the same time, however, it is also a *prophetic* prayer, in that, seizing upon the principal periods and stages, it sketches and announces with divine certitude the entire progress of the kingdom of God in development. None the less is it *kingly;* conscious of His internal victory over the world, and believing in the

consequences of this victory, Christ transports Himself, not to the stand-point of the Last Day or of the Ascension-Day, but to that of the deliverance upon Golgotha: *It is finished.* This royal feature of the Sacerdotal Prayer appears especially conspicuous in ver. 24. On the Sacerdotal Prayer, comp. also the ingenious words of Braune, p. 388; Stier, *Words of the Lord Jesus*, and others. We have still to direct attention to the fact that all doctrinal ideas find their expression here in the vivid representation of the march of the kingdom of God in development. The Trinity (the doctrine of the Spirit, though receding in the letter, advances all the more in point of fact), the divinity of Christ, the ideal foundation of the world. The lapse of the ungodly world into the power of Satan. The active obedience of Christ. His sacrifice. The completion of His work. The sending of His apostles. The form of the true Church in her unity. The gradual progress of the kingdom of God. The goal of the glorification of God in the eternal blessedness or heavenly glory of men.

3. If the decided self-offering of Christ in this Prayer be understood, a species of relapse into unclear reasoning or arbitrary imagining could alone render possible the assumption that Jesus did, in Gethsemane, call in question this offering or pray for an averting of death; as, similarly, it would evidence a want of exact Christologico-ethical thought to suppose that by the anticipation of the Passover Christ could have accelerated His death-journey by a whole day, thus wilfully forsaking the divine path and order prescribed through the law. On Christ's prayer in Gethsemane, see *Comm. on Matthew.*

4. Out of Christ's divinely rich prayer-life there emerge, as from an ocean, the pearls of those single prayers of His that are preserved to us: The prayer given in the Sermon on the Mount for the use of His people—*Our Father*; the ascription of praise to God at the departure from Galilee (Matt. xi. 25); the prayers at the grave of Lazarus, and within the precincts of the temple; our high-priestly prayer; the supplication in Gethsemane, and the prayer-words of the Crucified One—*Father, forgive them*—*Eli, Eli*—and the closing prayer, *Father, into Thy hands, etc.*, to which the exultant cry, *It is finished*, attaches itself, inasmuch as from one point of view it may be regarded as a word of prayer. Add to these the mentions of the prayings, the thanksgivings, the heavenward sighings of Christ, as also His summonses and encouragements to prayer, and He appears as the Prince of humanity even in the realm of prayer; in the manner, likewise, in which He has concealed His prayer-life, exhibiting it only as there was necessity for its presentment. If we regard His work as a tree that towers into heaven and overshadows the world, His prayer-life is the root of this tree; His overcoming of the world rests upon the infinite depth of His self-presentation before God, His self-devotion to God, His self-immersion in God, His self-certitude and power from God. In His prayer-life, the perfect truth of His human nature has also approved itself. The same who, as the Son of God, is complete revelation, is, as the Son of Man, complete religion.

5. The glorification of God through Christ, the redemption of the world. Christ distinguishes (*a*) that glorification of the Father which He has already accomplished (ver. 4); (*b*) the glorification of His own Person, now following thereupon (ver. 5), and (*c*) that which the latter glorification is to be instrumental in producing, the glorification of the Father in the Holy Ghost, which is also an actual glorification of the Holy Ghost. Glorification here is manifestly a presentation in the glory peculiar to the Glorified One, the glory *κατ' ἐξοχήν*, *i. e.* the unlimited power and appearing of the Spirit,—in accordance with the idea of Christ's life. *Glory is realized ideal beauty; the radiant exhibition of the dominion of the one Spirit in the rich, developed fulness of personal life.* Now if the glorification of God and Christ be the redemption of humanity, it follows that this redemption is likewise the foundation of its glorification, and appropriated redemption the germ of glorification (the Spirit of glory, 1 Pet. iv. 14; the earnest of glory, Eph. i. 14; Rom. viii. 29, 30). The most definite conception of this glorification appears Phil. iii. 21. If the vile—perishable—body be glorified as such, it is exempted from the creatural conditions of transitoriness, redeemed from a beginning and end in temporality, that pursuant to its eternal idea, it may, as a dislimited organ of the spirit, circle in infinitude as in itself. In the case of the perishable body, the ocean of air that seeks to absorb man, infinitely predominates at last over the canal of rejuvenating vital power that flows toward him; the earthly vital root ever languishes more and more. The body, when glorified, shall, above all things, be endowed with an endless faculty of rejuvenescence.

6. It corresponds to the idea of glorification that that *dynamical* and *personal* view of the world which is peculiar to Christianity in general and which is brought out with especial force in the Gospel of St. John, should appear in our chapter in its finished splendor. In Christ, the Apostles are dynamically comprehended; He is their Root and their Stem; in the Apostles, all future believers are dynamically comprehended (Rev. xxi. 14); these, again comprehend the whole Church, and in the Church the whole world is dynamically comprehended. What is matter here, compared with the personal life of Christ? Before this noble "visage" (*Angesichte*) the whole "weight of the world" (*Weltgewichte*) vanisheth. And because this view of the world is so dynamical, it is on that very account not merely a *view* of the world, but also a *grasping* and *overcoming* of the world (see Eph. i. 19 ff.). *Absolute-dynamical*—that, however, means at the same time *absolute-personal.* The worth and import of the *personal* life here appear in full light: The glorification of the Father, the restoration of His personal glory on which the whole kingdom of love is founded, is the issue and root of the whole work of redemption, —His name. Now the Son is glorified in His redeeming personality; then the personal life of the Apostles develops itself, and the *all* (the *πᾶν*) *which* the Father has given Christ, unfolds itself in the most definite *πάντες*, to *whom* Christ gives eternal life. And these (the *πάντες*) arrive at complete unity and oneness just on account of

their attaining complete personal articulation and self-distinction. Unsanctified individuals mingle themselves together without discipline and restraint in the same degree in which, as foes, they fall out; and religious denominations, also, loosely vibrate pell-mell into one another, in like measure as they abruptly fluctuate asunder. In their eccentric onesidedness they pitch into the onesidedness of an opposite denomination, instead of cultivating their peculiar charisma in clear articulation. The highest union in the kingdom of personal life is at once the highest self-distinction; and the converse also holds true. The dynamical kingdom, as the kingdom of absolute life, is the personal kingdom as the kingdom of light, and both, because it is the kingdom of love. Christ prays for the manifestation and consummation of the kingdom of love.

7. The world, in her disunity, is Babel; the Church of unity is the eternal, ideal Zion; the Holy Ghost is the Mediator of this union. One Body and one Spirit. See also Eph. iv. 13.

8. For the rest, we can but indicate the wealth of fundamental thoughts in this chapter, referring, in so doing, to the Exegetical and Critical division. These captions may, at the same time, serve as homiletical hints: ver. 1. Glorification of prayer: Prayer a fruit of true meditation and preaching.—Glorification of time: The hour of decision is at hand.—Christianity the glorification of Christ.—Christ's glorification the glorification of God (*in dei gloriam*).—Ver. 2. Christ's power over *all flesh* is to be developed in the bestowal of eternal life upon all persons.—The flesh, purified, shall in its turn develop into fair personalities.—Ver. 3. Trusting knowledge is faith; *cognitive, personal knowledge is love;* perfected, seeing knowledge is the felicity of the blessed; in all stages, however, it is life eternal, in respect of the beginning, progress and consummation of the same. It is agreeable to the idea of personal knowledge that we know God *and* Christ (distinctively) as well as God *through* Christ (Father and Son in their unity).—The divinity of Christ, and His humanity as the manifestation of that divinity.—Ver. 4. *It is finished;* Here the: "*It is finished,*" of the cross, is ideally included, but as the sealing of the work of Christ; while the mortal passion of Christ comes under consideration particularly as the work of the Father.—Ver. 5. The pre-existence of Christ. The self-divestment of Christ. The *status exaltationis* of the divine-human Christ. Christ, before the foundation of the world, the principle of its foundation, its Alpha and Omega.—Ver. 6. The Gospel a manifestation of the supreme name. The election of the disciples: *a.* Eternal, *b.* conditioned (they have kept His word), *c.* elected for the good of the world.—Ver. 7. Christianity alone pure, full, entire theism. Theism must be regenerated into Christianity, Christianity must discover itself in its theistic ideality.—Ver. 8. The complete life in the life-words of Christ.—Ver. 9. Dynamical importance of the Apostles. The Apostles the pure medium of the conversion of the world. The effect of Christ's work conditioned by its ideal and dynamic concentration.—Ver. 10. *All* that is Mine is Thine: The holiness of Christ. *All* that is Thine, is Mine: His glory. Christ's glorification in the Apostles, the foundation of His glorification for the world. (Luther says it is easier to say: All Mine is Thine, than the converse: All Thine is Mine. But only Christ could, in the ethical sense, say: All Mine is Thine).—Ver. 11. Christ's feeling of victory hovering over the world. His going to the Father pure intercession. The care of the Perfected One in the other world for the unperfected in this world. The preservation of the disciples a work of God's holiness. The strength of their preservation: His name. The purpose: Unity; personal kingdom of love.—Ver. 12. Direct, and temporarily mediated Providence. Christ, Providence become visible. Providence and freedom. The lost son and divine dispensation.—Ver. 13. The consolation of Christ's intercession the impulse of His people to prayer, even to the life of the Spirit, of perfect joy.—Ver. 14. At the word of God, the hatred of the ungodly world is developed.—Ver. 15. The Christian's renunciation of the world no flight from it, but a stand in it in order to the overcoming of it.—Ver. 16. Separation from the world, as the cause of the world's hatred, the common mark of Christ and Christians.—Ver. 17. The real ordination of the disciples of Jesus: 1. Through the truth; 2. in the word; 3. as an act of God.—Ver. 18. Their mission: 1. From Christ; 2. through Christ from God; 3. like Christ from God.—Ver. 19. The foundation of the entire Apostolic mission, of the entire Church, is the self-sacrifice of Christ.—Ver. 20. From the prayer of Christ on His own behalf there proceeded the petition for the disciples, from that the intercession for the whole body of the faithful.—Ver. 21. The whole Christian life characterized in accordance with its design: 1. As oneness; 2. like the oneness of the Father and Christ; 3. through oneness in God and Christ.—The glory of the triune God in the communion of the faithful. *The unity of the Church: the conversion of the world to the faith.*—Ver. 22. And the foundation of the glory of Christians. The glory of all Christians but *one* glory in the glory of Christ. Giving and embellished receiving again in giving, is the richness of life in the personal kingdom of love.—Ver. 23. *The glory of Christians, the leading of the world unto knowledge.*—Ver. 24. The completion of the manifestation of glory in the heavenly kingdom. The foundation of the heavenly kingdom. Its appearing at the end of time grounded, before the beginning of time, in the love of God to the Son. The reception of the inheritance on the part of the Son.—Ver. 25. The knowableness of God: 1. Simply unknowable for the world in its ungodliness; 2. conditionally knowable and known for the disciples in the beginnings of their life and faith; 3. absolutely knowable and known of Christ; this knowledge the goal of Christians, 1 Cor. xiii. 12. The steps of this knowledge are at once the steps of the kingdom of love and eternal life (see ver. 3).—Ver. 26. The consummation of the kingdom, a consummation in love through the consummate proclamation of the name of God. The great Epiphany. The perfected kingdom of love also the appearing of the imperishable beauty or glory.

HOMILETICAL AND PRACTICAL.

For details see the foregoing DOCTRINAL AND ETHICAL THOUGHTS. *Upon the whole Prayer:* The prayer of Christ as high-priestly.—As Messianic: prophetic, high-priestly and kingly at once.—The prayer for the consummation of the kingdom of heaven as a prayer for the consummation of the revelation of the Trinity: 1. The kingdom of the triune God; 2. the triune life in power (δύναμις), light (ideality) and love (personality: giving and receiving); 3. the three stepping-stones in the conversion of the world (believing on Christ, knowing Christ, knowing Christians); 4. the triple consummation: holiness, righteousness, glory. —The prayer of Christ: 1. For Himself; 2. for the disciples; 3. for believers generally (indirectly an intercession for the world, which shall be swallowed up by the kingdom of believers).—Heaven's foundation upon the righteousness of God.—*The three sections singly.* Christ's petition for Himself, *etc.* —The aim of the kingdom of love: salvation in the praise of God's name.

STARKE: LUTHER: The sum and cause of this chapter is as follows: a good sermon calls for a good prayer; that is, when a man has given utterance to the word, he should begin to groan and earnestly to entreat that it may have strength and produce fruit. I know not how strong in spirit others may be, but, let me be never so learned and full of genius, I cannot grow so holy as to gather devotion for prayer without hearing and handling the word of God.—ZEISIUS: Heart and eyes should simultaneously be raised to heaven.—Christian, if thou wouldst succeed in all that thou doest, set about each act with hearty prayer and end thus too.—CRAMER: God is a hidden God; had Christ not come into the world, He had remained a hidden God, but because Christ hath glorified and revealed Him, we can know God clearly in the Son.—*Power* denotes, in general, such power as is associated with right; in particular, it is employed in the sense of power to rule; hence magistrates are often called powers, 1 Cor. xv. 24; Eph. i. 21; iii. 10; Col. i. 16; Dan. vii. 14; see also Matt. xxviii. 18; Rev. xii. 10.—CANSTEIN: Whoso will not submit himself to Christ in the obedience of faith, to his everlasting salvation, is subjected to His power to everlasting perdition. —HEDINGER: Christ the fountain of life; thirst for that fountain!—*Ibid.:* Mark the chief ground of felicity, Is. liii. 11; 1 Cor. xiii. 12; 1 John iii. 2.—*Nova Bibl.:* If Jesus Himself had, in the redemption, no other final purpose than the honor and glorification of His Father, how much rather and more justly is it said concerning believers: *Whatsoever ye do, either in word or deed, etc.*, Col. iii. 17.—QUESNEL: God glorifies in heaven those who glorify Him on earth.—HEDINGER: Christ was faithful in His Father's house (Heb. iii. 2), having kept back nothing from us.—QUESNEL: Christ will have no servants in the ministry of the word but those whom His Father has elected thereunto and presented to Him for His own.—CANSTEIN: Our election to eternal life is something hidden in God; yet we may know it if we lay hold on Christ in true faith, perseveringly continuing therein.—*Ibid.:* The fellowship of believers gives a Christian the comfort and encouragement of knowing, when the devil assaults him, that he (the devil) is laying hold not on one finger but on the whole spiritual body of Christ, *i. e.* all the Christians in the world, nay, God and Christ Themselves.—How wonderful is it that Jesus, standing upon the threshold of His Passion, was yet overwhelmed with joy at the contemplation of the joy of those who were the cause of all His griefs! O how great is the strength of His love!—The hatred of the world is a genuine mark of a true Christian.—Preachers who, after the perverse fashion of the world, join in everything that is going on and are consequently favorites everywhere, are of no account.—ZEISIUS: Believing Christians, though *in* the world, are not *of* the world; they have not its mind, ways, habits, are not on the same footing with it; they possess the mind of Christ and follow His example alone.—HEDINGER: It is necessary for us to suffer in the world so long as we are able, and in duty bound, to be useful; God will call us away; we must not, in vexation and self-will, wish our own lives away. —We must recognize life in the world to be a benefit and be occupied in serving the world as long as we live.—ZEISIUS: A child of God, as long as he is in the world, is in peril of being seduced by it; hence praying and watching are highly necessary.—Believers must be crucified to the world and the world must be crucified to them, in imitation of Christ.—ZEISIUS: The dignity and bliss of believers is great. *How* great, is not discoverable here, but when it shall appear, it will be manifest that they are like the Lord.

GERLACH: We do not merely *receive* eternal life *through* the knowledge of God and Jesus Christ; this knowledge itself *is* life, *is* possession of the highest good. For this is not the shadowy knowledge of the sense sundered from the substance; it is the union of the knowing and the Known, in which, therefore, light, life and love unite.—As the Father and Son have been distinct from eternity and yet are One through the eternal Spirit of love, who proceedeth from both, so God hath, by the Son, created a world full of contrasts which His Spirit continually transfigureth into a glorious unity in love. Sin hath banished this harmonizing Spirit from man, hath perverted the contrasts into contradictions and rent men one from the other, as from God. But the work of Jesus Christ, the completion of His redemption, is that the Father's unity with the incarnate Son becometh a unity wherein the whole human race that believeth on the Son, is one with the Father.—This "sanctifying" of Christ's, therefore, embraces His whole active and passive obedience: the sacrifice of His will and the guilt-offering of His holy humanity laden with the sin of the world; by this sacrifice all of believing humanity is sanctified unto God as a sacrifice.—Jesus prays for future believers also, to the end that these may, with His then existing disciples, form one communion in holy love. With these words, the Lord declares the whole essence of His Church on earth. He came to restore unity to the disrupted human race, by means of their reconciliation to God.—This is a beholding whereby the beholder becometh one with the Beheld (1 John iii. 2, 3), whereby the glory of the Lord doth itself pass into him.

LISCO: Because it is the vocation of the disciples to diffuse heavenly life on earth, they may not live retired from the world, or, still less, quit it already by death; the more needful, therefore, is it that they should be preserved from all evil in the world.

BRAUNE: He who prays is not merely an artist erecting a monument to the grace of God; he is, at the same time, a work of art—the monument itself. Thus here the Redeemer who hath restored the image of God in humanity and doth restore it as the High Priest and Sacrifice of mankind.—The Prayer linked itself to His discourses. It is necessary for a good sermon to conclude with a good prayer. First Christ spake of God to His disciples; now He talketh of them to the Father. In this prayer is summed up that which the preceding discourses had unfolded.—Thither He raised His eyes, whither He would be taken by God.—The hour of suffering obscured Him in the eyes of those who looked upon Him as one tormented and stricken by God, and in the sight of His most faithful adherents. But He was confident that the Father *would glorify the Son*, would take Him to Himself, would give Him the glory of exalted efficacy.—In the world, unbelief and superstition had covered the Father's name with darkness. Out of that obscurity, the gospel of Jesus Christ, proclaimed in the power of the Spirit, should draw it forth into the true light.—In the beginning, the life of men was light; they, however, stretched forth their hands beyond life to grasp the light of knowledge; they desired to know, without being; to possess the knowledge of God without divine life. This is the old sin, new even to this day. Thus acting, they lost life and light. But now, through the light of truth, fragmentarily offered them in the Word of life, they should regain life.—Yea, a mind to do the will of God, helps a man to a clear knowledge of the truth that Christ and His doctrine are of God. Therefore despise no piety or fear of God, even though as yet they be not Christian.—"Heart and heart at one together." [*Herz und Herz vereint zusammen*,—one of the best hymns of Zinzendorf, based on this chapter.—P. S.]—"That, in sooth, is a true heavenly ladder, that rests upon earth, but whose top reaches to heaven, nay, to the throne of God, as the place where is the greatest unity. We, however, must not begin at the top, but must make sure of the first steps—we must see that we are first born anew of God through the word of truth, and thus become one with God and His life" (Rieger).

GOSSNER: Now the death-pass must be crossed. There Thou must crown *Thy Son* with honor and glory, that *Thou* mayest be praised and magnified in Him.—He giveth this life unto all whom the Father giveth Him, *i. e.*, all who, drawn by the Father, sundered from the world by preventing grace, suffer themselves to be attracted unto Him, and turn to Him in faith.—We have it from the mouth of Jesus that this, to know the Father and Him, is heaven on earth.—Hence, we have to teach men to know Jesus Christ; for the name of God is in Him, in Him dwelleth all fulness.—He saith: "*I have finished my course, etc.;* let come now what will. So it is with the day's work that is given a man,—whereunto a man is destined from his mother's womb. That is not cut short; though the pleasure of seeing its blessed results be something bated, the grand work to which the Saviour hath called a man, suffereth no retrenchment.—Almost all preachers, even the better sort, make of Christ a mere Teacher and Servant who bides outside of us, who does but teach us what is good; they do not say that He is to rule within us and Himself work good works in us.—"In Thy name have I kept them," says He. It is a bad thing for a shepherd to keep the flock in his own name only, as somewhat belonging to him, to his own glory, through his strength, and not as property entrusted to his care by God, and to God's glory, through God's grace and strength.—He hath left us perfect joy, and that His own. Thereby shall the work of sanctification be perfected in us, as David saith: *Let the glad Spirit keep me;* continue grace unto me.—Happy is he who knows that it is better to be hated by the world and loved by Christ, than to be loved by the world and rejected by Christ.—Christians, says Macarius, are children of another world, of the heavenly Adam, a new race, children of the Holy Ghost, of light, brothers of Christ; they are not of this world.—The "*as I*" can mean nothing else than that we too should be crucified to the world and the world to us, like Jesus, like Paul, like all true followers of Christ.—The word must sanctify us; it divides everything like a two-edged sword, and Satan, in his servants, is always seeking to make it a secondary affair, or to hustle it out of the way altogether.—Ver. 18. Men appeal in vain to these words of Christ and to the divine authority of their office, in support of their claim to be respected and heard like Christ, unless they are anointed by Christ, filled with His Spirit and the fulness of God, blessed, called and sent by Him, as He was sent by the Father, by means of an internal mission and anointing, not simply by outward calling and installation.—Who is not glad that Christ prayed for him before his Passion, in His high-priestly prayer? And He is always heard.—The highest pattern of unity is in heaven, between Father and Son, the copy is on earth.—Ver. 21. The case stands thus: every Christian must believe himself into Christ as deeply as if he were Christ. This constitutes everything, this constitutes faith, it constitutes all deeds, the walk, the virtues.

HEUBNER: The Father's cause was tarnished by the fall; Satan could rejoice at having seduced mankind; what had become of God's purpose in the creation? The Son came as Redeemer and put God's enemy to shame and made God glorious. The highest aim is to glorify God; he who does nothing towards that end, does nought.—Christ is Lord of the human race; He hath unlimited power and authority over it: far more than didactic authority. This authority, however, is for the good of men: Christ is to employ His power in making them happy.—*All things that Thou hast given Me*, My doctrine, My miraculous powers. To consider this *all* that was in Christ as of divine origin, is to believe on Christ.—Gradual progress to faith: Instruction, or external preaching, favorable reception, true knowledge, *i. e.*, heartfelt knowledge, the result of experience and the power of the Spirit.—HOLY FATHER; How can a Christian ear endure that this holiest of all titles should be given to a sinful man.—All joy, all felicity, is finally reduced, in respect of its deepest element, to love; from love flows joy. Hell is joyless because it is loveless.—Christ's prayer repudiates the foolish desire for exemption from the trials and conflicts of this world. It would indeed be by far the more comfortable thing to be transported at once to heavenly bliss, without a battle. Christ might thus have taken the Apostles immediately to heaven with Him. But how then would they have become Christ's Apostles? how would the world have been converted? how would they have been able, without labor, without conflict, without victory, to enjoy happiness in heaven? It likewise follows that the Essenic, Ascetic course is not the true one.—*In Thy truth.* 1. Through the truth: the Word of God is the means of sanctification; 2. in accordance with Thy truth: the Word of God is the rule of sanctification; 3. consecrate them to Thy truth: to the vocation of witnessing for the truth.—How does this prayer shame cold Christians! The Lord thought of the coming generations, and they think too little of Him.—There is but one Apostolic Christianity, and none beside; whoso will not have that, has none.—That unity of the Father and Son is, therefore, not simply a *type*, but a true and effective *cause*, of the oneness of Christians. They, belonging to the Father and the Son, united to the Father through the Son, remain one. As the children of one Father, united to Him through the First-born, they repose on a sure foundation of unity.—If the Church of Christ stood forth as a harmonious community of brethren, where nought but order, love and peace ruled, it would be so unique a phenomenon in our egotistical world that every one would be forced to acknowledge that here was a divine work, and to see in it the government of a higher Spirit, namely, the Spirit of Christ. All doubts as to, and accusations against, Christianity must perforce hold their peace.—*The world knoweth Thee not;* it has no idea that there is an ocean of love in God. Nevertheless, that does not do away with the love.

BESSER: There, on the holy mount, His countenance shone as the sun; here His soul shineth like the sun, His soul beameth like a calm, majestic light.—"It being certain that they are *Mine* and that I am their Lord, Master and Saviour, it is also certain and beyond doubt that they are *Thine,* nay, Thine not only now, but Thine from the begining, and that they come unto Me through Thee" (Luther).—"The Father the Root, Christ the Stem, the Holy Ghost the Sap, believers the branches that draw the Sap unto themselves, the Christian life the fruit of one Tree of the holy church" (Gerhard). —FREYLINGHAUSEN: The above-cited *Meditations* of Gerhard are furnished with an exceedingly significant frontispiece in two divisions. Above is the picture of the Old Testament high-priest burning incense at the altar of incense; underneath are the words: *Which is a shadow of things to come.* Beneath, a picture of the high-priestly praying Christ, surrounded by His disciples, with the inscription: *But the body itself* (the substance) *is in Christ,* Col. ii. 17.

SCHMIEDER, in the Introduction to his Meditations, depicts the solemn repose of the full moonlit night-heavens, up to which Christ, praying, gazed,—and the solemn repose in His soul. He is the High-priest who maketh us priests.—The fellowship of Jesus with the Father was a relationship appearing in Him simultaneously with His self-consciousness.—*The hour.* It is exceedingly noteworthy how Jesus, for everything that is to happen, knows, defines, and chooses time and hour—even that very instant to which the event belongs. (Entirely correct; being sensible of His eternity, He is sensible of His moment; the following is a fundamental thought of the Preacher Solomon: *All is vain,* for the reason that men in their vanity no longer have a perception of the moment, agreeably to the truth that everything has *its time.*)—Thus He invariably does and suffers that which is proper for each hour.—Glorification is the complete revelation of a form of life either abstractly or relatively perfect. A bud is glorified when it bursts its envelope and comes forth a flower.—The Son must earn this dominion which the Father has given Him, in order that it may be as truly His own as it is a gift from the Father. For all dominion is real autocracy so far only as it is acquired by individual prowess.—As the Father, in His Divine Kingdom, fills all the Divine Persons, being wholly in each One, and working in the Divine House that rules in eternal, creative joy, so Jesus would be and work in all men who are saved by Him, whom the Father has given Him, to the end that His joy may be perfect in them. And together with Him, the love in which the Father loves Him shall be in them (*i. e.,* the fellowship in the blessedness of God, the divine heritage of Christ's co-heirs).

[CRAVEN: from HILARY: Ver. 3. To know the only true God is *life,* but this *alone* does not constitute life: What else then is added? *And* JESUS CHRIST *whom Thou hast sent.*—Ver. 21. Unity is recommended by the great example of unity.——AUGUSTINE: Ver. 1. Our Lord, in the form of a servant, could have prayed in silence had He pleased; but He remembered that He had not only to *pray,* but to *teach.*—*Father, the hour is come,* shows that all time, and everything that He did or suffered to be done, was at His disposing, who is not subject to time.—*Father, the hour is come, glorify Thy Son;* the hour is come for sowing the seed, humility; defer not the fruit, glory.—The Son *glorified* the Father, when the Gospel of Christ spread the knowledge of the Father among the Gentiles.—*Glory* was defined among the ancients to be *fame* accompanied with *praise.*—When sight has made our faith truth, then eternity shall take possession of, and displace, our mortality.—Ver. 11. *That they may be one, as We are:* That they may be one in their *nature,* as We are one in Ours.—As the Father and the Son are one not only by equality of substance, but also in will, so they, between God and whom the Son is Mediator, may be one not only by the union of nature, but by the union of love.—Ver. 13. He says He spoke *in the world,* though He had just now said, *I am no more in the world:* inasmuch as He had not yet departed, He was still here; and inasmuch as He was going to depart, He was, in a certain sense, not here.—Ver. 17. *Sanctify them through Thy truth:* Thus were they to be kept from the evil.—Ver. 19. *That they also might be sanctified through the truth, i. e.*, in Me; inasmuch as the Word is truth, in which the Son of man was sanctified from the time that the Word was made flesh.—Ver. 21. They are in us and we in Them, so as that they are one in Their nature, we one in ours; they are in us, as God is in the temple; we in Them, as the creature is in its Creator.—Is not this unity, that peace eternal which is the *reward* of faith, rather than *faith itself?*—Ver. 23. *That they may be made perfect in one;* the reconciliation made by this Mediator, was carried on even to the enjoyment of everlasting blessedness.—As long as we believe what we do not see, we are not yet made perfect, as we shall be when we have merited to see what we believe.—*And hast loved them, as Thou hast loved Me;* There is no reason for God's loving His members, but that He loves Him; but since He hateth nothing that He hath made, who can adequately express how much He loves the members of His Only Begotten Son, and still more the Only Begotten Himself?—Ver. 24. It was not enough for Him to say, *I will that they may be where I am*, but He adds, *with Me:* to be *with* Him is the great good; even the miserable can be *where* He is, but only the happy can be *with* Him—as a blind man, though he is where the light is, yet is not himself *with* the light, but is absent from it in its presence, so not only the unbelieving, but the believing, though they cannot be where Christ is not, yet are not themselves *with* Christ by sight.—*That they may behold;* He says, not, that they may *believe;* it is the *reward* of faith which He speaks of, not *faith itself.*—Ver. 25. What is it to *know* Him, but *eternal life*, which He gave not to a condemned but to a reconciled world? For this reason the [*condemned*] *world* hath not known Thee; because Thou art just, and hast punished them with this ignorance of Thee; and for this reason the *reconciled world* knows Thee, because Thou art merciful, and hast vouchsafed this knowledge, not in consequence of their merits, but of Thy grace.—Ver. 26. *And I in them;* He is in us as in His temple; we in Him as our Head.——From CHRYSOSTOM: Ver. 1. Our Lord turns from *admonition* to *prayer;* thus teaching us in our tribulations to abandon all other things, and flee to God.—He lifted up His eyes to heaven to teach us intentness in our prayers: that we should stand with uplifted eyes, not of the body only, but of the mind.—Ver. 9. *I pray for them:* As the disciples were still sad in spite of all our Lord's consolations, henceforth He addresses Himself to the Father, to show the love which He had for them; He not only gives them what He has of His own, but entreats another for them, as a still further proof of His love.—Ver. 14. Again, our Lord gives a reason why the disciples are worthy of obtaining such favor from the Father; *I have given them Thy word, and the world hath hated them; i. e.*, they are had in hatred for Thy sake, and on account of Thy word.—Ver. 15. *Keep them from the evil: i. e.* not from dangers only, but from falling away from the faith.—Ver. 16. *They are not of the world;* because they have nothing in common with earth, they are made citizens of heaven.—Ver. 17. *Sanctify them in Thy truth; i. e.* make them holy, by the gift of the Holy Spirit, and sound doctrines: for sound doctrines give knowledge of God, and sanctify the soul.—*Thy word is truth, i. e.*, there is in it no lie, nor anything typical, or bodily.—*Sanctify them in Thy truth*, may mean, separate them for the ministry of the word, and preaching.—Ver. 19. *For their sakes I sanctify Myself, i. e.*, I offer myself as a sacrifice to Thee; for all sacrifices, and things that are offered to God, are called holy [sanctified].—*That they also may be sanctified through the truth, i. e.*, for I make them too an oblation to Thee; either meaning that He who was offered up was their Head, or that they would be offered up too; as the Apostle saith, *Present your bodies a living sacrifice, holy.*—Ver. 20. Another ground of consolation to them, that they were to be the cause of the salvation of others.—Ver. 21. For there is no scandal so great as division, whereas unity amongst believers is a great argument for believing; for if they quarrel, they will not be looked on as the disciples of a peace-making Master.—Ver. 22. By glory He means miracles, and doctrines, and unity; which last is the greatest glory.——From BEDE: Ver. 6. *And they have kept Thy word;* He calls Himself the Word of the Father, because the Father by Him created all things, and because He contains in Himself all words; as if to say, they have committed Me to memory so well, that they never will forget Me: Or, they have believed in Me.—Ver. 15. *Keep them from the evil:* every evil, but especially the evil of schism.——From THEOPHYLACT: Ver. 25. *O righteous Father, the world hath not known Thee:* as if to say, I would wish that all men obtained these good things which I have asked for the believing; but inasmuch as they have not known Thee, they shall not obtain the glory and crown.

[From BURKITT: Chap. xvii. If any part of Scripture be to be magnified above another, this chapter claims the pre-eminence; it contains the breathings out of Christ's soul for His Church and children before His departure; not for His disciples only, but for the succeeding Church to the end of the world.—Ver. 1. *These words spake Jesus:* that is, after He had finished His excellent sermon, He closes the exercise with a most fervent and affectionate prayer; teaching His ministers to add solemn prayer to all their instructions and exhortations.—*He lifted up His eyes to heaven:* The gestures which we use in prayer should be such as may express our reverence of God, and denote our affiance and trust in Him.—It is very sweet and comfortable in prayer, when we can come and call God *Father.*—*The hour is come:* that is, The hour of My sufferings, and Thy satisfaction; the hour of My victory and of Thy glory; the hour, the sad hour, determined in Thy decree: no calamity can touch us till God's hour is come; and when the sad hour is come, the best remedy is prayer, and the only person to fly unto for succor is our heavenly Father.—*Glorify thy Son, that Thy Son also may glorify Thee:* Note how the glory of the Father and the Son are inseparably linked together; it was the Father's design to glorify the Son, and it was the Son's desire to have glory *from* the Father, that He might bring glory *to* the Father.—Ver. 2. Observe 1. The dignity with which

Christ was invested; *power over all flesh;* 2. How Christ came to be invested with this power; it was given Him by His Father.—All mankind are under the power and authority of Jesus Christ as Mediator: He has 1. a *legislative* power, or a power to give laws to all mankind; and 2. a *judiciary* power, or a power to execute the laws that He hath given.—*That He might give eternal life to as many as God hath given Him:* Note 1. That all believers are given by God the Father unto Christ; they are given to Him as His *charge*, to redeem, sanctify, and save; and as His *reward*, Is. liii. 10; 2. All that are given to Christ, have life from Him; a life of justification and sanctification on earth, and a life of glory in heaven; 3. The life which Christ gives is *eternal* life; 4. That this eternal life is *a free gift* from Christ unto His people; though they do not work for *wages*, yet they shall not work for *nothing*.—Ver. 3. This is the true way and means to obtain eternal life, namely, by the true knowledge of God the Father, and of Jesus Christ the Mediator. —Learn, 1. That the beginning, increase, and perfection of eternal life lyeth in holy knowledge; 2. That no knowledge is sufficient to eternal life, but the knowledge of God, and Jesus Christ.—The knowledge of the only true God, and of Jesus Christ the Mediator, *is* the life of *grace*, and *the necessary way* to the life of *glory*.—Ver. 4. *I have glorified Thee on the earth:* The whole life of Christ, while here on earth, was a glorifying of His Father; by 1. The doctrine He preached; 2. The miracles He wrought; 3. The unspotted purity and innocency of His life; 4. His unparalleled sufferings at death.—*I have finished the work which Thou gavest Me to do:* He speaks of what He was resolved to do, as already done. Here note that 1. It is *work* that glorifies God; 2. Every man has his work assigned him by God; 3. This work must be finished here upon earth; 4. When we have done our proportion of work, we may expect our proportion of wages; 5. It is a blessed thing at the hour of death to be able to say in uprightness that we have glorified God, and have finished the work which He appointed us to do.—Ver. 5. Learn that, 1. Whoever expects to be glorified with God in heaven must glorify Him first here upon earth; 2. After we have glorified Him, we may expect to be glorified with Him, and by Him.—*With the glory which I had with Thee before the world was:* Here note that Christ—1. As *God*, had an essential glory with God the Father before the world was; 2. As *Mediator*, did so far humble Himself, that He needed to pray for His Father to bestow upon Him the glory which He wanted; namely, the glory of His ascension and exaltation.—Ver. 6. By the *name* of God, we are here to understand His nature, properties, attributes, designs and counsels for the salvation of mankind: Christ, as the Prophet of His Church, made all these known unto His people.—Learn that, 1. All believers are given unto Christ, as His purchase, and as His charge: as His subjects, as His children; as the wife of His bosom, as the members of His body; 2. None are given to Christ, but those that were first the Father's; 3. All those that are given unto Christ, do keep His word; they *keep* it in their *understandings*, they *hide* it in their *hearts*, they *feel the force* of it in their *souls*, they *express the power* of it in their *lives*.—Ver. 7. Observe, 1. The *faithfulness of Christ* in revealing the whole will of His Father to His disciples; 2. The *proficiency of the disciples* in the school of Christ.—Learn hence that, 1. Christ hath approved Himself a faithful messenger from His Father to His people, in that He hath *added nothing* to His message, and *taken nothing from it;* 2. It is our duty to know and believe on Christ, as the only Messenger and Mediator sent of God.—Ver. 8. Learn that, 1. The doctrine of the gospel, which was revealed by Christ, was received from the Father; 2. Faith is a receiving of the *Word* of Christ, and of *Christ* in and by the Word; 3. The ministers of the gospel are to preach that, and only that, which they have out of the Word of God.—Ver. 9. Learn that, 1. The Lord Jesus Christ is the great and gracious Intercessor; 2. All believers are under the fruit and benefit of Christ's intercession; 3. As all the members of Christ in general, so the ministers and ambassadors of Christ in special, have a peculiar interest in Christ's intercession; and great are the advantages of His intercession from (1) The person interceding, Christ: consider the *dignity* of His person, God-man; the *dearness* of His person, God's Son, (2) The manner of His intercession, not by way of entreaty, but meritorious claim, (3) The sublimity of the office; our Intercessor is near to God, even at His right hand, (4) The fruits of His intercession; it procures the acceptance and justification of our persons, the hearing and answering of our prayers, the pardon and forgiveness of our sins, our preservation in grace, and our hopes of eternal glory.—Ver. 10. We may understand this two ways: 1. Of all *persons*,—all My friends, all My disciples are Thine, as well as Mine. 2. All Thy *things* are Mine, and all My *things* are Thine; Christ and His Father are one, and They agree in one; They have the same essence and nature, the same attributes and will; Christ hath all things that the Father hath.—Thence note, That the Lord Jesus Christ is eminently glorified in and by all those that believe in Him, and belong unto Him.—Ver. 11. Note, 1. The title and appellation given to God, *Holy Father;* when we go to God in prayer, we must look upon Him as an *holy* Father, as essentially and originally holy, as infinitely and independently holy; 2. The supplication: *Keep through Thy name those whom Thou hast given Me*, the perseverance of the Saints is the effect of Christ's prayer; 3. The *end* of the supplication, *That they may be one as We are.*—Three things concur to the believer's perseverance; 1. On the *Father's* part, everlasting love and all sufficient power; 2. On the *Son's* part, everlasting merit and constant intercession; 3. On the *Spirit's* part, perpetual inhabitation and continued influence.—Note, 1. The heart of Christ is exceedingly set upon the unity of His members; 2. The believers' union with Christ and with one another, has some resemblance to that betwixt the Father and the Son: it is a union, (1) holy, (2) spiritual, (3) intimate, (4) indissoluble.—Ver. 12. Observe that, 1. Those who shall be saved, are given unto Christ and committed to His care and trust; 2. None of those that are given unto Christ shall be finally lost.—Ver. 13. There is a double care which Christ takes of His people;

namely, a care of their *graces*, and a care of their *joy and comfort*.—Learn that, 1. Christ is the author and original of the joy of His people: *My joy;* 2. It is Christ's will and desire that His people might be full of holy joy: *That My joy may be fulfilled in them;* 3. The great end of Christ's prayer and intercession was, and is, that His people's hearts might be full of joy.—Ver. 14. Learn that, 1. Christians, especially ministers, to whom Christ has given His word, must expect the world's hatred; 2. It is to the honor of believers that they are like unto Christ in being the objects of the world's hatred.—Vers. 15, 16. Observe 1. That the wisdom of Christ sees fit to continue His children and people in the world, notwithstanding all the perils and dangers of the world: He has work for them, and they are of use to Him, *for a time*, in the world; till their work be done, Christ's love will not, and the world's malice cannot, remove them hence; 2. Yet Christ prays that His Father will keep them from the *evil, i. e.*, the sins, temptations and snares of the world.—Note, 1. That a spiritual *victory* over evil is to be preferred before a total *exemption* from it; 2. How necessary divine aid is to our preservation and success, even in the holiest and best of enterprises, and how necessary it is to seek it by fervent prayer; 3. That such as sincerely devote themselves to Christ's service, are sure of His aid whilst so employed.—Ver. 17. Learn that, 1. Such as are already sanctified, ought to endeavor after higher degrees of sanctification; 2. The Word of God is the great instrument in God's hand for His people's sanctification; 3. The *Word* of God is the *truth* of God.—The Word of God is a divine truth, an eternal truth, an infallible truth, a holy truth. —Ver. 18. Observe, 1. Christ's *mission:* The Father *sent* Him into the world; Christ did not of Himself undertake the office of a Mediator; 2. *As* Christ's mission, *so* the Apostles' mission; *As Thou hast sent Me, so have I sent them:* Learn thence that none may undertake the office of the ministry, without an authoritative sending from Christ Himself; 3. Such as are so sent [by the ministers of Christ] are sent by Christ Himself; and it is the people's duty to reverence their persons, to respect their office, to receive their message.—Ver. 19. Christ's *sanctifying Himself* imports, 1. His setting Himself apart to be a sacrifice for sin; 2. His *dedication* of Himself to this holy use and service.—The great end for which Christ did thus sanctify Himself was that He might *sanctify His members;* that we should be consecrated to, and wholly set apart for Him.—Ver. 20. That, 1. All believers have a special interest in Christ's prayer; 2. In the sense of the gospel they are believers, who are wrought upon to believe in Christ through the word; 3. Such is Christ's care of, and love to, His own, that they were remembered by Him in His prayer, even before they had a being.—Ver. 21. The special mercy and particular blessing which Christ prays for, on behalf of believers, is a close and intimate union betwixt the Father, Himself and them, and also betwixt one another. —Note 1. The mystical union betwixt Christ and His members has some resemblance with that union which is betwixt the Father and the Son; 2. Unity amongst the ministers and members of Jesus Christ is of so great importance, that He did in their behalf principally pray for it.—Union amongst Christ's disciples is one special means to enlarge the kingdom [Church] of Christ, and to cause the world to have better thoughts of Him and His doctrine.—Ver. 22. Learn that, 1. God the Father hath bestowed much glory on Christ His Son, as He is man and Mediator of the church; 2. The same glory for kind and substance, though not for measure and degree, which Christ as Mediator has received from the Father, is communicated to true believers; 3. The great end of this communication was, and is, to oblige and enable His people to maintain a very strict union among themselves; 4. Unity amongst believers is part of that glory which Christ as Mediator hath obtained for them.—Ver. 23. Observe 1. As the Father is in Christ, so is Christ in believers, and they in Him; the Father is in Christ in respect of His divine nature, essence, and attributes; and Christ is in believers, by the inhabitation of His Holy Spirit; 2. The happiness of believers consisteth in their *oneness*, in being *one* with God through Christ, and *one* amongst themselves; 3. God the Father loved Christ His Son; (1) as God; (2) as Mediator, John x. 17; 4. God the Father loves believers, even as He loved Christ Himself; 5. Christ would have the world know, that God the Father loveth the children of men, as well as Himself.—Ver. 24. Our Saviour had prayed for His disciples' *sanctification* before, here He prays for their *glorification:* 1. *That they may be where He is; now* Christ is *with them* in His ordinances, in His word, and at His table; *ere long* they shall be *with Him*, as His friends, as His spouse, as His companions in His kingdom; 2. That they may be with Him where He is; that is more than the former: to be with Christ *where He is*, imports union and communion with Him.—Learn 1. All those that are given to Christ as His charge, and as His reward, shall certainly come to heaven to Him; 2. The work and employment of the saints in heaven chiefly consists in seeing and enjoying Christ's glory; for it will be a *possessive* sight; 3. The top and height of the saints' happiness in heaven consists in this, that they *shall be with Christ*.—Ver. 25. *O righteous Father;* righteous in making good Thy promises both to Me and them.—Observe what it is that our Saviour affirms concerning the wicked and unbelieving world, that they *have not known God*,—have no *saving* knowledge of God.—Christ is the original and fontal cause of all the saving knowledge that believers have of God.—Ver. 26. *And I have declared unto them Thy name, and will declare it; i. e.* I have made known unto them Thy nature, attributes, counsels, will and commands, and I will continue the manifestation of the same unto the end.—*That the love wherewith Thou hast loved Me, may be in them, and I in them;* It is not enough for the people of God that His love is *towards* them, but they must endeavor to have it *in* them; that is, experience it in the effects of it, and in the feeling of it in their own souls: the *safety* of a Christian lies in this, that God loves Him; but the *happiness* of a Christian consists in the *sensible apprehension* of this love.

[From M. Henry: Chap. xvii. Christ prayed this prayer in their hearing, so that it was a prayer 1. *After sermon;* when He had spoken from

God to them, He turned to speak to God for them; Those we *preach to*, we must *pray for*; 2. *After sacrament*; 3. Of a *family*: He not only, as a son of *Abraham, taught His household* (Gen. xviii. 19), but, as a son of *David, blessed His household* (2 Sam. vi. 20), prayed *for* them and *with* them; 4. Of *parting*; when we and our friends are parting, it is good to part with prayer, Acts xx. 36,—dying Jacob blessed the twelve patriarchs; dying Moses, the twelve tribes; and so, here, dying Jesus the twelve apostles; 5. That was *a preface to His sacrifice*, specifying the blessings designed to be purchased by His death for those that were His; 6. That was a specimen of His intercession.—All that have the Spirit of adoption, are taught to cry, *Abba, Father*, Rom. viii. 15; Gal. iv. 6: If God be our Father, we have liberty of access to Him, ground of confidence in Him, and great expectations from Him.—Christ calls Him *holy Father* (ver. 11); and *righteous Father* (ver. 25); it will be of great use to us in prayer, both for our direction and encouragement, to *call* God as we *hope to find* Him.—Christ began with prayer for Himself, and afterward prayed for His disciples; We must love and pray for our neighbor as ourselves, and therefore must in a right manner love and pray for ourselves first.—He was much shorter in His prayer for Himself than in His prayer for His disciples; Our prayer for the church must not be crowded into a corner of our prayer.—Ver. 1. The Father *glorified the Son* upon earth, 1. *In* His sufferings, by the signs and wonders which attended them; 2. *By* His sufferings: It was in His cross that He conquered Satan and death; His thorns were a crown, and Pilate in the inscription over His head wrote more than he thought; 3. Much more *after* His sufferings; the Father glorified the Son when He *raised Him from the dead*.—They that have received the *adoption* of sons, may in faith pray for the *inheritance* of sons; if sanctified, then glorified.—Good Christians in a trying hour, particularly a dying hour, may thus plead,—"*Now the hour is come*, stand by me."—*Father*, own Me in My sufferings, that I may honor Thee by them.—If God had not glorified *Christ crucified, by raising Him from the dead*, His whole undertaking had been crushed; therefore, *glorify Me, that I may glorify Thee*.—Hereby He hath taught us, 1. What to aim at in our prayers, in all our designs and desires, *viz.*, the honor of God; 2. What to expect and hope for.—Vers. 2, 3. See the power of the Mediator: 1. The *original* of His power; Thou hast given Him power; 2. The *extent* of His power, He has power over *all flesh, i. e.*, (1) *all* mankind, (2) mankind considered *as corrupt*; 3. The grand intention and design of this power; Here is the mystery of our salvation laid open; Here is (1) *the Father* making over the elect to the Redeemer; (2) the Son undertaking to secure the happiness of those that were given Him; (3) the subserviency of the Redeemer's universal dominion to this; 4. A further explication of this grand design (ver. 3): Here is (1) the *great end* which the Christian religion sets before us, *viz., eternal life*; (2) the *sure way* of attaining this blessed end, which is, by the right knowledge of *God and Jesus Christ*; *This is life eternal, to know Thee*; which may be taken two ways: *First*, Life eternal *lies in* the knowledge of *God and Jesus Christ*; the *present* principle of this life is the believing knowledge of God and Christ; the *future* perfection of that life will be the intuitive knowledge of God and Christ: *Secondly*, The knowledge of God and Christ *leads to* life eternal; this is the *way in which Christ gives* eternal life, by *the knowledge of Him that has called us* (2 Pet. i. 3); and this is *the way in which we come* to receive it.—The Christian religion shows the way to heaven by directing us, 1. *To God*, as the author and felicity of our being; 2. *To Jesus Christ*, as *the Mediator between God and man*.—They that are acquainted with God and Christ, are already in the suburbs of *life eternal*.—The Church's king is no usurper, as *the prince of this world* is.—Ver. 4. With what comfort Christ reflects on the life He had lived on earth; *I have glorified Thee, and finished My work*; it is as good as finished; He overlooks the poverty and disgrace He had. This is recorded, 1. For the *honor of Christ*, that His life upon earth did in all respects fully answer the end of His coming into the world; 2. For *example* to all; (1) We must make it our business to do the work God has appointed us to do; (2) We must *aim at the glory of God* in all; 3. For *encouragement* to all those that rest upon Him.—Ver. 5. All repetitions in prayer are not to be counted *vain* repetitions.—What His Father had *promised* Him, and He was *assured* of, yet He must *pray* for; *promises* are not designed to supersede *prayers*, but to be the guide of our desires and the ground of our hopes.—The brightest glories of the exalted Redeemer were to be displayed within the veil, where *the Father* manifests His glory.—Vers. 6-10. The apostleship and ministry, which are Christ's gift to the Church, were first the Father's gift to Jesus Christ.—Ver. 6. *Thou gavest them Me*, as *sheep* to the shepherd, to be *kept*; as *patients* to the physician, to be *cured*; as *children* to a tutor, to be *educated*.—Vers. 6, 8. Observe, 1. The *great design* of Christ's doctrine, which was *to manifest God's name, to declare Him*; 2. His *faithful discharge* of this undertaking: *I have* done it: His fidelity appears (1) in the *truth* of His doctrine; (2) in the *tendency* of His doctrine, which was to *manifest God's name*.—It is Christ's prerogative to manifest God's name to the souls of *the children of men*. Sooner or later, He will *manifest God's name to all that were given Him*, and will *give them His word* to be, 1. The seed of their new birth; 2. The support of their spiritual life; 3. The earnest of their everlasting bliss.—Vers. 6-8. What success the doctrine of Christ had among *those that were given Him*, in several particulars: 1. *They have received the words which I gave them*; 2. *They have kept Thy word*, have continued in it; have conformed to it; 3. They have *understood* the word—*have known that all things whatsoever Thou hast given Me are of Thee*; 4. They have *set their seal* to it; *They have known surely that I came out from God*.—Ver. 8. *Known surely*; It is a great satisfaction to us, in our reliance upon Christ, that He and all He is and has, all He said and did, all He is doing and will do, are of God, 1 Cor. i. 30: If the righteousness be of God's appointing, we shall be *justified*; if the grace be of His dispensing, *we shall be sanctified*.—See here, 1. What it is *to believe*; it is to *know surely*: We may *know surely* that which we neither do nor can know *fully;* 2. What it is *we are* to believe: *That Jesus Christ came out from God.*—Christ is a Master who delights in the proficiency of His scholars: See how willing He is to *make* the best of us, and to *say* the best of us; thereby encouraging our faith in Him, and teaching us charity to one another.—The due improvement of grace received, is a good plea, according to the tenor of the new covenant, for further grace.—Ver. 9. *They are Thine:* 1. All that receive Christ's word, and believe in Him, are taken into covenant relation to *the Father,* and are looked upon as *His;* 2. This is a good plea in prayer,—Christ here pleads it; we may plead it for ourselves.—Ver. 10. Those shall have an interest in Christ's intercession, in and by whom He is *glorified.*—That in which God and Christ are *glorified,* may, with humble confidence, be committed to God's special care.—Vers. 11-16. The particular petitions which Christ puts up for His disciples, 1. All relate to spiritual blessings in heavenly things; the prosperity *of the soul* is the best prosperity; 2. They are for such blessings as are suited to their *present* state and case, and their various exigencies and occasions; Christ's intercession is always *pertinent;* 3. He is large and full in the petitions, orders them before His Father, and *fills His mouth with arguments,* to teach us fervency and importunity in prayer, to be large in prayer, and dwell upon our errands at *the throne of grace,* wrestling as Jacob.—Note 1. The taking of good people out of *the world* is a thing by no means to be desired, but dreaded rather, and laid to heart, Is. lvii. 1; 2. Though Christ loves His disciples, He does not presently send for them to heaven, but leaves them for some time in this world, that they may do good, and glorify God upon earth, and be ripened for heaven.—It is more the honor of a Christian soldier by faith to *overcome the world,* than to *retreat from it;* and more for the honor of Christ to serve Him in a *city* than in a *cell.*—Ver. 11. It is the unspeakable comfort of all believers, that Christ Himself has committed them to the care of God Himself: Those cannot but be safe, whom the Almighty God keeps, and He cannot but keep those whom the Son of His love commits to Him.—He here puts them 1. Under the divine *protection; Keep* their lives, till they have done their work; *keep* their comforts, and let not them be broken in upon by the hardships they meet with; *keep* up their interest in *the world,* and let not that sink; 2. Under the divine *tuition; Keep them* in their integrity, keep them disciples, keep them close to their duty.—He speaks to God as a *holy Father;* In committing ourselves and others to the divine care, we may take encouragement, 1. From the attribute of His *holiness;* 2. From this relation of a *Father,* wherein He stands to us through Christ.—What we *receive* as our Father's *gifts,* we may comfortably *remit* to our Father's *care:* Father, keep the graces and comforts Thou hast given Me; the children Thou hast given Me; the ministry *I have received.*—Keep them *through Thine own name; i. e.,* 1. Keep them *for Thy name's sake;* so some—Thy name and honor are concerned in their preservation as well as Mine, for both will suffer by it if they either *revolt* or *sink;* 2. *In Thy name;* so others; the original is so, ἐν τῷ ὀνόματι; Keep them in the knowledge and fear of Thy name; keep them in the profession and service of Thy name whatever it costs them; 3. *By* or *through Thy name;* so others; Keep them by Thine own power, in Thine own hand: keep them Thyself.—*Keep them from the evil:* 1. The *evil one,* Satan; 2. The *evil thing,* sin; 3. Keep them from the evil of the world, and of their tribulation in it, so that it may have no sting in it, no malignity.—Ver. 12. Concerning all saints, it is implied that, 1. They are weak, and cannot keep themselves; 2. They are in God's sight valuable and worth keeping; 3. Their salvation is designed, for to that it is that they are kept, 1 Pet. i. 5; 4. They are the charge of the Lord Jesus.—Ver. 11. It should be a pleasure to those that have their home in the other world, to think of being *no more in this world;* for when we have done what we have to do in this world, and are made meet for that, what should court our stay?—They who love God, cannot but be pleased to think of coming to Him, though it be through the valley of the shadow of death.—When our Lord Jesus was going to the Father, He carried with Him a tender concern for *His own which are in the world: We* should have *such* a pity for those that are launching out into the world when we are got almost through it.—Ver. 13. Note, 1. Christ has not only *treasured up* comforts for His people, in providing for their future welfare, but has given out comforts to them, and said that which will be for their present satisfaction; 2. Christ's *intercession* for us is enough to *fulfil our joy in Him.*—Ver. 14. They that receive Christ's *good will* and *good word,* must expect the world's *ill will* and *ill word.*—Those that keep the word of Christ's patience, are entitled to special protection in the hour of temptation, Rev. iii. 10: That cause which makes a martyr, may well make a joyful sufferer.—They to whom the word of Christ comes in power, are *not of the world,* for it has this effect upon all that receive it in the love of it, that it *weans them from* the *wealth* of the world, and *turns them against* the *wickedness* of the world.—Ver. 16. *They* may in faith commit themselves to God's custody, 1. Who are *as Christ was in this world,* and tread in His steps; 2. Who do not engage themselves in the world's interest, nor devote themselves to its service.—Ver. 17. Note, 1. It is the prayer of Christ for all that are His that they may be sanctified; 2. Those that through grace are sanctified, have need to be sanctified more and more; not to go forward is to go backward; 3. It is God that *sanctifies* as well as God that *justifies,* 2 Cor. v. 5; 4. It is an encouragement to us in our prayers for *sanctifying grace,* that it is what Christ intercedes for, for us.—Jesus Christ intercedes for His *ministers* with a particular concern.—The great thing to be asked of God for gospel ministers is, that they may be sanctified, effectually separated from the world, entirely devoted to God, and experimentally acquainted with the influence of that word upon their own hearts, which they preach to others.—Vers. 18, 19. We have here two pleas or arguments to enforce the petition for the disciples' sanctification, 1. The *mission* they had from Him (ver. 18); 2. The *merit* they had from Him; *For their sakes I sanc-*

tify Myself.—Ver. 18. Whom Christ sends He will stand by, and interest Himself in those that are employed for Him; what He calls us out to, He will fit us out for, and bear us out in.—Vers. 20-23. Next to their *purity*, He prays for their *unity;* for the wisdom from above is *first* pure, then *peaceable.*—Ver. 20. Note, 1. Those, and those only, are interested in the mediation of Christ that do, or shall, believe in Him; 2. It is *through the word* that souls are brought to believe on Christ; 3. It is certainly and infallibly *known to Christ,* who *shall believe on Him;* 4. Jesus Christ intercedes not only for great and eminent believers, but for the meanest and weakest; 5. Jesus Christ in His mediation had an actual regard to those of the chosen remnant that were yet *unborn:* prayers are filed in heaven for them beforehand.—Ver. 21. The oneness prayed for includes three things: 1. That they might all be *incorporated in one body;* 2. That they might all be *animated by one Spirit;* 3. That they might all be *knit together* in one heart; that they *all may be one,* (1) in judgment and sentiment; not in *every little thing*—it is neither possible nor needful; (2) in disposition and inclination; (3) in their designs and aims; (4) in their desires and prayers; (5) in love and affection.—It is taken for granted that the *Father* and *Son* are *one;* this is insisted on in Christ's prayer for His disciples' oneness: 1. As its pattern; 2. As its centre—that they may be *one in us,* all meeting here; 3. As its plea.—Believers are one, in some measure, as God and Christ are one; for, 1. The union of believers is a *strict* and *close* union; they are united by a divine nature, by the power of divine grace, in pursuance of divine counsels; 2. It is a *holy* union, in the Holy Spirit, for holy ends; 3. It is, and will be at last, a *complete* union; Father and Son have the same attributes, properties, and perfections; so have believers now, as far as they are sanctified, and when grace shall be perfected in glory, they will be exactly consonant to each other, all changed into the same image.—Ver. 23. The words, *I in them, and Thou in Me,* show what that union is which is so necessary: *viz.,* 1. *Union with Christ;* **I** *in them;* 2. *Union with God* through Him; *Thou in Me;* 3. *Union with each other,* resulting from those; that they hereby may be *made perfect in one.*—Ver. 22. *The glory which Thou gavest Me, I have given them:* Christ gave it them, that they *might be one;* 1. To entitle them to the *privilege* of unity; 2. To engage them to the *duty* of unity; the more Christians are taken up with the glory Christ has given them, the less desirous they will be of vain-glory, and, consequently, less disposed to quarrel.—He pleads the happy influence their oneness would have upon others, showing, 1. His good will to the world of mankind in general; 2. The good fruit of the Church's *oneness:* it will be an evidence of the truth of Christianity and a means of bringing many to embrace it, (1) In *general,* it will recommend Christianity to the world; the *uniting* of Christians in *love* and *charity,* is the beauty of their profession, and invites others to join them; when Christianity, instead of causing quarrels about itself, makes all other strifes to cease, when it cools the fiery, smooths the rugged, and disposes men to be kind and loving, courteous and beneficent, to all men, studious to preserve and promote peace in all relations and societies, it will recommend itself to all; (2) In *particular,* it will beget in men good thoughts, (*a*) of Christ: they will know and believe that *Thou hast sent Me;* (*b*) of Christians; they will know that Thou hast loved them as Thou hast loved Me (ver. 23).—Ver. 24. A petition for the glorifying of all those that were given to Christ: observe the connection of this request with those foregoing; He had prayed that God would preserve, sanctify, and unite them; and now He prays that He would crown all His gifts with their glorification: In this method we must pray,—first for grace, and then for glory.—*Father, I will:* Here, as before, He addresses Himself to God as a Father, and therein we must do likewise; but when He says θέλω—*I will,* He speaks a language peculiar to Himself; He declares, 1. The authority of His intercession in general; He intercedes as a king, for He is a Priest upon His throne (like Melchizedek); 2. His particular authority in this matter; He had a power to *give eternal life.*—Three things make heaven: It is, 1. To *be where* Christ is; *where I am;* 2. To *be with* Him *where* He is; 3. To *behold His glory, which the Father has given Him.* Observe (1) The glory of the Redeemer is the brightness of heaven. (2) The felicity of the redeemed consists very much in the *beholding of that glory.*—The ground upon which we are to hope for heaven is no other than purely the mediation and intercession of Christ, because He hath said, *Father, I will.*—Ver. 25. *O righteous Father;* When He prayed that they might be sanctified, He calls Him *holy* Father; when He prays that they might be glorified, He calls Him *righteous* Father.—*These have known that Thou hast sent Me;* To know and believe in Jesus Christ, in the midst of a world that persists in ignorance and infidelity, is highly pleasing to God and shall certainly be crowned with distinguishing glory: Singular *faith* qualifies for singular *favors.*—Ver. 26. Observe 1. What Christ had done for them: *I have declared unto them Thy name:* Those whom Christ *recommends* to the *favor* of God, He first *leads* into an *acquaintance* with God; 2. What He intended to do yet further for them; *I will declare it;* 3. What He aimed at in all this; not to fill their heads with curious speculations, but to secure and advance their real happiness in two things: (1) Communion with God; (2) union with Christ in order hereunto; *and I in them.*—When God's love *to* us comes to be *in* us, it is like the virtue which the loadstone gives the needle, inclining it to move toward the pole.—It is the glory of the Redeemer to dwell in the redeemed; it is His *rest forever,* and He has desired it; Let us therefore make sure our union with Christ, and then take the comfort of His intercession.

[From Scott: Vers. 1-5. Fervent prayer forms the proper conclusion of religious instruction, and the preparation for approaching trials: and our hearts should habitually be lifted up to God, that He would glorify Himself in and by us; prosper our endeavors to honor Him; support us in resisting temptations; and carry us through all difficulties to His heavenly kingdom.—Ver. 12. Many have called Christ Lord, and seemed to be the children of God, who at length proved "sons of perdition." Such examples should excite to serious self-examination and prayer; but should not distress the believer, who, though he cannot do the things he would, is conscious of integrity in his professed repentance, and faith in Christ, and desire of living to His glory.—Ver. 15. The disciples of Christ should be *willing* to die, but not *impatiently desire* it.—Vers. 20-26. Union and communion with the Father and the Son, by the indwelling of the Holy Spirit, and harmony with one another, formed the substance of our Redeemer's prayer for all His disciples, to the end of time.——From A. CLARKE: Ver. 17. *Through Thy truth;* The doctrine that is not drawn from the truth of God can never save souls: God blesses no word but His own, because none is truth without mixture of error, but that which has proceeded from Himself.—Ver. 26. Christ's sermon on the *mount* shows men what they should *do*, so as to please God: *this* sermon (beginning at chap. xiii. 13) shows them *how* they are to do the things prescribed in the other: In the *former*, the reader sees a *strict morality*, which he fears he shall never be able to perform; in *this*, he sees all things are possible to him who believes, for that very God who made him, shall dwell in his heart, and enable him to do all things that He pleases to employ him in.——From A PLAIN COMMENTARY (Oxford): Ver. 1. Take notice of the precious indication of the gesture with which our Saviour pronounced the words which follow. (Comp. chap. xi. 41, and St. Mark vi. 41.) There are far more indications in our Lord's manner and gesture contained in the Gospels than a careless reader would suppose.—*Glorify Thy Son;* "Some things He knew should come to pass, and notwithstanding prayed for them; because He knew that the necessary means to effect them were His prayers." (HOOKER.)—Ver. 3. God is the life of the soul, as much as the soul is the life of the body: and we must not think of Eternal Life as a thing to be begun *hereafter;* but as something to be begun *now:* The Life of Glory is, in fact, the Life of Grace continued. (C. MARRIOTT.)—Ver. 4. The Son had glorified the Father upon the earth, by 1. Performing the great work which the Father had given Him to do; 2. His miracles; 3. His doctrine; 4. His pure and spotless life; 5. The call of the Twelve; 6. Laying the foundation of the Church.—Ver. 9. "In that prayer for Eternal Life, which our Saviour knew could not be made without effect, He excepteth them for whom He knew His sufferings would be frustrate, and commendeth unto God His own." (HOOKER.)—Ver. 15. Until our appointed earthly work is completed, Divine Love is concerned only to keep us from the power of the Enemy; *not* to take us out of the world.—Ver. 19. All is for our sakes!—Ver. 23. This communion of the Saints with the Son of God is, as most evident, so most remarkable. (Bishop PEARSON.)—Ver. 24. Rather, "*I wish;*" that is, "*I request:*" And O the unspeakable condescension of that wish on the lips of the Eternal Son! —even that He may be united throughout the ages of Eternity to the men whom the Father had given Him.

[From STIER: Chap. xvii.: This *Prayer* is the climax and consummation of all His discourses, pressing nearest to heaven and most immediately breathing of its mysteries,—a triumphantly and serenely bright *It is finished* before the darkness surrounded Him upon the cross, so that that must be first rightly interpreted by this!—"Every one of these words could have been spoken by Him *alone*, and by Him *only* at such a conjuncture." (THEREMIN.)—"Here is the *inwardness* of the East, the home of religion, seized and expressed with the *precision* of the West, the home of science." (BRAUNE.)—The most *glowing mystic* and the most *careful thinker* finds each his own language in these words, embracing both opposites in one.—The Lord, approaching the Father as His Son, proceeds from *Himself*—and His glorification now come, laying claim on that account to eternal life for all given to Him;—He then as Intercessor embraces all His disciples present and future—beginning with the commencement of His work within them, and continually enlarging the circle of His intercession until it reaches eternity and the full consummation of all;—and, finally, He carries back their glorification with becoming dignity to the first words concerning His own—*I in them!*—Ver. 1. The *first* word of the praying Lord is, *Father*—and nothing more. Not *our* Father, which He could never say; not even *My* Father, for that would be here too much.—The Son desires His own glorification not *egotistically*, but solely to *the end* that He again may glorify the Father, and give back to Him the might, honor, and glory which Himself should receive; and here once more we find that first petition after the invocation of the Father in heaven, a petition which includes all others—*Hallowed be Thy name.*—Ver. 2. Authority over all flesh, obtained by His becoming a man in the flesh, and the Head of our race, the Lord received with joy from His Father—"not as a burdensome commission, but as an authority conferred." (RIEGER.)—To become such a *possession* of Jesus (2 Thess. ii. 14)—is ever the condition for the reception of eternal life.—"Know this well, O man, that it is not given to thee to be thy own master; thou must have another Lord, the choice is between God and thine eternal enemy and His." (THEREMIN.)—That *real* life which is *eternal;* that fellowship with *God* which at once begins with living faith, and is consummated only in the full blessedness of eternal glory.—Ver. 3. "For to know Thee is perfect righteousness; yea, to know Thy power is the root of immortality." (WISDOM xv. 3.)—*Knowledge* means, in Scripture, not *apprehension, imagination, thinking* in cold speculation, or *feeling* in the unillumined warmth of false mysticism; nor is it *belief* as mere admission and credence, but a living, conscious possession of fellowship with Him.—*To know God*—the highest thing possible to the creature, or for which the creature was formed. When *that* is perfect, the *life* is consummate.—The two opposites to the knowledge of the true God here referred to, were in their historical manifestation at that time—1. *Gentile* idolatry, which knew not nor acknowledged even the one true God; 2. *Jewish* rejection of His Anointed in the person of Jesus: But in their internal and permanent principle, as the Lord here points to it for all futurity, they are—*Pantheistic* denial of the personal supermundane Creator, and deification of the creature, which is the root of all heathenism; and *Deistical* rationalism, which heeds not and rejects Christ.—"To take the Lord for our God is the *natural* part of the covenant; the *supernatural* part is, to take Christ for our Redeemer: The former is first necessary, and implied in the latter." (BAXTER's *Saints' Rest.*)—The babblers who find here *no more than* a praying mortal, have but a very slight perception of what the prerogative of God's honor *above* every praying creature demands. Was not Moses *sent* of God, and many others like him? But how would it run, Eternal life and blessedness consists in this, to know God and *Moses*—or God and *Paul!*—This is the only time that the Lord Himself unites thus simply and immediately His *Christ*-name with His *Jesus*-name;—but the occasion stands alone. The Lord here confirms, unfolds, explains, and glorifies the central word of the Old Testament, now fulfilled in Him; avows in the most solemn manner before the Father that He, *Jesus*, is the *only true Messiah.*—"Not to no purpose is it that the Lord does not simply say *Me*, but speaks of Himself in the third person; commemorating [declaring] Himself *His own proper name*, in order that He may intimate the *mystical meaning which it involves.*" (LAMPE.)—*Jesus*; This *name of salvation* (Luke ii. 21), first uttered by Gabriel, which combines a *name* common among the people with the sole and incomparable truth of its *signification*, which was borne in the Old Testament by typical persons, which in apostolic preaching is expounded even as the Angel of the Lord had expounded it (Acts iv. 12; ver. 30; Matt. i. 21)—is it not here fittingly used, where He who bears it presents Himself before the Father *in the full consciousness* of its power and meaning? St. Matthew's record of the *conception*, and St. John's of the *departure*, coincide in *the name of Jesus.*—Vers. 4, 5. To have the authority and power to *save*, according to the *meaning of His name*—this is the joy and the crown of His *Jesus-heart* at the present point of transition in His prayer, as He approaches the Father with the *name of Jesus*, that this name also may be *glorified* with and in Him.—Ver. 4. In this *finished*, before the fulfilment upon the cross, consists the pre-eminent wonder of this prayer, which *anticipates* the heavenly mediation and intercession.—"The foundation of the world was not laid, heaven was not yet created, when God planned for my best interest; His grace was extended to me before I had my being. It was His counsel that I should have *life* through His only begotten Son; Him would He provide as a Mediator for me, Him did He set forth as a propitiator, that through His blood I should be sanctified and saved." (HERMANN.)—Ver. 6. Christ first *preached* and testified *concerning the Father* (chap. xvi. 25)—in His own person He brought down and unfolded this great word, teaching man how he may, and why he should, call God his Father.—The question concerning the *name* of God had been hitherto answered by the inconceivable JEHOVAH, which the awe of the far-off worshippers dared not even pronounce, and which rather repelled, therefore, than satisfied the inquiry: but now *eternal being* is plainly revealed to be *eternal love.*—Beyond this name—*Father*, and its appropriate honor, the creature has nothing further to know, to confess, and to praise.—He announced Him *first* to be His own, the Son's, Father, and *then* ours, because He hath given to us the Son.—This is the permanent pre-eminence of the Adamic creature over all other "children of God," that they through Christ have *God* as in the most direct and essential manner their *Father.*—"*Thine they were;* They were the Father's, not only as His creatures and the heirs of the covenant with the fathers, but also as good hearts yielding to the discipline and drawing of God." (RIEGER.)—Ver. 8. Well for us, if we do not merely utter our own *we have believed* and *we have known*, but are also *acknowledged* before the Father by the ἀληθῶς of His Son!—Ver. 9. That which He had promised in Matt. x. 32, He begins now to fulfil; as well as what He had said in John xiv. 16—I will *ask* the Father for you.—"To pray for the world, and not to pray for the world, must both be right in their place." (LUTHER.)—As the typical high priest prayed only for Israel, bore only the twelve tribes on His breast-plate, so there is a corresponding prayer of the eternal High Priest only for the true people of God.—Ver. 10. *And I am glorified in them*, and all that which is Thine and Mine belongs *also to them;* so that every Christian may in the joyful confidence of faith, utter the same word to Christ, All that is Thine is Mine! (1 Cor. iv. 21-23.)—Ver. 11. *I am no more in the world;* although in some degree still remaining *in* them, He yet *leaves* His beloved disciples on going to the Father. And this thought touches His heart with the feeling of all *their* future *need.*—*Holy Father*, God is holy, that is, *exalted* in His ineffable and incomparable *praiseworthiness above all praise of* the creature, while He in pure love condescends to the creature, even to His *fallen* creatures, in order to re-establish in them *this* His honor and glory, that *He is love.* . . . Thus finally, God, as the Merciful One, who yet, in this self-communication of redeeming love, abideth righteous, true, the One God,—is *praiseworthy*, exalted, to be adored in deepest reverence, high above all praise (hence sometimes the נוֹרָא is connected with the קָדוֹשׁ)—but this holiness in its fullest and profoundest sense has its New Testament disclosure in the equally sublime and condescending *Father-name.* . . . Thus the formula which Christ here uses—*Holy Father*—condenses the Old and New Testament expressions into one, uniting the deepest word of the past revelation with the new name which was now to be revealed, and both being *one* in their meaning.—Christ, who bears in Himself and brings to the world the name of the Father, prays as if He should say, Keep them *in Me.*—*That they may be one;* The prayer glances forward to the great *end* of their preservation: One among themselves, because one with Me and Thee, with Us.—Ver. 12. Let no man depend upon the keeping of the Father and the Son, or upon the intercession of the High Priest, as upon an *irresistible grace* which will render this *being lost* impossible.—"Jesus caused it not, still less the Scripture, least of all God" (BRAUNE),—but Judas himself; although a child of Satan, he is at the same time the author and father of his own sin and his own perdition.—Ver. 13. That which the intercession of Jesus prayed for and assured to His own, is made in the hands of the Spirit a blessing distributed in ever-increasing measure to all.—Whosoever speaks and writes under the benediction of this discourse of Jesus increases and fulfils the *joy* of those who hear and read.—Ver. 14. The hatred of the world is the always resulting consequence, in the degree in which the Word has been given to us.—After the creation of the new man, which is now their proper *person*, after their union with Christ through the regeneration of the word, they are no longer of the world.—Ver. 15. *This* is the inmost reason why they must remain in the world: they must pursue the *conflict* unto *victory*.—Christ asks not that His disciples should be taken out of the world; then ask it not thyself, either for thyself or for others! Reply with the Apostle to thine own desire to depart, Nevertheless it is *better*, for it is more *needful*, to remain in the flesh and in the world. Content thyself with praying for thy *preservation*, until thou *hast* fulfilled all thy work, and *art* thyself made perfect. —The reasons for which it was better that they should remain: 1. Believers are to continue the witness and work of the Lord in the world; 2. Only in the struggle to accomplish this, are *we ourselves* perfected and *sanctified*.—"Men wonder when a believer falls; but they should much more wonder to see him hold fast to the end, and finish his course with joy." (HOFACKER.)—The great *prize*, the *full fruit* of our discipline is this, to be able to say throughout the conflict and at the end—But in all these we are *more than conquerors!* Rom. viii. 37.—*The evil* is really the same comprehensive term here as in the Lord's Prayer—sin, the *malitia mundana;* it includes all the miserable fruits and consequences of sin, from the equally *tempting* as profitable κακία (Matt. vi. 34), up to the tremendous ἀπώλεια of eternity.—Ver. 17. There is still something of the *world* in them; they are still *in the evil;* therefore they need to be *sanctified:* 1. for their own sake and in themselves; 2. as ver. 18 shows, for the sake of the world, and for their mission to it.—The great *means* of this sanctification is, the *word* of truth, just as in Acts xx. 32.—"*Thy* truth" and "*Thy* word" embrace even here every Old Testament word also, concerning which Ps. cxix. 160 gloried—*Thy word is true from the beginning*, or—The sum, the essential substance of Thy word is Truth.—But now it is obvious that "if the word of God is thus consecrated as a *sanctifying* medium," it receives this consecration as a living word, not regarded therefore as without and independent of the *Spirit*. It is the Son who sanctifies us in Himself; it is the Father who sanctifies us through the Son in the Spirit; specifically and conclusively it is thus the Spirit, as the living truth of God, who produces this sanctification.—Ver. 18. Christ does not merely *leave* them *in* the world, He *sends* them *to* it and *into* it! As He Himself in the flesh overcame through conflict, and by true obedience sowed the seed which was now to produce the full harvest of His glory—so also is it with us. Thus we have here the strongest reason why He will not take His own out of the world; why we should not wish to forsake the society of men, and be at rest *before the time;* why we should rather persevere in our mission, *as He did*.—Ver. 19. The common theory of atonement, which does not penetrate into the living oneness of the true humanity of Christ with the fallen children of Adam, will never be able to understand this memorable saying; for it leaves Jesus apart in His holiness, just where He, nevertheless, descending to and penetrating our humanity, *sanctifies* Himself for us. Does the ἁμαρτία by imputation lie only *upon* Him? Is it not rather, according to all Scripture, *in* His flesh, the same flesh of sin in the ὁμοίωμα of which He was sent and was born; so that in *His* flesh, this human nature and human person of the *incarnate* Son, *sin* was condemned and done away? [?]—In proportion as *sin* becomes to us, through the fellowship of His holy and willing Spirit, a *bitterness*, we also are sanctified *in the truth*, essentially *in truth*. The *truth* of God is the objective element and goal of actual, essential sanctification.—Vers. 20-26. He first *prays for* the *unity* of all who should believe in Him and the Father; passing altogether from praying (now become a θέλω, *I will*) into the final *promise* of vers. 25, 26. —Ver. 20. In this intercessory prayer, the beginning and pledge of that intercession which still prevails on high, every one who believeth has his place.—*Faith* itself is not prayed for or given; here, as in ver. 8, it is the *condition* of the validity and effect of the intercession.—All faith in all ages comes *through the word;* this, on the one hand, maintains the doctrine of prevenient grace, the grace of Him who calls, as universal for the world and as special for the individual, without which faith were entirely out of the question: while, on the other hand, it recognizes the freedom of our own decision, for *through the word* "means the free way of light and conviction." (BRAUNE.)—Ver. 21. What diversities are found among the members of the great body the Church, in external relation to the world, as well as in vocation, gifts, knowledge—and yet *all* are *one!* These two words most significantly meet here; this casts down the wall of partition between *Israel* and the Gentiles; as also all such distinctions as the ancient world recognized, according to Gal. iii. 28; Rom. i. 14; similarly, by anticipation, all the distinctions which the modern world, and the Christian world itself, has set up.—An enforced, external, deceptive unity is far from being the thing spoken of here; but the one Word on which faith rests, the one end of the one way in the imitation of the one Lord and Shepherd, the one Spirit by whom all have access to one Father, make the essential unity of all who believe, and according to the proportion of their faith, know and live in believing.—"The *being one* of believers is not only a being one after the *similitude* of the Father and the Son, but it is *bound up with* their being one; it is at the same time a being one *with* Father and Son, *since* God through Christ and His Spirit *essentially dwells in them*." 1 John i. 3 (MEYER). —The Restitution brings us abundantly more than man's original prerogative at the creation; although Mallet said well in his sermon, "Who can hear this petition from the heart and voice of Jesus—*That they may be one, as We are*—without thinking of the word, *Let Us make man an image of Ourselves?*"—The Lord (1) testifies now at the end *His own* desire and will that all the world might believe; (2) He suggests this aim of universal, all-seeking grace to *His Church;* and would teach His people to regard this as the goal, however unattainable in itself, of all the efforts of their united love—*ἵνα ὁ κόσμος πιστεύσῃ.*—That *unity* which alone gives power to its *missions*, and those *missions* which rest solely upon *unity*, are in their union the end of the Church.—An intimation from above, that the greatest obstacle to the world's believing is the want of manifest unity in faith and love on the part of the imperfect Church.—Ver. 22. *The glory which Thou hast given Me* is that same glory of grace and truth, of love, of unity with the Father, which, according to John i. 14, beamed forth to faith *from the humanity of Jesus;* and *this* He had truly given to His disciples upon earth already, because and so far as *He is in them.*—Even the slightest glimmering of heavenly light which begins to shine out of the countenance of a justified publican, is an outbeaming of His future glorification; and so is the still brighter angel-face of the crowned martyr at his trial.—Regard each other, at least, O believers, with respect! Learn, ye children of God, to stand in awe of your own dignity, that ye defile not yourselves with sin! Let your *thanksgivings* for what hath been already given, invigorate your prayer and effort after holiness and perfection!—And all this *through faith!* "A drop of faith is far more noble than a whole sea of mere science, though it be the historical science of the Divine word." (FRANCKE.)—Ver. 24. The Lord, when He reaches this point, elevates His tone, changes His petition into an *authorized demand*, and sets it before the hearers of His prayer in the form of a strong promise: *θέλω, I will*, is no other than a *testamentary word* of the Son, who in the unity of the Father, is *appointing* what He wills.—Our *love* teacheth us that to be *with Christ* would be in itself fully sufficient for blessedness; love desires, even in heaven, nothing beside for its unutterable joy;—as the same *love* here also speaks in Christ: "I will and must have all My children with Me." (FRANCKE.)—This is the resolution of the contest between *disinterested love* and the *regard to reward;* with the supremest majesty Christ here speaks of *His own* glory and the *beholding* it, as the highest blessedness of His glorified ones; comp. Ex. xxiii. 18.—He does not, however, say "*My* glory" otherwise than as He appoints it to be shared by *us.* *Behold* is an experiencing and tasting (as ch. viii. 51), for, according to ver. 22, the Lord had *given* to us already His glory.—Ver. 25. "Nothing is more wholesome and refreshing for every one of us, nothing more effectually secures the peace of the soul, than to say after the Saviour—Righteous Father! that is, when he can accept all—the death of his flesh, the life of his spirit, the destruction of his sin, the service of the living God, the loss of his portion in this life, with the corresponding heirship of God, and co-heirship with Christ—as grounded in the righteousness of the Father" (RIEGER)—and when he can also, like Christ in this last word of solace, accept it as right that its part in the tree of life and the holy city should be *taken away from the world.*—The *not knowing* is its own proper *guilt*, on account of which God can manifest Himself to it as only *just.*—The world, even the [nominally] Christian world, *knoweth not* the righteous Father, even to this day, knoweth not the Lord who revealeth Him—although naming and calling upon both, like the Jews with their God and their Messiah. *And these have known;* They knew Me as sent of Thee and as Thy Son (as Christ, the Son of the living God), and thus, through Me and in Me, *Thyself also* as My Father, holy and righteous—and this they know with Me, in opposition to the world from which they are saved.—Ver. 26. Yea, *as* He loveth Christ He loveth us, for He giveth Him up for us all.—*And will declare it;* It is to be noted that, through the Spirit, the Church of Christ is truly led to the knowledge of the *Father.*—*Love* (not faith, not eternal life, not glory)—only *love* is the last word here! let every one ponder this and feel it. "With this end of creation, redemption, and sanctification, the Redeemer closes His High-priestly prayer. Love created the world, love took compassion upon the sinful world, love will unite in one the sanctified. Love is the eternal essence of God, and the principle of all His dealings." (FIKENSCHER.)—The indwelling of His love is not simply "the *practical* end" of the knowledge of the name and nature of God, as it is very generally distinguished; but *the love being in them* is itself the living, consummate *knowledge.*—The love of the Father dwelleth in us only through the mediation of the Son; we know and we have the Father only as the Father of Christ, nor shall we possess Him throughout eternity otherwise: thus the *last word of all* after the last is, I IN THEM!—Christ in us, the love of the Father in us—is no other in its truth and power than the *communion of the Holy Ghost*, who bringeth through the grace of Christ the love of God to man.—Chap. xvii.: That all things which He prays for and promises may be Yea and Amen,—the Lord of glory went, after these words, to the woe of Gethsemane, to the death of the cross, and, through the death endured for our sins, to His holy and righteous Father. This death is the centre of all that grace and truth of which the word bears witness to faith; out of this death cometh life, and love, and sanctification, and unity, and eternal glory.

[From BARNES: They were proceeding to the garden of Gethsemane [?] (chap. xiv. 31); it adds much to the interest of this prayer that it was offered in the stillness of the night, in the open air, and in the peculiarly tender circumstances in which Jesus and His Apostles were.—Ver. 1. *Glorify Thy Son;* honor Thy Son, see ch. xi. 4; give to the world demonstration that I am Thy Son; so sustain Me, and so manifest Thy power in My death, resurrection and ascension, as to afford indubitable evidence that I am the Son of God.—Ver. 2. He has *power* over *all;* He can control, direct, sustain them. Wicked men are so far under His universal dominion, and so far restrained by His power, that they shall not be *able* to prevent His bestowing redemption on those who were given Him.—Ver. 3. *Might know*

Thee; The word *know* includes all the impressions on the mind and life which a just view of God and of the Saviour is fitted to produce. *To know God as He is,* is to know and regard Him as a lawgiver, a sovereign, a parent, a friend—To know Jesus Christ is to have a practical impression of Him *as He is,* that is, to suffer His character and work to make their due impression on the heart and life. Simply to have *heard* that there is a Saviour is not to *know* it.—Ver. 4. *I have finished the work;* How happy would it be if men would imitate His example, and not leave their great work to be done on a dying bed! Christians should have their work accomplished, and when that hour approaches have nothing to do but to die, and return to their Father in heaven.—Ver. 17. Truth is a representation of things as they are. The Saviour prayed that through those just views of God and of themselves they might be made holy. To *see things as they are* is to see God to be infinitely lovely and pure; His commands to be reasonable and just; heaven to be holy and desirable; His service to be easy, and religion pleasant, and sin odious; to see that life is short, that death is near, that the pride, pomp, pleasures, wealth and honors of this world are of little value, and that it is of infinite importance to be prepared to enter on the eternal state of being. He that sees all this, or *that looks on things as they are,* will desire to be holy; he will make it his great object to live near to God, and to glorify His name.—Ver. 19. *That they also, etc.* That they 1. Might have an *example* of the proper manner of laboring in the ministry; 2. Might be made pure by the *effect* of My sanctifying Myself, *i. e.,* by the shedding *of that blood which cleanses from all sin.*—Ver. 20. In the midst of any trials, we may remember that the Son of God *prayed for us.*—Ver. 21. *That they also may be one in us;* A union among all Christians founded on and resulting from a union to the same God and Saviour.—Ver. 23. *May be made perfect in one;* That their union may be *complete;* that there may be no *want* of union, no jars, discords, or contentions.—It is worthy of remark how entirely *the union of His people* occupied the mind of Jesus as He drew near to death.—All that is needed now, under the blessing of God, to convince the world *that God sent the Lord Jesus, is that very union among all Christians for which He prayed.*—Ver. 26. *I in them;* By My doctrines, and the influence of My Spirit—that my religion may show its power and produce its proper fruits in their minds. Gal. iv. 19.——From JACOBUS: Chap. xvii.: "First He prays for Himself, then for the whole Church, and for it He implores the four principal things of the Church—(1) the preservation of true doctrine, (2) concord in the Church, (3) the application of His sacrifice, (4) and the last and highest good, that the Church with Christ may be invested with life, joy and eternal glory." (MELANCHTHON.)—Ver. 2. He will lose *none* who are given to Him—and He will lose *nothing* that belongs to any of them (ch. x.), not even their bodies (ch. vi. 39).—Ver. 3. *This is life eternal—the* life eternal—not, this is the *way* to life eternal, but *this is it.*—"To know God, and to have experience of His graciousness, *is* the very participation of Him, and life results from the participation of God." (IRENÆUS.)—Our Lord uses the name by which He was known, *Jesus,* accompanied with the official title, *Christ*—thus solemnly recognizing these titles as embodying the treasures of that knowledge of which He here speaks—and giving a sweet sanction to this double title for the Church in all time.—Ver. 4. *Have finished;* "How doth He say that He hath finished the work of man's salvation since He hath not yet climbed the standard of the cross? Nay, but by the determination of His will, whereby He hath resolved to endure every article of His mysterious passion, He may truly proclaim that He hath finished the work." (POLYCARP.)—Ver. 5. There is shown here the oneness of Christ's person, in His three estates, before the world was—*on earth*—and afterward *in Heaven.* This glory of Christ He did not *receive,* but *possessed;* He HAD it originally, and always—and never began to have it.—Ver. 7. *They have known;* They have a knowledge derived from experience; they have that knowledge which is promised to those who follow on to know the Lord.—Ver. 8. Their reception of the truth came from His manifestation of it to them (ver. 6), and their reception of it was cordial, leading to obedience.—Ver. 9. It is not meant that He never could or would pray or ask any thing for the world as distinct from His people.—"The Lord knoweth them that are His," and this is the inscription on the seal of His foundation (2 Tim. ii. 19).—Ver. 10. *Thine are Mine;* How could any creature say this? What larger claim to Godhood could be made?—Ver. 11. *And now I am no more in the world;* Here we get a glimpse within the vail. We are given to see how He will make this the burden of His prayer in Heaven.—*Keep in Thy name;* Keep them in the knowledge and acknowledgment of Thy covenant titles and truths.—*That they may be one, as we are;* "Then will our unity be truly happy when it shall bear the image of God the Father, and of Christ, as the wax takes the form of the seal which is impressed upon it." (CALVIN).—Ver. 12. *I have kept;* I have *guarded*—or *kept as with a military guard.*—*The son of perdition;* It was no falling from grace, because he had no grace to fall from.—Ver. 13. It is not enough for Christ that His people be perfectly *safe* for eternity; He will have them also perfectly *happy.*—Ver. 15. We are not to seek our removal from the earth before the time—not to retire from active part in the affairs of this life—but we are to labor in our business here, seeking only to be preserved from the evil, and to grow in grace.—Ver. 17. "The revealed word of God is the only rule to direct us how we may glorify and enjoy Him." (WESTMINSTER CAT.)—Whatever contradicts this divine word is falsehood.—Ver. 19. *I sanctify Myself;* This, as applied to Christ, cannot refer to spiritual sanctification, but has necessarily the Old Testament sense of holy *self-consecration* to His sacrificial death.—Ver. 21. *One in us;* It is only by having fellowship with the Father and with His Son Jesus Christ, that they could be one.—This unity may consist with a variety of *form,* but it cannot consist with diversity of *spirit.* "*Union implies parts.*" (JAY.)—Ver. 23. The stalk and root of the Vine are one, so as that the branches should be one also, by having all of them a vital relation to the Vine, and deriving of its one life.—Ver. 24. When the Christian dies, we may regard it as being at this expressed "*I will*" of Christ. He claims that they shall have death to do them the service of introducing them to the beatific vision of their Lord.—*Will declare it;* This implies that He would continue His work of revealing the Father, by the mission of the Comforter, and that all these unfoldings of the Divine character, in all ages of the Church, should work in them a "hope that maketh not ashamed"—"Christ in them, the hope of glory."—From OWEN: Ver. 1. We are conducted, in the very opening of this sublime prayer, to the mysterious unity of the Father and Son, which is the great foundation upon which all that follows is based.—Ver. 6. The full and blessed import of the passage has reference to the covenanted inheritance of Jesus Christ, known, determined, and provided for, before the foundation of the world.—Ver. 8. Our Lord, by the word *surely* characterizes their knowledge as of a higher type than the *we know* of Nicodemus, ch. iii. 2.—Ver. 9. The intercessory prayer of Jesus embraces those only who are or are to be the actual subjects of His redeeming love.—*Through Thine own name;* literally, *in Thine own name*, the idea being that of dwelling or abiding in the protective power of God.—Ver. 12. There is a concealed argument *a fortiori;* if they stood in need of God's protecting care, while Jesus was personally with them, *much more* would its continuance be necessary, now that they were to be left by Him, to carry on the great work of evangelizing men.—Ver. 13. Our Lord uttered this intercessory prayer in the hearing of His disciples, in order that it might be a source of comfort in the dark hour of trial and affliction to them, and also to all who should come after them and be inheritors of like promises and blessings.—Ver. 15. This verse implies a conflict not only between His disciples and the world *without*, but also with the world *within*, according as indwelling sin gave force to the temptations by which they might be beset.—Ver. 16. As Jesus had been actuated by a supreme desire to do His Father's will, so they were influenced by a like heavenly spirit and temper. Their whole life and purpose was an antagonism of good with evil, truth with error, light with darkness.—Ver. 17. "They who are true disciples of Christ live and move in the word of truth as their element; they *breathe* it. This element, like all the means of grace, has a sanctifying tendency." (SCHAUFFLER.)—"The true sanctifying Word" (Incarnate Word), "by union to which men become holy, separate from the world, united to God, and partakers of the divine nature." (LEWIS.)—The living word of inspiration, that is, the revelation which the Incarnate Logos made of God, is the divinely appointed means of sanctification.—Ver. 19. The difference between this act (sanctification), as predicated of Him and of His disciples, is twofold: 1. He sanctifies Himself, 2. this very self-sanctification proves His personal holiness from the very beginning; but the disciples (1) were sanctified by the Spirit of God; (2) and this proves them to have been previously defiled by sin.—Ver. 20. This passage defines the true position of the preached Word in all which pertains to the salvation of men: "Faith cometh by hearing, and hearing by the Word of God." Rom. x. 14-17.—Ver. 21. The oneness of believers here spoken of, is one not of essence, but of love. It is the unity of the Spirit, resulting from their being "one body, one Spirit, one hope of [the believer's] calling, one Lord, one faith, one baptism, one God and Father of all, who is above all, and through all, and in all." (Eph. iv. 4-6).—The unity here prayed for, does not imply—1. an absolute sameness of opinion on matters of religious faith and practice among Christ's followers [Does it not require a *certain degree* of sameness?—E. R. C.]; 2. That silence should be kept when error is taught, or when a Christian brother goes astray; 3. The surrender of any essential point of belief, in order to effect a compromise of doctrinal views, and thereby seek to remove all denominational distinctions.... [Can any point of doctrine be *essential*, on which *evangelical* denominations disagree?—E. R. C.]—The Spirit of our Lord's petition is aimed against those sectarian prejudices and animosities, *etc.*, which have so often brought dishonor upon the religion of Christ.—*That the world may believe, etc.;* This is not so much the *purpose*, as the *result* of unity among Christians.—Ver. 22. The union of believers by the indwelling Spirit with the Father and Son from whom the Spirit proceeds, entitles them through grace to participate in the glory *given* to Christ.—The hidden spiritual life which they possess through faith in Him, and by which they become partakers of His glory, unites them all to Him, as the branches are united to the vine.—Ver. 23. *That they may be made perfect in one;* Moral perfection is not here referred to, but a completeness and perfection of unity, according to the pattern of that which subsisted between the Father and Son.—The evidence of the Father's love for believers, is here declared to be the great love which they manifest for one another, and the unity and harmony of purpose and aim which pervades their life.—Ver. 24. The verb *see*, in this connection, has the idea also of *partake;* "No mere spectator could *see* this glory." (ALFORD.)—Ver. 25. "He appeals to the righteousness of God against the evil world, and in favor of His people; see xvi. 10." (WEBSTER and WILKINSON.)—Ver. 26. *I in them;* As the Son was loved of the Father, His indwelling presence secured for His followers a participation in the Father's love.

[Ver. 21. *That they all may be one, etc.;* The unity of the Church here prayed for, was not (or not only) that of *essence* which *already* existed, and was *complete* and *invisible;* but that of *perfection* (ver. 23) which might be broken, was susceptible of *increase*,—and was *apparent* to the world.—The union contemplated was one immediately of *individuals*, and not of *denominations*.—That which Christ prayed for, it is the Church's duty to strive after.]

SIXTH SECTION.

The Lord in the circle of His foes, as the Light overtaken by the Darkness; the lofty Judge or the personal Judgment, whilst He is judged; victorious in His outward succumbing; how He carries out His judgment, to the victory of Light and Salvation.

(CHAPS. XVIII. AND XIX.)

I.

CHRIST AS THE JUDGMENT OF LIGHT UPON THE CONFUSED NOCTURNAL CONFLICT OF THE WORLD AGAINST AND OVER HIS PERSON; OVER AGAINST HIS BETRAYER, HIS APPREHENDERS, HIS VIOLENT HELPER. THE MAJESTY OF THE BETRAYED, IN CONTRAST TO THE NOTHINGNESS OF THE BETRAYER; THE VOLUNTARINESS OF THE SUFFERING, IN CONTRAST TO THE IMPOTENCE OF THE SEIZERS; THE REFERENCE TO THE DECREE OF THE FATHER, IN CONTRAST TO THE UNLAWFUL AID OF PETER. THE REPUDIATION OF PETER'S DEED OF VIOLENCE, AND THE VANITY AND INSIGNIFICANCE OF EMPLOYING VIOLENT MEANS FOR THE ACCOMPLISHMENT OF SPIRITUAL ENDS.

CHAP. XVIII. 1-11.

(Matt. xxvi. 36-56; Mark xiv. 32-52· Luke xxii. 39-53.)

1 When Jesus had spoken these words, he [Having spoken these words, Jesus]
went forth with his disciples over the brook Cedron, [the torrent Kidron][1] where
2 was a garden, into the which [into which] he entered, and his disciples. And
[But] Judas also, which[2] [who] betrayed him, knew the place; for Jesus oft-times
3 resorted thither with his disciples. Judas then, having received a band *of men* [the
band of soldiers, *i. e.*, the garrison of the fort,[3]] and officers from the chief priests
and Pharisees, cometh thither with lanterns and torches and weapons.[4]
4 Jesus therefore, knowing all things that should come [were coming, τὰ ἐρχόμενα]
5 upon him, went forth, and said[5] unto them, Whom seek ye [do ye seek]? They
answered him, Jesus of Nazareth [the Nazarene, τὸν Ναζωραῖον]. Jesus saith unto
them, I am *he* ['Εγώ εἰμι]. And [Now] Judas also, which [who] betrayed him,
6 stood with them. As soon then as he had said [he said, εἶπεν] unto them, I am *he*,
7 they went backward, and fell to the ground. Then asked he them again [Again
therefore he asked them], Whom seek ye [do ye seek]? And they said, Jesus of
8 Nazareth [the Nazarene]. Jesus answered, I have told you that I am *he:* if
9 therefore ye seek [are seeking] me, let these go their way: That the saying might
be fulfilled, which he spake, Of them which [those whom] thou gavest [hast given,
δέδωκάς] me have I lost none [I lost none, or, not a single one of them, οὐκ ἀπώλεσα
ἐξ αὐτῶν οὐδένα].
10 Then Simon Peter having a sword drew it, and smote the high priest's servant,
11 and cut off his right ear.[6] [And] The servant's name was Malchus. Then said
Jesus unto Peter, Put up thy [the][7] sword into the sheath: the cup which my [the][8]
Father hath given me, shall I not drink it?

TEXTUAL AND GRAMMATICAL.

[1] Ver. 1.—[The Recepta and Tischendorf read τῶν Κέδρων, in accordance with B. C. E. and many others; Griesbach, Lachmann in accordance with Codd. A. S. Δ., Jerome, Ambrose, *etc.* (conf. Joseph. *Antiq.*, viii. 1, 5) τοῦ Κεδρών. The plural seems to have originated in a misapprehension on the part of the transcribers: Cedar Brook instead of Black Brook. [In ed. viii. Tischendorf reads τοῦ κέδρου, on the authority of ℵ.* D. *a. b.* Sah. cop. æth.; Lachm. τοῦ Κεδρών with A. S. Δ.; but Tregelles, Alford, Westcott and Hort give the preference to the plural τῶν κέδρων with ℵ^c. B. C. L. X. Orig. Chrys. Cyr., *etc.* Josephus favors the singular, *Antiq.*, viii. 1, 5: τὸν χείμαῤῥον κεδρῶνος, *Bell. Jud.*, v. 2, 3: ἡ κεδρὼν ὠνόμασται. The plural form, τῶν κέδρων, brook of *cedars*, *Cedar Brook*, is found already in the Sept. version of 2 Sam. xv. 23, but the Alex. Cod. and the Zurich ed. read there: ἐν τῷ χειμάῤῥῳ τοῦ κέδρων. It is evidently a Greek corruption of the Hebrew קִדְרוֹן (*niger*, *Black Brook;* comp. the frequent Greek river-name Μέλας), under the impression that it means *cedars.* There is no evidence that cedars grew on the brook. John can hardly have sanctioned such a mistake, and therefore I would decide here from internal probability against the authority of MSS. The error may have been made by the first Greek copyist, who was ignorant of Hebrew.—P. S.]

[2] Ver. 2.—[Noyes and Am. B. U. render ὁ παραδιδοὺς αὐτόν, *his betrayer*. Alford retains the A. V., including *which*.—P. S.]

[3] Ver. 3.—[τὴν σπεῖραν refers to the well-known troop of soldiers or Roman cohort which was stationed in Jerusalem as garrison of Fort Antonia, Matt. xxvii. 27; Acts xxi. 31.—P. S.]

[4] Ver. 3.—[Probably more correct: *with torches* (μετὰ φανῶν), *and lamps* (λαμπάδων, lights fed with oil in lanterns) *and weapons* (ὅπλων, swords and staves),—the utensils of the military on a night march. λαμπάς, however, means also torch and lantern. The repetition of the καί is not superfluous, but rhetorical.—P. S.]

[5] Ver. 4.—B. C.*D. *etc.* ἐξῆλθεν καὶ λέγει (Lachmann, Tischendorf) instead of ἐξελθὼν εἶπεν.

[6] Ver. 10.—Tischendorf ὠτάριον, in accordance with B. C.* L. *etc.* (see Mark xiv. 47). [Cod. Sin. also sustains ὠτάριον, *auriculam*, versus ὠτίον, *aurem*, probably a correction from Matt.—P. S.]

[7] Ver. 11.—The Recepta: μάχαιράν σου. Σου is omitted in accordance with the decisive Codd. [ℵ. A. B. C. D., Alf. Tischend., *etc.*]

[8] Ver. 11.—[ὁ πατήρ, without μου, is the proper reading.—P. S.]

EXEGETICAL AND CRITICAL.

[Now follows the history of the Passion, chaps. xviii. and xix., and the Resurrection of our Lord, chaps. xx. and xxi., where we have the parallel accounts of the Synoptists. Yet John omits several items (as the agony in Gethsemane, anticipated in xii. 27, and xiii. 21; but he mentions the garden, xviii. 1), and supplies other interesting facts (as the commending of the mother of Jesus to John), and in the parallel accounts a number of minute, circumstantial details (xviii. 2, 10, 13, 24, 28; xix. 14, 20, 41, *etc.*) which betray the eye-witness of the scenes described. But it is wrong to say with Hengstenberg that John merely meant to give supplements to the Synoptic history of the Passion with such common traits as are necessary to show the connection, comp. the remarks of Godet, ii. p. 5, 69 f. —P. S.]

Ver. 1. **Jesus went forth** [ἐξῆλθεν]. Not precisely forth from the city (Meyer), but forth from the city precincts, which extended to the brook Kedron. 'Εξῆλθεν πέραν. *Leben Jesu*, ii. p. 1347 ff. [David, betrayed by Ahithophel, one of his body-guard, took the same course over Kedron in his flight from the rebellious Absalom, 2 Sam. xv. 23, and thus furnished a type to which Jesus Himself pointed, chap. xiii. 18.—P. S.]

Beyond the brook [or rather **torrent**] **Kidron** [or **Kedron**. See TEXT. NOTE]. Kidron, the name of a brook or torrent, χείμαῤῥος, [from χεῖμα and ῥέω, *winter-flowing*, *winter-torrent*, formed by the winter-rains, but dry in the summer.—P. S.]; also a wady, Joseph. *Antiq.* viii. 1, 5. קִדְרוֹן [from קָדַר, *to be black, dirty*], *the Black*, *the Black Brook* [from its color.] We must distinguish between the valley of Kedron and the Kedron itself, as well as between the Kedron as a torrent, and as a spring brook. "The vale of Kedron is the most important valley in the northern portion of the plateau of the wilderness of Judah. It takes its rise on the north side of the city of Jerusalem, upon the great water-shed between the Mediterranean and the Dead Sea, at an elevation of about 2,500 feet above the ocean; it surrounds the north and east sides of the city, turning by the well of Rogel, at a sharp angle to the southeast, toward the Dead Sea. Forming, at first, but a shallow, trough-shaped depression, it burrows deeper and deeper, and, from the point where it turns to the southeast, becomes a wild, untrodden, narrow chasm, opening south of the Ras el Feshka, towards the Dead Sea. No traveller has ever yet traversed its whole extent. In the middle of its course, between Jerusalem and the Dead Sea, there is a much-visited point, the cloister of St. Saba.*—The brook Kedron, which flows through the valley, has no regular water-course; it is only a winter-torrent [formed by the water which flows into the valley from the hills north and east of Jerusalem]. Over and above this, the valley does not lack perennial springs; on the eastern declivity of southern Moriah there is the well of Mary, *etc.*, and at the junction of Hinnom with the valley of the Kedron we find the well of Rogel". (L. Völter). According to Robinson, the Kedron does not flow unceasingly even in winter; one may stay several years in Jerusalem without seeing any water in this deep bed.† As the dividing brook between Jerusalem or Moriah, Zion and the Mount of Olives, the brook, like the valley, possesses some significancy. Upwards from the well of Rogel near Jerusalem, the valley is called the valley of Jehoshaphat ("the Lord judgeth"). According to the Jews (with reference to Joel iii. 2), as also according to the Mohammedans, the last judgment will be held in this valley. Simultaneously with Christ's passage of the Kedron, a passage infinitely more momentous than that of Cæsar over the Rubicon, doubtless the last judgment was principially decided, together with the redemption. Passages in which the Kedron is mentioned: 2 Sam. xv. 23; 1 Kings xv. 13; 2 Kings xxiii. 4, 6, 12; Neh. ii. 15; 1 Mac. xii. 37; Joseph. *Antiq.* xviii. 1, 5; ix. 7, 3; *De Bello Jud.* v. 6, 1. Comp. the article Kedron in Winer and that in Zeller's *Wörterbuch für das christliche Volk*; books of travel, particularly Robinson II. p. 35 [Am. ed. vol. I. 268-273; (Valley of K.), and I. 232, 273 (Brook of K.). Also art. *Kidron*, in Smith's *Dict. of the B.*, II. 1533 ff., Hackett & Abbot's ed., where Robinson's accurate description is quoted.—P. S.] As a torrent alone, the Kedron's waves were dark and turbid; and in the time of the temple-worship the blood of the sacrifices likewise flowed into it and darkened it; hence, doubtless, the name. It was probably the Stephen Gate or Mary Gate of the present day, through which Jesus had descended

* [Dean Stanley says that the Valley of the Kedron, especially in its greatest depth where it joins the Valley of Hinnom, gives full effect to the great peculiarity of Jerusalem, as seen from its eastern side—its situation as of a city rising out of a deep abyss, *Sinai & Pal.*, p. 188.—P. S.]

† [Since the time of Robinson, however, more copious torrents have been witnessed, probably in consequence of the numerous enclosures of mulberry and olive groves recently made by the Greek convent. For there is no doubt that the destruction of the forests which once covered the mountains and hills has diminished the rains in Palestine. The Kedron must have been once a much larger stream, or it would not have worked out such a chasm. Dr. Barclay and Lieutenant Warren express the opinion that the Kedron flows below the present surface of the ground. Warren discovered about 500 yards below the En-Rogel a flight of steps leading down to an ancient aqueduct now choked with silt, which he believes to have been connected with that well and the ancient system of water supply.—P. S.]

into the valley for the purpose of crossing the Kedron (*Leben Jesu*, ii. p. 1427).

There was a garden. On Gethsemane [*i. e.*, *Olive-Press*, from *gath*, *press*, and *schamna*, *oil*] see Comm. on *Matthew* [pp. 478, 482, Am. ed.].* The different designations are worth noting. Matthew: Jesus cometh unto a country-place called Gethsemane similarly Mark; Luke: *to the mount of Olives;* John: *there was a garden.*

[This notice of John to every reader of the Synoptic Gospels would at once suggest the scene of Gethsemane. On the doubtful typological reference to the garden of Eden, where the first Adam was tempted by the serpent and fell, while in Gethsemane the second Adam bruised the serpent's head, see the fathers, Lampe, Hengstenberg, and Wordsworth."†—P. S.]

Himself and His disciples.—The more minute account in Matthew and Mark.

Ver. 2. **But Judas also, His betrayer, knew the place.**—Thus John passes over the conflict in Gethsemane. It is his intention to exhibit it in its glorious issue, the majestic repose of Christ.—**For Jesus often resorted thither with His disciples.**—According to Luke, it was a habit of Jesus to go thither. The Synoptists jointly say that He there collected His thoughts in prayer. According to John, the place also served as a meeting-ground for Jesus and His disciples; probably He was wont to be met there by His adherents generally. The remark "refers to previous festal visits." Meyer. Comp. Comm. on *Mark* [p. 5, Am. ed. Dr. Lange conjectures there that Mark, whose mother had a house in Jerusalem, owned a country seat at the foot of the Mount of Olives, perhaps even the garden of Gethsemane.—P. S.] Instrumental in throwing light upon the base character of Judas is the fact of his reckoning that Jesus, in His divine strength of character and fidelity to prayer, would assuredly be found, even on this occasion, in Gethsemane.

Ver. 3. **Having received the band of soldiers and officers,** *etc.* [Ὁ *οὖν Ἰούδας λαβὼν τὴν σπεῖραν*—see Text. Notes—*καὶ ἐκ τῶν ἀρχιερέων κ. Φαρισαίων ὑπηρέτας ἔρχεται ἐκεῖ, κ. τ. λ.*]—See Comm. on *Matthew.* "According to Josephus, xx. 3, 4, the city governors were accustomed, at the feast, to station a *τάξις στρατιωτῶν* (in the Castle Antonia) near the avenues to the temple, in case of an insurrection; and for this reason —for fear, namely, that the adherents of Jesus might free Him by force—a detachment is here permitted to accompany the Jews. The Levitic *ὑπηρέται* of the Sanhedrin accomplish the arrest itself; they were sent out for a similar purpose, chap. vii. 45. Under these circumstances, it is not at all probable that the detachment of soldiers also pressed into the garden." (According to ver. 12, the thing is very probable, since they at once co-operate in the arrest.) "The strength of the cohorts conformed to circumstances. Some of those under Titus contained 1000 men, others 613 foot-soldiers and 120 horsemen. Moreover, in the usage of Polybius, *σπεῖρα* is equivalent to *manipulus*, the third of a cohort." Tholuck.

[There were ten *cohorts* or *companies* in every Roman legion, but varying in number according to circumstances. According to Josephus (*De Bello Jud.*, III., 4, 2) five of eighteen *σπεῖραι* contained 1000 men each, and the others 600. Robinson (*sub σπεῖρα*), with Kuinoel, understands here and ver. 12 the *temple guard* of Levites who performed the menial offices of the temple and kept watch by night. So also Baumgarten-Crusius and Bäumlein. But the *σπεῖρα* is here and ver. 6 expressly distinguished from the *ὑπηρέται ἐκ τῶν ἀρχιερέων κ. Φαρισαίων*, furnished by the Sanhedrin. The objection that Roman soldiers would have led Jesus to their own officers, not to the chief priests, does not hold; for Jesus was to be condemned first by the ecclesiastical authorities. It is not necessary to suppose that the whole garrison of the fortress Antonia, whether it consisted of 1000 or only of 300 men, was present; a small detachment with the captain (*χιλίαρχος*, ver. 12) was sufficient. Comp. note on Matt. xxvii. 27, p. 513. The combined power of the Romans and the Jews was brought into requisition against the one unarmed gentle Jesus. The military preparation (*μετὰ φανῶν καὶ λαμπάδων καὶ ὅπλων*—mark the accumulative *καί*) indicates the bad conscience of Judas and the Sanhedrin.—P. S.]

Ver. 4. **Jesus, therefore, stepped forth.**—Not out of the garden (Lampe, Meyer),—Mark pretty plainly decides against such an interpretation—nor out of the depths of the garden merely (De Wette, Tholuck [Alford: from the shade of the trees into the moonlight] and others), but, agreeably to His purpose, out of the circle of disciples, in advance of it, in order to protect it (*Leben Jesu*, II., p. 1456, Schweizer). This is indicated also by the design of the ques-

* [To the descriptions there given or referred to, I add that of Dean Stanley, *Sinai & Pal.*, p. 450. "Close beside the Church of the Virgin is a spot which, as it is omitted in Abbé Michon's catalogue of Holy Places, might perhaps have been passed over; yet a few words, and perhaps the fewer the better, must be devoted to the garden of Gethsemane. That the tradition reaches back to the age of Constantine is certain. How far it agrees with the slight indications of its position in the Gospel narrative will be judged by the impressions of each individual traveller. Some will think it too public; others will see an argument in its favor from its close proximity to the brook Kedron; none probably will be disposed to receive the traditional sites which surround it, the grotto of the Agony, the rocky bank of the three Apostles, the "terra damnata" of the Betrayal. But in spite of all the doubts that can be raised against their antiquity or the genuineness of their site, the eight aged olive-trees, if only by their manifest difference from all others in the mountain, have always struck even the most indifferent observer. They are now indeed less striking in the modern garden enclosure built round them by the Franciscan monks, than when they stood free and unprotected on the rough hill side; but they will remain, so long as their already protracted life is spared, the most venerable of their race on the surface of the earth; their gnarled trunks and scanty foliage will always be regarded as the most affecting of the sacred memorials in or about Jerusalem; the most nearly approaching to the everlasting hills themselves in the force with which they carry us back to the events of the Gospel History." Comp. also Hackett's supplementary notes of art. Gethsemane in Smith's *Dict.* ii. 908.—P. S.]

† [Cyril: "*Ut in paradiso malorum initium est factum, sic in horto Christi passio incepit, per quam a malis liberati in pristinum restituti sumus.*" Wordsworth: "Here is a striking contrast between the quest in the Garden of Eden for the first Adam, and this search in the garden of Gethsemane for the Second. The first Adam *hides himself* amongst the trees of the garden (Gen. iii. 8). He trembles before Him who seeks for him. The Second Adam *comes forth* and says *I am.* And, at the sound of His Voice, they who came to take Him, go back and fall to the ground. The first Adam inculpates Eve; the Second Adam pleads for His disciples. The first Adam is overcome by the Tempter and loses Paradise; the Second Adam overcomes Satan, and restores his Spouse, the Church, to Paradise and raises her to Heaven."—P. S.]

tion: Whom do ye seek? ver. 8. [Stier: "When men sought Jesus to make Him a King, He fled: now that they seek Him to put Him to death, He goes forth to meet them."—P. S.]—**Whom do ye seek?**—According to Hug, He put this question to the end that the temple-officers also might learn His name and that it might consequently be rendered impossible for Him to be put out of the way anonymously; the design, however, manifestly presents itself in what follows. They are to be dismayed at the distinct consciousness of their intention to seize Jesus, and, their commission being thus narrowly defined, they shall be in duty bound to let the disciples go.

Ver. 5. **But Judas also,** *etc.*—The band of disciples was stationed within the garden in two divisions, like a watch. The three intimates of Jesus were in the back-ground, the eight others near the entrance. From the stand-point of these latter, to whom Matthew belonged, the most striking occurrence was the pressing of the troop, with Judas at their head, into the garden; from the stand-point of the three, Jesus' hastening to meet the throng. To these external circumstances of position, supervenes a diversity of mental view; the Synoptic tradition and Mark, the disciple of Peter, regarding primarily the impudent boldness of the traitor, whilst it was the design of John to throw into relief the majestic preparedness of Christ and His fidelity to the disciples. Jesus, then, anticipated Judas' plot of betraying Him with a kiss, inasmuch as He rendered that plot entirely superfluous; this fact, however, forms no reason for supposing that Judas did not carry out the agreement and that the Judas-kiss is a tradition. It did but become a meaningless farce through Jesus' declaration of Himself. Hence, it is this that John wishes to indicate, *viz.*, that the Judas-kiss was frustrated in its design by the magnanimous self-presentation of Jesus, and at the same time, that Judas, together with the enemies, was felled to the ground through Christ's word. As the two brushed past each other, the kiss became an abortive, scarce-accomplished signal, and the traitor was cast back upon the line of the foes.

[Ἐγώ εἰμι, **I am He**. Words of cheer and comfort to the trembling disciples on the stormy lake, Mark vi. 50, and after the resurrection, Luke xxiv. 39; words of terror here to His enemies, overpowering the armed military and priestly band. So His rebuke, with the majesty of His presence, silenced the profane traffickers in the temple. Comp. also the impression made upon the ὑπηρέται, vii. 46. What will be the effect of the same *I am*, when spoken by the Lord of glory on the day of judgment! Augustine: *Quid judicaturus faciet, qui judicandus hoc fecit?* Bengel (on ver. 8): *Bis dicit:* EGO SUM; *si tertio dixisset, non cepissent illum. Tertio dicet* OLIM.—P. S.]

Ver. 6. **And fell to the ground** [ἀπῆλθαν εἰς τὰ ὀπίσω—started back in dismay—καὶ ἔπεσαν* χαμαί=χαμᾶζε].—Explanation of this fact:

1. A miracle of Jesus; by which He meant to prove the freedom of His self-surrender (ancient exposition).*

2. The fact is to be referred to the disciples who had retired and cast themselves upon the ground with a view to concealing themselves (Paulus)!

3. Mythical (Strauss).†

4. Psychological: there is no question of a prostration of all. The foremost ones were confounded at finding Jesus so suddenly—not sleeping, but waking—, presenting Himself so composedly; even before this, they were paralyzed, as it were, with awe of Him; now, when they would fain seize Him, a horror of awe overpowers them and, recoiling, they fall, one upon another (Lücke, Tholuck and others).‡

5. Here, also, it is an unjustifiable antithesis that causes the clashing of the miracle and its natural instrumentality, or of the objective, conscious agency of Christ and the subjective element of awe and fear (as, for instance, Meyer). The effect of the self-presentation of Christ could not arrive unexpectedly to Him, nor, hence, be undesigned. That is the miracle. Neither, however, can Jesus' miracle be regarded as a magical operation upon the bodies of them that fell; its channel was terror of conscience, as was the case in the death of Ananias, Acts v. (see *Leben Jesu*, p. 1457 ff.).§ Tholuck cites kindred instances, when before Mark Antony, Marius, Coligny, the murderers recoiled, panic-struck (p. 408; see, too, Heubner on this passage).‖ On New Testament ground the following belong here: Luke iv. 30; John viii. 59; vii. 44-46; x. 39; Matt. xxviii. 4; Acts v. 5, 10 in reference to a bad conscience; analogous phenomena occurred even in the circle of Jesus' friends, according to Luke v. 8; Matt. xxviii. 9, 17, *etc.*—Analogous effects of the manifestation of Jehovah, of the Angel of the Lord, or Christ, see in the Old Testament in the history of Balaam, Manoah, Isaiah, Daniel, as also in the New Testament at the commencement of Revelation.

Ver. 7. **Then asked He them again.**—This second question, in conjunction with the self-surrender of Jesus, has an effect upon the troop as elevating as that of the first question and the self-presentation of Jesus was depressing. This, also, is in analogy with the convulsing

* [ἀπῆλθαν and ἔπεσαν is the reading of ℵ. B. C., Tischend., Tregelles, Alf., Westcott and Hort. On this Alexandrian form see Winer, p. 71, 7th ed. The text. rec. has ἀπῆλθον and ἔπεσον.—P. S.]

* [So also Ebrard, Maier, Hengstenberg, Godet, Meyer, Luthardt, Brückner, Webster and Wilkinson, Wordsworth; some adding as another object: to prove His divine character. Luthardt, however, assumes that the miracle was psychologically *mediated*, and approaches the view of Lange (no. 5); Godet also (II. 575) lays the chief stress on the *moral* force, the same which in the temple made the enemies recoil. It was not a physical, but a moral miracle.—P. S.]

† [Strauss regards the scene as miraculous in the intention of the author, but as unhistorical. So also Scholten.—P. S.]

‡ [So also Olshausen, De Wette, Ebrard, Bäumlein, Barnes, Owen (not decided). Barnes thinks that the supposition of a miraculous power detracts greatly from the moral sublimity of the scene.—P. S.]

§ [Similarly Alford: The miracle was not specially intended by our Lord (?), but a result of the superhuman dignity of His person and the majestic calmness of His reply.—P. S.]

‖ [On the case of Mark Antony see Valerius Max., VIII. 9, 2; on Marius, Vellejus Pat. II. 19, 3; on Coligny, Serranus, *Com. de statu rel. in Gallia*, t. III. p. 32—as quoted by Tholuck (p. 380 of Krauth's translation), and by Meyer (p. 592). But these are at best very remote analogies from a different sphere.—P. S.]

and reanimating effects, as experienced by the Apocalyptists, of a divine revelation, Dan. x. 10; Rev. i. 17. These men (Daniel and John) were prostrated by the holiness of the Lord, in the consciousness of their sinfulness, lifted up again by His grace, in the element of their faith. Our case is somewhat similar,—the temple-officers being, on the one hand, the instruments of a godless, devilish plot, but also, on the other hand, the ministers of an existing order of things and the instruments of Divine Providence.

Ver. 8. **If, therefore, ye seek Me.**—The saying of Jesus is directly declarative of the security of the disciples, partly by way of logical deduction, partly as a command; it is, at the same time, indirectly the disciples' discharge from the present outward alliance of suffering. But the great utterance has also a deeper background. See Is. lxiii. 3. Bengel and others assume, without foundation, that some had already laid hands on the disciples. That there did exist an inclination for such a step, however, is evinced by the episode of the fleeing youth in Mark and by the maid who denounced Peter, in the history of the latter's denial.

Ver. 9. **That the saying might be fulfilled.**—Christ's declaration, chap. xvii. 12. The keeping of the disciples from being lost consisted finally in their preservation from captivity in the present situation, since the over-mighty temptation might have been the ruin of the souls of some among them. (This connection not recognized by Schweizer). [Alford: "An unquestionable proof, if any were wanted, that the words of ch. xvii. are no mere description of the mind of our Lord Jesus at the time, but His very words themselves. This is recognized even by De Wette. On the application of the saying, we may remark that the words unquestionably had a deeper meaning than any belonging to this occasion; but the remarks so often made in this commentary on the fulfillment of prophecies must be borne in mind;—that to '*fulfil*' a prophecy is not to *exhaust* its capability of being again and again fulfilled:—that the words of the Lord have many stages of unfolding;—and that the temporal deliverance of the Apostles now, doubtless was but a part in the great spiritual safe-keeping which the Lord asserted by anticipation in these words." See also a good note of Webster and Wilkinson *in loc.*—P. S.]

Ver. 10. **Simon, then—Peter.** [Σίμων οὖν Πέτρος. Lange: Simon now—Peter].—We bring out in the translation the trait that John inserts his οὖν of manifold import between the names Simon and Peter, thus emphasizing the Simon. To Simon it was natural to act in the way related. Comp. Comm. on *Matthew*, on this place; John xxi. 15. An explanation of the circumstance that John alone mentions the name of the disciple who was the author of the sword-blow, see in the Comm. on *Matthew* on this passage [p. 486, Am. ed.]. Similarly, John alone mentions the name of Malchus. [One of the circumstantial details so frequent in John's account of the history of the passion, which confirm his authorship. John knew the high-priest, ver. 15, and so probably also his servant Malchus (=King). The Synoptists who wrote earlier may have had prudential reasons for not mentioning the name.—P. S.] Peter wished, by this blow, to prove his readiness to risk his life for his Lord and to fulfil his vow, recorded chap. xiii. 37; in all probability it was also his design to give a signal to the friends of Jesus and the Lord Himself to rise in arms against the foe. Upon the particular circumstances comp. the Synoptists. [Peter's zeal was honest and well-meaning, but impulsive, hasty, imprudent, and mistaken in the selection of means. Hence the rebuke of our Lord, who here condemns for all time to come the use of carnal weapons and physical force in the defence of truth and promotion of His kingdom. The Romish church has imitated Peter in his weakness rather than his strength, and often invoked the arm of the secular power in the bloody persecution of heretics; thus making herself responsible for it in spite of her professed principle: *ecclesia non sitit sanguinem*. Comp. my *Hist. of the Apost. Church*, p. 677.—P. S.]

Ver. 11. **Jesus unto Peter.**—It is again significant that John here makes use only of the name Peter (without Simon). Christ's deliverance against the action of Peter, as given by John, does not exclude the words related by Matthew from conforming the more closely to the original expressions. The words of Jesus, as recorded by John, are expressive of the voluntary surrender of Jesus to the will of the Father, and they most decidedly look away from the doing of men. Mark passes over the direct disapproval awarded to Peter, his guide; Luke relates how Christ remedied the offense; Matthew brings out the theocratical points of Jesus' saying.—**The cup which My Father,** *etc.* Comp. Matt. xx. 22; xxvi. 39 [Comm., p. 479, Am. Ed.]. In His prayer He has sacredly bound Himself to drink the cup. ["*The cup* is a striking allusion to the prayer in Gethsemane; for the image does not elsewhere occur in our Evangelist." Alford. So also Paley, (*Evidences*, B. II., c. 4), Bengel, Webster and Wilkinson (comp. their note *in loc.*), Wordsworth, and others.—P. S.]

DOCTRINAL AND ETHICAL.

1. The *arrest of Jesus* in Gethsemane. John omits the directions of Jesus to His disciples as to their conduct in Gethsemane; the Passion of His soul; the reproof to His sleeping disciples; the kiss of Judas; the reference of Peter to the twelve legions of angels; the protest of Jesus against His seizers; the healing of Malchus recorded by Luke; the episode of the fugitive youth related by Mark. On the other hand, he gives prominence to the fact that Jesus went voluntarily to meet His apprehenders; that the multitude fell to the ground at the sight of His majesty; that He surrendered Himself prisoner, while securing a free exode to the disciples. He names Peter as the one who drew the sword, mentions the name of the servant, Malchus, who was wounded by him, and, with the words, "who drew the sword," refers the saying of Jesus, "shall I not drink the cup?" *etc.*, to His psychical passion. On Gethsemane, see Comm. on *Matthew*, p. 478, Am. Ed.

2. *Gethsemane*, as John paints it, presupposes the Gethsemane according to the Synoptists, and from the latter it is possible to deduce the former.

I. e., in the kingdom of God, a mighty assurance of victory admits the inference of a mighty conflict, and a mighty conflict that of a mighty assurance of victory.

3. The *passage of Jesus* over the brook *Kedron*, a step of the highest, world-historic import. An expression of His constrainedness in spirit, His freedom of will, His decision of heart.

4. *Paradise* and the *Garden*. The first and the second Adam. The serpent and the traitor. The defeat and the victory (attaching, in a greater degree, to the Synoptical version). The ancient typology, constituting the Garden of Gethsemane an antithesis of Paradise, is fully warranted here, so long as it does not, by enlarging upon minutiæ, degenerate into trifling.

5. The *sudden attack* upon the Lord in the sanctuary of prayer, a speaking sign: 1. That the hatred of the world was levelled at the praying heart of Christ and His flock,—that they fell upon Him on account of His piety; 2. that in this respect, also, He was to form the central point of the experience of the faithful: of the experience of Daniel (chap. vi. 7), of the first Christians, the Huguenots [Puritans, Covenanters], *etc.*

6. *Judas knew the place also.* How the spiritual experiences of false men and hypocrites redound to their ruin. He knew the *place*. But in what a base and imperfect way he knew the *Lord*, is proved by his equipment and march with the whole multitude.

7. In all religious persecutions, cohorts, legions and armies are transformed into gens-d'armes, police soldiers, myrmidons and executioners' assistants.

8. The drawing up of the world against Christ, and the sword-stroke of Peter for Him: Symbols of the impotence of His fleshly opposers, as of His fleshly defenders.

9. The *majesty* whereby the self-presentation of Christ casts His foes to the ground. A divine operation (see the Introduction), yet with a human instrumentality. See Note to ver. 6. At the same time an expression of His freedom in His surrender, which freedom, according to the Synoptists, He also declared by a decided protest.

10. Christ's submitting to be taken captive by His enemies, in order to the protection and deliverance of His people, a symbolic individual type, in which His faithfulness as a Redeemer is reflected.

HOMILETICAL AND PRACTICAL.

1. See Commentary on *Matthew, Mark, Luke.*—Gethsemane in profoundest gloom and brightest light (comparison of the Johannean version with the Synoptical).—Gethsemane as a place of victory: 1. Revelation of past victory, *a.* over inward temptation, *b.* over Judas (chap. xiii.). 2. Consummation of present victory, *a.* over the slanderous array and over treason (in that He voluntarily presents Himself to His enemies); *b.* over the haughtiness of the foe (by levelling them to the earth and ensuring the safety of the disciples); *c.* over the carnal zeal of the disciple. 3. A foretoken and life picture of all the future victories of Christ (free advance of the strong, secure shelterment of the weak, glorious correction of the passionate, dissipation of falsehood and treachery, disarming of violence, overcoming of the world through voluntary suffering).—The brook and the garden: 1. How insignificant! 2. How memorable!—Judas and Peter in the Gethsemane of the Lord.—*But Judas also knew the place.* How even this knowledge and recollection of his disciple-life becomes his ruin. The fearful judgment in the misuse of spiritual experiences.—The equipment of Judas, or how well and yet how poorly he knew his betrayed Lord: 1. His place of prayer and fidelity to prayer, but not the blessing of His prayer; 2. His power, but not His superiority and omnipotence; 3. His innocence, yet not His holiness; 4. His clemency, yet not His love and earnestness; 5. His human dignity, but not His divine majesty.—The betrayer of Christ a traitor out and out: 1. To the sanctuary, 2. to his fellow-disciples, 3. to his nation, 4. to humanity, 5. to himself.—Treason toward the sanctuary: 1. How all the secrets of the church of Christ are, by means of apostate members, betrayed to the world; 2. how all the plots of treason are brought to nought and transformed to a judgment upon the traitors.—The array of myrmidons against Jesus: 1. Called out by mendacious and vain fear; 2. terrible in its weapons and lamps, over against the Defenceless One; 3. made a laughing-stock through the light of truth with which Christ goes to meet it; 4. shown up in its impotence; 5. limited in its operation; 6. given free course in its plot, but only in order to the carrying out of the counsel of God.—How Christ baffles the plots of His foes by freely meeting and anticipating them [the plots 1. of craft (slander, falsehood), 2. of violence].—The majesty which Christ manifests in treading the way of His deepest humiliation.—The sublime freedom of spirit with which He resigns His outward freedom.—Why so calm, so grand in His surrender? Because He is conscious that He is not abandoning Himself to the impotence of His enemies, but confiding Himself to the omnipotence of His God.—The dignity of the pious in suffering, the foretoken of his triumph.—The terrors of Christ: 1. Origin: *a.* Terrors of divine holiness, *b.* terrors of human dignity. 2. Effect: In the conscience, in the psychical life, in the marrow and bone. 3. Signs: Tokens of inner judgment, foretokens of future judgment.—Whom seek ye?—If ye, then, seek Me, let these go.—Fulfilment of Scripture: 1. In the most universal sense, 2. in the most special sense.—The upshot of things in Gethsemane: Betrayed, surprised, made captive: 1. Christ seems betrayed, but the kingdom of darkness has betrayed itself; 2. He seems surprised, but henceforth He stands sovereign in the midst of the camp of the foe; 3. He seems a captive, but the adversary *is* the captive.—The sword of Simon and the cup of Christ.—Simon took the sword, Peter received the reprimand.—Christ's defence the defence of His people.

STARKE: ZEISIUS: That which the first Adam marred in the garden by the fall, the second Adam, Jesus Christ, regained and set in order in the garden by His guiltless passion.—The iniquity of the traitor was made all the more discernible by his betraying Christ to death in the very place where he had seen His deeds and heard the words of life.—The wicked man oft-times misuses his knowledge of the ingoings and outgoings of the righteous; let a man take care in whom he confides, Ps. lvii. 6.—The Lord Jesus has hallowed even the kind of suffering that His children endure when they must allow unfaithful souls a knowledge of their circumstances, Ps. xli. 6, 9.—No one hates Christ and His party more bitterly than a hypocrite who has thrown off the mask.—ZEISIUS: When Jesus, in His suffering, hath so oft evinced His stout-heartedness and advanced to meet His foes, why, O Christian mine, art thou in fear of the world and the devil, even whilst this conquering Lion of the Tribe of Judah is by thy side and fighteth for thee?—The first Adam, falling into the hands of divine justice, fled and hid himself, and God must needs call, saying: Adam, where art thou? but here the second Adam, being about to be delivered into the hands of His enemies, crieth out: Here am I.—What is more common now than Joab's greeting and Judas' kiss, Jacob's voice and Esau's hands?—Ver. 8: 1. Because He wished them preserved for a greater work; 2. to the end that men might not imagine that *His* death would not suffice for the redemption of mankind; 3. because they were not yet strong enough to withstand the like temptation; 4. He desired to prove that He had power and authority over His enemies.—Our fate does not depend upon the might or numbers of the enemy, but upon the permission which they receive from God, to injure us, 2 Chron. xxxii. 7.—Lord Jesus, when the world, death and the devil would fain swallow us up, speak Thou the word of command: Let these go, Ps. cv. 15.—OSIANDER: God setteth a bound to persecutions. —ZEISIUS: When Peter should have watched, he slept, and when he should have been quiet, he made resistance through carnal zeal; thus we always have by nature a sufficient leaning towards evil.—God overrules even the errors of His children, so that no greater harm shall result from them than He has resolved to permit, Gen. xx. 2, 6.

GOSSNER: In the garden of Eden man fell through lust and pride, in the garden of Gethsemane he was to be raised up again through mourning, anguish and humiliation.—What time their glory flashes in upon children of God and glimpses so heart-ravishing are theirs, they should not misuse this their blessedness, nor vaunt themselves of it.—When the Saviour saith: *Let my people go*, their sorest enemies must suffer this word to stand, and His people to go.—Thus, in the midst of the press, Christ looketh on the Father and taketh the suffering that men inflict upon Him, as coming, not from them, but out of the hand of the Father, without whose counsel and consent not a hair of our heads can be harmed.

HEUBNER: Over the brook Kedron, as David once fled before Absalom.—Ver. 4. This question attests (therefore) His innocence and undismayedness.—The morally good man will never deny his own identity, even though he be in mortal peril; conscious of his dignity he will freely say who he is, trusting in God. There is something debasing and dishonoring in a denial of one's identity.—These words, *Let these go*, are important to us also. "Jesus procures His disciples entire freedom and security; the power of this authoritative word shows itself even at the present day. The enemy had not left a disciple on earth if this word was not still in force. This word is the cause of the continued existence of disciples,—faithful ones, whom the world, against its will, must behold passing to and fro, and yet must *let go*." Burk, *Fingerzeig* II., p. 393.—*Shall I not, etc.* Violently to hold the righteous back from his suffering for duty's sake, is to hold him back from his glory and salvation.—Ver. 12. Bound as to the hands was Jesus; unbound in spirit.

[CRAVEN: From AUGUSTINE: Chap. xviii. vers. 1, 2. There the wolf in sheep's clothing, permitted by the deep counsel of the Master of the flock to go among the sheep, learned in what way to disperse the flock, and ensnare the Shepherd.—Ver. 6. Where now is the band of soldiers, where the terror and defence of arms? Without a blow, *one word* struck, drove back, prostrated a crowd fierce with hatred, terrible with arms. What shall He do when He cometh to judge, who did thus when He was going to be judged?—Ver. 8. So now having shown His power to them when they wished to take Him and could not, He lets them seize Him, that they might be unconscious agents of His will.—He commands His enemies, and they do what He commands; they permit them to go away, whom He would not have perish.—Ver. 11. Peter was to be admonished to have patience: and this was written for our learning.——From CHRYSOSTOM: Ver. 1. Why does not John say, When He had *prayed*, He entered? Because His prayer was a *speaking* for His disciples' sake.—He goes to the place which was known to the traitor; thus giving no trouble to those who were lying in wait for Him, and showing His disciples that He went voluntarily to die.—That it might not be thought that He went into a garden to hide Himself, it is added, *But Judas who betrayed Him knew the place: for Jesus often resorted thither with His disciples.*—Vers. 3-9. They had often sent elsewhere to take Him, but had not been able; whence it is evident that He gave Himself up voluntarily; as it follows, *Jesus, therefore, knowing all things—, went forth, etc.*—Ver. 8. Even to the last hour does He show His love for His own. ——From ALCUIN: Ver. 1. *Where there was a garden*, that the sin which was committed in a garden, He might blot out in a garden.——From HERBERT: Ver. 5.

> Judas, dost thou betray Me with a kiss?
> Canst thou find hell about My lips and miss
> Of life, just at the gates of life and bliss?

[From BURKITT: Ver. 3. How active was Judas, and how watchful was His bloody crew, even at that time when Christ's disciples could not keep their eyes open.—Ver. 4. Lord, how endearing are our obligations to Thyself, that when Thou knewest beforehand the bitterness of that cup which the justice of God was about to put into Thy hand, Thou didst not decline to drink it for our sakes.—Ver. 7. Obstinate and obdurate sinners will not be reclaimed by the most evident and convincing, by the most miraculous and surprising, appearances of God against them.—Ver. 8. Christ is so tender of His followers, that He will not put them upon trials, or call them forth to sufferings, till they are ripe and prepared for them.—Ver. 10. How doth a pious breast swell with indignation at the sight of an open insult offered unto the Saviour!—Ver. 11. The rebuke which Christ gave St. Peter for what he did; though his heart was sincere, yet his hand was rash; good intentions are no warrant for irregular actions.—*The cup which My Father hath given Me, shall I not drink it?* Learn 1. That oft-times the wisdom of God is pleased to put a very bitter cup of affliction into the hand of those to drink, whom He doth most sincerely love; 2. That when God doth so, it is their duty to drink it with submission.

[From M. Henry: Ver. 1. Our Lord Jesus took His work before Him: the office of the priest was to teach, and pray, and offer sacrifice; Christ, after teaching and praying, applies Himself to make atonement.—Having by His sermon [and prayer] prepared *His disciples* for this hour of trial, and by His prayer prepared *Himself* for it, He then courageously went out to meet it: when He had put on His armor, He entered the lists, and not till then.—Ver. 2. *Jesus oft-times resorted thither:* He would do as He was wont to do, and not alter His method, either to meet the cross or to miss it, when His hour was come.—Ver. 1. *Where there was a garden:* He would *set us an example* in the beginning of His passion, of retirement from the world.—*He went over the brook Cedron;* the notice taken of it intimates that there was something in it significant; and it points at 1. David's prophecy concerning the Messiah (Ps. cx. 7), that *He shall drink of the brook in the way;* 2. David's pattern, as a type of the Messiah; in his flight from Absalom, particular notice is taken of his *passing over the brook Cedron.*—He had *His disciples with Him,* 1. Because He used to take them with Him when He retired for prayer; 2. They must be witnesses of His sufferings, and His patience under them; 3. To show them their weakness: Christ sometimes brings His people into difficulties, that He may magnify Himself in their deliverance.—Ver. 2. Mention is made of *Judas' knowing the place,* 1. To aggravate his sin, that he would betray his Master notwithstanding his intimate acquaintance with Him: thus has Christ's holy religion been *wounded in the house of its friends,* as it could not have been anywhere else; many an apostate could not have been so profane as he is, if he had not been a professor; he could not have ridiculed Scriptures and ordinances, if he had not known them; 2. To magnify the love of Christ, that, though He knew where the traitor would seek Him, thither He went to be found of him; what He did, was not by constraint, but by consent. When others were going to bed, He was going to prayer, going to suffer.—Vers. 4-6. He received His enemies with all the mildness imaginable toward them, and all the calmness imaginable in Himself.—Ver. 5. *I am He;* He has hereby taught us to own Him, whatever it cost us; not to be *ashamed of Him or His words;* but even in difficult times, *to confess Christ crucified.*—Ver. 6. *They went backward;* they did not fall forward, as humbling themselves before Him, but backward, as standing it out to the utmost.—When He struck them down, He could have struck them dead, but He would not; because 1. *The hour* of His suffering *was come;* 2. He would give an instance of His patience and forbearance with the worst of men, and His compassionate love to His very enemies—in striking them down, and no more, He gave them both a call and space to repent.—Vers. 7-9. Having given His enemies a *repulse,* He gives His friends a *protection.*—Ver. 7. There are hearts so very hard in sin, that nothing will work upon them to reduce and reclaim.—Ver. 8. When Christ exposed Himself, He excused His disciples, because they were not, as yet, fit to suffer.—Herein Christ gives us 1. A great encouragement to follow Him; for though He has allotted us sufferings, yet He considers our frame; 2. A good example of love to our brethren and concern for their welfare.—Ver. 8. *Let these go their way;* He intended to give a specimen of His undertaking as Mediator; when He offered Himself to suffer and die, it was that we might escape.—Ver. 9. The safety and preservation of the saints are owing, not only to the divine grace in proportioning the strength to the trial, but to the divine providence in proportioning the trial to the strength.—Ver. 10. Peter's 1. Rashness; 2. Good-will; 3. Ill-conduct; He 1. had no warrant from His Master for what he did; 2. transgressed the duty of his place, and *resisted the powers that were;* 3. opposed His Master's suffering, notwithstanding the rebuke he had for it once; 4. broke the capitulation His master had lately made with the enemy; 5. foolishly exposed himself and his fellow-disciples to the fury of this enraged multitude; 6. he played the coward so soon after this (denying his Master), that we have reason to think that he would not have done this, but that he saw his Master cause them to fall on *the ground.*—God's over-ruling providence in the direction of the stroke, that it should do no more execution than *cut off his ear.*—Ver. 11. We must *pledge Christ* in the *cup* that He *drank of;* It is 1. but a *cup;* a small matter comparatively, be it what it will; 2. a cup that is *given us;* 3. given us by *a Father.*——From Scott: Vers. 1-9. Even the malice of our Lord's enemies did not render them more ready to crucify Him, than His love to sinners made Him ready to meet those sufferings.—Ver. 6. "The day of His wrath" will come, when all who oppose, yea, when all who do not obey, His Gospel, shall be driven backward and perish for ever. In the meantime He spares and warns His adversaries; yet neither His terror, nor His forbearance, will deter [sinful] men in general from their purpose.——From A Plain Commentary, (Oxford): Ver. 6. He lifts up for an instant the mantle which screened His Divinity, and lo, they are unable even to stand in His presence!—Ver. 8. This was because He must needs tread the winepress alone, and of the people there must be none with Him (Is. lxiii. 3); lest it should even enter into the dreams of any that the price of Man's Salvation was paid by some other Sacrifice besides that of Christ only.—Ver. 9. This is [at the first glance] a somewhat surprising statement: for our Saviour, when He uttered the words referred to, was speaking of *eternal,* not temporal death; [but] what might have been the conduct, what *would* have been the fate, of the others, if they had *now* been separated from their Lord, and dragged away to a terrible death.

[From Krummacher: Ver. 3. The superfluous torches and lanterns, in the light of the full moon, manifest their conscience-smitten fears.—*Officers from the chief priests and Pharisees;* It becomes, indeed, people of this class unconditionally [?] to obey the command of those who are set over them. Yet they are not mere machines, incapable of guilt in so doing, but answerable, as well as all other men, to God the final Judge, for their moral conduct; their obedience ought to be limited by the well-known maxim—"We must obey God rather than man;" and their duty it therefore was, in the present case, to prefer dying by the hand of the executioner, to the doubtful praise of having done their duty in the perpetration of the most heinous of crimes.—Vers. 5, 6. "*I am He!*" Great and significant expression! It was never uttered by the Saviour without being accompanied with the most powerful effects. "It is I!" exclaimed He to His astonished disciples, when walking on the waves of the sea; and as, at the sound, the raging storm immediately subsided, so a flood of peace and joy poured itself into the hearts of His followers. "I that speak unto thee am He!" said He to the Samaritan woman at Jacob's well; and immediately she left her water-pot and hastened back to Sychar, as the first evangelist to the borders of Samaria. "I am He!" was His testimony at the bar of the Sanhedrin; and the conviction that He was really the Messiah smote the minds of His judges so powerfully that it was only by means of the stage-trick of rending his clothes, that the high priest was able to save himself from the most painful embarrassment: and here, on hearing these words, the whole band of officials start, give way, stagger backward, and fall to the ground as if struck by an invisible flash of lightning, or blown upon by the breath of Omnipotence.—Their prostration in the dust before Him, points out to unbelievers the situation in which they will one day be found.—Ver. 8. *If ye seek me, let these go their way;* how well the Lord was able to preserve the most perfect self-possession in every situation, however terrible; and, with His anxiety to complete the work of redemption, to mingle the minute and inconsiderable with the stupendous and sublime, while girding Himself for His mysterious passage to the cross, He does not forget, in His adorable faithfulness, to rescue His disciples from the approaching storm.—Ver. 10. "Well done, Simon!" we are ready to exclaim, "only go on as thou hast begun." But that which appears to us as such an amiable trait in Peter, is only a confused mixture of self-love, arrogance, and folly; while the fire of our natural enthusiasm for Simon's act proceeds likewise from only short-sightedness and blindness.—Ver. 11. *The cup which My Father hath given Me, shall I not drink it?* In the cup was the entire curse of the inviolable law; all the horrors of conscious guilt, all the terrors of Satan's fiercest temptations, and all the sufferings which can befall both soul and body. It contained likewise the dreadful ingredients of abandonment by God, infernal agony, and a bloody death, to which the curse was attached. Christ has emptied it, and not a drop remains for His people. The satisfaction He rendered was complete, the reconciliation effected. "There is now no condemnation to them that are in Christ Jesus."

[From Barnes: Ver. 8. The wisdom, caution, and prudence of Jesus forsook Him in no peril, however sudden, and in no circumstances, however difficult or trying.——From Jacobus: Vers. 8, 9. Nothing can occur contrary to His eternal plan; not even the mad fury of His foes can overreach His wisdom, or overmatch His provision.——From Owen: Ver. 7. If it be asked how they could proceed to arrest and maltreat a person, before whom they had fallen prostrate as before a superior being, the answer is to be found in the transient influence which fear exerts upon the mind, and the probable fact, that this sudden repulse was represented by the leaders as effected by demoniacal agency at the instance of Jesus.

[Ver. 11. (Matt. xxvi. 52-54). The cause of Christ is not to be defended by carnal weapons.]

II.

CHRIST OVER AGAINST ANNAS AND CAIAPHAS. THE CLARITY AND SERENITY OF THE LORD OVER AGAINST THE INQUISITION OF THE HIGH-PRIEST AND MALTREATMENT ON THE PART OF THE SERVANT. THE TWO DISCIPLES IN THE HIGH-PRIESTLY PALACE, AND THE TOTTERING AND FALLING PETER.

Chapter XVIII. 12–27.

(Comp. Matt. xxvi. 57-75; Mark xiv. 53-72; Luke xxii. 54-65.)

12 Then the band and the captain [,] and [the] officers[1] of the Jews took Jesus, and
13 bound him. And led him away [led him][2] to Annas first; for he was father-in-law
to [of, τοῦ] Caiaphas, which was the high-priest that same year [who was high-
14 priest that year]. Now Caiaphas was he, which [But it was Caiaphas who] gave
counsel to the Jews, that it was expedient that one man should die[3] for the people.
15 And Simon Peter followed Jesus, and *so did* another disciple [And Simon Peter
and (the)[4] other disciple followed Jesus]: that disciple was known unto the high-
priest, and went in with Jesus into the palace [court-yard, αὐλήν] of the high-priest.

16 But Peter stood at the door without [was standing outside at the door]. Then went
out that [the] other disciple, which [who] was known unto the high-priest, and
17 spake unto her that kept the door, and brought in Peter. Then saith the damsel
[maid-servant] that kept the door unto Peter, Art not [*omit* not][5] thou also *one* of
18 this man's disciples? He saith, I am not. And the servants and [the] officers
stood [were standing] there, who had made [having made, πεποιηκότες] a fire of
coals, for it was cold; and they warmed [were warming] themselves: and Peter
stood [was standing] with them, and warmed [warming] himself.

19 The high-priest then asked Jesus of [about, or, concerning, περί] his disciples, and
20 of [about] his doctrine. Jesus answered him, I spake [have spoken, λελάληκα][6]
openly to the world; I ever [always] taught in the [a][7] synagogue, and in the tem-
ple, whither the Jews always resort [where all the Jews come together, assemble];[8]
21 and in secret have I said [I spoke, ἐλάλησα] nothing. Why askest thou me? ask
them which heard me [Ask those who have heard, τοὺς ἀκηκοότας], what I have
said [I spoke, ἐλάλησα] unto them: behold, they [these, οὗτοι] know what I said
22 [εἶπον]. And when he had thus spoken [said this], one of the officers which stood
by [who was standing by, παρεστηκώς] struck Jesus with the palm of his hand [or,
struck Jesus on the face, ἔδωκεν ῥάπισμα τῷ 'Ιησ.],[9] saying, Answerest thou the high-
23 priest so? Jesus answered him, If I have spoken [spoke, ἐλάλησα] evil, bear witness
of the evil: but if well, why smitest thou me?

24 Now Annas had sent him [Annas therefore sent him, ἀπέστειλεν οὖν][10] bound unto
25 Caiaphas the high-priest. And Simon Peter stood and warmed [was standing and
warming] himself. They said therefore unto him, Art not [*omit* not] thou also *one*
26 of his disciples? He denied *it* [*omit it*],[11] and said, I am not. One of the servants
of the high-priest, being *his* kinsman [being a kinsman of him] whose ear Peter cut
27 off, saith, Did not I see thee in the garden with him? Peter then denied again;
and immediately the [a] cock crew.

TEXTUAL AND GRAMMATICAL.

[1] Ver. 12.—[ἡ σπεῖρα καὶ ὁ χιλίαρχος are the detachment of the Roman garrison, οἱ ὑπηρέται, the levitical temple-guard. See notes on ver. 3. The omission of a comma and of the article before "officers" in the A. V., makes the impression that ὁ χιλίαρχος is alike dependent on τῶν 'Ιουδαίων as is οἱ ὑπηρέται.—P. S.]

[2] Ver. 13.—[ἀπήγαγον (A. C. ℵ^c. Vulg.) is not so well supported as ἤγαγον (ℵ.* B. D., Tischend.).—P. S.]

[3] Ver. 14.—Tischendorf [in former edd.] ἀπολέσθαι [*perish*] in accordance with A. C.** and others; Lachmann ἀποθανεῖν in accordance with B. C.* and others (Sin.). Meyer: ἀποθ. comes from chap. xi. 50. [In ed. VIII. Tischendorf reads ἀποθανεῖν, with ℵ. B. C.* D., and adds: "ἀποθανεῖν *potest ad* xi. 50 *accommodatum credi. At quum testimoniorum antiquissimorum pondere præstet. nec incredibile est ex illo* ἀπόληται xi. 50 *hoc loco* ἀπολέσθαι *ortum esse. Est iste locus ex eis ubi præstat probatissimos testes sequi quam conjecturæ fidere.*" Tregelles, Alford, Westcott and Hort, likewise agree on ἀποθανεῖν.—P. S.]

[4] Ver. 15.—The Recepta, Griesbach, Scholz, Tischendorf [formerly]: ὁ ἄλλος. The article is omitted by A. D., *etc.*, but attested by a majority of authorities. [Tischendorf, ed. VIII., Westcott and Hort omit, Alford brackets the article. Lange retains it. The insertion is more readily accounted for than the omission, and may have been conformed to xx. 2, 3, 4, 8, where the article occurs. There is no doubt, however, that no other than John is meant. In using this self-designation for the first time, he may have omitted the article.—P. S.]

[5] Ver. 17.—[Μή and μήτε, in interrogative sentences, imply (like the German *doch nicht?*) a negative answer, the English *not*, like the Greek οὐ and the Latin *nonne*, an affirmative answer. The παιδίσκη was apprehensive of an affirmative answer and wished politely to anticipate Peter's denial; or the negative form of the question reveals the feeling that she ought not to have admitted John as a disciple of Jesus except for his being an acquaintance of the high-priest.—P. S.]

[6] Ver. 20.—λελάληκα (Lachmann, Tischendorf) is most strongly attested, against ἐλάλησα.

[7] Ver. 20.—[The best authorities omit the article τῇ (text. rec.) before συναγωγῇ, very properly: for there are many synagogues, and but one temple.—P. S.]

[8] Ver. 20.—The reading πάντες (Griesbach, Lachmann) is established by A. B. C.* Sin., *etc.*, in opposition to a second πάντοτε (Tischendorf in accordance with E. G. H., *etc.*) and to παντοθεν. In ed. VIII., Tischend. reads likewise πάντες οἱ 'Ιουδ. without πάντοτε.—P. S.]

[9] Ver. 22.—[Uncertain whether with the hand (*Backenstreich*, Luther, Lange, Meyer) or with a rod (*Ruthenschlag*, Beza, Bengel, Godet). The former is more probable, as it was intended to be a punishment for saucy speech. Comp. Matt. xxvi. 67; Acts xxiii. 2. ῥάπισμα, from ῥάβδος, ῥαπίς, originally meant a blow from a rod or stick.—P. S.]

[10] Ver. 24.—The omission of οὖν (attested Codd. B. C.* L. X. Δ, Lachmann) appears to be exegetical. The Johannean οὖν, however, is quite characteristic here. Other exegetical apprehensions of the passage substituted δέ and καί. [Tischend., Alf., *etc.*, retain οὖν. The pluperf. rendering of ἀπέστειλεν is ungrammatical and in the interest of harmonistics. See p. 552.—P. S.]

[11] Ver. 25.—The οὖν [after ἠρνήσατο] is here not sufficiently attested (E. G. M., *etc.*); neither is it suitable.

EXEGETICAL AND CRITICAL.

Ver. 12. Then the band and the captain, *etc.* Manifestly, the Jewish guard and the Roman soldiers take Jesus prisoner in concert; the soldiers under their chiliarch even have the precedence on the occasion. Hence an incorrect distinction is made in saying; "not until this moment, when the prisoner must be led through the city, does the military troop rejoin the Jewish watch" (Tholuck). [Luthardt (II., 383): "He before whose aspect and ἐγώ εἰμι, the whole band had been terrified and cast to the ground, now suffers Himself to be taken, bound, and led away. . . . To apprehend and bind *One*, all gave their help, the cohort, the chiliarch, and the Jewish officers. . . . Only by the help of all did they feel themselves secure. And thus it was ordered, that the disciples might escape with the more safety. Jesus suffered Himself to be bound, to show thereby the complete surrender of His will, and also in this form of suffering to be our example (Gen. xxii. 9; Ps. cv. 18)."—P. S.]

Ver. 13. **Led him to Annas first.**—See Comm. on *Matthew*. On Annas see Comm. on *Luke*, III. 2 [p. 55, Am. Ed.], and the article Annas in Winer (at Josephus Ananos). [Annas (Ἄνανος) was appointed high-priest in his 37th year, A. D. 7, by Quirinus, the governor of Syria, but was obliged to give way to Ismael, A. D. 14. After two more changes, Joseph Caiaphas, the son-in-law of Annas (John xviii. 13; Joseph. *Antiqu.* xviii. 2, 1), was appointed to the office, and continued till A. D. 37. Annas seems to have retained the title and part of the power of that office. In Luke iii. 2, he is mentioned before Caiaphas, and in Acts iv. 6, he is called high-priest. Some hold that he was high-priest *de jure*, Caiaphas *de facto*. Wieseler maintains that both were at the head of the Jewish hierarchy, Caiaphas as actual high-priest, Annas as president of the Sanhedrin.—P. S.] The preliminary leading of Jesus to Annas recorded by John alone. Different suppositions: The house of Annas was situated near the gate, or they led Jesus, as in triumph, to Annas; Annas was the examiner (Ewald); he was president of the Sanhedrin (Lichtenstein and others). All destitute of evidence, confronted with the supposition suggested by John himself, *viz.*, that the Jews still regarded Annas as the true high-priest in a legitimistic sense, even after Caiaphas had been forced upon them as his successor (*Leben Jesu* II., p. 1468). The expression relative to Caiaphas: "high-priest of that year" (see chap. xi., ver. 49), appearing here for the second time, it would seem that the Evangelist had adopted it as an ironical characterization, current in the popular mouth, of the high-priesthood as desecrated by the Romans. With this observation, as well as with the very obvious notion that the high-priestly father-in-law and son-in-law occupied the same house as well as navigated the same boat, and that, accordingly, their common palace had a common *aula* or court-yard, in which Peter perpetrated the denial,* the difficulties that here present themselves are removed.

Meyer justly asserts (in company with Olshausen, Ebrard, Bleek, Baumg.-Crusius, Neander, Luthardt [Wieseler, Stier, Alford, also Chrysostom and Augustine]), that, according to John, the denial of Peter vers. 16-18, the examination vers. 19-21, and the maltreatment vers. 22. 23, took place in the dwelling of Annas; likewise justly, that it is impossible to follow the older harmonistics in assuming the leading to Caiaphas to be pre-supposed in ver. 15. Tholuck, on the other hand, persists in the assumption that the presentation before Annas receives nothing but a passing mention, as is discernible from the πρῶτον; the Aorist ver. 24 having therefore to be read as a Pluperfect (in accordance with Calvin, Lücke, De Wette, Hase and others),* in spite of Meyer's characterization of this as "violent" and Ebrard's and Bleek's as "neck-breaking." Luther takes for granted a blunder of the transcriber, who, as he thinks, should have made ver. 24 immediately follow ver. 14. Manifestly, however, the examination before Annas, as described by John, is an entirely different one from that before Caiaphas, as given by the Synoptists. For John the greatest weight attached to the pre-examination by Annas, for Matthew and Mark to the official chief examination by Caiaphas, for Luke to the legalizing final examination in the morning. See Comm. on *Matthew*. After the above remarks, the assumption of a discrepancy, entertained by Meyer, Baur and others, falls to the ground; such an assumption is also to be found in Euthym. Zigab., Casaubonus, Stier, Ebrard, p. 541. "It has been *fabricated* (says Meyer) that Annas and Caiaphas resided in one and the same house." But an extremely obvious, probable conjecture which, in the simplest manner, solves a difficulty, is something very different from a fabrication. [Augustine, Theophylact, Euthymius, Alford, Hengstenberg, Godet adopt the same easy conjecture. Annas and Caiaphas would naturally occupy different departments of the same (official) palace; and hence the sending from one to the other was quite possible and probable.—P. S.]

Ver. 14. **Now it was Caiaphas who gave counsel to the Jews.**—Wherefore this notice? The Evangelist, in relating that Jesus was led to Annas first, already announced that He would be brought before Caiaphas also. He, however, designs forthwith to intimate what fate impended over Jesus at the hands of both of them. It was an evil omen that the people intended taking Him before Caiaphas, him who had already pronounced sentence of death upon Him. But it is also characteristic of the enmity of old Annas that Jesus was led to him even before He was brought to Caiaphas; the announcement of this fact is appropriately accompanied by the statement that he was the father-in-law of that murderous Caiaphas.

Ver. 15. **And the other [another] disciple.**—Modest self-designation of John, as chap. xx. 2, 3, 4, 8, comp. chap. i. 40. The article is wanting only in A. D., *etc.* [also in B. א.* See Text. Notes.—P. S.]. On the omission of the article several untenable hypotheses are founded: 1. That it was an unknown disciple (Augustine, Calov., Gurlitt); 2. a citizen of Jerusalem (Grotius); 3. Judas Iscariot (Heumann). [Absurd. 4. James, the brother of John (P. Cassel, 1871).—P. S.] The notice that all the

* [Robinson, *Harmony*, p. 225: "An oriental house is usually built around a quadrangular interior court; into which there is a passage (sometimes arched) through the front part of the house, closed next the street by a heavy folding gate, with a smaller wicket for single persons, kept by a porter. In the text, the interior court, often paved or flagged, and open to the sky, is the αὐλή, where the attendants made a fire; and the passage beneath the front of the house, from the street to this court, is the προαύλιον or πυλών in Matt. xxvi. 71; Mark xiv. 68. The place where Jesus stood before the high-priest, may have been an open room or place of audience on the ground-floor, in the rear or on one side of the court; such rooms, open in front, being customary. It was close upon the court; for Jesus heard all that was going on around the fire, and turned and looked upon Peter: Luke xxii. 61."—P. S.]

* [Also E. V., Wordsworth, and even Robinson, *Harmony*, p. 226.—P. S.]

disciples had fled, does not conflict with the fact that they subsequently took heart again and that some of them returned. It is characteristic of the friendship of the two, Peter and John, that they here go voluntarily together, not on an official mission. Peter at first takes the lead. But at the street-door of the court (the *αὐλεία θύρα*),* their relative positions change. John is admitted into the court-yard, being known to the high-priest, while Peter remains without. See Comm. on *Matthew* [p. 491, Am. Ed.]. "John's acquaintance with the high-priest gains in probability if we may suppose, from chap. xix. 27, that he owned a house in Jerusalem. That the Jews had *portresses* instead of porters is shown also by Acts xii. 13." Tholuck. Joseph. *Antiq.* VII. 2, 1.

Ver. 16. **And brought in Peter.**—That is, John did this, not she who kept the door (as Grotius and others have it).

Ver. 17. **Art thou also?** [Μὴ καὶ σύ, as well as the ἄλλος, ver. 16].—"The *καί* contains the pre-supposition that John, whom she nevertheless had, for acquaintance' sake, admitted along with the rest, is a disciple of Jesus." Meyer. According to Mark, the girl does not say this until she has fixed her eyes upon Peter, according to Luke, not until she has examined him by the light. Hence it appears to result that she now grows doubtful as to whether she should have let him in, or whether she ought not to denounce him. This circumstance would, however, cast doubt on the supposition of Meyer, who holds the question of the maid to have been put in a totally unsuspecting mood. At all events she does not seem to have inferred the discipleship of Peter from the mere fact alone of his connection with John.—**(One) of the disciples of this man** [ἐκ τῶν μαθητῶν τοῦ ἀνθρώπου τούτου].—Contemptuously [Meyer]. Not compassionately (Chrysostom and others). Meyer conjectures that John went, together with Jesus and those who were about Him, *into the interior of the house, i. e.* out of the hall into the chamber of examination. This is improbable, though he occupied a position which enabled him to perceive what was going on in the chamber as well as what passed in the hall.

I am not [οὐκ εἰμί].—On the three different denials of Peter, see Comm. on *Matthew*, at the history in question, [p. 498, Am. ed.] "It may surprise us that John remains unmolested while Peter's temptations are repeated: but the reason of this should be sought less in the timorous embarrassment of this latter disciple than in the boldness with which he stepped in amongst the menials." Tholuck. Nevertheless, an *assumed* boldness is a characteristic symptom of fear.

Ver. 18. **Now Peter was standing with them** [ἦν . . . μετ' αὐτῶν ἑστώς]. The fact of his now *standing*, now *sitting*, seems to testify to his inward disquiet, equally with the temerity of his mingling in the crowd of servants and myrmidons and warming himself at their coal-fire.

Ver. 19. **The high-priest then.** Annas. The examination of Annas, in shrewd calculation, starts from the most general point. The Lord's disciples or adherents first form the subject of interrogation. Then follows inquiry as to the doctrine by which Jesus gained them. He desires to ascertain what is to be thought of, or, perchance, feared from, the followers of Jesus, hoping, from the answers of the latter, to gain foothold for an accusation. He, however, manifestly uses, as a stand-point, the malevolent assumption that Jesus has founded a *secret* association by means of *secret* teachings; this the answer of Jesus demonstrates. The distinction between this examination and the subsequent one by Caiaphas is obvious. At the latter, they sought to prove that He was a *public blasphemer* against the sanctuary, *etc.*

Ver. 20. **I have spoken frankly to the world.** [ἐγώ—emphatic, *some one who*—παῤῥησίᾳ λελάληκα τῷ κόσμῳ]. Meyer. *παῤῥησίᾳ* is to be apprehended subjectively: *without reserve, plainly*—not *publicly, openly*, which it does not mean. When accompanied, however, by *to the world*, the quality of publicity is, in an indirect manner, most strongly expressed. The term: **To the world**, means, in the first place, the Jewish world, and characterizes it in respect of the two central-points of publicity: in the synagogues and in the temple. **In a synagogue** [ἐν συναγωγῇ—without the article—there being many synagogues] is modified by πάντοτε, **at all times; in the temple** [ἐν τῷ ἱερῷ, the *one* temple at Jerusalem]; by the addition, **where all the Jews assemble** [ὅπου πάντες οἱ Ἰουδαῖοι συνέρχονται]. Both clauses signify: in complete connection with synagogue and temple; and so the assumption is made that the mountain, field, and lake sermons of Jesus have likewise preserved this connection.—**And in secret I spoke nothing** [καὶ ἐν κρυπτῷ ἐλάλησα οὐδέν]. These words do not conflict with Matt. x. 27, or with the fact that Jesus taught the disciples in confidential conversations. The warnings against the Pharisees in the sermon on the mount, for instance, He Himself publicly repeated in the temple, and, Matt. x. 27, characterized every confidential saying as destined for publicity. That which is here disaffirmed by Jesus is the assumption of mischievous sectarian or seditious secrecy; at the same time, the Lord characterizes the design of the old inquisitor's question and rends the web of his insinuation. The synagogue is spoken of collectively, as a unitous institution; hence, neither the synagogues in Jerusalem, nor the provincial synagogues, as Tholuck maintains, are exclusively referred to.

Ver. 21. **Why askest thou Me?** [τί με ἐρωτᾷς;]—The high-priest had deserved this sharp and thorough setting-down; it, however, also served to render his intention evident, to unmask and rebuke his craftiness. [The question seems to approve the principle of our judicature that the accused person should not be interrogated, but the proof of the charge be substantiated from the testimony of witnesses.]

Ver. 22. **One of the officers who was standing by.** [εἷς παρεστηκὼς τῶν ὑπηρετῶν ἔδωκεν ῥάπισμα τῷ Ἰησοῦ. On *ῥάπισμα* (a blow on the cheek with the hand, or

* [Also ἡ αὔλειος with or without θύρα. The αὐλή,—*atrium*, is the *court-yard*, around which an oriental house was built, a rectangular area in the open air, connected with the street by a προαύλιον, or vestibule (Mark xiv. 68), and πυλών or *portal* (Matt. xxvi. 71), in which was a θύρα, or wicket.—P. S.]

with the staff; only in later Greek) see TEXT. NOTE.—P. S.] This maltreatment of Jesus must be distinguished from that which He experienced on His examination before Caiaphas, subsequently to His condemnation (Matt. xxvi. 37); as, similarly, this last must in its turn be distinguished from the maltreatment narrated by Luke, chap. xxii. 63, 64; although Matthew has summed up in one the two latter acts. The maltreatments recorded by Luke occurred whilst Jesus, after His condemnation before Caiaphas in the night, was retained under arrest until the final examination which must, in accordance with the law, be held by day-time, on the following morning.

Is it thus that Thou answerest the high-priest?—The prohibition, Ex. xxii. 28, had been by the Jews extended into an ordinance instilling a bigoted veneration for superiors, and for the high-priest especially. In the present instance, the officer makes an application of this prohibition, with indiscretion, hypocritical eye-service, and brutality. Rupert: *fortis percussor, mollis adulator.* Comp. Acts xxiii. 2.

Ver. 23. **If I spoke evil.** [εἰ κακῶς ἐλάλησα].—In clear presence of mind, the answer of Christ corresponds to the situation. He is on trial. If He, therefore, here make an improper remark, the person who disapproves of it is at liberty to appear against Him as accuser and witness. Hence the μαρτύρησον does not mean simply: prove it [as Luther's version has it], but—come forward as a witness against it. Accusing and testifying are here thy business; not so judging, still less punishing before sentence is passed. With this admonition Christ awards him the right of accusation; with the following words, He reprimands him for the wrong of maltreatment. The entire deliverance shows how the saying Matt. v. 39 is to be interpreted and applied in spirit.* His reprimand indirectly touches the high-priest also, who allows the maltreatment.

Ver. 24. **Annas, therefore, despatched Him, bound** [ἀπέστειλεν οὖν αὐτὸν Ἀ. δεδεμένον πρὸς K.].—The pre-examination was at an end,—its result being the confounding of Annas, with his crafty inquisition. This, however, had made so little impression on him that he now sent the Lord bound (the signification is, doubtless: after he had caused the chains to be put upon Him again) to His formal examination before Caiaphas. In the fact of his forwarding Him chained, there lay a speaking sign of his desire for His death. Also the circumstance that it had been found impossible to stamp Jesus as a secret conspirator, by reason of His appeal to the publicity of His ministry, was made use of as a ground for summoning false witnesses against Him, who accused Him on account of a public declaration. It was a declaration made by Him in the ears of the rulers (John ii.), one which they had not forgotten and which they could easily pervert. [The pluperfect rendering of ἀπέστειλεν, *miserat, had sent* (E. V.) is ungrammatical (see Meyer, p. 599), inconsistent with οὖν (which for this reason was omitted by some MSS.), and owes its origin to the desire to harmonize John with the Synoptists. The apparent discrepancy disappears if we assume that Annas and his son-in-law Caiaphas occupied different departments in one and the same official palace, which is intrinsically all the more probable as they in some way shared the high-priestly dignity, the one perhaps as high-priest *de jure*, the other *de facto*. Comp. the notes on ver. 13.—P. S.]

Unto Caiaphas the high-priest.—On the now following official examination before Caiaphas, see Comm. on *Matthew* at this passage. On the third formal examination in the morning, see Comm. on *Luke*, p. 359, Am. Ed.

Ver. 25. **Now Simon Peter was still standing there and warming himself.**—The hall for both examination rooms must therefore have been the same. See note on ver. 13. Similarly Luke xxii. 54. Luke knows only of a house of the high-priest. Perhaps it was an official residence, of which Caiaphas had given up a part to his father-in-law.

They said therefore unto him.—This the second denial. According to Matthew it was at the moment when Peter wished to withdraw from the coal-fire in order to approach the entrance-hall; and the men questioned him at the instigation of another maid. See Matt. xxvi. 71; Mark xiv. 68; Luke xxii. 58.

Ver. 26. **One of the servants of the high-priest, being a kinsman.**—See Matthew, ver. 73; Mark, ver. 70; Luke, ver. 59. Meyer groundlessly affirms this servant to have stood outside of the garden awhile ago. Why may he not have been one of the seizers? Peter excited his notice in the garden; he does not seem to have observed—at all events not with precision—that it was Peter who dealt the sword-blow. John distinctly brings out the increase of danger in the charges. First it is a single maid who does but doubtingly question him. Then it is the officers around the coal-fire who more decidedly interrogate him. Finally a kinsman of Malchus whose ear he cut off, pretends to recognize him as one whom he has already seen in the garden with Jesus.—While John plainly depicts the intensifications of the temptations, he, in common with Luke, permits the intensifications of Peter's guilt, most vividly portrayed by Matthew (simple denial, abjuration, self-imprecation) and rendered prominent by Mark likewise, to recede from view. This gives a picture of the relation of Paul and John to Peter totally different from that invented by the Tübingen School. Matthew, the Apostle of the Jews, and Mark, the disciple of Peter, represent the magnitude of Peter's denial in a manner the most regardless; John and Luke manifest the greatest clemency; the Paulinist (Luke) is especially tender.

And immediately a cock crew.—Mark alone, ver. 68, has recorded the first cock-crow after the first denial. That crow also involved

* [Augustine: Christ shows that His precept Matt. v. 39 is to be followed *non ostentatione corporis, sed preparatione cordis.* An *angry* man may turn, in sullenness, the other cheek visibly to the smiter; better is he who makes a true answer with mildness, and prepares his heart in peace to endure greater sufferings. Luther: Christ forbids self-defence with the hand (violence), not with the tongue. See quotation in Meyer, p. 598). Godet: Jesus did not here fulfil literally His precept (Matt. v. 39); He owed to His innocence this answer full of sweetness and dignity. Alford: "It has been often and well observed, that our Lord here gives us the best interpretation of Matt. v. 39—that it does not exclude the remonstrating against unjust oppression, provided it be done calmly and patiently."—P. S.]

an aggravation of Peter's ease which John passes over. Similarly he passes over Peter's ineffectual attempt to withdraw—an attempt which exhibits him in a condition of such utter perplexity and helplessness.

DOCTRINAL AND ETHICAL

1. From John we learn the more minute *particulars* of the DENIAL OF PETER; especially its cause and the gradualness of its progress. As also the exceedingly important pre-examination by ANNAS, in which that sly old hierarch sought to ensnare the Lord in the reproach of secret conspiracy. On the other hand, our Evangelist passes over the principal examination by Caiaphas, and likewise the formal final session in the morning, which latter is intimated by Matthew and detailed by Luke. His narrative of the denial of Peter is very definite as to chronology and also locality; that denial runs through the lengthy period of Christ's examination before Annas and Caiaphas; the place is always the same (see the Exegetical note). By the Synoptists, on the contrary, the denial is summed up in respect of its end and issue, and in this form suitably follows, in Matthew and Mark, the principal examination before Caiaphas, while Luke, with equal correctness, makes it precede the morning examination.

2. The EXAMINATION OF JESUS BY ANNAS, whom the Romans had deposed, affords us a profound glimpse into the character and conduct of a legitimistic partyism. The Jews are forced to accept Caiaphas as the legal high-priest; but they do not cease to regard Annas as their legitimate head; Annas and Caiaphas, however, have accommodated themselves to this, the popular mind, and arranged their household affairs in a manner in keeping with the situation. And this old legitimistic secret-leaguer would stamp Christ as a revolutionary secret-leaguer!

3. The conjunction of the *Roman soldiers* with the *temple-guard* on the occasion of Christ's being taken prisoner, a symbol of the common share of the Gentile and the Jewish world in the crucifixion of Christ. See Luke xxiii. 12 and Acts iv. 26.

4. A stroke of John's greatness—his not thinking it necessary to justify himself in regard to his singular acquaintanceship in the house of the high-priest.

5. PETER AND JOHN in the high-priest's house. Or, *si duo faciunt idem, non est idem.* Peter was burdened with the consciousness of a civil offence against Malchus. This rendered his condition insecure. John, though meaning well, was at fault in not sufficiently entering into the dangerous situation of Peter.

6. The examination before Annas is a type of the ever-recurring plot of hierarchical governments to tax, first, Christianity generally, then Protestantism, further all decidedly evangelical social life with conspiracy, revolution, secret crimes and criminal complots. But as Christ defended Himself against this insinuation by appealing to His public ministry, so the like has been done and may be done by all His true confessors. Here we also have it demonstrated how decidedly Christianity has renounced all the impure, secret machinations of fanatical spirits and sects.

7. The saying called forth from Christ by the blow on the cheek, given Him by the eye-servant in the garb of a servant of justice, possesses not only a Christological but also a hermeneutical import. It indicates how His words, particularly Matt. v. 39, are in spirit to be interpreted. His remark, replete with composure, mental clearness and mild reproof, is like the offering of the other cheek.

8. The intensifications of PETER'S TEMPTATION are thrown into bold relief by John, his guilt being thus exhibited in a milder light. The first denial took place during the examination by Annas, the second and third during the examination before Caiaphas, after Christ had been led, bound, to the latter and when His prospects were, consequently, already very gloomy. Add to this that the third question exposed Peter to being recognized as the offender who had wounded Malchus. The *repentance of Peter* is set forth by John with sufficient distinctness in the later signs of his conversion. It is remarkable that John seems to have done nothing to warn Peter. Whether he was not near enough to him, or whether he entertained too high an opinion of his practical abilities, we will not venture to assert; at all events he appears to have been unwilling to exalt himself at Peter's expense in the version which he gives of the transaction.

9. The DENIAL OF PETER does not mean that he intended to renounce Jesus *inwardly*, but that he designed to escape a mortal peril by means of a so-called white lie. Thus, from a vocation to the morality of Christ, to apostolic faithfulness in confession, he momentarily sank to the level of ordinary, popular morality, which holds such evasions to be admissible, nay, clever. If we judge of David's trespasses by the absolute arbitrariness of oriental despots, they appear in a milder light than when exposed to the full rays of the Theocracy. So it is with the transgression of Peter, when judged according to popular and worldly conceptions. But in the light of Christ it was a deep fall.

HOMILETICAL AND PRACTICAL.

The capture of Jesus: 1. A consequence of His free surrender. 2. A sin of the united Roman and Jewish authorities of the ancient world. 3. A judgment, in which the glory of the ancient world does itself appear captive and bound.—The cord or bonds of Christ an indication of the bonds of the world.—The unanimity of Annas and Caiaphas.—The secret inquisitional trial by Annas, aiming at the ascertainment of secret transgressions on Christ's part: a picture of life.—The sufferings of Christ under hierarchic partyism.—How the worldly-wise State loves to shut one eye to the machinations of illegal, illustrious parties.—On the denial of Peter, see Comm. on *Matthew, Mark, Luke.*—Peter and John in the high-priest's house.—The measure of freedom of entrance into worldly circles, is diverse for Christians: 1. Not the same for every one; 2. not the same in all moods; 3. not the same in all external temptations.—Peter warmed himself: 1. Fact: He warmed himself and grew all the while colder.

2. Doctrine: We may not seek to grow warm by the fires of the Lord's enemies.—The examination before Annas, see Doctrinal Note, No. 6.—Comparison of the examination before Annas and that before Caiaphas. See Exeg. Note to first clause of ver. 25.—In the one examination He was assumed to be a secret sneak, in the other a public blasphemer.—The Lord's appeal to the publicity of His labors.—The Lord's intimation that the court of Annas was no authorized tribunal.—Annas found no pretext for accusing Jesus, and yet passed Him on bound to Caiaphas.—He sent Him bound for a sign: 1. The bad sign; 2. the sign-language of the bad.—The three spiritual examinations wherein Christ stood.—The first an unauthorized private examination, the second an examination with false witnesses, the third a mere mock examination.—How the world has warped justice in all forms over the head of Christ.—Christ in human judicatures; 1. As the Spirit's judgment upon them. 2. As the regeneration and sanctification of them. 3. As the final judgment upon them.—How Jesus confessed His disciples, whilst Peter denied Him.

Starke: Hands so powerful, so beneficent, are bound.—Our love of an unbound liberty has had to be atoned for by the bonds of the Son of God, Ps. ii. 3.—Connection and alliance by marriage is oft-times an occasion of damnation, because thereby men entangle themselves with people who do only evil, 2 Kings viii. 18.—It is Christ's presentation before the tribunal of men that we must thank for our liberation from the strict tribunal of God.—Stay away from that place where thou hast nothing to do; mere curiosity can readily get thee into danger and misfortune.—Let a man but step out of the way of God, and every step brings him nearer to his fall.—Quesnel: It is one of Satan's traps to smooth our way sometimes to such places as he would keep us in for his advantage.—Lange: It can easily happen that a man may act indiscreetly out of pure good will, and only injure another by his services.—Quesnel: Many a one thinks he stands fast as any column, and yet he is more easily shaken than a reed. O be not proud, but fear thee!—Osiander: We should avoid preachers who shun the light and teach secretly in corners what they may not publicly confess.—It does not conflict with modesty and humility to meet disguised enemies of the truth with undaunted frankness. Ver. 22. We witness the same spectacle here that occurred, 1 Kings xxii. 24.—An earnest presentation of a subject is a thorn in the eye to some people; they construe such presentation as immodesty, as a want of respect, because they are biased by prejudices. —Wicked masters have wicked servants; birds of a feather flock together.—Zeisius: Those who speak the truth, especially faithful preachers, are to this day smitten with Christ, covered with all manner of insult, derision, revilement, tribulation—and, withal, well-nigh forced to hold their peace, 2 Tim. iv. 3.—*Ibid.:* Though it is true that a Christian should, with a good conscience, suffer wrong, yet need he not extend to the world his approbation of her wrong, as she would gladly have him do; on the contrary, he should defend himself against it, yet with fitting meekness and modesty; therefore says Luther: he must divorce mouth and hand; he must not surrender his mouth to the enemy, so as to approve the wrong; but yet he must keep his hand quiet and not avenge himself, Acts xxvi. 25.—Christ, for the good of His members, has had to burst through the masks of false politeness.—The desire to shade away a fault committed, may become an occasion of fresh and greater sins.—Many a man, if he were not found in places where he hath nought to do, would keep out of numerous difficulties. Stay at home and do thine own business in the fear of God, trusting in Him, Prov. vii. 11 ff.—When Christ and His people are to be opposed, the slaves of Satan exert all their strength in unison, to the end that they may overwhelm and crush them, Ps. x. 2. [The appositeness of the passage cited not being apparent on reference to the English Bible, we subjoin a translation of the German rendering, which here, as in many other instances, differs considerably from the English. "Because the wicked exerciseth himself in pride, the miserable—afflicted—wretched—man must suffer. They cleave one to another and imagine maliciousness."]—We have cause to beware that we do not, by curious questions, plunge our neighbor into temptation to all kinds of lies and dissimulations. —What a faint-hearted wretch is man when conscience awakes. Every rustling leaf strikes him with fear and dismay.—If thou confess Jesus and deny thyself, together with the world, thou art blessed, but if thou deny Christ, the whole world cannot help thee to bliss—no, not if thou confess *it* a thousand times over.—Let him that standeth, take heed lest he fall, 1 Cor. x. 12.—If thou get not the start of sin, thou fallest from one sin into another, from a small one into a greater one, nay, even from the state of grace into the unblessed state of damnation.—Even the meanest creature, if it be God's will to use it as His instrument, may become a means of arousing the sinner.

Braune: John expressly remarks that Jesus was led *first to Annas*, the father-in-law of Caiaphas, high-priest under Augustus from the year 12 A. D. to 23, when Valerius Gratus, governor of Syria, deposed him; he was uncommonly crafty, and his secret acts were full of violence. In 24, his son Eleazar became high-priest for one year; at the end of the year 25 his son-in-law Joseph, called Caiaphas, received the office through the self-same governor who had deposed Annas. Caiaphas remained high-priest until 36—not, of a certainty, without the helpful influence of Annas—while the remaining high-priests followed one another like the shadows of clouds driven by the wind; for in the last 420 years of the temple, there ruled more than 300 high-priests. It is owing to the powerful influence of Annas that he is mentioned previous to Caiaphas, the ruling high-priest, and that Jesus is here led *first* to him. Ananus, the last of Annas' sons, having the same name as his father, had the apostle James put to death. This circumstance harmonizes with the family history. It was calculated that before this High Council—the sons of Aaron, the dignitaries of the temple—Jesus would answer with intimidation, and be caught in what He said. And how undaunted He stood there, how sublime! He would not cast pearls before swine. The legitimate answer was accounted disrespectful by the officers; one said: Oughtest Thou to answer the high-priest thus? It was in the form, then, that the error was thought to lie—in the mode of procedure. Great stress is put upon outward formality; a man may be permitted to speak the truth, but he must do it with grace and good breeding; behind these, however, so much untruth is concealed, that the truth itself becomes tainted and loses its virtue.—He is a betrayer of mankind, like Judas the betrayer of Christ, who desires a public office without possessing the necessary moral and mental qualifications therefor; nothing is so indispensable for such an office as humility and a respect for the dignity of men.—If it be a question of truth, proof is what is required. Only tyrants employ torture; even a police officer may be a tyrant, leaping over proofs in false official zeal.

GOSSNER: Peter, doubtless, thought it a piece of good fortune, and it was his misfortune. Thou art more fortunate in having a friend who preventeth thee from going in to men of the world than in possessing one who procureth thee access to them and introduceth thee into their dwellings.—This fire in the court of the high-priest could not impart fresh warmth to Peter's zeal and his fidelity to Jesus. If he had warmed himself by God in prayer, he would not have fallen.—Jesus was expected to deliver up a list of His disciples. Because disciples or pupils readily fall into some inadvertence, it was hoped that an accusation might thus be brought against Him. But the Saviour had already provided for the security of His disciples: Let these go! He said on the Mount of Olives. And what He says, does and must come to pass.—The Saviour saw through all this. He knew their hearts; and this clear glance into such fearfully perverted hearts—how it must have cut through and wounded His pure, holy, loving heart. Let him who experiences something similar, think of his Saviour and gather strength from Him to suffer after Him.—The enemies of the truth lie in wait. Christ acts openly.—Alas, what must He, what must the fairest visage in this world endure!—and yet He still maketh His face to shine upon us, and we are healed.—Officers of justice are never permitted to intermeddle in a case; here, however, against Jesus, they were free to do anything; they well knew how far they might go.—His answer was regarded as a sin and a violation of the priestly dignity; and Christ must suffer Himself to be treated as one who did not understand the laws of politeness; He must bear the blame of immodesty, just as the primitive Christians were always treated as unmannered boors when they frankly confessed the truth.—Am I not permitted to answer for Myself? Is it not demanded of Me? Why dost thou thus abuse Me for doing it?—The Saviour weareth the bonds and useth not His strength to burst them, as He easily could have done. Why not? Because it was not really the bonds that bound Him, but love and the impulse to free us from bonds, designing, by means of those very bonds of *His*, to break *our* chains from which we else should never have got free.—*On Malchus:* Thus God bringeth us again into the company of those we fain would never see more. Suddenly and unexpectedly we run into their hands: Therefore do thou cut off no person's ear, if thou wouldst never be dismayed at the sight of him.—Jesus shows that the cock, even, does not crow at hap-hazard, but that God is able, in His economy, to make use of his outcry as a good domestic medicine,—as at this time, when he had to preach repentance to the first Apostle.

HEUBNER: It was an unblest relationship betwixt Annas and Caiaphas; the ties were cords of sin. John mentions this in order to indicate that the sentence of such judges might be divined in advance. Caiaphas has enforced his wicked counsel. What a joy was that, that he might now feel?—Peter's following was the more presumptuous, since Jesus had said ver. 8: *Let them go.* It was a wrong following, entered upon in presumption and human strength. — Great houses of the world bring many dangers.—Against his will, John was instrumental to Peter's hurt. Introduction to the presence of the great often becomes an occasion of our sin. God put delays in Peter's way, in order to give him time for reflection.—The repairing to mixed companies in the homes of the great is to the weak generally a cause of their falling; intercourse with unsanctified men oft-times seduces Christians from the right path.—The accusations against Jesus were twofold: 1. To the effect that He had gathered Himself partizans,—He, who did but found a holy union, the kingdom of God; 2. that He had disseminated suspicious doctrines,—He, who taught heavenly truth.—Publicity was the character of Jesus' life and it is the character of Christianity. Christianity knows nothing of secret-mongery, mysteries of an order; it would be entirely public, because it diffuses *the truth* which is common property of all.—The conduct of the officer, conduct arising from malice and a desire to flatter, redounds to the accusation of the high-priest himself. That the officer dared indulge in such mutinous conduct before the eyes of the spiritual magistracy, betrays the spirit of that magistracy.—Ver. 23. This is a commentary upon Matt. v. 39. Christ shows how, even towards those who offer us the most bitter insult and wrong, we can unite earnest patience and love and make answer for ourselves.—Those hands, by Jesus extended only for the conferring of benefits, were bound.—John describes the waxing of the peril. The higher this mounts, the lower sinks the courage of Peter. First it was a maid, then men, now relatives of the wounded servant [who question him].

[CRAVEN: From AUGUSTINE: Ver. 17. Christ is not only denied by him who denies that He is Christ, but by him also who denies himself to be a Christian.—Ver. 23. What can be truer, gentler, kinder, than this answer?—Some one will ask here, why He did not do what He Himself commanded, *i. e.*, not make this answer, but give the other cheek to the smiter. But what if He did both, both answered gently, and gave, not His cheek only to the smiter, but His whole body to be nailed to the Cross? And herein He shows, that those precepts of patience are to be performed not by posture of the body, but by preparation of the heart; for it is possible that a man might give his cheek outwardly, and yet be angry at the same time.—Ver. 27. Lo! the prophecy of the Physician is fulfilled, the presumption of the sick man demonstrated.——From CHRYSOSTOM: Ver. 16. *But Peter stood at the door without;* Peter's *love* took him as far as the palace, but his *fear* prevented him entering in.—Ver. 17. What sayest thou, O Peter? Didst thou not say before, *I will lay down my life for Thy sake?* What then had happened, that thou givest way even when the damsel asks thee? It was not a soldier who asked thee, but a mean porteress.—Therefore did Divine Providence permit Peter first to fall, in order that he might be less severe to sinners from the remembrance of his own fall. Peter sinned, and obtained pardon, that judges might thereafter have that rule to go by in dispensing pardon.—Ver. 25. *And Simon Peter stood and warmed himself;* The Evangelist means that the once fervid disciple was now too torpid to move even when our Lord was carried away; showing how weak man's nature is when God forsakes him.—Vers. 15-18, 25-27. How hurtful it is to trust in self, and not to ascribe all to God.——From GREGORY: Ver. 18. The fire of love was smothered in Peter's breast, and he was warming himself before the coals of the persecutors, *i. e.*, with the love of this present life, whereby his weakness was increased.——From ALCUIN: Ver. 15. Peter *followed* his Master out of *devotion*, though *afar off*, on account of *fear*.—Ver. 19. He does not ask in order to *know the truth*, but to find out some charge against Him, on which to deliver Him to the Roman Governor to be condemned; but our Lord so tempers His answer, as neither to conceal the truth, nor yet to appear to defend Himself.

[From BURKITT: Vers. 12-14. How impossible it is for the greatest innocence and virtue to protect from slander and false accusation! And no person can be so innocent or good, whom false witness may not condemn.—Vers. 15-18, 25-27. How may the slavish fear of suffering drive the holiest and best of men to commit the foulest and worst of sins!—The occasion of Peter's fall: 1. His presumptuous confidence of his own strength and standing; *Though all men forsake Thee, yet will not I;* 2. His being in bad company.—He denied Him first with a *lie*, then with an *oath and curse.* Oh, how dangerous is it, not to resist the beginnings of sin! If we yield to one temptation, Satan will assault us with more and stronger.—The heinous and aggravating circumstances of Peter's sin: From 1. The character of his person; 2. The person whom he denies, his Master, his Saviour; 3. The time when he denied Him; soon after Christ had washed his feet; yea, soon after he had received the sacrament from Christ's own hand.—How unreasonable is their objection against coming to the Lord's table, that some who go to it dishonor Christ as soon as they come from it! Such examples ought not to discourage us from coming to the ordinance, but should excite and increase our watchfulness after we have been there.—Vers. 19-21. Christ never willingly affected *corners;* He taught openly, and propounded His doctrine publicly and plainly in the world.—Learn hence, That 1. It is not unusual for the best of doctrines to pass under the odious name of error and heresy; 2. The ministers of Christ who have truth on their side, may and ought to speak boldly and openly.—"Truth blushes at nothing, except at its being concealed."—Ver. 22. Christ did endure ignominious and contemptuous usage, *giving His cheek to the smiters*, to testify that shame and reproachful usage which was deserved by us, and to sanctify that condition to us, whenever it is allotted for us.—Ver. 23. Though our Saviour doth not *revenge* Himself, yet He *vindicates* Himself, and defends Himself both with law and reason; to stand up in defence of our own innocency, is not contrary to the duties of patience and forgiveness, or to the practice and example of our Lord Jesus.—Ver. 24. His condescending to go bound from one high-priest to another, and from one tribunal to another, teaches His people what delinquents they were before the tribunal of God, and what they deserved by reason of sin.——From M. HENRY: Ver. 12. To Christ's bonds we owe our liberty, His confinement was our enlargement. He was bound that 1. The types and prophecies of the Old Testament might herein be accomplished; 2. He might bind us to duty and obedience; His bonds *for* us are bonds *upon* us; 3. His bonds for us were designed to make our bonds for Him easy to us, if at any time we be so called out to suffer for Him.—Ver. 13. We had been *led away of our own* impetuous *lusts*, and *led captive by Satan at his will*, and, that we might be rescued, Christ was led away, led captive by Satan's agents and instruments.—*Caiaphas was high-priest that same year;* 1. When a *bad thing* was to be done by a high-priest, according to the fore-knowledge of God, Providence so ordered it that a *bad man* should be in the chair to do it; 2. When God would make it to appear what corruption there was in the heart of a *bad man*, He put him into a place of power; Many a man's *advancement* has lost him his *reputation*.—Ver. 15. We must take heed of tempting God by running upon difficulties beyond our strength, and venturing too far in the way of suffering: If our call be clear to expose ourselves, we may hope that God will enable us to honor Him; but if it be not, we may fear that God will leave us to shame ourselves.—*That disciple was known unto the high-priest;* as there are many who seem disciples, and are not so, so there are many who are disciples, and seem not so [at a casual glance]; we must not conclude a man to be no friend to Christ, merely because he has acquaintance and conversation with those that are His known enemies.—Ver. 16. The courtesies of our friends often prove a snare to us, through a misguided affection.—Ver. 17. Observe here 1. How slight the attack was: it was a silly maid, of no account, that challenged him; 2. How speedy the surrender was; without taking time to recollect himself, he suddenly answered, *I am not;* 3. Yet he goes further into the temptation, ver. 18.—*Peter stood and warmed himself;* 1. It was a *fault bad enough*, that he did not attend his Master, and appear for Him at the upper end of the hall, where He was now under examination; he might have been (1) a *witness for Him*, (2) a *witness to Him;* 2. It was much worse, that he joined himself with those that were His Master's enemies; *he stood with them, etc.*—Peter was much to be blamed, because 1. He *associated himself* with these wicked men; 2. He desired to be thought *one of them*, that he might not be suspected to be a disciple of Christ.

—Ver. 20. Christ sought no corners, for He feared no colors, nor said anything that He needed to be ashamed of.—Ver. 22. Wicked rulers will not want wicked servants, who will *help forward the affliction* of those whom their masters persecute.—Ver. 23. We learn 1. That in such cases we must not be our own avengers, nor judges in our own cause; 2. Our resentment of injuries done us must be always rational, and never passionate; 3. When called out to suffering, we must *accommodate ourselves* to the inconveniences of a suffering state, with patience, and by one indignity done us be prepared to receive another, and make the best of it.—Ver. 25. Peter staid to *warm himself;* but they that *warm themselves* with evil-doers, grow cold toward good people and good things; and they that are fond of the devil's fire-side, are in danger of the devil's fire.—Yielding to one temptation invites another, and perhaps a stronger; Satan redoubles his attacks when we give ground.—Ver. 26. They who by sin think to help themselves out of trouble, do but entangle and embarrass themselves the more: Dare to be brave, for truth will out—*a bird of the air* may perhaps *tell the matter* which we seek to conceal with a lie.—Notice is taken of this servant's being akin to Malchus; he that may need a *friend*, should not make a *foe.*—Ver. 27. *He denied again;* see here 1. The nature of sin in general; *the heart is hardened by the deceitfulness of it;* 2. Of the sin of lying in particular; it is a fruitful sin, and upon that account *exceeding sinful.—Immediately the cock crew;* see 1. The care Christ has of those that are His, notwithstanding their follies; though *they fall, they are not utterly cast down,* not *utterly cast off;* 2. The advantage of having faithful remembrancers near us, who, though they cannot tell us more than we know already, yet may remind us of that which we know, but have forgotten.—The crowing of the cock *to others* was an accidental thing, and had no significancy; but *to Peter* it was the voice of God, and had a blessed tendency to awaken his conscience, by putting him in mind of the word of Christ.——From SCOTT: Vers. 15-18, 25-27. Self-confident rashness differs from steady courage and patience of faith; and they who most readily venture into temptation, are often most easily overcome by it.—As Christ suffered every insult for the sake of Peter, even when Peter was denying Him; so He foresaw all our unfaithfulness and ingratitude, at the time when He shed His blood for our sins; this consideration should not only encourage our hope in His mercy, but also shame us out of our base requitals of such a Benefactor.—The meekness, patience and wisdom of the Son of God only served to increase the enmity of His persecutors; and their base usage illustrated His consummate excellency: This should teach us what to expect from the wicked, and how to behave towards them.

[From KRUMMACHER: Ver. 12. Behold Christ yonder bears your fetters. Jesus bound! What a spectacle! How many a prophetic type of the Old Testament finds its fulfilment in this fact! Isaac; the ram on Mount Moriah; the sacred ark of the covenant, when it had fallen into the hands of the Philistines; Joseph; the paschal lambs; Samson.—Jesus bound! Omnipotence in fetters! the Creator bound by the creature! the Lord of the world, the Captive of His mortal subjects!—Ver. 19. The world still acts like Annas; because it will not acknowledge that we possess the real and eternal truth of God, it stamps the latter as heretical, and brands us as a sect.—Ver. 20. "We may discern in Jesus all the marks of a true teacher—confidence, which delivers its testimony before the whole world; persevering continuance in that testimony at all times; and a siding with existing divine and human ordinances."—Ver. 22. The feeling of the family reflected itself in the soul of the menial who wore its livery.—How often are we treated in a similar manner, when the truth which we proclaim to the men of the world can no longer be assailed: how does hypocritical zeal for the preservation of the honor of authority start up against us, and how pompously it calls out to us, "Answerest thou the high-priest so?"—Vers. 15-18, 25-27. Peter reminds us of that class of our brethren, of whom we are wont to say that though they possess the burning heart, yet they are still in want of the light of the Holy Spirit; the new life is implanted in its germ, but the development itself is still far behind.—He did not yet know how much the noblest human feelings depend upon the change of circumstances, situations, and seasons; he was ignorant that one who could be enthusiastic for Jesus transfigured on Mount Tabor, possessed no pledge, from this feeling, that he would be equally zealous for Jesus ignominiously crucified on Mount Calvary.—It is only the Lord's gracious inspiration which produces true heroism. The simple disciple, in the armor of his own feeling of affection for his Master, thought himself abundantly able to cope with Satan and his crafty devices.—O what a disgrace for the disciple, *morally* to have convinced the troop that he could not be Jesus' friend, but had sworn fealty to the banner of his adversaries.—Simon Peter vowed and promised, certainly with the purest intentions, but neglected to watch and pray. Let him, therefore, that thinketh he standeth, take heed lest he fall. In the kingdom of God, indeed, a defeat may bring more blessings than a victory; and more costly fruits often spring from stumblings than from the most apparently successful strivings after holiness. But woe unto him whom this truth would render reckless!

[From BARNES: Ver. 21. Jesus here insisted on His *rights:* Learn 1. That though Jesus was willing to be reviled and persecuted, yet He also insisted that *justice* should be done Him; 2. He was conscious of innocence, and had been so open in His conduct, that He could appeal to the vast multitudes which had heard Him, as witnesses in His favor; 3. It is proper for us, when persecuted and reviled, meekly, but firmly, to insist on our rights, and to demand that justice should be done us; 4. Christians, like their Saviour, should so live that they may confidently appeal to all who have known them, as witnesses of the sincerity, purity, and rectitude of their lives.]

III.

CHRIST CONFRONTED WITH PILATE. 1. CONDUCT OF PILATE UPON THE FIRST CHARGE THAT JESUS IS A MALEFACTOR; 2. UPON THE ACCUSATION THAT JESUS PRETENDETH TO BE THE KING OF THE JEWS; 3. UPON THE ACCUSATION THAT JESUS HATH MADE HIMSELF THE SON OF GOD.—DECIDED FALL OF PILATE AT THE CHARGE THAT JESUS IS A REBEL AGAINST THE EMPEROR.—THE KINGDOM OF JESUS IN ANTITHESIS TO THE KINGDOM OF THIS WORLD. SYMBOLISM OF ROMANISM. JESUS THE KING IN THE KINGDOM OF TRUTH. THE VERDICT OF GUILTLESSNESS PRONOUNCED UPON JESUS. CHOICE OF THE MURDERER BARABBAS. JESUS IN THE CROWN OF THORNS AND PURPLE ROBE. VERDICT OF JESUS UPON PILATE. PILATE DISGUISES HIS DISCOMFITURE IN THE GARB OF DERISION. THE SENTENCE OF DEATH.

CHAPS. XVIII. 28—XIX. 16.

(Matt. chap. xxvi. (57) 59—xxvii. 31; Mark chap. xiv. 55—xv. 20; Luke chap. xxii. 63—xxiii. 25.)

28 ¶ Then led they [they lead, ἄγουσιν] Jesus from Caiaphas unto the hall of judg-
ment [to the prætorium, or the palace of the governor]: and it was early;[1] and
they themselves went not into the judgment hall [the palace] lest they should be de-
filed; but that they [that they might not be defiled, but] might eat the passover.
29 Pilate then [therefore] went out[2] unto them, and said, What accusation bring ye
30 against this man? They answered and said unto him, If he were not a malefactor,
31 we would not have delivered him up unto thee. Then said Pilate [Pilate therefore
said] unto them, Take ye him [take him yourselves], and judge him according to
your law. The Jews therefore said unto him, It is not lawful for us to put any
32 man [any one] to death: [.] That the saying of Jesus might be fulfilled, which
he spake, signifying what [kind of] death he should die.
33 Then Pilate entered into the judgment hall [the palace] again, and called Jesus,
34 and said unto him, Art thou the King of the Jews? Jesus answered him [*omit*
him], Sayest thou this thing of thyself, or did others tell it thee of me [tell thee
35 concerning me]? Pilate answered, Am I a Jew? Thine own nation and the chief
36 priests have [*omit* have] delivered thee unto me: what hast thou done? Jesus
answered, My kingdom is not of this world: if my kingdom were of this world,
then would my servants fight, that I should not be delivered to the Jews: but now
37 is my kingdom not from hence. Pilate therefore said unto him, Art thou a king
then? Jesus answered, Thou sayest that [Thou sayest it. For] I am a king.[4] To
this end was I[5] [have I been] born, and for this cause came I [have I come] into
the world, that I should [may] bear witness unto the truth. Every one that is of
38 the truth heareth my voice. Pilate saith unto him, What is truth? And when he
had said this, he went out again unto the Jews, and saith unto them, I find in him
39 no fault *at all* [no fault in him]. But ye have a custom, that I should release unto
you one at the passover: will ye therefore that I release unto you the King of the
40 Jews? Then cried they all [they all cried out][6] again, saying, Not this man, but
Barabbas. Now Barabbas was a robber.
1 Chap. XIX. Then Pilate therefore took Jesus and scourged *him*. And the sol-
2 diers platted a crown of thorns, and put *it* on his head, and they put on him a
3 purple robe, And [they approached him and, ἤρχοντο πρὸς αὐτὸν καὶ][7] said,
Hail, King of the Jews! and they smote him with their hands [smote him on
the face].[8]
4 Pilate therefore [And Pilate][9] went forth again and saith unto them, Behold, I
5 bring him forth unto you, that ye may know that I find no fault in him. Then
came Jesus forth [Jesus therefore came forth], wearing the crown of thorns, and
6 the purple robe. And *Pilate* [he][10] saith unto them, Behold the man![11] When
the chief priests therefore and [the] officers saw him, they cried out, saying, Crucify
him, crucify *him* [Crucify! crucify!][12] Pilate saith unto them, Take ye him [Take

7 him yourselves], and crucify *him:* for I find no fault in him. The Jews answered
him, We have a law, and by our[13] law he ought to die, because he made himself
the Son of God.
8 When Pilate therefore heard that [this] saying, he was the more afraid; And
9 went again into the judgment hall [the palace], and saith unto Jesus, Whence art
10 thou? But Jesus gave him no answer. Then[14] saith Pilate unto him, Speakest
thou not unto me? knowest thou not that I have power to crucify [release] thee,
11 and have power to release [crucify] thee?[15] Jesus answered, Thou couldest
[wouldest] have no power *at all* [*omit at all*] against me, except it were [had been]
given thee from above: therefore he that delivered me unto thee hath the greater
12 sin. And from thenceforth [Upon this, or, for the sake of this, ἐκ τούτου] Pilate
sought to release him: but the Jews cried out,[16] saying, If thou let this man go
[release this man] thou art not Cæsar's friend: whosoever [every one that] maketh
13 himself a king speaketh [declareth] against Cæsar. When Pilate therefore heard
that saying, [these words],[17] he brought Jesus forth, and sat down in the judgment
14 seat in a place that is called the Pavement, but in the Hebrew, Gabbatha. And
[Now] it was the preparation [day] of the passover, and [*omit* and, *and insert* it was][18]
15 about[19] the sixth[20] hour: and he saith unto the Jews, Behold your King! But
they cried out, Away with *him,* away with *him,* crucify him. Pilate saith unto
them, Shall I crucify your King? The chief priests answered, We have no king
16 but Cæsar. Then delivered he him therefore [Then therefore he delivered him up]
unto them to be crucified. And they took Jesus, and led *him* away.[21]

TEXTUAL AND GRAMMATICAL.

1 Chap. xviii. ver. 28.—Πρωΐ, not πρωΐα. [The former is sustained by ℵ. A. B. C., *etc.*, against the text. rec.—P. S.]

2 Ver. 29.—After Πιλᾶτος an ἔξω, according to B. C.* L. X. Sin. *etc.* Others give it after αὐτούς.

3 Ver. 34.—Most Codd. are without αὐτῷ.

4 Ver. 37.—[It is best to regard σὺ λέγεις as an affirmation (comp. σὺ εἶπας, Matt. xxvi. 25], and ὅτι as the reason for it. Lange: *Du sagst es. Ja ein König bin ich.* Noyes: *Thou sayest what is true; for I am a King.* So also Meyer, Alford, *etc.*—P. S.]

5 Ver. 37.—The second ἐγώ is omitted by B. D. L. *etc.* Probably because the transcribers considered it superfluous.

6 Ver. 40.—[πάντες is omitted by ℵ. B. L. X., Tischend., Westcott and Hort, but retained by Lange, Alford, with A. and Verss.—P. S.]

7 Chap. xix. ver. 3.—Codd. [ℵ] B. L. U. X., *etc.*, most versions, Augustine, *etc.*, instead of καὶ ἔλεγον, read: καὶ ἤρχοντο πρὸς αὐτὸν καὶ ἔλεγον (Lachmann, Tischendorf). [It was a mock-reverential approach as to a crowned monarch. Not understood by transcribers.—P. S.]

8 Ver. 3. [ἐδίδοσαν αὐτῷ ῥαπίσματα—uncertain whether with the hand or a rod or staff, probably the former. Lange: *Backenstreiche.* See Text. Notes on ch. xviii. 22.—P. S.]

9 Ver. 4.—Instead of ἐξῆλθεν οὖν, Lachmann reads καὶ ἐξῆλθεν, in accordance with A. B. K. L., *etc.*

10 Ver. 5.—[*Pilate* is omitted in the MSS. and inserted by the E. V. for clearness' sake.—P. S.]

11 Ver. 5.—['Ιδοὺ ὁ ἄνθρωπος: ℵ. B. L., *versus* ἴδε of text. rec., which is supported by A. D., but not by B., as Lachmann states. Comp. Tischend. ed. viii.—P. S.]

12 Ver. 6.—Most Codd., B. L. excepted, append αὐτόν (Lachmann) to the σταύρωσον of the Recepta. The passionate and characteristic exclamation was readily thus supplemented, however. [Alford, Tischend., Westcott and Hort omit αὐτόν, which was probably inserted from ver. 15, and from Mark and Luke.—P. S.]

13 Ver. 7.—Cod. B. and some others omit ἡμῶν (Lachmann). The context is in favor of its retention.

14 Ver. 10.—Οὖν is wanting in A. X. and in several translations (Tischendorf). Probably the form of the consequence presented by οὖν was considered remarkable here.

15 Ver. 10.—Codd. A. B., Lachmann, Tischendorf [Tregelles, Alford, Wescott and Hort] give the ἀπολῦσαι first. Probably a putative correction.

16 Ver. 12.—The stronger form ἐκραύγαζον instead of ἔκραζον, in accordance with Codd. A. B. L. M. Lachmann, Tischendorf.

17 Ver. 13.—Τῶν λόγων τούτων, according to Codd. A. B. L. Sin. *etc.* [instead of τοῦτον τὸν λόγον, text. rec.]

18 Ver. 14.—The reading ὥρα ἦν instead of ὥρα δέ, received by Lachmann and Tischendorf in accordance with A. B. D., *etc.* [So also the English critical edd.]

19 Ver. 14.—'Ως is more strongly attested than ὡσεί.

20 Ver. 14.—Most Codd., A. B. E. K., *etc.*, and the translations read ἕκτη; Codd. D. L. X., *etc.*, and the Alexandrian Chronicle differ from these; the Chronicle assures us that accurate copies and the authentic MS. preserved at Ephesus—τὸ ἰδιόχειρον—give τρίτη. A conformation to Mark xv. 25, due to the too literal apprehension of the Johannean expression. [See the full apparatus in Tischend. and the exegesis below.—P. S.]

21 Ver. 16.—Cod. A. *etc.* and the Recepta read: καὶ ἀπήγαγον. Codd. D. E. H. *etc.* read ἤγαγον. Codd. B. L. X. *etc.* the Itala and other translations, Lachmann, Tischendorf [Alford, Westcott and Hort] omit καὶ ἤγαγον. Omitted probably on account of the exegetical consideration that the word here refers to the Jews, while in Matt. xxvii. 31, it has reference to the soldiers.

EXEGETICAL AND CRITICAL.

[On the relation of John to the Synoptists in this passage see the clear statements in Doctrinal and Ethical, no. 1.—P. S.]

Ver. 28. **They, therefore, lead** [ἄγουσιν οὖν] **Jesus from Caiaphas.**—Since ver. 28 refers to ver. 24, the οὖν is here very expressive; it means that with the fact of Annas' sending the Lord bound to Caiaphas, everything further, even to the leading of Him into the heathen Prætorium, was decided. On the final session of the Sanhedrin in the morning see Comm. on *Matt.* at our passage.

To the Prætorium.—On the Prætorium see Comm. on *Matt.*, Note to ver. 27 [p. 513, Am. Ed.]. Not "before the morning twilight" as Tholuck supposes. See the Notes to *Matthew.* [The πραιτώριον (originally the tent of the general in the Roman camp) is the governor's mansion, whether it was the palace of Herod (the usual opinion), or more probably a building in the castle Antonia (Meyer, Ewald, Lange).—**And it was early** [ἦν δὲ πρωΐ], in the fourth night watch, towards the break of day.—P. S.]

Not into the Prætorium, that they might not be defiled but might eat the Passover [ἵνα μὴ μιανθῶσιν ἀλλὰ φάγωσιν τὸ πάσχα. The entrance of a Jew into the house of a Gentile made him levitically unclean till the close of that day (sunset). As the passover was not eaten before six o'clock, *i. e.* at the beginning of the next day, the defilement incurred in the morning would have ceased before the regular passover. This is a hint that φαγεῖν τὸ πάσχα must be taken here in a wider sense. See Matt., p. 455, and Lange below.—P. S.] This was a motive, but scarcely the only one; they, however, hypocritically took cover under it as the only one. If Pilate tried Jesus' cause in the palace, the Sanhedrists would lack the aid of the popular faction which they had driven together, and upon which they could securely count outside, in front of the palace.

Respecting John's pretended inconsistency with the Synoptists, see Comm. on *Matthew* [pp. 454 ff. 468]. Meyer again pleads at length in favor of the view which makes it result from our passage that there is a difference between John and the Synoptists; that according to John the paschal meal was still impendent on the evening after the crucifixion of Christ, while according to the Synoptists it had taken place the evening before. It is claimed that the feast began, according to the Synoptists, on Thursday evening, according to John, on Friday evening.

In order to a survey of the debates on this subject, we have first to ascertain the historical aspect of the case: *a.* the declarations of the New Testament, *b.* the controversies maintained by the ancient Church in regard to the Passover, *c.* the modern debates on the question of difference, *d.* the application of the discussion to the criticism of the New Testament Scriptures, particularly against the genuineness of John in the Tübingen School.

In respect to the different modern views we must consider

I. The assertion of the difference (Lücke, Neander, Krabbe, Theile, *etc.*, see Meyer [p. 601, 5th ed.]); and that generally in favor of John, it being assumed, in such case, that traces of the opposite view are also to be found in the Synoptists (Lücke, Bleek, Meyer, *etc.*); sometimes the side of the synoptical tradition is espoused (Baur, Schwegler).

II. Conceptions adverse to the difference.

First: Assumption of a double passover or banquet:

(*a*) The Jews deferred the passover; Jesus celebrated it at the legal time. The dominant view at the time of the Reformation [older Prot. divines], of late represented by Philippi [*Glaubenslehre*, I. p. 266 f. 2d ed.].

(*b*) Jesus kept the passover a day in advance of its time as μνημονευτικόν, Grotius, Hammond and others. (Casaubonus, Scaliger; placed by Meyer in the foregoing rubric.)

(*c*) The Caræans and Rabbinists did not agree concerning the time of the new moon (Iken).

(*d*) The δεῖπνον, John xiii., was not the paschal meal (Bengel, Wichelhaus).

Secondly: The Synoptists are to be explained in accordance with John:

(*a*) It is sought to obliterate the pretended difference in the Synoptists as much as possible by reference to Matthew xxvi. 5 (*not on the feast;* as if the Evangelist did not mean to say that this plan was frustrated), Mark xv. 21; Luke xxiii. 26.

(*b*) As a day of unleavened bread, the 14th Nisan also was celebrated as a feast by the Galileans; hence the Passover occurred on the evening of the 13th Nisan (Frisch, Rauch, Movers, Krafft, Maier [R. C.]).

Thirdly: John must be explained in accordance with the Synoptists: John speaks of another repast (Bengel, Wichelhaus). The eating of the passover denotes the eating of the *Khagiga;* the παρασκευή in John denotes the day of preparation for the Sabbath, the regular Friday as Sabbath-eve,—not the preparation-day previous to the first day of the passover (Wieseler, Tholuck and others). [The same view is maintained by Bynæus, Lightfoot, Reland, Olshausen, Hengstenberg, Luthardt, Hofmann, Riggenbach, Ebrard, Bäumlein, Robinson, Lange and myself. The most learned defence is given by Wieseler in his *Chronol. Synops.*, pp. 333 ff. and in Herzog's *Encycl.*, art. *Zeitrechnung*, vol. xxi. pp. 550 ff. Comp. also Lange on *Matthew*, pp. 454 ff. and Robinson's *Harmony*, pp. 216 ff., especially p. 218 where he fully discusses the phrase φαγεῖν τὸ πάσχα which ordinarily, but by no means necessarily means *to eat the paschal lamb on the 14th of Nisan,* but may mean also *to keep* the passover (2 Chr. xxx. 22, *they did eat the festival seven days*), or to eat the *paschal sacrifices,* called the *Khagigha.*—P. S.]

We hold to the assumption that φαγεῖν τὸ πάσχα, as an expression whose primitive force has been weakened by constant use, means: to observe or carry out the eating of the passover; *the like specific terms for a more general procedure grow into use everywhere in the ritual sphere.* As early as Exodus xii. 48 the terms: *to eat the passover,* and *to make* or *keep the passover* are used as reciprocal ideas. The expression: *to eat unleavened bread,* denotes the whole paschal celebration, Lev. xxiii. 6. *To appear before the Lord,* means: to perform divine service (Is. i. 12). *To spread forth the hands,* means: to pray (ver. 15). *To wash one's self,* means: to go through religious purification (ver. 16; John xiii. 10). The expressions: *to draw water* (see Is. xii. 3), *to light candles, to dwell in tents, etc.,* might become liturgical abbreviations with the Jews, as the terms: *to fast, to confess, to read mass,* and similar ones have done with the Roman Catholics.—It has been remarked that if the Jews had defiled themselves in the house of Pilate in the morning of the 14th Nisan (by entering a Gentile habitation, or a house where was leavened bread), they would still have been clean again after 6 o'clock in the evening. In opposition to this view, Lücke remarks: it is not proved, as Bynäus assumes, that entrance into a Gentile house defiled for the one day only. The contrary, however, is still less proved, and it is not supposable that contact with a Gentile house rendered unclean for a longer time than did contact with the carcass of a beast, which polluted only until the evening (Lev. xi. 40). We can suppose in general that all ordinary, merely levitical defilements continued only for one day; in cases of lengthier defilements, real sanitary considerations and the like were had in view. The plea that they were obliged to kill the Passover that afternoon, has been refuted by the observation that they could perform that duty by proxy. Lücke, indeed, mentions that in the case of a defilement in mass, substitution would be difficult to effect. It may be asked, however: when was the danger of defilement greater; if in the morning some few went into the Gentile house, or if the mass of the people, with the priests among them, ran bustling about upon Golgotha, the place of a skull, in the afternoon, at the very time when they are said to have slain the Passover? The case takes a much simpler aspect if we suppose that they were still mindful, in the morning, of the passover whereof they had partaken the evening before, and consequently desirous to keep themselves clean in order not to neutralize the benefit of the passover; whereas in the course of the day and toward its close, the passion attendant upon a turbulent execution rendered them more lax in their conduct.

In regard to the discussions upon this subject, see Meyer [p. 603 ff., 5th ed.]; Tholuck, p. 38 ff., and the account of the literature upon this topic in Lücke, p. 716.—On the paschal meal, see Comm. on *Matthew*.

[The critical and careful Dr. Robinson states his conclusion on this vexed question as follows (*Harmony*, p. 222): "After repeated and calm consideration, there rests upon my own mind a clear conviction, that there is nothing in the language of John, or in the attendant circumstances, which upon fair interpretation requires or permits us to believe, that the beloved disciple either intended to correct, or has in fact corrected or contradicted, the explicit and unquestionable testimony of Matthew, Mark and Luke." To this may be added a chronological consideration. According to Wieseler (to whom Lichtenstein, in Herzog's *Encycl.*, Vol. VI., 595 assents), Christ died Friday the 15th of Nisan A. U. C. 783, or A. D. 30. This was the 7th of April, and chronological calculations show that in the year 30, the 15th Nisan actually fell on a Friday, which was the case only once more (perhaps A. D. 34) between the years 28–36. See Wieseler's *Chron. Synopse*, p. 446, and in Herzog's *Encycl.* XXI., p. 550.—P. S.]

Ver. 29. **Pilate, therefore, went out unto them.**—On Pilate, see Comm. on *Matthew*, and that on *Luke*. "Bound to respect the Jewish customs (Joseph. *Antiq.*, XVI. 2, 3; *De Bello Jud.*, VI. 6, 2), the Procurator steps forth to them." Tholuck.

[Pontius Pilate was the sixth Roman governor (*ἡγεμών*), or, speaking more accurately, procurator (*ἐπίτροπος, procurator*) of Judæa, and held this office for ten years during the reign of Tiberius (A. D. 25 to 35). He is also mentioned by Tacitus in the famous passage: "The author of that name (*Christiani*) or sect was Christ, who was capitally punished under Tiberius by Pontius Pilate the procurator" (*Annal.* XV. 44). Josephus describes his administration as tyrannical and cruel: he insulted the Jews by introducing the images of Cæsar, gilt shields with the names of heathen deities, and misapplying the temple revenue to the construction of an aqueduct. He provoked several seditions and suppressed them by bloody violence. He was accused of maladministration, sent to Rome by Vitellius, President of Syria, and probably deposed. The latter accounts of an official report by Pilate of Christ's death to Tiberius and his suicide, are unreliable. The description of Josephus quite agrees with that of the Gospels, as has been satisfactorily shown in detail by the learned Lardner. Pilate had momentary impulses of justice and mercy; he openly pronounced the innocence of Christ, and made an attempt to rescue Him from the fanaticism of the Jews, whom he despised; but he was a selfish, unprincipled, worldly, Roman politician, skeptical or rather utterly indifferent to truth, cruel, weak and mean; and so he sacrificed innocence itself to the fear of losing his place and power, and, contrary to his better conviction, took part in the greatest crime ever committed. Yet after all his guilt was less than that of the Jewish priesthood who deliberately and malignantly delivered Christ into his hands and made him an instrument in the execution of their malignant hatred of their own Messiah (ch. xix. 11). The introduction of his name in the Apostles' and Nicene Creed, is intended not so much to single him out as specially guilty, as to mark the date of Christ's death under the hostile Roman world-power.—P. S.]

What accusation [*τίνα κατηγορίαν φέρετε*].—Though Pilate might have a general knowledge of the accusation, it was their place formally to present it here. Besides this, however, Pilate immediately observed, doubtless, that they came to him purposing, by a pompous and boisterous procession, to move him to confirm their sentence of death without more ado. His inquiry aims at thwarting this design from the beginning. Meyer.—"**Against this man** [*κατὰ τοῦ ἀνθρώπου τούτου*].—Spoken with indifference; not: against such a pious, celebrated man (Luther)."

Ver. 30. **If this person were not a malefactor** [*εἰ μὴ ἦν οὗτος κακοποιός*].—Here is contained the impetuous demand that Pilate should assent to their sentence of death without delay. Under the dominion of the Romans, the Jews had lost the *jus vitæ et necis* (according to the Talmud, forty years before the destruction of Jerusalem. Lightfoot). This they declared themselves, ver. 31. Consequently, the stoning of Stephen was a tumultuously illegal proceeding; as also the execution of James, according to Josephus (*Antiq.* xx. 9, 1). What still remained in the power of the Sanhedrin was 1: Disciplinary punishment pushed to the verge of capital punishment; 2. proposal for capital punishment. It made a difference whether their spiritual sentence of death was confirmed without further ceremony, or whether the governor, in accordance with Roman law, reserved to himself the right of cognizance and sentence. In the former case they could *stone* the condemned, according to Jewish custom; in the second case he was executed according to Roman custom, or, if extreme punishment was resorted to, crucified. The purpose of the Jews, therefore, is to obtain, by means of the impetuosity of their procession and demand, the ratification of their sentence. They had a twofold motive for this. In the first place, they were, no doubt, sensible of the difficulty of making the false accusation—charging Jesus with being a political criminal—good before Pilate, while they might guess that the latter would not recognize death as a punishment for merely religious or apparent transgressions. In the second place, their demand was at the same time intended to carry the right of a greater independence. He, therefore, is blindly to agree to their sentence. They seek, however, to make compensation for their bold demand by saying: we have delivered Him unto thee. One good turn deserves another. If we come before thy tribunal, that is an honor for thee, in return for which thou surely canst do us the honor to recognize our sentence without further ceremony. There was thus a close prospect of Christ's being stoned. But He had in spirit foreseen the turn affairs were now taking, and had announced His sufferings on the cross, chap. iii. 14; viii. 28; Matt. x. 38, *etc.* The cross was also included in the counsel of God, as the form of suffering in which Christ could manifest His glory quite otherwise than if subjected to a stoning (see Tholuck, p. 415).

Ver. 31. **Then take Him yourselves,** *etc.* [*λάβετε αὐτὸν ὑμεῖς, καὶ κατὰ τὸν νόμον ὑμῶν κρίνατε αὐτόν*].—*I. e.* if He is to pass for a criminal simply in accordance with your sentence, then execute Him also according to your law. According to Meyer, he means that they should try Him. But Pilate saw well that they had already done this. The *κρίνειν*, therefore, here denotes judicial proceedings in general, inclusive of punishment, but according to their law and right. The words certainly point derisively to the fact that they are not permitted to proceed to capital punishment (Lücke and others). Pilate meets fanatical presumption with frigid sarcasm.

The Jews therefore said unto him.—The *οὖν* denotes that Judaism must now come out openly. See note to ver. 30.—**It is not permitted us** [*ἡμῖν οὐκ ἔξεστιν ἀποκτεῖναι οὐδένα*].—Untenable limitations of this deliverance: 1. To execute capital punishment in the form of crucifixion (Chrysost.); 2. to execute a man on the feast-day (Semler); 3. to punish crimes of state (Krebs). That they now, in connection with this declaration of their death-sentence, brought forward the accusation against Jesus of political offences warranting death, results from the subsequent examination by Pilate ver. 34. Comp. Luke xxiii. 2. Meyer disallows the assumption of such an accusation, from a fear of "harmonistics." Pilate, he thinks, must have gathered this charge from the preceding demand for the guard. But a measure of police requires to be judicially formulated, and that by the accuser himself. Agreeably to the political accusation, a formal trial must now begin.

[Ver. 32. **That the saying of Jesus might be fulfilled,** *etc.*—See ch. xii. 32, 33; Matt. xx. 19, where Christ foretold His crucifixion. Had the Jews executed Him according to their law against false prophets and blasphemers, they would have *stoned* Him, as they repeatedly attempted to do (comp. ch. viii. 59; x. 31), and as they actually, in a tumultuary way, stoned Stephen (Acts vii.). Crucifixion was a Roman mode of punishment—the most cruel and disgraceful—for slaves, rebels and low criminals, such as pirates, assassins, deserters, but not for Roman citizens. Jesus on account of His Messianic claims must have appeared to the Roman governor as a rebel.—P. S.]

Ver. 33. **Art Thou the King of the Jews?**—The boundless perfidy of the Jewish accusation is distinctly reflected in Pilate's presentation of it. It is an ambiguous charge, forged out of Jesus' avowal that He is the Messiah; a charge embracing falsehood (since Jesus had no intention of being a political character), treason against their Messianic hope (which they abandoned in this case), and self-condemnation (since they hope for a political Messiah).—**Art Thou?** asks Pilate; not: sayest Thou that Thou art? The question need not necessarily be apprehended as purely derisive. Pilate might think thus: if His only offence was one of the tongue, He will deny that He is such a personage; but if He is a dangerous enthusiast, He will acknowledge the allegation. There is also, beyond a doubt, an incidental play of sarcasm.

Ver. 34. **Dost Thou say this of Thyself, or,** *etc.* [*'Απὸ σεαυτοῦ σὺ τοῦτο λέγεις ἢ ἄλλοι εἶπόν σοι περὶ ἐμοῦ*].—Design of the question. According to Olshausen, Neander (and my *Leben Jesu*, p. 1058) Jesus desires to ascertain in what sense Pilate puts the question: *whether in a Gentile-political* or *a Jewish-theocratical sense.** Meyer combats this assumption: 1. By the assertion that Jesus wished only to know the author of the accusation. The author, however, stood officially at the door. 2. By the declaration that it is not supposable that Pilate would thus separate the Messianic conceptions. He might, however, be taught thus to separate them. By the term: "King of the Jews," Pilate could understand nothing but a political seditionary urged by fanatical motives. The Sanhedrists knew this; but they also knew that Jesus claimed the Messiahship in another sense, and they now made use of the Messianic name to fit out a false accusation. Jesus could not acknowledge the Messianic conception of Pilate, but neither could He disown the theocratical Messianic conception. Hence, this distinction was to be made thoroughly clear. Like Meyer, Tholuck mistakes the decisive weight of Christ's distinction. It was necessary for Pilate to see that they were trying to humbug him by means of a perfidiously interpreted religious conception. And thus in the middle ages and in

*[So also Godet, Ewald, Alford. This is no doubt the proper view, and not set aside by the objections of Meyer (p. 610), who regards the question simply as intended to know the real author of the charge. Christ did not ask for information, which He did not need, but to bring out the distinction in the mind of Pilate, who seems to have suspected that Jesus was really what He was charged with being. This may be inferred also from the question, "Whence art Thou?" (xix. 8), his increasing desire to release Jesus (12), and his refusal to alter the inscription on the cross (22).—P. S.]

the time of the Reformation,—even down to the present day—the Hierarchs have, with evil consciousness, stamped reformation as revolution.

Ver. 35. **Am I a Jew?** [μήτι—looking to a negative answer—ἐγώ—a Roman governor—Ἰουδαῖός εἰμι].—With Roman pride he declares that he is not a Jew, *i. e.* that it is hence impossible that he should put the question in the Jewish sense;* he has but framed it in accordance with the statement made to him by the Prisoner's nation (τὸ ἔθνος τὸ σόν, sneeringly) and the high-priests. Compelled, however, to surmise the lurking of an ambiguity in this statement, he inquires, in a genuine Roman sense: **What hast Thou done?** [τί ἐποίησας].—Pilate's answer was manifestly inapplicable to the question: Art *thou* Mine accuser, or do the *Jews* accuse Me? It is appropriate, however, to the question: Hast thou, or have the Jews, formulated the accusation?

Ver. 36. **My kingdom is not of this world** [ἡ βασιλεία ἡ ἐμὴ οὐκ ἔστιν ἐκ τοῦ κόσμου τούτου. Ἐκ relates to origin and nature; yet Christ's kingdom, though not *of* this world, is yet *in* this world and *over* this world. Mark the emphatic repetition of *My*, and *this world*, as also the demonstrative ἐντεῦθεν in opposition to *cœlitus*.—P. S.].—This answer, the distinction between the purely theocratic and the purely political idea of a kingdom was manifestly contemplated from the very beginning, in the question of Jesus [ver. 34] and introduced by that question. First He acknowledges that He *has* a kingdom (*My kingdom*); passes on immediately, however, for Pilate's pacification, to the negative definition of His kingdom. It *is not of this world* as to its principle; it lays, therefore, in respect of its tendency, no claims to this world and does not, in respect of its character, come into collision with the existent secular empire of the Romans. Proof: If it *were* of this world, I should have fighters after the manner of the kingdoms of the world, and the very least that they could do would be, as worldly combatants, to prevent the base and contemptible resurrender of My person to the spiritual forum of the Jews.—**My servants** [οἱ ὑπηρέται οἱ ἐμοί].—Interpretations: 1. The servants that I *have*, disciples, angels (Lampe, Luthardt).† 2. The servants that I then *should* have (Meyer,‡ Tholuck [Lücke, Hengstenberg, Alford]). He, however, really has a kingdom, and He also really has servants. With such a fancy sketch: had I a worldly kingdom, and legions, My servants would liberate Me,—the innocence of Jesus would be poorly proved. But when He says: I have servants, but not one makes the slightest attempt at My liberation—this, to Pilate, who was acquainted with the nature of the disturbance, contains a striking proof of Jesus' innocence. The kingdom of which Christ speaks, however, does not wait for its beginning until the cessation of the kingdoms of the world (as Meyer asserts); neither does it itself become a world-kingdom (comp. Tholuck, p. 416). It conquers the world and makes the kingdoms of the world subject unto itself, in order to abolish and absorb the entire old form of the world in the kingdom of heaven.

But now is My kingdom not from hence, ἐντεῦθεν. Had Christ's kingdom been destined to be a worldly kingdom, it would have taken its rise at that very point in the crisis of the sufferings of the cross.

[This solemn declaration of Christ concerning the heavenly origin and unworldly character of His kingdom, settles in principle the question of Church and State in favor of separation and against penal laws for the punishment of heresy. Comp. Matt. xxii. 21, the wisest answer ever given to a question. Alford: "The word *now* (νῦν) has been absurdly pressed by the Romanist interpreters, to mean that at some time His kingdom would be ἐντεῦθεν—*i. e.*, ἐκ τοῦ κόσμου τούτου—as if its essential character could ever be changed: νῦν implies, 'as the case now stands,'—a *demonstratio ad oculos* from the fact that no servants of His had contended or were contending in His behalf; see similar usages of νῦν, ch. viii. 40; ix. 41; xv. 22," *etc.*—P. S.]

Ver. 37. **So, then,** [οὐκοῦν, *nonne igitur*] **Thou art a king** [βασιλεὺς εἶ σύ]?—Pilate asks, we doubt not, more out of curiosity and with the attention of an inquisitor, than with any mocking designs (Tholuck).

Yea, a king am I [σὺ λέγεις ὅτι βασιλεύς εἰμι ἐγώ. See TEXT. NOTE].—"So *Thou* art a king?" questions Pilate with ironical emphasis. "Thou sayest it," answers Jesus, with the accent of sublime self-assurance. And in face of the σύ He emphasizes the ἐγώ. Not only, however, does ὅτι recognize the utterance of Pilate—it likewise acknowledges the correctness of his deduction; from the kingdom of Jesus thou rightly inferrest His kingly dignity, says Jesus. Hence we represent ὅτι by *yea* (*Ja*).—Proof: **Thereunto have I been born and thereunto have I come into the world** [ἐγὼ εἰς τοῦτο γεγέννημαι καὶ εἰς τοῦτο ἐλήλυθα εἰς τὸν κόσμον].—According to Lücke and De Wette, Christ distinguishes His birth, and His official appearance. According to Meyer and Tholuck, the latter part of the sentence denotes the Divine Ambassador. Since, however, the birth also, as the birth of the Witness of the Truth, denotes a divine or divine-human birth, we likewise distinguish the expression of His ideal kingly nature (born), and of His historic Messianic mission (office). [Comp. here Alford].—**That I may bear witness unto the truth** [ἵνα μαρτυρήσω τῇ ἀληθείᾳ].—He is the faithful Witness, 2 Cor. i. 20; Rev. iii. 14.—**Every one that is of the truth** [πᾶς ὁ ὢν ἐκ τῆς ἀληθείας].—See John iii. 21. Chap. vi. 44; viii. 47; Rom. ii. 29.—**Heareth My voice** [ἀκούει μου τῆς φωνῆς].—Chap. x. 27. Why does He say this to Pilate? Calvin: He designs explaining why He finds so few adherents. Chrysost. and others: He is appealing to the Roman's consciousness, which is

* [Meyer just reversely: The answer of Pilate . . . indirectly denies the first, and consequently affirms the second question. But Lange is right. Pilate proudly and indignantly repudiates all connection with Jewish expectations, which he despised as sheer fanaticism.—P. S.]

† [Lampe: *Angels and disciples;* Luthardt and Stier: *angels;* Meyer: *disciples* only (ch. xii. 26; 1 Cor. iv. 1; 1 Tim. iv. 6), who are themselves not *of* this world, though *in* this world, ch. xvii. 16.—P. S.]

‡ [In the 5th ed., p. 611, Meyer rejects this view and understands by ὑπηρέται the disciples. See preceding footnote.—P. S.]

more susceptible than that of a Caiaphas. Bengel: *provocat a cæcitate Pilati ad captum fidelium.*—But manifestly He marks the moment in which Pilate is confronted with salvation, and the form under which salvation advances towards him. It is the form in which He is able to preach the Gospel to this man in this position. If thou art of the truth, if the impulse of truth is the vital impulse that influenceth thee, thou wilt know Me, and thou art saved.

Ver. 38. **What is truth?** [τί ἐστιν ἀλήθεια;]—The Evangelist plainly characterizes the meaning of the query by remarking that Pilate turned about upon uttering these words, and went out [καὶ τοῦτο εἰπὼν πάλιν ἐξῆλθεν]. No pause, no waiting for a reply, is spoken of. The word is thrown out; immediately he wheeled around upon his heel to tell the Jews without that he found no fault in Him. Thus is the patristic exposition, which makes him an eager inquirer after the truth (Chrysostom, Theodoret, Aretius and others) confuted, as also the assumption that he gave utterance to a feeling of disconsolateness (Olshausen). He has evidently no suspicion of subjective vital truth, and he understands, by truth, merely an objective school problem about which a practical man of business need not puzzle his wits. Not so much as a philosophizing skeptic is delineated—such an one as Pliny the elder (*ut solum certum sit, nihil esse certi*).* On the other hand, neither do we find that flight from truth, that was manifested in the case of the governor Felix, Acts xxiv. 25. The narrow, practical Roman mind that takes exception to every free investigation of truth, accounting such a fantasticalness from which it saves itself by observance of traditional ordinance, here expresses itself, as does, in measure, a Cicero as an Acataleptic [probabilist], the heathen Cæcilius in the *Octavius* of Minutius Felix, the Romish spirit continually, not only in its attitude toward the Reformation but also in modern times, as it stands confronted with Catholic philosophy.†

The question as to whence the Evangelist obtained his knowledge of this conversation, is difficult only when we forget that Christ's every step was watched by men who were of the truth; Strauss and Baur [and Scholten] alone have found the moment sufficiently obscure, in the light of the world's history, to induce them to assert this account to be a composition of the Evangelist, traceable to his peculiar tendency.

"Pilate's end corresponds with a life devoid of all foundation of objective [first of all, subjective] truth; according to classic authorities, he dies by suicide, in consequence of heavy misfortunes (Eusebius, *Hist. Eccles.* II. 7)." Tholuck.

I find no fault in Him [ἐγώ,—opposed to ὑμεῖς,—οὐδεμίαν εὑρίσκω ἐν αὐτῷ αἰτίαν].—The total result of the irrecoverable moment was his taking Jesus to be a good-natured but guiltless, perhaps rather tiresome, fanatic. With all this, his practical sense of justice finds clear utterance for an instant more—to be soon after caught in the net of a wretched policy. Soon after—for here, according to Luke, follows the sending of Jesus to the tribunal of Herod Antipas, Luke xxiii. 12. ["Pilate mocks both—the Witness of the Truth and the haters of the Truth. His conduct presents a pitiable specimen of the moral weakness of that spirit of worldly power, which reached its culminating point in the Roman empire." Alford.—P. S.]

Ver. 39. **But it is a custom of yours**, *etc.* [ἔστιν δὲ συνήθεια ὑμῖν, ἵνα ἕνα ἀπολύσω ὑμῖν ἐν τῷ πάσχα].—Pilate thinks to catch the Jews, and they catch him. Instead of simply administering justice and pronouncing the release of Jesus, he proposes to concede to them the ability of releasing Him themselves in right of a privilege obtained by them. The consequence of this half-measure is ruinous to the judge. It is, therefore, no good-natured love of justice that makes him resort to this expedient (Tholuck), but a preponderant consideration of policy. According to Matthew, he places Barabbas beside Jesus and bids the people choose, designing thus to make the acquittal of Jesus the more sure. The combination was probably first originated by the Jews, as John reports, and then formulated by Pilate (comp. Comm. on *Luke*). The Jewish custom of releasing a criminal was probably not an emanation from the paschal feast as a feast of reconciliation (Tholuck), but rather a dramatic Easter play, intended, perhaps, to illustrate the sparing of the Jewish first-born (see Comm. on *Matt.* at this passage).

At the passover [ἐν τῷ πάσχα. 'Εν is wanting in some MSS.].—"Pilate might thus express himself on the 14th as well as on the 15th." Meyer. *But according to the literal expression, the feast of the passover had really commenced.*

The king of the Jews [τὸν βασιλέα τῶν 'Ιουδ].—Meyer: "Unwise mocking bitterness." Perchance abortive cunning likewise. The King of the Jews He was considered by many among the people whose business it was to decide.

Ver. 40. **Then they cried out all again.**—The Evangelist's meaning seems to be either: they have cried, and cry again now; or: now that they again gave utterance to their sentiments, for the first time after the accusation, they did it with clamorous outcry. We apprehend the passage thus: they cried this time, and that *en masse* or with one voice.—**Saying: not this One but Barabbas** [μὴ τοῦτον, ἀλλὰ τὸν Βαραββᾶν. ἦν δὲ ὁ Βαραββᾶς λῃστής].—On Barabbas see Comm. on *Matthew.* It is the first practical fault of the Roman spirit to set criminals side by side with putative idealists, and to release the former rather than the latter. [Ewald suggests that Barabbas was the son of a Rabbi (Abba was a Rabbinic title of honor), and a leader in the insurrection (Mark xv. 7) against Pilate, arising out of his misappropriation of a part of the temple revenue to the construction of an aqueduct (Joseph. *De Bello Jud.* II. 9, § 4); and thus explains the eagerness

* [Meyer and Alford likewise derive the question of Pilate from indifferentism rather than skepticism. "It expresses, not without scoff and irony, that truth can never be found: and is an apt representative of the state of the polite Gentile mind at the time of the Lord's coming. It was rather an inability than an unwillingness to find the truth." Comp. the saying of Felix to Paul, Acts xxiv. 25.—P. S.]

† [Dr. Lange has in view Lammenais, Hermes, Günther, and other recent Roman Catholic philosophers, whose speculations have been condemned by the pope.—P. S.]

with which the Sanhedrin and the people demanded his release. On the significance of the name *Barabbas* (Son of the Father, with or without *Jesus* in the Synoptists) and the unconsciously representative character and release of this rebel and robber, as contrasted with the character and condemnation of the obedient and holy Jesus, see notes on Matt. xxvii. 16, p. 511, and the HOM. AND PRACT. below. *Ludit in humanis divina potentia rebus.*—P. S.]

Chap. xix. 1. **Then therefore Pilate took Jesus and scourged Him** [ἔλαβεν οὖν ὁ Πιλ. τὸν Ἰησ. καὶ ἐμαστίγωσεν].—The second wretched politic attempt of the Roman, according to John. He took, or received, Jesus and scourged Him. The sending of Jesus before Herod's tribunal, as also the hand-washing, likewise belong in this category. With this attempt he hopes to satisfy the vindictiveness of Jesus' foes, perhaps even to excite their compassion—and so much the more, since according to his ideas, Jesus, by this ignominious treatment, would be stripped of dignity in the eyes of the people and made of none effect. On the act of scourging see Comm. on *Matthew* [p. 512]. As also on the different signification assumed by the scourging according to the Synoptists and according to John.

[Pilate probably subjected Jesus to this disgraceful and horrible punishment in the vain hope of satisfying His accusers and moving them to compassion. The Roman mode of scourging is here meant, which was much more cruel than the Jewish; it was never inflicted upon Roman citizens, but only upon foreigners and slaves whose lives were considered of no account, either as a torture to extort a confession, or as a correction preparatory to crucifixion. The body was stripped, tied in a stooping posture to a low block or pillar, and the bare back lacerated by an unlimited number of lashes with rods or twisted thongs of leather, so that the poor sufferers frequently fainted and died on the spot. —P. S.]

Vers. 2, 3. **And the soldiers,** *etc.* [καὶ οἱ στρατιῶται πλέξαντες στέφανον ἐξ ἀκανθῶν, κ. τ. λ.].—See Comm. on *Matthew* [p. 514]. "The derisive blow on the cheek [ἐδίδουν αὐτῷ ῥαπίσματα] is substituted for the kiss."

Ver. 4. **I bring Him forth to you** [Ἴδε ἄγω ὑμῖν αὐτὸν ἔξω ἵνα γνῶτε, κ. τ. λ.]—According to Matthew, the scourging of the Lord had been consummated before the eyes of the people (not "in the court of the prætorium"). For after the scourging, the soldiers had led Him into the prætorium, probably in a mocking procession as though the king were brought into his castle. The scene probably took place in the fortress-court or in a hall. Therefore we read here: "I bring Him forth unto you."—**That ye may know.**—The Jews not possessing the right of capital punishment, the return of the person of Jesus to them was a declaration that He was free from the offence with which they charged Him. Pilate, however, utters his testimony unconditionally: **no fault** [οὐδεμίαν αἰτίαν].—The leading forth has been in different ways misinterpreted in regard to its intention,—by Gerhard, for instance: they should see how compliant he would be in punishing Him, if he found any fault in Him.

Ver. 5. **Behold, the man.** [Ἴδε, or rather Ἰδοὺ ὁ ἄνθρωπος, see TEXT. NOTES].—*Ecce Homo!* "But from the Lord cometh what the tongue shall speak." (Prov. xvi. 1 [Luther's Bible. "The preparation of the heart in man, and the answer of the tongue, is from the Lord." E. V.]). Pilate's words, unconsciously to himself, assume, like his superscription and the sentence of Caiaphas, a significance corresponding to the great situation. [An involuntary prophecy of heathenism, as the word of Caiaphas (ch. xi. 51, 52) was an involuntary prophecy of hostile Judaism.—P. S.] The word seems to express compassion; at all events it is designed to excite that emotion. There is no doubt as to the sense: there ye have Him again, and what a pitiable object! Take Him thus and let Him go. He forebodes not that Jesus is indeed the Man κατ' ἐξοχήν [the one perfect Man], who, through his wicked pliancy, steps forth so outraged in His outward appearance.

Ver. 6. **The high-priests and the officers.** —They cried as leaders—which does not exclude the joint crying of the assembled populace.

Take Him yourselves and crucify Him. —Pilate still makes a stand at the present stage, with a feeling of his own authority that causes him to deride the impotence of the Jews.

Ver. 7. **We have a law** [ἡμεῖς νόμον ἔχομεν].—The political accusation having borne no fruit, they now come out with the religious accusation in pursuance of which Jesus, at least according to *their* law, must die (as a blasphemer of God, namely, Lev. xxiv. 16, doubtless also as a false prophet, Deut. xviii. 20). The ἡμεῖς, *etc.*, defiantly arrayed against the ἐγώ—αἰτίαν of Pilate. They feel confident of Pilate's obligation to respect their law. See Joseph. *Antiq.*, 16, 2, 3.

Ver. 8. **When Pilate—he was the more afraid** [μᾶλλον ἐφοβήθη].—Their saying, in the first place, entirely missed the designed effect; it was productive of the opposite effect. Hitherto Pilate had been restrained by a *fear of conscience or of law* alone; now *religious fear* supervened, in connection with a *fear* of *Jesus' personality* itself, of which latter sentiment he now became fully conscious. According to Matthew, the message of his wife has already been received, hence is jointly influential.

Ver. 9. **Again into the pretorium** [καὶ εἰσῆλθεν εἰς τὸ πραιτώριον πάλιν]—We must supply in imagination the leading of Jesus before Pilate, in order to a fresh, private examination.—**Whence art Thou?** [πόθεν εἶ σύ].—The inquiry after the *whence* of Christ is indefinitely framed, in accordance with the Jews' accusation and Pilate's fear. Meyer: He pictures to himself the υἱὸς θεοῦ after the analogy of the heathen *heroes*, and fears the vengeance of the Jewish God Jehovah. Religious awe, in a moment of superstitious excitement, pictures to itself all manner of things, however, and nothing quite distinctly. Whether He were a Magus or a hero, an angel, after the religion of the land, or a divine apparition,—it now seemed very possible to him that there might be something super-terrestrial in the appearance of the Man;—and he had so unconcernedly caused Him to be scourged. In any case, celestial vengeance seemed to threaten him. Whether the πόθεν, *etc.*, is timid (Meyer) or cautiously sifting, is difficult to decide; fear and prudence may be united in it.

No answer ['Ο δὲ Ἰησοῦς ἀπόκρισιν οὐκ ἔδωκεν αὐτῷ].—Luthardt: He would not answer him, in order that He might not step in the way of God's will. An abstractly supernaturalistic view. If the answer had been a moral duty, no religious duty would have stood in the way of it. God had power, notwithstanding any answer of His, to accomplish His will. Under such a supposition as Luthardt's, Jesus would in no case have dared answer anything. He was silent, "as also before Herod and Caiaphas, because He had already testified enough for the susceptible; and for him who had turned his back upon the King of truth, neither could another testimony avail." Tholuck. Jesus could foresee that this transaction led to nothing. Pilate, with his question, abandoned his judicial position, for he was bound to acquit Jesus not on account of His danger-menacing Godhead, but on account of His *protection-demanding human innocence.* [Alford: "This silence was the most emphatic answer to all who had ears to hear it,—was a reference to what He had said before, ch. xviii. 37, and so a witness to His divine origin. Would any *mere man*, of true and upright character, have refused an answer to such a question, so put? Let the modern rationalist consider this."—P. S.]

Ver. 10. **Dost Thou not speak unto me?** [ἐμοὶ οὐ λαλεῖς].—Himself full of fear, he exacted considerations of fear from Jesus. He boasts of his power [ἐξουσίαν ἔχω] instead of remembering his duty, and of his freedom to release Jesus [ἀπολῦσαί σε], while the weight of temptation drives him in his impotence resistlessly forward. Ἐμοί has the emphasis of offended authority [pride of office], making efforts at once *terrifying* and *alluring*. *Crucify, release*, a more probable sequence than the converse. See the TEXTUAL NOTES. [The opposite order is better attested by external authority (א. A. B., *etc.*), and more natural, as *releasing* appeals more to the prisoner, and *crucifying* follows as the other alternative.—P. S.]

Ver. 11. **No power over Me unless it had been given,** *etc.* [οὐκ ἔχεις ἐξουσίαν οὐδεμίαν κατ' ἐμοῦ, εἰ μὴ ἦν σοι δεδομένον ἄνωθεν].—δεδομένον. Namely, the exercise of power—if *that* had not been *given* thee. [The neuter is more general than δεδομένη, and includes, as Meyer says, τὸ ἐξουσιάζειν κατ' ἐμοῦ.—P. S.].—**From above.**—Not: from the Roman emperor (Usteri), or from the Sanhedrin (Semler), but from God (chap. iii. 3, 31). [Grotius aptly: *inde scilicet, unde ortus sum;* ἄνωθεν is a precise anwer to the πόθεν of Pilate (ver. 10). It is equivalent to ἐκ θεοῦ or ἐκ τοῦ πατρός μου, but this Pilate would not have understood.—P. S.].—**No power.**—Ἐξουσία is interpreted:

1. As judicial authority, by Luther, Calvin, Baur and others. Thus, because thou hast this authority from above, the misuse of it is sin; the authors of this offence, however, the Jews, have the greater guilt.

2. Actual power, Beza, Gerhard, Tholuck: It is the providence of God that I, through the obduracy of My people, have fallen into thy hands. With this interpretation the διὰ τοῦτο [*on this account*, because of the power being given thee] is certainly better explained, yet this actual power rests upon the magisterial authority.

He that delivereth Me unto thee; ὁ παραδιδούς [the present, because the act is just going on].—Bengel, Meyer [Lampe, Alford, Ewald, Hengstenberg]: The high-priest [Caiaphas]; Tholuck collectively: The hardened Jewish nation. [Still others the Sanhedrin; some, unaptly, Judas who is now out of sight]. The declaration of Pilate ver. 35 is pertinent: Thy nation and the high-priests have delivered Thee unto me. Wherefore has the deliverer (ὁ παραδιδούς) the **greater sin** [μείζονα ἁμαρτίαν ἔχει]? Explanations:

1. Euthymius: Pilate's guilt rests more upon softness and weakness.

2. Grotius: Because he could not know, as well as the Jews, who Christ was.

3. Lampe: Because the Jews had not received this power from God.

4. Meyer: Because thou hast the disposal of Me not from any sovereign power of thine own, but by divine authorization.

But the abuse of his judicial authority does not excuse him. Decisive in the first place is the fact that Pilate is an ignorant Gentile, the deliverer Jewish; then, that the Jews claim, with a certain legal title, that he has but to execute their sentence. Pilate found himself in no clear position. He had to do, not with a Roman, but with a Jew, and not with a civil law, but with a religious accusation in regard to which the Jewish tribunal had already decided. This might readily mislead him in his simple judicial duty, and it was his fatality. His guilt would be still less than it really was, had he not been aware that they had delivered Jesus for envy, had not Jesus made so strong an impression on him, and had he not really known it to be his duty to release Him. Even in the case of the Jews there was also taken into account a consideration of excuse because of ignorance, which consideration exhibited the guilt of many of them as other than final obduracy. See Acts iii. 17; comp. Luke xxiii. 34. Meyer, in a note [p. 621], has with reason set aside the interpretation of Baur.

Ver. 12. **For the sake of this;** ἐκ τούτου.—Not: *from thenceforth* [E. V. and most commentators], but: for the sake of this saying [Meyer, Stier, Luthardt, comp. vi. 66.—P. S.]. It cast a bright accidental light upon his obscure, fateful, perilous situation, that for an instant marked the path of duty as a path of deliverance.—**Pilate sought to release Him.**—Ἐζήτει certainly cannot denote simply an increased striving (Lücke), it being expressive of a distinct act immediately provocative of the most excited outburst on the part of the Jews. But the interpretation: he demanded that He should be released (Meyer), gives rise to the supposition that Pilate must needs ask the Jews' sanction to the release of Jesus. This word, to which not sufficient regard is paid, means rather: he was really on the point of ordering the release of Christ. Perhaps he caused the guard to fall back, or he may have stated to the Jews that they might go home, that he would leave Jesus behind in the prætorium, under his own protection. At all events, here it is that the tragic knot was tied. The liberation of Jesus seems already decided.

But the Jews cried out, saying.—Now, in the uproar of the Jews, the whole storm of hell rises. At first the high-priests and officers led the voices,—now the entire mass is full of excitement and needs no starter. The demoniacal syllogism with which they debauch Pilate, scarcely originates, however, in the brain of the populace. The hierarchs take refuge in the political accusation, declaring: Jesus is a revolutionist against the emperor, and if thou let Him go, thou comest thyself under suspicion of treason to the emperor. Now the emperor was—Tiberius. The threat of being accused to this man of treason fells the weak courtling. On Pilate as manifoldly guilty, especially of extortions and outrages: Joseph., *Antiq.* XVIII. 3, 1 ff.; Philo, *De leg. ad Caj.*, 1033; on the suspicious character of Tiberius, Sueton., *Tib.*, 58; Tacit., *Ann.*, III. 38. *Majestatis crimen omnium accusationum complementum erat:*—Φίλος Καίσαρος, a predicate of honor, since the time of Augustus conferred, by the emperor himself and by others, partly upon prefects and legates, partly upon allies (Ernesti, *Suetonius, Excurs.* 15)." Tholuck. According to Meyer [and Alford], the term means simply: *loyal* to the emperor; unfavorable to this view is the technical use of the predicate: *amicus Cæsaris.* Even if Pilate did not formally possess the title, it is alluded to.—**Speaketh against**—is at variance with—**the emperor** (ἀντιλέγει). Meyer: He *declareth* against the emperor, not: he *rebelleth* (Kuinoel), *etc.* But *rebelling* is exactly what *declaring* against the sovereign means.

Ver. 13. **When Pilate therefore heard these words.**—Pilate's playing with the situation is past; now the situation plays with him. First he said—not asked—: what is *truth?* Now his frightened heart, to which the emperor's favor is the supreme law of life, says: what is *justice?* "He who fears not God above all things, is condemned to fear man." Tholuck.*—**He brought Jesus forth.**—Since the last examination, ver. 8 ff., he had left Him in the pretorium. —**And sat down in the judgment-seat** [ἐκάθισεν ἐπὶ βήματος εἰς τόπον λεγόμενον λιθόστρωτον]. — "Sentence was pronounced *sub divo*, not *ex æquo loco*, but *superiore;* there stood the judgment-seat on a floor of mosaic: *pavimentum, tessellatum* (Sueton. *Cæsar*, chap. 46)." Tholuck. [Such a tesselated pavement Julius Cæsar carried about on his expeditions, Suet. *Cæs.*, c. 46.]—**But in the Hebrew, Gabbatha.**—"The name Γαββ. must not be derived from גִּבְעָה, hill [so Hengstenberg], —against which derivation the double β would militate (comp. Γαβαθᾶ, Jos. *Antiq.* v. 1, 29), but from גַּב, ridge, hump." Meyer. Is it not, perhaps, still more probably an Aramaic modification of גַּבְהָה, *altum, altitudo?* [Alford from גָּבַהּ, *altus fuit*, Ewald from the root גָּבַע with a signification similar to λιθόστρωτον.—P. S.]

Ver. 14. **It was the preparation-day.**—Παρασκευὴ τοῦ πάσχα, see Comm. on *Matt.* [pp. 455, 468]; *John* on chap. xiii. [p. 405].

1. Friday in the passover-season, or paschal week, as a day of preparation for the Sabbath. Wieseler, p 336 f; Wichelhaus, p. 209 f. Only apparently a modification is Tholuck's explanation: The Paschal preparation-day as the preparation for the Sabbath falling in the Paschal season; since the terms Friday and Sabbath preparation-day were of necessity synonymous to the Jews, just as to the Germans the terms *Samstag* and *Sonnabend* are.

[This is the correct view, and is maintained also by Olshausen, Luthardt, Hengstenberg, Riggenbach, Robinson (*Harmony*, p. 219). The term παρασκευή here does not correspond (as Meyer, Lücke, Alford and others assert) to the Hebrew עֶרֶב הַפֶּסַח, "*the vigil of the Passover,*" "*passover-eve*" (mentioned in the Talmud, see Buxtorf, *Lex.*, p. 1765, but nowhere in the Bible), but to עֲרוּבְתָא, *eve*, as being the עֶרֶב הַשַּׁבָּת, *eve of the Sabbath* (see Buxtorf, *Lex.*, p. 1659). It is equivalent to προσάββατον, *fore-sabbath* (Mark xv 42; Judith viii. 6), or προεόρτιον, as Philo (*De vita contempl.*, p. 616) calls it. In other words, it is a technical Jewish name for *Friday*, just as the corresponding terms in the Syriac and Arabic, and as the German *Sonnabend* (Sunday-Eve) is used for *Samstag* (Saturday). It was so called from the Jewish habit of preparing the meals (הכין, παρασκευάζειν) on Friday for the Sabbath, since it was forbidden to kindle a fire on the Sabbath (Ex. xvi. 5; Joseph. *Antiq.* xvi. 6, 2). This is the uniform meaning of παρασκευή in all other passages of the New Testament where it occurs, *viz.*, in this very chapter, vers. 31, 32; Matt. xxvii. 62; Luke xxiii. 54; Mark xv. 42 (where it is expressly explained for non-Jewish readers, as being=προσάββατον). Why should our passage be an exception? The addition τοῦ πάσχα, which John always uses in the wider sense for the whole feast (not for the eating of the paschal lamb), makes no difference: it is simply the *Paschal Friday*, or *Easter-Friday*, as we speak of *Easter-Sunday, Easter-Monday, Easter-Tuesday*.* We have here a very significant hint that after all John is in perfect harmony with the Synoptists on the day of Christ's death, which was not the 14th, but the 15th of Nisan, or the first day of the paschal festival. John probably chose this very term to expose the awful inconsistency and crime of the Jews in putting the Lord and Saviour to death on the day when they should have prepared for the holy Sabbath—doubly sacred now as being at the same time the first day of the great passover.—P. S.]

2. Meyer following Lücke, Bleek, *etc.* [p. 623, comp. pp. 600 seq., 5th ed., where the discussions are]: "In order that the παρασκευή might

* [Of John Knox it is truly said: "He never feared the face of man." The reason was because he feared God. Only he is truly free and independent of men, who feels bound in God and dependent on Him.—P. S.]

* [Robinson, Tholuck, Wieseler and others, quote also as a parallel σάββατον τοῦ πάσχα in Ignatius *Ep. ad Phil.*, c. 13; but this is not the Sabbath of the Easter-week, but the Saturday preceding Easter-Sunday, Easter-eve.—P. S.]

not be apprehended as the weekly one, referable to the Sabbath (vers. 31, 42; Luke xxiii. 54; Mark xv. 42; Matt. xxvii. 62; Joseph. *Antiq.* xvi. 6, 2 al.), but that it might be regarded as connected with the feast-day of the *Passover*, John expressly adds τοῦ πάσχα. Undoubtedly it was a Friday, consequently Preparation-day for the Sabbath also—this reference, however, is not the one to be pointed out here; the true reference is to the *paschal feast* coming in on the evening of the day,—of which feast the first day fell, according to John, upon the Sabbath." [So also Alford.]

This view is contradicted:

(1) By the fact that in that case John would, shortly after, ver. 31 [ἐπεὶ παρασκευή ἦν, and ver. 42, διὰ τὴν παρασκευὴν τῶν Ἰουδ.], have used the word παρασκευή in another sense.

(2) That he then in ver. 31 would have been obliged to write παρασκευὴ τοῦ σαββάτου* in order to distinguish between the two senses.

(3) That, therefore, according to vers. 31, 42, παρασκευή had a thoroughly fixed signification and denoted the day of preparation for the Sabbath, in consequence of which fact, therefore, the παρασκευὴ τοῦ πάσχα is also to be interpreted as the day of preparation for the Sabbath of the paschal season.

(4) That John elsewhere uses the word πάσχα as a term for the ἑορτή, the paschal season. So, expressly, chap. ii. 23; vi. 4; xi. 55, 56; xviii. 39. And hence, assuredly, also here.

It was going on towards the [*es war gegen die*] **sixth hour** [ὥρα ἦν ὡς ἕκτη. This is the correct reading instead of ὥρα δὲ ὡσεὶ ἕκτη. —P. S.]—See Note on chap. i. 39 [p. 93.]; Comm. on *Matthew* at this passage [xxvii. 45, p. 525, Am. ed.]; *Mark* [xv. 25, p. 152]. According to Jewish reckoning it was on the way to 12 o'clock, *i. e.*, between 9 and 12 o'clock. On the difficulty of this notice, see the passages cited. [The difficulty is this, that according to John the hour of crucifixion was the *sixth*, *i. e.*, (counting with the Jews from sunrise) 12 o'clock of our time; while according to Mark xv. 25 it was the *third*, *i. e.*, 9 o'clock, A. M., with which the statement of Matt. xxvii. 45, and Luke xxiii. 44, agrees, that at the sixth hour or noon, when Jesus had already for some time been hanging on the cross, darkness covered the land for three hours, and that Jesus died about the ninth hour (*i.e.*, 3 P. M.); consequently according to the Synoptists the Saviour suffered for nearly six hours on the cross, according to John only about three hours.—P. S.] *Solutions* of the apparent contradiction:

1. Assumption of a writing-error (Euseb. and others): ϛ [6], instead of γ [3].

[So also Theophylact, Severus, Beza (ed. 5th), Bengel, Alford, Robinson, *Harmony*, p. 226, where Robinson says: "The ὥρα τρίτη of Mark, as the hour of crucifixion, is sustained by the whole course of the transactions and circumstances; as also by the fact stated by Matthew, Mark, and Luke, that the darkness commenced at the *sixth* hour, after Jesus had already for some time hung upon the cross. The reading ἕκτη in John is, therefore, probably an early error of transcription for τρίτη (ϛ for Γ). Indeed, this last reading is found in Cod. Bezæ and Cod. Reg. 62, as well as several other authorities; so that its external weight is marked by Griesbach as nearly or quite equal to that of the common reading, while the internal evidence in its favor is certainly far greater." But ἕκτη is undoubtedly the correct reading as far as *external* authority goes. See TEXT. NOTE, and Tischend. ed. VIII. *in loc.*—P. S.]

2. Roman reckoning is employed=6 A. M. (Rettig, Tholuck, Hug, and others). [So also Olshausen, Wieseler, Ewald, Townson, Wordsworth.—P. S.] But after the examination before Caiaphas, the first examination before Pilate, the examination before Herod (Luke xxiii. 9), the further proceedings in Pilate's presence, the scourging and mocking, it is impossible that it was only *approaching* or *about* 6 o'clock in the morning, since the final session in presence of Caiaphas did of itself presuppose the dawn of day, to make it legal. [Besides, this view creates the difficulty of too long a period (three hours) intervening between the sentence of death and the crucifixion. It is also very unlikely that John, with the Synoptical statements before him, should without any notice have introduced a different mode of reckoning, and with it an element of confusion rather than rectification.—P. S.]

3. It was about the sixth hour of the paschal feast, reckoned from midnight (Hofmann, Lichtenstein).* The passover, however, did not begin at midnight, but on the previous evening at about 6 o'clock; irrespective of the fact that this "would be an unprecedented way of reckoning hours, namely as belonging to the *feast*, not to the *day* (in opposition to chap. i. 39; iv. 6, 52)." Meyer.

4. "Again a difference from the Synoptists, according to whom (see Mark xv. 25, with which Matt. xxvii. 45; Luke xxiii. 44 agree) Jesus is crucified as early as 9 o'clock in the morning." (Meyer and others.)

5. The third hour of Mark is the third quarter of the day (Aret., Grot. [Calvin, Wetstein], and others), against which Mark xv. 33. ["And when the sixth hour was come, there was darkness over the whole land until the ninth hour. And at the ninth hour Jesus cried," *etc.*]

6. An indefinite computation of hours, according to which the sections of time between the third, sixth and ninth hours are indefinitely stated. Thus the third hour in Mark may mean: nine o'clock was past,—it was between nine and twelve o'clock when the crucifixion of Christ began; and this is the more probable since Mark regards the scourging as the prelude to the crucifixion, which, when the former took place, was really already decided (see ver. 15). And so the words of John: it was towards the sixth hour: it was past nine o'clock and approaching noon when Pilate—the scourging being accomplished, and the Scourged One having been presented to the populace—spoke the final words upon which

* [Or in ver. 14, ἦν δὲ παρασκευὴ τοῦ πάσχα, ὅ ἐστι προσάββατον τοῦ πάσχα, comp. Mark xv. 42.—P. S.]

* [In this case τοῦ πάσχα must be disconnected from παρασκευή, and connected with ὥρα in this way: ἦν δε παρασκευή, τοῦ πάσχα ὥρα ἦν ὡς ἕκτη, *i. e.*, it was preparation-day (Friday), about the sixth hour of the paschal feast (counting from midnight). Ingenious, but very artificial and without a parallel for such reckoning. Hofmann, of Erlangen, proposed this view in an article of the Erlangen *Zeitschrift f. Prot. und Kirche*, 1853, p. 260 ff., and again in his *Schriftbeweis*. Lichtenstein adopts it in his article *Jesus Christus*, in Herzog's *Theol. Encycl.*, Vol. VI., p. 595.—P. S.]

the procession to Golgotha immediately followed. John's employment of the *later* indefinite hour-date is accounted for by the thought; they now hastened to the close, because, with noon, the second, already more Sabbatic, half of the παρασκευή was approaching. Mark's choice, on the other hand, of the *earlier* indefinite hour-date is accounted for by the significant antithesis which he wishes to institute between the third and the sixth hour.

[This solution of the difficulty has been adopted by Godet, who remarks that the apostles did not count with the watch in their hands. So also Hengstenberg, who, however, very mechanically splits the difference and fixes the crucifixion at half-past ten! In this case the statements both of Mark and John would be wrong. Meyer rejects all attempts at reconciliation and gives John the preference over the Synoptists. But Lange's view has a strong support in the ὡς or ὡσεὶ of John, which excludes *strict* accuracy on his part and leaves room for *some* approach at least towards the third hour of Mark. At noon Christ must certainly have been already hanging on the cross; for this is the unanimous testimony of the Synoptists.—P. S.]

Behold, your king [Ἴδε ὁ βασιλεὺς ὑμῶν]!—Pilate, inwardly overcome, designs, by this mocking of the Jews, not only to *mask* his disgrace but also to *avenge* it; it may be that these words unfold even this threatening thought: your *King*, then, shall first be crucified, and after Him, *yourselves*. At all events, he shifts the guilt to their shoulders.

Ver. 15. **Away with Him, away with Him, crucify Him** [Ἆρον ἆρον, σταύρωσον αὐτόν]!—The words: ἆρον, ἆρον!* present to us something more than the meaning: Away with Him! away with Him! At this last moment there is still a mutual effort to shuffle off the legal responsibility upon each other. Pilate's meaning is: if He is to be executed, *ye* may execute Him. The meaning of the Jews is: *thou* shalt have Him, *thou* shalt crucify Him! It was only in this way that they could be assured of Pilate's inability to institute later a review of the proceedings. *The Hierarchs make the same claim again at the present day: the rude State, the Pilate of the Middle Ages, adjusted the terrors of the Inquisition in accordance with the laws then existing.* The brief, passionate exclamation is likewise expressive of the bitterness called forth by the word of Pilate: Behold, your King!

Shall I crucify your king?—This question of Pilate is an intimation of his last wavering in resolve—a wavering in all probability particularly induced by the message of his wife. See Comm. on *Matthew*. Not merely a "reverberation" of the preceding derisive words, but also a distincter expression of the same idea: If He is to be crucified as your King in your sense, He must, according to your law, die as a *religious* criminal. Hence the high-priest's reply.

We have no king but the emperor [Οὐκ ἔχομεν βασιλέα εἰ μὴ Καίσαρα].—*I. e.* He shall and must die as a political seditionary. At the same time it is the consummation of the godless perfidy with which they disclaim their own Messianic hope, deny the Messianic claims, traduce the Lord as a seditionary, whilst they themselves feign a zeal of the most loyal fidelity demonstrable by subjects, with which they would fain shame and terrify even the Roman governor. [Some of these very men who here made a hypocritical show of loyalty to carry their point and to make a tool of Pilate, perished afterwards miserably in rebellion against Cæsar. Bengel: *Jesum negant usque eo, ut omnino Christum negant.* Alford: "A degrading confession from the *chief priests* of that people of whom it was said, 'The Lord your God is your King,' 1 Sam. xii. 12."—P. S.]

Ver. 16. **Then therefore he delivered Him up unto them, to be crucified.**—The repeated threatening hint of the high-priest completes the conquest of Pilate. A compromise results, in pursuance of which Christ is delivered (παρέδωκεν not simply *yielded*, after Grotius and others) to the high-priests, to be taken to their place of execution, and is, nevertheless, crucified by Roman soldiers, according to Roman criminal law. It is to be presumed that Pilate combined the delivery of Jesus to the Jews with the symbolical act of washing his hands (according to Matthew). This compromise is one of the many legal contradictions in the history of the crucifixion, by means of which contradictions the *summum jus* of the ancient world is converted into the *summa injuria*. Comp. Comm. on *Matthew*, xxvii. 22 [pp. 512, 514, Am. Ed.]. Other contradictions: Declared innocent, and yet sent before another tribunal, and yet scourged. Scourged in order that He might be released, and yet afterwards crucified. Contradictions of the forum, of sentence, of cognizance, of the degree of punishment, of the form of punishment.

They therefore took Jesus [παρέλαβον οὖν τὸν Ἰησοῦν. Ver. 16 ought to close with σταυρωθῇ, and παρέλαβον begin the next section. So Tischendorf, Alford, Westcott and Hort.—P. S.] The *high-priests*, not (as De Wette thinks) the *soldiers*.—**And led Him away** [καὶ ἀπήγαγον—very doubtful, see Text. Notes.—P. S.] The taking was also consummated with the declaration: His blood be upon us, *etc.* (see Comm. on *Matt.*). On the site of Golgotha, outside of the city, see Comm. on *Matt.* [520 ff.] "The site of the place, without the city, is likewise attested by Heb. xii. 12." Tholuck.

DOCTRINAL AND ETHICAL.

1. By many supplementary touches John presents us with the clearest view of the incidents of the *secular trial* undergone by Jesus. To these supplementary traits belongs, above all, the gradation of the Jews' accusation.

(1) They charge Jesus with being an ecclesiastical criminal whom they have already sentenced, and whose sentence Pilate has but to confirm. (2) In the most ambiguous sense: With making Himself the King of the Jews. (3) With being an ecclesiastical criminal,—because He had made Himself the Son of God. (4) With being a political revolutionist,—because He claimed to be the King of the Jews.

*[Tischendorf, Alford and Westcott and Hort put no comma between the two ἆρον, which were no doubt spoken in rapid succession with all the vehemence of furious passion.—P. S.]

These form two accusations which they alternately bring forward: a Jewish one and a Roman political one. The first time each is couched in ambiguous and innuendo-like terms; the second time each is formulated in calumnious audacity.

Another of these supplementary traits is the conflict maintained between Pilate and the high-priests throughout the entire procedure—a conflict in which the personal character of Pilate, as well as that of the high-priests, is most clearly reflected; as is also the more general character of a vain, worldly state-craft in its haughty and nevertheless impotent struggle with a crafty hierarchical power and its fanatical tools in the popular life. Then those moments also stand out clearly, in which Christ is, as a delinquent, by the Jews delivered to, or pressed upon, Pilate; by Pilate delivered to, or pressed upon, the Jews, —down to the moment when a kind of compromise is effected. From vers. 28-31 Pilate refuses judgment. From vers. 32-38 he receives the Accused, granting Him a pre-examination; then, however, *he* does not simply acquit Him, but seeks to entrap the Jews and, by the offer of presenting Jesus to them for their paschal procession, which was annually graced by some recipient of governmental pardon, to move *them* to acquit Him with *éclat.* Pilate then for the second time receives Jesus, in order, for the gratification of the Jews, to perpetrate upon Him a police execution that was destitute of all judicial grounds,—viz. the scourging.

The expression *Ecce Homo* contains another return of the person of Jesus to the Jews. For the third time Pilate enters into judgment with Jesus upon the accusation: He made Himself the Son of God. He now designs setting Him free himself, but the Jews weaken his purpose by a threat accompanied with tumult; and he is now inwardly so discomfited that the last time he does not simply *deliver* the Accused to the Jews—he delivers Him *under sentence of crucifixion*, purposing a *formal* participation in the affair *himself*, while the *Jews* are to assume, and really do assume, the *actual* execution and responsibility of it. Both these facts are summed up in the words: "He delivered Him unto them that He might be crucified." As regards the contrasts of conduct, the stately, artificial repose of Pilate is overcome by cringing submissiveness; his political calculation by demoniacal craft and pertinacity; his effort of conscience by audacious menace; his attempt to turn the accusers into ridicule by treating them scornfully and mocking them, by fanatic popular agitation and a revolutionary, tumultuous petition, masking itself in pure zeal for the authority of the emperor.

The individual items for which, as new disclosures, thanks are due to John, are

a. The competence strife in regard to the trial;

b. The analysis of the ambiguous expression, *King of the Jews*, by the wisdom of the Lord—making manifest the vileness of the high-priests and the felony to the Messianic idea, of which they are guilty;

c. The antithesis of the Kingdom of Truth and the kingdom of this world, and the utterance of Pilate;

d. The circumstance that it is pre-eminently the Jews who are guilty of bringing the Lord into juxtaposition with Barabbas;

e. The real purpose of the scourging;

f. The effect which the charge that Jesus made Himself the Son of God, produced upon the soul of Pilate—the anguish of superstition, following hard upon the self-upliftment of unbelief;

g. The innuendo-like threat of the Jews to accuse Pilate to the emperor—as the weapon that prostrates him (Pilate);

h. The double masking: The rebellion of the Jews against their King and against the emperor's governor, in the mask of the most faithful Jewish piety and Roman subjection; Pilate's dejection, in the mask of a stately session for judgment, and a derisive treatment of the accusers and the whole Jewish nation;

i. The share of both—Pilate and the Jews—in the crucifixion.

John, in the close unity of his presentation, has however passed over, together with minor features, the trial in the morning (Matt. xxvii. 1); the dream of Pilate's wife (Matt. xxvii. 19); Pilate's washing of his hands, and the self-execration of the Jews (Matt. vers. 24 and 25); the reed (Matt. ver. 29); and the bespitting on the part of the soldiers (ver. 30). Similarly, the sending of Jesus to Herod, and the resultant friendship of Herod and Pilate (Luke xxiii. 6–12); finally, the notice that Barabbas had perpetrated a sedition in the city (Mark, Luke).

2. The *joint implication* of a *hierarchical Church* and a *despotic State* in the guilt of Christ's execution under pretext of His being a religious criminal:

(1) In losing the right of inflicting capital punishment, the hierarchs should have recognized the fact that their discipline could extend no further than to excommunication (Matt. xviii. 17). (2) With the assumption of rule over different national religions, the Roman State should have been constrained to penetrate to a purely political position and a distinction of matters religious and political,—to a principle of which the better men already had a presentiment (Acts xviii. 14 and 15). The two principles, however, the religious and the political, continue, on the one hand, involved, and, therefore, on the other hand, strained, because the Jewish hierarchy has not purified itself to a pure conception of the Church, nor the Roman power to a pure conception of the State.

This mingling of State and Church has been repeated from the time of Constantine, increasing more and more in the Middle Ages until the arrival of the Reformation. It still continues in the Greek economy of State and Church (Cæsaropapism), likewise in the Roman Ecclesiastical State,* as, partially, in the other Catholic States (Papal-Cæsarism). Christ and Christianity have always had to suffer under this confusion, the ground of which is a want of respect for the religious conscience.

(2) In taking for granted that disagreeable religious tendencies are to be punished, the hierarchy is fain to shuffle off the *execution* of punishment upon the despotism, the latter to shift the *responsibility* of punishment upon the hierarchy.

* [Overthrown in 1870, soon after the adoption of the blasphemous dogma of papal infallibility by the Vatican Council. —P. S.]

(3) Afterwards they both seek to excuse themselves; Pilate writes: "The King of the Jews," *i. e.* a *religious* motive has brought Him to the cross. The hierarchs wish the inscription to read: "He *said* that," *i. e.* He is a misleader of the people, and a disturber;—the motive is a *political* one.

In a similar manner ultramontane authors now try to impute the execution of heretics to the State of the Middle Ages.

(4) Pilate constituted himself and his Roman authority constable of the hierarchy, and from this time forth he rushes to perdition. Similar was the fate of the Maccabean house, and, since then, of several European dynasties. The clean sunderment of Church and State is a vital impulse of the spirit of Christianity, one of the greatest tasks of Christian times. See the author's essay: *Ueber die Neugestaltung des Verhältnisses zwischen Kirche und Staat.* Heidelberg, 1848.

3. The *fearful treason of the Jews to their Messianic idea*, consummated in the ambiguous accusation: "Jesus is the King of the Jews." A similar felony was committed by Josephus in applying the Messianic predictions of the Old Testament to Vespasian, *De Bello Jud.*, VI. 5, 4. See Gieseler, p. 47.

4. The *world-historical encounter of the Spirit of Christ with the genius of the Roman nation* on the occasion of the discourse concerning His kingdom (see EXEG. NOTES; and my *Leben Jesu*, II., 1508); analogous to His encounter with the genius of the Greek nation, John xii. 20 ff.

5. *Christ's kingdom not* OF *this world, but* IN *this world*, for it and over it. Christ the King in the Kingdom of Truth.

6. The *question of Pilate* no question, but a frivolous, unbelieving utterance. Characteristic of the Græco-Roman world-culture of his time.

7. Pilate surrendered *truth* first, and afterwards *justice*,—in consequence.

8. *Ecce Homo.* The scourging of Christ is intended by Pilate to save His life and, hence, to be an act of humanity. But as that governor's official administration is without consistency, his justice without any foundation of truth, his wit without wisdom, so his humanity is destitute of the fear of God, of strength and of blessing. Such a humanitarian idea gave issue to the African slave trade.

9. Pilate's superstitious fear at the saying: "Jesus made Himself the Son of God,"—a characteristic trait of the unbeliever. The indissoluble connection between unbelief and superstition. But after all, unbelieving Pilate is more believing than the superstitious high-priests in the consummate unbelief with which they reject Christ. Of the threefold terror of Pilate: his terror at the law, his terror of conscience, his religious terror—there appears no trace in these practical atheists, who have donned the mask of the holiest zeal.

10. The greater sins of the high-priests. Christ's sympathy with the judicial fate of the weak Pilate. In this, Christ's sentence upon Pilate, there lies a stronger *Ecce Homo!* than in the exclamation of Pilate. *Ecce Homo*—who believes he is *administering* divine government and justice, and stands impotent—the *tool* of divine judgment, destined *himself* to be the *prey* of judgment.

11. Ecclesiastical and political masks. See No. 1.

12. The hierarchy here begets a *revolution* and allies itself to the same, with a view to shaking the political authority. Hierarchy, popular insurrection, and political authority, in wicked alliance, sentence the King of the Kingdom of God and Protector of all holy order and authority, the High-priest and true Friend of the people, to death upon the cross, as a kindler of rebellion. See *Leben Jesu*, II., 1533.

13. *No King but the Emperor.* In that hour the besotted nation did, with hypocritical fanaticism, renounce, not its Messiah only, but also its Messianic hope, cherishing in its heart meanwhile rebellion against the emperor and the hope of a political Messiah. Yet even this judgment of hardening must, according to Rom. ix., redound to the salvation of the world—the Gentile world, primarily.

HOMILETICAL AND PRACTICAL.

See the DOCTRINAL NOTES, and Comm. on *Matthew, Mark* and *Luke*.

Christ at once being judged by, and judging, the world.—Christ at the bar of the Roman State.—Christ before Pilate, and Pilate before Christ.—How Christ's glance pierced through all the mazes of judgment: 1. Through all *entanglements*, to the *right*; 2. through all *concealments* and *misrepresentations*, to the *bottom*; 3. through all *ambiguities*, to the *purpose*; 4. through all *waverings*, to the *issue*.—How the judgment upon the *Lord* judgeth *itself*: 1. In its accusations; 2. in its examinations; 3. in the motives for its sentence.—The grave sign in the fact that the great prospect that existed of Christ's acquittal was immediately blighted: 1. The great prospect: *a.* Pilate at first repulses the accusers. *b.* He nevertheless holds the examination and declares the innocence of Jesus. *c.* He tries to adjust the matter with the scourging. *d.* He is convulsed with religious awe and already proceeds to release Jesus. 2. Blighted: *a.* By the stratagem of hypocrites; *b.* the audacity of fanaticism; *c.* the impotence and guilty consciousness of Pilate; *d.* the rule of Tiberius; *e.* the plots of Satan; *f.* the providence and judgment of God. 3. The grave sign: *a.* Of the depravity of the world; *b.* of the magnitude of human unrighteousness; *c.* of the majesty of divine righteousness; *d.* of the fixedness and depth of the Redemption.—As Roman State-spirit delivered the Lord Christ Himself to the will of the Hierarchy, so it subsequently pursued the same course with Christianity.—The light of the calm majesty of Christ alone illumines the dark scene of His condemnation.

SECTION FIRST—Chap. xviii. 28-40. The cunningly calculated appearing of the accusers: 1. Hypocritical: they keep the legal Passover holy, to the end that they may the more surely deliver up the true Paschal Lamb to the Gentiles; 2. Dissembling, naïve: they make as if the sentence were already decided; Pilate has nothing to do but to set the great seal to it; 3. Truckling: "we may not put any man to death;" 4. Slanderously and disclaimingly shameless: they design to entrap Pilate with the ambiguous phrase: "the King of the Jews;" 5. Crafty, bold: they choose a mob-hero, Barabbas, who has made a sedition (probably against the Roman authorities).—The competence conflict, or the embroilments between the Hierarchy and the despotic State, and the ultimate, wicked peace.—The counter-question of Christ (ver. 34) a word of the heavenly Judge (for instruction): 1. For the elucidation of the matter; 2. for the warning of Pilate; 3. for the illumination of the accusers.—The Roman interrogation: What hast Thou *done?*—The declaration of Jesus: My kingdom is not of this world: 1. As defence; 2. as accusation.—The kingdom of Christ in its spiritualness and heavenliness: 1. How it differs from the kingdom of the Romans; 2. but also from the government of the Priests. —The royal confession: A King am I.—The royal Kingdom of Truth: 1. The Kingdom of the King: Truth in its profoundest essence, as a revelation of God; in its highest power, as the Gospel; in its broadest extent, as the uniting bond of all life; in its bodily appearance, as the Person of Christ. 2. The King of the Kingdom: Christ, personal Truth itself, as the light centre of all life, thoroughly at one with itself, and therefore the Light of the world. 3. The title of the King: Perfect agreement of His birth and His mission (His office); His ideal and His historical vocation. 4. His government: The faithful Witness, with His testimony; the Host-leader of all faithful witnesses (martyrs). 5. Increase of the Kingdom: The Word received as His voice by all who are of the truth.—The word of Pilate: What is truth? 1. How it might have become the *saving* of his life (if he had spoken inquiringly and submitted himself to the answer); 2. How it became the *judgment* of his life (because he spoke it triflingly and scornfully, going out immediately.—What is truth? This question may be considered according to its divine meaning; 1. As the sneering exclamation of the impious scoffer; 2. as the mere declaration of a frivolous worldling (Pilate); 3. as the doubting question of an earnest investigator; 4. as the vital question of a longing heart.—The Pilate-question of the Roman spirit of tradition. (We must abide by the tradition, cried the Roman pagans to the Christians. How can ye think of such a thing as proclaiming new truths?) Pilate's declaration without: I find no fault in Him; in connection with the preceding utterance: What is truth?—Pilate's testimony to the innocence of Jesus. First attempt to release the Accused.—*But it is your custom;* How Pilate, with the first deviation from the right, had entered upon the road of calamity. *Barabbas*, see the Synoptists.

Section second, Chap. xix.1-16. The scourging of Christ, in respect to its two-fold signification: 1. In respect to Pilate's intention (made prominent by John), it was to avert the crucifixion. 2. In respect to the actual result, it formed (according to the statement of the Synoptists) the beginning of the crucial sufferings of Christ.—Second attempt to release the Accused. —Lo there, the Man! 1. The word in the sense of Pilate. 2. The word in respect of its higher signification.—The second accusation in respect to its contradiction of the first in the sense of the accusers.—Pilate's fear. Close connection between unbelief and superstition.—Second examination by Pilate, by reason of the charge: He made Himself the Son of God.—Jesus' silence in the second examination by Pilate compared with His silence before Caiaphas.—The haughtiness in Pilate's reproof (ver. 19), and the augustness in the answer of Christ.—Christ sees even in the power of Pilate and its misuse, pre-eminently an instrument and a work of Divine Providence.—The greater and the less great sinners, or Jesus Himself in judgment, the holy Judge in righteousness and clemency.—Pilate's resolution to release Jesus; or the last attempt, frustrated by the bold menace of the Jews. Why was it possible for this menace so to disturb him? 1. Because he was Pilate (on account of his extortions, destitute of a good conscience and of trust in God, and setting his earthly self-preservation above all things). 2. Because his sovereign was the emperor Tiberius (the cruel and suspicious tyrant who lent a ready ear to denunciations of all kinds). 3. Because he knew the Jewish priests (their deceitful cunning and fanatical boldness).—The priestly revolutionists with the bugbear of revolution in their mouths: 1. Revolutionists against the emperor (in their hearts;—against the authority of the governor). 2. Declaring Christ to be a revolutionist; And Pilate himself to be open to suspicion of this crime.—Gabbatha and Golgotha.—Pilate wraps himself in all the pomp of a judge, while his judicial dignity is drabbled in the dust.—The priests put on the mask of devotion to the emperor while they condemn their King to the cross.—The scoffs of a Pilate cannot break the power which the priests exercise over the blind populace.—Gentile-Roman policy overcome by the Jewish hierarchy.—The glory of Jerusalem and the glory of Rome sink away in one ordeal in which they judge the Lord of the world;—and with them the glory of Judaism and the glory of heathenism—the glory of the whole old world.—Agreement (concordance) of Pilate and the priests.—The suffering of the Lord in Pilate's tribunal: 1. In view of Pilate tottering to his fall; 2. in view of the priests of His nation in their obduracy and craftiness; 3. in view of the delusion of the infatuated, raging people.—The temptation of Christ in these sufferings, and His victory.

Starke: To chap. xviii. 28-40. The Most Holy, in suffering Himself to be delivered into the hands of the uncircumcised, did thereby (take upon Himself the shame of our spiritual foreskin and) purpose to procure for us poor Gentiles a right to the citizenship of Israel.—How stiff-necked men still are in their superstition; and on the contrary, how secure and careless about that which is really in accordance with God's word.—Hall: It is the way of all hypocrites to be exceedingly conscientious about things concerning which they really need have no scruples; but for things of which they should make scruple, they keep an accommodating conscience.—Cramer: It is a rickety proof—the pledging of one's own authority in human affairs: *We* say so, therefore 'tis true. Such are the vain-glorious,—they speak great blasphemy—slanders;—what they speak, must be spoken from heaven; what they say, must have weight on the earth, Ps. lxxiii. 8, 9 [another variation in translation].—QUESNEL: Judges should examine everything—and their own hearts more than all other things. —Christ's kingdom and the emperor's can well exist together. Worldly order and government are serviceable to the Church, and the Church, by her prayer and intercession, preserveth police and kingdom. Certainly: the better Christian, the better magistrate! the better Christian, the more blessed teacher! the better Christian, the more loyal subject!—True servants of Jesus must fight manfully for their King and His kingdom. —BIBL. WIRTEMB.: Dear Christian, what if thou be poor, despised, rejected in the world? for all that, thou art a king; thy Saviour hath made thee one, Rev. i. 6; v. 10. The kingdom is prepared thee from the beginning of the world, Matt. xxv. 34—with this thought breast the devil and the world.—ZEISIUS: Let all thy words and works proceed from truth, if thou wilt be Christ's subject, for thy King Christ is a King of Truth, Zech. viii. 19.—*Ibid.*: Politicians of the present day think with Pilate: What is truth? and hold such as suffer for its sake, to be fools, and, on the contrary, such as stoutly simulate, they account very clever and lucky.—*Ibid.*: So raging mad is the foolish and hardened world that it condemns the good and preserves the lives of the veriest knaves, preferring them, honoring them, and endowing them.—O what insane choice! a refractory subject is preferred to the King of Glory; a murderer, to the Prince of Life; a ravening wolf, to the Good Shepherd.—CRAMER: As it is an abomination to God to wrong the righteous, so it is in like manner an abomination in His eyes not to punish archknaves.

GERLACH: The true King and the true Kingdom are the King and the Kingdom of Truth, Truth in the fullest, deepest sense (comp. chap. i. 14), according to which this word includes perfect essentiality, agreement with itself, holiness. Every king except the King of Truth, has a limited dominion, is at the same time a subject and servant; but God's Truth and therefore His King and His Kingdom, are finally victorious over all opposition. On this very account, however, this dominion of Truth is no purely internal one, else it would not exercise sway over things external, and consequently it would itself be untrue, and not a thoroughly true, perfect dominion. All the kingdoms of the world shall serve this King when His testimony of the Truth shall have made all His foes His footstool. But every other weapon would itself be of falsehood and darkness. Christ was *born* such a King—in Him person and office are one—in this respect also He is nothing but Truth; and for this end He *came into the world* (*of* which He and His Kingdom are not. Ver. 36); His appearance, life and ministry have no other aim.—With the mid-day Sun in his face, Pilate shut his eyes and thought there was nothing but darkness about him. Christ stood before him, Himself the Truth, and he unbelievingly despaired of men's ever being able to know the truth. Pilate's question is no scoff, but the expression of the superficial, hopeless unbelief of a man of the world.

BRAUNE: *My kingdom, etc.;* It twines its blessing around all kingdoms, all circumstances; it is the flying bee, clinging with quiet diligence to the fast-fading flowers and their perishable glory, that it may extract honey from them for its kingdom of the future, creating, meanwhile, not the slightest disturbance in the garden of the world. But it is likewise the great power that in all the migrations of nations, in great wars, and the ruins of the kingdoms of the world, proves itself active in advancing the eternal kingdom of peace. It will not be confined to the heart and the world of thought, but will be set up in the living spirit which gives proof of itself in all situations and which ought to prove itself Christian.—It is founded upon truth—God's promises; it is erected by truth—testimony concerning them; it is enjoyed in truth—obedience towards them; truth is universally disseminated by it; in doctrine and life, ideas, feelings, words, deeds, relations, impulses, truth comes; vanity and falsehood are overcome.—"In the kingdoms of the world, the vanity, ambition and weakness of man are misused, roused and cherished, while truth in the conscience is hindered by unrighteousness. But in the kingdom of God, man's conscience, his sense of truth, and the truth active in that sense, are aided as a drawing to eternity" (RIEGER).—There are minds that ring loud and clear when the truth touches them, while others brought into contact with the truth continue dead and soundless. Purity of heart is the condition whereon depends clearness in the knowledge of God. The light-minded worldliness and dull skepticism of so-called culture lead to a despair of truth.

GOSSNER: They wish to make Christ a malefactor by means, simply, of their authority and office, which, notwithstanding, they had from Him alone. And He was constrained, and did will, to suffer it so to be. We will invert their proposition and say: Friend Pilate, if we were not malefactors, we would not have delivered the Innocent and Righteous One unto thee.—If we were not sinners, such things could and must never have befallen Christ.—With truth,—thought Pilate, like so many other men—a man does not get on in the world. The world shrugs its shoulders, saying: "Truth? Bah! A fellow can't be so particular."

HEUBNER: God's people delivers up its Saviour, its Crown, the sum of all the promises, to the Gentiles to be executed. What a spirit is this in comparison with the spirit of the waiting, hoping fathers! It happens in the morning, at the approach of the holiest of feasts,—at a time when the spirit should clearly see the right. The priests were moved, we doubt not, with the desire to cover Jesus with infamy in the sight of the people.—LAVATER: "Whenever a righteous person is sentenced and judged by an uncalled man, there stands a Jesus before Pilate." —RAMBACH says of Pilate: It is laudable in him that he examines Jesus according to the rule: *audiatur et altera pars*,—that *he himself* makes the investigation, conversing undisturbedly with Christ *alone*.—The Kingdom of Christ is not worldly, but the kingdom of the world becometh Godly and Christly (Bengel).—The truth that

Christ gives, is "truth unto a knowledge of the Father, truth unto an assurance of the forgiveness of sins, truth unto everlasting comfort through grace, truth and strength in godliness" (Rieger).—Truth's seat is least of all at the courts of the great in this world. A king of France complained that though he had all things else in his kingdom and at his court, he yet did lack truth, people to tell him the plain, unvarnished truth (the same).—But what was the innocence which in Pilate's eyes Jesus possessed? The innocence of a good-hearted fanatic.

STARKE: On chap. xix. 1-16. *Bibl. Wirt.* We must not do evil that good may come of it, Rom. iii. 8.—ZEISIUS: Let this: Lo, what a man! never depart out of thy thoughts; but let it be to thee a monition penitently to recognize the enormity of the sins wherewith thou broughtest thy Saviour to such a pass; a warning earnestly to guard against them henceforward, and a word of consolation, partly in view of the hideous picture of thine approaching death, partly for the time when the world shall make a spectacle and a monster of thee.—QUESNEL: A judge must not terrify others with his power; but must be in fear himself on account of the power which he hath received from God, and look to it that he use it aright.—ZEISIUS: When we must suffer wrong, there is no better means of calming our souls and inspiring them with patience and consolation than by turning our eyes utterly away from secondary causes and fixing them on God, 2 Sam. xvi. 10; Luke xxi. 18, 19.—One sin is indeed more grievous than another, and hence deserving of heavier punishment and condemnation, Ezek. xvi. 51, 52.—A frank confession of the truth hath great power and is never without blessing, Acts xxiv. 25.—Satan knows how to take hold of every man in the place where he is weakest, 2 Sam. xi. 2; John xiii. 2.—Satan understands making a masterly use of honor, consideration, favor, grace with great lords—with them he blinds the eyes of men and ensnares their hearts, thus bringing or keeping them under his dominion, chap. xii. 43.—HALL: A carnally-minded man is more anxious for his bodily prosperity and temporal honor than for his soul.—ZEISIUS: It is a sorrowful fact that the servants of great lords are far more afraid of their masters, than of God's displeasure; but cursed is the man that trusteth in men and, *etc.*, Jer. xvii. 5: Acts v. 29.—Truth is often made a mere laughing-stock,—yet the mocker must be defeated and truth victorious.

GERLACH: The heathen even, struck by the divine majesty of Jesus, must gain some inkling of the fact that He was really the Son of God—a fact, the presage of which augmented the sin of the high-priests and that of Pilate also.—Pilate nevertheless did not escape the fate that he here, by his sinful yieldingness, sought to avoid; three or four years after he was deposed by Vitellius, governor of Syria, and sent to Rome to answer to the charges of tyranny preferred against him by the Jews.—On ver. 15. With which they most solemnly renounce God, their King, and the Messiah whom they looked for from Him.—LISCO: Hence the question: *Whence art Thou? i. e.*, art Thou really of divine descent? Jesus is silent, not willing to deny His divine origin and yet unable to instruct the unreceptive Pilate concerning the truth.—In mockery of their rebellious tendencies that longed for a king of their own, yet now rejected Him whom God sent them, Pilate asked: *Shall I crucify your King?* Whereupon the Jews, feigning devotion and loyalty, say: none but the emperor do we recognize as our king.

BRAUNE: Thou art but the instrument of a supreme will—saith the Condemned unto the judge. It is the self-same thought of the Redeemer that He thus expressed to Peter (John xviii. 11)—Shall I not drink the cup My Father hath given Me? Here the Redeemer taketh His stand, even in the midst of the turbid tumult of Jewish passion and Gentile dissoluteness; the pure will of God remaineth serene for Him, as the sky letteth its blue be seen through clouds.—In the destruction of Jerusalem the blood of the fathers and the children flowed. And Pilate bore his load still earlier.

GOSSNER: That is a wicked pliancy men manifest when, like Pilate, to win people they yield the half of what they unjustly demand and consider that they discharge their duty inasmuch as they refuse the other half. Duty and fidelity towards God and one's conscience cannot be divided, else infidelity is already an accomplished fact.—Let him that carrieth his head on high and refuseth to bow his neck beneath the lowly yoke of Christ, look often upon the thorn-crowned and scorned head of his King.—O thou weak man! thou miserable judge! So oft dost thou publicly attest His innocence, and sufferest Him to be more and more cruelly maltreated, and even committest the innocent Lamb to the wolves again; instead of tearing Him from their clutches. Thou preachest unto deaf ears when thou discoursest to the wolves concerning the innocence of the Lamb.—He who yields once to godless, unscrupulous men and does their pleasure, must and will do it the second time, must do everything until their thirst is quenched.—*Behold, what a man!* how guiltless! and how wretched! So stood He there, the Only and Incomparable One, before His people! how must the angels have looked into it. And He, whither must He have looked, how must He have gazed up to His Father! how must His soul have prayed that eternal honor and glory might grow out of this, His disgrace.—Behold, that is the Man who restoreth men and maketh them again what man was in the beginning when he came from God's hands. Behold, that is the Man, the God incarnate, who maketh men partakers in the divine nature; that is the perfect Man, for all others are men no longer—they can and shall, however, become men once more through Him.—It is noteworthy that God's Son must die because He was God's Son, and *acknowledged and affirmed Himself to be the Son of God.*—A pious judge will never boast of his authority, for it is not his, but belongs to justice and law.—Pilate vaunted his power so, and yet was so impotent, so tottering, that every wind, every menace, cast him to the ground and dispersed his power.—He was always *endeavoring*, always intending and never performing. The foes strive too, and strive more earnestly and more zealously than thou with thy half will.—But thou, O pious soul, when the world, when sin tempteth thee and provoketh thee to do something hostile to God and Jesus, do thou ask: Shall I crucify my King?

HEUBNER: Christ's crown of thorns and the crowns of the princes of this world afford matter for careful comparison. In respect of outward appearance, the former is disgraceful and agonizing, and the latter gloriously radiant, envied; but in respect of reality, the former is bought with the wearer's own blood, the latter purchased oft-times with the blood of subjects; the former a token of the utterly self-sacrificing, all sorrows-enduring Martyr, the latter a sign of ambition that gratifies itself only; the former wins salvation and freedom for the human race, the latter often bring woes and bondage upon men; the former beams eternally before God and leads to heavenly glory, the latter soon fade away and procure for those that wear them no honor in the presence of God, but frequently rejection from that presence. (Comp. LAVATER *Pontius Pil.* iv. 21.)—Pilate is restless, he goes in and out.—*Behold, what a man! Ecce Homo!* Words of many meanings! (Comp. Lavater, *Pontius Pilatus*, iv. 24-78).—One of the choicest paintings in the Düsseldorf Gallery is (was) an *Ecce homo* with the Latin inscription: All this I did for thee; what doest thou for Me? Zinzendorf was greatly affected at the sight of this picture; he is minded that he would not be able himself to make much response to this query, and he prays his Saviour to pull him forcibly into the fellowship of His sufferings if he be inclined to remain without.—Ver. 11. Pilate had encroached upon the rights of the heavenly Father, Jesus protects the honor of His Father. Even Pilate's power Jesus recognizes as a divine ordinance. Everything is of God, even the power of an unjust authority. Good men are never delivered up to it unless God wills their delivery. A distinction must be made between the work of God and that of Pilate. The guilt of the High Council was greater than that of Pilate, because they had a better insight into religion, into God's counsel and promise, Jesus' deeds and holiness. At the same time the "*greater sin*" awards blame *implicite* to Pilate: he too had sin.—Earthly power is perilous; let not him who has it presume upon it, or him who has it not, desire it.—LUTHER, xvi. 61: "The Jews said, we have no king, and their saying has come to be such earnest, that they must (eternally?) be without a king."

KRUMMACHER. *The Suffering Christ, a Passion Book.* Bielefield, 1854 (Trans. into English by Samuel Jackson. Boston, 1868). Christ before Pilate.—Christ a King.—What is Truth?—The Lamb of God.—The Great Spectacle: *Ecce Homo! etc.*, pp. 378-690.

[CRAVEN; From AUGUSTINE: Chap. xviii. Ver. 28. O impious blindness! They feared to be defiled by the judgment hall of a foreign Prefect; to shed the blood of an innocent brother they feared not.—Ver. 30. Ask the freed from unclean spirits, the blind who saw, the dead who came to life again, and, what is greater than all, the fools who were made wise, and let them answer, whether Jesus was a malefactor. But they spoke, of whom He had Himself prophesied in the Psalms, *They rewarded Me evil for good.*—Ver. 36. All that are born again in Christ, are made a kingdom not of this world. Thus hath God taken us out of the power of darkness, and translated us into the kingdom of His dear Son.—Ver. 37. But when Christ bears witness to the truth, He bears witness to *Himself;* as He said above, *I am the truth.*—Chap. xix. 5. *And Pilate saith unto them, Behold the Man!* as if to say, If ye envy the King, spare the outcast. Ignominy overflows, let envy subside.—Ver. 11. So He answers. When He was silent, He was silent not as guilty or crafty, but as a sheep; when He answered, He taught as a shepherd.——From CHRYSOSTOM: Chap. xviii. ver. 36. He means that He does not derive His kingdom from the same source that earthly kings do; but that He hath His sovereignty from above; inasmuch as He is not mere man, but far greater and more glorious than man; *If My kingdom were of this world, then would my servants fight that I should not be delivered to the Jews;* here He shows the weakness of an earthly kingdom, that it has its strength from its servants, whereas that higher kingdom is sufficient to itself, and wanting in nothing.—When He says, *My kingdom is not from hence,* He does not deprive the world of His government and superintendence, but only shows that His government is not human and corruptible.—Chap. xix. 7. They kill Him for the very reason for which they ought to have worshipped Him.—Ver. 15. *We have no king but Cæsar;* With one accord they denied the kingdom of God, and God suffered them to fall into their own condemnation; for they rejected the kingdom of Christ, and called down upon their own heads that of Cæsar.——From BEDE: Chap. xix. 2. Though the soldiers did this in mockery, yet to us their acts have a meaning; for by the crown of thorns is signified the taking of our sins upon Him, the thorns which the earth of our body brings forth; and the purple robe signifies the flesh crucified.——From ALCUIN: Chap. xviii. Ver. 38. He did not wait to hear the reply, because he was unworthy to hear it.——From THEOPHYLACT: Chap. xviii. ver. 36. He says, *from hence,* not *here;* because He reigns in the world, and carries on the government of it, and disposes all things according to His will; but His kingdom is not from below, but from above, and before all ages.—Ver. 38. *Pilate said unto Him, What is truth?* For it had almost vanished from the world, and become unknown in consequence of the general unbelief.——From HERBERT: Chap. xviii. ver. 40.

> Thou who condemnest Jewish hate,
> For choosing Barabbas. a murderer,
> Before the Lord of glory;
> Look back upon thine own estate,
> Call home thine eye (that busy wanderer)—
> That choice may be thy story.

[From BURKITT: Chap. xviii. ver. 28. When persons are over-zealous for ceremonial observances, they are oftentimes too remiss with reference to moral duties.—Vers. 29, 30. When we lie under calumny and unjust imputation, we imitate Christ, who opened not His mouth but committed His cause to Him that judgeth uprightly. [He defended Himself before the High-Priest.]—Ver. 36. It is a clear evidence that Christ's kingdom is spiritual, inasmuch as it is not carried on by violence and force of arms, as worldly kingdoms are, but by spiritual means and methods.—Ver. 37. Observe 1. The dominion and sovereignty of Jesus Christ,—He has a kingdom: *My kingdom;* 2. The condition and qualification of this kingdom, negatively expressed: *not of this world;* 3. The use and end of this kingdom, that the truth may have place among the children of men, for their salvation: *to this end was I born, and came into the world, to bear witness unto the truth;* 4. The subjects of Christ's kingdom declared: *Every one that is of the truth, heareth My voice.*—Ver. 38. *What is truth?* A most noble and inportant question, had it been put forth with an honest heart, with a mind fairly disposed for information and satisfaction.—Ver. 40. No persons, how wicked and vile soever, are so odious in the eyes of the enemies of God as Christ Himself was, and His friends and followers now are.—Chap. xix. 1. It is a vain apology for sin, when persons pretend that it was not committed with their own consent.—Vers. 2, 3. What they did in jest, God permitted to be done in earnest.—Ver. 5. Thorns and briers shall the earth bring forth, Gen. iii. 18. Christ, by His bitter and bloody sufferings, has turned all the curses of His people into crowns and blessings. In spite of all malice, innocence shall find some friends and abettors; rather than Christ shall want witnesses, Pilate's mouth shall be opened for His justification.—Ver. 6. The chief priests and elders "persuaded the multitude:" Woe be to the common people, when their guides and leaders are corrupt; and woe be unto them much more, if they follow their wicked and pernicious counsels.—Vers. 7, 8. Serious thoughts of a Deity will strike terror even into a natural conscience, especially when the sinner is following a course which his own judgment cannot approve.—Ver. 10. It is the great sin and snare of men in power, to forget from Whom they derive their power, and to think that they may employ it as they please.—Ver. 11. *He that delivereth Me unto thee, hath the greater sin;* the greater means of light and knowledge persons sin against, the more aggravated is their guilt, and the more heightened will be their condemnation.—Ver. 12. Hypocrites within the pale of the visible church may be guilty of such tremendous acts of wickedness as the conscience of an Infidel and Pagan boggle at and protest against.—Conscience bids him spare, popularity bids him kill.—Vers. 12, 13. The natural consciences of men, and their innate notions of good and evil, may carry men on a great way in opposing that which is a bare-faced iniquity; but at last either fear or shame will over-rule, if there be not a superior and more noble principle.

[From M. Henry: Chap. xviii. 28. *Then led they Jesus from Caiaphas unto the hall of judgment;* They took this course that He might be put to death 1. More legally and regularly; 2. More safely; 3. With more reproach to Himself by *the death of the cross;* 4. With less reproach to them; thus many are more afraid of the *scandal* of an ill thing, than of the *sin* of it.—Two things are here observed concerning the prosecution: 1. Their policy and industry therein; 2. Their superstition and vile hypocrisy.—Ver. 29. Looking upon Pilate as a magistrate, here are three things commendable in him: 1. His diligent and close application to business; men in public trusts must not love their ease; 2. His condescension to the humor of the people, and receding from the honor of his place, to gratify their scruples; he goes *out to them;* for when it is for good, we should *become all things to all men;* 3. His adherence to the rule of justice in demanding the accusation, suspecting the prosecution to be malicious.—Ver. 31. If the Jews have no power *to put any man to death,* where is *the sceptre?* Yet they ask not, Where is the Shiloh?—Ver. 32. Even they who designed the defeating of Christ's sayings, beyond their intention were made serviceable to the fulfilling of them by an over-ruling hand of God.—It is likewise determined concerning us, though not discovered to us, *what death we shall die,* which should free us from all disquieting cares about that matter.—Ver. 35. *Am I a Jew?* Good names often suffer for the sake of the bad men that wear them. It is sad, that when a Turk is suspected of dishonesty, he should ask, "What! do you take me for a Christian?"—Christ, in His religion, still suffers by those that are of His *own nation,* even *the priests,* that profess relation to Him, but do not live up to their profession.—Ver. 36. *My kingdom is not of this world;* 1. Its rise is *not from this world;* it is not by succession, election, or conquest, but by the immediate and special designation of the divine will and counsel; 2. Its nature is not worldly; it is a kingdom within men; 3. Its guards and supports are not worldly; its weapons are spiritual; 4. Its tendency and design are not worldly; 5. Its subjects, though they are *in the world,* yet are not *of the world.*—Ver. 37. The *good confession* which our Lord Jesus *witnessed* before Pontius Pilate, 1 Tim. vi. 13.—Though Christ *took upon Him the form of a servant,* yet even then He justly claimed the honor and authority of *a king.*—Christ's errand into *the world,* and His business in *the world,* were *to bear witness to the truth:* 1. To reveal it, chap. i. 18; vii. 26; 2. To confirm it, Rom. xv. 8.—Learn 1. The foundation and power, the spirit and genius, of Christ's kingdom, is *truth,* divine *truth;* 2. The subjects of this kingdom are those *that are of the truth.*—Ver. 39. Pilate was willing to trim the matter and please all sides; and was governed more by worldly wisdom than by the rule of equity.—Ver. 40. The enemies of Christ's holy religion *cry* it down, and so hope to *run* it down; witness the outcry at Ephesus, Acts xix. 34.—There is cause to suspect a deficiency of reason and justice on that side which calls in the assistance of popular tumult.—*Now Barabbas was a robber;* Sin is *a robber,* every base lust is *a robber,* and yet foolishly chosen rather than Christ, who would truly enrich us.—Chap. xix. 1. This pain and shame Christ submitted to *for our sakes;* 1. That the Scripture might be fulfilled, Is. liii. 5, *etc.;* 2. *That by His stripes we might be* healed, 1 Pet. ii. 24; 3. *That stripes,* for His sake, might be sanctified, and made easy to His followers.—Vers. 1-3. See and admire 1. The *invincible patience of a sufferer;* 2. The *invincible love and kindness of a Saviour.*—He that bore these *sham honors,* was recompensed with *real honors,* and so shall we be, if we patiently *suffer shame* for Him. Ver. 5. Did He go forth thus bearing our reproach? Let us go forth to Him *bearing His reproach,* Heb. xiii. 13.—*Behold the Man;* It is good for every one of us, with an eye of faith to behold the Man, Christ Jesus in His sufferings, "Behold Him, and 1. Be suitably affected with the sight; 2. Mourn because of Him; 3. Love Him; be still *looking unto Jesus*."—Ver. 6. Did their hatred of Him sharpen their endeavors against Him, and shall not our love to Him quicken our endeavors for Him and His kingdom?—Pilate had not courage enough to act according to his conscience, and his cowardice betrayed him into a snare.—Ver. 7. In vain did they boast of their law, when they abused it to such bad purposes.—Ver. 8. Pilate fears lest he should run himself into a *premunire*.—Vers. 10, 11. When Pilate used his power, Christ silently submitted to it; but when he grew proud of it, He made him know himself.—Ver. 11. All sins are not equal; but the guilt of others will not acquit us, nor will it avail in the great day to say, that others were *worse than we*, for we are not to be judged by comparison, but must *bear our own burden*.—Ver. 12. It never does well, when our resolutions to do our duty are swallowed up in projects how to do it plausibly and conveniently. If Pilate's policy had not prevailed above his justice, he would not have been long seeking to release Him, but would have done it. —A few madmen may out-shout many wise men, and then fancy themselves to speak the sense (when it is but the nonsense) of a nation, or of all mankind.—It has always been the artifice of the enemies of religion, to represent it as hurtful to kings and provinces, when it would be highly beneficial to both.—Ver. 13. They that bind up their happiness in the favor of men, make themselves an easy prey to the temptations of Satan. —Ver. 15. Had not Christ interposed, and been thus *rejected of men*, we had been for ever *rejected of God*.—Ver. 16. *Then delivered he Him therefore unto them to be crucified;* It is common for those who think to keep themselves from greater sins by venturing upon lesser sins, to run into both. ——From SCOTT: Chap. xviii. 30, 31. Those who are scandalously unjust, frequently expect credit for their regard to justice; and are greatly affronted to be suspected of the least crime, while actually committing the greatest, 2 Sam. xx. 8-10, 20-22.—Ver. 38. Numbers give Jesus and His people a good word, who will not join them, or venture anything in His cause.—Numbers commit injustice for fear of their dependents, and from a desire of popularity.—Ver. 40. Let us beware of deliberately sparing our lusts, (those robbers of God, and murderers of the soul,) thus crucifying Christ afresh, and putting Him to open shame.—Chap. xix. 1-16. The conflict between convictions and corrupt affections, is often strong; but where faith is wanting, the world will get the victory.—Those rulers of every description, who have sat in judgment on Christ and His servants, will soon stand before His tribunal.——From A. CLARKE: Chap. xviii. 28-40. The most that we can say for Pilate, is, that he was disposed to justice, but was not inclined to hazard his comfort or safety in doing it. He was an easy, pliable man, who had no objection to doing a right thing, if it should cost him no trouble; but he felt no disposition to make any sacrifice, even in behalf of innocence, righteousness, and truth.——From A PLAIN COMMENTARY (Oxford): Chap. xviii. 36. Our Saviour does not say that He has no earthly kingdom; but that His kingdom is not of *earthly origin*.—Ver. 37. *Every one that is of the truth heareth My voice;* "Being of the truth" implies belonging to it; being mastered by it; taken up into it: it implies the being possessed by a principle which moulds that wherein it dwells to itself, as the weaker is held by the stronger; even the possession of the soul by the very Essence of Being and of Life, manifested in the person of the Son, and administered by the Holy Ghost.—Ver. 38. "Probably Pilate thought that Jesus professed only to add one more to the list of philosophies, or systems of ideas, and turned away from it in sickness of heart." (Archdeacon GRANT.)—Ver. 40. "His own, they among whom He had gone about all His life long, healing them, teaching them, feeding them, doing them all the good He could; it is *they* that cry, 'Not this Man, but Barabbas!'" (Bishop ANDREWS.)—Ch. xix. 2. *And the soldiers plaited a crown of thorns and put it on His head;* "A most unquestionable token this, that Christ's kingdom was not of this world, when He was crowned only with thorns and briars, which are the curse of the earth." (LIGHTFOOT.)—Ver. 5. *Behold the Man!* As if he said,—Behold the afflicted and tortured object of your malice and cruelty; "a worm, and no man." If ye have human hearts, ye cannot behold such a dismal spectacle without commiseration!—Ver. 6. Monstrous that a heathen should have had thus to remonstrate with the chief priests of a nation taught of God!—Vers. 8, 9. The heathen Procurator again puts the descendants of Abraham to shame. Like Gamaliel he is seized with a salutary apprehension "lest haply he be found even to fight against God."—Ver. 10. "Pilate further condemns himself in servilely yielding to a popular clamor, after so plainly declaring his own absolute, unfettered authority." (GROTIUS.)—Vers. 12, 13. Pilate fears less to put the Son of God to death, than to incur the Roman Emperor's displeasure.

[From KRUMMACHER: Ch. xviii. 28. They purposely push Him into the house they deemed unclean, and thus tangibly and symbolically expel Him as a publican and sinner from the commonwealth of Israel; but all this was to happen thus, in order that Christ's character as the sinner's Surety might become increasingly apparent, and every one perceive in Him the Man who, by virtue of a mysterious transfer, had taken upon Himself everything that was condemnatory in us.—Who is not acquainted with individuals who scrupulously abstain from worldly amusements, and carefully avoid coming into social contact with the worldly-minded, who not only vie with the world in the arts of dissimulation, uncharitable judgment of others, and hateful scandal, but even go beyond it?—The life of godliness is a harmonious organization, and not a sticking together of single acts of piety.—Ver. 30. Though they were endeavoring to murder innocence and do the devil's work, yet because *they* do it, it must be right and blameless.—Vers. 36, 37. Christ is a King; you are, therefore, not in error who wear His uniform, and have trusted your life and destiny to His hands.—He does not say that His Kingdom makes no claim eventually to the government of the whole world, or He would have denied more than was consistent with the truth; He only asserts that His government was not of *this* world, and clearly intimates by laying the emphasis on the word "*this*," that another æon than the present would certainly see His delegates seated on the thrones, and His word and Gospel the Magna Charta of all nations. It is particularly to be observed that in the sentence, "Now is My Kingdom not from hence," the word "now" evidently refers to a period in which His Kingdom should occupy a position very different from what it did at that time.—Those who hear His voice are citizens of His Kingdom.—The expression, *every one that is of the truth,* betokens an inward preparation for conversion which no one experiences without the operation of "preventing grace."—Ver. 38. *What is truth?* A seeking after truth belongs to human nature, and is wont to be the last feature of it that perishes.—In Pilate there was doubtless something of the proud philosopher, something of worn-out indifference, something of the professed skeptic, something of the frivolous free-thinker and scoffer, and something of the hasty, jealous and haughty blusterer; but still there is something beside this, something better and nobler—an unperverted, inquiring mind—a longing for deliverance. (If this last be true, would not Christ have answered?—E. R. C.).—Vers. 38, 39. Pilate stands as a warning example of the consequence of endeavoring to satisfy God and the world: We meet with Pilate under various forms; many a one has placed himself, like him, in a situation in which he must either set Barabbas free, or give up the Saviour, because he was deficient in courage to brave every danger for Christ's sake; many reckoning, like Pilate, on the instinctive moral feelings of the multitude, with whom they do not wish to be at variance, have cowardly asked, "Which will you choose, right or wrong?" and the unexpected reply has been thundered back, "We choose rebellion and treason."—Ver. 40. *Not this man, but Barabbas;* Such is the world's favor, and so little truth is there in the saying, "The voice of the people is the voice of God."—Barabbas does not stand before us merely as an individual; he represents, allegorically, the human race in its present condition bound in the fetters of the curse of the law till the day of judgment. Before he was presented with Jesus to the people's choice, every prospect of escape had been cut off; and such is also our case. It is now Barabbas or Jesus: if Jesus is set at liberty Barabbas is inevitably lost; if the former is rejected, then, hail to thee, Barabbas, thou art saved! His ruin is thy redemption; from His death springs thy life,—"God made Him to be sin for us who knew no sin, that we might be the righteousness of God in Him;" in Barabbas' deliverance we see our own.—Ch. xix. vers. 1-5. There is a closer connection between the garden of Eden and the Roman Prætorium than might at first sight be supposed; debts incurred in Eden are there liquidated, and sins committed in Paradise are there atoned for. What ought to have been the fate of Adam for lusting after the forbidden fruit, and for his impious infringement of God's prerogatives? At least, the *scourge* instead of sensual delight; a *crown of thorns* instead of the longed for diadem; and a *robe of mockery* instead of the imperial purple. —Does not Christ still wear, in a hundred different forms, the purple robe and crown of thorns in the world? Is He not exposed to public ridicule and treated as a liar and an enthusiast because He bears witness to His superhuman dignity? Is not His name, even to this day, proscribed by thousands, like scarcely any other? Does not an ironical smile dart across the lips of many, when it is mentioned with reverence and fervor?—The words, *Behold the Man,* point not only to what is past, they have also a condemning reference to the present. Alas, the world has become a Gabbatha! The thorn-crowned martyred form exhibited there mutely condemns us all without distinction.—*Behold the Man:* In the mock robe in which He stands before you, He gains victories which He never could have won in the sumptuous robe of His divine majesty; in it He overcomes eternal justice, the irrevocable law, sin, Satan, death: It is a strange ornament that decks His head—in this wreath He possesses and uses a power of which He could not boast while adorned only with the crown of Deity; in the latter He could say to the dying thief only "Be thou accursed;" in the former He is able to say to him, "This day shalt thou be with Me in Paradise;" in the former He certainly reigned, but over a hopelessly ruined race, devoted to destruction; in the diadem of thorns, He rules over a world replete with great and glorious anticipations: A feeble reed is His rod of office, but with the Sceptre of Omnipotence, which He wielded from the beginning, He did not perform the wonders which He works with this mark of abasement and weakness; true, the gates of hell opened for transgressors at a wave of the former; but when He sways the latter, the doors of the paradise they have forfeited open for them; with the former, He was Lord over mankind only as a lost race destined for the slaughter; with the latter, He now tends a flock of them called to eternal salvation. Can you mistake the Conqueror of the world in Him whom you see before you—the "stronger" who takes away the spoils and armor of the "strong man," and makes an end of all opposing authority? In the same attire in which He there yields Himself up to the world, He continues to overcome it; the sight of the suffering Saviour is still the mighty power which silently changes lions into lambs, breaks and melts the strong heart, and prepares the way for His most glorious achievements: Thus arrayed He exhibits Himself in the cell of the contrite penitent, and how is the heart of such an one relieved, for He bare our iniquities; to the sorely tempted, and renders their victory secure; to the grievously afflicted, and they exclaim, "Through the cross to the crown;" to His children despised and rejected by the world, and they exclaim, "We desire no other array from you than that in which you once clothed our Glorious Head;" to those grieved at base ingratitude and coldness, and their sorrow turns to deep confusion at their desire for human praise; to those of His flock seduced by the allurements of the world, and restores them.—Vers. 12-16. Pilate is compelled to take the part of the

Holy One to the setting aside of all private considerations, or to afford his sanction to the most cruel and bloody deed the world ever witnessed; The case is similar with us; if we refuse to do Him homage, we are compelled to aid in crucifying Him.—We find in Pilate a degree of humanity and susceptibility for something better; God, indeed, will judge him, but not with the lukewarm who disgust Him, and whom like the Laodiceans, He will spew out of His mouth.—Who could be able to form a correct idea of the spectacle, and yet believe that divine justice rules the world, if we were permitted to behold our Saviour only in His own person, and not at the same time as Mediator and High Priest!

[From BARNES: Ch. xviii. 38. *Pilate saith unto Him, What is truth?* Thousands ask the question in the same way. They have a fixed contempt for the Bible; they deride the instructions of religion; they are unwilling to *investigate*, and to wait at the gates of wisdom; and hence, like Pilate, they remain ignorant of the great Source of truth, and die in darkness and in error.—Ch. xix. 4. The highest evidence was given that the charges were false, even when He was condemned to die.—Ver. 6. When men are *determined* on evil, they cannot be reasoned with; thus sinners go in the way of wickedness down to death.—Ver. 11. How many men *in office* forget that *God* gives them their rank, and vainly think that it is owing to their own talents or merits, that they have risen to that elevation.—The providence of God was remarkable in so ordering affairs, that a man, flexible and yielding like Pilate, should be entrusted with power in Judea. He so orders affairs, that the *true character* of men shall be *brought out*, and makes use of that character to advance His own great purpose.—From JACOBUS: Ch. xviii. 38. *What is truth?* This is the kind of questioning which the world makes. It is rather a taunt thrown out against Christ and His religion—it waits for no answer.—*I find in Him no fault at all*; How many are willing to pronounce Him innocent, but rebel at the thought of relying on Him for salvation.—Ch. xix. 5. *Behold the Man!* Pilate pointed to Him as a spectacle calculated to move them.—Ver. 11. Christ acknowledges that Pilate's power is given him from on high.

[From OWEN: Ch. xviii. 37. This shows that the kingly domain of Jesus was in the domain of truth, that His followers were those who received the truth in the love of it, and that from all who were the subjects of truth, would be rendered to Him the most implicit obedience.—Ver. 38. The conversation had taken too serious a turn to suit Pilate's pleasure; he therefore waits for no reply.—"Pilate mocks both—the Witness to the Truth, and the haters of the Truth." (ALFORD.)—Ver. 40. "Thus was Jesus the goat upon which the Lord's lot fell, to be offered for a sin-offering." (LUTHARDT after KRAFFT.)—Ch. xix. 14. *Behold your King!* It is no longer, *Behold the Man!* to excite their sympathy and effect His release. Every emotion of tenderness, every principle of honor and justice, is now lost in the desire to evince his loyalty to Cæsar, and shield himself from an accusation like that threatened in ver. 12.—Ver. 15. *We have no king but Cæsar;* To such a depth of degradation did these chief men of the nation descend, in their hellish desire to rid themselves of Jesus.

[Chap. xviii. vers. 13, 24, 29, 40 (Matt. xxvii. 1; Mark xv. 1; Luke xxiii. 7). Our Lord was tried and condemned by every power having, or that might be supposed to have, authority over Him—Annas, Caiaphas, the Sanhedrin, Pilate, Herod, the Populace—1. That it might be apparent that He was condemned by every ecclesiastical and world power; 2. As prophetic of His future rejection by every conceivable form of human government.—Ver. 36. *My kingdom is not of this world*—NOW *is My kingdom not from hence;* My kingdom is not yet established; the present is, for Me and My disciples, the period of submission and patient endurance of wrong and suffering.*]

* [It is not denied that Christ, as God, had a kingdom which existed from the beginning, nor that at His ascension He was exalted "Head over all things," nor that His future earthly kingdom is to be *spiritual*, as well as *political;* it is simply denied that His *earthly* kingdom (the kingdom here referred to) was *then* (or now) established. To regard the νῦν as a particle of *inference*, and not of *time*, is to suppose that our Lord whispered into the ear of a *heathen*, in the *privacy* of the Prætorium (ver. 28), *the* great truth concerning His kingdom which He *concealed* from His *Apostles*, not twelve hours before, at the institution of the Supper, Luke xxii. 29; and again concealed throughout the forty days during which He gave them instruction concerning "the things pertaining to the kingdom of God." Acts i. 3, 6, 7!—E. R. C.]

IV.

CHRIST ON GOLGOTHA THE LIGHT OF SALVATION, OR THE GLORIFICATION OF THE CURSE OF THE OLD WORLD. CHRIST THE CROSS-BEARER. THE CRUCIFIED IN THE MIDST OF THE CRUCIFIED. THE SUPERSCRIPTION: THE KING OF THE JEWS, A WRITING OF DISGRACE CHANGING INTO A WRITING OF HONOR. THE BOOTY OF THE SOLDIERS, ALSO A FULFILMENT OF SCRIPTURE. THE INSTITUTION OF DEPARTING LOVE. THE LAST DRAUGHT. THE WORD OF VICTORY; IT IS FINISHED!

CHAP. XIX. 17–30.

(Matt. xxvii. 32-56; Mark xv. 20–41; Luke xxiii. 26-49).

And they [They therefore, οὖν] took Jesus and led him away.[1]
17 And he bearing his [own][2] cross went forth into a place called *the place* of a skull
[the so called Place of a Skull, εἰς τὸν λεγόμενον Κρανίου Τόπον] which is called
18 in the [*omit* the] Hebrew Golgotha:[3] Where they crucified him, and two others
with him, on either side one [and with him two others, one on each side], and Jesus
in the midst.
19 And Pilate wrote [also, καί] a title [or, an inscription], and put *it* on the cross.
And the writing was, JESUS OF NAZARETH [THE NAZARENE, ὁ Ναζω-
20 ραῖος] THE KING OF THE JEWS. This title then read many of the Jews;
for the place where Jesus was crucified was nigh to the city: and it was written
21 in Hebrew, *and* Greek, *and* Latin [in Hebrew, Roman, Greek].[4] Then [There-
fore] said the chief-priest of the Jews to Pilate, Write not, The King of the Jews;
22 but that he said, I am King of the Jews. Pilate answered, What I have written I
23 have written.
23 Then the soldiers, when they had crucified Jesus, took his [upper] garments, and
made four parts, to every soldier a part; and also *his* coat [the inner garment, tu-
nic, τὸν χιτῶνα]: now the coat was without seam [but the tunic was seamless,
24 ἄραφος], woven from the top throughout. They said therefore among themselves,
Let us not rend it, but cast lots for it, whose it shall be: that the Scripture might
be fulfilled, which saith, 'They parted my raiment [garments] among them, and for
my vesture they did cast lots.' [Ps. xxii. 18.] These things therefore the soldiers did.

25 Now there stood by the cross of Jesus his mother, and his mother's sister [Salome,
John's mother, see the Exeg.], Mary the *wife* of Cleophas [Clopas, ἡ τοῦ Κλωπᾶ], and
26 Mary [the, ἡ] Magdalene. When Jesus therefore saw [Jesus therefore seeing] his
mother, and the disciple standing by, whom he loved, he [*omit* he] saith unto his
27 mother, Woman, behold thy son! Then saith he to the disciple, Behold thy mother!
And from that hour that [the, ὁ] disciple took her unto his own *home*.

28 After this, Jesus knowing that all things were now accomplished [finished, τετέ-
λεσται, as ver. 30], that the Scripture might be fulfilled [accomplished, τελειωθῇ]
29 saith, I thirst. Now [*omit* Now][5] there was set a vessel full of vinegar: and they
filled a sponge with vinegar, and put *it* upon hyssop, and put *it* to his mouth [so
putting a sponge filled with the vinegar upon a stalk of hyssop, they raised it to
30 his mouth]. When Jesus therefore had received the vinegar, he said, It is finished:
and he bowed his head, and gave up the ghost [yielded up his spirit].

TEXTUAL AND GRAMMATICAL.

[1] Ver. 16.—[The words καὶ ἀπήγαγον after τὸν Ἰησοῦν are doubtful. See the TEXT. NOTE on ver. 16 in the preceding section, with which Dr. Lange connects this clause.—P. S.]

[2] Ver. 17.—The reading αὐτῷ τὸν σταυρόν, in accordance with B. L. X. Sin., Vulgate, Itala, Origen in Lachmann, Tischendorf. [αὐτῷ is *dat. commodi*, carrying the cross *for Himself*, or *His own* cross. The text. rec. reads τὸν σταυρὸν αὐτοῦ, *His cross*.—P. S.]

[3] Ver. 17.—[Different spellings: Γολγοθᾶ (Alford, Tischendorf), Γολγοθά (Westcott and Hort), Γολγοτά, Γολγόθ, *etc.* See Tischendorf. In Chaldee גָּלְגָּלְתָּא, *Gŭlgotha*, in Hebrew גֻּלְגֹּלֶת, *Gŭlgoleth*, in Greek κρανίον, *i. e.*, *Skull*. The Vulgate translates the word in all cases *Calvaria* (fem. *i. e.*, *skull*), from which our *Calvary* is derived. Comp. Jerome in Matt. xxvii. 33: "*Golgòtha, quod est Calvariæ locus.*" The E. V., following the Vulgate, uses *Calvary* only once, Luke xxiii. 33, for the

Greek κρανίον (a diminutive of κρᾶνον), *a skull.* In the three places where the term *Golgotha* occurs, *viz.*, Matt. xxvii. 33; Mark xv. 22; John xix. 17, the E. V. retains the Hebrew form, which, in our passage, is necessary on account of the Ἑβραϊστί. The popular expression "*Mount* Calvary," is probably of monastic origin and has no foundation in the Evangelists, where Golgotha is simply called τόπος, "a place," or "the Place of Skull." It was probably only a small, round and barren elevation in the shape of a skull, and derived its name from its globular form. Jerome (on Matt. xxvii. 33) informs us of the tradition that the place derived its name from Adam, the *head* (skull!) of the human family (hence, probably the skull introduced in early pictures of the crucifixion), but he himself discredits it, and conjectures that it was so called as a place of execution, on account of the *capita damnatorum.* But in this case the corresponding Greek name would have been τόπος κρανίων, "place of skulls," instead of τόπ. κρανίου, "pl. of *a* skull," still less "a skull," as in Hebrew and in the Greek of Luke xxiii. 33.—P. S.]

[4] Ver. 20.—Meyer: "The probabilities are in favor of the sequence Ἑβραϊστί, Ῥωμαϊστί, Ἑλληνιστί (thus Tischendorf, in accordance with B. L. X., Minuscules, *etc.*), from Pilate's standpoint." This very consideration may have given an exegetical rise to it. The Sin. supports it. [Treg., Alf., Westc. and H., adopt the same order. Lange, with Lachmann, retains the order of the text. rec., which is supported by A. D. Vulg. Syr.—P. S.]

[5] Ver. 29.—The οὖν is here omitted by Lachmann, in accordance with A. B. L. X. Lachmann, supported by B. L. X. *etc.*, gives an οὖν, instead of δὲ after οἱ.

EXEGETICAL AND CRITICAL.

[John's account of the crucifixion is brief and comprehensive, yet with several original details of the deepest import. On his relation to the Synoptists in this section, see the full analysis of Dr. Lange in *Doctr. & Ethic.* below, No. 1.—P. S.]

Ver. 17. **And bearing His own cross,** *etc.* Αὐτῷ [for Himself] τὸν σταυρόν emphasized. [See TEXT. NOTE, "As conquerors bear their own trophies, so Christ bears the symbol of His own victory."—P. S.] Thus He went forth [ἐξῆλθεν]. Out of the city, Heb xiii. 12.

Golgotha. See Comm. on *Matthew* xxvii. 33. [On the words *Golgotha, Cranion, Calvaria, Calvary, Mount* (?) *Calvary*, see my TEXTUAL NOTE 3. The vexed question of *locality* is fully discussed by Dr. Lange and myself in the *Commentary on Matthew*, pp. 520, 521, with reference to the principal arguments for and against the traditional site of the crucifixion, *i. e.*, the spot where now stands the Constantinian or, perhaps, post-Constantinian "Church of the Holy Sepulchre," which lies *within* the walls of the present city and in the north-western quarter, not far from the Damascus Gate. Robinson is the chief authority in opposition, G. Williams in defense, of the popular tradition. The former has still the best of the argument.* The other writers on the subject, Ritter, Raumer, Tobler, Winer, Schubert, Bergren, Arnold, Kraft, Friedlieb, Furrer, Lange, *etc.*, among the Germans, Wilson, Barclay, Finley, Olin, Lewin, Tristram, Stanley, Fergusson, *etc.*, among English and Americans, are divided in opinion or leave the matter doubtful. James Fergusson (art. *Jerusalem* in Smith's *Bible Dictionary*, and also in a special pamphlet *On the Site of the Holy Sepulchre, in answer to the Edinb. Rev.*) has recently propounded the startling theory that the place of crucifixion was Mount *Moriah*, on the very spot where now stands the Mosque of Omar, or as the Moslems call it, the Dome of the Rock; and, further, that this building is the identical church of the Holy Sepulchre which Constantine erected over the rocky tomb of Christ. But this theory, besides leaving the disappearance of Constantine's church and the substitution of the present Church of the Holy Sepulchre unexplained, is set aside by the extreme improbability that the temple area was outside of the city and a place of execution. Lange is disposed to identify Golgotha with the hill Goath, Jer. xxxi. 39, which was outside of the city, east of the Sheep Gate. My colleague, Prof. Dr. Hitchcock, informs me that by personal examination in 1870 he came independently to the same conclusion. Perhaps it is best that the real locality of crucifixion should be unknown: it is too holy to be desecrated by idolatrous superstitions and monkish impostures and quarrels such as, from the age of Constantine to this day, have disgraced the Church of the Holy Sepulchre, to the delight of Mohammedan Turks, and to the shame and grief of Christians. The apostles and evangelists barely allude to the places of our Lord's birth, death, and resurrection: they fixed their eyes of faith and love upon the great facts themselves, and upon the ever-living Christ in heaven. Only this is more or less certain from the Gospels, *viz.*: that the place of the crucifixion was *out* of the city (John xix. 17; Matt. xxviii. 11; comp. Heb. xiii. 12, ἔξω τῆς πύλης); yet *near* the city (John xix. 20); apparently near a thoroughfare and exposed to the gaze of the passing multitude (as may be inferred from Mark xv. 29 and John xix. 20); probably on a little conical elevation (hence probably the name: 'Skull,' or 'Place of a Skull'), but not on a mountain or hill (as the popular term *Mount* Calvary would imply); and that it was near the Lord's sepulchre (John xix. 41), which was in a garden and hewn in a rock (Matt. xxvii. 60).—P. S.]

* [The traditional site has been defended quite recently again by Furrer (art. *Golgatha* in Schenkel's *Bibel-Lexikon*, II., 508).—P. S.]

Ver. 18. **But Jesus in the midst.** [μέσον δὲ τὸν Ἰησοῦν]. This was Pilate's arrangement, and designed to mock the Jews (see 1 Kings xxii. 19). Meyer maintains that it was an arrangement of the Jews', the Jews being the crucifiers. Against this view we have to observe: 1. That the two thieves were not executed as Jewish heretics; 2. that the consummating of the crucifixion, as a Roman punitory act, must have been left to the Romans; 3. that it further reads: Pilate wrote *also*—namely, to complete the mockery of the Jews.

[Christ was crucified between the two robbers who represent the two classes of the human family: both guilty before God and justly condemned to death, but the one repenting, and saved by faith in the crucified Redeemer, the other impenitent, and rushing to ruin by unbelief. On the archæology of crucifixion, see the Notes on *Matthew*, pp. 522 f. Crucifixion was one of the most painful and disgraceful modes of death. It was unusual among the Jews, and applied among the Greeks and Romans (till the fourth century) only to slaves and gross criminals, as rebels and highway-robbers. Cicero calls it the most cruel and abominable punishment (*crudelissimum teterrimumque supplicium*). The cross consisted of two pieces of wood, generally put together transversely at right angles in the form of a T. The longer beam was planted in the earth, and provided with a projecting bar like a horn in the middle for the body to rest upon, which somewhat relieved the sufferings, and prevented the hands from being torn through. There were, however, various forms of the cross (*crux commissa, cr. immissa, cr. decussata*). The victim was first undressed, the arms tied with ropes to the cross-beam, the hands fastened with iron nails, the feet tied or nailed to the upright post. In this unnatural and immovable position of the body, he suffered intensely from thirst, hunger, inflammation of the wounds, and deep anguish in consequence of the rushing of the blood towards the head. Death followed slowly from loss of blood, thirst, and hunger, gradual exhaustion, and stiffening of the muscles, veins, and nerves. The loss of blood, however, was small, since the wounds in the hands and feet did not lacerate any large vessels, and were nearly closed by the nails. The sufferers lingered generally twelve hours,—sometimes, according to the strength of their constitution, to the second or third day. The bodies were left hanging on the cross until they decayed or were devoured by ravenous beasts and birds. But the Jews were accustomed to take them down and bury them. Constantine the Great, from motives of humanity, and especially from respect to the cross of Christ as the sign of victory (*Hoc signo vinces*), abolished crucifixion in the Roman empire, and since that time it has almost disappeared from Europe. What a wonderful change! Through the death of Christ the cross has been transformed from a symbol of shame into a symbol of glory and victory, and one of the richest themes of poetry. Well may we exclaim with Venantius Fortunatus, in his famous Passion-hymn, *Pange, lingua*:

Crux fidelis, inter omnes
Arbor una nobilis!
Nulla talem silva profert
Fronde, flore, germine:
Dulce lignum, dulces clavi,
Dulce pondus sustinens.

"Faithful cross! above all other,
One and only noble Tree!
None in foliage, none in blossom,
None in fruit thy peers may be:
Sweetest wood and sweetest iron,
Sweetest weight is hung on thee."—P. S.]

Ver. 19. **Pilate wrote also** [or, **Moreover Pilate wrote**, ἔγραψε δὲ καί].—After sentence was pronounced, and as a formulation of the same. On this account, however, it is as little the Pluperfect (Tholuck) as it is a formula manufactured during the crucifixion only. In a word, Pilate first arranged the manner of the execution—between two thieves—and then wrote the superscription. See Comm. on *Matthew*. Τίτλος [=ἐπιγραφή, from the Latin *titulus, inscription*], the customary Roman term for such superscriptions (Wetstein).

Jesus the Nazarene [Ἰησ. ὁ Ναζωραῖος ὁ Βασιλεὺς τῶν Ἰουδαίων, *Jesus Nazarenus Rex Judæorum*. All the four Evangelists give the inscription on the cross, but with slight variations, on which see Wordsworth *in loc.*—P. S.] The manifest double meaning of the superscription was the final expression of the suit. In the sense of the man Pilate, it meant: Jesus, the King of the Jewish fanatics, crucified in the midst of Jews, who should all thus be executed; in the sense of the Jews: Jesus, the seditionary, the King of rebels [and pseudo-prophets]; in the sense of the political judge: Jesus, for whose execution the Jews, with their ambiguous accusation, may answer; in the sense of the divine irony which ruled over the expression: Jesus, the Messiah, by the crucifixion become in very truth *the King of the people of God.*

Ver. 20. **Was read by many of the Jews.**—Whereby they were forced to reflect upon that treason to the Messianic idea, of which the high-priests were guilty.

The place was near the city.—On Sunday afternoon the populace are fond of walking out of the city, particularly in the direction of new suburbs. So the Jews on their festivals. Towards Golgotha the beginnings of the new city were forming,—Bezetha. *Leben Jesu*, ii. p. 1573.

In Hebrew, *etc.*—Here also the Evangelist has in view the triumph of the Divine Spirit over human sin and malice. The inscription, in this threefold form, must symbolize the preaching concerning the Crucified One in the three principal languages of the world: in the language of religion [Hebrew], of culture [Greek], and of the State [Latin—the language of law and government].*

Ver. 21. **Then said the high-priests to Pilate.**—A proposal to alter the title. They feel the sting of the inscription, and therefore prosecute their calumny. Jesus was to be more definitely characterized as a seditionary in the Roman sense, one whom Pilate himself had sentenced.

Ver. 22. **What I have written**, *etc.* [ὃ γέγραφα, γέγραφα. The first perfect denotes the past action, the second that it is complete and unchangeable.—P. S.]. Pilate feels secure again, and once more assumes the air of unshakeable authority and of the firm Roman. His declaration, however, contains at the same time the continuation of the idea that he lays the dark riddle of this crucifixion upon their consciences, that he does not acknowledge Jesus to be guilty in their sense, and that they need reckon upon no forbearance on his part. "Analogous *formulæ* from Rabbins, see in Lightfoot." Meyer. "Agreeably to his character ἀκαμπὴς τὴν φύσιν, as Philo calls him, Pilate adheres to his resolution." Tholuck.

Ver. 23. **Took His upper garments.**—"The only earthly leavings of the Redeemer do not fall to the share of His people, but, in accordance with Roman law, to the executors of the death-sentence. By the ἱμάτια may be understood the upper garment, the girdle, the sandals, perhaps the linen shirt; these are divided amongst the Roman guard, consisting of four men (Acts xii. 4)." Tholuck.

But the tunic, *etc.* [ἦν δὲ ὁ χιτὼν ἄραφος].—According to Isidor. Pelusiota, the like was worn by the lower classes in Galilee. This statement, however, might readily be abstracted from our passage. The Evangelist seems to see in this

* [Hamann ingeniously applied the inscription on the cross to the language of the New Testament which implies the three national elements, as it was written in *Greek* by *Jews* in a Jewish land, under the dominion of the *Romans*.—P. S.]

body-vest a homely work of art, wrought by loving hands. [χιτών, *tunica*, is an inner garment, worn to the skin like a shirt, mostly without sleeves, fastened round the neck with a clasp, and usually reaching to the knees. Sometimes two were worn for ornament or comfort. It was worn also by the Jewish high-priest and priests (but as an *outer* tunic, a broidered coat, *chethoneth thashpez*), and is described by Josephus, *Antiq.* l. iii. 7, § 4. The fathers (as also Roman commentators and Bishop Wordsworth) see in the seamless coat of Christ a symbol of the unity of the church.—P. S.]

Ver. 24. **In order that the Scripture might be fulfilled,** Ps. xxii. 19 (18), according to the Septuagint. A typical prophecy. See Comm. on *Matthew*. The apparent identicalness in the *parallelismus membrorum* of the Psalmist does not preclude our Evangelist's right to make the distinction he does—it being a question of the interpretation of an unconsciously prophetic, a typical, speech.

These things therefore the soldiers did. As the soldiers knew nothing of those words of the Psalmist, their fulfilment of them is the more strikingly a divine inspiration. The same idea as chap. xii. 16.

[Vers. 25-27. Peculiar to John. A scene of unique delicacy, tenderness and sublimity. A type of those pure and spiritual relationships (the sacred *Wahlverwandtschaften*) which have their origin in heaven and are deeper and stronger than those of blood and interest. The cross is the place where the holiest ties are formed, and where they are guarded against the disturbing influences of sin.

"*Das Kreuz ist es, das Herzen zieht und bindet,*
Wo Tiefverwandtes wunderbar sich findet."

A few simple touches reveal a world of mingled emotions of grief and comfort. The mother pierced in her soul by the sword (Luke ii. 35), the beloved disciple gazing at the cross, the dying Son and Lord uniting them in the tenderest relation! The first words furnished the keynote to that marvellous *Stabat Mater dolorosa* of Jacopône (1306), which, though disfigured by Mariolatry, describes with overpowering effect the intense sympathy with Mary's grief, and is the most pathetic, as the *Dies Iræ* is the most sublime, product of Latin hymnology. It is the text for some of the noblest musical compositions, which will never cease to stir the hearts of men.—P. S.]

Ver. 25. **Now there stood by the cross** [εἱστήκεισαν δὲ παρὰ τῷ σταυρῷ, in the Vulgate: *Stabat juxta crucem mater ejus*, from which the *Stabat Mater* took its rise, as the *Dies Iræ* from the Vulgate's rendering of Zeph. i. 15.—P. S.].—According to the Synoptists (Matthew, Mark), the women mentioned stand afar off. According to Lücke and Olshausen, they were there *previously*; according to Meyer, there is a difference which must be settled in John's favor. But it is manifestly necessary to distinguish two stages in the proceedings attendant upon the crucifixion: the tumult of the crucifixion itself, amidst which no friends could approach, and the subsequent sufferings on the cross. See *Comm. on Matthew* [p. 529].

We read with Wieseler (*Studien u. Kritiken*, 1840, p. 648): *His mother* (Mary) *and His mother's sister* (Salome); then *Mary—the wife of Clopas—and Mary Magdalene. Leben Jesu;* Introduction to this Comm. [p. 4]. So also Lücke, Ewald [Meyer and Alford]; in old times, the Syrian, Ethiopian and Persian translations,* as also the texts of Lachmann, *editio minor*, Tischendorf,† Muralt. [Also Westcott and Hort, who punctuate without a comma after Κλοπᾶ, thus: ἡ μήτηρ αὐτοῦ καὶ ἡ ἀδελφὴ τῆς μητρὸς αὐτοῦ, Μαρία ἡ τοῦ Κλ. καὶ Μαριὰμ ἡ Μαγδ.—P. S.]. The opposite side is taken by Luthardt, Ebrard [Hengstenberg, Godet] and others.

[Thus we have not *three* women (Mary, her sister Mary of Clopas, and Mary Magdalene), as is usually assumed, but *four*, arranged in two pairs: Mary and her sister (*viz.* Salome), Mary of Clopas and Mary the Magdalene. See the list of the apostles, Matt. x. 2 ff.; Luke vi. 16 ff. Consequently John, the son of Salome, was a cousin of Jesus and a nephew of His earthly mother. This double relationship explains the more readily the fact that Jesus intrusted her to John rather than to His half-brothers, who at the time were yet unbelieving. Apocryphal traditions make Salome now a daughter, now a sister, now a former wife, of Joseph.—P. S.]

Wieseler's hypothesis is upheld by the following facts:

1. It is not supposable that two sisters had the same name. [Some conjecture that Mary was only a step-sister. But I know of no example even of step-sisters or step-brothers bearing precisely the same name without an additional one to distinguish them. Hengstenberg escapes the difficulty by the arbitrary assumption that *sister* here denotes *sister-in-law*. —P. S.]

2. In a precisely similar manner John elsewhere paraphrases his own name. [Nor does he introduce his brother James by name.—P. S.]

3. According to Matt. xxvii. 56; Mark xv. 40, Salome really was among those women [who stood by the cross; and it is not likely that John should have omitted his own mother, the less so as he introduced himself.—P. S.]

The wife of Clopas [ἡ τοῦ Κλωπᾶ].—Clopas=Alpheus, Matt. x. 3. The mother of the so-called brethren of Jesus, *i. e.* His cousins.

[The identity of Κλωπᾶ (which sounds like an abridgement of Κλεόπατρος) with the Hebrew name Ἀλφαῖος, חַלְפַי (Matt. x. 3), is by no means so certain as Dr. Lange with most commentators (also Meyer) assumes, but quite doubtful on account of the difference of letters, and the improbability that John should use the Aramaic, and Matthew and Mark the Hellenistic form. Κλωπᾶς sounds rather like an abridgement of Κλεόπατρος, and may be the same with the Κλεόπας mentioned Luke xxiv. 18. But even in case of the identity of Clopas and Alpheus, it does not follow that James and Joses, the sons of Alpheus and a certain Mary (Matt. xxvii. 56; Mark xv. 40; xvi. 1; Luke xxiv. 10), were

* [These translations insert *and* (καί) between *sister of his mother* and *Mary*, thus making them two distinct persons.—P. S.]

† [In ed. viii., Tischendorf makes a comma after Κλωπᾶ. So does Alford, yet he adopts Wieseler's view.—P. S.]

cousins of Jesus, unless we identify this Mary with the sister of the mother of Jesus, which Lange does not. Nor is it certain that ἡ τοῦ means the *wife of*; it may also mean the *daughter of*, the Klopas mentioned Luke xxiv. 18 (as Ewald).—P. S.]

Ver. 26. **Woman, behold thy son** [Γύναι, ἴδε ὁ υἱός σου]!—*Woman* instead of *mother*. See chap. ii. 4. The word here denotes particularly the character of woman in her helplessness and need of comfort. It must be remembered, however, *that Mary deserved the name of "woman" in the ideal sense* also. As Christ was the Son of Man, or the Man, so she, though approximately only, not in the perfection of sinlessness, was the ideal woman. [The second Eve, *the Woman*, whose *Seed* here bruised the serpent's head, Gen. iii.—P. S.]. Thus the name "woman," the greeting of the woman who in spirit shares His crucial agony, is likewise a title of dignity. But besides this, Christ has sufficient reason for not exposing Mary to the mockery or persecution of the enemy by saluting her with the name of "mother."

The explanation recently (for instance in Piper's *Jahrbuch*, article "*Maria*") enlarged upon with ever-increasing grotesqueness, and which claims that with this saying Christ renounced His mother at the cross, goes, in its gradual development, from Luthardt, who is more precisely the author of it, back to Hofmann.* It is expressive of a Monophysite view which takes the bold flight of afterward annulling even the historical fact. People holding this view apparently conceive of the *status majestaticus*, not as the centre of the glorification of the human life, but as a sort of Oriental court raised to heaven. In connection with this view it would be better to represent the Logos in His birth as born not *of* Mary, but merely *through* her, in accordance with some of the ancients.

That it is the desire of Jesus to give Mary a son in His stead in a special sense, results from the fact that the Alphæides also were her sons.† And what sons! Nevertheless, Mary was to have a still richer compensation after the departure of Jesus than could be given by the Alphæides; John was destined to make this compensation. And he indeed stood alone by her in this moment, as her support; thus should he stand by her from this time forth. The thing, the unique adoptive relationship, already existed *de facto*, being born beneath the cross of Christ; consciousness, a name, and the sanction of Christ must be added to it. According to Tholuck, the ἀδελφοί were as yet unbelieving. In regard to this, see chap. vii. 5 [and my counter-notes, p. 241.—P. S.]. According to others, they were not so well off as John. But had there been question of a mere pecuniary provision for His mother, Christ would not have deferred its settlement until now. Mary needed a *son* in the sense of the higher soul-life, just as Jesus had Himself been refreshed by a *friend*. The friend of Jesus was fitted to be the son of Mary.

Behold thy mother [Ἴδε ἡ μήτηρ σου]!—We may primarily understand both sayings of Jesus in such a manner as to make them express the same idea: ye shall henceforth cleave together as mother and son. But not in vain are they divided into two sayings. If we apprehend them as *consolations*, the word: "Behold thy son!" signifies: in him shall be thy support; the word: "thy mother:" thou shalt become a sharer in her maternal blessing. If we apprehend them as *admonitions*, *commands*, the case presents a different aspect: the mother is enjoined to live for the son, the son for the mother. The one signification, however, is inseparable from the other. On both sides love and blessing are one in personal relationship.

[Alford: "The solemn and affecting commendation of her to John is doubly made,—and thus bound by the strongest injunctions on both. The Romanist idea, that the Lord *commended all His disciples as represented by the beloved one*, to the patronage of His mother, is simply absurd. The converse is true: He did solemnly commend the care of her, especially indeed to the beloved disciple, but in him to the whole cycle of disciples, among whom we find her, Acts iv. 14. No certain conclusion can be drawn from this commendation, as to the 'brethren of the Lord' believing on Him or not at this time. The reasons which influenced Him in His selection must ever be far beyond our penetration:—and *whatever relations to Him we suppose those brethren to have been*, it will remain equally mysterious why He passed them over, who were so closely connected with His mother. Still the presumption, that they did not then believe on Him, is one of which it is not easy to divest one's self; and at least may enter as an element into the consideration of the whole subject, beset as it is with uncertainty." John's relation to Mary as established beneath the Cross, was that of a sacred friendship and spiritual communion (comp. Matt. xii. 47–50), and interfered neither with John's relation and duty to his natural mother Salome, nor with Mary's relation to the "brethren" of Jesus, whatever view we may take of them. I have so often discussed this vexed question, especially in this vol. p. 241 and in the Com. on *Matthew*, pp. 456-460, that it is unnecessary to say more. —P. S.]

Took her unto his own home [ἔλαβεν ὁ μαθητὴς αὐτὴν εἰς τὰ ἴδια].—John gladly apprehended the word of Christ in that meaning also which carried an obligation with it. The expression: **from that hour**, cannot be weakened. Yet it is neither necessary to infer that John had a house of his own in Jerusalem, nor that he kept house for himself alone. "If he received Mary into his *dwelling*, into his *family circle*—consisting of Salome and perchance his brother, εἰς τὰ ἴδια would be perfectly correct." Meyer. [So also Alford. Ewald well

* [The original reads Hoffmann, evidently a printing error. Prof. Hofmann of Erlangen is not to be confounded with Dr. Hoffmann, General Superintendent and Court Preacher at Berlin. Steinmeyer (as quoted and opposed by Meyer, p. 630, note) adopts the view of Luthardt and asserts that the death of *the Redeemer of all men* solved the bonds of His earthly relationship. Of English commentators Alford says in the same sense: "The relationship in the flesh between the Lord and His mother was about to close; hence He commends her to another son who should care for and protect her."—P. S.]

† [According to Dr. Lange's peculiar theory on the adoption of the family of Mary's sister or sister-in-law into her own family—a view which I have frequently had occasion to oppose in connection with the cousin-theory concerning the brothers of Christ. Comp. pp. 115, 241, *Matthew*, pp. 456–460. —P. S.]

observes: "It was for the Apostle in his later years a sweet reward to recall vividly every such minute detail,—and for his readers it is, without his intention, a sign that he alone could have written all this (*dass nur er diess alles geschrieben haben könne*)." Against the misunderstanding of this most touching scene by such men as Scholten and Weisse, see the just remarks of Meyer, p. 630.—P. S.]

Ver. 28. **I thirst** [Μετὰ τοῦτο εἰδὼς ὁ Ἰησοῦς ὅτι ἤδη πάντα τετέλεσται, ἵνα τελειωθῇ ἡ γραφὴ, λέγει· Διψῶ].—Different views:

1. Prevailing ancient interpretation: ἵνα τελ. is referable to λέγει· διψῶ. Since He knew that all things were accomplished, He said, in order to fulfil the Scripture in that particular also: *I thirst* (Chrysostom, Theophylact and others). Beza: *Vehementissima quidem siti pressus, sed tamen de implendis singulis prophetiis nostraque salute potius quam de ulla siti sollicitus.* This manner of fulfilling the Scripture is in accordance neither with the view of the Lord nor the delineation of John (see ver. 24). Then, too, it would have to read thus: As He knew that the Scripture was fulfilled, with the exception of one particular, He said—in order that this one thing also might be fulfilled, *etc.*,—irrespective of the fact that in ver. 32 ff. additional unfulfilled particulars Nos. 2 and 3 would present themselves.

2. Intensified apprehension of the foregoing explanation: as vinegar was given Him to drink, the drink was demanded as *ultima pars passionum*, with reference to Ps. lxix. 22, which passage, as others also suppose, is here had in mind (Theodorus of Heraclea, Gerhard, Marheineke).

3. Christ did not drink for the sake of fulfilling the Scripture, but the Evangelist interprets His drinking as a fulfilment of Scripture; ἵνα τελειωθῇ ἡ γραφή is therefore a parenthesis, containing the explanation of the Evangelist (Piscator, Grotius, Lücke).

4. The final sentence (*ἵνα, etc.*) is not parenthetic, nor is it to be applied to what follows, but to that which precedes it: in the consciousness that His passion is finished, *i. e.* finished unto the accomplishment of the Scripture, He now says: "*I thirst*" (Michaelis, Semler, Knapp, Tholuck, Meyer and others). This interpretation seems to us the correct one. Hitherto Jesus has passed through one temptation and anxiety after another and, absorbed in the hot conflict in which He saw the fulfilment of the divine decree in accordance with the Scripture, has forgotten the burning thirst that has preyed upon Him since His last draught at the Supper. Now, with the presentiment of victory, His thirst makes itself felt, and He, being no legal ascetic, nor despising a service rendered by the hand of sinners, requests and partakes of the last, sorry refreshment. The expression: "that the Scripture might be accomplished," does not mean: for the bare fulfilling of the Scripture hath He passed through all these things,—but: in the fulfilling of Scripture as the expression of the divine counsel, He found that which was His perfect tranquillization and exaltation in view of all these things, Luke xxii. 22, Matt. xxvi. 54. According to Hofmann, Jesus demanded a refreshment conducive to the prolongation of life, in order thus to demonstrate the freedom of His departure. This would be drinking for a theologico-apologetic purpose. Tholuck more pertinently remarks that the *τελειοῦν* of the divine *βουλή* was but the very (likewise the very) *τελειοῦν* of the *γραφή*,—hence *τελειοῦν* instead of *πληροῦν*.

Ver. 29. **A vessel therefore was standing there** [σκεῦος ἔκειτο ὄξους—sour wine, or vinegar and water—μεστόν].—The Evangelist's *οὖν* might here mean: Jesus' glance had fallen upon the vessel containing the beverage and had suggested to Him the prospect of refreshment. From a strict interpretation of the word, however, a higher signification results. Christ's complaint, His last craving, must not fail of satisfaction. It was necessary, therefore, that provision should have been made before-hand; it was to be expected that satisfaction was nigh at hand. The *stupefying draught* that was offered Him at the beginning of His suffering (Matt. xxvii. 34; Mark xv. 23), Jesus had rejected. See Comm. on *Matthew*. But the pure, sour soldiers' wine, vinegar-wine, He now receives to His refreshment. "The most distressing thirst torments the crucified. The soldiers give Him some of the beverage [ὄξος] which they are wont to drink (*posca, vinum acidum*); saturating a sponge with it, they put the sponge upon a hyssop-stalk (which in the East attains a height of from one to one and a half feet. Ὑσσώπῳ, that is *καλάμῳ τοῦ ὑσσώπου*, see Matt. xxvii. 48), and thus convey it to His mouth as He hangs upon the slightly elevated cross." Matthew xxvii. 48 is a parallel passage. The touch in Luke xxiii. 36 really seems indicative of a third, derisive presentation of vinegar-wine on the part of the soldiers, situate between the first and the last. See Meyer on the passage, and Comm. on *Luke* xxiii. 26 [p. 373. Am. Ed.].

Ver. 30. **It is finished.**—Τετέλεσται. The expression of the consciousness, ver. 28. Bengel: *Hoc verbum in corde Jesu erat* ver. 28, *nunc ore profertur.* It is possible that He required the reviving refreshment to aid Him in pronouncing the last words. The sublime word, *finished*, refers to His work, as commanded Him according to the counsel of God (delineated in the Scripture).

And yielded up the (or His) **spirit** [καὶ κλίνας τὴν κεφαλὴν παρέδωκεν τὸ πνεῦμα].—Expressive of a *free* dying. The characteristic word for this exode is itself preserved by the Evangelist Luke: *Father, into Thy hands.* Comp. chap. x. 18. Gerhard and the older Lutheran exegetes declared that the death of Jesus was not a *suffering*, but a *deed*. Tholuck: "This can be said only in the *ethical* sense,—in which sense it can be predicated of all His suffering—not in the physical sense (comp. Thomasius, *Christol. Dogmatics*, II., p. 225 with 218); in itself it is merely the expression of self-surrender, trusting in God, as Ps. xxxi. 6, whence the expression is derived." But of a certainty, also the expression of a thoroughly unique, free dying which was at once suffering and deed in the ethico-physical sense. See chap. x. 18. ["The *παραδιδόναι* was strictly a voluntary and determinate act—no *coming on* of death, which had no power over Him." (Alford.) On the physical cause of Christ's death, comp. the remarks in *Comm. on Matthew*, p. 523, and the treatise of William Stroud, M. D., on the *Physical Cause of Christ's Death and its Relation to the Principles and Practice of Christianity.* Second ed. with Appendix by Sir James Y. Simpson, London, 1871 (504 pp.). Dr. Stroud endeavors to demonstrate that the immediate cause of the Saviour's death must be traced neither to the ordinary effects of crucifixion, nor the wound inflicted by the soldier's spear, nor an unusual degree of weakness, nor the interposition of supernatural influence, but to the vicarious agony of His mind culminating in the exclamation, "My God, My God," *etc.*, and producing *rupture of the heart*, which is intimated by a discharge of blood and water from His side, when it was afterwards pierced with a spear. "It was the death of a pure and perfect human being sustaining and discharging the penalty due to human depravity, and thereby acquiring an equitable claim to see the travail of His soul and to be satisfied, by becoming the author of eternal salvation to all that obey Him." See more of this below on ver. 34, p. 597. —P. S.]

DOCTRINAL AND ETHICAL.

1. In the history of the crucifixion of Jesus, as subsequently in that of His burial, John gives special prominence to the considerations of the *fulfilment of Biblical prophecies and types*. In correspondence with Scripture, Pilate was constrained to make the superscription: *The King of the Jews;* in accordance with Scripture, the division of the clothing took place, accompanied by the casting of lots for the body-vest; in further accordance, Jesus, at the approach of His death, felt that all things were accomplished, to the fulfilling of the Scripture; and thus the manner of His taking down from the cross must itself have reference to two passages of Scripture. But not for the sake of the fulfilment of the Scripture did all these things happen, but because in the providence of God they must happen, they were preceded by the presages and fore-glimpses of Scripture. The reference to Scripture, however, is designed to be expressive of two things: the objective veracity of God, who, in the ordering of the crucial sufferings, is consistent with Himself, and the unconditional trust of Christ and His people, that above all human arbitrariness and malice in the crucifixion, the providence and faithfulness of God were ruling.

Many items in the history of the crucifixion, the Evangelist assumes to be already familiar,—especially the history of Simon of Cyrene, the presentation of the intoxicating myrrh-wine, the mockings of the Crucified One, the conduct of the thieves, the darkening of the land, the earthquake, the rending of the vail in the temple, the testimony of the Gentile captain, Matthew's indication of extraordinary occurrences in the spirit-world, the agitation of the people, as recorded by Luke, as also the majority of the seven last words.

With pleasure, however, he dwells—first upon the trait of Christ's bravely and resolutely taking His cross on His own shoulders (αὐτῷ), upon the contest which Pilate and the Jews continued over the Crucified One, upon the significant superscription, and similar features. But for him there lay special preciousness in the recollection that Jesus, in His last hour, instituted filial relations between him, His friend, and His mother.

2. The word: *The King of the Jews*, was a fulfilment of the entire Old Testament—hence there are no particular citations here. According to the original accusation of the Jews, it was designed to denote His *mortal offence*. It then, in accordance with Pilate's meaning, denoted the *occasion of His death*, being intended as a mockery of, and sarcasm upon, the Jews. In the sense of the Scripture, however, it denotes His *divinely appointed destiny of death*, and in the sense of the Spirit, the *eternal gloriousness* and *fruit of His death*. Jesus of Nazareth, the King of the Jews: the word of the cross, glorified by the Spirit into a word about the cross. Pilate did not suspect that his writing, like his saying, *Ecce Homo*, did, under the providence of God, take significance, when he wrote, in the three most important languages of the world, this sermon over the cross.

3. The references to the *fulfilments of Scripture* in Christ's suffering are nought but celestial lights shining into the darkness of the crucial passion. All is spiritualized, or transillumined by the Spirit, in order to be by the Spirit glorified, as God's counsel, foreknowledge, ordinance, disposition, and judgment upon the blindness of the world,—glorified, I say, unto salvation.

4. If *Mary* is meant to be a symbol of the *Church*, then Christ, with His institution of this adoption, hath made His bosom-friends the veriest sons of the Church, and the Church their mother. Hence a form of the Church which is at extreme variance with the Johannean mind, cannot be the true one. Mary may, however, far rather be called a symbol of the *Theocracy*, which has been finally comprehended in her heart. In that sense the institution would mean: the Theocracy, *i. e.* the theocratic side of the Church, is always to have a spiritual son,—children of the Spirit; the children of the Spirit are always to have a *motherly* authority over them in the ecclesiastical communion.

5. As Peter, who recognized in Christ the Renewer of the old Theocracy, the King of the Divine Kingdom, was pre-eminently entrusted with the foundation and care of the Church of Christ, so to *John*, who in Christ saw pre-eminently the manifestation of the personal God, the portrait of eternal love, was confided the foundation and care of a *holy family* of the *friends of God* as the innermost vital focus within the Church.

6. The *thirst of Jesus*, His last suffering. A sign (1) that He has passed through all His sufferings and may now receive the draught of refreshment; (2) that He departs from earth and from those who have crucified Him, not proudly and coldly, but humbly, warmly and lovingly; (3) that He would be no pattern in self-chosen torments and penances; (4) that He still speaks in the consciousness of His divine spiritual power, as if it were at once a begging and a commanding; (5) that He is making preparation for the end.

7. *It is finished.* See the Homiletical Hints. Hebrews x. 14. The word as (1) a prophetic word (all scripture fulfilled); (2) a high-priestly

word (the expiatory sacrifice completed); (3) a kingly word (the kingdom of heaven founded); (4) a unitous word (the work of redemption accomplished as the founding of the new creation, the world of the eternal Spirit).

8. The share of John in the account of the seven last words of Jesus.

9. The three languages on the cross, the three ground-tongues of theology.

HOMILETICAL AND PRACTICAL.

See the Synoptists.—The grand fulfilments of the divine counsel in the Passion of Christ, attested by the most significant fulfilments of Scripture (vers. 31-37 must be considered in this connection).—Christ's suffering in its fundamental features: 1. As an *act of suffering*: the bearing of His cross and going forth (without the gate, Heb. xiii. 13; out of the old communion) unto Calvary; 2. as an *experience of suffering*—with the thieves, in the midst of the thieves; 3. as a *glorification of suffering*: Jesus of Nazareth, the King of the Jews (the King of sufferers, of the people of God, of kings), in all the languages of the world.—The superscription of Pilate: 1. As the word of Pilate: Continuation of his mockery of the Jews;—the Jews a robber-folk, whose Head is already crucified. 2. As a word of the Spirit, unconsciously to the writer: The Messiah, the King of the people of God. Or, 1. As an assumed title of guilt, the property of malefactors in the old world; 2. as a personal title of honor, the property of the King of righteousness in the new world. Or as the explanation and glorification (*Erklärung und Verklärung*) of the cross of Christ.—This superscription read many of the Jews, for the place was nigh unto the city: 1. The word concerning Christ is still read by many legal men; 2. for the place where He is testified of is nigh to the city. [The evangelical Church by the side of the Church of legality].—How the priests would fain alter the writing concerning Christ.—The demand of the priests and the declaration of Pilate.—Pilate and the soldiers are compelled to work together for the fulfilment of the Scripture.—Soldiers, also, are under the providence of God, even in slaying, and dividing spoil.

Contrast of Christ's adversaries and His friends at His crucifixion.—How they must glorify Him together; those unconsciously, these in grateful love.—Founding of the spiritual house of the mother and son beneath the cross.—The rich legacy of the poor Jesus.

The blissful presentiment of the dying Jesus that His day's work is accomplished in accordance with the Scripture (or in accordance with the counsel of God): 1. Expressed in the evening draught which the great Laborer taketh as He quitteth work; 2. expressed in His evening song before He goeth to sleep: It is finished.

It is finished: 1. *It*, not this and that: *all* that lays the foundation of the new, eternal world of God. 2. It *is*, not it *is being* (Heb. x. 14). 3. *Finished.* As a spiritual act, as a vital conflict, as a mortal suffering, as a triumph of Christ and the salvation of God—conducted to the goal τέλος).—The word, *It is finished*: 1. As the Evangel of Christ; 2. as the confession of the Church; 3. as the jubilation of the believing heart; 4. as an excitation to every work of faith; 5. as a prophecy of the Last Day.

STARKE: Christians must make many a painful pilgrimage out of the city, out of the land,—nay, even to the gallows and the stake, for the sake of their faith—but courage! press onward! ye have a noble Predecessor.—Take comfort, thou pious man, if thou art accounted godless; Jesus was numbered with the transgressors that thou mightest be declared the child of God and righteous, Is. liii. 12.—The vain lust of titles must be renounced in following the crucified Jesus. Though the world should crucify our honor and our good name; though she should nail above our head the superscription: this is a fool, a dreamer, an odd fellow, a heretic, *etc.*, we must be satisfied with being called the children of God and having our names written in heaven.—Christians, read the Holy Scriptures diligently; there ye find your King, and His nature, will, and benefits. Chap. v. 39.—ZEISIUS: The science of divers kinds of tongues, especially of the Hebrew and Greek, is to be recognized as a particular benefit of God, and is exceedingly useful for the investigation of Holy Scripture, that having been written in these two languages, 1 Cor. xii. 10.—Pilate may have diligently framed the superscription in ambiguity, knowing Jesus to be innocent. Underlying this fact, however, was a special providence of God, who took care that His Son should have the right superscription, since He suffered the death of the cross as the Messiah or anointed King of Israel. —Behold God's rule over the hearts of men; in this His sway over them He hath employed even His own enemies for the furtherance of His glory: yea, His foes must sometimes promote the glory of His children with the very things wherewith they have striven to dishonor them, Ps. cx. 2.—If the writing of an earthly judge cannot be altered, how much less shall that be erased which God Himself has written in a Testament and Word.—CRAMER: Christ is poor in the beginning, middle, and end of His life, that through His poverty He might make us rich.—ZEISIUS: The nearer Christ, the nearer the cross, and the heavier our afflictions.—OSIANDER: Fervent love to God and the Lord Jesus regardeth no danger.—With this speech on the cross, the Lord Jesus (1) intended to show how He beareth on His heart a care even for our bodily circumstances, and considereth such care a part of His mediatorial office; He therewith (2) designed to confirm the fifth commandment and to set all children a good example, as to how they should care for their poor and forsaken parents; He hath therewith (3) shown that it is not contrary to the sense of the fifth commandment if we extend its limits somewhat farther than the letter of it seemeth to require; He hath (4) designed to hallow the natural love existing between friends and relatives; He hath (5) sanctioned guardianships; He hath (6) approved of testaments; He hath (7) taught thereby how every one ought to strive to make this painful life more endurable to his neighbor by rendering him loving aid; He hath (8), particularly in the person of John, enjoined it upon the hearts of all the teachers of His Church to have a care for poor and destitute persons; He hath (9) shown how we should seek to accomplish through others the good that we ourselves are unable to perform; He hath (10) assured all whom He recognizeth as His mother and His brethren that He will not forsake or neglect them either.—Christ's eyes, amid the turmoil, are fixed upon believers, Ps. xxxiii. 18.—No man deriveth harm, but rather profit, from entering into the fellowship of Christ's shame and suffering.—HEDINGER: God provideth physically and spiritually for them that belong to Him.—CRAMER: A Christian should settle well his household affairs before he dieth.—CANSTEIN: It is love's way to interest itself for those it leaves destitute, and to endeavor to bring about by means of others such things as it cannot do itself.—LAMPE: It is right that those who are preparing themselves for death, should not forget to care for their families.—Happy is he that espouseth the cause of the widows and orphans and doeth them good; he doeth God's will and shall inherit the blessing, Ps. xli. 1 ff.; Ex. xxii. 22 ff.—Hear, dear Christian! that Jesus hath thirsted, and let it cause thee to guard the more vigilantly against all excess in drinking.—HALL: Christian mine, if thou too art tried with hunger and thirst in this world, comfort thyself with the thought that thy Saviour did also complain of the same on the cross. Ah, what a refreshment will this be to thee!—Τετέλεσται; In this one word everything appertaining to the purchase of our salvation is expressed and concluded. By this we see that the Master with the tongue of the learned, Is. l. 4, is before us,—He who can bring all things into one word, and yet it is *plena enuntiatio*, a complete declaration, a word above all words, a regular aphorism (as they call a concise saying, briefly and wittily expressed), short and yet intelligible: a true apophthegm (a momentous and pregnant saying). Upon hearing this declaration, *it is finished*, we are constrained to ask: what is finished? This question is easily answered if we do but consider the Person who made the declaration. It is accomplished—all that Christ was bound to do and to accomplish—and thus this word refers us to the whole course of His life. In consideration of the preceding 28th ver., the word τετέλεσται may be complemented after this fashion: *herewith is the Scripture*, in that which it hath prophesied concerning Me, *fulfilled*, Luke xviii. 31; xxii. 37. If we take into account the passages Heb. v. 9; x. 7, it may also be thus paraphrased: *Herewith is the counsel and will of God concerning our salvation accomplished*, namely, as regards the purchase of it; and in consideration of the declaration of Christ, Matt. v. 17, τετέλεσται means as much as: *Now is the law fulfilled.*—He now, as it were, nodded unto Death, bidding him come on; yea, He asserted by this bowing of His head, that He would become obedient to His Father unto death, Phil. ii. 8.—CRAMER: Hath Christ finished it?—then we need not achieve it.—ZEISIUS: Christ's *consummatum*, it is finished, hath been a blessed thing for us.—OSIANDER: Christ's death is our life; in dying we enter into true life, Heb. ii. 14.

GERLACH: The most horrible of all torments, the most burning thirst,—a circumstance expressly predicted of the suffering Messiah, Ps. xxii. 15; comp. Ps. lxix. 21.—LISCO: Pilate indignantly refuses the request of the Jews that Jesus should be characterized in the inscription as a deceiver.—The faithful love of those who clave to Jesus shunneth not that pain of deepest sympathy which is occasioned by the spectacle of His sufferings, Luke ii. 35.

BRAUNE: Conscious of his injustice and of the innocence of Jesus, angry with those who had driven him to commit that injustice, he says: *what I have written, I have written;* this is the formula of deciding magistrates:—With this decree the matter rests.—It was written in *Roman*—Latin—, the judicial tongue; in *Hebrew*, the popular tongue; in *Greek*, the tongue in general use.—Duties, those, even, that are apparently of the least account, must be fulfilled up to the very last breath. The Christian should die like a general, upon his feet, fighting, giving orders, 1 Tim. v. 8.—Thus the gap that death makes, is best filled. For love is strong as death (Song of Sol. viii. 6).—Think you, it would have been stronger, greater, worthier of His love, to repress the need He felt of quenching His burning thirst? Here we see how free His heart is from pride and rancor, passions by which many another apparently grows great and strong.—Whoso bindeth his soul and his soul's life to Christ's life, ways, walks, sufferings, can say, when faint in death: it is finished! What soul hath been converted unto God from its sins and is reconciled to Him, can exclaim: it is finished!—This word, *it is finished!* was uttered by Jesus, not at the close of His *activity*, in the high-priestly prayer, in Gethsemane, but at the end of His *suffering*.—But was He already risen for our justification? He had not yet sent the Comforter into the hearts of His people. But in the holy instant of death, by the light of eternity, His eye beheld the finished work of redemption, in its readiness for prosecution and spiritualization. Thus through suffering and tribulation is attained the triumph of the kingdom of God.

GOSSNER: What a procession! What a crosswalk! What a march! God's Only-begotten One, under the burden of the cross, the tree whereon the curse lay, marcheth to the bitterest death. *Thus* do men send Him back to His Father from whom He proceeded—laden with cross, curse and shame; as a malefactor. What a journey, followed by consequences most rich in blessing!—And He bare His cross! Why that was *our* cross, and He appropriated it to Himself, as though it were His own; He embraced it with such love and patience as it had been His life, and it brought Him death—but to *us life*.—Neither can the coat of Christ's righteousness be divided and cut into pieces—every soul must have it whole.—His nakedness on the cross is an evidence that He shunned no kind of humiliation for us.—The pagan Roman soldiers did not divide the coat of Christ, but Christians have made many rents and divisions over Christ's coat, that they might establish their own opinions and their own righteousness.—Those under the cross composed the family of the Saviour; it had melted away to so few; that was His little Church whereunto He reckoneth Himself, wherewith He abideth, with which His Spirit resteth on earth.

—His bowed head lifteth up the head of each one of us. He Himself inclined His head with the consciousness that He should soon raise it again, as He had foretold.

HEUBNER: God, whose hand guided the finger of Pilate, meant this superscription to be a challenge to all unbelieving Jews and all mankind to acknowledge this Jesus of Nazareth as their King. All languages, all tongues, are to resound with His praise and confess that He is Lord, to the glory of God the Father.—Pilate's firm determination is indicative of God's irrevocable decree. If all the world remonstrate against Christ's royal dignity—God hath willed it, and there is an end of it, Ps. ii.—Christ hung naked on the cross. This is very significant; He hung thus (1) In order to show how thoroughly the world had stripped Him of all that He owned, and covered Him with shame; (2) in order to present Himself to all as the Innocent and Pure One who can support the glances of all.—Mary, the mother of Jesus, stood beneath the cross: Now was fulfilled the prophecy of Simeon, Luke ii. 35.—What feelings must have pierced her maternal heart! This was the origin of the ancient church-hymn: *Stabat mater dolorosa.*—Of such strength is womanly nature capable. An example for all Christian men and women, admonishing them not to be ashamed of Jesus, often to go beneath His cross, that they may become worthy of those women who went before them. RAMBACH, *in loc.*, p. 1063, compares Mary and Eve. Eve stood in Paradise beside the pleasant tree of the knowledge of good and evil. Mary stands beside the ignominious tree of the cross. The former looked upon the forbidden tree, and its fruit conduced to her death; the latter looks upon the promised tree of life, and is refreshed by its fruit in her mortal anguish.—Our death too, when God calleth, must be voluntary. It is the Christian's art to die willingly.

[CRAVEN: From AMBROSE: Chap. xix. 26. Mary, as became the *Mother* of our Lord, stood before the cross, when the *Apostles* fled, and with pitiful eyes beheld the wounds of her Son.——From AUGUSTINE: Ver. 17. Great spectacle! to the profane a laughing-stock, to the pious a mystery. Profaneness sees a King bearing a cross instead of a sceptre; piety sees a King bearing a cross, thereon to nail Himself, and afterwards to nail it on the foreheads of kings.—Ver. 18. Even the cross was a judgment seat; for the Judge being the middle, one thief, who believed, was pardoned, the other, who mocked, was damned: a sign of what He would once do to the quick and dead,—place the one on His right hand, the other on His left.—Ver. 20. These three were the languages most known there: the Hebrew, on account of being used in the worship of the Jews; the Greek in consequence of the spread of Greek philosophy; the Latin, from the Roman empire being established everywhere.—Ver. 22. O ineffable working of Divine power, even in the hearts of ignorant men! Did not some hidden voice sound from within, and, if we may say so, with clamorous silence,—saying to Pilate in the prophetic words of the Psalm, *Alter not the inscription of the title?*—Vers. 26, 27. This truly is that hour of the which Jesus, when about to change the water into wine, said, *Mother* [Woman], *what have I to do with thee? Mine hour is not yet come.* Then, about to act divinely, He repelled the Mother of His humanity, of His infirmity, as if He knew her not: now, suffering humanly, He commands with humane affection, her of whom he was made Man. Here is a moral lesson. The good Teacher shows us by His example that pious sons should take care of their parents. The cross of the Sufferer is the chair of the Master.—Ver. 28. He who appeared Man, *suffered* all these things; He who was God, *ordered* them.——From CHRYSOSTOM: Ver. 17. He carried the badge of victory on His shoulders, as conquerors do.—Ver. 18. *And two others with Him;* What they did in wickedness was a gain to the truth. To convert a thief on the cross, and bring him into paradise, was no less a miracle than the rending of the rocks.—Vers. 23, 24. Behold the sureness of prophecy. The prophet foretold not only what they would part, but what they would not. They *parted* the raiment, but *cast lots* for the vesture.—Ver. 25. Observe how the weaker sex is the stronger; standing by the cross when the disciples fly.—Ver. 26. Though there were other women by, He makes no mention of any of them, but only of His Mother, to show us that we should specially honor our mothers.—Vers. 26-30. Observe how imperturbable He is during His crucifixion, talking to the disciple of His Mother, fulfilling prophecies, giving good hope to the thief; whereas, before His crucifixion, He seemed in fear. The weakness of His nature was shown there, the exceeding greatness of His power here. He teaches us too, herein, not to turn back, because we may feel disturbed at the difficulties before us; for when we are once actually under the trial, all will be light and easy for us.

[From BURKITT: Ver. 17. Why could not Christ bear His own cross, who was able to bear the sins of the whole world, when hanging upon the cross? 1. Probably, the Jews' malice provided Him a cross of an extraordinary greatness; 2. He was much debilitated and weakened, with His long watching and sweating the night before; 3. The sharp edges of the cross grating His late whipped and galled shoulders, might occasion the fresh bleeding of His wounds; 4. Thereby He gave the world a demonstration of the truth of His humanity, that He was in all things like unto us.—Ver. 18. It had been a sufficient disparagement to our blessed Redeemer to be sorted with the best of men; but to be numbered with the scum of mankind is such an indignity as confounds our thoughts.—Ver. 19. Pilate, who before was His *judge*, and pronounced Him innocent, is now His *herald* to proclaim His glory.—Pilate did that for Christ which none of His own disciples durst do. No thanks to him for this; because the highest services performed to Christ undesignedly shall neither be accepted nor rewarded by God.—Ver. 22. Surely the constancy of Pilate at this time must be attributed to special divine Providence. How wonderful was it that he who before was as inconstant as a reed, should now be fixed as a pillar of brass! [His so called *constancy* was nothing but the natural outworking of the *fear* excited by the threat to accuse him before Cæsar; his persistence in retaining the inscription would not only gall the Jews but be an effectual bar to any charge of his having neglected the Imperial interests. The true homiletical inferences from this passage are that 1. Those who attempt to accomplish their ends by improper influences, brought to bear on rulers, generally over-reach themselves; 2. God over-rules the arts of the wicked for their own punishment and His glory. E. R. C.]—Ver. 26. He calls her *woman*, and not *mother:* not that He was ashamed of, or unwilling to own her as His mother, but either 1. Fearing that calling her by that name should augment and increase her grief and trouble, or, 2. To intimate His change of state and condition, that, being ready to die and return to His Father in heaven, He was above all earthly relations.—Vers. 26, 27. The Lord never removes one comfort, and takes away the means of subsistence from His people, but He raises up another in the room of it.—Such as are beloved of Christ, shall be peculiarly honored by Him, and be employed in the highest services for Him.—Ver. 30. *It is finished:* 1. My Father's eternal counsel concerning Me is accomplished; 2. The scriptures are now fulfilled; 3. My sufferings are now ended; 4. The fury and malice of My enemies are now ended; 5. The work of man's redemption and salvation is perfected.—*He bowed His head, and gave up the ghost:* Christ was a volunteer in dying.

[From M. Henry: Ver. 17. Whatever cross He calls us out to bear at any time, we must remember that He bore the cross first, and by bearing it *for us*, bears it *off from us* in a great measure, for thus He hath made *His yoke easy*, *and His burden light.*—Ver. 18. Observe what death Christ died; 1. The death of the cross, a bloody, painful, shameful, cruel death; 2. He was *nailed* to the cross, as a sacrifice *bound* to the altar; 3. He was lifted up, as the brazen serpent, hung between heaven and earth, because we were unworthy of either, and abandoned by both; 4. His hands were stretched out to invite and embrace us; 5. He hung upon the tree some hours, dying gradually in the full use of reason and speech, that He might actually resign Himself a sacrifice. See Him bleeding, see Him struggling, see Him dying, see Him and love Him, love Him and live to Him, and study what we shall render.—Vers. 19, 20. God so ordered it that this (title) should be written in the three then most known tongues; intimating thereby that Jesus Christ should be a *Saviour to all nations*, and not to the Jews only; and also that every nation should hear *in their own tongue the wonderful works* of the Redeemer.—Vers. 21, 22. An earnest of what came to pass soon after, when the Gentiles submitted to *the kingdom of the Messiah,* which the unbelieving Jews had rebelled against.—Ver. 23. While Christ was in His dying agonies, the soldiers were merrily dividing His spoils.—Ver. 26. His speaking to her in this seemingly slight manner was designed to give check to the undue honors which He foresaw would be given her in the Romish Church.—Ver. 27. Those that truly love Christ, and are loved of Him, will be glad of an opportunity to do any service to Him, or His.—Ver. 29. To everlasting *thirst* we had been condemned, *had not Christ suffered* [thirsted] *for us.*—Christ would rather court an affront than see any prophecy unfulfilled. This should satisfy us under all our trials,—that the will of God is done, and the word of God accomplished.—Ver. 30. *It is finished;* that is 1. The malice of His persecutors; 2. The counsel and commandment of His Father; 3. The types and prophecies of the Old Testament; 4. The ceremonial law; 5. Sin; 6. His suffering; 7. His life; 8. The work of man's redemption.

[From Scott: Vers. 17-30. He was wounded and scourged that we might be healed; He was arrayed with scorn in the purple robe, that He might procure for us "the robe of righteousness;" He was crowned with thorns, that we might be "crowned with honor and immortality;" He stood speechless, that we might have an all-prevailing plea; He endured torture that we might have "a strong consolation;" He thirsted that we might drink of the waters of life; He bore the wrath of the Father, that we might enjoy His favor; He "was numbered with transgressors," that we might be made "equal to angels;" He died, that we might live forever!—Ver. 26. The surest interest in His love will not secure our exemption from the sharpest temporal sufferings.—Ver. 27. We ought to act as though we heard Jesus say from His cross concerning this and the other believer, "Behold My mother," "My brother," "My sister."——From A Plain Commentary (Oxford): Ver. 17. *And He bearing His cross went forth;* "The Jews themselves have referred this type (of Isaac) unto that custom: for upon the words, 'And Abraham took the wood of the burnt offering, and laid it upon Isaac his son,' they have this note,—'as a man *carries his cross upon his shoulders.*'" (Pearson.)—Vers. 19-22. "It was not for nothing that Pilate suddenly wrote, and resolutely maintained what he had written. That title on the cross did signify no less than that His royal power was active even there; for 'having spoiled principalities and powers, He made a show of them openly, triumphing over them in it; and through His death, destroyed him that had the power of death, that is, the devil.'" (Pearson.)—Ver. 23. And thus at the very foot of the cross of Christ was enacted the emblem of that triumph over our Saviour which the Powers of Darkness, it may well be supposed, by this time thought secure! They had slain their great enemy (the devils will have already assumed); and their wicked agents may now be instigated to "*divide the spoil.*"—"Because Christ's people cannot be rent and torn by divisions, His tunic, seamless and woven throughout, was not rent by them into whose hands it fell. Single,—united,—connected,—it shows the concord which should subsist among as many of ourselves as put on Christ. That vest of His declares to us, in a sacrament, the Unity of the Church." (Cyprian.)—Ver. 24. "Christ, like Joseph, was about to flee from this evil and adulterous world; and leave His garment in its hands." (Williams.)—Vers. 26, 27. O amazing privilege! thus to have been appointed by the Incarnate Word Himself to supply His place towards His bereaved mother! How stupendous a legacy was this for Divine Piety to bequeath, and for adoring love to inherit!—"The presence of the Godhead in our Lord's person did not efface and outshine the essential feelings of a human heart. It did but quicken and strengthen all those affections and sympathies which are still left as remnants of the heavenly image, and the groundwork of its renewal within us." (HOBHOUSE.)—"As GOD, our Saviour might have removed His human mother to the best of those 'many mansions' which are prepared for those that love Him. But it was *as* GOD He willed that she should stay awhile on earth: while *as Man*, He both provided a home for her such as He could never give her while He lived; and called the human feelings of a friend into play on her behalf, while He did so." (HOBHOUSE.)—Ver. 30. He was "reclining His head as on His Father's bosom." (ORIGEN.)

[From KRUMMACHER: Ver. 17. *And He bearing His cross, etc.* It is thus the unhappy world repels the Man who entered upon it heralded by angels!—It is thus she rewards Him for the unwearied love with which He poured upon her the abundance of all conceivable benefits and mercies.—Oh, who that is still inclined to doubt whether mankind was worthy of eternal perdition without the intervention of a Mediator, let him cast a look at this path of suffering and convince himself of the contrary! For why is the Holy One thus dragged along, unless it be that we loved sin too ardently not to hate a man, even to the death, who made Himself known as the deliverer from it.—Had He shrunk back from this fatal path, His road to suffering would have represented to us that on which, when dying, we should have quitted the world. Instead of soldiers, the emissaries of Satan would have escorted us; instead of the accursed tree, the curse of the law itself; instead of the fetters, the bands of eternal wrath would have encircled us, and despair have lashed us with its fiery scourge.—It may be that during our earthly pilgrimage we are led on similar paths to that on which we see Jesus, our Head, proceeding; but Christ has deprived our fearful path of its horrors, our burdens of their overpowering weight, our disgrace and need of their deadly stings, and placed us in a situation to say "Yea, though I walk through the valley of the shadow of death I will fear no evil, for Thou art with me."——*Golgotha*—Calvary—horrifying name—the appellation of the most momentous and awful spot upon the whole earth. Behold a naked and barren eminence, enriched only by the blood of criminals, and covered with the bones of executed rebels, incendiaries, prisoners, and other offscouring of the human race. An accursed spot, where love never rules, but where naked justice alone sits enthroned, with scales and sword, and from which every passer-by turns with abhorrence, a nocturnal rendezvous of jackals and hyenas. Only think, this place so full of horrors, becomes transformed into "the hill from whence cometh our help," and whose mysteries many kings and prophets desired to see and did not see them. Yes, upon this awful hill our roses shall blossom, and our springs of peace and salvation burst forth. The pillar of our refuge towers upon this height. The Bethany of our repose and eternal refreshment here displays itself to our view.—On that awful mount ends the earthly career of the Lord of Glory. Behold Him, the only green, sound, and fruitful tree upon earth, and at the root of this tree the axe is laid. What a testimony against the world, and what an annihilating contradiction to every thing that bears the name of God and Divine Providence, if the latter did not find its solution in the mystery of *the representative atonement.*—Ver. 18. *They crucified Him;* O what a dying bed for the King of kings! As often as we repose on the downy cushions of peace, or blissfully assemble in social brotherly circles, singing hymns of hope, let us not forget that the cause of the happiness we enjoy is solely to be found in the fact, that the Lord of Glory once extended Himself on the fatal tree for us.—The *earth* rejects the Prince of Life from its surface, and, as it seems, *heaven* also refuses Him: Though *rejected* by heaven and earth, yet He forms, *as such*, the connecting link between them both, and the Mediator of their eternal and renewed amity.—The moment the cross is elevated to its height, a purple stream falls from the wounds of the crucified Jesus, and bedews the place of torture and the sinful crowd which surrounds it. This is His legacy to His Church. This rosy dew works wonders. It falls upon spiritual deserts, and they blossom as the rose. We sprinkle it upon the door-posts of our hearts, and are secure against destroyers and avenging angels. This dew falls on the ice of the north pole, and the accumulated frozen mass of ages thaws beneath it. It streams down on the torrid zone, and the air becomes cool and pleasant. Where this rain falls, the gardens of God spring up, lilies bloom, and what was black becomes white in the purifying stream, and what was polluted becomes pure as the light of the sun.—For our justification nothing more is requisite than that, in the consciousness of our utter helplessness we lay hold on the horns of that altar, which is sprinkled with blood that "speaketh better things than that of Abel."—"I am crucified with Christ," exclaims the Apostle, and by these words points out the entire fruit which the cross bears for all believers. His meaning is, "They are not *His* sins for which the curse is there endured, but *mine*; for He who thus expires on the cross dies for me: Christ pays and suffers in my stead."—The *life* of the world springs only from the *death* of the Just One.—Ver. 19. "What sayest thou, Is this a King?" Do not shake thy head, but know that *thou* art wanting in discernment, not *He* in majesty.—Dost thou inquire where is the majesty of this King? Truly it exists, although for the time hidden, like the glittering gold of the ark beneath the rams' skins that covered it.—*Jesus of Nazareth*, THE KING of the Jews: Yes, it is He. Thou mayest recognize Him (as King) by the victories He achieves even on the fatal tree, the first of which is of a glorious twofold character—over *Himself* and over *the infernal tempter.* 1. Over *Himself*; 2. Over *Satan*; He suffers Himself to be wounded in the heel, but at the same time breaks the head of the old Serpent. 3. The greatest and most wonderful of all—the victory of the Lawgiver over the Law. There was no want of *wish* or *will* in heaven to save us; but the *right* to undertake the great work was wanting—the *law* put in its protest to our redemption. The *curse* had to be endured; He submitted to this and drank the cup of wrath—and when the voice of mercy was heard from heaven, the law had nothing to object.—Yes, He is a King! But where is His kingdom? He is founding it while hanging on the cross. The drops of blood which trickle down, are the price He paid to ransom His people, and the dying groans which issue from His breast, the joyful peal which announces the birthday of His Zion.—In His crown of thorns He governs the world of spirits and of hearts; and the greatest marvels by which He glorifies Himself on earth He performs with His pierced hands.—Ver. 20. The title was written in Greek, Latin, and Hebrew, the three theological languages, that all the world may read and understand.—Vers. 23, 24. A dying-bed presents itself to our view—an individual at the point of death—a legacy and the heirs; let us direct our attention first to the *Testator*, and then to His *legacy*, and *heirs:* 1. The *Testator;* Jesus of Nazareth—(1) the poorest of the poor, (2) the King of the Jews—the King of kings—the Son of the Living God—the Alpha and Omega, God blessed forever: 2. The *Legacy;* His clothing—(1) the upper garment which symbolizes the outwardly operating fullness of the Saviour's power and life, and in a second signification, the spiritual endowment intended for us—this is divisible; (2) the vesture or body-coat of the Man of sorrows which He used to wear under the mantle; beneath the resplendent robe of His wonderful and active life, the Saviour wore another, the garment of a perfect obedience—it is the robe of righteousness of the Son of God, which is symbolized by the coat without a seam (indivisible) for which the lot is cast at the foot of the cross; 3. The *heirs;* (1) the executioners, (2) *one* of the murderers inherits the costly robe,—this circumstance tells us that no wickedness, however great, excludes unconditionally from the inheritance; it only depends upon this, that the symbolical position of those executioners, with respect to the body should be essentially fulfilled in us—1. They know how to value the preciousness of the seamless vestment: 2. They perceive that only in its undivided whole it was of value; 3. They are satisfied to obtain possession gratuitously—without any merit of their own.—Vers. 25, 26. In the midst of rage and fury, love stands near Jesus in His dying moments and lifts up to Him its tearful and affectionate eye—behold a lovely little company in the midst of the bands of Belial, a hidden rosebud under wild and tangled bramble-bushes, a splendid wreath of lilies around the death-bed of the Redeemer.—In that mourning group you see only the first divinely quickened germs of the future kingdom of the Divine Sufferer.—Strange enough, with one exception, all of them are females: the strong are fled—the weak maintain their ground; the heroes despair—the timid, who did not presume to promise anything, overcome the world. If the man's is the splendid deed—the woman's is enduring patience; if to the former belongs the heroism which cuts the knot—to the latter (which is the greater of the two) belongs the silent self-sacrifice which is faithful unto death.—*The disciple whom He loved;* In these words the Apostle indicates what was his pride, his crown, and his highest boast. At the same time they point out the source whence he derived all his consolation, hope, and strength; this source was *love*—not the love with which he embraced the Lord, but that with which the Lord embraced him.—He who can sign himself the disciple whom Jesus loves has a sure guaranty for all that he needs, and for all that his heart can desire; he may call himself the man that is tossed with tempests, yet if he is "the disciple whom Jesus loves" what more will he have?—*Woman;* It becomes Him not to call her *Mother* now since this term in the Hebrew includes the idea of *Mistress,* while He was just preparing, as the Lord of lords, to ascend the throne of eternal majesty.—Vers. 26, 27. *Behold thy Son—Behold thy Mother;* These words contain the record of the institution of a new family relationship; in this fellowship Christ is the Head, and all His believing people form one great, closely-connected family: Let him who would envy John the pleasing task of being a support to the Mother of Jesus know that the way to the same honor lies open to him—Jesus has said, "Whosoever shall do the will of My Father which is in heaven, the same is My Mother and sister and brother," Matt. xii. 50.—Ver. 28. *I thirst:* What was the nature of the distress expressed by the cry?—1. Physical; 2. Does it not remind of the awful representation of the invisible world portrayed in the parable of Lazarus and Dives?—For what did He thirst? Not only for earthly water, but after the full restoration of His Father's countenance.—These words also solicited from mankind a charitable act.—That for which He chiefly thirsts is that He may gain us over to Himself—that transgressors may be freed from sin; those under the curse, absolved; those that are bound, liberated.—O that you could weep as Peter wept, and like David! Such tears are the drink-offering for which the Saviour still thirsts.—Ver. 30. *It is finished:* At the very moment when, for the Hero of Judah, all seems lost, His words declare that all is won and accomplished. Listen! at these words you hear fetters burst, and prison walls falling down; barriers as high as heaven are overthrown, and gates which had been closed for thousands of years again move on their hinges.—Every condition of the work of human redemption has been completed with the exception of one which was included in them.—If He has paid the ransom, how can a righteous God demand payment a second time?—With the heraldic and conquering cry, *It is finished,* He turned once more to the world. It was His farewell to earth—a farewell such as beseemed the Conqueror of Death, the Prince of Life, the Governor of all things. He then withdrew Himself entirely into connection with His God, and turned His face to Him alone.

[From JACOBUS: Vers. 26, 27. What a Son was this, true to His Father in Heaven, and to His mother on earth.——From OWEN: Ver. 18. *Jesus in the midst*—disgraceful eminence.—Vers. 26, 27. "The burden of the world's redemption with all its increasing horror of sin, lies upon His soul; boundless anticipations, now gradually receding and passing away, of the glory to be obtained had filled His spirit, yet He has room for the exercise of the minutest care." (STIER.)—Ver 28. Jesus was conscious that He was fulfilling a pre-determined series of sufferings, and manifested no impatient haste, that they should be endured other than in their allotted place and time.—Ver. 30. *It is finished;* "All things were done which the law required, all things established which prophecy predicted, all things abolished which were to be abrogated, all things obtained in order to be bestowed which had been the subject of promise. All things—down to the last drops of scornful compassion, and compassionate scorn, after receiving which Christ's lips uttered this great word—were suffered which were to be suffered; but therein, at the same time, all things were done and accomplished, nothing was left wanting. The theology of ages has striven to embrace this 'all' and to develop it; and strives to this day in vain to express it perfectly." (STIER.)

[Vers. 25, 26. *Now there stood by the cross, etc.* Is not this symbolic of the great *Apostasy* (2 Thess. ii. 3; Luke xviii. 8, *etc.*) when only a few shall remain faithful?—Ver. 26. *Woman;* "She was THE WOMAN whose *Seed* here bruises the serpent's head. What title, then, so fitting at the present juncture, as this—with its twofold weight of shame and glory? *Woman, Satan's* instrument in bringing *sin* and *death* into the world—thereby rendering this *cross* necessary: *Woman, God's* instrument in bringing Him into the world who is the *Righteousness* and *Life* thereof, whose *cross* shall be changed into a *crown* of rejoicing for Himself and His redeemed. Surely, it is no marvel if now, whilst the promise made to Eve is fulfilled to Mary, the same old word that meets us in the story of the fall, resounds from the lips of the Restorer, the suffering yet victorious Seed." (E. M.)—"Woman! Thy Saviour spake *thy* name in His last agony—not harshly, condemningly, as He in justice might have done, but lovingly, compassionately, with fostering care." (E. M.)]

V.

CHRIST THE GLORIFICATION OF DEATH, THE VERY LIFE IN DEATH. THE CORPSE OF JESUS, TO HIS FOES AN OBSCURE SIGN OF CALAMITY, TO HIS FRIENDS A MYSTERIOUS PASSOVER-SIGN (A SIGN THAT HE IS THE TRUE PASSOVER-LAMB AND THAT SOMETHING MIRACULOUS IS TRANSPIRING WITHIN HIM), TO HIS UNDECIDED DISCIPLES A DECISIVE, ANIMATING SIGN. THE HONORABLE BURIAL IN THE GARDEN AND IN THE NEW SEPULCHRE. THE FORETOKENS OF THE VICTORY OF CHRIST.

CHAP. XIX. 31-42.

(Matt. xxvii. 57-66; Mark xv. 42-47; Luke xxiii. 50-56.)

31 The Jews therefore, because it was the preparation [it was preparation day, παρασκευή, comp ver 42], that the bodies should [might] not remain upon the cross on
the sabbath day [sabbath], (for that sabbath day was a high day [for great was the
day of that sabbath, ἦν γὰρ μεγάλη ἡ ἡμέρα ἐκείνου τοῦ σαββάτου],) besought Pilate
32 that their legs might be broken, and *that* they might be taken away. Then came
the soldiers [The soldiers therefore came], and brake [broke] the legs of the first,
33 and of the other which [who] was crucified with him. But when they came to Je-
sus, and saw that he was dead already, they brake [broke] not his legs: But one of
the soldiers with a spear pierced his side, and forthwith came there [*omit* there, *or*
34 *read:* there came] out blood and water.
35 And he that saw *it* bare record [he that hath seen it, hath born witness, ὁ ἑωρακὼς μεμαρτύρηκεν], and his record [witness] is true [ἀληθινή][1]; and he knoweth that
he saith [what is] true [ἀληθῆ], that ye [also, καὶ ὑμεῖς] might believe [may believe,
36 πιστεύσητε]. For these things were done [came to pass], that the Scripture should
[might] be fulfilled, 'A bone of him shall not be broken.' [Ex. xii. 46; Num. ix.
37 12; Ps. xxxiv. 20.] And again another Scripture saith, 'They shall look on him
whom they pierced.' [Zech. xii. 10.]

38 And after this [these things, ταῦτα] Joseph[2] of Arimathea, being a disciple of
Jesus, but secretly [though in secret, or, concealing it, κεκρυμμένος δέ] for fear of the
Jews, besought Pilate that he might take away the body of Jesus: and Pilate gave
him leave. He came therefore, and took the body of Jesus [took away his body].[3]
39 And there came also Nicodemus, (which [who] at the first came to Jesus [to him, πρὸς
αὐτόν] by night) and brought [bringing, φέρων] a mixture of myrrh and aloes, about an
40 hundred pound *weight* [a hundred pounds, λίτρας, weight]. Then took they [They took
therefore] the body of Jesus, and wound it in linen clothes with the spices, as the
41 manner of the Jews is [as is the custom of the Jews] to bury. Now in the place
where he was crucified there was a garden; and in the garden a new sepulchre
[tomb], wherein was never man yet laid [in which no one had ever been laid].[4]

42 There laid they Jesus therefore because of the Jews' preparation *day* [day]; for the sepulchre [tomb] was nigh at hand.

TEXTUAL AND GRAMMATICAL.

[1] Ver. 35—[Cod. Sin. reads ἀληθής, but against most authorities.—P. S.]

[2] Ver. 38.—Ὁ Ἰωσὴφ ἀπὸ Ἀριμαθαίας. In support of the article A. J. Δ.; for the omission of the second ὁ before ἀπό A. B. D., *etc.* [Tischend., Alf., Westcott and Hort omit both articles, and read simply, with ℵ and B: Ἰωσὴφ ἀπὸ Ἀριμαθαίας.—P. S.]

[3] Ver. 38.—[I read with ℵ.[3a] B. L. X., *etc.*, Lachm., Treg., Alf., Westc. and Hort, ἦλθεν οὖν καὶ ἦρεν τὸ σῶμα αὐτοῦ. The text. rec. (with Vulg.) has τοῦ Ἰησοῦ instead of αὐτοῦ. Tischendorf ed. viii., follows the reading of ℵ.*: ἦλθον οὖν καὶ ἦρον αὐτόν: "*they* came therefore and took *him* away."—P. S.]

[4] Ver. 41.—[A. D. Orig., Tischend., Tregelles and Alf., read ἐτέθη, *was laid;* but ℵ. B. Cyr., Westcott read: ἦν τεθειμένος, *had been laid;* comp. Luke xxiii. 53.—P. S.]

EXEGETICAL AND CRITICAL.

Ver. 31. **The Jews therefore.**—The οὖν again characteristically indicates the next concern which troubled the Jews as Jews. The observance of the ceremonial law was their first thought after the work of the crucifixion was accomplished. Rupert: *Magnifici honoratores Dei, cum in conscientia mala reposuissent sanguinem Justi.*

That the bodies might not remain on the cross [ἵνα μὴ μείνῃ ἐπὶ τοῦ σταυροῦ τά σώματα].—On the Roman custom see the Commentary on *Matthew*. The Jewish ordinance in regard to the bodies of persons hanged on a tree Deut. xxi. 22 f.; Josephus, *De Bello Jud.*, IV. 5, 2.—**Because it was the Preparation day** [ἐπεὶ παρασκευὴ ἦν].—*I. e.* because preparations must be made for keeping holy the Sabbath, on which day no bodies were allowed to remain hanging on the tree.—**For great was the** (feast-) **day of that** (Paschal) **Sabbath** [ἦν γὰρ μεγάλη ἡ ἡμέρα ἐκείνου τοῦ σαββάτου].—(Comp. chap. vii. 37). Elucidating parenthesis. *I. e.* it was not a simple Sabbath of the current year, but its sanctity was increased by its falling in the Paschal season. This was true of the day in any case, whether, in accordance with the view of the disharmonists, the first paschal day was still to arrive and coincided with the Sabbath (Meyer and others), or whether, according to the view represented by us, the Sabbath in question fell upon the second Jewish passover-day. Meyer thinks that as the second passover-day it could have been called μεγάλη only because, in accordance with Lev. xxiii. 10, the feast of sheaves (Wieseler, *Synopse*, p. 344, p. 385) was celebrated on this day (16 Nisan). This reference, however, he asserts, John must have indicated. On the other hand, the first feast-day possessed, according to Lev. xxiii. 7-15, the character of a Sabbath also. But the case is simpler in its bearings. The Sabbath, being the principal holiday of the Jews, derived additional importance from every other festivity coincident with it, hence also from the second solemn passover-day. If, on the other hand, the passover-day had been the decisive motive, John would not have mentioned the Sabbath as a motive.

That their legs might be broken, *etc.* [ἵνα κατεαγῶσιν* αὐτῶν τὰ σκέλη καὶ ἀρθῶσιν].—Said in a perfectly general way, whence it follows that they were hastening the removal and as yet possessed no certain knowledge as to the death of Jesus. The shattering of the legs with clubs, *crucifragium* [σκελοκοπία], was a customary form of accelerating death—a procedure as harsh and brutal as crucifixion itself (Lactantius, *Instit.* IV. 26; Lipsius, *Ad Plaut.* II. 4, 63). It also appears as an independent punishment, Sueton., *Aug.* 67 [Seneca, *De Ira*, III. 32, *etc.*]. "The supervention of a *coup de grace*, by which (not by the *crucifragium* in itself) death was occasioned, cannot be proved, least of all from ver. 34 (contrary to Michaelis, Hug and others)." Thus Meyer [p. 633], while Tholuck, following Quintil., *Declam.* VI. 9, and other instances in Hug, declares in favor of the customariness of the death-stab in cases where death seemed to have already taken place, but where the soldier wished thoroughly to assure himself of the fact. In accordance with the presentation of our Gospel, the breaking of the legs must be conceived of as a deadly process. It is omitted, as the more difficult task, in cases where the stab of a lance is sufficient to complete the signs of death by means of an easy death-stroke.

* [The aor. with augm. syllab. from κατάγνυμι, see Buttmann, II. 97, Winer, p. 68 (§ 12).—P. S.]

Ver. 32. **The soldiers therefore came** [ἦλθον οὖν οἱ στρατιῶται, κ. τ. λ.].—Two soldiers simultaneously break the legs of the thief on the right and the thief on the left. With Jesus they consider this superfluous—therefore, to make assurance doubly sure, they pierce Him with the lance. His death is thus doubly and trebly warranted: once by the cognition of the soldiers, then by the mortal spear-stroke, finally by His burial on the part of His friends. From chap. xx. 27 Tholuck infers besides (less securely) that the wound was the breadth of a man's hand.—The soldier stood with his right hand opposite the left side of the Crucified One.

Ver. 34. **Blood and water** [καὶ ἐξῆλθεν εὐθὺς αἷμα καὶ ὕδωρ].—We must preface the explanations of this fact by the statement that the Evangelist looks upon it as one of great moment. See ver. 37. ["The strong asseverations of the Evangelist, show that he regarded the circumstance as very extraordinary, perhaps as supernatural. He writes of it like a person who hardly expected to be believed. Yet the effect he describes is exactly (?) that which we now know was most likely to result from preceding causes. Thus his accuracy of observation and the honesty and veracity of his testimony are most remarkably corroborated." Webster and Wilkinson.—P. S.]

Different explanations:

1. The modern explanation of the fact as a NATURAL phenomenon. This interpretation is

made the more difficult by the circumstance that the blood does not flow out of dead bodies, neither does it separate into blood and water [or placenta and serum] (as it does in a vessel after venesection).

First assumption: Death was produced by the spear-thrust, and the forth-flowing of the blood (or of a reddish lymph) must demonstrate Christ's corporeality, in contradiction of the Docetæ (Hammond, Kuinoel, Olshausen). This view is combated by the presupposition of the disciple and the ancient Church that Jesus was dead, and by the separation of blood and water. [See also against this view, Stroud, on the *Physical Cause of Christ's Death*, p. 141 f. It is certain, however, that, had Christ not been already dead, the infliction of such a wound in the heart by the spear of a Roman soldier must have produced death; and this fact in any case sets aside the Gnostic docetic view according to which Christ suffered and died only in appearance, as well as the older rationalistic view that Christ recovered from the effects of the crucifixion, and that His resurrection was merely an awakening from a trance.—P. S.]

Second assumption: The flow of blood and water from the body of a *dead* person is physiologically explained:

a. By the presence of extravasations, or blood-blisters, in which the globules and serum have become separated one from the other (Ebrard).

b. By the serum in the pericardium (Gruner, *De Jes. Christi morte vera non simulata, etc.*, Halle, 1805), to which yet other serous reservoirs on the side of the heart may be added (see Tholuck, p. 439). [The Gruners, two physicians, father and son, held that the blood issued from the heart, the water from the pericardium, *i. e.* the membrane which envelops the heart. So also Kipping (*De cruce et cruciariis*, pp. 187-195), Bishop Watson (*Apology for the Bible*), Barnes, Webster and Wilkinson, and Owen. To this theory it is objected that the quantity of liquid or reddish lymphatic humor in the pericardium is usually so minute as to be scarcely perceptible. "Haller states that a small quantity of water, not exceeding a few drachms, has frequently been found in the pericardium of executed persons; but, except under very peculiar and morbid circumstances, the eminent anatomists John and Charles Bell deny the occurrence altogether. . . . Naturally the pericardium exhibits scarcely anything which deserves the name of liquid; but after some forms of violent death, more especially when attended with obstructed circulation, it may contain a little serum, either pure or mixed with blood. . . . For the statement of the Gruners, that after death accompanied with anxiety the pericardium is full of water, there is no evidence." Stroud, l. c. p. 138, 139.—P. S.]

2. The apprehension of the fact as a MIRACLE (Origen and the ancient Church generally, Meyer, Luthardt). [Bengel: *quod sanguis exiit, mirum; quod etiam aqua, magis mirum; quod utrumque statim, uno tempore, et tamen distincte, maxime mirum.* So also Alford who, with Meyer, stops with the recognition of a miracle, without indulging in allegorizing.—P. S.]

3. Between the assumption of a miracle unassisted by any physiological instrumentality, and that of a natural phenomenon, there lies the assumption that we have to do with a PRIMITIVE PHENOMENON, *i. e.* a unique appearance based upon the unique situation. Meyer [p. 635] says: "A natural explanation in a higher sense is assigned for this phenomenon by Lange (*Leben Jesu*, II. p. 1614 f.); he assumes it to be explicable by the process of *transformation* which, as he affirms, the body of Christ was undergoing. A spinose conception in which there is not only an absence of clearness" (a fact equally true of the transformation itself, but which, nevertheless, does not render that transformation spinose), "but also imperiling the essential and necessary point of the actual *death* of Jesus" (*i. e.*, hazarding its being swallowed up in the resurrection), "and moreover representing the details of the assumed transformation as occurring in very sensuous and materialistic wise" (say, rather, in bodily and corporeal fashion). Meyer thinks he has warrant for citing against this view, 1 Cor. xv. 51-53. The following propositions may assist to an apprehension of the case: (1) After the death of Jesus, either corruption or transformation must have been preparing. (2) Corruption He did not see, hence it is transformation that was in course of preparation. (3) If this was preparing, the fact must of necessity make itself known by a sign transpiring in His wounded body,—a sign such as we are unacquainted with in other corpses. (4) That this sign is a *unicum*, concerning which we can find nothing in the history of extravasations, pericardia, *etc.* is a circumstance perfectly in order.

4. The MYTHICAL interpretation of Baur and others may be passed over (comp. Meyer [p. 637]).

5. [SYMBOLICAL and ALLEGORICAL] interpretations of the phenomenon [which may be connected with either of the preceding ones, especially with No. 2.—P. S.]. With reference to 1 John v. 6: Symbol of the two sacraments of grace: Apollinaris, Ambrose (*De Sacram. cp.* I. *aqua ut emundaret, sanguis ut redimeret,* Augustine, the R. Catholic exegetes, Luther).* Otherwise Baur: The death of Jesus symbolized as the source of spiritual life. Similarly Luthardt. The Evangelist has indeed said nothing of this meaning himself. He has laid stress upon the unexpectedness of the phenomenon, however.

[Other symbolical explanations: (1) Calvin: reference of the *blood* to *expiation;* of the water to *regeneration.* He, however, denies the *miraculous* character of the fact. Isaac Watts:

> "My Saviour's pierced side
> Poured out a double flood:
> By water we are purified
> And pardoned by the blood."

Toplady:

> "Let the water and the blood
> From Thy riven side which flowed,
> Be of sin the double cure,
> Cleanse me from its guilt and power."

(2) According to E. Swedenborg, *blood* signifies the proceeding Divine *truth* for the *spiritual* man,

* [So also Wordsworth (after the fathers): As Eve was taken from the side of sleeping Adam, so the church and the sacraments of the eucharist (*blood*) and baptism (*water*) emanated from the pierced side of the crucified Christ.—P. S.]

and *water* the Divine *truth* for the *natural* man. (*Apocalypse Explained*, No. 329).*—P. S.]

[Additional Remarks on the effusion of *blood* and *water*. This is properly a question for physicians to settle, but they differ as much as theologians. Comp. besides the dissertation of the Gruners already quoted, Thomas Bartholinus, *De Latere Christi aperto, etc.;* Hieronymus Bardus, *Epist. ad Thom. Bartholinum*, and the Reply of Bartholinus; William Stroud, M. D., *The Physical Cause of the Death of Christ*, 2d ed. with an Appendix by Sir James Y. Simpson, M. D. (London, 1871). The last work is probably the best and contains more curious information than any other. Dr. Stroud, as already mentioned on p. 587, traces the physical cause of the death of Christ to a sudden *rupture of the heart*, produced by intense agony of mind endured in behalf of sinners. He uses this verse as an argument for his theory. Rupture of the heart is followed by an effusion of blood (sometimes as much as a quart or much more) into the pericardium, where it quickly separates into its solid and liquid constituents, technically called *crassamentum* and *serum*, but in ordinary language *blood* and *water*. The soldier, in approaching the body of Christ and inflicting the wound for the purpose either to ascertain or to insure His death, would purposely aim at the heart, and, transfixing the lower part of the left side, would open the pericardium obliquely from below; that capsule being distended with crassamentum and serum, and consequently pressed against the side, its contents would, by force of gravity, be instantly and completely discharged through the wound, in a full stream of clear watery liquid intermixed with clotted blood, exactly corresponding to the sacred narrative: "and immediately there came forth blood and water." The difficulties of commentators have arisen mostly from the gratuitous assumption that the blood which flowed from the wound of Christ was liquid, and the water pure, and, to account for so marvellous an occurrence, recourse was had either to miraculous agency, or to other equally untenable suppositions. "Blood and water" simply denote the crassamentum and serum of blood which has separated into its constituents. See pp. 399 ff., and the instances adduced in illustration. Ewald (*Geschichte Christus*', 3d ed. 1867, p. 584 f.), without entering into the matter, likewise assumes that a sudden rupture of the heart (*ein plötzlicher Herzbruch*) was the immediate physical cause of the death of Christ, and explains from it the loud terrible cry of anguish on the cross.—P. S.]

Ver. 35. **And he that hath seen it hath borne witness** [[καὶ ὁ ἑωρακὼς μεμαρτύρηκεν].—According to Weisse, Schweizer, and others, a later reporter, distinguishing himself from John, here betrays himself. But it is the Evangelist who himself makes a distinction between an oral, evangelistic testimony, continued during many years, and his written iteration of the same at a later period—conscious that said testimony contains an extraordinary statement. He then distinguishes the *substance* of his testimony as essential truth (ἀληθινή), because the thing must so occur, as a fulfilment of the divine word, and the *form* of his testimony, ἀληθῆ. His testimony is, however, continually, and so in this instance also, designed to produce faith in Christ (see chap. xx. 31), namely, the confirmation and consummation of his readers' belief in the higher divine nature of Christ. Not, as some have supposed, *that ye may believe in the death of Jesus as an event which really transpired* (Beza and others); or *in the true corporeality of Christ*, in opposition to the Docetæ (Hammond, Paulus, and others). Meyer thinks that Gnosticism might have fastened even sooner upon the mysterious, enigmatical outflow (?).

Ver. 36. **A bone of Him shall not be broken** [Ὀστοῦν οὐ συντριβήσεται αὐτοῦ].—The first fulfilment of Scripture was of a *negative* sort: it was the fulfilment of the typical provision that not a bone of the paschal lamb should be broken, Ex. xii. 46; Nu. ix. 12. As the suffering Christ was the antitype of the paschal lamb (1 Cor. v. 7), it was necessary that this typical trait also should be fulfilled in Him.

Ver. 37. **Whom they pierced** [Ὄψονται εἰς ὃν ἐξεκέντησαν].—(Zech. xii. 10.) The εἰς ὃν by attraction in the place of εἰς ἐκεῖνον ὅν. Second, *positive* fulfilment of a Scriptural passage by the spear-thrust. The passage freely cited after the original text which the Septuagint has weakened ("Whom they have insulted"). Properly: They shall look up to Me אֵלַי Whom they have pierced. The reading אֵלָיו found in many manuscripts is probably an exegetical correction, as it seemed obvious that Jehovah cannot be pierced; hence likewise the figurative conception of the Septuagint. The passage in question is one of the exceedingly pregnant Messianic passages of the second half of Zechariah. The Messiah here appears in the light of the self-manifesting Jehovah Himself. The piercers are the Jews, standing, however, as representatives of the whole human race. "They have pierced Me," *i. e.* they have consummated their enmity against My highest manifestation and approach. "They shall look upon Me whom they have pierced," *i. e.* their eyes shall be opened in regard to their conduct and they shall perceive whom they have outraged,—they shall regret it, or it shall become a matter of regret to them. This prophecy has had a general fulfilment in the turning of the believing world to the Crucified One. It shall, however, be fulfilled in the most universal sense, in regard to the whole world, at the Last Judgment (Rev. i. 7). The beginning of this consternation of the world upon discovering that it has thrust at God, whilst it supposed itself to be piercing a criminal, in dealing the Messiah the heart-thrust, is significantly seen by the Evangelist in the fact that we have been considering. The spear-thrust was the final heart-blow and death-blow which, after many blows and stabs, the whole race of man inflicted upon the Messiah; it was therefore the concentrated symbol of His crucifixion in general. Hence, there immediately appeared a sign, such as is not met with in other

* [There is a Swedenborgian Commentary on the Gospel of John by Rev. J. Clowes, 3d ed. London, 1853. It has only recently come into my hands, but presents very little that might have been worth quoting in this work. It consists almost entirely of extracts from Swedenborg's writings, bearing on the "spiritual" sense of the spiritual Gospel.—P. S.]

corpses;—a sign in which the higher nature of Christ, the incipient manifestation of His glory, announced itself. That which is related concerning murdered persons, namely, that their wounds bleed afresh when the murderers approach their bodies, did actually happen here in the highest sense. That the phenomenon made one of the many signs that perplexed and dismayed the people at Golgotha, may be securely assumed from the prominent mention which this occurrence and its effect receive at the hands of John. This involves the complete overthrow of the *natural* [rationalistic] explanation. An ordinary appearance could not thus have operated. See viii. 28; xii. 32; Acts ii.

Ver. 38. **Joseph of Arimathea.**—Comp. Matt. xxvii. 57. After the Jews had induced Pilate to have the bodies taken down, Joseph presented his request and arrived at precisely the right moment to take the corpse which had been accorded him, down from the cross. So Meyer rightly, in opposition to De Wette who finds a difficulty here, as likewise in opposition to Lücke, who apprehends the *ἄρῃ* and *ἦρεν* as relating to the carrying away of the body which the soldiers had taken down. With this interpretation Meyer asserts that he has settled a difference which would otherwise exist, making this statement "unauthorized" by the side of Luke xxiii. 53; Mark xv. 46.

About a hundred pounds weight [*ὡς λίτρας ἑκατόν*].—See Comm. on *Matthew*, at the parallel passage. [A proof of the greatness of their love produced by the death of Christ. —P. S.]

Ver. 40. **As is the manner of the Jews** [*καθὼς ἔθος ἐστὶ τοῖς Ἰουδαίοις ἐνταφιάζειν*].—Contrast: The custom of the Egyptians, who took out the brain and bowels, or at least steeped the body for seventy days in natron. See Winer, "*Embalming*," Meyer. The Egyptian anointing was designed for the preservation of the bodies as mummies: the Jewish anointing formed a consecrated and beautiful transition of the corpse from death to corruption. On the fact that there is nothing surprising in the superabundance of one hundred pounds of aloes and myrrh for the anointing, see Tholuck.

Ver. 41. **In the place** [*ἐν τῷ τόπῳ*], *i. e.* in the district. According to Matt. xxvii. 60, it was Joseph's garden. Comp. Luke xxiii. 53; chap. xix. 30; Mark xi. 2.

Ver. 42. **On account of the preparation-day** [*διὰ τὴν παρασκευὴν τῶν Ἰουδ.*].—An intimation that if haste had not been urgent, they would have given Jesus more honorable burial in another place. Thus the very haste of the preparation-day was providential. Jesus should be interred in a new grave, in a manner the most extraordinary. The circumstance must serve at the same time to manifest Joseph's great alacrity in sacrifice.

DOCTRINAL AND ETHICAL.

1. The Johannean relation. John omits the trait of their rolling a great stone in front of the door of the sepulchre; he does not mention that Mary Magdalene and Mary the mother of James seated themselves over against the sepulchre; that the Jews, with the co-operation of Pilate, sealed the sepulchre on the Sabbath and set a military watch upon it (Matt.); that Pilate, before presenting Joseph with the body of Jesus, inquired of the centurion whether Jesus were dead (Mark); the approach of a greater number of acquaintances to view the death of Jesus; the inspection of the sepulchre by the women, and their Friday evening preparation of ointments for the formal interment of Jesus which they appointed to take place after the Sabbath (Luke).

On the other hand, he brings out the fact that Jesus was glorified in His death as the true Paschal Lamb, glorified no less by another mysterious fulfilment of Scripture, and specially glorified by the open emergence of His hitherto secret disciples, Joseph of Arimathea and Nicodemus, and the princely sepulture which they, in pious rivalry of love, have prepared for the Lord.

2. Great was the day of that Sabbath. A stroke of that Jewish hypocrisy which strains out gnats and swallows camels, similar to Chap. xviii. 28. In removing the bodies, however, in accordance with the instinct of an evil conscience, they are peculiarly interested in having the body of *Jesus* conveyed "out of sight and mind" of the people; in causing, along with the odious Man, the very name of Him, as also their work upon Him, to be hurried, with all possible expedition, beneath the sod. But here, as in the composition of the superscription, contingencies occur, which cross, modify and enfeeble their plots. They can not hinder Jesus, upon His descent from the cross, from being significantly distinguished from the thieves and honorably sepulchred.

3. Paschal Lamb. Ye shall break not a bone of Him. On the uncertainty of typology in regard to the meaning of this provision, see Tholuck, p. 430. We assume that the provision originally belonged to the expression of the *most hurried* preparation of the Paschal Lamb, as at the instant of flight or departure. Then at the same time it was expressive of the utterly undivided participation of the house-congregation or domestic church in fellowship and sacrament (Tholuck, p. 430). This type was fulfilled in Christ. The hurried removal from the cross—an expression of the Sufferer's speedy transportation to glory—prevented the breaking of the legs, and henceforth the *whole undivided* Christ should be the spiritual and vital food of the Church of His salvation.

4. Vers. 34 and 37. *Blood* and *water*. See the Exeg. Notes, and *Leben Jesu*, p. 1611.

5. The association of Joseph of Arimathea and Nicodemus: a sign showing how the complete development of malice and unrighteousness impels all nobler natures into the camp of Christ; and how the darkest hours of the kingdom of God are invariably the natal hour of a new discipleship. That glory of the Jewish world, to which they cleaved, being turned to shame in their eyes, they are become free from their earthly goods and know not how better to spend them than in the service of the love of Christ. One offers the abundance of his precious spices, which constituted an important household treasure among the Orientals; the

other offers his garden and his family-vault to be the resting-place of an excommunicate, outlawed, crucified Man; both sacrifice their safety, position, authority, their old associations and, greatest sacrifice of all, their old Jewish hierarchal pride, and their old Messianic hope and entire view of the world. To them all things are involved in midnight gloom; but the innocence and righteousness of Christ they see, shining as the broad day in the midst of this darkness.—Moral loathing and abhorrence of the mask of hypocritical godlessness are able to burst the strongest bonds of deference to human opinions, and to generate the highest sacrificial courage.

6. The pious OBSERVANCE OF THE SABBATH on the part of Jesus' friends, on the occasion of their burial of Him, a testimony against those who, with the charge of Sabbath-breaking, introduced His persecution unto death.

7. The REPOSE OF JESUS at once a slumber of death and a mystery of transformation unto resurrection.

HOMILETICAL AND PRACTICAL.

See the DOCT. NOTES and the Synoptists.

From the moment of Jesus' death, all things take a turn.—The glorification of Jesus begins with the glorification of His holy corpse: 1. Through special divine protection (break no bone); 2. through special heavenly signs (blood and water); 3. through special human reverence and care (the interment).—God watcheth over His own in death as in life.—How, in the funeral of the Just One, the victory of His life-battle is reflected.—The desire of the Jews to remove the bodies from Golgotha: The expression of (1) a legal, slavish zeal; (2) an hypocritical sanctimoniousness; (3) a bad conscience.—The last heart-thrust which Christ received from the world: 1. A collective expression of all that the world has done to Him: 2. a pursuing of His life into the jaws of death (a violation of His corpse); 3. and yet a "mercy-stroke," inasmuch as it is to secure His corpse from mutilation; 4. above all, a testimony of God to His death and unique nature (His transition to a new life).—The two great fulfilments connected with the one spear-thrust of an unsuspecting soldier: 1. The fulfilment of all the types of the Law in one feature (ver. 36). 2. The fulfilment of all the words of the Prophets in one single prophetic word.—Jesus, the unbroken Paschal Lamb for believing Israel, is at the same time the pierced Divine Image for unbelieving Israel.—The revealing of the Crucified One, the repentance of the world.—Nothing but the sight of Christ's breaking heart could melt the heart of sin.—The death of Jesus the life of the world: 1. His falling asleep, her awaking (as His eyes close, hers open); 2. the end of His heart-grief, the commencement of hers; 3. His corpse, her quickening.—The stately sepulture of the Lord, or the princely disciples of the Crucified One.—The thank-offerings which immediately glorify the redemptive and expiatory offering of Christ.—The operation of the cross of Christ: 1. Comprehension of the cross; 2. courage for the cross; 3. sacrifices to the cross; 4. witnesses to the cross.—The great calm after the great storm: 1. The quiet Sufferer. 2. The quiet grave. 3. The quiet Sabbath. 4. The quiet mystery of life (or becoming). 5. The quiet presentiment. 6. The quiet turning of all things.

STARKE: OSIANDER: See how hypocrites act! fierce sticklers are they for external matters and ordinances, but in the weightiest matters, those that concern the soul and salvation, they care not for the fear of God. Matt. xxiii. 23.—QUESNEL: In vain doth the sinner seek to bury the remembrance of his sins—sin shall ever rise up against him, Jer. xvii. 1; Gen. xlii. 21.—O how many think only how to conceal their sins, but not to be penitent for them! Job xxxi. 33, 34. A foot-soldier, and not a horseman, as painters are wont to depict the man who pierced Jesus.—CANSTEIN: Let us look in faith, love and gratitude unto Him whom we ourselves have pierced, in order that we may rejoice when He is seen of us with our bodily eyes, Heb. xii. 2.—QUESNEL: Jesus will come to judgment in the same flesh in which He was crucified, that He may confound His foes, chap. v. 27; Acts xvii. 31.—ZEISIUS: Thus God is able to raise up quickly unto His people, though they be, with Christ, forsaken of all men, persons who interest themselves for them with the greatest care and diligence, such as they would never have thought on. In sorest need, therefore, take heart, Jer. xxxviii. 7 ff.—The love of an upright friend remains constant even in death.——HEDINGER: Excellent compensation of weakness through strength! Abraham's faith was great, the thief's was great, the centurion's was great. The first saw Christ in the life, the second in dying, the last in death, amid many miracles. But there is nothing to surpass Joseph and Nicodemus—they believe on Him in the grave. O power of God in the faithful! O strength in the weak, we praise thee! 2 Cor. xii. 9.—Godly, wise and brave undertakings of a true Christian, though apparently never so bold and perilous, are furthered to a good end through the help of the Almighty.—Like to like, —one lover of Jesus joineth company with another. Mark this, O man, and do thou likewise, Sir. xiii. 20, 21.—BIBL. TUB.: O that yet other fearful Nicodemuses might at the cross and in the sepulchre of Jesus crucify and bury their fear of man; then would amendment be of rapid growth in all ranks, Ps. xxvii. 1; 1 Pet. iii. 13. —Though not many rich and noble are called, there still are some who willingly lay out their possessions in the service of Jesus, Luke vii. 5.—ZEISIUS: O how well do the rich do when they spend their riches on Christ, His glory and His needy members! *that they do good and grow rich in good works*, 1 Tim. vi. 18, 19.—OSIANDER: We must not carelessly cast away the bodies of Christians; such a course is contrary to love and the hope of resurrection; but we must honorably commit them to the earth.—Gardens are pictures of death and resurrection—graves do suit them well: it is therefore not unfit that church-yards should have trees planted along their sides, and that they should be made to resemble gardens—OSIANDER: Christ hath hallowed our graves and made sleeping-rooms of them, in which the bodies rest until they are awakened again unto everlasting life, Rom. vi. 4.

LISCO: Ver. 38. Publicly and boldly doth the hitherto timorous love to Jesus now come forward; it leapeth over all considerations and scruples and toucheth the dead body of Jesus without any dread of becoming defiled after the law, through contact with a corpse, and that the corpse of a reputed malefactor.

BRAUNE: The fear of man is overcome; so openly they act. Delay is at an end; they make haste. They are not ashamed before all witnesses to make common cause with the Galilean women.—Joseph had had it hewn out for himself and Jesus entereth it before him; thus Jesus consecrateth the graves of His people, to the end that they may dread them the less.

GOSSNER: The stab was given by one soldier only, and here it says: *They* have pierced Him. How is this? the soldier was but the instrument; *they, sinners,* all of them, from the first to the last, did guide the soldier's hand and the crime is imputed to them.—Love now breaketh through all fear of man, and where there was most to fear, fear vanisheth, so that he dreadlessly espouseth the cause of Him who was killed on the cross and rejected by the whole world,—espouseth it; I say, at a time when, to all appearance, there was nothing to hope for from Him whom, living, he was either ashamed or afraid openly to confess.—This of itself was a beautiful fruit of the death of Jesus, that His secret disciples were made open ones, the weak, strong.—The love of the Slain Lamb driveth out all fear.—Christ liked and deserved a new grave, because He was a Dead Man without an equal; for all the children of Adam die from guilt, He guiltlessly.

[CRAVEN: From AUGUSTINE: Ver. 34. That blood was shed for the remission of sins, that water tempers the cup of salvation.—*O death,* by which the dead are *quickened;* what can be purer than that blood, what more salutary than that wound!—Ver. 38. In performing this last office to our Lord, he showed a bold indifference to the Jews, though he had avoided our Lord's company when alive, for fear of incurring their hatred.—CHRYSOSTOM: Ver. 31. The Jews who strained at [out] a gnat and swallowed a camel, after their audacious wickedness, reason scrupulously about the day.—Ver. 34. When thou approachest the awful cup, approach as if thou wert about to drink out of Christ's side.—From THEOPHYLACT: Ver. 34. To please the Jews, they pierce Christ, thus insulting even His lifeless body. But the insult issues in a miracle; for a miracle it is that blood should flow from a dead body.—Ver. 40. Even now, in a certain sense, Christ is put to death by the avaricious, in the person of the poor man suffering famine. Be therefore a Joseph, and cover Christ's nakedness.—From HERBERT: Ver. 34. *Pierced His side;*

If ye have anything to send or write,
(I have no bag, but here is room)
Unto My Father's hand and sight
(Believe Me) it shall safely come.
That I shall mind, what you impart;
Look, you may put it very near My heart.
Or if hereafter any of My friends
Will use me in this kind, the door
Shall still be open; what he sends
I will present, and somewhat more,
Not to his hurt. Sighs will convey
Anything to Me. Hark, despair, away.

[From BURKITT: Ver. 31. Hence note the cursed hypocrisy of these Jews; they look upon themselves as strictly bound to observe an outward ceremony, but their consciences never scruple to violate the most weighty precepts of the moral law.—Ver. 34. No cruelty was omitted towards Christ, either dead or alive, which might testify the great desert of our sin, nor was there any needful evidence wanting, which might make clear the truth of His death.—Vers. 38-42. Grace doth not always make a public and open show where it is; but as there is much secret treasure unseen in the bowels of the earth, so is there much grace in the hearts of some saints, which the world takes little notice of.—We read of none of the apostles at Christ's funeral; fear had put them to flight; but Joseph and Nicodemus appeared boldly: If God strengthen the weak, and leave the strong to the prevalency of their own fears, the weak shall be as David, and the strong as tow.—Ver. 41. A *sepulchre* in a *garden,* to expiate Adam's sin committed in a garden.—Ver. 42. Of what use our Lord's burial is to us His followers: It shows us the amazing depth of His humiliation, *from* what and *to* what His love brought Him, even from the bosom of His Father to the bosom of the grave. It may also comfort us against the fears of death; the grave could not long keep Christ, it shall not always keep us; it was a loathsome prison before, it is a perfumed bed now; he whose head is in heaven, need not fear to put his feet into the grave. Awake and sing, thou that dwellest in the dust, for the enmity of the grave is slain by Christ.

[From M. HENRY: Ver. 31. Passover *Sabbaths* are *high days;* sacrament-days, supper-days, communion-days, are *high days,* and there ought to be more than ordinary preparation for them, that these may be *high days* indeed to us, as the *days of heaven.*—The pretended sanctity of hypocrites is abominable; they made no conscience of bringing an innocent and excellent person to the cross, and yet scrupled letting a dead body hang upon the cross.—Ver. 32. One of these *thieves* was a penitent, and had received from Christ an assurance that he should shortly be *with Him in paradise,* and yet died in the same pain and misery that the *other thief* did: the extremity of dying agonies is no obstruction to the living comforts that wait for holy souls on the other side of death.—Ver. 33. *Whatever devices are in men's hearts, the counsel of the Lord shall stand:*—It was fully designed to *break His legs,* but, God's counsel being otherwise, see how it was prevented.—Ver. 34. Through this window, opened in *Christ's side,* you may look into His heart, and see love flaming there, *love strong as death;* see our own names written there.—When *Christ, the second Adam, was fallen into a deep sleep upon the cross,* then was *His side* opened, and out of it was His Church taken, which, He espoused to Himself.—The blood and water that flowed out of it were significant: 1. Of the two great benefits which all believers partake of through Christ—justification and sanctification; *blood* for remission, *water,* for regeneration; *blood* for atonement, *water* for purification; 2. Of the two great ordinances of Baptism and the Lord's Supper.—Now was *the rock smitten* (1 Cor. x. 4), now was *the fountain opened* (Zech. xiii. 1), now were *the wells of salvation digged*, Is. xii. 3. Here is *the river, the streams whereof make glad the city of God*.—Ver. 36. *Christ our passover is sacrificed for us*, 1 Cor. v. 7. *He is the Lamb of God* (John i. 29), and, as *the true Passover, His bones* were kept *unbroken*.—Vers. 38-42. Come and see a burial that *conquered the grave*, and buried it; a burial that beautified the grave, and softened it for all believers!—Ver. 38. It was Joseph's *honor* that he was a *disciple of Christ*, his *weakness* that he was so *secretly*.—Some who in lesser trials have been timorous, yet in greater have been very courageous. — The impotent malice of those that can but censure, and revile, and clamor, is sometimes more formidable even to wise and good men than one would think.—When God has work to do, He can find out such as are proper to do it, and spirit them for it.—Vers. 39, 40. Since God designed honor for His body, they would put honor upon it.—Vers. 40, 42. In conformity to this example, we ought to have regard to the dead bodies of Christians. The resurrection of the saints will be in virtue of Christ's resurrection, and therefore in burying them we should have an eye to Christ's burial.—Ver. 41. In a garden Christ began His passion, and from a garden He would rise, and begin His exaltation.—He was buried in a *new sepulchre:* this was so ordered, 1. For honor; He that was born from a virgin-womb, must rise from a virgin-tomb; 2. For the confirming of the truth of His resurrection.—Ver. 42. What is to be done on the evening before the Sabbath, should be so contrived that it may neither intrench upon Sabbath-time, nor indispose us for Sabbath-work.

[From SCOTT: Vers. 31-42. Comparing the sacred oracles with the events which occur in the Church and in the world, our faith will be increased even by the most discouraging transaction.—From A PLAIN COMMENTARY (Oxford): "If the Jews that stood by said truly of Him at Lazarus' grave, Behold how He loved him! when He shed a few tears out of His eyes; much more truly may we say, Behold how He loved *us!* seeing Him shed both blood and water in great plenty out of His heart." (Bishop ANDREWES.)—Vers. 38-42. Surely, this entire history has consecrated expensive funerals, and given a solemn sanction to care bestowed on burial-places, forever!

[From KRUMMACHER: Ver. 34. In the water and the blood are represented the most essential blessings of salvation: the *water* has a remote reference to baptism, but it chiefly symbolizes the moral purifying power of the word of Christ; the *blood* points out the ransom paid for our guilt, as well as the atoning sacrifice.—The blood flowed separately from the water; *justification* must not be mingled with, much less exchanged for, personal amendment.—Vers. 38, 39. Marvellous things occur in the vicinity of the cross. Two individuals, belonging to the first ranks in society, who, when Jesus still walked abroad in the majesty of His supernatural acts did not venture to make known their favorable impression respecting Him,—now, that the termination of His course seems to have stamped Him as a pitiable enthusiast, honor Him as their King before all the people. The germ of faith which, all at once, manifests itself so gloriously and so fully developed, had long lain in their hearts; from out of the thunder-cloud that brooded over Calvary, abundant grace has proceeded.—Christ *crucified* must be the object of our affections; therefore detach Him from the accursed tree, and deposit Him in your hearts, as your only consolation in life and death.—Ver. 42. *There they laid Jesus;* The curse is removed from a sinful world, Deut. xxi. 22, 23.—Christ by His burial has consecrated and shed light upon the darkness of our graves.—From JACOBUS: Vers. 34, 35. Our faith weeps, yet triumphs, as it sees the death-blow fall upon our Substitute, for in this we see our release.]

[WORDSWORTH, on ver. 41: "Christ changes the valley of the shadow of death into a garden. Christ's human body was laid in a natural *garden*. His human soul was in a spiritual *garden* (Luke xxiii. 43), and by His death and burial He has prepared a *garden* for the souls and bodies of all who depart hence in the Lord; and He will make them to be like the dew of herbs (Isa. xxvi. 19), and to rise up and blossom in a glorious spring time. He provides Paradise, or a garden, for the departed soul (Luke xxiii. 43), and He makes the grave itself to be a garden of Paradise; from which at the great Day the bodies of the faithful, which have been sown in hope, will rise in vernal beauty, and be united for ever in unfading glory to their souls."—P. S.]

SEVENTH SECTION.

The finished victory of Christ over the world and the kingdom of darkness, and His manifestation in the circle of His disciples. Christ demonstrates His victory by banishing the last remnants of darkness, grief and unbelief from His Church and making it sure of His resurrection.

CHAP. XX.

I.

HOW THE RISEN ONE DOTH BY THE GRAVE-SIGNS PREPARE HIS PEOPLE FOR THE SIGNS OF HIS LIFE.

CHAP. XX. 1–10.

(Matt. xxviii. 1-15; Mark xvi. 1-11; Luke xxiv. 1-12.)

1 [And, or, But on] The first *day* of the week [sabbath week] cometh Mary [the
ἡ] Magdalene early, when [while] it was yet dark, unto the sepulchre [to the tomb],
2 and seeth the stone taken away from the sepulchre [out of the tomb]. Then she
runneth, and cometh to Simon Peter, and to the other disciple whom Jesus loved
[as a friend, ἐφίλει][2], and saith unto them, They have taken away the Lord[1] out of the
3 sepulchre [tomb], and we know not where they have laid him. Peter therefore
went forth [ἐξῆλθεν], and that other disciple, and came to the sepulchre [and were
4 going toward the tomb, καὶ ἤρχοντο εἰς τὸ μνημεῖον]. So they ran [And they
were running, ἔτρεχον δὲ] both together: and the other disciple did outrun [προέ-
5 δραμε] Peter, and came [ἦλθε] first to the sepulchre. And he stooping down, *and
looking in*, saw the linen clothes lying; yet went he not in. [And stooping down,
6 he seeth (παρακύψας[3] βλέπει) the linen clothes lying; yet he did not go in]. Then
cometh [also][4] Simon Peter following him, and went into the sepulchre, [tomb] and
seeth the linen clothes lie [and beholdeth the linen clothes lying, κ. θεωρεῖ[5] τὰ ὀθόνια
7 κείμενα, comp. ver. 11]. And the napkin, that was about his head, not lying with
8 the linen clothes, but wrapped together in a place by itself. Then [Then therefore,
τότε οὖν] went in also that [the, ὁ] other disciple, which [who] came first to the
9 sepulchre [tomb], and he saw, and believed. For as yet they knew not [or, For
not even yet did they know, οὐδέπω γὰρ ᾔδεισαν] the Scripture, that he must rise
10 again from the dead. Then [So] the disciples went away again unto their own
[*omit* own] home.

TEXTUAL AND GRAMMATICAL.

[1] Ver. 2.—[τὸν κύριον is the usual reading. Some Greek MSS., as Augustine observes (*Tract in Joa.* cxx. 6), insert μου, *dominum meum*.—P. S.]

[2] Ver. 2.—[*Loved as a friend*, ἐφίλει, comp. xi. 3. Otherwise ὃν ἠγάπα, xix. 26; xxi. 7, 20.—P. S.]

[3] Ver. 5.—[παρακύπτειν is *to stoop down* or *to bend forward*, in order to look at any thing more closely. The intention the E. V. has expressed here (and ver. 11) by adding in italics *and looking in*.—P. S.]

[4] Ver. 6.—[The first καί is omitted in the text. rec. with A., but is supported by ℵ.[3a] B. L. X. and the XI. century supplement of Cod. D. (see Alford).—P. S.]

[5] Ver. 6.—[The E. V. obliterates the difference between βλέπει (*sieht*), the cursory glance of John, ver. 5, and the stronger θεωρεῖ (*beschaut*), the intense gaze of Peter, ver. 6. See Tittman, *Synon.* p. 111 sq. 120 sq. The more minute distinction between κείμενα τὰ ὀθόνια, ver. 5, and τὰ ὀθόνια κείμενα, ver. 6, cannot be rendered in English and does not affect the sense. The position of ὀθόνια in ver. 6 corresponds to τὸ σουδάριον, ver. 7.—P. S.]

EXEGETICAL AND CRITICAL.

On the various presentations of the resurrection-history see Comm. on *Matthew* [p. 541, Am. Ed. The literature, p. 542]. In particular also Doedes, *De Jesu in vitam reditu*, 1841; Tholuck, *Glaubwürdigkeit der evang. Gesch.*, 5. *Abschnitt.* Ebrard, p. 575; the author's *Leben Jesu*, II. 3, p. 1669.

[On the chronology of the events of the Resurrection Meyer says (p. 643 note): "It is impossible to harmonize the differences between John and the Synoptists, and those between the latter, but the grand fact itself and the principal features of the history stand out all the more sure." So also Alford *in loc.*, who sees in the very failure of harmonistic attempts a strong corroboration of the truth of the evangelical narratives. "It is quite impossible that so astounding an event, coming upon various portions of the body of disciples from various quarters and in various forms, should not have been related, by four independent witnesses, in the scattered and fragmentary way in which we now find it. In the depth beneath this varied surface of narration rests the great central fact of the resurrection itself, unmoved and immovable. As it was *this* above all other things to which the Apostles bore their testimony, so in their testimony to this we have the most remarkable proof of each having faithfully elaborated into narrative those particular facts which came under his own eye or were repeated to himself by those concerned. Hence the great diversity in this portion of the narrative:—and hence I believe much that is now dark might be explained, were the facts themselves, in their order of occurrence, before us. Till that is the case (and I am willing to believe that it will be one of our delightful employments hereafter, to trace the *true* harmony of the Holy Gospels, under His teaching of whom they are the record), we must be content to walk by faith, and not by sight. We must also remember in this case, that our Evangelist is selecting his points of narrative with a special purpose,—to show us how the belief of the disciples was brought out and completed after the unbelief of Israel; comp. vers. 30, 31."—P. S.]

Ver. 1. **The first day of the Sabbath-week** [τῇ δὲ μιᾷ τῶν σαββάτων].—On the μία [=πρώτη, see Mark xvi. 9] τῶν σαββάτων [σάββατα=week], see Comm. on *Matthew*, chap. xxviii. 1 [p. 544]. [The first day of the week is now properly called, on account of the Lord's Resurrection, the *Lord's Day*, ἡ κυριακὴ ἡμέρα (Apoc. i. 10). It has taken the place of the Jewish Sabbath: the substance remained (weekly day of holy rest), the form changed (from the seventh to the first day of the week) with reference to the great fact of the Resurrection whereby our redemption or the new creation was completed. On that day the Lord appeared to His disciples with His peace-greeting, and on that day He sent His Holy Spirit, and founded the Christian Church. The Christian Sabbath blends the memories of creative and redemptive love, is the connecting link between paradise lost and paradise regained, the continuation of Pentecost, and the preparation and pledge of the eternal Sabbath-feast (σαββατισμός, Heb. iv. 9) in heaven.—P. S.]

Cometh Mary the Magdalene.—See Comm. on *Matthew*, chap. xxviii. [540 ff.], particularly chap. xxvii. 61 [534, 537]. [On *Magdalene* see my notes on John xi. 2, pp. 340, 341. Also the beautiful Easter hymn, "*Pone luctum, Magdalena!*" "Mary! put thy grief away," or, "Still thy sorrow, Magdalena," in Daniel's *Thes. hymnol.*, II. 365, and my *Christ in Song*, Lond. ed. p. 200 ff.—P. S]. The exclusive mention of the Magdalene finds its explanation not simply in the fact that John received the following report from her lips (Tholuck), but also in the desire of the Evangelist to make her peculiar experiences illustrative, in concrete form, of a chief manifestation of the Risen One; a similar motive induces his detailed description of the experience of Thomas. That she, moreover, did not go alone to the grave, is demonstrated by the οἴδαμεν ver. 2; though, according to Meyer, Brückner and Ebrard [Alford], this expression sprang from the fellow-feeling of those nearest to Jesus. Tholuck rightly rejects this interpretation of the plural, since she is speaking to disciples who are as yet ignorant of the grand fact which she announces—*viz.* the absence of the Lord's body from the sepulchre. Meyer groundlessly makes a counter-poise of the οὐκ οἶδα ver. 13. [In ver. 13 Mary Magdalene speaks in her own name].

Early, it being yet dark [πρωΐ, σκοτίας ἔτι οὔσης].—From this touch, compared with the account of Mark, chap. xvi. 2, "at the rising of the sun," it is clearly proved that she, in the impatience of her longing, must have hastened in advance of the other women, Mary the mother of James, and Salome. [So also Luthardt and Ewald]. See Comm. on *Mark* [p. 156 Am. Ed.]

The stone lifted away (moved away) **out of the tomb** [βλέπει τὸν λίθον ἠρμένον ἐκ τοῦ μνημείου—the stone had been fitted *into* the mouth of the tomb which was hewn in a rocky elevation, see Mark xv. 3, 4.—P. S.].—The stone now lies sideways by the opening of the tomb, which is conceived of as a perpendicular excavation. See Comm. on *Mark* [p. 156 Am. Ed.]

Ver. 2. **And cometh to Simon Peter, and to the other disciple.**—A characteristic historical trait. So soon as she perceives the opening of the sepulchre, like lightning comes the thought—the body is stolen;—so deep is her conception of the unfathomable iniquity and treachery of the foe. Women usually seek counsel and help from men. We need not (with Bengel) infer from the repetition of the καὶ πρός, that the two disciples were not together. Mary was in want not only of the one, but also of the other.

Whom Jesus loved [as a friend, ὃν ἐφίλει ὁ Ἰησοῦς].—Whom He honored with His particular friendship. *The other disciple:* See chap. i. 35-40; chap. xviii. 15; xx. 8. *Whom Jesus loved:* Chap. xiii. 23; xix. 26; xxi. 7; ver. 20.

They have taken away the Lord [ἦραν τὸν κύριον ἐκ τοῦ μνημείου].—A fore-judgment of fear in the love not yet perfect; an error, starting up and vanishing on the way to truth.

Ver. 4. **So they both were running together** [ἔτρεχον δὲ οἱ δύο ὁμοῦ. Mark the change of the aorists and the descriptive imperfects in vers. 3 and 4; comp. ch. iv. 30. The characteristic details, vers. 4–8, the liveliness, circumstantiality, and inner truth of this narrative betray unmistakably an eye-witness. Such things cannot be invented.—P. S.] A lively picture of their excitement. The going turns to running, the moderate running to a running with all their might, in which John takes the lead of Peter. The characteristicalness of these facts, presented in accordance with the lively recollection of John, is uninventibly striking and significant. We cannot, however, infer that Peter, as the elder, possessed less of *general* physical strength (Tholuck). Elasticity in *running* is a quality peculiar to youth. According to Lampe and Luthardt, Peter's consciousness of guilt helped to make him slower. This assumption, truly, is not vindicated by ver. 6. And yet at *that* moment, at sight of the empty sepulchre, the pressure on heart and conscience which weighed him down, perchance, at first, might be lifted.

Ver. 5. **Yet he did not go in** [οὐ μέντοι εἰσῆλθεν].—On the way to the tomb, John's pace was more winged than that of Peter. On reaching the grave, however, he seems to be fettered first by the fear of a sad discovery, then by awe, and his astonishment at the orderly disposed linen clothes, *i. e.* the sign of the foreboding of another issue than that conjectured by

Mary Magdalene. According to Ammon, his entrance was prevented by a fear of defilement; according to Meyer, by natural dread. The former view is contradicted by his stooping down; the latter by his narrow observation of the signs in the sepulchre. The contemplative disciple stands still, lost in meditation upon the new signs. Now, therefore, Peter steps forward, as the one endowed with more practical decision, and goes before him into the sepulchre. Precisely similar is the trait presented chap. xxi. 7, where John is the first to recognize the Lord, Peter the first to hasten to him by swimming. *Hence*, it would seem, Peter alone is mentioned Luke xxiv. 12. (By Strauss and Baur this trait is explained as originating in tendencies in favor of John.)—Aorist, Imperfect, and Present forms alternate right significantly in this lively narrative.—*And he beholdeth*, θεωρεῖ, in contradistinction to the βλέπει of John—the three signs in the sepulchre giving proof of a thoroughly tranquil occurrence, in contrast to a tumultuous ravishment: 1. The grave-clothes are not carried away as they naturally would have been if the body had been stolen. 2. The linen-clothes and the napkin, which latter enwrapped the head (see chap. xi. 44; Luke xix. 20), are separated and laid away in an orderly manner. 3. The napkin is even lying, wrapped together, in a place by itself.

Ver. 8. **Then went in, therefore, the other disciple also** [τότε οὖν εἰσῆλθε καὶ ὁ ἄλλος μαθητὴς ὁ ἐλθὼν πρῶτος εἰς τὸ μνημεῖον].—The precedence of Peter puts an end to John's fear, or rather, as we think, to his contemplative standing still. Hitherto he seems to have been disturbed by not seeing the head-cloth from his station on the outside of the sepulchre, because of its being laid in a separate place.

And he saw and believed [καὶ εἶδε καὶ ἐπίστευσεν].—These signs were sufficient to make him believe in the resurrection of Jesus. *He believed*, differently construed: 1. What Magdalene reported (Augustine, Theophylact, Erasmus, Luther, Bengel and others). 2. The resurrection signs (Chrysostom, Euthymius, Lücke and others).

Ver. 9. **For not even yet did they understand the scripture** [οὐδέπω γὰρ ᾔδεισαν τὴν γραφὴν ὅτι δεῖ αὐτὸν ἐκ νεκρῶν ἀναστῆναι—comp. Ps. xvi. 10; cx.; Isa. liii. 8, 10; Zech. vi. 12, 13; Acts ii. 24 ff.; viii. 32, 33].—The declarations of Jesus concerning His resurrection could not have become absolutely doubtful to them, except in reference to their literal meaning. A figurative interpretation so readily suggested itself to their little faith, recollecting, as they did, the figurative phraseology in which Jesus was wont to express Himself. Therefore we need not suppose, with Meyer, that His declarations were not so distinct as reported by the Synoptists. The Johannean ones see chap. ii. 21; viii. 28; x. 18; xii. 24, 32; the farewell-discourses. Their understanding of the Old Testament was not sufficiently advanced to induce them, on the strength of its predictions, to expect a literal resurrection of the Messiah. Yet but these signs, here given, were needed to give John the resurrection faith, and henceforth the meaning of the Scripture might become entirely clear to them. See Luke xxiv. 26 ff., 46; Acts i. 3. Tholuck: "Whilst this their πιστεύειν, though a religious one, did nevertheless rest on the sensuous substratum of appearance [ocular evidence], that upon the foundation of Scripture was the higher, for it mediated a consciousness of what the idea of a crucified Messiah demanded."

Ver. 10. **So the disciples went away again unto their home** [ἀπῆλθον οὖν πάλιν πρὸς αὑτοὺς οἱ μαθηταί].—Anxiously they awaited the further issue; John tranquillized at bottom. It is not stated that Peter also believed already. Probably the special appearance of Jesus, vouchsafed him on that Easter-day (Luke xxiv. 34; comp. ver. 12; 1 Cor. xv. 5), served not only for his personal tranquillization in respect of his fault, but also for the confirmation of his faith.

DOCTRINAL AND ETHICAL.

1. The *diversities*, like the *intertwinings*, of the single features of the *resurrection history* in the accounts of the four Evangelists, are the *highest proof* of the *truth* and the infinitely powerful *effect* of the *fact:* a portrait of the highest stirring of soul and spirit in humanity. A real Easter-motet. Thus do different combatants report concerning the culmination of the battle and the form of the victory.

2. The resurrection of Christ had not only to burst through the bonds of death, the closed gate of the sepulchre, and the seal and the guard of the world, but also the *grief* and *little faith* of the disciples. (See my book: *Der Herr ist wahrhaftig auferstanden: die Losung der christlichen Gemeinde unserer Zeit.* Zürich, 1852.) The belief in the resurrection, far from issuing, as a mythicized idea, from an enthusiastic *hope* of the disciples, as Strauss has affirmed, was obliged to force its passage through something entirely opposite, namely the *disconsolateness* of the disciples. Of a truth, supreme salvation is nigh unto extreme hopelessness, if the latter do not precipitately rush upon the sword but wait patiently for the Lord,—then, however, salvation comes to hopelessness always from *above*, as a *gift* of deliverance; hopelessness may prophesy of salvation, may prepare a worthy place for salvation, but it cannot be the parent of it. In face of the resurrection, however, unbelief concentrates and consummates itself, in seeking here to reduce the highest fact of the highest energy of life to a bare idea and symbolism of life; in seeking in this passage, where the union betwixt personal and actual life and the idea of life celebrates its consummation, to perpetuate the Adamitic conflict between idea and fact. See 1 Cor. xv.

3. The grand *subjective revolution*, prepared on the first Easter-day in the soul-life of the hopeless band of *disciples*, and upon which the establishment of the Christian Church rests, presupposes the grand *objective revolution* of things in the life of the *Lord: the resurrection.* And this *individual* revolution in the life of the *Lord* is at the same time, in respect of its dynamical working as well as its ideal value, the *universal* revolution of things in the life of *humanity*, Eph.

i. 19 ff. Christ's resurrection our resurrection. Ullmann: *Was setzt die Stiftung der Kirche Christi durch einen Gekreuzigten voraus? Stud. u. Krit.* 1832, III. 579.

4. The resurrection attested and glorified itself as a divine fact, most of all by the thorough change which it effected in the view of the cross-death and sufferings of Jesus, and, indirectly, in the view of the cross and death in general. By it the cross of the *curse* is become the cross of *reconciliation*,—the sign of the deepest *disgrace*, the sign of highest *honor*.

5. The portrait of the *Magdalene* in her transition from deepest desolation to supreme joy. She was fitted, in her loving grief for the Lord and His body, to become the first Easter messenger.

6. The hasting of the Magdalene to Peter and John, and the cleaving together of these two gives us an impression of the gentle, placable spirit which the suffering of Christ had developed in the hearts of the disciples. Peter is not shunned now by a Magdalene's and a John's enthusiasm for the Lord, although he has denied Him,—for he is a repentant Peter. In a similar manner the whole band of disciples bear with the doubting Thomas until he has arrived at the full resurrection faith.

7. The perplexed, excited, hurrying, running disciples are first composed by the order in the empty sepulchre of Jesus. They feel that there a calm spirit has ruled. And here is presented to us in concrete touches the whole contrast of the calm, mysterious resurrection of Jesus and the immeasurable commotion confronting it in the circle of disciples; primarily a commotion full of anguish,—stormy; then growing calmer, yet still fluttering. The life of the Risen One is infinitely calm and tranquil in its self-certitude, blissfully moving within itself, like God Himself. As Christ held it no robbery to be equal with God, neither did He think it robbery to be risen. His heart is become celestially tranquil and firm, the spiritual fixed star of the spirit-realm; hence the fixed point that, with mighty shock, moves and transforms the whole human world.

8. The characteristics of Peter and John (see EXEG. NOTE to ver. 5) on the way of their glorification.

9. The *first sign* of the resurrection is the stone rolled away; the annihilation of the wicked counsel of the world, the frustration of the league of the powers of this world, the annulment of all the old authorities that rise in rebellion against the truth and the faith. (Ps. ii.; Acts iv. 25 ff.; Eph. i. 21.) The *second sign* of the resurrection is the empty sepulchre. The grave kept not the body of Christ; that body is ravished from it along with His spirit. The personal principle is not swallowed up by matter; it elevates and preserves matter by its dynamic power, making it its heavenly organ. The *third sign* of the resurrection are the fairly disposed and ordered grave-clothes, as a sign of the ruling of the highest, clearest presence of mind amid the horrors of the night-dark sepulchre. The spark of faith of both Apostles kindles at this sign.

10. As the Scripture (of the Old Testament) prophetically points forward to the facts of the life of Jesus, so the life of Jesus points back to the Scripture concerning the future resurrection. The life of Jesus the key to the Old Testament. Special consideration must be directed to Scripture sayings such as Ps. ii.; Ps. xvi.; Ps. cx.; Is. liii. 11; Dan. ix. 25. To types such as Gen. xxii. Jonah. Sayings in regard to death, such as Is. xxv. 8; Hos. xiii. 14; comp. Acts ii. 25-34; chap. viii. 32, 33; chap. xiii. 33, 35.

11. Then the disciples went home again. The walk from the tomb of the Risen One a going home in a higher sense.

HOMILETICAL AND PRACTICAL.

See the Synoptists, Matthew, Mark, Luke. The DOCT. NOTES.

The portrait of the Magdalene in the light of the resurrection. The mourning Magdalene, ver. 1-11. The Magdalene rejoicing (as though heaven were already won), vers. 11-18. Magdalene at first the messenger of dismal alarms,—at last the messenger of heavenly joy.—Jerusalem's messenger of joy, comp. Is. xl. 1, 9.—The mistakes of a soul stirred with love must themselves become guiding stars to truth: 1. The mistakes of the disconsolate Magdalene, ver. 2; ver. 13; ver. 15. 2. The mistakes of the enraptured Magdalene (thinking herself to have already attained the supreme, the heavenly goal) ver. 17.—Magdalene and Thomas, or the saddest of the sad changed to the happiest of the happy: 1. Immeasurable grief takes the one out of the circle of female disciples, the other out of the circle of male disciples. 2. "Rabboni;" "My Lord and my God."—Magdalene and John in their conduct toward the fallen Peter, or how as mourners they are become tender-hearted, Matt. v.—How the disciples of Jesus go to His sepulchre: 1. How differently (Magdalene otherwise than the two men; Peter otherwise than John). 2. How unanimously (disciples, both male and female, and the women even in advance. Fallen ones and less guilty ones).—How the love of Christ hath made the first breach through the old fear of His people: 1. The fear of the world, the foes (guard). 2. The fear of the night, of the terrors of the grave. 3. The fear of spirits and of the other world itself.—The resurrection signs preceding the appearance of the Risen One (DOCT. NOTE 9): 1. As signs of the weakness of the disciples (of their need of this leading from faith to sight). 2. As signs of the wisdom of God (sight is not to bring about faith, but faith sight).—The first sign of the life of the Risen One, heavenly repose and presence of mind, John vi. 17 ff.—The linen clothes laid aside, or the signs of a change of apparel in the sleeping-chamber of the grave.—The investigating disciples (Peter in the sepulchre, Thomas about the body of the Lord).—The budding faith of the disciples: 1. Experimental faith, 2. Scriptural faith, 3. Spiritual faith.—Then the disciples went home again: 1. Tranquillized in regard to the mistake of Magdalene (her statement that the body was stolen). 2. Awaiting further disclosures. 3. Blessed and prepared at bottom to go home, by their budding faith.

STARKE: The plural σαββάτων is probably used here in reference to the seven weeks that were to be reckoned to Pentecost and that began to be reckoned from this day in particular: for these were peculiarly denominated weeks, and hence Pentecost was called the Feast of Weeks; it appears, therefore, from the above, that this day was at once the day subsequent to the great Paschal Sabbath, the beginning of the significant heptality of weeks,—which lasted until Pentecost, and represented the whole new economy and spiritual harvest,—and the third day after the death of Jesus.—True Christians find no time unseasonable for seeking Jesus; when the whole world is securely sleeping, they wake unto the Lord.—ZEISIUS: What a despondent, unbelieving thing the human heart is! many a time that which should bring comfort and joy, is productive but of terror and harm, Luke ii. 9.—Believers have fellowship one with another in joy and sadness.—Love demands that we should follow our friends to the grave, and it is edifying so to do; we must not remain there, however, but must wait on our calling, until we ourselves are carried to the grave, Sir. xxxviii.

GERLACH: Each one was initiated into this wondrous mystery in a peculiar manner: Magdalene, after a scrupulous trial by the angels and then by means of the first personal manifestation of Jesus; Peter and John, who should have been the first to believe, by the sight of the sepulchre; the weaker women only by the angels (?); the disciples on the way to Emmaus, with anxious, comfort-seeking, burning hearts, by the circumstance of Jesus' opening the Scripture to them; then all the still unbelieving disciples by Christ's appearance in their assembly. In each of these dispensations there lies a peculiar, tender regard for the persons whom it concerns.

BRAUNE: Our Sunday is the Lord's Resurrection Day, the first day of the creation, when light came into being. The New Testament exhibits distinct tokens of its observation; on it the Corinthian Church was commanded to lay up savings as collections for the church at Jerusalem (1 Cor. xvi. 2); on that day Paul journeyed not, but preached (Acts xx. 7, *on a Sabbath—the first day of the week.* [Luther's version has the word Sabbath in these two instances.])

GOSSNER: But the stone that had troubled her before, when it lay in front of the sepulchre, troubles her again, now that it is moved away.

HEUBNER: Mary Magdalene, one of the last to leave the grave, is the first to visit it again.—In great distress, seek counsel and help of upright brethren.—Love gave wings.

[CRAVEN: From GREGORY: Ver. 3. Peter and John ran before the others, for they loved most.—From THEOPHYLACT: Vers. 4-8. Peter is practical and prompt, John contemplative and intelligent, and learned in divine things. Now the *contemplative* man is generally beforehand in knowledge and intelligence; but the *practical*, by his fervor and activity, gets the advance of the other's perception, and sees first into the divine mystery.

[From BURKITT: Ver. 1. Though her heart did burn with an ardent zeal and affection to her crucified Lord, yet the commanded duties of the Sabbath were not omitted by her; she kept close, and silently spent that holy day in a mixture of grief and hope.—What magnanimity and courage is found in this weak woman; she followed Christ courageously, when His disciples left Him cowardly; she accompanied Him to His cross, she followed His hearse to the grave, when His disciples durst not appear; and now very early in the morning she goes to visit His sepulchre, fearing neither the darkness of the night, nor the presence of the watchmen. Learn thence, That courage is the special gift of God, and if He gives it to the feebler sex, even to timorous and fearful women, it is not in the power of man to make them afraid.—Ver. 2. But why had not the Virgin Mary, His disconsolate mother, this privilege conferred on her, rather than Mary Magdalene, who had been a grievous sinner? Doubtless this was for the comfort of all true penitents, and administers great consolation to them.—Vers. 5-7. When Christ arose from the grave, He left His grave-clothes behind Him; whereas, when Lazarus arose, he came forth with his grave-clothes about him; this teaches us, that Christ arose never to die more, but to live and reign forever; therefore He left His grave-clothes in the grave, as never to make use of them more.

[From M. HENRY: Ver. 1. Love to Christ, if it be *cordial*, will be *constant*.—Mary's love to Christ was *strong as death*, the death of the cross, for it stood by that; *cruel* [fast-holding] *as the grave*, for it made a visit to that, and was not deterred by its terrors.—We must study to do *honor* to Christ in those things wherein yet we cannot be *profitable* to Him.—Love to Christ will take off the terror of death and the grave. If we cannot come to Christ but through that darksome valley, even in that, if we love Him, we will *fear no evil*.—*Early;* They that love Christ will take the first opportunity of testifying their respect to Him.—Those who would seek Christ so as to find Him, must seek Him early; 1. *Solicitously*, with such a care as even breaks the sleep; 2. *Industriously*, we must deny ourselves and our own repose in pursuit of Christ; 3. *Betimes*, early in our days, early every day; *My voice shalt thou hear in the morning.*—They that diligently inquire after Christ *while it is yet dark*, shall have such *light* given them concerning Him as shall shine *more and more.*—*Surprising* comforts are the frequent encouragements of *early seekers*.—They that are most constant in their adherence to Christ, and most diligent in their inquiries after Him, have commonly the first and sweetest notices of the divine grace.—God ordinarily gives Himself and His comforts to us by *degrees;* to raise our expectations and quicken our inquiries.—Ver. 2. One would expect that the first thought that offered itself should have been, *Surely the Lord is risen.* When we come to reflect upon our own conduct in a *cloudy and dark day*, we shall stand amazed at our dullness and forgetfulness, that we could miss of such thoughts as afterward appear obvious.—Weak believers often make *that* the matter of their *complaint*, which is really just ground of *hope*, and matter of *joy*.—The communication of sorrows is one good improvement of the communion of saints.—Peter, though he had denied his Master, had not deserted his Master's friends; by this appears the sincerity of his repentance, that he associated with the disciple whom Jesus loved. And the disciples keeping up their intimacy with him as formerly, notwithstanding his fall, teaches us to *restore those with a spirit of meekness*, that have been faulty.—Ver. 3. It is well when those that are more *honored* than others with the *privileges* of disciples, are more *active* than others in the *duty* of disciples.—Do others tell us of the comfort and benefit of ordinances? Let us be engaged thereby to make trial of them.—Ver. 4. What haste we should make in a good work, and when we are going on a good errand: Peter and John consulted neither their ease nor their gravity, but *ran* to the sepulchre.—He that *got foremost* in this race, was the *disciple whom Jesus loved* in a special manner, and who therefore in a special manner loved Jesus. Sense of Christ's love to us, kindling love in us to Him again, will make us to *excel in virtue.*—He that was *cast behind* was *Peter*, who had denied his Master, and was in sorrow and shame for it, and this clogged him as a weight.—Ver. 5. The warmest affections are not always accompanied with the boldest resolutions; many are *swift* to run religion's *race* that are not *stout* to fight her *battles.*—Ver. 6. Though John out-ran him, Peter did not therefore turn back, or stand still, but *made after* him as fast as he could; and while John was with a deal of caution *looking in*, he came, and with a deal of courage *went into the sepulchre.*—Observe how God dispenses His gifts variously. John could out-run Peter, but Peter could out-dare John; some disciples are *quick*, and they are useful to quicken them that are *slow;* others are *bold* and they are useful to hearten them that are *timorous.*—Vers. 6, 7. When we rise from the death of sin to the life of righteousness, we must leave our grave-clothes behind us, must *put off* all our corruptions.—Ver. 8. It is good to be emboldened in a good work by the boldness of others.—John got the start of Peter in *believing;* Peter saw and *wondered* (Luke xxiv. 12), but John saw and *believed:* a mind disposed to contemplation may perhaps sooner receive the evidence of divine truth than a mind disposed to action. —Ver. 9. What was the reason of their slowness to believe? Because as yet they *knew not the scripture.*—Ver. 10. Where were the angels when Peter and John were at the sepulchre? This favor was showed to those who were early and constant in their inquiries after Christ, and was the reward of them that came first, and staid last, but denied to them that made a transient visit.

[From SCOTT: Ver 2. Under a large proportion of preaching, by men called Christian ministers, we are ready to say, "They have taken away the Lord and we know not where they have laid Him;" but the broken-hearted disciple cannot be thus contented, though others be filled with admiration of the preacher's eloquence, genius, or learning.——From A PLAIN COMMENTARY (Oxford): Ver. 1. "Good proof gave she of that love; she was last at His cross, and first at His grave: staid longest *there*, was soonest *here;* could not rest till she were up to seek Him: sought Him while it was yet dark, before she had light to seek Him by." (Bishop ANDREWES.)——From OWEN: Ver. 5. John's remaining without, may in part be attributed to the precedence, which, as the older and leading disciple, he modestly yielded to Peter.—Ver. 9. *That He* MUST *rise again from the dead;* the necessity was founded upon the immutable word and promise of God (Ps. xvi. 10), upon the principle of life inherent in Jesus as the Eternal Son of God, and upon the redemptive economy, by which Christ was to rise from the dead and become the first-fruits of them that are held in the power of the grave (1 Cor. xv. 20).]

II.

HOW THE RISEN ONE CHANGES MARY MAGDALENE'S DESOLATION INTO BLESSED PEACE AND MAKES HER HIS EASTER-MESSENGER.

CHAP. XX. 11–18.

(Matt. xxviii. 1-15; Mark xvi. 1-11; Luke xxiv. 1-12).

11 But Mary stood without at the sepulchre weeping [But Mary was standing (εἱ-
στήκει) without by the tomb weeping][1]: and as she wept, she stooped down, *and*
looked into the sepulchre [she stooped down into the tomb, παρέκυψεν εἰς τὸ μνημεῖον],
12 And seeth [beholdeth, θεωρεῖ, not βλέπει, see vers. 5 and 6] two angels in white sit-
ting, the one at the head, and the other at the feet, where the body of Jesus had
13 lain. And they say unto her, Woman, why weepest thou? She saith unto them,
Because they have taken away my Lord, and I know not where they have laid
14 him. And[2] when she had thus said [Having said this, ταῦτα εἰποῦσα], she turned
herself back, and saw [beholdeth, θεωρεῖ] Jesus standing, and knew not that it was
15 Jesus. Jesus saith unto her, Woman, why weepest thou? whom seekest thou? She,
supposing him to be the gardener [that it was the gardener, ὅτι ὁ κηπουρός ἐστι],
saith unto him, Sir, if thou have [hast] borne him hence, tell me where thou hast
16 laid him, and I will take him away. Jesus saith unto her, Mary. [!] She turned
herself, and saith unto him [in Hebrew][3] Rabboni; which is to say, Master [Rab-
17 boni! (which is to say, Teacher!)] Jesus saith unto her, Touch me not;[4] for I am

[have] not yet ascended to my[5] [the] Father: but go to my brethren, and say unto
them, I ascend unto my Father, [*omit* (,)] and your Father; [,] and *to* [*omit to*] my
God, [*omit* (,)] and your God.
18 Mary [the] Magdalene came [cometh, ἔρχεται] and told the disciples [bringing
tidings, ἀγγέλουσα, to the disciples] that she had seen the Lord, and *that* he had
spoken [said] these things unto her.

TEXTUAL AND GRAMMATICAL.

[1] Ver. 11.—The position of the words ἔξω κλαίουσα is in accordance with B. D. O. X., *etc.*, Tischendorf [The rec. reads κλαίουσα before ἔξω. εἰστήκει with B.* D. *etc.* Tisch. Treg. Alf. ἱστήκει: ℵ. A. B.,[3] *etc.*, Westcott. πρὸς τῷ μνημείῳ: A. B. D. Tisch. Alf. Westc. πρὸς τὸ μνημεῖον: *text rec.* ἐν τῷ μνημείῳ: ℵ. (See Tischendorf, Alford).—P. S.]

[2] Ver. 14.—Καί before ταῦτα [E. text. rec.] should be omitted in accordance with ℵ. A. B. D., *etc.* and the critical editions].

[3] Ver. 16.—The addition Ἑβραϊστί, in accordance with B. D. L. O. X. Δ. Sin., is received by Tischendorf [Tregelles, Alford, Westcott. Most MSS. read Ῥαββουνί (so Tischend. Alf. Treg.); some Ῥαββουνεί (so Westcott), some Ῥαββωνεί, some Ῥαβουνί.—P. S.]

[4] Ver. 17.—[Μή μου ἅπτου is the usual reading of the MSS. and Iren., Orig., *etc.*, but Cod. B. and Tert. put μού after ἅπτου, and Westcott inserts this on the margin.—P. S.]

[5] Ver. 17.—The first μου is wanting in B. D. X., Itala, Tischendorf. It was probably supplemented in imitation of the subsequent μου. [Treg. Alf. Westcott likewise read πρὸς τὸν πατέρα without μου.—P. S.]

EXEGETICAL AND CRITICAL.

Continuation of the history of the Magdalene. First manifestation of the Risen One.

Ver. 11. **But Mary was standing by the tomb.** [Μαριὰμ δὲ εἱστήκει (*al.* ἱστήκει) πρὸς τῷ μνημείῳ ἔξω κλαίουσα.]—Εἱστήκει: she was standing as if rooted to the spot. The Evangelist has omitted to mention that she immediately followed the two disciples. Whether she met them at the grave, the narrative says not. She comes, and again finds the empty tomb. She now stations herself in front of it, as though, all too late, she would become its guardian. It is the plastic expression of her thought, her grief.

Now as she wept [ὡς οὖν ἔκλαιεν].—Her weeping is in reference to her idea that the body of Jesus has been stolen; hence she glances ever and anon down toward the empty place where He has lain.

Ver. 12. **And she beholdeth two angels.** [καὶ θεωρεῖ δύο ἀγγέλους].—The angelic appearances in the resurrection history, a sign of the thoroughly new, wonderful epoch of this event. The truth and objectivity of her vision are supported by the slender impression which these appearances seem to make upon her in her present mood; the internal, subjective conditions, by the circumstance that the two apostles saw no angel, and the other women only one.

[Alford adopts the rather fanciful remark of Luthardt: The angels were in *white* because from the world of light; they *sit*, as not defending, but peacefully watching the Body; at the *head* and the *feet*, for the Body of the Lord was from head to foot in the charge of His Father and of His servants.—P. S.]

Ver. 14. **She turned back.** [ἐστράφη εἰς τὰ ὀπίσω], *i. e.*, to look towards the garden, and to see if some one would not appear and give her information.

And knew not that it was Jesus [οὐκ ᾔδει ὅτι Ἰησοῦς ἐστιν.—There is foundation on both sides for her non-recognition. On the one hand, Jesus has altered: He is the Risen, the Transformed One. The external feature which, in addition to the one already mentioned, some assume, is less certain. "She thinks the gardener (xix. 41) of Joseph of Arimathea is before her, and that he has assigned the body another place. The circumstance that the Risen One was clothed with the *subligaculum*, or loin-strip, which crucified persons wore, and the same also that field and garden laborers were in the habit of wearing, might incline her the more to this opinion." Tholuck (following Hug). Kuinoel, Paulus, and others have even clothed Him in the dress of the gardener. On the other hand, Magdalene's faculties were concentrated within; she was in a visionary mood rather than in one favorable to acute observation; irrespective of the fact that her mind was not in the slightest degree predisposed to expect the appearance of the Lord. In a similar manner, the eyes of the disciples journeying to Emmaus were holden. Meyer denies the holdenness of the eyes in the present case (Grotius); perhaps because he imagines it to be the fruit of some magical working. [Dräseke assigns as a reason because her tears wove a veil, and because the seeking after the dead prevents us from seeing the living. She was wholly absorbed in the thought of the absent Lord.—P. S.]

Ver. 15. **If thou hast borne Him hence** [εἰ σὺ ἐβάστασας αὐτόν].—She does not name Him. She takes it for granted that every one is thinking of Him only. Of course if the supposed gardener *had* carried away the Lord, he would understand her saying (Meyer); otherwise it were necessarily unintelligible to him. She will go, she will bring the body. Her assuming a posture with a view to hurrying away in a certain direction, is evident from the following: "she turned herself." We cannot infer from these words that she turned directly to the *grave* again. She gives herself credit for sufficient strength to enable her to carry the corpse and deposit it in the tomb again. For at this very time it should be receiving anointment at the hands of the women.

Ver. 16. **Mary** [Μαριάμ].—His voice had the same unique sound as before (see Luke xxiv. 35; comp. 30, 31); especially the call by name (Is. xliii. 1). Since the voice of every human being in a healthy condition is the expression of the man within him, we can infer the *impressiveness* of *Jesus'* voice without having a more definite conception of it. Recollections of things that address themselves to the ear are the most enduring, observes Strauss* in his *Glockentöne*. The manifestation of God begins with the hearing-wonder, and dies away in it. The expression of the voice is concentrated in the naming of a beloved name.

Rabboni [Ῥαββουνεί].—With the infinite expression of the salutation—*Mary*—with which Christ makes Himself known to her, the word of recognition corresponds—*Rabboni, my Teacher*. The Evangelist cannot help reproducing the original Hebrew word in its sonorousness; therefore the interpretation. The solemnity of the passage is not contained in the explanatory supplement, but in the Rabboni. We can infer from that which follows that she meantime has fallen at His feet and embraced them, "like those women in Matt. xxviii. 9, and the woman that was a sinner, Luke vii. 39." *I. e.*, her own self at the time.

Ver. 17. **Hold (Touch) Me not** [Μή μου ἅπτου.† *Noli me tangere.*—In explaining this, reference should be had to ver. 22, where Thomas is directed by the Lord: φέρε τὴν χεῖρά σου καὶ βάλε εἰς τὴν πλευράν μου, and Luke xxiv. 39, where He calls upon the disciples: ψηλαφήσατέ με. It is therefore not the act of touching, as such, which the Lord reproves, but the animus or motive of Mary. The scene has often been represented in pictures called *Noli me tangere*.—P. S.] Interpretations of the enigmatical μή μου ἅπτου:

1. "Handle (Touch) Me not" [in the literal sense]:

a. Strictly *supernaturalistic:* Jesus demands a greater reverence for His body now that it has become divine (Chrysostom, Erasmus and many others). Unseasonable devoutness and insufficient explanation of γάρ ("*for* I have not yet ascended").

b. Decidedly *natural*, in various apprehensions. Ammon: Jesus desired to spare her the touching of One levitically unclean; Paulus: His wounds still pained Him, therefore touching Him would have hurt Him!

c. Spiritualistic: Weisse: He was still bodiless, a mere spiritual apparition (a ghost).

d. Gnostic: Hilgenfeld: He as yet appeared only as a mere Man, being not yet reunited to the Logos, and therefore adoration was unseasonable. [Yet immediately afterwards He allows Himself to be called by Thomas: "My Lord and My God;" comp. also Matt. xxviii. 9.—P. S.]

e. Physiological. Because the new, glorified corporeality of Jesus was still so tender as to shun every vigorous grasp (Schleiermacher [and Olshausen, edd. 1 and 3]).

f. Psychological: Handle Me not for the purpose of examining whether it be really Myself in the body, or My glorified spirit. Meyer (following J. Fred. von Meyer‡), Lücke. [In this case the following words οὔπω γὰρ ἀναβέβηκα, κ. τ. λ., express the assurance of the Lord that He is still corporeally present with her, having not yet been translated to the Father in heaven.—P. S.]

2. "Hold Me not fast."

a. Supernaturalistic: Seek not thy comfort in My *present appearance by terrestrial contact*, but *by spiritual communion* (Aret., Grot., Neand. and others).

[Also Augustine (*Tract.* cxxi. c. 3). "'*Noli Me tangere:*' *id est, Noli in Me sic credere, quemadmodum adhuc sapis; noli tuum sensum huc usque pertendere quod pro te factus sum, nec transire ad illud per quod facta es. Quomodo enim non carnaliter adhuc in eum credebat, quem sicut hominem flebat?*" Leo the Great, *Serm.* 74 (*al.* 72), c. 4: "*Nolo ut ad Me corporaliter venias, nec ut me sensu carnis agnoscas: ad sublimiora te differo, majora tibi præparo: cum ad Patrem ascendero, tunc Me perfectius veriusque palpabis, apprehensura quod non tangis, et creditura quod non cernis.*" Calvin, Melancthon, De Wette, Tholuck, Luthardt, Hengstenberg, Godet hold substantially this same view. Alford: "She believed she had now gotten Him again, never to be parted from Him. This gesture He reproves as unsuited to the time, and the nature of His present appearance. 'Do not thus—for I am not yet restored fully to you in body—I have yet to ascend to the Father.' This implies in the background *another and truer touching* when He should have ascended to the Father." Wordsworth (who has a long note here): "Cleave not to Me in My bodily appearance; do not touch Me carnally, but learn to touch Me spiritually. When the power of the bodily touch ends, then the spiritual touch begins, and that touch most honors Christ and profits us." Wordsworth then applies the passage to Christ's presence in the eucharist which is spiritual, not carnal.—Hengstenberg (III. p. 303) conjectures that Mary, in the mistaken notion that the partition wall between Christ and her had now fallen, desired to *embrace* Him; this the Lord withstood, because the process of glorification was not yet completed, and the separation still continued in part. Godet: "ἅπτεσθαι is to touch in order to enjoy, *to attach one's self* to some one: This is not the moment to attach yourself to Me as I am before you in My human individuality." Comp. below sub *d.*—P. S.]

b. Historical: Tarry not with Me, but make haste and discharge the message; time enough later for handling, greeting, holding (Beza, Calovius, Bengel).

c. Spiritualistic-mythical: Jesus was on the point of ascending, and did not desire to be detained by Mary (Baur, Kinkel: One of the numerous ascensions occurring in the period of the forty days was about to be performed).

d. Christologico-psychological: Hold Me not as though we were in the perfection of the existence of that world beyond us, for *I* am not yet ascended, *etc.*, to say nothing of *thyself*. (*Leben Jesu* II., 1661; III., 744.* Hofmann, Luthardt, Tholuck. As regards the sense, similarly Luther and others at an earlier period.)† [Similar to explanation 2 *a*, above.—P. S.].

On the fact that the term ἅπτεσθαι does not barely mean *to touch, to handle*, but that it also particularly denotes a *hanging upon*, a *holding fast*, see

* [Late Professor of Practical Theology in the University of Berlin and Court-Chaplain and friend of Frederick IV. of Prussia. The *Glockentöne* were his first, the *Abend-Glockentöne* his last work.—P. S.]

† [ἅπτομαι occurs thirty-five times in the New Testament, and is uniformly translated *to touch* in the E. V. It is used of touching the hand, the garment, the body, food, *etc.*—P. S.]

‡ [Not the better known commentator, but also an eminent Biblical scholar (though a layman, Senator of Frankfort on the Maine) and reviser of Luther's German Bible.—P. S.]

* Tholuck's classification of J. P. Lange, p. 436, rests upon a mistake.

† The conjunctures, in despair of the text, σύ μου ἅπτου (Gersdorf) and μή συ πτόου, need merely be mentioned.

Tholuck, p. 434 [Krauth's transl. p. 411]. Tholuck divides the interpretations into two classes, one of which discovers the reason for the repulse in the *not yet glorified condition of Christ;* while the other maintains that it lies in the *glorified* state of the Lord. According to the distribution into ἅπτεσθαι *to lay hold of*, and *to hold fast*, the former is by preference interpreted as signifying the *catching hold* of the knees, *worshipping*. Yet not exclusively. The design of Jesus' speech was undoubtedly to limit the exuberance of Magdalene's rapture, to deprive her of the new illusion which is persuading her that every difficulty and danger of her life is laid behind her, that external intercourse with Jesus is now to continue and that it is the supreme thing,—and so to guide her feeling into a practical channel. Hence the commission.

To my brethren [πορεύου δὲ πρὸς τοὺς ἀδελφούς μου.]—So He calls the disciples by a new name of familiar co-ordination. Meyer: He means her to gather from this that His appearance is not as yet a super-terrestrial and glorified one. Glorification, however, does not put an end to the brotherly feeling. Bengel: The word is designed to speak peace to the disciples concerning their flight. Right, but too narrow. Christ breathes in the paradisaic peace of the new reconciliation. God is become the Father of the disciples; He greets them in the dignity of their new life—in which He will soon make them glad through the Spirit of adoption, as co-brothers in the new kingdom that is now founded, and as co-heirs. The relation of humanity to God is changed, the new Paradise is opened, together with the new Man there are born into the world His brethren *in spe*, He nevertheless remaining the Lord and King of them. Tholuck. It is the intimation of the relationship of reconciliation (Apollinaris, Luther, Bucer).

I ascend ['Αναβαίνω].—The imminent ascension spoken of as already present, since He even now finds Himself in the new heavenly state, or transition state, which is the condition of ascension. **To My Father and your Father** [πρὸς τὸν πατέρα μου καὶ πατέρα ὑμῶν].—He does not say to *our* (as also elsewhere *your Father*, *My Father*, Matt. vi. 9: after this manner pray *ye: Our Father*), for the relation in which He stands to the Father is, in its character of an eternal, immediate, principial relation, specifically different from their mediate relation to the Father. Still this positive assurance is herein contained: My Father is also your Father now; ye shall be glorified along with Me.—**To my God** [θεόν μου καὶ θεὸν ὑμῶν].—There is the same contrast again on both sides in His generalizations. His consciousness of God is specifically unique and the source of theirs (Eph. i. 3). But as in the resurrection, the Father has demonstrated Himself to be *His* almighty God, so in future, in their course of life and victory, He will prove Himself to be *their* God also.—Thus is Magdalene made the first Evangelist of the resurrection to the apostolic circle itself, the Lord having also first appeared to her.

Ver. 18. **Magdalene cometh** [Ἔρχεται Μαριὰμ ἡ Μαγδαληνὴ ἀγγέλουσα τοῖς μαθηταῖς ὅτι ἑώρακα τὸν κύριον καὶ ταῦτα εἶπεν αὐτῇ].—She is obedient to the commission. She first announces her joy that she has seen Him, then discharges His commission. According to Meyer, there is a difference between this commission and the passage Matt. xxviii. 10. Progress, however, from the most general disclosure to a more special one never constitutes a difference. Otherwise, the announcement of His imminent ascension would also present a difference from the directly following revelations of Jesus in the circle of disciples, as recorded by John himself.

DOCTRINAL AND ETHICAL.

1. *Mary Magdalene*, the first guardian of the Holy Sepulchre. The later and present guardians of it.

2. The *angelic* apparitions at the Birth, Passion, Resurrection, and Ascension of the Lord mark these moments as the great epochs in the life of Jesus. For the angelic world does, in general, emerge into view in the grand epochs of the Kingdom of God. Therefore particularly in the life of Abraham and in that of Moses; at the founding of the covenant-religion, and at the establishment of the Old Testament theocracy. For this reason, after the establishment of the New Covenant in the life of Jesus, there is a withdrawal of angelic apparitions in all the period through which the Church's history extends; their return, however, is promised for the end of the world. The psychological reason is contained in the fact that in all those moments the human world is brought into closest proximity to the spirit-world; that the whole form of the visible world vanishes, to a greater or less degree, from the deeply moved elect on this side the gulf, and in the deep twilight of this world there uncloses within them a ghostly vision for the spirit-world. See the author's *Positive Dogmatik*, p. 578 ff.

3. That the perception of the angels in their objective manifestation was still conditioned by the liberation of a visionary faculty on the part of those who beheld them, results from the history of the resurrection. Peter and John see no angel here, the other women see but one angel, Magdalene sees two angels. Similar relative degrees of visionary perception are announced chap. xii. 28, 29; likewise Acts ix. 7; chap. xxii. 9. Comp. Dan. x. 7.

4. Christ's superiority to the angels, a doctrine taught by Scripture, Matt. iv; chap. xxvi. 63; Eph. i. 21; Phil. ii. 10; Heb. ii. 5 ff., Mary Magdalene, who was scarcely dogmatically instructed therein, here scenically sets forth, in accordance with the instinct of Christian vital feeling.

5. The fact of Mary's recognizing the Lord by her *ear* rather than by her *eye* is entirely in agreement with the laws of manifestation; according to these laws, wonders which address themselves to the hearing are of earlier and more frequent occurrence and of later withdrawal than such as appeal to the sight. Here, however, it is at the same time a testimony to the spiritual and divine character of Magdalene's attachment to the Lord. She knows Him by the tone in which Christ calls her name. Through the human call she becomes aware of the divine call, the perception of which constitutes the most blissful experience of the elect. See Is. xliii. 1.

6. A dialogue most brief and yet most pregnant: *Mary; Rabboni.*

7. HOLD ME NOT. In no moment of blissful ecstasy may we forget that we are still on earth and still have a mission here. Even Mary must attain to a consciousness of the situation. The fact that Mary had not yet arrived at the goal was gently expressed by the Lord in the saying that He Himself had not yet reached it. At the same time there is here intimated the truth that spiritual communion with the Lord constitutes the essential part of a beatifying communion with Him, and is the condition of the bliss of beholding Him [face to face].

8. The message entrusted to Mary. It is addressed *to the brethren*. It is a message concerning the imminent perfecting of Christ. He does not speak of His resurrection; He speaks of His imminent ascension. His eye glances forward to the supreme goal. He designates His glorification as an ascension *to His Father*, in His character as the Son of God; *to His God*, in His character as the glorified Son of Man. This His ascension is, however, to redound to the advantage of His brethren as well as His own good. Hence the saying runs: "and to your Father," *etc.* It is to be observed that Christ connects His relation to God with that of His brethren, and also makes a distinction between the two.

9. The first Easter-message addressed by Christ to the apostolic circle itself, was discharged by a *woman*, a female disciple, who, without doubt, was formerly the great sinner. The first manifestation of Christ was apportioned to Magdalene, as was the first manifestation of the Angel of the Lord in the Old Testament to the Egyptian maid Hagar—doubtless for the reason that both, being in a condition most sorely needing consolation, first had need of the manifestation, and were moreover mentally disposed to receive it. [Hagar the bondmaid of Sarah, Magdalene once the bondmaid of sin.] "*Wenn wir in höchsten Nöthen sein.*"* ("When in the hour of utmost need.") At such a time is evolved the ability of perceiving the most wonderful help.

HOMILETICAL AND PRACTICAL.

See the DOCT. NOTES.

Mary Magdalene at the sepulchre of the Lord: 1. How disconsolate: a. she standeth chained to the spot, as the guardian of the sepulchre; b. she weepeth; c. she stoopeth down. 2. How comforted: a. she seeth the angels; b. she seeth the Lord; c. she is made a messenger of joy to the flock of disciples.—The spiritual unity in the great change experienced by Mary: 1. In all her desolation, love for the Lord remained the light of her life (her faith and her hope). 2. In all her bliss there remained the painful pressure of her longing after the consummation. —How the Lord crowneth love for Him: 1. She sought the Body of the Lord to anoint it and received the anointing of the Spirit from the Living One. 2. In her grief for the Body, she hoped in the Living One, and became a messenger of life to the whole Church of Christ in all ages.—The blessing of true mourning at the grave.—The saying, "Blessed are they that mourn"—most conspicuously fulfilled.—The angels at the feet and head of the dead and risen Lord.—While pious men weep, there is already prepared for them supreme consolation.—The threefold conversation of Mary indicative of three degrees of her Easter-joy: 1. With the angels, 2. with the Lord, 3. with the disciples.—The great school of the Spirit of Christ: 1. At first she thought it impossible to part from the body of Christ; 2. and soon she learns to let the Risen One Himself externally go home.—The mood of Mary when desirous of detaining the Lord, compared with the mood of Peter on the Mount of Transfiguration. —The message of the Risen One to His disciples: 1. Addressed to His brethren, 2. a message concerning His ascension on their behalf also, 3. the preparation for His appearing in the midst of them.—The first sermon about the Risen One: 1. Delivered by a soul that was nigh unto despair; 2. by a woman; 3. by a pardoned sinner.—How she discharges the message: 1. She speaks of her blessedness (I have seen the Lord). Then 2. she faithfully delivers the saying. Application: Thus in the true preaching of Christ, the testimony of experience and the commanded word must accompany each other.—The Christian life, until the consummation, an eternal alternation of beholding and renouncing (or of receiving and sacrificing; making holiday and working).—The mission to the brethren ever the precious heavenly fruit of the beholding of Christ's glory.

STARKE: Even pious souls do often err when they yield too much to those emotions which are good in themselves, Luke xxiv. 17 f.—O how many peek and pine without cause!—HALL: Holy desires always prosper, Prov. viii. 17.—To speak comfortably to the afflicted is praiseworthy, and in accordance with the custom of the angels, yea, of the great God Himself, Luke vii. 13; 1 Thess. v. 14.—*Ibid.:* Many a tender and humbled soul mourns over the loss of its Saviour and yet He, the while, is beside it, Cant. iii. 1-4.—HEDINGER: The greater and more intense the misery of a distressed soul, the nearer Christ is; but He is not immediately recognized in the darkness.—CANSTEIN: It stands to reason that believers, Jesus being risen, should not weep nor be sorrowful, but put in practice the words of St. Paul: "Rejoice in the Lord alway," *etc.*, Phil. iv. 4.—HALL: Jesus knoweth His sheep by name, chap. x. 3. Whoso is a true sheep of Jesus, knoweth also the voice of his Shepherd, chap. x. 4.—CANSTEIN: Christ's voice still presses upon our ears and pierces into our hearts when He calls us by name.—HEDINGER: Unto faithful hearts there suddenly ariseth a light of joy, Ps. xcvii. 11; yet must they moderate their longing and be satisfied with the brief glimpse granted them. The Lord will not have them hang upon His gifts and friendliness, but upon Himself and His love.—ZEISIUS: Eve, the first woman, brought transgression into the world; Mary, on the other hand, was the first preacher of restored, eternal righteousness.—BIBL. WIRT.: Through Christ's resurrection we are become His brethren and God's children. Now if we be children of God, we are also His heirs and joint-heirs with Christ,

* [Beginning of a German hymn by Paul Eber (1547), see Schaff's *German Hymn Book*, No. 336. English translation by Miss C. Winkworth.—P. S.]

our Brother, to eternal blessedness, Rom. viii. 17. —CRAMER: As woman was the first to serve the devil, so she must be the first to serve Christ, 1 Tim. ii. 14.—HALL: Unto the upright there ariseth light in the darkness, from the Gracious, Compassionate and Righteous One, Ps. cxii. 4.*—GERLACH: The inquiry of the angels concerning a thing which they know, is to be understood similarly with Christ's question to the blind men: what will ye that I should do unto you? Grief when uttered makes a man susceptible of consolation.—Before this speech of Jesus one manuscript inserts the words: "And she ran toward Him to lay hold of Him," which, even if John did not write it, we of course are to supply mentally.—*Father* has particular reference to His divinity, *God* to His humanity. Here, for the first time, He significantly calls them *brethren* (comp. Matt. xxviii. 10).

GOSSNER: Angels ministered unto the Lord after His temptation: they likewise ministered unto Him in His death and at His resurrection, as well as at His birth and His ascension. They were present everywhere—upon every occasion. —And behold, as Mary turneth away from every creature, even from the angels, she findeth and seeth *Jesus standing!* —We might at times become disconcerted at the greatness of the Lord and at our own amazing littleness and distance from Him, the while He is desiring to draw so near unto us and behaveth Himself so brotherly toward us. For the prevention of such feeling on our part there was no better means than His own positive declaration: I am your Brother, I am one of you, and I go, as such, unto our Father; for I have one God and Father with you; My Father is your Father; My God is your God; I indeed claim the pre-eminence, yet do pretend, notwithstanding, to be one of you.—Our Brother is the Supreme Good; the Supreme Good is our Brother!

HEUBNER: How brief is the season of tears; even whilst we weep, the Author of joy is at our side, ready to wipe away our tears.—Love hides itself in order that it may, on discovering itself, occasion us the more surprise and joy. What is this whole life of trial and misery—exile?—A hiding of the heavenly Father's love.—The measure of affliction the measure of joy.—He who tendeth the heavenly plants of His Father, *was* in a certain sense *the Gardener.*—Strive that Jesus may one day call thy name too, that thou mayest not belong to those spoken of in Ps. xvi. 4.—*Mary* and *Rabboni,*—just two words constitute the entire heart-conversation, but they are words full of power.—(JUSTINUS:) Moderate now thy craving for Me, for in heaven only shall our intimate, perfect connection begin,—earth is not the place of perfect union. Yonder alone shall the soul's longing for Jesus be satisfied. Do not now accompany Me, do not now follow Me as if the old intercourse still lasted.—"St. Peter and St. John have no more than Mary Magdalene and I and thou! Take them all in a lump,—they are all brethren together." (LUTHER.)—As yet we ascend not, but we shall one day ascend. Comp. REINHARD'S *Himmelfahrtspred.*, 1809 and THEREMIN, *Pred.*, 1819, III., 110-18.—Hüter, *Zeugnisse christlicher Wahrheit*, Bielefeld, 1858; Mary Magdalene's Easter-celebration: 1. The Easter-sorrow of Mary Magdalene; 2. her Easter-joy.—*Ibid.:* That none can rob us of the true Easter-joy: 1. The character or nature of Easter-joy; 2. the subject of Easter-joy, or the good whereat we rejoice on the Easter-feast.

[CRAVEN: From AUGUSTINE: Ver. 13. *And I know not where they have placed Him;* it was a still greater grief, that she did not know where to go to console her grief.——From GREGORY: Ver. 11. To have looked *once* is not enough for love.—Ver. 12. She sought the body and found it not; she *persevered* in seeking; and so it came to pass that she found. For holy longings ever gain strength by delay; did they not, they would not be *longings.*—Ver. 13. The very declarations of Scripture which excite our tears of love, wipe away those very tears, by promising us the sight of our Redeemer again.—Ver. 15. *Jesus saith unto her, Woman, why weepest thou?* He asks the cause of her grief, to set her longing still more. For the mere mentioning His name Whom she sought would inflame her love for Him.—Perhaps, however, the woman was right in believing Jesus to be the *gardener;* was not He the spiritual *Gardener*, who by the power of His love had sown strong seeds of virtue in her heart?—But how is it that, as soon as she sees the gardener, as she supposes Him to be, she says without having told Him who it was she was seeking, *Sir, if thou hast borne Him hence?* It arises from her love; when one loves a person, one never thinks that any one else can be ignorant of him.—Ver. 18. So the sin of mankind is buried in the very place whence it came forth. For whereas in Paradise the woman gave the man the deadly fruit, a woman from the sepulchre announced life to men; a woman delivers the message of Him who raises us from the dead, as a woman had delivered the words of the serpent who slew us.——From BEDE: Ver. 18. In that Mary Magdalene announced Christ's resurrection to the disciples, all, especially those to whom the office of preaching is committed, are admonished to be zealous in setting forth to others whatever is revealed from above.

[From BURKITT: Ver. 11. Note Mary's carriage and behaviour towards her Saviour; this is discovered by her patient attendance; *She stood without at the sepulchre;* by her passionate mourning, *weeping;* by her unwearied diligence, *she stooped down and looked into the sepulchre.*—Learn 1. True love to Christ suffers not itself to be stinted or limited, no, not by the greatest examples; the weakest woman that truly loves Christ, may piously strive with the greatest apostle in this point; 2. Strong love is valiant and undaunted, it will grapple and encounter with the strongest opposition; Mary fears nothing in seeking of her Lord, neither the darkness of the night, nor the terror of the soldiers, nor the malice of the Jews: Love is strong as death, and the flames thereof are vehement.—Ver. 12. Such as sincerely seek the Lord, shall certainly find, if not the very thing which they seek, yet that which is much better for them; Mary did not find Christ's *dead body*, but she finds two angels to testify that He was *risen.*—

* [The above is a literal rendering of the passage as it stands in Luther's Version.]

It is matter of comfort to the members of Christ, that angels do not wait upon the *head* only, but upon the *feet* also; and it ought to be matter of imitation also.—Ver. 13. The best company in the world will not satisfy or content such as are seeking for Jesus Christ, when they find not Him whom their souls seek; Mary now enjoyed the presence and company of two angels, but this did not satisfy her in the absence of Christ Himself.—Ver. 14. Christ may be present with, and very near unto, His people, and yet not be presently discerned by them; *Jesus stood by Mary, but she knew not that it was Jesus;* her not expecting a *living* Christ, was one cause why she did not discern Him.—Ver. 15. The soul of a sincere believer, 1. Is full of earnest and longing desires after Jesus Christ; 2. Is yet sometimes at a loss for Christ, and cannot tell where to find Him; 3. Whilst it is at a loss for Christ, its desires are often quicker and more stirring after Him.—Ver. 17. Our love to Jesus Christ is best shown, not by our human passionate affection to His bodily presence, but by our spiritual communion with Him by faith here on earth, in order to an immediate communion with Him face to face in heaven.—Christ calls His disciples *brethren*, after His exaltation and resurrection; thereby showing that the change of His *condition* had wrought no change in His *affection.*—God for Christ's sake has dignified believers with that near and dear relation of His being a Father to them in and through His Son.

[From M. HENRY: Ver. 11. Where there is a *true love* to Christ, there will be a constant adherence to Him, and a resolution with purpose of heart to cleave to Him.—Where there is a true desire of acquaintance with Christ, there will be a constant attendance on the means of knowledge.—They that seek Christ must *seek Him sorrowing* (Luke ii. 48), must weep, not for Him, but for themselves.—*Weeping* must not hinder *seeking;* though she *wept*, she *stooped down*, and *looked in.*—Those are likely to *seek and find*, that seek with *affection* and *in tears.*—Ver. 14. *The Lord is nigh to them that are of a broken heart* (Ps. xxxiv. 18), nearer than they are aware. They that seek Christ, though they do not see Him, may yet be sure He is not far from them.—Those that diligently seek the Lord, will *turn every way* in their inquiry after Him; *Mary turned herself back*, in hopes of some discoveries.—Ver. 15. *Whom seekest Thou?* When Christ knows that His people are seeking Him, yet He will know it *from themselves;* they must tell Him *whom they seek.—She, supposing Him to be the gardener, saith, etc.;* Troubled spirits, in a cloudy and dark day, are apt to misrepresent Christ to themselves, and to put wrong constructions upon the methods of His providence and grace.—Ver. 16. *Mary;* When those whom God *knew by name* in the counsels of His love (Ex. xxxiii. 12), *are called by name* in the efficacy of His grace, then *He reveals His Son in them*, as in Paul (Gal. i. 16).—*Rabboni;* Notwithstanding the freedom of communion which Christ is pleased to admit us to with Himself, we must remember that He is our *Master*, and to be approached with a *godly fear.*—Mary *turned herself* from the angels whom she had in her eye, to look unto Jesus; we must take off our regards from all creatures, even the brightest and best, to fix them upon Christ.—The soul *that hears Christ's voice*, and is turned to Him, calls Him, with joy and triumph, *My Master.*—Ver. 17. Mary must not stay to talk with her Master, but must carry His message; for it was a day of good tidings, which she must not engross the comfort of, but hand it to others.—*My brethren;* Though Christ be high, yet He is not haughty; notwithstanding His elevation, He disdains not to own His poor relations.—*My Father, and your Father; My God, and your God;* There are such an advancement of Christians and such a condescension of Christ, as bring them very near together.—Ver. 18. When God comforts us, it is with this design, that we may comfort others.

[From A PLAIN COMMENTARY (Oxford): Ver. 12. Christ's resting-place is therefore between two Angels, like the mercy-seat, of old. Even in His death, He is found to have dwelt, as in ancient days, "between the Cherubim."—Ver. 13. *Woman, why weepest thou?* "This case of Mary Magdalene is our case oftentimes: in the error of our conceit, to weep where we have no cause; to joy, where we have as little. Where we have cause to joy, we weep; and where to weep, we joy. False joys and false sorrows, false hopes and false fears, this life of ours is full of." (Bishop ANDREWES.)—Ver. 15. *Jesus saith unto her, Woman, why weepest thou?* "Now, seeing *Christ* asks it again a *second* time, we will think there is something in it, and stay a little at it. The rather, for that it is the very opening of His mouth; *the very first words that ever came from Him*, and that He spoke first of all, after His rising again from death. . . . . Thus say the Fathers; that Mary Magdalene standing by the grave's side, and there weeping, is thus brought in to represent unto us the state of all mankind before this Day, the Day of Christ's rising again; weeping over the dead as do the heathens, who have no hope. But Christ comes and asks 'Why weepest thou?' as much as to say, 'Weep not! There is no cause of weeping now.' Henceforth, none shall need to stand by the grave to weep there any more. . . . . So that this, 'Why weepest thou?' of Christ's, (a question very proper for the day of the Resurrection,) wipes away tears from all eyes; puts off our mourning weeds, girds us with gladness, and robes us all in 'white,' with the Angels." (Bishop ANDREWES.)—Ver. 17. Take notice that our Lord makes mention of *ascending*, twice; of *rising*, not at all. And it is to teach us that *Resurrection* is nothing, nor is any account to be made of it, if *Ascension* go not with it. . . . . "Never take care for Resurrection! *That* will come of itself, without any thought-taking of thine. Take thought for Ascension! set your minds there! Better lie still in our graves, better never rise, than *rise*, and, rising, not *ascend.*" (Bishop ANDREWES.)

[From BARNES: Ver. 17. Nothing was better fitted to afford them consolation than this assurance, that *His* God was *theirs.*—From JACOBUS: Vers. 13, 15. *Why weepest thou?* How different are these words as spoken by Jesus from the same words spoken even by His Angels. Friends often ask the same thing, in our moments of anguish; but they can give no relief, and no arguments of theirs can cure the inward wound. But our blessed Lord reveals Himself in words of grace that go to the heart's wound, and wonderfully heal.—Ver. 15. *Whom seekest thou?* Thus the adorable Saviour would *draw her out* to tell what she wants and whom she seeks for. So pleased is He to hear any poor sinner say, *I seek Jesus.*—Your Beloved is near you, though you have thought Him afar off. Who ever sought and did not find? But oh! instead of finding Him a corpse, you shall find Him a risen, living, glorious Redeemer.—Ver. 17. *Go to My brethren;* "This was a far greater honor than that which was denied her." The gracious Saviour denies us nothing but for our greater advantage.

[From OWEN: Ver. 15. *I will take Him away;* She takes all the responsibility upon herself. If no one else will share her pious duty, she is ready to discharge it independent and alone. Noble woman! The Church to the end of time shall embalm thy memory, and point to thee as the most loving and faithful of that devoted band, who

> "—While Apostles shrunk, could dangers brave,
> Last at His cross, and earliest at His grave."—

Ver. 17. "Do not stay here to embrace Me now, either to pay thy homage to Me, or to confirm thy faith, both which thou wilt have other opportunities of doing; for I am not yet withdrawn from your world, and ascended to the heavenly court of My Father, as you imagine I shall presently do, but I shall yet continue for a little while on earth, and give you further opportunities of seeing Me again; let nothing, therefore detain thee any longer, but go immediately to My dear brethren and say unto them," *etc.*—"Thou shalt possess Me again, but not as before, it shall be from this time and forever *in the Spirit.* The time of exalted and divine relationship is come." (STIER.)]

III.

HOW CHRIST FREES THE CIRCLE OF DISCIPLES FROM THE OLD FEAR, AND, BY THE BREATHING OF HIS SPIRIT, RAISES THEM TO A PRESENTIMENT OF THEIR APOSTOLIC CALLING.

CHAP. XX. 19–23.

(Mark xvi. 14; Luke xxiv. 36 ff.; John xx. 19-31, pericope for Quasi modo geniti).

19 Then the same day at evening, being the first *day* of the week, when the doors
were shut [When therefore it was evening on that day, the first of the
week, and the doors had been shut, or, the doors being shut, *οὔσης οὖν ὀψίας τῇ ἡμέρᾳ
ἐκείνῃ τῇ μιᾷ σαββάτων, καὶ τῶν θυρῶν κεκλεισμένων*], where the disciples were as-
sembled [*omit* assembled][1] for fear of the Jews, came Jesus and stood in the midst,
20 and saith unto them, Peace *be* unto you. And when he had so said, he shewed unto
them *his* hands and his side. [And having said this, he showed unto them both[2]
his hands and his side]. Then were the disciples glad [The disciples therefore were
21 glad], when they saw the Lord. Then said Jesus[3] [he said] to them again, Peace
22 *be* unto you: as *my* [the] Father hath sent me, even so send I you. And when he
had said this, he breathed on *them*, and saith unto them, Receive ye the Holy Ghost
23 [lit., Receive Holy Spirit, *Λάβετε πνεῦμα ἅγιον*[4]]: Whosesoever sins ye remit, they
are remitted [have been remitted, *ἀφέωνται*][5] unto them; *and* whosesoever *sins* [*omit*
sins] ye retain, they are retained [have been retained, *κεκράτηνται*].

TEXTUAL AND GRAMMATICAL.

[1] Ver. 19.—Συνηγμένοι [*assembled:* text. rec. with E. G. K. L. Vulg.] is omitted in accordance with ℵ. A. B. D., *etc.* Lachmann, Tischendorf. An exegetical addition. [Treg., Alf., Westc. likewise omit it.]

[2] Ver. 20.—[The text. rec. omits the καί before τὰς χεῖρας with ℵ. D.; but Lachm., Tischend. (in former edd., not in ed. viii.), Treg., Alf., Westc. retain it with A. B. Syr.—P. S.]

[3] Ver. 21.—[ὁ Ἰησοῦς is omitted by ℵ. D. L. X., Treg., Tischend.; bracketed by Alford and Westcott; retained by Lachmann and Lange with A. B.—P. S.]

[4] Ver. 22.—[The absence of the article before πνεῦμα may indicate the *partial* or *preparatory* inspiration, as distinct from the pentecostal effusion. See the EXEG.—P. S.]

[5] Ver. 23.—The reading ἀφέωνται in accordance with A. D. L. O. X., Lachmann—in opposition to the reading ἀφίενται, B. E. G. K., *etc.*, Tischendorf. On ἀφέωνται instead of ἀφεῖνται, see Winer, p. 91. [Tischend. ed. viii., Treg., Westc. and H. read ἀφέωνται, Alford ἀφίενται. ἀφέωνται is also found Matt. ix. 2, 5; Mark ii. 5; Luke v. 20, 23; vii. 47; 1 John ii. 12. The old grammarians differ as to this form, some declaring it to be identical with ἀφῶνται (as Homer has ἀφέῃ for ἀφῇ), others regarding it as the perf. pass. ἀφεῖνται. Winer adopts the latter view, *Gr.* p. 77, ed. vii. The bearing of this reading on the sense is important; see the EXEG.—P. S.]

EXEGETICAL AND CRITICAL.

The parallel-passage in Mark recounts how Jesus, after His entrance into the circle of disciples, rebuked their unbelief; the parallel in Luke makes the entrance of the Emmaus disciples into the circle of apostles precede the Lord's appearance, and makes Peter and the two journeyers to Emmaus exchange Easter-messages; Luke also hints at the gentle reproof of the disciples' unbelief,—the feature more powerfully brought out by Mark. He likewise reports, more explicitly than John, Jesus' invitation to the disciples to touch His hands and His feet, His eating before them, and His exposition of the Scripture concerning His sufferings and resurrection. Tholuck justly remarks that Luke xxiv. 44-49 bears a relation to vers. 22, 23 in our passage. Individual traits in this section of Luke may belong to a later meeting, or have been amplified later; assuredly, nothing but the section beginning with ver. 50 belongs to the last manifestation of Jesus. The most important thing remaining for John, was to supply the facts of Jesus' appearing to the disciples as they were sitting with shut doors, His announcing to them His return by bestowing upon them His peace-greeting (chap. xiv. 27), and His re-ratifying of their apostolic calling (forfeited by their flight), accompanying this act by a breathing upon them, which was preparatory to the outpouring of the Spirit.

Ver. 19. **When therefore it was evening on that day.** [Οὔσης οὖν ὀψίας τῇ ἡμέρᾳ ἐκείνῃ τῇ μιᾷ σαββάτων.]—The evening of that Sunday, the first resurrection day.

And the doors had been shut. [καὶ τῶν θυρῶν κεκλεισμένων ὅπου ἦσαν οἱ μαθηταί].—This circumstance is emphasized, as ver. 26; comp. Acts xii. 13.

1. Unfounded softening of the expression. Calvin and others, Baumg.-Crus.: The doors had suddenly opened *ad nutum divinæ majestatis ejus*. According to Lücke, the statement is even reducible to a mere unexpected, sudden appearing.

2. Unfounded intensification of the expression. He pressed bodily *through* the closed doors. In the interest of the [Lutheran] ubiquity-doctrine, Quenstädt.

3. A miraculous appearing, unqualified as to its manner, indicative of the higher condition in which He found Himself subsequently to His transformation (Luke xxiv. 31: ἄφαντος γενέσθαι; John xxi. 1; Mark xvi. 12: φανεροῦσθαι. F. Kühn: *Wie ging Christus durch die Grabesthür?* 1838. Tholuck). A. Tholuck: The description leads to the conception "of an unconfinedness to the limits of space"—bounds of locality.—Primarily it indicates nothing but a simple power of the glorified life of Christ to move unrestrainedly, to appear and disappear;—His local definedness, which is one with bodily circumscribedness, remaining the while undestroyed. According to Baur, an immaterial constitution was ascribed to Jesus; according to Meyer, the body of Christ was not yet glorified; as according to Lücke, who, in opposition to Olshausen (who distinguishes between the docetic and glorified body), remarks that a something intermediate betwixt the ethereal consistency of angels and material, corporeal solidity is to him inconceivable. Nevertheless, the idea of the body as dynamically transformed into the pure organ of the spirit is everywhere established in the New Testament (see 1 Cor. xv. 49).

Peace unto you [Εἰρήνη ὑμῖν].—The customary greeting is here filled with the weight of the resurrection-message and all that proclamation of salvation therewith connected; at the same time it is a fulfilment of the promise, chap. xiv. 27. See EXEG. NOTES there. [Ministers are messengers of *peace*.]

Ver. 20. **He showed unto them** [Ἔδειξεν καὶ τὰς χεῖρας καὶ τὴν πλευρὰν αὐτοῖς].—See Luke xxiv. 40. According to Meyer, a difference is constituted by the mention in that passage of the *feet* instead of the *side*.

Ver. 21. **As the Father hath sent Me** [καθὼς ἀπέσταλκέν με ὁ πατήρ, κἀγὼ πέμπω ὑμᾶς].—Comp. Matt. x.; John xiii.; Matt. xvi. 19; chap. xviii. The second εἰρήνη ὑμῖν solemn, more definitely proclamatory of the infinite import of the salutation,—not, however, a farewell-greeting, as Kuinoel and others have interpreted it.—**Even so send I you** [κἀγὼ πέμπω ὑμᾶς].—Analogy of dynamical authority. The Father now sends Him out of the kingdom of resurrection and reconciliation to them; so likewise the Son sends them out of this kingdom to the world. That therewith their re-institution into office is simultaneously expressed, in connection with an amplification of that office (henceforth they are witnesses for the Crucified and Risen One), is obvious, in accordance with the stronger analogy of chap. xxi. 15 ff. But as at the first bestowal of apostolic dignity, Peter took precedence of the others, so now the general restitution of the whole body precedes a more explicit restitution of Peter. Comp. chap. xvii. 18.

Ver. 22. **He breathed on them** [καὶ τοῦτο εἰπὼν ἐνεφύσησεν καὶ λέγει αὐτοῖς. The verb ἐμφυσάω occurs in the N. T. only here, but is used in the Sept. to express the act of God in the original infusion of the spirit of life into man (Gen. ii. 7: ἐνεφύσησεν εἰς τὸ πρόσωπον αὐτοῦ πνοὴν ζωῆς, καὶ ἐγένετο ὁ ἄνθρωπος εἰς ψυχὴν ζῶσαν). "This act is now by God incarnate repeated, sacramentally, representing the infusion of the new life, of which He is become by His glorified Humanity the source to His members: see Job xxxiii. 4; Ps. xxxiii. 6; 1 Cor. xv. 45" (Alford).—P. S.] Different interpretations:

1. Simply the prophetico-symbolical heralding of the Holy Ghost (Theod. Mopsueste, Bullinger, Lampe, *etc.*). This view is contradicted by: *a.* the act, *b.* the Aorist Imperative λάβετε, *c.* the remark that in this case the act were but a repetition of the promise contained in the farewell-discourses.

2. It is the *gratia ministerialis*, rather than the former *gratia sanctificationis*, not, however, as yet, the pentecostal communication or *gratia* χαρισματική (Theophylact, Maldonat and others).

3. It is *holy* spirit (πνεῦμα ἅγιον, without the article), but not yet *the* Holy Spirit, nor yet *the* Spirit of the new birth, of the world-mighty Jesus (Hofmann and Luthardt [also Gess]; see thereupon Tholuck and Meyer).

4. It is a quantitative, precursive communication of the Spirit, in accordance with Christ's not yet perfected state of glorification (Origen, Calvin, Neander, Stier, Tholuck. Meyer: A veritable ἀπαρχή of the Holy Ghost). [Similarly Bengel (*arrha pentecostes*), Brückner, Hengstenberg, Godet, Ewald, Alford. The full communication of the Holy Spirit did not take place be-

fore the day of Pentecost, comp. vii. 39; xvi. 7; Acts ii.—P. S.])

We have to consider on the one hand the afflation, and on the other hand the design of this bestowal of the Spirit. The afflation is an *afflatus* with the new life of the resurrection, and so the symbol, as the commencement, of the communication of His resurrection-life, *i. e.* life in His Holy Spirit. The degree of this communication, however, is determined in accordance with their present need; they must even now have power to gather the Resurrection-Church and to distinguish it from the world, in like manner as it, as the substratum of the people's Church shortly to be established, is to be thoroughly distinguished from the Israelitish Church. In respect of this consideration, this *gratia* is doubtless specially *ministerialis*. They have not yet the gift of communicating the Holy Ghost, but they do possess that of discerning the Holy Spirit when already communicated.

Ver. 23. **Whose sins ye remit** [ἄν τινων ἀφῆτε].—By proclaiming and promising to them forgiveness while ye receive them into your fellowship.—**They are (have been) remitted unto them** [ἀφέωνται αὐτοῖς].—See TEXT. NOTES. Meyer's antithesis: "They *become* (will be) remitted (according to the reading ἀφίενται) and they *are* (have been) retained (κεκράτηνται),* is to be refuted first by the Codd. which read ἀφέωνται [perf. pass.=ἀφεῖνται.—P. S.], secondly by the exegetical demand that the two terms should form a parallel. Their remitting of sin and retaining of sin will, as a prophetically ministerial act, rest upon corresponding acts of God, already accomplished in the Spirit,—not, however, have these acts as a result or, still less, effectuate them. They will be influenced in these acts by Christ; they will not influence Him.† The term, *remit sins* [ἀφιέναι], is akin to the term, *loose* [λύειν], Matt. xvi. 19; the term, *retain* [κρατεῖν], or *retain together*, is akin to the term, *bind* [δέειν]. See Comm. on *Matthew* at the passage designated, note (*Leben Jesu*, II., p. 889). The Lord does here but invert the expression, thereby indicating the now decided, New Testament stand-point, in which redemption [loosing], forgiveness, advances into the foreground. Here, then, as in those other passages, Matt. xvi. 19; xviii. 18, it is the *potestas clavium* in its broader sense, not merely, in accordance with the Heidelberg Catechism, the preaching of the holy Gospel and Christian penitential discipline (if it were confined to these, the latter branch would have to be considered as having reference also to reception into the Church: open the kingdom of heaven to believers), but in a still more extended sense in accordance with the *Artic. Smalc.*: *Mandatum docendi evangelium, remittendi peccata, administrandi sacramenta, prætera mandatum excommunicandi*; in which summing up the second and fourth items should really be regarded as expressed in the third: *administrandi sacramenta.* In reality the stations of the *potestas* are these: 1. The preaching of the gospel; 2. establishment of the preliminary conditions of reception; 3. reception into the Church; 4. penitential discipline in the real sense of the term. In a narrower sense it is undoubtedly the *potestas* of reception through baptism and of reception through repentance and absolution, together with the *potestas* of the opposite denial of reception, or exclusion. The symbolic prefiguration of the administration of the Church by the administration of the keys of the house of David, Is. xxii. 22, is, in consciously symbolic terms, continued in the Revelation (chap. iii. 7). See Tholuck, p. 441 ff.; Julius Müller, *Deutsche Zeitschrift*, 1852, p. 55 [on the power of the keys, in an essay on the *Divine Institution of the Ministry*, reprinted in Müller's *Dogmatische Abhandlungen* (1870), p. 496 ff.—P. S.].

DOCTRINAL AND ETHICAL.

1. Christ, the Risen One, first appeared unto *individual* souls, then to the *congregation* of the faithful. We find a repetition of this in the history of the Church.

2. The night of Christmas, the darkness of Good Friday, the evening of the Supper, the first Easter evening; glorious hours of the ever brighter shining of the Dayspring from on high (Luke i. 79). At evening time it shall be light, Zech. xiv. 7.

3. *How Christ, as the Risen One, bursts though the fear* of the company of *disciples*: (1) the fear of the Jews; (2) the fear of His own ghost-like apparition; (3) the fear of the whole world (ver. 21); (4) the fear of the power of sin and guilt (ver. 23); (5) the fear of the terrors of judgment ("whosoesoever sins ye retain," *etc.*).

4. The first Easter Church in its changing forms: *a.* a Church of secret, fugitive disciples, *b.* a Church of festive, glad believers, *c.* a Church of anointed and commissioned apostles.

5. *How Christ cometh into the midst of His people*: (1) in spite of closed doors; (2) with the salutation of peace; (3) with the firstling gift of the Spirit; (4) with the commission of the apostolic embassy; (5) with the bestowal of apostolic plenipotence.

6. The *entrance* of Jesus whilst the doors were *shut*, an evidence of His higher, *glorified corporeality*.

7. The *peace-greeting*, or the transformation of the every-day formula of salutation into the loveliest, richest Evangel by the mouth of Christ.

8. The *mission* of the *disciples* from Christ measured in accordance with the mission of Christ from the Father.

9. The *first gift of the Spirit*, or how, in the Easter feast of Christ, the last shadows of Good-Friday (*fear of the Jews*) come in contact with the first light of Pentecost (*He breathed on them*).

10. The inseparable connection of apostolic plenipotence with the apostolic embassy. See Matt. xvi. 10; chap. xviii. 18.

*[Similarly Bengel: ἀφίενται—κεκράτηνται, *remittuntur—retenta sunt: illud, præsens; hoc præteritum. Mundus* EST *sub peccato.*]

† [An important remark. Ministerial acts are not creative, but declarative of the preceding acts of Christ and the Holy Spirit. Dean Alford remarks *in loc.*, that ministers have the power of the keys "not by *successive delegation* from the Apostles,—*of which fiction I find in the New Testament no trace*" (—the italics are Alford's—), "but by their mission from Christ, the Bestower of the Spirit, for their office, when *orderly and legitimately conferred upon them by the various churches.* Not however to them exclusively,—though for decency and order it is expedient that the outward and formal declaration should be so:—but in proportion as *any disciple* shall have been filled with the Holy Spirit of wisdom, is the inner discernment, the κρίσις, his."—P. S.]

[11. Forgiveness of sins the fruit of the resurrection (and death of Christ). The triumph over death is also a triumph over sin—the cause of death.—P. S.]

HOMILETICAL AND PRACTICAL.

See Commentary on *Mark*, p. 163 f., *Luke*, p. 398 f. The Doct. Notes.

Quasi modo geniti: or Christ the First-born from the dead, Col. i. 18.—The transformation of the apostles' fear of the Jews into the loftiest feeling of triumph over the whole world (ver. 21).—How all things ensue from the peace of the Risen One: 1. The joy, the mirth of the disciples; 2. spiritual life; 3. the evangelic mission; 4. apostolic spiritual severity and clemency in the administration of the Gospel.—When the doors are shut to the world, then are they (in the highest sense) open to the Lord.—The union of familiarity and majesty in the first manifestation of the Risen One in the Church.—The first great fulfilment of the promise, Where two or three are gathered together in my name, there am I in the midst of them.—The day of Christ's heavenly birth from the dead, a birthday of all Christian blessings: 1. Of peace and joy in believing; 2. of Sunday and the feast-days (for now, for the first time, do the remaining festivals receive their true signification); 3. of religious worship (*cultus*), and of rest from labor, in the Spirit; 4. of the apostolic mission, and of preaching; 5. of New Testament discipline and social consecration.—The life-breath of Christ, the true mission to the world.—The judicial sentence of the apostolic Church: 1. In respect of its divine institution; 2. in respect of its historical obscuration; 3. in respect of its eternal import.—Or: 1. As a sacred power; 2. as an accountable right; 3. as a solemn duty.—The great word: Sent from Christ as Christ from the Father.

Starke: The experience of an afflicted and tempted person may be very different in the evening from what it was in the morning.—The lying in wait of the wicked must conduce to the best interests of the godly, in this respect also, viz. that the godly refrain themselves from them, and hence are not led away by intercourse with them, nor condemned with them.—Zeisius: What a precious and unspeakable fruit of the merit and resurrection of Christ, is peace with God in the conscience!—Yea, peace and joy in the Holy Ghost are two particular, precious fruits of the resurrection of Jesus and of His spiritual kingdom.—Hall: When Christ, the Morning Star, riseth upon the soul and discovereth Himself unto it, nothing but joy can spring up.—Zeisius: So soon as Christ rose from the dead, He instituted the office of the ministry: of what exceeding importance then must this office be.—Hall: He who desires that Christ should entrust to him the great embassy of His Gospel must likewise first receive His Spirit.—A testimony of the divinity of Jesus Christ, for the Holy Ghost is God, and therefore no one can give that Holy Ghost who is not himself God, chap. xv. 26.—In the evening and at night Jesus did take in hand many momentous things for our sake: He was born in the night, He suffered Himself to be taken prisoner in the night, He instituted the Lord's Supper in the night, and in the evening, when He was risen from the dead, He instituted the ministry of the New Testament. If we pondered these things every evening, we should make a holier use of the evening hours, and not perform so many works of darkness in the night!

Braune: In so far as we are sinful, Christ is sent unto us from the Father, but in so far as we are redeemed, we are sent, as His witnesses, unto others, that we may be co-laborers, not in our, but in His work. Amid the consciousness of our weakness and frailty, we should hold fast the sense of the loftiness of our calling as redeemed ones, and by the former feeling be but the more impelled to suffer ourselves to be redeemed and reconciled to God, to the end that the latter feeling may become true and strong; whoso but suffereth himself to be redeemed will draw others also into this beatific fellowship.—"He breathes on them;" like a *friend's breath* upon the cheek, shall the Holy Spirit of God come unto man's spirit.—Unto sanctified [consecrated] personalities the Redeemer commits the forgiveness of sins; these commissioned ones are a terror and vexation to the wicked, but friends to the good. That which the Redeemer here says concerning the remitting and retaining of sins may be compared with what He says of loosing and binding for the Kingdom of Heaven, Matt. xvi. 19; xviii. 18.—Sanctified [consecrated] personalities are, as St. Paul says of the Gospel, 2 Cor. ii. 16, unto some a savor of life unto life, unto others a savor of death unto death.

Gossner: He, therefore, who is sent from Christ, who is Christ's messenger, must needs have received the peace of Christ, which is higher than all reason, must likewise needs have received the Spirit of Christ, and this seal of the Spirit and of peace must give evidence of itself in him by the devolving of peace and anointing from him to others again, by others being filled and anointed therewith. All this is contained in that little word *as*.—But when ministers make their appearance who have nothing to recommend them save that they are puffed up by the spirit of this world, what will they accomplish? They will puff up others also with the same spirit of the world.

Heubner: *In the evening.* H. Müller, *Herzenssp.* p. 241: The Saviour will visit us in the evening. When the sun of the world hath set in our heart, the Sun of Righteousness ariseth.—Christians have often enough been obliged to assemble in secret; the Waldenses, for example, the Moravians, the Reformed in France, and others.—If Jesus come not into the assembly of Christians, it is cold, heartless, unfruitful.—Christ's peace-greeting was the spoil of victory—spoil which He won by death and resurrection.—Whoso hath followed Christ unto Golgotha, to him doth He shout His word of peace.—Augustine; *Cicatrices tituli gloriarum.*—Crucifixion and resurrection are inseparable—one is incomplete without the other. This is the sum of Christianity.—*The disciples were glad;* Behold the power of the appearing, the peace, of Jesus. From His peace comes joy.—Peace is indispensable to the mission of Jesus. A man must have Jesus' peace in his own heart if he would be a messenger of peace to others; he must first be redeemed himself, if he would preach redemption to others. Luther, in the postil to *Quasimodog.* Sunday, XI. 1040, writes this to all true Christians, after applying it to the Apostles and the ministry; they can meet these requisites, not by their own strength, but in Christ's name, in the might of the Holy Ghost.—SCHLEIERMACHER, *Pred.* iii. p. 563.—COUARD, ii. p. 326.—MARHEINEKE, ii. p. 45.

[CRAVEN: From AUGUSTINE: Ver. 19. If thou comprehendest the mode [of entering] it is no miracle: when reason fails, then is faith edified. —Ver. 20. The nails had pierced His hands, the lance had pierced His side. For the healing of doubting hearts, the marks of the wounds were still preserved.——From CHRYSOSTOM: Ver. 21. He shows the efficacy of the cross, by which He undoes all evil things, and gives all good things; which is peace.—To the women above there was announced *joy;* for that sex was in *sorrow,* and had received the *curse.*——From GREGORY: Ver. 21. I love you, now that I send you to persecution, with the same love wherewith My Father loved Me, when He sent Me to My sufferings.—Ver. 23. The disciples who were called to such works of humility, to what a height of glory are they led! Lo, not only have they salvation for themselves, but are admitted to the powers of the supreme Judgment-seat.——From BEDE: Ver. 21. A *repetition* is a *confirmation:* whether He repeats it because the grace of love is twofold, or because He it is who made of twain one.

[From BURKITT: Ver. 19. It has been no strange thing in the Church, that the best members of it have been put to frequent their assemblies with great fear, and been forced to meet in the night with great caution, because of the fury of the persecutors.—Let Christ's disciples meet together never so privately, and with never so much hazard and jeopardy, they shall have Christ's company with them.—Ver. 21. The repetition of, *Peace be unto you,* was not more than needful to signify His firm reconciliation to the disciples, notwithstanding their late cowardice in forsaking Him.—*As My Father hath sent Me, so send I you;* By the same authority, and for the same ends, in part; namely, to gather, govern, and instruct My Church.—Ver. 22. *He breathed on them, and said, Receive ye the Holy Ghost;* When Christ sends forth any about His work, He will furnish them with endowments answerable to their vast employment; and the best furniture they can have, is the Holy Spirit in His gifts and qualifications suitable to their work.—Ver. 23. There is a twofold power of remitting sins; the one *magisterial* and *authoritative;* this belongs to Christ alone: the other *ministerial* and *declarative;* this belongs to Christ's *ambassadors.*—"Christ first conferred the Holy Ghost upon His apostles, and then said, *Whose sins ye remit, they are remitted.* Thereby intimating that it is not they, but the Holy Ghost by them, that puts away sin; *For who can forgive sin, but God only?*" (AUGUSTINE). The power of forgiving sin, that man hath, is only to declare that if men be truly and really penitent, their sins are forgiven them for the sake of Christ's satisfaction.

[From M. HENRY: Ver. 19. *The disciples* of Christ, even in difficult times, must not *forsake the assembling of themselves together,* Heb. x. 25. —It is a comfort to Christ's *disciples,* when their solemn assemblies are reduced to privacy, that no doors can shut out Christ's presence from them.—His *speaking peace, makes peace, peace* with God, *peace* in your own consciences, *peace* with one another; all this *peace be with you;* not *peace with the world,* but *peace* in Christ.—Ver. 20. Conquerors glory in the marks of their wounds.—Christ's wounds were to speak on earth, that it was He Himself, and therefore He rose with them; they were to speak in heaven, in the intercession He must *ever live to make,* and therefore He ascended with them, and appeared in the midst of *the throne, a Lamb as it had been slain, and bleeding afresh,* Rev. v. 6. Nay, it should seem, He will come again with His scars, *that they may look on Him whom they pierced.*—When Christ manifests His love to believers by the comforts of His Spirit, assures them that *because He lives, they shall live also,* then *He shows them His hands and His side.*—A sight of Christ will gladden *the heart of a disciple* at any time; the more we *see* of Christ, the more we shall *rejoice* in Him; and our joy will never be perfect till we come there *where we shall see Him as He is.*—Ver. 21. Christ was now sending the disciples to publish *peace to the world* (Is. lii. 7); and He here not only *confers* it *upon* them for their own satisfaction, but *commits* it *to* them as a trust to be by them transmitted to all *the sons of peace,* Luke x. 5, 6.—*He sent them* authorized with a divine warrant, armed with a divine power; *sent them* as ambassadors to treat of *peace,* and as heralds to proclaim it; *sent them* as servants to *bid to the marriage:*—hence they were called *Apostles—men sent.*—Ver. 22. What Christ gives, we must receive, must submit ourselves and our whole souls to the quickening, sanctifying influences of the blessed Spirit; receive His motions, and comply with them; receive His powers, and make use of them; and they who thus obey His word as a precept, shall have the benefit of it as a promise; they shall receive the Holy Spirit as the guide of their way, and the earnest of their inheritance.—Ver. 23. Two ways the apostles and ministers of Christ *remit* and *retain* sin, and both as having authority: 1. By *sound doctrine;* 2. By a *strict discipline,* applying the general rule of the gospel to particular persons.

[From A PLAIN COMMENTARY (Oxford): Ver. 19. *Peace be unto you!* Can we forget that this was the salutation of SHILOH (that is, "Peace"), even "the Prince of Peace" Himself? of Him who is delared to be "our Peace:" who bequeathed His peace to the disciples; and promised that Peace should be their abiding portion; and directed them to salute with "Peace" every house into which they entered. Peace was the subject of the angels' carol on the night of the Lord's nativity: behold, Peace is the first word He pronounces in the hearing of His disciples now that He is risen from death.—Ver. 22. O most solemn and mysterious incident, as well as most solemn and prevailing words! The action of our Saviour here described may have shown emblematically (as AUGUSTINE suggests) that the HOLY GHOST *proceedeth from the* SON. It may further have served to show that this was He by the breath of whose mouth all the hosts of heaven were made; and especially (as CYRIL supposes), that Christ was the same who, after creating man in the beginning, "breathed into his nostrils the breath of life, and he became a living soul." But more than that is here intended. For it is to be thought that, at the time of man's creation, "together with his soul, or the principle of his natural life, he received also the grace of the Holy Spirit as a principle of the Divine Life to which he was also designed." (Bishop BULL). That is, the soul of man received from the very first "the peculiar impress of the Holy Spirit super-added," as CLEMENT of Alexandria writes. And Basil, expressly comparing the Divine insufflation upon Adam with that of Christ upon the Apostles, tells us that it was the same Son of God "by whom God gave the insufflation: then indeed, *together with* the soul, but now, *into* the soul." EUSEBIUS is even more explicit. "The Lord" (he says), "renews mankind. That grace which man enjoyed at first, because God breathed into his nostrils,—that same grace did Christ restore when He breathed into the face of the Apostles, and said, Receive the Holy Ghost."—At the first institution of certain mysteries of the Faith, there was not wanting the outward emblem of an inward grace; which grace was afterwards conveyed without any such visible demonstration. Thus, at the Baptism of Christ, "the Holy Ghost descended *in a bodily shape like a dove* upon Him." And now, at the ordination of His Apostles, our Lord is found to have "breathed into" their faces, when He would convey to them the gift of the same Blessed Spirit.

From BARNES: Ver. 19. True Christians will love to meet together for worship; nothing will prevent this.—Ver. 21. *As My Father hath sent Me;* As God sent Me to preach, to be persecuted, and to suffer; to make known His will, and to offer pardon to men; so I send you.——From JACOBUS: Ver. 19. *Glad;* So He had promised to them (ch. xvi. 20), "Your sorrow shall be turned into joy."]

IV.

HOW CHRIST PUTTETH THOMAS' UNBELIEF TO SHAME, AND CHANGETH THE DOUBTING DISCIPLE INTO THE MOST JOYFUL CONFESSOR.

CHAP. XX. 24–29.

(Chap. xx. 24-31, is the pericope for St. Thomas' Day).

24 But Thomas, one of the twelve, called Didymus, was not with them when Jesus
25 came. The other disciples therefore said unto him, We have seen the Lord. But
he said unto them, Except I shall see [I see, ἴδω] in his hands the print of the
nails, and put my finger into the print[1] of the nails, and thrust [put] my hand into
his side, I will not believe.
26 And after eight days again his disciples were within, and Thomas with them:
then came Jesus, [Jesus cometh, ἔρχεται], the doors being shut, and stood in the
27 midst, and said, Peace *be* unto you. Then saith he to Thomas, Reach hither thy
finger, and behold my hands; and reach hither thy hand, and thrust [put] *it* into
28 my side; and be [become, γίνου][2] not faithless, but believing. And Thomas[3] an-
29 swered and said unto him, My Lord and my God [!] Jesus saith unto him,
Thomas [*omit* Thomas][4] because thou hast seen me, thou hast believed: blessed *are*
they that have not seen, and *yet* have believed.

TEXTUAL AND GRAMMATICAL.

1 Ver. 25.—Lachmann, in accordance with Cod. A., *etc.*, Origen, Vulgate, reads here τόπον instead of τύπον. Meyer supposes the τύπον of the Recepta to be a mechanical repetition. But the reading τόπον can also have arisen from exegetical grounds. It weakens the solemnity of the expression. [Tischendorf, ed. 8, reads εἰς τὸν τόπον τῶν ἥλων, "into the *place* of the nails," but Alford, Westcott and Hort, like Lange, retain τύπον, *print.*—P. S.]

2 Ver. 27.—[Thomas was doubtful, but not unbelieving; he was anxious and ready to believe, and only waiting for tangible evidence. See EXEG.—P. S.]

3 Ver. 28.—The καί before ἀπεκρίθη, the ὁ before Θωμᾶς, are not firmly established.

4 Ver. 29.—[Θωμᾶ, which the text. rec. inserts after ἑώρακάς με, is omitted by A. B. C. D. ℵ.[3a], Tischend., Alf., Westcott.—P. S.]

EXEGETICAL AND CRITICAL.

The second appearance of Christ, on the first Sunday after the resurrection-day, in the midst of the disciples, at Jerusalem, is entirely in accordance with the festal circumstances. The Easter-Sunday was the third day of the paschal celebration. The next Friday, therefore, was the eighth. The disciples were not permitted to set out on their homeward journey on the Sabbath. On Sunday they either would not, or could not, set out, because this had now become their feast-day, and Thomas was not yet pacified (*Leben Jesu* II., p. 1704). It was probably the evening before their departure for Galilee, whither, as the place where all His disciples should see Him again, Christ had at first ordered the apostles. See Comm. on *Matthew*, chap. xxviii.

Ver. 24. **But Thomas, one of the twelve.** [Θωμᾶς δὲ εἷς ἐκ τῶν δώδεκα, ὁ λεγόμενος Δίδυμος].—See chap. xi. 16; chap. xiv. 5; Matt. chap. x. His absence from the circle of disciples on the first Easter Sunday gives rise to the inference that he was wandering about, solitary and gloomy.

Ver. 25. **But he said unto them,** *etc.* [ὁ δὲ εἶπεν αὐτοῖς· Ἐὰν μὴ ἴδω ἐν ταῖς χερσὶν αὐτοῦ τὸν τύπον τῶν ἥλων, καὶ βάλω τὸν δάκτυλόν μου εἰς τὸν τύπον* τῶν ἥλων, καὶ βάλω μου τὴν χεῖρα εἰς τὴν πλευρὰν αὐτοῦ, οὐ μὴ πιστεύσω]. We must distinguish between the strong *expression* of Thomas, and his *thought* itself. The testimony of his fellow-disciples does not suffice for him; he must first see the Risen One with his own eyes, and by touch convince himself of His corporality, and of the identity of that corporeality with the Crucified One, before he can believe. On the fact that nothing, therefore, can be deduced from the expression of Thomas militating against the nailing down of the *feet* of the Crucified One, comp. Tholuck, p. 442.

[Thomas has a place among the apostles, inferior indeed to John and Peter, yet an important one. He represents, within the Church, the principle: *intellectus præcedit fidem,* which is not necessarily incompatible with the higher principle: *fides præcedit intellectum.* He represents honest, earnest, inquiring, truth-loving skepticism, or that rationalism which anxiously craves tangible evidence, and embraces it with joy when presented. This is essentially distinct from the worldly, frivolous skepticism of indifference or hostility to truth, which ignores or opposes the truth in spite of evidence. The former wants knowledge in order to faith, the latter knowledge without or against faith. The inquiring spirit of Thomas, having a moral motive and a spiritual aim, is a wholesome, propelling principle in the Church, and indispensable in scientific theology; it dispels prejudice, ignorance and superstition, and promotes knowledge and intelligence. Yet, practically and spiritually, it is defective as compared with the childlike spirit of faith with which alone we can enter the kingdom of heaven, and hence it is gently rebuked by our Lord. For salvation we must go to Christ, not as reasoning logicians, or learned theologians, or pleading lawyers, or calculating merchants, but as the child goes to the mother's bosom, as heart goes to heart, and love to love—with unbounded confidence and trust. Faith is the true mother of true knowledge in divine things, and even in philosophy, which starts in *love* of wisdom, and consequently implies its existence. It is only in a very qualified sense, in matters of historical inquiry and philosophic and scientific research, that doubt may be called the father of knowledge, according to the principle of Cartesius: *De omnibus dubitandum est.*—P. S.]

Ver. 26. **And after eight days** [μεθ' ἡμέρας ὀκτώ].—That the disciples already attribute a particular importance to Sunday, is evidenced by the numeric completeness of their assembly.

[This is the beginning of the history of the Lord's Day, which to this day has never suffered a single interruption in Christian lands, except for a brief period of madness in France during the reign of terror. Sunday is here pointed out by our Lord Himself and honored by His special presence as *the day of religion, and public worship,* and so it will remain to the end of time. God's Word and God's Day are inseparable companions, and the pillars of God's Church.—P. S.]

That Thomas is an unbeliever willing to believe, his presence at this time seems to prove. Manifestly, the same place is meant as that in which they were eight days before. They were *within* again, in the same house. "Olshausen erroneously makes Galilee the scene of the appearance" (Meyer). "*To celebrate the Resurrection-day*" (Luthardt). Meyer: "There is nothing to indicate this." It seems at least to be indicated by the fact that they were still tarrying in Jerusalem on this day, and probably waiting for the Lord.

Ver. 27. **Therefore saith He to Thomas** [εἶτα λέγει τῷ Θωμᾷ].—Immediately after the peace-greeting Christ turns to Thomas, for it is with him that He has now to do, since he, in his doubting spirit, is a hindrance to the whole Church. Christ's acquaintance with Thomas' state of mind and singular demand is not to be referred to a mediate knowledge on the part of Christ (through the disciples, Lücke); it is the fruit of an immediate knowledge. — **Reach hither thy finger,** *etc.* [φέρε τὸν δάκτυλόν σου ὧδε καὶ ἴδε τὰς χεῖράς μου, καὶ φέρε τὴν χεῖρά σου καὶ βάλε εἰς τὴν πλευράν μου]. — A triumphant challenge which, with loving irony, accedes to his demand, in order to the infusing of a salutary shame into him who made it and who is now obliged to recognize the identity of personality by higher marks,—especially by the Lord's knowledge of the deplorable state of his soul, and by His voice. Bengel: *Si Pharisæus ita dixisset: "nisi videro," etc., nil impetrasset; sed discipulo pridem probato nil non datur.*

[The Lord is silent about the print of the *nails,* which would have recalled the malice of His *crucifiers,* and points simply to the wounds as the abiding monument of His dying love to Thomas and to all. The words "*Reach hither thy hand and put it into My side,*" seem to imply that the wound in His side was as large as a man's hand. Some infer also that His resurrection-body was bloodless. Wordsworth: "The wounds which Satan inflicted in malice and scorn on our Lord's crucified Body, have been converted by His controlling power and wisdom into proofs of His Resurrection, and marks of His personal identity. They have become indelible evidences of His power, graven, as it were, with an iron pen on the Rock of Ages, to be read by the eyes of Angels and men for eternity; and they remain for ever, as glorious trophies of His victory over death and sin, and over Satan himself."—P. S.]

* [Tischendorf reads τόπον, *place.* Grotius says: τύπος *videtur,* τόπος *impletur.*—P. S.]

And become not faithless [*καὶ μὴ γίνου ἄπιστος, ἀλλὰ πιστός*]—*γίνου*, not: *be* not faithless, Meyer. He had not been faithless hitherto, but he was in danger of becoming so.* Tholuck: "Religious belief which demands the support of sensuous perception runs the risk of making an entire loss of faith." Nevertheless, the *sincere heart that needs and craves belief*, receives even in the hour of temptation the right signs which transport it beyond the danger that threatens it. Such was the experience of Thomas. His faith was saved; the great sign of Christ's appearance quickly made the sickly plant burst forth into fairest bloom.

Ver. 28. **My Lord and my God!** [*ὁ κύριός μου καὶ ὁ θεός μου*! An address of Thomas to Christ (the nom. with the art. for the vocative, as often in the New Testament; compare Christ's address to His Father, Mark xv. 34: *ὁ θεός μου, ὁ θεός μου*. The highest apostolic confession of faith in the Lordship and Divinity of Christ,—an echo of the beginning of this Gospel: "The Word was God," i. 1, and an anticipation of its close, xx. 30, 31. Thomas, says Augustine, beheld and touched Christ as *Man*, and confessed Him to be *God*, whom he did not see nor touch.—P. S.] —Weakening interpretation of Theodore of Mopsuestia: "*Quasi pro miraculo facto deum collaudat.*" Alleging the expression to be addressed admiringly to God. Similarly the Socinians and Paulus [and Unitarians]. Against this view we cite 1. *εἶπεν αὐτῷ* [to Jesus, not to God], 2. the reference of the words: *ὁ κύριός μου* to Christ. Erasmus: *Agnovit Christus, utique repulsurus, si falso dictus fuisset Deus.*† The excitement of feeling in which Thomas utters the adoring word in glorification of Christ, does not lessen the definiteness of his acknowledgment of Christ's divinity; it detracts merely from the definiteness of his dogmatical conception of it.

Ver. 29. **Thou believest** [*Ὅτι ἑώρακάς με πεπίστευκας*.]—According to Lachmann and Meyer, [Ewald], *πεπίστευκας* should be read as a question. Lücke objects against this view: It infuses into the words a tone of doubt as to the faith of Thomas. The doubt might indeed be expressive of this thought: Thinkest thou now that thou didst believe because thou hast seen Me outwardly? Seeing did but help thy faith to be born. However, Jesus designs not merely to recognize the faith of Thomas (as He did the faith of the disciples, chap. xvi. 31), but also to institute a contrast between the road travelled by his faith and the faith of others. *Thou believest.* The Perfect; properly, *thou hast believed* [*πεπίστευκας*], hast become believing,—a believer.—**Blessed are** [*μακάριοι*]—properly **they that saw not, and believed**; [or, **who never saw, and yet became believers,** *οἱ μὴ ἰδόντες, καὶ πιστεύσαντες*].—Meyer: The Aorists indicate, not *habitude* (Lücke), but those who *have believed* [have become believers without first having viewed] from the time the *μακαριότης* is predicated of them.* The saying is so constructed as 1. to intimate a peculiar praise of the other disciples who first believed, as well as to touch them, likewise, in its blame; 2. it, however, does not exclude Thomas (from this blessedness) inasmuch as he too commenced to believe before he had seen;† it establishes 3. a general rule destined for the beatification of the believing Church of a later period; at bottom, however, it is 4. generally declarative of the innermost essence of faith. Tholuck discovers a distinction of a *degree of faith* higher than that supported by sensuous perception: "That faith, namely, which, supported by the Word and the inner demonstrative power of the Word, believes, as St. Paul has it, *παρ' ἐλπίδα ἐπ' ἐλπίδι*, Rom. iv. 18; comp. John iv. 48." There might be question of a higher *way of faith;* but the *degree of faith* attained by Thomas should certainly not be designated as a lower one. Baur seeks to contra-distinguish faith resting upon external events and that faith which is abstractly certain of what it holds; according to this view, Christ called blessed the *quasi*-faith of modern spiritualists, who claim that they are satisfied with mere abstract religious ideas and are able to do without those facts in which the ideas have been realized! Christianity, however, is the indissoluble synthesis of idea and fact, and an idea-belief which pretends to discredit the belief in facts is a kind of platonizing mythologism, wherever it may start up with grand mien in these days. Meyer more correctly distinguishes belief in something which has occurred, *with* and *without* one's own sensuous perception. Christ did not reject that *belief* which seeks and finds confirmation in the way of doubt and investigation; neither, therefore, did He reject the corresponding *way* of belief; He did, however, point out the danger of that way, in which it is possible for doubt to separate itself from a trust in spiritual experience, and, in consequence of the impulse after sensuous experience, to turn into unbelief and apostasy.

[Alford: "Wonderful indeed, and rich in blessing for us who have not seen Him, is this, the closing word of the Gospel. For these words cannot apply to the remaining Ten: they, like Thomas, had seen and believed." Stier: "All the appearances of the forty days were mere preparations for the believing without seeing." 1 Pet. i. 8, "Whom having not seen, ye love; in whom, though now ye see Him not, yet believing, ye rejoice with joy unspeakable and full of glory: receiving the end of your faith, *even* the salvation of *your* souls."—P. S.]

DOCTRINAL AND ETHICAL.

1. The *character* of *Thomas*, and its import for

* [So also Wordsworth: "Remark *γίνου*: Do not *become* unbelieving. Thomas was *doubtful*, not unbelieving. Our Lord warns us, through him, that if we miss opportunities of having our scruples removed, if we close our eyes to the evidences He gives us of truth, our *doubts* will be *hardened* into *unbelief*."—P. S.]

† [So also Meyer, Alford, and the best exegetes generally. The Socinian view is worse than absurd, it turns an act of adoration into an irrelevant and profane exclamation unrebuked by the Lord! There is no instance of such profane use of the name of God in exclamations.—P. S.]

* [Alford: "The aorists, as often in such sentences (see Luke i. 45) indicate the present state of those spoken of, grounded in the past."—P. S.]

† [And inasmuch as the other apostles also first saw before they believed. Bengel: "*Non negatur beatitudo Thomæ, sed rara et lauta prædicatur sors eorum, qui citra visum credunt, nam etiam cæteri apostoli, cum vidissent, demum credidere.*"—P. S.]

the Church. See the citations of the Exeg. Note on ver. 24 [and my note on ver. 25.—P. S.]

2. The correct element in Thomas' expectation: That the body of the *Risen One* would of necessity be indubitably recognizable by the stigmata of the *Crucified One*.

3. The *doubt* of Thomas: (1) wherein allied to unbelief; (2) wherein distinct from the same. Thomas comes into the congregation of the believing disciples.

4. The manifestation of Christ for Thomas. The confession of Thomas. The ascription of blessedness to those who see not and yet believe. See Exeg. Note to ver. 29.

5. *On the eighth day*, or the repeated sanction of *Sunday*.

[6. *Mary Magdalene* and *Thomas*. Wordsworth: "From the two examples of Mary Magdalene and St. Thomas respectively, as described by St. John in this chapter, we learn two several duties to Christ, risen from the dead and ascended into heaven. The case of *Mary Magdalene* (v. 17) was very different from that of *St. Thomas*. She acknowledged His bodily Resurrection, and clung with joy to His human Body risen from the grave, and was satisfied with His visible presence, and wished to retain *that*. She had yet to learn—and we by her—to see Him that is invisible; to touch Him by faith; to ascend to Him with heart and mind, and to cling to the hem of the garment of Him our great High Priest in heaven, and adore Him as God. Therefore our Lord said to her, 'Touch me not, *for* I am not ascended; touch me by faith. *That* is the touch, which I require; that is the touch, by which I am to be held, and by which you may have My Presence with you.' But St. Thomas would not believe that He was risen indeed; or, if risen, that He was risen in the *same human body* as that which he wore before, and at His crucifixion. This was, what he was to learn, and we by *him*, faith in our Lord's Resurrection; faith in our own future Resurrection; faith in the identity of our own bodies to rise hereafter. Therefore Christ, who had said '*Touch Me not*' to Mary, said '*Touch Me*' to St. Thomas. Thus we are taught the true faith in His Divinity, Humanity and Personality, by His providential and gracious correction of the too material yearnings of a woman's love, of the too spiritual doubts of an Apostle's fears."—P. S.]

HOMILETICAL AND PRACTICAL.

Thomas. His nature. His sin. His worth. His salvation. His Easter-festival. His confession. His example.—The Thomas-souls in the Church of disciples: 1. How they are a detention to the Church; 2. how they are worthy of its indulgence and clemency; 3. how they finally conduce to its confirmation in the faith.—The order of Christianity: 1 First believing without seeing; 2. then seeing in order to become perfect in believing.—Christ the Master, also Thomas' Master.—Also the Master of Thomas-natures.—The certainty of Christ's resurrection is mighty enough to shame every sincere doubter.—The difference betwixt solitude and solitude: 1. A solitude of Magdalene, who first saw the Lord (pure grief, constant seeking). 2. A solitude of Thomas who saw Him last (gloomy, repining and brooding).—Thomas' doubt converted into a blessing to the faith of Christendom.—Thomas the character-portrait of honest doubters. 1. He holds fast the possibility of belief; 2. he put himself in the way of attaining belief.

Starke: Zeisius: How perilous it is to forsake the assemblies of the saints! therefore doth the Apostle exhort: *Let us not forsake, etc.*, Heb. x. 25.—It is a blessed hour when, whilst men are fooling away the time with the world, Jesus doth please to come unto us, Matt. xxv. 10.—It is one of the duties of Christians gladly to guide others to Christ while themselves resorting to Him, 2 Cor. xi. 2.—Osiander: Those who are filled with spiritual joy, desire to make others sharers in the same, Phil. ii. 18, 28.—Canstein: It is a transcendent grace of God, that He makes so much allowance for the manner of speech of the weak and tempted, Job xxxviii. 1 f.—*Ibid:* Mark, on Sunday Christ did several times appear unto the Apostles, on Sunday the disciples were assembled together; and so the first day in the week has been from that time consecrate, as the Lord's Day, in memory of the resurrection of Christ and the ensuing outpouring of the Holy Ghost, Acts xx. 7; 1 Cor. xvi. 2; Rev. i. 10.—Jesus in the midst, all the disciples round about Him: one has as much part in Him as another, 1 Tim. ii. 4.—Canstein: God exercises the most watchful care over the weak and tempted, and is most eager to help them, Luke xxiv. 15.

Gerlach: He who pinneth faith to bodily sight, to the earthly and visible, doth himself expose it to change, since all things visible are temporal, and only the invisible is eternal, 2 Cor. iv. 18.—And so every faith that still hath need of sight, that still hath need of sensuous helps and props, cometh short of being a saving faith.

Braune: Thomas is just such a witness of the resurrection as we could desire.—Pope Leo the Great (440-461) was right in saying, with reference to the doubting of the disciples, and to that of Thomas in particular, that they doubted to the end that we might not need to doubt.—The disciples likewise believed not in the beginning; believed not on the strength of the tidings brought by the others; they believed not *for joy*. Thomas believed not—could not, would not, believe, *for sorrow*. Love for the Lord was the ground of that joy and of this sorrow,—not godless love of the world.—Thomas, doubtless, suffered many pangs in his faithless melancholy beside the comforted disciples—pangs inflicted upon him by his self-willed demand for proof. Doubts as to the legitimacy of his demand, as well as in regard to the statement of the disciples, augmented his grief.—Then entered Jesus with His familiar: *Peace be with you!* That is the salutation of the Risen One now and always. The greeting is for all, but for *one, in particular:* Jesus approaches Thomas, *etc.* Of so much importance does the Redeemer count the solitary individual who still believes not, though all the others are already believing.—Jesus does not censure inquiry, examination, investigation; He only reprehends the arbitrary and stubborn demand for proof, such as Thomas put forth.—He does not want credulity or thoughtless superstition, but neither does He like self-willed unbelief; He desires a faith that reposes upon the word of life and the idea of that truth which makes the spirit free.—Happy are all they in whose heart and life unbelief is but a passing shadow, driven away by the pursuing breath of the Spirit!

GOSSNER: When these words were so positively heard: "No man can live that seeth God," intercourse with God was very difficult. Enoch held close intercourse with God before the deluge, but forasmuch as he carried it to a greater extent than was possible for men, God took him, that he might come unto the true enjoyment of communion with Him. All this was different now,—all purely spiritual things became palpable in the forty days after Easter. Shadow gave place to substance. "Feel Me and see," *etc.*—The doors are bolted unto the world when the Lord visiteth His people.—The Saviour will let none of His people be lost. He waits for the slow, who come eight days behindhand with their faith. Yet the reprimand that He administered to Thomas, shows that He does not approve of the weakness and hardness of belief which mingled in the demand of that disciple; and it is at the same time an intimation to the effect that his hardness of belief might easily have degenerated into perfect unbelief.

HEUBNER: When a man is not found in the fellowship of the faithful, much good is speedily let slip. When a man mingles in the society of the wicked, much is speedily corrupted. *Be not unbelieving, etc.* This command manifestly presupposes that the exercise or non-exercise of faith is dependent upon a man's will.—Faith built on seeing is little worth. For this reason, however, no demand is here made for *blind* faith. There is a difference between skepticism and the spirit of examination.—"From the beginning God hath instructed His people by faith, but we are continually deviating further and further from this way of faith; wise men labor with all their strength to the end that not faith but knowledge may have the mastery in the case of every truth contained in the Holy Scriptures." (BENGEL.)

[CRAVEN: From AUGUSTINE: Ver. 27. He might, had He pleased, have wiped all spot and trace of wound from His glorified body; but He had reasons for retaining them. He showed them to Thomas, who would not believe except he saw and touched, and He will show them to His enemies, to convict them.——From CHRYSOSTOM: Ver. 25. As to believe directly, and any how, is the mark of too easy a mind, so is too much inquiring of a gross one: and this is Thomas' fault.—Ver. 27. Consider the mercy of the Lord, how for the sake of one soul, He exhibits His wounds. But He did not appear to him (Thomas) immediately, but waited till the eighth day, in order that the admonition being given in the presence of the disciples might kindle in him greater desire, and strengthen his faith for the future.—Ver. 27. Note how that before they receive the Holy Ghost faith wavers, but afterward is firm.—Ver. 29. If any one then says, Would that I had lived in those times, and seen Christ doing miracles! let him reflect, *Blessed are they that have not seen, and yet have believed.*——From GREGORY: Vers. 24, 25. It was not an accident that that particular disciple was not present. The Divine mercy ordained that a doubting disciple should, by feeling in his Master the wounds of the flesh, heal in us the wounds of unbelief. The unbelief of Thomas is more profitable to our faith than the belief of the other disciples; the touch by which he is brought to believe, confirming our minds in belief beyond all question. [He causeth not only the wrath of enemies, but the weakness and errors of believers, to serve Him.—E. R. C.]——From THEOPHYLACT: Ver. 28. He who had been before unbelieving, after touching the body showed himself the best divine; for he asserted the twofold nature and one Person of Christ; by saying *My Lord*, the human nature; by saying, *My God*, the divine; and by joining them both, confessed that one and the same Person was Lord and God. [The *skeptic* convinced is often the firmest and most intelligent believer.—E. R. C.]

[From BURKITT: Ver. 24. We know not what we lose, when we absent ourselves from the assembly of God's people. Such views of a crucified, raised Jesus may be communicated to others, as would have confirmed our faith and established our joy, had we been present.—Ver. 25. How strangely rooted unbelief is in the hearts of holy men, insomuch that they desire the objects of *faith* should fall under the *view* of their senses.—Ver. 28. The convincing condescension of Christ turns unbelief into a rapture of holy admiration and humble adoration.—Ver. 29. By how much our faith stands in less need of the external evidence of sense, the stronger and the more acceptable it is, provided what we believe be revealed in the word of God.

[From M. HENRY: Ver. 24. Absenters for a time must not be condemned as apostates forever; Thomas is not Judas.—Ver. 25. *We have seen the Lord;* The disciples of Christ should endeavor to *build up one another in their most holy faith*, both by *repeating* what they have *heard*, to those that were absent, that they may hear it at second hand; as also by communicating what they have *experienced.*—Ver. 26. A very melancholy week, we have reason to think, Thomas had of it, drooping, and in suspense, while the other disciples were *full of joy;* and it was owing to himself and his own folly: he that slips one tide, must stay a good while for another.—*Thomas with them;* When we have lost one opportunity, we should give the more earnest heed to lay hold on the next, that we may recover our losses. It is a *good* sign if such a loss *whet* our desires, and a *bad* sign if it *cool* them.—Observe, Christ did not appear to Thomas, for his satisfaction, till He found him in society with the rest of His disciples.—*Peace be unto you;* This was no vain repetition, but significant of the abundant and assured peace which Christ gives, and of the continuance of His blessings upon His people, for they *fail not*, but are *new every morning*, new every *meeting*. [The soul that hath heard its Saviour once speak *Peace* to it, craveth again and yet again, the comfortable word.—E. M.]—Ver. 27. There is not an unbelieving word in our tongues, no, nor thought in our minds, at any time, but it is known to the Lord Jesus, Ps. lxxviii. 21.—For the confirmation of our faith, He hath instituted an ordinance on purpose *to keep His death in remembrance*, and in that ordinance, wherein we *show the Lord's death*, we are called, as it were, to put our finger *into the print of the nails*.—Ver. 28. In faith there must be the consent of the will to *gospel-terms* as well as the assent of the understanding to *gospel-truths*.—*My*; This is the vital act of faith, He is *mine*, Cant. ii. 16.—Ver. 29. Christ owns Thomas as a believer. Sound and sincere believers, though they be slow and weak, shall be graciously accepted of the Lord Jesus.—"One proselyte is more acceptable to God than all the thousands of Israel that stood before Mt. Sinai; for they saw and received the law, but a proselyte sees not, and yet receives it." (A Rabbi quoted by LIGHTFOOT).

From SCOTT: Vers. 24-29. Unbelief is the source of almost all our sins and disquietudes. We all have too much copied the example of Thomas' incredulity, by refusing to believe the word of God, and rely on His help, even when our experience of His care has been abundant; and we are often apt to demand such proof of His truths, and of His will, as we have no right to expect.

[From A PLAIN COMMENTARY (Oxford): Ver. 25. It must have been a gaping and a ghastly wound,—*that* wound in our Saviour's side,—that St. Thomas should have proposed to "thrust his *hand*" therein!—Ver. 26. But when He thus appeared for the second time, we may be well assured that He designed *more* than the removal of unbelief from the mind of a single disciple. He vouchsafed this appearance for the sake of confirming the faith of all the others,—and of ourselves.—Ver. 27. Having "*convinced*" the disciple, He proceeds to "*rebuke*" him,—which now He may do with good effect; whereas before, rebuke would have been fruitless.—Ver. 28. "Minds of every natural complexion are called to the exercise of Christian faith. The principle of faith,—the disposition to receive the word of God as such, to embrace and to walk by it,—is not indeed the gift of nature, but of grace; but its operation in each individual mind is modified by that mind's peculiar cast or temperament; and to every class of mind there are sufficient motives presented for the willing admission of the truth whereby we are sanctified and saved." (DR. W. H. MILL.)—Ver. 29. The blessedness of faith without the evidence of sense,—*this* it is of which our Lord here assures us; and of this, St. John (concerning whom it is expressly related that "*he saw and believed*"), St. Peter, St. Thomas and all the rest, were perforce destitute. "Blessed are they who have not seen, and yet have believed: who, against the things of sense, the temptations of the world, and Satan, against the perplexities of the natural mind, the misgivings of a fearful, and the lacerations of a wounded, heart, have opposed a firm faith in facts remote in Time, but indelible and eternal in effect." (DR. W. H. MILL.)

[From BARNES: Ver. 25. Many are like Thomas. Many *now* are unwilling to believe because they do not *see* the Lord Jesus, and with just as little reason as Thomas had.——From JACOBUS: Ver. 24. Observe 1. How much is often lost by absence from a single social meeting; 2. This is often *excused* on the ground of divers hindrances, but is commonly *traceable* to the want of a lively piety; 3. Such absentees often miss the Saviour's appearing, and His wonderful communications of the Holy Spirit.——From OWEN: Ver. 29. If any are disposed to regard it as an inferior privilege, to accept this truth (of the resurrection) through *faith* rather than *sight*, this great utterance of Jesus should fully correct such an erroneous view.]

V.

DESIGN OF THE GOSPEL FACTS. TESTIMONY CONCERNING CHRIST, AND LIFE IN HIS NAME.

CHAP. XX. 30, 31.

30 And [moreover][1] many other signs truly[2] did Jesus in the presence of his disci-
31 ples, which are not written in this book: But these are [have been] written, that
ye might [may] believe that Jesus is the Christ, the Son of God; and that believing ye might [may] have life[3] through [in] his name.

TEXTUAL AND GRAMMATICAL.

1 Ver. 30.—[μὲν οὖν—*quidem igitur, yea and*, or *moreover*. Lange, *nun auch*. The meaning is, to guard against taking this Gospel as a complete account of the signs of Jesus.—P. S.]

2 Ver. 30.—[*Truly* is intended to give the force of καί after πολλά and before ἄλλα = *et quidem alia*, AND INDEED *many other signs*.—P. S.]

3 Ver. 31.—The addition αἰώνιον after ζωήν in C.* D. L. Sin., *etc.*, not satisfactorily established. [A. B. C.³ X., *etc.*, Vulg. Syr. Cyr., *etc.*, omit αἰώνιον, read ζωήν without αἰώνιον, and so do Tischend., Alf., Treg., Westc. Its insertion from other passages is more easily accounted for than its omission.—P. S.]

EXEGETICAL AND CRITICAL.

According to Lücke, De Wette, Meyer, John here closes his entire book, and chap. xxi. is an appendix. In our opinion, he here concludes the history of the Passion and Resurrection, insomuch as that history was designed to perfect the faith of the disciples—just as chap. xii. 37, he evidently closes the history of the public prophetic ministry of Jesus; as chap. i. 18, He manifestly closes the Prologue, and, similarly, chap. xxi. 24 the Epilogue. These different concluding formulas betoken a construction of the Gospel so well organized and thoroughly digested, that in view thereof, the conception which regards the verses under consideration as forming a conclusion to the entire Gospel must appear a too external conception of our Gospel.

[Ver. 30. It is a question how the expression: πολλὰ καὶ ἄλλα σημεῖα, *etc.*, should be interpreted. The word has been referred to resurrection signs, signs in attestation of the resurrection, by Chrysost., Theophylact, *etc.*, Kuinoel, Lücke, Olshausen, *etc.* Against this view it is remarked by Meyer and others: (1) The term σημεῖα is too general to support such an interpretation. The verse, however, does not touch upon the great mass of the σημεῖα, but upon such as were done by Jesus *in the presence of His disciples*, in the circle of the eleven in particular; τεκμήρια, Acts i. 3. (2) Πολλὰ καὶ ἄλλα is alleged to be contradictory to this interpretation; Christ, according to the Gospel as well as according to 1 Cor. xv., having appeared a few times only. But the words are not spoken of the appearances in themselves, but of the σημεῖα which occurred on the occasion of these appearances. To these σημεῖα, then, there must be reckoned His making of Himself known to Thomas by means of a miracle of knowledge, to Mary through the word of recognition: *Mary.* But besides these signs, recorded by St. John, yet others must be added to the list, *viz.:* His making of Himself known to the Emmaus disciples through the *breaking of bread;* to Peter, as to James, in a mode with which we are unacquainted; to the five hundred brethren in Galilee, by a majesty of sudden appearance which threw many of them upon their knees; to the disciples on the Mount of Olives, by His ascension; to Paul, by His manifestation from heaven. These instances certainly might justify the expression of the Evangelist; (3) however, ἐποίησεν is said to contradict this view. Tholuck remarks that this term cannot be used concerning appearances. It may, however, be applied to manifestations of miraculous knowledge, of celestial might, of divine Providence, which manifestations accompanied every appearance. Then (4) this view is said to be disfavored by the expression: ἐν τῷ βιβλ. τούτῳ, these words being alleged to prove that John has in view the contents *of his entire Gospel.* Since, however, the Evangelist is speaking of resurrection-signs, he has reference to that part of the book which contains statements relative to the resurrection.

So early a commentator as Euthymius introduced the other explanation of the σημεῖα (see Lücke, 802). He first interprets them correctly, as significant of the resurrection-signs, but then states that the word may also be *generally* construed, as signifying the whole mass of the wonderful signs of Christ, previous and subsequent to the resurrection. And thus do Jansen, Wolf, Bengel, Lampe, Tholuck, *etc.* (see Meyer, 661) now interpret the term. [So also Hengstenberg, Godet, Alford: Miracles in the most general sense, by which Jesus proved His Messiahship. —P. S.] This interpretation is contradicted by (1) The circumstance that John has already submitted his *résumé* relative to the earlier signs, chap. xii. 37; (2) the fact that he is here speaking of signs done by the Risen One in the presence of the disciples;—objections irrespective of the necessity involved by this interpretation, for regarding chap. xxi. as a foreign addition or clumsily adjusted appendix, and this in the absence of otherwise sufficient grounds.

Ver. 31. **But these have been written** [ταῦτα δὲ γεγραμμένα ἵνα, κ.τ.λ.].—These signs—namely, these manifestations of the δόξα of Christ. According to Tholuck and Meyer, the selections from the miracles performed by Jesus presented throughout the entire Gospel. Against this view, see the preceding Exeg. Note. Be it also observed that this Gospel was not written for the purpose of converting to the faith those who were not yet believers (Hilgenfeld), but with a view to confirming believing Christians in the faith. Hence, also, the expression πιστεύσητε is to be taken emphatically, like the exhortation to believe addressed to Thomas, and the chief emphasis lies upon: καὶ ἵνα πιστεύοντες, *etc.* They are to be confirmed in their faith in Christ by faith in the resurrection, and in that faith have perfect life. [Alford: "The mere *miracle-faith*, so often reproved by our Lord, is not that intended here. This is faith in *Himself*, as the Christ the Son of God; and the Evangelist means that enough is related in this book to be a ground for such a faith, by showing us His glory manifested forth.—P. S.]

The Christ, the Son of God. Both in the fullest meaning of the words, in accordance with the Prologue.

May have life in His name [ζωὴν ἔχητε ἐν τῷ ὀνόματι αὐτοῦ].—Entire, perfect life in the name perfected through the resurrection.

[The ὄνομα, the revealed being of Christ, divine essence in human form, is the object of faith, and the ground of the ζωή. The Gospel of John has indeed a tendency, but not such an one as the Tübingen School ascribes to it. Its tendency is the aim of all sound preaching and theological writing, namely, by the faithful exhibition of truth to produce and to strengthen faith in Christ, and thus to lead men to the possession of the true life which is identical with true happiness. To John, his task as an historian was the same with his task as an apostle—salvation in Christ.—P. S.].

DOCTRINAL AND ETHICAL.

1. Here, as well as chap. xxi. 25, the Evangelist has made a distinct deliverance concerning the principle of *his evangelical historiography,*—particularly of his presentation of the resurrection-history. His great anxiety was not to write down everything that he knew about Jesus; his aim was, rather, in a selection of significant facts to present his view of the glory of Christ, in order to the quickening, revival, and increase of faith in Christian readers, but especially in order to the furtherance of the full vitality and life-certitude of faith in the ideal knowledge (the *name*) of Christ.

The same is true, although not in the same degree, of the Synoptists. This is the character of religious, particularly of the evangelical, objective-subjective historiography; it is the first task of modern Gospel criticism to rise to an appreciation of this character. The atomistic conception of chroniclers, book-makers, transcribers, supplementers, human-tendency writers does not reach up to the Christological idea of the Evangelist.

2. *That ye may believe that Jesus is the Christ, the Son of God.* This they did already believe, and yet they must believe it now more fully than ever. A peculiar emphasis, however, rests upon the following: *And that, believing* [or, *as believers*], *ye may have life in His name.* The *name* of Christ in believers is the full, clear, ideal contemplation of Christ in lively knowledge; therewith the full truth, certainty, vigor, and blessedness of the new *life* is given.

3. That which John says of his own writings is true of *all* the *Gospels.* Their authors, therefore, are indeed tendency writers, but of a divine tendency, entirely opposed to the human, fraudulous, manifoldly egotistic tendencies which the Tübingen critics have dared impute to them, or, what is still worse, to the Holy Ghost who guided them.

4. The remark of John is in the broadest sense characteristic of *Holy Scripture* in general. It has a religious purpose, and is therefore written from a religious impulse, in a religious spirit, under the guidance of the Spirit of God. All the religious truth of Holy Writ, however, aims at the truth of God in Christ. Christ the marrow and star of Holy Scripture.

HOMILETICAL AND PRACTICAL.

The many signs of Jesus in His showings after the resurrection also.—The immeasurable fulness of the life of Jesus.—The simple presentation of the same in speaking signs.—The unity and diversity of the four evangelic portraits of Jesus.—In particular, of the Risen One.—Portrait of the Risen One by the hand of John.—Purpose of this resurrection-history.—Of this Gospel.—of the four Evangelists.—Of the whole of Sacred Writ.—How one must read the Holy Scriptures in the same spirit in which they are written.—How perseveringly and devoutly? Until faith has become perfect life in a clear knowledge of Christ.—How many sluggishly stand still in the beginnings of faith, without pressing onward to the full vital consciousness of a certain knowledge. We are to have *life in Christ's name.*

STARKE: The Holy Scriptures are not imperfect, but perfect unto salvation in all things pertaining to faith and life, 2 Tim. iii. 16, 17.—ZEISIUS: Learn here whereunto the Holy Scriptures (the greatest treasure upon earth) are given us by God,—namely, that from them we may learn to believe and be saved.

[CRAVEN: From CHRYSOSTOM: Ver. 31. *And that believing ye might have life through His name, i.e.* through Jesus, who is Life.—From BURKITT: Ver. 31. The great point concerning Christ, to be known and believed from the Scriptures, is this, that Jesus, the Son of the Virgin, is the promised Messiah, the Anointed of the Father, He in whom all the types and shadows of the law are accomplished; and that this Jesus is for nature co-essential, for dignity co-equal, and for duration co-eternal with the Father; one in essence, equal in power and glory. Thus believing that Jesus is the Son of God, and accompanying that belief with a holy life, if we believe well, and live well, we shall have life through His name.—From M. HENRY: Ver. 31. The duty of those that read and hear the Gospel: to believe, to embrace the doctrine of Christ, and that record given concerning Him, 1 John v. 11.—The great gospel-blessedness which we are to hope for—*That believing we shall have life through His name.*

[From A PLAIN COMMENTARY (Oxford): Ver. 31. "It is the real Incarnation of the Eternal Word,—the actual coming in the flesh of the Son of God, born, dead, and risen for our salvation,—which is the sole basis of our religion. This great fact, and not any particular proposition concerning it, in the totality of its objective character, and in the consequent totality of its applicable virtue and influence; this is the real *Article of a standing or falling Church.*" (Dr. W. H. MILL.)]

[From OWEN: Ver. 31. *In His name;* "Eternal life is obtained by believers in virtue of Him, upon the claim established by Him in whom they believe." (WEBSTER and WILKINSON.)]

III.

EPILOGUE TO THE GOSPEL. CHRIST'S POST-HISTORIC RULE IN THE WORLD UNTIL THE COMPLETED GLORIFICATION OF THE WORLD, OR UNTIL CHRIST'S COMING AGAIN; SYMBOLICALLY PRESENTED IN PARTICULAR ITEMS OF THE RESURRECTION-HISTORY.

Chapter XXI.

I.

THE MANIFESTATION OF THE RISEN ONE AT THE GALILEAN SEA, AS A SYMBOL OF THE FUTURE RELATION AND CONDUCT OF CHRIST TOWARDS THE APOSTOLIC CHURCH IN THIS WORLD.

Chap. XXI. 1-14.

1 After these things Jesus[1] shewed [he manifested] himself again to the disciples at
the sea [lake] of Tiberias; and on this wise shewed he *himself* [and he manifested
2 himself in this manner]. There were together Simon Peter, and Thomas called
Didymus, and Nathanael of Cana in Galilee, and the *sons* of Zebedee, and two other
3 [others] of his disciples. Simon Peter saith unto them, I go [ὑπάγω] a fishing.
They say unto him, We also go [come, ἐρχόμεθα] with thee. They went forth, and
entered into a [the, τό] ship immediately [*omit* immediately][2]; and [in] that night
4 they caught nothing. But when the morning was now come [when the morning was
already coming on, πρωΐας δὲ ἤδη γενομένης],[3] Jesus stood on[4] the shore; but the
5 disciples knew not that it was Jesus. Then Jesus saith unto them, Children, have
ye any meat [any fish, or, anything to eat, προσφάγιον]? They answered him, No.
6 And he said unto them, Cast the net on the right side of the ship, and ye shall
[will] find. They cast therefore, and now they were not able to draw it for the
7 multitude of [the, τῶν] fishes. Therefore that disciple whom Jesus loved saith unto
Peter, It is the Lord. Now when Simon Peter heard that it was the Lord, he girt
his fisher's coat *unto him* [girded on his outer garment], (for he was naked,) and did
8 cast [threw] himself into the sea [lake]. And the other disciples came in a little
ship [in the boat, τῷ πλοιαρίῳ], (for they were not far from land, but as it were
9 [only about] two hundred cubits,) dragging the net with [the] fishes. As soon then
as they were come to land [or, went on shore], they saw [see, βλέπουσιν] a fire of
10 coals there, and fish laid [lying, ἐπικείμενον] thereon, and bread. Jesus saith unto
11 them, Bring of the fish which ye have now caught. Simon Peter went up [on
board], and drew the net to land[5] full of great fishes, an hundred and fifty and
three: and for all there were so many, yet was not the net broken [the net was not
broken, or, rent].
12 Jesus saith unto them, Come *and* dine [breakfast, ἀριστήσατε].[6] And[7] none of
13 the disciples durst ask him, Who art thou? knowing that it was the Lord. Jesus
14 then cometh, and taketh [the] bread, and giveth them, and [the] fish likewise. This
is now the third time that Jesus shewed [manifested] himself to his disciples, after
that he was risen from the dead.

TEXTUAL AND GRAMMATICAL.

[1] Ver. 1.—['Ιησοῦς is retained by Tischend., Treg., Westc., in accordance with B. C., text. rec.; ὁ 'Ιησοῦς by Lachm., in accordance with ℵ. A. L. X., *etc.* Alford omits it with D. M. There is no good reason for its omission, but there is for its insertion in a reading lesson beginning with ἐφανέρωσε.—P. S.]

[2] Ver. 3.—Εὐθύς [A. C.[3] P. text. rec.] is to be omitted in accordance with [ℵ.] B. C.* D. L. X. Δ., *etc.*

[3] Ver. 4.—The reading γινομένης instead of γενομένης, in accordance with C.* E. L. (Tischendorf), is probably exegetical. The dawn may already have come, without its being yet day or morning. [Lachmann and Alford read γενομένης, (*cum mane factum esset*), which is supported by Cod. Sin., but Tregelles, Tischendorf, ed. viii., and Westcott and Hort γινομένης (*cum mane esset futurum*), which is supported by A. B. C.* E. L (γειν. A. B.). See Tischend.—P. S.]

[4] Ver. 4.—The preposition εἰς is supported by B. C. E., *etc.*, Tischendorf; ἐπί by A. D. L., *etc.*, Lachmann, Sin. Meyer: "ἐπί would more readily than εἰς be added as a gloss."

[5] Ver. 11.—Εἰς τὴν γῆν in accordance with A. C. L. P. X. Δ., Lachmann, Tischendoff. This may be a correction of the Recepta ἐπὶ τῆς γῆς, E. G. K. M., *etc.*

[6] Ver. 12.—[Lange: *esset das Morgenbrot, eat the morning meal*, ἀριστάω is *to take an early meal* (ἄριστον, *prandium, breakfast* or *lunch*), before the δεῖπνον or *chief meal* (corresponding to our *dinner*), which was taken late in the afternoon or early in the evening, after the heat of the day was over, as is the custom now in large cities, as Paris, London, New York.—P. S.]

[7] Ver. 12.—[The text. rec., with ℵ. A. D. L., inserts δέ after οὐδείς, and Tischendorf (ed. viii., not before) retains it. Alford and Westcott reject it in accordance with B. C.—P. S.]

EXEGETICAL AND CRITICAL.

On the GENUINENESS of Chap. xxi., see the Introduction, p. 31. Along with the genuineness, we maintain the organic appertinency of the chapter to the entire Gospel, in antithesis to the view which debases it to an appendix. See the Introduction, p. 46; *Leben Jesu*, III., p. 752. In respect to the discussions on the subject, see Lücke II., p. 805; Meyer [p. 662 ff.]; * Tholuck, p. 445 and others.

[The last chapter is generally regarded as a mere Appendix. Dr. Lange views it as the Epilogue which corresponds to the Prologue, (I. 1-18), and presents, in typical outline, the *post-resurrection history* of Christ, His perpetual, spiritual presence in, and guidance of, the Church; as the Prologue presents His history *before the Incarnation*, and the body of the Gospel, His *earthly history*. Lange's exegetical and doctrinal commentary of this plain, unassuming, yet most significant chapter, is exceedingly rich and ingenious, and leaves but little room for additions. Dr. F. W. Krummacher, the prince of German pulpit orators, told me in Elberfeld, on Easter Monday, 1844, after delivering a magnificent discourse on vers. 1-14, that he had prepared no less than fifteen different sermons on this section, and had found it inexhaustible in homiletical wealth. The other sections are equally rich. Ch. xx. is the Gospel for Easter Sunday. Ch. xxi. the Gospel for the Easter-Week, as irradiated by the Sun of the Resurrection. It is a picture of Christian life, and the life of the Church, with its contrasts and changes,—festive joy and hard work, poverty and abundance, failure and success, humility and loftiness, activity and rest, losing and finding the Lord, longing for Him and rejoicing in His presence.

On the *genuineness* of this chapter, I add the testimonies of an English and an American scholar. Canon Westcott (in his excellent *Introduction to the Study of the Gospels*, Boston ed., p. 258,) says: "This last chapter (xxi.) of his Gospel is in every way a most remarkable testimony to the influence of St. John's person and writings. Differences of language, no less than the abruptness of its introduction and its substance, seem to mark it clearly as an addition to the original narrative; and the universal concurrence of all outward evidence, no less certainly establishes its claim to a place in the canonical book. It is a ratification of the Gospel, and yet from the lips of him who wrote it; it allows time for the circulation of a wide-spread error, and yet corrects the error by the authoritative explanation of its origin. The testimony, though upon the extreme verge of the Apostolic period, yet falls within it, and the Apostle, in the consciousness (as it seems) of approaching death, confirms again his earlier record, and corrects the mistaken notion, which might have cast doubt upon the words of the Lord." Ezra Abbott, in his and Hackett's ed. of Smith's *Bibl. Dict.*, vol. II., p. 1430, note b., maintains, with the best German commentators, that the 21st ch. contains almost all the peculiarities of John's style, and that the points of difference are insignificant, compared with the striking agreement. He adds: "On the supposition, however, that the Gospel is not genuine, this Appendix presents a problem which seems to admit of no reasonable solution. What motive could there have been for adding such a supplement to a spurious work after the middle of the second century? Was it needful, fifty years or more after the Apostle's death, to correct a false report, that it was promised him that he should not die? Or what dogmatic purpose could this addition serve? And how is its minuteness of detail, and its extraordinary agreement in style with the rest of the Gospel to be explained? It may be said that it was designed to give credit to the forged Gospel, by a pretended attestation. But was the whole chapter needed for this? And what credit could a fictitious work of that period derive from an *anonymous* testimony? Had such been the object, moreover, how strange that the Apostle John should not be *named* as the author! The only plausible explanation, then, of vers. 24, 25, seems to be, that they are an attestation of the trustworthiness of the Gospel, by those who first put it into general circulation—companions and friends of the author, and well known to those to whom it was communicated; and the only plausible account of the first 23 verses of the chapter is, that they are a supplementary addition [?], which proceeded directly from the pen, or substantially from the dictation of the author of the rest of the Gospel." The Johannean origin of ch. xxi. is denied or doubted by Grotius, Clericus, Hammond, Semler, Paulus, Lücke, De Wette, Credner, Bleek, Baur, Keim, Scholten, *etc.*; defended by Wetstein, Lampe, Eichhorn, Kuinoel, Hug, Guericke, Tholuck, Schleiermacher, Olshausen, Luthardt, Ebrard, Hengstenberg, Godet, Alford, Westcott, Wordsworth, (who, in a long note, p. 362, maintains a view somewhat similar to that of Dr. Lange). The latest hypothesis brought out by Prof. Cassel, (1871), is that John wrote the 21st chapter, and endorsed the rest, which was originally written by his brother James. The first is true, the last is a worthless fancy.]

[The only argument worth mentioning against the Johannean origin of chap. xxi., is derived from a few rare and unimportant expressions, as *ἐρχεσθαι σὺν* (ver. 3) for the usual Johannean *ἀκολουθεῖν*; *πρωΐας γενομένης* (4) for *πρωΐ*; *τολμᾶν* and *ἐξατάζειν* (12); *φέρειν* (18) for *ἄγειν*. But these peculiarties are natural and easily explained from the context, and are more than counterbalanced by the number of Johannean words and phrases, as *μετὰ ταῦτα* (ver. 1), *ἡ θάλασσα τῆς* Τιβεριάδος (1), *ὀψάριον* (9, 10, 13), *παιδία* (5), *μέντοι* (4), the double *ἀμήν* (18). Ναθαναήλ (2) for Bartholomew, the form Θωμᾶς ὁ *λεγόμενος* Δίδυμος (2), *Σίμων* Πέτρος (2, 3, 7, 11, 15), *ὁ μαθητὴς ὃν ἠγάπα ὁ* Ἰησοῦς (7), as well as by the unanimous testimony of the manuscripts and ancient versions, which contain the whole chapter as an integral part of the Gospel. The only question is as to vers. 24 and 25, whether they are likewise from John, or an attestation by the hand of his surviving pupils and friends. Lange regards also these last two verses as Johannean

* [Meyer regards the whole of ch. xxi. as genuine, with the exception of ver. 25, (on which see below), and ably refutes the objections which, since Grotius, have been raised against the Johannean authorship.—P. S.]

with the exception of the phrase: "And *we* know that his testimony is true." They conclude the Epilogue, and correspond to the conclusion of the Prologue, i. 18, and the conclusion of the main body of the Gospel, xx. 30, 30.—P. S.]

Ver. 1. **After these things**—[Μετὰ ταῦτα].—*I. e.*, which, in Jerusalem, had already secured the confirmation of the disciples in the faith. [Several days must have elapsed since the last meeting, (xx. 26), for the disciples had in the meantime, according to the Lord's direction, returned to Galilee. (Matt. xxviii. 7, 10, 16; 1 Cor. xv. 6.) Afterwards they again proceeded to Jerusalem, to witness the ascension from Mount Olivet, (Luke xxiv. 50 ff.; Acts i. 1-12), and to be filled with the promised Spirit (Acts ii.).—P. S.]

Jesus manifested Himself [ἐφανέρωσεν ἑαυτόν].—Is an indication of His higher manner of appearing intended? De Wette finds in the expression the indication of a ghostly existence;—Luthardt that of a moving in a sphere of the invisible; this, Meyer impugns. The ghostliness, of course, cannot exclude His bodiliness, nor can His invisibility exclude His power of appearing. Nevertheless, we believe that something is meant here, other than the higher manner of appearing. In accordance with John's method of using πάλιν, the word seems indicative, not of His third manifestation after the resurrection, but of a second new, higher manifestation of His glory at the Lake of Gennesareth, in contradistinction to that first manifestation of His glory at the same Lake, of which we have an account in chap. vi.

At the Lake of Tiberias [ἐπὶ τῆς θαλάσσης τῆς Τιβεριάδος.]—The demonstrations of the Risen One still connect themselves with the old life-order of the disciples, especially the disciples in the wider sense. Agreeably to this order of life, from the Easter-feast [Passover] in Jerusalem they returned to Galilee, preparing themselves shortly afterwards for attendance upon the Feast of Pentecost. This old order of life, observed by the disciples, was, however, on the point of being dissolved, inasmuch as they brought their festal journeys into harmony with the new interest. Accordingly, after the Paschal Feast, they remained yet a Sunday in Jerusalem, and returned thither a long while before the Pentecostal Feast. But for the intervening time, Jesus had appointed His principal meeting with the circle of disciples, in the broader sense of that term, in Galilee, and His promise was fulfilled according to Matt. xxviii.; comp. 1 Cor. xv. That meeting, however, was doubtless preceded by Jesus' first manifestation in Galilee, at the lake, seven disciples being present. We find these busied again with their domestic trade; this circumstance points to the earliest period subsequent to their return home. They were, temporarily, without further occupation and instruction; they must wait for the Lord. The direction to tarry in Jerusalem (Luke xxiv. 49) applies to the period following the ascension.

Now He manifested Himself on this wise [ἐφανέρωσεν δὲ οὕτως].—In the following, stress is laid, not particularly upon Christ's issuing forth from invisibility, but upon the miraculous manner in which He made Himself known to the Apostles, and communed with them.

Ver. 2. **There were together** [ἦσαν ὁμοῦ κ. τ. λ. The witnesses of the Resurrection, the recipients of the Holy Ghost, returned to their humble work in Galilee, fishing together, probably for the last time! So festive joys and hard work alternate in the life of the Christian. —P. S.]—It is noteworthy that Thomas is here mentioned after Simon Peter, as the second disciple. Further we find Nathanael, or Bartholomew, and the two sons of Zebedee (John and James); together with these, two others of His disciples are enumerated without special designation. Our first inference would be, that these were Andrew, the brother of Peter, and Philip, the friend of Nathanael. From the circumstance that the disciples are not named, Meyer thinks fit to infer that they were disciples in the broader sense; ver. 1 seems to contradict this. John may have omitted the names of the two disciples for two reasons: 1. Because he would otherwise have been obliged to mention the sons of Zebedee by name, also; 2. Because, it was his desire, by speaking, at the close, of *two* disciples, to induce his readers to make the computation of the *seven.* Or is their anonymousness to serve the symbolical purpose of the Epilogue? Or was he unwilling, by naming the two, to give prominence to the four remaining ones, who had no part in this feast? Something enigmatical still attaches to this anonymousness. Contemplative natures, such as John's, are undoubtedly dreamily forgetful in certain moments and relations; it is, therefore, not necessary to infer the two nameless ones to have been disciples in the wider sense. Here only does he mention the sons of Zebedee together.

Ver. 3. **Simon Peter: I go a fishing** [ὑπάγω ἁλιεύειν].—Peter is foremost in outside enterprises also. And thoroughly decided in his own mind, without asking others; *I go.*—**We also go (come) with thee** [ἐρχόμεθα καὶ ἡμεῖς σὺν σοί].—The expression of their cordial, friendly cleaving to him.

And in that night they caught nothing [καὶ ἐν ἐκείνῃ τῇ νυκτὶ ἐπίασαν οὐδέν].—The night season is the most favorable time for catching fish, Luke v. 5. Yet there were unsuccessful nights; such an one was this. [A symbol of the utter failure of the fishers of men without Christ, as verse 6 illustrates their abundant success with Christ.—P. S.]

Ver. 4. **But when the morning had already dawned.**—[According to the other reading, *was about dawning.* See TEXT. NOTE.—P. S.] It was the time of the dawning.—**Jesus stood on the shore** [ἔστη Ἰησ. εἰς τὸν αἰγιαλόν].—He had taken His station on the shore (εἰς). They saw the form standing on the shore without recognizing it. Comp. John xx. 14; Luke xxiv. 16.

Ver. 5. **Children.**—Παιδία does not stand for the Johannean τεκνία (see chap. xiii. 33), not even in the sense of 1 John ii. 13. Jesus, wishing in His character of the Unknown One to address the fishermen first as a stranger, speaks to them in the universal, familiar language of seafaring men, with the dignity, we may conjecture, of a superior: Young men! Boys! 2 Macc. viii.

20; Nonnus, Euthym. Zigabenus; see *Leben Jesu* II., p. 1712; Tholuck.

Have ye any relish? or, have ye anything to eat? [μή τι προσφάγιον ἔχετε;]—Properly speaking, anything to eat with bread, προσφάγιον, [but especially *fish*, like the Attic ὄψον], namely, with their morning-bread, or breakfast.* By the sea, fish were their usual προσφάγιον with their bread. According to Tholuck, they regard the questioner as some one wishing to purchase fish for his own breakfast. The same is the opinion of Meyer; Jesus, on the other hand, takes for granted, as His last words show us, that they have caught nothing, and intimates that if the contrary were the case He would not need to interpose. It is manifest, however, that the question is primarily intended merely as an expression of human interest, and for the introduction of what follows.

Ver. 6. **Cast the net on the right side of the ship** [βάλετε εἰς τὰ δεξιὰ μέρη τοῦ πλοίου τὸ δίκτυον, καὶ εὑρήσετε].—Comp. Luke v. 4. There the Lord commands the disciples to launch out into the deep, here to cast the net on the right side of the ship, whence we might conclude that they had drawn the net after them on the other side, or, discouraged, had drawn it up out of the water with the intention of steering towards the shore.

No longer able to draw it up [οὐκέτι αὐτὸ ἑλκύσαι ἴσχυον].—To draw the net up over the water, or to themselves (ἑλκύειν)—a feat naturally more difficult than to drag it, closed, after them in the water itself (σύρειν).

Ver. 7. **It is the Lord** ['Ο Κύριός ἐστιν]. John first recognizes Him, with the mind's eye, by His manner of acting, and then, with the bodily ear, by His speech, as also, with the bodily glance, by His specific appearance.

Simon Peter then hearing that it was the Lord.—Again the characteristic picture of the two disciples, as in chap. xx. 4 ff. Each disciple is in advance of the other; John with the swift drawing of love, the eagle-glance of recognition, Peter with the spirited, decided act.—**For he was naked** [ἦν γὰρ γυμνός].—This assertion does not operate to the exclusion of the loin-cloth, or a fisherman's shirt, even. Reverence, however, commands him to put on the upper garment, ἐπενδύτης (מְעִיל), fisher's frock; this was without sleeves; it extended to the knees and was worn over the χιτών. He girded the garment on account of his swimming, for it was in this manner he reached the land; Grotius and others make him walk upon the water as aforetime.

Ver. 8. **As it were two hundred cubits,** or 300 feet = ½ stadium.

Ver. 9. **They saw a fire of coals laid.**—[Βλέπουσιν ἀνθρακιὰν κειμένην καὶ ὀψάριον ἐπικείμενον καὶ ἄρτον].—The coal-fire was laid, broiling fish were spread thereon as a *relish* (ὀψάριον), and moreover they saw *bread*. For καὶ ἄρτον, we doubt not, is to be referred simply to βλέπουσιν. Mysterious preparation. Interpretations:

1. Brought forth out of nothing: Chrysostom, Theophylact, Grotius, Calov and others.

2. Prepared by the ministry of angels: Nicephorus, Luthardt, *etc.*

3. Jesus either conveyed the meal thither Himself, or procured others to place it there: Meyer. Against this view, Tholuck: "Peter cannot have conveyed it thither, but neither can Jesus have procured it by means of others, if we must regard the perception of the Risen One not as an external, common, sensuous perception, but as conditioned by the inner sense" (?). Lücke: "A lack of clearness invests the miracle with an air of wild adventure." But had not Jesus friends everywhere along the lake? Could He not appear to them, and, in a mysterious manner, arrange something similar to the making ready of the she-ass in Bethphage and of the furnished room in Jerusalem? To this day Christ often, through the medium of wonderful providences, cares thus for the maintenance of His people by operating influentially upon foreboding souls. Here, therefore, as the Master and Father of the house, He has provided a breakfast for them (and that not merely in a vision). Comp. Luke xxiv. 30.

Ver. 10. **Bring of the fish.**—['Ενέγκατε ἀπὸ τῶν ὀψαρίων ὧν ἐπιάσατε νῦν].—Irrespective of the question whether the prepared repast is sufficient or not, they are commanded to add to it some of their own fish (which, however, they have caught in pursuance of His directions alone). Euthymius: In order to preserve the miraculous draught from all appearance of a φαντασία; Meyer: In order to the exigent completion of the meal. We think that it was likewise in order to the revelation of a new order of things. Here, as everywhere, the symbolical transparency of the story comes to light.

Ver. 11. **An hundred and fifty and three** [ἑκατὸν πεντήκοντα τριῶν].—The Evangelist's primary intention in reporting the number of the whole mass of great fishes was, manifestly, to render prominent the miraculousness of the fact that the net was nevertheless untorn. The trait that the number (153), as a number, is not symbolical, speaks very decidedly in favor of the historic truthfulness of the narrative in opposition to the assumption of its being a tradition (Strauss), or the work of an apocryphal narrator. The attempt has indeed been made to construe the number materially as a symbolical one. Ammonius: The number 100=the Gentiles, 50=the Jews, 3=the Trinity.* Jerome and Köstlin: Oppian counted 153 species of fish, ergo the universality of species=the universality of the nations entering the net of the Gospel. "Which statement, as far as Oppian is concerned, rests upon a mistake." Recently, some one has even conceived it to be his duty to work out the name of Simon [son of] Jonas, by means of numerical allegory (*Theol. Jahrb.* 1854, p. 135). We do not consider the *number* as symbolical, but the *num-*

* [No single English word adequately translates the Greek προσφάγιον and its German equivalent *Zukost*. The idea is that of some article of food added to what is regarded as the substantial part of the meal. The term *relish*, in one of its significations, more nearly expresses it than any other English word.—P. S.]

* [Other mystical explanations of the number in Wordsworth *in loc.*, who makes 153 expressive of the jubilee of the true Israel of beatified saints in heaven. Comp. also Meyer, p. 673. Calvin cuts off all such calculations by the sober remark: *Quantum ad piscium numerum spectat, non est aliquod in eo quærendum mysterium.*—P. S.]

bering does appear to us in that light. The elect, who form the main element of the Church, are great and *numbered* fishes. And great and numerous as the elect of the congregated mass may be, they are not the ones who break the net of the Church. It is the maxim of all the elect: first Christ, then the Church. John is moreover always fond of stating numbers; for instance, the 200 cubits, ver. 8; chap. vi. 10, *etc.*

Ver. 12. **(But) none of the disciples durst ask Him** [οὐδεὶς (δὲ) ἐτόλμα τῶν μαθητῶν ἐξετάσαι αὐτὸν Σὺ τίς εἶ; εἰδότες ὅτι ὁ Κύριός ἐστιν].—The ἐτόλμα is not pleonastic (Kuinoel), not expressive of *velle* (Lampe), or of a fear of doubt (Augustine and others), but of reverence, in connection with a quiet, blissful assurance in regard to the presence of Jesus (εἰδότες, *etc.*). [Comp. ch. iv. 27.—P. S.]. What was so particularly new to them at this manifestation of the Risen One was the feature of His partaking of a meal with them once more, like a house-father, after having miraculously prepared it for them.

Ver. 13. **Jesus cometh therefore** [ἔρχεται Ἰησοῦς].—As the disciples have been standing on this side of the coal fire, and have been called to approach by the Lord (δεῦτε, ver. 12), so the Lord has stood on the other side,—probably with that expression of reserve suitable to the unknown person in whose character He wished first to meet them,—and now He advances nearer and more familiarly to them.

And taketh the bread [καὶ λαμβάνει τὸν ἄρτον]—Why is the customary thanksgiving not mentioned? 1. Jesus wished to omit τὰ ἀνθρώπινα (Euthymius). 2. Luthardt; The table-communion of Jesus with His people is a silent one in this æon. 3. Meyer: The Evangelist is not describing a regular repast, such as is spoken of, Luke xxiv. 30, but a *breakfast*, that was partaken of standing. As it appears, it is also, however, the intention of Christ not to make Himself positively known as yet by the expression of the prayer of thanksgiving. And probably there is a symbolical reason for this. Peter who has denied Him, declaring that he knew Him not, must be made to recognize Him again, as the Anonymous One, by His conduct. At all events, the reserve of Jesus seems designed, by means of a continually increasing solemnity, to prepare the minds of the disciples for the ensuing act. Yet the manifestation has a purpose which touches the disciples in general; hence there follows a sort of conclusion, in order to the distinction of the general disciples' meal from the conference with Peter, and that concerning Peter and John.

Ver. 14. **This third time now Jesus manifested himself** [Τοῦτο ἤδη τρίτον ἐφανερώθη Ἰησ. τοῖς μαθηταῖς ἐγερθεὶς ἐκ νεκρῶν].—With these words John ranks the present manifestation of Jesus—as a more general one, allotted to the circle of disciples (incomplete though that was in numbers)—with the two manifestations recorded in chap. xx. Luthardt very properly remarks: "The appearings therein reported by John are by Paul summed up in εἶτα τοῖς δώδεκα, 1 Cor. xv. 5;" and only the well-known fear of harmonizing induces Meyer to maintain the existence of a difference which he decides in John's favor. Manifestly, Paul has no interest in citing repeatedly those appearances of Jesus of which *the same* persons were repeatedly spectators, intending, as he does, not to count the appearings of the Risen One, but to mention the witnesses as witnesses.

[Alford's remarks on this section are in the line of Lange's thoughts, and worthy of attention: "Without agreeing with all the allegorical interpretations of the Fathers, I cannot but see much depth and richness of meaning in this whole narrative. The Lord appears to His disciples busied about their occupation for their daily bread; speaks and acts in a manner wonderfully similar to His words and actions on a former memorable occasion, when we know that by their toiling long and taking nothing, but at His word enclosing a multitude of fishes, was set forth what should befall them as fishers of men. Can we miss that application at this far more important epoch of their apostolic mission? Besides, He graciously provides for their present wants, and invites them to be His guests: why but to show them that in their work hereafter they should never want but He would provide? And as connected with the parable, Matt. xiii. 47 ff., has the net *enclosing a great multitude and yet not broken*, no meaning? Has the 'taking the bread and giving to them and the fish likewise,' no meaning, which so closely binds together the miraculous feeding, and the institution of the Lord's Supper with their future meetings in His name and round His Table? Any one who recognizes the *teaching* character of the acts of the Lord, can hardly cast all such applications from him;—and those who do not, have yet the first rudiments of the Gospels to learn."—P. S.]

DOCTRINAL AND ETHICAL.

1. The significant manner in which John, seemingly by way of supplement, relates this single and unique meeting of the Risen One with the seven disciples by the Galilean Sea, culling it out of all the later showings of Jesus after His resurrection and emphasizing the individual, momentous items of the event, induces us to suppose that from the first he designed it to form *the conclusion of his Gospel*. That he at the same time, however, intended this conclusion as an Epilogue to the Gospel, is proved by the precursive close of the resurrection-history and the Gospel in its narrower sense, chap. xx. 31. If we now take into consideration how symbolically transparent the individual facts of this Epilogue are from beginning to end (especially the miraculous draught of fishes, the institution of Peter, the destination of John), we shall not hesitate to bring the Epilogue into an antithetic relation to the Prologue of the Gospel, chap. i. 1-18. And if John has there sketched Christ's pre-temporal rule in the world, finally represented, as it was, by John the Baptist, the recognition is obvious that he has designed to sketch here, in a speaking, evangelic fact, Christ's post-temporal rule in the world, represented by the heptade of the Apostles, particularly by the destination of Peter and John in respect of their typical import for the Church. See *Leben Jesu* ii. p. 1723.

2. *The resolve of Peter, to go a fishing.* A sym-

bol of the beginning of the apostolic mission. The *seven disciples* in a round, sacred number, a symbol of the apostolic Church. The Church is subdivided into an external, conspicuous part, and a mysteriously withdrawing, nameless part. Next to Peter are ranged Thomas, the apostolic searcher, and Nathanael, the representative of apostolic sincerity and simplicity. The sons of Zebedee retire into the back-ground; there is intimated, moreover, a nearer fellowship of John which forms the innermost, hidden, vital focus of the Church. Unanimity is the character of this fellowship. They go out together to catch fish. *Into the sea.* The sea a symbol of the world, of the life of the nations.

3. *The unsuccessful night.* A symbol of the times of waiting, of the apparently fruitless struggling and hoping, whereby the laborers of God are tried in their work. These trials are connected with the fact that the disciples must first be freed from their self-consciousness and brought to the point of fully renouncing their work and relinquishing all expectation of shining results. These humiliations, however, are connected with the necessity for distinguishing between an activity based upon human authority (Peter) and one drawing its inspiration from the word of Christ. A human and legal running produces no abiding fruit.

4. *The unknown Man on the shore.* Christ is always near His apostolic Church on this side of eternity. From the shore of the other world—the beyond—His eye is leveled upon their actions. And they are conscious of this fact in its general sense, but they do not immediately recognize the Lord in the new, concrete forms of life in which He approaches them, wishing to prepare them an apostolic blessing.

5. *Children, have ye nothing to eat?* Whenever the spirit of a new life-form of Christ discourses with the Church concerning her poverty, want of success, unavailing labor and fatigue, the moment of a new bestowal of blessing is being prepared.

6. *Cast the net.* It is always the *old* net that Christ tells His people to cast in a *new* way, in a *new* direction. This, Christ's instruction, alone indicates the true treasure of blessing, and obedience to Christ's instruction obtains the miraculous draught.

7. Christ has first unknown operated upon the Church by need and opportunity. His instruction has become of weight to her in the form of a pious, religious exhortation, or as a friendly counsel, and she has accorded it her confidence. In the result of miraculous blessing, however, the Lord is known as the author of that blessing. The Johannean eagle-glance first recognizes the Lord, Petrine fiery courage rushes through the flood to meet Him; the Church hastes to meet the Lord. But the true Petrine spirits in the Church are those who hurry on in advance of the Ship of the Church with their works and deeds. The one kind of spirits haste before it with the glance of recognition, the other by act; both, however, abide in full connection with the Ship.

8. *The ship not far from land.* Not far from the throne of the Lord and His coming.

9. *The coal-fire and repast on the shore.* There are continually recurring festive moments in the Church—moments when Christ holds a feast with His people, as though upon the heights of the new world. The goal is momentarily reached in a grand triumph, a grand manifestation of Christ. We would call to mind the time of Christ's resurrection itself, the year 70 (destruction of Jerusalem), 312; the years 1517, 1700, 1813 (the time of the liberation of Germany [eclipsed for Germany by 1870 and 1871]) and similar periods. In a wonderful way the Lord has ever prepared a refreshing repast for His weary ones.

10. *Bring of the fish.* The Lord prepares refreshment for His Church from a *synthesis* of His *gift of blessing* (for the preparation of which He has always ministering spirits) and their *labor of blessing* [*blessed labor*].

11. *Simon Peter drew the net to land.* Be of use! forward! to Christ! is the watchword of the Biblical Peter. It is not his intention to seize the net for himself, but to place it at the disposal of Christ. *The net was full of great fishes.* The word of the Church first catches the elect, those in a special degree receptive of salvation. The number 153. On the different interpretations see Exeg. Note *in loc.* We, as was previously stated, consider as symbolical, not the *number*, but the *numbering.* The elect are counted, man for man. See Jer. vii. 6; Rev. vii. 4. Thus also are the *Einherier*, the heroes of Odin in Valhalla, counted, according to German Mythology. ("'Five hundred doors and forty more methinks are in Valhalla.—Eight hundred heroes through each door shall issue forth against the wolf to combat.'" Therefore 800 × 540. Grimnismal). The Church is continually edified by the number of true subjective converts and believers who have received a new name, not by her unnumbered masses.—Nevertheless the net brake not. The truly faithful do not break the net. The great fishes swim lustily along in the draught of the net. The fishing net is broken by sea-reptiles, crabs, dead fish that weigh upon one point. Yet the true spiritual net of the eternal Church has never yet been broken.

12. *Come and partake of the repast.* Times of refreshing in the kingdom of God. Christ the Master of the House, who giveth the invitation to the feast. Reverential sense of His presence. Full sufficiency. It is a breakfast, however, in order to further labor. Blissful stillness of the Church in the Lord's nearness and in the assurance of His presence.

13. The *third* time, or the manifestations of the glorified Christ ever more glorious.

14. The present section shows us the Apostles Peter and John in the characters peculiar to them; the following sketches their destiny and lot in the Church.

HOMILETICAL AND PRACTICAL.

See the DOCT. NOTES. Christ's first meeting again with His disciples by the Sea of Galilee.—The old life in the new light of the resurrection: 1. The old persons (Peter, *etc.*); 2. the old occupation (going a fishing); 3. the old surroundings (the Sea of Galilee); 4. the old vicissitudes and the old need (caught nothing); 5. the old connection (Christ); 6. the old miracles (the draught of fishes); 7. the old feasts (the repast). Everything in a new light of life, peace and hope.—Christ at the sea of Galilee, formerly and now: 1. The sea formerly the scene of His first miracles, acts and sufferings; 2. now the mirror of His glory.

The two Easter-feasts in Galilee: 1. The Apostles' feast by the sea; 2. the Church's feast on the mountain (Matthew xxviii.).—Christ manifests Himself to the Apostles by the sea; for they must plunge into the sea of nations; to the Church, in the wider sense, on the mountain, for it is to be the firm city, stablished upon the mountain of the Lord.—The disciples, as sons of the resurrection, in their true unanimity: 1. How harmonious in their differences (all gladly following the foot of Peter, the glance of John). They all confess their need unanimously: "No;" but without complaint, ver. 5. There is no braggart among them and none who is disheartened. They are obedient in unison. Their faces are all set toward the Lord in one love; they are all filled and made happy with the one thought of His presence. 2. How rich in life and manifold in their unanimity (Peter, John; the disciples in the ship).—The Risen One in the gradualness of His glorious manifestation: 1. The strange form in the morning twilight on the shore; 2. the sympathizing question; 3. the confident direction; 4. the mysterious preparation of a fire; 5. the condescending community of goods (*bring hither of the fish*); 6. the glorious invitation; 7. the complete manifestation in its familiarity and sublimity.—Christ considered in respect to the riches of His life amongst His people: 1. Mysterious and familiar; 2. Master and Servant; 3. Host and Guest; 4. a heavenly Apparition and a festive Companion.—Transformation of the old form of life into the new in the kingdom of the Risen One: 1. The old calling becomes a new symbol of life; 2. the old home a new vestibule of heaven; 3. the old need a new divine blessing; 4. the old labor a new religious service; 5. the old partnership a new fellowship in Christ; 6. the old discipleship a new apostolate.—The heavenly refreshment of the disciples, the preparation for a solemn conversation and revelation.

STARKE: OSIANDER: Handicrafts are well-pleasing to God; and godly craftsmen should assist one another in love and harmony, Ps. cxxviii. 1, 2; Rom. xvi. 1, 2.—CRAMER: A work goes on well and speedily when we set about it with united hands and hearts. Concord nourishes men, discord consumes them, Gal. v. 15.—Temptation faileth not to be present in the assemblies of believers, Sir. ii. 1.—It seemeth often unto godly Christians as if their diligence and labor were utterly in vain, and yet such seasons are but meant by God for the trial of their faith, Is. lxv. 23.—OSIANDER: God knoweth the right time.—ZEISIUS: Although Jesus is still so near to His people, His presence is not always recognized by them, nor the secret grace heeded.—God's children are oft-times at a loss for food, but their Heavenly Father remedieth their case and nourisheth them, Matt. vi. 26, 27.—But He whose name is called *Counsellor* (Is. ix. 6), gave them good counsel as to how they should do.—Behold how Jesus can by His blessing in an instant repay His people for the painful toil that they have deemed lost.—ZEISIUS: When we faithfully wait on our calling, the Lord careth for our preservation meanwhile; and when no more means are in our possession, He can quickly provide them.—HEDINGER: How friendly and gracious are the ways of the Lord! even temporal blessings must speak of His love, Ps. xxv. 10.—ZEISIUS: The wonder-doing hand of the Lord knoweth neither measure nor limit, Ps. civ. 28.—*Ibid.*: Unto our bodies, after toil and labor endured, the Lord doth grant needful refreshment; and after the brief toilsomeness of this time, He will in heaven eternally regale our souls.—HEDINGER: Open, dear soul! the Lord would sup with thee, Rev. iii. 20.—ZEISIUS: So many appearances of the risen Jesus; so many seals of our perfect redemption and reconciliation with God, Rom. iv. 24.

GERLACH: The time was still when they, the Holy Ghost not yet being poured out upon them, must become sensible of the impotence of their own strength; Jesus still stood, like One partially unknown to them, beside their own efforts.—BRAUNE: "But how the Redeemer hath hallowed all things into symbols of the universal activity incumbent upon us all in His kingdom! The prince and his vicegerents, the mighty and armed warrior, the calculating merchant, the intelligent husbandman, the careful housefather, the tender mother, the faithful servant, the son, acquainted with his father's will, the hospitable householder, the peaceful gardener,—*everything* is drawn into this holy circle of refreshing pictures" (Schleiermacher).—In every calling Christ and His Spirit may be obtained, just *in* that calling; men need not fly to woods, vales, cloisters. The odor of sanctity can diffuse itself about every man's profession as it did over the occupation of the disciples at the sea of Gennesaret.—At *that* draught [Luke v. 4 ff.] Peter said: "Lord, depart from me, I am a sinful man;" he said this in the weakness of his faith and of his knowledge, and in the confusion of his mind, as though the nearness of the Holy One brought danger to him. This feeling he had surmounted; though conscious still of being a sinful man, he was more strongly convinced that the proximity of Jesus is always and everywhere salutary.—Of what value was the intimation of the calm John: "It is the Lord!" To note and point out the divine in life is a signal service of love.—*Yea, the Lord is my Shepherd, I shall not want* (Ps. xxiii. 1). Come, Lord Jesus, be our Guest; bless what Thou hast bestowed!*

GOSSNER: The right side is that of the elect. When the net is cast on that side, the fish enter into the net of themselves. The blessing that God puts in the mouth of the preacher along with His word, is really the source of all the fruit he produces.—*It is the Lord! said the disciple whom Jesus loved*,—he knew His Master first. A friend knows his friend by his walk, his step; so John knew the Lord by the fortunate draught of fishes. Ah, thought he, the Lord hath played us this loving trick; I know Him, that is His

* A German blessing invoked before meals: "*Komm', Herr Jesu, sei unser Gast, Und segne was Du uns bescheret hast.*"

way.—Peter forgot and deserted the net with the multitude of fishes—for all the trouble he had had with it—so soon as he saw his Lord again and knew Him.—Whoso cleaveth so to the Lord and feeleth himself to be so attracted by Him that he can leave all for the Lord's sake, he it is that loveth Him, ver. 7.—There is the table already spread. This was to paint His tender Providence vividly before their eyes, and to strengthen them in the faith, preparatory to their future calling, so that they might never feel afraid of lacking what was needful.—The net of the Church breaketh not—though never so many great fishes be in it—when it is drawn at the command of Jesus and by apostolic hands. But when men arbitrarily pull at the net, and one pulleth right and another left, it breaketh. And now, alas! what men usually call the net of the Lord is sorely broken. But the Lord hath His net, the which is not broken. The Lord knoweth His own.—Jesus here manifests Himself as the Host, the House-father of His little Church.

HEUBNER: Peter tarrieth not; he showeth his ardent love. Peter's natural disposition now became sanctified by love to Jesus. Thus shall all nature be sanctified through grace.

[CRAVEN: From AUGUSTINE: Ver. 3. The Apostles were not forbidden by their apostleship from earning their livelihood by a lawful craft, provided they had no other means of livelihood.—Ver. 11. In the first draught [Luke v. 6] the net was broken, to signify schisms; but here, to show that in that perfect peace of the blessed there would be no schisms, the Evangelist continues, *And for all they were so great, yet was not the net broken.*——From CHRYSOSTOM: Ver. 7. The recognition of Jesus brings out Peter and John in their different tempers of mind; the one *fervid*, the other *sublime;* the one *ready*, the other *penetrating.*——From GREGORY: Ver. 3. The craft which was exercised without sin before conversion, was no sin after it; wherefore after his conversion Peter returned to fishing; but Matthew sat not down again at the receipt of custom.—*They caught nothing;* the fishing was made to be very unlucky, in order to raise their astonishment at the miracle after.—Ver. 4. The disciples, inasmuch as they were still upon the waves of this mortal life, were laboring on the sea; but the Redeemer, having by His resurrection thrown off the corruption of the flesh, stood upon the shore.——From THEOPHYLACT: Ver. 3. In the night-time, before the presence of the Sun, Christ, the Prophets took nothing; for though they endeavored to correct the people, yet these often fell into idolatry.

[From BURKITT: Ver. 1. Jerusalem now becomes a forsaken place, a people abandoned to destruction: such places wherein Christ is most welcome to preach, shall be most honored with His presence.—Vers. 2, 3. All human labors and endeavors are in vain, unless Christ, by His presence and blessing, crown them with success. —Ver. 4. Christ is not always discerned by us when He is present with us; it is a *double* mercy to enjoy His company, and to know indeed that it is He.—Ver. 6. When Christ is about to do great things for His people, yet will He have them exert all possible endeavors of their own; and the want of former success must not discourage from future endeavors.—Ver. 7. *Cast himself into the sea;* It is not a sea of water, no, nor seas of blood, that can keep a zealous soul at a distance from Christ.—Vers. 12-14. Christ is still bone of our bone, and flesh of our flesh; He has taken possession of heaven in our nature, sitting there in our glorified humanity, clothed with that body which hung in its blood upon the cross.

[From M. HENRY: Vers. 1-14. Christ has many ways of making Himself known to His people; usually in His ordinances, but sometimes by His Spirit; He visits them when they are employed in common business.—Ver. 2. It is good for the disciples of Christ to be *much together;* not only in solemn religious assemblies, but in common conversation, and about common business; thus they both testify and increase their affection to, and delight in each other, and edify one another both by discourse and example. —*Thomas;* It is well, if losses by our neglects make us more careful afterward not to slip opportunities.—Ver. 3. It was commendable in them to *go a-fishing;* for they did it 1. To *redeem time*, and not be idle; 2. That they might help to maintain themselves, and not be burthensome to any.—*They caught nothing*; Even good men may come short of desired success in their honest undertakings: we may be in the way of our duty, and yet not prosper.—Ver. 4. *Jesus stood on the shore;* Christ's time of making Himself known to His people is when they are most *at a loss:* When they think they have *lost themselves*, He will let them know that they have not *lost Him.*—It is a comfort to us, when our passage is rough and stormy, that our Master is at shore, and we are hastening to Him.—*The disciples knew not that it was Jesus;* Christ is often *nearer* us than we *think He is*, and so we shall find afterward, to our comfort.—Ver. 5. Christ takes cognizance of the *temporal* wants of His people, and has promised them not only *grace* sufficient, but *food* convenient.—Christ looks into the cottages of the poor, and asks, *Children, have ye any meat?* —He has herein set us an example of compassionate concern for our brethren; there are many poor householders disabled for labor, or disappointed in it, that are reduced to straits, whom the rich should inquire after thus, *Have ye any meat?* For the most *necessitous* are commonly the least *clamorous.*—Ver. 6. *The right side;* Divine Providence extends itself to things most minute and contingent.—Those that are humble, diligent, and patient, though their labors may be *crossed*, shall be *crowned;* they sometimes live to see their affairs take a happy turn after many struggles and fruitless attempts.—There is nothing lost by observing Christ's orders.—Those are likely to speed well that follow the rule of the Word, the guidance of the Spirit, and the intimations of Providence; for that is *casting the net on the right side of the ship.*—When we are most at a loss, JEHOVAH-JIREH—*the Lord will provide.*—This miracle could not but put Peter in mind of a former one, Luke v. 4, *etc.*; later favors are designed to bring to mind former favors.— An encouragement to Christ's ministers to continue their diligence in their work; one happy draught, at length, may be sufficient to repay many years' toil at the Gospel net.—Ver. 7. They that have *been with Jesus* will be willing to swim through a stormy sea, a sea of blood, to *come to Him.*—Vers. 7-13. God dispenses His gifts variously: some *excel*, as Peter and John; others are but *ordinary* disciples;—yet both the *eminent* and the *obscure* shall *sit down together with Christ in glory;* nay, and perhaps, *the last shall be first;*—of those that do excel, some, like John, are eminently *contemplative;* others, like Peter, eminently *active* and *courageous;* some are useful as the Church's *eyes*, others as the Church's *hands*, and all for the good of the body.—If all the disciples had done as Peter did, what had become of their fish and their nets? And yet if Peter had done as they did, we had wanted this instance of holy zeal. Christ was well pleased with both, and so must we be.—There are several ways of bringing Christ's *disciples to shore* to Him from off *the sea* of this world; some are brought to Him by a violent death, as the martyrs, who *threw themselves into the sea*, in their zeal for Christ; others are brought to Him by a natural death, *dragging the net*, which is less terrible [but also less speedy]; but both meet at length on the safe and quiet shore with Christ.—Ver. 10. Christ would hereby teach us to use what we have; the benefits He bestows upon us are not to be *buried* and *laid up*, but to be *used* and *laid out.*—Ministers, who are *fishers of men*, must bring all they catch to their Master.—Ver. 11. *The net* of the Gospel has enclosed multitudes, *three thousand in one day*, and yet *is not broken;* it is still as mighty as ever to bring souls to God.—Ver. 12. Groundless doubts must be *stifled*, and not *started.*—Ver. 14. It is good to keep account of Christ's gracious visits; for *He keeps account of them*, and *they will be remembered* against us, if *we walk unworthily of them. This is now the third;* have we made a due improvement of *the first and second?* See 2 Cor. xii. 14. *This is the third*, perhaps it may be the *last.*

[From Scott: Vers. 1-14. Christ often permits His (ministerial) servants to labor for a time without visible success, to prove their faith and patience, to render them more observant of His directions, or more simply dependent on His assistance; and that their usefulness, when vouchsafed, may more evidently appear to be His work.——From A Plain Commentary (Oxford): Ver. 2. Never more will it be said that "Thomas, one of the Twelve, called Didymus, was not with them when Jesus came!"—"Wisdom" (that is Christ), is about to "build her House:" wherefore "she hath hewn out her *seven* pillars." Prov. ix. 1; comp. Gal. ii. 9.—Ver. 3. Verily, the discovery that their Lord and their God could suffer the men He loved to remain in such a low state and precarious condition, should teach Christians for evermore to submit cheerfully to poverty, as well as to behold with a feeling akin to reverence, the brother of low degree.—*They caught nothing;* The "ministers and stewards of His mysteries," in particular, are hereby taught that "except the Lord build the House, their labor is but lost that build it."—Ver. 4. *When the morning was now come,—Jesus stood on the shore;* It was a symbol of the Eternal Morning, when Jesus (who is "the hope of them that remain in the broad sea!" Ps. lxv. 5) will at last appear: for the Church as yet waiteth, "until the day break and the shadows flee away." No longer in the ship with His disciples,—He is seen standing on the fixed immovable shore! Thither "they shall go to Him, but thence He shall not return to them."—*Knew not that it was Jesus;* The eyes of all "*were holden* that they should not know Him." So enveloped was His risen Body with something that was Divine, something which He brought from the grave,—that it allowed not of human affection, but Divine Love to discern it. And it was done to accustom them to walk by *faith*, and not by *sight.* For thus it was that our Saviour was recognized by St. John *now.* The *miracle* was to be the evidence that it was He.—Ver. 6. The season for fishing prescribed by Nature, had already expired: it was now the season appointed by Grace. In truth, man's extremity is ever found to be God's opportunity. In the meantime, take notice that the necessity of human exertion is not to be *superseded* by the promise of Divine help. Paul must plant, and Apollos water, though God must give all the increase.—Not only *when* God commands, but *as* God directs, must the net be thrown, if we would secure the prize we long for.—In things to all appearance indifferent, a Divine command overcomes all other considerations, and must be implicitly obeyed, if we would inherit a blessing.—Ver. 7. "It is St. John whose instinct of love penetrates the disguise, and tells Peter that it is the Lord. It might strike the recollection of both, how a few short years before, the same Lord had, in His mortal days, given a similar direction,—a like miraculous draught following: though then, they drew the net; but now they could not: then, the net brake; but now, for all the greater multitude of fishes, when it was drawn to land, the net was unbroken: then, the ship began to sink, and Simon Peter, affrighted, besought the Lord to depart from him, a sinful man; whereas now, as soon as he heard that it was the Lord, and believed it was so, he plunged into the water to go to Him. These circumstances, symbolizing the greater power of the risen Lord, or rather, the greater power He obtained for the fishers of men when the mysteries of His Redemption were accomplished,—were not lost on St. John; who, ever calmer than St. Peter, while his emotions were the deepest, tranquilly remained with the rest in the vessel, till it was brought to shore." (Dr. W. H. Mill).—Ver. 8. *Two hundred cubits;* "So near are we, even in this troublous world, to the land of Everlasting Rest," and to Him who there abideth.—Ver. 12. What did this meal signify but that heavenly banquet, of which it is promised that the redeemed shall partake hereafter, when they shall "*sit down* with Abraham, and Isaac, and Jacob, in the kingdom of heaven?"—Ver. 13. The disciples do not *help themselves* to food. It is still Christ that taketh,—Christ that giveth! All the spiritual refreshment of heaven will still be *His* gift! The very bliss of the Saints will be altogether from *Him!* . . . . And yet, besides the fish miraculously provided for the refreshment of the disciples, we find that they were fed with some of the fish which they had themselves recently caught (ver. 10). O mystery of Divine Love, in reserve for those who have faithfully fed the flock of Christ committed to their care; if, throughout the ages, they shall be conscious of an augmentation of bliss from the souls of those to whom in life it was their privilege to minister!

[From BARNES: Vers. 2, 3. God has made *employment* indispensable to man, and if the field of labor is not open in one way, ministers should seek it in another.——From JACOBUS: Ver. 3. As fishers of men they would toil *all night*, and without Christ they could do nothing.—Ver. 6. Christian ministers, as fishers of men, must follow His positive directions as to *when* and *where* and *how*, without first demanding the *why* and *wherefore*.—Ver. 17. LOVE does always make the sweetest discoveries of Christ; ZEAL plunges even into the sea to reach (through fire and through water) the Master.—Ver. 10. Thus it is that *His grace goes before*, and *our works follow*. Happy day! when Christ's ministers may bring to heaven of the multitudes whom they have caught by His grace.—Ver. 11. So is it with the multitudes which we may catch as fishers of men. The "hundred and forty and four thousand" will all be brought safe to heaven.—From OWEN: Ver. 3. *Immediately;* They were *prompt* and *energetic* men, who would not let the hours of the night—the most advantageous time for fishing—pass away unimproved, when once they had made up their mind to spend it in the manner here spoken of. [They were also *persevering* men. E. R. C.]—Ver. 7. *Girt his fisher's coat unto him;* Note "the *reverence* which observes, even at such a moment of excited feeling, the petty proprieties of clothing." (STIER with DRAESEKE.)—Vers. 9-12. This twofold miracle of the draught of fishes, and the broiled fish and bread made ready for their repast when their labors were ended, symbolize the fidelity, zeal, and reliance upon Christ for success, with which the apostles and all who succeed them in the ministry of the word, were to labor in the work of saving souls, and the watchful providence with which He in whose service they are engaged, will supply all their temporal and spiritual wants.—"A type of that nearness and fellowship, to which the Lord would in future times condescend in His invisible relations with His people." (STIER.)—"The great and glorious ingathering from the sea of nations, which in the latter day shall be made to the Lord Jesus Christ, the end of which will be a *feast* of most gracious fellowship with Him, an antitype of the Lord's Supper, an *early meal* of the great resurrection morning which will be followed by a permanent day of eternal joy." (STIER.)]

II.

THE CONTINUING RULE OF CHRIST IN HIS CHURCH, REPRESENTED BY THE MINISTRY, WALK AND MARTYR-FATE OF PETER, OR THE DESTINY OF THE CHURCH IN RESPECT OF HER PREDOMINANTLY OFFICIAL AND EXTERNAL CHARACTER.

CHAP. XXI. 15–19.

15 So when they had dined [breakfasted, or, taken their morning meal, ἠρίστησαν],
Jesus saith to Simon Peter, Simon, *son* of Jonas [John, Ἰωάννου],[1] lovest [ἀγαπᾷς]
thou me more than these? He saith unto him, Yea, Lord; thou knowest that I
love [dearly love, φιλῶ][2] thee. He saith unto him, Feed [βόσκε] my lambs [τὰ
16 ἀρνία μου]. He saith to him again the [a] second time [δεύτερον], Simon, *son* of
Jonas [John], lovest [ἀγαπᾷς] thou me? He saith unto him, Yea, Lord; thou
knowest that I [dearly] love [φιλῶ] thee. He saith unto him, Feed [keep, tend,
17 ποίμαινε][3] my sheep [τὰ πρόβατά μου].[4] He saith unto him the third time [τὸ τρίτον],
Simon, *son* of Jonas [John], lovest thou me [dearly, φιλεῖς με]? Peter was grieved
because he said unto him the third time, Lovest thou me? [dearly, φιλεῖς με;]
And he said unto him, Lord, thou knowest all things; thou knowest that I love
thee [dearly, φιλῶ σε]. Jesus saith unto him, Feed [βόσκε] my sheep [my little
18 sheep, sheeplings, τὰ προβάτιά μου].[5] Verily, verily, I say unto thee, When
thou wast young, thou girdedst [didst gird] thyself, and walkedst [and didst
walk] whither thou wouldest: but when thou shalt be old, thou shalt stretch forth
thy hands, and another shall gird thee, and carry *thee* whither thou wouldest not.
19 This spake he signifying by what [kind or manner of] death he should [was to]
glorify God. And when he had spoken this [And having spoken this,] he saith
unto him, Follow me.

TEXTUAL AND GRAMMATICAL.

[1] Ver. 15.—On the reading Ἰωάνου instead of Ἰωνᾶ, vers. 15-17, see chap. i. 42. [p. 91, TEXT. NOTE 7. Lachm., Tischend., Treg., Alf., Westc. and H., read Ἰωάννου or Ἰωάνου here and vers. 16, 17, in accordance with א.[a] B. C.[1] D. L. Vulg. (*iohannis*), Jerome, Ambrose, *etc.* Ἰωνᾶ is from Matt. xv. 17. Lange adopts the latter, and translates *Simon Jonas*.—P. S.]

[2] Ver. 15.—[The significant difference between *ἀγαπᾶν* and *φιλεῖν* which runs through this section, cannot well be rendered in English, unless we translate *φιλῶ σε*: *I dearly love Thee.* Lange translates *ἀγαπᾶν lieben, φιλεῖν lieb haben. ἀγαπᾶν, diligere*, is used of the higher, reverential, constant, unwavering love, such as we ought to have to God as well as to man, and such as Christ had to John (ver. 20) and His church; *φιλεῖν, amare*, means personal, emotional love and friendship. The Vulgate renders the former always by *diligere*, the latter by *amare* and *osculari*. In the Hebrew and Syriac there are not the same shades of difference, but the Lord may have expressed it by an additional word or emphasis; at all events we have to account for the difference in the Greek of John. See more in the EXEG. NOTES.—P. S.]

[3] Ver. 16.—[The difference between *βόσκω* (*to feed, to pasture*) and *ποιμαίνω* (from *ποιμήν*; *to pasture, to tend, to provide for, to rule*, a flock or herd), is obliterated in the E. V. *βόσκω* occurs nine times in the N. T., and is always translated *to feed* in the E. V., except Matt. viii. 33 (*kept*). *ποιμαίνω* occurs eleven times and is rendered *to rule*, or *to feed*. *βόσκειν, βοσκή, βόσκημα, victus*, has reference mainly to the *feeding, nourishing* care ("*die ernährende Hütethätigkeit*," Meyer, p. 675), and applies therefore specially to the lambs, while *ποιμαίνειν* is more general, and covers the providing and governing activity ("*die fürsorglich regierende Thätigkeit*," Meyer); comp. Matt. ii. 6; Acts xx. 28; 1 Pet. v. 2; Apoc. ii. 27; vii. 17; xii. 5; xix. 15. See the EXEG. NOTES.—P. S.]

[4] Ver. 16.—[Π ρ ό β α τ α, *oves, sheep*, is sustained in this verse by Codd. ℵ. A. D. X. Γ. Δ. Λ. Π., and adopted by Lachmann, Tregelles, Meyer and Lange. π ρ ο β ά τ ι α, *oviculae, little sheep, sheeplings, Schäflein*, (which is the proper reading in ver. 17, see note 5) has the authority of B. C., and is adopted by Tischendorf, Alford and Westcott; the last, however, gives *πρόβατα* in the margin. The difference between *ἀρνία, πρόβατα, προβάτια* is significant; see the EXEG. NOTES.—P. S.]

[5] Ver. 17.—*Προβάτια*, Tischendorf, in accordance with Codd. A. C. Lachmann reads *πρόβατα*, with ℵ. D. X. text. rec., but Tischendorf, Tregelles, Alford and Westcott adopt *προβάτια* with A. B. C., Syr.; comp. Ambrose (quoted by Tisch.): *pasce agniculos meos, pasce agnos meos, pasce oviculas meas*). If *προβάτια* were better sustained in ver. 16, and *πρόβατα* in ver. 17, there would be a beautiful rising climax: *little lambs, sheeplings, sheep.*—P. S.]

EXEGETICAL AND CRITICAL.

GENERAL REMARKS.

The following transaction manifestly has reference to the three-fold denial of Peter, and takes the form of an apostolico-ethical trial, its object being the re-institution of that disciple.

[It is well to read the questions of our Lord, the answers of Peter, and the commands of Christ in parallel columns:

	Questions.	Answers.
I.	Ἀ γ α π ᾷ ς με π λ ε ῖ ο ν τούτων;	Ναί, Κύριε, σὺ οἶδας ὅτι φ ι λ ῶ σε.
II.	Ἀ γ α π ᾷ ς με;	Ναί, Κύριε, σὺ οἶδας ὅτι φ ι λ ῶ σε.
III.	Φ ι λ ε ῖ ς με;	Κύριε, π ά ν τ α σὺ οἶδας, σὺ γινώσκεις ὅτι φ ι λ ῶ σε.

Commands.

I.	Β ό σ κ ε	τὰ ἀ ρ ν ί α	μου.
II.	Π ο ί μ α ν ε	τὰ π ρ ό β α τ ά	μου.
III.	Β ό σ κ ε	τὰ π ρ ο β ά τ ι ά	μου.—P. S.]

The first consideration of significance is the THREE-FOLD INQUIRY OF JESUS together with THE THREE REPLIES OF PETER,—the counterpart of the three-fold temptation and denial. [This allusion (comp. ch. xiii. 38) is acknowledged by Augustine ("*redditur negationi trinæ trina confessio, ne minus amori lingua serviat quam timori*"), Wetstein ("*ut illi occasionem præberet, triplicis abnegationis maculam triplici professione eluendi*"), Bengel (who, in his brief, pointed way, remarks to τὸ τρίτον, ver. 17: "*numerus decretorius*"), Meyer, Alford, Godet, and others. It is vainly denied by Hengstenberg, who strangely says (iii. 342), that there is, in this whole section, not the least reference to Peter's denial, as this was completely done away with long before! This shows the disqualification of this harsh and angular, though learned and orthodox, divine to appreciate the nice and delicately fibred constitution of this Gospel.—P. S.]

Then the THREE-FOLD ADDRESS, "*Simon, son of Jonas* [*John*, see TEXT. NOTE.—P. S.]. Assuredly this is not simply an expression of solemnity and deeply stirred love (Meyer),—it is intended as a reminder of the natural descent and weakness of Peter which were productive of his fall; this meaning results surely from the antithesis, Matt. xvi. 17, 18: *Simon, son of Jonas* [*John*], and *Peter*, (see *Comm. on Matthew*, chap. x. and chap. xvi.).

Farther the SHADINGS of the thrice-repeated QUESTION:

(1) First, "*lovest thou Me more than these love Me*,"—with reference to the vow of Peter: "*Though all should be offended in Thee*," *etc.*, then the simple: "*Lovest thou Me?*" for the second and the third time.

(2) The change *ἀγαπᾷς με; ἀγαπᾷς με; φιλεῖς με*, *i. e.* "Lovest thou Me (ethically)?" "Art thou attached to Me as a friend (personally)?" The last question a searching entering into the twice-repeated assurance of Peter: *φιλῶ σε*.

Still farther the ANSWERS of Peter. After the first question, he avoids the danger of setting himself above his fellow-disciples, by evading the comparative in Jesus' question; on the other hand he specializes the *ἀγαπᾷς με* by replying: *φιλῶ σε*. It is a modification, in which he expresses himself partly with *more humility*, partly with *more fervor*, as if he meant to say: though I should be wanting in the divine measure of love that belongeth to Thee, I nevertheless am personally attached to Thee from the bottom of my heart. He answers the second question in the same manner. At the third question of Jesus, he is grieved that Jesus asks him for the third time: *φιλεῖς με*; and strengthens his former declarations, "*Lord, Thou knowest it!*" by the word: "*Lord, Thou knowest* ALL THINGS, *Thou knowest that I love Thee.*"

Of a very special significance, however, are the three DELIVERANCES of the Lord in reply to the three answers of Peter: 1. *β ό σ κ ε τ ὰ ἀ ρ ν ί α μ ο υ*, 2. *π ο ί μ α ι ν ε τ ὰ π ρ ό β α τ ά μ ο υ*, 3. *β ό σ κ ε τ ὰ π ρ ο β ά τ ι ά μ ο υ*. The nice, and yet important gradations in the distinction between *ἀρνία, lambs*, and *πρόβατα*, full-grown *sheep*, and *προβάτια* [see the TEXT. NOTES], full-grown sheep which are, nevertheless, to be treated tenderly like lambs; and the distinction between *β ό σ κ ε ι ν*, *to lead to pasture, to provide with food*, and *π ο ι μ α ί ν ε ι ν*, to *guide* and *govern as a shepherd*. The first and most necessary thing (intellectually it is also the easiest, though it presents peculiar difficulties to an imperious, high-soaring mind) is this: to provide for the lambs, *i. e.*, those of tender age in the faith, with spiritual sustenance, to lead them to the spiritual pasture (the office of a catechist). It is more difficult to guard and guide the full-grown sheep,—mature Christians,—to make them seek the right pasture, find the true spiritual food; most difficult of all: to offer to these full-aged members appropriate spiritual food.

The *Romish* Peter has made a κατακυριεύειν* of the βόσκειν and ποιμαίνειν; he has treated the προβάτια as ἀρνία, and has so thoroughly forgotten the instruction to provide spiritual nourishment for the πρόβατα, even as βόσκων, as to have, on the contrary, continually *withdrawn* such nourishment from them more and more, and *forbidden* it under various penalties.

Ver. 15. **Simon, son of John** [Σίμων Ἰωάννου. Lange reads *Jonas;* but see my TEXT. NOTES and *Comm. on Matthew* xvi. 17, p. 295, footnote.—P. S.] The objections of Meyer and even Tholuck: "Yet not as though the apostolic name were refused him (De Wette, Stier)," are without proof. According to them, the thrice-repeated address: "Simon, son of Jonas," [John], is merely expressive of solemnity. Solemnity, however, is always given with the momentous thought. [Godet agrees with Lange, who is right, that the address *Simon, son of John*, is intended to recall his natural character as distinct from that implied in his new and official name *Simon Peter.* So also Alford: "Σίμων Ἰωάννου a reminiscence probably of his own name and parentage, as distinguished from his apostolic name of honor, Cephas, or Peter, see chap. i. 43. Thus we have Σ. Βαριωνᾶ, Matt. xvi. 17, connected with the mention of his natural state of flesh and blood, which had not revealed to him the great truth just confessed—and Luke xxii. 31, 'Simon, Simon,' when he is reminded of his natural weakness. See also Mark xiv. 37, and Matt. xvii. 25, where the significance is not so plain." —P. S.]

Lovest thou Me more than these [ἀγαπᾷς με πλέον τούτων].—Strange interpretation: than these *things*, namely those appertaining to a fisher's life, τούτων construed as neuter, Bolten. The reference of the expression to Peter's setting up of himself above his fellow-Apostles, Matt. xxvi. 33, is groundlessly denied by Meyer. [Bengel: *Antea Petrus se plus his præstiturum dixerat* (Matt. xxvi. 33), *nunc autem simpliciter dicit 'amo te;' non addit, 'plus his.'*" So also Godet.—P. S.]

Thou knowest that I love Thee [Ναί, Κύριε, σὺ οἶδας ὅτι φιλῶ σε].—Φιλῶ σε—threefold expression of humility: 1. No making of comparisons. 2. Appeal to the knowledge of Christ. 3. Choice of the term of personal attachment.

[Observe that the Lord twice asks ἀγαπᾷς με, and once φιλεῖς με, while Peter three times assures the Lord φιλῶ σε. On the difference of the two terms, see the TEXT. NOTES, and Dr. Lange's preceding general remarks, to which I will add those of a few other commentators. Meyer: "Peter in his answer puts in the place of the ἀγαπᾷς (*diligis*) of the question, the expression of the *personal heart-motion* φιλῶ (*amo*, comp. xi. 3, 5; xx. 2), in justice to his inmost feeling." Alford: "The distinction between ἀγαπᾶν and φιλεῖν must not here be lost sight of, nor must we superficially say with Grotius, '*Promiscue hic usurpavit Johannes ἀγαπᾶν et φιλεῖν ut mox βόσκειν et ποιμαίνειν* (see below.). *Neque hic quærendæ sunt sublititates.*" If so, why do the Lord's two first questions contain ἀγαπᾷς, while Peter's answers have φιλῶ—whereas the third time the question and answer both have φιλεῖν? This does not look like accident. The distinction seems to be that ἀγαπᾶν is more used of that reverential love, grounded on high graces of character, which is borne towards God and man by the child of God;—whereas φιλεῖν expresses more the personal love of human affection. Peter therefore uses a less exalted word, and one implying a consciousness of his own weakness, but a persuasion and deep feeling of personal love. (Hence it will be seen that in the sublimest relations, where, all perfections existing, love can *only be personal*, φιλεῖν only can be used, see chap. v. 20). Then in the third question the Lord adopts the word of Peter's answer, the closer to press the meaning of it home to him." Godet: "*Le terme ἀγαπᾶν indique l'amour complet, profond, éternel, le mot φιλεῖν désigne le simple attachement personnel, l'inclination affectueuse. Ce dernier sentiment, il (Pierre) se l'attribue sans hésiter.*" Wordsworth: "Formerly Peter had professed ἀγαπᾶν, but it proved to be only a short-lived φιλεῖν. Now he only professes φιλεῖν, but Christ knows that it will be a long-lived ἀγαπᾶν, an ἀγάπη in old age (ver. 18), an ἀγάπη stronger than death."—P. S.]

Feed My little lambs. [Or *lambkins* (ἀρνίον dimint. of ἀρήν), Βόσκε τὰ ἀρνία μου, *Pasce agnos meos.* Christ speaks thus as the Arch-Shepherd (ἀρχιποιμήν (1 Pet. v. 4). Comp. here ver. 16: Ποίμανε (a more comprehensive term which includes βόσκειν) τὰ πρόβατά μου, *Custodi oves meas, Tend My sheep;* and ver. 17: Βόσκε τὰ προβάτιά μου, *Pasce oviculas meas, Feed My sheeplings.* See TEXT. NOTE. How Peter understood the Lord's trust, he shows himself, 1 Pet. v. 2, 3.—P. S.]—Love to Jesus, therefore, is the condition of the pastoral office to which he is now re-appointed. We may not, with Tholuck, obliterate the distinction of βόσκειν and ποιμαίνειν. Ποιμαίνειν is undoubtedly akin to *regere* (Bellarmine and Corn. a Lapide), but in an evangelical sense.—Τὰ ἀρνία, Rev. v. 6; not synonymous with τὰ πρόβατα, as Tholuck is inclined to suppose. The distinctions of Bellarmine and other Roman Catholic exegetes, according to whom the *lambs* denote the *laity*, the *sheep* the *clergy*, must undoubtedly be rejected; that distinctions do exist, however, is proved even by Is. xl. 11, and the distinction between immature and mature believers is obvious (Euthym. Zig., Wetstein and others); it suffers no diminution by the reading τὰ προβάτια in the third injunction, but only still further modification. Luthardt's interpretation: The tending of individuals, care of the whole flock, training up of individuals for the whole flock, is etymologically unfounded.

[Alford likewise insists on the nice shadings of meaning in the terms here used (on which see TEXT. NOTE): "We can hardly with any deep insight into the text hold βόσκειν and ποιμαίνειν to be synonymous (Grot. above, Lücke, De Wette, Trench), or ἀρνία, πρόβατα, and προβάτια. The sayings of the Lord have not surely been so carelessly reported as this would assume.

* [In the face of the expression of Peter to presbyters and bishops, not *to lord it over* God's heritage, but to feed the flock and to be ensamples to it (1 Pet. v. 2, 3).—P. S.]

Every thing here speaks for a *gradation* of meaning. The variety of reading certainly makes it difficult to point out exactly the steps of that gradation, and unnecessary to follow the various interpreters in their assignment of them: but that there *is such*, may be seen from Isa. xl. 11: 1 John ii. 12, 13. Perhaps the *feeding of the lambs* was the furnishing the apostolic testimony of the resurrection and facts of the Lord's life on earth to the first converts; The *shepherding* or ruling *the sheep*, the subsequent government of the Church as shown forth in the early part of the Acts; The *feeding of the προβάτια*, the choicest, the loved of the flock, the furnishing the now maturer Church of Christ with the wholesome food of the doctrine contained in his Epistles. But those must strangely miss the whole sense, who dream of an exclusive primatial power here granted or confirmed to him. A sufficient refutation of this silly idea, if it needed any other than the ἐλυπήθη of this passage, is found in the συμπρεσβύτεροι of 1 Pet. v. 1, where he refers apparently to this very charge: see note on Matt. xvi. 17 ff." Wordsworth: "The command βόσκε, *pasce*, is repeated: it stands first and last (vers. 15, 17) with ποίμαινε between, ver. 16. To provide wholesome food for Christ's sheep and lambs is the first and last thing: the love of the shepherd who tends, and leads, and guards, and lays down his life for the flock, is the central spring of all, which shows itself in outward acts." Godet rightly refers βόσκειν to the feeding of the flock, ποιμαίνειν to the general direction. The diminutives ἀρνία, *lambkins*, and προβάτια, *sheeplings*, are expressive of the tender affection of the Arch-Shepherd for His flock; comp. the term τεκνία, chap. xiii. 33. See also Bengel on vers. 15 and 16, who refers ἀρνία, προβάτια and πρόβατα to the different stages in Peter's public life, and in the history of the Church.—P. S.]

Ver. 17. **Lovest thou Me (dearly)?**—Φιλεῖς με; The change of expression in the third question, Tholuck [like Grotius] groundlessly makes a matter of indifference, considering the variation of ἀγαπᾶν and φιλεῖν as unintentional. [See the remarks above.—P. S.]

Lord, Thou knowest all things [Κύριε, πάντα σὺ οἶδας, σὺ γινώσκεις ὅτι φιλῶ σε].—Comp. chap. xvi. 30; Acts i. 24.

Ver. 18. **Verily, verily I say unto thee.**—Upon the solemn re-institution of Peter, follows the revelation of Jesus concerning the manner of his life, and his exode. The words of Jesus give the prophecy of Peter's future in a simple life-picture of the contrast between youth and old age. Peter is a vigorous man, in the middle years of life, occupying, therefore, a position betwixt youth and old age. The prophecy attaches itself to this fact, just as the contrast of youth and old age is frequently made a symbol in the Old Testament also (Is. xl. 30, 31; Ez. xvi.; Hos. xi. 1). The Lord employs the homeliest figure for the most mysterious disclosure. Yet allegorical traits mingle in the figure itself. That the young man girds himself, is agreeable to nature; it is likewise in accordance with nature that "a perfectly decrepid old man"* stretches out his hands for help and lets himself be girded and led by another. But the traits: Thou didst walk, as a young man, whither thou wouldest, as an old man thou shalt be led whither thou wouldest not, in themselves point to the prophetic meaning.

John gives the interpretation of the saying in ver. 19; he refers it to the martyrdom of Peter. This is the centre of the dark, significant saying; a meaning, however, that was not fully disclosed until Peter's martyrdom took place. It was, however, intended that this saying should primarily furnish Peter himself with a leading thought, and this thought is undoubtedly a word concerning the development and future of Peter's spiritual man—presented under the figure of the natural life—connected with the intimation of a fate big with suffering. Tholuck justly remarks that if the simile be intended to refer solely to the martyrdom of Peter, the protasis, the clause treating of his youth, seems really idle; and also incongruous, inasmuch as it indicates a whole period of his life, while the apodosis touches upon a moment only. But if, finally, in accordance with our conception, the Epilogue present a more general life-picture of the Church of Christ in the contrast of the Petrine and the Johannean type, then the saying will have a further application to the Petrine form of the Church.

When thou wast younger [ὅτε ἦς νεώτερος].—Meyer adds: "than now." The words however simply denote, doubtless, the younger man, characterizing him with the collateral idea of one youthfully strong, enterprising, self-willed. According to Meyer, the middle state of Peter is left uncharacterized. Its character, however, is that of transition, of gradual transformation from youth to old age. If, indeed, we here find only the martyrdom predicted, neither does the figure of the younger man constitute a trait of character. It undoubtedly denotes, however, the youthful conduct of Peter in his discipleship; not his state before he came to Christ (Gerh., Luthardt); nor does it include his present time of life. He girded himself in the acts of self-will of which the evangelical history testifies; he finally in self-will trod the way of denial.

But when thou hast grown old [ὅταν δὲ γηράσῃς], literally, *gray*.—Indicative at once of the last stage of Christian development (I John ii. 13) and of Peter's life's evening (2 Pet. i. 14).

Thou wilt stretch forth thy hands [ἐκτενεῖς τὰς χεῖράς σου].—An old man stretches out his hands for help foreign to himself. Accordingly, the outstretching of the hands is forthwith a symbol of submission to the power of another. The Christian grown gray in the faith resigns himself utterly to the leading of the Lord. (Acts xx. 22.—"When I am weak, then am I strong"). The aged Apostle carried out this submission by a submission to the power of Roman authority, in which God ruled over him. The term ἐκτενεῖς τὰς χεῖράς σου has, by the Church Fathers and some moderns, been referred to the extending of the hands on the

* (Meyer makes a note of interrogation at this expression, as if those who were not perfectly decrepid did also suffer themselves to be dressed and girded by others.)

cross (Maier, De Wette, Hilgenfeld, and others); similarly, the girding has been considered to mean the binding upon the cross (Tertullian*), or the girding of a cloth about the loins. This view is contradicted by the fact that the leading away does not occur until after the stretching forth of the hands. The effort has been made to meet this objection by the remark (Casaub., Wetst. and others) that cross-bearers, on being led forth, had their hands bound to the two sides of the cross. But this usage was not customary in the provinces. We need but hold fast this truth, namely, that the stretching forth of the hands, as a symbol of submission to another's power, is once more significantly and plastically reflected in the outstretching of the hands of a crucified martyr. The whole occurrence is, in reality, a single life-picture.

And another [καὶ ἄλλος].—The *other* unqualified: it is the figure of the objective might of Divine Providence, ruling through human instruments (John xix. 11).—**Will gird thee** [ζώσει σε].—Make thee ready for thy last journey;—in accordance with the figure of binding: he will fetter thee (the symbolical act Acts xxi. 11 means also, it is probable: the girdle, as the symbol of free will, shall be changed into a fetter, as a symbol of the unfree will of a prisoner).—**And will lead thee** [καὶ οἴσει].—That objective, earnest guidance which puts an end to self-will; more closely defined, apparently the leading away to martyrdom. Is a leading to the death of the cross distinctly intended? (Calvin, Beza, and others). Meyer finds only a *violent* death symbolized. However, it was the word of the Master, whose violent death had just consisted in crucifixion, and who had now purposely selected the figure of the outstretching of the hands, in order to express submission to the extremest fate. And death upon the cross was just this ("Even the ἐξεπέτασα τὰς χεῖράς μου, Is. lxv. 2, is referred by Barnabas, Ep. chap. xii.; Justin, *Dial. c. Tr.* C. 97, to the crucifixion of Christ." Tholuck). **Whither thou wouldest not** [ὅπου οὐ θέλεις], *i. e.* not as regards thy inner life and new man, which latter has just been active in the stretching forth of the hands, but as regards the old, expiring self-will of the natural life; comp. the legend of Peter's flight from prison at Rome. Calvin: *Nunquam enim tam soluto affectu obsequimur deo, quin caro velut funiculis quibusdam in contrarium nos retrahat.* Augustine: *Hunc invenit exitum ille negator et amator; præsumendo elatus, negando prostratus, flendo purgatus, confitendo probatus, patiendo coronatus.*—(The interpretation of the entire passage by Gurlitt and Paulus as a prophecy of actual senile weakness hardly needs mention).

Ver. 19. **Signifying by what manner of death** [σημαίνων ποίῳ θανάτῳ].—A Johannean expression, comp. chap. xii. 33; xviii. 32. By *what* (a) death,—bringing to view not only the kind of death, as martyrdom, namely, but also the distinguished species of *that* death. According to Tertullian (*Scorp.* 15, *De Præscr.* 35, and Euseb. *H. E.* III. 1), Peter was crucified. When John wrote, the crucifixion of Peter (67, or 68 A. D.) must already have been an event in ecclesiastical history well known in the Christian churches. Had Peter still been living, John would not thus have publicly interpreted the dark saying of Christ, even though he were himself perfectly cognizant of its meaning.—**He was to glorify God** [δοξάσει τὸν θεόν].—Martyrdom has a reflex lustre from the crucial death of Christ; it redounds in a peculiar degree to the glory of God. Hence the expression: δοξάζειν τὸν θεόν was later a customary term for martyrdom (Suicer, *Thes.* i. p. 949). [To suffer for Christ is to glorify God; but there is a martyrdom of life as well as of death; by the former John, by the latter Peter and Paul glorified God.—P. S.].

Follow me. [Ἀκολούθει μοι. This, in a wider sense, is the sum and substance, the beginning and end of Christian life, as an imitation of the life of Christ in its sinless perfection, its divine-human character, its prophetic, priestly, and kingly office, and in its states of humiliation and exaltation from the cross to the crown. —P. S.] Comp. chap. xiii. 36. Different interpretations:

1. Follow me in doctrine and till death (Cyril, Theophylact);
2. In the death of the cross (Euthym.);
3. In a martyr's death (Meyer);
4. As ecumenical bishop or teacher (Chrysostom);
5. Reference at once to the guidance of the Church and to martyrdom (Ewald);
6. The words are to be taken literally: the Redeemer leads the disciple aside in order to a confidential communication (Kuinoel, Paulus, Thol., and others). Meyer in objection to this view: The words would thereby be stripped of all significance.

The first question to be asked is, what they mean when considered in connection with the context; this done, the immediately subsequent: **Peter turned himself about and saw,** *etc.* **following** [ἐπιστραφεὶς ὁ Πέτρος βλέπει τὸν μαθητὴν ὃν ἠγάπα ὁ Ἰησοῦς ἀκολουθοῦντα, ver. 20] is decisive in favor of the primarily literal sense. It is to be considered, moreover, that Peter could not understand this saying of Jesus as distinctly referring to martyrdom, if he did not understand the previous saying as referring to the same. We suppose, however, the significance of this literal sense to have lain in the fact that Jesus retired to the background of the scene, as if for departure to the invisible world, and hence that the summons to Peter was a trial. The literal expression, therefore, has likewise a symbolical background. He must prepare himself for the possibility of the immediate decision of his fate; *i. e.* stand a test of absolute submission. (*Leben Jesu*, ii. pp. 17, 19. Luthardt). This assumption does not exclude the design of a further communication. On the contrary, such a communication was probably intended, since the imminent walk could not be a merely symbolical one. Had the communication, however, as strictly confidential, been designed to exclude John, that disciple would doubtless not have followed too.

* [*Scorp.* 15: "*Tunc Petrus ab altero vincitur, cum cruci adstringitur.*" Comp. the traditionary account of Peter's Martyrdom in Euseb. II. 25; III. 1, and the notes of Heinichen.—P. S.]

DOCTRINAL AND ETHICAL.

1. *The re-instatement of Peter in his ministry*, a life-picture of the appointment of the ecclesiastical ministry in general, as the first ground-form through which Christ wills to be present in His Church in the world, and by means of which He chooses to rule in the Church.

a. Every calling and institution [ordination] is in reality a *re-reception* and *re-instatement*, no man having kept his gift of grace pure, and himself clean from denial.

b. Every calling pre-supposes a *previous* discipleship, experience of Christ, leading, humiliation, and refreshment.

c. Every calling takes place in an assembled apostolic congregation of believers.

d. No calling ensues without previous trial (*Examen rigorosum.*)

e. The main question is always the question of Christ: "*Lovest thou Me?*" with a forbearing recollection of the old nature ("Simon, son of Jonas"), its errors and dangers. Love to Christ is the decisive fundamental condition of the pastoral office.

f. To the *ethical* love for Christ, resting upon *piety* (ἀγαπᾶν), there must be added a *personal* love for Him, resting upon historically grounded *knowledge* (φιλεῖν).

g. The trial must lead the examinate to earnest self-examination, resulting in his confusion and sorrow; it must make him certain of his love for Christ and of his vocation, occasioning prayerful appeal on his part to Christ's privity to the condition of his soul.

h. It must be proved from the first that, with all his certainty of his vocation, he renounces all self-upliftment above those who are called along with him (he consequently renounces pride, envy, rivalry, false human emulation). The examiner, however, must know that he is to act by order of, and in the spirit of, the Lord.

Finally, institution [the act of installation or investment] has, above all things, to give prominence to the feeding of the lambs, the catechising of those of tender age, the preliminary condition of which is the missionary *halieutics* [*aptness to fish* for men]. Only on this basis does it become an introduction into the real pastorate or presbyterial episcopate, or into the office of guiding the sheep, *i. e.* the adult Church. Neither can it stop at this, however; it finally becomes an installation in the evangelical Doctorate, the providing of the sheep, as adult sheeplings that need the spiritual nourishment of advanced knowledge, with strong meat, 1 Cor. iii. 2; Heb. v. 12, 13. See Ex. NOTE 1.

2. An ecclesiastical ministry that exalts itself above other ministries ("more than these"); that fails to hold fast the love of Christ as its fundamental condition, that pretends to regard Christ's sheep (*My* lambs, *My* sheep, *My* sheeplings) as *its own*, that chooses to know of *immature lambs* only, not of *mature sheep*, and that desires but to *lead* (ποιμαίνειν) the whole flock, or rather to exercise lordship over it from on high (κατακυριεύειν), not to *feed* it (βόσκειν) in the green meadows of evangelical knowledge, does by these characteristics prove itself a sombre antitype or caricature of the Petrine ecclesiastical ministry.

3. The *gradation of evangelical functions* indicated by Christ, is not to be a gradation of *hierarchical dignities;* this is proved by the fact that Peter is forced to evade, as a temptation, the question: 'Lovest thou Me more than these?' But if anything ought to establish a hierarchical gradation, it would be the declaration, 'I love Thee better than others;' but not: 'Thou hast granted me prerogatives above others,' or, 'The heathen world-city of Rome will give me these prerogatives,' or, The reminiscence, called up by the ἀρνία, of the old prerogatives of the levitic high-priests or the Roman pontifices. But who would dare declare unto the Lord: 'I love Thee better than all others?' Moreover, the institution of Peter is a re-instatement, of which, in this solemn form, only he, as the fallen one, had need, in order to a full restitution to the apostolic circle which, in general, had received the new sanction of the old calling on the very first Easter-evening (chap. xx. 21).

Hence this formal explication of the Petrine ministry is likewise an explication of the ministry received by all the Apostles. It applies to all the officially called servants of Christ to the end of time.

4. The announcement of *Peter's destiny*, which succeeded the sanction of his calling, was primarily a prophetic revelation, to the effect that he was called to follow Christ in His sufferings, and that he should be trained up by the guidance of God. It further proved to be a more decided announcement of his martyrdom. In accordance with the symbolical character of this Chapter, however, it is at the same time a life-picture of the leading which the Lord bestows upon every individual servant in his vocation; finally, in its most universal application it is also, we doubt not, a prophecy that the official Church will incur judgment previous to the coming of the Lord. See Matt. xxiv. 48; 2 Thess. ii. 4; Rev. xii. 1; Comp. Chap. xvii.; Chap. xix. 7; Chap. xiii. 1. Comp. ver. 11.

5. *Follow Me.* One of the most mysterious moments in the whole resurrection-history. In a symbolical act, Peter must follow the Lord into the background of the scene, as if he were now to be translated with Him from the visible earth across the boundaries of the spirit-realm. Thus is the unconditional following, the readiness for death, of the servant of Christ, presented in a symbolical act. The type of martyrdom in the Church. See EXEG. NOTE *in loc.*

HOMILETICAL AND PRACTICAL.

See the DOCT. NOTES. The ecclesiastical ministry after Christ's heart.—Apostolic ordination after Christ's example.—How the Lord hath made Simon (son of) Jonas to be Simon Peter again.—The ministerial vocation in the Church conditioned by a holy examination: 1. By three questions in one. Infinite importance (always: *Lovest thou Me?*); 2. by one question in three. Perfect distinctness.—Love for Christ the decisive characteristic of His called servant: 1. As the condition of the recognition that His (His sheep) are His; 2. as the condition of true discrimination between lambs and sheep, as likewise of the sheep as sheep and as sheeplings (as adults and yet as having to be led further. Rightly dividing the word; ὀρθοτομεῖν 2 Tim. ii. 15); 3. as the condition of true pastoral fidelity (in which a single ποιμαίνειν is accompanied by a twice-repeated βόσκειν).—The right examination of the official spirit must be to it an occasion of self-examination (and so of confusion, prayer, certitude of self).—Peter's humility, the first token of his ripeness for the ministry,—his love for Jesus, the second,—his knowledge of Christ as the Trier of the heart, the third,—but, however, his love for Jesus, the one and all (as the root of his humility and of his knowledge). —Why no question is made of faith in this transaction. Because it must be present in a developed form: 1. In the form of humility, 2. of love, 3. of knowledge.—*Verily, verily:* On the ministry in respect of its youthful, and in respect of its matured, character (girding one's self, choosing one's own ways, making great pretensions; denying one's self, suffering one's self to be led, submitting to the guidance of the Lord). —Christ the Master of His servants: 1. In the establishment of their vocation; 2. in the foresight of their fate.—How the right conduct of the ministry should approve itself a government in which Christ wills to be present with the Church: 1. Christ in His works; 2. Christ in His suffering. —How the whole business of a servant of Christ is comprehended in the business of *following* Christ.—How Christ will be present with the Church and the world in the *following* of His people [in His people's imitation of Him].

STARKE: HEDINGER: But what shall a shepherd of the sheep do without love? such [as are without love] are thieves and murderers, who, like the wolves, spare not the flocks.—OSIANDER: The apostolic office consisteth not in worldly *dominion*, but in the *feeding* of the *sheep* and *lambs*, which thing, Peter, as well as the other apostles, was obliged to do, so that he consequently was devoid of superiority to them, 1 Pet. v. 2, 3.—ZEISIUS: Christ having first recommended the lambs to Peter's feeding, it results that Christian teachers should consider youth and simplicity as specially recommended to their care.—O how Jesus loves the souls of men, inasmuch as He will commit them to the feeding of none but those who first sincerely love Him.—Preachers should distinguish between lambs and sheep, *i. e.* children, youths and old persons, communicating to each his food: to the lambs, milk, to the adult in Christianity, strong meat, Heb. v. 12 ff.—He that hath sinned much, ought often to examine his heart, as to whether it sincerely loves its God, or whether its repentance is nought but hypocrisy.—ZEISIUS: Jesus is the Searcher of the hearts and reins—comfort thyself therewith in every cross, temptation, and persecution: but beware lest thou follow sin in thy thoughts, words and works, for there is nothing hid before Him, nor doth ought remain unpunished, Rev. ii. 23.—LANGE: The Lord Jesus, by connecting the question concerning love toward Him with the announcement of Peter's imminent sufferings, indicates that by the willing assumption of sufferings inflicted for His name's sake, the sincerity and faithfulness of love, and, consequently, also the steadfastness of faith, are to be proved.—ZEISIUS: To die for Christ's sake, disgraceful as it may appear in the eyes of the world, is equally honorable and precious in the sight of God and all the faithful, for thereby is God praised, Ps. cxvi. 15.—And sure, how can there be a death more glorious than one that is suffered for God's and Christ's sake, the King of all kings!—The cross which believers bear for love of their Saviour, hath a right fair name,—it is called the laud and praise of God, Phil. i. 20.

GERLACH: It was easier for a man like Peter to act, dare, sacrifice, than to wait, suffer, passively stand still. Jesus therefore promises him a high place in His Church, in doing and suffering; but in a doing in which he had shown himself so unskilful by his denial, and in a suffering which was in the extreme repugnant to his nature.—LISCO: In *youth*, in the fulness of intellectual power, zealous (but also in many respects self-willed) activity for the Lord is shown; in *old age*, however, manifold hindrances (but also purifications) are at work, and the highest pitch of self-denial is death for Christ.

BRAUNE: Living love to Christ impels to the most earnest participation in His work, and all the knowledge of the human heart, without love to Christ, leads to craftiness and makes a man a rogue. The Apostles are qualified only by their love for the Saviour.—*Feed My lambs—feed My sheep*, tender youth and vigorous age.—This, too, the Lord says three times with emphasis. Love makes the shepherd; Peter was to be a shepherd, like his Lord; the Lord elevates him to that office by this examination and humiliation. —When he was an old man, he wrote to the elders of his church (1 Pet. v. 2, 3): Feed the flock of Christ, *etc.*—Peter bears this intimation in mind in his second epistle (chap. i. 14).—This kept Peter's enthusiasm for the Risen One young till he himself was old, for he exclaims, 1 Pet. i. 3, 4: Blessed be God and the Father of our Lord Jesus Christ, *etc.*—He knew that he should follow the Lord through shame to glory; to him the cross became a token of honor.—Vigorous souls are not terrified by a future full of dangers, beyond the stormy night, they see the glorious morning of eternity.—His life accords with his word, 1 Pet. iv. 12, 19.

GOSSNER: This question is easily answered with "yes;" but if we think again, many a consideration will present itself.—Just so much as we lack in simple love, we fail of in daily bliss.—If thou wouldst be a true pastor and shepherd, love for Me must bring the thing about—else is it impossible. For a large measure of love is needed to serve the bodies and souls of men, and often to incur, in so doing, much danger, and to experience the grossest ingratitude.—Hence it is the extreme of temerity to take upon one's self, or to seek, the office and ministry of a shepherd in the Church of Christ, without feeling love toward Jesus and solicitude for His flock.—When a man is still young, God hath no very high opinion of his abilities; but when one hath been longer acquainted with Him, He maketh one a larger sharer in His sufferings.—What a doctrine! What a religion! The Lord prophesieth to His disciples torture and death, and inviteth them to follow Him, and they do follow Him! They prefer to lay down their lives rather than leave Him.

Heubner: The practice of Christ was entirely different from the subsequently invented church-penance, according to the canons of which, as Zinzendorf says, Peter would have been forced to kneel outside of the church-door for at least fifteen years.—The main thing is *personal* love, true, real love for the Person of Jesus. It is this very thing that many are horrified at; they cannot relish it at all; they scent directly I know not what manner of pietistic and mystical rubbish, and seek to dilute it and beat it down and circum-interpret it into a mere cold esteem, or keeping of His commandments.—The schoolmen apprehended the thrice-repeated feeding as feeding by doctrine, by example, by hospitality. The generality of men are concerned only about the unimportant *worldly* examination, but the passing of a *heart*-examination before Jesus does not enter into their heads.—How utterly distinct a character a man bears so long as he is bent upon being his own master; he follows his own self-will, the natural will; how different the man when his will has been taken away by grace and he belongs to God. Then the self-will of the flesh is entirely captive to the will of the Spirit.

[Craven: From Augustine: Ver. 15. Our Lord asked this, knowing it: He knew that Peter not only loved Him, but loved Him more than all the rest [?]. While our Lord was being condemned to death, Peter feared, and denied Him. But by His resurrection Christ implanted love in his heart, and drove away fear. Peter denied, because he feared to die: but when our Lord was risen from the dead, and by His death destroyed death, what should he fear?—*Feed My lambs;* As if there were no way of Peter's showing his love for Him, but by being a faithful shepherd, under the Chief Shepherd.—Ver. 17. *Jesus saith unto him, Feed My sheep;* As if to say, Be it the office of love to feed the Lord's flock, as it was the resolution of fear to deny the Shepherd.—They who feed Christ's sheep as if they were their own, not Christ's, show plainly that they love themselves, not Christ; that they are moved by lust of glory, power, gain, not by the love of obeying, ministering, pleasing God. Let us love therefore, not ourselves, but Him, and in feeding His sheep, seek not our own, but the things that are His.—If we call our sheep *ours*, as they [sectarists] call them *theirs*, Christ hath lost His sheep.—Vers. 18, 19. Whatever be the pain of death, it ought to be conquered by the strength of love for Him, who being our Life, voluntarily also underwent death for us.—If there is no pain in death, or very little, the glory of martyrdom would not be great.—He who denied and loved, died in perfect love for Him, for whom he had promised to die with wrong haste.—It was necessary that Christ should first die for Peter's salvation, and then Peter die for Christ's Gospel.

[From Chrysostom: Vers. 15-17. If thou lovest Me, have rule over thy brethren [?], show forth that love which thou hast evidenced throughout, and that life which thou saidst thou wouldst lay down for Me, lay down for the sheep.—Ver. 18. Christ reminds Peter of his former life, because whereas in worldly matters a young man has powers, an old man none; in spiritual things, on the contrary, virtue is brighter, manliness stronger, in old age; age is no hindrance to grace.—He says, *Whither thou wouldest not,* with reference to the natural reluctance of the soul to be separated from the body; an instinct implanted by God to prevent men putting an end to themselves.——From Alcuin: Vers. 15-17. To feed the sheep is to support the believers in Christ from falling from the faith, to provide earthly sustenance for those under us, to preach and exemplify withal our preaching by our lives, to resist adversaries, to correct wanderers.

[From Burkitt: Vers. 15-17. Christ puts Peter upon a threefold profession of his love unto Him, answerable to his threefold denial of Him. True repentance ought to be, and will be, as eminent in the fruit and effects of it, as the saint's fall hath been.—Ministers who are called to take charge of Christ's flock, have need of much love to Jesus Christ.—The best evidence of a minister's love to Jesus Christ, is his conscientious care to *feed, i. e.,* teach, instruct and govern the whole flock of Christ; lambs and sheep, weak and strong; the feeblest in the fold were purchased by the great Shepherd.—Such as would be faithful in their ministerial charge, ought to look upon their people as committed to them by Christ Himself, as loved of Him, and committed to their care by Him.—Ver. 15. Note the great modesty of Peter in his reply: once he vaunted, *Though all men forsake Thee, yet will not I;* but now his fall had taught him humility.—It is a blessed thing, when we can and dare appeal to God's knowledge.—Ver. 18. The ministers of Jesus Christ, when they undertake the charge of His flock, must prepare for *suffering* work.—*Whither thou wouldest not;* Human nature in Christ's ministers, as well as in other men, reluctates sufferings, has an antipathy against a violent death.—*When thou shalt be old;* The timing of the saints' sufferings is in Christ's hands.—Ver. 19. The sufferings of the saints in general, and of the ministers of Christ in particular, do redound much to the glory of God.

[From M. Henry: Vers. 15-17. Herein Christ has given us an encouraging instance of His tenderness towards penitents, and has taught us, in like manner, to *restore such as are fallen with a spirit of meekness.*—We must not reckon it an affront to have our sincerity questioned, when we ourselves have done that which makes it questionable.—Peter was now upon his probation as a penitent; but the question is not, "*Simon,* how much hast *thou wept?* How often hast *thou fasted and afflicted thy soul?*" but, "*Dost thou love Me?*" *Much is forgiven her,* not because *she wept much,* but because *she loved much.*—Nothing but *the love of Christ* will constrain ministers to go cheerfully through the difficulties and discouragements they meet with in their work, 2 Cor. v. 13, 14.—Ver. 15. "*Lovest thou Me more than thou lovest these,* more than *thou lovest these persons?*" Those do not love Christ aright, that do not love Him better than the best friend they have in the world. Or, "*more than thou lovest these things,* these boats and nets;" those only *love* Christ indeed, that *love* Him better than all the delights of sense and all the profits of this world.—"*Lovest thou Me more than thou lovest these* occupations thou art now employed in? If so, leave them, to employ thyself wholly in feeding My flock." (WHITBY).—"*Lovest thou Me more than these. love Me, more than* any of the rest of *the disciples love Me?*" We should all study to excel in our love to Christ; it is no breach of the peace to strive which shall *love* Christ best; nor any breach of good manners, to go before others in this *love.*—Peter does not pretend to *love Christ more than* the rest of *the disciples* did. —Though we must aim to be better than others, yet we must, *in lowliness of mind, esteem others better than ourselves;* for we know more evil of ourselves than we do of any of our brethren.—Those who can truly say, through grace, that *they love Jesus Christ,* may take the comfort of their interest in Him, notwithstanding their daily infirmities. —Ver. 17. It is a terror to a hypocrite, to think that Christ *knows all things;* but it is a comfort to a sincere Christian, that he has that to appeal to; *My witness is in heaven, my record is on high.* Christ knows us better than we know ourselves, though we know not our own uprightness, He does.—*Peter was grieved,* when Christ asked Him *the third time, Lovest thou Me?* Because it put him 1. In mind of his threefold denial of Christ; 2. In fear, lest his Master foresaw some further miscarriage of his.—Vers. 15-17. The Church of Christ is *His flock:* in this *flock* some are *lambs,* young and tender and weak, others are *sheep,* grown to some strength and maturity; the shepherd here takes care of both, and of the *lambs* first.—It is the duty of all Christ's ministers, *to feed His lambs and sheep* 1. *Teach* them; for the doctrine of the Gospel is spiritual food; 2. *Lead* them *to the green pastures,* presiding in their religious assemblies, and ministering all the ordinances to them; 3. By personal application to their respective state and case; not only *lay meat before them,* but *feed them* with it, that are wilful and will not, or weak and cannot, *feed themselves.* —*When Christ ascended on high, He gave pastors;* left His flock with them that loved Him, and would take care of them for His sake.—*Simon Peter;* a commission given to one convicted of a crime is supposed to amount to a pardon.—Ver. 18. When trouble comes, we are apt to aggravate it with this, that it has been otherwise; and to fret the more at the grievances of restraint, sickness and poverty, because we have known the sweets of liberty, health, and plenty. But we may turn it the other way, and reason thus with ourselves: "How many years of prosperity have I enjoyed more than I deserved and improved!" —Ver. 19. There is *one* way *into* the world, but *many* ways *out,* and God has determined which way we shall go.—It is the great concern of every good man, whatever death he dies, to *glorify God* in it.—When we die *patiently,* submitting to *the will of God; cheerfully,* rejoicing in hope of the glory of God; and *usefully,* witnessing to the truth and goodness of religion, and encouraging others, we *glorify God* in dying.—*Follow Me;* Expect to be treated as I have been, and to tread the same bloody path that I have trod before thee; *for the disciple is not greater than his Lord.*—They that faithfully *follow Christ in grace* shall certainly *follow Him to glory.*

[From SCOTT: Vers. 15-17. Our Lord will readily pardon the sins of His believing servants: but He will rebuke them, in one way or other; that they may be more sensible how greatly He abhors their offences, notwithstanding His mercy to their souls.—Those who "love the Lord Jesus in sincerity," have a consciousness of it, notwithstanding all their defects.—Those who have been greatly tempted, and have had humiliating experience of their frailty and sinfulness, and who have had much forgiven them, generally prove the most tender and attentive pastors, and the best guides of young converts.—The Lord often leaves those whom He loves to pass through painful conflicts, as well as much experience of His compassion, in order to render them more gentle to their weak brethren, and the lambs of His flock.

[From A PLAIN COMMENTARY (Oxford): Ver. 15. Ἀγαπᾷς με; *Lovest thou Me?* "At this moment, when all the pulses in the heart of the now penitent Apostle are beating with an earnest affection toward his Lord, this word on that Lord's lips sounds too cold. Besides the question itself, which grieves and hurts Peter, there is an additional pang in the form which the question takes, sounding as though it were intended to put him at a comparative distance from his Lord, and to keep him there; or at least, as not permitting him to approach so near to Him as he fain would. He therefore in His answer substitutes for it the word of a more personal love,—'Thou knowest that I love Thee dearly.' When Christ repeats the question in the same words as at the first, Peter in his reply again substitutes his 'I love Thee dearly' for the 'lovest thou' of his Lord. And now at length he has conquered: for when his Master puts the question to him for the third time, He does it with the word which Peter feels will alone express all that is in his heart; and instead of the twice repeated 'Lovest thou Me?' His word is, 'Dost thou *love Me dearly?*' The question, grievous in itself to Peter, as seeming to imply a doubt in his love, is not any longer made more grievous still, by the peculiar shape which it assumes." (TRENCH.)—*Feed My lambs;* The lambs are to be *fed.* Their daily portion of *food* (all that is needed for the soul's health and strength, all that is included in that petition "Give us this day *our daily bread,*" is here especially spoken of.—Those "lambs," saith "the great Shepherd of the sheep," are "Mine." O salutary thought for the pastor of souls, that the "sheep" and the "lambs" are not *his* but *Christ's!* Not *his;* —therefore, like Jacob with the flock of Laban, he should be prepared to give account for all. Not *his;*—therefore must there be One above him, to whom they are a care as well as to himself; even "the Chief Shepherd," who careth alike for *him* and for *them.*—"Woe be to the shepherds of Israel that do feed themselves! Should not the shepherds feed the flock?" (Ezek. xxxiv. 2).—Ver. 16. Before, it was "Feed;" now, it is "Tend" or "Shepherd," *i. e.* "Perform all a shepherd's duties" by them; "Feed the flock, *like a shepherd;*" do all that should be done by a "*shepherd of the sheep.*" Call thine own sheep by name, and lead them out; and when thou puttest forth thine own sheep, go before them, that the sheep (knowing thy voice) may follow thee. Consider St. John x. 3, 4.—Ver. 17. The

Divine Speaker "seems to say that, in a Pastor, the first, the second, the third requisite, is *love of Christ*." (WILLIAMS.)—*Feed My sheep;* It is no longer "*Tend*," or "*Shepherd*," My sheep,—as in ver. 16; but "*Feed*" them,—the same word which was used above, in ver. 15, with reference to the little lambs. The same catechetical training, therefore,—the same careful attention to the soul's natural cravings and acquired needs, which was enjoined on behalf of the "lambs" of the fold,—is here enjoined on behalf of the "sheep" also.—"Feed the flock of God which is among you, taking the oversight thereof, not by constraint, but willingly; not for filthy lucre, but of a ready mind; neither as being lords over God's heritage, but being ensamples to the flock. And when the Chief Shepherd shall appear, ye shall receive a crown of glory that fadeth not away." (1 Pet. v. 1-4.)

[From BARNES: Ver. 15. *Thou knowest that I love Thee;* The expression of a humbled soul, a soul made sensible of its weakness and need of strength, yet with evidence of true attachment to the Saviour. It is not the most confident pretensions that constitute the highest proof of love to Christ.—*Feed My lambs;* It is not merely, therefore, the *privilege*,—it is the solemn *duty* of ministers of the gospel to countenance and patronize Sunday-schools.——From JACOBUS: Vers. 15-17. The test of ministerial love to Christ is a faithful care of the flock.—*Thou knowest all things;* The Divine Omniscience ought not to be a terror to the true Christian, but a comfort; for His all-searching eye can trace His own likeness wherever it is to be found, in the deepest depths of the soul.——From OWEN: Vers. 15-17. "There was no formal rebuke uttered, for the matter was already forgiven; this asking about his love was at farthest a most gentle and affectionate reproof." (STIER.)—The gradation "1. *Feed My lambs, i. e.* help the weak; 2. *Guide and guard My sheep, i. e.* counsel the strong; 3. *Feed My sheep, i. e.* help the strong, for they too need feeding with the divine food of the word." (CROSBY.)—A descending gradation, the *lambs*, a term of endearment, being given first, and then in the repetition of the charge, the less emphatic term, *sheep*." (WEBSTER AND WILKINSON.)—"Ministers ought to look upon Christ's people as very seriously recommended to them, and therefore should very seriously mind their work about them; for therefore is this charge thrice laid on Peter, that he may mind it much." (HUTCHESON.)—Ver. 18. The phrase *thou wouldest not*, refers to the shrinking back of weak humanity from a violent death, but not to the unwillingness of Peter to die for Jesus.]

III.

THE CONTINUING RULE OF CHRIST IN HIS CHURCH, REPRESENTED BY THE MINISTRY, SPIRITUAL LIFE AND PATRIARCHAL AGE OF JOHN; OR THE DESTINY OF THE CHURCH IN RESPECT OF HER PREDOMINANTLY INTERNAL CHARACTER AND IMMORTAL SPIRITUAL LIFE.

CHAP. XXI. 20-23.

(CHAP. XXI. 20-24, pericope for the third day after Christmas or for St. John the Evangelist's day.)

20 Then [*omit* Then][1] Peter, turning about [turning round], seeth the disciple whom
Jesus loved following; which [who] also leaned on his breast at supper, and said,
21 Lord, which [who] is he that betrayeth thee? Peter [therefore][2] seeing him saith to
Jesus, Lord, and what *shall* this man *do* [or, But how will it be with him? *οὗτος δὲ*
22 *τί*]? Jesus saith unto him, If I will that he tarry till I come, what *is that* to thee?[3]
23 follow [Follow] thou me.[4] Then went this saying [This report therefore went]
abroad among the brethren, that that disciple should not die [dieth not, was not to
die, *οὐκ ἀποθνήσκει*]: yet Jesus said not unto him, He shall not die [dieth not]; but,
If I will that he tarry till I come, what *is that* to thee?

TEXTUAL AND GRAMMATICAL.

[1] Ver. 20.—[The text. rec. inserts δέ after ἐπιστραφεὶς, with ℵ. D., so also Lange; but A. B. C. Vulg. omit it, so also Lachm., Tischend., Alf., Westc.—P. S.]

[2] Ver. 21.—[The text. rec. omits οὖν after τοῦτον, which is well supported by Orig., ℵ. B. C. D. Vulg. Syr., and adopted by the critical edd.—P. S.]

[3] Ver. 22.—[Noyes: "*If it be my will (θέλω) that he remain till I come, what is it to thee?*"]

[4] Ver. 22.—[Alford, to bring out the emphatic position of σύ and μοι more fully, translates: "*Do thou follow Me.*"—P. S.]

EXEGETICAL AND CRITICAL.

Ver. 20. **Following** (also) [ἀκολουθοῦντα].—The following of John is to be explained as the result of the involuntary drawing of love. It proves, however, that John did not understand the Lord as wishing to make Peter the recipient of an exclusively confidential communication.

Who also leaned on His breast at the

supper [ὃς καὶ ἀνέπεσεν ἐν τῷ δείπνῳ ἐπὶ τὸ στῆθος αὐτοῦ].—Wherefore this addition? Interpretations:

1. It is intended to bring to mind the incident chap. xiii. 23 ff., when John inquired of the Lord on Peter's behalf, and to demonstrate the fact that Peter has now grown far bolder, insomuch that he himself questions Christ, and that in behalf of John (Chrysostom and others).

2. It is designed as an intimation to this effect; namely that, peradventure, a lot so full of sufferings as Peter's might not be intended for the disciple so pre-eminently loved by Jesus (Meyer). As if Jesus in partiality protected His particular friends from sufferings!

3. It is intended to assign the motive for John's following.* John, in referring to the fact that he was the confidant of Jesus at the Last Supper, doubtless means to intimate that it was allowable for him now, *as* the confidant of Jesus, freely to join Him. Peter himself had possibly understood the summons of Jesus as prefacing an instantaneous being "girded" by "another" for an entrance into the other world; John understood it as the prelude to a love-test to be administered at Christ's withdrawal into concealment.

Ver. 21. **But how will it be with this (man)?**† οὗτος δὲ τί; [*sc.* ἔσται].

Meaning of the question:

1. In accordance with the interpretation of the *following* as accomplished by *martyrdom:* How shall it be with this my fellow-combatant (Euthymius)?

2. In accordance with the *literal* interpretation of the *following:* Is he to be with us now? (Paulus).

3. What sort of a fate shall this man have in his calling? (Tholuck, Luthardt).

4. If Peter saw in the mysterious walk a test of joyful following, his first thought would be: John, without being called, exposes himself to a moment of difficulty. The question: Shall this man go too? had at the same time, then, the background: What shall become of this man?

Motive of the question:

1. Special love for John (Chrysostom, Erasmus, Luthardt).

2. A question prompted by curiosity and a certain jealousy (Lücke, Meyer).

3. Disapprobation of a supposed unauthorized accompanying (Paulus and others).

4. Curiosity and interest as to John's fate. "A want of concentration, an excess of natural vivacity, was certainly involved in Peter's ability to turn away his eyes so quickly from himself and his own destiny, and fasten them upon another." Tholuck.

The self-consciousness with which Peter receives the disclosure and summons of the Lord, turns to *compassion* for *John* whose present and future task Jesus apparently fails to appoint. Between Jesus and John everything is understood of itself, tacitly, as it were, while between Jesus and Peter everything has to be expressed, discussed, in a degree stipulated. Now thinks Peter,—in all noble-mindedness, we may say,—the same course must be pursued with John, else will he come short in somewhat: he, therefore, must receive his instructions for now and for the future. Hence Christ, in His reproof, appeals to His will, not to a distinct instruction; while, indeed, indicating the substance of His will. [The words τί πρὸς σέ in the next verse imply a gentle rebuke (Bengel: *hoc Petri curiositatem in ordinem redigit*), and remind Peter of the distinctness of each man's position and calling. Hence "Do *thou* follow *Me*," instead of inquiring after *him*. See Meyer and Alford.—P. S.]

Ver. 22. **If I will that he remain** [Ἐὰν αὐτὸν θέλω μένειν ἕως ἔρχομαι, τί πρός σέ;]—As we do not read that Jesus sent John back, or that He returned with Peter and John from the mysterious walk, we must (contrary to our first edition) admit that Tholuck is right in here rejecting the literal interpretation: "If I choose to leave him behind until I return from My walk with thee (Mark, *Exerc. exeg.* Similarly Paulus)."

In these words, however, Christ enwraps the prophecy concerning John. *That he remain—tarry,*—μένειν "the opposite of ἀκολουθεῖν which was to be accomplished through *martyrdom;* therefore: *to be preserved alive.* Comp. Phil. i. 25; 1 Cor. xv. 6." Meyer.

Till I come [ἕως ἔρχομαι].

1. To lead him out of Galilee to apostolic activity (Theophyl.).

2. In the destruction of Jerusalem (Wetstein and others)*.

3. Reference to the near Parousia of Christ (Lücke, [De Wette], Meyer).

4. In the destruction of Jerusalem as the beginning of the Parousia of Christ (Luthardt). [So also Bengel, Stier and Alford: "After the destruction of Jerusalem began that mighty series of events of which the Apocalypse is the prophetic record, and which is in the complex known as the *coming of the Lord*, ending, as it shall, with His glorious and personal Advent." Bengel: "*Joannes tum, quum Apocalypsin scripsit, Dominum venire scripsit.*"—P. S.]

5. Legendary interpretation: As expressive of the mysterious surviving of the disciple until the end of the world. (Vulg.: *Sic cum volo manere*); see the Introduction [p. 12].

6. Hypothetical: Until the last coming (Rev. xxii. 20). Tholuck: "The sentence hypothetically declares that not even the longest extension of the life-term of Peter's fellow-disciple ought to be the occasion of jealousy." [So also Trench, *Miracles*, p. 466, as quoted by Alford.—P. S.] Supposing the saying to be *hypothetical*, however, its prophetic meaning would be weakened.

7. The coming [of Jesus] to take [John to heaven] through the medium of an easy [natural] death (*adventus gratiosus in articulo mortis.* Rupert, Grotius, Olshausen and others). [So also Lampe, Ewald, Wordsworth.] In opposition to this view Tholuck remarks: The characteristic καὶ παραλήψομαι αὐτόν is wanting. Nevertheless this interpretation alone forms a real antithesis; if ἀκολουθεῖν here mean: to follow the home-returning Jesus through the

* [So also Alford, who sees in this description of the beloved disciple a strong token of John's hand having written this chapter. See chap. xiii. 23.—P. S.]

† [Lange: *Was soll aber dieser?*]

* [Next to this might be ranked the unfounded view of Hengstenberg: the time of the decisive struggle between Christ and Rome, which commenced under Domitian.—P. S.]

medium of martyrdom, and *μένειν*, on the other hand signify: to remain alive,—then to remain alive until I come, means also, until I come to take him. The destruction of Jerusalem, for instance, forms no contrast to martyrdom; neither does the Parousia itself. Such a contrast *is* presented, however, by a natural death. Natural death is the *individual type*, continuing throughout New Testament times, of the Parousia for the individual Christian (Matt. xxiv. 44; John xiv. 3, *etc.*); and this Parousia of Christ in the death of believers, is a warranty to them of their participation in the general Parousia (1 Cor. xv. 51.; 1 Thess. iv. 15). Simultaneously with John's remaining until the coming of Christ in the hour of his natural death, there is indicated, however, the remaining of the Johannean type until the Parousia of Christ.

Ver. 23. **This saying therefore went abroad** [*Ἐξῆλθεν οὖν οὗτος ὁ λόγος εἰς τοὺς ἀδελφοὺς ὅτι ὁ μαθητὴς ἐκεῖνος οὐκ ἀποθνήσκει*].—The above mentioned tradition, which not even the Gospel has been able utterly to do away with. See the Introduction. According to Baur, that tradition grew out of the Revelation; the statement is entirely without foundation. The tradition to the effect that John did but slumber in the grave and moved the earth with his breath, was a synthesis of the fact of his death and the precipitate apodictic interpretation of Christ's word.

Yet Jesus said not unto him [*οὐκ εἶπεν δὲ αὐτῷ ὁ Ἰησοῦς*].—This defense of Christ's word against a precipitate interpretation is of the highest importance. It warrants the sure conclusion that John was still living when this was written; that consequently, it must have been written by him. Had John been dead, another author would have expressed himself positively against the interpretation of the brethren, giving, very probably, a different interpretation at the same time. The disciple, however, would not anticipate the mysterious purport of Christ's saying which was as yet unfulfilled.

["So also Alford, whose note may be added: The following words are to me a proof that this chapter was written during John's life-time. If written by another person after John's death, we should certainly, in the refutation of this error, have read, *ἀπέθανεν γὰρ, καὶ ἐτάφη*, as in Acts ii. 29." This notion of John's not having died, was prevalent in the ancient Church,—so that Augustine himself seems almost to credit the story of the earth of John's tomb heaving with his breath. Tract cxxiv. 2. "The English sect of the 'Seekers' under Cromwell expected the reappearance of the Apostle as the forerunner of the coming of Christ." Tholuck. See Trench on the *Miracles*, ed. 2, p. 467, note. The simple recapitulation of the words of the Lord shows that their sense remained dark to the writer, who ventured on no explanation of them; merely setting his own side of the apostolic duty over against that of Peter, who probably had already by following his Master through the Cross, glorified God, whereas the beloved disciple was, whatever that meant, to tarry till He came." Wordsworth makes the following practical remark on ver. 23: "The Holy Spirit, by *commenting* here on a *fulfilled* prophecy, that concerning Peter, teaches us to attend to the fulfilment of prophecy in our own times. And by *only correcting* an *error* with regard to an *unfulfilled* prophecy,—that concerning St. John, He teaches us not to speculate curiously on *unfulfilled prophecies;* but to wait patiently, till Christ comes to us in the events of history, and interprets His own prophecies by fulfilling them."—P. S.]

DOCTRINAL AND ETHICAL.

1. The foregoing section should, above all, be valued as an eloquent token of the *authenticity* of this Gospel. Every later writer would, in one way or another, have labored after additional emphasis. See the last EXEG. NOTE.

2. The word of Jesus concerning *John* has been fulfilled, in a literal sense, in the circumstance of his dying a natural death at an advanced age. And it is in accordance with this fact, therefore, that we have to apply the saying in respect of its primary signification. That it, however, as well as the saying concerning Peter, was at the same time intended to designate John as a type of the post-temporal presence of Christ in the Church, is proved by the very fact that men gave vent to the feeling of the lofty significance of the saying, whose ideal sense they came short of, in mythical allegations touching the continuous on-living of John. See EXEG. NOTE to ver. 22. Further communications on this subject, as also concerning the dark counterpart of this tradition, the tradition of the Wandering Jew, see in Heubner, *Joh.* p. 512.

3. The higher sense of the saying, then, is expressive of a *Johannean form of Christianity*, just as the previous saying is significant of a Petrine form of the same. The words mean, therefore:

(1) There shall always be friends of God, friends of Christ, inward—subjective,—intuitive Christians, in accordance with the characteristic of John, representative of the innermost presence of Christ in the Church.

(2) In this form, the Christian spiritual life shall remain until Christ returns.

(3) The more the Petrine characteristic of the Church recedes, the more prominent will her Johannean characteristic become. The Church shall attain to maturity. She shall be a bride adorned with her ornaments, Rev. xix. 7, 8.

4. PAULINE Christianity may be regarded as a form of transition from the PETRINE type to the JOHANNEAN. And so far as this, the Schellingean distinction of the three Christian ages is correct. Only we must not identify Petrinism with Roman Catholicism, Paulinism with Protestantism (though in Protestantism, Paulinism has found its triumphant expression), and least of all must we make a synthesis of Protestantism and Roman Catholicism, affirming said synthesis to represent Johannean Christianity.

The Petrine characteristic is the trait of the Church as influenced by law; as the *confessing* Church; the Pauline is the trait of the Church as influenced by the freedom of faith; as the *witnessing* Church; the Johannean, the trait of the Church as filled with the ideality of faith, *working* and *keeping joyful holiday*, the Church of the light, love and life of Christ, *i. e.* the Adorned Bride. These three degrees of development, however, denote but the one unitous post-temporal presence of the Spirit of Christ in the Church, in accordance with the ground-forms of that presence. Now the two primitively distinct ground-forms are Peter and John. See the discussions on this subject: *Apostolisches Zeitalter*, II., p. 649, and the concluding section of Schaff's *History of the Apostolic Church*.

5. John's free joining in the following which Christ commanded Peter is likewise a characteristic of the Johannean essence. It is the involuntary drawing of love's impulse and friendship's right; the perfect humanity of the life of faith. The expression of this ripe spiritual fellowship with the glorified Lord makes so ghostly and yet so human an impression upon the world, that John passes, almost untouched, through its persecutions. He is exiled, but not killed. His keenest sufferings, however, are prepared him by the misconceptions of external circles of [religious] fellowship themselves, these latter stamping the Petrine as the statutory essence. He too, in his own way, is nailed to the cross like Peter, but not with heathen nails—ah no! with Christian or Judo-Christian; and, insomuch as this is true, with silver nails.

6. Here, then, belongs also the entire import of all Christian mysticism and speculation, in respect of their pure, ideal form.

HOMILETICAL AND PRACTICAL.

The solemnization of the resurrection of Jesus: A call to follow Him.—The following of Jesus not simply a following of the Crucified One, but also of the Risen One.—The disciples' following of the Lord: 1. In its unity, 2. in its diversity.—How Peter, as he follows the Lord, hears the rustle of John's foot behind him.—The question of Peter: Lord, but what shall this man do? 1. In the mouth of Peter himself: well-meant and yet not wholly warranted; 2. in the mouth of those who boast of Peter: ill-meant and unwarrantable.—How the most zealous servants of Christ frequently fail to understand His most intimate friends.—John, the friend of Jesus, the patriarch of all the friends of God and of Christ.—Christ's presence in the world and Church through the medium of the love of His friends.—Friendship with Christ on earth an undying spring, enduring until the summer-time at the end of the world.—*If I will that he tarry:* Christ's will the fate of His people (if we live, we live unto the Lord, *etc.*)—How the Lord has appointed such different careers to His people, yet deciding for all aright.—Christ can insure the longest life.—"*What is that to thee?*" In what sense we should concern ourselves about our Christian colleague, and in what sense we should avoid so doing: 1. As to his spiritual welfare, but not as to the external form thereof; 2. as to the will of God concerning his way, not as to a human regulation of his way; 3. in divine sympathy, not in human comparison or in human rivalry.—Christ's conference with Peter in regard to the destiny of John: 1. The question of Peter; 2. the answer of Christ; 3. the proud interpretation of the disciples; 4. the modest correction of John.—The remaining of John until Christ's coming again: 1. In its historical sense; 2. in its symbolical import.

STARKE: LANGE: It becomes evident from this, that when Christ said to Peter, Follow Me, He advanced a few paces from him, desiring, in a prophetic manner, in conformity to which a secret matter was sometimes presented in outward gestures, to lead Peter, while claiming from him a bodily following for a short distance only, to a spiritual following, and, in particular, to a following to the death of the cross.—ZEISIUS: We all have, alas, an innate propensity to concern ourselves unnecessarily about others, rather than about ourselves. Therefore flee curiosity, Sir. III., 22. It is one of the infirmities of believers to discover a kind of jealousy when they perceive others to possess gifts of grace, either physical or spiritual, in a greater degree than themselves, Jon. iv. 1 f.—BIBL. WIRT.: Let every man wait on his vocation, not troubling himself as to what God will do or decree with others.—LAMPE: Moreover, we perceive from these words 1. The humility of John, in not being willing to have so great honor ascribed to him; 2. his solicitude for the brethren, whom he sought to free from error.

GERLACH: John worked inward in the Church rather than outward.—BRAUNE: Inscrutable and mysterious are the ways by which God leads us, until we are come to the end of them. Therefore abide by the testimony of Scripture, and attend every man to his own affairs.—GOSSNER: Why is it only to me that such things are said? That man gets off more easily. Before one can turn round, people are ready with questions like this: What shall this one and that one do?

JOHANNES MUELLER, *Lebensgeschichte* 1806, p. 34, writes: "The opinion now starting up again that the disciple whom Jesus loved, did not die, is found, if I mistake not, in Sulpitius Severus, also *Hist. S., Lib.* II. I have frequently met with it in Greek legends, monologues, and chronicles, with this addition, *viz.*, that the dust upon his grave is moved by the breath of his mouth." P. 106: "In a work of the Patriarch Ephraim, of Antioch (p. 545, Photius, num. 229, p. 418 of the Augsburg Edition 1604) it is positively affirmed that John is still living; that he has vanished, and that in his grave nought was found but a delicious odor and a precious spring of healing balm. George of Alexandria informs us (Photius *num.* 96, p. 139) that to the monk Hesychius, a Syrian, there appeared St. Peter and St. John, and that the latter delivered a book to the young monk, who was afterwards called Chrysostom. Of the tradition's having come into our parts also, thou wilt find a proof in Hübner's *Salzburg*, Part. I., p. 317."—He who has promised to follow the Saviour can do nothing else than await His orders, composing himself to rest and be active as His Lord wills, and more than once to labor till he is weary.

HEUBNER: The question as to ourselves should concern us so entirely to the exclusion of all else, as to keep us quiet when hundreds are threatening to get precedence of us. We, perhaps, think ourselves ripe (to go home), but there are reasons why God decrees otherwise with us.—Ver. 23: It results from this verse that the apostles could not have been of the decided opinion that they would live to see the coming of Christ; otherwise they could not have ascribed such a destiny to John as a special prerogative.—The spirit of John shall never perish; it shall ever renew itself—never shall there be wanting loving and beloved Johannean souls.

[CRAVEN: From AUGUSTINE: Ver. 22. Let action be perfected by following the example of My Passion, but let contemplation wait inchoate till at My coming it be completed.—From CHRYSOSTOM: Ver. 22. Attend to the work committed to thee, and do IT: if I will that he abide here, what is that to thee?

[From BURKITT: Vers. 20-22. There are two great vanities in man with reference to knowledge,—the one a *neglect* to know what it is our duty to know; the other, a *curiosity* to know what it doth not belong to us to know.—Ver. 23. How much the wisdom of God ought to be admired, in giving us a written word, and tying us to it, when we see erroneous traditions so soon on foot in the world, and our Saviour's own speeches so much mistaken, and that by wise and holy men themselves in the purest times.—How great is the vanity and uncertainty of oral tradition!

[From M. HENRY: Ver. 21. Peter seems more concerned for another than for himself: so apt are we to be busy in other men's matters, but negligent in the concerns of our own souls.—He seems more concerned about *event* than about *duty*.—Ver. 22. Though Christ calls out some of His disciples to resist unto blood, yet not all. Though the crown of martyrdom is bright and glorious, yet the *beloved disciple* comes short of it.—It is the will of Christ, that His disciples should mind their own present duty, and not be curious in their inquiries about future events, concerning either themselves or others.—If we will closely attend to the duty of following Christ, we shall find neither heart nor time to meddle with that which does not belong to us.—Ver. 23. Hence learn, The aptness of men to misinterpret the sayings of Christ. The grossest errors have sometimes shrouded themselves under the umbrage of incontestable truths; and the Scriptures themselves have been wrested by the unlearned and unstable.

[From SCOTT: Ver. 22: *Follow thou Me;* If we attend to this voice, even "death itself will be gain to us," and we shall be ready for His coming.—[From KEBLE: Vers. 21, 22.

"Lord, and what shall this man do?
Ask'st thou, Christian, for thy friend?
If his love for Christ be true,
Christ hath told thee of his end:
This is he whom God approves,
This is he whom Jesus loves.

Ask not of him more than this,
Leave it in his Saviour's breast,
Whether, early called to bliss,
He in youth shall find his rest,
Or armed in his station wait
Till his Lord be at the gate."

[From A PLAIN COMMENTARY (Oxford): Ver. 22. Our Lord's words to Peter are made up of *rebuke* and *counsel*. *What is that to thee?*—which of us has not deserved the *rebuke? Follow thou Me!* which of us does not require the *counsel?* The heart and eye are thus called away from the problem which perplexes, the prospect which discourages, the thoughts which distract and paralyze; and a plain duty is proposed instead. Not *speculation*, is enjoined, but *practice;* not *knowledge*, but *goodness;* not *another man's* matters, but *our own*.—"This was a transient stumbling in one who, but lately recovered of a great disease, did not walk firmly. But it is the common track of most, to wear out their days with impertinent inquiries. There is a natural desire in men to know the things of others, and to neglect their own; and to be more concerned about things to come, than about things present." (LEIGHTON.)

[From BARNES: Ver. 22. Hence we learn that 1. Our main business is to *follow*, and imitate the Lord Jesus Christ; 2. There are many subjects of religion on which a vain and impertinent curiosity is exercised; 3. Jesus will take care of *all* His beloved disciples, and we should not be unduly solicitous about them; 4. We should go forward to whatever He calls us, not envying the lot of any other man, and anxious only to do the will of God.

[From JACOBUS: Ver. 22. The intimation was that "John was to wait patiently, to linger on year after year in loneliness and weariness of spirit, to abide persecution, oppression and wrong (Rev. i. 9), to endure the enmity of the wicked (1 John iii. 13), and the sight of heresies abounding in the Church (1 John ii. 18, 19-26), as if to exemplify in himself all classes of the faithful, and the various modes of drinking the cup of Christ."—*Thou* (emphatic); "They, measuring themselves by themselves, and comparing themselves among themselves, are not wise." 2 Cor. x. 12.—Each *must do his own duty*, which is not another's, and whether another shall do his own duty or not.—Christian liberality is cramped with many by the constant asking of this question, "What shall this man do?" when the question should be, "What shall I do?"—Ver. 23. Let us fall back upon God's *word*—study its precise terms—and bring out its very language more and more to the public understanding: and thus will many an error be stripped of its disguises, many a perversion of God's will be exposed, and the Church shall "grow up in all things unto Him who is the Head."

[From OWEN: Ver. 23. "John was earlier than the other disciples prepared for the death of martyrdom, as the most perfect sacrifice of obedience to God, and of love to God and man; but that was the very reason why he was not to taste the martyr's death. John consummated in his life and natural death what the martyrs sealed in their final sacrifice, namely, the victorious manifestation of the love of God and man." (STIER.)]

IV.

THE TESTIMONY OF JOHN AND THE TESTIMONY OF THE CHURCH. INFINITUDE OF THE EVANGELICAL HISTORY.

CHAP. XXI. 24, 25.

24 This is the disciple which [who] testifieth [ὁ μαρτυρῶν] of these things, and wrote
[who wrote, ὁ γράψας][1] these things: and we know that his testimony is true.[2]
25 [3]And there are also many other things which[4] Jesus did, the which, if they should
be written every one, I suppose that even the world itself could not contain[5] the
books that should be written. Amen. [*omit* Amen.][6]

TEXTUAL AND GRAMMATICAL.

1 Ver. 24.—[The article before γράψας is omitted by ℵ[1]. A. C. X. Orig., Tischend., inserted by B. D. lat. (*et* QUI *scripsit.*) Lachm., Treg., Alf., West. Cod. B. inserts καὶ before μαρτυρῶν.—P. S.]

2 Ver. 24.—[Dr. Lange brackets the last clause: καὶ οἴδαμεν ὅτι ἀληθής αὐτοῦ ἡ μαρτυρία ἐστίν, considering it an addition of the elders of Ephesus and friends of John, while he ascribes all the rest, including ver. 25, to John. See EXEG.—P. S.]

3 Ver. 25.—This verse is wanting in Cod. 63 [?],—a circumstance of no importance, however. (On the Sin. see Tischend.) [Lachmann, Tregelles, Alford, and Westcott retain ver. 25, except the concluding ἀμήν, Westcott, however, separates it from the preceding text. Tischendorf alone, ed. VIII., excludes it from the text on the sole authority of the Sinaitic MS. which indeed contains the verse, but, as *he asserts*, written by another hand, see his note, p. 965. But in the large quasi-fac-simile ed. of the Cod. which I have used all along, there is no perceptible difference. He then also corrects an error with regard to Cod. 63, which was quoted by Mill, Wetstein, Griesbach, Lange (in the preceding remark), *etc.*, in favor of omission, but according to Scrivener, the last page of that Cod. with the 25th verse is lost. Tischendorf here gives too much weight to Cod. Sin., which he had the good fortune to discover. The omission, if such could be proven, has little weight in view of the many instances of carelessness on the part of the copyist, and of the filling up of the lacuna by the first corrector, who, according to Tischendorf, was cotemporary with the copyist. All other known MSS. contain ver. 25, though many state in a note that it was regarded by some as a later addition.—P. S.]

4 Ver. 25.—The reading ἅ in accordance with Codd. ℵ. B. D.* *etc.*, Lachmann [Treg., Alf., West., instead of text rec. ὅσα which is retained by A. C.[2] D. and expresses the *quantitative* relation, *quæ et quanta, quotquot, what and how many;* comp. Rev. i. 2.—P. S.]

5 Ver. 25.—[Lachm., Alfd. χωρῆσαι, with A. B. C.[2] D. text. rec.; Treg., Tisch., West. χωρήσειν, with ℵ. B. C*.—P. S.]

6 Ver. 25.—The ἀμήν of the Recepta (Codd. E. G. H. K. M. *etc.*) is wanting in Codd. [ℵ.] A. B. C. D. *etc.* [*Amen* is a liturgical or devotional addition, and justly omitted by Lachm., Treg., Alf., Westc. and H.—P. S.] On the various subscriptions: εὐαγγέλιον κατὰ Ἰωάννην (A. C. E. [ℵ[a]]); κατα Ἰωάννην (B.) *etc.*, comp. Tischendorf. K. M. U. X. [also ℵ*. Γ] have no subscription. [Tischendorf states that the subscription in ℵ is not written by the same hand, but by ℵ corr.[1a] On the Latin subscriptions, see Tischend. p. 967.—P. S.]

EXEGETICAL AND CRITICAL.

Ver 24. **This is the disciple** [Οὗτός ἐστιν ὁ μαθητής].—Self-designation of John, as in chap. xix. 26. [A conclusion corresponding to the one chap. xx. 31, and traced to John also by Meyer and Alford.—P. S.]

Of these things [ὁ μαρτυρῶν περὶ τούτων].—Referring to the contents of the 21st chapter.—**And who wrote these things** [καὶ ὁ γράψας ταῦτα].—Particularly, also, to the setting of the Christians right in regard to the tradition which had commenced to gather form. [Mark the difference of the tenses: μαρτυρῶν—the testimony continues, γράψας—the writing is an accomplished act.—P. S.]

We know that his testimony [καὶ οἴδαμεν ὅτι ἀληθής αὐτοῦ ἡ μαρτυρία ἐστίν.—Different interpretations:

1. Οἶδα [I know] μέν (Chrysostom, Theophylact). An exegetical conjecture (similarly Beza's οἶδεν).

2. An indication of the ungenuineness of the conclusion or of the whole chapter (modern criticism).

3. John made himself one with his readers (Meyer). [So also Alford; comp. i. 14; 1 John iv. 14, 16; v. 18.]

4. Probably a later addition from the Ephesian church. Not because, as according to Lücke, "John never wrote in the first person, either of the plural or of the singular." See on the contrary, chap. i. 14. But the corroboration of his own testimony with the words: *We know that his testimony is true*, would be too strikingly singular. The expression chap. xix. 35 runs differently. We have therefore bracketed the words "we know," *etc.*, considering them to be the only later Ephesian addition in the whole chapter.

[Meyer regards only ver. 25 as a later addition; Tholuck, Luthardt, Godet, *etc.*, vers. 24 and 25; Lücke, Bleek, Ewald, *etc.*, the whole chapter; Lange, Alford and Wordsworth accept the whole as Johannean,—Lange, however, excepting the second clause of ver. 24.—P. S.]

Ver. 25. **But there are also many other things** [Ἔστι δὲ καὶ ἄλλα πολλά].—Meyer: "Apocryphal conclusion of the whole Gospel—after the addition of the Johannean supplement vers. 1-24." The Evangelist thinks it important that he should remind his readers that he has not written as a chronicler, but has selected and arranged things in conformity to an organizing principle, as did also his predecessors, though not in the equal power of a concentrated, unitous, ideal view.* That this note

* [So also Alford: "The purpose of this verse seems to be to assert and vindicate the fragmentary character of the

of the Gospel has not at all an apocryphal aspect, but would, on the contrary, be qualified, were more attention accorded it, to strip our modern criticism of many apocryphal opinions (particularly, of the continually recurring idea that the Evangelists were chroniclers, that their writings were grounded upon one another, *etc.*), is evident.

If they should be written every one . . one by one [ἅτινα (*quippe quæ, utpote quæ*, referring to the large number) ἐὰν γράφηται καθ' ἕν (piece for piece), οὐδ' αὐτὸν οἶμαι τὸν κόσμον (*ne ipsum quidem mundum*) χωρήσειν* τὰ γραφόμενα βιβλία. Comp. a somewhat analogous expression Eccl. xii. 12: "Of making many books (or chapters) there is no end." Different interpretations of χωρεῖν, *capere:* 1. Locally: Unable to hold (*capacitas loci*). Restricted by Ebrard: No place in literature. 2. Intellectually: Unable to understand (*capacitas intellectus*). Jerome, Augustine, Calov, Bengel ("*hoc non de capacitate geometrica, sed morali accipiendum est*"). 3. Figuratively and hyperbolically: Any number of books would not exhaust the subject. Similarly Godet: "*Divin de sa nature, l'objet de l'histoire évangélique est plus grand que le monde et que toutes les narrations que le monde pourrait contenir. L'écrivain exprime, par une image matérielle, le vif sentiment qu'il a de la richesse infinie de cette histoire.*"—P. S.] According to the conclusion of the Evangelist, the world itself would be unable to contain the books that would then be written continually (γραφόμενα). Even Tholuck agrees with Meyer (who refers to similar hyperboles in Fabricius *ad Cod. Apocryph.* I., p. 321) in thinking this proposition hyperbolical. The apparent hyperbolism of the expression, however, very clearly illustrates the pure infiniteness in the life-development of the Logos, by a quantitative, local measure. We make use of a hundred similar expressions without their hyperbolism being deemed improper or apocryphal, for instance: "*O dass ich tausend Zungen hätte*" ("O that I had a thousand tongues")—"*Den aller Weltkreis nie umschloss*" ("Whom the whole world did ne'er enclose")†—"The whole world lieth in wickedness—in the Evil One," *etc.* Weitzel has entered the lists in defence of the propriety of the expression, *Studien u. Kritiken* 1849, p. 633; comp. my *Leben Jesu* III., p. 760. Luthardt: "For only an absolute external compass corresponds with the absolute contents of the person and life of Christ;" whereupon Meyer remarks: "Inevident to me!" "*Aber, Freunde, im Raum wohnt das Erhabene nicht*" ("But, O friends, the sublime dwelleth not in space"), says Schiller elucidatively. The Evangelist, however, in submitting his book to the Church, may well come forward with an unwonted οἶμαι, in order, by a strong expression, to dissuade the reader from the chronistic apprehension of the Gospel, and to urge him to the historico-symbolical view which recognizes in the organically articulated selection of ideally transparent facts, the historical life-picture of the infinite fulness of the life of Jesus.*

This symbolical character, presented in pure but speaking facts, is possessed, in a peculiar degree, by the closing chapter, to which the closing words primarily have reference. The interpretation of Jerome, Augustine and others: The world would be spiritually incapable of grasping such books,—would apply even to the four small Gospels, though in sooth a Gospel developed *in infinitum* would pass the comprehension not only of the present *world*, but also of *Christendom* as it here exists. Here, however, emphasis is laid not upon the æonic unfathomableness of the life of Jesus, but upon its ideal infinitude, in the symbolical explicitness of the evangelical history.†

DOCTRINAL AND ETHICAL.

1. The absolutely *dynamical* view of the world, as the specifically *Christian view of it*, is the fundamental feature and the key of the Johannean Gospel, of Johannean theology. The personal principle is the royal life-principle of the world. The personality of God in the personality of Christ, annihilates the power of the anti-personal, Satanic essence, and appoints the impersonal world to the service of life; it is diffused in the personality of the Apostles, in order that it may lift the whole world out of the abyss into the light of glorification, in which the world, as the old world, vanishes, in order to shine forth again as the eternal House of the Father, the eternal City of God. In conformity to this dynamical view, Christ's pre-temporal rule in the world is finally summed up in the testimony of John the Baptist; His post-temporal rule, in the ministry of the twelve Apostles; the draught of fishes of the seven; the simple contrast of the following disciple and the tarrying one; finally, in the

Gospel, considered merely as a historical narrative:—for that the doings of the Lord were so many—His life so rich in matter of record,—that, in a popular hyperbole, we can hardly imagine the world containing them all, if singly written down; thus setting forth the superfluity and cumberousness of anything like a perfect detail, in the strongest terms, and in terms which certainly look as if fault had been found with this Gospel for want of completeness, by some objectors."—P. S.]

* [Or, according to the other reading infin. aor. χωρῆσαι, which after οἶμαι without ἄν is pure Greek, and expresses more strongly the faith in the certainty of the fact stated than the fut. χωρήσειν.—P. S.]

† [Lines of two celebrated German hymns. To these may be added similar expressions in English hymns, as,

"Oh! for a thousand tongues to sing," *etc.*

"Had I a thousand hearts to give," *etc.*

"Were the whole realm of nature mine," *etc.*

But these and similar expressions are desires poetically expressed, while here we have a statement in prose.—P. S.]

* [Wordsworth puts into the first person singular οἶμαι, which John nowhere else uses in the Gospel, the intention of the writer to guard against the inference that ver. 25 was written by a person different from John, who wrote in the plural οἴδαμεν in the preceding verse. But this would have been done more effectually by using the singular in both cases. Godet conjectures that the subject of the οἶμαι is one of the apostles present with John at Ephesus, probably Andrew, who, with John, was the oldest disciple of Christ (ch. i.).—P. S.]

† "*Vom Himmel steigend Jesus bracht*
Des Evangeliums ewige Schrift,
Den Jüngern las Er sie Tag und Nacht;
Ein göttlich Wort, es wirkt und trifft.
Er stieg zurück, nahm's wieder mit,
Sie aber hatten's gut gefühlt,
Und Jeder schrieb so Schritt für Schritt,
Wie er's in seinem Sinn behielt.
Verschieden: Es hat nichts zu bedeuten
Sie hatten nicht gleiche Fähigkeiten;
Doch damit können sich die Christen
Bis zu dem jüngsten Tage fristen."

(GOETHE).]

type of a friendship with Christ which remains until the Lord comes.

With this dynamical character, then, the apostolic presentation of the evangelical history also corresponds. That history is not chronistically, but æonically, executed; not atomistically expanded, but principially concentrated; the whole infinitude and fulness of the signs of Jesus must be reflected in a concentric selection of speaking facts, translumined by the idea. Not in outward extension—in transparent concentration, the expression of eternal life is accomplished.

2. The great distance between John's view of the essence of evangelical historiography and the opinions or prejudices of modern criticism, becomes evident from the foregoing, and from the last Exeg. Note.

3. Even the Christian *Gramma* may err in the way of profuse book-making. Against this the Christian spirit of a John opposes its final words of warning; the like did the Preacher Solomon in the Old Testament (Eccles. xii. 12), and also Plato in Phædrus 60. The Christian spirit-word does not aim at converting the world into a vast library of sacred writings, but into the Divine House of the adorned Bride of Christ and of the marriage of the Bridegroom. To this end, Christian literature, with its testimony concerning Christ, is indeed to work, drawing all literature into His service; but the more it extends itself through the world, the more it should concentrate itself, shaping itself into the transparent life-picture of the glory of God in Christ.

HOMILETICAL AND PRACTICAL.

The testimony of the friend of Jesus concerning his Lord and Master.—Together with the faithful testimony concerning Christ, the testifying disciple unconsciously immortalizes himself.—And we know that his testimony is true: 1. We know: *a.* we believe it, *b.* we not only believe it, we know it, *c.* we not only know it (in the sense of the world's knowledge), we experience it. 2. We know, concerning his testimony, that it is sealed with the water and blood of Christ. 3. That it is true: *a.* true in spite of all the objections and contradictions of the world, *b.* true in the might of the Spirit who hath overcome the world.—How it is impossible, and yet possible, to depict the glory of Christ: 1. Impossible by the multitude of words, discourses and writings; 2. possible by the simple word of the Spirit concerning His great signs.—The evangelical life-picture of the Lord: 1. In respect of its finite form; 2. in respect of its infinite contents; 3. in respect of its New Testament, eternally new operation.

Starke: That which by grace we have received from God and done for the honor of God, we may well make known to others, taking care only that all boastfulness on account of our own persons is avoided, 1 Cor. xi.

Braune: "An individual once appeared on earth who, merely by moral omnipotence, conquered remote times and founded an eternity of His own. It is that calm Spirit whom we call Jesus Christ. Only quiet teaching and quiet striving formed the melodies wherewith this higher Orpheus tamed human beasts and converted rocks into sanctuaries of God. And yet out of so divine a life,—as it were, out of a thirty years' war against a perverse, insensible people,—we are familiar with but a few weeks. What transactions, what words of His may have been swallowed up from our knowledge before He became acquainted with the four writers of His history, those men by nature so dissimilar! If, then, out of so divine a life-book only scattered leaves have fluttered to us, so that perhaps greater deeds and words of that life are forgotten (?) than were detailed, repine not, nor pass judgment over the ship-wreck of little works and men, but recognize in that Christianity which nevertheless blossomed afterwards, the fulness with which the (All) Spirit yearly suffers the perishing blossoms to exceed in number those that thrive, without therefore forfeiting a future spring" (Jean Paul).

Schleiermacher: "For a long time there has been a fable current among men, and even in these days it is (still) frequently heard; unbelief invented it, and little faith receives it. Thus it runs: 'There shall come a time, and perhaps it is already here, when His right shall befall even this Jesus of Nazareth. Every human memory is fruitful but for a certain period; much doth the human race owe to Him, great things hath God accomplished by Him, yet He was but one of us, and His hour of oblivion, too, must strike. If He was in earnest in desiring to make the world absolutely free, He must likewise have willed to make it free from Himself, that God might be all in all. Then men would not only perceive that they have strength enough in themselves to fulfil the divine will, but in the true understanding of the same, they would be able to exceed His measure, if they did but wish. Yes, only when the Christian name is forgotten, shall a universal kingdom of love and truth arise, in which no germ more of enmity shall lie, such as has been sown from the beginning betwixt those that believe on this Jesus and the rest of the children of men.' But it shall not be realized,—this fable; since the days of His flesh, the Redeemer's image has been indelibly stamped on the race of men! Even though the letter might perish, which is holy only because it preserves us the image, the image itself shall last for ever; too deeply is it graven upon men ever to be effaced, and what the disciple said, shall always be truth: 'Lord, whither shall we go? Thou alone hast words of eternal life!'"

Heubner: The pernicious making and reading of books has been greatly prejudicial to the reading of the Book of Life, and to the Christian life. Luther himself on this account often wished his books done away with, *Works* i. 1938; xiv. 420; xv. *Anh.*, p. 90 xxi. 1031; xxii. 85.

Yet doubtless only in a qualified sense. The books of faith should promote life,—hence should be, as living books, strictly articulated organisms of life. Their foundation and aim is the Book of Life. This is above all true of the Holy Scriptures, particularly of the Gospels, most particularly of our Gospel.

[Craven: From Burkitt: Ver. 25. The wonderful activity, industry, and diligence of the Lord Jesus Christ; He was never idle, but His whole life was spent in doing good.

[From M. Henry: Ver. 25. If it be asked why the gospels are not larger; it may be answered, I. It was not because *they had exhausted their subject;* II. But 1. It was not *needful* to write *more;* 2. It was not *possible* to write *all;* 3. It was not *advisable* to write *much.*

[Schaff: Vers. 24, 25. Though but little has been written on the life of Christ by the Evangelists, that little is of more account than all the literature of the world, and has been more productive of books, as well as thoughts and deeds, than any number of biographies of sages and saints of ancient and modern times. The Gospels, and the Bible generally, rise like Mount Ararat high above the flood of literature; they are the sacred library for all nations, the literary sanctuary for scholars and the common people; they combine word and work, letter and spirit, earth and heaven, time and eternity. The eloquent tribute of an English divine* to the influence of the Bible applies especially to the Gospel of John, and may appropriately conclude this Commentary. "This collection of books has been to the world what no other book has ever been to a nation. States have been founded on its principles. Kings rule by a compact based on it. Men hold the Bible in their hands when they prepare to give solemn evidence affecting life, death, or property; the sick man is almost afraid to die unless the Book be within reach of his hands; the battle-ship goes into action with one on board whose office is to expound it; its prayers, its psalms are the language which we use when we speak to God; eighteen centuries have found no holier, no diviner language. If ever there has been a prayer or a hymn enshrined in the heart of a nation, you are sure to find its basis in the Bible. There is no new religious idea given to the world, but it is merely the development of something given in the Bible. The very translation of it has fixed language and settled the idioms of speech. Germany and England speak as they speak because the Bible was translated. It has made the most illiterate peasant more familiar with the history, customs, and geography of ancient Palestine, than with the localities of his own country. Men who know nothing of the Grampians, of Snowdon, or of Skiddaw, are at home in Zion, the lake of Gennesaret, or among the rills of Carmel. People who know little about London know by heart the palaces in Jerusalem, where those blessed feet trod which were nailed to the Cross. Men who know nothing of the architecture of a Christian cathedral, can yet tell you all about the pattern of the Holy Temple. Even this shows us the influence of the Bible. The orator holds a thousand men for half-an-hour breathless—a thousand men as one, listening to his single word. But this Word of God has held a thousand nations for thrice a thousand years spell-bound; held them by an abiding power, even the universality of its truth; and we feel it to be no more a collection of books, but *the* Book."—P. S.]

* [I saw it in a respectable Magazine attributed to the Rev. F. Robertson, the late gifted preacher of Brighton, but I have been unable to verify the quotation and cannot vouch for its accuracy.—P. S.]